Collins
internet-linked
dictionary of

Synonyms
&
Antonyms

GW00669962

William Collins' dream of knowledge for all began with the publication of his first book in 1819. A self-educated mill worker, he not only enriched millions of lives, but also founded a flourishing publishing house. Today, staying true to this spirit, Collins books are packed with inspiration, innovation, and practical expertise. They place you at the centre of a world of possibility and give you exactly what you need to explore it.

Language is the key to this exploration, and at the heart of Collins Dictionaries is language as it is really used. New words, phrases, and meanings spring up every day, and all of them are captured and analysed by the Collins Word Web. Constantly updated, and with over 2.5 billion entries, this living language resource is unique to our dictionaries.

Words are tools for life. And a Collins Dictionary makes them work for you.

Collins. Do more

Collins
internet-linked
dictionary of

Synonyms

&

Antonyms

Collins

HarperCollins Publishers
Westerhill Road
Bishopbriggs
Glasgow
G64 2QT

First Edition 2005

© HarperCollins Publishers 2005

UK Edition ISBN 0–00–719466-8

Collins® is a registered trademark of
HarperCollins Publishers Limited

www.collins.co.uk

A catalogue record for this book is
available from the British Library.

Designed by Mark Thomson

Typeset by Wordcraft

Printed in Great Britain by Clays Ltd, St Ives plc

Acknowledgements
We would like to thank those authors and
publishers who kindly gave permission for
copyright material to be used in the Collins Word
Web. We would also like to thank Times
Newspapers Ltd for providing valuable data.

All rights reserved. No part of this publication
may be reproduced, stored in a retrieval system or
transmitted, in any form or by any means,
electronic, mechanical, photocopying, recording or
otherwise, without the prior permission of the
publisher. This book is sold subject to the
conditions that it shall not, by way of trade or
otherwise, be lent, re-sold, hired out or otherwise
circulated without the publisher's prior consent in
any form of binding or cover other than that in
which it is published and without a similar
condition including this condition being imposed
on the subsequent purchase.

HarperCollins do not accept responsibility for the
content or reliability of the web addresses featured
within this dictionary.

CONTENTS

EDITORIAL STAFF

EDITORS
Justin Crozier
Lorna Gilmour
Elspeth Summers

COMPUTING SUPPORT
Thomas Callan
Nigel Rochford

FOR THE PUBLISHERS
Morven Dooner
Elaine Higgleton
Lorna Knight

The written word plays a huge part in our lives. Thanks to e-mail and the internet, verbal communication is faster and farther-reaching than ever before, putting a premium on writing skills. The ability to write clearly and accurately is vital for success in many fields, and is a real advantage whoever you are and whatever you do.

Nothing kills prose quicker than repetition. A sound principle for any writer is to avoid using same word twice in a sentence, unless absolutely necessary. This sounds easy enough, but when faced with a tight deadline or busy schedule, it can be very difficult. That's where this *internet-linked dictionary of Synonyms & Antonyms* comes in. With over 150,000 alternatives and opposites, it's the ideal means of recharging your vocabulary and refreshing your writing. When you wish to avoid repeating a word, simply look it up to find a host of equivalent terms. These synonyms are labelled, where necessary, to indicate the context in which the word is generally used, thus alerting you to the dangers of using inappropriate language.

The synonyms in this book provide one way of resolving an impasse; the antonyms give you a different option: rephrasing your sentence so that it uses an opposite with a negative, rather than an equivalent. So, rather than saying:

the team's performance was half-hearted

you might write:

the team was less than spirited

The main text is augmented by the *Literally Speaking* supplement, which contains detailed information on choosing the right word, and avoiding embarrassing clichés and clangers. The supplement also contains links to useful URLs to improve your writing and enhance your wordpower.

Even the best wordsmiths get stumped occasionally – but help is at hand. The Collins *internet-linked dictionary of Synonyms & Antonyms* provides a swift detour past writer's block, and a route to powerful writing that works.

Main Entry Words	Main entry words are printed in bold type: **altogether**
Parts of Speech	Parts of speech are shown in italics. Where a word has several senses for one part of speech, the senses are numbered: **altogether** *adverb* 1
Synonyms	The key synonym for each sense is given in small capitals, with other alternatives given in roman: **altogether** *adverb* 1 ABSOLUTELY quite, completely, totally, perfectly,fully, thoroughly, wholly, utterly, downright, one hundred per cent (*informal*), undisputedly, lock, stock and barrel 2 COMPLETELY, all, fully, entirely, comprehensively, thoroughly, wholly, utterly, downright, one hundred per cent (*informal*)
Antonyms	Opposites are preceded by two left-facing arrows and ANTONYM in small capitals: <<ANTONYM partially
Labels	Labels have been added, where necessary, to denote register, subject field, or region. Regional labels have been abbreviated: *Austral*: Australia, *Brit*: Britain, *Canad*: Canada, *NZ*: New Zealand, *Scot*: Scotland, *US*: United States

Aa

aback *adverb* ▷▷ **taken aback** SURPRISED, thrown, shocked, stunned, confused, astonished, staggered, startled, bewildered, astounded, disconcerted, bowled over (*informal*), stupefied, floored (*informal*), knocked for six, dumbfounded, left open-mouthed, nonplussed, flabbergasted (*informal*)

abandon *verb* **1** LEAVE, strand, ditch, leave behind, walk out on, forsake, jilt, run out on, throw over, turn your back on, desert, dump, leave high and dry, leave in the lurch **2** STOP, drop, give up, halt, cease, cut out, pack in (*Brit informal*), discontinue, leave off, desist from << ANTONYM continue **3** GIVE UP, resign from, yield, surrender, relinquish, renounce, waive, cede, forgo, abdicate << ANTONYM keep **4** (takes *ship* as object) EVACUATE, quit, withdraw from, vacate, depart from << ANTONYM maintain ▷ *noun* RECKLESSNESS, dash, wildness, wantonness, unrestraint, careless freedom << ANTONYM restraint

abandoned *adjective* **1** UNOCCUPIED, empty, deserted, vacant, derelict, uninhabited << ANTONYM occupied **2** DESERTED, dropped, rejected, neglected, stranded, ditched, discarded, relinquished, left, forsaken, cast off, jilted, cast aside, cast out, cast away **3** UNINHIBITED, wild, uncontrolled, unbridled, unrestrained, unconstrained << ANTONYM inhibited

abandonment *noun* **1** DESERTION, leaving, forsaking, jilting **2** EVACUATION, leaving, quitting, departure, withdrawal **3** STOPPING, cessation, discontinuation **4** RENUNCIATION, giving up, surrender, waiver, abdication, cession, relinquishment

abate *verb* **1** DECREASE, decline, relax, ease, sink, fade, weaken, diminish, dwindle, lessen, slow, wane, subside, ebb, let up,

slacken, attenuate, taper off << ANTONYM increase **2** REDUCE, slow, relax, ease, relieve, moderate, weaken, dull, diminish, decrease, lessen, alleviate, quell, mitigate, attenuate << ANTONYM increase

abatement *noun* **1** DECREASE, slowing, decline, easing, sinking, fading, weakening, relaxation, dwindling, lessening, waning, subsiding, ebbing, cessation, let-up, slackening, diminution, tapering off, attenuation **2** REDUCTION, slowing, relief, easing, weakening, dulling, decrease, lessening, cutback, quelling, moderation, remission, slackening, mitigation, diminution, curtailment, alleviation, attenuation, extenuation

abattoir *noun* SLAUGHTERHOUSE, shambles, butchery

abbey *noun* MONASTERY, convent, priory, cloister, nunnery, friary

abbreviate *verb* SHORTEN, reduce, contract, trim, cut, prune, summarize, compress, condense, abridge << ANTONYM expand

abbreviated *adjective* SHORTENED, shorter, reduced, brief, potted, trimmed, pruned, cut, summarized, compressed, concise, condensed, abridged << ANTONYM expanded

abbreviation *noun* SHORTENING, reduction, résumé, trimming, summary, contraction, compression, synopsis, précis, abridgment

abdicate *verb* **1** RESIGN, retire, quit, step down (*informal*) **2** GIVE UP, yield, hand over, surrender, relinquish, renounce, waive, vacate, cede, abjure **3** RENOUNCE, give up, abandon, surrender, relinquish, waive, forgo, abnegate

abdication *noun* **1** RESIGNATION, quitting, retirement, retiral (*chiefly Scot*) **2** GIVING UP, yielding, surrender, waiving, renunciation, cession, relinquishment, abjuration

abdomen *noun* STOMACH, guts (*slang*), belly, tummy (*informal*), midriff, midsection, makutu (*NZ*), puku (*NZ*)

abdominal *adjective* GASTRIC, intestinal, visceral

abduct *verb* KIDNAP, seize, carry off, run off with, run away with, make off with, snatch (*slang*)

abduction *noun* KIDNAPPING, seizure, carrying off

aberrant *adjective* 1 ABNORMAL, odd, strange, extraordinary, curious, weird, peculiar, eccentric, queer, irregular, erratic, deviant, off-the-wall (*slang*), oddball (*informal*), anomalous, untypical, wacko (*slang*), outré, daggy (*Austral & NZ informal*) 2 DEPRAVED, corrupt, perverted, perverse, degenerate, deviant, debased, debauched

aberration *noun* ANOMALY, exception, defect, abnormality, inconsistency, deviation, quirk, peculiarity, divergence, departure, irregularity, incongruity

abet *verb* 1 HELP, aid, encourage, sustain, assist, uphold, back, second, incite, egg on, succour 2 ENCOURAGE, further, forward, promote, urge, boost, prompt, spur, foster, incite, connive at

abetting *noun* HELP, backing, support, aid, assistance, encouragement, abetment, abettal

abeyance *noun* ▷▷ in abeyance SHELVED, pending, on ice (*informal*), in cold storage (*informal*), hanging fire, suspended

abhor *verb* HATE, loathe, despise, detest, shrink from, shudder at, recoil from, be repelled by, have an aversion to, abominate, execrate, regard with repugnance *or* horror << ANTONYM love

abhorrent *adjective* HATEFUL, hated, offensive, disgusting, horrible, revolting, obscene, distasteful, horrid, repellent, obnoxious, despicable, repulsive, heinous, odious, repugnant, loathsome, abominable, execrable, detestable

abide *verb* 1 TOLERATE, suffer, accept, bear, endure, brook, hack (*slang*), put up with, take, stand, stomach, thole (*Scot*) 2 LAST, continue, remain, survive, carry on, endure, persist, keep on ▷▷ abide by something OBEY, follow, agree to, carry out, observe, fulfil, stand by, act on, comply with, hold to, heed, submit to, conform to, keep to, adhere to, mind

abiding *adjective* ENDURING, lasting, continuing, remaining, surviving, permanent, constant, prevailing, persisting, persistent, eternal, tenacious, firm, fast, everlasting, unending, unchanging << ANTONYM brief

ability *noun* 1 CAPABILITY, power, potential, facility, capacity, qualification, competence, proficiency, competency, potentiality << ANTONYM inability 2 SKILL, talent, know-how (*informal*), gift, expertise, faculty, flair, competence, energy, accomplishment, knack, aptitude, proficiency, dexterity, cleverness, potentiality, adroitness, adeptness

abject *adjective* 1 WRETCHED, miserable, hopeless, dismal, outcast, pitiful, forlorn, deplorable, pitiable 2 SERVILE, humble, craven, cringing, fawning, submissive, grovelling, subservient, slavish, mean, low, obsequious << ANTONYM dignified 3 DESPICABLE, base, degraded, worthless, vile, sordid, debased, reprehensible, contemptible, dishonourable, ignoble, detestable, scungy (*Austral & NZ*)

ablaze *adjective* 1 ON FIRE, burning, flaming, blazing, fiery, alight, aflame, afire 2 BRIGHT, brilliant, flashing, glowing, sparkling, illuminated, gleaming, radiant, luminous, incandescent, aglow 3 PASSIONATE, excited, stimulated, fierce, enthusiastic, aroused, animated, frenzied, fervent, impassioned, fervid

able *adjective* CAPABLE, experienced, fit, skilled, expert, powerful, masterly, effective, qualified, talented, gifted, efficient, clever, practised, accomplished, competent, skilful, adept, masterful, strong, proficient, adroit, highly endowed << ANTONYM incapable

able-bodied *adjective* STRONG, firm, sound, fit, powerful, healthy, strapping, hardy, robust, vigorous, sturdy, hale, stout, staunch, hearty, lusty, right as rain (*Brit informal*), tough, capable, sturdy, Herculean, fighting fit, sinewy, fit as a fiddle << ANTONYM weak

abnormal *adjective* UNUSUAL, different, odd, strange, surprising, extraordinary, remarkable, bizarre, unexpected, curious, weird, exceptional, peculiar, eccentric, unfamiliar, queer, irregular, phenomenal, uncommon, erratic, monstrous, singular, unnatural, deviant, unconventional, off-the-wall (*slang*), oddball (*informal*), out of the ordinary, left-field (*informal*), anomalous, atypical, aberrant, untypical, wacko (*slang*), outré, daggy (*Austral & NZ informal*) << ANTONYM normal

abnormality *noun* 1 STRANGENESS, deviation, eccentricity, aberration, peculiarity, idiosyncrasy, irregularity, weirdness, singularity, oddness, waywardness, unorthodoxy, unexpectedness, queerness, unnaturalness, bizarreness, unusualness, extraordinariness, aberrance, atypicalness, uncommonness, untypicalness, curiousness 2 ANOMALY, flaw, rarity, deviation, oddity, aberration, exception, peculiarity, deformity, monstrosity, irregularity, malformation

abnormally *adverb* UNUSUALLY, oddly, strangely, extremely, exceptionally, extraordinarily, overly, excessively, peculiarly, particularly, bizarrely, disproportionately, singularly, fantastically, unnaturally, uncannily, inordinately, uncommonly, prodigiously, freakishly, atypically, subnormally, supernormally

abode *noun* HOME, house, quarters, lodging, pad (*slang*), residence, habitat, dwelling, habitation, domicile, dwelling place

abolish *verb* DO AWAY WITH, end, destroy, eliminate, shed, cancel, axe (*informal*), get rid of, ditch (*slang*), dissolve, junk (*informal*), suppress, overturn, throw out, discard, wipe out, overthrow, void, terminate, drop, trash (*slang*), repeal, eradicate, put an end to, quash, extinguish, dispense with, revoke, stamp out, obliterate, subvert, jettison, repudiate, annihilate, rescind, exterminate, invalidate, bring to an end, annul, nullify, blot out, expunge, abrogate, vitiate, extirpate, kennet (*Austral slang*), jeff (*Austral slang*) << ANTONYM establish

abolition *noun* ERADICATION, ending, end, withdrawal, destruction, removal, overturning, wiping out, overthrow, voiding, extinction, repeal, elimination, cancellation, suppression, quashing, termination, stamping out, subversion, extermination, annihilation, blotting out, repudiation, erasure, annulment, obliteration, revocation, effacement, nullification, abrogation, rescission, extirpation, invalidation, vitiation, expunction

abominable *adjective* DETESTABLE, shocking, terrible, offensive, foul, disgusting, horrible, revolting, obscene, vile, horrid, repellent, atrocious, obnoxious, despicable, repulsive, base, heinous, hellish, odious, hateful, repugnant, reprehensible, loathsome, abhorrent, contemptible, villainous, nauseous, wretched, accursed, execrable, godawful (*slang*) << ANTONYM pleasant

abomination *noun* 1 OUTRAGE, bête noire, horror, evil, shame, plague, curse, disgrace, crime, atrocity, torment, anathema, barbarism, bugbear 2 HATRED, hate, horror, disgust, dislike, loathing, distaste, animosity, aversion, revulsion, antagonism, antipathy, enmity, ill will, animus, abhorrence, repugnance, odium, detestation, execration

aboriginal *adjective* INDIGENOUS, first, earliest, original, primary, ancient, native, primitive, pristine, primordial, primeval, autochthonous

aborigine *noun* ORIGINAL INHABITANT, native, aboriginal, indigene

abort *verb* 1 TERMINATE (*a pregnancy*), miscarry 2 STOP, end, finish, check, arrest, halt, cease, bring *or* come to a halt *or* standstill, axe (*informal*), pull up, terminate, call off, break off, cut short, pack in (*Brit informal*), discontinue, desist

abortion *noun* 1 TERMINATION, feticide, aborticide, miscarriage, deliberate miscarriage 2 FAILURE, disappointment, fiasco, misadventure, vain effort 3 MONSTROSITY

abortive *adjective* FAILED, failing, useless, vain, unsuccessful, idle, ineffective, futile, fruitless, unproductive, ineffectual, miscarried, unavailing, bootless

abound *verb* BE PLENTIFUL, thrive, flourish, be numerous, proliferate, be abundant, be thick on the ground, superabound ▷▷ **abound with** *or* **in something** OVERFLOW WITH, be packed with, teem with, be crowded with, swell with, crawl with, swarm with, be jammed with, be infested with, be thronged with, luxuriate with

about *preposition* 1 REGARDING, on, re, concerning, touching, dealing with, respecting, referring to, relating to, concerned with, connected with, relative to, with respect to, as regards, anent (*Scot*) 2 AROUND, over, through, round, throughout, all over 3 NEAR, around, close to, bordering, nearby, beside, close by, adjacent to, just round the corner from, in the neighbourhood of, alongside of, contiguous to, within sniffing distance of (*informal*), at close quarters to, a hop, skip and a jump away from (*informal*) ▷ *adverb* 1 APPROXIMATELY, around, almost, nearing, nearly, approaching, close to, roughly, just about, more or less, in the region of, in the vicinity of, not far off 2 EVERYWHERE, around, all over, here and there, on all sides, in all directions, to and fro, from place to place, hither and thither ▷▷ **about to** ON THE POINT OF, ready to, intending to, on the verge or brink of

about-turn noun CHANGE OF DIRECTION, reverse, reversal, turnaround, U-turn, right about (turn), about-face, volte-face, turnabout, paradigm shift ▷ verb CHANGE DIRECTION, reverse, about-face, volte-face, face the opposite direction, turn about or around, turn through 180 degrees, do or perform a U-turn or volte-face

above preposition 1 OVER, upon, beyond, on top of, exceeding, higher than, atop << ANTONYM under 2 SENIOR TO, over, ahead of, in charge of, higher than, surpassing, superior to, more powerful than << ANTONYM subordinate to 3 BEFORE, more than, rather than, beyond, instead of, sooner than, in preference to ▷ adverb OVERHEAD, upward, in the sky, on high, in heaven, atop, aloft, up above, skyward ▷ adjective PRECEDING, earlier, previous, prior, foregoing, aforementioned, aforesaid

abrasion noun 1 (medical) GRAZE, scratch, trauma (pathology), scrape, scuff, chafe, surface injury 2 RUBBING, wear, scratching, scraping, grating, friction, scouring, attrition, corrosion, wearing down, erosion, scuffing, chafing, grinding down, wearing away, abrading

abrasive adjective 1 HARSH, cutting, biting, tough, sharp, severe, bitter, rough, hard, nasty, cruel, annoying, brutal, stern, irritating, unpleasant, grating, abusive, galling, unkind, hurtful, caustic, vitriolic, pitiless, unfeeling, comfortless 2 ROUGH, scratching, scraping, grating, scuffing, chafing, scratchy, frictional, erosive ▷ noun SCOURER, grinder, burnisher, scarifier, abradant

abreast adverb ALONGSIDE, level, beside, in a row, side by side, neck and neck, shoulder to shoulder ▷▷ **abreast of** or **with** INFORMED ABOUT, in touch with, familiar with, acquainted with, up to date with, knowledgeable about, conversant with, up to speed with (informal), in the picture about, au courant with, au fait with, keeping your finger on the pulse of

abridge verb SHORTEN, reduce, contract, trim, clip, diminish, decrease, abstract, digest, cut down, cut back, cut, prune, concentrate, lessen, summarize, compress, curtail, condense, abbreviate, truncate, epitomize, downsize, précis, synopsize (US) << ANTONYM expand

abridged adjective SHORTENED, shorter, reduced, brief, potted (informal), trimmed, diminished, pruned, summarized, cut, compressed, curtailed, concise, condensed, abbreviated << ANTONYM expanded

abroad adverb 1 OVERSEAS, out of the country, beyond the sea, in foreign lands 2 ABOUT, everywhere, circulating, at large, here and there, current, all over, in circulation

abrupt adjective 1 SUDDEN, unexpected, hurried, rapid, surprising, quick, swift, rash, precipitate, hasty, impulsive, headlong, unforeseen, unanticipated << ANTONYM slow 2 CURT, direct, brief, sharp, rough, short, clipped, blunt, rude, tart, impatient, brisk, concise, snappy, terse, gruff, succinct, pithy, brusque, offhand, impolite, monosyllabic, ungracious, discourteous, uncivil, unceremonious, snappish << ANTONYM polite 3 STEEP, sharp, sheer, sudden, precipitous << ANTONYM gradual

abruptly adverb 1 SUDDENLY, short, unexpectedly, all of a sudden, hastily, precipitately, all at once, hurriedly << ANTONYM gradually 2 CURTLY, bluntly, rudely, briskly, tersely, shortly, sharply, brusquely, gruffly, snappily << ANTONYM politely

abscess noun BOIL, infection, swelling, blister, ulcer, inflammation, gathering, whitlow, blain, carbuncle, pustule, bubo, furuncle (pathology), gumboil, parulis (pathology)

abscond verb ESCAPE, flee, get away, bolt, fly, disappear, skip, run off, slip away, clear out, flit (informal), make off, break free or out, decamp, hook it (slang), do a runner (slang), steal away, sneak away, do a bunk (Brit slang), fly the coop (US & Canad informal), skedaddle (informal), take a powder (US & Canad slang), go on the lam (US & Canad slang), make your getaway, do a Skase (Austral informal), make or effect your escape

absence noun 1 TIME OFF, leave, break, vacation, recess, truancy, absenteeism, nonappearance, nonattendance 2 LACK, deficiency, deprivation, omission, scarcity, want, need, shortage, dearth, privation, unavailability, nonexistence

absent adjective 1 AWAY, missing, gone, lacking, elsewhere, unavailable, not present, truant, nonexistent, nonattendant << ANTONYM present 2 ABSENT-MINDED, blank, unconscious, abstracted, vague, distracted, unaware, musing, vacant, preoccupied, empty, absorbed, bemused, oblivious, dreamy, daydreaming, faraway, unthinking, heedless, inattentive, unheeding << ANTONYM alert ▷▷ **absent yourself** STAY AWAY, withdraw, depart, keep away, truant, abscond, play truant, slope off (*informal*), bunk off (*slang*), remove yourself

absentee *noun* NONATTENDER, stay-at-home, truant, no-show, stayaway

absent-minded *adjective* FORGETFUL, absorbed, abstracted, vague, absent, distracted, unaware, musing, preoccupied, careless, bemused, oblivious, dreamy, faraway, engrossed, unthinking, neglectful, heedless, inattentive, unmindful, unheeding, apt to forget, in a brown study, ditzy *or* ditsy (*slang*) << ANTONYM alert

absolute *adjective* 1 COMPLETE, total, perfect, entire, pure, sheer, utter, outright, thorough, downright, consummate, unqualified, full-on (*informal*), out-and-out, unadulterated, unmitigated, dyed-in-the-wool, thoroughgoing, unalloyed, unmixed, arrant, deep-dyed (*usually derogatory*) 2 SUPREME, sovereign, unlimited, ultimate, full, utmost, unconditional, unqualified, predominant, superlative, unrestricted, pre-eminent, unrestrained, tyrannical, peerless, unsurpassed, unquestionable, matchless, peremptory, unbounded 3 AUTOCRATIC, supreme, unlimited, autonomous, arbitrary, dictatorial, all-powerful, imperious, domineering, tyrannical, despotic, absolutist, tyrannous, autarchical 4 DEFINITE, sure, certain, positive, guaranteed, actual, assured, genuine, exact, precise, decisive, conclusive, unequivocal, unambiguous, infallible, categorical, unquestionable, dinkum (*Austral & NZ informal*), nailed-on (*slang*)

absolutely *adverb* 1 COMPLETELY, totally, perfectly, quite, fully, entirely, purely, altogether, thoroughly, wholly, utterly, consummately, every inch, to the hilt, a hundred per cent, one hundred per cent, unmitigatedly, lock, stock and barrel << ANTONYM somewhat 2 DEFINITELY, surely, certainly, clearly, obviously, plainly, truly, precisely, exactly, genuinely, positively, decidedly, decisively, without doubt, unquestionably, undeniably, categorically, without question, unequivocally, conclusively, unambiguously, beyond any doubt, infallibly

absolution *noun* FORGIVENESS, release, freedom, liberation, discharge, amnesty, mercy, pardon, indulgence, exemption, acquittal, remission, vindication, deliverance, dispensation, exoneration, exculpation, shriving, condonation

absolve *verb* EXCUSE, free, clear, release, deliver, loose, forgive, discharge, liberate, pardon, exempt, acquit, vindicate, remit, let off, set free, exonerate, exculpate << ANTONYM condemn

absorb *verb* 1 SOAK UP, drink in, devour, suck up, receive, digest, imbibe, ingest, osmose 2 ENGROSS, hold, involve, fill, arrest, fix, occupy, engage, fascinate, preoccupy, engulf, fill up, immerse, rivet, captivate, monopolize, enwrap

absorbed *adjective* ENGROSSED, lost, involved, fixed, concentrating, occupied, engaged, gripped, fascinated, caught up, intrigued, wrapped up, preoccupied, immersed, riveted, captivated, enthralled, rapt, up to your ears

absorbent *adjective* POROUS, receptive, imbibing, spongy, permeable, absorptive, blotting, penetrable, pervious, assimilative

absorbing *adjective* FASCINATING, interesting, engaging, gripping, arresting, compelling, intriguing, enticing, preoccupying, enchanting, seductive, riveting, captivating, alluring, bewitching, engrossing, spellbinding << ANTONYM boring

absorption *noun* 1 SOAKING UP, consumption, digestion, sucking up, osmosis 2 IMMERSION, holding, involvement, concentration, occupation, engagement, fascination, preoccupation, intentness, captivation, raptness

abstain from *verb* REFRAIN FROM, avoid, decline, give up, stop, refuse, cease, do without, shun, renounce, eschew, leave off, keep from, forgo, withhold from, forbear, desist from, deny yourself, kick (*informal*) << ANTONYM abandon yourself to

abstention *noun* 1 ABSTAINING, non-voting, refusal to vote 2 ABSTINENCE, refraining, avoidance, forbearance, eschewal, desistance, nonindulgence

abstinence *noun* ABSTENTION, continence, temperance, self-denial, self-restraint, forbearance, refraining, avoidance, moderation, sobriety, asceticism, teetotalism, abstemiousness, soberness << ANTONYM self-indulgence

abstract *adjective* THEORETICAL, general,

complex, academic, intellectual, subtle, profound, philosophical, speculative, unrealistic, conceptual, indefinite, deep, separate, occult, hypothetical, generalized, impractical, arcane, notional, abstruse, recondite, theoretic, conjectural, unpractical, nonconcrete << ANTONYM actual ▷ *noun* SUMMARY, résumé, outline, extract, essence, summing-up, digest, epitome, rundown, condensation, compendium, synopsis, précis, recapitulation, review, abridgment << ANTONYM expansion ▷ *verb* EXTRACT, draw, pull, remove, separate, withdraw, isolate, pull out, take out, take away, detach, dissociate, pluck out << ANTONYM add

abstracted *adjective* PREOCCUPIED, withdrawn, remote, absorbed, intent, absent, distracted, unaware, wrapped up, bemused, immersed, oblivious, dreamy, daydreaming, faraway, engrossed, rapt, absent-minded, heedless, inattentive, distrait, woolgathering

abstraction *noun* 1 CONCEPT, thought, idea, view, theory, impression, formula, notion, hypothesis, generalization, theorem, generality 2 ABSENT-MINDEDNESS, musing, preoccupation, daydreaming, vagueness, remoteness, absence, inattention, dreaminess, obliviousness, absence of mind, pensiveness, woolgathering, distractedness, bemusedness

absurd *adjective* RIDICULOUS, crazy (*informal*), silly, incredible, outrageous, foolish, unbelievable, daft (*informal*), hilarious, ludicrous, meaningless, unreasonable, irrational, senseless, preposterous, laughable, funny, stupid, farcical, illogical, incongruous, comical, zany, idiotic, nonsensical, inane, dumb-ass (*slang*) << ANTONYM sensible

absurdity *noun* RIDICULOUSNESS, nonsense, folly, stupidity, foolishness, silliness, idiocy, irrationality, incongruity, meaninglessness, daftness (*informal*), senselessness, illogicality, ludicrousness, unreasonableness, preposterousness, farcicality, craziness (*informal*), bêtise (*rare*), farcicalness, illogicalness

absurdly *adverb* RIDICULOUSLY, incredibly, unbelievably, foolishly, ludicrously, unreasonably, incongruously, laughably, irrationally, implausibly, preposterously, illogically, inanely, senselessly, idiotically, inconceivably, farcically

abundance *noun* 1 PLENTY, heap (*informal*),

bounty, exuberance, profusion, plethora, affluence, fullness, opulence, plenitude, fruitfulness, copiousness, ampleness, cornucopia, plenteousness, plentifulness << ANTONYM shortage 2 WEALTH, money, funds, capital, cash, riches, resources, assets, fortune, possessions, prosperity, big money, wad (*US & Canad slang*), affluence, big bucks (*informal, chiefly US*), opulence, megabucks (*US & Canad slang*), tidy sum (*informal*), lucre, pretty penny (*informal*), pelf, top whack (*informal*)

abundant *adjective* PLENTIFUL, full, rich, liberal, generous, lavish, ample, infinite, overflowing, exuberant, teeming, copious, inexhaustible, bountiful, luxuriant, profuse, rank, well-provided, well-supplied, bounteous, plenteous << ANTONYM scarce

abundantly *adverb* PLENTIFULLY, greatly, freely, amply, richly, liberally, fully, thoroughly, substantially, lavishly, extensively, generously, profusely, copiously, exuberantly, in plentiful supply, luxuriantly, unstintingly, bountifully, bounteously, plenteously, in great *or* large numbers << ANTONYM sparsely

abuse *noun* 1 MALTREATMENT, wrong, damage, injury, hurt, harm, spoiling, bullying, exploitation, oppression, imposition, mistreatment, manhandling, ill-treatment, rough handling 2 INSULTS, blame, slights, curses, put-downs, libel, censure, reproach, scolding, defamation, indignities, offence, tirade, derision, slander, rudeness, vilification, invective, swear words, opprobrium, insolence, upbraiding, aspersions, character assassination, disparagement, vituperation, castigation, contumely, revilement, traducement, calumniation 3 MISUSE, corruption, perversion, misapplication, misemployment, misusage ▷ *verb* 1 ILL-TREAT, wrong, damage, hurt, injure, harm, mar, oppress, maul, molest, impose upon, manhandle, rough up, brutalize, maltreat, handle roughly, knock about *or* around << ANTONYM care for 2 INSULT, injure, offend, curse, put down, smear, libel, slate (*informal, chiefly Brit*), slag (off) (*slang*), malign, scold, swear at, disparage, castigate, revile, vilify, slander, defame, upbraid, slight, inveigh against, call names, traduce, calumniate, vituperate << ANTONYM praise

abusive *adjective* 1 VIOLENT, wild, rough, cruel, savage, brutal, vicious, destructive, harmful, maddened, hurtful, unrestrained, impetuous, homicidal, intemperate, raging, furious, injurious, maniacal << ANTONYM kind 2 INSULTING, offensive, rude, degrading, scathing, maligning, scolding, affronting, contemptuous, disparaging, castigating, reviling, vilifying, invective, scurrilous, defamatory, insolent, derisive, censorious, slighting, libellous, upbraiding, vituperative, reproachful, slanderous, traducing, opprobrious, calumniating, contumelious << ANTONYM complimentary

abut *verb* ADJOIN, join, touch, border, neighbour, link to, attach to, combine with, connect with, couple with, communicate with, annex, meet, unite with, verge on, impinge, append, affix to

abysmal *adjective* DREADFUL, bad, terrible, awful, appalling, dismal, dire, ghastly, hideous, atrocious, godawful (*informal*)

abyss *noun* CHASM, gulf, split, crack, gap, pit, opening, breach, hollow, void, gorge, crater, cavity, ravine, cleft, fissure, crevasse, bottomless depth, abysm

academic *adjective* 1 SCHOLASTIC, school, university, college, educational, campus, collegiate 2 SCHOLARLY, learned, intellectual, literary, erudite, highbrow, studious, lettered 3 THEORETICAL, ideal, abstract, speculative, hypothetical, impractical, notional, conjectural ▷ *noun* SCHOLAR, intellectual, don, student, master, professor, fellow, pupil, lecturer, tutor, scholastic, bookworm, man of letters, egghead (*informal*), savant, academician, acca (*Austral slang*), bluestocking (*usually disparaging*), schoolman

academy *noun* COLLEGE, school, university, institution, institute, establishment, seminary, centre of learning, whare wananga (*NZ*)

accede to *verb* 1 AGREE TO, accept, grant, endorse, consent to, give in to, surrender to, yield to, concede to, acquiesce in, assent to, comply with, concur to 2 (takes *throne* as object) INHERIT, come to, assume, succeed, come into, attain, succeed to (*as heir*), enter upon, fall heir to

accelerate *verb* 1 INCREASE, grow, advance, extend, expand, build up, strengthen, raise, swell, intensify, enlarge, escalate, multiply, inflate, magnify, proliferate, snowball << ANTONYM fall 2 EXPEDITE, press, forward, promote, spur, further, stimulate, hurry, step up (*informal*), speed up, facilitate, hasten, precipitate, quicken << ANTONYM

delay 3 SPEED UP, speed, advance, quicken, get under way, gather momentum, get moving, pick up speed, put your foot down (*informal*), open up the throttle, put on speed << ANTONYM slow down

acceleration *noun* HASTENING, hurrying, stepping up (*informal*), expedition, speeding up, stimulation, advancement, promotion, spurring, quickening

accent *noun* PRONUNCIATION, tone, articulation, inflection, brogue, intonation, diction, modulation, elocution, enunciation, accentuation ▷ *verb* EMPHASIZE, stress, highlight, underline, bring home, underscore, accentuate, give emphasis to, call *or* draw attention to

accentuate *verb* EMPHASIZE, stress, highlight, accent, underline, bring home, underscore, foreground, give emphasis to, call *or* draw attention to << ANTONYM minimize

accept *verb* 1 RECEIVE, take, gain, pick up, secure, collect, have, get, obtain, acquire 2 TAKE ON, try, begin, attempt, bear, assume, tackle, acknowledge, undertake, embark on, set about, commence, avow, enter upon << ANTONYM reject 3 ACKNOWLEDGE, believe, allow, admit, adopt, approve, recognize, yield, concede, swallow (*informal*), buy (*slang*), affirm, profess, consent to, buy into (*slang*), cooperate with, take on board, accede, acquiesce, concur with 4 STAND, take, experience, suffer, bear, allow, weather, cope with, tolerate, sustain, put up with, wear (*Brit slang*), stomach, endure, undergo, brook, hack (*slang*), abide, withstand, bow to, yield to, countenance, like it or lump it (*informal*)

acceptability *noun* ADEQUACY, fitness, suitability, propriety, appropriateness, admissibility, permissibility, acceptableness, satisfactoriness << ANTONYM unacceptability

acceptable *adjective* 1 SATISFACTORY, fair, all right, suitable, sufficient, good enough, standard, adequate, so-so (*informal*), tolerable, up to scratch (*informal*), passable, up to the mark << ANTONYM unsatisfactory 2 PLEASANT, pleasing, welcome, satisfying, grateful, refreshing, delightful, gratifying, agreeable, pleasurable

acceptance *noun* 1 ACCEPTING, taking, receiving, obtaining, acquiring, reception, receipt 2 ACKNOWLEDGEMENT, agreement, belief, approval, recognition, admission, consent, consensus, adoption, affirmation, assent, credence, accession, approbation, concurrence, accedence, stamp *or* seal of approval **3** TAKING ON, admission, assumption, acknowledgement, undertaking, avowal **4** SUBMISSION, yielding, resignation, concession, compliance, deference, passivity, acquiescence

accepted *adjective* AGREED, received, common, standard, established, traditional, confirmed, regular, usual, approved, acknowledged, recognized, sanctioned, acceptable, universal, authorized, customary, agreed upon, time-honoured << ANTONYM unconventional

access *noun* **1** ADMISSION, entry, passage, entrée, admittance, ingress **2** ENTRANCE, road, door, approach, entry, path, gate, opening, way in, passage, avenue, doorway, gateway, portal, passageway

accessibility *noun* **1** APPROACHABILITY, availability, readiness, nearness, handiness **2** AVAILABILITY, possibility, attainability, obtainability

accessible *adjective* HANDY, near, nearby, at hand, within reach, at your fingertips, reachable, achievable, get-at-able (*informal*), a hop, skip and a jump away << ANTONYM inaccessible

accession *noun* ▷▷ **accession to** SUCCESSION TO, attainment of, inheritance of, elevation to, taking up of, assumption of, taking over of, taking on of

accessory *noun* **1** EXTRA, addition, supplement, convenience, attachment, add-on, component, extension, adjunct, appendage, appurtenance **2** ACCOMPLICE, partner, ally, associate (*in crime*), assistant, helper, colleague, collaborator, confederate, henchman, abettor ▷ *adjective* SUPPLEMENTARY, extra, additional, accompanying, secondary, subordinate, complementary, auxiliary, abetting, supplemental, contributory, ancillary

accident *noun* **1** CRASH, smash, wreck, collision, pile-up (*informal*), smash-up (*informal*) **2** MISFORTUNE, blow, disaster, tragedy, setback, calamity, mishap, misadventure, mischance, stroke of bad luck **3** CHANCE, fortune, luck, fate, hazard, coincidence, fluke, fortuity

accidental *adjective* **1** UNINTENTIONAL, unexpected, incidental, unforeseen, unintended, unplanned, unpremeditated << ANTONYM deliberate **2** CHANCE, random, casual, unintentional, unintended, unplanned, fortuitous, inadvert ent,

serendipitous, unlooked-for, uncalculated, contingent

accidentally *adverb* UNINTENTIONALLY, casually, unexpectedly, incidentally, by accident, by chance, inadvertently, unwittingly, randomly, unconsciously, by mistake, haphazardly, fortuitously, adventitiously << ANTONYM deliberately

acclaim *verb* PRAISE, celebrate, honour, cheer, admire, hail, applaud, compliment, salute, approve, congratulate, clap, pay tribute to, commend, exalt, laud, extol, crack up (*informal*), eulogize ▷ *noun* PRAISE, honour, celebration, approval, tribute, applause, cheering, clapping, ovation, accolades, plaudits, kudos, commendation, exaltation, approbation, acclamation, eulogizing, panegyric, encomium << ANTONYM criticism

acclaimed *adjective* CELEBRATED, famous, acknowledged, praised, outstanding, distinguished, admired, renowned, noted, highly rated, eminent, revered, famed, illustrious, well received, much vaunted, highly esteemed, much touted, well thought of, lionized, highly thought of << ANTONYM criticized

accolade *noun* **1** HONOUR, award, recognition, tribute **2** PRAISE, approval, acclaim, applause, compliment, homage, laud (*literary*), eulogy, congratulation, commendation, acclamation (*formal*), recognition, tribute, ovation, plaudit

accommodate *verb* **1** HOUSE, put up, take in, lodge, board, quarter, shelter, entertain, harbour, cater for, billet **2** HELP, support, aid, encourage, assist, befriend, cooperate with, abet, lend a hand to, lend a helping hand to, give a leg up to (*informal*) **3** ADAPT, match, fit, fashion, settle, alter, adjust, modify, compose, comply, accustom, reconcile, harmonize

accommodating *adjective* OBLIGING, willing, kind, friendly, helpful, polite, cooperative, agreeable, amiable, courteous, considerate, hospitable, unselfish, eager to please, complaisant << ANTONYM unhelpful

accommodation *noun* **1** HOUSING, homes, houses, board, quartering, quarters, digs (*Brit informal*), shelter, sheltering, lodging(s), dwellings **2** ADAPTATION, change, settlement, compromise, composition, adjustment, transformation, reconciliation, compliance, modification, alteration, conformity

accompaniment *noun* **1** BACKING MUSIC,

backing, support, obbligato **2** SUPPLEMENT, extra, addition, extension, companion, accessory, complement, decoration, frill, adjunct, appendage, adornment

accompany *verb* **1** GO WITH, lead, partner, protect, guide, attend, conduct, escort, shepherd, convoy, usher, chaperon **2** OCCUR WITH, belong to, come with, supplement, coincide with, join with, coexist with, go together with, follow, go cheek by jowl with

accompanying *adjective* ADDITIONAL, added, extra, related, associate, associated, joint, fellow, connected, attached, accessory, attendant, complementary, supplementary, supplemental, concurrent, concomitant, appended

accomplice *noun* PARTNER IN CRIME, ally, associate, assistant, companion, accessory, comrade, helper, colleague, collaborator, confederate, henchman, coadjutor, abettor

accomplish *verb* REALIZE, produce, effect, finish, complete, manage, achieve, perform, carry out, conclude, fulfil, execute, bring about, attain, consummate, bring off (*informal*), do, effectuate << ANTONYM fail

accomplished *adjective* SKILLED, able, professional, expert, masterly, talented, gifted, polished, practised, cultivated, skilful, adept, consummate, proficient << ANTONYM unskilled

accomplishment *noun* **1** ACHIEVEMENT, feat, attainment, act, stroke, triumph, coup, exploit, deed **2** *often plural* TALENT, ability, skill, gift, achievement, craft, faculty, capability, forte, attainment, proficiency **3** ACCOMPLISHING, effecting, finishing, carrying out, achievement, conclusion, bringing about, execution, completion, realization, fulfilment, attainment, consummation

accord *noun* **1** TREATY, contract, agreement, arrangement, settlement, pact, deal (*informal*) **2** SYMPATHY, agreement, concert, harmony, accordance, unison, rapport, conformity, assent, unanimity, concurrence << ANTONYM conflict ▷ *verb* GRANT, give, award, render, assign, present with, endow with, bestow on, confer on, vouchsafe, impart with << ANTONYM refuse ▷▷ **accord with something** AGREE WITH, match, coincide with, fit with, square with, correspond with, conform with, concur with, tally with, be in tune with (*informal*), harmonize with, assent with

accordance *noun* ▷▷ **in accordance with** IN AGREEMENT WITH, consistent with, in harmony with, in concert with, in sympathy with, in conformity with, in assent with, in congruence with

accordingly *adverb* **1** CONSEQUENTLY, so, thus, therefore, hence, subsequently, in consequence, ergo, as a result **2** APPROPRIATELY, correspondingly, properly, suitably, fitly

accost *verb* CONFRONT, challenge, address, stop, approach, oppose, halt, greet, hail, solicit (*as a prostitute*), buttonhole

account *noun* **1** DESCRIPTION, report, record, story, history, detail, statement, relation, version, tale, explanation, narrative, chronicle, portrayal, recital, depiction, narration **2** IMPORTANCE, standing, concern, value, note, benefit, use, profit, worth, weight, advantage, rank, import, honour, consequence, substance, merit, significance, distinction, esteem, usefulness, repute, momentousness **3** (*commerce*) LEDGER, charge, bill, statement, balance, tally, invoice, computation ▷ *verb* CONSIDER, rate, value, judge, estimate, think, hold, believe, count, reckon, assess, weigh, calculate, esteem, deem, compute, gauge, appraise, regard as ▷▷ **account for something 1** CONSTITUTE, make, make up, compose, comprise **2** EXPLAIN, excuse, justify, clarify, give a reason for, give an explanation for, illuminate, clear up, answer for, rationalize, elucidate **3** PUT OUT OF ACTION, kill, destroy, put paid to, incapacitate ▷▷ **on account of** BY REASON OF, because of, owing to, on the basis of, for the sake of, on the grounds of

accountability *noun* RESPONSIBILITY, liability, culpability, answerability, chargeability

accountable *adjective* ANSWERABLE, subject, responsible, obliged, liable, amenable, obligated, chargeable

accountant *noun* AUDITOR, book-keeper, bean counter (*informal*)

accounting *noun* ACCOUNTANCY, auditing, book-keeping

accoutrements *plural noun* PARAPHERNALIA, fittings, dress, material, clothing, stuff, equipment, tackle, gear, things, kit, outfit, trimmings, fixtures, array, decorations, baggage, apparatus, furnishings, trappings, garb, adornments, ornamentation, bells and whistles, impedimenta, appurtenances, equipage

accredit *verb* **1** APPROVE, support, back, commission, champion, favour, guarantee,

9

promote, recommend, appoint, recognize, sanction, advocate, license, endorse, warrant, authorize, ratify, empower, certify, entrust, vouch for, depute **2** ATTRIBUTE, credit, assign, ascribe, trace to, put down to, lay at the door of

accredited *adjective* AUTHORIZED, official, commissioned, guaranteed, appointed, recognized, sanctioned, licensed, endorsed, empowered, certified, vouched for, deputed, deputized

accrue *verb* ACCUMULATE, issue, increase, grow, collect, gather, flow, build up, enlarge, follow, ensue, pile up, amass, spring up, stockpile

accumulate *verb* BUILD UP, increase, grow, be stored, collect, gather, pile up, amass, stockpile, hoard, accrue, cumulate << ANTONYM disperse

accumulation *noun* **1** COLLECTION, increase, stock, store, mass, build-up, pile, stack, heap, rick, stockpile, hoard **2** GROWTH, collection, gathering, build-up, aggregation, conglomeration, augmentation

accuracy *noun* EXACTNESS, precision, fidelity, authenticity, correctness, closeness, truth, verity, nicety, veracity, faithfulness, truthfulness, niceness, exactitude, strictness, meticulousness, carefulness, scrupulousness, preciseness, faultlessness, accurateness << ANTONYM inaccuracy

accurate *adjective* **1** PRECISE, right, close, regular, correct, careful, strict, exact, faithful, explicit, authentic, spot-on, just, clear-cut, meticulous, truthful, faultless, scrupulous, unerring, veracious << ANTONYM inaccurate **2** CORRECT, right, true, exact, faithful, spot-on (*Brit informal*), faultless, on the money (*US*)

accurately *adverb* **1** PRECISELY, rightly, correctly, closely, carefully, truly, properly, strictly, literally, exactly, faithfully, meticulously, to the letter, justly, scrupulously, truthfully, authentically, unerringly, faultlessly, veraciously **2** EXACTLY, rightly, closely, correctly, definitely, truly, properly, precisely, nicely, strictly, faithfully, explicitly, unequivocally, scrupulously, truthfully

accusation *noun* CHARGE, complaint, allegation, indictment, impeachment, recrimination, citation, denunciation, attribution, imputation, arraignment, incrimination

accuse *verb* **1** POINT A *or* THE FINGER

AT, blame for, denounce, attribute to, hold responsible for, impute blame to << ANTONYM exonerate **2** CHARGE WITH, indict for, impeach for, arraign for, cite, tax with, censure with, incriminate for, recriminate for << ANTONYM absolve

accustom *verb* FAMILIARIZE, train, coach, discipline, adapt, instruct, make used, school, season, acquaint, inure, habituate, acclimatize, make conversant

accustomed *adjective* **1** USED, trained, familiar, disciplined, given to, adapted, acquainted, in the habit of, familiarized, seasoned, inured, habituated, exercised, acclimatized << ANTONYM unaccustomed **2** USUAL, established, expected, general, common, standard, set, traditional, normal, fixed, regular, ordinary, familiar, conventional, routine, everyday, customary, habitual, wonted << ANTONYM unusual

ace *noun* **1** (*cards, dice*) ONE, single point **2** (*informal*) EXPERT, star, champion, authority, winner, professional, master, pro (*informal*), specialist, genius, guru, buff (*informal*), wizard (*informal*), whizz (*informal*), virtuoso, connoisseur, hotshot (*informal*), past master, dab hand (*Brit informal*), maven (*US*) ▷ *adjective* (*informal*) GREAT, good, brilliant, mean (*slang*), fine, champion, expert, masterly, wonderful, excellent, cracking (*Brit informal*), outstanding, superb, fantastic (*informal*), tremendous (*informal*), marvellous (*informal*), terrific (*informal*), mega (*slang*), awesome (*slang*), dope (*slang*), admirable, virtuoso, first-rate, brill (*informal*), bitchin' (*US slang*), chillin' (*US slang*), booshit (*Austral slang*), exo (*Austral slang*), sik (*Austral slang*), ka pai (*NZ*), rad (*informal*), phat (*slang*), schmick (*Austral informal*)

acerbic *adjective* SHARP, cutting, biting, severe, acid, bitter, nasty, harsh, stern, rude, scathing, acrimonious, barbed, unkind, unfriendly, sarcastic, sardonic, caustic, churlish, vitriolic, trenchant, acrid, brusque, rancorous, mordant

ache *verb* **1** HURT, suffer, burn, pain, smart, sting, pound, throb, be tender, twinge, be sore **2** SUFFER, hurt, grieve, sorrow, agonize, be in pain, go through the mill (*informal*), mourn, feel wretched ▷ *noun* **1** PAIN, discomfort, suffering, hurt, smart, smarting, cramp, throb, throbbing, irritation, tenderness, pounding, spasm, pang, twinge, soreness, throe (*rare*) **2** ANGUISH, suffering, pain, torture, distress, grief, misery, mourning, torment, sorrow, woe, heartache, heartbreak

achievable *adjective* ATTAINABLE, obtainable, winnable, reachable, realizable, within your grasp, graspable, gettable, acquirable, possible, accessible, probable, feasible, practicable, accomplishable

achieve *verb* ACCOMPLISH, reach, fulfil, finish, complete, gain, perform, earn, do, get, win, carry out, realize, obtain, conclude, acquire, execute, bring about, attain, consummate, procure, bring off (*informal*), effectuate, put the tin lid on

achievement *noun* 1 ACCOMPLISHMENT, effort, feat, deed, stroke, triumph, coup, exploit, act, attainment, feather in your cap 2 FULFILMENT, effecting, performance, production, execution, implementation, completion, accomplishment, realization, attainment, acquirement, carrying out *or* through

achiever *noun* SUCCESS, winner, dynamo, high-flyer, doer, go-getter (*informal*), organizer, active person, overachiever, man *or* woman of action, wheeler-dealer (*informal*)

aching *adjective* 1 PAINFUL, suffering, hurting, tired, smarting, pounding, raw, tender, sore, throbbing, harrowing, inflamed, excruciating, agonizing 2 LONGING, anxious, eager, pining, hungering, craving, yearning, languishing, thirsting, ardent, avid, wishful, wistful, hankering, desirous

acid *adjective* 1 SOUR, sharp, tart, pungent, biting, acidic, acerbic, acrid, acetic, vinegary, acidulous, acidulated, vinegarish, acerb << ANTONYM sweet 2 SHARP, cutting, biting, severe, bitter, harsh, stinging, scathing, acrimonious, barbed, pungent, hurtful, sarcastic, sardonic, caustic, vitriolic, acerbic, trenchant, mordant, mordacious << ANTONYM kindly

acidity *noun* SOURNESS, bitterness, sharpness, pungency, tartness, acerbity, acridness, acidulousness, acridity, vinegariness, vinegarishness

acknowledge *verb* 1 ADMIT, own up, allow, accept, reveal, grant, declare, recognize, yield, concede, confess, disclose, affirm, profess, divulge, accede, acquiesce, 'fess up (*US slang*) << ANTONYM deny 2 GREET, address, notice, recognize, salute, nod to, accost, tip your hat to << ANTONYM snub 3 REPLY TO, answer, notice, recognize, respond to, come back to, react to, write

back to, retort to << ANTONYM ignore

acknowledged *adjective* ACCEPTED, admitted, established, confirmed, declared, approved, recognized, well-known, sanctioned, confessed, authorized, professed, accredited, agreed upon

acknowledgment *or* **acknowledgement** *noun* 1 RECOGNITION, allowing, understanding, yielding, profession, admission, awareness, acceptance, confession, realization, accession, acquiescence 2 GREETING, welcome, notice, recognition, reception, hail, hailing, salute, salutation 3 APPRECIATION, answer, thanks, credit, response, reply, reaction, recognition, gratitude, indebtedness, thankfulness, gratefulness

acme *noun* HEIGHT, top, crown, summit, peak, climax, crest, optimum, high point, pinnacle, culmination, zenith, apex, apogee, vertex << ANTONYM depths

acolyte *noun* 1 FOLLOWER, fan, supporter, pupil, convert, believer, admirer, backer, partisan, disciple, devotee, worshipper, apostle, cohort (*chiefly US*), adherent, henchman, habitué, votary 2 ATTENDANT, assistant, follower, helper, altar boy

acquaint *verb* TELL, reveal, advise, inform, communicate, disclose, notify, enlighten, divulge, familiarize, apprise, let (someone) know

acquaintance *noun* 1 ASSOCIATE, contact, ally, colleague, comrade, confrère << ANTONYM intimate 2 RELATIONSHIP, association, exchange, connection, intimacy, fellowship, familiarity, companionship, social contact, cognizance, conversance, conversancy << ANTONYM unfamiliarity

acquainted *adjective* ▷▷ **acquainted with** FAMILIAR WITH, aware of, in on, experienced in, conscious of, informed of, alive to, privy to, knowledgeable about, versed in, conversant with, apprised of, cognizant of, up to speed with, *au fait* with

acquiesce *verb* SUBMIT, agree, accept, approve, yield, bend, surrender, consent, tolerate, comply, give in, conform, succumb, go along with, bow to, cave in (*informal*), concur, assent, capitulate, accede, play ball (*informal*), toe the line, hoist the white flag << ANTONYM resist

acquiescence *noun* AGREEMENT, yielding, approval, acceptance, consent, harmony, giving in, submission, compliance, obedience, conformity, assent, accession, concord, concurrence

acquire *verb* GET, win, buy, receive, land, score (*slang*), gain, achieve, earn, pick up, bag, secure, collect, gather, realize, obtain, attain, amass, procure, come into possession of << ANTONYM lose

acquisition *noun* **1** ACQUIRING, gaining, achievement, procurement, attainment, acquirement, obtainment **2** PURCHASE, buy, investment, property, gain, prize, asset, possession

acquisitive *adjective* GREEDY, grabbing, grasping, hungry, selfish, avid, predatory, rapacious, avaricious, desirous, covetous << ANTONYM generous

acquit *verb* **1** CLEAR, free, release, deliver, excuse, relieve, discharge, liberate, vindicate, exonerate, absolve, exculpate << ANTONYM find guilty ▷▷ **acquit yourself** BEHAVE, bear yourself, conduct yourself, comport yourself

acquittal *noun* CLEARANCE, freeing, release, relief, liberation, discharge, pardon, setting free, vindication, deliverance, absolution, exoneration, exculpation

acrid *adjective* **1** PUNGENT, biting, strong, burning, sharp, acid, bitter, harsh, stinging, irritating, caustic, astringent, vitriolic, highly flavoured, acerb **2** HARSH, cutting, biting, sharp, bitter, nasty, acrimonious, caustic, vitriolic, trenchant, mordant, mordacious

acrimonious *adjective* BITTER, cutting, biting, sharp, severe, hostile, crabbed, sarcastic, embittered, caustic, petulant, spiteful, churlish, astringent, vitriolic, acerbic, trenchant, irascible, testy, censorious, rancorous, mordant, peevish, splenetic, mordacious << ANTONYM good-tempered

acrimony *noun* BITTERNESS, harshness, rancour, ill will, virulence, sarcasm, pungency, asperity, tartness, astringency, irascibility, peevishness, acerbity, churlishness, trenchancy, mordancy << ANTONYM goodwill

acrobat *noun* GYMNAST, balancer, tumbler, tightrope walker, rope walker, funambulist

across *preposition* **1** OVER, on the other *or* far side of, past, beyond **2** THROUGHOUT, over, all over, right through, all through, covering, straddling, everywhere in, through the whole of, from end to end of, over the length and breadth of ▷ *adverb* FROM SIDE TO SIDE, athwart, transversely, crossways *or* crosswise

across-the-board *adjective* GENERAL, full, complete, total, sweeping, broad, widespread, comprehensive, universal, blanket, thorough, wholesale, panoramic, indiscriminate, all-inclusive, wall-to-wall, all-embracing, overarching, all-encompassing, thoroughgoing, without exception *or* omission, one-size-fits-all << ANTONYM limited

act *verb* **1** DO SOMETHING, perform, move, function, go about, conduct yourself, undertake something **2** PLAY, seem to be, pose as, pretend to be, posture as, imitate, sham, feign, characterize, enact, personify, impersonate, play the part of **3** PERFORM, mimic, mime ▷ *noun* **1** DEED, action, step, performance, operation, doing, move, blow, achievement, stroke, undertaking, exploit, execution, feat, accomplishment, exertion **2** PRETENCE, show, front, performance, display, attitude, pose, stance, fake, posture, façade, sham, veneer, counterfeit, feigning, affectation, dissimulation **3** LAW, bill, measure, resolution, decree, statute, ordinance, enactment, edict **4** PERFORMANCE, show, turn, production, routine, presentation, gig (*informal*), sketch ▷▷ **act for someone** STAND IN FOR, serve, represent, replace, substitute for, cover for, take the place of, fill in for, deputize for, function in place of ▷▷ **act on** *or* **upon something 1** OBEY, follow, carry out, observe, embrace, execute, comply with, heed, conform to, adhere to, abide by, yield to, act upon, be ruled by, act in accordance with, do what is expected **2** AFFECT, change, influence, impact, transform, alter, modify ▷▷ **act up** MISBEHAVE, carry on, cause trouble, mess about, be naughty, horse around (*informal*), give trouble, give someone grief (*Brit & S African*), give bother

acting *noun* PERFORMANCE, playing, performing, theatre, dramatics, portraying, enacting, portrayal, impersonation, characterization, stagecraft ▷ *adjective* TEMPORARY, substitute, intervening, interim, provisional, surrogate, stopgap, pro tem

action *noun* **1** DEED, move, act, performance, blow, exercise, achievement, stroke, undertaking, exploit, feat, accomplishment, exertion **2** MEASURE, act, step, operation, manoeuvre **3** LAWSUIT, case, cause, trial, suit, argument, proceeding, dispute, contest, prosecution, litigation **4** ENERGY, activity, spirit, force, vitality, vigour, liveliness, vim **5** EFFECT, working, work, force, power, process, effort, operation, activity, movement, influence, functioning, motion, exertion **6** BATTLE, war, fight, fighting, conflict, clash, contest, encounter, combat, engagement, hostilities, warfare, fray, skirmish, sortie, affray

activate *verb* START, move, trigger (off), stimulate, turn on, set off, initiate, switch on, propel, rouse, prod, get going, mobilize, kick-start (*informal*), set in motion, impel, galvanize, set going, actuate << ANTONYM stop

activation *noun* START, triggering, turning on, switching on, animation, arousal, initiation, mobilization, setting in motion, actuation

active *adjective* **1** BUSY, involved, occupied, engaged, tiring, lively, energetic, bustling, restless, on the move, strenuous, tireless, on the go (*informal*) << ANTONYM sluggish **2** ENERGETIC, strong, spirited, quick, vital, alert, dynamic, lively, vigorous, potent, animated, vibrant, forceful, nimble, diligent, industrious, sprightly, vivacious, on the go (*informal*), alive and kicking, spry, full of beans (*informal*), bright-eyed and bushy-tailed (*informal*) << ANTONYM inactive **3** IN OPERATION, working, live, running, moving, acting, functioning, stirring, at work, in business, in action, operative, in force, effectual, astir

activist *noun* MILITANT, partisan, organizer, warrior

activity *noun* **1** ACTION, work, life, labour, movement, energy, exercise, spirit, enterprise, motion, bustle, animation, vigour, hustle, exertion, hurly-burly, liveliness, activeness << ANTONYM inaction **2** PURSUIT, act, project, scheme, task, pleasure, interest, enterprise, undertaking, occupation, hobby, deed, endeavour, pastime, avocation

actor *or* **actress** *noun* PERFORMER, player, artiste, leading man *or* lady, Thespian, luvvie (*informal*), trouper, thesp (*informal*), play-actor, dramatic artist, tragedian *or* tragedienne

actual *adjective* **1** GENUINE, real, true, confirmed, authentic, verified, truthful, bona fide, dinkum (*Austral & NZ informal*) << ANTONYM unreal **2** REAL, substantial, concrete, definite, tangible << ANTONYM theoretical

actuality *noun* **1** REALITY, truth, substance, verity, materiality, realness, substantiality, factuality, corporeality **2** FACT, truth, reality, verity

actually *adverb* REALLY, in fact, indeed, essentially, truly, literally, genuinely, in reality, in truth, in actuality, in point of fact, veritably, as a matter of fact ▷ see **actual**

acumen *noun* JUDGMENT, intelligence, perception, wisdom, insight, wit, ingenuity, sharpness, cleverness, keenness, shrewdness, discernment, perspicacity, sagacity, smartness, smarts (*slang, chiefly US*), astuteness, acuteness, perspicuity

acute *adjective* **1** SERIOUS, important, dangerous, critical, crucial, alarming, severe, grave, sudden, urgent, decisive **2** SHARP, shooting, powerful, violent, severe, intense, overwhelming, distressing, stabbing, cutting, fierce, piercing, racking, exquisite, poignant, harrowing, overpowering, shrill, excruciating **3** PERCEPTIVE, sharp, keen, smart, sensitive, clever, subtle, piercing, penetrating, discriminating, discerning, ingenious, astute, intuitive, canny, incisive, insightful, observant, perspicacious << ANTONYM slow

adage *noun* SAYING, motto, maxim, proverb, dictum, precept, by-word, saw, axiom, aphorism, apophthegm

adamant *adjective* DETERMINED, firm, fixed, stiff, rigid, set, relentless, stubborn, uncompromising, insistent, resolute, inflexible, unrelenting, inexorable, unyielding, intransigent, immovable, unbending, obdurate, unshakable << ANTONYM flexible

adapt *verb* **1** ADJUST, change, match, alter, modify, accommodate, comply, conform, reconcile, harmonize, familiarize, habituate, acclimatize **2** CONVERT, change, prepare, fit, fashion, make, shape, suit, qualify, transform, alter, modify, tailor, remodel, tweak (*informal*), metamorphose, customize

adaptability *noun* FLEXIBILITY, versatility, resilience, variability, convertibility, plasticity, malleability, pliability, changeability, pliancy, adjustability, compliancy, modifiability, adaptableness, alterability

adaptable *adjective* **1** FLEXIBLE, variable, versatile, resilient, easy-going, changeable, modifiable, conformable **2** ADJUSTABLE, flexible, compliant, malleable, pliant, plastic, modifiable, alterable

adaptation *noun* **1** ACCLIMATIZATION, naturalization, habituation, familiarization, accustomedness **2** CONVERSION, change, shift, variation, adjustment, transformation, modification, alteration, remodelling, reworking, refitting

add *verb* **1** COUNT UP, total, reckon, sum up, compute, add up, tot up << ANTONYM take away **2** INCLUDE, attach, supplement, increase by, adjoin, annex, amplify, augment, affix, append, enlarge by ▷▷ **add to something** INCREASE, boost, expand, strengthen, enhance, step up (*informal*), intensify, raise, advance, spread, extend, heighten, enlarge, escalate, multiply, inflate, magnify, amplify, augment, proliferate ▷▷ **add up 1** COUNT UP, add, total, count, reckon, calculate, sum up, compute, tally, tot up, add together **2** MAKE SENSE, hold up, be reasonable, ring true, be plausible, stand to reason, hold water, bear examination, bear investigation ▷▷ **add up to something** MEAN, reveal, indicate, imply, amount to, signify

addict *noun* **1** JUNKIE (*informal*), abuser, user (*informal*), druggie (*informal*), freak (*informal*), fiend (*informal*), mainliner (*slang*), smackhead (*slang*), space cadet (*slang*), pill-popper (*informal*), head (*slang*), pothead (*slang*), dope-fiend (*slang*), cokehead (*slang*), acidhead (*slang*), hashhead (*slang*) **2** FAN, lover, nut (*slang*), follower, enthusiast, freak (*informal*), admirer, buff (*informal*), junkie (*informal*), devotee, fiend (*informal*), adherent, rooter (*US*), zealot, groupie (*slang*), aficionado

addicted *adjective* HOOKED, dependent

addiction *noun* **1** DEPENDENCE, need, habit, weakness, obsession, attachment, craving, vulnerability, subordination, enslavement, subservience, overreliance **2** *with* **to** LOVE OF, passion for, attachment to, fondness for, zeal for, fervour for, ardour for

addictive *adjective* HABIT-FORMING, compelling, compulsive, causing addiction *or* dependency, moreish *or* morish (*informal*)

addition *noun* **1** EXTRA, supplement, complement, adjunct, increase, gain, bonus, extension, accessory, additive, appendix, increment, appendage, addendum **2** INCLUSION, adding, increasing, extension, attachment, adjoining, insertion, incorporation, annexation, accession, affixing, augmentation << ANTONYM removal **3** COUNTING UP, totalling, reckoning, summing up, adding up, computation, totting up, summation << ANTONYM subtraction ▷▷ **in addition to** AS WELL AS, along with, on top of, besides,

to boot, additionally, over and above, to say nothing of, into the bargain

additional *adjective* EXTRA, more, new, other, added, increased, further, fresh, spare, supplementary, auxiliary, ancillary, appended

additive *noun* ADDED INGREDIENT, artificial *or* synthetic ingredient, E number, extra, supplement

addled *adjective* CONFUSED, silly, foolish, at sea, bewildered, mixed-up, muddled, perplexed, flustered, befuddled

address *noun* **1** DIRECTION, label, inscription, superscription **2** LOCATION, home, place, house, point, position, situation, site, spot, venue, lodging, pad (*slang*), residence, dwelling, whereabouts, abode, locus, locale, domicile **3** SPEECH, talk, lecture, discourse, sermon, dissertation, harangue, homily, oration, spiel (*informal*), disquisition, korero (*NZ*) ▷ *verb* **1** GIVE A SPEECH TO, talk to, speak to, lecture, discourse, harangue, give a talk to, spout to, hold forth to, expound to, orate to, sermonize to **2** SPEAK TO, talk to, greet, hail, salute, invoke, communicate with, accost, approach, converse with, apostrophize ▷▷ **address yourself to something** CONCENTRATE ON, turn to, focus on, take up, look to, undertake, engage in, take care of, attend to, knuckle down to, devote yourself to, apply yourself to

adept *adjective* SKILFUL, able, skilled, expert, masterly, practised, accomplished, versed, masterful, proficient, adroit, dexterous << ANTONYM unskilled ▷ *noun* EXPERT, master, genius, buff (*informal*), whizz (*informal*), hotshot (*informal*), rocket scientist (*informal, chiefly US*), dab hand (*Brit informal*), maven (*US*)

adequacy *noun* SUFFICIENCY, capability, competence, suitability, tolerability, fairness, commensurateness, requisiteness, satisfactoriness

adequate *adjective* **1** PASSABLE, acceptable, middling, average, fair, ordinary, moderate, satisfactory, competent, mediocre, so-so (*informal*), tolerable, up to scratch (*informal*), presentable, unexceptional << ANTONYM inadequate **2** SUFFICIENT, enough, capable, suitable, requisite << ANTONYM insufficient

adherent *noun* SUPPORTER, fan, advocate, follower, admirer, partisan, disciple, protagonist, devotee, henchman, hanger-on, upholder, sectary << ANTONYM opponent ▷ *adjective* ADHERING, holding, sticking, clinging, sticky, tacky, adhesive, tenacious, glutinous, gummy, gluey, mucilaginous

adhere to *verb* 1 FOLLOW, keep, maintain, respect, observe, be true to, fulfil, obey, heed, keep to, abide by, be loyal to, mind, be constant to, be faithful to 2 BE FAITHFUL TO, follow, support, respect, observe, be true to, obey, be devoted to, be attached to, keep to, be loyal to 3 STICK TO, attach to, cling to, unite to, glue to, fix to, fasten to, hold fast to, paste to, cement to, cleave to, glue on to, stick fast to, cohere to

adhesion *noun* STICKING, grip, attachment, cohesion, coherence, adherence, adhesiveness

adhesive *noun* GLUE, cement, gum, paste, mucilage ▷ *adjective* STICKY, holding, sticking, attaching, clinging, adhering, tacky, cohesive, tenacious, glutinous, gummy, gluey, mucilaginous

ad hoc *adjective* MAKESHIFT, emergency, improvised, impromptu, expedient, stopgap, jury-rigged (*chiefly nautical*) << ANTONYM permanent

adjacent *adjective* ADJOINING, neighbouring, nearby, abutting << ANTONYM far away

adjoin *verb* CONNECT WITH *or* TO, join, neighbour (on), link with, attach to, combine with, couple with, communicate with, touch on, border on, annex, approximate, unite with, verge on, impinge on, append, affix to, interconnect with

adjoining *adjective* CONNECTING, nearby, joined, joining, touching, bordering, neighbouring, next door, adjacent, interconnecting, abutting, contiguous

adjourn *verb* POSTPONE, delay, suspend, interrupt, put off, stay, defer, recess, discontinue, put on the back burner (*informal*), prorogue, take a rain check on (*US & Canad informal*) << ANTONYM continue

adjournment *noun* POSTPONEMENT, delay, suspension, putting off, stay, recess, interruption, deferment, deferral, discontinuation, prorogation

adjudge *verb* JUDGE, determine, declare, decide, assign, pronounce, decree, apportion, adjudicate

adjudicate *verb* 1 DECIDE, judge, determine, settle, mediate, adjudge, arbitrate 2 JUDGE, referee, umpire

adjudication *noun* JUDGMENT, finding, ruling, decision, settlement, conclusion, verdict, determination, arbitration, pronouncement, adjudgment

adjudicator *noun* JUDGE, referee, umpire, umpie (*Austral slang*), arbiter, arbitrator, moderator

adjunct *noun* ADDITION, supplement, accessory, complement, auxiliary, add-on, appendage, addendum, appurtenance

adjust *verb* 1 ADAPT, change, settle, convert, alter, accommodate, dispose, get used, accustom, conform, reconcile, harmonize, acclimatize, familiarize yourself, attune 2 CHANGE, order, reform, fix, arrange, alter, adapt, revise, modify, set, regulate, amend, reconcile, remodel, redress, rectify, recast, customize, make conform 3 MODIFY, arrange, fix, tune (up), alter, adapt, remodel, tweak (*informal*), customize

adjustable *adjective* ALTERABLE, flexible, adaptable, malleable, movable, tractable, modifiable, mouldable

adjustment *noun* 1 ALTERATION, setting, change, ordering, fixing, arrangement, tuning, repair, conversion, modifying, adaptation, modification, remodelling, redress, refinement, rectification 2 ACCLIMATIZATION, settling in, orientation, familiarization, change, regulation, settlement, amendment, reconciliation, adaptation, accustoming, revision, modification, naturalization, acculturation, harmonization, habituation, acclimation, inurement

administer *verb* 1 MANAGE, run, control, rule, direct, handle, conduct, command, govern, oversee, supervise, preside over, be in charge of, superintend 2 DISPENSE, give, share, provide, apply, distribute, assign, allocate, allot, dole out, apportion, deal out 3 EXECUTE, do, give, provide, apply, perform, carry out, impose, realize, implement, enforce, render, discharge, enact, dispense, mete out, bring off

administration *noun* 1 MANAGEMENT, government, running, control, performance, handling, direction, conduct, application, command, provision, distribution, governing, administering, execution, overseeing, supervision, manipulation, governance, dispensation, superintendence 2 DIRECTORS, board, executive(s), bosses (*informal*), management, employers, directorate 3 GOVERNMENT, authority, executive, leadership, ministry, regime, governing body

administrative *adjective* MANAGERIAL, executive, management, directing, regulatory, governmental, organizational, supervisory, directorial, gubernatorial (*chiefly US*)

administrator *noun* MANAGER, head, official, director, officer, executive, minister, boss (*informal*), agent, governor, controller, supervisor, bureaucrat, superintendent, gaffer (*informal, chiefly Brit*), organizer, mandarin, functionary, overseer, baas (*S African*)

admirable *adjective* PRAISEWORTHY, good, great, fine, capital, noted, choice, champion, prime, select, wonderful, excellent, brilliant, rare, cracking (*Brit informal*), outstanding, valuable, superb, distinguished, superior, sterling, worthy, first-class, notable, sovereign, dope (*slang*), world-class, exquisite, exemplary, first-rate, superlative, commendable, top-notch (*informal*), brill (*informal*), laudable, meritorious, estimable, tiptop, A1 or A-one (*informal*), bitchin' (*US slang*), chillin' (*US slang*), booshit (*Austral slang*), exo (*Austral slang*), sik (*Austral slang*), ka pai (*NZ*), rad (*informal*), phat (*slang*), schmick (*Austral informal*) << ANTONYM deplorable

admiration *noun* REGARD, surprise, wonder, respect, delight, pleasure, praise, approval, recognition, affection, esteem, appreciation, amazement, astonishment, reverence, deference, adoration, veneration, wonderment, approbation

admire *verb* 1 RESPECT, value, prize, honour, praise, appreciate, esteem, approve of, revere, venerate, take your hat off to, have a good *or* high opinion of, think highly of << ANTONYM despise 2 ADORE, like, love, desire, take to, go for, fancy (*Brit informal*), treasure, worship, cherish, glorify, look up to, dote on, hold dear, be captivated by, have an eye for, find attractive, idolize, take a liking to, be infatuated with, be enamoured of, lavish affection on 3 MARVEL AT, look at, appreciate, delight in, gaze at, wonder at, be amazed by, take pleasure in, gape at, be awed by, goggle at, be filled with surprise by

admirer *noun* 1 FAN, supporter, follower, enthusiast, partisan, disciple, buff (*informal*), protagonist, devotee, worshipper, adherent, votary 2 SUITOR, lover, boyfriend, sweetheart, beau, wooer

admissible *adjective* PERMISSIBLE, allowed, permitted, acceptable, tolerated, tolerable, passable, allowable << ANTONYM inadmissible

admission *noun* 1 ADMITTANCE, access, entry, introduction, entrance, acceptance, initiation, entrée, ingress 2 CONFESSION, admitting, profession, declaration, revelation, concession, allowance, disclosure, acknowledgement, affirmation, unburdening, avowal, divulgence, unbosoming

admit *verb* 1 CONFESS, own up, confide, profess, own up, come clean (*informal*), avow, come out of the closet, sing (*slang, chiefly US*), cough (*slang*), spill your guts (*slang*), 'fess up (*US slang*) 2 ALLOW, agree, accept, reveal, grant, declare, acknowledge, recognize, concede, disclose, affirm, divulge << ANTONYM deny 3 LET IN, allow, receive, accept, introduce, take in, initiate, give access to, allow to enter << ANTONYM keep out

admittance *noun* ACCESS, entry, way in, passage, entrance, reception, acceptance

admittedly *adverb* IT MUST BE ADMITTED, certainly, undeniably, it must be said, to be fair *or* honest, avowedly, it cannot be denied, it must be allowed, confessedly, it must be confessed, allowedly

admonish *verb* 1 REPRIMAND, caution, censure, rebuke, scold, berate, check, chide, tear into (*informal*), tell off (*informal*), reprove, upbraid, read the riot act to someone, carpet (*informal*), chew out (*US & Canad informal*), tear someone off a strip (*Brit informal*), give someone a rocket (*Brit & NZ informal*), slap someone on the wrist, rap someone over the knuckles << ANTONYM praise 2 ADVISE, suggest, warn, urge, recommend, counsel, caution, prescribe, exhort, enjoin, forewarn

admonition *noun* REPRIMAND, warning, advice, counsel, caution, rebuke, reproach, scolding, berating, chiding, telling off (*informal*), upbraiding, reproof, remonstrance

ado *noun* FUSS, to-do, trouble, delay, bother, stir, confusion, excitement, disturbance, bustle, flurry, agitation, commotion, pother

adolescence *noun* TEENS, youth, minority, boyhood, girlhood, juvenescence

adolescent *adjective* 1 YOUNG, growing, junior, teenage, juvenile, youthful, childish, immature, boyish, undeveloped, girlish, puerile, in the springtime of life 2 TEENAGE, young, teen (*informal*), juvenile, youthful, immature ▷ *noun* TEENAGER, girl, boy, kid (*informal*), youth, lad, minor, young man, youngster, young woman, juvenile, young person, lass, young adult

adopt *verb* 1 TAKE ON, follow, support, choose, accept, maintain, assume, select, take over, approve, appropriate, take up, embrace, engage in, endorse, ratify, become involved in, espouse 2 TAKE IN, raise, nurse, mother, rear, foster, bring up, take care of << ANTONYM abandon

adoption *noun* 1 FOSTERING, adopting, taking in, fosterage 2 EMBRACING, choice, taking on, taking up, support, taking over, selection, approval, following, assumption, maintenance, acceptance, endorsement, appropriation, ratification, approbation, espousal

adorable *adjective* LOVABLE, pleasing, appealing, dear, sweet, attractive, charming, precious, darling, fetching, delightful, cute, captivating, cutesy (*informal, chiefly US*) << ANTONYM hateful

adoration *noun* LOVE, honour, worship, worshipping, esteem, admiration, reverence, estimation, exaltation, veneration, glorification, idolatry, idolization

adore *verb* LOVE, honour, admire, worship, esteem, cherish, bow to, revere, dote on, idolize << ANTONYM hate

adoring *adjective* ADMIRING, loving, devoted, worshipping, fond, affectionate, ardent, doting, venerating, enamoured, reverential, reverent, idolizing, adulatory << ANTONYM hating

adorn *verb* DECORATE, enhance, deck, trim, grace, array, enrich, garnish, ornament, embellish, emblazon, festoon, bedeck, beautify, engarland

adornment *noun* 1 DECORATION, trimming, supplement, accessory, ornament, frill, festoon, embellishment, frippery 2 BEAUTIFICATION, decorating, decoration, embellishment, ornamentation

adrift *adjective* 1 DRIFTING, afloat, cast off, unmoored, aweigh, unanchored 2 AIMLESS, goalless, directionless, purposeless ▷ *adverb* WRONG, astray, off course, amiss, off target, wide of the mark

adroit *adjective* SKILFUL, able, skilled, expert, bright (*informal*), clever, apt, cunning, ingenious, adept, deft, nimble, masterful, proficient, artful, quick-witted, dexterous << ANTONYM unskilful

adulation *noun* EXTRAVAGANT FLATTERY, worship, fawning, sycophancy, fulsome praise, blandishment, bootlicking (*informal*), servile flattery << ANTONYM ridicule

adult *noun* GROWN-UP, mature person, person of mature age, grown *or* grown-up person, man *or* woman ▷ *adjective* 1 FULLY GROWN, mature, grown-up, of age, ripe, fully fledged, fully developed, full grown 2 PORNOGRAPHIC, blue, dirty, offensive, sexy, erotic, porn (*informal*), obscene, taboo, filthy, indecent, sensual, hard-core, lewd, carnal, porno (*informal*), X-rated (*informal*), salacious, prurient, smutty

adulterer *or* **adulteress** *noun* CHEAT (*informal*), love rat (*slang*), love cheat (*slang*), fornicator

adulterous *adjective* UNFAITHFUL, cheating (*informal*), extramarital, fornicating, unchaste

adultery *noun* UNFAITHFULNESS, infidelity, cheating (*informal*), fornication, playing the field (*slang*), extramarital sex, playing away from home (*slang*), illicit sex, unchastity, extramarital relations, extracurricular sex (*informal*), extramarital congress, having an affair *or* a fling << ANTONYM faithfulness

advance *verb* 1 PROGRESS, proceed, go ahead, move up, come forward, go forward, press on, gain ground, make inroads, make headway, make your way, cover ground, make strides, move onward << ANTONYM retreat 2 ACCELERATE, speed, promote, hurry (up), step up (*informal*), hasten, precipitate, quicken, bring forward, push forward, expedite, send forward 3 IMPROVE, rise, grow, develop, reform, pick up, progress, thrive, upgrade, multiply, prosper, make strides 4 SUGGEST, offer, present, propose, allege, cite, advocate, submit, prescribe, put forward, proffer, adduce, offer as a suggestion << ANTONYM withhold 5 LEND, loan, accommodate someone with, supply on credit << ANTONYM withhold payment ▷ *noun* 1 CREDIT 2 DOWN PAYMENT, credit, fee, deposit, retainer, prepayment 3 LOAN, credit 4 INCREASE (*in price*) 5 ATTACK, charge, strike, rush, assault, raid, invasion, offensive, onslaught, advancement, foray, incursion, forward movement, onward movement 6 IMPROVEMENT, development, gain, growth, breakthrough, advancement, step, headway, inroads, betterment, furtherance, forward movement, amelioration, onward movement ▷ *modifier* PRIOR, early, previous, beforehand ▷▷ **in advance** BEFOREHAND, earlier, ahead, previously, in the lead, in the forefront

advanced *adjective* SOPHISTICATED, foremost, modern, revolutionary, up-to-date, higher, leading, recent, prime, forward, ahead, supreme, extreme, principal, progressive, paramount, state-of-the-art, avant-garde, precocious, pre-eminent, up-to-the-minute, ahead of the times << ANTONYM backward

advancement *noun* 1 PROMOTION, rise, gain, growth, advance, progress, improvement, betterment, preferment, amelioration 2 PROGRESS, advance, headway, forward movement, onward movement

advantage *noun* 1 BENEFIT, use, start, help, service, aid, profit, favour, asset, assistance, blessing, utility, boon, ace in the hole, ace up your sleeve << ANTONYM disadvantage 2 LEAD, control, edge, sway, dominance, superiority, upper hand, precedence, primacy, pre-eminence 3 SUPERIORITY, good, worth, gain, comfort, welfare, enjoyment, mileage (*informal*)

advantageous *adjective* 1 BENEFICIAL, useful, valuable, helpful, profitable, of service, convenient, worthwhile, expedient << ANTONYM unfavourable 2 SUPERIOR, dominating, commanding, dominant, important, powerful, favourable, fortuitous

advent *noun* COMING, approach, appearance, arrival, entrance, onset, occurrence, visitation

adventure *noun* VENTURE, experience, chance, risk, incident, enterprise, speculation, undertaking, exploit, fling, hazard, occurrence, contingency, caper, escapade ▷ *verb* VENTURE, risk, brave, dare

adventurer *noun* 1 MERCENARY, rogue, gambler, speculator, opportunist, charlatan, fortune-hunter 2 VENTURER, hero, traveller, heroine, wanderer, voyager, daredevil, soldier of fortune, swashbuckler, knight-errant

adventurous *adjective* DARING, dangerous, enterprising, bold, risky, rash, have-a-go (*informal*), hazardous, reckless, audacious, intrepid, foolhardy, daredevil, headstrong, venturesome, adventuresome, temerarious (*rare*) << ANTONYM cautious

adversary *noun* OPPONENT, rival, opposer, enemy, competitor, foe, contestant, antagonist << ANTONYM ally

adverse *adjective* 1 HARMFUL, damaging, conflicting, dangerous, opposite, negative, destructive, detrimental, hurtful, antagonistic, injurious, inimical, inopportune, disadvantageous, unpropitious, inexpedient << ANTONYM beneficial 2 UNFAVOURABLE, bad, threatening, hostile, unfortunate, unlucky, ominous, unfriendly, untimely, unsuited, ill-suited, inopportune, disadvantageous, unseasonable 3 NEGATIVE, opposing, reluctant, hostile, contrary, dissenting, unwilling, unfriendly, unsympathetic, ill-disposed

adversity *noun* HARDSHIP, trouble, distress, suffering, trial, disaster, reverse, misery, hard times, catastrophe, sorrow, woe, misfortune, bad luck, deep water, calamity, mishap, affliction, wretchedness, ill-fortune, ill-luck

advert *noun* (*Brit informal*) ADVERTISEMENT, bill, notice, display, commercial, ad (*informal*), announcement, promotion, publicity, poster, plug (*informal*), puff, circular, placard, blurb

advertise *verb* PUBLICIZE, promote, plug (*informal*), announce, publish, push (*informal*), display, declare, broadcast, advise, inform, praise, proclaim, puff, hype, notify, tout, flaunt, crack up (*informal*), promulgate, make known, apprise, beat the drum (*informal*), blazon, bring to public notice

advertisement *noun* ADVERT (*Brit informal*), bill, notice, display, commercial, ad (*informal*), announcement, promotion, publicity, poster, plug (*informal*), puff, circular, placard, blurb

advice *noun* 1 GUIDANCE, help, opinion, direction, suggestion, instruction, counsel, counselling, recommendation, injunction, admonition 2 INSTRUCTION, notification, view, information, warning, teaching, notice, word, intelligence

advisable *adjective* WISE, seemly, sound, suggested, fitting, fit, politic, recommended, appropriate, suitable, sensible, proper, profitable, desirable, apt, prudent, expedient, judicious << ANTONYM unwise

advise *verb* 1 RECOMMEND, suggest, urge, counsel, advocate, caution, prescribe, commend, admonish, enjoin 2 NOTIFY, tell, report, announce, warn, declare, inform, acquaint, make known, apprise, let (someone) know

adviser *noun* COUNSELLOR, authority, teacher, coach, guide, lawyer, consultant, solicitor, counsel, aide, tutor, guru, mentor, helper, confidant, right-hand man

advisory *adjective* ADVISING, helping, recommending, counselling, consultative

advocacy *noun* RECOMMENDATION, support, defence, championing, backing, proposal, urging, promotion, campaigning for, upholding, encouragement, justification, argument for, advancement, pleading for, propagation, espousal, promulgation, boosterism, spokesmanship

advocate *verb* RECOMMEND, support, champion, encourage, propose, favour, defend, promote, urge, advise, justify, endorse, campaign for, prescribe, speak for, uphold, press for, argue for, commend, plead for, espouse, countenance, hold a brief for (*informal*) << ANTONYM oppose ▷ *noun* 1 SUPPORTER, spokesman, champion, defender, speaker, pleader, campaigner, promoter, counsellor, backer, proponent, apostle, apologist, upholder, proposer 2 (*law*) LAWYER, attorney, solicitor, counsel, barrister

aegis *noun* SUPPORT, backing, wing, favour, protection, shelter, sponsorship, patronage, advocacy, auspices, guardianship

aesthetic *adjective* ORNAMENTAL, artistic, pleasing, pretty, fancy, enhancing, decorative, tasteful, beautifying, nonfunctional

affable *adjective* FRIENDLY, kindly, civil, warm, pleasant, mild, obliging, benign, gracious, benevolent, good-humoured, amiable, courteous, amicable, cordial, sociable, genial, congenial, urbane, approachable, good-natured << ANTONYM unfriendly

affair *noun* 1 MATTER, thing, business, question, issue, happening, concern, event, subject, project, activity, incident, proceeding, circumstance, episode, topic, undertaking, transaction, occurrence 2 RELATIONSHIP, romance, intrigue, fling, liaison, flirtation, amour, dalliance

affect¹ *verb* 1 INFLUENCE, involve, concern, impact, transform, alter, modify, change, manipulate, act on, sway, prevail over, bear upon, impinge upon 2 EMOTIONALLY MOVE, touch, upset, overcome, stir, disturb, perturb, impress on, tug at your heartstrings (*often facetious*) ▷ see **effect**

affect² *verb* PUT ON, assume, adopt, pretend, imitate, simulate, contrive, aspire to, sham, counterfeit, feign

affectation *noun* PRETENCE, show, posing, posturing, act, display, appearance, pose, façade, simulation, sham, pretension, veneer, artifice, mannerism, insincerity, pretentiousness, hokum (*slang, chiefly US & Canad*), artificiality, fakery, affectedness, assumed manners, false display, unnatural imitation

affected¹ *adjective* PRETENDED, artificial, contrived, put-on, assumed, mannered, studied, precious, stiff, simulated, mincing, sham, unnatural, pompous, pretentious, counterfeit, feigned, spurious, conceited, insincere, camp (*informal*), la-di-da (*informal*), arty-farty (*informal*), phoney *or* phony (*informal*) << ANTONYM genuine

affected² *adjective* TOUCHED, influenced, concerned, troubled, damaged, hurt, injured, upset, impressed, stirred, altered, changed, distressed, stimulated, melted, impaired, afflicted, deeply moved << ANTONYM untouched

affecting *adjective* EMOTIONALLY MOVING, touching, sad, pathetic, poignant, saddening, pitiful, pitiable, piteous

affection *noun* FONDNESS, liking, feeling, love, care, desire, passion, warmth, attachment, goodwill, devotion, kindness, inclination, tenderness, propensity, friendliness, amity, aroha (*NZ*)

affectionate *adjective* FOND, loving, kind, caring, warm, friendly, attached, devoted, tender, doting, warm-hearted << ANTONYM cool

affiliate *verb* ASSOCIATE, unite, join, link, ally, combine, connect, incorporate, annex, confederate, amalgamate, band together

affiliated *adjective* ASSOCIATED, united, joined, linked, allied, connected, incorporated, confederated, amalgamated, federated, conjoined

affiliation *noun* ASSOCIATION, union, joining, league, relationship, connection, alliance, combination, coalition, merging, confederation, incorporation, amalgamation, banding together

affinity *noun* 1 ATTRACTION, liking, leaning, sympathy, inclination, rapport, fondness, partiality, aroha (*NZ*) << ANTONYM hostility 2 SIMILARITY, relationship, relation, connection, alliance, correspondence, analogy, resemblance, closeness, likeness, compatibility, kinship << ANTONYM difference

affirm *verb* 1 DECLARE, state, maintain, swear, assert, testify, pronounce, certify, attest, avow, aver, asseverate, avouch << ANTONYM deny 2 CONFIRM, prove, sanction, endorse, ratify, verify, validate, bear out, substantiate, corroborate, authenticate << ANTONYM refute

affirmation *noun* 1 DECLARATION, statement, assertion, oath, certification, pronouncement, avowal, asseveration, averment **2** CONFIRMATION, testimony, ratification, attestation, avouchment

affirmative *adjective* AGREEING, confirming, positive, approving, consenting, favourable, concurring, assenting, corroborative << ANTONYM negative

affix *verb* ATTACH, add, join, stick on, bind, put on, tag, glue, paste, tack, fasten, annex, append, subjoin << ANTONYM remove

afflict *verb* TORMENT, trouble, pain, hurt, wound, burden, distress, rack, try, plague, grieve, harass, ail, oppress, beset, smite

affliction *noun* MISFORTUNE, suffering, trouble, trial, disease, pain, distress, grief, misery, plague, curse, ordeal, sickness, torment, hardship, sorrow, woe, adversity, calamity, scourge, tribulation, wretchedness

affluence *noun* WEALTH, riches, plenty, fortune, prosperity, abundance, big money, exuberance, profusion, big bucks (*informal, chiefly US*), opulence, megabucks (*US & Canad slang*), pretty penny (*informal*), wad (*US & Canad slang*)

affluent *adjective* WEALTHY, rich, prosperous, loaded (*slang*), well-off, opulent, well-heeled (*informal*), well-to-do, moneyed << ANTONYM poor

afford *verb* **1** HAVE THE MONEY FOR, manage, bear, pay for, spare, stand, stretch to **2** BEAR, stand, sustain, allow yourself **3** GIVE, offer, provide, produce, supply, grant, yield, render, furnish, bestow, impart

affordable *adjective* INEXPENSIVE, fair, cheap, reasonable, moderate, modest, low-price, low-cost, economical << ANTONYM expensive

affront *verb* OFFEND, anger, provoke, outrage, insult, annoy, vex, displease, pique, put *or* get your back up, slight ▷ *noun* INSULT, wrong, injury, abuse, offence, slight, outrage, provocation, slur, indignity, slap in the face (*informal*), vexation

affronted *adjective* OFFENDED, cross, angry, upset, slighted, outraged, insulted, annoyed, stung, incensed, indignant, irate, miffed (*informal*), displeased, peeved (*informal*), piqued (*Austral slang*), tooshie (*Austral slang*)

afloat *adjective* **1** FLOATING, on the surface, buoyant, keeping your head above water, unsubmerged << ANTONYM sunken **2** SOLVENT, in business, above water << ANTONYM bankrupt

afoot *adjective* GOING ON, happening, current, operating, abroad, brewing, hatching, circulating, up (*informal*), about, in preparation, in progress, afloat, in the wind, on the go (*informal*), astir

afraid *adjective* **1** SCARED, frightened, nervous, anxious, terrified, shaken, alarmed, startled, suspicious, intimidated, fearful, cowardly, timid, apprehensive, petrified, panicky, panic-stricken, timorous, faint-hearted << ANTONYM unafraid **2** RELUCTANT, slow, frightened, scared, unwilling, backward, hesitant, recalcitrant, loath, disinclined, unenthusiastic, indisposed **3** SORRY, apologetic, regretful, sad, distressed, unhappy << ANTONYM pleased

afresh *adverb* AGAIN, newly, once again, once more, over again, anew

after *preposition* **1** AT THE END OF, following, subsequent to << ANTONYM before **2** FOLLOWING, chasing, pursuing, on the hunt for, on the tail of (*informal*), on the track of ▷ *adverb* FOLLOWING, later, next, succeeding, afterwards, subsequently, thereafter

aftereffect *noun usually plural* CONSEQUENCE, wake, trail, aftermath, hangover (*informal*), spin-off, repercussion, afterglow, aftershock, delayed response

aftermath *noun* EFFECTS, end, results, wake, consequences, outcome, sequel, end result, upshot, aftereffects

afterwards *or* **afterward** *adverb* LATER, after, then, after that, subsequently, thereafter, following that, at a later date *or* time

again *adverb* **1** ONCE MORE, another time, anew, afresh **2** ALSO, in addition, moreover, besides, furthermore ▷▷ **there again** *or* **then again** ON THE OTHER HAND, in contrast, on the contrary, conversely

against *preposition* **1** BESIDE, on, up against, in contact with, abutting, close up to **2** OPPOSED TO, anti (*informal*), opposing, counter, contra (*informal*), hostile to, in opposition to, averse to, opposite to, not in accord with **3** IN OPPOSITION TO, resisting, versus, counter to, in the opposite direction of **4** IN PREPARATION FOR, in case of, in anticipation of, in expectation of, in provision for

age *noun* **1** YEARS, days, generation, lifetime, stage of life, length of life, length of existence **2** OLD AGE, experience, maturity, completion, seniority, fullness, majority, maturation, senility, decline (*of life*), advancing years, declining years, senescence, full growth, matureness << ANTONYM youth **3** TIME, day(s), period, generation, era, epoch ▷ *plural noun* (*informal*) A LONG TIME *or* WHILE, years, centuries, for ever (*informal*), aeons, donkey's years (*informal*), yonks (*informal*), a month of Sundays (*informal*), an age *or* eternity

▷ *verb* **1** GROW OLD, decline, weather, fade, deteriorate, wither **2** MATURE, season, condition, soften, mellow, ripen

aged *adjective* OLD, getting on, grey, ancient, antique, elderly, past it (*informal*), age-old, antiquated, hoary, superannuated, senescent, cobwebby << ANTONYM young

ageing *or* **aging** *adjective* GROWING OLD *or* OLDER, declining, maturing, deteriorating, mellowing, in decline, senile, long in the tooth, senescent, getting on *or* past it (*informal*) ▷ *noun* GROWING OLD, decline, decay, deterioration, degeneration, maturation, senility, senescence

ageless *adjective* ETERNAL, enduring, abiding, perennial, timeless, immortal, unchanging, deathless, unfading << ANTONYM momentary

agency *noun* **1** BUSINESS, company, office, firm, department, organization, enterprise, establishment, bureau **2** (*old-fashioned*) MEDIUM, work, means, force, power, action, operation, activity, influence, vehicle, instrument, intervention, mechanism, efficiency, mediation, auspices, intercession, instrumentality

agenda *noun* PROGRAMME, list, plan, schedule, diary, calendar, timetable

agent *noun* **1** REPRESENTATIVE, deputy, substitute, advocate, rep (*informal*), broker, delegate, factor, negotiator, envoy, trustee, proxy, surrogate, go-between, emissary **2** AUTHOR, officer, worker, actor, vehicle, instrument, operator, performer, operative, catalyst, executor, doer, perpetuator **3** FORCE, means, power, cause, instrument

aggravate *verb* **1** MAKE WORSE, exaggerate, intensify, worsen, heighten, exacerbate, magnify, inflame, increase, add insult to injury, fan the flames of << ANTONYM improve **2** (*informal*) ANNOY, bother, provoke, needle (*informal*), irritate, tease, hassle (*informal*), gall, exasperate, nettle, pester, vex, irk, get under your skin (*informal*), get on your nerves (*informal*), nark (*Brit, Austral & NZ slang*), get up your nose (*informal*), be on your back (*slang*), rub (someone) up the wrong way (*informal*), get in your hair (*informal*), get on your wick (*Brit slang*), hack you off (*informal*) << ANTONYM please

aggravating *adjective* **1** (*informal*) ANNOYING, provoking, irritating, teasing, galling, exasperating, vexing, irksome **2** WORSENING, exaggerating, intensifying, heightening, exacerbating, magnifying, inflaming

aggravation *noun* **1** (*informal*) ANNOYANCE, grief (*informal*), teasing, irritation, hassle (*informal*), provocation, gall, exasperation, vexation, irksomeness **2** WORSENING, heightening, inflaming, exaggeration, intensification, magnification, exacerbation

aggregate *noun* TOTAL, body, whole, amount, collection, mass, sum, combination, pile, mixture, bulk, lump, heap, accumulation, assemblage, agglomeration ▷ *adjective* COLLECTIVE, added, mixed, combined, collected, corporate, assembled, accumulated, composite, cumulative ▷ *verb* COMBINE, mix, collect, assemble, heap, accumulate, pile, amass

aggregation *noun* COLLECTION, body, mass, combination, pile, mixture, bulk, lump, heap, accumulation, assemblage, agglomeration

aggression *noun* **1** HOSTILITY, malice, antagonism, antipathy, aggressiveness, ill will, belligerence, destructiveness, malevolence, pugnacity **2** ATTACK, campaign, injury, assault, offence, raid, invasion, offensive, onslaught, foray, encroachment

aggressive *adjective* **1** HOSTILE, offensive, destructive, belligerent, unkind, unfriendly, malevolent, contrary, antagonistic, pugnacious, bellicose, quarrelsome, aggers (*Austral slang*), biffo (*Austral slang*), inimical, rancorous, ill-disposed << ANTONYM friendly **2** FORCEFUL, powerful, convincing, effective, enterprising, dynamic, bold, militant, pushing, vigorous, energetic, persuasive, assertive, zealous, pushy (*informal*), in-your-face (*slang*) << ANTONYM submissive

aggressor *noun* ATTACKER, assaulter, invader, assailant

aggrieved *adjective* HURT, wronged, injured, harmed, disturbed, distressed, unhappy, afflicted, saddened, woeful, peeved (*informal*), ill-used

aghast *adjective* HORRIFIED, shocked, amazed, stunned, appalled, astonished, startled, astounded, confounded, awestruck, horror-struck, thunder-struck

agile *adjective* **1** NIMBLE, active, quick, lively, swift, brisk, supple, sprightly, lithe, limber, spry, lissom(e) << ANTONYM slow **2** ACUTE, sharp, quick, bright (*informal*), prompt, alert, clever, lively, nimble, quick-witted

agility *noun* **1** NIMBLENESS, activity, suppleness, quickness, swiftness, liveliness, briskness, litheness, sprightliness, spryness **2** ACUTENESS, sharpness, alertness, cleverness, quickness, liveliness, promptness, quick-wittedness, promptitude

agitate *verb* **1** STIR, beat, mix, shake, disturb, toss, rouse, churn **2** UPSET, worry, trouble, disturb, excite, alarm, stimulate, distract, rouse, ruffle, inflame, incite, unnerve, disconcert, disquiet, fluster, perturb, faze, work someone up, give someone grief (*Brit & S African*) << ANTONYM calm

agitated *adjective* UPSET, worried, troubled, disturbed, shaken, excited, alarmed, nervous, anxious, distressed, rattled (*informal*), distracted, uneasy, unsettled, worked up, ruffled, unnerved, disconcerted, disquieted, edgy, flustered, perturbed, on edge, fazed, ill at ease, hot under the collar (*informal*), in a flap (*informal*), hot and bothered (*informal*), antsy (*informal*), angsty, all of a flutter (*informal*), discomposed << ANTONYM calm

agitation *noun* **1** TURBULENCE, rocking, shaking, stirring, stir, tossing, disturbance, upheaval, churning, convulsion **2** TURMOIL, worry, trouble, upset, alarm, confusion, excitement, disturbance, distraction, upheaval, stimulation, flurry, outcry, clamour, arousal, ferment, disquiet, commotion, fluster, lather (*informal*), incitement, tumult, discomposure, tizzy, tizz or tiz-woz (*informal*)

agitator *noun* TROUBLEMAKER, revolutionary, inciter, firebrand, instigator, demagogue, rabble-rouser, agent provocateur, stirrer (*informal*)

ago *adverb* PREVIOUSLY, back, before, since, earlier, formerly

agonize *verb* SUFFER, labour, worry, struggle, strain, strive, writhe, be distressed, be in agony, go through the mill, be in anguish

agonized *adjective* TORTURED, suffering, wounded, distressed, racked, tormented, anguished, broken-hearted, grief-stricken, wretched

agonizing *adjective* PAINFUL, bitter, distressing, harrowing, heartbreaking, grievous, excruciating, hellish, heart-rending, gut-wrenching, torturous

agony *noun* SUFFERING, pain, distress, misery, torture, discomfort, torment, hardship, woe, anguish, pangs, affliction, throes

agrarian *adjective* AGRICULTURAL, country, land, farming, rural, rustic, agrestic << ANTONYM urban

agree *verb* **1** CONCUR, engage, be as one, sympathize, assent, see eye to eye, be of the same opinion, be of the same mind << ANTONYM disagree **2** CORRESPOND, match, accord, answer, fit, suit, square, coincide, tally, conform, chime, harmonize ▷▷ **agree on something** SHAKE HANDS ON, reach agreement on, settle on, negotiate, work out, arrive at, yield to, thrash out, accede to, concede to ▷▷ **agree to something** CONSENT TO, grant, approve, permit, accede to, assent to, acquiesce to, comply to, concur to ▷▷ **agree with someone** SUIT, get on with, be good for, befit

agreeable *adjective* **1** PLEASANT, pleasing, satisfying, acceptable, delightful, enjoyable, gratifying, pleasurable, congenial, to your liking, to your taste, likable or likeable << ANTONYM unpleasant **2** FRIENDLY, nice, pleasant, sociable, affable, congenial, good-natured, likable or likeable **3** CONSENTING, willing, agreeing, approving, sympathetic, complying, responsive, concurring, amenable, in accord, well-disposed, acquiescent

agreed *adjective* SETTLED, given, established, guaranteed, fixed, arranged, definite, stipulated, predetermined << ANTONYM indefinite ▷ *interjection* ALL RIGHT, done, settled, it's a bargain or deal, O.K. or okay (*informal*), you're on (*informal*), ka pai (*NZ*)

agreement *noun* **1** TREATY, contract, bond, arrangement, alliance, deal (*informal*), understanding, settlement, bargain, pact, compact, covenant, entente **2** CONCURRENCE, harmony, compliance, union, agreeing, concession, consent, unison, assent, concord, acquiescence << ANTONYM disagreement **3** CORRESPONDENCE, agreeing, accord, similarity, consistency, analogy, accordance, correlation, affinity, conformity, compatibility, congruity, suitableness << ANTONYM difference

agricultural *adjective* FARMING, country, rural, rustic, agrarian, agronomic, agronomical, agrestic

agriculture *noun* FARMING, culture, cultivation, husbandry, tillage, agronomy, agronomics

aground *adverb* BEACHED, grounded, stuck, shipwrecked, foundered, stranded, ashore, marooned, on the rocks, high and dry

ahead *adverb* **1** FORWARDS, in front, on, in advance, onwards, towards the front, frontwards **2** AT AN ADVANTAGE, in advance, in the lead **3** IN THE LEAD, winning, leading, at the head, to the fore, at an advantage **4** IN FRONT, before, in advance, onwards, in the lead, in the vanguard

aid *noun* **1** HELP, backing, support, benefit, favour, relief, promotion, assistance, encouragement, helping hand, succour << ANTONYM hindrance **2** HELPER, supporter, assistant, aide, adjutant, aide-de-camp, second, abettor ▷ *verb* **1** HELP, second, support, serve, sustain, assist, relieve, avail, subsidize, abet, succour, be of service to, lend a hand to, give a leg up to (*informal*) << ANTONYM hinder **2** PROMOTE, help, further, forward, encourage, favour, facilitate, pave the way for, expedite, smooth the path of, assist the progress of

aide *noun* ASSISTANT, supporter, deputy, attendant, helper, henchman, right-hand man, adjutant, second, helpmate, coadjutor (*rare*)

ail *verb* **1** (*literary*) TROUBLE, worry, bother, distress, pain, upset, annoy, irritate, sicken, afflict, be the matter with **2** BE ILL, be sick, be unwell, feel unwell, be indisposed, be *or* feel off colour

ailing *adjective* **1** WEAK, failing, poor, flawed, unstable, feeble, unsatisfactory, deficient, unsound **2** ILL, suffering, poorly, diseased, sick, weak, crook (*Austral & NZ informal*), feeble, invalid, debilitated, sickly, unwell, infirm, off colour, under the weather (*informal*), indisposed

ailment *noun* ILLNESS, disease, complaint, disorder, sickness, affliction, malady, infirmity, lurgy (*informal*)

aim *verb* **1** TRY FOR, want, seek, work for, plan for, strive, aspire to, wish for, have designs on, set your sights on **2** POINT, level, train, direct, sight, take aim (at) ▷ *noun* INTENTION, end, point, plan, course, mark, goal, design, target, wish, scheme, purpose, direction, desire, object, objective, ambition, intent, aspiration, Holy Grail (*informal*)

aimless *adjective* PURPOSELESS, random, stray, pointless, erratic, wayward, frivolous, chance, goalless, haphazard, vagrant, directionless, unguided, undirected << ANTONYM purposeful

air *noun* **1** WIND, blast, breath, breeze, puff, whiff, draught, gust, waft, zephyr, air-current, current of air **2** ATMOSPHERE, sky, heavens, aerosphere **3** TUNE, song, theme, melody, strain, lay, aria **4** MANNER, feeling, effect, style, quality, character, bearing, appearance, look, aspect, atmosphere, tone, mood, impression, flavour, aura, ambience, demeanour, vibe (*slang*) ▷ *verb* **1** PUBLICIZE, tell, reveal, exhibit, communicate, voice, express, display, declare, expose, disclose, proclaim, utter, circulate, make public, divulge, disseminate, ventilate, make known, give vent to, take the wraps off **2** VENTILATE, expose, freshen, aerate

airborne *adjective* FLYING, floating, soaring, in the air, hovering, gliding, in flight, on the wing, wind-borne, volitant

aircraft *noun* PLANE, jet, aeroplane, airplane (*US & Canad*), airliner, kite (*Brit slang*), flying machine

airfield *noun* AIRPORT, airstrip, aerodrome, landing strip, air station, airdrome (*US*)

airily *adverb* LIGHT-HEARTEDLY, happily, blithely, gaily, animatedly, breezily, jauntily, buoyantly, high-spiritedly

airing *noun* **1** VENTILATION, drying, freshening, aeration **2** EXPOSURE, display, expression, publicity, vent, utterance, dissemination

airless *adjective* STUFFY, close, heavy, stifling, oppressive, stale, breathless, suffocating, sultry, muggy, unventilated << ANTONYM airy

airplane *noun* (*US & Canad*) PLANE, aircraft, jet, aeroplane, airliner, kite (*Brit slang*), flying machine

airport *noun* AIRFIELD, aerodrome, airdrome (*US*)

airs *plural noun* AFFECTATION, arrogance, pretensions, pomposity, swank (*informal*), hauteur, haughtiness, superciliousness, affectedness

airy *adjective* **1** WELL-VENTILATED, open, light, fresh, spacious, windy, lofty, breezy, uncluttered, draughty, gusty, blowy << ANTONYM stuffy **2** LIGHT-HEARTED, light, happy, gay, lively, cheerful, animated, merry, upbeat (*informal*), buoyant, graceful, cheery, genial, high-spirited, jaunty, chirpy (*informal*), sprightly, debonair, nonchalant, blithe, frolicsome << ANTONYM gloomy **3** INSUBSTANTIAL, imaginary, visionary, flimsy, fanciful, ethereal, immaterial, illusory, wispy, weightless, incorporeal, vaporous << ANTONYM real

aisle *noun* PASSAGEWAY, path, lane, passage, corridor, alley, gangway

ajar *adjective* OPEN, gaping, agape, partly open, unclosed

akin *adjective* ▷▷ **akin to** SIMILAR TO, like, related to, corresponding to, parallel to, comparable to, allied with, analogous to, affiliated with, of a piece with, kin to, cognate with, congenial with, connected with *or* to

alacrity *noun* EAGERNESS, enthusiasm, willingness, readiness, speed, zeal, gaiety, alertness, hilarity, cheerfulness, quickness, liveliness, briskness, promptness, avidity, joyousness, sprightliness << ANTONYM reluctance

alarm *noun* 1 FEAR, horror, panic, anxiety, distress, terror, dread, dismay, fright, unease, apprehension, nervousness, consternation, trepidation, uneasiness << ANTONYM calmness 2 DANGER SIGNAL, warning, bell, alert, siren, alarm bell, hooter, distress signal, tocsin ▷ *verb* FRIGHTEN, shock, scare, panic, distress, terrify, startle, rattle, dismay, daunt, unnerve, terrorize, put the wind up (*informal*), give (someone) a turn (*informal*), make (someone's) hair stand on end << ANTONYM calm

alarmed *adjective* FRIGHTENED, troubled, shocked, scared, nervous, disturbed, anxious, distressed, terrified, startled, dismayed, uneasy, fearful, daunted, unnerved, apprehensive, in a panic << ANTONYM calm

alarming *adjective* FRIGHTENING, shocking, scaring, disturbing, distressing, terrifying, appalling, startling, dreadful, horrifying, menacing, intimidating, dismaying, scary (*informal*), fearful, daunting, fearsome, unnerving, hair-raising, bloodcurdling

albeit *conjunction* EVEN THOUGH, though, although, even if, notwithstanding, tho' (*US poetic*)

album *noun* 1 RECORD, recording, CD, single, release, disc, waxing (*informal*), LP, vinyl, EP, forty-five, platter (*US slang*), seventy-eight, gramophone record, black disc 2 BOOK, collection, scrapbook

alchemy *noun* MAGIC, witchcraft, wizardry, sorcery, makutu (*NZ*)

alcohol *noun* 1 DRINK, spirits, liquor, intoxicant, juice (*informal*), booze (*informal*), the bottle (*informal*), grog (*informal, chiefly Austral & NZ*), the hard stuff (*informal*), strong drink, Dutch courage (*informal*), firewater, John Barleycorn, hooch *or* hootch (*informal, chiefly US & Canad*) 2 ETHANOL, ethyl alcohol

alcoholic *noun* DRUNKARD, drinker, drunk, boozer (*informal*), toper, soak (*slang*), lush (*slang*), sponge (*informal*), carouser, sot, tippler, wino (*informal*), inebriate,

dipsomaniac, hard drinker, tosspot (*informal*), alky (*slang*), alko *or* alco (*Austral slang*) ▷ *adjective* INTOXICATING, hard, strong, stiff, brewed, fermented, distilled, vinous, inebriating, spirituous, inebriant

alcove *noun* RECESS, corner, bay, niche, bower, compartment, cubicle, nook, cubbyhole

alert *adjective* 1 ATTENTIVE, careful, awake, wary, vigilant, perceptive, watchful, ready, on the lookout, circumspect, observant, on guard, wide-awake, on your toes, on the watch, keeping a weather eye on, heedful << ANTONYM careless 2 QUICK-WITTED, spirited, quick, bright, sharp, active, lively, brisk, on the ball (*informal*), nimble, agile, sprightly, bright-eyed and bushy-tailed (*informal*) ▷ *noun* WARNING, signal, alarm, siren << ANTONYM all clear ▷ *verb* WARN, signal, inform, alarm, notify, tip off, forewarn << ANTONYM lull

alertness *noun* WATCHFULNESS, vigilance, agility, wariness, quickness, liveliness, readiness, circumspection, attentiveness, spiritedness, briskness, nimbleness, perceptiveness, carefulness, sprightliness, promptitude, activeness, heedfulness

alias *noun* PSEUDONYM, pen name, assumed name, stage name, nom de guerre, nom de plume ▷ *adverb* ALSO KNOWN AS, otherwise, also called, otherwise known as, a.k.a. (*informal*)

alibi *noun* EXCUSE, reason, defence, explanation, plea, justification, pretext

alien *noun* FOREIGNER, incomer, immigrant, stranger, outsider, newcomer, asylum seeker, outlander << ANTONYM citizen ▷ *adjective* 1 FOREIGN, outside, strange, imported, overseas, unknown, exotic, unfamiliar, not native, not naturalized 2 STRANGE, new, foreign, novel, remote, unknown, exotic, unfamiliar, estranged, outlandish, untried, unexplored << ANTONYM similar ▷▷ **alien to** UNFAMILIAR TO, opposed to, contrary to, separated from, conflicting with, incompatible with, inappropriate to, repugnant to, adverse to

alienate *verb* ANTAGONIZE, anger, annoy, offend, irritate, hassle (*informal*), gall, repel, estrange, lose the affection of, disaffect, hack off (*informal*)

alienation *noun* ESTRANGEMENT, setting against, divorce, withdrawal, separation, turning away, indifference, breaking off, diversion, rupture, disaffection, remoteness

alight¹ *verb* 1 GET OFF, descend, get down,

disembark, dismount **2** LAND, light, settle, come down, descend, perch, touch down, come to rest << ANTONYM take off

alight² *adjective* **1** LIT UP, bright, brilliant, shining, illuminated, fiery **2** ON FIRE, ignited, set ablaze, lit, burning, aflame, blazing, flaming, flaring

align *verb* **1** ALLY, side, join, associate, affiliate, cooperate, sympathize **2** LINE UP, even, order, range, sequence, regulate, straighten, coordinate, even up, make parallel, arrange in line

alignment *noun* **1** ALLIANCE, union, association, agreement, sympathy, cooperation, affiliation **2** LINING UP, line, order, ranging, arrangement, evening, sequence, regulating, adjustment, coordination, straightening up, evening up

alike *adjective* SIMILAR, close, the same, equal, equivalent, uniform, parallel, resembling, identical, corresponding, akin, duplicate, analogous, homogeneous, of a piece, cut from the same cloth, like two peas in a pod << ANTONYM different ▷ *adverb* SIMILARLY, identically, equally, uniformly, correspondingly, analogously << ANTONYM differently

alive *adjective* **1** LIVING, breathing, animate, having life, subsisting, existing, functioning, alive and kicking, in the land of the living (*informal*) << ANTONYM dead **2** IN EXISTENCE, existing, functioning, active, operative, in force, on-going, prevalent, existent, extant << ANTONYM inoperative **3** LIVELY, spirited, active, vital, alert, eager, quick, awake, vigorous, cheerful, energetic, animated, brisk, agile, perky, chirpy (*informal*), sprightly, vivacious, full of life, spry, full of beans (*informal*), zestful << ANTONYM dull ▷▷ **alive to** AWARE OF, sensitive to, susceptible to, alert to, eager for, awake to, cognizant of, sensible of

all *determiner* **1** THE WHOLE AMOUNT, everything, the whole, the total, the sum, the total amount, the aggregate, the totality, the sum total, the entirety, the entire amount, the complete amount **2** EVERY, each, every single, every one of, each and every ▷ *adjective* COMPLETE, greatest, full, total, perfect, entire, utter ▷ *adverb* COMPLETELY, totally, fully, entirely, absolutely, altogether, wholly, utterly

allay *verb* REDUCE, quiet, relax, ease, calm, smooth, relieve, check, moderate, dull, diminish, compose, soften, blunt, soothe,

subdue, lessen, alleviate, appease, quell, mitigate, assuage, pacify, mollify

allegation *noun* CLAIM, charge, statement, profession, declaration, plea, accusation, assertion, affirmation, deposition, avowal, asseveration, averment

allege *verb* CLAIM, hold, charge, challenge, state, maintain, advance, declare, assert, uphold, put forward, affirm, profess, depose, avow, aver, asseverate << ANTONYM deny

alleged *adjective* CLAIMED, supposed, declared, assumed, so-called, apparent, rumoured, stated, described, asserted, designated, presumed, affirmed, professed, reputed, hypothetical, putative, presupposed, averred, unproved

allegedly *adverb* SUPPOSEDLY, apparently, reportedly, by all accounts, reputedly, purportedly

allegiance *noun* LOYALTY, duty, obligation, devotion, fidelity, homage, obedience, adherence, constancy, faithfulness, troth (*archaic*), fealty << ANTONYM disloyalty

allegorical *adjective* SYMBOLIC, figurative, symbolizing, emblematic, parabolic

allegory *noun* SYMBOL, story, tale, myth, symbolism, emblem, fable, parable, apologue

allergic *adjective* SENSITIVE, affected, susceptible, sensitized, hypersensitive ▷▷ **allergic to** (*informal*) AVERSE TO, opposed to, hostile to, loath to, disinclined to, antipathetic to

allergy *noun* **1** SENSITIVITY, reaction, susceptibility, antipathy, hypersensitivity, sensitiveness **2** (*informal*) DISLIKE, hatred, hostility, aversion, loathing, disgust, antipathy, animosity, displeasure, antagonism, distaste, enmity, opposition, repugnance, disinclination

alleviate *verb* EASE, reduce, relieve, moderate, smooth, dull, diminish, soften, check, blunt, soothe, subdue, lessen, lighten, quell, allay, mitigate, abate, slacken, assuage, quench, mollify, slake, palliate ▷ see **ameliorate**

alley *noun* PASSAGE, walk, lane, pathway, alleyway, passageway, backstreet

alliance *noun* UNION, league, association, agreement, marriage, connection, combination, coalition, treaty, partnership, federation, pact, compact, confederation, affinity, affiliation, confederacy, concordat << ANTONYM division

allied *adjective* **1** UNITED, joined, linked, related, married, joint, combined, bound, integrated, unified, affiliated, leagued, confederate, amalgamated, cooperating, in league, hand in glove (*informal*), in cahoots (*US informal*) **2** CONNECTED, joined, linked, tied, related, associated, syndicated, affiliated, kindred

all-important *adjective* ESSENTIAL, central, significant, key, necessary, vital, critical, crucial, pivotal, momentous, consequential

allocate *verb* ASSIGN, grant, distribute, designate, set aside, earmark, give out, consign, allow, budget, allot, mete, share out, apportion, appropriate

allocation *noun* **1** ALLOWANCE, share, measure, grant, portion, quota, lot, ration, stint, stipend **2** ASSIGNMENT, allowance, rationing, allotment, apportionment, appropriation

allot *verb* ASSIGN, allocate, designate, set aside, earmark, mete, share out, apportion, budget, appropriate

allotment *noun* **1** PLOT, patch, tract, kitchen garden **2** ASSIGNMENT, share, measure, grant, allowance, portion, quota, lot, ration, allocation, stint, appropriation, stipend, apportionment

allotted *verb* ASSIGNED, given, allocated, designated, set aside, earmarked, apportioned

all-out *or* **all out** *adjective* TOTAL, full, complete, determined, supreme, maximum, outright, thorough, unlimited, full-scale, optimum, exhaustive, resolute, full-on (*informal*), unrestrained, unremitting, thoroughgoing, unstinted << ANTONYM half-hearted ▷ *adverb* ENERGETICALLY, hard, strongly, sharply, heavily, severely, fiercely, vigorously, intensely, violently, powerfully, forcibly, forcefully, with all your might, with might and main

allow *verb* **1** PERMIT, approve, enable, sanction, endure, license, brook, endorse, warrant, tolerate, put up with (*informal*), authorize, stand, suffer, bear << ANTONYM prohibit **2** LET, permit, sanction, authorize, license, tolerate, consent to, countenance, concede to, assent to, give leave to, give the green light for, give a blank cheque to << ANTONYM forbid **3** GIVE, provide, grant, spare, devote, assign, allocate, set aside, deduct, earmark, remit, allot **4** ACKNOWLEDGE, accept, admit, grant, recognize, yield, concede, confess, acquiesce ▷▷ **allow for something** TAKE INTO ACCOUNT, consider, plan for, accommodate, provide for, arrange for, foresee, make provision for,

make allowances for, make concessions for, keep in mind, set something aside for, take into consideration

allowable *adjective* PERMISSIBLE, all right, approved, appropriate, suitable, acceptable, tolerable, admissible, sufferable, sanctionable

allowance *noun* **1** PORTION, lot, share, amount, measure, grant, pension, subsidy, quota, allocation, stint, annuity, allotment, remittance, stipend, apportionment **2** POCKET MONEY, grant, fee, payment, consideration, ration, handout, remittance **3** CONCESSION, discount, reduction, repayment, deduction, rebate

alloy *noun* MIXTURE, combination, compound, blend, hybrid, composite, amalgam, meld, admixture

all right *adjective* **1** SATISFACTORY, O.K. *or* okay (*informal*), average, fair, sufficient, standard, acceptable, good enough, adequate, so-so (*informal*), up to scratch (*informal*), passable, up to standard, up to the mark, unobjectionable << ANTONYM unsatisfactory **2** WELL, O.K. *or* okay (*informal*), strong, whole, sound, fit, safe, healthy, hale, unharmed, out of the woods, uninjured, unimpaired, up to par << ANTONYM ill ▷ *adverb* SATISFACTORILY, O.K. *or* okay (*informal*), reasonably, well enough, adequately, suitably, acceptably, passably, unobjectionably ▷ see **alright**

allude to *verb* REFER TO, suggest, mention, speak of, imply, intimate, hint at, remark on, insinuate, touch upon ▷ see **elude**

allure *noun* ATTRACTIVENESS, appeal, charm, attraction, lure, temptation, glamour, persuasion, enchantment, enticement, seductiveness ▷ *verb* ATTRACT, persuade, charm, win over, tempt, lure, seduce, entice, enchant, lead on, coax, captivate, beguile, cajole, decoy, inveigle

alluring *adjective* ATTRACTIVE, fascinating, enchanting, seductive, tempting, sexy, intriguing, fetching, glamorous, captivating, beguiling, bewitching, come-hither << ANTONYM unattractive

allusion *noun* REFERENCE, mention, suggestion, hint, implication, innuendo, intimation, insinuation, casual remark, indirect reference

ally *noun* PARTNER, friend, colleague, associate, mate, accessory, comrade, helper, collaborator, accomplice, confederate, co-worker, bedfellow, cobber (*Austral & NZ* old-fashioned *informal*), coadjutor, abettor, E hoa (NZ) << ANTONYM opponent >> **ally yourself with something** *or* **someone** UNITE WITH, join, associate with, connect with, unify, league with, affiliate with, collaborate with, join forces with, confederate, band together with

almighty *adjective* 1 ALL-POWERFUL, supreme, absolute, unlimited, invincible, omnipotent << ANTONYM powerless 2 (*informal*) GREAT, terrible, enormous, desperate, severe, intense, awful, loud, excessive << ANTONYM slight

almost *adverb* NEARLY, about, approaching, close to, virtually, practically, roughly, all but, just about, not quite, on the brink of, not far from, approximately, well-nigh, as good as

alms *plural noun* (*old-fashioned*) DONATION, relief, gift, charity, bounty, benefaction, koha (NZ)

aloft *adverb* 1 IN THE AIR, up, higher, above, overhead, in the sky, on high, high up, up above 2 UPWARD, skyward, heavenward

alone *adjective* 1 SOLITARY, isolated, sole, separate, apart, abandoned, detached, by yourself, unattended, unaccompanied, out on a limb, unescorted, on your tod (*slang*) << ANTONYM accompanied 2 LONELY, abandoned, deserted, isolated, solitary, estranged, desolate, forsaken, forlorn, destitute, lonesome (*chiefly US & Canad*), friendless ▷ *adverb* 1 SOLELY, only, individually, singly, exclusively, uniquely 2 BY YOURSELF, independently, unaided, unaccompanied, without help, on your own, unassisted, without assistance, under your own steam << ANTONYM with help

aloof *adjective* DISTANT, cold, reserved, cool, formal, remote, forbidding, detached, indifferent, chilly, unfriendly, unsympathetic, uninterested, haughty, unresponsive, supercilious, unapproachable, unsociable, standoffish << ANTONYM friendly

aloud *adverb* OUT LOUD, clearly, plainly, distinctly, audibly, intelligibly

alphabet *noun* LETTERS, script, writing system, syllabary

already *adverb* BEFORE NOW, before, previously, at present, by now, by then, even now, by this time, just now, by that time, heretofore, as of now

alright ▷ see **all right**

also *adverb* AND, too, further, plus, along with, in addition, as well, moreover, besides, furthermore, what's more, on top of that, to boot, additionally, into the bargain, as well as

alter *verb* 1 MODIFY, change, reform, shift, vary, transform, adjust, adapt, revise, amend, diversify, remodel, tweak (*informal*), recast, reshape, metamorphose, transmute 2 CHANGE, turn, vary, transform, adjust, adapt, metamorphose

alteration *noun* 1 CHANGE, adjustment, shift, amendment, conversion, modification 2 ADJUSTMENT, change, amendment, variation, conversion, transformation, adaptation, difference, revision, modification, remodelling, reformation, diversification, metamorphosis, variance, reshaping, transmutation

altercation *noun* ARGUMENT, row, clash, disagreement, dispute, controversy, contention, quarrel, squabble, wrangle, bickering, discord, dissension

alternate *verb* 1 INTERCHANGE, change, alter, fluctuate, intersperse, take turns, oscillate, chop and change, follow one another, follow in turn 2 INTERSPERSE, interchange, exchange, swap, stagger, rotate ▷ *adjective* 1 ALTERNATING, interchanging, every other, rotating, every second, sequential 2 SUBSTITUTE, alternative, other, different, replacement, complementary ▷ *noun* (US) SUBSTITUTE, reserve, deputy, relief, replacement, stand-by, makeshift

alternating *adjective* INTERCHANGING, changing, shifting, swinging, rotating, fluctuating, occurring by turns, oscillating, vacillating, seesawing

alternative *noun* SUBSTITUTE, choice, other (*of two*), option, preference, recourse ▷ *adjective* DIFFERENT, other, substitute, alternate

alternatively *adverb* OR, instead, otherwise, on the other hand, if not, then again, as an alternative, by way of alternative, as another option

although *conjunction* THOUGH, while, even if, even though, whilst, albeit, despite the fact that, notwithstanding, even supposing, tho' (US *poetic*)

altitude *noun* HEIGHT, summit, peak, elevation, loftiness

altogether *adverb* 1 ABSOLUTELY, quite, completely, totally, perfectly, fully, thoroughly, wholly, utterly, downright, one hundred per cent (*informal*), undisputedly, lock, stock and barrel 2 COMPLETELY, all, fully, entirely, comprehensively, thoroughly, wholly, every inch, one hundred per cent (*informal*), in every respect << ANTONYM partially **3** ON THE WHOLE, generally, mostly, in general, collectively, all things considered, on average, for the most part, all in all, on balance, in toto (*Latin*), as a whole **4** IN TOTAL, in all, all told, taken together, in sum, everything included, in toto (*Latin*)

altruism *noun* SELFLESSNESS, charity, consideration, goodwill, generosity, self-sacrifice, philanthropy, benevolence, magnanimity, humanitarianism, unselfishness, beneficence, charitableness, greatheartedness, bigheartedness << ANTONYM self-interest

altruistic *adjective* SELFLESS, generous, humanitarian, charitable, benevolent, considerate, self-sacrificing, philanthropic, unselfish, public-spirited << ANTONYM self-interested

always *adverb* **1** HABITUALLY, regularly, every time, inevitably, consistently, invariably, aye (*Scot*), perpetually, without exception, customarily, unfailingly, on every occasion, day in, day out << ANTONYM seldom **2** FOREVER, for keeps, eternally, for all time, evermore, till the cows come home (*informal*), till Doomsday **3** CONTINUALLY, constantly, all the time, forever, repeatedly, aye (*Scot*), endlessly, persistently, eternally, perpetually, incessantly, interminably, unceasingly, everlastingly, in perpetuum (*Latin*)

amalgam *noun* COMBINATION, mixture, compound, blend, union, composite, fusion, alloy, amalgamation, meld, admixture

amalgamate *verb* COMBINE, unite, ally, compound, blend, incorporate, integrate, merge, fuse, mingle, alloy, coalesce, meld, commingle, intermix << ANTONYM divide

amalgamation *noun* COMBINATION, union, joining, mixing, alliance, coalition, merger, mixture, compound, blend, integration, composite, fusion, mingling, alloy, amalgamating, incorporation, amalgam, meld, admixture, commingling

amass *verb* COLLECT, gather, assemble, compile, accumulate, aggregate, pile up, garner, hoard, scrape together, rake up, heap up

amateur *noun* NONPROFESSIONAL, outsider, layman, dilettante, layperson, non-specialist, dabbler

amateurish *adjective* UNPROFESSIONAL,

amateur, crude, bungling, clumsy, inexpert, unaccomplished, unskilful << ANTONYM professional

amaze *verb* ASTONISH, surprise, shock, stun, alarm, stagger, startle, bewilder, astound, daze, confound, stupefy, flabbergast, bowl someone over (*informal*), boggle someone's mind, dumbfound

amazement *noun* ASTONISHMENT, surprise, wonder, shock, confusion, admiration, awe, marvel, bewilderment, wonderment, perplexity, stupefaction

amazing *adjective* ASTONISHING, striking, surprising, brilliant, stunning, impressive, overwhelming, staggering, sensational (*informal*), bewildering, breathtaking, astounding, eye-opening, wondrous (*archaic* or *literary*), mind-boggling, jaw-dropping, stupefying

ambassador *noun* REPRESENTATIVE, minister, agent, deputy, diplomat, envoy, consul, attaché, emissary, legate, plenipotentiary

ambience *noun* ATMOSPHERE, feel, setting, air, quality, character, spirit, surroundings, tone, mood, impression, flavour, temper, tenor, aura, complexion, vibes (*slang*), vibrations (*slang*), milieu

ambiguity *noun* VAGUENESS, doubt, puzzle, uncertainty, obscurity, enigma, equivocation, inconclusiveness, indefiniteness, dubiety, dubiousness, tergiversation, indeterminateness, equivocality, doubtfulness, equivocacy

ambiguous *adjective* UNCLEAR, puzzling, uncertain, obscure, vague, doubtful, dubious, enigmatic, indefinite, inconclusive, cryptic, indeterminate, equivocal, Delphic, oracular, enigmatical, clear as mud (*informal*) << ANTONYM clear

ambition *noun* **1** GOAL, end, hope, design, dream, target, aim, wish, purpose, desire, intention, objective, intent, aspiration, Holy Grail (*informal*) **2** ENTERPRISE, longing, drive, fire, spirit, desire, passion, enthusiasm, warmth, striving, initiative, aspiration, yearning, devotion, zeal, verve, zest, fervour, eagerness, gusto, hankering, get-up-and-go (*informal*), ardour, keenness, avidity, fervency

ambitious *adjective* **1** ENTERPRISING, spirited, keen, active, daring, eager, intent, enthusiastic, hopeful, striving, vigorous, aspiring, energetic, adventurous, avid, zealous, intrepid, resourceful, purposeful, desirous << ANTONYM unambitious **2** DEMANDING, trying, hard, taxing, difficult, challenging, tough, severe, impressive, exhausting, exacting, bold, elaborate, formidable, energetic, strenuous, pretentious, arduous, grandiose, industrious << ANTONYM modest

ambivalence *noun* INDECISION, doubt, opposition, conflict, uncertainty, contradiction, wavering, fluctuation, hesitancy, equivocation, vacillation, irresolution

ambivalent *adjective* UNDECIDED, mixed, conflicting, opposed, uncertain, doubtful, unsure, contradictory, wavering, unresolved, fluctuating, hesitant, inconclusive, debatable, equivocal, vacillating, warring, irresolute << ANTONYM definite

amble *verb* STROLL, walk, wander, ramble, meander, saunter, dawdle, mosey (*informal*)

ambush *verb* TRAP, attack, surprise, deceive, dupe, ensnare, waylay, ambuscade, bushwhack (*US*) ▷ *noun* TRAP, snare, attack, lure, waylaying, ambuscade

ameliorate *verb* IMPROVE, better, benefit, reform, advance, promote, amend, elevate, raise, mend, mitigate, make better, assuage, meliorate

amenable *adjective* RECEPTIVE, open, susceptible, responsive, agreeable, compliant, tractable, acquiescent, persuadable, able to be influenced << ANTONYM stubborn

amend *verb* CHANGE, improve, reform, fix, correct, repair, edit, alter, enhance, update, revise, modify, remedy, rewrite, mend, rectify, tweak (*informal*), ameliorate, redraw

amendment *noun* 1 ADDITION, change, adjustment, attachment, adaptation, revision, modification, alteration, remodelling, reformation, clarification, adjunct, addendum 2 CHANGE, improvement, repair, edit, remedy, correction, revision, modification, alteration, mending, enhancement, reform, betterment, rectification, amelioration, emendation

amends *plural noun* (usually in *make amends*) COMPENSATION, apology, restoration, redress, reparation, indemnity, restitution, atonement, recompense, expiation, requital

amenity *noun* 1 FACILITY, service, advantage, comfort, convenience 2 REFINEMENT, politeness, affability, amiability, courtesy, mildness, pleasantness, suavity, agreeableness, complaisance << ANTONYM rudeness

American *adjective* YANKEE *or* YANK, US ▷ *noun* YANKEE *or* YANK, Yankee Doodle

amiable *adjective* PLEASANT, kind, kindly, pleasing, friendly, attractive, engaging, charming, obliging, delightful, cheerful, benign, winning, agreeable, good-humoured, lovable, sociable, genial, affable, congenial, winsome, good-natured, sweet-tempered, likable *or* likeable << ANTONYM unfriendly

amicable *adjective* FRIENDLY, kindly, brotherly, civil, neighbourly, peaceful, polite, harmonious, good-humoured, amiable, courteous, cordial, sociable, fraternal, peaceable << ANTONYM unfriendly

amid *or* **amidst** *preposition* 1 DURING, among, at a time of, in an atmosphere of 2 IN THE MIDDLE OF, among, surrounded by, amongst, in the midst of, in the thick of

amiss *adjective* WRONG, mistaken, confused, false, inappropriate, rotten, incorrect, faulty, inaccurate, unsuitable, improper, defective, out of order, awry, erroneous, untoward, fallacious << ANTONYM right ▷▷ **take something amiss** TAKE AS AN INSULT, take wrongly, take as offensive, take out of turn

ammunition *noun* MUNITIONS, rounds, shot, shells, powder, explosives, cartridges, armaments, materiel, shot and shell

amnesty *noun* GENERAL PARDON, mercy, pardoning, immunity, forgiveness, reprieve, oblivion, remission (*of penalty*), clemency, dispensation, absolution, condonation

amok *or* **amuck** *adverb* ▷▷ **run amok** GO MAD, go wild, turn violent, go berserk, lose control, go insane, go into a frenzy

among *or* **amongst** *preposition* 1 IN THE MIDST OF, with, together with, in the middle of, amid, surrounded by, amidst, in the thick of 2 IN THE GROUP OF, one of, part of, included in, in the company of, in the class of, in the number of 3 BETWEEN, to 4 WITH ONE ANOTHER, mutually, by all of, by the whole of, by the joint action of

amoral *adjective* UNETHICAL, nonmoral, unvirtuous

amorous *adjective* LOVING, in love, tender, passionate, fond, erotic, affectionate, ardent, impassioned, doting, enamoured, lustful, attached, lovesick, amatory << ANTONYM cold

amorphous *adjective* SHAPELESS, vague, irregular, nondescript, indeterminate, unstructured, nebulous, formless, inchoate, characterless, unformed, unshaped, unshapen << ANTONYM definite

amount *noun* **1** QUANTITY, lot, measure, size, supply, mass, volume, capacity, extent, bulk, number, magnitude, expanse **2** TOTAL, whole, mass, addition, sum, lot, extent, aggregate, entirety, totality, sum total
▷▷ **amount to something 1** ADD UP TO, mean, total, equal, constitute, comprise, aggregate, purport, be equivalent to **2** COME TO, become, grow to, develop into, advance to, progress to, mature into

amour *noun* LOVE AFFAIR, relationship, affair, romance, intrigue, liaison, affaire de coeur (*French*)

ample *adjective* **1** PLENTY OF, great, rich, liberal, broad, generous, lavish, spacious, abounding, abundant, plentiful, expansive, copious, roomy, unrestricted, voluminous, capacious, profuse, commodious, plenteous << ANTONYM insufficient **2** LARGE, great, big, full, wide, broad, extensive, generous, abundant, voluminous, bountiful

amplification *noun* **1** INCREASE, boosting, stretching, strengthening, expansion, extension, widening, raising, heightening, deepening, lengthening, enlargement, intensification, magnification, dilation, augmentation **2** EXPLANATION, development, expansion, supplementing, fleshing out, elaboration, rounding out, augmentation, expatiation

amplify *verb* **1** EXPAND, raise, extend, boost, stretch, strengthen, increase, widen, intensify, heighten, deepen, enlarge, lengthen, magnify, augment, dilate << ANTONYM reduce **2** GO INTO DETAIL, develop, explain, expand, supplement, elaborate, augment, flesh out, round out, enlarge on, expatiate << ANTONYM simplify

amplitude *noun* **1** EXTENT, reach, range, size, mass, sweep, dimension, bulk, scope, width, magnitude, compass, greatness, breadth, expanse, vastness, spaciousness, bigness, largeness, hugeness, capaciousness **2** FULLNESS, abundance, richness, plethora, profusion, completeness, plenitude, copiousness, ampleness

amply *adverb* FULLY, well, greatly, completely, richly, liberally, thoroughly, substantially, lavishly, extensively, generously, abundantly, profusely, copiously, plentifully, unstintingly, bountifully, without stinting, plenteously, capaciously << ANTONYM insufficiently

amputate *verb* CUT OFF, remove, separate, sever, curtail, truncate, lop off

amuck ▷ see amok

amuse *verb* **1** ENTERTAIN, please, delight, charm, cheer, tickle, gratify, beguile, enliven, regale, gladden << ANTONYM bore **2** OCCUPY, interest, involve, engage, entertain, absorb, divert, engross

amusement *noun* **1** ENJOYMENT, delight, entertainment, cheer, laughter, mirth, hilarity, merriment, gladdening, beguilement, regalement << ANTONYM boredom **2** DIVERSION, interest, sport, pleasing, fun, pleasure, recreation, entertainment, gratification **3** PASTIME, game, sport, joke, entertainment, hobby, recreation, distraction, diversion, lark, prank

amusing *adjective* FUNNY, humorous, gratifying, laughable, farcical, comical, droll, interesting, pleasing, charming, cheering, entertaining, comic, pleasant, lively, diverting, delightful, enjoyable, cheerful, witty, merry, gladdening, facetious, jocular, rib-tickling, waggish << ANTONYM boring

anaemic *adjective* **1** PALE, weak, dull, frail, feeble, wan, sickly, bloodless, colourless, infirm, pallid, ashen, characterless, enervated, like death warmed up (*informal*) << ANTONYM rosy **2** WEAK, feeble

anaesthetic *noun* PAINKILLER, narcotic, sedative, opiate, anodyne, analgesic, soporific, stupefacient, stupefactive
▷ *adjective* PAIN-KILLING, dulling, numbing, narcotic, sedative, opiate, deadening, anodyne, analgesic, soporific, sleep-inducing, stupefacient, stupefactive

analogous *adjective* SIMILAR, like, related, equivalent, parallel, resembling, alike, corresponding, comparable, akin, homologous << ANTONYM different

analogy *noun* SIMILARITY, relation, comparison, parallel, correspondence, resemblance, correlation, likeness, equivalence, homology, similitude

analyse *verb* **1** EXAMINE, test, study, research, judge, estimate, survey, investigate, interpret, evaluate, inspect, work over **2** BREAK DOWN, consider, study, separate, divide, resolve, dissolve, dissect, think through, assay, anatomize

analysis *noun* **1** STUDY, reasoning, opinion, judgment, interpretation, evaluation, estimation, dissection **2** EXAMINATION, test, division, inquiry, investigation, resolution, interpretation, breakdown, scanning,

separation, evaluation, scrutiny, sifting,
anatomy, dissolution, dissection, assay,
perusal, anatomization

analytic *or* **analytical** *adjective* RATIONAL,
questioning, testing, detailed, searching,
organized, exact, precise, logical, systematic,
inquiring, diagnostic, investigative,
dissecting, explanatory, discrete, inquisitive,
interpretive, studious, interpretative,
expository

anarchic *adjective* LAWLESS, rioting, confused,
disordered, revolutionary, chaotic,
rebellious, riotous, disorganized, misruled,
ungoverned, misgoverned << ANTONYM
law-abiding

anarchist *noun* REVOLUTIONARY, rebel,
terrorist, insurgent, nihilist

anarchy *noun* LAWLESSNESS, revolution,
riot, disorder, confusion, chaos, rebellion,
misrule, disorganization, misgovernment
<< ANTONYM order

anathema *noun* ABOMINATION, bête noire,
enemy, pariah, bane, bugbear

anatomy *noun* 1 STRUCTURE, build, make-
up, frame, framework, composition
2 EXAMINATION, study, division, inquiry,
investigation, analysis, dismemberment,
dissection

ancestor *noun* FOREFATHER, predecessor,
precursor, forerunner, forebear, antecedent,
progenitor, tupuna *or* tipuna (*NZ*)
<< ANTONYM descendant

ancestral *adjective* INHERITED, hereditary,
patriarchal, antecedent, forefatherly,
genealogical, lineal, ancestorial

ancestry *noun* ORIGIN, house, family, line,
race, stock, blood, ancestors, descent,
pedigree, extraction, lineage, forebears,
antecedents, parentage, forefathers,
genealogy, derivation, progenitors

anchor *noun* MOORING, hook (*nautical*), bower
(*nautical*), kedge, drogue, sheet anchor ▷ *verb*
1 MOOR, harbour, dock, tie up, kedge 2 DOCK,
moor, harbour, drop anchor, kedge, cast
anchor, drop the hook, let go the anchor, lay
anchor, come to anchor 3 SECURE, tie, fix,
bind, chain, attach, bolt, fasten, affix

anchorage *noun* BERTH, haven, port, harbour,
dock, quay, dockage, moorage, harbourage

ancient *adjective* 1 CLASSICAL, old, former,
past, bygone, primordial, primeval, olden
2 VERY OLD, early, aged, antique, obsolete,
archaic, age-old, bygone, antiquated,
hoary, olden, superannuated, antediluvian,
timeworn, old as the hills 3 OLD-

FASHIONED, dated, outdated, obsolete, out
of date, unfashionable, outmoded, passé
<< ANTONYM up-to-date

ancillary *adjective* SUPPLEMENTARY,
supporting, extra, additional, secondary,
subsidiary, accessory, subordinate, auxiliary,
contributory << ANTONYM major

and *conjunction* 1 ALSO, including, along with,
together with, in addition to, as well as
2 MOREOVER, plus, furthermore

androgynous *adjective* HERMAPHRODITE,
bisexual, androgyne, hermaphroditic,
epicene

android *noun* (*science fiction*) ROBOT,
automaton, humanoid, cyborg, mechanical
man, bionic man *or* woman

anecdote *noun* STORY, tale, sketch, short story,
yarn, reminiscence, urban myth, urban
legend

anew *adverb* AGAIN, once again, once more,
over again, from the beginning, from
scratch, another time, afresh

angel *noun* 1 DIVINE MESSENGER, spirit,
cherub, archangel, seraph, spiritual being,
guardian spirit 2 (*informal*) DEAR, ideal,
beauty, saint, treasure, darling, dream, jewel,
gem, paragon

angelic *adjective* 1 PURE, beautiful, lovely,
innocent, entrancing, virtuous, saintly,
adorable, beatific 2 HEAVENLY, celestial,
ethereal, cherubic, seraphic << ANTONYM
demonic

anger *noun* RAGE, passion, outrage, temper,
fury, resentment, irritation, wrath,
indignation, annoyance, agitation, ire,
antagonism, displeasure, exasperation,
irritability, spleen, pique, ill temper,
vehemence, vexation, high dudgeon, ill
humour, choler << ANTONYM calmness
▷ *verb* ENRAGE, provoke, outrage, annoy,
offend, excite, irritate, infuriate, hassle
(*informal*), aggravate (*informal*), incense,
fret, gall, madden, exasperate, nettle,
vex, affront, displease, rile, pique, get on
someone's nerves (*informal*), antagonize,
get someone's back up, put someone's back
up, nark (*Brit, Austral & NZ slang*), make
someone's blood boil, get in someone's hair
(*informal*), get someone's dander up (*informal*)
<< ANTONYM soothe

angle *noun* 1 GRADIENT, bank, slope, incline,
inclination 2 INTERSECTION, point, edge,
corner, knee, bend, elbow, crook, crotch,
nook, cusp 3 POINT OF VIEW, position,
approach, direction, aspect, perspective,

outlook, viewpoint, slant, standpoint, take (*informal*), side

angler *noun* FISHERMAN, fisher, piscator *or* piscatrix

angling *noun* FISHING

angry *adjective* FURIOUS, cross, heated, mad (*informal*), raging, provoked, outraged, annoyed, passionate, irritated, raving, hacked (off) (*US slang*), choked, infuriated, hot, incensed, enraged, ranting, exasperated, irritable, resentful, nettled, snappy, indignant, irate, tumultuous, displeased, uptight (*informal*), riled, up in arms, incandescent, ill-tempered, irascible, antagonized, waspish, piqued, hot under the collar (*informal*), on the warpath, hopping mad (*informal*), foaming at the mouth, choleric, splenetic, wrathful, at daggers drawn, in high dudgeon, as black as thunder, ireful, tooshie (*Austral slang*), off the air (*Austral slang*) << ANTONYM calm

angst *noun* ANXIETY, worry, distress, torment, unease, apprehension, agitation, malaise, perturbation, vexation, fretfulness, disquietude, inquietude << ANTONYM peace of mind

anguish *noun* SUFFERING, pain, torture, distress, grief, misery, agony, torment, sorrow, woe, heartache, heartbreak, pang, throe

anguished *adjective* SUFFERING, wounded, tortured, distressed, tormented, afflicted, agonized, grief-stricken, wretched, brokenhearted

angular *adjective* SKINNY, spare, lean, gaunt, bony, lanky, scrawny, lank, rangy, rawboned, macilent (*rare*)

animal *noun* 1 CREATURE, beast, brute 2 BRUTE, devil, monster, savage, beast, bastard (*informal, offensive*), villain, barbarian, swine (*informal*), wild man ▷ *adjective* PHYSICAL, gross, fleshly, bodily, sensual, carnal, brutish, bestial

animate *adjective* LIVING, live, moving, alive, breathing, alive and kicking ▷ *verb* ENLIVEN, encourage, excite, urge, inspire, stir, spark, move, fire, spur, stimulate, revive, activate, rouse, prod, quicken, incite, instigate, kick-start (*informal*), impel, energize, kindle, embolden, liven up, breathe life into, invigorate, gladden, gee up, vitalize, vivify, inspirit << ANTONYM inhibit

animated *adjective* LIVELY, spirited, quick, excited, active, vital, dynamic, enthusiastic, passionate, vivid, vigorous, energetic, vibrant, brisk, buoyant, ardent, airy, fervent, zealous, elated, ebullient, sparky, sprightly, vivacious, gay, alive and kicking, full of beans (*informal*), zestful << ANTONYM listless

animation *noun* LIVELINESS, life, action, activity, energy, spirit, passion, enthusiasm, excitement, pep, sparkle, vitality, vigour, zeal, verve, zest, fervour, high spirits, dynamism, buoyancy, elation, exhilaration, gaiety, ardour, vibrancy, brio, zing (*informal*), vivacity, ebullience, briskness, airiness, sprightliness, pizzazz *or* pizazz (*informal*)

animosity *noun* HOSTILITY, hate, hatred, resentment, bitterness, malice, antagonism, antipathy, enmity, acrimony, rancour, bad blood, ill will, animus, malevolence, virulence, malignity << ANTONYM friendliness

animus *noun* ILL WILL, hate, hostility, hatred, resentment, bitterness, malice, animosity, antagonism, antipathy, enmity, acrimony, rancour, bad blood, malevolence, virulence, malignity

annals *plural noun* RECORDS, history, accounts, registers, journals, memorials, archives, chronicles

annex *verb* 1 SEIZE, take over, appropriate, acquire, occupy, conquer, expropriate, arrogate 2 JOIN, unite, add, connect, attach, tack, adjoin, fasten, affix, append, subjoin << ANTONYM detach

annexation *noun* SEIZURE, takeover, occupation, conquest, appropriation, annexing, expropriation, arrogation

annexe *noun* 1 EXTENSION, wing, ell, supplementary building 2 APPENDIX, addition, supplement, attachment, adjunct, addendum, affixment

annihilate *verb* DESTROY, abolish, wipe out, erase, eradicate, extinguish, obliterate, liquidate, root out, exterminate, nullify, extirpate, wipe from the face of the earth, kennel (*Austral slang*), jeff (*Austral slang*)

annihilation *noun* DESTRUCTION, wiping out, abolition, extinction, extinguishing, liquidation, rooting out, extermination, eradication, erasure, obliteration, nullification, extirpation

anniversary *noun* JUBILEE, remembrance, commemoration

annotate *verb* MAKE NOTES ON, explain, note, illustrate, comment on, interpret, gloss, footnote, commentate, elucidate, make observations on

annotation *noun* NOTE, comment,

explanation, observation, interpretation, illustration, commentary, gloss, footnote, exegesis, explication, elucidation

announce *verb* **1** MAKE KNOWN, tell, report, reveal, publish, declare, advertise, broadcast, disclose, intimate, proclaim, trumpet, make public, publicize, divulge, promulgate, propound, shout from the rooftops (*informal*) << ANTONYM keep secret **2** BE A SIGN OF, signal, herald, warn of, signify, augur, harbinger, presage, foretell, portend, betoken

announcement *noun* **1** STATEMENT, communication, broadcast, explanation, publication, declaration, advertisement, testimony, disclosure, bulletin, communiqué, proclamation, utterance, intimation, promulgation, divulgence **2** DECLARATION, report, reporting, publication, revelation, disclosure, proclamation, intimation, promulgation, divulgence

announcer *noun* PRESENTER, newscaster, reporter, commentator, broadcaster, newsreader, master of ceremonies, anchor man, anchor

annoy *verb* IRRITATE, trouble, bore, anger, harry, bother, disturb, provoke, get (*informal*), bug (*informal*), needle (*informal*), plague, tease, harass, hassle (*informal*), aggravate (*informal*), badger, gall, madden, ruffle, exasperate, nettle, molest, pester, vex, displease, irk, bedevil, rile, peeve, get under your skin (*informal*), get on your nerves (*informal*), nark (*Brit, Austral & NZ slang*), get up your nose (*informal*), give someone grief (*Brit & S African*), make your blood boil, rub someone up the wrong way (*informal*), get your goat (*slang*), get in your hair (*informal*), get on your wick (*Brit slang*), get your dander up (*informal*), get your back up, incommode, put your back up, hack you off (*informal*) << ANTONYM soothe

annoyance *noun* **1** IRRITATION, trouble, anger, bother, grief (*informal*), harassment, disturbance, hassle (*informal*), nuisance, provocation, displeasure, exasperation, aggravation, vexation, bedevilment **2** NUISANCE, bother, pain (*informal*), bind (*informal*), bore, drag (*informal*), plague, tease, pest, gall, pain in the neck (*informal*)

annoyed *adjective* IRRITATED, bothered, harassed, hassled (*informal*), aggravated (*informal*), maddened, ruffled, exasperated, nettled, vexed, miffed (*informal*), displeased, irked, riled, harried, peeved (*informal*), piqued, browned off (*informal*)

annoying *adjective* IRRITATING, boring, disturbing, provoking, teasing, harassing, aggravating, troublesome, galling, maddening, exasperating, displeasing, bedevilling, peeving (*informal*), irksome, bothersome, vexatious << ANTONYM delightful

annual *adjective* **1** ONCE A YEAR, yearly **2** YEARLONG, yearly

annually *adverb* **1** ONCE A YEAR, yearly, each year, every year, per year, by the year, every twelve months, per annum, year after year **2** PER YEAR, yearly, each year, every year, by the year, per annum

annul *verb* INVALIDATE, reverse, cancel, abolish, void, repeal, recall, revoke, retract, negate, rescind, nullify, obviate, abrogate, countermand, declare *or* render null and void << ANTONYM restore

anodyne *adjective* BLAND, dull, boring, insipid, unexciting, uninspiring, uninteresting, mind-numbing (*informal*) ▷ *noun* PAINKILLER, narcotic, palliative, analgesic, pain reliever

anoint *verb* **1** SMEAR, oil, rub, grease, spread over, daub, embrocate **2** CONSECRATE, bless, sanctify, hallow, anele (*archaic*)

anomalous *adjective* UNUSUAL, odd, rare, bizarre, exceptional, peculiar, eccentric, abnormal, irregular, inconsistent, off-the-wall (*slang*), incongruous, deviating, oddball (*informal*), atypical, aberrant, outré << ANTONYM normal

anomaly *noun* IRREGULARITY, departure, exception, abnormality, rarity, inconsistency, deviation, eccentricity, oddity, aberration, peculiarity, incongruity

anon *adverb* (*archaic or literary*) SOON, presently, shortly, promptly, before long, forthwith, betimes (*archaic*), erelong (*archaic or poetic*), in a couple of shakes (*informal*)

anonymity *noun* **1** NAMELESSNESS, innominateness **2** UNREMARKABILITY *or* UNREMARKABLENESS, characterlessness, unsingularity

anonymous *adjective* **1** UNNAMED, unknown, unidentified, nameless, unacknowledged, incognito, unauthenticated, innominate << ANTONYM identified **2** UNSIGNED, uncredited, unattributed, unattested << ANTONYM signed **3** NONDESCRIPT, impersonal, faceless, colourless, undistinguished, unexceptional, characterless

answer *verb* 1 REPLY, explain, respond, resolve, acknowledge, react, return, retort, rejoin, refute << ANTONYM ask 2 SATISFY, meet, serve, fit, fill, suit, solve, fulfil, suffice, measure up to ▷ *noun* 1 REPLY, response, reaction, resolution, explanation, plea, comeback, retort, report, return, defence, acknowledgement, riposte, counterattack, refutation, rejoinder << ANTONYM question 2 SOLUTION, resolution, explanation 3 REMEDY, solution, vindication ▷▷ **answer to someone** BE RESPONSIBLE TO, obey, work under, be ruled by, be managed by, be subordinate to, be accountable to, be answerable to

answerable *adjective* RESPONSIBLE FOR *or* TO, to blame for, liable for *or* to, accountable for *or* to, chargeable for, subject to

answer back *verb* BE IMPERTINENT, argue, dispute, disagree, retort, contradict, rebut, talk back, be cheeky

antagonism *noun* HOSTILITY, competition, opposition, conflict, rivalry, contention, friction, discord, antipathy, dissension << ANTONYM friendship

antagonist *noun* OPPONENT, rival, opposer, enemy, competitor, contender, foe, adversary

antagonistic *adjective* HOSTILE, opposed, resistant, at odds, incompatible, set against, averse, unfriendly, at variance, inimical, antipathetic, ill-disposed

antagonize *verb* ANNOY, anger, insult, offend, irritate, alienate, hassle (*informal*), aggravate (*informal*), gall, repel, estrange, get under your skin (*informal*), get on your nerves (*informal*), nark (*Brit, Austral & NZ slang*), get up your nose (*informal*), be on your back (*slang*), rub (you) up the wrong way (*informal*), disaffect, get in your hair (*informal*), get on your wick (*Brit slang*), hack you off (*informal*) << ANTONYM pacify

antecedent *adjective* PRECEDING, earlier, former, previous, prior, preliminary, foregoing, anterior, precursory << ANTONYM subsequent

anterior *adjective* 1 FRONT, forward, fore, frontward 2 EARLIER, former, previous, prior, preceding, introductory, foregoing, antecedent

anthem *noun* SONG OF PRAISE, carol, chant, hymn, psalm, paean, chorale, canticle

anthology *noun* COLLECTION, choice, selection, treasury, digest, compilation, garland, compendium, miscellany, analects

anticipate *verb* 1 EXPECT, predict, forecast, prepare for, look for, hope for, envisage, foresee, bank on, apprehend, foretell, think likely, count upon 2 AWAIT, look forward to, count the hours until

anticipation *noun* EXPECTANCY, hope, expectation, apprehension, foresight, premonition, preconception, foretaste, prescience, forethought, presentiment

anticlimax *noun* DISAPPOINTMENT, letdown, comedown (*informal*), bathos << ANTONYM climax

antics *plural noun* CLOWNING, tricks, stunts, mischief, larks, capers, pranks, frolics, escapades, foolishness, silliness, playfulness, skylarking, horseplay, buffoonery, tomfoolery, monkey tricks

antidote *noun* REMEDY, cure, preventive, corrective, neutralizer, nostrum, countermeasure, antitoxin, antivenin, counteragent

antipathy *noun* HOSTILITY, opposition, disgust, dislike, hatred, loathing, distaste, animosity, aversion, antagonism, enmity, rancour, bad blood, incompatibility, ill will, animus, repulsion, abhorrence, repugnance, odium, contrariety << ANTONYM affinity

antiquated *adjective* OBSOLETE, old, aged, ancient, antique, old-fashioned, elderly, dated, past it (*informal*), out-of-date, archaic, outmoded, passé, old hat, hoary, superannuated, antediluvian, outworn, cobwebby, old as the hills << ANTONYM up-to-date

antique *noun* PERIOD PIECE, relic, bygone, heirloom, collector's item, museum piece, object of virtu ▷ *adjective* 1 VINTAGE, classic, antiquarian, olden 2 OLD-FASHIONED, old, aged, ancient, remote, elderly, primitive, outdated, obsolete, archaic, bygone, primordial, primeval, immemorial, superannuated

antiquity *noun* 1 DISTANT PAST, ancient times, time immemorial, olden days 2 OLD AGE, age, oldness, ancientness, elderliness

antiseptic *adjective* HYGIENIC, clean, pure, sterile, sanitary, uncontaminated, unpolluted, germ-free, aseptic << ANTONYM unhygienic ▷ *noun* DISINFECTANT, purifier, bactericide, germicide

antisocial *adjective* 1 UNSOCIABLE, reserved, retiring, withdrawn, alienated, unfriendly, uncommunicative, misanthropic, asocial << ANTONYM sociable 2 DISRUPTIVE, disorderly, hostile, menacing, rebellious, belligerent, antagonistic, uncooperative

antithesis *noun* **1** OPPOSITE, contrast, reverse, contrary, converse, inverse, antipode **2** CONTRAST, opposition, contradiction, reversal, inversion, contrariety, contraposition

anxiety *noun* UNEASINESS, concern, care, worry, doubt, tension, alarm, distress, suspicion, angst, unease, apprehension, misgiving, suspense, nervousness, disquiet, trepidation, foreboding, restlessness, solicitude, perturbation, watchfulness, fretfulness, disquietude, apprehensiveness, dubiety << ANTONYM confidence

anxious *adjective* **1** EAGER, keen, intent, yearning, impatient, itching, ardent, avid, expectant, desirous << ANTONYM reluctant **2** UNEASY, concerned, worried, troubled, upset, careful, wired (*slang*), nervous, disturbed, distressed, uncomfortable, tense, fearful, unsettled, restless, neurotic, agitated, taut, disquieted, apprehensive, edgy, watchful, jittery (*informal*), perturbed, on edge, ill at ease, twitchy (*informal*), solicitous, overwrought, fretful, on tenterhooks, in suspense, hot and bothered, unquiet (*chiefly literary*), like a fish out of water, antsy (*informal*), angsty, on pins and needles, discomposed << ANTONYM confident

apace *adverb* (*literary*) QUICKLY, rapidly, swiftly, speedily, without delay, at full speed, expeditiously, posthaste, with dispatch

apart *adverb* **1** TO PIECES, to bits, asunder, into parts **2** AWAY FROM EACH OTHER, distant from each other **3** ASIDE, away, alone, independently, separately, singly, excluded, isolated, cut off, to one side, to yourself, by itself, aloof, to itself, by yourself, out on a limb ▷▷ **apart from** EXCEPT FOR, excepting, other than, excluding, besides, not including, aside from, but, save, bar, not counting

apartment *noun* **1** (*US*) FLAT, room, suite, compartment, penthouse, duplex (*US & Canad*), crib, bachelor apartment (*Canad*) **2** ROOMS, quarters, chambers, accommodation, living quarters

apathetic *adjective* UNINTERESTED, passive, indifferent, sluggish, unmoved, stoic, stoical, unconcerned, listless, cold, cool, impassive, unresponsive, phlegmatic, unfeeling, unemotional, torpid, emotionless, insensible << ANTONYM interested

apathy *noun* LACK OF INTEREST, indifference, inertia, coolness, passivity, coldness,

stoicism, nonchalance, torpor, phlegm, sluggishness, listlessness, unconcern, insensibility, unresponsiveness, impassivity, passiveness, impassibility, unfeelingness, emotionlessness, uninterestedness << ANTONYM interest

ape *verb* IMITATE, copy, mirror, echo, mock, parrot, mimic, parody, caricature, affect, counterfeit

aperture *noun* OPENING, space, hole, crack, gap, rent, passage, breach, slot, vent, rift, slit, cleft, eye, chink, fissure, orifice, perforation, eyelet, interstice

apex *noun* **1** CULMINATION, top, crown, height, climax, highest point, zenith, apogee, acme << ANTONYM depths **2** HIGHEST POINT, point, top, tip, summit, peak, crest, pinnacle, vertex << ANTONYM lowest point

aphorism *noun* SAYING, maxim, gnome, adage, proverb, dictum, precept, axiom, apothegm, saw

aphrodisiac *noun* LOVE POTION, philtre ▷ *adjective* EROTIC *or* EROTICAL, exciting, stimulating, arousing, venereal

apiece *adverb* EACH, individually, separately, for each, to each, respectively, from each, severally << ANTONYM all together

aplenty *adjective* IN PLENTY, to spare, galore, in abundance, in quantity, in profusion, à gogo (*informal*) ▷ *adverb* PLENTIFULLY, in abundance, abundantly, in quantity, in plenty, copiously, plenteously

aplomb *noun* SELF-POSSESSION, confidence, stability, self-confidence, composure, poise, coolness, calmness, equanimity, balance, self-assurance, sang-froid, level-headedness << ANTONYM self-consciousness

apocalypse *noun* DESTRUCTION, holocaust, havoc, devastation, carnage, conflagration, cataclysm

apocryphal *adjective* DUBIOUS, legendary, doubtful, questionable, mythical, spurious, fictitious, unsubstantiated, equivocal, unverified, unauthenticated, uncanonical << ANTONYM factual

apogee *noun* HIGHEST POINT, top, tip, crown, summit, height, peak, climax, crest, pinnacle, culmination, zenith, apex, acme, vertex

apologetic *adjective* REGRETFUL, sorry, rueful, contrite, remorseful, penitent

apologize *verb* SAY SORRY, express regret, ask forgiveness, make an apology, beg pardon, say you are sorry

apology *noun* REGRET, explanation, excuse,

confession, extenuation ▷▷ **apology for something** *or* **someone** MOCKERY OF, excuse for, imitation of, caricature of, travesty of, poor substitute for

apostle *noun* 1 EVANGELIST, herald, missionary, preacher, messenger, proselytizer 2 SUPPORTER, champion, advocate, pioneer, proponent, propagandist, propagator

apotheosis *noun* DEIFICATION, elevation, exaltation, glorification, idealization, idolization

appal *verb* HORRIFY, shock, alarm, frighten, scare, terrify, outrage, disgust, dishearten, revolt, intimidate, dismay, daunt, sicken, astound, harrow, unnerve, petrify, scandalize, make your hair stand on end (*informal*)

appalled *adjective* HORRIFIED, shocked, stunned, alarmed, frightened, scared, terrified, outraged, dismayed, daunted, astounded, unnerved, disquieted, petrified, disheartened

appalling *adjective* 1 HORRIFYING, shocking, terrible, alarming, frightening, scaring, awful, terrifying, horrible, grim, dreadful, intimidating, dismaying, horrific, fearful, daunting, dire, astounding, ghastly, hideous, shameful, harrowing, vile, unnerving, petrifying, horrid, unspeakable, frightful, nightmarish, abominable, disheartening, godawful (*slang*), hellacious (*US slang*) << ANTONYM reassuring 2 AWFUL, terrible, tremendous, distressing, horrible, dreadful, horrendous, ghastly, godawful (*slang*)

apparatus *noun* 1 ORGANIZATION, system, network, structure, bureaucracy, hierarchy, setup (*informal*), chain of command 2 EQUIPMENT, machine, tackle, gear, means, materials, device, tools, implements, mechanism, outfit, machinery, appliance, utensils, contraption (*informal*)

apparel *noun* (*old-fashioned*) CLOTHING, dress, clothes, equipment, gear (*informal*), habit, outfit, costume, threads (*slang*), array (*poetic*), garments, robes, trappings, attire, garb, accoutrements, vestments, raiment (*archaic* or *poetic*), schmutter (*slang*), habiliments

apparent *adjective* 1 SEEMING, supposed, alleged, outward, exterior, superficial, ostensible, specious << ANTONYM actual 2 OBVIOUS, marked, clear, plain, visible, bold, patent, evident, distinct, open, understandable, manifest, noticeable, blatant, conspicuous, overt, unmistakable, palpable, undeniable, discernible, salient, self-evident, indisputable, much in evidence, undisguised, unconcealed, indubitable, staring you in the face (*informal*), plain as the nose on your face << ANTONYM unclear

apparently *adverb* SEEMINGLY, outwardly, ostensibly, speciously

apparition *noun* GHOST, spirit, shade (*literary*), phantom, spectre, spook (*informal*), wraith, chimera, revenant, visitant, eidolon, atua (*NZ*), kehua (*NZ*)

appeal *verb* PLEAD, call, ask, apply, refer, request, sue, lobby, pray, beg, petition, solicit, implore, beseech, entreat, importune, adjure, supplicate << ANTONYM refuse ▷ *noun* 1 PLEA, call, application, request, prayer, petition, overture, invocation, solicitation, entreaty, supplication, suit, cry from the heart, adjuration << ANTONYM refusal 2 ATTRACTION, charm, fascination, charisma, beauty, attractiveness, allure, magnetism, enchantment, seductiveness, interestingness, engagingness, pleasingness << ANTONYM repulsiveness ▷▷ **appeal to someone** ATTRACT, interest, draw, please, invite, engage, charm, fascinate, tempt, lure, entice, enchant, captivate, allure, bewitch

appealing *adjective* ATTRACTIVE, inviting, engaging, charming, winning, desirable, endearing, alluring, winsome, prepossessing << ANTONYM repellent

appear *verb* 1 SEEM, be clear, be obvious, be evident, look (like *or* as if), be apparent, be plain, be manifest, be patent 2 LOOK (LIKE *or* AS IF), seem, occur, look to be, come across as, strike you as 3 COME INTO VIEW, emerge, occur, attend, surface, come out, turn out, arise, turn up, be present, loom, show (*informal*), issue, develop, arrive, show up (*informal*), come to light, crop up (*informal*), materialize, come forth, come into sight, show your face << ANTONYM disappear 4 COME INTO BEING, come out, be published, be developed, be created, be invented, become available, come into existence 5 PERFORM, play, act, enter, come on, take part, play a part, be exhibited, come onstage

appearance *noun* 1 LOOK, face, form, air, figure, image, looks, bearing, aspect, manner, expression, demeanour, mien (*literary*) 2 ARRIVAL, appearing, presence, turning up, introduction, showing up (*informal*), emergence, advent 3 IMPRESSION, air, front, image, illusion, guise, façade, pretence, veneer, semblance, outward show

appease *verb* **1** PACIFY, satisfy, calm, soothe, quiet, placate, mollify, conciliate << ANTONYM anger **2** EASE, satisfy, calm, relieve, diminish, compose, quiet, blunt, soothe, subdue, lessen, alleviate, lull, quell, allay, mitigate, assuage, quench, tranquillize

appeasement *noun* **1** PACIFICATION, compromise, accommodation, concession, conciliation, acceding, propitiation, mollification, placation **2** EASING, relieving, satisfaction, softening, blunting, soothing, quieting, lessening, lulling, quelling, solace, quenching, mitigation, abatement, alleviation, assuagement, tranquillization

appellation *noun (formal)* NAME, term, style, title, address, description, designation, epithet, sobriquet

append *verb (formal)* ADD, attach, join, hang, adjoin, fasten, annex, tag on, affix, tack on, subjoin << ANTONYM detach

appendage *noun* ATTACHMENT, addition, supplement, accessory, appendix, auxiliary, affix, ancillary, adjunct, annexe, addendum, appurtenance

appendix *noun* SUPPLEMENT, add-on, postscript, adjunct, appendage, addendum, addition, codicil

appetite *noun* **1** HUNGER **2** DESIRE, liking, longing, demand, taste, passion, stomach, hunger, willingness, relish, craving, yearning, inclination, zeal, zest, propensity, hankering, proclivity, appetence, appetency << ANTONYM distaste

appetizer *noun* HORS D'OEUVRE, titbit, antipasto, canapé

applaud *verb* **1** CLAP, encourage, praise, cheer, hail, acclaim, laud, give (someone) a big hand << ANTONYM boo **2** PRAISE, celebrate, approve, acclaim, compliment, salute, commend, extol, crack up (*informal*), big up (*slang, chiefly Caribbean*), eulogize << ANTONYM criticize

applause *noun* OVATION, praise, cheering, cheers, approval, acclaim, clapping, accolade, big hand, commendation, hand-clapping, approbation, acclamation, eulogizing, plaudit

appliance *noun* DEVICE, machine, tool, instrument, implement, mechanism, apparatus, gadget, waldo

applicable *adjective* APPROPRIATE, fitting, fit, suited, useful, suitable, relevant, to the point, apt, pertinent, befitting, apposite, apropos, germane, to the purpose << ANTONYM inappropriate

applicant *noun* CANDIDATE, entrant, claimant, suitor, petitioner, aspirant, inquirer, job-seeker, suppliant, postulant

application *noun* **1** REQUEST, claim, demand, appeal, suit, inquiry, plea, petition, requisition, solicitation **2** RELEVANCE, use, value, practice, bearing, exercise, purpose, function, appropriateness, aptness, pertinence, appositeness, germaneness **3** EFFORT, work, study, industry, labour, trouble, attention, struggle, pains, commitment, hard work, endeavour, dedication, toil, diligence, perseverance, travail (*literary*), attentiveness, assiduity, blood, sweat, and tears (*informal*)

apply *verb* **1** REQUEST, seek, appeal, put in, petition, inquire, solicit, claim, sue, requisition, make application **2** BE RELEVANT, concern, relate, refer, be fitting, be appropriate, be significant, fit, suit, pertain, be applicable, bear upon, appertain **3** USE, exercise, carry out, employ, engage, implement, practise, execute, assign, administer, exert, enact, utilize, bring to bear, put to use, bring into play **4** PUT ON, work in, cover with, lay on, paint on, anoint, spread on, rub in, smear on, shampoo in, bring into contact with ▷▷ **apply yourself** WORK HARD, concentrate, study, pay attention, try, commit yourself, buckle down (*informal*), be assiduous, devote yourself, be diligent, dedicate yourself, make an effort, address yourself, be industrious, persevere

appoint *verb* **1** ASSIGN, name, choose, commission, select, elect, install, delegate, nominate << ANTONYM fire **2** DECIDE, set, choose, establish, determine, settle, fix, arrange, specify, assign, designate, allot << ANTONYM cancel

appointed *adjective* **1** DECIDED, set, chosen, established, determined, settled, fixed, arranged, assigned, designated, allotted **2** ASSIGNED, named, chosen, commissioned, selected, elected, installed, delegated, nominated **3** EQUIPPED, provided, supplied, furnished, fitted out

appointment *noun* **1** SELECTION, naming, election, choosing, choice, commissioning, delegation, nomination, installation, assignment, allotment, designation **2** JOB, office, position, post, situation, place, station, employment, assignment, berth (*informal*) **3** MEETING, interview, date, session, arrangement, consultation, engagement, fixture, rendezvous, tryst (*archaic*), assignation 4 APPOINTEE, candidate, representative, delegate, nominee, office-holder

apportion *verb* DIVIDE, share, deal, distribute, assign, allocate, dispense, give out, allot, mete out, dole out, measure out, parcel out, ration out

apposite *adjective* APPROPRIATE, fitting, suited, suitable, relevant, proper, to the point, apt, applicable, pertinent, befitting, apropos, germane, to the purpose, appertaining << ANTONYM inappropriate

appraisal *noun* 1 ASSESSMENT, opinion, estimate, judgment, evaluation, estimation, sizing up (*informal*), recce (*slang*) 2 VALUATION, pricing, rating, survey, reckoning, assay

appraise *verb* ASSESS, judge, review, estimate, survey, price, rate, value, evaluate, inspect, gauge, size up (*informal*), eye up, assay, recce (*slang*)

appreciable *adjective* SIGNIFICANT, marked, obvious, considerable, substantial, visible, evident, pronounced, definite, noticeable, clear-cut, discernible, measurable, material, recognizable, detectable, perceptible, distinguishable, ascertainable, perceivable << ANTONYM insignificant

appreciably *adverb* SIGNIFICANTLY, obviously, definitely, considerably, substantially, evidently, visibly, markedly, noticeably, palpably, perceptively, measurably, recognizably, discernibly, detectably, distinguishably, perceivably, ascertainably

appreciate *verb* 1 ENJOY, like, value, regard, respect, prize, admire, treasure, esteem, relish, cherish, savour, rate highly << ANTONYM scorn 2 BE AWARE OF, know, understand, estimate, realize, acknowledge, recognize, perceive, comprehend, take account of, be sensitive to, be conscious of, sympathize with, be alive to, be cognizant of << ANTONYM be unaware of 3 BE GRATEFUL FOR, be obliged for, be thankful for, give thanks for, be indebted for, be in debt for, be appreciative of << ANTONYM be ungrateful for 4 INCREASE, rise, grow, gain, improve, mount, enhance, soar, inflate << ANTONYM fall

appreciation *noun* 1 ADMIRATION, liking, respect, assessment, esteem, relish, valuation, enjoyment, appraisal, estimation, responsiveness 2 GRATITUDE, thanks, recognition, obligation, acknowledgment, indebtedness, thankfulness, gratefulness << ANTONYM ingratitude 3 AWARENESS, understanding, regard, knowledge, recognition, perception, sympathy, consciousness, sensitivity, realization, comprehension, familiarity, mindfulness, cognizance << ANTONYM ignorance 4 INCREASE, rise, gain, growth, inflation, improvement, escalation, enhancement << ANTONYM fall 5 REVIEW, report, notice, analysis, criticism, praise, assessment, recognition, tribute, evaluation, critique, acclamation

appreciative *adjective* 1 ENTHUSIASTIC, understanding, pleased, aware, sensitive, conscious, admiring, sympathetic, supportive, responsive, knowledgeable, respectful, mindful, perceptive, in the know (*informal*), cognizant, regardful 2 GRATEFUL, obliged, thankful, indebted, beholden

apprehend *verb* 1 ARREST, catch, lift (*slang*), nick (*slang, chiefly Brit*), capture, seize, run in (*slang*), take, nail (*informal*), bust (*informal*), collar (*informal*), pinch (*informal*), nab (*informal*), take prisoner, feel your collar (*slang*) << ANTONYM release 2 UNDERSTAND, know, think, believe, imagine, realize, recognize, appreciate, perceive, grasp, conceive, comprehend, get the message, get the picture << ANTONYM be unaware of

apprehension *noun* 1 ANXIETY, concern, fear, worry, doubt, alarm, suspicion, dread, unease, mistrust, misgiving, disquiet, premonition, trepidation, foreboding, uneasiness, pins and needles, apprehensiveness << ANTONYM confidence 2 ARREST, catching, capture, taking, seizure << ANTONYM release 3 AWARENESS, understanding, knowledge, intelligence, ken, perception, grasp, comprehension << ANTONYM incomprehension

apprehensive *adjective* ANXIOUS, concerned, worried, afraid, alarmed, nervous, suspicious, doubtful, uneasy, fearful, neurotic, disquieted, foreboding, twitchy (*informal*), mistrustful, antsy (*informal*) << ANTONYM confident

apprentice *noun* TRAINEE, student, pupil, novice, beginner, learner, neophyte, tyro, probationer << ANTONYM master

apprenticeship *noun* TRAINEESHIP, probation, studentship, novitiate *or* noviciate

apprise *verb* MAKE AWARE, tell, warn, advise, inform, communicate, notify, enlighten, acquaint, give notice, make cognizant ▷ see **appraise**

approach *verb* **1** MOVE TOWARDS, come to, reach, near, advance, catch up, meet, come close, gain on, converge on, come near, push forward, draw near, creep up on **2** MAKE A PROPOSAL TO, speak to, apply to, appeal to, proposition, solicit, sound out, make overtures to, make advances to, broach the matter with **3** SET ABOUT, tackle, undertake, embark on, get down to, launch into, begin work on, commence on, make a start on, enter upon **4** APPROXIMATE, touch, be like, compare with, resemble, come close to, border on, verge on, be comparable to, come near to ▷ *noun* **1** ADVANCE, coming, nearing, appearance, arrival, advent, drawing near **2** ACCESS, way, drive, road, passage, entrance, avenue, passageway **3** *often plural* PROPOSAL, offer, appeal, advance, application, invitation, proposition, overture **4** WAY, means, course, style, attitude, method, technique, manner, procedure, mode, modus operandi **5** APPROXIMATION, likeness, semblance

approachable *adjective* **1** FRIENDLY, open, cordial, sociable, affable, congenial << ANTONYM unfriendly **2** ACCESSIBLE, attainable, reachable, get-at-able (*informal*), come-at-able (*informal*) << ANTONYM inaccessible

appropriate *adjective* SUITABLE, right, fitting, fit, suited, correct, belonging, relevant, proper, to the point, in keeping, apt, applicable, pertinent, befitting, well-suited, well-timed, apposite, apropos, opportune, becoming, seemly, felicitous, germane, to the purpose, appurtenant, congruous << ANTONYM unsuitable ▷ *verb* **1** SEIZE, take, claim, assume, take over, acquire, confiscate, annex, usurp, impound, pre-empt, commandeer, take possession of, expropriate, arrogate << ANTONYM relinquish **2** ALLOCATE, allow, budget, devote, assign, designate, set aside, earmark, allot, share out, apportion << ANTONYM withhold **3** STEAL, take, nick (*slang, chiefly Brit*), pocket, pinch (*informal*), pirate, poach, swipe (*slang*), lift (*informal*), heist (*US slang*), embezzle, blag (*slang*), pilfer, misappropriate, snitch (*slang*), purloin, filch, plagiarize, thieve, peculate

appropriateness *noun* SUITABILITY, fitness, relevance, correctness, felicity, rightness, applicability, timeliness, aptness, pertinence, fittingness, seemliness, appositeness, properness, germaneness, opportuneness, becomingness, congruousness, felicitousness, well-suitedness

appropriation *noun* **1** SETTING ASIDE, assignment, allocation, earmarking, allotment, apportionment **2** SEIZURE, taking, takeover, assumption, annexation, confiscation, commandeering, expropriation, pre-emption, usurpation, impoundment, arrogation

approval *noun* **1** CONSENT, agreement, sanction, licence, blessing, permission, recommendation, concession, confirmation, mandate, endorsement, leave, compliance, the go-ahead (*informal*), countenance, ratification, the green light, assent, authorization, validation, acquiescence, imprimatur, concurrence, O.K. *or* okay (*informal*) **2** FAVOUR, liking, regard, respect, praise, esteem, acclaim, appreciation, encouragement, admiration, applause, commendation, approbation, good opinion << ANTONYM disapproval

approve *verb* AGREE TO, second, allow, pass, accept, confirm, recommend, permit, sanction, advocate, bless, endorse, uphold, mandate, authorize, ratify, go along with, subscribe to, consent to, buy into (*informal*), validate, countenance, rubber stamp, accede to, give the go-ahead to (*informal*), give the green light to, assent to, concur in, O.K. *or* okay (*informal*) << ANTONYM veto ▷▷ **approve of something** *or* **someone** FAVOUR, like, support, respect, praise, appreciate, agree with, admire, endorse, esteem, acclaim, applaud, commend, be pleased with, have a good opinion of, regard highly, think highly of

approving *adjective* FAVOURABLE, admiring, applauding, respectful, appreciative, commendatory, acclamatory

approximate *adjective* ROUGH, close, general, near, estimated, loose, vague, hazy, sketchy, amorphous, imprecise, inexact, almost exact, almost accurate << ANTONYM exact ▷▷ **approximate to** RESEMBLE, reach, approach, touch, come close to, border on, come near, verge on

approximately *adverb* ALMOST, about, around, generally, nearly, close to, relatively, roughly, loosely, just about, more or less, in the region of, in the vicinity of, not far off, in the neighbourhood of

approximation *noun* GUESS, estimate, conjecture, estimation, guesswork, rough idea, rough calculation, ballpark figure (*informal*), ballpark estimate (*informal*)

a priori *adjective* DEDUCED, deductive, inferential

apron *noun* PINNY (*informal*), overall, pinafore

apropos *adjective* APPROPRIATE, right, seemly, fitting, fit, related, correct, belonging, suitable, relevant, proper, to the point, apt, applicable, pertinent, befitting, apposite, opportune, germane, to the purpose ▷▷ **apropos of** CONCERNING, about, re, regarding, respecting, on the subject of, in respect of, as to, with reference to, in re, in the matter of, as regards, in *or* with regard to

apt *adjective* **1** APPROPRIATE, timely, right, seemly, fitting, fit, related, correct, belonging, suitable, relevant, proper, to the point, applicable, pertinent, befitting, apposite, apropos, opportune, germane, to the purpose << ANTONYM inappropriate **2** INCLINED, likely, ready, disposed, prone, liable, given, predisposed, of a mind **3** GIFTED, skilled, expert, quick, bright, talented, sharp, capable, smart, prompt, clever, intelligent, accomplished, ingenious, skilful, astute, adroit, teachable << ANTONYM slow

aptitude *noun* GIFT, ability, talent, capacity, intelligence, leaning, bent, tendency, faculty, capability, flair, inclination, disposition, knack, propensity, proficiency, predilection, cleverness, proclivity, quickness, giftedness, proneness, aptness

arable *adjective* PRODUCTIVE, fertile, fruitful, fecund, cultivable, farmable, ploughable, tillable

arbiter *noun* **1** JUDGE, referee, umpire, umpie (*Austral slang*), arbitrator, adjudicator **2** AUTHORITY, expert, master, governor, ruler, dictator, controller, lord, pundit

arbitrary *adjective* **1** RANDOM, chance, optional, subjective, unreasonable, inconsistent, erratic, discretionary, personal, fanciful, wilful, whimsical, capricious << ANTONYM logical **2** DICTATORIAL, absolute, unlimited, uncontrolled, autocratic, dogmatic, imperious, domineering, unrestrained, overbearing, tyrannical, summary, magisterial, despotic, high-handed, peremptory, tyrannous

arbitrate *verb* DECIDE, judge, determine, settle, referee, umpire, mediate, adjudicate, adjudge, pass judgment, sit in judgment

arbitration *noun* DECISION, settlement, judgment, determination, adjudication, arbitrament

arbitrator *noun* JUDGE, referee, umpire, umpie (*Austral slang*), arbiter, adjudicator

arc *noun* CURVE, bend, bow, arch, crescent, half-moon

arcade *noun* GALLERY, mall, cloister, portico, colonnade, covered walk, peristyle

arcane *adjective* MYSTERIOUS, secret, hidden, esoteric, occult, recondite, cabbalistic

arch[1] *noun* **1** ARCHWAY, curve, dome, span, vault **2** CURVE, bend, bow, crook, arc, hunch, sweep, hump, curvature, semicircle ▷ *verb* CURVE, bridge, bend, bow, span, arc

arch[2] *adjective* PLAYFUL, joking, teasing, humorous, sly, mischievous, saucy, tongue-in-cheek, jesting, jokey, pert, good-natured, roguish, frolicsome, waggish

archaic *adjective* **1** OLD, ancient, antique, primitive, bygone, olden (*archaic*) << ANTONYM modern **2** OLD-FASHIONED, obsolete, out of date, antiquated, outmoded, passé, old hat, behind the times, superannuated << ANTONYM up-to-date

arched *adjective* CURVED, domed, vaulted

archer *noun* BOWMAN (*archaic*), toxophilite (*formal*)

archetypal *or* **archetypical** *adjective* TYPICAL, standard, model, original, normal, classic, ideal, exemplary, paradigmatic, prototypal, prototypic *or* prototypical

archetype *noun* PRIME EXAMPLE, standard, model, original, pattern, classic, ideal, norm, form, prototype, paradigm, exemplar

architect *noun* **1** DESIGNER, planner, draughtsman, master builder **2** CREATOR, father, shaper, engineer, author, maker, designer, founder, deviser, planner, inventor, contriver, originator, prime mover, instigator, initiator

architecture *noun* **1** DESIGN, planning, building, construction, architectonics **2** CONSTRUCTION, design, style **3** STRUCTURE, design, shape, make-up, construction, framework, layout, anatomy

archive *noun* RECORD OFFICE, museum, registry, repository ▷ *plural noun* RECORDS, papers, accounts, rolls, documents, files, registers, deeds, chronicles, annals

arctic *adjective* (*informal*) FREEZING, cold, frozen, icy, chilly, frosty, glacial, frigid, gelid, frost-bound, cold as ice

Arctic *adjective* POLAR, far-northern, hyperborean

ardent *adjective* **1** ENTHUSIASTIC, keen, eager, avid, zealous, keen as mustard << ANTONYM indifferent **2** PASSIONATE, warm, spirited, intense, flaming, fierce, fiery, hot, fervent, impassioned, ablaze, lusty, vehement, amorous, hot-blooded, warm-blooded, fervid << ANTONYM cold

ardour *noun* **1** PASSION, feeling, fire, heat, spirit, intensity, warmth, devotion, fervour, vehemence, fierceness **2** ENTHUSIASM, zeal, eagerness, earnestness, keenness, avidity

arduous *adjective* DIFFICULT, trying, hard, tough, tiring, severe, painful, exhausting, punishing, harsh, taxing, heavy, steep, formidable, fatiguing, rigorous, troublesome, gruelling, strenuous, onerous, laborious, burdensome, backbreaking, toilsome << ANTONYM easy

area *noun* **1** REGION, land, quarter, division, sector, district, stretch, territory, zone, plot, province, patch, neighbourhood, sphere, turf (*US slang*), realm, domain, tract, locality, neck of the woods (*informal*) **2** PART, section, sector, portion **3** RANGE, reach, size, sweep, extent, scope, sphere, domain, width, compass, breadth, parameters (*informal*), latitude, expanse, radius, ambit **4** REALM, part, department, field, province, arena, sphere, domain

arena *noun* **1** RING, ground, stage, field, theatre, bowl, pitch, stadium, enclosure, park (*US & Canad*), coliseum, amphitheatre **2** SCENE, world, area, stage, field, theatre, sector, territory, province, forum, scope, sphere, realm, domain

arguably *adverb* POSSIBLY, potentially, conceivably, plausibly, feasibly, questionably, debatably, deniably, disputably, contestably, controvertibly, dubitably, refutably

argue *verb* **1** QUARREL, fight, row, clash, dispute, disagree, feud, squabble, spar, wrangle, bicker, have an argument, cross swords, be at sixes and sevens, fight like cat and dog, go at it hammer and tongs, bandy words, altercate **2** DISCUSS, debate, dispute, thrash out, exchange views on, controvert **3** CLAIM, question, reason, challenge, insist, maintain, hold, allege, plead, assert, contend, uphold, profess, remonstrate, expostulate **4** DEMONSTRATE, show, suggest, display, indicate, imply, exhibit, denote, evince

argument *noun* **1** REASON, case, reasoning, ground(s), defence, excuse, logic, justification, rationale, polemic, dialectic, line of reasoning, argumentation **2** DEBATE, questioning, claim, row, discussion, dispute, controversy, pleading, plea, contention, assertion, polemic, altercation, remonstrance, expostulation, remonstration **3** QUARREL, fight, row, clash, dispute, controversy, disagreement, misunderstanding, feud, barney (*informal*), squabble, wrangle, bickering, difference of opinion, tiff, altercation << ANTONYM agreement

argumentative *adjective* QUARRELSOME, contrary, contentious, belligerent, combative, opinionated, litigious, disputatious << ANTONYM easy-going

arid *adjective* **1** DRY, desert, dried up, barren, sterile, torrid, parched, waterless, moistureless << ANTONYM lush **2** BORING, dull, tedious, dreary, dry, tiresome, lifeless, colourless, uninteresting, flat, uninspired, vapid, spiritless, jejune, as dry as dust << ANTONYM exciting

arise *verb* **1** HAPPEN, start, begin, follow, issue, result, appear, develop, emerge, occur, spring, set in, stem, originate, ensue, come about, commence, come to light, emanate, crop up (*informal*), come into being, materialize **2** (*old-fashioned*) GET TO YOUR FEET, get up, rise, stand up, spring up, leap up **3** GET UP, wake up, awaken, get out of bed **4** ASCEND, rise, lift, mount, climb, tower, soar, move upward

aristocracy *noun* UPPER CLASS, elite, nobility, gentry, peerage, ruling class, patricians, upper crust (*informal*), noblesse (*literary*), haut monde (*French*), patriciate, body of nobles << ANTONYM commoners

aristocrat *noun* NOBLE, lord, lady, peer, patrician, grandee, nobleman, aristo (*informal*), childe (*archaic*), noblewoman, peeress

aristocratic *adjective* **1** UPPER-CLASS, lordly, titled, gentle (*archaic*), elite, gentlemanly, noble, patrician, blue-blooded, well-born, highborn << ANTONYM common **2** REFINED, fine, polished, elegant, stylish, dignified, haughty, courtly, snobbish, well-bred << ANTONYM vulgar

arm¹ *noun* **1** UPPER LIMB, limb, appendage **2** BRANCH, part, office, department, division, section, wing, sector, extension, detachment, offshoot, subdivision, subsection **3** AUTHORITY, might, force, power, strength, command, sway, potency

arm² *verb* **1** EQUIP, provide, supply, outfit, rig, array, furnish, issue with, deck out, accoutre **2** PROVIDE, prime, prepare, protect, guard, strengthen, outfit, equip, brace, fortify, forearm, make ready, gird your loins, jack up (*NZ*) ▷ *plural noun* WEAPONS, guns, firearms, weaponry, armaments, ordnance, munitions, instruments of war

armada *noun* FLEET, navy, squadron, flotilla

armaments *plural noun* WEAPONS, arms, guns, ammunition, weaponry, ordnance, munitions, materiel

armed *adjective* CARRYING WEAPONS, provided, prepared, supplied, ready, protected, guarded, strengthened, equipped, primed, arrayed, furnished, fortified, in arms, forearmed, fitted out, under arms, girded, rigged out, tooled up (*slang*), accoutred

armistice *noun* TRUCE, peace, ceasefire, suspension of hostilities

armour *noun* PROTECTION, covering, shield, sheathing, armour plate, chain mail, protective covering

armoured *adjective* PROTECTED, mailed, reinforced, toughened, bulletproof, armour-plated, steel-plated, ironclad, bombproof

armoury or *US* **armory** *noun* ARSENAL, magazine, ammunition dump, arms depot, ordnance depot

army *noun* 1 SOLDIERS, military, troops, armed force, legions, infantry, military force, land forces, land force, soldiery 2 VAST NUMBER, host, gang, mob, flock, array, legion, swarm, sea, pack, horde, multitude, throng

aroma *noun* SCENT, smell, perfume, fragrance, bouquet, savour, odour, redolence

aromatic *adjective* FRAGRANT, perfumed, spicy, savoury, pungent, balmy, redolent, sweet-smelling, sweet-scented, odoriferous << ANTONYM smelly

around *preposition* 1 APPROXIMATELY, about, nearly, close to, roughly, just about, in the region of, circa (*used with dates*), in the vicinity of, not far off, in the neighbourhood of 2 SURROUNDING, about, enclosing, encompassing, framing, encircling, on all sides of, on every side of, environing ▷ *adverb* 1 EVERYWHERE, about, throughout, all over, here and there, on all sides, in all directions, to and fro 2 NEAR, close, nearby, handy, at hand, close by, close at hand

arousal *noun* STIMULATION, movement, response, reaction, excitement, animation, stirring up, provocation, inflammation, agitation, exhilaration, incitement, enlivenment

arouse *verb* 1 STIMULATE, encourage, inspire, prompt, spark, spur, foster, provoke, rouse, stir up, inflame, incite, instigate, whip up,

summon up, whet, kindle, foment, call forth << ANTONYM quell 2 INFLAME, move, warm, excite, spur, provoke, animate, prod, stir up, agitate, quicken, enliven, goad, foment 3 AWAKEN, wake up, rouse, waken

arraign *verb* ACCUSE, charge, prosecute, denounce, indict, impeach, incriminate, call to account, take to task

arrange *verb* 1 PLAN, agree, prepare, determine, schedule, organize, construct, devise, contrive, fix up, jack up (*NZ informal*) 2 PUT IN ORDER, group, form, order, sort, class, position, range, file, rank, line up, organize, set out, sequence, exhibit, sort out (*informal*), array, classify, tidy, marshal, align, categorize, systematize, jack up (*NZ informal*) << ANTONYM disorganize 3 ADAPT, score, orchestrate, harmonize, instrument

arrangement *noun* 1 *often plural* PLAN, planning, provision, preparation 2 AGREEMENT, contract, settlement, appointment, compromise, deal (*informal*), pact, compact, covenant 3 DISPLAY, grouping, system, order, ordering, design, ranging, structure, rank, organization, exhibition, line-up, presentation, array, marshalling, classification, disposition, alignment, setup (*informal*) 4 ADAPTATION, score, version, interpretation, instrumentation, orchestration, harmonization

array *noun* 1 ARRANGEMENT, show, order, supply, display, collection, exhibition, line-up, mixture, parade, formation, presentation, spectacle, marshalling, muster, disposition 2 (*poetic*) CLOTHING, dress, clothes, threads (*slang*), garments, apparel, attire, garb, finery, regalia, raiment (*archaic* or *poetic*), schmutter (*slang*) ▷ *verb* 1 ARRANGE, show, group, order, present, range, display, line up, sequence, parade, exhibit, unveil, dispose, draw up, marshal, lay out, muster, align, form up, place in order, set in line (*military*) 2 DRESS, supply, clothe, wrap, deck, outfit, decorate, equip, robe, get ready, adorn, apparel (*archaic*), festoon, attire, fit out, garb, bedeck, caparison, accoutre

arrest *verb* 1 CAPTURE, catch, lift (*slang*), nick (*slang, chiefly Brit*), seize, run in (*slang*), nail (*informal*), bust (*informal*), collar (*informal*), take, detain, pinch (*informal*), nab (*informal*), apprehend, take prisoner, take into custody, lay hold of << ANTONYM release 2 STOP, end, hold, limit, check, block, slow, delay, halt, stall, stay, interrupt, suppress, restrain, hamper, inhibit, hinder, obstruct, retard, impede << ANTONYM speed up **3** FASCINATE, hold, involve, catch, occupy, engage, grip, absorb, entrance, intrigue, rivet, enthral, mesmerize, engross, spellbind ▷ *noun* **1** CAPTURE, bust (*informal*), detention, seizure, apprehension << ANTONYM release **2** STOPPAGE, halt, suppression, obstruction, inhibition, blockage, hindrance << ANTONYM acceleration

arresting *adjective* STRIKING, surprising, engaging, dramatic, stunning, impressive, extraordinary, outstanding, remarkable, noticeable, conspicuous, salient, jaw-dropping << ANTONYM unremarkable

arrival *noun* **1** APPEARANCE, coming, arriving, entrance, advent, materialization **2** COMING, happening, taking place, dawn, emergence, occurrence, materialization **3** NEWCOMER, arriver, incomer, visitor, caller, entrant, comer, visitant

arrive *verb* **1** COME, appear, enter, turn up, show up (*informal*), materialize, draw near << ANTONYM depart **2** OCCUR, happen, take place, ensue, transpire, fall, befall **3** (*informal*) SUCCEED, make it (*informal*), triumph, do well, thrive, flourish, be successful, make good, prosper, cut it (*informal*), reach the top, become famous, make the grade (*informal*), get to the top, crack it (*informal*), hit the jackpot (*informal*), turn out well, make your mark (*informal*), achieve recognition, do all right for yourself (*informal*) ▷▷ **arrive at something** REACH, make, get to, enter, land at, get as far as

arrogance *noun* CONCEIT, pride, swagger, pretension, presumption, bluster, hubris, pomposity, insolence, hauteur, pretentiousness, high-handedness, haughtiness, loftiness, imperiousness, pompousness, superciliousness, lordliness, conceitedness, contemptuousness, scornfulness, uppishness (*Brit informal*), disdainfulness, overweeningness << ANTONYM modesty

arrogant *adjective* CONCEITED, lordly, assuming, proud, swaggering, pompous, pretentious, stuck up (*informal*), cocky, contemptuous, blustering, imperious, overbearing, haughty, scornful, puffed up, egotistical, disdainful, self-important, presumptuous, high-handed, insolent, supercilious, high and mighty (*informal*), overweening, immodest, swollen-headed, bigheaded (*informal*), uppish (*Brit informal*) << ANTONYM modest

arrow *noun* **1** DART, flight, reed (*archaic*), bolt, shaft (*archaic*), quarrel **2** POINTER, indicator, marker

arsenal *noun* **1** STORE, stock, supply, magazine, stockpile **2** ARMOURY, storehouse, ammunition dump, arms depot, ordnance depot

art *noun* **1** ARTWORK, style of art, fine art, creativity **2** SKILL, knowledge, method, facility, craft, profession, expertise, competence, accomplishment, mastery, knack, ingenuity, finesse, aptitude, artistry, artifice (*archaic*), virtuosity, dexterity, cleverness, adroitness

artful *adjective* **1** CUNNING, designing, scheming, sharp, smart, clever, subtle, intriguing, tricky, shrewd, sly, wily, politic, crafty, foxy, deceitful << ANTONYM straightforward **2** SKILFUL, masterly, smart, clever, subtle, ingenious, adept, resourceful, proficient, adroit, dexterous << ANTONYM clumsy

article *noun* **1** FEATURE, story, paper, piece, item, creation, essay, composition, discourse, treatise **2** THING, piece, unit, item, object, device, tool, implement, commodity, gadget, utensil **3** CLAUSE, point, part, heading, head, matter, detail, piece, particular, division, section, item, passage, portion, paragraph, proviso

articulate *adjective* EXPRESSIVE, clear, effective, vocal, meaningful, understandable, coherent, persuasive, fluent, eloquent, lucid, comprehensible, communicative, intelligible << ANTONYM incoherent ▷ *verb* **1** EXPRESS, say, tell, state, word, speak, declare, phrase, communicate, assert, pronounce, utter, couch, put across, enunciate, put into words, verbalize, asseverate **2** PRONOUNCE, say, talk, speak, voice, utter, enunciate, vocalize, enounce

articulation *noun* **1** EXPRESSION, delivery, pronunciation, saying, talking, voicing, speaking, utterance, diction, enunciation, vocalization, verbalization **2** VOICING, statement, expression, verbalization **3** JOINT, coupling, jointing, connection, hinge, juncture

artifice *noun* **1** CUNNING, scheming, trick, device, craft, tactic, manoeuvre, deception, hoax, expedient, ruse, guile, trickery, duplicity, subterfuge, stratagem, contrivance, chicanery, wile, craftiness, artfulness, slyness, machination

2 CLEVERNESS, skill, facility, invention, ingenuity, finesse, inventiveness, deftness, adroitness

artificial *adjective* **1** SYNTHETIC, manufactured, plastic, man-made, non-natural **2** INSINCERE, forced, affected, assumed, phoney *or* phony (*informal*), put on, false, pretended, hollow, contrived, unnatural, feigned, spurious, meretricious << ANTONYM genuine **3** FAKE, mock, imitation, bogus, simulated, phoney *or* phony (*informal*), sham, pseudo (*informal*), fabricated, counterfeit, spurious, ersatz, specious << ANTONYM authentic

artillery *noun* BIG GUNS, battery, cannon, ordnance, gunnery, cannonry

artisan *noun* CRAFTSMAN, technician, mechanic, journeyman, artificer, handicraftsman, skilled workman

artist *noun* CREATOR, master, maker, craftsman, artisan (*obsolete*), fine artist

artiste *noun* PERFORMER, player, entertainer, Thespian, trouper, play-actor

artistic *adjective* **1** CREATIVE, cultured, original, sensitive, sophisticated, refined, imaginative, aesthetic, discerning, eloquent, arty (*informal*) << ANTONYM untalented **2** BEAUTIFUL, fine, pleasing, lovely, creative, elegant, stylish, cultivated, imaginative, decorative, aesthetic, exquisite, graceful, expressive, ornamental, tasteful << ANTONYM unattractive

artistry *noun* SKILL, art, style, taste, talent, craft, genius, creativity, touch, flair, brilliance, sensibility, accomplishment, mastery, finesse, craftsmanship, proficiency, virtuosity, workmanship, artistic ability

artless *adjective* **1** NATURAL, simple, fair, frank, plain, pure, open, round, true, direct, genuine, humble, straightforward, sincere, honest, candid, unaffected, upfront (*informal*), unpretentious, unadorned, dinkum (*Austral & NZ informal*), guileless, uncontrived, undesigning << ANTONYM artificial **2** UNSKILLED, awkward, crude, primitive, rude, bungling, incompetent, clumsy, inept, untalented, maladroit << ANTONYM artful

arty *adjective* (*informal*) ARTISTIC, arty-farty (*informal*), arty-crafty (*informal*)

as *conjunction* **1** WHEN, while, just as, at the time that, during the time that **2** IN THE WAY THAT, like, in the manner that **3** SINCE, because, seeing that, considering that, on account of the fact that ▷ *preposition* IN THE ROLE OF, being, under the name of, in the character of ▷▷ **as for** *or* **to** WITH REGARD TO, about, re, concerning, regarding, respecting, relating to, with respect to, on the subject of, with reference to, in reference to, in the matter of, apropos of, as regards, anent (*Scot*) ▷▷ **as it were** IN A WAY, to some extent, so to speak, in a manner of speaking, so to say

ascend *verb* **1** CLIMB, scale, mount, go up << ANTONYM go down **2** SLOPE UPWARDS, come up, rise up << ANTONYM slope downwards **3** MOVE UP, rise, go up << ANTONYM move down **4** FLOAT UP, rise, climb, tower, go up, take off, soar, lift off, fly up << ANTONYM descend

ascendancy *or* **ascendence** *noun* INFLUENCE, power, control, rule, authority, command, reign, sovereignty, sway, dominance, domination, superiority, supremacy, mastery, dominion, upper hand, hegemony, prevalence, pre-eminence, predominance, rangatiratanga (*NZ*) << ANTONYM inferiority

ascendant *or* **ascendent** *adjective* INFLUENTIAL, controlling, ruling, powerful, commanding, supreme, superior, dominant, prevailing, authoritative, predominant, uppermost, pre-eminent ▷▷ **in the ascendant** RISING, increasing, growing, powerful, mounting, climbing, dominating, commanding, supreme, dominant, influential, prevailing, flourishing, ascending, up-and-coming, on the rise, uppermost, on the way up

ascension *noun* **1** RISE, rising, mounting, climb, ascending, ascent, moving upwards **2** SUCCESSION, taking over, assumption, inheritance, elevation, entering upon

ascent *noun* **1** CLIMBING, scaling, mounting, climb, clambering, ascending, ascension **2** UPWARD SLOPE, rise, incline, ramp, gradient, rising ground, acclivity **3** RISE, rising, climb, ascension, upward movement

ascertain *verb* FIND OUT, learn, discover, determine, confirm, settle, identify, establish, fix, verify, make certain, suss (out) (*slang*), ferret out

ascetic *noun* RECLUSE, monk, nun, abstainer, hermit, anchorite, self-denier << ANTONYM hedonist ▷ *adjective* SELF-DENYING, severe, plain, harsh, stern, rigorous, austere, Spartan, self-disciplined, celibate, puritanical, frugal, abstemious, abstinent << ANTONYM self-indulgent

ascribe *verb* ATTRIBUTE, credit, refer, charge, assign, put down, set down, impute

asexual *adjective* SEXLESS, neutral, neuter

ashamed *adjective* **1** EMBARRASSED, sorry, guilty, upset, distressed, shy, humbled, humiliated, blushing, self-conscious, red-faced, chagrined, flustered, mortified, sheepish, bashful, prudish, crestfallen, discomfited, remorseful, abashed, shamefaced, conscience-stricken, discountenanced << ANTONYM proud **2** RELUCTANT, afraid, embarrassed, scared, unwilling, loath, disinclined

ashen *adjective* PALE, white, grey, wan, livid, pasty, leaden, colourless, pallid, anaemic, ashy, like death warmed up (*informal*) << ANTONYM rosy

ashore *adverb* ON LAND, on the beach, on the shore, aground, to the shore, on dry land, shorewards, landwards

aside *adverb* TO ONE SIDE, away, alone, separately, apart, alongside, beside, out of the way, on one side, to the side, in isolation, in reserve, out of mind ▷ *noun* INTERPOLATION, remark, parenthesis, digression, interposition, confidential remark

ask *verb* **1** INQUIRE, question, quiz, query, interrogate << ANTONYM answer **2** REQUEST, apply to, appeal to, plead with, demand, urge, sue, pray, beg, petition, crave, solicit, implore, enjoin, beseech, entreat, supplicate **3** INVITE, bid, summon

askance *adverb* **1** SUSPICIOUSLY, doubtfully, dubiously, sceptically, disapprovingly, distrustfully, mistrustfully **2** OUT OF THE CORNER OF YOUR EYE, sideways, indirectly, awry, obliquely, with a side glance

askew *adjective* CROOKED, awry, oblique, lopsided, off-centre, cockeyed (*informal*), skewwhiff (*Brit informal*) << ANTONYM straight ▷ *adverb* CROOKEDLY, to one side, awry, obliquely, off-centre, aslant << ANTONYM straight

asleep *adjective* SLEEPING, napping, dormant, crashed out (*slang*), dozing, slumbering, snoozing (*informal*), fast asleep, sound asleep, out for the count, dead to the world (*informal*), in a deep sleep

aspect *noun* **1** FEATURE, point, side, factor, angle, characteristic, facet **2** POSITION, view, situation, scene, bearing, direction, prospect, exposure, point of view, outlook **3** APPEARANCE, look, air, condition, quality, bearing, attitude, cast, manner, expression, countenance, demeanour, mien (*literary*)

aspirant *noun* CANDIDATE, applicant, hopeful,

aspirer, seeker, suitor, postulant ▷ *adjective* HOPEFUL, longing, ambitious, eager, striving, aspiring, endeavouring, wishful

aspiration *noun* AIM, longing, end, plan, hope, goal, design, dream, wish, desire, object, intention, objective, ambition, craving, endeavour, yearning, eagerness, Holy Grail (*informal*), hankering

aspire to *verb* AIM FOR, desire, pursue, hope for, long for, crave, seek out, wish for, dream about, yearn for, hunger for, hanker after, be eager for, set your heart on, set your sights on, be ambitious for

aspiring *adjective* HOPEFUL, longing, would-be, ambitious, eager, striving, endeavouring, wannabe (*informal*), wishful, aspirant

ass *noun* **1** DONKEY, moke (*slang*), jennet **2** FOOL, dope (*informal*), jerk (*slang, chiefly US & Canad*), idiot, plank (*Brit slang*), berk (*Brit slang*), wally (*slang*), prat (*slang*), charlie (*Brit informal*), plonker (*slang*), coot, geek (*slang*), twit (*informal, chiefly Brit*), bonehead (*slang*), dunce, oaf, simpleton, airhead (*slang*), jackass, dipstick (*Brit slang*), gonzo (*slang*), schmuck (*US slang*), dork (*slang*), nitwit (*informal*), dolt, blockhead, ninny, divvy (*Brit slang*), pillock (*Brit slang*), halfwit, nincompoop, dweeb (*US slang*), putz (*US slang*), fathead (*informal*), weenie (*US informal*), eejit (*Scot & Irish*), dumb-ass (*slang*), numpty (*Scot informal*), doofus (*slang, chiefly US*), daftie (*informal*), nerd *or* nurd (*slang*), numbskull *or* numskull, twerp *or* twirp (*informal*), dorba *or* dorb (*Austral slang*), bogan (*Austral slang*)

assail *verb* **1** CRITICIZE, abuse, blast, put down, malign, berate, revile, vilify, tear into (*informal*), diss (*slang, chiefly US*), impugn, go for the jugular, lambast(e) **2** ATTACK, charge, assault, invade, set about, beset, fall upon, set upon, lay into (*informal*), maltreat, belabour

assailant *noun* ATTACKER, assaulter, invader, aggressor, assailer

assassin *noun* MURDERER, killer, slayer, liquidator, executioner, hit man (*slang*), eliminator (*slang*), hatchet man (*slang*)

assassinate *verb* MURDER, kill, eliminate (*slang*), take out (*slang*), terminate, hit (*slang*), slay, blow away (*slang, chiefly US*), liquidate

assassination *noun* MURDER, killing, slaughter, purge, hit (*slang*), removal, elimination (*slang*), slaying, homicide, liquidation

assault *noun* ATTACK, campaign, strike, rush,

storm, storming, raid, invasion, charge, offensive, onset, onslaught, foray, incursion, act of aggression, inroad << ANTONYM defence ▷ *verb* STRIKE, attack, beat, knock, punch, belt (*informal*), bang, batter, clip (*informal*), slap, bash (*informal*), deck (*slang*), sock (*slang*), chin (*slang*), smack, thump, set about, lay one on (*slang*), clout (*informal*), cuff, flog, whack, lob, beset, clobber (*slang*), smite (*archaic*), wallop (*informal*), swat, fall upon, set upon, lay into (*informal*), tonk (*slang*), lambast(e), belabour, beat *or* knock seven bells out of (*informal*)

assay *verb* ANALYSE, examine, investigate, assess, weigh, evaluate, inspect, try, appraise

assemblage *noun* GROUP, company, meeting, body, crowd, collection, mass, gathering, rally, assembly, flock, congregation, accumulation, multitude, throng, hui (NZ), conclave, aggregation, convocation, runanga (NZ)

assemble *verb* 1 GATHER, meet, collect, rally, flock, accumulate, come together, muster, convene, congregate, foregather << ANTONYM scatter 2 BRING TOGETHER, collect, gather, rally, summon, accumulate, round up, marshal, come together, muster, convene, amass, congregate, call together, foregather, convoke 3 PUT TOGETHER, make, join, set up, manufacture, build up, connect, construct, erect, piece together, fabricate, fit together << ANTONYM take apart

assembly *noun* 1 GATHERING, group, meeting, body, council, conference, crowd, congress, audience, collection, mass, diet, rally, convention, flock, company, house, congregation, accumulation, multitude, throng, synod, hui (NZ), assemblage, conclave, aggregation, convocation, runanga (NZ) 2 PUTTING TOGETHER, joining, setting up, manufacture, construction, building up, connecting, erection, piecing together, fabrication, fitting together

assent *noun* AGREEMENT, accord, sanction, approval, permission, acceptance, consent, compliance, accession, acquiescence, concurrence << ANTONYM refusal ▷▷ **assent to something** AGREE TO, allow, accept, grant, approve, permit, sanction, O.K., comply with, go along with, subscribe to, consent to, say yes to, accede to, fall in with, acquiesce in, concur with, give the green light to

assert *verb* 1 STATE, argue, maintain, declare, allege, swear, pronounce, contend, affirm, profess, attest, predicate, postulate, avow, aver, asseverate, avouch (*archaic*) << ANTONYM deny 2 INSIST UPON, stress, defend, uphold, put forward, vindicate, press, stand up for << ANTONYM retract ▷▷ **assert yourself** BE FORCEFUL, put your foot down (*informal*), put yourself forward, make your presence felt, exert your influence

assertion *noun* 1 STATEMENT, claim, allegation, profession, declaration, contention, affirmation, pronouncement, avowal, attestation, predication, asseveration 2 INSISTENCE, defence, stressing, maintenance, vindication

assertive *adjective* CONFIDENT, firm, demanding, decided, forward, can-do (*informal*), positive, aggressive, decisive, forceful, emphatic, insistent, feisty (*informal, chiefly US & Canad*), pushy (*informal*), in-your-face (*Brit slang*), dogmatic, strong-willed, domineering, overbearing, self-assured << ANTONYM meek

assertiveness *noun* CONFIDENCE, insistence, aggressiveness, firmness, decisiveness, dogmatism, forcefulness, positiveness, pushiness (*informal*), forwardness, self-assuredness, decidedness, domineeringness << ANTONYM meekness

assess *verb* 1 JUDGE, determine, estimate, fix, analyse, evaluate, rate, value, check out, compute, gauge, weigh up, appraise, size up (*informal*), eye up 2 EVALUATE, rate, tax, value, demand, estimate, fix, impose, levy

assessment *noun* 1 JUDGMENT, analysis, determination, evaluation, valuation, appraisal, estimation, rating, opinion, estimate, computation 2 EVALUATION, rating, rate, charge, tax, demand, fee, duty, toll, levy, tariff, taxation, valuation, impost

asset *noun* BENEFIT, help, service, aid, advantage, strength, resource, attraction, blessing, boon, good point, strong point, ace in the hole, feather in your cap, ace up your sleeve << ANTONYM disadvantage

assiduous *adjective* DILIGENT, constant, steady, hard-working, persistent, attentive, persevering, laborious, industrious, indefatigable, studious, unflagging, untiring, sedulous, unwearied << ANTONYM lazy

assign *verb* 1 GIVE, set, grant, allocate, give out, consign, allot, apportion 2 ALLOCATE, give, determine, fix, appoint, distribute, earmark, mete 3 SELECT FOR, post, commission, elect, appoint, delegate, nominate, name, designate, choose for, stipulate for **4** ATTRIBUTE, credit, put down, set down, ascribe, accredit

assignment *noun* **1** TASK, work, job, charge, position, post, commission, exercise, responsibility, duty, mission, appointment, undertaking, occupation, chore **2** SELECTION, choice, option, appointment, delegation, nomination, designation **3** GIVING, issuing, grant, distribution, allocation, earmarking, allotment, designation, consignment, dealing out, assignation (*law, chiefly Scot*), apportionment

assimilate *verb* **1** ADJUST, fit, adapt, accommodate, accustom, conform, mingle, blend in, become like, homogenize, acclimatize, intermix, become similar, acculturate **2** LEARN, absorb, take in, incorporate, digest, imbibe (*literary*), ingest

assist *verb* **1** HELP, back, support, further, benefit, aid, encourage, work with, work for, relieve, collaborate with, cooperate with, abet, expedite, succour, lend a hand to, lend a helping hand to, give a leg up to (*informal*) **2** FACILITATE, help, further, serve, aid, forward, promote, boost, ease, sustain, reinforce, speed up, pave the way for, make easy, expedite, oil the wheels of, smooth the path of, assist the progress of << ANTONYM hinder

assistance *noun* HELP, backing, service, support, benefit, aid, relief, boost, promotion, cooperation, encouragement, collaboration, reinforcement, helping hand, sustenance, succour, furtherance, abetment << ANTONYM hindrance

assistant *noun* HELPER, partner, ally, colleague, associate, supporter, deputy, subsidiary, aide, aider, second, accessory, attendant, backer, protagonist, collaborator, accomplice, confederate, auxiliary, henchman, right-hand man, adjutant, helpmate, coadjutor (*rare*), abettor, cooperator

associate *verb* **1** CONNECT, couple, league, link, mix, relate, pair, ally, identify, unite, join, combine, attach, affiliate, fasten, correlate, confederate, yoke, affix, lump together, cohere, mention in the same breath, conjoin, think of together << ANTONYM separate **2** SOCIALIZE, mix, hang (*informal, chiefly US*), accompany, hang out (*informal*), run around (*informal*), mingle, be friends, befriend, consort, hang about, hobnob, fraternize << ANTONYM avoid ▷ *noun* PARTNER, friend, ally, colleague, mate

(*informal*), companion, comrade, affiliate, collaborator, confederate, co-worker, workmate, main man (*slang, chiefly US*), cobber (*Austral & NZ old-fashioned informal*), confrère, compeer, E hoa (*NZ*)

associated *adjective* CONNECTED, united, joined, leagued, linked, tied, related, allied, combined, involved, bound, syndicated, affiliated, correlated, confederated, yoked

association *noun* **1** GROUP, company, club, order, union, class, society, league, band, set, troop, pack, camp, collection, gathering, organization, circle, corporation, alliance, coalition, partnership, federation, bunch, formation, faction, cluster, syndicate, congregation, batch, confederation, cooperative, fraternity, affiliation, posse (*slang*), clique, confederacy, assemblage **2** FRIENDSHIP, relationship, link, tie, relations, bond, connection, partnership, attachment, intimacy, liaison, fellowship, affinity, familiarity, affiliation, companionship, comradeship, fraternization **3** CONNECTION, union, joining, linking, tie, mixing, relation, bond, pairing, combination, mixture, blend, identification, correlation, linkage, yoking, juxtaposition, lumping together, concomitance

assorted *adjective* VARIOUS, different, mixed, varied, diverse, diversified, miscellaneous, sundry, motley, variegated, manifold, heterogeneous << ANTONYM similar

assortment *noun* VARIETY, choice, collection, selection, mixture, diversity, array, jumble, medley, mixed bag (*informal*), potpourri, mélange (*French*), miscellany, mishmash, farrago, hotchpotch, salmagundi, pick 'n' mix

assuage *verb* **1** RELIEVE, ease, calm, moderate, temper, soothe, lessen, alleviate, lighten, allay, mitigate, quench, palliate << ANTONYM increase **2** CALM, still, quiet, relax, satisfy, soften, soothe, appease, lull, pacify, mollify, tranquillize << ANTONYM provoke

assume *verb* **1** PRESUME, think, believe, expect, accept, suppose, imagine, suspect, guess (*informal, chiefly US & Canad*), take it, fancy, take for granted, infer, conjecture, postulate, surmise, presuppose << ANTONYM know **2** TAKE ON, begin, accept, manage, bear, handle, shoulder, take over, don, acquire, put on, take up, embrace, undertake, set about, attend to, take responsibility for, embark upon, enter upon **3** SIMULATE, affect, adopt, put on, imitate, mimic, sham, counterfeit, feign, impersonate **4** TAKE OVER, take, appropriate, acquire, seize, hijack, confiscate, wrest, usurp, lay claim to, pre-empt, commandeer, requisition, expropriate, arrogate << ANTONYM give up

assumed *adjective* FALSE, affected, made-up, pretended, fake, imitation, bogus, simulated, sham, counterfeit, feigned, spurious, fictitious, make-believe, pseudonymous, phoney *or* phony (*informal*) << ANTONYM real

assumption *noun* **1** PRESUMPTION, theory, opinion, belief, guess, expectation, fancy, suspicion, premise, acceptance, hypothesis, anticipation, inference, conjecture, surmise, supposition, presupposition, premiss, postulation **2** TAKING ON, managing, handling, shouldering, putting on, taking up, takeover, acquisition **3** SEIZURE, taking, takeover, acquisition, appropriation, wresting, confiscation, commandeering, expropriation, pre-empting, usurpation, arrogation

assurance *noun* **1** PROMISE, statement, guarantee, commitment, pledge, profession, vow, declaration, assertion, oath, affirmation, protestation, word, word of honour << ANTONYM lie **2** CONFIDENCE, conviction, courage, certainty, self-confidence, poise, assertiveness, security, faith, coolness, nerve, aplomb, boldness, self-reliance, firmness, self-assurance, certitude, sureness, self-possession, positiveness, assuredness << ANTONYM self-doubt

assure *verb* **1** CONVINCE, encourage, persuade, satisfy, comfort, prove to, reassure, soothe, hearten, embolden, win someone over, bring someone round **2** MAKE CERTAIN, ensure, confirm, guarantee, secure, make sure, complete, seal, clinch **3** PROMISE TO, pledge to, vow to, guarantee to, swear to, attest to, confirm to, certify to, affirm to, give your word to, declare confidently to

assured *adjective* **1** CONFIDENT, certain, positive, bold, poised, assertive, complacent, fearless, audacious, pushy (*informal*), brazen, self-confident, self-assured, self-possessed, overconfident, dauntless, sure of yourself << ANTONYM self-conscious **2** CERTAIN, sure, ensured, confirmed, settled, guaranteed, fixed, secure, sealed, clinched, made certain, sound, in the bag (*slang*),

dependable, beyond doubt, irrefutable, unquestionable, indubitable, nailed-on (*slang*) << ANTONYM doubtful

astonish *verb* AMAZE, surprise, stun, stagger, bewilder, astound, daze, confound, stupefy, boggle the mind, dumbfound, flabbergast (*informal*)

astonished *adjective* AMAZED, surprised, staggered, bewildered, astounded, dazed, stunned, confounded, perplexed, gobsmacked (*informal*), dumbfounded, flabbergasted (*informal*), stupefied

astonishing *adjective* AMAZING, striking, surprising, brilliant, stunning, impressive, overwhelming, staggering, startling, sensational (*informal*), bewildering, breathtaking, astounding, eye-opening, wondrous (*archaic or literary*), jaw-dropping, stupefying

astonishment *noun* AMAZEMENT, surprise, wonder, confusion, awe, consternation, bewilderment, wonderment, stupefaction

astound *verb* AMAZE, surprise, overwhelm, astonish, stagger, bewilder, daze, confound, stupefy, stun, take your breath away, boggle the mind, dumbfound, flabbergast (*informal*)

astounding *adjective* AMAZING, striking, surprising, brilliant, impressive, astonishing, staggering, sensational (*informal*), bewildering, stunning, breathtaking, wondrous (*archaic or literary*), jaw-dropping, stupefying

astray *adjective or adverb* OFF THE RIGHT TRACK, adrift, off course, off the mark, amiss ▷▷ **lead someone astray** LEAD INTO SIN, lead into error, lead into bad ways, lead into wrong

astringent *adjective* **1** CONTRACTIVE, contractile, styptic **2** SEVERE, strict, exacting, harsh, grim, stern, hard, rigid, rigorous, stringent, austere, caustic, acerbic

astrology *noun* STARGAZING, astromancy, horoscopy

astronaut *noun* SPACE TRAVELLER, cosmonaut, spaceman, spacewoman, space pilot

astronomical *or* **astronomic** *adjective* HUGE, great, giant, massive, vast, enormous, immense, titanic, infinite, gigantic, monumental, colossal, boundless, galactic, Gargantuan, immeasurable

astute *adjective* INTELLIGENT, politic, bright, sharp, keen, calculating, clever, subtle, penetrating, knowing, shrewd, cunning, discerning, sly, on the ball (*informal*), canny, perceptive, wily, crafty, artful, insightful, foxy, adroit, sagacious << ANTONYM stupid

asunder *adverb or adjective (literary)* TO PIECES, apart, torn, rent, to bits, to shreds, in pieces, into pieces

asylum *noun* 1 (*old-fashioned*) MENTAL HOSPITAL, hospital, institution, psychiatric hospital, madhouse (*informal*), funny farm (*facetious*), loony bin (*slang*), nuthouse (*slang*), rubber room (*US slang*), laughing academy (*US slang*) 2 REFUGE, security, haven, safety, protection, preserve, shelter, retreat, harbour, sanctuary

atheism *noun* NONBELIEF, disbelief, scepticism, infidelity, paganism, unbelief, freethinking, godlessness, irreligion, heathenism

atheist *noun* NONBELIEVER, pagan, sceptic, disbeliever, heathen, infidel, unbeliever, freethinker, irreligionist

athlete *noun* SPORTSPERSON, player, runner, competitor, contender, sportsman, contestant, gymnast, games player, sportswoman

athletic *adjective* FIT, strong, powerful, healthy, active, trim, strapping, robust, vigorous, energetic, muscular, sturdy, husky (*informal*), lusty, herculean, sinewy, brawny, able-bodied, well-proportioned << ANTONYM feeble

athletics *plural noun* SPORTS, games, races, exercises, contests, sporting events, gymnastics, track and field events, games of strength

atmosphere *noun* 1 AIR, sky, heavens, aerosphere 2 FEELING, feel, air, quality, character, environment, spirit, surroundings, tone, mood, climate, flavour, aura, ambience, vibes (*slang*)

atom *noun* PARTICLE, bit, spot, trace, scrap, molecule, grain, dot, fragment, fraction, shred, crumb, mite, jot, speck, morsel, mote, whit, tittle, iota, scintilla (*rare*)

atone *verb* MAKE AMENDS, pay, do penance, make reparation, make redress

atonement *noun* AMENDS, payment, compensation, satisfaction, redress, reparation, restitution, penance, recompense, expiation, propitiation

atrocious *adjective* 1 (*informal*) SHOCKING, terrible, appalling, horrible, horrifying, grievous, execrable, detestable << ANTONYM fine 2 CRUEL, savage, brutal, vicious, ruthless, infamous, monstrous, wicked, barbaric, inhuman, diabolical, heinous, flagrant, infernal, fiendish, villainous, nefarious,

godawful (*slang*), hellacious (*US slang*) << ANTONYM kind

atrocity *noun* 1 ACT OF CRUELTY, wrong, crime, horror, offence, evil, outrage, outrage, cruelty, brutality, obscenity, wrongdoing, enormity, monstrosity, transgression, abomination, barbarity, villainy 2 CRUELTY, wrong, horror, brutality, wrongdoing, enormity, savagery, ruthlessness, wickedness, inhumanity, infamy, transgression, barbarity, viciousness, villainy, baseness, monstrousness, heinousness, nefariousness, shockingness, atrociousness, fiendishness, barbarousness, grievousness, villainousness

atrophy *verb* 1 WASTE AWAY, waste, shrink, diminish, deteriorate, decay, dwindle, wither, wilt, degenerate, shrivel 2 DECLINE, waste, fade, shrink, diminish, deteriorate, dwindle, wither, wilt, degenerate, shrivel, waste away ▷ *noun* 1 WASTING AWAY, decline, wasting, decay, decaying, withering, deterioration, meltdown (*informal*), shrivelling, degeneration, diminution 2 WASTING, decline, decay, decaying, withering, deterioration, meltdown (*informal*), shrivelling, degeneration, diminution, wasting away

attach *verb* 1 AFFIX, stick, secure, bind, unite, add, join, couple, link, tie, fix, connect, lash, glue, adhere, fasten, annex, truss, yoke, append, make fast, cohere, subjoin << ANTONYM detach 2 ASCRIBE, connect, attribute, assign, place, associate, lay on, accredit, invest with, impute ▷▷ **attach yourself to** *or* **be attached to something** JOIN, accompany, associate with, combine with, join forces with, latch on to, unite with, sign up with, become associated with, sign on with, affiliate yourself with

attached *adjective* SPOKEN FOR, married, partnered, engaged, accompanied ▷▷ **attached to** FOND OF, devoted to, affectionate towards, full of regard for

attachment *noun* 1 FONDNESS, liking, feeling, love, relationship, regard, bond, friendship, attraction, loyalty, affection, devotion, fidelity, affinity, tenderness, reverence, predilection, possessiveness, partiality, aroha (*NZ*) << ANTONYM aversion 2 ACCESSORY, fitting, extra, addition, component, extension, supplement, fixture, auxiliary, adaptor *or* adapter, supplementary part, add-on, adjunct, appendage, accoutrement, appurtenance

attack *verb* **1** ASSAULT, strike (at), mug, set about, ambush, assail, tear into, fall upon, set upon, lay into (*informal*) << ANTONYM defend **2** INVADE, occupy, raid, infringe, charge, rush, storm, encroach **3** CRITICIZE, blame, abuse, blast, pan (*informal*), condemn, knock (*informal*), slam (*slang*), put down, slate (*informal*), have a go (at) (*informal*), censure, malign, berate, disparage, revile, vilify, tear into (*informal*), slag off (*Brit slang*), diss (*slang, chiefly US*), find fault with, impugn, go for the jugular, lambast(e), pick holes in, excoriate, bite someone's head off, snap someone's head off, pick to pieces ▷ *noun* **1** ASSAULT, charge, campaign, strike, rush, raid, invasion, offensive, aggression, blitz, onset, onslaught, foray, incursion, inroad << ANTONYM defence **2** CRITICISM, panning (*informal*), slating (*informal*), censure, disapproval, slagging (*slang*), abuse, knocking (*informal*), bad press, vilification, denigration, calumny, character assassination, disparagement, impugnment **3** BOUT, fit, access, spell, stroke, seizure, spasm, convulsion, paroxysm

attacker *noun* ASSAILANT, assaulter, raider, intruder, invader, aggressor, mugger

attain *verb* **1** OBTAIN, get, win, reach, effect, land, score (*slang*), complete, gain, achieve, earn, secure, realize, acquire, fulfil, accomplish, grasp, reap, procure **2** REACH, achieve, realize, acquire, arrive at, accomplish

attainable *adjective* ACHIEVABLE, possible, likely, potential, accessible, probable, at hand, feasible, within reach, practicable, obtainable, reachable, realizable, graspable, gettable, procurable, accomplishable << ANTONYM unattainable

attainment *noun* **1** ACHIEVEMENT, getting, winning, reaching, gaining, obtaining, acquisition, feat, completion, reaping, accomplishment, realization, fulfilment, arrival at, procurement, acquirement **2** SKILL, art, ability, talent, gift, achievement, capability, competence, accomplishment, mastery, proficiency

attempt *verb* TRY, seek, aim, struggle, tackle, take on, experiment, venture, undertake, essay, strive, endeavour, have a go at (*informal*), make an effort, make an attempt, have a crack at, have a shot at (*informal*), try your hand at, do your best to, jump through hoops (*informal*), have a stab at (*informal*), take the bit between your teeth ▷ *noun* **1** TRY, go (*informal*), shot (*informal*), effort, trial, bid, experiment, crack (*informal*), venture, undertaking, essay, stab (*informal*), endeavour **2** ATTACK, assault

attempted *adjective* TRIED, ventured, undertaken, endeavoured, assayed

attend *verb* **1** BE PRESENT, go to, visit, be at, be there, be here, frequent, haunt, appear at, turn up at, patronize, show up at (*informal*), show yourself, put in an appearance at, present yourself at << ANTONYM be absent **2** PAY ATTENTION, listen, follow, hear, mark, mind, watch, note, regard, notice, observe, look on, heed, take to heart, pay heed, hearken (*archaic*) << ANTONYM ignore **3** ESCORT, conduct, guard, shadow, accompany, companion, shepherd, convoy, usher, squire, chaperon ▷▷ **attend to someone** LOOK AFTER, help, mind, aid, tend, nurse, care for, take care of, minister to, administer to ▷▷ **attend to something** APPLY YOURSELF TO, concentrate on, look after, take care of, see to, get to work on, devote yourself to, occupy yourself with

attendance *noun* **1** PRESENCE, being there, attending, appearance **2** TURNOUT, audience, gate, congregation, house, crowd, throng, number present

attendant *noun* ASSISTANT, guide, guard, servant, companion, aide, escort, follower, steward, waiter, usher, warden, helper, auxiliary, custodian, page, menial, concierge, underling, lackey, chaperon, flunky ▷ *adjective* ACCOMPANYING, related, associated, accessory, consequent, resultant, concomitant

attention *noun* **1** THINKING, thought, mind, notice, consideration, concentration, observation, scrutiny, heed, deliberation, contemplation, thoughtfulness, attentiveness, intentness, heedfulness **2** CARE, support, concern, treatment, looking after, succour, ministration **3** AWARENESS, regard, notice, recognition, consideration, observation, consciousness << ANTONYM inattention ▷ *plural noun* COURTESY, compliments, regard, respect, care, consideration, deference, politeness, civility, gallantry, mindfulness, assiduities << ANTONYM discourtesy

attentive *adjective* **1** INTENT, listening, concentrating, careful, alert, awake, mindful, watchful, observant, studious, on your toes, heedful, regardful << ANTONYM heedless **2** CONSIDERATE, kind, civil, devoted, helpful, obliging, accommodating, polite, thoughtful, gracious, conscientious, respectful, courteous, gallant << ANTONYM neglectful

attenuate *verb* WEAKEN, reduce, contract, lower, diminish, decrease, dilute, lessen, sap, water down, adulterate, enfeeble, enervate, devaluate

attenuated *adjective* 1 SLENDER, extended, thinned, slimmed, refined, stretched out, lengthened, drawn out, spun out, elongated, rarefied 2 WEAKENED, reduced, contracted, lowered, diminished, decreased, dilute, diluted, lessened, devalued, sapped, watered down, adulterated, enfeebled, enervated

attest *verb* TESTIFY, show, prove, confirm, display, declare, witness, demonstrate, seal, swear, exhibit, warrant, assert, manifest, give evidence, invoke, ratify, affirm, certify, verify, bear out, substantiate, corroborate, bear witness, authenticate, vouch for, evince, aver, adjure << ANTONYM disprove

attic *noun* LOFT, garret, roof space

attire *noun* CLOTHES, wear, dress, clothing, gear (*informal*), habit, uniform, outfit, costume, threads (*slang*), array (*poetic*), garments, robes, apparel, garb, accoutrements, raiment (*archaic or poetic*), vestment, schmutter (*slang*), habiliments

attitude *noun* 1 OPINION, thinking, feeling, thought, view, position, approach, belief, mood, perspective, point of view, stance, outlook, viewpoint, slant, frame of mind 2 MANNER, air, condition, bearing, aspect, carriage, disposition, demeanour, mien (*literary*) 3 POSITION, bearing, pose, stance, carriage, posture

attorney *noun* LAWYER, solicitor, counsel, advocate, barrister, counsellor, legal adviser

attract *verb* 1 ALLURE, interest, draw, invite, persuade, engage, charm, appeal to, fascinate, win over, tempt, lure (*informal*), induce, incline, seduce, entice, enchant, endear, lead on, coax, captivate, beguile, cajole, bewitch, decoy, inveigle, pull, catch (someone's) eye << ANTONYM repel 2 PULL, draw, magnetize

attraction *noun* 1 APPEAL, interest, draw, pull (*informal*), come-on (*informal*), charm, incentive, invitation, lure, bait, temptation, fascination, attractiveness, allure, inducement, magnetism, enchantment, endearment, enticement, captivation, temptingness, pleasingness 2 PULL, draw, magnetism

attractive *adjective* 1 SEDUCTIVE, charming, tempting, interesting, pleasing, pretty, fair, beautiful, inviting, engaging, likable *or* likeable, lovely, winning, sexy (*informal*), pleasant, handsome, fetching, good-looking, glamorous, gorgeous, magnetic, cute, irresistible, enticing, provocative, captivating, beguiling, alluring, bonny, winsome, comely, prepossessing << ANTONYM unattractive 2 APPEALING, pleasing, inviting, fascinating, tempting, enticing, agreeable, irresistible << ANTONYM unappealing

attributable *adjective* ASCRIBABLE, accountable, applicable, traceable, explicable, assignable, imputable, blamable *or* blameable, placeable, referable *or* referrable

attribute *verb* ASCRIBE, apply, credit, blame, refer, trace, assign, charge, allocate, put down, set down, allot, impute ▷ *noun* QUALITY, point, mark, sign, note, feature, property, character, element, aspect, symbol, characteristic, indication, distinction, virtue, trait, hallmark, facet, quirk, peculiarity, idiosyncrasy

attribution *noun* ASCRIPTION, charge, credit, blame, assignment, attachment, placement, referral, assignation, imputation

attrition *noun* WEARING DOWN, harrying, weakening, harassment, thinning out, attenuation, debilitation

attuned *adjective* ACCUSTOMED, adjusted, coordinated, in tune, in harmony, in accord, harmonized, familiarized, acclimatized

atypical *adjective* UNUSUAL, exceptional, uncommon, singular, deviant, unconventional, unique, unorthodox, uncharacteristic, out of the ordinary, unrepresentative, out of keeping, uncustomary, nonconforming, unconforming << ANTONYM normal

auburn *adjective* REDDISH-BROWN, tawny, russet, henna, rust-coloured, copper-coloured, chestnut-coloured, Titian red, nutbrown

audacious *adjective* 1 DARING, enterprising, brave, bold, risky, rash, adventurous, reckless, courageous, fearless, intrepid, valiant, daredevil, death-defying, dauntless, venturesome << ANTONYM timid 2 CHEEKY, presumptuous, impertinent, insolent, impudent, forward, fresh (*informal*), assuming, rude, defiant, brazen, in-your-face (*Brit slang*), shameless, sassy (*US informal*), pert, disrespectful << ANTONYM tactful

audacity *noun* 1 DARING, nerve, courage, guts (*informal*), bravery, boldness, recklessness, face (*informal*), front, enterprise, valour, fearlessness, rashness, adventurousness, intrepidity, audaciousness, dauntlessness, venturesomeness 2 CHEEK, nerve, defiance, gall (*informal*), presumption, rudeness, chutzpah (*US & Canad informal*), insolence, impertinence, neck (*informal*), impudence, effrontery, brass neck (*Brit informal*), shamelessness, sassiness (*US informal*), forwardness, pertness, audaciousness, disrespectfulness

audible *adjective* CLEAR, distinct, discernible, detectable, perceptible, hearable << ANTONYM inaudible

audience *noun* 1 SPECTATORS, company, house, crowd, gathering, gallery, assembly, viewers, listeners, patrons, congregation, turnout, onlookers, throng, assemblage 2 PUBLIC, market, following, fans, devotees, fanbase, aficionados 3 INTERVIEW, meeting, hearing, exchange, reception, consultation

audit (*accounting*) *verb* INSPECT, check, review, balance, survey, examine, investigate, go through, assess, go over, evaluate, vet, verify, appraise, scrutinize, inquire into ▷ *noun* INSPECTION, check, checking, review, balancing, search, survey, investigation, examination, scan, scrutiny, supervision, surveillance, look-over, verification, once-over (*informal*), checkup, superintendence

augment *verb* INCREASE, grow, raise, extend, boost, expand, add to, build up, strengthen, enhance, reinforce, swell, intensify, heighten, enlarge, multiply, inflate, magnify, amplify, dilate << ANTONYM diminish

augur *verb* BODE, promise, predict, herald, signify, foreshadow, prophesy, harbinger, presage, prefigure, portend, betoken, be an omen of

august *adjective* NOBLE, great, kingly, grand, excellent, imposing, impressive, superb, distinguished, magnificent, glorious, splendid, elevated, eminent, majestic, dignified, regal, stately, high-ranking, monumental, solemn, lofty, exalted

aura *noun* AIR, feeling, feel, quality, atmosphere, tone, suggestion, mood, scent, aroma, odour, ambience, vibes (*slang*), vibrations (*slang*), emanation

auspices *plural noun* SUPPORT, backing, control, charge, care, authority, championship, influence, protection, guidance, sponsorship, supervision, patronage, advocacy, countenance, aegis

auspicious *adjective* FAVOURABLE, timely, happy, promising, encouraging, bright, lucky, hopeful, fortunate, prosperous, rosy, opportune, propitious, felicitous << ANTONYM unpromising

austere *adjective* 1 STERN, hard, serious, cold, severe, formal, grave, strict, exacting, harsh, stiff, forbidding, grim, rigorous, solemn, stringent, inflexible, unrelenting, unfeeling << ANTONYM kindly 2 PLAIN, simple, severe, spare, harsh, stark, bleak, subdued, economical, Spartan, unadorned, unornamented << ANTONYM luxurious 3 ASCETIC, strict, continent, exacting, rigid, sober, economical, solemn, Spartan, unrelenting, self-disciplined, puritanical, chaste, strait-laced, abstemious, self-denying, abstinent << ANTONYM abandoned

austerity *noun* 1 PLAINNESS, economy, simplicity, severity, starkness, spareness, Spartanism 2 ASCETICISM, economy, rigidity, abstinence, self-discipline, chastity, sobriety, continence, puritanism, solemnity, self-denial, strictness, abstemiousness, chasteness, exactingness, Spartanism

authentic *adjective* 1 REAL, true, original, actual, pure, genuine, valid, faithful, undisputed, veritable, lawful, on the level (*informal*), bona fide, dinkum (*Austral & NZ informal*), pukka, the real McCoy, true-to-life << ANTONYM fake 2 ACCURATE, true, certain, reliable, legitimate, authoritative, factual, truthful, dependable, trustworthy, veracious << ANTONYM fictitious

authenticate *verb* 1 VERIFY, guarantee, warrant, authorize, certify, avouch << ANTONYM invalidate 2 VOUCH FOR, confirm, endorse, validate, attest

authenticity *noun* 1 GENUINENESS, purity, realness, veritableness 2 ACCURACY, truth, certainty, validity, reliability, legitimacy, verity, actuality, faithfulness, truthfulness, dependability, trustworthiness, authoritativeness, factualness

author *noun* 1 WRITER, composer, novelist, hack, creator, columnist, scribbler, scribe, essayist, wordsmith, penpusher, littérateur, man *or* woman of letters 2 CREATOR, father, parent, mother, maker, producer, framer, designer, founder, architect, planner, inventor, mover, originator, prime mover, doer, initiator, begetter, fabricator

authoritarian *adjective* STRICT, severe,

absolute, harsh, rigid, autocratic, dictatorial, dogmatic, imperious, domineering, unyielding, tyrannical, disciplinarian, despotic, doctrinaire << ANTONYM lenient ▷ *noun* DISCIPLINARIAN, dictator, tyrant, despot, autocrat, absolutist

authoritative *adjective* **1** COMMANDING, lordly, masterly, imposing, dominating, confident, decisive, imperative, assertive, autocratic, dictatorial, dogmatic, imperious, self-assured, peremptory << ANTONYM timid **2** OFFICIAL, approved, sanctioned, legitimate, sovereign, authorized, commanding << ANTONYM unofficial **3** RELIABLE, learned, sound, true, accurate, valid, scholarly, faithful, authentic, definitive, factual, truthful, veritable, dependable, trustworthy << ANTONYM unreliable

authority *noun* **1** *usually plural* POWERS THAT BE, government, police, officials, the state, management, administration, the system, the Establishment, Big Brother (*informal*), officialdom **2** PREROGATIVE, right, influence, might, force, power, control, charge, rule, government, weight, strength, direction, command, licence, privilege, warrant, say-so, sway, domination, jurisdiction, supremacy, dominion, ascendancy, mana (*NZ*) **3** EXPERT, specialist, professional, master, ace (*informal*), scholar, guru, buff (*informal*), wizard, whizz (*informal*), virtuoso, connoisseur, arbiter, hotshot (*informal*), fundi (*S African*) **4** COMMAND, power, control, rule, management, direction, grasp, sway, domination, mastery, dominion **5** PERMISSION, leave, permit, sanction, licence, approval, go-ahead (*informal*), liberty, consent, warrant, say-so, tolerance, justification, green light, assent, authorization, dispensation, carte blanche, a blank cheque, sufferance

authorization *noun* PERMISSION, right, leave, power, authority, ability, strength, permit, sanction, licence, approval, warrant, say-so, credentials, a blank cheque

authorize *verb* **1** EMPOWER, commission, enable, entitle, mandate, accredit, give authority to **2** PERMIT, allow, suffer, grant, confirm, agree to, approve, sanction, endure, license, endorse, warrant, tolerate, ratify, consent to, countenance, accredit, vouch for, give leave, give the green light for, give a blank cheque to, give authority for << ANTONYM forbid

authorized *adjective* OFFICIAL, commissioned, approved, licensed, ratified, signed and sealed

autobiography *noun* LIFE STORY, record, history, résumé, memoirs

autocracy *noun* DICTATORSHIP, tyranny, despotism, absolutism

autocrat *noun* DICTATOR, tyrant, despot, absolutist

autocratic *adjective* DICTATORIAL, absolute, unlimited, all-powerful, imperious, domineering, tyrannical, despotic, tyrannous

automatic *adjective* **1** MECHANICAL, robot, automated, mechanized, push-button, self-regulating, self-propelling, self-activating, self-moving, self-acting << ANTONYM done by hand **2** INVOLUNTARY, natural, unconscious, mechanical, spontaneous, reflex, instinctive, instinctual, unwilled << ANTONYM conscious **3** INEVITABLE, certain, necessary, assured, routine, unavoidable, inescapable

autonomous *adjective* SELF-RULING, free, independent, sovereign, self-sufficient, self-governing, self-determining

autonomy *noun* INDEPENDENCE, freedom, sovereignty, self-determination, self-government, self-rule, self-sufficiency, home rule, rangatiratanga (*NZ*) << ANTONYM dependency

autopsy *noun* POSTMORTEM, dissection, postmortem examination, necropsy

auxiliary *adjective* **1** SUPPLEMENTARY, reserve, emergency, substitute, secondary, back-up, subsidiary, fall-back **2** SUPPORTING, helping, aiding, assisting, accessory, ancillary << ANTONYM primary ▷ *noun* HELPER, partner, ally, associate, supporter, assistant, companion, accessory, subordinate, protagonist, accomplice, confederate, henchman

avail *noun* BENEFIT, use, help, good, service, aid, profit, advantage, purpose, assistance, utility, effectiveness, mileage (*informal*), usefulness, efficacy ▷▷ **avail yourself of something** MAKE USE OF, use, employ, exploit, take advantage of, profit from, make the most of, utilize, have recourse to, turn to account

availability *noun* ACCESSIBILITY, readiness, handiness, attainability, obtainability

available *adjective* ACCESSIBLE, ready, to hand, convenient, handy, vacant, on hand, at hand, free, applicable, to be had, achievable, obtainable, on tap (*informal*), attainable, at your fingertips, at your disposal, ready for use << ANTONYM in use

avalanche *noun* 1 SNOW-SLIDE, landslide, landslip, snow-slip 2 LARGE AMOUNT, barrage, torrent, deluge, inundation

avant-garde *adjective* PROGRESSIVE, pioneering, way-out (*informal*), experimental, innovative, unconventional, far-out (*slang*), ground-breaking, innovatory << ANTONYM conservative

avarice *noun* GREED, meanness, penny-pinching, parsimony, acquisitiveness, rapacity, cupidity, stinginess, covetousness, miserliness, greediness, niggardliness, graspingness, close-fistedness, penuriousness << ANTONYM liberality

avenge *verb* GET REVENGE FOR, revenge, repay, retaliate for, take revenge for, hit back for, requite, pay (someone) back for, get even for (*informal*), even the score for, get your own back for, take vengeance for, take satisfaction for, pay (someone) back in his *or* her own coin for

avenue *noun* STREET, way, course, drive, road, pass, approach, channel, access, entry, route, path, passage, entrance, alley, pathway, boulevard, driveway, thoroughfare

average *noun* STANDARD, normal, usual, par, mode, mean, rule, medium, norm, run of the mill, midpoint ▷ *adjective* 1 USUAL, common, standard, general, normal, regular, ordinary, typical, commonplace, unexceptional << ANTONYM unusual 2 MEAN, middle, medium, intermediate, median << ANTONYM minimum 3 MEDIOCRE, fair, ordinary, moderate, pedestrian, indifferent, not bad, middling, insignificant, so-so (*informal*), banal, second-rate, middle-of-the-road, tolerable, run-of-the-mill, passable, undistinguished, uninspired, unexceptional, bog-standard (*Brit & Irish slang*), no great shakes (*informal*), fair to middling (*informal*) ▷ *verb* MAKE ON AVERAGE, be on average, even out to, do on average, balance out to ▷▷ **on average** USUALLY, generally, normally, typically, for the most part, as a rule

averse *adjective* OPPOSED, reluctant, hostile, unwilling, backward, unfavourable, loath, disinclined, inimical, indisposed, antipathetic, ill-disposed << ANTONYM favourable

aversion *noun* HATRED, hate, horror, disgust, hostility, opposition, dislike, reluctance, loathing, distaste, animosity, revulsion, antipathy, repulsion, abhorrence, disinclination, repugnance, odium, detestation, indisposition << ANTONYM love

avert *verb* 1 WARD OFF, avoid, prevent, frustrate, fend off, preclude, stave off, forestall 2 TURN AWAY, turn, turn aside

aviation *noun* FLYING, flight, aeronautics, powered flight

aviator *noun* PILOT, flyer, airman, airwoman, aeronaut

avid *adjective* 1 ENTHUSIASTIC, keen, devoted, intense, eager, passionate, ardent, fanatical, fervent, zealous, keen as mustard << ANTONYM indifferent 2 INSATIABLE, hungry, greedy, thirsty, grasping, voracious, acquisitive, ravenous, rapacious, avaricious, covetous, athirst

avoid *verb* 1 PREVENT, stop, frustrate, hamper, foil, inhibit, head off, avert, thwart, intercept, hinder, obstruct, impede, ward off, stave off, forestall, defend against 2 REFRAIN FROM, bypass, dodge, eschew, escape, duck (out of) (*informal*), fight shy of, shirk from 3 KEEP AWAY FROM, dodge, shun, evade, steer clear of, sidestep, circumvent, bypass, body-swerve (*Scot*), give a wide berth to

avoidable *adjective* 1 PREVENTABLE, stoppable, avertible *or* avertable << ANTONYM unpreventable 2 ESCAPABLE, evadable << ANTONYM inevitable

avoidance *noun* 1 REFRAINING, dodging, shirking, eschewal 2 PREVENTION, safeguard, precaution, anticipation, thwarting, elimination, deterrence, forestalling, prophylaxis, preclusion, obviation

avow *verb* STATE, maintain, declare, allege, recognize, swear, assert, proclaim, affirm, profess, aver, asseverate

avowed *adjective* DECLARED, open, admitted, acknowledged, confessed, sworn, professed, self-proclaimed

await *verb* 1 WAIT FOR, expect, look for, look forward to, anticipate, stay for 2 BE IN STORE FOR, wait for, be ready for, lie in wait for, be in readiness for

awake *verb* 1 WAKE UP, come to, wake, stir, awaken, rouse 2 ALERT, excite, stimulate, provoke, revive, arouse, activate, awaken, fan, animate, stir up, incite, kick-start (*informal*), enliven, kindle, breathe life into, call forth, vivify 3 STIMULATE, excite, provoke, activate, alert, animate, fan, stir up, incite, kick-start (*informal*), enliven, kindle, breathe life into, call forth, vivify ▷ *adjective* 1 NOT SLEEPING, sleepless, wide-awake, aware, waking, conscious, aroused, awakened, restless, restive, wakeful, bright-eyed and bushy-tailed << ANTONYM asleep **2** ALERT, aware, on the lookout, alive, attentive, on the alert, observant, watchful, on guard, on your toes, heedful, vigilant ▷ see **wake**

award *verb* **1** PRESENT WITH, give, grant, gift, distribute, render, assign, decree, hand out, confer, endow, bestow, allot, apportion, adjudge **2** GRANT, give, render, assign, decree, accord, confer, adjudge ▷ *noun* **1** GRANT, subsidy, scholarship, hand-out, endowment, stipend **2** PRIZE, gift, trophy, decoration, grant, bonsela (*S African*), koha (*NZ*) **3** (*law*) SETTLEMENT, payment, compensation

aware *adjective* INFORMED, enlightened, knowledgeable, learned, expert, versed, up to date, in the picture, in the know (*informal*), erudite, well-read, au fait (*French*), in the loop, well-briefed, au courant (*French*), clued-up (*informal*) << ANTONYM ignorant ▷▷ **aware of** KNOWING ABOUT, familiar with, conscious of, wise to (*slang*), alert to, mindful of, acquainted with, alive to, awake to, privy to, hip to (*slang*), appreciative of, attentive to, conversant with, apprised of, cognizant of, sensible of

awareness *noun* ▷▷ **awareness of** KNOWLEDGE OF, understanding of, appreciation of, recognition of, attention to, perception of, consciousness of, acquaintance with, enlightenment with, sensibility to, realization of, familiarity with, mindfulness of, cognizance of, sentience of

away *adjective* ABSENT, out, gone, elsewhere, abroad, not there, not here, not present, on vacation, not at home ▷ *adverb* **1** OFF, elsewhere, abroad, hence, from here **2** ASIDE, out of the way, to one side **3** AT A DISTANCE, far, apart, remote, isolated **4** CONTINUOUSLY, repeatedly, relentlessly, incessantly, interminably, unremittingly, uninterruptedly

awe *noun* WONDER, fear, respect, reverence, horror, terror, dread, admiration, amazement, astonishment, veneration << ANTONYM contempt ▷ *verb* IMPRESS, amaze, stun, frighten, terrify, cow, astonish, horrify, intimidate, daunt

awed *adjective* IMPRESSED, shocked, amazed, afraid, stunned, frightened, terrified, cowed, astonished, horrified, intimidated, fearful, daunted, dumbfounded, wonder-struck

awe-inspiring *adjective* IMPRESSIVE, striking, wonderful, amazing, stunning (*informal*), magnificent, astonishing, intimidating, awesome, daunting, breathtaking, fearsome, wondrous (*archaic* or *literary*), jaw-dropping << ANTONYM unimpressive

awesome *adjective* AWE-INSPIRING, striking, shocking, imposing, terrible, amazing, stunning, wonderful, alarming, impressive, frightening, awful, overwhelming, terrifying, magnificent, astonishing, horrible, dreadful, formidable, horrifying, intimidating, fearful, daunting, breathtaking, majestic, solemn, fearsome, wondrous (*archaic* or *literary*), redoubtable, jaw-dropping, stupefying

awestruck or **awe-stricken** *adjective* IMPRESSED, shocked, amazed, stunned, afraid, frightened, terrified, cowed, astonished, horrified, intimidated, fearful, awed, daunted, awe-inspired, dumbfounded, struck dumb, wonder-struck

awful *adjective* **1** DISGUSTING, terrible, tremendous, offensive, gross, nasty, foul, horrible, dreadful, unpleasant, revolting, stinking, sickening, hideous, vulgar, vile, distasteful, horrid, frightful, nauseating, odious, repugnant, loathsome, abominable, nauseous, detestable, godawful (*slang*), hellacious (*US slang*), festy (*Austral slang*), yucko (*Austral slang*) **2** BAD, poor, terrible, appalling, foul, rubbish (*slang*), dreadful, unpleasant, dire, horrendous, ghastly, from hell (*informal*), atrocious, deplorable, abysmal, frightful, hellacious (*US slang*) << ANTONYM wonderful **3** SHOCKING, serious, alarming, distressing, dreadful, horrifying, horrific, hideous, harrowing, gruesome **4** UNWELL, poorly (*informal*), ill, terrible, sick, ugly, crook (*Austral & NZ informal*), unhealthy, unsightly, queasy, out of sorts (*informal*), off-colour, under the weather (*informal*), green about the gills

awfully *adverb* **1** (*informal*) VERY, extremely, terribly, exceptionally, quite, very much, seriously (*informal*), greatly, immensely, exceedingly, excessively, dreadfully **2** BADLY, woefully, dreadfully, inadequately, disgracefully, wretchedly, unforgivably, shoddily, reprehensibly, disreputably

awhile *adverb* FOR A WHILE, briefly, for a moment, for a short time, for a little while

awkward *adjective* **1** EMBARRASSING, difficult, compromising, sensitive, embarrassed, painful, distressing, delicate, uncomfortable, tricky, trying, humiliating, unpleasant, sticky (*informal*), troublesome, perplexing, disconcerting, inconvenient, thorny, untimely, ill at ease, discomfiting, ticklish, inopportune, toe-curling (*slang*), barro (*Austral slang*), cringeworthy (*Brit informal*) << ANTONYM comfortable **2** INCONVENIENT, difficult, troublesome, cumbersome, unwieldy, unmanageable, clunky (*informal*), unhandy << ANTONYM convenient **3** CLUMSY, stiff, rude, blundering, coarse, bungling, lumbering, inept, unskilled, bumbling, unwieldy, ponderous, ungainly, gauche, gawky, uncouth, unrefined, artless, inelegant, uncoordinated, graceless, cack-handed (*informal*), unpolished, clownish, oafish, inexpert, maladroit, ill-bred, all thumbs, ungraceful, skill-less, unskilful, butterfingered (*informal*), unhandy, ham-fisted *or* ham-handed (*informal*), unco (*Austral slang*) << ANTONYM graceful **4** UNCOOPERATIVE, trying, difficult, annoying, unpredictable, unreasonable, stubborn, troublesome, perverse, prickly, exasperating, irritable, intractable, vexing, unhelpful, touchy, obstinate, obstructive, bloody-minded (*Brit informal*), chippy (*informal*), vexatious, hard to handle, disobliging

awkwardness *noun* **1** CLUMSINESS, stiffness, rudeness, coarseness, ineptness, ill-breeding, artlessness, gaucheness, inelegance, gaucherie, gracelessness, oafishness, gawkiness, uncouthness, maladroitness, ungainliness, clownishness, inexpertness, uncoordination, unskilfulness, unskilledness **2** EMBARRASSMENT, difficulty, discomfort, delicacy, unpleasantness, inconvenience, stickiness (*informal*), painfulness, ticklishness, uphill (*S*

African), thorniness, inopportuneness, perplexingness, untimeliness

awry *adverb* ASKEW, to one side, off course, out of line, obliquely, unevenly, off-centre, cockeyed (*informal*), out of true, crookedly, skew-whiff (*informal*) ▷ *adjective* ASKEW, twisted, crooked, to one side, uneven, off course, out of line, asymmetrical, off-centre, cockeyed (*informal*), misaligned, out of true, skew-whiff (*informal*) ▷ *adverb or adjective* WRONG, amiss

axe *noun* HATCHET, chopper, tomahawk, cleaver, adze ▷ *verb* **1** (*informal*) ABANDON, end, pull, eliminate, cancel, scrap, wind up, turn off (*informal*), relegate, cut back, terminate, dispense with, discontinue, pull the plug on **2** (*informal*) DISMISS, fire (*informal*), sack (*informal*), remove, get rid of, discharge, throw out, oust, give (someone) their marching orders, give the boot to (*slang*), give the bullet to (*Brit slang*), give the push to, kennet (*Austral slang*), jeff (*Austral slang*) ▷▷ **an axe to grind** PET SUBJECT, grievance, ulterior motive, private purpose, personal consideration, private ends ▷▷ **the axe** (*informal*) THE SACK (*informal*), dismissal, discharge, wind-up, the boot (*slang*), cancellation, cutback, termination, the chop (*slang*), the (old) heave-ho (*informal*), the order of the boot (*slang*)

axiom *noun* PRINCIPLE, fundamental, maxim, gnome, adage, postulate, dictum, precept, aphorism, truism, apophthegm

axis *noun* PIVOT, shaft, axle, spindle, centre line

axle *noun* SHAFT, pin, rod, axis, pivot, spindle, arbor, mandrel

azure *adjective* SKY BLUE, blue, clear blue, ultramarine, cerulean, sky-coloured

baas *noun* (*S African*) MASTER, bo (*informal*), chief, ruler, commander, head, overlord, overseer

babble *verb* 1 GABBLE, chatter, gush, spout, waffle (*informal, chiefly Brit*), splutter, gaggle, burble, prattle, gibber, rabbit on (*Brit informal*), jabber, prate, earbash (*Austral & NZ slang*) 2 GURGLE, lap, bubble, splash, murmur, ripple, burble, plash ▷ *noun* 1 GABBLE, chatter, burble, prattle, blabber 2 GIBBERISH, waffle (*informal, chiefly Brit*), drivel, twaddle

babe *noun* BABY, child, innocent, infant, bairn (*Scot & N English*), tacker (*Austral slang*), suckling, newborn child, babe in arms, nursling

baby *noun* CHILD, infant, babe, wean (*Scot*), little one, bairn (*Scot & N English*), suckling, newborn child, babe in arms, sprog (*slang*), neonate, rug rat (*US & Canad informal*), ankle biter (*Austral slang*), tacker (*Austral slang*) ▷ *adjective* SMALL, little, minute, tiny, mini, wee, miniature, dwarf, diminutive, petite, midget, teeny (*informal*), pocket-sized, undersized, teeny-weeny (*informal*), Lilliputian, teensy-weensy (*informal*), pygmy or pigmy ▷ *verb* SPOIL, pamper, cosset, coddle, pet, humour, indulge, spoon-feed, mollycoddle, overindulge, wrap up in cotton wool (*informal*)

back *noun* 1 SPINE, backbone, vertebrae, spinal column, vertebral column 2 REAR, back end << ANTONYM front 3 REVERSE, rear, other side, wrong side, underside, flip side, verso ▷ *adjective* 1 REAR << ANTONYM front 2 REARMOST, hind, hindmost 3 PREVIOUS, earlier, former, past, elapsed << ANTONYM future 4 TAIL, end, rear, posterior ▷ *verb* 1 SUPPORT, help, second, aid, champion, encourage, favour, defend, promote, sanction, sustain, assist, advocate, endorse, side with, stand up for, espouse, stand behind, countenance, abet, stick up for (*informal*), take up the cudgels for << ANTONYM oppose 2 SUBSIDIZE, help, support, finance, sponsor, assist, underwrite ▷▷ **back down** GIVE IN, collapse, withdraw, yield, concede, submit, surrender, comply, cave in (*informal*), capitulate, accede, admit defeat, back-pedal ▷▷ **back out** WITHDRAW, retire, give up, pull out, retreat, drop out, renege, cop out (*slang*), chicken out (*informal*), detach yourself ▷▷ **back someone up** SUPPORT, second, aid, assist, stand by, bolster ▷▷ **behind someone's back** SECRETLY, covertly, surreptitiously, furtively, conspiratorially, sneakily, deceitfully

backbone *noun* 1 SPINAL COLUMN, spine, vertebrae, vertebral column 2 FOUNDATION, support, base, basis, mainstay, bedrock 3 STRENGTH OF CHARACTER, will, character, bottle (*Brit slang*), resolution, resolve, nerve, daring, courage, determination, guts, pluck, stamina, grit, bravery, fortitude, toughness, tenacity, willpower, mettle, boldness, firmness, spunk (*informal*), fearlessness, steadfastness, moral fibre, hardihood, dauntlessness

backer *noun* 1 SUPPORTER, second, ally, angel (*informal*), patron, promoter, subscriber, underwriter, helper, benefactor 2 ADVOCATE, supporter, patron, sponsor, promoter, protagonist

backfire *verb* FAIL, founder, flop (*informal*), rebound, fall through, fall flat, boomerang, miscarry, misfire, go belly-up (*slang*), turn out badly, meet with disaster

background *noun* 1 UPBRINGING, history, culture, environment, tradition, circumstances, breeding, milieu 2 EXPERIENCE, grounding, education, preparation, qualifications, credentials

3 CIRCUMSTANCES, history, conditions, situation, atmosphere, environment, framework, ambience, milieu, frame of reference

backing noun **1** SUPPORT, seconding, championing, promotion, sanction, approval, blessing, encouragement, endorsement, patronage, accompaniment, advocacy, moral support, espousal **2** ASSISTANCE, support, help, funds, aid, grant, subsidy, sponsorship, patronage

backlash noun REACTION, response, resistance, resentment, retaliation, repercussion, counterblast, counteraction, retroaction

backlog noun BUILD-UP, stock, excess, accumulation, accretion

backside noun (informal) BUTTOCKS, behind (informal), seat, bottom, rear, tail (informal), cheeks (informal), butt (US & Canad informal), bum (Brit slang), buns (US slang), rump, rear end, posterior, haunches, hindquarters, derrière (euphemistic), tush, fundament, gluteus maximus (anatomy), coit (Austral slang), nates (technical name), jacksy (Brit slang), keister or keester (slang, chiefly US)

backtrack verb **1** often with **on** RETRACT, withdraw, retreat, draw back, recant **2** RETRACE YOUR STEPS, go back, reverse, retreat, move back, back-pedal

backup noun **1** SUPPORT, backing, help, aid, reserves, assistance, reinforcement, auxiliaries **2** SUBSTITUTE, reserve, relief, stand-in, replacement, stand-by, understudy, second string, locum

backward adjective **1** REVERSE, inverted, inverse, back to front, rearward << ANTONYM forward **2** UNDERDEVELOPED, undeveloped **3** SLOW, behind, stupid, retarded, deficient, underdeveloped, subnormal, half-witted, behindhand, slow-witted, intellectually handicapped (Austral)

backwardness noun **1** LACK OF DEVELOPMENT, underdevelopment **2** SLOWNESS, learning difficulties, underdevelopment, retardation, arrested development << ANTONYM brightness

backwards or **backward** adverb TOWARDS THE REAR, behind you, in reverse, rearwards

backwoods plural noun STICKS (informal), outback, back country (US), back of beyond, backlands (US)

bacteria plural noun MICROORGANISMS, viruses, bugs (slang), germs, microbes, pathogens, bacilli

bad adjective **1** HARMFUL, damaging, dangerous, disastrous, destructive, unhealthy, detrimental, hurtful, ruinous, deleterious, injurious, disadvantageous << ANTONYM beneficial **2** SEVERE, serious, terrible, acute, extreme, intense, painful, distressing, fierce, harsh **3** UNFAVOURABLE, troubling, distressing, unfortunate, grim, discouraging, unpleasant, gloomy, adverse **4** INFERIOR, poor, inadequate, pathetic, faulty, duff (Brit informal), unsatisfactory, mediocre, defective, second-class, deficient, imperfect, second-rate, shoddy, low-grade, erroneous, substandard, low-rent (informal, chiefly US), two-bit (US & Canad slang), crappy (slang), end-of-the-pier (Brit informal), poxy (slang), dime-a-dozen (informal), bush-league (Austral & NZ informal), tinhorn (US slang), half-pie (NZ informal), bodger or bodgie (Austral slang), strictly for the birds (informal) << ANTONYM satisfactory **5** INCOMPETENT, poor, useless, incapable, unfit, inexpert **6** GRIM, severe, hard, tough **7** WICKED, criminal, evil, corrupt, worthless, base, vile, immoral, delinquent, sinful, depraved, debased, amoral, egregious, villainous, unprincipled, iniquitous, nefarious, dissolute, maleficent << ANTONYM virtuous **8** NAUGHTY, defiant, perverse, wayward, mischievous, wicked, unruly, impish, undisciplined, roguish, disobedient << ANTONYM well-behaved **9** GUILTY, sorry, ashamed, apologetic, rueful, sheepish, contrite, remorseful, regretful, shamefaced, conscience-stricken **10** ROTTEN, off, rank, sour, rancid, mouldy, fetid, putrid, festy (Austral slang) ▷▷ **not bad** (informal) O.K. or OKAY, fine, middling, average, fair, all right, acceptable, moderate, adequate, respectable, satisfactory, so-so, tolerable, passable, fair to middling (informal)

baddie or **baddy** noun (informal) VILLAIN, criminal, rogue, bad guy, scoundrel, miscreant, antihero, evildoer, wrong 'un (Austral slang) << ANTONYM goodie or goody

badge noun **1** IMAGE, brand, stamp, identification, crest, emblem, insignia **2** MARK, sign, token

badger verb PESTER, worry, harry, bother, bug (informal), bully, plague, hound, get at, harass, nag, hassle (informal), chivvy, importune, bend someone's ear (informal), be on someone's back (slang)

badly adverb **1** POORLY, incorrectly, carelessly, inadequately, erroneously, imperfectly,

ineptly, shoddily, defectively, faultily
<< ANTONYM well **2** SEVERELY, greatly,
deeply, seriously, gravely, desperately,
sorely, dangerously, intensely, painfully,
acutely, exceedingly **3** UNFAVOURABLY,
unsuccessfully

badness *noun* WICKEDNESS, wrong, evil,
corruption, sin, impropriety, immorality,
villainy, naughtiness, sinfulness, foulness,
baseness, rottenness, vileness, shamefulness
<< ANTONYM virtue

bad-tempered *adjective* IRRITABLE, cross,
angry, tense, crabbed, fiery, grumbling,
snarling, prickly, exasperated, edgy, snappy,
sullen, touchy, surly, petulant, sulky, ill-
tempered, irascible, cantankerous, tetchy,
ratty (*Brit & NZ informal*), tooshie (*Austral
slang*), testy, chippy (*informal*), fretful,
grouchy (*informal*), querulous, peevish,
crabby, huffy, dyspeptic, choleric, splenetic,
crotchety (*informal*), oversensitive, snappish,
ill-humoured, liverish, narky (*Brit slang*), out
of humour << ANTONYM good-tempered

baffle *verb* PUZZLE, beat (*slang*), amaze,
confuse, stump, bewilder, astound, elude,
confound, perplex, disconcert, mystify,
flummox, boggle the mind of, dumbfound
<< ANTONYM explain

baffling *adjective* PUZZLING, strange,
confusing, weird, mysterious, unclear,
bewildering, elusive, enigmatic, perplexing,
incomprehensible, mystifying, inexplicable,
unaccountable, unfathomable << ANTONYM
understandable

bag *noun* SACK, container, poke (*Scot*), sac,
receptacle ▷ *verb* **1** GET, take, land, score
(*slang*), gain, pick up, capture, acquire, get
hold of, come by, procure, make sure of,
win possession of **2** CATCH, get, kill, shoot,
capture, acquire, trap

baggage *noun* LUGGAGE, things, cases,
bags, equipment, gear, trunks, suitcases,
belongings, paraphernalia, accoutrements,
impedimenta

baggy *adjective* LOOSE, hanging, slack,
loosened, bulging, not fitting, sagging,
sloppy, floppy, billowing, roomy, slackened,
ill-fitting, droopy, oversize, not tight
<< ANTONYM tight

bail¹ *noun* (*law*) SECURITY, bond, guarantee,
pledge, warranty, surety, guaranty ▷▷ **bail
out** ESCAPE, withdraw, get away, retreat,
make your getaway, break free *or* out, make
or effect your escape ▷▷ **bail something** *or*
someone out (*informal*) SAVE, help, free,

release, aid, deliver, recover, rescue, get out,
relieve, liberate, salvage, set free, save the
life of, extricate, save (someone's) bacon (*Brit
informal*)

bail² *or* **bale** *verb* SCOOP, empty, dip, ladle,
drain off

bait *noun* LURE, attraction, incentive, carrot
(*informal*), temptation, bribe, magnet,
snare, inducement, decoy, carrot and
stick, enticement, allurement ▷ *verb* TEASE,
provoke, annoy, irritate, guy (*informal*),
bother, needle (*informal*), plague (*informal*),
mock, rag, rib (*informal*), wind up (*Brit slang*),
hound, torment, harass, ridicule, taunt,
hassle (*informal*), aggravate (*informal*), badger,
gall, persecute, pester, goad, irk, bedevil, take
the mickey out of (*informal*), chaff, gibe, get
on your nerves (*informal*), nark (*Brit, Austral
& NZ slang*), be on your back (*slang*), get in
your hair (*informal*), get *or* take a rise out of,
hack you off (*informal*)

baked *adjective* DRY, desert, seared, dried
up, scorched, barren, sterile, arid,
torrid, desiccated, sun-baked, waterless,
moistureless

bakkie *noun* (*S African*) TRUCK, pick-up, van,
lorry, pick-up truck

balance *verb* **1** STABILIZE, level, steady
<< ANTONYM overbalance **2** OFFSET, match,
square, make up for, compensate for,
counteract, neutralize, counterbalance,
even up, equalize, counterpoise **3** WEIGH,
consider, compare, estimate, contrast,
assess, evaluate, set against, juxtapose
4 (*accounting*) CALCULATE, rate, judge, total,
determine, estimate, settle, count, square,
reckon, work out, compute, gauge, tally ▷
noun **1** EQUILIBRIUM, stability, steadiness,
evenness, equipoise, counterpoise
<< ANTONYM instability **2** STABILITY,
equanimity, constancy, steadiness
3 PARITY, equity, fairness, impartiality,
equality, correspondence, equivalence
4 REMAINDER, rest, difference, surplus,
residue **5** COMPOSURE, stability, restraint,
self-control, poise, self-discipline, coolness,
calmness, equanimity, self-restraint,
steadiness, self-possession, self-mastery,
strength of mind *or* will

balance sheet *noun* STATEMENT, report,
account, budget, ledger, financial statement,
credits and debits sheet

balcony *noun* **1** TERRACE, veranda **2** UPPER
CIRCLE, gods, gallery

bald *adjective* **1** HAIRLESS, bare, shorn,

clean-shaven, tonsured, depilated, glabrous (*biology*), baldheaded, baldpated **2** PLAIN, direct, simple, straight, frank, severe, bare, straightforward, blunt, rude, outright, downright, forthright, unadorned, unvarnished, straight from the shoulder

balding *adjective* LOSING YOUR HAIR, receding, thin on top, becoming bald

baldness *noun* HAIRLESSNESS, alopecia (*pathology*), baldheadedness, baldpatedness, glabrousness (*biology*)

bale ▷ see **bail**2

baleful *adjective* MENACING, threatening, dangerous, frightening, evil, deadly, forbidding, intimidating, harmful, sinister, ominous, malignant, hurtful, vindictive, pernicious, mournful, malevolent, noxious, venomous, ruinous, intimidatory, minatory, maleficent, bodeful, louring *or* lowering, minacious << ANTONYM friendly

balk *or* **baulk** *verb usually with* at RECOIL, resist, hesitate, dodge, falter, evade, shy away, flinch, quail, shirk, shrink, draw back, jib << ANTONYM accept

ball *noun* **1** SPHERE, drop, globe, pellet, orb, globule, spheroid **2** PROJECTILE, shot, missile, bullet, ammunition, slug, pellet, grapeshot

ballast *noun* COUNTERBALANCE, balance, weight, stability, equilibrium, sandbag, counterweight, stabilizer

balloon *verb* EXPAND, rise, increase, extend, swell, blow up, enlarge, inflate, bulge, billow, dilate, be inflated, puff out, become larger, distend, bloat, grow rapidly

ballot *noun* VOTE, election, voting, poll, polling, referendum, show of hands

balm *noun* **1** OINTMENT, cream, lotion, salve, emollient, balsam, liniment, embrocation, unguent **2** COMFORT, support, relief, cheer, consolation, solace, palliative, anodyne, succour, restorative, curative

balmy *adjective* **1** MILD, warm, calm, moderate, pleasant, clement, tranquil, temperate, summery << ANTONYM rough **2** ▷ see **barmy**

bamboozle *verb* (*informal*) **1** CHEAT, do (*informal*), kid (*informal*), skin (*slang*), trick, fool, take in (*informal*), con (*informal*), stiff, sting (*informal*), mislead, rip off (*slang*), thwart, deceive, fleece, hoax, defraud, dupe, beguile, gull (*archaic*), delude, swindle, stitch up (*slang*), victimize, hoodwink, double-cross (*informal*), diddle (*informal*), take for a ride (*informal*), do the dirty on (*Brit informal*), bilk, pull a fast one on (*informal*), cozen

2 PUZZLE, confuse, stump, baffle, bewilder, confound, perplex, mystify, befuddle, flummox, nonplus

ban *verb* **1** PROHIBIT, black, bar, block, restrict, veto, forbid, boycott, suppress, outlaw, banish, disallow, proscribe, debar, blackball, interdict << ANTONYM permit **2** BAR, prohibit, exclude, forbid, disqualify, preclude, debar, declare ineligible ▷ *noun* PROHIBITION, block, restriction, veto, boycott, embargo, injunction, censorship, taboo, suppression, stoppage, disqualification, interdiction, interdict, proscription, disallowance, rahui (*NZ*), restraining order (*US law*) << ANTONYM permission

banal *adjective* UNORIGINAL, stock, ordinary, boring, tired, routine, dull, everyday, stereotypical, pedestrian, commonplace, mundane, tedious, vanilla (*slang*), dreary, stale, tiresome, monotonous, humdrum, threadbare, trite, unimaginative, uneventful, uninteresting, clichéd, old hat, mind-numbing, hackneyed, ho-hum (*informal*), vapid, repetitious, wearisome, platitudinous, cliché-ridden, unvaried << ANTONYM original

banality *noun* **1** UNORIGINALITY, triviality, vapidity, triteness **2** CLICHÉ, commonplace, platitude, truism, bromide (*informal*), trite phrase

band[1] *noun* **1** ENSEMBLE, group, orchestra, combo **2** GANG, company, group, set, party, team, lot, club, body, association, crowd, troop, pack, camp, squad, crew (*informal*), assembly, mob, horde, troupe, posse (*informal*), clique, coterie, bevy ▷▷ **band together** UNITE, group, join, league, ally, associate, gather, pool, merge, consolidate, affiliate, collaborate, join forces, cooperate, confederate, pull together, join together, federate, close ranks, club together

band[2] *noun* **1** HEADBAND, tie, strip, ribbon, fillet **2** BANDAGE, tie, binding, strip, belt, strap, cord, swathe, fetter

bandage *noun* DRESSING, plaster, compress, gauze ▷ *verb* DRESS, cover, bind, swathe

bandit *noun* ROBBER, gunman, crook, outlaw, pirate, raider, gangster, plunderer, mugger (*informal*), hijacker, looter, highwayman, racketeer, desperado, marauder, brigand, freebooter, footpad

bandy *verb* EXCHANGE, trade, pass, throw, truck, swap, toss, shuffle, commute, interchange, barter, reciprocate

bane *noun* PLAGUE, bête noire, trial, disaster, evil, ruin, burden, destruction, despair, misery, curse, pest, torment, woe, nuisance, downfall, calamity, scourge, affliction << ANTONYM blessing

bang *noun* **1** EXPLOSION, report, shot, pop, clash, crack, blast, burst, boom, slam, discharge, thump, clap, thud, clang, peal, detonation **2** BLOW, hit, box, knock, stroke, punch, belt (*informal*), rap, bump, bash (*informal*), sock (*slang*), smack, thump, buffet, clout (*informal*), cuff, clump (*slang*), whack, wallop (*informal*), slosh (*Brit slang*), tonk (*informal*), clomp (*slang*) ▷ *verb* **1** RESOUND, beat, crash, burst, boom, echo, drum, explode, thunder, thump, throb, thud, clang **2** BUMP, knock, elbow, jostle **3** *often with* **on** HIT, pound, beat, strike, crash, knock, belt (*informal*), hammer, slam, rap, bump, bash (*informal*), thump, clatter, pummel, tonk (*informal*), beat *or* knock seven bells out of (*informal*) ▷ *adverb* EXACTLY, just, straight, square, squarely, precisely, slap, smack, plumb (*informal*)

banish *verb* **1** EXCLUDE, bar, ban, dismiss, expel, throw out, oust, drive away, eject, evict, shut out, ostracize **2** EXPEL, transport, exile, outlaw, deport, drive away, expatriate, excommunicate << ANTONYM admit **3** GET RID OF, remove, eliminate, eradicate, shake off, dislodge, see the back of

banishment *noun* EXPULSION, exile, dismissal, removal, discharge, transportation, exclusion, deportation, eviction, ejection, extrusion, proscription, expatriation, debarment

banisters *plural noun* RAILING, rail, balustrade, handrail, balusters

bank¹ *noun* **1** FINANCIAL INSTITUTION, repository, depository **2** STORE, fund, stock, source, supply, reserve, pool, reservoir, accumulation, stockpile, hoard, storehouse ▷ *verb* DEPOSIT, keep, save ▷▷ **bank on something** RELY ON, trust (in), depend on, look to, believe in, count on, be sure of, lean on, be confident of, have confidence in, swear by, reckon on, repose trust in

bank² *noun* **1** SIDE, edge, margin, shore, brink, lakeside, waterside **2** MOUND, banking, rise, hill, mass, pile, heap, ridge, dune, embankment, knoll, hillock, kopje *or* koppie (*S African*) ▷ *verb* TILT, tip, pitch, heel, slope, incline, slant, cant, camber

bank³ *noun* ROW, group, line, train, range, series, file, rank, arrangement, sequence, succession, array, tier

bankrupt *adjective* INSOLVENT, broke (*informal*), spent, ruined, wiped out (*informal*), impoverished, beggared, in the red, on the rocks, destitute, gone bust (*informal*), in receivership, gone to the wall, in the hands of the receivers, on your uppers, in queer street << ANTONYM solvent

bankruptcy *noun* INSOLVENCY, failure, crash, disaster, ruin, liquidation, indebtedness

banner *noun* **1** FLAG, standard, colours, jack, pennant, ensign, streamer, pennon **2** PLACARD

banquet *noun* FEAST, spread (*informal*), dinner, meal, entertainment, revel, blowout (*slang*), repast, slap-up meal (*Brit informal*), hakari (*NZ*)

banter *noun* JOKING, kidding (*informal*), ribbing (*informal*), teasing, jeering, mockery, derision, jesting, chaff, pleasantry, repartee, wordplay, badinage, chaffing, raillery, persiflage ▷ *verb* JOKE, kid (*informal*), rib (*informal*), tease, taunt, jeer, josh (*slang, chiefly US & Canad*), jest, take the mickey (*informal*), chaff

baptism *noun* **1** (*Christianity*) CHRISTENING, sprinkling, purification, immersion **2** INITIATION, beginning, debut, introduction, admission, dedication, inauguration, induction, inception, rite of passage, commencement, investiture, baptism of fire, instatement

baptize *verb* **1** (*Christianity*) CHRISTEN, cleanse, immerse, purify, besprinkle **2** INITIATE, admit, introduce, invest, recruit, enrol, induct, indoctrinate, instate

bar *noun* **1** PUBLIC HOUSE, pub (*informal, chiefly Brit*), counter, inn, local (*Brit informal*), lounge, saloon, tavern, canteen, watering hole (*facetious slang*), boozer (*Brit, Austral & NZ informal*), beer parlour (*Canad*), roadhouse, hostelry (*archaic or facetious*), alehouse (*archaic*), taproom **2** ROD, staff, stick, stake, rail, pole, paling, shaft, baton, mace, batten, palisade, crosspiece **3** OBSTACLE, block, barrier, hurdle, hitch, barricade, snag, deterrent, obstruction, stumbling block, impediment, hindrance, interdict << ANTONYM aid ▷ *verb* **1** LOCK, block, secure, chain, attach, anchor, bolt, blockade, barricade, fortify, fasten, latch, obstruct, make firm, make fast **2** BLOCK, restrict, hold up, restrain, hamper, thwart, hinder, obstruct, impede, shut off **3** EXCLUDE, ban, forbid, prohibit, keep out of, disallow, shut out of, ostracize, debar, blackball, interdict, black << ANTONYM admit

barb *noun* 1 POINT, spur, spike, thorn, bristle, quill, prickle, tine, prong 2 DIG, abuse, slight, insult, put-down, snub, sneer, scoff, rebuff, affront, slap in the face (*informal*), gibe, aspersion

barbarian *noun* 1 SAVAGE, monster, beast, brute, yahoo, swine, ogre, sadist 2 LOUT, hooligan, illiterate, vandal, yahoo, bigot, philistine, ned (*Scot slang*), hoon (*Austral & NZ*), cougan (*Austral slang*), scozza (*Austral slang*), bogan (*Austral slang*), ruffian, ignoramus, boor, lowbrow, vulgarian ▷ *adjective* UNCIVILIZED, wild, rough, savage, crude, primitive, vulgar, illiterate, barbaric, philistine, uneducated, unsophisticated, barbarous, boorish, uncouth, uncultivated, lowbrow, uncultured, unmannered << ANTONYM civilized

barbaric *adjective* 1 BRUTAL, fierce, cruel, savage, crude, vicious, ruthless, coarse, vulgar, heartless, inhuman, merciless, bloodthirsty, remorseless, barbarous, pitiless, uncouth 2 UNCIVILIZED, wild, savage, primitive, rude, barbarian, barbarous << ANTONYM civilized

barbarism *noun* CRUELTY, outrage, atrocity, brutality, savagery, ruthlessness, wickedness, inhumanity, barbarity, viciousness, coarseness, crudity, monstrousness, heinousness, fiendishness, barbarousness

barbarity *noun* 1 VICIOUSNESS, horror, cruelty, brutality, ferocity, savagery, ruthlessness, inhumanity 2 ATROCITY, cruelty, horror, inhumanity

barbarous *adjective* 1 UNCIVILIZED, wild, rough, gross, savage, primitive, rude, coarse, vulgar, barbarian, philistine, uneducated, brutish, unsophisticated, uncouth, uncultivated, unpolished, uncultured, unmannered 2 BRUTAL, cruel, savage, vicious, ruthless, ferocious, monstrous, barbaric, heartless, inhuman, merciless, remorseless, pitiless

barbed *adjective* 1 CUTTING, pointed, biting, critical, acid, hostile, nasty, harsh, savage, brutal, searing, withering, scathing, unkind, hurtful, belittling, sarcastic, caustic, scornful, vitriolic, trenchant, acrid, catty (*informal*), mordant, mordacious 2 SPIKED, pointed, toothed, hooked, notched, prickly, jagged, thorny, pronged, spiny, snaggy

bard *noun* (*archaic*) POET, singer, rhymer, minstrel, lyricist, troubadour

bare *adjective* 1 NAKED, nude, stripped, exposed, uncovered, shorn, undressed, divested, denuded, in the raw (*informal*), disrobed, unclothed, buck naked (*slang*), unclad, scuddy (*slang*), without a stitch on (*informal*), in the bare scud (*slang*), naked as the day you were born (*informal*) << ANTONYM dressed 2 SIMPLE, basic, severe, spare, stark, austere, spartan, unadorned, unfussy, unvarnished, unembellished, unornamented, unpatterned << ANTONYM adorned 3 EMPTY, wanting, mean, lacking, deserted, vacant, void, scarce, barren, uninhabited, unoccupied, scanty, unfurnished << ANTONYM full 4 PLAIN, hard, simple, cold, basic, essential, obvious, sheer, patent, evident, stark, manifest, bald, literal, overt, unembellished

barely *adverb* ONLY JUST, just, hardly, scarcely, at a push, almost not << ANTONYM completely

bargain *noun* 1 GOOD BUY, discount purchase, good deal, good value, steal (*informal*), snip (*informal*), giveaway, cheap purchase 2 AGREEMENT, deal (*informal*), understanding, promise, contract, negotiation, arrangement, settlement, treaty, pledge, convention, transaction, engagement, pact, compact, covenant, stipulation ▷ *verb* 1 HAGGLE, deal, sell, trade, traffic, barter, drive a hard bargain 2 NEGOTIATE, deal, contract, mediate, covenant, stipulate, arbitrate, transact, cut a deal ▷▷ **bargain for** *or* **on something** ANTICIPATE, expect, look for, imagine, predict, plan for, forecast, hope for, contemplate, be prepared for, foresee, foretell, count upon

barge *noun* CANAL BOAT, lighter, narrow boat, scow, flatboat ▷▷ **barge in (on something** *or* **someone)** (*informal*) INTERRUPT, break in (on), muscle in (on) (*informal*), intrude (on), infringe (on), burst in (on), butt in (on), impose yourself (on), force your way in (on), elbow your way in (on) ▷▷ **barge into someone** BUMP INTO, drive into, press, push against, shoulder, thrust, elbow into, shove into, collide with, jostle with, cannon into

bark¹ *verb* 1 YAP, bay, howl, snarl, growl, yelp, woof 2 SHOUT, snap, yell, snarl, growl, bawl, bluster, raise your voice ▷ *noun* YAP, bay, howl, snarl, growl, yelp, woof

bark² *noun* COVERING, casing, cover, skin, protection, layer, crust, housing, cortex (*anatomy, botany*), rind, husk ▷ *verb* SCRAPE, skin, strip, rub, scratch, shave, graze, scuff, flay, abrade

barmy or **balmy** adjective (slang) **1** STUPID, bizarre, foolish, silly, daft (informal), irresponsible, irrational, senseless, preposterous, impractical, idiotic, inane, fatuous, dumb-ass (slang) **2** INSANE, odd, crazy, stupid, silly, nuts (slang), loony (slang), nutty (slang), goofy (informal), idiotic, loopy (informal), crackpot (informal), out to lunch (informal), dippy, out of your mind, gonzo (slang), doolally (slang), off your trolley (slang), round the twist (Brit slang), up the pole (informal), off your rocker (slang), off the air (Austral slang), wacko or whacko (informal), porangi (NZ) << ANTONYM sane

baroque adjective ORNATE, fancy, bizarre, elegant, decorated, elaborate, extravagant, flamboyant, grotesque, convoluted, flowery, rococo, florid, bedecked, overelaborate, overdecorated

barrack verb (informal) HECKLE, abuse, mock, bait, criticize, boo, taunt, jeer, shout down, diss (slang, chiefly US)

barracks plural noun CAMP, quarters, garrison, encampment, billet, cantonment, casern

barrage noun **1** BOMBARDMENT, attack, bombing, assault, shelling, battery, volley, blitz, salvo, strafe, fusillade, cannonade, curtain of fire **2** TORRENT, attack, mass, storm, assault, burst, stream, hail, outburst, rain, spate, onslaught, deluge, plethora, profusion

barren adjective **1** DESOLATE, empty, desert, waste **2** UNPRODUCTIVE, dry, useless, fruitless, arid, unprofitable, unfruitful << ANTONYM fertile **3** DULL, boring, commonplace, tedious, dreary, stale, lacklustre, monotonous, uninspiring, humdrum, uninteresting, vapid, unrewarding, as dry as dust << ANTONYM interesting **4** (old-fashioned) INFERTILE, sterile, childless, unproductive, nonproductive, infecund, unprolific

barricade noun BARRIER, wall, railing, fence, blockade, obstruction, rampart, fortification, bulwark, palisade, stockade ▷ verb BAR, block, defend, secure, lock, bolt, blockade, fortify, fasten, latch, obstruct

barrier noun BARRICADE, wall, bar, block, railing, fence, pale, boundary, obstacle, ditch, blockade, obstruction, rampart, bulwark, palisade, stockade

barter verb TRADE, sell, exchange, switch, traffic, bargain, swap, haggle, drive a hard bargain

base¹ noun **1** BOTTOM, floor, lowest part, deepest part << ANTONYM top **2** SUPPORT, stand, foot, rest, bed, bottom, foundation, pedestal, groundwork **3** FOUNDATION, institution, organization, establishment, starting point **4** CENTRE, post, station, camp, settlement, headquarters **5** HOME, house, territory, pad (slang), residence, home ground, abode, stamping ground, dwelling place **6** ESSENCE, source, basis, concentrate, root, core, extract ▷ verb **1** GROUND, found, build, rest, establish, depend, root, construct, derive, hinge **2** PLACE, set, post, station, establish, fix, locate, install, garrison

base² adjective DISHONOURABLE, evil, corrupt, infamous, disgraceful, vulgar, shameful, vile, immoral, scandalous, wicked, sordid, abject, despicable, depraved, ignominious, disreputable, contemptible, villainous, ignoble, discreditable, scungy (Austral & NZ) << ANTONYM honourable

baseless adjective UNFOUNDED, false, fabricated, unconfirmed, spurious, unjustified, unproven, unsubstantiated, groundless, unsupported, trumped up, without foundation, unjustifiable, uncorroborated, ungrounded, without basis << ANTONYM well-founded

bash verb HIT, break, beat, strike, knock, smash, punch, belt (informal), crush, deck (slang), batter, slap, sock (slang), chin (slang), smack, thump, clout (informal), whack (informal), biff (slang), clobber (slang), wallop (informal), slosh (Brit slang), tonk (informal), lay one on (slang), beat or knock seven bells out of (informal)

bashful adjective SHY, reserved, retiring, nervous, modest, shrinking, blushing, constrained, timid, self-conscious, coy, reticent, self-effacing, diffident, sheepish, mousy, timorous, abashed, shamefaced, easily embarrassed, overmodest << ANTONYM forward

basic adjective **1** FUNDAMENTAL, main, key, essential, primary, vital, principal, constitutional, cardinal, inherent, elementary, indispensable, innate, intrinsic, elemental, immanent **2** VITAL, needed, important, key, necessary, essential, primary, crucial, fundamental, elementary, indispensable, requisite **3** ESSENTIAL, central, key, vital, fundamental, underlying, indispensable << ANTONYM secondary **4** MAIN, key, essential, primary **5** PLAIN, simple, classic, severe, straightforward, Spartan, uncluttered, unadorned, unfussy, bog-standard (*informal*), unembellished ▷ *plural noun* ESSENTIALS, facts, principles, fundamentals, practicalities, requisites, nuts and bolts (*informal*), hard facts, nitty-gritty (*informal*), rudiments, brass tacks (*informal*), necessaries

basically *adverb* ESSENTIALLY, firstly, mainly, mostly, principally, fundamentally, primarily, at heart, inherently, intrinsically, at bottom, in substance, au fond (*French*)

basis *noun* 1 ARRANGEMENT, way, system, footing, agreement 2 FOUNDATION, support, base, ground, footing, theory, bottom, principle, premise, groundwork, principal element, chief ingredient

bask *verb* LIE, relax, lounge, sprawl, loaf, lie about, swim in, sunbathe, recline, loll, laze, outspan (*S African*), warm yourself, toast yourself ▷▷ **bask in** ENJOY, relish, delight in, savour, revel in, wallow in, rejoice in, luxuriate in, indulge yourself in, take joy in, take pleasure in *or* from

bass *adjective* DEEP, low, resonant, sonorous, low-pitched, deep-toned

bastion *noun* STRONGHOLD, support, defence, rock, prop, refuge, fortress, mainstay, citadel, bulwark, tower of strength, fastness

batch *noun* GROUP, set, lot, crowd, pack, collection, quantity, bunch, accumulation, assortment, consignment, assemblage, aggregation

bath *noun* WASH, cleaning, washing, soaping, shower, soak, cleansing, scrub, scrubbing, bathe, shampoo, sponging, douse, douche, ablution ▷ *verb* CLEAN, wash, soap, shower, soak, cleanse, scrub, bathe, tub, sponge, rinse, douse, scrub down, lave (*archaic*)

bathe *verb* 1 SWIM 2 WASH, clean, bath, soap, shower, soak, cleanse, scrub, tub, sponge, rinse, scrub down, lave (*archaic*) 3 CLEANSE, clean, wash, soak, rinse 4 COVER, flood, steep, engulf, immerse, overrun, suffuse, wash over ▷ *noun* (*Brit*) SWIM, dip, dook (*Scot*)

bathroom *noun* LAVATORY, toilet, loo (*Brit informal*), washroom, can (*US & Canad slang*), john (*slang, chiefly US & Canad*), head(s) (*nautical slang*), shower, convenience (*chiefly Brit*), bog (*slang*), bogger (*Austral slang*), brasco (*Austral slang*), privy, cloakroom (*Brit*), latrine, rest room, powder room, dunny (*Austral & NZ old-fashioned*), water closet, khazi (*slang*), comfort station (*US*), pissoir (*French*), Gents *or* Ladies, little boy's

room *or* little girl's room (*informal*), (public) convenience, W.C.

baton *noun* STICK, club, staff, stake, pole, rod, crook, cane, mace, wand, truncheon, sceptre, mere (*NZ*), patu (*NZ*)

battalion *noun* COMPANY, army, force, team, host, division, troop, brigade, regiment, legion, contingent, squadron, military force, horde, multitude, throng

batten *verb usually with* **down** FASTEN, unite, fix, secure, lock, bind, chain, connect, attach, seal, tighten, anchor, bolt, clamp down, affix, nail down, make firm, make fast, fasten down

batter *verb* 1 BEAT, hit, strike, knock, assault, smash, punch, belt (*informal*), deck (*slang*), bang, bash (*informal*), lash, thrash, pound, lick (*informal*), buffet, flog, maul, pelt, clobber (*slang*), smite, wallop (*informal*), pummel, tonk (*informal*), cudgel, thwack, lambast(e), belabour, dash against, beat the living daylights out of, lay one on (*slang*), drub, beat *or* knock seven bells out of (*informal*) 2 DAMAGE, destroy, hurt, injure, harm, ruin, crush, mar, wreck, total (*slang*), shatter, weaken, bruise, demolish, shiver, trash (*slang*), maul, mutilate, mangle, mangulate (*Austral slang*), disfigure, deface, play (merry) hell with (*informal*)

battered *adjective* 1 BEATEN, injured, harmed, crushed, bruised, squashed, beat-up (*informal*), oppressed, manhandled, black-and-blue, ill-treated, maltreated 2 DAMAGED, broken-down, wrecked, beat-up (*informal*), ramshackle, dilapidated

battery *noun* 1 ARTILLERY, ordnance, gunnery, gun emplacement, cannonry 2 SERIES, set, course, chain, string, sequence, suite, succession 3 (*criminal law*) BEATING, attack, assault, aggression, thumping, onslaught, physical violence

battle *noun* 1 FIGHT, war, attack, action, struggle, conflict, clash, set-to (*informal*), encounter, combat, scrap (*informal*), biffo (*Austral slang*), engagement, warfare, fray, duel, skirmish, head-to-head, tussle, scuffle, fracas, scrimmage, sparring match, bagarre (*French*), melee *or* mêlée, boilover (*Austral*) << ANTONYM peace 2 CONFLICT, campaign, struggle, debate, clash, dispute, contest, controversy, disagreement, crusade, strife, head-to-head, agitation 3 CAMPAIGN, drive, movement, push, struggle ▷ *verb* 1 WRESTLE, war, fight, argue, dispute, contest, combat, contend, feud, grapple, agitate, clamour, scuffle, lock horns **2** STRUGGLE, work, labour, strain, strive, go for it (*informal*), toil, make every effort, go all out (*informal*), bend over backwards (*informal*), go for broke (*slang*), bust a gut (*informal*), give it your best shot (*informal*), break your neck (*informal*), exert yourself, make an all-out effort (*informal*), work like a Trojan, knock yourself out (*informal*), do your damnedest (*informal*), give it your all (*informal*), rupture yourself (*informal*)

battle cry *noun* **1** SLOGAN, motto, watchword, catch phrase, tag-line, catchword, catchcry (*Austral*) **2** WAR CRY, rallying cry, war whoop

battlefield *noun* BATTLEGROUND, front, field, combat zone, field of battle

battleship *noun* WARSHIP, gunboat, man-of-war, ship of the line, capital ship

batty *adjective* CRAZY, odd, mad, eccentric, bats (*slang*), nuts (*slang*), barking (*slang*), peculiar, daft (*informal*), crackers (*Brit slang*), queer (*informal*), insane, lunatic, loony (*slang*), barmy (*slang*), off-the-wall (*slang*), touched, nutty (*informal*), potty (*Brit informal*), oddball (*informal*), off the rails, cracked (*slang*), bonkers (*slang, chiefly Brit*), cranky (*US, Canad & Irish informal*), dotty (*slang, chiefly Brit*), loopy (*informal*), crackpot (*informal*), out to lunch (*informal*), barking mad (*slang*), out of your mind, outré, gonzo (*slang*), screwy (*informal*), doolally (*slang*), off your trolley (*slang*), off the air (*Austral slang*), round the twist (*Brit slang*), up the pole (*informal*), off your rocker (*slang*), not the full shilling (*informal*), as daft as a brush (*informal, chiefly Brit*), wacko *or* whacko (*slang*), porangi (*NZ*), daggy (*Austral & NZ informal*)

bauble *noun* TRINKET, ornament, trifle, toy, plaything, bagatelle, gimcrack, gewgaw, knick-knack, bibelot, kickshaw

bawdy *adjective* RUDE, blue, dirty, gross, crude, erotic, obscene, coarse, filthy, indecent, vulgar, improper, steamy (*informal*), pornographic, raunchy (*US slang*), suggestive, racy, lewd, risqué, X-rated (*informal*), salacious, prurient, lascivious, smutty, lustful, lecherous, ribald, libidinous, licentious, indelicate, near the knuckle (*informal*), indecorous << ANTONYM clean

bawl *verb* **1** SHOUT, call, scream, roar, yell, howl, bellow, bay, clamour, holler (*informal*), raise your voice, halloo, hollo, vociferate **2** CRY, weep, sob, wail, whine, whimper, whinge (*informal*), keen, greet (*Scot archaic*), squall, blubber, snivel, shed tears, yowl,

mewl, howl your eyes out

bay[1] *noun* INLET, sound, gulf, entrance, creek, cove, fjord, arm (of the sea), bight, ingress, natural harbour, sea loch (*Scot*), firth *or* frith (*Scot*)

bay[2] *noun* RECESS, opening, corner, niche, compartment, nook, alcove, embrasure

bay[3] *verb* HOWL, cry, roar (*used of hounds*), bark, lament, cry out, wail, growl, bellow, quest (*used of hounds*), bell, clamour, yelp ▷ *noun* CRY, bell, roar (*used of hounds*), bark, lament, howl, wail, growl, bellow, clamour, yelp ▷▷ **at bay** AWAY, off, at arm's length

bayonet *verb* STAB, cut, wound, knife, slash, pierce, run through, spear, transfix, impale, lacerate, stick

bazaar *noun* **1** MARKET, exchange, fair, marketplace, mart **2** FAIR, fête, gala, festival, garden party, bring-and-buy

be *verb* **1** BE ALIVE, live, exist, survive, breathe, last, be present, continue, endure, be living, be extant, happen **2** TAKE PLACE, happen, occur, arise, come about, transpire (*informal*), befall, come to pass

beach *noun* SHORE, coast, sands, margin, strand, seaside, shingle, lakeside, water's edge, lido, foreshore, seashore, plage, littoral, sea (*chiefly US*)

beached *adjective* STRANDED, grounded, abandoned, deserted, wrecked, ashore, marooned, aground, high and dry

beacon *noun* **1** SIGNAL, sign, rocket, beam, flare, bonfire, smoke signal, signal fire **2** LIGHTHOUSE, pharos, watchtower

bead *noun* DROP, tear, bubble, pearl, dot, drip, blob, droplet, globule, driblet ▷ *plural noun* NECKLACE, pearls, pendant, choker, necklet, chaplet

beady *adjective* BRIGHT, powerful, concentrated, sharp, intense, shining, glittering, gleaming, glinting

beak *noun* **1** BILL, nib, neb (*archaic or dialect*), mandible **2** (*slang*) NOSE, snout, hooter (*slang*), snitch (*slang*), conk (*slang*), neb (*archaic or dialect*), proboscis, schnozzle (*slang, chiefly US*)

beam *verb* **1** SMILE, grin **2** TRANSMIT, show, air, broadcast, cable, send out, relay, televise, radio, emit, put on the air **3** RADIATE, flash, shine, glow, glitter, glare, gleam, emit light, give off light ▷ *noun* **1** RAY, bar, flash, stream, glow, radiation, streak, emission, shaft, gleam, glint, glimmer **2** RAFTER, support, timber, spar, plank, girder, joist **3** SMILE, grin

beaming *adjective* 1 SMILING, happy, grinning, pleasant, sunny, cheerful, cheery, joyful, chirpy (*informal*), light-hearted 2 RADIATING, bright, brilliant, flashing, shining, glowing, sparkling, glittering, gleaming, glimmering, radiant, glistening, scintillating, burnished, lustrous

bear *verb* 1 CARRY, take, move, bring, lift, transfer, conduct, transport, haul, transmit, convey, relay, tote (*informal*), hump (*Brit slang*), lug << ANTONYM put down 2 SUPPORT, shoulder, sustain, endure, uphold, withstand, bear up under << ANTONYM give up 3 DISPLAY, have, show, hold, carry, possess, exhibit 4 SUFFER, feel, experience, go through, sustain, stomach, endure, undergo, admit, brook, hack (*slang*), abide, put up with (*informal*) 5 BRING YOURSELF TO, allow, accept, permit, endure, tolerate, hack (*informal*), countenance 6 PRODUCE, develop, generate, yield, bring forth 7 GIVE BIRTH TO, produce, deliver, breed, bring forth, beget 8 EXHIBIT, hold, maintain, entertain, harbour, cherish 9 CONDUCT, carry, move, deport ▷▷ **bear down on someone** ADVANCE ON, attack, approach, move towards, close in on, converge on, move in on, come near to, draw near to ▷▷ **bear down on something or someone** PRESS DOWN, push, strain, crush, compress, weigh down, encumber ▷▷ **bear on something** BE RELEVANT TO, involve, concern, affect, regard, refer to, be part of, relate to, belong to, apply to, be appropriate to, befit, pertain to, touch upon, appertain to ▷▷ **bear something out** SUPPORT, prove, confirm, justify, endorse, uphold, vindicate, validate, substantiate, corroborate, legitimize ▷▷ **bear with someone** BE PATIENT WITH, suffer, wait for, hold on (*informal*), stand by, tolerate, put up with (*informal*), make allowances for, hang fire

bearable *adjective* TOLERABLE, acceptable, sustainable, manageable, passable, admissible, supportable, endurable, sufferable << ANTONYM intolerable

beard *noun* WHISKERS, bristles, stubble, five-o'clock shadow

bearded *adjective* UNSHAVEN, hairy, whiskered, stubbly, bushy, shaggy, hirsute, bristly, bewhiskered

bearer *noun* 1 AGENT, carrier, courier, herald, envoy, messenger, conveyor, emissary, harbinger 2 CARRIER, runner, servant, porter 3 PAYEE, beneficiary, consignee

bearing *noun* 1 *usually with* **on** *or* **upon** RELEVANCE, relation, application, connection, import, reference, significance, pertinence, appurtenance << ANTONYM irrelevance 2 MANNER, attitude, conduct, appearance, aspect, presence, behaviour, tone, carriage, posture, demeanour, deportment, mien, air, comportment 3 (*nautical*) POSITION, course, direction, point of compass ▷ *plural noun* WAY, course, position, situation, track, aim, direction, location, orientation, whereabouts

bearish *adjective* (*stock exchange*) FALLING, declining, slumping

beast *noun* 1 ANIMAL, creature, brute 2 BRUTE, monster, savage, barbarian, fiend, swine, ogre, ghoul, sadist

beastly *adjective* (*informal*) 1 UNPLEASANT, mean, terrible, awful, nasty, foul, rotten, horrid, disagreeable, irksome << ANTONYM pleasant 2 (CRUEL, mean, nasty, harsh, savage, brutal, coarse, monstrous, malicious, insensitive, sadistic, unfriendly, unsympathetic, uncaring, spiteful, thoughtless, brutish, barbarous, unfeeling, inconsiderate, bestial, uncharitable, unchristian, hardhearted << ANTONYM humane

beat *verb* 1 BATTER, break, hit, strike, knock, punch, belt (*informal*), whip, deck (*slang*), bruise, bash (*informal*), sock (*slang*), lash, chin (*slang*), pound, smack, thrash, cane, thump, lick (*informal*), buffet, clout (*informal*), flog, whack (*informal*), maul, clobber (*slang*), wallop (*informal*), tonk (*informal*), cudgel, thwack (*informal*), lambast(e), lay one on (*slang*), drub, beat *or* knock seven bells out of (*informal*) 2 POUND, strike, hammer, batter, thrash, pelt 3 THROB, pulse, tick, thump, tremble, pound, quake, quiver, vibrate, pulsate, palpitate 4 HIT, strike, bang 5 FLAP, thrash, flutter, agitate, wag, swish 6 DEFEAT, outdo, trounce, overcome, stuff (*slang*), master, tank (*slang*), crush, overwhelm, conquer, lick (*informal*), undo, subdue, excel, surpass, overpower, outstrip, clobber (*slang*), vanquish, outrun, subjugate, run rings around (*informal*), wipe the floor with (*informal*), knock spots off (*informal*), make mincemeat of (*informal*), pip at the post, outplay, blow out of the water (*slang*), put in the shade (*informal*), bring to their knees ▷ *noun* 1 THROB, pounding, pulse, thumping, vibration, pulsating, palpitation, pulsation 2 ROUTE, way, course, rounds, path, circuit

▷▷ **beat it** (*slang*) GO AWAY, leave, depart, get lost (*informal*), shoo, exit, go to hell (*informal*), hook it (*slang*), scarper (*Brit slang*), pack your bags (*informal*), make tracks, hop it (*slang*), scram (*informal*), get on your bike (*Brit slang*), skedaddle (*informal*), sling your hook (*Brit slang*), vamoose (*slang, chiefly US*), voetsek (*S African offensive*), rack off (*Austral & NZ slang*)
▷▷ **beat someone up** (*informal*) ASSAULT, attack, batter, thrash, set about, do over (*Brit, Austral & NZ slang*), work over (*slang*), clobber (*slang*), assail, set upon, lay into (*informal*), put the boot in (*slang*), lambast(e), duff up (*Brit slang*), beat the living daylights out of (*informal*), knock about *or* around, fill in (*Brit slang*), beat *or* knock seven bells out of (*informal*)

beaten *adjective* **1** WELL-TRODDEN, worn, trodden, trampled, well-used, much travelled **2** STIRRED, mixed, whipped, blended, whisked, frothy, foamy **3** SHAPED, worked, formed, stamped, hammered, forged **4** DEFEATED, overcome, frustrated, overwhelmed, cowed, thwarted, vanquished, disheartened

beating *noun* **1** THRASHING, hiding (*informal*), belting (*informal*), whipping (*slang*), slapping, tanning, lashing, smacking, caning, pasting (*slang*), flogging, drubbing, corporal punishment, chastisement **2** DEFEAT, ruin, overthrow, pasting (*slang*), conquest, rout, downfall

beau *noun* (*Chiefly US*) BOYFRIEND, man, guy (*informal*), date, lover, young man, steady, escort, admirer, fiancé, sweetheart, suitor, swain, toy boy, leman (*archaic*), fancy man (*slang*)

beautiful *adjective* ATTRACTIVE, pretty, lovely, stunning (*informal*), charming, tempting, pleasant, handsome, fetching, good-looking, gorgeous, fine, pleasing, fair, magnetic, delightful, cute, exquisite, enticing, seductive, graceful, captivating, appealing, radiant, alluring, drop-dead (*slang*), ravishing, bonny, winsome, comely, prepossessing << ANTONYM ugly

beautify *verb* MAKE BEAUTIFUL, enhance, decorate, enrich, adorn, garnish, ornament, gild, embellish, grace, festoon, bedeck, glamorize

beauty *noun* **1** ATTRACTIVENESS, charm, grace, bloom, glamour, fairness, elegance, symmetry (*formal or literary*), allure, loveliness, handsomeness, pulchritude, comeliness, exquisiteness, seemliness

<< ANTONYM ugliness **2** GOOD-LOOKER, looker (*informal, chiefly US*), lovely (*slang*), sensation, dazzler, belle, goddess, Venus, peach (*informal*), cracker (*slang*), wow (*slang, chiefly US*), dolly (*slang*), knockout (*informal*), heart-throb, stunner (*informal*), charmer, smasher (*informal*), humdinger (*slang*), glamour puss, beaut (*Austral & NZ slang*) **3** ADVANTAGE, good, use, benefit, profit, gain, asset, attraction, blessing, good thing, utility, excellence, boon << ANTONYM disadvantage

becalmed *adjective* STILL, stuck, settled, stranded, motionless

because *conjunction* SINCE, as, in that
▷▷ **because of** AS A RESULT OF, on account of, by reason of, thanks to, owing to

beckon *verb* **1** GESTURE, sign, wave, indicate, signal, nod, motion, summon, gesticulate **2** LURE, call, draw, pull, attract, invite, tempt, entice, coax, allure

become *verb* **1** COME TO BE, develop into, be transformed into, grow into, change into, evolve into, alter to, mature into, metamorphose into, ripen into **2** SUIT, fit, enhance, flatter, ornament, embellish, grace, harmonize with, set off ▷▷ **become of something** *or* **someone** HAPPEN TO, befall, betide

becoming *adjective* **1** FLATTERING, pretty, attractive, enhancing, neat, graceful, tasteful, well-chosen, comely << ANTONYM unflattering **2** APPROPRIATE, right, seemly, fitting, fit, correct, suitable, decent, proper, worthy, in keeping, compatible, befitting, decorous, comme il faut (*French*), congruous, meet (*archaic*) << ANTONYM inappropriate

bed *noun* **1** BEDSTEAD, couch, berth, cot (*informal*), pallet, divan **2** PLOT, area, row, strip, patch, ground, land, garden, border **3** BOTTOM, ground, floor **4** BASE, footing, basis, bottom, foundation, underpinning, groundwork, bedrock, substructure, substratum ▷ *verb* FIX, set, found, base, plant, establish, settle, root, sink, insert, implant, embed ▷▷ **bed down** SLEEP, lie down, retire, turn in (*informal*), settle down, kip (*Brit slang*), hit the hay (*slang*)

bedclothes *plural noun* BEDDING, covers, sheets, blankets, linen, pillow, quilt, duvet, pillowcase, bed linen, coverlet, eiderdown

bedding *noun* BEDCLOTHES, covers, sheets, blankets, linen, pillow, quilt, duvet, pillowcase, bed linen, coverlet, eiderdown

bedeck *verb* DECORATE, grace, trim, array, enrich, adorn, garnish, ornament, embellish, festoon, beautify, bedight (*archaic*), bedizen (*archaic*), engarland

bedevil *verb* PLAGUE, worry, trouble, frustrate, torture, irritate, torment, harass, hassle (*informal*), aggravate (*informal*), afflict, pester, vex, irk

bedlam *noun* PANDEMONIUM, noise, confusion, chaos, turmoil, clamour, furore, uproar, commotion, rumpus, babel, tumult, hubbub, ruction (*informal*), hullabaloo, hue and cry, ruckus (*informal*)

bedraggled *adjective* MESSY, soiled, dirty, disordered, stained, dripping, muddied, muddy, drenched, ruffled, untidy, sodden, sullied, dishevelled, rumpled, unkempt, tousled, disarranged, disarrayed, daggy (*Austral & NZ informal*)

bedridden *adjective* CONFINED TO BED, confined, incapacitated, laid up (*informal*), flat on your back

bedrock *noun* **1** FIRST PRINCIPLE, rule, basis, basics, principle, essentials, roots, core, fundamentals, cornerstone, nuts and bolts (*informal*), sine qua non (*Latin*), rudiment **2** BOTTOM, bed, foundation, underpinning, rock bottom, substructure, substratum

beef *noun* (*slang*) COMPLAINT, dispute, grievance, problem, grumble, criticism, objection, dissatisfaction, annoyance, grouse, gripe (*informal*), protestation, grouch (*informal*), remonstrance

beefy *adjective* (*informal*) BRAWNY, strong, powerful, athletic, strapping, robust, hefty (*informal*), muscular, sturdy, stalwart, bulky, burly, stocky, hulking, well-built, herculean, sinewy, thickset << ANTONYM scrawny

beehive *noun* HIVE, colony, comb, swarm, honeycomb, apiary

beer *noun* ALE, brew, swipes (*Brit slang*), wallop (*Brit slang*), hop juice, amber fluid *or* nectar (*Austral informal*), tinnie *or* tinny (*Austral slang*)

beer parlour *noun* (*Canad*) TAVERN, inn, bar, pub (*informal, chiefly Brit*), public house, watering hole (*facetious slang*), boozer (*Brit, Austral & NZ informal*), beverage room (*Canad*), hostelry, alehouse (*archaic*), taproom

befall *verb* (*archaic or literary*) HAPPEN TO, fall upon, occur in, take place in, ensue in, transpire in (*informal*), materialize in, come to pass in

befit *verb* BE APPROPRIATE FOR, become, suit, be fitting for, be suitable for, be seemly for, behove (*US*)

befitting *adjective* APPROPRIATE TO, right for,

suitable for, fitting for, fit for, becoming to, seemly for, proper for, apposite to, meet (*archaic*) << ANTONYM unsuitable for

before *preposition* **1** EARLIER THAN, ahead of, prior to, in advance of << ANTONYM after **2** IN FRONT OF, ahead of, in advance of, to the fore of **3** IN THE PRESENCE OF, in front of **4** AHEAD OF, in front of, in advance of ▷ *adverb* **1** PREVIOUSLY, earlier, sooner, in advance, formerly << ANTONYM after **2** IN THE PAST, earlier, once, previously, formerly, at one time, hitherto, beforehand, a while ago, heretofore, in days *or* years gone by

beforehand *adverb* IN ADVANCE, before, earlier, already, sooner, ahead, previously, in anticipation, before now, ahead of time

befriend *verb* MAKE FRIENDS WITH, back, help, support, benefit, aid, encourage, welcome, favour, advise, sustain, assist, stand by, uphold, side with, patronize, succour

befuddle *verb* CONFUSE, puzzle, baffle, bewilder, muddle, daze, perplex, mystify, disorient, faze, stupefy, flummox, bemuse, intoxicate << ANTONYM make clear

befuddled *adjective* CONFUSED, upset, puzzled, baffled, at sea, bewildered, muddled, dazed, perplexed, taken aback, intoxicated, disorientated, disorganized, muzzy (*US informal*), groggy (*informal*), flummoxed, woozy (*informal*), at sixes and sevens, fuddled, inebriated, thrown off balance, discombobulated (*informal, chiefly US & Canad*), not with it (*informal*), not knowing if you are coming or going

beg *verb* **1** IMPLORE, plead with, beseech, desire, request, pray, petition, conjure, crave, solicit, entreat, importune, supplicate, go on bended knee to **2** SCROUNGE, bum (*informal*), blag (*slang*), touch (someone) for (*slang*), mooch (*slang*), cadge, forage for, hunt around (for), sponge on (someone) for, freeload (*slang*), seek charity, call for alms, solicit charity << ANTONYM give **3** DODGE, avoid, get out of, duck (*informal*), hedge, parry, shun, evade, elude, fudge, fend off, eschew, flannel (*Brit informal*), sidestep, shirk, equivocate, body-swerve (*Scot*)

beget *verb* (*old-fashioned*) **1** CAUSE, bring, produce, create, effect, lead to, occasion, result in, generate, provoke, induce, bring about, give rise to, precipitate, incite, engender **2** FATHER, breed, generate, sire, get, propagate, procreate

beggar *noun* TRAMP, bankrupt, bum (*informal*), derelict, drifter, down-and-out, pauper, vagrant, hobo (*chiefly US*), vagabond, bag lady (*chiefly US*), dosser (*Brit slang*), derro (*Austral slang*), starveling ▷ *verb* DEFY, challenge, defeat, frustrate, foil, baffle, thwart, withstand, surpass, elude, repel

begin *verb* 1 START, commence, proceed << ANTONYM stop 2 COMMENCE, start, initiate, embark on, set about, instigate, inaugurate, institute, make a beginning, set on foot 3 START TALKING, start, initiate, commence, begin business, get or start the ball rolling 4 COME INTO EXISTENCE, start, appear, emerge, spring, be born, arise, dawn, be developed, be created, originate, commence, be invented, become available, crop up (*informal*), come into being 5 EMERGE, start, spring, stem, derive, issue, originate << ANTONYM end

beginner *noun* NOVICE, student, pupil, convert, recruit, amateur, initiate, newcomer, starter, trainee, apprentice, cub, fledgling, learner, freshman, neophyte, tyro, probationer, greenhorn (*informal*), novitiate, tenderfoot, proselyte << ANTONYM expert

beginning *noun* 1 START, opening, break (*informal*), chance, source, opportunity, birth, origin, introduction, outset, starting point, onset, overture, initiation, inauguration, inception, commencement, opening move << ANTONYM end 2 OUTSET, start, opening, birth, onset, prelude, preface, commencement, kickoff (*informal*) 3 *often plural* ORIGINS, family, beginnings, stock, birth, roots, heritage, descent, pedigree, extraction, ancestry, lineage, parentage, stirps

begrudge *verb* 1 RESENT, envy, grudge, be jealous of 2 BE BITTER ABOUT, object to, be angry about, give reluctantly, bear a grudge about, be in a huff about, give stingily, have hard feelings about

beguile *verb* 1 CHARM, please, attract, delight, occupy, cheer, fascinate, entertain, absorb, entrance, win over, amuse, divert, distract, enchant, captivate, solace, allure, bewitch, mesmerize, engross, enrapture, tickle the fancy of 2 FOOL, trick, take in, cheat, con (*informal*), mislead, impose on, deceive, dupe, gull (*archaic*), delude, bamboozle, hoodwink, take for a ride (*informal*), befool << ANTONYM enlighten

beguiling *adjective* CHARMING, interesting, pleasing, attractive, engaging, lovely, entertaining, pleasant, intriguing, diverting, delightful, irresistible, enchanting,

seductive, captivating, enthralling, winning, eye-catching, alluring, bewitching, delectable, winsome, likable or likeable

behalf *noun* 1 ▷▷ **on behalf of something** or **someone** or **on something** or **someone's behalf** 1 AS A REPRESENTATIVE OF, representing, in the name of, as a spokesperson for 2 FOR THE BENEFIT OF, for the sake of, in support of, on the side of, in the interests of, on account of, for the good of, in defence of, to the advantage of, for the profit of

behave *verb* 1 ACT, react, conduct yourself, acquit yourself, comport yourself 2 *often reflexive* BE WELL-BEHAVED, be good, be polite, mind your manners, keep your nose clean, act correctly, act politely, conduct yourself properly << ANTONYM misbehave

behaviour *noun* 1 CONDUCT, ways, actions, bearing, attitude, manner, manners, carriage, demeanour, deportment, mien (*literary*), comportment 2 ACTION, working, running, performance, operation, practice, conduct, functioning

behead *verb* DECAPITATE, execute, guillotine

behest *noun* ▷▷ **at someone's behest** AT SOMEONE'S COMMAND, by someone's order, at someone's demand, at someone's wish, by someone's decree, at someone's bidding, at someone's instruction, by someone's mandate, at someone's dictate, at someone's commandment

behind *preposition* 1 AT THE REAR OF, at the back of, at the heels of 2 AFTER, following 3 SUPPORTING, for, backing, on the side of, in agreement with 4 CAUSING, responsible for, the cause of, initiating, at the bottom of, to blame for, instigating 5 LATER THAN, after ▷ *adverb* 1 THE BACK, the rear 2 AFTER, next, following, afterwards, subsequently, in the wake (of) << ANTONYM in advance of 3 BEHIND SCHEDULE, delayed, running late, behind time << ANTONYM ahead 4 OVERDUE, in debt, in arrears, behindhand ▷ *noun* (*informal*) BOTTOM, seat, bum (*Brit slang*), butt (*US & Canad informal*), buns (*US slang*), buttocks, rump, posterior, tail (*informal*), derrière (*euphemistic*), tush (*US slang*), jacksy (*Brit slang*)

behold *verb* (*archaic* or *literary*) LOOK AT, see, view, eye, consider, study, watch, check, regard, survey, witness, clock (*Brit slang*), examine, observe, perceive, gaze, scan, contemplate, check out (*informal*), inspect, discern, eyeball (*slang*), scrutinize, recce (*slang*), get a load of (*informal*), take a gander at (*informal*), take a dekko at (*Brit slang*), feast your eyes upon

beholden *adjective* INDEBTED, bound, owing, grateful, obliged, in debt, obligated, under obligation

beige *noun or adjective* FAWN, coffee, cream, sand, neutral, mushroom, tan, biscuit, camel, buff, cinnamon, khaki, oatmeal, ecru, café au lait (*French*)

being *noun* 1 INDIVIDUAL, thing, body, animal, creature, human being, beast, mortal, living thing 2 LIFE, living, reality, animation, actuality << ANTONYM nonexistence 3 SOUL, spirit, presence, substance, creature, essence, organism, entity

belated *adjective* LATE, delayed, overdue, late in the day, tardy, behind time, unpunctual, behindhand

belch *verb* 1 BURP, eructate, eruct 2 EMIT, discharge, erupt, send out, throw out, vent, vomit, issue, give out, gush, eject, diffuse, emanate, exude, give off, exhale, cast out, disgorge, give vent to, send forth, spew forth, breathe forth

beleaguered *adjective* 1 HARASSED, troubled, plagued, tormented, hassled (*informal*), aggravated (*informal*), badgered, persecuted, pestered, vexed, put upon 2 BESIEGED, surrounded, blockaded, encompassed, beset, encircled, assailed, hemmed in, hedged in, environed

belie *verb* 1 MISREPRESENT, disguise, conceal, distort, misinterpret, falsify, gloss over 2 DISPROVE, deny, expose, discredit, contradict, refute, repudiate, negate, invalidate, rebut, give the lie to, make a nonsense of, gainsay (*archaic or literary*), prove false, blow out of the water (*slang*), controvert, confute

belief *noun* 1 TRUST, confidence, conviction, reliance << ANTONYM disbelief 2 FAITH, principles, doctrine, ideology, creed, dogma, tenet, credence, credo 3 OPINION, feeling, idea, view, theory, impression, assessment, notion, judgment, point of view, sentiment, persuasion, presumption

believable *adjective* CREDIBLE, possible, likely, acceptable, reliable, authentic, probable, plausible, imaginable, trustworthy, creditable << ANTONYM unbelievable

believe *verb* 1 THINK, consider, judge, suppose, maintain, estimate, imagine, assume, gather, guess (*informal, chiefly US & Canad*), reckon, conclude, deem, speculate,

presume, conjecture, postulate, surmise 2 ACCEPT, hold, buy (*slang*), trust, credit, depend on, rely on, swallow (*informal*), count on, buy into (*slang*), have faith in, swear by, be certain of, be convinced of, place confidence in, presume true, take as gospel, take on (*US*) << ANTONYM disbelieve ▷▷ **believe in something** ADVOCATE, champion, approve of, swear by

believer *noun* FOLLOWER, supporter, convert, disciple, protagonist, devotee, worshipper, apostle, adherent, zealot, upholder, proselyte << ANTONYM sceptic

belittle *verb* RUN DOWN, dismiss, diminish, put down, underestimate, discredit, ridicule, scorn, rubbish (*informal*), degrade, minimize, downgrade, undervalue, knock (*informal*), deride, malign, detract from, denigrate, scoff at, disparage, decry, sneer at, underrate, deprecate, depreciate, defame, derogate << ANTONYM praise

belle *noun* BEAUTY, looker (*informal*), lovely, good-looker, goddess, Venus, peach (*informal*), cracker (*informal*), stunner (*informal*), charmer

bellicose *adjective* AGGRESSIVE, offensive, hostile, destructive, defiant, provocative, belligerent, combative, antagonistic, pugnacious, hawkish, warlike, quarrelsome, militaristic, sabre-rattling, jingoistic, warmongering

belligerence *noun* AGGRESSIVENESS, hostility, animosity, antagonism, destructiveness, pugnacity, combativeness, offensiveness, unfriendliness

belligerent *adjective* AGGRESSIVE, hostile, contentious, combative, unfriendly, antagonistic, pugnacious, argumentative, bellicose, quarrelsome, aggers (*Austral slang*), biffo (*Austral slang*), litigious << ANTONYM friendly ▷ *noun* FIGHTER, battler, militant, contender, contestant, combatant, antagonist, warring nation, disputant

bellow *verb* SHOUT, call, cry (out), scream, roar, yell, howl, shriek, clamour, bawl, holler (*informal*) ▷ *noun* SHOUT, call, cry, scream, roar, yell, howl, shriek, bell, clamour, bawl

belly *noun* STOMACH, insides (*informal*), gut, abdomen, tummy, paunch, vitals, breadbasket (*slang*), potbelly, corporation (*informal*), puku (*NZ*)

belong *verb* GO WITH, fit into, be part of, relate to, attach to, be connected with, pertain to, have as a proper place

belonging *noun* FELLOWSHIP, relationship,

association, loyalty, acceptance, attachment, inclusion, affinity, rapport, affiliation, kinship

belongings *plural noun* POSSESSIONS, goods, things, effects, property, stuff, gear, paraphernalia, personal property, accoutrements, chattels, goods and chattels

beloved *adjective* DEAR, loved, valued, prized, dearest, sweet, admired, treasured, precious, darling, worshipped, adored, cherished, revered

below *preposition* **1** UNDER, underneath, lower than **2** LESS THAN, lower than **3** SUBORDINATE TO, subject to, inferior to, lesser than ▷ *adverb* **1** LOWER, down, under, beneath, underneath **2** BENEATH, following, at the end, underneath, at the bottom, further on

belt *noun* **1** WAISTBAND, band, sash, girdle, girth, cummerbund, cincture **2** CONVEYOR BELT, band, loop, fan belt, drive belt **3** (*geography*) ZONE, area, region, section, sector, district, stretch, strip, layer, patch, portion, tract ▷▷ **below the belt** (*informal*) UNFAIR, foul, crooked (*informal*), cowardly, sly, fraudulent, unjust, dishonest, deceptive, unscrupulous, devious, unethical, sneaky, furtive, deceitful, surreptitious, dishonourable, unsporting, unsportsmanlike, underhanded, not playing the game (*informal*)

bemoan *verb* LAMENT, regret, complain about, rue, deplore, grieve for, weep for, bewail, cry over spilt milk, express sorrow about, moan over

bemused *adjective* PUZZLED, stunned, confused, stumped, baffled, at sea, bewildered, muddled, preoccupied, dazed, perplexed, mystified, engrossed, clueless, stupefied, nonplussed, absent-minded, flummoxed, half-drunk, fuddled

bench *noun* **1** SEAT, stall, pew **2** WORKTABLE, stand, table, counter, slab, trestle table, workbench ▷▷ **the bench** COURT, judge, judges, magistrate, magistrates, tribunal, judiciary, courtroom

benchmark *noun* REFERENCE POINT, gauge, yardstick, measure, level, example, standard, model, reference, par, criterion, norm, touchstone

bend *verb* **1** TWIST, turn, wind, lean, hook, bow, curve, arch, incline, arc, deflect, warp, buckle, coil, flex, stoop, veer, swerve, diverge, contort, inflect, incurvate **2** SUBMIT, yield, bow, surrender, give in, give way, cede,

capitulate, resign yourself **3** FORCE, direct, influence, shape, persuade, compel, mould, sway ▷ *noun* CURVE, turn, corner, hook, twist, angle, bow, loop, arc, zigzag, camber

beneath *preposition* **1** UNDER, below, underneath, lower than << ANTONYM over **2** INFERIOR TO, below **3** UNWORTHY OF, unfitting for, unsuitable for, inappropriate for, unbefitting ▷ *adverb* UNDERNEATH, below, in a lower place

benefactor *noun* SUPPORTER, friend, champion, defender, sponsor, angel (*informal*), patron, promoter, contributor, backer, helper, subsidizer, philanthropist, upholder, well-wisher

beneficial *adjective* FAVOURABLE, useful, valuable, helpful, profitable, benign, wholesome, advantageous, expedient, salutary, healthful, serviceable, salubrious, gainful << ANTONYM harmful

beneficiary *noun* **1** RECIPIENT, receiver, payee, assignee, legatee **2** HEIR, inheritor

benefit *noun* **1** GOOD, use, help, profit, gain, favour, utility, boon, mileage (*informal*), avail << ANTONYM harm **2** ADVANTAGE, interest, aid, gain, favour, assistance, betterment ▷ *verb* **1** PROFIT FROM, make the most of, gain from, do well out of, reap benefits from, turn to your advantage **2** HELP, serve, aid, profit, improve, advance, advantage, enhance, assist, avail << ANTONYM harm

benevolence *noun* KINDNESS, understanding, charity, grace, sympathy, humanity, tolerance, goodness, goodwill, compassion, generosity, indulgence, decency, altruism, clemency, gentleness, philanthropy, magnanimity, fellow feeling, beneficence, kindliness, kind-heartedness, aroha (NZ) << ANTONYM ill will

benevolent *adjective* KIND, good, kindly, understanding, caring, liberal, generous, obliging, sympathetic, humanitarian, charitable, benign, humane, compassionate, gracious, indulgent, amiable, amicable, lenient, cordial, considerate, affable, congenial, altruistic, philanthropic, bountiful, beneficent, well-disposed, kind-hearted, warm-hearted, bounteous, tender-hearted

benighted *adjective* UNCIVILIZED, crude, primitive, backward, uncultivated, unenlightened

benign *adjective* **1** BENEVOLENT, kind, kindly, warm, liberal, friendly, generous, obliging, sympathetic, favourable,

compassionate, gracious, amiable, genial,
affable, complaisant << ANTONYM unkind
2 (*medical*) HARMLESS, innocent, superficial,
innocuous, curable, inoffensive, not
dangerous, remediable << ANTONYM
malignant **3** FAVOURABLE, good,
encouraging, warm, moderate, beneficial,
clement, advantageous, salutary, auspicious,
propitious << ANTONYM unfavourable

bent *adjective* **1** MISSHAPEN, twisted, angled,
bowed, curved, arched, crooked, crippled,
distorted, warped, deformed, tortuous,
disfigured, out of shape << ANTONYM
straight **2** STOOPED, bowed, arched, hunched
▷ *noun* INCLINATION, ability, taste, facility,
talent, leaning, tendency, preference,
faculty, forte, flair, knack, penchant, bag
(*slang*), propensity, aptitude, predisposition,
predilection, proclivity, turn of mind
▷▷ **bent on** INTENT ON, set on, fixed on,
predisposed to, resolved to, insistent on

bequeath *verb* **1** LEAVE, will, give, grant,
commit, transmit, hand down, endow,
bestow, entrust, leave to by will **2** GIVE, offer,
accord, grant, afford, contribute, yield, lend,
pass on, transmit, confer, bestow, impart

bequest *noun* LEGACY, gift, settlement,
heritage, trust, endowment, estate,
inheritance, dower, bestowal, koha (*NZ*)

berate *verb* SCOLD, rebuke, reprimand,
reproach, blast, carpet (*informal*), put down,
criticize, slate (*informal, chiefly Brit*), censure,
castigate, revile, chide, harangue, tear into
(*informal*), tell off (*informal*), rail at, read
the riot act to, reprove, upbraid, slap on
the wrist, lambast(e) (*informal*), bawl out (*informal*),
excoriate, rap over the knuckles, chew out
(*US & Canad informal*), tear (someone) off a
strip (*Brit informal*), give a rocket (*Brit & NZ
informal*), vituperate << ANTONYM praise

bereavement *noun* LOSS, death, misfortune,
deprivation, affliction, tribulation

bereft *adjective* ▷▷ **bereft of** DEPRIVED OF,
without, minus, lacking in, devoid of, cut off
from, parted from, sans (*archaic*), robbed of,
empty of, denuded of

berg *noun* (*S African*) MOUNTAIN, peak, mount,
height, ben (*Scot*), horn, ridge, fell (*Brit*), alp,
pinnacle, elevation, eminence

berserk *adjective* CRAZY, wild, mad, frantic, ape
(*slang*), insane, barro (*Austral slang*), off the
air (*Austral slang*), porangi (*NZ*)

berth *noun* **1** BUNK, bed, cot (*nautical*),
hammock, billet **2** (*nautical*) ANCHORAGE,
haven, slip, port, harbour, dock, pier, wharf,

quay ▷ *verb* (*nautical*) ANCHOR, land, dock,
moor, tie up, drop anchor

beseech *verb* BEG, ask, petition, call upon,
plead with, solicit, implore, entreat,
importune, adjure, supplicate

beset *verb* PLAGUE, trouble, embarrass,
torture, haunt, torment, harass, afflict,
badger, perplex, pester, vex, entangle,
bedevil

besetting *adjective* CHRONIC, persistent, long-
standing, prevalent, habitual, ingrained,
deep-seated, incurable, deep-rooted,
inveterate, incorrigible, ineradicable

beside *preposition* NEXT TO, near, close to,
neighbouring, alongside, overlooking, next
door to, adjacent to, at the side of, abreast
of, cheek by jowl with ▷▷ **beside yourself**
DISTRAUGHT, desperate, mad, distressed,
frantic, frenzied, hysterical, insane, crazed,
demented, unbalanced, uncontrolled,
deranged, berserk, delirious, unhinged, very
anxious, overwrought, apoplectic, out of
your mind, at the end of your tether

besides *preposition* APART FROM, barring,
excepting, other than, excluding, as well (as),
in addition to, over and above ▷ *adverb* ALSO,
too, further, otherwise, in addition, as well,
moreover, furthermore, what's more, into
the bargain ▷ see **beside**

besiege *verb* **1** HARASS, worry, trouble, harry,
bother, disturb, plague, hound, hassle
(*informal*), badger, pester, importune, bend
someone's ear (*informal*), give someone grief
(*Brit & S African*), beleaguer **2** SURROUND,
confine, enclose, blockade, encompass,
beset, encircle, close in on, hem in, shut in,
lay siege to, hedge in, environ, beleaguer,
invest (*rare*)

besotted *adjective* INFATUATED, charmed,
captivated, beguiled, doting, smitten,
bewitched, bowled over (*informal*),
spellbound, enamoured, hypnotized, swept
off your feet

bespeak *verb* ENGAGE, solicit, prearrange,
order beforehand

best *adjective* **1** FINEST, leading, chief,
supreme, principal, first, foremost,
superlative, pre-eminent, unsurpassed, most
accomplished, most skilful, most excellent
2 MOST FITTING, right, most desirable, most
apt, most advantageous, most correct ▷ *noun*
UTMOST, most, greatest, hardest, highest
endeavour ▷ *adverb* MOST HIGHLY, most
fully, most deeply ▷▷ **the best** THE FINEST,
the pick, the choice, the flower, the cream,

the elite, the crème de la crème (*French*)

bestow *verb* PRESENT, give, accord, award, grant, commit, hand out, lavish, confer, endow, entrust, impart, allot, honour with, apportion << ANTONYM obtain

bestseller *noun* SUCCESS, hit (*informal*), winner, smash (*informal*), belter (*slang*), sensation, blockbuster (*informal*), wow (*slang*), market leader, smash hit (*informal*), chart-topper (*informal*), runaway success, number one << ANTONYM failure

bestselling *adjective* SUCCESSFUL, top, hit (*informal*), smash (*informal*), flourishing, lucrative, smash-hit (*informal*), chart-topping (*informal*), moneymaking, number one, highly successful

bet *verb* GAMBLE, chance, stake, venture, hazard, speculate, punt (*chiefly Brit*), wager, put money, risk money, pledge money, put your shirt ▷ *noun* GAMBLE, risk, stake, venture, pledge, speculation, hazard, flutter (*informal*), ante, punt, wager, long shot

betray *verb* **1** BE DISLOYAL TO, break with, grass on (*Brit slang*), dob in (*Austral slang*), double-cross (*informal*), stab in the back, be unfaithful to, sell down the river (*informal*), grass up (*slang*), shop (*slang, chiefly Brit*), put the finger on (*informal*), inform on *or* against **2** GIVE AWAY, tell, show, reveal, expose, disclose, uncover, manifest, divulge, blurt out, unmask, lay bare, tell on, let slip, evince

betrayal *noun* DISLOYALTY, sell-out (*informal*), deception, treason, treachery, trickery, duplicity, double-cross (*informal*), double-dealing, breach of trust, perfidy, unfaithfulness, falseness, inconstancy << ANTONYM loyalty

better *adverb* **1** TO A GREATER DEGREE, more completely, more thoroughly **2** IN A MORE EXCELLENT MANNER, more effectively, more attractively, more advantageously, more competently, in a superior way << ANTONYM worse ▷ *adjective* **1** WELL, stronger, improving, progressing, recovering, healthier, cured, mending, fitter, fully recovered, on the mend (*informal*), more healthy, less ill << ANTONYM worse **2** SUPERIOR, finer, worthier, higher-quality, surpassing, preferable, more appropriate, more useful, more valuable, more suitable, more desirable, streets ahead, more fitting, more expert << ANTONYM inferior ▷ *verb* **1** BEAT, top, exceed, excel, surpass, outstrip, outdo, improve on *or* upon, cap (*informal*) **2** IMPROVE, forward, reform, advance,

promote, correct, amend, mend, rectify, augment, ameliorate, meliorate ▷▷ **get the better of someone** DEFEAT, beat, surpass, triumph over, outdo, trounce, outwit, best, subjugate, prevail over, outsmart (*informal*), get the upper hand over, score off, run rings around (*informal*), wipe the floor with (*informal*), make mincemeat of (*informal*), blow out of the water (*slang*)

betterment *noun* IMPROVEMENT, gain, advancement, enhancement, edification, amelioration, melioration

between *preposition* AMIDST, among, mid, in the middle of, betwixt

beverage *noun* DRINK, liquid, liquor, refreshment, draught, bevvy (*dialect*), libation (*facetious*), thirst quencher, potable, potation

beverage room *noun* (*Canad*) TAVERN, inn, bar, pub (*informal, chiefly Brit*), public house, watering hole (*facetious slang*), boozer (*Brit, Austral & NZ informal*), beer parlour (*Canad*), hostelry, alehouse (*archaic*), taproom

bevy *noun* GROUP, company, set, party, band, crowd, troop, pack, collection, gathering, gang, bunch (*informal*), cluster, congregation, clump, troupe, posse (*slang*), clique, coterie, assemblage

beware *verb* **1** BE CAREFUL, look out, watch out, be wary, be cautious, take heed, guard against something **2** AVOID, mind, shun, refrain from, steer clear of, guard against

bewilder *verb* CONFOUND, surprise, stun, confuse, puzzle, baffle, mix up, daze, perplex, mystify, stupefy, befuddle, flummox, bemuse, dumbfound, nonplus, flabbergast (*informal*)

bewildered *adjective* CONFUSED, surprised, stunned, puzzled, uncertain, startled, baffled, at sea, awed, muddled, dizzy, dazed, perplexed, disconcerted, at a loss, mystified, taken aback, speechless, giddy, disorientated, bamboozled (*informal*), nonplussed, flummoxed, at sixes and sevens, thrown off balance, discombobulated (*informal, chiefly US & Canad*)

bewildering *adjective* CONFUSING, surprising, amazing, stunning, puzzling, astonishing, staggering, baffling, astounding, perplexing, mystifying, stupefying

bewitch *verb* ENCHANT, attract, charm, fascinate, absorb, entrance, captivate, beguile, allure, ravish, mesmerize, hypnotize, cast a spell on, enrapture, spellbind << ANTONYM repulse

bewitched *adjective* ENCHANTED, charmed,

transformed, fascinated, entranced, possessed, captivated, enthralled, beguiled, ravished, spellbound, mesmerized, enamoured, hypnotized, enraptured, under a spell

beyond *preposition* **1** ON THE OTHER SIDE OF, outwith (*Scot*) **2** AFTER, over, past, above **3** PAST, outwith (*Scot*) **4** EXCEPT FOR, but, save, apart from, other than, excluding, besides, aside from **5** EXCEEDING, surpassing, superior to, out of reach of **6** OUTSIDE, over, above, outwith (*Scot*)

bias *noun* **1** PREJUDICE, leaning, bent, tendency, inclination, penchant, intolerance, bigotry, propensity, favouritism, predisposition, nepotism, unfairness, predilection, proclivity, partiality, narrow-mindedness, proneness, one-sidedness << ANTONYM impartiality **2** SLANT, cross, angle, diagonal line ▷ *verb* INFLUENCE, colour, weight, prejudice, distort, sway, warp, slant, predispose

biased *adjective* PREJUDICED, weighted, one-sided, partial, distorted, swayed, warped, slanted, embittered, predisposed, jaundiced

bicker *verb* QUARREL, fight, argue, row (*informal*), clash, dispute, scrap (*informal*), disagree, fall out (*informal*), squabble, spar, wrangle, cross swords, fight like cat and dog, go at it hammer and tongs, altercate << ANTONYM agree

bid *noun* **1** ATTEMPT, try, effort, venture, undertaking, go (*informal*), shot (*informal*), stab (*informal*), crack (*informal*), endeavour **2** OFFER, price, attempt, amount, advance, proposal, sum, tender, proposition, submission ▷ *verb* **1** MAKE AN OFFER, offer, propose, submit, tender, proffer **2** WISH, say, call, tell, greet **3** TELL, call, ask, order, charge, require, direct, desire, invite, command, summon, instruct, solicit, enjoin

bidding *noun* **1** ORDER, call, charge, demand, request, command, instruction, invitation, canon, beck, injunction, summons, behest, beck and call **2** OFFER, proposal, auction, tender

big *adjective* **1** LARGE, great, huge, giant, massive, vast, enormous, considerable, substantial, extensive, immense, spacious, gigantic, monumental, mammoth, bulky, burly, colossal, stellar (*informal*), prodigious, hulking, ponderous, voluminous, elephantine, ginormous (*informal*), humongous *or* humungous (*US slang*), sizable *or* sizeable << ANTONYM

small **2** IMPORTANT, serious, significant, grave, urgent, paramount, big-time (*informal*), far-reaching, momentous, major league (*informal*), weighty << ANTONYM unimportant **3** POWERFUL, important, prime, principal, prominent, dominant, influential, paramount, eminent, puissant, skookum (*Canad*) **4** GROWN-UP, adult, grown, mature, elder, full-grown << ANTONYM young **5** GENEROUS, good, princely, noble, heroic, gracious, benevolent, disinterested, altruistic, unselfish, magnanimous, big-hearted

bighead *noun* (*informal*) BOASTER, know-all (*informal*), swaggerer, self-seeker, egomaniac, egotist, braggart, braggadocio, narcissist, swell-head (*informal*), blowhard (*informal*), self-admirer, figjam (*Austral slang*)

bigheaded *adjective* BOASTFUL, arrogant, swaggering, bragging, cocky, vaunting, conceited, puffed-up, bumptious, immodest, crowing, overconfident, vainglorious, swollen-headed, egotistic, full of yourself, too big for your boots *or* breeches

bigot *noun* FANATIC, racist, extremist, sectarian, maniac, fiend (*informal*), zealot, persecutor, dogmatist

bigoted *adjective* INTOLERANT, twisted, prejudiced, biased, warped, sectarian, dogmatic, opinionated, narrow-minded, obstinate, illiberal << ANTONYM tolerant

bigotry *noun* INTOLERANCE, discrimination, racism, prejudice, bias, ignorance, injustice, sexism, unfairness, fanaticism, sectarianism, racialism, dogmatism, provincialism, narrow-mindedness, mindlessness, pig-ignorance (*slang*) << ANTONYM tolerance

bigwig *noun* (*informal*) IMPORTANT PERSON, somebody, celebrity, heavyweight (*informal*), notable, big name, mogul, big gun (*informal*), dignitary, celeb (*informal*), big shot (*informal*), personage, nob (*slang*), big cheese (*old-fashioned slang*), big noise (*informal*), big hitter (*informal*), heavy hitter (*informal*), panjandrum, notability, V.I.P. << ANTONYM nonentity

bile *noun* BITTERNESS, anger, hostility, resentment, animosity, venom, irritability, spleen, acrimony, pique, nastiness, rancour, virulence, asperity, ill humour, irascibility, peevishness, churlishness

bill¹ *noun* **1** CHARGES, rate, costs, score, account, damage (*informal*), statement, reckoning, expense, tally, invoice, note of charge **2** ACT OF PARLIAMENT, measure, proposal, piece of legislation, projected law **3** LIST, listing, programme, card, schedule, agenda, catalogue, inventory, roster, syllabus **4** ADVERTISEMENT, notice, poster, leaflet, bulletin, circular, handout, placard, handbill, playbill ▷ *verb* **1** CHARGE, debit, invoice, send a statement to, send an invoice to **2** ADVERTISE, post, announce, push (*informal*), declare, promote, plug (*informal*), proclaim, tout, flaunt, publicize, crack up (*informal*), give advance notice of

bill² *noun* BEAK, nib, neb (*archaic or dialect*), mandible

billet *verb* QUARTER, post, station, locate, install, accommodate, berth, garrison ▷ *noun* QUARTERS, accommodation, lodging, barracks

billow *verb* SURGE, roll, expand, swell, balloon, belly, bulge, dilate, puff up, bloat ▷ *noun* SURGE, wave, flow, rush, flood, cloud, gush, deluge, upsurge, outpouring, uprush

bind *verb* **1** OBLIGE, make, force, require, engage, compel, prescribe, constrain, necessitate, impel, obligate **2** TIE, unite, join, stick, secure, attach, wrap, rope, knot, strap, lash, glue, tie up, hitch, paste, fasten, truss, make fast << ANTONYM untie **3** RESTRICT, limit, handicap, confine, detain, restrain, hamper, inhibit, hinder, impede, hem in, keep within bounds *or* limits **4** FUSE, join, stick, bond, cement, adhere **5** BANDAGE, cover, dress, wrap, swathe, encase ▷ *noun* (*informal*) NUISANCE, inconvenience, hassle (*informal*), drag (*informal*), spot (*informal*), difficulty, bore, dilemma, pest, hot water (*informal*), uphill (*S African*), predicament, annoyance, quandary, pain in the neck (*informal*), pain in the backside, pain in the butt (*informal*)

binding *adjective* COMPULSORY, necessary, mandatory, imperative, obligatory, conclusive, irrevocable, unalterable, indissoluble << ANTONYM optional

binge *noun* (*informal*) BOUT, session, spell, fling, feast, stint, spree, orgy, bender (*informal*), jag (*slang*), beano (*Brit slang*), blind (*slang*)

biography *noun* LIFE STORY, life, record, account, profile, memoir, CV, life history, curriculum vitae

bird *noun* FEATHERED FRIEND, fowl, songbird

birth *noun* **1** CHILDBIRTH, delivery, nativity, parturition << ANTONYM death **2** BEGINNING, start, rise, source, origin, emergence, outset, genesis, initiation,

inauguration, inception, commencement, fountainhead **3** ANCESTRY, line, race, stock, blood, background, breeding, strain, descent, pedigree, extraction, lineage, forebears, parentage, genealogy, derivation

bisect *verb* CUT IN TWO, cross, separate, split, halve, cut across, intersect, cut in half, split down the middle, divide in two, bifurcate

bisexual *adjective* BI (*slang*), ambidextrous (*slang*), swinging both ways (*slang*), AC/DC (*slang*)

bit¹ *noun* **1** SLICE, segment, fragment, crumb, mouthful, small piece, morsel **2** PIECE, scrap, small piece **3** JOT, whit, tittle, iota **4** PART, moment, period **5** LITTLE WHILE, time, second, minute, moment, spell, instant, tick (*Brit informal*), jiffy (*informal*)

bit² *noun* CURB, check, brake, restraint, snaffle

bitchy *adjective* (*informal*) SPITEFUL, mean, nasty, cruel, vicious, malicious, barbed, vindictive, malevolent, venomous, snide, rancorous, catty (*informal*), backbiting, shrewish, ill-natured, vixenish, snarky (*informal*) << ANTONYM nice

bite *verb* **1** NIP, cut, tear, wound, grip, snap, crush, rend, pierce, champ, pinch, chew, crunch, clamp, nibble, gnaw, masticate **2** EAT, burn, smart, sting, erode, tingle, eat away, corrode, wear away ▷ *noun* **1** SNACK, food, piece, taste, refreshment, mouthful, morsel, titbit, light meal **2** WOUND, sting, pinch, nip, prick **3** EDGE, interest, force, punch (*informal*), sting, zest, sharpness, keenness, pungency, incisiveness, acuteness **4** KICK (*informal*), edge, punch (*informal*), spice, relish, zest, tang, sharpness, piquancy, pungency, spiciness

biting *adjective* **1** PIERCING, cutting, cold, sharp, freezing, frozen, bitter, raw, chill, harsh, penetrating, arctic, nipping, icy, blighting, chilly, wintry, gelid, cold as ice **2** SARCASTIC, cutting, sharp, severe, stinging, withering, scathing, acrimonious, incisive, virulent, caustic, vitriolic, trenchant, mordant, mordacious

bitter *adjective* **1** GRIEVOUS, hard, severe, distressing, fierce, harsh, cruel, savage, ruthless, dire, relentless, poignant, ferocious, galling, unrelenting, merciless, remorseless, gut-wrenching, vexatious, hard-hearted << ANTONYM pleasant **2** RESENTFUL, hurt, wounded, angry, offended, sour, put out, sore, choked, crabbed, acrimonious, aggrieved, sullen, miffed (*informal*), embittered, begrudging, peeved (*informal*),

piqued, rancorous << ANTONYM happy
3 FREEZING, biting, severe, intense, raw,
fierce, chill, stinging, penetrating, arctic, icy,
polar, Siberian, glacial, wintry << ANTONYM
mild **4** SOUR, biting, sharp, acid, harsh,
unpleasant, tart, astringent, acrid,
unsweetened, vinegary, acidulated, acerb
<< ANTONYM sweet

bitterly *adverb* **1** RESENTFULLY, sourly,
sorely, tartly, grudgingly, sullenly, testily,
acrimoniously, caustically, mordantly,
irascibly **2** INTENSELY, freezing, severely,
fiercely, icy, bitingly

bitterness *noun* **1** RESENTMENT, hurt, anger,
hostility, indignation, animosity, venom,
acrimony, pique, rancour, ill feeling, bad
blood, ill will, umbrage, vexation, asperity
2 SOURNESS, acidity, sharpness, tartness,
acerbity, vinegariness

bizarre *adjective* STRANGE, odd, unusual,
extraordinary, fantastic, curious, weird, way-
out (*informal*), peculiar, eccentric, abnormal,
ludicrous, queer (*informal*), irregular, rum
(*Brit slang*), uncommon, singular, grotesque,
perplexing, uncanny, mystifying, off-the-
wall (*slang*), outlandish, comical, oddball
(*informal*), off the rails, zany, unaccountable,
off-beat, left-field (*informal*), freakish, wacko
(*slang*), outré, cockamamie (*slang, chiefly US*),
daggy (*Austral & NZ informal*) << ANTONYM
normal

black *adjective* **1** DARK, raven, ebony, sable, jet,
dusky, pitch-black, inky, swarthy, stygian,
coal-black, pitchy, murky << ANTONYM
light **2** GLOOMY, sad, depressing, distressing,
horrible, grim, bleak, hopeless, dismal,
ominous, sombre, morbid, mournful,
morose, lugubrious, joyless, funereal,
doleful, cheerless << ANTONYM happy
3 TERRIBLE, bad, devastating, tragic, fatal,
unfortunate, dreadful, destructive, unlucky,
harmful, adverse, dire, catastrophic, hapless,
detrimental, untoward, ruinous, calamitous,
cataclysmic, ill-starred, unpropitious,
ill-fated, cataclysmal **4** WICKED, bad, evil,
corrupt, vicious, immoral, depraved,
debased, amoral, villainous, unprincipled,
nefarious, dissolute, iniquitous, irreligious,
impious, unrighteous << ANTONYM good
5 ANGRY, cross, furious, hostile, sour,
menacing, moody, resentful, glowering,
sulky, baleful, louring *or* lowering
<< ANTONYM happy **6** DIRTY, soiled, stained,
filthy, muddy, blackened, grubby, dingy,
grimy, sooty, mucky, scuzzy (*slang, chiefly*

US), begrimed, festy (*Austral slang*), mud-
encrusted, miry << ANTONYM clean ▷▷ **black
out** PASS OUT, drop, collapse, faint, swoon,
lose consciousness, keel over (*informal*), flake
out (*informal*), become unconscious ▷▷ **black
something out** DARKEN, cover, shade,
conceal, obscure, eclipse, dim, blacken,
obfuscate, make dark, make darker, make
dim ▷▷ **in the black** IN CREDIT, solid, solvent,
in funds, financially sound, without debt,
unindebted

blacken *verb* **1** DARKEN, deepen, grow black
2 MAKE DARK, shadow, shade, obscure,
overshadow, make darker, make dim
3 DISCREDIT, stain, disgrace, smear, knock
(*informal*), degrade, rubbish (*informal*), taint,
tarnish, censure, slur, slag (off) (*slang*),
malign, reproach, denigrate, disparage,
decry, vilify, slander, sully, dishonour,
defile, defame, bad-mouth (*slang, chiefly US
& Canad*), traduce, bring into disrepute,
smirch, calumniate

blacklist *verb* EXCLUDE, bar, ban, reject, rule
out, veto, boycott, embargo, expel, vote
against, preclude, disallow, repudiate,
proscribe, ostracize, debar, blackball

black magic *noun* WITCHCRAFT, magic,
witching, voodoo, the occult, wizardry,
enchantment, sorcery, occultism,
incantation, black art, witchery, necromancy,
diabolism, sortilege, makutu (*NZ*)

blackmail *noun* THREAT, intimidation,
ransom, compulsion, protection (*informal*),
coercion, extortion, pay-off (*informal*),
shakedown, hush money (*slang*), exaction
▷ *verb* THREATEN, force, squeeze, compel,
exact, intimidate, wring, coerce, milk, wrest,
dragoon, extort, bleed (*informal*), press-gang,
hold to ransom

blackness *noun* DARKNESS, shade, gloom,
dusk, obscurity, nightfall, murk, dimness,
murkiness, duskiness, shadiness, melanism,
swarthiness, inkiness, nigrescence, nigritude
(*rare*) << ANTONYM light

blackout *noun* **1** NONCOMMUNICATION,
secrecy, censorship, suppression,
radio silence **2** POWER CUT, power
failure **3** UNCONSCIOUSNESS, collapse,
faint, oblivion, swoon (*literary*), loss of
consciousness, syncope (*pathology*)

black sheep *noun* DISGRACE, rebel, maverick,
outcast, renegade, dropout, prodigal,
individualist, nonconformist, ne'er-do-well,
reprobate, wastrel, bad egg (*old-fashioned
informal*)

blame *verb* **1** HOLD RESPONSIBLE, accuse, denounce, indict, impeach, incriminate, impute, recriminate, point a *or* the finger at << ANTONYM absolve **2** ATTRIBUTE TO, credit to, assign to, put down to, impute to **3** (used in negative constructions) CRITICIZE, charge, tax, blast, condemn, put down, disapprove of, censure, reproach, chide, admonish, tear into (*informal*), find fault with, reprove, upbraid, lambast(e), reprehend, express disapprobation of << ANTONYM praise ▷ *noun* RESPONSIBILITY, liability, rap (*slang*), accountability, onus, culpability, answerability << ANTONYM praise

blameless *adjective* INNOCENT, clear, clean, upright, stainless, honest, immaculate, impeccable, virtuous, faultless, squeaky-clean, unblemished, unsullied, uninvolved, unimpeachable, untarnished, above suspicion, irreproachable, guiltless, unspotted, unoffending << ANTONYM guilty

blanch *verb* TURN PALE, fade, pale, drain, bleach, wan, whiten, go white, become pallid, become *or* grow white

bland *adjective* **1** DULL, boring, weak, plain, flat, commonplace, tedious, vanilla (*informal*), dreary, tiresome, monotonous, run-of-the-mill, uninspiring, humdrum, unimaginative, uninteresting, insipid, unexciting, ho-hum (*informal*), vapid, unstimulating, undistinctive << ANTONYM exciting **2** TASTELESS, weak, watered-down, insipid, flavourless, thin, unstimulating, undistinctive

blank *adjective* **1** UNMARKED, white, clear, clean, empty, plain, bare, void, spotless, unfilled, uncompleted << ANTONYM marked **2** EXPRESSIONLESS, empty, dull, vague, hollow, vacant, lifeless, deadpan, straight-faced, vacuous, impassive, inscrutable, inane, wooden, poker-faced (*informal*) << ANTONYM expressive **3** PUZZLED, lost, confused, stumped, doubtful, baffled, stuck, at sea, bewildered, muddled, mixed up, confounded, perplexed, disconcerted, at a loss, mystified, clueless, dumbfounded, nonplussed, uncomprehending, flummoxed **4** ABSOLUTE, complete, total, utter, outright, thorough, downright, consummate, unqualified, out and out, unmitigated, unmixed ▷ *noun* **1** EMPTY SPACE, space, gap **2** VOID, vacuum, vacancy, emptiness, nothingness, vacuity, tabula rasa

blanket *noun* **1** COVER, rug, coverlet, afghan **2** COVERING, cover, bed, sheet, coating, coat, layer, film, carpet, cloak, mantle, thickness ▷ *verb* COAT, cover, hide, surround, cloud, mask, conceal, obscure, eclipse, cloak ▷ *adjective* COMPREHENSIVE, full, complete, wide, sweeping, broad, extensive, wide-ranging, thorough, inclusive, exhaustive, all-inclusive, all-embracing

blare *verb* BLAST, scream, boom, roar, thunder, trumpet, resound, hoot, toot, reverberate, sound out, honk, clang, peal

blarney *noun* FLATTERY, coaxing, exaggeration, fawning, adulation, wheedling, spiel, sweet talk (*informal*), flannel (*Brit informal*), soft soap (*informal*), sycophancy, servility, obsequiousness, cajolery, blandishment, fulsomeness, toadyism, overpraise, false praise, honeyed words

blasé *adjective* NONCHALANT, cool, bored, distant, regardless, detached, weary, indifferent, careless, lukewarm, glutted, jaded, unmoved, unconcerned, impervious, uncaring, uninterested, apathetic, offhand, world-weary, heedless, satiated, unexcited, surfeited, cloyed << ANTONYM interested

blasphemous *adjective* IRREVERENT, cheeky (*informal*), contemptuous, profane, disrespectful, godless, ungodly, sacrilegious, irreligious, impious << ANTONYM reverent

blasphemy *noun* IRREVERENCE, swearing, cursing, indignity (*to God*), desecration, sacrilege, profanity, impiety, profanation, execration, profaneness, impiousness

blast *noun* **1** EXPLOSION, crash, burst, discharge, blow-up, eruption, detonation **2** GUST, rush, storm, breeze, puff, gale, flurry, tempest, squall, strong breeze **3** BLARE, blow, scream, trumpet, wail, resound, clamour, hoot, toot, honk, clang, peal ▷ *verb* **1** BLOW UP, bomb, destroy, burst, ruin, break up, explode, shatter, demolish, rupture, dynamite, put paid to, blow sky-high **2** CRITICIZE, attack, put down, censure, berate, castigate, tear into (*informal*), flay, rail at, lambast(e), chew out (*US & Canad informal*)

blasted *adjective* (*slang*) DAMNED (*chiefly US*), confounded, hateful, infernal, detestable

blastoff *noun* LAUNCH, launching, take off, discharge, projection, lift-off, propelling, sendoff

blatant *adjective* OBVIOUS, open, clear, plain, naked, sheer, patent, evident, pronounced, straightforward, outright, glaring, manifest, bald, transparent, noticeable, conspicuous, overt, unmistakable, flaunting, palpable, undeniable, brazen, flagrant, indisputable, ostentatious, unmitigated, cut-and-dried (*informal*), undisguised, obtrusive, unsubtle, unconcealed << ANTONYM subtle

blaze *verb* 1 BURN, glow, flare, flicker, be on fire, go up in flames, be ablaze, fire, flash, flame 2 SHINE, flash, beam, glow, flare, glare, gleam, shimmer, radiate 3 FLARE UP, rage, boil, explode, fume, seethe, be livid, be incandescent ▷ *noun* 1 INFERNO, fire, flames, bonfire, combustion, conflagration 2 FLASH, glow, glitter, flare, glare, gleam, brilliance, radiance

bleach *verb* LIGHTEN, wash out, blanch, peroxide, whiten, blench, etiolate

bleak *adjective* 1 DISMAL, black, dark, depressing, grim, discouraging, gloomy, hopeless, dreary, sombre, unpromising, disheartening, joyless, cheerless, comfortless << ANTONYM cheerful 2 EXPOSED, open, empty, raw, bare, stark, barren, desolate, gaunt, windswept, weather-beaten, unsheltered << ANTONYM sheltered 3 STORMY, cold, severe, bitter, rough, harsh, chilly, windy, tempestuous, intemperate

bleary *adjective* DIM, blurred, fogged, murky, fuzzy, watery, misty, hazy, foggy, blurry, ill-defined, indistinct, rheumy

bleed *verb* 1 LOSE BLOOD, flow, weep, trickle, gush, exude, spurt, shed blood 2 BLEND, run, meet, unite, mix, combine, flow, fuse, mingle, converge, ooze, seep, amalgamate, meld, intermix 3 (*informal*) EXTORT, milk, squeeze, drain, exhaust, fleece

blemish *noun* 1 MARK, line, spot, scratch, bruise, scar, blur, defect, flaw, blot, smudge, imperfection, speck, blotch, disfigurement, pock, smirch << ANTONYM perfection 2 DEFECT, fault, weakness, stain, disgrace, deficiency, shortcoming, taint, inadequacy, dishonour, demerit ▷ *verb* DISHONOUR, mark, damage, spot, injure, ruin, mar, spoil, stain, blur, disgrace, impair, taint, tarnish, blot, smudge, disfigure, sully, deface, blotch, besmirch, smirch << ANTONYM enhance

blend *verb* 1 MIX, join, combine, compound, incorporate, merge, put together, fuse, unite, mingle, alloy, synthesize, amalgamate, interweave, coalesce, intermingle, meld, intermix, commingle, commix 2 GO WELL, match, fit, suit, go with, correspond, complement, coordinate, tone in, harmonize, cohere 3 COMBINE, mix,

link, integrate, merge, put together, fuse, unite, synthesize, marry, amalgamate ▷ *noun* MIXTURE, cross, mix, combination, compound, brew, composite, union, fusion, synthesis, alloy, medley, concoction, amalgam, amalgamation, meld, mélange (*French*), conglomeration, admixture

bless *verb* 1 SANCTIFY, dedicate, ordain, exalt, anoint, consecrate, hallow, invoke happiness on << ANTONYM curse 2 ENDOW, give to, provide for, grant for, favour, grace, bestow to << ANTONYM afflict 3 PRAISE, thank, worship, glorify, magnify, exalt, extol, pay homage to, give thanks to

blessed *adjective* 1 ENDOWED, supplied, granted, favoured, lucky, fortunate, furnished, bestowed, jammy (*Brit slang*) 2 HAPPY, contented, glad, merry, heartening, joyous, joyful, blissful 3 HOLY, sacred, divine, adored, revered, hallowed, sanctified, beatified

blessing *noun* 1 BENEFIT, help, service, profit, gain, advantage, favour, gift, windfall, kindness, boon, good fortune, bounty, godsend, manna from heaven << ANTONYM disadvantage 2 APPROVAL, backing, support, agreement, regard, favour, sanction, go-ahead (*informal*), permission, leave, consent, mandate, endorsement, green light, ratification, assent, authorization, good wishes, acquiescence, approbation, concurrence, O.K. or okay (*informal*) << ANTONYM disapproval 3 BENEDICTION, grace, dedication, thanksgiving, invocation, commendation, consecration, benison << ANTONYM curse

blight *noun* 1 CURSE, suffering, evil, depression, corruption, distress, pollution, misery, plague, hardship, woe, misfortune, contamination, adversity, scourge, affliction, bane, wretchedness << ANTONYM blessing 2 DISEASE, plague, pest, fungus, contamination, mildew, contagion, infestation, pestilence, canker, cancer ▷ *verb* FRUSTRATE, destroy, ruin, crush, mar, dash, wreck, spoil, crool or cruel (*Austral slang*), scar, undo, mess up, annihilate, nullify, put a damper on

blind *adjective* 1 SIGHTLESS, unsighted, unseeing, eyeless, visionless, stone-blind << ANTONYM sighted 2 *usually followed by* to UNAWARE OF, unconscious of, deaf to, ignorant of, indifferent to, insensitive to, oblivious of, unconcerned about, inconsiderate of, neglectful of, heedless of,

insensible of, unmindful of, disregardful
of << ANTONYM aware **3** UNQUESTIONING,
prejudiced, wholesale, indiscriminate,
uncritical, unreasoning, undiscriminating
4 HIDDEN, concealed, obscured, dim,
unseen, tucked away << ANTONYM open
5 DEAD-END, closed, dark, obstructed,
leading nowhere, without exit
6 UNTHINKING, wild, violent, rash, reckless,
irrational, hasty, senseless, mindless,
uncontrollable, uncontrolled, unchecked,
impetuous, intemperate, unconstrained
▷ see **disabled**

blinding *adjective* **1** BRIGHT, brilliant, intense,
shining, glowing, blazing, dazzling, vivid,
glaring, gleaming, beaming, effulgent,
bedazzling **2** AMAZING, striking, surprising,
stunning, impressive, astonishing,
staggering, sensational (*informal*),
breathtaking, wondrous (*archaic* or *literary*),
jaw-dropping, gee-whizz (*slang*)

blindly *adverb* **1** THOUGHTLESSLY, carelessly,
recklessly, indiscriminately, unreasonably,
impulsively, senselessly, heedlessly,
regardlessly **2** WILDLY, aimlessly, madly,
frantically, confusedly

blink *verb* **1** FLUTTER, wink, bat **2** FLASH,
flicker, sparkle, wink, shimmer, twinkle,
glimmer, scintillate ▷▷ **on the blink** (*slang*)
NOT WORKING (PROPERLY), faulty, defective,
playing up, out of action, malfunctioning,
out of order, on the fritz (*US slang*)

blinkered *adjective* NARROW-MINDED, narrow,
one-sided, prejudiced, biased, partial,
discriminatory, parochial, constricted,
insular, hidebound, one-eyed, lopsided
<< ANTONYM broad-minded

bliss *noun* **1** JOY, ecstasy, euphoria, rapture,
nirvana, felicity, gladness, blissfulness,
delight, pleasure, heaven, satisfaction,
happiness, paradise << ANTONYM
misery **2** BEATITUDE, ecstasy, exaltation,
blessedness, felicity, holy joy

blissful *adjective* **1** DELIGHTFUL, pleasing,
satisfying, heavenly (*informal*), enjoyable,
gratifying, pleasurable **2** HAPPY, joyful,
satisfied, ecstatic, joyous, euphoric,
rapturous

blister *noun* SORE, boil, swelling, cyst, pimple,
wen, blain, carbuncle, pustule, bleb, furuncle
(*pathology*)

blitz *noun* ATTACK, strike, assault, raid,
offensive, onslaught, bombardment,
bombing campaign, blitzkrieg

blizzard *noun* SNOWSTORM, storm, tempest

bloated *adjective* **1** PUFFED UP, swollen
<< ANTONYM shrivelled **2** TOO FULL

blob *noun* DROP, ball, mass, pearl, lump, bead,
dab, droplet, globule, glob, dewdrop

bloc *noun* GROUP, union, league, ring, alliance,
coalition, axis, combine

block *noun* **1** PIECE, bar, square, mass, cake,
brick, lump, chunk, cube, hunk, nugget,
ingot **2** OBSTRUCTION, bar, barrier, obstacle,
impediment, hindrance ▷ *verb* **1** OBSTRUCT,
close, stop, cut off, plug, choke, clog, shut
off, stop up, bung up (*informal*) << ANTONYM
clear **2** OBSCURE, bar, cut off, interrupt,
obstruct, get in the way of, shut off **3** SHUT
OFF, stop, bar, cut off, head off, hamper,
obstruct, get in the way of

blockade *noun* STOPPAGE, block, barrier,
restriction, obstacle, barricade, obstruction,
impediment, hindrance, encirclement

blockage *noun* OBSTRUCTION, block, blocking,
stoppage, impediment, occlusion

bloke *noun* (*informal*) MAN, person, individual,
customer (*informal*), character (*informal*), guy
(*informal*), fellow, punter (*informal*), chap, boy,
bod (*informal*)

blonde *or* **blond** *adjective* **1** FAIR, light, light-
coloured, flaxen **2** FAIR-HAIRED, golden-
haired, tow-headed

blood *noun* **1** LIFEBLOOD, gore, vital fluid
2 FAMILY, relations, birth, descent,
extraction, ancestry, lineage, kinship,
kindred ▷▷ **bad blood** HOSTILITY, anger,
offence, resentment, bitterness, animosity,
antagonism, enmity, bad feeling, rancour,
hard feelings, ill will, animus, dudgeon
(*archaic*), disgruntlement, chip on your
shoulder

bloodless *adjective* PALE, white, wan, sickly,
pasty, colourless, pallid, anaemic, ashen,
chalky, sallow, ashy, like death warmed up
(*informal*)

bloodshed *noun* KILLING, murder, massacre,
slaughter, slaying, carnage, butchery, blood-
letting, blood bath

bloodthirsty *adjective* CRUEL, savage, brutal,
vicious, ruthless, ferocious, murderous,
heartless, inhuman, merciless, cut-throat,
remorseless, warlike, barbarous, pitiless

bloody *adjective* **1** CRUEL, fierce, savage, brutal,
vicious, ferocious, cut-throat, warlike,
barbarous, sanguinary **2** BLOODSTAINED, raw,
bleeding, blood-soaked, blood-spattered

bloody-minded *adjective* (*Brit informal*)
DIFFICULT, contrary, annoying, awkward,
unreasonable, stubborn, perverse,

exasperating, intractable, unhelpful, obstructive, cussed (*informal*), uncooperative, disobliging << ANTONYM helpful

bloom *noun* **1** FLOWER, bud, blossom **2** PRIME, flower, beauty, height, peak, flourishing, maturity, perfection, best days, heyday, zenith, full flowering **3** GLOW, flush, blush, freshness, lustre, radiance, rosiness << ANTONYM pallor ▷ *verb* **1** FLOWER, blossom, open, bud << ANTONYM wither **2** GROW, develop, wax **3** SUCCEED, flourish, thrive, prosper, fare well << ANTONYM fail

blossom *noun* FLOWER, bloom, bud, efflorescence, floret ▷ *verb* **1** BLOOM, grow, develop, mature **2** SUCCEED, progress, thrive, flourish, prosper **3** FLOWER, bloom, bud

blot *noun* **1** DISGRACE, spot, fault, stain, scar, defect, flaw, taint, blemish, demerit, smirch, blot on your escutcheon **2** SPOT, mark, patch, smear, smudge, speck, blotch, splodge, stain ▷ *verb* SOAK UP, take up, absorb, dry up ▷▷ **blot something out 1** OBLITERATE, hide, shadow, disguise, obscure, blur, eclipse, block out, efface, obfuscate **2** ERASE, cancel, excise, obliterate, expunge

blotch *noun* MARK, spot, patch, splash, stain, blot, smudge, blemish, splodge, smirch, smutch

blow[1] *verb* **1** MOVE, carry, drive, bear, sweep, fling, whisk, buffet, whirl, waft **2** BE CARRIED, hover, flutter, flit, flitter **3** EXHALE, breathe, pant, puff, breathe out, expel air **4** PLAY, sound, pipe, trumpet, blare, toot ▷▷ **blow over** DIE DOWN, end, pass, finish, cease, be forgotten, subside ▷▷ **blow someone away 1** BOWL OVER, amaze, stun, stagger, astound, electrify (*informal*), stupefy, flabbergast **2** OPEN FIRE ON, kill, blast (*slang*), bring down, zap (*slang*), pick off, pump full of lead (*slang*) ▷▷ **blow something out** PUT OUT, extinguish, snuff out ▷▷ **blow something up 1** EXPLODE, bomb, blast, dynamite, detonate, blow sky-high **2** INFLATE, pump up, fill, expand, swell, enlarge, puff up, distend **3** EXAGGERATE, heighten, enlarge on, inflate, embroider, magnify, amplify, overstate, embellish, blow out of (all) proportion, make a mountain out of a molehill, make a production out of, make a federal case of (*US informal*), hyperbolize **4** MAGNIFY, increase, extend, stretch, expand, widen, broaden, lengthen, amplify, elongate, dilate, make larger ▷▷ **blow up 1** EXPLODE, burst, go off, shatter, erupt, detonate **2** (*informal*) LOSE

YOUR TEMPER, rage, erupt, lose it (*informal*), crack up (*informal*), see red (*informal*), lose the plot (*informal*), become angry, go ballistic (*slang, chiefly US*), hit the roof (*informal*), blow a fuse (*slang, chiefly US*), fly off the handle (*informal*), become enraged, go off the deep end (*informal*), wig out (*slang*), go up the wall (*slang*), go crook (*Austral & NZ slang*), flip your lid (*slang*), blow your top **3** FLARE UP, widen, heighten, enlarge, magnify ▷▷ **blow your top** (*informal*) LOSE YOUR TEMPER, explode, blow up (*informal*), lose it (*informal*), see red (*informal*), lose the plot (*informal*), have a fit (*informal*), throw a tantrum, fly off the handle (*informal*), go spare (*Brit slang*), fly into a temper, flip your lid (*slang*), do your nut (*Brit slang*)

blow[2] *noun* **1** KNOCK, stroke, punch, belt (*informal*), bang, rap, bash (*informal*), sock (*slang*), smack, thump, buffet, clout (*informal*), whack (*informal*), wallop (*informal*), slosh (*Brit slang*), tonk (*informal*), clump (*slang*), clomp (*slang*) **2** SETBACK, shock, upset, disaster, reverse, disappointment, catastrophe, misfortune, jolt, bombshell, calamity, affliction, whammy (*informal, chiefly US*), choker (*informal*), sucker punch, bummer (*slang*), bolt from the blue, comedown (*informal*)

blowout *noun* **1** (*slang*) BINGE (*informal*), party, feast, rave (*Brit slang*), spree, beano (*Brit slang*), rave-up (*Brit slang*), carousal, carouse, hooley *or* hoolie (*chiefly Irish & NZ*) **2** PUNCTURE, burst, flat, flat tyre, flattie (*NZ*)

bludge *verb* (*Austral & NZ informal*) SLACK, skive (*Brit informal*), idle, shirk, gold-brick (*US slang*), bob off (*Brit slang*), scrimshank (*Brit military slang*)

bludgeon *verb* **1** CLUB, batter, beat, strike, belt (*informal*), clobber (*slang*), pound, cosh (*Brit*), cudgel, beat *or* knock seven bells out of (*informal*) **2** BULLY, force, coerce, intimidate, railroad (*informal*), hector, coerce, bulldoze (*informal*), dragoon, steamroller, browbeat, tyrannize ▷ *noun* CLUB, stick, baton, truncheon, cosh (*Brit*), cudgel, shillelagh, bastinado, mere (*NZ*), patu (*NZ*)

blue *adjective* **1** DEPRESSED, low, sad, unhappy, fed up, gloomy, dismal, melancholy, glum, dejected, despondent, downcast, down in the dumps (*informal*), down in the mouth, low-spirited, down-hearted << ANTONYM happy **2** SMUTTY, dirty, naughty, obscene, indecent, vulgar, lewd, risqué, X-rated (*informal*), bawdy, near the knuckle (*informal*) << ANTONYM respectable ▷ *plural noun* DEPRESSION, gloom, melancholy, unhappiness, despondency, the hump (*Brit informal*), dejection, moodiness, low spirits, the dumps (*informal*), doldrums, gloominess, glumness

blueprint *noun* 1 SCHEME, plan, design, system, idea, programme, proposal, strategy, pattern, suggestion, procedure, plot, draft, outline, sketch, proposition, prototype, layout, pilot scheme 2 PLAN, scheme, project, pattern, draft, outline, sketch, layout

bluff¹ *noun* DECEPTION, show, lie, fraud, fake, sham, pretence, deceit, bravado, bluster, humbug, subterfuge, feint, mere show ▷ *verb* DECEIVE, lie, trick, fool, pretend, cheat, con, fake, mislead, sham, dupe, feign, delude, humbug, bamboozle (*informal*), hoodwink, double-cross (*informal*), pull the wool over someone's eyes

bluff² *noun* PRECIPICE, bank, peak, cliff, ridge, crag, escarpment, promontory, scarp ▷ *adjective* HEARTY, open, frank, blunt, sincere, outspoken, honest, downright, cordial, genial, affable, ebullient, jovial, plain-spoken, good-natured, unreserved, back-slapping << ANTONYM tactful

blunder *noun* MISTAKE, slip, fault, error, boob (*Brit slang*), oversight, gaffe, slip-up (*informal*), indiscretion, impropriety, howler (*informal*), bloomer (*Brit informal*), clanger (*informal*), faux pas, boo-boo (*informal*), gaucherie, barry or Barry Crocker (*Austral slang*) << ANTONYM correctness ▷ *verb* 1 MAKE A MISTAKE, blow it (*slang*), err, slip up (*informal*), cock up (*Brit slang*), miscalculate, foul up, drop a clanger (*informal*), put your foot in it (*informal*), drop a brick (*Brit informal*), screw up (*informal*) << ANTONYM be correct 2 STUMBLE, fall, reel, stagger, flounder, lurch, lose your balance

blunt *adjective* 1 FRANK, forthright, straightforward, explicit, rude, outspoken, bluff, downright, upfront (*informal*), trenchant, brusque, plain-spoken, tactless, impolite, discourteous, unpolished, uncivil, straight from the shoulder << ANTONYM tactful 2 DULL, rounded, dulled, edgeless, unsharpened << ANTONYM sharp ▷ *verb* DULL, weaken, soften, numb, dampen, water down, deaden, take the edge off << ANTONYM stimulate

blur *noun* HAZE, confusion, fog, obscurity, dimness, cloudiness, blear, blurredness, indistinctness ▷ *verb* 1 BECOME INDISTINCT,

soften, become vague, become hazy, become fuzzy 2 OBSCURE, make indistinct, mask, soften, muddy, obfuscate, make vague, befog, make hazy

blurred *adjective* INDISTINCT, faint, vague, unclear, dim, fuzzy, misty, hazy, foggy, blurry, out of focus, ill-defined, lacking definition

blush *verb* TURN RED, colour, burn, flame, glow, flush, crimson, redden, go red (as a beetroot), turn scarlet << ANTONYM turn pale ▷ *noun* REDDENING, colour, glow, flush, pink tinge, rosiness, ruddiness, rosy tint

bluster *verb* BOAST, swagger, talk big (*slang*) ▷ *noun* HOT AIR, boasting, bluff, swagger, swaggering (*informal*), bravado, bombast

blustery *adjective* GUSTY, wild, violent, stormy, windy, tempestuous, inclement, squally, blusterous

board *noun* 1 PLANK, panel, timber, slat, piece of timber 2 COUNCIL, directors, committee, congress, ministry, advisers, panel, assembly, chamber, trustees, governing body, synod, directorate, quango, advisory group, conclave 3 MEALS, provisions, victuals, daily meals ▷ *verb* GET ON, enter, mount, embark, entrain, embus, enplane << ANTONYM get off

boast *verb* 1 BRAG, crow, vaunt, bluster, talk big (*slang*), blow your own trumpet, show off, be proud of, flaunt, congratulate yourself on, flatter yourself, pride yourself on, skite (*Austral & NZ informal*) << ANTONYM cover up 2 POSSESS, offer, present, exhibit ▷ *noun* BRAGGING, vaunting, rodomontade (*literary*), gasconade (*rare*) << ANTONYM disclaimer

boat *noun* VESSEL, ship, craft, barge (*informal*), barque (*poetic*) ▷▷ **in the same boat** IN THE SAME SITUATION, alike, even, together, equal, on a par, on equal *or* even terms, on the same *or* equal footing ▷▷ **miss the boat** MISS YOUR CHANCE *or* OPPORTUNITY, miss out, be too late, lose out, blow your chance (*informal*) ▷▷ **rock the boat** (*informal*) CAUSE TROUBLE, protest, object, dissent, make waves (*informal*), throw a spanner in the works, upset the apple cart

bob *verb* BOUNCE, duck, leap, hop, weave, skip, jerk, wobble, quiver, oscillate, waggle ▷▷ **bob up** SPRING UP, rise, appear, emerge, surface, pop up, jump up, bounce up

bode *verb* AUGUR, portend, threaten, predict, signify, foreshadow, presage, betoken, be an omen, forebode

bodily *adjective* PHYSICAL, material, actual,

substantial, fleshly, tangible, corporal, carnal, corporeal

body *noun* **1** PHYSIQUE, build, form, figure, shape, make-up, frame, constitution **2** TORSO, trunk **3** CORPSE, dead body, remains, stiff (*slang*), relics, carcass, cadaver **4** ORGANIZATION, company, group, society, league, association, band, congress, institution, corporation, federation, outfit (*informal*), syndicate, bloc, confederation **5** MAIN PART, matter, material, mass, substance, bulk, essence **6** EXPANSE, mass, sweep **7** MASS, company, press, army, host, crowd, majority, assembly, mob, herd, swarm, horde, multitude, throng, bevy **8** CONSISTENCY, substance, texture, density, richness, firmness, solidity, viscosity

boffin *noun* (*Brit informal*) EXPERT, authority, brain(s) (*informal*), intellectual, genius, guru, inventor, thinker, wizard, mastermind, intellect, egghead, wonk (*informal*), brainbox, bluestocking (*usually disparaging*), maven (*US*), fundi (*S African*)

bog *noun* MARSH, moss (*Scot & N English dialect*), swamp, slough, wetlands, fen, mire, quagmire, morass, marshland, peat bog, pakihi (*NZ*), muskeg (*Canad*) ▷▷ **bog something** *or* **someone down** HOLD UP, stick, delay, halt, stall, slow down, impede, slow up

bogey *noun* **1** BUGBEAR, bête noire, horror, nightmare, bugaboo **2** SPIRIT, ghost, phantom, spectre, spook (*informal*), apparition, imp, sprite, goblin, bogeyman, hobgoblin, eidolon, atua (*NZ*), kehua (*NZ*)

boggle *verb* CONFUSE, surprise, shock, amaze, stun, stagger, bewilder, astound, daze, confound, stupefy, dumbfound

bogus *adjective* FAKE, false, artificial, forged, dummy, imitation, sham, fraudulent, pseudo (*informal*), counterfeit, spurious, ersatz, phoney *or* phony (*informal*), assumed << ANTONYM genuine

Bohemian *adjective often not cap.* UNCONVENTIONAL, alternative, artistic, exotic, way-out (*informal*), eccentric, avant-garde, off-the-wall (*slang*), unorthodox, arty (*informal*), oddball (*informal*), offbeat, left bank, nonconformist, outré << ANTONYM conventional ▷ *noun often not cap.* NONCONFORMIST, rebel, radical, eccentric, maverick, hippy, dropout, individualist, beatnik, iconoclast

boil[1] *verb* **1** SIMMER, bubble, foam, churn, seethe, fizz, froth, effervesce **2** BE FURIOUS, storm, rage, rave, fume, be angry, crack up

(*informal*), see red (*informal*), go ballistic (*slang, chiefly US*), be indignant, fulminate, foam at the mouth (*informal*), blow a fuse (*slang, chiefly US*), fly off the handle (*informal*), go off the deep end (*informal*), wig out (*slang*), go up the wall (*slang*) ▷▷ **boil something down** REDUCE, concentrate, precipitate (*chemistry*), thicken, condense, decoct

boil[2] *noun* PUSTULE, gathering, swelling, blister, blain, carbuncle, furuncle (*pathology*)

boisterous *adjective* **1** UNRULY, wild, disorderly, loud, noisy, wayward, rowdy, wilful, riotous, unrestrained, rollicking, impetuous, rumbustious, uproarious, obstreperous, clamorous << ANTONYM self-controlled **2** STORMY, rough, raging, turbulent, tumultuous, tempestuous, blustery, gusty, squally << ANTONYM calm

bold *adjective* **1** FEARLESS, enterprising, brave, daring, heroic, adventurous, courageous, gritty, gallant, gutsy (*slang*), audacious, intrepid, valiant, plucky, undaunted, unafraid, unflinching, dauntless, lion-hearted, valorous << ANTONYM timid **2** IMPUDENT, forward, fresh (*informal*), confident, rude, cheeky, brash, feisty (*informal, chiefly US & Canad*), saucy, pushy (*informal*), brazen, in-your-face (*Brit slang*), shameless, sassy (*US informal*), unabashed, pert, insolent, barefaced, spirited, forceful << ANTONYM shy **3** BRIGHT, conspicuous, strong, striking, loud, prominent, lively, pronounced, colourful, vivid, flashy, eye-catching, salient, showy << ANTONYM soft

bolster *verb* SUPPORT, help, aid, maintain, boost, strengthen, assist, prop, reinforce, hold up, cushion, brace, shore up, augment, buttress, buoy up, give a leg up to (*informal*)

bolt *noun* **1** PIN, rod, peg, rivet **2** BAR, catch, lock, latch, fastener, sliding bar **3** ARROW, missile, shaft, dart, projectile **4** DASH, race, flight, spring, rush, bound, sprint, dart, spurt ▷ *verb* **1** LOCK, close, bar, secure, fasten, latch **2** DASH, run, fly, spring, jump, rush, bound, leap, sprint, hurtle **3** GOBBLE, stuff, wolf, cram, gorge, devour, gulp, guzzle, swallow whole

bomb *noun* EXPLOSIVE, charge, mine, shell, missile, device, rocket, grenade, torpedo, bombshell, projectile ▷ *verb* BLOW UP, attack, destroy, assault, shell, blast, blitz, bombard, torpedo, open fire on, strafe, fire upon, blow sky-high

bombard *verb* **1** ATTACK, assault, batter, barrage, besiege, beset, assail **2** BOMB, shell, blast, blitz, open fire, strafe, fire upon

bombardment *noun* BOMBING, attack, fire, assault, shelling, blitz, barrage, flak, strafe, fusillade, cannonade

bombast *noun* POMPOSITY, ranting, bragging, hot air (*informal*), bluster, grandiosity, braggadocio, grandiloquence, rodomontade (*literary*), gasconade (*rare*), extravagant boasting, magniloquence

bombastic *adjective* GRANDILOQUENT, inflated, ranting, windy, high-flown, pompous, grandiose, histrionic, wordy, verbose, declamatory, fustian, magniloquent

bona fide *adjective* GENUINE, real, true, legal, actual, legitimate, authentic, honest, veritable, lawful, on the level (*informal*), kosher (*informal*), dinkum (*Austral & NZ informal*), the real McCoy << ANTONYM bogus

bond *noun* **1** TIE, union, coupling, link, association, relation, connection, alliance, attachment, affinity, affiliation **2** FASTENING, band, tie, binding, chain, cord, shackle, fetter, manacle **3** AGREEMENT, word, promise, contract, guarantee, pledge, obligation, compact, covenant ▷ *verb* **1** FORM FRIENDSHIPS, connect **2** FIX, hold, bind, connect, glue, gum, fuse, stick, paste, fasten

bondage *noun* SLAVERY, imprisonment, captivity, confinement, yoke, duress, servitude, enslavement, subjugation, serfdom, subjection, vassalage, thraldom, enthralment

bonny *adjective* (*Scot & N English dialect*) BEAUTIFUL, pretty, fair, sweet, appealing, attractive, lovely, charming, handsome, good-looking, gorgeous, radiant, alluring, comely

bonus *noun* **1** EXTRA, benefit, commission, prize, gift, reward, premium, dividend, hand-out, perk (*Brit informal*), bounty, gratuity, honorarium **2** ADVANTAGE, benefit, gain, extra, plus, asset, perk (*Brit informal*), icing on the cake

bony *adjective* THIN, lean, skinny, angular, gaunt, skeletal, haggard, emaciated, scrawny, undernourished, cadaverous, rawboned, macilent (*rare*)

book *noun* **1** WORK, title, volume, publication, manual, paperback, textbook, tract, hardback, tome **2** NOTEBOOK, album, journal, diary, pad, record book, Filofax (*trademark*), notepad, exercise book, jotter, memorandum book ▷ *verb* RESERVE, schedule, engage, line up, organize, charter,

arrange for, procure, make reservations ▷▷ **book in** REGISTER, enter, enrol

booking *noun* (*Chiefly Brit*) RESERVATION, date, appointment

bookish *adjective* STUDIOUS, learned, academic, intellectual, literary, scholarly, erudite, pedantic, well-read, donnish

booklet *noun* BROCHURE, leaflet, hand-out, pamphlet, folder, mailshot, handbill

boom *noun* **1** EXPANSION, increase, development, growth, advance, jump, boost, improvement, spurt, upsurge, upturn, upswing << ANTONYM decline **2** BANG, report, shot, crash, clash, blast, burst, explosion, roar, thunder, rumble, clap, peal, detonation ▷ *verb* **1** INCREASE, flourish, grow, develop, succeed, expand, strengthen, do well, swell, thrive, intensify, prosper, burgeon, spurt << ANTONYM fall **2** BANG, roll, crash, blast, echo, drum, explode, roar, thunder, rumble, resound, reverberate, peal

boomerang *verb* REBOUND, backfire, come home to roost

boon *noun* **1** BENEFIT, advantage, blessing, godsend, gift **2** (*archaic*) GIFT, present, grant, favour, donation, hand-out, gratuity, benefaction

boorish *adjective* LOUTISH, gross, crude, rude, hick (*informal, chiefly US & Canad*), coarse, vulgar, rustic, barbaric, churlish, uneducated, bearish, uncouth, unrefined, uncivilized, clownish, oafish, ill-bred, lubberly << ANTONYM refined

boost *verb* INCREASE, develop, raise, expand, add to, build up, heighten, enlarge, inflate, magnify, amplify, augment, jack up << ANTONYM decrease ▷ *noun* **1** RISE, increase, advance, jump, addition, improvement, expansion, upsurge, upturn, increment, upswing, upward turn << ANTONYM fall **2** ENCOURAGEMENT, help

boot *verb* KICK, punt, put the boot in(to) (*slang*), drop-kick ▷▷ **boot someone out** (*informal*) DISMISS, sack (*informal*), expel, throw out, oust, relegate, kick out, eject, kiss off (*slang, chiefly US & Canad*), show someone the door, give someone the boot (*slang*), give someone their marching orders, give someone the bullet (*Brit slang*), give someone the bum's rush (*slang*), throw someone out on their ear (*informal*), give someone the heave or push (*informal*)

bootleg *adjective* ILLICIT, illegal, outlawed, pirate, unofficial, black-market, unlicensed, under-the-table, unauthorized, contraband,

hooky (*slang*), under-the-counter
<< ANTONYM official

booty *noun* PLUNDER, winnings, gains, haul,
spoils, prey, loot, takings, pillage, swag
(*slang*), boodle (*slang, chiefly US*)

booze *verb* (*informal*) DRINK, indulge, get
drunk, tipple, imbibe, tope, carouse, bevvy
(*dialect*), get plastered, drink like a fish, get
soused, get tanked up (*informal*), go on a
binge *or* bender (*informal*), hit the booze *or*
bottle (*informal*)

boozer *noun* (*informal*) **1** PUB, local (*Brit
informal*), bar (*informal, chiefly Brit*), inn,
tavern, beer parlour (*Canad*), beverage
room (*Canad*), public house, watering
hole (*facetious slang*), roadhouse, hostelry,
alehouse (*archaic*), taproom **2** DRINKER, toper,
drunk, soak (*slang*), alcoholic, lush (*slang*),
drunkard, sot, tippler, wino (*informal*), alko
or alco (*Austral slang*), inebriate

border *noun* **1** FRONTIER, line, marches, limit,
bounds, boundary, perimeter, borderline,
borderland **2** EDGE, lip, margin, skirt, verge,
rim, hem, brim, flange ▷ *verb* EDGE, bound,
decorate, trim, fringe, rim, hem ▷▷ **border
on something** COME CLOSE TO, approach, be
like, resemble, be similar to, approximate,
come near

borderline *adjective* MARGINAL, bordering,
doubtful, peripheral, indefinite,
indeterminate, equivocal, inexact,
unclassifiable

bore¹ *verb* DRILL, mine, sink, tunnel, pierce,
penetrate, burrow, puncture, perforate,
gouge out

bore² *verb* TIRE, exhaust, annoy, fatigue, weary,
wear out, jade, wear down, be tedious, pall
on, send to sleep << ANTONYM excite ▷ *noun*
NUISANCE, pain (*informal*), drag (*informal*),
headache (*informal*), yawn (*informal*), anorak
(*informal*), pain in the neck (*informal*),
dullard, dull person, tiresome person,
wearisome talker

bored *adjective* FED UP, tired, hacked (off) (*US
slang*), wearied, weary, uninterested, sick
and tired (*informal*), listless, browned-off
(*informal*), brassed off (*Brit slang*), ennuied,
hoha (*NZ*)

boredom *noun* TEDIUM, apathy, doldrums,
weariness, monotony, dullness, sameness,
ennui, flatness, world-weariness,
tediousness, irksomeness << ANTONYM
excitement

boring *adjective* UNINTERESTING, dull, tedious,
stale, tiresome, monotonous, old, dead, flat,

routine, humdrum, insipid, mind-numbing,
unexciting, ho-hum (*informal*), repetitious,
wearisome, unvaried

born *verb* BROUGHT INTO THIS WORLD,
delivered

borrow *verb* **1** TAKE ON LOAN, touch (someone)
for (*slang*), scrounge (*informal*), blag (*slang*),
mooch (*slang*), cadge, use temporarily, take
and return << ANTONYM lend **2** STEAL,
take, use, copy, adopt, appropriate, acquire,
pinch (*informal*), pirate, poach, pilfer, filch,
plagiarize

bosom *noun* **1** BREAST, chest, front, bust, teats,
thorax **2** MIDST, centre, heart, protection,
circle, shelter **3** HEART, feelings, spirit,
soul, emotions, sympathies, sentiments,
affections ▷ *adjective* INTIMATE, close, warm,
dear, friendly, confidential, cherished, boon,
very dear

boss *noun* MANAGER, head, leader, director,
chief, executive, owner, master, governor
(*informal*), employer, administrator,
supervisor, superintendent, gaffer (*informal,
chiefly Brit*), foreman, overseer, kingpin, big
cheese (*old-fashioned slang*), baas (*S African*),
numero uno (*informal*), Mister Big (*slang,
chiefly US*), sherang (*Austral & NZ*) ▷▷ **boss
someone around** (*informal*) ORDER AROUND,
dominate, bully, intimidate, oppress, dictate
to, terrorize, put upon, push around (*slang*),
browbeat, ride roughshod over, tyrannize,
rule with an iron hand

bossy *adjective* (*informal*) DOMINEERING,
lordly, arrogant, authoritarian, oppressive,
hectoring, autocratic, dictatorial, coercive,
imperious, overbearing, tyrannical, despotic,
high-handed

botch *verb* SPOIL, mar, bungle, fumble, screw
up (*informal*), mess up, cock up (*Brit slang*),
mismanage, muff, make a nonsense of
(*informal*), bodge (*informal*), make a pig's ear
of (*informal*), flub (*US slang*), crool *or* cruel
(*Austral slang*) ▷ *noun* MESS, failure, blunder,
miscarriage, bungle, bungling, fumble, hash,
cock-up (*Brit slang*), pig's ear (*informal*), pig's
breakfast (*informal*)

bother *verb* **1** TROUBLE, concern, worry,
upset, alarm, disturb, distress, annoy,
dismay, gall, disconcert, vex, perturb, faze,
put *or* get someone's back up **2** PESTER,
plague, irritate, put out, harass, nag, hassle
(*informal*), inconvenience, molest, breathe
down someone's neck, get on your nerves
(*informal*), nark (*Brit, Austral & NZ slang*),
bend someone's ear (*informal*), give someone

grief (*Brit & S African*), get on your wick (*Brit slang*) << ANTONYM help ▷ *noun* TROUBLE, problem, worry, difficulty, strain, grief (*Brit & S African*), fuss, pest, irritation, hassle (*informal*), nuisance, flurry, uphill (*S African*), inconvenience, annoyance, aggravation, vexation << ANTONYM help

bottleneck *noun* BLOCK, hold-up, obstacle, congestion, obstruction, impediment, blockage, snarl-up (*informal, chiefly Brit*), (traffic) jam

bottle shop *noun* (*Austral & NZ*) OFF-LICENCE (*Brit*), liquor store (*US & Canad*), bottle store (*S African*), package store (*US & Canad*), offie or offy (*Brit informal*)

bottle store *noun* (*S African*) OFF-LICENCE (*Brit*), liquor store (*US & Canad*), bottle shop (*Austral & NZ*), package store (*US & Canad*), offie or offy (*Brit informal*)

bottom *noun* 1 LOWEST PART, base, foot, bed, floor, basis, foundation, depths, support, pedestal, deepest part << ANTONYM top 2 UNDERSIDE, sole, underneath, lower side 3 (*informal*) BUTTOCKS, behind (*informal*), rear, butt (*US & Canad informal*), bum (*Brit slang*), buns (*US slang*), backside, rump, seat, tail (*informal*), rear end, posterior, derrière (*euphemistic*), tush (*US slang*), fundament, jacksy (*Brit slang*) ▷ *adjective* LOWEST, last, base, ground, basement, undermost << ANTONYM higher

bottomless *adjective* 1 UNLIMITED, endless, infinite, limitless, boundless, inexhaustible, immeasurable, unbounded, illimitable 2 DEEP, profound, yawning, boundless, unfathomable, immeasurable, fathomless, abyssal

bounce *verb* 1 REBOUND, return, thump, recoil, ricochet, spring back, resile 2 BOUND, spring, jump, leap, skip, caper, prance, gambol, jounce 3 (*slang*) THROW OUT, fire (*informal*), turn out, expel, oust, relegate, kick out (*informal*), drive out, eject, evict, boot out (*informal*), show someone the door, give someone the bum's rush (*slang*), throw someone out on their ear (*informal*) ▷ *noun* 1 SPRINGINESS, give, spring, bound, rebound, resilience, elasticity, recoil 2 (*informal*) LIFE, go (*informal*), energy, pep, sparkle, zip (*informal*), vitality, animation, vigour, exuberance, dynamism, brio, vivacity, liveliness, vim (*slang*), lustiness, vivaciousness

bouncing *adjective* LIVELY, healthy, thriving, blooming, robust, vigorous, energetic, perky, sprightly, alive and kicking, fighting fit, full of beans (*informal*), fit as a fiddle (*informal*), bright-eyed and bushy-tailed

bouncy *adjective* 1 LIVELY, active, enthusiastic, energetic, bubbly, exuberant, irrepressible, ebullient, perky, chirpy (*informal*), sprightly, vivacious, effervescent, chipper (*informal*), full of beans (*informal*), zestful, full of pep (*informal*), bright-eyed and bushy-tailed << ANTONYM listless 2 SPRINGY, flexible, elastic, resilient, rubbery, spongy << ANTONYM flat

bound[1] *adjective* 1 COMPELLED, obliged, forced, committed, pledged, constrained, obligated, beholden, duty-bound 2 TIED, fixed, secured, attached, lashed, tied up, fastened, trussed, pinioned, made fast 3 CERTAIN, sure, fated, doomed, destined

bound[2] *verb* LEAP, bob, spring, jump, bounce, skip, vault, pounce ▷ *noun* LEAP, bob, spring, jump, bounce, hurdle, skip, vault, pounce, caper, prance, lope, frisk, gambol

bound[3] *verb* 1 SURROUND, confine, enclose, terminate, encircle, circumscribe, hem in, demarcate, delimit 2 LIMIT, fix, define, restrict, confine, restrain, circumscribe, demarcate, delimit

boundary *noun* 1 FRONTIER, edge, border, march, barrier, margin, brink 2 EDGES, limits, bounds, pale, confines, fringes, verges, precinct, extremities 3 DIVIDING LINE, borderline

boundless *adjective* UNLIMITED, vast, endless, immense, infinite, untold, limitless, unending, inexhaustible, incalculable, immeasurable, unbounded, unconfined, measureless, illimitable << ANTONYM limited

bounds *plural noun* BOUNDARY, line, limit, edge, border, march, margin, pale, confine, fringe, verge, rim, perimeter, periphery

bountiful *adjective* 1 PLENTIFUL, generous, lavish, ample, prolific, abundant, exuberant, copious, luxuriant, bounteous, plenteous 2 GENEROUS, kind, princely, liberal, charitable, hospitable, prodigal, open-handed, unstinting, beneficent, bounteous, munificent, ungrudging

bounty *noun* 1 GENEROSITY, charity, assistance, kindness, philanthropy, benevolence, beneficence, liberality, almsgiving, open-handedness, largesse or largess 2 ABUNDANCE, plenty, exuberance, profusion, affluence, plenitude, copiousness, plenteousness 3 REWARD, present, grant, prize, payment, gift, compensation, bonus, premium, donation, recompense, gratuity, meed (*archaic*), largesse *or* largess, koha (*NZ*)

bouquet *noun* 1 BUNCH OF FLOWERS, spray, garland, wreath, posy, buttonhole, corsage, nosegay, boutonniere 2 AROMA, smell, scent, perfume, fragrance, savour, odour, redolence

bourgeois *adjective* MIDDLE-CLASS, traditional, conventional, materialistic, hidebound, Pooterish

bout *noun* 1 PERIOD, time, term, fit, session, stretch, spell, turn, patch, interval, stint 2 ROUND, run, course, series, session, cycle, sequence, stint, spree 3 FIGHT, match, battle, competition, struggle, contest, set-to, encounter, engagement, head-to-head, boxing match

bovine *adjective* DULL, heavy, slow, thick, stupid, dull, dense, sluggish, lifeless, inactive, inert, lethargic, dozy (*Brit informal*), listless, unresponsive, stolid, torpid, slothful

bow¹ *verb* BEND, bob, nod, incline, stoop, droop, genuflect, make obeisance ▷ *noun* BENDING, bob, nod, inclination, salaam, obeisance, kowtow, genuflection ▷▷ **bow out** GIVE UP, retire, withdraw, get out, resign, quit, pull out, step down (*informal*), back out, throw in the towel, cop out (*slang*), throw in the sponge, call it a day *or* night ▷▷ **bow to something** *or* **someone** GIVE IN TO, accept, comply with, succumb to, submit to, surrender to, yield to, defer to, concede to, acquiesce to, kowtow to

bow² *noun* (*nautical*) PROW, head, stem, fore, beak .

bowels *plural noun* 1 GUTS, insides (*informal*), intestines, innards (*informal*), entrails, viscera, vitals 2 DEPTHS, hold, middle, inside, deep, interior, core, belly, midst, remotest part, deepest part, furthest part, innermost part

bower *noun* ARBOUR, grotto, alcove, summerhouse, shady recess, leafy shelter

bowl¹ *noun* BASIN, plate, dish, vessel

bowl² *verb* 1 THROW, hurl, launch, cast, pitch, toss, fling, chuck (*informal*), lob (*informal*) 2 *often with* **along** DRIVE, shoot, speed, tear, barrel (along) (*informal, chiefly US & Canad*), trundle ▷▷ **bowl someone over** 1 KNOCK DOWN, fell, floor, deck (*slang*), overturn, overthrow, bring down 2 (*informal*) SURPRISE, amaze, stun, overwhelm, astonish, stagger, startle, astound, take (someone) aback, stupefy, strike (someone) dumb, throw off balance, sweep (someone) off their feet,

dumbfound

box¹ *noun* CONTAINER, case, chest, trunk, pack, package, carton, casket, receptacle, ark (*dialect*), portmanteau, coffret, kist (*Scot & N English dialect*) ▷ *verb* PACK, package, wrap, encase, bundle up ▷▷ **box something** *or* **someone in** CONFINE, contain, surround, trap, restrict, isolate, cage, enclose, restrain, imprison, shut up, incarcerate, hem in, shut in, coop up

box² *verb* 1 FIGHT, spar, exchange blows 2 PUNCH, hit, strike, belt (*informal*), deck (*slang*), slap, sock (*slang*), buffet, clout (*informal*), cuff, whack (*informal*), wallop (*informal*), chin (*slang*), tonk (*informal*), thwack (*informal*), lay one on (*slang*)

boxer *noun* FIGHTER, pugilist, prizefighter, sparrer

boxing *noun* PRIZEFIGHTING, the ring, sparring, fisticuffs, the fight game (*informal*), pugilism

boy *noun* LAD, kid (*informal*), youth, fellow, youngster, chap (*informal*), schoolboy, junior, laddie (*Scot*), stripling

boycott *verb* EMBARGO, reject, snub, refrain from, spurn, blacklist, black, cold-shoulder, ostracize, blackball << ANTONYM support

boyfriend *noun* SWEETHEART, man, lover, young man, steady, beloved, valentine, admirer, suitor, beau, date, swain, toy boy, truelove, leman (*archaic*), inamorato

boyish *adjective* YOUTHFUL, young, innocent, adolescent, juvenile, childish, immature

brace *verb* 1 STEADY, support, balance, secure, stabilize 2 SUPPORT, strengthen, steady, prop, reinforce, hold up, tighten, shove, bolster, fortify, buttress, shove up ▷ *noun* SUPPORT, stay, prop, bracer, bolster, bracket, reinforcement, strut, truss, buttress, stanchion

bracing *adjective* REFRESHING, fresh, cool, stimulating, reviving, lively, crisp, vigorous, rousing, brisk, uplifting, exhilarating, fortifying, chilly, rejuvenating, invigorating, energizing, healthful, restorative, tonic, rejuvenative << ANTONYM tiring

brag *verb* BOAST, crow, swagger, vaunt, bluster, talk big (*slang*), blow your own trumpet, blow your own horn (*US & Canad*)

braid *verb* INTERWEAVE, weave, lace, intertwine, plait, entwine, twine, ravel, interlace

brain *noun* 1 CEREBRUM, mind, grey matter (*informal*) 2 (*informal*) INTELLECTUAL, genius, scholar, sage, pundit, mastermind, intellect,

prodigy, highbrow, egghead (*informal*),
brainbox, bluestocking (*usually disparaging*)
▷ *plural noun* INTELLIGENCE, mind, reason,
understanding, sense, capacity, smarts (*slang*,
chiefly US), wit, intellect, savvy (*slang*), nous
(*Brit slang*), suss (*slang*), shrewdness, sagacity

brainwashing *noun* INDOCTRINATION,
conditioning, persuasion, re-education

brainwave *noun* IDEA, thought, bright idea,
stroke of genius

brainy *adjective* (*informal*) INTELLIGENT, quick,
bright, sharp, brilliant, acute, smart, alert,
clever, rational, knowing, quick-witted

brake *noun* CONTROL, check, curb, restraint,
constraint, rein ▷ *verb* SLOW, decelerate,
reduce speed

branch *noun* **1** BOUGH, shoot, arm, spray,
limb, sprig, offshoot, prong, ramification
2 OFFICE, department, unit, wing, chapter,
bureau, local office **3** DIVISION, part, section,
subdivision, subsection **4** DISCIPLINE,
section, subdivision ▷▷ **branch out** EXPAND,
diversify

brand *noun* **1** TRADEMARK **2** LABEL, mark, sign,
stamp, symbol, logo, trademark, marker,
hallmark, emblem **3** STIGMA, mark, stain,
disgrace, taint, slur, blot, infamy, smirch
▷ *verb* **1** STIGMATIZE, mark, label, expose,
denounce, disgrace, discredit, censure,
pillory, defame **2** MARK, burn, label, stamp,
scar

brandish *verb* WAVE, raise, display, shake,
swing, exhibit, flourish, wield, flaunt

brash *adjective* BOLD, forward, rude,
arrogant, cocky, pushy (*informal*), brazen,
presumptuous, impertinent, insolent,
impudent, bumptious, cocksure,
overconfident, hubristic, full of yourself
<< ANTONYM timid

brassy *adjective* **1** STRIDENT, loud, harsh,
piercing, jarring, noisy, grating, raucous,
blaring, shrill, jangling, dissonant,
cacophonous **2** BRAZEN, forward, bold,
brash, saucy, pushy (*informal*), pert, insolent,
impudent, loud-mouthed, barefaced
3 FLASHY, loud, blatant, vulgar, gaudy,
garish, jazzy (*informal*), showy, obtrusive
<< ANTONYM discreet

brat *noun* YOUNGSTER, kid (*informal*),
urchin, imp, rascal, spoilt child, devil,
puppy (*informal*), cub, scallywag (*informal*),
whippersnapper, guttersnipe

bravado *noun* SWAGGER, boast, boasting,
swaggering, vaunting, bluster,
swashbuckling, bombast, braggadocio,
boastfulness, fanfaronade (*rare*)

brave *adjective* COURAGEOUS, daring, bold,
heroic, adventurous, gritty, fearless,
resolute, gallant, gutsy (*slang*), audacious,
intrepid, valiant, plucky, undaunted,
unafraid, unflinching, dauntless, lion-
hearted, valorous << ANTONYM timid ▷
verb CONFRONT, face, suffer, challenge, bear,
tackle, dare, endure, defy, withstand, stand
up to << ANTONYM give in to

bravery *noun* COURAGE, nerve, daring, pluck,
spirit, bottle (*Brit slang*), guts (*informal*),
grit, fortitude, heroism, mettle, boldness,
bravura, gallantry, valour, spunk (*informal*),
hardiness, fearlessness, intrepidity,
indomitability, hardihood, dauntlessness,
doughtiness, pluckiness, lion-heartedness
<< ANTONYM cowardice

bravo *interjection* CONGRATULATIONS, well
done

bravura *noun* BRILLIANCE, energy, spirit,
display, punch (*informal*), dash, animation,
vigour, verve, panache, boldness, virtuosity,
élan, exhibitionism, brio, ostentation

brawl *noun* FIGHT, battle, row (*informal*), clash,
disorder, scrap (*informal*), fray, squabble,
wrangle, skirmish, scuffle, punch-up (*Brit
informal*), free-for-all (*informal*), fracas,
altercation, rumpus, broil, tumult, affray
(*law*), shindig (*informal*), donnybrook, ruckus
(*informal*), scrimmage, shindy (*informal*), biffo
(*Austral slang*), bagarre (*French*), melee or
mêlée ▷ *verb* FIGHT, battle, scrap (*informal*),
wrestle, wrangle, tussle, scuffle, go at it
hammer and tongs, fight like Kilkenny cats,
altercate

brawn *noun* MUSCLE, might, power, strength,
muscles, beef (*informal*), flesh, vigour,
robustness, muscularity, beefiness (*informal*),
brawniness

bray *verb* **1** NEIGH, bellow, screech, heehaw
2 ROAR, trumpet, bellow, hoot ▷ *noun*
1 NEIGH, bellow, screech, heehaw **2** ROAR,
cry, shout, bellow, screech, hoot, bawl, harsh
sound

brazen *adjective* BOLD, forward, defiant,
brash, saucy, audacious, pushy (*informal*),
shameless, unabashed, pert, unashamed,
insolent, impudent, immodest, barefaced,
brassy (*informal*) << ANTONYM shy ▷▷ **brazen
it out** BE UNASHAMED, persevere, be defiant,
confront something, be impenitent, outface,
outstare

breach *noun* **1** NONOBSERVANCE, abuse,
violation, infringement, trespass,

disobedience, transgression, contravention, infraction, noncompliance << ANTONYM compliance **2** DISAGREEMENT, difference, division, separation, falling-out (*informal*), quarrel, alienation, variance, severance, disaffection, schism, parting of the ways, estrangement, dissension **3** OPENING, crack, break, hole, split, gap, rent, rift, rupture, aperture, chasm, cleft, fissure

bread *noun* **1** FOOD, provisions, fare, necessities, subsistence, kai (*NZ informal*), nourishment, sustenance, victuals, nutriment, viands, aliment **2** (*slang*) MONEY, funds, cash, finance, necessary (*informal*), silver, tin (*slang*), brass (*N English dialect*), dough (*slang*), dosh (*Brit & Austral slang*), needful (*informal*), shekels (*informal*), dibs (*slang*), ackers (*slang*), spondulicks (*slang*), rhino (*Brit slang*)

breadth *noun* **1** WIDTH, spread, beam, span, latitude, broadness, wideness **2** EXTENT, area, reach, range, measure, size, scale, spread, sweep, scope, magnitude, compass, expanse, vastness, amplitude, comprehensiveness, extensiveness

break *verb* **1** SHATTER, separate, destroy, split, divide, crack, snap, smash, crush, fragment, demolish, sever, trash (*slang*), disintegrate, splinter, smash to smithereens, shiver << ANTONYM repair **2** FRACTURE, crack, smash **3** BURST, tear, split **4** DISOBEY, breach, defy, violate, disregard, flout, infringe, contravene, transgress, go counter to, infract (*law*) << ANTONYM obey **5** STOP, cut, check, suspend, interrupt, cut short, discontinue **6** DISTURB, interrupt **7** END, stop, cut, drop, give up, abandon, suspend, interrupt, terminate, put an end to, discontinue, pull the plug on **8** WEAKEN, undermine, cow, tame, subdue, demoralize, dispirit **9** RUIN, destroy, crush, humiliate, bring down, bankrupt, degrade, impoverish, demote, make bankrupt, bring to ruin **10** PAUSE, stop briefly, stop, rest, halt, cease, take a break, have a breather (*informal*) **11** INTERRUPT, stop, suspend **12** CUSHION, reduce, ease, moderate, diminish, temper, soften, lessen, alleviate, lighten **13** BE REVEALED, come out, be reported, be published, be announced, be made public, be proclaimed, be let out, be imparted, be divulged, come out in the wash **14** REVEAL, tell, announce, declare, disclose, proclaim, divulge, make known **15** BEAT, top, better, exceed, go beyond, excel, surpass, outstrip, outdo, cap (*informal*) **16** (always

used of *dawn*) HAPPEN, appear, emerge, occur, erupt, burst out, come forth suddenly ▷ *noun* **1** FRACTURE, opening, tear, hole, split, crack, gap, rent, breach, rift, rupture, gash, cleft, fissure **2** INTERVAL, pause, recess, interlude, intermission, entr'acte **3** HOLIDAY, leave, vacation, time off, recess, awayday, schoolie (*Austral*), acumulated day off *or* ADO (*Austral*) **4** (*informal*) STROKE OF LUCK, chance, opportunity, advantage, fortune, opening **5** BREACH, split, dispute, separation, rift, rupture, alienation, disaffection, schism, estrangement ▷▷ **break away** GET AWAY, escape, flee, run away, break free, break loose, make your escape ▷▷ **break down 1** STOP WORKING, stop, seize up, conk out (*informal*), go kaput (*informal*), go phut, cark it (*Austral & NZ slang*) **2** FAIL, collapse, fall through, be unsuccessful, come unstuck, run aground, come to grief, come a cropper (*informal*) **3** BE OVERCOME, crack up (*informal*), go to pieces ▷▷ **break in 1** BREAK AND ENTER, enter, gain access **2** INTERRUPT, intervene, interfere, intrude, burst in, interject, butt in, barge in, interpose, put your oar in, put your two cents in (*US slang*) ▷▷ **break off** STOP TALKING, pause, stumble, falter, fumble, hem and haw *or* hum and haw ▷▷ **break out 1** BEGIN, start, happen, occur, arise, set in, commence, spring up **2** ESCAPE, flee, bolt, burst out, get free, break loose, abscond, do a bunk (*Brit slang*), do a Skase (*Austral informal*) **3** ERUPT, gush, flare up, burst out, burst forth, pour forth ▷▷ **break someone in** INITIATE, train, accustom, habituate ▷▷ **break something in** PREPARE, condition, tame ▷▷ **break something off** DETACH, separate, divide, cut off, pull off, sever, part, remove, splinter, tear off, snap off ▷▷ **break something up** STOP, end, suspend, disrupt, dismantle, disperse, terminate, disband, diffuse ▷▷ **break through** SUCCEED, make it (*informal*), achieve, do well, flourish, cut it (*informal*), get to the top, crack it (*informal*), make your mark (*informal*), shine forth ▷▷ **break through something** PENETRATE, go through, get past, burst through ▷▷ **break up 1** FINISH, be suspended, adjourn, recess **2** SPLIT UP, separate, part, divorce, end a relationship **3** SCATTER, separate, divide, dissolve ▷▷ **break with something** *or* **someone** SEPARATE FROM, drop (*informal*), reject, ditch (*slang*), renounce, depart from, break away from, part company with, repudiate, jilt

breakage *noun* BREAK, cut, tear, crack, rent, breach, fracture, rift, rupture, cleft, fissure

breakaway *adjective* REBEL, revolutionary, rebellious, dissenting, insurgent, seceding, secessionist, heretical, mutinous, insubordinate, insurrectionary, schismatic

breakdown *noun* 1 COLLAPSE, crackup (*informal*) 2 ANALYSIS, classification, dissection, categorization, detailed list, itemization

breaker *noun* WAVE, roller, comber, billow, white horse, whitecap

break-in *noun* BURGLARY, robbery, breaking and entering, home invasion (*Austral & NZ*)

breakneck *adjective* DANGEROUS, rapid, excessive, rash, reckless, precipitate, headlong, express

breakthrough *noun* DEVELOPMENT, advance, progress, improvement, discovery, find, finding, invention, step forward, leap forwards, turn of events, quantum leap

break-up *noun* 1 SEPARATION, split, divorce, breakdown, ending, parting, breaking, splitting, wind-up, rift, disintegration, dissolution, termination 2 DISSOLUTION, division, splitting, disintegration

breakwater *noun* SEA WALL, spur, mole, jetty, groyne

breast *noun* 1 HEART, feelings, thoughts, soul, being, emotions, core, sentiments, seat of the affections 2 BOSOM

breath *noun* 1 INHALATION, breathing, pant, gasp, gulp, wheeze, exhalation, respiration 2 GUST, sigh, puff, flutter, flurry, whiff, draught, waft, zephyr, slight movement, faint breeze 3 TRACE, suggestion, hint, whisper, suspicion, murmur, undertone, intimation 4 REST, breather 5 LIFE, energy, existence, vitality, animation, life force, lifeblood, mauri (*NZ*)

breathe *verb* 1 INHALE AND EXHALE, pant, gasp, puff, gulp, wheeze, respire, draw in breath 2 WHISPER, say, voice, express, sigh, utter, articulate, murmur 3 INSTIL, inspire, pass on, inject, impart, infuse, imbue

breather *noun* (*informal*) REST, break, halt, pause, recess, breathing space, breath of air

breathless *adjective* 1 OUT OF BREATH, winded, exhausted, panting, gasping, choking, gulping, wheezing, out of whack (*informal*), short-winded 2 EXCITED, anxious, curious, eager, enthusiastic, impatient, agog, on tenterhooks, in suspense

breathtaking *adjective* AMAZING, striking, exciting, brilliant, dramatic, stunning (*informal*), impressive, thrilling, overwhelming, magnificent, astonishing, sensational, awesome, wondrous (*archaic or literary*), awe-inspiring, jaw-dropping, heart-stirring

breed *noun* 1 VARIETY, race, stock, type, species, strain, pedigree 2 KIND, sort, type, variety, brand, stamp ▷ *verb* 1 REAR, tend, keep, raise, maintain, farm, look after, care for, bring up, nurture, nourish 2 REPRODUCE, multiply, propagate, procreate, produce offspring, bear young, bring forth young, generate offspring, beget offspring, develop 3 PRODUCE, cause, create, occasion, generate, bring about, arouse, originate, give rise to, stir up

breeding *noun* REFINEMENT, style, culture, taste, manners, polish, grace, courtesy, elegance, sophistication, delicacy, cultivation, politeness, civility, gentility, graciousness, urbanity, politesse

breeze *noun* LIGHT WIND, air, whiff, draught, gust, waft, zephyr, breath of wind, current of air, puff of air, capful of wind ▷ *verb* SWEEP, move briskly, pass, trip, sail, hurry, sally, glide, flit

breezy *adjective* 1 CAREFREE, casual, lively, sparkling, sunny, informal, cheerful, animated, upbeat (*informal*), buoyant, airy, easy-going, genial, jaunty, chirpy (*informal*), sparky, sprightly, vivacious, debonair, blithe, free and easy, full of beans (*informal*), light, light-hearted << ANTONYM serious 2 WINDY, fresh, airy, blustery, blowing, gusty, squally, blowy, blusterous << ANTONYM calm

brevity *noun* 1 SHORTNESS, transience, impermanence, ephemerality, briefness, transitoriness 2 CONCISENESS, economy, crispness, concision, terseness, succinctness, curtness, pithiness << ANTONYM wordiness

brew *verb* 1 BOIL, make, soak, steep, stew, infuse (*tea*) 2 MAKE, ferment, prepare by fermentation 3 START, develop, gather, foment 4 DEVELOP, form, gather, foment ▷ *noun* DRINK, preparation, mixture, blend, liquor, beverage, infusion, concoction, fermentation, distillation

bribe *noun* INDUCEMENT, incentive, pay-off (*informal*), graft (*informal*), sweetener (*slang*), kickback (*US*), sop, backhander (*slang*), enticement, hush money (*slang*), payola (*informal*), allurement, corrupting gift, reward for treachery ▷ *verb* BUY OFF, reward, pay off (*informal*), lure, corrupt, get at, square, suborn, grease the palm *or* hand of (*slang*), influence by gifts, oil the palm of (*slang*)

bribery *noun* CORRUPTION, graft (*informal*), inducement, buying off, payola (*informal*), crookedness (*informal*), palm-greasing (*slang*), subornation

bric-a-brac *noun* KNICK-KNACKS, ornaments, trinkets, baubles, curios, objets d'art (*French*), gewgaws, bibelots, kickshaws, objects of virtu

bridal *adjective* MATRIMONIAL, marriage, wedding, marital, bride's, nuptial, conjugal, spousal, connubial, hymeneal

bride *noun* WIFE, newly-wed, marriage partner, wifey (*informal*)

bridegroom *noun* HUSBAND, groom, newly-wed, marriage partner

bridge *noun* 1 ARCH, span, viaduct, flyover, overpass 2 LINK, tie, bond, connection ▷ *verb* 1 SPAN, cross, go over, cross over, traverse, reach across, extend across, arch over 2 RECONCILE, unite, resolve

bridle *noun* REIN, curb, control, check, restraint, trammels ▷ *verb* 1 GET ANGRY, draw (yourself) up, bristle, seethe, see red, be infuriated, rear up, be indignant, be maddened, raise your hackles, get your dander up (*slang*), get your back up 2 CURB, control, master, govern, moderate, restrain, rein, subdue, repress, constrain, keep in check, check, keep a tight rein on, keep on a string

brief *adjective* 1 SHORT, fast, quick, temporary, fleeting, swift, short-lived, little, hasty, momentary, ephemeral, quickie (*informal*), transitory << ANTONYM long 2 CONCISE, short, limited, to the point, crisp, compressed, terse, curt, laconic, succinct, clipped, pithy, thumbnail, monosyllabic << ANTONYM long 3 CURT, short, sharp, blunt, abrupt, brusque ▷ *verb* INFORM, prime, prepare, advise, fill in (*informal*), instruct, clue in (*informal*), gen up (*Brit informal*), put in the picture (*informal*), give a rundown, keep posted, give the gen (*Brit informal*) ▷ *noun* 1 SUMMARY, résumé, outline, sketch, abstract, summing-up, digest, epitome, rundown, synopsis, précis, recapitulation, abridgment 2 CASE, defence, argument, data, contention

briefing *noun* 1 CONFERENCE, meeting, priming 2 INSTRUCTIONS, information, priming, directions, instruction, preparation, guidance, preamble, rundown

briefly *adverb* 1 QUICKLY, shortly, precisely, casually, temporarily, abruptly, hastily, briskly, momentarily, hurriedly, curtly, summarily, fleetingly, cursorily 2 IN OUTLINE, in brief, in passing, in a nutshell, concisely, in a few words

brigade *noun* 1 CORPS, company, force, unit, division, troop, squad, crew, team, outfit, regiment, contingent, squadron, detachment 2 GROUP, party, body, band, camp, squad, organization, crew, bunch (*informal*)

bright *adjective* 1 VIVID, rich, brilliant, intense, glowing, colourful, highly-coloured 2 SHINING, flashing, beaming, glowing, blazing, sparkling, glittering, dazzling, illuminated, gleaming, shimmering, twinkling, radiant, luminous, glistening, resplendent, scintillating, lustrous, lambent, effulgent 3 (*informal*) INTELLIGENT, smart, clever, knowing, thinking, quick, aware, sharp, keen, acute, alert, rational, penetrating, enlightened, apt, astute, brainy, wide-awake, clear-headed, perspicacious, quick-witted << ANTONYM stupid 4 (*informal*) CLEVER, brilliant, smart, sensible, cunning, ingenious, inventive, canny 5 CHEERFUL, happy, glad, lively, jolly, merry, upbeat (*informal*), joyous, joyful, genial, chirpy (*informal*), sparky, vivacious, full of beans (*informal*), gay, light-hearted 6 PROMISING, good, encouraging, excellent, golden, optimistic, hopeful, favourable, prosperous, rosy, auspicious, propitious, palmy 7 SUNNY, clear, fair, pleasant, clement, lucid, cloudless, unclouded, sunlit << ANTONYM cloudy

brighten *verb* 1 CHEER UP, rally, take heart, perk up, buck up (*informal*), become cheerful << ANTONYM become gloomy 2 LIGHT UP, shine, glow, gleam, clear up, lighten, enliven << ANTONYM dim 3 ENLIVEN, animate, make brighter, vitalize 4 BECOME BRIGHTER, light up, glow, gleam, clear up

brightness *noun* 1 VIVIDNESS, intensity, brilliance, splendour, resplendence 2 (*informal*) INTELLIGENCE, intellect, brains (*informal*), awareness, sharpness, alertness, cleverness, quickness, acuity, brain power, smarts (*slang, chiefly US*), smartness

brilliance *or* **brilliancy** *noun* 1 CLEVERNESS, talent, wisdom, distinction, genius, excellence, greatness, aptitude, inventiveness, acuity, giftedness, braininess << ANTONYM stupidity 2 BRIGHTNESS, blaze, intensity, sparkle, glitter, dazzle, gleam, sheen, lustre, radiance, luminosity,

vividness, resplendence, effulgence, refulgence << ANTONYM darkness
3 SPLENDOUR, glamour, grandeur, magnificence, éclat, gorgeousness, illustriousness, pizzazz *or* pizazz (*informal*), gilt

brilliant *adjective* **1** INTELLIGENT, sharp, intellectual, alert, clever, quick, acute, profound, rational, penetrating, discerning, inventive, astute, brainy, perspicacious, quick-witted << ANTONYM stupid
2 EXPERT, masterly, talented, gifted, accomplished << ANTONYM untalented
3 SPLENDID, grand, famous, celebrated, rare, supreme, outstanding, remarkable, superb, magnificent, sterling, glorious, exceptional, notable, renowned, heroic, admirable, eminent, sublime, illustrious
4 BRIGHT, shining, intense, sparkling, glittering, dazzling, vivid, radiant, luminous, ablaze, resplendent, scintillating, lustrous, coruscating, refulgent, lambent
<< ANTONYM dark

brim *noun* RIM, edge, border, lip, margin, verge, brink, flange ▷ *verb* **1** BE FULL, spill, well over, run over, overflow, spill over, brim over **2** FILL, well over, fill up, overflow

brine *noun* SALT WATER, saline solution, pickling solution

bring *verb* **1** FETCH, take, carry, bear, transfer, deliver, transport, import, convey **2** TAKE, guide, conduct, accompany, escort, usher **3** CAUSE, produce, create, effect, occasion, result in, contribute to, inflict, wreak, engender **4** MAKE, force, influence, convince, persuade, prompt, compel, induce, move, dispose, sway, prevail on *or* upon ▷▷ **bring someone up** REAR, raise, support, train, develop, teach, nurse, breed, foster, educate, care for, nurture ▷▷ **bring something about** CAUSE, produce, create, effect, manage, achieve, occasion, realize, generate, accomplish, give rise to, make happen, effectuate, bring to pass ▷▷ **bring something down 1** OVERTURN, reduce, undermine, overthrow, abase **2** REDUCE, cut, drop, lower, slash, decrease **3** CUT DOWN, level, fell, hew, lop, raze **4** DEMOLISH, level, destroy, dismantle, flatten, knock down, pull down, tear down, bulldoze, raze, kennet (*Austral slang*), jeff (*Austral slang*) ▷▷ **bring something in 1** INTRODUCE, start, found, launch, establish, set up, institute, organize, pioneer, initiate, usher in, inaugurate **2** PRODUCE, return, net, realize, generate, be worth, yield,

gross, fetch, accrue ▷▷ **bring something off** ACCOMPLISH, achieve, perform, carry out, succeed, execute, discharge, pull off, carry off, bring to pass ▷▷ **bring something up** MENTION, raise, introduce, point out, refer to, allude to, broach, call attention to, speak about *or* of

brink *noun* EDGE, point, limit, border, lip, margin, boundary, skirt, frontier, fringe, verge, threshold, rim, brim

brio *noun* ENERGY, spirit, enthusiasm, dash, pep, zip (*informal*), animation, vigour, verve, zest, panache, gusto, get-up-and-go (*informal*), élan, vivacity, liveliness

brisk *adjective* **1** QUICK, lively, energetic, active, vigorous, animated, bustling, speedy, nimble, agile, sprightly, vivacious, spry
<< ANTONYM slow **2** SHORT, sharp, brief, blunt, rude, tart, abrupt, no-nonsense, terse, gruff, pithy, brusque, offhand, monosyllabic, ungracious, uncivil, snappish
3 INVIGORATING, fresh, biting, sharp, keen, stimulating, crisp, bracing, refreshing, exhilarating, nippy << ANTONYM tiring

briskly *adverb* **1** QUICKLY, smartly, promptly, rapidly, readily, actively, efficiently, vigorously, energetically, pronto (*informal*), nimbly, posthaste **2** RAPIDLY, quickly, apace, pdq (*slang*) **3** BRUSQUELY, firmly, decisively, incisively

bristle *noun* HAIR, spine, thorn, whisker, barb, stubble, prickle ▷ *verb* **1** STAND UP, rise, prickle, stand on end, horripilate **2** BE ANGRY, rage, seethe, flare up, bridle, see red, be infuriated, spit (*informal*), go ballistic (*slang, chiefly US*), be maddened, wig out (*slang*), get your dander up (*slang*) **3** ABOUND, crawl, be alive, hum, swarm, teem, be thick

Briton *noun* BRIT (*informal*), limey (*US & Canad slang*), Briter, pommy *or* pom (*Austral & NZ slang*), Anglo-Saxon

brittle *adjective* **1** FRAGILE, delicate, crisp, crumbling, frail, crumbly, breakable, shivery, friable, frangible, shatterable << ANTONYM tough **2** TENSE, nervous, edgy, stiff, wired (*slang*), irritable, curt

broach *verb* **1** BRING UP, approach, introduce, mention, speak of, talk of, open up, hint at, touch on, raise the subject of **2** OPEN, crack, pierce, puncture, uncork

broad *adjective* **1** WIDE, large, ample, generous, expansive **2** LARGE, huge, comfortable, vast, extensive, ample, spacious, expansive, roomy, voluminous, capacious, uncrowded, commodious, beamy (*of a ship*), sizable *or* sizeable << ANTONYM narrow **3** FULL, general, comprehensive, complete, wide, global, catholic, sweeping, extensive, wide-ranging, umbrella, thorough, unlimited, inclusive, far-reaching, exhaustive, all-inclusive, all-embracing, overarching, encyclopedic **4** UNIVERSAL, general, common, wide, sweeping, worldwide, widespread, wide-ranging, far-reaching **5** GENERAL, loose, vague, approximate, indefinite, ill-defined, inexact, nonspecific, unspecific, undetailed **6** CLEAR, open, full, plain **7** VULGAR, blue, dirty, gross, crude, rude, naughty, coarse, indecent, improper, suggestive, risqué, boorish, uncouth, unrefined, ribald, indelicate, near the knuckle (*informal*), indecorous, unmannerly

broadcast *noun* TRANSMISSION, show, programme, telecast ▷ *verb* **1** TRANSMIT, show, send, air, radio, cable, beam, send out, relay, televise, disseminate, put on the air **2** MAKE PUBLIC, report, announce, publish, spread, advertise, proclaim, circulate, disseminate, promulgate, shout from the rooftops (*informal*)

broaden *verb* EXPAND, increase, develop, spread, extend, stretch, open up, swell, supplement, widen, enlarge, augment << ANTONYM restrict

broadly *adverb* **1** WIDELY, greatly, hugely, vastly, extensively, expansively **2** GENERALLY, commonly, widely, universally, popularly << ANTONYM narrowly

broadside *noun* ATTACK, criticism, censure, swipe, denunciation, diatribe, philippic

brochure *noun* BOOKLET, advertisement, leaflet, hand-out, circular, pamphlet, folder, mailshot, handbill

broekies *plural noun* (*S African informal*) UNDERPANTS, pants, briefs, drawers, knickers, panties, boxer shorts, Y-fronts (*trademark*), underdaks (*Austral slang*)

broke *adjective* (*informal*) PENNILESS, short, ruined, bust (*informal*), bankrupt, impoverished, in the red, cleaned out (*slang*), insolvent, down and out, skint (*Brit slang*), strapped for cash (*informal*), dirt-poor (*informal*), flat broke (*informal*), penurious, on your uppers, stony-broke (*Brit slang*), in queer street, without two pennies to rub together (*informal*), without a penny to your name << ANTONYM rich

broken *adjective* **1** INTERRUPTED, disturbed, incomplete, erratic, disconnected, intermittent, fragmentary, spasmodic,

discontinuous **2** IMPERFECT, halting, hesitating, stammering, disjointed **3** SMASHED, destroyed, burst, shattered, fragmented, fractured, demolished, severed, ruptured, rent, separated, shivered **4** DEFECTIVE, not working, ruined, imperfect, out of order, not functioning, on the blink (*slang*), on its last legs, kaput (*informal*) **5** VIOLATED, forgotten, ignored, disregarded, not kept, infringed, retracted, disobeyed, dishonoured, transgressed, traduced **6** DEFEATED, beaten, crushed, humbled, crippled, tamed, subdued, oppressed, overpowered, vanquished, demoralized, browbeaten

broken-down *adjective* NOT IN WORKING ORDER, old, worn out, out of order, dilapidated, not functioning, out of commission, on the blink (*slang*), inoperative, kaput (*informal*), in disrepair, on the fritz (*US slang*)

brokenhearted *adjective* HEARTBROKEN, devastated, disappointed, despairing, miserable, choked, desolate, mournful, prostrated, grief-stricken, sorrowful, wretched, disconsolate, inconsolable, crestfallen, down in the dumps (*informal*), heart-sick

broker *noun* DEALER, marketer, agent, trader, supplier, merchant, entrepreneur, negotiator, chandler, mediator, intermediary, wholesaler, middleman, factor, purveyor, go-between, tradesman, merchandiser

bronze *adjective* REDDISH-BROWN, copper, tan, rust, chestnut, brownish, copper-coloured, yellowish-brown, reddish-tan, metallic brown

brood *noun* **1** OFFSPRING, young, issue, breed, infants, clutch, hatch, litter, chicks, progeny **2** CHILDREN, family, offspring, progeny, nearest and dearest, flesh and blood, ainga (*NZ*) ▷ *verb* THINK, obsess, muse, ponder, fret, meditate, agonize, mull over, mope, ruminate, eat your heart out, dwell upon, repine

brook¹ *noun* STREAM, burn (*Scot & N English*), rivulet, gill (*dialect*), beck, watercourse, rill, streamlet, runnel (*literary*)

brook² *verb* TOLERATE, stand, allow, suffer, accept, bear, stomach, endure, swallow, hack (*slang*), abide, put up with (*informal*), withstand, countenance, support, thole (*dialect*)

brothel *noun* WHOREHOUSE, red-light district,

bordello, cathouse (*US slang*), house of ill repute, knocking shop (*slang*), bawdy house (*archaic*), house of prostitution, bagnio, house of ill fame, stews (*archaic*)

brother *noun* 1 MALE SIBLING 2 COMRADE, partner, colleague, associate, mate, pal (*informal*), companion, cock (*Brit informal*), chum (*informal*), fellow member, confrère, compeer 3 MONK, cleric, friar, monastic, religious, regular

brotherhood *noun* 1 FELLOWSHIP, kinship, companionship, comradeship, friendliness, camaraderie, brotherliness 2 ASSOCIATION, order, union, community, society, league, alliance, clan, guild, fraternity, clique, coterie

brotherly *adjective* FRATERNAL, friendly, neighbourly, sympathetic, affectionate, benevolent, kind, amicable, altruistic, philanthropic

brow *noun* 1 FOREHEAD, temple 2 TOP, summit, peak, edge, tip, crown, verge, brink, rim, crest, brim

brown *adjective* 1 BRUNETTE, dark, bay, coffee, chocolate, brick, toasted, ginger, rust, chestnut, hazel, dun, auburn, tawny, umber, donkey brown, fuscous 2 TANNED, browned, bronze, bronzed, tan, dusky, sunburnt ▷ *verb* FRY, cook, grill, sear, sauté

browse *verb* 1 SKIM, scan, glance at, survey, look through, look round, dip into, leaf through, peruse, flip through, examine cursorily 2 GRAZE, eat, feed, crop, pasture, nibble

bruise *noun* DISCOLORATION, mark, injury, trauma (*pathology*), blemish, black mark, contusion, black-and-blue mark ▷ *verb* 1 HURT, injure, mark, blacken 2 DAMAGE, mark, mar, blemish, discolour 3 INJURE, hurt, pain, wound, slight, insult, sting, offend, grieve, displease, rile, pique

bruiser *noun* (*informal*) TOUGH, heavy (*slang*), rough (*informal*), bully, thug, gorilla (*informal*), hard man, rowdy, tough guy, hoodlum, bully boy, ruffian, roughneck (*slang*)

brunt *noun* FULL FORCE, force, pressure, violence, shock, stress, impact, strain, burden, thrust

brush¹ *noun* 1 BROOM, sweeper, besom 2 CONFLICT, fight, clash, set-to (*informal*), scrap (*informal*), confrontation, skirmish, tussle, fracas, spot of bother (*informal*), slight engagement 3 ENCOUNTER, meeting, confrontation, rendezvous ▷ *verb* 1 CLEAN, wash, polish, buff 2 TOUCH, come into

contact with, sweep, kiss, stroke, glance, flick, scrape, graze, caress ▷▷ **brush someone off** (*slang*) IGNORE, cut, reject, dismiss, slight, blank (*slang*), put down, snub, disregard, scorn, disdain, spurn, rebuff, repudiate, disown, cold-shoulder, kiss off (*slang, chiefly US & Canad*), send to Coventry ▷▷ **brush something aside** DISMISS, ignore, discount, override, disregard, sweep aside, have no time for, kiss off (*slang, chiefly US & Canad*) ▷▷ **brush something up** *or* **brush up on something** REVISE, study, go over, cram, polish up, read up on, relearn, bone up on (*informal*), refresh your memory

brush² *noun* SHRUBS, bushes, scrub, underwood, undergrowth, thicket, copse, brushwood

brusque *adjective* CURT, short, sharp, blunt, tart, abrupt, hasty, terse, surly, gruff, impolite, monosyllabic, discourteous, unmannerly << ANTONYM polite

brutal *adjective* 1 CRUEL, harsh, savage, grim, vicious, ruthless, ferocious, callous, sadistic, heartless, atrocious, inhuman, merciless, cold-blooded, inhumane, brutish, bloodthirsty, remorseless, barbarous, pitiless, uncivilized, hard-hearted << ANTONYM kind 2 HARSH, tough, severe, rough, rude, indifferent, insensitive, callous, merciless, unconcerned, uncaring, gruff, bearish, tactless, unfeeling, impolite, uncivil, unmannerly << ANTONYM sensitive

brutality *noun* CRUELTY, atrocity, ferocity, savagery, ruthlessness, barbarism, inhumanity, barbarity, viciousness, brutishness, bloodthirstiness, savageness

brutally *adverb* CRUELLY, fiercely, savagely, ruthlessly, viciously, mercilessly, ferociously, remorselessly, in cold blood, callously, murderously, pitilessly, heartlessly, inhumanly, barbarously, brutishly, barbarically, hardheartedly

brute *noun* 1 SAVAGE, devil, monster, beast, barbarian, fiend, swine, ogre, ghoul, sadist 2 BEAST, animal, creature, wild animal ▷ *adjective* PHYSICAL, bodily, mindless, instinctive, senseless, unthinking

brutish *adjective* COARSE, stupid, gross, cruel, savage, crude, vulgar, barbarian, crass, boorish, uncouth, loutish, subhuman, swinish

bubble *noun* AIR BALL, drop, bead, blister, blob, droplet, globule, vesicle ▷ *verb* 1 BOIL, seethe 2 FOAM, fizz, froth, churn, agitate, percolate, effervesce 3 GURGLE, splash, murmur, trickle, ripple, babble, trill, burble, lap, purl, plash

bubbly *adjective* **1** LIVELY, happy, excited, animated, merry, bouncy, elated, sparky, alive and kicking, full of beans (*informal*) **2** FROTHY, sparkling, fizzy, effervescent, carbonated, foamy, sudsy, lathery

buccaneer *noun* PIRATE, privateer, corsair, freebooter, sea-rover

buckle *noun* FASTENER, catch, clip, clasp, hasp ▷ *verb* **1** FASTEN, close, secure, hook, clasp **2** DISTORT, bend, warp, crumple, contort **3** COLLAPSE, bend, twist, fold, give way, subside, cave in, crumple ▷▷ **buckle down** (*informal*) APPLY YOURSELF, set to, fall to, pitch in, get busy, get cracking (*informal*), exert yourself, put your shoulder to the wheel

bud *noun* SHOOT, branch, sprout, twig, sprig, offshoot, scion ▷ *verb* DEVELOP, grow, shoot, sprout, burgeon, burst forth, pullulate

budding *adjective* DEVELOPING, beginning, growing, promising, potential, burgeoning, fledgling, embryonic

buddy *noun* (*Chiefly US & Canad*) FRIEND, mate (*informal*), pal, companion, comrade, chum (*informal*), crony, main man (*slang, chiefly US*), homeboy (*slang, chiefly US*), cobber (*Austral & NZ old-fashioned informal*), E hoa (*NZ*)

budge *verb* **1** YIELD, change, bend, concede, surrender, comply, give way, capitulate **2** PERSUADE, influence, convince, sway **3** MOVE, roll, slide, stir, give way, change position **4** DISLODGE, move, push, roll, remove, transfer, shift, slide, stir, propel

budget *noun* ALLOWANCE, means, funds, income, finances, resources, allocation ▷ *verb* PLAN, estimate, allocate, cost, ration, apportion, cost out

buff¹ *adjective* FAWN, cream, tan, beige, yellowish, ecru, straw-coloured, sand-coloured, yellowish-brown, biscuit-coloured, camel-coloured, oatmeal-coloured ▷ *verb* POLISH, clean, smooth, brush, shine, rub, wax, brighten, burnish ▷▷ **in the buff** NAKED, bare, nude, in the raw (*informal*), unclothed, in the altogether (*informal*), buck naked (*slang*), unclad, in your birthday suit (*informal*), scuddy (*slang*), without a stitch on (*informal*), with bare skin, in the bare scud (*slang*)

buff² *noun* (*informal*) EXPERT, fan, addict, enthusiast, freak (*informal*), admirer, whizz (*informal*), devotee, connoisseur, fiend (*informal*), grandmaster, hotshot (*informal*),

aficionado, wonk (*informal*), maven (*US*), fundi (*S African*)

buffer *noun* SAFEGUARD, screen, shield, cushion, intermediary, bulwark

buffet¹ *noun* **1** SMORGASBORD, counter, cold table **2** SNACK BAR, café, cafeteria, brasserie, salad bar, refreshment counter

buffet² *verb* KNOCK, push, bang, rap, slap, bump, smack, shove, thump, cuff, jolt, wallop (*informal*), box

buffoon *noun* CLOWN, fool, comic, comedian, wag, joker, jester, dag (*NZ informal*), harlequin, droll, silly billy (*informal*), joculator *or (fem.)* joculatrix

bug *noun* **1** (*informal*) ILLNESS, disease, complaint, virus, infection, disorder, disability, sickness, ailment, malaise, affliction, malady, lurgy (*informal*) **2** FAULT, failing, virus, error, defect, flaw, blemish, imperfection, glitch, gremlin **3** (*informal*) MANIA, passion, rage, obsession, craze, fad, thing (*informal*) ▷ *verb* **1** TAP, eavesdrop, listen in on, wiretap **2** (*informal*) ANNOY, bother, disturb, needle (*informal*), plague, irritate, harass, hassle (*informal*), aggravate (*informal*), badger, gall, nettle, pester, vex, irk, get under your skin (*informal*), get on your nerves (*informal*), nark (*Brit, Austral & NZ slang*), get up your nose (*informal*), be on your back (*slang*), get in your hair (*informal*), get on your wick (*Brit slang*), hack you off (*informal*)

build *verb* **1** CONSTRUCT, make, raise, put up, assemble, erect, fabricate, form << ANTONYM demolish **2** ESTABLISH, start, begin, found, base, set up, institute, constitute, initiate, originate, formulate, inaugurate << ANTONYM finish **3** DEVELOP, increase, improve, extend, strengthen, intensify, enlarge, amplify, augment << ANTONYM decrease ▷ *noun* PHYSIQUE, form, body, figure, shape, structure, frame ▷▷ **build something up** INCREASE, develop, improve, extend, expand, add to, strengthen, enhance, reinforce, intensify, heighten, fortify, amplify, augment

building *noun* STRUCTURE, house, construction, dwelling, erection, edifice, domicile, pile

build-up *noun* **1** INCREASE, development, growth, expansion, accumulation, enlargement, escalation, upsurge, intensification, augmentation **2** ACCUMULATION, accretion **3** HYPE, promotion, publicity, plug (*informal*), puff, razzmatazz (*slang*), brouhaha, ballyhoo

(*informal*)

built-in *adjective* ESSENTIAL, integral, included, incorporated, inherent, implicit, in-built, intrinsic, inseparable, immanent

bulbous *adjective* BULGING, rounded, swelling, swollen, bloated, convex

bulge *verb* 1 SWELL OUT, project, expand, swell, stand out, stick out, protrude, puff out, distend, bag 2 STICK OUT, stand out, protrude ▷ *noun* 1 LUMP, swelling, bump, projection, hump, protuberance, protrusion << ANTONYM hollow 2 INCREASE, rise, boost, surge, intensification

bulk *noun* 1 SIZE, volume, dimensions, magnitude, substance, vastness, amplitude, immensity, bigness, largeness, massiveness 2 WEIGHT, size, mass, heaviness, poundage, portliness 3 MAJORITY, mass, most, body, quantity, best part, major part, lion's share, better part, generality, preponderance, main part, plurality, nearly all, greater number ▷▷ **bulk large** BE IMPORTANT, dominate, loom, stand out, loom large, carry weight, preponderate, threaten

bulky *adjective* LARGE, big, huge, heavy, massive, enormous, substantial, immense, mega (*slang*), very large, mammoth, colossal, cumbersome, weighty, hulking, unwieldy, ponderous, voluminous, unmanageable, elephantine, massy, ginormous (*informal*), humongous *or* humungous (*US slang*) << ANTONYM small

bulldoze *verb* 1 DEMOLISH, level, destroy, flatten, knock down, tear down, raze, kennet (*Austral slang*), jeff (*Austral slang*) 2 (*informal*) PUSH, force, drive, thrust, shove, propel 3 (*informal*) FORCE, bully, intimidate, railroad (*informal*), cow, hector, coerce, dragoon, browbeat, put the screws on

bullet *noun* PROJECTILE, ball, shot, missile, slug, pellet

bulletin *noun* REPORT, account, statement, message, communication, announcement, dispatch, communiqué, notification, news flash

bully *noun* PERSECUTOR, tough, oppressor, tormentor, bully boy, browbeater, coercer, ruffian, intimidator ▷ *verb* 1 PERSECUTE, intimidate, torment, hound, oppress, pick on, victimize, terrorize, push around (*slang*), ill-treat, ride roughshod over, maltreat, tyrannize, overbear 2 FORCE, coerce, railroad (*informal*), bulldoze (*informal*), dragoon, pressurize, browbeat, cow, hector, press-gang, domineer, bullyrag

bulwark *noun* 1 FORTIFICATION, defence, bastion, buttress, rampart, redoubt, outwork 2 DEFENCE, support, safeguard, security, guard, buffer, mainstay

bumbling *adjective* CLUMSY, awkward, blundering, bungling, incompetent, inefficient, lumbering, inept, maladroit, unco (*Austral slang*) << ANTONYM efficient

bump *verb* 1 KNOCK, hit, strike, crash, smash, slam, bang 2 JERK, shake, bounce, rattle, jar, jog, lurch, jolt, jostle, jounce ▷ *noun* 1 KNOCK, hit, blow, shock, impact, rap, collision, thump 2 THUD, crash, knock, smash, bang, smack, thump, clump, wallop (*informal*), clunk, clonk 3 LUMP, swelling, bulge, hump, node, nodule, protuberance, contusion ▷▷ **bump into someone** (*informal*) MEET, encounter, come across, run into, run across, meet up with, chance upon, happen upon, light upon ▷▷ **bump someone off** (*slang*) MURDER, kill, assassinate, remove, do in (*slang*), eliminate, take out (*slang*), wipe out (*informal*), dispatch, finish off, do away with, blow away (*slang, chiefly US*), knock off (*slang*), liquidate, rub out (*US slang*)

bumper *adjective* EXCEPTIONAL, excellent, exo (*Austral slang*), massive, unusual, mega (*slang*), jumbo (*informal*), abundant, whacking (*informal, chiefly Brit*), spanking (*informal*), whopping (*informal*), bountiful

bumpy *adjective* 1 UNEVEN, rough, pitted, irregular, rutted, lumpy, potholed, knobby 2 JOLTING, jarring, bouncy, choppy, jerky, bone-breaking, jolty

bunch *noun* 1 (*informal*) GROUP, band, crowd, party, team, troop, gathering, crew (*informal*), gang, knot, mob, flock, swarm, multitude, posse (*informal*), bevy 2 BOUQUET, spray, sheaf 3 CLUSTER, clump ▷▷ **bunch together** *or* **up** GROUP, crowd, mass, collect, assemble, cluster, flock, herd, huddle, congregate

bundle *noun* BUNCH, group, collection, mass, pile, quantity, stack, heap, rick, batch, accumulation, assortment ▷ *verb* PUSH, thrust, shove, throw, rush, hurry, hasten, jostle, hustle ▷▷ **bundle someone up** WRAP UP, swathe, muffle up, clothe warmly ▷▷ **bundle something up** PACKAGE, tie, pack, bind, wrap, tie up, bale, fasten, truss, tie together, palletize

bungle *verb* MESS UP, blow (*slang*), ruin, spoil, blunder, fudge, screw up (*informal*), botch, cock up (*Brit slang*), miscalculate, make a mess of, mismanage, muff, foul up, make a nonsense of (*informal*), bodge (*informal*), make a pig's ear of (*informal*), flub (*US slang*), crool *or* cruel (*Austral slang*), louse up (*slang*) << ANTONYM accomplish

bungling *adjective* INCOMPETENT, blundering, awkward, clumsy, inept, botching, cack-handed (*informal*), maladroit, ham-handed (*informal*), unskilful, ham-fisted (*informal*), unco (*Austral slang*)

bunk¹ *noun* ▷▷ **do a bunk** (*Brit slang*) RUN AWAY, flee, bolt, clear out (*informal*), beat it (*slang*), abscond, decamp, do a runner (*slang*), run for it (*informal*), cut and run (*informal*), scram (*informal*), fly the coop (*US & Canad informal*), skedaddle (*informal*), take a powder (*US & Canad slang*), take it on the lam (*US & Canad slang*), do a Skase (*Austral informal*)

bunk² *or* **bunkum** *noun* (*informal*) NONSENSE, rubbish, rot, crap (*slang*), garbage (*informal*), trash, hot air (*informal*), tosh (*slang, chiefly Brit*), bilge (*informal*), twaddle, tripe (*informal*), guff (*slang*), havers (*Scot*), moonshine, baloney (*informal*), hogwash, bizzo (*Austral slang*), bull's wool (*Austral & NZ slang*), hokum (*slang, chiefly US & Canad*), piffle (*informal*), tomfoolery, poppycock (*informal*), balderdash, bosh (*informal*), eyewash (*informal*), kak (*S African taboo slang*), stuff and nonsense, hooey (*slang*), tommyrot, horsefeathers (*US slang*), tarradiddle

buoy *noun* FLOAT, guide, signal, marker, beacon ▷▷ **buoy someone up** ENCOURAGE, support, boost, cheer, sustain, hearten, cheer up, keep afloat, gee up

buoyancy *noun* **1** FLOATABILITY, lightness, weightlessness **2** CHEERFULNESS, bounce (*informal*), pep, animation, good humour, high spirits, zing (*informal*), liveliness, spiritedness, cheeriness, sunniness

buoyant *adjective* **1** CHEERFUL, happy, bright, lively, sunny, animated, upbeat (*informal*), joyful, carefree, bouncy, breezy, genial, jaunty, chirpy (*informal*), sparky, vivacious, debonair, blithe, full of beans (*informal*), peppy (*informal*), light-hearted << ANTONYM gloomy **2** FLOATING, light, floatable

burden *noun* **1** TROUBLE, care, worry, trial, weight, responsibility, stress, strain, anxiety, sorrow, grievance, affliction, onus, albatross, millstone, encumbrance **2** LOAD, weight, cargo, freight, bale, consignment, encumbrance ▷ *verb* WEIGH DOWN, worry, load, tax, strain, bother, overwhelm, handicap, oppress, inconvenience, overload, saddle with, encumber, trammel, incommode

burdensome *adjective* TROUBLESOME, trying, taxing, difficult, heavy, crushing, exacting, oppressive, weighty, onerous, irksome

bureau *noun* **1** AGENCY **2** OFFICE, department, section, branch, station, unit, division, subdivision **3** DESK, writing desk

bureaucracy *noun* **1** GOVERNMENT, officials, authorities, administration, ministry, the system, civil service, directorate, officialdom, corridors of power **2** RED TAPE, regulations, officialdom, officialese, bumbledom

bureaucrat *noun* OFFICIAL, minister, officer, administrator, civil servant, public servant, functionary, apparatchik, office-holder, mandarin

burglar *noun* HOUSEBREAKER, thief, robber, pilferer, filcher, cat burglar, sneak thief, picklock

burglary *noun* BREAKING AND ENTERING, housebreaking, break-in, home invasion (*Austral & NZ*)

burial *noun* FUNERAL, interment, burying, obsequies, entombment, inhumation, exequies, sepulture

burial ground *noun* GRAVEYARD, cemetery, churchyard, necropolis, God's acre

burlesque *noun* PARODY, mockery, satire, caricature, send-up (*Brit informal*), spoof (*informal*), travesty, takeoff (*informal*) ▷ *adjective* SATIRICAL, comic, mocking, mock, farcical, travestying, ironical, parodic, mock-heroic, caricatural, hudibrastic

burly *adjective* BRAWNY, strong, powerful, big, strapping, hefty, muscular, sturdy, stout, bulky, stocky, hulking, beefy (*informal*), well-built, thickset << ANTONYM scrawny

burn *verb* **1** BE ON FIRE, blaze, be ablaze, smoke, flame, glow, flare, flicker, go up in flames **2** SET ON FIRE, light, ignite, kindle, incinerate, reduce to ashes **3** SCORCH, toast, sear, char, singe, brand **4** STING, hurt, smart, tingle, bite, pain **5** BE PASSIONATE, blaze, be excited, be aroused, be inflamed **6** SEETHE, fume, be angry, simmer, smoulder

burning *adjective* **1** INTENSE, passionate, earnest, eager, frantic, frenzied, ardent, fervent, impassioned, zealous, vehement, all-consuming, fervid << ANTONYM mild **2** CRUCIAL, important, pressing, significant, essential, vital, critical, acute, compelling, urgent

burnish *verb* POLISH, shine, buff, brighten, rub up, furbish << ANTONYM scuff

burrow *noun* HOLE, shelter, tunnel, den, lair, retreat ▷ *verb* **1** DIG, tunnel, excavate **2** DELVE, search, dig, probe, ferret, rummage, forage, fossick (*Austral & NZ*)

burst *verb* **1** EXPLODE, blow up, break, split, crack, shatter, fragment, shiver, disintegrate, puncture, rupture **2** RUSH, run, break, break out, erupt, spout, gush forth **3** BARGE, charge, rush, shove ▷ *noun* **1** RUSH, surge, fit, outbreak, outburst, spate, gush, torrent, eruption, spurt, outpouring **2** EXPLOSION, crack, blast, blasting, bang, discharge

bury *verb* **1** INTER, lay to rest, entomb, sepulchre, consign to the grave, inearth, inhume, inurn << ANTONYM dig up **2** HIDE, cover, conceal, stash (*informal*), secrete, cache, stow away << ANTONYM uncover **3** SINK, embed, immerse, enfold **4** FORGET, draw a veil over, think no more of, put in the past, not give another thought to **5** ENGROSS, involve, occupy, interest, busy, engage, absorb, preoccupy, immerse

bush *noun* SHRUB, plant, hedge, thicket, shrubbery ▷▷ **the bush** THE WILDS, brush, scrub, woodland, backwoods, back country (*US*), scrubland, backlands (*US*)

bushy *adjective* THICK, bristling, spreading, rough, stiff, fuzzy, fluffy, unruly, shaggy, wiry, luxuriant, bristly

busily *adverb* ACTIVELY, briskly, intently, earnestly, strenuously, speedily, purposefully, diligently, energetically, assiduously, industriously

business *noun* **1** TRADE, selling, trading, industry, manufacturing, commerce, dealings, merchandising **2** ESTABLISHMENT, company, firm, concern, organization, corporation, venture, enterprise **3** PROFESSION, work, calling, job, line, trade, career, function, employment, craft, occupation, pursuit, vocation, métier **4** MATTER, issue, subject, point, problem, question, responsibility, task, duty, function, topic, assignment **5** CONCERN, affair

businesslike *adjective* EFFICIENT, professional, practical, regular, correct, organized, routine, thorough, systematic, orderly, matter-of-fact, methodical, well-ordered, workaday << ANTONYM inefficient

businessman *or* **businesswoman** *noun* EXECUTIVE, director, manager, merchant, capitalist, administrator, entrepreneur, tycoon, industrialist, financier, tradesman, homme d'affaires (*French*)

bust¹ *noun* BOSOM, breasts, chest, front

bust² (*informal*) *verb* **1** BREAK, smash, split, burst, shatter, fracture, rupture, break into fragments **2** ARREST, catch, lift (*slang*), raid, cop (*slang*), nail (*informal*), collar (*informal*), nab (*informal*), feel your collar (*slang*) ▷ *noun* ARREST, capture, raid, cop (*slang*) ▷▷ **go bust** GO BANKRUPT, fail, break, be ruined, become insolvent

bustle *verb* HURRY, tear, rush, dash, scramble, fuss, flutter, beetle, hasten, scuttle, scurry, scamper << ANTONYM idle ▷ *noun* ACTIVITY, to-do, stir, excitement, hurry, fuss, flurry, haste, agitation, commotion, ado, tumult, hurly-burly, pother << ANTONYM inactivity

bustling *adjective* BUSY, full, crowded, rushing, active, stirring, lively, buzzing, energetic, humming, swarming, thronged, hustling, teeming, astir

busy *adjective* **1** ACTIVE, brisk, diligent, industrious, assiduous, rushed off your feet << ANTONYM idle **2** OCCUPIED WITH, working, engaged in, on duty, employed in, hard at work, engrossed in, in harness, on active service << ANTONYM unoccupied **3** HECTIC, full, active, tiring, exacting, energetic, strenuous, on the go (*informal*) ▷▷ **busy yourself** OCCUPY YOURSELF, be engrossed, immerse yourself, involve yourself, amuse yourself, absorb yourself, employ yourself, engage yourself, keep busy *or* occupied

but *conjunction* HOWEVER, still, yet, nevertheless ▷ *preposition* EXCEPT (FOR), save, bar, barring, excepting, excluding, with the exception of ▷ *adverb* ONLY, just, simply, merely

butcher *noun* MURDERER, killer, slaughterer, slayer, destroyer, liquidator, executioner, cut-throat, exterminator ▷ *verb* **1** SLAUGHTER, prepare, carve, cut up, dress, cut, clean, joint **2** KILL, slaughter, massacre, destroy, cut down, assassinate, slay, liquidate, exterminate, put to the sword **3** MESS UP, destroy, ruin, wreck, spoil, mutilate, botch, bodge (*informal*)

butchery *noun* SLAUGHTER, killing, murder, massacre, bloodshed, carnage, mass murder, blood-letting, blood bath

butt¹ *noun* **1** END, handle, shaft, stock, shank, hilt, haft **2** STUB, end, base, foot, tip, tail, leftover, fag end (*informal*)

butt² *noun* TARGET, victim, object, point, mark, subject, dupe, laughing stock, Aunt Sally

butt³ *verb* KNOCK, push, bump, punch, buck, thrust, ram, shove, poke, buffet, prod, jab, bunt ▷▷ **butt in 1** INTERFERE, meddle, intrude, heckle, barge in (*informal*), stick your nose in, put your oar in **2** INTERRUPT, cut in, break in, chip in (*informal*), put your two cents in (*US slang*)

butt⁴ *noun* CASK, drum, barrel, cylinder

butter *noun* ▷▷ **butter someone up** FLATTER, coax, cajole, pander to, blarney, wheedle, suck up to (*informal*), soft-soap, fawn on *or* upon

buttocks *noun* BOTTOM, behind (*informal*), bum (*Brit slang*), backside (*informal*), seat, rear, tail (*informal*), butt (*US & Canad informal*), buns (*US slang*), rump, posterior, haunches, hindquarters, derrière (*euphemistic*), tush (*US slang*), fundament, gluteus maximus (*anatomy*), jacksy (*Brit slang*)

buttonhole *verb* DETAIN, catch, grab, intercept, accost, waylay, take aside

buttress *noun* SUPPORT, shore, prop, brace, pier, reinforcement, strut, mainstay, stanchion, stay, abutment ▷ *verb* SUPPORT, sustain, strengthen, shore, prop, reinforce, back up, brace, uphold, bolster, prop up, shore up, augment

buxom *adjective* PLUMP, ample, voluptuous, busty, well-rounded, curvaceous, comely, bosomy, full-bosomed << ANTONYM slender

buy *verb* PURCHASE, get, score (*slang*), secure, pay for, obtain, acquire, invest in, shop for, procure << ANTONYM sell ▷ *noun* PURCHASE, deal, bargain, acquisition, steal (*informal*), snip (*informal*), giveaway ▷▷ **buy someone off** BRIBE, square, fix (*informal*), pay off (*informal*), lure, corrupt, get at, suborn, grease

someone's palm (*slang*), influence by gifts, oil the palm of (*slang*)

buzz *verb* HUM, whizz, drone, whir ▷ *noun* **1** HUM, buzzing, murmur, drone, whir, bombilation *or* bombination (*literary*) **2** GOSSIP, news, report, latest (*informal*), word, scandal, rumour, whisper, dirt (*US slang*), gen (*Brit informal*), hearsay, scuttlebutt (*US slang*), goss (*informal*)

by *preposition* **1** THROUGH, under the aegis of, through the agency of **2** VIA, over, by way of **3** NEAR, past, along, close to, closest to, neighbouring, next to, beside, nearest to, adjoining, adjacent to ▷ *adverb* NEARBY, close, handy, at hand, within reach ▷▷ **by and by** PRESENTLY, shortly, soon, eventually, one day, before long, in a while, anon, in the course of time, erelong (*archaic or poetic*)

bygone *adjective* PAST, former, previous, lost, forgotten, ancient, of old, one-time, departed, extinct, gone by, erstwhile, antiquated, of yore, olden, past recall, sunk in oblivion << ANTONYM future

bypass *verb* **1** GET ROUND, avoid, evade, circumvent, outmanoeuvre, body-swerve (*Scot*) **2** GO ROUND, skirt, circumvent, depart from, deviate from, pass round, detour round << ANTONYM cross

bystander *noun* ONLOOKER, passer-by, spectator, witness, observer, viewer, looker-on, watcher, eyewitness << ANTONYM participant

byword *noun* SAYING, slogan, motto, maxim, gnome, adage, proverb, epithet, dictum, precept, aphorism, saw, apophthegm

Cc

cab *noun* TAXI, minicab, taxicab, hackney, hackney carriage

cabal *noun* **1** CLIQUE, set, party, league, camp, coalition, faction, caucus, junta, coterie, schism, confederacy, conclave **2** PLOT, scheme, intrigue, conspiracy, machination

cabin *noun* **1** ROOM, berth, quarters, compartment, deckhouse **2** HUT, shed, cottage, lodge, cot (*archaic*), shack, chalet, shanty, hovel, bothy, whare (*NZ*)

cabinet *noun* CUPBOARD, case, locker, dresser, closet, press, chiffonier

Cabinet *noun* COUNCIL, committee, administration, ministry, assembly, board

cache *noun* STORE, fund, supply, reserve, treasury, accumulation, stockpile, hoard, stash (*informal*)

cackle *verb* LAUGH, giggle, chuckle ▷ *noun* LAUGH, giggle, chuckle

cacophony *noun* DISCORD, racket, din, dissonance, disharmony, stridency

cad *noun* (*Old-fashioned, informal*) SCOUNDREL (*slang*), rat (*informal*), bounder (*Brit old-fashioned slang*), cur, knave, rotter (*slang, chiefly Brit*), heel, scumbag (*slang*), churl, dastard (*archaic*), wrong 'un (*Austral slang*)

cadence *noun* **1** INTONATION, accent, inflection, modulation **2** RHYTHM, beat, measure (*Prosody*), metre, pulse, throb, tempo, swing, lilt

café *noun* SNACK BAR, restaurant, cafeteria, coffee shop, brasserie, coffee bar, tearoom, lunchroom, eatery *or* eaterie

cage *noun* ENCLOSURE, pen, coop, hutch, pound, corral (*US*) ▷ *verb* SHUT UP, confine, restrain, imprison, lock up, mew, incarcerate, fence in, impound, coop up, immure, pound

cagey *or* **cagy** *adjective* (*informal*) GUARDED, reserved, careful, cautious, restrained, wary, discreet, shrewd, wily, reticent, noncommittal, chary << ANTONYM careless

cajole *verb* PERSUADE, tempt, lure, flatter, manoeuvre, seduce, entice, coax, beguile, wheedle, sweet-talk (*informal*), inveigle

cake *noun* BLOCK, bar, slab, lump, cube, loaf, mass ▷ *verb* SOLIDIFY, dry, consolidate, harden, thicken, congeal, coagulate, ossify, encrust

calamitous *adjective* DISASTROUS, terrible, devastating, tragic, fatal, deadly, dreadful, dire, catastrophic, woeful, ruinous, cataclysmic << ANTONYM fortunate

calamity *noun* DISASTER, tragedy, ruin, distress, reversal of fortune, hardship, catastrophe, woe, misfortune, downfall, adversity, scourge, mishap, affliction, trial, tribulation, misadventure, cataclysm, wretchedness, mischance << ANTONYM benefit

calculate *verb* **1** WORK OUT, value, judge, determine, estimate, count, reckon, weigh, consider, compute, rate, gauge, enumerate, figure **2** PLAN, design, aim, intend, frame, arrange, formulate, contrive

calculated *adjective* DELIBERATE, planned, considered, studied, intended, intentional, designed, aimed, purposeful, premeditated << ANTONYM unplanned

calculating *adjective* SCHEMING, designing, sharp, shrewd, cunning, contriving, sly, canny, devious, manipulative, crafty, Machiavellian << ANTONYM direct

calculation *noun* **1** COMPUTATION, working out, reckoning, figuring, estimate, forecast, judgment, estimation, result, answer **2** PLANNING, intention, deliberation, foresight, contrivance, forethought, circumspection, premeditation

calibrate *verb* MEASURE, gauge

calibre *or US* **caliber** *noun* **1** WORTH, quality, ability, talent, gifts, capacity, merit, distinction, faculty, endowment, stature **2** DIAMETER, bore, gauge, measure

call *verb* **1** NAME, entitle, dub, designate, term, style, label, describe as, christen, denominate **2** CONSIDER, think, judge, estimate, describe as, refer to as, regard as **3** CRY, announce, shout, scream, proclaim, yell, cry out, whoop << ANTONYM whisper **4** PHONE, contact, telephone, ring (up) (*informal, chiefly Brit*), give (someone) a bell (*Brit slang*) **5** HAIL, address, summon, contact, halloo **6** SUMMON, gather, invite, rally, assemble, muster, convene, convoke, collect << ANTONYM dismiss **7** WAKEN, arouse, awaken, rouse ▷ *noun* **1** VISIT **2** REQUEST, order, demand, appeal, notice, command, announcement, invitation, plea, summons, supplication **3** (usually used in a negative construction) NEED, cause, reason, grounds, occasion, excuse, justification, claim **4** ATTRACTION, draw, pull (*informal*), appeal, lure, attractiveness, allure, magnetism **5** CRY, shout, scream, yell, whoop << ANTONYM whisper ▷▷ **call for someone** FETCH, pick up, collect, uplift (*Scot*) ▷▷ **call for something 1** DEMAND, order, request, insist on, cry out for **2** REQUIRE, need, involve, demand, occasion, entail, necessitate ▷▷ **call on someone 1** REQUEST, ask, bid, invite, appeal to, summon, invoke, call upon, entreat, supplicate **2** VISIT, look up, drop in on, look in on, see ▷▷ **call someone up 1** TELEPHONE, phone, ring (*chiefly Brit*), buzz (*informal*), dial, call up, give someone a ring (*informal, chiefly Brit*), put a call through to, give someone a call, give someone a buzz (*informal*), give someone a bell (*Brit slang*), give someone a tinkle (*Brit informal*), get on the blower to (*informal*) **2** ENLIST, draft, recruit, muster

calling *noun* PROFESSION, work, business, line, trade, career, mission, employment, province, occupation, pursuit, vocation, walk of life, life's work, métier

callous *adjective* HEARTLESS, cold, harsh, hardened, indifferent, insensitive, hard-boiled (*informal*), unsympathetic, uncaring, soulless, hard-bitten, unfeeling, obdurate, case-hardened, hardhearted << ANTONYM compassionate

callousness *noun* HEARTLESSNESS, insensitivity, hardness, coldness, harshness, obduracy, soullessness, hardheartedness, obdurateness

callow *adjective* INEXPERIENCED, juvenile, naïve, immature, raw, untried, green, unsophisticated, puerile, guileless, jejune, unfledged

calm *adjective* **1** COOL, relaxed, composed, sedate, undisturbed, collected, unmoved, dispassionate, unfazed (*informal*), impassive, unflappable (*informal*), unruffled, unemotional, self-possessed, imperturbable, equable, keeping your cool, unexcited, unexcitable, as cool as a cucumber << ANTONYM excited **2** STILL, quiet, smooth, peaceful, mild, serene, tranquil, placid, halcyon, balmy, restful, windless, pacific << ANTONYM rough ▷ *noun* **1** PEACEFULNESS, peace, serenity, calmness **2** STILLNESS, peace, quiet, hush, serenity, tranquillity, repose, calmness, peacefulness **3** PEACE, calmness << ANTONYM disturbance ▷ *verb* **1** SOOTHE, settle, quiet, relax, appease, still, allay, assuage, quieten << ANTONYM excite **2** PLACATE, hush, pacify, mollify << ANTONYM aggravate

calmly *adverb* COOLLY, casually, sedately, serenely, nonchalantly, impassively, dispassionately, placidly, unflinchingly, equably, imperturbably, tranquilly, composedly, collectedly, self-possessedly

camaraderie *noun* COMRADESHIP, fellowship, brotherhood, companionship, togetherness, esprit de corps, good-fellowship, companionability

camouflage *noun* **1** PROTECTIVE COLOURING, mimicry, false appearance, deceptive markings **2** DISGUISE, front, cover, screen, blind, mask, cloak, guise, masquerade, subterfuge, concealment ▷ *verb* DISGUISE, cover, screen, hide, mask, conceal, obscure, veil, cloak, obfuscate << ANTONYM reveal

camp¹ *noun* **1** CAMP SITE, tents, encampment, camping ground **2** BIVOUAC, cantonment (*Military*)

camp² *adjective* (*informal*) **1** EFFEMINATE, campy (*informal*), camped up (*informal*), poncy (*slang*) **2** AFFECTED, mannered, artificial, posturing, ostentatious, campy (*informal*), camped up (*informal*)

campaign *noun* **1** DRIVE, appeal, movement, push (*informal*), offensive, crusade **2** OPERATION, drive, attack, movement, push, offensive, expedition, crusade, jihad

campaigner *noun* DEMONSTRATOR, champion, advocate, activist, reformer, crusader

canal *noun* WATERWAY, channel, passage, conduit, duct, watercourse

cancel *verb* 1 CALL OFF, drop, abandon, forget about 2 ANNUL, abolish, repeal, abort, quash, do away with, revoke, repudiate, rescind, obviate, abrogate, countermand, eliminate ▷▷ **cancel something out** COUNTERBALANCE, offset, make up for, compensate for, redeem, neutralize, nullify, obviate, balance out

cancellation *noun* 1 ABANDONMENT, abandoning 2 ANNULMENT, abolition, repeal, elimination, quashing, revocation

cancer *noun* 1 GROWTH, tumour, carcinoma (*Pathology*), malignancy 2 EVIL, corruption, rot, sickness, blight, pestilence, canker

candid *adjective* 1 HONEST, just, open, truthful, fair, plain, straightforward, blunt, sincere, outspoken, downright, impartial, forthright, upfront (*informal*), unequivocal, unbiased, guileless, unprejudiced, free, round, frank << ANTONYM diplomatic 2 INFORMAL, impromptu, uncontrived, unposed

candidate *noun* CONTENDER, competitor, applicant, nominee, entrant, claimant, contestant, suitor, aspirant, possibility, runner

candour *noun* HONESTY, simplicity, fairness, sincerity, impartiality, frankness, directness, truthfulness, outspokenness, forthrightness, straightforwardness, ingenuousness, artlessness, guilelessness, openness, unequivocalness, naïveté << ANTONYM dishonesty

cannabis *noun* MARIJUANA, pot (*slang*), dope (*slang*), hash (*slang*), blow (*slang*), smoke (*informal*), stuff (*slang*), leaf (*slang*), tea (*US slang*), grass (*slang*), chronic (*US slang*), weed (*slang*), hemp, gage (*US dated slang*), hashish, mary jane (*US slang*), ganja, bhang, kif, sinsemilla, dagga (*S African*), charas

cannon *noun* GUN, big gun, artillery piece, field gun, mortar

canny *adjective* SHREWD, knowing, sharp, acute, careful, wise, clever, subtle, cautious, prudent, astute, on the ball (*informal*), artful, judicious, circumspect, perspicacious, sagacious, worldly-wise << ANTONYM inept

canon *noun* 1 RULE, standard, principle, regulation, formula, criterion, dictate, statute, yardstick, precept 2 LIST, index, catalogue, syllabus, roll

canopy *noun* AWNING, covering, shade, shelter, sunshade

cant[1] *noun* 1 HYPOCRISY, pretence, lip service, humbug, insincerity, pretentiousness, sanctimoniousness, pious platitudes, affected piety, sham holiness 2 JARGON, slang, vernacular, patter, lingo, argot

cant[2] *verb* TILT, angle, slope, incline, slant, bevel, rise

cantankerous *adjective* BAD-TEMPERED, contrary, perverse, irritable, crusty, grumpy, disagreeable, cranky (*US, Canad & Irish informal*), irascible, tetchy, ratty (*Brit & NZ informal*), testy, quarrelsome, waspish, grouchy (*informal*), peevish, crabby, choleric, crotchety (*informal*), ill-humoured, captious, difficult <<< ANTONYM cheerful

canter *verb* JOG, lope ▷ *noun* JOG, lope, easy gait, dogtrot

canvass *verb* 1 CAMPAIGN, solicit votes, electioneer 2 POLL, study, examine, investigate, analyse, scan, inspect, sift, scrutinize

canyon *noun* GORGE, pass, gulf, valley, clough (*dialect*), gully, ravine, defile, gulch (*US & Canad*), coulee (*US*)

cap *verb* 1 (*informal*) BEAT, top, better, exceed, eclipse, lick (*informal*), surpass, transcend, outstrip, outdo, run rings around (*informal*), put in the shade, overtop 2 TOP, cover, crown

capability *noun* ABILITY, means, power, potential, facility, capacity, qualification(s), faculty, competence, proficiency, wherewithal, potentiality << ANTONYM inability

capable *adjective* 1 ABLE, fitted, suited, adapted, adequate << ANTONYM incapable 2 ACCOMPLISHED, experienced, masterly, qualified, talented, gifted, efficient, clever, intelligent, competent, apt, skilful, adept, proficient << ANTONYM incompetent

capacious *adjective* SPACIOUS, wide, broad, vast, substantial, comprehensive, extensive, generous, ample, expansive, roomy, voluminous, commodious, sizable *or* sizeable << ANTONYM limited

capacity *noun* 1 ABILITY, power, strength, facility, gift, intelligence, efficiency, genius, faculty, capability, forte, readiness, aptitude, aptness, competence *or* competency 2 SIZE, room, range, space, volume, extent, dimensions, scope, magnitude, compass, amplitude **3** FUNCTION, position, role, post, appointment, province, sphere, service, office

cape *noun* HEADLAND, point, head, peninsula, ness (*archaic*), promontory

caper *verb* DANCE, trip, spring, jump, bound, leap, bounce, hop, skip, romp, frolic, cavort, frisk, gambol ▷ *noun* ESCAPADE, sport, stunt, mischief, lark (*informal*), prank, jest, practical joke, high jinks, antics, jape, shenanigan (*informal*)

capital *noun* MONEY, funds, stock, investment(s), property, cash, finance, finances, financing, resources, assets, wealth, principal, means, wherewithal ▷ *adjective* (*Old-fashioned*) FIRST-RATE, fine, excellent, superb, sterling, splendid, world-class

capitalism *noun* PRIVATE ENTERPRISE, free enterprise, private ownership, laissez faire *or* laisser faire

capitalize *verb* SELL, put up for sale, trade, dispose of ▷▷ **capitalize on something** TAKE ADVANTAGE OF, exploit, benefit from, profit from, make the most of, gain from, cash in on (*informal*)

capitulate *verb* GIVE IN, yield, concede, submit, surrender, comply, give up, come to terms, succumb, cave in (*informal*), relent << ANTONYM resist

capitulation *noun* SURRENDER, yielding, submission, cave-in (*informal*)

caprice *noun* WHIM, notion, impulse, freak, fad, quirk, vagary, whimsy, humour, fancy, fickleness, inconstancy, fitfulness, changeableness

capricious *adjective* UNPREDICTABLE, variable, unstable, inconsistent, erratic, quirky, fickle, impulsive, mercurial, freakish, fitful, inconstant << ANTONYM consistent

capsize *verb* OVERTURN, turn over, invert, tip over, keel over, turn turtle, upset

capsule *noun* **1** PILL, tablet, lozenge, bolus **2** (*Botany*) POD, case, shell, vessel, sheath, receptacle, seed case

captain *noun* **1** LEADER, boss, master, skipper, chieftain, head, number one (*informal*), chief **2** COMMANDER, officer, skipper, (senior) pilot

captivate *verb* CHARM, attract, fascinate, absorb, entrance, dazzle, seduce, enchant, enthral, beguile, allure, bewitch, ravish, enslave, mesmerize, ensnare, hypnotize, enrapture, sweep off your feet, enamour, infatuate << ANTONYM repel

captive *adjective* CONFINED, caged, imprisoned, locked up, enslaved, incarcerated, ensnared, subjugated, penned, restricted ▷ *noun* PRISONER, hostage, convict, prisoner of war, detainee, internee

captivity *noun* CONFINEMENT, custody, detention, imprisonment, incarceration, internment, durance (*archaic*), restraint

captor *noun* JAILER *or* GAOLER, guard, keeper, custodian

capture *verb* CATCH, arrest, take, bag, secure, seize, nail (*informal*), collar (*informal*), nab (*informal*), apprehend, lift (*slang*), take prisoner, take into custody, feel your collar (*slang*) << ANTONYM release ▷ *noun* ARREST, catching, trapping, imprisonment, seizure, apprehension, taking, taking captive

car *noun* **1** VEHICLE, motor, wheels (*informal*), auto (*US*), automobile, jalopy (*informal*), motorcar, machine **2** (*US & Canad*) (RAILWAY) CARRIAGE, coach, cable car, dining car, sleeping car, buffet car, van

carcass *noun* **1** BODY, remains, corpse, skeleton, dead body, cadaver (*Medical*) **2** REMAINS, shell, framework, debris, remnants, hulk

cardinal *adjective* PRINCIPAL, first, highest, greatest, leading, important, chief, main, prime, central, key, essential, primary, fundamental, paramount, foremost, pre-eminent << ANTONYM secondary

care *verb* BE CONCERNED, mind, bother, be interested, be bothered, give a damn, concern yourself ▷ *noun* **1** CUSTODY, keeping, control, charge, management, protection, supervision, guardianship, safekeeping, ministration **2** CAUTION, attention, regard, pains, consideration, heed, prudence, vigilance, forethought, circumspection, watchfulness, meticulousness, carefulness << ANTONYM carelessness **3** WORRY, concern, pressure, trouble, responsibility, stress, burden, anxiety, hardship, woe, disquiet, affliction, tribulation, perplexity, vexation << ANTONYM pleasure ▷▷ **care for someone 1** LOOK AFTER, mind, tend, attend, nurse, minister to, watch over **2** LOVE, desire, be fond of, want, prize, find congenial ▷▷ **care for something** *or* **someone** LIKE, enjoy, take to, relish, be fond of, be keen on, be partial to ▷▷ **take care of something** *or* **someone 1** LOOK AFTER, mind, watch, protect, tend, nurse, care for, provide for **2** DEAL WITH, manage, cope with, see to, handle

career *noun* **1** OCCUPATION, calling, employment, pursuit, vocation, livelihood, life's work **2** PROGRESS, course, path, procedure, passage ▷ *verb* RUSH, race, speed, tear, dash, barrel (along) (*informal, chiefly US & Canad*), bolt, hurtle, burn rubber (*informal*)

carefree *adjective* UNTROUBLED, happy, cheerful, careless, buoyant, airy, radiant, easy-going, cheery, breezy, halcyon, sunny, jaunty, chirpy (*informal*), happy-go-lucky, blithe, insouciant, light-hearted ≪ ANTONYM unhappy

careful *adjective* **1** CAUTIOUS, painstaking, scrupulous, fastidious, circumspect, punctilious, chary, heedful, thoughtful, discreet ≪ ANTONYM careless **2** THOROUGH, full, particular, accurate, precise, intensive, in-depth, meticulous, conscientious, attentive, exhaustive, painstaking, scrupulous, assiduous ≪ ANTONYM casual **3** PRUDENT, sparing, economical, canny, provident, frugal, thrifty

careless *adjective* **1** SLAPDASH, irresponsible, sloppy (*informal*), cavalier, offhand, neglectful, slipshod, lackadaisical, inattentive ≪ ANTONYM careful **2** NEGLIGENT, hasty, unconcerned, cursory, perfunctory, thoughtless, indiscreet, unthinking, forgetful, absent-minded, inconsiderate, heedless, remiss, incautious, unmindful ≪ ANTONYM careful **3** NONCHALANT, casual, offhand, artless, unstudied ≪ ANTONYM careful

carelessness *noun* NEGLIGENCE, neglect, omission, indiscretion, inaccuracy, irresponsibility, slackness, inattention, sloppiness (*informal*), laxity, thoughtlessness, laxness, remissness

caress *noun* STROKE, pat, kiss, embrace, hug, cuddle, fondling ▷ *verb* STROKE, cuddle, fondle, pet, embrace, hug, nuzzle, neck (*informal*), kiss

caretaker *noun* WARDEN, keeper, porter, superintendent, curator, custodian, watchman, janitor, concierge ▷ *adjective* TEMPORARY, holding, short-term, interim

cargo *noun* LOAD, goods, contents, shipment, freight, merchandise, baggage, ware, consignment, tonnage, lading

caricature *noun* PARODY, cartoon, distortion, satire, send-up (*Brit informal*), travesty, takeoff (*informal*), lampoon, burlesque,

mimicry, farce ▷ *verb* PARODY, take off (*informal*), mock, distort, ridicule, mimic, send up (*Brit informal*), lampoon, burlesque, satirize

caring *adjective* COMPASSIONATE, loving, kindly, warm, soft, sensitive, tender, sympathetic, responsive, receptive, considerate, warmhearted, tenderhearted, softhearted, touchy-feely (*informal*)

carnage *noun* SLAUGHTER, murder, massacre, holocaust, havoc, bloodshed, shambles, mass murder, butchery, blood bath

carnal *adjective* SEXUAL, animal, sexy (*informal*), fleshly, erotic, sensual, randy (*informal, chiefly Brit*), steamy (*informal*), raunchy (*slang*), sensuous, voluptuous, lewd, wanton, amorous, salacious, prurient, impure, lascivious, lustful, lecherous, libidinous, licentious, unchaste

carnival *noun* FESTIVAL, fair, fête, celebration, gala, jubilee, jamboree, Mardi Gras, revelry, merrymaking, fiesta, holiday

carol *noun* SONG, noël, hymn, Christmas song, canticle

carouse *verb* DRINK, booze (*informal*), revel, imbibe, quaff, pub-crawl (*informal, chiefly Brit*), bevvy (*dialect*), make merry, bend the elbow (*informal*), roister

carp *verb* FIND FAULT, complain, beef (*slang*), criticize, nag, censure, reproach, quibble, cavil, pick holes, kvetch (*US slang*) ≪ ANTONYM praise

carpenter *noun* JOINER, cabinet-maker, woodworker

carping *adjective* FAULT-FINDING, critical, nagging, picky (*informal*), nit-picking (*informal*), hard to please, cavilling, captious

carriage *noun* **1** VEHICLE, coach, trap, gig, cab, wagon, hackney, conveyance **2** TRANSPORTATION, transport, delivery, conveying, freight, conveyance, carrying **3** BEARING, posture, gait, deportment, air

carry *verb* **1** CONVEY, take, move, bring, bear, lift, transfer, conduct, transport, haul, transmit, fetch, relay, cart, tote (*informal*), hump (*Brit slang*), lug **2** TRANSPORT, take, transfer, transmit **3** SUPPORT, stand, bear, maintain, shoulder, sustain, hold up, suffer, uphold, bolster, underpin **4** TRANSMIT, transfer, spread, pass on **5** PUBLISH, include, release, display, print, broadcast, communicate, disseminate, give **6** WIN, gain, secure, capture, accomplish ▷▷ **carry on 1** CONTINUE, last, endure, persist, keep

going, persevere **2** (*informal*) MAKE A FUSS,
act up (*informal*), misbehave, create (*slang*),
raise Cain ▷▷ **carry something on** ENGAGE
IN, conduct, carry out, undertake, embark
on, enter into ▷▷ **carry something out**
PERFORM, effect, achieve, realize, implement,
fulfil, accomplish, execute, discharge,
consummate, carry through

carry-on *noun* (*informal, chiefly Brit*) FUSS,
disturbance, racket, fracas, commotion,
rumpus, tumult, hubbub, shindy (*informal*)

carton *noun* BOX, case, pack, package,
container

cartoon *noun* **1** DRAWING, parody, satire,
caricature, comic strip, takeoff (*informal*),
lampoon, sketch **2** ANIMATION, animated
film, animated cartoon

cartridge *noun* **1** SHELL, round,
charge **2** CONTAINER, case, magazine,
cassette, cylinder, capsule

carve *verb* **1** SCULPT, form, cut, chip,
sculpture, whittle, chisel, hew,
fashion **2** ETCH, engrave, inscribe, fashion,
slash

carving *noun* SCULPTURE

cascade *noun* WATERFALL, falls, torrent,
flood, shower, fountain, avalanche, deluge,
downpour, outpouring, cataract ▷ *verb*
FLOW, fall, flood, pour, plunge, surge, spill,
tumble, descend, overflow, gush, teem, pitch

case¹ *noun* **1** SITUATION, event,
circumstance(s), state, position, condition,
context, dilemma, plight, contingency,
predicament **2** INSTANCE, example,
occasion, specimen, occurrence **3** (*Law*)
LAWSUIT, process, trial, suit, proceedings,
dispute, cause, action

case² *noun* **1** CABINET, box, chest,
holder **2** CONTAINER, compact, capsule,
carton, cartridge, canister, casket,
receptacle **3** SUITCASE, bag, grip, trunk,
holdall, portmanteau, valise **4** CRATE,
box **5** COVERING, casing, cover, shell,
wrapping, jacket, envelope, capsule, folder,
sheath, wrapper, integument

cash *noun* MONEY, change, funds, notes,
ready (*informal*), the necessary (*informal*),
resources, currency, silver, bread (*slang*),
coin, tin (*slang*), brass (*Northern English
dialect*), dough (*slang*), rhino (*Brit slang*),
banknotes, bullion, dosh (*Brit & Austral
slang*), wherewithal, coinage, needful
(*informal*), specie, shekels (*informal*),
dibs (*slang*), ready money, ackers (*slang*),
spondulicks (*slang*)

cashier¹ *noun* TELLER, accountant, clerk,
treasurer, bank clerk, purser, bursar, banker

cashier² *verb* DISMISS, discharge, expel, cast
off, drum out, give the boot to (*slang*)

casing *noun* COVERING, case, cover, shell,
container, integument

cask *noun* BARREL, drum, cylinder, keg

casket *noun* BOX, case, chest, coffer, ark
(*dialect*), jewel box, kist (*Scot & Northern
English dialect*)

cast *noun* **1** ACTORS, company,
players, characters, troupe, dramatis
personae **2** TYPE, turn, sort, kind, style,
stamp ▷ *verb* **1** CHOOSE, name, pick, select,
appoint, assign, allot **2** BESTOW, give, level,
accord, direct, confer **3** GIVE OUT, spread,
deposit, shed, distribute, scatter, emit,
radiate, bestow, diffuse **4** THROW, project,
launch, pitch, shed, shy, toss, thrust, hurl,
fling, chuck (*informal*), sling, lob, impel,
drive, drop **5** MOULD, set, found, form,
model, shape ▷▷ **cast someone down**
DISCOURAGE, depress, desolate, dishearten,
dispirit, deject

caste *noun* CLASS, order, race, station, rank,
status, stratum, social order, lineage

castigate *verb* REPRIMAND, blast, carpet
(*informal*), put down, criticize, lash, slate
(*informal, chiefly Brit*), censure, rebuke, scold,
berate, dress down (*informal*), chastise,
chasten, tear into (*informal*), diss (*slang, chiefly
US*), read the riot act, slap on the wrist,
lambast(e), bawl (someone) out (*informal*),
excoriate, rap over the knuckles, haul over
the coals (*informal*), chew out (*US & Canad
informal*), tear (someone) off a strip (*Brit
informal*), give a rocket (*Brit & NZ informal*)

cast-iron *adjective* CERTAIN, established,
settled, guaranteed, fixed, definite, copper-
bottomed, idiot-proof, nailed-on (*slang*)

castle *noun* FORTRESS, keep, palace, tower,
peel, chateau, stronghold, citadel, fastness

castrate *verb* NEUTER, unman, emasculate,
geld

casual *adjective* **1** CARELESS, relaxed,
informal, indifferent, unconcerned,
apathetic, blasé, offhand, nonchalant,
insouciant, lackadaisical << ANTONYM
serious **2** CHANCE, unexpected, random,
accidental, incidental, unforeseen,
unintentional, fortuitous (*informal*),
serendipitous, unpremeditated
<< ANTONYM planned **3** INFORMAL,
leisure, sporty, non-dressy << ANTONYM
formal

casualty *noun* 1 FATALITY, death, loss, wounded 2 VICTIM, sufferer

cat *noun* FELINE, pussy (*informal*), moggy (*slang*), puss (*informal*), ballarat (*Austral informal*), tabby

cataclysm *noun* DISASTER, collapse, catastrophe, upheaval, debacle, devastation, calamity

cataclysmic *adjective* DISASTROUS, devastating, catastrophic, calamitous

catalogue *or US* **catalog** *noun* LIST, record, schedule, index, register, directory, inventory, gazetteer ▷ *verb* LIST, file, index, register, classify, inventory, tabulate, alphabetize

catapult *noun* SLING, slingshot (*US*), trebuchet, ballista ▷ *verb* SHOOT, pitch, plunge, toss, hurl, propel, hurtle, heave

cataract *noun* 1 (*Medical*) OPACITY (*of the eye*) 2 WATERFALL, falls, rapids, cascade, torrent, deluge, downpour, Niagara

catastrophe *noun* DISASTER, tragedy, calamity, meltdown (*informal*), cataclysm, trouble, trial, blow, failure, reverse, misfortune, devastation, adversity, mishap, affliction, whammy (*informal, chiefly US*), bummer (*slang*), mischance, fiasco

catastrophic *adjective* DISASTROUS, devastating, tragic, calamitous, cataclysmic

catch *verb* 1 CAPTURE, arrest, trap, seize, nail (*informal*), nab (*informal*), snare, lift (*slang*), apprehend, ensnare, entrap, feel your collar (*slang*) << ANTONYM free 2 TRAP, capture, snare, entangle, ensnare, entrap 3 SEIZE, get, grab, snatch 4 GRAB, take, grip, seize, grasp, clutch, lay hold of << ANTONYM release 5 DISCOVER, surprise, find out, expose, detect, catch in the act, take unawares 6 CONTRACT, get, develop, suffer from, incur, succumb to, go down with << ANTONYM escape ▷ *noun* 1 FASTENER, hook, clip, bolt, latch, clasp, hasp, hook and eye, snib (*Scot*), sneck (*dialect, chiefly Scot & Northern English*) 2 (*informal*) DRAWBACK, trick, trap, disadvantage, hitch, snag, stumbling block, fly in the ointment << ANTONYM advantage ▷▷ **catch on** 1 (*informal*) UNDERSTAND, see, find out, grasp, see through, comprehend, twig (*Brit informal*), get the picture, see the light of day 2 BECOME POPULAR, take off, become trendy, come into fashion

catchcry *noun* (*Austral*) CATCHPHRASE, slogan, saying, quotation, motto

catching *adjective* INFECTIOUS, contagious, transferable, communicable, infective, transmittable << ANTONYM non-infectious

catch phrase *noun* SLOGAN, saying, quotation, motto, catchcry (*Austral*)

catchy *adjective* MEMORABLE, haunting, unforgettable, captivating

categorical *adjective* ABSOLUTE, direct, express, positive, explicit, unconditional, emphatic, downright, unequivocal, unqualified, unambiguous, unreserved << ANTONYM vague

category *noun* CLASS, grouping, heading, head, order, sort, list, department, type, division, section, rank, grade, classification

cater *verb* ▷▷ **cater for something** *or* **someone** 1 PROVIDE FOR, supply, provision, purvey, victual 2 TAKE INTO ACCOUNT, consider, bear in mind, make allowance for, have regard for ▷▷ **cater to something** *or* **someone** INDULGE, spoil, minister to, pamper, gratify, pander to, coddle, mollycoddle

catharsis *noun* RELEASE, cleansing, purging, purification

catholic *adjective* WIDE, general, liberal, global, varied, comprehensive, universal, world-wide, tolerant, eclectic, all-inclusive, ecumenical, all-embracing, broad-minded, unbigoted, unsectarian << ANTONYM limited

cattle *plural noun* COWS, stock, beasts, livestock, bovines

caucus *noun* GROUP, division, section, camp, sector, lobby, bloc, contingent, pressure group, junta, public-interest group (*US & Canad*)

cause *noun* 1 ORIGIN, source, agency, spring, agent, maker, producer, root, beginning, creator, genesis, originator, prime mover, mainspring << ANTONYM result 2 REASON, call, need, grounds, basis, incentive, motive, motivation, justification, inducement 3 AIM, movement, purpose, principle, object, ideal, enterprise, end ▷ *verb* PRODUCE, begin, create, effect, lead to, occasion, result in, generate, provoke, compel, motivate, induce, bring about, give rise to, precipitate, incite, engender << ANTONYM prevent

caustic *adjective* 1 BURNING, corrosive, corroding, astringent, vitriolic, acrid 2 SARCASTIC, biting, keen, cutting, severe, stinging, scathing, acrimonious, pungent, vitriolic, trenchant, mordant << ANTONYM kind

caution noun 1 CARE, discretion, heed, prudence, vigilance, alertness, forethought, circumspection, watchfulness, belt and braces, carefulness, heedfulness << ANTONYM carelessness 2 REPRIMAND, warning, injunction, admonition ▷ verb 1 WARN, urge, advise, alert, tip off, forewarn, put you on your guard 2 REPRIMAND, warn, admonish, give an injunction to

cautious adjective CAREFUL, guarded, alert, wary, discreet, tentative, prudent, vigilant, watchful, judicious, circumspect, cagey (informal), on your toes, chary, belt-and-braces, keeping a weather eye on << ANTONYM careless

cautiously adverb CAREFULLY, alertly, discreetly, tentatively, warily, prudently, judiciously, guardedly, circumspectly, watchfully, vigilantly, cagily (informal), mindfully

cavalcade noun PARADE, train, procession, march-past

cavalier adjective OFFHAND, lordly, arrogant, lofty, curt, condescending, haughty, scornful, disdainful, insolent, supercilious

cavalry noun HORSEMEN, horse, mounted troops << ANTONYM infantrymen

cave noun HOLLOW, cavern, grotto, den, cavity

caveat noun WARNING, caution, admonition, qualification, proviso, reservation, condition

cavern noun CAVE, hollow, grotto, underground chamber

cavernous adjective VAST, wide, huge, enormous, extensive, immense, spacious, expansive, capacious, commodious

cavity noun HOLLOW, hole, gap, pit, dent, crater

cavort verb FROLIC, sport, romp, caper, prance, frisk, gambol

cease verb 1 STOP, end, finish, be over, come to an end, peter out, die away << ANTONYM start 2 DISCONTINUE, end, stop, fail, finish, give up, conclude, suspend, halt, terminate, break off, refrain, leave off, give over (informal), bring to an end, desist, belay (Nautical) << ANTONYM begin

ceaseless adjective CONTINUAL, constant, endless, continuous, eternal, perennial, perpetual, never-ending, interminable, incessant, everlasting, unending, unremitting, nonstop, untiring << ANTONYM occasional

cede verb SURRENDER, grant, transfer, abandon, yield, concede, hand over, relinquish, renounce, make over, abdicate

celebrate verb 1 REJOICE, party, enjoy yourself, carouse, live it up (informal), whoop it up (informal), make merry, paint the town red (informal), go on a spree, put the flags out, roister, kill the fatted calf 2 COMMEMORATE, honour, observe, toast, drink to, keep 3 PERFORM, observe, preside over, officiate at, solemnize 4 PRAISE, honour, commend (informal), glorify, publicize, exalt, laud, extol, eulogize

celebrated adjective RENOWNED, popular, famous, outstanding, distinguished, well-known, prominent, glorious, acclaimed, notable, eminent, revered, famed, illustrious, pre-eminent, lionized << ANTONYM unknown

celebration noun 1 PARTY, festival, gala, jubilee, festivity, rave (Brit slang), beano (Brit slang), revelry, red-letter day, rave-up (Brit slang), merrymaking, carousal, -fest (in combination), hooley or hoolie (chiefly Irish & NZ) 2 COMMEMORATION, honouring, remembrance 3 PERFORMANCE, observance, solemnization

celebrity noun 1 PERSONALITY, name, star, superstar, big name, dignitary, luminary, bigwig (informal), celeb (informal), face (informal), big shot (informal), personage, megastar (informal), V.I.P. << ANTONYM nobody 2 FAME, reputation, honour, glory, popularity, distinction, prestige, prominence, stardom, renown, pre-eminence, repute, éclat, notability << ANTONYM obscurity

celestial adjective 1 ASTRONOMICAL, planetary, stellar, astral, extraterrestrial 2 HEAVENLY, spiritual, divine, eternal, sublime, immortal, supernatural, astral, ethereal, angelic, godlike, seraphic

celibacy noun CHASTITY, purity, virginity, continence, singleness

celibate adjective CHASTE, single, pure, virgin, continent

cell noun 1 ROOM, chamber, lock-up, compartment, cavity, cubicle, dungeon, stall 2 UNIT, group, section, core, nucleus, caucus, coterie

cement noun 1 MORTAR, plaster, paste 2 SEALANT, glue, gum, adhesive, binder ▷ verb STICK, join, bond, attach, seal, glue, plaster, gum, weld, solder

cemetery noun GRAVEYARD, churchyard,

burial ground, necropolis, God's acre

censor *verb* EXPURGATE, cut, blue-pencil, bowdlerize

censorship *noun* EXPURGATION, blue pencil, purgation, bowdlerization *or* bowdlerisation, sanitization *or* sanitisation

censure *verb* CRITICIZE, blame, abuse, condemn, carpet (*informal*), denounce, put down, slate (*informal, chiefly US*), rebuke, reprimand, reproach, scold, berate, castigate, chide, tear into (*informal*), diss (*slang, chiefly US*), blast, read (someone) the riot act, reprove, upbraid, slap (someone) on the wrist, lambast(e), bawl (someone) out (*informal*), excoriate, rap (someone) over the knuckles, chew (someone) out (*US & Canad informal*), tear (someone) off a strip (*Brit informal*), give (someone) a rocket (*Brit & NZ informal*), reprehend << ANTONYM applaud ▷ *noun* DISAPPROVAL, criticism, blame, condemnation, rebuke, reprimand, reproach, dressing down (*informal*), stick (*slang*), stricture, reproof, castigation, obloquy, remonstrance << ANTONYM approval

central *adjective* **1** INNER, middle, mid, interior << ANTONYM outer **2** MAIN, chief, key, essential, primary, principal, fundamental, focal << ANTONYM minor

centralize *verb* UNIFY, concentrate, incorporate, compact, streamline, converge, condense, amalgamate, rationalize

centre *noun* MIDDLE, heart, focus, core, nucleus, hub, pivot, kernel, crux, bull's-eye, midpoint << ANTONYM edge ▷▷ **centre on something** *or* **someone** FOCUS, concentrate, cluster, revolve, converge

centrepiece *noun* FOCUS, highlight, hub, star

ceremonial *adjective* FORMAL, public, official, ritual, stately, solemn, liturgical, courtly, ritualistic << ANTONYM informal ▷ *noun* RITUAL, ceremony, rite, formality, solemnity

ceremony *noun* **1** RITUAL, service, rite, observance, commemoration, solemnities **2** FORMALITY, ceremonial, propriety, decorum, formal courtesy

certain *adjective* **1** SURE, convinced, positive, confident, satisfied, assured, free from doubt << ANTONYM unsure **2** BOUND, sure, fated, destined << ANTONYM unlikely **3** INEVITABLE, unavoidable, inescapable, inexorable, ineluctable **4** KNOWN, true, positive, plain, ascertained, unmistakable, conclusive, undoubted, unequivocal,

undeniable, irrefutable, unquestionable, incontrovertible, indubitable, nailed-on (*slang*) << ANTONYM doubtful **5** FIXED, decided, established, settled, definite << ANTONYM indefinite **6** PARTICULAR, special, individual, specific

certainly *adverb* DEFINITELY, surely, truly, absolutely, undoubtedly, positively, decidedly, without doubt, unquestionably, undeniably, without question, unequivocally, indisputably, assuredly, indubitably, doubtlessly, come hell or high water, irrefutably

certainty *noun* **1** CONFIDENCE, trust, faith, conviction, assurance, certitude, sureness, positiveness << ANTONYM doubt **2** INEVITABILITY << ANTONYM uncertainty **3** FACT, truth, reality, sure thing (*informal*), surety, banker

certificate *noun* DOCUMENT, licence, warrant, voucher, diploma, testimonial, authorization, credential(s)

certify *verb* CONFIRM, show, declare, guarantee, witness, assure, endorse, testify, notify, verify, ascertain, validate, attest, corroborate, avow, authenticate, vouch for, aver

cessation *noun* CEASING, ending, break, halt, halting, pause, suspension, interruption, respite, standstill, stoppage, termination, let-up (*informal*), remission, abeyance, discontinuance, stay

chafe *verb* **1** RUB, scratch, scrape, rasp, abrade **2** BE ANNOYED, rage, fume, be angry, fret, be offended, be irritated, be incensed, be impatient, be exasperated, be inflamed, be ruffled, be vexed, be narked (*Brit, Austral & NZ slang*)

chaff *noun* HUSKS, remains, refuse, waste, hulls, rubbish, trash, dregs

chagrin *noun* ANNOYANCE, embarrassment, humiliation, dissatisfaction, disquiet, displeasure, mortification, discomfiture, vexation, discomposure ▷ *verb* ANNOY, embarrass, humiliate, disquiet, vex, displease, mortify, discomfit, dissatisfy, discompose

chain *noun* **1** TETHER, coupling, link, bond, shackle, fetter, manacle **2** SERIES, set, train, string, sequence, succession, progression, concatenation ▷ *verb* BIND, confine, restrain, handcuff, shackle, tether, fetter, manacle

chairman *or* **chairwoman** *noun*
1 DIRECTOR, president, chief, executive,

chairperson **2** MASTER OF CEREMONIES, spokesman, chair, speaker, MC, chairperson

chalk up *verb* (*informal*) **1** SCORE, win, gain, achieve, accumulate, attain **2** RECORD, mark, enter, credit, register, log, tally

challenge *noun* **1** DARE, provocation, summons to contest, wero (*NZ*) **2** TEST, trial, opposition, confrontation, defiance, ultimatum, face-off (*slang*) ▷ *verb* **1** DISPUTE, question, tackle, confront, defy, object to, disagree with, take issue with, impugn **2** DARE, invite, provoke, defy, summon, call out, throw down the gauntlet **3** TEST, try, tax **4** QUESTION, interrogate, accost

chamber *noun* **1** HALL, room **2** COUNCIL, assembly, legislature, legislative body **3** ROOM, bedroom, apartment, enclosure, cubicle **4** COMPARTMENT, hollow, cavity

champion *noun* **1** WINNER, hero, victor, conqueror, title holder, warrior **2** DEFENDER, guardian, patron, backer, protector, upholder, vindicator ▷ *verb* SUPPORT, back, defend, promote, advocate, fight for, uphold, espouse, stick up for (*informal*)

chance *noun* **1** PROBABILITY, odds, possibility, prospect, liability, likelihood << ANTONYM certainty **2** OPPORTUNITY, opening, occasion, time, scope, window **3** ACCIDENT, fortune, luck, fate, destiny, coincidence, misfortune, providence << ANTONYM design **4** RISK, speculation, gamble, hazard ▷ *adjective* ACCIDENTAL, random, casual, incidental, unforeseen, unintentional, fortuitous, inadvertent, serendipitous, unforeseeable, unlooked-for << ANTONYM planned ▷ *verb* **1** HAPPEN **2** RISK, try, stake, venture, gamble, hazard, wager **change** *noun* **1** ALTERATION, innovation, transformation, modification, mutation, metamorphosis, permutation, transmutation, difference, revolution, transition **2** VARIETY, break (*informal*), departure, variation, novelty, diversion, whole new ball game (*informal*) << ANTONYM monotony **3** EXCHANGE, trade, conversion, swap, substitution, interchange ▷ *verb* **1** ALTER, reform, transform, adjust, moderate, revise, modify, remodel, reorganize, restyle, convert << ANTONYM keep **2** SHIFT, vary, transform, alter, modify, diversify, fluctuate, mutate, metamorphose, transmute << ANTONYM stay **3** EXCHANGE, trade,

replace, substitute, swap, interchange

changeable *adjective* VARIABLE, shifting, mobile, uncertain, volatile, unsettled, unpredictable, versatile, unstable, irregular, erratic, wavering, uneven, unreliable, fickle, temperamental, whimsical, mercurial, capricious, unsteady, protean, vacillating, fitful, mutable, inconstant << ANTONYM constant

channel *noun* **1** MEANS, way, course, approach, medium, route, path, avenue **2** STRAIT, sound, route, passage, canal, waterway, main **3** DUCT, chamber, artery, groove, gutter, furrow, conduit ▷ *verb* DIRECT, guide, conduct, transmit, convey

chant *noun* SONG, carol, chorus, melody, psalm ▷ *verb* SING, chorus, recite, intone, carol

chaos *noun* DISORDER, confusion, mayhem, anarchy, lawlessness, pandemonium, entropy, bedlam, tumult, disorganization << ANTONYM orderliness

chaotic *adjective* DISORDERED, confused, uncontrolled, anarchic, tumultuous, lawless, riotous, topsy-turvy, disorganized, purposeless

chap *noun* (*informal*) FELLOW, man, person, individual, type, sort, customer (*informal*), character, guy (*informal*), bloke (*Brit informal*), cove (*slang*), dude (*US & Canad informal*)

chapter *noun* **1** SECTION, part, stage, division, episode, topic, segment, instalment **2** PERIOD, time, stage, phase

char *verb* SCORCH, sear, singe

character *noun* **1** PERSONALITY, nature, make-up, cast, constitution, bent, attributes, temper, temperament, complexion, disposition, individuality, marked traits **2** NATURE, kind, quality, constitution, calibre **3** (*informal*) PERSON, sort, individual, type, guy (*informal*), fellow **4** REPUTATION, honour, integrity, good name, rectitude **5** ROLE, part, persona **6** ECCENTRIC, card (*informal*), original, nut (*slang*), flake (*slang, chiefly US*), oddity, oddball (*informal*), odd bod (*informal*), queer fish (*Brit informal*), wacko *or* whacko (*informal*) **7** SYMBOL, mark, sign, letter, figure, type, device, logo, emblem, rune, cipher, hieroglyph

characteristic *noun* FEATURE, mark, quality, property, attribute, faculty, trait, quirk, peculiarity, idiosyncrasy ▷ *adjective* TYPICAL, special, individual, specific, representative, distinguishing, distinctive, peculiar, singular, idiosyncratic, symptomatic << ANTONYM rare

characterize *verb* DISTINGUISH, mark, identify, brand, inform, stamp, typify

charade *noun* PRETENCE, farce, parody, pantomime, fake

charge *verb* 1 ACCUSE, indict, impeach, incriminate, arraign << ANTONYM acquit 2 ATTACK, assault, assail << ANTONYM retreat 3 RUSH, storm, stampede 4 FILL, load, instil, suffuse, lade ▷ *noun* 1 PRICE, rate, cost, amount, payment, expense, toll, expenditure, outlay, damage (*informal*) 2 ACCUSATION, allegation, indictment, imputation << ANTONYM acquittal 3 CARE, trust, responsibility, custody, safekeeping 4 DUTY, office, concern, responsibility, remit 5 WARD, pupil, protégé, dependant 6 ATTACK, rush, assault, onset, onslaught, stampede, sortie << ANTONYM retreat

charisma *noun* CHARM, appeal, personality, attraction, lure, allure, magnetism, force of personality

charismatic *adjective* CHARMING, appealing, attractive, influential, magnetic, enticing, alluring

charitable *adjective* 1 BENEVOLENT, liberal, generous, lavish, philanthropic, bountiful, beneficent << ANTONYM mean 2 KIND, understanding, forgiving, sympathetic, favourable, tolerant, indulgent, lenient, considerate, magnanimous, broad-minded << ANTONYM unkind

charity *noun* 1 CHARITABLE ORGANIZATION, fund, movement, trust, endowment 2 DONATIONS, help, relief, gift, contributions, assistance, hand-out, philanthropy, alms-giving, benefaction, largesse *or* largess, koha (*NZ*) << ANTONYM meanness 3 KINDNESS, love, pity, humanity, affection, goodness, goodwill, compassion, generosity, indulgence, bounty, altruism, benevolence, fellow feeling, bountifulness, tenderheartedness, aroha (*NZ*) << ANTONYM ill will

charlatan *noun* FRAUD, cheat, fake, sham, pretender, quack, con man (*informal*), impostor, fraudster, swindler, mountebank, grifter (*slang, chiefly US & Canad*), phoney *or* phony (*informal*), rorter (*Austral slang*), rogue trader

charm *noun* 1 ATTRACTION, appeal, fascination, allure, magnetism, desirability, allurement << ANTONYM

repulsiveness 2 TRINKET 3 TALISMAN, amulet, lucky piece, good-luck piece, fetish 4 SPELL, magic, enchantment, sorcery, makutu (*NZ*) ▷ *verb* 1 ATTRACT, win, please, delight, fascinate, absorb, entrance, win over, enchant, captivate, beguile, allure, bewitch, ravish, mesmerize, enrapture, enamour << ANTONYM repel 2 PERSUADE, seduce, coax, beguile, cajole, sweet-talk (*informal*)

charming *adjective* ATTRACTIVE, pleasing, appealing, engaging, lovely, winning, pleasant, fetching, delightful, cute, irresistible, seductive, captivating, eye-catching, bewitching, delectable, winsome, likable *or* likeable << ANTONYM unpleasant

chart *noun* TABLE, diagram, blueprint, graph, tabulation, plan, map ▷ *verb* 1 PLOT, map out, delineate, sketch, draft, graph, tabulate 2 MONITOR, follow, record, note, document, register, trace, outline, log, graph, tabulate

charter *noun* 1 DOCUMENT, right, contract, bond, permit, licence, concession, privilege, franchise, deed, prerogative, indenture 2 CONSTITUTION, laws, rules, code ▷ *verb* 1 HIRE, commission, employ, rent, lease 2 AUTHORIZE, permit, sanction, entitle, license, empower, give authority

chase *verb* 1 PURSUE, follow, track, hunt, run after, course 2 DRIVE AWAY, drive, expel, hound, send away, send packing, put to flight 3 (*informal*) RUSH, run, race, shoot, fly, speed, dash, sprint, bolt, dart, hotfoot ▷ *noun* PURSUIT, race, hunt, hunting

chasm *noun* 1 GULF, opening, crack, gap, rent, hollow, void, gorge, crater, cavity, abyss, ravine, cleft, fissure, crevasse 2 GAP, division, gulf, split, breach, rift, alienation, hiatus

chassis *noun* FRAME, framework, fuselage, bodywork, substructure

chaste *adjective* 1 PURE, moral, decent, innocent, immaculate, wholesome, virtuous, virginal, unsullied, uncontaminated, undefiled, incorrupt << ANTONYM promiscuous 2 SIMPLE, quiet, elegant, modest, refined, restrained, austere, unaffected, decorous

chasten *verb* SUBDUE, discipline, cow, curb, humble, soften, humiliate, tame, afflict, repress, put in your place

chastise *verb* SCOLD, blame, correct, discipline, lecture, carpet (*informal*), nag, censure, rebuke, reprimand, reproach,

berate, tick (someone) off (*informal*),
castigate, chide, tell off (*informal*), find fault
with, remonstrate with, bring (someone)
to book, take (someone) to task, reprove,
upbraid, bawl (someone) out (*informal*),
give (someone) a talking-to (*informal*), haul
(someone) over the coals (*informal*), chew
(someone) out (*US & Canad informal*), give
(someone) a dressing-down, give (someone)
a rocket (*Brit & NZ informal*), give (someone)
a row << ANTONYM praise

chastity *noun* PURITY, virtue, innocence,
modesty, virginity, celibacy, continence,
maidenhood << ANTONYM promiscuity

chat *verb* TALK, gossip, jaw (*slang*), natter,
blather, schmooze (*slang*), blether (*Scot*),
shoot the breeze (*US slang*), chew the rag
or fat (*slang*) ▷ *noun* TALK, tête-à-tête,
conversation, gossip, heart-to-heart, natter,
blather, schmooze (*slang*), blether (*Scot*),
chinwag (*Brit informal*), confab (*informal*),
craic (*Irish informal*), korero (*NZ*)

chatter *verb* PRATTLE, chat, rabbit on (*Brit
informal*), babble, gab (*informal*), natter,
tattle, jabber, blather, schmooze (*slang*),
blether (*Scot*), run off at the mouth (*US
slang*), prate, gossip ▷ *noun* PRATTLE, chat,
rabbit (*Brit informal*), gossip, babble, twaddle,
gab (*informal*), natter, tattle, jabber, blather,
blether (*Scot*)

chatty *adjective* TALKATIVE, informal,
effusive, garrulous, gabby (*informal*), gossipy,
newsy (*informal*) << ANTONYM quiet

cheap *adjective* 1 INEXPENSIVE, sale,
economy, reduced, keen, reasonable,
bargain, low-priced, low-cost, cut-price,
economical, cheapo (*informal*) << ANTONYM
expensive 2 INFERIOR, poor, worthless,
second-rate, shoddy, tawdry, tatty, trashy,
substandard, low-rent (*informal, chiefly
US*), two-bit (*US & Canad slang*), crappy
(*slang*), two a penny, rubbishy, dime-a-
dozen (*informal*), tinhorn (*US slang*), bodger
or bodgie (*Austral slang*) << ANTONYM
good 3 (*informal*) DESPICABLE, mean, low,
base, vulgar, sordid, contemptible, scurvy,
scungy (*Austral & NZ*) << ANTONYM decent

cheapen *verb* DEGRADE, lower, discredit,
devalue, demean, belittle, depreciate, debase,
derogate

cheat *verb* 1 DECEIVE, skin (*slang*), trick, fool,
take in (*informal*), con (*informal*), stiff (*slang*),
sting (*informal*), mislead, rip off (*slang*), fleece,
hoax, defraud, dupe, beguile, gull (*archaic*),
do (*informal*), swindle, stitch up (*slang*),

victimize, bamboozle (*informal*), hoodwink,
double-cross (*informal*), diddle (*informal*),
take for a ride (*informal*), bilk, pull a fast
one on (*informal*), screw (*informal*), finagle
(*informal*) 2 FOIL, check, defeat, prevent,
frustrate, deprive, baffle, thwart ▷ *noun*
DECEIVER, sharper, cheater, shark, charlatan,
trickster, con man (*informal*), impostor,
fraudster, double-crosser (*informal*),
swindler, grifter (*slang, chiefly US & Canad*),
rorter (*Austral slang*), chiseller (*informal*),
rogue trader

check *verb* 1 *often with* out EXAMINE, test,
study, look at, research, note, confirm,
investigate, monitor, probe, tick, vet, inspect,
look over, verify, work over, scrutinize,
make sure of, inquire into, take a dekko at
(*Brit slang*) << ANTONYM overlook 2 STOP,
control, limit, arrest, delay, halt, curb,
bar, restrain, inhibit, rein, thwart, hinder,
repress, obstruct, retard, impede, bridle,
stem the flow of, nip in the bud, put a
spoke in someone's wheel << ANTONYM
further ▷ *noun* 1 EXAMINATION, test,
research, investigation, inspection, scrutiny,
once-over (*informal*) 2 CONTROL, limitation,
restraint, constraint, rein, obstacle,
curb, obstruction, stoppage, inhibition,
impediment, hindrance, damper

cheek *noun* (*informal*) IMPUDENCE, face
(*informal*), front, nerve, sauce (*informal*),
gall (*informal*), disrespect, audacity, neck
(*informal*), lip (*slang*), temerity, chutzpah (*US
& Canad informal*), insolence, impertinence,
effrontery, brass neck (*Brit informal*),
brazenness, sassiness (*US informal*)

cheeky *adjective* IMPUDENT, rude, forward,
fresh (*informal*), insulting, saucy, audacious,
sassy (*US informal*), pert, disrespectful,
impertinent, insolent, lippy (*US & Canad
slang*) << ANTONYM respectful

cheer *verb* 1 APPLAUD, hail, acclaim, clap,
hurrah << ANTONYM boo 2 HEARTEN,
encourage, warm, comfort, elevate, animate,
console, uplift, brighten, exhilarate, solace,
enliven, cheer up, buoy up, gladden, elate,
inspirit << ANTONYM dishearten ▷ *noun*
1 APPLAUSE, ovation 2 CHEERFULNESS,
comfort, joy, optimism, animation, glee,
solace, buoyancy, mirth, gaiety, merriment,
liveliness, gladness, hopefulness, merrymaking ▷▷ **cheer someone up** COMFORT,
encourage, brighten, hearten, enliven,
gladden, gee up, jolly along (*informal*)
▷▷ **cheer up** TAKE HEART, rally, perk up,

buck up (*informal*)

cheerful *adjective* **1** HAPPY, bright, contented, glad, optimistic, bucked (*informal*), enthusiastic, sparkling, gay, sunny, jolly, animated, merry, upbeat (*informal*), buoyant, hearty, cheery, joyful, jovial, genial, jaunty, chirpy (*informal*), sprightly, blithe, light-hearted << ANTONYM sad **2** PLEASANT, bright, sunny, gay, enlivening << ANTONYM gloomy

cheerfulness *noun* HAPPINESS, good humour, exuberance, high spirits, buoyancy, gaiety, good cheer, gladness, geniality, light-heartedness, jauntiness, joyousness

cheery *adjective* CHEERFUL, happy, pleasant, lively, sunny, upbeat (*informal*), good-humoured, carefree, breezy, genial, chirpy (*informal*), jovial, full of beans (*informal*)

chemical *noun* COMPOUND, drug, substance, synthetic substance, potion

chemist *noun* PHARMACIST, apothecary (*obsolete*), pharmacologist, dispenser

cherish *verb* **1** CLING TO, prize, treasure, hold dear, cleave to << ANTONYM despise **2** CARE FOR, love, support, comfort, look after, shelter, treasure, nurture, cosset, hold dear << ANTONYM neglect **3** HARBOUR, nurse, sustain, foster, entertain

chest *noun* **1** BREAST, front **2** BOX, case, trunk, crate, coffer, ark (*dialect*), casket, strongbox **chew** *verb* MUNCH, bite, grind, champ, crunch, gnaw, chomp, masticate ▷▷ **chew something over** CONSIDER, weigh up, ponder, mull (over), meditate on, reflect upon, muse on, ruminate, deliberate upon

chewy *adjective* TOUGH, fibrous, leathery, as tough as old boots

chic *adjective* STYLISH, smart, elegant, fashionable, trendy (*Brit informal*), up-to-date, modish, à la mode, voguish (*informal*), schmick (*Austral informal*) << ANTONYM unfashionable

chide *verb* SCOLD, blame, lecture, carpet (*informal*), put down, criticize, slate (*informal, chiefly Brit*), censure, rebuke, reprimand, reproach, berate, tick (someone) off (*informal*), admonish, tear into (*informal*), blast, tell (someone) off (*informal*), find fault with, diss (*slang, chiefly US*), read (someone) the riot act, reprove, upbraid, slap (someone) on the wrist, lambast(e), bawl (someone) out (*informal*), rap (someone) over the knuckles, chew (someone) out (*US & Canad informal*), tear (someone) off a strip (*Brit informal*),

give (someone) a rocket (*Brit & NZ informal*), reprehend, give (someone) a row (*Scot informal*)

chief *noun* HEAD, leader, director, manager, lord, boss (*informal*), captain, master, governor, commander, principal, superior, ruler, superintendent, chieftain, ringleader, baas (*S African*), ariki (*NZ*), sherang (*Austral & NZ*) << ANTONYM subordinate ▷ *adjective* PRIMARY, highest, leading, main, prime, capital, central, key, essential, premier, supreme, most important, outstanding, principal, prevailing, cardinal, paramount, big-time (*informal*), foremost, major league (*informal*), predominant, uppermost, pre-eminent, especial << ANTONYM minor

chiefly *adverb* **1** ESPECIALLY, essentially, principally, primarily, above all **2** MAINLY, largely, usually, mostly, in general, on the whole, predominantly, in the main

child *noun* **1** YOUNGSTER, baby, kid (*informal*), minor, infant, babe, juvenile, toddler, tot, wean (*Scot*), little one, brat, bairn (*Scot*), suckling, nipper (*informal*), chit, babe in arms, sprog (*slang*), munchkin (*informal, chiefly US*), rug rat (*slang*), nursling, littlie (*Austral informal*), ankle-biter (*Austral slang*), tacker (*Austral slang*) **2** OFFSPRING, issue, descendant, progeny **childbirth** *noun* CHILD-BEARING, labour, delivery, lying-in, confinement, parturition **childhood** *noun* YOUTH, minority, infancy, schooldays, immaturity, boyhood *or* girlhood

childish *adjective* **1** YOUTHFUL, young, boyish *or* girlish **2** IMMATURE, silly, juvenile, foolish, trifling, frivolous, infantile, puerile << ANTONYM mature

childlike *adjective* INNOCENT, trusting, simple, naive, credulous, artless, ingenuous, guileless, unfeigned, trustful

chill *verb* **1** COOL, refrigerate, freeze **2** DISHEARTEN, depress, discourage, dismay, dampen, deject ▷ *noun* **1** COLDNESS, bite, nip, sharpness, coolness, rawness, crispness, frigidity **2** SHIVER, frisson, goose pimples, goose flesh ▷ *adjective* CHILLY, biting, sharp, freezing, raw, bleak, chilly, wintry, frigid, parky (*Brit informal*)

chilly *adjective* **1** COOL, fresh, sharp, crisp, penetrating, brisk, breezy, draughty, nippy, parky (*Brit informal*), blowy << ANTONYM warm **2** UNFRIENDLY, hostile, unsympathetic, frigid, unresponsive, unwelcoming, cold as ice << ANTONYM friendly

chime *verb* RING ▷ *noun* SOUND, boom, toll, jingle, dong, tinkle, clang, peal

chimera *noun* ILLUSION, dream, fantasy, delusion, spectre, snare, hallucination, figment, ignis fatuus, will-o'-the-wisp

china¹ *noun* POTTERY, ceramics, ware, porcelain, crockery, tableware, service

china² *noun* (*Brit & S African informal*) FRIEND, pal, mate (*informal*), buddy (*informal*), companion, best friend, intimate, cock (*Brit informal*), close friend, comrade, chum (*informal*), crony, main man (*slang, chiefly US*), soul mate, homeboy (*slang, chiefly US*), cobber (*Austral & NZ old-fashioned informal*), bosom friend, boon companion, E hoa (*NZ*)

chink *noun* OPENING, crack, gap, rift, aperture, cleft, crevice, fissure, cranny

chip *noun* 1 FRAGMENT, scrap, shaving, flake, paring, wafer, sliver, shard 2 SCRATCH, nick, flaw, notch, dent 3 COUNTER, disc, token ▷ *verb* 1 NICK, damage, gash 2 CHISEL, whittle ▷▷ **chip in** (*informal*) 1 CONTRIBUTE, pay, donate, subscribe, go Dutch (*informal*) 2 INTERPOSE, put in, interrupt, interject, butt in, put your oar in

chirp *verb* CHIRRUP, pipe, peep, warble, twitter, cheep, tweet

chirpy *adjective* (*informal*) CHEERFUL, happy, bright, enthusiastic, lively, sparkling, sunny, jolly, animated, buoyant, radiant, jaunty, sprightly, in high spirits, blithe, full of beans (*informal*), light-hearted

chivalry *noun* 1 COURTESY, politeness, gallantry, courtliness, gentlemanliness 2 KNIGHT-ERRANTRY, knighthood, gallantry, courtliness

choice *noun* 1 RANGE, variety, selection, assortment 2 SELECTION, preference, election, pick 3 OPTION, say, alternative ▷ *adjective* BEST, bad (*slang*), special, prime, nice, prize, select, excellent, elect, crucial (*slang*), exclusive, elite, superior, exquisite, def (*slang*), booshit (*Austral slang*), exo (*Austral slang*), sik (*Austral slang*), hand-picked, dainty, rad (*informal*), phat (*slang*), schmick (*Austral informal*)

choke *verb* 1 SUFFOCATE, stifle, smother, overpower, asphyxiate 2 STRANGLE, throttle, asphyxiate 3 BLOCK, dam, clog, obstruct, bung, constrict, occlude, congest, close, stop, bar

choose *verb* 1 PICK, take, prefer, select, elect, adopt, opt for, designate, single out, espouse, settle on, fix on, cherry-pick, settle upon, predestine << ANTONYM reject 2 WISH,

want, desire, see fit

choosy *adjective* (*informal*) FUSSY, particular, exacting, discriminating, selective, fastidious, picky (*informal*), finicky, faddy << ANTONYM indiscriminating

chop *verb* CUT, fell, axe, slash, hack, sever, shear, cleave, hew, lop, truncate ▷▷ **chop something up** CUT UP, divide, fragment, cube, dice, mince ▷▷ **the chop** (*Brit & Austral slang*) THE SACK, sacking (*informal*), dismissal, the boot (*slang*), your cards (*informal*), the axe (*informal*), termination, the (old) heave-ho (*informal*), the order of the boot (*slang*)

choppy *adjective* ROUGH, broken, ruffled, tempestuous, blustery, squally << ANTONYM calm

chore *noun* TASK, job, duty, burden, hassle (*informal*), fag (*informal*), errand, no picnic

chortle *verb* CHUCKLE, laugh, cackle, guffaw ▷ *noun* CHUCKLE, laugh, cackle, guffaw

chorus *noun* 1 REFRAIN, response, strain, burden 2 CHOIR, singers, ensemble, vocalists, choristers ▷▷ **in chorus** IN UNISON, as one, all together, in concert, in harmony, in accord, with one voice

christen *verb* 1 BAPTIZE, name 2 NAME, call, term, style, title, dub, designate

Christmas *noun* THE FESTIVE SEASON, Noël, Xmas (*informal*), Yule (*archaic*), Yuletide (*archaic*)

chronic *adjective* 1 PERSISTENT, constant, continual, deep-seated, incurable, deep-rooted, ineradicable 2 (*informal*) DREADFUL, awful, appalling, atrocious, abysmal

chronicle *verb* RECORD, tell, report, enter, relate, register, recount, set down, narrate, put on record ▷ *noun* RECORD, story, history, account, register, journal, diary, narrative, annals

chronicler *noun* RECORDER, reporter, historian, narrator, scribe, diarist, annalist

chronological *adjective* SEQUENTIAL, ordered, historical, progressive, consecutive, in sequence << ANTONYM random

chubby *adjective* PLUMP, stout, fleshy, tubby, flabby, portly, buxom, roly-poly, rotund, round, podgy << ANTONYM skinny

chuck *verb* (*informal*) 1 THROW, cast, pitch, shy, toss, hurl, fling, sling, heave 2 *often with* **away** *or* **out** THROW OUT, dump (*informal*), scrap, get rid of, bin (*informal*), ditch (*slang*), junk (*informal*), discard, dispose of, dispense with, jettison 3 GIVE UP *or* OVER, leave, stop, abandon, cease, resign from, pack in, jack in **4** (*US, Austral & NZ informal*) VOMIT, throw up (*informal*), spew, heave (*slang*), puke (*slang*), barf (*US slang*), chunder (*slang, chiefly Austral*), upchuck (*US slang*), do a technicolour yawn, toss your cookies (*US slang*)

chuckle *verb* LAUGH, giggle, snigger, chortle, titter ▷ *noun* LAUGH, giggle, snigger, chortle, titter

chum *noun* (*informal*) FRIEND, mate (*informal*), pal (*informal*), companion, cock (*Brit informal*), comrade, crony, main man (*slang, chiefly US*), cobber (*Austral & NZ old-fashioned informal*), E hoa (*NZ*)

chummy *adjective* (*informal*) FRIENDLY, close, thick (*informal*), pally (*informal*), intimate, affectionate, buddy-buddy (*slang, chiefly US & Canad*), palsy-walsy (*informal*), matey *or* maty (*Brit informal*)

chunk *noun* PIECE, block, mass, portion, lump, slab, hunk, nugget, wad, dollop (*informal*), wodge (*Brit informal*)

chunky *adjective* THICKSET, stocky, beefy (*informal*), stubby, dumpy

church *noun* CHAPEL, temple, cathedral, kirk (*Scot*), minster, tabernacle, place of worship, house of God **churlish** *adjective* RUDE, harsh, vulgar, sullen, surly, morose, brusque, ill-tempered, boorish, uncouth, impolite, loutish, oafish, uncivil, unmannerly << ANTONYM polite

churn *verb* **1** STIR UP, beat, disturb, swirl, agitate **2** SWIRL, boil, toss, foam, seethe, froth

cigarette *noun* FAG (*Brit slang*), smoke, gasper (*slang*), ciggy (*informal*), coffin nail (*slang*), cancer stick (*slang*)

cinema *noun* **1** PICTURES, movies, picture-house, flicks (*slang*) **2** FILMS, pictures, movies, the big screen (*informal*), motion pictures, the silver screen

cipher *noun* **1** CODE, coded message, cryptogram **2** NOBODY, nonentity

circa *preposition* APPROXIMATELY, about, around, roughly, in the region of, round about

circle *noun* **1** RING, round, band, disc, loop, hoop, cordon, perimeter, halo **2** GROUP, company, set, school, club, order, class, society, crowd, assembly, fellowship, fraternity, clique, coterie **3** SPHERE, world, area, range, field, scene, orbit, realm, milieu ▷ *verb* **1** GO ROUND, ring, surround, belt, curve, enclose, encompass, compass, envelop, encircle, circumscribe, hem in,

gird, circumnavigate, enwreath **2** WHEEL, spiral, revolve, rotate, whirl, pivot

circuit *noun* **1** COURSE, round, tour, track, route, journey **2** RACETRACK, course, track, racecourse **3** LAP, round, tour, revolution, orbit, perambulation

circuitous *adjective* **1** INDIRECT, winding, rambling, roundabout, meandering, tortuous, labyrinthine << ANTONYM direct **2** OBLIQUE, indirect

circular *adjective* **1** ROUND, ring-shaped, discoid **2** CIRCUITOUS, cyclical, orbital ▷ *noun* ADVERTISEMENT, notice, ad (*informal*), announcement, advert (*Brit informal*), press release

circulate *verb* **1** SPREAD, issue, publish, broadcast, distribute, diffuse, publicize, propagate, disseminate, promulgate, make known **2** FLOW, revolve, rotate, radiate

circulation *noun* **1** DISTRIBUTION, currency, readership **2** BLOODSTREAM, blood flow **3** FLOW, circling, motion, rotation **4** SPREAD, distribution, transmission, dissemination

circumference *noun* EDGE, limits, border, bounds, outline, boundary, fringe, verge, rim, perimeter, periphery, extremity

circumscribe *verb* RESTRICT, limit, define, confine, restrain, delineate, hem in, demarcate, delimit, straiten

circumspect *adjective* CAUTIOUS, politic, guarded, careful, wary, discriminating, discreet, sage, prudent, canny, attentive, vigilant, watchful, judicious, observant, sagacious, heedful << ANTONYM rash

circumstance *noun* **1** *usually plural* SITUATION, condition, scenario, contingency, state of affairs, lie of the land **2** *usually plural* DETAIL, fact, event, particular, respect, factor **3** *usually plural* SITUATION, state, means, position, station, resources, status, lifestyle **4** CHANCE, the times, accident, fortune, luck, fate, destiny, misfortune, providence

circumstantial *adjective* **1** INDIRECT, contingent, incidental, inferential, presumptive, conjectural, founded on circumstances **2** DETAILED, particular, specific

circumvent *verb* **1** (*Formal*) EVADE, bypass, elude, steer clear of, sidestep **2** OUTWIT, trick, mislead, thwart, deceive, dupe, beguile, outflank, hoodwink

cistern *noun* TANK, vat, basin, reservoir, sink

citadel *noun* FORTRESS, keep, tower,

stronghold, bastion, fortification, fastness

citation noun **1** COMMENDATION, award, mention **2** QUOTATION, quote, reference, passage, illustration, excerpt

cite verb **1** QUOTE, name, evidence, advance, mention, extract, specify, allude to, enumerate, adduce **2** (*Law*) SUMMON, call, subpoena

citizen noun INHABITANT, resident, dweller, ratepayer, denizen, subject, freeman, burgher, townsman **city** noun TOWN, metropolis, municipality, conurbation, megalopolis **civic** adjective PUBLIC, community, borough, municipal, communal, local

civil adjective **1** CIVIC, home, political, domestic, interior, municipal << ANTONYM state **2** POLITE, obliging, accommodating, civilized, courteous, considerate, affable, courtly, well-bred, complaisant, well-mannered << ANTONYM rude

civility noun POLITENESS, consideration, courtesy, tact, good manners, graciousness, cordiality, affability, amiability, complaisance, courteousness

civilization noun **1** SOCIETY, people, community, nation, polity **2** CULTURE, development, education, progress, enlightenment, sophistication, advancement, cultivation, refinement

civilize verb CULTIVATE, improve, polish, educate, refine, tame, enlighten, humanize, sophisticate

civilized adjective **1** CULTURED, educated, sophisticated, enlightened, humane << ANTONYM primitive **2** POLITE, mannerly, tolerant, gracious, courteous, affable, well-behaved, well-mannered

clad adjective DRESSED, clothed, arrayed, draped, fitted out, decked out, attired, rigged out (*informal*), covered

claim verb **1** ASSERT, insist, maintain, allege, uphold, profess, hold **2** TAKE, receive, pick up, collect, lay claim to **3** DEMAND, call for, ask for, insist on ▷ noun **1** ASSERTION, statement, allegation, declaration, contention, pretension, affirmation, protestation **2** DEMAND, application, request, petition, call **3** RIGHT, title, entitlement

claimant noun APPLICANT, pretender, petitioner, supplicant, suppliant

clairvoyant adjective PSYCHIC, visionary, prophetic, prescient, telepathic, fey, second-sighted, extrasensory, oracular, sibylline

▷ noun PSYCHIC, diviner, prophet, visionary, oracle, seer, augur, fortune-teller, soothsayer, sibyl, prophetess, telepath

clamber verb CLIMB, scale, scramble, claw, shin, scrabble

clammy adjective **1** MOIST, sweating, damp, sticky, sweaty, slimy **2** DAMP, humid, dank, muggy, close

clamour noun NOISE, shouting, racket, outcry, din, uproar, agitation, blare, commotion, babel, hubbub, brouhaha, hullabaloo, shout

clamp noun VICE, press, grip, bracket, fastener ▷ verb FASTEN, fix, secure, clinch, brace, make fast

clan noun **1** FAMILY, house, group, order, race, society, band, tribe, sept, fraternity, brotherhood, sodality, ainga (*NZ*), ngai *or* ngati (*NZ*) **2** GROUP, set, crowd, circle, crew (*informal*), gang, faction, coterie, schism, cabal

clandestine adjective SECRET, private, hidden, underground, concealed, closet, covert, sly, furtive, underhand, surreptitious, stealthy, cloak-and-dagger, under-the-counter

clang verb RING, toll, resound, chime, reverberate, jangle, clank, bong, clash ▷ noun RINGING, clash, jangle, knell, clank, reverberation, ding-dong, clangour

clap verb **1** APPLAUD, cheer, acclaim, give (someone) a big hand << ANTONYM boo **2** STRIKE, pat, punch, bang, thrust, slap, whack, wallop (*informal*), thwack

clarification noun EXPLANATION, interpretation, exposition, illumination, simplification, elucidation

clarify verb **1** EXPLAIN, resolve, interpret, illuminate, clear up, simplify, make plain, elucidate, explicate, clear the air about, throw *or* shed light on **2** REFINE, cleanse, purify

clarity noun **1** CLEARNESS, precision, simplicity, transparency, lucidity, explicitness, intelligibility, obviousness, straightforwardness, comprehensibility << ANTONYM obscurity **2** TRANSPARENCY, clearness << ANTONYM cloudiness

clash verb **1** CONFLICT, grapple, wrangle, lock horns, cross swords, war, feud, quarrel **2** DISAGREE, conflict, vary, counter, differ, depart, contradict, diverge, deviate, run counter to, be dissimilar, be discordant **3** NOT GO, jar, not match, be discordant **4** CRASH, bang, rattle, jar, clatter, jangle, clang, clank ▷ noun

1 CONFLICT, fight, brush, confrontation, collision, showdown (*informal*), boilover (*Austral*) 2 DISAGREEMENT, difference, division, argument, dispute, dissent, difference of opinion

clasp *verb* GRASP, hold, press, grip, seize, squeeze, embrace, clutch, hug, enfold ▷ *noun* 1 GRASP, hold, grip, embrace, hug 2 FASTENING, catch, grip, hook, snap, pin, clip, buckle, brooch, fastener, hasp, press stud

class *noun* 1 GROUP, grouping, set, order, league, division, rank, caste, status, sphere 2 TYPE, set, sort, kind, collection, species, grade, category, stamp, genre, classification, denomination, genus ▷ *verb* CLASSIFY, group, rate, rank, brand, label, grade, designate, categorize, codify ▷ see **family**

classic *adjective* 1 TYPICAL, standard, model, regular, usual, ideal, characteristic, definitive, archetypal, exemplary, quintessential, time-honoured, paradigmatic, dinki-di (*Austral informal*) 2 MASTERLY, best, finest, master, world-class, consummate, first-rate << ANTONYM second-rate 3 LASTING, enduring, abiding, immortal, undying, ageless, deathless ▷ *noun* STANDARD, masterpiece, prototype, paradigm, exemplar, masterwork, model

classification *noun* 1 CATEGORIZATION, grading, cataloguing, taxonomy, codification, sorting, analysis, arrangement 2 CLASS, grouping, heading, head, order, sort, list, department, type, division, section, rank, grade

classify *verb* CATEGORIZE, sort, file, rank, arrange, grade, catalogue, codify, pigeonhole, tabulate, systematize

classy *adjective* (*informal*) HIGH-CLASS, select, exclusive, superior, elegant, stylish, posh (*informal, chiefly Brit*), swish (*informal, chiefly Brit*), up-market, urbane, swanky (*informal*), top-drawer, ritzy (*slang*), high-toned, schmick (*Austral informal*)

clause *noun* SECTION, condition, article, item, chapter, rider, provision, passage, point, part, heading, paragraph, specification, proviso, stipulation

claw *noun* 1 NAIL, talon 2 PINCER, nipper ▷ *verb* SCRATCH, tear, dig, rip, scrape, graze, maul, scrabble, mangle, mangulate (*Austral slang*), lacerate

clean *adjective* 1 HYGIENIC, natural, fresh, sterile, pure, purified, antiseptic, sterilized, unadulterated, uncontaminated, unpolluted, decontaminated << ANTONYM contaminated 2 SPOTLESS, fresh, washed, immaculate, laundered, impeccable, flawless, sanitary, faultless, squeaky-clean, hygienic, unblemished, unsullied, unstained, unsoiled, unspotted << ANTONYM dirty 3 MORAL, good, pure, decent, innocent, respectable, upright, honourable, impeccable, exemplary, virtuous, chaste, undefiled << ANTONYM immoral 4 COMPLETE, final, whole, total, perfect, entire, decisive, thorough, conclusive, unimpaired 5 NEAT, simple, elegant, trim, delicate, tidy, graceful, uncluttered << ANTONYM untidy ▷ *verb* CLEANSE, wash, bath, sweep, dust, wipe, vacuum, scrub, sponge, rinse, mop, launder, scour, purify, do up, swab, disinfect, deodorize, sanitize << ANTONYM dirty

clean-cut *adjective* NEAT, trim, tidy, chiselled

cleanliness *noun* CLEANNESS, purity, freshness, whiteness, sterility, spotlessness

cleanse *verb* 1 PURIFY, clear, purge 2 ABSOLVE, clear, purge, purify 3 CLEAN, wash, rinse, scour

cleanser *noun* DETERGENT, soap, solvent, disinfectant, soap powder, purifier, scourer, wash

clear *adjective* 1 COMPREHENSIBLE, explicit, articulate, understandable, coherent, lucid, user-friendly, intelligible << ANTONYM confused 2 DISTINCT, audible, perceptible << ANTONYM indistinct 3 OBVIOUS, plain, apparent, bold, patent, evident, distinct, pronounced, definite, manifest, blatant, conspicuous, unmistakable, express, palpable, unequivocal, recognizable, unambiguous, unquestionable, cut-and-dried (*informal*), incontrovertible << ANTONYM ambiguous 4 CERTAIN, sure, convinced, positive, satisfied, resolved, explicit, definite, decided << ANTONYM confused 5 TRANSPARENT, see-through, translucent, crystalline, glassy, limpid, pellucid << ANTONYM opaque 6 UNOBSTRUCTED, open, free, empty, unhindered, unimpeded, unhampered << ANTONYM blocked 7 BRIGHT, fine, fair, shining, sunny, luminous, halcyon, cloudless, undimmed, light, unclouded << ANTONYM cloudy 8 UNTROUBLED, clean, pure, innocent, stainless, immaculate, unblemished, untarnished, guiltless, sinless,

undefiled ▷ *verb* **1** UNBLOCK, unclog,
free, loosen, extricate, disengage, open,
disentangle **2** REMOVE, clean, wipe, cleanse,
tidy (up), sweep away **3** BRIGHTEN, break
up, lighten **4** PASS OVER, jump, leap, vault,
miss **5** ABSOLVE, acquit, vindicate, exonerate
<< ANTONYM blame ▷▷ **clear out** (*informal*)
GO AWAY, leave, retire, withdraw, depart,
beat it (*slang*), decamp, hook it (*slang*), slope
off, pack your bags (*informal*), make tracks,
take yourself off, make yourself scarce, rack
off (*Austral & NZ slang*) ▷▷ **clear something
out 1** EMPTY, sort, tidy up **2** GET RID OF,
remove, dump, dispose of, throw away *or* out
▷▷ **clear something up 1** TIDY (UP), order,
straighten, rearrange, put in order **2** SOLVE,
explain, resolve, clarify, unravel, straighten
out, elucidate

clearance *noun* **1** EVACUATION,
emptying, withdrawal, removal, eviction,
depopulation **2** PERMISSION, consent,
endorsement, green light, authorization,
blank cheque, go-ahead (*informal*), leave,
sanction, O.K. *or* okay (*informal*) **3** SPACE,
gap, margin, allowance, headroom

clear-cut *adjective* STRAIGHTFORWARD,
specific, plain, precise, black-and-
white, explicit, definite, unequivocal,
unambiguous, cut-and-dried (*informal*)

clearing *noun* GLADE, space, dell

clearly *adverb* **1** OBVIOUSLY, undoubtedly,
evidently, distinctly, markedly, overtly,
undeniably, beyond doubt, incontrovertibly,
incontestably, openly **2** LEGIBLY,
distinctly **3** AUDIBLY, distinctly, intelligibly,
comprehensibly

cleave *verb* SPLIT, open, divide, crack, slice,
rend, sever, part, hew, tear asunder, sunder

cleft *noun* OPENING, break, crack, gap, rent,
breach, fracture, rift, chink, crevice, fissure,
cranny

clemency *noun* MERCY, pity, humanity,
compassion, kindness, forgiveness,
indulgence, leniency, forbearance, quarter

clement *adjective* MILD, fine, fair, calm,
temperate, balmy

clergy *noun* PRIESTHOOD, ministry, clerics,
clergymen, churchmen, the cloth, holy
orders, ecclesiastics

clergyman *noun* MINISTER, priest, vicar,
parson, reverend (*informal*), rabbi, pastor,
chaplain, cleric, rector, curate, father,
churchman, padre, man of God, man of the
cloth, divine

clerical *adjective* **1** ADMINISTRATIVE, office,

bureaucratic, secretarial, book-keeping,
stenographic **2** ECCLESIASTICAL, priestly,
pastoral, sacerdotal

clever *adjective* **1** INTELLIGENT, quick,
bright, talented, gifted, keen, capable, smart,
sensible, rational, witty, apt, discerning,
knowledgeable, astute, brainy (*informal*),
quick-witted, sagacious, knowing, deep,
expert << ANTONYM stupid **2** SHREWD,
bright, cunning, ingenious, inventive,
astute, resourceful, canny << ANTONYM
unimaginative **3** SKILFUL, able, talented,
gifted, capable, inventive, adroit, dexterous
<< ANTONYM inept

cleverness *noun* **1** INTELLIGENCE, sense,
brains, wit, brightness, nous (*Brit slang*), suss
(*slang*), quickness, gumption (*Brit informal*),
sagacity, smartness, astuteness, quick wits,
smarts (*slang, chiefly US*) **2** SHREWDNESS,
sharpness, resourcefulness,
canniness **3** DEXTERITY, ability, talent, gift,
flair, ingenuity, adroitness

cliché *noun* PLATITUDE, stereotype,
commonplace, banality, truism, bromide,
old saw, hackneyed phrase, chestnut
(*informal*)

click *noun* SNAP, beat, tick, clack ▷ *verb*
1 SNAP, beat, tick, clack **2** (*informal*) BECOME
CLEAR, come home (to), make sense, fall into
place **3** (*Slang*) GET ON, be compatible, hit
it off (*informal*), be on the same wavelength,
get on like a house on fire (*informal*), take to
each other, feel a rapport

client *noun* CUSTOMER, consumer, buyer,
patron, shopper, habitué, patient

clientele *noun* CUSTOMERS, market, business,
following, trade, regulars, clients, patronage

cliff *noun* ROCK FACE, overhang, crag,
precipice, escarpment, face, scar, bluff

climactic *adjective* CRUCIAL, central, critical,
peak, decisive, paramount, pivotal

climate *noun* **1** WEATHER, country, region,
temperature, clime **2** ATMOSPHERE,
environment, spirit, surroundings, tone,
mood, trend, flavour, feeling, tendency,
temper, ambience, vibes (*slang*)

climax *noun* CULMINATION, head, top,
summit, height, highlight, peak, pay-off
(*informal*), crest, high point, zenith, apogee,
high spot (*informal*), acme, ne plus ultra
(*Latin*) ▷ *verb* CULMINATE, end, finish,
conclude, peak, come to a head

climb *verb* **1** ASCEND, scale, mount, go up,
clamber, shin up **2** CLAMBER, descend,
scramble, dismount **3** RISE, go up, soar,

ascend, fly up ▷▷ **climb down** BACK DOWN,
withdraw, yield, concede, retreat, surrender,
give in, cave in (*informal*), retract, admit
defeat, back-pedal, eat your words, eat crow
(*US informal*)

clinch *verb* **1** SECURE, close, confirm,
conclude, seal, verify, sew up (*informal*), set
the seal on **2** SETTLE, decide, determine, tip
the balance

cling *verb* **1** CLUTCH, grip, embrace, grasp,
hug, hold on to, clasp **2** STICK TO, attach to,
adhere to, fasten to, twine round ▷▷ **cling to
something** ADHERE TO, maintain, stand by,
cherish, abide by, be true to, be loyal to, be
faithful to, cleave to

clinical *adjective* UNEMOTIONAL, cold,
scientific, objective, detached, analytic,
impersonal, antiseptic, disinterested,
dispassionate, emotionless

clip¹ *verb* **1** TRIM, cut, crop, dock,
prune, shorten, shear, cut short, snip,
pare **2** (*informal*) SMACK, strike, box,
knock, punch, belt (*informal*), thump, clout
(*informal*), cuff, whack, wallop (*informal*),
skelp (*dialect*) ▷ *noun* **1** (*informal*) SMACK,
strike, box, knock, punch, belt (*informal*),
thump, clout (*informal*), cuff, whack, wallop
(*informal*), skelp (*dialect*) **2** (*informal*) SPEED,
rate, pace, gallop, lick (*informal*), velocity

clip² *verb* ATTACH, fix, secure, connect, pin,
staple, fasten, affix, hold

clipping *noun* CUTTING, passage, extract,
excerpt, piece, article

clique *noun* GROUP, set, crowd, pack, circle,
crew (*informal*), gang, faction, mob, clan,
posse (*informal*), coterie, schism, cabal

cloak *noun* **1** CAPE, coat, wrap,
mantle **2** COVERING, layer, blanket,
shroud **3** DISGUISE, front, cover, screen,
blind, mask, shield, cover-up, façade, pretext,
smoke screen ▷ *verb* **1** COVER, coat, wrap,
blanket, shroud, envelop **2** HIDE, cover,
screen, mask, disguise, conceal, obscure,
veil, camouflage

clobber¹ *verb* (*Slang*) BATTER, beat, assault,
smash, bash (*informal*), lash, thrash, pound,
beat up (*informal*), wallop (*informal*), pummel,
rough up (*informal*), lambast(e), belabour,
duff up (*informal*), beat *or* knock seven bells
out of (*informal*)

clobber² *noun* (*Brit slang*) BELONGINGS,
things, effects, property, stuff, gear,
possessions, paraphernalia, accoutrements,
chattels

clog *verb* OBSTRUCT, block, jam, hamper,
hinder, impede, bung, stop up, dam up,
occlude, congest

cloistered *adjective* SHELTERED, protected,
restricted, shielded, confined, insulated,
secluded, reclusive, shut off, sequestered,
withdrawn, cloistral << ANTONYM public

close¹ *verb* **1** SHUT, lock, push to, fasten,
secure << ANTONYM open **2** SHUT DOWN,
finish, cease, discontinue **3** WIND UP,
finish, axe (*informal*), shut down, terminate,
discontinue, mothball **4** BLOCK UP, bar, seal,
shut up << ANTONYM open **5** END, finish,
complete, conclude, wind up, culminate,
terminate << ANTONYM begin **6** CLINCH,
confirm, secure, conclude, seal, verify,
sew up (*informal*), set the seal on **7** COME
TOGETHER, join, connect << ANTONYM
separate ▷ *noun* END, ending, finish,
conclusion, completion, finale, culmination,
denouement

close² *adjective* **1** NEAR, neighbouring,
nearby, handy, adjacent, adjoining, hard
by, just round the corner, within striking
distance (*informal*), cheek by jowl, proximate,
within spitting distance (*informal*), within
sniffing distance, a hop, skip and a jump
away << ANTONYM far **2** INTIMATE,
loving, friendly, familiar, thick (*informal*),
attached, devoted, confidential, inseparable,
dear << ANTONYM distant **3** NOTICEABLE,
marked, strong, distinct,
pronounced **4** CAREFUL, detailed, searching,
concentrated, keen, intense, minute, alert,
intent, thorough, rigorous, attentive,
painstaking, assiduous **5** EVEN, level,
neck and neck, fifty-fifty (*informal*), evenly
matched, equally balanced **6** IMMINENT,
near, approaching, impending, at hand,
upcoming, nigh, just round the corner
<< ANTONYM far away **7** STIFLING,
confined, oppressive, stale, suffocating,
stuffy, humid, sweltering, airless, muggy,
unventilated, heavy, thick << ANTONYM
airy **8** ACCURATE, strict, exact, precise,
faithful, literal, conscientious

closed *adjective* **1** SHUT, locked,
sealed, fastened << ANTONYM
open **2** SHUT DOWN, out of business,
out of service **3** EXCLUSIVE, select,
restricted **4** FINISHED, over, ended, decided,
settled, concluded, resolved, terminated

closet *noun* (*US*) CUPBOARD, cabinet, recess,
cubicle, cubbyhole ▷ *adjective* SECRET,
private, hidden, unknown, concealed, covert,
unrevealed

closure *noun* CLOSING, end, finish, conclusion, stoppage, termination, cessation

clot *verb* CONGEAL, thicken, curdle, coalesce, jell, coagulate

cloth *noun* FABRIC, material, textiles, dry goods, stuff

clothe *verb* DRESS, outfit, rig, array, robe, drape, get ready, swathe, apparel, attire, fit out, garb, doll up (*slang*), accoutre, cover, deck << ANTONYM undress

clothes *plural noun* CLOTHING, wear, dress, gear (*informal*), habits, get-up (*informal*), outfit, costume, threads (*slang*), wardrobe, ensemble, garments, duds (*informal*), apparel, clobber (*Brit slang*), attire, garb, togs (*informal*), vestments, glad rags (*informal*), raiment (*archaic or poetic*), rigout (*informal*)

clothing *noun* CLOTHES, wear, dress, gear (*informal*), habits, get-up (*informal*), outfit, costume, threads (*slang*), wardrobe, ensemble, garments, duds (*informal*), apparel, clobber (*Brit slang*), attire, garb, togs (*informal*), vestments, glad rags (*informal*), raiment (*archaic or poetic*), rigout (*informal*)

cloud *noun* 1 MIST, fog, haze, obscurity, vapour, nebula, murk, darkness, gloom 2 BILLOW, mass, shower, puff ▷ *verb* 1 CONFUSE, obscure, distort, impair, muddle, disorient 2 DARKEN, dim, be overshadowed, be overcast

cloudy *adjective* 1 DULL, dark, dim, gloomy, dismal, sombre, overcast, leaden, sunless, louring *or* lowering << ANTONYM clear 2 OPAQUE, muddy, murky 3 VAGUE, confused, obscure, blurred, unclear, hazy, indistinct << ANTONYM plain

clout (*informal*) *verb* HIT, strike, punch, deck (*slang*), slap, sock (*slang*), chin (*slang*), smack, thump, cuff, clobber (*slang*), wallop (*informal*), box, wham, lay one on (*slang*), skelp (*dialect*) ▷ *noun* 1 THUMP, blow, crack, punch, slap, sock (*slang*), cuff, wallop (*informal*), skelp (*dialect*) 2 INFLUENCE, power, standing, authority, pull, weight, bottom, prestige, mana (*NZ*)

cloven *adjective* SPLIT, divided, cleft, bisected

clown *noun* 1 COMEDIAN, fool, harlequin, jester, buffoon, pierrot, dolt 2 JOKER, comic, prankster 3 FOOL, dope (*informal*), jerk (*slang, chiefly US & Canad*), idiot, ass, berk (*Brit slang*), prat (*slang*), moron, twit (*informal, chiefly Brit*), imbecile (*informal*), ignoramus, jackass, dolt, blockhead, ninny, putz (*US slang*), eejit (*Scot & Irish*), doofus (*slang, chiefly US*), dorba *or* dorb (*Austral slang*),

bogan (*Austral slang*), lamebrain (*informal*), numbskull *or* numskull ▷ *verb usually with* **around** PLAY THE FOOL, mess about, jest, act the fool, act the goat, play the goat

cloying *adjective* 1 SICKLY, nauseating, icky (*informal*), treacly, oversweet, excessive 2 OVER-SENTIMENTAL, sickly, nauseating, mushy, twee, slushy, mawkish, icky (*informal*), treacly, oversweet

club *noun* 1 ASSOCIATION, company, group, union, society, circle, lodge, guild, fraternity, set, order, sodality 2 STICK, bat, bludgeon, truncheon, cosh (*Brit*), cudgel ▷ *verb* BEAT, strike, hammer, batter, bash, clout (*informal*), bludgeon, clobber (*slang*), pummel, cosh (*Brit*), beat *or* knock seven bells out of (*informal*)

clue *noun* INDICATION, lead, sign, evidence, tip, suggestion, trace, hint, suspicion, pointer, tip-off, inkling, intimation

clueless *adjective* STUPID, thick, dull, naive, dim, dense, dumb (*informal*), simple-minded, dozy (*Brit informal*), simple, slow, witless, dopey (*informal*), moronic, unintelligent, half-witted, slow on the uptake (*informal*)

clump *noun* CLUSTER, group, bunch, bundle, shock ▷ *verb* STOMP, stamp, stump, thump, lumber, tramp, plod, thud, clomp

clumsiness *noun* INSENSITIVITY, heavy-handedness, tactlessness, gaucheness, lack of tact, uncouthness << ANTONYM sensitivity

clumsy *adjective* 1 AWKWARD, blundering, bungling, lumbering, inept, bumbling, ponderous, ungainly, gauche, accident-prone, gawky, heavy, uncoordinated, cack-handed (*informal*), inexpert, maladroit, ham-handed (*informal*), like a bull in a china shop, klutzy (*US & Canad slang*), unskilful, butterfingered (*informal*), ham-fisted (*informal*), unco (*Austral slang*) << ANTONYM skilful 2 UNWIELDY, ill-shaped, unhandy, clunky (*informal*)

cluster *noun* GATHERING, group, collection, bunch, knot, clump, assemblage ▷ *verb* GATHER, group, collect, bunch, assemble, flock, huddle

clutch *verb* 1 HOLD, grip, embrace, grasp, cling to, clasp 2 SEIZE, catch, grab, grasp, snatch ▷ *plural noun* POWER, hands, control, grip, possession, grasp, custody, sway, keeping, claws

clutter *noun* UNTIDINESS, mess, disorder, confusion, litter, muddle, disarray, jumble, hotchpotch << ANTONYM order

▷ *verb* LITTER, scatter, strew, mess up
<< ANTONYM tidy

cluttered *adjective* UNTIDY, confused, disordered, littered, messy, muddled, jumbled, disarrayed

coach *noun* **1** INSTRUCTOR, teacher, trainer, tutor, handler **2** BUS, charabanc ▷ *verb* INSTRUCT, train, prepare, exercise, drill, tutor, cram

coalesce *verb* BLEND, unite, mix, combine, incorporate, integrate, merge, consolidate, come together, fuse, amalgamate, meld, cohere

coalition *noun* ALLIANCE, union, league, association, combination, merger, integration, compact, conjunction, bloc, confederation, fusion, affiliation, amalgam, amalgamation, confederacy

coarse *adjective* **1** ROUGH, crude, unfinished, homespun, impure, unrefined, rough-hewn, unprocessed, unpolished, coarse-grained, unpurified << ANTONYM smooth **2** VULGAR, offensive, rude, indecent, improper, raunchy (*slang*), earthy, foul-mouthed, bawdy, impure, smutty, impolite, ribald, immodest, indelicate **3** LOUTISH, rough, brutish, boorish, uncivil << ANTONYM well-mannered

coast *noun* SHORE, border, beach, strand, seaside, coastline, seaboard ▷ *verb* CRUISE, sail, drift, taxi, glide, freewheel **coat** *noun* **1** FUR, hair, skin, hide, wool, fleece, pelt **2** LAYER, covering, coating, overlay ▷ *verb* COVER, spread, plaster, smear

coating *noun* LAYER, covering, finish, skin, sheet, coat, dusting, blanket, membrane, glaze, film, varnish, veneer, patina, lamination

coat of arms *noun* HERALDRY, crest, insignia, escutcheon, blazonry

coax *verb* PERSUADE, cajole, talk into, wheedle, sweet-talk (*informal*), prevail upon, inveigle, soft-soap (*informal*), twist (someone's) arm, flatter, entice, beguile, allure << ANTONYM bully

cobber *noun* (*Austral & NZ old-fashioned informal*) FRIEND, pal, mate (*informal*), buddy (*informal*), china (*Brit & S African informal*), best friend, intimate, cock (*Brit informal*), close friend, comrade, chum (*informal*), crony, alter ego, main man (*slang, chiefly US*), soul mate, homeboy (*slang, chiefly US*), bosom friend, boon companion, E hoa (*NZ*)

cock *noun* COCKEREL, rooster, chanticleer ▷ *verb* RAISE, prick up, perk up

cocktail *noun* MIXTURE, combination, compound, blend, concoction, mix, amalgamation, admixture

cocky¹ *adjective* OVERCONFIDENT, arrogant, brash, swaggering, conceited, egotistical, cocksure, swollen-headed, vain, full of yourself << ANTONYM modest

cocky² *or* **cockie** *noun* (*Austral & NZ informal*) FARMER, smallholder, crofter (*Scot*), grazier, agriculturalist, rancher, husbandman

cocoon *verb* **1** WRAP, swathe, envelop, swaddle, pad **2** PROTECT, shelter, cushion, insulate, screen

coddle *verb* PAMPER, spoil, indulge, cosset, baby, nurse, pet, wet-nurse (*informal*), mollycoddle

code *noun* **1** PRINCIPLES, rules, manners, custom, convention, ethics, maxim, etiquette, system, kawa (*NZ*), tikanga (*NZ*) **2** CIPHER, cryptograph

codify *verb* SYSTEMATIZE, catalogue, classify, summarize, tabulate, collect, organize

coerce *verb* FORCE, compel, bully, intimidate, railroad (*informal*), constrain, bulldoze (*informal*), dragoon, pressurize, browbeat, press-gang, twist (someone's) arm (*informal*), drive

coercion *noun* FORCE, pressure, threats, bullying, constraint, intimidation, compulsion, duress, browbeating, strong-arm tactics (*informal*)

cogent *adjective* CONVINCING, strong, powerful, effective, compelling, urgent, influential, potent, irresistible, compulsive, forceful, conclusive, weighty, forcible

cognition *noun* PERCEPTION, reasoning, understanding, intelligence, awareness, insight, comprehension, apprehension, discernment

coherence *noun* CONSISTENCY, rationality, concordance, consonance, congruity, union, agreement, connection, unity, correspondence

coherent *adjective* **1** CONSISTENT, reasoned, organized, rational, logical, meaningful, systematic, orderly << ANTONYM inconsistent **2** ARTICULATE, lucid, comprehensible, intelligible << ANTONYM unintelligible

cohort *noun* GROUP, set, band, contingent, batch

coil *verb* **1** WIND, twist, curl, loop, spiral, twine **2** CURL, wind, twist, snake, loop, entwine, twine, wreathe, convolute

coin *noun* MONEY, change, cash, silver,

copper, dosh (*Brit & Austral slang*), specie, kembla (*Austral slang*) ▷ *verb* INVENT, create, make up, frame, forge, conceive, originate, formulate, fabricate, think up **coincide** *verb* **1** OCCUR SIMULTANEOUSLY, coexist, synchronize, be concurrent **2** AGREE, match, accord, square, correspond, tally, concur, harmonize << ANTONYM disagree

coincidence *noun* CHANCE, accident, luck, fluke, eventuality, stroke of luck, happy accident, fortuity

coincidental *adjective* ACCIDENTAL, unintentional, unintended, unplanned, fortuitous, fluky (*informal*), chance, casual << ANTONYM deliberate

cold *adjective* **1** CHILLY, biting, freezing, bitter, raw, chill, harsh, bleak, arctic, icy, frosty, wintry, frigid, inclement, parky (*Brit informal*), cool << ANTONYM hot **2** FREEZING, frozen, chilled, numb, chilly, shivery, benumbed, frozen to the marrow **3** DISTANT, reserved, indifferent, aloof, glacial, cold-blooded, apathetic, frigid, unresponsive, unfeeling, passionless, undemonstrative, standoffish << ANTONYM emotional **4** UNFRIENDLY, indifferent, stony, lukewarm, glacial, unmoved, unsympathetic, apathetic, frigid, inhospitable, unresponsive << ANTONYM friendly ▷ *noun* COLDNESS, chill, frigidity, chilliness, frostiness, iciness

cold-blooded *adjective* CALLOUS, cruel, savage, brutal, ruthless, steely, heartless, inhuman, merciless, unmoved, dispassionate, barbarous, pitiless, unfeeling, unemotional, stony-hearted << ANTONYM caring

collaborate *verb* **1** WORK TOGETHER, team up, join forces, cooperate, play ball (*informal*), participate **2** CONSPIRE, cooperate, collude, fraternize

collaboration *noun* **1** TEAMWORK, partnership, cooperation, association, alliance, concert **2** CONSPIRING, cooperation, collusion, fraternization

collaborator *noun* **1** CO-WORKER, partner, colleague, associate, team-mate, confederate **2** TRAITOR, turncoat, quisling, collaborationist, fraternizer

collapse *verb* **1** FALL DOWN, fall, give way, subside, cave in, crumple, fall apart at the seams **2** FAIL, fold, founder, break down, fall through, come to nothing, go belly-up (*informal*) **3** FAINT, break down, pass out, black out, swoon (*literary*), crack up (*informal*), keel over (*informal*), flake out (*informal*) ▷ *noun* **1** FALLING DOWN, ruin, falling apart, cave-in, disintegration, subsidence **2** FAILURE, slump, breakdown, flop, downfall **3** FAINT, breakdown, blackout, prostration

collar *verb* (*informal*) SEIZE, catch, arrest, appropriate, grab, capture, nail (*informal*), nab (*informal*), apprehend, lay hands on

collate *verb* COLLECT, gather, organize, assemble, compose, adduce, systematize

collateral *noun* SECURITY, guarantee, deposit, assurance, surety, pledge

colleague *noun* FELLOW WORKER, partner, ally, associate, assistant, team-mate, companion, comrade, helper, collaborator, confederate, auxiliary, workmate, confrère

collect *verb* **1** GATHER, save, assemble, heap, accumulate, aggregate, amass, stockpile, hoard << ANTONYM scatter **2** RAISE, secure, gather, obtain, acquire, muster, solicit **3** ASSEMBLE, meet, rally, cluster, come together, convene, converge, congregate, flock together << ANTONYM disperse

collected *adjective* CALM, together (*slang*), cool, confident, composed, poised, serene, sedate, self-controlled, unfazed (*informal*), unperturbed, unruffled, self-possessed, keeping your cool, unperturbable, as cool as a cucumber << ANTONYM nervous

collection *noun* **1** ACCUMULATION, set, store, mass, pile, heap, stockpile, hoard, congeries **2** COMPILATION, accumulation, anthology **3** GROUP, company, crowd, gathering, assembly, cluster, congregation, assortment, assemblage **4** GATHERING, acquisition, accumulation **5** CONTRIBUTION, donation, alms **6** OFFERING, offertory

collective *adjective* **1** JOINT, united, shared, common, combined, corporate, concerted, unified, cooperative << ANTONYM individual **2** COMBINED, aggregate, composite, cumulative << ANTONYM separate

collide *verb* **1** CRASH, clash, meet head-on, come into collision **2** CONFLICT, clash, be incompatible, be at variance

collision *noun* **1** CRASH, impact, accident, smash, bump, pile-up (*informal*), prang (*informal*) **2** CONFLICT, opposition, clash, clashing, encounter, disagreement, incompatibility

colloquial *adjective* INFORMAL, familiar, everyday, vernacular, conversational, demotic, idiomatic

collude *verb* CONSPIRE, scheme, plot, intrigue, collaborate, contrive, abet, connive, be in cahoots (*informal*), machinate

collusion *noun* CONSPIRACY, intrigue, deceit, complicity, connivance, secret understanding

colonist *noun* SETTLER, immigrant, pioneer, colonial, homesteader (*US*), colonizer, frontiersman

colonize *verb* SETTLE, populate, put down roots in, people, pioneer, open up

colonnade *noun* CLOISTERS, arcade, portico, covered walk

colony *noun* SETTLEMENT, territory, province, possession, dependency, outpost, dominion, satellite state, community

colossal *adjective* HUGE, massive, vast, enormous, immense, titanic, gigantic, monumental, monstrous, mammoth, mountainous, stellar (*informal*), prodigious, gargantuan, herculean, elephantine, humongous *or* humungous (*US slang*)
<< ANTONYM tiny

colour *or US* **color** *noun* 1 HUE, tone, shade, tint, tinge, tincture, colourway 2 PAINT, stain, dye, tint, pigment, tincture, coloration, colourwash, colorant 3 LIVELINESS, life, interest, excitement, animation, zest ▷ *plural noun* 1 FLAG, standard, banner, emblem, ensign 2 NATURE, quality, character, aspect, personality, stamp, traits, temperament ▷ *verb* 1 BLUSH, flush, crimson, redden, go crimson, burn, go as red as a beetroot 2 INFLUENCE, affect, prejudice, distort, pervert, taint, slant 3 EXAGGERATE, disguise, embroider, misrepresent, falsify, gloss over

colourful *adjective* 1 BRIGHT, rich, brilliant, intense, vivid, vibrant, psychedelic, motley, variegated, jazzy (*informal*), multicoloured, Day-glo (*trademark*), kaleidoscopic
<< ANTONYM drab 2 INTERESTING, rich, unusual, stimulating, graphic, lively, distinctive, vivid, picturesque, characterful
<< ANTONYM boring

colourless *adjective* 1 UNCOLOURED, faded, neutral, bleached, washed out, achromatic 2 ASHEN, washed out, wan, sickly, anaemic << ANTONYM radiant 3 UNINTERESTING, dull, tame, dreary, drab, lacklustre, vacuous, insipid, vapid, characterless, unmemorable
<< ANTONYM interesting

column *noun* 1 PILLAR, support, post, shaft, upright, obelisk 2 LINE, train, row, file, rank, string, queue, procession, cavalcade

columnist *noun* JOURNALIST, correspondent, editor, reporter, critic, reviewer, gossip columnist, journo (*slang*)

coma *noun* UNCONSCIOUSNESS, trance, oblivion, lethargy, stupor, torpor, insensibility

comatose *adjective* 1 UNCONSCIOUS, in a coma, out cold, insensible 2 INERT, stupefied, out cold, somnolent, torpid, insensible, dead to the world (*informal*), drugged

comb *verb* 1 UNTANGLE, arrange, groom, dress 2 SEARCH, hunt through, sweep, rake, sift, scour, rummage, ransack, forage, fossick (*Austral & NZ*), go through with a fine-tooth comb

combat *noun* FIGHT, war, action, battle, conflict, engagement, warfare, skirmish
<< ANTONYM peace ▷ *verb* FIGHT, battle against, oppose, contest, engage, cope with, resist, defy, withstand, struggle against, contend with, do battle with, strive against
<< ANTONYM support

combatant *noun* FIGHTER, soldier, warrior, contender, gladiator, belligerent, antagonist, fighting man, serviceman *or* servicewoman ▷ *adjective* FIGHTING, warring, battling, conflicting, opposing, contending, belligerent, combative

combative *adjective* AGGRESSIVE, militant, contentious, belligerent, antagonistic, pugnacious, warlike, bellicose, truculent, quarrelsome << ANTONYM nonaggressive

combination *noun* 1 MIXTURE, mix, compound, blend, composite, amalgam, amalgamation, meld, coalescence 2 ASSOCIATION, union, alliance, coalition, merger, federation, consortium, unification, syndicate, confederation, cartel, confederacy, cabal

combine *verb* 1 AMALGAMATE, marry, mix, bond, bind, compound, blend, incorporate, integrate, merge, put together, fuse, synthesize << ANTONYM separate 2 JOIN TOGETHER, link, connect, integrate, merge, fuse, amalgamate, meld 3 UNITE, associate, team up, unify, get together, collaborate, join forces, cooperate, join together, pool resources << ANTONYM split up

combustible *adjective* FLAMMABLE, explosive, incendiary, inflammable

come *verb* 1 APPROACH, near, advance, move towards, draw near 2 ARRIVE, move, appear, enter, turn up (*informal*), show up (*informal*), materialize **3** REACH, extend **4** HAPPEN, fall, occur, take place, come about, come to pass **5** BE AVAILABLE, be made, be offered, be produced, be on offer ▷▷ **come about** HAPPEN, result, occur, take place, arise, transpire (*informal*), befall, come to pass ▷▷ **come across as something** *or* **someone** SEEM, look, seem to be, appear to be, give the impression of being ▷▷ **come across someone** MEET, encounter, run into, bump into (*informal*) ▷▷ **come across something** FIND, discover, notice, unearth, stumble upon, hit upon, chance upon, happen upon, light upon ▷▷ **come at someone** ATTACK, charge, rush, go for, assault, fly at, assail, fall upon, rush at ▷▷ **come back** RETURN, reappear, re-enter ▷▷ **come between someone** SEPARATE, part, divide, alienate, estrange, set at odds ▷▷ **come by something** GET, win, land, score (*slang*), secure, obtain, acquire, get hold of, procure, take possession of ▷▷ **come down 1** DECREASE, fall, drop, reduce, go down, diminish, lessen, become lower **2** FALL, descend ▷▷ **come down on someone** REPRIMAND, blast, carpet (*informal*), put down, criticize, jump on (*informal*), rebuke, dress (someone) down (*informal*), tear into (*informal*), diss (*slang, chiefly US*), read (someone) the riot act, lambast(e), bawl (someone) out (*informal*), rap (someone) over the knuckles, chew (someone) out (*US & Canad informal*), tear (someone) off a strip (*Brit informal*), give (someone) a rocket (*Brit & NZ informal*) ▷▷ **come down on something** (with one or other side of an argument as object) DECIDE ON, choose, favour ▷▷ **come down to something** AMOUNT TO, boil down to ▷▷ **come down with something** (with illness as object) CATCH, get, take, contract, fall victim to, fall ill, be stricken with, take sick, sicken with ▷▷ **come forward** VOLUNTEER, step forward, present yourself, offer your services ▷▷ **come from something 1** BE FROM, originate, hail from, be a native of **2** BE OBTAINED, be from, issue, emerge, flow, arise, originate, emanate ▷▷ **come in 1** ARRIVE, enter, appear, show up (*informal*), cross the threshold **2** FINISH ▷▷ **come in for something** (with criticism or blame as object) RECEIVE, get, suffer, endure, be subjected to, bear the brunt of, be the object of ▷▷ **come into something** (with money or property as object) INHERIT, be left, acquire, succeed to, be bequeathed, fall heir to

▷▷ **come off** (*informal*) SUCCEED, work out, be successful, pan out (*informal*), turn out well ▷▷ **come on 1** PROGRESS, develop, improve, advance, proceed, make headway **2** BEGIN, appear, take place ▷▷ **come out 1** BE PUBLISHED, appear, be released, be issued, be launched **2** BE REVEALED, emerge, be reported, be announced, become apparent, come to light, be divulged **3** TURN OUT, result, end up, work out, pan out (*informal*) ▷▷ **come out with something** SAY, speak, utter, let out ▷▷ **come round** *or* **around 1** CALL, visit, drop in, stop by, pop in **2** CHANGE YOUR OPINION, yield, concede, mellow, relent, accede, acquiesce **3** REGAIN CONSCIOUSNESS, come to, recover, rally, revive ▷▷ **come through** SUCCEED, triumph, prevail, make the grade (*informal*) ▷▷ **come through something** (with a negative or bad experience as object) SURVIVE, overcome, endure, withstand, weather, pull through ▷▷ **come to** REVIVE, recover, rally, come round, regain consciousness ▷▷ **come to something** AMOUNT TO, total, add up to ▷▷ **come up** HAPPEN, occur, arise, turn up, spring up, crop up ▷▷ **come up to something** MEASURE UP TO, meet, match, approach, rival, equal, compare with, resemble, admit of comparison with, stand *or* bear comparison with ▷▷ **come up with something** PRODUCE, offer, provide, present, suggest, advance, propose, submit, furnish

comeback *noun* **1** (*informal*) RETURN, revival, rebound, resurgence, rally, recovery, triumph **2** RESPONSE, reply, retort, retaliation, riposte, rejoinder

comedian *noun* COMIC, laugh (*informal*), wit, clown, funny man, humorist, wag, joker, jester, dag (*NZ informal*), card (*informal*)

comedy *noun* **1** LIGHT ENTERTAINMENT, sitcom (*informal*), soap opera (*slang*), soapie *or* soapy (*Austral*) << ANTONYM tragedy **2** HUMOUR, fun, joking, farce, jesting, slapstick, wisecracking, hilarity, witticisms, facetiousness, chaffing << ANTONYM seriousness

comfort *noun* **1** EASE, luxury, wellbeing, opulence **2** CONSOLATION, cheer, encouragement, succour, help, support, aid, relief, ease, compensation, alleviation << ANTONYM annoyance ▷ *verb* CONSOLE, encourage, ease, cheer, strengthen, relieve, reassure, soothe, hearten, solace, assuage, gladden, commiserate with << ANTONYM distress

comfortable *adjective* **1** LOOSE-FITTING, loose, adequate, ample, snug, roomy, commodious << ANTONYM tight-fitting **2** PLEASANT, homely, easy, relaxing, delightful, enjoyable, cosy, agreeable, restful << ANTONYM unpleasant **3** AT EASE, happy, at home, contented, relaxed, serene << ANTONYM uncomfortable **4** (*informal*) WELL-OFF, prosperous, affluent, well-to-do, comfortably-off, in clover (*informal*)

comforting *adjective* CONSOLING, encouraging, cheering, reassuring, soothing, heart-warming, inspiriting << ANTONYM upsetting

comic *adjective* FUNNY, amusing, witty, humorous, farcical, comical, light, joking, droll, facetious, jocular, waggish << ANTONYM sad ▷ *noun* COMEDIAN, funny man, humorist, wit, clown, wag, jester, dag (*NZ informal*), buffoon

comical *adjective* FUNNY, entertaining, comic, silly, amusing, ridiculous, diverting, absurd, hilarious, ludicrous, humorous, priceless, laughable, farcical, whimsical, zany, droll, risible, side-splitting

coming *adjective* **1** APPROACHING, next, future, near, due, forthcoming, imminent, in store, impending, at hand, upcoming, on the cards, in the wind, nigh, just round the corner **2** UP-AND-COMING, future, promising, aspiring ▷ *noun* ARRIVAL, approach, advent, accession

command *verb* **1** ORDER, tell, charge, demand, require, direct, bid, compel, enjoin << ANTONYM beg **2** HAVE AUTHORITY OVER, lead, head, control, rule, manage, handle, dominate, govern, administer, supervise, be in charge of, reign over << ANTONYM be subordinate to ▷ *noun* **1** ORDER, demand, direction, instruction, requirement, decree, bidding, mandate, canon, directive, injunction, fiat, ultimatum, commandment, edict, behest, precept **2** DOMINATION, control, rule, grasp, sway, mastery, dominion, upper hand, power, government **3** MANAGEMENT, power, control, charge, authority, direction, supervision

commandeer *verb* SEIZE, appropriate, hijack, confiscate, requisition, sequester, expropriate, sequestrate

commander *noun* LEADER, director, chief, officer, boss, head, captain, bass (*S African*), ruler, commander-in-chief, commanding officer, C in C, C.O., sherang (*Austral & NZ*)

commanding *adjective* **1** DOMINANT, controlling, dominating, superior, decisive, advantageous **2** AUTHORITATIVE, imposing, impressive, compelling, assertive, forceful, autocratic, peremptory << ANTONYM unassertive

commemorate *verb* CELEBRATE, remember, honour, recognize, salute, pay tribute to, immortalize, memorialize << ANTONYM ignore

commemoration *noun* **1** CEREMONY, tribute, memorial service, testimonial **2** REMEMBRANCE, honour, tribute

commemorative *adjective* MEMORIAL, celebratory

commence *verb* **1** EMBARK ON, start, open, begin, initiate, originate, instigate, inaugurate, enter upon << ANTONYM stop **2** START, open, begin, go ahead << ANTONYM end

commencement *noun* BEGINNING, start, opening, launch, birth, origin, dawn, outset, onset, initiation, inauguration, inception, embarkation

commend *verb* **1** PRAISE, acclaim, applaud, compliment, extol, approve, big up (*slang, chiefly Caribbean*), eulogize, speak highly of << ANTONYM criticize **2** RECOMMEND, suggest, approve, advocate, endorse, vouch for, put in a good word for

commendable *adjective* PRAISEWORTHY, deserving, worthy, admirable, exemplary, creditable, laudable, meritorious, estimable

commendation *noun* PRAISE, credit, approval, acclaim, encouragement, Brownie points, approbation, acclamation, good opinion, panegyric, encomium

commensurate *adjective* **1** EQUIVALENT, consistent, corresponding, comparable, compatible, in accord, proportionate, coextensive **2** APPROPRIATE, fitting, fit, due, sufficient, adequate

comment *verb* **1** REMARK, say, note, mention, point out, observe, utter, opine, interpose **2** *usually with* on REMARK ON, explain, talk about, discuss, speak about, say something about, allude to, elucidate, make a comment on ▷ *noun* **1** REMARK, statement, observation **2** NOTE, criticism, explanation, illustration, commentary, exposition, annotation, elucidation

commentary *noun* **1** NARRATION, report, review, explanation, description, voice-over **2** ANALYSIS, notes, review, critique, treatise

commentator *noun* **1** REPORTER, special correspondent, sportscaster, commenter **2** CRITIC, interpreter, annotator

commercial *adjective* **1** MERCANTILE, business, trade, trading, sales **2** PROFITABLE, popular, in demand, marketable, saleable **3** MATERIALISTIC, mercenary, profit-making, venal, monetary, exploited, pecuniary

commiserate *verb often with* **with** SYMPATHIZE, pity, feel for, console, condole

commission *verb* APPOINT, order, contract, select, engage, delegate, nominate, authorize, empower, depute ▷ *noun* **1** DUTY, authority, trust, charge, task, function, mission, employment, appointment, warrant, mandate, errand **2** FEE, cut, compensation, percentage, allowance, royalties, brokerage, rake-off (*slang*) **3** COMMITTEE, board, representatives, commissioners, delegation, deputation, body of commissioners

commit *verb* **1** DO, perform, carry out, execute, enact, perpetrate **2** GIVE, deliver, engage, deposit, hand over, commend, entrust, consign << ANTONYM withhold **3** PUT IN CUSTODY, confine, imprison, consign << ANTONYM release ▷▷ **commit yourself to something** PLEDGE TO, promise to, bind yourself to, make yourself liable for, obligate yourself to

commitment *noun* **1** DEDICATION, loyalty, devotion, adherence << ANTONYM indecisiveness **2** RESPONSIBILITY, tie, duty, obligation, liability, engagement **3** PLEDGE, promise, guarantee, undertaking, vow, assurance, word << ANTONYM disavowal

committee *noun* GROUP, commission, panel, delegation, subcommittee, deputation ▷ see **family**

commodity *noun usually plural* GOODS, produce, stock, products, merchandise, wares

common *adjective* **1** USUAL, standard, daily, regular, ordinary, familiar, plain, conventional, routine, frequent, everyday, customary, commonplace, vanilla (*slang*), habitual, run-of-the-mill, humdrum, stock, workaday, bog-standard (*Brit & Irish slang*), a dime a dozen << ANTONYM rare **2** POPULAR, general, accepted, standard, routine, widespread, universal, prevailing, prevalent **3** SHARED, collective **4** ORDINARY, average, simple, typical, undistinguished, dinki-di (*Austral informal*) << ANTONYM

important **5** VULGAR, low, inferior, coarse, plebeian << ANTONYM refined **6** COLLECTIVE, public, community, social, communal << ANTONYM personal

commonplace *adjective* EVERYDAY, common, ordinary, widespread, pedestrian, customary, mundane, vanilla (*slang*), banal, run-of-the-mill, humdrum, dime-a-dozen (*informal*) << ANTONYM rare ▷ *noun* CLICHÉ, platitude, banality, truism

common sense *noun* GOOD SENSE, sound judgment, level-headedness, practicality, prudence, nous (*Brit slang*), soundness, reasonableness, gumption (*Brit informal*), horse sense, native intelligence, mother wit, smarts (*slang, chiefly US*), wit

common-sense *adjective* SENSIBLE, sound, practical, reasonable, realistic, shrewd, down-to-earth, matter-of-fact, sane, astute, judicious, level-headed, hard-headed << ANTONYM foolish

commotion *noun* DISTURBANCE, to-do, riot, disorder, excitement, fuss, turmoil, racket, upheaval, bustle, furore, uproar, ferment, agitation, ado, rumpus, tumult, hubbub, hurly-burly, brouhaha, hullabaloo, hue and cry

communal *adjective* **1** COMMUNITY, neighbourhood **2** PUBLIC, shared, general, joint, collective, communistic << ANTONYM private

commune *noun* COMMUNITY, collective, cooperative, kibbutz

commune with *verb* **1** CONTEMPLATE, ponder, reflect on, muse on, meditate on **2** TALK TO, communicate with, discuss with, confer with, converse with, discourse with, parley with

communicable *adjective* INFECTIOUS, catching, contagious, transferable, transmittable

communicate *verb* **1** CONTACT, talk, speak, phone, correspond, make contact, be in touch, ring up (*informal, chiefly Brit*), be in contact, get in contact **2** MAKE KNOWN, report, announce, reveal, publish, declare, spread, disclose, pass on, proclaim, transmit, convey, impart, divulge, disseminate << ANTONYM keep secret **3** PASS ON, transfer, spread, transmit

communication *noun* **1** CONTACT, conversation, correspondence, intercourse, link, relations, connection **2** PASSING ON, spread, circulation, transmission, disclosure, imparting, dissemination, conveyance **3** MESSAGE, news, report, word, information, statement, intelligence, announcement, disclosure, dispatch ▷ *plural noun* CONNECTIONS, travel, links, transport, routes

communicative *adjective* TALKATIVE, open, frank, forthcoming, outgoing, informative, candid, expansive, chatty, voluble, loquacious, unreserved << ANTONYM reserved

communion *noun* AFFINITY, accord, agreement, unity, sympathy, harmony, intercourse, fellowship, communing, closeness, rapport, converse, togetherness, concord

Communion *noun* (*Christianity*) EUCHARIST, Mass, Sacrament, Lord's Supper

communiqué *noun* ANNOUNCEMENT, report, bulletin, dispatch, news flash, official communication

communism *noun usually cap.* SOCIALISM, Marxism, Stalinism, collectivism, Bolshevism, Marxism-Leninism, state socialism, Maoism, Trotskyism, Eurocommunism, Titoism

communist *noun often cap.* SOCIALIST, Red (*informal*), Marxist, Bolshevik, collectivist

community *noun* **1** SOCIETY, people, public, association, population, residents, commonwealth, general public, populace, body politic, state, company **2** DISTRICT, area, quarter, region, sector, parish, neighbourhood, vicinity, locality, locale, neck of the woods (*informal*)

commute *verb* **1** TRAVEL **2** (*Law*) REDUCE, cut, modify, shorten, alleviate, curtail, remit, mitigate

commuter *noun* DAILY TRAVELLER, passenger, suburbanite

compact[1] *adjective* **1** CLOSELY PACKED, firm, solid, thick, dense, compressed, condensed, impenetrable, impermeable, pressed together << ANTONYM loose **2** CONCISE, brief, to the point, succinct, terse, laconic, pithy, epigrammatic, pointed << ANTONYM lengthy ▷ *verb* PACK CLOSELY, stuff, cram, compress, condense, tamp << ANTONYM loosen

compact[2] *noun* AGREEMENT, deal, understanding, contract, bond, arrangement, alliance, treaty, bargain, pact, covenant, entente, concordat

companion *noun* **1** FRIEND, partner, ally, colleague, associate, mate (*informal*), gossip (*archaic*), buddy (*informal*), comrade,

accomplice, crony, confederate, consort, main man (*slang, chiefly US*), homeboy (*slang, chiefly US*), cobber (*Austral & NZ old-fashioned informal*) **2** ASSISTANT, aide, escort, attendant **3** COMPLEMENT, match, fellow, mate, twin, counterpart

companionship *noun* FELLOWSHIP, company, friendship, fraternity, rapport, camaraderie, togetherness, comradeship, amity, esprit de corps, conviviality

company *noun* **1** BUSINESS, firm, association, corporation, partnership, establishment, syndicate, house, concern **2** GROUP, troupe, set, community, league, band, crowd, camp, collection, gathering, circle, crew, assembly, convention, ensemble, throng, coterie, bevy, assemblage, party, body **3** TROOP, unit, squad, team **4** COMPANIONSHIP, society, presence, fellowship **5** GUESTS, party, visitors, callers

comparable *adjective* **1** EQUAL, equivalent, on a par, tantamount, a match, proportionate, commensurate, as good << ANTONYM unequal **2** SIMILAR, related, alike, corresponding, akin, analogous, of a piece, cognate, cut from the same cloth

comparative *adjective* RELATIVE, qualified, by comparison, approximate

compare *verb* CONTRAST, balance, weigh, set against, collate, juxtapose ▷▷ **compare to something** LIKEN TO, parallel, identify with, equate to, correlate to, mention in the same breath as ▷▷ **compare with something** BE AS GOOD AS, match, approach, equal, compete with, come up to, vie, be on a par with, be the equal of, approximate to, hold a candle to, bear comparison, be in the same class as

comparison *noun* **1** CONTRAST, distinction, differentiation, juxtaposition, collation **2** SIMILARITY, analogy, resemblance, correlation, likeness, comparability

compartment *noun* **1** SECTION, carriage, berth **2** BAY, chamber, booth, locker, niche, cubicle, alcove, pigeonhole, cubbyhole, cell **3** CATEGORY, area, department, division, section, subdivision

compass *noun* RANGE, field, area, reach, scope, sphere, limit, stretch, bound, extent, zone, boundary, realm

compassion *noun* SYMPATHY, understanding, charity, pity, humanity, mercy, heart, quarter, sorrow, kindness, tenderness, condolence, clemency, commiseration, fellow feeling, soft-

heartedness, tender-heartedness, aroha (NZ)
<< ANTONYM indifference

compassionate *adjective* SYMPATHETIC,
kindly, understanding, tender, pitying,
humanitarian, charitable, humane,
indulgent, benevolent, lenient, merciful,
kind-hearted, tender-hearted << ANTONYM
uncaring

compatibility *noun* 1 AGREEMENT,
consistency, accordance, affinity, conformity,
concord, congruity, accord 2 LIKE-
MINDEDNESS, harmony, empathy, rapport,
single-mindedness, amity, sympathy,
congeniality

compatible *adjective* 1 CONSISTENT,
in keeping, consonant, congenial,
congruent, reconcilable, congruous,
accordant, agreeable << ANTONYM
inappropriate 2 LIKE-MINDED, harmonious,
in harmony, in accord, of one mind,
of the same mind, en rapport (*French*)
<< ANTONYM incompatible

compatriot *noun* FELLOW COUNTRYMAN,
countryman, fellow citizen

compel *verb* FORCE, make, urge, enforce,
railroad (*informal*), drive, oblige, constrain,
hustle (*slang*), necessitate, coerce, bulldoze
(*informal*), impel, dragoon

compelling *adjective* 1 CONVINCING, telling,
powerful, forceful, conclusive, weighty,
cogent, irrefutable 2 FASCINATING, gripping,
irresistible, enchanting, enthralling,
hypnotic, spellbinding, mesmeric
<< ANTONYM boring

compendium *noun* COLLECTION, summary,
abstract, digest, compilation, epitome,
synopsis, précis

compensate *verb* 1 RECOMPENSE, repay,
refund, reimburse, indemnify, make
restitution, requite, remunerate, satisfy,
make good 2 MAKE AMENDS FOR, make
up for, atone for, pay for, do penance for,
cancel out, make reparation for, make
redress for 3 BALANCE, cancel (out), offset,
make up for, redress, counteract, neutralize,
counterbalance

compensation *noun* 1 REPARATION, damages,
payment, recompense, indemnification,
offset, remuneration, indemnity, restitution,
reimbursement, requital 2 RECOMPENSE,
amends, reparation, restitution, atonement

compete *verb* 1 CONTEND, fight, rival, vie,
challenge, struggle, contest, strive, pit
yourself against 2 TAKE PART, participate,
be in the running, be a competitor, be a

contestant, play

competence *noun* 1 ABILITY, skill,
talent, capacity, expertise, proficiency,
competency, capability << ANTONYM
incompetence 2 FITNESS, suitability,
adequacy, appropriateness << ANTONYM
inadequacy

competent *adjective* 1 ABLE, skilled, capable,
clever, endowed, proficient << ANTONYM
incompetent 2 FIT, qualified, equal,
appropriate, suitable, sufficient, adequate
<< ANTONYM unqualified

competition *noun* 1 RIVALRY, opposition,
struggle, contest, contention, strife,
one-upmanship (*informal*) 2 OPPOSITION,
field, rivals, challengers 3 CONTEST, event,
championship, tournament, head-to-head

competitive *adjective* 1 CUT-THROAT,
aggressive, fierce, ruthless, relentless,
antagonistic, dog-eat-dog 2 AMBITIOUS,
pushing, opposing, aggressive, vying,
contentious, combative

competitor *noun* 1 RIVAL,
competition, opposition, adversary,
antagonist 2 CONTESTANT, participant,
contender, challenger, entrant, player,
opponent

compilation *noun* COLLECTION, treasury,
accumulation, anthology, assortment,
assemblage

compile *verb* PUT TOGETHER, collect, gather,
organize, accumulate, marshal, garner,
amass, cull, anthologize

complacency *noun* SMUGNESS, satisfaction,
gratification, contentment, self-
congratulation, self-satisfaction

complacent *adjective* SMUG, self-satisfied,
pleased with yourself, resting on your
laurels, pleased, contented, satisfied,
gratified, serene, unconcerned, self-
righteous, self-assured, self-contented
<< ANTONYM insecure

complain *verb* FIND FAULT, moan, grumble,
whinge (*informal*), beef (*slang*), carp, fuss,
bitch (*slang*), groan, grieve, lament, whine,
growl, deplore, grouse, gripe (*informal*),
bemoan, bleat, put the boot in (*slang*), bewail,
kick up a fuss (*informal*), grouch (*informal*),
bellyache (*slang*), kvetch (*US slang*)

complaint *noun* 1 PROTEST, accusation,
objection, grievance, remonstrance,
charge 2 GRUMBLE, criticism, beef (*slang*),
moan, bitch (*slang*), lament, grievance,
wail, dissatisfaction, annoyance, grouse,
gripe (*informal*), grouch (*informal*), plaint,

fault-finding **3** DISORDER, problem, trouble, disease, upset, illness, sickness, ailment, affliction, malady, indisposition

complement *verb* ENHANCE, complete, improve, boost, crown, add to, set off, heighten, augment, round off ▷ *noun* **1** ACCOMPANIMENT, companion, accessory, completion, finishing touch, rounding-off, adjunct, supplement **2** TOTAL, capacity, quota, aggregate, contingent, entirety

complementary *adjective* MATCHING, companion, corresponding, compatible, reciprocal, interrelating, interdependent, harmonizing << ANTONYM incompatible

complete *adjective* **1** TOTAL, perfect, absolute, utter, outright, thorough, consummate, out-and-out, unmitigated, dyed-in-the-wool, thoroughgoing, deep-dyed (*usually derogatory*) **2** WHOLE, full, entire << ANTONYM partial **3** ENTIRE, full, whole, intact, unbroken, faultless, undivided, unimpaired << ANTONYM incomplete **4** UNABRIDGED, full, entire **5** FINISHED, done, ended, completed, achieved, concluded, fulfilled, accomplished << ANTONYM unfinished ▷ *verb* **1** PERFECT, accomplish, finish off, round off, crown, cap << ANTONYM spoil **2** FINISH, conclude, fulfil, accomplish, do, end, close, achieve, perform, settle, realize, execute, discharge, wrap up (*informal*), terminate, finalize << ANTONYM start

completely *adverb* TOTALLY, entirely, wholly, utterly, quite, perfectly, fully, solidly, absolutely, altogether, thoroughly, in full, every inch, en masse, heart and soul, a hundred per cent, one hundred per cent, from beginning to end, down to the ground, root and branch, in toto (*Latin*), from A to Z, hook, line and sinker, lock, stock and barrel

completion *noun* FINISHING, end, close, conclusion, accomplishment, realization, fulfilment, culmination, attainment, fruition, consummation, finalization

complex *adjective* **1** COMPOUND, compounded, multiple, composite, manifold, heterogeneous, multifarious **2** COMPLICATED, difficult, involved, mixed, elaborate, tangled, mingled, intricate, tortuous, convoluted, knotty, labyrinthine, circuitous << ANTONYM simple ▷ *noun* **1** STRUCTURE, system, scheme, network, organization, aggregate, composite, synthesis **2** (*informal*) OBSESSION, preoccupation, phobia, fixation, fixed idea,

idée fixe (*French*)

complexion *noun* **1** SKIN, colour, colouring, hue, skin tone, pigmentation **2** NATURE, character, make-up, cast, stamp, disposition

complexity *noun* COMPLICATION, involvement, intricacy, entanglement, convolution

compliance *noun* **1** CONFORMITY, agreement, obedience, assent, observance, concurrence << ANTONYM disobedience **2** SUBMISSIVENESS, yielding, submission, obedience, deference, passivity, acquiescence, complaisance, consent << ANTONYM defiance

compliant *adjective* OBEDIENT, willing, accepting, yielding, obliging, accommodating, passive, cooperative, agreeable, submissive, conformist, deferential, acquiescent, complaisant, conformable

complicate *verb* MAKE DIFFICULT, confuse, muddle, embroil, entangle, make intricate, involve << ANTONYM simplify

complicated *adjective* **1** INVOLVED, difficult, puzzling, troublesome, problematic, perplexing << ANTONYM simple **2** COMPLEX, involved, elaborate, intricate, Byzantine << ANTONYM understandable **3** (*of attitudes, etc*) CONVOLUTED, labyrinthine ▷ see **complex**

complication *noun* **1** PROBLEM, difficulty, obstacle, drawback, snag, uphill (*S African*), stumbling block, aggravation **2** COMPLEXITY, combination, mixture, web, confusion, intricacy, entanglement

complicity *noun* COLLUSION, conspiracy, collaboration, connivance, abetment

compliment *noun* PRAISE, honour, tribute, courtesy, admiration, bouquet, flattery, eulogy << ANTONYM criticism ▷ *plural noun* **1** GREETINGS, regards, respects, good wishes, salutation << ANTONYM insult **2** CONGRATULATIONS, praise, commendation ▷ *verb* PRAISE, flatter, salute, congratulate, pay tribute to, commend, laud, extol, crack up (*informal*), pat on the back, sing the praises of, wax lyrical about, big up (*slang, chiefly Caribbean*), speak highly of << ANTONYM criticize

complimentary *adjective* **1** FLATTERING, approving, appreciative, congratulatory, eulogistic, commendatory << ANTONYM critical **2** FREE, donated, courtesy, honorary, free of charge, on the house, gratuitous, gratis

comply *verb* OBEY, follow, respect, agree to, satisfy, observe, fulfil, submit to, conform to, adhere to, abide by, consent to, yield to, defer to, accede to, act in accordance with, perform, acquiesce with << ANTONYM defy

component *noun* PART, piece, unit, item, element, ingredient, constituent ▷ *adjective* CONSTITUENT, composing, inherent, intrinsic

compose *verb* **1** PUT TOGETHER, make up, constitute, comprise, make, build, form, fashion, construct, compound << ANTONYM destroy **2** CREATE, write, produce, imagine, frame, invent, devise, contrive **3** ARRANGE, make up, construct, put together, order, organize ▷▷ **compose yourself** CALM YOURSELF, be still, control yourself, settle yourself, collect yourself, pull yourself together

composed *adjective* CALM, together (*slang*), cool, collected, relaxed, confident, poised, at ease, laid-back (*informal*), serene, tranquil, sedate, self-controlled, level-headed, unfazed (*informal*), unflappable, unruffled, self-possessed, imperturbable, unworried, keeping your cool, as cool as a cucumber << ANTONYM agitated

composite *adjective* COMPOUND, mixed, combined, complex, blended, conglomerate, synthesized ▷ *noun* COMPOUND, blend, conglomerate, fusion, synthesis, amalgam, meld

composition *noun* **1** DESIGN, form, structure, make-up, organization, arrangement, constitution, formation, layout, configuration **2** CREATION, work, piece, production, opus, masterpiece, chef-d'oeuvre (*French*) **3** ESSAY, writing, study, exercise, treatise, literary work **4** ARRANGEMENT, balance, proportion, harmony, symmetry, concord, consonance, placing **5** PRODUCTION, creation, making, fashioning, formation, putting together, invention, compilation, formulation

compost *noun* FERTILIZER, mulch, humus

composure *noun* CALMNESS, calm, poise, self-possession, cool (*slang*), ease, dignity, serenity, tranquillity, coolness, aplomb, equanimity, self-assurance, sang-froid, placidity, sedateness << ANTONYM agitation

compound *noun* COMBINATION, mixture, blend, composite, conglomerate, fusion, synthesis, alloy, medley, amalgam, meld, composition << ANTONYM element ▷ *adjective* COMPLEX, multiple, composite, conglomerate, intricate, not simple << ANTONYM simple ▷ *verb* **1** INTENSIFY, add to, complicate, worsen, heighten, exacerbate, aggravate, magnify, augment, add insult to injury << ANTONYM lessen **2** COMBINE, unite, mix, blend, mingle, synthesize, concoct, amalgamate, coalesce, intermingle, meld << ANTONYM divide

comprehend *verb* UNDERSTAND, see, take in, perceive, grasp, conceive, make out, discern, assimilate, see the light, fathom, apprehend, get the hang of (*informal*), get the picture, know << ANTONYM misunderstand

comprehensible *adjective* UNDERSTANDABLE, clear, plain, explicit, coherent, user-friendly, intelligible

comprehension *noun* UNDERSTANDING, grasp, conception, realization, sense, knowledge, intelligence, judgment, perception, discernment << ANTONYM incomprehension

comprehensive *adjective* BROAD, full, complete, wide, catholic, sweeping, extensive, blanket, umbrella, thorough, inclusive, exhaustive, all-inclusive, all-embracing, overarching, encyclopedic << ANTONYM limited

compress *verb* **1** SQUEEZE, crush, squash, constrict, press, crowd, wedge, cram **2** CONDENSE, contract, concentrate, compact, shorten, summarize, abbreviate

compressed *adjective* **1** SQUEEZED, concentrated, compact, compacted, consolidated, squashed, flattened, constricted **2** REDUCED, compacted, shortened, abridged

compression *noun* SQUEEZING, pressing, crushing, consolidation, condensation, constriction

comprise *verb* **1** BE COMPOSED OF, include, contain, consist of, take in, embrace, encompass, comprehend **2** MAKE UP, form, constitute, compose

compromise *noun* GIVE-AND-TAKE, agreement, settlement, accommodation, concession, adjustment, trade-off, middle ground, half measures << ANTONYM disagreement ▷ *verb* **1** MEET HALFWAY, concede, make concessions, give and take, strike a balance, strike a happy medium, go fifty-fifty (*informal*) << ANTONYM disagree **2** UNDERMINE, expose, embarrass, weaken, prejudice, endanger, discredit, implicate, jeopardize, dishonour, imperil << ANTONYM support

compulsion *noun* **1** URGE, need, obsession, necessity, preoccupation, drive **2** FORCE, pressure, obligation, constraint, urgency, coercion, duress, demand

compulsive *adjective* **1** OBSESSIVE, confirmed, chronic, persistent, addictive, uncontrollable, incurable, inveterate, incorrigible **2** FASCINATING, gripping, absorbing, compelling, captivating, enthralling, hypnotic, engrossing, spellbinding **3** IRRESISTIBLE, overwhelming, compelling, urgent, neurotic, besetting, uncontrollable, driving

compulsory *adjective* OBLIGATORY, forced, required, binding, mandatory, imperative, requisite, de rigueur (*French*) << ANTONYM voluntary

compute *verb* CALCULATE, rate, figure, total, measure, estimate, count, reckon, sum, figure out, add up, tally, enumerate

comrade *noun* COMPANION, friend, partner, ally, colleague, associate, fellow, mate (*informal*), pal (*informal*), buddy (*informal*), compatriot, crony, confederate, co-worker, main man (*slang, chiefly US*), homeboy (*slang, chiefly US*), cobber (*Austral & NZ old-fashioned informal*), compeer

comradeship *noun* FELLOWSHIP, solidarity, fraternity, brotherhood, companionship, camaraderie, kotahitanga (*NZ*)

con (*informal*) *verb* SWINDLE, trick, cheat, rip off (*slang*), kid (*informal*), skin (*slang*), stiff (*slang*), mislead, deceive, hoax, defraud, dupe, gull (*archaic*), rook (*slang*), humbug, bamboozle (*informal*), hoodwink, double-cross (*informal*), diddle (*informal*), take for a ride (*informal*), inveigle, do the dirty on (*Brit informal*), bilk, sell a pup, pull a fast one on (*informal*) ▷ *noun* SWINDLE, trick, fraud, deception, scam (*slang*), sting (*informal*), bluff, fastie (*Austral slang*)

concave *adjective* HOLLOW, cupped, depressed, scooped, hollowed, excavated, sunken, indented << ANTONYM convex

conceal *verb* **1** HIDE, bury, stash (*informal*), secrete, cover, screen, disguise, obscure, camouflage << ANTONYM reveal **2** KEEP SECRET, hide, disguise, mask, suppress, veil, dissemble, draw a veil over, keep dark, keep under your hat << ANTONYM show

concealed *adjective* HIDDEN, covered, secret, screened, masked, obscured, covert, unseen, tucked away, secreted, under wraps, inconspicuous

concealment *noun* **1** COVER, hiding, camouflage, hiding place **2** COVER-UP, disguise, keeping secret << ANTONYM disclosure

concede *verb* **1** ADMIT, allow, accept, acknowledge, own, grant, confess << ANTONYM deny **2** GIVE UP, yield, hand over, surrender, relinquish, cede << ANTONYM conquer

conceit *noun* **1** SELF-IMPORTANCE, vanity, arrogance, complacency, pride, swagger, narcissism, egotism, self-love, amour-propre, vainglory **2** (*Archaic*) IMAGE, idea, concept, metaphor, imagery, figure of speech, trope

conceited *adjective* SELF-IMPORTANT, vain, arrogant, stuck up (*informal*), cocky, narcissistic, puffed up, egotistical, overweening, immodest, vainglorious, swollen-headed, bigheaded (*informal*), full of yourself, too big for your boots *or* breeches << ANTONYM modest

conceivable *adjective* IMAGINABLE, possible, credible, believable, thinkable << ANTONYM inconceivable

conceive *verb* **1** IMAGINE, envisage, comprehend, visualize, think, believe, suppose, fancy, appreciate, grasp, apprehend **2** THINK UP, form, produce, create, develop, design, project, purpose, devise, formulate, contrive **3** BECOME PREGNANT, get pregnant, become impregnated

concentrate *verb* **1** FOCUS YOUR ATTENTION, focus, pay attention, be engrossed, apply yourself << ANTONYM pay no attention **2** FOCUS, centre, converge, bring to bear **3** GATHER, collect, cluster, accumulate, congregate << ANTONYM scatter

concentrated *adjective* **1** CONDENSED, rich, undiluted, reduced, evaporated, thickened, boiled down **2** INTENSE, hard, deep, intensive, all-out (*informal*)

concentration *noun* **1** ATTENTION, application, absorption, single-mindedness, intentness << ANTONYM inattention **2** FOCUSING, centring, consolidation, convergence, bringing to bear, intensification, centralization **3** CONVERGENCE, collection, mass, cluster, accumulation, aggregation << ANTONYM scattering

concept *noun* IDEA, view, image, theory,

impression, notion, conception, hypothesis, abstraction, conceptualization

conception *noun* **1** UNDERSTANDING, idea, picture, impression, perception, clue, appreciation, comprehension, inkling **2** IDEA, plan, design, image, concept, notion **3** IMPREGNATION, insemination, fertilization, germination **4** ORIGIN, beginning, launching, birth, formation, invention, outset, initiation, inception

concern *noun* **1** ANXIETY, fear, worry, distress, unease, apprehension, misgiving, disquiet **2** WORRY, care, anxiety **3** AFFAIR, issue, matter, consideration **4** CARE, interest, regard, consideration, solicitude, attentiveness **5** BUSINESS, job, charge, matter, department, field, affair, responsibility, task, mission, pigeon (*informal*) **6** COMPANY, house, business, firm, organization, corporation, enterprise, establishment **7** IMPORTANCE, interest, bearing, relevance ▷ *verb* **1** WORRY, trouble, bother, disturb, distress, disquiet, perturb, make uneasy, make anxious **2** BE ABOUT, cover, deal with, go into, relate to, have to do with **3** BE RELEVANT TO, involve, affect, regard, apply to, bear on, have something to do with, pertain to, interest, touch

concerned *adjective* **1** INVOLVED, interested, active, mixed up, implicated, privy to **2** WORRIED, troubled, upset, bothered, disturbed, anxious, distressed, uneasy << ANTONYM indifferent **3** CARING, attentive, solicitous

concerning *preposition* REGARDING, about, re, touching, respecting, relating to, on the subject of, as to, with reference to, in the matter of, apropos of, as regards

concert ▷▷ in concert TOGETHER, jointly, unanimously, in unison, in league, in collaboration, shoulder to shoulder, concertedly

concerted *adjective* COORDINATED, united, joint, combined, collaborative << ANTONYM separate

concession *noun* **1** COMPROMISE, agreement, settlement, accommodation, adjustment, trade-off, give-and-take, half measures **2** PRIVILEGE, right, permit, licence, franchise, entitlement, indulgence, prerogative **3** REDUCTION, saving, grant, discount, allowance **4** SURRENDER, yielding, conceding, renunciation, relinquishment

conciliation *noun* PACIFICATION, reconciliation, disarming, appeasement,

propitiation, mollification, soothing, placation

conciliatory *adjective* PACIFYING, pacific, disarming, appeasing, mollifying, peaceable, placatory, soothing

concise *adjective* BRIEF, short, to the point, compact, summary, compressed, condensed, terse, laconic, succinct, pithy, synoptic, epigrammatic, compendious << ANTONYM rambling

conclave *noun* (SECRET *or* PRIVATE) MEETING, council, conference, congress, session, cabinet, assembly, parley, runanga (*NZ*)

conclude *verb* **1** DECIDE, judge, establish, suppose, determine, assume, gather, reckon (*informal*), work out, infer, deduce, surmise **2** COME TO AN END, end, close, finish, wind up, draw to a close << ANTONYM begin **3** BRING TO AN END, end, close, finish, complete, wind up, terminate, round off << ANTONYM begin **4** ACCOMPLISH, effect, settle, bring about, fix, carry out, resolve, clinch, pull off, bring off (*informal*)

conclusion *noun* **1** DECISION, agreement, opinion, settlement, resolution, conviction, verdict, judgment, deduction, inference **2** END, ending, close, finish, completion, finale, termination, bitter end, result **3** OUTCOME, result, upshot, consequence, sequel, culmination, end result, issue ▷▷ in conclusion FINALLY, lastly, in closing, to sum up

conclusive *adjective* DECISIVE, final, convincing, clinching, definite, definitive, irrefutable, unanswerable, unarguable, ultimate << ANTONYM inconclusive

concoct *verb* MAKE UP, design, prepare, manufacture, plot, invent, devise, brew, hatch, formulate, contrive, fabricate, think up, cook up (*informal*), trump up, project

concoction *noun* MIXTURE, preparation, compound, brew, combination, creation, blend

concord *noun* TREATY, agreement, convention, compact, protocol, entente, concordat

concourse *noun* CROWD, collection, gathering, assembly, crush, multitude, throng, convergence, hui (*NZ*), assemblage, meeting, runanga (*NZ*)

concrete *noun* CEMENT (*not in technical usage*) ▷ *adjective* **1** SPECIFIC, precise, explicit, definite, clear-cut, unequivocal, unambiguous << ANTONYM vague **2** REAL, material, actual, substantial, sensible, tangible, factual << ANTONYM abstract

concubine noun (Old-fashioned) MISTRESS, courtesan, kept woman

concur verb AGREE, accord, approve, assent, accede, acquiesce

concurrent adjective SIMULTANEOUS, coexisting, concomitant, contemporaneous, coincident, synchronous, concerted

concussion noun 1 SHOCK, brain injury 2 IMPACT, crash, shaking, clash, jarring, collision, jolt, jolting

condemn verb 1 DENOUNCE, damn, criticize, disapprove, censure, reprove, upbraid, excoriate, reprehend, blame << ANTONYM approve 2 SENTENCE, convict, damn, doom, pass sentence on << ANTONYM acquit

condemnation noun DENUNCIATION, blame, censure, disapproval, reproach, stricture, reproof, denouncement

condensation noun 1 DISTILLATION, precipitation, liquefaction 2 ABRIDGMENT, summary, abstract, digest, contraction, synopsis, précis, encapsulation

condense verb 1 ABRIDGE, contract, concentrate, compact, shorten, summarize, compress, encapsulate, abbreviate, epitomize, précis << ANTONYM expand 2 CONCENTRATE, reduce, precipitate (Chemistry), thicken, boil down, solidify, coagulate << ANTONYM dilute

condensed adjective 1 ABRIDGED, concentrated, compressed, potted, shortened, summarized, slimmed-down, encapsulated 2 CONCENTRATED, reduced, thickened, boiled down, precipitated (Chemistry)

condescend verb 1 PATRONIZE, talk down to, treat like a child, treat as inferior, treat condescendingly 2 DEIGN, see fit, lower yourself, be courteous enough, bend, submit, stoop, unbend (informal), vouchsafe, come down off your high horse (informal), humble or demean yourself

condescending adjective PATRONIZING, lordly, superior, lofty, snooty (informal), snobbish, disdainful, supercilious, toffee-nosed (slang, chiefly Brit), on your high horse (informal)

condescension noun PATRONIZING ATTITUDE, superiority, disdain, haughtiness, loftiness, superciliousness, lordliness, airs

condition noun 1 STATE, order, shape, nick (Brit informal), trim 2 SITUATION, state, position, status, circumstances, plight, status quo (Latin), case, predicament 3 REQUIREMENT, terms, rider, provision, restriction, qualification, limitation, modification, requisite, prerequisite, proviso, stipulation, rule, demand 4 HEALTH, shape, fitness, trim, form, kilter, state of health, fettle, order 5 AILMENT, problem, complaint, weakness, malady, infirmity ▷ plural noun CIRCUMSTANCES, situation, environment, surroundings, way of life, milieu ▷ verb TRAIN, teach, educate, adapt, accustom, inure, habituate

conditional adjective DEPENDENT, limited, qualified, contingent, provisional, with reservations << ANTONYM unconditional

conditioning noun TRAINING, education, teaching, accustoming, habituation

condom noun SHEATH, safe (US & Canad slang), rubber (US slang), blob (Brit slang), scumbag (US slang), Frenchie (slang), flunky (slang), French letter (slang), rubber johnny (Brit slang), French tickler (slang)

condone verb OVERLOOK, excuse, forgive, pardon, disregard, turn a blind eye to, wink at, look the other way, make allowance for, let pass << ANTONYM condemn

conducive adjective FAVOURABLE, helpful, productive, contributory, calculated to produce, leading, tending

conduct verb 1 CARRY OUT, run, control, manage, direct, handle, organize, govern, regulate, administer, supervise, preside over 2 ACCOMPANY, lead, escort, guide, attend, steer, convey, usher, pilot ▷ noun 1 MANAGEMENT, running, control, handling, administration, direction, leadership, organization, guidance, supervision 2 BEHAVIOUR, ways, bearing, attitude, manners, carriage, demeanour, deportment, mien (literary), comportment ▷▷ **conduct yourself** BEHAVE YOURSELF, act, carry yourself, acquit yourself, deport yourself, comport yourself

conduit noun PASSAGE, channel, tube, pipe, canal, duct, main

confederacy noun UNION, league, alliance, coalition, federation, compact, confederation, covenant, bund

confederate noun ASSOCIATE, partner, ally, colleague, accessory, accomplice, abettor ▷ adjective ALLIED, federal, associated, combined, federated, in alliance

confer verb 1 DISCUSS, talk, consult, deliberate, discourse, converse, parley **2** GRANT, give, present, accord, award, hand out, bestow, vouchsafe

conference *noun* MEETING, congress, discussion, convention, forum, consultation, seminar, symposium, hui (*NZ*), convocation, colloquium

confess *verb* **1** ADMIT, acknowledge, disclose, confide, own up, come clean (*informal*), divulge, blurt out, come out of the closet, make a clean breast of, get (something) off your chest (*informal*), spill your guts (*slang*), 'fess up (*US*), sing (*slang, chiefly US*) << ANTONYM cover up **2** DECLARE, own up, allow, prove, reveal, grant, confirm, concede, assert, manifest, affirm, profess, attest, evince, aver

confession *noun* ADMISSION, revelation, disclosure, acknowledgment, avowal, divulgence, exposure, unbosoming

confidant *or* **confidante** *noun* CLOSE FRIEND, familiar, intimate, crony, alter ego, bosom friend

confide *verb* TELL, admit, reveal, confess, whisper, disclose, impart, divulge, breathe

confidence *noun* **1** TRUST, belief, faith, dependence, reliance, credence << ANTONYM distrust **2** SELF-ASSURANCE, courage, assurance, aplomb, boldness, self-reliance, self-possession, nerve << ANTONYM shyness **3** SECRET ▷▷ **in confidence** IN SECRECY, privately, confidentially, between you and me (and the gatepost), (just) between ourselves

confident *adjective* **1** CERTAIN, sure, convinced, positive, secure, satisfied, counting on << ANTONYM unsure **2** SELF-ASSURED, positive, assured, bold, self-confident, self-reliant, self-possessed, sure of yourself, can-do (*informal*) << ANTONYM insecure

confidential *adjective* **1** SECRET, private, intimate, classified, privy, off the record, hush-hush (*informal*) **2** SECRETIVE, low, soft, hushed

confidentially *adverb* IN SECRET, privately, personally, behind closed doors, in confidence, in camera, between ourselves, sub rosa

configuration *noun* ARRANGEMENT, form, shape, cast, outline, contour, conformation, figure

confine *verb* **1** IMPRISON, enclose, shut up, intern, incarcerate, circumscribe, hem in, immure, keep, cage **2** RESTRICT, limit ▷ *plural noun* LIMITS, bounds, boundaries,

compass, precincts, circumference, edge, pale

confined *adjective* RESTRICTED, small, limited, narrow, enclosed, cramped

confinement *noun* **1** IMPRISONMENT, custody, detention, incarceration, internment, porridge (*slang*) **2** CHILDBIRTH, labour, travail, childbed, accouchement (*French*), time

confirm *verb* **1** PROVE, support, establish, back up, verify, validate, bear out, substantiate, corroborate, authenticate **2** RATIFY, establish, approve, sanction, endorse, authorize, certify, validate, authenticate **3** STRENGTHEN, establish, settle, fix, secure, assure, reinforce, clinch, verify, fortify

confirmation *noun* **1** PROOF, evidence, testimony, verification, ratification, validation, corroboration, authentication, substantiation << ANTONYM repudiation **2** AFFIRMATION, approval, acceptance, endorsement, ratification, assent, agreement << ANTONYM disapproval

confirmed *adjective* LONG-ESTABLISHED, seasoned, rooted, chronic, hardened, habitual, ingrained, inveterate, inured, dyed-in-the-wool

confiscate *verb* SEIZE, appropriate, impound, commandeer, sequester, expropriate << ANTONYM give back

confiscation *noun* SEIZURE, appropriation, impounding, forfeiture, expropriation, sequestration, takeover

conflagration *noun* FIRE, blaze, holocaust, inferno, wildfire

conflict *noun* **1** DISPUTE, difference, opposition, hostility, disagreement, friction, strife, fighting, antagonism, variance, discord, bad blood, dissension, divided loyalties << ANTONYM agreement **2** STRUGGLE, battle, clash, strife **3** BATTLE, war, fight, clash, contest, set-to (*informal*), encounter, combat, engagement, warfare, collision, contention, strife, head-to-head, fracas, boilover (*Austral*) << ANTONYM peace ▷ *verb* BE INCOMPATIBLE, clash, differ, disagree, contend, strive, collide, be at variance << ANTONYM agree

conflicting *adjective* INCOMPATIBLE, opposed, opposing, clashing, contrary, contradictory, inconsistent, paradoxical, discordant << ANTONYM agreeing

congregate

conform *verb* **1** FIT IN, follow, yield, adjust, adapt, comply, obey, fall in, toe the line, follow the crowd, run with the pack, follow convention **2** *with* **with** FULFIL, meet, match, suit, satisfy, agree with, obey, abide by, accord with, square with, correspond with, tally with, harmonize with

conformation *noun* SHAPE, build, form, structure, arrangement, outline, framework, anatomy, configuration

conformist *noun* TRADITIONALIST, conservative, reactionary, Babbitt (*US*), stickler, yes man, stick-in-the-mud (*informal*), conventionalist

conformity *noun* **1** COMPLIANCE, agreement, accordance, observance, conformance, obedience **2** CONVENTIONALITY, compliance, allegiance, orthodoxy, observance, traditionalism, Babbittry (*US*)

confound *verb* **1** BEWILDER, baffle, amaze, confuse, astonish, startle, mix up, astound, perplex, surprise, mystify, flummox, boggle the mind, be all Greek to (*informal*), dumbfound, nonplus, flabbergast (*informal*) **2** DISPROVE, contradict, refute, negate, destroy, ruin, overwhelm, explode, overthrow, demolish, annihilate, give the lie to, make a nonsense of, prove false, blow out of the water (*slang*), controvert, confute

confront *verb* **1** TACKLE, deal with, cope with, brave, beard, face up to, meet head-on **2** TROUBLE, face, afflict, perplex, perturb, bedevil **3** CHALLENGE, face, oppose, tackle, encounter, defy, call out, stand up to, come face to face with, accost, face off (*slang*) << ANTONYM evade

confrontation *noun* CONFLICT, fight, crisis, contest, set-to (*informal*), encounter, showdown (*informal*), head-to-head, face-off (*slang*), boilover (*Austral*)

confuse *verb* **1** MIX UP WITH, take for, mistake for, muddle with **2** BEWILDER, puzzle, baffle, perplex, mystify, fluster, faze, flummox, bemuse, be all Greek to (*informal*), nonplus **3** OBSCURE, cloud, complicate, muddle, darken, make more difficult, muddy the waters

confused *adjective* **1** BEWILDERED, puzzled, baffled, at sea, muddled, dazed, perplexed, at a loss, taken aback, disorientated, muzzy (*US informal*), nonplussed, flummoxed, at sixes and sevens, thrown off balance, discombobulated (*informal, chiefly US & Canad*), not with it (*informal*), not knowing if you are coming or going << ANTONYM enlightened **2** DISORDERLY, disordered, chaotic, mixed up, jumbled, untidy, out of order, in disarray, topsy-turvy, disorganized, higgledy-piggledy (*informal*), at sixes and sevens, disarranged, disarrayed << ANTONYM tidy

confusing *adjective* BEWILDERING, complicated, puzzling, misleading, unclear, baffling, muddling, contradictory, ambiguous, inconsistent, perplexing, clear as mud (*informal*) << ANTONYM clear

confusion *noun* **1** BEWILDERMENT, doubt, uncertainty, puzzlement, perplexity, mystification, bafflement, perturbation << ANTONYM enlightenment **2** DISORDER, chaos, turmoil, upheaval, muddle, bustle, shambles, disarray, commotion, disorganization, disarrangement << ANTONYM order **3** PUZZLEMENT, bewilderment, perplexity, bafflement, mystification, perturbation

congeal *verb* THICKEN, set, freeze, harden, clot, stiffen, condense, solidify, curdle, jell, coagulate

congenial *adjective* PLEASANT, kindly, pleasing, friendly, agreeable, cordial, sociable, genial, affable, convivial, companionable, favourable, complaisant

congenital *adjective* **1** INBORN, innate, inherent, hereditary, natural, constitutional, inherited, inbred **2** (*informal*) COMPLETE, confirmed, chronic, utter, hardened, thorough, habitual, incurable, inveterate, incorrigible, deep-dyed (*usually derogatory*)

congested *adjective* **1** PACKED (OUT), crowded, overcrowded, teeming **2** CLOGGED, jammed, blocked-up, overfilled, stuffed, packed, crammed, overflowing, stuffed-up << ANTONYM clear

congestion *noun* OVERCROWDING, crowding, mass, jam, clogging, bottleneck, snarl-up (*informal, chiefly Brit*)

conglomerate *noun* CORPORATION, multinational, corporate body, business, association, consortium, aggregate, agglomerate

congratulate *verb* COMPLIMENT, pat on the back, wish joy to

congratulations *plural noun* GOOD WISHES, greetings, compliments, best wishes, pat on the back, felicitations ▷ *interjection* GOOD WISHES, greetings, compliments, best wishes, felicitations

congregate *verb* COME TOGETHER, meet, mass, collect, gather, concentrate, rally,

133

assemble, flock, muster, convene, converge, throng, rendezvous, foregather, convoke << ANTONYM disperse

congregation *noun* PARISHIONERS, host, brethren, crowd, assembly, parish, flock, fellowship, multitude, throng, laity, flock

congress *noun* **1** MEETING, council, conference, diet, assembly, convention, conclave, legislative assembly, convocation, hui (*NZ*), runanga (*NZ*) **2** LEGISLATURE, house, council, parliament, representatives, delegates, quango, legislative assembly, chamber of deputies, House of Representatives (*NZ*)

conical *or* **conic** *adjective* CONE-SHAPED, pointed, tapered, tapering, pyramidal, funnel-shaped

conjecture *noun* GUESS, theory, fancy, notion, speculation, assumption, hypothesis, inference, presumption, surmise, theorizing, guesswork, supposition, shot in the dark, guesstimate (*informal*) ▷ *verb* GUESS, speculate, surmise, theorize, suppose, imagine, assume, fancy, infer, hypothesize

conjunction *noun* COMBINATION, union, joining, association, coincidence, juxtaposition, concurrence

conjure *verb* **1** PRODUCE, generate, bring about, give rise to, make, create, effect, produce as if by magic **2** *often with* **up** SUMMON UP, raise, invoke, rouse, call upon ▷▷ **conjure something up** BRING TO MIND, recall, evoke, recreate, recollect, produce as if by magic

conjuring *noun* MAGIC, juggling, trickery, sleight of hand

connect *verb* **1** LINK, join, couple, attach, fasten, affix, unite <<< ANTONYM separate **2** ASSOCIATE, unite, join, couple, league, link, mix, relate, pair, ally, identify, combine, affiliate, correlate, confederate, lump together, mention in the same breath, think of together

connected *adjective* LINKED, united, joined, coupled, related, allied, associated, combined, bracketed, affiliated, akin, banded together

connection *noun* **1** ASSOCIATION, relationship, link, relation, bond, correspondence, relevance, tie-in, correlation, interrelation **2** COMMUNICATION, alliance, commerce, attachment, intercourse, liaison, affinity, affiliation, uniono **3** LINK, coupling, junction, fastening, tie **4** CONTACT,

friend, relation, ally, associate, relative, acquaintance, kin, kindred, kinsman, kith **5** CONTEXT, relation, reference, frame of reference

connivance *noun* COLLUSION, intrigue, conspiring, complicity, abetting, tacit consent, abetment

connive *verb* CONSPIRE, scheme, plot, intrigue, collude

connoisseur *noun* EXPERT, authority, judge, specialist, buff (*informal*), devotee, whiz (*informal*), arbiter, aficionado, savant, maven (*US*), appreciator, cognoscente, fundi (*S African*)

connotation *noun* IMPLICATION, colouring, association, suggestion, significance, nuance, undertone

connote *verb* IMPLY, suggest, indicate, intimate, signify, hint at, betoken, involve

conquer *verb* **1** SEIZE, obtain, acquire, occupy, overrun, annex, win **2** DEFEAT, overcome, overthrow, beat, stuff (*slang*), master, tank (*slang*), triumph, crush, humble, lick (*informal*), undo, subdue, rout, overpower, quell, get the better of, clobber (*slang*), vanquish, subjugate, prevail over, checkmate, run rings around (*informal*), wipe the floor with (*informal*), make mincemeat of (*informal*), put in their place, blow out of the water (*slang*), bring to their knees << ANTONYM lose to **3** OVERCOME, beat, defeat, master, rise above, overpower, get the better of, surmount, best

conqueror *noun* WINNER, champion, master, victor, conquistador, lord

conquest *noun* **1** TAKEOVER, coup, acquisition, invasion, occupation, appropriation, annexation, subjugation, subjection **2** DEFEAT, victory, triumph, overthrow, pasting (*slang*), rout, mastery, vanquishment **3** SEDUCTION **4** CATCH, prize, supporter, acquisition, follower, admirer, worshipper, adherent, fan, feather in your cap

conscience *noun* **1** PRINCIPLES, scruples, moral sense, sense of right and wrong, still small voice **2** GUILT, shame, regret, remorse, contrition, self-reproach, self-condemnation ▷▷ **in all conscience** IN FAIRNESS, rightly, certainly, fairly, truly, honestly, in truth, assuredly

conscientious *adjective* THOROUGH, particular, careful, exact, faithful, meticulous, painstaking, diligent, punctilious << ANTONYM careless

conscious *adjective* **1** *often with* **of** AWARE OF, wise to (*slang*), alert to, responsive to, cognizant of, sensible of, clued-up on (*informal*), percipient of << ANTONYM unaware **2** DELIBERATE, knowing, reasoning, studied, responsible, calculated, rational, reflective, self-conscious, intentional, wilful, premeditated << ANTONYM unintentional **3** AWAKE, wide-awake, sentient, alive << ANTONYM asleep

consciousness *noun* AWARENESS, understanding, knowledge, recognition, enlightenment, sensibility, realization, apprehension

consecrate *verb* SANCTIFY, dedicate, ordain, exalt, venerate, set apart, hallow, devote

consecutive *adjective* SUCCESSIVE, running, following, succeeding, in turn, uninterrupted, chronological, sequential, in sequence, seriatim

consensus *noun* AGREEMENT, general agreement, unanimity, common consent, unity, harmony, assent, concord, concurrence, kotahitanga (*NZ*)

consent *noun* AGREEMENT, sanction, approval, go-ahead (*informal*), permission, compliance, green light, assent, acquiescence, concurrence, O.K. *or* okay (*informal*) << ANTONYM refusal ▷ *verb* AGREE, approve, yield, permit, comply, concur, assent, accede, acquiesce, play ball (*informal*) << ANTONYM refuse

consequence *noun* **1** RESULT, effect, outcome, repercussion, end, issue, event, sequel, end result, upshot **2** IMPORTANCE, interest, concern, moment, value, account, note, weight, import, significance, portent **3** STATUS, standing, bottom, rank, distinction, eminence, repute, notability ▷▷ **in consequence** CONSEQUENTLY, as a result, so, then, thus, therefore, hence, accordingly, for that reason, thence, ergo

consequent *adjective* FOLLOWING, resulting, subsequent, successive, ensuing, resultant, sequential

consequential *adjective* **1** RESULTING, subsequent, successive, ensuing, indirect, consequent, resultant, sequential, following **2** IMPORTANT, serious, significant, grave, far-reaching, momentous, weighty, eventful

consequently *adverb* AS A RESULT, thus, therefore, necessarily, hence, subsequently, accordingly, for that reason, thence, ergo

conservation *noun* **1** PRESERVATION, saving, protection, maintenance, custody, safeguarding, upkeep, guardianship, safekeeping **2** ECONOMY, saving, thrift, husbandry, careful management, thriftiness

conservative *adjective* TRADITIONAL, guarded, quiet, conventional, moderate, cautious, sober, reactionary, die-hard, middle-of-the-road, hidebound << ANTONYM radical ▷ *noun* TRADITIONALIST, moderate, reactionary, die-hard, middle-of-the-roader, stick-in-the-mud (*informal*) << ANTONYM radical

Conservative *adjective* TORY, Republican (*US*), right-wing ▷ *noun* TORY, Republican (*US*), right-winger

conservatory *noun* GREENHOUSE, hothouse, glasshouse

conserve *verb* **1** SAVE, husband, take care of, hoard, store up, go easy on, use sparingly << ANTONYM waste **2** PROTECT, keep, save, preserve

consider *verb* **1** THINK, see, believe, rate, judge, suppose, deem, view as, look upon, regard as, hold to be, adjudge **2** THINK ABOUT, study, reflect on, examine, weigh, contemplate, deliberate, muse, ponder, revolve, meditate, work over, mull over, eye up, ruminate, chew over, cogitate, turn over in your mind **3** BEAR IN MIND, remember, regard, respect, think about, care for, take into account, reckon with, take into consideration, make allowance for, keep in view

considerable *adjective* LARGE, goodly, much, great, marked, comfortable, substantial, reasonable, tidy, lavish, ample, noticeable, abundant, plentiful, tolerable, appreciable, sizable *or* sizeable << ANTONYM small

considerably *adverb* GREATLY, very much, seriously (*informal*), significantly, remarkably, substantially, markedly, noticeably, appreciably

considerate *adjective* THOUGHTFUL, kind, kindly, concerned, obliging, attentive, mindful, unselfish, solicitous << ANTONYM inconsiderate

consideration *noun* **1** THOUGHT, study, review, attention, regard, analysis, examination, reflection, scrutiny, deliberation, contemplation, perusal, cogitation **2** THOUGHTFULNESS, concern, respect, kindness, friendliness, tact, solicitude, kindliness, considerateness **3** FACTOR, point, issue, concern, element, aspect, determinant **4** PAYMENT, fee, reward, remuneration, recompense, perquisite, tip ▷▷ **take something into consideration** BEAR IN MIND, consider, remember, think about, weigh, take into account, make allowance for, keep in view

considering *preposition* TAKING INTO ACCOUNT, in the light of, bearing in mind, in view of, keeping in mind, taking into consideration ▷ *adverb* (*informal*) ALL THINGS CONSIDERED, all in all, taking everything into consideration, taking everything into account

consign *verb* **1** PUT AWAY, commit, deposit, relegate **2** DELIVER, ship, transfer, transmit, convey

consignment *noun* SHIPMENT, delivery, batch, goods

consist *verb* ▷▷ **consist in something** LIE IN, involve, reside in, be expressed by, subsist in, be found *or* contained in ▷▷ **consist of something** BE MADE UP OF, include, contain, incorporate, amount to, comprise, be composed of

consistency *noun* **1** AGREEMENT, harmony, correspondence, accordance, regularity, coherence, compatibility, uniformity, constancy, steadiness, steadfastness, evenness, congruity **2** TEXTURE, density, thickness, firmness, viscosity, compactness

consistent *adjective* **1** STEADY, even, regular, stable, constant, persistent, dependable, unchanging, true to type, undeviating << ANTONYM erratic **2** COMPATIBLE, agreeing, in keeping, harmonious, in harmony, consonant, in accord, congruent, congruous, accordant << ANTONYM incompatible **3** COHERENT, logical, compatible, harmonious, consonant, all of a piece << ANTONYM contradictory

consolation *noun* COMFORT, help, support, relief, ease, cheer, encouragement, solace, succour, alleviation, assuagement

console *verb* COMFORT, cheer, relieve, soothe, support, encourage, calm, solace, assuage, succour, express sympathy for << ANTONYM distress

consolidate *verb* **1** STRENGTHEN, secure, reinforce, cement, fortify, stabilize **2** COMBINE, unite, join, marry, merge, unify, amalgamate, federate, conjoin

consolidation *noun* **1** STRENGTHENING, reinforcement, fortification, stabilization **2** COMBINATION, union, association, alliance, merger, federation, amalgamation

consort *verb* ASSOCIATE WITH, mix with, mingle with, hang with (*informal, chiefly US*), go around with, keep company with, fraternize with, hang about, around *or* out with ▷ *noun* SPOUSE, wife, husband, partner, associate, fellow, companion, significant other (*US informal*), wahine (*NZ*), wifey (*informal*)

conspicuous *adjective* OBVIOUS, clear, apparent, visible, patent, evident, manifest, noticeable, blatant, discernible, salient, perceptible, easily seen << ANTONYM inconspicuous

conspiracy *noun* PLOT, scheme, intrigue, collusion, confederacy, cabal, frame-up (*slang*), machination, league

conspirator *noun* PLOTTER, intriguer, conspirer, traitor, schemer

conspire *verb* **1** PLOT, scheme, intrigue, devise, manoeuvre, contrive, machinate, plan, hatch treason **2** WORK TOGETHER, combine, contribute, cooperate, concur, tend, conduce

constancy *noun* **1** STEADINESS, stability, regularity, uniformity, perseverance, firmness, permanence **2** FAITHFULNESS, loyalty, devotion, fidelity, dependability, trustworthiness, steadfastness

constant *adjective* **1** CONTINUOUS, sustained, endless, persistent, eternal, relentless, perpetual, continual, never-ending, habitual, uninterrupted, interminable, unrelenting, incessant, everlasting, ceaseless, unremitting, nonstop << ANTONYM occasional **2** UNCHANGING, even, fixed, regular, permanent, stable, steady, uniform, continual, unbroken, immutable, immovable, invariable, unalterable, unvarying, firm << ANTONYM changing **3** FAITHFUL, true, devoted, loyal, stalwart, staunch, dependable, trustworthy, trusty, steadfast, unfailing, tried-and-true << ANTONYM undependable

constantly *adverb* CONTINUOUSLY, always, all the time, invariably, continually, aye (*Scot*), endlessly, relentlessly, persistently, perpetually, night and day, incessantly, nonstop, interminably, everlastingly, morning, noon and night << ANTONYM occasionally

consternation *noun* DISMAY, shock, alarm, horror, panic, anxiety, distress, confusion, terror, dread, fright, amazement, fear, bewilderment, trepidation

constituent *noun* 1 VOTER, elector, member of the electorate 2 COMPONENT, element, ingredient, part, unit, factor, principle ▷ *adjective* COMPONENT, basic, essential, integral, elemental

constitute *verb* 1 REPRESENT, be, consist of, embody, exemplify, be equivalent to 2 MAKE UP, make, form, compose, comprise 3 SET UP, found, name, create, commission, establish, appoint, delegate, nominate, enact, authorize, empower, ordain, depute

constitution *noun* 1 STATE OF HEALTH, build, body, make-up, frame, physique, physical condition 2 STRUCTURE, form, nature, make-up, organization, establishment, formation, composition, character, temper, temperament, disposition

constitutional *adjective* LEGITIMATE, official, legal, chartered, statutory, vested

constrain *verb* 1 RESTRICT, confine, curb, restrain, rein, constrict, hem in, straiten, check, chain 2 FORCE, pressure, urge, bind, compel, oblige, necessitate, coerce, impel, pressurize, drive

constraint *noun* 1 RESTRICTION, limitation, curb, rein, deterrent, hindrance, damper, check 2 FORCE, pressure, necessity, restraint, compulsion, coercion 3 REPRESSION, reservation, embarrassment, restraint, inhibition, timidity, diffidence, bashfulness

constrict *verb* 1 SQUEEZE, contract, narrow, restrict, shrink, tighten, pinch, choke, cramp, strangle, compress, strangulate 2 LIMIT, restrict, confine, curb, inhibit, delimit, straiten

constriction *noun* TIGHTNESS, pressure, narrowing, reduction, squeezing, restriction, constraint, cramp, compression, blockage, limitation, impediment, stricture

construct *verb* 1 BUILD, make, form, create, design, raise, establish, set up, fashion, shape, engineer, frame, manufacture, put up, assemble, put together, erect, fabricate << ANTONYM demolish 2 CREATE, make, form, set up, organize, compose, put together, formulate

construction *noun* 1 BUILDING, assembly, creation, formation, composition, erection, fabrication 2 STRUCTURE, building, edifice, form, figure, shape 3 (*Formal*) INTERPRETATION, meaning, reading, sense, explanation, rendering, take (*informal, chiefly US*), inference

constructive *adjective* HELPFUL, positive, useful, practical, valuable, productive

<< ANTONYM unproductive

construe *verb* INTERPRET, take, read, explain

consult *verb* 1 ASK, refer to, turn to, interrogate, take counsel, ask advice of, pick (someone's) brains, question 2 CONFER, talk, debate, deliberate, commune, compare notes, consider 3 REFER TO, check in, look in

consultant *noun* SPECIALIST, adviser, counsellor, authority

consultation *noun* 1 DISCUSSION, talk, council, conference, dialogue 2 MEETING, interview, session, appointment, examination, deliberation, hearing

consume *verb* 1 EAT, swallow, devour, put away, gobble (up), eat up, guzzle, polish off (*informal*) 2 USE UP, use, spend, waste, employ, absorb, drain, exhaust, deplete, squander, utilize, dissipate, expend, eat up, fritter away 3 DESTROY, devastate, demolish, ravage, annihilate, lay waste 4 *often passive* OBSESS, dominate, absorb, preoccupy, devour, eat up, monopolize, engross

consumer *noun* BUYER, customer, user, shopper, purchaser

consuming *adjective* OVERWHELMING, gripping, absorbing, compelling, devouring, engrossing, immoderate

consummate *adjective* 1 SKILLED, perfect, supreme, polished, superb, practised, accomplished, matchless 2 COMPLETE, total, supreme, extreme, ultimate, absolute, utter, conspicuous, unqualified, deep-dyed (*usually derogatory*) ▷ *verb* COMPLETE, finish, achieve, conclude, perform, perfect, carry out, crown, fulfil, end, accomplish, effectuate, put the tin lid on << ANTONYM initiate

consummation *noun* COMPLETION, end, achievement, perfection, realization, fulfilment, culmination

consumption *noun* 1 USING UP, use, loss, waste, drain, consuming, expenditure, exhaustion, depletion, utilization, dissipation 2 (*Old-fashioned*) TUBERCULOSIS, atrophy, T.B., emaciation

contact *noun* 1 COMMUNICATION, link, association, connection, correspondence, intercourse 2 TOUCH, contiguity 3 CONNECTION, colleague, associate, liaison, acquaintance, confederate ▷ *verb* GET *or* BE IN TOUCH WITH, call, reach, approach, phone, ring (up) (*informal, chiefly Brit*), write to, speak to, communicate with, get hold of, touch base with (*US & Canad informal*)

contagion *noun* SPREAD, spreading,

communication, passage, proliferation, diffusion, transference, dissemination, dispersal, transmittal

contagious *adjective* INFECTIOUS, catching, spreading, epidemic, communicable, transmissible

contain *verb* 1 HOLD, incorporate, accommodate, enclose, have capacity for 2 INCLUDE, consist of, embrace, comprise, embody, comprehend 3 RESTRAIN, control, hold in, curb, suppress, hold back, stifle, repress, keep a tight rein on

container *noun* HOLDER, vessel, repository, receptacle

contaminate *verb* POLLUTE, infect, stain, corrupt, taint, sully, defile, adulterate, befoul, soil << ANTONYM purify

contaminated *adjective* POLLUTED, dirtied, poisoned, infected, stained, corrupted, tainted, sullied, defiled, soiled, adulterated

contamination *noun* POLLUTION, dirtying, infection, corruption, poisoning, decay, taint, filth, impurity, contagion, adulteration, foulness, defilement

contemplate *verb* 1 CONSIDER, plan, think of, propose, intend, envisage, foresee, have in view *or* in mind 2 THINK ABOUT, consider, ponder, mull over, reflect upon, ruminate (upon), meditate on, brood over, muse over, deliberate over, revolve *or* turn over in your mind 3 LOOK AT, examine, observe, check out (*informal*), inspect, gaze at, behold, eye up, view, study, regard, survey, stare at, scrutinize, eye

contemplation *noun* 1 THOUGHT, consideration, reflection, musing, meditation, pondering, deliberation, reverie, rumination, cogitation 2 OBSERVATION, viewing, looking at, survey, examination, inspection, scrutiny, gazing at

contemplative *adjective* THOUGHTFUL, reflective, introspective, rapt, meditative, pensive, ruminative, in a brown study, intent, musing, deep *or* lost in thought

contemporary *adjective* 1 MODERN, latest, recent, current, with it (*informal*), trendy (*Brit informal*), up-to-date, present-day, in fashion, up-to-the-minute, à la mode, newfangled, happening (*informal*), present, ultramodern << ANTONYM old-fashioned 2 COEXISTING, concurrent, contemporaneous, synchronous, coexistent ▷ *noun* PEER, fellow, equal

contempt *noun* SCORN, disdain, mockery, derision, disrespect, disregard

<< ANTONYM respect

contemptible *adjective* DESPICABLE, mean, low, base, cheap, worthless, shameful, shabby, vile, degenerate, low-down (*informal*), paltry, pitiful, abject, ignominious, measly, scurvy, detestable, odious << ANTONYM admirable

contemptuous *adjective* SCORNFUL, insulting, arrogant, withering, sneering, cavalier, condescending, haughty, disdainful, insolent, derisive, supercilious, high and mighty, on your high horse (*informal*) << ANTONYM respectful

contend *verb* 1 ARGUE, hold, maintain, allege, assert, affirm, avow, avere 2 COMPETE, fight, struggle, clash, contest, strive, vie, grapple, jostle, skirmish

contender *noun* COMPETITOR, rival, candidate, applicant, hopeful, contestant, aspirant

content[1] *noun* 1 SUBJECT MATTER, ideas, matter, material, theme, text, substance, essence, gist 2 AMOUNT, measure, size, load, volume, capacity ▷ *plural noun* CONSTITUENTS, elements, load, ingredients 2 SUBJECTS, chapters, themes, topics, subject matter, divisions

content[2] *adjective* SATISFIED, happy, pleased, contented, comfortable, fulfilled, at ease, gratified, agreeable, willing to accept ▷ *noun* SATISFACTION, peace, ease, pleasure, comfort, peace of mind, gratification, contentment ▷▷ **content yourself with something** SATISFY YOURSELF WITH, be happy with, be satisfied with, be content with

contented *adjective* SATISFIED, happy, pleased, content, comfortable, glad, cheerful, at ease, thankful, gratified, serene, at peace << ANTONYM discontented

contention *noun* 1 ASSERTION, claim, stand, idea, view, position, opinion, argument, belief, allegation, profession, declaration, thesis, affirmationo 2 DISPUTE, hostility, disagreement, feuding, strife, wrangling, discord, enmity, dissension

contentious *adjective* ARGUMENTATIVE, wrangling, perverse, bickering, combative, pugnacious, quarrelsome, litigious, querulous, cavilling, disputatious, factious, captious

contentment *noun* SATISFACTION, peace, content, ease, pleasure, comfort, happiness, fulfilment, gratification, serenity, equanimity, gladness, repletion, contentedness << ANTONYM discontent

contest *noun* **1** COMPETITION, game, match, trial, tournament, head-to-head **2** STRUGGLE, fight, battle, debate, conflict, dispute, encounter, controversy, combat, discord ▷ *verb* **1** COMPETE IN, take part in, fight in, go in for, contend for, vie in **2** OPPOSE, question, challenge, argue, debate, dispute, object to, litigate, call in *or* into question

contestant *noun* COMPETITOR, candidate, participant, contender, entrant, player, aspirant

context *noun* **1** CIRCUMSTANCES, times, conditions, situation, ambience **2** FRAME OF REFERENCE, background, framework, relation, connection

contingency *noun* POSSIBILITY, happening, chance, event, incident, accident, emergency, uncertainty, eventuality, juncture

contingent *noun* GROUP, detachment, deputation, set, body, section, bunch (*informal*), quota, batch ▷ *adjective* CHANCE, random, casual, uncertain, accidental, haphazard, fortuitous ▷▷ **contingent on** DEPENDENT ON, subject to, controlled by, conditional on

continual *adjective* **1** CONSTANT, endless, continuous, eternal, perpetual, uninterrupted, interminable, incessant, everlasting, unremitting, unceasing << ANTONYM erratic **2** FREQUENT, regular, repeated, repetitive, recurrent, oft-repeated << ANTONYM occasional

continually *adverb* **1** CONSTANTLY, always, all the time, forever, aye (*Scot*), endlessly, eternally, incessantly, nonstop, interminably, everlastingly **2** REPEATEDLY, often, frequently, many times, over and over, again and again, time and (time) again, persistently, time after time, many a time and oft (*archaic or poetic*)

continuance *noun* PERPETUATION, lasting, carrying on, keeping up, endurance, continuation, prolongation

continuation *noun* **1** CONTINUING, lasting, carrying on, maintenance, keeping up, endurance, perpetuation, prolongation **2** ADDITION, extension, supplement, sequel, resumption, postscript

continue *verb* **1** KEEP ON, go on, maintain, pursue, sustain, carry on, stick to, keep up, prolong, persist in, keep at, persevere, stick at, press on with << ANTONYM stop **2** GO ON, advance, progress, proceed, carry on,

keep going **3** RESUME, return to, take up again, proceed, carry on, recommence, pick up where you left off << ANTONYM stop **4** REMAIN, last, stay, rest, survive, carry on, live on, endure, stay on, persist, abide << ANTONYM quit

continuing *adjective* LASTING, sustained, enduring, ongoing, in progress

continuity *noun* COHESION, flow, connection, sequence, succession, progression, wholeness, interrelationship

continuous *adjective* CONSTANT, continued, extended, prolonged, unbroken, uninterrupted, unceasing << ANTONYM occasional

contort *verb* TWIST, knot, distort, warp, deform, misshape

contortion *noun* TWIST, distortion, deformity, convolution, bend, knot, warp

contour *noun* OUTLINE, profile, lines, form, figure, shape, relief, curve, silhouette

contraband *adjective* SMUGGLED, illegal, illicit, black-market, hot (*informal*), banned, forbidden, prohibited, unlawful, bootleg, bootlegged, interdicted

contract *noun* AGREEMENT, deal (*informal*), commission, commitment, arrangement, understanding, settlement, treaty, bargain, convention, engagement, pact, compact, covenant, bond, stipulation, concordat ▷ *verb* **1** AGREE, arrange, negotiate, engage, pledge, bargain, undertake, come to terms, shake hands, covenant, make a deal, commit yourself, enter into an agreement << ANTONYM refuse **2** CONSTRICT, confine, tighten, shorten, wither, compress, condense, shrivel **3** TIGHTEN, narrow, knit, purse, shorten, pucker << ANTONYM stretch **4** LESSEN, reduce, shrink, diminish, decrease, dwindle << ANTONYM increase **5** CATCH, get, develop, acquire, incur, be infected with, go down with, be afflicted with << ANTONYM avoid

contraction *noun* **1** TIGHTENING, narrowing, tensing, shortening, drawing in, constricting, shrinkage **2** ABBREVIATION, reduction, shortening, compression, diminution, constriction, elision

contradict *verb* **1** DISPUTE, deny, challenge, belie, fly in the face of, make a nonsense of, be at variance with **2** NEGATE, deny, oppose, counter, contravene, rebut, impugn, controvert << ANTONYM confirm

contradiction *noun* **1** CONFLICT, inconsistency, contravention, incongruity, confutation **2** NEGATION, opposite, denial, antithesis

contradictory *adjective* INCONSISTENT, conflicting, opposed, opposite, contrary, incompatible, paradoxical, irreconcilable, antithetical, discrepant

contraption *noun* (*informal*) DEVICE, instrument, mechanism, apparatus, gadget, contrivance, rig

contrary *adjective* **1** OPPOSITE, different, opposed, clashing, counter, reverse, differing, adverse, contradictory, inconsistent, diametrically opposed, antithetical << ANTONYM in agreement **2** PERVERSE, difficult, awkward, wayward, intractable, wilful, obstinate, cussed (*informal*), stroppy (*Brit slang*), cantankerous, disobliging, unaccommodating, thrawn (*Scot & Northern English dialect*) << ANTONYM cooperative ▷ *noun* OPPOSITE, reverse, converse, antithesis ▷▷ **on the contrary** QUITE THE OPPOSITE *or* REVERSE, on the other hand, in contrast, conversely

contrast *noun* DIFFERENCE, opposition, comparison, distinction, foil, disparity, differentiation, divergence, dissimilarity, contrariety ▷ *verb* **1** DIFFERENTIATE, compare, oppose, distinguish, set in opposition **2** DIFFER, be contrary, be distinct, be at variance, be dissimilar

contravene *verb* **1** (*Formal*) BREAK, violate, go against, infringe, disobey, transgress **2** CONFLICT WITH, cross, oppose, interfere with, thwart, contradict, hinder, go against, refute, counteract

contravention *noun* **1** BREACH, violation, infringement, trespass, disobedience, transgression, infraction **2** CONFLICT, interference, contradiction, hindrance, rebuttal, refutation, disputation, counteraction

contribute *verb* GIVE, provide, supply, donate, furnish, subscribe, chip in (*informal*), bestow ▷▷ **contribute to something** BE PARTLY RESPONSIBLE FOR, lead to, be instrumental in, be conducive to, conduce to, help

contribution *noun* GIFT, offering, grant, donation, input, subscription, bestowal, koha (*NZ*)

contributor *noun* **1** DONOR, supporter, patron, subscriber, backer, bestower, giver **2** WRITER, correspondent, reporter, journalist, freelance, freelancer, journo

(*slang*)

contrite *adjective* SORRY, humble, chastened, sorrowful, repentant, remorseful, regretful, penitent, conscience-stricken, in sackcloth and ashes

contrition *noun* REGRET, sorrow, remorse, repentance, compunction, penitence, self-reproach

contrivance *noun* **1** DEVICE, machine, equipment, gear, instrument, implement, mechanism, invention, appliance, apparatus, gadget, contraption **2** STRATAGEM, plan, design, measure, scheme, trick, plot, dodge, expedient, ruse, artifice, machination

contrive *verb* **1** DEVISE, plan, fabricate, create, design, scheme, engineer, frame, manufacture, plot, construct, invent, improvise, concoct, wangle (*informal*) **2** MANAGE, succeed, arrange, manoeuvre

contrived *adjective* FORCED, planned, laboured, strained, artificial, elaborate, unnatural, overdone, recherché << ANTONYM natural

control *noun* **1** POWER, government, rule, authority, management, direction, command, discipline, guidance, supervision, jurisdiction, supremacy, mastery, superintendence, charge **2** RESTRAINT, check, regulation, brake, limitation, curb **3** SELF-DISCIPLINE, cool, calmness, self-restraint, restraint, coolness, self-mastery, self-command **4** SWITCH, instrument, button, dial, lever, knob ▷ *plural noun* INSTRUMENTS, dash, dials, console, dashboard, control panel ▷ *verb* **1** HAVE POWER OVER, lead, rule, manage, boss (*informal*), direct, handle, conduct, dominate, command, pilot, govern, steer, administer, oversee, supervise, manipulate, call the shots, call the tune, reign over, keep a tight rein on, have charge of, superintend, have (someone) in your pocket, keep (someone) on a string **2** LIMIT, restrict, curb, delimit **3** RESTRAIN, limit, check, contain, master, curb, hold back, subdue, repress, constrain, bridle, rein in

controversial *adjective* DISPUTED, contended, contentious, at issue, debatable, polemic, under discussion, open to question, disputable

controversy *noun* ARGUMENT, debate, row, discussion, dispute, contention, quarrel, squabble, strife, wrangle, wrangling, polemic, altercation, dissension

conundrum *noun* PUZZLE, problem, riddle, enigma, teaser, poser, brain-teaser (*informal*)

convalesce *verb* RECOVER, rest, rally, rehabilitate, recuperate, improve

convalescence *noun* RECOVERY, rehabilitation, recuperation, return to health, improvement

convalescent *adjective* RECOVERING, getting better, recuperating, on the mend, improving, mending

convene *verb* 1 CALL, gather, assemble, summon, bring together, muster, convoke 2 MEET, gather, rally, assemble, come together, muster, congregate

convenience *noun* 1 BENEFIT, good, interest, advantage 2 SUITABILITY, fitness, appropriateness, opportuneness 3 USEFULNESS, utility, serviceability, handiness << ANTONYM uselessness 4 ACCESSIBILITY, availability, nearness, handiness 5 APPLIANCE, facility, comfort, amenity, labour-saving device, help ▷▷ **at your convenience** AT A SUITABLE TIME, at your leisure, in your own time, whenever you like, in your spare time, in a spare moment

convenient *adjective* 1 SUITABLE, fitting, fit, handy, satisfactory 2 USEFUL, practical, handy, serviceable, labour-saving << ANTONYM useless 3 NEARBY, available, accessible, handy, at hand, within reach, close at hand, just round the corner << ANTONYM inaccessible 4 APPROPRIATE, timely, suited, suitable, beneficial, well-timed, opportune, seasonable, helpful

convent *noun* NUNNERY, religious community, religious house

convention *noun* 1 CUSTOM, practice, tradition, code, usage, protocol, formality, etiquette, propriety, kawa (*NZ*), tikanga (*NZ*), rule 2 AGREEMENT, contract, treaty, bargain, pact, compact, protocol, stipulation, concordat 3 ASSEMBLY, meeting, council, conference, congress, convocation, hui (*NZ*), runanga (*NZ*)

conventional *adjective* 1 PROPER, conservative, correct, formal, respectable, bourgeois, genteel, staid, conformist, decorous, Pooterish 2 ORDINARY, standard, normal, regular, usual, vanilla (*slang*), habitual, bog-standard (*Brit & Irish slang*), common 3 TRADITIONAL, accepted, prevailing, orthodox, customary, prevalent, hidebound, wonted 4 UNORIGINAL, routine, stereotyped, pedestrian, commonplace, banal, prosaic, run-of-the-mill, hackneyed, vanilla (*slang*) << ANTONYM unconventional

converge *verb* COME TOGETHER, meet, join, combine, gather, merge, coincide, mingle, intersect ▷▷ **converge on something** CLOSE IN ON, arrive at, move towards, home in on, come together at

convergence *noun* MEETING, junction, intersection, confluence, concentration, blending, merging, coincidence, conjunction, mingling, concurrence, conflux

conversation *noun* TALK, exchange, discussion, dialogue, tête-à-tête, conference, communication, chat, gossip, intercourse, discourse, communion, converse, powwow, colloquy, chinwag (*Brit informal*), confabulation, confab (*informal*), craic (*Irish informal*), korero (*NZ*)

conversational *adjective* CHATTY, informal, communicative, colloquial

converse[1] *verb* TALK, speak, chat, communicate, discourse, confer, commune, exchange views, shoot the breeze (*slang, chiefly US & Canad*)

converse[2] *noun* OPPOSITE, reverse, contrary, other side of the coin, obverse, antithesis ▷ *adjective* OPPOSITE, counter, reverse, contrary

conversion *noun* 1 CHANGE, transformation, metamorphosis, transfiguration, transmutation, transmogrification (*jocular*) 2 ADAPTATION, reconstruction, modification, alteration, remodelling, reorganization 3 REFORMATION, rebirth, change of heart, proselytization

convert *verb* 1 CHANGE, turn, transform, alter, metamorphose, transpose, transmute, transmogrify (*jocular*) 2 ADAPT, modify, remodel, reorganize, customize, restyle 3 REFORM, save, convince, proselytize, bring to God ▷ *noun* NEOPHYTE, disciple, proselyte, catechumen

convertible *adjective* CHANGEABLE, interchangeable, exchangeable, adjustable, adaptable

convex *adjective* ROUNDED, bulging, protuberant, gibbous, outcurved << ANTONYM concave

convey *verb* 1 COMMUNICATE, impart, reveal, relate, disclose, make known, tell 2 CARRY, transport, move, bring, support, bear, conduct, transmit, fetch

conveyance *noun* 1 (*Old-fashioned*) VEHICLE,

transport **2** TRANSPORTATION, movement, transfer, transport, transmission, carriage, transference

convict *verb* FIND GUILTY, sentence, condemn, imprison, pronounce guilty ▷ *noun* PRISONER, criminal, con (*slang*), lag (*slang*), villain, felon, jailbird, malefactor

conviction *noun* **1** BELIEF, view, opinion, principle, faith, persuasion, creed, tenet, kaupapa (*NZ*) **2** CERTAINTY, confidence, assurance, fervour, firmness, earnestness, certitude

convince *verb* **1** ASSURE, persuade, satisfy, prove to, reassure **2** PERSUADE, induce, coax, talk into, prevail upon, inveigle, twist (someone's) arm, bring round to the idea of

convincing *adjective* PERSUASIVE, credible, conclusive, incontrovertible, telling, likely, powerful, impressive, probable, plausible, cogent << ANTONYM unconvincing

convivial *adjective* SOCIABLE, friendly, lively, cheerful, jolly, merry, festive, hearty, genial, fun-loving, jovial, back-slapping, gay, partyish (*informal*)

convocation *noun* (*Formal*) MEETING, congress, convention, synod, diet, assembly, concourse, council, assemblage, conclave, hui (*NZ*), runanga (*NZ*)

convoy *verb* ESCORT, conduct, accompany, shepherd, protect, attend, guard, pilot, usher

convulse *verb* **1** SHAKE, twist, agitate, contort **2** TWIST, contort, work

convulsion *noun* **1** SPASM, fit, shaking, seizure, contraction, tremor, cramp, contortion, paroxysm **2** UPHEAVAL, disturbance, furore, turbulence, agitation, commotion, tumult

cool *adjective* **1** COLD, chilled, chilling, refreshing, chilly, nippy << ANTONYM warm **2** CALM, together (*slang*), collected, relaxed, composed, laid-back (*informal*), serene, sedate, self-controlled, placid, level-headed, dispassionate, unfazed (*informal*), unruffled, unemotional, self-possessed, imperturbable, unexcited << ANTONYM agitated **3** UNFRIENDLY, reserved, distant, indifferent, aloof, lukewarm, unconcerned, uninterested, frigid, unresponsive, offhand, unenthusiastic, uncommunicative, unwelcoming, standoffish <<<ANTONYM friendly **4** UNENTHUSIASTIC, indifferent, lukewarm, uninterested, apathetic, unresponsive, unwelcoming **5** (*informal*) FASHIONABLE, with it (*informal*), hip (*slang*), stylish, trendy (*Brit informal*), chic,

up-to-date, urbane, up-to-the-minute, voguish (*informal*), trendsetting, schmick (*Austral informal*) **6** IMPUDENT, bold, cheeky, audacious, brazen, shameless, presumptuous, impertinent ▷ *verb* **1** LOSE HEAT, cool off << ANTONYM warm (up) **2** MAKE COOL, freeze, chill, refrigerate, cool off << ANTONYM warm (up) **3** CALM (DOWN), lessen, abate **4** LESSEN, calm (down), quiet, moderate, temper, dampen, allay, abate, assuage ▷ *noun* **1** COLDNESS, chill, coolness **2** (*Slang*) CALMNESS, control, temper, composure, self-control, poise, self-discipline, self-possession

coolness *noun* **1** COLDNESS, freshness, chilliness, nippiness << ANTONYM warmness **2** CALMNESS, control, composure, self-control, self-discipline, self-possession, level-headedness, imperturbability, sedateness, placidness << ANTONYM agitation **3** UNFRIENDLINESS, reserve, distance, indifference, apathy, remoteness, aloofness, frigidity, unconcern, unresponsiveness, frostiness, offhandedness << ANTONYM friendliness **4** IMPUDENCE, audacity, boldness, insolence, impertinence, shamelessness, cheekiness, brazenness, presumptuousness, audaciousness

coop *noun* PEN, pound, box, cage, enclosure, hutch, corral (*chiefly US & Canad*) ▷▷ **coop someone up** CONFINE, imprison, shut up, impound, pound, pen, cage, immure

cooperate *verb* **1** WORK TOGETHER, collaborate, coordinate, join forces, conspire, concur, pull together, pool resources, combine your efforts << ANTONYM conflict **2** HELP, contribute to, assist, go along with, aid, pitch in, abet, play ball (with) (*informal*), lend a helping hand << ANTONYM oppose

cooperation *noun* **1** TEAMWORK, concert, unity, collaboration, give-and-take, combined effort, esprit de corps, concurrence, kotahitanga (*NZ*) << ANTONYM opposition **2** HELP, assistance, participation, responsiveness, helpfulness << ANTONYM hindrance

cooperative *adjective* **1** SHARED, united, joint, combined, concerted, collective, unified, coordinated, collaborative **2** HELPFUL, obliging, accommodating, supportive, responsive, onside (*informal*)

coordinate *verb* **1** ORGANIZE, synchronize, integrate, bring together, mesh, correlate, systematize **2** MATCH, blend, harmonize

▷▷ **coordinate with** GO WITH, match, blend with, harmonize with

cope *verb* MANAGE, get by (*informal*), struggle through, rise to the occasion, survive, carry on, make out (*informal*), make the grade, hold your own ▷▷ **cope with something** DEAL WITH, handle, struggle with, grapple with, wrestle with, contend with, tangle with, tussle with, weather

copious *adjective* ABUNDANT, liberal, generous, lavish, full, rich, extensive, ample, overflowing, plentiful, exuberant, bountiful, luxuriant, profuse, bounteous, superabundant, plenteous

cop out *verb* (*Slang*) AVOID, dodge, abandon, withdraw from, desert, quit, skip, renounce, revoke, renege, skive (*Brit slang*), bludge (*Austral & NZ informal*)

cop-out *noun* (*Slang*) PRETENCE, dodge, pretext, fraud, alibi

copulate *verb* HAVE INTERCOURSE, have sex

copy *noun* REPRODUCTION, duplicate, photocopy, carbon copy, image, print, fax, representation, fake, replica, imitation, forgery, counterfeit, Xerox (*trademark*), transcription, likeness, replication, facsimile, Photostat (*trademark*) << ANTONYM original ▷ *verb* 1 REPRODUCE, replicate, duplicate, photocopy, transcribe, counterfeit, Xerox (*trademark*), Photostat (*trademark*) << ANTONYM create 2 IMITATE, act like, emulate, behave like, follow, repeat, mirror, echo, parrot, ape, mimic, simulate, follow suit, follow the example of

cord *noun* ROPE, line, string, twine

cordial *adjective* 1 WARM, welcoming, friendly, cheerful, affectionate, hearty, agreeable, sociable, genial, affable, congenial, warm-hearted << ANTONYM unfriendly 2 WHOLEHEARTED, earnest, sincere, heartfelt

cordon *noun* CHAIN, line, ring, barrier, picket line ▷▷ **cordon something off** SURROUND, isolate, close off, fence off, separate, enclose, picket, encircle

core *noun* 1 CENTRE 2 HEART, essence, nucleus, kernel, crux, gist, nub, pith

corner *noun* 1 ANGLE, joint, crook 2 BEND, curve 3 SPACE, hole, niche, recess, cavity, hideaway, nook, cranny, hide-out, hidey-hole (*informal*) 4 TIGHT SPOT, predicament, tricky situation, spot (*informal*), hole (*informal*), hot water (*informal*), pickle (*informal*) ▷ *verb* 1 TRAP, catch, run to earth, bring to bay 2 (usually with *market* as object)

MONOPOLIZE, take over, dominate, control, hog (*slang*), engross, exercise *or* have a monopoly of

cornerstone *noun* BASIS, key, premise, starting point, bedrock

corny *adjective* (*Slang*) 1 UNORIGINAL, banal, trite, hackneyed, dull, old-fashioned, stereotyped, commonplace, feeble, stale, old hat 2 SENTIMENTAL, mushy (*informal*), maudlin, slushy (*informal*), mawkish, schmaltzy (*slang*)

corollary *noun* CONSEQUENCE, result, effect, outcome, sequel, end result, upshot

corporal *adjective* BODILY, physical, fleshly, anatomical, carnal, corporeal (*archaic*), material

corporate *adjective* COLLECTIVE, collaborative, united, shared, allied, joint, combined, pooled, merged, communal

corporation *noun* 1 BUSINESS, company, concern, firm, society, association, organization, enterprise, establishment, corporate body 2 TOWN COUNCIL, council, municipal authorities, civic authorities

corps *noun* TEAM, unit, regiment, detachment, company, body, band, division, troop, squad, crew, contingent, squadron

corpse *noun* BODY, remains, carcass, cadaver, stiff (*slang*)

corpus *noun* COLLECTION, body, whole, compilation, entirety, oeuvre (*French*), complete works

corral *verb* (*US & Canad*) ENCLOSE, confine, cage, fence in, impound, pen in, coop up

correct *adjective* 1 ACCURATE, right, true, exact, precise, flawless, faultless, on the right lines, O.K. or okay (*informal*) << ANTONYM inaccurate 2 RIGHT, standard, regular, appropriate, acceptable, strict, proper, precise 3 PROPER, seemly, standard, fitting, diplomatic, kosher (*informal*) << ANTONYM inappropriate ▷ *verb* 1 RECTIFY, remedy, redress, right, improve, reform, cure, adjust, regulate, amend, set the record straight, emend << ANTONYM spoil 2 REBUKE, discipline, reprimand, chide, admonish, chastise, chasten, reprove, punish << ANTONYM praise

correction *noun* 1 RECTIFICATION, improvement, amendment, adjustment, modification, alteration, emendation 2 PUNISHMENT, discipline, reformation, admonition, chastisement, reproof, castigation

corrective *adjective* 1 REMEDIAL,

therapeutic, palliative, restorative, rehabilitative **2** DISCIPLINARY, punitive, penal, reformatory

correctly *adverb* RIGHTLY, right, perfectly, properly, precisely, accurately, aright

correctness *noun* **1** TRUTH, accuracy, precision, exactitude, exactness, faultlessness **2** DECORUM, propriety, good manners, civility, good breeding, bon ton (*French*)

correlate *verb* **1** CORRESPOND, parallel, be connected, equate, tie in, match **2** CONNECT, compare, associate, tie in, coordinate, match

correlation *noun* CORRESPONDENCE, link, relation, connection, equivalence

correspond *verb* **1** BE CONSISTENT, match, agree, accord, fit, square, coincide, complement, be related, tally, conform, correlate, dovetail, harmonize << ANTONYM differ **2** COMMUNICATE, write, keep in touch, exchange letters

correspondence *noun* **1** COMMUNICATION, writing, contact **2** LETTERS, post, mail **3** RELATION, match, agreement, fitness, comparison, harmony, coincidence, similarity, analogy, correlation, conformity, comparability, concurrence, congruity

correspondent *noun* **1** REPORTER, journalist, contributor, special correspondent, journo (*slang*), hack **2** LETTER WRITER, pen friend *or* pen pal

corresponding *adjective* EQUIVALENT, matching, similar, related, correspondent, identical, complementary, synonymous, reciprocal, analogous, interrelated, correlative

corridor *noun* PASSAGE, alley, aisle, hallway, passageway

corroborate *verb* SUPPORT, establish, confirm, document, sustain, back up, endorse, ratify, validate, bear out, substantiate, authenticate << ANTONYM contradict

corrode *verb* EAT AWAY, waste, consume, corrupt, deteriorate, erode, rust, gnaw, oxidize

corrosive *adjective* CORRODING, wasting, caustic, vitriolic, acrid, erosive

corrugated *adjective* FURROWED, channelled, ridged, grooved, wrinkled, creased, fluted, rumpled, puckered, crinkled

corrupt *adjective* **1** DISHONEST, bent (*slang*), crooked (*informal*), rotten, shady (*informal*), fraudulent, unscrupulous, unethical, venal, unprincipled << ANTONYM honest **2** DEPRAVED, abandoned, vicious, degenerate, debased, demoralized, profligate, dishonoured, defiled, dissolute **3** DISTORTED, doctored, altered, falsified ▷ *verb* **1** BRIBE, square, fix (*informal*), buy off, suborn, grease (someone's) palm (*slang*) **2** DEPRAVE, pervert, subvert, debase, demoralize, debauch << ANTONYM reform **3** DISTORT, doctor, tamper with

corruption *noun* **1** DISHONESTY, fraud, fiddling (*informal*), graft (*informal*), bribery, extortion, profiteering, breach of trust, venality, shady dealings (*informal*), shadiness **2** DEPRAVITY, vice, evil, degradation, perversion, decadence, impurity, wickedness, degeneration, immorality, iniquity, profligacy, viciousness, sinfulness, turpitude, baseness **3** DISTORTION, doctoring, falsification

corset *noun* GIRDLE, bodice, foundation garment, panty girdle, stays (*rare*)

cortege *noun* PROCESSION, train, entourage, cavalcade, retinue, suite

cosmetic *adjective* SUPERFICIAL, surface, touching-up, nonessential

cosmic *adjective* **1** EXTRATERRESTRIAL, stellar **2** UNIVERSAL, general, omnipresent, all-embracing, overarching **3** VAST, huge, immense, infinite, grandiose, limitless, measureless

cosmonaut *noun* ASTRONAUT, spaceman, space pilot, space cadet

cosmopolitan *adjective* SOPHISTICATED, worldly, cultured, refined, cultivated, urbane, well-travelled, worldly-wise << ANTONYM unsophisticated

cosmos *noun* UNIVERSE, world, creation, macrocosm

cosset *verb* PAMPER, baby, pet, coddle, mollycoddle, wrap up in cotton wool (*informal*)

cost *noun* **1** PRICE, worth, expense, rate, charge, figure, damage (*informal*), amount, payment, expenditure, outlay **2** LOSS, suffering, damage, injury, penalty, hurt, expense, harm, sacrifice, deprivation, detriment ▷ *plural noun* EXPENSES, spending, expenditure, overheads, outgoings, outlay, budget ▷ *verb* **1** SELL AT, come to, set (someone) back (*informal*), be priced at, command a price of **2** LOSE, deprive of, cheat of ▷▷ **at all costs** NO MATTER WHAT, regardless, whatever happens, at any price, come what may, without fail

costly *adjective* **1** EXPENSIVE, dear, stiff, excessive, steep (*informal*), highly-priced, exorbitant, extortionate << ANTONYM inexpensive **2** SPLENDID, rich, valuable, precious, gorgeous, lavish, luxurious, sumptuous, priceless, opulent **3** DAMAGING, disastrous, harmful, catastrophic, loss-making, ruinous, deleterious

costume *noun* OUTFIT, dress, clothing, get-up (*informal*), uniform, ensemble, robes, livery, apparel, attire, garb, national dress

cosy *adjective* **1** COMFORTABLE, homely, warm, intimate, snug, comfy (*informal*), sheltered **2** SNUG, warm, secure, comfortable, sheltered, comfy (*informal*), tucked up, cuddled up, snuggled down **3** INTIMATE, friendly, informal

coterie *noun* CLIQUE, group, set, camp, circle, gang, outfit (*informal*), posse (*informal*), cabal

cottage *noun* CABIN, lodge, hut, shack, chalet, but-and-ben (*Scot*), cot, whare (*NZ*)

couch *noun* SOFA, bed, chesterfield, ottoman, settee, divan, chaise longue, day bed ▷ *verb* EXPRESS, word, frame, phrase, utter, set forth

cough *verb* CLEAR YOUR THROAT, bark, hawk, hack, hem ▷ *noun* FROG *or* TICKLE IN YOUR THROAT, bark, hack ▷▷ **cough up** (*informal*) FORK OUT, deliver, hand over, surrender, come across (*informal*), shell out (*informal*), ante up (*informal*, *chiefly US*)

council *noun* **1** COMMITTEE, governing body, board, panel, quango **2** GOVERNING BODY, house, parliament, congress, cabinet, ministry, diet, panel, assembly, chamber, convention, synod, conclave, convocation, conference, runanga (*NZ*)

counsel *noun* **1** ADVICE, information, warning, direction, suggestion, recommendation, caution, guidance, admonition **2** LEGAL ADVISER, lawyer, attorney, solicitor, advocate, barrister ▷ *verb* ADVISE, recommend, advocate, prescribe, warn, urge, caution, instruct, exhort, admonish

count *verb* **1** *often with* **up** ADD (UP), total, reckon (up), tot up, score, check, estimate, calculate, compute, tally, number, enumerate, cast up **2** MATTER, be important, cut any ice (*informal*), carry weight, tell, rate, weigh, signify, enter into consideration **3** CONSIDER, judge, regard, deem, think of, rate, esteem, look upon, impute **4** INCLUDE, number among, take into account *or* consideration ▷ *noun*

CALCULATION, poll, reckoning, sum, tally, numbering, computation, enumeration ▷▷ **count on** *or* **upon something** *or* **someone** DEPEND ON, trust, rely on, bank on, take for granted, lean on, reckon on, take on trust, believe in, pin your faith on ▷▷ **count someone out** (*informal*) LEAVE OUT, except, exclude, disregard, pass over, leave out of account

countenance *noun* (*Literary*) FACE, features, expression, look, appearance, aspect, visage, mien, physiognomy ▷ *verb* TOLERATE, sanction, endorse, condone, support, encourage, approve, endure, brook, stand for (*informal*), hack (*slang*), put up with (*informal*)

counter *verb* **1** OPPOSE, meet, block, resist, offset, parry, deflect, repel, rebuff, fend off, counteract, ward off, stave off, repulse, obviate, hold at bay **2** RETALIATE, return, answer, reply, respond, come back, retort, hit back, rejoin, strike back << ANTONYM yield ▷ *adverb* OPPOSITE TO, against, versus, conversely, in defiance of, at variance with, contrarily, contrariwise << ANTONYM in accordance with ▷ *adjective* OPPOSING, conflicting, opposed, contrasting, opposite, contrary, adverse, contradictory, obverse, against << ANTONYM similar

counteract *verb* **1** ACT AGAINST, check, defeat, prevent, oppose, resist, frustrate, foil, thwart, hinder, cross **2** OFFSET, negate, neutralize, invalidate, counterbalance, annul, obviate, countervail

counterbalance *verb* OFFSET, balance out, compensate for, make up for, counterpoise, countervail

counterfeit *adjective* FAKE, copied, false, forged, imitation, bogus, simulated, sham, fraudulent, feigned, spurious, ersatz, phoney *or* phony (*informal*), pseud *or* pseudo (*informal*) << ANTONYM genuine ▷ *noun* FAKE, copy, reproduction, imitation, sham, forgery, phoney *or* phony (*informal*), fraud << ANTONYM the real thing ▷ *verb* FAKE, copy, forge, imitate, simulate, sham, fabricate, feign

counterpart *noun* OPPOSITE NUMBER, equal, twin, equivalent, peer, match, fellow, mate

countless *adjective* INNUMERABLE, legion, infinite, myriad, untold, limitless, incalculable, immeasurable, numberless, uncounted, multitudinous, endless, measureless << ANTONYM limited

country *noun* **1** NATION, state, land, commonwealth, kingdom, realm, sovereign state, people **2** PEOPLE, community, nation, society, citizens, voters, inhabitants, grass roots, electors, populace, citizenry, public **3** COUNTRYSIDE, rural areas, provinces, outdoors, sticks (*informal*), farmland, outback (*Austral & NZ*), the middle of nowhere, green belt, wide open spaces (*informal*), backwoods, back country (*US*), the back of beyond, bush (*NZ & S African*), backlands (*US*), boondocks (*US slang*) << ANTONYM town **4** TERRITORY, part, land, region, terrain **5** NATIVE LAND, nationality, homeland, motherland, fatherland, patria (*Latin*), Hawaiki (*NZ*), Godzone (*Austral informal*) ▷ *adjective* RURAL, pastoral, rustic, agrarian, bucolic, Arcadian << ANTONYM urban

countryman *noun* **1** COMPATRIOT, fellow citizen **2** YOKEL, farmer, peasant, provincial, hick (*informal, chiefly US & Canad*), rustic, swain, hillbilly, bucolic, country dweller, hayseed (*US & Canad informal*), clodhopper (*informal*), cockie (*NZ*), (country) bumpkin

countryside *noun* COUNTRY, rural areas, outdoors, farmland, outback (*Austral & NZ*), green belt, wide open spaces (*informal*), sticks (*informal*)

county *noun* PROVINCE, district, shire ▷ *adjective* (*informal*) UPPER-CLASS, upper-crust (*informal*), tweedy, plummy (*informal*), green-wellie, huntin', shootin', and fishin' (*informal*)

coup *noun* MASTERSTROKE, feat, stunt, action, stroke, exploit, manoeuvre, deed, accomplishment, tour de force (*French*), stratagem, stroke of genius

coup d'état *noun* OVERTHROW, takeover, coup, rebellion, putsch, seizure of power, palace revolution

couple *noun* PAIR, two, brace, span (*of horses or oxen*), duo, twain (*archaic*), twosome ▷▷ **couple something to something** LINK TO, connect to, pair with, unite with, join to, hitch to, buckle to, clasp to, yoke to, conjoin to

coupon *noun* SLIP, ticket, certificate, token, voucher, card, detachable portion

courage *noun* BRAVERY, nerve, fortitude, boldness, bottle (*Brit slang*), resolution, daring, guts (*informal*), pluck, grit, heroism, mettle, firmness, gallantry, valour, spunk (*informal*), fearlessness, intrepidity << ANTONYM cowardice

courageous *adjective* BRAVE, daring, bold, plucky, hardy, heroic, gritty, stalwart, fearless, resolute, gallant, audacious, intrepid, valiant, indomitable, dauntless, ballsy (*taboo slang*), lion-hearted, valorous, stouthearted << ANTONYM cowardly

courier *noun* **1** MESSENGER, runner, carrier, bearer, herald, envoy, emissary **2** GUIDE, representative, escort, conductor, chaperon, cicerone, dragoman

course *noun* **1** ROUTE, way, line, road, track, channel, direction, path, passage, trail, orbit, tack, trajectory **2** PROCEDURE, plan, policy, programme, method, conduct, behaviour, manner, mode, regimen **3** PROGRESSION, order, unfolding, development, movement, advance, progress, flow, sequence, succession, continuity, advancement, furtherance, march **4** CLASSES, course of study, programme, schedule, lectures, curriculum, studies **5** RACECOURSE, race, circuit, cinder track, lap **6** PERIOD, time, duration, term, passing, sweep, passage, lapse ▷ *verb* **1** RUN, flow, stream, gush, race, speed, surge, dash, tumble, scud, move apace **2** HUNT, follow, chase, pursue ▷▷ **in due course** IN TIME, finally, eventually, in the end, sooner or later, in the course of time ▷▷ **of course** NATURALLY, certainly, obviously, definitely, undoubtedly, needless to say, without a doubt, indubitably

court *noun* **1** LAW COURT, bar, bench, tribunal, court of justice, seat of judgment **2** PALACE, hall, castle, manor **3** ROYAL HOUSEHOLD, train, suite, attendants, entourage, retinue, cortege ▷ *verb* **1** CULTIVATE, seek, flatter, solicit, pander to, curry favour with, fawn upon **2** INVITE, seek, attract, prompt, provoke, bring about, incite **3** WOO, go (out) with, go steady with (*informal*), date, chase, pursue, take out, make love to, run after, walk out with, keep company with, pay court to, set your cap at, pay your addresses to

courteous *adjective* POLITE, civil, respectful, mannerly, polished, refined, gracious, gallant, affable, urbane, courtly, well-bred, well-mannered << ANTONYM discourteous

courtesan *noun* (*History*) MISTRESS, prostitute, whore, call girl, working girl (*facetious slang*), kept woman, harlot, paramour, scarlet woman, fille de joie (*French*)

courtesy *noun* **1** POLITENESS, grace, good manners, civility, gallantry, good breeding, graciousness, affability, urbanity, courtliness **2** FAVOUR, consideration, generosity, kindness, indulgence, benevolence

courtier noun ATTENDANT, follower, squire, train-bearer

courtly adjective CEREMONIOUS, civil, formal, obliging, refined, polite, dignified, stately, aristocratic, gallant, affable, urbane, decorous, chivalrous, highbred

courtship noun WOOING, courting, suit, romance, engagement, keeping company

courtyard noun YARD, square, piazza, quadrangle, area, plaza, enclosure, cloister, quad (*informal*), peristyle

cove noun BAY, sound, creek, inlet, bayou, firth or frith (*Scot*), anchorage

covenant noun 1 PROMISE, contract, agreement, commitment, arrangement, treaty, pledge, bargain, convention, pact, compact, concordat, trust 2 (*Law*) DEED, contract, bond

cover verb 1 CONCEAL, cover up, screen, hide, shade, curtain, mask, disguise, obscure, hood, veil, cloak, shroud, camouflage, enshroud << ANTONYM reveal 2 CLOTHE, invest, dress, wrap, envelop << ANTONYM uncover 3 OVERLAY, blanket, eclipse, mantle, canopy, overspread, layer 4 COAT, cake, plaster, smear, envelop, spread, encase, daub, overspread 5 SUBMERGE, flood, engulf, overrun, wash over 6 TRAVEL OVER, cross, traverse, pass through or over, range 7 PROTECT, guard, defend, shelter, shield, watch over 8 INSURE, compensate, provide for, offset, balance, make good, make up for, take account of, counterbalance 9 DEAL WITH, refer to, provide for, take account of, include, involve, contain, embrace, incorporate, comprise, embody, encompass, comprehend << ANTONYM exclude 10 CONSIDER, deal with, examine, investigate, detail, describe, survey, refer to, tell of, recount 11 REPORT ON, write about, commentate on, give an account of, relate, tell of, narrate, write up 12 PAY FOR, fund, provide for, offset, be enough for ▷ noun 1 PROTECTION, shelter, shield, refuge, defence, woods, guard, sanctuary, camouflage, hiding place, undergrowth, concealment 2 INSURANCE, payment, protection, compensation, indemnity, reimbursement 3 COVERING, case, top, cap, coating, envelope, lid, canopy, sheath, wrapper, awning 4 BEDCLOTHES, bedding, sheet, blanket, quilt, duvet, eiderdown 5 JACKET, case, binding,

wrapper 6 DISGUISE, front, screen, mask, cover-up, veil, cloak, façade, pretence, pretext, window-dressing, smoke screen
▷▷ **cover for someone** STAND IN FOR, take over for, substitute for, relieve, double for, fill in for, hold the fort for (*informal*)
▷▷ **cover something up** CONCEAL, hide, suppress, repress, keep secret, whitewash (*informal*), hush up, sweep under the carpet, draw a veil over, keep silent about, cover your tracks, keep dark, feign ignorance about, keep under your hat (*informal*)

coverage noun REPORTING, treatment, analysis, description, reportage

covering noun COVER, coating, casing, wrapping, layer, blanket ▷ adjective EXPLANATORY, accompanying, introductory, descriptive

covert adjective SECRET, private, hidden, disguised, concealed, veiled, sly, clandestine, underhand, unsuspected, surreptitious, stealthy

cover-up noun CONCEALMENT, conspiracy, whitewash (*informal*), complicity, front, smoke screen

covet verb LONG FOR, desire, fancy (*informal*), envy, crave, aspire to, yearn for, thirst for, begrudge, hanker after, lust after, set your heart on, have your eye on, would give your eyeteeth for

cow verb INTIMIDATE, daunt, frighten, scare, bully, dismay, awe, subdue, unnerve, overawe, terrorize, browbeat, psych out (*informal*), dishearten

coward noun WIMP, chicken (*slang*), scaredy-cat (*informal*), sneak, pussy (*slang, chiefly US*), yellow-belly (*slang*)

cowardice noun FAINT-HEARTEDNESS, weakness, softness, fearfulness, pusillanimity, spinelessness, timorousness

cowardly adjective FAINT-HEARTED, scared, spineless, gutless (*informal*), base, soft, yellow (*informal*), weak, chicken (*slang*), shrinking, fearful, craven, abject, dastardly, timorous, weak-kneed (*informal*), pusillanimous, chicken-hearted, lily-livered, white-livered, sookie (*NZ*) << ANTONYM brave

cowboy noun COWHAND, drover, herder, rancher, stockman, cattleman, herdsman, gaucho (*S American*), buckaroo (*US*), ranchero (*US*), cowpuncher (*US informal*), broncobuster (*US*), wrangler (*US*)

cower verb CRINGE, shrink, tremble, crouch, flinch, quail, draw back, grovel

coy adjective 1 MODEST, retiring, shy,

shrinking, arch, timid, self-effacing, demure, flirtatious, bashful, prudish, skittish, coquettish, kittenish, overmodest << ANTONYM bold **2** UNCOMMUNICATIVE, mum, secretive, reserved, quiet, silent, evasive, taciturn, unforthcoming, tight-lipped, close-lipped

crack *verb* **1** SPLIT, break, burst, snap, fracture, splinter, craze, rive **2** SNAP, ring, crash, burst, explode, crackle, pop, detonate **3** (*informal*) HIT, clip (*informal*), slap, smack, thump, buffet, clout (*informal*), cuff, whack, wallop (*informal*), chop **4** BREAK, cleave **5** SOLVE, work out, resolve, interpret, clarify, clear up, fathom, decipher, suss (out) (*slang*), get to the bottom of, disentangle, elucidate, get the answer to **6** BREAK DOWN, collapse, yield, give in, give way, succumb, lose control, be overcome, go to pieces ▷ *noun* **1** BREAK, chink, gap, breach, fracture, rift, cleft, crevice, fissure, cranny, interstice **2** SPLIT, break, chip, breach, fracture, rupture, cleft **3** SNAP, pop, crash, burst, explosion, clap, report **4** (*informal*) BLOW, slap, smack, thump, buffet, clout (*informal*), cuff, whack, wallop (*informal*), clip (*informal*) **5** (*informal*) ATTEMPT, go (*informal*), try, shot, opportunity, stab (*informal*) **6** (*informal*) JOKE, dig, insult, gag (*informal*), quip, jibe, wisecrack, witticism, funny remark, smart-alecky remark ▷ *adjective* (*Slang*) FIRST-CLASS, choice, excellent, ace, elite, superior, world-class, first-rate, hand-picked ▷▷ **crack up** (*informal*) **1** HAVE A BREAKDOWN, collapse, break down, go crazy (*informal*), go berserk, freak out (*informal*), go to pieces, go ape (*slang*), fly off the handle (*informal*), come apart at the seams (*informal*), throw a wobbly (*slang*), go off the deep end (*informal*), go out of your mind, flip your lid (*slang*), go off your rocker (*slang*), go off your head (*slang*) **2** BURST OUT LAUGHING, laugh, fall about (laughing), guffaw, roar with laughter, be in stitches, split your sides

crackdown *noun* CLAMPDOWN, crushing, repression, suppression

cracked *adjective* **1** BROKEN, damaged, split, chipped, flawed, faulty, crazed, defective, imperfect, fissured **2** (*informal*) CRAZY, nuts (*slang*), eccentric, nutty (*slang*), touched, bats (*slang or informal*), daft (*informal*), batty (*slang*), insane, loony (*slang*), off-the-wall (*slang*), oddball (*informal*), loopy (*informal*), crackpot (*informal*), out to lunch (*informal*),

round the bend (*slang*), out of your mind, gonzo (*slang*), doolally (*slang*), off your trolley (*slang*), off the air (*Austral slang*), round the twist (*Brit slang*), up the pole (*informal*), off your rocker (*slang*), crackbrained, off your head *or* nut (*slang*), wacko *or* whacko (*informal*), porangi (*NZ*), daggy (*Austral & NZ informal*)

cradle *noun* **1** CRIB, cot, Moses basket, bassinet **2** BIRTHPLACE, beginning, source, spring, origin, fount, fountainhead, wellspring ▷ *verb* HOLD, support, rock, nurse, nestle

craft *noun* **1** VESSEL, boat, ship, plane, aircraft, spacecraft, barque **2** OCCUPATION, work, calling, business, line, trade, employment, pursuit, vocation, handiwork, handicraft **3** SKILL, art, ability, technique, know-how (*informal*), expertise, knack, aptitude, artistry, dexterity, workmanship **4** CUNNING, ingenuity, guile, cleverness, scheme, subtlety, deceit, ruse, artifice, trickery, wiles, duplicity, subterfuge, contrivance, shrewdness, artfulness

craftsman *noun* SKILLED WORKER, artisan, master, maker, wright, technician, artificer, smith

craftsmanship *noun* WORKMANSHIP, technique, expertise, mastery, artistry

crafty *adjective* CUNNING, scheming, sly, devious, knowing, designing, sharp, calculating, subtle, tricky, shrewd, astute, fraudulent, canny, wily, insidious, artful, foxy, deceitful, duplicitous, tricksy, guileful << ANTONYM open

crag *noun* ROCK, peak, bluff, pinnacle, tor, aiguille

craggy *adjective* ROCKY, broken, rough, rugged, uneven, jagged, stony, precipitous, jaggy (*Scot*)

cram *verb* **1** STUFF, force, jam, ram, shove, compress, compact **2** PACK, fill, stuff **3** SQUEEZE, press, crowd, pack, crush, pack in, fill to overflowing, overfill, overcrowd **4** STUDY, revise, swot, bone up (*informal*), grind, swot up, mug up (*slang*)

cramp[1] *noun* SPASM, pain, ache, contraction, pang, stiffness, stitch, convulsion, twinge, crick, shooting pain

cramp[2] *verb* RESTRICT, hamper, inhibit, hinder, check, handicap, confine, hamstring, constrain, obstruct, impede, shackle, circumscribe, encumber

cramped *adjective* RESTRICTED, confined, overcrowded, crowded, packed, narrow, squeezed, uncomfortable, awkward, closed in, congested, circumscribed, jammed in, hemmed in << ANTONYM spacious

crank *noun* (*informal*) ECCENTRIC, freak (*informal*), oddball (*informal*), weirdo *or* weirdie (*informal*), case (*informal*), character (*informal*), nut (*slang*), flake (*slang, chiefly US*), screwball (*slang, chiefly US & Canad*), odd fish (*informal*), kook (*US & Canad informal*), queer fish (*Brit informal*), rum customer (*Brit slang*), wacko *or* whacko (*informal*)

cranky *adjective* (*US, Canad & Irish informal*) ECCENTRIC, wacky (*slang*), oddball (*informal*), freakish, odd, strange, funny (*informal*), bizarre, peculiar, queer (*informal*), rum (*Brit slang*), quirky, idiosyncratic, off-the-wall (*slang*), freaky (*slang*), outré, wacko *or* whacko (*informal*), daggy (*Austral & NZ informal*)

cranny *noun* CREVICE, opening, hole, crack, gap, breach, rift, nook, cleft, chink, fissure, interstice

crash *noun* 1 COLLISION, accident, smash, wreck, prang (*informal*), bump, pile-up (*informal*), smash-up 2 SMASH, clash, boom, smashing, bang, thunder, thump, racket, din, clatter, clattering, thud, clang 3 COLLAPSE, failure, depression, ruin, bankruptcy, downfall ▷ *verb* 1 FALL, pitch, plunge, sprawl, topple, lurch, hurtle, come a cropper (*informal*), overbalance, fall headlong 2 PLUNGE, hurtle, precipitate yourself 3 SMASH, break, break up, shatter, fragment, fracture, shiver, disintegrate, splinter, dash to pieces 4 COLLAPSE, fail, go under, be ruined, go bust (*informal*), fold up, go broke (*informal*), go to the wall, go belly up (*informal*), smash, fold ▷ *adjective* INTENSIVE, concentrated, immediate, urgent, round-the-clock, emergency ▷▷ **crash into** COLLIDE WITH, hit, bump into, bang into, run into, drive into, plough into, hurtle into

crass *adjective* INSENSITIVE, stupid, gross, blundering, dense, coarse, witless, boorish, obtuse, unrefined, asinine, indelicate, oafish, lumpish, doltish << ANTONYM sensitive

crate *noun* CONTAINER, case, box, packing case, tea chest ▷ *verb* BOX, pack, enclose, pack up, encase, case

crater *noun* HOLLOW, hole, depression, dip, cavity, shell hole

crave *verb* 1 LONG FOR, yearn for, hanker after, be dying for, want, need, require, desire, fancy (*informal*), hope for, cry out for (*informal*), thirst for, pine for, lust after, pant

for, sigh for, set your heart on, hunger after, eat your heart out over, would give your eyeteeth for 2 BEG, ask for, seek, petition, pray for, plead for, solicit, implore, beseech, entreat, supplicate

craven *adjective* COWARDLY, weak, scared, fearful, abject, dastardly, mean-spirited, timorous, pusillanimous, chicken-hearted, yellow (*informal*), lily-livered

craving *noun* LONGING, hope, desire, urge, yen (*informal*), hunger, appetite, ache, lust, yearning, thirst, hankering

crawl *verb* 1 CREEP, slither, go on all fours, move on hands and knees, inch, drag, wriggle, writhe, move at a snail's pace, worm your way, advance slowly, pull *or* drag yourself along << ANTONYM run 2 GROVEL, creep, cringe, humble yourself, abase yourself ▷▷ **be crawling with something** BE FULL OF, teem with, be alive with, swarm with, be overrun with (*slang*), be lousy with ▷▷ **crawl to someone** FAWN ON, pander to, suck up to (*slang*), toady to, truckle to, lick someone's boots (*slang*)

craze *noun* FAD, thing, fashion, trend, passion, rage, enthusiasm, mode, vogue, novelty, preoccupation, mania, infatuation, the latest thing (*informal*)

crazed *adjective* MAD, crazy, raving, insane, lunatic, demented, unbalanced, deranged, berserk, unhinged, berko (*Austral slang*), off the air (*Austral slang*), porangi (*NZ*)

crazy *adjective* 1 STRANGE, odd, bizarre, fantastic, silly, weird, ridiculous, outrageous, peculiar, eccentric, rum (*Brit slang*), oddball (*informal*), cockamamie (*slang, chiefly US*), wacko *or* whacko (*informal*), off the air (*Austral slang*), porangi (*NZ*), daggy (*Austral & NZ informal*) << ANTONYM normal 2 (*informal*) RIDICULOUS, wild, absurd, inappropriate, foolish, ludicrous, irresponsible, unrealistic, unwise, senseless, preposterous, potty (*Brit informal*), short-sighted, unworkable, foolhardy, idiotic, nonsensical, half-baked (*informal*), inane, fatuous, ill-conceived, quixotic, imprudent, impracticable, cockeyed (*informal*), cockamamie (*slang, chiefly US*), porangi (*NZ*) << ANTONYM sensible 3 INSANE, mad, unbalanced, deranged, touched, cracked (*slang*), mental (*slang*), nuts (*slang*), barking (*slang*), daft (*informal*), batty (*slang*), crazed, lunatic, demented, cuckoo (*informal*), barmy (*slang*), off-the-wall (*slang*), off the air (*Austral slang*), nutty (*slang*), potty (*Brit informal*), berserk, delirious, bonkers (*slang, chiefly Brit*), idiotic, unhinged, loopy (*informal*), crackpot (*informal*), out to lunch (*informal*), round the bend (*slang*), barking mad (*slang*), out of your mind, maniacal, not all there (*informal*), doolally (*slang*), off your head (*slang*), off your trolley (*slang*), round the twist (*Brit slang*), up the pole (*informal*), of unsound mind, not right in the head, off your rocker (*slang*), not the full shilling (*informal*), a bit lacking upstairs (*informal*), as daft as a brush (*informal, chiefly Brit*), mad as a hatter, mad as a March hare, nutty as a fruitcake (*slang*), porangi (*NZ*) << ANTONYM sane **4** FANATICAL, wild (*informal*), mad, devoted, enthusiastic, passionate, hysterical, ardent, very keen, zealous, smitten, infatuated, enamoured << ANTONYM uninterested ▷ see **mad**

creak *verb* SQUEAK, grind, scrape, groan, grate, screech, squeal, scratch, rasp

creaky *adjective* SQUEAKY, creaking, squeaking, unoiled, grating, rusty, rasping, raspy

cream *noun* **1** LOTION, ointment, oil, essence, cosmetic, paste, emulsion, salve, liniment, unguent **2** BEST, elite, prime, pick, flower, crème de la crème (*French*) ▷ *adjective* OFF-WHITE, ivory, yellowish-white

creamy *adjective* **1** MILKY, buttery **2** SMOOTH, soft, creamed, lush, oily, velvety, rich

crease *noun* **1** FOLD, ruck, line, tuck, ridge, groove, pucker, corrugation **2** WRINKLE, line, crow's-foot ▷ *verb* **1** CRUMPLE, rumple, pucker, crinkle, fold, ridge, double up, crimp, ruck up, corrugate **2** WRINKLE, crumple, screw up

create *verb* **1** CAUSE, lead to, occasion, bring about **2** MAKE, form, produce, develop, design, generate, invent, coin, compose, devise, initiate, hatch, originate, formulate, give birth to, spawn, dream up (*informal*), concoct, beget, give life to, bring into being *or* existence << ANTONYM destroy **3** APPOINT, make, found, establish, set up, invest, install, constitute

creation *noun* **1** UNIVERSE, world, life, nature, cosmos, natural world, living world, all living things **2** INVENTION, production, concept, achievement, brainchild (*informal*), concoction, handiwork, pièce de résistance (*French*), magnum opus, chef-d'oeuvre (*French*) **3** MAKING, generation, formation, conception, genesis **4** SETTING UP, development, production, institution, foundation, constitution, establishment, formation, laying down, inception, origination

creative *adjective* IMAGINATIVE, gifted, artistic, inventive, original, inspired, clever, productive, fertile, ingenious, visionary

creativity *noun* IMAGINATION, talent, inspiration, productivity, fertility, ingenuity, originality, inventiveness, cleverness, fecundity

creator *noun* **1** MAKER, father, author, framer, designer, architect, inventor, originator, initiator, begetter **2** *usually with cap.* GOD, Maker

creature *noun* **1** LIVING THING, being, animal, beast, brute, critter (*US dialect*), quadruped, dumb animal, lower animal **2** PERSON, man, woman, individual, character, fellow, soul, human being, mortal, body **3** MINION, tool, instrument (*informal*), puppet, cohort (*chiefly US*), dependant, retainer, hanger-on, lackey

credence *noun* **1** CREDIBILITY, credit, plausibility, believability **2** BELIEF, trust, confidence, faith, acceptance, assurance, certainty, dependence, reliance

credentials *plural noun* **1** QUALIFICATIONS, ability, skill, capacity, fitness, attribute, capability, endowment(s), accomplishment, eligibility, aptitude, suitability **2** CERTIFICATION, document, reference(s), papers, title, card, licence, recommendation, passport, warrant, voucher, deed, testament, diploma, testimonial, authorization, missive, letters of credence, attestation, letter of recommendation *or* introduction

credibility *noun* BELIEVABILITY, reliability, plausibility, trustworthiness, tenability

credible *adjective* **1** BELIEVABLE, possible, likely, reasonable, probable, plausible, conceivable, imaginable, tenable, verisimilar << ANTONYM unbelievable **2** RELIABLE, honest, dependable, trustworthy, sincere, trusty << ANTONYM unreliable

credit *noun* **1** PRAISE, honour, recognition, glory, thanks, approval, fame, tribute, merit, acclaim, acknowledgment, kudos, commendation, Brownie points **2** SOURCE OF SATISFACTION *or* PRIDE, asset, honour, feather in your cap **3** PRESTIGE, reputation, standing, position, character, influence, regard, status, esteem, clout (*informal*), good name, estimation, repute **4** BELIEF, trust, confidence, faith, reliance, credence ▷ *verb*

BELIEVE, rely on, have faith in, trust, buy (*slang*), accept, depend on, swallow (*informal*), fall for, bank on ▷▷ **credit someone with something** ATTRIBUTE TO, assign to, ascribe to, accredit to, impute to, chalk up to (*informal*) ▷▷ **credit something to someone** ATTRIBUTE TO, ascribe to, accredit to, impute to, chalk up to (*informal*) ▷▷ **on credit** ON ACCOUNT, by instalments, on tick (*informal*), on hire-purchase, on the slate (*informal*), by deferred payment, on (the) H.P.

creditable *adjective* PRAISEWORTHY, worthy, respectable, admirable, honourable, exemplary, reputable, commendable, laudable, meritorious, estimable

credulity *noun* GULLIBILITY, naïveté *or* naivety, blind faith, credulousness

creed *noun* BELIEF, principles, profession (*of faith*), doctrine, canon, persuasion, dogma, tenet, credo, catechism, articles of faith

creek *noun* **1** INLET, bay, cove, bight, firth *or* frith (*Scot*) **2** (*US, Canad, Austral & NZ*) STREAM, brook, tributary, bayou, rivulet, watercourse, streamlet, runnel

creep *verb* **1** CRAWL, worm, wriggle, squirm, slither, writhe, drag yourself, edge, inch, crawl on all fours **2** SNEAK, steal, tiptoe, slink, skulk ▷ *noun* (*Slang*) BOOTLICKER (*informal*), sneak, sycophant, crawler (*slang*), toady ▷▷ **give someone the creeps** (*informal*) DISGUST, frighten, scare, repel, repulse, make your hair stand on end, make you squirm

creeper *noun* CLIMBING PLANT, runner, vine (*chiefly US*), climber, rambler, trailing plant

creepy *adjective* (*informal*) DISTURBING, threatening, frightening, terrifying, weird, forbidding, horrible, menacing, unpleasant, scary (*informal*), sinister, ominous, eerie, macabre, nightmarish, hair-raising, awful

crescent *noun* MENISCUS, sickle, new moon, half-moon, old moon, sickle-shape

crest *noun* **1** TOP, summit, peak, ridge, highest point, pinnacle, apex, head, crown, height **2** TUFT, crown, comb, plume, mane, tassel, topknot, cockscomb **3** EMBLEM, badge, symbol, insignia, charge, bearings, device

crestfallen *adjective* DISAPPOINTED, depressed, discouraged, dejected, despondent, downcast, disheartened, disconsolate, downhearted, sick as a parrot (*informal*), choked << ANTONYM elated

crevice *noun* GAP, opening, hole, split, crack, rent, fracture, rift, slit, cleft, chink, fissure,

cranny, interstice

crew *noun* **1** (SHIP'S) COMPANY, hands, (ship's) complement **2** TEAM, company, party, squad, gang, corps, working party, posse **3** (*informal*) CROWD, set, lot, bunch (*informal*), band, troop, pack, camp, gang, mob, herd, swarm, company, horde, posse (*informal*), assemblage

crib *noun* **1** CRADLE, bed, cot, bassinet, Moses basket **2** (*informal*) TRANSLATION, notes, key, trot (*US slang*) **3** MANGER, box, stall, rack, bunker ▷ *verb* (*informal*) COPY, cheat, pirate, pilfer, purloin, plagiarize, pass off as your own work

crick (*informal*) *noun* SPASM, cramp, convulsion, twinge ▷ *verb* RICK, jar, wrench

crime *noun* **1** OFFENCE, job (*informal*), wrong, fault, outrage, atrocity, violation, trespass, felony, misdemeanour, misdeed, transgression, unlawful act **2** LAWBREAKING, corruption, delinquency, illegality, wrong, vice, sin, guilt, misconduct, wrongdoing, wickedness, iniquity, villainy, unrighteousness, malefaction

criminal *noun* LAWBREAKER, convict, con (*slang*), offender, crook (*informal*), lag (*slang*), villain, culprit, sinner, delinquent, felon, con man (*informal*), rorter (*Austral slang*), jailbird, malefactor, evildoer, transgressor, skelm (*S African*), rogue trader ▷ *adjective* **1** UNLAWFUL, illicit, lawless, wrong, illegal, corrupt, crooked (*informal*), vicious, immoral, wicked, culpable, under-the-table, villainous, nefarious, iniquitous, indictable, felonious, bent (*slang*) << ANTONYM lawful **2** (*informal*) DISGRACEFUL, ridiculous, foolish, senseless, scandalous, preposterous, deplorable

criminality *noun* ILLEGALITY, crime, corruption, delinquency, wrongdoing, lawlessness, wickedness, depravity, culpability, villainy, sinfulness, turpitude

cringe *verb* **1** SHRINK, flinch, quail, recoil, start, shy, tremble, quiver, cower, draw back, blench **2** WINCE, squirm, writhe

crinkle *noun* CREASE, wrinkle, crumple, ruffle, twist, fold, curl, rumple, pucker, crimp

cripple *verb* **1** DISABLE, paralyse, lame, debilitate, mutilate, maim, incapacitate, enfeeble, weaken, hamstring **2** DAMAGE, destroy, ruin, bring to a standstill, halt, spoil, cramp, impair, put paid to, vitiate, put out of action << ANTONYM help

crippled *adjective* DISABLED, handicapped,

challenged, paralysed, lame, deformed, incapacitated, bedridden, housebound, enfeebled ▷ see **disabled**

crisis *noun* **1** EMERGENCY, plight, catastrophe, predicament, pass, trouble, disaster, mess, dilemma, strait, deep water, meltdown (*informal*), extremity, quandary, dire straits, exigency, critical situation **2** CRITICAL POINT, climax, point of no return, height, confrontation, crunch (*informal*), turning point, culmination, crux, moment of truth, climacteric, tipping point

crisp *adjective* **1** FIRM, crunchy, crispy, crumbly, fresh, brittle, unwilted << ANTONYM soft **2** BRACING, fresh, refreshing, brisk, invigorating << ANTONYM warm **3** CLEAN, smart, trim, neat, tidy, orderly, spruce, snappy, clean-cut, well-groomed, well-pressed **4** BRIEF, clear, short, tart, incisive, terse, succinct, pithy, brusque

criterion *noun* STANDARD, test, rule, measure, principle, proof, par, norm, canon, gauge, yardstick, touchstone, bench mark

critic *noun* **1** JUDGE, authority, expert, analyst, commentator, pundit, reviewer, connoisseur, arbiter, expositor **2** FAULT-FINDER, attacker, detractor, knocker (*informal*)

critical *adjective* **1** CRUCIAL, decisive, momentous, deciding, pressing, serious, vital, psychological, urgent, all-important, pivotal, high-priority, now or never << ANTONYM unimportant **2** GRAVE, serious, dangerous, acute, risky, hairy (*slang*), precarious, perilous << ANTONYM safe **3** DISPARAGING, disapproving, scathing, derogatory, nit-picking (*informal*), censorious, cavilling, fault-finding, captious, carping, niggling << ANTONYM complimentary **4** ANALYTICAL, penetrating, discriminating, discerning, diagnostic, perceptive, judicious, accurate, precise << ANTONYM undiscriminating

criticism *noun* **1** FAULT-FINDING, censure, disapproval, disparagement, stick (*slang*), knocking (*informal*), panning (*informal*), slamming (*slang*), slating (*informal*), flak (*informal*), slagging (*slang*), strictures, bad press, denigration, brickbats (*informal*), character assassination, critical remarks, animadversion **2** ANALYSIS, review, notice, assessment, judgment, commentary, evaluation, appreciation, appraisal, critique, elucidation

criticize *verb* FIND FAULT WITH, censure, disapprove of, knock (*informal*), blast, pan (*informal*), condemn, slam (*slang*), carp, put down, slate (*informal*), have a go (at) (*informal*), disparage, tear into (*informal*), diss (*slang, chiefly US*), nag at, lambast(e), pick holes in, pick (someone *or* something) to pieces, give (someone *or* something) a bad press, pass strictures upon << ANTONYM praise

critique *noun* ESSAY, review, analysis, assessment, examination, commentary, appraisal, treatise

croak *verb* **1** GRUNT, squawk, caw **2** RASP, gasp, grunt, wheeze, utter *or* speak harshly, utter *or* speak huskily, utter *or* speak throatily **3** (*Slang*) DIE, expire, pass away, perish, buy it (*US slang*), check out (*US slang*), kick it (*slang*), go belly-up (*slang*), peg out (*informal*), kick the bucket (*informal*), buy the farm (*US slang*), peg it (*informal*), cark it (*Austral & NZ slang*), pop your clogs (*informal*), hop the twig (*informal*)

crone *noun* OLD WOMAN, witch, hag, old bag (*derogatory slang*), old bat (*slang*), kuia (*NZ*)

crony *noun* FRIEND, china (*Brit slang*), colleague, associate, mate (*informal*), pal (*informal*), companion, cock (*Brit informal*), buddy (*informal*), comrade, chum (*informal*), accomplice, ally, sidekick (*slang*), main man (*slang, chiefly US*), homeboy (*slang, chiefly US*), cobber (*Austral & NZ old-fashioned informal*)

crook *noun* (*informal*) CRIMINAL, rogue, cheat, thief, shark, lag (*slang*), villain, robber, racketeer, fraudster, swindler, knave (*archaic*), grifter (*slang, chiefly US & Canad*), chiseller (*informal*), skelm (*S African*) ▷ *verb* BEND, hook, angle, bow, curve, curl, cock, flex ▷ *adjective* (*Austral & NZ informal*) ILL, sick, poorly (*informal*), funny (*informal*), weak, ailing, queer, frail, feeble, unhealthy, seedy (*informal*), sickly, unwell, laid up (*informal*), queasy, infirm, out of sorts (*informal*), dicky (*Brit informal*), nauseous, off-colour, under the weather (*informal*), at death's door, indisposed, peaky, on the sick list (*informal*), green about the gills ▷▷ **go (off) crook** (*Austral & NZ informal*) LOSE YOUR TEMPER, be furious, rage, go mad, lose it (*informal*), seethe, crack up (*informal*), see red (*informal*), lose the plot (*informal*), go ballistic (*slang, chiefly US*), blow a fuse (*slang, chiefly US*), fly off the handle (*informal*), be incandescent, go off the deep end (*informal*), throw a fit (*informal*), wig out (*slang*), go up the wall (*slang*), blow your top, lose your rag (*slang*), be beside yourself, flip your lid (*slang*)

crooked *adjective* **1** BENT, twisted, bowed, curved, irregular, warped, deviating, out of shape, misshapen << ANTONYM straight **2** DEFORMED, crippled, distorted, disfigured **3** AT AN ANGLE, angled, tilted, to one side, uneven, slanted, slanting, squint, awry, lopsided, askew, asymmetric, off-centre, skewwhiff (*Brit informal*), unsymmetrical **4** (*informal*) DISHONEST, criminal, illegal, corrupt, dubious, questionable, unlawful, shady (*informal*), fraudulent, unscrupulous, under-the-table, bent (*slang*), shifty, deceitful, underhand, unprincipled, dishonourable, nefarious, knavish << ANTONYM honest

croon *verb* **1** SING, warble **2** SAY SOFTLY, breathe, hum, purr

crop *noun* YIELD, produce, gathering, fruits, harvest, vintage, reaping, season's growth ▷ *verb* **1** HARVEST, pick, collect, gather, bring in, reap, bring home, garner, mow **2** GRAZE, eat, browse, feed on, nibble **3** CUT, reduce, trim, clip, dock, prune, shorten, shear, snip, pare, lop ▷▷ **crop up** (*informal*) HAPPEN, appear, emerge, occur, arise, turn up, spring up

cross *verb* **1** GO ACROSS, pass over, traverse, cut across, move across, travel across **2** SPAN, bridge, ford, go across, extend over **3** INTERSECT, meet, intertwine, crisscross **4** OPPOSE, interfere with, hinder, obstruct, deny, block, resist, frustrate, foil, thwart, impede **5** INTERBREED, mix, blend, cross-pollinate, crossbreed, hybridize, cross-fertilize, intercross ▷ *noun* **1** CRUCIFIX **2** TROUBLE, worry, trial, load, burden, grief, misery, woe, misfortune, affliction, tribulation **3** MIXTURE, combination, blend, amalgam, amalgamation **4** CROSSBREED, hybrid ▷ *adjective* ANGRY, impatient, irritable, annoyed, put out, hacked (off) (*informal*), crusty, snappy, grumpy, vexed, sullen, surly, fractious, petulant, disagreeable, short, churlish, peeved (*informal*), ill-tempered, irascible, cantankerous, tetchy, ratty (*Brit & NZ informal*), tooshie (*Austral slang*), testy, fretful, waspish, in a bad mood, grouchy (*informal*), querulous, shirty (*slang, chiefly Brit*), peevish, splenetic, crotchety (*informal*), snappish, ill-humoured, captious, pettish, out of humour, hoha (*NZ*) << ANTONYM good-humoured ▷▷ **cross something out** *or* **off** STRIKE OFF *or* OUT, eliminate, cancel,

delete, blue-pencil, score off *or* out

cross-examine *verb* QUESTION, grill (*informal*), quiz, interrogate, catechize, pump

crotch *noun* GROIN, lap, crutch

crouch *verb* BEND DOWN, kneel, squat, stoop, bow, duck, hunch

crow *verb* GLOAT, triumph, boast, swagger, brag, vaunt, bluster, exult, blow your own trumpet

crowd *noun* **1** MULTITUDE, mass, assembly, throng, company, press, army, host, pack, mob, flock, herd, swarm, horde, rabble, concourse, bevy **2** GROUP, set, lot, circle, gang, bunch (*informal*), clique **3** AUDIENCE, spectators, house, gate, attendance ▷ *verb* **1** FLOCK, press, push, mass, collect, gather, stream, surge, cluster, muster, huddle, swarm, throng, congregate, foregather **2** SQUEEZE, pack, pile, bundle, cram **3** CONGEST, pack, cram **4** (*informal*) JOSTLE, batter, butt, push, elbow, shove ▷▷ **the crowd** THE MASSES, the people, the public, the mob, the rank and file, the populace, the rabble, the proletariat, the hoi polloi, the riffraff, the vulgar herd

crowded *adjective* PACKED, full, busy, mobbed, cramped, swarming, overflowing, thronged, teeming, congested, populous, jam-packed, crushed

crown *noun* **1** CORONET, tiara, diadem, circlet, coronal (*poetic*), chaplet **2** LAUREL WREATH, trophy, distinction, prize, honour, garland, laurels, wreath, kudos **3** HIGH POINT, head, top, tip, summit, crest, pinnacle, apex ▷ *verb* **1** INSTALL, invest, honour, dignify, ordain, inaugurate **2** TOP, cap, be on top of, surmount **3** CAP, finish, complete, perfect, fulfil, consummate, round off, put the finishing touch to, put the tin lid on, be the climax *or* culmination of **4** (*Slang*) STRIKE, belt (*informal*), bash, hit over the head, box, punch, cuff, biff (*slang*), wallop ▷▷ **the Crown 1** MONARCH, ruler, sovereign, rex (*Latin*), emperor *or* empress, king *or* queen **2** MONARCHY, sovereignty, royalty

crucial *adjective* **1** (*informal*) VITAL, important, pressing, essential, urgent, momentous, high-priority **2** CRITICAL, central, key, psychological, decisive, pivotal, now or never

crucify *verb* **1** EXECUTE, put to death, nail to a cross **2** (*Slang*) PAN (*informal*), rubbish (*informal*), ridicule, slag (off) (*slang*), lampoon, wipe the floor with (*informal*), tear to pieces **3** TORTURE, rack, torment, harrow

crude *adjective* **1** ROUGH, undeveloped, basic, outline, unfinished, makeshift, sketchy, unformed **2** SIMPLE, rudimentary, basic, primitive, coarse, clumsy, rough-and-ready, rough-hewn **3** VULGAR, dirty, rude, obscene, coarse, indecent, crass, tasteless, lewd, X-rated (*informal*), boorish, smutty, uncouth, gross << ANTONYM tasteful **4** UNREFINED, natural, raw, unprocessed, unpolished, unprepared << ANTONYM processed

crudely *adverb* **1** ROUGHLY, basically, sketchily **2** SIMPLY, roughly, basically, coarsely, clumsily **3** VULGARLY, rudely, coarsely, crassly, indecently, obscenely, lewdly, impolitely, tastelessly

cruel *adjective* **1** BRUTAL, ruthless, callous, sadistic, inhumane, hard, fell (*archaic*), severe, harsh, savage, grim, vicious, relentless, murderous, monstrous, unnatural, unkind, heartless, atrocious, inhuman, merciless, cold-blooded, malevolent, hellish, depraved, spiteful, brutish, bloodthirsty, remorseless, barbarous, pitiless, unfeeling, hard-hearted, stony-hearted << ANTONYM kind **2** BITTER, severe, painful, ruthless, traumatic, grievous, unrelenting, merciless, pitiless

cruelly *adverb* **1** BRUTALLY, severely, savagely, viciously, mercilessly, in cold blood, callously, monstrously, unmercifully, sadistically, pitilessly, spitefully, heartlessly, barbarously **2** BITTERLY, deeply, severely, mortally, painfully, ruthlessly, mercilessly, grievously, pitilessly, traumatically

cruelty *noun* BRUTALITY, spite, severity, savagery, ruthlessness, sadism, depravity, harshness, inhumanity, barbarity, callousness, viciousness, bestiality, heartlessness, spitefulness, bloodthirstiness, mercilessness, fiendishness, hardheartedness

cruise *noun* SAIL, voyage, boat trip, sea trip ▷ *verb* **1** SAIL, coast, voyage **2** TRAVEL ALONG, coast, drift, keep a steady pace

crumb *noun* **1** BIT, grain, particle, fragment, shred, speck, sliver, morsel **2** MORSEL, scrap, atom, shred, mite, snippet, sliver, soupçon (*French*)

crumble *verb* **1** DISINTEGRATE, collapse, break up, deteriorate, decay, fall apart, perish, degenerate, decompose, tumble down, moulder, go to pieces **2** CRUSH, fragment, crumb, pulverize, pound, grind, powder, granulate **3** COLLAPSE, break down,

deteriorate, decay, fall apart, degenerate, go to pieces, go to wrack and ruin

crummy *adjective* (*Slang*) SECOND-RATE, cheap, inferior, substandard, poor, pants (*informal*), miserable, rotten (*informal*), duff (*Brit informal*), lousy (*slang*), shoddy, trashy, low-rent (*informal, chiefly US*), for the birds (*informal*), third-rate, contemptible, two-bit (*US & Canad slang*), crappy (*slang*), rubbishy, poxy (*slang*), dime-a-dozen (*informal*), bodger or bodgie (*Austral slang*), bush-league (*Austral & NZ informal*), tinhorn (*US slang*), of a sort or of sorts, strictly for the birds (*informal*)

crumple *verb* **1** CRUSH, squash, screw up, scrumple **2** CREASE, wrinkle, rumple, ruffle, pucker e **3** COLLAPSE, sink, go down, fall **4** BREAK DOWN, fall, collapse, give way, cave in, go to pieces **5** SCREW UP, pucker

crunch *verb* CHOMP, champ, munch, masticate, chew noisily, grind ▷▷ **the crunch** (*informal*) CRITICAL POINT, test, crisis, emergency, crux, moment of truth, hour of decision

crusade *noun* **1** CAMPAIGN, drive, movement, cause, push **2** HOLY WAR, jihad ▷ *verb* CAMPAIGN, fight, push, struggle, lobby, agitate, work

crusader *noun* CAMPAIGNER, champion, advocate, activist, reformer

crush *verb* **1** SQUASH, pound, break, smash, squeeze, crumble, crunch, mash, compress, press, crumple, pulverize **2** CREASE, wrinkle, crumple, rumple, scrumple, ruffle l **3** OVERCOME, overwhelm, put down, subdue, overpower, quash, quell, extinguish, stamp out, vanquish, conquer **4** DEMORALIZE, depress, devastate, discourage, humble, put down (*slang*), humiliate, squash, flatten, deflate, mortify, psych out (*informal*), dishearten, dispirit, deject **5** SQUEEZE, press, embrace, hug, enfold ▷ *noun* CROWD, mob, horde, throng, press, pack, mass, jam, herd, huddle, swarm, multitude, rabble

crust *noun* LAYER, covering, coating, incrustation, film, outside, skin, surface, shell, coat, caking, scab, concretion

crusty *adjective* **1** CRISPY, well-baked, crisp, well-done, brittle, friable, hard, short **2** IRRITABLE, short, cross, prickly, touchy, curt, surly, gruff, brusque, cantankerous, tetchy, ratty (*Brit & NZ informal*), testy, chippy (*informal*), short-tempered, peevish, crabby, choleric, splenetic, ill-humoured, captious, snappish *or* snappy

crux *noun* CRUCIAL POINT, heart, core, essence, nub, decisive point

cry *verb* **1** WEEP, sob, bawl, shed tears, keen, greet (*Scot archaic*), wail, whine, whimper, whinge (*informal*), blubber, snivel, yowl, howl your eyes out << ANTONYM laugh **2** SHOUT, call, scream, roar, hail, yell, howl, call out, exclaim, shriek, bellow, whoop, screech, bawl, holler (*informal*), ejaculate, sing out, halloo, vociferate << ANTONYM whisper **3** ANNOUNCE, hawk, advertise, proclaim, bark (*informal*), trumpet, shout from the rooftops (*informal*) ▷ *noun* **1** WEEP, greet (*Scot archaic*), sob, howl, bawl, blubber, snivel **2** SHOUT, call, scream, roar, yell, howl, shriek, bellow, whoop, screech, hoot, ejaculation, bawl, holler (*informal*), exclamation, squawk, yelp, yoo-hoo **3** WEEPING, sobbing, blubbering, snivelling ▷▷ **cry off** (*informal*) BACK OUT, withdraw, quit, cop out (*slang*), beg off, excuse yourself

crypt *noun* VAULT, tomb, catacomb

cryptic *adjective* MYSTERIOUS, dark, coded, puzzling, obscure, vague, veiled, ambiguous, enigmatic, perplexing, arcane, equivocal, abstruse, Delphic, oracular

crystallize *verb* HARDEN, solidify, coalesce, form crystals

cub *noun* YOUNG, baby, offspring, whelp

cuddle *verb* **1** HUG, embrace, clasp, fondle, cosset **2** PET, hug, canoodle (*slang*), bill and coo ▷▷ **cuddle up** SNUGGLE, nestle

cuddly *adjective* SOFT, plump, buxom, curvaceous, warm

cue *noun* SIGNAL, sign, nod, hint, prompt, reminder, suggestion

cuff¹ *noun* ▷▷ **off the cuff** (*informal*) **1** IMPROMPTU, spontaneous, improvised, offhand, unrehearsed, extempore **2** WITHOUT PREPARATION, spontaneously, impromptu, offhand, on the spur of the moment, ad lib, extempore, off the top of your head

cuff² *noun* SMACK, blow, knock, punch, thump, box, belt (*informal*), rap, slap, clout (*informal*), whack, biff (*slang*)

cul-de-sac *noun* DEAD END, blind alley

cull *verb* SELECT, collect, gather, amass, choose, pick, pick up, pluck, glean, cherry-pick

culminate *verb* END UP, end, close, finish, conclude, wind up, climax, terminate, come to a head, come to a climax, rise to a crescendo

culmination *noun* CLIMAX, conclusion, completion, finale, consummation

culpability *noun* FAULT, blame, responsibility, liability, accountability

culpable *adjective* BLAMEWORTHY, wrong, guilty, to blame, liable, in the wrong, at fault, sinful, answerable, found wanting, reprehensible << ANTONYM blameless

culprit *noun* OFFENDER, criminal, villain, sinner, delinquent, felon, person responsible, guilty party, wrongdoer, miscreant, evildoer, transgressor

cult *noun* **1** SECT, following, body, faction, party, school, church, faith, religion, denomination, clique, hauhau (*NZ*) **2** CRAZE, fashion, trend, fad **3** OBSESSION, worship, admiration, devotion, reverence, veneration, idolization

cultivate *verb* **1** FARM, work, plant, tend, till, harvest, plough, bring under cultivation **2** DEVELOP, establish, acquire, foster, devote yourself to, pursue **3** COURT, associate with, seek out, run after, consort with, butter up, dance attendance upon, seek someone's company *or* friendship, take trouble *or* pains with **4** FOSTER, further, forward, encourage **5** IMPROVE, better, train, discipline, polish, refine, elevate, enrich, civilize

cultivated *adjective* REFINED, cultured, advanced, polished, educated, sophisticated, accomplished, discriminating, enlightened, discerning, civilized, genteel, well-educated, urbane, erudite, well-bred

cultivation *noun* **1** FARMING, working, gardening, tilling, ploughing, husbandry, agronomy **2** GROWING, planting, production, farming **3** DEVELOPMENT, fostering, pursuit, devotion to **4** PROMOTION, support, encouragement, nurture, patronage, advancement, advocacy, enhancement, furtherance **5** REFINEMENT, letters, learning, education, culture, taste, breeding, manners, polish, discrimination, civilization, enlightenment, sophistication, good taste, civility, gentility, discernment

cultural *adjective* **1** ETHNIC, national, native, folk, racial **2** ARTISTIC, educational, elevating, aesthetic, enriching, broadening, enlightening, developmental, civilizing, edifying, educative

culture *noun* **1** THE ARTS **2** CIVILIZATION, society, customs, way of life **3** LIFESTYLE, habit, way of life, mores **4** REFINEMENT, education, breeding, polish, enlightenment, accomplishment, sophistication, good taste, erudition, gentility, urbanity

cultured *adjective* REFINED, advanced, polished, intellectual, educated, sophisticated, accomplished, scholarly, enlightened, knowledgeable, well-informed, genteel, urbane, erudite, highbrow, well-bred, well-read << ANTONYM uneducated

culvert *noun* DRAIN, channel, gutter, conduit, watercourse

cumbersome *adjective* 1 AWKWARD, heavy, hefty (*informal*), clumsy, bulky, weighty, impractical, inconvenient, burdensome, unmanageable, clunky (*informal*) << ANTONYM easy to use 2 INEFFICIENT, unwieldy, badly organized << ANTONYM efficient

cumulative *adjective* COLLECTIVE, increasing, aggregate, amassed, accruing, snowballing, accumulative

cunning *adjective* 1 CRAFTY, sly, devious, artful, sharp, subtle, tricky, shrewd, astute, canny, wily, Machiavellian, shifty, foxy, guileful << ANTONYM frank 2 INGENIOUS, subtle, imaginative, shrewd, sly, astute, devious, artful, Machiavellian 3 SKILFUL, clever, deft, adroit, dexterous << ANTONYM clumsy ▷ *noun* 1 CRAFTINESS, guile, trickery, shrewdness, deviousness, artfulness, slyness, wiliness << ANTONYM candour 2 SKILL, art, ability, craft, subtlety, ingenuity, finesse, artifice, dexterity, cleverness, deftness, astuteness, adroitness << ANTONYM clumsiness

cup *noun* 1 MUG, goblet, chalice, teacup, beaker, demitasse, bowl 2 TROPHY

cupboard *noun* CABINET, closet, locker, press

curative *adjective* RESTORATIVE, healing, therapeutic, tonic, corrective, medicinal, remedial, salutary, healthful, health-giving

curb *verb* RESTRAIN, control, check, contain, restrict, moderate, suppress, inhibit, subdue, hinder, repress, constrain, retard, impede, stem the flow of, keep a tight rein on ▷ *noun* RESTRAINT, control, check, brake, limitation, rein, deterrent, bridle

curdle *verb* CONGEAL, clot, thicken, condense, turn sour, solidify, coagulate << ANTONYM dissolve

cure *verb* 1 MAKE BETTER, correct, heal, relieve, remedy, mend, rehabilitate, help, ease 2 RESTORE TO HEALTH, restore, heal 3 PRESERVE, smoke, dry, salt, pickle, kipper ▷ *noun* REMEDY, treatment,

medicine, healing, antidote, corrective, panacea, restorative, nostrum

cure-all *noun* PANACEA, elixir, nostrum, elixir vitae (*Latin*)

curio *noun* COLLECTOR'S ITEM, antique, trinket, knick-knack, bibelot

curiosity *noun* 1 INQUISITIVENESS, interest, prying, snooping (*informal*), nosiness (*informal*) 2 ODDITY, wonder, sight, phenomenon, spectacle, freak, marvel, novelty, rarity 3 COLLECTOR'S ITEM, trinket, curio, knick-knack, objet d'art (*French*), bibelot

curious *adjective* 1 INQUISITIVE, interested, questioning, searching, inquiring, peering, puzzled, peeping, meddling, prying, snoopy (*informal*), nosy (*informal*) << ANTONYM uninterested 2 STRANGE, unusual, bizarre, odd, novel, wonderful, rare, unique, extraordinary, puzzling, unexpected, exotic, mysterious, marvellous, peculiar, queer (*informal*), rum (*Brit slang*), singular, unconventional, quaint, unorthodox << ANTONYM ordinary

curl *noun* 1 RINGLET, lock 2 TWIST, spiral, coil, kink, whorl, curlicue ▷ *verb* 1 CRIMP, wave, perm, frizz 2 TWIRL, turn, bend, twist, curve, loop, spiral, coil, meander, writhe, corkscrew, wreathe 3 WIND, entwine, twine

curly *adjective* WAVY, waved, curled, curling, fuzzy, kinky, permed, corkscrew, crimped, frizzy

currency *noun* 1 MONEY, coinage, legal tender, medium of exchange, bills, notes, coins 2 ACCEPTANCE, exposure, popularity, circulation, vogue, prevalence

current *noun* 1 FLOW, course, undertow, jet, stream, tide, progression, river, tideway 2 DRAUGHT, flow, breeze, puff 3 MOOD, feeling, spirit, atmosphere, trend, tendency, drift, inclination, vibe (*slang*), undercurrent ▷ *adjective* 1 PRESENT, fashionable, ongoing, up-to-date, in, now (*informal*), happening (*informal*), contemporary, in the news, sexy (*informal*), trendy (*Brit informal*), topical, present-day, in fashion, in vogue, up-to-the-minute << ANTONYM out-of-date 2 PREVALENT, general, common, accepted, popular, widespread, in the air, prevailing, circulating, going around, customary, rife, in circulation

curse *verb* 1 SWEAR, cuss (*informal*), blaspheme, use bad language, turn the air blue (*informal*), be foul-mouthed, take the

Lord's name in vain **2** ABUSE, damn, scold,
swear at, revile, vilify, fulminate, execrate,
vituperate, imprecate **3** PUT A CURSE
ON, damn, doom, jinx, excommunicate,
execrate, put a jinx on, accurse, imprecate,
anathematize **4** AFFLICT, trouble,
burden ▷ *noun* **1** OATH, obscenity,
blasphemy, expletive, profanity,
imprecation, swearword **2** MALEDICTION,
jinx, anathema, hoodoo (*informal*), evil
eye, excommunication, imprecation,
execration **3** AFFLICTION, evil, plague,
scourge, cross, trouble, disaster, burden,
ordeal, torment, hardship, misfortune,
calamity, tribulation, bane, vexation
cursed *adjective* UNDER A CURSE, damned,
doomed, jinxed, bedevilled, fey (*Scot*), star-
crossed, accursed, ill-fated
cursory *adjective* BRIEF, passing, rapid,
casual, summary, slight, hurried, careless,
superficial, hasty, perfunctory, desultory,
offhand, slapdash
curt *adjective* TERSE, short, brief, sharp,
summary, blunt, rude, tart, abrupt, gruff,
brusque, offhand, ungracious, uncivil,
unceremonious, snappish
curtail *verb* REDUCE, cut, diminish, decrease,
dock, cut back, shorten, lessen, cut short,
pare down, retrench
curtain *noun* HANGING, drape (*chiefly US*),
portière ▷▷ **curtain something off** CONCEAL,
screen, hide, veil, drape, shroud, shut off
curvaceous *adjective* (*informal*) SHAPELY,
voluptuous, curvy, busty, well-rounded,
buxom, full-figures, bosomy, well-stacked
(*Brit slang*), Rubenesque
curvature *noun* CURVING, bend, curve,
arching, arc
curve *noun* BEND, turn, loop, arc, curvature,
camber ▷ *verb* BEND, turn, wind, twist,
bow, arch, snake, arc, coil, swerve **curved**
adjective BENT, rounded, sweeping, twisted,
bowed, arched, arced, humped, serpentine,
sinuous, twisty
cushion *noun* PILLOW, pad, bolster, headrest,
beanbag, scatter cushion, hassock ▷ *verb*
1 PROTECT, support, bolster, cradle,
buttress **2** SOFTEN, dampen, muffle,
mitigate, deaden, suppress, stifle
cushy *adjective* (*informal*) EASY, soft,
comfortable, undemanding, jammy (*Brit
slang*)
custodian *noun* KEEPER, guardian,
superintendent, warden, caretaker, curator,
protector, warder, watchman, overseer

custody *noun* **1** CARE, charge,
protection, supervision, preservation,
auspices, aegis, tutelage, guardianship,
safekeeping, keeping, trusteeship,
custodianship **2** IMPRISONMENT, detention,
confinement, incarceration
custom *noun* **1** TRADITION, practice,
convention, ritual, form, policy, rule,
style, fashion, usage, formality, etiquette,
observance, praxis, unwritten law,
kaupapa (*NZ*) **2** HABIT, way, practice,
manner, procedure, routine, mode,
wont **3** CUSTOMERS, business, trade,
patronage
customarily *adverb* USUALLY, generally,
commonly, regularly, normally, traditionally,
ordinarily, habitually, in the ordinary way,
as a rule
customary *adjective* **1** USUAL, general,
common, accepted, established, traditional,
normal, ordinary, familiar, acknowledged,
conventional, routine, everyday
<< ANTONYM unusual **2** ACCUSTOMED,
regular, usual, habitual, wonted
customer *noun* CLIENT, consumer, regular
(*informal*), buyer, patron, shopper, purchaser,
habitué
customs *plural noun* IMPORT CHARGES, tax,
duty, toll, tariff
cut *verb* **1** SLIT, saw, score, nick, slice, slash,
pierce, hack, penetrate, notch **2** CHOP,
split, divide, slice, segment, dissect, cleave,
part **3** CARVE, slice **4** SEVER, cut in two,
sunder **5** SHAPE, carve, engrave, chisel,
form, score, fashion, chip, sculpture, whittle,
sculpt, inscribe, hew **6** SLASH, nick, wound,
lance, gash, lacerate, incise **7** CLIP, mow,
trim, dock, prune, snip, pare, lop **8** TRIM,
shave, hack, snip **9** REDUCE, lower, slim
(down), diminish, slash, decrease, cut
back, rationalize, ease up on, downsize,
kennet (*Austral slang*), jeff (*Austral slang*)
<< ANTONYM increase **10** ABRIDGE, edit,
shorten, curtail, condense, abbreviate,
précis << ANTONYM extend **11** DELETE,
take out, expurgate **12** HURT, wound,
upset, sting, grieve, pain, hurt someone's
feelings **13** (*informal*) IGNORE, avoid,
slight, blank (*slang*), snub, spurn, freeze
(someone) out (*informal*), cold-shoulder,
turn your back on, send to Coventry, look
straight through (someone) << ANTONYM
greet **14** CROSS, interrupt, intersect, bisect
▷ *noun* **1** INCISION, nick, rent, stroke, rip,
slash, groove, slit, snip **2** GASH, nick, wound,

slash, graze, laceration **3** REDUCTION, fall, lowering, slash, decrease, cutback, diminution **4** (*informal*) SHARE, piece, slice, percentage, portion, kickback (*chiefly US*), rake-off (*slang*) **5** STYLE, look, form, fashion, shape, mode, configuration ▷▷ **a cut above something** *or* **someone** (*informal*) SUPERIOR TO, better than, more efficient than, more reliable than, streets ahead of, more useful than, more capable than, more competent than ▷▷ **be cut out for something** BE SUITED FOR, be designed for, be fitted for, be suitable for, be adapted for, be equipped for, be adequate for, be eligible for, be competent for, be qualified for ▷▷ **cut in** INTERRUPT, break in, butt in, interpose ▷▷ **cut someone down to size** MAKE (SOMEONE) LOOK SMALL, humble, humiliate, bring (someone) low, take (someone) down a peg (*informal*), abash, crush, put (someone) in their place, take the wind out of (someone's) sails ▷▷ **cut someone off 1** SEPARATE, isolate, sever, keep apart **2** INTERRUPT, stop, break in, butt in, interpose **3** DISINHERIT, renounce, disown ▷▷ **cut someone out** (*informal*) EXCLUDE, eliminate, oust, displace, supersede, supplant ▷▷ **cut someone up** SLASH, injure, wound, knife, lacerate ▷▷ **cut something back 1** REDUCE, check, lower, slash, decrease, curb, lessen, economize, downsize, retrench, draw *or* pull in your horns (*informal*), kennet (*Austral slang*), jeff (*Austral slang*) **2** TRIM, prune, shorten ▷▷ **cut something down 1** REDUCE, moderate, decrease, lessen, lower **2** FELL, level, hew, lop ▷▷ **cut something off** DISCONTINUE, disconnect, suspend, halt, obstruct, bring to an end ▷▷ **cut something out 1** REMOVE, extract, censor, delete, edit out **2** STOP, cease, refrain from, pack in, kick (*informal*), give up, sever ▷▷ **be cut up** BE UPSET, be disturbed, be distressed, be stricken, be agitated, be heartbroken, be desolated, be dejected, be wretched ▷▷ **cut something up** CHOP, divide, slice, carve, dice, mince

cutback *noun* REDUCTION, cut, retrenchment, economy, decrease, lessening

cute *adjective* APPEALING, sweet, attractive, engaging, charming, delightful, lovable, winsome, winning, cutesy (*informal, chiefly US*)

cut-price *adjective* CHEAP, sale, reduced, bargain, cut-rate (*chiefly US*), cheapo (*informal*)

cut-throat *adjective* **1** COMPETITIVE, fierce, ruthless, relentless, unprincipled, dog-eat-dog **2** MURDEROUS, violent, bloody, cruel, savage, ferocious, bloodthirsty, barbarous, homicidal, thuggish, death-dealing

cutting *adjective* **1** HURTFUL, wounding, severe, acid, bitter, malicious, scathing, acrimonious, barbed, sarcastic, sardonic, caustic, vitriolic, trenchant, pointed << ANTONYM kind **2** PIERCING, biting, sharp, keen, bitter, raw, chilling, stinging, penetrating, numbing << ANTONYM pleasant

cycle *noun* SERIES OF EVENTS, round (*of years*), circle, revolution, rotation

cyclone *noun* TYPHOON, hurricane, tornado, whirlwind, tempest, twister (*US informal*), storm

cynic *noun* SCEPTIC, doubter, pessimist, misanthrope, misanthropist, scoffer

cynical *adjective* **1** SCEPTICAL, mocking, ironic, sneering, pessimistic, scoffing, contemptuous, sarcastic, sardonic, scornful, distrustful, derisive, misanthropic << ANTONYM trusting **2** UNBELIEVING, sceptical, disillusioned, pessimistic, disbelieving, mistrustful << ANTONYM optimistic

cynicism *noun* **1** SCEPTICISM, pessimism, sarcasm, misanthropy, sardonicism **2** DISBELIEF, doubt, scepticism, mistrust

cyst *noun* SAC, growth, blister, wen, vesicle

dab *verb* **1** PAT, touch, tap, wipe, blot, swab **2** APPLY, daub, stipple ▷ *noun* **1** SPOT, bit, drop, pat, fleck, smudge, speck, dollop (*informal*), smidgen *or* smidgin (*informal, chiefly US & Canad*) **2** TOUCH, stroke, flick, smudge

dabble *verb usually with* **in** *or with* PLAY (AT *or* WITH), potter, tinker (with), trifle (with), dip into, dally (with)

daft *adjective* (*informal, chiefly Brit*) **1** STUPID, simple, crazy, silly, absurd, foolish, giddy, goofy, idiotic, inane, loopy (*informal*), witless, crackpot (*informal*), out to lunch (*informal*), dopey (*informal*), scatty (*Brit informal*), asinine, gonzo (*slang*), doolally (*slang*), off your head (*informal*), off your trolley (*slang*), up the pole (*informal*), dumb-ass (*slang*), wacko *or* whacko (*slang*), off the air (*Austral slang*) **2** CRAZY, mad, mental (*slang*), touched, nuts (*slang*), barking (*slang*), crackers (*Brit slang*), insane, lunatic, demented, nutty (*slang*), deranged, unhinged, round the bend (*Brit slang*), barking mad (*slang*), not right in the head, not the full shilling (*informal*), off the air (*Austral slang*), porangi (*NZ*) ▷▷ **daft about** ENTHUSIASTIC ABOUT, mad about, crazy about (*informal*), doting on, besotted with, sweet on, nuts about (*slang*), potty about (*Brit informal*), infatuated by, dotty about (*slang, chiefly Brit*), nutty about (*informal*)

dag *noun* (*NZ informal*) JOKER, comic, wag, wit, comedian, clown, kidder (*informal*), jester, humorist, prankster ▷▷ **rattle your dags** (*NZ informal*) HURRY UP, get a move on, step on it (*informal*), get your skates on (*informal*), make haste

dagga *noun* (*S African*) CANNABIS, marijuana, pot (*slang*), dope (*slang*), hash (*slang*), black (*slang*), blow (*slang*), smoke (*informal*), stuff (*slang*), leaf (*slang*), tea (*US slang*), grass (*slang*), chronic (*US slang*), weed (*slang*), hemp, gage (*US dated slang*), hashish, mary jane (*US slang*), ganja, bhang, kif, wacky baccy (*slang*), sinsemilla, charas

dagger *noun* KNIFE, bayonet, dirk, stiletto, poniard, skean ▷▷ **at daggers drawn** ON BAD TERMS, at odds, at war, at loggerheads, up in arms, at enmity ▷▷ **look daggers at someone** GLARE, frown, scowl, glower, look black, lour *or* lower

daggy *adjective* (*Austral & NZ informal*) **1** UNTIDY, unkempt, dishevelled, tousled, disordered, messy, ruffled, scruffy, rumpled, bedraggled, ratty (*informal*), straggly, windblown, disarranged, mussed up (*informal*) **2** ECCENTRIC, odd, strange, bizarre, weird, peculiar, abnormal, queer (*informal*), irregular, uncommon, quirky, singular, unconventional, idiosyncratic, off-the-wall (*slang*), outlandish, whimsical, rum (*Brit slang*), capricious, anomalous, freakish, aberrant, wacko (*slang*), outré

daily *adjective* **1** EVERYDAY, regular, circadian (*biology*), diurnal, quotidian **2** DAY-TO-DAY, common, ordinary, routine, everyday, commonplace, quotidian ▷ *adverb* EVERY DAY, day by day, day after day, once a day, per diem

dainty *adjective* **1** DELICATE, pretty, charming, fine, elegant, neat, exquisite, graceful, petite << ANTONYM clumsy **2** DELECTABLE, choice, delicious, tender, tasty, savoury, palatable, toothsome **3** PARTICULAR, nice, refined, fussy, scrupulous, fastidious, choosy, picky (*informal*), finicky, finical

dais *noun* PLATFORM, stage, podium, rostrum, estrade

dale *noun* VALLEY, glen, vale, dell, dingle, strath (*Scot*), coomb

dalliance *noun* (*old-fashioned*) DABBLING,

playing, toying, trifling

dally *verb* WASTE TIME, delay, fool (about *or* around), linger, hang about, loiter, while away, dawdle, fritter away, procrastinate, tarry, dilly-dally (*informal*), drag your feet *or* heels << ANTONYM hurry (up) ▷▷ **dally with someone** FLIRT WITH, tease, lead on, toy with, play around with, fool (about *or* around) with, trifle with, play fast and loose with (*informal*), frivol with (*informal*)

dam *noun* BARRIER, wall, barrage, obstruction, embankment, hindrance ▷ *verb* BLOCK UP, block, hold in, restrict, check, confine, choke, hold back, barricade, obstruct

damage *noun* 1 DESTRUCTION, harm, loss, injury, suffering, hurt, ruin, crushing, wrecking, shattering, devastation, detriment, mutilation, impairment, annihilation, ruination << ANTONYM improvement 2 (*informal*) COST, price, charge, rate, bill, figure, amount, total, payment, expense, outlay ▷ *plural noun* (*law*) COMPENSATION, fine, payment, satisfaction, amends, reparation, indemnity, restitution, reimbursement, atonement, recompense, indemnification, meed (*archaic*), requital ▷ *verb* SPOIL, hurt, injure, smash, harm, ruin, crush, devastate, mar, wreck, shatter, weaken, gut, demolish, undo, trash (*slang*), total (*slang*), impair, ravage, mutilate, annihilate, incapacitate, raze, deface, play (merry) hell with (*informal*) << ANTONYM fix

damaging *adjective* HARMFUL, detrimental, hurtful, ruinous, prejudicial, deleterious, injurious, disadvantageous << ANTONYM helpful

dame *noun* 1 *with cap.* LADY, baroness, dowager, grande dame (*French*), noblewoman, peeress 2 (*slang, chiefly US & Canad*) WOMAN, girl, lady, female, bird (*slang*), maiden (*archaic*), miss, chick (*slang*), maid (*archaic*), gal (*slang*), lass, lassie (*informal*), wench (*facetious*), charlie (*Austral slang*), chook (*Austral slang*), wahine (*NZ*)

damn *verb* CRITICIZE, condemn, blast, pan (*informal*), slam (*slang*), denounce, put down, slate (*informal*), censure, castigate, tear into (*informal*), diss (*slang, chiefly US*), inveigh against, lambast(e), excoriate, denunciate << ANTONYM praise ▷▷ **not give a damn** (*informal*) NOT CARE, not mind, be indifferent, not give a hoot, not care a jot, not give two hoots, not care a whit, not care a brass farthing, not give a tinker's curse *or* damn (*slang*)

damnation *noun* (*theology*) CONDEMNATION, damning, sending to hell, consigning to perdition

damned *adjective* (*slang*) INFERNAL, accursed, detestable, revolting, infamous, confounded, despicable, abhorred, hateful, loathsome, abominable, freaking (*slang, chiefly US*)

damning *adjective* INCRIMINATING, implicating, condemnatory, dooming, accusatorial, damnatory, implicative

damp *adjective* MOIST, wet, dripping, soggy, humid, sodden, dank, sopping, clammy, dewy, muggy, drizzly, vaporous << ANTONYM dry ▷ *noun* MOISTURE, liquid, humidity, drizzle, dew, dampness, wetness, dankness, clamminess, mugginess << ANTONYM dryness ▷ *verb* MOISTEN, wet, soak, dampen, lick, moisturize, humidify ▷▷ **damp something down** CURB, reduce, check, cool, moderate, dash, chill, dull, diminish, discourage, restrain, inhibit, stifle, allay, deaden, pour cold water on

dampen *verb* 1 REDUCE, check, moderate, dash, dull, restrain, deter, stifle, lessen, smother, muffle, deaden 2 MOISTEN, wet, spray, make damp, bedew, besprinkle

damper *noun* DISCOURAGEMENT, cloud, chill, curb, restraint, gloom, cold water (*informal*), pall

dampness *noun* MOISTNESS, damp, moisture, humidity, wetness, sogginess, dankness, clamminess, mugginess << ANTONYM dryness

dance *verb* 1 PRANCE, rock, trip, swing, spin, hop, skip, sway, whirl, caper, jig, frolic, cavort, gambol, bob up and down, cut a rug (*informal*) 2 CAPER, trip, spring, jump, bound, leap, bounce, hop, skip, romp, frolic, cavort, gambol ▷ *noun* BALL, social, hop (*informal*), disco, knees-up (*Brit informal*), discotheque, dancing party, B and S (*Austral informal*)

dancer *noun* BALLERINA, hoofer (*slang*), Terpsichorean

dandy *noun* FOP, beau, swell (*informal*), blood (*rare*), buck (*archaic*), blade (*archaic*), peacock, dude (*US & Canad informal*), toff (*Brit slang*), macaroni (*obsolete*), man about town, popinjay, coxcomb ▷ *adjective* (*informal*) EXCELLENT, great, fine, capital, splendid, first-rate

danger *noun* 1 JEOPARDY, vulnerability, insecurity, precariousness, endangerment 2 HAZARD, risk, threat, menace, peril, pitfall

dangerous *adjective* PERILOUS, threatening, risky, hazardous, exposed, alarming, vulnerable, nasty, ugly, menacing, insecure, hairy (*slang*), unsafe, precarious, treacherous, breakneck, parlous (*archaic*), fraught with danger, chancy (*informal*), unchancy (*Scot*) << ANTONYM safe

dangerously *adverb* PERILOUSLY, alarmingly, carelessly, precariously, recklessly, daringly, riskily, harmfully, hazardously, unsafely, unsecurely

dangle *verb* 1 HANG, swing, trail, sway, flap, hang down, depend 2 OFFER, flourish, brandish, flaunt, tempt someone with, lure someone with, entice someone with, tantalize someone with

dangling *adjective* HANGING, swinging, loose, trailing, swaying, disconnected, drooping, unconnected

dank *adjective* DAMP, dripping, moist, soggy, clammy, dewy

dapper *adjective* (only ever used with reference to *men*, not *women*) NEAT, nice, smart, trim, stylish, spruce, dainty, natty (*informal*), well-groomed, well turned out, trig (*archaic or dialect*), soigné << ANTONYM untidy

dappled *adjective* MOTTLED, spotted, speckled, pied, flecked, variegated, checkered, freckled, stippled, piebald, brindled

dare *verb* 1 RISK DOING, venture, presume, make bold (*archaic*), hazard doing, brave doing 2 CHALLENGE, provoke, defy, taunt, goad, throw down the gauntlet

daredevil *noun* ADVENTURER, show-off (*informal*), madcap, desperado, exhibitionist, stunt man, hot dog (*chiefly US*), adrenalin junky (*slang*) ▷ *adjective* DARING, bold, adventurous, reckless, audacious, madcap, death-defying

daring *adjective* BRAVE, bold, adventurous, rash, have-a-go (*informal*), reckless, fearless, audacious, intrepid, impulsive, valiant, plucky, game (*informal*), daredevil, venturesome, (as) game as Ned Kelly (*Austral slang*) << ANTONYM timid ▷ *noun* BRAVERY, nerve (*informal*), courage, face (*informal*), spirit, bottle (*Brit slang*), guts (*informal*), pluck, grit, audacity, boldness, temerity, derring-do (*archaic*), spunk (*informal*), fearlessness, rashness, intrepidity << ANTONYM timidity

dark *adjective* 1 DIM, murky, shady, shadowy, grey, cloudy, dingy, overcast, dusky, unlit, pitch-black, indistinct, poorly lit, sunless, tenebrous, darksome (*literary*), pitchy, unilluminated 2 BLACK, brunette, ebony, dark-skinned, sable, dusky, swarthy << ANTONYM fair 3 EVIL, foul, horrible, sinister, infamous, vile, satanic, wicked, atrocious, sinful, hellish, infernal, nefarious, damnable 4 SECRET, deep, hidden, mysterious, concealed, obscure, mystic, enigmatic, puzzling, occult, arcane, cryptic, abstruse, recondite, Delphic 5 GLOOMY, sad, grim, miserable, low, bleak, moody, dismal, pessimistic, melancholy, sombre, morbid, glum, mournful, morose, joyless, doleful, cheerless << ANTONYM cheerful 6 ANGRY, threatening, forbidding, frowning, ominous, dour, scowling, sullen, glum, glowering, sulky ▷ *noun* 1 DARKNESS, shadows, gloom, dusk, obscurity, murk, dimness, semi-darkness, murkiness 2 NIGHT, twilight, evening, evo (*Austral slang*), dusk, night-time, nightfall

darken *verb* 1 CLOUD, shadow, shade, obscure, eclipse, dim, deepen, overshadow, blacken, becloud << ANTONYM brighten 2 MAKE DARK, shade, blacken, make darker, deepen 3 BECOME GLOOMY, blacken, become angry, look black, go crook (*Austral & NZ slang*), grow troubled << ANTONYM become cheerful 4 SADDEN, upset, cloud, blacken, cast a pall over, cast a gloom upon

darkness *noun* DARK, shadows, shade, gloom, obscurity, blackness, murk, dimness, murkiness, duskiness, shadiness

darling *noun* 1 BELOVED, love, dear, dearest, angel, treasure, precious, loved one, sweetheart, sweetie, truelove, dear one 2 FAVOURITE, pet, spoilt child, apple of your eye, blue-eyed boy, fair-haired boy (*US*) ▷ *adjective* 1 BELOVED, dear, dearest, sweet, treasured, precious, adored, cherished, revered 2 ADORABLE, sweet, attractive, lovely, charming, cute, enchanting, captivating

darn *verb* MEND, repair, patch, stitch, sew up, cobble up ▷ *noun* MEND, patch, reinforcement, invisible repair

dart *verb* DASH, run, race, shoot, fly, speed, spring, tear, rush, bound, flash, hurry, sprint, bolt, hasten, whizz, haste, flit, scoot

dash *verb* 1 RUSH, run, race, shoot, fly, career, speed, spring, tear, bound, hurry, barrel (along) (*informal, chiefly US & Canad*), sprint, bolt, dart, hasten, scurry, haste, stampede, burn rubber (*informal*), make haste, hotfoot << ANTONYM dawdle 2 THROW, cast, pitch, slam, toss, hurl, fling, chuck (*informal*), propel, project, sling, lob (*informal*) 3 CRASH, break, smash, shatter, shiver, splinter

4 DISAPPOINT, ruin, frustrate, spoil, foil, undo, thwart, dampen, confound, crool *or* cruel (*Austral slang*) ▷ *noun* **1** RUSH, run, race, sprint, bolt, dart, spurt, sortie **2** DROP, little, bit, shot (*informal*), touch, spot, suggestion, trace, hint, pinch, sprinkling, tot, trickle, nip, tinge, soupçon (*French*) << ANTONYM lot **3** STYLE, spirit, flair, flourish, vigour, verve, panache, élan, brio, vivacity

dashing *adjective* (*old-fashioned*) STYLISH, smart, elegant, dazzling, flamboyant, sporty, swish (*informal, chiefly Brit*), urbane, jaunty, dapper, showy

dastardly *adjective* (*old-fashioned*) DESPICABLE, mean, low, base, sneaking, cowardly, craven, vile, abject, sneaky, contemptible, underhand, weak-kneed (*informal*), faint-hearted, spiritless, recreant (*archaic*), caitiff (*archaic*), niddering (*archaic*)

data *noun* **1** DETAILS, facts, figures, materials, documents, intelligence, statistics, gen (*Brit informal*), dope (*informal*), info (*informal*) **2** (*computing*) INFORMATION, input

date *noun* **1** TIME, stage, period **2** APPOINTMENT, meeting, arrangement, commitment, engagement, rendezvous, tryst, assignation **3** PARTNER, escort, friend, steady (*informal*) ▷ *verb* **1** PUT A DATE ON, determine the date of, assign a date to, fix the period of **2** BECOME DATED, become old-fashioned, obsolesce ▷▷ **date from** *or* **date back to** (with a *time* or *date* as object) COME FROM, belong to, originate in, exist from, bear a date of ▷▷ **to date** UP TO NOW, yet, so far, until now, now, as yet, thus far, up to this point, up to the present

dated *adjective* OLD-FASHIONED, outdated, out of date, obsolete, archaic, unfashionable, antiquated, outmoded, passé, out, old hat, untrendy (*Brit informal*), démodé (*French*), out of the ark (*informal*) << ANTONYM modern

daub *verb* SMEAR, dirty, splatter, stain, spatter, sully, deface, smirch, begrime, besmear, bedaub, paint, coat, stain, plaster, slap on (*informal*) ▷ *noun* SMEAR, spot, stain, blot, blotch, splodge, splotch, smirch

daughter *noun* **1** FEMALE CHILD, girl **2** DESCENDANT, girl

daunt *verb* DISCOURAGE, alarm, shake, frighten, scare, terrify, cow, intimidate, deter, dismay, put off, subdue, overawe, frighten off, dishearten, dispirit << ANTONYM reassure

daunted *adjective* INTIMIDATED, alarmed, shaken, frightened, overcome, cowed, discouraged, deterred, dismayed, put off, disillusioned, unnerved, demoralized, dispirited, downcast

daunting *adjective* INTIMIDATING, alarming, frightening, discouraging, awesome, unnerving, disconcerting, demoralizing, off-putting (*Brit informal*), disheartening << ANTONYM reassuring

dawdle *verb* **1** WASTE TIME, potter, trail, lag, idle, loaf, hang about, dally, loiter, dilly-dally (*informal*), drag your feet *or* heels << ANTONYM hurry **2** LINGER, idle, dally, take your time, procrastinate, drag your feet *or* heels

dawn *noun* **1** DAYBREAK, morning, sunrise, dawning, daylight, aurora (*poetic*), crack of dawn, sunup, cockcrow, dayspring (*poetic*) **2** (*literary*) BEGINNING, start, birth, rise, origin, dawning, unfolding, emergence, outset, onset, advent, genesis, inception ▷ *verb* **1** BEGIN, start, open, rise, develop, emerge, unfold, originate **2** GROW LIGHT, break, brighten, lighten ▷▷ **dawn on** *or* **upon someone** HIT, strike, occur to, register (*informal*), become apparent, come to mind, cross your mind, come into your head, flash across your mind

day *noun* **1** TWENTY-FOUR HOURS, working day **2** DAYTIME, daylight, daylight hours **3** DATE, particular day **4** TIME, age, era, prime, period, generation, heyday, epoch ▷▷ **call it a day** STOP, finish, cease, pack up (*informal*), leave off, knock off (*informal*), desist, pack it in (*slang*), shut up shop, jack it in, chuck it in (*informal*), give up *or* over ▷▷ **day after day** CONTINUALLY, regularly, relentlessly, persistently, incessantly, nonstop, unremittingly, monotonously, unfalteringly ▷▷ **day by day** GRADUALLY, slowly, progressively, daily, steadily, bit by bit, little by little, by degrees

daybreak *noun* DAWN, morning, sunrise, first light, crack of dawn, break of day, sunup, cockcrow, dayspring (*poetic*)

daydream *noun* FANTASY, dream, imagining, fancy, reverie, figment of the imagination WISH, pipe dream, fond hope, castle in the air *or* in Spain ▷ *verb* FANTASIZE, dream, imagine, envision, stargaze

daylight *noun* **1** SUNLIGHT, sunshine, light of day **2** DAYTIME, broad daylight, daylight hours

day-to-day *adjective* EVERYDAY, regular, usual, routine, accustomed, customary, habitual, run-of-the-mill, wonted

daze *verb* 1 STUN, shock, paralyse, numb, stupefy, benumb 2 CONFUSE, surprise, amaze, blind, astonish, stagger, startle, dazzle, bewilder, astound, perplex, flummox, dumbfound, nonplus, flabbergast (*informal*), befog ▷ *noun* (usually used in the phrase *in a daze*) SHOCK, confusion, distraction, trance, bewilderment, stupor, trancelike state

dazed *adjective* SHOCKED, stunned, confused, staggered, baffled, at sea, bewildered, muddled, numbed, dizzy, bemused, perplexed, disorientated, flabbergasted (*informal*), dopey (*slang*), groggy (*informal*), stupefied, nonplussed, light-headed, flummoxed, punch-drunk, woozy (*informal*), fuddled

dazzle *verb* 1 IMPRESS, amaze, fascinate, overwhelm, astonish, awe, overpower, bowl over (*informal*), overawe, hypnotize, stupefy, take your breath away, strike dumb 2 BLIND, confuse, daze, bedazzle ▷ *noun* SPLENDOUR, sparkle, glitter, flash, brilliance, magnificence, razzmatazz (*slang*), razzle-dazzle (*slang*), éclat

dazzling *adjective* SPLENDID, brilliant, stunning, superb, divine, glorious, sparkling, glittering, sensational (*informal*), sublime, virtuoso, drop-dead (*slang*), ravishing, scintillating << ANTONYM ordinary

dead *adjective* 1 DECEASED, gone, departed, late, perished, extinct, defunct, passed away, pushing up (the) daisies << ANTONYM alive 2 INANIMATE, still, barren, sterile, stagnant, lifeless, inert, uninhabited 3 BORING, dull, dreary, flat, plain, stale, tasteless, humdrum, uninteresting, insipid, ho-hum (*informal*), vapid, dead-and-alive 4 NOT WORKING, useless, inactive, inoperative << ANTONYM working 5 OBSOLETE, old, antique, discarded, extinct, archaic, disused 6 SPIRITLESS, cold, dull, wooden, glazed, indifferent, callous, lukewarm, inhuman, unsympathetic, apathetic, frigid, glassy, unresponsive, unfeeling, torpid << ANTONYM lively 7 NUMB, frozen, paralysed, insensitive, inert, deadened, immobilized, unfeeling, torpid, insensible, benumbed 8 (usually used of *centre, silence,* or *stop*) TOTAL, complete, perfect, entire, absolute, utter, outright, thorough, downright, unqualified 9 (*informal*) EXHAUSTED, tired, worn out, spent, wasted, done in (*informal*), all in (*slang*), drained, wiped out (*informal*), sapped, knackered (*slang*), prostrated, clapped out (*Brit, Austral & NZ informal*), tired out, ready to drop, dog-tired (*informal*), zonked (*slang*), dead tired, dead beat (*informal*), shagged out (*Brit slang*), worn to a frazzle (*informal*), on your last legs (*informal*), creamcrackered (*Brit slang*) ▷ *noun* MIDDLE, heart, depth, thick, midst ▷ *adverb* EXACTLY, quite, completely, totally, directly, perfectly, fully, entirely, absolutely, thoroughly, wholly, utterly, consummately, wholeheartedly, unconditionally, to the hilt, one hundred per cent, unmitigatedly

deadbeat *noun* (*informal, chiefly US & Canad*) LAYABOUT, bum (*informal*), waster, lounger, piker (*Austral & NZ slang*), sponge (*informal*), parasite, drone, loafer, slacker (*informal*), scrounger (*informal*), skiver (*Brit slang*), idler, freeloader (*slang*), good-for-nothing, sponger (*informal*), wastrel, bludger (*Austral & NZ informal*), cadger, quandong (*Austral slang*)

deaden *verb* 1 REDUCE, dull, diminish, check, weaken, cushion, damp, suppress, blunt, paralyse, impair, numb, lessen, alleviate, smother, dampen, anaesthetize, benumb 2 SUPPRESS, reduce, dull, diminish, cushion, damp, mute, stifle, hush, lessen, smother, dampen, muffle, quieten

deadline *noun* TIME LIMIT, cutoff point, target date *or* time, limit

deadlock *noun* 1 IMPASSE, stalemate, standstill, halt, cessation, gridlock, standoff, full stop 2 TIE, draw, stalemate, impasse, standstill, gridlock, standoff, dead heat

deadly *adjective* 1 LETHAL, fatal, deathly, dangerous, devastating, destructive, mortal, murderous, poisonous, malignant, virulent, pernicious, noxious, venomous, baleful, death-dealing, baneful 2 (*informal*) BORING, dull, tedious, flat, monotonous, uninteresting, mind-numbing, unexciting, ho-hum (*informal*), wearisome, as dry as dust 3 DEATHLY, white, pale, ghostly, ghastly, wan, pasty, colourless, pallid, anaemic, ashen, sallow, whitish, cadaverous, waxen, ashy, deathlike, wheyfaced

deadpan *adjective* EXPRESSIONLESS, empty, blank, wooden, straight-faced, vacuous, impassive, inscrutable, poker-faced, inexpressive

deaf *adjective* 1 HARD OF HEARING, without hearing, stone deaf 2 OBLIVIOUS, indifferent, unmoved, unconcerned, unsympathetic, impervious, unresponsive, heedless, unhearing ▷ see **disabled**

deafen *verb* MAKE DEAF, split *or* burst the eardrums

deafening *adjective* EAR-SPLITTING, intense, piercing, ringing, booming, overpowering, resounding, dinning, thunderous, ear-piercing

deal *noun* 1 (*informal*) AGREEMENT, understanding, contract, business, negotiation, arrangement, bargain, transaction, pact 2 AMOUNT, quantity, measure, degree, mass, volume, share, portion, bulk ▷▷ **deal in something** SELL, trade in, stock, traffic in, buy and sell ▷▷ **deal something out** DISTRIBUTE, give, administer, share, divide, assign, allocate, dispense, bestow, allot, mete out, dole out, apportion ▷▷ **deal with something** BE CONCERNED WITH, involve, concern, touch, regard, apply to, bear on, pertain to, be relevant to, treat of ▷▷ **deal with something** *or* **someone** 1 HANDLE, manage, treat, cope with, take care of, see to, attend to, get to grips with, come to grips with 2 BEHAVE TOWARDS, act towards, conduct yourself towards

dealer *noun* TRADER, marketer, merchant, supplier, wholesaler, purveyor, tradesman, merchandiser

dealings *plural noun* BUSINESS, selling, trading, trade, traffic, truck, bargaining, commerce, transactions, business relations

dear *adjective* 1 BELOVED, close, valued, favourite, respected, prized, dearest, sweet, treasured, precious, darling, intimate, esteemed, cherished, revered << ANTONYM hated 2 EXPENSIVE, costly, high-priced, excessive, pricey (*informal*), at a premium, overpriced, exorbitant << ANTONYM cheap ▷ *noun* DARLING, love, dearest, sweet, angel, treasure, precious, beloved, loved one, sweetheart, truelove

dearly *adverb* 1 VERY MUCH, greatly, extremely, profoundly 2 AT GREAT COST, dear, at a high price, at a heavy cost

dearth *noun* LACK, want, need, absence, poverty, shortage, deficiency, famine, inadequacy, scarcity, paucity, insufficiency, sparsity, scantiness, exiguousness

death *noun* 1 DYING, demise, bereavement, end, passing, release, loss, departure, curtains (*informal*), cessation, expiration, decease, quietus << ANTONYM birth 2 DESTRUCTION, ending, finish, ruin, wiping out, undoing, extinction, elimination, downfall, extermination, annihilation, obliteration, ruination << ANTONYM beginning 3 *sometimes capital* THE GRIM REAPER, the Dark Angel

deathly *adjective* 1 DEATHLIKE, white, pale, ghastly, wan, gaunt, haggard, bloodless, pallid, ashen, sallow, cadaverous, ashy, like death warmed up (*informal*) 2 FATAL, terminal, deadly, terrible, destructive, lethal, mortal, malignant, incurable, pernicious

debacle *or* **débâcle** *noun* DISASTER, catastrophe, fiasco

debar *verb* BAR, exclude, prohibit, black, stop, keep out, preclude, shut out, blackball, interdict, refuse admission to

debase *verb* 1 (*formal*) CORRUPT, contaminate, devalue, pollute, impair, taint, depreciate, defile, adulterate, vitiate, bastardize << ANTONYM purify 2 DEGRADE, reduce, lower, shame, humble, disgrace, humiliate, demean, drag down, dishonour, cheapen, abase << ANTONYM exalt

debased *adjective* 1 CORRUPT, devalued, reduced, lowered, mixed, contaminated, polluted, depreciated, impure, adulterated 2 DEGRADED, corrupt, fallen, low, base, abandoned, perverted, vile, sordid, depraved, debauched, scungy (*Austral & NZ*) << ANTONYM virtuous

debatable *adjective* DOUBTFUL, uncertain, dubious, controversial, unsettled, questionable, undecided, borderline, in dispute, moot, arguable, iffy (*informal*), open to question, disputable

debate *noun* DISCUSSION, talk, argument, dispute, analysis, conversation, consideration, controversy, dialogue, contention, deliberation, polemic, altercation, disputation ▷ *verb* 1 DISCUSS, question, talk about, argue about, dispute, examine, contest, deliberate, contend, wrangle, thrash out, controvert 2 CONSIDER, reflect, think about, weigh, contemplate, deliberate, ponder, revolve, mull over, ruminate, give thought to, cogitate, meditate upon

debauched *adjective* CORRUPT, abandoned, perverted, degraded, degenerate, immoral, dissipated, sleazy, depraved, wanton, debased, profligate, dissolute, licentious, pervy (*slang*)

debauchery *noun* DEPRAVITY, excess, lust, revel, indulgence, orgy, incontinence, gluttony, dissipation, licentiousness, intemperance, overindulgence, lewdness, dissoluteness, carousal

debilitate *verb* WEAKEN, exhaust, wear out, sap, incapacitate, prostrate, enfeeble, enervate, devitalize << ANTONYM invigorate

debilitating *adjective* WEAKENING, tiring, exhausting, draining, fatiguing, wearing, sapping, incapacitating, enervating, enfeebling, devitalizing << ANTONYM invigorating

debonair *adjective* ELEGANT, charming, dashing, smooth, refined, courteous, affable, suave, urbane, well-bred

debrief *verb* INTERROGATE, question, examine, probe, quiz, cross-examine

debris *noun* REMAINS, bits, pieces, waste, ruins, wreck, rubbish, fragments, litter, rubble, wreckage, brash, detritus, dross

debt *noun* DEBIT, bill, score, due, duty, commitment, obligation, liability, arrears
▷▷ **in debt** OWING, liable, accountable, in the red (*informal*), in arrears, beholden, in hock (*informal, chiefly US*)

debtor *noun* BORROWER, mortgagor

debunk *verb* (*informal*) EXPOSE, show up, mock, ridicule, puncture, deflate, disparage, lampoon, cut down to size

debut *noun* **1** ENTRANCE, beginning, launch, launching, introduction, first appearance, inauguration **2** PRESENTATION, coming out, introduction, first appearance, launching, initiation

decadence *noun* DEGENERATION, decline, corruption, fall, decay, deterioration, dissolution, perversion, dissipation, debasement, retrogression

decadent *adjective* DEGENERATE, abandoned, corrupt, degraded, immoral, self-indulgent, depraved, debased, debauched, dissolute << ANTONYM moral

decamp *verb* MAKE OFF, fly, escape, desert, flee, bolt, run away, flit (*informal*), abscond, hook it (*slang*), sneak off, do a runner (*slang*), scarper (*Brit slang*), steal away, do a bunk (*Brit slang*), fly the coop (*US & Canad informal*), skedaddle (*informal*), hightail it (*informal, chiefly US*), take a powder (*US & Canad slang*), take it on the lam (*US & Canad slang*), do a Skase (*Austral informal*)

decant *verb* (*formal*) TRANSFER, tap, drain, pour out, draw off, let flow

decapitate *verb* BEHEAD, execute, guillotine

decay *verb* **1** ROT, break down, disintegrate, spoil, crumble, deteriorate, perish, degenerate, fester, decompose, mortify, moulder, go bad, putrefy **2** DECLINE, sink, break down, diminish, dissolve, crumble, deteriorate, fall off, dwindle, lessen, wane, disintegrate, degenerate << ANTONYM grow ▷ *noun* **1** ROT, rotting, deterioration, corruption, mould, blight, perishing, disintegration, corrosion, decomposition, gangrene, mortification, canker, caries, putrefaction, putrescence, cariosity, putridity **2** DECLINE, collapse, deterioration, failing, fading, decadence, degeneration, degeneracy << ANTONYM growth

decayed *adjective* ROTTEN, bad, decaying, wasted, spoiled, perished, festering, decomposed, corroded, unsound, putrid, putrefied, putrescent, carrion, carious

decaying *adjective* ROTTING, deteriorating, disintegrating, crumbling, perishing, wasting away, wearing away, gangrenous, putrefacient

deceased *adjective* DEAD, late, departed, lost, gone, expired, defunct, lifeless, pushing up daisies (*informal*)

deceit *noun* LYING, fraud, cheating, deception, hypocrisy, cunning, pretence, treachery, dishonesty, guile, artifice, trickery, misrepresentation, duplicity, subterfuge, feint, double-dealing, chicanery, wile, dissimulation, craftiness, imposture, fraudulence, slyness, deceitfulness, underhandedness << ANTONYM honesty

deceitful *adjective* DISHONEST, false, deceiving, fraudulent, treacherous, deceptive, hypocritical, counterfeit, crafty, sneaky, illusory, two-faced, disingenuous, untrustworthy, underhand, insincere, double-dealing, duplicitous, fallacious, guileful, knavish (*archaic*)

deceive *verb* TAKE IN, trick, fool (*informal*), cheat, con (*informal*), kid (*informal*), stiff (*slang*), sting (*informal*), mislead, betray, lead (someone) on (*informal*), hoax, dupe, beguile, delude, swindle, outwit, ensnare, bamboozle (*informal*), hoodwink, entrap, double-cross (*informal*), take (someone) for a ride (*informal*), pull a fast one on (*slang*), cozen, pull the wool over (someone's) eyes

decency *noun* **1** PROPRIETY, correctness, decorum, fitness, good form, respectability, etiquette, appropriateness, seemliness **2** COURTESY, grace, politeness, good manners, civility, good breeding, graciousness, urbanity, courteousness, gallantry

decent *adjective* **1** SATISFACTORY, average, fair, all right, reasonable, suitable, sufficient, acceptable, good enough, adequate, competent, ample, tolerable, up to scratch, passable, up to standard, up to the mark << ANTONYM unsatisfactory **2** PROPER, becoming, seemly, fitting, fit, appropriate, suitable, respectable, befitting, decorous, comme il faut (*French*) << ANTONYM improper **3** (*informal*) GOOD, kind, friendly, neighbourly, generous, helpful, obliging, accommodating, sympathetic, comradely, benign, gracious, benevolent, courteous, amiable, amicable, sociable, genial, peaceable, companionable, well-disposed **4** RESPECTABLE, nice, pure, proper, modest, polite, chaste, presentable, decorous

deception *noun* **1** TRICKERY, fraud, deceit, hypocrisy, cunning, treachery, guile, duplicity, insincerity, legerdemain, dissimulation, craftiness, fraudulence, deceitfulness, deceptiveness << ANTONYM honesty **2** TRICK, lie, fraud, cheat, bluff, sham, snare, hoax, decoy, ruse, artifice, subterfuge, canard, feint, stratagem, porky (*Brit slang*), pork pie (*Brit slang*), wile, hokum (*slang, chiefly US & Canad*), leg-pull (*Brit informal*), imposture, snow job (*slang, chiefly US & Canad*), fastie (*Austral slang*)

deceptive *adjective* **1** MISLEADING, false, fake, mock, ambiguous, unreliable, spurious, illusory, specious, fallacious, delusive **2** DISHONEST, deceiving, fraudulent, treacherous, hypocritical, crafty, sneaky, two-faced, disingenuous, deceitful, untrustworthy, underhand, insincere, duplicitous, guileful

decide *verb* **1** MAKE A DECISION, make up your mind, reach *or* come to a decision, end, choose, determine, purpose, elect, conclude, commit yourself, come to a conclusion << ANTONYM hesitate **2** RESOLVE, answer, determine, settle, conclude, decree, clear up, ordain, adjudicate, adjudge, arbitrate **3** SETTLE, determine, conclude, resolve

decided *adjective* **1** DEFINITE, certain, positive, absolute, distinct, pronounced, clear-cut, undisputed, unequivocal, undeniable, unambiguous, indisputable, categorical, unquestionable << ANTONYM doubtful **2** DETERMINED, firm, decisive, assertive, emphatic, resolute, strong-willed, unhesitating, unfaltering << ANTONYM irresolute

decidedly *adverb* DEFINITELY, clearly, certainly, absolutely, positively, distinctly, downright, decisively, unequivocally, unmistakably

deciding *adjective* DETERMINING, chief, prime, significant, critical, crucial, principal, influential, decisive, conclusive

decimate *verb* DESTROY, devastate, wipe out, ravage, eradicate, annihilate, put paid to, lay waste, wreak havoc on

decipher *verb* **1** DECODE, crack, solve, understand, explain, reveal, figure out (*informal*), unravel, suss (out) (*slang*) **2** FIGURE OUT, read, understand, interpret (*informal*), make out, unravel, deduce, construe, suss (out) (*slang*)

decision *noun* **1** JUDGMENT, finding, ruling, order, result, sentence, settlement, resolution, conclusion, outcome, verdict, decree, arbitration **2** DECISIVENESS, purpose, resolution, resolve, determination, firmness, forcefulness, purposefulness, resoluteness, strength of mind *or* will

decisive *adjective* **1** CRUCIAL, significant, critical, final, positive, absolute, influential, definite, definitive, momentous, conclusive, fateful << ANTONYM uncertain **2** RESOLUTE, decided, firm, determined, forceful, uncompromising, incisive, trenchant, strong-minded << ANTONYM indecisive

deck *verb* DECORATE, dress, trim, clothe, grace, array, garland, adorn, ornament, embellish, apparel (*archaic*), festoon, attire, bedeck, beautify, bedight (*archaic*), bedizen (*archaic*), engarland ▷▷ **deck someone** *or* **something out** DRESS UP, doll up (*slang*), prettify, trick out, rig out, pretty up, prink, tog up *or* out

declaim *verb* SPEAK, lecture, proclaim, recite, rant, harangue, hold forth, spiel (*informal*), orate, perorate ▷▷ **declaim against something** *or* **someone** PROTEST AGAINST, attack, rail at *or* against, denounce, decry, inveigh against

declaration *noun* **1** ANNOUNCEMENT, proclamation, decree, notice, manifesto, notification, edict, pronouncement, promulgation, pronunciamento **2** AFFIRMATION, profession, assertion, revelation, disclosure, acknowledgment, protestation, avowal, averment **3** STATEMENT, testimony, deposition, attestation

declare *verb* **1** STATE, claim, announce, voice, express, maintain, confirm, assert, proclaim, pronounce, utter, notify, affirm, profess, avow, aver, asseverate **2** TESTIFY, state, witness, swear, assert, affirm, certify, attest, bear witness, vouch, give testimony, asseverate **3** MAKE KNOWN, tell, reveal, show, broadcast, confess, communicate, disclose, convey, manifest, make public

decline *verb* **1** FALL, fail, drop, contract, lower, sink, flag, fade, shrink, diminish, decrease, slow down, fall off, dwindle, lessen, wane, ebb, slacken << ANTONYM rise **2** DETERIORATE, fade, weaken, pine, decay, worsen, lapse, languish, degenerate, droop << ANTONYM improve **3** REFUSE, reject, turn down, avoid, deny, spurn, abstain, forgo, send your regrets, say 'no' << ANTONYM accept ▷ *noun* **1** DEPRESSION, recession, slump, falling off, downturn, dwindling, lessening, diminution, abatement << ANTONYM rise **2** DETERIORATION, fall, failing, slump, weakening, decay, worsening, descent, downturn, disintegration, degeneration, atrophy, decrepitude, retrogression, enfeeblement << ANTONYM improvement

decode *verb* **1** DECIPHER, crack, work out, solve, interpret, unscramble, decrypt, descramble << ANTONYM encode **2** UNDERSTAND, explain, interpret, make sense of, construe, decipher, elucidate, throw light on, explicate

decompose *verb* **1** ROT, spoil, corrupt, crumble, decay, perish, fester, corrode, moulder, go bad, putrefy **2** BREAK DOWN, break up, crumble, deteriorate, fall apart, disintegrate, degenerate

decomposition *noun* ROT, corruption, decay, rotting, perishing, mortification, putrefaction, putrescence, putridity

decor *or* **décor** *noun* DECORATION, colour scheme, ornamentation, furnishing style

decorate *verb* **1** ADORN, deck, trim, embroider, garnish, ornament, embellish, festoon, bedeck, beautify, grace, engarland **2** DO UP, paper, paint, wallpaper, renovate (*informal*), furbish **3** PIN A MEDAL ON, cite, confer an honour on *or* upon

decoration *noun* **1** ADORNMENT, trimming, garnishing, enhancement, elaboration, embellishment, ornamentation, beautification **2** ORNAMENT, trimmings, garnish, frill, scroll, spangle, festoon, trinket, bauble, flounce, arabesque, curlicue, furbelow, falderal, cartouch(e) **3** MEDAL, award, order, star, colours, ribbon, badge, emblem, garter

decorative *adjective* ORNAMENTAL, fancy, pretty, attractive, enhancing, adorning, for show, embellishing, showy, beautifying, nonfunctional, arty-crafty

decorum *noun* PROPRIETY, decency, etiquette, breeding, protocol, respectability, politeness, good manners, good grace, gentility, deportment, courtliness, politesse,

punctilio, seemliness << ANTONYM impropriety

decoy *noun* LURE, attraction, bait, trap, inducement, enticement, ensnarement

decrease *verb* **1** DROP, decline, lessen, contract, lower, ease, shrink, diminish, fall off, dwindle, wane, subside, abate, peter out, slacken **2** REDUCE, cut, lower, contract, depress, moderate, weaken, diminish, turn down, slow down, cut down, shorten, dilute, impair, lessen, curtail, wind down, abate, tone down, truncate, abridge, downsize << ANTONYM increase ▷ *noun* LESSENING, decline, reduction, loss, falling off, downturn, dwindling, contraction, ebb, cutback, subsidence, curtailment, shrinkage, diminution, abatement << ANTONYM growth

decree *noun* **1** LAW, order, ruling, act, demand, command, regulation, mandate, canon, statute, covenant, ordinance, proclamation, enactment, edict, dictum, precept **2** JUDGMENT, finding, order, result, ruling, decision, award, conclusion, verdict, arbitration ▷ *verb* ORDER, rule, command, decide, demand, establish, determine, proclaim, dictate, prescribe, pronounce, lay down, enact, ordain

decrepit *adjective* **1** RUINED, broken-down, battered, crumbling, run-down, deteriorated, decaying, beat-up (*informal*), shabby, worn-out, ramshackle, dilapidated, antiquated, rickety, weather-beaten, tumbledown **2** WEAK, aged, frail, wasted, fragile, crippled, feeble, past it, debilitated, incapacitated, infirm, superannuated, doddering

decry *verb* CONDEMN, blame, abuse, blast, denounce, put down, criticize, run down, discredit, censure, detract, denigrate, belittle, disparage, rail against, depreciate, tear into (*informal*), diss (*slang, chiefly US*), lambast(e), traduce, excoriate, derogate, cry down, asperse

dedicate *verb* **1** DEVOTE, give, apply, commit, concern, occupy, pledge, surrender, give over **2** OFFER, address, assign, inscribe **3** CONSECRATE, bless, sanctify, set apart, hallow

dedicated *adjective* COMMITTED, devoted, sworn, enthusiastic, single-minded, zealous, purposeful, given over to, wholehearted << ANTONYM indifferent

dedication *noun* **1** COMMITMENT, loyalty, devotion, allegiance, adherence, single-mindedness, faithfulness, wholeheartedness, devotedness << ANTONYM indifference **2** INSCRIPTION, message, address

deduce *verb* WORK OUT, reason, understand, gather, conclude, derive, infer, glean

deduct *verb* SUBTRACT, remove, take off, withdraw, take out, take from, take away, reduce by, knock off (*informal*), decrease by << ANTONYM add

deduction *noun* **1** CONCLUSION, finding, verdict, judgment, assumption, inference, corollary **2** REASONING, thinking, thought, reason, analysis, logic, cogitation, ratiocination **3** DISCOUNT, reduction, cut, concession, allowance, decrease, rebate, diminution **4** SUBTRACTION, reduction, allowance, concession

deed *noun* **1** ACTION, act, performance, achievement, exploit, feat **2** (*law*) DOCUMENT, title, contract, title deed, indenture

deem *verb* CONSIDER, think, believe, hold, account, judge, suppose, regard, estimate, imagine, reckon, esteem, conceive

deep *adjective* **1** BIG, wide, broad, profound, yawning, cavernous, bottomless, unfathomable, fathomless, abyssal << ANTONYM shallow **2** INTENSE, great, serious (*informal*), acute, extreme, grave, profound, heartfelt, unqualified, abject, deeply felt, heartrending << ANTONYM superficial **3** SOUND, peaceful, profound, unbroken, undisturbed, untroubled **4** *with* in ABSORBED IN, lost in, gripped by, intent on, preoccupied with, carried away by, immersed in, engrossed in, rapt by **5** WISE, learned, searching, keen, critical, acute, profound, penetrating, discriminating, shrewd, discerning, astute, perceptive, incisive, perspicacious, sagacious << ANTONYM simple **6** DARK, strong, rich, warm, intense, vivid << ANTONYM light **7** LOW, booming, bass, full, mellow, resonant, sonorous, mellifluous, dulcet, low-pitched, full-toned << ANTONYM high **8** ASTUTE, knowing, clever, designing, scheming, sharp, smart, intelligent, discriminating, shrewd, cunning, discerning, canny, devious, perceptive, insidious, artful, far-sighted, far-seeing, perspicacious, sagacious << ANTONYM simple **9** SECRET, hidden, unknown, mysterious, concealed, obscure, abstract, veiled, esoteric, mystifying, impenetrable, arcane, abstruse, recondite ▷ *noun* MIDDLE, heart, midst, dead, thick, culmination ▷ *adverb* **1** FAR, a long way, a

good way, miles, deeply, far down, a great distance **2** LATE, far ▷▷ **the deep** (*poetic*) THE OCEAN, the sea, the waves, the main, the drink (*informal*), the high seas, the briny (*informal*)

deepen *verb* **1** INTENSIFY, increase, grow, strengthen, reinforce, escalate, magnify, augment **2** DIG OUT, excavate, scoop out, hollow out, scrape out

deeply *adverb* THOROUGHLY, completely, seriously, sadly, severely, gravely, profoundly, intensely, to the heart, passionately, acutely, to the core, feelingly, movingly, distressingly, to the quick, affectingly

deep-rooted *or* **deep-seated** *adjective* FIXED, confirmed, rooted, settled, entrenched, ingrained, inveterate, dyed-in-the-wool, ineradicable << ANTONYM superficial

deface *verb* VANDALIZE, damage, destroy, total (*slang*), injure, mar, spoil, trash (*slang*), impair, tarnish, obliterate, mutilate, deform, blemish, disfigure, sully

de facto *adverb* IN FACT, really, actually, in effect, in reality ▷ *adjective* ACTUAL, real, existing

defamation *noun* SLANDER, smear, libel, scandal, slur, vilification, opprobrium, denigration, calumny, character assassination, disparagement, obloquy, aspersion, traducement

defamatory *adjective* SLANDEROUS, insulting, abusive, denigrating, disparaging, vilifying, derogatory, injurious, libellous, vituperative, calumnious, contumelious

defame *verb* SLANDER, smear, libel, discredit, knock (*informal*), rubbish (*informal*), disgrace, blacken, slag (off) (*slang*), detract, malign, denigrate, disparage, vilify, dishonour, stigmatize, bad-mouth (*slang, chiefly US & Canad*), besmirch, traduce, cast aspersions on, speak evil of, cast a slur on, calumniate, vituperate, asperse

default *noun* **1** (usually in phrase *by default* or *in default of*) FAILURE, want, lack, fault, absence, neglect, defect, deficiency, lapse, omission, dereliction **2** NONPAYMENT, evasion ▷ *verb* FAIL TO PAY, dodge, evade, rat (*informal*), neglect, levant (*Brit*), welch *or* welsh (*slang*)

defeat *verb* **1** BEAT, crush, overwhelm, conquer, stuff (*slang*), master, worst, tank (*slang*), overthrow, lick (*informal*), undo, subdue, rout, overpower, quell, trounce, clobber (*slang*), vanquish, repulse, subjugate, run rings around (*informal*), wipe the floor with (*informal*), make mincemeat of (*informal*), pip at the post, outplay, blow out of the water (*slang*) << ANTONYM surrender **2** FRUSTRATE, foil, thwart, ruin, baffle, confound, balk, get the better of, forestall, stymie ▷ *noun* **1** CONQUEST, beating, overthrow, pasting (*slang*), rout, debacle, trouncing, repulse, vanquishment << ANTONYM victory **2** FRUSTRATION, failure, reverse, disappointment, setback, thwarting

defeated *adjective* BEATEN, crushed, conquered, worsted, routed, overcome, overwhelmed, thrashed, licked (*informal*), thwarted, overpowered, balked, trounced, vanquished, checkmated, bested << ANTONYM victorious

defeatist *noun* PESSIMIST, sceptic, scoffer, doubter, quitter, prophet of doom, yielder ▷ *adjective* PESSIMISTIC, resigned, despairing, hopeless, foreboding, despondent, fatalistic

defecate *verb* EXCRETE, eliminate, discharge, evacuate (*physiology*), dump (*slang, chiefly US*), pass a motion, move the bowels, empty the bowels, open the bowels, egest, void excrement

defect *noun* DEFICIENCY, want, failing, lack, mistake, fault, error, absence, weakness, flaw, shortcoming, inadequacy, imperfection, frailty, foible ▷ *verb* DESERT, rebel, quit, revolt, change sides, apostatize, tergiversate

defection *noun* DESERTION, revolt, rebellion, abandonment, dereliction, backsliding, apostasy

defective *adjective* **1** FAULTY, broken, not working, flawed, imperfect, out of order, on the blink (*slang*) << ANTONYM perfect **2** DEFICIENT, lacking, short, inadequate, insufficient, incomplete, scant << ANTONYM adequate

defector *noun* DESERTER, renegade, turncoat, apostate, recreant (*archaic*), runagate (*archaic*), tergiversator

defence *or US* **defense** *noun* **1** PROTECTION, cover, security, guard, shelter, refuge, resistance, safeguard, immunity **2** ARMAMENTS, weapons **3** ARGUMENT, explanation, excuse, plea, apology, justification, vindication, rationalization, apologia, exoneration, exculpation, extenuation **4** PLEA (*law*), case, claim, pleading, declaration, testimony, denial, alibi, vindication, rebuttal ▷ *plural noun* SHIELD, barricade, fortification, bastion, buttress, rampart, bulwark, fastness,

fortified pa (*NZ*)

defenceless *or US* **defenseless** *adjective* HELPLESS, exposed, vulnerable, naked, endangered, powerless, wide open, unarmed, unprotected, unguarded << ANTONYM safe

defend *verb* **1** PROTECT, cover, guard, screen, secure, preserve, look after, shelter, shield, harbour, safeguard, fortify, ward off, watch over, stick up for (*informal*), keep safe, give sanctuary **2** SUPPORT, champion, justify, maintain, sustain, plead for, endorse, assert, stand by, uphold, vindicate, stand up for, espouse, speak up for, stick up for (*informal*)

defendant *noun* ACCUSED, respondent, appellant, litigant, prisoner at the bar

defender *noun* **1** SUPPORTER, champion, advocate, sponsor, follower, patron, apologist, upholder, vindicator **2** PROTECTOR, guard, guardian, escort, bodyguard, guardian angel

defensible *adjective* JUSTIFIABLE, right, sound, reasonable, acceptable, sensible, valid, legitimate, plausible, permissible, well-founded, tenable, excusable, pardonable, vindicable << ANTONYM unjustifiable

defensive *adjective* **1** PROTECTIVE, defending, opposing, safeguarding, watchful, on the defensive, on guard **2** OVERSENSITIVE, uptight (*informal*)

defensively *adverb* IN SELF-DEFENCE, in defence, suspiciously, on the defensive

defer¹ *verb* POSTPONE, delay, put off, suspend, shelve, set aside, adjourn, hold over, procrastinate, put on ice (*informal*), put on the back burner (*informal*), protract, take a rain check on (*US & Canad informal*), prorogue

defer² *with* **to** COMPLY WITH, give way to, submit to, bow to, give in to, yield to, accede to, capitulate to

deference *noun* **1** RESPECT, regard, consideration, attention, honour, esteem, courtesy, homage, reverence, politeness, civility, veneration, thoughtfulness << ANTONYM disrespect **2** OBEDIENCE, yielding, submission, compliance, capitulation, acquiescence, obeisance, complaisance << ANTONYM disobedience

deferential *adjective* RESPECTFUL, civil, polite, courteous, considerate, obedient, submissive, dutiful, ingratiating, reverential, obsequious, complaisant, obeisant, regardful

defiance *noun* RESISTANCE, challenge, opposition, confrontation, contempt, disregard, provocation, disobedience, insolence, insubordination, rebelliousness, recalcitrance, contumacy << ANTONYM obedience

defiant *adjective* RESISTING, challenging, rebellious, daring, aggressive, bold, provocative, audacious, recalcitrant, antagonistic, insolent, mutinous, disobedient, refractory, insubordinate, contumacious << ANTONYM obedient

deficiency *noun* **1** LACK, want, deficit, absence, shortage, deprivation, inadequacy, scarcity, dearth, privation, insufficiency, scantiness << ANTONYM sufficiency **2** FAILING, fault, weakness, defect, flaw, drawback, shortcoming, imperfection, frailty, demerit

deficient *adjective* **1** LACKING, wanting, needing, short, inadequate, insufficient, scarce, scant, meagre, skimpy, scanty, exiguous **2** UNSATISFACTORY, weak, flawed, inferior, impaired, faulty, incomplete, defective, imperfect

deficit *noun* SHORTFALL, shortage, deficiency, loss, default, arrears

defile *verb* **1** DEGRADE, stain, disgrace, sully, debase, dishonour, besmirch, smirch **2** DESECRATE, violate, contaminate, abuse, pollute, profane, dishonour, despoil, treat sacrilegiously **3** DIRTY, soil, contaminate, smear, pollute, taint, tarnish, make foul, smirch, befoul

define *verb* **1** MARK OUT, outline, limit, bound, delineate, circumscribe, demarcate, delimit **2** DESCRIBE, interpret, characterize, explain, spell out, expound **3** ESTABLISH, detail, determine, specify, designate

definite *adjective* **1** SPECIFIC, exact, precise, clear, particular, express, determined, fixed, black-and-white, explicit, clear-cut, cut-and-dried (*informal*), clearly defined << ANTONYM vague **2** CLEAR, explicit, black-and-white, clear-cut, unequivocal, unambiguous, guaranteed, cut-and-dried (*informal*) **3** NOTICEABLE, marked, clear, decided, striking, noted, particular, obvious, dramatic, considerable, remarkable, apparent, evident, distinct, notable, manifest, conspicuous **4** CERTAIN, decided, sure, settled, convinced, positive, confident, assured << ANTONYM uncertain

definitely *adverb* CERTAINLY, clearly, obviously, surely, easily, plainly, absolutely, positively, decidedly, needless to say, without doubt, unquestionably, undeniably, categorically, without question,

unequivocally, unmistakably, far and away, without fail, beyond any doubt, indubitably, come hell or high water (*informal*)

definition *noun* **1** DESCRIPTION, interpretation, explanation, clarification, exposition, explication, elucidation, statement of meaning **2** SHARPNESS, focus, clarity, contrast, precision, distinctness

definitive *adjective* **1** FINAL, convincing, absolute, clinching, decisive, definite, conclusive, irrefutable **2** AUTHORITATIVE, greatest, ultimate, reliable, most significant, exhaustive, superlative, mother of all (*informal*) ▷ see **definite**

deflate *verb* **1** HUMILIATE, humble, squash, put down (*slang*), disconcert, chasten, mortify, dispirit **2** PUNCTURE, flatten, empty << ANTONYM inflate **3** COLLAPSE, go down, contract, empty, shrink, void, flatten << ANTONYM expand **4** (*economics*) REDUCE, depress, decrease, diminish, devalue, depreciate

deflect *verb* TURN ASIDE, turn, bend, twist, sidetrack

deflection *noun* DEVIATION, bending, veering, swerving, divergence, turning aside, refraction, declination

deform *verb* **1** DISFIGURE, twist, injure, cripple, ruin, mar, spoil, mutilate, maim, deface **2** DISTORT, twist, warp, buckle, mangle, contort, gnarl, misshape, malform

deformation *noun* DISTORTION, warping, contortion, malformation, disfiguration, misshapenness

deformed *adjective* DISTORTED, bent, twisted, crooked, crippled, warped, maimed, marred, mangled, disfigured, misshapen, malformed, misbegotten

deformity *noun* **1** ABNORMALITY, defect, malformation, disfigurement **2** DISTORTION, irregularity, misshapenness, misproportion

defraud *verb* CHEAT, rob, con (*informal*), do (*slang*), skin (*slang*), stiff (*slang*), rip off (*slang*), fleece, swindle, stitch up (*slang*), rook (*slang*), diddle (*informal*), bilk, gyp (*slang*), pull a fast one on (*informal*), cozen

defray *verb* (used with *costs* or *expenses* as object) PAY, meet, cover, clear, settle, discharge

deft *adjective* SKILFUL, able, expert, clever, neat, handy, adept, nimble, proficient, agile, adroit, dexterous << ANTONYM clumsy

defunct *adjective* **1** DEAD, extinct, gone, departed, expired, deceased, bygone, nonexistent **2** NOT FUNCTIONING, obsolete, out of commission, inoperative

defuse *verb* 1 CALM, settle, cool, contain, smooth, stabilize, damp down, take the heat *or* sting out of << ANTONYM aggravate 2 DEACTIVATE, disable, disarm, make safe << ANTONYM activate ▷ see **diffuse**

defy *verb* 1 RESIST, oppose, confront, face, brave, beard, disregard, stand up to, spurn, flout, disobey, hold out against, put up a fight against, hurl defiance at, contemn 2 CHALLENGE, dare, provoke 3 FOIL, defeat, escape, frustrate, be beyond, baffle, thwart, elude, confound

degenerate *verb* DECLINE, slip, sink, decrease, deteriorate, worsen, rot, decay, lapse, fall off, regress, go to pot, retrogress ▷ *adjective* DEPRAVED, base, corrupt, fallen, low, perverted, degraded, degenerated, immoral, decadent, debased, debauched, dissolute, pervy (*slang*)

degeneration *noun* DETERIORATION, decline, dissolution, descent, regression, dissipation, degeneracy, debasement

degradation *noun* 1 DISGRACE, shame, humiliation, discredit, ignominy, dishonour, mortification 2 DETERIORATION, decline, decadence, degeneration, perversion, degeneracy, debasement, abasement

degrade *verb* 1 DEMEAN, disgrace, humiliate, injure, shame, corrupt, humble, discredit, pervert, debase, dishonour, cheapen << ANTONYM ennoble 2 DEMOTE, reduce, lower, downgrade, depose, cashier << ANTONYM promote

degraded *adjective* 1 HUMILIATED, embarrassed, shamed, mortified, debased, discomfited, abased 2 CORRUPT, low, base, abandoned, vicious, vile, sordid, decadent, despicable, depraved, debased, profligate, disreputable, debauched, dissolute, scungy (*Austral & NZ*)

degrading *adjective* DEMEANING, lowering, humiliating, disgraceful, shameful, unworthy, debasing, undignified, contemptible, cheapening, dishonourable, infra dig (*informal*)

degree *noun* 1 AMOUNT, measure, rate, stage, extent, grade, proportion, gradation 2 (*archaic*) RANK, order, standing, level, class, position, station, status, grade, caste, nobility, echelon ▷▷ **by degrees** LITTLE BY LITTLE, slowly, gradually, moderately, gently, piecemeal, bit by bit, imperceptibly, inch by inch, unhurriedly

dehydrate *verb* DRY, evaporate, parch, desiccate, exsiccate

deign *verb* CONDESCEND, consent, stoop, see fit, think fit, lower yourself, deem it worthy

deity *noun* GOD, goddess, immortal, divinity, godhead, divine being, supreme being, celestial being, atua (*NZ*)

dejected *adjective* DOWNHEARTED, down, low, blue, sad, depressed, miserable, gloomy, dismal, melancholy, glum, despondent, downcast, morose, disheartened, wretched, disconsolate, crestfallen, doleful, down in the dumps (*informal*), cast down, sick as a parrot (*informal*), woebegone, low-spirited << ANTONYM cheerful

delay *verb* 1 PUT OFF, suspend, postpone, stall, shelve, prolong, defer, hold over, temporize, put on the back burner (*informal*), protract, take a rain check on (*US & Canad informal*) 2 HOLD UP, detain, hold back, stop, arrest, halt, hinder, obstruct, retard, impede, bog down, set back, slow up << ANTONYM speed (up) 3 LINGER, lag, loiter, dawdle, tarry, dilly-dally (*informal*), drag your feet *or* heels (*informal*) ▷ *noun* 1 HOLD-UP, wait, check, setback, interruption, obstruction, stoppage, impediment, hindrance 2 DAWDLING, lingering, loitering, procrastination, tarrying, dilly-dallying (*informal*)

delectable *adjective* 1 DELICIOUS, tasty, luscious, inviting, satisfying, pleasant, delightful, enjoyable, lush, enticing, gratifying, dainty, yummy (*slang*), scrumptious (*informal*), appetizing, toothsome, lekker (*S African slang*), yummo (*Austral slang*) << ANTONYM disgusting 2 CHARMING, pleasant, delightful, agreeable, adorable

delegate *noun* REPRESENTATIVE, agent, deputy, ambassador, commissioner, envoy, proxy, depute (*Scot*), legate, spokesman *or* spokeswoman ▷ *verb* 1 ENTRUST, transfer, hand over, give, pass on, assign, relegate, consign, devolve 2 APPOINT, commission, select, contract, engage, nominate, designate, mandate, authorize, empower, accredit, depute

delegation *noun* 1 DEPUTATION, envoys, contingent, commission, embassy, legation 2 COMMISSIONING, relegation, assignment, devolution, committal, deputizing, entrustment

delete *verb* REMOVE, cancel, cut out, erase, edit, excise, strike out, obliterate, efface, blot out, cross out, expunge, dele, rub out, edit out, blue-pencil

deliberate *adjective* **1** INTENTIONAL, meant, planned, considered, studied, designed, intended, conscious, calculated, thoughtful, wilful, purposeful, premeditated, prearranged, done on purpose << ANTONYM accidental **2** CAREFUL, measured, slow, cautious, wary, thoughtful, prudent, circumspect, methodical, unhurried, heedful << ANTONYM hurried ▷ *verb* CONSIDER, think, ponder, discuss, debate, reflect, consult, weigh, meditate, mull over, ruminate, cogitate

deliberately *adverb* INTENTIONALLY, on purpose, consciously, emphatically, knowingly, resolutely, pointedly, determinedly, wilfully, by design, studiously, in cold blood, wittingly, calculatingly

deliberation *noun* **1** CONSIDERATION, thought, reflection, study, speculation, calculation, meditation, forethought, circumspection, cogitation **2** *usually plural* DISCUSSION, talk, conference, exchange, debate, analysis, conversation, dialogue, consultation, seminar, symposium, colloquy, confabulation

delicacy *noun* **1** FRAGILITY, frailty, brittleness, flimsiness, frailness, frangibility **2** DAINTINESS, charm, grace, elegance, neatness, prettiness, slenderness, exquisiteness **3** DIFFICULTY, sensitivity, stickiness (*informal*), precariousness, critical nature, touchiness, ticklishness **4** SENSITIVITY, understanding, consideration, judgment, perception, diplomacy, discretion, skill, finesse, tact, thoughtfulness, savoir-faire, adroitness, sensitiveness **5** TREAT, luxury, goody, savoury, dainty, morsel, titbit, choice item, juicy bit, bonne bouche (*French*) **6** LIGHTNESS, accuracy, precision, elegance, sensibility, purity, subtlety, refinement, finesse, nicety, fineness, exquisiteness

delicate *adjective* **1** FINE, detailed, elegant, exquisite, graceful **2** SUBTLE, fine, nice, soft, delicious, faint, refined, muted, subdued, pastel, understated, dainty << ANTONYM bright **3** FRAGILE, weak, frail, brittle, tender, flimsy, dainty, breakable, frangible << ANTONYM strong **4** DIFFICULT, critical, sensitive, complicated, sticky (*informal*), problematic, precarious, thorny, touchy, knotty, ticklish **5** SKILLED, accurate, precise, deft **6** FASTIDIOUS, nice, critical, pure, Victorian, proper, refined, discriminating, stuffy, scrupulous, prim, puritanical,

squeamish, prudish, prissy (*informal*), strait-laced, schoolmarmish (*Brit informal*), old-maidish (*informal*) << ANTONYM crude **7** DIPLOMATIC, sensitive, careful, subtle, thoughtful, discreet, prudent, considerate, judicious, tactful << ANTONYM insensitive

delicately *adverb* **1** FINELY, lightly, subtly, softly, carefully, precisely, elegantly, gracefully, deftly, exquisitely, skilfully, daintily **2** TACTFULLY, carefully, subtly, discreetly, thoughtfully, diplomatically, sensitively, prudently, judiciously, considerately

delicious *adjective* **1** DELECTABLE, tasty, luscious, choice, savoury, palatable, dainty, mouthwatering, yummy (*slang*), scrumptious (*informal*), appetizing, toothsome, ambrosial, lekker (*S African slang*), nectareous, yummo (*Austral slang*) << ANTONYM unpleasant **2** DELIGHTFUL, pleasing, charming, heavenly, thrilling, entertaining, pleasant, enjoyable, exquisite, captivating, agreeable, pleasurable, rapturous, delectable

delight *verb* PLEASE, satisfy, content, thrill, charm, cheer, amuse, divert, enchant, rejoice, gratify, ravish, gladden, give pleasure to, tickle pink (*informal*) << ANTONYM displease ▷ *noun* PLEASURE, joy, satisfaction, comfort, happiness, ecstasy, enjoyment, bliss, felicity, glee, gratification, rapture, gladness << ANTONYM displeasure
▷▷ **delight in** *or* **take (a) delight in something** *or* **someone** LIKE, love, enjoy, appreciate, relish, indulge in, savour, revel in, take pleasure in, glory in, luxuriate in

delighted *adjective* PLEASED, happy, charmed, thrilled, enchanted, ecstatic, captivated, jubilant, joyous, elated, over the moon (*informal*), overjoyed, rapt, gladdened, cock-a-hoop, blissed out, in seventh heaven, sent, stoked (*Austral & NZ informal*)

delightful *adjective* PLEASANT, pleasing, charming, engaging, heavenly, thrilling, fascinating, entertaining, amusing, enjoyable, enchanting, captivating, gratifying, agreeable, pleasurable, ravishing, rapturous << ANTONYM unpleasant

delineate *verb* OUTLINE, describe, draw, picture, paint, chart, trace, portray, sketch, render, depict, characterize, map out

delinquency *noun* CRIME, misconduct, wrongdoing, fault, offence, misdemeanour, misdeed, misbehaviour, villainy, lawbreaking

delinquent *noun* CRIMINAL, offender,

villain, culprit, young offender, wrongdoer,
juvenile delinquent, miscreant, malefactor,
lawbreaker

delirious *adjective* **1** MAD, crazy, raving, insane,
demented, deranged, incoherent, unhinged,
light-headed << ANTONYM rational
2 ECSTATIC, wild, excited, frantic, frenzied,
hysterical, carried away, blissed out, beside
yourself, sent, Corybantic << ANTONYM
calm

delirium *noun* **1** MADNESS, raving, insanity,
lunacy, derangement **2** FRENZY, passion,
rage, fever, fury, ecstasy, hysteria

deliver *verb* **1** BRING, carry, bear, transport,
distribute, convey, cart **2** *sometimes with* **over**
or **up** HAND OVER, present, commit, give
up, yield, surrender, turn over, relinquish,
make over **3** GIVE, read, present, announce,
publish, declare, proclaim, pronounce, utter,
give forth **4** STRIKE, give, deal, launch, throw,
direct, aim, administer, inflict **5** RELEASE,
free, save, rescue, loose, discharge, liberate,
acquit, redeem, ransom, emancipate

deliverance *noun* RELEASE, rescue,
liberation, salvation, redemption, ransom,
emancipation

delivery *noun* **1** HANDING OVER, transfer,
distribution, transmission, dispatch,
consignment, conveyance, transmittal
2 CONSIGNMENT, goods, shipment,
batch **3** SPEECH, speaking, expression,
pronunciation, utterance, articulation,
intonation, diction, elocution, enunciation,
vocalization **4** CHILDBIRTH, labour,
confinement, parturition

delude *verb* DECEIVE, kid (*informal*), fool,
trick, take in (*informal*), cheat, con (*informal*),
mislead, impose on, hoax, dupe, beguile,
gull (*archaic*), bamboozle (*informal*),
hoodwink, take someone for a ride
(*informal*), pull the wool over someone's eyes,
lead someone up the garden path (*informal*),
cozen, misguide

deluge *noun* **1** RUSH, flood, avalanche, barrage,
spate, torrent **2** FLOOD, spate, overflowing,
torrent, downpour, cataclysm, inundation ▷
verb **1** OVERWHELM, swamp, engulf, overload,
overrun, inundate **2** FLOOD, drown, swamp,
submerge, soak, drench, inundate, douse

delusion *noun* MISCONCEPTION, mistaken
idea, misapprehension, fancy, illusion,
deception, hallucination, fallacy, self-
deception, false impression, phantasm,
misbelief

deluxe *or* **de luxe** *adjective* LUXURIOUS, grand,

select, special, expensive, rich, exclusive,
superior, elegant, costly, splendid, gorgeous,
sumptuous, plush (*informal*), opulent,
palatial, splendiferous (*facetious*)

delve *verb* **1** RESEARCH, investigate, explore,
examine, probe, look into, burrow into,
dig into **2** RUMMAGE, search, look, burrow,
ransack, forage, dig, fossick (*Austral & NZ*)

demagogue *noun* AGITATOR, firebrand,
haranguer, rabble-rouser, soapbox orator

demand *verb* **1** REQUEST, ask (for), order,
expect, claim, seek, call for, insist on,
exact, appeal for, solicit **2** CHALLENGE, ask,
question, inquire **3** REQUIRE, take, want,
need, involve, call for, entail, necessitate,
cry out for << ANTONYM provide ▷ *noun*
1 REQUEST, order, charge, bidding **2** NEED,
want, call, market, claim, requirement,
necessity ▷▷ **in demand** SOUGHT AFTER,
needed, popular, favoured, requested, in
favour, fashionable, well-liked, in vogue, like
gold dust

demanding *adjective* DIFFICULT, trying,
hard, taxing, wearing, challenging, tough,
exhausting, exacting, exigent << ANTONYM
easy

demarcation *noun* **1** LIMIT, bound, margin,
boundary, confine, enclosure, pale
2 DELIMITATION, division, distinction,
separation, differentiation

demean *verb* DEGRADE, lower, debase,
humble, abase ▷▷ **demean yourself** LOWER
YOURSELF, humiliate yourself, humble
yourself, debase yourself, downgrade
yourself, abase yourself, belittle yourself,
degrade yourself

demeanour *or* US **demeanor** *noun*
1 BEHAVIOUR, conduct, manner **2** BEARING,
air, manner, carriage, deportment, mien,
comportment

demented *adjective* MAD, crazy, foolish, daft
(*informal*), frenzied, distraught, manic,
insane, crazed, lunatic, unbalanced,
deranged, idiotic, unhinged, dotty (*slang*,
chiefly Brit), loopy (*informal*), crackpot
(*informal*), out to lunch (*informal*), barking
mad (*slang*), barking (*slang*), maniacal,
gonzo (*slang*), doolally (*slang*), off your
trolley (*slang*), up the pole (*informal*), non
compos mentis (*Latin*), not the full shilling
(*informal*), crackbrained, wacko *or* whacko
(*slang*), off the air (*Austral slang*), porangi (*NZ*)
<< ANTONYM sane

demise *noun* **1** FAILURE, end, fall, defeat,
collapse, ruin, breakdown, overthrow,

downfall, dissolution, termination
2 (*euphemistic*) DEATH, end, dying, passing, departure, expiration, decease

democracy *noun* SELF-GOVERNMENT, republic, commonwealth, representative government, government by the people

Democrat *noun* LEFT-WINGER

democratic *adjective* SELF-GOVERNING, popular, republican, representative, autonomous, populist, egalitarian

demolish *verb* **1** KNOCK DOWN, level, destroy, ruin, overturn, dismantle, flatten, trash (*slang*), total (*slang*), tear down, bulldoze, raze, pulverize << ANTONYM build **2** DESTROY, wreck, overturn, overthrow, undo, blow out of the water (*slang*) **3** (*facetious*) DEVOUR, eat, consume, swallow, bolt, gorge, put away, gobble up, guzzle, polish off (*informal*), gulp down, wolf down, pig out on (*slang*)

demolition *noun* KNOCKING DOWN, levelling, destruction, explosion, wrecking, tearing down, bulldozing, razing

demon *noun* **1** EVIL SPIRIT, devil, fiend, goblin, ghoul, malignant spirit, atua (*NZ*), wairua (*NZ*) **2** WIZARD, master, ace (*informal*), addict, fanatic, fiend **3** MONSTER, beast, villain, rogue, barbarian, brute, ogre

demoniac, demonic *or* **demoniacal** *adjective* **1** DEVILISH, satanic, diabolical, hellish, infernal, fiendish, diabolic **2** FRENZIED, mad, furious, frantic, hectic, manic, crazed, frenetic, maniacal, like one possessed

demonstrable *adjective* PROVABLE, obvious, evident, certain, positive, unmistakable, palpable, undeniable, self-evident, verifiable, irrefutable, incontrovertible, axiomatic, indubitable, attestable, evincible

demonstrate *verb* **1** PROVE, show, establish, indicate, make clear, manifest, evidence, testify to, evince, show clearly **2** SHOW, evidence, express, display, indicate, exhibit, manifest, make clear *or* plain **3** MARCH, protest, rally, object, parade, picket, say no to, remonstrate, take up the cudgels, express disapproval, hikoi (*NZ*) **4** DESCRIBE, show, explain, teach, illustrate

demonstration *noun* **1** MARCH, protest, rally, sit-in, parade, procession, demo (*informal*), picket, mass lobby, hikoi (*NZ*) **2** DISPLAY, show, performance, explanation, description, presentation, demo (*informal*), exposition **3** INDICATION, proof, testimony, confirmation, affirmation, validation, substantiation, attestation **4** EXHIBITION, display, expression, illustration

demoralize *verb* DISHEARTEN, undermine, discourage, shake, depress, weaken, rattle (*informal*), daunt, unnerve, disconcert, psych out (*informal*), dispirit, deject << ANTONYM encourage

demoralized *adjective* DISHEARTENED, undermined, discouraged, broken, depressed, crushed, weakened, subdued, unnerved, unmanned, dispirited, downcast, sick as a parrot (*informal*)

demoralizing *adjective* DISHEARTENING, discouraging, depressing, crushing, disappointing, daunting, dampening, dispiriting << ANTONYM encouraging

demote *verb* DOWNGRADE, relegate, degrade, kick downstairs (*slang*), declass, disrate (*naval*), lower in rank << ANTONYM promote

demur *verb* OBJECT, refuse, protest, doubt, dispute, pause, disagree, hesitate, waver, balk, take exception, cavil ▷ *noun* (always used in a negative construction) OBJECTION, protest, dissent, hesitation, misgiving, qualm, scruple, compunction, demurral, demurrer

demure *adjective* (usually used of a young woman) SHY, reserved, modest, retiring, reticent, unassuming, diffident, decorous << ANTONYM brazen

den *noun* **1** LAIR, hole, shelter, cave, haunt, cavern, hide-out **2** (*Chiefly US*) STUDY, retreat, sanctuary, hideaway, cloister, sanctum, cubbyhole, snuggery

denial *noun* **1** NEGATION, dismissal, contradiction, dissent, disclaimer, retraction, repudiation, disavowal, adjuration << ANTONYM admission **2** REFUSAL, veto, rejection, prohibition, rebuff, repulse

denigrate *verb* DISPARAGE, run down, slag (off) (*slang*), knock (*informal*), rubbish (*informal*), blacken, malign, belittle, decry, revile, vilify, slander, defame, bad-mouth (*slang, chiefly US & Canad*), besmirch, impugn, calumniate, asperse << ANTONYM praise

denizen *noun* INHABITANT, resident, citizen, occupant, dweller

denomination *noun* **1** RELIGIOUS GROUP, belief, sect, persuasion, creed, school, hauhau (*NZ*) **2** UNIT, value, size, grade

denote *verb* INDICATE, show, mean, mark, express, import, imply, designate, signify, typify, betoken

denouement *or* **dénouement** *noun* OUTCOME, end, result, consequence, resolution, conclusion, end result, upshot

denounce *verb* 1 CONDEMN, attack, censure, decry, castigate, revile, vilify, proscribe, stigmatize, impugn, excoriate, declaim against 2 REPORT, dob in (*Austral slang*)

dense *adjective* 1 THICK, close, heavy, solid, substantial, compact, compressed, condensed, impenetrable, close-knit, thickset << ANTONYM thin 2 HEAVY, thick, substantial, opaque, impenetrable 3 (*informal*) STUPID, slow, thick, dull, dumb (*informal*), crass, dozy (*Brit informal*), dozy (*Brit informal*), stolid, dopey (*informal*), moronic, obtuse, brainless, blockheaded, braindead (*informal*), dumb-ass (*informal*), dead from the neck up (*informal*), thickheaded, blockish, dim-witted (*informal*), slow-witted, thick-witted << ANTONYM bright

density *noun* 1 TIGHTNESS, closeness, thickness, compactness, impenetrability, denseness, crowdedness 2 MASS, body, bulk, consistency, solidity

dent *noun* HOLLOW, chip, indentation, depression, impression, pit, dip, crater, ding (*Austral & NZ dated informal*), dimple, concavity ▷ *verb* MAKE A DENT IN, press in, gouge, depress, hollow, imprint, push in, dint, make concave

denude *verb* STRIP, expose, bare, uncover, divest, lay bare

denunciation *noun* 1 CONDEMNATION, criticism, accusation, censure, stick (*slang*), invective, character assassination, stigmatization, castigation, obloquy, denouncement, fulmination 2 IMPLICATION, accusation, indictment, incrimination, denouncement, inculpation

deny *verb* 1 CONTRADICT, oppose, counter, disagree with, rebuff, negate, rebut, refute, gainsay (*archaic or literary*) << ANTONYM admit 2 RENOUNCE, reject, discard, revoke, retract, repudiate, renege, disown, rebut, disavow, recant, disclaim, abjure, abnegate, refuse to acknowledge *or* recognize 3 REFUSE, decline, forbid, reject, rule out, veto, turn down, prohibit, withhold, preclude, disallow, negate, begrudge, interdict << ANTONYM permit

deodorant *noun* 1 ANTIPERSPIRANT, deodorizer 2 DEODORIZER, disinfectant, air freshener, fumigant

depart *verb* 1 LEAVE, go, withdraw, retire, disappear, quit, retreat, exit, go away, vanish, absent (yourself), start out, migrate, set forth, take (your) leave, decamp, hook it (*slang*), slope off, pack your bags (*informal*),

make tracks, rack off (*Austral & NZ slang*) << ANTONYM arrive 2 DEVIATE, vary, differ, stray, veer, swerve, diverge, digress, turn aside 3 (*Chiefly US*) RESIGN, leave, quit, step down (*informal*), give in your notice, call it a day *or* night, vacate your post

departed *adjective* (*euphemistic*) DEAD, late, deceased, expired, perished

department *noun* 1 SECTION, office, unit, station, division, branch, bureau, subdivision 2 (*informal*) AREA, line, responsibility, function, province, sphere, realm, domain, speciality

departure *noun* 1 LEAVING, going, retirement, withdrawal, exit, going away, removal, exodus, leave-taking << ANTONYM arrival 2 RETIREMENT, going, withdrawal, exit, going away, removal 3 SHIFT, change, difference, variation, innovation, novelty, veering, deviation, branching out, divergence, digression

dependable *adjective* RELIABLE, sure, responsible, steady, faithful, staunch, reputable, trustworthy, trusty, unfailing << ANTONYM undependable

dependant *noun* RELATIVE, rellie (*Austral slang*), child, minor, subordinate, cohort (*chiefly US*), protégé, henchman, retainer, hanger-on, minion, vassal

dependence *or sometimes US* **dependance** *noun* RELIANCE, trust, hope, confidence, belief, faith, expectation, assurance

dependency *or sometimes US* **dependancy** *noun* 1 OVERRELIANCE, attachment 2 ADDICTION, dependence, craving, need, habit, obsession, enslavement, overreliance

dependent *or sometimes US* **dependant** *adjective* 1 RELIANT, vulnerable, helpless, powerless, weak, defenceless << ANTONYM independent 2 DETERMINED BY, depending on, subject to, influenced by, relative to, liable to, conditional on, contingent on ▷▷ **dependent on** *or* **upon** RELIANT ON, relying on, counting on ▷ see **dependant**

depend on *verb* 1 BE DETERMINED BY, be based on, be subject to, hang on, rest on, revolve around, hinge on, be subordinate to, be contingent on 2 COUNT ON, turn to, trust in, bank on, lean on, rely upon, confide in, build upon, calculate on, reckon on

depict *verb* 1 ILLUSTRATE, portray, picture, paint, outline, draw, sketch, render, reproduce, sculpt, delineate, limn 2 DESCRIBE, present, represent, detail, outline, sketch, characterize

depiction *noun* 1 PICTURE, drawing, image, outline, illustration, sketch, likeness, delineation 2 REPRESENTATION, description, portrait, illustration, sketch, portrayal

deplete *verb* USE UP, reduce, drain, exhaust, consume, empty, decrease, evacuate, lessen, impoverish, expend << ANTONYM increase

depleted *adjective* USED (UP), drained, exhausted, consumed, spent, reduced, emptied, weakened, decreased, lessened, worn out, depreciated

depletion *noun* USING UP, reduction, drain, consumption, lowering, decrease, expenditure, deficiency, dwindling, lessening, exhaustion, diminution

deplorable *adjective* 1 TERRIBLE, distressing, dreadful, sad, unfortunate, disastrous, miserable, dire, melancholy, heartbreaking, grievous, regrettable, lamentable, calamitous, wretched, pitiable << ANTONYM excellent 2 DISGRACEFUL, shameful, scandalous, reprehensible, disreputable, dishonourable, execrable, blameworthy, opprobrious << ANTONYM admirable

deplore *verb* 1 DISAPPROVE OF, condemn, object to, denounce, censure, abhor, deprecate, take a dim view of, excoriate 2 LAMENT, regret, mourn, rue, bemoan, grieve for, bewail, sorrow over

deploy *verb* (used of troops or military resources) USE, station, set up, position, arrange, set out, dispose, utilize, spread out, distribute

deployment *noun* (used of troops or military resources) USE, stationing, spread, organization, arrangement, positioning, disposition, setup, utilization

deport *verb* EXPEL, exile, throw out, oust, banish, expatriate, extradite, evict, send packing, show you the door

deportation *noun* EXPULSION, exile, removal, transportation, exclusion, extradition, eviction, ejection, banishment, expatriation, debarment

depose *verb* OUST, dismiss, displace, degrade, downgrade, cashier, demote, dethrone, remove from office

deposit *verb* 1 PUT, place, lay, drop, settle 2 STORE, keep, put, bank, save, lodge, entrust, consign, hoard, stash (*informal*), lock away, put in storage ▷ *noun* 1 DOWN PAYMENT, security, stake, pledge, warranty, instalment, retainer, part payment 2 ACCUMULATION, growth, mass, build-up, layer 3 SEDIMENT, grounds, residue, lees, precipitate,

deposition, silt, dregs, alluvium, settlings

deposition *noun* 1 (*law*) SWORN STATEMENT, evidence, testimony, declaration, affidavit 2 REMOVAL, dismissal, ousting, toppling, expulsion, displacement, unseating, dethronement

depository *noun* STOREHOUSE, store, warehouse, depot, repository, safe-deposit box

depot *noun* 1 ARSENAL, warehouse, storehouse, repository, depository, dump 2 (*US & Canad*) BUS STATION, station, garage, terminus

deprave *verb* CORRUPT, pervert, degrade, seduce, subvert, debase, demoralize, debauch, brutalize, lead astray, vitiate

depraved *adjective* CORRUPT, abandoned, perverted, evil, vicious, degraded, vile, degenerate, immoral, wicked, shameless, sinful, lewd, debased, profligate, debauched, lascivious, dissolute, licentious, pervy (*slang*) << ANTONYM moral

depravity *noun* CORRUPTION, vice, evil, criminality, wickedness, immorality, iniquity, profligacy, debauchery, viciousness, degeneracy, sinfulness, debasement, turpitude, baseness, depravation, vitiation

deprecate *verb* DISPARAGE, criticize, run down, discredit, scorn, deride, detract, malign, denigrate, belittle, vilify, depreciate, knock (*informal*), diss (*slang, chiefly US*), bad-mouth (*slang, chiefly US & Canad*), lambast(e) ▷ see **depreciate**

depreciate *verb* 1 DECREASE, reduce, lessen, devalue, deflate, lower in value, devaluate << ANTONYM augment 2 LOSE VALUE, devalue, devaluate << ANTONYM appreciate

depreciation *noun* DEVALUATION, fall, drop, depression, slump, deflation

depress *verb* 1 SADDEN, upset, distress, chill, discourage, grieve, daunt, oppress, desolate, weigh down, cast down, bring tears to your eyes, make sad, dishearten, dispirit, make your heart bleed, aggrieve, deject, make despondent, cast a gloom upon << ANTONYM cheer 2 LOWER, cut, reduce, diminish, decrease, impair, lessen << ANTONYM raise 3 DEVALUE, depreciate, cheapen, devaluate 4 PRESS DOWN, push, squeeze, lower, flatten, compress, push down, bear down on

depressed *adjective* 1 SAD, down, low, blue, unhappy, discouraged, fed up, moody, gloomy, pessimistic, melancholy, sombre, glum, mournful, dejected, despondent, dispirited, downcast, morose, disconsolate, crestfallen, doleful, downhearted, heavy-hearted, down in the dumps (*informal*), cheerless, woebegone, down in the mouth (*informal*), low-spirited 2 POVERTY-STRICKEN, poor, deprived, distressed, disadvantaged, run-down, impoverished, needy, destitute, down at heel 3 LOWERED, devalued, weakened, impaired, depreciated, cheapened 4 SUNKEN, hollow, recessed, set back, indented, concave

depressing *adjective* BLEAK, black, sad, distressing, discouraging, gloomy, daunting, hopeless, dismal, melancholy, dreary, harrowing, saddening, sombre, heartbreaking, dispiriting, disheartening, funereal, dejecting

depression *noun* 1 DESPAIR, misery, sadness, dumps (*informal*), the blues, melancholy, unhappiness, hopelessness, despondency, the hump (*Brit informal*), bleakness, melancholia, dejection, wretchedness, low spirits, gloominess, dolefulness, cheerlessness, downheartedness 2 RECESSION, slump, economic decline, stagnation, inactivity, hard *or* bad times 3 HOLLOW, pit, dip, bowl, valley, sink, impression, dent, sag, cavity, excavation, indentation, dimple, concavity

deprivation *noun* 1 LACK, denial, withdrawal, removal, expropriation, divestment, dispossession, deprival 2 WANT, need, hardship, suffering, distress, disadvantage, oppression, detriment, privation, destitution

deprive *verb* DISPOSSESS, rob, strip, divest, expropriate, despoil, bereave

deprived *adjective* POOR, disadvantaged, needy, in need, lacking, bereft, destitute, in want, denuded, down at heel, necessitous << ANTONYM prosperous

depth *noun* 1 DEEPNESS, drop, measure, extent, profundity, profoundness 2 STRENGTH, intensity, seriousness, severity, extremity, keenness, intenseness 3 INSIGHT, intelligence, wisdom, penetration, profundity, acuity, discernment, perspicacity, sagacity, astuteness, profoundness, perspicuity << ANTONYM superficiality 4 BREADTH, degree, magnitude, amplitude 5 INTENSITY, strength, warmth, richness, brightness, vibrancy, vividness 6 COMPLEXITY, intricacy, elaboration, obscurity, abstruseness, reconditeness ▷ *plural noun* 1 DEEPEST PART,

middle, midst, remotest part, furthest part, innermost part 2 MOST INTENSE PART, pit, void, abyss, chasm, deepest part, furthest part, bottomless depth

deputy *noun* SUBSTITUTE, representative, ambassador, agent, commissioner, delegate, lieutenant, proxy, surrogate, second-in-command, nuncio, legate, vicegerent, number two ▷ *modifier* ASSISTANT, subordinate, depute (*Scot*)

deranged *adjective* MAD, crazy, insane, distracted, frantic, frenzied, irrational, maddened, crazed, lunatic, demented, unbalanced, berserk, delirious, unhinged, loopy (*informal*), crackpot (*informal*), out to lunch (*informal*), barking mad (*slang*), barking (*slang*), gonzo (*slang*), doolally (*slang*), off your trolley (*slang*), up the pole (*informal*), not the full shilling (*informal*), wacko *or* whacko (*slang*), berko (*Austral slang*), off the air (*Austral slang*), porangi (*NZ*) << ANTONYM sane

derelict *adjective* 1 ABANDONED, deserted, ruined, neglected, discarded, forsaken, dilapidated 2 (only used with *duty*) NEGLIGENT, slack, irresponsible, careless, lax, remiss ▷ *noun* TRAMP, bum (*informal*), outcast, drifter, down-and-out, vagrant, hobo (*chiefly US*), vagabond, bag lady, dosser (*Brit slang*), derro (*Austral slang*)

dereliction *noun* 1 ABANDONMENT, desertion, renunciation, relinquishment 2 (only used with *duty*) NEGLIGENCE, failure, neglect, evasion, delinquency, abdication, faithlessness, nonperformance, remissness

deride *verb* MOCK, ridicule, scorn, knock (*informal*), insult, taunt, sneer, jeer, disdain, scoff, detract, flout, disparage, chaff, gibe, pooh-pooh, contemn

derision *noun* MOCKERY, laughter, contempt, ridicule, scorn, insult, sneering, disdain, scoffing, disrespect, denigration, disparagement, contumely, raillery

derisory *adjective* RIDICULOUS, insulting, outrageous, ludicrous, preposterous, laughable, contemptible

derivation *noun* ORIGIN, source, basis, beginning, root, foundation, descent, ancestry, genealogy, etymology

derivative *adjective* UNORIGINAL, copied, second-hand, rehashed, imitative, plagiarized, uninventive, plagiaristic << ANTONYM original ▷ *noun* BY-PRODUCT, spin-off, offshoot, descendant, derivation, outgrowth

derive *verb* OBTAIN, get, receive, draw, gain, collect, gather, extract, elicit, glean, procure ▷▷ **derive from something** COME FROM, stem from, arise from, flow from, spring from, emanate from, proceed from, descend from, issue from, originate from

derogatory *adjective* DISPARAGING, damaging, offensive, slighting, detracting, belittling, unfavourable, unflattering, dishonouring, defamatory, injurious, discreditable, uncomplimentary, depreciative << ANTONYM complimentary

descend *verb* 1 FALL, drop, sink, go down, plunge, dive, tumble, plummet, subside, move down << ANTONYM rise 2 GO DOWN, come down, walk down, move down, climb down 3 SLOPE, dip, incline, slant, gravitate ▷▷ **be descended from** ORIGINATE FROM, derive from, spring from, proceed from, issue from ▷▷ **descend on something** *or* **someone** ATTACK, assault, raid, invade, swoop, pounce, assail, arrive, come in force ▷▷ **descend to something** LOWER YOURSELF TO, stoop to, condescend to, abase yourself by

descendant *noun* SUCCESSOR, child, issue, son, daughter, heir, offspring, progeny, scion, inheritor << ANTONYM ancestor

descent *noun* 1 FALL, drop, plunge, coming down, swoop 2 SLOPE, drop, dip, incline, slant, declination, declivity 3 DECLINE, deterioration, degradation, decadence, degeneration, debasement 4 ORIGIN, extraction, ancestry, lineage, family tree, parentage, heredity, genealogy, derivation

describe *verb* 1 RELATE, tell, report, present, detail, explain, express, illustrate, specify, chronicle, recount, recite, impart, narrate, set forth, give an account of 2 PORTRAY, depict, characterize, define, sketch 3 TRACE, draw, outline, mark out, delineate

description *noun* 1 ACCOUNT, report, explanation, representation, sketch, narrative, portrayal, depiction, narration, characterization, delineation 2 CALLING, naming, branding, labelling, dubbing, designation 3 KIND, sort, type, order, class, variety, brand, species, breed, category, kidney, genre, genus, ilk

descriptive *adjective* GRAPHIC, vivid, expressive, picturesque, detailed, explanatory, pictorial, illustrative, depictive

desecrate *verb* PROFANE, dishonour, defile, violate, contaminate, pollute, pervert, despoil, blaspheme, commit sacrilege

<< ANTONYM revere

desert[1] *noun* WILDERNESS, waste, wilds, wasteland ▷ *adjective* BARREN, dry, waste, wild, empty, bare, lonely, solitary, desolate, arid, unproductive, infertile, uninhabited, uncultivated, unfruitful, untilled

desert[2] *verb* 1 ABANDON, leave, give up, quit (*informal*), withdraw from, move out of, relinquish, renounce, vacate, forsake, go away from, leave empty, relinquish possession of 2 LEAVE, abandon, strand, betray, maroon, walk out on (*informal*), forsake, jilt, run out on (*informal*), throw over, leave stranded, leave high and dry, leave (someone) in the lurch << ANTONYM take care of 3 ABSCOND, defect, decamp, go over the hill (*military slang*)

deserted *adjective* 1 EMPTY, abandoned, desolate, neglected, lonely, vacant, derelict, bereft, unoccupied, godforsaken 2 ABANDONED, neglected, forsaken, lonely, forlorn, cast off, left stranded, left in the lurch, unfriended

deserter *noun* DEFECTOR, runaway, fugitive, traitor, renegade, truant, escapee, absconder, apostate

desertion *noun* 1 ABANDONMENT, betrayal, forsaking, dereliction, relinquishment 2 DEFECTION, apostasy 3 ABSCONDING, flight, escape (*informal*), evasion, truancy

deserts ▷▷ **just deserts** DUE, payment, reward, punishment, right, return, retribution, recompense, come-uppance (*slang*), meed (*archaic*), requital, guerdon (*poetic*)

deserve *verb* MERIT, warrant, be entitled to, have a right to, win, rate, earn, justify, be worthy of, have a claim to

deserved *adjective* WELL-EARNED, just, right, meet (*archaic*), fitting, due, fair, earned, appropriate, justified, suitable, merited, proper, warranted, rightful, justifiable, condign

deservedly *adverb* RIGHTLY, fittingly, fairly, appropriately, properly, duly, justifiably, justly, by rights, rightfully, according to your due, condignly << ANTONYM undeservedly

deserving *adjective* WORTHY, righteous, commendable, laudable, praiseworthy, meritorious, estimable << ANTONYM undeserving

design *verb* 1 PLAN, describe, draw, draft, trace, outline, invent, devise, sketch, formulate, contrive, think out, delineate 2 CREATE, make, plan, project, fashion, scheme, propose, invent, devise, tailor, draw up, conceive, originate, contrive, fabricate, think up **3** INTEND, mean, plan, aim, purpose ▷ noun **1** PATTERN, form, figure, style, shape, organization, arrangement, construction, motif, configuration **2** PLAN, drawing, model, scheme, draft, outline, sketch, blueprint, delineation **3** INTENTION, end, point, aim, goal, target, purpose, object, objective, intent

designate *verb* **1** NAME, call, term, style, label, entitle, dub, nominate, christen **2** SPECIFY, describe, indicate, define, characterize, stipulate, denote **3** CHOOSE, reserve, select, label, flag, assign, allocate, set aside **4** APPOINT, name, choose, commission, select, elect, delegate, nominate, assign, depute

designation *noun* **1** NAME, title, label, description, denomination, epithet **2** APPOINTMENT, specification, classification **3** ELECTION, choice, selection, appointment, nomination

designer *noun* **1** COUTURIER, stylist **2** PRODUCER, architect, deviser, creator, planner, inventor, artificer, originator

designing *adjective* SCHEMING, plotting, intriguing, crooked (*informal*), shrewd, conspiring, cunning, sly, astute, treacherous, unscrupulous, devious, wily, crafty, artful, conniving, Machiavellian, deceitful

desirability *noun* WORTH, value, benefit, profit, advantage, merit, usefulness

desirable *adjective* **1** ADVANTAGEOUS, useful, valuable, helpful, profitable, of service, convenient, worthwhile, beneficial, preferable, advisable << ANTONYM disadvantageous **2** POPULAR << ANTONYM unpopular **3** ATTRACTIVE, appealing, beautiful, winning, interesting, pleasing, pretty, fair, inviting, engaging, lovely, charming, fascinating, sexy (*informal*), handsome, fetching, good-looking, eligible, glamorous, gorgeous, magnetic, cute, enticing, seductive, captivating, alluring, adorable, bonny, winsome, comely << ANTONYM unattractive

desire *verb* **1** WANT, long for, crave, fancy, hope for, ache for, covet, aspire to, wish for, yearn for, thirst for, hanker after, set your heart on, desiderate **2** (*formal*) REQUEST, ask, petition, solicit, entreat, importune ▷ noun **1** WISH, want, longing, need, hope, urge, yen (*informal*), hunger, appetite, aspiration, ache, craving, yearning, inclination, thirst, hankering **2** LUST, passion, libido, appetite, lechery, carnality, lasciviousness, concupiscence, randiness (*informal, chiefly Brit*), lustfulness

desired *adjective* REQUIRED, necessary, correct, appropriate, right, expected, fitting, particular, express, accurate, proper, exact

desist *verb* STOP, cease, refrain from, end, kick (*informal*), give up, suspend, break off, abstain, discontinue, leave off, have done with, give over (*informal*), forbear, belay (*nautical*)

desolate *adjective* **1** UNINHABITED, deserted, bare, waste, wild, ruined, bleak, solitary, barren, dreary, godforsaken, unfrequented << ANTONYM inhabited **2** MISERABLE, depressed, lonely, lonesome (*chiefly US & Canad*), gloomy, dismal, melancholy, forlorn, bereft, dejected, despondent, downcast, wretched, disconsolate, down in the dumps (*informal*), cheerless, comfortless, companionless << ANTONYM happy ▷ verb **1** DEJECT, depress, distress, discourage, dismay, grieve, daunt, dishearten << ANTONYM cheer **2** DESTROY, ruin, devastate, ravage, lay low, lay waste, despoil, depopulate

desolation *noun* **1** MISERY, distress, despair, gloom, sadness, woe, anguish, melancholy, unhappiness, dejection, wretchedness, gloominess **2** BLEAKNESS, isolation, loneliness, solitude, wildness, barrenness, solitariness, forlornness, desolateness **3** RUIN, destruction, havoc, devastation, ruination

despair *verb* LOSE HOPE, give up, lose heart, be despondent, be dejected ▷ noun DESPONDENCY, depression, misery, gloom, desperation, anguish, melancholy, hopelessness, dejection, wretchedness, disheartenment

despairing *adjective* HOPELESS, desperate, depressed, anxious, miserable, frantic, dismal, suicidal, melancholy, dejected, broken-hearted, despondent, downcast, grief-stricken, wretched, disconsolate, inconsolable, down in the dumps (*informal*), at the end of your tether

despatch ▷ see **dispatch**

desperado *noun* CRIMINAL, thug, outlaw, villain, gangster, gunman, bandit, mugger (*informal*), cut-throat, hoodlum (*chiefly US*), ruffian, heavy (*slang*), lawbreaker, skelm (*S African*)

desperate *adjective* **1** HOPELESS, despairing, in despair, forlorn, abject, dejected,

despondent, demoralized, wretched,
disconsolate, inconsolable, downhearted,
at the end of your tether **2** GRAVE, great,
pressing, serious, critical, acute, severe,
extreme, urgent, dire, drastic, very
grave **3** LAST-DITCH, dangerous, daring,
determined, wild, violent, furious, risky,
frantic, rash, hazardous, precipitate, hasty,
audacious, madcap, foolhardy, headstrong,
impetuous, death-defying

desperately adverb GRAVELY, badly, seriously,
severely, dangerously, perilously

desperation noun **1** MISERY, worry, trouble,
pain, anxiety, torture, despair, agony,
sorrow, distraction, anguish, unhappiness,
heartache, hopelessness, despondency
2 RECKLESSNESS, madness, defiance, frenzy,
impetuosity, rashness, foolhardiness,
heedlessness

despicable adjective CONTEMPTIBLE, mean,
low, base, cheap, infamous, degrading,
worthless, disgraceful, shameful, vile,
sordid, pitiful, abject, hateful, reprehensible,
ignominious, disreputable, wretched, scurvy,
detestable, scungy (Austral & NZ), beyond
contempt << ANTONYM admirable

despise verb LOOK DOWN ON, loathe, scorn,
disdain, spurn, undervalue, deride, detest,
revile, abhor, have a down on (informal),
contemn << ANTONYM admire

despite preposition IN SPITE OF, in the face of,
regardless of, even with, notwithstanding, in
defiance of, in the teeth of, undeterred by, in
contempt of

despondency noun DEJECTION, depression,
despair, misery, gloom, sadness, desperation,
melancholy, hopelessness, the hump (Brit
informal), discouragement, wretchedness,
low spirits, disconsolateness, dispiritedness,
downheartedness

despondent adjective DEJECTED, sad,
depressed, down, low, blue, despairing,
discouraged, miserable, gloomy, hopeless,
dismal, melancholy, in despair, glum,
dispirited, downcast, morose, disheartened,
sorrowful, wretched, disconsolate, doleful,
downhearted, down in the dumps (informal),
sick as a parrot (informal), woebegone, low-
spirited << ANTONYM cheerful

despot noun TYRANT, dictator, oppressor,
autocrat, monocrat

despotic adjective TYRANNICAL, authoritarian,
dictatorial, absolute, arrogant, oppressive,
autocratic, imperious, domineering,
monocratic

despotism noun TYRANNY, dictatorship,
oppression, totalitarianism, autocracy,
absolutism, autarchy, monocracy

dessert noun PUDDING, sweet (informal), afters
(Brit informal), second course, last course,
sweet course

destination noun STOP, station, haven,
harbour, resting-place, terminus, journey's
end, landing-place

destined adjective FATED, meant, intended,
designed, certain, bound, doomed, ordained,
predestined, foreordained ▷▷ **destined for**
BOUND FOR, booked for, directed towards,
scheduled for, routed for, heading for,
assigned to, en route to, on the road to

destiny noun **1** FATE, fortune, lot, portion,
doom, nemesis, divine decree **2** usually
cap. FORTUNE, chance, karma, providence,
kismet, predestination, divine will

destitute adjective PENNILESS, poor,
impoverished, distressed, needy, on the
rocks, insolvent, poverty-stricken, down
and out, indigent, impecunious, dirt-poor
(informal), on the breadline (informal), flat
broke (informal), short, penurious, on
your uppers, necessitous, in queer street
(informal), moneyless, without two pennies
to rub together (informal) ▷▷ **destitute of**
LACKING, wanting, without, in need of,
deprived of, devoid of, bereft of, empty of,
drained of, deficient in, depleted in

destroy verb **1** RUIN, smash, crush, waste,
devastate, break down, wreck, shatter, gut,
wipe out, dispatch, dismantle, demolish,
trash (slang), total (slang), ravage, slay,
eradicate, torpedo, extinguish, desolate,
annihilate, put paid to, raze, blow to bits,
extirpate, blow sky-high **2** SLAUGHTER, kill,
exterminate

destruction noun **1** RUIN, havoc, wreckage,
crushing, wrecking, shattering, undoing,
demolition, devastation, annihilation,
ruination **2** MASSACRE, overwhelming,
slaughter, overthrow, extinction, end,
downfall, liquidation, obliteration,
extermination, eradication **3** SLAUGHTER

destructive adjective **1** DEVASTATING,
fatal, deadly, lethal, harmful, damaging,
catastrophic, detrimental, hurtful,
pernicious, noxious, ruinous, calamitous,
cataclysmic, baleful, deleterious, injurious,
baneful, maleficent **2** NEGATIVE, hostile,
discouraging, undermining, contrary,
vicious, adverse, discrediting, disparaging,
antagonistic, derogatory

desultory *adjective* RANDOM, vague, irregular, loose, rambling, inconsistent, erratic, disconnected, haphazard, cursory, aimless, off and on, fitful, spasmodic, discursive, unsystematic, inconstant, maundering, unmethodical

detach *verb* **1** SEPARATE, free, remove, divide, isolate, cut off, sever, loosen, segregate, disconnect, tear off, disengage, disentangle, unfasten, disunite, uncouple, unhitch, disjoin, unbridle << ANTONYM attach **2** FREE, remove, separate, isolate, cut off, segregate, disengage

detached *adjective* **1** OBJECTIVE, neutral, impartial, reserved, aloof, impersonal, disinterested, unbiased, dispassionate, uncommitted, uninvolved, unprejudiced << ANTONYM subjective **2** SEPARATE, free, severed, disconnected, loosened, discrete, unconnected, undivided, disjoined

detachment *noun* **1** INDIFFERENCE, fairness, neutrality, objectivity, impartiality, coolness, remoteness, nonchalance, aloofness, unconcern, disinterestedness, nonpartisanship **2** (*military*) UNIT, party, force, body, detail, squad, patrol, task force

detail *noun* **1** POINT, fact, feature, particular, respect, factor, count, item, instance, element, aspect, specific, component, facet, technicality **2** FINE POINT, part, particular, nicety, minutiae, triviality **3** (*military*) PARTY, force, body, duty, squad, assignment, fatigue, detachment ▷ *verb* **1** LIST, describe, relate, catalogue, portray, specify, depict, recount, rehearse, recite, narrate, delineate, enumerate, itemize, tabulate, particularize **2** APPOINT, name, choose, commission, select, elect, delegate, nominate, assign, allocate, charge ▷▷ **in detail** COMPREHENSIVELY, completely, fully, thoroughly, extensively, inside out, exhaustively, point by point, item by item

detailed *adjective* **1** COMPREHENSIVE, full, complete, minute, particular, specific, extensive, exact, thorough, meticulous, exhaustive, all-embracing, itemized, encyclopedic, blow-by-blow, particularized << ANTONYM brief **2** COMPLICATED, involved, complex, fancy, elaborate, intricate, meticulous, convoluted

detain *verb* **1** HOLD, arrest, confine, restrain, imprison, intern, take prisoner, take into custody, hold in custody **2** DELAY, keep, stop, hold up, hamper, hinder, retard, impede, keep back, slow up *or* down

detect *verb* **1** DISCOVER, find, reveal, catch, expose, disclose, uncover, track down, unmask **2** NOTICE, see, spot, catch, note, identify, observe, remark, recognize, distinguish, perceive, scent, discern, ascertain, descry

detection *noun* DISCOVERY, exposure, uncovering, tracking down, unearthing, unmasking, ferreting out

detective *noun* INVESTIGATOR, cop (*slang*), copper (*slang*), dick (*slang, chiefly US*), constable, tec (*slang*), private eye, sleuth (*informal*), private investigator, gumshoe (*US slang*), bizzy (*slang*), C.I.D. man

detention *noun* IMPRISONMENT, custody, restraint, keeping in, quarantine, confinement, porridge (*slang*), incarceration << ANTONYM release

deter *verb* **1** DISCOURAGE, inhibit, put off, frighten, intimidate, daunt, hinder, dissuade, talk out of **2** PREVENT, stop, check, curb, damp, restrain, prohibit, hinder, debar

detergent *noun* CLEANER, cleanser ▷ *adjective* CLEANSING, cleaning, purifying, abstergent, detersive

deteriorate *verb* **1** DECLINE, worsen, degenerate, slump, degrade, depreciate, go downhill, go to the dogs (*informal*), go to pot << ANTONYM improve **2** DISINTEGRATE, decay, spoil, fade, break down, weaken, crumble, fall apart, ebb, decompose, wear away, retrogress

deterioration *noun* **1** DECLINE, fall, drop, slump, worsening, downturn, depreciation, degradation, degeneration, debasement, retrogression, vitiation, dégringolade (*French*) **2** DISINTEGRATION, corrosion, atrophy

determination *noun* **1** RESOLUTION, purpose, resolve, drive, energy, conviction, courage, dedication, backbone, fortitude, persistence, tenacity, perseverance, willpower, boldness, firmness, staying power, stubbornness, constancy, single-mindedness, earnestness, obstinacy, steadfastness, doggedness, relentlessness, resoluteness, indomitability, staunchness << ANTONYM indecision **2** DECISION, ruling, settlement, resolution, resolve, conclusion, verdict, judgment

determine *verb* **1** AFFECT, control, decide, rule, condition, direct, influence, shape, govern, regulate, ordain **2** SETTLE, learn, establish, discover, check, find out, work out, detect, certify, verify, ascertain **3** DECIDE ON, choose, establish, purpose, fix, elect, resolve

4 DECIDE, purpose, conclude, resolve, make up your mind

determined *adjective* RESOLUTE, firm, dogged, fixed, constant, bold, intent, persistent, relentless, stalwart, persevering, single-minded, purposeful, tenacious, undaunted, strong-willed, steadfast, unwavering, immovable, unflinching, strong-minded

determining *adjective* DECIDING, important, settling, essential, critical, crucial, decisive, final, definitive, conclusive

deterrent *noun* DISCOURAGEMENT, obstacle, curb, restraint, impediment, check, hindrance, disincentive, defensive measures, determent << ANTONYM incentive

detest *verb* HATE, loathe, despise, abhor, be hostile to, recoil from, be repelled by, have an aversion to, abominate, dislike intensely, execrate, feel aversion towards, feel disgust towards, feel hostility towards, feel repugnance towards << ANTONYM love

dethrone *verb* DEPOSE, overthrow, oust, unseat, uncrown

detonate *verb* SET OFF, trigger, explode, discharge, blow up, touch off

detonation *noun* EXPLOSION, blast, bang, report, boom, discharge, fulmination

detour *noun* DIVERSION, bypass, deviation, circuitous route, roundabout way, indirect course

detract from *verb* **1** LESSEN, reduce, diminish, lower, take away from, derogate, devaluate << ANTONYM enhance **2** DIVERT, shift, distract, deflect, draw *or* lead away from

detractor *noun* SLANDERER, belittler, disparager, defamer, traducer, muckraker, scandalmonger, denigrator, backbiter, derogator (*rare*)

detriment *noun* DAMAGE, loss, harm, injury, hurt, prejudice, disadvantage, impairment, disservice

detrimental *adjective* DAMAGING, destructive, harmful, adverse, pernicious, unfavourable, prejudicial, baleful, deleterious, injurious, inimical, disadvantageous << ANTONYM beneficial

devastate *verb* **1** DESTROY, waste, ruin, sack, wreck, spoil, demolish, trash (*slang*), level, total (*slang*), ravage, plunder, desolate, pillage, raze, lay waste, despoil **2** (*informal*) SHATTER, overwhelm, confound, floor (*informal*)

devastating *adjective* **1** DESTRUCTIVE, damaging, catastrophic, harmful, detrimental, pernicious, ruinous, calamitous, cataclysmic, deleterious, injurious, maleficent **2** TRAUMATIC, shocking, upsetting, disturbing, painful, scarring **3** SAVAGE, cutting, overwhelming, withering, overpowering, satirical, incisive, sardonic, caustic, vitriolic, trenchant, mordant

devastation *noun* DESTRUCTION, ruin, havoc, ravages, demolition, plunder, pillage, desolation, depredation, ruination, spoliation

develop *verb* **1** GROW, advance, progress, mature, evolve, flourish, blossom, ripen **2** RESULT, follow, arise, issue, happen, spring, stem, derive, break out, ensue, come about, be a direct result of **3** ESTABLISH, set up, promote, generate, undertake, initiate, embark on, cultivate, instigate, inaugurate, set in motion **4** FORM, start, begin, contract, establish, pick up, breed, acquire, generate, foster, originate **5** EXPAND, extend, work out, elaborate, unfold, enlarge, broaden, amplify, augment, dilate upon

development *noun* **1** GROWTH, increase, growing, advance, progress, spread, expansion, extension, evolution, widening, maturing, unfolding, unravelling, advancement, progression, thickening, enlargement **2** ESTABLISHMENT, forming, generation, institution, invention, initiation, inauguration, instigation, origination **3** EVENT, change, happening, issue, result, situation, incident, circumstance, improvement, outcome, phenomenon, evolution, unfolding, occurrence, upshot, turn of events, evolvement

deviant *adjective* PERVERTED, sick (*informal*), twisted, bent (*slang*), abnormal, queer (*informal or derogatory*), warped, perverse, wayward, kinky (*slang*), devious, deviate, freaky (*slang*), aberrant, pervy (*slang*), sicko (*informal*) << ANTONYM normal ▷ *noun* PERVERT, freak, queer (*informal or derogatory*), misfit, sicko (*informal*), odd type

deviate *verb* DIFFER, vary, depart, part, turn, bend, drift, wander, stray, veer, swerve, meander, diverge, digress, turn aside

deviation *noun* DEPARTURE, change, variation, shift, alteration, discrepancy, inconsistency, disparity, aberration, variance, divergence, fluctuation, irregularity, digression

device *noun* **1** GADGET, machine, tool, instrument, implement, invention, appliance, apparatus, gimmick, utensil, contraption, contrivance, waldo, gizmo *or* gismo (*slang, chiefly US & Canad*) **2** PLOY, scheme, strategy, plan, design, project, shift, trick, manoeuvre, stunt, dodge, expedient, ruse, artifice, gambit, stratagem, wile

devil *noun* **1** EVIL SPIRIT, demon, fiend, ghoul, hellhound, atua (*NZ*), wairua (*NZ*) **2** BRUTE, monster, savage, beast, villain, rogue, barbarian, fiend, terror, swine, ogre **3** PERSON, individual, soul, creature, thing, human being, beggar **4** SCAMP, monkey (*informal*), rogue, imp, rascal, tyke (*informal*), scoundrel, scallywag (*informal*), mischief-maker, whippersnapper, toerag (*slang*), pickle (*Brit informal*), nointer (*Austral slang*) ▷▷ the Devil SATAN, Lucifer, Prince of Darkness, Old One, Deuce, Old Gentleman (*informal*), Lord of the Flies, Old Harry (*informal*), Mephistopheles, Evil One, Beelzebub, Old Nick (*informal*), Mephisto, Belial, Clootie (*Scot*), deil (*Scot*), Apollyon, Old Scratch (*informal*), Foul Fiend, Wicked One, archfiend, Old Hornie (*informal*), Abbadon

devilish *adjective* **1** FIENDISH, diabolical, wicked, satanic, atrocious, hellish, infernal, accursed, execrable, detestable, damnable, diabolic **2** DIFFICULT, involved, complex, complicated, baffling, intricate, perplexing, thorny, knotty, problematical, ticklish

devious *adjective* **1** SLY, scheming, calculating, tricky, crooked (*informal*), indirect, treacherous, dishonest, wily, insidious, evasive, deceitful, underhand, insincere, surreptitious, double-dealing, not straightforward << ANTONYM straightforward **2** INDIRECT, roundabout, wandering, crooked, rambling, tortuous, deviating, circuitous, excursive << ANTONYM direct

devise *verb* WORK OUT, plan, form, design, imagine, frame, arrange, plot, construct, invent, conceive, formulate, contrive, dream up, concoct, think up

devoid *adjective* with of LACKING IN, without, free from, wanting in, sans (*archaic*), bereft of, empty of, deficient in, denuded of, barren of

devolution *noun* TRANSFER OF POWER, decentralization, distribution of power, surrender of power, relinquishment of power

devolve *verb* with on, upon, to, *etc.* TRANSFER, entrust, consign, depute

devote *verb* DEDICATE, give, commit, apply, reserve, pledge, surrender, assign, allot, give over, consecrate, set apart

devoted *adjective* DEDICATED, loving, committed, concerned, caring, true, constant, loyal, faithful, fond, ardent, staunch, devout, steadfast << ANTONYM disloyal

devotee *noun* **1** ENTHUSIAST, fan, supporter, follower, addict, admirer, buff (*informal*), fanatic, adherent, aficionado **2** FOLLOWER, student, supporter, pupil, convert, believer, partisan, disciple, learner, apostle, adherent, votary, proselyte, catechumen

devotion *noun* **1** LOVE, passion, affection, intensity, attachment, zeal, fondness, fervour, adoration, ardour, earnestness **2** DEDICATION, commitment, loyalty, allegiance, fidelity, adherence, constancy, faithfulness << ANTONYM indifference **3** WORSHIP, reverence, spirituality, holiness, piety, sanctity, adoration, godliness, religiousness, devoutness << ANTONYM irreverence ▷ *plural noun* PRAYERS, religious observance, church service, divine office

devotional *adjective* RELIGIOUS, spiritual, holy, sacred, devout, pious, reverential

devour *verb* **1** EAT, consume, swallow, bolt, dispatch, cram, stuff, wolf, gorge, gulp, gobble, guzzle, polish off (*informal*), pig out on (*slang*) **2** ENJOY, go through, absorb, appreciate, take in, relish, drink in, delight in, revel in, be preoccupied with, feast on, be engrossed by, read compulsively or voraciously

devouring *adjective* OVERWHELMING, powerful, intense, flaming, consuming, excessive, passionate, insatiable

devout *adjective* **1** RELIGIOUS, godly, pious, pure, holy, orthodox, saintly, reverent, prayerful << ANTONYM irreverent **2** SINCERE, serious, deep, earnest, genuine, devoted, intense, passionate, profound, ardent, fervent, heartfelt, zealous, dinkum (*Austral & NZ informal*) << ANTONYM indifferent

dexterity *noun* **1** SKILL, expertise, mastery, touch, facility, craft, knack, finesse, artistry, proficiency, smoothness, neatness, deftness, nimbleness, adroitness, effortlessness, handiness << ANTONYM incompetence **2** CLEVERNESS, art, ability, ingenuity, readiness, aptitude, adroitness, aptness, expertness, skilfulness

diabolical *adjective* **1** (*informal*) DREADFUL, shocking, terrible, appalling, nasty, tricky, unpleasant, outrageous, vile, excruciating, atrocious, abysmal, damnable **2** WICKED, cruel, savage, monstrous, malicious, satanic, from hell (*informal*), malignant, unspeakable, inhuman, implacable, malevolent, hellish, devilish, infernal, fiendish, ungodly, black-hearted, demoniac, hellacious (*US slang*)

diagnose *verb* IDENTIFY, determine, recognize, distinguish, interpret, pronounce, pinpoint

diagnosis *noun* **1** IDENTIFICATION, discovery, recognition, detection **2** OPINION, conclusion, interpretation, pronouncement

diagnostic *adjective* SYMPTOMATIC, particular, distinguishing, distinctive, peculiar, indicative, idiosyncratic, recognizable, demonstrative

diagonal *adjective* SLANTING, angled, oblique, cross, crosswise, crossways, cater-cornered (*US informal*), cornerways

diagonally *adverb* ASLANT, obliquely, on the cross, at an angle, crosswise, on the bias, cornerwise

diagram *noun* PLAN, figure, drawing, chart, outline, representation, sketch, layout, graph

dialect *noun* LANGUAGE, speech, tongue, jargon, idiom, vernacular, brogue, lingo (*informal*), patois, provincialism, localism

dialectic *noun* DEBATE, reasoning, discussion, logic, contention, polemics, disputation, argumentation, ratiocination

dialogue *noun* **1** DISCUSSION, conference, exchange, debate, confabulation **2** CONVERSATION, discussion, communication, discourse, converse, colloquy, confabulation, duologue, interlocution **3** SCRIPT, conversation, lines, spoken part

diametrically *adverb* COMPLETELY, totally, entirely, absolutely, utterly

diarrhoea *or US* **diarrhea** *noun* THE RUNS, the trots (*informal*), dysentery, looseness, the skits (*informal*), Montezuma's revenge (*informal*), gippy tummy, holiday tummy, Spanish tummy, the skitters (*informal*)

diary *noun* **1** JOURNAL, chronicle, day-to-day account **2** ENGAGEMENT BOOK, Filofax (*trademark*), appointment book

diatribe *noun* TIRADE, abuse, criticism, denunciation, reviling, stricture, harangue, invective, vituperation, stream of abuse, verbal onslaught, philippic

dicey *adjective* (*informal, chiefly Brit*) DANGEROUS, difficult, tricky, risky, hairy (*slang*), ticklish, chancy (*informal*)

dichotomy *noun* DIVISION, split, separation, disjunction

dicky *adjective* (*Brit informal*) WEAK, queer (*informal*), shaky, unreliable, unsteady, unsound, fluttery

dictate *verb* SPEAK, say, utter, read out ▷ *noun* **1** COMMAND, order, decree, word, demand, direction, requirement, bidding, mandate, injunction, statute, fiat, ultimatum, ordinance, edict, behest **2** PRINCIPLE, law, rule, standard, code, criterion, ethic, canon, maxim, dictum, precept, axiom, moral law ▷▷ **dictate to someone** ORDER (ABOUT), direct, lay down the law to, pronounce to

dictator *noun* ABSOLUTE RULER, tyrant, despot, oppressor, autocrat, absolutist, martinet

dictatorial *adjective* **1** ABSOLUTE, unlimited, totalitarian, autocratic, unrestricted, tyrannical, despotic << ANTONYM democratic **2** DOMINEERING, authoritarian, oppressive, bossy (*informal*), imperious, overbearing, magisterial, iron-handed, dogmatical << ANTONYM servile

dictatorship *noun* ABSOLUTE RULE, tyranny, totalitarianism, authoritarianism, reign of terror, despotism, autocracy, absolutism

diction *noun* PRONUNCIATION, speech, articulation, delivery, fluency, inflection, intonation, elocution, enunciation

dictionary *noun* WORDBOOK, vocabulary, glossary, encyclopedia, lexicon, concordance

dictum *noun* **1** SAYING, saw, maxim, adage, proverb, precept, axiom, gnome **2** DECREE, order, demand, statement, command, dictate, canon, fiat, edict, pronouncement

didactic *adjective* **1** INSTRUCTIVE, educational, enlightening, moral, edifying, homiletic, preceptive **2** PEDANTIC, academic, formal, pompous, schoolmasterly, erudite, bookish, abstruse, moralizing, priggish, pedagogic

die *verb* **1** PASS AWAY, depart, expire, perish, buy it (*US slang*), check out (*US slang*), kick it (*slang*), croak (*slang*), give up the ghost, go belly-up (*slang*), snuff it (*slang*), peg out (*informal*), kick the bucket (*slang*), buy the farm (*US slang*), peg it (*informal*), decease, cark it (*Austral & NZ slang*), pop your clogs (*informal*), breathe your last, hop the twig (*slang*) << ANTONYM live **2** STOP, fail, halt, break down, run down, stop working, peter out, fizzle out, lose power, seize up, conk out (*informal*), go kaput (*informal*), go phut, fade out *or* away **3** DWINDLE, end, decline, pass, disappear, sink, fade, weaken, diminish, vanish, decrease, decay, lapse, wither, wilt, lessen, wane, subside, ebb, die down, die out, abate, peter out, die away, grow less

<< ANTONYM increase >> **be dying for something** LONG FOR, want, desire, crave, yearn for, hunger for, pine for, hanker after, be eager for, ache for, swoon over, languish for, set your heart on >> **be dying of something** (*informal*) BE OVERCOME WITH, succumb to, collapse with

die-hard *or* **diehard** *noun* REACTIONARY, fanatic, zealot, intransigent, stick-in-the-mud (*informal*), old fogey, ultraconservative

diet¹ *noun* **1** FOOD, provisions, fare, rations, subsistence, kai (*NZ informal*), nourishment, sustenance, victuals, commons, edibles, comestibles, nutriment, viands, aliment **2** FAST, regime, abstinence, regimen, dietary regime ▷ *verb* SLIM, fast, lose weight, abstain, eat sparingly << ANTONYM overindulge

diet² *noun often cap.* COUNCIL, meeting, parliament, sitting, congress, chamber, convention, legislature, legislative assembly

dieter *noun* SLIMMER, weight watcher, calorie counter, faster, reducer

differ *verb* **1** BE DISSIMILAR, contradict, contrast with, vary, counter, belie, depart from, diverge, negate, fly in the face of, run counter to, be distinct, stand apart, make a nonsense of, be at variance with << ANTONYM accord **2** DISAGREE, clash, dispute, dissent << ANTONYM agree

difference *noun* **1** DISSIMILARITY, contrast, variation, change, variety, exception, distinction, diversity, alteration, discrepancy, disparity, deviation, differentiation, peculiarity, divergence, singularity, particularity, distinctness, unlikeness << ANTONYM similarity **2** REMAINDER, rest, balance, remains, excess **3** DISAGREEMENT, conflict, argument, row, clash, dispute, set-to (*informal*), controversy, contention, quarrel, strife, wrangle, tiff, contretemps, discordance, contrariety << ANTONYM agreement

different *adjective* **1** DISSIMILAR, opposed, contrasting, changed, clashing, unlike, altered, diverse, at odds, inconsistent, disparate, deviating, divergent, at variance, discrepant, streets apart **2** VARIOUS, some, many, several, varied, numerous, diverse, divers (*archaic*), assorted, miscellaneous, sundry, manifold, multifarious **3** UNUSUAL, unique, special, strange, rare, extraordinary, bizarre, distinctive, something else, peculiar, uncommon, singular, unconventional, out of the ordinary, left-field (*informal*), atypical **4** OTHER, another, separate, individual,

distinct, discrete

differential *adjective* DISTINCTIVE, distinguishing, discriminative, diacritical ▷ *noun* DIFFERENCE, discrepancy, disparity, amount of difference

differentiate *verb* **1** DISTINGUISH, separate, discriminate, contrast, discern, mark off, make a distinction, tell apart, set off *or* apart **2** MAKE DIFFERENT, separate, distinguish, characterize, single out, segregate, individualize, mark off, set apart, set off *or* apart **3** BECOME DIFFERENT, change, convert, transform, alter, adapt, modify

differently *adverb* DISSIMILARLY, otherwise, in another way, in contrary fashion << ANTONYM similarly

difficult *adjective* **1** HARD, tough, taxing, demanding, challenging, painful, exacting, formidable, uphill, strenuous, problematic, arduous, onerous, laborious, burdensome, wearisome, no picnic (*informal*), toilsome, like getting blood out of a stone << ANTONYM easy **2** PROBLEMATICAL, involved, complex, complicated, delicate, obscure, abstract, baffling, intricate, perplexing, thorny, knotty, abstruse, ticklish, enigmatical << ANTONYM simple **3** TROUBLESOME, trying, awkward, demanding, rigid, stubborn, perverse, fussy, tiresome, intractable, fastidious, fractious, unyielding, obstinate, intransigent, unmanageable, unbending, uncooperative, hard to please, refractory, obstreperous, pig-headed, bull-headed, unaccommodating, unamenable << ANTONYM cooperative **4** TOUGH, trying, hard, dark, grim, straitened, full of hardship << ANTONYM easy

difficulty *noun* **1** PROBLEM, trouble, obstacle, hurdle, dilemma, hazard, complication, hassle (*informal*), snag, uphill (*S African*), predicament, pitfall, stumbling block, impediment, hindrance, tribulation, quandary, can of worms (*informal*), point at issue, disputed point **2** HARDSHIP, labour, pain, strain, awkwardness, painfulness, strenuousness, arduousness, laboriousness

diffident *adjective* SHY, reserved, withdrawn, reluctant, modest, shrinking, doubtful, backward, unsure, insecure, constrained, timid, self-conscious, hesitant, meek, unassuming, unobtrusive, self-effacing, sheepish, bashful, timorous, unassertive

diffuse *verb* SPREAD, distribute, scatter, circulate, disperse, dispense, dispel,

dissipate, propagate, disseminate ▷ *adjective*
1 SPREAD-OUT, scattered, dispersed,
unconcentrated << ANTONYM concentrated
2 RAMBLING, loose, vague, meandering,
waffling (*informal*), long-winded, wordy,
discursive, verbose, prolix, maundering,
digressive, diffusive, circumlocutory
<< ANTONYM concise

diffusion *noun* SPREADING, distribution,
scattering, circulation, expansion,
propagation, dissemination, dispersal,
dispersion, dissipation

dig *verb* **1** HOLLOW OUT, mine, pierce, quarry,
excavate, gouge, scoop out **2** DELVE, tunnel,
burrow, grub **3** TURN OVER, till, break up,
hoe **4** SEARCH, hunt, root, delve, forage, dig
down, fossick (*Austral & NZ*) **5** POKE, drive,
push, stick, punch, stab, thrust, shove,
prod, jab **6** (*informal*) LIKE, enjoy, go for,
appreciate, groove (*dated slang*), delight in, be
fond of, be keen on, be partial to **7** (*informal*)
UNDERSTAND, follow ▷ *noun* **1** CUTTING
REMARK, crack (*slang*), insult, taunt, sneer,
jeer, quip, barb, wisecrack (*informal*), gibe
2 POKE, thrust, butt, nudge, prod, jab, punch
▷▷ **dig in** (*informal*) BEGIN *or* START EATING,
tuck in (*informal*)

digest *verb* **1** INGEST, absorb, incorporate,
dissolve, assimilate **2** TAKE IN, master,
absorb, grasp, drink in, soak up, devour,
assimilate ▷ *noun* SUMMARY, résumé,
abstract, epitome, condensation,
compendium, synopsis, précis, abridgment

digestion *noun* INGESTION, absorption,
incorporation, assimilation

digit *noun* FINGER, toe

dignified *adjective* DISTINGUISHED, august,
reserved, imposing, formal, grave, noble,
upright, stately, solemn, lofty, exalted,
decorous << ANTONYM undignified

dignify *verb* DISTINGUISH, honour, grace,
raise, advance, promote, elevate, glorify,
exalt, ennoble, aggrandize

dignitary *noun* PUBLIC FIGURE, worthy,
notable, high-up (*informal*), bigwig (*informal*),
celeb (*informal*), personage, pillar of society,
pillar of the church, notability, pillar of the
state, V.I.P.

dignity *noun* **1** DECORUM, breeding, gravity,
majesty, grandeur, respectability, nobility,
propriety, solemnity, gentility, courtliness,
loftiness, stateliness **2** SELF-IMPORTANCE,
pride, self-esteem, self-respect, self-regard,
self-possession, amour-propre (*French*)

digress *verb* WANDER, drift, stray, depart,

ramble, meander, diverge, deviate, turn
aside, be diffuse, expatiate, go off at a
tangent, get off the point *or* subject

dilapidated *adjective* RUINED, fallen in,
broken-down, battered, neglected,
crumbling, run-down, decayed, decaying,
falling apart, beat-up (*informal*), shaky,
shabby, worn-out, ramshackle, in ruins,
rickety, decrepit, tumbledown, uncared for,
gone to rack and ruin

dilate *verb* ENLARGE, extend, stretch, expand,
swell, widen, broaden, puff out, distend
<< ANTONYM contract

dilemma *noun* PREDICAMENT, problem,
difficulty, spot (*informal*), fix (*informal*), mess,
puzzle, jam (*informal*), embarrassment,
plight, strait, pickle (*informal*), how-do-you-
do (*informal*), quandary, perplexity, tight
corner *or* spot ▷▷ **on the horns of a dilemma**
BETWEEN THE DEVIL AND THE DEEP BLUE
SEA, between a rock and a hard place
(*informal*), between Scylla and Charybdis

dilettante *noun* AMATEUR, aesthete, dabbler,
trifler, nonprofessional

diligence *noun* APPLICATION, industry, care,
activity, attention, perseverance, earnestness,
attentiveness, assiduity, intentness,
assiduousness, laboriousness, heedfulness,
sedulousness

diligent *adjective* HARD-WORKING, careful,
conscientious, earnest, active, busy,
persistent, attentive, persevering, tireless,
painstaking, laborious, industrious,
indefatigable, studious, assiduous, sedulous
<< ANTONYM indifferent

dilute *verb* **1** WATER DOWN, thin (out), weaken,
adulterate, make thinner, cut (*informal*)
<< ANTONYM condense **2** REDUCE, weaken,
diminish, temper, decrease, lessen, diffuse,
mitigate, attenuate << ANTONYM intensify

diluted *adjective* WATERED DOWN, thinned,
weak, weakened, dilute, watery, adulterated,
cut (*informal*), wishy-washy (*informal*)

dim *adjective* **1** DULL, weak, pale, muted,
subdued, feeble, murky, opaque, dingy,
subfusc **2** POORLY LIT, dark, gloomy, murky,
shady, shadowy, dusky, crepuscular, darkish,
tenebrous, unilluminated, caliginous
(*archaic*) **3** CLOUDY, grey, gloomy, dismal,
overcast, leaden << ANTONYM bright
4 UNCLEAR, obscured, faint, blurred,
fuzzy, shadowy, hazy, indistinguishable,
bleary, undefined, out of focus, ill-defined,
indistinct, indiscernible << ANTONYM
distinct **5** OBSCURE, remote, vague, confused,

shadowy, imperfect, hazy, intangible, indistinct **6** UNFAVOURABLE, bad, black, depressing, discouraging, gloomy, dismal, sombre, unpromising, dispiriting, disheartening **7** (*informal*) STUPID, slow, thick, dull, dense, dumb (*informal*), daft (*informal*), dozy (*Brit informal*), obtuse, unintelligent, asinine, slow on the uptake (*informal*), braindead (*informal*), doltish << ANTONYM bright ▷ *verb* **1** TURN DOWN, lower, fade, dull, bedim **2** GROW *or* BECOME FAINT, fade, dull, grow *or* become dim **3** DARKEN, dull, cloud over

dimension *noun* **1** ASPECT, side, feature, angle, facet **2** EXTENT, size, magnitude, importance, scope, greatness, amplitude, largeness ▷ *plural noun* PROPORTIONS, range, size, scale, measure, volume, capacity, bulk, measurement, amplitude, bigness

diminish *verb* **1** DECREASE, decline, lessen, contract, weaken, shrink, dwindle, wane, recede, subside, ebb, taper, die out, fade away, abate, peter out << ANTONYM grow **2** REDUCE, cut, decrease, lessen, contract, lower, weaken, curtail, abate, retrench << ANTONYM increase **3** BELITTLE, scorn, devalue, undervalue, deride, demean, denigrate, scoff at, disparage, decry, sneer at, underrate, deprecate, depreciate, cheapen, derogate

diminution *noun* **1** DECREASE, decline, lessening, weakening, decay, contraction, abatement **2** REDUCTION, cut, decrease, weakening, deduction, contraction, lessening, cutback, retrenchment, abatement, curtailment

diminutive *adjective* SMALL, little, tiny, minute, pocket(-sized), mini, wee, miniature, petite, midget, undersized, teeny-weeny, Lilliputian, bantam, teensy-weensy, pygmy *or* pigmy << ANTONYM giant

din *noun* NOISE, row, racket, crash, clash, shout, outcry, clamour, clatter, uproar, commotion, pandemonium, babel, hubbub, hullabaloo, clangour << ANTONYM silence

dine *verb* EAT, lunch, feast, sup, chow down (*slang*) ▷▷ **dine on** *or* **off something** EAT, consume, feed on

dingy *adjective* DISCOLOURED, soiled, dirty, shabby, faded, seedy, grimy

dinkum *adjective* (*Austral & NZ informal*) GENUINE, honest, natural, frank, sincere, candid, upfront (*informal*), artless, guileless

dinky *adjective* (*Brit informal*) CUTE, small, neat, mini, trim, miniature, petite, dainty, natty

(*informal*), cutesy (*informal, chiefly US*)

dinner *noun* **1** MEAL, main meal, spread (*informal*), repast, blowout (*slang*), collation, refection **2** BANQUET, feast, blowout (*slang*), repast, beanfeast (*Brit informal*), carousal, hakari (*NZ*)

dinosaur *noun* FUDDY-DUDDY, anachronism, dodo (*informal*), stick-in-the-mud (*informal*), antique (*informal*), fossil (*informal*), relic (*informal*), back number (*informal*)

dint ▷▷ **by dint of** BY MEANS OF, using, by virtue of, by force of

diocese *noun* BISHOPRIC, see

dip *verb* **1** PLUNGE, immerse, bathe, duck, rinse, douse, dunk, souse **2** DROP (DOWN), set, fall, lower, disappear, sink, fade, slump, descend, tilt, subside, sag, droop **3** SLOPE, drop (down), descend, fall, decline, pitch, sink, incline, drop away ▷ *noun* **1** PLUNGE, ducking, soaking, drenching, immersion, douche, submersion **2** NOD, drop, lowering, slump, sag **3** HOLLOW, hole, depression, pit, basin, dent, trough, indentation, concavity **4** MIXTURE, solution, preparation, suspension, infusion, concoction, dilution ▷▷ **dip into something 1** SAMPLE, try, skim, play at, glance at, run over, browse, dabble, peruse, surf (*computing*) **2** DRAW UPON, use, employ, extract, take from, make use of, fall back on, reach into, have recourse to

diplomacy *noun* **1** STATESMANSHIP, statecraft, international negotiation **2** TACT, skill, sensitivity, craft, discretion, subtlety, delicacy, finesse, savoir-faire, artfulness << ANTONYM tactlessness

diplomat *noun* OFFICIAL, ambassador, envoy, statesman, consul, attaché, emissary, chargé d'affaires

diplomatic *adjective* **1** CONSULAR, official, foreign-office, ambassadorial, foreign-politic **2** TACTFUL, politic, sensitive, subtle, delicate, polite, discreet, prudent, adept, considerate, judicious, treating with kid gloves << ANTONYM tactless

dire *adjective* DESPERATE, pressing, crying, critical, terrible, crucial, alarming, extreme, awful, appalling, urgent, cruel, horrible, disastrous, grim, dreadful, gloomy, fearful, dismal, drastic, catastrophic, ominous, horrid, woeful, ruinous, calamitous, cataclysmic, portentous, godawful (*slang*), exigent, bodeful

direct *verb* **1** AIM, point, turn, level, train, focus, fix, cast **2** GUIDE, show, lead, point the way, point in the direction of 3 CONTROL, run, manage, lead, rule, guide, handle, conduct, advise, govern, regulate, administer, oversee, supervise, dispose, preside over, mastermind, call the shots, call the tune, superintend 4 ORDER, command, instruct, charge, demand, require, bid, enjoin, adjure 5 ADDRESS, send, mail, route, label, superscribe ▷ *adjective* 1 QUICKEST, shortest 2 STRAIGHT, through << ANTONYM circuitous 3 FIRST-HAND, personal, immediate << ANTONYM indirect 4 CLEAR, specific, plain, absolute, distinct, definite, explicit, downright, point-blank, unequivocal, unqualified, unambiguous, categorical << ANTONYM ambiguous 5 STRAIGHTFORWARD, open, straight, frank, blunt, sincere, outspoken, honest, matter-of-fact, downright, candid, forthright, truthful, upfront (*informal*), man-to-man, plain-spoken << ANTONYM indirect 6 VERBATIM, exact, word-for-word, strict, accurate, faithful, letter-for-letter ▷ *adverb* NON-STOP, straight

direction *noun* 1 WAY, course, line, road, track, bearing, route, path 2 TENDENCY, bent, current, trend, leaning, drift, bias, orientation, tack, tenor, proclivity 3 MANAGEMENT, government, control, charge, administration, leadership, command, guidance, supervision, governance, oversight, superintendence

directions *plural noun* INSTRUCTIONS, rules, information, plan, briefing, regulations, recommendations, indication, guidelines, guidance

directive *noun* ORDER, ruling, regulation, charge, notice, command, instruction, dictate, decree, mandate, canon, injunction, imperative, fiat, ordinance, edict

directly *adverb* 1 STRAIGHT, unswervingly, without deviation, by the shortest route, in a beeline 2 IMMEDIATELY, promptly, instantly, right away, straightaway, speedily, instantaneously, pronto (*informal*), pdq (*slang*) 3 AT ONCE, presently, soon, quickly, as soon as possible, in a second, straightaway, forthwith, posthaste 4 HONESTLY, openly, frankly, plainly, face-to-face, overtly, point-blank, unequivocally, truthfully, candidly, unreservedly, straightforwardly, straight from the shoulder (*informal*), without prevarication

directness *noun* HONESTY, candour, frankness, sincerity, plain speaking, bluntness, outspokenness, forthrightness, straightforwardness

director *noun* CONTROLLER, head, leader, manager, chief, executive, chairman, boss (*informal*), producer, governor, principal, administrator, supervisor, organizer, baas (*S African*), helmer, sherang (*Austral & NZ*)

dirge *noun* LAMENT, requiem, elegy, death march, threnody, dead march, funeral song, coronach (*Scot & Irish*)

dirt *noun* 1 FILTH, muck, grime, dust, mud, stain, tarnish, smudge, mire, impurity, slob (*Irish*), crud (*slang*), grot (*slang*) 2 SOIL, ground, earth, clay, turf, clod, loam, loam

dirty *adjective* 1 FILTHY, soiled, grubby, nasty, foul, muddy, polluted, messy, sullied, grimy, unclean, mucky, grotty (*slang*), grungy (*slang, chiefly US & Canad*), scuzzy (*slang, chiefly US*), begrimed, festy (*Austral slang*) << ANTONYM clean 2 DISHONEST, illegal, unfair, cheating, corrupt, crooked, deceiving, fraudulent, treacherous, deceptive, unscrupulous, crafty, deceitful, double-dealing, unsporting, knavish (*archaic*) << ANTONYM honest 3 OBSCENE, rude, coarse, indecent, blue, offensive, gross, filthy, vulgar, pornographic, sleazy, suggestive, lewd, risqué, X-rated (*informal*), bawdy, salacious, smutty, off-colour, unwholesome << ANTONYM decent 4 DESPICABLE, mean, low, base, cheap, nasty, cowardly, beggarly, worthless, shameful, shabby, vile, sordid, low-down (*informal*), abject, squalid, ignominious, contemptible, wretched, scurvy, detestable, scungy (*Austral & NZ*) ▷ *verb* SOIL, foul, stain, spoil, smear, muddy, pollute, blacken, mess up, smudge, sully, defile, smirch, begrime << ANTONYM clean

disability *noun* HANDICAP, affliction, disorder, defect, impairment, disablement, infirmity

disable *verb* HANDICAP, weaken, cripple, damage, hamstring, paralyse, impair, debilitate, incapacitate, prostrate, unman, immobilize, put out of action, enfeeble, render inoperative, render *hors de combat*

disabled *adjective* DIFFERENTLY ABLED, physically challenged, handicapped, challenged, weakened, crippled, paralysed, lame, mutilated, maimed, incapacitated, infirm, bedridden << ANTONYM able-bodied

disabuse *verb* (usually in phrase *disabuse someone of an idea or notion*) ENLIGHTEN, correct, set right, open the eyes of, set straight, shatter (someone's) illusions, free from error, undeceive

disadvantage *noun* **1** DRAWBACK, trouble, burden, weakness, handicap, liability, minus (*informal*), flaw, hardship, nuisance, snag, inconvenience, downside, impediment, hindrance, privation, weak point, fly in the ointment (*informal*) << ANTONYM advantage **2** HARM, loss, damage, injury, hurt, prejudice, detriment, disservice << ANTONYM benefit ▷▷ **at a disadvantage** EXPOSED, vulnerable, wide open, unprotected, defenceless, open to attack, assailable

disadvantaged *adjective* DEPRIVED, struggling, impoverished, discriminated against, underprivileged

disaffected *adjective* ALIENATED, resentful, discontented, hostile, estranged, dissatisfied, rebellious, antagonistic, disloyal, seditious, mutinous, uncompliant, unsubmissive

disaffection *noun* ALIENATION, resentment, discontent, hostility, dislike, disagreement, dissatisfaction, animosity, aversion, antagonism, antipathy, disloyalty, estrangement, ill will, repugnance, unfriendliness

disagree *verb* **1** DIFFER (IN OPINION), argue, debate, clash, dispute, contest, fall out (*informal*), contend, dissent, quarrel, wrangle, bicker, take issue with, have words (*informal*), cross swords, be at sixes and sevens << ANTONYM agree **2** *with* with MAKE ILL, upset, sicken, trouble, hurt, bother, distress, discomfort, nauseate, be injurious to ▷▷ **disagree with something** *or* **someone** OPPOSE, object to, dissent from

disagreeable *adjective* **1** NASTY, offensive, disgusting, unpleasant, distasteful, horrid, repellent, unsavoury, obnoxious, unpalatable, displeasing, repulsive, objectionable, repugnant, uninviting, yucky *or* yukky (*slang*), yucko (*Austral slang*) << ANTONYM pleasant **2** ILL-NATURED, difficult, nasty, cross, contrary, unpleasant, rude, irritable, unfriendly, bad-tempered, surly, churlish, brusque, tetchy, ratty (*Brit & NZ informal*), peevish, ungracious, disobliging, unlikable *or* unlikeable << ANTONYM good-natured

disagreement *noun* ARGUMENT, row, difference, division, debate, conflict, clash, dispute, falling out, misunderstanding, dissent, quarrel, squabble, strife, wrangle, discord, tiff, altercation << ANTONYM agreement

disallow *verb* REJECT, refuse, ban, dismiss,

cancel, veto, forbid, embargo, prohibit, rebuff, repudiate, disown, proscribe, disavow, disclaim, abjure

disappear *verb* **1** VANISH, recede, drop out of sight, vanish off the face of the earth, evanesce, be lost to view *or* sight << ANTONYM appear **2** PASS, wane, ebb, fade away **3** FLEE, bolt, run away, fly, escape, split (*slang*), retire, withdraw, take off (*informal*), get away, vanish, depart, go, make off, abscond, take flight, do a runner (*slang*), scarper (*Brit slang*), slope off, cut and run (*informal*), beat a hasty retreat, make your escape, make your getaway **4** BE LOST, be taken, be stolen, go missing, be mislaid **5** CEASE, end, fade, vanish, dissolve, expire, evaporate, perish, die out, pass away, cease to exist, melt away, leave no trace, cease to be known

disappearance *noun* **1** VANISHING, going, passing, disappearing, fading, melting, eclipse, evaporation, evanescence **2** FLIGHT, departure, desertion, disappearing trick **3** LOSS, losing, mislaying

disappoint *verb* **1** LET DOWN, dismay, fail, dash, disillusion, sadden, vex, chagrin, dishearten, disenchant, dissatisfy, disgruntle **2** FRUSTRATE, foil, thwart, defeat, baffle, balk

disappointed *adjective* LET DOWN, upset, distressed, discouraged, depressed, choked, disillusioned, discontented, dejected, disheartened, disgruntled, dissatisfied, downcast, saddened, disenchanted, despondent, downhearted, cast down << ANTONYM satisfied

disappointing *adjective* UNSATISFACTORY, inadequate, discouraging, sorry, upsetting, sad, depressing, unhappy, unexpected, pathetic, inferior, insufficient, lame, disconcerting, second-rate, unworthy, not much cop (*Brit slang*)

disappointment *noun* **1** REGRET, distress, discontent, dissatisfaction, disillusionment, displeasure, chagrin, disenchantment, dejection, despondency, discouragement, mortification, unfulfilment **2** LETDOWN, blow, disaster, failure, setback, fiasco, misfortune, calamity, whammy (*informal, chiefly US*), choker (*informal*), washout (*informal*) **3** FRUSTRATION, failure, ill-success

disapproval *noun* DISPLEASURE, criticism, objection, condemnation, dissatisfaction, censure, reproach, denunciation, deprecation, disapprobation, stick (*slang*)

disapprove *verb* **1** CONDEMN, object to, dislike,

censure, deplore, deprecate, frown on,
take exception to, take a dim view of, find
unacceptable, have a down on (*informal*),
discountenance, look down your nose
at (*informal*), raise an *or* your eyebrow at
<< ANTONYM approve **2** TURN DOWN, reject,
veto, set aside, spurn, disallow << ANTONYM
endorse

disapproving *adjective* CRITICAL,
discouraging, frowning, disparaging,
censorious, reproachful, deprecatory,
condemnatory, denunciatory,
disapprobatory << ANTONYM approving

disarm *verb* **1** DEMILITARIZE, disband,
demobilize, deactivate **2** WIN OVER, persuade

disarmament *noun* ARMS REDUCTION,
demobilization, arms limitation,
demilitarization, de-escalation

disarming *adjective* CHARMING, winning,
irresistible, persuasive, likable *or* likeable

disarray *noun* **1** CONFUSION, upset, disorder,
indiscipline, disunity, disharmony,
disorganization, unruliness, discomposure,
disorderliness << ANTONYM order
2 UNTIDINESS, state, mess, chaos, tangle,
mix-up, muddle, clutter, shambles, jumble,
hotchpotch, hodgepodge (*US*), dishevelment,
pig's breakfast (*informal*) << ANTONYM
tidiness

disaster *noun* **1** CATASTROPHE, trouble, blow,
accident, stroke, reverse, tragedy, ruin,
misfortune, adversity, calamity, mishap,
whammy (*informal, chiefly US*), misadventure,
cataclysm, act of God, bummer (*slang*),
ruination, mischance **2** FAILURE, mess, flop
(*informal*), catastrophe, rout, debacle, cock-up
(*Brit slang*), washout (*informal*)

disastrous *adjective* **1** TERRIBLE, devastating,
tragic, fatal, unfortunate, dreadful,
destructive, unlucky, harmful, adverse,
dire, catastrophic, detrimental, untoward,
ruinous, calamitous, cataclysmic, ill-
starred, unpropitious, ill-fated, cataclysmal
2 UNSUCCESSFUL, devastating, tragic,
calamitous, cataclysmic

disavow *verb* DENY, reject, contradict, retract,
repudiate, disown, rebut, disclaim, forswear,
gainsay (*archaic or literary*), abjure

disband *verb* **1** DISMISS, separate, break up,
scatter, dissolve, let go, disperse, send home,
demobilize **2** BREAK UP, separate, scatter,
disperse, part company, go (their) separate
ways

disbelief *noun* SCEPTICISM, doubt, distrust,
mistrust, incredulity, unbelief, dubiety

<< ANTONYM belief

disbelieve *verb* DOUBT, reject, discount,
suspect, discredit, not accept, mistrust, not
buy (*slang*), repudiate, scoff at, not credit, not
swallow (*informal*), give no credence to

disburse *verb* PAY OUT, spend, lay out, fork
out (*slang*), expend, shell out (*informal*)

disbursement *noun* PAYMENT, spending,
expenditure, disposal, outlay

disc *noun* **1** CIRCLE, plate, saucer, discus
2 (*old-fashioned*) RECORD, vinyl, gramophone
record, phonograph record (*US & Canad*),
platter (*US slang*)

discard *verb* GET RID OF, drop, remove,
throw away *or* out, reject, abandon, dump
(*informal*), shed, scrap, axe (*informal*), ditch
(*slang*), junk (*informal*), chuck (*informal*),
dispose of, relinquish, dispense with,
jettison, repudiate, cast aside << ANTONYM
keep

discern *verb* SEE, perceive, make out, notice,
observe, recognize, behold, catch sight of,
suss (out) (*slang*), espy, descry

discernible *adjective* CLEAR, obvious,
apparent, plain, visible, distinct, noticeable,
recognizable, detectable, observable,
perceptible, distinguishable, appreciable,
discoverable

discerning *adjective* DISCRIMINATING,
knowing, sharp, critical, acute, sensitive,
wise, intelligent, subtle, piercing,
penetrating, shrewd, ingenious, astute,
perceptive, judicious, clear-sighted,
percipient, perspicacious, sagacious

discharge *verb* **1** RELEASE, free, clear, liberate,
pardon, let go, acquit, allow to go, set free,
exonerate, absolve **2** DISMISS, sack (*informal*),
fire (*informal*), remove, expel, discard, oust,
eject, cashier, give (someone) the boot
(*slang*), give (someone) the sack (*informal*),
kennet (*Austral slang*), jeff (*Austral slang*)
3 CARRY OUT, perform, fulfil, accomplish,
do, effect, realize, observe, implement,
execute, carry through **4** PAY, meet, clear,
settle, square (up), honour, satisfy, relieve,
liquidate **5** POUR FORTH, release, empty,
leak, emit, dispense, void, gush, ooze,
exude, give off, excrete, disembogue **6** FIRE,
shoot, set off, explode, let off, detonate,
let loose (*informal*) ▷ *noun* **1** RELEASE,
liberation, clearance, pardon, acquittal,
remittance, exoneration **2** DISMISSAL, notice,
removal, the boot (*slang*), expulsion, the
sack (*informal*), the push (*slang*), marching
orders (*informal*), ejection, demobilization,

kiss-off (*slang, chiefly US & Canad*), the bum's rush (*slang*), the (old) heave-ho (*informal*), the order of the boot (*slang*), congé, your books *or* cards (*informal*) **3** EMISSION, flow, ooze, secretion, excretion, pus, seepage, suppuration **4** FIRING, report, shot, blast, burst, explosion, discharging, volley, salvo, detonation, fusillade **5** CARRYING OUT, performance, achievement, execution, accomplishment, fulfilment, observance

disciple *noun* **1** APOSTLE **2** FOLLOWER, student, supporter, pupil, convert, believer, partisan, devotee, apostle, adherent, proselyte, votary, catechumen << ANTONYM teacher

disciplinarian *noun* AUTHORITARIAN, tyrant, despot, stickler, taskmaster, martinet, drill sergeant, strict teacher, hard master

discipline *noun* **1** CONTROL, rule, authority, direction, regulation, supervision, orderliness, strictness **2** SELF-CONTROL, control, restraint, self-discipline, coolness, cool, willpower, calmness, self-restraint, orderliness, self-mastery, strength of mind *or* will **3** TRAINING, practice, exercise, method, regulation, drill, regimen **4** FIELD OF STUDY, area, subject, theme, topic, course, curriculum, speciality, subject matter, branch of knowledge, field of inquiry *or* reference ▷ *verb* **1** PUNISH, correct, reprimand, castigate, chastise, chasten, penalize, bring to book, reprove **2** TRAIN, control, govern, check, educate, regulate, instruct, restrain

disclaim *verb* **1** DENY, decline, reject, disallow, retract, repudiate, renege, rebut, disavow, abnegate, disaffirm **2** RENOUNCE, reject, abandon, relinquish, disown, abdicate, forswear, abjure

disclaimer *noun* DENIAL, rejection, renunciation, retraction, repudiation, disavowal, abjuration

disclose *verb* **1** MAKE KNOWN, tell, reveal, publish, relate, broadcast, leak, confess, communicate, unveil, utter, make public, impart, divulge, out (*informal*), let slip, spill the beans about (*informal*), blow wide open (*slang*), get off your chest (*informal*), spill your guts about (*slang*) << ANTONYM keep secret **2** SHOW, reveal, expose, discover, exhibit, unveil, uncover, lay bare, bring to light, take the wraps off << ANTONYM hide

disclosure *noun* **1** REVELATION, exposé, announcement, publication, leak, admission, declaration, confession, acknowledgment **2** UNCOVERING,

publication, exposure, revelation, divulgence

discolour *or US* **discolor** *verb* **1** MARK, soil, mar, fade, stain, streak, tinge **2** STAIN, fade, streak, rust, tarnish

discoloured *or US* **discolored** *adjective* STAINED, tainted, tarnished, faded, pale, washed out, wan, blotched, besmirched, foxed, etiolated

discomfort *noun* **1** PAIN, suffering, hurt, smarting, ache, throbbing, irritation, tenderness, pang, malaise, twinge, soreness << ANTONYM comfort **2** UNEASINESS, worry, anxiety, doubt, alarm, distress, suspicion, apprehension, misgiving, nervousness, disquiet, agitation, qualms, trepidation, perturbation, apprehensiveness, dubiety, inquietude << ANTONYM reassurance **3** INCONVENIENCE, trouble, difficulty, bother, hardship, irritation, hassle (*informal*), nuisance, uphill (*S African*), annoyance, awkwardness, unpleasantness, vexation ▷ *verb* MAKE UNCOMFORTABLE, worry, trouble, shake, alarm, disturb, distress, unsettle, ruffle, unnerve, disquiet, perturb, discomfit, discompose << ANTONYM reassure

disconcert *verb* DISTURB, worry, trouble, upset, confuse, rattle (*informal*), baffle, put off, unsettle, bewilder, shake up (*informal*), undo, flurry, agitate, ruffle, perplex, unnerve, unbalance, take aback, fluster, perturb, faze, flummox, throw off balance, nonplus, abash, discompose, put out of countenance

disconcerted *adjective* DISTURBED, worried, troubled, thrown (*informal*), upset, confused, embarrassed, annoyed, rattled (*informal*), distracted, at sea, unsettled, bewildered, shook up (*informal*), flurried, ruffled, taken aback, flustered, perturbed, fazed, nonplussed, flummoxed, caught off balance, out of countenance

disconcerting *adjective* DISTURBING, upsetting, alarming, confusing, embarrassing, awkward, distracting, dismaying, baffling, bewildering, perplexing, off-putting (*Brit informal*), bothersome

disconnect *verb* **1** CUT OFF **2** DETACH, separate, part, divide, sever, disengage, take apart, uncouple

disconnected *adjective* **1** UNRELATED **2** CONFUSED, mixed-up, rambling, irrational, jumbled, unintelligible, illogical, incoherent, disjointed, garbled, uncoordinated

disconsolate *adjective* **1** INCONSOLABLE, crushed, despairing, miserable, hopeless, heartbroken, desolate, forlorn, woeful, grief-stricken, wretched **2** SAD, low, unhappy, miserable, gloomy, dismal, melancholy, forlorn, woeful, dejected, wretched, down in the dumps (*informal*)

discontent *noun* DISSATISFACTION, unhappiness, displeasure, regret, envy, restlessness, uneasiness, vexation, discontentment, fretfulness

discontented *adjective* DISSATISFIED, complaining, unhappy, miserable, fed up, disgruntled, disaffected, vexed, displeased, fretful, cheesed off (*Brit slang*), brassed off (*Brit slang*), with a chip on your shoulder (*informal*) << ANTONYM satisfied

discontinue *verb* STOP, end, finish, drop, kick (*informal*), give up, abandon, suspend, quit, halt, pause, cease, axe (*informal*), interrupt, terminate, break off, put an end to, refrain from, leave off, pull the plug on, belay (*nautical*)

discontinued *adjective* STOPPED, ended, finished, abandoned, halted, terminated, no longer made, given up *or* over

discontinuity *noun* LACK OF UNITY, disconnection, incoherence, disunion, lack of coherence, disjointedness, disconnectedness

discord *noun* DISAGREEMENT, division, conflict, difference, opposition, row, clashing, dispute, contention, friction, strife, wrangling, variance, disunity, dissension, incompatibility, discordance, lack of concord << ANTONYM agreement

discordant *adjective* **1** DISAGREEING, conflicting, clashing, different, opposite, contrary, at odds, contradictory, inconsistent, incompatible, incongruous, divergent **2** HARSH, jarring, grating, strident, shrill, jangling, dissonant, cacophonous, inharmonious, unmelodious

discount *verb* **1** MARK DOWN, reduce, lower **2** DISREGARD, reject, ignore, overlook, discard, set aside, dispel, pass over, repudiate, disbelieve, brush off (*slang*), lay aside, pooh-pooh ▷ *noun* DEDUCTION, cut, reduction, concession, allowance, rebate, cut price

discourage *verb* **1** DISHEARTEN, daunt, deter, crush, put off, depress, cow, dash, intimidate, dismay, unnerve, unman, overawe, demoralize, cast down, put a damper on, psych out (*informal*), dispirit, deject << ANTONYM hearten **2** PUT OFF, deter, prevent, dissuade, talk out of,

discountenance << ANTONYM encourage

discouraged *adjective* PUT OFF, deterred, daunted, dashed, dismayed, pessimistic, dispirited, downcast, disheartened, crestfallen, sick as a parrot (*informal*)

discouragement *noun* **1** DETERRENT, opposition, obstacle, curb, check, setback, restraint, constraint, impediment, hindrance, damper, disincentive **2** DEPRESSION, disappointment, despair, pessimism, hopelessness, despondency, loss of confidence, dejection, discomfiture, low spirits, downheartedness

discouraging *adjective* DISHEARTENING, disappointing, depressing, daunting, dampening, unfavourable, off-putting (*Brit informal*), dispiriting, unpropitious

discourse *noun* **1** CONVERSATION, talk, discussion, speech, communication, chat, dialogue, converse **2** SPEECH, talk, address, essay, lecture, sermon, treatise, dissertation, homily, oration, disquisition, whaikorero (*NZ*)

discover *verb* **1** FIND OUT, see, learn, reveal, spot, determine, notice, realize, recognize, perceive, detect, disclose, uncover, discern, ascertain, suss (out) (*slang*), get wise to (*informal*) **2** FIND, come across, uncover, unearth, turn up, dig up, come upon, bring to light, light upon **3** INVENT, design, pioneer, devise, originate, contrive, conceive of

discoverer *noun* **1** EXPLORER, pioneer **2** INVENTOR, author, originator, initiator

discovery *noun* **1** FINDING OUT, news, announcement, revelation, realization **2** INVENTION, launch, institution, introduction, pioneering, innovation, initiation, inauguration, induction, coinage, origination **3** BREAKTHROUGH, find, finding, development, advance, leap, coup, invention, step forward, godsend, quantum leap **4** FINDING, turning up, locating, revelation, uncovering, disclosure, detection, espial

discredit *verb* **1** DISGRACE, blame, shame, smear, stain, humiliate, degrade, taint, slur, detract from, disparage, vilify, slander, sully, dishonour, stigmatize, defame, bring into disrepute, bring shame upon << ANTONYM honour **2** DISPUTE, question, challenge, deny, reject, discount, distrust, mistrust, repudiate, cast doubt on *or* upon, disbelieve, pooh-pooh ▷ *noun* DISGRACE, scandal, shame, disrepute, smear, stigma, censure, slur, ignominy, dishonour, imputation, odium, ill-repute, aspersion << ANTONYM honour

discredited *adjective* REJECTED, exposed, exploded, discarded, obsolete, refuted, debunked, outworn

discreet *adjective* TACTFUL, diplomatic, politic, reserved, guarded, careful, sensible, cautious, wary, discerning, prudent, considerate, judicious, circumspect, sagacious << ANTONYM tactless ▷ see **discrete**

discrepancy *noun* DISAGREEMENT, difference, variation, conflict, contradiction, inconsistency, disparity, variance, divergence, dissonance, incongruity, dissimilarity, discordance, contrariety

discrete *adjective* SEPARATE, individual, distinct, detached, disconnected, unattached, discontinuous

discretion *noun* 1 TACT, care, consideration, judgment, caution, diplomacy, good sense, prudence, acumen, wariness, discernment, circumspection, sagacity, carefulness, judiciousness, heedfulness << ANTONYM tactlessness 2 CHOICE, will, wish, liking, mind, option, pleasure, preference, inclination, disposition, predilection, volition

discretionary *adjective* OPTIONAL, arbitrary (*law*), unrestricted, elective, open to choice, nonmandatory

discriminate *verb* DIFFERENTIATE, distinguish, discern, separate, assess, evaluate, tell the difference, draw a distinction ▷▷ **discriminate against someone** TREAT DIFFERENTLY, single out, victimize, disfavour, treat as inferior, show bias against, show prejudice against

discriminating *adjective* DISCERNING, particular, keen, critical, acute, sensitive, refined, cultivated, selective, astute, tasteful, fastidious << ANTONYM undiscriminating

discrimination *noun* 1 PREJUDICE, bias, injustice, intolerance, bigotry, favouritism, unfairness, inequity 2 DISCERNMENT, taste, judgment, perception, insight, penetration, subtlety, refinement, acumen, keenness, sagacity, acuteness, clearness

discriminatory *adjective* PREJUDICED, biased, partial, weighted, favouring, one-sided, partisan, unjust, preferential, prejudicial, inequitable

discuss *verb* TALK ABOUT, consider, debate, review, go into, examine, argue about, thrash out, ventilate, reason about, exchange views

on, deliberate about, weigh up the pros and cons of, converse about, confer about

discussion *noun* 1 TALK, debate, argument, conference, exchange, review, conversation, consideration, dialogue, consultation, seminar, discourse, deliberation, symposium, colloquy, confabulation, korero (*NZ*) 2 EXAMINATION, investigation, analysis, scrutiny, dissection

disdain *noun* CONTEMPT, dislike, scorn, arrogance, indifference, sneering, derision, hauteur, snobbishness, contumely, haughtiness, superciliousness ▷ *verb* SCORN, reject, despise, slight, disregard, spurn, undervalue, deride, look down on, belittle, sneer at, pooh-pooh, contemn, look down your nose at (*informal*), misprize

disdainful *adjective* CONTEMPTUOUS, scornful, arrogant, superior, proud, sneering, aloof, haughty, derisive, supercilious, high and mighty (*informal*), hoity-toity (*informal*), turning up your nose (at), on your high horse (*informal*), looking down your nose (at)

disease *noun* 1 ILLNESS, condition, complaint, upset, infection, disorder, sickness, ailment, affliction, malady, infirmity, indisposition, lurgy (*informal*) 2 EVIL, disorder, plague, curse, cancer, blight, contamination, scourge, affliction, bane, contagion, malady, canker

diseased *adjective* UNHEALTHY, sick, infected, rotten, ailing, tainted, sickly, unwell, crook (*Austral & NZ informal*), unsound, unwholesome

disembark *verb* LAND, get off, alight, arrive, step out, go ashore

disembodied *adjective* GHOSTLY, phantom, spectral

disenchanted *adjective* DISILLUSIONED, disappointed, soured, cynical, indifferent, sick, let down, blasé, jaundiced, undeceived

disenchantment *noun* DISILLUSIONMENT, disappointment, disillusion, rude awakening

disengage *verb* 1 RELEASE, free, separate, ease, liberate, loosen, set free, extricate, untie, disentangle, unloose, unbridle 2 DETACH, withdraw

disengaged *adjective* UNCONNECTED, separate, apart, detached, unattached

disengagement *noun* DISCONNECTION, withdrawal, separation, detachment, disentanglement

disentangle *verb* 1 RESOLVE, clear (up), work out, sort out, clarify, simplify 2 FREE, separate, loose, detach, sever, disconnect, extricate, disengage **3** UNTANGLE, unravel, untwist, unsnarl

disfigure *verb* **1** DAMAGE, scar, mutilate, maim, injure, wound, deform **2** MAR, distort, blemish, deface, make ugly, disfeature

disgorge *verb* EMIT, discharge, send out, expel, throw out, vent, throw up, eject, spout, spew, belch, send forth

disgrace *noun* **1** SHAME, contempt, discredit, degradation, disrepute, ignominy, dishonour, infamy, opprobrium, odium, disfavour, obloquy, disesteem << ANTONYM honour **2** SCANDAL, stain, stigma, blot, blemish ▷ *verb* SHAME, stain, humiliate, discredit, degrade, taint, sully, dishonour, stigmatize, defame, abase, bring shame upon << ANTONYM honour

disgraced *adjective* SHAMED, humiliated, discredited, branded, degraded, mortified, in disgrace, dishonoured, stigmatized, under a cloud, in the doghouse (*informal*)

disgraceful *adjective* SHAMEFUL, shocking, scandalous, mean, low, infamous, degrading, unworthy, ignominious, disreputable, contemptible, dishonourable, detestable, discreditable, blameworthy, opprobrious

disgruntled *adjective* DISCONTENTED, dissatisfied, annoyed, irritated, put out, hacked (off) (*US slang*), grumpy, vexed, sullen, displeased, petulant, sulky, peeved, malcontent, testy, peevish, huffy, cheesed off (*Brit slang*), hoha (*NZ*)

disguise *verb* HIDE, cover, conceal, screen, mask, suppress, withhold, veil, cloak, shroud, camouflage, keep secret, hush up, draw a veil over, keep dark, keep under your hat ▷ *noun* COSTUME, get-up (*informal*), mask, camouflage, false appearance

disguised *adjective* **1** IN DISGUISE, masked, camouflaged, undercover, incognito, unrecognizable **2** FALSE, assumed, pretend, artificial, forged, fake, mock, imitation, sham, pseudo (*informal*), counterfeit, feigned, phoney *or* phony (*informal*)

disgust *verb* **1** SICKEN, outrage, offend, revolt, put off, repel, nauseate, gross out (*US slang*), turn your stomach, fill with loathing, cause aversion << ANTONYM delight **2** OUTRAGE, shock, anger, hurt, fury, resentment, wrath, indignation

disgusted *adjective* **1** OUTRAGED, appalled, offended, sickened, scandalized **2** SICKENED, repelled, repulsed, nauseated

disgusting *adjective* **1** SICKENING, foul,

revolting, gross, repellent, nauseating, repugnant, loathsome, festy (*Austral slang*), yucko (*Austral slang*) **2** APPALLING, shocking, awful, offensive, dreadful, horrifying

dish *noun* **1** BOWL, plate, platter, salver **2** FOOD, fare, recipe ▷▷ **dish something out** (*informal*) DISTRIBUTE, assign, allocate, designate, set aside, hand out, earmark, inflict, mete out, dole out, share out, apportion ▷▷ **dish something up** SERVE UP, serve, produce, present, hand out, ladle out, spoon out

disharmony *noun* DISCORD, conflict, clash, friction, discordance, disaccord, inharmoniousness

disheartened *adjective* DISCOURAGED, depressed, crushed, dismayed, choked, daunted, dejected, dispirited, downcast, crestfallen, downhearted, sick as a parrot (*informal*)

dishevelled *or US* **disheveled** *adjective* UNTIDY, disordered, messy, ruffled, rumpled, bedraggled, unkempt, tousled, hanging loose, blowsy, uncombed, disarranged, disarrayed, frowzy, daggy (*Austral & NZ informal*) << ANTONYM tidy

dishonest *adjective* DECEITFUL, corrupt, crooked (*informal*), designing, lying, bent (*slang*), false, unfair, cheating, deceiving, shady (*informal*), fraudulent, treacherous, deceptive, unscrupulous, crafty, swindling, disreputable, untrustworthy, double-dealing, unprincipled, mendacious, perfidious, untruthful, guileful, knavish (*archaic*) << ANTONYM honest

dishonesty *noun* DECEIT, fraud, corruption, cheating, graft (*informal*), treachery, trickery, criminality, duplicity, falsehood, chicanery, falsity, sharp practice, perfidy, mendacity, fraudulence, crookedness, wiliness, unscrupulousness, improbity

dishonour *or US* **dishonor** *verb* DISGRACE, shame, discredit, corrupt, degrade, blacken, sully, debase, debauch, defame, abase << ANTONYM respect ▷ *noun* DISGRACE, scandal, shame, discredit, degradation, disrepute, reproach, ignominy, infamy, opprobrium, odium, disfavour, abasement, obloquy << ANTONYM honour

disillusion *verb* SHATTER THE ILLUSIONS OF, disabuse, bring down to earth, open the eyes of, disenchant, undeceive

disillusioned *adjective* DISENCHANTED, disappointed, enlightened, indifferent, disabused, sadder and wiser, undeceived

disillusionment *noun* DISENCHANTMENT,

disappointment, disillusion, enlightenment, rude awakening, lost innocence

disincentive *noun* DISCOURAGEMENT, deterrent, impediment, damper, dissuasion, determent

disinclined *adjective* RELUCTANT, unwilling, averse, opposed, resistant, hesitant, balking, loath, not in the mood, indisposed, antipathetic

disinfect *verb* STERILIZE, purify, decontaminate, clean, cleanse, fumigate, deodorize, sanitize << ANTONYM contaminate

disinfectant *noun* ANTISEPTIC, sterilizer, germicide, sanitizer

disintegrate *verb* BREAK UP, crumble, fall apart, separate, shatter, splinter, break apart, fall to pieces, go to pieces, disunite

disinterest *noun* INDIFFERENCE, apathy, lack of interest, disregard, detachment, absence of feeling

disinterested *adjective* 1 IMPARTIAL, objective, neutral, detached, equitable, impersonal, unbiased, even-handed, unselfish, uninvolved, unprejudiced, free from self-interest << ANTONYM biased 2 INDIFFERENT, apathetic, uninterested

disjointed *adjective* 1 INCOHERENT, confused, disordered, rambling, disconnected, unconnected, loose, aimless, fitful, spasmodic 2 DISCONNECTED, separated, divided, split, displaced, dislocated, disunited

dislike *verb* HATE, object to, loathe, despise, shun, scorn, disapprove of, detest, abhor, recoil from, take a dim view of, be repelled by, be averse to, disfavour, have an aversion to, abominate, have a down on (*informal*), disrelish, have no taste *or* stomach for, not be able to bear *or* abide *or* stand << ANTONYM like ▷ *noun* HATRED, disgust, hostility, loathing, disapproval, distaste, animosity, aversion, antagonism, displeasure, antipathy, enmity, animus, disinclination, repugnance, odium, detestation, disapprobation << ANTONYM liking

dislocate *verb* 1 PUT OUT OF JOINT, disconnect, disengage, unhinge, disunite, disjoint, disarticulate 2 DISRUPT, disturb, disorder

dislocation *noun* 1 DISRUPTION, disorder, disturbance, disarray, disorganization 2 PUTTING OUT OF JOINT, unhinging, disengagement, disconnection,

disarticulation

dislodge *verb* 1 DISPLACE, remove, disturb, dig out, uproot, extricate, disentangle, knock loose 2 OUST, remove, expel, throw out, displace, topple, force out, eject, depose, unseat

disloyal *adjective* TREACHEROUS, false, unfaithful, subversive, two-faced, faithless, untrustworthy, perfidious, apostate, traitorous << ANTONYM loyal

disloyalty *noun* TREACHERY, infidelity, breach of trust, double-dealing, falsity, perfidy, unfaithfulness, falseness, betrayal of trust, inconstancy, deceitfulness, breaking of faith, Punic faith

dismal *adjective* 1 BAD, awful, dreadful, rotten (*informal*), terrible, poor, dire, duff (*Brit informal*), abysmal, frightful, godawful (*slang*) 2 SAD, gloomy, melancholy, black, dark, depressing, discouraging, bleak, dreary, sombre, forlorn, despondent, lugubrious, sorrowful, wretched, funereal, cheerless, dolorous << ANTONYM happy 3 GLOOMY, depressing, dull, dreary, lugubrious, cheerless << ANTONYM cheerful

dismantle *verb* TAKE APART, strip, demolish, raze, disassemble, unrig, take to pieces *or* bits

dismay *verb* 1 ALARM, frighten, scare, panic, distress, terrify, appal, startle, horrify, paralyse, unnerve, put the wind up (someone) (*informal*), give (someone) a turn (*informal*), affright, fill (someone) with consternation 2 DISAPPOINT, upset, sadden, dash, discourage, put off, daunt, disillusion, let down, vex, chagrin, dishearten, dispirit, disenchant, disgruntle ▷ *noun* 1 ALARM, fear, horror, panic, anxiety, distress, terror, dread, fright, unease, apprehension, nervousness, agitation, consternation, trepidation, uneasiness 2 DISAPPOINTMENT, upset, distress, frustration, dissatisfaction, disillusionment, chagrin, disenchantment, discouragement, mortification

dismember *verb* CUT INTO PIECES, divide, rend, sever, mutilate, dissect, dislocate, amputate, disjoint, anatomize, dislimb

dismiss *verb* 1 REJECT, disregard, spurn, repudiate, pooh-pooh 2 BANISH, drop, dispel, shelve, discard, set aside, eradicate, cast out, lay aside, put out of your mind 3 SACK, fire (*informal*), remove (*informal*), axe (*informal*), discharge, oust, lay off, kick out (*informal*), cashier, send packing (*informal*), give notice to, kiss off (*slang, chiefly US &*

Canad), give (someone) their marching orders, give (someone) the push (*informal*), give (someone) the elbow, give the boot to (*slang*), give the bullet to (*Brit slang*), kennet (*Austral slang*), jeff (*Austral slang*) **4** LET GO, free, release, discharge, dissolve, liberate, disperse, disband, send away

dismissal *noun* THE SACK, removal, discharge, notice, the boot (*slang*), expulsion (*informal*), the push (*slang*), marching orders (*informal*), kiss-off (*slang, chiefly US & Canad*), the bum's rush (*slang*), the (old) heave-ho (*informal*), the order of the boot (*slang*), your books *or* cards (*informal*)

dismount *verb* GET OFF, descend, get down, alight, light

disobedience *noun* DEFIANCE, mutiny, indiscipline, revolt, insubordination, waywardness, infraction, recalcitrance, noncompliance, unruliness, nonobservance

disobey *verb* **1** DEFY, ignore, rebel, resist, disregard, refuse to obey, dig your heels in (*informal*), go counter to **2** INFRINGE, defy, refuse to obey, flout, violate, contravene, overstep, transgress, go counter to

disorder *noun* **1** ILLNESS, disease, complaint, condition, sickness, ailment, affliction, malady, infirmity, indisposition
2 UNTIDINESS, mess, confusion, chaos, muddle, state, clutter, shambles, disarray, jumble, irregularity, disorganization, hotchpotch, derangement, hodgepodge (*US*), pig's breakfast (*informal*), disorderliness **3** DISTURBANCE, fight, riot, turmoil, unrest, quarrel, upheaval, brawl, clamour, uproar, turbulence, fracas, commotion, rumpus, tumult, hubbub, shindig (*informal*), hullabaloo, scrimmage, unruliness, shindy (*informal*), bagarre (*French*), biffo (*Austral slang*)

disorderly *adjective* **1** UNTIDY, confused, chaotic, messy, irregular, jumbled, indiscriminate, shambolic (*informal*), disorganized, higgledy-piggledy (*informal*), unsystematic << ANTONYM tidy **2** UNRULY, disruptive, rowdy, turbulent, unlawful, stormy, rebellious, boisterous, tumultuous, lawless, riotous, unmanageable, ungovernable, refractory, obstreperous, indisciplined

disorganized *adjective* MUDDLED, confused, disordered, shuffled, chaotic, jumbled, haphazard, unorganized, unsystematic, unmethodical

disorientate *or* **disorient** *verb* CONFUSE,

upset, perplex, dislocate, cause to lose your bearings

disorientated *or* **disoriented** *adjective* CONFUSED, lost, unsettled, bewildered, mixed up, perplexed, all at sea

disown *verb* DENY, reject, abandon, renounce, disallow, retract, repudiate, cast off, rebut, disavow, disclaim, abnegate, refuse to acknowledge *or* recognize

disparage *verb* RUN DOWN, dismiss, put down, criticize, underestimate, discredit, ridicule, scorn, minimize, disdain, undervalue, deride, slag (off) (*slang*), knock (*informal*), blast, rubbish (*informal*), malign, detract from, denigrate, belittle, decry, underrate, vilify, slander, deprecate, depreciate, tear into (*informal*), diss (*slang, chiefly US*), defame, bad-mouth (*slang, chiefly US & Canad*), lambast(e), traduce, derogate, asperse

disparaging *adjective* CONTEMPTUOUS, damaging, critical, slighting, offensive, insulting, abusive, scathing, dismissive, belittling, unfavourable, derogatory, unflattering, scornful, disdainful, defamatory, derisive, libellous, slanderous, deprecatory, uncomplimentary, fault-finding, contumelious << ANTONYM complimentary

disparate *adjective* DIFFERENT, contrasting, unlike, contrary, distinct, diverse, at odds, dissimilar, discordant, at variance, discrepant

disparity *noun* DIFFERENCE, gap, inequality, distinction, imbalance, discrepancy, incongruity, unevenness, dissimilarity, disproportion, unlikeness, dissimilitude

dispassionate *adjective* **1** UNEMOTIONAL, cool, collected, calm, moderate, composed, sober, serene, unmoved, temperate, unfazed (*informal*), unruffled, imperturbable, unexcited, unexcitable << ANTONYM emotional **2** OBJECTIVE, fair, neutral, detached, indifferent, impartial, impersonal, disinterested, unbiased, uninvolved, unprejudiced << ANTONYM biased

dispatch *or* **despatch** *verb* **1** SEND, transmit, forward, express, communicate, consign, remit **2** KILL, murder, destroy, do in (*slang*), eliminate (*slang*), take out (*slang*), execute, butcher, slaughter, assassinate, slay, finish off, put an end to, do away with, blow away (*slang, chiefly US*), liquidate, annihilate, exterminate, take (someone's) life, bump off (*slang*) **3** CARRY OUT, perform, fulfil, effect, finish, achieve, settle, dismiss, conclude, accomplish, execute, discharge, dispose of, expedite, make short work of (*informal*) ▷ *noun* 1 MESSAGE, news, report, story, letter, account, piece, item, document, communication, instruction, bulletin, communiqué, missive 2 SPEED, haste, promptness, alacrity, rapidity, quickness, swiftness, briskness, expedition, celerity, promptitude, precipitateness

dispel *verb* DRIVE AWAY, dismiss, eliminate, resolve, scatter, expel, disperse, banish, rout, allay, dissipate, chase away

dispensation *noun* 1 EXEMPTION, licence, exception, permission, privilege, relaxation, immunity, relief, indulgence, reprieve, remission 2 DISTRIBUTION, supplying, dealing out, appointment, endowment, allotment, consignment, disbursement, apportionment, bestowal, conferment

dispense *verb* 1 DISTRIBUTE, assign, allocate, allot, mete out, dole out, share out, apportion, deal out, disburse 2 PREPARE, measure, supply, mix 3 ADMINISTER, direct, operate, carry out, implement, undertake, enforce, execute, apply, discharge 4 EXEMPT, except, excuse, release, relieve, reprieve, let off (*informal*), exonerate ▷▷ **dispense with something** *or* **someone** 1 DO AWAY WITH, ignore, give up, cancel, abolish, omit, disregard, pass over, brush aside, forgo, render needless 2 DO WITHOUT, get rid of, dispose of, relinquish, shake off

dispersal *noun* 1 SCATTERING, spread, distribution, dissemination, dissipation 2 SPREAD, broadcast, circulation, diffusion, dissemination

disperse *verb* 1 SCATTER, spread, distribute, circulate, strew, diffuse, dissipate, disseminate, throw about 2 BREAK UP, separate, dismiss, disappear, send off, vanish, scatter, dissolve, rout, dispel, disband, part company, demobilize, go (their) separate ways << ANTONYM gather 3 DISSOLVE, disappear, vanish, evaporate, break up, dissipate, melt away, evanesce ▷ see **disburse**

dispirited *adjective* DISHEARTENED, depressed, discouraged, down, low, sad, gloomy, glum, dejected, in the doldrums, despondent, downcast, morose, crestfallen, sick as a parrot (*informal*)

dispiriting *adjective* DISHEARTENING, disappointing, depressing, crushing, discouraging, daunting, sickening, saddening, demoralizing << ANTONYM

reassuring

displace *verb* 1 REPLACE, succeed, take over from, supersede, oust, usurp, supplant, take the place of, crowd out, fill *or* step into (someone's) boots 2 FORCE OUT, turn out, expel, throw out, oust, unsettle, kick out (*informal*), eject, evict, dislodge, boot out (*informal*), dispossess, turf out (*informal*) 3 MOVE, shift, disturb, budge, misplace, disarrange, derange 4 REMOVE, fire (*informal*), dismiss, sack (*informal*), discharge, oust, depose, cashier, dethrone, remove from office

display *verb* 1 SHOW, present, exhibit, unveil, open to view, take the wraps off, put on view << ANTONYM conceal 2 EXPOSE, show, reveal, bare, exhibit, uncover, lay bare, expose to view 3 DEMONSTRATE, show, reveal, register, expose, disclose, betray, manifest, divulge, make known, evidence, evince 4 SHOW OFF, parade, exhibit, sport (*informal*), flash (*informal*), boast, flourish, brandish, flaunt, vaunt, make a (great) show of, disport, make an exhibition of ▷ *noun* 1 PROOF, exhibition, demonstration, evidence, expression, exposure, illustration, revelation, testimony, confirmation, manifestation, affirmation, substantiation 2 EXHIBITION, show, demonstration, presentation, showing, array, expo (*informal*), exposition 3 OSTENTATION, show, dash, flourish, fanfare, pomp 4 SHOW, exhibition, demonstration, parade, spectacle, pageant, pageantry

displease *verb* ANNOY, upset, anger, provoke, offend, irritate, put out, hassle (*informal*), aggravate (*informal*), incense, gall, exasperate, nettle, vex, irk, rile, pique, nark (*Brit, Austral & NZ slang*), dissatisfy, put your back up, hack you off (*informal*)

displeasure *noun* ANNOYANCE, anger, resentment, irritation, offence, dislike, wrath, dissatisfaction, disapproval, indignation, distaste, pique, vexation, disgruntlement, disfavour, disapprobation << ANTONYM satisfaction

disposable *adjective* 1 THROWAWAY, paper, nonreturnable 2 AVAILABLE, expendable, free for use, consumable, spendable, at your service

disposal *noun* THROWING AWAY, dumping (*informal*), scrapping, removal, discarding, clearance, jettisoning, ejection, riddance, relinquishment ▷▷ **at your disposal** AVAILABLE, ready, to hand, accessible, convenient, handy, on hand, at hand, obtainable, on tap, expendable, at your fingertips, at your service, free for use, ready for use, consumable, spendable

dispose *verb* 1 ARRANGE, put, place, group, set, order, stand, range, settle, fix, rank, distribute, array 2 LEAD, move, condition, influence, prompt, tempt, adapt, motivate, bias, induce, incline, predispose, actuate ▷▷ **dispose of someone** KILL, murder, destroy, do in (*slang*), take out (*slang*), execute, slaughter, dispatch, assassinate, slay, do away with, knock off (*slang*), liquidate, neutralize, exterminate, take (someone's) life, bump off (*slang*), wipe from the face of the earth (*informal*) ▷▷ **dispose of something** 1 GET RID OF, destroy, dump (*informal*), scrap, bin (*informal*), junk (*informal*), chuck (*informal*), discard, unload, dispense with, jettison, get shot of, throw out *or* away 2 DEAL WITH, manage, treat, handle, settle, cope with, take care of, see to, finish with, attend to, get to grips with 3 GIVE, give up, part with, bestow, transfer, make over

disposed *adjective* INCLINED, given, likely, subject, ready, prone, liable, apt, predisposed, tending towards, of a mind to

disposition *noun* 1 CHARACTER, nature, spirit, make-up, constitution, temper, temperament 2 TENDENCY, inclination, propensity, habit, leaning, bent, bias, readiness, predisposition, proclivity, proneness 3 (*archaic*) ARRANGEMENT, grouping, ordering, organization, distribution, disposal, placement

dispossess *verb* STRIP, deprive

dispossessed *adjective* DESTITUTE, landless

disproportionate *adjective* EXCESSIVE, too much, unreasonable, uneven, unequal, unbalanced, out of proportion, inordinate, incommensurate

disprove *verb* PROVE FALSE, discredit, refute, contradict, negate, invalidate, rebut, give the lie to, make a nonsense of, blow out of the water (*slang*), controvert, confute ≪ ANTONYM prove

dispute *verb* 1 CONTEST, question, challenge, deny, doubt, oppose, object to, contradict, rebut, impugn, controvert, call in *or* into question 2 ARGUE, fight, clash, row, disagree, fall out (*informal*), contend, feud, quarrel, brawl, squabble, spar, wrangle, bicker, have an argument, cross swords, be at sixes and sevens, fight like cat and dog, go at it hammer and tongs, altercate ▷

noun 1 DISAGREEMENT, conflict, argument, falling out, dissent, friction, strife, discord, altercation 2 ARGUMENT, row, clash, controversy, disturbance, contention, feud, quarrel, brawl, squabble, wrangle, difference of opinion, tiff, dissension, shindig (*informal*), shindy (*informal*), bagarre (*French*)

disqualification *noun* BAN, exclusion, elimination, rejection, ineligibility, debarment, disenablement, disentitlement

disqualified *adjective* ELIMINATED, knocked out, out of the running, debarred, ineligible

disqualify *verb* BAN, rule out, prohibit, preclude, debar, declare ineligible, disentitle

disquiet *noun* UNEASINESS, concern, fear, worry, alarm, anxiety, distress, unrest, angst, nervousness, trepidation, foreboding, restlessness, fretfulness, disquietude ▷ *verb* MAKE UNEASY, concern, worry, trouble, upset, bother, disturb, distress, annoy, plague, unsettle, harass, hassle (*informal*), agitate, vex, perturb, discompose, incommode

disquieting *adjective* WORRYING, troubling, upsetting, disturbing, distressing, annoying, irritating, unsettling, harrowing, unnerving, disconcerting, vexing, perturbing, bothersome

disregard *verb* IGNORE, discount, take no notice of, overlook, neglect, pass over, turn a blind eye to, disobey, laugh off, make light of, pay no attention to, pay no heed to, leave out of account, brush aside *or* away ≪ ANTONYM pay attention to ▷ *noun* IGNORING, neglect, contempt, indifference, negligence, disdain, disrespect, heedlessness

disrepair *noun* DILAPIDATION, collapse, decay, deterioration, ruination ▷▷ **in disrepair** OUT OF ORDER, broken, decayed, worn-out, decrepit, not functioning, out of commission, on the blink (*slang*), bust (*informal*), kaput (*informal*)

disreputable *adjective* DISCREDITABLE, mean, low, base, shocking, disorderly, notorious, vicious, infamous, disgraceful, shameful, vile, shady (*informal*), scandalous, ignominious, contemptible, louche, unprincipled, dishonourable, opprobrious ≪ ANTONYM respectable

disrepute *noun* DISCREDIT, shame, disgrace, unpopularity, ignominy, dishonour, infamy, disfavour, ill repute, obloquy, ill favour, disesteem

disrespect *noun* CONTEMPT, cheek, disregard, rudeness, lack of respect, irreverence, insolence, impertinence, impudence, discourtesy, incivility, impoliteness, lese-majesty, unmanctliness << ANTONYM respect

disrespectful *adjective* CONTEMPTUOUS, insulting, rude, cheeky, irreverent, bad-mannered, impertinent, insolent, impolite, impudent, discourteous, uncivil, ill-bred

disrupt *verb* 1 INTERRUPT, stop, upset, hold up, interfere with, unsettle, obstruct, cut short, intrude on, break up *or* into 2 DISTURB, upset, confuse, disorder, spoil, unsettle, agitate, disorganize, disarrange, derange, throw into disorder

disruption *noun* DISTURBANCE, disorder, confusion, interference, disarray, interruption, stoppage, disorderliness

disruptive *adjective* DISTURBING, upsetting, disorderly, unsettling, troublesome, unruly, obstreperous, troublemaking << ANTONYM well-behaved

dissatisfaction *noun* DISCONTENT, frustration, resentment, regret, distress, disappointment, dismay, irritation, unhappiness, annoyance, displeasure, exasperation, chagrin

dissatisfied *adjective* DISCONTENTED, frustrated, unhappy, disappointed, fed up, disgruntled, not satisfied, unfulfilled, displeased, unsatisfied, ungratified << ANTONYM satisfied

dissect *verb* 1 CUT UP *or* APART, dismember, lay open, anatomize 2 ANALYSE, study, investigate, research, explore, break down, inspect, scrutinize

dissection *noun* 1 CUTTING UP, anatomy, autopsy, dismemberment, postmortem (examination), necropsy, anatomization 2 ANALYSIS, examination, breakdown, research, investigation, inspection, scrutiny

disseminate *verb* SPREAD, publish, broadcast, distribute, scatter, proclaim, circulate, sow, disperse, diffuse, publicize, dissipate, propagate, promulgate

dissemination *noun* SPREAD, publishing, broadcasting, publication, distribution, circulation, diffusion, propagation, promulgation

dissension *noun* DISAGREEMENT, conflict, dissent, dispute, contention, quarrelling, friction, strife, discord, discordance, conflict of opinion

dissent *noun* DISAGREEMENT, opposition, protest, resistance, refusal, objection, discord, demur, dissension, dissidence,

nonconformity, remonstrance ▷▷ **dissent from something** DISAGREE WITH, object to, protest against, refuse to accept << ANTONYM assent

dissenter *noun* OBJECTOR, dissident, nonconformist, protestant, disputant

dissenting *adjective* DISAGREEING, protesting, opposing, conflicting, differing, dissident

dissertation *noun* THESIS, essay, discourse, critique, exposition, treatise, disquisition

disservice *noun* WRONG, injury, harm, injustice, disfavour, unkindness, bad turn, ill turn << ANTONYM good turn

dissident *adjective* DISSENTING, disagreeing, nonconformist, heterodox, schismatic, dissentient ▷ *noun* PROTESTER, rebel, dissenter, demonstrator, agitator, recusant, protest marcher

dissimilar *adjective* DIFFERENT, unlike, various, varied, diverse, assorted, unrelated, disparate, miscellaneous, sundry, divergent, manifold, heterogeneous, mismatched, multifarious, not similar, not alike, not capable of comparison << ANTONYM alike

dissipate *verb* DISAPPEAR, fade, vanish, dissolve, disperse, evaporate, diffuse, melt away, evanesce

dissipated *adjective* 1 DEBAUCHED, abandoned, self-indulgent, profligate, intemperate, dissolute, rakish 2 SQUANDERED, spent, wasted, exhausted, consumed, scattered

dissociate *or* **disassociate** *verb* SEPARATE, distance, divorce, isolate, detach, segregate, disconnect, set apart ▷▷ **dissociate yourself from something** *or* **someone** BREAK AWAY FROM, part company with, break off relations with

dissociation *noun* SEPARATION, break, division, distancing, divorce, isolation, segregation, detachment, severance, disengagement, disconnection, disunion

dissolution *noun* 1 ENDING, end, finish, conclusion, suspension, dismissal, termination, adjournment, disbandment, discontinuation << ANTONYM union 2 BREAKING UP, parting, divorce, separation, disintegration

dissolve *verb* 1 MELT, soften, thaw, flux, liquefy, deliquesce 2 END, dismiss, suspend, axe (*informal*), break up, wind up, overthrow, terminate, discontinue, dismantle, disband, disunite 3 DISAPPEAR, fade, vanish, break down, crumble, disperse, dwindle, evaporate, disintegrate, perish, diffuse, dissipate, decompose, melt away, waste away, evanesce

▷▷ **dissolve into** or **in something** (with *tears* or *laughter* as object) BREAK INTO, burst into, give way to, launch into

dissonance or **dissonancy** *noun*
DISCORDANCE, discord, jangle, cacophony, jarring, harshness, lack of harmony, unmelodiousness

distance *noun* 1 SPACE, length, extent, range, stretch, gap, interval, separation, span, width 2 REMOTENESS 3 ALOOFNESS, reserve, detachment, restraint, indifference, stiffness, coolness, coldness, remoteness, frigidity, uninvolvement, standoffishness
▷▷ **go the distance** FINISH, stay the course, complete, see through, bring to an end ▷▷ **in the distance** FAR OFF, far away, the horizon, afar, yonder

distant *adjective* 1 FAR-OFF, far, remote, removed, abroad, out-of-the-way, far-flung, faraway, outlying, afar << ANTONYM close 2 REMOTE, slight 3 RESERVED, cold, withdrawn, cool, formal, remote, stiff, restrained, detached, indifferent, aloof, unfriendly, reticent, haughty, unapproachable, standoffish << ANTONYM friendly 4 FARAWAY, blank, abstracted, vague, absorbed, distracted, unaware, musing, vacant, preoccupied, bemused, oblivious, dreamy, daydreaming, absent-minded, inattentive

distaste *noun* DISLIKE, horror, disgust, loathing, aversion, revulsion, displeasure, antipathy, abhorrence, disinclination, repugnance, odium, disfavour, detestation, disrelish

distasteful *adjective* UNPLEASANT, offensive, obscene, undesirable, unsavoury, obnoxious, unpalatable, displeasing, repulsive, objectionable, disagreeable, repugnant, loathsome, abhorrent, nauseous, uninviting << ANTONYM enjoyable

distil *verb* 1 PURIFY, refine, evaporate, condense, sublimate, vaporize 2 EXTRACT, express, squeeze, obtain, take out, draw out, separate out, press out

distillation *noun* ESSENCE, extract, elixir, spirit, quintessence

distinct *adjective* 1 DIFFERENT, individual, separate, disconnected, discrete, dissimilar, unconnected, unattached << ANTONYM similar 2 STRIKING, sharp, dramatic, stunning (*informal*), outstanding, bold, noticeable, well-defined 3 DEFINITE, marked, clear, decided, obvious, sharp, plain, apparent, patent, evident, black-and-white,

manifest, noticeable, conspicuous, clear-cut, unmistakable, palpable, recognizable, unambiguous, observable, perceptible, appreciable << ANTONYM vague

distinction *noun* 1 DIFFERENCE, contrast, variation, differential, discrepancy, disparity, deviation, differentiation, fine line, distinctness, dissimilarity 2 EXCELLENCE, note, quality, worth, account, rank, reputation, importance, consequence, fame, celebrity, merit, superiority, prominence, greatness, eminence, renown, repute
3 FEATURE, quality, characteristic, name, mark, individuality, peculiarity, singularity, distinctiveness, particularity 4 MERIT, credit, honour, integrity, excellence, righteousness, rectitude, uprightness

distinctive *adjective* CHARACTERISTIC, special, individual, specific, unique, typical, extraordinary, distinguishing, peculiar, singular, idiosyncratic << ANTONYM ordinary

distinctly *adverb* 1 DEFINITELY, clearly, obviously, sharply, plainly, patently, manifestly, decidedly, markedly, noticeably, unmistakably, palpably 2 CLEARLY, plainly, precisely

distinguish *verb* 1 DIFFERENTIATE, determine, separate, discriminate, decide, judge, discern, ascertain, tell the difference, make a distinction, tell apart, tell between 2 CHARACTERIZE, mark, separate, single out, individualize, set apart 3 MAKE OUT, recognize, perceive, know, see, tell, pick out, discern

distinguishable *adjective* 1 RECOGNIZABLE, noticeable, conspicuous, discernible, obvious, evident, manifest, perceptible, well-marked 2 CONSPICUOUS, clear, strong, bright, plain, bold, pronounced, colourful, vivid, eye-catching, salient

distinguished *adjective* EMINENT, great, important, noted, famous, celebrated, well-known, prominent, esteemed, acclaimed, notable, renowned, prestigious, elevated, big-time (*informal*), famed, conspicuous, illustrious, major league (*informal*) << ANTONYM unknown

distinguishing *adjective* CHARACTERISTIC, marked, distinctive, typical, peculiar, differentiating, individualistic

distort *verb* 1 MISREPRESENT, twist, bias, disguise, pervert, slant, colour, misinterpret, falsify, garble 2 DEFORM, bend, twist, warp, buckle, mangle, mangulate (*Austral slang*), disfigure, contort, gnarl, misshape, malform

distorted *adjective* DEFORMED, bent, twisted, crooked, irregular, warped, buckled, disfigured, contorted, misshapen

distortion *noun* **1** MISREPRESENTATION, bias, slant, perversion, falsification, colouring **2** DEFORMITY, bend, twist, warp, buckle, contortion, malformation, crookedness, twistedness

distract *verb* **1** DIVERT, sidetrack, draw away, turn aside, lead astray, lead away **2** AMUSE, occupy, entertain, beguile, engross **3** AGITATE, trouble, disturb, confuse, puzzle, torment, bewilder, madden, confound, perplex, disconcert, derange, discompose ▷ see **detract**

distracted *adjective* **1** AGITATED, troubled, confused, puzzled, at sea, bewildered, bemused, confounded, perplexed, flustered, in a flap (*informal*) **2** FRANTIC, wild, mad, crazy, desperate, raving, frenzied, distraught, insane, deranged, grief-stricken, overwrought, at the end of your tether

distraction *noun* **1** DISTURBANCE, interference, diversion, interruption **2** ENTERTAINMENT, recreation, amusement, diversion, pastime, divertissement, beguilement **3** FRENZY, desperation, mania, insanity, delirium, derangement

distraught *adjective* FRANTIC, wild, desperate, mad, anxious, distressed, raving, distracted, hysterical, worked-up, agitated, crazed, overwrought, out of your mind, at the end of your tether, wrought-up, beside yourself

distress *verb* UPSET, worry, trouble, pain, wound, bother, disturb, dismay, grieve, torment, harass, afflict, harrow, agitate, sadden, perplex, disconcert, agonize, fluster, perturb, faze, throw (someone) off balance ▷ *noun* **1** SUFFERING, pain, worry, anxiety, torture, grief, misery, agony, sadness, discomfort, torment, sorrow, woe, anguish, heartache, affliction, desolation, wretchedness **2** NEED, suffering, trouble, trial, difficulties, poverty, misery, hard times, hardship, straits, misfortune, adversity, calamity, affliction, privation, destitution, ill-fortune, ill-luck, indigence

distressed *adjective* **1** UPSET, worried, troubled, anxious, distracted, tormented, distraught, afflicted, agitated, saddened, wretched **2** POVERTY-STRICKEN, poor, impoverished, needy, destitute, indigent, down at heel, straitened, penurious

distressing *adjective* UPSETTING, worrying, disturbing, painful, affecting, sad, afflicting, harrowing, grievous, hurtful, lamentable, heart-breaking, nerve-racking, gut-wrenching, distressful

distribute *verb* **1** HAND OUT, dispense, give out, dish out (*informal*), disseminate, deal out, disburse, pass round **2** CIRCULATE, deliver, convey **3** SHARE, give, deal, divide, assign, administer, allocate, dispose, dispense, allot, mete out, dole out, apportion, measure out **4** SPREAD, scatter, disperse, diffuse, disseminate, strew

distribution *noun* **1** DELIVERY, mailing, transport, transportation, handling **2** (*economics*) SHARING, division, assignment, rationing, allocation, partition, allotment, dispensation, apportionment **3** SPREADING, circulation, diffusion, scattering, propagation, dissemination, dispersal, dispersion **4** SPREAD, organization, arrangement, location, placement, disposition

district *noun* AREA, community, region, sector, quarter, ward, parish, neighbourhood, vicinity, locality, locale, neck of the woods (*informal*)

distrust *verb* SUSPECT, doubt, discredit, be wary of, wonder about, mistrust, disbelieve, be suspicious of, be sceptical of, misbelieve << ANTONYM trust ▷ *noun* SUSPICION, question, doubt, disbelief, scepticism, mistrust, misgiving, qualm, wariness, lack of faith, dubiety << ANTONYM trust

distrustful *adjective* SUSPICIOUS, doubting, wary, cynical, doubtful, sceptical, uneasy, dubious, distrusting, disbelieving, leery (*slang*), mistrustful, chary

disturb *verb* **1** INTERRUPT, trouble, bother, startle, plague, disrupt, put out, interfere with, rouse, hassle, inconvenience, pester, intrude on, butt in on **2** UPSET, concern, worry, trouble, shake, excite, alarm, confuse, distress, distract, dismay, unsettle, agitate, ruffle, confound, unnerve, vex, fluster, perturb, derange, discompose << ANTONYM calm **3** MUDDLE, disorder, mix up, mess up, disorganize, jumble up, disarrange, muss (*US & Canad*)

disturbance *noun* **1** DISORDER, bother (*informal*), turmoil, riot, upheaval, fray, brawl, uproar, agitation, fracas, commotion, rumpus, tumult, hubbub, shindig (*informal*), ruction (*informal*), ruckus (*informal*), shindy (*informal*) **2** UPSET, bother, disorder, confusion, distraction, intrusion, interruption, annoyance, agitation, hindrance, perturbation, derangement **3** PROBLEM, upset, disorder, trouble

disturbed *adjective* **1** (*psychiatry*) UNBALANCED, troubled, disordered, unstable, neurotic, upset, deranged, unsound, maladjusted << ANTONYM balanced **2** WORRIED, concerned, troubled, upset, bothered, nervous, anxious, uneasy << ANTONYM calm

disturbing *adjective* WORRYING, troubling, upsetting, alarming, frightening, distressing, startling, discouraging, dismaying, unsettling, harrowing, agitating, disconcerting, disquieting, perturbing

ditch *noun* CHANNEL, drain, trench, dyke, furrow, gully, moat, watercourse ▷ *verb* **1** (*slang*) GET RID OF, dump (*informal*), scrap, discard, dispose of, dispense with, jettison, throw out *or* overboard **2** (*slang*) LEAVE, drop, abandon, dump (*informal*), axe (*informal*), get rid of, bin (*informal*), chuck (*informal*), forsake, jilt

dither (*Chiefly Brit*) *verb* VACILLATE, hesitate, waver, haver, falter, hum and haw, faff about (*Brit informal*), shillyshally (*informal*), swither (*Scot*) << ANTONYM decide ▷ *noun* FLUTTER, flap (*informal*), fluster, bother, stew (*informal*), twitter (*informal*), tizzy (*informal*), pother, tiz-woz (*informal*)

diva *noun* SINGER, opera singer, prima donna

dive *verb* **1** PLUNGE, drop, jump, pitch, leap, duck, dip, descend, plummet **2** GO UNDERWATER, submerge **3** NOSE-DIVE, fall, plunge, crash, pitch, swoop, plummet ▷ *noun* **1** PLUNGE, spring, jump, leap, dash, header (*informal*), swoop, lunge, nose dive **2** (*slang*) SLEAZY BAR, joint (*slang*), honky-tonk (*US slang*)

diverge *verb* **1** SEPARATE, part, split, branch, divide, fork, divaricate **2** CONFLICT, differ, disagree, dissent, be at odds, be at variance **3** DEVIATE, depart, stray, wander, meander, turn aside

divergence *noun* DIFFERENCE, varying, departure, disparity, deviation, separation

divergent *adjective* DIFFERENT, conflicting, differing, disagreeing, diverse, separate, varying, variant, diverging, dissimilar, deviating

diverse *adjective* **1** VARIOUS, mixed, varied, diversified, assorted, miscellaneous, several, sundry, motley, manifold, heterogeneous, of every description **2** DIFFERENT, contrasting, unlike, varying, differing, separate, distinct, disparate, discrete, dissimilar, divergent, discrepant

diversify *verb* VARY, change, expand, transform, alter, spread out, branch out

diversion *noun* **1** DISTRACTION, deviation, deflection, digression **2** PASTIME, play, game, sport, delight, pleasure, entertainment, hobby, relaxation, recreation, enjoyment, distraction, amusement, gratification, divertissement, beguilement **3** (*Chiefly Brit*) DETOUR, deviation, circuitous route, roundabout way, indirect course **4** (*Chiefly Brit*) DEVIATION, departure, straying, divergence, digression

diversity *noun* **1** DIFFERENCE, diversification, variety, divergence, multiplicity, heterogeneity, variegation, diverseness **2** RANGE, variety, scope, sphere

divert *verb* **1** REDIRECT, switch, avert, deflect, deviate, sidetrack, turn aside **2** DISTRACT, shift, deflect, detract, sidetrack, lead astray, draw *or* lead away **3** ENTERTAIN, delight, amuse, please, charm, gratify, beguile, regale

diverting *adjective* ENTERTAINING, amusing, enjoyable, fun, pleasant, humorous, beguiling

divest *verb* **1** DEPRIVE, strip, dispossess, despoil **2** STRIP, remove, take off, undress, denude, disrobe, unclothe

divide *verb* **1** SEPARATE, part, split, cut (up), sever, shear, segregate, cleave, subdivide, bisect, sunder << ANTONYM join **2** SHARE, distribute, allocate, portion, dispense, allot, mete, dole out, apportion, deal out, measure out, divvy (up) (*informal*) **3** SPLIT, break up, alienate, embroil, come between, disunite, estrange, sow dissension, cause to disagree, set at variance *or* odds, set *or* pit against one another ▷▷ **divide something up** GROUP, sort, separate, arrange, grade, classify, categorize

dividend *noun* BONUS, share, cut (*informal*), gain, extra, plus, portion, divvy (*informal*)

divination *noun* PREDICTION, divining, prophecy, presage, foretelling, clairvoyance, fortune-telling, prognostication, augury, soothsaying, sortilege

divine *adjective* **1** HEAVENLY, spiritual, holy, immortal, supernatural, celestial, angelic, superhuman, godlike, cherubic, seraphic, supernal (*literary*), paradisaical **2** SACRED, religious, holy, spiritual, blessed, revered, venerable, hallowed, consecrated, sanctified **3** (*informal*) WONDERFUL, perfect, beautiful, excellent, lovely, stunning (*informal*), glorious, marvellous, splendid, gorgeous, delightful, exquisite, radiant, superlative, ravishing ▷ *noun* PRIEST, minister, vicar, reverend, pastor, cleric, clergyman, curate, churchman, padre (*informal*), holy man, man of God, man of the cloth, ecclesiastic, father confessor ▷ *verb* 1 GUESS, understand, suppose, suspect, perceive, discern, infer, deduce, apprehend, conjecture, surmise, foretell, intuit, prognosticate 2 DOWSE (*for water or minerals*)

divinity *noun* 1 THEOLOGY, religion, religious studies 2 GODLINESS, holiness, sanctity, godhead, divine nature, godhood 3 DEITY, spirit, genius, guardian spirit, daemon, god *or* goddess, atua (*NZ*)

division *noun* 1 SEPARATION, dividing, splitting up, detaching, partition, cutting up, bisection 2 SHARING, sharing, distribution, assignment, rationing, allocation, allotment, apportionment 3 DISAGREEMENT, split, breach, feud, rift, rupture, abyss, chasm, variance, discord, difference of opinion, estrangement, disunion << ANTONYM unity 4 DIVIDING LINE, border, boundary, divide, partition, demarcation, divider 5 DEPARTMENT, group, head, sector, branch, subdivision 6 PART, bit, piece, section, sector, class, category, segment, portion, fraction, compartment

divisive *adjective* DISRUPTIVE, unsettling, alienating, troublesome, controversial, contentious

divorce *noun* 1 SEPARATION, split, break-up, parting, split-up, rift, dissolution, severance, estrangement, annulment, decree nisi, disunion 2 BREACH, break, split, falling-out (*informal*), disagreement, feud, rift, bust-up (*informal*), rupture, abyss, chasm, schism, estrangement ▷ *verb* 1 SPLIT UP, separate, part company, annul your marriage, dissolve your marriage 2 SEPARATE, divide, isolate, detach, distance, sever, disconnect, dissociate, set apart, disunite, sunder

divulge *verb* MAKE KNOWN, tell, reveal, publish, declare, expose, leak, confess, exhibit, communicate, spill (*informal*), disclose, proclaim, betray, uncover, impart, promulgate, let slip, blow wide open (*slang*), get off your chest (*informal*), out (*informal*), spill your guts about (*slang*) << ANTONYM keep secret

dizzy *adjective* 1 GIDDY, faint, light-headed, swimming, reeling, staggering, shaky, wobbly, off balance, unsteady, vertiginous, woozy (*informal*), weak at the knees 2 CONFUSED, dazzled, at sea, bewildered, muddled, bemused, dazed, disorientated, befuddled, light-headed, punch-drunk, fuddled 3 (*informal*) SCATTERBRAINED, silly, foolish, frivolous, giddy, capricious, forgetful, flighty, light-headed, scatty (*Brit informal*), empty-headed, bird-brained (*informal*), featherbrained, ditzy *or* ditsy (*slang*) 4 STEEP, towering, soaring, lofty, sky-high, vertiginous

do *verb* 1 PERFORM, work, achieve, carry out, produce, effect, complete, conclude, undertake, accomplish, execute, discharge, pull off, transact 2 BEHAVE, act, conduct yourself, deport yourself, bear yourself, acquit yourself 3 MAKE, prepare, fix, arrange, look after, organize, be responsible for, see to, get ready, make ready 4 SOLVE, work out, resolve, figure out, decode, decipher, puzzle out 5 GET ON, manage, fare, proceed, make out, prosper, get along 6 PRESENT, give, show, act, produce, stage, perform, mount, put on 7 BE ADEQUATE, be enough, be sufficient, answer, serve, suit, content, satisfy, suffice, be of use, pass muster, cut the mustard, fill the bill (*informal*), meet requirements 8 (*informal*) CHEAT, trick, con (*informal*), skin (*slang*), stiff (*slang*), deceive, fleece, hoax, defraud, dupe, swindle, diddle (*informal*), take (someone) for a ride (*informal*), pull a fast one on (*informal*), cozen 9 PRODUCE, make, create, develop, manufacture, construct, invent, fabricate 10 (*informal*) VISIT, tour in *or* around, look at, cover, explore, take in (*informal*), stop in, journey through *or* around, travel in *or* around ▷ *noun* (*informal, chiefly Brit & NZ*) PARTY, gathering, function, social, event, affair, at-home, occasion, celebration, reception, bash (*informal*), rave (*Brit slang*), get-together (*informal*), festivity, knees-up (*Brit informal*), beano (*Brit slang*), social gathering, shindig (*informal*), soirée, rave-up (*Brit slang*), hooley *or* hoolie (*chiefly Irish & NZ*) ▷▷ **do away with someone** KILL, murder, do in (*slang*), destroy, take out (*slang*), dispatch, slay, blow away (*slang, chiefly US*), knock off (*slang*), liquidate, exterminate, take (someone's) life, bump off (*slang*) ▷▷ **do away with something** GET RID OF, remove, eliminate, axe (*informal*), abolish, junk (*informal*), pull, chuck (*informal*), discard, put an end to, dispense with, discontinue, put paid to, pull the plug on ▷▷ **do's and don'ts** (*informal*) RULES, code, regulations, standards, instructions, customs, convention, usage, protocol, formalities, etiquette, p's and q's, good *or* proper behaviour ▷▷ **do someone in** (*slang*) **1** KILL, murder, destroy, eliminate (*slang*), take out (*slang*), execute, butcher, slaughter, dispatch, assassinate, slay, do away with, blow away (*slang, chiefly US*), knock off (*slang*), liquidate, annihilate, neutralize, take (someone's) life, bump off (*slang*) **2** EXHAUST, tire, drain, shatter (*informal*), weaken, fatigue, weary, fag (*informal*), sap, wear out, tire out, knacker (*slang*) ▷▷ **do without something** *or* **someone** MANAGE WITHOUT, give up, dispense with, forgo, kick (*informal*), sacrifice, abstain from, get along without

docile *adjective* OBEDIENT, manageable, compliant, amenable, submissive, pliant, tractable, biddable, ductile, teachable (*rare*) << ANTONYM difficult

dock¹ *noun* PORT, haven, harbour, pier, wharf, quay, waterfront, anchorage ▷ *verb* **1** MOOR, land, anchor, put in, tie up, berth, drop anchor **2** (*of spacecraft*) LINK UP, unite, join, couple, rendezvous, hook up

dock² *verb* **1** CUT, reduce, decrease, diminish, lessen << ANTONYM increase **2** DEDUCT, subtract **3** CUT OFF, crop, clip, shorten, curtail, cut short

docket *noun* **1** (*Chiefly Brit*) LABEL, bill, ticket, certificate, tag, voucher, tab, receipt, tally, chit, chitty, counterfoil **2** (*US law*) FILE, index, register

doctor *noun* PHYSICIAN, medic (*informal*), general practitioner, medical practitioner, G.P. ▷ *verb* **1** CHANGE, alter, interfere with, disguise, pervert, fudge, tamper with, tinker with, misrepresent, falsify, meddle with, mess about with **2** ADD TO, spike, cut, mix something with something, dilute, water down, adulterate

doctrinaire *adjective* **1** DOGMATIC, rigid, fanatical, inflexible **2** IMPRACTICAL, theoretical, speculative, ideological, unrealistic, hypothetical, unpragmatic

doctrine *noun* TEACHING, principle, belief, opinion, article, concept, conviction, canon, creed, dogma, tenet, precept, article of faith, kaupapa (*NZ*)

document *noun* PAPER, form, certificate, report, record, testimonial, authorization, legal form ▷ *verb* SUPPORT, back up, certify, verify, detail, instance, validate, substantiate, corroborate, authenticate, give weight to, particularize

doddle *noun* (*Brit informal*) PIECE OF CAKE

(*informal*), picnic (*informal*), child's play (*informal*), pushover (*slang or informal*), no sweat (*slang*), cinch (*slang*), cakewalk (*informal*), money for old rope, bludge (*Austral & NZ informal*)

dodge *verb* **1** DUCK, dart, swerve, sidestep, shoot, shift, turn aside, body-swerve (*Scot*) **2** EVADE, avoid, escape, get away from, elude, body-swerve (*Scot*), slip through the net of **3** AVOID, hedge, parry, get out of, evade, shirk ▷ *noun* TRICK, scheme, ploy, trap, device, fraud, con (*slang*), manoeuvre, deception, scam (*slang*), gimmick, hoax, wheeze (*Brit slang*), deceit, ruse, artifice, subterfuge, canard, feint, stratagem, contrivance, machination, fastie (*Austral slang*)

dodgy *adjective* **1** (*Brit, Austral & NZ informal*) NASTY, offensive, unpleasant, revolting, distasteful, repellent, unsavoury, obnoxious, repulsive, objectionable, repugnant, shonky (*Austral & NZ informal*) **2** (*Brit, Austral & NZ informal*) RISKY, difficult, tricky, dangerous, delicate, uncertain, problematic(al), unreliable, dicky (*Brit informal*), dicey (*informal, chiefly Brit*), ticklish, chancy (*informal*), shonky (*Austral & NZ informal*)

doer *noun* ACHIEVER, organizer, powerhouse (*slang*), dynamo, live wire (*slang*), go-getter (*informal*), active person, wheeler-dealer (*informal*)

doff *verb* **1** TIP, raise, remove, lift, take off **2** TAKE OFF, remove, shed, discard, throw off, cast off, slip out of, slip off

dog *noun* **1** HOUND, canine, bitch, puppy, pup, mongrel, tyke, mutt (*slang*), pooch (*slang*), cur, man's best friend, kuri *or* goorie (*NZ*), brak (*S African*) **2** (*informal*) SCOUNDREL, villain, cur, heel (*slang*), knave (*archaic*), blackguard ▷ *verb* **1** PLAGUE, follow, trouble, haunt, hound, torment, afflict **2** PURSUE, follow, track, chase, shadow, harry, tail (*informal*), trail, hound, stalk, go after, give chase to ▷▷ **dog-eat-dog** RUTHLESS, fierce, vicious, ferocious, cut-throat, with no holds barred

dogged *adjective* DETERMINED, steady, persistent, stubborn, firm, staunch, persevering, resolute, single-minded, tenacious, steadfast, unyielding, obstinate, indefatigable, immovable, stiff-necked, unshakable, unflagging, pertinacious << ANTONYM irresolute

dogma *noun* DOCTRINE, teachings, principle, opinion, article, belief, creed, tenet, precept, credo, article of faith, kaupapa (*NZ*)

dogmatic *adjective* 1 OPINIONATED, arrogant, assertive, arbitrary, emphatic, downright, dictatorial, imperious, overbearing, categorical, magisterial, doctrinaire, obdurate, peremptory 2 DOCTRINAL, authoritative, categorical, canonical, oracular, ex cathedra

doing *noun* 1 CARRYING OUT *or* THROUGH, performance, execution, implementation 2 HANDIWORK, act, action, achievement, exploit, deed

doings *plural noun* DEEDS, actions, exploits, concerns, events, affairs, happenings, proceedings, transactions, dealings, goings-on (*informal*)

doldrums ▷▷ **the doldrums** BLUES, depression, dumps (*informal*), gloom, boredom, apathy, inertia, stagnation, inactivity, tedium, dullness, the hump (*Brit informal*), ennui, torpor, lassitude, listlessness

dole *noun* SHARE, grant, gift, allowance, portion, donation, quota, parcel, handout, modicum, pittance, alms, gratuity, koha (*NZ*) ▷▷ **dole something out** GIVE OUT, share, deal out, distribute, divide, assign, administer, allocate, hand out, dispense, allot, mete, apportion

dollop *noun* 1 LUMP, blob 2 HELPING, serving, portion, scoop, gob

domain *noun* AREA, field, department, discipline, sphere, realm, speciality

domestic *adjective* 1 HOME, internal, native, indigenous, not foreign 2 HOUSEHOLD, home, family, private, domiciliary 3 HOME-LOVING, homely, housewifely, stay-at-home, domesticated 4 DOMESTICATED, trained, tame, house, pet, house-trained ▷ *noun* SERVANT, help, maid, woman (*informal*), daily, char (*informal*), charwoman, daily help

domesticate *or sometimes US* **domesticize** *verb* 1 TAME, break, train, house-train, gentle 2 NATURALIZE, accustom, familiarize, habituate, acclimatize

domesticated *adjective* 1 TAME, broken (in), tamed << ANTONYM wild 2 HOME-LOVING, homely, domestic, housewifely, house-trained (*jocular*)

domesticity *noun* HOME LIFE, housekeeping, domestication, homemaking, housewifery, home-lovingness

dominance *noun* CONTROL, government, power, rule, authority, command, sway, domination, supremacy, mastery, ascendancy, paramountcy

dominant *adjective* 1 MAIN, chief, primary, outstanding, principal, prominent, influential, prevailing, paramount, prevalent, predominant, pre-eminent << ANTONYM minor 2 CONTROLLING, leading, ruling, commanding, supreme, governing, superior, presiding, authoritative, ascendant

dominate *verb* 1 CONTROL, lead, rule, direct, master, govern, monopolize, tyrannize, have the upper hand over, lead by the nose (*informal*), overbear, have the whip hand over, domineer, keep under your thumb, have the upper hand (in), rule the roost (in) 2 TOWER ABOVE, overlook, survey, stand over, loom over, stand head and shoulders above, bestride

domination *noun* CONTROL, power, rule, authority, influence, command, sway, dictatorship, repression, oppression, suppression, supremacy, mastery, tyranny, ascendancy, subordination, despotism, subjection

domineering *adjective* OVERBEARING, arrogant, authoritarian, oppressive, autocratic, masterful, dictatorial, coercive, bossy (*informal*), imperious, tyrannical, magisterial, despotic, high-handed, iron-handed << ANTONYM submissive

dominion *noun* 1 CONTROL, government, power, rule, authority, command, sovereignty, sway, domination, jurisdiction, supremacy, mastery, ascendancy, mana (*NZ*) 2 KINGDOM, territory, province, country, region, empire, patch, turf (*US slang*), realm, domain

don *verb* PUT ON, get into, dress in, pull on, change into, get dressed in, clothe yourself in, slip on *or* into

donate *verb* GIVE, present, contribute, grant, commit, gift, hand out, subscribe, endow, chip in (*informal*), bestow, entrust, impart, bequeath, make a gift of

donation *noun* CONTRIBUTION, gift, subscription, offering, present, grant, hand-out, boon, alms, stipend, gratuity, benefaction, largesse *or* largess, koha (*NZ*)

done *interjection* AGREED, you're on (*informal*), O.K. *or* okay (*informal*), it's a bargain, it's a deal, ka pai (*NZ*) ▷ *adjective* 1 FINISHED, completed, accomplished, over, through, ended, perfected, realized, concluded, executed, terminated, consummated, in the can (*informal*) 2 COOKED, ready, cooked enough, cooked to a turn, cooked sufficiently 3 ACCEPTABLE, proper,

conventional, protocol, de rigueur (*French*)
▷▷ **done for** (*informal*) FINISHED, lost, beaten,
defeated, destroyed, ruined, broken, dashed,
wrecked, doomed, foiled, undone ▷▷ **done
in** *or* **up** (*informal*) EXHAUSTED, bushed
(*informal*), all in (*slang*), worn out, dead
(*informal*), knackered (*slang*), clapped out
(*Austral & NZ informal*), tired out, ready to
drop, dog-tired (*informal*), zonked (*slang*),
dead beat (*informal*), fagged out (*informal*),
worn to a frazzle (*informal*), on your last
legs, creamcrackered (*Brit slang*) ▷▷ **have**
or **be done with something** *or* **someone**
BE THROUGH WITH, give up, be finished
with, throw over, wash your hands of, end
relations with
donor *noun* GIVER, contributor, benefactor,
philanthropist, grantor (*law*), donator,
almsgiver << ANTONYM recipient
doom *noun* DESTRUCTION, ruin, catastrophe,
death, downfall ▷ *verb* CONDEMN, sentence,
consign, foreordain, destine, predestine,
preordain
doomed *adjective* HOPELESS, condemned, ill-
fated, fated, unhappy, unfortunate, cursed,
unlucky, blighted, hapless, bedevilled,
luckless, ill-starred, star-crossed, ill-omened
door *noun* OPENING, entry, entrance, exit,
doorway, ingress, egress ▷▷ **out of doors**
IN THE OPEN AIR, outside, outdoors, out,
alfresco ▷▷ **show someone the door** THROW
OUT, remove, eject, evict, turn out, bounce
(*slang*), oust, drive out, boot out (*informal*),
ask to leave, show out, throw out on your ear
(*informal*)
do-or-die *adjective* DESPERATE, risky,
hazardous, going for broke, win-or-bust,
death-or-glory, kill-or-cure
dope *noun* 1 (*slang*) DRUGS, narcotics, opiates,
dadah (*Austral slang*) 2 (*informal*) IDIOT, fool,
jerk (*slang, chiefly US & Canad*), plank (*Brit
slang*), charlie (*Brit informal*), berk (*Brit slang*),
wally (*slang*), prat (*slang*), plonker (*slang*),
coot, geek (*slang*), twit (*informal, chiefly Brit*),
dunce, oaf, simpleton, dimwit (*informal*),
dipstick (*Brit slang*), gonzo (*slang*), schmuck
(*US slang*), dork (*slang*), nitwit (*informal*),
dolt, blockhead, divvy (*Brit slang*), pillock
(*Brit slang*), dweeb (*US slang*), putz (*US slang*),
fathead (*informal*), eejit (*Scot & Irish*), dumb-
ass (*slang*), numpty (*Scot informal*), lamebrain
(*informal*), nerd *or* nurd (*slang*), numbskull
or numskull, dorba *or* dorb (*Austral
slang*), bogan (*Austral slang*) 3 (*informal*)
INFORMATION, facts, details, material,

news, intelligence, gen (*Brit informal*), info
(*informal*), inside information, lowdown
(*informal*) ▷ *verb* DRUG, doctor, knock
out, inject, sedate, stupefy, anaesthetize,
narcotize
dopey *or* **dopy** *adjective* (*informal*) 1 DROWSY,
dazed, groggy (*informal*), drugged, muzzy,
stupefied, half-asleep, woozy (*informal*)
2 STUPID, simple, slow, thick, silly, foolish,
dense, dumb (*informal*), senseless, goofy
(*informal*), idiotic, dozy (*Brit informal*),
asinine, dumb-ass (*slang*)
dormant *adjective* LATENT, inactive, lurking,
quiescent, unrealized, unexpressed,
inoperative
dorp *noun* (*S African*) TOWN, village,
settlement, municipality, kainga *or* kaika
(*NZ*)
dose *noun* 1 (*medical*) MEASURE, amount,
allowance, portion, prescription, ration,
draught, dosage, potion 2 QUANTITY,
measure, supply, portion
dot *noun* SPOT, point, mark, circle, atom, dab,
mite, fleck, jot, speck, full stop, speckle,
mote, iota ▷ *verb* SPOT, stud, fleck, speckle
▷▷ **on the dot** ON TIME, promptly, precisely,
exactly (*informal*), to the minute, on the
button (*informal*), punctually
dote with on *or* **upon** *verb* ADORE, prize,
treasure, admire, hold dear, idolize, lavish
affection on
doting *adjective* ADORING, devoted, fond,
foolish, indulgent, lovesick
dotty *adjective* (*slang, chiefly Brit*) CRAZY,
touched, peculiar, eccentric, batty (*slang*),
off-the-wall (*slang*), potty (*Brit informal*),
oddball (*informal*), loopy (*informal*), crackpot
(*informal*), out to lunch (*informal*), outré,
doolally (*slang*), off your trolley (*slang*), up
the pole (*informal*), wacko *or* whacko (*slang*),
off the air (*Austral slang*), porangi (*NZ*), daggy
(*Austral & NZ informal*)
double *adjective* 1 MATCHING, coupled,
doubled, paired, twin, duplicate, in
pairs, binate (*botany*) 2 DECEITFUL, false,
fraudulent, deceiving, treacherous,
dishonest, deceptive, hypocritical,
counterfeit, two-faced, disingenuous,
insincere, double-dealing, duplicitous,
perfidious, knavish (*archaic*), Janus-faced
3 DUAL, enigmatic, cryptic, twofold,
Delphic, enigmatical ▷ *noun* TWIN,
lookalike, spitting image, copy, fellow, mate,
counterpart, clone, replica, ringer (*slang*),
impersonator (*informal*), dead ringer (*slang*),

Doppelgänger, duplicate ▷ *verb* 1 MULTIPLY BY TWO, duplicate, increase twofold, repeat, enlarge, magnify 2 FOLD UP *or* OVER 3 *with as* FUNCTION AS, serve as ▷▷ **at** *or* **on the double** AT ONCE, now, immediately, directly, quickly, promptly, right now, straight away, right away, briskly, without delay, pronto (*informal*), at full speed, in double-quick time, this instant, this very minute, pdq (*slang*), posthaste, tout de suite (*French*)

double-cross *verb* BETRAY, trick, cheat, mislead, two-time (*informal*), defraud, swindle, hoodwink, sell down the river (*informal*), cozen

doubly *adverb* TWICE AS, in two ways, twofold, as much again, in double measure

doubt *noun* 1 UNCERTAINTY, confusion, hesitation, dilemma, scepticism, misgiving, suspense, indecision, bewilderment, lack of confidence, hesitancy, perplexity, vacillation, lack of conviction, irresolution, dubiety << ANTONYM certainty 2 SUSPICION, scepticism, distrust, fear, apprehension, mistrust, misgivings, disquiet, qualms, incredulity, lack of faith << ANTONYM belief ▷ *verb* 1 BE UNCERTAIN, be sceptical, be dubious 2 WAVER, hesitate, vacillate, sway, fluctuate, dither (*chiefly Brit*), haver, oscillate, chop and change, blow hot and cold (*informal*), keep changing your mind, shillyshally (*informal*), be irresolute *or* indecisive, swither (*Scot*) 3 DISBELIEVE, question, suspect, query, distrust, mistrust, lack confidence in, misgive << ANTONYM believe ▷▷ **no doubt** CERTAINLY, surely, probably, admittedly, doubtless, assuredly, doubtlessly

doubter *noun* SCEPTIC, questioner, disbeliever, agnostic, unbeliever, doubting Thomas

doubtful *adjective* 1 UNLIKELY, unclear, dubious, unsettled, dodgy (*Brit, Austral & NZ informal*), questionable, ambiguous, improbable, indefinite, unconfirmed, inconclusive, debatable, indeterminate, iffy (*informal*), equivocal, inexact << ANTONYM certain 2 UNSURE, uncertain, hesitant, suspicious, hesitating, sceptical, unsettled, tentative, wavering, unresolved, perplexed, undecided, unconvinced, vacillating, leery (*slang*), distrustful, in two minds (*informal*), irresolute << ANTONYM certain 3 QUESTIONABLE, suspect, suspicious, crooked, dubious, dodgy (*Brit, Austral & NZ informal*), slippery, shady (*informal*),

unscrupulous, fishy (*informal*), shifty, disreputable, untrustworthy, shonky (*Austral & NZ informal*)

doubtless *adverb* PROBABLY, presumably, most likely

doughty *adjective* (*old-fashioned*) INTREPID, brave, daring, bold, hardy, heroic, courageous, gritty, fearless, resolute, gallant, valiant, redoubtable, dauntless, valorous, stouthearted

dour *adjective* GLOOMY, forbidding, grim, sour, dismal, dreary, sullen, unfriendly, morose << ANTONYM cheery

douse *or* **dowse** *verb* 1 PUT OUT, smother, blow out, extinguish, snuff (out) 2 DRENCH, soak, steep, saturate, duck, submerge, immerse, dunk, souse, plunge into water

dovetail *verb* CORRESPOND, match, agree, accord, coincide, tally, conform, harmonize

dowdy *adjective* FRUMPY, old-fashioned, shabby, drab, tacky (*US informal*), unfashionable, dingy, frumpish, ill-dressed, frowzy << ANTONYM chic

down *adjective* DEPRESSED, low, sad, blue, unhappy, discouraged, miserable, fed up, dismal, pessimistic, melancholy, glum, dejected, despondent, dispirited, downcast, morose, disheartened, crestfallen, downhearted, down in the dumps (*informal*), sick as a parrot (*informal*), low-spirited ▷ *verb* 1 (*informal*) SWALLOW, drink (down), drain, gulp (down), put away (*informal*), toss off 2 BRING DOWN, fell, knock down, throw, trip, floor, tackle, deck (*slang*), overthrow, prostrate

down-and-out *adjective* DESTITUTE, ruined, impoverished, derelict, penniless, dirt-poor (*informal*), flat broke (*informal*), on your uppers (*informal*), without two pennies to rub together (*informal*) ▷ *noun* TRAMP, bum (*informal*), beggar, derelict, outcast, pauper, vagrant, vagabond, bag lady, dosser (*Brit slang*), derro (*Austral slang*)

downbeat *adjective* (*informal*) 1 LOW-KEY, muted, subdued, sober, sombre 2 GLOOMY, negative, depressed, pessimistic, unfavourable << ANTONYM cheerful

downcast *adjective* DEJECTED, sad, depressed, unhappy, disappointed, discouraged, miserable, dismayed, choked, daunted, dismal, despondent, dispirited, disheartened, disconsolate, crestfallen, down in the dumps (*informal*), cheerless, sick as a parrot (*informal*) << ANTONYM cheerful

downfall *noun* RUIN, fall, destruction,

collapse, breakdown, disgrace, overthrow, descent, undoing, comeuppance (*slang*), comedown

downgrade *verb* 1 DEMOTE, degrade, take down a peg (*informal*), lower *or* reduce in rank << ANTONYM promote 2 RUN DOWN, denigrate, disparage, detract from, decry

down-market *adjective* SECOND-RATE, cheap, inferior, tacky (*informal*), shoddy, low-grade, tawdry, low-quality, two-bit (*US & Canad slang*), cheap and nasty (*informal*), lowbrow, bush-league (*Austral & NZ informal*), bodger *or* bodgie (*Austral slang*) << ANTONYM first-rate

downpour *noun* RAINSTORM, flood, deluge, torrential rain, cloudburst, inundation

downright *adjective* COMPLETE, absolute, utter, total, positive, clear, plain, simple, explicit, outright, blatant, unequivocal, unqualified, out-and-out, categorical, undisguised, thoroughgoing, arrant, deep-dyed (*usually derogatory*)

downside *noun* DRAWBACK, disadvantage, snag, problem, trouble, minus (*informal*), flip side, other side of the coin (*informal*), bad *or* weak point << ANTONYM benefit

down-to-earth *adjective* SENSIBLE, practical, realistic, common-sense, matter-of-fact, sane, no-nonsense, hard-headed, unsentimental, plain-spoken

downtrodden *adjective* OPPRESSED, abused, exploited, subservient, subjugated, tyrannized

downward *adjective* DESCENDING, declining, heading down, earthward

doze *verb* NAP, sleep, slumber, nod, kip (*Brit slang*), snooze (*informal*), catnap, drowse, sleep lightly, zizz (*Brit informal*) ▷ *noun* NAP, kip (*Brit slang*), snooze (*informal*), siesta, little sleep, catnap, forty winks (*informal*), shuteye (*slang*), zizz (*Brit informal*)

dozy *adjective* (*Brit informal*) STUPID, simple, slow, silly, daft (*informal*), senseless, goofy (*informal*), witless, not all there, slow-witted

drab *adjective* DULL, grey, gloomy, dismal, dreary, shabby, sombre, lacklustre, flat, dingy, colourless, uninspired, vapid, cheerless << ANTONYM bright

Draconian *adjective sometimes not cap.* SEVERE, hard, harsh, stern, drastic, stringent, punitive, austere, pitiless

draft *noun* 1 OUTLINE, plan, sketch, version, rough, abstract, delineation, preliminary form 2 MONEY ORDER, bill (of exchange), cheque, postal order ▷ *verb* OUTLINE, write,

plan, produce, create, design, draw, frame, compose, devise, sketch, draw up, formulate, contrive, delineate

drag *verb* 1 PULL, draw, haul, trail, tow, tug, jerk, yank, hale, lug 2 LAG, trail, linger, loiter, straggle, dawdle, hang back, tarry, draggle 3 GO SLOWLY, inch, creep, crawl, advance slowly ▷ *noun* (*informal*) NUISANCE, pain (*informal*), bore, bother, pest, hassle (*informal*), inconvenience, annoyance, pain in the neck, pain in the backside, pain in the butt (*informal*) ▷▷ **drag on** LAST, continue, carry on, remain, endure, persist, linger, abide ▷▷ **drag yourself** GO SLOWLY, creep, crawl, inch, shuffle, shamble, limp along, move at a snail's pace, advance slowly

dragoon *verb* FORCE, drive, compel, bully, intimidate, railroad (*informal*), constrain, coerce, impel, strong-arm (*informal*), browbeat

drain *noun* 1 SEWER, channel, pipe, sink, outlet, ditch, trench, conduit, duct, culvert, watercourse 2 REDUCTION, strain, drag, expenditure, exhaustion, sapping, depletion ▷ *verb* 1 REMOVE, draw, empty, withdraw, milk, tap, pump, bleed, evacuate 2 EMPTY 3 FLOW OUT, leak, discharge, trickle, ooze, seep, exude, well out, effuse 4 DRINK UP, swallow, finish, put away (*informal*), quaff, gulp down 5 EXHAUST, tire, wear out, strain, weaken, fatigue, weary, debilitate, prostrate, tax, tire out, enfeeble, enervate 6 CONSUME, waste, exhaust, empty, deplete, use up, sap, dissipate, swallow up ▷▷ **down the drain** GONE, lost, wasted, ruined, gone for good

drainage *noun* SEWERAGE, waste, sewage

dram *noun* MEASURE, shot (*informal*), drop, glass, tot, slug, snort (*slang*), snifter (*informal*)

drama *noun* 1 PLAY, show, stage show, stage play, dramatization, theatrical piece 2 THEATRE, acting, dramatic art, stagecraft, dramaturgy, Thespian art 3 EXCITEMENT, crisis, dramatics, spectacle, turmoil, histrionics, theatrics

dramatic *adjective* 1 EXCITING, emotional, thrilling, tense, startling, sensational, breathtaking, electrifying, melodramatic, climactic, high-octane (*informal*), shock-horror (*facetious*), suspenseful 2 THEATRICAL, Thespian, dramaturgical, dramaturgic 3 EXPRESSIVE 4 POWERFUL, striking, stunning (*informal*), impressive, effective, vivid, jaw-dropping << ANTONYM ordinary

dramatist *noun* PLAYWRIGHT, screenwriter, scriptwriter, dramaturge

dramatize *or* **dramatise** *verb* EXAGGERATE, overdo, overstate, lay it on (thick) (*slang*), play-act, play to the gallery, make a performance of

drape *verb* **1** COVER, wrap, fold, array, adorn, swathe **2** HANG, drop, dangle, suspend, lean, droop, let fall

drastic *adjective* EXTREME, strong, radical, desperate, severe, harsh, dire, forceful

draught *or* US **draft** *noun* **1** BREEZE, current, movement, flow, puff, influx, gust, current of air **2** DRINK

draw *verb* **1** SKETCH, design, outline, trace, portray, paint, depict, mark out, map out, delineate **2** PULL, drag, haul, tow, tug **3** INHALE, breathe in, pull, inspire, suck, respire **4** EXTRACT, take, remove, drain **5** CHOOSE, pick, select, take, single out **6** DEDUCE, make, get, take, derive, infer **7** ATTRACT, engage **8** ENTICE, bring in ▷ *noun* **1** TIE, deadlock, stalemate, impasse, dead heat **2** (*informal*) APPEAL, interest, pull (*informal*), charm, attraction, lure, temptation, fascination, attractiveness, allure, magnetism, enchantment, enticement, captivation, temptingness ▷▷ **draw back** RECOIL, withdraw, retreat, shrink, falter, back off, shy away, flinch, retract, quail, start back ▷▷ **draw on** *or* **upon something** MAKE USE OF, use, employ, rely on, exploit, extract, take from, fall back on, have recourse to ▷▷ **draw something out** STRETCH OUT, extend, lengthen, elongate, attenuate ▷▷ **draw something up** DRAFT, write, produce, create, prepare, frame, compose, devise, formulate, contrive ▷▷ **draw up** HALT, stop, pull up, stop short, come to a stop

drawback *noun* DISADVANTAGE, trouble, difficulty, fault, handicap, obstacle, defect, deficiency, flaw, hitch, nuisance, snag, downside, stumbling block, impediment, detriment, imperfection, hindrance, fly in the ointment (*informal*) << ANTONYM advantage

drawing *noun* PICTURE, illustration, representation, cartoon, sketch, portrayal, depiction, study, outline, delineation

drawl *verb* SPEAK *or* SAY SLOWLY

drawn *adjective* TENSE, worn, strained, stressed, tired, pinched, fatigued, harassed, fraught, sapped, harrowed, haggard

dread *verb* FEAR, shrink from, cringe at the thought of, quail from, shudder to think about, have cold feet about (*informal*), anticipate with horror, tremble to think about ▷ *noun* FEAR, alarm, horror, terror, dismay, fright, apprehension, consternation, trepidation, apprehensiveness, affright

dreadful *adjective* **1** TERRIBLE, shocking, awful, alarming, distressing, appalling, tragic, horrible, formidable, fearful, dire, horrendous, hideous, monstrous, from hell (*informal*), grievous, atrocious, frightful, godawful (*slang*), hellacious (US *slang*) **2** SERIOUS, terrible, awful, appalling, horrendous, monstrous, unspeakable, abysmal **3** AWFUL, terrible, horrendous, frightful

dream *noun* **1** VISION, illusion, delusion, hallucination, reverie **2** AMBITION, wish, fantasy, desire, Holy Grail (*informal*), pipe dream **3** DAYDREAM **4** DELIGHT, pleasure, joy, beauty, treasure, gem, marvel, pearler (*Austral slang*), beaut (*Austral & NZ slang*) ▷ *verb* **1** HAVE DREAMS, hallucinate **2** DAYDREAM, stargaze, build castles in the air *or* in Spain ▷▷ **dream of something** *or* **someone** DAYDREAM ABOUT, fantasize about ▷▷ **dream something up** INVENT, create, imagine, devise, hatch, contrive, concoct, think up, cook up (*informal*), spin

dreamer *noun* IDEALIST, visionary, daydreamer, utopian, theorizer, fantasizer, romancer, Don Quixote, escapist, Walter Mitty, fantasist, fantast

dreamy *adjective* **1** VAGUE, abstracted, absent, musing, preoccupied, daydreaming, faraway, pensive, in a reverie, with your head in the clouds **2** RELAXING, calming, romantic, gentle, soothing, lulling **3** IMPRACTICAL, vague, imaginary, speculative, visionary, fanciful, quixotic, dreamlike, airy-fairy << ANTONYM realistic

dreary *adjective* **1** DULL, boring, tedious, routine, drab, tiresome, lifeless, monotonous, humdrum, colourless, uneventful, uninteresting, mind-numbing, ho-hum (*informal*), wearisome, as dry as dust << ANTONYM exciting **2** DISMAL, depressing, bleak, sad, lonely, gloomy, solitary, melancholy, sombre, forlorn, glum, mournful, lonesome (*chiefly US & Canad*), downcast, sorrowful, wretched, joyless, funereal, doleful, cheerless, drear, comfortless

dredge up *verb* (*informal*) DIG UP, raise, rake up, discover, uncover, draw up, unearth, drag up, fish up

dregs *plural noun* SEDIMENT, grounds, lees,

waste, deposit, trash, residue, scum, dross, residuum, scourings, draff ▷▷ **the dregs** (*Brit informal*) SCUM, outcasts, rabble, down-and-outs, good-for-nothings, riffraff, canaille (*French*), ragtag and bobtail

drench *verb* SOAK, flood, wet, duck, drown, steep, swamp, saturate, inundate, souse, imbrue

dress *noun* 1 FROCK, gown, garment, robe 2 CLOTHING, clothes, gear (*informal*), costume, threads (*slang*), garments, apparel, attire, garb, togs, raiment (*archaic or poetic*), vestment, schmutter (*slang*), habiliment ▷ *verb* 1 PUT ON CLOTHES, don clothes, slip on *or* into something << ANTONYM undress 2 CLOTHE 3 BANDAGE, treat, plaster, bind up 4 DECORATE, deck, adorn, trim, array, drape, ornament, embellish, festoon, bedeck, furbish, rig out 5 ARRANGE, do (up), groom, set, prepare, comb (out), get ready ▷▷ **dress someone down** (*informal*) REPRIMAND, rebuke, scold, berate, castigate, tear into (*informal*), tell off (*informal*), read the riot act, reprove, upbraid, slap on the wrist, carpet (*informal*), bawl out (*informal*), rap over the knuckles, haul over the coals, chew out (*US & Canad informal*), tear (someone) off a strip (*Brit informal*), give a rocket (*Brit & NZ informal*) ▷▷ **dress up** 1 PUT ON FANCY DRESS, wear a costume, disguise yourself 2 DRESS FORMALLY, dress for dinner, doll yourself up (*slang*), put on your best bib and tucker (*informal*), put on your glad rags (*informal*)

dressmaker *noun* SEAMSTRESS, tailor, couturier, sewing woman, modiste

dribble *verb* 1 RUN, drip, trickle, drop, leak, ooze, seep, fall in drops 2 DROOL, drivel, slaver, slobber, drip saliva

drift *verb* 1 FLOAT, go (aimlessly), bob, coast, slip, sail, slide, glide, meander, waft, be carried along, move gently 2 WANDER, stroll, stray, roam, meander, rove, range, straggle, traipse (*informal*), stravaig (*Scot & N English dialect*), peregrinate 3 STRAY, wander, roam, meander, digress, get sidetracked, go off at a tangent, get off the point 4 PILE UP, gather, accumulate, amass, bank up ▷ *noun* 1 PILE, bank, mass, heap, mound, accumulation 2 MEANING, point, gist, aim, direction, object, import, intention, implication, tendency, significance, thrust, tenor, purport

drifter *noun* WANDERER, bum (*informal*), tramp, itinerant, vagrant, hobo (*US*), vagabond, rolling stone, bag lady (*chiefly US*), derro (*Austral slang*)

drill *noun* 1 BIT, borer, gimlet, rotary tool, boring tool 2 TRAINING, exercise, discipline, instruction, preparation, repetition 3 (*informal*) PRACTICE ▷ *verb* 1 BORE, pierce, penetrate, sink in, puncture, perforate 2 TRAIN, coach, teach, exercise, discipline, practise, instruct, rehearse

drink *verb* 1 SWALLOW, drain, sip, suck, gulp, sup, swig (*informal*), swill, guzzle, imbibe, quaff, partake of, toss off 2 BOOZE (*informal*), tipple, tope, hit the bottle (*informal*), bevvy (*dialect*), bend the elbow (*informal*), go on a binge *or* bender (*informal*) ▷ *noun* 1 GLASS, cup, swallow, sip, draught, gulp, swig (*informal*), taste, tipple, snifter (*informal*), noggin 2 BEVERAGE, refreshment, potion, liquid, thirst quencher 3 ALCOHOL, booze (*informal*), liquor, spirits, the bottle (*informal*), Dutch courage, hooch *or* hootch (*informal, chiefly US & Canad*) ▷▷ **drink something in** ABSORB, take in, digest, pay attention to, soak up, devour, assimilate, be fascinated by, imbibe ▷▷ **drink to something** TOAST, salute, pledge the health of ▷▷ **the drink** (*informal*) THE SEA, the main, the deep, the ocean, the briny (*informal*)

drinker *noun* ALCOHOLIC, drunk, boozer (*informal*), soak (*slang*), lush (*slang*), toper, sponge (*informal*), guzzler, drunkard, sot, tippler, wino (*informal*), inebriate, dipsomaniac, bibber, alko *or* alco (*Austral slang*)

drip *verb* DROP, splash, sprinkle, trickle, dribble, exude, drizzle, plop ▷ *noun* 1 DROP, bead, trickle, dribble, droplet, globule, pearl, driblet 2 (*informal*) WEAKLING, wet (*Brit informal*), weed (*informal*), softie (*informal*), mummy's boy (*informal*), namby-pamby, ninny, milksop

drive *verb* 1 GO (BY CAR), ride (by car), motor, travel by car 2 OPERATE, manage, direct, guide, handle, steer 3 PUSH, propel 4 THRUST, push, sink, dig, hammer, plunge, stab, ram 5 HERD, urge, impel 6 FORCE, press, prompt, spur, compel, motivate, oblige, railroad (*informal*), prod, constrain, prick, coerce, goad, impel, dragoon, actuate 7 WORK, overwork, overburden ▷ *noun* 1 RUN, ride, trip, journey, spin (*informal*), hurl (*Scot*), outing, excursion, jaunt 2 INITIATIVE, push (*informal*), energy, enterprise, ambition, pep, motivation, zip (*informal*), vigour, get-up-and-go (*informal*) 3 CAMPAIGN, push (*informal*), crusade, action, effort, appeal, advance, surge ▷▷ **drive at something**

(*informal*) MEAN, suggest, intend, refer to, imply, intimate, get at, hint at, have in mind, allude to, insinuate

drivel *verb* BABBLE, ramble, waffle (*informal, chiefly Brit*), gab (*informal*), gas (*informal*), maunder, blether, prate ▷ *noun* NONSENSE, rubbish, garbage (*informal*), rot, crap (*slang*), trash, bunk (*informal*), blah (*slang*), hot air (*informal*), tosh (*slang, chiefly Brit*), waffle (*informal, chiefly Brit*), prating, pap, bilge (*informal*), twaddle, tripe (*informal*), dross, gibberish, guff (*slang*), moonshine, hogwash, hokum (*slang, chiefly US & Canad*), piffle (*informal*), poppycock (*informal*), balderdash, bosh (*informal*), eyewash (*informal*), tommyrot, horsefeathers (*US slang*), bunkum *or* buncombe (*chiefly US*), bizzo (*Austral slang*), bull's wool (*Austral & NZ slang*)

drizzle *noun* FINE RAIN, Scotch mist, smir (*Scot*) ▷ *verb* RAIN, shower, spit, spray, sprinkle, mizzle (*dialect*), spot *or* spit with rain

droll *adjective* AMUSING, odd, funny, entertaining, comic, ridiculous, diverting, eccentric, ludicrous, humorous, quaint, off-the-wall (*slang*), laughable, farcical, whimsical, comical, oddball (*informal*), risible, jocular, clownish, waggish

drone¹ *noun* PARASITE, skiver (*Brit slang*), idler, lounger, leech, loafer, couch potato (*slang*), scrounger (*informal*), sponger (*informal*), sluggard, bludger (*Austral & NZ informal*), quandong (*Austral slang*)

drone² *verb* 1 HUM, buzz, vibrate, purr, whirr, thrum 2 *often with* **on** SPEAK MONOTONOUSLY, drawl, chant, spout, intone, talk interminably ▷ *noun* HUM, buzz, purr, vibration, whirr, whirring, thrum

droning *adjective* MONOTONOUS, boring, tedious, drawling, soporific

drool *verb* 1 DRIVEL, dribble, salivate, slaver, slobber, water at the mouth 2 *often with* **over** GLOAT OVER, pet, gush, make much of, rave about (*informal*), dote on, slobber over

droop *verb* SAG, drop, hang (down), sink, bend, dangle, fall down

droopy *adjective* SAGGING, limp, wilting, stooped, floppy, drooping, languid, flabby, languorous, pendulous, lassitudinous

drop *verb* 1 FALL, lower, decline, diminish 2 *often with* **away** DECLINE, fall, sink 3 PLUNGE, fall, dive, tumble, descend, plummet 4 DRIP, trickle, dribble, fall in drops 5 SINK, fall, descend, droop 6 SET DOWN, leave, deposit, unload, let off 7 QUIT,

give up, abandon, cease, axe (*informal*), kick (*informal*), terminate, relinquish, remit, discontinue, forsake 8 ABANDON, desert, forsake, repudiate, leave, jilt, throw over ▷ *noun* 1 DECREASE, fall, cut, lowering, decline, reduction, slump, fall-off, downturn, deterioration, cutback, diminution, decrement 2 DROPLET, bead, globule, bubble, pearl, drip, driblet 3 DASH, shot (*informal*), spot, taste, trace, pinch, sip, tot, trickle, nip, dab, mouthful 4 FALL, plunge, descent, abyss, chasm, precipice ▷▷ **drop in** (*informal*) VISIT, call, stop, turn up, look up, call in, look in, pop in (*informal*) ▷▷ **drop off** (*informal*) 1 FALL ASLEEP, nod (off), doze (off), snooze (*informal*), catnap, drowse, have forty winks (*informal*) 2 DECREASE, lower, decline, shrink, diminish, fall off, dwindle, lessen, wane, subside, slacken ▷▷ **drop out** LEAVE, stop, give up, withdraw, quit, pull out, back out, renege, throw in the towel, cop out (*slang*), fall by the wayside ▷▷ **drop out of something** DISCONTINUE, give up, abandon, quit, cease, terminate, forsake ▷▷ **drop someone off** SET DOWN, leave, deliver, let off, allow to alight

droppings *plural noun* EXCREMENT, stool, manure, dung, faeces, guano, excreta, doo-doo (*informal*), ordure, kak (*S African taboo slang*)

dross 1 RUBBISH, remains, refuse, lees, waste, debris, dregs 2 NONSENSE, garbage (*chiefly US*), drivel, twaddle, pants (*slang*), rot, crap (*slang*), trash, hot air (*informal*), tosh (*slang, chiefly Brit*), pap, bilge (*informal*), tripe (*informal*), gibberish, guff (*slang*), havers (*Scot*), moonshine, claptrap (*informal*), hogwash, hokum (*slang, chiefly US & Canad*), codswallop (*Brit slang*), piffle (*informal*), poppycock (*informal*), balderdash, bosh (*informal*), wack (*US slang*), eyewash (*informal*), stuff and nonsense, flapdoodle (*slang*), tommyrot, horsefeathers (*US slang*), bunkum *or* buncombe (*chiefly US*), bizzo (*Austral slang*), bull's wool (*Austral & NZ slang*)

drought *noun* 1 WATER SHORTAGE, dryness, dry weather, dry spell, aridity, drouth (*Scot*), parchedness << ANTONYM flood 2 SHORTAGE, lack, deficit, deficiency, want, need, shortfall, scarcity, dearth, insufficiency << ANTONYM abundance

drove *noun often plural* HERD, company, crowds, collection, gathering, mob, flocks, swarm, horde, multitude, throng

drown *verb* 1 GO DOWN, go under 2 DRENCH,

flood, soak, steep, swamp, saturate, engulf, submerge, immerse, inundate, deluge **3** *often with* **out** OVERWHELM, overcome, wipe out, overpower, obliterate, swallow up

drowsiness *noun* SLEEPINESS, tiredness, lethargy, torpor, sluggishness, languor, somnolence, heavy eyelids, doziness, torpidity << ANTONYM wakefulness

drowsy *adjective* **1** SLEEPY, tired, lethargic, heavy, nodding, dazed, dozy, comatose, dopey (*slang*), half asleep, somnolent, torpid << ANTONYM awake **2** PEACEFUL, quiet, sleepy, soothing, lulling, dreamy, restful, soporific

drubbing *noun* BEATING, defeat, hammering (*informal*), pounding, whipping, thrashing, licking (*informal*), pasting (*slang*), flogging, trouncing, clobbering (*informal*), walloping (*informal*), pummelling

drudge *noun* MENIAL, worker, servant, slave, toiler, dogsbody (*informal*), plodder, factotum, scullion (*archaic*), skivvy (*chiefly Brit*), maid *or* man of all work

drudgery *noun* LABOUR, grind (*informal*), sweat (*informal*), hard work, slavery, chore, fag (*informal*), toil, slog, donkey-work, sweated labour, menial labour, skivvying (*Brit*)

drug *noun* **1** MEDICATION, medicine, remedy, physic, medicament **2** DOPE (*slang*), narcotic (*slang*), stimulant, opiate, dadah (*Austral slang*) ▷ *verb* KNOCK OUT, dope (*slang*), numb, deaden, stupefy, anaesthetize

drug addict *noun* JUNKIE (*informal*), tripper (*informal*), crack-head (*informal*), acid head (*informal*), dope-fiend (*slang*), hop-head (*informal*), head (*informal*)

drugged *adjective* STONED, high (*informal*), flying (*slang*), bombed (*slang*), tripping (*informal or slang*), wasted (*slang*), smashed (*slang*), wrecked (*slang*), turned on (*slang*), out of it (*slang*), doped (*slang*), under the influence (*informal*), on a trip (*informal*), spaced out (*slang*), comatose, stupefied, out of your mind (*slang*), zonked (*slang*), out to it (*Austral & NZ slang*)

drum *verb* POUND, beat, tap, rap, lash, thrash, tattoo, throb, pulsate, reverberate ▷▷ **drum something into someone** DRIVE, hammer, instil, din, harp on about ▷▷ **drum something up** SEEK, attract, request, ask for, obtain, bid for, petition, round up, solicit, canvass

drunk *adjective* INTOXICATED, loaded (*slang, chiefly US & Canad*), tight (*informal*), canned (*slang*), flying (*slang*), bombed (*slang*), stoned (*slang*), wasted (*slang*), smashed (*slang*), steaming (*slang*), wrecked (*slang*), soaked (*informal*), out of it (*slang*), plastered (*slang*), drunken, blitzed (*slang*), lit up (*slang*), merry (*Brit informal*), stewed (*slang*), pickled (*informal*), bladdered (*slang*), under the influence (*informal*), sloshed (*slang*), tipsy, maudlin, well-oiled (*slang*), legless (*informal*), paralytic (*informal*), tired and emotional (*euphemistic*), steamboats (*Scot slang*), tiddly (*slang, chiefly Brit*), zonked (*slang*), blotto (*slang*), fuddled, inebriated, out to it (*Austral & NZ slang*), sottish, tanked up (*slang*), bacchic, half seas over (*informal*), bevvied (*dialect*), babalas (*S African*), fu' (*Scot*), pie-eyed (*slang*) ▷ *noun* DRUNKARD, alcoholic, lush (*slang*), boozer (*informal*), toper, sot, soak (*slang*), wino (*informal*), inebriate, alko *or* alco (*Austral slang*)

drunkard *noun* DRUNK, alcoholic, soak (*slang*), drinker, lush (*slang*), carouser, sot, tippler, toper, wino (*informal*), dipsomaniac, alko *or* alco (*Austral slang*)

drunken *adjective* **1** INTOXICATED, smashed (*slang*), drunk, flying (*slang*), bombed (*slang*), wasted (*slang*), steaming (*slang*), wrecked (*slang*), out of it (*slang*), boozing (*informal*), blitzed (*slang*), lit up (*slang*), bladdered (*slang*), under the influence (*informal*), tippling, toping, red-nosed, legless (*informal*), paralytic (*informal*), steamboats (*Scot slang*), zonked (*slang*), bibulous, blotto (*slang*), inebriate, out to it (*Austral & NZ slang*), sottish, bevvied (*dialect*), (gin-)sodden **2** BOOZY, dissipated (*informal*), riotous, debauched, dionysian, orgiastic, bacchanalian, bacchic, saturnalian

drunkenness *noun* INTOXICATION, alcoholism, intemperance, inebriation, dipsomania, tipsiness, insobriety, bibulousness, sottishness

dry *adjective* **1** DEHYDRATED, dried-up, arid, torrid, parched, desiccated, waterless, juiceless, sapless, moistureless << ANTONYM wet **2** DRIED, crisp, withered, brittle, shrivelled, crispy, parched, desiccated, sun-baked **3** THIRSTY, parched **4** SARCASTIC, cutting, sharp, keen, cynical, low-key, sly, sardonic, deadpan, droll, ironical, quietly humorous **5** DULL, boring, tedious, commonplace, dreary, tiresome, monotonous, run-of-the-mill, humdrum, unimaginative, uninteresting, mind-numbing, ho-hum (*informal*) << ANTONYM interesting **6** PLAIN, simple, bare, basic,

pure, stark, unembellished ▷ *verb* 1 DRAIN,
make dry 2 *often with* out DEHYDRATE, make
dry, desiccate, sear, parch, dehumidify
<< ANTONYM wet ▷▷ **dry out** *or* **up** BECOME
DRY, harden, wither, mummify, shrivel up,
wizen

dryness *noun* 1 ARIDITY, drought,
dehydration, aridness, dehumidification,
waterlessness, moisturelessness,
parchedness 2 THIRSTINESS, thirst,
parchedness

dual *adjective* TWOFOLD, double, twin,
matched, coupled, paired, duplicate, binary,
duplex

duality *noun* DUALISM, dichotomy, polarity,
doubleness, biformity, duplexity

dub *verb* NAME, call, term, style, label,
nickname, designate, christen, denominate

dubious *adjective* 1 SUSPECT, suspicious,
crooked, dodgy (*Brit, Austral & NZ informal*),
questionable, unreliable, shady (*informal*),
unscrupulous, fishy (*informal*), disreputable,
untrustworthy, undependable << ANTONYM
trustworthy 2 UNSURE, uncertain, suspicious,
hesitating, doubtful, sceptical, tentative,
wavering, hesitant, undecided, unconvinced,
iffy (*informal*), leery (*slang*), distrustful, in
two minds (*informal*) << ANTONYM sure
3 DOUBTFUL, questionable, ambiguous,
debatable, moot, arguable, equivocal, open
to question, disputable

duck *verb* 1 BOB, drop, lower, bend, bow,
dodge, crouch, stoop 2 (*informal*) DODGE,
avoid, escape, evade, elude, sidestep,
circumvent, shirk, body-swerve (*Scot*)
3 DUNK, wet, plunge, dip, submerge,
immerse, douse, souse

duct *noun* PIPE, channel, passage, tube, canal,
funnel, conduit

dud (*informal*) *noun* FAILURE, flop (*informal*),
washout (*informal*), clinker (*slang, chiefly
US*), clunker (*informal*) ▷ *adjective* FAULTY,
broken, failed, damaged, bust (*informal*), not
working, useless, flawed, impaired, duff (*Brit
informal*), worthless, defective, imperfect,
malfunctioning, out of order, unsound,
not functioning, valueless, on the blink,
inoperative, kaput (*informal*)

due *adjective* 1 EXPECTED, scheduled, expected
to arrive 2 FITTING, deserved, appropriate,
just, right, becoming, fit, justified, suitable,
merited, proper, obligatory, rightful,
requisite, well-earned, bounden 3 PAYABLE,
outstanding, owed, owing, unpaid, in
arrears ▷ *noun* RIGHT(s), privilege, deserts,

merits, prerogative, comeuppance (*informal*)
▷ *adverb* DIRECTLY, dead, straight, exactly,
undeviatingly

duel *noun* 1 SINGLE COMBAT, affair of honour
2 CONTEST, fight, competition, clash,
encounter, engagement, rivalry ▷ *verb* FIGHT,
struggle, clash, compete, contest, contend,
vie with, lock horns

dues *plural noun* MEMBERSHIP FEE, charges,
fee, contribution, levy

duff *adjective* (*Brit, Austral & NZ informal*) BAD,
poor, useless, pathetic, inferior, worthless,
unsatisfactory, defective, deficient,
imperfect, substandard, low-rent (*informal,
chiefly US*), poxy (*slang*), pants (*informal*),
bodger *or* bodgie (*Austral slang*)

duffer *noun* (*informal*) CLOT, blunderer (*Brit
informal*), booby, clod, oaf, bungler, galoot
(*slang, chiefly US*), lubber, lummox (*informal*)

dulcet *adjective* SWEET, pleasing, musical,
charming, pleasant, honeyed, delightful,
soothing, agreeable, harmonious,
melodious, mellifluous, euphonious,
mellifluent

dull *adjective* 1 BORING, tedious, dreary,
flat, dry, plain, commonplace, tiresome,
monotonous, prosaic, run-of-the-
mill, humdrum, unimaginative, dozy,
uninteresting, mind-numbing, ho-hum
(*informal*), vapid, as dry as dust << ANTONYM
exciting 2 LIFELESS, dead, heavy, slow,
indifferent, sluggish, insensitive, apathetic,
listless, unresponsive, passionless,
insensible << ANTONYM lively 3 DRAB,
faded, muted, subdued, feeble, murky,
sombre, toned-down, subfusc 4 CLOUDY,
dim, gloomy, dismal, overcast, leaden,
turbid << ANTONYM bright 5 MUTED, faint,
suppressed, subdued, stifled, indistinct
6 BLUNT, dulled, blunted, not keen, not
sharp, edgeless, unsharpened << ANTONYM
sharp ▷ *verb* 1 RELIEVE, blunt, lessen,
moderate, soften, alleviate, allay, mitigate,
assuage, take the edge off, palliate 2 CLOUD
OVER, darken, grow dim, become cloudy
3 DAMPEN, reduce, check, depress, moderate,
discourage, stifle, lessen, smother, sadden,
dishearten, dispirit, deject

dullness *noun* 1 TEDIOUSNESS, monotony,
banality, flatness, dreariness, vapidity,
insipidity << ANTONYM interest
2 STUPIDITY, thickness, slowness, dimness,
obtuseness, doziness (*Brit informal*), dim-
wittedness, dopiness (*slang*) << ANTONYM
intelligence 3 DRABNESS, greyness, dimness,

gloominess, dinginess, colourlessness << ANTONYM brilliance

duly *adverb* **1** PROPERLY, fittingly, correctly, appropriately, accordingly, suitably, deservedly, rightfully, decorously, befittingly **2** ON TIME, promptly, in good time, punctually, at the proper time

dumb *adjective* **1** UNABLE TO SPEAK, mute << ANTONYM articulate **2** SILENT, mute, speechless, inarticulate, tongue-tied, wordless, voiceless, soundless, at a loss for words, mum **3** (*informal*) STUPID, thick, dull, foolish, dense, dozy (*Brit informal*), dim, obtuse, unintelligent, asinine, braindead (*informal*), dim-witted (*informal*) << ANTONYM clever

dumbfounded *adjective* AMAZED, stunned, astonished, confused, overcome, overwhelmed, staggered, thrown, startled, at sea, dumb, bewildered, astounded, breathless, confounded, taken aback, speechless, bowled over (*informal*), gobsmacked (*Brit slang*), flabbergasted (*informal*), nonplussed, lost for words, flummoxed, thunderstruck, knocked sideways (*informal*), knocked for six (*informal*)

dummy *noun* **1** MODEL, figure, mannequin, form, manikin, lay figure **2** IMITATION, copy, duplicate, sham, counterfeit, replica **3** (*slang*) FOOL, jerk (*slang, chiefly US & Canad*), idiot, plank (*Brit slang*), charlie (*Brit informal*), berk (*Brit slang*), wally (*slang*), prat (*slang*), plonker (*slang*), coot, geek (*slang*), dunce, oaf, simpleton, dullard, dimwit (*informal*), dipstick (*Brit slang*), gonzo (*slang*), schmuck (*US slang*), dork (*slang*), nitwit (*informal*), dolt, blockhead, divvy (*Brit slang*), pillock (*Brit slang*), dweeb (*US slang*), fathead (*informal*), weenie (*US informal*), eejit (*Scot & Irish*), dumb-ass (*slang*), numpty (*Scot informal*), doofus (*slang, chiefly US*), lamebrain (*informal*), nerd or nurd (*slang*), numbskull or numskull, dorba or dorb (*Austral slang*), bogan (*Austral slang*) ▷ *modifier* IMITATION, false, fake, artificial, mock, bogus, simulated, sham, phoney or phony (*informal*)

dummy run *noun* PRACTICE, trial, dry run

dump *verb* **1** DROP, deposit, throw down, let fall, fling down **2** GET RID OF, tip, discharge, dispose of, unload, jettison, empty out, coup (*Scot*), throw away or out **3** SCRAP, axe (*informal*), get rid of, abolish, junk (*informal*), put an end to, discontinue, jettison, put paid to ▷ *noun* **1** RUBBISH TIP, tip, junkyard, rubbish heap, refuse heap **2** (*informal*)

PIGSTY, hole (*informal*), joint (*slang*), slum, shack, shanty, hovel

dumps *plural noun* ▷▷ **down in the dumps** DOWN, low, blue, sad, unhappy, low-spirited, discouraged, fed up, moody, pessimistic, melancholy, glum, dejected, despondent, dispirited, downcast, morose, crestfallen, downhearted

dumpy *adjective* PODGY, homely, short, plump, squat, stout, chunky, chubby, tubby, roly-poly, pudgy, squab, fubsy (*archaic or dialect*)

dunce *noun* SIMPLETON, moron, duffer (*informal*), bonehead (*slang*), loon (*informal*), goose (*informal*), ass, donkey, oaf, dullard, dimwit (*informal*), ignoramus, nitwit (*informal*), dolt, blockhead, halfwit, nincompoop, fathead (*informal*), dunderhead, lamebrain (*informal*), thickhead, numbskull or numskull

dungeon *noun* PRISON, cell, cage, vault, lockup, oubliette, calaboose (*US informal*), donjon, boob (*Austral slang*)

dunny *noun* (*Austral & NZ old-fashioned informal*) TOILET, lavatory, bathroom, loo (*Brit informal*), W.C., bog (*slang*), Gents or Ladies, can (*US & Canad slang*), john (*slang, chiefly US & Canad*), head(s) (*nautical slang*), throne (*informal*), closet, privy, cloakroom (*Brit*), urinal, latrine, washroom, powder room, crapper (*taboo slang*), water closet, khazi (*slang*), pissoir (*French*), little boy's room or little girl's room (*informal*), (public) convenience, bogger (*Austral slang*), brasco (*Austral slang*)

dupe *noun* VICTIM, mug (*Brit slang*), sucker (*slang*), pigeon (*slang*), sap (*slang*), gull, pushover (*slang*), fall guy (*informal*), simpleton ▷ *verb* DECEIVE, trick, cheat, con (*informal*), kid (*informal*), rip off (*slang*), hoax, defraud, beguile, gull (*archaic*), delude, swindle, outwit, bamboozle (*informal*), hoodwink, take for a ride (*informal*), pull a fast one on (*informal*), cozen

duplicate *adjective* IDENTICAL, matched, matching, twin, corresponding, twofold ▷ *noun* **1** COPY, facsimile **2** PHOTOCOPY, copy, reproduction, replica, Xerox (*trademark*), carbon copy, Photostat (*trademark*) ▷ *verb* **1** REPEAT, reproduce, echo, copy, clone, replicate **2** COPY, photocopy, Xerox (*trademark*), Photostat (*trademark*)

duplicity *noun* DECEIT, fraud, deception, hypocrisy, dishonesty, guile, artifice, falsehood, double-dealing, chicanery, perfidy, dissimulation << ANTONYM honesty

durable *adjective* 1 HARD-WEARING, strong, tough, sound, substantial, reliable, resistant, sturdy, long-lasting << ANTONYM fragile 2 ENDURING, lasting, permanent, continuing, firm, fast, fixed, constant, abiding, dependable, unwavering, unfaltering

duration *noun* LENGTH, time, period, term, stretch, extent, spell, span, time frame, timeline

duress *noun* (usually in phrase *under duress*) PRESSURE, threat, constraint, compulsion, coercion

dusk *noun* 1 TWILIGHT, evening, evo (*Austral slang*), nightfall, sunset, dark, sundown, eventide, gloaming (*Scot poetic*) << ANTONYM dawn 2 (*poetic*) SHADE, darkness, gloom, obscurity, murk, shadowiness

dusky *adjective* 1 DIM, twilight, shady, shadowy, gloomy, murky, cloudy, overcast, crepuscular, darkish, twilit, tenebrous, caliginous (*archaic*) 2 DARK, swarthy, dark-complexioned

dust *noun* 1 GRIME, grit, powder, powdery dirt 2 EARTH, ground, soil, dirt 3 PARTICLES, fine fragments ▷ *verb* SPRINKLE, cover, powder, spread, spray, scatter, sift, dredge

dusty *adjective* 1 DIRTY, grubby, unclean, unswept, undusted 2 POWDERY, sandy, chalky, crumbly, granular, friable

dutiful *adjective* CONSCIENTIOUS, devoted, obedient, respectful, compliant, submissive, docile, deferential, reverential, filial, punctilious, duteous (*archaic*) << ANTONYM disrespectful

duty *noun* 1 RESPONSIBILITY, job, task, work, calling, business, service, office, charge, role, function, mission, province, obligation, assignment, pigeon (*informal*), onus 2 TAX, customs, toll, levy, tariff, excise, due, impost ▷▷ **off duty** OFF WORK, off, free, on holiday, at leisure ▷▷ **on duty** AT WORK, busy, engaged, on active service

dwarf *noun* GNOME, midget, Lilliputian, Tom Thumb, munchkin (*informal, chiefly US*), homunculus, manikin, hop-o'-my-thumb, pygmy *or* pigmy ▷ *modifier* MINIATURE, small, baby, tiny, pocket, dwarfed, diminutive, petite, bonsai, pint-sized, undersized, teeny-weeny, Lilliputian, teensy-weensy ▷ *verb* 1 TOWER ABOVE *or* OVER, dominate, overlook, stand over, loom over, stand head and shoulders above 2 ECLIPSE, tower above *or* over, put in the shade, diminish

dwell *verb* (*formal* or *literary*) LIVE, stay, reside, rest, quarter, settle, lodge, abide, hang out (*informal*), sojourn, establish yourself ▷▷ **dwell on** *or* **upon something** GO ON ABOUT, emphasize (*informal*), elaborate on, linger over, harp on about, be engrossed in, expatiate on, continue to think about, tarry over

dwelling *noun* (*formal* or *literary*) HOME, house, residence, abode, quarters, establishment, lodging, pad (*slang*), habitation, domicile, dwelling house, whare (*NZ*)

dwindle *verb* LESSEN, fall, decline, contract, sink, fade, weaken, shrink, diminish, decrease, decay, wither, wane, subside, ebb, die down, die out, abate, shrivel, peter out, die away, waste away, taper off, grow less << ANTONYM increase

dye *noun* COLOURING, colour, pigment, stain, tint, tinge, colorant ▷ *verb* COLOUR, stain, tint, tinge, pigment, tincture

dying *adjective* 1 NEAR DEATH, going, failing, fading, doomed, expiring, ebbing, near the end, moribund, fading fast, in extremis (*Latin*), at death's door, not long for this world, on your deathbed, breathing your last 2 FINAL, last, parting, departing 3 FAILING, declining, sinking, foundering, diminishing, decreasing, dwindling, subsiding

dynamic *adjective* ENERGETIC, spirited, powerful, active, vital, driving, electric, go-ahead, lively, magnetic, vigorous, animated, high-powered, forceful, go-getting (*informal*), tireless, indefatigable, high-octane (*informal*), zippy (*informal*), full of beans (*informal*) << ANTONYM apathetic

dynamism *noun* ENERGY, go (*informal*), drive, push (*informal*), initiative, enterprise, pep, zip (*informal*), vigour, zap (*slang*), get-up-and-go (*informal*), brio, liveliness, forcefulness

dynasty *noun* EMPIRE, house, rule, regime, sovereignty

each *adjective* EVERY, every single ▷ *pronoun* EVERY ONE, all, each one, each and every one, one and all ▷ *adverb* APIECE, individually, singly, for each, to each, respectively, per person, from each, per head, per capita

eager *adjective* **1** *often with* **to** *or* **for** ANXIOUS, keen, raring, hungry, intent, yearning, impatient, itching, thirsty, zealous << ANTONYM unenthusiastic **2** KEEN, interested, earnest, intense, enthusiastic, passionate, ardent, avid (*informal*), fervent, zealous, fervid, keen as mustard, bright-eyed and bushy-tailed (*informal*) << ANTONYM uninterested

eagerness *noun* **1** LONGING, anxiety, hunger, yearning, zeal, impatience, impetuosity, avidity **2** PASSION, interest, enthusiasm, intensity, fervour, ardour, earnestness, keenness, heartiness, thirst, intentness

ear *noun* **1** SENSITIVITY, taste, discrimination, appreciation, musical perception **2** ATTENTION, hearing, regard, notice, consideration, observation, awareness, heed ▷▷ **lend an ear** LISTEN, pay attention, heed, take notice, pay heed, hearken (*archaic*), give ear

early *adverb* **1** IN GOOD TIME, beforehand, ahead of schedule, in advance, with time to spare, betimes (*archaic*) << ANTONYM late **2** TOO SOON, before the usual time, prematurely, ahead of time << ANTONYM late ▷ *adjective* **1** FIRST, opening, earliest, initial, introductory **2** PREMATURE, forward, advanced, untimely, unseasonable << ANTONYM belated **3** PRIMITIVE, first, earliest, young, original, undeveloped, primordial, primeval << ANTONYM developed

earmark *verb* **1** SET ASIDE, reserve, label, flag, tag, allocate, designate, mark out, keep back **2** MARK OUT, identify, designate

earn *verb* **1** BE PAID, make, get, receive, draw, gain, net, collect, bring in, gross, procure, clear, get paid, take home **2** DESERVE, win, gain, attain, justify, merit, warrant, be entitled to, reap, be worthy of

earnest *adjective* **1** SERIOUS, keen, grave, intense, steady, dedicated, eager, enthusiastic, passionate, sincere, thoughtful, solemn, ardent, fervent, impassioned, zealous, staid, keen as mustard << ANTONYM frivolous **2** DETERMINED, firm, dogged, constant, urgent, intent, persistent, ardent, persevering, resolute, heartfelt, zealous, vehement, wholehearted << ANTONYM half-hearted

earnestness *noun* **1** SERIOUSNESS, resolution, passion, enthusiasm, warmth, gravity, urgency, zeal, sincerity, fervour, eagerness, ardour, keenness **2** DETERMINATION, resolve, urgency, zeal, ardour, vehemence

earnings *plural noun* INCOME, pay, wages, revenue, reward, proceeds, salary, receipts, return, remuneration, takings, stipend, take-home pay, emolument, gross pay, net pay

earth *noun* **1** WORLD, planet, globe, sphere, orb, earthly sphere, terrestrial sphere **2** GROUND, land, dry land, terra firma **3** SOIL, ground, land, dust, mould, clay, dirt, turf, sod, silt, topsoil, clod, loam

earthenware *noun* CROCKERY, pots, ceramics, pottery, terracotta, crocks, faience, maiolica

earthly *adjective* **1** WORLDLY, material, physical, secular, mortal, mundane, terrestrial, temporal, human, materialistic, profane, telluric, sublunary, non-spiritual, tellurian, terrene << ANTONYM spiritual **2** SENSUAL, worldly, base, physical, gross, low, fleshly, bodily, vile, sordid, carnal **3** (*informal*) POSSIBLE, likely, practical, feasible, conceivable, imaginable

earthy *adjective* 1 CRUDE, coarse, raunchy (*slang*), lusty, bawdy, ribald 2 CLAYLIKE, soil-like

ease *noun* 1 STRAIGHTFORWARDNESS, simplicity, readiness 2 COMFORT, luxury, leisure, relaxation, prosperity, affluence, rest, repose, restfulness << ANTONYM hardship 3 PEACE OF MIND, peace, content, quiet, comfort, happiness, enjoyment, serenity, tranquillity, contentment, calmness, quietude << ANTONYM agitation 4 NATURALNESS, informality, freedom, liberty, unaffectedness, unconstraint, unreservedness, relaxedness << ANTONYM awkwardness ▷ *verb* 1 RELIEVE, calm, moderate, soothe, lessen, alleviate, appease, lighten, lower, allay, relax, still, mitigate, assuage, pacify, mollify, tranquillize, palliate << ANTONYM aggravate 2 *often with* **off** *or* **up** REDUCE, moderate, weaken, diminish, decrease, slow down, dwindle, lessen, die down, abate, slacken, grow less, de-escalate 3 MOVE CAREFULLY, edge, guide, slip, inch, slide, creep, squeeze, steer, manoeuvre 4 FACILITATE, further, aid, forward, smooth, assist, speed up, simplify, make easier, expedite, lessen the labour of << ANTONYM hinder

easily *adverb* 1 WITHOUT A DOUBT, clearly, surely, certainly, obviously, definitely, plainly, absolutely, undoubtedly, unquestionably, undeniably, unequivocally, far and away, indisputably, beyond question, indubitably, doubtlessly 2 WITHOUT DIFFICULTY, smoothly, readily, comfortably, effortlessly, simply, with ease, straightforwardly, without trouble, standing on your head, with your eyes closed *or* shut

easy *adjective* 1 SIMPLE, straightforward, no trouble, not difficult, effortless, painless, clear, light, uncomplicated, child's play (*informal*), plain sailing, undemanding, a pushover (*slang*), a piece of cake (*informal*), no bother, a bed of roses, easy-peasy (*slang*) << ANTONYM hard 2 UNTROUBLED, contented, relaxed, satisfied, calm, peaceful, serene, tranquil, quiet, undisturbed, unworried 3 RELAXED, friendly, open, natural, pleasant, casual, informal, laid-back (*informal*), graceful, gracious, unaffected, easy-going, affable, unpretentious, unforced, undemanding, unconstrained, unceremonious << ANTONYM stiff 4 CAREFREE, comfortable, leisurely,

trouble-free, untroubled, cushy (*informal*) << ANTONYM difficult 5 TOLERANT, light, liberal, soft, flexible, mild, laid-back (*informal*), indulgent, easy-going, lenient, permissive, unoppressive << ANTONYM strict 6 (*informal*) ACCOMMODATING, yielding, manageable, easy-going, compliant, amenable, submissive, docile, pliant, tractable, biddable << ANTONYM difficult 7 VULNERABLE, soft, naive, susceptible, gullible, exploitable 8 LEISURELY, relaxed, comfortable, moderate, unhurried, undemanding

easy-going *adjective* RELAXED, easy, liberal, calm, flexible, mild, casual, tolerant, laid-back (*informal*), indulgent, serene, lenient, carefree, placid, unconcerned, amenable, permissive, happy-go-lucky, unhurried, nonchalant, insouciant, even-tempered, easy-peasy (*slang*) << ANTONYM tense

eat *verb* 1 CONSUME, swallow, chew, scoff (*slang*), devour, munch, tuck into (*informal*), put away, gobble, polish off (*informal*), wolf down 2 HAVE A MEAL, lunch, breakfast, dine, snack, feed, graze (*informal*), have lunch, have dinner, have breakfast, nosh (*slang*), take food, have supper, break bread, chow down (*slang*), take nourishment

eavesdrop *verb* LISTEN IN, spy, overhear, bug (*informal*), pry, tap in, snoop (*informal*), earwig (*informal*)

ebb *verb* 1 FLOW BACK, go out, withdraw, sink, retreat, fall back, wane, recede, fall away 2 DECLINE, drop, sink, flag, weaken, shrink, diminish, decrease, deteriorate, decay, dwindle, lessen, subside, degenerate, fall away, fade away, abate, peter out, slacken ▷ *noun* FLOWING BACK, going out, withdrawal, retreat, wane, waning, regression, low water, low tide, ebb tide, outgoing tide, falling tide, receding tide

ebony *adjective* BLACK, dark, jet, raven, sable, pitch-black, jet-black, inky, swarthy, coal-black

ebullient *adjective* EXUBERANT, excited, enthusiastic, buoyant, exhilarated, elated, irrepressible, vivacious, effervescent, effusive, in high spirits, zestful

eccentric *adjective* ODD, strange, bizarre, weird, peculiar, abnormal, queer (*informal*), irregular, uncommon, quirky, singular, unconventional, idiosyncratic, off-the-wall (*slang*), outlandish, whimsical, rum (*Brit slang*), capricious, anomalous, freakish, aberrant, wacko (*slang*), outré, daggy (*Austral*

& *NZ informal*) << ANTONYM normal ▷ *noun* CRANK (*informal*), character (*informal*), nut (*slang*), freak (*informal*), flake (*slang, chiefly US*), oddity, oddball (*informal*), loose cannon, nonconformist, wacko (*slang*), case (*informal*), screwball (*slang, chiefly US & Canad*), card (*informal*), odd fish (*informal*), kook (*US & Canad informal*), queer fish (*Brit informal*), rum customer (*Brit slang*), weirdo *or* weirdie (*informal*)

eccentricity *noun* 1 ODDITY, peculiarity, strangeness, irregularity, weirdness, singularity, oddness, waywardness, nonconformity, capriciousness, unconventionality, queerness (*informal*), bizarreness, whimsicality, freakishness, outlandishness 2 FOIBLE, anomaly, abnormality, quirk, oddity, aberration, peculiarity, idiosyncrasy

ecclesiastical *adjective* CLERICAL, religious, church, churchly, priestly, spiritual, holy, divine, pastoral, sacerdotal

echelon *noun* LEVEL, place, office, position, step, degree, rank, grade, tier, rung

echo *noun* 1 REVERBERATION, ringing, repetition, answer, resonance, resounding 2 COPY, reflection, clone, reproduction, imitation, duplicate, double, reiteration 3 REMINDER, suggestion, trace, hint, recollection, vestige, evocation, intimation ▷ *verb* 1 REVERBERATE, repeat, resound, ring, resonate 2 RECALL, reflect, copy, mirror, resemble, reproduce, parrot, imitate, reiterate, ape

eclectic *adjective* DIVERSE, general, broad, varied, comprehensive, extensive, wide-ranging, selective, diversified, manifold, heterogeneous, catholic, all-embracing, liberal, many-sided, multifarious, dilettantish

eclipse *noun* 1 OBSCURING, covering, blocking, shading, dimming, extinction, darkening, blotting out, occultation 2 DECLINE, fall, loss, failure, weakening, deterioration, degeneration, diminution ▷ *verb* 1 SURPASS, exceed, overshadow, excel, transcend, outdo, outclass, outshine, leave *or* put in the shade (*informal*) 2 OBSCURE, cover, block, cloud, conceal, dim, veil, darken, shroud, extinguish, blot out

economic *adjective* 1 FINANCIAL, business, trade, industrial, commercial, mercantile 2 MONETARY, financial, material, fiscal, budgetary, bread-and-butter (*informal*), pecuniary 3 (*Brit*) PROFITABLE, successful,

commercial, rewarding, productive, lucrative, worthwhile, viable, solvent, cost-effective, money-making, profit-making, remunerative 4 (*informal*) ECONOMICAL, fair, cheap, reasonable, modest, low-priced, inexpensive

economical *adjective* 1 ECONOMIC, fair, cheap, reasonable, modest, low-priced, inexpensive << ANTONYM expensive 2 THRIFTY, sparing, careful, prudent, provident, frugal, parsimonious, scrimping, economizing << ANTONYM extravagant 3 EFFICIENT, sparing, cost-effective, money-saving, time-saving, work-saving, unwasteful << ANTONYM wasteful

economics *noun* FINANCE, commerce, the dismal science

economy *noun* 1 FINANCIAL SYSTEM, financial state 2 THRIFT, saving, restraint, prudence, providence, husbandry, retrenchment, frugality, parsimony, thriftiness, sparingness

ecstasy *noun* RAPTURE, delight, joy, enthusiasm, frenzy, bliss, trance, euphoria, fervour, elation, rhapsody, exaltation, transport, ravishment << ANTONYM agony

ecstatic *adjective* RAPTUROUS, entranced, enthusiastic, frenzied, joyous, fervent, joyful, elated, over the moon (*informal*), overjoyed, blissful, delirious, euphoric, enraptured, on cloud nine (*informal*), cock-a-hoop, blissed out, transported, rhapsodic, sent, walking on air, in seventh heaven, floating on air, in exaltation, in transports of delight, stoked (*Austral & NZ informal*)

ecumenical, oecumenical, ecumenic *or* **oecumenic** *adjective* UNIFYING, universal, non-denominational, non-sectarian, general

eddy *noun* SWIRL, whirlpool, vortex, undertow, tideway, counter-current, counterflow ▷ *verb* SWIRL, turn, roll, spin, twist, surge, revolve, whirl, billow

edge *noun* 1 BORDER, side, line, limit, bound, lip, margin, outline, boundary, fringe, verge, brink, threshold, rim, brim, perimeter, contour, periphery, flange 2 VERGE, point, brink, threshold 3 ADVANTAGE, lead, dominance, superiority, upper hand, head start, ascendancy, whip hand 4 POWER, interest, force, bite, effectiveness, animation, zest, incisiveness, powerful quality 5 SHARPNESS, point, sting, urgency, bitterness, keenness, pungency, acuteness ▷ *verb* 1 INCH, ease, creep, worm, slink, steal, sidle, work, move slowly 2 BORDER, shape,

bind, trim, fringe, rim, hem, pipe ▷▷ **on
edge** TENSE, excited, wired (*slang*), nervous,
eager, impatient, irritable, apprehensive,
edgy, uptight (*informal*), ill at ease, twitchy
(*informal*), tetchy, on tenterhooks, keyed up,
antsy (*informal*), adrenalized

edgy *adjective* NERVOUS, wired (*slang*), anxious,
tense, neurotic, irritable, touchy, uptight
(*informal*), on edge, nervy (*Brit informal*), ill
at ease, restive, twitchy (*informal*), irascible,
tetchy, chippy (*informal*), on tenterhooks,
keyed up, antsy (*informal*), on pins and
needles, adrenalized

edible *adjective* SAFE TO EAT, harmless,
wholesome, palatable, digestible,
eatable, comestible (*rare*), fit to eat, good
<< ANTONYM inedible

edict *noun* DECREE, law, act, order, ruling,
demand, command, regulation, dictate,
mandate, canon, manifesto, injunction,
statute, fiat, ordinance, proclamation,
enactment, dictum, pronouncement, ukase
(*rare*), pronunciamento

edifice *noun* BUILDING, house, structure,
construction, pile, erection, habitation

edify *verb* INSTRUCT, school, teach, inform,
guide, improve, educate, nurture, elevate,
enlighten, uplift

edifying *adjective* INSTRUCTIVE, improving,
inspiring, elevating, enlightening, uplifting,
instructional

edit *verb* 1 REVISE, check, improve, correct,
polish, adapt, rewrite, censor, condense,
annotate, rephrase, redraft, copy-edit,
emend, prepare for publication, redact
2 PUT TOGETHER, select, arrange, organize,
assemble, compose, rearrange, reorder
3 BE IN CHARGE OF, control, direct, be
responsible for, be the editor of

edition *noun* 1 PRINTING, publication 2 COPY,
impression, number 3 VERSION, volume,
issue 4 PROGRAMME (*TV, radio*)

educate *verb* TEACH, school, train, coach,
develop, improve, exercise, inform,
discipline, rear, foster, mature, drill, tutor,
instruct, cultivate, enlighten, civilize, edify,
indoctrinate

educated *adjective* 1 CULTURED, lettered,
intellectual, learned, informed, experienced,
polished, literary, sophisticated, refined,
cultivated, enlightened, knowledgeable,
civilized, tasteful, urbane, erudite, well-
bred << ANTONYM uncultured 2 TAUGHT,
schooled, coached, informed, tutored,
instructed, nurtured, well-informed, well-

read, well-taught << ANTONYM uneducated

education *noun* 1 TEACHING, schooling,
training, development, coaching,
improvement, discipline, instruction,
drilling, tutoring, nurture, tuition,
enlightenment, erudition, indoctrination,
edification 2 LEARNING, schooling,
culture, breeding, scholarship, civilization,
cultivation, refinement

educational *adjective* 1 ACADEMIC, school,
learning, teaching, scholastic, pedagogical,
pedagogic 2 INSTRUCTIVE, useful, cultural,
illuminating, enlightening, informative,
instructional, didactic, edifying, educative,
heuristic

educator *noun* TEACHER, professor,
lecturer, don, coach, guide, fellow, trainer,
tutor, instructor, mentor, schoolteacher,
pedagogue, edifier, educationalist
or educationist, schoolmaster *or*
schoolmistress, master *or* mistress

eerie *adjective* UNCANNY, strange, frightening,
ghostly, weird, mysterious, scary (*informal*),
sinister, uneasy, fearful, awesome, unearthly,
supernatural, unnatural, spooky (*informal*),
creepy (*informal*), spectral, eldritch (*poetic*),
preternatural

efface *verb* OBLITERATE, remove, destroy,
cancel, wipe out, erase, eradicate, excise,
delete, annihilate, raze, blot out, cross out,
expunge, rub out, extirpate

effect *noun* 1 RESULT, consequence,
conclusion, outcome, event, issue,
aftermath, fruit, end result, upshot
2 IMPRESSION, feeling, impact, influence
3 PURPOSE, meaning, impression, sense,
import, drift, intent, essence, thread, tenor,
purport 4 IMPLEMENTATION, force, action,
performance, operation, enforcement,
execution ▷ *verb* BRING ABOUT, make, cause,
produce, create, complete, achieve, perform,
carry out, fulfil, accomplish, execute, initiate,
give rise to, consummate, actuate, effectuate
▷▷ **in effect** IN FACT, really, actually,
essentially, virtually, effectively, in reality, in
truth, as good as, in actual fact, to all intents
and purposes, in all but name, in actuality,
for practical purposes ▷▷ **put, bring** *or* **carry
into effect** IMPLEMENT, perform, carry out,
fulfil, enforce, execute, bring about, put
into action, put into operation, bring into
force ▷▷ **take effect** PRODUCE RESULTS, work,
begin, come into force, become operative

effective *adjective* 1 EFFICIENT, successful,
useful, active, capable, valuable, helpful,

adequate, productive, operative, competent, serviceable, efficacious, effectual << ANTONYM ineffective 2 POWERFUL, strong, convincing, persuasive, telling, impressive, compelling, potent, forceful, striking, emphatic, weighty, forcible, cogent << ANTONYM weak 3 VIRTUAL, essential, practical, implied, implicit, tacit, unacknowledged 4 IN OPERATION, official, current, legal, real, active, actual, in effect, valid, operative, in force, in execution << ANTONYM inoperative

effectiveness *noun* POWER, effect, efficiency, success, strength, capability, use, validity, usefulness, potency, efficacy, fruitfulness, productiveness

effects *plural noun* BELONGINGS, goods, things, property, stuff, gear, furniture, possessions, trappings, paraphernalia, personal property, accoutrements, chattels, movables

effeminate *adjective* WOMANLY, affected, camp (*informal*), soft, weak, feminine, unmanly, sissy, effete, foppish, womanish, wussy (*slang*), womanlike, poofy (*slang*), wimpish *or* wimpy (*informal*) << ANTONYM manly

effervescent *adjective* 1 FIZZY, bubbling, sparkling, bubbly, foaming, fizzing, fermenting, frothing, frothy, aerated, carbonated, foamy, gassy << ANTONYM still 2 LIVELY, excited, dynamic, enthusiastic, sparkling, energetic, animated, merry, buoyant, exhilarated, bubbly, exuberant, high-spirited, irrepressible, ebullient, chirpy, vital, scintillating, vivacious, zingy (*informal*) << ANTONYM dull

effete *adjective* WEAK, cowardly, feeble, ineffectual, decrepit, spineless, enfeebled, weak-kneed (*informal*), enervated, overrefined, chicken-hearted, wimpish *or* wimpy (*informal*)

efficacy *noun* EFFECTIVENESS, efficiency, power, value, success, strength, virtue, vigour, use, usefulness, potency, fruitfulness, productiveness, efficaciousness

efficiency *noun* 1 EFFECTIVENESS, power, economy, productivity, organization, efficacy, cost-effectiveness, orderliness 2 COMPETENCE, ability, skill, expertise, capability, readiness, professionalism, proficiency, adeptness, skilfulness

efficient *adjective* 1 EFFECTIVE, successful, structured, productive, powerful, systematic, streamlined, cost-effective, methodical, well-organized, well-planned, labour-saving, effectual << ANTONYM inefficient 2 COMPETENT, able, professional, capable, organized, productive, skilful, adept, ready, proficient, businesslike, well-organized, workmanlike << ANTONYM incompetent

effigy *noun* LIKENESS, figure, image, model, guy, carving, representation, statue, icon, idol, dummy, statuette

effluent *noun* WASTE, discharge, flow, emission, sewage, pollutant, outpouring, outflow, exhalation, issue, emanation, liquid waste, efflux, effluvium, effluence

effort *noun* 1 ATTEMPT, try, endeavour, shot (*informal*), bid, essay, go (*informal*), stab (*informal*) 2 EXERTION, work, labour, trouble, force, energy, struggle, stress, application, strain, striving, graft, toil, hard graft, travail (*literary*), elbow grease (*facetious*), blood, sweat, and tears (*informal*) 3 ACHIEVEMENT, act, performance, product, job, production, creation, feat, deed, accomplishment, attainment

effortless *adjective* 1 EASY, simple, flowing, smooth, graceful, painless, uncomplicated, trouble-free, facile, undemanding, easy-peasy (*slang*), untroublesome, unexacting << ANTONYM difficult 2 NATURAL, simple, spontaneous, instinctive, intuitive

effusive *adjective* DEMONSTRATIVE, enthusiastic, lavish, extravagant, overflowing, gushing, exuberant, expansive, ebullient, free-flowing, unrestrained, talkative, fulsome, profuse, unreserved

egg *noun* OVUM, gamete, germ cell ▷▷ **egg someone on** INCITE, push, encourage, urge, prompt, spur, provoke, prod, goad, exhort

egocentric *adjective* SELF-CENTRED, vain, selfish, narcissistic, self-absorbed, egotistical, inward-looking, self-important, self-obsessed, self-seeking, egoistic, egoistical

egotism *or* **egoism** *noun* SELF-CENTREDNESS, self-esteem, vanity, superiority, self-interest, selfishness, narcissism, self-importance, self-regard, self-love, self-seeking, self-absorption, self-obsession, egocentricity, egomania, self-praise, vainglory, self-conceit, self-admiration, conceitedness

ejaculate *verb* 1 HAVE AN ORGASM, climax, emit semen 2 DISCHARGE, release, emit, shoot out, eject, spurt 3 (*literary*) EXCLAIM, declare, shout, call out, cry out, burst out, blurt out

ejaculation *noun* DISCHARGE, release, emission, ejection

eject *verb* **1** THROW OUT, remove, turn out, expel (*slang*), exile, oust, banish, deport, drive out, evict, boot out (*informal*), force to leave, chuck out (*informal*), bounce, turf out (*informal*), give the bum's rush (*slang*), show someone the door, throw someone out on their ear (*informal*) **2** DISMISS, sack (*informal*), fire (*informal*), remove, get rid of, discharge, expel, throw out, oust, kick out (*informal*), kennet (*Austral slang*), jeff (*Austral slang*) **3** DISCHARGE, expel, emit, give off **4** BAIL OUT, escape, get out

ejection *noun* **1** EXPULSION, removal, ouster (*law*), deportation, eviction, banishment, exile **2** DISMISSAL, sacking (*informal*), firing (*informal*), removal, discharge, the boot (*slang*), expulsion, the sack (*informal*), dislodgement **3** EMISSION, throwing out, expulsion, spouting, casting out, disgorgement

eke out *verb* BE SPARING WITH, stretch out, be economical with, economize on, husband, be frugal with ▷▷ **eke out a living** SUPPORT YOURSELF, survive, get by, make ends meet, scrimp, save, scrimp and save

elaborate *adjective* **1** COMPLICATED, detailed, studied, laboured, perfected, complex, careful, exact, precise, thorough, intricate, skilful, painstaking **2** ORNATE, detailed, involved, complex, fancy, complicated, decorated, extravagant, intricate, baroque, ornamented, fussy, embellished, showy, ostentatious, florid << ANTONYM plain ▷ *verb* **1** DEVELOP, improve, enhance, polish, complicate, decorate, refine, garnish, ornament, flesh out **2** *usually with* **on** *or* **upon** EXPAND UPON, extend upon, enlarge on, amplify upon, embellish, flesh out, add detail to << ANTONYM simplify

élan *noun* STYLE, spirit, dash, flair, animation, vigour, verve, zest, panache, esprit, brio, vivacity, impetuosity

elapse *verb* PASS, go, go by, lapse, pass by, slip away, roll on, slip by, roll by, glide by

elastic *adjective* **1** FLEXIBLE, yielding, supple, rubbery, pliable, plastic, springy, pliant, tensile, stretchy, ductile, stretchable << ANTONYM rigid **2** ADAPTABLE, yielding, variable, flexible, accommodating, tolerant, adjustable, supple, complaisant << ANTONYM inflexible

elasticity *noun* **1** FLEXIBILITY, suppleness, plasticity, give (*informal*), pliability, ductility, springiness, pliancy, stretchiness, rubberiness **2** ADAPTABILITY,

accommodation, flexibility, tolerance, variability, suppleness, complaisance, adjustability, compliantness

elated *adjective* JOYFUL, excited, delighted, proud, cheered, thrilled, elevated, animated, roused, exhilarated, ecstatic, jubilant, joyous, over the moon (*informal*), overjoyed, blissful, euphoric, rapt, gleeful, sent, puffed up, exultant, in high spirits, on cloud nine (*informal*), cock-a-hoop, blissed out, in seventh heaven, floating *or* walking on air, stoked (*Austral & NZ informal*) << ANTONYM dejected

elation *noun* JOY, delight, thrill, excitement, ecstasy, bliss, euphoria, glee, rapture, high spirits, exhilaration, jubilation, exaltation, exultation, joyfulness, joyousness

elbow *noun* JOINT, turn, corner, bend, angle, curve ▷ *verb* PUSH, force, crowd, shoulder, knock, bump, shove, nudge, jostle, hustle ▷▷ **at your elbow** WITHIN REACH, near, to hand, handy, at hand, close by

elder *adjective* OLDER, first, senior, first-born, earlier born ▷ *noun* **1** OLDER PERSON, senior **2** (*Presbyterianism*) CHURCH OFFICIAL, leader, office bearer, presbyter

elect *verb* **1** VOTE FOR, choose, pick, determine, select, appoint, opt for, designate, pick out, settle on, decide upon **2** CHOOSE, decide, prefer, select, opt ▷ *adjective* **1** SELECTED, chosen, picked, choice, preferred, select, elite, hand-picked **2** FUTURE, to-be, coming, next, appointed, designate, prospective

election *noun* **1** VOTE, poll, ballot, determination, referendum, franchise, plebiscite, show of hands **2** APPOINTMENT, choosing, picking, choice, selection

elector *noun* VOTER, chooser, selector, constituent, member of the electorate, member of a constituency, enfranchised person

electric *adjective* **1** ELECTRIC-POWERED, powered, cordless, battery-operated, electrically-charged, mains-operated **2** CHARGED, exciting, stirring, thrilling, stimulating, dynamic, tense, rousing, electrifying, adrenalized

electrify *verb* **1** THRILL, shock, excite, amaze, stir, stimulate, astonish, startle, arouse, animate, rouse, astound, jolt, fire, galvanize, take your breath away << ANTONYM bore **2** WIRE UP, wire, supply electricity to, convert to electricity

elegance *noun* STYLE, taste, beauty,

grace, dignity, sophistication,
grandeur, refinement, polish, gentility,
sumptuousness, courtliness, gracefulness,
tastefulness, exquisiteness

elegant *adjective* 1 STYLISH, fine, beautiful,
sophisticated, delicate, artistic, handsome,
fashionable, refined, cultivated, chic,
luxurious, exquisite, nice, discerning,
graceful, polished, sumptuous, genteel,
choice, tasteful, urbane, courtly, modish,
comely, à la mode, schmick (*Austral informal*)
<< ANTONYM inelegant 2 INGENIOUS,
simple, effective, appropriate, clever, neat,
apt

elegiac *adjective* (*literary*) LAMENTING,
sad, melancholy, nostalgic, mournful,
plaintive, melancholic, sorrowful, funereal,
valedictory, keening, dirgeful, threnodial,
threnodic

elegy *noun* LAMENT, requiem, dirge, plaint
(*archaic*), threnody, keen, funeral song,
coronach (*Scot & Irish*), funeral poem

element *noun* 1 COMPONENT, part, feature,
unit, section, factor, principle, aspect,
foundation, ingredient, constituent,
subdivision 2 GROUP, faction, clique, set,
party, circle 3 TRACE, suggestion, hint, dash,
suspicion, tinge, smattering, soupçon ▷
plural noun WEATHER CONDITIONS, climate,
the weather, wind and rain, atmospheric
conditions, powers of nature, atmospheric
forces ▷▷ **in your element** IN A SITUATION
YOU ENJOY, in your natural environment, in
familiar surroundings

elemental *adjective* 1 PRIMAL, original,
primitive, primordial 2 ATMOSPHERIC,
natural, meteorological

elementary *adjective* 1 BASIC, essential,
primary, initial, fundamental, introductory,
preparatory, rudimentary, elemental, bog-
standard (*informal*) << ANTONYM advanced
2 SIMPLE, clear, easy, plain, straightforward,
rudimentary, uncomplicated, facile,
undemanding, unexacting << ANTONYM
complicated

elevate *verb* 1 PROMOTE, raise, advance,
upgrade, exalt, kick upstairs (*informal*),
aggrandize, give advancement to 2 INCREASE,
lift, raise, step up, intensify, move up, hoist,
raise high 3 RAISE, lift, heighten, uplift,
hoist, lift up, raise up, hike up, upraise
4 CHEER, raise, excite, boost, animate, rouse,
uplift, brighten, exhilarate, hearten, lift up,
perk up, buoy up, gladden, elate

elevated *adjective* 1 EXALTED, high, important,

august, grand, superior, noble, dignified,
high-ranking, lofty 2 HIGH-MINDED, high,
fine, grand, noble, inflated, dignified,
sublime, lofty, high-flown, pompous,
exalted, bombastic << ANTONYM humble
3 RAISED, high, lifted up, upraised

elevation *noun* 1 SIDE, back, face, front,
aspect 2 ALTITUDE, height 3 PROMOTION,
upgrading, advancement, exaltation,
preferment, aggrandizement 4 RISE, hill,
mountain, height, mound, berg (*S African*),
high ground, higher ground, eminence,
hillock, rising ground, acclivity

elicit *verb* 1 BRING ABOUT, cause, derive, bring
out, evoke, give rise to, draw out, bring forth,
bring to light, call forth 2 OBTAIN, extract,
exact, evoke, wrest, draw out, extort, educe

eligible *adjective* 1 ENTITLED, fit, qualified,
suited, suitable << ANTONYM ineligible
2 AVAILABLE, free, single, unmarried,
unattached

eliminate *verb* 1 REMOVE, end, stop, withdraw,
get rid of, abolish, cut out, dispose of,
terminate, banish, eradicate, put an end
to, do away with, dispense with, stamp out,
exterminate, get shot of, wipe from the face
of the earth 2 KNOCK OUT, drop, reject,
exclude, axe (*informal*), get rid of, expel, leave
out, throw out, omit, put out, eject 3 (*slang*)
MURDER, kill, do in (*slang*), take out (*slang*),
terminate, slay, blow away (*slang, chiefly US*),
liquidate, annihilate, exterminate, bump off
(*slang*), rub out (*US slang*), waste (*informal*)

elite *noun* ARISTOCRACY, best, pick, elect,
cream, upper class, nobility, gentry, high
society, crème de la crème (*French*), flower,
nonpareil << ANTONYM rabble ▷ *adjective*
LEADING, best, finest, pick, choice, selected,
elect, crack (*slang*), supreme, exclusive,
privileged, first-class, foremost, first-rate,
pre-eminent, most excellent

elitist *adjective* SNOBBISH, exclusive, superior,
arrogant, selective, pretentious, stuck-up
(*informal*), patronizing, condescending,
snooty (*informal*), uppity, high and mighty
(*informal*), hoity-toity (*informal*), high-hat
(*informal, chiefly US*), uppish (*Brit informal*)

elixir *noun* 1 PANACEA, cure-all, nostrum,
sovereign remedy 2 SYRUP, essence, solution,
concentrate, mixture, extract, potion,
distillation, tincture, distillate

elliptical *adjective* OBLIQUE, concentrated,
obscure, compact, indirect, ambiguous,
concise, condensed, terse, cryptic, laconic,
abstruse, recondite

elongate *verb* LENGTHEN, extend, stretch (out), make longer

elongated *adjective* EXTENDED, long, stretched

elope *verb* RUN AWAY, leave, escape, disappear, bolt, run off, slip away, abscond, decamp, sneak off, steal away, do a bunk (*informal*)

eloquence *noun* **1** FLUENCY, effectiveness, oratory, expressiveness, persuasiveness, forcefulness, gracefulness, powerfulness, whaikorero (*NZ*) **2** EXPRESSIVENESS, significance, meaningfulness, pointedness

eloquent *adjective* **1** SILVER-TONGUED, moving, powerful, effective, stirring, articulate, persuasive, graceful, forceful, fluent, expressive, well-expressed << ANTONYM inarticulate **2** EXPRESSIVE, telling, pointed, revealing, significant, pregnant, vivid, meaningful, indicative, suggestive

elsewhere *adverb* IN *or* TO ANOTHER PLACE, away, abroad, hence (*archaic*), somewhere else, not here, in other places, in *or* to a different place

elucidate *verb* CLARIFY, explain, illustrate, interpret, make clear, unfold, illuminate, spell out, clear up, gloss, expound, make plain, annotate, explicate, shed *or* throw light upon

elude *verb* **1** EVADE, escape, lose, avoid, flee, duck (*informal*), dodge, get away from, shake off, run away from, circumvent, outrun, body-swerve (*Scot*) **2** ESCAPE, baffle, frustrate, puzzle, stump, foil, be beyond (someone), thwart, confound

elusive *adjective* **1** DIFFICULT TO CATCH, tricky, slippery, difficult to find, evasive, shifty **2** INDEFINABLE, puzzling, fleeting, subtle, baffling, indefinite, transient, intangible, indescribable, transitory, indistinct

emaciated *adjective* SKELETAL, thin, weak, lean, pinched, skinny, wasted, gaunt, bony, haggard, atrophied, scrawny, attenuate, attenuated, undernourished, scraggy, half-starved, cadaverous, macilent (*rare*)

emanate *verb* **1** GIVE OUT, send out, emit, radiate, exude, issue, give off, exhale, send forth **2** *often with* **from** FLOW, emerge, spring, proceed, arise, stem, derive, originate, issue, come forth

emancipate *verb* FREE, release, liberate, set free, deliver, discharge, let out, let loose, untie, unchain, enfranchise, unshackle, disencumber, unfetter, unbridle, disenthral, manumit << ANTONYM enslave

emancipation *noun* LIBERATION, freedom, freeing, release, liberty, discharge, liberating, setting free, letting loose, untying, deliverance, unchaining, manumission, enfranchisement, unshackling, unfettering << ANTONYM slavery

emasculate *verb* WEAKEN, soften, cripple, impoverish, debilitate, reduce the power of, enfeeble, make feeble, enervate, deprive of force

embalm *verb* PRESERVE, lay out, mummify

embargo *noun* BAN, bar, block, barrier, restriction, boycott, restraint, check, prohibition, moratorium, stoppage, impediment, blockage, hindrance, interdiction, interdict, proscription, rahui (*NZ*) ▷ *verb* BLOCK, stop, bar, ban, restrict, boycott, check, prohibit, impede, blacklist, proscribe, ostracize, debar, interdict

embark *verb* GO ABOARD, climb aboard, board ship, step aboard, go on board, take ship << ANTONYM get off >> **embark on something** BEGIN, start, launch, enter, engage, take up, set out, undertake, initiate, set about, plunge into, commence, broach

embarrass *verb* SHAME, distress, show up (*informal*), humiliate, disconcert, chagrin, fluster, mortify, faze, discomfit, make uncomfortable, make awkward, discountenance, nonplus, abash, discompose, make ashamed, put out of countenance

embarrassed *adjective* ASHAMED, upset, shamed, uncomfortable, shown-up, awkward, abashed, humiliated, uneasy, unsettled, self-conscious, thrown, disconcerted, red-faced, chagrined, flustered, mortified, sheepish, discomfited, discountenanced, caught with egg on your face, not knowing where to put yourself, put out of countenance

embarrassing *adjective* HUMILIATING, upsetting, compromising, shaming, distressing, delicate, uncomfortable, awkward, tricky, sensitive, troublesome, shameful, disconcerting, touchy, mortifying, discomfiting, toe-curling (*slang*), cringe-making (*Brit informal*), cringeworthy (*Brit informal*), barro (*Austral slang*)

embarrassment *noun* **1** SHAME, distress, showing up (*informal*), humiliation, discomfort, unease, chagrin, self-consciousness, awkwardness, mortification, discomfiture, bashfulness, discomposure **2** PROBLEM, difficulty, nuisance, source of trouble, thorn in your flesh **3** PREDICAMENT, problem, difficulty (*informal*), mess, jam (*informal*), plight, scrape (*informal*), pickle (*informal*)

embed *or* **imbed** *verb often with* **in** FIX, set, plant, root, sink, lodge, insert, implant, drive in, dig in, hammer in, ram in

embellish *verb* **1** DECORATE, enhance, adorn, dress, grace, deck, trim, dress up, enrich, garnish, ornament, gild, festoon, bedeck, tart up (*slang*), beautify **2** ELABORATE, colour, exaggerate, dress up, embroider, varnish

embellishment *noun* **1** DECORATION, garnishing, ornament, gilding, enhancement, enrichment, adornment, ornamentation, trimming, beautification **2** ELABORATION, exaggeration, embroidery

ember *noun usually plural* CINDERS, ashes, residue, live coals

embezzle *verb* MISAPPROPRIATE, steal, appropriate, rob, pocket, nick (*slang, chiefly Brit*), pinch (*informal*), rip off (*slang*), siphon off, pilfer, purloin, filch, help yourself to, thieve, defalcate (*law*), peculate

embezzlement *noun* MISAPPROPRIATION, stealing, robbing, fraud, pocketing, theft, robbery, nicking (*slang, chiefly Brit*), pinching (*informal*), appropriation, siphoning off, thieving, pilfering, larceny, purloining, filching, pilferage, peculation, defalcation (*law*)

embittered *adjective* RESENTFUL, angry, acid, bitter, sour, soured, alienated, disillusioned, disaffected, venomous, rancorous, at daggers drawn (*informal*), nursing a grudge, with a chip on your shoulder (*informal*)

emblazon *verb* DECORATE, show, display, present, colour, paint, illuminate, adorn, ornament, embellish, blazon

emblem *noun* **1** CREST, mark, design, image, figure, seal, shield, badge, insignia, coat of arms, heraldic device, sigil (*rare*) **2** REPRESENTATION, symbol, mark, sign, type, token

emblematic *or* **emblematical** *adjective* **1** SYMBOLIC, significant, figurative, allegorical **2** CHARACTERISTIC, representative, typical, symptomatic

embodiment *noun* PERSONIFICATION, example, model, type, ideal, expression, symbol, representation, manifestation, realization, incarnation, paradigm, epitome, incorporation, paragon, perfect example, exemplar, quintessence, actualization, exemplification, reification

embody *verb* **1** PERSONIFY, represent, express, realize, incorporate, stand for, manifest, exemplify, symbolize, typify, incarnate, actualize, reify, concretize **2** *often with* **in** INCORPORATE, include, contain, combine, collect, concentrate, organize, take in, integrate, consolidate, bring together, encompass, comprehend, codify, systematize

embolden *verb* ENCOURAGE, cheer, stir, strengthen, nerve, stimulate, reassure, fire, animate, rouse, inflame, hearten, invigorate, gee up, make brave, give courage, vitalize, inspirit

embrace *verb* **1** HUG, hold, cuddle, seize, squeeze, grasp, clasp, envelop, encircle, enfold, canoodle (*slang*), take *or* hold in your arms **2** ACCEPT, support, receive, welcome, adopt, grab, take up, seize, make use of, espouse, take on board, welcome with open arms, avail yourself of, receive enthusiastically **3** INCLUDE, involve, cover, deal with, contain, take in, incorporate, comprise, enclose, provide for, take into account, embody, encompass, comprehend, subsume ▷ *noun* HUG, hold, cuddle, squeeze, clinch (*slang*), clasp, canoodle (*slang*)

embroil *verb* INVOLVE, complicate, mix up, implicate, entangle, mire, ensnare, encumber, enmesh

embryo *noun* **1** FETUS, unborn child, fertilized egg **2** GERM, beginning, source, root, seed, nucleus, rudiment

embryonic *or* **embryonal** *adjective* RUDIMENTARY, early, beginning, primary, budding, fledgling, immature, seminal, nascent, undeveloped, incipient, inchoate, unformed, germinal << ANTONYM advanced

emerge *verb* **1** COME OUT, appear, come up, surface, rise, proceed, arise, turn up, spring up, emanate, materialize, issue, come into view, come forth, become visible, manifest yourself << ANTONYM withdraw **2** BECOME APPARENT, develop, come out, turn up, become known, come to light, crop up, transpire, materialize, become evident, come out in the wash

emergence *noun* **1** COMING, development, arrival, surfacing, rise, appearance, arising, turning up, issue, dawn, advent, emanation, materialization **2** DISCLOSURE, publishing, broadcasting, broadcast, publication, declaration, revelation, becoming known, becoming apparent, coming to light, becoming evident

emergency *noun* CRISIS, danger, difficulty, accident, disaster, necessity, pinch, plight, scrape (*informal*), strait, catastrophe, predicament, calamity, extremity, quandary, exigency, critical situation, urgent situation ▷ *adjective* 1 URGENT, crisis, immediate 2 ALTERNATIVE, extra, additional, substitute, replacement, temporary, makeshift, stopgap

emergent *adjective* DEVELOPING, coming, beginning, rising, appearing, budding, burgeoning, fledgling, nascent, incipient

emigrate *verb* MOVE ABROAD, move, relocate, migrate, remove, resettle, leave your country

emigration *noun* DEPARTURE, removal, migration, exodus, relocation, resettlement

eminence *noun* 1 PROMINENCE, reputation, importance, fame, celebrity, distinction, note, esteem, rank, dignity, prestige, superiority, greatness, renown, pre-eminence, repute, notability, illustriousness 2 HIGH GROUND, bank, rise, hill, summit, height, mound, elevation, knoll, hillock, kopje *or* koppie (*S African*)

eminent *adjective* PROMINENT, high, great, important, noted, respected, grand, famous, celebrated, outstanding, distinguished, well-known, superior, esteemed, notable, renowned, prestigious, elevated, paramount, big-time (*informal*), foremost, high-ranking, conspicuous, illustrious, major league (*informal*), exalted, noteworthy, pre-eminent << ANTONYM unknown

emissary *noun* ENVOY, agent, deputy, representative, ambassador, diplomat, delegate, courier, herald, messenger, consul, attaché, go-between, legate

emission *noun* GIVING OFF *or* OUT, release, shedding, leak, radiation, discharge, transmission, venting, issue, diffusion, utterance, ejaculation, outflow, issuance, ejection, exhalation, emanation, exudation

emit *verb* 1 GIVE OFF, release, shed, leak, transmit, discharge, send out, throw out, vent, issue, give out, radiate, eject, pour out, diffuse, emanate, exude, exhale, breathe out, cast out, give vent to, send forth << ANTONYM absorb 2 UTTER, produce, voice, give out, let out

emotion *noun* 1 FEELING, spirit, soul, passion, excitement, sensation, sentiment, agitation, fervour, ardour, vehemence, perturbation 2 INSTINCT, sentiment, sensibility, intuition, tenderness, gut feeling, soft-heartedness

emotional *adjective* 1 PSYCHOLOGICAL, private, personal, hidden, spiritual, inner 2 MOVING, touching, affecting, exciting, stirring, thrilling, sentimental, poignant, emotive, heart-rending, heart-warming, tear-jerking (*informal*) 3 EMOTIVE, sensitive, controversial, delicate, contentious, heated, inflammatory, touchy 4 PASSIONATE, enthusiastic, sentimental, fiery, feeling, susceptible, responsive, ardent, fervent, zealous, temperamental, excitable, demonstrative, hot-blooded, fervid, touchy-feely (*informal*) << ANTONYM dispassionate

emotive *adjective* 1 SENSITIVE, controversial, delicate, contentious, inflammatory, touchy 2 MOVING, touching, affecting, emotional, exciting, stirring, thrilling, sentimental, poignant, heart-rending, heart-warming, tear-jerking (*informal*)

empathize ▷▷ **empathize with** IDENTIFY WITH, understand, relate to, feel for, sympathize with, have a rapport with, feel at one with, be on the same wavelength as

emphasis *noun* 1 IMPORTANCE, attention, weight, significance, stress, strength, priority, moment, intensity, insistence, prominence, underscoring, pre-eminence 2 STRESS, accent, accentuation, force, weight

emphasize *verb* 1 HIGHLIGHT, stress, insist, underline, draw attention to, dwell on, underscore, weight, play up, make a point of, give priority to, press home, give prominence to, prioritize << ANTONYM minimize 2 STRESS, accent, accentuate, lay stress on, put the accent on

emphatic *adjective* 1 FORCEFUL, decided, certain, direct, earnest, positive, absolute, distinct, definite, vigorous, energetic, unmistakable, insistent, unequivocal, vehement, forcible, categorical << ANTONYM hesitant 2 SIGNIFICANT, marked, strong, striking, powerful, telling, storming (*informal*), impressive, pronounced, decisive, resounding, momentous, conclusive << ANTONYM insignificant

empire *noun* 1 KINGDOM, territory, province, federation, commonwealth, realm, domain, imperium (*rare*) 2 ORGANIZATION, company, business, firm, concern, corporation, consortium, syndicate, multinational, conglomeration

empirical *adjective* FIRST-HAND, direct, observed, practical, actual, experimental, pragmatic, factual, experiential << ANTONYM hypothetical

employ *verb* 1 HIRE, commission, appoint, take on, retain, engage, recruit, sign up, enlist, enrol, have on the payroll 2 USE, apply, exercise, exert, make use of, utilize, ply, bring to bear, put to use, bring into play, avail yourself of **3** SPEND, fill, occupy, involve, engage, take up, make use of, use up

employed *adjective* **1** WORKING, in work, having a job, in employment, in a job, earning your living << ANTONYM out of work **2** BUSY, active, occupied, engaged, hard at work, in harness, rushed off your feet << ANTONYM idle

employee *or US* **employe** *noun* WORKER, labourer, workman, staff member, member of staff, hand, wage-earner, white-collar worker, blue-collar worker, hired hand, job-holder, member of the workforce

employer *noun* **1** BOSS (*informal*), manager, head, leader, director, chief, executive, owner, owner, master, chief executive, governor (*informal*), skipper, managing director, administrator, patron, supervisor, superintendent, gaffer (*informal, chiefly Brit*), foreman, proprietor, manageress, overseer, kingpin, honcho (*informal*), big cheese (*slang or old-fashioned*), baas (*S African*), numero uno (*informal*), Mister Big (*slang, chiefly US*), sherang (*Austral & NZ*) **2** COMPANY, business, firm, organization, establishment, outfit (*informal*)

employment *noun* **1** JOB, work, business, position, trade, post, situation, employ, calling, profession, occupation, pursuit, vocation, métier **2** TAKING ON, commissioning, appointing, hire, hiring, retaining, engaging, appointment, recruiting, engagement, recruitment, enlisting, enrolling, enlistment **3** USE, application, exertion, exercise, utilization

emporium *noun* (*old-fashioned*) SHOP, market, store, supermarket, outlet, warehouse, department store, mart, boutique, bazaar, retail outlet, superstore, hypermarket

empower *verb* **1** AUTHORIZE, allow, commission, qualify, permit, sanction, entitle, delegate, license, warrant, give power to, give authority to, invest with power **2** ENABLE, equip, emancipate, give means to, enfranchise

emptiness *noun* **1** FUTILITY, banality, worthlessness, hollowness, pointlessness, meaninglessness, barrenness, senselessness, aimlessness, purposelessness, unsatisfactoriness, valuelessness **2** MEANINGLESSNESS, vanity, banality, frivolity, idleness, unreality, silliness, triviality, ineffectiveness, cheapness, insincerity, worthlessness, hollowness, inanity, unsubstantiality, trivialness, vainness **3** VOID, gap, vacuum, empty space, nothingness, blank space, free space, vacuity **4** BARENESS, waste, desolation, destitution, blankness, barrenness, desertedness, vacantness **5** BLANKNESS, vacancy, vacuity, impassivity, vacuousness, expressionlessness, stoniness, unintelligence, absentness, vacantness

empty *adjective* **1** BARE, clear, abandoned, deserted, vacant, free, void, desolate, destitute, uninhabited, unoccupied, waste, unfurnished, untenanted, without contents << ANTONYM full **2** MEANINGLESS, cheap, hollow, vain, idle, trivial, ineffective, futile, insubstantial, insincere **3** WORTHLESS, meaningless, hollow, pointless, unsatisfactory, futile, unreal, senseless, frivolous, fruitless, aimless, inane, valueless, purposeless, otiose, bootless << ANTONYM meaningful **4** BLANK, absent, vacant, stony, deadpan, vacuous, impassive, expressionless, unintelligent ▷ *verb* **1** CLEAR, drain, gut, void, unload, pour out, unpack, unburden, remove the contents of << ANTONYM fill **2** EXHAUST, consume the contents of, void, deplete, use up << ANTONYM replenish **3** EVACUATE, clear, vacate

emulate *verb* IMITATE, follow, copy, mirror, echo, mimic, take after, follow in the footsteps of, follow the example of, take a leaf out of someone's book, model yourself on

emulation *noun* IMITATION, following, copying, mirroring, reproduction, mimicry

enable *verb* **1** ALLOW, permit, facilitate, empower, give someone the opportunity, give someone the means << ANTONYM prevent **2** AUTHORIZE, allow, commission, permit, qualify, sanction, entitle, license, warrant, empower, give someone the right << ANTONYM stop

enact *verb* **1** ESTABLISH, order, pass, command, approve, sanction, proclaim, decree, authorize, ratify, ordain, validate, legislate, make law **2** PERFORM, play, act, present, stage, represent, put on, portray, depict, act out, play the part of, appear as *or* in, personate

enactment *or* **enaction** *noun* **1** PASSING, legislation, sanction, approval, establishment, proclamation, ratification, authorization, validation, making law **2** DECREE, order, law, act, ruling, bill, measure, command, legislation, regulation, resolution, dictate, canon, statute, ordinance, commandment, edict, bylaw **3** PORTRAYAL, staging, performance, playing, acting, performing, representation, depiction, play-acting, personation

enamoured ▷▷ **enamoured with** IN LOVE WITH, taken with, charmed by, fascinated by, entranced by, fond of, enchanted by, captivated by, enthralled by, smitten with, besotted with, bewitched by, crazy about (*informal*), infatuated with, enraptured by, wild about (*informal*), swept off your feet by, nuts on or about (*slang*)

encampment *noun* CAMP, base, post, station, quarters, campsite, bivouac, camping ground, cantonment

encapsulate or **incapsulate** *verb* SUM UP, digest, summarize, compress, condense, abbreviate, epitomize, abridge, précis

enchant *verb* FASCINATE, delight, charm, entrance, dazzle, captivate, enthral, beguile, bewitch, ravish, mesmerize, hypnotize, cast a spell on, enrapture, enamour, spellbind

enchanting *adjective* DELIGHTFUL, fascinating, appealing, attractive, lovely, charming, entrancing, pleasant, endearing, captivating, alluring, bewitching, ravishing, winsome, Orphean

enchantment *noun* **1** CHARM, fascination, delight, beauty, joy, attraction, bliss, allure, transport, rapture, mesmerism, ravishment, captivation, beguilement, allurement **2** SPELL, magic, charm, witchcraft, voodoo, wizardry, sorcery, occultism, incantation, necromancy, conjuration, makutu (*NZ*)

encircle *verb* SURROUND, ring, circle, enclose, encompass, compass, envelop, girdle, circumscribe, hem in, enfold, environ, gird in, begird (*poetic*), enwreath

enclose or **inclose** *verb* **1** SURROUND, cover, circle, bound, wrap, fence, pound, pen, hedge, confine, close in, encompass, wall in, encircle, encase, fence in, impound, circumscribe, hem in, shut in, environ **2** SEND WITH, include, put in, insert

encompass *verb* **1** INCLUDE, hold, involve, cover, admit, deal with, contain, take in, embrace, incorporate, comprise, embody, comprehend, subsume **2** SURROUND, circle, enclose, close in, envelop, encircle, fence in, ring, girdle, circumscribe, hem in, shut in, environ, enwreath

encounter *verb* **1** EXPERIENCE, meet, face, suffer, have, go through, sustain, endure, undergo, run into, live through **2** MEET, confront, come across, run into (*informal*), bump into (*informal*), run across, come upon, chance upon, meet by chance, happen on or upon **3** BATTLE WITH, attack, fight, oppose, engage with, confront, combat, clash with, contend with, strive against, struggle with, grapple with, face off (*slang*), do battle with, cross swords with, come into conflict with, meet head on ▷ *noun* **1** MEETING, brush, confrontation, rendezvous, chance meeting **2** BATTLE, fight, action, conflict, clash, dispute, contest, set-to (*informal*), run-in (*informal*), combat, confrontation, engagement, collision, skirmish, head-to-head, face-off (*slang*)

encourage *verb* **1** INSPIRE, comfort, rally, cheer, stimulate, reassure, animate, console, rouse, hearten, cheer up, embolden, buoy up, pep up, boost someone's morale, give hope to, buck up (*informal*), gee up, lift the spirits of, give confidence to, inspirit << ANTONYM discourage **2** URGE, persuade, prompt, spur, coax, incite, egg on, abet << ANTONYM dissuade **3** PROMOTE, back, help, support, increase, further, aid, forward, advance, favour, boost, strengthen, foster, advocate, stimulate, endorse, commend, succour << ANTONYM prevent

encouragement *noun* **1** INSPIRATION, help, support, aid, favour, comfort, comforting, cheer, cheering, consolation, reassurance, morale boosting, succour **2** URGING, prompting, stimulus, persuasion, coaxing, egging on, incitement **3** PROMOTION, backing, support, boost, endorsement, stimulation, advocacy, furtherance

encouraging *adjective* PROMISING, good, bright, comforting, cheering, stimulating, reassuring, hopeful, satisfactory, cheerful, favourable, rosy, heartening, auspicious, propitious << ANTONYM discouraging

encroach *verb often with* **on** *or* **upon** INTRUDE, invade, trespass, infringe, usurp, impinge, trench, overstep, make inroads, impose yourself

encroachment *noun* INTRUSION, invasion, violation, infringement, trespass, incursion, usurpation, inroad, impingement

encumber *verb* **1** BURDEN, load, embarrass, saddle, oppress, obstruct, retard, weigh down **2** HAMPER, restrict, handicap, slow down, cramp, inhibit, clog, hinder, inconvenience, overload, impede, weigh down, trammel, incommode

encyclopedic or **encyclopaedic** *adjective*

COMPREHENSIVE, full, complete, vast, universal, wide-ranging, thorough, in-depth, exhaustive, all-inclusive, all-embracing, all-encompassing, thoroughgoing

end *noun* 1 CLOSE, ending, finish, expiry, expiration << ANTONYM beginning 2 CONCLUSION, ending, climax, completion, finale, culmination, denouement, consummation << ANTONYM start 3 FINISH, close, stop, resolution, conclusion, closure, wind-up, completion, termination, cessation 4 EXTREMITY, limit, edge, border, bound, extent, extreme, margin, boundary, terminus 5 TIP, point, head, peak, extremity 6 PURPOSE, point, reason, goal, design, target, aim, object, mission, intention, objective, drift, intent, aspiration 7 OUTCOME, result, consequence, resolution, conclusion, completion, issue, sequel, end result, attainment, upshot, consummation 8 DEATH, dying, ruin, destruction, passing on, doom, demise, extinction, dissolution, passing away, extermination, annihilation, expiration, ruination 9 REMNANT, butt, bit, stub, scrap, fragment, stump, remainder, leftover, tail end, oddment, tag end ▷ *verb* 1 STOP, finish, complete, resolve, halt, cease, axe (*informal*), dissolve, wind up, terminate, call off, discontinue, put paid to, bring to an end, pull the plug on, call a halt to, nip in the bud, belay (*nautical*) << ANTONYM start 2 FINISH, close, conclude, wind up, culminate, terminate, come to an end, draw to a close << ANTONYM begin 3 DESTROY, take, kill, abolish, put an end to, do away with, extinguish, annihilate, exterminate, put to death ▷▷ **end up** 1 FINISH UP, stop, wind up, come to a halt, fetch up (*informal*) 2 TURN OUT TO BE, finish as, finish up, pan out as (*informal*), become eventually

endanger *verb* PUT AT RISK, risk, threaten, compromise, hazard, jeopardize, imperil, put in danger, expose to danger << ANTONYM save

endear *verb* ATTRACT, draw, bind, engage, charm, attach, win, incline, captivate

endearing *adjective* ATTRACTIVE, winning, pleasing, appealing, sweet, engaging, charming, pleasant, cute, enticing, captivating, lovable, alluring, adorable, winsome, cutesy (*informal, chiefly US*)

endeavour (*formal*) *verb* TRY, labour, attempt, aim, struggle, venture, undertake, essay, strive, aspire, have a go, go for it (*informal*), make an effort, have a shot (*informal*), have

a crack (*informal*), take pains, bend over backwards (*informal*), do your best, go for broke (*slang*), bust a gut (*informal*), give it your best shot (*informal*), jump through hoops (*informal*), have a stab (*informal*), break your neck (*informal*), make an all-out effort (*informal*), knock yourself out (*informal*), do your damnedest (*informal*), give it your all (*informal*), rupture yourself (*informal*) ▷ *noun* ATTEMPT, try, shot (*informal*), effort, trial, go (*informal*), aim, bid, crack (*informal*), venture, enterprise, undertaking, essay, stab (*informal*)

ended *adjective* FINISHED, done, over, through, closed, past, complete, done with, settled, all over (bar the shouting), no more, concluded, accomplished, wrapped-up (*informal*), at an end, finis

ending *noun* FINISH, end, close, resolution, conclusion, summing up, wind-up, completion, finale, termination, culmination, cessation, denouement, last part, consummation << ANTONYM start

endless *adjective* 1 ETERNAL, constant, infinite, perpetual, continual, immortal, unbroken, unlimited, uninterrupted, limitless, interminable, incessant, boundless, everlasting, unending, ceaseless, inexhaustible, undying, unceasing, unbounded, measureless, unfading << ANTONYM temporary 2 INTERMINABLE, constant, persistent, perpetual, never-ending, incessant, monotonous, overlong 3 CONTINUOUS, unbroken, uninterrupted, undivided, without end

endorse *or* **indorse** *verb* 1 APPROVE, back, support, champion, favour, promote, recommend, sanction, sustain, advocate, warrant, prescribe, uphold, authorize, ratify, affirm, approve of, subscribe to, espouse, vouch for, throw your weight behind 2 SIGN, initial, countersign, sign on the back of, superscribe, undersign

endorsement *or* **indorsement** *noun* APPROVAL, backing, support, championing, favour, promotion, sanction, recommendation, acceptance, agreement, warrant, confirmation, upholding, subscription, fiat, advocacy, affirmation, ratification, authorization, seal of approval, approbation, espousal, O.K. *or* okay (*informal*)

endow *verb* 1 FINANCE, fund, pay for, award, grant, invest in, confer, settle on, bestow, make over, bequeath, purvey, donate money to 2 IMBUE, steep, bathe, saturate, pervade, instil, infuse, permeate, impregnate, inculcate

endowed *adjective usually with* **with** PROVIDED, favoured, graced, blessed, supplied, furnished, enriched

endowment *noun* **1** PROVISION, fund, funding, award, income, grant, gift, contribution, revenue, subsidy, presentation, donation, legacy, hand-out, boon, bequest, stipend, bestowal, benefaction, largesse *or* largess, koha (NZ) **2** *usually plural* TALENT, power, feature, quality, ability, gift, capacity, characteristic, attribute, qualification, genius, faculty, capability, flair, aptitude

endurance *noun* **1** STAYING POWER, strength, resolution, resignation, determination, patience, submission, stamina, fortitude, persistence, tenacity, perseverance, toleration, sufferance, doggedness, stickability (*informal*), pertinacity **2** PERMANENCE, stability, continuity, duration, continuation, longevity, durability, continuance, immutability, lastingness

endure *verb* **1** EXPERIENCE, suffer, bear, weather, meet, go through, encounter, cope with, sustain, brave, undergo, withstand, live through, thole (*Scot*) **2** PUT UP WITH, stand, suffer, bear, allow, accept, stick (*slang*), take (*informal*), permit, stomach, swallow, brook, tolerate, hack (*slang*), abide, submit to, countenance, stick out (*informal*), take patiently **3** LAST, live, continue, remain, stay, hold, stand, go on, survive, live on, prevail, persist, abide, be durable, wear well

enduring *adjective* LONG-LASTING, lasting, living, continuing, remaining, firm, surviving, permanent, constant, steady, prevailing, persisting, abiding, perennial, durable, immortal, steadfast, unwavering, immovable, imperishable, unfaltering << ANTONYM brief

enemy *noun* FOE, rival, opponent, the opposition, competitor, the other side, adversary, antagonist

energetic *adjective* **1** FORCEFUL, strong, determined, powerful, storming (*informal*), active, aggressive, dynamic, vigorous, potent, hard-hitting, high-powered, strenuous, punchy (*informal*), forcible, high-octane (*informal*) **2** LIVELY, spirited, active, dynamic, vigorous, animated, brisk, tireless, bouncy, indefatigable, alive and kicking, zippy (*informal*), full of beans (*informal*), bright-eyed and bushy-tailed (*informal*) << ANTONYM lethargic **3** STRENUOUS, hard, taxing, demanding, tough, exhausting,

vigorous, arduous

energize *or* **energise** *verb* **1** MOTIVATE, stimulate, drive, stir, activate, animate, enthuse, quicken, enliven, galvanize, liven up, pep up, invigorate, vitalize, inspirit **2** STIMULATE, operate, trigger, turn on, start up, activate, switch on, kick-start, electrify, actuate

energy *noun* **1** STRENGTH, might, force, power, activity, intensity, stamina, exertion, forcefulness **2** LIVELINESS, life, drive, fire, spirit, determination, pep, go (*informal*), zip (*informal*), vitality, animation, vigour, verve, zest, resilience, get-up-and-go (*informal*), élan, brio, vivacity, vim (*slang*) **3** POWER

enfold *or* **infold** *verb* **1** WRAP, surround, enclose, wrap up, encompass, shroud, immerse, swathe, envelop, sheathe, enwrap **2** EMBRACE, hold, fold, hug, cuddle, clasp

enforce *verb* **1** CARRY OUT, apply, implement, fulfil, execute, administer, put into effect, put into action, put into operation, put in force **2** IMPOSE, force, require, urge, insist on, compel, exact, oblige, constrain, coerce

enforced *adjective* IMPOSED, required, necessary, compelled, dictated, prescribed, compulsory, mandatory, constrained, ordained, obligatory, unavoidable, involuntary

enforcement *noun* **1** ADMINISTRATION, carrying out, application, prosecution, execution, implementation, reinforcement, fulfilment **2** IMPOSITION, requirement, obligation, insistence, exaction

engage *verb* **1** PARTICIPATE IN, join in, take part in, undertake, practise, embark on, enter into, become involved in, set about, partake of **2** CAPTIVATE, win, draw, catch, arrest, fix, attract, capture, charm, attach, fascinate, enchant, allure, enamour **3** OCCUPY, involve, draw, busy, grip, absorb, tie up, preoccupy, immerse, engross **4** EMPLOY, commission, appoint, take on, hire, retain, recruit, enlist, enrol, put on the payroll << ANTONYM dismiss **5** BOOK, reserve, secure, hire, rent, charter, lease, prearrange **6** INTERLOCK, join, interact, mesh, interconnect, dovetail **7** SET GOING, apply, trigger, activate, switch on, energize, bring into operation **8** (*military*) BEGIN BATTLE WITH, attack, take on, encounter, combat, fall on, battle with, meet, fight with, assail, face off (*slang*), wage war on, join battle with, give battle to, come to close quarters with

engaged *adjective* 1 OCCUPIED, working, involved, committed, employed, busy, absorbed, tied up, preoccupied, engrossed 2 BETROTHED, promised, pledged, affianced, promised in marriage << ANTONYM unattached 3 IN USE, busy, tied up, unavailable << ANTONYM free

engagement *noun* 1 APPOINTMENT, meeting, interview, date, commitment, arrangement, rendezvous 2 BETROTHAL, marriage contract, troth (*archaic*), agreement to marry 3 BATTLE, fight, conflict, action, struggle, clash, contest, encounter, combat, confrontation, skirmish, face-off (*slang*) 4 PARTICIPATION, joining, taking part, involvement 5 JOB, work, post, situation, commission, employment, appointment, gig (*informal*), stint

engaging *adjective* CHARMING, interesting, pleasing, appealing, attractive, lovely, fascinating, entertaining, winning, pleasant, fetching (*informal*), delightful, cute, enchanting, captivating, agreeable, lovable, winsome, cutesy (*informal, chiefly US*), likable *or* likeable << ANTONYM unpleasant

engender *verb* PRODUCE, make, cause, create, lead to, occasion, excite, result in, breed, generate, provoke, induce, bring about, arouse, give rise to, precipitate, incite, instigate, foment, beget

engine *noun* MACHINE, motor, mechanism, generator, dynamo

engineer *noun* 1 DESIGNER, producer, architect, developer, deviser, creator, planner, inventor, stylist, artificer, originator, couturier 2 WORKER, specialist, operator, practitioner, operative, driver, conductor, technician, handler, skilled employee ▷ *verb* 1 DESIGN, plan, create, construct, devise, originate 2 BRING ABOUT, plan, control, cause, effect, manage, set up (*informal*), scheme, arrange, plot, manoeuvre, encompass, mastermind, orchestrate, contrive, concoct, wangle (*informal*), finagle (*informal*)

engrave *verb* CARVE, cut, etch, inscribe, chisel, incise, chase, enchase (*rare*), grave (*archaic*)

engraved *adjective* FIXED, set, printed, impressed, lodged, embedded, imprinted, etched, ingrained, infixed

engraving *noun* 1 PRINT, block, impression, carving, etching, inscription, plate, woodcut, dry point 2 CUTTING, carving, etching, inscribing, chiselling, inscription, chasing, dry point, enchasing (*rare*)

engrossed *adjective* ABSORBED, lost, involved, occupied, deep, engaged, gripped, fascinated, caught up, intrigued, intent, preoccupied, immersed, riveted, captivated, enthralled, rapt

engrossing *adjective* ABSORBING, interesting, arresting, engaging, gripping, fascinating, compelling, intriguing, riveting, captivating, enthralling

engulf *or* **ingulf** *verb* 1 IMMERSE, bury, flood (out), plunge, consume, drown, swamp, encompass, submerge, overrun, inundate, deluge, envelop, swallow up 2 OVERWHELM, overcome, crush, absorb, swamp, engross

enhance *verb* IMPROVE, better, increase, raise, lift, boost, add to, strengthen, reinforce, swell, intensify, heighten, elevate, magnify, augment, exalt, embellish, ameliorate << ANTONYM reduce

enhancement *noun* IMPROVEMENT, strengthening, heightening, enrichment, increment, embellishment, boost, betterment, augmentation, amelioration

enigma *noun* MYSTERY, problem, puzzle, riddle, paradox, conundrum, teaser

enigmatic *or* **enigmatical** *adjective* MYSTERIOUS, puzzling, obscure, baffling, ambiguous, perplexing, incomprehensible, mystifying, inexplicable, unintelligible, paradoxical, cryptic, inscrutable, unfathomable, indecipherable, recondite, Delphic, oracular, sphinxlike << ANTONYM straightforward

enjoin *verb* 1 ORDER, charge, warn, urge, require, direct, bid, command, advise, counsel, prescribe, instruct, call upon 2 (*law*) PROHIBIT, bar, ban, forbid, restrain, preclude, disallow, proscribe, interdict, place an injunction on

enjoy *verb* 1 TAKE PLEASURE IN *or* FROM, like, love, appreciate, relish, delight in, revel in, be pleased with, be fond of, be keen on, rejoice in, be entertained by, find pleasure in, find satisfaction in, take joy in << ANTONYM hate 2 HAVE, use, own, experience, possess, have the benefit of, reap the benefits of, have the use of, be blessed *or* favoured with ▷▷ **enjoy yourself** HAVE A GOOD TIME, be happy, have fun, have a field day (*informal*), have a ball (*informal*), live life to the full, make merry, let your hair down

enjoyable *adjective* PLEASURABLE, good, great, fine, pleasing, nice, satisfying, lovely, entertaining, pleasant, amusing, delicious, delightful, gratifying, agreeable, delectable, to your liking << ANTONYM unpleasant

enjoyment *noun* 1 PLEASURE, liking, fun, delight, entertainment, joy, satisfaction, happiness, relish, recreation, amusement, indulgence, diversion, zest, gratification, gusto, gladness, delectation, beer and skittles (*informal*) 2 BENEFIT, use, advantage, favour, possession, blessing

enlarge *verb* 1 EXPAND, increase, extend, add to, build up, widen, intensify, blow up (*informal*), heighten, broaden, inflate, lengthen, magnify, amplify, augment, make bigger, elongate, make larger << ANTONYM reduce 2 GROW, increase, extend, stretch, expand, swell, wax, multiply, inflate, lengthen, diffuse, elongate, dilate, become bigger, puff up, grow larger, grow bigger, become larger, distend, bloat ▷▷ **enlarge on something** EXPAND ON, develop, add to, fill out, elaborate on, flesh out, expatiate on, give further details about

enlighten *verb* INFORM, tell, teach, advise, counsel, educate, instruct, illuminate, make aware, edify, apprise, let know, cause to understand

enlightened *adjective* INFORMED, aware, liberal, reasonable, educated, sophisticated, refined, cultivated, open-minded, knowledgeable, literate, broad-minded << ANTONYM ignorant

enlightenment *noun* UNDERSTANDING, information, learning, education, teaching, knowledge, instruction, awareness, wisdom, insight, literacy, sophistication, comprehension, cultivation, refinement, open-mindedness, edification, broad-mindedness

enlist *verb* 1 JOIN UP, join, enter (into), register, volunteer, sign up, enrol 2 OBTAIN, get, gain, secure, engage, procure

enliven *verb* CHEER UP, excite, inspire, cheer, spark, enhance, stimulate, wake up, animate, fire, rouse, brighten, exhilarate, quicken, hearten, perk up, liven up, buoy up, pep up, invigorate, gladden, vitalize, vivify, inspirit, make more exciting, make more lively << ANTONYM subdue

en masse *adverb* ALL TOGETHER, together, as one, as a whole, ensemble, as a group, in a group, all at once, in a mass, as a body, in a body

enmity *noun* HOSTILITY, hate, spite, hatred, bitterness, friction, malice, animosity, aversion, venom, antagonism, antipathy, acrimony, rancour, bad blood, ill will, animus, malevolence, malignity << ANTONYM friendship

ennoble *verb* 1 DIGNIFY, honour, enhance, elevate, magnify, raise, glorify, exalt, aggrandize 2 RAISE TO THE PEERAGE, kick upstairs (*informal*), make noble

ennui *noun* (*literary*) BOREDOM, dissatisfaction, tiredness, the doldrums, lethargy, tedium, lassitude, listlessness

enormity *noun* 1 (*informal*) HUGENESS, extent, magnitude, greatness, vastness, immensity, massiveness, enormousness, extensiveness 2 WICKEDNESS, disgrace, atrocity, depravity, viciousness, villainy, turpitude, outrageousness, baseness, vileness, evilness, monstrousness, heinousness, nefariousness, atrociousness 3 ATROCITY, crime, horror, evil, outrage, disgrace, monstrosity, abomination, barbarity, villainy

enormous *adjective* HUGE, massive, vast, extensive, tremendous, gross, excessive, immense, titanic, jumbo (*informal*), gigantic, monstrous, mammoth, colossal, mountainous, stellar (*informal*), prodigious, gargantuan, elephantine, astronomic, ginormous (*informal*), Brobdingnagian, humongous *or* humungous (*US slang*) << ANTONYM tiny

enough *adjective* SUFFICIENT, adequate, ample, abundant, as much as you need, as much as is necessary ▷ *pronoun* SUFFICIENCY, plenty, sufficient, abundance, adequacy, right amount, ample supply ▷ *adverb* SUFFICIENTLY, amply, fairly, moderately, reasonably, adequately, satisfactorily, abundantly, tolerably, passably

enquire ▷ see **inquire**

enquiry ▷ see **inquiry**

enrage *verb* ANGER, provoke, irritate, infuriate, aggravate (*informal*), incense, gall, madden, inflame, exasperate, incite, antagonize, make you angry, nark (*Brit, Austral & NZ slang*), make your blood boil, get your back up, make you see red (*informal*), put your back up << ANTONYM calm

enraged *adjective* FURIOUS, cross, wild, angry, angered, mad (*informal*), raging, irritated, fuming, choked, infuriated, aggravated (*informal*), incensed, inflamed, exasperated, very angry, irate, livid (*informal*), incandescent, on the warpath, fit to be tied (*slang*), boiling mad, raging mad, tooshie (*Austral slang*), off the air (*Austral slang*)

enraptured *adjective* ENCHANTED, delighted, charmed, fascinated, absorbed, entranced, captivated, transported, enthralled, beguiled, bewitched, ravished, spellbound, enamoured

enrich *verb* 1 ENHANCE, develop, improve, boost, supplement, refine, cultivate, heighten, endow, augment, ameliorate, aggrandize 2 MAKE RICH, make wealthy, make affluent, make prosperous, make well-off

enrol *or US* **enroll** *verb* 1 ENLIST, register, be accepted, be admitted, join up, matriculate, put your name down for, sign up *or* on 2 RECRUIT, take on, engage, enlist

enrolment *or US* **enrollment** *noun* ENLISTMENT, admission, acceptance, engagement, registration, recruitment, matriculation, signing on *or* up

en route *adverb* ON *or* ALONG THE WAY, travelling, on the road, in transit, on the journey

ensemble *noun* 1 GROUP, company, band, troupe, cast, orchestra, chorus, supporting cast 2 COLLECTION, set, body, whole, total, sum, combination, entity, aggregate, entirety, totality, assemblage, conglomeration 3 OUTFIT, suit, get-up (*informal*), costume

enshrine *verb* PRESERVE, protect, treasure, cherish, revere, exalt, consecrate, embalm, sanctify, hallow, apotheosize

ensign *noun* FLAG, standard, colours, banner, badge, pennant, streamer, jack, pennon

enslave *verb* SUBJUGATE, bind, dominate, trap, suppress, enthral, yoke, tyrannize, sell into slavery, reduce to slavery, enchain

ensnare *verb* TRAP, catch, capture, seize, snarl, embroil, net, snare, entangle, entrap, enmesh

ensue *verb* FOLLOW, result, develop, succeed, proceed, arise, stem, derive, come after, issue, befall, flow, come next, come to pass (*archaic*), supervene, be consequent on, turn out *or* up << ANTONYM come first

ensure *or especially US* **insure** *verb* 1 MAKE CERTAIN, guarantee, secure, make sure, confirm, warrant, certify 2 PROTECT, defend, secure, safeguard, guard, make safe

entail *verb* INVOLVE, require, cause, produce, demand, lead to, call for, occasion, need, impose, result in, bring about, give rise to, encompass, necessitate

entangle *verb* 1 TANGLE, catch, trap, twist, knot, mat, mix up, snag, snarl, snare, jumble, ravel, trammel, enmesh << ANTONYM disentangle 2 EMBROIL, involve, complicate, mix up, muddle, implicate, bog down, enmesh

entanglement *noun* BECOMING ENTANGLED, mix-up, becoming enmeshed, becoming ensnared, becoming jumbled, entrapment, snarl-up (*informal, chiefly Brit*), ensnarement

enter *verb* 1 COME *or* GO IN *or* INTO, arrive, set foot in somewhere, cross the threshold of somewhere, make an entrance << ANTONYM exit 2 PENETRATE, get in, insert into, pierce, pass into, perforate 3 JOIN, start work at, begin work at, sign up for, enrol in, become a member of, enlist in, commit yourself to << ANTONYM leave 4 PARTICIPATE IN, join (in), be involved in, get involved in, play a part in, partake in, associate yourself with, start to be in 5 BEGIN, start, take up, move into, set about, commence, set out on, embark upon 6 COMPETE IN, contest, take part in, join in, fight, sign up for, go in for 7 RECORD, note, register, log, list, write down, take down, inscribe, set down, put in writing 8 SUBMIT, offer, present, table, register, lodge, tender, put forward, proffer

enterprise *noun* 1 FIRM, company, business, concern, operation, organization, establishment, commercial undertaking 2 VENTURE, operation, project, adventure, undertaking, programme, pursuit, endeavour 3 INITIATIVE, energy, spirit, resource, daring, enthusiasm, push (*informal*), imagination, drive, pep, readiness, vigour, zeal, ingenuity, originality, eagerness, audacity, boldness, get-up-and-go (*informal*), alertness, resourcefulness, gumption (*informal*), adventurousness, imaginativeness

enterprising *adjective* RESOURCEFUL, original, spirited, keen, active, daring, alert, eager, bold, enthusiastic, vigorous, imaginative, energetic, adventurous, ingenious, up-and-coming, audacious, zealous, intrepid, venturesome

entertain *verb* 1 AMUSE, interest, please, delight, occupy, charm, enthral, cheer, divert, recreate (*rare*), regale, give pleasure to 2 SHOW HOSPITALITY TO, receive, accommodate, treat, put up, lodge, be host to, have company of, invite round, ask round, invite to a meal, ask for a meal 3 CONSIDER, support, maintain, imagine, think about, hold, foster, harbour, contemplate, conceive of, ponder, cherish, bear in mind, keep in mind, think over, muse over, give thought to, cogitate on, allow yourself to consider

entertaining *adjective* ENJOYABLE, interesting, pleasing, funny, charming, cheering, pleasant, amusing, diverting, delightful, witty, humorous, pleasurable, recreative (*rare*)

entertainment *noun* 1 ENJOYMENT, fun, pleasure, leisure, satisfaction, relaxation, recreation, enjoyment, distraction, amusement, diversion 2 PASTIME, show, sport, performance, play, treat, presentation, leisure activity, beer and skittles

enthral *or US* **enthrall** *verb* ENGROSS, charm, grip, fascinate, absorb, entrance, intrigue, enchant, rivet, captivate, beguile, ravish, mesmerize, hypnotize, enrapture, hold spellbound, spellbind

enthralling *adjective* ENGROSSING, charming, gripping, fascinating, entrancing, compelling, intriguing, compulsive, enchanting, riveting, captivating, beguiling, mesmerizing, hypnotizing, spellbinding

enthusiasm *noun* 1 KEENNESS, interest, passion, excitement, warmth, motivation, relish, devotion, zeal, zest, fervour, eagerness, ardour, vehemence, earnestness, zing (*informal*), avidity 2 INTEREST, passion, rage, hobby, obsession, craze, fad (*informal*), mania, hobbyhorse

enthusiast *noun* FAN, supporter, lover, follower, addict, freak (*informal*), admirer, buff (*informal*), fanatic, devotee, fiend (*informal*), adherent, zealot, aficionado

enthusiastic *adjective* KEEN, earnest, spirited, committed, excited, devoted, warm, eager, lively, passionate, vigorous, ardent, hearty, exuberant, avid, fervent, zealous, ebullient, vehement, wholehearted, full of beans (*informal*), fervid, keen as mustard, bright-eyed and bushy-tailed (*informal*) << ANTONYM apathetic

entice *verb* LURE, attract, invite, persuade, draw, tempt, induce, seduce, lead on, coax, beguile, allure, cajole, decoy, wheedle, prevail on, inveigle, dangle a carrot in front of

enticing *adjective* ATTRACTIVE, appealing, inviting, charming, fascinating, tempting, intriguing, irresistible, persuasive, seductive, captivating, beguiling, alluring << ANTONYM unattractive

entire *adjective* 1 CONTINUOUS, unified, unbroken, uninterrupted, undivided 2 WHOLE, full, complete, total 3 ABSOLUTE, full, total, utter, outright, thorough, unqualified, unrestricted, undiminished, unmitigated, unreserved 4 INTACT, whole, perfect, unmarked, unbroken, sound, unharmed, undamaged, without a scratch, unmarred

entirely *adverb* 1 COMPLETELY, totally, perfectly, absolutely, fully, altogether, thoroughly, wholly, utterly, every inch, without exception, unreservedly, in every respect, without reservation, lock, stock and barrel << ANTONYM partly 2 ONLY, exclusively, solely

entirety *noun* WHOLE, total, sum, unity, aggregate, totality

entitle *verb* 1 GIVE THE RIGHT TO, allow, enable, permit, sanction, license, qualify for, warrant, authorize, empower, enfranchise, make eligible 2 CALL, name, title, term, style, label, dub, designate, characterize, christen, give the title of, denominate

entity *noun* 1 THING, being, body, individual, object, presence, existence, substance, quantity, creature, organism 2 ESSENTIAL NATURE, being, existence, essence, quintessence, real nature, quiddity (*philosophy*)

entomb *verb* BURY, inter, lay to rest, sepulchre, place in a tomb, inhume, inurn

entourage *noun* RETINUE, company, following, staff, court, train, suite, escort, cortege

entrails *plural noun* INTESTINES, insides (*informal*), guts, bowels, offal, internal organs, innards (*informal*), vital organs, viscera

entrance[1] *noun* 1 WAY IN, opening, door, approach, access, entry, gate, passage, avenue, doorway, portal, inlet, ingress, means of access << ANTONYM exit 2 APPEARANCE, coming in, entry, arrival, introduction, ingress << ANTONYM exit 3 ADMISSION, access, entry, entrée, admittance, permission to enter, ingress, right of entry

entrance[2] *verb* 1 ENCHANT, delight, charm, absorb, fascinate, dazzle, captivate, transport, enthral, beguile, bewitch, ravish, gladden, enrapture, spellbind << ANTONYM bore 2 MESMERIZE, bewitch, hypnotize, put a spell on, cast a spell on, put in a trance

entrant *noun* 1 NEWCOMER, novice, initiate, beginner, trainee, apprentice, convert, new member, fresher, neophyte, tyro, probationer 2 COMPETITOR, player, candidate, entry, participant, applicant, contender, contestant

entrap *noun* TRICK, lure, seduce, entice,

deceive, implicate, lead on, embroil, beguile, allure, entangle, ensnare, inveigle, set a trap for, enmesh ▷ *verb* CATCH, net, capture, trap, snare, entangle, ensnare

entreaty *noun* PLEA, appeal, suit, request, prayer, petition, exhortation, solicitation, supplication, importunity, earnest request

entrench *or* **intrench** *verb* FIX, set, establish, plant, seat, settle, root, install, lodge, anchor, implant, embed, dig in, ensconce, ingrain

entrenched *or* **intrenched** *adjective* FIXED, set, firm, rooted, well-established, ingrained, deep-seated, deep-rooted, indelible, unshakeable *or* unshakable, ineradicable

entrepreneur *noun* BUSINESSMAN *or* BUSINESSWOMAN, tycoon, director, executive, contractor, industrialist, financier, speculator, magnate, impresario, business executive

entrust *or* **intrust** *verb* 1 GIVE CUSTODY OF, trust, deliver, commit, delegate, hand over, turn over, confide, commend, consign 2 *usually with* **with** ASSIGN, charge, trust, invest, authorize

entry *noun* 1 ADMISSION, access, entrance, admittance, entrée, permission to enter, right of entry 2 COMING IN, entering, appearance, arrival, entrance << ANTONYM exit 3 INTRODUCTION, presentation, initiation, inauguration, induction, debut, investiture 4 RECORD, listing, account, note, minute, statement, item, registration, memo, memorandum, jotting 5 COMPETITOR, player, attempt, effort, candidate, participant, challenger, submission, entrant, contestant 6 WAY IN, opening, door, approach, access, gate, passage, entrance, avenue, doorway, portal, inlet, passageway, ingress, means of access

entwine *or* **intwine** *verb* TWIST, surround, embrace, weave, knit, braid, encircle, wind, intertwine, interweave, plait, twine, ravel, interlace, entwist (*archaic*) << ANTONYM disentangle

enumerate *verb* 1 LIST, tell, name, detail, relate, mention, quote, cite, specify, spell out, recount, recite, itemize, recapitulate 2 COUNT, calculate, sum up, total, reckon, compute, add up, tally, number

enunciate *verb* 1 PRONOUNCE, say, speak, voice, sound, utter, articulate, vocalize, enounce (*formal*) 2 STATE, declare, proclaim, pronounce, publish, promulgate, propound

envelop *verb* ENCLOSE, cover, hide, surround, wrap around, embrace, blanket, conceal, obscure, veil, encompass, engulf, cloak, shroud, swathe, encircle, encase, swaddle, sheathe, enfold, enwrap

envelope *noun* WRAPPING, casing, case, covering, cover, skin, shell, coating, jacket, sleeve, sheath, wrapper

enviable *adjective* DESIRABLE, favoured, privileged, fortunate, lucky, blessed, advantageous, to die for (*informal*), much to be desired, covetable << ANTONYM undesirable

envious *adjective* COVETOUS, jealous, grudging, malicious, resentful, green-eyed, begrudging, spiteful, jaundiced, green with envy

environment *noun* 1 SURROUNDINGS, setting, conditions, situation, medium, scene, circumstances, territory, background, atmosphere, context, habitat, domain, milieu, locale 2 (*ecology*) HABITAT, home, surroundings, territory, terrain, locality, natural home

environmental *adjective* ECOLOGICAL, green

environmentalist *noun* CONSERVATIONIST, ecologist, green, friend of the earth

environs *plural noun* SURROUNDING AREA, surroundings, district, suburbs, neighbourhood, outskirts, precincts, vicinity, locality, purlieus

envisage *verb* 1 IMAGINE, contemplate, conceive (of), visualize, picture, fancy, think up, conceptualize 2 FORESEE, see, expect, predict, anticipate, envision

envision *verb* CONCEIVE OF, expect, imagine, predict, anticipate, see, contemplate, envisage, foresee, visualize

envoy *noun* 1 AMBASSADOR, minister, diplomat, emissary, legate, plenipotentiary 2 MESSENGER, agent, deputy, representative, delegate, courier, intermediary, emissary

envy *noun* COVETOUSNESS, spite, hatred, resentment, jealousy, bitterness, malice, ill will, malignity, resentfulness, enviousness (*informal*) ▷ *verb* 1 BE JEALOUS (OF), resent, begrudge, be envious (of) 2 COVET, desire, crave, aspire to, yearn for, hanker after

ephemeral *adjective* TRANSIENT, short, passing, brief, temporary, fleeting, short-lived, fugitive, flitting, momentary, transitory, evanescent, impermanent, fugacious << ANTONYM eternal

epidemic *adjective* WIDESPREAD, wide-ranging, general, sweeping, prevailing, rampant, prevalent, rife, pandemic ▷ *noun* 1 OUTBREAK, plague, growth, spread, scourge, contagion **2** SPATE, plague, outbreak, wave, rash, eruption, upsurge

epilogue *noun* CONCLUSION, postscript, coda, afterword, concluding speech << ANTONYM prologue

episode *noun* **1** EVENT, experience, happening, matter, affair, incident, circumstance, adventure, business, occurrence, escapade **2** INSTALMENT, part, act, scene, section, chapter, passage

episodic *or* **episodical** *adjective* **1** IRREGULAR, occasional, sporadic, intermittent **2** RAMBLING, irregular, disconnected, anecdotal, disjointed, wandering, discursive, digressive

epistle *noun* LETTER, note, message, communication, missive

epitaph *noun* **1** COMMEMORATION, elegy, obituary **2** INSCRIPTION, engraving

epithet *noun* NAME, title, description, tag, nickname, designation, appellation, sobriquet, moniker *or* monicker (*slang*), obscenity, blasphemy, swear word, imprecation

epitome *noun* PERSONIFICATION, essence, embodiment, type, representation, norm, archetype, exemplar, typical example, quintessence

epitomize *or* **epitomise** *verb* TYPIFY, represent, illustrate, embody, exemplify, symbolize, personify, incarnate

epoch *noun* ERA, time, age, period, date, aeon

equal *adjective* **1** *often with* **to** *or* **with** IDENTICAL, the same, matched, matching, like, equivalent, uniform, alike, corresponding, tantamount, one and the same, proportionate, commensurate << ANTONYM unequal **2** FAIR, just, impartial, egalitarian, unbiased, even-handed, equable << ANTONYM unfair **3** EVEN, balanced, fifty-fifty (*informal*), evenly matched, evenly balanced, evenly proportioned << ANTONYM uneven **4** *with* **to** CAPABLE OF, adequate for ▷ *noun* MATCH, equivalent, fellow, twin, mate, peer, parallel, counterpart, compeer ▷ *verb* **1** AMOUNT TO, make, come to, total, balance with, agree with, level with, parallel, tie with, equate with, correspond to, be equal to, square with, be tantamount to, equalize, tally with, be level with, be even with << ANTONYM be unequal to **2** BE EQUAL TO, match, reach, rival, come up to, be level with, be even with **3** BE AS GOOD AS, match, compare with, equate with, measure up to, be as great as

equality *noun* **1** FAIRNESS, equal opportunity, equal treatment, egalitarianism, fair treatment, justness << ANTONYM inequality **2** SAMENESS, balance, identity, similarity, correspondence, parity, likeness, uniformity, equivalence, evenness, coequality, equatability << ANTONYM disparity

equalize *or* **equalise** *verb* **1** MAKE EQUAL, match, level, balance, square, equal, smooth, equate, standardize, even out, even up, regularize, make level **2** DRAW LEVEL, level the score, square the score, make the score level

equanimity *noun* COMPOSURE, peace, calm, poise, serenity, tranquillity, coolness, aplomb, calmness, phlegm, steadiness, presence of mind, sang-froid, self-possession, placidity, level-headedness, imperturbability

equate *verb* **1** IDENTIFY, associate, connect, compare, relate, mention in the same breath, think of in connection with, think of together **2** MAKE EQUAL, match, balance, square, even up, equalize

equation *noun* EQUATING, match, agreement, balancing, pairing, comparison, parallel, equality, correspondence, likeness, equivalence, equalization

equestrian *adjective* RIDING, mounted, horse riding

equilibrium *noun* **1** STABILITY, balance, symmetry, steadiness, evenness, equipoise, counterpoise **2** COMPOSURE, calm, stability, poise, serenity, coolness, calmness, equanimity, steadiness, self-possession, collectedness

equip *verb* **1** SUPPLY, provide, stock, dress, outfit, arm, rig, array, furnish, endow, attire, fit out, deck out, kit out, fit up, accoutre **2** PREPARE, qualify, educate, get ready, endow

equipment *noun* APPARATUS, stock, supplies, material, stuff, tackle, gear, tools, provisions, kit, rig, baggage, paraphernalia, accoutrements, appurtenances, equipage

equitable *adjective* EVEN-HANDED, just, right, fair, due, reasonable, proper, honest, impartial, rightful, unbiased, dispassionate, proportionate, unprejudiced, nondiscriminatory

equity *noun* FAIRNESS, justice, integrity, honesty, fair play, righteousness, impartiality, rectitude, reasonableness, even-handedness, fair-mindedness, uprightness, equitableness << ANTONYM unfairness

equivalence *or* **equivalency** *noun* EQUALITY,

correspondence, agreement, similarity, identity, parallel, match, parity, conformity, likeness, sameness, parallelism, evenness, synonymy, alikeness, interchangeableness

equivalent *adjective* EQUAL, even, same, comparable, parallel, identical, alike, corresponding, correspondent, synonymous, of a kind, tantamount, interchangeable, of a piece with, commensurate, homologous << ANTONYM different ▷ *noun* EQUAL, counterpart, correspondent, twin, peer, parallel, match, opposite number

equivocal *adjective* AMBIGUOUS, uncertain, misleading, obscure, suspicious, vague, doubtful, dubious, questionable, ambivalent, indefinite, evasive, oblique, indeterminate, prevaricating, oracular << ANTONYM clear

era *noun* AGE, time, period, stage, date, generation, cycle, epoch, aeon, day *or* days

eradicate *verb* WIPE OUT, eliminate, remove, destroy, get rid of, abolish, erase, excise, extinguish, stamp out, obliterate, uproot, weed out, annihilate, put paid to, root out, efface, exterminate, expunge, extirpate, wipe from the face of the earth

eradication *noun* WIPING OUT, abolition, destruction, elimination, removal, extinction, extermination, annihilation, erasure, obliteration, effacement, extirpation, expunction

erase *verb* 1 DELETE, cancel out, wipe out, remove, eradicate, excise, obliterate, efface, blot out, expunge 2 RUB OUT, remove, wipe out, delete, scratch out

erect *adjective* UPRIGHT, raised, straight, standing, stiff, firm, rigid, vertical, elevated, perpendicular, pricked-up << ANTONYM bent ▷ *verb* 1 BUILD, raise, set up, lift, pitch, mount, stand up, rear, construct, put up, assemble, put together, elevate << ANTONYM demolish 2 FOUND, establish, form, create, set up, institute, organize, put up, initiate

erection *noun* 1 HARD-ON (*slang*), erect penis 2 BUILDING, setting-up, manufacture, construction, assembly, creation, establishment, elevation, fabrication

ergo *conjunction* THEREFORE, so, then, thus, hence, consequently, accordingly, for that reason, in consequence

erode *verb* 1 DISINTEGRATE, crumble, deteriorate, corrode, break up, grind down, waste away, wear down *or* away 2 DESTROY, consume, spoil, crumble, eat away, corrode, break up, grind down, abrade, wear down *or* away 3 WEAKEN, destroy, undermine,

diminish, impair, lessen, wear away

erosion *noun* 1 DISINTEGRATION, deterioration, corrosion, corrasion, wearing down *or* away, grinding down 2 DETERIORATION, wearing, undermining, destruction, consumption, weakening, spoiling, attrition, eating away, abrasion, grinding down, wearing down *or* away

erotic *adjective* SEXUAL, sexy (*informal*), crude, explicit, rousing, sensual, seductive, vulgar, stimulating, steamy (*informal*), suggestive, aphrodisiac, voluptuous, carnal, titillating, bawdy, lustful, sexually arousing, erogenous, amatory

err *verb* 1 MAKE A MISTAKE, mistake, go wrong, blunder, slip up (*informal*), misjudge, be incorrect, be inaccurate, miscalculate, go astray, be in error, put your foot in it (*informal*), misapprehend, blot your copybook (*informal*), drop a brick *or* clanger (*informal*) 2 SIN, fall, offend, lapse, trespass, do wrong, deviate, misbehave, go astray, transgress, be out of order, blot your copybook (*informal*)

errand *noun* JOB, charge, commission, message, task, mission

errant *adjective* SINNING, offending, straying, wayward, deviant, erring, aberrant

erratic *adjective* UNPREDICTABLE, variable, unstable, irregular, shifting, eccentric, abnormal, inconsistent, uneven, unreliable, wayward, capricious, desultory, changeable, aberrant, fitful, inconstant << ANTONYM regular

erroneous *adjective* INCORRECT, wrong, mistaken, false, flawed, faulty, inaccurate, untrue, invalid, unfounded, spurious, amiss, unsound, wide of the mark, inexact, fallacious << ANTONYM correct

error *noun* MISTAKE, slip, fault, blunder, flaw, boob (*Brit slang*), delusion, oversight, misconception, fallacy, inaccuracy, howler (*informal*), bloomer (*Brit informal*), boner (*slang*), miscalculation, misapprehension, solecism, erratum, barry *or* Barry Crocker (*Austral slang*)

ersatz *adjective* ARTIFICIAL, substitute, pretend, fake, imitation, synthetic, bogus, simulated, sham, counterfeit, spurious, phoney *or* phony (*informal*)

erstwhile *adjective* FORMER, old, late, previous, once, past, ex (*informal*), one-time, sometime, bygone, quondam

erudite *adjective* LEARNED, lettered, cultured, educated, scholarly, cultivated, knowledgeable, literate, well-educated, well-read << ANTONYM uneducated

erudition *noun* LEARNING, education, knowledge, scholarship, letters, lore, academic knowledge

erupt *verb* 1 EXPLODE, blow up, flare up, emit lava 2 GUSH, burst out, be ejected, burst forth, pour forth, belch forth, spew forth *or* out 3 START, break out, begin, explode, flare up, burst out, boil over 4 (*medical*) BREAK OUT, appear, flare up

eruption *noun* 1 EXPLOSION, discharge, outburst, venting, ejection 2 FLARE-UP, outbreak, sally 3 (*medical*) INFLAMMATION, outbreak, rash, flare-up

escalate *verb* 1 GROW, increase, extend, intensify, expand, surge, be increased, mount, heighten << ANTONYM decrease 2 INCREASE, develop, extend, intensify, expand, build up, step up, heighten, enlarge, magnify, amplify << ANTONYM lessen

escalation *noun* INCREASE, rise, build-up, expansion, heightening, developing, acceleration, upsurge, intensification, amplification

escapade *noun* ADVENTURE, fling, stunt, romp, trick, scrape (*informal*), spree, mischief, lark (*informal*), caper, prank, antic

escape *verb* 1 GET AWAY, flee, take off, fly, bolt, skip, slip away, abscond, decamp, hook it (*slang*), do a runner (*slang*), do a bunk (*Brit slang*), fly the coop (*US & Canad informal*), make a break for it, slip through your fingers, skedaddle (*informal*), take a powder (*US & Canad slang*), make your getaway, take it on the lam (*US & Canad slang*), break free *or* out, make *or* effect your escape, run away *or* off, do a Skase (*Austral informal*) 2 AVOID, miss, evade, dodge, shun, elude, duck, steer clear of, circumvent, body-swerve (*Scot*) 3 BE FORGOTTEN BY, be beyond (someone), baffle, elude, puzzle, stump 4 *usually with* **from** LEAK OUT, flow out, drain away, discharge, gush out, emanate, seep out, exude, spurt out, spill out, pour forth ▷ *noun* 1 GETAWAY, break, flight, break-out, bolt, decampment 2 AVOIDANCE, evasion, circumvention, elusion 3 RELAXATION, relief, recreation, distraction, diversion, pastime 4 LEAK, emission, discharge, outpouring, gush, spurt, outflow, leakage, drain, seepage, issue, emanation, efflux, effluence, outpour

eschew *verb* AVOID, give up, abandon, have nothing to do with, shun, elude, renounce, refrain from, forgo, abstain from, fight shy of, forswear, abjure, kick (*informal*), swear off, give a wide berth to, keep *or* steer clear of

escort *noun* 1 GUARD, protection, safeguard, bodyguard, company, train, convoy, entourage, retinue, cortege 2 COMPANION, partner, attendant, guide, squire (*rare*), protector, beau, chaperon ▷ *verb* ACCOMPANY, lead, partner, conduct, guide, guard, shepherd, convoy, usher, squire, hold (someone's) hand, chaperon

esoteric *adjective* OBSCURE, private, secret, hidden, inner, mysterious, mystical, mystic, occult, arcane, cryptic, inscrutable, abstruse, recondite, cabbalistic

especially *adverb* 1 NOTABLY, largely, chiefly, mainly, mostly, principally, strikingly, conspicuously, outstandingly 2 VERY, specially, particularly, signally, extremely, remarkably, unusually, exceptionally, extraordinarily, markedly, supremely, uncommonly 3 PARTICULARLY, expressly, exclusively, precisely, specifically, uniquely, peculiarly, singularly

espionage *noun* SPYING, intelligence, surveillance, counter-intelligence, undercover work

espouse *verb* SUPPORT, back, champion, promote, maintain, defend, adopt, take up, advocate, embrace, uphold, stand up for

espy *verb* CATCH SIGHT OF, see, discover, spot, notice, sight, observe, spy, perceive, detect, glimpse, make out, discern, behold, catch a glimpse of, descry

essay *noun* 1 COMPOSITION, study, paper, article, piece, assignment, discourse, tract, treatise, dissertation, disquisition 2 (*formal*) ATTEMPT, go (*informal*), try, effort, shot (*informal*), trial, struggle, bid, test, experiment, crack (*informal*), venture, undertaking, stab (*informal*), endeavour, exertion ▷ *verb* (*formal*) ATTEMPT, try, test, take on, undertake, strive for, endeavour, have a go at, try out, have a shot at (*informal*), have a crack at (*informal*), have a bash at (*informal*)

essence *noun* 1 FUNDAMENTAL NATURE, nature, being, life, meaning, heart, spirit, principle, soul, core, substance, significance, entity, bottom line, essential part, kernel, crux, lifeblood, pith, quintessence, basic characteristic, quiddity 2 CONCENTRATE, spirits, extract, elixir, tincture, distillate ▷▷ **in essence** ESSENTIALLY, materially, virtually, basically, fundamentally, in effect, substantially, in the main, to all intents and

purposes, in substance ▷▷ **of the essence**
VITALLY IMPORTANT, essential, vital, critical,
crucial, key, indispensable, of the utmost
importance
essential *adjective* 1 VITAL, important,
needed, necessary, critical, crucial, key,
indispensable, requisite, vitally important,
must-have << ANTONYM unimportant
2 FUNDAMENTAL, main, basic, radical, key,
principal, constitutional, cardinal, inherent,
elementary, innate, intrinsic, elemental,
immanent << ANTONYM secondary
3 CONCENTRATED, extracted, refined, volatile,
rectified, distilled ▷ *noun* PREREQUISITE,
principle, fundamental, necessity, must,
basic, requisite, vital part, sine qua non
(*Latin*), rudiment, must-have
establish *verb* 1 SET UP, found, start, create,
institute, organize, install, constitute,
inaugurate 2 PROVE, show, confirm,
demonstrate, ratify, certify, verify, validate,
substantiate, corroborate, authenticate
3 SECURE, form, base, ground, plant, settle,
fix, root, implant, entrench, ensconce, put
down roots
establishment *noun* 1 CREATION, founding,
setting up, foundation, institution,
organization, formation, installation,
inauguration, enactment 2 ORGANIZATION,
company, business, firm, house, concern,
operation, structure, institution, institute,
corporation, enterprise, outfit (*informal*),
premises, setup (*informal*) 3 OFFICE, house,
building, plant, quarters, factory
Establishment *noun* ▷▷ **the Establishment**
THE AUTHORITIES, the system, the powers
that be, the ruling class, the established
order, institutionalized authority
estate *noun* 1 LANDS, property, area, grounds,
domain, manor, holdings, demesne,
homestead (*US & Canad*) 2 (*Chiefly Brit*)
AREA, centre, park, development, site,
zone, plot 3 (*law*) PROPERTY, capital, assets,
fortune, goods, effects, wealth, possessions,
belongings
esteem *verb* RESPECT, admire, think highly
of, like, love, value, prize, honour, treasure,
cherish, revere, reverence, be fond of,
venerate, regard highly, take off your
hat to ▷ *noun* RESPECT, regard, honour,
consideration, admiration, reverence,
estimation, veneration
estimate *verb* 1 CALCULATE ROUGHLY, value,
guess, judge, reckon, assess, evaluate, gauge,
number, appraise 2 THINK, believe, consider,

rate, judge, hold, rank, guess, reckon, assess,
conjecture, surmise ▷ *noun* 1 APPROXIMATE
CALCULATION, guess, reckoning, assessment,
judgment, evaluation, valuation, appraisal,
educated guess, guesstimate (*informal*),
rough calculation, ballpark figure (*informal*),
approximate cost, approximate price,
ballpark estimate (*informal*), appraisement
2 ASSESSMENT, opinion, belief, appraisal,
evaluation, conjecture, appraisement,
judgment, estimation, surmise
estimation *noun* 1 OPINION, view, regard,
belief, honour, credit, consideration,
judgment, esteem, evaluation, admiration,
reverence, veneration, good opinion,
considered opinion 2 ESTIMATE, reckoning,
assessment, appreciation, valuation,
appraisal, guesstimate (*informal*), ballpark
figure (*informal*)
estrangement *noun* ALIENATION, parting,
division, split, withdrawal, break-up,
breach, hostility, separation, withholding,
disaffection, disunity, dissociation,
antagonization
estuary *noun* INLET, mouth, creek, firth, fjord
et cetera *or* **etcetera** *adverb* AND SO ON, and
so forth, etc.
etch *verb* 1 ENGRAVE, cut, impress, stamp,
carve, imprint, inscribe, furrow, incise,
ingrain 2 CORRODE, eat into, burn into
etching *noun* PRINT, impression, carving,
engraving, imprint, inscription
eternal *adjective* 1 EVERLASTING, lasting,
permanent, enduring, endless, perennial,
perpetual, timeless, immortal, unending,
unchanging, immutable, indestructible,
undying, without end, unceasing,
imperishable, deathless, sempiternal
(*literary*) << ANTONYM transitory
2 INTERMINABLE, constant, endless, abiding,
infinite, continual, immortal, never-ending,
everlasting, ceaseless, unremitting, deathless
<< ANTONYM occasional
eternity *noun* 1 THE AFTERLIFE, heaven,
paradise, the next world, the hereafter
2 PERPETUITY, immortality, infinity,
timelessness, endlessness, infinitude, time
without end 3 AGES, years, an age, centuries,
for ever (*informal*), aeons, donkey's years
(*informal*), yonks (*informal*), a month of
Sundays (*informal*), a long time *or* while, an
age *or* eternity
ethereal *adjective* 1 INSUBSTANTIAL, light,
fairy, aerial, airy, intangible, rarefied,
impalpable 2 SPIRITUAL, heavenly, unearthly,

sublime, celestial, unworldly, empyreal

ethical *adjective* **1** MORAL, behavioural
2 RIGHT, morally right, morally acceptable, good, just, fitting, fair, responsible, principled, correct, decent, proper, upright, honourable, honest, righteous, virtuous
<< ANTONYM unethical

ethics *plural noun* MORAL CODE, standards, principles, morals, conscience, morality, moral values, moral principles, moral philosophy, rules of conduct, moral beliefs, tikanga (NZ)

ethnic *or* **ethnical** *adjective* CULTURAL, national, traditional, native, folk, racial, genetic, indigenous

ethos *noun* SPIRIT, character, attitude, beliefs, ethic, tenor, disposition

etiquette *noun* GOOD *or* PROPER BEHAVIOUR, manners, rules, code, customs, convention, courtesy, usage, protocol, formalities, propriety, politeness, good manners, decorum, civility, politesse, p's and q's, polite behaviour, kawa (NZ), tikanga (NZ)

eulogy *noun* PRAISE, tribute, acclaim, compliment, applause, accolade, paean, commendation, exaltation, glorification, acclamation, panegyric, encomium, plaudit, laudation

euphoria *noun* ELATION, joy, ecstasy, bliss, glee, rapture, high spirits, exhilaration, jubilation, intoxication, transport, exaltation, joyousness << ANTONYM despondency

evacuate *verb* **1** REMOVE, clear, withdraw, expel, move out, send to a safe place
2 ABANDON, leave, clear, desert, quit, depart (from), withdraw from, pull out of, move out of, relinquish, vacate, forsake, decamp from

evacuation *noun* **1** REMOVAL, departure, withdrawal, clearance, flight, expulsion, exodus **2** ABANDONMENT, withdrawal from, pulling out of, moving out, clearance from, vacation from

evade *verb* **1** AVOID, escape, dodge, get away from, shun, elude, eschew, steer clear of, sidestep, circumvent, duck, shirk, slip through the net of, escape the clutches of, body-swerve (*Scot*) << ANTONYM face
2 AVOID ANSWERING, parry, circumvent, fend off, balk, cop out of (*slang*), fence, fudge, hedge, prevaricate, flannel (*Brit informal*), beat about the bush about, equivocate

evaluate *verb* ASSESS, rate, value, judge, estimate, rank, reckon, weigh, calculate, gauge, weigh up, appraise, size up (*informal*),

assay

evaluation *noun* ASSESSMENT, rating, judgment, calculation, valuation, appraisal, estimation

evangelical (*Christianity*) *adjective* CRUSADING, converting, missionary, zealous, revivalist, proselytizing, propagandizing

evaporate *verb* **1** DISAPPEAR, vaporize, dematerialize, evanesce, melt, vanish, dissolve, disperse, dry up, dispel, dissipate, fade away, melt away **2** DRY UP, dry, dehydrate, vaporize, desiccate **3** FADE AWAY, disappear, fade, melt, vanish, dissolve, disperse, dissipate, melt away

evaporation *noun* **1** VAPORIZATION, vanishing, disappearance, dispelling, dissolution, fading away, melting away, dispersal, dissipation, evanescence, dematerialization
2 DRYING UP, drying, dehydration, desiccation, vaporization

evasion *noun* **1** AVOIDANCE, escape, dodging, shirking, cop-out (*slang*), circumvention, elusion **2** DECEPTION, shuffling, cunning, fudging, pretext, ruse, artifice, trickery, subterfuge, equivocation, prevarication, sophistry, evasiveness, obliqueness, sophism

evasive *adjective* **1** DECEPTIVE, misleading, indirect, cunning, slippery, tricky, shuffling, devious, oblique, shifty, cagey (*informal*), deceitful, dissembling, prevaricating, equivocating, sophistical, casuistic, casuistical << ANTONYM straightforward
2 AVOIDING, escaping, circumventing

eve *noun* **1** NIGHT BEFORE, day before, vigil
2 BRINK, point, edge, verge, threshold

even *adjective* **1** REGULAR, stable, constant, steady, smooth, uniform, unbroken, uninterrupted, unwavering, unvarying, metrical << ANTONYM variable **2** LEVEL, straight, flat, plane, smooth, true, steady, uniform, parallel, flush, horizontal, plumb
<< ANTONYM uneven **3** EQUAL, like, the same, matching, similar, uniform, parallel, identical, comparable, commensurate, coequal << ANTONYM unequal **4** EQUALLY MATCHED, level, tied, drawn, on a par, neck and neck, fifty-fifty (*informal*), equalized, all square, equally balanced << ANTONYM ill-matched **5** SQUARE, quits, on the same level, on an equal footing **6** CALM, stable, steady, composed, peaceful, serene, cool, tranquil, well-balanced, placid, undisturbed, unruffled, imperturbable, equable, even-tempered, unexcitable, equanimous
<< ANTONYM excitable **7** FAIR, just,

balanced, equitable, impartial, disinterested, unbiased, dispassionate, fair and square, unprejudiced << ANTONYM unfair ▷
adverb **1** DESPITE, in spite of, disregarding, notwithstanding, in spite of the fact that, regardless of the fact that **2** ALL THE MORE, much, still, yet, to a greater extent, to a greater degree ▷▷ **even as** WHILE, just as, whilst, at the same time that, at the same time as, exactly as, during the time that ▷▷ **even so** NEVERTHELESS, still, however, yet, despite that, in spite of (that), nonetheless, all the same, notwithstanding that, be that as it may ▷▷ **even something out** MAKE *or* BECOME LEVEL, align, level, square, smooth, steady, flatten, stabilize, balance out, regularize ▷▷ **even something up** EQUALIZE, match, balance, equal ▷▷ **get even (with)** (*informal*) PAY BACK, repay, reciprocate, even the score, requite, get your own back, settle the score, take vengeance, take an eye for an eye, be revenged *or* revenge yourself, give tit for tat, pay (someone) back in their own coin, return like for like

even-handed *adjective* FAIR, just, balanced, equitable, impartial, disinterested, unbiased, fair and square, unprejudiced

evening *noun* DUSK (*archaic*), night, sunset, twilight, sundown, eve, vesper (*archaic*), eventide (*archaic or poetic*), gloaming (*Scot poetic*), e'en (*archaic or poetic*), close of day, crepuscule, even, evo (*Austral slang*)

event *noun* **1** INCIDENT, happening, experience, matter, affair, occasion, proceeding, fact, business, circumstance, episode, adventure, milestone, occurrence, escapade **2** COMPETITION, game, tournament, contest, bout ▷▷ **in any event** *or* **at all events** WHATEVER HAPPENS, regardless, in any case, no matter what, at any rate, come what may ▷▷ **in the event of** IN THE EVENTUALITY, in the situation of, in the likelihood of

eventful *adjective* EXCITING, active, busy, dramatic, remarkable, historic, full, lively, memorable, notable, momentous, fateful, noteworthy, consequential << ANTONYM dull

eventual *adjective* FINAL, later, resulting, future, overall, concluding, ultimate, prospective, ensuing, consequent

eventuality *noun* POSSIBILITY, event, likelihood, probability, case, chance, contingency

eventually *adverb* IN THE END, finally, one day, after all, some time, ultimately, at the end of the day, in the long run, sooner or later, some day, when all is said and done, in the fullness of time, in the course of time

ever *adverb* **1** AT ANY TIME, at all, in any case, at any point, by any chance, on any occasion, at any period **2** ALWAYS, for ever, at all times, relentlessly, eternally, evermore, unceasingly, to the end of time, everlastingly, unendingly, aye (*Scot*) **3** CONSTANTLY, continually, endlessly, perpetually, incessantly, unceasingly, unendingly

everlasting *adjective* **1** ETERNAL, endless, abiding, infinite, perpetual, timeless, immortal, never-ending, indestructible, undying, imperishable, deathless << ANTONYM transitory **2** CONTINUAL, constant, endless, continuous, never-ending, interminable, incessant, ceaseless, unremitting, unceasing

every *adjective* EACH, each and every, every single

everybody *pronoun* EVERYONE, each one, the whole world, each person, every person, all and sundry, one and all ▷ see **everyone**

everyday *adjective* **1** DAILY, day-to-day, diurnal, quotidian << ANTONYM occasional **2** ORDINARY, common, usual, familiar, conventional, routine, dull, stock, accustomed, customary, commonplace, mundane, vanilla (*slang*), banal, habitual, run-of-the-mill, unimaginative, workaday, unexceptional, bog-standard (*Brit & Irish slang*), common or garden (*informal*), dime-a-dozen (*informal*), wonted << ANTONYM unusual

everyone *pronoun* EVERYBODY, each one, the whole world, each person, every person, all and sundry, one and all

everything *pronoun* ALL, the whole, the total, the lot, the sum, the whole lot, the aggregate, the entirety, each thing, the whole caboodle (*informal*), the whole kit and caboodle (*informal*)

everywhere *adverb* **1** ALL OVER, all around, the world over, high and low, in each place, in every nook and cranny, far and wide *or* near, to *or* in every place **2** ALL AROUND, all over, in each place, in every nook and cranny, ubiquitously, far and wide *or* near, to *or* in every place

evict *verb* EXPEL, remove, turn out, put out, throw out, oust, kick out (*informal*), eject, dislodge, boot out (*informal*), force to leave, dispossess, chuck out (*informal*), show the door (to), turf out (*informal*), throw on to the streets

eviction *noun* EXPULSION, removal, clearance, ouster (*law*), ejection, dispossession, dislodgement

evidence *noun* 1 PROOF, grounds, data, demonstration, confirmation, verification, corroboration, authentication, substantiation 2 SIGN(s), mark, suggestion, trace, indication, token, manifestation 3 (*law*) TESTIMONY, statement, witness, declaration, submission, affirmation, deposition, avowal, attestation, averment ▷ *verb* SHOW, prove, reveal, display, indicate, witness, demonstrate, exhibit, manifest, signify, denote, testify to, evince

evident *adjective* OBVIOUS, clear, plain, apparent, visible, patent, manifest, tangible, noticeable, blatant, conspicuous, unmistakable, palpable, salient, indisputable, perceptible, incontrovertible, incontestable, plain as the nose on your face << ANTONYM hidden

evidently *adverb* 1 OBVIOUSLY, clearly, plainly, patently, undoubtedly, manifestly, doubtless, without question, unmistakably, indisputably, doubtlessly, incontrovertibly, incontestably 2 APPARENTLY, it seems, seemingly, outwardly, it would seem, ostensibly, so it seems, to all appearances

evil *adjective* 1 WICKED, bad, wrong, corrupt, vicious, vile, malicious, base, immoral, malignant, sinful, unholy, malevolent, heinous, depraved, villainous, nefarious, iniquitous, reprobate, maleficent 2 HARMFUL, painful, disastrous, destructive, dire, catastrophic, mischievous, detrimental, hurtful, woeful, pernicious, ruinous, sorrowful, deleterious, injurious, baneful (*archaic*) 3 DEMONIC, satanic, diabolical, hellish, devilish, infernal, fiendish 4 OFFENSIVE, nasty, foul, unpleasant, vile, noxious, disagreeable, putrid, pestilential, mephitic 5 UNFORTUNATE, unlucky, unfavourable, ruinous, calamitous, inauspicious ▷ *noun* 1 WICKEDNESS, bad, wrong, vice, corruption, sin, wrongdoing, depravity, immorality, iniquity, badness, viciousness, villainy, sinfulness, turpitude, baseness, malignity, heinousness, maleficence 2 HARM, suffering, pain, hurt, misery, sorrow, woe 3 ACT OF CRUELTY, crime, ill, horror, outrage, cruelty, brutality, misfortune, mischief, affliction, monstrosity,

abomination, barbarity, villainy

evince *verb* (*formal*) SHOW, evidence, reveal, establish, express, display, indicate, demonstrate, exhibit, make clear, manifest, signify, attest, bespeak, betoken, make evident

evoke *verb* 1 AROUSE, cause, excite, stimulate, induce, awaken, give rise to, stir up, rekindle, summon up << ANTONYM suppress 2 PROVOKE, produce, elicit, call to mind, call forth, educe (*rare*)

evolution *noun* 1 (*biology*) RISE, development, adaptation, natural selection, Darwinism, survival of the fittest, evolvement 2 DEVELOPMENT, growth, advance, progress, working out, expansion, extension, unfolding, progression, enlargement, maturation, unrolling

evolve *verb* 1 DEVELOP, metamorphose, adapt yourself 2 GROW, develop, advance, progress, mature 3 WORK OUT, develop, progress, expand, elaborate, unfold, enlarge, unroll

exacerbate *verb* IRRITATE, excite, provoke, infuriate, aggravate (*informal*), enrage, madden, inflame, exasperate, vex, embitter, add insult to injury, fan the flames of, envenom

exact *adjective* 1 ACCURATE, very, correct, true, particular, right, express, specific, careful, precise, identical, authentic, faithful, explicit, definite, literal, unequivocal, faultless, on the money (*US*), unerring, veracious << ANTONYM approximate 2 METICULOUS, severe, careful, strict, exacting, precise, rigorous, painstaking, scrupulous, methodical, orderly, punctilious ▷ *verb* 1 DEMAND, claim, require, call for, force, impose, command, squeeze, extract, compel, wring, wrest, insist upon, extort 2 INFLICT, apply, impose, administer, mete out, deal out

exacting *adjective* 1 DEMANDING, hard, taxing, difficult, tough, painstaking << ANTONYM easy 2 STRICT, severe, harsh, stern, rigid, rigorous, stringent, oppressive, imperious, unsparing

exactly *adverb* 1 ACCURATELY, correctly, definitely, truly, precisely, strictly, literally, faithfully, explicitly, rigorously, unequivocally, scrupulously, truthfully, methodically, unerringly, faultlessly, veraciously 2 PRECISELY, just, expressly, prompt (*informal*), specifically, bang on (*informal*), to the letter, on the button (*informal*) ▷ *sentence substitute* PRECISELY, yes, quite, of course, certainly, indeed, truly, that's right, absolutely, spot-on (*Brit informal*), just so, quite so, ya (*S African*), as you say, you got it (*informal*), assuredly, yebo (*S African informal*) ▷▷ **not exactly** (*ironical*) NOT AT ALL, hardly, not really, not quite, certainly not, by no means, in no way, not by any means, in no manner

exaggerate *verb* OVERSTATE, emphasize, enlarge, inflate, embroider, magnify, overdo, amplify, exalt, embellish, overestimate, overemphasize, pile it on about (*informal*), blow up out of all proportion, lay it on thick about (*informal*), lay it on with a trowel about (*informal*), make a production (out) of (*informal*), make a federal case of (*US informal*), hyperbolize

exaggerated *adjective* OVERSTATED, extreme, excessive, over the top (*informal*), inflated, extravagant, overdone, tall (*informal*), amplified, hyped, pretentious, exalted, overestimated, overblown, fulsome, hyperbolic, highly coloured, O.T.T. (*slang*)

exaggeration *noun* OVERSTATEMENT, inflation, emphasis, excess, enlargement, pretension, extravagance, hyperbole, magnification, amplification, embellishment, exaltation, pretentiousness, overemphasis, overestimation << ANTONYM understatement

exalt *verb* 1 PRAISE, acclaim, applaud, pay tribute to, bless, worship, magnify (*archaic*), glorify, reverence, laud, extol, crack up (*informal*), pay homage to, idolize, apotheosize, set on a pedestal 2 UPLIFT, raise, lift, excite, delight, inspire, thrill, stimulate, arouse, heighten, elevate, animate, exhilarate, electrify, fire the imagination of, fill with joy, elate, inspirit

exaltation *noun* 1 ELATION, delight, joy, excitement, inspiration, ecstasy, stimulation, bliss, transport, animation, elevation, rapture, exhilaration, jubilation, exultation, joyousness 2 PRAISE, tribute, worship, acclaim, applause, glory, blessing, homage, reverence, magnification, apotheosis, glorification, acclamation, panegyric, idolization, extolment, lionization, laudation

exalted *adjective* 1 HIGH-RANKING, high, grand, honoured, intellectual, noble, prestigious, august, elevated, eminent, dignified, lofty 2 NOBLE, ideal, superior, elevated, intellectual, uplifting, sublime, lofty, high-minded 3 ELATED, excited,

inspired, stimulated, elevated, animated, uplifted, transported, exhilarated, ecstatic, jubilant, joyous, joyful, over the moon (*informal*), blissful, rapturous, exultant, in high spirits, on cloud nine (*informal*), cock-a-hoop, in seventh heaven, inspirited, stoked (*Austral & NZ informal*)

examination *noun* 1 (*medical*) CHECKUP, analysis, going-over (*informal*), exploration, health check, check, medical, once-over (*informal*) 2 EXAM, test, research, paper, investigation, practical, assessment, quiz, evaluation, oral, appraisal, catechism

examine *verb* 1 INSPECT, test, consider, study, check, research, review, survey, investigate, explore, probe, analyse, scan, vet, check out, ponder, look over, look at, sift through, work over, pore over, appraise, scrutinize, peruse, take stock of, assay, recce (*slang*), look at carefully, go over *or* through 2 (*medical*) CHECK, analyse, check over 3 (*education*) TEST, question, assess, quiz, evaluate, appraise, catechize 4 (*law*) QUESTION, quiz, interrogate, cross-examine, grill (*informal*), give the third degree to (*informal*)

example *noun* 1 INSTANCE, specimen, case, sample, illustration, case in point, particular case, particular instance, typical case, exemplification, representative case 2 ILLUSTRATION, model, ideal, standard, norm, precedent, pattern, prototype, paradigm, archetype, paragon, exemplar 3 WARNING, lesson, caution, deterrent, admonition ▷▷ **for example** AS AN ILLUSTRATION, like, such as, for instance, to illustrate, by way of illustration, exempli gratia (*Latin*), e.g., to cite an instance

exasperate *verb* IRRITATE, anger, provoke, annoy, rouse, infuriate, hassle (*informal*), exacerbate, aggravate (*informal*), incense, enrage, gall, madden, inflame, bug (*informal*), nettle, get to (*informal*), vex, embitter, irk, rile (*informal*), pique, rankle, peeve (*informal*), needle (*informal*), get on your nerves (*informal*), try the patience of, nark (*Brit, Austral & NZ slang*), get in your hair (*informal*), get on your wick (*Brit slang*), hack you off (*informal*) << ANTONYM calm

exasperating *adjective* IRRITATING, provoking, annoying, infuriating, aggravating (*informal*), galling, maddening, vexing, irksome, enough to drive you up the wall (*informal*), enough to try the patience of a saint

exasperation *noun* IRRITATION, anger, rage, fury, wrath, provocation, passion, annoyance, ire (*literary*), pique, aggravation (*informal*), vexation, exacerbation

excavate *verb* 1 DIG UP, mine, dig, tunnel, scoop, cut, hollow, trench, burrow, quarry, delve, gouge 2 UNEARTH, expose, uncover, dig out, exhume, lay bare, bring to light, bring to the surface, disinter

excavation *noun* HOLE, mine, pit, ditch, shaft, cutting, cut, hollow, trench, burrow, quarry, dig, trough, cavity, dugout, diggings

exceed *verb* 1 SURPASS, better, pass, eclipse, beat, cap (*informal*), top, be over, be more than, overtake, go beyond, excel, transcend, be greater than, outstrip, outdo, outreach, be larger than, outshine, surmount, be superior to, outrun, run rings around (*informal*), outdistance, knock spots off (*informal*), put in the shade (*informal*) 2 GO OVER THE LIMIT OF, go beyond, overstep, go beyond the bounds of

exceeding *adjective* EXTRAORDINARY, great, huge, vast, enormous, superior, excessive, exceptional, surpassing, superlative, pre-eminent, streets ahead

exceedingly *adverb* EXTREMELY, very, highly, greatly, especially, hugely, seriously (*informal*), vastly, unusually, enormously, exceptionally, extraordinarily, excessively, superlatively, inordinately, to a fault, to the nth degree, surpassingly

excel *verb* BE SUPERIOR TO, better, pass, eclipse, beat, top, cap (*informal*), exceed, go beyond, surpass, transcend, outdo, outshine, surmount, run rings around (*informal*), put in the shade (*informal*), outrival ▷▷ **excel in** *or* **at something** BE GOOD AT, be master of, predominate in, shine at, be proficient in, show talent in, be skilful at, have (something) down to a fine art, be talented at

excellence *noun* HIGH QUALITY, worth, merit, distinction, virtue, goodness, perfection, superiority, purity, greatness, supremacy, eminence, virtuosity, transcendence, pre-eminence, fineness

excellent *adjective* OUTSTANDING, good, great, fine, prime, capital, noted, choice, champion, cool (*informal*), select, brilliant, very good, cracking (*Brit informal*), crucial (*slang*), mean (*slang*), superb, distinguished, fantastic, magnificent, superior, sterling, worthy, first-class, marvellous, exceptional, terrific, splendid, notable, mega (*slang*), topping (*Brit slang*), sovereign, dope (*slang*), world-class, exquisite, admirable,

exemplary, wicked (*slang*), first-rate, def (*slang*), superlative, top-notch (*informal*), brill (*informal*), pre-eminent, meritorious, estimable, tiptop, bodacious (*slang, chiefly US*), boffo (*slang*), jim-dandy (*slang*), A1 or A-one (*informal*), bitchin' (*US slang*), chillin' (*US slang*), booshit (*Austral slang*), exo (*Austral slang*), sik (*Austral slang*), rad (*informal*), phat (*slang*), schmick (*Austral informal*) << ANTONYM terrible

except *preposition often with* **for** APART FROM, but for, saving, bar, barring, excepting, other than, excluding, omitting, with the exception of, aside from, save (*archaic*), not counting, exclusive of ▷ *verb* EXCLUDE, rule out, leave out, omit, disregard, pass over

exception *noun* SPECIAL CASE, departure, freak, anomaly, inconsistency, deviation, quirk, oddity, peculiarity, irregularity ▷▷ **take exception** *usually with* **to** OBJECT TO, disagree with, take offence at, take umbrage at, be resentful of, be offended at, demur at, quibble at

exceptional *adjective* 1 REMARKABLE, special, excellent, extraordinary, outstanding, superior, first-class, marvellous, notable, phenomenal, first-rate, prodigious, unsurpassed, one in a million, bodacious (*slang, chiefly US*), unexcelled << ANTONYM average 2 UNUSUAL, special, odd, strange, rare, extraordinary, unprecedented, peculiar, abnormal, irregular, uncommon, inconsistent, singular, deviant, anomalous, atypical, aberrant << ANTONYM ordinary

excerpt *noun* EXTRACT, part, piece, section, selection, passage, portion, fragment, quotation, citation, pericope ▷ *verb* EXTRACT, take, select, quote, cite, pick out, cull

excess *noun* 1 SURFEIT, surplus, overdose, overflow, overload, plethora, glut, overabundance, superabundance, superfluity << ANTONYM shortage 2 OVERINDULGENCE, extravagance, profligacy, debauchery, dissipation, intemperance, indulgence, prodigality, extreme behaviour, immoral behaviour, dissoluteness, immoderation, exorbitance, unrestraint << ANTONYM moderation ▷ *adjective* SPARE, remaining, extra, additional, surplus, unwanted, redundant, residual, leftover, superfluous, unneeded

excessive *adjective* 1 IMMODERATE, too much, enormous, extreme, exaggerated, over the top (*slang*), extravagant, needless, unreasonable, disproportionate, undue, uncontrolled, superfluous, prodigal, unrestrained, profligate, inordinate, fulsome, intemperate, unconscionable, overmuch, O.T.T. (*slang*) **2** INORDINATE, unfair, unreasonable, disproportionate, undue, unwarranted, exorbitant, over the odds, extortionate, immoderate

exchange *verb* INTERCHANGE, change, trade, switch, swap, truck, barter, reciprocate, bandy, give to each other, give to one another ▷ *noun* **1** CONVERSATION, talk, word, discussion, chat, dialogue, natter, powwow **2** INTERCHANGE, dealing, trade, switch, swap, traffic, trafficking, truck, swapping, substitution, barter, bartering, reciprocity, tit for tat, quid pro quo **3** MARKET, money market, Bourse

excise¹ *noun* TAX, duty, customs, toll, levy, tariff, surcharge, impost

excise² *verb* **1** DELETE, cut, remove, erase, destroy, eradicate, strike out, exterminate, cross out, expunge, extirpate, wipe from the face of the earth **2** CUT OFF *or* OUT *or* AWAY, remove, take out, extract

excitable *adjective* NERVOUS, emotional, violent, sensitive, tense, passionate, volatile, hasty, edgy, temperamental, touchy, mercurial, uptight (*informal*), irascible, testy, hot-headed, chippy (*informal*), hot-tempered, quick-tempered, highly strung, adrenalized << ANTONYM calm

excite *verb* **1** THRILL, inspire, stir, stimulate, provoke, awaken, animate, move, fire, rouse, exhilarate, agitate, quicken, inflame, enliven, galvanize, foment **2** AROUSE, stimulate, provoke, evoke, rouse, stir up, fire, elicit, work up, incite, instigate, whet, kindle, waken **3** TITILLATE, thrill, stimulate, turn on (*slang*), arouse, get going (*informal*), electrify

excited *adjective* **1** THRILLED, stirred, stimulated, enthusiastic, high (*informal*), moved, wild, aroused, awakened, animated, roused, tumultuous, aflame **2** AGITATED, worried, stressed, alarmed, nervous, disturbed, tense, flurried, worked up, feverish, overwrought, hot and bothered (*informal*), discomposed, adrenalized

excitement *noun* **1** EXHILARATION, action, activity, passion, heat, thrill, adventure, enthusiasm, fever, warmth, flurry, animation, furore, ferment, agitation, commotion, elation, ado, tumult, perturbation, discomposure **2** PLEASURE, thrill, sensation, stimulation, tingle, kick (*informal*)

exciting *adjective* **1** STIMULATING, inspiring, dramatic, gripping, stirring, thrilling, moving, sensational, rousing, exhilarating, electrifying, intoxicating, rip-roaring (*informal*) << ANTONYM boring **2** TITILLATING, stimulating, sexy (*informal*), arousing, erotic, provocative

exclaim *verb* CRY OUT, call, declare, cry, shout, proclaim, yell, utter, call out, ejaculate, vociferate

exclamation *noun* CRY, call, shout, yell, outcry, utterance, ejaculation, expletive, interjection, vociferation

exclude *verb* **1** KEEP OUT, bar, ban, veto, refuse, forbid, boycott, embargo, prohibit, disallow, shut out, proscribe, black, refuse to admit, ostracize, debar, blackball, interdict, prevent from entering << ANTONYM let in **2** OMIT, reject, eliminate, rule out, miss out, leave out, preclude, repudiate << ANTONYM include **3** ELIMINATE, reject, ignore, rule out, except, leave out, set aside, omit, pass over, not count, repudiate, count out

exclusion *noun* **1** BAN, bar, veto, refusal, boycott, embargo, prohibition, disqualification, interdict, proscription, debarment, preclusion, forbiddance, nonadmission **2** ELIMINATION, exception, missing out, rejection, leaving out, omission, repudiation

exclusive *adjective* **1** SELECT, fashionable, stylish, private, limited, choice, narrow, closed, restricted, elegant, posh (*informal, chiefly Brit*), chic, selfish, classy (*slang*), restrictive, aristocratic, high-class, swish (*informal, chiefly Brit*), up-market, snobbish, top-drawer, ritzy (*slang*), high-toned, clannish, discriminative, cliquish << ANTONYM unrestricted **2** SOLE, only, full, whole, single, private, complete, total, entire, unique, absolute, undivided, unshared << ANTONYM shared **3** ENTIRE, full, whole, complete, total, absolute, undivided **4** LIMITED, unique, restricted, confined, peculiar ▷▷ **exclusive of** EXCEPT FOR, excepting, excluding, ruling out, not including, omitting, not counting, leaving aside, debarring

excommunicate *verb* (*RC Church*) EXPEL, ban, remove, exclude, denounce, banish, eject, repudiate, proscribe, cast out, unchurch, anathematize

excrement *noun* FAECES, dung, stool, droppings, motion, mess (*especially of a domestic animal*), defecation, excreta, ordure, kak (*S African taboo slang*), night soil

excrete *verb* DEFECATE, discharge, expel, evacuate, eliminate, void, eject, exude, egest

excruciating *adjective* AGONIZING, acute, severe, extreme, burning, violent, intense, piercing, racking, searing, tormenting, exquisite, harrowing, unbearable, insufferable, torturous, unendurable

excursion *noun* TRIP, airing, tour, journey, outing, expedition, ramble, day trip, jaunt, pleasure trip

excuse *verb* 1 JUSTIFY, explain, defend, vindicate, condone, mitigate, apologize for, make excuses for << ANTONYM blame 2 FORGIVE, pardon, overlook, tolerate, indulge, acquit, pass over, turn a blind eye to, exonerate, absolve, bear with, wink at, make allowances for, extenuate, exculpate 3 FREE, relieve, liberate, exempt, release, spare, discharge, let off, absolve << ANTONYM convict ▷ *noun* 1 JUSTIFICATION, reason, explanation, defence, grounds, plea, apology, pretext, vindication, mitigation, mitigating circumstances, extenuation << ANTONYM accusation 2 PRETEXT, evasion, pretence, cover-up, expedient, get-out, cop-out (*slang*), subterfuge 3 (*informal*) POOR SUBSTITUTE, apology, mockery, travesty

execute *verb* 1 PUT TO DEATH, kill, shoot, hang, behead, decapitate, guillotine, electrocute 2 CARRY OUT, effect, finish, complete, achieve, realize, do, implement, fulfil, enforce, accomplish, render, discharge, administer, prosecute, enact, consummate, put into effect, bring off 3 PERFORM, do, carry out, accomplish

execution *noun* 1 KILLING, hanging, the death penalty, the rope, capital punishment, beheading, the electric chair, the guillotine, the noose, the scaffold, electrocution, decapitation, the firing squad, necktie party (*informal*) 2 CARRYING OUT, performance, operation, administration, achievement, effect, prosecution, rendering, discharge, enforcement, implementation, completion, accomplishment, realization, enactment, bringing off, consummation 3 PERFORMANCE, style, delivery, manner, technique, mode, presentation, rendition

executioner *noun* HANGMAN, firing squad, headsman, public executioner, Jack Ketch

executive *noun* 1 ADMINISTRATOR, official, director, manager, chairman, managing director, controller, chief executive officer, senior manager, chairwoman, chairperson 2 ADMINISTRATION, government, directors, management, leadership, hierarchy, directorate ▷ *adjective* ADMINISTRATIVE, controlling, directing, governing, regulating, decision-making, managerial

exemplar *noun* 1 MODEL, example, standard, ideal, criterion, paradigm, epitome, paragon 2 EXAMPLE, instance, illustration, type, specimen, prototype, typical example, representative example, exemplification

exemplary *adjective* 1 IDEAL, good, fine, model, excellent, sterling, admirable, honourable, commendable, laudable, praiseworthy, meritorious, estimable, punctilious 2 TYPICAL, representative, characteristic, illustrative 3 WARNING, harsh, cautionary, admonitory, monitory

exemplify *verb* SHOW, represent, display, demonstrate, instance, illustrate, exhibit, depict, manifest, evidence, embody, serve as an example of

exempt *verb* GRANT IMMUNITY, free, except, excuse, release, spare, relieve, discharge, liberate, let off, exonerate, absolve ▷ *adjective* IMMUNE, free, excepted, excused, released, spared, clear, discharged, liberated, not subject to, absolved, not liable to << ANTONYM liable

exemption *noun* IMMUNITY, freedom, privilege, relief, exception, discharge, release, dispensation, absolution, exoneration

exercise *verb* 1 PUT TO USE, use, apply, employ, practise, exert, enjoy, wield, utilize, bring to bear, avail yourself of 2 TRAIN, work out, practise, drill, keep fit, inure, do exercises 3 WORRY, concern, occupy, try, trouble, pain, disturb, burden, distress, preoccupy, agitate, perplex, vex, perturb ▷ *noun* 1 USE, practice, application, operation, employment, discharge, implementation, enjoyment, accomplishment, fulfilment, exertion, utilization 2 EXERTION, training, activity, action, work, labour, effort, movement, discipline, toil, physical activity 3 (*military*) MANOEUVRE, campaign, operation, movement, deployment 4 TASK, problem, lesson, assignment, work, schooling, practice, schoolwork

exert *verb* APPLY, use, exercise, employ, wield, make use of, utilize, expend, bring to bear, put forth, bring into play ▷▷ **exert yourself** MAKE AN EFFORT, work, labour, struggle, strain, strive, endeavour, go for it (*informal*), try hard, toil, bend over backwards (*informal*), do your best, go for broke (*slang*), bust a gut (*informal*), spare no effort, make a great effort, give it your best shot (*informal*), break your neck (*informal*), apply yourself, put yourself out, make an all-out effort (*informal*), get your finger out (*Brit informal*), pull your finger out (*Brit informal*), knock yourself out (*informal*), do your damnedest (*informal*), give it your all (*informal*), rupture yourself (*informal*)

exertion *noun* 1 EFFORT, action, exercise, struggle, industry, labour, trial, pains, stretch, strain, endeavour, toil, travail (*literary*), elbow grease (*facetious*) 2 USE, exercise, application, employment, bringing to bear, utilization

exhale *verb* GIVE OFF, emit, steam, discharge, send out, evaporate, issue, eject, emanate

exhaust *verb* 1 TIRE OUT, tire, fatigue, drain, disable, weaken, cripple, weary, sap, wear out, debilitate, prostrate, enfeeble, make tired, enervate 2 USE UP, spend, finish, consume, waste, go through, run through, deplete, squander, dissipate, expend

exhausted *adjective* 1 WORN OUT, tired out, drained, spent, beat (*slang*), bushed (*informal*), dead (*informal*), wasted, done in (*informal*), weak, all in (*slang*), disabled, crippled, fatigued, wiped out (*informal*), sapped, debilitated, jaded, knackered (*slang*), prostrated, clapped out (*Brit, Austral & NZ informal*), effete, enfeebled, enervated, ready to drop, dog-tired (*informal*), zonked (*slang*), dead tired, dead beat (*informal*), shagged out (*Brit slang*), fagged out (*informal*), worn to a frazzle (*informal*), on your last legs (*informal*), creamcrackered (*Brit slang*), out on your feet (*informal*) << ANTONYM invigorated 2 USED UP, consumed, spent, finished, gone, depleted, dissipated, expended, at an end << ANTONYM replenished

exhausting *adjective* TIRING, hard, testing, taxing, difficult, draining, punishing, crippling, fatiguing, wearying, gruelling, sapping, debilitating, strenuous, arduous, laborious, enervating, backbreaking

exhaustion *noun* 1 TIREDNESS, fatigue, weariness, lassitude, feebleness, prostration, debilitation, enervation 2 DEPLETION, emptying, consumption, using up

exhaustive *adjective* THOROUGH, detailed, complete, full, total, sweeping, comprehensive, extensive, intensive, full-scale, in-depth, far-reaching, all-inclusive,

all-embracing, encyclopedic, thoroughgoing << ANTONYM superficial

exhibit *verb* 1 SHOW, reveal, display, demonstrate, air, evidence, express, indicate, disclose, manifest, evince, make clear *or* plain 2 DISPLAY, show, present, set out, parade, unveil, flaunt, put on view ▷ *noun* OBJECT, piece, model, article, illustration

exhibition *noun* 1 SHOW, display, exhibit, showing, fair, representation, presentation, spectacle, showcase, expo (*informal*), exposition 2 DISPLAY, show, performance, demonstration, airing, revelation, manifestation

exhilarate *verb* EXCITE, delight, cheer, thrill, stimulate, animate, exalt, lift, enliven, invigorate, gladden, elate, inspirit, pep *or* perk up

exhilarating *adjective* EXCITING, thrilling, stimulating, breathtaking, cheering, exalting, enlivening, invigorating, gladdening, vitalizing, exhilarant

exhilaration *noun* EXCITEMENT, delight, joy, happiness, animation, high spirits, elation, mirth, gaiety, hilarity, exaltation, cheerfulness, vivacity, liveliness, gladness, joyfulness, sprightliness, gleefulness << ANTONYM depression

exhort *verb* (*formal*) URGE, warn, encourage, advise, bid, persuade, prompt, spur, press, counsel, caution, call upon, incite, goad, admonish, enjoin, beseech, entreat

exhortation *noun* (*formal*) URGING, warning, advice, counsel, lecture, caution, bidding, encouragement, sermon, persuasion, goading, incitement, admonition, beseeching, entreaty, clarion call, enjoinder (*rare*)

exhume *verb* DIG UP, unearth, disinter, unbury, disentomb << ANTONYM bury

exile *noun* 1 BANISHMENT, expulsion, deportation, eviction, separation, ostracism, proscription, expatriation 2 EXPATRIATE, refugee, outcast, émigré, deportee ▷ *verb* BANISH, expel, throw out, deport, oust, drive out, eject, expatriate, proscribe, cast out, ostracize

exiled *adjective* BANISHED, deported, expatriate, outcast, refugee, ostracized, expat

exist *verb* 1 LIVE, be present, be living, last, survive, breathe, endure, be in existence, be, be extant, have breath 2 OCCUR, happen, stand, remain, obtain, be present, prevail, abide 3 SURVIVE, stay alive, make ends meet, subsist, eke out a living, scrape by, scrimp and save, support yourself, keep your head above water, get along *or* by

existence *noun* **1** REALITY, being, life, survival, duration, endurance, continuation, subsistence, actuality, continuance **2** LIFE, situation, way of life, life style **3** CREATION, life, the world, reality, the human condition, this mortal coil

existent *adjective* IN EXISTENCE, living, existing, surviving, around, standing, remaining, present, current, alive, enduring, prevailing, abiding, to the fore (*Scot*), extant

existing *adjective* IN EXISTENCE, living, present, surviving, remaining, available, alive, in operation, extant, alive and kicking << ANTONYM gone

exit *noun* **1** WAY OUT, door, gate, outlet, doorway, vent, gateway, escape route, passage out, egress << ANTONYM entry **2** DEPARTURE, withdrawal, retreat, farewell, going, retirement, goodbye, exodus, evacuation, decamping, leave-taking, adieu ▷ *verb* DEPART, leave, go out, withdraw, retire, quit, retreat, go away, say goodbye, bid farewell, make tracks, take your leave, go offstage (*theatre*) << ANTONYM enter

exodus *noun* DEPARTURE, withdrawal, retreat, leaving, flight, retirement, exit, migration, evacuation

exonerate *verb* ACQUIT, clear, excuse, pardon, justify, discharge, vindicate, absolve, exculpate

exorbitant *adjective* EXCESSIVE, high, expensive, extreme, ridiculous, outrageous, extravagant, unreasonable, undue, preposterous, unwarranted, inordinate, extortionate, unconscionable, immoderate << ANTONYM reasonable

exorcise *or* **exorcize** *verb* **1** DRIVE OUT, expel, cast out, adjure **2** PURIFY, free, cleanse

exorcism *noun* **1** DRIVING OUT, expulsion, deliverance, casting out, adjuration **2** PURIFICATION, freeing, cleansing

exotic *adjective* **1** UNUSUAL, different, striking, strange, extraordinary, bizarre, fascinating, curious, mysterious, colourful, glamorous, peculiar, unfamiliar, outlandish << ANTONYM ordinary **2** FOREIGN, alien, tropical, external, extraneous, naturalized, extrinsic, not native

expand *verb* **1** GET BIGGER, increase, grow, extend, swell, widen, blow up, wax, heighten, enlarge, multiply, inflate, thicken, fill out, lengthen, fatten, dilate, become bigger, puff up, become larger, distend << ANTONYM

contract **2** MAKE BIGGER, increase, develop, extend, widen, blow up, heighten, enlarge, multiply, broaden, inflate, thicken, fill out, lengthen, magnify, amplify, augment, dilate, make larger, distend, bloat, protract << ANTONYM reduce **3** SPREAD (OUT), open (out), stretch (out), unfold, unravel, diffuse, unfurl, unroll, outspread ▷▷ **expand on something** GO INTO DETAIL ABOUT, embellish, elaborate on, develop, flesh out, expound on, enlarge on, expatiate on, add detail to

expanse *noun* AREA, range, field, space, stretch, sweep, extent, plain, tract, breadth

expansion *noun* **1** INCREASE, development, growth, spread, diffusion, magnification, multiplication, amplification, augmentation **2** ENLARGEMENT, inflation, increase, growth, swelling, unfolding, expanse, unfurling, opening out, distension

expansive *adjective* **1** WIDE, broad, extensive, spacious, sweeping **2** COMPREHENSIVE, extensive, broad, wide, widespread, wide-ranging, thorough, inclusive, far-reaching, voluminous, all-embracing **3** TALKATIVE, open, friendly, outgoing, free, easy, warm, sociable, genial, affable, communicative, effusive, garrulous, loquacious, unreserved

expatriate *adjective* EXILED, refugee, banished, emigrant, émigré, expat ▷ *noun* EXILE, refugee, emigrant, émigré

expect *verb* **1** THINK, believe, suppose, assume, trust, imagine, reckon, forecast, calculate, presume, foresee, conjecture, surmise, think likely **2** ANTICIPATE, look forward to, predict, envisage, await, hope for, contemplate, bargain for, look ahead to **3** REQUIRE, demand, want, wish, look for, call for, ask for, hope for, insist on, count on, rely upon

expectancy *noun* **1** LIKELIHOOD, prospect, tendency, outlook, probability **2** EXPECTATION, hope, anticipation, waiting, belief, looking forward, assumption, prediction, probability, suspense, presumption, conjecture, surmise, supposition

expectant *adjective* **1** EXPECTING, excited, anticipating, anxious, ready, awaiting, eager, hopeful, apprehensive, watchful, in suspense **2** PREGNANT, expecting (*informal*), gravid, enceinte

expectation *noun* **1** *usually plural* PROJECTION, supposition, assumption, calculation, belief, forecast, assurance, likelihood, probability, presumption, conjecture, surmise, presupposition **2** ANTICIPATION, hope, possibility, prospect, chance, fear, promise, looking forward, excitement, prediction, outlook, expectancy, apprehension, suspense **3** *usually plural* REQUIREMENT, demand, want, wish, insistence, reliance

expected *adjective* ANTICIPATED, wanted, promised, looked-for, predicted, forecast, awaited, hoped-for, counted on, long-awaited

expecting *adjective (informal)* PREGNANT, with child, expectant, in the club (*Brit slang*), in the family way (*informal*), gravid, enceinte

expediency *or* **expedience** *noun* SUITABILITY, benefit, fitness, utility, effectiveness, convenience, profitability, practicality, usefulness, prudence, pragmatism, propriety, desirability, appropriateness, utilitarianism, helpfulness, advisability, aptness, judiciousness, properness, meetness, advantageousness

expedient *adjective* ADVANTAGEOUS, effective, useful, profitable, fit, politic, appropriate, practical, suitable, helpful, proper, convenient, desirable, worthwhile, beneficial, pragmatic, prudent, advisable, utilitarian, judicious, opportune << ANTONYM unwise ▷ *noun* MEANS, measure, scheme, method, resource, resort, device, manoeuvre, expediency, stratagem, contrivance, stopgap

expedite *verb* SPEED (UP), forward, promote, advance, press, urge, rush, assist, hurry, accelerate, dispatch, facilitate, hasten, precipitate, quicken << ANTONYM hold up

expedition *noun* **1** JOURNEY, exploration, mission, voyage, tour, enterprise, undertaking, quest, trek **2** TEAM, crew, party, group, company, travellers, explorers, voyagers, wayfarers **3** TRIP, tour, outing, excursion, jaunt

expel *verb* **1** THROW OUT, exclude, ban, bar, dismiss, discharge, relegate, kick out (*informal*), ask to leave, send packing, turf out (*informal*), black, debar, drum out, blackball, give the bum's rush (*slang*), show you the door, throw out on your ear (*informal*) << ANTONYM let in **2** BANISH, exile, oust, deport, expatriate, evict, force to leave, proscribe << ANTONYM take in **3** DRIVE OUT, discharge, throw out, force out, let out, eject, issue, dislodge, spew, belch, cast out

expend *verb* **1** USE (UP), employ, go through (*informal*), exhaust, consume, dissipate

2 SPEND, pay out, lay out (*informal*), fork out (*slang*), shell out, disburse

expendable *adjective* DISPENSABLE, unnecessary, unimportant, replaceable, nonessential, inessential << ANTONYM indispensable

expenditure *noun* **1** SPENDING, payment, expense, outgoings, cost, charge, outlay, disbursement **2** CONSUMPTION, use, using, application, output

expense *noun* COST, charge, expenditure, payment, spending, output, toll, consumption, outlay, disbursement ▷▷ **at the expense of** WITH THE SACRIFICE OF, with the loss of, at the cost of, at the price of

expensive *adjective* COSTLY, high-priced, lavish, extravagant, rich, dear, stiff, excessive, steep (*informal*), pricey, overpriced, exorbitant << ANTONYM cheap

experience *noun* **1** KNOWLEDGE, understanding, practice, skill, evidence, trial, contact, expertise, know-how (*informal*), proof, involvement, exposure, observation, participation, familiarity, practical knowledge **2** EVENT, affair, incident, happening, test, trial, encounter, episode, adventure, ordeal, occurrence ▷ *verb* UNDERGO, have, know, feel, try, meet, face, suffer, taste, go through, observe, sample, encounter, sustain, perceive, endure, participate in, run into, live through, behold, come up against, apprehend, become familiar with

experienced *adjective* **1** KNOWLEDGEABLE, trained, professional, skilled, tried, tested, seasoned, expert, master, qualified, familiar, capable, veteran, practised, accomplished, competent, skilful, adept, well-versed << ANTONYM inexperienced **2** WORLDLY-WISE, knowing, worldly, wise, mature, sophisticated

experiment *noun* **1** TEST, trial, investigation, examination, venture, procedure, demonstration, observation, try-out, assay, trial run, scientific test, dummy run **2** RESEARCH, investigation, analysis, observation, research and development, experimentation, trial and error ▷ *verb* TEST, investigate, trial, research, try, examine, pilot, sample, verify, put to the test, assay

experimental *adjective* **1** TEST, trial, pilot, preliminary, provisional, tentative, speculative, empirical, exploratory, trial-and-error, fact-finding, probationary **2** INNOVATIVE, new, original, radical, creative, ingenious, avant-garde, inventive, ground-breaking

expert *noun* SPECIALIST, authority, professional, master, pro (*informal*), ace (*informal*), genius, guru, pundit, buff (*informal*), wizard, adept, whizz (*informal*), maestro, virtuoso, connoisseur, hotshot (*informal*), past master, dab hand (*Brit informal*), wonk (*informal*), maven (*US*), fundi (*S African*) << ANTONYM amateur ▷ *adjective* SKILFUL, trained, experienced, able, professional, skilled, master, masterly, qualified, talented, outstanding, clever, practised, accomplished, handy, competent, apt, adept, knowledgeable, virtuoso, deft, proficient, facile, adroit, dexterous << ANTONYM unskilled

expertise *noun* SKILL, knowledge, know-how (*informal*), facility, grip, craft, judgment, grasp, mastery, knack, proficiency, dexterity, cleverness, deftness, adroitness, aptness, expertness, knowing inside out, ableness, masterliness, skilfulness

expiration *noun* EXPIRY, end, finish, conclusion, close, termination, cessation

expire *verb* 1 BECOME INVALID, end, finish, conclude, close, stop, run out, cease, lapse, terminate, come to an end, be no longer valid 2 DIE, decease, depart, buy it (*US slang*), check out (*US slang*), perish, kick it (*slang*), croak (*slang*), go belly-up (*slang*), snuff it (*informal*), peg out (*informal*), kick the bucket (*informal*), peg it (*informal*), depart this life, meet your maker, cark it (*Austral & NZ slang*), pop your clogs (*informal*), pass away *or* on

expiry *noun* EXPIRATION, ending, end, conclusion, close, demise, lapsing, lapse, termination, cessation

explain *verb* 1 MAKE CLEAR *or* PLAIN, describe, demonstrate, illustrate, teach, define, solve, resolve, interpret, disclose, unfold, clarify, clear up, simplify, expound, elucidate, put into words, throw light on, explicate (*formal*), give the details of 2 ACCOUNT FOR, excuse, justify, give a reason for, give an explanation for

explanation *noun* 1 REASON, meaning, cause, sense, answer, account, excuse, motive, justification, vindication, mitigation, the why and wherefore 2 DESCRIPTION, report, definition, demonstration, teaching, resolution, interpretation, illustration, clarification, exposition, simplification, explication, elucidation

explanatory *or* **explanative** *adjective*

DESCRIPTIVE, interpretive, illustrative, interpretative, demonstrative, justifying, expository, illuminative, elucidatory, explicative

explicit *adjective* 1 CLEAR, obvious, specific, direct, certain, express, plain, absolute, exact, precise, straightforward, definite, overt, unequivocal, unqualified, unambiguous, categorical << ANTONYM vague 2 FRANK, direct, open, specific, positive, plain, patent, graphic, distinct, outspoken, upfront (*informal*), unambiguous, unrestricted, unrestrained, uncensored, unreserved << ANTONYM indirect

explode *verb* 1 BLOW UP, erupt, burst, go off, shatter, shiver 2 DETONATE, set off, discharge, let off 3 LOSE YOUR TEMPER, rage, erupt, blow up (*informal*), lose it (*informal*), crack up (*informal*), see red (*informal*), lose the plot (*informal*), become angry, have a fit (*informal*), go ballistic (*slang, chiefly US*), hit the roof (*informal*), throw a tantrum, blow a fuse (*slang, chiefly US*), go berserk (*slang*), go mad (*slang*), fly off the handle (*informal*), go spare (*Brit slang*), become enraged, go off the deep end (*informal*), go up the wall (*slang*), blow your top (*informal*), go crook (*Austral & NZ slang*), fly into a temper, flip your lid (*slang*), do your nut (*Brit slang*) 4 INCREASE, grow, develop, extend, advance, shoot up, soar, boost, expand, build up, swell, step up (*informal*), escalate, multiply, proliferate, snowball, aggrandize 5 DISPROVE, discredit, refute, belie, demolish, repudiate, put paid to, invalidate, debunk, prove impossible, prove wrong, give the lie to, blow out of the water (*slang*)

exploit *noun* FEAT, act, achievement, enterprise, adventure, stunt, deed, accomplishment, attainment, escapade ▷ *verb* 1 TAKE ADVANTAGE OF, abuse, use, manipulate, milk, misuse, dump on (*slang, chiefly US*), ill-treat, play on *or* upon 2 MAKE THE BEST USE OF, use, make use of, utilize, cash in on (*informal*), capitalize on, put to use, make capital out of, use to advantage, use to good advantage, live off the backs of, turn to account, profit by *or* from

exploitation *noun* 1 MISUSE, abuse, manipulation, imposition, using, ill-treatment 2 CAPITALIZATION, utilization, using to good advantage, trading upon

exploration *noun* 1 EXPEDITION, tour, trip, survey, travel, journey, reconnaissance, recce (*slang*) 2 INVESTIGATION, study, research, survey, search, inquiry, analysis, examination, probe, inspection, scrutiny, once-over (*informal*)

exploratory *adjective* INVESTIGATIVE, trial, searching, probing, experimental, analytic, fact-finding

explore *verb* 1 TRAVEL AROUND, tour, survey, scout, traverse, range over, recce (*slang*), reconnoitre, case (*slang*), have *or* take a look around 2 INVESTIGATE, consider, research, survey, search, prospect, examine, probe, analyse, look into, inspect, work over, scrutinize, inquire into

explosion *noun* 1 BLAST, crack, burst, bang, discharge, report, blowing up, outburst, clap, detonation 2 INCREASE, rise, development, growth, boost, expansion, enlargement, escalation, upturn 3 OUTBURST, fit, storm, attack, surge, flare-up, eruption, paroxysm 4 OUTBREAK, flare-up, eruption, upsurge

explosive *adjective* 1 UNSTABLE, dangerous, volatile, hazardous, unsafe, perilous, combustible, inflammable 2 DANGEROUS, worrying, strained, anxious, charged, ugly, tense, hazardous, stressful, perilous, nerve-racking, overwrought 3 FIERY, violent, volatile, stormy, touchy, vehement, chippy (*informal*) ▷ *noun* BOMB, mine, shell, missile, rocket, grenade, charge, torpedo, incendiary

exponent *noun* 1 ADVOCATE, champion, supporter, defender, spokesman, spokeswoman, promoter, backer, spokesperson, proponent, propagandist, upholder 2 PERFORMER, player, interpreter, presenter, executant

expose *verb* 1 UNCOVER, show, reveal, display, exhibit, present, unveil, manifest, lay bare, take the wraps off, put on view << ANTONYM hide 2 REVEAL, disclose, uncover, air, detect, betray, show up, denounce, unearth, let out, divulge, unmask, lay bare, make known, bring to light, out (*informal*), smoke out, blow wide open (*slang*) << ANTONYM keep secret 3 MAKE VULNERABLE, subject, leave open, lay open ▷▷ **expose someone to something** INTRODUCE TO, acquaint with, bring into contact with, familiarize with, make familiar with, make conversant with

exposé *noun* EXPOSURE, revelation, uncovering, disclosure, divulgence

exposed *adjective* 1 UNCONCEALED, revealed, bare, exhibited, unveiled, shown, uncovered, on display, on show, on view, laid bare, made manifest 2 UNSHELTERED, open, unprotected, open to the elements

3 VULNERABLE, open, subject, in danger, liable, susceptible, wide open, left open, laid bare, in peril, laid open

exposition *noun* 1 EXPLANATION, account, description, interpretation, illustration, presentation, commentary, critique, exegesis, explication, elucidation 2 EXHIBITION, show, fair, display, demonstration, presentation, expo (*informal*)

exposure *noun* 1 VULNERABILITY, subjection, susceptibility, laying open 2 HYPOTHERMIA, frostbite, extreme cold, intense cold 3 REVELATION, exposé, uncovering, disclosure, airing, manifestation, detection, divulging, denunciation, unmasking, divulgence 4 PUBLICITY, promotion, attention, advertising, plugging (*informal*), propaganda, hype, pushing, media hype 5 UNCOVERING, showing, display, exhibition, baring, revelation, presentation, unveiling, manifestation 6 CONTACT, experience, awareness, acquaintance, familiarity

expound *verb* EXPLAIN, describe, illustrate, interpret, unfold, spell out, set forth, elucidate, explicate (*formal*)

express *verb* 1 STATE, communicate, convey, articulate, say, tell, put, word, speak, voice, declare, phrase, assert, pronounce, utter, couch, put across, enunciate, put into words, give voice to, verbalize, asseverate 2 SHOW, indicate, exhibit, demonstrate, reveal, disclose, intimate, convey, testify to, depict, designate, manifest, embody, signify, symbolize, denote, divulge, bespeak, make known, evince ▷ *adjective* 1 EXPLICIT, clear, direct, precise, pointed, certain, plain, accurate, exact, distinct, definite, outright, unambiguous, categorical 2 SPECIFIC, exclusive, particular, sole, special, deliberate, singular, clear-cut, especial 3 FAST, direct, quick, rapid, priority, prompt, swift, high-speed, speedy, quickie (*informal*), nonstop, expeditious

expression *noun* 1 STATEMENT, declaration, announcement, communication, mention, assertion, utterance, articulation, pronouncement, enunciation, verbalization, asseveration 2 INDICATION, demonstration, exhibition, display, showing, show, sign, symbol, representation, token, manifestation, embodiment 3 LOOK, countenance, face, air, appearance, aspect, mien (*literary*) 4 INTONATION, style, delivery, phrasing, emphasis, execution, diction 5 PHRASE, saying, word, wording, term, language, speech, remark, maxim, idiom, adage, choice of words, turn of phrase, phraseology, locution, set phrase

expressionless *adjective* BLANK, empty, deadpan, straight-faced, wooden, dull, vacuous, inscrutable, poker-faced (*informal*)

expressive *adjective* **1** VIVID, strong, striking, telling, moving, lively, sympathetic, energetic, poignant, emphatic, eloquent, forcible << ANTONYM impassive **2** *with of* MEANINGFUL, indicative, suggestive, demonstrative, revealing, significant, allusive

expressly *adverb* **1** EXPLICITLY, clearly, plainly, absolutely, positively, definitely, outright, manifestly, distinctly, decidedly, categorically, pointedly, unequivocally, unmistakably, in no uncertain terms, unambiguously **2** SPECIFICALLY, specially, especially, particularly, purposely, exclusively, precisely, solely, exactly, deliberately, intentionally, on purpose

expropriate *verb* (*formal*) SEIZE, take, appropriate, confiscate, assume, take over, take away, commandeer, requisition, arrogate

expropriation *noun* (*formal*) SEIZURE, takeover, impounding, confiscation, commandeering, requisitioning, sequestration, disseisin (*law*)

expulsion *noun* **1** EJECTION, exclusion, dismissal, removal, exile, discharge, eviction, banishment, extrusion, proscription, expatriation, debarment, dislodgment **2** DISCHARGE, emptying, emission, voiding, spewing, secretion, excretion, ejection, seepage, suppuration

expunge *verb* (*formal*) ERASE, remove, destroy, abolish, cancel, get rid of, wipe out, eradicate, excise, delete, extinguish, strike out, obliterate, annihilate, efface, exterminate, annul, raze, blot out, extirpate

exquisite *adjective* **1** BEAUTIFUL, elegant, graceful, pleasing, attractive, lovely, charming, comely << ANTONYM unattractive **2** FINE, beautiful, lovely, elegant, precious, delicate, dainty **3** INTENSE, acute, severe, sharp, keen, extreme, piercing, poignant, excruciating **4** REFINED, cultivated, discriminating, sensitive, polished, selective, discerning, impeccable, meticulous, consummate, appreciative, fastidious **5** EXCELLENT, fine, outstanding, superb, choice, perfect, select, delicious, divine, splendid, admirable, consummate, flawless, superlative, incomparable, peerless,

matchless << ANTONYM imperfect

extant *adjective* IN EXISTENCE, existing, remaining, surviving, living, existent, subsisting, undestroyed

extend *verb* **1** SPREAD OUT, reach, stretch, continue, carry on **2** STRETCH, stretch out, spread out, unfurl, straighten out, unroll **3** LAST, continue, go on, stretch, carry on **4** PROTRUDE, project, stand out, bulge, stick out, hang, overhang, jut out **5** REACH, spread, go as far as **6** WIDEN, increase, develop, expand, spread, add to, enhance, supplement, enlarge, broaden, diversify, amplify, augment << ANTONYM reduce **7** MAKE LONGER, prolong, lengthen, draw out, spin out, elongate, drag out, protract << ANTONYM shorten **8** OFFER, give, hold out, present, grant, advance, yield, reach out, confer, stretch out, stick out, bestow, impart, proffer, put forth << ANTONYM withdraw

extended *adjective* **1** LENGTHENED, long, prolonged, protracted, stretched out, drawn-out, unfurled, elongated, unrolled **2** BROAD, wide, expanded, extensive, widespread, comprehensive, large-scale, enlarged, far-reaching **3** OUTSTRETCHED, conferred, stretched out, proffered

extension *noun* **1** ANNEXE, wing, addition, supplement, branch, appendix, add-on, adjunct, appendage, ell, addendum **2** LENGTHENING, extra time, continuation, postponement, prolongation, additional period of time, protraction **3** DEVELOPMENT, expansion, widening, increase, stretching, broadening, continuation, enlargement, diversification, amplification, elongation, augmentation

extensive *adjective* **1** LARGE, considerable, substantial, spacious, wide, sweeping, broad, expansive, capacious, commodious << ANTONYM confined **2** COMPREHENSIVE, complete, thorough, lengthy, long, wide, wholesale, pervasive, protracted, all-inclusive << ANTONYM restricted **3** GREAT, large, huge, extended, vast, widespread, comprehensive, universal, large-scale, far-reaching, prevalent, far-flung, all-inclusive, voluminous, humongous *or* humungous (*US slang*) << ANTONYM limited

extent *noun* **1** MAGNITUDE, amount, degree, scale, level, measure, stretch, quantity, bulk, duration, expanse, amplitude **2** SIZE, area, range, length, reach, bounds, sweep, sphere, width, compass, breadth, ambit

exterior *noun* OUTSIDE, face, surface, covering,

finish, skin, appearance, aspect, shell,
coating, façade, outside surface ▷ *adjective*
OUTER, outside, external, surface, outward,
superficial, outermost << ANTONYM inner

exterminate *verb* DESTROY, kill, eliminate,
abolish, eradicate, annihilate, extirpate

extermination *noun* DESTRUCTION, murder,
massacre, slaughter, killing, wiping out,
genocide, elimination, mass murder,
annihilation, eradication, extirpation

external *adjective* 1 OUTER, outside, surface,
apparent, visible, outward, exterior,
superficial, outermost << ANTONYM
internal 2 FOREIGN, international, alien,
exotic, exterior, extraneous, extrinsic
<< ANTONYM domestic 3 OUTSIDE, visiting,
independent, extramural << ANTONYM
inside

extinct *adjective* 1 DEAD, lost, gone, vanished,
defunct << ANTONYM living 2 INACTIVE,
extinguished, doused, out, snuffed out,
quenched

extinction *noun* DYING OUT, death,
destruction, abolition, oblivion,
extermination, annihilation, eradication,
obliteration, excision, extirpation

extinguish *verb* 1 PUT OUT, stifle, smother,
blow out, douse, snuff out, quench
2 DESTROY, end, kill, remove, eliminate,
obscure, abolish, suppress, wipe out,
erase, eradicate, annihilate, put paid to,
exterminate, expunge, extirpate

extol *verb* PRAISE, acclaim, applaud, pay
tribute to, celebrate, commend, magnify
(*archaic*), glorify, exalt, laud, crack up
(*informal*), sing the praises of, eulogize, cry
up, panegyrize

extort *verb* EXTRACT, force, squeeze, exact,
bully, bleed (*informal*), blackmail, wring,
coerce, wrest

extortion *noun* BLACKMAIL, force, oppression,
compulsion, coercion, shakedown (*US slang*),
rapacity, exaction

extortionate *adjective* EXORBITANT, excessive,
outrageous, unreasonable, inflated,
extravagant, preposterous, sky-high,
inordinate, immoderate << ANTONYM
reasonable

extra *adjective* 1 ADDITIONAL, more, new,
other, added, further, fresh, accessory,
supplementary, auxiliary, add-on,
supplemental, ancillary << ANTONYM
vital 2 SURPLUS, excess, reserve, spare,
unnecessary, redundant, needless,
unused, leftover, superfluous, extraneous,

unneeded, inessential, supernumerary,
supererogatory ▷ *noun* ADDITION, bonus,
supplement, accessory, complement,
add-on, affix, adjunct, appendage,
addendum, supernumerary, appurtenance
<< ANTONYM necessity ▷ *adverb* 1 IN
ADDITION, additionally, over and above
2 EXCEPTIONALLY, very, specially, especially,
particularly, extremely, remarkably,
unusually, extraordinarily, uncommonly

extract *verb* 1 OBTAIN, take out, distil,
squeeze out, draw out, express, separate out,
press out 2 TAKE OUT, draw, pull, remove,
withdraw, pull out, bring out 3 PULL OUT,
remove, take out, draw, uproot, pluck out,
extirpate 4 ELICIT, get, obtain, force, draw,
gather, derive, exact, bring out, evoke, reap,
wring, glean, coerce, wrest 5 SELECT, quote,
cite, abstract, choose, cut out, reproduce,
cull, copy out ▷ *noun* 1 PASSAGE, selection,
excerpt, cutting, clipping, abstract,
quotation, citation 2 ESSENCE, solution,
concentrate, juice, distillation, decoction,
distillate

extraction *noun* 1 ORIGIN, family, ancestry,
descent, race, stock, blood, birth, pedigree,
lineage, parentage, derivation 2 TAKING
OUT, drawing, pulling, withdrawal, removal,
uprooting, extirpation 3 DISTILLATION,
separation, derivation

extraneous *adjective* 1 NONESSENTIAL,
unnecessary, extra, additional, redundant,
needless, peripheral, supplementary,
incidental, superfluous, unneeded,
inessential, adventitious, unessential
2 IRRELEVANT, inappropriate, unrelated,
unconnected, immaterial, beside the point,
impertinent, inadmissible, off the subject,
inapplicable, inapt, inapposite

extraordinary *adjective* 1 REMARKABLE,
special, wonderful, outstanding, rare,
amazing, fantastic, astonishing, marvellous,
exceptional, notable, serious (*informal*),
phenomenal, singular, wondrous (*archaic*
or *literary*), out of this world (*informal*),
extremely good << ANTONYM unremarkable
2 UNUSUAL, surprising, odd, strange,
unique, remarkable, bizarre, curious,
weird, unprecedented, peculiar, unfamiliar,
uncommon, unheard-of, unwonted
<< ANTONYM ordinary

extravagance *noun* 1 OVERSPENDING,
squandering, profusion, profligacy,
wastefulness, waste, lavishness, prodigality,
improvidence 2 LUXURY, treat, indulgence,

extra, frill, nonessential 3 EXCESS, folly, exaggeration, absurdity, recklessness, wildness, dissipation, outrageousness, unreasonableness, preposterousness, immoderation, exorbitance, unrestraint

extravagant *adjective* 1 WASTEFUL, excessive, lavish, prodigal, profligate, spendthrift, imprudent, improvident << ANTONYM economical 2 OVERPRICED, expensive, costly 3 EXORBITANT, excessive, steep (*informal*), unreasonable, inordinate, extortionate << ANTONYM reasonable 4 EXCESSIVE, exaggerated, outrageous, wild, fantastic, absurd, foolish, over the top (*slang*), unreasonable, preposterous, fanciful, unrestrained, inordinate, outré, immoderate, O.T.T. (*slang*) << ANTONYM moderate 5 SHOWY, elaborate, flamboyant, impressive, fancy, flashy, ornate, pretentious, grandiose, gaudy, garish, ostentatious << ANTONYM restrained

extravaganza *noun* SPECTACULAR, show, spectacle, display, pageant, flight of fancy

extreme *adjective* 1 GREAT, high, highest, greatest, worst, supreme, acute, severe, maximum, intense, ultimate, utmost, mother of all (*informal*), uttermost << ANTONYM mild 2 SEVERE, radical, strict, harsh, stern, rigid, dire, drastic, uncompromising, unbending 3 RADICAL, unusual, excessive, exceptional, exaggerated, outrageous, over the top (*slang*), unreasonable, uncommon, unconventional, fanatical, zealous, out-and-out, inordinate, egregious, intemperate, immoderate, O.T.T. (*slang*) << ANTONYM moderate 4 FARTHEST, furthest, far, final, last, ultimate, remotest, terminal, utmost, far-off, faraway, outermost, most distant, uttermost << ANTONYM nearest ▷ *noun* LIMIT, end, edge, opposite, pole, ultimate, boundary, antithesis, extremity, acme

extremely *adverb* VERY, highly, greatly, particularly, severely, terribly, ultra, utterly, unusually, exceptionally, extraordinarily, intensely, tremendously, markedly, awfully (*informal*), acutely, exceedingly, excessively, inordinately, uncommonly, to a fault, to the nth degree, to or in the extreme

extremist *noun* RADICAL, activist, militant, enthusiast, fanatic, devotee, die-hard, bigot, zealot, energumen ▷ *adjective* EXTREME, wild, mad, enthusiastic, passionate, frenzied, obsessive, fanatical, fervent, zealous, bigoted, rabid, immoderate, overenthusiastic

extremity *noun* 1 LIMIT, end, edge, border, top, tip, bound, minimum, extreme, maximum, pole, margin, boundary, terminal, frontier, verge, brink, rim, brim, pinnacle, termination, nadir, zenith, apex, terminus, apogee, farthest point, furthest point, acme 2 DEPTH, height, excess, climax, consummation, acuteness 3 CRISIS, trouble, emergency, disaster, setback, pinch, plight, hardship, adversity, dire straits, exigency, extreme suffering ▷ *plural noun* HANDS AND FEET, limbs, fingers and toes

extricate *verb* 1 WITHDRAW, relieve, free, clear, deliver, liberate, wriggle out of, get (someone) off the hook (*slang*), disembarrass 2 FREE, clear, release, remove, rescue, get out, disengage, disentangle ▷ see **extract**

extrovert or **extravert** (*psychology*) *noun* OUTGOING PERSON, mingler, socializer, mixer, life and soul of the party << ANTONYM introvert ▷ *adjective* SOCIABLE, social, lively, outgoing, hearty, exuberant, amiable, gregarious << ANTONYM introverted

exuberance *noun* 1 HIGH SPIRITS, energy, enthusiasm, vitality, life, spirit, excitement, pep, animation, vigour, zest, eagerness, buoyancy, exhilaration, cheerfulness, brio, vivacity, ebullience, liveliness, effervescence, sprightliness 2 LUXURIANCE, abundance, richness, profusion, plenitude, lushness, superabundance, lavishness, rankness, copiousness

exuberant *adjective* 1 HIGH-SPIRITED, spirited, enthusiastic, lively, excited, eager, sparkling, vigorous, cheerful, energetic, animated, upbeat (*informal*), buoyant, exhilarated, elated, ebullient, chirpy (*informal*), sprightly, vivacious, effervescent, full of life, full of beans (*informal*), zestful << ANTONYM subdued 2 LUXURIANT, rich, lavish, abundant, lush, overflowing, plentiful, teeming, copious, profuse, superabundant, plenteous 3 FULSOME, excessive, exaggerated, lavish, overdone, superfluous, prodigal, effusive

exude *verb* 1 RADIATE, show, display, exhibit, manifest, emanate 2 EMIT, leak, discharge, ooze, emanate, issue, secrete, excrete 3 SEEP, leak, sweat, bleed, weep, trickle, ooze, emanate, issue, filter through, well forth

exult *verb* 1 BE JOYFUL, be delighted, rejoice, be overjoyed, celebrate, be elated, be jubilant, jump for joy, make merry, be in high spirits, jubilate 2 *often with* **over** REVEL, glory in, boast, crow, taunt, brag, vaunt, drool, gloat, take delight in

exultant *adjective* JOYFUL, delighted, flushed, triumphant, revelling, rejoicing, jubilant, joyous, transported, elated, over the moon (*informal*), overjoyed, rapt, gleeful, exulting, cock-a-hoop, stoked (*Austral & NZ informal*)

eye *noun* **1** EYEBALL, optic (*informal*), peeper (*slang*), orb (*poetic*), organ of vision, organ of sight **2** *often plural* EYESIGHT, sight, vision, observation, perception, ability to see, range of vision, power of seeing **3** APPRECIATION, taste, recognition, judgment, discrimination, perception, discernment **4** OBSERVANCE, observation, supervision, surveillance, attention, notice, inspection, heed, vigil, watch, lookout, vigilance, alertness, watchfulness **5** CENTRE, heart, middle, mid, core, nucleus ▷ *verb* LOOK AT, view, study, watch, check, regard, survey, clock (*Brit slang*), observe, stare at, scan, contemplate, check out (*informal*), inspect, glance at, gaze at, behold (*archaic or literary*), eyeball (*slang*), scrutinize, peruse, get a load of (*informal*), take a dekko at (*Brit slang*), have *or* take a look at ▷▷ **an eye for an eye** RETALIATION, justice, revenge, vengeance, reprisal, retribution, requital, lex talionis ▷▷ **turn a blind eye to** *or* **close your eyes to** IGNORE, reject, overlook, disregard, pass over, take no notice of, be oblivious to, pay no attention to, turn your back on, turn a deaf ear to, bury your head in the sand ▷▷ **eye something** *or* **someone up** OGLE, leer at, make eyes at, give (someone) the (glad) eye ▷▷ **see eye to eye (with)** AGREE (WITH), accord (with), get on (with), fall in (with), coincide (with), go along (with), subscribe (to), be united (with), concur (with), harmonize (with), speak the same language (as), be on the same wavelength (as), be of the same mind (as), be in unison (with) ▷▷ **set, clap** *or* **lay eyes on someone** SEE, meet, notice, observe, encounter, come across, run into, behold ▷▷ **up to your eyes (in)** VERY BUSY (WITH), overwhelmed (with), caught up (in), inundated (by), wrapped up (in), engaged (in), flooded out (by), fully occupied (with), up to here (with), up to your elbows (in)

eye-catching *adjective* STRIKING, arresting, attractive, dramatic, spectacular, captivating, showy

eyesight *noun* VISION, sight, observation, perception, ability to see, range of vision, power of seeing, power of sight

eyesore *noun* MESS, blight, blot, blemish, sight (*informal*), horror, disgrace, atrocity, ugliness, monstrosity, disfigurement

eyewitness *noun* OBSERVER, witness, spectator, looker-on, viewer, passer-by, watcher, onlooker, bystander

Ff

fable *noun* **1** LEGEND, myth, parable, allegory, story, tale, apologue **2** FICTION, lie, fantasy, myth, romance, invention, yarn (*informal*), fabrication, falsehood, fib, figment, untruth, fairy story (*informal*), urban myth, white lie, tall story (*informal*), urban legend << ANTONYM fact

fabled *adjective* LEGENDARY, fictional, famed, mythical, storied, famous, fabulous

fabric *noun* **1** CLOTH, material, stuff, textile, web **2** FRAMEWORK, structure, make-up, organization, frame, foundations, construction, constitution, infrastructure **3** STRUCTURE, foundations, construction, framework, infrastructure

fabricate *verb* **1** MAKE UP, invent, concoct, falsify, form, coin, devise, forge, fake, feign, trump up **2** MANUFACTURE, make, build, form, fashion, shape, frame, construct, assemble, erect

fabrication *noun* **1** FORGERY, lie, fiction, myth, fake, invention, fable, concoction, falsehood, figment, untruth, porky (*Brit slang*), fairy story (*informal*), pork pie (*Brit slang*), cock-and-bull story (*informal*) **2** MANUFACTURE, production, construction, assembly, erection, assemblage, building

fabulous *adjective* **1** (*informal*) WONDERFUL, excellent, brilliant, superb, spectacular, fantastic (*informal*), marvellous, sensational (*informal*), first-rate, brill (*informal*), magic (*informal*), out-of-this-world (*informal*) << ANTONYM ordinary **2** ASTOUNDING, amazing, extraordinary, remarkable, incredible, astonishing, legendary, immense, unbelievable, breathtaking, phenomenal, inconceivable **3** LEGENDARY, imaginary, mythical, fictitious, made-up, fantastic, invented, unreal, mythological, apocryphal

façade *noun* **1** FRONT, face, exterior, frontage

2 SHOW, front, appearance, mask, exterior, guise, pretence, veneer, semblance

face *noun* **1** COUNTENANCE, features, kisser (*slang*), profile, dial (*Brit slang*), mug (*slang*), visage, physiognomy, lineaments, phiz *or* phizog (*slang*) **2** EXPRESSION, look, air, appearance, aspect, countenance **3** SIDE, front, cover, outside, surface, aspect, exterior, right side, elevation, facet, vertical surface **4** (*informal*) IMPUDENCE, front, confidence, audacity, nerve, neck (*informal*), sauce (*informal*), cheek (*informal*), assurance, gall (*informal*), presumption, boldness, chutzpah (*US & Canad informal*), sass (*US & Canad informal*), effrontery, brass neck (*Brit informal*), sassiness (*US informal*) ▷ *verb* **1** *often with* **to**, **towards**, *or* **on** LOOK ONTO, overlook, be opposite, look out on, front onto, give towards *or* onto **2** CONFRONT, meet, encounter, deal with, oppose, tackle, cope with, experience, brave, defy, come up against, be confronted by, face off (*slang*) ▷▷ **face up to** ACCEPT, deal with, tackle, acknowledge, cope with, confront, come to terms with, meet head-on, reconcile yourself to ▷▷ **make** *or* **pull a face at someone** SCOWL, frown, pout, grimace, smirk, moue (*French*) ▷▷ **on the face of it** TO ALL APPEARANCES, apparently, seemingly, outwardly, at first sight, at face value, to the eye ▷▷ **show your face** TURN UP, come, appear, be seen, show up (*informal*), put in *or* make an appearance, approach

faceless *adjective* IMPERSONAL, remote, unknown, unidentified, anonymous

face-lift *noun* **1** RENOVATION, improvement, restoration, refurbishing, modernization, redecoration **2** COSMETIC SURGERY, plastic surgery

facet *noun* **1** ASPECT, part, face, side, phase,

angle **2** FACE, side, surface, plane, slant

facile *adjective* **1** SUPERFICIAL, shallow, slick, glib, hasty, cursory **2** EFFORTLESS, easy, simple, quick, ready, smooth, skilful, adept, fluent, uncomplicated, proficient, adroit, dexterous, light << ANTONYM difficult

facilitate *verb* FURTHER, help, forward, promote, ease, speed up, pave the way for, make easy, expedite, oil the wheels of, smooth the path of, assist the progress of << ANTONYM hinder

facility *noun* **1** *often plural* AMENITY, means, aid, opportunity, advantage, resource, equipment, provision, convenience, appliance **2** OPPORTUNITY, possibility, convenience **3** ABILITY, skill, talent, gift, craft, efficiency, knack, fluency, proficiency, dexterity, quickness, adroitness, expertness, skilfulness **4** EASE, readiness, fluency, smoothness, effortlessness << ANTONYM difficulty

facsimile *noun* COPY, print, carbon, reproduction, replica, transcript, duplicate, photocopy, Xerox (*trademark*), carbon copy, Photostat (*trademark*), fax

fact *noun* **1** TRUTH, reality, gospel (truth), certainty, verity, actuality, naked truth << ANTONYM fiction **2** DETAIL, point, feature, particular, item, specific, circumstance **3** (*usually in phrase after* or *before the fact*) (*criminal law*) EVENT, happening, act, performance, incident, deed, occurrence, fait accompli (*French*) ▷ *plural noun* INFORMATION, details, data, the score (*informal*), gen (*Brit informal*), info (*informal*), the whole story, ins and outs, the lowdown (*informal*) ▷▷ **as a matter of fact** *or* **in fact** *or* **in point of fact** ACTUALLY, really, indeed, truly, in reality, in truth, to tell the truth, in actual fact, in point of fact

faction *noun* **1** GROUP, set, party, division, section, camp, sector, minority, combination, coalition, gang, lobby, bloc, contingent, pressure group, caucus, junta, clique, coterie, schism, confederacy, splinter group, cabal, ginger group, public-interest group (*US & Canad*) **2** DISSENSION, division, conflict, rebellion, disagreement, friction, strife, turbulence, variance, discord, infighting, disunity, sedition, tumult, disharmony, divisiveness << ANTONYM agreement

factor *noun* ELEMENT, thing, point, part, cause, influence, item, aspect, circumstance, characteristic, consideration, component, determinant

factory *noun* WORKS, plant, mill, workshop, assembly line, shop floor, manufactory (*obsolete*)

factual *adjective* TRUE, objective, authentic, unbiased, close, real, sure, correct, genuine, accurate, exact, precise, faithful, credible, matter-of-fact, literal, veritable, circumstantial, unadorned, dinkum (*Austral & NZ informal*), true-to-life << ANTONYM fictitious

faculty *noun* **1** ABILITY, power, skill, facility, talent, gift, capacity, bent, capability, readiness, knack, propensity, aptitude, dexterity, cleverness, adroitness, turn << ANTONYM failing **2** DEPARTMENT, school, discipline, profession, branch of learning **3** TEACHING STAFF, staff, teachers, professors, lecturers (*chiefly US*) **4** POWER, reason, sense, intelligence, mental ability, physical ability

fad *noun* CRAZE, fashion, trend, fancy, rage, mode, vogue, whim, mania, affectation

fade *verb* **1** BECOME PALE, dull, dim, bleach, wash out, blanch, discolour, blench, lose colour, lose lustre, decolour **2** MAKE PALE, dull, dim, bleach, wash out, blanch, discolour, decolour **3** GROW DIM, dim, fade away, become less loud **4** *usually with* **away** *or* **out** DWINDLE, disappear, vanish, melt away, fall, fail, decline, flag, dissolve, dim, disperse, wither, wilt, wane, perish, ebb, languish, die out, droop, shrivel, die away, waste away, vanish into thin air, become unimportant, evanesce, etiolate

faded *adjective* DISCOLOURED, pale, bleached, washed out, dull, dim, indistinct, etiolated, lustreless

fading *adjective* DECLINING, dying, disappearing, vanishing, decreasing, on the decline

faeces *or esp US* **feces** *plural noun* EXCREMENT, stools, excreta, bodily waste, dung, droppings, ordure

fail *verb* **1** BE UNSUCCESSFUL, founder, fall flat, come to nothing, fall, miss, go down, break down, flop (*informal*), be defeated, fall short, fall through, fall short of, fizzle out (*informal*), come unstuck, run aground, miscarry, be in vain, misfire, fall by the wayside, go astray, come to grief, come a cropper (*informal*), bite the dust, go up in smoke, go belly-up (*slang*), come to naught, lay an egg (*slang, chiefly US & Canad*), go by the board, not make the grade (*informal*), go down like a lead balloon (*informal*), turn out badly, fall flat on your face, meet with disaster, be found lacking *or* wanting << ANTONYM succeed **2** DISAPPOINT, abandon, desert, neglect, omit, let down, forsake, turn your back on, be disloyal to, break your word, forget **3** STOP WORKING, stop, die, give up, break down, cease, stall, cut out, malfunction, conk out (*informal*), go on the blink (*informal*), go phut **4** WITHER, perish, sag, droop, waste away, shrivel up **5** GO BANKRUPT, crash, collapse, fold (*informal*), close down, go under, go bust (*informal*), go out of business, be wound up, go broke (*informal*), go to the wall, go into receivership, go into liquidation, become insolvent, smash **6** DECLINE, fade, weaken, deteriorate, dwindle, sicken, degenerate, fall apart at the seams, be on your last legs (*informal*) **7** GIVE OUT, disappear, fade, dim, dwindle, wane, gutter, languish, peter out, die away, grow dim, sink ▷▷ **without fail** WITHOUT EXCEPTION, regularly, constantly, invariably, religiously, unfailingly, conscientiously, like clockwork, punctually, dependably

failing *noun* SHORTCOMING, failure, fault, error, weakness, defect, deficiency, lapse, flaw, miscarriage, drawback, misfortune, blemish, imperfection, frailty, foible, blind spot << ANTONYM strength ▷ *preposition* IN THE ABSENCE OF, lacking, in default of

failure *noun* **1** LACK OF SUCCESS, defeat, collapse, abortion, wreck, frustration, breakdown, overthrow, miscarriage, fiasco, downfall << ANTONYM success **2** LOSER, disappointment, no-good, flop (*informal*), write-off, incompetent, no-hoper (*chiefly Austral*), dud (*informal*), clinker (*slang, chiefly US*), black sheep, washout (*informal*), clunker (*informal*), dead duck (*slang*), ne'er-do-well, nonstarter **3** NEGLIGENCE, neglect, deficiency, default, shortcoming, omission, oversight, dereliction, nonperformance, nonobservance, nonsuccess, remissness << ANTONYM observance **4** BREAKDOWN, stalling, cutting out, malfunction, crash, disruption, stoppage, mishap, conking out (*informal*) **5** FAILING, deterioration, decay, loss, decline **6** BANKRUPTCY, crash, collapse, ruin, folding (*informal*), closure, winding up, downfall, going under, liquidation, insolvency << ANTONYM prosperity

faint *adjective* **1** DIM, low, light, soft, thin, faded, whispered, distant, dull, delicate, vague, unclear, muted, subdued, faltering, hushed, bleached, feeble, indefinite, muffled, hazy, ill-defined, indistinct << ANTONYM clear **2** SLIGHT, weak, feeble, unenthusiastic, remote, slim, vague, slender **3** TIMID, weak, feeble, lame, unconvincing, unenthusiastic, timorous, faint-hearted, spiritless, half-hearted, lily-livered << ANTONYM brave **4** DIZZY, giddy, light-headed, vertiginous, weak, exhausted, fatigued, faltering, wobbly, drooping, languid, lethargic, muzzy, woozy (*informal*), weak at the knees, enervated << ANTONYM energetic ▷ *verb* PASS OUT, black out, lose consciousness, keel over (*informal*), fail, go out, collapse, fade, weaken, languish, swoon (*literary*), flake out (*informal*) ▷ *noun* BLACKOUT, collapse, coma, swoon (*literary*), unconsciousness, syncope (*pathology*)

faintly *adverb* **1** SLIGHTLY, rather, a little, somewhat, dimly **2** SOFTLY, weakly, feebly, in a whisper, indistinctly, unclearly

fair¹ *adjective* **1** UNBIASED, impartial, even-handed, unprejudiced, just, clean, square, equal, objective, reasonable, proper, legitimate, upright, honourable, honest, equitable, lawful, trustworthy, on the level (*informal*), disinterested, dispassionate, above board, according to the rules << ANTONYM unfair **2** RESPECTABLE, middling, average, reasonable, decent, acceptable, moderate, adequate, satisfactory, not bad, mediocre, so-so (*informal*), tolerable, passable, O.K. *or* okay (*informal*), all right **3** LIGHT, golden, blonde, blond, yellowish, fair-haired, light-coloured, flaxen-haired, towheaded, tow-haired **4** LIGHT-COMPLEXIONED, white, pale **5** FINE, clear, dry, bright, pleasant, sunny, favourable, clement, cloudless, unclouded, sunshiny **6** BEAUTIFUL, pretty, attractive, lovely, handsome, good-looking, bonny, comely, beauteous, well-favoured << ANTONYM ugly ▷▷ **fair and square** HONESTLY, straight, legally, on the level (*informal*), by the book, lawfully, above board, according to the rules, without cheating

fair² *noun* **1** CARNIVAL, fête, gala, bazaar **2** EXHIBITION, show, market, festival, mart, expo (*informal*), exposition

fairly *adverb* **1** EQUITABLY, objectively, legitimately, honestly, justly, lawfully, without prejudice, dispassionately, impartially, even-handedly, without bias **2** MODERATELY, rather, quite, somewhat, reasonably, adequately, pretty well, tolerably, passably **3** POSITIVELY, really, simply, absolutely, in a manner of speaking, veritably **4** DESERVEDLY, objectively, honestly, justifiably, justly, impartially, equitably, without fear or favour, properly

fair-minded *adjective* IMPARTIAL, just, fair, reasonable, open-minded, disinterested, unbiased, even-handed, unprejudiced

fairness *noun* IMPARTIALITY, justice, equity, legitimacy, decency, disinterestedness, uprightness, rightfulness, equitableness

fairy *noun* SPRITE, elf, brownie, hob, pixie, puck, imp, leprechaun, peri, Robin Goodfellow

fairy tale *or* **fairy story** *noun* **1** FOLK TALE, romance, traditional story **2** LIE, fantasy, fiction, invention, fabrication, untruth, porky (*Brit slang*), pork pie (*Brit slang*), urban myth, tall story, urban legend, cock-and-bull story (*informal*)

faith *noun* **1** CONFIDENCE, trust, credit, conviction, assurance, dependence, reliance, credence << ANTONYM distrust **2** RELIGION, church, belief, persuasion, creed, communion, denomination, dogma << ANTONYM agnosticism

faithful *adjective* **1** LOYAL, true, committed, constant, attached, devoted, dedicated, reliable, staunch, truthful, dependable, trusty, steadfast, unwavering, true-blue, immovable, unswerving << ANTONYM disloyal **2** ACCURATE, just, close, true, strict, exact, precise >> **the faithful** BELIEVERS, brethren, followers, congregation, adherents, the elect, communicants

faithfulness *noun* LOYALTY, devotion, fidelity, constancy, dependability, trustworthiness, fealty, adherence

faithless *adjective* DISLOYAL, unreliable, unfaithful, untrustworthy, doubting, false, untrue, treacherous, dishonest, fickle, perfidious, untruthful, traitorous, unbelieving, inconstant, false-hearted, recreant (*archaic*)

fake *verb* **1** FORGE, copy, reproduce, fabricate, counterfeit, falsify **2** SHAM, affect, assume, put on, pretend, simulate, feign, go through the motions of ▷ *noun* **1** FORGERY, copy, fraud, reproduction, dummy, imitation, hoax, counterfeit **2** CHARLATAN, deceiver, sham, quack, mountebank, phoney *or* phony (*informal*) ▷ *adjective* ARTIFICIAL, false, forged, counterfeit, affected, assumed, put-on, pretend (*informal*), mock, imitation, sham, pseudo (*informal*), feigned, pinchbeck,

phoney *or* phony (*informal*) << ANTONYM genuine

fall *verb* **1** DROP, plunge, tumble, plummet, trip, settle, crash, collapse, pitch, sink, go down, come down, dive, stumble, descend, topple, subside, cascade, trip over, drop down, nose-dive, come a cropper (*informal*), keel over, go head over heels << ANTONYM rise **2** DECREASE, drop, decline, go down, flag, slump, diminish, fall off, dwindle, lessen, subside, ebb, abate, depreciate, become lower << ANTONYM increase **3** BE OVERTHROWN, be taken, surrender, succumb, yield, submit, give way, capitulate, be conquered, give in *or* up, pass into enemy hands << ANTONYM triumph **4** BE KILLED, die, be lost, perish, be slain, be a casualty, meet your end << ANTONYM survive **5** OCCUR, happen, come about, chance, take place, fall out, befall, come to pass ▷ *noun* **1** DROP, slip, plunge, dive, spill, tumble, descent, plummet, nose dive **2** DECREASE, drop, lowering, decline, reduction, slump, dip, falling off, dwindling, lessening, diminution, cut **3** COLLAPSE, defeat, surrender, downfall, death, failure, ruin, resignation, destruction, overthrow, submission, capitulation **4** SLOPE, incline, descent, downgrade, slant, declivity ▷ *plural noun* WATERFALL, rapids, cascade, cataract, linn (*Scot*), force (*N English dialect*) >> **fall apart 1** BREAK UP, crumble, disintegrate, fall to bits, go to seed, come apart at the seams, break into pieces, go *or* come to pieces, shatter **2** BREAK DOWN, dissolve, disperse, disband, lose cohesion **3** GO TO PIECES, break down, crack up (*informal*), have a breakdown, crumble >> **fall away 1** SLOPE, drop, go down, incline, incline downwards **2** DECREASE, drop, diminish, fall off, dwindle, lessen >> **fall back** RETREAT, retire, withdraw, move back, recede, pull back, back off, recoil, draw back >> **fall back on something** *or* **someone** RESORT TO, have recourse to, employ, turn to, make use of, call upon, press into service >> **fall behind 1** LAG, trail, be left behind, drop back, get left behind, lose your place **2** BE IN ARREARS, be late, not keep up >> **fall down** *often with* **on** (*informal*) FAIL, disappoint, go wrong, fall short, fail to make the grade, prove unsuccessful >> **fall for someone** FALL IN LOVE WITH, become infatuated with, be smitten by, be swept off your feet by, desire, fancy (*Brit informal*), succumb to the charms of, lose your head over ▷▷ **fall for something** BE FOOLED BY, be deceived by, be taken in by, be duped by, buy (*slang*), accept, swallow (*informal*), take on board, give credence to ▷▷ **fall in** COLLAPSE, sink, cave in, crash in, fall to the ground, fall apart at the seams, come down about your ears ▷▷ **fall in with someone** *often with* **with** MAKE FRIENDS WITH, go around with, become friendly with, hang about with (*informal*) ▷▷ **fall in with something** GO ALONG WITH, support, accept, agree with, comply with, submit to, yield to, buy into (*informal*), cooperate with, assent, take on board, concur with ▷▷ **fall off 1** TUMBLE, topple, plummet, be unseated, come a cropper *or* purler (*informal*), take a fall *or* tumble **2** DECREASE, drop, reduce, decline, fade, slump, weaken, shrink, diminish, dwindle, lessen, wane, subside, fall away, peter out, slacken, tail off (*informal*), ebb away, go down *or* downhill ▷▷ **fall on** *or* **upon something** *or* **someone** ATTACK, assault, snatch, assail, tear into (*informal*), lay into, descend upon, pitch into (*informal*), belabour, let fly at, set upon *or* about ▷▷ **fall out** (*informal*) ARGUE, fight, row, clash, differ, disagree, quarrel, squabble, have a row, have words, come to blows, cross swords, altercate ▷▷ **fall short** *often with* **of** BE LACKING, miss, fail, disappoint, be wanting, be inadequate, be deficient, fall down on (*informal*), prove inadequate, not come up to expectations *or* scratch (*informal*) ▷▷ **fall through** FAIL, be unsuccessful, come to nothing, fizzle out (*informal*), miscarry, go awry, go by the board ▷▷ **fall to someone** BE THE RESPONSIBILITY OF, be up to, come down to, devolve upon ▷▷ **fall to something** BEGIN, start, set to, set about, commence, apply yourself to

fallacy *noun* ERROR, mistake, illusion, flaw, deception, delusion, inconsistency, misconception, deceit, falsehood, untruth, misapprehension, sophistry, casuistry, sophism, faultiness

fallen *adjective* **1** KILLED, lost, dead, slaughtered, slain, perished **2** DISHONOURED, lost, loose, shamed, ruined, disgraced, immoral, sinful, unchaste

fallible *adjective* IMPERFECT, weak, uncertain, ignorant, mortal, frail, erring, prone to error << ANTONYM infallible

fallout *noun* CONSEQUENCES, results, effects, outcome, repercussions, upshot

fallow *adjective* **1** UNCULTIVATED, unused, undeveloped, unplanted, untilled

2 INACTIVE, resting, idle, dormant, inert

false *adjective* **1** INCORRECT, wrong, mistaken, misleading, faulty, inaccurate, invalid, improper, unfounded, erroneous, inexact << ANTONYM correct **2** UNTRUE, fraudulent, unreal, concocted, fictitious, trumped up, fallacious, untruthful, truthless << ANTONYM true **3** ARTIFICIAL, forged, fake, mock, reproduction, synthetic, replica, imitation, bogus, simulated, sham, pseudo (*informal*), counterfeit, feigned, spurious, ersatz, pretended << ANTONYM real **4** TREACHEROUS, lying, deceiving, unreliable, two-timing (*informal*), dishonest, deceptive, hypocritical, unfaithful, two-faced, disloyal, unsound, deceitful, faithless, untrustworthy, insincere, double-dealing, dishonourable, duplicitous, mendacious, perfidious, treasonable, traitorous, inconstant, delusive, false-hearted << ANTONYM loyal

falsehood *noun* **1** UNTRUTHFULNESS, deception, deceit, dishonesty, prevarication, mendacity, dissimulation, perjury, inveracity (*rare*) **2** LIE, story, fiction, fabrication, fib, untruth, porky (*Brit slang*), pork pie (*Brit slang*), misstatement

falsify *verb* ALTER, forge, fake, tamper with, doctor, cook (*slang*), distort, pervert, belie, counterfeit, misrepresent, garble, misstate

falter *verb* **1** HESITATE, delay, waver, vacillate, break << ANTONYM persevere **2** TUMBLE, shake, tremble, totter **3** STUTTER, pause, stumble, hesitate, stammer, speak haltingly

faltering *adjective* HESITANT, broken, weak, uncertain, stumbling, tentative, stammering, timid, irresolute

fame *noun* PROMINENCE, glory, celebrity, stardom, name, credit, reputation, honour, prestige, stature, eminence, renown, repute, public esteem, illustriousness << ANTONYM obscurity

famed *adjective* RENOWNED, celebrated, recognized, well-known, acclaimed, widely-known

familiar *adjective* **1** WELL-KNOWN, household, everyday, recognized, common, stock, domestic, repeated, ordinary, conventional, routine, frequent, accustomed, customary, mundane, reeognizable, common or garden (*informal*) << ANTONYM unfamiliar **2** FRIENDLY, close, dear, intimate, confidential, amicable, chummy (*informal*), buddy-buddy (*slang, chiefly US & Canad*), palsy-walsy (*informal*) << ANTONYM formal **3** RELAXED, open, easy, friendly, free, near, comfortable, intimate, casual, informal, amicable, cordial, free-and-easy, unreserved, unconstrained, unceremonious, hail-fellow-well-met **4** DISRESPECTFUL, forward, bold, presuming, intrusive, presumptuous, impudent, overfamiliar ▷▷ **familiar with** ACQUAINTED WITH, aware of, introduced to, conscious of, at home with, no stranger to, informed about, abreast of, knowledgeable about, versed in, well up in, proficient in, conversant with, on speaking terms with, in the know about, *au courant* with, *au fait* with

familiarity *noun* **1** ACQUAINTANCE, experience, understanding, knowledge, awareness, grasp, acquaintanceship << ANTONYM unfamiliarity **2** FRIENDLINESS, friendship, intimacy, closeness, freedom, ease, openness, fellowship, informality, sociability, naturalness, absence of reserve, unceremoniousness << ANTONYM formality **3** DISRESPECT, forwardness, overfamiliarity, liberties, liberty, cheek, presumption, boldness << ANTONYM respect

familiarize *or* **familiarise** *verb* ACCUSTOM, instruct, habituate, make used to, school, season, train, prime, coach, get to know (about), inure, bring into common use, make conversant

family *noun* **1** RELATIONS, people, children, issue, relatives, household, folk (*informal*), offspring, descendants, brood, kin, nuclear family, progeny, kindred, next of kin, kinsmen, ménage, kith and kin, your nearest and dearest, kinsfolk, your own flesh and blood, ainga (*NZ*), rellies (*Austral slang*) **2** CHILDREN, kids (*informal*), offspring, little ones, munchkins (*informal, chiefly US*), littlies (*Austral informal*) **3** ANCESTORS, forebears, parentage, forefathers, house, line, race, blood, birth, strain, tribe, sept, clan, descent, dynasty, pedigree, extraction, ancestry, lineage, genealogy, line of descent, stemma, stirps **4** SPECIES, group, class, system, order, kind, network, genre, classification, subdivision, subclass

family tree *noun* LINEAGE, genealogy, line of descent, ancestral tree, line, descent, pedigree, extraction, ancestry, blood line, stemma, stirps, whakapapa (*NZ*)

famine *noun* HUNGER, want, starvation, deprivation, scarcity, dearth, destitution

famous *adjective* WELL-KNOWN, celebrated, acclaimed, notable, noted, excellent, signal, honoured, remarkable, distinguished, prominent, glorious, legendary, renowned, eminent, conspicuous, illustrious, much-publicized, lionized, far-famed << ANTONYM unknown

fan¹ *noun* BLOWER, ventilator, air conditioner, vane, punkah (*in India*), blade, propeller ▷ *verb* **1** BLOW, cool, refresh, air-condition, ventilate, air-cool, winnow (*rare*) **2** STIMULATE, increase, excite, provoke, arouse, rouse, stir up, work up, agitate, whip up, add fuel to the flames, impassion, enkindle **3** *often with* **out** SPREAD OUT, spread, lay out, disperse, unfurl, open out, space out

fan² *noun* **1** SUPPORTER, lover, follower, enthusiast, admirer, groupie (*slang*), rooter (*US*) **2** DEVOTEE, addict, freak (*informal*), buff (*informal*), fiend (*informal*), adherent, zealot, aficionado

fanatic *noun* EXTREMIST, activist, militant, addict, enthusiast, buff (*informal*), visionary, devotee, bigot, zealot, energumen

fanatical *adjective* OBSESSIVE, burning, wild, mad, extreme, enthusiastic, passionate, frenzied, visionary, fervent, zealous, bigoted, rabid, immoderate, overenthusiastic

fanaticism *noun* IMMODERATION, enthusiasm, madness, devotion, dedication, zeal, bigotry, extremism, infatuation, single-mindedness, zealotry, obsessiveness, monomania, overenthusiasm

fancier *noun* EXPERT, amateur, breeder, connoisseur, aficionado

fanciful *adjective* UNREAL, wild, ideal, romantic, fantastic, curious, fabulous, imaginative, imaginary, poetic, extravagant, visionary, fairy-tale, mythical, whimsical, capricious, chimerical << ANTONYM unimaginative

fancy *adjective* **1** ELABORATE, decorated, decorative, extravagant, intricate, baroque, ornamented, ornamental, ornate, elegant, fanciful, embellished << ANTONYM plain **2** EXPENSIVE, high-quality, classy, flashy, swish (*informal*), showy, ostentatious ▷ *noun* **1** WHIM, thought, idea, desire, urge, notion, humour, impulse, inclination, caprice **2** DELUSION, dream, vision, fantasy, nightmare, daydream, chimera, phantasm ▷ *verb* **1** (*informal*) WISH FOR, want, desire, would like, hope for, dream of, relish, long for, crave, be attracted to, yearn for, thirst for, hanker after, have a yen for **2** (*Brit informal*) BE ATTRACTED TO, find attractive, desire, lust after, like, prefer, favour, take to, go for, be captivated by, have an eye for, have a thing about (*informal*), have eyes for, take a liking to **3** SUPPOSE, think, believe, imagine, guess (*informal, chiefly US & Canad*), reckon, conceive, infer, conjecture, surmise, think likely, be inclined to think ▷▷ **fancy yourself** THINK YOU ARE GOD'S GIFT, have a high opinion of yourself, think you are the cat's whiskers ▷▷ **take a fancy to something or someone** START LIKING, like, want, be fond of, hanker after, have a partiality for

fanfare *noun* TRUMPET CALL, flourish, trump (*archaic*), tucket (*archaic*), fanfaronade

fang *noun* TOOTH, tusk

fantasize *or* **fantasise** *verb* DAYDREAM, imagine, invent, romance, envision, hallucinate, see visions, live in a dream world, build castles in the air, give free rein to the imagination

fantastic *adjective* **1** (*informal*) WONDERFUL, great, excellent, very good, mean (*slang*), topping (*Brit slang*), cracking (*Brit informal*), crucial (*slang*), smashing (*informal*), superb, tremendous (*informal*), magnificent, marvellous, terrific (*informal*), sensational (*informal*), mega (*slang*), awesome (*slang*), dope (*slang*), world-class, first-rate, def (*slang*), brill (*informal*), out of this world (*informal*), boffo (*slang*), jim-dandy (*slang*), bitchin' (*US slang*), chillin' (*US slang*), booshit (*Austral slang*), exo (*Austral slang*), sik (*Austral slang*), rad (*informal*), phat (*slang*), schmick (*Austral informal*) << ANTONYM ordinary **2** (*informal*) ENORMOUS, great, huge, vast, severe, extreme, overwhelming, tremendous, immense **3** STRANGE, bizarre, weird, exotic, peculiar, imaginative, queer, grotesque, quaint, unreal, fanciful, outlandish, whimsical, freakish, chimerical, phantasmagorical **4** IMPLAUSIBLE, unlikely, incredible, absurd, irrational, preposterous, capricious, cock-and-bull (*informal*), cockamamie (*slang, chiefly US*), mad

fantasy *or* **phantasy** *noun* **1** DAYDREAM, dream, wish, fancy, delusion, reverie, flight of fancy, pipe dream **2** IMAGINATION, fancy, invention, creativity, originality

far *adverb* **1** A LONG WAY, miles, deep, a good way, afar, a great distance **2** MUCH, greatly, very much, extremely, significantly, considerably, decidedly, markedly, incomparably ▷ *adjective often with* **off** REMOTE, distant, far-flung, faraway, long, removed, out-of-the-way, far-off, far-removed, outlying, off the beaten track

<< ANTONYM near ▷▷ **by far** *or* **far and away** VERY MUCH, easily, immeasurably, by a long way, incomparably, to a great degree, by a long shot, by a long chalk (*informal*), by a great amount ▷▷ **far and wide** EXTENSIVELY, everywhere, worldwide, far and near, widely, broadly, in all places, in every nook and cranny, here, there and everywhere ▷▷ **far from** NOT AT ALL, not, by no means, absolutely not ▷▷ **so far 1** UP TO A POINT, to a certain extent, to a limited extent **2** UP TO NOW, to date, until now, thus far, up to the present

faraway *adjective* **1** DISTANT, far, remote, far-off, far-removed, far-flung, outlying, beyond the horizon **2** DREAMY, lost, distant, abstracted, vague, absent

farce *noun* **1** COMEDY, satire, slapstick, burlesque, buffoonery, broad comedy **2** MOCKERY, joke, nonsense, parody, shambles, sham, absurdity, travesty, ridiculousness

farcical *adjective* **1** LUDICROUS, ridiculous, diverting, absurd, preposterous, laughable, nonsensical, derisory, risible **2** COMIC, funny, amusing, slapstick, droll, custard-pie

fare *noun* **1** CHARGE, price, ticket price, transport cost, ticket money, passage money **2** FOOD, meals, diet, provisions, board, commons, table, feed, menu, rations, tack (*informal*), kai (*NZ informal*), nourishment, sustenance, victuals, nosebag (*slang*), nutriment, vittles (*obsolete or dialect*), eatables **3** PASSENGER, customer, pick-up (*informal*), traveller ▷ *verb* **1** GET ON, do, manage, make out, prosper, get along **2** *used impersonally* HAPPEN, go, turn out, proceed, pan out (*informal*)

farewell *interjection* GOODBYE, bye (*informal*), so long, see you, take care, good morning, bye-bye (*informal*), good day, all the best, good night, good evening, good afternoon, see you later, ciao (*Italian*), have a nice day (*US*), adieu (*French*), au revoir (*French*), be seeing you, auf Wiedersehen (*German*), adios (*Spanish*), mind how you go, haere ra (*NZ*) ▷ *noun* GOODBYE, parting, departure, leave-taking, adieu, valediction, sendoff (*informal*), adieux *or* adieus

far-fetched *adjective* UNCONVINCING, unlikely, strained, fantastic, incredible, doubtful, unbelievable, dubious, unrealistic, improbable, unnatural, preposterous, implausible, hard to swallow (*informal*), cock-and-bull (*informal*) << ANTONYM believable

farm *noun* SMALLHOLDING, holding, ranch (*chiefly US & Canad*), farmstead, land, station (*Austral & NZ*), acres, vineyard, plantation, croft (*Scot*), grange, homestead, acreage ▷ *verb* CULTIVATE, work, plant, operate, till the soil, grow crops on, bring under cultivation, keep animals on, practise husbandry

farmer *noun* AGRICULTURIST, yeoman, smallholder, crofter (*Scot*), grazier, agriculturalist, rancher, agronomist, husbandman, cockie *or* cocky (*Austral & NZ informal*)

farming *noun* AGRICULTURE, cultivation, husbandry, land management, agronomy, tilling

far-out *adjective* STRANGE, wild, unusual, bizarre, weird, avant-garde, unconventional, off-the-wall (*slang*), outlandish, outré, advanced

far-reaching *adjective* EXTENSIVE, important, significant, sweeping, broad, widespread, pervasive, momentous

far-sighted *adjective* PRUDENT, acute, wise, cautious, sage, shrewd, discerning, canny, provident, judicious, prescient, far-seeing, politic

fascinate *verb* ENTRANCE, delight, charm, absorb, intrigue, enchant, rivet, captivate, enthral, beguile, allure, bewitch, ravish, transfix, mesmerize, hypnotize, engross, enrapture, interest greatly, enamour, hold spellbound, spellbind, infatuate << ANTONYM bore

fascinated *adjective* ENTRANCED, charmed, absorbed, very interested, captivated, hooked on, enthralled, beguiled, smitten, bewitched, engrossed, spellbound, infatuated, hypnotized, under a spell

fascinating *adjective* CAPTIVATING, engaging, gripping, compelling, intriguing, very interesting, irresistible, enticing, enchanting, seductive, riveting, alluring, bewitching, ravishing, engrossing << ANTONYM boring

fascination *noun* ATTRACTION, pull, spell, magic, charm, lure, glamour, allure, magnetism, enchantment, sorcery

Fascism *noun sometimes not cap.* AUTHORITARIANISM, dictatorship, totalitarianism, despotism, autocracy, absolutism, Hitlerism

fashion *noun* 1 STYLE, look, trend, rage, custom, convention, mode, vogue, usage, craze, fad, latest style, prevailing taste, latest 2 METHOD, way, style, approach, manner, mode ▷ *verb* 1 MAKE, shape, cast, construct, work, form, create, design, manufacture, forge, mould, contrive, fabricate 2 FIT, adapt, tailor, suit, adjust, accommodate ▷▷ **after a fashion** TO SOME EXTENT, somehow, in a way, moderately, to a certain extent, to a degree, somehow or other, in a manner of speaking

fashionable *adjective* POPULAR, in fashion, trendy (*Brit informal*), cool (*slang*), in (*informal*), latest, happening (*informal*), current, modern, with it (*informal*), usual, smart, hip (*slang*), prevailing, stylish, chic, up-to-date, customary, genteel, in vogue, all the rage, voguish (*informal*), trendsetting, all the go (*informal*), schmick (*Austral informal*) << ANTONYM unfashionable

fast¹ *adjective* 1 QUICK, flying, winged, rapid, fleet, hurried, accelerated, swift, speedy, brisk, hasty, nimble, mercurial, sprightly, nippy (*Brit informal*) << ANTONYM slow 2 FIXED, firm, sound, stuck, secure, tight, jammed, fortified, fastened, impregnable, immovable << ANTONYM unstable 3 DISSIPATED, wild, exciting, loose, extravagant, reckless, immoral, promiscuous, giddy, self-indulgent, wanton, profligate, impure, intemperate, dissolute, rakish, licentious, gadabout (*informal*) 4 CLOSE, lasting, firm, permanent, constant, devoted, loyal, faithful, stalwart, staunch, steadfast, unwavering ▷ *adverb* 1 QUICKLY, rapidly, swiftly, hastily, hurriedly, speedily, presto, apace, in haste, like a shot (*informal*), at full speed, hell for leather (*informal*), like lightning, hotfoot, like a flash, at a rate of knots, like the clappers (*Brit informal*), like a bat out of hell (*slang*), pdq (*slang*), like nobody's business (*informal*), posthaste, like greased lightning (*informal*), with all haste << ANTONYM slowly 2 FIRMLY, staunchly, resolutely, steadfastly, determinedly, unwaveringly, unchangeably 3 SECURELY, firmly, tightly, fixedly 4 FIXEDLY, firmly, soundly, deeply, securely, tightly 5 RECKLESSLY, wildly, loosely, extravagantly, promiscuously, rakishly, intemperately

fast² *verb* GO HUNGRY, abstain, go without food, deny yourself, practise abstention, refrain from food *or* eating ▷ *noun* FASTING, diet, abstinence

fasten *verb* 1 SECURE, close, lock, chain, seal, bolt, do up 2 TIE, bind, lace, tie up 3 FIX, join, link, connect, grip, attach, anchor, affix,

make firm, make fast **4** *often with* **on** *or* **upon**
CONCENTRATE, focus, fix **5** DIRECT, aim,
focus, fix, concentrate, bend, rivet

fastening *noun* TIE, union, coupling, link,
linking, bond, joint, binding, connection,
attachment, junction, zip, fusion, clasp,
concatenation, ligature, affixation

fastidious *adjective* PARTICULAR, meticulous,
fussy, overdelicate, difficult, nice, critical,
discriminating, dainty, squeamish, choosy,
picky (*informal*), hard to please, finicky,
punctilious, pernickety, hypercritical,
overnice << ANTONYM careless

fat *noun* FATNESS, flesh, bulk, obesity, cellulite,
weight problem, flab, blubber, paunch,
fatty tissue, adipose tissue, corpulence, beef
(*informal*) ▷ *adjective* **1** OVERWEIGHT, large,
heavy, plump, gross, stout, obese, fleshy,
beefy (*informal*), tubby, portly, roly-poly,
rotund, podgy, corpulent, elephantine,
broad in the beam (*informal*), solid
<< ANTONYM thin **2** LARGE, rich, substantial,
thriving, flourishing, profitable, productive,
lucrative, fertile, lush, prosperous, affluent,
fruitful, cushy (*slang*), jammy (*Brit slang*),
remunerative << ANTONYM scanty **3** FATTY,
greasy, lipid, adipose, oleaginous, suety, oily
<< ANTONYM lean ▷▷ **a fat chance** (*slang*) NO
CHANCE, (a) slim chance, very little chance,
not much chance

fatal *adjective* **1** DISASTROUS, devastating,
crippling, lethal, catastrophic, ruinous,
calamitous, baleful, baneful << ANTONYM
minor **2** DECISIVE, final, determining,
critical, crucial, fateful **3** LETHAL, deadly,
mortal, causing death, final, killing,
terminal, destructive, malignant, incurable,
pernicious << ANTONYM harmless

fatalism *noun* RESIGNATION, acceptance,
passivity, determinism, stoicism,
necessitarianism, predestinarianism

fatality *noun* CASUALTY, death, loss, victim

fate *noun* **1** DESTINY, chance, fortune, luck,
the stars, weird (*archaic*), providence,
nemesis, kismet, predestination, divine
will **2** FORTUNE, destiny, lot, portion, cup,
horoscope **3** OUTCOME, future, destiny, end,
issue, upshot **4** DOWNFALL, end, death, ruin,
destruction, doom, demise

fated *adjective* DESTINED, doomed,
predestined, preordained, foreordained,
pre-elected

fateful *adjective* **1** CRUCIAL, important,
significant, critical, decisive, momentous,
portentous << ANTONYM unimportant

2 DISASTROUS, fatal, deadly, destructive,
lethal, ominous, ruinous

father *noun* **1** DADDY (*informal*), dad
(*informal*), male parent, patriarch, pop (*US
informal*), governor (*informal*), old man (*Brit
informal*), pa (*informal*), old boy (*informal*),
papa (*old-fashioned informal*), sire, pater,
biological father, foster father, begetter,
paterfamilias, birth father **2** FOUNDER,
author, maker, architect, creator, inventor,
originator, prime mover, initiator **3** *often
plural* FOREFATHER, predecessor, ancestor,
forebear, progenitor, tupuna *or* tipuna
(*NZ*) **4** *usually plural* LEADER, senator,
elder, patron, patriarch, guiding light,
city father, kaumatua (*NZ*) ▷ *verb* **1** SIRE,
parent, conceive, bring to life, beget,
procreate, bring into being, give life to, get
2 ORIGINATE, found, create, establish, author,
institute, invent, engender

Father *noun* PRIEST, minister, vicar, parson,
pastor, cleric, churchman, padre (*informal*),
confessor, abbé, curé, man of God

fatherland *noun* HOMELAND, motherland,
old country, native land, land of your birth,
land of your fathers, whenua (*NZ*), Godzone
(*Austral informal*)

fatherly *adjective* PATERNAL, kind, kindly,
tender, protective, supportive, benign,
affectionate, indulgent, patriarchal,
benevolent, forbearing

fathom *verb* UNDERSTAND, grasp,
comprehend, interpret, get to the bottom of

fatigue *noun* TIREDNESS, lethargy, weariness,
ennui, heaviness, debility, languor,
listlessness, overtiredness << ANTONYM
freshness ▷ *verb* TIRE, exhaust, weaken,
weary, drain, fag (out) (*informal*), whack
(*Brit informal*), wear out, jade, take it out
of (*informal*), poop (*informal*), tire out,
knacker (*slang*), drain of energy, overtire
<< ANTONYM refresh

fatigued *adjective* TIRED, exhausted, weary,
tired out, bushed (*informal*), wasted, all in
(*slang*), fagged (out) (*informal*), whacked (*Brit
informal*), jaded, knackered (*slang*), clapped
out (*Austral & NZ informal*), overtired,
zonked (*slang*), dead beat (*informal*), jiggered
(*informal*), on your last legs, creamcrackered
(*Brit informal*)

fatten *verb* **1** GROW FAT, spread, expand, swell,
thrive, broaden, thicken, put on weight,
gain weight, coarsen, become fat, become
fatter **2** FEED UP, feed, stuff, build up, cram,
nourish, distend, bloat, overfeed

fatty *adjective* GREASY, fat, creamy, oily, adipose, oleaginous, suety, rich

fatuous *adjective* FOOLISH, stupid, silly, dull, absurd, dense, ludicrous, lunatic, mindless, idiotic, vacuous, inane, witless, puerile, moronic, brainless, asinine, weak-minded, dumb-ass (*slang*)

faucet *noun* (*US & Canad*) TAP, spout, spigot, stopcock, valve

fault *noun* 1 RESPONSIBILITY, liability, guilt, accountability, culpability 2 MISTAKE, slip, error, offence, blunder, lapse, negligence, omission, boob (*Brit slang*), oversight, slip-up, indiscretion, inaccuracy, howler (*informal*), glitch (*informal*), error of judgment, boo-boo (*informal*), barry *or* Barry Crocker (*Austral slang*) 3 FAILING, lack, weakness, defect, deficiency, flaw, drawback, shortcoming, snag, blemish, imperfection, Achilles heel, weak point, infirmity, demerit << ANTONYM strength ▷ *verb* CRITICIZE, blame, complain, condemn, moan about, censure, hold (someone) responsible, hold (someone) accountable, find fault with, call to account, impugn, find lacking, hold (someone) to blame ▷▷ **at fault** GUILTY, responsible, to blame, accountable, in the wrong, culpable, answerable, blamable ▷▷ **find fault with something** *or* **someone** CRITICIZE, complain about, whinge about (*informal*), whine about (*informal*), quibble, diss (*slang, chiefly US*), carp at, take to task, pick holes in, grouse about (*informal*), haul over the coals (*informal*), pull to pieces ▷▷ **to a fault** EXCESSIVELY, overly (*US*), unduly, ridiculously, in the extreme, needlessly, out of all proportion, preposterously, overmuch, immoderately

faultless *adjective* FLAWLESS, model, perfect, classic, correct, accurate, faithful, impeccable, exemplary, foolproof, unblemished

faulty *adjective* 1 DEFECTIVE, damaged, not working, malfunctioning, broken, bad, flawed, impaired, imperfect, blemished, out of order, on the blink 2 INCORRECT, wrong, flawed, inaccurate, bad, weak, invalid, erroneous, unsound, imprecise, fallacious

faux pas *noun* GAFFE, blunder, indiscretion, impropriety, bloomer (*Brit informal*), boob (*Brit slang*), clanger (*informal*), solecism, breach of etiquette, gaucherie

favour *or US* **favor** *noun* 1 APPROVAL, grace, esteem, goodwill, kindness, friendliness, commendation, partiality, approbation, kind regard << ANTONYM disapproval 2 FAVOURITISM, preference, bias, nepotism, preferential treatment, partisanship, jobs for the boys (*informal*), partiality, one-sidedness 3 SUPPORT, backing, aid, championship, promotion, assistance, patronage, espousal, good opinion 4 GOOD TURN, service, benefit, courtesy, kindness, indulgence, boon, good deed, kind act, obligement (*Scot archaic*) << ANTONYM wrong 5 MEMENTO, present, gift, token, souvenir, keepsake, love-token ▷ *verb* 1 PREFER, opt for, like better, incline towards, choose, pick, desire, select, elect, adopt, go for, fancy, single out, plump for, be partial to << ANTONYM object to 2 INDULGE, reward, spoil, esteem, side with, pamper, befriend, be partial to, smile upon, pull strings for (*informal*), have in your good books, treat with partiality, value 3 SUPPORT, like, back, choose, champion, encourage, approve, fancy, advocate, opt for, subscribe to, commend, stand up for, espouse, be in favour of, countenance, patronize << ANTONYM oppose 4 HELP, benefit, aid, advance, promote, assist, accommodate, facilitate, abet, succour, do a kindness to 5 OBLIGE, please, honour, accommodate, benefit ▷▷ **in favour of** FOR, backing, supporting, behind, pro, all for (*informal*), on the side of, right behind

favourable *or US* **favorable** *adjective* 1 POSITIVE, kind, understanding, encouraging, welcoming, friendly, approving, praising, reassuring, enthusiastic, sympathetic, benign, commending, complimentary, agreeable, amicable, well-disposed, commendatory << ANTONYM disapproving 2 AFFIRMATIVE, agreeing, confirming, positive, assenting, corroborative 3 ADVANTAGEOUS, timely, good, promising, fit, encouraging, fair, appropriate, suitable, helpful, hopeful, convenient, beneficial, auspicious, opportune, propitious << ANTONYM disadvantageous

favourably *or US* **favorably** *adverb* 1 POSITIVELY, well, enthusiastically, helpfully, graciously, approvingly, agreeably, with approval, without prejudice, genially, with approbation, in a kindly manner, with cordiality 2 ADVANTAGEOUSLY, well, fortunately, conveniently, profitably, to your advantage, auspiciously, opportunely

favourite *or US* **favorite** *adjective* PREFERRED, favoured, best-loved, most-liked, special,

choice, dearest, pet, esteemed, fave (*informal*)
▷ *noun* DARLING, pet, preference, blue-eyed
boy (*informal*), pick, choice, dear, beloved,
idol, fave (*informal*), teacher's pet, the apple
of your eye

favouritism *or US* **favoritism** *noun* BIAS,
preference, nepotism, preferential
treatment, partisanship, jobs for the
boys (*informal*), partiality, one-sidedness
<< ANTONYM impartiality

fawn[1] *adjective* BEIGE, neutral, buff, yellowish-
brown, greyish-brown

fawn[2] *verb usually with* **on** *or* **upon** INGRATIATE
YOURSELF, court, flatter, pander to, creep,
crawl, kneel, cringe, grovel, curry favour,
toady, pay court, kowtow, bow and scrape,
dance attendance, truckle, be obsequious, be
servile, lick (someone's) boots

fawning *adjective* OBSEQUIOUS, crawling,
flattering, cringing, abject, grovelling,
prostrate, deferential, sycophantic, servile,
slavish, bowing and scraping, bootlicking
(*informal*)

fear *noun* 1 DREAD, horror, panic, terror,
dismay, awe, fright, tremors, qualms,
consternation, alarm, trepidation,
timidity, fearfulness, blue funk (*informal*),
apprehensiveness, cravenness 2 BUGBEAR,
bête noire, horror, nightmare, anxiety,
terror, dread, spectre, phobia, bogey, thing
(*informal*) 3 ANXIETY, concern, worry, doubt,
nerves (*informal*), distress, suspicion, willies
(*informal*), creeps (*informal*), butterflies
(*informal*), funk (*informal*), angst, unease,
apprehension, misgiving(s), nervousness,
agitation, foreboding(s), uneasiness,
solicitude, blue funk (*informal*), heebie-
jeebies (*informal*), collywobbles (*informal*),
disquietude 4 AWE, wonder, respect,
worship, dread, reverence, veneration ▷
verb 1 BE AFRAID OF, dread, be scared of,
be frightened of, shudder at, be fearful
of, be apprehensive about, tremble at, be
terrified by, have a horror of, take fright at,
have a phobia about, have qualms about,
live in dread of, be in a blue funk about
(*informal*), have butterflies in your stomach
about (*informal*), shake in your shoes about
2 REVERE, respect, reverence, venerate,
stand in awe of 3 REGRET, feel, suspect, have
a feeling, have a hunch, have a sneaking
suspicion, have a funny feeling ▷▷ **fear for
something** *or* **someone** WORRY ABOUT, be
concerned about, be anxious about, tremble
for, be distressed about, feel concern for, be
disquieted over

fearful *adjective* 1 SCARED, afraid, alarmed,
frightened, nervous, terrified, apprehensive,
petrified, jittery (*informal*) << ANTONYM
unafraid 2 TIMID, afraid, frightened, scared,
alarmed, wired (*slang*), nervous, anxious,
shrinking, tense, intimidated, uneasy,
neurotic, hesitant, apprehensive, jittery
(*informal*), panicky, nervy (*Brit informal*),
diffident, jumpy, timorous, pusillanimous,
faint-hearted << ANTONYM brave 3 (*informal*)
FRIGHTFUL, shocking, terrible, awful,
distressing, appalling, horrible, grim,
dreadful, horrific, dire, horrendous, ghastly,
hideous, monstrous, harrowing, gruesome,
grievous, unspeakable, atrocious, hair-
raising, hellacious (*US slang*)

fearfully *adverb* 1 NERVOUSLY, uneasily,
timidly, apprehensively, diffidently, in
fear and trembling, timorously, with
bated breath, with many misgivings *or*
forebodings, with your heart in your
mouth 2 (*informal*) VERY, terribly, horribly,
tremendously, awfully, exceedingly,
excessively, dreadfully, frightfully

fearless *adjective* INTREPID, confident,
brave, daring, bold, heroic, courageous,
gallant, gutsy (*slang*), valiant, plucky, game
(*informal*), doughty, undaunted, indomitable,
unabashed, unafraid, unflinching, dauntless,
lion-hearted, valorous, (as) game as Ned
Kelly (*Austral slang*)

fearsome *adjective* FORMIDABLE, alarming,
frightening, awful, terrifying, appalling,
horrifying, menacing, dismaying, awesome,
daunting, horrendous, unnerving, hair-
raising, awe-inspiring, baleful, hellacious
(*US slang*)

feasibility *noun* POSSIBILITY, viability,
usefulness, expediency, practicability,
workability

feasible *adjective* PRACTICABLE, possible,
reasonable, viable, workable, achievable,
attainable, realizable, likely << ANTONYM
impracticable

feast *noun* 1 BANQUET, repast, spread
(*informal*), dinner, entertainment, barbecue,
revel, junket, beano (*Brit slang*), blowout
(*slang*), carouse, slap-up meal (*Brit informal*),
beanfeast (*Brit informal*), jollification,
carousal, festive board, treat, hakari (*NZ*)
2 FESTIVAL, holiday, fête, celebration, holy
day, red-letter day, religious festival, saint's
day, -fest, gala day 3 TREAT, delight, pleasure,
enjoyment, gratification, cornucopia ▷ *verb*

EAT YOUR FILL, wine and dine, overindulge, eat to your heart's content, stuff yourself, consume, indulge, gorge, devour, pig out (*slang*), stuff your face (*slang*), fare sumptuously, gormandize ▷▷ **feast your eyes on something** LOOK AT WITH DELIGHT, gaze at, devour with your eyes

feat *noun* ACCOMPLISHMENT, act, performance, achievement, enterprise, undertaking, exploit, deed, attainment, feather in your cap

feather *noun* PLUME

feathery *adjective* DOWNY, soft, feathered, fluffy, plumed, wispy, plumy, plumate *or* plumose (*botany, zoology*), light

feature *noun* 1 ASPECT, quality, characteristic, attribute, point, mark, property, factor, trait, hallmark, facet, peculiarity 2 ARTICLE, report, story, piece, comment, item, column 3 HIGHLIGHT, draw, attraction, innovation, speciality, specialty, main item, crowd puller (*informal*), special attraction, special ▷ *plural noun* FACE, countenance, physiognomy, lineament ▷ *verb* 1 SPOTLIGHT, present, promote, set off, emphasize, play up, accentuate, foreground, call attention to, give prominence to, give the full works (*slang*) 2 STAR, appear, headline, participate, play a part

febrile *adjective* (*formal*) FEVERISH, hot, fevered, flushed, fiery, inflamed, delirious, pyretic (*medical*)

feckless *adjective* IRRESPONSIBLE, useless, hopeless, incompetent, feeble, worthless, futile, ineffectual, aimless, good-for-nothing, shiftless, weak

federation *noun* UNION, league, association, alliance, combination, coalition, partnership, consortium, syndicate, confederation, amalgamation, confederacy, entente, Bund (*German*), copartnership, federacy

fed up *adjective* CHEESED OFF, down, depressed, bored, tired, annoyed, hacked (off) (*US slang*), weary, gloomy, blue, dismal, discontented, dissatisfied, glum, sick and tired (*informal*), browned-off (*informal*), down in the mouth (*informal*), brassed off (*Brit slang*), hoha (*NZ*)

fee *noun* CHARGE, pay, price, cost, bill, account, payment, wage, reward, hire, salary, compensation, toll, remuneration, recompense, emolument, honorarium, meed (*archaic*)

feeble *adjective* 1 WEAK, failing, exhausted, weakened, delicate, faint, powerless, frail, debilitated, sickly, languid, puny, weedy (*informal*), infirm, effete, enfeebled, doddering, enervated, etiolated, shilpit (*Scot*) << ANTONYM strong 2 INADEQUATE, weak, pathetic, insufficient, incompetent, ineffective, inefficient, lame, insignificant, ineffectual, indecisive 3 UNCONVINCING, poor, thin, weak, slight, tame, pathetic, lame, flimsy, paltry, flat << ANTONYM effective

feed *verb* 1 CATER FOR, provide for, nourish, provide with food, supply, sustain, nurture, cook for, wine and dine, victual, provision 2 GRAZE, eat, browse, pasture 3 EAT, drink milk, take nourishment 4 SUPPLY, take, send, carry, convey, impart 5 DISCLOSE, give, tell, reveal, supply, communicate, pass on, impart, divulge, make known 6 ENCOURAGE, boost, fuel, strengthen, foster, minister to, bolster, fortify, augment, make stronger ▷ *noun* 1 FOOD, fodder, forage, silage, provender, pasturage 2 (*informal*) MEAL, spread (*informal*), dinner, lunch, tea, breakfast, feast, supper, tuck-in (*informal*), nosh (*slang*), repast, nosh-up (*Brit slang*) ▷▷ **feed on something** LIVE ON, depend on, devour, exist on, partake of, subsist on

feel *verb* 1 EXPERIENCE, suffer, bear, go through, endure, undergo, have a sensation of, have 2 TOUCH, handle, manipulate, run your hands over, finger, stroke, paw, maul, caress, fondle 3 BE AWARE OF, have a sensation of, be sensible of, enjoy 4 PERCEIVE, sense, detect, discern, know, experience, notice, observe 5 GROPE, explore, fumble, sound 6 SENSE, be aware, be convinced, have a feeling, have the impression, intuit, have a hunch, feel in your bones 7 BELIEVE, consider, judge, deem, think, hold, be of the opinion that 8 SEEM, appear, strike you as 9 NOTICE, note, observe, perceive, detect, discern ▷ *noun* 1 TEXTURE, finish, touch, surface, surface quality 2 IMPRESSION, feeling, air, sense, quality, atmosphere, mood, aura, ambience, vibes (*slang*) ▷▷ **feel for someone** FEEL COMPASSION FOR, pity, feel sorry for, sympathize with, be moved by, be sorry for, empathize, commiserate with, bleed for, feel sympathy for, condole with ▷▷ **feel like something** WANT, desire, would like, fancy, wish for, could do with, feel the need for, feel inclined, feel up to, have the inclination for

feeler ▷▷ **put out feelers** APPROACH, probe,

test of the waters, overture, trial, launch a trial balloon

feeling *noun* **1** EMOTION, sentiment **2** OPINION, view, attitude, belief, point of view, instinct, inclination **3** PASSION, heat, emotion, intensity, warmth, sentimentality **4** ARDOUR, love, care, affection, warmth, tenderness, fondness, fervour **5** SYMPATHY, understanding, concern, pity, appreciation, sensitivity, compassion, sorrow, sensibility, empathy, fellow feeling **6** SENSATION, sense, impression, awareness **7** SENSE OF TOUCH, sense, perception, sensation, feel, touch **8** IMPRESSION, idea, sense, notion, suspicion, consciousness, hunch, apprehension, inkling, presentiment **9** ATMOSPHERE, mood, aura, ambience, feel, air, quality, vibes (*slang*) ▷ *plural noun* EMOTIONS, ego, self-esteem, sensibilities, susceptibilities, sensitivities ▷▷ **bad feeling** HOSTILITY, anger, dislike, resentment, bitterness, distrust, enmity, ill feeling, ill will, upset

feign *verb* PRETEND, affect, assume, put on, devise, forge, fake, imitate, simulate, sham, act, fabricate, counterfeit, give the appearance of, dissemble, make a show of

feigned *adjective* PRETENDED, affected, assumed, false, artificial, fake, imitation, simulated, sham, pseudo (*informal*), fabricated, counterfeit, spurious, ersatz, insincere

feint *noun* BLUFF, manoeuvre, dodge, mock attack, play, blind, distraction, pretence, expedient, ruse, artifice, gambit, subterfuge, stratagem, wile

feisty *adjective* (*informal*) FIERY, spirited, bold, plucky, vivacious, (as) game as Ned Kelly (*Austral slang*)

felicity *noun* **1** HAPPINESS, joy, ecstasy, bliss, delectation, blessedness, blissfulness **2** APTNESS, grace, effectiveness, suitability, propriety, appropriateness, applicability, becomingness, suitableness

feline *adjective* **1** CATLIKE, leonine **2** GRACEFUL, flowing, smooth, elegant, sleek, slinky, sinuous, stealthy

fell *verb* **1** CUT DOWN, cut, level, demolish, flatten, knock down, hew, raze **2** KNOCK DOWN, floor, flatten, strike down, prostrate, deck (*slang*)

fellow *noun* **1** (*old-fashioned*) MAN, boy, person, individual, customer (*informal*), character, guy (*informal*), bloke (*Brit informal*), punter (*informal*), chap (*informal*) **2** ASSOCIATE, colleague, peer, co-worker, member, friend, partner, equal, companion, comrade, crony, compeer ▷ *modifier* CO-, similar, related, allied, associate, associated, affiliated, akin, like

fellowship *noun* **1** SOCIETY, club, league, association, organization, guild, fraternity, brotherhood, sisterhood, order, sodality **2** CAMARADERIE, intimacy, communion, familiarity, brotherhood, companionship, sociability, amity, kindliness, fraternization, companionability, intercourse

feminine *adjective* **1** WOMANLY, pretty, soft, gentle, tender, modest, delicate, graceful, girlie, girlish, ladylike << ANTONYM masculine **2** EFFEMINATE, camp (*informal*), weak, unmanly, effete, womanish, unmasculine

femininity *noun* WOMANLINESS, delicacy, softness, womanhood, gentleness, girlishness, feminineness, muliebrity

fen *noun* MARSH, moss (*Scot*), swamp, bog, slough, quagmire, holm (*dialect*), morass, pakihi (*NZ*), muskeg (*Canad*)

fence *noun* BARRIER, wall, defence, guard, railings, paling, shield, hedge, barricade, hedgerow, rampart, palisade, stockade, barbed wire ▷ *verb with* **in** *or* **off** ENCLOSE, surround, bound, hedge, pound, protect, separate, guard, defend, secure, pen, restrict, confine, fortify, encircle, coop, impound, circumscribe ▷▷ **sit on the fence** BE UNCOMMITTED, be uncertain, be undecided, vacillate, be in two minds, blow hot and cold (*informal*), be irresolute, avoid committing yourself

fend ▷▷ **fend for yourself** LOOK AFTER YOURSELF, support yourself, sustain yourself, take care of yourself, provide for yourself, make do, make provision for yourself, shift for yourself ▷▷ **fend something** *or* **someone off** **1** DEFLECT, resist, parry, avert, ward off, stave off, turn aside, hold *or* keep at bay **2** BEAT OFF, resist, parry, avert, deflect, repel, drive back, ward off, stave off, repulse, keep off, turn aside, hold *or* keep at bay

feral *adjective* **1** WILD, untamed, uncultivated, undomesticated, unbroken **2** SAVAGE, fierce, brutal, ferocious, fell, wild, vicious, bestial

ferment *noun* COMMOTION, turmoil, unrest, turbulence, trouble, heat, excitement, glow, fever, disruption, frenzy, stew, furore, uproar, agitation, tumult, hubbub, brouhaha, imbroglio, state of unrest << ANTONYM tranquillity ▷ *verb* **1** BREW, froth, concoct, effervesce, work, rise, heat, boil, bubble, foam, seethe, leaven 2 STIR UP, excite, provoke, rouse, agitate, inflame, incite

ferocious adjective 1 FIERCE, violent, savage, ravening, predatory, feral, rapacious, wild << ANTONYM gentle 2 CRUEL, bitter, brutal, vicious, ruthless, relentless, barbaric, merciless, brutish, bloodthirsty, barbarous, pitiless, tigerish

ferocity noun SAVAGERY, violence, cruelty, brutality, ruthlessness, inhumanity, wildness, barbarity, viciousness, fierceness, rapacity, bloodthirstiness, savageness, ferociousness

ferry noun FERRY BOAT, boat, ship, passenger boat, packet boat, packet ▷ verb TRANSPORT, bring, carry, ship, take, run, shuttle, convey, chauffeur

fertile adjective PRODUCTIVE, rich, flowering, lush, fat, yielding, prolific, abundant, plentiful, fruitful, teeming, luxuriant, generative, fecund, fruit-bearing, flowing with milk and honey, plenteous << ANTONYM barren

fertility noun FRUITFULNESS, abundance, richness, fecundity, luxuriance, productiveness

fertilization or **fertilisation** noun INSEMINATION, propagation, procreation, implantation, pollination, impregnation

fertilize or **fertilise** verb 1 INSEMINATE, impregnate, pollinate, make pregnant, fructify, make fruitful, fecundate 2 ENRICH, feed, compost, manure, mulch, top-dress, dress, fertigate (Austral)

fertilizer or **fertiliser** noun COMPOST, muck, manure, dung, guano, marl, bone meal, dressing

fervent adjective ARDENT, earnest, enthusiastic, fervid, passionate, warm, excited, emotional, intense, flaming, eager, animated, fiery, ecstatic, devout, heartfelt, impassioned, zealous, vehement, perfervid (literary) << ANTONYM apathetic

fervour or US **fervor** noun ARDOUR, passion, enthusiasm, excitement, intensity, warmth, animation, zeal, eagerness, vehemence, earnestness, fervency

fester verb 1 INTENSIFY, gall, smoulder, chafe, irk, rankle, aggravate 2 PUTREFY, decay, become infected, become inflamed, suppurate, ulcerate, maturate, gather

festering adjective SEPTIC, infected, poisonous, inflamed, pussy, suppurating, ulcerated, purulent, maturating, gathering

festival noun 1 CELEBRATION, fair, carnival, gala, treat, fête, entertainment, jubilee, fiesta, festivities, jamboree, -fest, field day 2 HOLY DAY, holiday, feast, commemoration, feast day, red-letter day, saint's day, fiesta, fête, anniversary

festive adjective CELEBRATORY, happy, holiday, carnival, jolly, merry, gala, hearty, jubilant, cheery, joyous, joyful, jovial, convivial, gleeful, back-slapping, Christmassy, mirthful, sportive, light-hearted, festal, gay << ANTONYM mournful

festivity noun 1 MERRYMAKING, fun, pleasure, amusement, mirth, gaiety, merriment, revelry, conviviality, joviality, joyfulness, jollification, sport 2 often plural CELEBRATION, party, festival, entertainment, rave (Brit slang), beano (Brit slang), fun and games, rave-up (Brit slang), jollification, festive event, carousal, festive proceedings, hooley or hoolie (chiefly Irish & NZ)

festoon noun DECORATION, garland, swathe, wreath, swag, lei, chaplet ▷ verb DECORATE, deck, array, drape, garland, swathe, bedeck, wreathe, beribbon, engarland, hang

fetch verb 1 BRING, pick up, collect, go and get, get, carry, deliver, conduct, transport, go for, obtain, escort, convey, retrieve 2 SELL FOR, make, raise, earn, realize, go for, yield, bring in ▷▷ **fetch up** (informal) END UP, reach, arrive, turn up, come, stop, land, halt, finish up

fetching adjective (informal) ATTRACTIVE, sweet, charming, enchanting, fascinating, intriguing, cute, enticing, captivating, alluring, winsome

fête or **fete** noun FAIR, festival, gala, bazaar, garden party, sale of work ▷ verb ENTERTAIN, welcome, honour, make much of, wine and dine, hold a reception for (someone), lionize, bring out the red carpet for (someone), kill the fatted calf for (someone), treat

fetish noun 1 FIXATION, obsession, mania, thing (informal), idée fixe (French) 2 TALISMAN, amulet, cult object

fetter plural noun 1 RESTRAINTS, checks, curbs, constraints, captivity, obstructions, bondage, hindrances 2 CHAINS, bonds, irons, shackles, manacles, leg irons, gyves (archaic), bilboes ▷ verb 1 RESTRICT, bind, confine, curb, restrain, hamstring, hamper, encumber, clip someone's wings, trammel, straiten 2 CHAIN, tie, tie up, shackle, hobble, hold captive, manacle, gyve (archaic), put a straitjacket on

feud noun HOSTILITY, row, conflict, argument, faction, falling out, disagreement, rivalry, contention, quarrel, grudge, strife, bickering, vendetta, discord, enmity, broil, bad blood, estrangement, dissension ▷ *verb* QUARREL, row, clash, dispute, fall out, contend, brawl, war, squabble, duel, bicker, be at odds, be at daggers drawn

fever *noun* 1 AGUE, high temperature, feverishness, pyrexia (*medical*) 2 EXCITEMENT, heat, passion, intensity, flush, turmoil, ecstasy, frenzy, ferment, agitation, fervour, restlessness, delirium

fevered *adjective* FRANTIC, excited, desperate, distracted, frenzied, impatient, obsessive, restless, agitated, frenetic, overwrought

feverish *or* **feverous** *adjective* 1 FRANTIC, excited, desperate, distracted, frenzied, impatient, obsessive, restless, agitated, frenetic, overwrought << ANTONYM calm 2 HOT, burning, flaming, fevered, flushed, hectic, inflamed, febrile, pyretic (*medical*)

few *adjective* NOT MANY, one or two, hardly any, scarcely any, rare, thin, scattered, insufficient, scarce, scant, meagre, negligible, sporadic, sparse, infrequent, scanty, inconsiderable << ANTONYM many ▷ *pronoun* A SMALL NUMBER, a handful, a sprinkling, a scattering, some, scarcely any ▷▷ **few and far between** SCARCE, rare, unusual, scattered, irregular, uncommon, in short supply, hard to come by, infrequent, thin on the ground, widely spaced, seldom met with

fiancé *or* **fiancée** *noun* HUSBAND- *or* WIFE-TO-BE, intended, betrothed, prospective spouse, future husband *or* wife

fiasco *noun* FLOP, failure, disaster, ruin, mess (*informal*), catastrophe, rout, debacle, cock-up (*Brit slang*), washout (*informal*)

fib *noun* LIE, story, fiction, untruth, whopper (*informal*), porky (*Brit slang*), pork pie (*Brit slang*), white lie, prevarication

fibre *or* US **fiber** *noun* THREAD, strand, filament, tendril, pile, texture, staple, wisp, fibril ▷▷ **moral fibre** STRENGTH OF CHARACTER, strength, resolution, resolve, stamina, backbone, toughness

fickle *adjective* CAPRICIOUS, variable, volatile, unpredictable, unstable, unfaithful, temperamental, mercurial, unsteady, faithless, changeable, quicksilver, vacillating, fitful, flighty, blowing hot and cold, mutable, irresolute, inconstant << ANTONYM constant

fiction *noun* 1 TALE, story, novel, legend, myth, romance, fable, storytelling,

narration, creative writing, work of imagination 2 IMAGINATION, fancy, fantasy, creativity 3 LIE, fancy, fantasy, invention, improvisation, fabrication, concoction, falsehood, untruth, porky (*Brit slang*), pork pie (*Brit slang*), urban myth, tall story, urban legend, cock and bull story (*informal*), figment of the imagination

fictional *adjective* IMAGINARY, made-up, invented, legendary, unreal, nonexistent

fictitious *adjective* 1 FALSE, made-up, bogus, untrue, non-existent, fabricated, counterfeit, feigned, spurious, apocryphal << ANTONYM true 2 IMAGINARY, imagined, made-up, assumed, invented, artificial, improvised, mythical, unreal, fanciful, make-believe

fiddle *noun* 1 (*Brit informal*) FRAUD, racket, scam (*slang*), piece of sharp practice, fix, sting (*informal*), graft (*informal*), swindle, wangle (*informal*) 2 (*informal*) VIOLIN ▷ *verb* (*informal*) 1 *often with* with FIDGET, play, finger, toy, tamper, trifle, mess about *or* around 2 *often with* with TINKER, adjust, interfere, mess about *or* around 3 CHEAT, cook (*informal*), fix, manoeuvre (*informal*), graft (*informal*), diddle (*informal*), wangle (*informal*), gerrymander, finagle (*informal*)

fiddling *adjective* TRIVIAL, small, petty, trifling, insignificant, unimportant, pettifogging, futile

fidelity *noun* 1 LOYALTY, faith, integrity, devotion, allegiance, constancy, faithfulness, dependability, trustworthiness, troth (*archaic*), fealty, staunchness, devotedness, lealty (*archaic, Scot*), true-heartedness << ANTONYM disloyalty 2 ACCURACY, precision, correspondence, closeness, adherence, faithfulness, exactitude, exactness, scrupulousness, preciseness << ANTONYM inaccuracy

fidget *verb* MOVE RESTLESSLY, fiddle (*informal*), bustle, twitch, fret, squirm, chafe, jiggle, jitter (*informal*), be like a cat on hot bricks (*informal*), worry

field *noun* 1 MEADOW, land, green, lea (*poetic*), pasture, mead (*archaic*), greensward (*archaic or literary*) 2 SPECIALITY, line, area, department, environment, territory, discipline, province, pale, confines, sphere, domain, specialty, sphere of influence, purview, metier, sphere of activity, bailiwick, sphere of interest, sphere of study 3 LINE, reach, range, limits, bounds, sweep, scope 4 COMPETITORS, competition, candidates, runners, applicants, entrants, contestants ▷

verb **1** (*informal*) DEAL WITH, answer, handle, respond to, reply to, deflect, turn aside **2** (*sport*) RETRIEVE, return, stop, catch, pick up

fiend *noun* **1** BRUTE, monster, savage, beast, degenerate, barbarian, ogre, ghoul **2** (*informal*) ENTHUSIAST, fan, addict, freak (*informal*), fanatic, maniac, energumen **3** DEMON, devil, evil spirit, hellhound, atua (*NZ*)

fiendish *adjective* **1** (*informal*) DIFFICULT, involved, complex, puzzling, baffling, intricate, thorny, knotty **2** WICKED, cruel, savage, monstrous, malicious, satanic, malignant, unspeakable, atrocious, inhuman, diabolical, implacable, malevolent, hellish, devilish, infernal, accursed, ungodly, black-hearted, demoniac

fierce *adjective* **1** FEROCIOUS, wild, dangerous, cruel, savage, brutal, aggressive, menacing, vicious, fiery, murderous, uncontrollable, feral, untamed, barbarous, fell (*archaic*), threatening, baleful, truculent, tigerish, aggers (*Austral slang*), biffo (*Austral slang*) << ANTONYM gentle **2** INTENSE, strong, keen, passionate, relentless, cut-throat **3** STORMY, strong, powerful, violent, intense, raging, furious, howling, uncontrollable, boisterous, tumultuous, tempestuous, blustery, inclement << ANTONYM tranquil

fiercely *adverb* FEROCIOUSLY, savagely, passionately, furiously, viciously, menacingly, tooth and nail, in a frenzy, like cat and dog, frenziedly, tigerishly, with no holds barred, tempestuously, with bared teeth, uncontrolledly

fiery *adjective* **1** BURNING, flaming, glowing, blazing, on fire, red-hot, ablaze, in flames, aflame, afire **2** EXCITABLE, violent, fierce, passionate, irritable, impetuous, irascible, peppery, hot-headed, choleric

fiesta *noun* CARNIVAL, party, holiday, fair, fête, festival, celebration, feast, revel, jubilee, festivity, jamboree, Mardi Gras, revelry, Saturnalia, saint's day, merrymaking, carousal, bacchanal *or* bacchanalia, gala

fight *verb* **1** OPPOSE, campaign against, dispute, contest, resist, defy, contend, withstand, stand up to, take issue with, make a stand against **2** STRIVE, battle, push, struggle, contend **3** BATTLE, assault, combat, war with, go to war, do battle, wage war, take up arms, bear arms against, engage in hostilities, carry on war, engage **4** ENGAGE IN, conduct, wage, pursue, carry on **5** TAKE THE FIELD, cross swords, taste battle **6** BRAWL, clash, scrap (*informal*), exchange blows, struggle, row, tilt, wrestle, feud, grapple, tussle, joust, come to blows, lock horns, fight like Kilkenny cats **7** BOX, spar with, exchange blows with ▷ *noun* **1** BATTLE, campaign, movement, struggle **2** CONFLICT, war, action, clash, contest, encounter, brush, combat, engagement, hostilities, skirmish, passage of arms **3** BRAWL, set-to (*informal*), riot, scrap (*informal*), confrontation, rumble (*US & NZ slang*), fray, duel, skirmish, head-to-head, tussle, scuffle, free-for-all (*informal*), fracas, altercation, dogfight, joust, dissension, affray (*law*), shindig (*informal*), scrimmage, sparring match, exchange of blows, shindy (*informal*), melee *or* mêlée, biffo (*Austral slang*), boilover (*Austral*) **4** ROW, argument, dispute, quarrel, squabble **5** MATCH, contest, bout, battle, competition, struggle, set-to, encounter, engagement, head-to-head, boxing match **6** RESISTANCE, spirit, pluck, militancy, mettle, belligerence, will to resist, gameness, pluckiness ▷▷ **fight shy of something** AVOID, shun, steer clear of, duck out of (*informal*), keep at arm's length, hang back from, keep aloof from

fighter *noun* **1** COMBATANT, battler, militant, contender, contestant, belligerent, antagonist, disputant **2** BOXER, wrestler, bruiser (*informal*), pugilist, prize fighter **3** SOLDIER, warrior, fighting man, man-at-arms

figment *noun* INVENTION, production, fancy, creation, fiction, fable, improvisation, fabrication, falsehood

figurative *adjective* SYMBOLICAL, representative, abstract, allegorical, typical, tropical (*rhetoric*), imaginative, ornate, descriptive, fanciful, pictorial, metaphorical, flowery, florid, poetical, emblematical << ANTONYM literal

figure *noun* **1** DIGIT, character, symbol, number, numeral, cipher **2** OUTLINE, form, shape, shadow, profile, silhouette **3** SHAPE, build, body, frame, proportions, chassis (*slang*), torso, physique **4** PERSONAGE, force, face (*informal*), leader, person, individual, character, presence, somebody, personality, celebrity, worthy, notable, big name, dignitary, notability **5** DIAGRAM, drawing, picture, illustration, representation, sketch, emblem **6** DESIGN, shape, pattern, device, motif, depiction **7** PRICE, cost, value, amount, total, sum ▷ *verb* **1** (*informal*) MAKE

SENSE, follow, be expected, add up, go without saying, seem reasonable **2** *usually with* **in** FEATURE, act, appear, contribute to, be included, be mentioned, play a part, be featured, have a place in, be conspicuous **3** CALCULATE, work out, compute, tot up, add, total, count, reckon, sum, tally ▷▷ **figure on something** (*US, Canad & NZ informal*) PLAN ON, depend on, rely on, count on, bargain on ▷▷ **figure something out** (*informal*) CALCULATE, reckon, work out, compute ▷▷ **figure something** *or* **someone out** UNDERSTAND, make out, fathom, make head or tail of (*informal*), see, solve, resolve, comprehend, make sense of, decipher, think through, suss (out) (*slang*)

figurehead *noun* NOMINAL HEAD, leader in name only, titular head, front man, name, token, dummy, puppet, mouthpiece, cipher, nonentity, straw man (*chiefly US*), man of straw

figure of speech *noun* EXPRESSION, image, turn of phrase, trope

filament *noun* STRAND, string, wire, fibre, thread, staple, wisp, cilium (*biology, zoology*), fibril, pile

file¹ *noun* **1** FOLDER, case, portfolio, binder **2** DOSSIER, record, information, data, documents, case history, report, case **3** LINE, row, chain, string, column, queue, procession ▷ *verb* **1** ARRANGE, order, classify, put in place, slot in (*informal*), categorize, pigeonhole, put in order **2** REGISTER, record, enter, log, put on record **3** MARCH, troop, parade, walk in line, walk behind one another

file² *verb* SMOOTH, shape, polish, rub, refine, scrape, rasp, burnish, rub down, abrade

filibuster *noun* OBSTRUCTION, delay, postponement, hindrance, procrastination ▷ *verb* OBSTRUCT, prevent, delay, put off, hinder, play for time, procrastinate

filigree *noun* WIREWORK, lace, lattice, tracery, lacework

fill *verb* **1** TOP UP, fill up, make full, become full, brim over **2** SWELL, expand, inflate, become bloated, extend, balloon, fatten **3** PACK, crowd, squeeze, cram, throng **4** STOCK, supply, store, pack, load, furnish, replenish **5** PLUG, close, stop, seal, cork, bung, block up, stop up **6** SATURATE, charge, pervade, permeate, imbue, impregnate, suffuse, overspread **7** FULFIL, hold, perform, carry out, occupy, take up, execute, discharge, officiate **8** *often with*

up SATISFY, stuff, gorge, glut, satiate, sate ▷▷ **fill in for someone** REPLACE, represent, substitute for, cover for, take over from, act for, stand in for, sub for, deputize for ▷▷ **fill someone in** (*informal*) INFORM, acquaint, advise of, apprise of, bring up to date with, update with, put wise to (*slang*), give the facts *or* background of ▷▷ **fill something in** COMPLETE, answer, fill up, fill out (*US*) ▷▷ **your fill** SUFFICIENT, enough, plenty, ample, all you want, a sufficiency

filling *noun* STUFFING, padding, filler, wadding, inside, insides, contents, innards (*informal*) ▷ *adjective* SATISFYING, heavy, square, substantial, ample

fillip *noun* BOOST, push, spur, spice, incentive, stimulus, prod, zest, goad

film *noun* **1** MOVIE, picture, flick (*slang*), motion picture **2** CINEMA, the movies **3** LAYER, covering, cover, skin, coating, coat, dusting, tissue, membrane, scum, gauze, integument, pellicle **4** HAZE, cloud, blur, mist, veil, opacity, haziness, mistiness ▷ *verb* **1** PHOTOGRAPH, record, shoot, video, videotape, take **2** ADAPT FOR THE SCREEN, make into a film

filter *noun* SIEVE, mesh, gauze, strainer, membrane, riddle, sifter ▷ *verb* **1** TRICKLE, leach, seep, percolate, well, escape, leak, penetrate, ooze, dribble, exude **2** *with* **through** PURIFY, treat, strain, refine, riddle, sift, sieve, winnow, filtrate, screen

filth *noun* **1** DIRT, refuse, pollution, muck, garbage, sewage, contamination, dung, sludge, squalor, grime, faeces, slime, excrement, nastiness, carrion, excreta, crud (*slang*), foulness, putrefaction, ordure, defilement, grot (*slang*), filthiness, uncleanness, putrescence, foul matter **2** OBSCENITY, corruption, pornography, indecency, impurity, vulgarity, smut, vileness, dirty-mindedness

filthy *adjective* **1** DIRTY, nasty, foul, polluted, vile, squalid, slimy, unclean, putrid, faecal, scummy, scuzzy (*slang, chiefly US*), feculent, festy (*Austral slang*) **2** GRIMY, black, muddy, smoky, blackened, grubby, sooty, unwashed, mucky, scuzzy (*slang, chiefly US*), begrimed, mud-encrusted, miry, festy (*Austral slang*) **3** OBSCENE, foul, corrupt, coarse, indecent, pornographic, suggestive, lewd, depraved, foul-mouthed, X-rated (*informal*), bawdy, impure, smutty, licentious, dirty-minded **4** DESPICABLE, mean, low, base, offensive, vicious, vile, contemptible, scurvy

final *adjective* **1** LAST, latest, end, closing, finishing, concluding, ultimate, terminal, last-minute, eventual, terminating
<< ANTONYM first **2** IRREVOCABLE, absolute, decisive, definitive, decided, finished, settled, definite, conclusive, irrefutable, incontrovertible, unalterable, determinate

finale *noun* CLIMAX, ending, close, conclusion, culmination, denouement, last part, epilogue, last act, crowning glory, finis
<< ANTONYM opening

finality *noun* CONCLUSIVENESS, resolution, decisiveness, certitude, definiteness, irrevocability, inevitableness, unavoidability, decidedness

finalize *or* **finalise** *verb* COMPLETE, settle, conclude, tie up, decide, agree, work out, clinch, wrap up (*informal*), shake hands, sew up (*informal*), complete the arrangements for

finally *adverb* **1** EVENTUALLY, at last, in the end, ultimately, at the last, at the end of the day, in the long run, at length, at the last moment, at long last, when all is said and done, in the fullness of time, after a long time **2** LASTLY, in the end, ultimately **3** IN CONCLUSION, lastly, in closing, to conclude, to sum up, in summary **4** CONCLUSIVELY, for good, permanently, for ever, completely, definitely, once and for all, decisively, convincingly, inexorably, irrevocably, for all time, inescapably, beyond the shadow of a doubt

finance *noun* ECONOMICS, business, money, banking, accounts, investment, commerce, financial affairs, money management ▷ *plural noun* RESOURCES, money, funds, capital, cash, affairs, budgeting, assets, cash flow, financial affairs, money management, wherewithal, financial condition ▷ *verb* FUND, back, support, pay for, guarantee, float, invest in, underwrite, endow, subsidize, bankroll (*US*), set up in business, provide security for, provide money for

financial *adjective* ECONOMIC, business, money, budgeting, budgetary, commercial, monetary, fiscal, pecuniary

find *verb* **1** DISCOVER, turn up, uncover, unearth, spot, expose, come up with, locate, detect, come across, track down, catch sight of, stumble upon, hit upon, espy, ferret out, chance upon, light upon, put your finger on, lay your hand on, run to ground, run to earth, descry << ANTONYM lose **2** REGAIN, recover, get back, retrieve, repossess **3** OBTAIN, get, come by, procure, win, gain,

achieve, earn, acquire, attain **4** ENCOUNTER, meet, recognize **5** OBSERVE, learn, note, discover, notice, realize, remark, come up with, arrive at, perceive, detect, become aware of, experience, ascertain **6** FEEL, have, experience, sense, obtain, know **7** PROVIDE, supply, contribute, furnish, cough up (*informal*), purvey, be responsible for, bring ▷ *noun* DISCOVERY, catch, asset, bargain, acquisition, good buy ▷▷ **find someone out** DETECT, catch, unmask, rumble (*Brit informal*), reveal, expose, disclose, uncover, suss (out) (*slang*), bring to light ▷▷ **find something out** LEARN, discover, realize, observe, perceive, detect, become aware, come to know, note

finding *noun* (*law*) JUDGMENT, ruling, decision, award, conclusion, verdict, recommendation, decree, pronouncement

fine¹ *adjective* **1** EXCELLENT, good, great, striking, choice, beautiful, masterly, select, rare, very good, supreme, impressive, outstanding, magnificent, superior, accomplished, sterling, first-class, divine, exceptional, splendid, world-class, exquisite, admirable, skilful, ornate, first-rate, showy << ANTONYM poor **2** SATISFACTORY, good, all right, suitable, acceptable, convenient, agreeable, hunky-dory (*informal*), fair, O.K. *or* okay (*informal*) **3** THIN, small, light, narrow, wispy **4** DELICATE, light, thin, sheer, lightweight, flimsy, wispy, gossamer, diaphanous, gauzy, chiffony << ANTONYM coarse **5** STYLISH, expensive, elegant, refined, tasteful, quality, schmick (*Austral informal*) **6** EXQUISITE, delicate, fragile, dainty **7** MINUTE, exact, precise, nice **8** KEEN, minute, nice, quick, sharp, critical, acute, sensitive, subtle, precise, refined, discriminating, tenuous, fastidious, hairsplitting **9** BRILLIANT, quick, keen, alert, clever, intelligent, penetrating, astute **10** SHARP, keen, polished, honed, razor-sharp, cutting **11** GOOD-LOOKING, striking, pretty, attractive, lovely, smart, handsome, stylish, bonny, well-favoured **12** SUNNY, clear, fair, dry, bright, pleasant, clement, balmy, cloudless << ANTONYM cloudy **13** PURE, clear, refined, unadulterated, unalloyed, unpolluted, solid, sterling

fine² *noun* PENALTY, damages, punishment, forfeit, financial penalty, amercement (*obsolete*) ▷ *verb* PENALIZE, charge, punish

finery *noun* SPLENDOUR, trappings, frippery, glad rags (*informal*), gear (*informal*), decorations, ornaments, trinkets, Sunday best, gewgaws, showiness, best bib and tucker (*informal*)

finesse *noun* 1 SKILL, style, know-how (*informal*), polish, craft, sophistication, cleverness, quickness, adroitness, adeptness 2 DIPLOMACY, discretion, subtlety, delicacy, tact, savoir-faire, artfulness, adeptness ▷ *verb* MANOEUVRE, steer, manipulate, bluff

finger *verb* TOUCH, feel, handle, play with, manipulate, paw (*informal*), maul, toy with, fiddle with (*informal*), meddle with, play about with ▷▷ **put your finger on something** IDENTIFY, place, remember, discover, indicate, recall, find out, locate, pin down, bring to mind, hit upon, hit the nail on the head

finish *verb* 1 STOP, close, complete, achieve, conclude, cease, accomplish, execute, discharge, culminate, wrap up (*informal*), terminate, round off, bring to a close *or* conclusion << ANTONYM start 2 GET DONE, complete, put the finishing touch(es) to, finalize, do, deal with, settle, conclude, fulfil, carry through, get out of the way, make short work of 3 END, stop, conclude, wind up, terminate 4 CONSUME, dispose of, devour, polish off, drink, eat, drain, get through, dispatch, deplete 5 USE UP, use, spend, empty, exhaust, expend 6 COAT, polish, stain, texture, wax, varnish, gild, veneer, lacquer, smooth off, face 7 *often with* **off** DESTROY, defeat, overcome, bring down, best, worst, ruin, get rid of, dispose of, rout, put an end to, overpower, annihilate, put paid to, move in for the kill, drive to the wall, administer *or* give the coup de grâce 8 *often with* **off** KILL, murder, destroy, do in (*slang*), take out (*slang*), massacre, butcher, slaughter, dispatch, slay, eradicate, do away with, blow away (*slang, chiefly US*), knock off (*slang*), annihilate, exterminate, take (someone's) life, bump off (*slang*) ▷ *noun* 1 END, ending, close, closing, conclusion, run-in, winding up (*informal*), wind-up, completion, finale, termination, culmination, cessation, last stage(s), denouement, finalization << ANTONYM beginning 2 SURFACE, appearance, polish, shine, grain, texture, glaze, veneer, lacquer, lustre, smoothness, patina

finished *adjective* 1 OVER, done, completed, achieved, through, ended, closed, full, final, complete, in the past, concluded, shut, accomplished, executed, tied up, wrapped up (*informal*), terminated, sewn up (*informal*), finalized, over and done with << ANTONYM begun 2 RUINED, done for (*informal*), doomed, bankrupt, through, lost, gone, defeated, devastated, wrecked, wiped out, undone, washed up (*informal, chiefly US*), wound up, liquidated

finite *adjective* LIMITED, bounded, restricted, demarcated, conditioned, circumscribed, delimited, terminable, subject to limitations << ANTONYM infinite

fire *noun* 1 FLAMES, blaze, combustion, inferno, conflagration, holocaust 2 PASSION, force, light, energy, heat, spirit, enthusiasm, excitement, dash, intensity, sparkle, life, vitality, animation, vigour, zeal, splendour, verve, fervour, eagerness, dynamism, lustre, radiance, virtuosity, élan, ardour, brio, vivacity, impetuosity, burning passion, scintillation, fervency, pizzazz *or* pizazz (*informal*) 3 BOMBARDMENT, shooting, firing, shelling, hail, volley, barrage, gunfire, sniping, flak, salvo, fusillade, cannonade ▷ *verb* 1 LET OFF, shoot, launch, shell, loose, set off, discharge, hurl, eject, detonate, let loose (*informal*), touch off 2 SHOOT, explode, discharge, detonate, pull the trigger 3 (*informal*) DISMISS, sack (*informal*), get rid of, discharge, lay off, make redundant, cashier, give notice, show the door, give the boot (*slang*), kiss off (*slang, chiefly US & Canad*), give the push, give the bullet (*Brit slang*), give marching orders, give someone their cards, give the sack to (*informal*), kennet (*Austral slang*), jeff (*Austral slang*) 4 INSPIRE, excite, stir, stimulate, motivate, irritate, arouse, awaken, animate, rouse, stir up, quicken, inflame, incite, electrify, enliven, spur on, galvanize, inspirit, impassion 5 SET FIRE TO, torch, ignite, set on fire, kindle, set alight, set ablaze, put a match to, set aflame, enkindle, light ▷▷ **on fire** 1 BURNING, flaming, blazing, alight, ablaze, in flames, aflame, fiery 2 ARDENT, excited, inspired, eager, enthusiastic, passionate, fervent

firearm *noun* GUN, weapon, handgun, revolver, shooter (*slang*), piece (*slang*), rod (*slang*), pistol, heater (*US slang*)

firebrand *noun* RABBLE-ROUSER, activist, incendiary, fomenter, instigator, agitator, demagogue, tub-thumper, soapbox orator

fireworks *plural noun* 1 PYROTECHNICS, illuminations, feux d'artifice 2 (*informal*) TROUBLE, row, storm, rage, temper, wax (*informal, chiefly Brit*), uproar, hysterics, paroxysms, fit of rage

firm[1] *adjective* **1** HARD, solid, compact, dense, set, concentrated, stiff, compacted, rigid, compressed, inflexible, solidified, unyielding, congealed, inelastic, jelled, close-grained, jellified << ANTONYM soft **2** SECURE, strong, fixed, secured, rooted, stable, steady, anchored, braced, robust, cemented, fast, sturdy, embedded, fastened, riveted, taut, stationary, motionless, immovable, unmoving, unshakeable, unfluctuating << ANTONYM unstable **3** STRONG, close, tight, steady **4** STRICT, unwavering, unswerving, unshakeable, constant, stalwart, resolute, inflexible, steadfast, unyielding, immovable, unflinching, unbending, obdurate, unalterable, unfaltering **5** DETERMINED, true, settled, fixed, resolved, strict, definite, set on, adamant, stalwart, staunch, resolute, inflexible, steadfast, unyielding, unwavering, immovable, unflinching, unswerving, unbending, obdurate, unshakeable, unalterable, unshaken, unfaltering << ANTONYM wavering **6** DEFINITE, hard, clear, confirmed, settled, fixed, hard-and-fast, cut-and-dried (*informal*)

firm[2] *noun* COMPANY, business, concern, association, organization, house, corporation, venture, enterprise, partnership, establishment, undertaking, outfit (*informal*), consortium, conglomerate

firmament *noun* SKY, skies, heaven, heavens, the blue, vault, welkin (*archaic*), empyrean (*poetic*), vault of heaven, rangi (NZ)

firmly *adverb* **1** SECURELY, safely, tightly **2** IMMOVABLY, securely, steadily, like a rock, unflinchingly, enduringly, motionlessly, unshakeably **3** STEADILY, securely, tightly, unflinchingly **4** RESOLUTELY, strictly, staunchly, steadfastly, determinedly, through thick and thin, with decision, with a rod of iron, definitely, unwaveringly, unchangeably

firmness *noun* **1** HARDNESS, resistance, density, rigidity, stiffness, solidity, inflexibility, compactness, fixedness, inelasticity **2** STEADINESS, tension, stability, tightness, soundness, tautness, tensile strength, immovability **3** STRENGTH, tightness, steadiness **4** RESOLVE, resolution, constancy, inflexibility, steadfastness, obduracy, strictness, strength of will, fixity, fixedness, staunchness

first *adjective* **1** EARLIEST, initial, opening, introductory, original, maiden, primitive, primordial, primeval, pristine **2** TOP, best, winning, premier **3** ELEMENTARY, key, basic, primary, fundamental, cardinal, rudimentary, elemental **4** FOREMOST, highest, greatest, leading, head, ruling, chief, prime, supreme, principal, paramount, overriding, pre-eminent ▷ *noun* **1** NOVELTY, innovation, originality, new experience **2** *usually in phrase* **from the first** START, beginning, outset, the very beginning, introduction, starting point, inception, commencement, the word 'go' (*informal*) ▷ *adverb* TO BEGIN WITH, firstly, initially, at the beginning, in the first place, beforehand, to start with, at the outset, before all else

first class *or* **first-class** *adjective* EXCELLENT, great, very good, superb, topping (*Brit slang*), top, tops (*slang*), bad (*slang*), prime, capital, choice, champion, cool (*informal*), brilliant, crack (*slang*), mean (*slang*), cracking (*Brit informal*), crucial (*slang*), outstanding, premium, ace (*informal*), marvellous, exceptional, mega (*slang*), sovereign, dope (*slang*), world-class, blue-chip, top-flight, top-class, five-star, exemplary, wicked (*slang*), first-rate, def (*slang*), superlative, second to none, top-notch (*informal*), brill (*informal*), top-drawer, matchless, tiptop, boffo (*slang*), jim-dandy (*slang*), twenty-four carat, A1 *or* A-one (*informal*), bitchin' (*US slang*), chillin' (*US slang*), booshit (*Austral slang*), exo (*Austral slang*), sik (*Austral slang*), rad (*informal*), phat (*slang*), schmick (*Austral informal*) << ANTONYM terrible

first-hand *adjective* DIRECT, personal, immediate, face-to-face, straight from the horse's mouth ▷▷ **at first hand** DIRECTLY, personally, immediately, face-to-face, straight from the horse's mouth

first-rate (*informal*) *adjective* EXCELLENT, outstanding, first class, exceptional, mean (*slang*), topping (*Brit slang*), top, tops (*slang*), prime, cool (*informal*), crack (*slang*), cracking (*Brit informal*), crucial (*slang*), exclusive, superb, mega (*slang*), sovereign, dope (*slang*), world-class, admirable, wicked (*slang*), def (*slang*), superlative, second to none, top-notch (*informal*), brill (*informal*), tiptop, bodacious (*slang, chiefly US*), boffo (*slang*), jim-dandy (*slang*), A1 *or* A-one (*informal*), bitchin' (*US slang*), chillin' (*US slang*), booshit (*Austral slang*), exo (*Austral slang*), sik (*Austral slang*), rad (*informal*), phat (*slang*), schmick (*Austral informal*)

fiscal *adjective* FINANCIAL, money, economic, monetary, budgetary, pecuniary, tax

fish *verb* 1 ANGLE, net, cast, trawl 2 LOOK (FOR), search, delve, ferret, rummage, fossick (*Austral & NZ*) ▷▷ **fish for something** SEEK, look for, angle for, try to get, hope for, hunt for, hint at, elicit, solicit, invite, search for ▷▷ **fish something out** *verb* PULL OUT, produce, take out, extract, bring out, extricate, haul out, find

fishy *adjective* 1 FISHLIKE, piscine, piscatorial, piscatory 2 (*informal*) SUSPICIOUS, odd, suspect, unlikely, funny (*informal*), doubtful, dubious, dodgy (*Brit, Austral & NZ informal*), queer, rum (*Brit slang*), questionable, improbable, implausible, cock-and-bull (*informal*), shonky (*Austral & NZ informal*)

fission *noun* SPLITTING, parting, breaking, division, rending, rupture, cleavage, schism, scission

fissure *noun* CRACK, opening, hole, split, gap, rent, fault, breach, break, fracture, rift, slit, rupture, cleavage, cleft, chink, crevice, cranny, interstice

fit¹ *verb* 1 ADAPT, fashion, shape, arrange, alter, adjust, modify, tweak (*informal*), customize 2 PLACE, position, insert 3 ATTACH, join, connect, interlock 4 SUIT, meet, match, belong to, agree with, go with, conform to, correspond to, accord with, be appropriate to, concur with, tally with, dovetail with, be consonant with 5 EQUIP, provide, arm, prepare, outfit, accommodate, fit out, kit out, rig out, accoutre ▷ *adjective* 1 APPROPRIATE, qualified, suitable, competent, right, becoming, meet (*archaic*), seemly, trained, able, prepared, fitting, fitted, ready, skilled, correct, deserving, capable, adapted, proper, equipped, good enough, adequate, worthy, convenient, apt, well-suited, expedient, apposite << ANTONYM inappropriate 2 HEALTHY, strong, robust, sturdy, well, trim, strapping, hale, in good shape, in good condition, in good health, toned up, as right as rain, in good trim, able-bodied << ANTONYM unfit

fit² *noun* 1 (*pathology*) SEIZURE, attack, bout, spasm, convulsion, paroxysm 2 BOUT, burst, outbreak, outburst, spell ▷▷ **have a fit** (*informal*) GO MAD, explode, blow up (*informal*), lose it (*informal*), see red (*informal*), lose the plot (*informal*), throw a tantrum, fly off the handle (*informal*), go spare (*Brit slang*), blow your top (*informal*), fly into a temper, flip your lid (*slang*), do your nut (*Brit slang*)

▷▷ **in** *or* **by fits and starts** SPASMODICALLY, sporadically, erratically, fitfully, on and off, irregularly, intermittently, off and on, unsystematically

fitful *adjective* IRREGULAR, broken, disturbed, erratic, variable, flickering, unstable, uneven, fluctuating, sporadic, intermittent, impulsive, haphazard, desultory, spasmodic, inconstant << ANTONYM regular

fitfully *adverb* IRREGULARLY, on and off, intermittently, sporadically, off and on, erratically, in fits and starts, spasmodically, in snatches, desultorily, by fits and starts, interruptedly

fitness *noun* 1 APPROPRIATENESS, qualifications, adaptation, competence, readiness, eligibility, suitability, propriety, preparedness, applicability, aptness, pertinence, seemliness 2 HEALTH, strength, good health, vigour, good condition, wellness, robustness

fitted *adjective* BUILT-IN, permanent

fitting *adjective* APPROPRIATE, suitable, proper, apt, right, becoming, meet (*archaic*), seemly, correct, decent, desirable, apposite, decorous, comme il faut (*French*) << ANTONYM unsuitable ▷ *noun* ACCESSORY, part, piece, unit, connection, component, attachment ▷ *plural noun* FURNISHINGS, extras, equipment, fixtures, appointments, furniture, trimmings, accessories, conveniences, accoutrements, bells and whistles, fitments, appurtenances

fix *verb* 1 PLACE, join, stick, attach, set, position, couple, plant, link, establish, tie, settle, secure, bind, root, connect, locate, pin, install, anchor, glue, cement, implant, embed, fasten, make fast 2 *often with* **up** DECIDE, set, name, choose, limit, establish, determine, settle, appoint, arrange, define, conclude, resolve, arrive at, specify, agree on 3 *often with* **up** ARRANGE, organize, sort out, see to, make arrangements for 4 REPAIR, mend, service, sort, correct, restore, adjust, regulate, see to, overhaul, patch up, get working, put right, put to rights 5 FOCUS, direct at, level at, fasten on, rivet on 6 (*informal*) RIG, set up (*informal*), influence, manipulate, bribe, manoeuvre, fiddle (*informal*), pull strings (*informal*) 7 STABILIZE, set, consolidate, harden, thicken, stiffen, solidify, congeal, rigidify ▷ *noun* (*informal*) MESS, spot (*informal*), corner, hole (*slang*), difficulty, jam (*informal*), dilemma, embarrassment, plight, hot water (*informal*), pickle (*informal*), uphill (*S African*), predicament, difficult situation, quandary, tight spot, ticklish situation ▷▷ **fix someone up** *often with* **with** PROVIDE, supply, accommodate, bring about, furnish, lay on, arrange for ▷▷ **fix something up** ARRANGE, plan, settle, fix, organize, sort out, agree on, make arrangements for

fixated *adjective* OBSESSED, fascinated, preoccupied, captivated, attached, devoted, absorbed, caught up in, single-minded, smitten, taken up with, besotted, wrapped up in, engrossed, spellbound, infatuated, mesmerized, hypnotized, hung up on (*slang*), monomaniacal, prepossessed << ANTONYM uninterested

fixation *noun* OBSESSION, complex, addiction, hang-up (*informal*), preoccupation, mania, infatuation, idée fixe (*French*), thing (*informal*)

fixed *adjective* **1** INFLEXIBLE, set, steady, resolute, unwavering, unflinching, unblinking, unbending, undeviating << ANTONYM wavering **2** IMMOVABLE, set, established, secure, rooted, permanent, attached, anchored, rigid, made fast << ANTONYM mobile **3** AGREED, set, planned, decided, established, settled, arranged, resolved, specified, definite **4** (*informal*) RIGGED, framed, put-up, manipulated, packed

fizz *verb* **1** BUBBLE, froth, fizzle, effervesce, produce bubbles **2** SPUTTER, buzz, sparkle, hiss, crackle

fizzle *verb* (*informal*) *often with* **out** DIE AWAY, fail, collapse, fold (*informal*), abort, fall through, peter out, come to nothing, miss the mark, end in disappointment

fizzy *adjective* BUBBLY, bubbling, sparkling, effervescent, carbonated, gassy

flab *noun* FAT, flesh, flabbiness, fleshiness, weight, beef (*informal*), heaviness, slackness, plumpness, loose flesh

flabbergasted *adjective* ASTONISHED, amazed, stunned, overcome, overwhelmed, staggered, astounded, dazed, confounded, disconcerted, speechless, bowled over (*informal*), gobsmacked (*Brit slang*), dumbfounded, nonplussed, lost for words, struck dumb, abashed, rendered speechless

flabby *adjective* **1** LIMP, hanging, loose, slack, unfit, sagging, sloppy, baggy, floppy, lax, drooping, flaccid, pendulous, toneless, yielding << ANTONYM firm **2** WEAK, ineffective, feeble, impotent, wasteful, ineffectual, disorganized, spineless, effete,

boneless, nerveless, enervated, wussy (*slang*), wimpish *or* wimpy (*informal*)

flaccid *adjective* LIMP, soft, weak, loose, slack, lax, drooping, flabby, nerveless

flag¹ *noun* BANNER, standard, colours, jack, pennant, ensign, streamer, pennon, banderole, gonfalon ▷ *verb* **1** MARK, identify, indicate, label, tab, pick out, note, docket **2** *often with* **down** HAIL, stop, signal, salute, wave down

flag² *verb* WEAKEN, fall, die, fail, decline, sink, fade, slump, pine, faint, weary, fall off, succumb, falter, wilt, wane, ebb, sag, languish, abate, droop, peter out, taper off, feel the pace, lose your strength

flagging *adjective* WEAKENING, failing, declining, waning, giving up, tiring, sinking, fading, decreasing, slowing down, deteriorating, wearying, faltering, wilting, ebbing

flagrant *adjective* OUTRAGEOUS, open, blatant, barefaced, shocking, crying, enormous, awful, bold, dreadful, notorious, glaring, infamous, scandalous, flaunting, atrocious, brazen, shameless, out-and-out, heinous, ostentatious, egregious, undisguised, immodest, arrant, flagitious << ANTONYM slight

flagstone *noun* PAVING STONE, flag, slab, block

flail *verb* THRASH, beat, windmill, thresh

flair *noun* **1** ABILITY, feel, talent, gift, genius, faculty, accomplishment, mastery, knack, aptitude **2** (*informal*) STYLE, taste, dash, chic, elegance, panache, discernment, stylishness

flak (*informal*) *noun* CRITICISM, stick (*slang*), opposition, abuse, complaints, hostility, condemnation, censure, disapproval, bad press, denigration, brickbats (*informal*), disparagement, fault-finding, disapprobation

flake *noun* CHIP, scale, layer, peeling, shaving, disk, wafer, sliver, lamina, squama (*biology*) ▷ *verb* CHIP, scale (off), peel (off), blister, desquamate

flamboyance *noun* SHOWINESS, show, style, dash, sparkle, chic, flair, verve, swagger, extravagance, panache, pomp, glitz (*informal*), élan, bravura, swank (*informal*), theatricality, exhibitionism, brio, ostentation, stylishness, flashiness, flamboyancy, floridity, pizzazz *or* pizazz (*informal*) << ANTONYM restraint

flamboyant *adjective* **1** CAMP (*informal*), dashing, theatrical, swashbuckling **2** SHOWY, rich, elaborate, over the top (*informal*), extravagant, baroque, ornate, ostentatious, rococo **3** COLOURFUL, striking, exciting, brilliant, glamorous, stylish, dazzling, glitzy (*slang*), showy, florid

flame *noun* **1** FIRE, light, spark, glow, blaze, brightness, inferno **2** PASSION, fire, enthusiasm, intensity, affection, warmth, fervour, ardour, keenness, fervency **3** (*informal*) SWEETHEART, partner, lover, girlfriend, boyfriend, beloved, heart-throb (*Brit*), beau, ladylove ▷ *verb* BURN, flash, shine, glow, blaze, flare, glare

flaming *adjective* **1** BURNING, blazing, fiery, ignited, red, brilliant, raging, glowing, red-hot, ablaze, in flames, afire **2** INTENSE, angry, raging, impassioned, hot, aroused, vivid, frenzied, ardent, scintillating, vehement

flammable *adjective* COMBUSTIBLE, incendiary, inflammable, ignitable

flank *noun* **1** SIDE, quarter, hip, thigh, loin, haunch, ham **2** WING, side, sector, aspect ▷ *verb* BORDER, line, wall, screen, edge, circle, bound, skirt, fringe, book-end

flannel (*Brit informal*) *noun* WAFFLE, flattery, blarney, sweet talk (*US informal*), baloney (*informal*), equivocation, hedging, prevarication, weasel words (*informal, chiefly US*), soft soap (*informal*) ▷ *verb* PREVARICATE, hedge, flatter, waffle (*informal, chiefly Brit*), blarney, sweet-talk (*informal*), soft-soap (*informal*), equivocate, butter up, pull the wool over (*someone's*) eyes

flap *verb* **1** FLUTTER, wave, swing, swish, flail **2** BEAT, wave, thrash, flutter, agitate, wag, vibrate, shake, thresh **3** (*informal*) PANIC, fuss, dither (*chiefly Brit*) ▷ *noun* **1** COVER, covering, tail, fold, skirt, tab, overlap, fly, apron, lapel, lappet **2** FLUTTER, beating, waving, shaking, swinging, bang, banging, swish **3** (*informal*) PANIC, state (*informal*), agitation, commotion, sweat (*informal*), stew (*informal*), dither (*chiefly Brit*), fluster, twitter (*informal*), tizzy (*informal*)

flare *verb* **1** BLAZE, flame, dazzle, glare, flicker, flutter, waver, burn up **2** WIDEN, spread, broaden, spread out, dilate, splay ▷ *noun* **1** FLAME, burst, flash, blaze, dazzle, glare, flicker ▷▷ **flare up 1** BURN, explode, blaze, be on fire, go up in flames, be alight, flame (*informal*) **2** LOSE YOUR TEMPER, explode, lose it (*informal*), lose control, lose the plot (*informal*), throw a tantrum, fly off the handle (*informal*), lose your cool (*informal*), blow your top (*informal*), fly into a temper

flash *noun* **1** BLAZE, ray, burst, spark, beam, sparkle, streak, flare, dazzle, shaft, glare, gleam, flicker, shimmer, twinkle, scintillation, coruscation **2** BURST, show, sign, touch, display, rush, demonstration, surge, outbreak, outburst, manifestation **3** *usually in phrase* **in a flash** MOMENT, second, instant, split second, trice, jiffy (*informal*), the twinkling of an eye, a twinkling, two shakes of a lamb's tail (*informal*), the bat of an eye (*informal*) ▷ *verb* **1** BLAZE, shine, beam, sparkle, glitter, flare, glare, gleam, light up, flicker, shimmer, twinkle, glint, glisten, scintillate, coruscate **2** SPEED, race, shoot, fly, tear, sweep, dash, barrel (along) (*informal, chiefly US & Canad*), whistle, sprint, bolt, streak, dart, zoom, burn rubber (*informal*) **3** (*informal*) SHOW QUICKLY, display, expose, exhibit, flourish, show off, flaunt ▷ *adjective* (*informal*) OSTENTATIOUS, smart, glamorous, trendy, showy, cheap

flashy *adjective* SHOWY, loud, over the top (*informal*), flamboyant, brash, tacky (*informal*), flaunting, glitzy (*slang*), tasteless, naff (*Brit slang*), gaudy, garish, jazzy (*informal*), tawdry, ostentatious, snazzy (*informal*), glittery, meretricious, cheap and nasty, in poor taste, tinselly << ANTONYM plain

flat¹ *adjective* **1** EVEN, level, levelled, plane, smooth, uniform, horizontal, unbroken, planar << ANTONYM uneven **2** HORIZONTAL, prone, outstretched, reclining, prostrate, laid low, supine, recumbent, lying full length << ANTONYM upright **3** PUNCTURED, collapsed, burst, blown out, deflated, empty **4** USED UP, finished, empty, drained, expired **5** ABSOLUTE, firm, direct, straight, positive, fixed, plain, final, explicit, definite, outright, unconditional, downright, unmistakable, unequivocal, unqualified, out-and-out, categorical, peremptory **6** DULL, dead, empty, boring, depressing, pointless, tedious, stale, lacklustre, tiresome, lifeless, monotonous, uninteresting, insipid, unexciting, spiritless << ANTONYM exciting **7** WITHOUT ENERGY, empty, weak, tired, depressed, drained, weary, worn out, dispirited, downhearted, tired out **8** MONOTONOUS, boring, uniform, dull, tedious, droning, tiresome, unchanging, colourless, toneless, samey (*informal*), uninflected, unvaried ▷ *noun often plural* PLAIN, strand, shallow, marsh, swamp, shoal, lowland, mud flat ▷ *adverb* COMPLETELY, directly, absolutely, categorically, precisely, exactly, utterly, outright, point blank, unequivocally ▷▷ **flat out** (*informal*) AT FULL SPEED, all out, to the full, hell for leather (*informal*), as hard as possible, at full tilt, at full gallop, posthaste, for all you are worth, under full steam

flat² *noun* APARTMENT, rooms, quarters, digs, suite, penthouse, living quarters, duplex (*US & Canad*), bachelor apartment (*Canad*)

flatly *adverb* ABSOLUTELY, completely, positively, categorically, unequivocally, unhesitatingly

flatten *verb* **1** *sometimes with* **out** LEVEL, roll, plaster, squash, compress, trample, iron out, even out, smooth off **2** *sometimes with* **out** DESTROY, level, ruin, demolish, knock down, pull down, tear down, throw down, bulldoze, raze, remove, kennet (*Austral slang*), jeff (*Austral slang*) **3** (*informal*) KNOCK DOWN, fell, floor, deck (*slang*), bowl over, prostrate, knock off your feet **4** (*informal*) CRUSH, beat, defeat, trounce, master, worst, overwhelm, conquer, lick (*informal*), undo, subdue, rout, overpower, quell, clobber (*slang*), vanquish, run rings around (*informal*), wipe the floor with (*informal*), make mincemeat of (*informal*), blow out of the water (*slang*)

flatter *verb* **1** PRAISE, compliment, pander to, sweet-talk (*informal*), court, humour, puff, flannel (*Brit informal*), fawn, cajole, lay it on (thick) (*slang*), wheedle, inveigle, soft-soap (*informal*), butter up, blandish **2** SUIT, become, enhance, set off, embellish, do something for, show to advantage

flattering *adjective* **1** BECOMING, kind, effective, enhancing, well-chosen << ANTONYM unflattering **2** INGRATIATING, complimentary, gratifying, fawning, sugary, fulsome, laudatory, adulatory, honeyed, honey-tongued << ANTONYM uncomplimentary

flattery *noun* OBSEQUIOUSNESS, fawning, adulation, sweet-talk (*informal*), flannel (*Brit informal*), blarney, soft-soap (*informal*), sycophancy, servility, cajolery, blandishment, fulsomeness, toadyism, false praise, honeyed words

flatulence *noun* WIND, borborygmus (*medical*), eructation

flaunt *verb* SHOW OFF, display, boast, parade, exhibit, flourish, brandish, vaunt, make a (great) show of, sport (*informal*), disport, make an exhibition of, flash about

flavour *or* (*US*) **flavor** *noun* **1** TASTE, seasoning, flavouring, savour, extract, essence, relish, smack, aroma, odour, zest, tang, zing (*informal*), piquancy, tastiness << ANTONYM blandness **2** QUALITY, feeling, feel, style,

property, touch, character, aspect, tone, suggestion, stamp, essence, tinge, soupçon (*French*) ▷ *verb* SEASON, spice, add flavour to, enrich, infuse, imbue, pep up, leaven, ginger up, lace

flavouring *or* (*US*) **flavoring** *noun* ESSENCE, extract, zest, tincture, spirit

flaw *noun* **1** WEAKNESS, failing, defect, weak spot, spot, fault, scar, blemish, imperfection, speck, disfigurement, chink in your armour **2** CRACK, break, split, breach, tear, rent, fracture, rift, cleft, crevice, fissure, scission

flawed *adjective* **1** DAMAGED, defective, imperfect, blemished, broken, cracked, chipped, faulty **2** ERRONEOUS, incorrect, inaccurate, invalid, wrong, mistaken, false, faulty, untrue, unfounded, spurious, amiss, unsound, wide of the mark, inexact, fallacious

flawless *adjective* PERFECT, impeccable, faultless, spotless, unblemished, unsullied

flay *verb* **1** SKIN, strip, peel, scrape, excoriate, remove the skin from **2** UPBRAID, slam (*slang*), castigate, revile, tear into (*informal*), diss (*slang, chiefly US*), excoriate, tear a strip off, execrate, pull to pieces (*informal*), give a tongue-lashing, criticize severely

fleck *noun* MARK, speck, streak, spot, dot, pinpoint, speckle ▷ *verb* SPECKLE, mark, spot, dust, dot, streak, dapple, stipple, mottle, variegate, bespeckle, besprinkle

fledgling *or* **fledgeling** *noun* CHICK, nestling, young bird

flee *verb* RUN AWAY, leave, escape, bolt, fly, avoid, split (*slang*), take off (*informal*), get away, vanish, depart, run off, shun, make off, abscond, decamp, take flight, hook it (*slang*), do a runner (*slang*), scarper (*Brit slang*), slope off, cut and run (*informal*), make a run for it, beat a hasty retreat, turn tail, fly the coop (*US & Canad informal*), make a quick exit, skedaddle (*informal*), make yourself scarce (*informal*), take a powder (*US & Canad slang*), make your escape, make your getaway, take it on the lam (*US & Canad slang*), take to your heels

fleece *noun* WOOL, hair, coat, fur, coat of wool ▷ *verb* CHEAT, skin (*slang*), steal, rob, con (*informal*), rifle, stiff (*slang*), soak (*US & Canad slang*), bleed (*informal*), rip off (*slang*), plunder, defraud, overcharge, swindle, rook (*slang*), diddle (*informal*), take for a ride (*informal*), despoil, take to the cleaners (*slang*), sell a pup, cozen, mulct

fleet¹ *noun* NAVY, vessels, task force, squadron,

warships, flotilla, armada, naval force, sea power, argosy

fleet² *adjective* SWIFT, flying, fast, quick, winged, rapid, speedy, nimble, mercurial, meteoric, nimble-footed

fleeting *adjective* MOMENTARY, short, passing, flying, brief, temporary, short-lived, fugitive, transient, flitting, ephemeral, transitory, evanescent, fugacious, here today, gone tomorrow << ANTONYM lasting

flesh *noun* 1 FAT, muscle, beef (*informal*), tissue, body, brawn 2 (*informal*) FATNESS, fat, adipose tissue, corpulence, weight 3 MEAT, food 4 PHYSICAL NATURE, sensuality, physicality, carnality, body, human nature, flesh and blood, animality, sinful nature ▷▷ **your own flesh and blood** FAMILY, blood, relations, relatives, kin, kindred, kith and kin, blood relations, kinsfolk, ainga (*NZ*), rellies (*Austral slang*)

fleshy *adjective* PLUMP, fat, chubby, obese, hefty, overweight, ample, stout, chunky, meaty, beefy (*informal*), tubby, podgy, brawny, corpulent, well-padded

flex *verb* BEND, contract, stretch, angle, curve, tighten, crook, move

flexibility *noun* 1 ELASTICITY, pliability, springiness, pliancy, tensility, give (*informal*) 2 ADAPTABILITY, openness, versatility, adjustability 3 COMPLAISANCE, accommodation, give and take, amenability

flexible *adjective* 1 PLIABLE, plastic, yielding, elastic, supple, lithe, limber, springy, willowy, pliant, tensile, stretchy, whippy, lissom(e), ductile, bendable, mouldable << ANTONYM rigid 2 ADAPTABLE, open, variable, adjustable, discretionary << ANTONYM inflexible 3 COMPLIANT, accommodating, manageable, amenable, docile, tractable, biddable, complaisant, responsive, gentle << ANTONYM unyielding

flick *verb* 1 JERK, pull, tug, lurch, jolt 2 STRIKE, tap, jab, remove quickly, hit, touch, stroke, rap, flip, peck, whisk, dab, fillip ▷ *noun* TAP, touch, sweep, stroke, rap, flip, peck, whisk, jab ▷▷ **flick through something** BROWSE, glance at, skim, leaf through, flip through, thumb through, skip through

flicker *verb* 1 TWINKLE, flash, sparkle, flare, shimmer, gutter, glimmer 2 FLUTTER, waver, quiver, vibrate ▷ *noun* 1 GLIMMER, flash, spark, flare, gleam 2 TRACE, drop, breath, spark, atom, glimmer, vestige, iota

flier ▷ see **flyer**

flight¹ *noun* 1 JOURNEY, trip, voyage

2 AVIATION, flying, air transport, aeronautics, aerial navigation 3 FLYING, winging, mounting, soaring, ability to fly 4 FLOCK, group, unit, cloud, formation, squadron, swarm, flying group

flight² *noun* ESCAPE, fleeing, departure, retreat, exit, running away, exodus, getaway, absconding ▷▷ **put to flight** DRIVE OFF, scatter, disperse, rout, stampede, scare off, send packing, chase off ▷▷ **take (to) flight** RUN AWAY *or* OFF, flee, bolt, abscond, decamp, do a runner (*slang*), turn tail, do a bunk (*Brit slang*), fly the coop (*US & Canad informal*), beat a retreat, light out (*informal*), skedaddle (*informal*), make a hasty retreat, take a powder (*US & Canad slang*), withdraw hastily, take it on the lam (*US & Canad slang*), do a Skase (*Austral informal*)

flighty *adjective* FRIVOLOUS, wild, volatile, unstable, irresponsible, dizzy, fickle, unbalanced, impulsive, mercurial, giddy, capricious, unsteady, thoughtless, changeable, impetuous, skittish, light-headed, harebrained, scatterbrained, ditzy *or* ditsy (*slang*)

flimsy *adjective* 1 FRAGILE, weak, slight, delicate, shallow, shaky, frail, superficial, makeshift, rickety, insubstantial, gimcrack, unsubstantial << ANTONYM sturdy 2 THIN, light, sheer, transparent, chiffon, gossamer, gauzy 3 UNCONVINCING, poor, thin, weak, inadequate, pathetic, transparent, trivial, feeble, unsatisfactory, frivolous, tenuous, implausible

flinch *verb* 1 WINCE, start, duck, shrink, cringe, quail, recoil, cower, blench 2 *often with* **from** SHY AWAY, shrink, withdraw, flee, retreat, back off, swerve, shirk, draw back, baulk

fling *verb* THROW, toss, hurl, chuck (*informal*), launch, cast, pitch, send, shy, jerk, propel, sling, precipitate, lob (*informal*), catapult, heave, let fly ▷ *noun* 1 BINGE, good time, bash, bit of fun, party, rave (*Brit slang*), spree, indulgence (*informal*), beano (*Brit slang*), night on the town, rave-up (*Brit slang*), hooley *or* hoolie (*chiefly Irish & NZ*) 2 TRY, go (*informal*), attempt, shot (*informal*), trial, crack (*informal*), venture, gamble, stab (*informal*), bash (*informal*), whirl (*informal*)

flip *verb* 1 FLICK, switch, snap, jerk 2 SPIN, turn, overturn, turn over, roll over, twist 3 TOSS, throw, cast, pitch, flick, fling, sling ▷ *noun* TOSS, throw, cast, pitch, spin, snap, twist, flick, jerk

flippant *adjective* FRIVOLOUS, rude, cheeky,

irreverent, flip (*informal*), superficial, saucy, glib, pert, disrespectful, offhand, impertinent, impudent << ANTONYM serious

flirt *verb* 1 CHAT UP, lead on (*informal*), dally with, make advances at, make eyes at, coquet, philander, make sheep's eyes at 2 *usually with* **with** TOY WITH, consider, entertain, play with, dabble in, trifle with, give a thought to, expose yourself to ▷ *noun* TEASE, philanderer, coquette, heart-breaker, wanton, trifler

flirtation *noun* TEASING, philandering, dalliance, coquetry, toying, intrigue, trifling

flirtatious *adjective* TEASING, flirty, coquettish, amorous, come-on (*informal*), arch, enticing, provocative, coy, come-hither, sportive

flit *verb* FLY, dash, dart, skim, pass, speed, wing, flash, fleet, whisk, flutter

float *verb* 1 GLIDE, sail, drift, move gently, bob, coast, slide, be carried, slip along 2 BE BUOYANT, stay afloat, be *or* lie on the surface, rest on water, hang, hover, poise, displace water << ANTONYM sink 3 LAUNCH, offer, sell, set up, promote, get going, push off << ANTONYM dissolve

floating *adjective* 1 UNCOMMITTED, wavering, undecided, indecisive, vacillating, sitting on the fence (*informal*), unaffiliated, independent 2 FREE, wandering, variable, fluctuating, unattached, migratory, movable, unfixed

flock *noun* 1 HERD, group, flight, drove, colony, gaggle, skein 2 CROWD, company, group, host, collection, mass, gathering, assembly, convoy, herd, congregation, horde, multitude, throng, bevy ▷ *verb* 1 STREAM, crowd, mass, swarm, throng 2 GATHER, group, crowd, mass, collect, assemble, herd, huddle, converge, throng, congregate, troop

flog *verb* BEAT, whip, lash, thrash, whack, scourge, hit hard, trounce, castigate, chastise, flay, lambast(e), flagellate, punish severely, beat *or* knock seven bells out of (*informal*)

flogging *noun* BEATING, hiding (*informal*), whipping, lashing, thrashing, caning, scourging, trouncing, flagellation, horsewhipping

flood *noun* 1 DELUGE, downpour, flash flood, inundation, tide, overflow, torrent, spate, freshet 2 TORRENT, flow, rush, stream, tide, abundance, multitude, glut, outpouring, profusion 3 SERIES, stream, avalanche, barrage, spate, torrent 4 OUTPOURING, rush,

stream, surge, torrent ▷ *verb* 1 IMMERSE, swamp, submerge, inundate, deluge, drown, cover with water 2 POUR OVER, swamp, run over, overflow, inundate, brim over 3 ENGULF, flow into, rush into, sweep into, overwhelm, surge into, swarm into, pour into, gush into 4 SATURATE, fill, choke, swamp, glut, oversupply, overfill 5 STREAM, flow, rush, pour, surge

floor *noun* 1 GROUND 2 STOREY, level, stage, tier ▷ *verb* 1 (*informal*) DISCONCERT, stump, baffle, confound, beat, throw (*informal*), defeat, puzzle, conquer, overthrow, bewilder, perplex, bowl over (*informal*), faze, discomfit, bring up short, dumbfound, nonplus 2 KNOCK DOWN, fell, knock over, prostrate, deck (*slang*)

flop *verb* 1 SLUMP, fall, drop, collapse, sink, tumble, topple 2 HANG DOWN, hang, dangle, sag, droop, hang limply 3 (*informal*) FAIL, close, bomb (*US & Canad slang*), fold (*informal*), founder, fall short, fall flat, come to nothing, come unstuck, misfire, go belly-up (*slang*), go down like a lead balloon (*informal*) << ANTONYM succeed ▷ *noun* (*informal*) FAILURE, disaster, loser, fiasco, debacle, washout (*informal*), cockup (*Brit slang*), nonstarter << ANTONYM success

floppy *adjective* DROOPY, soft, loose, hanging, limp, flapping, sagging, baggy, flip-flop, flaccid, pendulous

floral *adjective* FLOWERY, flower-patterned

florid *adjective* 1 FLOWERY, high-flown, figurative, grandiloquent, euphuistic 2 ORNATE, busy, flamboyant, baroque, fussy, embellished, flowery, overelaborate << ANTONYM plain 3 FLUSHED, ruddy, rubicund, high-coloured, high-complexioned, blowsy << ANTONYM pale

flotsam *noun* 1 DEBRIS, rubbish, wreckage, detritus, jetsam 2 RUBBISH, sweepings, debris, junk, odds and ends

flounce *verb often with* **out, away, out,** *etc.* BOUNCE, storm, stamp, go quickly, throw, spring, toss, fling, jerk

flounder *verb* 1 FALTER, struggle, stall, slow down, run into trouble, come unstuck (*informal*), be in difficulties, hit a bad patch 2 DITHER, struggle, blunder, be confused, falter, be in the dark, be out of your depth 3 STRUGGLE, toss, thrash, plunge, stumble, tumble, muddle, fumble, grope, wallow

flourish *verb* 1 THRIVE, increase, develop, advance, progress, boom, bloom, blossom, prosper, burgeon << ANTONYM fail

2 SUCCEED, do well, be successful, move ahead, get ahead, go places (*informal*), go great guns (*slang*), go up in the world **3** GROW, thrive, develop, flower, succeed, get on, bloom, blossom, prosper, bear fruit, be vigorous, be in your prime **4** WAVE, brandish, sweep, swish, display, shake, swing, wield, flutter, wag, flaunt, vaunt, twirl ▷ *noun* **1** WAVE, sweep, brandish, swish, shaking, swing, dash, brandishing, twirling, twirl, showy gesture **2** SHOW, display, parade, fanfare **3** CURLICUE, sweep, decoration, swirl, plume, embellishment, ornamentation

flourishing *adjective* THRIVING, successful, doing well, blooming, mushrooming, prospering, rampant, burgeoning, on a roll, going places, going strong, in the pink, in top form, on the up and up (*informal*)

flout *verb* DEFY, scorn, spurn, scoff at, outrage, insult, mock, scout (*archaic*), ridicule, taunt, deride, sneer at, jeer at, laugh in the face of, show contempt for, gibe at, treat with disdain << ANTONYM respect ▷ see **flaunt**

flow *verb* **1** RUN, course, rush, sweep, move, issue, pass, roll, flood, pour, slide, proceed, stream, run out, surge, spill, go along, circulate, swirl, glide, ripple, cascade, whirl, overflow, gush, inundate, deluge, spurt, teem, spew, squirt, purl, well forth **2** POUR, move, sweep, flood, stream, overflow **3** ISSUE, follow, result, emerge, spring, pour, proceed, arise, derive, ensue, emanate ▷ *noun* **1** STREAM, current, movement, motion, course, issue, flood, drift, tide, spate, gush, flux, outpouring, outflow, undertow, tideway **2** OUTPOURING, flood, stream, succession, train, plenty, abundance, deluge, plethora, outflow, effusion, emanation

flower *noun* **1** BLOOM, blossom, efflorescence **2** ELITE, best, prime, finest, pick, choice, cream, height, crème de la crème (*French*), choicest part **3** HEIGHT, prime, peak, vigour, freshness, greatest *or* finest point ▷ *verb* **1** BLOOM, open, mature, flourish, unfold, blossom, burgeon, effloresce **2** BLOSSOM, grow, develop, progress, mature, thrive, flourish, bloom, bud, prosper

flowering *adjective* BLOOMING, in flower, in bloom, in blossom, out, open, ready, blossoming, florescent, abloom

flowery *adjective* **1** FLORAL, flower-patterned **2** ORNATE, fancy, rhetorical, high-flown, embellished, figurative, florid, overwrought, euphuistic, baroque << ANTONYM plain

flowing *adjective* **1** STREAMING, rushing, gushing, teeming, falling, full, rolling, sweeping, flooded, fluid, prolific, abundant, overrun, brimming over **2** SLEEK, smooth, fluid, unbroken, uninterrupted **3** FLUENT, easy, natural, continuous, effortless, uninterrupted, free-flowing, cursive, rich

fluctuate *verb* **1** CHANGE, swing, vary, alter, hesitate, alternate, waver, veer, rise and fall, go up and down, ebb and flow, seesaw **2** SHIFT, undulate, oscillate, vacillate

fluctuation *noun* CHANGE, shift, swing, variation, instability, alteration, wavering, oscillation, alternation, vacillation, unsteadiness, inconstancy

fluency *noun* EASE, control, facility, command, assurance, readiness, smoothness, slickness, glibness, volubility, articulateness

fluent *adjective* EFFORTLESS, natural, articulate, well-versed, glib, facile, voluble, smooth-spoken

fluff *noun* FUZZ, down, pile, dust, fibre, threads, nap, lint, oose (*Scot*), dustball ▷ *verb* (*informal*) MESS UP, spoil, bungle, screw up (*informal*), cock up (*Brit slang*), foul up (*informal*), make a nonsense of, be unsuccessful in, make a mess off, muddle, crool *or* cruel (*Austral slang*)

fluffy *adjective* SOFT, fuzzy, feathery, downy, fleecy, flossy

fluid *noun* LIQUID, solution, juice, liquor, sap ▷ *adjective* **1** CHANGEABLE, mobile, flexible, volatile, unstable, adjustable, fluctuating, indefinite, shifting, floating, adaptable, mercurial, protean, mutable << ANTONYM fixed **2** LIQUID, running, flowing, watery, molten, melted, runny, liquefied, in solution, aqueous << ANTONYM solid

fluke *noun* STROKE OF LUCK, accident, coincidence, chance occurrence, chance, stroke, blessing, freak, windfall, quirk, lucky break, serendipity, quirk of fate, fortuity, break

flunk (*informal, US & Canad*) *verb* FAIL, screw up (*informal*), flop in (*informal*), plough (*Brit slang*), be unsuccessful in, not make the grade at (*informal*), not come up to scratch in (*informal*), not come up to the mark in (*informal*)

flurry *noun* **1** COMMOTION, stir, bustle, flutter, to-do, excitement, hurry, fuss, disturbance, flap, whirl, furore, ferment, agitation, fluster, ado, tumult **2** BURST, spell, bout, outbreak, spurt **3** GUST, shower, gale, swirl, squall, storm

flush¹ *verb* **1** BLUSH, colour, burn, flame, glow,

crimson, redden, suffuse, turn red, go red, colour up, go as red as a beetroot **2** CLEANSE, wash out, swab, rinse out, flood, drench, syringe, swill, hose down, douche **3** EXPEL, drive, eject, dislodge ▷ *noun* **1** BLUSH, colour, glow, reddening, redness, rosiness **2** BLOOM, glow, vigour, freshness

flush² *adjective* **1** LEVEL, even, true, flat, square, plane **2** (*informal*) WEALTHY, rich, rolling (*slang*), well-off, in the money (*informal*), in funds, well-heeled (*informal*), replete, moneyed, well-supplied **3** AFFLUENT, liberal, generous, lavish, abundant, overflowing, plentiful, prodigal, full ▷ *adverb* LEVEL, even, touching, squarely, in contact, hard (against)

flush³ *verb* *often with* **out** DRIVE OUT, force, dislodge, put to flight, start, discover, disturb, uncover, rouse

flushed *adjective* **1** *often with* **with** EXHILARATED, excited, aroused, elated, high (*informal*), inspired, thrilled, animated, enthused, intoxicated, stoked (*Austral & NZ informal*) **2** BLUSHING, red, hot, burning, embarrassed, glowing, rosy, crimson, feverish, ruddy, rubicund

fluster *verb* UPSET, bother, disturb, ruffle, heat, excite, confuse, hurry, rattle (*informal*), bustle, hassle (*informal*), flurry, agitate, confound, unnerve, perturb, throw off balance, make nervous

fluted *adjective* (*architecture*) GROOVED, channelled, furrowed, corrugated

flutter *verb* **1** BEAT, bat, flap, tremble, shiver, flicker, ripple, waver, fluctuate, agitate, ruffle, quiver, vibrate, palpitate **2** FLIT, hover, flitter ▷ *noun* **1** TREMOR, tremble, shiver, shudder, palpitation **2** VIBRATION, twitching, quiver, quivering **3** AGITATION, state (*informal*), confusion, excitement, flap (*informal*), tremble, flurry, dither (*chiefly Brit*), commotion, fluster, tumult, perturbation, state of nervous excitement

flux *noun* **1** INSTABILITY, change, transition, unrest, modification, alteration, mutation, fluctuation, mutability **2** FLOW, movement, motion, fluidity

fly¹ *verb* **1** TAKE WING, soar, glide, take to the air, wing, mount, sail, hover, flutter, flit **2** PILOT, control, operate, steer, manoeuvre, navigate, be at the controls, aviate **3** AIRLIFT, send by plane, take by plane, take in an aircraft **4** FLUTTER, wave, float, flap **5** DISPLAY, show, flourish, brandish **6** RUSH, race, shoot, career, speed, tear, dash, hurry, barrel (along) (*informal, chiefly US & Canad*),

sprint, bolt, dart, zoom, hare (*Brit informal*), hasten, whizz (*informal*), scoot, scamper, burn rubber (*informal*), be off like a shot (*informal*) **7** PASS SWIFTLY, pass, glide, slip away, roll on, flit, elapse, run its course, go quickly **8** LEAVE, disappear, get away, depart, run, escape, flee, take off, run from, shun, clear out (*informal*), light out (*informal*), abscond, decamp, take flight, do a runner (*slang*), run for it, cut and run (*informal*), fly the coop (*US & Canad informal*), beat a retreat, make a quick exit, make a getaway, show a clean pair of heels, skedaddle (*informal*), hightail (*informal, chiefly US*), take a powder (*US & Canad slang*), hasten away, make your escape, take it on the lam (*US & Canad slang*), take to your heels ▷▷ **let fly** (*informal*) LOSE YOUR TEMPER, lash out, burst forth, keep nothing back, give free rein, let (someone) have it ▷▷ **let something fly** THROW, launch, cast, hurl, shoot, fire, fling, chuck (*informal*), sling, lob (*informal*), hurtle, let off, heave

fly² *noun* ▷▷ **fly in the ointment** PROBLEM, difficulty, rub, flaw, hitch, drawback, snag, small problem

fly³ *adjective* (*slang, chiefly Brit*) CUNNING, knowing, sharp, smart, careful, shrewd, astute, on the ball (*informal*), canny, wide-awake, nobody's fool, not born yesterday

flyer *or* **flier** *noun* **1** (*old-fashioned*) PILOT, aeronaut, airman *or* airwoman, aviator *or* aviatrix **2** AIR TRAVELLER, air passenger **3** HANDBILL, bill, notice, leaf, release, literature (*informal*), leaflet, advert (*Brit informal*), circular, booklet, pamphlet, handout, throwaway (*US*), promotional material, publicity material **4** (*informal*) JUMP, spring, bound, leap, hurdle, vault, jeté, flying *or* running jump

flying *adjective* **1** AIRBORNE, waving, winging, floating, streaming, soaring, in the air, hovering, flapping, gliding, fluttering, wind-borne, volitant **2** FAST, running, express, speedy, winged, mobile, rapid, fleet, mercurial **3** HURRIED, brief, rushed, fleeting, short-lived, hasty, transitory, fugacious

foam *noun* FROTH, spray, bubbles, lather, suds, spume, head ▷ *verb* BUBBLE, boil, fizz, froth, lather, effervesce

fob ▷▷ **fob someone off** PUT OFF, deceive, appease, flannel (*Brit informal*), give (someone) the run-around (*informal*), stall, equivocate with ▷▷ **fob something off on someone** PASS OFF, dump, get rid of, inflict, unload, foist, palm off

focus *noun* **1** CENTRE, focal point, central point, core, bull's eye, centre of attraction, centre of activity, cynosure **2** FOCAL POINT, heart, target, headquarters, hub, meeting place ▷ *verb* **1** *often with* **on** CONCENTRATE, centre, spotlight, zero in on (*informal*), meet, join, direct, aim, pinpoint, converge, rivet, bring to bear, zoom in **2** FIX, train, direct, aim

fodder *noun* FEED, food, rations, tack (*informal*), foodstuff, kai (*NZ informal*), forage, victuals, provender, vittles (*obsolete* or *dialect*)

foe *noun* (*formal or literary*) ENEMY, rival, opponent, adversary, antagonist, foeman (*archaic*) << ANTONYM friend

fog *noun* **1** MIST, gloom, haze, smog, murk, miasma, murkiness, peasouper (*informal*) **2** STUPOR, confusion, trance, daze, haze, disorientation ▷ *verb* **1** MIST OVER *or* UP, cloud over, steam up, become misty **2** DAZE, cloud, dim, muddle, blind, confuse, obscure, bewilder, darken, perplex, stupefy, befuddle, muddy the waters, obfuscate, blear, becloud, bedim

foggy *adjective* **1** MISTY, grey, murky, cloudy, obscure, blurred, dim, hazy, nebulous, indistinct, soupy, smoggy, vaporous, brumous (*rare*) << ANTONYM clear **2** UNCLEAR, confused, clouded, stupid, obscure, vague, dim, bewildered, muddled, dazed, cloudy, stupefied, indistinct, befuddled, dark << ANTONYM sharp

foible *noun* IDIOSYNCRASY, failing, fault, weakness, defect, quirk, imperfection, peculiarity, weak point, infirmity

foil¹ *verb* THWART, stop, check, defeat, disappoint, counter, frustrate, hamper, baffle, elude, balk, circumvent, outwit, nullify, checkmate, nip in the bud, put a spoke in (someone's) wheel (*Brit*)

foil² *noun* COMPLEMENT, setting, relief, contrast, background, antithesis

foist ▷▷ **foist something on** *or* **upon someone** FORCE

fold *verb* **1** BEND, double, gather, tuck, overlap, crease, pleat, intertwine, double over, turn under **2** *often with* **up** (*informal*) GO BANKRUPT, close, fail, crash, collapse, founder, shut down, go under, be ruined, go bust (*informal*), go to the wall, go belly-up (*slang*) **3** *with* **in** WRAP, envelop, entwine, enfold **4** *often with* **up** *or* **in** WRAP UP, wrap, enclose, envelop, do up, enfold ▷ *noun* CREASE, turn, gather, bend, layer, overlap, wrinkle, pleat, ruffle, furrow, knife-edge, double thickness, folded portion

folder *noun* FILE, portfolio, envelope, dossier, binder

folk *noun* **1** PEOPLE, persons, humans, individuals, men and women, human beings, humanity, inhabitants, mankind, mortals **2** *usually plural* (*informal*) FAMILY, parents, relations, relatives, tribe, clan, kin, kindred, ainga (*NZ*), rellies (*Austral slang*)

follow *verb* **1** ACCOMPANY, attend, escort, come after, go behind, tag along behind, bring up the rear, come behind, come *or* go with, tread on the heels of **2** PURSUE, track, dog, hunt, chase, shadow, tail (*informal*), trail, hound, stalk, run after << ANTONYM avoid **3** COME AFTER, go after, come next << ANTONYM precede **4** RESULT, issue, develop, spring, flow, proceed, arise, ensue, emanate, be consequent, supervene **5** OBEY, observe, comply with, adhere to, mind, watch, note, regard, stick to, heed, conform to, keep to, pay attention to, be guided by, act according to, act in accordance with, give allegiance to << ANTONYM ignore **6** COPY, imitate, emulate, mimic, model, adopt, live up to, take a leaf out of someone's book, take as an example, pattern yourself upon **7** SUCCEED, replace, come after, take over from, come next, supersede, supplant, take the place of, step into the shoes of **8** UNDERSTAND, get, see, catch, realize, appreciate, take in, grasp, catch on (*informal*), keep up with, comprehend, fathom, get the hang of (*informal*), get the picture **9** KEEP UP WITH, support, be interested in, cultivate, be devoted to, be a fan of, keep abreast of, be a devotee *or* supporter of ▷▷ **follow something through** COMPLETE, conclude, pursue, see through, consummate, bring to a conclusion

follower *noun* **1** SUPPORTER, fan, representative, convert, believer, admirer, backer, partisan, disciple, protagonist, devotee, worshipper, apostle, pupil, cohort (*chiefly US*), adherent, henchman, groupie (*slang*), habitué, votary << ANTONYM leader **2** ATTENDANT, assistant, companion, helper, sidekick (*slang*), henchman, retainer (*history*), hanger-on, minion, lackey << ANTONYM opponent

following *adjective* **1** NEXT, subsequent, successive, ensuing, coming, later, succeeding, specified, consequent, consequential **2** COMING, about to be mentioned ▷ *noun* SUPPORTERS, backing, public, support, train, fans, audience, circle, suite, patronage, clientele, entourage, coterie, retinue

folly *noun* FOOLISHNESS, bêtise (*rare*), nonsense, madness, stupidity, absurdity, indiscretion, lunacy, recklessness, silliness, idiocy, irrationality, imprudence, rashness, imbecility, fatuity, preposterousness, daftness (*informal*), desipience << ANTONYM wisdom

foment *verb* STIR UP, raise, encourage, promote, excite, spur, foster, stimulate, provoke, brew, arouse, rouse, agitate, quicken, incite, instigate, whip up, goad, abet, sow the seeds of, fan the flames

fond *adjective* **1** LOVING, caring, warm, devoted, tender, adoring, affectionate, indulgent, doting, amorous << ANTONYM indifferent **2** UNREALISTIC, empty, naive, vain, foolish, deluded, indiscreet, credulous, overoptimistic, delusive, delusory, absurd << ANTONYM sensible ▷▷ **fond of 1** ATTACHED TO, in love with, keen on, attracted to, having a soft spot for, enamoured of **2** KEEN ON, into (*informal*), hooked on, partial to, having a soft spot for, having a taste for, addicted to, having a liking for, predisposed towards, having a fancy for

fondle *verb* CARESS, pet, cuddle, touch gently, pat, stroke, dandle

fondly *adverb* **1** LOVINGLY, tenderly, affectionately, amorously, dearly, possessively, with affection, indulgently, adoringly **2** UNREALISTICALLY, stupidly, vainly, foolishly, naively, credulously

fondness *noun* **1** DEVOTION, love, affection, warmth, attachment, kindness, tenderness, care, aroha (*NZ*) << ANTONYM dislike **2** LIKING, love, taste, fancy, attraction, weakness, preference, attachment, penchant, susceptibility, predisposition, soft spot, predilection, partiality

food *noun* NOURISHMENT, cooking, provisions, fare, board, commons, table, eats (*slang*), stores, feed, diet, meat, bread, menu, tuck (*informal*), tucker (*Austral & NZ informal*), rations, nutrition, cuisine, tack (*informal*), refreshment, scoff (*slang*), nibbles, grub (*slang*), foodstuffs, subsistence, kai (*NZ informal*), larder, chow (*informal*), sustenance, nosh (*slang*), daily bread, victuals, edibles, comestibles, provender, nosebag (*slang*), pabulum (*rare*), nutriment, vittles (*obsolete or dialect*), viands, aliment, eatables (*slang*),

survival rations

fool *noun* **1** SIMPLETON, idiot, mug (*Brit slang*), berk (*Brit slang*), charlie (*Brit informal*), silly, goose (*informal*), dope (*informal*), jerk (*slang, chiefly US & Canad*), dummy (*slang*), ass (*US & Canad taboo slang*), clot (*Brit informal*), plank (*Brit slang*), sap (*slang*), wally (*slang*), illiterate, prat (*slang*), plonker (*slang*), coot, moron, nit (*informal*), git (*Brit slang*), geek (*slang*), twit (*informal, chiefly Brit*), bonehead (*slang*), chump (*informal*), dunce, imbecile (*informal*), loon, clod, cretin, oaf, bozo (*US slang*), dullard, dimwit (*informal*), ignoramus, dumbo (*slang*), jackass, dipstick (*Brit slang*), gonzo (*slang*), schmuck (*US slang*), dork (*slang*), nitwit (*informal*), dolt, blockhead, ninny, divvy (*Brit slang*), bird-brain (*informal*), pillock (*Brit slang*), halfwit, nincompoop, dweeb (*US slang*), putz (*US slang*), fathead (*informal*), weenie (*US informal*), schlep (*US slang*), eejit (*Scot & Irish*), dumb-ass (*slang*), pea-brain (*slang*), dunderhead, numpty (*Scot informal*), doofus (*slang, chiefly US*), lamebrain (*informal*), mooncalf, thickhead, clodpate (*archaic*), nerd or nurd (*slang*), numbskull or numskull, twerp or twirp (*informal*), dorba or dorb (*Austral slang*), bogan (*Austral slang*) << ANTONYM genius **2** DUPE, butt, mug (*Brit slang*), sucker (*slang*), gull (*archaic*), stooge (*slang*), laughing stock, pushover (*informal*), fall guy (*informal*), chump (*informal*), greenhorn (*informal*), easy mark (*informal*) **3** JESTER, comic, clown, harlequin, motley, buffoon, pierrot, court jester, punchinello, joculator or (*fem.*) joculatrix, merry-andrew ▷ *verb* DECEIVE, cheat, mislead, delude, kid (*informal*), trick, take in, con (*informal*), stiff (*slang*), have (someone) on, bluff, hoax, dupe, beguile, gull (*archaic*), swindle, make a fool of, bamboozle, hoodwink, take for a ride (*informal*), put one over on (*informal*), play a trick on, pull a fast one on (*informal*) ▷▷ **fool around with something** (*informal*) PLAY AROUND WITH, play with, tamper with, toy with, mess around with, meddle with, trifle with, fiddle around with (*informal*), monkey around with

foolhardy *adjective* RASH, risky, irresponsible, reckless, precipitate, unwise, impulsive, madcap, impetuous, hot-headed, imprudent, incautious, venturesome, venturous, temerarious << ANTONYM cautious

foolish *adjective* **1** UNWISE, silly, absurd, rash, unreasonable, senseless, short-sighted, ill-advised, foolhardy, nonsensical, inane, indiscreet, ill-judged, ill-considered, imprudent, unintelligent, asinine, injudicious, incautious << ANTONYM sensible **2** SILLY, stupid, mad, daft (*informal*), simple, weak, crazy, ridiculous, dumb (*informal*), ludicrous, senseless, barmy (*slang*), potty (*Brit informal*), goofy (*informal*), idiotic, half-baked (*informal*), dotty (*slang*), inane, fatuous, loopy (*informal*), witless, crackpot (*informal*), moronic, brainless, half-witted, imbecilic, off your head (*informal*), braindead (*informal*), harebrained, as daft as a brush (*informal, chiefly Brit*), dumb-ass (*slang*), doltish

foolishly *adverb* UNWISELY, stupidly, mistakenly, absurdly, like a fool, idiotically, incautiously, imprudently, ill-advisedly, indiscreetly, short-sightedly, injudiciously, without due consideration

foolishness *noun* **1** STUPIDITY, irresponsibility, recklessness, idiocy, weakness, absurdity, indiscretion, silliness, inanity, imprudence, rashness, foolhardiness, folly, bêtise (*rare*) **2** NONSENSE, carrying-on (*informal, chiefly Brit*), rubbish, trash, bunk (*informal*), claptrap (*informal*), rigmarole, foolery, bunkum *or* buncombe (*chiefly US*)

foolproof *adjective* INFALLIBLE, certain, safe, guaranteed, never-failing, unassailable, sure-fire (*informal*), unbreakable

footing *noun* **1** BASIS, foundation, foothold, base position, ground, settlement, establishment, installation, groundwork **2** RELATIONSHIP, terms, position, basis, state, standing, condition, relations, rank, status, grade **3** FOOTHOLD, hold, grip, toehold, support

footpath *noun* (*Austral & NZ*) PAVEMENT, sidewalk (*US & Canad*)

footstep *noun* **1** STEP, tread, footfall **2** FOOTPRINT, mark, track, trace, outline, imprint, indentation, footmark

footwear *noun* FOOTGEAR, boots, shoes, slippers, sandals

forage *noun* (*for cattle, etc*) FODDER, food, feed, foodstuffs, provender ▷ *verb* SEARCH, hunt, scavenge, cast about, seek, explore, raid, scour, plunder, look round, rummage, ransack, scrounge (*informal*), fossick (*Austral & NZ*)

foray *noun* RAID, sally, incursion, inroad, attack, assault, invasion, swoop, reconnaissance, sortie, irruption

forbearance *noun* **1** PATIENCE, resignation, restraint, tolerance, indulgence, long-suffering, moderation, self-control, leniency, temperance, mildness, lenity, longanimity (*rare*) << ANTONYM impatience **2** ABSTINENCE, refraining, avoidance

forbid *verb* PROHIBIT, ban, disallow, proscribe, exclude, rule out, veto, outlaw, inhibit, hinder, preclude, make illegal, debar, interdict << ANTONYM permit

forbidden *adjective* PROHIBITED, banned, vetoed, outlawed, taboo, out of bounds, proscribed, verboten (*German*)

forbidding *adjective* THREATENING, severe, frightening, hostile, grim, menacing, sinister, daunting, ominous, unfriendly, foreboding, baleful, bodeful << ANTONYM inviting

force *noun* **1** COMPULSION, pressure, violence, enforcement, constraint, oppression, coercion, duress, arm-twisting (*informal*) **2** POWER, might, pressure, energy, stress, strength, impact, muscle, momentum, impulse, stimulus, vigour, potency, dynamism, life << ANTONYM weakness **3** INFLUENCE, power, effect, authority, weight, strength, punch (*informal*), significance, effectiveness, validity, efficacy, soundness, persuasiveness, cogency, bite **4** INTENSITY, vigour, vehemence, fierceness, drive, emphasis, persistence **5** ARMY, unit, division, corps, company, body, host, troop, squad, patrol, regiment, battalion, legion, squadron, detachment ▷ *verb* **1** COMPEL, make, drive, press, pressure, urge, overcome, oblige, railroad (*informal*), constrain, necessitate, coerce, impel, strong-arm (*informal*), dragoon, pressurize, press-gang, put the squeeze on (*informal*), obligate, twist (someone's) arm, put the screws on (*informal*), bring pressure to bear upon **2** IMPOSE, foist **3** PUSH, thrust, propel **4** BREAK OPEN, blast, wrench, prise, wrest, use violence on **5** EXTORT, drag, exact, wring << ANTONYM coax ▷▷ **in force 1** VALID, working, current, effective, binding, operative, operational, in operation, on the statute book **2** IN GREAT NUMBERS, all together, in full strength

forced *adjective* **1** COMPULSORY, enforced, slave, unwilling, mandatory, obligatory, involuntary, conscripted << ANTONYM voluntary **2** FALSE, affected, strained, wooden, stiff, artificial, contrived, unnatural, insincere, laboured << ANTONYM natural

forceful *adjective* **1** DYNAMIC, powerful,

vigorous, potent, assertive << ANTONYM weak **2** POWERFUL, strong, convincing, effective, compelling, persuasive, weighty, pithy, cogent, telling

forcible *adjective* **1** VIOLENT, armed, aggressive, compulsory, drastic, coercive **2** COMPELLING, strong, powerful, effective, active, impressive, efficient, valid, mighty, potent, energetic, forceful, weighty, cogent

forcibly *adverb* BY FORCE, compulsorily, under protest, against your will, under compulsion, by main force, willy-nilly

forebear *or* **forbear** *noun* ANCESTOR, father, predecessor, forerunner, forefather, progenitor, tupuna *or* tipuna (NZ)

foreboding *noun* **1** DREAD, fear, anxiety, chill, unease, apprehension, misgiving, premonition, presentiment, apprehensiveness **2** OMEN, warning, prediction, portent, sign, token, foreshadowing, presage, prognostication, augury, foretoken

forecast *verb* PREDICT, anticipate, foresee, foretell, call, plan, estimate, calculate, divine, prophesy, augur, forewarn, prognosticate, vaticinate (*rare*) ▷ *noun* PREDICTION, projection, anticipation, prognosis, planning, guess, outlook, prophecy, foresight, conjecture, forewarning, forethought

forefather *noun* ANCESTOR, father, predecessor, forerunner, forebear, progenitor, procreator, primogenitor, tupuna *or* tipuna (NZ)

forefront *noun* LEAD, centre, front, fore, spearhead, prominence, vanguard, foreground, leading position, van

forego ▷ see **forgo**

foregoing *adjective* PRECEDING, former, above, previous, prior, antecedent, anterior, just mentioned, previously stated

foreground *noun* **1** FRONT, focus, forefront **2** PROMINENCE, limelight, fore, forefront

foreign *adjective* **1** ALIEN, overseas, exotic, unknown, outside, strange, imported, borrowed, remote, distant, external, unfamiliar, far off, outlandish, beyond your ken << ANTONYM native **2** UNASSIMILABLE, external, extraneous, outside **3** UNCHARACTERISTIC, inappropriate, unrelated, incongruous, inapposite, irrelevant

foreigner *noun* ALIEN, incomer, immigrant, non-native, stranger, newcomer, settler, outlander

foremost *adjective* LEADING, best, first, highest, front, chief, prime, primary, supreme, initial, most important, principal, paramount, inaugural, pre-eminent, headmost

forerunner *noun* **1** OMEN, sign, indication, token, premonition, portent, augury, prognostic, foretoken, harbinger **2** PRECURSOR, predecessor, ancestor, prototype, forebear, progenitor, herald

foresee *verb* PREDICT, forecast, anticipate, envisage, prophesy, foretell, forebode, vaticinate (*rare*), divine

foreshadow *verb* PREDICT, suggest, promise, indicate, signal, imply, bode, prophesy, augur, presage, prefigure, portend, betoken, adumbrate, forebode

foresight *noun* FORETHOUGHT, prudence, circumspection, far-sightedness, care, provision, caution, precaution, anticipation, preparedness, prescience, premeditation, prevision (*rare*) << ANTONYM hindsight

forestall *verb* PREVENT, stop, frustrate, anticipate, head off, parry, thwart, intercept, hinder, preclude, balk, circumvent, obviate, nip in the bud, provide against

forestry *noun* WOODCRAFT, silviculture, arboriculture, dendrology (*botany*), woodmanship

foretaste *noun* SAMPLE, example, indication, preview, trailer, prelude, whiff, foretoken, warning

foretell *verb* PREDICT, forecast, prophesy, portend, call, signify, bode, foreshadow, augur, presage, forewarn, prognosticate, adumbrate, forebode, foreshow, soothsay, vaticinate (*rare*)

forever *or* for ever *adverb* **1** EVERMORE, always, ever, for good, for keeps, for all time, in perpetuity, for good and all (*informal*), till the cows come home (*informal*), world without end, till the end of time, till Doomsday **2** CONSTANTLY, always, all the time, continually, endlessly, persistently, eternally, perpetually, incessantly, interminably, unremittingly, everlastingly

forewarn *verb* ALERT, advise, caution, tip off, apprise, give fair warning, put on guard, put on the qui vive

foreword *noun* INTRODUCTION, preliminary, preface, preamble, prologue, prolegomenon

forfeit *noun* PENALTY, fine, damages, forfeiture, loss, mulct, amercement (*obsolete*) ▷ *verb* RELINQUISH, lose, give up, surrender, renounce, be deprived of, say goodbye to, be stripped of

forfeiture *noun* LOSS, giving up, surrender, forfeiting, confiscation, sequestration (*law*), relinquishment

forge *verb* **1** FORM, build, create, establish, set up, fashion, shape, frame, construct, invent, devise, mould, contrive, fabricate, hammer out, make, work **2** FAKE, copy, reproduce, imitate, counterfeit, feign, falsify, coin **3** CREATE, make, work, found, form, model, fashion, shape, cast, turn out, construct, devise, mould, contrive, fabricate, hammer out, beat into shape

forged *adjective* **1** FAKE, copy, false, counterfeit, pretend, artificial, mock, pirated, reproduction, synthetic, imitation, bogus, simulated, duplicate, quasi, sham, fraudulent, pseudo, fabricated, copycat (*informal*), falsified, ersatz, unoriginal, ungenuine, phony *or* phoney (*informal*) << ANTONYM genuine **2** FORMED, worked, founded, modelled, fashioned, shaped, cast, framed, stamped, crafted, moulded, minted, hammered out, beat out, beaten into shape

forger *noun* COUNTERFEITER, copier, copyist, falsifier, coiner

forgery *noun* **1** FALSIFICATION, faking, pirating, counterfeiting, fraudulence, fraudulent imitation, coining **2** FAKE, imitation, sham, counterfeit, falsification, phoney *or* phony (*informal*)

forget *verb* **1** FAIL TO REMEMBER, not remember, not recollect, let slip from the memory, fail to bring to mind << ANTONYM remember **2** NEGLECT, overlook, omit, not remember, be remiss, fail to remember **3** LEAVE BEHIND, lose, lose sight of, mislay **4** DISMISS FROM YOUR MIND, ignore, overlook, stop thinking about, let bygones be bygones, consign to oblivion, put out of your mind

forgetful *adjective* ABSENT-MINDED, vague, careless, neglectful, oblivious, lax, negligent, dreamy, slapdash, heedless, slipshod, inattentive, unmindful, apt to forget, having a memory like a sieve << ANTONYM mindful

forgetfulness *noun* ABSENT-MINDEDNESS, oblivion, inattention, carelessness, abstraction, laxity, laxness, dreaminess, obliviousness, lapse of memory, heedlessness, woolgathering

forgive *verb* EXCUSE, pardon, bear no malice towards, not hold something against, understand, acquit, condone, remit, let off (*informal*), turn a blind eye to, exonerate,

absolve, bury the hatchet, let bygones be bygones, turn a deaf ear to, accept (someone's) apology << ANTONYM blame

forgiveness *noun* PARDON, mercy, absolution, exoneration, overlooking, amnesty, acquittal, remission, condonation

forgiving *adjective* LENIENT, tolerant, compassionate, clement, patient, mild, humane, gracious, long-suffering, merciful, magnanimous, forbearing, willing to forgive, soft-hearted

forgo *or* **forego** *verb* GIVE UP, sacrifice, surrender, do without, kick (*informal*), abandon, resign, yield, relinquish, renounce, waive, say goodbye to, cede, abjure, leave alone *or* out

fork *verb* BRANCH, part, separate, split, divide, diverge, subdivide, branch off, go separate ways, bifurcate

forked *adjective* BRANCHING, split, branched, divided, angled, pronged, zigzag, tined, Y-shaped, bifurcate(d)

forlorn *adjective* **1** MISERABLE, helpless, pathetic, pitiful, lost, forgotten, abandoned, unhappy, lonely, lonesome (*chiefly US & Canad*), homeless, forsaken, bereft, destitute, wretched, disconsolate, friendless, down in the dumps (*informal*), pitiable, cheerless, woebegone, comfortless << ANTONYM cheerful **2** ABANDONED, deserted, ruined, bleak, dreary, desolate, godforsaken, waste **3** HOPELESS, useless, vain, pointless, futile, no-win, unattainable, impracticable, unachievable, impossible, not having a prayer

form *noun* **1** TYPE, sort, kind, variety, way, system, order, class, style, practice, method, species, manner, stamp, description **2** SHAPE, formation, configuration, construction, cut, model, fashion, structure, pattern, cast, appearance, stamp, mould **3** STRUCTURE, plan, order, organization, arrangement, construction, proportion, format, framework, harmony, symmetry, orderliness **4** BUILD, being, body, figure, shape, frame, outline, anatomy, silhouette, physique, person **5** CONDITION, health, shape, nick (*informal*), fitness, trim, good condition, good spirits, fettle **6** DOCUMENT, paper, sheet, questionnaire, application **7** PROCEDURE, behaviour, manners, etiquette, use, rule, conduct, ceremony, custom, convention, ritual, done thing, usage, protocol, formality, wont, right practice, kawa (*NZ*), tikanga (*NZ*) **8** (*education, chiefly*)

Brit) CLASS, year, set, rank, grade, stream
9 MODE, character, shape, appearance, arrangement, manifestation, guise, semblance, design ▷ *verb* **1** ARRANGE, combine, line up, organize, assemble, dispose, draw up **2** MAKE, produce, model, fashion, build, create, shape, manufacture, stamp, construct, assemble, forge, mould, fabricate **3** CONSTITUTE, make up, compose, comprise, serve as, make **4** ESTABLISH, start, found, launch, set up, invent, devise, put together, bring about, contrive **5** TAKE SHAPE, grow, develop, materialize, rise, appear, settle, show up (*informal*), accumulate, come into being, crystallize, become visible **6** DRAW UP, design, devise, formulate, plan, pattern, frame, organize, think up **7** DEVELOP, pick up, acquire, cultivate, contract, get into (*informal*) **8** TRAIN, develop, shape, mould, school, teach, guide, discipline, rear, educate, bring up, instruct

formal *adjective* **1** SERIOUS, stiff, detached, aloof, official, reserved, correct, conventional, remote, exact, precise, starched, prim, unbending, punctilious, ceremonious << ANTONYM informal **2** OFFICIAL, express, explicit, authorized, set, legal, fixed, regular, approved, strict, endorsed, prescribed, rigid, certified, solemn, lawful, methodical, pro forma (*Latin*) **3** CEREMONIAL, traditional, solemn, ritualistic, dressy **4** CONVENTIONAL, established, traditional

formality *noun* **1** CORRECTNESS, seriousness, decorum, ceremoniousness, protocol, etiquette, politesse, p's and q's, punctilio **2** CONVENTION, form, conventionality, matter of form, procedure, ceremony, custom, gesture, ritual, rite

format *noun* ARRANGEMENT, form, style, make-up, look, plan, design, type, appearance, construction, presentation, layout

formation *noun* **1** ESTABLISHMENT, founding, forming, setting up, starting, production, generation, organization, manufacture, constitution **2** DEVELOPMENT, shaping, constitution, evolution, moulding, composition, compilation, accumulation, genesis, crystallization **3** ARRANGEMENT, grouping, figure, design, structure, pattern, rank, organization, array, disposition, configuration

formative *adjective* **1** DEVELOPMENTAL,

sensitive, susceptible, impressionable, malleable, pliant, mouldable **2** INFLUENTIAL, determinative, controlling, important, shaping, significant, moulding, decisive, developmental

former *adjective* **1** PREVIOUS, one-time, erstwhile, ex-, late, earlier, prior, sometime, foregoing, antecedent, anterior, quondam, whilom (*archaic*), ci-devant (*French*) << ANTONYM current **2** PAST, earlier, long ago, bygone, old, ancient, departed, old-time, long gone, of yore << ANTONYM present **3** AFOREMENTIONED, above, first mentioned, aforesaid, preceding, foregoing

formerly *adverb* PREVIOUSLY, earlier, in the past, at one time, before, lately, once, already, heretofore, aforetime (*archaic*)

formidable *adjective* **1** DIFFICULT, taxing, challenging, overwhelming, staggering, daunting, mammoth, colossal, arduous, very great, onerous, toilsome << ANTONYM easy **2** IMPRESSIVE, great, powerful, tremendous, mighty, terrific, awesome, invincible, indomitable, redoubtable, puissant **3** INTIMIDATING, threatening, dangerous, terrifying, appalling, horrible, dreadful, menacing, dismaying, fearful, daunting, frightful, baleful, shocking << ANTONYM encouraging

formula *noun* **1** METHOD, plan, policy, rule, principle, procedure, recipe, prescription, blueprint, precept, modus operandi, way **2** FORM OF WORDS, code, phrase, formulary, set expression **3** MIXTURE, preparation, compound, composition, concoction, tincture, medicine

formulate *verb* **1** DEVISE, plan, develop, prepare, work out, invent, evolve, coin, forge, draw up, originate, map out **2** EXPRESS, detail, frame, define, specify, articulate, set down, codify, put into words, systematize, particularize, give form to

forsake *verb* **1** DESERT, leave, abandon, quit, strand, jettison, repudiate, cast off, disown, jilt, throw over, leave in the lurch **2** GIVE UP, set aside, relinquish, forgo, kick (*informal*), yield, surrender, renounce, have done with, stop using, abdicate, stop having, turn your back on, forswear **3** ABANDON, leave, go away from, take your leave of

forsaken *adjective* **1** ABANDONED, ignored, lonely, lonesome (*chiefly US & Canad*), stranded, ditched, left behind, marooned, outcast, forlorn, cast off, jilted, friendless, left in the lurch **2** DESERTED, abandoned, isolated, solitary, desolate, forlorn, destitute, disowned, godforsaken

fort *noun* FORTRESS, keep, station, camp, tower, castle, garrison, stronghold, citadel, fortification, redoubt, fastness, blockhouse, fortified pa (*NZ*) ▷▷ **hold the fort** (*informal*) TAKE RESPONSIBILITY, cover, stand in, carry on, take over the reins, maintain the status quo, deputize, keep things moving, keep things on an even keel

forte *noun* SPECIALITY, strength, talent, strong point, métier, long suit (*informal*), gift << ANTONYM weak point

forth *adverb* (*formal* or *old-fashioned*) **1** FORWARD, out, away, ahead, onward, outward **2** OUT, into the open, out of concealment

forthcoming *adjective* **1** APPROACHING, coming, expected, future, imminent, prospective, impending, upcoming **2** AVAILABLE, ready, accessible, at hand, in evidence, obtainable, on tap (*informal*) **3** COMMUNICATIVE, open, free, informative, expansive, sociable, chatty, talkative, unreserved

forthright *adjective* OUTSPOKEN, open, direct, frank, straightforward, blunt, downright, candid, upfront (*informal*), plain-spoken, straight from the shoulder (*informal*) << ANTONYM secretive

forthwith *adverb* IMMEDIATELY, directly, instantly, at once, right away, straightaway, without delay, tout de suite (*French*), quickly

fortification *noun* **1** REINFORCEMENT, protecting, securing, protection, strengthening, reinforcing, embattlement **2** DEFENCE, keep, protection, castle, fort, fortress, stronghold, bastion, citadel, bulwark, fastness, fortified pa (*NZ*) **3** STRENGTHENING, supplementing, reinforcement

fortify *verb* **1** PROTECT, defend, secure, strengthen, reinforce, support, brace, garrison, shore up, augment, buttress, make stronger, embattle **2** STRENGTHEN, add alcohol to **3** SUSTAIN, encourage, confirm, cheer, strengthen, reassure, brace, stiffen, hearten, embolden, invigorate << ANTONYM dishearten

fortitude *noun* COURAGE, strength, resolution, determination, guts (*informal*), patience, pluck, grit, endurance, bravery, backbone, perseverance, firmness, staying power, valour, fearlessness, strength of mind, intrepidity, hardihood, dauntlessness,

stoutheartedness

fortress *noun* CASTLE, fort, stronghold, citadel, redoubt, fastness, fortified pa (*NZ*)

fortuitous *adjective* **1** CHANCE, lucky, random, casual, contingent, accidental, arbitrary, incidental, unforeseen, unplanned **2** LUCKY, happy, fortunate, serendipitous, providential, fluky (*informal*)

fortunate *adjective* **1** LUCKY, happy, favoured, bright, golden, rosy, on a roll, jammy (*Brit slang*), in luck, having a charmed life, born with a silver spoon in your mouth << ANTONYM unfortunate **2** PROVIDENTIAL, auspicious, fortuitous, felicitous, timely, promising, encouraging, helpful, profitable, convenient, favourable, advantageous, expedient, opportune, propitious

fortunately *adverb* LUCKILY, happily, as luck would have it, providentially, by good luck, by a happy chance

fortune *noun* **1** LARGE SUM OF MONEY, bomb (*Brit slang*), packet (*slang*), bundle (*slang*), big money, big bucks (*informal, chiefly US*), megabucks (*US & Canad slang*), an arm and a leg (*informal*), king's ransom, pretty penny (*informal*), top whack (*informal*) **2** WEALTH, means, property, riches, resources, assets, pile (*informal*), possessions, treasure, prosperity, mint, gold mine, wad (*US & Canad slang*), affluence, opulence, tidy sum (*informal*) << ANTONYM poverty **3** LUCK, accident, fluke (*informal*), stroke of luck, serendipity, hap (*archaic*), twist of fate, run of luck **4** CHANCE, fate, destiny, providence, the stars, Lady Luck, kismet, fortuity **5** *often plural* DESTINY, life, lot, experiences, history, condition, success, means, circumstances, expectation, adventures

forum *noun* **1** MEETING, conference, assembly, meeting place, court, body, council, parliament, congress, gathering, diet, senate, rally, convention, tribunal (*archaic* or *literary*), seminar, get-together (*informal*), congregation, caucus (*chiefly US & Canad*), synod, convergence, symposium, hui (*NZ*), moot, assemblage, conclave, convocation, consistory (*in various Churches*), ecclesia (*in Church use*), colloquium, folkmoot (*in medieval England*), runanga (*NZ*) **2** PUBLIC SQUARE, court, square, chamber, platform, arena, pulpit, meeting place, amphitheatre, stage, rostrum, agora (*in ancient Greece*)

forward *adjective* **1** LEADING, first, head, front, advance, foremost, fore **2** FUTURE, early, advanced, progressive, premature,

prospective, onward, forward-looking
3 PRESUMPTUOUS, confident, familiar, bold, fresh (*informal*), assuming, presuming, cheeky, brash, pushy (*informal*), brazen, shameless, sassy (*US informal*), pert, impertinent, impudent, bare-faced, overweening, immodest, brass-necked (*Brit informal*), overfamiliar, brazen-faced, overassertive << ANTONYM shy ▷ *adverb* INTO THE OPEN, out, to light, to the front, to the surface, into consideration, into view, into prominence ▷ *verb* **1** FURTHER, back, help, support, aid, encourage, speed, advance, favour, promote, foster, assist, hurry, hasten, expedite << ANTONYM retard **2** SEND ON, send, post, pass on, ship, route, transmit, dispatch, freight, redirect

forwards *or* **forward** *adverb* **1** FORTH, on, ahead, onwards << ANTONYM backward(s) **2** ON, onward, onwards

fossick *verb* (*Austral & NZ*) SEARCH, hunt, explore, ferret, check, forage, rummage

foster *verb* **1** BRING UP, mother, raise, nurse, look after, rear, care for, take care of, nurture **2** DEVELOP, support, further, encourage, feed, promote, stimulate, uphold, nurture, cultivate, foment << ANTONYM suppress **3** CHERISH, sustain, entertain, harbour, accommodate, nourish

foul *adjective* **1** DIRTY, rank, offensive, nasty, disgusting, unpleasant, revolting, contaminated, rotten, polluted, stinking, filthy, tainted, grubby, repellent, squalid, repulsive, sullied, grimy, nauseating, loathsome, unclean, impure, grotty (*slang*), fetid, grungy (*slang, chiefly US & Canad*), putrid, malodorous, noisome, scuzzy (*slang, chiefly US*), mephitic, olid, yucky *or* yukky (*slang*), festy (*Austral slang*), yucko (*Austral slang*) << ANTONYM clean **2** OBSCENE, crude, indecent, foul-mouthed, low, blue, dirty, gross, abusive, coarse, filthy, vulgar, lewd, profane, blasphemous, scurrilous, smutty, scatological **3** STORMY, bad, wild, rough, wet, rainy, murky, foggy, disagreeable, blustery **4** UNFAIR, illegal, dirty, crooked, shady (*informal*), fraudulent, unjust, dishonest, unscrupulous, underhand, inequitable, unsportsmanlike **5** OFFENSIVE, bad, base, wrong, evil, notorious, corrupt, vicious, infamous, disgraceful, shameful, vile, immoral, scandalous, wicked, sinful, despicable, heinous, hateful, abhorrent, egregious, abominable, dishonourable, nefarious, iniquitous, detestable

<< ANTONYM admirable ▷ *verb* **1** DIRTY, soil, stain, contaminate, smear, pollute, taint, sully, defile, besmirch, smirch, begrime, besmear << ANTONYM clean **2** CLOG, block, jam, choke **3** ENTANGLE, catch, twist, snarl, ensnare, tangle up ▷▷ **foul something up** BUNGLE, spoil, botch, mess up, cock up (*Brit slang*), make a mess of, mismanage, make a nonsense of, muck up, clean up, make a pig's ear of (*informal*), put a spanner in the works (*Brit informal*), flub (*US slang*), crool *or* cruel (*Austral slang*)

foul play *noun* CRIME, fraud, corruption, deception, treachery, criminal activity, duplicity, dirty work, double-dealing, skulduggery, chicanery, villainy, sharp practice, perfidy, roguery, dishonest behaviour

found *verb* **1** ESTABLISH, start, set up, begin, create, institute, organize, construct, constitute, originate, endow, inaugurate, bring into being **2** ERECT, build, construct, raise, settle

foundation *noun* **1** BASIS, heart, root, mainstay, beginning, support, ground, rest, key, principle, fundamental, premise, starting point, principal element **2** *often plural* SUBSTRUCTURE, underpinning, groundwork, bedrock, base, footing, bottom **3** SETTING UP, institution, instituting, organization, settlement, establishment, initiating, originating, starting, endowment, inauguration

founded ▷▷ **founded on** BASED ON, built on, rooted in, grounded on, established on

founder[1] *noun* INITIATOR, father, establisher, author, maker, framer, designer, architect, builder, creator, beginner, generator, inventor, organizer, patriarch, benefactor, originator, constructor, institutor

founder[2] *verb* **1** FAIL, collapse, break down, abort, fall through, be unsuccessful, come to nothing, come unstuck, miscarry, misfire, fall by the wayside, come to grief, bite the dust, go belly-up (*slang*), go down like a lead balloon (*informal*) **2** SINK, go down, be lost, submerge, capsize, go to the bottom

fountain *noun* **1** FONT, spring, reservoir, spout, fount, water feature, well **2** JET, stream, spray, gush **3** SOURCE, fount, wellspring, wellhead, beginning, rise, cause, origin, genesis, commencement, derivation, fountainhead

fowl *noun* POULTRY

foxy *adjective* CRAFTY, knowing, sharp, tricky,

shrewd, cunning, sly, astute, canny, devious, wily, artful, guileful

foyer *noun* ENTRANCE HALL, lobby, reception area, vestibule, anteroom, antechamber

fracas *noun* BRAWL, fight, trouble, row, riot, disturbance, quarrel, uproar, skirmish, scuffle, free-for-all (*informal*), rumpus, aggro (*slang*), affray (*law*), shindig (*informal*), donnybrook, scrimmage, shindy (*informal*), bagarre (*French*), melee *or* mêlée, biffo (*Austral slang*)

fraction *noun* **1** BIT, little bit, mite, jot, tiny amount, iota, scintilla **2** PERCENTAGE, share, cut, division, section, proportion, slice, ratio, portion, quota, subdivision, moiety **3** FRAGMENT, part, piece, section, sector, selection, segment

fractious *adjective* IRRITABLE, cross, awkward, unruly, touchy, recalcitrant, petulant, tetchy, ratty (*Brit & NZ informal*), testy, chippy (*informal*), fretful, grouchy (*informal*), querulous, peevish, refractory, crabby, captious, froward (*archaic*), pettish << ANTONYM affable

fracture *noun* **1** BREAK, split, crack **2** CLEFT, opening, split, crack, gap, rent, breach, rift, rupture, crevice, fissure, schism ▷ *verb* **1** BREAK, crack **2** SPLIT, separate, divide, rend, fragment, splinter, rupture

fragile *adjective* **1** UNSTABLE, weak, vulnerable, delicate, uncertain, insecure, precarious, flimsy **2** FINE, weak, delicate, frail, feeble, brittle, flimsy, dainty, easily broken, breakable, frangible << ANTONYM durable **3** UNWELL, poorly, weak, delicate, crook (*Austral & NZ informal*), shaky, frail, feeble, sickly, unsteady, infirm

fragility *noun* WEAKNESS, delicacy, frailty, infirmity, feebleness, brittleness, frangibility

fragment *noun* PIECE, part, bit, scrap, particle, portion, fraction, shiver, shred, remnant, speck, sliver, wisp, morsel, oddment, chip ▷ *verb* **1** BREAK, split, shatter, crumble, shiver, disintegrate, splinter, come apart, break into pieces, come to pieces << ANTONYM fuse **2** BREAK UP, divide, split up, disunite

fragmentary *adjective* INCOMPLETE, broken, scattered, partial, disconnected, discrete, sketchy, piecemeal, incoherent, scrappy, disjointed, bitty, unsystematic

fragrance *or* **fragrancy** *noun* **1** SCENT, smell, perfume, bouquet, aroma, balm, sweet smell, sweet odour, redolence, fragrancy << ANTONYM stink **2** PERFUME, scent, cologne, eau de toilette, eau de Cologne, toilet water, Cologne water

fragrant *adjective* AROMATIC, perfumed, balmy, redolent, sweet-smelling, sweet-scented, odorous, ambrosial, odoriferous << ANTONYM stinking

frail *adjective* **1** FEEBLE, weak, puny, decrepit, infirm << ANTONYM strong **2** FLIMSY, weak, vulnerable, delicate, fragile, brittle, unsound, wispy, insubstantial, breakable, frangible, slight

frailty *noun* **1** WEAKNESS, susceptibility, fallibility, peccability << ANTONYM strength **2** INFIRMITY, poor health, feebleness, puniness, frailness **3** FAULT, failing, vice, weakness, defect, deficiency, flaw, shortcoming, blemish, imperfection, foible, weak point, peccadillo, chink in your armour << ANTONYM strong point

frame *noun* **1** MOUNTING, setting, surround, mount **2** CASING, framework, structure, shell, system, form, construction, fabric, skeleton, chassis **3** PHYSIQUE, build, form, body, figure, skeleton, anatomy, carcass, morphology ▷ *verb* **1** MOUNT, case, enclose **2** SURROUND, ring, enclose, close in, encompass, envelop, encircle, fence in, hem in **3** DEVISE, plan, form, shape, institute, draft, compose, sketch, forge, put together, conceive, hatch, draw up, formulate, contrive, map out, concoct, cook up, block out ▷▷ **frame of mind** MOOD, state, spirit, attitude, humour, temper, outlook, disposition, mind-set, fettle

framework *noun* **1** SYSTEM, plan, order, scheme, arrangement, fabric, schema, frame of reference, the bare bones **2** STRUCTURE, body, frame, foundation, shell, fabric, skeleton

franchise *noun* **1** AUTHORIZATION, right, permit, licence, charter, privilege, prerogative **2** VOTE, voting rights, suffrage

frank *adjective* **1** CANDID, open, free, round, direct, plain, straightforward, blunt, outright, sincere, outspoken, honest, downright, truthful, forthright, upfront (*informal*), unrestricted, plain-spoken, unreserved, artless, ingenuous, straight from the shoulder (*informal*) << ANTONYM secretive **2** UNCONCEALED, open, undisguised, dinkum (*Austral & NZ informal*)

frankly *adverb* **1** HONESTLY, sincerely, in truth, candidly, to tell you the truth, to be frank, to be honest **2** OPENLY, freely, directly, straight, plainly, bluntly, overtly, candidly, without reserve, straight from the shoulder

frankness *noun* OUTSPOKENNESS, openness, candour, truthfulness, plain speaking, bluntness, forthrightness, laying it on the line, ingenuousness, absence of reserve

frantic *adjective* **1** FRENZIED, wild, mad, raging, furious, raving, distracted, distraught, berserk, uptight (*informal*), overwrought, at the end of your tether, beside yourself, at your wits' end, berko (*Austral slang*) << ANTONYM calm **2** HECTIC, desperate, frenzied, fraught (*informal*), frenetic

fraternity *noun* **1** COMPANIONSHIP, fellowship, brotherhood, kinship, camaraderie, comradeship **2** CIRCLE, company, set, order, clan, guild **3** (*US & Canad*) BROTHERHOOD, club, union, society, league, association, sodality

fraud *noun* **1** DECEPTION, deceit, treachery, swindling, guile, trickery, duplicity, double-dealing, chicanery, sharp practice, imposture, fraudulence, spuriousness << ANTONYM honesty **2** SCAM, craft, cheat, sting (*informal*), deception (*slang*), artifice, humbug, canard, stratagems, chicane **3** HOAX, trick, cheat, con (*informal*), deception, sham, spoof (*informal*), prank, swindle, ruse, practical joke, joke, fast one (*informal*), imposture, fastie (*Austral slang*) **4** (*informal*) IMPOSTOR, cheat, fake, bluffer, sham, hoax, hoaxer, forgery, counterfeit, pretender, charlatan, quack, fraudster, swindler, mountebank, grifter (*slang, chiefly US & Canad*), double-dealer, phoney *or* phony (*informal*)

fraudulent *adjective* DECEITFUL, false, crooked (*informal*), untrue, sham, treacherous, dishonest, deceptive, counterfeit, spurious, crafty, swindling, double-dealing, duplicitous, knavish, phoney *or* phony (*informal*), criminal << ANTONYM genuine

fraught *adjective* **1** (*informal*) TENSE, trying, difficult, distressing, tricky, emotionally charged **2** *usually with* **with** AGITATED, wired (*slang*), anxious, distressed, tense, distracted, emotive, uptight (*informal*), emotionally charged, strung-up, on tenterhooks, hag-ridden, adrenalized >> **fraught with** FILLED WITH, full of, charged with, accompanied by, attended by, stuffed with, laden with, heavy with, bristling with, replete with, abounding with

fray¹ *noun* FIGHT, battle, row, conflict, clash, set-to (*informal*), riot, combat, disturbance, rumble (*US & NZ slang*), quarrel, brawl, skirmish, scuffle, rumpus, broil, affray (*law*), shindig (*informal*), donnybrook, battle royal, ruckus (*informal*), scrimmage, shindy (*informal*), bagarre (*French*), melee *or* mêlée, biffo (*Austral slang*), boilover (*Austral*)

fray² *verb* WEAR THIN, wear, rub, fret, wear out, chafe, wear away, become threadbare

frayed *adjective* **1** WORN, ragged, worn out, tattered, threadbare, worn thin, out at elbows **2** STRAINED, stressed, tense, edgy, uptight (*informal*), frazzled

freak *modifier* ABNORMAL, chance, unusual, unexpected, exceptional, unpredictable, queer, erratic, unparalleled, unforeseen, fortuitous, unaccountable, atypical, aberrant, fluky (*informal*), odd, bizarre ▷ *noun* **1** (*informal*) ENTHUSIAST, fan, nut (*slang*), addict, buff (*informal*), fanatic, devotee, fiend (*informal*), aficionado **2** ABERRATION, eccentric, anomaly, abnormality, sport (*biology*), monster, mutant, oddity, monstrosity, malformation, rara avis (*Latin*), queer fish (*Brit informal*), teratism **3** (*informal*) WEIRDO *or* WEIRDIE (*informal*), eccentric, oddity, case (*informal*), character (*informal*), nut (*slang*), flake (*slang, chiefly US*), oddball (*informal*), nonconformist, screwball (*slang, chiefly US & Canad*), odd fish (*informal*), kook (*US & Canad informal*), queer fish (*Brit informal*)

freakish *adjective* ODD, strange, fantastic, weird, abnormal, monstrous, grotesque, unnatural, unconventional, outlandish, freaky (*slang*), aberrant, outré, malformed, preternatural, teratoid (*biology*)

freaky *adjective* WEIRD, odd, wild, strange, crazy, bizarre, abnormal, queer, rum (*Brit slang*), unconventional, far-out (*slang*), freakish

free *adjective* **1** COMPLIMENTARY, for free (*informal*), for nothing, unpaid, for love, free of charge, on the house, without charge, gratuitous, at no cost, gratis, buckshee (*Brit slang*) **2** ALLOWED, permitted, unrestricted, unimpeded, open, clear, able, loose, unattached, unregulated, disengaged, untrammelled, unobstructed, unhampered, unengaged **3** AT LIBERTY, loose, liberated, at large, off the hook (*slang*), on the loose << ANTONYM confined **4** INDEPENDENT, unfettered, unrestrained, uncommitted, footloose, unconstrained, unengaged, not tied down **5** AVAILABLE, extra, empty, spare, vacant, unused, uninhabited, unoccupied, untaken **6** *often with* **of** *or* **with** GENEROUS, willing, liberal, eager, lavish, charitable, hospitable, prodigal, bountiful, open-handed, unstinting, unsparing, bounteous, munificent, big (*informal*) << ANTONYM mean 7 AUTONOMOUS, independent, democratic, sovereign, self-ruling, self-governing, emancipated, self-determining, autarchic 8 RELAXED, open, easy, forward, natural, frank, liberal, familiar, loose, casual, informal, spontaneous, laid-back (*informal*), easy-going (*informal*), lax, uninhibited, unforced, free and easy, unbidden, unconstrained, unceremonious << ANTONYM formal ▷ *adverb* FREELY, easily, loosely, smoothly, idly ▷ *verb* 1 *often ends with* **of** *or* **from** CLEAR, deliver, disengage, cut loose, release, rescue, rid, relieve, exempt, undo, redeem, ransom, extricate, unburden, unshackle 2 RELEASE, liberate, let out, set free, deliver, loose, discharge, unleash, let go, untie, emancipate, unchain, turn loose, uncage, set at liberty, unfetter, disenthrall, unbridle, manumit << ANTONYM confine 3 DISENTANGLE, extricate, disengage, detach, separate, loose, unfold, unravel, disconnect, untangle, untwist, unsnarl ▷▷ **free and easy** RELAXED, liberal, casual, informal, tolerant, laid-back (*informal*), easy-going, lax, lenient, uninhibited, unceremonious ▷▷ **free of** *or* **from** UNAFFECTED BY, without, above, lacking (in), beyond, clear of, devoid of, exempt from, immune to, sans (*archaic*), safe from, untouched by, deficient in, unencumbered by, not liable to

freedom *noun* 1 INDEPENDENCE, democracy, sovereignty, autonomy, self-determination, emancipation, self-government, home rule, autarchy, rangatiratanga (*NZ*) 2 LIBERTY, release, discharge, emancipation, deliverance, manumission << ANTONYM captivity 3 *usually with* **from** EXEMPTION, release, relief, privilege, immunity, impunity 4 LICENCE, latitude, a free hand, free rein, play, power, range, opportunity, ability, facility, scope, flexibility, discretion, leeway, carte blanche, blank cheque, elbowroom << ANTONYM restriction 5 OPENNESS, ease, directness, naturalness, abandon, familiarity, candour, frankness, informality, casualness, ingenuousness, lack of restraint *or* reserve, unconstraint << ANTONYM restraint

free-for-all *noun* (*informal*) FIGHT, row, riot, brawl, fracas, affray (*law*), dust-up (*informal*), shindig (*informal*), donnybrook, scrimmage, shindy (*informal*), bagarre (*French*), melee *or* mêlée, biffo (*Austral slang*)

freely *adverb* 1 ABUNDANTLY, liberally, lavishly, like water, extravagantly, copiously, unstintingly, with a free hand, bountifully, open-handedly, amply 2 OPENLY, frankly, plainly, candidly, unreservedly, straightforwardly, without reserve 3 WILLINGLY, readily, voluntarily, spontaneously, without prompting, of your own free will, of your own accord 4 EASILY, cleanly, loosely, smoothly, readily 5 WITHOUT RESTRAINT, voluntarily, willingly, unchallenged, as you please, without being forced, without let or hindrance

freeway *noun* (*US & Austral*) MOTORWAY (*Brit*), autobahn (*German*), autoroute (*French*), autostrada (*Italian*)

freewheel *verb* COAST, drift, glide, relax your efforts, rest on your oars, float

freeze *verb* 1 ICE OVER *or* UP, harden, stiffen, solidify, congeal, become solid, glaciate 2 CHILL, benumb 3 FIX, hold, limit, hold up, peg 4 SUSPEND, stop, shelve, curb, cut short, discontinue

freezing *adjective* (*informal*) 1 ICY, biting, bitter, raw, chill, chilled, penetrating, arctic, numbing, polar, Siberian, frosty, glacial, wintry, parky (*Brit informal*), cold as ice, frost-bound, cutting 2 FROZEN, chilled, numb, chilly, very cold, shivery, benumbed, frozen to the marrow

freight *noun* 1 TRANSPORTATION, traffic, delivery, carriage, shipment, haulage, conveyance, transport 2 CARGO, goods, contents, load, lading, delivery, burden, haul, bulk, shipment, merchandise, bales, consignment, payload, tonnage

French *adjective* GALLIC

frenetic *adjective* FRANTIC, wild, excited, crazy, frenzied, distraught, obsessive, fanatical, demented, unbalanced, overwrought, maniacal

frenzied *adjective* UNCONTROLLED, wild, excited, mad, crazy, furious, frantic, distraught, hysterical, agitated, frenetic, feverish, rabid, maniacal

frenzy *noun* 1 FIT, burst, bout, outburst, spasm, convulsion, paroxysm 2 FURY, transport, passion, rage, madness, turmoil, distraction, seizure, hysteria, mania, insanity, agitation, aberration, lunacy, delirium, paroxysm, derangement << ANTONYM calm

frequency *noun* RECURRENCE, repetition, constancy, periodicity, commonness, frequentness, prevalence

frequent *adjective* COMMON, repeated, usual, familiar, constant, everyday, persistent, reiterated, recurring, customary, continual, recurrent, habitual, incessant << ANTONYM infrequent ▷ *verb* VISIT, attend, haunt, be found at, patronize, hang out at (*informal*), visit often, go to regularly, be a regular customer of << ANTONYM keep away

frequently *adverb* OFTEN, commonly, repeatedly, many times, very often, oft (*archaic or poetic*), over and over again, habitually, customarily, oftentimes (*archaic*), not infrequently, many a time, much << ANTONYM infrequently

fresh *adjective* **1** ADDITIONAL, more, new, other, added, further, extra, renewed, supplementary, auxiliary **2** NATURAL, raw, crude, unsalted, unprocessed, uncured, unpreserved, undried, green << ANTONYM preserved **3** NEW, original, novel, unusual, latest, different, recent, modern, up-to-date, this season's, unconventional, unorthodox, ground-breaking, left-field (*informal*), new-fangled, modernistic << ANTONYM old **4** INVIGORATING, clear, clean, bright, sweet, pure, stiff, crisp, sparkling, bracing, refreshing, brisk, spanking, unpolluted << ANTONYM stale **5** COOL, cold, refreshing, brisk, chilly, nippy **6** VIVID, bright, verdant, undimmed, unfaded << ANTONYM old **7** ROSY, clear, fair, bright, healthy, glowing, hardy, blooming, wholesome, ruddy, florid, dewy, good << ANTONYM pallid **8** LIVELY, rested, bright, keen, vital, restored, alert, bouncing, revived, refreshed, vigorous, energetic, sprightly, invigorated, spry, chipper (*informal*), full of beans (*informal*), like a new man, full of vim and vigour (*informal*), unwearied, bright-eyed and bushy-tailed (*informal*) << ANTONYM weary **9** INEXPERIENCED, new, young, green, natural, raw, youthful, unqualified, callow, untrained, untried, artless, uncultivated, wet behind the ears << ANTONYM experienced **10** (*informal*) CHEEKY (*informal*), bold, brazen, impertinent, forward, familiar, flip (*informal*), saucy, audacious, sassy (*US informal*), pert, disrespectful, presumptuous, insolent, impudent, smart-alecky (*informal*) << ANTONYM well-mannered

freshen *verb* REFRESH, restore, rouse, enliven, revitalize, spruce up, liven up, freshen up, titivate

freshness *noun* **1** NOVELTY, creativity, originality, inventiveness, newness, innovativeness **2** CLEANNESS, shine, glow, bloom, sparkle, vigour, brightness, wholesomeness, clearness, dewiness

fret *verb* **1** WORRY, anguish, brood, agonize, obsess, lose sleep, upset yourself, distress yourself **2** ANNOY, trouble, bother, disturb, distress, provoke, irritate, grieve, torment, harass, nag, gall, agitate, ruffle, nettle, vex, goad, chagrin, irk, rile, pique, peeve (*informal*), rankle with

friction *noun* **1** CONFLICT, opposition, hostility, resentment, disagreement, rivalry, discontent, wrangling, bickering, animosity, antagonism, discord, bad feeling, bad blood, dissension, incompatibility, disharmony, dispute **2** RESISTANCE, rubbing, scraping, grating, irritation, erosion, fretting, attrition, rasping, chafing, abrasion, wearing away **3** RUBBING, scraping, grating, fretting, rasping, chafing, abrasion

friend *noun* **1** COMPANION, pal, mate (*informal*), buddy (*informal*), partner, china (*Brit & S African informal*), familiar, best friend, intimate, cock (*Brit informal*), close friend, comrade, chum (*informal*), crony, alter ego, confidant, playmate, confidante, main man (*slang, chiefly US*), soul mate, homeboy (*slang, chiefly US*), cobber (*Austral & NZ*), E hoa (*NZ old-fashioned informal*), bosom friend, boon companion, Achates << ANTONYM foe **2** SUPPORTER, ally, associate, sponsor, advocate, patron, backer, partisan, protagonist, benefactor, adherent, well-wisher

friendliness *noun* AMIABILITY, warmth, sociability, conviviality, neighbourliness, affability, geniality, kindliness, congeniality, companionability, mateyness *or* matiness (*Brit informal*), open arms

friendly *adjective* **1** AMIABLE, kind, kindly, welcoming, warm, neighbourly, thick (*informal*), attached, pally (*informal*), helpful, sympathetic, fond, outgoing, comradely, confiding, affectionate, receptive, benevolent, attentive, sociable, genial, affable, fraternal, good, close, on good terms, chummy (*informal*), peaceable, companionable, clubby, well-disposed, buddy-buddy (*slang, chiefly US & Canad*), palsy-walsy (*informal*), matey *or* maty (*Brit informal*), on visiting terms **2** AMICABLE, warm, familiar, pleasant, intimate, informal, benign, conciliatory, cordial, congenial, convivial << ANTONYM unfriendly

friendship *noun* **1** ATTACHMENT,

relationship, bond, alliance, link, association, tie 2 FRIENDLINESS, affection, harmony, goodwill, intimacy, affinity, familiarity, closeness, rapport, fondness, companionship, concord, benevolence, comradeship, amity, good-fellowship << ANTONYM unfriendliness 3 CLOSENESS, love, regard, affection, intimacy, fondness, companionship, comradeship

fright noun 1 FEAR, shock, alarm, horror, panic, terror, dread, dismay, quaking, apprehension, consternation, trepidation, cold sweat, fear and trembling, (blue) funk (informal) << ANTONYM courage 2 SCARE, start, turn, surprise, shock, jolt, the creeps (informal), the shivers, the willies (slang), the heebie-jeebies (slang) 3 (informal) SIGHT (informal), mess (informal), eyesore, scarecrow, frump

frighten verb SCARE, shock, alarm, terrify, cow, appal, startle, intimidate, dismay, daunt, unnerve, petrify, unman, terrorize, scare (someone) stiff, put the wind up (someone) (informal), scare the living daylights out of (someone) (informal), make your hair stand on end (informal), get the wind up, make your blood run cold, throw into a panic, affright (archaic), freeze your blood, make (someone) jump out of his skin (informal), throw into a fright << ANTONYM reassure

frightened adjective AFRAID, alarmed, scared, terrified, shocked, frozen, cowed, startled, dismayed, unnerved, petrified, flustered, panicky, terrorized, in a panic, scared stiff, in a cold sweat, abashed, terror-stricken, affrighted (archaic), in fear and trepidation, numb with fear

frightening adjective TERRIFYING, shocking, alarming, appalling, startling, dreadful, horrifying, menacing, intimidating, dismaying, scary (informal), fearful, daunting, fearsome, unnerving, spooky (informal), hair-raising, baleful, spine-chilling, bloodcurdling

frightful adjective 1 TERRIBLE, shocking, alarming, awful, appalling, horrible, grim, terrifying, dreadful, dread, fearful, traumatic, dire, horrendous, ghastly, hideous, harrowing, gruesome, unnerving, lurid, from hell (informal), grisly, macabre, petrifying, horrid, unspeakable, godawful (slang), hellacious (US slang) << ANTONYM pleasant 2 DREADFUL, great, terrible, extreme, awful, annoying, unpleasant, disagreeable, insufferable << ANTONYM

slight

frigid adjective 1 FREEZING, cold, frozen, icy, chill, arctic, Siberian, frosty, cool, glacial, wintry, gelid, frost-bound, hyperboreal << ANTONYM hot 2 CHILLY, formal, stiff, forbidding, rigid, passive, icy, austere, aloof, lifeless, repellent, unresponsive, unfeeling, unbending, unapproachable, passionless, unloving, cold as ice, cold-hearted << ANTONYM warm

frill noun 1 RUFFLE, gathering, tuck, ruff, flounce, ruche, ruching, furbelow, purfle 2 often plural TRIMMINGS, extras, additions, fuss, jazz (slang), dressing up, decoration(s), bits and pieces, icing on the cake, finery, embellishments, affectation(s), ornamentation, ostentation, frippery, bells and whistles, tomfoolery, gewgaws, superfluities, fanciness, frilliness, fandangles

frilly adjective RUFFLED, fancy, lacy, frothy, ruched, flouncy

fringe noun 1 BORDER, edging, edge, binding, trimming, hem, frill, tassel, flounce 2 EDGE, limits, border, margin, march, marches, outskirts, perimeter, periphery, borderline ▷ modifier UNOFFICIAL, alternative, radical, innovative, avant-garde, unconventional, unorthodox ▷ verb BORDER, edge, surround, bound, skirt, trim, enclose, flank

fringed adjective 1 BORDERED, edged, befringed 2 EDGED, bordered, margined, outlined

frisk verb 1 (informal) SEARCH, check, inspect, run over, shake down (US slang), body-search 2 FROLIC, play, sport, dance, trip, jump, bounce, hop, skip, romp, caper, prance, cavort, gambol, rollick, curvet

frisky adjective LIVELY, spirited, romping, playful, bouncy, high-spirited, rollicking, in high spirits, full of beans (informal), coltish, kittenish, frolicsome, ludic (literary), sportive, full of joie de vivre << ANTONYM sedate

fritter verb usually with **away** SQUANDER, waste, run through, dissipate, misspend, idle away, fool away, spend like water

frivolous adjective 1 FLIPPANT, foolish, dizzy, superficial, silly, flip (informal), juvenile, idle, childish, giddy, puerile, flighty, ill-considered, empty-headed, light-hearted, nonserious, light-minded, ditzy or ditsy (slang) << ANTONYM serious 2 TRIVIAL, petty, trifling, unimportant, light, minor, shallow, pointless, extravagant, peripheral, niggling, paltry, impractical, nickel-and-dime (*US slang*), footling (*informal*) << ANTONYM important

frivolousness *or* **frivolity** *noun* FLIPPANCY, fun, nonsense, folly, trifling, lightness, jest, gaiety, silliness, triviality, superficiality, levity, shallowness, childishness, giddiness, flummery, light-heartedness, puerility, flightiness, frivolousness << ANTONYM seriousness

frizzy *adjective* TIGHT-CURLED, crisp, corrugated, wiry, crimped, frizzed

frolic *noun* MERRIMENT, sport, fun, amusement, gaiety, fun and games, skylarking (*informal*), high jinks, drollery ▷ *verb* PLAY, romp, lark, caper, cavort, frisk, gambol, make merry, rollick, cut capers, sport

front *noun* **1** HEAD, start, lead, beginning, top, fore, forefront **2** EXTERIOR, facing, face, façade, frontage, anterior, obverse, forepart **3** FOREGROUND, fore, forefront, nearest part **4** (*military*) FRONT LINE, trenches, vanguard, firing line, van **5** APPEARANCE, show, face, air, bearing, aspect, manner, expression, exterior, countenance, demeanour, mien **6** (*informal*) DISGUISE, cover, blind, mask, cover-up, cloak, façade, pretext ▷ *adjective* **1** FOREMOST, at the front << ANTONYM back **2** LEADING, first, lead, head, foremost, topmost, headmost ▷ *verb often with* **on** *or* **onto** FACE ONTO, overlook, look out on, have a view of, look over *or* onto

frontier *noun* BORDER, limit, edge, bound, boundary, confines, verge, perimeter, borderline, dividing line, borderland, marches

frost *noun* HOARFROST, freeze, freeze-up, Jack Frost, rime

frosty *adjective* **1** COLD, frozen, icy, chilly, wintry, parky (*Brit informal*) **2** ICY, ice-capped, icicled, hoar (*rare*), rimy **3** UNFRIENDLY, discouraging, icy, frigid, off-putting (*Brit informal*), unenthusiastic, unwelcoming, standoffish, cold as ice

froth *noun* FOAM, head, bubbles, lather, suds, spume, effervescence, scum ▷ *verb* FIZZ, foam, come to a head, lather, bubble over, effervesce

frothy *adjective* **1** FOAMY, foaming, bubbly, effervescent, sudsy, spumous, spumescent, spumy **2** TRIVIAL, light, empty, slight, unnecessary, vain, petty, trifling, frivolous, frilly, unsubstantial

frown *verb* GLARE, scowl, glower, make a face,

look daggers, knit your brows, give a dirty look, lour *or* lower ▷ *noun* SCOWL, glare, glower, dirty look ▷▷ **frown on** DISAPPROVE OF, dislike, discourage, take a dim view of, look askance at, discountenance, view with disfavour, not take kindly to, show disapproval *or* displeasure

frozen *adjective* **1** ICY, hard, solid, frosted, arctic, ice-covered, icebound **2** CHILLED, cold, iced, refrigerated, ice-cold **3** ICE-COLD, freezing, numb, very cold, frigid, frozen stiff, chilled to the marrow **4** MOTIONLESS, rooted, petrified, stock-still, turned to stone, stopped dead in your tracks **5** FIXED, held, stopped, limited, suspended, pegged (*of prices*)

frugal *adjective* **1** THRIFTY, sparing, careful, prudent, provident, parsimonious, abstemious, penny-wise, saving, cheeseparing << ANTONYM wasteful **2** MEAGRE, economical, niggardly

fruit *noun* **1** (*botany*) PRODUCE, crop, yield, harvest **2** *often plural* RESULT, reward, outcome, end result, return, effect, benefit, profit, advantage, consequence

fruitful *adjective* **1** USEFUL, successful, effective, rewarding, profitable, productive, worthwhile, beneficial, advantageous, well-spent, gainful << ANTONYM useless **2** FERTILE, fecund, fructiferous << ANTONYM barren **3** PRODUCTIVE, prolific, abundant, plentiful, rich, flush, spawning, copious, profuse, plenteous

fruition *noun* FULFILMENT, maturity, completion, perfection, enjoyment, realization, attainment, maturation, consummation, ripeness, actualization, materialization

fruitless *adjective* USELESS, vain, unsuccessful, in vain, pointless, futile, unproductive, abortive, to no avail, ineffectual, unprofitable, to no effect, unavailing, unfruitful, profitless, bootless << ANTONYM fruitful

fruity *adjective* **1** RICH, full, mellow **2** RESONANT, full, deep, rich, vibrant, mellow **3** (*informal, chiefly Brit*) RISQUÉ, indecent, suggestive, racy, blue, hot, sexy, ripe, spicy (*informal*), vulgar, juicy, titillating, bawdy, salacious, smutty, indelicate, near the knuckle (*informal*)

frumpy *or* **frumpish** *adjective* DOWDY, dated, dreary, out of date, drab, unfashionable, dingy, mumsy, badly-dressed

frustrate *verb* **1** DISCOURAGE, anger, depress,

annoy, infuriate, exasperate, dishearten, dissatisfy << ANTONYM encourage **2** THWART, stop, check, block, defeat, disappoint, counter, confront, spoil, foil, baffle, inhibit, hobble, balk, circumvent, forestall, neutralize, stymie, nullify, render null and void, crool *or* cruel (*Austral slang*) << ANTONYM further

frustrated *adjective* DISAPPOINTED, discouraged, infuriated, discontented, exasperated, resentful, embittered, irked, disheartened, carrying a chip on your shoulder (*informal*)

frustration *noun* **1** ANNOYANCE, disappointment, resentment, irritation, grievance, dissatisfaction, exasperation, vexation **2** OBSTRUCTION, blocking, curbing, foiling, failure, spoiling, thwarting, contravention, circumvention, nonfulfilment, nonsuccess

fudge *verb* MISREPRESENT, avoid, dodge, evade, hedge, stall, fake, flannel (*Brit informal*), patch up, falsify, equivocate

fuel *noun* **1** NOURISHMENT, food, kai (*NZ informal*), sustenance **2** INCITEMENT, encouragement, ammunition, provocation, food, material, incentive, fodder ▷ *verb* INFLAME, power, charge, fire, fan, encourage, feed, boost, sustain, stimulate, nourish, incite, whip up, stoke up

fugitive *noun* RUNAWAY, refugee, deserter, escapee, runagate (*archaic*)

fulfil *or US* **fulfill** *verb* **1** CARRY OUT, perform, execute, discharge, keep, effect, finish, complete, achieve, conclude, accomplish, bring to completion << ANTONYM neglect **2** ACHIEVE, realize, satisfy, attain, consummate, bring to fruition, perfect **3** SATISFY, please, content, cheer, refresh, gratify, make happy **4** COMPLY WITH, meet, fill, satisfy, observe, obey, conform to, answer

fulfilment *or US* **fullfilment** *noun* ACHIEVEMENT, effecting, implementation, carrying out *or* through, end, crowning, discharge, discharging, completion, perfection, accomplishment, realization, attainment, observance, consummation

full *adjective* **1** FILLED, stocked, brimming, replete, complete, entire, loaded, sufficient, intact, gorged, saturated, bursting at the seams, brimful **2** CRAMMED, crowded, packed, crushed, jammed, in use, congested, chock-full, chock-a-block << ANTONYM empty **3** OCCUPIED, taken, in use, unavailable **4** SATIATED, satisfied, having had enough,

replete, sated **5** EXTENSIVE, detailed, complete, broad, generous, adequate, ample, abundant, plentiful, copious, plenary, plenteous << ANTONYM incomplete **6** COMPREHENSIVE, complete, thorough, exhaustive, all-inclusive, all-embracing, unabridged **7** ROUNDED, strong, rich, powerful, intense, pungent **8** PLUMP, rounded, voluptuous, shapely, well-rounded, buxom, curvaceous **9** VOLUMINOUS, large, loose, baggy, billowing, puffy, capacious, loose-fitting, balloon-like << ANTONYM tight **10** (*music*) RICH, strong, deep, loud, distinct, resonant, sonorous, clear << ANTONYM thin ▷▷ **in full** COMPLETELY, fully, in total, without exception, in its entirety, in toto (*Latin*) ▷▷ **to the full** THOROUGHLY, completely, fully, entirely, to the limit, without reservation, to the utmost

full-blooded *adjective* WHOLEHEARTED, full, complete, sweeping, thorough, uncompromising, exhaustive, all-embracing

full-blown *adjective* **1** FULLY DEVELOPED, total, full-scale, fully fledged, full, whole, developed, complete, advanced, entire, full-sized, fully grown, fully formed << ANTONYM undeveloped **2** IN FULL BLOOM, full, flowering, unfolded, blossoming, opened out

full-bodied *adjective* RICH, strong, heavy, heady, mellow, fruity, redolent, full-flavoured, well-matured

fullness *or US* **fulness** *noun* **1** PLENTY, glut, saturation, sufficiency, profusion, satiety, repletion, copiousness, ampleness, adequateness **2** COMPLETENESS, wealth, entirety, totality, wholeness, vastness, plenitude, comprehensiveness, broadness, extensiveness **3** ROUNDNESS, voluptuousness, curvaceousness, swelling, enlargement, dilation, distension, tumescence **4** (*music*) RICHNESS, strength, resonance, loudness, clearness

full-scale *adjective* MAJOR, extensive, wide-ranging, all-out, sweeping, comprehensive, proper, thorough, in-depth, exhaustive, all-encompassing, thoroughgoing, full-dress

fully *adverb* **1** COMPLETELY, totally, perfectly, entirely, absolutely, altogether, thoroughly, intimately, wholly, positively, utterly, every inch, heart and soul, to the hilt, one hundred per cent, in all respects, from first to last, lock, stock and barrel **2** IN ALL RESPECTS, completely, totally, entirely, altogether, thoroughly, wholly

3 ADEQUATELY, amply, comprehensively, sufficiently, enough, satisfactorily, abundantly, plentifully **4** AT LEAST, quite, without (any) exaggeration, without a word of a lie (*informal*)

fully-fledged *or* **full-fledged** *adjective* EXPERIENCED, trained, senior, professional, qualified, mature, proficient, time-served

fulsome *adjective* EXTRAVAGANT, excessive, over the top, sickening, overdone, fawning, nauseating, inordinate, ingratiating, cloying, insincere, saccharine, sycophantic, unctuous, smarmy (*Brit informal*), immoderate, adulatory, gross

fumble *verb* **1** *often with* **for** *or* **with** GROPE, flounder, paw (*informal*), scrabble, feel around **2** BUNGLE, spoil, botch, mess up, cock up (*Brit slang*), mishandle, mismanage, muff, make a hash of (*informal*), make a nonsense of, bodge (*informal*), misfield, crool *or* cruel (*Austral slang*)

fume *verb* RAGE, boil, seethe, see red (*informal*), storm, rave, rant, smoulder, crack up (*informal*), go ballistic (*slang, chiefly US*), champ at the bit (*informal*), blow a fuse (*slang, chiefly US*), fly off the handle (*informal*), get hot under the collar (*informal*), go off the deep end (*informal*), wig out (*slang*), go up the wall (*slang*), get steamed up about (*slang*) ▷ *noun* **1** *often plural* SMOKE, gas, exhaust, pollution, haze, vapour, smog, miasma, exhalation, effluvium **2** STENCH, stink, whiff (*Brit slang*), reek, pong (*Brit informal*), foul smell, niff (*Brit slang*), malodour, mephitis, fetor, noisomeness

fuming *adjective* FURIOUS, angry, raging, choked, roused, incensed, enraged, seething, up in arms, incandescent, in a rage, on the warpath (*informal*), foaming at the mouth, at boiling point (*informal*), all steamed up (*slang*), tooshie (*Austral slang*)

fun *noun* **1** AMUSEMENT, sport, treat, pleasure, entertainment, cheer, good time, recreation, enjoyment, romp, distraction, diversion, frolic, junketing, merriment, whoopee (*informal*), high jinks, living it up, jollity, beer and skittles (*informal*), merrymaking, jollification **2** JOKING, clowning, merriment, playfulness, play, game, sport, nonsense, teasing, jesting, skylarking (*informal*), horseplay, buffoonery, tomfoolery, jocularity, foolery **3** ENJOYMENT, pleasure, joy, cheer, mirth, gaiety << ANTONYM gloom ▷ *modifier* ENJOYABLE, entertaining, pleasant, amusing, lively, diverting, witty, convivial ▷▷ **for** *or* **in**

fun FOR A JOKE, tongue in cheek, jokingly, playfully, for a laugh, mischievously, in jest, teasingly, with a straight face, facetiously, light-heartedly, roguishly, with a gleam *or* twinkle in your eye ▷▷ **make fun of something** *or* **someone** MOCK, tease, ridicule, poke fun at, take off, rag, rib (*informal*), laugh at, taunt, mimic, parody, deride, send up (*Brit informal*), scoff at, sneer at, lampoon, make a fool of, pour scorn on, take the mickey out of (*Brit informal*), satirize, pull someone's leg, hold up to ridicule, make a monkey of, make sport of, make the butt of, make game of

function *noun* **1** PURPOSE, business, job, concern, use, part, office, charge, role, post, operation, situation, activity, exercise, responsibility, task, duty, mission, employment, capacity, province, occupation, raison d'être (*French*) **2** RECEPTION, party, affair, gathering, bash (*informal*), lig (*Brit slang*), social occasion, soiree, do (*informal*) ▷ *verb* **1** WORK, run, operate, perform, be in business, be in running order, be in operation *or* action, go **2** *with* **as** ACT, serve, operate, perform, behave, officiate, act the part of, do duty, have the role of, be in commission, be in operation *or* action, serve your turn

functional *adjective* **1** PRACTICAL, utility, utilitarian, serviceable, hard-wearing, useful **2** WORKING, operative, operational, in working order, going, prepared, ready, viable, up and running, workable, usable

functionary *noun* OFFICER, official, dignitary, office holder, office bearer, employee

fund *noun* **1** RESERVE, stock, supply, store, collection, pool, foundation, endowment, tontine **2** STORE, stock, source, supply, mine, reserve, treasury, vein, reservoir, accumulation, hoard, repository ▷ *verb* FINANCE, back, support, pay for, promote, float, endow, subsidize, stake, capitalize, provide money for, put up the money for

fundamental *adjective* **1** CENTRAL, first, most important, prime, key, necessary, basic, essential, primary, vital, radical, principal, cardinal, integral, indispensable, intrinsic << ANTONYM incidental **2** BASIC, essential, underlying, organic, profound, elementary, rudimentary

fundamentally *adverb* **1** BASICALLY, at heart, at bottom **2** ESSENTIALLY, radically, basically, primarily, profoundly, intrinsically

fundi *noun* (*S African*) EXPERT, authority,

specialist, professional, master, pro (*informal*), ace (*informal*), genius, guru, pundit, buff (*informal*), maestro, virtuoso, boffin (*Brit informal*), hotshot (*informal*), past master, dab hand (*Brit informal*), wonk (*informal*), maven (*US*)

funds *plural noun* MONEY, capital, cash, finance, means, savings, necessary (*informal*), resources, assets, silver, bread (*slang*), wealth, tin (*slang*), brass (*N English dialect*), dough (*slang*), rhino (*Brit slang*), the ready (*informal*), dosh (*Brit & Austral slang*), hard cash, the wherewithal, needful (*informal*), shekels (*informal*), dibs (*slang*), ready money, ackers (*slang*), spondulicks (*slang*)

funeral *noun* BURIAL, committal, laying to rest, cremation, interment, obsequies, entombment, inhumation

funereal *adjective* GLOOMY, dark, sad, grave, depressing, dismal, lamenting, solemn, dreary, sombre, woeful, mournful, lugubrious, sepulchral, dirge-like, deathlike

funk *verb* CHICKEN OUT OF, dodge, recoil from, take fright, flinch from, duck out of (*informal*), turn tail (*informal*)

funnel *verb* 1 CONDUCT, direct, channel, convey, move, pass, pour, filter 2 CHANNEL, direct, pour, filter, convey

funny *adjective* 1 HUMOROUS, amusing, comical, entertaining, killing (*informal*), rich, comic, silly, ridiculous, diverting, absurd, jolly, witty, hilarious, ludicrous, laughable, farcical, slapstick, riotous, droll, risible, facetious, jocular, side-splitting, waggish, jocose << ANTONYM unfunny 2 COMIC, comical, a scream, a card (*informal*), a caution (*informal*) 3 PECULIAR, odd, strange, unusual, remarkable, bizarre, puzzling, curious, weird, mysterious, suspicious, dubious, queer, rum (*Brit slang*), quirky, perplexing 4 (*informal*) ILL, poorly (*informal*), queasy, sick, odd, crook (*Austral & NZ informal*), ailing, queer, unhealthy, seedy (*informal*), unwell, out of sorts (*informal*), off-colour (*informal*), under the weather (*informal*)

furious *adjective* 1 ANGRY, mad, raging, boiling, fuming, choked, frantic, frenzied, infuriated, incensed, enraged, maddened, inflamed, very angry, cross, livid (*informal*), up in arms, incandescent, on the warpath (*informal*), foaming at the mouth, wrathful, in high dudgeon, wroth (*archaic*), fit to be tied (*slang*), beside yourself, tooshie (*Austral slang*) << ANTONYM pleased 2 VIOLENT, wild, intense, fierce, savage, turbulent, stormy, agitated, boisterous, tumultuous, vehement, unrestrained, tempestuous, impetuous, ungovernable

furnish *verb* 1 DECORATE, fit, fit out, appoint, provide, stock, supply, store, provision, outfit, equip, fit up, purvey 2 SUPPLY, give, offer, provide, present, reveal, grant, afford, hand out, endow, bestow

furniture *noun* HOUSEHOLD GOODS, furnishings, fittings, house fittings, goods, things (*informal*), effects, equipment, appointments, possessions, appliances, chattels, movable property, movables

furore *or US* **furor** *noun* COMMOTION, to-do, stir, excitement, fury, disturbance, flap (*informal*), outburst, frenzy, outcry, uproar, brouhaha, hullabaloo

furrow *noun* 1 GROOVE, line, channel, hollow, trench, seam, crease, fluting, rut, corrugation 2 WRINKLE, line, crease, crinkle, crow's-foot, gather, fold, crumple, rumple, pucker, corrugation ▷ *verb* WRINKLE, knit, draw together, crease, seam, flute, corrugate

further *adverb* IN ADDITION, moreover, besides, furthermore, also, yet, on top of, what's more, to boot, additionally, over and above, as well as, into the bargain ▷ *adjective* ADDITIONAL, more, new, other, extra, fresh, supplementary ▷ *verb* PROMOTE, help, develop, aid, forward, champion, push, encourage, speed, advance, work for, foster, contribute to, assist, plug (*informal*), facilitate, pave the way for, hasten, patronize, expedite, succour, lend support to << ANTONYM hinder ▷ see **farther**

furthermore *adverb* MOREOVER, further, in addition, besides, too, as well, not to mention, what's more, to boot, additionally, into the bargain

furthest *adjective* MOST DISTANT, extreme, ultimate, remotest, outermost, uttermost, furthermost, outmost ▷ see **farthest**

furtive *adjective* SLY, secret, hidden, sneaking, covert, cloaked, behind someone's back, secretive, clandestine, sneaky, under-the-table, slinking, conspiratorial, skulking, underhand, surreptitious, stealthy << ANTONYM open

fury *noun* 1 ANGER, passion, rage, madness, frenzy, wrath, ire, red mist (*informal*), impetuosity << ANTONYM calmness 2 VIOLENCE, force, power, intensity, severity, turbulence, ferocity, savagery, vehemence, fierceness, tempestuousness << ANTONYM peace

fuse *verb* 1 JOIN, unite, combine, blend, integrate, merge, put together, dissolve, amalgamate, federate, coalesce, intermingle, meld, run together, commingle, intermix, agglutinate << ANTONYM separate 2 BOND, join, stick, melt, weld, smelt, solder

fusion *noun* MERGING, uniting, union, merger, federation, mixture, blend, blending, integration, synthesis, amalgamation, coalescence, commingling, commixture

fuss *noun* 1 COMMOTION, to-do, worry, upset, bother, stir, confusion, excitement, hurry, flap (*informal*), bustle, flutter, flurry, agitation, fidget, fluster, ado, hue and cry, palaver, storm in a teacup (*Brit*), pother 2 BOTHER, trouble, struggle, hassle (*informal*), nuisance, inconvenience, hindrance 3 COMPLAINT, row, protest, objection, trouble, display, argument, difficulty, upset, bother, unrest, hassle (*informal*), squabble, furore, altercation ▷ *verb* WORRY, flap (*informal*), bustle, fret, niggle, fidget, chafe, take pains, make a meal of (*informal*), be agitated, labour over, get worked up, get in a stew (*informal*), make a thing of (*informal*)

fussy *adjective* 1 PARTICULAR, difficult, exacting, discriminating, fastidious, dainty, squeamish, choosy (*informal*), picky (*informal*), nit-picking (*informal*), hard to please, finicky, pernickety, faddish, faddy, old-maidish, old womanish, overparticular 2 OVERELABORATE, busy, cluttered, rococo, overdecorated, overembellished

futile *adjective* 1 USELESS, vain, unsuccessful, pointless, empty, hollow, in vain, worthless, barren, sterile, fruitless, forlorn, unproductive, abortive, to no avail, ineffectual, unprofitable, valueless, unavailing, otiose, profitless, nugatory, without rhyme or reason, bootless << ANTONYM useful 2 TRIVIAL, pointless, trifling, unimportant << ANTONYM important

futility *noun* 1 USELESSNESS, ineffectiveness, pointlessness, fruitlessness, emptiness, hollowness, spitting in the wind, bootlessness 2 TRIVIALITY, vanity, pointlessness, unimportance

future *noun* 1 TIME TO COME, hereafter, what lies ahead 2 PROSPECT, expectation, outlook ▷ *adjective* FORTHCOMING, to be, coming, later, expected, approaching, to come, succeeding, fated, ultimate, subsequent, destined, prospective, eventual, ensuing, impending, unborn, in the offing << ANTONYM past

fuzz *noun* FLUFF, down, hair, pile, fibre, nap, floss, lint

fuzzy *adjective* 1 FRIZZY, fluffy, woolly, downy, flossy, down-covered, linty, napped 2 INDISTINCT, faint, blurred, vague, distorted, unclear, shadowy, bleary, unfocused, out of focus, ill-defined << ANTONYM distinct

gadget *noun* DEVICE, thing, appliance, machine, tool, implement, invention, instrument, novelty, apparatus, gimmick, utensil, contraption (*informal*), gizmo (*slang, chiefly US & Canad*), contrivance

gaffe *noun* BLUNDER, mistake, error, indiscretion, lapse, boob (*Brit slang*), slip-up (*informal*), slip, howler, bloomer (*informal*), clanger (*informal*), faux pas, boo-boo (*informal*), solecism, gaucherie, barry *or* Barry Crocker (*Austral slang*)

gag¹ *noun* MUZZLE, tie, restraint ▷ *verb* 1 SUPPRESS, silence, subdue, muffle, curb, stifle, muzzle, quieten 2 RETCH, choke, heave

gag² *noun* (*informal*) JOKE, crack (*slang*), funny (*informal*), quip, pun, jest, wisecrack (*informal*), sally, witticism

gaiety *noun* 1 CHEERFULNESS, glee, good humour, buoyancy, happiness, animation, exuberance, high spirits, elation, exhilaration, hilarity, merriment, joie de vivre (*French*), good cheer, vivacity, jollity, liveliness, gladness, effervescence, light-heartedness, joyousness << ANTONYM misery 2 MERRYMAKING, celebration, revels, festivity, fun, mirth, revelry, conviviality, jollification, carousal

gaily *adverb* 1 CHEERFULLY, happily, gleefully, brightly, blithely, merrily, joyfully, cheerily, jauntily, light-heartedly, chirpily (*informal*) 2 COLOURFULLY, brightly, vividly, flamboyantly, gaudily, brilliantly, flashily, showily

gain *verb* 1 ACQUIRE, get, receive, achieve, earn, pick up, win, secure, collect, gather, obtain, build up, attain, glean, procure 2 PROFIT, make, earn, get, win, clear, land, score (*slang*), achieve, net, bag, secure, collect, gather, realize, obtain, capture, acquire, bring in, harvest, attain, reap, glean, procure << ANTONYM lose 3 PUT ON, increase in, gather, build up 4 ATTAIN, earn, get, achieve, win, reach, get to, secure, obtain, acquire, arrive at, procure ▷ *noun* 1 RISE, increase, growth, advance, improvement, upsurge, upturn, increment, upswing 2 PROFIT, income, earnings, proceeds, winnings, return, produce, benefit, advantage, yield, dividend, acquisition, attainment, lucre, emolument << ANTONYM loss ▷ *plural noun* PROFITS, earnings, revenue, proceeds, winnings, takings, pickings, booty ▷▷ **gain on something** *or* **someone** GET NEARER TO, close in on, approach, catch up with, narrow the gap on

gainful *adjective* PROFITABLE, rewarding, productive, lucrative, paying, useful, valuable, worthwhile, beneficial, fruitful, advantageous, expedient, remunerative, moneymaking

gainsay *verb* DENY, dispute, disagree with, contradict, contravene, rebut, controvert << ANTONYM confirm

gait *noun* WALK, step, bearing, pace, stride, carriage, tread, manner of walking

gala *noun* FESTIVAL, party, fête, celebration, carnival, festivity, pageant, jamboree ▷ *adjective* FESTIVE, merry, joyous, joyful, celebratory, convivial, gay, festal

galaxy *noun* STAR SYSTEM, solar system, nebula

gale *noun* 1 STORM, hurricane, tornado, cyclone, whirlwind, blast, gust, typhoon, tempest, squall 2 (*informal*) OUTBURST, scream, roar, fit, storm, shout, burst, explosion, outbreak, howl, shriek, eruption, peal, paroxysm

gall¹ *verb* ANNOY, provoke, irritate, aggravate (*informal*), get (*informal*), trouble, bother, disturb, plague, madden, ruffle, exasperate, nettle, vex, displease, irk, rile (*informal*), peeve (*informal*), get under your skin (*informal*), get on your nerves (*informal*), nark (*Brit, Austral & NZ slang*), get up your nose (*informal*), make your blood boil, rub up the wrong way, get on your wick (*Brit slang*), get your back up, put your back up, hack you off (*informal*)

gall² *noun* GROWTH, lump, excrescence

gallant *adjective* **1** BRAVE, daring, bold, heroic, courageous, dashing, noble, manly, gritty, fearless, intrepid, valiant, plucky, doughty, dauntless, lion-hearted, valorous, manful, mettlesome << ANTONYM cowardly **2** COURTEOUS, mannerly, gentlemanly, polite, gracious, attentive, courtly, chivalrous << ANTONYM discourteous

gallantry *noun* **1** BRAVERY, spirit, daring, courage, nerve, guts (*informal*), pluck, grit, heroism, mettle, boldness, manliness, valour, derring-do (*archaic*), fearlessness, intrepidity, valiance, courageousness, dauntlessness, doughtiness << ANTONYM cowardice **2** COURTESY, politeness, chivalry, attentiveness, graciousness, courtliness, gentlemanliness, courteousness << ANTONYM discourtesy

galling *adjective* ANNOYING, provoking, irritating, aggravating (*informal*), disturbing, humiliating, maddening, exasperating, vexing, displeasing, rankling, irksome, vexatious, nettlesome

gallop *verb* **1** RUN, race, shoot, career, speed, bolt, stampede **2** DASH, run, race, shoot, fly, career, speed, tear, rush, barrel (along) (*informal, chiefly US & Canad*), sprint, dart, zoom

galore *adverb* IN ABUNDANCE, everywhere, to spare, all over the place, aplenty, in great numbers, in profusion, in great quantity, à gogo (*informal*)

galvanize *verb* STIMULATE, encourage, inspire, prompt, move, fire, shock, excite, wake, stir, spur, provoke, startle, arouse, awaken, rouse, prod, jolt, kick-start, electrify, goad, impel, invigorate

gamble *noun* **1** RISK, chance, venture, lottery, speculation, uncertainty, leap in the dark << ANTONYM certainty **2** BET, flutter (*informal*), punt (*chiefly Brit*), wager ▷ *verb* **1** *often with* **on** TAKE A CHANCE, back, speculate, take the plunge, stick your neck out (*informal*), put your faith *or* trust in **2** RISK, chance, stake, venture, hazard, wager **3** BET, play, game, stake, speculate, back,

punt, wager, put money on, have a flutter (*informal*), try your luck, put your shirt on, lay *or* make a bet

game¹ *noun* **1** PASTIME, sport, activity, entertainment, recreation, distraction, amusement, diversion << ANTONYM job **2** MATCH, meeting, event, competition, tournament, clash, contest, round, head-to-head **3** AMUSEMENT, joke, entertainment, diversion, lark **4** ACTIVITY, business, line, situation, proceeding, enterprise, undertaking, occupation, pursuit **5** WILD ANIMALS *or* BIRDS, prey, quarry **6** SCHEME, plan, design, strategy, trick, plot, tactic, manoeuvre, dodge, ploy, scam, stratagem, fastie (*Austral slang*) ▷ *adjective* **1** WILLING, prepared, ready, keen, eager, interested, inclined, disposed, up for it (*informal*), desirous **2** BRAVE, courageous, dogged, spirited, daring, bold, persistent, gritty, fearless, feisty (*informal, chiefly US & Canad*), persevering, intrepid, valiant, plucky, unflinching, dauntless, (as) game as Ned Kelly (*Austral slang*) << ANTONYM cowardly

game² *adjective* LAME, injured, disabled, crippled, defective, bad, maimed, deformed, gammy (*Brit slang*)

gamut *noun* RANGE, series, collection, variety, lot, field, scale, sweep, catalogue, scope, compass, assortment

gang *noun* GROUP, crowd, pack, company, party, lot, band, crew (*informal*), bunch, mob, horde

gangster *noun* HOODLUM (*chiefly US*), crook (*informal*), thug, bandit, heavy (*slang*), tough, hood (*US slang*), robber, gang member, mobster (*US slang*), racketeer, desperado, ruffian, brigand, wise guy (*US*), tsotsi (*S African*)

gaol ▷ see **jail**

gap *noun* **1** OPENING, space, hole, break, split, divide, crack, rent, breach, slot, vent, rift, aperture, cleft, chink, crevice, fissure, cranny, perforation, interstice **2** INTERVAL, pause, recess, interruption, respite, lull, interlude, breathing space, hiatus, intermission, lacuna, entr'acte **3** DIFFERENCE, gulf, contrast, disagreement, discrepancy, inconsistency, disparity, divergence

gape *verb* **1** STARE, wonder, goggle, gawp (*Brit slang*), gawk **2** OPEN, split, crack, yawn

gaping *adjective* WIDE, great, open, broad, vast, yawning, wide open, cavernous

garb *noun* CLOTHES, dress, clothing, gear (*slang*), wear, habit, get-up (*informal*), uniform, outfit, costume, threads (*slang*), array, ensemble, garments, robes, duds (*informal*), apparel, clobber (*Brit slang*), attire, togs (*informal*), vestments, raiment (*archaic*), rigout (*informal*)

garbage *noun* 1 JUNK, rubbish, litter, trash (*chiefly US*), refuse, waste, sweepings, scraps, debris, muck, filth, swill, slops, offal, detritus, dross, odds and ends, flotsam and jetsam, grot (*slang*), leavings, dreck (*slang, chiefly US*), scourings, offscourings 2 NONSENSE, rot, crap (*slang*), trash, hot air (*informal*), tosh (*informal*), pap, bilge (*informal*), drivel, twaddle, tripe (*informal*), gibberish, guff (*slang*), moonshine, claptrap (*informal*), hogwash, hokum (*slang, chiefly US & Canad*), codswallop (*Brit slang*), piffle (*informal*), poppycock (*informal*), balderdash, bosh (*informal*), eyewash (*informal*), kak (*S African slang*), stuff and nonsense, bunkum or buncombe (*chiefly US*), bizzo (*Austral slang*), bull's wool (*Austral & NZ slang*)

garbled *adjective* JUMBLED, confused, distorted, mixed up, muddled, incomprehensible, unintelligible

garden *noun* GROUNDS, park, plot, patch, lawn, allotment, yard (*US & Canad*), forest park (*NZ*)

gargantuan *adjective* HUGE, big, large, giant, massive, towering, vast, enormous, extensive, tremendous, immense, mega (*slang*), titanic, jumbo (*informal*), gigantic, monumental, monstrous, mammoth, colossal, mountainous, prodigious, stupendous, elephantine, ginormous (*informal*), Brobdingnagian, humongous or humungous (*US slang*) << ANTONYM tiny

garish *adjective* GAUDY, bright, glaring, vulgar, brilliant, flash (*informal*), loud, brash, tacky (*informal*), flashy, tasteless, naff (*Brit slang*), jazzy (*informal*), tawdry, showy, brassy, raffish << ANTONYM dull

garland *noun* WREATH, band, bays, crown, honours, loop, laurels, festoon, coronet, coronal, chaplet ▷ *verb* ADORN, crown, deck, festoon, wreathe

garment *noun often plural* CLOTHES, wear, dress, clothing, gear (*slang*), habit, get-up (*informal*), uniform, outfit, costume, threads (*slang*), array, robes, duds (*informal*), apparel, clobber (*Brit slang*), attire, garb, togs, vestments, articles of clothing, raiment (*archaic*), rigout (*informal*), habiliment

garnish *noun* DECORATION, ornament, embellishment, adornment, ornamentation,

trimming, trim ▷ *verb* DECORATE, adorn, ornament, embellish, deck, festoon, trim, bedeck << ANTONYM strip

garrison *noun* 1 TROOPS, group, unit, section, command, armed force, detachment 2 FORT, fortress, camp, base, post, station, stronghold, fortification, encampment, fortified pa (*NZ*) ▷ *verb* STATION, position, post, mount, install, assign, put on duty

garrulous *adjective* 1 TALKATIVE, gossiping, chattering, babbling, gushing, chatty, long-winded, effusive, gabby (*informal*), prattling, voluble, gossipy, loquacious, verbose, mouthy << ANTONYM taciturn 2 RAMBLING, lengthy, diffuse, long-winded, wordy, discursive, windy, overlong, verbose, prolix, prosy << ANTONYM concise

gas *noun* 1 FUMES, vapour 2 (*US, Canad & NZ*) PETROL, gasoline (*trademark*)

gash *noun* CUT, tear, split, wound, rent, slash, slit, gouge, incision, laceration ▷ *verb* CUT, tear, split, wound, rend, slash, slit, gouge, lacerate

gasp *verb* PANT, blow, puff, choke, gulp, fight for breath, catch your breath ▷ *noun* PANT, puff, gulp, intake of breath, sharp intake of breath

gate *noun* BARRIER, opening, door, access, port (*Scot*), entrance, exit, gateway, portal, egress

gather *verb* 1 CONGREGATE, assemble, get together, collect, group, meet, mass, rally, flock, come together, muster, convene, converge, rendezvous, foregather << ANTONYM scatter 2 ASSEMBLE, group, collect, round up, marshal, bring together, muster, convene, call together << ANTONYM disperse 3 COLLECT, assemble, accumulate, round up, mass, heap, marshal, bring together, muster, pile up, garner, amass, stockpile, hoard, stack up 4 PICK, harvest, pluck, reap, garner, glean 5 BUILD UP, rise, increase, grow, develop, expand, swell, intensify, wax, heighten, deepen, enlarge, thicken 6 UNDERSTAND, believe, hear, learn, assume, take it, conclude, presume, be informed, infer, deduce, surmise, be led to believe 7 FOLD, tuck, pleat, ruffle, pucker, shirr

gathering *noun* ASSEMBLY, group, crowd, meeting, conference, company, party, congress, mass, rally, convention, knot, flock, get-together (*informal*), congregation, muster, turnout, multitude, throng, hui (*NZ*), concourse, assemblage, conclave, convocation, runanga (NZ)

gauche *adjective* AWKWARD, clumsy, inept, unsophisticated, inelegant, graceless, unpolished, uncultured, maladroit, ill-bred, ill-mannered, lacking in social graces << ANTONYM sophisticated

gaudy *adjective* GARISH, bright, glaring, vulgar, brilliant, flash (*informal*), loud, brash, tacky (*informal*), flashy, tasteless, jazzy (*informal*), tawdry, showy, gay, ostentatious, raffish << ANTONYM dull

gauge *verb* 1 MEASURE, calculate, evaluate, value, size, determine, count, weigh, compute, ascertain, quantify 2 JUDGE, estimate, guess, assess, evaluate, rate, appraise, reckon, adjudge ▷ *noun* METER, indicator, dial, measuring instrument

gaunt *adjective* 1 THIN, lean, skinny, skeletal, wasted, drawn, spare, pinched, angular, bony, lanky, haggard, emaciated, scrawny, skin and bone, scraggy, cadaverous, rawboned << ANTONYM plump 2 BLEAK, bare, harsh, forbidding, grim, stark, dismal, dreary, desolate, forlorn << ANTONYM inviting

gawky *adjective* AWKWARD, clumsy, lumbering, ungainly, gauche, uncouth, loutish, graceless, clownish, oafish, maladroit, lumpish, ungraceful, unco (*Austral slang*) <<^ANTONYM graceful

gay *adjective* 1 HOMOSEXUAL, camp (*informal*), lesbian, pink (*informal*), queer (*informal or derogatory*), same-sex, sapphic, moffie (*S African slang*) 2 CHEERFUL, happy, bright, glad, lively, sparkling, sunny, jolly, animated, merry, upbeat (*informal*), buoyant, cheery, joyous, joyful, carefree, jaunty, chirpy (*informal*), vivacious, jovial, gleeful, debonair, blithe, insouciant, full of beans (*informal*), light-hearted << ANTONYM sad 3 COLOURFUL, rich, bright, brilliant, vivid, flamboyant, flashy, gaudy, garish, showy << ANTONYM drab ▷ *noun* HOMOSEXUAL, lesbian, fairy (*slang*), queer (*informal or derogatory*), faggot (*slang, chiefly US & Canad*), auntie *or* aunty (*Austral slang*), lily (*Austral slang*) << ANTONYM heterosexual

gaze *verb* STARE, look, view, watch, regard, contemplate, gape, eyeball (*slang*), ogle, look fixedly ▷ *noun* STARE, look, fixed look

gazette *noun* NEWSPAPER, paper, journal, organ, periodical, news-sheet

g'day *or* **gidday** *interjection* (*Austral & NZ*) HELLO, hi (*informal*), greetings, how do you do?, good morning, good evening, good afternoon, welcome, kia ora (NZ)

gear *noun* 1 MECHANISM, works, action, gearing, machinery, cogs, cogwheels, gearwheels 2 EQUIPMENT, supplies, tackle, tools, instruments, outfit, rigging, rig, accessories, apparatus, trappings, paraphernalia, accoutrements, appurtenances, equipage 3 POSSESSIONS, things, effects, stuff, kit, luggage, baggage, belongings, paraphernalia, personal property, chattels 4 CLOTHING, wear, dress, clothes, habit, outfit, costume, threads (*slang*), array, garments, apparel, attire, garb, togs, rigout ▷ *verb with* **to** *or* **towards** EQUIP, fit, suit, adjust, adapt, rig, tailor

gem *noun* 1 PRECIOUS STONE, jewel, stone, semiprecious stone 2 TREASURE, pick, prize, jewel, flower, pearl, masterpiece, paragon, humdinger (*slang*), taonga (NZ)

genealogy *noun* ANCESTRY, descent, pedigree, line, origin, extraction, lineage, family tree, parentage, derivation, blood line

general *adjective* 1 WIDESPREAD, accepted, popular, public, common, broad, extensive, universal, prevailing, prevalent << ANTONYM individual 2 OVERALL, complete, total, global, comprehensive, blanket, inclusive, all-embracing, overarching << ANTONYM restricted 3 UNIVERSAL, overall, widespread, collective, across-the-board, all-inclusive << ANTONYM exceptional 4 VAGUE, broad, loose, blanket, sweeping, unclear, inaccurate, approximate, woolly, indefinite, hazy, imprecise, ill-defined, inexact, unspecific, undetailed << ANTONYM specific

generality *noun* 1 GENERALIZATION, abstraction, sweeping statement, vague notion, loose statement 2 IMPRECISENESS, vagueness, looseness, lack of detail, inexactitude, woolliness, indefiniteness, approximateness, inexactness, lack of preciseness

generally *adverb* 1 BROADLY, mainly, mostly, principally, on the whole, predominantly, in the main, for the most part 2 USUALLY, commonly, typically, regularly, normally, on average, on the whole, for the most part, almost always, in most cases, by and large, ordinarily, as a rule, habitually, conventionally, customarily << ANTONYM occasionally 3 COMMONLY, widely, publicly, universally, extensively, popularly, conventionally, customarily << ANTONYM individually

generate *verb* PRODUCE, create, make, form,

cause, initiate, bring about, originate, give rise to, engender, whip up << ANTONYM end

generation *noun* 1 AGE GROUP, peer group 2 AGE, period, era, time, days, lifetime, span, epoch

generic *adjective* COLLECTIVE, general, common, wide, sweeping, comprehensive, universal, blanket, inclusive, all-encompassing << ANTONYM specific

generosity *noun* 1 LIBERALITY, charity, bounty, munificence, beneficence, largesse *or* largess 2 MAGNANIMITY, goodness, kindness, benevolence, selflessness, charity, unselfishness, high-mindedness, nobleness

generous *adjective* 1 LIBERAL, lavish, free, charitable, free-handed, hospitable, prodigal, bountiful, open-handed, unstinting, beneficent, princely, bounteous, munificent, ungrudging << ANTONYM mean 2 MAGNANIMOUS, kind, noble, benevolent, good, big, high-minded, unselfish, big-hearted, ungrudging 3 PLENTIFUL, lavish, ample, abundant, full, rich, liberal, overflowing, copious, bountiful, unstinting, profuse, bounteous (*literary*), plenteous << ANTONYM meagre

genesis *noun* BEGINNING, source, root, origin, start, generation, birth, creation, dawn, formation, outset, starting point, engendering, inception, commencement, propagation << ANTONYM end

genial *adjective* FRIENDLY, kind, kindly, pleasant, warm, cheerful, jolly, hearty, agreeable, cheery, amiable, cordial, affable, congenial, jovial, convivial, good-natured, warm-hearted << ANTONYM unfriendly

genitals *plural noun* SEX ORGANS, privates, loins, genitalia, private parts, reproductive organs, pudenda

genius *noun* 1 BRILLIANCE, ability, talent, capacity, gift, bent, faculty, excellence, endowment, flair, inclination, knack, propensity, aptitude, cleverness, creative power 2 MASTER, expert, mastermind, brain (*informal*), buff (*informal*), intellect (*informal*), adept, maestro, virtuoso, whiz (*informal*), hotshot (*informal*), rocket scientist (*informal, chiefly US*), wonk (*informal*), brainbox, maven (*US*), master-hand, fundi (*S African*) << ANTONYM dunce

genre *noun* TYPE, group, school, form, order, sort, kind, class, style, character, fashion, brand, species, category, stamp, classification, genus, subdivision

genteel *adjective* REFINED, cultured, mannerly, elegant, formal, gentlemanly, respectable, polite, cultivated, courteous, courtly, well-bred, ladylike, well-mannered << ANTONYM unmannerly

gentility *noun* 1 REFINEMENT, culture, breeding, courtesy, elegance, formality, respectability, cultivation, politeness, good manners, courtliness 2 BLUE BLOOD, high birth, rank, good family, good breeding, gentle birth

gentle *adjective* 1 KIND, loving, kindly, peaceful, soft, quiet, pacific, tender, mild, benign, humane, compassionate, amiable, meek, lenient, placid, merciful, kind-hearted, sweet-tempered, tender-hearted << ANTONYM unkind 2 SLOW, easy, slight, deliberate, moderate, gradual, imperceptible 3 MODERATE, low, light, easy, soft, calm, slight, mild, soothing, clement, temperate, balmy << ANTONYM violent

gentlemanly *adjective* CHIVALROUS, mannerly, obliging, refined, polite, civil, cultivated, courteous, gallant, genteel, suave, well-bred, well-mannered

gentleness *noun* TENDERNESS, compassion, kindness, consideration, sympathy, sweetness, softness, mildness, kindliness

gentry *noun* NOBILITY, lords, elite, nobles, upper class, aristocracy, peerage, ruling class, patricians, upper crust (*informal*), gentility, gentlefolk

genuine *adjective* 1 AUTHENTIC, real, original, actual, sound, true, pure, sterling, valid, legitimate, honest, veritable, bona fide, dinkum (*Austral & NZ informal*), the real McCoy << ANTONYM counterfeit 2 HEARTFELT, sincere, honest, earnest, real, true, frank, unaffected, wholehearted, unadulterated, unalloyed, unfeigned << ANTONYM affected 3 SINCERE, straightforward, honest, natural, frank, candid, upfront (*informal*), dinkum (*Austral & NZ informal*), artless, guileless << ANTONYM hypocritical

genus *noun* TYPE, sort, kind, group, set, order, race, class, breed, category, genre, classification

germ *noun* 1 MICROBE, virus, bug (*informal*), bacterium, bacillus, microorganism 2 BEGINNING, root, seed, origin, spark, bud, embryo, rudiment

germinate *verb* SPROUT, grow, shoot, develop, generate, swell, bud, vegetate

gestation *noun* INCUBATION, development, growth, pregnancy, evolution, ripening, maturation

gesticulate verb SIGNAL, sign, wave, indicate, motion, gesture, beckon, make a sign

gesture noun SIGN, action, signal, motion, indication, gesticulation ▷ verb SIGNAL, sign, wave, indicate, motion, beckon, gesticulate

get verb 1 BECOME, grow, turn, wax, come to be 2 PERSUADE, convince, win over, induce, influence, sway, entice, coax, incite, impel, talk into, wheedle, prevail upon 3 ARRIVE, come, reach, make it (informal) 4 MANAGE, fix, succeed, arrange, contrive, wangle (informal) 5 (informal) ANNOY, upset, anger, bother, disturb, trouble, bug (informal), irritate, aggravate (informal), gall, madden, exasperate, nettle, vex, irk, rile, pique, get on your nerves (informal), nark (Brit, Austral & NZ slang), get up your nose (informal), give someone grief (Brit & S African), make your blood boil, get your goat (slang), get on your wick (Brit slang), get your back up, hack you off (informal) 6 OBTAIN, receive, gain, acquire, win, land, score (slang), achieve, net, pick up, bag, secure, attain, reap, get hold of, come by, glean, procure, get your hands on, come into possession of 7 FETCH, bring, collect 8 UNDERSTAND, follow, catch, see, notice, realize, appreciate, be aware of, take in, perceive, grasp, comprehend, fathom, apprehend, suss (out) (slang), get the hang of (informal), get your head round 9 CATCH, develop, contract, succumb to, fall victim to, go down with, come down with, become infected with, be afflicted with, be smitten by 10 ARREST, catch, grab, capture, trap, seize, take, nail (informal), collar (informal), nab (informal), apprehend, take prisoner, take into custody, lay hold of 11 CONTACT, reach, communicate with, get hold of, get in touch with 12 PUZZLE, confuse, baffle, bewilder, confound, perplex, mystify, stump, beat (slang), flummox, nonplus 13 (informal) MOVE, touch, affect, excite, stir, stimulate, arouse, have an impact on, have an effect on, tug at (someone's) heartstrings (often facetious) ▷▷ **get across something** CROSS, negotiate, pass over, traverse, ford ▷▷ **get at someone** 1 CRITICIZE, attack, blame, put down, knock (informal), carp, have a go (at) (informal), taunt, nag, hassle (informal), pick on, disparage, diss (slang, chiefly US), find fault with, put the boot into (slang), nark (Brit, Austral & NZ slang), be on your back (slang) 2 CORRUPT, influence, bribe, tamper with, buy off, fix (informal), suborn ▷▷ **get at something** 1 REACH, touch, grasp, get (a) hold of, stretch to verb 2 FIND OUT, get, learn, reach, reveal, discover, acquire, detect, uncover, attain, get hold of, gain access to, come to grips with 3 IMPLY, mean, suggest, hint, intimate, lead up to, insinuate ▷▷ **get away** ESCAPE, leave, disappear, flee, depart, fly, slip away, abscond, decamp, hook it (slang), do a runner (slang), slope off, do a bunk (Brit slang), fly the coop (US & Canad informal), skedaddle (informal), take a powder (US & Canad slang), make good your escape, make your getaway, take it on the lam (US & Canad slang), break free or out, run away or off, do a Skase (Austral informal) ▷▷ **get back** RETURN, arrive home, come back or home ▷▷ **get back at someone** RETALIATE, pay (someone) back, hit back at, take revenge on, get even with, strike back at, even the score with, exact retribution on, get your own back on, make reprisal with, be avenged on, settle the score with, give (someone) a taste of his or her own medicine, give tit for tat, take or wreak vengeance on ▷▷ **get by** MANAGE, survive, cope, fare, get through, exist, make out, get along, make do, subsist, muddle through, keep your head above water, make both ends meet ▷▷ **get in** ARRIVE, come in, appear, land ▷▷ **get off** 1 BE ABSOLVED, be acquitted, escape punishment, walk (slang, chiefly US) 2 LEAVE, go, move, take off (informal), depart, slope off, make tracks, set out or off 3 DESCEND, leave, exit, step down, alight, disembark, dismount ▷▷ **get on** 1 BE FRIENDLY, agree, get along, concur, be compatible, hit it off (informal), harmonize, be on good terms 2 PROGRESS, manage, cope, fare, advance, succeed, make out (informal), prosper, cut it (informal), get along 3 BOARD, enter, mount, climb, embark, ascend ▷▷ **get out** LEAVE, escape, withdraw, quit, take off (informal), exit, go, break out, go away, depart, evacuate, vacate, clear out (informal), abscond, decamp, hook it (slang), free yourself, do a bunk (Brit slang), extricate yourself, sling your hook (Brit slang), rack off (Austral & NZ slang), do a Skase (Austral informal) ▷▷ **get out of something** AVOID, dodge, evade, escape, shirk, body-swerve (Scot) ▷▷ **get over something** 1 RECOVER FROM, survive, get better from, come round, bounce back, mend, get well, recuperate, turn the corner, pull through, get back on your feet, feel yourself again, regain your health or strength 2 OVERCOME, deal with, solve, resolve, defeat, master, lick (*informal*), shake off, rise above, get the better of, surmount **3** CROSS, pass, pass over, traverse, get across, move across, ford, go across ▷▷ **get round someone** (*informal*) WIN OVER, persuade, charm, influence, convince, convert, sway, coax, cajole, wheedle, prevail upon, bring round, talk round ▷▷ **get round something** OVERCOME, deal with, solve, resolve, defeat, master, bypass, lick (*informal*), shake off, rise above, get the better of, circumvent, surmount ▷▷ **get something across** COMMUNICATE, publish, spread, pass on, transmit, convey, impart, get (something) through, disseminate, bring home, make known, put over, make clear *or* understood ▷▷ **get something back** REGAIN, recover, retrieve, take back, recoup, repossess ▷▷ **get something over** COMMUNICATE, spread, pass on, convey, impart, make known, get *or* put across, make clear *or* understood ▷▷ **get together** MEET, unite, join, collect, gather, rally, assemble, muster, convene, converge, congregate ▷▷ **get up** ARISE, stand (up), rise, get to your feet

getaway *noun* ESCAPE, break, flight, break-out, decampment

get-together *noun* GATHERING, party, celebration, reception, meeting, social, function, bash (*informal*), rave (*Brit slang*), festivity, do (*informal*), knees-up (*Brit informal*), beano (*Brit slang*), social gathering, shindig (*informal*), soirée, rave-up (*Brit slang*), hooley *or* hoolie (*chiefly Irish & NZ*)

ghastly *adjective* HORRIBLE, shocking, terrible, awful, grim, dreadful, horrendous, hideous, from hell (*informal*), horrid (*informal*), repulsive, frightful, loathsome, godawful (*slang*) << ANTONYM lovely

ghost *noun* **1** SPIRIT, soul, phantom, spectre, spook (*informal*), apparition, wraith, shade (*literary*), phantasm, atua (*NZ*), kehua (*NZ*), wairua (*NZ*) **2** TRACE, shadow, suggestion, hint, suspicion, glimmer, semblance

ghostly *adjective* UNEARTHLY, weird, phantom, eerie, supernatural, uncanny, spooky (*informal*), spectral, eldritch (*poetic*), phantasmal

ghoulish *adjective* MACABRE, sick (*informal*), disgusting, hideous, gruesome, grisly, horrid, morbid, unwholesome

giant *adjective* HUGE, great, large, vast, enormous, extensive, tremendous, immense, titanic, jumbo (*informal*), gigantic, monumental, monstrous,

mammoth, colossal, mountainous, stellar (*informal*), prodigious, stupendous, gargantuan, elephantine, ginormous (*informal*), Brobdingnagian, humongous *or* humungous (*US slang*) << ANTONYM tiny ▷ *noun* OGRE, monster, titan, colossus, leviathan, behemoth

gibber *verb* GABBLE, chatter, babble, waffle (*informal, chiefly Brit*), prattle, jabber, blab, rabbit on (*Brit informal*), blather, blabber, earbash (*Austral & NZ slang*)

gibberish *noun* NONSENSE, crap (*slang*), garbage (*informal*), hot air (*informal*), tosh (*slang, chiefly Brit*), babble, pap, bilge (*informal*), drivel, twaddle, tripe (*informal*), guff (*slang*), prattle, mumbo jumbo, moonshine, jabber, gabble, gobbledegook (*informal*), hogwash, hokum (*slang, chiefly US & Canad*), blather, double talk, piffle (*informal*), all Greek (*informal*), poppycock (*informal*), balderdash, bosh (*informal*), yammer (*informal*), eyewash (*informal*), tommyrot, horsefeathers (*US slang*), bunkum *or* buncombe (*chiefly US*), bizzo (*Austral slang*), bull's wool (*Austral & NZ slang*)

gibe ▷ see **jibe**

giddy *adjective* **1** DIZZY, reeling, faint, unsteady, light-headed, vertiginous **2** FLIGHTY, silly, volatile, irresponsible, reckless, dizzy, careless, frivolous, impulsive, capricious, thoughtless, impetuous, skittish, heedless, scatterbrained, ditzy *or* ditsy (*slang*) << ANTONYM serious

gift *noun* **1** DONATION, offering, present, contribution, grant, legacy, hand-out, endowment, boon, bequest, gratuity, prezzie (*informal*), bonsela (*S African*), largesse *or* largess, koha (*NZ*) **2** TALENT, ability, capacity, genius, power, bent, faculty, capability, forte, flair, knack, aptitude

gifted *adjective* TALENTED, able, skilled, expert, masterly, brilliant, capable, clever, accomplished, proficient, adroit << ANTONYM talentless

gigantic *adjective* HUGE, great, large, giant, massive, vast, enormous, extensive, tremendous, immense, titanic, jumbo (*informal*), monumental, monstrous, mammoth, colossal, mountainous, stellar (*informal*), prodigious, stupendous, gargantuan, herculean, elephantine, ginormous (*informal*), Brobdingnagian, humongous *or* humungous (*US slang*) << ANTONYM tiny

giggle *verb* LAUGH, chuckle, snigger, chortle,

titter, twitter, tee-hee ▷ *noun* LAUGH, chuckle, snigger, chortle, titter, twitter

gimmick *noun* STUNT, trick, device, scheme, manoeuvre, dodge, ploy, gambit, stratagem, contrivance

gingerly *adverb* CAUTIOUSLY, carefully, reluctantly, suspiciously, tentatively, warily, hesitantly, timidly, circumspectly, cagily (*informal*), charily << ANTONYM carelessly

gird *verb* 1 GIRDLE, bind, belt 2 SURROUND, ring, pen, enclose, encompass, encircle, hem in, enfold, engird 3 PREPARE, ready, steel, brace, fortify, make *or* get ready

girdle *noun* BELT, band, sash, waistband, cummerbund ▷ *verb* SURROUND, ring, bound, enclose, encompass, hem, encircle, fence in, gird

girl *noun* FEMALE CHILD, schoolgirl, lass, lassie (*informal*), miss, maiden (*archaic*), maid (*archaic*)

girth *noun* SIZE, measure, proportions, dimensions, bulk, measurement(s), circumference

gist *noun* ESSENCE, meaning, point, idea, sense, import, core, substance, drift, significance, nub, pith, quintessence

give *verb* 1 PERFORM, do, carry out, execute 2 COMMUNICATE, announce, publish, transmit, pronounce, utter, emit, issue, be a source of, impart 3 PRODUCE, make, cause, occasion, engender 4 PRESENT, contribute, donate, provide, supply, award, grant, deliver, commit, administer, furnish, confer, bestow, entrust, consign, make over, hand over *or* out << ANTONYM take 5 COLLAPSE, fall, break, sink, bend 6 CONCEDE, allow, grant 7 SURRENDER, yield, devote, hand over, relinquish, part with, cede 8 DEMONSTRATE, show, offer, provide, evidence, display, indicate, manifest, set forth ▷▷ **give in** ADMIT DEFEAT, yield, concede, collapse, quit, submit, surrender, comply, succumb, cave in (*informal*), capitulate ▷▷ **give something away** REVEAL, expose, leak, disclose, betray, uncover, let out, divulge, let slip, let the cat out of the bag (*informal*) ▷▷ **give something off** *or* **out** EMIT, produce, release, discharge, send out, throw out, vent, exude, exhale ▷▷ **give something out** 1 DISTRIBUTE, issue, deliver, circulate, hand out, dispense, dole out, pass round 2 MAKE KNOWN, announce, publish, broadcast, communicate, transmit, utter, notify, impart, disseminate, shout from the rooftops (*informal*) ▷▷ **give something up** 1 ABANDON, stop, quit, kick

(*informal*), cease, cut out, renounce, leave off, say goodbye to, desist, kiss (something) goodbye, forswear 2 QUIT, leave, resign, step down from (*informal*) 3 HAND OVER, yield, surrender, relinquish, waive

given *adjective* 1 SPECIFIED, particular, specific, designated, stated, predetermined 2 INCLINED, addicted, disposed, prone, liable

glacial *adjective* 1 ICY, biting, cold, freezing, frozen, bitter, raw, chill, piercing, arctic, polar, chilly, frosty, wintry 2 UNFRIENDLY, hostile, cold, icy, frosty, antagonistic, frigid, inimical

glad *adjective* 1 HAPPY, pleased, delighted, contented, cheerful, gratified, joyful, overjoyed, chuffed (*slang*), gleeful << ANTONYM unhappy 2 (*archaic*) PLEASING, happy, cheering, pleasant, delightful, cheerful, merry, gratifying, cheery, joyous, felicitous

gladly *adverb* 1 HAPPILY, cheerfully, gleefully, merrily, gaily, joyfully, joyously, jovially 2 WILLINGLY, freely, happily, readily, cheerfully, with pleasure, with (a) good grace << ANTONYM reluctantly

glamorous *adjective* 1 ATTRACTIVE, beautiful, lovely, charming, entrancing, elegant, dazzling, enchanting, captivating, alluring, bewitching << ANTONYM unglamorous 2 EXCITING, glittering, prestigious, glossy, glitzy (*slang*) << ANTONYM unglamorous

glamour *noun* 1 CHARM, appeal, beauty, attraction, fascination, allure, magnetism, enchantment, bewitchment 2 EXCITEMENT, magic, thrill, romance, prestige, glitz (*slang*)

glance *verb* 1 PEEK, look, view, check, clock (*Brit informal*), gaze, glimpse, check out (*informal*), peep, take a dekko at (*Brit slang*) << ANTONYM scrutinize 2 *with* **over, through,** *etc.* SCAN, browse, dip into, leaf through, flip through, thumb through, skim through, riffle through, run over *or* through, surf (*computing*) ▷ *noun* PEEK, look, glimpse, peep, squint, butcher's (*Brit slang*), quick look, gander (*informal*), brief look, dekko (*slang*), shufti (*Brit slang*) << ANTONYM good look

glare *verb* 1 SCOWL, frown, glower, look daggers, stare angrily, give a dirty look, lour *or* lower 2 DAZZLE, blaze, flare, flame ▷ *noun* 1 SCOWL, frown, glower, dirty look, black look, angry stare, lour *or* lower 2 DAZZLE, glow, blaze, flare, flame, brilliance

glaring *adjective* OBVIOUS, open, outstanding, patent, visible, gross, outrageous, manifest, blatant, conspicuous, overt, audacious, flagrant, rank, egregious, unconcealed << ANTONYM inconspicuous

glassy *adjective* **1** SMOOTH, clear, slick, shiny, glossy, transparent, slippery **2** EXPRESSIONLESS, cold, fixed, empty, dull, blank, glazed, vacant, dazed, lifeless

glaze *noun* COAT, finish, polish, shine, gloss, varnish, enamel, lacquer, lustre, patina ▷ *verb* COAT, polish, gloss, varnish, enamel, lacquer, burnish, furbish

gleam *verb* SHINE, flash, glow, sparkle, glitter, flare, shimmer, glint, glimmer, glisten, scintillate ▷ *noun* **1** GLIMMER, flash, beam, glow, sparkle **2** TRACE, ray, suggestion, hint, flicker, glimmer, inkling

gleaming *adjective* SHINING, bright, brilliant, glowing, sparkling, glimmering, glistening, scintillating, burnished, lustrous << ANTONYM dull

glean *verb* GATHER, learn, pick up, collect, harvest, accumulate, reap, garner, amass, cull

glee *noun* DELIGHT, joy, triumph, exuberance, elation, exhilaration, mirth, hilarity, merriment, exultation, gladness, joyfulness, joyousness << ANTONYM gloom

gleeful *adjective* DELIGHTED, happy, pleased, cheerful, merry, triumphant, gratified, exuberant, jubilant, joyous, joyful, elated, overjoyed, chirpy (*informal*), exultant, cock-a-hoop, mirthful, stoked (*Austral & NZ informal*)

glib *adjective* SMOOTH, easy, ready, quick, slick, plausible, slippery, fluent, suave, artful, insincere, fast-talking, smooth-tongued << ANTONYM sincere

glide *verb* SLIP, sail, slide, skim

glimmer *verb* GLEAM, shine, glow, sparkle, glitter, blink, flicker, shimmer, twinkle, glisten ▷ *noun* **1** GLOW, ray, sparkle, gleam, blink, flicker, shimmer, twinkle **2** TRACE, ray, suggestion, hint, grain, gleam, flicker, inkling

glimpse *noun* LOOK, sighting, sight, glance, peep, peek, squint, butcher's (*Brit slang*), quick look, gander (*informal*), brief view, shufti (*Brit slang*) ▷ *verb* CATCH SIGHT OF, spot, sight, view, clock (*Brit informal*), spy, espy

glint *verb* GLEAM, flash, shine, sparkle, glitter, twinkle, glimmer ▷ *noun* GLEAM, flash, shine, sparkle, glitter, twinkle, twinkling, glimmer

glisten *verb* GLEAM, flash, shine, sparkle, glitter, shimmer, twinkle, glint, glimmer, scintillate

glitch *noun* PROBLEM, difficulty, fault, flaw,

bug (*informal*), hitch, snag, uphill (*S African*), interruption, blip, malfunction, kink, gremlin, fly in the ointment

glitter *verb* SHINE, flash, sparkle, flare, glare, gleam, shimmer, twinkle, glint, glimmer, glisten, scintillate ▷ *noun* **1** GLAMOUR, show, display, gilt, splendour, tinsel, pageantry, gaudiness, showiness **2** SPARKLE, flash, shine, beam, glare, gleam, brilliance, sheen, shimmer, brightness, lustre, radiance, scintillation

gloat *verb* RELISH, triumph, glory, crow, revel in, vaunt, drool, exult, rub your hands

global *adjective* **1** WORLDWIDE, world, international, universal, planetary **2** COMPREHENSIVE, general, total, thorough, unlimited, exhaustive, all-inclusive, all-encompassing, encyclopedic, unbounded << ANTONYM limited

globe *noun* PLANET, world, earth, sphere, orb

gloom *noun* **1** DARKNESS, dark, shadow, cloud, shade, twilight, dusk, obscurity, blackness, dullness, murk, dimness, murkiness, cloudiness, gloominess, duskiness << ANTONYM light **2** DEPRESSION, despair, misery, sadness, sorrow, blues, woe, melancholy, unhappiness, desolation, despondency, dejection, low spirits, downheartedness << ANTONYM happiness

gloomy *adjective* **1** DARK, dull, dim, dismal, black, grey, obscure, murky, dreary, sombre, shadowy, overcast, dusky << ANTONYM light **2** MISERABLE, down, sad, dismal, low, blue, pessimistic, melancholy, glum, dejected, despondent, dispirited, downcast, joyless, downhearted, down in the dumps (*informal*), cheerless, down in the mouth, in low spirits << ANTONYM happy **3** DEPRESSING, bad, dismal, dreary, black, saddening, sombre, dispiriting, disheartening, funereal, cheerless, comfortless

glorify *verb* **1** PRAISE, celebrate, magnify, laud, extol, crack up (*informal*), eulogize, sing *or* sound the praises of << ANTONYM condemn **2** WORSHIP, honour, bless, adore, revere, exalt, pay homage to, venerate, sanctify, immortalize << ANTONYM dishonour **3** ENHANCE, raise, elevate, adorn, dignify, magnify, augment, lift up, ennoble, add lustre to, aggrandize << ANTONYM degrade

glorious *adjective* **1** SPLENDID, beautiful, bright, brilliant, shining, superb, divine, gorgeous, dazzling, radiant, resplendent, splendiferous (*facetious*) << ANTONYM dull **2** DELIGHTFUL, fine, wonderful, excellent, heavenly (*informal*), marvellous, splendid, gorgeous, pleasurable, splendiferous (*facetious*) **3** ILLUSTRIOUS, famous, celebrated, distinguished, noted, grand, excellent, honoured, magnificent, noble, renowned, elevated, eminent, triumphant, majestic, famed, sublime << ANTONYM ordinary

glory *noun* **1** HONOUR, praise, fame, celebrity, distinction, acclaim, prestige, immortality, eminence, kudos, renown, exaltation, illustriousness << ANTONYM shame **2** SPLENDOUR, majesty, greatness, grandeur, nobility, pomp, magnificence, pageantry, éclat, sublimity **3** BEAUTY, brilliance, lustre, radiance, gorgeousness, resplendence **4** WORSHIP, praise, blessing, gratitude, thanksgiving, homage, adoration, veneration ▷ *verb* TRIUMPH, boast, relish, revel, crow, drool, gloat, exult, take delight, pride yourself

gloss¹ *noun* **1** SHINE, gleam, sheen, polish, brilliance, varnish, brightness, veneer, lustre, burnish, patina **2** FAÇADE, show, front, surface, appearance, mask, semblance

gloss² *noun* INTERPRETATION, comment, note, explanation, commentary, translation, footnote, elucidation ▷ *verb* INTERPRET, explain, comment, translate, construe, annotate, elucidate

glossy *adjective* SHINY, polished, shining, glazed, bright, brilliant, smooth, sleek, silky, burnished, glassy, silken, lustrous << ANTONYM dull

glow *noun* **1** LIGHT, gleam, splendour, glimmer, brilliance, brightness, radiance, luminosity, vividness, incandescence, phosphorescence << ANTONYM dullness **2** COLOUR, bloom, flush, blush, reddening, rosiness << ANTONYM pallor ▷ *verb* **1** SHINE, burn, gleam, brighten, glimmer, smoulder **2** BE PINK, colour, flush, blush **3** BE SUFFUSED, thrill, radiate, tingle

glower *verb* SCOWL, glare, frown, look daggers, give a dirty look, lour *or* lower ▷ *noun* SCOWL, glare, frown, dirty look, black look, angry stare, lour *or* lower

glowing *adjective* **1** COMPLIMENTARY, enthusiastic, rave (*informal*), ecstatic, rhapsodic, laudatory, adulatory << ANTONYM scathing **2** BRIGHT, vivid, vibrant, rich, warm, radiant, luminous << ANTONYM dull

glue *noun* ADHESIVE, cement, gum, paste ▷ *verb* STICK, fix, seal, cement, gum, paste, affix

glum *adjective* GLOOMY, miserable, dismal, down, low, melancholy, dejected, downcast, morose, doleful, downhearted, down in the dumps (*informal*), down in the mouth, in low spirits << ANTONYM cheerful

glut *noun* SURFEIT, excess, surplus, plethora, saturation, oversupply, overabundance, superabundance << ANTONYM scarcity ▷ *verb* **1** SATURATE, flood, choke, clog, overload, inundate, deluge, oversupply **2** OVERFILL, fill, stuff, cram, satiate

glutinous *adjective* STICKY, adhesive, cohesive, gooey, viscous, gummy, gluey, viscid

glutton *noun* GOURMAND, gorger, gannet (*slang*), gobbler, pig (*informal*)

gluttonous *adjective* GREEDY, insatiable, voracious, ravenous, rapacious, piggish, hoggish

gluttony *noun* GREED, rapacity, voracity, greediness, voraciousness, piggishness

gnarled *adjective* **1** TWISTED, knotted, contorted, knotty **2** WRINKLED, rough, rugged, leathery

gnaw *verb* **1** BITE, chew, nibble, munch **2** DISTRESS, worry, trouble, harry, haunt, plague, nag, fret **3** ERODE, consume, devour, eat away *or* into, wear away *or* down

go *verb* **1** MOVE, travel, advance, journey, proceed, pass, fare (*archaic*), set off << ANTONYM stay **2** LEAVE, withdraw, depart, move out, decamp, slope off, make tracks **3** LEAD, run, reach, spread, extend, stretch, connect, span, give access **4** ELAPSE, pass, flow, fly by, expire, lapse, slip away **5** BE GIVEN, be spent, be awarded, be allotted **6** DIE, perish, pass away, buy it (*US slang*), expire, check out (*US slang*), kick it (*slang*), croak (*slang*), give up the ghost, snuff it (*informal*), peg out (*informal*), kick the bucket (*slang*), peg it (*informal*), cark it (*Austral & NZ slang*), pop your clogs (*informal*) **7** PROCEED, develop, turn out, work out, fare, fall out, pan out (*informal*) **8** FUNCTION, work, run, move, operate, perform << ANTONYM fail **9** MATCH, blend, correspond, fit, suit, chime, harmonize **10** SERVE, help, tend ▷ *noun* **1** ATTEMPT, try, effort, bid, shot (*informal*), crack (*informal*), essay, stab (*informal*), whirl (*informal*), whack (*informal*) **2** TURN, shot (*informal*), spell, stint **3** (*informal*) ENERGY, life, drive, spirit, pep, vitality, vigour, verve, force, get-up-and-go (*informal*), oomph (*informal*), brio, vivacity ▷▷ **go about something 1** TACKLE, begin, approach, undertake, set about **2** ENGAGE IN, perform, conduct, pursue, practise, ply, carry on with, apply yourself to, busy or occupy yourself with ▷▷ **go along with something** AGREE, follow, cooperate, concur, assent, acquiesce ▷▷ **go at something** SET ABOUT, start, begin, tackle, set to, get down to, wade into, get to work on, make a start on, get cracking on (*informal*), address yourself to, get weaving on (*informal*) ▷▷ **go away** LEAVE, withdraw, exit, depart, move out, go to hell (*informal*), decamp, hook it (*slang*), slope off, pack your bags (*informal*), make tracks, get on your bike (*Brit slang*), bog off (*Brit slang*), sling your hook (*Brit slang*), rack off (*Austral & NZ slang*) ▷▷ **go back** RETURN ▷▷ **go back on something** REPUDIATE, break, forsake, retract, renege on, desert, back out of, change your mind about ▷▷ **go by** PASS, proceed, elapse, flow on, move onward ▷▷ **go by something** OBEY, follow, adopt, observe, comply with, heed, submit to, be guided by, take as guide ▷▷ **go down 1** FALL, drop, decline, slump, decrease, fall off, dwindle, lessen, ebb, depreciate, become lower **2** SET, sink **3** SINK, founder, go under, be submerged ▷▷ **go for someone 1** PREFER, like, choose, favour, admire, be attracted to, be fond of, hold with **2** ATTACK, assault, assail, spring upon, rush upon, launch yourself at, set about or upon **3** SCOLD, attack, blast, criticize, flame (*informal*), put down, tear into (*informal*), diss (*slang, chiefly US*), impugn, lambast(e) ▷▷ **go in for something** PARTICIPATE IN, pursue, take part in, undertake, embrace, practise, engage in ▷▷ **go into something 1** INVESTIGATE, consider, study, research, discuss, review, examine, pursue, probe, analyse, look into, delve into, work over, scrutinize, inquire into **2** ENTER, begin, participate in ▷▷ **go off 1** DEPART, leave, quit, go away, move out, decamp, hook it (*slang*), slope off, pack your bags (*informal*), rack off (*Austral & NZ slang*) **2** EXPLODE, fire, blow up, detonate **3** SOUND, ring, toll, chime, peal **4** TAKE PLACE, happen, occur, come off (*informal*), come about **5** (*informal*) GO BAD, turn, spoil, rot, go stale ▷▷ **go on 1** HAPPEN, occur, take place **2** CONTINUE, last, stay, proceed, carry on, keep going **3** *often with* **about** RAMBLE ON, carry on, chatter, waffle (*informal, chiefly Brit*), witter (on) (*informal*), rabbit on (*Brit informal*), prattle, blether, earbash (*Austral & NZ slang*) ▷▷ **go on doing something** or **go on with something** CONTINUE, pursue, proceed, carry on, stick to, persist, keep on, keep at, persevere, stick

at ▷▷ **go out 1** SEE SOMEONE, court, date (*informal, chiefly US*), woo, go steady (*informal*), be romantically involved with *verb* **2** BE EXTINGUISHED, die out, fade out ▷▷ **go over something 1** EXAMINE, study, review, revise, inspect, work over **2** REHEARSE, read, scan, reiterate, skim over, peruse ▷▷ **go through something 1** SUFFER, experience, bear, endure, brave, undergo, tolerate, withstand **2** SEARCH, look through, rummage through, rifle through, hunt through, fossick through (*Austral & NZ*), ferret about in **3** EXAMINE, check, search, explore, look through, work over **4** USE UP, exhaust, consume, squander ▷▷ **go through with something** CARRY ON, continue, pursue, keep on, persevere ▷▷ **go together 1** HARMONIZE, match, agree, accord, fit, make a pair **2** (*informal*) GO OUT, court, date (*informal, chiefly US*), go steady (*informal*) ▷▷ **go under 1** FAIL, die, sink, go down, fold (*informal*), founder, succumb, go bankrupt **2** SINK, go down, founder, submerge ▷▷ **go up** INCREASE, rise, mount, soar, get higher ▷▷ **go with something** MATCH, suit, blend, correspond with, agree with, fit, complement, harmonize ▷▷ **go without something** BE DEPRIVED OF, want, lack, be denied, do without, abstain, go short, deny yourself ▷▷ **no go** IMPOSSIBLE, not on (*informal*), vain, hopeless, futile

goad *verb* URGE, drive, prompt, spur, stimulate, provoke, arouse, propel, prod, prick, incite, instigate, egg on, exhort, impel ▷ *noun* INCENTIVE, urge, spur, motivation, pressure, stimulus, stimulation, impetus, incitement

go-ahead *noun* (*informal*) PERMISSION, consent, green light, assent, leave, authorization, O.K. or okay (*informal*) ▷ *adjective* ENTERPRISING, pioneering, ambitious, progressive, go-getting (*informal*), up-and-coming

goal *noun* AIM, end, target, purpose, object, intention, objective, ambition, destination, Holy Grail (*informal*)

gob *noun* PIECE, lump, chunk, hunk, nugget, blob, wad, clod, wodge (*Brit informal*)

gobble *verb* DEVOUR, swallow, gulp, guzzle, wolf, bolt, cram in, gorge on, pig out on (*slang*), stuff yourself with

go-between *noun* INTERMEDIARY, agent, medium, broker, factor, dealer, liaison, mediator, middleman

god *noun* DEITY, immortal, divinity, divine being, supreme being, atua (*NZ*)

godforsaken *adjective* DESOLATE, abandoned, deserted, remote, neglected, lonely, bleak, gloomy, backward, dismal, dreary, forlorn, wretched

godless *adjective* WICKED, depraved, profane, unprincipled, atheistic, ungodly, irreligious, impious, unrighteous

godlike *adjective* DIVINE, heavenly, celestial, superhuman

godly *adjective* DEVOUT, religious, holy, righteous, pious, good, saintly, god-fearing

godsend *noun* BLESSING, help, benefit, asset, boon

gogga *noun* (*S African*) INSECT, bug, creepy-crawly (*Brit informal*)

goggle *verb* STARE, gape, gawp (*slang*), gawk

going-over *noun* **1** EXAMINATION, study, check, review, survey, investigation, analysis, inspection, scrutiny, perusal **2** THRASHING, attack, beating, whipping, thumping, pasting (*slang*), buffeting, drubbing (*informal*) **3** DRESSING-DOWN, talking-to (*informal*), lecture, rebuke, reprimand, scolding, chiding, tongue-lashing, chastisement, castigation

golden *adjective* **1** YELLOW, bright, brilliant, blonde, blond, flaxen << ANTONYM dark **2** SUCCESSFUL, glorious, prosperous, best, rich, flourishing, halcyon << ANTONYM worst **3** PROMISING, excellent, valuable, favourable, advantageous, auspicious, opportune, propitious << ANTONYM unfavourable

gone *adjective* **1** MISSING, lost, away, vanished, absent, astray **2** USED UP, spent, finished, consumed **3** PAST, over, ended, finished, elapsed

good *adjective* **1** EXCELLENT, great, fine, pleasing, capital, choice, crucial (*slang*), acceptable, pleasant, worthy, first-class, divine, splendid, satisfactory, superb, enjoyable, awesome (*slang*), dope (*slang*), world-class, admirable, agreeable, super (*informal*), pleasurable, wicked (*slang*), bad (*slang*), first-rate, tiptop, bitchin' (*US slang*), booshit (*Austral slang*), exo (*Austral slang*), sik (*Austral slang*), rad (*informal*), phat (*slang*), schmick (*Austral informal*) << ANTONYM bad **2** PROFICIENT, able, skilled, capable, expert, talented, efficient, clever, accomplished, reliable, first-class, satisfactory, competent, thorough, adept, first-rate, adroit, dexterous << ANTONYM bad **3** BENEFICIAL, useful, healthy, helpful, favourable, wholesome, advantageous,

salutary, salubrious << ANTONYM harmful **4** HONOURABLE, moral, worthy, ethical, upright, admirable, honest, righteous, exemplary, right, virtuous, trustworthy, altruistic, praiseworthy, estimable << ANTONYM bad **5** WELL-BEHAVED, seemly, mannerly, proper, polite, orderly, obedient, dutiful, decorous, well-mannered << ANTONYM naughty **6** KIND, kindly, friendly, obliging, charitable, humane, gracious, benevolent, merciful, beneficent, well-disposed, kind-hearted << ANTONYM unkind **7** TRUE, real, genuine, proper, reliable, dependable, sound, trustworthy, dinkum (*Austral & NZ informal*) **8** FULL, long, whole, complete, entire, solid, extensive << ANTONYM scant **9** CONSIDERABLE, large, substantial, sufficient, adequate, ample **10** VALID, convincing, compelling, legitimate, authentic, persuasive, sound, bona fide << ANTONYM invalid **11** BEST, newest, special, finest, nicest, smartest, fancy, most valuable, most precious **12** EDIBLE, untainted, uncorrupted, eatable, fit to eat << ANTONYM bad **13** CONVENIENT, timely, fitting, fit, appropriate, suitable, well-timed, opportune << ANTONYM inconvenient ▷ *noun* **1** BENEFIT, interest, gain, advantage, use, service, profit, welfare, behalf, usefulness, wellbeing << ANTONYM disadvantage **2** VIRTUE, goodness, righteousness, worth, merit, excellence, morality, probity, rectitude, uprightness << ANTONYM evil ▷▷ **for good** PERMANENTLY, finally, for ever, once and for all, irrevocably, never to return, sine die (*Latin*)

goodbye *noun* FAREWELL, parting, leave-taking ▷ *interjection* FAREWELL, see you, see you later, ciao (*Italian*), cheerio, adieu, ta-ta, au revoir (*French*), auf Wiedersehen (*German*), adios (*Spanish*), haere ra (*NZ*)

good-humoured *adjective* GENIAL, happy, pleasant, cheerful, amiable, affable, congenial, good-tempered

good-looking *adjective* ATTRACTIVE, pretty, fair, beautiful, lovely, handsome, gorgeous, bonny, personable, comely, well-favoured

good-natured *adjective* AMIABLE, kind, kindly, friendly, generous, helpful, obliging, tolerant, agreeable, benevolent, good-hearted, magnanimous, well-disposed, warm-hearted

goodness *noun* **1** VIRTUE, honour, merit, integrity, morality, honesty, righteousness, probity, rectitude, uprightness << ANTONYM badness 2 EXCELLENCE, value, quality, worth, merit, superiority 3 NUTRITION, benefit, advantage, nourishment, wholesomeness, salubriousness 4 KINDNESS, charity, humanity, goodwill, mercy, compassion, generosity, friendliness, benevolence, graciousness, beneficence, kindliness, humaneness, kind-heartedness

goods *plural noun* 1 MERCHANDISE, stock, products, stuff, commodities, wares 2 PROPERTY, things, effects, gear, furniture, movables, possessions, furnishings, belongings, trappings, paraphernalia, chattels, appurtenances

goodwill *noun* FRIENDLINESS, favour, friendship, benevolence, amity, kindliness

gooey *adjective* 1 STICKY, soft, tacky, viscous, glutinous, gummy, icky (*informal*), gluey, gloopy, gungy 2 SENTIMENTAL, romantic, sloppy, soppy, maudlin, syrupy (*informal*), slushy (*informal*), mawkish, tear-jerking (*informal*), icky (*informal*)

gore[1] *noun* BLOOD, slaughter, bloodshed, carnage, butchery

gore[2] *verb* PIERCE, wound, stab, spit, transfix, impale

gorge *noun* RAVINE, canyon, pass, clough (*dialect*), chasm, cleft, fissure, defile, gulch (*US & Canad*) ▷ *verb* 1 OVEREAT, bolt, devour, gobble, wolf, swallow, gulp, guzzle, pig out (*slang*) 2 *usually reflexive* STUFF, fill, feed, cram, glut, surfeit, satiate, sate

gorgeous *adjective* 1 MAGNIFICENT, grand, beautiful, superb, spectacular, splendid, glittering, dazzling, luxurious, sumptuous, opulent << ANTONYM shabby 2 (*informal*) BEAUTIFUL, attractive, lovely, stunning (*informal*), elegant, handsome, good-looking, exquisite, drop-dead (*slang*), ravishing << ANTONYM dull

gory *adjective* 1 GRISLY, bloody, murderous, bloodthirsty 2 BLOODY, bloodstained, blood-soaked

gospel *noun* 1 DOCTRINE, news, teachings, message, revelation, creed, credo, tidings 2 TRUTH, fact, certainty, the last word, verity

gossip *noun* 1 IDLE TALK, scandal, hearsay, tittle-tattle, buzz, dirt (*US slang*), goss (*informal*), jaw (*slang*), gen (*Brit informal*), small talk, chitchat, blether, scuttlebutt (*US slang*), chinwag (*Brit informal*) 2 BUSYBODY, babbler, prattler, chatterbox (*informal*), blether, chatterer, scandalmonger, gossipmonger, tattletale (*chiefly US & Canad*)

▷ *verb* CHAT, chatter, blather, schmooze (*slang*), jaw (*slang*), dish the dirt (*informal*), blether, shoot the breeze (*slang, chiefly US*), chew the fat *or* rag (*slang*)

gouge *verb* SCOOP, cut, score, dig (out), scratch, hollow (out), claw, chisel, gash, incise ▷ *noun* GASH, cut, scratch, hollow, score, scoop, notch, groove, trench, furrow, incision

gourmet *noun* CONNOISSEUR, foodie (*informal*), bon vivant (*French*), epicure, gastronome

govern *verb* 1 RULE, lead, control, command, manage, direct, guide, handle, conduct, order, reign over, administer, oversee, supervise, be in power over, call the shots, call the tune, hold sway over, superintend 2 DETERMINE, decide, guide, rule, influence, underlie, sway 3 RESTRAIN, control, check, contain, master, discipline, regulate, curb, inhibit, tame, subdue, get the better of, bridle, hold in check, keep a tight rein on

government *noun* 1 ADMINISTRATION, executive, ministry, regime, governing body, powers-that-be 2 RULE, state, law, authority, administration, sovereignty, governance, dominion, polity, statecraft ▷ see **family**

governmental *adjective* ADMINISTRATIVE, state, political, official, executive, ministerial, sovereign, bureaucratic

governor *noun* LEADER, administrator, ruler, head, minister, director, manager, chief, officer, executive, boss (*informal*), commander, controller, supervisor, superintendent, mandarin, comptroller, functionary, overseer, baas (*S African*)

gown *noun* DRESS, costume, garment, robe, frock, garb, habit

grab *verb* SNATCH, catch, seize, capture, bag, grip, grasp, clutch, snap up, pluck, latch on to, catch *or* take hold of

grace *noun* 1 ELEGANCE, finesse, poise, ease, polish, refinement, fluency, suppleness, gracefulness << ANTONYM ungainliness 2 MANNERS, decency, cultivation, etiquette, breeding, consideration, propriety, tact, decorum, mannerliness << ANTONYM bad manners 3 INDULGENCE, mercy, pardon, compassion, quarter, charity, forgiveness, reprieve, clemency, leniency 4 BENEVOLENCE, favour, goodness, goodwill, generosity, kindness, beneficence, kindliness << ANTONYM ill will 5 PRAYER, thanks, blessing, thanksgiving, benediction 6 FAVOUR, regard, respect, approval, esteem, approbation, good opinion << ANTONYM disfavour ▷ *verb* 1 ADORN, enhance, decorate, enrich, set off, garnish, ornament, deck, embellish, bedeck, beautify 2 HONOUR, favour, distinguish, elevate, dignify, glorify << ANTONYM insult

graceful *adjective* ELEGANT, easy, flowing, smooth, fine, pleasing, beautiful, agile, symmetrical, gracile (*rare*) << ANTONYM inelegant

graceless *adjective* 1 INELEGANT, forced, awkward, clumsy, ungainly, unco (*Austral slang*) 2 ILL-MANNERED, crude, rude, coarse, vulgar, rough, improper, shameless, unsophisticated, gauche, barbarous, boorish, gawky, uncouth, loutish, indecorous, unmannerly

gracious *adjective* COURTEOUS, polite, civil, accommodating, kind, kindly, pleasing, friendly, obliging, amiable, cordial, hospitable, courtly, chivalrous, well-mannered << ANTONYM ungracious

grade *verb* CLASSIFY, rate, order, class, group, sort, value, range, rank, brand, arrange, evaluate ▷ *noun* 1 CLASS, condition, quality, brand 2 MARK, degree, place, order 3 LEVEL, position, rank, group, order, class, stage, step, station, category, rung, echelon ▷▷ **make the grade** (*informal*) SUCCEED, measure up, win through, pass muster, come up to scratch (*informal*), come through with flying colours, prove acceptable, measure up to expectations

gradient *noun* SLOPE, hill, rise, grade, incline, bank

gradual *adjective* STEADY, even, slow, regular, gentle, moderate, progressive, piecemeal, unhurried << ANTONYM sudden

gradually *adverb* STEADILY, slowly, moderately, progressively, gently, step by step, evenly, piecemeal, bit by bit, little by little, by degrees, piece by piece, unhurriedly, drop by drop

graduate *verb* 1 MARK OFF, grade, proportion, regulate, gauge, calibrate, measure out 2 CLASSIFY, rank, grade, group, order, sort, range, arrange, sequence

graft1 *noun* SHOOT, bud, implant, sprout, splice, scion ▷ *verb* JOIN, insert, transplant, implant, splice, affix

graft2 (*informal*) *noun* LABOUR, work, industry, effort, struggle, sweat, toil, slog, exertion, blood, sweat, and tears (*informal*) ▷ *verb* WORK, labour, struggle, sweat (*informal*), grind (*informal*), slave, strive, toil, drudge

grain *noun* 1 SEED, kernel, grist 2 CEREAL, corn

3 BIT, piece, trace, spark, scrap, suspicion, molecule, particle, fragment, atom, ounce, crumb, mite, jot, speck, morsel, granule, modicum, mote, whit, iota 4 TEXTURE, pattern, surface, fibre, weave, nap

grammar *noun* SYNTAX, rules of language

grammatical *adjective* SYNTACTIC, linguistic

grand *adjective* 1 IMPRESSIVE, great, large, magnificent, striking, fine, princely, imposing, superb, glorious, noble, splendid, gorgeous, luxurious, eminent, majestic, regal, stately, monumental, sublime, sumptuous, grandiose, opulent, palatial, ostentatious, splendiferous (*facetious*) << ANTONYM unimposing 2 AMBITIOUS, great, glorious, lofty, grandiose, exalted, ostentatious 3 SUPERIOR, great, lordly, noble, elevated, eminent, majestic, dignified, stately, lofty, august, illustrious, pompous, pretentious, haughty 4 EXCELLENT, great (*informal*), fine, wonderful, very good, brilliant, outstanding, smashing (*informal*), superb, first-class, divine, marvellous (*informal*), terrific (*informal*), splendid, awesome (*slang*), world-class, admirable, super (*informal*), first-rate, splendiferous (*facetious*) << ANTONYM bad 5 CHIEF, highest, lead, leading, head, main, supreme, principal, big-time (*informal*), major league (*informal*), pre-eminent << ANTONYM inferior

grandeur *noun* SPLENDOUR, glory, majesty, nobility, pomp, state, magnificence, sumptuousness, sublimity, stateliness

grandiose *adjective* 1 PRETENTIOUS, ambitious, extravagant, flamboyant, high-flown, pompous, showy, ostentatious, bombastic << ANTONYM unpretentious 2 IMPOSING, grand, impressive, magnificent, majestic, stately, monumental, lofty << ANTONYM humble

grant *noun* AWARD, allowance, donation, endowment, gift, concession, subsidy, hand-out, allocation, bounty, allotment, bequest, stipend ▷ *verb* 1 GIVE, allow, present, award, accord, permit, assign, allocate, hand out, confer on, bestow on, impart on, allot, vouchsafe 2 ACCEPT, allow, admit, acknowledge, concede, cede, accede

granule *noun* GRAIN, scrap, molecule, particle, fragment, atom, crumb, jot, speck, iota

graphic *adjective* 1 VIVID, clear, detailed, striking, telling, explicit, picturesque, forceful, expressive, descriptive, illustrative, well-drawn << ANTONYM vague

2 PICTORIAL, seen, drawn, visible, visual, representational, illustrative, diagrammatic << ANTONYM impressionistic

grapple verb 1 DEAL, tackle, cope, face, fight, battle, struggle, take on, engage, encounter, confront, combat, contend, wrestle, tussle, get to grips, do battle, address yourself to 2 STRUGGLE, fight, combat, wrestle, battle, clash, contend, strive, tussle, scuffle, come to grips

grasp verb 1 GRIP, hold, catch, grab, seize, snatch, clutch, clinch, clasp, lay or take hold of 2 UNDERSTAND, realize, take in, get, see, follow, catch on, comprehend, get the message about, get the picture about, catch or get the drift of ▷ noun 1 GRIP, hold, possession, embrace, clutches, clasp 2 UNDERSTANDING, knowledge, grip, perception, awareness, realization, mastery, comprehension 3 REACH, power, control, range, sweep, capacity, scope, sway, compass, mastery

grasping adjective GREEDY, acquisitive, rapacious, mean, selfish, stingy, penny-pinching (informal), venal, miserly, avaricious, niggardly, covetous, tightfisted, close-fisted, snoep (S African informal) << ANTONYM generous

grate verb 1 SHRED, mince, pulverize 2 SCRAPE, grind, rub, scratch, creak, rasp ▷▷ **grate on someone** or **grate on someone's nerves** ANNOY, irritate, aggravate (informal), gall, exasperate, nettle, jar, vex, chafe, irk, rankle, peeve, get under your skin (informal), get up your nose (informal), get on your nerves (informal), nark (Brit, Austral & NZ slang), set your teeth on edge, get on your wick (Brit slang), rub you up the wrong way, hack you off (informal)

grateful adjective THANKFUL, obliged, in (someone's) debt, indebted, appreciative, beholden

gratification noun 1 SATISFACTION, delight, pleasure, joy, thrill, relish, enjoyment, glee, kick or kicks (informal) << ANTONYM disappointment 2 INDULGENCE, satisfaction, fulfilment << ANTONYM denial

gratify verb PLEASE, delight, satisfy, thrill, give pleasure, gladden

grating[1] noun GRILLE, grid, grate, lattice, trellis, gridiron

grating[2] adjective IRRITATING, grinding, harsh, annoying, jarring, unpleasant, scraping, raucous, strident, squeaky, rasping, discordant, disagreeable, irksome

<< ANTONYM pleasing

gratitude noun THANKFULNESS, thanks, recognition, obligation, appreciation, indebtedness, sense of obligation, gratefulness << ANTONYM ingratitude

gratuitous adjective UNJUSTIFIED, unnecessary, needless, unfounded, unwarranted, superfluous, wanton, unprovoked, groundless, baseless, uncalled-for, unmerited, causeless << ANTONYM justifiable

gratuity noun TIP, present, gift, reward, bonus, donation, boon, bounty, recompense, perquisite, baksheesh, benefaction, pourboire (French), bonsela (S African), largesse or largess

grave[1] noun TOMB, vault, crypt, mausoleum, sepulchre, pit, last resting place, burying place

grave[2] adjective 1 SERIOUS, important, significant, critical, pressing, threatening, dangerous, vital, crucial, acute, severe, urgent, hazardous, life-and-death, momentous, perilous, weighty, leaden, of great consequence << ANTONYM trifling 2 SOLEMN, sober, gloomy, dull, thoughtful, subdued, sombre, dour, grim-faced, long-faced, unsmiling << ANTONYM carefree

graveyard noun CEMETERY, churchyard, burial ground, charnel house, necropolis, boneyard (informal), God's acre (literary)

gravitas noun SERIOUSNESS, gravity, solemnity

gravitate verb with **to** or **towards** BE DRAWN, move, tend, lean, be pulled, incline, be attracted, be influenced

gravity noun 1 SERIOUSNESS, importance, consequence, significance, urgency, severity, acuteness, moment, weightiness, momentousness, perilousness, hazardousness << ANTONYM triviality 2 SOLEMNITY, gloom, seriousness, gravitas, thoughtfulness, grimness << ANTONYM frivolity

graze[1] verb FEED, crop, browse, pasture

graze[2] verb 1 SCRATCH, skin, bark, scrape, chafe, abrade 2 TOUCH, brush, rub, scrape, shave, skim, kiss, glance off ▷ noun SCRATCH, scrape, abrasion

greasy adjective 1 FATTY, slick, slippery, oily, slimy, oleaginous 2 SYCOPHANTIC, fawning, grovelling, ingratiating, smooth, slick, oily, unctuous, smarmy (Brit informal), toadying

great adjective 1 LARGE, big, huge, vast, enormous, extensive, tremendous, immense, gigantic, mammoth, bulky, colossal, prodigious, stupendous, voluminous, elephantine, ginormous (*informal*), humongous *or* humungous (*US slang*) << ANTONYM small **2** EXTREME, considerable, excessive, high, decided, pronounced, extravagant, prodigious, inordinate **3** MAJOR, lead, leading, chief, main, capital, grand, primary, principal, prominent, superior, paramount, big-time (*informal*), major league (*informal*) **4** IMPORTANT, serious, significant, critical, crucial, heavy, grave, momentous, weighty, consequential << ANTONYM unimportant **5** FAMOUS, celebrated, outstanding, excellent, remarkable, distinguished, prominent, glorious, notable, renowned, eminent, famed, illustrious, exalted, noteworthy **6** EXPERT, skilled, talented, skilful, good, able, masterly, crack (*slang*), superb, world-class, adept, stellar (*informal*), superlative, proficient, adroit << ANTONYM unskilled **7** (*informal*) EXCELLENT, good, fine, wonderful, mean (*slang*), topping (*Brit slang*), cracking (*Brit informal*), superb, fantastic (*informal*), tremendous (*informal*), marvellous (*informal*), terrific (*informal*), mega (*slang*), sovereign, awesome (*slang*), dope (*slang*), admirable, first-rate, def (*informal*), brill (*informal*), boffo (*slang*), bitchin', chillin' (*US slang*), booshit (*Austral slang*), exo (*Austral slang*), sik (*Austral slang*), rad (*informal*), phat (*slang*), schmick (*Austral informal*) << ANTONYM poor **8** VERY, really, particularly, truly, extremely, awfully (*informal*), exceedingly **9** ENTHUSIASTIC, keen, active, devoted, zealous

greatly *adverb* VERY MUCH, much, hugely, vastly, extremely, highly, seriously (*informal*), notably, considerably, remarkably, enormously, immensely, tremendously, markedly, powerfully, exceedingly, mightily, abundantly, by much, by leaps and bounds, to the nth degree

greatness *noun* **1** GRANDEUR, glory, majesty, splendour, power, pomp, magnificence **2** FAME, glory, celebrity, distinction, eminence, note, lustre, renown, illustriousness

greed *or* **greediness** *noun* **1** GLUTTONY, voracity, insatiableness, ravenousness **2** AVARICE, longing, desire, hunger, craving, eagerness, selfishness, acquisitiveness, rapacity, cupidity, covetousness, insatiableness << ANTONYM generosity

greedy *adjective* **1** GLUTTONOUS, insatiable, voracious, ravenous, piggish, hoggish **2** AVARICIOUS, grasping, selfish, insatiable, acquisitive, rapacious, materialistic, desirous, covetous << ANTONYM generous

Greek *adjective* HELLENIC ▷ *noun* HELLENE

green *adjective* **1** VERDANT, leafy, grassy **2** ECOLOGICAL, conservationist, environment-friendly, ecologically sound, eco-friendly, ozone-friendly, non-polluting **3** UNRIPE, fresh, raw, immature **4** INEXPERIENCED, new, innocent, raw, naive, ignorant, immature, gullible, callow, untrained, unsophisticated, credulous, ingenuous, unpolished, wet behind the ears (*informal*) **5** JEALOUS, grudging, resentful, envious, covetous **6** NAUSEOUS, ill, sick, pale, unhealthy, wan, under the weather ▷ *noun* **1** *with capital* ENVIRONMENTALIST, conservationist **2** LAWN, common, turf, sward, grassplot

green light *noun* AUTHORIZATION, sanction, approval, go-ahead (*informal*), blessing, permission, confirmation, clearance, imprimatur, O.K. or okay (*informal*)

greet *verb* **1** SALUTE, hail, nod to, say hello to, address, accost, tip your hat to **2** WELCOME, meet, receive, karanga (*NZ*), mihi (*NZ*) **3** RECEIVE, take, respond to, react to

greeting *noun* WELCOME, reception, hail, salute, address, salutation, hongi (*NZ*), kia ora (*NZ*) ▷ *plural noun* BEST WISHES, regards, respects, compliments, good wishes, salutations

gregarious *adjective* OUTGOING, friendly, social, cordial, sociable, affable, convivial, companionable << ANTONYM unsociable

grey *adjective* **1** DULL, dark, dim, gloomy, cloudy, murky, drab, misty, foggy, overcast, sunless **2** BORING, dull, anonymous, faceless, colourless, nondescript, characterless **3** OLD, aged, ancient, mature, elderly, venerable, hoary **4** PALE, wan, livid, bloodless, colourless, pallid, ashen, like death warmed up (*informal*) **5** AMBIGUOUS, uncertain, neutral, unclear, debatable

gridlock *noun* **1** TRAFFIC JAM **2** DEADLOCK, halt, stalemate, impasse, standstill, full stop

grief *noun* SADNESS, suffering, pain, regret, distress, misery, agony, mourning, sorrow, woe, anguish, remorse, bereavement, heartache, heartbreak, mournfulness << ANTONYM joy ▷▷ **come to grief** (*informal*) FAIL, founder, break down, come unstuck, miscarry, fall flat on your face, meet with disaster

grievance noun COMPLAINT, protest, beef (*slang*), gripe (*informal*), axe to grind, chip on your shoulder (*informal*)

grieve verb 1 MOURN, suffer, weep, ache, lament, sorrow, wail 2 SADDEN, hurt, injure, distress, wound, crush, pain, afflict, upset, agonize, break the heart of, make your heart bleed << ANTONYM gladden

grievous adjective 1 DEPLORABLE, shocking, appalling, dreadful, outrageous, glaring, intolerable, monstrous, shameful, unbearable, atrocious, heinous, lamentable, egregious << ANTONYM pleasant 2 SEVERE, damaging, heavy, wounding, grave, painful, distressing, dreadful, harmful, calamitous, injurious << ANTONYM mild

grim adjective TERRIBLE, shocking, severe, harsh, forbidding, horrible, formidable, sinister, ghastly, hideous, gruesome (*slang*), grisly, horrid, frightful, godawful

grimace verb SCOWL, frown, sneer, wince, lour or lower, make a face or faces ▷ noun SCOWL, frown, sneer, wince, face, wry face

grime noun DIRT, filth, soot, smut, grot (*slang*)

grimy adjective DIRTY, polluted, filthy, soiled, foul, grubby, sooty, unclean, grotty (*slang*), smutty, scuzzy (*slang*), begrimed, festy (*Austral slang*)

grind verb 1 CRUSH, mill, powder, grate, pulverize, pound, kibble, abrade, granulate 2 PRESS, push, crush, jam, mash, force down 3 GRATE, scrape, grit, gnash 4 SHARPEN, file, polish, sand, smooth, whet ▷ noun (*informal*) HARD WORK , labour, effort, task, sweat (*informal*), chore, toil, drudgery ▷▷ **grind someone down** OPPRESS, suppress, harass, subdue, hound, bring down, plague, persecute, subjugate, trample underfoot, tyrannize (over)

grip verb 1 GRASP, hold, catch, seize, clutch, clasp, latch on to, take hold of 2 ENGROSS, fascinate, absorb, entrance, hold, catch up, compel, rivet, enthral, mesmerize, spellbind ▷ noun 1 CLASP, hold, grasp, handclasp (*US*) 2 CONTROL, rule, influence, command, power, possession, sway, dominance, domination, mastery 3 HOLD, purchase, friction, traction 4 UNDERSTANDING, sense, command, perception, awareness, grasp, appreciation, mastery, comprehension, discernment ▷▷ **come or get to grips with something** TACKLE, deal with, handle, take on, meet, encounter, cope with, confront, undertake, grasp, face up to, grapple with, close with, contend with

gripe (*informal*) verb COMPLAIN, moan, groan, grumble, beef (*slang*), carp, bitch (*slang*), nag, whine, grouse, bleat, grouch (*informal*), bellyache (*slang*), kvetch (*US slang*) ▷ noun COMPLAINT, protest, objection, beef (*slang*), moan, grumble, grievance, grouse, grouch (*informal*)

gripping adjective FASCINATING, exciting, thrilling, entrancing, compelling, compulsive, riveting, enthralling, engrossing, spellbinding, unputdownable (*informal*)

grisly adjective GRUESOME, shocking, terrible, awful, terrifying, appalling, horrible, grim, dreadful, sickening, ghastly, hideous, macabre, horrid, frightful, abominable, hellacious (*US slang*) << ANTONYM pleasant

grit noun 1 GRAVEL, sand, dust, pebbles 2 COURAGE, spirit, resolution, determination, nerve, guts (*informal*), pluck, backbone, fortitude, toughness, tenacity, perseverance, mettle, doggedness, hardihood ▷ verb CLENCH, grind, grate, gnash

gritty adjective 1 ROUGH, sandy, dusty, abrasive, rasping, grainy, gravelly, granular 2 COURAGEOUS, game, dogged, determined, tough, spirited, brave, hardy, feisty (*informal, chiefly US & Canad*), resolute, tenacious, plucky, steadfast, mettlesome, (as) game as Ned Kelly (*Austral slang*)

grizzle verb WHINE, fret, whimper, whinge (*informal*), snivel, girn (*Scot*)

grizzled adjective GREY, greying, grey-haired, grizzly, hoary, grey-headed

groan verb 1 MOAN, cry, sigh 2 (*informal*) COMPLAIN, object, moan, grumble, gripe (*informal*), beef (*slang*), carp, bitch (*slang*), lament, whine, grouse, bemoan, whinge (*informal*), grouch (*informal*), bellyache (*slang*) ▷ noun 1 MOAN, cry, sigh, whine 2 (*informal*) COMPLAINT, protest, objection, grumble, beef (*slang*), grouse, gripe (*informal*), grouch (*informal*)

groggy adjective DIZZY, faint, stunned, confused, reeling, shaky, dazed, wobbly, weak, unsteady, muzzy, stupefied, befuddled, punch-drunk, woozy (*informal*)

groom noun 1 STABLEMAN, stableboy, hostler or ostler (*archaic*) 2 NEWLY-WED, husband, bridegroom, marriage partner ▷ verb 1 BRUSH, clean, tend, rub down, curry 2 SMARTEN UP, dress, clean, turn out, get up (*informal*), tidy, preen, spruce up, primp, gussy up (*slang, chiefly US*) 3 TRAIN, prime, prepare, coach, ready, educate, drill, nurture, make ready

groove *noun* INDENTATION, cut, hollow, score, channel, trench, flute, gutter, trough, furrow, rut

grope *verb* FEEL, search, fumble, flounder, fish, finger, scrabble, cast about, fossick (*Austral* & *NZ*)

gross *adjective* 1 FLAGRANT, obvious, glaring, blatant, serious, shocking, rank, plain, sheer, utter, outrageous, manifest, shameful, downright, grievous, unqualified, heinous, egregious, unmitigated, arrant << ANTONYM qualified 2 VULGAR, offensive, crude, rude, obscene, low, coarse, indecent, improper, unseemly, lewd, X-rated (*informal*), impure, smutty, ribald, indelicate << ANTONYM decent 3 COARSE, crass, tasteless, unsophisticated, ignorant, insensitive, callous, boorish, unfeeling, unrefined, uncultured, undiscriminating, imperceptive << ANTONYM cultivated 4 FAT, obese, overweight, great, big, large, heavy, massive, dense, bulky, hulking, corpulent, lumpish << ANTONYM slim 5 TOTAL, whole, entire, aggregate, before tax, before deductions << ANTONYM net ▷ *verb* EARN, make, take, bring in, rake in (*informal*)

grotesque *adjective* 1 UNNATURAL, bizarre, weird, odd, strange, fantastic, distorted, fanciful, deformed, outlandish, whimsical, freakish, misshapen, malformed << ANTONYM natural 2 ABSURD, ridiculous, ludicrous, preposterous, incongruous << ANTONYM natural

grouch *verb* COMPLAIN, moan, grumble, beef (*slang*), carp, bitch (*slang*), whine, grouse, gripe (*informal*), whinge (*informal*), bleat, find fault, bellyache (*slang*), kvetch (*US slang*) ▷ *noun* 1 MOANER, complainer, grumbler, whiner, grouser, malcontent, curmudgeon, crosspatch (*informal*), crab (*informal*), faultfinder 2 COMPLAINT, protest, objection, grievance, moan, grumble, beef (*slang*), grouse, gripe (*informal*)

grouchy *adjective* BAD-TEMPERED, cross, irritable, grumpy, discontented, grumbling, surly, petulant, sulky, ill-tempered, irascible, cantankerous, tetchy, ratty (*Brit* & *NZ informal*), testy, querulous, peevish, huffy, liverish

ground *noun* 1 EARTH, land, dry land, terra firma 2 ARENA, pitch, stadium, park (*informal*), field, enclosure ▷ *plural noun* 1 ESTATE, holding, land, fields, gardens, property, district, territory, domain 2 REASON, cause, basis, argument, call, base, occasion, foundation, excuse, premise, motive, justification, rationale, inducement 3 DREGS, lees, deposit, sediment ▷ *verb* 1 BASE, found, establish, set, settle, fix 2 INSTRUCT, train, prepare, coach, teach, inform, initiate, tutor, acquaint with, familiarize with

groundless *adjective* BASELESS, false, unfounded, unjustified, unproven, empty, unauthorized, unsubstantiated, unsupported, uncorroborated << ANTONYM well-founded

groundwork *noun* PRELIMINARIES, basis, foundation, base, footing, preparation, fundamentals, cornerstone, underpinnings, spadework

group *noun* 1 CROWD, company, party, band, troop, pack, gathering, gang, bunch, congregation, posse (*slang*), bevy, assemblage 2 CLUSTER, formation, clump, aggregation ▷ *verb* 1 ARRANGE, order, sort, class, range, gather, organize, assemble, put together, classify, marshal, bracket, assort 2 UNITE, associate, gather, cluster, get together, congregate, band together

grouse *verb* COMPLAIN, moan, grumble, gripe (*informal*), beef (*slang*), carp, bitch (*slang*), whine, whinge (*informal*), bleat, find fault, grouch (*informal*), bellyache (*slang*), kvetch (*US slang*) ▷ *noun* COMPLAINT, protest, objection, moan, grievance, grumble, gripe (*informal*), beef (*slang*), grouch (*informal*)

grove *noun* WOOD, woodland, plantation, covert, thicket, copse, brake, coppice, spinney

grovel *verb* HUMBLE YOURSELF, creep, crawl, flatter, fawn, pander, cower, toady, kowtow, bow and scrape, lick someone's boots, demean yourself, abase yourself << ANTONYM hold your head high

grow *verb* 1 DEVELOP, fill out, get bigger, get taller << ANTONYM shrink 2 GET BIGGER, spread, swell, extend, stretch, expand, widen, enlarge, multiply, thicken 3 SPRING UP, shoot up, develop, flourish, sprout, germinate, vegetate 4 CULTIVATE, produce, raise, farm, breed, nurture, propagate 5 BECOME, get, turn, come to be 6 ORIGINATE, spring, arise, stem, issue 7 IMPROVE, advance, progress, succeed, expand, thrive, flourish, prosper

grown-up *noun* ADULT, man, woman ▷ *adjective* MATURE, adult, of age, fully-grown

growth noun 1 INCREASE, development, expansion, extension, growing, heightening, proliferation, enlargement, multiplication << ANTONYM decline 2 PROGRESS, success, improvement, expansion, advance, prosperity, advancement << ANTONYM failure 3 VEGETATION, development, production, sprouting, germination, shooting 4 (medical) TUMOUR, cancer, swelling, lump, carcinoma (pathology), sarcoma (medical), excrescence

grub noun 1 LARVA, maggot, caterpillar 2 (slang) FOOD, feed, rations, tack (informal), eats (slang), kai (NZ informal), sustenance, nosh (slang), victuals, nosebag (slang), vittles (obsolete or dialect) ▷ verb 1 SEARCH, hunt, scour, ferret, rummage, forage, fossick (Austral & NZ) 2 DIG, search, root (informal), probe, burrow, rootle (Brit)

grubby adjective DIRTY, soiled, filthy, squalid, messy, shabby, seedy, scruffy, sordid, untidy, grimy, unwashed, unkempt, mucky, smutty, grungy (slang, chiefly US & Canad), slovenly, manky (Scot dialect), scuzzy (slang), scungy (Austral & NZ), frowzy, besmeared, festy (Austral slang)

grudge noun RESENTMENT, bitterness, grievance, malice, hate, spite, dislike, animosity, aversion, venom, antipathy, enmity, rancour, hard feelings, ill will, animus, malevolence << ANTONYM goodwill ▷ verb RESENT, mind, envy, covet, begrudge << ANTONYM welcome

gruelling adjective EXHAUSTING, demanding, difficult, tiring, trying, hard, taxing, grinding, severe, crushing, fierce, punishing, harsh, stiff, brutal, fatiguing, strenuous, arduous, laborious, backbreaking << ANTONYM easy

gruesome adjective HORRIFIC, shocking, terrible, awful, horrible, grim, horrifying, fearful, obscene, horrendous, ghastly, hideous, from hell (informal), grisly, macabre, horrid, repulsive, repugnant, loathsome, abominable, spine-chilling, hellacious (US slang) << ANTONYM pleasant

gruff adjective 1 HOARSE, rough, harsh, rasping, husky, low, croaking, throaty, guttural << ANTONYM mellifluous 2 SURLY, rough, rude, grumpy, blunt, crabbed, crusty, sullen, bad-tempered, curt, churlish, brusque, impolite, grouchy (informal), ungracious, discourteous, uncivil, ill-humoured, unmannerly, ill-natured << ANTONYM polite

grumble verb 1 COMPLAIN, moan, gripe (informal), whinge (informal), beef (slang), carp, bitch (slang), whine, grouse, bleat, grouch (informal), bellyache (slang), kvetch (US slang), repine 2 RUMBLE, growl, gurgle ▷ noun 1 COMPLAINT, protest, objection, moan, grievance, grouse, gripe (informal), grouch (informal), beef (slang) 2 RUMBLE, growl, gurgle

grumpy adjective IRRITABLE, cross, bad-tempered, grumbling, crabbed, edgy, surly, petulant, ill-tempered, cantankerous, tetchy, ratty (Brit & NZ informal), testy, grouchy (informal), querulous, peevish, huffy, crotchety (informal), liverish

guarantee verb 1 ENSURE, secure, assure, warrant, insure, make certain 2 PROMISE, pledge, undertake, swear ▷ noun 1 PROMISE, word, pledge, undertaking, assurance, certainty, covenant, word of honour 2 WARRANTY, contract, bond, guaranty

guarantor noun UNDERWRITER, guarantee, supporter, sponsor, backer, surety, warrantor

guard verb PROTECT, watch, defend, secure, police, mind, cover, screen, preserve, shelter, shield, patrol, oversee, safeguard, watch over ▷ noun 1 SENTRY, warder, warden, custodian, watch, patrol, lookout, watchman, sentinel 2 ESCORT, patrol, convoy 3 SHIELD, security, defence, screen, protection, pad, safeguard, bumper, buffer, rampart, bulwark ▷▷ off (your) guard UNPREPARED, napping, unwary, unready, with your defences down ▷▷ on (your) guard VIGILANT, cautious, wary, prepared, ready, alert, watchful, on the lookout, circumspect, on the alert, on the qui vive

guarded adjective CAUTIOUS, reserved, careful, suspicious, restrained, wary, discreet, prudent, reticent, circumspect, cagey (informal), leery (slang), noncommittal

guardian noun KEEPER, champion, defender, guard, trustee, warden, curator, protector, warder, custodian, preserver

guerrilla noun FREEDOM FIGHTER, partisan, irregular, underground fighter, member of the underground or resistance

guess verb 1 ESTIMATE, predict, work out, speculate, fathom, conjecture, postulate, surmise, hazard a guess, hypothesize << ANTONYM know 2 SUPPOSE, think, believe, suspect, judge, imagine, reckon, fancy, conjecture, dare say ▷ noun 1 ESTIMATE, reckoning, speculation, judgment, hypothesis, conjecture, surmise,

shot in the dark, ballpark figure (*informal*)
<< ANTONYM certainty **2** SUPPOSITION,
feeling, idea, theory, notion, suspicion,
hypothesis

guesswork *noun* SPECULATION, theory,
presumption, conjecture, estimation,
surmise, supposition

guest *noun* VISITOR, company, caller,
manu(w)hiri (*NZ*)

guff *noun* (*informal*) NONSENSE, rubbish, rot,
crap (*slang*), garbage (*informal*), trash, hot air
(*informal*), tosh (*slang, chiefly Brit*), pap, bilge
(*informal*), humbug, drivel, tripe (*informal*),
moonshine, hogwash, hokum (*slang, chiefly
US & Canad*), piffle (*informal*), poppycock
(*informal*), balderdash, bosh (*informal*),
eyewash (*informal*), kak (*S African taboo slang*),
empty talk, tommyrot, horsefeathers (*US
slang*), bunkum *or* buncombe (*chiefly US*),
bizzo (*Austral slang*), bull's wool (*Austral &
NZ slang*)

guidance *noun* ADVICE, direction,
leadership, instruction, government, help,
control, management, teaching, counsel,
counselling, auspices

guide *noun* **1** HANDBOOK, manual, guidebook,
instructions, catalogue **2** DIRECTORY, street
map **3** ESCORT, leader, controller, attendant,
usher, chaperon, torchbearer, dragoman
4 POINTER, sign, signal, mark, key, clue,
landmark, marker, beacon, signpost,
guiding light, lodestar **5** MODEL, example,
standard, ideal, master, inspiration,
criterion, paradigm, exemplar, lodestar ▷
verb **1** LEAD, direct, escort, conduct, pilot,
accompany, steer, shepherd, convoy, usher,
show the way **2** STEER, control, manage,
direct, handle, command, manoeuvre
3 SUPERVISE, train, rule, teach, influence,
advise, counsel, govern, educate, regulate,
instruct, oversee, sway, superintend

guild *noun* SOCIETY, union, league,
association, company, club, order,
organization, corporation, lodge, fellowship,
fraternity, brotherhood

guile *noun* CUNNING, craft, deception,
deceit, trickery, duplicity, cleverness,
art, gamesmanship (*informal*), craftiness,
artfulness, slyness, trickiness, wiliness
<< ANTONYM honesty

guilt *noun* **1** SHAME, regret, remorse,
contrition, guilty conscience, bad
conscience, self-reproach, self-
condemnation, guiltiness << ANTONYM
pride **2** CULPABILITY, blame, responsibility,

misconduct, delinquency, criminality,
wickedness, iniquity, sinfulness,
blameworthiness, guiltiness << ANTONYM
innocence

guilty *adjective* **1** ASHAMED, sorry, rueful,
sheepish, contrite, remorseful, regretful,
shamefaced, hangdog, conscience-
stricken << ANTONYM proud **2** CULPABLE,
responsible, convicted, to blame, offending,
erring, at fault, reprehensible, iniquitous,
felonious, blameworthy << ANTONYM
innocent

guise *noun* **1** FORM, appearance, dress,
fashion, shape, aspect, mode, semblance
2 PRETENCE, show, mask, disguise, face,
front, aspect, façade, semblance

gulch *noun* (*US & Canad*) RAVINE, canyon,
defile, gorge, gully, pass

gulf *noun* **1** BAY, bight, sea inlet **2** CHASM,
opening, split, gap, rent, breach, separation,
void, rift, abyss, cleft

gullible *adjective* TRUSTING, innocent,
naive, unsuspecting, green, simple, silly,
foolish, unsophisticated, credulous, born
yesterday, wet behind the ears (*informal*),
easily taken in, unsceptical, as green as grass
<< ANTONYM suspicious

gully *noun* RAVINE, canyon, gorge, chasm,
channel, fissure, defile, watercourse

gulp *verb* **1** SWALLOW, bolt, devour, gobble,
knock back (*informal*), wolf, swig (*informal*),
swill, guzzle, quaff **2** GASP, swallow, choke
▷ *noun* SWALLOW, draught, mouthful, swig
(*informal*)

gum *noun* GLUE, adhesive, resin, cement,
paste ▷ *verb* STICK, glue, affix, cement, paste,
clog

gun *noun* FIREARM, shooter (*slang*), piece
(*slang*), rod (*slang*), heater (*US slang*), handgun

gunman *noun* ARMED MAN, hit man (*slang*),
gunslinger (*US slang*)

gurgle *verb* RIPPLE, lap, bubble, splash,
murmur, babble, burble, purl, plash ▷ *noun*
BURBLE, chuckle, ripple, babble

guru *noun* **1** AUTHORITY, expert, leader,
master, pundit, arbiter, Svengali,
torchbearer, fundi (*S African*) **2** TEACHER,
mentor, sage, master, tutor, mahatma,
guiding light, swami, maharishi

gush *verb* **1** FLOW, run, rush, flood, pour,
jet, burst, stream, cascade, issue, spurt,
spout **2** ENTHUSE, rave, spout, overstate,
rhapsodize, effuse ▷ *noun* STREAM, flow, rush,
flood, jet, burst, issue, outburst, cascade,
torrent, spurt, spout, outflow

gust *noun* 1 BLAST, blow, rush, breeze, puff, gale, flurry, squall 2 SURGE, fit, storm, burst, explosion, gale, outburst, eruption, paroxysm ▷ *verb* BLOW, blast, puff, squall

gusto *noun* RELISH, enthusiasm, appetite, appreciation, liking, delight, pleasure, enjoyment, savour, zeal, verve, zest, fervour, exhilaration, brio, zing (*informal*) << ANTONYM apathy

gusty *adjective* WINDY, stormy, breezy, blustering, tempestuous, blustery, inclement, squally, blowy

gut *noun* (*informal*) PAUNCH, belly, spare tyre (*Brit slang*), potbelly, puku (*NZ*) ▷ *verb* 1 DISEMBOWEL, draw, dress, clean, eviscerate 2 RAVAGE, strip, empty, sack, rifle, plunder, clean out, ransack, pillage, despoil ▷ *adjective* INSTINCTIVE, natural, basic, emotional, spontaneous, innate, intuitive, involuntary, heartfelt, deep-seated, unthinking

guts *plural noun* 1 INTESTINES, insides (*informal*), stomach, belly, bowels, inwards, innards (*informal*), entrails 2 (*informal*) COURAGE, spirit, nerve, daring, pluck, grit, backbone, willpower, bottle (*slang*), audacity, mettle, boldness, spunk (*informal*), forcefulness, hardihood

gutsy *adjective* BRAVE, determined, spirited, bold, have-a-go (*informal*), courageous, gritty, staunch, feisty (*informal, chiefly US & Canad*), game (*informal*), resolute, gallant, plucky, indomitable, mettlesome, (as) game as Ned Kelly (*Austral slang*)

gutter *noun* DRAIN, channel, tube, pipe, ditch, trench, trough, conduit, duct, sluice

guy *noun* (*informal*) MAN, person, fellow, lad, cat (*dated slang*), bloke (*Brit informal*), chap

guzzle *verb* DEVOUR, drink, bolt, wolf, cram, gorge, gobble, knock back (*informal*), swill, quaff, tope, pig out on (*slang*), stuff yourself with

Gypsy *or* **Gipsy** *noun* TRAVELLER, roamer, wanderer, Bohemian, rover, rambler, nomad, vagrant, Romany, vagabond

gyrate *verb* ROTATE, circle, spin, spiral, revolve, whirl, twirl, pirouette

habit *noun* **1** MANNERISM, custom, way, practice, manner, characteristic, tendency, quirk, propensity, foible, proclivity **2** CUSTOM, rule, practice, tradition, routine, convention, mode, usage, wont, second nature **3** ADDICTION, weakness, obsession, dependence, compulsion, fixation **4** DRESS, costume, garment, apparel, garb, habiliment, riding dress

habitat *noun* HOME, environment, surroundings, element, territory, domain, terrain, locality, home ground, abode, habitation, natural home

habitation *noun* **1** OCCUPATION, living in, residence, tenancy, occupancy, residency, inhabitance, inhabitancy **2** (*formal*) DWELLING, home, house, residence, quarters, lodging, pad (*slang*), abode, living quarters, domicile, dwelling house

habitual *adjective* **1** CUSTOMARY, normal, usual, common, standard, natural, traditional, fixed, regular, ordinary, familiar, routine, accustomed, wonted << ANTONYM unusual **2** PERSISTENT, established, confirmed, constant, frequent, chronic, hardened, recurrent, ingrained, inveterate << ANTONYM occasional

hack¹ *verb* **1** CUT, chop, slash, mutilate, mangle, mangulate (*Austral slang*), gash, hew, lacerate **2** (*informal*) COUGH, bark, wheeze, rasp ▷ *noun* (*informal*) COUGH, bark, wheeze, rasp

hack² *noun* **1** REPORTER, writer, correspondent, journalist, scribbler, contributor, literary hack, penny-a-liner, Grub Street writer **2** YES-MAN, lackey, toady, flunky ▷ *adjective* UNORIGINAL, pedestrian, mediocre, poor, tired, stereotyped, banal, undistinguished, uninspired

hackles ▷▷ **raise someone's hackles** *or* **make someone's hackles rise** ANGER, annoy, infuriate, cause resentment, rub someone up the wrong way, make someone see red (*informal*), get someone's dander up (*slang*), hack you off (*informal*)

hackneyed *adjective* CLICHÉD, stock, tired, common, stereotyped, pedestrian, played out (*informal*), commonplace, worn-out, stale, overworked, banal, run-of-the-mill, threadbare, trite, unoriginal, timeworn << ANTONYM original

Hades *noun* UNDERWORLD, hell, nether regions, lower world, infernal regions, realm of Pluto, (the) inferno

hag *noun* WITCH, virago, shrew, vixen, crone, fury, harridan, beldam (*archaic*), termagant

haggard *adjective* GAUNT, wasted, drawn, thin, pinched, wrinkled, ghastly, wan, emaciated, shrunken, careworn, hollow-eyed << ANTONYM robust

haggle *verb* **1** BARGAIN, barter, beat down, drive a hard bargain, dicker (*chiefly US*), chaffer, palter, higgle **2** WRANGLE, dispute, quarrel, squabble, bicker

hail¹ *noun* **1** HAILSTONES, sleet, hailstorm, frozen rain **2** SHOWER, rain, storm, battery, volley, barrage, bombardment, pelting, downpour, salvo, broadside ▷ *verb* **1** RAIN, shower, pelt **2** BATTER, rain, barrage, bombard, pelt, rain down on, beat down upon

hail² *verb* **1** ACCLAIM, honour, acknowledge, cheer, applaud, glorify, exalt << ANTONYM condemn **2** SALUTE, call, greet, address, welcome, speak to, shout to, say hello to, accost, sing out, halloo << ANTONYM snub **3** FLAG DOWN, summon, signal to, wave down ▷▷ **hail from somewhere** COME FROM, be born in, originate in, be a native of, have your roots in

hair noun LOCKS, mane, tresses, shock, mop, head of hair ▷▷ **let your hair down** LET YOURSELF GO, relax, chill out (*slang, chiefly US*), let off steam (*informal*), let it all hang out (*informal*), mellow out (*informal*), veg out (*slang, chiefly US*), outspan (*S African*) ▷▷ **not turn a hair** REMAIN CALM, keep your cool (*slang*), not bat an eyelid, keep your hair on (*Brit informal*) ▷▷ **split hairs** QUIBBLE, find fault, cavil, overrefine, pettifog

hairdresser noun STYLIST, barber, coiffeur or coiffeuse, friseur

hair-raising adjective FRIGHTENING, shocking, alarming, thrilling, exciting, terrifying, startling, horrifying, scary, breathtaking, creepy, petrifying, spine-chilling, bloodcurdling

hairstyle noun HAIRCUT, hairdo, coiffure, cut, style

hairy adjective 1 SHAGGY, woolly, furry, stubbly, bushy, bearded, unshaven, hirsute, fleecy, bewhiskered, pileous (*biology*), pilose (*biology*) 2 (*slang*) DANGEROUS, scary, risky, unpredictable, hazardous, perilous

halcyon adjective 1 HAPPY, golden, flourishing, prosperous, carefree, palmy 2 PEACEFUL, still, quiet, calm, gentle, mild, serene, tranquil, placid, pacific, undisturbed, unruffled

hale adjective (*old-fashioned*) HEALTHY, well, strong, sound, fit, flourishing, blooming, robust, vigorous, hearty, in the pink, in fine fettle, right as rain (*Brit informal*), able-bodied

half noun FIFTY PER CENT, equal part ▷ adjective PARTIAL, limited, fractional, divided, moderate, halved, incomplete ▷ adverb PARTIALLY, partly, incompletely, slightly, all but, barely, in part, inadequately, after a fashion, pretty nearly

half-baked adjective (*informal*) STUPID, impractical, crazy, silly, foolish, senseless, short-sighted, inane, loopy (*informal*), ill-conceived, crackpot (*informal*), ill-judged, brainless, unformed, poorly planned, harebrained, dumb-ass (*slang*), unthought out or through

half-hearted adjective UNENTHUSIASTIC, indifferent, apathetic, cool, neutral, passive, lacklustre, lukewarm, uninterested, perfunctory, listless, spiritless << ANTONYM enthusiastic

halfway adverb 1 MIDWAY, to the midpoint, to or in the middle 2 (*informal*) PARTIALLY, partly, moderately, rather, nearly ▷ adjective MIDWAY, middle, mid, central, intermediate, equidistant ▷▷ **meet someone halfway** COMPROMISE, accommodate, come to terms, reach a compromise, strike a balance, trade off with, find the middle ground

hall noun 1 PASSAGE, lobby, corridor, hallway, foyer, entry, passageway, entrance hall, vestibule 2 MEETING PLACE, chamber, auditorium, concert hall, assembly room

hallmark noun 1 TRADEMARK, indication, badge, emblem, sure sign, telltale sign 2 (*Brit*) MARK, sign, device, stamp, seal, symbol, signet, authentication

hallowed adjective SANCTIFIED, holy, blessed, sacred, honoured, dedicated, revered, consecrated, sacrosanct, inviolable, beatified

hallucinate verb IMAGINE, trip (*informal*), envision, daydream, fantasize, freak out (*informal*), have hallucinations

hallucination noun ILLUSION, dream, vision, fantasy, delusion, mirage, apparition, phantasmagoria, figment of the imagination

hallucinogenic adjective PSYCHEDELIC, mind-blowing (*informal*), psychoactive, hallucinatory, psychotropic, mind-expanding

halo noun RING OF LIGHT, aura, corona, radiance, nimbus, halation (*philosophy*), aureole or aureola

halt verb 1 STOP, draw up, pull up, break off, stand still, wait, rest, call it a day, belay (*nautical*) << ANTONYM continue 2 COME TO AN END, stop, cease 3 HOLD BACK, end, check, block, arrest, stem, curb, terminate, obstruct, staunch, cut short, impede, bring to an end, stem the flow, nip in the bud << ANTONYM aid ▷ noun STOP, end, close, break, stand, arrest, pause, interruption, impasse, standstill, stoppage, termination << ANTONYM continuation

halting adjective FALTERING, stumbling, awkward, hesitant, laboured, stammering, imperfect, stuttering

halve verb 1 CUT IN HALF, reduce by fifty per cent, decrease by fifty per cent, lessen by fifty per cent 2 SPLIT IN TWO, cut in half, bisect, divide in two, share equally, divide equally

hammer verb 1 HIT, drive, knock, beat, strike, tap, bang 2 *often with* **into** IMPRESS UPON, repeat, drive home, drum into, grind into, din into, drub into 3 (*informal*) DEFEAT, beat, thrash, stuff (*slang*), master, worst, tank (*slang*), lick (*informal*), slate (*informal*), trounce, clobber (*slang*), run rings around (*informal*), wipe the floor with (*informal*), blow out of the water (*slang*), drub ▷▷ **hammer away at something** WORK, keep on, persevere, grind, persist, stick at, plug away (*informal*), drudge, pound away, peg away (*chiefly Brit*), beaver away (*Brit informal*)

hamper *verb* HINDER, handicap, hold up, prevent, restrict, frustrate, curb, slow down, restrain, hamstring, interfere with, cramp, thwart, obstruct, impede, hobble, fetter, encumber, trammel << ANTONYM help

hamstring *verb* THWART, stop, block, prevent, ruin, frustrate, handicap, curb, foil, obstruct, impede, balk, fetter

hamstrung *adjective* INCAPACITATED, disabled, crippled, helpless, paralysed, at a loss, hors de combat (*French*)

hand *noun* 1 PALM, fist, paw (*informal*), mitt (*slang*), hook, meathook (*slang*) 2 INFLUENCE, part, share, agency, direction, participation 3 ASSISTANCE, help, aid, support, helping hand 4 WORKER, employee, labourer, workman, operative, craftsman, artisan, hired man, hireling 5 ROUND OF APPLAUSE, clap, ovation, big hand 6 WRITING, script, handwriting, calligraphy, longhand, penmanship, chirography ▷ *verb* 1 GIVE, pass, hand over, present to, deliver 2 HELP, guide, conduct, lead, aid, assist, convey ▷▷ **at** or **on hand** WITHIN REACH, nearby, handy, close, available, ready, on tap (*informal*), at your fingertips ▷▷ **hand in glove** IN ASSOCIATION, in partnership, in league, in collaboration, in cooperation, in cahoots (*informal*) ▷▷ **hand over fist** SWIFTLY, easily, steadily, by leaps and bounds ▷▷ **hand something down** PASS ON or DOWN, pass, transfer, bequeath, will, give, grant, gift, endow ▷▷ **hand something on** PASS ON or DOWN, pass, transfer, bequeath, will, give, grant, relinquish ▷▷ **hand something** or **someone over** 1 GIVE, present, deliver, donate 2 TURN OVER, release, transfer, deliver, yield, surrender ▷▷ **hands down** EASILY, effortlessly, with ease, comfortably, without difficulty, with no trouble, standing on your head, with one hand tied behind your back, with no contest, with your eyes closed or shut ▷▷ **in hand** 1 IN RESERVE, ready, put by, available for use 2 UNDER CONTROL, in order, receiving attention ▷▷ **lay hands on someone** 1 ATTACK, assault, set on, beat up, work over (*slang*), lay into (*informal*) 2 BLESS (*Christianity*), confirm, ordain, consecrate ▷▷ **lay hands on something** GET HOLD OF, get,

obtain, gain, grab, acquire, seize, grasp

handbook *noun* GUIDEBOOK, guide, manual, instruction book, Baedeker, vade mecum

handcuff *verb* SHACKLE, secure, restrain, fetter, manacle ▷ *plural noun* SHACKLES, cuffs (*informal*), fetters, manacles, bracelets (*slang*)

handful *noun* FEW, sprinkling, small amount, small quantity, smattering, small number << ANTONYM a lot

handgun *noun* PISTOL, automatic, revolver, shooter (*informal*), piece (*US slang*), rod (*US slang*), derringer

handicap *noun* 1 DISABILITY, defect, impairment, physical abnormality 2 DISADVANTAGE, block, barrier, restriction, obstacle, limitation, hazard, drawback, shortcoming, stumbling block, impediment, albatross, hindrance, millstone, encumbrance << ANTONYM advantage 3 ADVANTAGE, penalty, head start ▷ *verb* HINDER, limit, restrict, burden, hamstring, hamper, hold back, retard, impede, hobble, encumber, place at a disadvantage << ANTONYM help

handicraft *noun* SKILL, art, craft, handiwork

handily *adverb* 1 CONVENIENTLY, readily, suitably, helpfully, advantageously, accessibly 2 SKILFULLY, expertly, cleverly, deftly, adroitly, capably, proficiently, dexterously

handiwork *noun* CREATION, product, production, achievement, result, design, invention, artefact, handicraft, handwork

handkerchief *noun* HANKY (*informal*), tissue, mouchoir, snot rag (*slang*), nose rag (*slang*)

handle *noun* GRIP, knob, hilt, haft, stock, handgrip, helve ▷ *verb* 1 MANAGE, deal with, tackle, cope with 2 DEAL WITH, manage, take care of, administer, conduct, supervise 3 CONTROL, manage, direct, operate, guide, use, steer, manipulate, manoeuvre, wield 4 HOLD, feel, touch, pick up, finger, grasp, poke, paw (*informal*), maul, fondle 5 DEAL IN, market, sell, trade in, carry, stock, traffic in 6 DISCUSS, report, treat, review, tackle, examine, discourse on ▷▷ **fly off the handle** (*informal*) LOSE YOUR TEMPER, explode, lose it (*informal*), lose the plot (*informal*), let fly (*informal*), go ballistic (*slang, chiefly US*), fly into a rage, have a tantrum, wig out (*slang*), lose your cool (*slang*), blow your top, flip your lid (*slang*), hit or go through the roof (*informal*)

handling *noun* MANAGEMENT, running, treatment, approach, administration, conduct, manipulation

hand-out *noun* **1** *often plural* CHARITY, dole, alms, pogey (*Canad*) **2** PRESS RELEASE, bulletin, circular, mailshot **3** LEAFLET, literature (*informal*), bulletin, flyer, pamphlet, printed matter **4** GIVEAWAY, freebie (*informal*), free gift, free sample

hand-picked *adjective* SELECTED, chosen, choice, select, elect, elite, recherché << ANTONYM random

handsome *adjective* **1** GOOD-LOOKING, attractive, gorgeous, fine, stunning, elegant, personable, nice-looking, dishy (*informal, chiefly Brit*), comely, fanciable, well-proportioned << ANTONYM ugly **2** GENEROUS, large, princely, liberal, considerable, lavish, ample, abundant, plentiful, bountiful, sizable *or* sizeable << ANTONYM mean

handsomely *adverb* GENEROUSLY, amply, richly, liberally, lavishly, abundantly, plentifully, bountifully, munificently

handwriting *noun* WRITING, hand, script, fist, scrawl, calligraphy, longhand, penmanship, chirography

handy *adjective* **1** USEFUL, practical, helpful, neat, convenient, easy to use, manageable, user-friendly, serviceable << ANTONYM useless **2** CONVENIENT, close, near, available, nearby, accessible, on hand, at hand, within reach, just round the corner, at your fingertips << ANTONYM inconvenient **3** SKILFUL, skilled, expert, clever, adept, ready, deft, nimble, proficient, adroit, dexterous << ANTONYM unskilled

handyman *noun* ODD-JOBMAN, jack-of-all-trades, handy Andy (*informal*), DIY expert

hang *verb* **1** DANGLE, swing, suspend, be pendent **2** LOWER, suspend, dangle, let down, let droop **3** LEAN, incline, loll, bend forward, bow, bend downward **4** DROOP, drop, dangle, trail, sag **5** DECORATE, cover, fix, attach, deck, furnish, drape, fasten **6** EXECUTE, lynch, string up (*informal*), gibbet, send to the gallows **7** HOVER, float, drift, linger, remain ▷▷ **get the hang of something** GRASP, understand, learn, master, comprehend, catch on to, acquire the technique of, get the knack *or* technique of ▷▷ **hang about** *or* **around** LOITER, frequent, haunt, linger, roam, loaf, waste time, dally, dawdle, skulk, tarry, dilly-dally (*informal*) ▷▷ **hang around with someone** ASSOCIATE WITH, go around with, mix with, hang with (*informal, chiefly US*), hang out with (*informal*)

▷▷ **hang back** BE RELUCTANT, hesitate, hold back, recoil, demur, be backward ▷▷ **hang fire** PUT OFF, delay, stall, be slow, vacillate, hang back, procrastinate ▷▷ **hang on** (*informal*) **1** WAIT, stop, hold on, hold the line, remain **2** CONTINUE, remain, go on, carry on, endure, hold on, persist, hold out, persevere, stay the course **3** GRASP, grip, clutch, cling, hold fast ▷▷ **hang on** *or* **upon something 1** DEPEND ON, turn on, rest on, be subject to, hinge on, be determined by, be dependent on, be conditional on, be contingent on **2** LISTEN ATTENTIVELY TO, pay attention to, be rapt, give ear to

hanger-on *noun* PARASITE, follower, cohort (*chiefly US*), leech, dependant, minion, lackey, sycophant, freeloader (*slang*), sponger (*informal*), ligger (*slang*), quandong (*Austral slang*)

hanging *adjective* SUSPENDED, swinging, dangling, loose, flopping, flapping, floppy, drooping, unattached, unsupported, pendent

hang-out *noun* HAUNT, joint (*slang*), resort, dive (*slang*), den

hangover *noun* AFTEREFFECTS, morning after (*informal*), head (*informal*), crapulence

hang-up *noun* (*informal*) PREOCCUPATION, thing (*informal*), problem, block, difficulty, obsession, mania, inhibition, phobia, fixation

hank *noun* COIL, roll, length, bunch, piece, loop, clump, skein

hanker after *or* **for** *verb* DESIRE, want, long for, hope for, crave, covet, wish for, yearn for, pine for, lust after, eat your heart out, ache for, yen for (*informal*), itch for, set your heart on, hunger for *or* after, thirst for *or* after

hankering *noun* DESIRE, longing, wish, hope, urge, yen (*informal*), pining, hunger, ache, craving, yearning, itch, thirst

haphazard *adjective* **1** UNSYSTEMATIC, disorderly, disorganized, casual, careless, indiscriminate, aimless, slapdash, slipshod, hit or miss (*informal*), unmethodical << ANTONYM systematic **2** RANDOM, chance, accidental, arbitrary, fluky (*informal*) << ANTONYM planned

hapless *adjective* UNLUCKY, unfortunate, cursed, unhappy, miserable, jinxed, luckless, wretched, ill-starred, ill-fated

happen *verb* **1** OCCUR, take place, come about, follow, result, appear, develop, arise, come off (*informal*), ensue, crop up (*informal*), transpire (*informal*), materialize, present itself, come to pass, see the light of day, eventuate **2** CHANCE, turn out (*informal*), have the fortune to be **3** BEFALL, overtake, become of, betide ▷▷ **happen on** *or* **upon something** FIND, encounter, run into, come upon, turn up, stumble on, hit upon, chance upon, light upon, blunder on, discover unexpectedly

happening *noun* EVENT, incident, occasion, case, experience, chance, affair, scene, accident, proceeding, episode, adventure, phenomenon, occurrence, escapade

happily *adverb* **1** LUCKILY, fortunately, providentially, favourably, auspiciously, opportunely, propitiously, seasonably **2** JOYFULLY, cheerfully, gleefully, blithely, merrily, gaily, joyously, delightedly **3** WILLINGLY, freely, gladly, enthusiastically, heartily, with pleasure, contentedly, lief (*rare*)

happiness *noun* PLEASURE, delight, joy, cheer, satisfaction, prosperity, ecstasy, enjoyment, bliss, felicity, exuberance, contentment, wellbeing, high spirits, elation, gaiety, jubilation, merriment, cheerfulness, gladness, beatitude, cheeriness, blessedness, light-heartedness << ANTONYM unhappiness

happy *adjective* **1** PLEASED, delighted, content, contented, thrilled, glad, blessed, blest, sunny, cheerful, jolly, merry, ecstatic, gratified, jubilant, joyous, joyful, elated, over the moon (*informal*), overjoyed, blissful, rapt, blithe, on cloud nine (*informal*), cock-a-hoop, walking on air (*informal*), floating on air, stoked (*Austral & NZ informal*) **2** CONTENTED, blessed, blest, joyful, blissful, blithe << ANTONYM sad **3** FORTUNATE, lucky, timely, appropriate, convenient, favourable, auspicious, propitious, apt, befitting, advantageous, well-timed, opportune, felicitous, seasonable << ANTONYM unfortunate

happy-go-lucky *adjective* CAREFREE, casual, easy-going, irresponsible, unconcerned, untroubled, nonchalant, blithe, heedless, insouciant, devil-may-care, improvident, light-hearted << ANTONYM serious

harangue *verb* RANT AT, address, lecture, exhort, preach to, declaim, hold forth, spout at (*informal*) ▷ *noun* RANT, address, speech, lecture, tirade, polemic, broadside, diatribe, homily, exhortation, oration, spiel (*informal*), declamation, philippic

harass *verb* ANNOY, trouble, bother, worry, harry, disturb, devil (*informal*), plague, bait, hound, torment, hassle (*informal*), badger,

persecute, exasperate, pester, vex, breathe down someone's neck, chivvy (*Brit*), give someone grief (*Brit & S African*), be on your back (*slang*), beleaguer

harassed *adjective* HASSLED, worried, troubled, strained, harried, under pressure, plagued, tormented, distraught (*informal*), vexed, under stress, careworn

harassment *noun* HASSLE, trouble, bother, grief (*informal*), torment, irritation, persecution (*informal*), nuisance, badgering, annoyance, pestering, aggravation (*informal*), molestation, vexation, bedevilment

harbinger *noun* (*literary*) SIGN, indication, herald, messenger, omen, precursor, forerunner, portent, foretoken

harbour *noun* **1** PORT, haven, dock, mooring, marina, pier, wharf, anchorage, jetty, pontoon, slipway **2** SANCTUARY, haven, shelter, retreat, asylum, refuge, oasis, covert, safe haven, sanctum ▷ *verb* **1** HOLD, bear, maintain, nurse, retain, foster, entertain, nurture, cling to, cherish, brood over **2** SHELTER, protect, hide, relieve, lodge, shield, conceal, secrete, provide refuge, give asylum to

hard *adjective* **1** TOUGH, strong, firm, solid, stiff, compact, rigid, resistant, dense, compressed, stony, impenetrable, inflexible, unyielding, rocklike << ANTONYM soft **2** DIFFICULT, involved, complex, complicated, puzzling, tangled, baffling, intricate, perplexing, impenetrable, thorny, knotty, unfathomable, ticklish << ANTONYM easy **3** EXHAUSTING, tough, exacting, formidable, fatiguing, wearying, rigorous, uphill, gruelling, strenuous, arduous, laborious, burdensome, Herculean, backbreaking, toilsome << ANTONYM easy **4** FORCEFUL, strong, powerful, driving, heavy, sharp, violent, smart, tremendous, fierce, vigorous, hefty **5** HARSH, severe, strict, cold, exacting, cruel, grim, stern, ruthless, stubborn, unjust, callous, unkind, unrelenting, implacable, unsympathetic, pitiless, unfeeling, obdurate, unsparing, affectless, hardhearted << ANTONYM kind **6** GRIM, dark, painful, distressing, harsh, disastrous, unpleasant, intolerable, grievous, disagreeable, calamitous **7** DEFINITE, reliable, verified, cold, plain, actual, bare, undeniable, indisputable, verifiable, unquestionable, unvarnished ▷ *adverb* **1** STRENUOUSLY, steadily, persistently, earnestly, determinedly, doggedly, diligently, energetically, assiduously, industriously, untiringly **2** INTENTLY, closely, carefully, sharply, keenly **3** FORCEFULLY, strongly, heavily, sharply, severely, fiercely, vigorously, intensely, violently, powerfully, forcibly, with all your might, with might and main << ANTONYM softly **4** WITH DIFFICULTY, painfully, laboriously

hard-bitten *adjective* (*informal*) TOUGH, realistic, cynical, practical, shrewd, down-to-earth, matter-of-fact, hard-nosed (*informal*), hard-headed, unsentimental, hard-boiled (*informal*), case-hardened, badass (*slang, chiefly US*) << ANTONYM idealistic

hard-boiled *adjective* (*informal*) TOUGH, practical, realistic, cynical, shrewd, down-to-earth, matter-of-fact, hard-nosed (*informal*), hard-headed, hard-bitten (*informal*), unsentimental, case-hardened, badass (*slang, chiefly US*) << ANTONYM idealistic

hard-core *adjective* **1** DYED-IN-THE-WOOL, extreme, dedicated, rigid, staunch, die-hard, steadfast, obstinate, intransigent **2** EXPLICIT, obscene, pornographic, X-rated (*informal*)

harden *verb* **1** SOLIDIFY, set, freeze, cake, bake, clot, thicken, stiffen, crystallize, congeal, coagulate, anneal **2** ACCUSTOM, season, toughen, train, brutalize, inure, habituate, case-harden **3** REINFORCE, strengthen, fortify, steel, nerve, brace, toughen, buttress, gird, indurate

hardened *adjective* **1** HABITUAL, set, fixed, chronic, shameless, inveterate, incorrigible, reprobate, irredeemable, badass (*slang, chiefly US*) << ANTONYM occasional **2** SEASONED, experienced, accustomed, toughened, inured, habituated << ANTONYM naive

hard-headed *adjective* SHREWD, tough, practical, cool, sensible, realistic, pragmatic, astute, hard-boiled (*informal*), hard-bitten, level-headed, unsentimental, badass (*slang, chiefly US*) << ANTONYM idealistic

hard-hearted *adjective* UNSYMPATHETIC, hard, cold, cruel, indifferent, insensitive, callous, stony, unkind, heartless, inhuman, merciless, intolerant, uncaring, pitiless, unfeeling, unforgiving, hard as nails, affectless << ANTONYM kind

hardly *adverb* **1** BARELY, only just, scarcely, just, faintly, with difficulty, infrequently, with effort, at a push (*Brit informal*), almost not << ANTONYM completely **2** ONLY JUST, just, only, barely, not quite, scarcely **3** NOT AT ALL, not, no way, by no means ▷ see **scarcely**

hard-nosed *adjective* (*informal*) TOUGH, practical, realistic, shrewd, pragmatic, down-to-earth, hardline, uncompromising, businesslike, hard-headed, unsentimental, badass (*slang, chiefly US*)

hard-pressed *adjective* **1** UNDER PRESSURE, pushed (*informal*), harried, in difficulties, up against it (*informal*), with your back to the wall **2** PUSHED (*informal*), in difficulties, up against it (*informal*)

hardship *noun* SUFFERING, want, need, trouble, trial, difficulty, burden, misery, torment, oppression, persecution, grievance, misfortune, austerity, adversity, calamity, affliction, tribulation, privation, destitution << ANTONYM ease

hard up *adjective* POOR, broke (*informal*), short, bust (*informal*), bankrupt, impoverished, in the red (*informal*), cleaned out (*slang*), penniless, out of pocket, down and out, skint (*Brit slang*), strapped for cash (*informal*), impecunious, dirt-poor (*informal*), on the breadline, flat broke (*informal*), on your uppers (*informal*), in queer street, without two pennies to rub together (*informal*), short of cash *or* funds << ANTONYM wealthy

hardy *adjective* **1** STRONG, tough, robust, sound, fit, healthy, vigorous, rugged, sturdy, hale, stout, stalwart, hearty, lusty, in fine fettle << ANTONYM frail **2** COURAGEOUS, brave, daring, bold, heroic, manly, gritty, feisty (*informal, chiefly US & Canad*), resolute, intrepid, valiant, plucky, valorous, stouthearted << ANTONYM feeble

harem *noun* WOMEN'S QUARTERS, seraglio, zenana (*in eastern countries*), gynaeceum (*in ancient Greece*)

hark *verb* LISTEN, attend, pay attention, hearken (*archaic*), give ear, hear, mark, notice, give heed ▷▷ **hark back to something 1** RECALL, recollect, call to mind, cause you to remember, cause you to recollect **2** RETURN TO, remember, recall, revert to, look back to, think back to, recollect, regress to

harlot *noun* (*literary*) PROSTITUTE, tart (*informal*), whore, slag (*Brit slang*), pro (*slang*), tramp (*slang*), call girl, working girl (*facetious slang*), slapper (*Brit slang*), hussy, streetwalker, loose woman, fallen woman, scrubber (*Brit & Austral slang*), strumpet

harm *verb* **1** INJURE, hurt, wound, abuse, molest, ill-treat, maltreat, lay a finger on, ill-use << ANTONYM heal **2** DAMAGE, hurt, ruin, mar, spoil, impair, blemish ▷ *noun* **1** INJURY, suffering, damage, ill, hurt, distress **2** DAMAGE, loss, ill, hurt, misfortune, mischief, detriment, impairment, disservice << ANTONYM good **3** SIN, wrong, evil, wickedness, immorality, iniquity, sinfulness, vice << ANTONYM goodness

harmful *adjective* DAMAGING, dangerous, negative, evil, destructive, hazardous, unhealthy, detrimental, hurtful, pernicious, noxious, baleful, deleterious, injurious, unwholesome, disadvantageous, baneful, maleficent << ANTONYM harmless

harmless *adjective* **1** SAFE, benign, wholesome, innocuous, not dangerous, nontoxic, innoxious << ANTONYM dangerous **2** INOFFENSIVE, innocent, innocuous, gentle, tame, unobjectionable

harmonious *adjective* **1** FRIENDLY, amicable, cordial, sympathetic, compatible, agreeable, in harmony, in unison, fraternal, congenial, in accord, concordant, of one mind, en rapport (*French*) << ANTONYM unfriendly **2** COMPATIBLE, matching, coordinated, correspondent, agreeable, consistent, consonant, congruous << ANTONYM incompatible **3** MELODIOUS, musical, harmonic, harmonizing, tuneful, concordant, mellifluous, dulcet, sweet-sounding, euphonious, euphonic, symphonious (*literary*) << ANTONYM discordant

harmonize *verb* **1** MATCH, accord, suit, blend, correspond, tally, chime, coordinate, go together, tone in, cohere, attune, be of one mind, be in unison **2** COORDINATE, match, agree, blend, tally, reconcile, attune

harmony *noun* **1** ACCORD, order, understanding, peace, agreement, friendship, unity, sympathy, consensus, cooperation, goodwill, rapport, conformity, compatibility, assent, unanimity, concord, amity, amicability, like-mindedness << ANTONYM conflict **2** TUNE, melody, unison, tunefulness, euphony, melodiousness << ANTONYM discord **3** BALANCE, consistency, fitness, correspondence, coordination, symmetry, compatibility, suitability, concord, parallelism, consonance, congruity << ANTONYM incongruity

harness *verb* **1** EXPLOIT, control, channel, apply, employ, utilize, mobilize, make productive, turn to account, render useful **2** PUT IN HARNESS, couple, saddle, yoke, hitch up ▷ *noun* EQUIPMENT, tackle, gear, tack, trappings ▷▷ **in harness 1** WORKING,

together, in a team **2** AT WORK, working, employed, active, busy, in action

harp *verb* GO ON, reiterate, dwell on, labour, press, repeat, rub in

harried *adjective* HARASSED, worried, troubled, bothered, anxious, distressed, plagued, tormented, hassled (*informal*), agitated, beset, hard-pressed, hag-ridden

harrowing *adjective* DISTRESSING, disturbing, alarming, frightening, painful, terrifying, chilling, traumatic, tormenting, heartbreaking, excruciating, agonizing, nerve-racking, heart-rending, gut-wrenching

harry *verb* PESTER, trouble, bother, disturb, worry, annoy, plague, tease, torment, harass, hassle (*informal*), badger, persecute, molest, vex, bedevil, breathe down someone's neck, chivvy, give someone grief (*Brit & S African*), be on your back (*slang*), get in your hair (*informal*)

harsh *adjective* **1** SEVERE, hard, tough, grim, stark, stringent, austere, Spartan, inhospitable, comfortless **2** BLEAK, cold, freezing, severe, bitter, icy **3** CRUEL, savage, brutal, ruthless, relentless, unrelenting, barbarous, pitiless **4** HARD, sharp, severe, bitter, cruel, stern, unpleasant, abusive, unkind, pitiless, unfeeling << ANTONYM kind **5** DRASTIC, hard, severe, stringent, punitive, austere, Draconian, punitory **6** RAUCOUS, rough, jarring, grating, strident, rasping, discordant, croaking, guttural, dissonant, unmelodious << ANTONYM soft

harshly *adverb* SEVERELY, roughly, cruelly, strictly, grimly, sternly, brutally

harshness *noun* BITTERNESS, acrimony, ill-temper, sourness, asperity, acerbity

harvest *noun* **1** HARVESTING, picking, gathering, collecting, reaping, harvest-time **2** CROP, yield, year's growth, produce ▷ *verb* **1** GATHER, pick, collect, bring in, pluck, reap **2** COLLECT, get, gain, earn, obtain, acquire, accumulate, garner, amass

hash *noun* ▷▷ **make a hash of** (*informal*) MESS UP, muddle, bungle, botch, cock up (*Brit slang*), mishandle, mismanage, make a nonsense of (*informal*), bodge (*informal*), make a pig's ear of (*informal*), flub (*US slang*)

hassle (*informal*) *noun* TROUBLE, problem, difficulty, upset, bother, grief (*informal*), trial, struggle, uphill (*S African*), inconvenience ▷ *verb* BOTHER, bug (*informal*), annoy, harry, hound, harass, badger, pester, get on your nerves (*informal*), be on your back (*slang*), get in your hair (*informal*), breath down someone's neck

hassled *adjective* BOTHERED, pressured, worried, stressed, under pressure, hounded, uptight, browbeaten, hunted, hot and bothered

haste *noun* SPEED, rapidity, urgency, expedition, dispatch, velocity, alacrity, quickness, swiftness, briskness, nimbleness, fleetness, celerity, promptitude, rapidness << ANTONYM slowness

hasten *verb* **1** HURRY (UP), speed (up), advance, urge, step up (*informal*), accelerate, press, dispatch, precipitate, quicken, push forward, expedite << ANTONYM slow down **2** RUSH, run, race, fly, speed, tear (along), dash, hurry (up), barrel (along) (*informal, chiefly US & Canad*), sprint, bolt, beetle, scuttle, scurry, haste, burn rubber (*informal*), step on it (*informal*), make haste, get your skates on (*informal*) << ANTONYM dawdle

hastily *adverb* **1** QUICKLY, fast, rapidly, promptly, straightaway, speedily, apace, pronto (*informal*), double-quick, hotfoot, pdq (*slang*), posthaste **2** HURRIEDLY, rashly, precipitately, recklessly, too quickly, on the spur of the moment, impulsively, impetuously, heedlessly

hasty *adjective* **1** SPEEDY, fast, quick, prompt, rapid, fleet, hurried, urgent, swift, brisk, expeditious << ANTONYM leisurely **2** BRIEF, short, quick, passing, rushed, fleeting, superficial, cursory, perfunctory, transitory << ANTONYM long **3** RASH, premature, reckless, precipitate, impulsive, headlong, foolhardy, thoughtless, impetuous, indiscreet, imprudent, heedless, incautious, unduly quick << ANTONYM cautious

hatch *verb* **1** INCUBATE, breed, sit on, brood, bring forth **2** DEVISE, plan, design, project, scheme, manufacture, plot, invent, put together, conceive, brew, formulate, contrive, dream up (*informal*), concoct, think up, cook up (*informal*), trump up

hatchet *noun* AXE, machete, tomahawk, cleaver

hate *verb* **1** DETEST, loathe, despise, dislike, be sick of, abhor, be hostile to, recoil from, be repelled by, have an aversion to, abominate, not be able to bear, execrate << ANTONYM love **2** DISLIKE, detest, shrink from, recoil from, have no stomach for, not be able to bear << ANTONYM like **3** BE UNWILLING, regret, be reluctant, hesitate, be sorry, be loath, feel disinclined ▷ *noun* DISLIKE,

hostility, hatred, loathing, animosity, aversion, antagonism, antipathy, enmity, abomination, animus, abhorrence, odium, detestation, execration << ANTONYM love

hateful *adjective* HORRIBLE, despicable, offensive, foul, disgusting, forbidding, revolting, obscene, vile, repellent, obnoxious, repulsive, heinous, odious, repugnant, loathsome, abhorrent, abominable, execrable, detestable << ANTONYM pleasant

hatred *noun* HATE, dislike, animosity, aversion, revulsion, antagonism, antipathy, enmity, abomination, ill will, animus, repugnance, odium, detestation, execration << ANTONYM love

haughty *adjective* PROUD, arrogant, lofty, high, stuck-up (*informal*), contemptuous, conceited, imperious, snooty (*informal*), scornful, snobbish, disdainful, supercilious, high and mighty (*informal*), overweening, hoity-toity (*informal*), on your high horse (*informal*), uppish (*Brit informal*) << ANTONYM humble

haul *verb* **1** DRAG, draw, pull, hale, heave **2** PULL, trail, convey, tow, move, carry, transport, tug, cart, hump (*Brit slang*), lug ▷ *noun* YIELD, gain, spoils, find, catch, harvest, loot, takings, booty

haunt *verb* **1** PLAGUE, trouble, obsess, torment, come back to, possess, stay with, recur, beset, prey on, weigh on **2** VISIT, hang around *or* about, frequent, linger in, resort to, patronize, repair to, spend time in, loiter in, be a regular in **3** APPEAR IN, materialize in ▷ *noun* MEETING PLACE, resort, hangout (*informal*), den, rendezvous, stamping ground, gathering place

haunted *adjective* **1** POSSESSED, ghostly, cursed, eerie, spooky (*informal*), jinxed **2** PREOCCUPIED, worried, troubled, plagued, obsessed, tormented

haunting *adjective* EVOCATIVE, poignant, unforgettable, indelible

have *verb* **1** OWN, keep, possess, hold, retain, occupy, boast, be the owner of **2** GET, obtain, take, receive, accept, gain, secure, acquire, procure, take receipt of **3** SUFFER, experience, undergo, sustain, endure, be suffering from **4** GIVE BIRTH TO, bear, deliver, bring forth, beget, bring into the world **5** PUT UP WITH (*informal*), allow, permit, consider, think about, entertain, tolerate **6** EXPERIENCE, go through, undergo, meet with, come across, run into, be faced

with ▷▷ **have had it** (*informal*) BE EXHAUSTED,
be knackered (*Brit informal*), be finished,
be pooped (*US slang*) ▷▷ **have someone on**
TEASE, kid (*informal*), wind up (*Brit slang*),
trick, deceive, take the mickey out of
(*informal*), pull someone's leg, play a joke
on, jerk *or* yank someone's chain (*informal*)
▷▷ **have something on 1** WEAR, be wearing,
be dressed in, be clothed in, be attired in
2 HAVE SOMETHING PLANNED, be committed
to, be engaged to, have something on the
agenda ▷▷ **have to 1** *with* **to** MUST, should,
be forced, ought, be obliged, be bound, have
got to, be compelled **2** HAVE GOT TO, must

haven *noun* **1** SANCTUARY, shelter, retreat,
asylum, refuge, oasis, sanctum **2** HARBOUR,
port, anchorage, road (*nautical*)

havoc *noun* **1** DEVASTATION, damage,
destruction, waste, ruin, wreck, slaughter,
ravages, carnage, desolation, rack and
ruin, despoliation **2** (*informal*) DISORDER,
confusion, chaos, disruption, mayhem,
shambles ▷▷ **play havoc with something**
WRECK, destroy, devastate, disrupt, demolish,
disorganize, bring into chaos

hawk *verb* PEDDLE, market, sell, push, traffic,
tout (*informal*), vend

hawker *noun* PEDLAR, tout, vendor, travelling
salesman, crier, huckster, barrow boy (*Brit*),
door-to-door salesman

haywire *adjective* **1** OUT OF ORDER, out of
commission, on the blink (*slang*), on the
fritz (*slang*) **2** (*of people*) CRAZY, wild, mad,
potty (*Brit informal*), berserk, bonkers (*slang,
chiefly Brit*), loopy (*informal*), mad as a hatter,
berko (*Austral slang*), off the air (*Austral
slang*), porangi (*NZ*)

hazard *noun* DANGER, risk, threat,
problem, menace, peril, jeopardy, pitfall,
endangerment, imperilment ▷ *verb*
JEOPARDIZE, risk, endanger, threaten,
expose, imperil, put in jeopardy ▷▷ **hazard a
guess** GUESS, conjecture, suppose, speculate,
presume, take a guess

hazardous *adjective* DANGEROUS, risky,
difficult, uncertain, unpredictable, insecure,
hairy (*slang*), unsafe, precarious, perilous,
parlous (*archaic or humorous*), dicey (*informal,
chiefly Brit*), fraught with danger, chancy
(*informal*) ≪ ANTONYM safe

haze *noun* MIST, film, cloud, steam, fog,
obscurity, vapour, smog, dimness,
smokiness

hazy *adjective* **1** MISTY, faint, dim, dull,
obscure, veiled, smoky, cloudy, foggy,

overcast, blurry, nebulous ≪ ANTONYM
bright **2** VAGUE, uncertain, unclear,
muddled, fuzzy, indefinite, loose,
muzzy, nebulous, ill-defined, indistinct
≪ ANTONYM clear

head *noun* **1** SKULL, crown, pate, bean (*US
& Canad slang*), nut (*slang*), loaf (*slang*),
cranium, conk (*slang*), noggin, noddle
(*informal, chiefly Brit*) **2** MIND, reasoning,
understanding, thought, sense, brain,
brains (*informal*), intelligence, wisdom, wits,
common sense, loaf (*Brit informal*), intellect,
rationality, grey matter, brainpower, mental
capacity **3** ABILITY, mind, talent, capacity,
faculty, flair, mentality, aptitude **4** FRONT,
beginning, top, first place, fore, forefront
5 FOREFRONT, cutting edge, vanguard,
van **6** TOP, crown, summit, height, peak,
crest, pinnacle, apex, vertex **7** (*informal*)
HEAD TEACHER, principal, headmaster
or headmistress **8** LEADER, president,
director, manager, chief, boss (*informal*),
captain, master, premier, commander,
principal, supervisor, superintendent,
chieftain, sherang (*Austral & NZ*) **9** CLIMAX,
crisis, turning point, culmination, end,
conclusion, tipping point **10** SOURCE, start,
beginning, rise, origin, commencement,
well head **11** (*geography*) HEADLAND, point,
cape, promontory, foreland ▷ *adjective* CHIEF,
main, leading, first, highest, front, prime,
premier, supreme, principal, arch, foremost,
pre-eminent, topmost ▷ *verb* **1** LEAD,
precede, be the leader of, be *or* go first, be *or*
go at the front of, lead the way **2** TOP, lead,
crown, cap **3** BE IN CHARGE OF, run, manage,
lead, control, rule, direct, guide, command,
govern, supervise ▷▷ **go to your head**
1 INTOXICATE, befuddle, inebriate, addle,
stupefy, fuddle, put (someone) under the
table (*informal*) **2** MAKE SOMEONE CONCEITED,
puff someone up, make someone full
of themselves ▷▷ **head for something** *or*
someone MAKE FOR, aim for, set off for, go
to, turn to, set out for, make a beeline for,
start towards, steer for ▷▷ **head over heels**
COMPLETELY, thoroughly, utterly, intensely,
wholeheartedly, uncontrollably ▷▷ **head
someone off** INTERCEPT, divert, deflect, cut
someone off, interpose, block someone off
▷▷ **head something off** PREVENT, stop, avert,
parry, fend off, ward off, forestall ▷▷ **put your
heads together** (*informal*) CONSULT, confer,
discuss, deliberate, talk (something) over,
powwow, confab (*informal*), confabulate

headache *noun* 1 MIGRAINE, head (*informal*), neuralgia, cephalalgia (*medical*) 2 (*informal*) PROBLEM, worry, trouble, bother, nuisance, inconvenience, bane, vexation

headfirst *or* **head first** *adverb* 1 HEADLONG, head foremost 2 RECKLESSLY, rashly, hastily, precipitately, without thinking, carelessly, heedlessly, without forethought

heading *noun* 1 TITLE, name, caption, headline, rubric 2 CATEGORY, class, section, division

headland *noun* PROMONTORY, point, head, cape, cliff, bluff, mull (*Scot*), foreland, bill

headlong *adverb* 1 HASTILY, hurriedly, helter-skelter, pell-mell, heedlessly 2 HEADFIRST, head-on, headforemost 3 RASHLY, wildly, hastily, precipitately, head first, thoughtlessly, impetuously, heedlessly, without forethought ▷ *adjective* HASTY, reckless, precipitate, dangerous, impulsive, thoughtless, breakneck, impetuous, inconsiderate

headmaster *or* **headmistress** *noun* PRINCIPAL, head, head teacher, rector

headstrong *adjective* STUBBORN, wilful, obstinate, contrary, perverse, unruly, intractable, stiff-necked, ungovernable, self-willed, pig-headed, mulish, froward (*archaic*) << ANTONYM manageable

headway *noun* PROGRESS, ground, inroads, strides

heady *adjective* 1 EXCITING, thrilling, stimulating, exhilarating, overwhelming, intoxicating 2 INTOXICATING, strong, potent, inebriating, spirituous

heal *verb* 1 *sometimes with* up MEND, get better, get well, cure, regenerate, show improvement 2 CURE, restore, mend, make better, remedy, make good, make well << ANTONYM injure 3 PATCH UP, settle, reconcile, put right, harmonize, conciliate

healing *adjective* RESTORING, medicinal, therapeutic, remedial, restorative, curative, analeptic, sanative

health *noun* 1 CONDITION, state, form, shape, tone, constitution, fettle 2 WELLBEING, strength, fitness, vigour, good condition, wellness, soundness, robustness, healthiness, salubrity, haleness << ANTONYM illness 3 STATE, condition, shape

healthful *adjective* HEALTHY, beneficial, good for you, bracing, nourishing, wholesome, nutritious, invigorating, salutary, salubrious, health-giving

healthy *adjective* 1 WELL, sound, fit, strong, active, flourishing, hardy, blooming, robust, vigorous, sturdy, hale, hearty, in good shape (*informal*), in good condition, in the pink, alive and kicking, fighting fit, in fine form, in fine fettle, hale and hearty, fit as a fiddle (*informal*), right as rain (*Brit informal*), physically fit, in fine feather << ANTONYM ill 2 WHOLESOME, beneficial, nourishing, good for you, nutritious, salutary, hygienic, healthful, salubrious, health-giving << ANTONYM unwholesome 3 INVIGORATING, bracing, beneficial, good for you, salutary, healthful, salubrious

heap *noun* 1 PILE, lot, collection, store, mountain, mass, stack, rick, mound, accumulation, stockpile, hoard, aggregation 2 *often plural* (*informal*) A LOT, lots (*informal*), plenty, masses, load(s) (*informal*), ocean(s), great deal, quantities, tons, stack(s), lashings (*Brit informal*), abundance, oodles (*informal*) ▷ *verb sometimes with* up PILE, store, collect, gather, stack, accumulate, mound, amass, stockpile, hoard, bank ▷▷ **heap something on someone** LOAD WITH, burden with, confer on, assign to, bestow on, shower upon

hear *verb* 1 OVERHEAR, catch, detect 2 LISTEN TO, heed, attend to, eavesdrop on, listen in to, give attention to, hearken to (*archaic*), hark to, be all ears for (*informal*) 3 (*law*) TRY, judge, examine, investigate 4 LEARN, discover, find out, understand, pick up, gather, be informed, ascertain, be told of, get wind of (*informal*), hear tell (*dialect*)

hearing *noun* 1 SENSE OF HEARING, auditory perception, ear, aural faculty 2 INQUIRY, trial, investigation, industrial tribunal 3 CHANCE TO SPEAK, interview, audience, audition 4 EARSHOT, reach, range, hearing distance, auditory range

hearsay *noun* RUMOUR, talk, gossip, report, buzz, dirt (*US slang*), goss (*informal*), word of mouth, tittle-tattle, talk of the town, scuttlebutt (*slang, chiefly US*), idle talk, mere talk, on dit (*French*)

heart *noun* 1 EMOTIONS, feelings, sentiments, love, affection 2 NATURE, character, soul, constitution, essence, temperament, inclination, disposition 3 TENDERNESS, feeling(s), love, understanding, concern, sympathy, pity, humanity, affection, compassion, kindness, empathy, benevolence, concern for others 4 ROOT, core, essence, centre, nucleus, marrow, hub, kernel, crux, gist, central part, nitty-gritty (*informal*), nub, pith, quintessence

5 COURAGE, will, spirit, mind, purpose, bottle (*Brit informal*), resolution, resolve, nerve, stomach, enthusiasm, determination, guts (*informal*), spine, pluck, bravery, backbone, fortitude, mettle, boldness, spunk (*informal*) ▷▷ **by heart** FROM *or* BY MEMORY, verbatim, word for word, pat, word-perfect, by rote, off by heart, off pat, parrot-fashion (*informal*) ▷▷ **from (the bottom of) your heart** DEEPLY, heartily, fervently, heart and soul, devoutly, with all your heart ▷▷ **take heart** BE ENCOURAGED, be comforted, cheer up, perk up, brighten up, be heartened, buck up (*informal*), derive comfort

heartache *noun* SORROW, suffering, pain, torture, distress, despair, grief, agony, torment, bitterness, anguish, remorse, heartbreak, affliction, heartsickness

heartbreak *noun* GRIEF, suffering, pain, despair, misery, sorrow, anguish, desolation

heartbreaking *adjective* SAD, distressing, tragic, bitter, poignant, harrowing, desolating, grievous, pitiful, agonizing, heart-rending, gut-wrenching << ANTONYM happy

hearten *verb* ENCOURAGE, inspire, cheer, comfort, assure, stimulate, reassure, animate, console, rouse, incite, embolden, buoy up, buck up (*informal*), raise someone's spirits, revivify, gee up, inspirit

heartfelt *adjective* SINCERE, deep, earnest, warm, genuine, profound, honest, ardent, devout, hearty, fervent, cordial, wholehearted, dinkum (*Austral & NZ informal*), unfeigned << ANTONYM insincere

heartily *adverb* **1** SINCERELY, feelingly, deeply, warmly, genuinely, profoundly, cordially, unfeignedly **2** ENTHUSIASTICALLY, vigorously, eagerly, resolutely, earnestly, zealously **3** THOROUGHLY, very, completely, totally, absolutely

heartless *adjective* CRUEL, hard, callous, cold, harsh, brutal, unkind, inhuman, merciless, cold-blooded, uncaring, pitiless, unfeeling, cold-hearted, affectless, hardhearted << ANTONYM compassionate

heart-rending *adjective* MOVING, sad, distressing, affecting, tragic, pathetic, poignant, harrowing, heartbreaking, pitiful, gut-wrenching, piteous

heart-to-heart *adjective* INTIMATE, honest, candid, open, personal, sincere, truthful, unreserved ▷ *noun* TÊTE-À-TÊTE, cosy chat, one-to-one, private conversation, private chat

heart-warming *adjective* MOVING, touching, affecting, pleasing, encouraging, warming, rewarding, satisfying, cheering, gratifying, heartening

hearty *adjective* **1** FRIENDLY, genial, warm, generous, eager, enthusiastic, ardent, cordial, affable, ebullient, jovial, effusive, unreserved, back-slapping << ANTONYM cool **2** WHOLEHEARTED, sincere, heartfelt, real, true, earnest, genuine, honest, unfeigned << ANTONYM insincere **3** SUBSTANTIAL, filling, ample, square, solid, nourishing, sizable *or* sizeable **4** HEALTHY, well, strong, sound, active, hardy, robust, vigorous, energetic, hale, alive and kicking, right as rain (*Brit informal*) << ANTONYM frail

heat *verb* **1** *sometimes with* **up** WARM (UP), cook, boil, roast, reheat, make hot << ANTONYM chill **2** INTENSIFY, increase, heighten, deepen, escalate ▷ *noun* **1** WARMTH, hotness, temperature, swelter, sultriness, fieriness, torridity, warmness, calefaction << ANTONYM cold **2** HOT WEATHER, warmth, closeness, high temperature, heatwave, warm weather, hot climate, hot spell, mugginess **3** PASSION, excitement, intensity, violence, fever, fury, warmth, zeal, agitation, fervour, ardour, vehemence, earnestness, impetuosity << ANTONYM calmness ▷▷ **heat up** WARM UP, get hotter, become hot, rise in temperature, become warm, grow hot

heated *adjective* **1** IMPASSIONED, intense, spirited, excited, angry, violent, bitter, raging, furious, fierce, lively, passionate, animated, frenzied, fiery, stormy, vehement, tempestuous << ANTONYM calm **2** WOUND UP, worked up, keyed up, het up (*informal*)

heathen *noun* **1** PAGAN, infidel, unbeliever, idolater, idolatress **2** BARBARIAN, savage, philistine, oaf, ignoramus, boor ▷ *adjective* **1** PAGAN, infidel, godless, irreligious, idolatrous, heathenish **2** UNCIVILIZED, savage, primitive, barbaric, brutish, unenlightened, uncultured

heave *verb* **1** LIFT, raise, pull (up), drag (up), haul (up), tug, lever, hoist, heft (*informal*) **2** THROW, fling, toss, send, cast, pitch, hurl, sling **3** SURGE, rise, swell, billow **4** VOMIT, be sick, throw up (*informal*), chuck (up) (*slang, chiefly US*), chuck (*Austral & NZ informal*), gag, spew, retch, barf (*US slang*), chunder (*slang, chiefly Austral*), upchuck (*US slang*), do a technicolour yawn (*slang*), toss your cookies (*US slang*) **5** BREATHE, sigh, puff, groan, sob, breathe heavily, suspire (*archaic*), utter wearily

heaven *noun* **1** PARADISE, next world, hereafter, nirvana (*Buddhism, Hinduism*), bliss, Zion (*Christianity*), Valhalla (*Norse myth*), Happy Valley, happy hunting ground (*Native American legend*), life to come, life everlasting, abode of God, Elysium *or* Elysian fields (*Greek myth*) **2** (*informal*) HAPPINESS, paradise, ecstasy, bliss, felicity, utopia, contentment, rapture, enchantment, dreamland, seventh heaven, transport, sheer bliss ▷▷ **the heavens** (*old-fashioned*) SKY, ether, firmament, celestial sphere, welkin (*archaic*), empyrean (*poetic*)

heavenly *adjective* **1** CELESTIAL, holy, divine, blessed, blest, immortal, supernatural, angelic, extraterrestrial, superhuman, godlike, beatific, cherubic, seraphic, supernal (*literary*), empyrean (*poetic*), paradisaical << ANTONYM earthly **2** (*informal*) WONDERFUL, lovely, delightful, beautiful, entrancing, divine (*informal*), glorious, exquisite, sublime, alluring, blissful, ravishing, rapturous << ANTONYM awful

heavily *adverb* **1** EXCESSIVELY, to excess, very much, a great deal, frequently, considerably, copiously, without restraint, immoderately, intemperately **2** DENSELY, closely, thickly, compactly **3** HARD, clumsily, awkwardly, weightily

heaviness *noun* **1** WEIGHT, gravity, ponderousness, heftiness **2** SADNESS, depression, gloom, seriousness, melancholy, despondency, dejection, gloominess, glumness

heavy *adjective* **1** WEIGHTY, large, massive, hefty, bulky, ponderous << ANTONYM light **2** INTENSIVE, severe, serious, concentrated, fierce, excessive, relentless **3** CONSIDERABLE, large, huge, substantial, abundant, copious, profuse << ANTONYM slight **4** ONEROUS, hard, difficult, severe, harsh, tedious, intolerable, oppressive, grievous, burdensome, wearisome, vexatious << ANTONYM easy **5** SLUGGISH, slow, dull, wooden, stupid, inactive, inert, apathetic, drowsy, listless, indolent, torpid << ANTONYM alert **6** HARD, demanding, difficult, physical, strenuous, laborious **7** OVERCAST, dull, gloomy, cloudy, leaden, louring *or* lowering **8** SAD, depressed, gloomy, grieving, melancholy, dejected, despondent, downcast, sorrowful,

disconsolate, crestfallen << ANTONYM happy **9** SERIOUS, grave, solemn, difficult, deep, complex, profound, weighty << ANTONYM trivial

heavy-handed *adjective* **1** OPPRESSIVE, harsh, Draconian, autocratic, domineering, overbearing **2** CLUMSY, awkward, bungling, inept, graceless, inexpert, maladroit, ham-handed (*informal*), like a bull in a china shop (*informal*), ham-fisted (*informal*) << ANTONYM skilful

heckle *verb* JEER, interrupt, shout down, disrupt, bait, barrack (*informal*), boo, taunt, pester

hectic *adjective* FRANTIC, chaotic, frenzied, heated, wild, excited, furious, fevered, animated, turbulent, flurrying, frenetic, boisterous, feverish, tumultuous, flustering, riotous, rumbustious << ANTONYM peaceful

hector *verb* BULLY, harass, browbeat, worry, threaten, menace, intimidate, ride roughshod over, bullyrag

hedge *noun* GUARD, cover, protection, compensation, shield, safeguard, counterbalance, insurance cover ▷ *verb* **1** PREVARICATE, evade, sidestep, duck, dodge, flannel (*Brit informal*), waffle (*informal, chiefly Brit*), quibble, beg the question, pussyfoot (*informal*), equivocate, temporize, be noncommittal **2** ENCLOSE, edge, border, surround, fence ▷▷ **hedge against something** PROTECT, insure, guard, safeguard, shield, cover, fortify ▷▷ **hedge someone in** HAMPER, restrict, handicap, hamstring, hinder, hem in ▷▷ **hedge something in** SURROUND, enclose, encompass, encircle, ring, fence in, girdle, hem in ▷▷ **hedge something or someone about** RESTRICT, confine, hinder, hem in, hem around, hem about

hedonism *noun* PLEASURE-SEEKING, gratification, sensuality, self-indulgence, dolce vita, pursuit of pleasure, luxuriousness, sensualism, sybaritism, epicureanism, epicurism

hedonistic *adjective* PLEASURE-SEEKING, self-indulgent, luxurious, voluptuous, sybaritic, epicurean, bacchanalian

heed *verb* PAY ATTENTION TO, listen to, take notice of, follow, mark, mind, consider, note, regard, attend, observe, obey, bear in mind, be guided by, take to heart, give ear to << ANTONYM ignore ▷ *noun* THOUGHT, care, mind, note, attention, regard, respect, notice, consideration, watchfulness << ANTONYM disregard

heedless *adjective* CARELESS, reckless, negligent, rash, precipitate, oblivious, foolhardy, thoughtless, unthinking, imprudent, neglectful, inattentive, incautious, unmindful, unobservant << ANTONYM careful

heel *noun* 1 END, stump, remainder, crust, rump, stub 2 (*slang*) SWINE, cad (*Brit informal*), scoundrel, scally (*Northwest English dialect*), bounder (*Brit old-fashioned slang*), rotter (*slang, chiefly Brit*), scumbag (*slang*), blackguard, wrong 'un (*Austral slang*) ▷▷ **take to your heels** FLEE, escape, run away *or* off, take flight, hook it (*slang*), turn tail, show a clean pair of heels, skedaddle (*informal*), vamoose (*slang, chiefly US*)

hefty *adjective* (*informal*) 1 BIG, strong, massive, strapping, robust, muscular, burly, husky (*informal*), hulking, beefy (*informal*), brawny << ANTONYM small 2 FORCEFUL, heavy, powerful, vigorous (*slang*) << ANTONYM gentle 3 HEAVY, large, massive, substantial, tremendous, awkward, ample, bulky, colossal, cumbersome, weighty, unwieldy, ponderous << ANTONYM light 4 LARGE, massive, substantial, excessive, inflated, sizeable, astronomical (*informal*), extortionate

height *noun* 1 TALLNESS, stature, highness, loftiness << ANTONYM shortness 2 ALTITUDE, measurement, highness, elevation, tallness << ANTONYM depth 3 PEAK, top, hill, mountain, crown, summit, crest, pinnacle, elevation, apex, apogee, vertex << ANTONYM valley 4 CULMINATION, climax, zenith, limit, maximum, ultimate, extremity, uttermost, ne plus ultra (*Latin*), utmost degree << ANTONYM low point

heighten *verb* INTENSIFY, increase, add to, improve, strengthen, enhance, sharpen, aggravate, magnify, amplify, augment

heinous *adjective* SHOCKING, evil, monstrous, grave, awful, vicious, outrageous, revolting, infamous, hideous, unspeakable, atrocious, flagrant, odious, hateful, abhorrent, abominable, villainous, nefarious, iniquitous, execrable

heir *noun* SUCCESSOR, beneficiary, inheritor, heiress (*fem*), scion, next in line, inheritress *or* inheritrix (*fem*)

hell *noun* 1 THE UNDERWORLD, the abyss, Hades (*Greek myth*), hellfire, the inferno, fire and brimstone, the bottomless pit, Gehenna (*New Testament, Judaism*), the nether world, the lower world, Tartarus (*Greek myth*), the infernal regions, the bad fire (*informal*), Acheron (*Greek myth*), Abaddon, the abode of the damned 2 (*informal*) TORMENT, suffering, agony, trial, nightmare, misery, ordeal, anguish, affliction, martyrdom, wretchedness ▷▷ **hell for leather** HEADLONG, speedily, quickly, swiftly, hurriedly, at the double, full-tilt, pell-mell, hotfoot, at a rate of knots, like a bat out of hell (*slang*), posthaste

hellbent *adjective* (*informal*) INTENT, set, determined, settled, fixed, resolved, bent

hellish *adjective* 1 (*informal*) ATROCIOUS, terrible, dreadful, cruel, vicious, monstrous, wicked, inhuman, barbarous, abominable, nefarious, accursed, execrable, detestable << ANTONYM wonderful 2 DEVILISH, fiendish, diabolical, infernal, damned, damnable, demoniacal

hello *interjection* HI (*informal*), greetings, how do you do?, good morning, good evening, good afternoon, welcome, kia ora (*NZ*), gidday *or* g'day (*Austral & NZ*)

helm *noun* (*nautical*) TILLER, wheel, rudder, steering gear ▷▷ **at the helm** IN CHARGE, in control, in command, directing, at the wheel, in the saddle, in the driving seat

help *verb* 1 *sometimes with* out AID, back, support, second, encourage, promote, assist, relieve, stand by, befriend, cooperate with, abet, lend a hand, succour, lend a helping hand, give someone a leg up (*informal*) << ANTONYM hinder 2 IMPROVE, ease, heal, cure, relieve, remedy, facilitate, alleviate, mitigate, ameliorate << ANTONYM make worse 3 ASSIST, aid, support, give a leg up (*informal*) 4 RESIST, refrain from, avoid, control, prevent, withstand, eschew, keep from, abstain from, forbear ▷ *noun* 1 ASSISTANCE, aid, support, service, advice, promotion, guidance, cooperation, helping hand << ANTONYM hindrance 2 REMEDY, cure, relief, corrective, balm, salve, succour, restorative 3 ASSISTANT, hand, worker, employee, helper

helper *noun* ASSISTANT, partner, ally, colleague, supporter, mate, deputy, second, subsidiary, aide, aider, attendant, collaborator, auxiliary, henchman, right-hand man, adjutant, helpmate, coadjutor, abettor

helpful *adjective* 1 COOPERATIVE, accommodating, kind, caring, friendly, neighbourly, sympathetic, supportive, benevolent, considerate, beneficent

2 USEFUL, practical, productive, profitable, constructive, serviceable 3 BENEFICIAL, advantageous, expedient, favourable

helpfulness noun 1 COOPERATION, kindness, support, assistance, sympathy, friendliness, rallying round, neighbourliness, good neighbourliness 2 USEFULNESS, benefit, advantage

helping noun PORTION, serving, ration, piece, dollop (informal), plateful

helpless adjective 1 VULNERABLE, exposed, unprotected, defenceless, abandoned, dependent, stranded, wide open, forlorn, destitute << ANTONYM invulnerable 2 POWERLESS, weak, disabled, incapable, challenged, paralysed, incompetent, unfit, feeble, debilitated, impotent, infirm << ANTONYM powerful

helplessness noun VULNERABILITY, weakness, impotence, powerlessness, disability, infirmity, feebleness, forlornness, defencelessness

helter-skelter adjective HAPHAZARD, confused, disordered, random, muddled, jumbled, topsy-turvy, hit-or-miss, higgledy-piggledy (informal) ▷ adverb WILDLY, rashly, anyhow, headlong, recklessly, carelessly, pell-mell

hem noun EDGE, border, margin, trimming, fringe ▷▷ **hem something** or **someone in** 1 SURROUND, edge, border, skirt, confine, enclose, shut in, hedge in, environ 2 RESTRICT, confine, beset, circumscribe

hence adverb THEREFORE, thus, consequently, for this reason, in consequence, ergo, on that account

henceforth adverb FROM NOW ON, in the future, hereafter, hence, hereinafter, from this day forward

henchman noun ATTENDANT, supporter, heavy (slang), associate, aide, follower, subordinate, bodyguard, minder (slang), crony, sidekick (slang), cohort (chiefly US), right-hand man, minion, satellite, myrmidon

henpecked adjective DOMINATED, subjugated, browbeaten, subject, bullied, timid, cringing, meek, treated like dirt, led by the nose, tied to someone's apron strings << ANTONYM domineering

herald verb 1 INDICATE, promise, precede, pave the way, usher in, harbinger, presage, portend, foretoken 2 ANNOUNCE, publish, advertise, proclaim, broadcast, trumpet, publicize ▷ noun 1 (often literary) FORERUNNER, sign, signal, indication, token,

omen, precursor, harbinger 2 MESSENGER, courier, proclaimer, announcer, crier, town crier, bearer of tidings

herculean adjective 1 ARDUOUS, hard, demanding, difficult, heavy, tough, exhausting, formidable, gruelling, strenuous, prodigious, onerous, laborious, toilsome 2 STRONG, muscular, powerful, athletic, strapping, mighty, rugged, sturdy, stalwart, husky (informal), sinewy, brawny

herd noun 1 FLOCK, crowd, collection, mass, drove, crush, mob, swarm, horde, multitude, throng, assemblage, press 2 (often disparaging) MOB, the masses, rabble, populace, the hoi polloi, the plebs, riffraff ▷ verb 1 LEAD, drive, force, direct, guide, shepherd 2 DRIVE, lead, force, guide, shepherd

hereafter adverb IN FUTURE, after this, from now on, henceforth, henceforward, hence ▷▷ **the hereafter** AFTERLIFE, next world, life after death, future life, the beyond

hereditary adjective 1 GENETIC, inborn, inbred, transmissible, inheritable 2 (law) INHERITED, handed down, passed down, willed, family, traditional, transmitted, ancestral, bequeathed, patrimonial

heredity noun GENETICS, inheritance, genetic make-up, congenital traits

heresy noun UNORTHODOXY, apostasy, dissidence, impiety, revisionism, iconoclasm, heterodoxy

heretic noun NONCONFORMIST, dissident, separatist, sectarian, renegade, revisionist, dissenter, apostate, schismatic

heretical adjective 1 CONTROVERSIAL, unorthodox, revisionist, freethinking 2 UNORTHODOX, revisionist, iconoclastic, heterodox, impious, idolatrous, schismatic, freethinking

heritage noun INHERITANCE, legacy, birthright, lot, share, estate, tradition, portion, endowment, bequest, patrimony

hermit noun RECLUSE, monk, loner (informal), solitary, anchorite, anchoress, stylite, eremite

hero noun 1 PROTAGONIST, leading man, lead actor, male lead, principal male character 2 STAR, champion, celebrity, victor, superstar, great man, heart-throb (Brit), conqueror, exemplar, celeb (informal), megastar (informal), popular figure, man of the hour 3 IDOL, favourite, pin-up (slang), fave (informal)

heroic adjective 1 COURAGEOUS, brave,

daring, bold, fearless, gallant, intrepid, valiant, doughty, undaunted, dauntless, lion-hearted, valorous, stouthearted << ANTONYM cowardly **2** LEGENDARY, classical, mythological, Homeric **3** EPIC, grand, classic, extravagant, exaggerated, elevated, inflated, high-flown, grandiose << ANTONYM simple

heroine *noun* **1** PROTAGONIST, leading lady, diva, prima donna, female lead, lead actress, principal female character **2** STAR, celebrity, goddess, celeb (*informal*), megastar (*informal*), woman of the hour **3** IDOL, favourite, pin-up (*slang*), fave (*informal*)

heroism *noun* BRAVERY, daring, courage, spirit, fortitude, boldness, gallantry, valour, fearlessness, intrepidity, courageousness

hero-worship *noun* ADMIRATION, idolization, adulation, adoration, veneration, idealization, putting on a pedestal

hesitant *adjective* UNCERTAIN, reluctant, shy, halting, doubtful, sceptical, unsure, hesitating, wavering, timid, diffident, lacking confidence, vacillating, hanging back, irresolute, half-hearted << ANTONYM confident

hesitate *verb* **1** WAVER, delay, pause, haver (*Brit*), wait, doubt, falter, be uncertain, dither (*chiefly Brit*), vacillate, equivocate, temporize, hum and haw, shillyshally (*informal*), swither (*Scot dialect*) << ANTONYM be decisive **2** BE RELUCTANT, be unwilling, shrink from, think twice, boggle, scruple, demur, hang back, be disinclined, balk *or* baulk << ANTONYM be determined

hesitation *noun* **1** DELAY, pausing, uncertainty, stalling, dithering, indecision, hesitancy, doubt, vacillation, temporizing, shilly-shallying, irresolution, hemming and hawing, dubiety **2** RELUCTANCE, reservation(s), misgiving(s), ambivalence, qualm(s), unwillingness, scruple(s), compunction, demurral

heterogeneous *adjective* VARIED, different, mixed, contrasting, unlike, diverse, diversified, assorted, unrelated, disparate, miscellaneous, motley, incongruous, dissimilar, divergent, manifold, discrepant

hew *verb* CUT, chop, axe, hack, split, lop **2** (*old-fashioned*) CARVE, make, form, fashion, shape, model, sculpture, sculpt

heyday *noun* PRIME, time, day, flowering, pink, bloom, high point, zenith, salad days, prime of life

hiatus *noun* PAUSE, break, interval, space, gap, breach, blank, lapse, interruption, respite, chasm, discontinuity, lacuna, entr'acte

hibernate *verb* SLEEP, lie dormant, winter, overwinter, vegetate, remain torpid, sleep snug

hidden *adjective* **1** SECRET, veiled, dark, mysterious, obscure, mystical, mystic, shrouded, occult, latent, cryptic, hermetic, ulterior, abstruse, recondite, hermetical **2** CONCEALED, covered, secret, covert, unseen, clandestine, secreted, under wraps, unrevealed

hide¹ *verb* **1** CONCEAL, stash (*informal*), secrete, cache, put out of sight << ANTONYM display **2** GO INTO HIDING, take cover, keep out of sight, hole up, lie low, go underground, go to ground, go to earth **3** KEEP SECRET, suppress, withhold, keep quiet about, hush up, draw a veil over, keep dark, keep under your hat << ANTONYM disclose **4** OBSCURE, cover, screen, bury, shelter, mask, disguise, conceal, eclipse, veil, cloak, shroud, camouflage, blot out << ANTONYM reveal

hide² *noun* SKIN, fell, leather, pelt

hideaway *noun* HIDING PLACE, haven, retreat, refuge, sanctuary, hide-out, nest, sequestered nook

hidebound *adjective* CONVENTIONAL, set, rigid, narrow, puritan, narrow-minded, strait-laced, brassbound, ultraconservative, set in your ways << ANTONYM broad-minded

hideous *adjective* **1** UGLY, revolting, ghastly, monstrous, grotesque, gruesome, grisly, unsightly, repulsive << ANTONYM beautiful **2** TERRIFYING, shocking, terrible, awful, appalling, disgusting, horrible, dreadful, horrific, obscene, sickening, horrendous, macabre, horrid, odious, loathsome, abominable, detestable, godawful (*slang*)

hide-out *noun* HIDING PLACE, shelter, den, hideaway, lair, secret place

hiding *noun* (*informal*) BEATING, whipping, thrashing, tanning (*slang*), caning, licking (*informal*), flogging, spanking, walloping (*informal*), drubbing, lathering (*informal*), whaling, larruping (*Brit dialect*)

hierarchy *noun* GRADING, ranking, social order, pecking order, class system, social stratum

higgledy-piggledy (*informal*) *adjective* HAPHAZARD, muddled, jumbled, indiscriminate, topsy-turvy, helter-skelter, pell-mell ▷ *adverb* HAPHAZARDLY, all over the place, anyhow, topsy-turvy, helter-skelter, all over the shop (*informal*), pell-mell, confusedly, any old how

high *adjective* 1 TALL, towering, soaring, steep, elevated, lofty << ANTONYM short 2 EXTREME, great, acute, severe, extraordinary, excessive << ANTONYM low 3 STRONG, violent, extreme, blustery, squally, sharp 4 EXPENSIVE, dear, steep (*informal*), costly, stiff, high-priced, exorbitant 5 IMPORTANT, leading, ruling, chief, powerful, significant, distinguished, prominent, superior, influential, notable, big-time (*informal*), eminent, major league (*informal*), exalted, consequential, skookum (*Canad*) << ANTONYM lowly 6 NOTABLE, important, leading, famous, significant, celebrated, distinguished, renowned, eminent, pre-eminent 7 HIGH-PITCHED, piercing, shrill, penetrating, treble, soprano, strident, sharp, acute, piping << ANTONYM deep 8 CHEERFUL, excited, merry, exhilarated, exuberant, joyful, bouncy (*informal*), boisterous, elated, light-hearted, stoked (*Austral & NZ informal*) << ANTONYM dejected 9 (*informal*) INTOXICATED, stoned (*slang*), spaced out (*slang*), tripping (*informal*), turned on (*slang*), on a trip (*informal*), delirious, euphoric, freaked out (*informal*), hyped up (*slang*), inebriated 10 LUXURIOUS, rich, grand, lavish, extravagant, opulent, hedonistic ▷ *adverb* WAY UP, aloft, far up, to a great height ▷ *noun* 1 PEAK, height, top, summit, crest, record level, apex 2 (*informal*) INTOXICATION, trip (*informal*), euphoria, delirium, ecstasy ▷▷ **high and dry** ABANDONED, stranded, helpless, forsaken, bereft, destitute, in the lurch ▷▷ **high and mighty** (*informal*) SELF-IMPORTANT, superior, arrogant, stuck-up (*informal*), conceited, imperious, overbearing, haughty, snobbish, disdainful

highbrow (*often disparaging*) *adjective* INTELLECTUAL, cultured, sophisticated, deep, cultivated, brainy (*informal*), highbrowed, bookish << ANTONYM unintellectual ▷ *noun* INTELLECTUAL, scholar, egghead (*informal*), brain (*informal*), mastermind, Brahmin (*US*), aesthete, savant, brainbox (*slang*) << ANTONYM philistine

high-class *adjective* HIGH-QUALITY, top (*slang*), choice, select, exclusive, elite, superior, posh (*informal, chiefly Brit*), classy (*slang*), top-flight, upper-class, swish (*informal, chiefly Brit*), first-rate, up-market, top-drawer, ritzy (*slang*), tip-top, high-toned, A1 *or* A-one (*informal*) << ANTONYM inferior

higher-up *noun* (*informal*) SUPERIOR, senior, manager, director, executive, boss, gaffer (*informal, chiefly Brit*), baas (*S African*), sherang (*Austral & NZ*)

high-flown *adjective* EXTRAVAGANT, elaborate, pretentious, exaggerated, inflated, lofty, grandiose, overblown, florid, high-falutin (*informal*), arty-farty (*informal*), magniloquent << ANTONYM straightforward

high-handed *adjective* DICTATORIAL, domineering, overbearing, arbitrary, oppressive, autocratic, bossy (*informal*), imperious, tyrannical, despotic, peremptory

highlight *verb* EMPHASIZE, stress, accent, feature, set off, show up, underline, spotlight, play up, accentuate, foreground, focus attention on, call attention to, give prominence to, bring to the fore << ANTONYM play down ▷ *noun* HIGH POINT, peak, climax, feature, focus, best part, focal point, main feature, high spot, memorable part << ANTONYM low point

highly *adverb* 1 EXTREMELY, very, greatly, seriously (*informal*), vastly, exceptionally, extraordinarily, immensely, decidedly, tremendously, supremely, eminently 2 FAVOURABLY, well, warmly, enthusiastically, approvingly, appreciatively

highly-strung *adjective* NERVOUS, stressed, tense, sensitive, wired (*slang*), restless, neurotic, taut, edgy, temperamental, excitable, nervy (*Brit informal*), twitchy (*informal*), on tenterhooks, easily upset, on pins and needles, adrenalized << ANTONYM relaxed

high-minded *adjective* PRINCIPLED, moral, worthy, noble, good, fair, pure, ethical, upright, elevated, honourable, righteous, idealistic, virtuous, magnanimous << ANTONYM dishonourable

high-powered *adjective* DYNAMIC, driving, powerful, enterprising, effective, go-ahead, aggressive, vigorous, energetic, forceful, fast-track, go-getting (*informal*), high-octane (*informal*), highly capable

high-pressure *adjective* (*informal*) FORCEFUL, aggressive, compelling, intensive, persistent, persuasive, high-powered, insistent, bludgeoning, pushy (*informal*), in-your-face (*slang*), coercive, importunate

high-spirited *adjective* LIVELY, spirited, vivacious, vital, daring, dashing, bold, energetic, animated, vibrant, exuberant, bouncy, boisterous, fun-loving, ebullient, sparky, effervescent, alive and kicking, full of life, spunky (*informal*), full of beans (*informal*), frolicsome, mettlesome

hijack *or* **highjack** *verb* SEIZE, take over, commandeer, expropriate, skyjack

hike *noun* WALK, march, trek, ramble, tramp, traipse, journey on foot ▷ *verb* WALK, march, trek, ramble, tramp, leg it (*informal*), backpack, hoof it (*slang*) ▷▷ **hike something up** HITCH UP, raise, lift, pull up, jack up

hiker *noun* WALKER, rambler, backpacker, wayfarer, hillwalker

hilarious *adjective* **1** FUNNY, entertaining, amusing, hysterical, humorous, exhilarating, comical, side-splitting **2** MERRY, uproarious, happy, gay, noisy, jolly, joyous, joyful, jovial, rollicking, convivial, mirthful << ANTONYM serious

hilarity *noun* MERRIMENT, high spirits, mirth, gaiety, laughter, amusement, glee, exuberance, exhilaration, cheerfulness, jollity, levity, conviviality, joviality, boisterousness, joyousness, jollification

hill *noun* **1** MOUNT, down (*archaic*), fell, height, mound, prominence, elevation, eminence, hilltop, tor, knoll, hillock, brae (*Scot*), kopje *or* koppie (*S African*) **2** SLOPE, incline, gradient, rise, climb, brae (*Scot*), acclivity

hilly *adjective* MOUNTAINOUS, rolling, steep, undulating

hilt *noun* HANDLE, grip, haft, handgrip, helve ▷▷ **to the hilt** (*informal*) FULLY, completely, totally, entirely, wholly

hind *adjective* BACK, rear, hinder, posterior, caudal (*anatomy*)

hinder *verb* OBSTRUCT, stop, check, block, prevent, arrest, delay, oppose, frustrate, handicap, interrupt, slow down, deter, hamstring, hamper, thwart, retard, impede, hobble, stymie, encumber, throw a spanner in the works, trammel, hold up *or* back << ANTONYM help

hindrance *noun* OBSTACLE, check, bar, block, difficulty, drag, barrier, restriction, handicap, limitation, hazard, restraint, hitch, drawback, snag, deterrent, interruption, obstruction, stoppage, stumbling block, impediment, encumbrance, trammel << ANTONYM help

hinge on *verb* DEPEND ON, be subject to, hang on, turn on, rest on, revolve around, be contingent on, pivot on

hint *noun* **1** CLUE, mention, suggestion, implication, indication, reminder, tip-off, pointer, allusion, innuendo, inkling, intimation, insinuation, word to the

wise **2** ADVICE, help, tip(s), suggestion(s), pointer(s) **3** TRACE, touch, suggestion, taste, breath, dash, whisper, suspicion, tinge, whiff, speck, undertone, soupçon (*French*) ▷ *verb sometimes with* at SUGGEST, mention, indicate, imply, intimate, tip off, let it be known, insinuate, allude to the fact, tip the wink (*informal*)

hip *adjective* (*slang*) TRENDY (*Brit informal*), with it, fashionable, in, aware, informed, wise (*slang*), clued-up (*informal*)

hippy *or* **hippie** *noun* FLOWER CHILD, bohemian, dropout, free spirit, beatnik, basketweaver (*Austral derogatory slang*)

hire *verb* **1** EMPLOY, commission, take on, engage, appoint, sign up, enlist **2** RENT, charter, lease, let, engage ▷ *noun* **1** RENTAL, hiring, rent, lease **2** CHARGE, rental, price, cost, fee

hirsute *adjective* (*formal*) HAIRY, bearded, shaggy, unshaven, bristly, bewhiskered, hispid (*biology*)

hiss *verb* **1** WHISTLE, wheeze, rasp, whiz, whirr, sibilate **2** JEER, mock, ridicule, deride, decry, revile ▷ *noun* FIZZ, buzz, hissing, fizzing, sibilance, sibilation

historian *noun* CHRONICLER, recorder, biographer, antiquarian, historiographer, annalist, chronologist

historic *adjective* SIGNIFICANT, notable, momentous, famous, celebrated, extraordinary, outstanding, remarkable, ground-breaking, consequential, red-letter, epoch-making << ANTONYM unimportant

historical *adjective* FACTUAL, real, documented, actual, authentic, chronicled, attested, archival, verifiable << ANTONYM contemporary ▷ see **historic**

history *noun* **1** THE PAST, the old days, antiquity, yesterday, the good old days, yesteryear, ancient history, olden days, days of old, days of yore, bygone times **2** CHRONICLE, record, story, account, relation, narrative, saga, recital, narration, annals, recapitulation

histrionic *adjective* THEATRICAL, affected, dramatic, forced, camp (*informal*), actorly, artificial, unnatural, melodramatic, actressy ▷ *plural noun* DRAMATICS, scene, tantrums, performance, temperament, theatricality, staginess, hissy fit (*informal*)

hit *verb* **1** STRIKE, beat, knock, punch, belt (*informal*), deck (*slang*), bang, batter, clip (*informal*), slap, bash (*informal*), sock (*slang*), chin (*slang*), smack, thump, clout (*informal*), cuff, flog, whack, clobber (*slang*), smite (*archaic*), wallop (*informal*), swat, lay one on (*slang*), beat *or* knock seven bells out of (*informal*) **2** COLLIDE WITH, run into, bump into, clash with, smash into, crash against, bang into, meet head-on **3** AFFECT, damage, harm, ruin, devastate, overwhelm, touch, impact on, impinge on, leave a mark on, make an impact *or* impression on **4** REACH, strike, gain, achieve, secure, arrive at, accomplish, attain ▷ *noun* **1** SHOT, blow, impact, collision **2** BLOW, knock, stroke, belt (*informal*), rap, slap, bump, smack, clout (*informal*), cuff, swipe (*informal*), wallop (*informal*) **3** SUCCESS, winner, triumph, smash (*informal*), sensation, sellout, smasheroo (*informal*) ▷▷ **hit it off** (*informal*) GET ON (WELL) WITH, take to, click (*slang*), warm to, be on good terms, get on like a house on fire (*informal*) ▷▷ **hit on** *or* **upon something** THINK UP, discover, arrive at, guess, realize, invent, come upon, stumble on, chance upon, light upon, strike upon ▷▷ **hit out at someone** ATTACK, condemn, denounce, lash out, castigate, rail against, assail, inveigh against, strike out at

hit-and-miss *or* **hit-or-miss** *adjective* HAPHAZARD, random, uneven, casual, indiscriminate, cursory, perfunctory, aimless, disorganized, undirected, scattershot << ANTONYM systematic

hitch *noun* PROBLEM, catch, trouble, check, difficulty, delay, hold-up, obstacle, hazard, drawback, hassle (*informal*), snag, uphill (*S African*), stoppage, mishap, impediment, hindrance ▷ *verb* **1** (*informal*) HITCHHIKE, thumb a lift **2** FASTEN, join, attach, unite, couple, tie, connect, harness, tether, yoke, make fast ▷▷ **hitch something up** PULL UP, tug, jerk, yank, hoick

hither *adverb* (*old-fashioned*) HERE, over here, to this place, close, closer, near, nearer, nigh (*archaic*)

hitherto *adverb* (*formal*) PREVIOUSLY, so far, until now, thus far, up to now, till now, heretofore

hive *noun* **1** COLONY, swarm **2** CENTRE, hub, powerhouse (*slang*)

hoard *verb* SAVE, store, collect, gather, treasure, accumulate, garner, amass, stockpile, buy up, put away, hive, cache, lay up, put by, stash away (*informal*) ▷ *noun* STORE, fund, supply, reserve, mass, pile, heap, fall-back, accumulation, stockpile, stash, cache, treasure-trove

hoarse *adjective* ROUGH, harsh, husky, grating, growling, raucous, rasping, gruff, throaty, gravelly, guttural, croaky << ANTONYM clear

hoary *adjective* **1** OLD, aged, ancient, antique, venerable, antiquated **2** WHITE-HAIRED, white, grey, silvery, frosty, grey-haired, grizzled, hoar

hoax *noun* TRICK, joke, fraud, con (*informal*), deception, spoof (*informal*), prank, swindle, ruse, practical joke, canard, fast one (*informal*), imposture, fastie (*Austral slang*) ▷ *verb* DECEIVE, trick, fool, take in (*informal*), con (*slang*), wind up (*Brit slang*), kid (*informal*), bluff, dupe, gull (*archaic*), delude, swindle, bamboozle (*informal*), gammon (*Brit informal*), hoodwink, take (someone) for a ride (*informal*), befool, hornswoggle (*slang*)

hobble *verb* **1** LIMP, stagger, stumble, shuffle, falter, shamble, totter, dodder, halt **2** RESTRICT, hamstring, shackle, fetter

hobby *noun* PASTIME, relaxation, leisure pursuit, sideline, diversion, avocation, favourite occupation, (leisure) activity

hobnob *verb* SOCIALIZE, mix, associate, hang out (*informal*), mingle, consort, hang about, keep company, fraternize

hog *verb* (*slang*) MONOPOLIZE, dominate, tie up, corner, corner the market in, be a dog in the manger

hoist *verb* RAISE, lift, erect, elevate, heave, upraise ▷ *noun* LIFT, crane, elevator, winch, tackle

hold *verb* **1** CARRY, keep, grip, grasp, cling to, clasp **2** SUPPORT, take, bear, shoulder, sustain, prop, brace << ANTONYM give way **3** EMBRACE, grasp, clutch, hug, squeeze, cradle, clasp, enfold **4** RESTRAIN, constrain, check, bind, curb, hamper, hinder << ANTONYM release **5** DETAIN, arrest, confine, imprison, impound, pound, hold in custody, put in jail << ANTONYM release **6** ACCOMMODATE, take, contain, seat, comprise, have a capacity for **7** CONSIDER, think, believe, view, judge, regard, maintain, assume, reckon, esteem, deem, presume, entertain the idea << ANTONYM deny **8** OCCUPY, have, fill, maintain, retain, possess, hold down (*informal*) **9** CONDUCT, convene, have, call, run, celebrate, carry on, assemble, preside over, officiate at, solemnize << ANTONYM cancel **10** *sometimes with* **up** CONTINUE, last, remain, stay, wear, resist, endure, persist, persevere **11** APPLY, exist, be the case, stand up, operate, be in force, remain true, hold good, remain

valid ▷ *noun* **1** GRIP, grasp, clutch, clasp
2 FOOTHOLD, footing, purchase, leverage,
vantage, anchorage **3** CONTROL, authority,
influence, pull (*informal*), sway, dominance,
clout (*informal*), mastery, dominion,
ascendancy, mana (*NZ*) ▷▷ **hold back** DESIST,
forbear, hesitate, stop yourself, restrain
yourself, refrain from doing something
▷▷ **hold forth** SPEAK, go on, discourse,
lecture, preach, spout (*informal*), harangue,
declaim, spiel (*informal*), descant, orate,
speechify, korero (*NZ*) ▷▷ **hold off** PUT OFF,
delay, postpone, defer, avoid, refrain, keep
from ▷▷ **hold on** (*informal*) WAIT (A MINUTE),
hang on (*informal*), sit tight (*informal*), hold
your horses (*informal*), just a moment *or*
second ▷▷ **hold onto something** *or* **someone**
1 GRAB, hold, grip, clutch, cling to **2** RETAIN,
keep, hang onto, not give away, keep
possession of ▷▷ **hold out** LAST, continue,
carry on, endure, hang on, persist, persevere,
stay the course, stand fast ▷▷ **hold out**
against something *or* **someone** WITHSTAND,
resist, fend off, keep at bay, fight ▷▷ **hold**
someone back HINDER, prevent, restrain,
check, hamstring, hamper, inhibit, thwart,
obstruct, impede ▷▷ **hold someone up**
DELAY, slow down, hinder, stop, detain,
retard, impede, set back ▷▷ **hold something**
back 1 RESTRAIN, check, curb, control,
suppress, rein (in), repress, stem the flow
of **2** WITHHOLD, hold in, suppress, stifle,
repress, keep the lid on (*informal*), keep
back ▷▷ **hold something out** OFFER, give,
present, extend, proffer ▷▷ **hold something**
over POSTPONE, delay, suspend, put off,
defer, adjourn, waive, take a rain check on
(*US & Canad informal*) ▷▷ **hold something up**
1 DISPLAY, show, exhibit, flourish, show off,
hold aloft, present **2** SUPPORT, prop, brace,
bolster, sustain, shore up, buttress, jack up
3 ROB, mug (*informal*), stick up (*slang, chiefly*
US), waylay ▷▷ **hold something** *or* **someone**
off FEND OFF, repel, rebuff, stave off, repulse,
keep off ▷▷ **hold up** LAST, survive, endure,
bear up, wear ▷▷ **hold with something**
APPROVE OF, be in favour of, support,
subscribe to, countenance, agree to *or* with,
take kindly to

holder *noun* **1** OWNER, bearer, possessor,
keeper, purchaser, occupant, proprietor,
custodian, incumbent **2** CASE, cover,
container, sheath, receptacle, housing

holding *noun often plural* PROPERTY,
securities, investments, resources, estate,
assets, possessions, stocks and shares, land
interests

hold-up *noun* **1** ROBBERY, theft, mugging
(*informal*), stick-up (*slang, chiefly US*) **2** DELAY,
wait, hitch, trouble, difficulty, setback,
snag, traffic jam, obstruction, stoppage,
bottleneck

hole *noun* **1** CAVITY, depression, pit, hollow,
pocket, chamber, cave, shaft, cavern,
excavation **2** OPENING, split, crack, break,
tear, gap, rent, breach, outlet, vent, puncture,
aperture, fissure, orifice, perforation
3 BURROW, nest, den, earth, shelter, retreat,
covert, lair **4** FAULT, error, flaw, defect,
loophole, discrepancy, inconsistency,
fallacy **5** (*informal*) HOVEL, dump (*informal*),
dive (*slang*), slum, joint (*slang*) **6** (*informal*)
PREDICAMENT, spot (*informal*), fix (*informal*),
mess, jam (*informal*), dilemma, scrape
(*informal*), tangle, hot water (*informal*),
quandary, tight spot, imbroglio ▷▷ **hole up**
HIDE, shelter, take refuge, go into hiding,
take cover, go to earth

holiday *noun* **1** VACATION, leave, break, time
off, recess, away day, schoolie (*Austral*),
accumulated day off *or* ADO (*Austral*)
2 FESTIVAL, bank holiday, festivity, public
holiday, fête, celebration, anniversary, feast,
red-letter day, name day, saint's day, gala

holiness *noun* SANCTITY, spirituality,
sacredness, purity, divinity, righteousness,
piety, godliness, saintliness, blessedness,
religiousness, devoutness, virtuousness

holler (*informal*) *verb sometimes with* **out** YELL,
call, cry, shout, cheer, roar, hail, bellow,
whoop, clamour, bawl, hurrah, halloo,
huzzah (*archaic*) ▷ *noun* YELL, call, cry, shout,
cheer, roar, hail, bellow, whoop, clamour,
bawl, hurrah, halloo, huzzah (*archaic*)

hollow *adjective* **1** EMPTY, vacant, void,
unfilled, not solid << ANTONYM solid
2 SUNKEN, depressed, cavernous, indented,
concave, deep-set << ANTONYM rounded
3 WORTHLESS, empty, useless, vain,
meaningless, pointless, futile, fruitless,
specious, Pyrrhic, unavailing << ANTONYM
meaningful **4** INSINCERE, false, artificial,
cynical, hypocritical, hollow-hearted
5 DULL, low, deep, flat, rumbling, muted,
muffled, expressionless, sepulchral, toneless,
reverberant << ANTONYM vibrant ▷ *noun*
1 CAVITY, cup, hole, bowl, depression, pit,
cave, den, basin, dent, crater, trough, cavern,
excavation, indentation, dimple, concavity
<< ANTONYM mound **2** VALLEY, dale, glen,

dell, dingle << ANTONYM hill ▷ *verb often followed by* **out** SCOOP OUT, dig out, excavate, gouge out, channel, groove, furrow

holocaust *noun* 1 DEVASTATION, destruction, carnage, genocide, inferno, annihilation, conflagration 2 GENOCIDE, massacre, carnage, mass murder, annihilation, pogrom

holy *adjective* 1 SACRED, blessed, hallowed, dedicated, venerable, consecrated, venerated, sacrosanct, sanctified << ANTONYM unsanctified 2 DEVOUT, godly, religious, pure, divine, faithful, righteous, pious, virtuous, hallowed, saintly, god-fearing << ANTONYM sinful

homage *noun* 1 RESPECT, honour, worship, esteem, admiration, awe, devotion, reverence, duty, deference, adulation, adoration << ANTONYM contempt 2 ALLEGIANCE, service, tribute, loyalty, devotion, fidelity, faithfulness, obeisance, troth (*archaic*), fealty

home *noun* 1 DWELLING, house, residence, abode, habitation, pad (*slang*), domicile, dwelling place 2 BIRTHPLACE, household, homeland, home town, homestead, native land, Godzone (*Austral informal*) 3 TERRITORY, environment, habitat, range, element, haunt, home ground, abode, habitation, stamping ground ▷ *adjective* DOMESTIC, national, local, central, internal, native, inland ▷▷ **at home** 1 IN, present, available 2 AT EASE, relaxed, comfortable, content, at peace ▷▷ **at home in, on,** *or* **with** FAMILIAR WITH, experienced in, skilled in, proficient in, conversant with, au fait with, knowledgeable of, well-versed in ▷▷ **bring something home to someone** MAKE CLEAR, emphasize, drive home, press home, impress upon ▷ see **hone**

homeland *noun* NATIVE LAND, birthplace, motherland, fatherland, country of origin, mother country, Godzone (*Austral informal*)

homeless *adjective* DESTITUTE, exiled, displaced, dispossessed, unsettled, outcast, abandoned, down-and-out

homely *adjective* 1 COMFORTABLE, welcoming, friendly, domestic, familiar, informal, cosy, comfy (*informal*), homespun, downhome (*slang, chiefly US*), homelike, homy 2 PLAIN, simple, natural, ordinary, modest, everyday, down-to-earth, unaffected, unassuming, unpretentious, unfussy << ANTONYM elaborate 3 (*US*) UNATTRACTIVE, plain, ugly, not striking, unprepossessing, not beautiful, no oil painting (*informal*), ill-favoured

homespun *adjective* UNSOPHISTICATED, homely, plain, rough, rude, coarse, home-made, rustic, artless, inelegant, unpolished

homicidal *adjective* MURDEROUS, deadly, lethal, maniacal, death-dealing

homicide *noun* MURDER, killing, manslaughter, slaying, bloodshed

homily *noun* SERMON, talk, address, speech, lecture, preaching, discourse, oration, declamation

homogeneous *or* **homogenous** *adjective* UNIFORM, similar, consistent, identical, alike, comparable, akin, analogous, kindred, unvarying, cognate << ANTONYM diverse

homosexual *adjective* GAY, lesbian, queer (*informal or derogatory*), camp (*informal*), pink (*informal*), same-sex, homoerotic, sapphic, moffie (*S African slang*) ▷ *noun* GAY, lesbian, queer (*informal or derogatory*), moffie (*S African slang*), auntie *or* aunty (*Austral slang*), lily (*Austral slang*)

homy *or* **homey** *adjective* (*Chiefly US*) HOMELY, comfortable, welcoming, domestic, friendly, familiar, cosy, comfy (*informal*), homespun, downhome (*slang, chiefly US*), homelike

hone *verb* 1 IMPROVE, better, polish, enhance, upgrade, refine, sharpen, augment, help 2 SHARPEN, point, grind, edge, file, polish, whet, strop

honest *adjective* 1 TRUSTWORTHY, decent, upright, reliable, ethical, honourable, conscientious, reputable, truthful, virtuous, law-abiding, trusty, scrupulous, high-minded, veracious << ANTONYM dishonest 2 OPEN, direct, frank, plain, straightforward, outright, sincere, candid, forthright, upfront (*informal*), undisguised, round, ingenuous, unfeigned << ANTONYM secretive 3 GENUINE, real, true, straight, fair, proper, authentic, equitable, impartial, on the level (*informal*), bona fide, dinkum (*Austral & NZ informal*), above board, fair and square, on the up and up, honest to goodness << ANTONYM false

honestly *adverb* 1 ETHICALLY, legitimately, legally, in good faith, on the level (*informal*), lawfully, honourably, by fair means, with clean hands 2 FRANKLY, plainly, candidly, straight (out), truthfully, to your face, in plain English, in all sincerity

honesty *noun* 1 INTEGRITY, honour, virtue, morality, fidelity, probity, rectitude, veracity, faithfulness, truthfulness, trustworthiness, straightness, incorruptibility, scrupulousness, uprightness, reputability

2 FRANKNESS, openness, sincerity, candour, bluntness, outspokenness, genuineness, plainness, straightforwardness

honeyed *adjective* **1** FLATTERING, sweet, soothing, enticing, mellow, seductive, agreeable, sweetened, cajoling, alluring, melodious, unctuous, dulcet **2** (*poetic*) SWEET, sweetened, luscious, sugary, syrupy, toothsome

honorary *adjective* NOMINAL, unofficial, titular, ex officio, honoris causa (*Latin*), in name *or* title only

honour *noun* **1** INTEGRITY, principles, morality, honesty, goodness, fairness, decency, righteousness, probity, rectitude, trustworthiness, uprightness << ANTONYM dishonour **2** PRESTIGE, credit, reputation, glory, fame, distinction, esteem, dignity, elevation, eminence, renown, repute, high standing << ANTONYM disgrace **3** REPUTATION, standing, prestige, image, status, stature, good name, kudos, cachet **4** ACCLAIM, regard, respect, praise, recognition, compliments, homage, accolades, reverence, deference, adoration, commendation, veneration << ANTONYM contempt **5** PRIVILEGE, credit, favour, pleasure, compliment, source of pride *or* satisfaction **6** (*old-fashioned*) VIRGINITY, virtue, innocence, purity, modesty, chastity ▷ *verb* **1** ACCLAIM, celebrate, praise, decorate, compliment, commemorate, dignify, commend, glorify, exalt, laud, lionize **2** RESPECT, value, esteem, prize, appreciate, admire, worship, adore, revere, glorify, reverence, exalt, venerate, hallow << ANTONYM scorn **3** FULFIL, keep, carry out, observe, discharge, live up to, be true to, be as good as (*informal*), be faithful to **4** PAY, take, accept, clear, pass, cash, credit, acknowledge << ANTONYM refuse

honourable *adjective* **1** PRINCIPLED, moral, ethical, just, true, fair, upright, honest, virtuous, trustworthy, trusty, high-minded, upstanding **2** PROPER, right, respectable, righteous, virtuous, creditable **3** PRESTIGIOUS, great, noble, noted, distinguished, notable, renowned, eminent, illustrious, venerable

hoodoo *noun* (*informal*) JINX, curse, bad luck, voodoo, nemesis, hex (*US & Canad informal*), evil eye, evil star

hoodwink *verb* DECEIVE, trick, fool, cheat, con (*informal*), kid (*informal*), mislead, hoax, dupe, gull (*archaic*), delude, swindle, rook

(*slang*), bamboozle (*informal*), take for a ride (*informal*), lead up the garden path (*informal*), sell a pup, pull a fast one on (*informal*), cozen, befool

hook *noun* FASTENER, catch, link, lock, holder, peg, clasp, hasp ▷ *verb* **1** FASTEN, fix, secure, catch, clasp, hasp **2** CATCH, land, trap, entrap ▷▷ **by hook or by crook** BY ANY MEANS, somehow, somehow or other, someway, by fair means or foul ▷▷ **hook, line, and sinker** (*informal*) COMPLETELY, totally, entirely, thoroughly, wholly, utterly, through and through, lock, stock and barrel ▷▷ **off the hook** (*informal*) LET OFF, cleared, acquitted, vindicated, in the clear, exonerated, under no obligation, allowed to walk (*slang, chiefly US*)

hooked *adjective* **1** BENT, curved, beaked, aquiline, beaky, hook-shaped, hamate (*rare*), hooklike, falcate (*biology*), unciform (*anatomy, etc*), uncinate (*biology*) **2** (*informal*) OBSESSED, addicted, taken, devoted, turned on (*slang*), enamoured **3** (*informal*) ADDICTED, dependent, using (*informal*), having a habit

hooligan *noun* DELINQUENT, tough, vandal, casual, ned (*Scot slang*), rowdy, hoon (*Austral & NZ*), hoodlum (*chiefly US*), ruffian, lager lout, yob or yobbo (*Brit slang*), cougan (*Austral slang*), scozza (*Austral slang*), bogan (*Austral slang*)

hooliganism *noun* DELINQUENCY, violence, disorder, vandalism, rowdiness, loutishness, yobbishness

hoop *noun* RING, band, loop, wheel, round, girdle, circlet

hoot *noun* **1** CRY, shout, howl, scream, shriek, whoop **2** TOOT, beep, honk **3** JEER, yell, boo, catcall **4** (*informal*) LAUGH, scream (*informal*), caution (*informal*), card (*informal*) ▷ *verb* **1** JEER, boo, howl, yell, catcall **2** CRY, call, screech, tu-whit tu-whoo **3** TOOT, sound, blast, blare, beep, honk **4** SHOUT, cry, yell, scream, shriek, whoop

hop *verb* JUMP, spring, bound, leap, skip, vault, caper ▷ *noun* JUMP, step, spring, bound, leap, bounce, skip, vault

hope *verb* BELIEVE, expect, trust, rely, look forward to, anticipate, contemplate, count on, foresee, keep your fingers crossed, cross your fingers ▷ *noun* BELIEF, confidence, expectation, longing, dream, desire, faith, ambition, assumption, anticipation, expectancy, light at the end of the tunnel << ANTONYM despair

hopeful *adjective* **1** OPTIMISTIC, confident,

assured, looking forward to, anticipating, buoyant, sanguine, expectant << ANTONYM despairing 2 PROMISING, encouraging, bright, reassuring, cheerful, rosy, heartening, auspicious, propitious << ANTONYM unpromising

hopefully *adverb* 1 OPTIMISTICALLY, confidently, expectantly, with anticipation, sanguinely 2 (*informal*) IT IS HOPED, probably, all being well, God willing, conceivably, feasibly, expectedly

hopeless *adjective* 1 PESSIMISTIC, desperate, despairing, forlorn, in despair, abject, dejected, despondent, demoralized, defeatist, disconsolate, downhearted << ANTONYM hopeful 2 IMPOSSIBLE, pointless, futile, useless, vain, forlorn, no-win, unattainable, impracticable, unachievable, not having a prayer 3 (*informal*) NO GOOD, inadequate, useless (*informal*), poor, pants (*informal*), pathetic, inferior, incompetent, ineffectual 4 INCURABLE, irreversible, irreparable, lost, helpless, irremediable, past remedy, remediless << ANTONYM curable

hopelessly *adverb* 1 WITHOUT HOPE, desperately, in despair, despairingly, irredeemably, irremediably, beyond all hope 2 COMPLETELY, totally, extremely, desperately, terribly, utterly, tremendously, awfully, impossibly, frightfully

horde *noun* CROWD, mob, swarm, press, host, band, troop, pack, crew, drove, gang, multitude, throng

horizon *noun* 1 SKYLINE, view, vista, field *or* range of vision 2 SCOPE, perspective, range, prospect, stretch, ken, sphere, realm, compass, ambit, purview

horizontal *adjective* LEVEL, flat, plane, parallel, supine

horny *adjective* (*informal*) AROUSED, excited, turned on (*slang*), randy (*informal, chiefly Brit*), raunchy (*slang*), amorous, lustful

horrible *adjective* 1 (*informal*) DREADFUL, terrible, awful, nasty, cruel, beastly (*informal*), mean, unpleasant, ghastly (*informal*), unkind, horrid, disagreeable << ANTONYM wonderful 2 TERRIBLE, awful, appalling, terrifying, shocking, grim, dreadful, revolting, fearful, obscene, ghastly, hideous, shameful, gruesome, from hell (*informal*), grisly, horrid, repulsive, frightful, heinous, loathsome, abhorrent, abominable, hellacious (*US slang*)

horrid *adjective* (*informal*) 1 UNPLEASANT,

terrible, awful, offensive, nasty, disgusting, horrible, dreadful, obscene, disagreeable, yucky *or* yukky (*slang*), yucko (*Austral slang*) 2 NASTY, dreadful, horrible, mean, unkind, cruel, beastly (*informal*)

horrific *adjective* HORRIFYING, shocking, appalling, frightening, awful, terrifying, grim, dreadful, horrendous, ghastly, from hell (*informal*), grisly, frightful, hellacious (*US slang*)

horrify *verb* 1 TERRIFY, alarm, frighten, scare, intimidate, petrify, terrorize, put the wind up (*informal*), gross out (*US slang*), make your hair stand on end, affright << ANTONYM comfort 2 SHOCK, appal, disgust, dismay, sicken, outrage << ANTONYM delight

horror *noun* 1 TERROR, fear, alarm, panic, dread, dismay, awe, fright, apprehension, consternation, trepidation 2 HATRED, disgust, loathing, aversion, revulsion, antipathy, abomination, abhorrence, repugnance, odium, detestation << ANTONYM love

horse *noun* NAG, mount, mare, colt, filly, stallion, gelding, jade, pony, yearling, steed (*archaic or literary*), dobbin, moke (*Austral slang*), hobby (*archaic or dialect*), yarraman *or* yarramin (*Austral*), gee-gee (*slang*), cuddy *or* cuddie (*dialect, chiefly Scot*), studhorse *or* stud ▷▷ **horse around** *or* **about** (*informal*) PLAY AROUND *or* ABOUT, fool about *or* around, clown, misbehave, play the fool, roughhouse (*slang*), play the goat, monkey about *or* around, indulge in horseplay, lark about *or* around

horseman *noun* RIDER, equestrian

hospitable *adjective* WELCOMING, kind, friendly, liberal, generous, gracious, amicable, cordial, sociable, genial, bountiful << ANTONYM inhospitable

hospitality *noun* WELCOME, warmth, kindness, friendliness, sociability, conviviality, neighbourliness, cordiality, heartiness, hospitableness

host¹ *or* **hostess** *noun* 1 MASTER OF CEREMONIES, proprietor, innkeeper, landlord *or* landlady 2 PRESENTER, compere (*Brit*), anchorman *or* anchorwoman ▷ *verb* PRESENT, introduce, compere (*Brit*), front (*informal*)

host² *noun* 1 MULTITUDE, lot, load (*informal*), wealth, array, myriad, great quantity, large number 2 CROWD, army, pack, drove, mob, herd, legion, swarm, horde, throng

hostage *noun* CAPTIVE, prisoner, pledge,

pawn, security, surety

hostile *adjective* **1** ANTAGONISTIC, anti (*informal*), opposed, opposite, contrary, inimical, ill-disposed **2** UNFRIENDLY, belligerent, antagonistic, unkind, malevolent, warlike, bellicose, inimical, rancorous, ill-disposed << ANTONYM friendly **3** INHOSPITABLE, adverse, alien, uncongenial, unsympathetic, unwelcoming, unpropitious << ANTONYM hospitable

hostility *noun* **1** UNFRIENDLINESS, hatred, animosity, spite, bitterness, malice, venom, antagonism, enmity, abhorrence, malevolence, detestation << ANTONYM friendliness **2** OPPOSITION, resentment, antipathy, aversion, antagonism, ill feeling, bad blood, ill-will, animus << ANTONYM approval ▷ *plural noun* WARFARE, war, fighting, conflict, combat, armed conflict, state of war << ANTONYM peace

hot *adjective* **1** HEATED, burning, boiling, steaming, flaming, roasting, searing, blistering, fiery, scorching, scalding, piping hot **2** WARM, close, stifling, humid, torrid, sultry, sweltering, balmy, muggy << ANTONYM cold **3** SPICY, pungent, peppery, piquant, biting, sharp, acrid << ANTONYM mild **4** INTENSE, passionate, heated, spirited, excited, fierce, lively, animated, ardent, inflamed, fervent, impassioned, fervid **5** NEW, latest, fresh, recent, up to date, just out, up to the minute, bang up to date (*informal*), hot off the press << ANTONYM old **6** POPULAR, hip, fashionable, cool, in demand, sought-after, must-see, in vogue << ANTONYM unpopular **7** FIERCE, intense, strong, keen, competitive, cut-throat **8** FIERY, violent, raging, passionate, stormy, touchy, vehement, impetuous, irascible << ANTONYM calm

hot air *noun* EMPTY TALK, rant, guff (*slang*), bombast, wind, gas (*informal*), verbiage, claptrap (*informal*), blather, bunkum (*chiefly US*), blether, bosh (*informal*), tall talk (*informal*)

hotbed *noun* BREEDING GROUND, nest, den

hot-headed *adjective* VOLATILE, rash, fiery, reckless, precipitate, hasty, unruly, foolhardy, impetuous, hot-tempered, quick-tempered

hothouse *noun* GREENHOUSE, conservatory, glasshouse, orangery

hotly *adverb* **1** FIERCELY, passionately, angrily, vehemently, indignantly, with indignation, heatedly, impetuously **2** CLOSELY, enthusiastically, eagerly, with enthusiasm, hotfoot

hound *verb* **1** HARASS, harry, bother, provoke, annoy, torment, hassle (*informal*), prod, badger, persecute, pester, goad, keep after **2** FORCE, drive, pressure, push, chase, railroad (*informal*), propel, impel, pressurize

house *noun* **1** HOME, residence, dwelling, building, pad (*slang*), homestead, edifice, abode, habitation, domicile, whare (*NZ*) **2** HOUSEHOLD, family, ménage **3** FIRM, company, business, concern, organization, partnership, establishment, outfit (*informal*) **4** ASSEMBLY, parliament, Commons, legislative body **5** RESTAURANT, inn, hotel, pub (*Brit informal*), tavern, public house, hostelry **6** DYNASTY, line, race, tribe, clan, ancestry, lineage, family tree, kindred ▷ *verb* **1** ACCOMMODATE, board, quarter, take in, put up, lodge, harbour, billet, domicile **2** CONTAIN, keep, hold, cover, store, protect, shelter **3** TAKE, accommodate, sleep, provide shelter for, give a bed to ▷▷ **on the house** FREE, for free (*informal*), for nothing, free of charge, gratis, without expense

household *noun* FAMILY, home, house, ménage, family circle, ainga (*NZ*) ▷ *modifier* DOMESTIC, family, domiciliary

householder *noun* OCCUPANT, resident, tenant, proprietor, homeowner, freeholder, leaseholder

housekeeping *noun* HOUSEHOLD MANAGEMENT, homemaking (*US*), home economy, housewifery, housecraft

housing *noun* **1** ACCOMMODATION, homes, houses, dwellings, domiciles **2** CASE, casing, covering, cover, shell, jacket, holder, container, capsule, sheath, encasement

hovel *noun* HUT, hole, shed, cabin, den, slum, shack, shanty, whare (*NZ*)

hover *verb* **1** FLOAT, fly, hang, drift, be suspended, flutter, poise **2** LINGER, loiter, wait nearby, hang about *or* around (*informal*) **3** WAVER, alternate, fluctuate, haver (*Brit*), falter, dither (*chiefly Brit*), oscillate, vacillate, seesaw, swither (*Scot dialect*)

however *adverb* BUT, nevertheless, still, though, yet, even though, on the other hand, nonetheless, notwithstanding, anyhow, be that as it may

howl *verb* **1** BAY, cry, bark, yelp, quest (*used of hounds*) **2** CRY, shout, scream, roar, weep, yell, cry out, wail, shriek, bellow, bawl, yelp ▷ *noun* **1** BAYING, cry, bay, bark, barking, yelp, yelping, yowl **2** CRY, scream, roar, bay, wail, outcry, shriek, bellow, clamour, hoot, bawl, yelp, yowl

howler noun (*informal*) MISTAKE, error, blunder, boob (*Brit slang*), bloomer (*Brit informal*), clanger (*informal*), malapropism, schoolboy howler, booboo (*informal*), barry *or* Barry Crocker (*Austral slang*)

hub noun CENTRE, heart, focus, core, middle, focal point, pivot, nerve centre

hubbub noun **1** NOISE, racket, din, uproar, cacophony, pandemonium, babel, tumult, hurly-burly **2** HUE AND CRY, confusion, disturbance, riot, disorder, clamour, rumpus, bedlam, brouhaha, ruction (*informal*), hullabaloo, ruckus (*informal*)

hubris noun PRIDE, vanity, arrogance, conceit, self-importance, haughtiness, conceitedness

huddle verb **1** CURL UP, crouch, hunch up, nestle, snuggle, make yourself small **2** CROWD, press, gather, collect, squeeze, cluster, flock, herd, throng ▷ noun **1** CROWD, mass, bunch, cluster, heap, muddle, jumble **2** (*informal*) DISCUSSION, conference, meeting, hui (*NZ*), powwow, confab (*informal*), korero (*NZ*)

hue noun **1** COLOUR, tone, shade, dye, tint, tinge, tincture **2** ASPECT, light, cast, complexion

huff noun SULK, temper, bad mood, passion, rage, pet, pique, foulie (*Austral slang*)

hug verb **1** EMBRACE, hold (onto), cuddle, squeeze, cling, clasp, enfold, hold close, take in your arms **2** FOLLOW CLOSELY, keep close, stay near, cling to, follow the course of ▷ noun EMBRACE, squeeze, bear hug, clinch (*slang*), clasp

huge adjective ENORMOUS, great, giant, large, massive, vast, extensive, tremendous, immense, mega (*slang*), titanic, jumbo (*informal*), gigantic, monumental, mammoth, bulky, colossal, mountainous, stellar (*informal*), prodigious, stupendous, gargantuan, elephantine, ginormous (*informal*), Brobdingnagian, humongous *or* humungous (*US slang*) << ANTONYM tiny

hugely adverb IMMENSELY, enormously, massively, prodigiously, monumentally, stupendously

hui noun (*NZ*) MEETING, gathering, assembly, meet, conference, congress, session, rally, convention, get-together (*informal*), reunion, congregation, conclave, convocation, powwow

hulk noun WRECK, shell, hull, shipwreck, frame

hulking adjective UNGAINLY, massive, lumbering, gross, awkward, clumsy, bulky, cumbersome, overgrown, unwieldy, ponderous, clunky (*informal*), oafish, lumpish, lubberly, unco (*Austral slang*)

hull noun **1** FRAMEWORK, casing, body, covering, frame, skeleton **2** HUSK, skin, shell, peel, pod, rind, shuck ▷ verb TRIM, peel, skin, shell, husk, shuck

hum verb **1** DRONE, buzz, murmur, throb, vibrate, purr, croon, thrum, whir **2** (*informal*) BE BUSY, buzz, bustle, move, stir, pulse, be active, vibrate, pulsate

human adjective **1** MORTAL, anthropoid, manlike << ANTONYM nonhuman **2** KIND, natural, vulnerable, kindly, understandable, humane, compassionate, considerate, approachable << ANTONYM inhuman ▷ noun HUMAN BEING, person, individual, body, creature, mortal, man *or* woman << ANTONYM nonhuman

humane adjective KIND, compassionate, good, kindly, understanding, gentle, forgiving, tender, mild, sympathetic, charitable, benign, clement, benevolent, lenient, merciful, good-natured, forbearing, kind-hearted << ANTONYM cruel

humanitarian adjective **1** COMPASSIONATE, charitable, humane, benevolent, altruistic, beneficent **2** CHARITABLE, philanthropic, public-spirited ▷ noun PHILANTHROPIST, benefactor, Good Samaritan, altruist

humanity noun **1** THE HUMAN RACE, man, mankind, people, men, mortals, humankind, Homo sapiens **2** HUMAN NATURE, mortality, humanness **3** KINDNESS, charity, compassion, understanding, sympathy, mercy, tolerance, tenderness, philanthropy, benevolence, fellow feeling, benignity, brotherly love, kind-heartedness ▷ plural noun ARTS, liberal arts, classics, classical studies, literae humaniores

humble adjective **1** MODEST, meek, unassuming, unpretentious, submissive, self-effacing, unostentatious << ANTONYM proud **2** LOWLY, common, poor, mean, low, simple, ordinary, modest, obscure, commonplace, insignificant, unimportant, unpretentious, undistinguished, plebeian, low-born << ANTONYM distinguished ▷ verb HUMILIATE, shame, disgrace, break, reduce, lower, sink, crush, put down (*slang*), bring down, subdue, degrade, demean, chagrin, chasten, mortify, debase, put (someone) in their place, abase, take (someone) down a peg (*informal*), abash << ANTONYM exalt

humbly *adverb* MEEKLY, modestly, respectfully, cap in hand, diffidently, deferentially, submissively, unassumingly, obsequiously, subserviently, on bended knee, servilely

humbug *noun* NONSENSE, rubbish, trash, hypocrisy, cant, baloney (*informal*), claptrap (*informal*), quackery, eyewash (*informal*), charlatanry

humdrum *adjective* DULL, ordinary, boring, routine, commonplace, mundane, tedious, dreary, banal, tiresome, monotonous, uneventful, uninteresting, mind-numbing, ho-hum (*informal*), repetitious, wearisome, unvaried << ANTONYM exciting

humid *adjective* DAMP, sticky, moist, wet, steamy, sultry, dank, clammy, muggy << ANTONYM dry

humidity *noun* DAMP, moisture, dampness, wetness, moistness, sogginess, dankness, clamminess, mugginess, humidness

humiliate *verb* EMBARRASS, shame, humble, crush, disgrace, put down, subdue, degrade, chagrin, chasten, mortify, debase, discomfit, bring low, put (someone) in their place, take the wind out of someone's sails, abase, take down a peg (*informal*), abash, make (someone) eat humble pie << ANTONYM honour

humiliating *adjective* EMBARRASSING, shaming, humbling, mortifying, crushing, disgracing, degrading, ignominious, toe-curling (*slang*), cringe-making (*Brit informal*), cringeworthy (*Brit informal*), barro (*Austral slang*)

humiliation *noun* EMBARRASSMENT, shame, disgrace, humbling, put-down, degradation, affront, indignity, chagrin, ignominy, dishonour, mortification, loss of face, abasement, self-abasement

humility *noun* MODESTY, diffidence, meekness, submissiveness, servility, self-abasement, humbleness, lowliness, unpretentiousness, lack of pride << ANTONYM pride

humorist *noun* COMEDIAN, comic, wit, eccentric, wag, joker, card (*informal*), jester, dag (*NZ informal*), funny man

humorous *adjective* FUNNY, comic, amusing, entertaining, witty, merry, hilarious, ludicrous, laughable, farcical, whimsical, comical, droll, facetious, jocular, side-splitting, waggish, jocose << ANTONYM serious

humour *noun* 1 COMEDY, funniness, fun, amusement, funny side, jocularity, facetiousness, ludicrousness, drollery, comical aspect << ANTONYM seriousness 2 MOOD, spirits, temper, disposition, frame of mind 3 JOKING, jokes, comedy, wit, gags (*informal*), farce, jesting, jests, wisecracks (*informal*), witticisms, wittiness ▷ *verb* INDULGE, accommodate, go along with, spoil, flatter, pamper, pander to, mollify, cosset, fawn on << ANTONYM oppose

humourless *adjective* SERIOUS, intense, solemn, straight, dry, dour, unfunny, po-faced, unsmiling, heavy-going, unamused, unamusing

hump *noun* LUMP, bump, projection, bulge, mound, hunch, knob, protuberance, protrusion ▷ *verb* (*informal*) CARRY, lug, heave, hoist, shoulder

hunch *noun* FEELING, idea, impression, suspicion, intuition, premonition, inkling, presentiment ▷ *verb* CROUCH, bend, stoop, curve, arch, huddle, draw in, squat, hump

hunger *noun* 1 APPETITE, emptiness, voracity, hungriness, ravenousness 2 STARVATION, famine, malnutrition, undernourishment 3 DESIRE, appetite, craving, yen (*informal*), ache, lust, yearning, itch, thirst, greediness ▷▷ **hunger for** or **after something** WANT, desire, crave, hope for, long for, wish for, yearn for, pine for, hanker after, ache for, thirst after, itch after

hungry *adjective* 1 STARVING, ravenous, famished, starved, empty, hollow, voracious, peckish (*informal, chiefly Brit*), famishing 2 EAGER, keen, craving, yearning, greedy, avid, desirous, covetous, athirst

hunk *noun* LUMP, piece, chunk, block, mass, wedge, slab, nugget, wodge (*Brit informal*), gobbet

hunt *verb* STALK, track, chase, pursue, trail, hound, gun for ▷ *noun* SEARCH, hunting, investigation, chase, pursuit, quest ▷▷ **hunt for something** or **someone** SEARCH FOR, look for, try to find, seek for, forage for, rummage for, scour for, look high and low, fossick for (*Austral & NZ*), go in quest of, ferret about for

hunted *adjective* HARASSED, desperate, harried, tormented, stricken, distraught, persecuted, terror-stricken

hunter *noun* HUNTSMAN or HUNTRESS, Diana, Herne, Orion, Nimrod, jaeger (*rare*), Artemis, sportsman or sportswoman

hurdle *noun* 1 OBSTACLE, block, difficulty,

barrier, handicap, hazard, complication, snag, uphill (*S African*), obstruction, stumbling block, impediment, hindrance **2** FENCE, wall, hedge, block, barrier, barricade

hurl *verb* THROW, fling, chuck (*informal*), send, fire, project, launch, cast, pitch, shy, toss, propel, sling, heave, let fly (with)

hurly-burly *noun* COMMOTION, confusion, chaos, turmoil, disorder, upheaval, furore, uproar, turbulence, pandemonium, bedlam, tumult, hubbub, brouhaha << ANTONYM order

hurricane *noun* STORM, gale, tornado, cyclone, typhoon, tempest, twister (*US informal*), windstorm, willy-willy (*Austral*)

hurried *adjective* **1** HASTY, quick, brief, rushed, short, swift, speedy, precipitate, quickie (*informal*), breakneck **2** RUSHED, perfunctory, hectic, speedy, superficial, hasty, cursory, slapdash

hurriedly *adverb* HASTILY, quickly, briskly, speedily, in a rush, at the double, hurry-scurry

hurry *verb* **1** RUSH, fly, dash, barrel (along) (*informal, chiefly US & Canad*), scurry, scoot, burn rubber (*informal*) << ANTONYM dawdle **2** MAKE HASTE, rush, lose no time, get a move on (*informal*), step on it (*informal*), get your skates on (*informal*) **3** *sometimes with* **up** SPEED (UP), accelerate, hasten, quicken, hustle, urge, push on, goad, expedite << ANTONYM slow down ▷ *noun* RUSH, haste, speed, urgency, bustle, flurry, commotion, precipitation, quickness, celerity, promptitude << ANTONYM slowness

hurt *verb* **1** INJURE, damage, wound, cut, disable, bruise, scrape, impair, gash << ANTONYM heal **2** ACHE, be sore, be painful, burn, smart, sting, throb, be tender **3** HARM, injure, molest, ill-treat, maltreat, lay a finger on **4** UPSET, distress, pain, wound, annoy, sting, grieve, afflict, sadden, cut to the quick, aggrieve ▷ *noun* **1** DISTRESS, suffering, pain, grief, misery, agony, sadness, sorrow, woe, anguish, heartache, wretchedness << ANTONYM happiness **2** HARM, trouble, damage, wrong, loss, injury, misfortune, mischief, affliction ▷ *adjective* **1** INJURED, wounded, damaged, harmed, cut, scratched, bruised, scarred, scraped, grazed << ANTONYM healed **2** UPSET, pained, injured, wounded, sad, crushed, offended, aggrieved, miffed (*informal*), rueful, piqued, tooshie (*Austral slang*) << ANTONYM calmed

hurtful *adjective* UNKIND, upsetting, distressing, mean, cutting, damaging, wounding, nasty, cruel, destructive, harmful, malicious, mischievous, detrimental, pernicious, spiteful, prejudicial, injurious, disadvantageous, maleficent

hurtle *verb* RUSH, charge, race, shoot, fly, speed, tear, crash, plunge, barrel (along) (*informal, chiefly US & Canad*), scramble, spurt, stampede, scoot, burn rubber (*informal*), rush headlong, go hell for leather (*informal*)

husband *noun* PARTNER, man (*informal*), spouse, hubby (*informal*), mate, old man (*informal*), bridegroom, significant other (*US informal*), better half (*humorous*) ▷ *verb* CONSERVE, budget, use sparingly, save, store, hoard, economize on, use economically, manage thriftily << ANTONYM squander

husbandry *noun* **1** FARMING, agriculture, cultivation, land management, tillage, agronomy **2** THRIFT, economy, good housekeeping, frugality, careful management

hush *verb* QUIETEN, still, silence, suppress, mute, muzzle, shush ▷ *noun* QUIET, silence, calm, still (*poetic*), peace, tranquillity, stillness, peacefulness ▷▷ **hush something up** COVER UP, conceal, suppress, sit on (*informal*), squash, smother, keep secret, sweep under the carpet (*informal*), draw a veil over, keep dark

hush-hush *adjective* (*informal*) SECRET, confidential, classified, top-secret, restricted, under wraps

husk *noun* RIND, shell, hull, covering, bark, chaff, shuck

husky *adjective* **1** HOARSE, rough, harsh, raucous, rasping, croaking, gruff, throaty, guttural, croaky **2** (*informal*) MUSCULAR, powerful, strapping, rugged, hefty, burly, stocky, beefy (*informal*), brawny, thickset

hustle *verb* **1** JOSTLE, force, push, crowd, rush, hurry, thrust, elbow, shove, jog, bustle, impel **2** HURRY, hasten, get a move on (*informal*)

hut *noun* **1** CABIN, shack, shanty, hovel, whare (*NZ*) **2** SHED, outhouse, lean-to, lockup

hybrid *noun* **1** CROSSBREED, cross, mixture, compound, composite, mule, amalgam, mongrel, half-breed, half-blood **2** MIXTURE, compound, composite, amalgam

hygiene *noun* CLEANLINESS, sanitation, disinfection, sterility, sanitary measures, hygienics

hygienic *adjective* CLEAN, healthy, sanitary,

pure, sterile, salutary, disinfected, germ-free, aseptic << ANTONYM dirty

hymn *noun* **1** RELIGIOUS SONG, song of praise, carol, chant, anthem, psalm, paean, canticle, doxology **2** SONG OF PRAISE, anthem, paean

hype *noun* PUBLICITY, promotion, build-up, plugging (*informal*), puffing, racket, razzmatazz (*slang*), brouhaha, ballyhoo (*informal*)

hyperbole *noun* EXAGGERATION, hype (*informal*), overstatement, enlargement, magnification, amplification

hypnotic *adjective* MESMERIC, soothing, narcotic, opiate, soporific, sleep-inducing, somniferous

hypnotize *verb* **1** MESMERIZE, put in a trance, put to sleep **2** FASCINATE, absorb, entrance, magnetize, spellbind

hypochondriac *noun* NEUROTIC, valetudinarian

hypocrisy *noun* INSINCERITY, pretence, deceit, deception, cant, duplicity, dissembling, falsity, imposture, sanctimoniousness, phoniness (*informal*), deceitfulness, pharisaism, speciousness, two-facedness, phariseeism << ANTONYM sincerity

hypocrite *noun* FRAUD, deceiver, pretender, charlatan, impostor, pharisee, dissembler, Tartuffe, Pecksniff, Holy Willie, whited sepulchre, phoney *or* phony (*informal*)

hypocritical *adjective* INSINCERE, false, fraudulent, hollow, deceptive, spurious, two-faced, deceitful, sanctimonious, specious, duplicitous, dissembling, canting, Janus-faced, pharisaical, phoney *or* phony (*informal*)

hypodermic *noun* SYRINGE, needle, works (*slang*)

hypothesis *noun* THEORY, premise, proposition, assumption, thesis, postulate, supposition, premiss

hypothetical *adjective* THEORETICAL, supposed, academic, assumed, imaginary, speculative, putative, conjectural << ANTONYM real

hysteria *noun* FRENZY, panic, madness, agitation, delirium, hysterics, unreason

hysterical *adjective* **1** FRENZIED, mad, frantic, raving, distracted, distraught, crazed, uncontrollable, berserk, overwrought, convulsive, beside yourself, berko (*Austral slang*) << ANTONYM calm **2** (*informal*) HILARIOUS, uproarious, side-splitting, farcical, comical, wildly funny << ANTONYM serious

ice ▷▷ **break the ice** KICK OFF (*informal*), lead the way, take the plunge (*informal*), make a start, begin a relationship, initiate the proceedings, start *or* set the ball rolling (*informal*) ▷▷ **skate on thin ice** BE AT RISK, be vulnerable, be unsafe, be in jeopardy, be out on a limb, be open to attack, be sticking your neck out (*informal*)

icy *adjective* **1** COLD, freezing, bitter, biting, raw, chill, chilling, arctic, chilly, frosty, glacial, ice-cold, frozen over, frost-bound << ANTONYM hot **2** SLIPPERY, glassy, slippy (*informal or dialect*), like a sheet of glass, rimy **3** UNFRIENDLY, cold, distant, hostile, forbidding, indifferent, aloof, stony, steely, frosty, glacial, frigid, unwelcoming << ANTONYM friendly

idea *noun* **1** PLAN, scheme, proposal, design, theory, strategy, method, solution, suggestion, recommendation, proposition **2** NOTION, thought, view, understanding, teaching, opinion, belief, conclusion, hypothesis, impression, conviction, judgment, interpretation, sentiment, doctrine, conception, viewpoint **3** IMPRESSION, estimate, guess, hint, notion, clue, conjecture, surmise, inkling, approximation, intimation, ballpark figure **4** UNDERSTANDING, thought, view, sense, opinion, concept, impression, judgment, perception, conception, abstraction, estimation **5** INTENTION, aim, purpose, object, end, plan, reason, goal, design, objective, motive

ideal *noun* **1** *often plural* PRINCIPLE, standard, ideology, morals, conviction, integrity, scruples, probity, moral value, rectitude, sense of duty, sense of honour, uprightness **2** EPITOME, standard, dream, pattern, perfection, last word, paragon, nonpareil, standard of perfection **3** MODEL, example, criterion, prototype, paradigm, archetype, exemplar ▷ *adjective* **1** PERFECT, best, model, classic, supreme, ultimate, archetypal, exemplary, consummate, optimal, quintessential << ANTONYM imperfect **2** IMAGINARY, impractical, Utopian, romantic, fantastic, fabulous, poetic, visionary, fairy-tale, mythical, unreal, fanciful, unattainable, ivory-towered, imagal (*psychoanalysis*) << ANTONYM actual **3** HYPOTHETICAL, academic, intellectual, abstract, theoretical, speculative, conceptual, metaphysical, transcendental, notional

idealist *noun* ROMANTIC, visionary, dreamer, Utopian

idealistic *adjective* PERFECTIONIST, romantic, optimistic, visionary, Utopian, quixotic, impracticable, starry-eyed << ANTONYM realistic

idealize *verb* ROMANTICIZE, glorify, exalt, worship, magnify, ennoble, deify, put on a pedestal, apotheosize

ideally *adverb* IN A PERFECT WORLD, in theory, preferably, if possible, all things being equal, under the best of circumstances, if you had your way, in a Utopia

identical *adjective* ALIKE, like, the same, matching, equal, twin, equivalent, corresponding, duplicate, synonymous, indistinguishable, analogous, interchangeable, a dead ringer (*slang*), the dead spit (*informal*), like two peas in a pod << ANTONYM different

identifiable *adjective* RECOGNIZABLE, noticeable, known, unmistakable, discernible, detectable, distinguishable, ascertainable

identification *noun* **1** DISCOVERY, recognition, determining, establishment, diagnosis,

confirmation, detection, divination
2 RECOGNITION, naming, labelling, distinguishing, cataloguing, classifying, confirmation, pinpointing, establishment of identity **3** CONNECTION, relationship, link, association, tie, partnership, affinity, familiarity, interconnection, interrelation **4** UNDERSTANDING, relationship, involvement, unity, sympathy, empathy, rapport, fellow feeling **5** ID, papers, credentials, licence, warrant, identity card, proof of identity, letters of introduction

identify *verb* **1** RECOGNIZE, place, name, remember, spot, label, flag, catalogue, tag, diagnose, classify, make out, pinpoint, recollect, put your finger on (*informal*) **2** ESTABLISH, spot, confirm, finger (*informal, chiefly US*), demonstrate, pick out, single out, certify, verify, validate, mark out, substantiate, corroborate ▷▷ **identify something** *or* **someone with something** *or* **someone** EQUATE WITH, associate with, think of in connection with, put in the same category as ▷▷ **identify with someone** RELATE TO, understand, respond to, feel for, ally with, empathize with, speak the same language as, put yourself in the place *or* shoes of, see through another's eyes, be on the same wavelength as

identity *noun* INDIVIDUALITY, self, character, personality, existence, distinction, originality, peculiarity, uniqueness, oneness, singularity, separateness, distinctiveness, selfhood, particularity

ideology *noun* BELIEF(S), ideas, principles, ideals, opinion, philosophy, doctrine, creed, dogma, tenets, world view, credence, articles of faith, Weltanschauung (*German*)

idiocy *noun* FOOLISHNESS, insanity, lunacy, tomfoolery, inanity, imbecility, senselessness, cretinism, fatuity, abject stupidity, asininity, fatuousness << ANTONYM wisdom

idiom *noun* **1** PHRASE, expression, turn of phrase, locution, set phrase **2** LANGUAGE, talk, style, usage, jargon, vernacular, parlance, mode of expression

idiosyncrasy *noun* PECULIARITY, habit, characteristic, quirk, eccentricity, oddity, mannerism, affectation, trick, singularity, personal trait

idiosyncratic *adjective* DISTINCTIVE, special, individual, typical, distinguishing, distinct, peculiar, individualistic

idiot *noun* FOOL, jerk (*slang, chiefly US &*

Canad), ass, plank (*Brit slang*), charlie (*Brit informal*), berk (*Brit slang*), wally (*slang*), prat (*slang*), plonker (*slang*), moron, geek (*slang*), twit (*informal, chiefly Brit*), chump, imbecile, cretin, oaf, simpleton, airhead (*slang*), dimwit (*informal*), dipstick (*Brit slang*), gonzo (*slang*), schmuck (*US slang*), dork (*slang*), nitwit (*informal*), blockhead, divvy (*Brit slang*), pillock (*Brit slang*), halfwit, nincompoop, dweeb (*US slang*), putz (*US slang*), eejit (*Scot & Irish*), dumb-ass (*slang*), dunderhead, numpty (*Scot informal*), doofus (*slang, chiefly US*), lamebrain (*informal*), mooncalf, nerd *or* nurd (*slang*), numbskull *or* numskull, galah (*Austral & NZ informal*), dorba *or* dorb (*Austral slang*), bogan (*Austral slang*)

idiotic *adjective* FOOLISH, crazy, stupid, dumb (*informal*), daft (*informal*), insane, lunatic, senseless, foolhardy, inane, fatuous, loopy (*informal*), crackpot (*informal*), moronic, imbecile, unintelligent, asinine, imbecilic, braindead (*informal*), harebrained, dumb-ass (*slang*), halfwitted << ANTONYM wise

idle *adjective* **1** UNOCCUPIED, unemployed, redundant, jobless, out of work, out of action, inactive, at leisure, between jobs, unwaged, at a loose end << ANTONYM occupied **2** UNUSED, stationary, inactive, out of order, ticking over, gathering dust, mothballed, out of service, out of action *or* operation **3** LAZY, slow, slack, sluggish, lax, negligent, inactive, inert, lethargic, indolent, lackadaisical, good-for-nothing, remiss, workshy, slothful, shiftless << ANTONYM busy **4** USELESS, vain, pointless, hopeless, unsuccessful, ineffective, worthless, futile, fruitless, unproductive, abortive, ineffectual, groundless, of no use, valueless, disadvantageous, unavailing, otiose, of no avail, profitless, bootless << ANTONYM useful **5** TRIVIAL, superficial, insignificant, frivolous, silly, unnecessary, irrelevant, foolish, unhelpful, flippant, puerile, flighty, ill-considered, empty-headed, nugatory << ANTONYM meaningful ▷ *verb often with* **away** FRITTER, while, waste, fool, lounge, potter, loaf, dally, loiter, dawdle, laze

idleness *noun* **1** INACTIVITY, unemployment, leisure, inaction, time on your hands **2** LOAFING, inertia, sloth, pottering, trifling, laziness, time-wasting, lazing, torpor, sluggishness, skiving (*Brit slang*), vegetating, dilly-dallying (*informal*), shiftlessness

idly *adverb* LAZILY, casually, passively, languidly, unthinkingly, sluggishly, languorously, lethargically, apathetically, indolently, inertly, lackadaisically, inactively, shiftlessly, slothfully << ANTONYM energetically

idol *noun* **1** HERO, superstar, pin-up, favourite, pet, darling, beloved (*slang*), fave (*informal*) **2** GRAVEN IMAGE, god, image, deity, pagan symbol

idolize *verb* WORSHIP, love, adore, admire, revere, glorify, exalt, look up to, venerate, hero-worship, deify, bow down before, dote upon, apotheosize, worship to excess

idyllic *adjective* HEAVENLY, idealized, ideal, charming, peaceful, pastoral, picturesque, rustic, Utopian, halcyon, out of this world, unspoiled, arcadian

if *conjunction* **1** PROVIDED, assuming, given that, providing, allowing, admitting, supposing, granting, in case, presuming, on the assumption that, on condition that, as long as **2** WHEN, whenever, every time, any time **3** WHETHER ▷ *noun* DOUBT, condition, uncertainty, provision, constraint, hesitation, vagueness, stipulation

iffy *adjective* UNCERTAIN, doubtful, unpredictable, conditional, undecided, up in the air, problematical, chancy (*informal*), in the lap of the gods

ignite *verb* **1** CATCH FIRE, burn, burst into flames, fire, inflame, flare up, take fire **2** SET FIRE TO, light, set alight, torch, kindle, touch off, put a match to (*informal*)

ignoble *adjective* **1** DISHONOURABLE, low, base, mean, petty, infamous, degraded, craven, disgraceful, shabby, vile, degenerate, abject, unworthy, shameless, despicable, heinous, dastardly, contemptible, wretched **2** LOWLY, mean, low, base, common, peasant, vulgar, plebeian, humble, lowborn (*rare*), baseborn (*archaic*)

ignominious *adjective* HUMILIATING, disgraceful, shameful, sorry, scandalous, abject, despicable, mortifying, undignified, disreputable, dishonourable, inglorious, discreditable, indecorous << ANTONYM honourable

ignominy *noun* DISGRACE, shame, humiliation, contempt, discredit, stigma, disrepute, dishonour, infamy, mortification, bad odour << ANTONYM honour

ignorance *noun* **1** LACK OF EDUCATION, stupidity, foolishness, blindness, illiteracy, benightedness, unenlightenment, unintelligence, mental darkness << ANTONYM knowledge **2** *with* **of**

UNAWARENESS OF, inexperience of, unfamiliarity with, innocence of, unconsciousness of, greenness about, oblivion about, nescience of (*literary*)

ignorant *adjective* **1** UNEDUCATED, unaware, naive, green, illiterate, inexperienced, innocent, untrained, unlearned, unread, untutored, uncultivated, wet behind the ears (*informal*), unlettered, untaught, unknowledgeable, uncomprehending, unscholarly, as green as grass << ANTONYM educated **2** INSENSITIVE, gross, crude, rude, shallow, superficial, crass **3** *with* **of** UNINFORMED OF, unaware of, oblivious to, blind to, innocent of, in the dark about, unconscious of, unschooled in, out of the loop of, inexperienced of, uninitiated about, unknowing of, unenlightened about << ANTONYM informed

ignore *verb* **1** PAY NO ATTENTION TO, neglect, disregard, slight, overlook, scorn, spurn, rebuff, take no notice of, be oblivious to << ANTONYM pay attention to **2** OVERLOOK, discount, disregard, reject, neglect, shrug off, pass over, brush aside, turn a blind eye to, turn a deaf ear to, shut your eyes to **3** SNUB, cut (*informal*), slight, blank (*slang*), rebuff, cold-shoulder, turn your back on, give (someone) the cold shoulder, send (someone) to Coventry, give (someone) the brush-off

ilk *noun* TYPE, sort, kind, class, style, character, variety, brand, breed, stamp, description, kidney, disposition

ill *adjective* **1** UNWELL, sick, poorly (*informal*), diseased, funny (*informal*), weak, crook (*Austral & NZ slang*), ailing, queer, frail, feeble, unhealthy, seedy (*informal*), sickly, laid up (*informal*), queasy, infirm, out of sorts (*informal*), dicky (*Brit informal*), nauseous, off-colour, under the weather (*informal*), at death's door, indisposed, peaky, on the sick list (*informal*), valetudinarian, green about the gills, not up to snuff (*informal*) << ANTONYM healthy **2** HARMFUL, bad, damaging, evil, foul, unfortunate, destructive, unlucky, vile, detrimental, hurtful, pernicious, noxious, ruinous, deleterious, injurious, iniquitous, disadvantageous, maleficent << ANTONYM favourable **3** HOSTILE, malicious, acrimonious, cross, harsh, adverse, belligerent, unkind, hurtful, unfriendly, malevolent, antagonistic, hateful, bellicose, cantankerous, inimical, rancorous, ill-disposed << ANTONYM kind **4** BAD, threatening, disturbing, menacing, unlucky, sinister, gloomy, dire, ominous, unhealthy, unfavourable, foreboding, unpromising, inauspicious, unwholesome, unpropitious, bodeful ▷ *noun* **1** PROBLEM, trouble, suffering, worry, trial, injury, pain, hurt, strain, harm, distress, misery, hardship, woe, misfortune, affliction, tribulation, unpleasantness **2** HARM, suffering, damage, hurt, evil, destruction, grief, trauma, anguish, mischief, malice << ANTONYM good ▷ *adverb* **1** BADLY, unfortunately, unfavourably, inauspiciously **2** HARDLY, barely, scarcely, just, only just, by no means, at a push << ANTONYM well **3** ILLEGALLY, criminally, unlawfully, fraudulently, dishonestly, illicitly, illegitimately, unscrupulously, foully **4** INSUFFICIENTLY, badly, poorly, inadequately, imperfectly, deficiently

ill-advised *adjective* MISGUIDED, inappropriate, foolish, rash, reckless, unwise, short-sighted, unseemly, foolhardy, thoughtless, indiscreet, ill-judged, ill-considered, imprudent, wrong-headed, injudicious, incautious, impolitic, overhasty << ANTONYM wise

ill at ease *adjective* UNCOMFORTABLE, nervous, tense, strange, wired (*slang*), disturbed, anxious, awkward, uneasy, unsettled, faltering, unsure, restless, out of place, neurotic, self-conscious, hesitant, disquieted, edgy, on edge, twitchy (*informal*), on tenterhooks, fidgety, unquiet, like a fish out of water, antsy (*informal*), unrelaxed, on pins and needles (*informal*) << ANTONYM comfortable

ill-considered *adjective* UNWISE, rash, imprudent, careless, precipitate, hasty, heedless, injudicious, improvident, overhasty

ill-defined *adjective* UNCLEAR, vague, indistinct, blurred, dim, fuzzy, shadowy, woolly, nebulous << ANTONYM clear

illegal *adjective* UNLAWFUL, banned, forbidden, prohibited, criminal, outlawed, unofficial, illicit, unconstitutional, lawless, wrongful, off limits, unlicensed, under-the-table, unauthorized, proscribed, under-the-counter, actionable (*law*), felonious << ANTONYM legal

illegality *noun* CRIME, wrong, felony, criminality, lawlessness, illegitimacy, wrongness, unlawfulness, illicitness

illegible *adjective* INDECIPHERABLE, unreadable, faint, crabbed, scrawled, hieroglyphic, hard to make out, undecipherable, obscure << ANTONYM legible

illegitimacy *noun* **1** BASTARDY, bastardism **2** ILLEGALITY, unconstitutionality, unlawfulness, illicitness, irregularity

illegitimate *adjective* **1** BORN OUT OF WEDLOCK, natural, bastard, love, misbegotten (*literary*), baseborn (*archaic*) **2** UNLAWFUL, illegal, illicit, improper, unconstitutional, under-the-table, unauthorized, unsanctioned << ANTONYM legal **3** INVALID, incorrect, illogical, spurious, unsound

ill-fated *adjective* DOOMED, unfortunate, unlucky, unhappy, blighted, hapless, luckless, ill-starred, star-crossed, ill-omened

ill feeling *noun* HOSTILITY, resentment, bitterness, offence, indignation, animosity, antagonism, enmity, rancour, bad blood, hard feelings, ill will, animus, dudgeon (*archaic*), chip on your shoulder << ANTONYM goodwill

illiberal *adjective* INTOLERANT, prejudiced, bigoted, narrow-minded, small-minded, reactionary, hidebound, uncharitable, ungenerous << ANTONYM tolerant

illicit *adjective* **1** ILLEGAL, criminal, prohibited, unlawful, black-market, illegitimate, off limits, unlicensed, unauthorized, bootleg, contraband, felonious << ANTONYM legal **2** FORBIDDEN, improper, immoral, wrong, guilty, clandestine, furtive

illiteracy *noun* LACK OF EDUCATION, ignorance, benightedness, illiterateness

illiterate *adjective* UNEDUCATED, ignorant, unlettered, unable to read and write, analphabetic << ANTONYM educated

ill-judged *adjective* MISGUIDED, foolish, rash, unwise, short-sighted, ill-advised, ill-considered, wrong-headed, injudicious, overhasty

ill-mannered *adjective* RUDE, impolite, discourteous, coarse, churlish, boorish, insolent, uncouth, loutish, uncivil, ill-bred, badly behaved, ill-behaved, unmannerly << ANTONYM polite

illness *noun* SICKNESS, ill health, malaise, attack, disease, complaint, infection, disorder, bug (*informal*), disability, ailment, affliction, poor health, malady, infirmity, indisposition, lurgy (*informal*)

illogical *adjective* IRRATIONAL, absurd, unreasonable, meaningless, incorrect, faulty, inconsistent, invalid, senseless, spurious, inconclusive, unsound, unscientific, specious, fallacious, sophistical << ANTONYM logical

ill-tempered *adjective* CROSS, irritable, grumpy, irascible, sharp, annoyed, impatient, touchy, bad-tempered, curt, spiteful, tetchy, ratty (*Brit & NZ informal*), testy, chippy (*informal*), choleric, ill-humoured, liverish << ANTONYM good-natured

ill-treat *verb* ABUSE, injure, harm, wrong, damage, harry, harass, misuse, oppress, dump on (*slang, chiefly US*), mishandle, maltreat, ill-use, handle roughly, knock about *or* around

ill-treatment *noun* ABUSE, harm, mistreatment, damage, injury, misuse, ill-use, rough handling

illuminate *verb* 1 LIGHT UP, light, brighten, irradiate, illumine (*literary*) << ANTONYM darken 2 EXPLAIN, interpret, make clear, clarify, clear up, enlighten, shed light on, elucidate, explicate, give insight into << ANTONYM obscure 3 DECORATE, illustrate, adorn, ornament

illuminating *adjective* INFORMATIVE, revealing, enlightening, helpful, explanatory, instructive << ANTONYM confusing

illumination *noun* 1 LIGHT, lighting, lights, ray, beam, lighting up, brightening, brightness, radiance 2 ENLIGHTENMENT, understanding, insight, perception, awareness, revelation, inspiration, clarification, edification ▷ *plural noun* (*chiefly Brit*) LIGHTS, decorations, fairy lights

illusion *noun* 1 DELUSION, misconception, misapprehension, fancy, deception, fallacy, self-deception, false impression, false belief, misbelief 2 FALSE IMPRESSION, feeling, appearance, impression, fancy, deception, imitation, sham, pretence, semblance, fallacy << ANTONYM reality 3 FANTASY, vision, hallucination, trick, spectre, mirage, semblance, daydream, apparition, chimera, figment of the imagination, phantasm, ignis fatuus, will-o'-the-wisp

illusory *or* **illusive** *adjective* UNREAL, false, misleading, untrue, seeming, mistaken, apparent, sham, deceptive, deceitful, hallucinatory, fallacious, chimerical, delusive << ANTONYM real

illustrate *verb* 1 DEMONSTRATE, show, exhibit, emphasize, exemplify, explicate 2 EXPLAIN, describe, interpret, sum up, make clear,

clarify, summarize, bring home, point up, make plain, elucidate 3 ADORN, ornament, embellish

illustrated *adjective* PICTURED, decorated, illuminated, embellished, pictorial, with illustrations

illustration *noun* 1 EXAMPLE, case, instance, sample, explanation, demonstration, interpretation, specimen, analogy, clarification, case in point, exemplar, elucidation, exemplification 2 PICTURE, drawing, painting, image, print, plate, figure, portrait, representation, sketch, decoration, portrayal, likeness, adornment

illustrative *adjective* 1 REPRESENTATIVE, typical, descriptive, explanatory, interpretive, expository, explicatory, illustrational 2 PICTORIAL, graphic, diagrammatic, delineative

illustrious *adjective* FAMOUS, great, noted, celebrated, signal, brilliant, remarkable, distinguished, prominent, glorious, noble, splendid, notable, renowned, eminent, famed, exalted << ANTONYM obscure

ill will *noun* HOSTILITY, spite, dislike, hatred, envy, resentment, grudge, malice, animosity, aversion, venom, antagonism, antipathy, enmity, acrimony, rancour, bad blood, hard feelings, animus, malevolence, unfriendliness << ANTONYM goodwill

image *noun* 1 THOUGHT, idea, vision, concept, impression, perception, conception, mental picture, conceptualization 2 FIGURE OF SPEECH, metaphor, simile, conceit, trope 3 REFLECTION, appearance, likeness, mirror image 4 FIGURE, idol, icon, fetish, talisman 5 REPLICA, copy, reproduction, counterpart, spit (*informal, chiefly Brit*), clone, facsimile, spitting image (*informal*), similitude, Doppelgänger, (dead) ringer (*slang*), double 6 PICTURE, photo, photograph, representation, reproduction, snapshot

imaginable *adjective* POSSIBLE, conceivable, likely, credible, plausible, believable, under the sun, comprehensible, thinkable, within the bounds of possibility, supposable << ANTONYM unimaginable

imaginary *adjective* FICTIONAL, made-up, invented, supposed, imagined, assumed, ideal, fancied, legendary, visionary, shadowy, unreal, hypothetical, fanciful, fictitious, mythological, illusory, nonexistent, dreamlike, hallucinatory, illusive, chimerical, unsubstantial, phantasmal, suppositious, imagal (*psychoanalysis*)

<< ANTONYM real

imagination *noun* **1** CREATIVITY, vision, invention, ingenuity, enterprise, insight, inspiration, wit, originality, inventiveness, resourcefulness **2** MIND'S EYE, fancy

imaginative *adjective* CREATIVE, original, inspired, enterprising, fantastic, clever, stimulating, vivid, ingenious, visionary, inventive, fanciful, dreamy, whimsical, poetical << ANTONYM unimaginative

imagine *verb* **1** ENVISAGE, see, picture, plan, create, project, think of, scheme, frame, invent, devise, conjure up, envision, visualize, dream up (*informal*), think up, conceive of, conceptualize, fantasize about, see in the mind's eye, form a mental picture of **2** BELIEVE, think, suppose, assume, suspect, gather, guess (*informal, chiefly US & Canad*), realize, take it, reckon, fancy, deem, speculate, presume, take for granted, infer, deduce, apprehend, conjecture, surmise

imbalance *noun* UNEVENNESS, bias, inequality, unfairness, partiality, disproportion, lopsidedness, top-heaviness, lack of proportion

imbibe *verb* (*formal*) **1** DRINK, consume, knock back (*informal*), sink (*informal*), swallow, suck, swig (*informal*), quaff **2** ABSORB, receive, take in, gain, gather, acquire, assimilate, ingest

imbue *verb* INSTIL, infuse, steep, bathe, saturate, pervade, permeate, impregnate, inculcate

imitate *verb* **1** COPY, follow, repeat, echo, emulate, ape, simulate, mirror, follow suit, duplicate, counterfeit, follow in the footsteps of, take a leaf out of (someone's) book **2** DO AN IMPRESSION OF, take off (*informal*), mimic, do (*informal*), affect, copy, mock, parody, caricature, send up (*Brit informal*), spoof (*informal*), impersonate, burlesque, personate

imitation *noun* **1** REPLICA, fake, reproduction, sham, forgery, carbon copy (*informal*), counterfeit, counterfeiting, likeness, duplication **2** COPYING, echoing, resemblance, aping, simulation, mimicry **3** IMPRESSION, parody, mockery, takeoff (*informal*), impersonation ▷ *adjective* ARTIFICIAL, mock, reproduction, dummy, synthetic, man-made, simulated, sham, pseudo (*informal*), ersatz, repro, phoney *or* phony (*informal*) << ANTONYM real

imitator *noun* IMPERSONATOR, mimic, impressionist, copycat, echo, follower, parrot (*informal*), copier, carbon copy (*informal*)

immaculate *adjective* **1** CLEAN, impeccable, spotless, trim, neat, spruce, squeaky-clean, spick-and-span, neat as a new pin << ANTONYM dirty **2** PURE, perfect, innocent, impeccable, virtuous, flawless, faultless, squeaky-clean, guiltless, above reproach, sinless, incorrupt << ANTONYM corrupt **3** PERFECT, flawless, impeccable, stainless, faultless, unblemished, unsullied, uncontaminated, unpolluted, untarnished, unexceptionable, undefiled << ANTONYM tainted

immaterial *adjective* IRRELEVANT, insignificant, unimportant, unnecessary, trivial, trifling, inconsequential, extraneous, inconsiderable, of no importance, of no consequence, inessential, a matter of indifference, of little account, inapposite << ANTONYM significant

immature *adjective* **1** YOUNG, adolescent, undeveloped, green, raw, premature, unfinished, imperfect, untimely, unripe, unformed, unseasonable, unfledged **2** CHILDISH, juvenile, infantile, puerile, callow, babyish, wet behind the ears (*informal*), jejune << ANTONYM adult

immaturity *noun* **1** RAWNESS, imperfection, greenness, unpreparedness, unripeness **2** CHILDISHNESS, puerility, callowness, juvenility, babyishness

immeasurable *adjective* INCALCULABLE, vast, immense, endless, unlimited, infinite, limitless, boundless, bottomless, inexhaustible, unfathomable, unbounded, inestimable, measureless, illimitable << ANTONYM finite

immediate *adjective* **1** INSTANT, prompt, instantaneous, quick, on-the-spot, split-second << ANTONYM later **2** CURRENT, present, pressing, existing, actual, urgent, on hand, extant **3** NEAREST, next, direct, close, near, adjacent, contiguous, proximate << ANTONYM far

immediately *adverb* AT ONCE, now, instantly, straight away, directly, promptly, right now, right away, there and then, speedily, without delay, without hesitation, instantaneously, forthwith, pronto (*informal*), unhesitatingly, this instant, on the nail, this very minute, posthaste, tout de suite (*French*), before you could say Jack Robinson (*informal*)

immemorial *adjective* AGE-OLD, ancient, long-standing, traditional, fixed, rooted, archaic, time-honoured, of yore, olden (*archaic*)

immense *adjective* HUGE, great, massive,

vast, large, giant, enormous, extensive, tremendous, mega (*slang*), titanic, infinite, jumbo (*informal*), very big, gigantic, monumental, monstrous, mammoth, colossal, mountainous, stellar (*informal*), prodigious, interminable, stupendous, king-size, king-sized, immeasurable, elephantine, ginormous (*informal*), Brobdingnagian, illimitable, humongous *or* humungous (*US slang*) << ANTONYM tiny

immerse *verb* 1 ENGROSS, involve, absorb, busy, occupy, engage 2 PLUNGE, dip, submerge, sink, duck, bathe, douse, dunk, submerse

immersed *adjective* ENGROSSED, involved, absorbed, deep, busy, occupied, taken up, buried, consumed, wrapped up, bound up, rapt, spellbound, mesmerized, in a brown study

immersion *noun* 1 INVOLVEMENT, concentration, preoccupation, absorption 2 DIPPING, submerging, plunging, ducking, dousing, dunking

immigrant *noun* SETTLER, incomer, alien, stranger, outsider, newcomer, migrant, emigrant

imminent *adjective* NEAR, coming, close, approaching, threatening, gathering, on the way, in the air, forthcoming, looming, menacing, brewing, impending, at hand, upcoming, on the cards, on the horizon, in the pipeline, nigh (*archaic*), in the offing, fast-approaching, just round the corner, near-at-hand << ANTONYM remote

immobile *adjective* MOTIONLESS, still, stationary, fixed, rooted, frozen, stable, halted, stiff, rigid, static, riveted, lifeless, inert, at rest, inanimate, immovable, immobilized, at a standstill, unmoving, stock-still, like a statue, immotile << ANTONYM mobile

immobility *noun* STILLNESS, firmness, steadiness, stability, fixity, inertness, immovability, motionlessness, absence of movement

immobilize *verb* PARALYSE, stop, freeze, halt, disable, cripple, lay up (*informal*), bring to a standstill, put out of action, render inoperative

immoral *adjective* WICKED, bad, wrong, abandoned, evil, corrupt, vicious, obscene, indecent, vile, degenerate, dishonest, pornographic, sinful, unethical, lewd, depraved, impure, debauched, unprincipled, nefarious, dissolute, iniquitous, reprobate, licentious, of easy virtue, unchaste << ANTONYM moral ▷ see **amoral**

immorality *noun* WICKEDNESS, wrong, vice, evil, corruption, sin, depravity, iniquity, debauchery, badness, licentiousness, turpitude, dissoluteness << ANTONYM morality

immortal *adjective* 1 TIMELESS, eternal, everlasting, lasting, traditional, classic, constant, enduring, persistent, abiding, perennial, ageless, unfading << ANTONYM ephemeral 2 UNDYING, eternal, perpetual, indestructible, death-defying, imperishable, deathless << ANTONYM mortal ▷ *noun* 1 HERO, genius, paragon, great 2 GOD, goddess, deity, Olympian, divine being, immortal being, atua (*NZ*)

immortality *noun* 1 ETERNITY, perpetuity, everlasting life, timelessness, incorruptibility, indestructibility, endlessness, deathlessness 2 FAME, glory, celebrity, greatness, renown, glorification, gloriousness

immovable *adjective* 1 FIXED, set, fast, firm, stuck, secure, rooted, stable, jammed, stationary, immutable, unbudgeable 2 INFLEXIBLE, adamant, resolute, steadfast, constant, unyielding, unwavering, impassive, obdurate, unshakable, unchangeable, unshaken, stony-hearted, unimpressionable << ANTONYM flexible

immune ▷▷ **immune from** EXEMPT FROM, free from, let off (*informal*), not subject to, not liable to ▷▷ **immune to** 1 RESISTANT TO, free from, protected from, safe from, not open to, spared from, secure against, invulnerable to, insusceptible to 2 UNAFFECTED BY, not affected by, invulnerable to, insusceptible to

immunity *noun* 1 EXEMPTION, amnesty, indemnity, release, freedom, liberty, privilege, prerogative, invulnerability, exoneration 2 *with* to RESISTANCE, protection, resilience, inoculation, immunization << ANTONYM susceptibility

immunize *verb* VACCINATE, inoculate, protect, safeguard

immutable *adjective* UNCHANGING, fixed, permanent, stable, constant, enduring, abiding, perpetual, inflexible, steadfast, sacrosanct, immovable, ageless, invariable, unalterable, unchangeable, changeless

imp *noun* 1 DEMON, devil, sprite 2 RASCAL, rogue, brat, urchin, minx, scamp, pickle (*Brit informal*), gamin, nointer (*Austral slang*)

impact *noun* 1 EFFECT, influence,

consequences, impression, repercussions, ramifications **2** COLLISION, force, contact, shock, crash, knock, stroke, smash, bump, thump, jolt ▷ *verb* HIT, strike, crash, clash, crush, ram, smack, collide

impair *verb* WORSEN, reduce, damage, injure, harm, mar, undermine, weaken, spoil, diminish, decrease, blunt, deteriorate, lessen, hinder, debilitate, vitiate, enfeeble, enervate << ANTONYM improve

impaired *adjective* DAMAGED, flawed, faulty, defective, imperfect, unsound

impale *verb* PIERCE, stick, run through, spike, lance, spear, skewer, spit, transfix

impart *verb* **1** COMMUNICATE, pass on, convey, tell, reveal, discover, relate, disclose, divulge, make known **2** GIVE, accord, lend, bestow, offer, grant, afford, contribute, yield, confer

impartial *adjective* NEUTRAL, objective, detached, just, fair, equal, open-minded, equitable, disinterested, unbiased, even-handed, nonpartisan, unprejudiced, without fear or favour, nondiscriminating << ANTONYM unfair

impartiality *noun* NEUTRALITY, equity, fairness, equality, detachment, objectivity, disinterest, open-mindedness, even-handedness, disinterestedness, dispassion, nonpartisanship, lack of bias << ANTONYM unfairness

impassable *adjective* BLOCKED, closed, obstructed, impenetrable, unnavigable

impasse *noun* DEADLOCK, stalemate, standstill, dead end, standoff, blind alley (*informal*)

impassioned *adjective* INTENSE, heated, passionate, warm, excited, inspired, violent, stirring, flaming, furious, glowing, blazing, vivid, animated, rousing, fiery, worked up, ardent, inflamed, fervent, ablaze, vehement, fervid << ANTONYM cool

impassive *adjective* UNEMOTIONAL, unmoved, emotionless, reserved, cool, calm, composed, indifferent, self-contained, serene, callous, aloof, stoical, unconcerned, apathetic, dispassionate, unfazed (*informal*), inscrutable, stolid, unruffled, phlegmatic, unfeeling, poker-faced (*informal*), imperturbable, insensible, impassible (*rare*), unexcitable, insusceptible, unimpressible

impatience *noun* **1** IRRITABILITY, shortness, edginess, intolerance, quick temper, snappiness, irritableness << ANTONYM patience **2** EAGERNESS, longing, enthusiasm, hunger, yearning, thirst, zeal, fervour,

ardour, vehemence, earnestness, keenness, impetuosity, heartiness, avidity, intentness, greediness **3** HASTE, hurry, impetuosity, rashness, hastiness

impatient *adjective* **1** CROSS, tense, annoyed, irritated, prickly, edgy, touchy, bad-tempered, intolerant, petulant, ill-tempered, cantankerous, ratty (*Brit & NZ informal*), chippy (*informal*), hot-tempered, quick-tempered, crotchety (*informal*), ill-humoured, narky (*Brit slang*), out of humour **2** IRRITABLE, fiery, abrupt, hasty, snappy, indignant, curt, vehement, brusque, irascible, testy << ANTONYM easy-going **3** EAGER, longing, keen, hot, earnest, raring, anxious, hungry, intent, enthusiastic, yearning, greedy, restless, ardent, avid, fervent, zealous, chafing, vehement, fretful, straining at the leash, fervid, keen as mustard, like a cat on hot bricks (*informal*), athirst << ANTONYM calm

impeach *verb* CHARGE, accuse, prosecute, blame, denounce, indict, censure, bring to trial, arraign

impeachment *noun* ACCUSATION, prosecution, indictment, arraignment

impeccable *adjective* FAULTLESS, perfect, pure, exact, precise, exquisite, stainless, immaculate, flawless, squeaky-clean, unerring, unblemished, unimpeachable, irreproachable, sinless, incorrupt << ANTONYM flawed

impede *verb* HINDER, stop, slow (down), check, bar, block, delay, hold up, brake, disrupt, curb, restrain, hamper, thwart, clog, obstruct, retard, encumber, cumber, throw a spanner in the works of (*Brit informal*) << ANTONYM help

impediment *noun* OBSTACLE, barrier, check, bar, block, difficulty, hazard, curb, snag, obstruction, stumbling block, hindrance, encumbrance, fly in the ointment, millstone around your neck << ANTONYM aid

impel *verb* FORCE, move, compel, drive, require, push, influence, urge, inspire, prompt, spur, stimulate, motivate, oblige, induce, prod, constrain, incite, instigate, goad, actuate << ANTONYM discourage

impending *adjective* LOOMING, coming, approaching, near, nearing, threatening, forthcoming, brewing, imminent, hovering, upcoming, on the horizon, in the pipeline, in the offing

impenetrable *adjective* **1** IMPASSABLE, solid, impervious, thick, dense,

hermetic, impermeable, inviolable, unpierceable << ANTONYM passable
2 INCOMPREHENSIBLE, obscure, baffling, dark, hidden, mysterious, enigmatic, arcane, inexplicable, unintelligible, inscrutable, unfathomable, indiscernible, cabbalistic, enigmatical << ANTONYM understandable

imperative *adjective* URGENT, essential, pressing, vital, crucial, compulsory, indispensable, obligatory, exigent << ANTONYM unnecessary

imperceptible *adjective* UNDETECTABLE, slight, subtle, small, minute, fine, tiny, faint, invisible, gradual, shadowy, microscopic, indistinguishable, inaudible, infinitesimal, teeny-weeny, unnoticeable, insensible, impalpable, indiscernible, teensy-weensy, inappreciable << ANTONYM perceptible

imperceptibly *adverb* INVISIBLY, slowly, subtly, little by little, unobtrusively, unseen, by a hair's-breadth, unnoticeably, indiscernibly, inappreciably

imperfect *adjective* FLAWED, impaired, faulty, broken, limited, damaged, partial, unfinished, incomplete, defective, patchy, immature, deficient, rudimentary, sketchy, undeveloped, inexact << ANTONYM perfect

imperfection *noun* **1** BLEMISH, fault, defect, flaw, stain **2** FAULT, failing, weakness, defect, deficiency, flaw, shortcoming, inadequacy, frailty, foible, weak point **3** INCOMPLETENESS, deficiency, inadequacy, frailty, insufficiency << ANTONYM perfection

imperial *adjective* ROYAL, regal, kingly, queenly, princely, sovereign, majestic, monarchial, monarchal

imperil *verb* ENDANGER, risk, hazard, jeopardize << ANTONYM protect

imperious *adjective* DOMINEERING, dictatorial, bossy (*informal*), haughty, lordly, commanding, arrogant, authoritative, autocratic, overbearing, tyrannical, magisterial, despotic, high-handed, overweening, tyrannous

impermanent *adjective* TEMPORARY, passing, brief, fleeting, elusive, mortal, short-lived, flying, fugitive, transient, momentary, ephemeral, transitory, perishable, fly-by-night (*informal*), evanescent, inconstant, fugacious, here today, gone tomorrow (*informal*)

impersonal *adjective* **1** INHUMAN, cold, remote, bureaucratic **2** DETACHED, neutral, dispassionate, cold, formal, aloof, businesslike << ANTONYM intimate

impersonate *verb* **1** IMITATE, pose as (*informal*), masquerade as, enact, ape, act out, pass yourself off as **2** MIMIC, take off (*informal*), do (*informal*), ape, parody, caricature, do an impression of, personate

impersonation *noun* IMITATION, impression, parody, caricature, takeoff (*informal*), mimicry

impertinent *adjective* **1** RUDE, forward, cheeky (*informal*), saucy (*informal*), fresh (*informal*), bold, flip (*informal*), brazen, sassy (*US informal*), pert, disrespectful, presumptuous, insolent, impolite, impudent, lippy (*US & Canad slang*), discourteous, uncivil, unmannerly << ANTONYM polite
2 INAPPROPRIATE, irrelevant, incongruous, inapplicable << ANTONYM appropriate

imperturbable *adjective* CALM, cool, collected, composed, complacent, serene, tranquil, sedate, undisturbed, unmoved, stoic, stoical, unfazed (*informal*), unflappable (*informal*), unruffled, self-possessed, nerveless, unexcitable, equanimous << ANTONYM agitated

impervious *adjective* **1** UNAFFECTED, immune, unmoved, closed, untouched, proof, invulnerable, unreceptive, unswayable **2** RESISTANT, sealed, impenetrable, invulnerable, impassable, hermetic, impermeable, imperviable

impetuous *adjective* RASH, hasty, impulsive, violent, furious, fierce, eager, passionate, spontaneous, precipitate, ardent, impassioned, headlong, unplanned, unbridled, vehement, unrestrained, spur-of-the-moment, unthinking, unpremeditated, unreflecting << ANTONYM cautious

impetus *noun* **1** INCENTIVE, push, spur, motivation, impulse, stimulus, catalyst, goad, impulsion **2** FORCE, power, energy, momentum

impinge ▷▷ **impinge on** *or* **upon something** INVADE, violate, encroach on, trespass on, infringe on, make inroads on, obtrude on ▷▷ **impinge on** *or* **upon something** *or* **someone** AFFECT, influence, relate to, impact on, touch, touch upon, have a bearing on, bear upon

impish *adjective* MISCHIEVOUS, devilish, roguish, rascally, elfin, puckish, waggish, sportive, prankish

implacable *adjective* RUTHLESS, cruel, relentless, uncompromising, intractable, inflexible, unrelenting, merciless, unforgiving, inexorable, unyielding, remorseless, pitiless, unbending, unappeasable << ANTONYM merciful

implant *verb* 1 INSERT, place, plant, fix, root, sow, graft, embed, ingraft 2 INSTIL, sow, infuse, inculcate, infix

implausible *adjective* IMPROBABLE, unlikely, weak, incredible, unbelievable, dubious, suspect, unreasonable, flimsy, unconvincing, far-fetched, cock-and-bull (*informal*)

implement *verb* CARRY OUT, effect, carry through, complete, apply, perform, realize, fulfil, enforce, execute, discharge, bring about, enact, put into action *or* effect << ANTONYM hinder ▷ *noun* TOOL, machine, device, instrument, appliance, apparatus, gadget, utensil, contraption, contrivance, agent

implementation *noun* CARRYING OUT, effecting, execution, performance, performing, discharge, enforcement, accomplishment, realization, fulfilment

implicate *verb* INCRIMINATE, involve, compromise, embroil, entangle, inculpate << ANTONYM dissociate ▷▷ **implicate something** *or* **someone in something** INVOLVE IN, associate with, connect with, tie up with

implicated *adjective* INVOLVED, suspected, incriminated, under suspicion

implication *noun* 1 SUGGESTION, hint, inference, meaning, conclusion, significance, presumption, overtone, innuendo, intimation, insinuation, signification 2 INVOLVEMENT, association, connection, incrimination, entanglement 3 CONSEQUENCE, result, development, ramification, complication, upshot

implicit *adjective* 1 IMPLIED, understood, suggested, hinted at, taken for granted, unspoken, inferred, tacit, undeclared, insinuated, unstated, unsaid, unexpressed << ANTONYM explicit 2 INHERENT, contained, underlying, intrinsic, latent, ingrained, inbuilt 3 ABSOLUTE, full, complete, total, firm, fixed, entire, constant, utter, outright, consummate, unqualified, out-and-out, steadfast, wholehearted, unadulterated, unreserved, unshakable, unshaken, unhesitating

implicitly *adverb* ABSOLUTELY, completely, utterly, unconditionally, unreservedly, firmly, unhesitatingly, without reservation

implied *adjective* SUGGESTED, inherent, indirect, hinted at, implicit, unspoken,

tacit, undeclared, insinuated, unstated, unexpressed

implore *verb* BEG, beseech, entreat, conjure, plead with, solicit, pray to, importune, crave of, supplicate, go on bended knee to

imply *verb* 1 SUGGEST, hint, insinuate, indicate, signal, intimate, signify, connote, give (someone) to understand 2 INVOLVE, mean, entail, include, require, indicate, import, point to, signify, denote, presuppose, betoken ▷ see **infer**

impolite *adjective* BAD-MANNERED, rude, disrespectful, rough, churlish, boorish, insolent, uncouth, unrefined, loutish, ungentlemanly, ungracious, discourteous, indelicate, uncivil, unladylike, indecorous, ungallant, ill-bred, unmannerly, ill-mannered << ANTONYM polite

import *verb* BRING IN, buy in, ship in, land, introduce ▷ *noun* (*formal*) 1 SIGNIFICANCE, concern, value, worth, weight, consequence, substance, moment, magnitude, usefulness, momentousness 2 MEANING, implication, significance, sense, message, bearing, intention, explanation, substance, drift, interpretation, thrust, purport, upshot, gist, signification

importance *noun* 1 SIGNIFICANCE, interest, concern, matter, moment, value, worth, weight, import, consequence, substance, relevance, usefulness, momentousness 2 PRESTIGE, standing, status, rule, authority, influence, distinction, esteem, prominence, supremacy, mastery, dominion, eminence, ascendancy, pre-eminence, mana (*NZ*)

important *adjective* 1 SIGNIFICANT, critical, substantial, grave, urgent, serious, material, signal, primary, meaningful, far-reaching, momentous, seminal, weighty, of substance, salient, noteworthy << ANTONYM unimportant 2 *often with* **to** VALUED, loved, prized, dear, essential, valuable, of interest, treasured, precious, esteemed, cherished, of concern, highly regarded 3 POWERFUL, leading, prominent, commanding, supreme, outstanding, high-level, dominant, influential, notable, big-time (*informal*), foremost, eminent, high-ranking, authoritative, major league (*informal*), of note, noteworthy, pre-eminent, skookum (*Canad*)

impose ▷▷ **impose on someone** INTRUDE ON, exploit, take advantage of, use, trouble, abuse, bother, encroach on, horn in (*informal*), trespass on, gate-crash (*informal*),

take liberties with, butt in on, presume upon, force yourself on, obtrude on
▷▷ **impose something on** or **upon someone** 1 LEVY, apply, introduce, put, place, set, charge, establish, lay, fix, institute, exact, decree, ordain 2 INFLICT, force, enforce, visit, press, apply, thrust, dictate, saddle (someone) with, foist

imposing adjective IMPRESSIVE, striking, grand, august, powerful, effective, commanding, awesome, majestic, dignified, stately, forcible << ANTONYM unimposing

imposition noun 1 APPLICATION, introduction, levying, decree, laying on 2 INTRUSION, liberty, presumption, cheek (informal), encroachment 3 CHARGE, tax, duty, burden, levy

impossibility noun HOPELESSNESS, inability, impracticability, inconceivability

impossible adjective 1 NOT POSSIBLE, out of the question, impracticable, unfeasible, beyond the bounds of possibility 2 UNACHIEVABLE, hopeless, out of the question, vain, unthinkable, inconceivable, far-fetched, unworkable, implausible, unattainable, unobtainable, beyond you, not to be thought of << ANTONYM possible 3 ABSURD, crazy (informal), ridiculous, unacceptable, outrageous, ludicrous, unreasonable, unsuitable, intolerable, preposterous, laughable, farcical, illogical, insoluble, unanswerable, inadmissible, ungovernable

impostor noun FRAUD, cheat, fake, impersonator, rogue, deceiver, sham, pretender, hypocrite, charlatan, quack, trickster, knave (archaic), phoney or phony (informal)

impotence noun POWERLESSNESS, inability, helplessness, weakness, disability, incompetence, inadequacy, paralysis, inefficiency, frailty, incapacity, infirmity, ineffectiveness, uselessness, feebleness, enervation, inefficacy << ANTONYM powerfulness

impotent adjective POWERLESS, weak, helpless, unable, disabled, incapable, paralysed, frail, incompetent, ineffective, feeble, incapacitated, unmanned, infirm, emasculate, nerveless, enervated << ANTONYM powerful

impoverish verb 1 BANKRUPT, ruin, beggar, break, pauperize 2 DEPLETE, drain, exhaust, diminish, use up, sap, wear out, reduce

impoverished adjective 1 POOR, needy, destitute, ruined, distressed, bankrupt, poverty-stricken, indigent, impecunious, straitened, penurious, necessitous, in reduced or straitened circumstances << ANTONYM rich 2 DEPLETED, spent, reduced, empty, drained, exhausted, played out, worn out, denuded

impracticable adjective UNFEASIBLE, impossible, out of the question, unworkable, unattainable, unachievable << ANTONYM practicable

impractical adjective 1 UNWORKABLE, impracticable, unrealistic, inoperable, impossible, unserviceable, nonviable << ANTONYM practical 2 IDEALISTIC, wild, romantic, unrealistic, visionary, unbusinesslike, starry-eyed << ANTONYM realistic

imprecise adjective INDEFINITE, estimated, rough, vague, loose, careless, ambiguous, inaccurate, sloppy (informal), woolly, hazy, indeterminate, wide of the mark, equivocal, ill-defined, inexact, inexplicit, blurred round the edges << ANTONYM precise

impregnable adjective INVULNERABLE, strong, secure, unbeatable, invincible, impenetrable, unassailable, indestructible, immovable, unshakable, unconquerable << ANTONYM vulnerable

impregnate verb 1 SATURATE, soak, steep, fill, seep, pervade, infuse, permeate, imbue, suffuse, percolate, imbrue (rare) 2 INSEMINATE, fertilize, make pregnant, fructify, fecundate, get with child

impress verb EXCITE, move, strike, touch, affect, influence, inspire, grab (informal), amaze, overcome, stir, overwhelm, astonish, dazzle, sway, awe, overawe, make an impression on ▷▷ **impress something on** or **upon someone** STRESS, bring home to, instil in, drum into, knock into, emphasize to, fix in, inculcate in, ingrain in

impression noun 1 IDEA, feeling, thought, sense, opinion, view, assessment, judgment, reaction, belief, concept, fancy, notion, conviction, suspicion, hunch, apprehension, inkling, funny feeling (informal) 2 EFFECT, influence, impact, sway 3 IMITATION, parody, impersonation, mockery, send-up (Brit informal), takeoff (informal) 4 MARK, imprint, stamp, stamping, depression, outline, hollow, dent, impress, indentation ▷▷ **make an impression** CAUSE A STIR, stand out, make an impact, be conspicuous, find favour, make a hit (informal), arouse comment, excite notice

impressionable *adjective* SUGGESTIBLE, vulnerable, susceptible, open, sensitive, responsive, receptive, gullible, ingenuous << ANTONYM blasé

impressive *adjective* GRAND, striking, splendid, good, great (*informal*), fine, affecting, powerful, exciting, wonderful, excellent, dramatic, outstanding, stirring, superb, first-class, marvellous (*informal*), terrific (*informal*), awesome, world-class, admirable, first-rate, forcible << ANTONYM unimpressive

imprint *noun* MARK, print, impression, stamp, indentation ▷ *verb* ENGRAVE, print, stamp, impress, etch, emboss

imprison *verb* JAIL, confine, detain, lock up, constrain, put away, intern, incarcerate, send down (*informal*), send to prison, impound, put under lock and key, immure << ANTONYM free

imprisoned *adjective* JAILED, confined, locked up, inside (*slang*), in jail, captive, behind bars, put away, interned, incarcerated, in irons, under lock and key, immured

imprisonment *noun* CONFINEMENT, custody, detention, captivity, incarceration, internment, duress

improbable *adjective* 1 DOUBTFUL, unlikely, uncertain, unbelievable, dubious, questionable, fanciful, far-fetched, implausible << ANTONYM probable 2 UNCONVINCING, weak, unbelievable, preposterous << ANTONYM convincing

impromptu *adjective* SPONTANEOUS, improvised, unprepared, off-the-cuff (*informal*), offhand, ad-lib, unscripted, unrehearsed, unpremeditated, extempore, unstudied, extemporaneous, extemporized << ANTONYM rehearsed

improper *adjective* 1 INAPPROPRIATE, unfit, unsuitable, out of place, unwarranted, incongruous, unsuited, ill-timed, uncalled-for, inopportune, inapplicable, unseasonable, inapt, infelicitous, inapposite, malapropos << ANTONYM appropriate 2 INDECENT, vulgar, suggestive, unseemly, untoward, risqué, smutty, unbecoming, unfitting, impolite, off-colour, indelicate, indecorous << ANTONYM decent 3 INCORRECT, wrong, inaccurate, false, irregular, erroneous

impropriety *noun* 1 INDECENCY, vulgarity, immodesty, bad taste, incongruity, unsuitability, indecorum << ANTONYM

propriety 2 LAPSE, mistake, slip, blunder, gaffe, bloomer (*Brit informal*), faux pas, solecism, gaucherie

improve *verb* 1 ENHANCE, better, add to, upgrade, amend, mend, augment, embellish, touch up, ameliorate, polish up << ANTONYM worsen 2 GET BETTER, pick up, look up (*informal*), develop, advance, perk up, take a turn for the better (*informal*) 3 RECUPERATE, recover, rally, mend, make progress, turn the corner, gain ground, gain strength, convalesce, be on the mend, grow better, make strides, take on a new lease of life (*informal*)

improvement *noun* 1 ENHANCEMENT, increase, gain, boost, amendment, correction, heightening, advancement, enrichment, face-lift, embellishment, betterment, rectification, augmentation, amelioration 2 ADVANCE, development, progress, recovery, reformåtion, upswing, furtherance

improvisation *noun* 1 INVENTION, spontaneity, ad-libbing, extemporizing 2 AD-LIB

improvise *verb* 1 DEVISE, contrive, make do, concoct, throw together 2 AD-LIB, invent, vamp, busk, wing it (*informal*), play it by ear (*informal*), extemporize, speak off the cuff (*informal*)

improvised *adjective* UNPREPARED, spontaneous, makeshift, spur-of-the-moment, off-the-cuff (*informal*), ad-lib, unrehearsed, extempore, extemporaneous, extemporized

imprudent *adjective* UNWISE, foolish, rash, irresponsible, reckless, careless, ill-advised, foolhardy, indiscreet, unthinking, ill-judged, ill-considered, inconsiderate, heedless, injudicious, incautious, improvident, impolitic, overhasty, temerarious << ANTONYM prudent

impudence *noun* BOLDNESS, nerve (*informal*), cheek (*informal*), face (*informal*), front, neck (*informal*), gall (*informal*), lip (*slang*), presumption, audacity, rudeness, chutzpah (*US & Canad informal*), insolence, impertinence, effrontery, brass neck (*Brit informal*), shamelessness, sauciness, brazenness, sassiness (*US informal*), pertness, bumptiousness

impudent *adjective* BOLD, rude, cheeky (*informal*), forward, fresh (*informal*), saucy (*informal*), cocky (*informal*), audacious, brazen, shameless, sassy (*US informal*), pert, presumptuous, impertinent, insolent, lippy (*US & Canad slang*), bumptious, immodest, bold-faced << ANTONYM polite

impulse *noun* **1** URGE, longing, desire, drive, wish, fancy, notion, yen (*informal*), instinct, yearning, inclination, itch, whim, compulsion, caprice **2** FORCE, pressure, push, movement, surge, motive, thrust, momentum, stimulus, catalyst, impetus ▷▷ **on impulse** IMPULSIVELY, of your own accord, freely, voluntarily, instinctively, impromptu, off the cuff (*informal*), in the heat of the moment, off your own bat, quite unprompted

impulsive *adjective* INSTINCTIVE, emotional, unpredictable, quick, passionate, rash, spontaneous, precipitate, intuitive, hasty, headlong, impetuous, devil-may-care, unconsidered, unpremeditated << ANTONYM cautious

impunity *noun* IMMUNITY, freedom, licence, permission, liberty, security, exemption, dispensation, nonliability

impure *adjective* **1** UNREFINED, mixed, alloyed, debased, adulterated, admixed **2** IMMORAL, corrupt, obscene, indecent, gross, coarse, lewd, carnal, X-rated (*informal*), salacious, unclean, prurient, lascivious, smutty, lustful, ribald, immodest, licentious, indelicate, unchaste << ANTONYM moral **3** UNCLEAN, dirty, foul, infected, contaminated, polluted, filthy, tainted, sullied, defiled, unwholesome, vitiated, festy (*Austral slang*) << ANTONYM clean

impurity *noun* **1** *often plural* DIRT, pollutant, scum, grime, contaminant, dross, bits, foreign body, foreign matter **2** CONTAMINATION, infection, pollution, taint, filth, foulness, defilement, dirtiness, uncleanness, befoulment **3** IMMORALITY, corruption, obscenity, indecency, vulgarity, prurience, coarseness, licentiousness, immodesty, carnality, lewdness, grossness, salaciousness, lasciviousness, unchastity, smuttiness

impute *verb* ATTRIBUTE, assign, ascribe, credit, refer, accredit

inaccessible *adjective* OUT-OF-REACH, remote, out-of-the-way, unattainable, impassable, unreachable, unapproachable, un-get-at-able (*informal*) << ANTONYM accessible

inaccuracy *noun* **1** IMPRECISION, unreliability, incorrectness, unfaithfulness, erroneousness, inexactness **2** ERROR, mistake, slip, fault, defect, blunder, lapse,

boob (*Brit slang*), literal (*printing*), howler (*informal*), miscalculation, typo (*informal, printing*), erratum, corrigendum, barry *or* Barry Crocker (*Austral slang*)

inaccurate *adjective* INCORRECT, wrong, mistaken, wild, faulty, careless, unreliable, defective, unfaithful, erroneous, unsound, imprecise, wide of the mark, out, inexact, off-base (*US & Canad informal*), off-beam (*informal*), discrepant, way off-beam (*informal*) << ANTONYM accurate

inaction *noun* INACTIVITY, inertia, idleness, immobility, torpor, dormancy, torpidity

inactive *adjective* **1** UNUSED, idle, dormant, latent, inert, immobile, mothballed, out of service, inoperative, abeyant << ANTONYM used **2** IDLE, unemployed, out of work, jobless, unoccupied, kicking your heels << ANTONYM employed **3** LAZY, passive, slow, quiet, dull, low-key (*informal*), sluggish, lethargic, sedentary, indolent, somnolent, torpid, slothful << ANTONYM active

inactivity *noun* IMMOBILITY, unemployment, inaction, passivity, hibernation, dormancy << ANTONYM mobility

inadequacy *noun* **1** SHORTAGE, poverty, dearth, paucity, insufficiency, incompleteness, meagreness, skimpiness, scantiness, inadequateness **2** INCOMPETENCE, inability, deficiency, incapacity, ineffectiveness, incompetency, unfitness, inefficacy, defectiveness, inaptness, faultiness, unsuitableness **3** SHORTCOMING, failing, lack, weakness, shortage, defect, imperfection

inadequate *adjective* **1** INSUFFICIENT, short, scarce, meagre, poor, lacking, incomplete, scant, sparse, skimpy, sketchy, insubstantial, scanty, niggardly, incommensurate << ANTONYM adequate **2** INCAPABLE, incompetent, pathetic, faulty, unfitted, defective, unequal, deficient, imperfect, unqualified, not up to scratch (*informal*), inapt << ANTONYM capable

inadequately *adverb* INSUFFICIENTLY, poorly, thinly, sparsely, scantily, imperfectly, sketchily, skimpily, meagrely

inadvertent *adjective* UNINTENTIONAL, accidental, unintended, chance, careless, negligent, unwitting, unplanned, thoughtless, unthinking, heedless, unpremeditated, unheeding

inadvertently *adverb* UNINTENTIONALLY, accidentally, by accident, mistakenly, unwittingly, by mistake, involuntarily

<< ANTONYM deliberately

inalienable *adjective* SACROSANCT, absolute, unassailable, inherent, entailed (*law*), non-negotiable, inviolable, nontransferable, untransferable

inane *adjective* SENSELESS, stupid, silly, empty, daft (*informal*), worthless, futile, trifling, frivolous, mindless, goofy (*informal*), idiotic, vacuous, fatuous, puerile, vapid, unintelligent, asinine, imbecilic, devoid of intelligence << ANTONYM sensible

inanimate *adjective* LIFELESS, inert, dead, cold, extinct, defunct, inactive, soulless, quiescent, spiritless, insensate, insentient << ANTONYM animate

inaugural *adjective* FIRST, opening, initial, maiden, introductory, dedicatory

inaugurate *verb* 1 INVEST, install, induct, instate 2 OPEN, commission, dedicate, ordain 3 LAUNCH, begin, introduce, institute, set up, kick off (*informal*), initiate, originate, commence, get under way, usher in, set in motion

inauguration *noun* 1 INVESTITURE, installation, induction 2 OPENING, launch, birth, inception, commencement 3 LAUNCH, launching, setting up, institution, initiation

inborn *adjective* NATURAL, inherited, inherent, hereditary, instinctive, innate, intuitive, ingrained, congenital, inbred, native, immanent, in your blood, connate

inbred *adjective* INNATE, natural, constitutional, native, ingrained, inherent, deep-seated, immanent

inbuilt *adjective* INTEGRAL, built-in, incorporated, component

incalculable *adjective* VAST, enormous, immense, countless, infinite, innumerable, untold, limitless, boundless, inestimable, numberless, uncountable, measureless, without number, incomputable

incandescent *adjective* GLOWING, brilliant, shining, red-hot, radiant, luminous, white-hot, Day-Glo, phosphorescent

incantation *noun* CHANT, spell, charm, formula, invocation, hex (*US & Canad informal*), abracadabra, conjuration

incapacitate *verb* DISABLE, cripple, paralyse, scupper (*Brit slang*), prostrate, immobilize, put someone out of action (*informal*), lay someone up (*informal*)

incapacitated *adjective* DISABLED, challenged, unfit, out of action (*informal*), laid up (*informal*), immobilized, indisposed, hors de combat (*French*)

incapacity *noun* INABILITY, weakness, inadequacy, impotence, powerlessness, ineffectiveness, feebleness, incompetency, unfitness, incapability

incarcerate *verb* IMPRISON, confine, detain, lock up, restrict, restrain, intern, send down (*Brit*), impound, coop up, throw in jail, put under lock and key, immure, jail *or* gaol

incarceration *noun* CONFINEMENT, restraint, imprisonment, detention, captivity, bondage, internment

incarnate *adjective* 1 PERSONIFIED, embodied, typified 2 MADE FLESH, in the flesh, in human form, in bodily form

incarnation *noun* EMBODIMENT, manifestation, epitome, type, impersonation, personification, avatar, exemplification, bodily form

incendiary *adjective* INFLAMMATORY, provocative, subversive, seditious, rabble-rousing, dissentious

incense[1] *noun* PERFUME, scent, fragrance, bouquet, aroma, balm, redolence

incense[2] *verb* ANGER, infuriate, enrage, excite, provoke, irritate, gall, madden, inflame, exasperate, rile (*informal*), raise the hackles of, nark (*Brit, Austral & NZ slang*), make your blood boil (*informal*), rub you up the wrong way, make your hackles rise, get your hackles up, make you see red (*informal*)

incensed *adjective* ANGRY, mad (*informal*), furious, cross, fuming, choked, infuriated, enraged, maddened, exasperated, indignant, irate, up in arms, incandescent, steamed up (*slang*), hot under the collar (*informal*), on the warpath (*informal*), wrathful, ireful (*literary*), tooshie (*Austral slang*), off the air (*Austral slang*)

incentive *noun* INDUCEMENT, motive, encouragement, urge, come-on (*informal*), spur, lure, bait, motivation, carrot (*informal*), impulse, stimulus, impetus, stimulant, goad, incitement, enticement << ANTONYM disincentive

inception *noun* BEGINNING, start, rise, birth, origin, dawn, outset, initiation, inauguration, commencement, kickoff (*informal*) << ANTONYM end

incessant *adjective* CONSTANT, endless, continuous, persistent, eternal, relentless, perpetual, continual, unbroken, never-ending, interminable, unrelenting, everlasting, unending, ceaseless, unremitting, nonstop, unceasing << ANTONYM intermittent

incessantly *adverb* ALL THE TIME, constantly, continually, endlessly, persistently, eternally, perpetually, nonstop, ceaselessly, without a break, interminably, everlastingly

incidence *noun* PREVALENCE, frequency, occurrence, rate, amount, degree, extent

incident *noun* **1** DISTURBANCE, scene, clash, disorder, confrontation, brawl, uproar, skirmish, mishap, fracas, commotion, contretemps **2** HAPPENING, event, affair, business, fact, matter, occasion, circumstance, episode, occurrence, escapade **3** ADVENTURE, drama, excitement, crisis, spectacle, theatrics

incidental *adjective* **1** SECONDARY, subsidiary, subordinate, minor, occasional, ancillary, nonessential << ANTONYM essential **2** ACCOMPANYING, related, attendant, contingent, contributory, concomitant

incidentally *adverb* **1** BY THE WAY, in passing, en passant, parenthetically, by the bye **2** ACCIDENTALLY, casually, by chance, coincidentally, fortuitously, by happenstance

incinerate *verb* **1** BURN UP, carbonize **2** CREMATE, burn up, reduce to ashes, consume by fire

incipient *adjective* BEGINNING, starting, developing, originating, commencing, embryonic, nascent, inchoate, inceptive

incision *noun* CUT, opening, slash, notch, slit, gash

incisive *adjective* PENETRATING, sharp, keen, acute, piercing, trenchant, perspicacious << ANTONYM dull

incite *verb* PROVOKE, encourage, drive, excite, prompt, urge, spur, stimulate, set on, animate, rouse, prod, stir up, inflame, instigate, whip up, egg on, goad, impel, foment, put up to, agitate for *or* against << ANTONYM discourage

incitement *noun* PROVOCATION, prompting, encouragement, spur, motive, motivation, impulse, stimulus, impetus, agitation, inducement, goad, instigation, clarion call

inclination *noun* **1** DESIRE, longing, wish, need, aspiration, craving, yearning, hankering **2** TENDENCY, liking, taste, turn, fancy, leaning, bent, stomach, prejudice, bias, affection, thirst, disposition, penchant, fondness, propensity, aptitude, predisposition, predilection, proclivity, partiality, turn of mind, proneness << ANTONYM aversion **3** BOW, bending, nod, bowing

incline *verb* **1** PREDISPOSE, influence, tend, persuade, prejudice, bias, sway, turn, dispose **2** BEND, lower, nod, bow, stoop, nutate (*rare*) ▷ *noun* SLOPE, rise, dip, grade, descent, ramp, ascent, gradient, declivity, acclivity

inclined *adjective* **1** DISPOSED, given, prone, likely, subject, liable, apt, predisposed, tending towards **2** WILLING, minded, ready, disposed, of a mind (*informal*)

inclose ▷ see **enclose**

include *verb* **1** CONTAIN, involve, incorporate, cover, consist of, take in, embrace, comprise, take into account, embody, encompass, comprehend, subsume << ANTONYM exclude **2** COUNT, introduce, make a part of, number among **3** ADD, enter, put in, insert

including *preposition* CONTAINING, with, counting, plus, together with, as well as, inclusive of

inclusion *noun* ADDITION, incorporation, introduction, insertion << ANTONYM exclusion

inclusive *adjective* COMPREHENSIVE, full, overall, general, global, sweeping, all-in, blanket, umbrella, across-the-board, all-together, catch-all (*chiefly US*), all-embracing, overarching, in toto (*Latin*) << ANTONYM limited

incognito *adjective* IN DISGUISE, unknown, disguised, unrecognized, under an assumed name

incoherent *adjective* UNINTELLIGIBLE, wild, confused, disordered, wandering, muddled, rambling, inconsistent, jumbled, stammering, disconnected, stuttering, unconnected, disjointed, inarticulate, uncoordinated << ANTONYM coherent

income *noun* REVENUE, gains, earnings, means, pay, interest, returns, profits, wages, rewards, yield, proceeds, salary, receipts, takings

incoming *adjective* **1** ARRIVING, landing, approaching, entering, returning, homeward << ANTONYM departing **2** NEW, next, succeeding, elected, elect

incomparable *adjective* UNEQUALLED, supreme, unparalleled, paramount, superlative, transcendent, unrivalled, inimitable, unmatched, peerless, matchless, beyond compare

incompatibility *noun* INCONSISTENCY, conflict, discrepancy, antagonism, incongruity, irreconcilability, disparateness, uncongeniality

incompatible *adjective* INCONSISTENT, conflicting, contradictory, unsuitable, disparate, incongruous, discordant, antagonistic, irreconcilable, unsuited, mismatched, discrepant, uncongenial, antipathetic, ill-assorted, inconsonant << ANTONYM compatible

incompetence *noun* INEPTITUDE, inability, inadequacy, incapacity, ineffectiveness, uselessness, insufficiency, ineptness, incompetency, unfitness, incapability, skill-lessness

incompetent *adjective* INEPT, useless, incapable, unable, cowboy (*informal*), floundering, bungling, unfit, unfitted, ineffectual, incapacitated, inexpert, skill-less, unskilful << ANTONYM competent

incomplete *adjective* UNFINISHED, partial, insufficient, wanting, short, lacking, undone, defective, deficient, imperfect, undeveloped, fragmentary, unaccomplished, unexecuted, half-pie (*NZ informal*) << ANTONYM complete

incomprehensible *adjective* 1 UNINTELLIGIBLE << ANTONYM comprehensible 2 OBSCURE, puzzling, mysterious, baffling, enigmatic, perplexing, opaque, impenetrable, inscrutable, unfathomable, above your head, beyond comprehension, all Greek to you (*informal*), beyond your grasp << ANTONYM understandable

inconceivable *adjective* UNIMAGINABLE, impossible, incredible, staggering (*informal*), unbelievable, unthinkable, out of the question, incomprehensible, unheard-of, mind-boggling (*informal*), beyond belief, unknowable, not to be thought of << ANTONYM conceivable

inconclusive *adjective* UNCERTAIN, vague, ambiguous, open, indecisive, unsettled, undecided, unconvincing, up in the air (*informal*), indeterminate

incongruity *noun* INAPPROPRIATENESS, discrepancy, inconsistency, disparity, incompatibility, unsuitability, inaptness, inharmoniousness

incongruous *adjective* INAPPROPRIATE, absurd, out of place, conflicting, contrary, contradictory, inconsistent, unsuitable, improper, incompatible, discordant, incoherent, extraneous, unsuited, unbecoming, out of keeping, inapt, disconsonant << ANTONYM appropriate

inconsequential *adjective* UNIMPORTANT, trivial, insignificant, minor, petty, trifling, negligible, paltry, immaterial, measly, inconsiderable, nickel-and-dime (*US slang*),

of no significance

inconsiderable *adjective* INSIGNIFICANT, small, slight, light, minor, petty, trivial, trifling, negligible, unimportant, small-time (*informal*), inconsequential, exiguous

inconsiderate *adjective* SELFISH, rude, insensitive, self-centred, careless, unkind, intolerant, thoughtless, unthinking, tactless, uncharitable, ungracious, indelicate << ANTONYM considerate

inconsistency *noun* 1 UNRELIABILITY, instability, unpredictability, fickleness, unsteadiness 2 INCOMPATIBILITY, paradox, discrepancy, disparity, disagreement, variance, divergence, incongruity, contrariety, inconsonance

inconsistent *adjective* 1 CHANGEABLE, variable, unpredictable, unstable, irregular, erratic, uneven, fickle, capricious, unsteady, inconstant << ANTONYM consistent 2 INCOMPATIBLE, conflicting, contrary, at odds, contradictory, in conflict, incongruous, discordant, incoherent, out of step, irreconcilable, at variance, discrepant, inconstant << ANTONYM compatible

inconsolable *adjective* HEARTBROKEN, devastated, despairing, desolate, wretched, heartsick, brokenhearted, sick at heart, prostrate with grief

inconspicuous *adjective* 1 UNOBTRUSIVE, hidden, unnoticeable, retiring, quiet, ordinary, plain, muted, camouflaged, insignificant, unassuming, unostentatious << ANTONYM noticeable 2 PLAIN, ordinary, modest, unobtrusive, unnoticeable

incontrovertible *adjective* INDISPUTABLE, sure, certain, established, positive, undeniable, irrefutable, unquestionable, unshakable, beyond dispute, incontestable, indubitable, nailed-on (*slang*)

inconvenience *noun* 1 TROUBLE, difficulty, bother, upset, fuss, disadvantage, disturbance, disruption, drawback, hassle (*informal*), nuisance, downside, annoyance, hindrance, awkwardness, vexation, uphill (*S African*) 2 AWKWARDNESS, unfitness, unwieldiness, cumbersomeness, unhandiness, unsuitableness, untimeliness ▷ *verb* TROUBLE, bother, disturb, upset, disrupt, put (someone) out, hassle (*informal*), irk, discommode, give (someone) bother *or* trouble, make (someone) go out of his way, put (someone) to trouble

inconvenient *adjective* 1 TROUBLESOME, annoying, awkward, embarrassing, disturbing, unsuitable, tiresome, untimely, bothersome, vexatious, inopportune, disadvantageous, unseasonable << ANTONYM convenient **2** DIFFICULT, awkward, unmanageable, cumbersome, unwieldy, unhandy

incorporate *verb* **1** INCLUDE, contain, take in, embrace, integrate, embody, encompass, assimilate, comprise of **2** INTEGRATE, include, absorb, unite, merge, accommodate, knit, fuse, assimilate, amalgamate, subsume, coalesce, harmonize, meld **3** BLEND, mix, combine, compound, consolidate, fuse, mingle, meld

incorporation *noun* MERGER, federation, blend, integration, unifying, inclusion, fusion, absorption, assimilation, amalgamation, coalescence

incorrect *adjective* FALSE, wrong, mistaken, flawed, faulty, unfitting, inaccurate, untrue, improper, erroneous, out, wide of the mark (*informal*), specious, inexact, off-base (*US & Canad informal*), off-beam (*informal*), way off-beam (*informal*) << ANTONYM correct

incorrigible *adjective* INCURABLE, hardened, hopeless, intractable, inveterate, unreformed, irredeemable

increase *verb* **1** RAISE, extend, boost, expand, develop, advance, add to, strengthen, enhance, step up (*informal*), widen, prolong, intensify, heighten, elevate, enlarge, multiply, inflate, magnify, amplify, augment, aggrandize << ANTONYM decrease **2** GROW, develop, spread, mount, expand, build up, swell, wax, enlarge, escalate, multiply, fill out, get bigger, proliferate, snowball, dilate << ANTONYM shrink ▷ *noun* GROWTH, rise, boost, development, gain, addition, expansion, extension, heightening, proliferation, enlargement, escalation, upsurge, upturn, increment, intensification, augmentation, aggrandizement ▷▷ **on the increase** GROWING, increasing, spreading, expanding, escalating, multiplying, developing, on the rise, proliferating

increasingly *adverb* PROGRESSIVELY, more and more, to an increasing extent, continuously more

incredible *adjective* **1** (*informal*) AMAZING, great, wonderful, brilliant, stunning, extraordinary, overwhelming, ace (*informal*), astonishing, staggering, marvellous, sensational (*informal*), mega (*slang*), breathtaking, astounding, far-out (*slang*), prodigious, awe-inspiring, superhuman,

rad (*informal*) **2** UNBELIEVABLE, impossible, absurd, unthinkable, questionable, improbable, inconceivable, preposterous, unconvincing, unimaginable, outlandish, far-fetched, implausible, beyond belief, cock-and-bull (*informal*), not able to hold water

incredulity *noun* DISBELIEF, doubt, scepticism, distrust, unbelief

incredulous *adjective* DISBELIEVING, doubting, sceptical, suspicious, doubtful, dubious, unconvinced, distrustful, mistrustful, unbelieving << ANTONYM credulous

increment *noun* INCREASE, gain, addition, supplement, step up, advancement, enlargement, accretion, accrual, augmentation, accruement

incriminate *verb* IMPLICATE, involve, accuse, blame, indict, point the finger at (*informal*), stigmatize, arraign, blacken the name of, inculpate

incumbent *noun* HOLDER, keeper, bearer, custodian ▷ *adjective* (*formal*) OBLIGATORY, required, necessary, essential, binding, compulsory, mandatory, imperative

incur *verb* SUSTAIN, experience, suffer, gain, earn, collect, meet with, provoke, run up, induce, arouse, expose yourself to, lay yourself open to, bring upon yourself

incurable *adjective* **1** FATAL, terminal, inoperable, irrecoverable, irremediable, remediless **2** INCORRIGIBLE, hopeless, inveterate, dyed-in-the-wool

incursion *noun* FORAY, raid, invasion, penetration, infiltration, inroad, irruption

indebted *adjective* GRATEFUL, obliged, in debt, obligated, beholden, under an obligation

indecency *noun* OBSCENITY, impurity, lewdness, impropriety, pornography, vulgarity, coarseness, crudity, licentiousness, foulness, outrageousness, immodesty, grossness, vileness, bawdiness, unseemliness, indelicacy, smuttiness, indecorum << ANTONYM decency

indecent *adjective* **1** OBSCENE, lewd, dirty, blue, offensive, outrageous, inappropriate, rude, gross, foul, crude, coarse, filthy, vile, improper, pornographic, salacious, impure, smutty, immodest, licentious, scatological, indelicate << ANTONYM decent **2** UNBECOMING, unsuitable, vulgar, improper, tasteless, unseemly, undignified, disreputable, unrefined, discreditable, indelicate, indecorous, unbefitting << ANTONYM proper

indecision *noun* HESITATION, doubt, uncertainty, wavering, ambivalence, dithering (*chiefly Brit*), hesitancy, indecisiveness, vacillation, shilly-shallying (*informal*), irresolution

indecisive *adjective* **1** HESITATING, uncertain, wavering, doubtful, faltering, tentative, undecided, dithering (*chiefly Brit*), vacillating, in two minds (*informal*), undetermined, pussyfooting (*informal*), irresolute << ANTONYM decisive **2** INCONCLUSIVE, unclear, undecided, indefinite, indeterminate << ANTONYM conclusive

indeed *adverb* **1** CERTAINLY, yes, definitely, surely, truly, absolutely, undoubtedly, positively, decidedly, without doubt, undeniably, without question, unequivocally, indisputably, assuredly, doubtlessly **2** REALLY, actually, in fact, certainly, undoubtedly, genuinely, in reality, to be sure, in truth, categorically, verily (*archaic*), in actuality, in point of fact, veritably

indefatigable *adjective* TIRELESS, dogged, persevering, patient, relentless, diligent, inexhaustible, unremitting, assiduous, unflagging, untiring, sedulous, pertinacious, unwearying, unwearied

indefensible *adjective* UNFORGIVABLE, wrong, inexcusable, unjustifiable, untenable, unpardonable, insupportable, unwarrantable << ANTONYM defensible

indefinite *adjective* **1** UNCERTAIN, general, vague, unclear, unsettled, loose, unlimited, evasive, indeterminate, imprecise, undefined, equivocal, ill-defined, indistinct, undetermined, inexact, unfixed, oracular << ANTONYM settled **2** UNCLEAR, unknown, uncertain, obscure, doubtful, ambiguous, indeterminate, imprecise, undefined, ill-defined, indistinct, undetermined, inexact, unfixed << ANTONYM specific

indefinitely *adverb* ENDLESSLY, continually, for ever, ad infinitum, sine die (*Latin*), till the cows come home (*informal*)

indelible *adjective* PERMANENT, lasting, enduring, ingrained, indestructible, ineradicable, ineffaceable, inexpungible, inextirpable << ANTONYM temporary

indemnify *verb* **1** INSURE, protect, guarantee, secure, endorse, underwrite **2** COMPENSATE, pay, reimburse, satisfy, repair, repay, requite, remunerate

indemnity *noun* **1** INSURANCE, security, guarantee, protection **2** COMPENSATION, remuneration, reparation, satisfaction, redress, restitution, reimbursement, requital **3** (*law*) EXEMPTION, immunity, impunity, privilege

indent *verb* **1** NOTCH, cut, score, mark, nick, pink, scallop, dint, serrate **2** ORDER, request, ask for, requisition

indentation *noun* NOTCH, cut, nick, depression, pit, dip, bash (*informal*), hollow, dent, jag, dimple

independence *noun* FREEDOM, liberty, autonomy, separation, sovereignty, self-determination, self-government, self-rule, self-sufficiency, self-reliance, home rule, autarchy, rangatiratanga (*NZ*) << ANTONYM subjugation

independent *adjective* **1** SEPARATE, unrelated, unconnected, unattached, uncontrolled, unconstrained << ANTONYM controlled **2** SELF-SUFFICIENT, free, liberated, unconventional, self-contained, individualistic, unaided, self-reliant, self-supporting **3** SELF-GOVERNING, free, autonomous, separated, liberated, sovereign, self-determining, nonaligned, decontrolled, autarchic << ANTONYM subject

independently *adverb* SEPARATELY, alone, solo, on your own, by yourself, unaided, individually, autonomously, under your own steam

indescribable *adjective* UNUTTERABLE, indefinable, beyond words, ineffable, inexpressible, beyond description, incommunicable, beggaring description

indestructible *adjective* PERMANENT, durable, unbreakable, lasting, enduring, abiding, immortal, everlasting, indelible, incorruptible, imperishable, indissoluble, unfading, nonperishable << ANTONYM breakable

indeterminate *adjective* UNCERTAIN, indefinite, unspecified, vague, inconclusive, imprecise, undefined, undetermined, inexact, unfixed, unstipulated << ANTONYM fixed

index *noun* INDICATION, guide, sign, mark, note, evidence, signal, symptom, hint, clue, token

indicate *verb* **1** SHOW, suggest, reveal, display, signal, demonstrate, point to, imply, disclose, manifest, signify, denote, bespeak, make known, be symptomatic of, evince, betoken **2** IMPLY, suggest, hint, intimate, signify, insinuate, give someone to understand **3** POINT TO, point out, specify, gesture towards, designate **4** REGISTER, show, record, mark, read, express, display, demonstrate

indication *noun* SIGN, mark, evidence, warning, note, signal, suggestion, symptom, hint, clue, manifestation, omen, inkling, portent, intimation, forewarning, wake-up call

indicative *adjective* SUGGESTIVE, significant, symptomatic, pointing to, exhibitive, indicatory, indicial

indicator *noun* SIGN, mark, measure, guide, display, index, signal, symbol, meter, gauge, marker, benchmark, pointer, signpost, barometer

indict *verb* CHARGE, accuse, prosecute, summon, impeach, arraign, serve with a summons

indictment *noun* CHARGE, allegation, prosecution, accusation, impeachment, summons, arraignment

indifference *noun* **1** DISREGARD, apathy, lack of interest, negligence, detachment, coolness, carelessness, coldness, nonchalance, callousness, aloofness, inattention, unconcern, absence of feeling, heedlessness << ANTONYM concern **2** IRRELEVANCE, insignificance, triviality, unimportance

indifferent *adjective* **1** UNCONCERNED, distant, detached, cold, cool, regardless, careless, callous, aloof, unimpressed, unmoved, unsympathetic, impervious, uncaring, uninterested, apathetic, unresponsive, heedless, inattentive << ANTONYM concerned **2** MEDIOCRE, middling, average, fair, ordinary, moderate, insignificant, unimportant, so-so (*informal*), immaterial, passable, undistinguished, uninspired, of no consequence, no great shakes (*informal*), half-pie (*NZ informal*) << ANTONYM excellent

indigenous *adjective* NATIVE, original, aboriginal, home-grown, autochthonous

indigent *adjective* (*formal*) DESTITUTE, poor, impoverished, needy, penniless, poverty-stricken, down and out, in want, down at heel (*informal*), impecunious, dirt-poor, straitened, on the breadline, short, flat broke (*informal*), penurious, necessitous << ANTONYM wealthy

indigestion *noun* UPSET STOMACH, heartburn, dyspepsia, dyspepsy

indignant *adjective* RESENTFUL, angry, mad (*informal*), heated, provoked, furious, annoyed, hacked (off) (*US slang*), sore

(*informal*), fuming (*informal*), choked, incensed, disgruntled, exasperated, irate, livid (*informal*), seeing red (*informal*), miffed (*informal*), riled, up in arms (*informal*), peeved (*informal*), in a huff, hot under the collar (*informal*), huffy (*informal*), wrathful, narked (*Brit, Austral & NZ slang*), in high dudgeon, tooshie (*Austral slang*), off the air (*Austral slang*)

indignation *noun* RESENTMENT, anger, rage, fury, wrath, ire (*literary*), exasperation, pique, umbrage, righteous anger

indignity *noun* HUMILIATION, abuse, outrage, injury, slight, insult, snub, reproach, affront, disrespect, dishonour, opprobrium, obloquy, contumely

indirect *adjective* **1** RELATED, accompanying, secondary, subsidiary, contingent, collateral, incidental, unintended, ancillary, concomitant **2** CIRCUITOUS, winding, roundabout, curving, wandering, rambling, deviant, meandering, tortuous, zigzag, long-drawn-out, circumlocutory << ANTONYM direct

indirectly *adverb* **1** BY IMPLICATION, in a roundabout way, circumlocutorily **2** OBLIQUELY, in a roundabout way, evasively, not in so many words, circuitously, periphrastically

indiscreet *adjective* TACTLESS, foolish, rash, reckless, unwise, hasty, ill-advised, unthinking, ill-judged, ill-considered, imprudent, heedless, injudicious, incautious, undiplomatic, impolitic << ANTONYM discreet

indiscretion *noun* **1** FOLLY, foolishness, recklessness, imprudence, rashness, tactlessness, gaucherie **2** MISTAKE, slip, error, lapse, folly, boob (*Brit slang*), gaffe, bloomer (*Brit informal*), faux pas, barry *or* Barry Crocker (*Austral slang*)

indiscriminate *adjective* RANDOM, general, wholesale, mixed, sweeping, confused, chaotic, careless, mingled, jumbled, miscellaneous, promiscuous, motley, haphazard, uncritical, aimless, desultory, hit or miss (*informal*), higgledy-piggledy (*informal*), undiscriminating, unsystematic, unselective, undistinguishable, unmethodical, scattershot << ANTONYM systematic

indispensable *adjective* ESSENTIAL, necessary, needed, key, vital, crucial, imperative, requisite, needful, must-have << ANTONYM dispensable

indistinct *adjective* **1** UNCLEAR, confused, obscure, faint, blurred, vague, doubtful, ambiguous, fuzzy, shadowy, indefinite, misty, hazy, unintelligible, indistinguishable, indeterminate, bleary, undefined, out of focus, ill-defined, indiscernible << ANTONYM distinct **2** MUFFLED, confused, faint, dim, weak, indistinguishable, indiscernible

indistinguishable *adjective* IDENTICAL, the same, cut from the same cloth, like as two peas in a pod (*informal*)

individual *adjective* **1** SEPARATE, single, independent, isolated, lone, solitary, discrete << ANTONYM collective **2** UNIQUE, special, fresh, novel, exclusive, distinct, singular, idiosyncratic, unorthodox << ANTONYM conventional ▷ *noun* PERSON, being, human, party, body (*informal*), type, unit, character, soul, creature, human being, mortal, personage, living soul

individualism *noun* INDEPENDENCE, self-interest, originality, self-reliance, egoism, egocentricity, self-direction, freethinking

individualist *noun* MAVERICK, nonconformist, independent, original, loner, lone wolf, freethinker

individuality *noun* CHARACTER, personality, uniqueness, distinction, distinctiveness, originality, peculiarity, singularity, separateness, discreteness

individually *adverb* SEPARATELY, independently, singly, one by one, one at a time, severally

indoctrinate *verb* BRAINWASH, school, train, teach, drill, initiate, instruct, imbue

indoctrination *noun* BRAINWASHING, schooling, training, instruction, drilling, inculcation

indomitable *adjective* INVINCIBLE, resolute, steadfast, set, staunch, unbeatable, unyielding, unflinching, unconquerable, untameable << ANTONYM weak

indorse ▷ see **endorse**

indorsement ▷ see **endorsement**

induce *verb* **1** CAUSE, produce, create, begin, effect, lead to, occasion, generate, provoke, motivate, set off, bring about, give rise to, precipitate, incite, instigate, engender, set in motion << ANTONYM prevent **2** PERSUADE, encourage, influence, get, move, press, draw, convince, urge, prompt, sway, entice, coax, incite, impel, talk someone into, prevail upon, actuate << ANTONYM dissuade

inducement *noun* INCENTIVE, motive, cause,

influence, reward, come-on (*informal*), spur, consideration, attraction, lure, bait, carrot (*informal*), encouragement, impulse, stimulus, incitement, clarion call

induct *verb* INSTALL, admit, introduce, allow, swear, initiate, inaugurate

induction *noun* INSTALLATION, institution, introduction, initiation, inauguration, investiture

indulge *verb* **1** GRATIFY, satisfy, fulfil, feed, give way to, yield to, cater to, pander to, regale, gladden, satiate **2** SPOIL, pamper, cosset, baby, favour, humour, give in to, coddle, spoon-feed, mollycoddle, fawn on, overindulge ▷▷ **indulge yourself** TREAT YOURSELF, splash out, spoil yourself, luxuriate in something, overindulge yourself

indulgence *noun* **1** LUXURY, treat, extravagance, favour, privilege **2** LENIENCY, pampering, spoiling, kindness, fondness, permissiveness, partiality **3** INTEMPERANCE, excess, extravagance, debauchery, dissipation, overindulgence, prodigality, immoderation, dissoluteness, intemperateness << ANTONYM temperance **4** GRATIFICATION, satisfaction, fulfilment, appeasement, satiation

indulgent *adjective* LENIENT, liberal, kind, kindly, understanding, gentle, tender, mild, fond, favourable, tolerant, gratifying, easy-going, compliant, permissive, forbearing << ANTONYM strict

industrialist *noun* CAPITALIST, tycoon, magnate, boss, producer, manufacturer, baron, financier, captain of industry, big businessman

industrious *adjective* HARD-WORKING, diligent, active, busy, steady, productive, energetic, conscientious, tireless, zealous, laborious, assiduous, sedulous << ANTONYM lazy

industry *noun* **1** BUSINESS, production, manufacturing, trade, trading, commerce, commercial enterprise **2** TRADE, world, business, service, line, field, craft, profession, occupation **3** DILIGENCE, effort, labour, hard work, trouble, activity, application, striving, endeavour, toil, vigour, zeal, persistence, assiduity, tirelessness

ineffable *adjective* INDESCRIBABLE, unspeakable, indefinable, beyond words, unutterable, inexpressible, incommunicable

ineffective *adjective* **1** UNPRODUCTIVE, useless, futile, vain, unsuccessful, pointless, fruitless, to no avail, ineffectual, unprofitable, to no effect, unavailing, unfruitful, profitless, bootless, inefficacious << ANTONYM effective **2** INEFFICIENT, inadequate, useless, poor, weak, pathetic, powerless, unfit, feeble, worthless, inept, impotent, ineffectual

ineffectual *adjective* **1** UNPRODUCTIVE, useless, ineffective, vain, unsuccessful, pointless, futile, fruitless, to no avail, unprofitable, to no effect, unavailing, unfruitful, profitless, bootless, inefficacious **2** INEFFICIENT, useless, powerless, poor, weak, inadequate, pathetic, unfit, ineffective, feeble, worthless, inept, impotent

inefficiency *noun* INCOMPETENCE, slackness, sloppiness, disorganization, carelessness

inefficient *adjective* **1** WASTEFUL, uneconomical, profligate, ruinous, improvident, unthrifty, inefficacious **2** INCOMPETENT, incapable, inept, weak, bungling, feeble, sloppy, ineffectual, disorganized, slipshod, inexpert << ANTONYM efficient

ineligible *adjective* UNQUALIFIED, ruled out, unacceptable, disqualified, incompetent (*law*), unfit, unfitted, unsuitable, undesirable, objectionable, unequipped

inept *adjective* **1** INCOMPETENT, bungling, clumsy, cowboy (*informal*), awkward, bumbling, gauche, cack-handed (*informal*), inexpert, maladroit, unskilful, unhandy, unworkmanlike << ANTONYM competent **2** UNSUITABLE, inappropriate, out of place, ridiculous, absurd, meaningless, pointless, unfit, improper, inapt, infelicitous, malapropos << ANTONYM appropriate

ineptitude *noun* INCOMPETENCE, inefficiency, inability, incapacity, clumsiness, unfitness, gaucheness, inexpertness, unhandiness

inequality *noun* DISPARITY, prejudice, difference, bias, diversity, irregularity, unevenness, lack of balance, disproportion, imparity, preferentiality

inert *adjective* INACTIVE, still, motionless, dead, passive, slack, static, dormant, lifeless, leaden, immobile, inanimate, unresponsive, unmoving, quiescent, torpid, unreactive, slumberous (*chiefly poetic*) << ANTONYM moving

inertia *noun* INACTIVITY, apathy, lethargy, passivity, stillness, laziness, sloth, idleness, stupor, drowsiness, dullness, immobility, torpor, sluggishness, indolence, lassitude, languor, listlessness, deadness, unresponsiveness << ANTONYM activity

inescapable *adjective* UNAVOIDABLE, inevitable, certain, sure, fated, destined, inexorable, ineluctable, ineludible (*rare*)

inevitable *adjective* UNAVOIDABLE, inescapable, inexorable, sure, certain, necessary, settled, fixed, assured, fated, decreed, destined, ordained, predetermined, predestined, preordained, ineluctable, unpreventable << ANTONYM avoidable

inevitably *adverb* UNAVOIDABLY, naturally, necessarily, surely, certainly, as a result, automatically, consequently, of necessity, perforce, inescapably, as a necessary consequence

inexcusable *adjective* UNFORGIVABLE, indefensible, unjustifiable, outrageous, unpardonable, unwarrantable, inexpiable << ANTONYM excusable

inexhaustible *adjective* **1** ENDLESS, infinite, never-ending, limitless, boundless, bottomless, unbounded, measureless, illimitable << ANTONYM limited **2** TIRELESS, undaunted, indefatigable, unfailing, unflagging, untiring, unwearying, unwearied << ANTONYM tiring

inexorable *adjective* UNRELENTING, relentless, implacable, hard, severe, harsh, cruel, adamant, inescapable, inflexible, merciless, unyielding, immovable, remorseless, pitiless, unbending, obdurate, ineluctable, unappeasable << ANTONYM relenting

inexorably *adverb* RELENTLESSLY, inevitably, irresistibly, remorselessly, implacably, unrelentingly

inexpensive *adjective* CHEAP, reasonable, low-priced, budget, bargain, modest, low-cost, economical << ANTONYM expensive

inexperience *noun* UNFAMILIARITY, ignorance, newness, rawness, greenness, callowness, unexpertness

inexperienced *adjective* NEW, unskilled, untrained, green, fresh, amateur, raw, unfamiliar, unused, callow, immature, unaccustomed, untried, unschooled, wet behind the ears (*informal*), unacquainted, unseasoned, unpractised, unversed, unfledged << ANTONYM experienced

inexplicable *adjective* UNACCOUNTABLE, strange, mysterious, baffling, enigmatic, incomprehensible, mystifying, unintelligible, insoluble, inscrutable, unfathomable, beyond comprehension << ANTONYM explicable

inextricably *adverb* INSEPARABLY, totally, intricately, irretrievably, indissolubly, indistinguishably

infallibility *noun* 1 SUPREMACY, perfection, omniscience, impeccability, faultlessness, irrefutability, unerringness 2 RELIABILITY, safety, dependability, trustworthiness, sureness

infallible *adjective* 1 PERFECT, impeccable, faultless, unerring, omniscient, unimpeachable << ANTONYM fallible 2 SURE, certain, reliable, unbeatable, dependable, trustworthy, foolproof, sure-fire (*informal*), unfailing << ANTONYM unreliable

infamous *adjective* NOTORIOUS, base, shocking, outrageous, disgraceful, monstrous, shameful, vile, scandalous, wicked, atrocious, heinous, odious, hateful, loathsome, ignominious, disreputable, egregious, abominable, villainous, dishonourable, nefarious, iniquitous, detestable, opprobrious, ill-famed, flagitious << ANTONYM esteemed

infamy *noun* NOTORIETY, scandal, shame, disgrace, atrocity, discredit, stigma, disrepute, ignominy, dishonour, abomination, opprobrium, villainy, odium, outrageousness, obloquy

infancy *noun* 1 EARLY CHILDHOOD, babyhood 2 BEGINNINGS, start, birth, roots, seeds, origins, dawn, early stages, emergence, outset, cradle, inception << ANTONYM end

infant *noun* BABY, child, babe, toddler, tot, wean (*Scot*), little one, bairn (*Scot*), suckling, newborn child, babe in arms, sprog (*slang*), munchkin (*informal, chiefly US*), neonate, rug rat (*slang*), littlie (*Austral informal*), ankle-biter (*Austral slang*), tacker (*Austral slang*) ▷ *adjective* EARLY, new, developing, young, growing, initial, dawning, fledgling, newborn, immature, embryonic, emergent, nascent, unfledged

infantile *adjective* CHILDISH, immature, puerile, babyish, young, weak << ANTONYM mature

infatuated *adjective* OBSESSED, fascinated, captivated, possessed, carried away, inflamed, beguiled, smitten (*informal*), besotted, bewitched, intoxicated, crazy about (*informal*), spellbound, enamoured, enraptured, under the spell of, head over heels in love with, swept off your feet

infatuation *noun* OBSESSION, thing (*informal*), passion, crush (*informal*), madness, folly, fixation, foolishness

infect *verb* 1 CONTAMINATE, transmit disease to, spread disease to or among 2 POLLUTE,

dirty, poison, foul, corrupt, contaminate, taint, defile, vitiate 3 AFFECT, move, touch, influence, upset, overcome, stir, disturb

infection *noun* DISEASE, condition, complaint, illness, virus, disorder, corruption, poison, pollution, contamination, contagion, defilement, septicity

infectious *adjective* CATCHING, spreading, contagious, communicable, poisoning, corrupting, contaminating, polluting, virulent, defiling, infective, vitiating, pestilential, transmittable

infer *verb* DEDUCE, understand, gather, conclude, derive, presume, conjecture, surmise, read between the lines, put two and two together

inference *noun* DEDUCTION, conclusion, assumption, reading, consequence, presumption, conjecture, surmise, corollary

inferior *adjective* 1 LOWER, junior, minor, secondary, subsidiary, lesser, humble, subordinate, lowly, less important, menial << ANTONYM superior 2 SUBSTANDARD, bad, poor, mean, worse, poorer, pants (*informal*), flawed, rotten, dire, indifferent, duff (*Brit informal*), mediocre, second-class, deficient, imperfect, second-rate, shoddy, low-grade, unsound, downmarket, low-rent (*informal, chiefly US*), for the birds (*informal*), wretched, two-bit (*US & Canad slang*), crappy (*slang*), no great shakes (*informal*), poxy (*slang*), dime-a-dozen (*informal*), bush-league (*Austral & NZ informal*), not much cop (*Brit slang*), tinhorn (*US slang*), half-pie (*NZ informal*), of a sort or of sorts, strictly for the birds (*informal*), bodger or bodgie (*Austral slang*) << ANTONYM excellent ▷ *noun* UNDERLING, junior, subordinate, lesser, menial, minion

inferiority *noun* SUBSERVIENCE, subordination, lowliness, servitude, abasement, inferior status or standing << ANTONYM superiority

infernal *adjective* 1 (*informal*) DAMNED, malevolent, hellish, devilish, accursed, damnable 2 HELLISH, lower, underworld, nether, Stygian, Hadean, Plutonian, chthonian, Tartarean (*literary*) << ANTONYM heavenly

infertile *adjective* 1 STERILE, barren, infecund 2 BARREN, unproductive, nonproductive, unfruitful, infecund << ANTONYM fertile

infertility *noun* STERILITY, barrenness, unproductiveness, unfruitfulness, infecundity

infest *verb* OVERRUN, flood, invade, penetrate,

ravage, swarm, throng, beset, permeate

infested *adjective* OVERRUN, plagued, crawling, swarming, ridden, alive, ravaged, lousy (*slang*), beset, pervaded, teeming

infidel *noun* UNBELIEVER, sceptic, atheist, heretic, agnostic, heathen, nonconformist, freethinker, nonbeliever

infidelity *noun* UNFAITHFULNESS, cheating (*informal*), adultery, betrayal, duplicity, disloyalty, bad faith, perfidy, falseness, faithlessness, false-heartedness

infiltrate *verb* PENETRATE, pervade, permeate, creep in, percolate, filter through to, make inroads into, sneak into (*informal*), insinuate yourself, work or worm your way into

infinite *adjective* 1 VAST, enormous, immense, wide, countless, innumerable, untold, stupendous, incalculable, immeasurable, inestimable, numberless, uncounted, measureless, uncalculable 2 ENORMOUS, total, supreme, absolute, all-embracing, unbounded 3 LIMITLESS, endless, unlimited, eternal, perpetual, never-ending, interminable, boundless, everlasting, bottomless, unending, inexhaustible, immeasurable, without end, unbounded, numberless, measureless, illimitable, without number << ANTONYM finite

infinity *noun* ETERNITY, vastness, immensity, perpetuity, endlessness, infinitude, boundlessness

infirm *adjective* 1 FRAIL, weak, feeble, failing, ailing, debilitated, decrepit, enfeebled, doddery, doddering << ANTONYM robust 2 IRRESOLUTE, weak, faltering, unstable, shaky, insecure, wavering, wobbly, indecisive, unsound, vacillating

inflame *verb* 1 ENRAGE, stimulate, provoke, fire, heat, excite, anger, arouse, rouse, infuriate, ignite, incense, madden, agitate, kindle, rile, foment, intoxicate, make your blood boil, impassion << ANTONYM calm 2 AGGRAVATE, increase, intensify, worsen, exacerbate, fan

inflamed *adjective* SWOLLEN, sore, red, hot, angry, infected, fevered, festering, chafing, septic

inflammable *adjective* FLAMMABLE, explosive, volatile, incendiary, combustible ▷ see **flammable**

inflammation *noun* SWELLING, soreness, burning, heat, sore, rash, tenderness, redness, painfulness

inflammatory *adjective* PROVOCATIVE, incendiary, explosive, fiery, inflaming, insurgent, anarchic, rabid, riotous, intemperate, seditious, rabble-rousing, demagogic, like a red rag to a bull, instigative

inflate *verb* 1 BLOW UP, pump up, swell, balloon, dilate, distend, aerate, bloat, puff up or out << ANTONYM deflate 2 INCREASE, boost, expand, enlarge, escalate, amplify << ANTONYM diminish 3 EXAGGERATE, embroider, embellish, emphasize, enlarge, magnify, overdo, amplify, exalt, overstate, overestimate, overemphasize, blow out of all proportion, aggrandize, hyperbolize

inflated *adjective* EXAGGERATED, excessive, swollen, amplified, hyped, exalted, overblown

inflation *noun* INCREASE, expansion, extension, swelling, escalation, enlargement, intensification

inflection *noun* 1 INTONATION, stress, emphasis, beat, measure, rhythm, cadence, modulation, accentuation 2 (*grammar*) CONJUGATION, declension

inflexibility *noun* OBSTINACY, persistence, intransigence, obduracy, fixity, steeliness

inflexible *adjective* 1 FIXED, set, established, rooted, rigid, immovable, unadaptable 2 OBSTINATE, strict, relentless, firm, fixed, iron, adamant, rigorous, stubborn, stringent, uncompromising, resolute, steely, intractable, inexorable, implacable, steadfast, hard and fast, unyielding, immutable, immovable, unbending, obdurate, stiff-necked, dyed-in-the-wool, unchangeable, brassbound, set in your ways << ANTONYM flexible 3 STIFF, hard, rigid, hardened, taut, inelastic, nonflexible << ANTONYM pliable

inflict *verb* IMPOSE, exact, administer, visit, apply, deliver, levy, wreak, mete or deal out

influence *noun* 1 CONTROL, power, authority, direction, command, domination, supremacy, mastery, ascendancy, mana (NZ) 2 POWER, force, authority, pull (*informal*), weight, strength, connections, importance, prestige, clout (*informal*), leverage, good offices 3 SPELL, hold, power, rule, weight, magic, sway, allure, magnetism, enchantment ▷ *verb* 1 AFFECT, have an effect on, have an impact on, control, concern, direct, guide, impact on, modify, bear upon, impinge upon, act or work upon 2 PERSUADE, move, prompt, urge, counsel, induce, incline, dispose, arouse, sway, rouse, entice, coax, incite, instigate, predispose, impel, prevail upon 3 CARRY WEIGHT WITH, cut any ice with (*informal*), pull strings with (*informal*), bring pressure to bear upon, make yourself felt with

influential *adjective* **1** IMPORTANT, powerful, moving, telling, leading, strong, guiding, inspiring, prestigious, meaningful, potent, persuasive, authoritative, momentous, weighty << ANTONYM unimportant **2** INSTRUMENTAL, important, significant, controlling, guiding, effective, crucial, persuasive, forcible, efficacious

influx *noun* ARRIVAL, flow, rush, invasion, convergence, inflow, incursion, inundation, inrush

infold ▷ see **enfold**

inform *verb* **1** TELL, advise, let someone know, notify, brief, instruct, enlighten, acquaint, leak to, communicate to, fill someone in, keep someone posted, apprise, clue someone in (*informal*), put someone in the picture (*informal*), tip someone off, send word to, give someone to understand, make someone conversant (with) **2** INFUSE, characterize, permeate, animate, saturate, typify, imbue, suffuse ▷▷ **inform on someone** BETRAY, report, denounce, shop (*slang, chiefly Brit*), peach (*slang*), give someone away, incriminate, tell on (*informal*), blow the whistle on (*informal*), grass on (*Brit slang*), double-cross (*informal*), rat on (*informal*), spill the beans on (*informal*), stab someone in the back, nark (*Brit, Austral & NZ slang*), blab about, squeal on (*slang*), snitch on (*slang*), put the finger on (*informal*), sell someone down the river (*informal*), blow the gaff on (*Brit slang*), tell all on, inculpate, dob someone in (*Austral & NZ slang*)

informal *adjective* **1** NATURAL, relaxed, casual, familiar, unofficial, laid-back, easy-going, colloquial, unconstrained, unceremonious **2** RELAXED, easy, comfortable, simple, natural, casual, cosy, laid-back (*informal*), mellow, leisurely, easy-going << ANTONYM formal **3** CASUAL, comfortable, leisure, everyday, simple **4** UNOFFICIAL, irregular, unconstrained, unceremonious << ANTONYM official

informality *noun* FAMILIARITY, naturalness, casualness, ease, relaxation, simplicity, lack of ceremony

information *noun* FACTS, details, material, news, latest (*informal*), report, word, message, notice, advice, knowledge, data, intelligence, instruction, counsel, the score (*informal*), gen (*Brit informal*), dope (*informal*), info (*informal*),

inside story, blurb, lowdown (*informal*), tidings, drum (*Austral informal*)

informative *adjective* INSTRUCTIVE, revealing, educational, forthcoming, illuminating, enlightening, chatty, communicative, edifying, gossipy, newsy

informed *adjective* KNOWLEDGEABLE, up to date, enlightened, learned, primed, posted, expert, briefed, familiar, versed, acquainted, in the picture, up, abreast, in the know (*informal*), erudite, well-read, conversant, au fait (*French*), in the loop, genned up (*Brit informal*), au courant (*French*), keeping your finger on the pulse

informer *noun* BETRAYER, grass (*Brit slang*), sneak, squealer (*slang*), Judas, accuser, stool pigeon, nark (*Brit, Austral & NZ slang*), fizgig (*Austral slang*)

infrequent *adjective* OCCASIONAL, rare, uncommon, unusual, sporadic, few and far between, once in a blue moon << ANTONYM frequent

infringe *verb* BREAK, violate, contravene, disobey, transgress ▷▷ **infringe on** *or* **upon** INTRUDE ON, compromise, undermine, limit, weaken, diminish, disrupt, curb, encroach on, trespass on

infringement *noun* CONTRAVENTION, breach, violation, trespass, transgression, infraction, noncompliance, nonobservance

infuriate *verb* ENRAGE, anger, provoke, irritate, incense, gall, madden, exasperate, rile, nark (*Brit, Austral & NZ slang*), be like a red rag to a bull, make your blood boil, get your goat (*slang*), make your hackles rise, raise your hackles, get your back up, make you see red (*informal*), put your back up << ANTONYM soothe

infuriating *adjective* ANNOYING, irritating, aggravating (*informal*), provoking, galling, maddening, exasperating, irksome, vexatious, pestilential

infuse *verb* BREW, soak, steep, saturate, immerse, macerate

ingenious *adjective* CREATIVE, original, brilliant, clever, masterly, bright, subtle, fertile, shrewd, inventive, skilful, crafty, resourceful, adroit, dexterous << ANTONYM unimaginative

ingenuity *noun* ORIGINALITY, genius, inventiveness, skill, gift, faculty, flair, knack, sharpness, cleverness, resourcefulness, shrewdness, adroitness, ingeniousness << ANTONYM dullness

ingrained *or* **engrained** *adjective* FIXED,

rooted, deep-seated, fundamental, constitutional, inherent, hereditary, in the blood, intrinsic, deep-rooted, indelible, inveterate, inborn, inbred, inbuilt, ineradicable, brassbound

ingratiate *verb* ▷▷ **ingratiate yourself with someone** GET ON THE RIGHT SIDE OF, court, win over, flatter, pander to, crawl to, play up to, get in with, suck up to (*informal*), curry favour with, grovel to, keep someone sweet, lick someone's boots, fawn to, toady to, seek someone's favour, rub someone up the right way (*informal*), be a yes man to, insinuate yourself with

ingratiating *adjective* SYCOPHANTIC, servile, obsequious, crawling, humble, flattering, fawning, unctuous, toadying, bootlicking (*informal*), timeserving

ingredient *noun* COMPONENT, part, element, feature, piece, unit, item, aspect, attribute, constituent

inhabit *verb* LIVE IN, people, occupy, populate, reside in, tenant, lodge in, dwell in, colonize, take up residence in, abide in, make your home in

inhabitant *noun* OCCUPANT, resident, citizen, local, native, tenant, inmate, dweller, occupier, denizen, indigene, indweller

inhabited *adjective* POPULATED, peopled, occupied, held, developed, settled, tenanted, colonized

inhalation *noun* BREATHING, breath, inspiration, inhaling

inhale *verb* BREATHE IN, gasp, draw in, suck in, respire << ANTONYM exhale

inherent *adjective* INTRINSIC, natural, basic, central, essential, native, fundamental, underlying, hereditary, instinctive, innate, ingrained, elemental, congenital, inborn, inbred, inbuilt, immanent, connate << ANTONYM extraneous

inherit *verb* BE LEFT, come into, be willed, accede to, succeed to, be bequeathed, fall heir to

inheritance *noun* LEGACY, estate, heritage, provision, endowment, bequest, birthright, patrimony

inheritor *noun* HEIR, successor, recipient, beneficiary, legatee

inhibit *verb* **1** HINDER, stop, prevent, check, bar, arrest, frustrate, curb, restrain, constrain, obstruct, impede, bridle, stem the flow of, throw a spanner in the works of, hold back *or* in << ANTONYM further **2** PREVENT, stop, bar, frustrate, forbid,

prohibit, debar << ANTONYM allow

inhibited *adjective* SHY, reserved, guarded, withdrawn, frustrated, subdued, repressed, constrained, self-conscious, reticent, uptight (*informal*) << ANTONYM uninhibited

inhibition *noun* **1** SHYNESS, reserve, restraint, hang-up (*informal*), modesty, nervousness, reticence, self-consciousness, timidity, diffidence, bashfulness, mental blockage, timidness **2** OBSTACLE, check, bar, block, barrier, restriction, hazard, restraint, hitch, drawback, snag, deterrent, obstruction, stumbling block, impediment, hindrance, encumbrance, interdict

inhospitable *adjective* **1** BLEAK, empty, bare, hostile, lonely, forbidding, barren, sterile, desolate, unfavourable, uninhabitable, godforsaken **2** UNFRIENDLY, unwelcoming, uncongenial, cool, unkind, xenophobic, ungenerous, unsociable, unreceptive << ANTONYM hospitable

inhuman *adjective* CRUEL, savage, brutal, vicious, ruthless, barbaric, heartless, merciless, diabolical, cold-blooded, remorseless, barbarous, fiendish, pitiless, unfeeling, bestial << ANTONYM humane

inhumane *adjective* CRUEL, savage, brutal, severe, harsh, grim, unkind, heartless, atrocious, unsympathetic, hellish, depraved, barbarous, pitiless, unfeeling, uncompassionate

inhumanity *noun* CRUELTY, atrocity, brutality, ruthlessness, barbarism, viciousness, heartlessness, unkindness, brutishness, cold-bloodedness, pitilessness, cold-heartedness, hardheartedness

inimical *adjective* HOSTILE, opposed, contrary, destructive, harmful, adverse, hurtful, unfriendly, unfavourable, antagonistic, injurious, unwelcoming, ill-disposed << ANTONYM helpful

inimitable *adjective* UNIQUE, unparalleled, unrivalled, incomparable, supreme, consummate, unmatched, peerless, unequalled, matchless, unsurpassable, nonpareil, unexampled

iniquity *noun* WICKEDNESS, wrong, crime, evil, sin, offence, injustice, wrongdoing, misdeed, infamy, abomination, sinfulness, baseness, unrighteousness, heinousness, evildoing << ANTONYM goodness

initial *adjective* OPENING, first, early, earliest, beginning, primary, maiden, inaugural, commencing, introductory, embryonic, incipient, inchoate, inceptive << ANTONYM final

initially *adverb* AT FIRST, first, firstly, originally, primarily, at the start, in the first place, to begin with, at the outset, in the beginning, in the early stages, at *or* in the beginning

initiate *verb* **1** BEGIN, start, open, launch, establish, institute, pioneer, kick off (*informal*), bring about, embark on, originate, set about, get under way, instigate, kick-start, inaugurate, set in motion, trigger off, lay the foundations of, commence on, set going, break the ice on, set the ball rolling on **2** INTRODUCE, admit, enlist, enrol, launch, establish, invest, recruit, induct, instate ▷ *noun* NOVICE, member, pupil, convert, amateur, newcomer, beginner, trainee, apprentice, entrant, learner, neophyte, tyro, probationer, novitiate, proselyte ▷▷ **initiate someone into something** INSTRUCT IN, train in, coach in, acquaint with, drill in, make aware of, teach about, tutor in, indoctrinate, prime in, familiarize with

initiation *noun* **1** INTRODUCTION, installation, inauguration, inception, commencement **2** ENTRANCE, debut, introduction, admission, inauguration, induction, inception, enrolment, investiture, baptism of fire, instatement

initiative *noun* **1** ADVANTAGE, start, lead, upper hand **2** ENTERPRISE, drive, push (*informal*), energy, spirit, resource, leadership, ambition, daring, enthusiasm, pep, vigour, zeal, originality, eagerness, dynamism, boldness, inventiveness, get-up-and-go (*informal*), resourcefulness, gumption (*informal*), adventurousness

inject *verb* **1** VACCINATE, shoot (*informal*), administer, jab (*informal*), shoot up (*informal*), mainline (*informal*), inoculate **2** INTRODUCE, bring in, insert, instil, infuse, breathe, interject

injection *noun* **1** VACCINATION, shot (*informal*), jab (*informal*), dose, vaccine, booster, immunization, inoculation **2** INTRODUCTION, investment, insertion, advancement, dose, infusion, interjection

injunction *noun* ORDER, ruling, command, instruction, dictate, mandate, precept, exhortation, admonition

injure *verb* **1** HURT, wound, harm, break, damage, smash, crush, mar, disable, shatter, bruise, impair, mutilate, maim, mangle, mangulate (*Austral slang*), incapacitate **2** DAMAGE, harm, ruin, wreck, weaken, spoil, impair, crool *or* cruel (*Austral slang*) **3** UNDERMINE, damage, mar, blight, tarnish, blacken, besmirch, vitiate

injured *adjective* **1** HURT, damaged, wounded, broken, cut, crushed, disabled, challenged, weakened, bruised, scarred, crook (*Austral & NZ slang*), fractured, lamed, mutilated, maimed, mangled **2** WRONGED, abused, harmed, insulted, offended, tainted, tarnished, blackened, maligned, vilified, mistreated, dishonoured, defamed, ill-treated, maltreated, ill-used **3** UPSET, hurt, wounded, troubled, bothered, undermined, distressed, unhappy, stung, put out, grieved, hassled (*informal*), disgruntled, displeased, reproachful, cut to the quick

injurious *adjective* HARMFUL, bad, damaging, corrupting, destructive, adverse, unhealthy, detrimental, hurtful, pernicious, noxious, ruinous, deleterious, iniquitous, disadvantageous, baneful (*archaic*), maleficent, unconducive

injury *noun* **1** WOUND, cut, damage, slash, trauma (*pathology*), sore, gash, lesion, abrasion, laceration **2** HARM, suffering, damage, ill, hurt, disability, misfortune, affliction, impairment, disfigurement **3** WRONG, abuse, offence, insult, injustice, grievance, affront, detriment, disservice

injustice *noun* **1** UNFAIRNESS, discrimination, prejudice, bias, inequality, oppression, intolerance, bigotry, favouritism, inequity, chauvinism, iniquity, partisanship, partiality, narrow-mindedness, one-sidedness, unlawfulness, unjustness << ANTONYM justice **2** WRONG, injury, crime, abuse, error, offence, sin, grievance, infringement, trespass, misdeed, transgression, infraction, bad *or* evil deed

inkling *noun* SUSPICION, idea, hint, suggestion, notion, indication, whisper, clue, conception, glimmering, intimation, faintest *or* foggiest idea

inland *adjective* INTERIOR, internal, upcountry

inlet *noun* BAY, creek, cove, passage, entrance, fjord, bight, ingress, sea loch (*Scot*), arm of the sea, firth *or* frith (*Scot*)

innards *plural noun* **1** INTESTINES, insides (*informal*), guts, entrails, viscera, vitals **2** WORKS, mechanism, guts (*informal*)

innate *adjective* INBORN, natural, inherent, essential, native, constitutional, inherited, indigenous, instinctive, intuitive, intrinsic, ingrained, congenital, inbred, immanent, in your blood, connate << ANTONYM acquired

inner *adjective* **1** INSIDE, internal, interior, inward << ANTONYM outer **2** CENTRAL, middle, internal, interior **3** INTIMATE, close, personal, near, private, friendly, confidential, cherished, bosom **4** HIDDEN, deep, secret, underlying, obscure, repressed, esoteric, unrevealed << ANTONYM obvious

innkeeper *noun* PUBLICAN, hotelier, mine host, host *or* hostess, landlord *or* landlady

innocence *noun* **1** NAIVETÉ, simplicity, inexperience, freshness, credulity, gullibility, ingenuousness, artlessness, unworldliness, guilelessness, credulousness, simpleness, trustfulness, unsophistication, naiveness << ANTONYM worldliness **2** BLAMELESSNESS, righteousness, clean hands, uprightness, sinlessness, irreproachability, guiltlessness << ANTONYM guilt **3** CHASTITY, virtue, purity, modesty, virginity, celibacy, continence, maidenhood, stainlessness **4** IGNORANCE, oblivion, lack of knowledge, inexperience, unfamiliarity, greenness, unawareness, nescience (*literary*)

innocent *adjective* **1** NOT GUILTY, in the clear, blameless, clear, clean, honest, faultless, squeaky-clean, uninvolved, irreproachable, guiltless, unoffending << ANTONYM guilty **2** NAIVE, open, trusting, simple, natural, frank, confiding, candid, unaffected, childlike, gullible, unpretentious, unsophisticated, unworldly, credulous, artless, ingenuous, guileless, wet behind the ears (*informal*), unsuspicious << ANTONYM worldly **3** HARMLESS, innocuous, inoffensive, well-meant, unobjectionable, unmalicious, well-intentioned << ANTONYM malicious **4** PURE, stainless, immaculate, moral, virgin, decent, upright, impeccable, righteous, pristine, wholesome, spotless, demure, chaste, unblemished, virginal, unsullied, sinless, incorrupt << ANTONYM impure ▷ *noun* CHILD, novice, greenhorn (*informal*), babe in arms (*informal*), ingénue *or* (*masc.*) ingénu ▷▷ **innocent of** FREE FROM, clear of, unaware of, ignorant of, untouched by, unfamiliar with, empty of, lacking, unacquainted with, nescient of

innocuous *adjective* HARMLESS, safe, innocent, inoffensive, innoxious

innovation *noun* **1** CHANGE, revolution, departure, introduction, variation, transformation, upheaval, alteration **2** NEWNESS, novelty, originality, freshness, modernism, modernization, uniqueness

innovative *adjective* NOVEL, new, original, different, fresh, unusual, unfamiliar, uncommon, inventive, singular, ground-breaking, left-field (*informal*), transformational, variational

innovator *noun* MODERNIZER, introducer, inventor, changer, transformer

innuendo *noun* INSINUATION, suggestion, hint, implication, whisper, overtone, intimation, imputation, aspersion

innumerable *adjective* COUNTLESS, many, numerous, infinite, myriad, untold, incalculable, numberless, unnumbered, multitudinous, beyond number << ANTONYM limited

inordinate *adjective* EXCESSIVE, unreasonable, disproportionate, extravagant, undue, preposterous, unwarranted, exorbitant, unrestrained, intemperate, unconscionable, immoderate << ANTONYM moderate

inorganic *adjective* ARTIFICIAL, chemical, man-made, mineral

inquest *noun* INQUIRY, investigation, probe, inquisition

inquire *or* **enquire** *verb* ASK, question, query, quiz, seek information of, request information of ▷▷ **inquire into** INVESTIGATE, study, examine, consider, research, search, explore, look into, inspect, probe into, scrutinize, make inquiries into

inquiry *or* **enquiry** *noun* **1** QUESTION, query, investigation **2** INVESTIGATION, hearing, study, review, search, survey, analysis, examination, probe, inspection, exploration, scrutiny, inquest **3** RESEARCH, investigation, analysis, examination, inspection, exploration, scrutiny, interrogation

inquisition *noun* INVESTIGATION, questioning, examination, inquiry, grilling (*informal*), quizzing, inquest, cross-examination, third degree (*informal*)

inquisitive *adjective* CURIOUS, questioning, inquiring, peering, probing, intrusive, prying, snooping (*informal*), scrutinizing, snoopy (*informal*), nosy (*informal*), nosy-parkering (*informal*) << ANTONYM uninterested

insane *adjective* **1** MAD, crazy, nuts (*slang*), cracked (*slang*), mental (*slang*), barking (*slang*), crackers (*Brit slang*), mentally ill, crazed, demented, cuckoo (*informal*), deranged, loopy (*informal*), round the bend (*informal*), barking mad (*slang*), out of your mind, gaga (*informal*), screwy (*informal*), doolally (*slang*), off your trolley (*slang*), round the twist (*informal*), of unsound mind, not right in the head, non compos mentis (*Latin*), off your rocker (*slang*), not the full shilling (*informal*), mentally disordered, off the air (*Austral slang*), porangi (*NZ*) << ANTONYM sane 2 STUPID, foolish, daft (*informal*), bizarre, irresponsible, irrational, lunatic, senseless, preposterous, impractical, idiotic, inane, fatuous, dumb-ass (*slang*) << ANTONYM reasonable ▷ see **mad**

insanity *noun* 1 MADNESS, mental illness, dementia, aberration, mental disorder, delirium, craziness, mental derangement, psychiatric disorder, psychiatric illness << ANTONYM sanity 2 STUPIDITY, folly, lunacy, irresponsibility, senselessness, preposterousness << ANTONYM sense

insatiable *adjective* UNQUENCHABLE, greedy, voracious, ravenous, rapacious, intemperate, gluttonous, unappeasable, insatiate, quenchless, edacious << ANTONYM satiable

inscribe *verb* 1 CARVE, cut, etch, engrave, impress, imprint 2 DEDICATE, sign, address

inscription *noun* ENGRAVING, words, lettering, label, legend, saying

inscrutable *adjective* 1 ENIGMATIC, blank, impenetrable, deadpan, unreadable, poker-faced (*informal*), sphinxlike << ANTONYM transparent 2 MYSTERIOUS, incomprehensible, inexplicable, hidden, unintelligible, unfathomable, unexplainable, undiscoverable << ANTONYM comprehensible

insect *noun* BUG, creepy-crawly (*Brit informal*), gogga (*S African informal*)

insecure *adjective* 1 UNCONFIDENT, worried, anxious, afraid, shy, uncertain, unsure, timid, self-conscious, hesitant, meek, self-effacing, diffident, unassertive << ANTONYM confident 2 UNSAFE, dangerous, exposed, vulnerable, hazardous, wide-open, perilous, unprotected, defenceless, unguarded, open to attack, unshielded, ill-protected << ANTONYM safe 3 UNRELIABLE, unstable, unsafe, precarious, unsteady, unsound << ANTONYM secure UNRELIABLE

insecurity *noun* 1 ANXIETY, fear, worry, uncertainty, unsureness << ANTONYM confidence 2 VULNERABILITY, risk, danger, weakness, uncertainty, hazard, peril, defencelessness << ANTONYM safety 3 INSTABILITY, uncertainty, unreliability, precariousness, weakness, shakiness, unsteadiness, dubiety, frailness << ANTONYM stability

insensitive *adjective* UNFEELING, indifferent, unconcerned, uncaring, tough, hardened, callous, crass, unresponsive, thick-skinned, obtuse, tactless, imperceptive, unsusceptible << ANTONYM sensitive ▷▷ **insensitive to** UNAFFECTED BY, immune to, impervious to, dead to, unmoved by, proof against

inseparable *adjective* 1 DEVOTED, close, intimate, bosom 2 INDIVISIBLE, inalienable, conjoined, indissoluble, inseverable

insert *verb* PUT, place, set, position, work in, slip, slide, slot, thrust, stick in, wedge, tuck in

insertion *noun* 1 INCLUSION, introduction, interpolation 2 INSERT, addition, inclusion, supplement, implant, inset

inside *noun* INTERIOR, contents, core, nucleus, inner part, inner side ▷ *plural noun* (*informal*) STOMACH, gut, guts, belly, bowels, internal organs, innards (*informal*), entrails, viscera, vitals ▷ *adjective* 1 INNER, internal, interior, inward, innermost << ANTONYM outside 2 CONFIDENTIAL, private, secret, internal, exclusive, restricted, privileged, classified ▷ *adverb* INDOORS, in, within, under cover

insidious *adjective* STEALTHY, subtle, cunning, designing, smooth, tricky, crooked, sneaking, slick, sly, treacherous, deceptive, wily, crafty, artful, disingenuous, Machiavellian, deceitful, surreptitious, duplicitous, guileful << ANTONYM straightforward

insight *noun* 1 INTELLIGENCE, understanding, perception, sense, knowledge, vision, judgment, awareness, grasp, appreciation, intuition, penetration, comprehension, acumen, discernment, perspicacity 2 *with* **into** UNDERSTANDING, perception, awareness, experience, description, introduction, observation, judgment, revelation, comprehension, intuitiveness

insightful *adjective* PERCEPTIVE, shrewd, discerning, understanding, wise, penetrating, knowledgeable, astute, observant, perspicacious, sagacious

insignia *noun* BADGE, symbol, decoration, crest, earmark, emblem, ensign, distinguishing mark

insignificance *noun* UNIMPORTANCE, irrelevance, triviality, pettiness, worthlessness, meaninglessness, inconsequence, immateriality, paltriness, negligibility << ANTONYM importance

insignificant *adjective* UNIMPORTANT, minor, irrelevant, petty, trivial, meaningless, trifling, meagre, negligible, flimsy, paltry, immaterial, inconsequential, nondescript, measly, scanty, inconsiderable, of no consequence, nonessential, small potatoes, nickel-and-dime (*US slang*), of no account, nugatory, unsubstantial, not worth mentioning, of no moment << ANTONYM important

insincere *adjective* DECEITFUL, lying, false, pretended, hollow, untrue, dishonest, deceptive, devious, hypocritical, unfaithful, evasive, two-faced, disingenuous, faithless, double-dealing, duplicitous, dissembling, mendacious, perfidious, untruthful, dissimulating, Janus-faced << ANTONYM sincere

insinuate *verb* IMPLY, suggest, hint, indicate, intimate, allude

insipid *adjective* **1** TASTELESS, bland, flavourless, watered down, watery, wishy-washy (*informal*), unappetizing, savourless << ANTONYM tasty **2** BLAND, boring, dull, flat, dry, weak, stupid, limp, tame, pointless, tedious, stale, drab, banal, tiresome, lifeless, prosaic, trite, unimaginative, colourless, uninteresting, anaemic, wishy-washy (*informal*), ho-hum (*informal*), vapid, wearisome, characterless, spiritless, jejune, prosy << ANTONYM exciting

insist *verb* **1** PERSIST, press (someone), be firm, stand firm, stand your ground, lay down the law, put your foot down (*informal*), not take no for an answer, brook no refusal, take or make a stand **2** DEMAND, order, urge, require, command, dictate, entreat **3** ASSERT, state, maintain, hold, claim, declare, repeat, vow, swear, contend, affirm, reiterate, profess, avow, aver, asseverate

insistence *noun* **1** DEMAND, urging, command, pressing, dictate, entreaty, importunity, insistency **2** ASSERTION, claim, statement, declaration, contention, persistence, affirmation, pronouncement, reiteration, avowal, attestation

insistent *adjective* **1** EMPHATIC, persistent, demanding, pressing, dogged, urgent, forceful, persevering, unrelenting, peremptory, importunate, exigent **2** PERSISTENT, repeated, constant, repetitive, incessant, unremitting

insolence *noun* RUDENESS, cheek (*informal*), disrespect, front, abuse, sauce (*informal*), gall (*informal*), audacity, boldness, chutzpah (*US & Canad informal*), insubordination, impertinence, impudence, effrontery, backchat (*informal*), incivility, sassiness

(*US informal*), pertness, contemptuousness << ANTONYM politeness

insolent *adjective* RUDE, cheeky, impertinent, fresh (*informal*), bold, insulting, abusive, saucy, contemptuous, pert, impudent, uncivil, insubordinate, brazen-faced << ANTONYM polite

insoluble *adjective* INEXPLICABLE, mysterious, baffling, obscure, mystifying, impenetrable, unaccountable, unfathomable, indecipherable, unsolvable << ANTONYM explicable

insolvency *noun* BANKRUPTCY, failure, ruin, liquidation

insolvent *adjective* BANKRUPT, ruined, on the rocks (*informal*), broke (*informal*), failed, gone bust (*informal*), in receivership, gone to the wall, in the hands of the receivers, in queer street (*informal*)

insomnia *noun* SLEEPLESSNESS, restlessness, wakefulness

insouciance *noun* NONCHALANCE, light-heartedness, jauntiness, airiness, breeziness, carefreeness

inspect *verb* **1** EXAMINE, check, look at, view, eye, survey, observe, scan, check out (*informal*), look over, eyeball (*slang*), scrutinize, give (something or someone) the once-over (*informal*), take a dekko at (*Brit slang*), go over or through **2** CHECK, examine, investigate, study, look at, research, search, survey, assess, probe, audit, vet, oversee, supervise, check out (*informal*), look over, work over, superintend, give (something or someone) the once-over (*informal*), go over or through

inspection *noun* **1** EXAMINATION, investigation, scrutiny, scan, look-over, once-over (*informal*) **2** CHECK, search, investigation, review, survey, examination, scan, scrutiny, supervision, surveillance, look-over, once-over (*informal*), checkup, recce (*slang*), superintendence

inspector *noun* EXAMINER, investigator, supervisor, monitor, superintendent, auditor, censor, surveyor, scrutinizer, checker, overseer, scrutineer

inspiration *noun* **1** IMAGINATION, creativity, ingenuity, talent, insight, genius, productivity, fertility, stimulation, originality, inventiveness, cleverness, fecundity, imaginativeness **2** MOTIVATION, example, influence, model, boost, spur, incentive, revelation, encouragement, stimulus, catalyst, stimulation, inducement,

incitement, instigation, afflatus
<< ANTONYM deterrent **3** INFLUENCE, spur,
stimulus, muse
inspire *verb* **1** MOTIVATE, move, cause,
stimulate, encourage, influence, persuade,
spur, be responsible for, animate, rouse,
instil, infuse, hearten, enliven, imbue, spark
off, energize, galvanize, gee up, inspirit, fire
or touch the imagination of << ANTONYM
discourage **2** GIVE RISE TO, cause, produce,
result in, prompt, stir, spawn, engender
inspired *adjective* **1** BRILLIANT, wonderful,
impressive, exciting, outstanding, thrilling,
memorable, dazzling, enthralling,
superlative, of genius **2** STIMULATED,
possessed, aroused, uplifted, exhilarated,
stirred up, enthused, exalted, elated,
galvanized
inspiring *adjective* UPLIFTING, encouraging,
exciting, moving, affecting, stirring,
stimulating, rousing, exhilarating,
heartening << ANTONYM uninspiring
instability *noun* **1** UNCERTAINTY, insecurity,
weakness, imbalance, vulnerability,
wavering, volatility, unpredictability,
restlessness, fluidity, fluctuation,
disequilibrium, transience, impermanence,
precariousness, mutability, shakiness,
unsteadiness, inconstancy << ANTONYM
stability **2** IMBALANCE, weakness, volatility,
variability, frailty, unpredictability,
oscillation, vacillation, capriciousness,
unsteadiness, flightiness, fitfulness,
changeableness
install *verb* **1** SET UP, put in, place, position,
station, establish, lay, fix, locate, lodge
2 INSTITUTE, establish, introduce, invest,
ordain, inaugurate, induct, instate **3** SETTLE,
position, plant, establish, lodge, ensconce
installation *noun* **1** SETTING UP, fitting,
instalment, placing, positioning,
establishment **2** APPOINTMENT, ordination,
inauguration, induction, investiture,
instatement **3** (*military*) BASE, centre, post,
station, camp, settlement, establishment,
headquarters
instalment *noun* **1** PAYMENT, repayment, part
payment **2** PART, section, chapter, episode,
portion, division
instance *noun* **1** EXAMPLE, case, occurrence,
occasion, sample, illustration, precedent,
case in point, exemplification **2** INSISTENCE,
demand, urging, pressure, stress,
application, request, prompting, impulse,
behest, incitement, instigation, solicitation,

entreaty, importunity ▷ *verb* NAME, mention,
identify, point out, advance, quote, finger
(*informal, chiefly US*), refer to, point to, cite,
specify, invoke, allude to, adduce, namedrop
instant *noun* **1** MOMENT, second, minute,
shake (*informal*), flash, tick (*Brit informal*), no
time, twinkling, split second, jiffy (*informal*),
trice, twinkling of an eye (*informal*), two
shakes (*informal*), two shakes of a lamb's tail
(*informal*), bat of an eye (*informal*) **2** TIME,
point, hour, moment, stage, occasion, phase,
juncture ▷ *adjective* **1** IMMEDIATE, prompt,
instantaneous, direct, quick, urgent, on-
the-spot, split-second **2** READY-MADE, fast,
convenience, ready-mixed, ready-cooked,
precooked
instantaneous *adjective* IMMEDIATE, prompt,
instant, direct, on-the-spot
instantaneously *adverb* IMMEDIATELY,
instantly, at once, straight away, promptly,
on the spot, forthwith, in the same breath,
then and there, pronto (*informal*), in the
twinkling of an eye (*informal*), on the instant,
in a fraction of a second, posthaste, quick as
lightning, in the bat of an eye (*informal*)
instantly *adverb* IMMEDIATELY, at once,
straight away, now, directly, on the spot,
right away, there and then, without delay,
instantaneously, forthwith, this minute,
pronto (*informal*), posthaste, instanter (*law*),
tout de suite (*French*)
instead *adverb* RATHER, alternatively,
preferably, in preference, in lieu, on second
thoughts ▷▷ **instead of** IN PLACE OF, rather
than, in preference to, in lieu of, in contrast
with, as an alternative *or* equivalent to
instigate *verb* PROVOKE, start, encourage,
move, influence, prompt, trigger, spur,
stimulate, set off, initiate, bring about,
rouse, prod, stir up, get going, incite,
kick-start, whip up, impel, kindle, foment,
actuate << ANTONYM suppress
instigation *noun* PROMPTING, urging,
bidding, incentive, encouragement, behest,
incitement
instigator *noun* RINGLEADER, inciter,
motivator, leader, spur, goad, troublemaker,
incendiary, firebrand, prime mover,
fomenter, agitator, stirrer (*informal*),
mischief-maker
instil *or* **instill** *verb* INTRODUCE, implant,
engender, infuse, imbue, impress, insinuate,
sow the seeds, inculcate, engraft, infix
instinct *noun* **1** NATURAL INCLINATION,
feeling, urge, talent, tendency, faculty,

inclination, intuition, knack, aptitude, predisposition, sixth sense, proclivity, gut reaction (*informal*), second sight **2** TALENT, skill, gift, capacity, bent, genius, faculty, knack, aptitude **3** INTUITION, feeling, impulse, gut feeling (*informal*), sixth sense

instinctive *adjective* NATURAL, inborn, automatic, unconscious, mechanical, native, inherent, spontaneous, reflex, innate, intuitive, subconscious, involuntary, visceral, unthinking, instinctual, unlearned, unpremeditated, intuitional << ANTONYM acquired

instinctively *adverb* INTUITIVELY, naturally, automatically, without thinking, involuntarily, by instinct, in your bones

institute *noun* ESTABLISHMENT, body, centre, school, university, society, association, college, institution, organization, foundation, academy, guild, conservatory, fellowship, seminary, seat of learning ▷ *verb* ESTABLISH, start, begin, found, launch, set up, introduce, settle, fix, invest, organize, install, pioneer, constitute, initiate, originate, enact, commence, inaugurate, set in motion, bring into being, put into operation << ANTONYM end

institution *noun* **1** ESTABLISHMENT, body, centre, school, university, society, association, college, institute, organization, foundation, academy, guild, conservatory, fellowship, seminary, seat of learning **2** CUSTOM, practice, tradition, law, rule, procedure, convention, ritual, fixture, rite **3** CREATION, introduction, establishment, investment, debut, foundation, formation, installation, initiation, inauguration, enactment, inception, commencement, investiture

institutional *adjective* CONVENTIONAL, accepted, established, formal, establishment (*informal*), organized, routine, orthodox, bureaucratic, procedural, societal

instruct *verb* **1** ORDER, tell, direct, charge, bid, command, mandate, enjoin **2** TEACH, school, train, direct, coach, guide, discipline, educate, drill, tutor, enlighten, give lessons in **3** TELL, advise, inform, counsel, notify, brief, acquaint, apprise

instruction *noun* **1** ORDER, ruling, command, rule, demand, direction, regulation, dictate, decree, mandate, directive, injunction, behest **2** TEACHING, schooling, training, classes, grounding, education, coaching, lesson(s), discipline, preparation, drilling, guidance, tutoring, tuition, enlightenment, apprenticeship, tutorials, tutelage ▷ *plural noun* INFORMATION, rules, advice, directions, recommendations, guidance, specifications

instructive *adjective* INFORMATIVE, revealing, useful, educational, helpful, illuminating, enlightening, instructional, cautionary, didactic, edifying

instructor *noun* TEACHER, coach, guide, adviser, trainer, demonstrator, tutor, guru, mentor, educator, pedagogue, preceptor (*rare*), master *or* mistress, schoolmaster *or* schoolmistress

instrument *noun* **1** TOOL, device, implement, mechanism, appliance, apparatus, gadget, utensil, contraption (*informal*), contrivance, waldo **2** AGENT, means, force, cause, medium, agency, factor, channel, vehicle, mechanism, organ **3** (*informal*) PUPPET, tool, pawn, toy, creature, dupe, stooge (*slang*), plaything, cat's-paw

instrumental *adjective* ACTIVE, involved, influential, useful, helpful, conducive, contributory, of help *or* service

insubstantial *adjective* **1** FLIMSY, thin, weak, slight, frail, feeble, tenuous << ANTONYM substantial **2** IMAGINARY, unreal, fanciful, immaterial, ephemeral, illusory, incorporeal, chimerical

insufferable *adjective* UNBEARABLE, impossible, intolerable, dreadful, outrageous, unspeakable, detestable, insupportable, unendurable, past bearing, more than flesh and blood can stand, enough to test the patience of a saint, enough to try the patience of Job << ANTONYM bearable

insufficient *adjective* INADEQUATE, incomplete, scant, meagre, short, sparse, deficient, lacking, unqualified, insubstantial, incommensurate << ANTONYM ample

insular *adjective* NARROW-MINDED, prejudiced, provincial, closed, limited, narrow, petty, parochial, blinkered, circumscribed, inward-looking, illiberal, parish-pump << ANTONYM broad-minded

insulate *verb* ISOLATE, protect, screen, defend, shelter, shield, cut off, cushion, cocoon, close off, sequester, wrap up in cotton wool

insult *verb* OFFEND, abuse, injure, wound, slight, outrage, put down, humiliate, libel, snub, slag (off) (*slang*), malign, affront, denigrate, disparage, revile, slander, displease, defame, hurt (someone's) feelings, call names, give offence to << ANTONYM praise ▷ noun 1 JIBE, slight, put-down, abuse, snub, barb, affront, indignity, contumely, abusive remark, aspersion 2 OFFENCE, slight, outrage, snub, slur, affront, rudeness, slap in the face (informal), kick in the teeth (informal), insolence, aspersion

insulting adjective OFFENSIVE, rude, abusive, slighting, degrading, affronting, contemptuous, disparaging, scurrilous, insolent << ANTONYM complimentary

insuperable adjective INSURMOUNTABLE, invincible, impassable, unconquerable << ANTONYM surmountable

insurance noun 1 ASSURANCE, cover, security, protection, coverage, safeguard, indemnity, indemnification 2 PROTECTION, security, guarantee, provision, shelter, safeguard, warranty

insure verb 1 ASSURE, cover, protect, guarantee, warrant, underwrite, indemnify 2 PROTECT, cover, safeguard

insurgent noun REBEL, revolutionary, revolter, rioter, resister, mutineer, revolutionist, insurrectionist ▷ adjective REBELLIOUS, revolutionary, mutinous, revolting, riotous, seditious, disobedient, insubordinate, insurrectionary

insurmountable adjective INSUPERABLE, impossible, overwhelming, hopeless, invincible, impassable, unconquerable

insurrection noun REBELLION, rising, revolution, riot, coup, revolt, uprising, mutiny, insurgency, putsch, sedition

intact adjective UNDAMAGED, whole, complete, sound, perfect, entire, virgin, untouched, unscathed, unbroken, flawless, unhurt, faultless, unharmed, uninjured, unimpaired, undefiled, all in one piece, together, scatheless, unviolated << ANTONYM damaged

intangible adjective ABSTRACT, vague, invisible, dim, elusive, shadowy, airy, unreal, indefinite, ethereal, evanescent, incorporeal, impalpable, unsubstantial

integral adjective 1 ESSENTIAL, basic, fundamental, necessary, component, constituent, indispensable, intrinsic, requisite, elemental << ANTONYM inessential 2 WHOLE, full, complete, entire, intact, undivided << ANTONYM partial

integrate verb JOIN, unite, combine, blend, incorporate, merge, accommodate, knit, fuse, mesh, assimilate, amalgamate, coalesce, harmonize, meld, intermix << ANTONYM separate

integrity noun 1 HONESTY, principle, honour, virtue, goodness, morality, purity, righteousness, probity, rectitude, truthfulness, trustworthiness, incorruptibility, uprightness, scrupulousness, reputability << ANTONYM dishonesty 2 UNITY, unification, cohesion, coherence, wholeness, soundness, completeness << ANTONYM fragility

intellect noun 1 INTELLIGENCE, mind, reason, understanding, sense, brains (informal), judgment 2 (informal) THINKER, intellectual, genius, mind, brain (informal), intelligence, rocket scientist (informal, chiefly US), egghead (informal)

intellectual adjective SCHOLARLY, learned, academic, lettered, intelligent, rational, cerebral, erudite, scholastic, highbrow, well-read, studious, bookish << ANTONYM stupid ▷ noun ACADEMIC, expert, genius, thinker, master, brain (informal), mastermind, maestro, highbrow, rocket scientist (informal, chiefly US), egghead (informal), brainbox, bluestocking (usually disparaging), master-hand, fundi (S African), acca (Austral slang) << ANTONYM idiot

intelligence noun 1 INTELLECT, understanding, brains (informal), mind, reason, sense, knowledge, capacity, smarts (slang, chiefly US), judgment, wit, perception, awareness, insight, penetration, comprehension, brightness, aptitude, acumen, nous (Brit slang), alertness, cleverness, quickness, discernment, grey matter (informal), brain power << ANTONYM stupidity 2 INFORMATION, news, facts, report, findings, word, notice, advice, knowledge, data, disclosure, gen (Brit informal), tip-off, low-down (informal), notification << ANTONYM misinformation

intelligent adjective CLEVER, bright, smart, knowing, quick, sharp, acute, alert, rational, penetrating, enlightened, apt, discerning, knowledgeable, astute, well-informed, brainy (informal), perspicacious, quick-witted, sagacious << ANTONYM stupid

intelligentsia noun INTELLECTUALS, highbrows, literati, masterminds, the learned, eggheads (informal), illuminati

intelligible adjective UNDERSTANDABLE, clear, distinct, lucid, comprehensible << ANTONYM unintelligible

intemperate adjective EXCESSIVE, extreme, over the top (slang), wild, violent, severe, passionate, extravagant, uncontrollable, self-indulgent, unbridled, prodigal, unrestrained, tempestuous, profligate, inordinate, incontinent, ungovernable, immoderate, O.T.T. (*slang*) << ANTONYM temperate

intend *verb* **1** PLAN, mean, aim, determine, scheme, propose, purpose, contemplate, envisage, foresee, be resolved *or* determined, have in mind *or* view **2** *often with* **for** DESTINE, mean, design, earmark, consign, aim, mark out, set apart

intended *adjective* PLANNED, proposed ▷ *noun* (*informal*) BETROTHED, fiancé *or* fiancée, future wife *or* husband, husband- *or* wife-to-be

intense *adjective* **1** EXTREME, great, severe, fierce, serious (*informal*), deep, powerful, concentrated, supreme, acute, harsh, excessive, profound, exquisite, drastic, forceful, protracted, unqualified, agonizing, mother of all (*informal*) << ANTONYM mild **2** FIERCE, close, tough **3** PASSIONATE, burning, earnest, emotional, keen, flaming, consuming, fierce, eager, enthusiastic, heightened, energetic, animated, ardent, fanatical, fervent, heartfelt, impassioned, vehement, forcible, fervid << ANTONYM indifferent

intensely *adverb* **1** VERY, highly, extremely, greatly, strongly, severely, terribly, ultra, utterly, unusually, exceptionally, extraordinarily, markedly, awfully (*informal*), acutely, exceedingly, excessively, inordinately, uncommonly, to the nth degree, to *or* in the extreme **2** DEEPLY, seriously (*informal*), profoundly, passionately

intensify *verb* **1** INCREASE, boost, raise, extend, concentrate, add to, strengthen, enhance, compound, reinforce, step up (*informal*), emphasize, widen, heighten, sharpen, magnify, amplify, augment, redouble << ANTONYM decrease **2** ESCALATE, increase, extend, widen, heighten, deepen, quicken

intensity *noun* **1** FORCE, power, strength, severity, extremity, fierceness **2** PASSION, emotion, fervour, force, power, fire, energy, strength, depth, concentration, excess, severity, vigour, potency, extremity, fanaticism, ardour, vehemence, earnestness, keenness, fierceness, fervency, intenseness

intensive *adjective* CONCENTRATED, thorough, exhaustive, full, demanding, detailed, complete, serious, concerted, comprehensive, vigorous, all-out, in-depth, strenuous, painstaking, all-embracing,

assiduous, thoroughgoing ▷ see **intense**

intent *adjective* ABSORBED, focused, fixed, earnest, committed, concentrated, occupied, fascinated, steady, alert, wrapped up, preoccupied, enthralled, attentive, watchful, engrossed, steadfast, rapt, enrapt << ANTONYM indifferent ▷ *noun* INTENTION, aim, purpose, meaning, end, plan, goal, design, target, object, resolution, resolve, objective, ambition, aspiration << ANTONYM chance ▷▷ **intent on something** SET ON, committed to, eager to, bent on, fixated on, hellbent on (*informal*), insistent about, determined about, resolute about, inflexible about, resolved about ▷▷ **to all intents and purposes** IN EFFECT, essentially, effectively, really, actually, in fact, virtually, in reality, in truth, in actuality, for practical purposes

intention *noun* AIM, plan, idea, goal, end, design, target, wish, scheme, purpose, object, objective, determination, intent

intentional *adjective* DELIBERATE, meant, planned, studied, designed, purposed, intended, calculated, wilful, premeditated, prearranged, done on purpose, preconcerted << ANTONYM unintentional

intentionally *adverb* DELIBERATELY, on purpose, wilfully, by design, designedly

intently *adverb* ATTENTIVELY, closely, hard, keenly, steadily, fixedly, searchingly, watchfully ▷ see **intensely**

inter *verb* BURY, lay to rest, entomb, sepulchre, consign to the grave, inhume, inurn

intercede *verb* MEDIATE, speak, plead, intervene, arbitrate, advocate, interpose

intercept *verb* CATCH, take, stop, check, block, arrest, seize, cut off, interrupt, head off, deflect, obstruct

interchange *noun* EXCHANGE, give and take, alternation, reciprocation ▷ *verb* EXCHANGE, switch, swap, alternate, trade, barter, reciprocate, bandy

interchangeable *adjective* IDENTICAL, the same, equivalent, synonymous, reciprocal, exchangeable, transposable, commutable

intercourse *noun* **1** SEXUAL INTERCOURSE, sex (*informal*), lovemaking, the other (*informal*), congress, screwing (*taboo slang*), intimacy, shagging (*Brit taboo slang*), sexual relations, sexual act, nookie (*slang*), copulation, coitus, carnal knowledge, intimate relations, rumpy-pumpy (*slang*), legover (*slang*), coition, rumpo (*slang*) **2** CONTACT, relationships, communication, association, relations, trade, traffic, connection, truck, commerce, dealings, correspondence, communion, converse, intercommunication

interest *noun* 1 IMPORTANCE, concern, significance, moment, note, weight, import, consequence, substance, relevance, momentousness << ANTONYM insignificance 2 ATTENTION, regard, curiosity, notice, suspicion, scrutiny, heed, absorption, attentiveness, inquisitiveness, engrossment << ANTONYM disregard 3 *often plural* HOBBY, activity, pursuit, entertainment, relaxation, recreation, amusement, preoccupation, diversion, pastime, leisure activity 4 *often plural* ADVANTAGE, good, benefit, profit, gain, boot (*dialect*) 5 *often plural* BUSINESS, concern, matter, affair 6 STAKE, investment ▷ *verb* 1 AROUSE YOUR CURIOSITY, engage, appeal to, fascinate, move, involve, touch, affect, attract, grip, entertain, absorb, intrigue, amuse, divert, rivet, captivate, catch your eye, hold your attention, engross << ANTONYM bore 2 *with* in SELL, persuade to buy ▷▷ **in the interest(s) of** FOR THE SAKE OF, on behalf of, on the part of, to the advantage of

interested *adjective* 1 CURIOUS, into (*informal*), moved, affected, attracted, excited, drawn, keen, gripped, fascinated, stimulated, intent, responsive, riveted, captivated, attentive << ANTONYM uninterested 2 INVOLVED, concerned, affected, prejudiced, biased, partial, partisan, implicated, predisposed

interesting *adjective* INTRIGUING, fascinating, absorbing, pleasing, appealing, attractive, engaging, unusual, gripping, stirring, entertaining, entrancing, stimulating, curious, compelling, amusing, compulsive, riveting, captivating, enthralling, beguiling, thought-provoking, engrossing, spellbinding << ANTONYM uninteresting

interface *noun* CONNECTION, link, boundary, border, frontier ▷ *verb* CONNECT, couple, link, combine, join together

interfere *verb* MEDDLE, intervene, intrude, butt in, get involved, tamper, pry, encroach, intercede, stick your nose in (*informal*), stick your oar in (*informal*), poke your nose in (*informal*), intermeddle, put your two cents in (*US slang*) ▷▷ **interfere with something** *or* **someone** CONFLICT WITH, affect, get in the way of, check, block, clash, frustrate, handicap, hamper, disrupt, cramp, inhibit, thwart, hinder, obstruct, impede, baulk, trammel, be a drag upon (*informal*)

interference *noun* INTRUSION, intervention, meddling, opposition, conflict, obstruction, prying, impedance, meddlesomeness, intermeddling

interfering *adjective* MEDDLING, intrusive, prying, obtrusive, meddlesome, interruptive

interim *adjective* TEMPORARY, provisional, makeshift, acting, passing, intervening, caretaker, improvised, transient, stopgap, pro tem ▷ *noun* INTERVAL, meanwhile, meantime, respite, interregnum, entr'acte

interior *noun* 1 INSIDE, centre, heart, middle, contents, depths, core, belly, nucleus, bowels, bosom, innards (*informal*) 2 (*geography*) HEARTLAND, centre, hinterland, upcountry ▷ *adjective* 1 INSIDE, internal, inner << ANTONYM exterior 2 MENTAL, emotional, psychological, private, personal, secret, hidden, spiritual, intimate, inner, inward, instinctive, impulsive 3 DOMESTIC, home, national, civil, internal

interject *verb* INTERRUPT WITH, put in, interpose, introduce, throw in, interpolate

interjection *noun* EXCLAMATION, cry, ejaculation, interpolation, interposition

interloper *noun* TRESPASSER, intruder, gate-crasher (*informal*), uninvited guest, meddler, unwanted visitor, intermeddler

interlude *noun* INTERVAL, break, spell, stop, rest, halt, episode, pause, respite, stoppage, breathing space, hiatus, intermission, entr'acte

intermediary *noun* MEDIATOR, agent, middleman, broker, entrepreneur, go-between

intermediate *adjective* MIDDLE, mid, halfway, in-between (*informal*), midway, intervening, transitional, intermediary, median, interposed

interminable *adjective* ENDLESS, long, never-ending, dragging, unlimited, infinite, perpetual, protracted, limitless, boundless, everlasting, ceaseless, long-winded, long-drawn-out, immeasurable, wearisome, unbounded << ANTONYM limited

intermission *noun* INTERVAL, break, pause, stop, rest, suspension, recess, interruption, respite, lull, stoppage, interlude, cessation, let-up (*informal*), breathing space, entr'acte

intermittent *adjective* PERIODIC, broken, occasional, recurring, irregular, punctuated, sporadic, recurrent, stop-go (*informal*), fitful, spasmodic, discontinuous << ANTONYM continuous

intern *verb* IMPRISON, hold, confine, detain, hold in custody

internal *adjective* **1** DOMESTIC, home, national, local, civic, in-house, intramural **2** INNER, inside, interior << ANTONYM external **3** EMOTIONAL, mental, private, secret, subjective << ANTONYM revealed

international *adjective* GLOBAL, world, worldwide, universal, cosmopolitan, planetary, intercontinental

Internet *noun* ▷▷ **the Internet** THE INFORMATION SUPERHIGHWAY, the net (*informal*), the web (*informal*), the World Wide Web, cyberspace

interplay *noun* INTERACTION, give-and-take, reciprocity, reciprocation, meshing

interpret *verb* **1** TAKE, understand, read, explain, regard, construe **2** TRANSLATE, convert, paraphrase, adapt, transliterate **3** EXPLAIN, define, clarify, spell out, make sense of, decode, decipher, expound, elucidate, throw light on, explicate **4** UNDERSTAND, read, explain, crack, solve, figure out (*informal*), comprehend, decode, deduce, decipher, suss out (*slang*) **5** PORTRAY, present, perform, render, depict, enact, act out

interpretation *noun* **1** EXPLANATION, meaning, reading, understanding, sense, analysis, construction, exposition, explication, elucidation, signification **2** PERFORMANCE, portrayal, presentation, rendering, reading, execution, rendition, depiction **3** READING, study, review, version, analysis, explanation, examination, diagnosis, evaluation, exposition, exegesis, explication, elucidation

interpreter *noun* TRANSLATOR, linguist, metaphrast, paraphrast

interrogate *verb* QUESTION, ask, examine, investigate, pump, grill (*informal*), quiz, cross-examine, cross-question, put the screws on (*informal*), catechize, give (someone) the third degree (*informal*)

interrogation *noun* QUESTIONING, inquiry, examination, probing, grilling (*informal*), cross-examination, inquisition, third degree (*informal*), cross-questioning

interrupt *verb* **1** INTRUDE, disturb, intervene, interfere (with), break in, heckle, butt in, barge in (*informal*), break (someone's) train of thought **2** SUSPEND, break, stop, end, cut, stay, check, delay, cease, cut off, postpone, shelve, put off, defer, break off, adjourn, cut short, discontinue

interruption *noun* **1** DISRUPTION, break, halt, obstacle, disturbance, hitch, intrusion, obstruction, impediment, hindrance

2 STOPPAGE, stop, pause, suspension, cessation, severance, hiatus, disconnection, discontinuance

intersect *verb* CROSS, meet, cut, divide, cut across, bisect, crisscross

intersection *noun* JUNCTION, crossing, crossroads

intersperse *verb* SCATTER, sprinkle, intermix, pepper, interlard, bestrew

interval *noun* **1** PERIOD, time, spell, term, season, space, stretch, pause, span **2** BREAK, interlude, intermission, rest, gap, pause, respite, lull, entr'acte **3** DELAY, wait, gap, interim, hold-up, meanwhile, meantime, stoppage, hiatus **4** STRETCH, area, space, distance, gap

intervene *verb* **1** STEP IN (*informal*), interfere, mediate, intrude, intercede, arbitrate, interpose, take a hand (*informal*) **2** INTERRUPT, involve yourself, put your oar in, interpose yourself, put your two cents in (*US slang*) **3** HAPPEN, occur, take place, follow, succeed, arise, ensue, befall, materialize, come to pass, supervene

intervention *noun* MEDIATION, involvement, interference, intrusion, arbitration, conciliation, intercession, interposition, agency

interview *noun* **1** MEETING, examination, evaluation, oral (examination), interrogation **2** AUDIENCE, talk, conference, exchange, dialogue, consultation, press conference ▷ *verb* **1** EXAMINE, talk to, sound out **2** QUESTION, interrogate, examine, investigate, ask, pump, grill (*informal*), quiz, cross-examine, cross-question, put the screws on (*informal*), catechize, give (someone) the third degree (*informal*)

interviewer *noun* QUESTIONER, reporter, investigator, examiner, interrogator, interlocutor

intestinal *adjective* ABDOMINAL, visceral, duodenal, gut (*informal*), inner, coeliac, stomachic

intestine *noun usu pl* GUTS, insides (*informal*), bowels, internal organs, innards (*informal*), entrails, vitals

intimacy *noun* FAMILIARITY, closeness, understanding, confidence, confidentiality, fraternization << ANTONYM aloofness

intimate¹ *adjective* **1** CLOSE, dear, loving, near, warm, friendly, familiar, thick (*informal*), devoted, confidential, cherished, bosom, inseparable, nearest and dearest << ANTONYM distant **2** PRIVATE, personal, confidential, special, individual, particular, secret, exclusive, privy << ANTONYM public **3** DETAILED, minute, full, experienced, personal, deep, particular, specific, immediate, comprehensive, exact, elaborate, profound, penetrating, thorough, in-depth, intricate, first-hand, exhaustive **4** COSY, relaxed, friendly, informal, harmonious, snug, comfy (*informal*), warm ▷ *noun* FRIEND, close friend, buddy (*informal*), mate (*informal*), pal, comrade, chum (*informal*), mucker (*Brit slang*), crony, main man (*slang, chiefly US*), china (*Brit slang*), homeboy (*slang, chiefly US*), cobber (*Austral & NZ old-fashioned informal*), bosom friend, familiar, confidant *or* confidante, (constant) companion, E hoa (*NZ*) << ANTONYM stranger

intimate² *verb* **1** SUGGEST, indicate, hint, imply, warn, allude, let it be known, insinuate, give (someone) to understand, drop a hint, tip (someone) the wink (*Brit informal*) **2** ANNOUNCE, state, declare, communicate, impart, make known

intimately *adverb* **1** CLOSELY, very well, personally, warmly, familiarly, tenderly, affectionately, confidentially, confidingly **2** FULLY, very well, thoroughly, in detail, inside out, to the core, through and through

intimation *noun* **1** HINT, warning, suggestion, indication, allusion, inkling, insinuation **2** ANNOUNCEMENT, notice, communication, declaration

intimidate *verb* FRIGHTEN, pressure, threaten, alarm, scare, terrify, cow, bully, plague, menace, hound, awe, daunt, harass, subdue, oppress, persecute, lean on (*informal*), coerce, overawe, scare off (*informal*), terrorize, pressurize, browbeat, twist someone's arm (*informal*), tyrannize, dishearten, dispirit, affright (*archaic*), domineer

intimidation *noun* BULLYING, pressure, threat(s), menaces, coercion, arm-twisting (*informal*), browbeating, terrorization

intonation *noun* **1** TONE, inflection, cadence, modulation, accentuation **2** INCANTATION, spell, charm, formula, chant, invocation, hex (*US & Canad informal*), conjuration

intone *verb* CHANT, sing, recite, croon, intonate

intoxicating *adjective* **1** ALCOHOLIC, strong, intoxicant, spirituous, inebriant **2** EXCITING, thrilling, stimulating, sexy (*informal*), heady, exhilarating

intoxication *noun* **1** DRUNKENNESS, inebriation, tipsiness, inebriety, insobriety

2 EXCITEMENT, euphoria, elation, exhilaration, infatuation, delirium, exaltation

intractable *adjective* DIFFICULT, contrary, awkward, wild, stubborn, perverse, wayward, unruly, uncontrollable, wilful, incurable, fractious, unyielding, obstinate, intransigent, headstrong, unmanageable, undisciplined, cantankerous, unbending, obdurate, uncooperative, stiff-necked, ungovernable, self-willed, refractory, pig-headed, bull-headed

intransigent *adjective* UNCOMPROMISING, intractable, tough, stubborn, hardline, tenacious, unyielding, obstinate, immovable, unbending, obdurate, stiff-necked, inflexible, unbudgeable << ANTONYM compliant

intrenched ▷ see **entrenched**

intrepid *adjective* FEARLESS, brave, daring, bold, heroic, game (*informal*), have-a-go (*informal*), courageous, stalwart, resolute, gallant, audacious, valiant, plucky, doughty, undaunted, unafraid, unflinching, nerveless, dauntless, lion-hearted, valorous, stouthearted, (as) game as Ned Kelly (*Austral slang*) << ANTONYM fearful

intricacy *noun* COMPLEXITY, involvement, complication, elaborateness, obscurity, entanglement, convolutions, involution, intricateness, knottiness

intricate *adjective* COMPLICATED, involved, complex, difficult, fancy, sophisticated, elaborate, obscure, tangled, baroque, perplexing, tortuous, Byzantine, convoluted, rococo, knotty, labyrinthine, daedal (*literary*) << ANTONYM simple

intrigue *noun* **1** PLOT, scheme, conspiracy, manoeuvre, manipulation, collusion, ruse, trickery, cabal, stratagem, double-dealing, chicanery, sharp practice, wile, knavery, machination **2** AFFAIR, romance, intimacy, liaison, amour ▷ *verb* **1** INTEREST, fascinate, arouse the curiosity of, attract, charm, rivet, titillate, pique, tickle your fancy **2** PLOT, scheme, manoeuvre, conspire, connive, machinate

intriguing *adjective* INTERESTING, fascinating, absorbing, exciting, engaging, gripping, stirring, stimulating, curious, compelling, amusing, diverting, provocative, beguiling, thought-provoking, titillating, engrossing, tantalizing

intrinsic *adjective* ESSENTIAL, real, true, central, natural, basic, radical, native,

genuine, fundamental, constitutional,
built-in, underlying, inherent, elemental,
congenital, inborn, inbred << ANTONYM
extrinsic

intrinsically *adverb* ESSENTIALLY, basically,
fundamentally, constitutionally, as such, in
itself, at heart, by definition, per se

introduce *verb* 1 BRING IN, establish, set
up, start, begin, found, develop, launch,
institute, organize, pioneer, initiate,
originate, commence, get going, instigate,
phase in, usher in, inaugurate, set in
motion, bring into being 2 PRESENT,
acquaint, make known, familiarize, do
the honours, make the introductions
3 ANNOUNCE, present, open, launch, precede,
lead into, preface, lead off 4 SUGGEST, offer,
air, table, advance, propose, recommend,
float, submit, bring up, put forward, set
forth, ventilate, broach, moot 5 ADD, insert,
inject, throw in (*informal*), infuse, interpose,
interpolate

introduction *noun* 1 LAUNCH, institution,
establishment, start, opening, beginning,
pioneering, presentation, initiation,
inauguration, induction, commencement,
instigation << ANTONYM elimination
2 OPENING, prelude, preface, lead-in,
preliminaries, overture, preamble, foreword,
prologue, intro (*informal*), commencement,
opening remarks, proem, opening passage,
prolegomena, prolegomenon, exordium
<< ANTONYM conclusion 3 INSERTION,
addition, injection, interpolation
<< ANTONYM extraction

introductory *adjective* 1 PRELIMINARY,
elementary, first, early, initial, inaugural,
preparatory, initiatory, prefatory, precursory
<< ANTONYM concluding 2 STARTING,
opening, initial, early

introspection *noun* SELF-EXAMINATION,
brooding, self-analysis, navel-gazing (*slang*),
introversion, heart-searching

introspective *adjective* INWARD-LOOKING,
introverted, brooding, contemplative,
meditative, subjective, pensive, inner-
directed

introverted *adjective* INTROSPECTIVE,
withdrawn, inward-looking, self-contained,
self-centred, indrawn, inner-directed

intrude *verb* BUTT IN, encroach, push in,
obtrude, thrust yourself in *or* forward, put
your two cents in (*US slang*) ▷▷ **intrude on
something** *or* **someone** 1 INTERFERE WITH,
interrupt, impinge on, encroach on, meddle

with, infringe on 2 TRESPASS ON, invade,
infringe on, obtrude on

intruder *noun* TRESPASSER, burglar, invader,
squatter, prowler, interloper, infiltrator,
gate-crasher (*informal*)

intrusion *noun* 1 INTERRUPTION, interference,
infringement, trespass, encroachment
2 INVASION, breach, infringement,
infiltration, encroachment, infraction,
usurpation

intrusive *adjective* 1 INTERFERING, disturbing,
invasive, unwanted, presumptuous,
uncalled-for, importunate 2 PUSHY
(*informal*), forward, interfering, unwanted,
impertinent, nosy (*informal*), officious,
meddlesome

intrust ▷ see entrust

intuition *noun* 1 INSTINCT, perception,
insight, sixth sense, discernment 2 FEELING,
idea, impression, suspicion, premonition,
inkling, presentiment

intuitive *adjective* INSTINCTIVE, spontaneous,
innate, involuntary, instinctual, untaught,
unreflecting

intuitively *adverb* INSTINCTIVELY,
automatically, spontaneously, involuntarily,
innately, instinctually

inundate *verb* 1 OVERWHELM, flood, swamp,
engulf, overflow, overrun, glut 2 FLOOD,
engulf, submerge, drown, overflow,
immerse, deluge

invade *verb* 1 ATTACK, storm, assault, capture,
occupy, seize, raid, overwhelm, violate,
conquer, overrun, annex, march into,
assail, descend upon, infringe on, burst
in on, make inroads on 2 INFEST, swarm,
overrun, flood, infect, ravage, beset, pervade,
permeate, overspread

invader *noun* ATTACKER, raider, plunderer,
aggressor, looter, trespasser

invalid[1] *noun* PATIENT, sufferer, convalescent,
valetudinarian ▷ *adjective* DISABLED,
challenged, ill, sick, poorly (*informal*), weak,
ailing, frail, feeble, sickly, infirm, bedridden,
valetudinarian

invalid[2] *adjective* 1 NULL AND VOID, void,
worthless, untrue, null, not binding,
inoperative, nugatory << ANTONYM valid
2 UNFOUNDED, false, untrue, illogical,
irrational, unsound, unscientific, baseless,
fallacious, ill-founded << ANTONYM sound

invalidate *verb* NULLIFY, cancel, annul,
undermine, weaken, overthrow, undo,
quash, overrule, rescind, abrogate, render
null and void << ANTONYM validate

invalidity *noun* FALSITY, fallacy, unsoundness, inconsistency, irrationality, illogicality, speciousness, sophism, fallaciousness

invaluable *adjective* PRECIOUS, valuable, priceless, costly, inestimable, beyond price, worth your *or* its weight in gold << ANTONYM worthless

invariably *adverb* ALWAYS, regularly, constantly, every time, inevitably, repeatedly, consistently, ever, continually, aye (*Scot*), eternally, habitually, perpetually, without exception, customarily, unfailingly, on every occasion, unceasingly, day in, day out

invasion *noun* 1 ATTACK, assault, capture, takeover, raid, offensive, occupation, conquering, seizure, onslaught, foray, appropriation, sortie, annexation, incursion, expropriation, inroad, irruption, arrogation 2 INTRUSION, breach, violation, disturbance, disruption, infringement, overstepping, infiltration, encroachment, infraction, usurpation

invective *noun* ABUSE, censure, tirade, reproach, berating, denunciation, diatribe, vilification, tongue-lashing, billingsgate, vituperation, castigation, obloquy, contumely, philippic(s), revilement

invent *verb* 1 CREATE, make, produce, develop, design, discover, imagine, manufacture, generate, come up with (*informal*), coin, devise, conceive, originate, formulate, spawn, contrive, improvise, dream up (*informal*), concoct, think up 2 MAKE UP, devise, concoct, forge, fake, fabricate, feign, falsify, cook up (*informal*), trump up

invention *noun* 1 CREATION, machine, device, design, development, instrument, discovery, innovation, gadget, brainchild (*informal*), contraption, contrivance 2 DEVELOPMENT, design, production, setting up, foundation, construction, constitution, creation, discovery, introduction, establishment, pioneering, formation, innovation, conception, masterminding, formulation, inception, contrivance, origination 3 FICTION, story, fantasy, lie, yarn, fabrication, concoction, falsehood, fib (*informal*), untruth, urban myth, prevarication, tall story (*informal*), urban legend, figment *or* product of (someone's) imagination 4 CREATIVITY, vision, imagination, initiative, enterprise, inspiration, genius, brilliance, ingenuity, originality, inventiveness, resourcefulness, creativeness, ingeniousness, imaginativeness

inventive *adjective* CREATIVE, original, innovative, imaginative, gifted, inspired, fertile, ingenious, ground-breaking, resourceful << ANTONYM uninspired

inventor *noun* CREATOR, father, maker, author, framer, designer, architect, coiner, originator

inventory *noun* LIST, record, catalogue, listing, account, roll, file, schedule, register, description, log, directory, tally, roster, stock book

inverse *adjective* 1 OPPOSITE, reverse, reversed, contrary, inverted, converse, transposed 2 REVERSE, opposite, reversed, inverted, transposed

inversion *noun* REVERSAL, opposite, antithesis, transposition, contrary, contrariety, contraposition, transposal, antipode

invert *verb* OVERTURN, upturn, turn upside down, upset, reverse, capsize, transpose, introvert, turn inside out, turn turtle, invaginate (*pathology*), overset, intussuscept (*pathology*)

invest *verb* 1 SPEND, expend, advance, venture, put in, devote, lay out, sink in, use up, plough in 2 CHARGE, fill, steep, saturate, endow, pervade, infuse, imbue, suffuse, endue 3 EMPOWER, provide, charge, sanction, license, authorize, vest 4 INSTALL, establish, ordain, crown, inaugurate, anoint, consecrate, adopt, induct, enthrone, instate ▷▷ **invest in something** BUY, get, purchase, score (*slang*), pay for, obtain, acquire, procure

investigate *verb* EXAMINE, study, research, consider, go into, explore, search for, analyse, look into, inspect, look over, sift, probe into, work over, scrutinize, inquire into, make inquiries about, enquire into

investigation *noun* EXAMINATION, study, inquiry, hearing, research, review, search, survey, analysis, probe, inspection, exploration, scrutiny, inquest, fact finding, recce (*slang*)

investigative *adjective* FACT-FINDING, researching, investigating, research, inspecting

investigator *noun* EXAMINER, researcher, inspector, monitor, detective, analyser, explorer, reviewer, scrutinizer, checker, inquirer, scrutineer

investment *noun* 1 INVESTING, backing, funding, financing, contribution, speculation, transaction, expenditure, outlay 2 STAKE, interest, share, concern, portion, ante (*informal*) 3 BUY, asset, acquisition, venture, risk, speculation, gamble

inveterate *adjective* **1** CHRONIC, confirmed, incurable, hardened, established, long-standing, hard-core, habitual, obstinate, incorrigible, dyed-in-the-wool, ineradicable, deep-dyed (*usually derogatory*) **2** DEEP-ROOTED, entrenched, ingrained, deep-seated, incurable, established **3** STAUNCH, long-standing, dyed-in-the-wool, deep-dyed (*usually derogatory*)

invidious *adjective* UNDESIRABLE, unpleasant, hateful, thankless << ANTONYM pleasant

invigorating *adjective* REFRESHING, stimulating, bracing, fresh, tonic, uplifting, exhilarating, rejuvenating, energizing, healthful, restorative, salubrious, rejuvenative

invincible *adjective* UNBEATABLE, unassailable, indomitable, unyielding, indestructible, impregnable, insuperable, invulnerable, unconquerable, unsurmountable << ANTONYM vulnerable

invisible *adjective* **1** UNSEEN, imperceptible, indiscernible, unseeable, unperceivable << ANTONYM visible **2** HIDDEN, concealed, obscured, secret, disguised, inconspicuous, unobserved, unnoticeable, inappreciable

invitation *noun* **1** REQUEST, call, invite (*informal*), bidding, summons **2** INDUCEMENT, come-on (*informal*), temptation, challenge, provocation, open door, overture, incitement, enticement, allurement

invite *verb* **1** ASK, bid, summon, request the pleasure of (someone's) company **2** REQUEST, seek, look for, call for, ask for, bid for, appeal for, petition, solicit **3** ENCOURAGE, attract, cause, draw, lead to, court, ask for (*informal*), generate, foster, tempt, provoke, induce, bring on, solicit, engender, allure, call forth, leave the door open to

inviting *adjective* TEMPTING, appealing, attractive, pleasing, welcoming, warm, engaging, fascinating, intriguing, magnetic, delightful, enticing, seductive, captivating, beguiling, alluring, mouthwatering << ANTONYM uninviting

invocation *noun* **1** APPEAL, request, petition, beseeching, solicitation, entreaty **2** PRAYER, chant, supplication, orison, karakia (*NZ*)

invoke *verb* **1** APPLY, use, implement, call in, initiate, resort to, put into effect **2** CALL UPON, appeal to, pray to, petition, conjure, solicit, beseech, entreat, adjure, supplicate

involuntary *adjective* UNINTENTIONAL, automatic, unconscious, spontaneous, reflex, instinctive, uncontrolled, unthinking, instinctual, blind, unconditioned << ANTONYM voluntary

involve *verb* **1** ENTAIL, mean, demand, require, call for, occasion, result in, imply, give rise to, encompass, necessitate **2** INCLUDE, contain, take in, embrace, cover, incorporate, draw in, comprise of, number among **3** IMPLICATE, tangle, mix up, embroil, link, entangle, incriminate, mire, stitch up (*slang*), enmesh, inculpate (*formal*) **4** CONCERN, draw in, associate, connect, bear on

involved *adjective* COMPLICATED, complex, intricate, hard, difficult, confused, confusing, sophisticated, elaborate, tangled, bewildering, jumbled, entangled, tortuous, Byzantine, convoluted, knotty, unfathomable, labyrinthine << ANTONYM straightforward

involvement *noun* CONNECTION, interest, relationship, concern, association, commitment, friendship, attachment

invulnerable *adjective* SAFE, secure, invincible, impenetrable, unassailable, indestructible, insusceptible << ANTONYM vulnerable

inward *adjective* **1** INCOMING, entering, penetrating, inbound, inflowing, ingoing, inpouring **2** INTERNAL, inner, private, personal, inside, secret, hidden, interior, confidential, privy, innermost, inmost << ANTONYM outward

inwardly *adverb* PRIVATELY, secretly, to yourself, within, inside, at heart, deep down, in your head, in your inmost heart

iota *noun* BIT, particle, atom, trace, hint, scrap, grain, mite, jot, speck, whit, tittle

irascible *adjective* BAD-TEMPERED, cross, irritable, crabbed, touchy, cantankerous, peppery, tetchy, ratty (*Brit & NZ informal*), testy, chippy (*informal*), short-tempered, hot-tempered, quick-tempered, choleric, narky (*Brit slang*)

irate *adjective* ANGRY, cross, furious, angered, mad (*informal*), provoked, annoyed, irritated, fuming (*informal*), choked, infuriated, incensed, enraged, worked up, exasperated, indignant, livid, riled, up in arms, incandescent, hacked off (*US slang*), piqued, hot under the collar (*informal*), wrathful, fit to be tied (*slang*), as black as thunder, tooshie (*Austral slang*), off the air (*Austral slang*)

ire *noun literary* ANGER, rage, fury, wrath, passion, indignation, annoyance, displeasure, exasperation, choler

Ireland *noun* HIBERNIA (*Latin*)

iridescent *adjective* SHIMMERING, pearly, opalescent, shot, opaline, prismatic, rainbow-coloured, polychromatic, nacreous

Irish *adjective* HIBERNIAN, green

irk *verb* IRRITATE, annoy, aggravate (*informal*), provoke, bug (*informal*), put out (*informal*), gall, ruffle, nettle, vex, rile, peeve (*informal*), get on your nerves (*informal*), nark (*Brit, Austral & NZ slang*), miff (*informal*), be on your back (*slang*), get in your hair (*informal*), rub you up the wrong way (*informal*), put your nose out of joint (*informal*), get your back up, put your back up, hack you off (*informal*)

irksome *adjective* IRRITATING, trying, annoying, aggravating, troublesome, unwelcome, exasperating, tiresome, vexing, disagreeable, burdensome, wearisome, bothersome, vexatious << ANTONYM pleasant

iron *modifier* FERROUS, ferric, irony ▷ *adjective* INFLEXIBLE, hard, strong, tough, steel, rigid, adamant, unconditional, steely, implacable, indomitable, unyielding, immovable, unbreakable, unbending, obdurate << ANTONYM weak ▷▷ **iron something out** SETTLE, resolve, sort out, eliminate, get rid of, reconcile, clear up, simplify, unravel, erase, eradicate, put right, straighten out, harmonize, expedite, smooth over

ironic *or* **ironical** *adjective* **1** SARCASTIC, dry, sharp, acid, bitter, stinging, mocking, sneering, scoffing, wry, scathing, satirical, tongue-in-cheek, sardonic, caustic, double-edged, acerbic, trenchant, mordant, mordacious **2** PARADOXICAL, absurd, contradictory, puzzling, baffling, ambiguous, inconsistent, confounding, enigmatic, illogical, incongruous

irons *plural noun* CHAINS, shackles, fetters, manacles, bonds

irony *noun* **1** SARCASM, mockery, ridicule, bitterness, scorn, satire, cynicism, derision, causticity, mordancy **2** PARADOX, ambiguity, absurdity, incongruity, contrariness

irrational *adjective* **1** ILLOGICAL, crazy, silly, absurd, foolish, unreasonable, unwise, preposterous, idiotic, nonsensical, unsound, unthinking, injudicious, unreasoning << ANTONYM rational **2** SENSELESS, wild, crazy, unstable, insane, mindless, demented, aberrant, brainless, off the air (*Austral slang*)

irrationality *noun* SENSELESSNESS, madness, insanity, absurdity, lunacy, lack of judgment, illogicality, unreasonableness, preposterousness, unsoundness, brainlessness

irreconcilable *adjective* **1** IMPLACABLE, uncompromising, inflexible, inexorable, intransigent, unappeasable **2** INCOMPATIBLE, conflicting, opposed, inconsistent, incongruous, diametrically opposed

irrefutable *adjective* UNDENIABLE, sure, certain, irresistible, invincible, unassailable, indisputable, unanswerable, unquestionable, incontrovertible, beyond question, incontestable, indubitable, apodictic, irrefragable

irregular *adjective* **1** VARIABLE, inconsistent, erratic, shifting, occasional, random, casual, shaky, wavering, uneven, fluctuating, eccentric, patchy, sporadic, intermittent, haphazard, unsteady, desultory, fitful, spasmodic, unsystematic, inconstant, nonuniform, unmethodical, scattershot << ANTONYM steady **2** UNEVEN, broken, rough, twisted, twisting, curving, pitted, ragged, crooked, unequal, jagged, bumpy, lumpy, serpentine, contorted, lopsided, craggy, indented, asymmetrical, serrated, holey, unsymmetrical << ANTONYM even **3** INAPPROPRIATE, unconventional, improper, unethical, odd, unusual, extraordinary, disorderly, exceptional, peculiar, unofficial, abnormal, queer, rum (*Brit slang*), back-door, unsuitable, unorthodox, out-of-order, unprofessional, anomalous **4** UNOFFICIAL, underground, guerrilla, volunteer, resistance, partisan, rogue, paramilitary, mercenary

irregularity *noun* **1** INCONSISTENCY, randomness, disorganization, unsteadiness, unpunctuality, haphazardness, disorderliness, lack of method, desultoriness **2** UNEVENNESS, deformity, asymmetry, crookedness, contortion, patchiness, lopsidedness, raggedness, lack of symmetry, spottiness, jaggedness **3** MALPRACTICE, anomaly, breach, abnormality, deviation, oddity, aberration, malfunction, peculiarity, singularity, unorthodoxy, unconventionality

irregularly *adverb* ERRATICALLY, occasionally, now and again, intermittently, off and on, anyhow, unevenly, fitfully, haphazardly, eccentrically, spasmodically, jerkily, in snatches, out of sequence, by fits and starts, disconnectedly, unmethodically, unpunctually

irrelevance *or* **irrelevancy** *noun*
INAPPROPRIATENESS, inapplicability,
inaptness, unconnectedness, pointlessness,
non sequitur, inconsequence,
extraneousness, inappositeness
<< ANTONYM relevance

irrelevant *adjective* UNCONNECTED, unrelated,
unimportant, inappropriate, peripheral,
insignificant, negligible, immaterial,
extraneous, beside the point, impertinent,
neither here nor there, inapplicable, inapt,
inapposite, inconsequent << ANTONYM
relevant

irreparable *adjective* BEYOND REPAIR,
irreversible, incurable, irretrievable,
irrecoverable, irremediable

irreplaceable *adjective* INDISPENSABLE,
unique, invaluable, priceless

irrepressible *adjective* UNSTOPPABLE, buoyant,
uncontrollable, boisterous, ebullient,
effervescent, unmanageable, unquenchable,
bubbling over, uncontainable,
unrestrainable, insuppressible

irresistible *adjective* 1 OVERWHELMING,
compelling, overpowering, urgent, potent,
imperative, compulsive, uncontrollable,
overmastering 2 SEDUCTIVE, inviting,
tempting, enticing, provocative, fascinating,
enchanting, captivating, beguiling, alluring,
bewitching, ravishing 3 INESCAPABLE,
inevitable, unavoidable, sure, certain, fated,
destined, inexorable, ineluctable

irrespective of *preposition* DESPITE, in spite of,
regardless of, discounting, notwithstanding,
without reference to, without regard to

irresponsible *adjective* THOUGHTLESS,
reckless, careless, wild, unreliable, giddy,
untrustworthy, flighty, ill-considered,
good-for-nothing, shiftless, harebrained,
undependable, harum-scarum,
scatterbrained, featherbrained << ANTONYM
responsible

irreverence *noun* DISRESPECT, cheek (*informal*),
impertinence, sauce (*informal*), mockery,
derision, lack of respect, impudence,
flippancy, cheekiness (*informal*)

irreverent *adjective* DISRESPECTFUL,
cheeky (*informal*), impertinent, fresh
(*informal*), mocking, flip (*informal*), saucy,
contemptuous, tongue-in-cheek, sassy (*US
informal*), flippant, iconoclastic, derisive,
impudent << ANTONYM reverent

irreversible *adjective* IRREVOCABLE, incurable,
irreparable, final, unalterable

irrevocable *adjective* FIXED, settled,
irreversible, fated, predetermined,
immutable, invariable, irretrievable,
predestined, unalterable, unchangeable,
changeless, irremediable, unreversible

irrigate *verb* WATER, wet, moisten, flood,
inundate, fertigate (*Austral*)

irritability *noun* BAD TEMPER, impatience, ill
humour, prickliness, tetchiness, irascibility,
peevishness, testiness, touchiness
<< ANTONYM good humour

irritable *adjective* BAD-TEMPERED, cross,
snappy, hot, tense, crabbed, fiery, snarling,
prickly, exasperated, edgy, touchy, petulant,
ill-tempered, irascible, cantankerous, tetchy,
ratty (*Brit & NZ informal*), testy, chippy
(*informal*), fretful, peevish, crabby, dyspeptic,
choleric, crotchety (*informal*), oversensitive,
snappish, ill-humoured, narky (*Brit slang*),
out of humour << ANTONYM even-
tempered

irritate *verb* 1 ANNOY, anger, bother, provoke,
offend, needle (*informal*), harass, infuriate,
aggravate (*informal*), incense, fret, enrage,
gall, ruffle, inflame, exasperate, nettle,
pester, vex, irk, pique, rankle with, get under
your skin (*informal*), nark (*Brit, Austral & NZ slang*),
drive you up the wall (*slang*), rub you up the
wrong way (*informal*), get your goat (*slang*),
try your patience, get in your hair (*informal*),
get on your wick (*informal*), get your dander
up (*informal*), raise your hackles, get your
back up, get your hackles up, put your back
up, hack you off (*informal*) << ANTONYM
placate 2 INFLAME, pain, rub, scratch, scrape,
grate, graze, fret, gall, chafe, abrade

irritated *adjective* ANNOYED, cross, angry,
bothered, put out, hacked (off) (*US slang*),
harassed, impatient, ruffled, exasperated,
irritable, nettled, vexed, displeased,
flustered, peeved (*informal*), piqued, out of
humour, tooshie (*Austral slang*), hoha (*NZ*)

irritating *adjective* ANNOYING, trying,
provoking, infuriating, upsetting,
disturbing, nagging, aggravating (*informal*),
troublesome, galling, maddening,
disquieting, displeasing, worrisome,
irksome, vexatious, pestilential
<< ANTONYM pleasing

irritation *noun* 1 ANNOYANCE, anger, fury,
resentment, wrath, gall, indignation,
impatience, displeasure, exasperation,
chagrin, irritability, ill temper, shortness,
vexation, ill humour, testiness, crossness,

snappiness, infuriation << ANTONYM pleasure **2** NUISANCE, annoyance, irritant, pain (*informal*), drag (*informal*), bother, plague, menace, tease, pest, hassle, provocation, gall, goad, aggravation (*informal*), pain in the neck (*informal*), thorn in your flesh

island *noun* ISLE, inch (*Scot & Irish*), atoll, holm (*dialect*), islet, ait *or* eyot (*dialect*), cay *or* key

isolate *verb* **1** SEPARATE, break up, cut off, detach, split up, insulate, segregate, disconnect, divorce, sequester, set apart, disunite, estrange **2** QUARANTINE, separate, exclude, cut off, detach, keep in solitude

isolated *adjective* REMOTE, far, distant, lonely, out-of-the-way, hidden, retired, far-off, secluded, inaccessible, faraway, outlying, in the middle of nowhere, off the beaten track, backwoods, godforsaken, incommunicado, unfrequented

isolation *noun* SEPARATION, withdrawal, loneliness, segregation, detachment, quarantine, solitude, exile, self-sufficiency, seclusion, remoteness, disconnection, insularity

issue *noun* **1** TOPIC, point, matter, problem, business, case, question, concern, subject, affair, argument, theme, controversy, can of worms (*informal*) **2** POINT, question, concern, bone of contention, matter of contention, point in question **3** EDITION, printing, copy, impression, publication, number, instalment, imprint, version **4** CHILDREN, young, offspring, babies, kids (*informal*), seed (*chiefly biblical*), successors, heirs, descendants, progeny, scions << ANTONYM parent **5** DISTRIBUTION, issuing, supply, supplying, delivery, publication, circulation, sending out, dissemination, dispersal, issuance ▷ *verb* **1** GIVE OUT, release, publish, announce, deliver, spread, broadcast, distribute, communicate, proclaim, put

out, circulate, emit, impart, disseminate, promulgate, put in circulation **2** EMERGE, come out, proceed, rise, spring, flow, arise, stem, originate, emanate, exude, come forth, be a consequence of ▷▷ **at issue** UNDER DISCUSSION, in question, in dispute, under consideration, to be decided, for debate

▷▷ **take issue with something** *or* **someone** DISAGREE WITH, question, challenge, oppose, dispute, object to, argue with, take exception to, raise an objection to

itch *verb* **1** PRICKLE, tickle, tingle, crawl **2** LONG, ache, crave, burn, pine, pant, hunger, lust, yearn, hanker ▷ *noun* **1** IRRITATION, tingling, prickling, itchiness **2** DESIRE, longing, craving, passion, yen (*informal*), hunger, lust, yearning, hankering, restlessness

itchy *adjective* IMPATIENT, eager, restless, unsettled, edgy, restive, fidgety

item *noun* **1** ARTICLE, thing, object, piece, unit, component **2** MATTER, point, issue, case, question, concern, detail, subject, feature, particular, affair, aspect, entry, theme, consideration, topic **3** REPORT, story, piece, account, note, feature, notice, article, paragraph, bulletin, dispatch, communiqué, write-up

itemize *verb* LIST, record, detail, count, document, instance, set out, specify, inventory, number, enumerate, particularize

itinerant *adjective* WANDERING, travelling, journeying, unsettled, Gypsy, roaming, roving, nomadic, migratory, vagrant, peripatetic, vagabond, ambulatory, wayfaring << ANTONYM settled

itinerary *noun* SCHEDULE, line, programme, tour, route, journey, circuit, timetable

ivory tower *noun* SECLUSION, remoteness, unreality, retreat, refuge, cloister, sanctum, splendid isolation, world of your own

jab *verb* POKE, dig, punch, thrust, tap, stab, nudge, prod, lunge ▷ *noun* POKE, dig, punch, thrust, tap, stab, nudge, prod, lunge

jacket *noun* COVERING, casing, case, cover, skin, shell, coat, wrapping, envelope, capsule, folder, sheath, wrapper, encasement, housing

jackpot *noun* PRIZE, winnings, award, pool, reward, pot, kitty, bonanza, pot of gold at the end of the rainbow

jack up *verb* **1** HOIST, raise, elevate, winch up, lift, rear, uplift, lift up, heave, haul up, hike up, upraise **2** INCREASE, raise, put up, augment, advance, boost, expand, add to, enhance, step up (*informal*), intensify, enlarge, escalate, inflate, amplify

jaded *adjective* **1** TIRED, bored, weary, worn out, done in (*informal*), clapped out (*Brit, Austral & NZ informal*), spent, drained, exhausted, shattered, dulled, fatigued, fed up, wearied, fagged (out) (*informal*), sapped, uninterested, listless, tired-out, enervated, zonked (*slang*), over-tired, ennuied, hoha (*NZ*) << ANTONYM fresh **2** SATIATED, sated, surfeited, cloyed, gorged, glutted

jagged *adjective* UNEVEN, pointed, craggy, broken, toothed, rough, ragged, ridged, spiked, notched, barbed, cleft, indented, serrated, snaggy, denticulate << ANTONYM rounded

jail *or* **gaol** *noun* PRISON, penitentiary (*US*), jailhouse (*Southern US*), penal institution, can (*slang*), inside, cooler (*slang*), confinement, dungeon, clink (*slang*), glasshouse (*military informal*), brig (*chiefly US*), borstal, calaboose (*US informal*), choky (*slang*), pound, nick (*Brit slang*), stir (*slang*), jug (*slang*), slammer (*slang*), lockup, reformatory, quod (*slang*), poky *or* pokey (*US & Canad slang*), boob (*Austral slang*) ▷

verb IMPRISON, confine, detain, lock up, constrain, put away, intern, incarcerate, send down, send to prison, impound, put under lock and key, immure

jailbird *or* **gaolbird** *noun* PRISONER, convict, con (*slang*), lag (*slang*), trusty, felon, malefactor, ticket-of-leave man (*Historical*)

jailer *or* **gaoler** *noun* GUARD, keeper, warden, screw (*slang*), captor, warder, turnkey (*archaic*)

jam *noun* **1** TAILBACK, queue, hold-up, bottleneck, snarl-up, line, chain, congestion, obstruction, stoppage, gridlock **2** (*informal*) PREDICAMENT, tight spot, scrape (*informal*), corner, state, situation, trouble, spot (*informal*), hole (*slang*), fix (*informal*), bind, emergency, mess, dilemma, pinch, plight, strait, hot water, pickle (*informal*), deep water, quandary ▷ *verb* **1** PACK, force, press, stuff, squeeze, compact, ram, wedge, cram, compress **2** CROWD, cram, throng, crush, press, mass, surge, flock, swarm, congregate **3** CONGEST, block, clog, stick, halt, stall, obstruct

jamboree *noun* FESTIVAL, party, fête, celebration, blast (*US slang*), rave (*Brit slang*), carnival, spree, jubilee, festivity, beano (*Brit slang*), merriment, revelry, carouse, rave-up (*Brit slang*), carousal, frolic, hooley *or* hoolie (*chiefly Irish & NZ*)

jangle *verb* RATTLE, ring, clash, clatter, chime, ping, vibrate, jingle, ding, clank ▷ *noun* CLASH, clang, cacophony, reverberation, rattle, jar, racket, din, dissonance, clangour << ANTONYM quiet

janitor *noun* CARETAKER, porter, custodian, concierge, doorkeeper

jar¹ *noun* POT, container, flask, receptacle, vessel, drum, vase, jug, pitcher, urn, crock, canister, repository, decanter, carafe, flagon

jar² *verb* **1** *usually with* **on** IRRITATE, grind, clash, annoy, offend, rattle, gall, nettle, jangle, irk, grate on, get on your nerves (*informal*), nark (*Brit, Austral & NZ slang*), discompose **2** *sometimes with* **with** CLASH, conflict, contrast, differ, disagree, interfere, contend, collide, oppose **3** JOLT, rock, shake, disturb, bump, rattle, grate, agitate, vibrate, rasp, convulse

jargon *noun* PARLANCE, slang, idiom, patter, tongue, usage, dialect, cant, lingo (*informal*), patois, argot

jaundiced *adjective* CYNICAL, bitter, hostile, prejudiced, biased, suspicious, partial, jealous, distorted, sceptical, resentful, envious, bigoted, spiteful, preconceived << ANTONYM optimistic

jaunt *noun* OUTING, tour, trip, stroll, expedition, excursion, ramble, promenade, airing

jaunty *adjective* **1** SPRIGHTLY, buoyant, carefree, high-spirited, gay, lively, airy, breezy, perky, sparky, self-confident << ANTONYM serious **2** SMART, trim, gay, dapper, spruce, showy

jaw *plural noun* OPENING, gates, entrance, aperture, mouth, abyss, maw, orifice, ingress ▷ *verb* (*slang*) TALK, chat, rabbit (on) (*Brit informal*), gossip, chatter, spout, babble, natter, schmooze (*slang*), shoot the breeze (*US slang*), run off at the mouth (*slang*), chew the fat *or* rag (*slang*)

jealous *adjective* **1** SUSPICIOUS, suspecting, guarded, protective, wary, doubtful, sceptical, attentive, anxious, apprehensive, vigilant, watchful, zealous, possessive, solicitous, distrustful, mistrustful, unbelieving << ANTONYM trusting **2** ENVIOUS, grudging, resentful, begrudging, green, intolerant, green-eyed, invidious, green with envy, desirous, covetous, emulous << ANTONYM satisfied

jealousy *noun* SUSPICION, distrust, mistrust, possessiveness, doubt, spite, resentment, wariness, ill-will, dubiety

jeer *verb* MOCK, hector, deride, heckle, knock (*informal*), barrack, ridicule, taunt, sneer, scoff, banter, flout, gibe, cock a snook at (*Brit*), contemn (*formal*) << ANTONYM cheer ▷ *noun* MOCKERY, abuse, ridicule, taunt, sneer, hiss, boo, scoff, hoot, derision, gibe, catcall, obloquy, aspersion << ANTONYM applause

jeopardize *verb* ENDANGER, threaten, put at risk, put in jeopardy, risk, expose, gamble, hazard, menace, imperil, put on the line

jeopardy *noun* DANGER, risk, peril,

vulnerability, venture, exposure, liability, hazard, insecurity, pitfall, precariousness, endangerment

jerk *verb* JOLT, bang, bump, lurch, shake ▷ *noun* LURCH, movement, thrust, twitch, jolt, throw

jerky *adjective* BUMPY, rough, jolting, jumpy, shaky, bouncy, uncontrolled, twitchy, fitful, spasmodic, convulsive, tremulous << ANTONYM smooth

jest *noun* JOKE, play, crack (*slang*), sally, gag (*informal*), quip, josh (*slang, chiefly US & Canad*), banter, hoax, prank, wisecrack (*informal*), pleasantry, witticism, jape, bon mot ▷ *verb* JOKE, kid (*informal*), mock, tease, sneer, jeer, quip, josh (*slang, chiefly US & Canad*), scoff, banter, deride, chaff, gibe

jester *noun* FOOL, clown, harlequin, zany, madcap, prankster, buffoon, pantaloon, mummer

jet *noun* STREAM, current, spring, flow, rush, flood, burst, spray, fountain, cascade, gush, spurt, spout, squirt ▷ *verb* **1** FLY, wing, cruise, soar, zoom **2** STREAM, course, issue, shoot, flow, rush, surge, spill, gush, emanated, spout, spew, squirt

jet-black *adjective* BLACK, jet, raven, ebony, sable, pitch-black, inky, coal-black

jet-setting *adjective* FASHIONABLE, rich, sophisticated, trendy (*Brit informal*), cosmopolitan, well-off, high-society, ritzy (*slang*), trendsetting

jettison *verb* **1** ABANDON, reject, desert, dump, shed, scrap, throw out, discard, throw away, relinquish, forsake, slough off, throw on the scrapheap **2** EXPEL, dump, unload, throw overboard, eject, heave

jetty *noun* PIER, dock, wharf, mole, quay, breakwater, groyne

jewel *noun* **1** GEMSTONE, gem, precious stone, brilliant, ornament, trinket, sparkler (*informal*), rock (*slang*) **2** TREASURE, wonder, prize, darling, pearl, gem, paragon, pride and joy, taonga (*NZ*)

jewellery *noun* JEWELS, treasure, gems, trinkets, precious stones, ornaments, finery, regalia

jibe *or* **gibe** *noun* JEER, sneer, dig (*informal*), crack, taunt, snide remark ▷ *verb* JEER, mock, sneer, taunt

jig *verb* SKIP, bob, prance, jiggle, shake, bounce, twitch, wobble, caper, wiggle, jounce

jiggle *verb* **1** SHAKE, jerk, agitate, joggle **2** JERK, bounce, jog, fidget, shake, twitch, wiggle, jig, shimmy, joggle

jilt *verb* REJECT, drop, disappoint, abandon, desert, ditch (*slang*), betray, discard, deceive, forsake, throw over, coquette, leave (someone) in the lurch

jingle *verb* RING, rattle, clatter, chime, jangle, tinkle, clink, clank, tintinnabulate ▷ *noun* **1** RATTLE, ringing, tinkle, clang, clink, reverberation, clangour **2** SONG, tune, melody, ditty, chorus, slogan, verse, limerick, refrain, doggerel

jinx *noun* CURSE, plague, voodoo, nemesis, black magic, hoodoo (*informal*), hex (*US & Canad informal*), evil eye ▷ *verb* CURSE, bewitch, hex (*US & Canad informal*)

jitters *plural noun* NERVES, anxiety, butterflies (in your stomach) (*informal*), nervousness, the shakes (*informal*), fidgets, cold feet (*informal*), the willies (*informal*), tenseness, heebie-jeebies (*slang*)

jittery *adjective* NERVOUS, anxious, jumpy, twitchy (*informal*), wired (*slang*), trembling, shaky, neurotic, agitated, quivering, hyper (*informal*), fidgety, antsy (*informal*) << ANTONYM calm

job *noun* **1** POSITION, post, function, capacity, work, posting, calling, place, business, office, trade, field, career, situation, activity, employment, appointment, craft, profession, occupation, placement, vocation, livelihood, métier **2** TASK, concern, duty, charge, work, business, role, operation, affair, responsibility, function, contribution, venture, enterprise, undertaking, pursuit, assignment, stint, chore, errand

jobless *adjective* UNEMPLOYED, redundant, out of work, on the dole (*Brit informal*), inactive, out of a job, unoccupied, idle

jockey *verb* MANOEUVRE, manage, engineer, negotiate, trim, manipulate, cajole, insinuate, wheedle, finagle (*informal*)

jog *verb* **1** RUN, trot, canter, lope, dogtrot **2** NUDGE, push, shake, prod **3** STIMULATE, remind, prompt, stir, arouse, activate, nudge, prod

join *verb* **1** ENROL IN, enter, sign up for, become a member of, enlist in **2** CONNECT, unite, couple, link, marry, tie, combine, attach, knit, cement, adhere, fasten, annex, add, splice, yoke, append << ANTONYM detach **3** MEET, touch, border, extend, butt, adjoin, conjoin, reach << ANTONYM part

joint *adjective* SHARED, mutual, collective, communal, united, joined, allied, combined, corporate, concerted, consolidated, cooperative, reciprocal, collaborative ▷ *noun*

JUNCTION, union, link, connection, knot, brace, bracket, seam, hinge, weld, linkage, intersection, node, articulation, nexus

jointly *adverb* COLLECTIVELY, together, in conjunction, as one, in common, mutually, in partnership, in league, unitedly << ANTONYM separately

joke *noun* **1** JEST, gag (*informal*), wisecrack (*informal*), witticism, crack (*informal*), sally, quip, josh (*slang, chiefly US & Canad*), pun, quirk, one-liner (*informal*), jape **2** LAUGH, jest, fun, josh (*slang, chiefly US & Canad*), lark, sport, frolic, whimsy, jape **3** PRANK, trick, practical joke, lark (*informal*), caper, frolic, escapade, antic, jape **4** LAUGHING STOCK, butt, clown, buffoon, simpleton ▷ *verb* JEST, kid (*informal*), fool, mock, wind up (*Brit slang*), tease, ridicule, taunt, quip, josh (*slang, chiefly US & Canad*), banter, deride, frolic, chaff, gambol, play the fool, play a trick

joker *noun* COMEDIAN, comic, wit, clown, wag, kidder (*informal*), jester, prankster, buffoon, trickster, humorist

jokey *adjective* PLAYFUL, funny, amusing, teasing, humorous, mischievous, jesting, wisecracking, droll, facetious, waggish, prankish, nonserious << ANTONYM humourless

jolly *adjective* HAPPY, bright, funny, lively, hopeful, sunny, cheerful, merry, vibrant, hilarious, festive, upbeat (*informal*), bubbly, gay, airy, playful, exuberant, jubilant, cheery, good-humoured, joyous, joyful, carefree, breezy, genial, ebullient, chirpy (*informal*), sprightly, jovial, convivial, effervescent, frolicsome, ludic (*literary*), mirthful, sportive, light-hearted, jocund, gladsome (*archaic*), blithesome << ANTONYM miserable

jolt *verb* **1** JERK, push, shake, knock, jar, shove, jog, jostle **2** SURPRISE, upset, stun, disturb, astonish, stagger, startle, perturb, discompose ▷ *noun* **1** JERK, start, jump, shake, bump, jar, jog, lurch, quiver **2** SURPRISE, blow, shock, setback, reversal, bombshell, thunderbolt, whammy (*informal, chiefly US*), bolt from the blue

jostle *verb* PUSH, press, crowd, shake, squeeze, thrust, butt, elbow, bump, scramble, shove, jog, jolt, throng, hustle, joggle

jot *verb* usually with **down** NOTE DOWN, record, list, note, register, tally, scribble ▷ *noun* BIT, detail, ace, scrap, grain, particle, atom, fraction, trifle, mite, tad (*informal, chiefly US*), speck, morsel, whit, tittle, iota, scintilla, smidgen *or* smidgin (*informal, chiefly US &*

Canad)

journal _noun_ **1** MAGAZINE, record, review, register, publication, bulletin, chronicle, gazette, periodical, zine (_informal_) **2** NEWSPAPER, paper, daily, weekly, monthly, tabloid **3** DIARY, record, history, log, notebook, chronicle, annals, yearbook, commonplace book, daybook

journalist _noun_ REPORTER, writer, correspondent, newsman _or_ newswoman, stringer, commentator, broadcaster, hack (_derogatory_), columnist, contributor, scribe (_informal_), pressman, journo (_slang_), newshound (_informal_), newspaperman _or_ newspaperwoman

journey _noun_ **1** TRIP, drive, tour, flight, excursion, progress, cruise, passage, trek, outing, expedition, voyage, ramble, jaunt, peregrination, travel **2** PROGRESS, passage, voyage, pilgrimage, odyssey ▷ _verb_ TRAVEL, go, move, walk, fly, range, cross, tour, progress, proceed, fare, wander, trek, voyage, roam, ramble, traverse, rove, wend, go walkabout (_Austral_), peregrinate

jovial _adjective_ CHEERFUL, happy, jolly, animated, glad, merry, hilarious, buoyant, airy, jubilant, cheery, cordial, convivial, blithe, gay, mirthful, jocund, jocose << ANTONYM solemn

joy _noun_ **1** DELIGHT, pleasure, triumph, satisfaction, happiness, ecstasy, enjoyment, bliss, transport, euphoria, festivity, felicity, glee, exuberance, rapture, elation, exhilaration, radiance, gaiety, jubilation, hilarity, exaltation, ebullience, exultation, gladness, joyfulness, ravishment << ANTONYM sorrow **2** TREASURE, wonder, treat, prize, delight, pride, charm, thrill

joyful _adjective_ **1** PLEASING, satisfying, engaging, charming, delightful, enjoyable, gratifying, agreeable, pleasurable **2** DELIGHTED, happy, satisfied, glad, jolly, merry, gratified, pleased, jubilant, elated, over the moon (_informal_), jovial, rapt, enraptured, on cloud nine (_informal_), cock-a-hoop, floating on air, light-hearted, jocund, gladsome (_archaic_), blithesome, stoked (_Austral & NZ informal_)

joyless _adjective_ UNHAPPY, sad, depressing, miserable, gloomy, dismal, dreary, dejected, dispirited, downcast, down in the dumps (_informal_), cheerless

joyous _adjective_ JOYFUL, cheerful, merry, festive, heartening, rapturous, blithe

jubilant _adjective_ OVERJOYED, excited, thrilled, glad, triumphant, rejoicing, exuberant, joyous, elated, over the moon (_informal_), euphoric, triumphal, enraptured, exultant, cock-a-hoop, rhapsodic, stoked (_Austral & NZ informal_) << ANTONYM downcast

jubilation _noun_ JOY, triumph, celebration, excitement, ecstasy, jubilee, festivity, elation, jamboree, exultation

jubilee _noun_ CELEBRATION, holiday, fête, festival, carnival, festivity, gala

judge _noun_ **1** MAGISTRATE, justice, beak (_Brit slang_), His, Her _or_ Your Honour **2** REFEREE, expert, specialist, umpire, umpie (_Austral slang_), mediator, examiner, connoisseur, assessor, arbiter, appraiser, arbitrator, moderator, adjudicator, evaluator, authority **3** CRITIC, assessor, arbiter, appraiser, evaluator ▷ _verb_ **1** ADJUDICATE, referee, umpire, mediate, officiate, adjudge, arbitrate **2** EVALUATE, rate, consider, appreciate, view, class, value, review, rank, examine, esteem, criticize, ascertain, surmise **3** ESTIMATE, guess, assess, calculate, evaluate, gauge, appraise **4** FIND, rule, pass, pronounce, decree, adjudge

judgment _noun_ **1** OPINION, view, estimate, belief, assessment, conviction, diagnosis, valuation, deduction, appraisal **2** VERDICT, finding, result, ruling, decision, sentence, conclusion, determination, decree, order, arbitration, adjudication, pronouncement **3** SENSE, common sense, good sense, judiciousness, reason, understanding, taste, intelligence, smarts (_slang, chiefly US_), discrimination, perception, awareness, wisdom, wit, penetration, prudence, sharpness, acumen, shrewdness, discernment, perspicacity, sagacity, astuteness, percipience

judgmental _adjective_ CONDEMNATORY, self-righteous, censorious, pharisaic, critical

judicial _adjective_ LEGAL, official, judiciary, juridical

judicious _adjective_ SENSIBLE, considered, reasonable, discerning, sound, politic, acute, informed, diplomatic, careful, wise, cautious, rational, sober, discriminating, thoughtful, discreet, sage, enlightened, shrewd, prudent, sane, skilful, astute, expedient, circumspect, well-advised, well-judged, sagacious, sapient << ANTONYM injudicious

jug _noun_ CONTAINER, pitcher, urn, carafe, creamer (_US & Canad_), vessel, jar, crock, ewer

juggle _verb_ MANIPULATE, change, doctor

(*informal*), fix (*informal*), alter, modify, disguise, manoeuvre, tamper with, misrepresent, falsify

juice *noun* **1** LIQUID, extract, fluid, liquor, sap, nectar **2** SECRETION, serum

juicy *adjective* **1** MOIST, lush, watery, succulent, sappy **2** INTERESTING, colourful, sensational, vivid, provocative, spicy (*informal*), suggestive, racy, risqué

jumble *noun* MUDDLE, mixture, mess, disorder, confusion, chaos, litter, clutter, disarray, medley, mélange (*French*), miscellany, mishmash, farrago, hotchpotch (*US*), hodgepodge, gallimaufry, pig's breakfast (*informal*), disarrangement ▷ *verb* MIX, mistake, confuse, disorder, shuffle, tangle, muddle, confound, entangle, ravel, disorganize, disarrange, dishevel

jumbo *adjective* GIANT, large, huge, immense, mega (*informal*), gigantic, oversized, elephantine, ginormous (*informal*), humongous *or* humungous (*US slang*) << ANTONYM tiny

jump *verb* **1** LEAP, dance, spring, bound, bounce, hop, skip, caper, prance, gambol **2** VAULT, clear, hurdle, go over, sail over, hop over **3** SPRING, bound, leap, bounce **4** RECOIL, start, jolt, flinch, shake, jerk, quake, shudder, twitch, wince **5** INCREASE, rise, climb, escalate, gain, advance, boost, mount, soar, surge, spiral, hike, ascend **6** MISS, avoid, skip, omit, evade, digress ▷ *noun* **1** LEAP, spring, skip, bound, buck, hop, vault, caper **2** RISE, increase, escalation, upswing, advance, boost, elevation, upsurge, upturn, increment, augmentation **3** JOLT, start, movement, shock, shake, jar, jerk, lurch, twitch, swerve, spasm **4** HURDLE, gate, barrier, fence, obstacle, barricade, rail

jumped-up *adjective* (*informal*) CONCEITED, arrogant, pompous, stuck-up, cocky, overbearing, puffed up, presumptuous, insolent, immodest, toffee-nosed, self-opinionated, too big for your boots *or* breeches

jumper *noun* SWEATER, top, jersey, cardigan, woolly, pullover

jumpy *adjective* NERVOUS, anxious, tense, shaky, restless, neurotic, agitated, hyper (*informal*), apprehensive, jittery (*informal*), on edge, twitchy (*informal*), fidgety, timorous, antsy (*informal*), wired (*slang*) << ANTONYM calm

juncture *noun* MOMENT, time, point, crisis, occasion, emergency, strait, contingency, predicament, crux, exigency, conjuncture

junior *adjective* **1** MINOR, lower, secondary, lesser, subordinate, inferior **2** YOUNGER << ANTONYM senior

junk *noun* RUBBISH, refuse, waste, scrap, litter, debris, crap (*slang*), garbage (*chiefly US*), trash, clutter, rummage, dross, odds and ends, oddments, flotsam and jetsam, leavings, dreck (*slang, chiefly US*)

junkie *or* **junky** *noun* (*informal*) ADDICT, user, drug addict, druggie (*informal*), head (*slang*), freak (*informal*), mainliner (*slang*), smackhead (*slang*), pill-popper (*slang*), pothead (*slang*), cokehead (*slang*), acidhead (*slang*), hashhead (*slang*), weedhead (*slang*)

junta *noun* CABAL, council, faction, league, set, party, ring, camp, crew, combination, assembly, gang, clique, coterie, schism, confederacy, convocation

jurisdiction *noun* **1** AUTHORITY, say, power, control, rule, influence, command, sway, dominion, prerogative, mana (*NZ*) **2** RANGE, area, field, district, bounds, zone, province, circuit, scope, orbit, sphere, compass, dominion

just *adverb* **1** RECENTLY, lately, only now **2** MERELY, but, only, simply, solely, no more than, nothing but **3** BARELY, hardly, only just, scarcely, at most, by a whisker, at a push, by the skin of your teeth **4** EXACTLY, really, quite, completely, totally, perfectly, entirely, truly, absolutely, precisely, altogether, positively ▷ *adjective* **1** FAIR, good, legitimate, honourable, right, square, pure, decent, upright, honest, equitable, righteous, conscientious, impartial, virtuous, lawful, blameless, unbiased, fair-minded, unprejudiced << ANTONYM unfair **2** FITTING, due, correct, deserved, appropriate, justified, reasonable, suitable, decent, sensible, merited, proper, legitimate, desirable, apt, rightful, well-deserved, condign << ANTONYM inappropriate ▷▷ **just about** PRACTICALLY, almost, nearly, close to, virtually, all but, not quite, well-nigh

justice *noun* **1** FAIRNESS, equity, integrity, honesty, decency, impartiality, rectitude, reasonableness, uprightness, justness, rightfulness, right << ANTONYM injustice **2** JUSTNESS, fairness, legitimacy, reasonableness, right, integrity, honesty, legality, rectitude, rightfulness **3** JUDGE, magistrate, beak (*Brit slang*), His, Her *or* Your Honour

justifiable *adjective* REASONABLE, right,

sound, fit, acceptable, sensible, proper, valid, legitimate, understandable, lawful, well-founded, defensible, tenable, excusable, warrantable, vindicable << ANTONYM indefensible

justification *noun* REASON, grounds, defence, basis, excuse, approval, plea, warrant, apology, rationale, vindication, rationalization, absolution, exoneration, explanation, exculpation, extenuation

justify *verb* EXPLAIN, support, warrant, bear out, legitimize, establish, maintain, confirm, defend, approve, excuse, sustain, uphold, acquit, vindicate, validate, substantiate, exonerate, legalize, absolve, exculpate

justly *adverb* JUSTIFIABLY, rightly, correctly, properly, legitimately, rightfully, with good reason, lawfully

jut *verb* STICK OUT, project, extend, protrude, poke, bulge, overhang, impend

juvenile *noun* CHILD, youth, minor, girl, boy, teenager, infant, adolescent << ANTONYM adult ▷ *adjective* **1** YOUNG, junior, adolescent, youthful, immature << ANTONYM adult **2** IMMATURE, childish, infantile, puerile, young, youthful, inexperienced, boyish, callow, undeveloped, unsophisticated, girlish, babyish, jejune

juxtaposition *noun* PROXIMITY, adjacency, contact, closeness, vicinity, nearness, contiguity, propinquity

kai *noun* (*NZ informal*) FOOD, grub (*slang*), provisions, fare, board, commons, eats (*slang*), feed, diet, meat, bread, tuck (*informal*), tucker (*Austral & NZ informal*), rations, nutrition, tack (*informal*), refreshment, scoff (*slang*), nibbles, foodstuffs, nourishment, chow (*informal*), sustenance, nosh (*slang*), daily bread, victuals, edibles, comestibles, provender, nosebag (*slang*), pabulum (*rare*), nutriment, vittles (*obsolete* or *dialect*), viands, aliment, eatables (*slang*)

kak *noun* (*S African taboo*) **1** FAECES, excrement, stool, muck, manure, dung, droppings, waste matter **2** RUBBISH, nonsense, garbage (*informal*), rot, crap (*taboo slang*), drivel, tripe (*informal*), claptrap (*informal*), poppycock (*informal*), pants, bizzo (*Austral slang*), bull's wool (*Austral & NZ slang*)

kaleidoscopic *adjective* **1** MANY-COLOURED, multi-coloured, harlequin, psychedelic, motley, variegated, prismatic, varicoloured **2** CHANGEABLE, shifting, varied, mobile, variable, fluid, uncertain, volatile, unpredictable, unstable, fluctuating, indefinite, unsteady, protean, mutable, impermanent, inconstant **3** COMPLICATED, complex, confused, confusing, disordered, puzzling, unclear, baffling, bewildering, chaotic, muddled, intricate, jumbled, convoluted, disorganized, disarranged

kamikaze *modifier* SELF-DESTRUCTIVE, suicidal, foolhardy

keel over *verb* **1** (*informal*) COLLAPSE, faint, pass out, black out (*informal*), swoon (*literary*) **2** CAPSIZE, list, upset, founder, overturn, turn over, lean over, tip over, topple over, turn turtle

keen¹ *adjective* **1** EAGER, earnest, spirited, devoted, intense, fierce, enthusiastic, passionate, ardent, avid, fervent, impassioned, zealous, ebullient, wholehearted, fervid, bright-eyed and bushy-tailed (*informal*) << ANTONYM unenthusiastic **2** EARNEST, fierce, intense, vehement, burning, flaming, consuming, eager, passionate, heightened, energetic, ardent, fanatical, fervent, impassioned, fervid **3** SHARP, satirical, incisive, trenchant, pointed, cutting, biting, edged, acute, acid, stinging, piercing, penetrating, searing, tart, withering, scathing, pungent, sarcastic, sardonic, caustic, astringent, vitriolic, acerbic, mordant, razor-like, finely honed << ANTONYM dull **4** PERCEPTIVE, quick, sharp, brilliant, acute, smart, wise, clever, subtle, piercing, penetrating, discriminating, shrewd, discerning, ingenious, astute, intuitive, canny, incisive, insightful, observant, perspicacious, sapient << ANTONYM obtuse **5** PENETRATING, clear, powerful, sharp, acute, sensitive, piercing, discerning, perceptive, observant **6** INTENSE, strong, fierce, relentless, cut-throat

keen² *verb* LAMENT, cry, weep, sob, mourn, grieve, howl, sorrow, wail, whine, whimper, bewail

keep *verb* **1** *usually with* **from** PREVENT, hold back, deter, inhibit, block, stall, restrain, hamstring, hamper, withhold, hinder, retard, impede, shackle, keep back **2** *sometimes with* **on** CONTINUE, go on, carry on, persist in, persevere in, remain **3** HOLD ON TO, maintain, retain, keep possession of, save, preserve, nurture, cherish, conserve << ANTONYM lose **4** STORE, put, place, house, hold, deposit, pile, stack, heap, amass, stow **5** CARRY, stock, have, hold, sell, supply, handle, trade in, deal in **6** COMPLY WITH, carry out, honour, fulfil, hold, follow, mind, respect, observe, respond to, embrace, execute, obey, heed, conform to, adhere to, abide by, act upon << ANTONYM disregard **7** SUPPORT, maintain, sustain, provide for, mind, fund, board, finance, feed, look after, foster, shelter, care for, take care of, nurture, safeguard, cherish, nourish, subsidize **8** RAISE, own, maintain, tend, farm, breed, look after, rear, care for, bring up, nurture, nourish **9** MANAGE, run, administer, be in charge (of), rule, direct, handle, govern, oversee, supervise, preside over, superintend **10** DELAY, detain, hinder, impede, stop, limit, check, arrest, curb, constrain, obstruct, retard, set back << ANTONYM release **11** ASSOCIATE WITH, mix with, mingle with, hang out with (*informal*), hang with (*informal, chiefly US*), be friends with, consort with, run around with (*informal*), hobnob with, socialize with, hang about with, fraternize with ▷ *noun* **1** BOARD, food, maintenance, upkeep, means, living, support, nurture, livelihood, subsistence, kai (*NZ informal*), nourishment, sustenance **2** TOWER, castle, stronghold, dungeon, citadel, fastness, donjon ▷▷ **keep at it** PERSIST, continue, carry on, keep going, stick with it, stay with it, be steadfast, grind it out, persevere, remain with it ▷▷ **keep something back 1** HOLD BACK, hold, save, set aside, husband, store, retain, preserve, hang on to, conserve, stockpile, hoard, lay up, put by **2** SUPPRESS, hide, reserve, conceal, restrain, cover up, withhold, stifle, censor, repress, smother, muffle, muzzle, keep something under your hat **3** RESTRAIN, control, limit, check, delay, restrict, curb, prohibit, withhold, hold back, constrain, retard, keep a tight rein on ▷▷ **keep something up 1** CONTINUE, make, maintain, carry on, persist in, persevere with **2** MAINTAIN, sustain, uphold, perpetuate, retain, preserve, prolong ▷▷ **keep up** KEEP PACE, match, compete, contend, emulate, persevere

keeper *noun* CURATOR, guardian, steward, superintendent, attendant, caretaker, overseer, preserver

keeping *noun* CARE, keep, charge, trust, protection, possession, maintenance, custody, patronage, guardianship, safekeeping ▷▷ **in keeping with** IN AGREEMENT WITH, consistent with, in harmony with, in accord with, in compliance with, in conformity with, in balance with, in correspondence with, in proportion with, in congruity with, in observance with

keepsake *noun* SOUVENIR, symbol, token, reminder, relic, remembrance, emblem, memento, favour

keg *noun* BARREL, drum, vat, cask, firkin, tun, hogshead

ken ▷▷ **beyond someone's ken** BEYOND THE KNOWLEDGE OF, beyond the comprehension of, beyond the understanding of, beyond the acquaintance of, beyond the awareness of, beyond the cognizance of

kernel *noun* ESSENCE, core, substance, gist, grain, marrow, germ, nub, pith

key *noun* **1** OPENER, door key, latchkey **2** ANSWER, means, secret, solution, path, formula, passage, clue, cue, pointer, sign ▷ *modifier* ESSENTIAL, leading, major, main, important, chief, necessary, basic, vital, crucial, principal, fundamental, decisive, indispensable, pivotal, must-have << ANTONYM minor

keynote *noun* HEART, centre, theme, core, substance, essence, marrow, kernel, gist, pith

keystone *noun* BASIS, principle, core, crux, ground, source, spring, root, motive, cornerstone, lynchpin, mainspring, fundament, quoin

kia ora *interjection* (*NZ*) HELLO, hi (*informal*), greetings, gidday *or* g'day (*Austral & NZ*), how do you do?, good morning, good evening, good afternoon, welcome

kick *verb* **1** BOOT, strike, knock, punt, put the boot in(to) (*slang*) **2** (*informal*) GIVE UP, break, stop, abandon, quit, cease, eschew, leave off, desist from, end ▷ *noun* **1** (*informal*) THRILL, glow, buzz (*slang*), tingle, high (*slang*), sensation **2** (*informal*) PUNGENCY, force, power, edge, strength, snap (*informal*), punch, intensity, pep, sparkle, vitality, verve, zest, potency, tang, piquancy ▷▷ **kick someone out** (*informal*) DISMISS, remove, reject, get rid of, discharge, expel, oust, eject, evict, toss out, give the boot (*slang*), sack (*informal*), kiss off (*slang, chiefly US & Canad*), give (someone) their marching orders, give the push, give the bum's rush (*slang*), show you the door, throw you out on your ear (*informal*), kennet (*Austral slang*), jeff (*Austral slang*) ▷▷ **kick something off** (*informal*) BEGIN, start, open, commence, launch, initiate, get under way, kick-start, get on the road

kickback *noun* BRIBE, payoff, backhander (*slang*), enticement, share, cut (*informal*), payment, gift, reward, incentive, graft (*informal*), sweetener (*slang*), inducement,

sop, recompense, hush money (*slang*), payola
(*informal*), allurement

kick-off *noun* (*informal*) START, opening,
beginning, commencement, outset, starting
point, inception

kid[1] *noun* (*informal*) CHILD, girl, boy, baby,
lad, teenager, youngster, infant, adolescent,
juvenile, toddler, tot, lass, wean, little one,
bairn, stripling, sprog (*slang*), munchkin
(*informal, chiefly US*), rug rat (*US & Canad
informal*), littlie (*Austral informal*), ankle-biter
(*Austral slang*), tacker (*Austral slang*)

kid[2] *verb* TEASE, joke, trick, fool, pretend,
mock, rag (*Brit*), wind up (*Brit slang*), ridicule,
hoax, beguile, gull (*archaic*), delude, jest,
bamboozle, hoodwink, cozen, jerk *or* yank
someone's chain (*informal*)

kidnap *verb* ABDUCT, remove, steal, capture,
seize, snatch (*slang*), hijack, run off with, run
away with, make off with, hold to ransom

kill *verb* 1 SLAY, murder, execute, slaughter,
destroy, waste (*informal*), do in (*slang*),
take out (*slang*), massacre, butcher,
wipe out (*informal*), dispatch, cut down,
erase, assassinate, eradicate, whack
(*informal*), do away with, blow away
(*slang, chiefly US*), obliterate, knock off
(*slang*), liquidate, decimate, annihilate,
neutralize, exterminate, croak, mow down,
take (someone's) life, bump off (*slang*),
extirpate, wipe from the face of the earth
(*informal*) 2 (*informal*) DESTROY, defeat,
crush, scotch, still, stop, total (*slang*), ruin,
halt, cancel, wreck, shatter, veto, suppress,
dismantle, stifle, trash (*slang*), ravage,
eradicate, smother, quash, quell, extinguish,
annihilate, put paid to

killer *noun* MURDERER, slaughterer, slayer,
hit man (*slang*), butcher, gunman,
assassin, destroyer, liquidator, terminator,
executioner, exterminator

killing *noun* MURDER, massacre, slaughter,
execution, dispatch, manslaughter,
elimination, slaying, homicide, bloodshed,
carnage, fatality, liquidation, extermination,
annihilation, eradication, butchery, necktie
party (*informal*) ▷ *adjective* 1 (*informal*)
TIRING, hard, testing, taxing, difficult,
draining, exhausting, punishing, crippling,
fatiguing, gruelling, sapping, debilitating,
strenuous, arduous, laborious, enervating,
backbreaking 2 DEADLY, deathly, dangerous,
fatal, destructive, lethal, mortal, murderous,
death-dealing ▷▷ **make a killing** (*informal*)
PROFIT, gain, clean up (*informal*), be lucky,

be successful, make a fortune, strike it rich
(*informal*), make a bomb (*slang*), rake it in
(*informal*), have a windfall

killjoy *noun* SPOILSPORT, dampener, damper,
wet blanket (*informal*)

kin *noun* FAMILY, people, relations, relatives,
connections, kindred, kinsmen, kith,
kinsfolk, ainga (*NZ*), rellies (*Austral slang*)

kind[1] *adjective* CONSIDERATE, good, loving,
kindly, understanding, concerned,
friendly, neighbourly, gentle, generous,
mild, obliging, sympathetic, charitable,
thoughtful, benign, humane, affectionate,
compassionate, clement, gracious,
indulgent, benevolent, attentive, amiable,
courteous, amicable, lenient, cordial,
congenial, philanthropic, unselfish,
propitious, beneficent, kind-hearted,
bounteous, tender-hearted << ANTONYM
unkind

kind[2] *noun* 1 CLASS, sort, type, variety, brand,
grade, category, genre, classification,
league 2 SORT, set, type, ilk, family, race,
species, breed, genus 3 NATURE, sort, type,
manner, style, quality, character, make-
up, habit, stamp, description, mould,
essence, temperament, persuasion, calibre,
disposition

kind-hearted *adjective* SYMPATHETIC,
kind, generous, helpful, tender, humane,
compassionate, gracious, amicable,
considerate, altruistic, good-natured,
tender-hearted << ANTONYM hard-hearted

kindle *verb* 1 AROUSE, excite, inspire, stir,
thrill, stimulate, provoke, induce, awaken,
animate, rouse, sharpen, inflame, incite,
foment, bestir, enkindle 2 LIGHT, start,
ignite, fire, spark, torch, inflame, set fire to,
set a match to << ANTONYM extinguish

kindly *adjective* BENEVOLENT, kind, caring,
nice, warm, gentle, helpful, pleasant, mild,
sympathetic, beneficial, polite, favourable,
benign, humane, compassionate, hearty,
cordial, considerate, genial, affable, good-
natured, beneficent, well-disposed, kind-
hearted, warm-hearted << ANTONYM cruel ▷
adverb BENEVOLENTLY, politely, generously,
thoughtfully, tenderly, lovingly, cordially,
affectionately, helpfully, graciously,
obligingly, agreeably, indulgently, selflessly,
unselfishly, compassionately, considerately
<< ANTONYM unkindly

kindness *noun* 1 GOODWILL, understanding,
charity, grace, humanity, affection,
patience, tolerance, goodness, compassion,

hospitality, generosity, indulgence, decency, tenderness, clemency, gentleness, philanthropy, benevolence, magnanimity, fellow-feeling, amiability, beneficence, kindliness << ANTONYM malice 2 GOOD DEED, help, service, aid, favour, assistance, bounty, benefaction

kindred *noun* FAMILY, relations, relatives, connections, flesh, kin, lineage, kinsmen, kinsfolk, ainga (*NZ*), rellies (*Austral slang*) ▷ *adjective* 1 SIMILAR, like, related, allied, corresponding, affiliated, akin, kin, cognate, matching 2 LIKE-MINDED, similar, compatible, understanding, similar, friendly, sympathetic, responsive, agreeable, in tune, congenial, like, companionable

king *noun* RULER, monarch, sovereign, crowned head, leader, lord, prince, Crown, emperor, majesty, head of state, consort, His Majesty, overlord

kingdom *noun* 1 COUNTRY, state, nation, land, division, territory, province, empire, commonwealth, realm, domain, tract, dominion, sovereign state 2 DOMAIN, territory, province, realm, area, department, field, zone, arena, sphere

kink *noun* 1 TWIST, bend, wrinkle, knot, tangle, coil, corkscrew, entanglement, crimp, frizz 2 QUIRK, eccentricity, foible, idiosyncrasy, whim, fetish, vagary, singularity, crotchet 3 FLAW, difficulty, defect, complication, tangle, knot, hitch, imperfection

kinky *adjective* 1 (*slang*) PERVERTED, warped, deviant, unnatural, degenerated, unsavoury, unhealthy, depraved, licentious, pervy (*slang*) 2 (*informal*) WEIRD, odd, strange, bizarre, peculiar, eccentric, queer, quirky, unconventional, off-the-wall (*slang*), outlandish, oddball (*informal*), wacko (*slang*), outré 3 TWISTED, curled, curly, frizzy, tangled, coiled, crimped, frizzled

kinship *noun* 1 RELATIONSHIP, kin, family ties, consanguinity, ties of blood, blood relationship 2 SIMILARITY, relationship, association, bearing, connection, alliance, correspondence, affinity

kinsman *or* **kinswoman** *noun* RELATIVE, relation, blood relative, fellow tribesman, fellow clansman, rellie (*Austral slang*)

kiosk *noun* BOOTH, stand, counter, stall, newsstand, bookstall

kiss *verb* 1 PECK (*informal*), osculate, snog (*Brit slang*), neck (*informal*), smooch (*informal*), canoodle (*slang*) 2 BRUSH, touch, shave,

scrape, graze, caress, glance off, stroke ▷ *noun* PECK (*informal*), snog (*Brit slang*), smacker (*slang*), smooch (*informal*), French kiss, osculation

kit *noun* 1 EQUIPMENT, supplies, materials, tackle, tools, instruments, provisions, implements, rig, apparatus, trappings, utensils, paraphernalia, accoutrements, appurtenances 2 GEAR, things, effects, dress, clothes, clothing, stuff, equipment, uniform, outfit, rig, costume, garments, baggage, equipage ▷▷ **kit something** *or* **someone out** *or* **up** EQUIP, fit, supply, provide with, arm, stock, outfit, costume, furnish, fix up, fit out, deck out, accoutre

kitchen *noun* COOKHOUSE, galley, kitchenette, scullery

knack *noun* SKILL, art, ability, facility, talent, gift, capacity, trick, bent, craft, genius, expertise, forte, flair, competence, ingenuity, propensity, aptitude, dexterity, cleverness, quickness, adroitness, expertness, handiness, skilfulness << ANTONYM ineptitude

knackered *adjective* (*Brit slang*) 1 EXHAUSTED, worn out, tired out, drained, beat (*slang*), done in (*informal*), all in (*slang*), debilitated, prostrated, enervated, ready to drop, dog-tired (*informal*), zonked (*slang*), dead tired, dead beat (*slang*) 2 BROKEN, not working, out of order, not functioning, done in (*informal*), ruined, worn out, on the blink (*slang*), on its last legs

knavish *adjective* (*archaic*) DISHONEST, tricky, fraudulent, deceptive, unscrupulous, rascally, scoundrelly, deceitful, villainous, unprincipled, dishonourable, roguish << ANTONYM honourable

knead *verb* SQUEEZE, work, massage, manipulate, form, press, shape, stroke, blend, rub, mould

kneel *verb* GENUFLECT, bow, stoop, curtsy *or* curtsey, bow down, kowtow, get down on your knees, make obeisance

knell *noun* RING, sound, toll, chime, clang, peal

knickers *plural noun* UNDERWEAR, smalls, briefs, drawers, panties, bloomers

knife *noun* BLADE, carver, cutter, cutting tool ▷ *verb* CUT, wound, stab, slash, thrust, gore, pierce, spear, jab, bayonet, impale, lacerate

knit *verb* 1 JOIN, unite, link, tie, bond, ally, combine, secure, bind, connect, merge, weave, fasten, meld 2 HEAL, unite, join, link, bind, connect, loop, mend, fasten, intertwine, interlace 3 FURROW, tighten, knot, wrinkle, crease, screw up, pucker, scrunch up

knob *noun* BALL, stud, nub, protuberance, boss, bunch, swell, knot, bulk, lump, bump, projection, snag, hump, protrusion, knurl

knock *verb* 1 BANG, beat, strike, tap, rap, bash (*informal*), thump, buffet, pummel 2 HIT, strike, punch, belt (*informal*), deck (*slang*), slap, chin (*slang*), smack, thump, clap, cuff, smite (*archaic*), thwack, lay one on (*slang*), beat *or* knock seven bells out of (*informal*) 3 (*informal*) CRITICIZE, condemn, put down, run down, abuse, blast, pan (*informal*), slam (*slang*), slate (*informal*), have a go (at) (*informal*), censure, slag (off) (*slang*), denigrate, belittle, disparage, deprecate, diss (*slang, chiefly US*), find fault with, carp at, lambast(e), pick holes in, cast aspersions on, cavil at, pick to pieces, give (someone *or* something) a bad press ▷ *noun* 1 KNOCKING, pounding, beating, tap, hammering, bang, banging, rap, thump, thud 2 BANG, blow, impact, jar, collision, jolt, smash 3 BLOW, hit, punch, crack, belt (*informal*), clip, slap, bash, smack, thump, clout (*informal*), cuff, box 4 (*informal*) SETBACK, check, defeat, blow, upset, reverse, disappointment, hold-up, hitch, reversal, misfortune, rebuff, whammy (*informal, chiefly US*), bummer (*slang*) ▷▷ **knock about** *or* **around** WANDER, travel, roam, rove, range, drift, stray, ramble, straggle, traipse, go walkabout (*Austral*), stravaig (*Scot & N English dialect*) ▷▷ **knock about** *or* **around with someone** MIX WITH, associate with, mingle with, hang out with (*informal*), hang with (*informal, chiefly US*), be friends with, consort with, run around with (*informal*), hobnob with, socialize with, accompany, hang about with, fraternize with ▷▷ **knock off** (*informal*) STOP WORK, get out, conclude, shut down, terminate, call it a day (*informal*), finish work, clock off, clock out ▷▷ **knock someone about** *or* **around** HIT, attack, beat, strike, damage, abuse, hurt, injure, wound, assault, harm, batter, slap, bruise, thrash, beat up (*informal*), buffet, maul, work over (*slang*), clobber (*slang*), mistreat, manhandle, maltreat, lambast(e), slap around (*informal*), beat *or* knock seven bells out of (*informal*) ▷▷ **knock someone down** RUN OVER, hit, run down, knock over, mow down ▷▷ **knock someone off** (*slang*) KILL, murder, do in (*slang*), slaughter, destroy, waste (*informal*), take out (*slang*), execute, massacre, butcher, wipe

out (*informal*), dispatch, cut down, erase, assassinate, slay, eradicate, whack (*informal*), do away with, blow away (*slang, chiefly US*), obliterate, liquidate, decimate, annihilate, neutralize, exterminate, croak, mow down, take (someone's) life, bump off (*slang*), extirpate, wipe from the face of the earth (*informal*) ▷▷ **knock someone out** 1 FLOOR, knock unconscious, knock senseless, render unconscious, level, stun, daze 2 ELIMINATE, beat, defeat, trounce, vanquish 3 (*informal*) IMPRESS, move, strike, touch, affect, influence, excite, inspire, grab (*informal*), stir, overwhelm, sway, make an impression on ▷▷ **knock something down** DEMOLISH, destroy, flatten, tear down, level, total (*slang*), fell, ruin, dismantle, trash (*slang*), bulldoze, raze, pulverize, kennet (*Austral slang*), jeff (*Austral slang*) ▷▷ **knock something off** 1 (*slang*) STEAL, take, nick (*slang, chiefly Brit*), thieve, rob, pinch, cabbage (*Brit slang*), blag (*slang*), pilfer, purloin, filch 2 REMOVE, take away, deduct, debit, subtract

knockabout *adjective* BOISTEROUS, riotous, rollicking, rough-and-tumble, rumbustious, rambunctious (*informal*), harum-scarum, farcical, slapstick

knockout *noun* 1 KILLER BLOW, coup de grâce (*French*), kayo (*slang*), KO *or* K.O. (*slang*) 2 (*informal*) SUCCESS, hit, winner, triumph, smash, sensation, smash hit, stunner (*informal*), smasheroo (*informal*) << ANTONYM failure

knoll HILLOCK

knot *noun* 1 CONNECTION, tie, bond, joint, bow, loop, braid, splice, rosette, ligature 2 GROUP, company, set, band, crowd, pack, squad, circle, crew (*informal*), gang, mob, clique, assemblage ▷ *verb* TIE, secure, bind, complicate, weave, loop, knit, tether, entangle

knotty *adjective* 1 PUZZLING, hard, difficult, complex, complicated, tricky, baffling, intricate, troublesome, perplexing, mystifying, thorny, problematical 2 KNOTTED, rough, rugged, bumpy, gnarled, knobby, nodular

know *verb* 1 HAVE KNOWLEDGE OF, see, understand, recognize, perceive, be aware of, be conscious of 2 BE ACQUAINTED WITH, recognize, associate with, be familiar with, be friends with, be friendly with, have knowledge of, have dealings with, socialize with, fraternize with, be pals with << ANTONYM be unfamiliar with

3 *sometimes with* **about** *or* **of** BE FAMILIAR WITH, experience, understand, ken (*Scot*), comprehend, fathom, apprehend, have knowledge of, be acquainted with, feel certain of, have dealings in, be versed in << ANTONYM be ignorant of **4** RECOGNIZE, remember, identify, recall, place, spot, notice, distinguish, perceive, make out, discern, differentiate, recollect

know-all *noun* (*informal*) SMART ALECK, wise guy (*informal*), smarty (*informal*), clever-clogs (*informal*), clever Dick (*informal*), smarty-pants (*informal*), smartarse (*slang*), wiseacre, smarty-boots (*informal*)

know-how *noun* (*informal*) EXPERTISE, experience, ability, skill, knowledge, facility, talent, command, craft, grasp, faculty, capability, flair, knack, ingenuity, aptitude, proficiency, dexterity, cleverness, deftness, savoir-faire, adroitness, ableness

knowing *adjective* MEANINGFUL, significant, expressive, eloquent, enigmatic, suggestive

knowingly *adverb* DELIBERATELY, purposely, consciously, intentionally, on purpose, wilfully, wittingly

knowledge *noun* **1** UNDERSTANDING, sense, intelligence, judgment, perception, awareness, insight, grasp, appreciation, penetration, comprehension, discernment **2** LEARNING, schooling, education, science, intelligence, instruction, wisdom, scholarship, tuition, enlightenment, erudition << ANTONYM ignorance **3** CONSCIOUSNESS, recognition, awareness, apprehension, cognition, discernment << ANTONYM unawareness **4** ACQUAINTANCE, information, notice, intimacy, familiarity, cognizance << ANTONYM unfamiliarity

knowledgeable *adjective* **1** WELL-INFORMED, acquainted, conversant, au fait (*French*), experienced, understanding, aware, familiar, conscious, in the know (*informal*), cognizant, in the loop, au courant (*French*), clued-up (*informal*) **2** INTELLIGENT, lettered, learned, educated, scholarly, erudite

known *adjective* FAMOUS, well-known, celebrated, popular, common, admitted, noted, published, obvious, familiar, acknowledged, recognized, plain, confessed, patent, manifest, avowed << ANTONYM unknown

koppie *or* **kopje** *noun* (*S African*) HILL, down (*archaic*), fell, mount, height, mound, prominence, elevation, eminence, hilltop, tor, knoll, hillock, brae (*Scot*)

kudos *noun* PRESTIGE, regard, honour, praise, glory, fame, distinction, esteem, acclaim, applause, plaudits, renown, repute, notability, laudation

Ll

label *noun* **1** TAG, ticket, tab, marker, flag, tally, sticker, docket (*chiefly Brit*) **2** EPITHET, description, classification, characterization **3** BRAND, company, mark, trademark, brand name, trade name ▷ *verb* **1** TAG, mark, stamp, ticket, flag, tab, tally, sticker, docket (*chiefly Brit*) **2** BRAND, classify, describe, class, call, name, identify, define, designate, characterize, categorize, pigeonhole

laborious *adjective* **1** HARD, difficult, tiring, exhausting, wearing, sweat, tough, fatiguing, uphill, strenuous, arduous, tiresome, onerous, burdensome, herculean, wearisome, backbreaking, toilsome << ANTONYM easy **2** INDUSTRIOUS, hard-working, diligent, tireless, persevering, painstaking, indefatigable, assiduous, unflagging, sedulous **3** (*of literary style, etc*) FORCED, laboured, strained, ponderous, not fluent << ANTONYM natural

labour *noun* **1** TOIL, effort, industry, grind (*informal*), pains, sweat (*informal*), slog (*informal*), exertion, drudgery, travail, donkey-work << ANTONYM leisure **2** WORKERS, employees, workforce, labourers, hands, workmen **3** WORK, effort, employment, toil, industry **4** CHILDBIRTH, birth, delivery, contractions, pains, throes, travail, labour pains, parturition **5** CHORE, job, task, undertaking ▷ *verb* **1** WORK, toil, strive, work hard, grind (*informal*), sweat (*informal*), slave, endeavour, plod away, drudge, travail, slog away (*informal*), exert yourself, peg along *or* away (*chiefly Brit*), plug along *or* away (*informal*) << ANTONYM rest **2** STRUGGLE, work, strain, work hard, strive, go for it (*informal*), grapple, toil, make an effort, make every effort, do your best, exert yourself, work like a Trojan **3** OVEREMPHASIZE, stress, elaborate,

exaggerate, strain, dwell on, overdo, go on about, make a production (out) of (*informal*), make a federal case of (*US informal*) **4** *usually with* **under** BE DISADVANTAGED BY, suffer from, be a victim of, be burdened by

Labour *adjective* LEFT-WING, Democrat (*US*)

laboured *adjective* **1** DIFFICULT, forced, strained, heavy, awkward **2** CONTRIVED, studied, affected, awkward, unnatural, overdone, ponderous, overwrought

labourer *noun* WORKER, workman, working man, manual worker, hand, blue-collar worker, drudge, unskilled worker, navvy (*Brit informal*), labouring man

labyrinth *noun* MAZE, jungle, tangle, coil, snarl, entanglement

labyrinthine *adjective* MAZELIKE, winding, tangled, intricate, tortuous, convoluted, mazy

lace *noun* **1** NETTING, net, filigree, tatting, meshwork, openwork **2** CORD, tie, string, lacing, thong, shoelace, bootlace ▷ *verb* **1** FASTEN, tie, tie up, do up, secure, bind, close, attach, thread **2** MIX, drug, doctor, add to, spike, contaminate, fortify, adulterate **3** INTERTWINE, interweave, entwine, twine, interlink

lacerate *verb* **1** TEAR, cut, wound, rend, rip, slash, claw, maim, mangle, mangulate (*Austral slang*), gash, jag **2** HURT, wound, rend, torture, distress, torment, afflict, harrow

laceration *noun* CUT, injury, tear, wound, rent, rip, slash, trauma (*pathology*), gash, mutilation

lack *noun* SHORTAGE, want, absence, deficiency, need, shortcoming, deprivation, inadequacy, scarcity, dearth, privation, shortness, destitution, insufficiency, scantiness << ANTONYM abundance ▷

verb MISS, want, need, require, not have, be without, be short of, be in need of, be deficient in << ANTONYM have

lackey *noun* HANGER-ON, fawner, pawn, attendant, tool, instrument, parasite, cohort (*chiefly US*), valet, menial, minion, footman, sycophant, yes-man, manservant, toady, flunky, flatterer, varlet (*archaic*)

lacking *adjective* DEFICIENT, wanting, needing, missing, inadequate, minus (*informal*), flawed, impaired, sans (*archaic*)

lacklustre *adjective* FLAT, boring, dull, dim, dry, muted, sombre, drab, lifeless, prosaic, leaden, unimaginative, uninspired, unexciting, vapid, lustreless

laconic *adjective* TERSE, short, brief, clipped, to the point, crisp, compact, concise, curt, succinct, pithy, monosyllabic, sententious << ANTONYM long-winded

lacy *adjective* FILIGREE, open, fine, sheer, delicate, frilly, gossamer, gauzy, net-like, lace-like, meshy

lad *noun* BOY, kid (*informal*), guy (*informal*), youth, fellow, youngster, chap (*informal*), juvenile, shaver (*informal*), nipper (*informal*), laddie (*Scot*), stripling

laden *adjective* LOADED, burdened, hampered, weighted, full, charged, taxed, oppressed, fraught, weighed down, encumbered

lady *noun* 1 GENTLEWOMAN, duchess, noble, dame, baroness, countess, aristocrat, viscountess, noblewoman, peeress 2 WOMAN, female, girl, miss, maiden (*archaic*), maid (*archaic*), lass, damsel, lassie (*informal*), charlie (*Austral slang*), chook (*Austral slang*), wahine (*NZ*)

ladylike *adjective* REFINED, cultured, sophisticated, elegant, proper, modest, respectable, polite, genteel, courtly, well-bred, decorous << ANTONYM unladylike

lag *verb* 1 HANG BACK, delay, drag (behind), trail, linger, be behind, idle, saunter, loiter, straggle, dawdle, tarry, drag your feet (*informal*) 2 DROP, fail, diminish, decrease, flag, fall off, wane, ebb, slacken, lose strength

laggard *noun* STRAGGLER, lounger, lingerer, piker (*Austral & NZ slang*), snail, saunterer, loafer, loiterer, dawdler, skiver (*Brit slang*), idler, slowcoach (*Brit informal*), sluggard, bludger (*Austral & NZ informal*), slowpoke (*US & Canad informal*)

laid-back *adjective* RELAXED, calm, casual, together (*slang*), at ease, easy-going, unflappable (*informal*), unhurried, free and easy, easy-peasy (*slang*) << ANTONYM tense

lair *noun* 1 NEST, den, hole, burrow, resting place 2 HIDE-OUT (*informal*), retreat, refuge, den, sanctuary

laissez faire *or* **laisser faire** *noun* NONINTERVENTION, free trade, individualism, free enterprise, live and let live

lake *noun* POND, pool, reservoir, loch (*Scot*), lagoon, mere, lough (*Irish*), tarn

lame *adjective* 1 DISABLED, handicapped, crippled, limping, defective, hobbling, game, halt (*archaic*) 2 UNCONVINCING, poor, pathetic, inadequate, thin, weak, insufficient, feeble, unsatisfactory, flimsy

lament *verb* BEMOAN, grieve, mourn, weep over, complain about, regret, wail about, deplore, bewail ▷ *noun* 1 COMPLAINT, moaning, moan, keening, wail, wailing, lamentation, plaint, ululation 2 DIRGE, requiem, elegy, threnody, monody, coronach (*Scot & Irish*)

lamentable *adjective* 1 REGRETTABLE, distressing, tragic, unfortunate, harrowing, grievous, woeful, deplorable, mournful, sorrowful, gut-wrenching 2 DISAPPOINTING, poor, miserable, unsatisfactory, mean, low quality, meagre, pitiful, wretched, not much cop (*Brit slang*)

lamentation *noun* SORROW, grief, weeping, mourning, moan, grieving, sobbing, keening, lament, wailing, dirge, plaint, ululation

laminated *adjective* COVERED, coated, overlaid, veneered, faced

lampoon *verb* RIDICULE, mock, mimic, parody, caricature, send up (*Brit informal*), take off (*informal*), make fun of, squib, burlesque, satirize, pasquinade ▷ *noun* SATIRE, parody, caricature, send-up (*Brit informal*), takeoff (*informal*), skit, squib, burlesque, pasquinade

land *noun* 1 GROUND, earth, dry land, terra firma 2 SOIL, ground, earth, clay, dirt, sod, loam 3 COUNTRYSIDE, farming, farmland, rural districts 4 (*law*) PROPERTY, grounds, estate, acres, real estate, realty, acreage, real property, homestead (*US & Canad*) 5 COUNTRY, nation, region, state, district, territory, province, kingdom, realm, tract, motherland, fatherland ▷ *verb* 1 ARRIVE, dock, put down, moor, berth, alight, touch down, disembark, come to rest, debark 2 (*informal*) GAIN, get, win, score (*slang*), secure, obtain, acquire ▷▷ **land up** END UP, arrive, turn up, wind up, finish up, fetch up

(*informal*)

landing *noun* **1** COMING IN, arrival, touchdown, disembarkation, disembarkment **2** PLATFORM, jetty, quayside, landing stage

landlord *noun* **1** OWNER, landowner, proprietor, freeholder, lessor, landholder **2** INNKEEPER, host, hotelier, hotel-keeper

landmark *noun* **1** FEATURE, spectacle, monument **2** MILESTONE, turning point, watershed, critical point, tipping point **3** BOUNDARY MARKER, cairn, benchmark, signpost, milepost

landscape *noun* SCENERY, country, view, land, scene, prospect, countryside, outlook, terrain, panorama, vista

landslide *noun* LANDSLIP, avalanche, rockfall

lane *noun* ROAD, street, track, path, strip, way, passage, trail, pathway, footpath, passageway, thoroughfare

language *noun* **1** TONGUE, speech, vocabulary, dialect, idiom, vernacular, patter, lingo (*informal*), patois, lingua franca **2** SPEECH, communication, expression, speaking, talk, talking, conversation, discourse, interchange, utterance, parlance, vocalization, verbalization **3** STYLE, wording, expression, phrasing, vocabulary, usage, parlance, diction, phraseology

languid *adjective* INACTIVE, lazy, indifferent, lethargic, weary, sluggish, inert, uninterested, listless, unenthusiastic, languorous, lackadaisical, torpid, spiritless << ANTONYM energetic

languish *verb* **1** DECLINE, waste away, fade away, wither away, flag, weaken, wilt, sicken << ANTONYM flourish **2** (*literary*) WASTE AWAY, suffer, rot, be abandoned, be neglected, be disregarded << ANTONYM thrive **3** *often with* **for** PINE, want, long, desire, sigh, hunger, yearn, hanker, eat your heart out over, suspire

languishing *adjective* FADING, failing, declining, flagging, sinking, weakening, deteriorating, withering, wilting, sickening, drooping, droopy, wasting away

lank *adjective* **1** LIMP, lifeless, long, dull, straggling, lustreless **2** THIN, lean, slim, slender, skinny, spare, gaunt, lanky, emaciated, scrawny, attenuated, scraggy, rawboned

lanky *adjective* GANGLING, thin, tall, spare, angular, gaunt, bony, weedy (*informal*), scrawny, rangy, scraggy, rawboned, loose-jointed << ANTONYM chubby

lap¹ *noun* CIRCUIT, course, round, tour, leg, distance, stretch, circle, orbit, loop

lap² *verb* **1** RIPPLE, wash, splash, slap, swish, gurgle, slosh, purl, plash **2** DRINK, sip, lick, swallow, gulp, sup ▷▷ **lap something up** RELISH, like, enjoy, appreciate, delight in, savour, revel in, wallow in, accept eagerly

lapse *noun* **1** DECLINE, fall, drop, descent, deterioration, relapse, backsliding **2** MISTAKE, failing, fault, failure, error, slip, negligence, omission, oversight, indiscretion **3** INTERVAL, break, gap, passage, pause, interruption, lull, breathing space, intermission ▷ *verb* **1** SLIP, fall, decline, sink, drop, slide, deteriorate, degenerate **2** END, stop, run out, expire, terminate, become obsolete, become void

lapsed *adjective* **1** EXPIRED, ended, finished, run out, invalid, out of date, discontinued, unrenewed **2** BACKSLIDING, uncommitted, lacking faith, nonpractising

large *adjective* **1** BIG, great, huge, heavy, giant, massive, vast, enormous, tall, considerable, substantial, strapping, immense (*informal*), hefty, gigantic, monumental, bulky, chunky, burly, colossal, hulking, goodly, man-size, brawny, elephantine, thickset, ginormous (*informal*), humongous *or* humungous (*US slang*), sizable *or* sizeable << ANTONYM small **2** MASSIVE, great, big, huge, giant, vast, enormous, considerable, substantial, immense, tidy (*informal*), jumbo (*informal*), gigantic, monumental, mammoth, colossal, gargantuan, stellar (*informal*), king-size, ginormous (*informal*), humongous *or* humungous (*US slang*), sizable *or* sizeable << ANTONYM small **3** PLENTIFUL, full, grand, liberal, sweeping, broad, comprehensive, extensive, generous, lavish, ample, spacious, abundant, grandiose, copious, roomy, bountiful, capacious, profuse << ANTONYM scanty ▷▷ **at large 1** IN GENERAL, generally, chiefly, mainly, as a whole, in the main **2** FREE, roaming, on the run, fugitive, at liberty, on the loose, unchained, unconfined ▷▷ **by and large** ON THE WHOLE, generally, mostly, in general, all things considered, predominantly, in the main, for the most part, all in all, as a rule, taking everything into consideration

largely *adverb* MAINLY, generally, chiefly, widely, mostly, principally, primarily, considerably, predominantly, extensively, by and large, as a rule, to a large extent, to a great extent

large-scale *adjective* WIDE-RANGING, global, sweeping, broad, wide, vast, extensive, wholesale, far-reaching

largesse *or* **largess** *noun* 1 GENEROSITY, charity, bounty, philanthropy, munificence, liberality, alms-giving, benefaction, open-handedness 2 GIFT, present, grant, donation, endowment, bounty, bequest

lark (*informal*) *noun* PRANK, game, fun, fling, romp, spree, revel, mischief, caper, frolic, escapade, skylark, gambol, antic, jape, rollick ▷▷ **lark about** FOOL AROUND, play around, romp around, have fun, caper, frolic, cavort, gambol, muck around, make mischief, lark around, rollick, cut capers

lascivious *adjective* 1 LUSTFUL, sensual, immoral, randy (*informal, chiefly Brit*), horny (*slang*), voluptuous, lewd, wanton, salacious, prurient, lecherous, libidinous, licentious, unchaste 2 BAWDY, dirty, offensive, crude, obscene, coarse, indecent, blue, vulgar, immoral, pornographic, suggestive, X-rated (*informal*), scurrilous, smutty, ribald

lash¹ *verb* 1 POUND, beat, strike, hammer, drum, smack (*dialect*) 2 CENSURE, attack, blast, put down, criticize, slate (*informal, chiefly Brit*), ridicule, scold, berate, castigate, lampoon, tear into (*informal*), flay, upbraid, satirize, lambast(e), belabour 3 WHIP, beat, thrash, birch, flog, lam (*slang*), scourge, chastise, lambast(e), flagellate, horsewhip ▷ *noun* BLOW, hit, strike, stroke, stripe, swipe (*informal*)

lash² *verb* FASTEN, join, tie, secure, bind, rope, strap, make fast

lass *noun* GIRL, young woman, miss, bird (*slang*), maiden, chick (*slang*), maid, damsel, colleen (*Irish*), lassie (*informal*), wench (*facetious*), charlie (*Austral slang*), chook (*Austral slang*)

last¹ *adjective* 1 MOST RECENT, latest, previous 2 HINDMOST, furthest, final, at the end, remotest, furthest behind, most distant, rearmost, aftermost << ANTONYM foremost 3 FINAL, closing, concluding, ultimate, utmost << ANTONYM first ▷ *adverb* IN *or* AT THE END, after, behind, in the rear, bringing up the rear ▷ *noun* END, ending, close, finish, conclusion, completion, finale, termination ▷▷ **at last** FINALLY, eventually, in the end, ultimately, at the end of the day, at length, at long last, in conclusion, in the fullness of time ▷▷ **the last word** 1 FINAL DECISION, final say, final statement, conclusive comment 2 LEADING, best, first, highest, finest, cream, supreme, elite, first-class, foremost, first-rate, superlative, pre-eminent, unsurpassed, crème de la crème (*French*), most excellent

last² *verb* CONTINUE, keep, remain, survive, wear, carry on, endure, hold on, persist, keep on, hold out, abide << ANTONYM end

last-ditch *adjective* FINAL, frantic, desperate, struggling, straining, heroic, all-out (*informal*)

lasting *adjective* CONTINUING, long-term, permanent, enduring, remaining, eternal, abiding, long-standing, perennial, lifelong, durable, perpetual, long-lasting, deep-rooted, indelible, unending, undying, unceasing << ANTONYM passing

lastly *conjunction* FINALLY, to conclude, at last, in the end, ultimately, all in all, to sum up, in conclusion

latch *noun* FASTENING, catch, bar, lock, hook, bolt, clamp, hasp, sneck (*dialect*) ▷ *verb* FASTEN, bar, secure, lock, bolt, make fast, sneck (*dialect*)

late *adjective* 1 OVERDUE, delayed, last-minute, belated, tardy, behind time, unpunctual, behindhand << ANTONYM early 2 DEAD, deceased, departed, passed on, old, former, previous, preceding, defunct << ANTONYM alive 3 RECENT, new, advanced, fresh << ANTONYM old ▷ *adverb* BEHIND TIME, belatedly, tardily, behindhand, dilatorily, unpunctually << ANTONYM early

lately *adverb* RECENTLY, of late, just now, in recent times, not long ago, latterly

lateness *noun* DELAY, late date, retardation, tardiness, unpunctuality, belatedness, advanced hour

latent *adjective* HIDDEN, secret, concealed, invisible, lurking, veiled, inherent, unseen, dormant, undeveloped, quiescent, immanent, unrealized, unexpressed << ANTONYM obvious

later *adverb* AFTERWARDS, after, next, eventually, in time, subsequently, later on, thereafter, in a while, in due course, at a later date, by and by, at a later time ▷ *adjective* SUBSEQUENT, next, following, ensuing

lateral *adjective* SIDEWAYS, side, flanking, edgeways, sideward

latest *adjective* UP-TO-DATE, current, fresh, newest, happening (*informal*), modern, most recent, up-to-the-minute

lather *noun* 1 FROTH, soap, bubbles, foam, suds, soapsuds 2 (*informal*) FLUSTER, state (*informal*), sweat, fever, fuss, flap (*informal*), stew (*informal*), dither (*chiefly Brit*), twitter (*informal*), tizzy (*informal*), pother ▷ *verb* FROTH, soap, foam

latitude *noun* SCOPE, liberty, indulgence, freedom, play, room, space, licence, leeway, laxity, elbowroom, unrestrictedness

latter *noun* SECOND, last, last-mentioned, second-mentioned ▷ *adjective* LAST, later, latest, ending, closing, final, concluding << ANTONYM earlier

latterly *adverb* RECENTLY, lately, of late, hitherto

lattice *noun* GRID, network, web, grating, mesh, grille, trellis, fretwork, tracery, latticework, openwork, reticulation

laud *verb* (*literary*) PRAISE, celebrate, honour, acclaim, approve, magnify (*archaic*), glorify, extol, sing or sound the praises of

laudable *adjective* PRAISEWORTHY, excellent, worthy, admirable, of note, commendable, creditable, meritorious, estimable << ANTONYM blameworthy

laugh *verb* CHUCKLE, giggle, snigger, crack up (*informal*), cackle, chortle, guffaw, titter, roar, bust a gut (*informal*), be convulsed (*informal*), be in stitches, crease up (*informal*), split your sides, be rolling in the aisles (*informal*) ▷ *noun* 1 CHORTLE, giggle, chuckle, snigger, guffaw, titter, belly laugh, roar, shriek 2 (*informal*) JOKE, scream (*informal*), hoot (*informal*), lark, prank 3 (*informal*) CLOWN, character (*informal*), scream (*informal*), comic, caution (*informal*), wit, comedian, entertainer, card (*informal*), wag, joker, hoot (*informal*), humorist ▷▷ **laugh at something** *or* **someone** MAKE FUN OF, mock, tease, ridicule, taunt, jeer, deride, scoff at, belittle, lampoon, take the mickey out of (*informal*), pour scorn on, make a mock of ▷▷ **laugh something off** DISREGARD, ignore, dismiss, overlook, shrug off, minimize, brush aside, make light of, pooh-pooh

laughable *adjective* 1 RIDICULOUS, absurd, ludicrous, preposterous, farcical, nonsensical, derisory, risible, derisive, worthy of scorn 2 FUNNY, amusing, hilarious, humorous, diverting, comical, droll, mirthful

laughing stock *noun* FIGURE OF FUN, target, victim, butt, fair game, Aunt Sally (*Brit*), everybody's fool

laughter *noun* 1 CHUCKLING, laughing, giggling, chortling, guffawing, tittering, cachinnation 2 AMUSEMENT, entertainment, humour, glee, fun, mirth, hilarity, merriment

launch *verb* 1 PROPEL, fire, dispatch, discharge, project, send off, set in motion, send into orbit 2 BEGIN, start, open, initiate, introduce, found, set up, originate, commence, get under way, instigate, inaugurate, embark upon ▷ *noun* 1 PROPELLING, projection, sendoff 2 BEGINNING, start, introduction, initiation, opening, founding, setting-up, inauguration, commencement, instigation ▷▷ **launch into something** START ENTHUSIASTICALLY, begin, initiate, embark on, instigate, inaugurate, embark upon

launder *verb* 1 WASH, clean, dry-clean, tub, wash and iron, wash and press 2 PROCESS, doctor, manipulate

laurel ▷▷ **rest on your laurels** SIT BACK, relax, take it easy, relax your efforts

lavatory *noun* TOILET, bathroom, loo (*Brit informal*), bog (*slang*), can (*US & Canad slang*), john (*slang, chiefly US & Canad*), head(s) (*nautical slang*), throne (*informal*), closet, privy, cloakroom (*Brit*), urinal, latrine, washroom, powder room, ablutions (*military informal*), crapper (*taboo slang*), water closet, khazi (*slang*), pissoir (*French*), Gents or Ladies, little boy's room or little girl's room (*informal*), (public) convenience, W.C., dunny (*Austral & NZ old-fashioned informal*), bogger (*Austral slang*), brasco (*Austral slang*)

lavish *adjective* 1 GRAND, magnificent, splendid, lush, abundant, sumptuous, exuberant, opulent, copious, luxuriant, profuse << ANTONYM stingy 2 EXTRAVAGANT, wild, excessive, exaggerated, unreasonable, wasteful, prodigal, unrestrained, intemperate, immoderate, improvident, thriftless << ANTONYM thrifty 3 GENEROUS, free, liberal, bountiful, effusive, open-handed, unstinting, munificent << ANTONYM stingy ▷ *verb* SHOWER, pour, heap, deluge, dissipate << ANTONYM stint

law *noun* 1 CONSTITUTION, code, legislation, charter, jurisprudence 2 STATUTE, act, bill, rule, demand, order, command, code, regulation, resolution, decree, canon, covenant, ordinance, commandment, enactment, edict 3 PRINCIPLE, standard, code, formula, criterion, canon, precept, axiom, kaupapa (*NZ*) 4 THE LEGAL PROFESSION, the bar, barristers ▷▷ **lay down the law** BE DOGMATIC, call the shots (*informal*), pontificate, rule the roost, crack the whip, boss around, dogmatize, order about *or* around

law-abiding *adjective* OBEDIENT, good, peaceful, honourable, orderly, honest, lawful, compliant, dutiful, peaceable

lawful *adjective* LEGAL, constitutional, just, proper, valid, warranted, legitimate, authorized, rightful, permissible, legalized, allowable, licit << ANTONYM unlawful

lawless *adjective* DISORDERLY, wild, unruly, rebellious, chaotic, reckless, insurgent, anarchic, riotous, unrestrained, seditious, mutinous, insubordinate, ungoverned << ANTONYM law-abiding

lawlessness *noun* ANARCHY, disorder, chaos, reign of terror, mob rule, mobocracy, ochlocracy

lawsuit *noun* CASE, cause, action, trial, suit, argument, proceedings, dispute, contest, prosecution, legal action, indictment, litigation, industrial tribunal, legal proceedings

lawyer *noun* LEGAL ADVISER, attorney, solicitor, counsel, advocate, barrister, counsellor, legal representative

lax *adjective* SLACK, casual, careless, sloppy (*informal*), easy-going, negligent, lenient, slapdash, neglectful, slipshod, remiss, easy-peasy (*slang*), overindulgent << ANTONYM strict

laxative *noun* PURGATIVE, salts, purge, cathartic, physic (*rare*), aperient

lay¹ *verb* **1** PLACE, put, set, spread, plant, establish, settle, leave, deposit, put down, set down, posit **2** DEVISE, plan, design, prepare, work out, plot, hatch, contrive, concoct **3** PRODUCE, bear, deposit **4** ARRANGE, prepare, make, organize, position, locate, set out, devise, put together, dispose, draw up **5** ATTRIBUTE, charge, assign, allocate, allot, ascribe, impute **6** PUT FORWARD, offer, present, advance, lodge, submit, bring forward **7** BET, stake, venture, gamble, chance, risk, hazard, wager, give odds ▷▷ **lay into someone** (*informal*) ATTACK, hit, set about, hit out at, assail, tear into, pitch into (*informal*), go for the jugular, lambast(e), belabour, lash into, let fly at ▷▷ **lay off** (*informal*) STOP, give up, quit, cut it out, leave alone, pack in, abstain, leave off, give over (*informal*), let up, get off someone's back (*informal*), give it a rest (*informal*) ▷▷ **lay someone off** DISMISS, fire (*informal*), release, drop, sack (*informal*), pay off, discharge, oust, let go, make redundant, give notice to, give the boot to (*slang*), give the sack to (*informal*), give someone their cards, kennet

(*Austral slang*), jeff (*Austral slang*) ▷▷ **lay someone out** (*informal*) KNOCK OUT, fell, floor, knock unconscious, knock for six, kayo (*slang*) ▷▷ **lay someone up** (*informal*) CONFINE (TO BED), hospitalize, incapacitate ▷▷ **lay something aside** ABANDON, reject, dismiss, postpone, shelve, put off, renounce, put aside, cast aside ▷▷ **lay something bare** REVEAL, show, expose, disclose, unveil, divulge ▷▷ **lay something down 1** STIPULATE, state, establish, prescribe, assume, formulate, affirm, ordain, set down, postulate **2** SACRIFICE, give up, yield, surrender, turn over, relinquish ▷▷ **lay something in** STORE (UP), collect, build up, accumulate, buy in, amass, stockpile, hoard, stock up, heap up ▷▷ **lay something on** PROVIDE, prepare, supply, organize, give, cater (for), furnish, purvey ▷▷ **lay something out 1** ARRANGE, order, design, display, exhibit, put out, spread out **2** (*informal*) SPEND, pay, invest, fork out (*slang*), expend, shell out (*informal*), disburse

lay² *adjective* **1** NONCLERICAL, secular, non-ordained, laic, laical **2** NONSPECIALIST, amateur, unqualified, untrained, inexpert, nonprofessional

layer *noun* **1** COVERING, film, cover, sheet, coating, coat, blanket, mantle **2** TIER, level, seam, stratum

layman *noun* NONPROFESSIONAL, amateur, outsider, lay person, non-expert, nonspecialist

lay-off *noun* UNEMPLOYMENT, firing (*informal*), sacking (*informal*), dismissal, discharge

layout *noun* ARRANGEMENT, design, draft, outline, format, plan, formation, geography

laze *verb* **1** IDLE, lounge, hang around, loaf, stand around, loll **2** *often with* **away** KILL TIME, waste time, fritter away, pass time, while away the hours, veg out (*slang, chiefly US*), fool away

laziness *noun* IDLENESS, negligence, inactivity, slowness, sloth, sluggishness, slackness, indolence, tardiness, dilatoriness, slothfulness, do-nothingness, faineance

lazy *adjective* **1** IDLE, inactive, indolent, slack, negligent, inert, remiss, workshy, slothful, shiftless << ANTONYM industrious **2** LETHARGIC, languorous, slow-moving, languid, sleepy, sluggish, drowsy, somnolent, torpid << ANTONYM quick

leach *verb* EXTRACT, strain, drain, filter, seep, percolate, filtrate, lixiviate (*chemistry*)

lead *verb* **1** GO IN FRONT (OF), head, be in front

(of), be at the head (of), walk in front (of) **2** GUIDE, conduct, steer, escort, precede, usher, pilot, show the way **3** CONNECT TO, link, open onto **4** BE AHEAD (OF), be first, exceed, be winning, excel, surpass, come first, transcend, outstrip, outdo, blaze a trail **5** COMMAND, rule, govern, preside over, head, control, manage, direct, supervise, be in charge of, head up **6** LIVE, have, spend, experience, pass, undergo **7** RESULT IN, cause, produce, contribute, generate, bring about, bring on, give rise to, conduce **8** CAUSE, prompt, persuade, move, draw, influence, motivate, prevail, induce, incline, dispose ▷ *noun* **1** FIRST PLACE, winning position, primary position, vanguard, van **2** ADVANTAGE, start, advance, edge, margin, winning margin **3** EXAMPLE, direction, leadership, guidance, model, pattern **4** CLUE, tip, suggestion, trace, hint, guide, indication, pointer, tip-off **5** LEADING ROLE, principal, protagonist, title role, star part, principal part **6** LEASH, line, cord, rein, tether ▷ *adjective* MAIN, prime, top, leading, first, head, chief, premier, primary, most important, principal, foremost ▷▷ **lead off** BEGIN, start, open, set out, kick off (*informal*), initiate, commence, get going, get under way, inaugurate, start the ball rolling (*informal*) ▷▷ **lead someone on** ENTICE, tempt, lure, mislead, draw on, seduce, deceive, beguile, delude, hoodwink, inveigle, string along (*informal*) ▷▷ **lead up to something** INTRODUCE, approach, prepare for, intimate, pave the way for, prepare the way, make advances, make overtures, work round to

leaden *adjective* **1** GREY, dingy, overcast, sombre, lacklustre, dark grey, greyish, lustreless, louring *or* lowering **2** LABOURED, wooden, stiff, sluggish, plodding, stilted, humdrum **3** LIFELESS, dull, gloomy, dismal, dreary, languid, listless, spiritless **4** HEAVY, lead, crushing, oppressive, cumbersome, inert, onerous, burdensome

leader *noun* PRINCIPAL, president, head, chief, boss (*informal*), director, manager, chairman, captain, chair, premier, governor, commander, superior, ruler, conductor, controller, counsellor, supervisor, superintendent, big name, big gun (*informal*), chairwoman, chieftain, bigwig (*informal*), ringleader, chairperson, big shot (*informal*), overseer, big cheese (*slang* or *old-fashioned*), big noise (*informal*), big hitter (*informal*), baas (*S African*), torchbearer, number one, sherang

(*Austral & NZ*) << ANTONYM follower

leadership *noun* **1** AUTHORITY, control, influence, command, premiership, captaincy, governance, headship, superintendency **2** GUIDANCE, government, authority, management, administration, direction, supervision, domination, directorship, superintendency

leading *adjective* PRINCIPAL, top, major, main, first, highest, greatest, ruling, chief, prime, key, primary, supreme, most important, outstanding, governing, superior, dominant, foremost, pre-eminent, unsurpassed, number one << ANTONYM minor

leaf *noun* **1** FROND, flag, needle, pad, blade, bract, cotyledon, foliole **2** PAGE, sheet, folio ▷▷ **leaf through something** (with *book, magazine* etc. as object) SKIM, glance through, scan, browse, look through, dip into, flick through, flip through, thumb through, riffle through ▷▷ **turn over a new leaf** REFORM, change, improve, amend, make a fresh start, begin anew, change your ways, mend your ways

leaflet *noun* BOOKLET, notice, advert (*Brit informal*), brochure, bill, circular, flyer, tract, pamphlet, handout, mailshot, handbill

leafy *adjective* GREEN, leaved, leafed, shaded, shady, summery, verdant, bosky (*literary*), springlike, in foliage

league *noun* **1** ASSOCIATION, union, alliance, coalition, group, order, band, corporation, combination, partnership, federation, compact, consortium, guild, confederation, fellowship, fraternity, confederacy **2** CLASS, group, level, category, ability group ▷▷ **in league with someone** COLLABORATING WITH, leagued with, allied with, conspiring with, working together with, in cooperation with, in cahoots with (*informal*), hand in glove with

leak *verb* **1** ESCAPE, pass, spill, release, discharge, drip, trickle, ooze, seep, exude, percolate **2** DISCLOSE, tell, reveal, pass on, give away, make public, divulge, let slip, make known, spill the beans (*informal*), blab (*informal*), let the cat out of the bag, blow wide open (*slang*) ▷ *noun* **1** LEAKAGE, leaking, discharge, drip, oozing, seepage, percolation **2** HOLE, opening, crack, puncture, aperture, chink, crevice, fissure, perforation **3** DISCLOSURE, exposé, exposure, admission, revelation, uncovering, betrayal, unearthing, divulgence

leaky *adjective* LEAKING, split, cracked,

punctured, porous, waterlogged, perforated, holey, not watertight

lean¹ *verb* **1** BEND, tip, slope, incline, tilt, heel, slant **2** REST, prop, be supported, recline, repose **3** TEND, prefer, favour, incline, be prone to, gravitate, be disposed to, have a propensity to ▷▷ **lean on someone** DEPEND ON, trust, rely on, cling to, count on, confide in, have faith in

lean² *adjective* THIN, slim, slender, skinny, angular, trim, spare, gaunt, bony, lanky, wiry, emaciated, scrawny, svelte, lank, rangy, scraggy, macilent (*rare*) << ANTONYM fat

leaning *noun* TENDENCY, liking for, bias, inclination, taste, bent, disposition, penchant, propensity, aptitude, predilection, proclivity, partiality, proneness

leap *verb* **1** JUMP, spring, bound, bounce, hop, skip, caper, cavort, frisk, gambol **2** VAULT, clear, jump, bound, spring ▷ *noun* **1** JUMP, spring, bound, hop, skip, vault, caper, frisk **2** RISE, change, increase, soaring, surge, escalation, upsurge, upswing ▷▷ **leap at something** ACCEPT EAGERLY, seize on, jump at

learn *verb* **1** MASTER, grasp, acquire, pick up, take in, attain, become able, familiarize yourself with **2** DISCOVER, hear, understand, gain knowledge, find out about, become aware, discern, ascertain, come to know, suss (out) (*slang*) **3** MEMORIZE, commit to memory, learn by heart, learn by rote, get (something) word-perfect, learn parrot-fashion, get off pat, con (*archaic*)

learned *adjective* SCHOLARLY, experienced, lettered, cultured, skilled, expert, academic, intellectual, versed, literate, well-informed, erudite, highbrow, well-read << ANTONYM uneducated

learner *noun* STUDENT, pupil, scholar, novice, beginner, trainee, apprentice, disciple, neophyte, tyro << ANTONYM expert

learning *noun* KNOWLEDGE, study, education, schooling, research, scholarship, tuition, enlightenment

lease *verb* HIRE, rent, let, loan, charter, rent out, hire out

leash *noun* **1** LEAD, line, restraint, cord, rein, tether **2** RESTRAINT, hold, control, check, curb ▷ *verb* TETHER, control, secure, restrain, tie up, hold back, fasten

least *adjective* SMALLEST, meanest, fewest, minutest, lowest, tiniest, minimum, slightest, minimal ▷▷ **at least** AT THE MINIMUM, at the very least, not less than

leathery *adjective* TOUGH, hard, rough, hardened, rugged, wrinkled, durable, leathern (*archaic*), coriaceous, leatherlike

leave¹ *verb* **1** DEPART FROM, withdraw from, go from, escape from, desert, quit, flee, exit, pull out of, retire from, move out of, disappear from, run away from, forsake, flit (*informal*), set out from, go away from, hook it (*slang*), pack your bags (*informal*), make tracks, abscond from, decamp from, sling your hook (*Brit slang*), slope off from, take your leave of, do a bunk from (*Brit slang*), take yourself off from (*informal*) << ANTONYM arrive **2** QUIT, give up, get out of, resign from, drop out of **3** GIVE UP, abandon, desert, dump (*informal*), drop, surrender, ditch (*informal*), chuck (*informal*), discard, relinquish, renounce, jilt (*informal*), cast aside, forbear, leave in the lurch << ANTONYM stay with **4** ENTRUST, commit, delegate, refer, hand over, assign, consign, allot, cede, give over **5** BEQUEATH, will, transfer, endow, transmit, confer, hand down, devise (*law*), demise **6** FORGET, lay down, leave behind, mislay **7** CAUSE, produce, result in, generate, deposit ▷▷ **leave off something** STOP, end, finish, give up, cease, halt, break off, refrain from, abstain from, discontinue, knock off (*informal*), give over (*informal*), kick (*informal*), desist, keep off, belay (*nautical*) ▷▷ **leave something or someone out** OMIT, exclude, miss out, forget, except, reject, ignore, overlook, neglect, skip, disregard, bar, cast aside, count out

leave² *noun* **1** HOLIDAY, break, vacation, time off, sabbatical, leave of absence, furlough, schoolie (*Austral*), accumulated day off *or* ADO (*Austral*) **2** PERMISSION, freedom, sanction, liberty, concession, consent, allowance, warrant, authorization, dispensation << ANTONYM refusal **3** DEPARTURE, parting, withdrawal, goodbye, farewell, retirement, leave-taking, adieu, valediction << ANTONYM arrival

leave-taking *noun* DEPARTURE, going, leaving, parting, goodbye, farewell, valediction, sendoff (*informal*)

lecherous *adjective* LUSTFUL, randy (*informal, chiefly Brit*), raunchy (*slang*), lewd, wanton, carnal, salacious, prurient, lascivious, libidinous, licentious, lubricious (*literary*), concupiscent, goatish (*archaic or literary*), unchaste, ruttish << ANTONYM puritanical

lechery *noun* LUSTFULNESS, lust, licentiousness, salaciousness, sensuality, profligacy, debauchery, prurience, womanizing, carnality, lewdness, wantonness, lasciviousness, libertinism, concupiscence, randiness (*informal, chiefly Brit*), leching (*informal*), rakishness, lubricity, libidinousness, lecherousness

lecture *noun* 1 TALK, address, speech, lesson, instruction, presentation, discourse, sermon, exposition, harangue, oration, disquisition 2 TELLING-OFF (*informal*), rebuke, reprimand, talking-to (*informal*), heat (*slang, chiefly US & Canad*), going-over (*informal*), wigging (*Brit slang*), censure, scolding, chiding, dressing-down (*informal*), reproof, castigation ▷ *verb* 1 TALK, speak, teach, address, discourse, spout, expound, harangue, give a talk, hold forth, expatiate 2 TELL OFF (*informal*), berate, scold, reprimand, carpet (*informal*), censure, castigate, chide, admonish, tear into (*informal*), read someone the riot act, reprove, bawl someone out (*informal*), chew someone out (*US & Canad informal*), tear someone off a strip (*Brit informal*), give someone a rocket (*Brit & NZ informal*), give someone a talking-to (*informal*), give someone a dressing-down (*informal*), give someone a telling-off (*informal*)

ledge *noun* SHELF, step, ridge, projection, mantle, sill

lee *noun* SHELTER, cover, screen, protection, shadow, shade, shield, refuge

leech *noun* PARASITE, hanger-on, sycophant, freeloader (*slang*), sponger (*informal*), ligger (*slang*), bloodsucker (*informal*), quandong (*Austral slang*)

leer *verb* GRIN, eye, stare, wink, squint, goggle, smirk, drool, gloat, ogle ▷ *noun* GRIN, stare, wink, squint, smirk, drool, gloat, ogle

leery *adjective* (*slang*) WARY, cautious, uncertain, suspicious, doubting, careful, shy, sceptical, dubious, unsure, distrustful, on your guard, chary

lees *plural noun* SEDIMENT, grounds, refuse, deposit, precipitate, dregs, settlings

leeway *noun* ROOM, play, space, margin, scope, latitude, elbowroom

left *adjective* 1 LEFT-HAND, port, larboard (*nautical*) 2 (*of politics*) SOCIALIST, liberal, radical, progressive, left-wing, leftist

leftover *noun* REMNANT, leaving, remains, scrap, oddment ▷ *adjective* SURPLUS, remaining, extra, excess, unwanted, unused, uneaten

left-wing *adjective* SOCIALIST, communist,

red (*informal*), radical, leftist, liberal, revolutionary, militant, Marxist, Bolshevik, Leninist, collectivist, Trotskyite

left-winger *noun* SOCIALIST, communist, red (*informal*), radical, revolutionary, militant, Marxist, Bolshevik, Leninist, Trotskyite

leg *noun* 1 LIMB, member, shank, lower limb, pin (*informal*), stump (*informal*) 2 SUPPORT, prop, brace, upright 3 STAGE, part, section, stretch, lap, segment, portion ▷▷ **leg it** (*informal*) RUN, walk, escape, flee, hurry, run away, make off, make tracks, hotfoot, go on foot, skedaddle (*informal*) ▷▷ **not have a leg to stand on** (*informal*) HAVE NO BASIS, be vulnerable, be undermined, be invalid, be illogical, be defenceless, lack support, be full of holes ▷▷ **on its or your last legs** WORN OUT, dying, failing, exhausted, giving up the ghost, at death's door, about to collapse, about to fail, about to break down ▷▷ **pull someone's leg** (*informal*) TEASE, joke, trick, fool, kid (*informal*), have (someone) on, rag, rib (*informal*), wind up (*Brit slang*), deceive, hoax, make fun of, poke fun at, twit, chaff, lead someone up the garden path, jerk or yank someone's chain (*informal*) ▷▷ **shake a leg** (*informal*) HURRY, rush, move it, hasten, get cracking (*informal*), get a move on (*informal*), look lively (*informal*), stir your stumps (*informal*) ▷▷ **stretch your legs** TAKE A WALK, exercise, stroll, promenade, move about, go for a walk, take the air

legacy *noun* BEQUEST, inheritance, endowment, gift, estate, devise (*law*), heirloom

legal *adjective* 1 JUDICIAL, judiciary, forensic, juridical, jurisdictive 2 LAWFUL, allowed, sanctioned, constitutional, proper, valid, legitimate, authorized, rightful, permissible, legalized, allowable, within the law, licit

legalistic *adjective* HAIRSPLITTING, narrow, strict, contentious, literal, narrow-minded, polemical, litigious, disputatious

legality *noun* LAWFULNESS, validity, legitimacy, accordance with the law, permissibility, rightfulness, admissibleness

legalize *or* **legalise** *verb* PERMIT, allow, approve, sanction, license, legitimate, authorize, validate, legitimize, make legal, decriminalize

legal tender *noun* CURRENCY, money, medium, payment, specie

legend *noun* 1 MYTH, story, tale, fiction, narrative, saga, fable, folk tale, urban myth, urban legend, folk story 2 CELEBRITY, star, phenomenon, genius, spectacle, wonder, big name, marvel, prodigy, luminary, celeb (*informal*), megastar (*informal*) **3** INSCRIPTION, title, caption, device, device, motto, rubric

legendary *adjective* **1** FAMOUS, celebrated, well-known, acclaimed, renowned, famed, immortal, illustrious << ANTONYM unknown **2** MYTHICAL, fabled, traditional, romantic, fabulous, fanciful, fictitious, storybook, apocryphal << ANTONYM factual

legible *adjective* READABLE, clear, plain, bold, neat, distinct, easy to read, easily read, decipherable

legion *noun* **1** ARMY, company, force, division, troop, brigade **2** MULTITUDE, host, mass, drove, number, horde, myriad, throng ▷ *adjective* VERY MANY, numerous, countless, myriad, numberless, multitudinous

legislate *verb* MAKE LAWS, establish laws, prescribe, enact laws, pass laws, ordain, codify laws, put laws in force

legislation *noun* **1** LAW, act, ruling, rule, bill, measure, regulation, charter, statute **2** LAWMAKING, regulation, prescription, enactment, codification

legislative *adjective* LAW-MAKING, parliamentary, congressional, judicial, ordaining, law-giving, juridical, jurisdictive

legislator *noun* LAWMAKER, parliamentarian, lawgiver

legislature *noun* PARLIAMENT, house, congress, diet, senate, assembly, chamber, law-making body

legitimate *adjective* **1** LAWFUL, real, true, legal, acknowledged, sanctioned, genuine, proper, authentic, statutory, authorized, rightful, kosher (*informal*), dinkum (*Austral & NZ informal*), legit (*slang*), licit << ANTONYM unlawful **2** REASONABLE, just, correct, sensible, valid, warranted, logical, justifiable, well-founded, admissible << ANTONYM unreasonable ▷ *verb* LEGITIMIZE, allow, permit, sanction, authorize, legalize, give the green light to, legitimatize, pronounce lawful

legitimize *or* **legitimise** *verb* LEGALIZE, permit, sanction, legitimate, authorize, give the green light to, pronounce lawful

leisure *noun* SPARE, free, rest, holiday, quiet, ease, retirement, relaxation, vacation, recreation, time off, breathing space, spare moments << ANTONYM work ▷▷ **at one's leisure** IN YOUR OWN (GOOD) TIME, in due course, at your convenience, unhurriedly, when it suits you, without hurry, at an

unhurried pace, when you get round to it (*informal*)

leisurely *adjective* UNHURRIED, relaxed, slow, easy, comfortable, gentle, lazy, laid-back (*informal*), restful << ANTONYM hurried ▷ *adverb* UNHURRIEDLY, slowly, easily, comfortably, lazily, at your leisure, at your convenience, lingeringly, indolently, without haste << ANTONYM hurriedly

lekker *adjective* (*S African slang*) DELICIOUS, tasty, luscious, choice, savoury, palatable, dainty, delectable, mouthwatering, yummy (*slang*), scrumptious (*informal*), appetizing, toothsome, ambrosial, yummo (*Austral slang*)

lend *verb* **1** LOAN, advance, sub (*Brit informal*), accommodate one with **2** GIVE, provide, add, present, supply, grant, afford, contribute, hand out, furnish, confer, bestow, impart ▷▷ **lend itself to something** BE APPROPRIATE FOR, suit, be suitable for, fit, be appropriate to, be adaptable to, present opportunities of, be serviceable for

length *noun* **1** DISTANCE, reach, measure, extent, span, longitude **2** DURATION, term, period, space, stretch, span, expanse **3** PIECE, measure, section, segment, portion **4** LENGTHINESS, extent, elongation, wordiness, verbosity, prolixity, long-windedness, extensiveness, protractedness ▷▷ **at length 1** AT LAST, finally, eventually, in time, in the end, at long last **2** FOR A LONG TIME, completely, fully, thoroughly, for hours, in detail, for ages, in depth, to the full, exhaustively, interminably

lengthen *verb* **1** EXTEND, continue, increase, stretch, expand, elongate, make longer << ANTONYM shorten **2** PROTRACT, extend, prolong, draw out, spin out, make longer << ANTONYM cut down

lengthy *adjective* **1** PROTRACTED, long, prolonged, very long, tedious, lengthened, diffuse, drawn-out, interminable, long-winded, long-drawn-out, overlong, verbose, prolix **2** VERY LONG, rambling, interminable, long-winded, wordy, discursive, extended, overlong, verbose, prolix << ANTONYM brief

leniency *or* **lenience** *noun* MERCY, compassion, clemency, quarter, pity, tolerance, indulgence, tenderness, moderation, gentleness, forbearance, mildness, lenity

lenient *adjective* MERCIFUL, sparing, gentle, forgiving, kind, tender, mild, tolerant, compassionate, clement, indulgent, forbearing << ANTONYM severe

leper noun OUTCAST, reject, untouchable, pariah, lazar (*archaic*)

lesbian adjective HOMOSEXUAL, gay, les (*slang*), butch (*slang*), sapphic, lesbo (*slang*), tribadic ▷ noun LEZZIE (*slang*), les (*slang*), butch (*slang*), lesbo (*slang*)

lesion noun INJURY, hurt, wound, bruise, trauma (*pathology*), sore, impairment, abrasion, contusion

less adjective SMALLER, shorter, slighter, not so much ▷ adverb TO A SMALLER EXTENT, little, barely, not much, not so much, meagrely ▷ preposition MINUS, without, lacking, excepting, subtracting

lessen verb 1 REDUCE, lower, diminish, decrease, relax, ease, narrow, moderate, weaken, erode, impair, degrade, minimize, curtail, lighten, wind down, abridge, de-escalate << ANTONYM increase 2 GROW LESS, diminish, decrease, contract, ease, weaken, shrink, slow down, dwindle, lighten, wind down, die down, abate, slacken

lesser adjective LOWER, slighter, secondary, subsidiary, subordinate, inferior, less important << ANTONYM greater

lesson noun 1 CLASS, schooling, period, teaching, coaching, session, instruction, lecture, seminar, tutoring, tutorial 2 EXAMPLE, warning, model, message, moral, deterrent, precept, exemplar 3 EXERCISE, reading, practice, task, lecture, drill, assignment, homework, recitation 4 BIBLE READING, reading, text, Bible passage, Scripture passage

let verb 1 ENABLE, make, allow, cause, grant, permit 2 ALLOW, grant, permit, warrant, authorize, give the go-ahead, give permission, suffer (*archaic*), give the green light, give leave, give the O.K. or okay (*informal*) 3 LEASE, hire, rent, rent out, hire out, sublease ▷▷ **let on** (*informal*) 1 REVEAL, disclose, say, tell, admit, give away, divulge, let slip, make known, let the cat out of the bag (*informal*) 2 PRETEND, make out, feign, simulate, affect, profess, counterfeit, make believe, dissemble, dissimulate ▷▷ **let someone down** DISAPPOINT, fail, abandon, desert, disillusion, fall short, leave stranded, leave in the lurch, disenchant, dissatisfy ▷▷ **let someone off** (*informal*) EXCUSE, release, discharge, pardon, spare, forgive, exempt, dispense, exonerate, absolve, grant an amnesty to ▷▷ **let something down** DEFLATE, empty, exhaust, flatten, puncture ▷▷ **let something off** 1 FIRE, explode, set

off, discharge, detonate 2 EMIT, release, leak, exude, give off ▷▷ **let something out** 1 RELEASE, discharge 2 EMIT, make, produce, give vent to 3 REVEAL, tell, make known, let slip, leak, disclose, let fall, take the wraps off ▷▷ **let something or someone in** ADMIT, include, receive, welcome, greet, take in, incorporate, give access to, allow to enter ▷▷ **let up** STOP, diminish, decrease, subside, relax, ease (up), moderate, lessen, abate, slacken

letdown noun DISAPPOINTMENT, disillusionment, frustration, anticlimax, setback, washout (*informal*), comedown (*informal*), disgruntlement

lethal adjective DEADLY, terminal, fatal, deathly, dangerous, devastating, destructive, mortal, murderous, poisonous, virulent, pernicious, noxious, baneful << ANTONYM harmless

lethargic adjective SLUGGISH, slow, lazy, sleepy, heavy, dull, indifferent, debilitated, inactive, inert, languid, apathetic, drowsy, listless, comatose, stupefied, unenthusiastic, somnolent, torpid, slothful, enervated, unenergetic << ANTONYM energetic

lethargy noun SLUGGISHNESS, inertia, inaction, slowness, indifference, apathy, sloth, stupor, drowsiness, dullness, torpor, sleepiness, lassitude, languor, listlessness, torpidity, hebetude (*rare*) << ANTONYM energy

letter noun 1 MESSAGE, line, answer, note, reply, communication, dispatch, acknowledgment, billet (*archaic*), missive, epistle 2 CHARACTER, mark, sign, symbol ▷▷ **to the letter** PRECISELY, strictly, literally, exactly, faithfully, accurately, word for word, punctiliously

letters plural noun LEARNING, education, culture, literature, humanities, scholarship, erudition, belles-lettres

let-up noun (*informal*) LESSENING, break, pause, interval, recess, respite, lull, cessation, remission, breathing space, slackening, abatement

level noun 1 POSITION, standard, degree, grade, standing, stage, rank, status 2 HEIGHT, altitude, elevation, vertical position 3 FLAT SURFACE, plane, horizontal ▷ adjective 1 EQUAL, in line, aligned, balanced, on a line, at the same height 2 HORIZONTAL, even, flat, plane, smooth, uniform, as flat as a pancake << ANTONYM slanted 3 EVEN, tied, equal, drawn, neck and neck, all square, level pegging ▷ *verb* **1** EQUALIZE, balance, even up **2** DESTROY, devastate, wreck, demolish, flatten, knock down, pull down, tear down, bulldoze, raze, lay waste to, kennet (*Austral slang*), jeff (*Austral slang*) << ANTONYM build **3** DIRECT, point, turn, train, aim, focus, beam **4** FLATTEN, plane, smooth, make flat, even off *or* out ▷▷ **level with someone** (*informal*) BE HONEST, be open, be frank, come clean (*informal*), be straightforward, be up front (*slang*), be above board, keep nothing back ▷▷ **on the level** (*informal*) HONEST, genuine, sincere, open, straight, fair, square, straightforward, up front (*slang*), dinkum (*Austral & NZ informal*), above board

level-headed *adjective* CALM, balanced, reasonable, composed, together (*slang*), cool, collected, steady, sensible, sane, dependable, unflappable (*informal*), self-possessed, even-tempered

lever *noun* HANDLE, bar, crowbar, jemmy, handspike ▷ *verb* PRISE, move, force, raise, pry (*US*), jemmy

leverage *noun* **1** INFLUENCE, authority, pull (*informal*), weight, rank, clout (*informal*), purchasing power, ascendancy **2** FORCE, hold, pull, strength, grip, grasp

leviathan *noun* MONSTER, whale, mammoth, Titan, hulk, colossus, behemoth

levy *noun* TAX, fee, toll, tariff, duty, assessment, excise, imposition, impost, exaction ▷ *verb* IMPOSE, charge, tax, collect, gather, demand, exact

lewd *adjective* INDECENT, obscene, vulgar, dirty, blue, loose, vile, pornographic, wicked, wanton, X-rated (*informal*), profligate, bawdy, salacious, impure, lascivious, smutty, lustful, libidinous, licentious, unchaste

lexicon *noun* VOCABULARY, dictionary, glossary, word list, wordbook

liabilities *plural noun* DEBTS, expenditure, debit, arrears, obligations, accounts payable

liability *noun* **1** DISADVANTAGE, burden, drawback, inconvenience, drag, handicap, minus (*informal*), nuisance, impediment, albatross, hindrance, millstone, encumbrance **2** RESPONSIBILITY, accountability, culpability, obligation, onus, answerability

liable *adjective* **1** LIKELY, tending, inclined, disposed, prone, apt **2** VULNERABLE, subject, exposed, prone, susceptible, open, at risk of **3** RESPONSIBLE, accountable, amenable, answerable, bound, obligated, chargeable

liaise *verb* COMMUNICATE, link up, connect,

intermediate, mediate, interchange, hook up, keep contact

liaison *noun* **1** CONTACT, communication, connection, interchange **2** INTERMEDIARY, contact, hook-up, go-between **3** AFFAIR, romance, intrigue, fling, love affair, amour, entanglement, illicit romance

liar *noun* FALSIFIER, storyteller (*informal*), perjurer, fibber, fabricator, prevaricator

libel *noun* DEFAMATION, slander, misrepresentation, denigration, smear, calumny, vituperation, obloquy, aspersion ▷ *verb* DEFAME, smear, slur, blacken, malign, denigrate, revile, vilify, slander, traduce, derogate, calumniate, drag (someone's) name through the mud

liberal *adjective* **1** TOLERANT, enlightened, open-minded, permissive, advanced, catholic, humanitarian, right-on (*informal*), indulgent, easy-going, unbiased, high-minded, broad-minded, unprejudiced, unbigoted, politically correct *or* PC << ANTONYM intolerant **2** PROGRESSIVE, radical, reformist, libertarian, advanced, right-on (*informal*), forward-looking, humanistic, free-thinking, latitudinarian, politically correct *or* PC << ANTONYM conservative **3** ABUNDANT, generous, handsome, lavish, ample, rich, plentiful, copious, bountiful, profuse, munificent << ANTONYM limited **4** GENEROUS, kind, charitable, extravagant, free-handed, prodigal, altruistic, open-hearted, bountiful, magnanimous, open-handed, unstinting, beneficent, bounteous << ANTONYM stingy **5** FLEXIBLE, general, broad, rough, free, loose, lenient, not close, inexact, not strict, not literal << ANTONYM strict

liberalism *noun* PROGRESSIVISM, radicalism, humanitarianism, libertarianism, freethinking, latitudinarianism

liberalize *verb* RELAX, ease, moderate, modify, stretch, soften, broaden, loosen, mitigate, slacken, ameliorate

liberate *verb* FREE, release, rescue, save, deliver, discharge, redeem, let out, set free, let loose, untie, emancipate, unchain, unbind, manumit << ANTONYM imprison

liberator *noun* DELIVERER, saviour, rescuer, redeemer, freer, emancipator, manumitter

liberty *noun* **1** INDEPENDENCE, sovereignty, liberation, autonomy, immunity, self-determination, emancipation, self-government, self-rule **2** FREEDOM, liberation, redemption, emancipation, deliverance,

manumission, enfranchisement,
unshackling, unfettering << ANTONYM
restraint ▷▷ **at liberty 1** FREE, escaped,
unlimited, at large, not confined, untied,
on the loose, unchained, unbound **2** ABLE,
free, allowed, permitted, entitled, authorized
▷▷ **take liberties** or **a liberty** NOT SHOW
ENOUGH RESPECT, show disrespect, act
presumptuously, behave too familiarly,
behave impertinently
libretto noun WORDS, book, lines, text, script,
lyrics
licence noun **1** CERTIFICATE, document,
permit, charter, warrant **2** PERMISSION,
the right, authority, leave, sanction,
liberty, privilege, immunity, entitlement,
exemption, prerogative, authorization,
dispensation, a free hand, carte
blanche, blank cheque << ANTONYM
denial **3** FREEDOM, creativity, latitude,
independence, liberty, deviation, leeway,
free rein, looseness << ANTONYM
restraint **4** LAXITY, abandon, disorder,
excess, indulgence, anarchy, lawlessness,
impropriety, irresponsibility, profligacy,
licentiousness, unruliness, immoderation
<< ANTONYM moderation
license verb PERMIT, commission, enable,
sanction, allow, entitle, warrant, authorize,
empower, certify, accredit, give a blank
cheque to << ANTONYM forbid
lick verb **1** TASTE, lap, tongue, touch, wash,
brush **2** (informal) BEAT, defeat, overcome,
best, top, stuff (slang), tank (slang), undo,
rout, excel, surpass, outstrip, outdo, trounce,
clobber (slang), vanquish, run rings around
(informal), wipe the floor with (informal), blow
out of the water (slang) **3** (of flames) FLICKER,
touch, flick, dart, ripple, ignite, play over,
kindle ▷ noun **1** DAB, little, bit, touch, taste,
sample, stroke, brush, speck **2** (informal)
PACE, rate, speed, clip (informal)
licking noun THRASHING, beating, hiding
(informal), whipping, tanning (slang),
flogging, spanking, drubbing
lie¹ noun FALSEHOOD, deceit, fabrication, fib,
fiction, invention, deception, untruth, porky
(Brit slang), pork pie (Brit slang), white lie,
falsification, prevarication, falsity, mendacity
▷ verb FIB, fabricate, invent, misrepresent,
falsify, tell a lie, prevaricate, perjure, not
tell the truth, equivocate, dissimulate, tell
untruths, not speak the truth, say something
untrue, forswear yourself ▷▷ **give the lie
to something** DISPROVE, expose, discredit,

contradict, refute, negate, invalidate, rebut,
make a nonsense of, prove false, controvert,
confute
lie² verb **1** RECLINE, rest, lounge, couch,
sprawl, stretch out, be prone, loll, repose,
be prostrate, be supine, be recumbent **2** BE
PLACED, be, rest, exist, extend, be situated
3 BE SITUATED, sit, be located, be positioned
4 usually with **in** EXIST, be present, consist,
dwell, reside, pertain, inhere **5** BE BURIED,
remain, rest, be, be found, belong, be
located, be interred, be entombed **6** usually
with **on** or **upon** WEIGH, press, rest, burden,
oppress
liege noun FEUDAL LORD, master, superior,
sovereign, chieftain, overlord, seigneur,
suzerain
lieu ▷▷ **in lieu of** INSTEAD OF, in place of
life noun **1** BEING, existence, breath, entity,
vitality, animation, viability, sentience
2 LIVING THINGS, creatures, wildlife,
organisms, living beings **3** EXISTENCE, being,
lifetime, time, days, course, span, duration,
continuance **4** WAY OF LIFE, situation,
conduct, behaviour, life style **5** LIVELINESS,
activity, energy, spirit, go (informal), pep,
sparkle, vitality, animation, vigour, verve,
zest, high spirits, get-up-and-go (informal),
oomph (informal), brio, vivacity **6** BIOGRAPHY,
story, history, career, profile, confessions,
autobiography, memoirs, life story **7** SPIRIT,
heart, soul, essence, core, lifeblood, moving
spirit, vital spark, animating spirit, élan vital
(French) **8** PERSON, human, individual, soul,
human being, mortal
lifeblood noun ANIMATING FORCE, life,
heart, inspiration, guts (informal), essence,
stimulus, driving force, vital spark
lifeless adjective **1** DEAD, unconscious, extinct,
deceased, cold, defunct, inert, inanimate,
comatose, out cold, out for the count,
insensible, in a faint, insensate, dead to
the world (informal) << ANTONYM alive
2 BARREN, empty, desert, bare, waste, sterile,
unproductive, uninhabited **3** DULL, cold,
flat, hollow, heavy, slow, wooden, stiff,
passive, static, pointless, sluggish, lacklustre,
lethargic, colourless, listless, torpid,
spiritless << ANTONYM lively
lifelike adjective REALISTIC, faithful, authentic,
natural, exact, graphic, vivid, photographic,
true-to-life, undistorted
lifelong adjective LONG-LASTING, enduring,
lasting, permanent, constant, lifetime, for
life, persistent, long-standing, perennial,

deep-rooted, for all your life

lifetime *noun* EXISTENCE, time, day(s), course, period, span, life span, your natural life, all your born days

lift *verb* **1** RAISE, pick up, hoist, draw up, elevate, uplift, heave up, buoy up, raise high, bear aloft, upheave, upraise << ANTONYM lower **2** REVOKE, end, remove, withdraw, stop, relax, cancel, terminate, rescind, annul, countermand << ANTONYM impose **3** EXALT, raise, advance, promote, boost, enhance, upgrade, elevate, dignify, cheer up, perk up, ameliorate, buoy up << ANTONYM depress **4** DISAPPEAR, clear, vanish, disperse, dissipate, rise, be dispelled **5** (*informal*) STEAL, take, copy, appropriate, nick (*slang, chiefly Brit*), pocket, pinch (*informal*), pirate, cabbage (*Brit slang*), crib (*informal*), half-inch (*old-fashioned slang*), blag (*slang*), pilfer, purloin, plagiarize, thieve ▷ *noun* **1** BOOST, encouragement, stimulus, reassurance, uplift, pick-me-up, fillip, shot in the arm (*informal*), gee-up << ANTONYM blow **2** ELEVATOR (*chiefly US*), hoist, paternoster **3** RIDE, run, drive, transport, hitch (*informal*), car ride ▷▷ **lift off** TAKE OFF, be launched, blast off, take to the air

light¹ *noun* **1** BRIGHTNESS, illumination, luminosity, luminescence, ray of light, flash of light, shining, glow, blaze, sparkle, glare, gleam, brilliance, glint, lustre, radiance, incandescence, phosphorescence, scintillation, effulgence, lambency, refulgence << ANTONYM dark **2** LAMP, bulb, torch, candle, flare, beacon, lighthouse, lantern, taper **3** MATCH, spark, flame, lighter **4** ASPECT, approach, attitude, context, angle, point of view, interpretation, viewpoint, slant, standpoint, vantage point **5** UNDERSTANDING, knowledge, awareness, insight, information, explanation, illustration, enlightenment, comprehension, illumination, elucidation << ANTONYM mystery **6** DAYBREAK, morning, dawn, sun, sunrise, sunshine, sunlight, daylight, daytime, sunbeam, morn (*poetic*), cockcrow, broad day ▷ *adjective* **1** BRIGHT, brilliant, shining, glowing, sunny, illuminated, luminous, well-lighted, well-lit, lustrous, aglow, well-illuminated << ANTONYM dark **2** PALE, fair, faded, blonde, blond, bleached, pastel, light-coloured, whitish, light-toned, light-hued << ANTONYM dark ▷ *verb* **1** ILLUMINATE, light up, brighten, lighten, put on, turn on, clarify, switch on, floodlight, irradiate, illumine, flood with light << ANTONYM darken **2** IGNITE, inflame, fire, torch, kindle, touch off, set alight, set a match to << ANTONYM put out ▷▷ **bring something to light** REVEAL, expose, unveil, show, discover, disclose, show up, uncover, unearth, lay bare ▷▷ **come to light** BE REVEALED, appear, come out, turn up, be discovered, become known, become apparent, be disclosed, transpire ▷▷ **in the light of something** CONSIDERING, because of, taking into account, bearing in mind, in view of, taking into consideration, with knowledge of ▷▷ **light up 1** CHEER, shine, blaze, sparkle, animate, brighten, lighten, irradiate **2** SHINE, flash, beam, blaze, sparkle, flare, glare, gleam, flicker

light² *adjective* **1** INSUBSTANTIAL, thin, delicate, lightweight, easy, slight, portable, buoyant, airy, flimsy, underweight, not heavy, transportable, lightsome, imponderous << ANTONYM heavy **2** WEAK, soft, gentle, moderate, slight, mild, faint, indistinct << ANTONYM strong **3** CRUMBLY, loose, sandy, porous, spongy, friable << ANTONYM hard **4** DIGESTIBLE, small, restricted, modest, frugal, not rich, not heavy << ANTONYM substantial **5** UNDEMANDING, easy, simple, moderate, manageable, effortless, cushy (*informal*), untaxing, unexacting << ANTONYM strenuous **6** INSIGNIFICANT, small, minute, tiny, slight, petty, trivial, trifling, inconsequential, inconsiderable, unsubstantial << ANTONYM serious **7** LIGHT-HEARTED, pleasing, funny, entertaining, amusing, diverting, witty, trivial, superficial, humorous, gay, trifling, frivolous, unserious << ANTONYM serious **8** CAREFREE, happy, bright, lively, sunny, cheerful, animated, merry, gay, airy, frivolous, cheery, untroubled, blithe, light-hearted **9** NIMBLE, graceful, airy, deft, agile, sprightly, lithe, limber, lissom, light-footed, sylphlike << ANTONYM clumsy **10** DIZZY, reeling, faint, volatile, giddy, unsteady, light-headed ▷▷ **light on** or **upon something 1** SETTLE, land, perch, alight **2** COME ACROSS, find, discover, encounter, stumble on, hit upon, happen upon ▷▷ **light out** (*US*) RUN AWAY, escape, depart, make off, abscond, quit, do a runner (*slang*), scarper (*Brit slang*), do a bunk (*Brit slang*), fly the coop (*US & Canad informal*), skedaddle (*informal*), take a powder (*US & Canad slang*), take it on the lam (*US & Canad slang*), do a Skase (*Austral informal*)

lighten¹ *verb* BRIGHTEN, flash, shine, illuminate, gleam, light up, irradiate, become light, make bright

lighten² *verb* **1** EASE, relieve, alleviate, allay, reduce, facilitate, lessen, mitigate, assuage << ANTONYM intensify **2** CHEER, lift, revive, brighten, hearten, perk up, buoy up, gladden, elate << ANTONYM depress **3** MAKE LIGHTER, ease, disburden, reduce in weight

light-headed *adjective* **1** FAINT, dizzy, hazy, giddy, delirious, unsteady, vertiginous, woozy (*informal*) **2** FRIVOLOUS, silly, shallow, foolish, superficial, trifling, inane, flippant, flighty, bird-brained (*informal*), featherbrained, rattlebrained (*slang*)

light-hearted *adjective* CAREFREE, happy, bright, glad, sunny, cheerful, jolly, merry, upbeat (*informal*), playful, joyous, joyful, genial, chirpy (*informal*), jovial, untroubled, gleeful, happy-go-lucky, gay, effervescent, blithe, insouciant, frolicsome, ludic (*literary*), jocund, blithesome (*literary*) << ANTONYM gloomy

lightly *adverb* **1** MODERATELY, thinly, slightly, sparsely, sparingly << ANTONYM heavily **2** GENTLY, softly, slightly, faintly, delicately, gingerly, airily, timidly << ANTONYM forcefully **3** CARELESSLY, indifferently, breezily, thoughtlessly, flippantly, frivolously, heedlessly, slightingly << ANTONYM seriously **4** EASILY, simply, readily, effortlessly, unthinkingly, without thought, flippantly, heedlessly << ANTONYM with difficulty

lightweight *adjective* **1** THIN, fine, delicate, sheer, flimsy, gossamer, diaphanous, filmy, unsubstantial **2** UNIMPORTANT, shallow, trivial, insignificant, slight, petty, worthless, trifling, flimsy, paltry, inconsequential, undemanding, insubstantial, nickel-and-dime (*US slang*), of no account << ANTONYM significant

like¹ *adjective* SIMILAR TO, same as, allied to, equivalent to, parallel to, resembling, identical to, alike, corresponding to, comparable to, akin to, approximating, analogous to, cognate to << ANTONYM different ▷ *noun* EQUAL, equivalent, parallel, match, twin, counterpart << ANTONYM opposite

like² *verb* **1** ENJOY, love, adore (*informal*), delight in, go for, dig (*slang*), relish, savour, revel in, be fond of, be keen on, be partial to, have a preference for, have a weakness for << ANTONYM dislike **2** ADMIRE, approve of, appreciate, prize, take to, esteem, cherish, hold dear, take a shine to (*informal*), think well of << ANTONYM dislike **3** WISH, want, choose, prefer, desire, select, fancy, care, feel inclined ▷ *noun usually plural* LIKING, favourite, preference, cup of tea (*informal*), predilection, partiality

likelihood *noun* PROBABILITY, chance, possibility, prospect, liability, good chance, strong possibility, reasonableness, likeliness

likely *adjective* **1** INCLINED, disposed, prone, liable, tending, apt **2** PROBABLE, expected, anticipated, odds-on, on the cards, to be expected **3** PLAUSIBLE, possible, reasonable, credible, feasible, believable, verisimilar **4** APPROPRIATE, promising, pleasing, fit, fair, favourite, qualified, suitable, acceptable, proper, hopeful, agreeable, up-and-coming, befitting ▷ *adverb* PROBABLY, no doubt, presumably, in all probability, like enough (*informal*), doubtlessly, like as not (*informal*)

like-minded *adjective* AGREEING, compatible, harmonious, in harmony, unanimous, in accord, of one mind, of the same mind, en rapport (*French*)

liken *verb* COMPARE, match, relate, parallel, equate, juxtapose, mention in the same breath, set beside

likeness *noun* **1** RESEMBLANCE, similarity, correspondence, affinity, similitude **2** PORTRAIT, study, picture, model, image, photograph, copy, counterpart, representation, reproduction, replica, depiction, facsimile, effigy, delineation **3** APPEARANCE, form, guise, semblance

likewise *adverb* **1** ALSO, too, as well, further, in addition, moreover, besides, furthermore **2** SIMILARLY, the same, in the same way, in similar fashion, in like manner

liking *noun* FONDNESS, love, taste, desire, bent, stomach, attraction, weakness, tendency, preference, bias, affection, appreciation, inclination, thirst, affinity, penchant, propensity, soft spot, predilection, partiality, proneness << ANTONYM dislike

lilt *noun* RHYTHM, intonation, cadence, beat, pitch, swing, sway

limb *noun* **1** PART, member, arm, leg, wing, extension, extremity, appendage **2** BRANCH, spur, projection, offshoot, bough

limber *adjective* PLIANT, flexible, supple, agile, plastic, graceful, elastic, lithe, pliable, lissom(e), loose-jointed, loose-limbed

▷▷ **limber up** LOOSEN UP, prepare, exercise, warm up, get ready

limelight *noun* PUBLICITY, recognition, fame, the spotlight, attention, prominence, stardom, public eye, public notice, glare of publicity

limit *noun* **1** END, bound, ultimate, deadline, utmost, breaking point, termination, extremity, greatest extent, the bitter end, end point, cutoff point, furthest bound **2** BOUNDARY, end, edge, border, extent, pale, confines, frontier, precinct, perimeter, periphery **3** LIMITATION, maximum, restriction, ceiling, restraint ▷ *verb* RESTRICT, control, check, fix, bound, confine, specify, curb, restrain, ration, hinder, circumscribe, hem in, demarcate, delimit, put a brake on, keep within limits, straiten ▷▷ **the limit** (*informal*) THE END, it (*informal*), enough, the last straw, the straw that broke the camel's back

limitation *noun* **1** RESTRICTION, control, check, block, curb, restraint, constraint, obstruction, impediment **2** WEAKNESS, failing, qualification, reservation, defect, disadvantage, flaw, drawback, shortcoming, snag, imperfection

limited *adjective* **1** RESTRICTED, controlled, fixed, defined, checked, bounded, confined, curbed, hampered, constrained, finite, circumscribed << ANTONYM unlimited **2** NARROW, little, small, restricted, slight, inadequate, minimal, insufficient, unsatisfactory, scant

limitless *adjective* INFINITE, endless, unlimited, never-ending, vast, immense, countless, untold, boundless, unending, inexhaustible, undefined, immeasurable, unbounded, numberless, measureless, illimitable, uncalculable

limp¹ *verb* HOBBLE, stagger, stumble, shuffle, halt (*archaic*), hop, falter, shamble, totter, dodder, hirple (*Scot*) ▷ *noun* LAMENESS, hobble, hirple (*Scot*)

limp² *adjective* **1** FLOPPY, soft, relaxed, loose, flexible, slack, lax, drooping, flabby, limber, pliable, flaccid << ANTONYM stiff **2** WEAK, tired, exhausted, worn out, spent, debilitated, lethargic, enervated << ANTONYM strong

limpid *adjective* **1** CLEAR, bright, pure, transparent, translucent, crystal-clear, crystalline, pellucid **2** UNDERSTANDABLE, clear, lucid, unambiguous, comprehensible, intelligible, perspicuous

line¹ *noun* **1** STROKE, mark, rule, score, bar, band, channel, dash, scratch, slash, underline, streak, stripe, groove **2** WRINKLE, mark, crease, furrow, crow's foot **3** ROW, queue, rank, file, series, column, sequence, convoy, procession, crocodile (*Brit*) **4** STRING, cable, wire, strand, rope, thread, cord, filament, wisp **5** TRAJECTORY, way, course, track, channel, direction, route, path, axis **6** OUTLINE, shape, figure, style, cut, features, appearance, profile, silhouette, configuration, contour **7** BOUNDARY, mark, limit, edge, border, frontier, partition, borderline, demarcation **8** (*military*) FORMATION, front, position, front line, trenches, firing line **9** APPROACH, policy, position, way, course, practice, scheme, method, technique, procedure, tactic, avenue, ideology, course of action **10** OCCUPATION, work, calling, interest, business, job, area, trade, department, field, career, activity, bag (*slang*), employment, province, profession, pursuit, forte, vocation, specialization **11** LINEAGE, family, breed, succession, race, stock, strain, descent, ancestry, parentage **12** NOTE, message, letter, memo, report, word, card, e-mail, postcard ▷ *verb* **1** BORDER, edge, bound, fringe, rank, skirt, verge, rim **2** MARK, draw, crease, furrow, cut, rule, score, trace, underline, inscribe ▷▷ **draw the line at something** OBJECT TO, prohibit, stop short at, set a limit at, put your foot down over ▷▷ **in line** IN ACCORD, in agreement, in harmony, in step, in conformity ▷▷ **in line for** DUE FOR, being considered for, a candidate for, shortlisted for, in the running for, on the short list for, next in succession to ▷▷ **line something up 1** ALIGN, order, range, arrange, sequence, array, regiment, dispose, marshal, straighten, straighten up, put in a line **2** PREPARE, schedule, organize, secure, obtain, come up with, assemble, get together, lay on, procure, jack up (*NZ informal*) ▷▷ **line up** QUEUE UP, file, fall in, form a queue, form ranks

line² *verb* FILL, face, cover, reinforce, encase, inlay, interline, ceil

lineage *noun* DESCENT, family, line, succession, house, stock, birth, breed, pedigree, extraction, ancestry, forebears, progeny, heredity, forefathers, genealogy

lined *adjective* **1** WRINKLED, worn, furrowed, wizened **2** RULED, feint

lines *plural noun* PRINCIPLE, plan, example,

model, pattern, procedure, convention

line-up noun ARRANGEMENT, team, row, selection, array

linger verb 1 CONTINUE, last, remain, stay, carry on, endure, persist, abide 2 HANG ON, last, survive, cling to life, die slowly 3 STAY, remain, stop, wait, delay, lag, hang around, idle, dally, loiter, take your time, wait around, dawdle, hang in the air, procrastinate, tarry, drag your feet or heels

lingering adjective SLOW, prolonged, protracted, long-drawn-out, remaining, dragging, persistent

lingo noun (informal) LANGUAGE, jargon, dialect, talk, speech, tongue, idiom, vernacular, patter, cant, patois, argot

link noun 1 CONNECTION, relationship, association, tie-up, affinity, affiliation, vinculum 2 RELATIONSHIP, association, tie, bond, connection, attachment, liaison, affinity, affiliation 3 COMPONENT, part, piece, division, element, constituent ▷ verb 1 ASSOCIATE, relate, identify, connect, bracket 2 CONNECT, join, unite, couple, tie, bind, attach, fasten, yoke << ANTONYM separate

lion noun HERO, champion, fighter, warrior, conqueror, lionheart, brave person

lip noun 1 EDGE, rim, brim, margin, brink, flange 2 (slang) IMPUDENCE, rudeness, insolence, impertinence, sauce (informal), cheek (informal), effrontery, backchat (informal), brass neck (informal) ▷▷ **smack** or **lick your lips** GLOAT, drool, slaver

liquefy verb MELT, dissolve, thaw, liquidize, run, fuse, flux, deliquesce

liquid noun FLUID, solution, juice, liquor, sap ▷ adjective 1 FLUID, running, flowing, wet, melted, thawed, watery, molten, runny, liquefied, aqueous 2 CLEAR, bright, brilliant, shining, transparent, translucent, limpid 3 SMOOTH, clear, soft, flowing, sweet, pure, melting, fluent, melodious, mellifluous, dulcet, mellifluent 4 (of assets) CONVERTIBLE, disposable, negotiable, realizable

liquidate verb 1 DISSOLVE, cancel, abolish, terminate, annul 2 CONVERT TO CASH, cash, realize, sell off, sell up 3 KILL, murder, remove, destroy, do in (slang), silence, eliminate, take out (slang), get rid of, wipe out (informal), dispatch, finish off, do away with, blow away (slang, chiefly US), annihilate, exterminate, bump off (slang), rub out (US slang)

liquor noun 1 ALCOHOL, drink, spirits, booze (informal), grog, hard stuff (informal), strong drink, Dutch courage (informal), intoxicant, juice (informal), hooch or hootch (informal, chiefly US & Canad) 2 JUICE, stock, liquid, extract, gravy, infusion, broth

list¹ noun INVENTORY, record, listing, series, roll, file, schedule, index, register, catalogue, directory, tally, invoice, syllabus, tabulation, leet (Scot) ▷ verb ITEMIZE, record, note, enter, file, schedule, index, register, catalogue, write down, enrol, set down, enumerate, note down, tabulate

list² verb LEAN, tip, heel, incline, tilt, cant, heel over, careen ▷ noun TILT, leaning, slant, cant

listen verb 1 HEAR, attend, pay attention, hark, be attentive, be all ears, lend an ear, hearken (archaic), prick up your ears, give ear, keep your ears open, pin back your ears (informal) 2 PAY ATTENTION, observe, obey, mind, concentrate, heed, take notice, take note of, take heed of, do as you are told, give heed to

listless adjective LANGUID, sluggish, lifeless, lethargic, heavy, limp, vacant, indifferent, languishing, inert, apathetic, lymphatic, impassive, supine, indolent, torpid, inattentive, enervated, spiritless, mopish << ANTONYM energetic

litany noun 1 RECITAL, list, tale, catalogue, account, repetition, refrain, recitation, enumeration 2 PRAYER, petition, invocation, supplication, set words

literacy noun EDUCATION, learning, knowledge, scholarship, cultivation, proficiency, articulacy, ability to read and write, articulateness

literal adjective 1 EXACT, close, strict, accurate, faithful, verbatim, word for word 2 UNIMAGINATIVE, boring, dull, down-to-earth, matter-of-fact, factual, prosaic, colourless, uninspired, prosy 3 ACTUAL, real, true, simple, plain, genuine, gospel, bona fide, unvarnished, unexaggerated

literally adverb EXACTLY, really, closely, actually, simply, plainly, truly, precisely, strictly, faithfully, to the letter, verbatim, word for word

literary adjective WELL-READ, lettered, learned, formal, intellectual, scholarly, literate, erudite, bookish

literate adjective EDUCATED, lettered, learned, cultured, informed, scholarly, cultivated, knowledgeable, well-informed, erudite, well-read

literature noun 1 WRITINGS, letters, compositions, lore, creative writing,

written works, belles-lettres 2 (*informal*)
INFORMATION, publicity, leaflet, brochure,
circular, pamphlet, handout, mailshot,
handbill

lithe *adjective* SUPPLE, flexible, agile, limber,
pliable, pliant, lissom(e), loose-jointed,
loose-limbed

litigant *noun* CLAIMANT, party, plaintiff,
contestant, litigator, disputant

litigation *noun* LAWSUIT, case, action, process,
disputing, prosecution, contending

litigious *adjective* CONTENTIOUS, belligerent,
argumentative, quarrelsome, disputatious

litter *noun* 1 RUBBISH, refuse, waste,
fragments, junk, debris, shreds, garbage
(*chiefly US*), trash, muck, detritus, grot (*slang*)
2 JUMBLE, mess, disorder, confusion, scatter,
tangle, muddle, clutter, disarray, untidiness
3 BROOD, family, young, offspring, progeny
4 BEDDING, couch, mulch, floor cover,
straw-bed 5 STRETCHER, palanquin ▷ *verb*
1 CLUTTER, mess up, clutter up, be scattered
about, disorder, disarrange, derange, muss
(*US & Canad*) 2 SCATTER, spread, shower,
strew

little *adjective* 1 NOT MUCH, small, insufficient,
scant, meagre, sparse, skimpy, measly, hardly
any << ANTONYM ample 2 SMALL, minute,
short, tiny, mini, wee, compact, miniature,
dwarf, slender, diminutive, petite, dainty,
elfin, bijou, infinitesimal, teeny-weeny,
Lilliputian, munchkin (*informal, chiefly
US*), teensy-weensy, pygmy *or* pigmy
<< ANTONYM big 3 YOUNG, small, junior,
infant, immature, undeveloped, babyish
4 UNIMPORTANT, minor, petty, trivial,
trifling, insignificant, negligible, paltry,
inconsiderable << ANTONYM important
5 MEAN, base, cheap, petty, narrow-minded,
small-minded, illiberal ▷ *adverb* 1 HARDLY,
barely, not quite, not much, only just,
scarcely << ANTONYM much 2 RARELY,
seldom, scarcely, not often, infrequently,
hardly ever << ANTONYM always ▷ *noun*
BIT, touch, spot, trace, hint, dash, particle,
fragment, pinch, small amount, dab, trifle,
tad (*informal, chiefly US*), snippet, speck,
modicum << ANTONYM lot ▷▷ **a little** TO A
SMALL EXTENT, slightly, to some extent, to a
certain extent, to a small degree

liturgical *adjective* CEREMONIAL, ritual,
solemn, sacramental, formal, eucharistic

liturgy *noun* CEREMONY, service, ritual,
services, celebration, formula, worship, rite,
sacrament, form of worship

live[1] *verb* 1 DWELL, board, settle, lodge, occupy,
abide, inhabit, hang out (*informal*), stay
(*chiefly Scot*), reside, have as your home, have
your home in 2 EXIST, last, prevail, be, have
being, breathe, persist, be alive, have life,
draw breath, remain alive 3 SURVIVE, remain
alive, feed yourself, get along, make a living,
earn a living, make ends meet, subsist, eke
out a living, support yourself, maintain
yourself 4 THRIVE, be happy, flourish,
prosper, have fun, enjoy life, enjoy yourself,
luxuriate, live life to the full, make the most
of life

live[2] *adjective* 1 LIVING, alive, breathing,
animate, existent, vital, quick (*archaic*)
2 ACTIVE, connected, switched on,
unexploded 3 TOPICAL, important,
pressing, current, hot, burning, active, vital,
controversial, unsettled, prevalent, pertinent
▷▷ **live wire** (*informal*) DYNAMO, hustler (*US
& Canad slang*), ball of fire (*informal*), life
and soul of the party, go-getter (*informal*),
self-starter

livelihood *noun* OCCUPATION, work,
employment, means, living, job,
maintenance, subsistence, bread and butter
(*informal*), sustenance, (means of) support,
(source of) income

lively *adjective* 1 ANIMATED, spirited, quick,
keen, active, alert, dynamic, sparkling,
vigorous, cheerful, energetic, outgoing,
merry, upbeat (*informal*), brisk, bubbly,
nimble, agile, perky, chirpy (*informal*),
sparky, sprightly, vivacious, frisky, gay,
alive and kicking, spry, chipper (*informal*),
blithe, full of beans (*informal*), frolicsome,
full of pep (*informal*), blithesome, bright-
eyed and bushy-tailed << ANTONYM dull
2 BUSY, crowded, stirring, buzzing, bustling,
moving, eventful << ANTONYM slow
3 VIVID, strong, striking, bright, exciting,
stimulating, bold, colourful, refreshing,
forceful, racy, invigorating << ANTONYM
dull 4 ENTHUSIASTIC, strong, keen,
stimulating, eager, formidable, vigorous,
animated, weighty

liven up *verb* 1 STIR, brighten, hot up
(*informal*), cheer up, perk up, buck up
(*informal*) 2 CHEER UP, animate, rouse,
enliven, perk up, brighten up, pep up, buck
up (*informal*), put life into, vitalize, vivify

livery *noun* COSTUME, dress, clothing, suit,
uniform, attire, garb, regalia, vestments,
raiment (*archaic or poetic*)

livid *adjective* 1 (*informal*) ANGRY, cross, furious,

outraged, mad (*informal*), boiling, fuming, choked, infuriated, incensed, enraged, exasperated, indignant, incandescent, hot under the collar (*informal*), fit to be tied (*slang*), beside yourself, as black as thunder, tooshie (*Austral slang*), off the air (*Austral slang*) << ANTONYM delighted **2** DISCOLOURED, angry, purple, bruised, black-and-blue, contused

living *noun* **1** LIVELIHOOD, work, job, maintenance, occupation, subsistence, bread and butter (*informal*), sustenance, (means of) support, (source of) income **2** LIFESTYLE, ways, situation, conduct, behaviour, customs, lifestyle, way of life, mode of living ▷ *adjective* **1** ALIVE, existing, moving, active, vital, breathing, lively, vigorous, animated, animate, alive and kicking, in the land of the living (*informal*), quick (*archaic*) << ANTONYM dead **2** CURRENT, continuing, present, developing, active, contemporary, persisting, ongoing, operative, in use, extant << ANTONYM obsolete

load *verb* **1** FILL, stuff, pack, pile, stack, heap, cram, freight, lade **2** MAKE READY, charge, prime, prepare to fire ▷ *noun* **1** CARGO, lading, delivery, haul, shipment, batch, freight, bale, consignment **2** OPPRESSION, charge, pressure, worry, trouble, weight, responsibility, burden, affliction, onus, albatross, millstone, encumbrance, incubus ▷▷ **load someone down** BURDEN, worry, trouble, hamper, oppress, weigh down, saddle with, encumber, snow under

loaded *adjective* **1** LADEN, full, charged, filled, weighted, burdened, freighted **2** CHARGED, armed, primed, at the ready, ready to shoot or fire **3** TRICKY, charged, sensitive, delicate, manipulative, emotive, insidious, artful, prejudicial, tendentious **4** BIASED, weighted, rigged, distorted **5** (*slang*) RICH, wealthy, affluent, well off, rolling (*slang*), flush (*informal*), well-heeled (*informal*), well-to-do, moneyed

loaf¹ *noun* **1** LUMP, block, cake, cube, slab **2** (*slang*) HEAD, mind, sense, common sense, block (*informal*), nous (*Brit slang*), chump (*Brit slang*), gumption (*Brit informal*), noddle (*informal, chiefly Brit*)

loaf² *verb* IDLE, hang around, take it easy, lie around, loiter, loll, laze, lounge around, veg out (*slang, chiefly US*), be indolent

loafer *noun* IDLER, lounger, bum (*informal*), piker (*Austral & NZ slang*), drone (*Brit*), shirker, couch potato (*slang*), time-waster,

layabout, skiver (*Brit slang*), ne'er-do-well, wastrel, bludger (*Austral & NZ informal*), lazybones (*informal*)

loan *noun* ADVANCE, credit, mortgage, accommodation, allowance, touch (*slang*), overdraft ▷ *verb* LEND, allow, credit, advance, accommodate, let out

loath *or* **loth** *adjective* UNWILLING, against, opposed, counter, resisting, reluctant, backward, averse, disinclined, indisposed << ANTONYM willing

loathe *verb* HATE, dislike, despise, detest, abhor, abominate, have a strong aversion to, find disgusting, execrate, feel repugnance towards, not be able to bear or abide

loathing *noun* HATRED, hate, horror, disgust, aversion, revulsion, antipathy, abomination, repulsion, abhorrence, repugnance, odium, detestation, execration

loathsome *adjective* HATEFUL, offensive, nasty, disgusting, horrible, revolting, obscene, vile, obnoxious, repulsive, nauseating, odious, repugnant, abhorrent, abominable, execrable, detestable, yucky or yukky (*slang*), yucko (*Austral slang*) << ANTONYM delightful

lob *verb* THROW, launch, toss, hurl, lift, pitch, shy (*informal*), fling, loft

lobby *verb* CAMPAIGN, press, pressure, push, influence, promote, urge, persuade, appeal, petition, pull strings (*Brit informal*), exert influence, bring pressure to bear, solicit votes ▷ *noun* **1** PRESSURE GROUP, group, camp, faction, lobbyists, interest group, special-interest group, ginger group, public-interest group (*US & Canad*) **2** CORRIDOR, hall, passage, entrance, porch, hallway, foyer, passageway, entrance hall, vestibule

lobola *noun* (*S African*) DOWRY, portion, marriage settlement, dot (*archaic*)

local *adjective* **1** COMMUNITY, district, regional, provincial, parish, neighbourhood, small-town (*chiefly US*), parochial, parish pump **2** CONFINED, limited, narrow, restricted ▷ *noun* RESIDENT, native, inhabitant, character (*informal*), local yokel (*disparaging*)

locale *noun* SITE, place, setting, position, spot, scene, location, venue, locality, locus

locality *noun* **1** NEIGHBOURHOOD, area, region, district, vicinity, neck of the woods (*informal*) **2** SITE, place, setting, position, spot, scene, location, locale

localize *verb* RESTRICT, limit, contain, concentrate, confine, restrain, circumscribe, delimit

locate *verb* **1** FIND, discover, detect, come across, track down, pinpoint, unearth, pin down, lay your hands on, run to earth *or* ground **2** PLACE, put, set, position, seat, site, establish, settle, fix, situate

location *noun* PLACE, point, setting, position, situation, spot, venue, whereabouts, locus, locale

lock¹ *verb* **1** FASTEN, close, secure, shut, bar, seal, bolt, latch, sneck (*dialect*) **2** UNITE, join, link, engage, mesh, clench, entangle, interlock, entwine **3** EMBRACE, press, grasp, clutch, hug, enclose, grapple, clasp, encircle ▷ *noun* FASTENING, catch, bolt, clasp, padlock ▷▷ **lock someone out** SHUT OUT, bar, ban, exclude, keep out, debar, refuse admittance to ▷▷ **lock someone up** IMPRISON, jail, confine, cage, detain, shut up, incarcerate, send down (*informal*), send to prison, put behind bars

lock² *noun* STRAND, curl, tuft, tress, ringlet

lodge *noun* **1** CABIN, house, shelter, cottage, hut, chalet, gatehouse, hunting lodge **2** SOCIETY, group, club, association, section, wing, chapter, branch, assemblage ▷ *verb* **1** REGISTER, put, place, set, lay, enter, file, deposit, submit, put on record **2** STAY, room, stop, board, reside, sojourn **3** ACCOMMODATE, house, shelter, put up, entertain, harbour, quarter, billet **4** STICK, remain, catch, implant, come to rest, become fixed, imbed

lodger *noun* TENANT, roomer, guest, resident, boarder, paying guest

lodging *noun often plural* ACCOMMODATION, rooms, boarding, apartments, quarters, digs (*Brit informal*), shelter, residence, dwelling, abode, habitation, bachelor apartment (*Canad*)

lofty *adjective* **1** NOBLE, grand, distinguished, superior, imposing, renowned, elevated, majestic, dignified, stately, sublime, illustrious, exalted << ANTONYM humble **2** HIGH, raised, towering, tall, soaring, elevated, sky-high << ANTONYM low **3** HAUGHTY, lordly, proud, arrogant, patronizing, condescending, snooty (*informal*), disdainful, supercilious, high and mighty (*informal*), toffee-nosed (*slang, chiefly Brit*) << ANTONYM modest

log *noun* **1** STUMP, block, branch, chunk, trunk, bole, piece of timber **2** RECORD, listing, account, register, journal, chart, diary, tally, logbook, daybook ▷ *verb* RECORD, report, enter, book, note, register, chart, put down, tally, set down, make a note of

loggerhead ▷▷ **at loggerheads** QUARRELLING, opposed, feuding, at odds, estranged, in dispute, at each other's throats, at daggers drawn, at enmity

logic *noun* **1** SCIENCE OF REASONING, deduction, dialectics, argumentation, ratiocination, syllogistic reasoning **2** CONNECTION, rationale, coherence, relationship, link, chain of thought **3** REASON, reasoning, sense, good reason, good sense, sound judgment

logical *adjective* **1** RATIONAL, clear, reasoned, reasonable, sound, relevant, consistent, valid, coherent, pertinent, well-organized, cogent, well-reasoned, deducible << ANTONYM illogical **2** REASONABLE, obvious, sensible, most likely, natural, necessary, wise, plausible, judicious << ANTONYM unlikely

logistics *noun* ORGANIZATION, management, strategy, engineering, plans, masterminding, coordination, orchestration

loiter *verb* LINGER, idle, loaf, saunter, delay, stroll, lag, dally, loll, dawdle, skulk, dilly-dally (*informal*), hang about *or* around

loll *verb* **1** LOUNGE, relax, lean, slump, flop, sprawl, loaf, slouch, recline, outspan (*S African*) **2** DROOP, drop, hang, flop, flap, dangle, sag, hang loosely

lone *adjective* **1** SOLITARY, single, separate, one, only, sole, by yourself, unaccompanied **2** ISOLATED, deserted, remote, secluded, lonesome (*chiefly US & Canad*), godforsaken

loneliness *noun* SOLITUDE, isolation, desolation, seclusion, aloneness, dreariness, solitariness, forlornness, lonesomeness (*chiefly US & Canad*), desertedness

lonely *adjective* **1** SOLITARY, alone, isolated, abandoned, lone, withdrawn, single, estranged, outcast, forsaken, forlorn, destitute, by yourself, lonesome (*chiefly US & Canad*), friendless, companionless << ANTONYM accompanied **2** DESOLATE, deserted, remote, isolated, solitary, out-of-the-way, secluded, uninhabited, sequestered, off the beaten track (*informal*), godforsaken, unfrequented << ANTONYM crowded

loner *noun* (*informal*) INDIVIDUALIST, outsider, solitary, maverick, hermit, recluse, misanthrope, lone wolf

lonesome *adjective* (*Chiefly US & Canad*) LONELY, deserted, isolated, lone, gloomy, dreary, desolate, forlorn, friendless, cheerless, companionless

long¹ *adjective* **1** ELONGATED, extended, stretched, expanded, extensive, lengthy, far-reaching, spread out << ANTONYM short **2** PROLONGED, slow, dragging, lengthy, lingering, protracted, interminable, spun out, long-drawn-out << ANTONYM brief

long² *verb* DESIRE, want, wish, burn, dream of, pine, hunger, ache, lust, crave, yearn, covet, itch, hanker, set your heart on, eat your heart out over

long-drawn-out *adjective* PROLONGED, marathon, lengthy, protracted, interminable, spun out, dragged out, overlong, overextended

longing *noun* DESIRE, hope, wish, burning, urge, ambition, hunger, yen (*informal*), hungering, aspiration, ache, craving, yearning, coveting, itch, thirst, hankering << ANTONYM indifference ▷ *adjective* YEARNING, anxious, eager, burning, hungry, pining, craving, languishing, ardent, avid, wishful, wistful, desirous << ANTONYM indifferent

long-lived *adjective* LONG-LASTING, enduring, full of years, old as Methuselah, longevous

long-standing *adjective* ESTABLISHED, fixed, enduring, abiding, long-lasting, long-lived, long-established, time-honoured

long-suffering *adjective* UNCOMPLAINING, patient, resigned, forgiving, tolerant, easy-going, stoical, forbearing

long-winded *adjective* RAMBLING, prolonged, lengthy, tedious, diffuse, tiresome, wordy, long-drawn-out, garrulous, discursive, repetitious, overlong, verbose, prolix << ANTONYM brief

look *verb* **1** SEE, view, consider, watch, eye, study, check, regard, survey, clock (*Brit slang*), examine, observe, stare, glance, gaze, scan, check out (*informal*), inspect, gape, peep, behold (*archaic*), goggle, eyeball (*slang*), scrutinize, ogle, gawp (*Brit slang*), gawk, recce (*slang*), get a load of (*informal*), take a gander at (*informal*), rubberneck (*slang*), take a dekko at (*Brit slang*), feast your eyes upon **2** SEARCH, seek, hunt, forage, fossick (*Austral & NZ*) **3** CONSIDER, contemplate **4** FACE, overlook, front on, give onto **5** HOPE, expect, await, anticipate, reckon on **6** SEEM, appear, display, seem to be, look like, exhibit, manifest, strike you as ▷ *noun* **1** GLIMPSE, view, glance, observation, review, survey, sight, examination, gaze, inspection, peek, squint (*informal*), butcher's (*Brit slang*),

gander (*informal*), once-over (*informal*), recce (*slang*), eyeful (*informal*), look-see (*slang*), shufti (*Brit slang*) **2** APPEARANCE, effect, bearing, face, air, style, fashion, cast, aspect, manner, expression, impression, complexion, guise, countenance, semblance, demeanour, mien (*literary*) ▷▷ **look after something** *or* **someone** TAKE CARE OF, mind, watch, protect, tend, guard, nurse, care for, supervise, sit with, attend to, keep an eye on, take charge of ▷▷ **look down on** *or* **upon someone** DISDAIN, despise, scorn, sneer at, spurn, hold in contempt, treat with contempt, turn your nose up (at) (*informal*), contemn (*formal*), look down your nose at (*informal*), misprize ▷▷ **look forward to something** ANTICIPATE, expect, look for, wait for, await, hope for, long for, count on, count the days until, set your heart on ▷▷ **look out for something** BE CAREFUL OF, beware, watch out for, pay attention to, be wary of, be alert to, be vigilant about, keep an eye out for, be on guard for, keep your eyes open for, keep your eyes peeled for, keep your eyes skinned for, be on the qui vive for ▷▷ **look over something** EXAMINE, view, check, monitor, scan, check out (*informal*), inspect, look through, eyeball (*slang*), work over, flick through, peruse, cast an eye over, take a dekko at (*Brit slang*) ▷▷ **look someone up** VISIT, call on, go to see, pay a visit to, drop in on (*informal*), look in on ▷▷ **look something up** RESEARCH, find, search for, hunt for, track down, seek out ▷▷ **look up** IMPROVE, develop, advance, pick up, progress, come along, get better, shape up (*informal*), perk up, ameliorate, show improvement ▷▷ **look up to someone** RESPECT, honour, admire, esteem, revere, defer to, have a high opinion of, regard highly, think highly of

lookalike *noun* DOUBLE, twin, clone, replica, spit (*informal, chiefly Brit*), ringer (*slang*), spitting image (*informal*), dead ringer (*slang*), living image, exact match, spit and image (*informal*)

lookout *noun* **1** WATCHMAN, guard, sentry, sentinel, vedette (*military*) **2** WATCH, guard, vigil, qui vive **3** WATCHTOWER, post, tower, beacon, observatory, citadel, observation post **4** (*informal*) CONCERN, business, worry, funeral (*informal*), pigeon (*Brit informal*)

loom *verb* **1** APPEAR, emerge, hover, take shape, threaten, bulk, menace, come into view, become visible **2** OVERHANG, rise, mount, dominate, tower, soar, overshadow, hang over, rise up, overtop

loop *noun* CURVE, ring, circle, bend, twist, curl, spiral, hoop, coil, loophole, twirl, kink, noose, whorl, eyelet, convolution ▷ *verb* TWIST, turn, join, roll, circle, connect, bend, fold, knot, curl, spiral, coil, braid, encircle, wind round, curve round

loophole *noun* LET-OUT, escape, excuse, plea, avoidance, evasion, pretence, pretext, subterfuge, means of escape

loose *adjective* **1** FREE, detached, insecure, unfettered, released, floating, wobbly, unsecured, unrestricted, untied, unattached, movable, unfastened, unbound, unconfined **2** SLACK, easy, hanging, relaxed, loosened, not fitting, sloppy, baggy, slackened, loose-fitting, not tight << ANTONYM tight **3** (*old-fashioned*) PROMISCUOUS, fast, abandoned, immoral, dissipated, lewd, wanton, profligate, disreputable, debauched, dissolute, libertine, licentious, unchaste << ANTONYM chaste **4** VAGUE, random, inaccurate, disordered, rambling, diffuse, indefinite, disconnected, imprecise, ill-defined, indistinct, inexact << ANTONYM precise ▷ *verb* FREE, release, ease, liberate, detach, unleash, let go, undo, loosen, disconnect, set free, slacken, untie, disengage, unfasten, unbind, unloose, unbridle << ANTONYM fasten

loosen *verb* UNTIE, undo, release, separate, detach, let out, unstick, slacken, unbind, work free, work loose, unloose ▷▷ **loosen up** RELAX, chill (*slang*), soften, unwind, go easy (*informal*), lighten up (*slang*), hang loose, outspan (*S African*), ease up *or* off

loot *verb* PLUNDER, rob, raid, sack, rifle, ravage, ransack, pillage, despoil ▷ *noun* PLUNDER, goods, prize, haul, spoils, booty, swag (*slang*)

lop *verb* CUT, crop, chop, trim, clip, dock, hack, detach, prune, shorten, sever, curtail, truncate

lope *verb* STRIDE, spring, bound, gallop, canter, lollop

lopsided *adjective* CROOKED, one-sided, tilting, warped, uneven, unequal, disproportionate, squint, unbalanced, off balance, awry, askew, out of shape, asymmetrical, cockeyed, out of true, skewwhiff (*Brit informal*)

lord *noun* **1** PEER, nobleman, count, duke, gentleman, earl, noble, baron, aristocrat, viscount, childe (*archaic*) **2** RULER, leader, chief, king, prince, master, governor, commander, superior, monarch, sovereign, liege, overlord, potentate, seigneur ▷▷ **lord it over someone** BOSS AROUND *or* ABOUT (*informal*), order around, threaten, bully, menace, intimidate, hector, bluster, browbeat, ride roughshod over, pull rank on, tyrannize, put on airs, be overbearing, act big (*slang*), overbear, play the lord, domineer ▷▷ **the Lord** *or* **Our Lord** JESUS CHRIST, God, Christ, Messiah, Jehovah, the Almighty, the Galilean, the Good Shepherd, the Nazarene

lore *noun* TRADITIONS, sayings, experience, saws, teaching, beliefs, wisdom, doctrine, mythos, folk-wisdom, traditional wisdom

lose *verb* **1** BE DEFEATED, be beaten, lose out, be worsted, come to grief, come a cropper (*informal*), be the loser, suffer defeat, get the worst of, take a licking (*informal*) **2** MISLAY, miss, drop, forget, displace, be deprived of, fail to keep, lose track of, suffer the loss of, misplace **3** FORFEIT, miss, fail, yield, default, be deprived of, pass up (*informal*), lose out on (*informal*) **4** WASTE, consume, squander, drain, exhaust, lavish, deplete, use up, dissipate, expend, misspend **5** STRAY FROM, miss, confuse, wander from **6** ESCAPE FROM, pass, leave behind, evade, lap, duck, dodge, shake off, elude, slip away from, outstrip, throw off, outrun, outdistance, give someone the slip

loser *noun* FAILURE, flop (*informal*), underdog, also-ran, no-hoper (*Austral slang*), dud (*informal*), lemon (*slang*), clinker (*slang, chiefly US*), washout (*informal*), non-achiever

loss *noun* **1** LOSING, waste, disappearance, deprivation, squandering, drain, forfeiture << ANTONYM gain **2** *sometimes plural* DEFICIT, debt, deficiency, debit, depletion, shrinkage, losings << ANTONYM gain **3** DAMAGE, cost, injury, hurt, harm, disadvantage, detriment, impairment << ANTONYM advantage ▷ *plural noun* CASUALTIES, dead, victims, death toll, fatalities, number killed, number wounded ▷▷ **at a loss** CONFUSED, puzzled, baffled, bewildered, stuck (*informal*), helpless, stumped, perplexed, mystified, nonplussed, at your wits' end

lost *adjective* **1** MISSING, missed, disappeared, vanished, strayed, wayward, forfeited, misplaced, mislaid **2** BEWILDERED, confused, puzzled, baffled, helpless, ignorant, perplexed, mystified, clueless (*slang*) **3** WASTED, consumed, neglected, misused, squandered, forfeited, dissipated, misdirected, frittered away, misspent, misapplied **4** GONE, finished, destroyed, vanished, extinct, defunct, died out **5** PAST, former, gone, dead, forgotten, lapsed, extinct, obsolete, out-of-date, bygone, unremembered **6** ENGROSSED, taken up, absorbed, entranced, abstracted, absent, distracted, preoccupied, immersed, dreamy, rapt, spellbound **7** FALLEN, corrupt, depraved, wanton, abandoned, damned, profligate, dissolute, licentious, unchaste, irreclaimable

lot noun **1** BUNCH (informal), group, crowd, crew, set, band, quantity, assortment, consignment **2** DESTINY, situation, circumstances, fortune, chance, accident, fate, portion, doom, hazard, plight **3** SHARE, group, set, piece, collection, portion, parcel, batch ▷▷ **a lot** or **lots 1** PLENTY, scores, masses (informal), load(s) (informal), ocean(s), wealth, piles (informal), a great deal, quantities, stack(s), heap(s), a good deal, a large amount, abundance, reams (informal), oodles (informal) **2** OFTEN, regularly, a great deal, frequently, a good deal ▷▷ **draw lots** CHOOSE, pick, select, toss up, draw straws (informal), throw dice, spin a coin ▷▷ **throw in your lot with someone** JOIN WITH, support, join forces with, make common cause with, align yourself with, ally or align yourself with, join fortunes with

loth ▷ see **loath**

lotion noun CREAM, solution, balm, salve, liniment, embrocation

lottery noun **1** RAFFLE, draw, lotto (Brit, NZ & S African), sweepstake **2** GAMBLE, chance, risk, venture, hazard, toss-up (informal)

loud adjective **1** NOISY, strong, booming, roaring, piercing, thundering, forte (music), turbulent, resounding, deafening, thunderous, rowdy, blaring, strident, boisterous, tumultuous, vociferous, vehement, sonorous, ear-splitting, obstreperous, stentorian, clamorous, ear-piercing, high-sounding << ANTONYM quiet **2** GARISH, bold, glaring, flamboyant, vulgar, brash, tacky (informal), flashy, lurid, tasteless, naff (Brit slang), gaudy, tawdry, showy, ostentatious, brassy << ANTONYM sombre **3** LOUD-MOUTHED, offensive, crude, coarse, vulgar, brash, crass, raucous, brazen (informal) << ANTONYM quiet

loudly adverb NOISILY, vigorously, vehemently, vociferously, uproariously, lustily, shrilly, fortissimo (music), at full volume, deafeningly, at the top of your voice, clamorously

lounge verb RELAX, pass time, hang out (informal), idle, loaf, potter, sprawl, lie about, waste time, recline, take it easy, saunter, loiter, loll, dawdle, laze, kill time, make yourself at home, veg out (slang, chiefly US), outspan (S African), fritter time away ▷ noun SITTING ROOM, living room, parlour, drawing room, front room, reception room, television room

louring or **lowering** adjective **1** DARKENING, threatening, forbidding, menacing, black, heavy, dark, grey, clouded, gloomy, ominous, cloudy, overcast, foreboding **2** GLOWERING, forbidding, grim, frowning, brooding, scowling, sullen, surly

lousy adjective (slang) **1** INFERIOR, bad, poor, terrible, awful, no good, miserable, rotten (informal), duff, second-rate, shoddy, low-rent (informal, chiefly US), for the birds (informal), two-bit (US & Canad slang), slovenly, poxy (slang), dime-a-dozen (informal), bush-league (Austral & NZ informal), not much cop (Brit slang), tinhorn (US slang), of a sort or of sorts, strictly for the birds (informal), bodger or bodgie (Austral slang) **2** MEAN, low, base, dirty, vicious, rotten (informal), vile, despicable, hateful, contemptible **3** with WELL-SUPPLIED WITH, rolling in (slang), not short of, amply supplied with

lout noun OAF, boor, bear, ned (Scot slang), yahoo, hoon (Austral & NZ slang), clod, bumpkin, gawk, dolt, churl, lubber, lummox (informal), clumsy idiot, yob or yobbo (Brit slang), cougan (Austral slang), scozza (Austral slang), bogan (Austral slang)

lovable or **loveable** adjective ENDEARING, attractive, engaging, charming, winning, pleasing, sweet, lovely, fetching (informal), delightful, cute, enchanting, captivating, cuddly, amiable, adorable, winsome, likable or likeable << ANTONYM detestable

love verb **1** ADORE, care for, treasure, cherish, prize, worship, be devoted to, be attached to, be in love with, dote on, hold dear, think the world of, idolize, feel affection for, have affection for, adulate << ANTONYM hate **2** ENJOY, like, desire, fancy, appreciate, relish, delight in, savour, take pleasure in, have a soft spot for, be partial to, have a weakness for << ANTONYM dislike **3** CUDDLE, neck (informal), kiss, pet, embrace, caress, fondle, canoodle (slang) ▷ noun **1** PASSION, liking, regard, friendship, affection, warmth, attachment, intimacy, devotion, tenderness, fondness, rapture, adulation, adoration, infatuation, ardour, endearment, aroha (NZ), amity << ANTONYM hatred **2** *with of* LIKING FOR, taste for, delight in, bent for, weakness for, relish for, enjoyment, devotion to, penchant for, inclination for, zest for, fondness for, soft spot for, partiality to **3** BELOVED, dear, dearest, sweet, lover, angel, darling, honey, loved one, sweetheart, truelove, dear one, leman (*archaic*), inamorata *or* inamorato << ANTONYM enemy **4** SYMPATHY, understanding, heart, charity, pity, humanity, warmth, mercy, sorrow, kindness, tenderness, friendliness, condolence, commiseration, fellow feeling, soft-heartedness, tender-heartedness, aroha (NZ) ▷▷ **fall in love with someone** LOSE YOUR HEART TO, fall for, be taken with, take a shine to (*informal*), become infatuated with, fall head over heels in love with, be swept off your feet by, bestow your affections on ▷▷ **for love** WITHOUT PAYMENT, freely, for nothing, free of charge, gratis, pleasurably ▷▷ **for love or money** BY ANY MEANS, ever, under any conditions ▷▷ **in love** ENAMOURED, charmed, captivated, smitten, wild (*informal*), mad (*informal*), crazy (*informal*), enthralled, besotted, infatuated, enraptured ▷▷ **make love** HAVE SEXUAL INTERCOURSE, have sex, go to bed, sleep together, do it (*informal*), mate, have sexual relations, have it off (*slang*), have it away (*slang*)

love affair *noun* ROMANCE, relationship, affair, intrigue, liaison, amour, affaire de coeur (*French*)

loveless *adjective* **1** UNLOVING, hard, cold, icy, insensitive, unfriendly, heartless, frigid, unresponsive, unfeeling, cold-hearted **2** UNLOVED, disliked, forsaken, lovelorn, friendless, unappreciated, unvalued, uncherished

lovelorn *adjective* LOVESICK, mooning, slighted, pining, yearning, languishing, spurned, jilted, moping, unrequited, crossed in love

lovely *adjective* **1** BEAUTIFUL, appealing, attractive, charming, winning, pretty, sweet, handsome, good-looking, exquisite, admirable, enchanting, graceful, captivating, amiable, adorable, comely << ANTONYM ugly **2** WONDERFUL, pleasing, nice, pleasant, engaging, marvellous, delightful, enjoyable, gratifying, agreeable << ANTONYM horrible

lovemaking *noun* SEXUAL INTERCOURSE, intercourse, intimacy, sexual relations,

the other (*informal*), mating, nookie (*slang*), copulation, coitus, act of love, carnal knowledge, rumpy-pumpy (*slang*), coition, sexual union *or* congress, rumpo (*slang*)

lover *noun* SWEETHEART, beloved, loved one, beau, flame (*informal*), mistress, admirer, suitor, swain (*archaic*), woman friend, lady friend, man friend, toy boy, paramour, leman (*archaic*), fancy bit (*slang*), boyfriend *or* girlfriend, fancy man *or* fancy woman (*slang*), fiancé *or* fiancée, inamorata *or* inamorato

loving *adjective* **1** AFFECTIONATE, kind, warm, dear, friendly, devoted, tender, fond, ardent, cordial, doting, amorous, solicitous, demonstrative, warm-hearted << ANTONYM cruel **2** TENDER, kind, caring, warm, gentle, sympathetic, considerate

low[1] *adjective* **1** SMALL, little, short, stunted, squat, fubsy (*archaic or dialect*) << ANTONYM tall **2** LOW-LYING, deep, depressed, shallow, subsided, sunken, ground-level << ANTONYM high **3** INEXPENSIVE, cheap, reasonable, bargain, moderate, modest, cut-price, economical, bargain-basement **4** MEAGRE, little, small, reduced, depleted, scant, trifling, insignificant, sparse, paltry, measly << ANTONYM significant **5** INFERIOR, bad, poor, inadequate, pathetic, worthless, unsatisfactory, mediocre, deficient, second-rate, shoddy, low-grade, puny, substandard, low-rent (*informal, chiefly US*), half-pie (*NZ informal*), bodger *or* bodgie (*Austral slang*) **6** QUIET, soft, gentle, whispered, muted, subdued, hushed, muffled << ANTONYM loud **7** DEJECTED, down, blue, sad, depressed, unhappy, miserable, fed up, moody, gloomy, dismal, forlorn, glum, despondent, downcast, morose, disheartened, downhearted, down in the dumps (*informal*), sick as a parrot (*informal*), cheesed off (*informal*), brassed off (*Brit slang*) << ANTONYM happy **8** COARSE, common, rough, gross, crude, rude, obscene, disgraceful, vulgar, undignified, disreputable, unbecoming, unrefined, dishonourable, ill-bred **9** CONTEMPTIBLE, mean, base, nasty, cowardly, degraded, vulgar, vile, sordid, abject, unworthy, despicable, depraved, menial, reprehensible, dastardly, scurvy, servile, unprincipled, dishonourable, ignoble << ANTONYM honourable **10** LOWLY, poor, simple, plain, peasant, obscure, humble, meek, unpretentious, plebeian, lowborn **11** ILL, weak, exhausted, frail, dying, reduced, sinking, stricken, feeble, debilitated, prostrate << ANTONYM strong ▷▷ **lie low** HIDE, lurk, hole up, hide away, keep a low profile, hide out, go underground, skulk, go into hiding, take cover, keep out of sight, go to earth, conceal yourself

low² *verb* MOO, bellow

low-down *noun* (*informal*) INFORMATION, intelligence, info (*informal*), inside story, gen (*Brit informal*), dope (*informal*) ▷ *adjective* MEAN, low, base, cheap (*informal*), nasty, ugly, despicable, reprehensible, contemptible, underhand, scurvy

lower *adjective* **1** SUBORDINATE, under, smaller, junior, minor, secondary, lesser, low-level, inferior, second-class **2** REDUCED, cut, diminished, decreased, lessened, curtailed, pared down << ANTONYM increased ▷ *verb* **1** DROP, sink, depress, let down, submerge, take down, let fall, make lower << ANTONYM raise **2** LESSEN, cut, reduce, moderate, diminish, slash, decrease, prune, minimize, curtail, abate << ANTONYM increase **3** DEMEAN, humble, disgrace, humiliate, degrade, devalue, downgrade, belittle, condescend, debase, deign, abase **4** QUIETEN, soften, hush, tone down

lowering ▷ see **louring**

low-key *adjective* SUBDUED, quiet, restrained, muted, played down, understated, muffled, toned down, low-pitched

lowly *adjective* **1** LOWBORN, obscure, subordinate, inferior, mean, proletarian, ignoble, plebeian **2** UNPRETENTIOUS, common, poor, average, simple, ordinary, plain, modest, homespun

low-tech *adjective* UNSOPHISTICATED, simple, basic, elementary << ANTONYM high-tech *or* hi-tech

loyal *adjective* FAITHFUL, true, devoted, dependable, constant, attached, patriotic, staunch, trustworthy, trusty, steadfast, dutiful, unwavering, true-blue, immovable, unswerving, tried and true, true-hearted << ANTONYM disloyal

loyalty *noun* FAITHFULNESS, commitment, devotion, allegiance, reliability, fidelity, homage, patriotism, obedience, constancy, dependability, trustworthiness, steadfastness, troth (*archaic*), fealty, staunchness, trueness, trustiness, true-heartedness

lozenge *noun* TABLET, pastille, troche, cough drop, jujube

lubricate *verb* OIL, grease, smear, smooth the way, oil the wheels, make smooth, make slippery

lucid *adjective* **1** CLEAR, obvious, plain, evident, distinct, explicit, transparent, clear-cut, crystal clear, comprehensible, intelligible, limpid, pellucid << ANTONYM vague **2** CLEAR-HEADED, sound, reasonable, sensible, rational, sober, all there, sane, compos mentis (*Latin*), in your right mind << ANTONYM confused

luck *noun* **1** GOOD FORTUNE, success, advantage, prosperity, break (*informal*), stroke of luck, blessing, windfall, good luck, fluke, godsend, serendipity **2** FORTUNE, lot, stars, chance, accident, fate, hazard, destiny, hap (*archaic*), twist of fate, fortuity

luckily *adverb* FORTUNATELY, happily, by chance, as luck would have it, fortuitously, opportunely, as it chanced

luckless *adjective* UNLUCKY, unfortunate, unsuccessful, hapless, unhappy, disastrous, cursed, hopeless, jinxed, calamitous, ill-starred, star-crossed, unpropitious, ill-fated

lucky *adjective* **1** FORTUNATE, successful, favoured, charmed, blessed, prosperous, jammy (*Brit slang*), serendipitous << ANTONYM unlucky **2** FORTUITOUS, timely, fortunate, auspicious, opportune, propitious, providential, adventitious << ANTONYM unlucky

lucrative *adjective* PROFITABLE, rewarding, productive, fruitful, paying, high-income, well-paid, money-making, advantageous, gainful, remunerative

ludicrous *adjective* RIDICULOUS, crazy, absurd, preposterous, odd, funny, comic, silly, laughable, farcical, outlandish, incongruous, comical, zany, nonsensical, droll, burlesque, cockamamie (*slang, chiefly US*) << ANTONYM sensible

lug *verb* DRAG, carry, pull, haul, tow, yank, hump (*Brit slang*), heave

luggage *noun* BAGGAGE, things, cases, bags, gear, trunks, suitcases, paraphernalia, impedimenta

lugubrious *adjective* GLOOMY, serious, sad, dismal, melancholy, dreary, sombre, woeful, mournful, morose, sorrowful, funereal, doleful, woebegone, dirgelike

lukewarm *adjective* **1** TEPID, warm, blood-warm **2** HALF-HEARTED, cold, cool, indifferent, unconcerned, uninterested, apathetic, unresponsive, phlegmatic, unenthusiastic, laodicean

lull *noun* RESPITE, pause, quiet, silence, calm,

hush, tranquillity, stillness, let-up (*informal*), calmness ▷ *verb* CALM, soothe, subdue, still, quiet, compose, hush, quell, allay, pacify, lullaby, tranquillize, rock to sleep

lullaby *noun* CRADLESONG, berceuse

lumber¹ *verb* (*Brit informal*) BURDEN, land, load, saddle, impose upon, encumber ▷ *noun* (*Brit*) JUNK, refuse, rubbish, discards, trash, clutter, jumble, white elephants, castoffs, trumpery

lumber² *verb* PLOD, shuffle, shamble, trudge, stump, clump, waddle, trundle, lump along

lumbering *adjective* AWKWARD, heavy, blundering, bumbling, hulking, unwieldy, ponderous, ungainly, elephantine, heavy-footed, lubberly

luminary *noun* CELEBRITY, star, expert, somebody, lion, worthy, notable, big name, dignitary, leading light, celeb (*informal*), personage, megastar (*informal*), fundi (*S African*), V.I.P.

luminous *adjective* BRIGHT, lighted, lit, brilliant, shining, glowing, vivid, illuminated, radiant, resplendent, lustrous, luminescent

lump¹ *noun* 1 PIECE, group, ball, spot, block, mass, cake, bunch, cluster, chunk, wedge, dab, hunk, nugget, gob, clod, gobbet 2 SWELLING, growth, bump, tumour, bulge, hump, protuberance, protrusion, tumescence ▷ *verb* GROUP, throw, mass, combine, collect, unite, pool, bunch, consolidate, aggregate, batch, conglomerate, coalesce, agglutinate

lump² *verb* ▷▷ **lump it** PUT UP WITH IT, take it, stand it, bear it, suffer it, hack it (*slang*), tolerate it, endure it, brook it

lumpy *adjective* BUMPY, clotted, uneven, knobbly, grainy, curdled, granular, full of lumps

lunacy *noun* 1 FOOLISHNESS, madness, folly, stupidity, absurdity, aberration, idiocy, craziness, tomfoolery, imbecility, foolhardiness, senselessness << ANTONYM sense 2 INSANITY, madness, mania, dementia, psychosis, idiocy, derangement << ANTONYM sanity

lunatic *noun* MADMAN, maniac, psychopath, nut (*slang*), loony (*slang*), nutter (*Brit slang*), nutcase (*slang*), headcase (*informal*), headbanger (*informal*) ▷ *adjective* MAD, crazy, insane, irrational, nuts (*slang*), barking (*slang*), daft, demented, barmy (*slang*), deranged, bonkers (*slang, chiefly Brit*), unhinged, loopy (*informal*), crackpot

(*informal*), out to lunch (*informal*), barking mad (*slang*), maniacal, gonzo (*slang*), up the pole (*informal*), crackbrained, wacko or whacko (*informal*), off the air (*Austral slang*) ▷ see mad

lunge *verb* POUNCE, charge, bound, dive, leap, plunge, dash, thrust, poke, jab ▷ *noun* THRUST, charge, pounce, pass, spring, swing, jab, swipe (*informal*)

lurch *verb* 1 TILT, roll, pitch, list, rock, lean, heel 2 STAGGER, reel, stumble, weave, sway, totter

lure *verb* TEMPT, draw, attract, invite, trick, seduce, entice, beckon, lead on, allure, decoy, ensnare, inveigle ▷ *noun* TEMPTATION, attraction, incentive, bait, carrot (*informal*), magnet, inducement, decoy, enticement, siren song, allurement

lurid *adjective* 1 SENSATIONAL, shocking, disgusting, graphic, violent, savage, startling, grim, exaggerated, revolting, explicit, vivid, ghastly, gruesome, grisly, macabre, melodramatic, yellow (*of journalism*), gory, unrestrained, shock-horror (*facetious*) << ANTONYM mild 2 GLARING, bright, bloody, intense, flaming, vivid, fiery, livid, sanguine, glowering, overbright << ANTONYM pale

lurk *verb* HIDE, sneak, crouch, prowl, snoop, lie in wait, slink, skulk, conceal yourself, move with stealth, go furtively

luscious *adjective* 1 SEXY, attractive, arousing, erotic, inviting, provocative, seductive, cuddly, sensuous, alluring, voluptuous, kissable, beddable 2 DELICIOUS, sweet, juicy, rich, honeyed, savoury, succulent, palatable, mouth-watering, delectable, yummy (*slang*), scrumptious (*informal*), appetizing, toothsome, yummo (*Austral slang*)

lush *adjective* 1 ABUNDANT, green, flourishing, lavish, dense, prolific, rank, teeming, overgrown, verdant 2 LUXURIOUS, grand, elaborate, lavish, extravagant, sumptuous, plush (*informal*), ornate, opulent, palatial, ritzy (*slang*) 3 SUCCULENT, fresh, tender, ripe, juicy

lust *noun* 1 LECHERY, sensuality, licentiousness, carnality, the hots (*slang*), libido, lewdness, wantonness, salaciousness, lasciviousness, concupiscence, randiness (*informal, chiefly Brit*) 2 DESIRE, longing, passion, appetite, craving, greed, thirst, cupidity, covetousness, avidity, appetence ▷▷ **lust for** or **after someone** DESIRE, want, crave, need, yearn for, covet, slaver over, lech after (*informal*), be consumed with desire for, hunger for *or* after ▷▷ **lust for** *or* **after something** DESIRE, crave, yearn for, covet

lustful *adjective* LASCIVIOUS, sexy (*informal*), passionate, erotic, craving, sensual, randy (*informal, chiefly Brit*), raunchy (*slang*), horny (*slang*), hankering, lewd, wanton, carnal, prurient, lecherous, hot-blooded, libidinous, licentious, concupiscent, unchaste

lustre *noun* 1 SPARKLE, shine, glow, glitter, dazzle, gleam, gloss, brilliance, sheen, shimmer, glint, brightness, radiance, burnish, resplendence, lambency, luminousness 2 GLORY, honour, fame, distinction, prestige, renown, illustriousness

lustrous *adjective* SHINING, bright, glowing, sparkling, dazzling, shiny, gleaming, glossy, shimmering, radiant, luminous, glistening, burnished

lusty *adjective* VIGOROUS, strong, powerful, healthy, strapping, robust, rugged, energetic, sturdy, hale, stout, stalwart, hearty, virile, red-blooded (*informal*), brawny

luxuriant *adjective* 1 LUSH, rich, dense, abundant, excessive, thriving, flourishing, rank, productive, lavish, ample, fertile, prolific, overflowing, plentiful, exuberant, fruitful, teeming, copious, prodigal, riotous, profuse, fecund, superabundant, plenteous << ANTONYM sparse 2 ELABORATE, fancy,

decorated, extravagant, flamboyant, baroque, sumptuous, ornate, festooned, flowery, rococo, florid, corinthian << ANTONYM plain ▷ see **luxurious**

luxuriate *verb* 1 ENJOY, delight, indulge, relish, revel, bask, wallow 2 LIVE IN LUXURY, take it easy, live the life of Riley, have the time of your life, be in clover

luxurious *adjective* 1 SUMPTUOUS, expensive, comfortable, magnificent, costly, splendid, lavish, plush (*informal*), opulent, ritzy (*slang*), de luxe, well-appointed 2 SELF-INDULGENT, pleasure-loving, sensual, pampered, voluptuous, sybaritic, epicurean << ANTONYM austere

luxury *noun* 1 OPULENCE, splendour, richness, extravagance, affluence, hedonism, a bed of roses, voluptuousness, the life of Riley, sumptuousness << ANTONYM poverty 2 EXTRAVAGANCE, treat, extra, indulgence, frill, nonessential << ANTONYM necessity 3 PLEASURE, delight, comfort, satisfaction, enjoyment, bliss, indulgence, gratification, wellbeing << ANTONYM discomfort

lyric *adjective* 1 (*of poetry*) SONGLIKE, musical, lyrical, expressive, melodic 2 (*of a voice*) MELODIC, clear, clear, light, flowing, graceful, mellifluous, dulcet

lyrical *adjective* ENTHUSIASTIC, emotional, inspired, poetic, carried away, ecstatic, expressive, impassioned, rapturous, effusive, rhapsodic

macabre *adjective* GRUESOME, grim, ghastly, frightening, ghostly, weird, dreadful, unearthly, hideous, eerie, grisly, horrid, morbid, frightful, ghoulish << ANTONYM delightful

Machiavellian *adjective* SCHEMING, cynical, shrewd, cunning, designing, intriguing, sly, astute, unscrupulous, wily, opportunist, crafty, artful, amoral, foxy, deceitful, underhand, double-dealing, perfidious

machine *noun* 1 APPLIANCE, device, apparatus, engine, tool, instrument, mechanism, gadget, contraption, gizmo (*informal*), contrivance 2 SYSTEM, agency, structure, organization, machinery, setup (*informal*)

machinery *noun* 1 EQUIPMENT, gear, instruments, apparatus, works, technology, tackle, tools, mechanism(s), gadgetry 2 ADMINISTRATION, system, organization, agency, machine, structure, channels, procedure

macho *adjective* MANLY, masculine, butch (*slang*), chauvinist, virile, he-man

mad *adjective* 1 INSANE, mental (*slang*), crazy (*informal*), nuts (*slang*), bananas (*slang*), barking (*slang*), raving, distracted, frantic, frenzied, unstable, crackers (*Brit slang*), batty (*slang*), crazed, lunatic, loony (*slang*), psychotic, demented, cuckoo (*informal*), unbalanced, barmy (*slang*), nutty (*slang*), deranged, delirious, rabid, bonkers (*slang, chiefly Brit*), flaky (*US slang*), unhinged, loopy (*informal*), crackpot (*informal*), out to lunch (*informal*), round the bend (*Brit slang*), aberrant, barking mad (*slang*), out of your mind, gonzo (*slang*), screwy (*informal*), doolally (*slang*), off your head (*slang*), off your trolley (*slang*), round the twist (*Brit slang*), up the pole (*informal*), of unsound mind, as daft as a brush (*informal, chiefly Brit*), having lost your marbles (*informal*), not right in the head, non compos mentis (*Latin*), off your rocker (*slang*), not the full shilling (*informal*), off your nut (*slang*), off your chump (*slang*), wacko *or* whacko (*informal*), off the air (*Austral slang*) << ANTONYM sane 2 FOOLISH, absurd, wild, stupid, daft (*informal*), ludicrous, unreasonable, irrational, unsafe, senseless, preposterous, foolhardy, nonsensical, unsound, inane, imprudent, asinine << ANTONYM sensible 3 (*informal*) ANGRY, cross, furious, irritated, fuming, choked, infuriated, raging, ape (*slang*), incensed, enraged, exasperated, irate, livid (*informal*), berserk, seeing red (*informal*), incandescent, wrathful, fit to be tied (*slang*), in a wax (*informal, chiefly Brit*), berko (*Austral slang*), tooshie (*Austral slang*), off the air (*Austral slang*) << ANTONYM calm 4 *usually with* **about** ENTHUSIASTIC, wild, crazy (*informal*), nuts (*slang*), keen, hooked, devoted, in love with, fond, daft (*informal*), ardent, fanatical, avid, impassioned, zealous, infatuated, dotty (*slang, chiefly Brit*), enamoured << ANTONYM nonchalant 5 FRENZIED, wild, excited, energetic, abandoned, agitated, frenetic, uncontrolled, boisterous, full-on (*informal*), ebullient, gay, riotous, unrestrained

madcap *adjective* RECKLESS, rash, impulsive, ill-advised, wild, crazy, foolhardy, thoughtless, crackpot (*informal*), hot-headed, imprudent, heedless, hare-brained ▷ *noun* DAREDEVIL, tearaway, wild man, hothead

madden *verb* INFURIATE, irritate, incense, enrage, upset, provoke, annoy, aggravate (*informal*), gall, craze, inflame, exasperate, vex, unhinge, drive you crazy, nark (*Brit, Austral & NZ slang*), drive you round the bend (*Brit slang*), make your blood boil, drive you to distraction (*informal*), get your goat (*slang*), drive you round the twist (*Brit slang*), get your dander up (*informal*), make your hackles rise, raise your hackles, drive you off your head (*slang*), drive you out of your mind, get your back up, get your hackles up, make you see red (*informal*), put your back up, hack you off (*informal*) << ANTONYM calm

made-up *adjective* 1 PAINTED, powdered, rouged, done up 2 FALSE, invented, imaginary, fictional, untrue, mythical, unreal, fabricated, make-believe, trumped-up, specious

madly *adverb* 1 (*informal*) PASSIONATELY, wildly, desperately, intensely, exceedingly, extremely, excessively, to distraction, devotedly 2 FOOLISHLY, wildly, absurdly, ludicrously, unreasonably, irrationally, senselessly, nonsensically 3 ENERGETICALLY, quickly, wildly, rapidly, hastily, furiously, excitedly, hurriedly, recklessly, speedily, like mad (*informal*), hell for leather, like lightning, hotfoot, like the clappers (*Brit informal*), like nobody's business (*informal*), like greased lightning (*informal*) 4 INSANELY, frantically, hysterically, crazily, deliriously, distractedly, rabidly, frenziedly, dementedly

madman *or* **madwoman** *noun* LUNATIC, psycho (*slang*), maniac, loony (*slang*), nut (*slang*), psychotic, psychopath, nutter (*Brit slang*), nutcase (*slang*), headcase (*informal*), mental case (*slang*), headbanger (*informal*) ▷ see **mad**

madness *noun* 1 INSANITY, mental illness, delusion, mania, dementia, distraction, aberration, psychosis, lunacy, craziness, derangement, psychopathy 2 FOOLISHNESS, nonsense, folly, absurdity, idiocy, wildness, daftness (*informal*), foolhardiness, preposterousness 3 FRENZY, riot, furore, uproar, abandon, excitement, agitation, intoxication, unrestraint

maelstrom *noun* 1 WHIRLPOOL, swirl, eddy, vortex, Charybdis (*literary*) 2 TURMOIL, disorder, confusion, chaos, upheaval, uproar, pandemonium, bedlam, tumult

maestro *noun* MASTER, expert, genius, virtuoso, wonk (*informal*), fundi (*S African*)

magazine *noun* JOURNAL, paper, publication, supplement, rag (*informal*), issue, glossy (*informal*), pamphlet, periodical, fanzine (*informal*)

magic *noun* 1 SORCERY, wizardry, witchcraft, enchantment, occultism, black art,

spells, necromancy, sortilege, theurgy 2 CONJURING, illusion, trickery, sleight of hand, hocus-pocus, jiggery-pokery (*informal, chiefly Brit*), legerdemain, prestidigitation, jugglery 3 CHARM, power, glamour, fascination, magnetism, enchantment, allurement ▷ *adjective* MIRACULOUS, entrancing, charming, fascinating, marvellous, magical, magnetic, enchanting, bewitching, spellbinding, sorcerous

magician *noun* 1 CONJUROR, illusionist, prestidigitator 2 SORCERER, witch, wizard, illusionist, warlock, necromancer, thaumaturge (*rare*), theurgist, archimage (*rare*), enchanter *or* enchantress 3 MIRACLE-WORKER, genius, marvel, wizard, virtuoso, wonder-worker, spellbinder

magisterial *adjective* AUTHORITATIVE, lordly, commanding, masterful, imperious << ANTONYM subservient

magistrate *noun* JUDGE, justice, provost (*Scot*), bailie (*Scot*), justice of the peace, J.P.

magnanimous *adjective* GENEROUS, kind, noble, selfless, big, free, kindly, handsome, charitable, high-minded, bountiful, unselfish, open-handed, big-hearted, unstinting, beneficent, great-hearted, munificent, ungrudging << ANTONYM petty

magnate *noun* TYCOON, leader, chief, fat cat (*slang, chiefly US*), baron, notable, mogul, bigwig (*informal*), grandee, big shot (*informal*), captain of industry, big wheel (*slang*), big cheese (*slang* or *old-fashioned*), plutocrat, big noise (*informal*), big hitter (*informal*), magnifico, heavy hitter (*informal*), nabob (*informal*), Mister Big (*slang, chiefly US*), V.I.P.

magnetic *adjective* ATTRACTIVE, irresistible, seductive, captivating, charming, fascinating, entrancing, charismatic, enchanting, hypnotic, alluring, mesmerizing << ANTONYM repulsive

magnetism *noun* CHARM, appeal, attraction, power, draw, pull, spell, magic, fascination, charisma, attractiveness, allure, enchantment, hypnotism, drawing power, seductiveness, mesmerism, captivatingness

magnification *noun* 1 ENLARGEMENT, increase, inflation, boost, expansion, blow-up (*informal*), intensification, amplification, dilation, augmentation 2 EXAGGERATION, build-up, heightening, deepening, enhancement, aggrandizement

magnificence *noun* SPLENDOUR, glory, majesty, grandeur, brilliance, nobility, gorgeousness, sumptuousness, sublimity, resplendence

magnificent *adjective* **1** SPLENDID, striking, grand, impressive, august, rich, princely, imposing, elegant, divine (*informal*), glorious, noble, gorgeous, lavish, elevated, luxurious, majestic, regal, stately, sublime, sumptuous, grandiose, exalted, opulent, transcendent, resplendent, splendiferous (*facetious*) << ANTONYM ordinary **2** BRILLIANT, fine, excellent, outstanding, superb, superior, splendid

magnify *verb* **1** ENLARGE, increase, boost, expand, intensify, blow up (*informal*), heighten, amplify, augment, dilate << ANTONYM reduce **2** MAKE WORSE, exaggerate, intensify, worsen, heighten, deepen, exacerbate, aggravate, increase, inflame, fan the flames of **3** EXAGGERATE, overdo, overstate, build up, enhance, blow up, inflate, overestimate, dramatize, overrate, overplay, overemphasize, blow up out of all proportion, aggrandize, make a production (out) of (*informal*), make a federal case of (*US informal*) << ANTONYM understate

magnitude *noun* **1** IMPORTANCE, consequence, significance, mark, moment, note, weight, proportion, dimension, greatness, grandeur, eminence << ANTONYM unimportance **2** IMMENSITY, size, extent, enormity, strength, volume, vastness, bigness, largeness, hugeness << ANTONYM smallness **3** INTENSITY, measure, capacity, amplitude

maid *noun* **1** SERVANT, chambermaid, housemaid, menial, handmaiden (*archaic*), maidservant, female servant, domestic (*archaic*), parlourmaid, serving-maid **2** (*archaic or literary*) GIRL, maiden, lass, miss, nymph (*poetic*), damsel, lassie (*informal*), wench

maiden *noun* (*archaic or literary*) GIRL, maid, lass, damsel, miss, virgin, nymph (*poetic*), lassie (*informal*), wench ▷ *modifier* **1** FIRST, initial, inaugural, introductory, initiatory **2** UNMARRIED, pure, virgin, intact, chaste, virginal, unwed, undefiled

mail *noun* **1** LETTERS, post, packages, parcels, correspondence **2** POSTAL SERVICE, post, postal system ▷ *verb* **1** POST, send, forward, dispatch, send by mail *or* post **2** E-MAIL, send, forward

maim *verb* CRIPPLE, hurt, injure, wound, mar, disable, hamstring, impair, lame, mutilate, mangle, incapacitate, put out of action, mangulate (*Austral slang*)

main *adjective* CHIEF, leading, major, prime, head, special, central, particular, necessary, essential, premier, primary, vital, critical, crucial, supreme, outstanding, principal, cardinal, paramount, foremost, predominant, pre-eminent, must-have << ANTONYM minor ▷ *plural noun* **1** PIPELINE, channel, pipe, conduit, duct **2** CABLE, line, electricity supply, mains supply ▷▷ **in the main** ON THE WHOLE, generally, mainly, mostly, in general, for the most part

mainly *adverb* CHIEFLY, mostly, largely, generally, usually, principally, in general, primarily, above all, substantially, on the whole, predominantly, in the main, for the most part, most of all, first and foremost, to the greatest extent

mainstay *noun* PILLAR, backbone, bulwark, prop, anchor, buttress, lynchpin, chief support

mainstream *adjective* CONVENTIONAL, general, established, received, accepted, central, current, core, prevailing, orthodox << ANTONYM unconventional

maintain *verb* **1** CONTINUE, retain, preserve, sustain, carry on, keep, keep up, prolong, uphold, nurture, conserve, perpetuate << ANTONYM end **2** ASSERT, state, hold, claim, insist, declare, allege, contend, affirm, profess, avow, aver, asseverate << ANTONYM disavow **3** LOOK AFTER, care for, take care of, finance, conserve, keep in good condition

maintenance *noun* **1** UPKEEP, keeping, care, supply, repairs, provision, conservation, nurture, preservation **2** ALLOWANCE, living, support, keep, food, livelihood, subsistence, upkeep, sustenance, alimony, aliment **3** CONTINUATION, carrying-on, continuance, support, perpetuation, prolongation, sustainment, retainment

majestic *adjective* GRAND, magnificent, impressive, superb, kingly, royal, august, princely, imposing, imperial, noble, splendid, elevated, awesome, dignified, regal, stately, monumental, sublime, lofty, pompous, grandiose, exalted, splendiferous (*facetious*) << ANTONYM modest

majesty *noun* GRANDEUR, glory, splendour, magnificence, dignity, nobility, sublimity, loftiness, impressiveness, awesomeness, exaltedness << ANTONYM triviality

major *adjective* **1** IMPORTANT, vital, critical, significant, great, serious, radical, crucial, outstanding, grave, extensive, notable, weighty, pre-eminent **2** MAIN, higher,

greater, bigger, lead, leading, head, larger, better, chief, senior, supreme, superior, elder, uppermost << ANTONYM minor
majority noun 1 MOST, more, mass, bulk, best part, better part, lion's share, preponderance, plurality, greater number 2 ADULTHOOD, maturity, age of consent, seniority, manhood or womanhood
make verb 1 PRODUCE, cause, create, effect, lead to, occasion, generate, bring about, give rise to, engender, beget 2 PERFORM, do, act out, effect, carry out, engage in, execute, prosecute 3 FORCE, cause, press, compel, drive, require, oblige, induce, railroad (informal), constrain, coerce, impel, dragoon, pressurize, prevail upon 4 APPOINT, name, select, elect, invest, install, nominate, assign, designate, hire as, cast as, employ as, ordain, vote in as, recruit as, engage as, enlist as 5 CREATE, build, produce, manufacture, form, model, fashion, shape, frame, construct, assemble, compose, forge, mould, put together, originate, fabricate 6 ENACT, form, pass, establish, fix, institute, frame, devise, lay down, draw up 7 EARN, get, gain, net, win, clear, secure, realize, obtain, acquire, bring in, take in, fetch 8 AMOUNT TO, total, constitute, add up to, count as, tot up to (informal) 9 GET TO, reach, catch, arrive at, meet, arrive in time for 10 CALCULATE, judge, estimate, determine, think, suppose, reckon, work out, compute, gauge, count up, put a figure on ▷ noun BRAND, sort, style, model, build, form, mark, kind, type, variety, construction, marque ▷▷ **make as if** PRETEND, affect, give the impression that, feign, feint, make a show of, act as if or though ▷▷ **make away or off with something** STEAL, nick (slang, chiefly Brit), pinch (informal), nab (informal), carry off, swipe (slang), knock off (slang), pilfer, cart off (slang), purloin, filch ▷▷ **make believe** PRETEND, play, enact, feign, play-act, act as if or though ▷▷ **make do** MANAGE, cope, improvise, muddle through, get along or by, scrape along or by ▷▷ **make for something** 1 HEAD FOR, aim for, head towards, set out for, be bound for, make a beeline for, steer (a course) for, proceed towards 2 CONTRIBUTE TO, produce, further, forward, advance, promote, foster, facilitate, be conducive to ▷▷ **make it** (informal) 1 SUCCEED, be successful, prosper, be a success, arrive (informal), get on, make good, cut it (informal), get ahead, make the

grade (informal), crack it (informal), make it big, get somewhere, distinguish yourself 2 GET BETTER, survive, recover, rally, come through, pull through ▷▷ **make off** FLEE, clear out (informal), abscond, fly, bolt, decamp, hook it (slang), do a runner (slang), run for it (informal), slope off, cut and run (informal), beat a hasty retreat, fly the coop (US & Canad informal), make away, skedaddle (informal), take a powder (US & Canad slang), take to your heels, run away or off ▷▷ **make out** FARE, manage, do, succeed, cope, get on, proceed, thrive, prosper ▷▷ **make something out** 1 SEE, observe, distinguish, perceive, recognize, detect, glimpse, pick out, discern, catch sight of, espy, descry 2 UNDERSTAND, see, work out, grasp, perceive, follow, realize, comprehend, fathom, decipher, suss (out) (slang), get the drift of 3 WRITE OUT, complete, draft, draw up, inscribe, fill in or out 4 PRETEND, claim, suggest, maintain, declare, allege, hint, imply, intimate, assert, insinuate, let on, make as if 5 PROVE, show, describe, represent, demonstrate, justify ▷▷ **make something up** INVENT, create, construct, compose, write, frame, manufacture, coin, devise, hatch, originate, formulate, dream up, fabricate, concoct, cook up (informal), trump up ▷▷ **make up** SETTLE YOUR DIFFERENCES, shake hands, make peace, bury the hatchet, call it quits, forgive and forget, mend fences, become reconciled, declare a truce, be friends again ▷▷ **make up for something** COMPENSATE FOR, redress, make amends for, atone for, balance out, offset, expiate, requite, make reparation for, make recompense for ▷▷ **make up something** 1 FORM, account for, constitute, compose, comprise 2 COMPLETE, meet, supply, fill, round off ▷▷ **make up to someone** (informal) FLIRT WITH, be all over, come on to, chase after, court, pursue, woo, run after, chat up (informal), curry favour with, make overtures to, make eyes at
make-believe noun FANTASY, imagination, pretence, charade, unreality, dream, play-acting << ANTONYM reality ▷ adjective IMAGINARY, dream, imagined, made-up, fantasy, pretend, pretended, mock, sham, unreal, fantasized << ANTONYM real
maker noun MANUFACTURER, producer, builder, constructor, fabricator
Maker noun GOD, Creator, Prime Mover
makeshift adjective TEMPORARY, provisional, make-do, substitute, jury (chiefly nautical),

expedient, rough and ready, stopgap

make-up *noun* **1** COSMETICS, paint (*informal*), powder, face (*informal*), greasepaint (*theatre*), war paint (*informal*), maquillage (*French*) **2** NATURE, character, constitution, temperament, make, build, figure, stamp, temper, disposition, frame of mind, cast of mind **3** STRUCTURE, organization, arrangement, form, construction, assembly, constitution, format, formation, composition, configuration

making *noun* CREATION, production, manufacture, construction, assembly, forging, composition, fabrication ▷ *plural noun* BEGINNINGS, qualities, potential, stuff, basics, materials, capacity, ingredients, essence, capability, potentiality ▷▷ **in the making** BUDDING, potential, up and coming, emergent, coming, growing, developing, promising, burgeoning, nascent, incipient

malady *noun* DISEASE, complaint, illness, disorder, sickness, ailment, affliction, infirmity, ill, indisposition, lurgy (*informal*)

malaise *noun* UNEASE, illness, depression, anxiety, weakness, sickness, discomfort, melancholy, angst, disquiet, doldrums, lassitude, enervation

malcontent *noun* TROUBLEMAKER, rebel, complainer, grumbler, grouser, agitator, stirrer (*informal*), mischief-maker, grouch (*informal*), fault-finder ▷ *adjective* DISCONTENTED, unhappy, disgruntled, dissatisfied, disgusted, rebellious, resentful, disaffected, restive, unsatisfied, ill-disposed, factious

male *adjective* MASCULINE, manly, macho, virile, manlike, manful << ANTONYM female

malevolent *adjective* SPITEFUL, hostile, vicious, malicious, malign, malignant, vindictive, pernicious, vengeful, hateful (*archaic*), baleful, rancorous, evil-minded, maleficent, ill-natured << ANTONYM benevolent

malfunction *verb* BREAK DOWN, fail, go wrong, play up (*Brit informal*), stop working, be defective, conk out (*informal*), develop a fault ▷ *noun* FAULT, failure, breakdown, defect, flaw, impairment, glitch

malice *noun* SPITE, animosity, enmity, hate, hatred, bitterness, venom, spleen, rancour, bad blood, ill will, animus, malevolence, vindictiveness, evil intent, malignity, spitefulness, vengefulness, maliciousness

malicious *adjective* SPITEFUL, malevolent, malignant, vicious, bitter, resentful, pernicious, vengeful, bitchy (*informal*), hateful, baleful, injurious, rancorous, catty (*informal*), shrewish, ill-disposed, evil-minded, ill-natured << ANTONYM benevolent

malign *verb* DISPARAGE, abuse, run down, libel, knock (*informal*), injure, rubbish (*informal*), smear, blacken (someone's name), slag (off) (*slang*), denigrate, revile, vilify, slander, defame, bad-mouth (*slang, chiefly US & Canad*), traduce, speak ill of, derogate, do a hatchet job on (*informal*), calumniate, asperse << ANTONYM praise ▷ *adjective* EVIL, bad, destructive, harmful, hostile, vicious, malignant, wicked, hurtful, pernicious, malevolent, baleful, deleterious, injurious, baneful, maleficent << ANTONYM good

malignant *adjective* **1** (*medical*) UNCONTROLLABLE, dangerous, evil, fatal, deadly, cancerous, virulent, irremediable **2** HOSTILE, harmful, bitter, vicious, destructive, malicious, malign, hurtful, pernicious, malevolent, spiteful, baleful, injurious, inimical, maleficent, of evil intent << ANTONYM benign

malleable *adjective* **1** MANAGEABLE, adaptable, compliant, impressionable, pliable, tractable, biddable, governable, like putty in your hands **2** WORKABLE, soft, plastic, tensile, ductile

malpractice *noun* MISCONDUCT, abuse, negligence, mismanagement, misbehaviour, dereliction

mammoth *adjective* COLOSSAL, huge, giant, massive, vast, enormous, mighty, immense, titanic, jumbo (*informal*), gigantic, monumental, mountainous, stellar (*informal*), prodigious, stupendous, gargantuan, elephantine, ginormous (*informal*), Brobdingnagian, humongous *or* humungous (*US slang*) << ANTONYM tiny

man *noun* **1** MALE, guy (*informal*), fellow (*informal*), gentleman, bloke (*Brit informal*), chap (*Brit informal*), dude (*US informal*), geezer (*informal*), adult male **2** HUMAN, human being, body, person, individual, adult, being, somebody, soul, personage **3** MANKIND, humanity, people, mortals, human race, humankind, Homo sapiens **4** PARTNER, boy, husband, lover, mate, boyfriend, old man, groom, spouse, sweetheart, beau, significant other (*US*) ▷ *verb* STAFF, people, fill, crew, occupy, garrison, furnish with men ▷▷ **to a man** WITHOUT EXCEPTION, as one, every one, unanimously, each and every one, one and all, bar none

mana *noun* (*NZ*) AUTHORITY, influence, power, might, force, weight, strength, domination, sway, standing, status, importance, esteem, stature, eminence

manacle *noun* HANDCUFF, bond, chain, shackle, tie, iron, fetter, gyve (*archaic*) ▷ *verb* HANDCUFF, bind, confine, restrain, check, chain, curb, hamper, inhibit, constrain, shackle, fetter, tie someone's hands, put in chains, clap *or* put in irons

manage *verb* **1** BE IN CHARGE OF, run, handle, rule, direct, conduct, command, govern, administer, oversee, supervise, preside over, be head of, call the shots in, superintend, call the tune in **2** ORGANIZE, use, handle, govern, regulate **3** COPE, survive, shift, succeed, get on, carry on, fare, get through, make out, cut it (*informal*), get along, make do, get by (*informal*), crack it (*informal*), muddle through **4** PERFORM, do, deal with, achieve, carry out, undertake, cope with, accomplish, contrive, finish off, bring about *or* off **5** CONTROL, influence, guide, handle, master, dominate, manipulate **6** STEER, operate, pilot

manageable *adjective* EASY, convenient, handy, user-friendly, wieldy << ANTONYM difficult

management *noun* **1** ADMINISTRATION, control, rule, government, running, charge, care, operation, handling, direction, conduct, command, guidance, supervision, manipulation, governance, superintendence **2** DIRECTORS, board, executive(s), bosses (*informal*), administration, employers, directorate

manager *noun* SUPERVISOR, head, director, executive, boss (*informal*), governor, administrator, conductor, controller, superintendent, gaffer (*informal, chiefly Brit*), proprietor, organizer, comptroller, overseer, baas (*S African*), sherang (*Austral & NZ*)

mandate *noun* COMMAND, order, charge, authority, commission, sanction, instruction, warrant, decree, bidding, canon, directive, injunction, fiat, edict, authorization, precept

mandatory *adjective* COMPULSORY, required, binding, obligatory, requisite << ANTONYM optional

manfully *adverb* BRAVELY, boldly, vigorously, stoutly, hard, strongly, desperately, courageously, stalwartly, powerfully, resolutely, determinedly, heroically, valiantly, nobly, gallantly, like the devil, to the best of your ability, like a Trojan, intrepidly, like one possessed, with might and main

mangle *verb* CRUSH, mutilate, maim, deform, cut, total (*slang*), tear, destroy, ruin, mar, rend, wreck, spoil, butcher, cripple, hack, distort, trash (*slang*), maul, disfigure, lacerate, mangulate (*Austral slang*)

manhandle *verb* **1** ROUGH UP, pull, push, paw (*informal*), maul, handle roughly, knock about *or* around **2** HAUL, carry, pull, push, lift, manoeuvre, tug, shove, hump (*Brit slang*), heave

manhood *noun* MANLINESS, masculinity, spirit, strength, resolution, courage, determination, maturity, bravery, fortitude, mettle, firmness, virility, valour, hardihood, manfulness

mania *noun* **1** OBSESSION, passion, thing (*informal*), desire, rage, enthusiasm, craving, preoccupation, craze, fad (*informal*), fetish, fixation, partiality **2** MADNESS, disorder, frenzy, insanity, dementia, aberration, lunacy, delirium, craziness, derangement

maniac *noun* **1** MADMAN *or* MADWOMAN, psycho (*slang*), lunatic, loony (*slang*), psychopath, nutter (*Brit slang*), nutcase (*slang*), headcase (*informal*), headbanger (*informal*) **2** FANATIC, fan, enthusiast, freak (*informal*), fiend (*informal*)

manifest *adjective* OBVIOUS, apparent, patent, evident, open, clear, plain, visible, bold, distinct, glaring, noticeable, blatant, conspicuous, unmistakable, palpable, salient << ANTONYM concealed ▷ *verb* DISPLAY, show, reveal, establish, express, prove, declare, demonstrate, expose, exhibit, set forth, make plain, evince << ANTONYM conceal

manifestation *noun* **1** SIGN, symptom, indication, mark, example, evidence, instance, proof, token, testimony **2** DISPLAY, show, exhibition, expression, demonstration, appearance, exposure, revelation, disclosure, materialization

manifold *adjective* (*formal*) NUMEROUS, many, various, varied, multiple, diverse, multiplied, diversified, abundant, assorted, copious, multifarious, multitudinous, multifold

manipulate *verb* **1** INFLUENCE, control, direct, guide, conduct, negotiate, exploit, steer, manoeuvre, do a number on (*chiefly US*), twist around your little finger **2** WORK, use, operate, handle, employ, wield

mankind *noun* PEOPLE, man, humanity, human race, humankind, Homo sapiens

manliness *noun* VIRILITY, masculinity, manhood, machismo, courage, bravery, vigour, heroism, mettle, boldness, firmness, valour, fearlessness, intrepidity, hardihood

manly *adjective* VIRILE, male, masculine, macho, strong, powerful, brave, daring, bold, strapping, hardy, heroic, robust, vigorous, muscular, courageous, fearless, butch (*slang*), resolute, gallant, valiant, well-built, red-blooded (*informal*), dauntless, stout-hearted, valorous, manful << ANTONYM effeminate

man-made *adjective* ARTIFICIAL, manufactured, plastic (*slang*), mock, synthetic, ersatz

manner *noun* 1 STYLE, way, fashion, method, means, form, process, approach, practice, procedure, habit, custom, routine, mode, genre, tack, tenor, usage, wont 2 BEHAVIOUR, look, air, bearing, conduct, appearance, aspect, presence, tone, demeanour, deportment, mien (*literary*), comportment 3 TYPE, form, sort, kind, nature, variety, brand, breed, category ▷ *plural noun* 1 CONDUCT, bearing, behaviour, breeding, carriage, demeanour, deportment, comportment 2 POLITENESS, courtesy, etiquette, refinement, polish, decorum, p's and q's 3 PROTOCOL, ceremony, customs, formalities, good form, proprieties, the done thing, social graces, politesse

mannered *adjective* AFFECTED, put-on, posed, artificial, pseudo (*informal*), pretentious, stilted, arty-farty (*informal*) << ANTONYM natural

mannerism *noun* HABIT, characteristic, trait, quirk, peculiarity, foible, idiosyncrasy

manoeuvre *verb* 1 STEER, direct, guide, pilot, work, move, drive, handle, negotiate, jockey, manipulate, navigate 2 SCHEME, plot, plan, intrigue, wangle (*informal*), machinate 3 MANIPULATE, arrange, organize, devise, manage, set up, engineer, fix, orchestrate, contrive, stage-manage ▷ *noun* 1 STRATAGEM, move, plan, action, movement, scheme, trick, plot, tactic, intrigue, dodge, ploy, ruse, artifice, subterfuge, machination 2 *often plural* MOVEMENT, operation, exercise, deployment, war game

mansion *noun* RESIDENCE, manor, hall, villa, dwelling, abode, habitation, seat

mantle *noun* 1 COVERING, cover, screen, cloud, curtain, envelope, blanket, veil, shroud,

canopy, pall 2 (*archaic*) CLOAK, wrap, cape, hood, shawl ▷ *verb* COVER, hide, blanket, cloud, wrap, screen, mask, disguise, veil, cloak, shroud, envelop, overspread

manual *adjective* 1 PHYSICAL, human, done by hand 2 HAND-OPERATED, hand, non-automatic ▷ *noun* HANDBOOK, guide, instructions, bible, guidebook, workbook

manufacture *verb* 1 MAKE, build, produce, construct, form, create, process, shape, turn out, assemble, compose, forge, mould, put together, fabricate, mass-produce 2 CONCOCT, make up, invent, devise, hatch, fabricate, think up, cook up (*informal*), trump up ▷ *noun* MAKING, production, construction, assembly, creation, produce, fabrication, mass-production

manufacturer *noun* MAKER, producer, builder, creator, industrialist, factory-owner, constructor, fabricator

manure *noun* COMPOST, muck, fertilizer, dung, droppings, excrement, ordure

many *adjective* NUMEROUS, various, varied, countless, abundant, myriad, innumerable, sundry, copious, manifold, umpteen (*informal*), profuse, multifarious, multitudinous, multifold, divers (*archaic*) ▷ *pronoun* A LOT, lots (*informal*), plenty, a mass, scores, piles (*informal*), tons (*informal*), heaps (*informal*), large numbers, a multitude, umpteen (*informal*), a horde, a thousand and one, a gazillion (*informal*) ▷▷ **the many** THE MASSES, the people, the crowd, the majority, the rank and file, the multitude, (the) hoi polloi

mar *verb* 1 HARM, damage, hurt, spoil, stain, blight, taint, tarnish, blot, sully, vitiate, put a damper on 2 RUIN, injure, spoil, scar, flaw, impair, mutilate, detract from, maim, deform, blemish, mangle, disfigure, deface << ANTONYM improve

marauder *noun* RAIDER, outlaw, bandit, pirate, robber, ravager, plunderer, pillager, buccaneer, brigand, corsair, sea wolf, freebooter, reiver (*dialect*)

march *verb* 1 PARADE, walk, file, pace, stride, tread, tramp, swagger, footslog 2 WALK, strut, storm, sweep, stride, stalk, flounce ▷ *noun* 1 WALK, trek, hike, tramp, slog, yomp (*Brit informal*), routemarch 2 DEMONSTRATION, parade, procession, demo (*informal*) 3 PROGRESS, development, advance, evolution, progression

margin *noun* 1 ROOM, space, surplus, allowance, scope, play, compass, latitude, leeway, extra room, elbowroom **2** EDGE, side, limit, border, bound, boundary, confine, verge, brink, rim, brim, perimeter, periphery

marginal *adjective* **1** INSIGNIFICANT, small, low, minor, slight, minimal, negligible **2** BORDERLINE, bordering, on the edge, peripheral

marijuana *noun* CANNABIS, pot (*slang*), weed (*slang*), dope (*slang*), blow (*slang*), smoke (*informal*), stuff (*slang*), leaf (*slang*), tea (*US slang*), grass (*slang*), chronic (*US slang*), hemp, hash (*slang*), gage (*US dated slang*), hashish, mary jane (*US slang*), ganja, bhang, kif, wacky baccy (*slang*), sinsemilla, dagga (*S African*), charas

marine *adjective* NAUTICAL, sea, maritime, oceanic, naval, saltwater, seafaring, ocean-going, seagoing, pelagic, thalassic

mariner *noun* SAILOR, seaman, sea dog, seafarer, hand, salt, tar, navigator, gob (*US slang*), matelot (*slang, chiefly Brit*), Jack Tar, seafaring man, bluejacket

marital *adjective* MATRIMONIAL, married, wedded, nuptial, conjugal, spousal, connubial

maritime *adjective* **1** NAUTICAL, marine, naval, sea, oceanic, seafaring **2** COASTAL, seaside, littoral

mark *noun* **1** SPOT, stain, streak, smudge, line, nick, impression, scratch, bruise, scar, dent, blot, blemish, blotch, pock, splotch, smirch **2** CHARACTERISTIC, feature, symptom, standard, quality, measure, stamp, par, attribute, criterion, norm, trait, badge, hallmark, yardstick, peculiarity **3** INDICATION, sign, note, evidence, symbol, proof, token **4** BRAND, impression, label, stamp, print, device, flag, seal, symbol, token, earmark, emblem, insignia, signet **5** IMPRESSION, effect, influence, impact, trace, imprint, vestiges **6** TARGET, goal, aim, purpose, end, object, objective ▷ *verb* **1** SCAR, scratch, dent, imprint, nick, brand, impress, stain, bruise, streak, blot, smudge, blemish, blotch, splotch, smirch **2** LABEL, identify, brand, flag, stamp, characterize **3** GRADE, correct, assess, evaluate, appraise **4** DISTINGUISH, show, illustrate, exemplify, denote, evince, betoken **5** OBSERVE, mind, note, regard, notice, attend to, pay attention to, pay heed to, hearken to (*archaic*) ▷▷ **make your mark** SUCCEED, make it (*informal*), make good, prosper, be a success, achieve recognition, get on in the world, make something of yourself, find a place in the sun, make a success of yourself

marked *adjective* NOTICEABLE, clear, decided, striking, noted, obvious, signal, dramatic, considerable, outstanding, remarkable, apparent, prominent, patent, evident, distinct, pronounced, notable, manifest, blatant, conspicuous, salient << ANTONYM imperceptible

markedly *adverb* NOTICEABLY, greatly, clearly, obviously, seriously (*informal*), signally, patently, notably, considerably, remarkably, evidently, manifestly, distinctly, decidedly, strikingly, conspicuously, to a great extent, outstandingly

market *noun* FAIR, mart, bazaar, souk (*Arabic*) ▷ *verb* SELL, promote, retail, peddle, vend, offer for sale

marketable *adjective* SOUGHT AFTER, wanted, in demand, saleable, merchantable, vendible

marksman *or* **markswoman** *noun* SHARPSHOOTER, good shot, crack shot (*informal*), dead shot (*informal*), deadeye (*informal, chiefly US*)

maroon *verb* ABANDON, leave, desert, strand, leave high and dry (*informal*), cast away, cast ashore

marriage *noun* **1** WEDDING, match, nuptials, wedlock, wedding ceremony, matrimony, espousal, nuptial rites **2** UNION, coupling, link, association, alliance, merger, confederation, amalgamation

married *adjective* **1** WEDDED, one, united, joined, wed, hitched (*slang*), spliced (*informal*) **2** MARITAL, wifely, husbandly, nuptial, matrimonial, conjugal, spousal, connubial

marry *verb* **1** TIE THE KNOT (*informal*), wed, take the plunge (*informal*), walk down the aisle (*informal*), get hitched (*slang*), get spliced (*informal*), become man and wife, plight your troth (*old-fashioned*) **2** UNITE, match, join, link, tie, bond, ally, merge, knit, unify, splice, yoke

marsh *noun* SWAMP, moss (*Scot & N English dialect*), bog, slough, fen, quagmire, morass, muskeg (*Canad*)

marshal *verb* **1** CONDUCT, take, lead, guide, steer, escort, shepherd, usher **2** ARRANGE, group, order, collect, gather, line up, organize, assemble, deploy, array, dispose, draw up, muster, align

martial *adjective* MILITARY, soldierly, brave, heroic, belligerent, warlike, bellicose

martyrdom *noun* PERSECUTION, suffering, torture, agony, ordeal, torment, anguish << ANTONYM bliss

marvel *verb* BE AMAZED, wonder, gaze, gape, goggle, be awed, be filled with surprise ▷ *noun* 1 WONDER, phenomenon, miracle, portent 2 GENIUS, whizz (*informal*), prodigy

marvellous *adjective* EXCELLENT, great (*informal*), mean (*slang*), topping (*Brit slang*), wonderful, brilliant, bad (*slang*), cracking (*Brit informal*), amazing, crucial (*slang*), extraordinary, remarkable, smashing (*informal*), superb, spectacular, fantastic (*informal*), magnificent, astonishing, fabulous (*informal*), divine (*informal*), glorious, terrific (*informal*), splendid, sensational (*informal*), mega (*slang*), sovereign, awesome (*slang*), breathtaking, phenomenal, astounding, singular, miraculous, colossal, super (*informal*), wicked (*informal*), def (*slang*), prodigious, wondrous (*archaic or literary*), brill (*informal*), stupendous, jaw-dropping, bodacious (*slang, chiefly US*), boffo (*slang*), jim-dandy (*slang*), chillin' (*US slang*), booshit (*Austral slang*), exo (*Austral slang*), sik (*Austral slang*), rad (*informal*), phat (*slang*), schmick (*Austral informal*) << ANTONYM terrible

masculine *adjective* 1 MALE, manly, mannish, manlike, virile, manful 2 STRONG, powerful, bold, brave, strapping, hardy, robust, vigorous, muscular, macho, butch (*slang*), resolute, gallant, well-built, red-blooded (*informal*), stout-hearted

mask *noun* 1 DISGUISE, visor, vizard (*archaic*), stocking mask, false face, domino (*rare*) 2 FAÇADE, disguise, show, front, cover, screen, blind, cover-up, veil, cloak, guise, camouflage, veneer, semblance, concealment ▷ *verb* DISGUISE, hide, conceal, obscure, cover (up), screen, blanket, veil, cloak, mantle, camouflage, enshroud

masquerade *verb* POSE, pretend to be, impersonate, profess to be, pass yourself off, simulate, disguise yourself ▷ *noun* 1 PRETENCE, disguise, deception, front (*informal*), cover, screen, put-on (*slang*), mask, cover-up, cloak, guise, subterfuge, dissimulation, imposture 2 MASKED BALL, revel, mummery, fancy dress party, costume ball, masked party

mass *noun* 1 LOT, collection, load, combination, pile, quantity, bunch, stack, heap, rick, batch, accumulation, stockpile, assemblage, aggregation, conglomeration 2 PIECE, block, lump, chunk, hunk, concretion 3 MAJORITY, body, bulk, best part, greater part, almost all, lion's share, preponderance 4 CROWD, group, body, pack, lot, army, host, band, troop, drove, crush, bunch (*informal*), mob, flock, herd, number, horde, multitude, throng, rabble, assemblage 5 SIZE, matter, weight, extent, dimensions, bulk, magnitude, greatness ▷ *adjective* LARGE-SCALE, general, popular, widespread, extensive, universal, wholesale, indiscriminate, pandemic ▷ *verb* GATHER, assemble, accumulate, collect, rally, mob, muster, swarm, amass, throng, congregate, foregather ▷▷ **the masses** THE MULTITUDE, the crowd, the mob, the common people, the great unwashed (*derogatory*), the hoi polloi, the commonalty

massacre *noun* SLAUGHTER, killing, murder, holocaust, carnage, extermination, annihilation, butchery, mass slaughter, blood bath ▷ *verb* SLAUGHTER, kill, murder, butcher, take out (*slang*), wipe out, slay, blow away (*slang, chiefly US*), annihilate, exterminate, mow down, cut to pieces

massage *noun* RUB-DOWN, rubbing, manipulation, kneading, reflexology, shiatsu, acupressure, chiropractic treatment, palpation ▷ *verb* 1 RUB DOWN, rub, manipulate, knead, pummel, palpate 2 MANIPULATE, alter, distort, doctor, cook (*informal*), fix (*informal*), rig, fiddle (*informal*), tamper with, tinker with, misrepresent, fiddle with, falsify

massive *adjective* HUGE, great, big, heavy, imposing, vast, enormous, solid, impressive, substantial, extensive, monster, immense, hefty, titanic, gigantic, monumental, whacking (*informal*), mammoth, bulky, colossal, whopping (*informal*), weighty, stellar (*informal*), hulking, ponderous, gargantuan, elephantine, ginormous (*informal*), humongous *or* humungous (*US slang*) << ANTONYM tiny

master *noun* 1 LORD, ruler, commander, chief, director, manager, boss (*informal*), head, owner, captain, governor, employer, principal, skipper (*informal*), controller, superintendent, overlord, overseer, baas (*S African*) << ANTONYM servant 2 EXPERT, maestro, pro (*informal*), ace (*informal*), genius, wizard, adept, virtuoso, grandmaster, doyen, past master, dab hand (*Brit informal*), wonk (*informal*), maven (*US*), fundi (*S African*) << ANTONYM amateur 3 TEACHER, tutor, instructor, schoolmaster, pedagogue, preceptor << ANTONYM student ▷ *adjective* MAIN, principal, chief, prime, grand, great, foremost, predominant << ANTONYM lesser ▷ *verb* **1** LEARN, understand, pick up, acquire, grasp, get the hang of (*informal*), become proficient in, know inside out, know backwards **2** OVERCOME, defeat, suppress, conquer, check, curb, tame, lick (*informal*), subdue, overpower, quash, quell, triumph over, bridle, vanquish, subjugate << ANTONYM give in to **3** CONTROL, manage, direct, dominate, rule, command, govern, regulate

masterful *adjective* **1** SKILFUL, skilled, expert, finished, fine, masterly, excellent, crack (*informal*), supreme, clever, superior, world-class, exquisite, adept, consummate, first-rate, deft, superlative, adroit, dexterous << ANTONYM unskilled **2** DOMINEERING, authoritative, dictatorial, bossy (*informal*), arrogant, imperious, overbearing, tyrannical, magisterial, despotic, high-handed, peremptory, overweening, self-willed << ANTONYM meek

masterly *adjective* SKILFUL, skilled, expert, finished, fine, excellent, crack (*informal*), supreme, clever, superior, world-class, exquisite, adept, consummate, first-rate, superlative, masterful, adroit, dexterous ▷ see **masterful**

mastermind *verb* PLAN, manage, direct, organize, devise, conceive, be the brains behind (*informal*) ▷ *noun* ORGANIZER, director, manager, authority, engineer, brain(s) (*informal*), architect, genius, planner, intellect, virtuoso, rocket scientist (*informal, chiefly US*), brainbox

masterpiece *noun* CLASSIC, tour de force (*French*), pièce de résistance (*French*), magnum opus, master work, jewel, chef-d'oeuvre (*French*)

mastery *noun* **1** UNDERSTANDING, knowledge, comprehension, ability, skill, know-how, command, grip, grasp, expertise, prowess, familiarity, attainment, finesse, proficiency, virtuosity, dexterity, cleverness, deftness, acquirement **2** CONTROL, authority, command, rule, victory, triumph, sway, domination, superiority, conquest, supremacy, dominion, upper hand, ascendancy, pre-eminence, mana (*NZ*), whip hand

masturbation *noun* SELF-ABUSE, onanism, playing with yourself (*slang*), autoeroticism

match *noun* **1** GAME, test, competition, trial, tie, contest, fixture, bout, head-to-head **2** COMPANION, mate, equal, equivalent, counterpart, fellow, complement **3** REPLICA, double, copy, twin, equal, spit (*informal, chiefly Brit*), duplicate, lookalike, ringer (*slang*), spitting image (*informal*), dead ringer (*slang*), spit and image (*informal*) **4** MARRIAGE, union, couple, pair, pairing, item (*informal*), alliance, combination, partnership, duet, affiliation **5** EQUAL, rival, equivalent, peer, competitor, counterpart ▷ *verb* **1** CORRESPOND WITH, suit, go with, complement, fit with, accompany, team with, blend with, tone with, harmonize with, coordinate with **2** TAILOR, fit, suit, adapt **3** CORRESPOND, agree, accord, square, coincide, tally, conform, match up, be compatible, harmonize, be consonant **4** PAIR, unite, join, couple, link, marry, ally, combine, mate, yoke **5** RIVAL, equal, compete with, compare with, emulate, contend with, measure up to ▷▷ **match something or someone against something or someone** PIT AGAINST, set against, play off against, put in opposition to

matching *adjective* IDENTICAL, like, same, double, paired, equal, toning, twin, equivalent, parallel, corresponding, comparable, duplicate, coordinating, analogous << ANTONYM different

matchless *adjective* UNEQUALLED, unique, unparalleled, unrivalled, perfect, supreme, exquisite, consummate, superlative, inimitable, incomparable, unmatched, peerless, unsurpassed << ANTONYM average

mate *noun* **1** (*informal*) FRIEND, pal (*informal*), companion, buddy (*informal*), china (*Brit slang*), cock (*Brit informal*), comrade, chum (*informal*), mucker (*Brit informal*), crony, main man (*slang, chiefly US*), homeboy (*slang, chiefly US*), cobber (*Austral & NZ old-fashioned informal*), E hoa (*NZ*) **2** PARTNER, lover, companion, spouse, consort, significant other (*US informal*), better half (*humorous*), helpmeet, husband *or* wife **3** DOUBLE, match, fellow, twin, counterpart, companion **4** ASSISTANT, subordinate, apprentice, helper, accomplice, sidekick (*informal*) **5** COLLEAGUE, associate, companion, co-worker, fellow-worker, compeer ▷ *verb* **1** PAIR, couple, breed, copulate **2** MARRY, match, wed, get married, shack up (*informal*) **3** JOIN, match, couple, pair, yoke

material *noun* **1** SUBSTANCE, body, matter, stuff, elements, constituents **2** CLOTH, stuff, fabric, textile **3** INFORMATION, work, details, facts, notes, evidence, particulars, data, info (*informal*), subject matter, documentation

▷ *adjective* **1** PHYSICAL, worldly, solid, substantial, concrete, fleshly, bodily, tangible, palpable, corporeal, nonspiritual **2** RELEVANT, important, significant, essential, vital, key, serious, grave, meaningful, applicable, indispensable, momentous, weighty, pertinent, consequential, apposite, apropos, germane

materialize *verb* **1** OCCUR, happen, take place, turn up, come about, take shape, come into being, come to pass **2** APPEAR, arrive, emerge, surface, turn up, loom, show up (*informal*), pop up (*informal*), put in an appearance

materially *adverb* SIGNIFICANTLY, much, greatly, considerably, essentially, seriously, gravely, substantially << ANTONYM insignificantly

maternal *adjective* MOTHERLY, protective, nurturing, maternalistic

maternity *noun* MOTHERHOOD, parenthood, motherliness

matey *adjective* (*Brit informal*) FRIENDLY, intimate, comradely, thick (*informal*), pally (*informal*), amiable, sociable, chummy (*informal*), free-and-easy, companionable, clubby, buddy-buddy (*slang, chiefly US & Canad*), hail-fellow-well-met, palsy-walsy (*informal*)

matrimonial *adjective* MARITAL, married, wedding, wedded, nuptial, conjugal, spousal, connubial, hymeneal

matrimony *noun* MARRIAGE, nuptials, wedlock, wedding ceremony, marital rites

matted *adjective* TANGLED, knotted, unkempt, knotty, tousled, ratty, uncombed

matter *noun* **1** SITUATION, thing, issue, concern, business, question, event, subject, affair, incident, proceeding, episode, topic, transaction, occurrence **2** SUBSTANCE, material, body, stuff **3** CONTENT, sense, subject, argument, text, substance, burden, thesis, purport, gist, pith **4** (*medical*) PUS, discharge, secretion, suppuration, purulence **5** IMPORTANCE, interest, moment, note, weight, import, consequence, significance ▷ *verb* BE IMPORTANT, make a difference, count, be relevant, make any difference, mean anything, have influence, carry weight, cut any ice (*informal*), be of consequence, be of account

matter-of-fact *adjective* UNSENTIMENTAL, flat, dry, plain, dull, sober, down-to-earth, mundane, lifeless, prosaic, deadpan, unimaginative, unvarnished, emotionless, unembellished

mature *verb* DEVELOP, grow up, bloom, blossom, come of age, become adult, age, reach adulthood, maturate ▷ *adjective* **1** MATURED, seasoned, ripe, mellow, ripened **2** GROWN-UP, adult, grown, of age, full-blown, fully fledged, fully developed, full-grown << ANTONYM immature

maturity *noun* **1** ADULTHOOD, majority, completion, puberty, coming of age, fullness, full bloom, full growth, pubescence, manhood *or* womanhood << ANTONYM immaturity **2** RIPENESS, perfection, maturation

maudlin *adjective* SENTIMENTAL, tearful, mushy (*informal*), soppy (*Brit informal*), weepy (*informal*), slushy (*informal*), mawkish, lachrymose, icky (*informal*), overemotional

maul *verb* **1** MANGLE, claw, lacerate, tear, mangulate (*Austral slang*) **2** ILL-TREAT, beat, abuse, batter, thrash, beat up (*informal*), molest, work over (*slang*), pummel, manhandle, rough up, handle roughly, knock about *or* around, beat *or* knock seven bells out of (*informal*)

maverick *noun* REBEL, radical, dissenter, individualist, protester, eccentric, heretic, nonconformist, iconoclast, dissentient << ANTONYM traditionalist ▷ *adjective* REBEL, radical, dissenting, individualistic, eccentric, heretical, iconoclastic, nonconformist

maw *noun* MOUTH, crop, throat, jaws, gullet, craw

maxim *noun* SAYING, motto, adage, proverb, rule, saw, gnome, dictum, axiom, aphorism, byword, apophthegm

maximum *adjective* GREATEST, highest, supreme, paramount, utmost, most, maximal, topmost << ANTONYM minimal ▷ *noun* TOP, most, peak, ceiling, crest, utmost, upper limit, uttermost << ANTONYM minimum

maybe *adverb* PERHAPS, possibly, it could be, conceivably, perchance (*archaic*), mayhap (*archaic*), peradventure (*archaic*)

mayhem *noun* CHAOS, trouble, violence, disorder, destruction, confusion, havoc, fracas, commotion

maze *noun* WEB, puzzle, confusion, tangle, snarl, mesh, labyrinth, imbroglio, convolutions, complex network

meadow *noun* FIELD, pasture, grassland, ley, lea (*poetic*)

meagre *adjective* INSUBSTANTIAL, little, small, poor, spare, slight, inadequate, pathetic, slender, scant, sparse, deficient, paltry, skimpy, puny, measly, scanty, exiguous, scrimpy

mean¹ *verb* **1** SIGNIFY, say, suggest, indicate, represent, express, stand for, convey, spell out, purport, symbolize, denote, connote, betoken **2** IMPLY, suggest, intend, indicate, refer to, intimate, get at (*informal*), hint at, have in mind, drive at (*informal*), allude to, insinuate **3** PRESAGE, promise, herald, foreshadow, augur, foretell, portend, betoken, adumbrate **4** RESULT IN, cause, produce, effect, lead to, involve, bring about, give rise to, entail, engender, necessitate **5** INTEND, want, plan, expect, design, aim, wish, think, propose, purpose, desire, set out, contemplate, aspire, have plans, have in mind **6** DESTINE, make, design, suit, fate, predestine, preordain

mean² *adjective* **1** MISERLY, stingy, parsimonious, niggardly, close (*informal*), near (*informal*), tight, selfish, beggarly, mercenary, skimpy, penny-pinching, ungenerous, penurious, tight-fisted, mingy (*Brit informal*), snoep (*S African informal*) << ANTONYM generous **2** DISHONOURABLE, base, petty, degraded, disgraceful, shameful, shabby, vile, degenerate, callous, sordid, abject, despicable, narrow-minded, contemptible, wretched, scurvy, ignoble, hard-hearted, scungy (*Austral & NZ*), low-minded << ANTONYM honourable **3** (*informal*) MALICIOUS, hostile, nasty, sour, unpleasant, rude, unfriendly, bad-tempered, disagreeable, churlish, ill-tempered, cantankerous << ANTONYM kind **4** SHABBY, poor, miserable, run-down, beggarly, seedy, scruffy, sordid, paltry, squalid, tawdry, low-rent (*informal, chiefly US*), contemptible, wretched, down-at-heel, grungy (*slang, chiefly US*), scuzzy (*slang, chiefly US*) << ANTONYM superb **5** LOWLY, low, common, ordinary, modest, base, obscure, humble, inferior, vulgar, menial, proletarian, undistinguished, servile, ignoble, plebeian, lowborn, baseborn (*archaic*) << ANTONYM noble

mean³ *noun* AVERAGE, middle, balance, norm, median, midpoint ▷ *adjective* AVERAGE, middle, middling, standard, medium, normal, intermediate, median, medial

meander *verb* **1** WIND, turn, snake, zigzag **2** WANDER, stroll, stray, ramble, stravaig (*Scot & N English dialect*) ▷ *noun* CURVE, bend, turn, twist, loop, coil, zigzag

meandering *adjective* WINDING, wandering, snaking, tortuous, convoluted, serpentine, circuitous << ANTONYM straight

meaning *noun* **1** SIGNIFICANCE, message, explanation, substance, value, import, implication, drift, interpretation, essence, purport, connotation, upshot, gist, signification **2** DEFINITION, sense, interpretation, explication, elucidation, denotation **3** PURPOSE, point, end, idea, goal, design, aim, object, intention **4** FORCE, use, point, effect, value, worth, consequence, thrust, validity, usefulness, efficacy ▷ *adjective* EXPRESSIVE, meaningful, pointed, revealing, significant, speaking, pregnant, suggestive, telltale

meaningful *adjective* **1** SIGNIFICANT, important, serious, material, useful, relevant, valid, worthwhile, purposeful << ANTONYM trivial **2** EXPRESSIVE, suggestive, meaning, pointed, speaking, pregnant

meaningless *adjective* NONSENSICAL, senseless, inconsequential, inane, insubstantial << ANTONYM worthwhile

meanness *noun* **1** MISERLINESS, parsimony, stinginess, tight-fistedness, niggardliness, selfishness, minginess (*Brit informal*), penuriousness **2** PETTINESS, degradation, degeneracy, wretchedness, narrow-mindedness, shabbiness, baseness, vileness, sordidness, shamefulness, scurviness, abjectness, low-mindedness, ignobility, despicableness, disgracefulness, dishonourableness **3** MALICE, hostility, bad temper, rudeness, nastiness, unpleasantness, ill temper, sourness, unfriendliness, maliciousness, cantankerousness, churlishness, disagreeableness **4** SHABBINESS, squalor, insignificance, pettiness, wretchedness, seediness, tawdriness, sordidness, scruffiness, humbleness, poorness, paltriness, beggarliness, contemptibleness

means *plural noun* **1** METHOD, way, course, process, medium, measure, agency, channel, instrument, avenue, mode, expedient **2** MONEY, funds, capital, property, riches, income, resources, estate, fortune, wealth, substance, affluence, wherewithal ▷▷ **by all means** CERTAINLY, surely, of course, definitely, absolutely, positively, doubtlessly ▷▷ **by means of** BY WAY OF, using, through, via, utilizing, with the aid of, by dint of ▷▷ **by no means** IN NO WAY, no way, not at all, definitely not, not in the least, on no account, not in the slightest, not the least bit, absolutely not

meantime *or* **meanwhile** *adverb* AT THE SAME TIME, in the meantime, simultaneously, for the present, concurrently, in the meanwhile

meanwhile *or* **meantime** *adverb* FOR NOW, in the meantime, for the moment, in the interim, for then, in the interval, in the meanwhile, in the intervening time

measly *adjective* (*informal*) MEAGRE, miserable, pathetic, paltry, mean, poor, petty, beggarly, pitiful, skimpy, puny, stingy, contemptible, scanty, miserly, niggardly, ungenerous, mingy (*Brit informal*), snoep (*S African informal*)

measurable *adjective* 1 PERCEPTIBLE, material, significant, distinct, palpable, discernible, detectable 2 QUANTIFIABLE, material, quantitative, assessable, determinable, computable, gaugeable, mensurable

measure *verb* QUANTIFY, rate, judge, determine, value, size, estimate, survey, assess, weigh, calculate, evaluate, compute, gauge, mark out, appraise, calibrate ▷ *noun* 1 QUANTITY, share, amount, degree, reach, range, size, capacity, extent, proportion, allowance, portion, scope, quota, ration, magnitude, allotment, amplitude 2 STANDARD, example, model, test, par, criterion, norm, benchmark, barometer, yardstick, touchstone, litmus test 3 ACTION, act, step, procedure, means, course, control, proceeding, initiative, manoeuvre, legal action, deed, expedient 4 GAUGE, rule, scale, metre, ruler, yardstick 5 LAW, act, bill, legislation, resolution, statute, enactment ▷▷ **for good measure** IN ADDITION, as well, besides, to boot, as an extra, into the bargain, as a bonus ▷▷ **measure up** COME UP TO STANDARD, be fit, be adequate, be capable, be suitable, make the grade (*informal*), be suited, be satisfactory, come up to scratch (*informal*), cut the mustard (*US slang*), fulfil the expectations, fit *or* fill the bill ▷▷ **measure up to something** *or* **someone** ACHIEVE, meet, match, rival, equal, compare to, come up to, be equal to, vie with, be on a level with

measured *adjective* 1 STEADY, even, slow, regular, dignified, stately, solemn, leisurely, sedate, unhurried 2 CONSIDERED, planned, reasoned, studied, calculated, deliberate, sober, premeditated, well-thought-out 3 QUANTIFIED, standard, exact, regulated, precise, gauged, verified, predetermined, modulated

measurement *noun* 1 SIZE, length, dimension, area, amount, weight, volume, capacity, extent, height, depth, width, magnitude, amplitude 2 CALCULATION, assessment, evaluation, estimation, survey, judgment, valuation, appraisal, computation, calibration, mensuration, metage

meat *noun* 1 FOOD, provisions, nourishment, sustenance, eats (*slang*), fare, flesh, rations, grub (*slang*), subsistence, kai (*NZ informal*), chow (*informal*), nosh (*slang*), victuals, comestibles, provender, nutriment, viands 2 GIST, point, heart, core, substance, essence, nucleus, marrow, kernel, nub, pith

meaty *adjective* 1 SUBSTANTIAL, rich, nourishing, hearty 2 BRAWNY, muscular, heavy, solid, strapping, sturdy, burly, husky (*informal*), fleshy, beefy (*informal*), heavily built 3 INTERESTING, rich, significant, substantial, profound, meaningful, pithy

mechanical *adjective* 1 AUTOMATIC, automated, mechanized, power-driven, motor-driven, machine-driven << ANTONYM manual 2 UNTHINKING, routine, automatic, matter-of-fact, cold, unconscious, instinctive, lacklustre, involuntary, impersonal, habitual, cursory, perfunctory, unfeeling, machine-like, emotionless, spiritless << ANTONYM conscious

mechanism *noun* 1 WORKINGS, motor, gears, works, action, components, machinery, innards (*informal*) 2 PROCESS, workings, way, means, system, performance, operation, medium, agency, method, functioning, technique, procedure, execution, methodology 3 MACHINE, system, structure, device, tool, instrument, appliance, apparatus, contrivance

meddle *verb* INTERFERE, intervene, tamper, intrude, pry, butt in, interpose, stick your nose in (*informal*), put your oar in, intermeddle, put your two cents in (*US slang*)

mediate *verb* INTERVENE, moderate, step in (*informal*), intercede, settle, referee, resolve, umpire, reconcile, arbitrate, interpose, conciliate, make peace, restore harmony, act as middleman, bring to terms, bring to an agreement

mediation *noun* ARBITRATION, intervention, reconciliation, conciliation, good offices, intercession, interposition

mediator *noun* NEGOTIATOR, arbitrator, judge, referee, advocate, umpire, intermediary, middleman, arbiter, peacemaker, go-between, moderator, interceder, honest broker

medicinal *adjective* THERAPEUTIC, medical, healing, remedial, restorative, curative, analeptic, roborant, sanative

medicine *noun* REMEDY, drug, cure, prescription, medication, nostrum, physic, medicament

medieval *adjective* (*informal*) OLD-FASHIONED, antique, primitive, obsolete, out-of-date, archaic, prehistoric, antiquated, anachronistic, antediluvian, unenlightened, out of the ark

mediocre *adjective* SECOND-RATE, average, ordinary, indifferent, middling, pedestrian, inferior, commonplace, vanilla (*slang*), insignificant, so-so (*informal*), banal, tolerable, run-of-the-mill, passable, undistinguished, uninspired, bog-standard (*Brit & Irish slang*), no great shakes (*informal*), half-pie (*NZ informal*), fair to middling (*informal*) << ANTONYM excellent

mediocrity *noun* 1 INSIGNIFICANCE, indifference, inferiority, meanness, ordinariness, unimportance, poorness 2 NONENTITY, nobody, lightweight (*informal*), second-rater, cipher

meditate *verb* REFLECT, think, consider, contemplate, deliberate, muse, ponder, ruminate, cogitate, be in a brown study ▷▷ **meditate on something** CONSIDER, study, contemplate, ponder, reflect on, mull over, think over, chew over, deliberate on, weigh, turn something over in your mind

meditation *noun* REFLECTION, thought, concentration, study, musing, pondering, contemplation, reverie, ruminating, rumination, cogitation, cerebration, a brown study

meditative *adjective* REFLECTIVE, thoughtful, contemplative, studious, pensive, deliberative, ruminative, cogitative

medium *adjective* AVERAGE, mean, middle, middling, fair, intermediate, midway, mediocre, median, medial << ANTONYM extraordinary ▷ *noun* 1 SPIRITUALIST, seer, clairvoyant, fortune teller, spiritist, channeller 2 MIDDLE, mean, centre, average, compromise, middle ground, middle way, midpoint, middle course, middle path

medley *noun* MIXTURE, confusion, jumble, assortment, patchwork, pastiche, mixed bag (*informal*), potpourri, mélange (*French*), miscellany, mishmash, farrago, hotchpotch,

hodgepodge, salmagundi, olio, gallimaufry, omnium-gatherum

meek *adjective* 1 SUBMISSIVE, soft, yielding, gentle, peaceful, modest, mild, patient, humble, timid, long-suffering, compliant, unassuming, unpretentious, docile, deferential, forbearing, acquiescent << ANTONYM overbearing 2 SPINELESS, weak, tame, boneless, weak-kneed (*informal*), spiritless, unresisting, wussy (*slang*), wimpish *or* wimpy (*informal*)

meet *verb* 1 ENCOUNTER, come across, run into, happen on, find, contact, confront, bump into (*informal*), run across, chance on, come face to face with << ANTONYM avoid 2 GATHER, collect, assemble, get together, rally, come together, muster, convene, congregate, foregather << ANTONYM disperse 3 FULFIL, match (up to), answer, perform, handle, carry out, equal, satisfy, cope with, discharge, comply with, come up to, conform to, gratify, measure up to << ANTONYM fall short of 4 EXPERIENCE, face, suffer, bear, go through, encounter, endure, undergo 5 CONVERGE, unite, join, cross, touch, connect, come together, link up, adjoin, intersect, abut << ANTONYM diverge

meeting *noun* 1 CONFERENCE, gathering, assembly, meet, congress, session, rally, convention, get-together (*informal*), reunion, congregation, hui (*NZ*), conclave, convocation, powwow 2 ENCOUNTER, introduction, confrontation, engagement, rendezvous, tryst, assignation 3 CONVERGENCE, union, crossing, conjunction, junction, intersection, concourse, confluence

melancholy *adjective* SAD, down, depressed, unhappy, low, blue, miserable, moody, gloomy, dismal, sombre, woeful, glum, mournful, dejected, despondent, dispirited, melancholic, downcast, lugubrious, pensive, sorrowful, disconsolate, joyless, doleful, downhearted, heavy-hearted, down in the dumps (*informal*), woebegone, down in the mouth, low-spirited << ANTONYM happy ▷ *noun* SADNESS, depression, misery, gloom, sorrow, woe, blues, unhappiness, despondency, the hump (*Brit informal*), dejection, low spirits, gloominess, pensiveness << ANTONYM happiness

melee *or* **mêlée** *noun* FIGHT, fray, brawl, skirmish, tussle, scuffle, free-for-all (*informal*), fracas, set-to (*informal*), rumpus, broil, affray (*law*), shindig (*informal*), donnybrook, ruction (*informal*), battle royal, ruckus (*informal*), scrimmage, stramash (*Scot*), shindy (*informal*), bagarre (*French*), biffo (*Austral slang*)

mellow *adjective* **1** TUNEFUL, full, rich, soft, melodious, mellifluous, dulcet, well-tuned, euphonic **2** FULL-FLAVOURED, rounded, rich, sweet, smooth, delicate, juicy **3** RIPE, perfect, mature, ripened, well-matured << ANTONYM unripe **4** RELAXED, happy, cheerful, jolly, elevated, merry (*Brit informal*), expansive, cordial, genial, jovial ▷ *verb* **1** RELAX, improve, settle, calm, mature, soften, sweeten **2** SEASON, develop, improve, perfect, ripen

melodramatic *adjective* THEATRICAL, actorly, extravagant, histrionic, sensational, hammy (*informal*), actressy, stagy, overemotional, overdramatic

melody *noun* **1** TUNE, song, theme, refrain, air, music, strain, descant **2** TUNEFULNESS, music, harmony, musicality, euphony, melodiousness

melt *verb* **1** DISSOLVE, run, soften, fuse, thaw, diffuse, flux, defrost, liquefy, unfreeze, deliquesce **2** *often with* **away** DISAPPEAR, fade, vanish, dissolve, disperse, evaporate, evanesce **3** SOFTEN, touch, relax, disarm, mollify

member *noun* REPRESENTATIVE, associate, supporter, fellow, subscriber, comrade, disciple

membership *noun* **1** PARTICIPATION, belonging, fellowship, enrolment **2** MEMBERS, body, associates, fellows

memento *noun* SOUVENIR, trophy, memorial, token, reminder, relic, remembrance, keepsake

memoir *noun* ACCOUNT, life, record, register, journal, essay, biography, narrative, monograph

memoirs *plural noun* AUTOBIOGRAPHY, diary, life story, life, experiences, memories, journals, recollections, reminiscences

memorable *adjective* NOTEWORTHY, celebrated, impressive, historic, important, special, striking, famous, significant, signal, extraordinary, remarkable, distinguished, haunting, notable, timeless, unforgettable, momentous, illustrious, catchy, indelible, unfading << ANTONYM forgettable

memorandum *noun* NOTE, minute, message, communication, reminder, memo, jotting

memorial *noun* **1** MONUMENT, cairn,

shrine, plaque, cenotaph **2** PETITION, address, statement, memorandum ▷ *adjective* COMMEMORATIVE, remembrance, monumental

memorize *verb* REMEMBER, learn, commit to memory, learn by heart, learn by rote, get by heart, con (*archaic*)

memory *noun* **1** RECALL, mind, retention, ability to remember, powers of recall, powers of retention **2** RECOLLECTION, reminder, reminiscence, impression, echo, remembrance **3** COMMEMORATION, respect, honour, recognition, tribute, remembrance, observance

menace *noun* **1** DANGER, risk, threat, hazard, peril, jeopardy **2** (*informal*) NUISANCE, plague, pest, annoyance, troublemaker, mischief-maker **3** THREAT, warning, intimidation, ill-omen, ominousness, commination ▷ *verb* BULLY, threaten, intimidate, terrorize, alarm, frighten, scare, browbeat, utter threats to

menacing *adjective* THREATENING, dangerous, alarming, frightening, forbidding, looming, intimidating, ominous, baleful, intimidatory, minatory, bodeful, louring *or* lowering, minacious << ANTONYM encouraging

mend *verb* **1** REPAIR, fix, restore, renew, patch up, renovate, refit, retouch **2** DARN, repair, patch, stitch, sew **3** HEAL, improve, recover, cure, remedy, get better, be all right, be cured, recuperate, pull through, convalesce **4** IMPROVE, better, reform, correct, revise, amend, rectify, ameliorate, emend ▷▷ **on the mend** CONVALESCENT, improving, recovering, getting better, recuperating, convalescing

menial *adjective* LOW-STATUS, degrading, lowly, unskilled, low, base, sorry, boring, routine, dull, humble, mean, vile, demeaning, fawning, abject, grovelling, humdrum, subservient, ignominious, sycophantic, servile, slavish, ignoble, obsequious << ANTONYM high ▷ *noun* SERVANT, domestic, attendant, lackey, labourer, serf, underling, drudge, vassal (*archaic*), dogsbody (*informal*), flunky, skivvy (*chiefly Brit*), varlet (*archaic*) << ANTONYM master

menstruation *noun* PERIOD, menstrual cycle, menses, courses (*physiology*), flow (*informal*), monthly (*informal*), the curse (*informal*), catamenia (*physiology*)

mental *adjective* **1** INTELLECTUAL, rational, theoretical, cognitive, brain, conceptual, cerebral **2** (*slang*) INSANE, mad, disturbed, unstable, mentally ill, lunatic, psychotic, unbalanced, deranged, round the bend (*Brit slang*), as daft as a brush (*informal, chiefly Brit*), not right in the head

mentality *noun* ATTITUDE, character, personality, psychology, make-up, outlook, disposition, way of thinking, frame of mind, turn of mind, cast of mind

mentally *adverb* PSYCHOLOGICALLY, intellectually, rationally, inwardly, subjectively

mention *verb* REFER TO, point out, acknowledge, bring up, state, report, reveal, declare, cite, communicate, disclose, intimate, tell of, recount, hint at, impart, allude to, divulge, broach, call attention to, make known, touch upon, adduce, speak about or of ▷ *noun* **1** often with **of** REFERENCE, announcement, observation, indication, remark, notification, allusion **2** ACKNOWLEDGMENT, recognition, tribute, citation, honourable mention ▷▷ **not to mention** TO SAY NOTHING OF, besides, not counting, as well as

mentor *noun* GUIDE, teacher, coach, adviser, tutor, instructor, counsellor, guru

menu *noun* BILL OF FARE, tariff (*chiefly Brit*), set menu, table d'hôte, carte du jour (*French*)

mercantile *adjective* **1** COMMERCIAL, business, trade, trading, merchant **2** PROFIT-MAKING, money-orientated

mercenary *noun* HIRELING, freelance (*history*), soldier of fortune, condottiere (*history*), free companion (*history*) ▷ *adjective* **1** GREEDY, grasping, acquisitive, venal, avaricious, covetous, money-grubbing (*informal*), bribable << ANTONYM generous **2** HIRED, paid, bought, venal

merchandise *noun* GOODS, produce, stock, products, truck, commodities, staples, wares, stock in trade, vendibles ▷ *verb* TRADE, market, sell, retail, distribute, deal in, buy and sell, traffic in, vend, do business in

merchant *noun* TRADESMAN, dealer, trader, broker, retailer, supplier, seller, salesman, vendor, shopkeeper, trafficker, wholesaler, purveyor

merciful *adjective* COMPASSIONATE, forgiving, sympathetic, kind, liberal, soft, sparing, generous, mild, pitying, humane, clement, gracious, lenient, beneficent, forbearing, tender-hearted, benignant << ANTONYM merciless

merciless *adjective* CRUEL, ruthless, hard,

severe, harsh, relentless, callous, heartless, unforgiving, fell (*archaic*), inexorable, implacable, unsympathetic, inhumane, barbarous, pitiless, unfeeling, unsparing, hard-hearted, unmerciful, unappeasable, unpitying

mercurial *adjective* CAPRICIOUS, volatile, unpredictable, erratic, variable, unstable, fickle, temperamental, impulsive, irrepressible, changeable, quicksilver, flighty, inconstant << ANTONYM consistent

mercy *noun* **1** COMPASSION, charity, pity, forgiveness, quarter, favour, grace, kindness, clemency, leniency, benevolence, forbearance << ANTONYM cruelty **2** BLESSING, relief, boon, godsend, piece of luck, benison (*archaic*) ▷▷ **at the mercy of something** or **someone 1** DEFENCELESS AGAINST, subject to, open to, exposed to, vulnerable to, threatened by, susceptible to, prey to, an easy target for, naked before, unprotected against **2** IN THE POWER OF, under the control of, in the clutches of, under the heel of

mere *adjective* **1** SIMPLE, merely, no more than, nothing more than, just, common, plain, pure, pure and simple, unadulterated, unmitigated, unmixed **2** BARE, slender, trifling, meagre, just, only, basic, no more than, minimal, scant, paltry, skimpy, scanty

merge *verb* **1** COMBINE, blend, fuse, amalgamate, unite, join, mix, consolidate, mingle, converge, coalesce, melt into, meld, intermix << ANTONYM separate **2** JOIN, unite, combine, consolidate, fuse << ANTONYM separate **3** MELT, blend, incorporate, mingle, tone with, be swallowed up by, become lost in

merger *noun* UNION, fusion, consolidation, amalgamation, combination, coalition, incorporation

merit *noun* ADVANTAGE, value, quality, worth, strength, asset, virtue, good point, strong point, worthiness ▷ *verb* DESERVE, warrant, be entitled to, earn, incur, have a right to, be worthy of, have a claim to

merited *adjective* DESERVED, justified, warranted, just, earned, appropriate, entitled, rightful, condign, rightly due

merriment *noun* FUN, amusement, glee, mirth, sport, laughter, festivity, frolic, gaiety, hilarity, revelry, jollity, levity, liveliness, conviviality, joviality, jocularity, merrymaking

merry *adjective* **1** CHEERFUL, happy, upbeat

(*informal*), carefree, glad, jolly, festive, joyous,
joyful, genial, fun-loving, chirpy (*informal*),
vivacious, rollicking, convivial, gleeful,
blithe, frolicsome, mirthful, sportive,
light-hearted, jocund, gay, blithesome
<< ANTONYM gloomy **2** (*Brit informal*) TIPSY,
happy, elevated (*informal*), mellow, tiddly
(*slang, chiefly Brit*), squiffy (*Brit informal*)
▷▷ **make merry** HAVE FUN, celebrate, revel,
have a good time, feast, frolic, enjoy yourself,
carouse, make whoopee (*informal*)

mesh *noun* **1** NET, netting, network, web,
tracery **2** TRAP, web, tangle, toils, snare,
entanglement ▷ *verb* **1** ENGAGE, combine,
connect, knit, come together, coordinate,
interlock, dovetail, fit together, harmonize
2 ENTANGLE, catch, net, trap, tangle, snare,
ensnare, enmesh

mesmerize *verb* ENTRANCE, fascinate,
absorb, captivate, grip, enthral, hypnotize,
magnetize, hold spellbound, spellbind

mess *noun* **1** UNTIDINESS, disorder,
confusion, chaos, turmoil, litter, clutter,
disarray, jumble, disorganization, grot
(*slang*), dirtiness **2** SHAMBLES, botch, hash,
cock-up (*Brit slang*), state, bodge (*informal*),
pig's breakfast (*informal*) **3** DIFFICULTY,
dilemma, plight, spot (*informal*), hole
(*informal*), fix (*informal*), jam (*informal*), hot
water (*informal*), stew (*informal*), mix-up,
muddle, pickle (*informal*), uphill (*S African*),
predicament, deep water, perplexity, tight
spot, imbroglio, fine kettle of fish (*informal*)
▷▷ **mess about** *or* **around 1** POTTER ABOUT,
dabble, amuse yourself, footle (*informal*),
fool about *or* around, muck about *or* around
(*informal*), play about *or* around **2** MEDDLE,
play, interfere, toy, fiddle (*informal*), tamper,
tinker, trifle, fool about *or* around ▷▷ **mess
something up 1** BOTCH, bungle, make a hash
of (*informal*), make a nonsense of, make a
pig's ear of (*informal*), cock something up
(*Brit slang*), muck something up (*Brit slang*),
muddle something up **2** DIRTY, foul, litter,
pollute, clutter, besmirch, disarrange,
befoul, dishevel ▷▷ **mess with something** *or*
someone INTERFERE WITH, play with, fiddle
with (*informal*), tamper with, tinker with,
meddle with

message *noun* **1** COMMUNICATION, note,
bulletin, word, letter, notice, memo,
dispatch, memorandum, communiqué,
missive, intimation, tidings **2** POINT,
meaning, idea, moral, theme, import,
purport ▷▷ **get the message** UNDERSTAND,

see, get it, catch on (*informal*), comprehend,
twig (*Brit informal*), get the point, take the
hint

messenger *noun* COURIER, agent, runner,
carrier, herald, envoy, bearer, go-between,
emissary, harbinger, delivery boy, errand boy

messy *adjective* **1** DISORGANIZED, sloppy
(*informal*), untidy, slovenly **2** DIRTY, grubby,
grimy, scuzzy (*slang, chiefly US*) **3** UNTIDY,
disordered, littered, chaotic, muddled,
cluttered, shambolic, disorganized, daggy
(*Austral & NZ informal*) << ANTONYM tidy
4 DISHEVELLED, ruffled, untidy, rumpled,
bedraggled, unkempt, tousled, uncombed,
daggy (*Austral & NZ informal*) **5** CONFUSING,
difficult, complex, confused, tangled,
chaotic, tortuous

metamorphose *verb* TRANSFORM, change,
alter, remake, convert, remodel, mutate,
reshape, be reborn, transmute, transfigure,
transmogrify (*jocular*), transubstantiate

metamorphosis *noun* TRANSFORMATION,
conversion, alteration, change, mutation,
rebirth, changeover, transfiguration,
transmutation, transubstantiation,
transmogrification (*jocular*)

metaphor *noun* FIGURE OF SPEECH, image,
symbol, analogy, emblem, conceit (*literary*),
allegory, trope, figurative expression

metaphorical *adjective* FIGURATIVE, symbolic,
emblematic, allegorical, emblematical,
tropical (*rhetoric*)

metaphysical *adjective* **1** ABSTRACT,
intellectual, theoretical, deep, basic,
essential, ideal, fundamental, universal,
profound, philosophical, speculative, high-
flown, esoteric, transcendental, abstruse,
recondite, oversubtle **2** SUPERNATURAL,
spiritual, unreal, intangible, immaterial,
incorporeal, impalpable, unsubstantial

meteoric *adjective* SPECTACULAR, sudden,
overnight, rapid, fast, brief, brilliant,
flashing, fleeting, swift, dazzling, speedy,
transient, momentary, ephemeral
<< ANTONYM gradual

mete out *verb* DISTRIBUTE, portion, assign,
administer, ration, dispense, allot, dole out,
share out, apportion, deal out, measure out,
parcel out, divide out

method *noun* **1** MANNER, process, approach,
technique, way, plan, course, system, form,
rule, programme, style, practice, fashion,
scheme, arrangement, procedure, routine,
mode, modus operandi **2** ORDERLINESS,
planning, order, system, form, design,

structure, purpose, pattern, organization, regularity

methodical *adjective* ORDERLY, planned, ordered, structured, regular, disciplined, organized, efficient, precise, neat, deliberate, tidy, systematic, meticulous, painstaking, businesslike, well-regulated << ANTONYM haphazard

meticulous *adjective* THOROUGH, detailed, particular, strict, exact, precise, microscopic, fussy, painstaking, perfectionist, scrupulous, fastidious, punctilious << ANTONYM careless

metropolis *noun* CITY, town, capital, big city, municipality, conurbation, megalopolis

mettle *noun* 1 COURAGE, spirit, resolution, resolve, life, heart, fire, bottle (*Brit slang*), nerve, daring, guts (*informal*), pluck, grit, bravery, fortitude, vigour, boldness, gallantry, ardour, valour, spunk (*informal*), indomitability, hardihood, gameness 2 CHARACTER, quality, nature, make-up, stamp, temper, kidney, temperament, calibre, disposition

microbe *noun* MICROORGANISM, virus, bug (*informal*), germ, bacterium, bacillus

microscopic *adjective* TINY, minute, invisible, negligible, minuscule, imperceptible, infinitesimal, teeny-weeny, teensy-weensy << ANTONYM huge

midday *noun* NOON, twelve o'clock, noonday, noontime, twelve noon, noontide

middle *noun* 1 CENTRE, heart, inside, thick, core, midst, nucleus, hub, halfway point, midpoint, midsection 2 WAIST, gut, belly, tummy (*informal*), waistline, midriff, paunch, midsection ▷ *adjective* 1 CENTRAL, medium, inside, mid, intervening, inner, halfway, intermediate, median, medial 2 INTERMEDIATE, inside, intervening, inner

middle-class *adjective* BOURGEOIS, traditional, conventional, suburban, petit-bourgeois

middleman *noun* INTERMEDIARY, broker, entrepreneur, distributor, go-between

middling *adjective* 1 MEDIOCRE, all right, indifferent, so-so (*informal*), unremarkable, tolerable, run-of-the-mill, passable, serviceable, unexceptional, half-pie (*NZ informal*), O.K. *or* okay (*informal*) 2 MODERATE, medium, average, fair, ordinary, modest, adequate, bog-standard (*Brit & Irish slang*)

midget *noun* DWARF, shrimp (*informal*), gnome, Tom Thumb, munchkin (*informal, chiefly US*), homunculus, manikin, homuncule, pygmy *or* pigmy ▷ *adjective*

1 BABY, small, tiny, miniature, dwarf, teeny-weeny, teensy-weensy 2 DIMINUTIVE, little, pocket-sized, Lilliputian, dwarfish, pygmy *or* pigmy

midnight *noun* TWELVE O'CLOCK, middle of the night, dead of night, twelve o'clock at night, the witching hour

midst *noun* MIDDLE, centre, heart, interior, thick, depths, core, hub, bosom ▷▷ **in the midst of** 1 DURING, in the middle of, amidst 2 AMONG, in the middle of, surrounded by, amidst, in the thick of, enveloped by

midway *adverb* HALFWAY, in the middle of, part-way, equidistant, at the midpoint, betwixt and between

miffed *adjective* UPSET, hurt, annoyed, offended, irritated, put out, hacked (off) (*US slang*), resentful, nettled, aggrieved, vexed, displeased, irked, in a huff, piqued, narked (*Brit, Austral & NZ slang*), tooshie (*Austral slang*)

might *noun* POWER, force, energy, ability, strength, capacity, efficiency, capability, sway, clout (*informal*), vigour, prowess, potency, efficacy, valour, puissance

mightily *adverb* 1 VERY, highly, greatly, hugely, very much, seriously (*informal*), extremely, intensely, decidedly, exceedingly 2 POWERFULLY, vigorously, strongly, forcefully, energetically, with all your strength, with all your might and main

mighty *adjective* 1 POWERFUL, strong, strapping, robust, hardy, vigorous, potent, sturdy, stout, forceful, stalwart, doughty, lusty, indomitable, manful, puissant << ANTONYM weak 2 GREAT, large, huge, grand, massive, towering, vast, enormous, tremendous, immense, titanic, gigantic, monumental, bulky, colossal, stellar (*informal*), prodigious, stupendous, elephantine, ginormous (*informal*), humongous *or* humungous (*US slang*) << ANTONYM tiny

migrant *noun* WANDERER, immigrant, traveller, gypsy, tinker, rover, transient, nomad, emigrant, itinerant, drifter, vagrant ▷ *adjective* ITINERANT, wandering, drifting, roving, travelling, shifting, immigrant, gypsy, transient, nomadic, migratory, vagrant

migrate *verb* MOVE, travel, journey, wander, shift, drift, trek, voyage, roam, emigrate, rove

migration *noun* WANDERING, journey, voyage, travel, movement, shift, trek, emigration, roving

migratory *adjective* NOMADIC, travelling, wandering, migrant, itinerant, unsettled, shifting, gypsy, roving, transient, vagrant, peripatetic

mild *adjective* **1** GENTLE, kind, easy, soft, pacific, calm, moderate, forgiving, tender, pleasant, mellow, compassionate, indulgent, serene, easy-going, amiable, meek, placid, docile, merciful, peaceable, forbearing, equable, easy-oasy (*slang*) << ANTONYM harsh **2** TEMPERATE, warm, calm, moderate, clement, tranquil, balmy << ANTONYM cold **3** BLAND, thin, smooth, tasteless, insipid, flavourless **4** SOOTHING, mollifying, emollient, demulcent, lenitive

milieu *noun* SURROUNDINGS, setting, scene, environment, element, background, location, sphere, locale, mise en scène (*French*)

militant *adjective* AGGRESSIVE, warring, fighting, active, combating, contending, vigorous, assertive, in arms, embattled, belligerent, combative << ANTONYM peaceful ▷ *noun* ACTIVIST, radical, fighter, partisan, belligerent, combatant

military *adjective* WARLIKE, armed, soldierly, martial, soldierlike ▷▷ **the military** THE ARMED FORCES, the forces, the services, the army

militate ▷▷ **militate against something** COUNTERACT, conflict with, contend with, count against, oppose, counter, resist, be detrimental to, weigh against, tell against ▷ see **mitigate**

militia *noun* RESERVE(S), National Guard (*US*), Territorial Army (*Brit*), yeomanry (*history*), fencibles (*history*), trainband (*history*)

milk *verb* EXPLOIT, use, pump, squeeze, drain, take advantage of, bleed, impose on, wring, fleece, suck dry

milky *adjective* WHITE, clouded, opaque, cloudy, alabaster, whitish, milk-white

mill *noun* **1** GRINDER, crusher, quern **2** FACTORY, works, shop, plant, workshop, foundry ▷ *verb* GRIND, pound, press, crush, powder, grate, pulverize, granulate, comminute ▷▷ **mill about** *or* **around** SWARM, crowd, stream, surge, seethe, throng

millstone *noun* BURDEN, weight, load, albatross, drag, affliction, dead weight, encumbrance

mime *noun* DUMB SHOW, gesture, pantomime, mummery ▷ *verb* ACT OUT, represent, gesture, simulate, pantomime

mimic *verb* **1** IMITATE, do (*informal*), take off (*informal*), ape, parody, caricature, impersonate **2** RESEMBLE, look like, mirror, echo, simulate, take on the appearance of ▷ *noun* IMITATOR, impressionist, copycat (*informal*), impersonator, caricaturist, parodist, parrot

mimicry *noun* IMITATION, impression, impersonation, copying, imitating, mimicking, parody, caricature, mockery, burlesque, apery

mince *verb* **1** CUT, grind, crumble, dice, hash, chop up **2** POSTURE, pose, ponce (*slang*), attitudinize **3** TONE DOWN, spare, moderate, weaken, diminish, soften, hold back, extenuate, palliate, euphemize

mincing *adjective* AFFECTED, nice, camp (*informal*), precious, pretentious, dainty, sissy, effeminate, foppish, poncy (*slang*), arty-farty (*informal*), lah-di-dah (*informal*), niminy-piminy

mind *noun* **1** BRAIN, head, imagination, psyche, subconscious **2** MEMORY, recollection, remembrance, powers of recollection **3** ATTENTION, thinking, thoughts, concentration **4** INTELLIGENCE, reason, reasoning, understanding, sense, spirit, brain(s) (*informal*), wits, mentality, intellect, grey matter (*informal*), ratiocination **5** THINKER, academic, intellectual, genius, brain (*informal*), scholar, sage, intellect, rocket scientist (*informal, chiefly US*), brainbox, acca (*Austral slang*) **6** INTENTION, will, wish, desire, urge, fancy, purpose, leaning, bent, notion, tendency, inclination, disposition **7** SANITY, reason, senses, judgment, wits, marbles (*informal*), rationality, mental balance ▷ *verb* **1** TAKE OFFENCE AT, dislike, care about, object to, resent, disapprove of, be bothered by, look askance at, be affronted by **2** BE CAREFUL, watch, take care, be wary, be cautious, be on your guard **3** BE SURE, ensure, make sure, be careful, make certain **4** LOOK AFTER, watch, protect, tend, guard, take care of, attend to, keep an eye on, have *or* take charge of **5** PAY ATTENTION TO, follow, mark, watch, note, regard, respect, notice, attend to, listen to, observe, comply with, obey, heed, adhere to, take heed of, pay heed to ▷▷ **in** *or* **of two minds** UNDECIDED, uncertain, unsure, wavering, hesitant, dithering (*chiefly Brit*), vacillating, swithering (*Scot*), shillyshallying (*informal*) ▷▷ **make up your mind** DECIDE, choose, determine, resolve, reach a decision, come to a decision ▷▷ **mind out** BE CAREFUL, watch out, take care, look out, beware, pay attention, keep your eyes open, be on your guard

mindful *adjective with of* AWARE, careful, conscious, alert, sensible, wary, thoughtful, attentive, respectful, watchful, alive to, cognizant, chary, heedful, regardful << ANTONYM heedless

mindless *adjective* **1** UNTHINKING, gratuitous, thoughtless, careless, oblivious, brutish, inane, witless, heedless, unmindful, dumb-ass (*slang*) << ANTONYM reasoning **2** UNINTELLIGENT, stupid, foolish, careless, negligent, idiotic, thoughtless, inane, witless, forgetful, moronic, obtuse, neglectful, asinine, imbecilic, braindead (*informal*), dumb-ass (*slang*), dead from the neck up (*informal*) **3** MECHANICAL, automatic, monotonous, mind-numbing, brainless

mind's eye ▷▷ **in your mind's eye** IN YOUR IMAGINATION, in your head, in your mind

mine *noun* **1** PIT, deposit, shaft, vein, colliery, excavation, coalfield, lode **2** SOURCE, store, fund, stock, supply, reserve, treasury, wealth, abundance, hoard ▷ *verb* **1** DIG UP, extract, quarry, unearth, delve, excavate, hew, dig for **2** LAY MINES IN *or* UNDER, sow with mines

miner *noun* COALMINER, pitman (*Brit*), collier (*Brit*)

mingle *verb* **1** MIX, combine, blend, merge, unite, join, marry, compound, alloy, interweave, coalesce, intermingle, meld, commingle, intermix, admix << ANTONYM separate **2** ASSOCIATE, circulate, hang out (*informal*), consort, socialize, rub shoulders (*informal*), hobnob, fraternize, hang about *or* around << ANTONYM dissociate

miniature *adjective* SMALL, little, minute, baby, reduced, tiny, pocket, toy, mini, wee, dwarf, scaled-down, diminutive, minuscule, midget, teeny-weeny, Lilliputian, teensy-weensy, pygmy *or* pigmy << ANTONYM giant

minimal *adjective* MINIMUM, smallest, least, slightest, token, nominal, negligible, least possible, littlest

minimize *verb* **1** REDUCE, decrease, shrink, diminish, prune, curtail, attenuate, downsize, miniaturize << ANTONYM increase **2** PLAY DOWN, discount, underestimate, belittle, disparage, decry, underrate, deprecate, depreciate, make light *or* little of << ANTONYM praise

minimum *adjective* LOWEST, smallest, least, slightest, minimal, least possible, littlest << ANTONYM maximum ▷ *noun* LOWEST,

least, depth, slightest, lowest level, nadir, bottom level

minion *noun* FOLLOWER, henchman, underling, lackey, favourite, pet, creature, darling, parasite, cohort (*chiefly US*), dependant, hanger-on, sycophant, yes man, toady, hireling, flunky, flatterer, lickspittle, bootlicker (*informal*)

minister *noun* **1** OFFICIAL, ambassador, diplomat, delegate, executive, administrator, envoy, cabinet member, office-holder, plenipotentiary **2** CLERGYMAN, priest, divine, vicar, parson, preacher, pastor, chaplain, cleric, rector, curate, churchman, padre (*informal*), ecclesiastic ▷▷ **minister to** ATTEND TO, serve, tend to, answer to, accommodate, take care of, cater to, pander to, administer to, be solicitous of

ministry *noun* **1** DEPARTMENT, office, bureau, government department **2** ADMINISTRATION, government, council, cabinet **3** THE PRIESTHOOD, the church, the cloth, the pulpit, holy orders

minor *adjective* SMALL, lesser, subordinate, smaller, light, slight, secondary, petty, inferior, trivial, trifling, insignificant, negligible, unimportant, paltry, inconsequential, inconsiderable, nickel-and-dime (*US slang*) << ANTONYM major

minstrel *noun* MUSICIAN, singer, harper, bard, troubadour, songstress, jongleur

mint *verb* **1** MAKE, produce, strike, cast, stamp, punch, coin **2** INVENT, produce, fashion, make up, construct, coin, devise, forge, fabricate, think up ▷ *noun* FORTUNE, million, bomb (*Brit slang*), pile (*informal*), packet (*slang*), bundle (*slang*), heap (*informal*), King's ransom, top whack (*informal*) ▷ *adjective* PERFECT, excellent, first-class, brand-new, fresh, unmarked, undamaged, unblemished, untarnished

minuscule *adjective* TINY, little, minute, fine, very small, miniature, microscopic, diminutive, infinitesimal, teeny-weeny, Lilliputian, teensy-weensy

minute¹ *noun* **1** SIXTY SECONDS, sixtieth of an hour **2** MOMENT, second, bit, shake (*informal*), flash, instant, tick (*Brit informal*), sec (*informal*), short time, little while, jiffy (*informal*), trice ▷▷ **up to the minute** LATEST, in, newest, now (*informal*), with it (*informal*), smart, stylish, trendiest, trendy (*Brit informal*), vogue, up to date, modish, (most) fashionable, schmick (*Austral informal*)

minute² *adjective* **1** SMALL, little, tiny,

miniature, slender, fine, microscopic, diminutive, minuscule, infinitesimal, teeny-weeny, Lilliputian, teensy-weensy << ANTONYM huge **2** NEGLIGIBLE, slight, petty, trivial, trifling, unimportant, paltry, puny, piddling (*informal*), inconsiderable, picayune (*US*) << ANTONYM significant **3** PRECISE, close, detailed, critical, exact, meticulous, exhaustive, painstaking, punctilious << ANTONYM imprecise

minutely *adverb* PRECISELY, closely, exactly, in detail, critically, meticulously, painstakingly, exhaustively, with a fine-tooth comb

minutes *plural noun* RECORD, notes, proceedings, transactions, transcript, memorandum

minutiae *plural noun* DETAILS, particulars, subtleties, trifles, trivia, niceties, finer points, ins and outs

miracle *noun* WONDER, phenomenon, sensation, marvel, amazing achievement, astonishing feat

miraculous *adjective* WONDERFUL, amazing, extraordinary, incredible, astonishing, marvellous, magical, unbelievable, phenomenal, astounding, inexplicable, wondrous (*archaic or literary*), unaccountable, superhuman << ANTONYM ordinary

mirage *noun* ILLUSION, vision, hallucination, pipe dream, chimera, optical illusion, phantasm

mire *noun* **1** MUD, dirt, muck, ooze, sludge, slime, slob (*Irish*), gloop (*informal*), grot (*slang*) **2** SWAMP, marsh, bog, fen, quagmire, morass, wetland, pakihi (*NZ*), muskeg (*Canad*) ▷ *verb* **1** SOIL, dirty, muddy, besmirch, begrime, bespatter **2** ENTANGLE, involve, mix up, catch up, bog down, tangle up, enmesh

mirror *noun* LOOKING-GLASS, glass (*Brit*), reflector, speculum ▷ *verb* REFLECT, show, follow, match, represent, copy, repeat, echo, parallel, depict, reproduce, emulate

mirror image *noun* REFLECTION, double, image, copy, twin, representation, clone, replica, likeness, spitting image (*informal*), dead ringer (*informal*), exact likeness

mirth *noun* MERRIMENT, amusement, fun, pleasure, laughter, rejoicing, festivity, glee, frolic, sport, gaiety, hilarity, cheerfulness, revelry, jollity, levity, gladness, joviality, jocularity, merrymaking, joyousness

misadventure *noun* MISFORTUNE, accident, disaster, failure, reverse, setback, catastrophe, debacle, bad luck, calamity, mishap, bad break (*informal*), ill fortune, ill luck, mischance

misapprehension *noun* MISUNDERSTANDING, mistake, error, delusion, misconception, fallacy, misreading, false impression, misinterpretation, false belief, misconstruction, wrong idea *or* impression

misappropriate *verb* STEAL, embezzle, pocket, misuse, swindle, misspend, misapply, defalcate (*law*)

misbehave *verb* BE NAUGHTY, be bad, act up (*informal*), muck about (*Brit slang*), get up to mischief (*informal*), carry on (*informal*), be insubordinate << ANTONYM behave

misbehaviour *noun* MISCONDUCT, mischief, misdemeanour, shenanigans (*informal*), impropriety, acting up (*informal*), bad behaviour, misdeeds, rudeness, indiscipline, insubordination, naughtiness, monkey business (*informal*), incivility

miscalculate *verb* **1** MISJUDGE, get something wrong, underestimate, underrate, overestimate, overrate **2** CALCULATE WRONGLY, blunder, make a mistake, get it wrong, err, slip up

miscarriage *noun* **1** SPONTANEOUS ABORTION; still birth **2** FAILURE, error, breakdown, mismanagement, undoing, thwarting, mishap, botch (*informal*), perversion, misfire, mischance, nonsuccess

miscarry *verb* **1** HAVE A MISCARRIAGE, lose your baby, have a spontaneous abortion **2** FAIL, go wrong, fall through, come to nothing, misfire, go astray, go awry, come to grief, go amiss, go pear-shaped (*informal*), gang agley (*Scot*)

miscellaneous *adjective* MIXED, various, varied, diverse, confused, diversified, mingled, assorted, jumbled, sundry, motley, indiscriminate, manifold, heterogeneous, multifarious, multiform

mischief *noun* **1** MISBEHAVIOUR, trouble, naughtiness, pranks, shenanigans (*informal*), monkey business (*informal*), waywardness, devilment, impishness, roguishness, roguery **2** HARM, trouble, damage, injury, hurt, evil, disadvantage, disruption, misfortune, detriment

mischievous *adjective* **1** NAUGHTY, bad, troublesome, wayward, exasperating, playful, rascally, impish, roguish, vexatious, puckish, frolicsome, arch, ludic (*literary*), sportive, badly behaved **2** MALICIOUS, damaging, vicious, destructive, harmful, troublesome, malignant, detrimental, hurtful, pernicious, spiteful, deleterious, injurious

misconception *noun* DELUSION, error, misunderstanding, fallacy, misapprehension, mistaken belief, wrong idea, wrong end of the stick, misconstruction

misconduct *noun* IMMORALITY, wrongdoing, mismanagement, malpractice, misdemeanour, delinquency, impropriety, transgression, misbehaviour, dereliction, naughtiness, malfeasance (*law*), unethical behaviour, malversation (*rare*)

misconstrue *verb* MISINTERPRET, misunderstand, misjudge, misread, mistake, misapprehend, get a false impression of, misconceive, mistranslate, get your lines crossed about, make a wrong interpretation of

misdeed *noun often plural* OFFENCE, wrong, crime, fault, sin, misconduct, trespass, misdemeanour, transgression, villainy

misdemeanour *noun* OFFENCE, misconduct, infringement, trespass, misdeed, transgression, misbehaviour, peccadillo

miserable *adjective* 1 SAD, down, low, depressed, distressed, gloomy, dismal, afflicted, melancholy, heartbroken, desolate, forlorn, mournful, dejected, broken-hearted, despondent, downcast, sorrowful, wretched, disconsolate, crestfallen, doleful, down in the dumps (*informal*), woebegone, down in the mouth (*informal*) << ANTONYM happy 2 PATHETIC, low, sorry, disgraceful, mean, shameful, shabby, abject, despicable, deplorable, lamentable, contemptible, scurvy, pitiable, detestable, piteous << ANTONYM respectable

miserly *adjective* MEAN, stingy, penny-pinching (*informal*), parsimonious, close, near, grasping, beggarly, illiberal, avaricious, niggardly, ungenerous, covetous, penurious, tightfisted, close-fisted, mingy (*Brit informal*), snoep (*S African informal*) << ANTONYM generous

misery *noun* 1 UNHAPPINESS, distress, despair, grief, suffering, depression, torture, agony, gloom, sadness, discomfort, torment, hardship, sorrow, woe, anguish, melancholy, desolation, wretchedness << ANTONYM happiness 2 POVERTY, want, need, squalor, privation, penury, destitution, wretchedness, sordidness, indigence << ANTONYM luxury 3 (*Brit informal*) MOANER, pessimist, killjoy, spoilsport, grouch (*informal*), prophet of doom, wet blanket (*informal*), sourpuss (*informal*), wowser (*Austral & NZ slang*)

4 MISFORTUNE, trouble, trial, disaster, load, burden, curse, ordeal, hardship, catastrophe, sorrow, woe, calamity, affliction, tribulation, bitter pill (*informal*)

misfire *verb* FAIL, go wrong, fall through, miscarry, go pear-shaped (*informal*), fail to go off, go phut (*informal*)

misfit *noun* NONCONFORMIST, eccentric, flake (*slang, chiefly US*), oddball (*informal*), fish out of water (*informal*), square peg (in a round hole) (*informal*)

misfortune *noun* 1 *often plural* BAD LUCK, adversity, hard luck, ill luck, infelicity, evil fortune, bad trot (*Austral slang*) 2 MISHAP, loss, trouble, trial, blow, failure, accident, disaster, reverse, tragedy, harm, misery, setback, hardship, calamity, affliction, tribulation, whammy (*informal, chiefly US*), misadventure, bummer (*slang*), mischance, stroke of bad luck, evil chance << ANTONYM good luck

misgiving *noun* UNEASE, worry, doubt, anxiety, suspicion, uncertainty, reservation, hesitation, distrust, apprehension, qualm, trepidation, scruple, dubiety

misguided *adjective* UNWISE, mistaken, foolish, misled, misplaced, deluded, ill-advised, imprudent, injudicious, labouring under a delusion *or* misapprehension

mishandle *verb* MISMANAGE, bungle, botch, mess up (*informal*), screw (up) (*informal*), make a mess of, muff, make a hash of (*informal*), make a nonsense of, bodge (*informal*), flub (*US slang*)

mishap *noun* ACCIDENT, disaster, misfortune, stroke of bad luck, adversity, calamity, misadventure, contretemps, mischance, infelicity, evil chance, evil fortune

misinform *verb* MISLEAD, deceive, misdirect, misguide, give someone a bum steer (*informal, chiefly US*)

misinterpret *verb* MISUNDERSTAND, mistake, distort, misrepresent, misjudge, falsify, pervert, misread, misconstrue, get wrong, misapprehend, misconceive

misjudge *verb* MISCALCULATE, be wrong about, underestimate, underrate, overestimate, overrate, get the wrong idea about

mislay *verb* LOSE, misplace, miss, be unable to find, lose track of, be unable to put *or* lay your hand on, forget the whereabouts of

mislead *verb* DECEIVE, fool, delude, take someone in (*informal*), bluff, beguile, misdirect, misinform, hoodwink, lead someone astray, pull the wool over someone's eyes (*informal*), take someone for a ride (*informal*), misguide, give someone a bum steer (*informal, chiefly US*)

misleading *adjective* CONFUSING, false, ambiguous, deceptive, spurious, evasive, disingenuous, tricky (*informal*), deceitful, specious, delusive, delusory, sophistical, casuistical, unstraightforward << ANTONYM straightforward

mismatched *adjective* INCOMPATIBLE, clashing, irregular, disparate, incongruous, discordant, unsuited, ill-assorted, unreconcilable, misallied

misquote *verb* MISREPRESENT, twist, distort, pervert, muddle, mangle, falsify, garble, misreport, misstate, quote *or* take out of context

misrepresent *verb* DISTORT, disguise, pervert, belie, twist, misinterpret, falsify, garble, misstate

miss¹ *verb* 1 FAIL TO NOTICE, mistake, overlook, pass over 2 MISUNDERSTAND, fail to appreciate 3 LONG FOR, wish for, yearn for, want, need, hunger for, pine for, long to see, ache for, feel the loss of, regret the absence of 4 BE LATE FOR, fail to catch *or* get 5 NOT GO TO, skip, cut, omit, be absent from, fail to attend, skive off (*informal*), play truant from, bludge (*Austral & NZ informal*), absent yourself from 6 AVOID, beat, escape, skirt, duck, cheat, bypass, dodge, evade, get round, elude, steer clear of, sidestep, circumvent, find a way round, give a wide berth to ▷ *noun* MISTAKE, failure, fault, error, blunder, omission, oversight

miss² *noun* GIRL, maiden, maid, schoolgirl, young lady, lass, damsel, spinster, lassie (*informal*)

misshapen *adjective* DEFORMED, twisted, crippled, distorted, ugly, crooked, warped, grotesque, wry, unsightly, contorted, ungainly, malformed, ill-made, unshapely, ill-proportioned

missile *noun* PROJECTILE, weapon, shell, rocket

missing *adjective* LOST, misplaced, not present, gone, left behind, astray, unaccounted for, mislaid, nowhere to be found

mission *noun* 1 ASSIGNMENT, job, labour, operation, work, commission, trip, message (*Scot*), task, undertaking, expedition, chore, errand 2 TASK, work, calling, business, job, office, charge, goal, operation, commission,

trust, aim, purpose, duty, undertaking, pursuit, quest, assignment, vocation, errand

missionary *noun* EVANGELIST, preacher, apostle, converter, propagandist, proselytizer

missive *noun* LETTER, report, note, message, communication, dispatch, memorandum, epistle

mist *noun* FOG, cloud, steam, spray, film, haze, vapour, drizzle, smog, dew, condensation, haar (*Eastern Brit*), smur *or* smir (*Scot*) ▷▷ **mist over** *or* **up** STEAM (UP), cloud, obscure, blur, fog, film, blear, becloud, befog

mistake *noun* 1 ERROR, blunder, oversight, slip, misunderstanding, boob (*Brit slang*), misconception, gaffe (*informal*), slip-up (*informal*), bloomer (*Brit informal*), clanger (*informal*), miscalculation, error of judgment, faux pas, false move, boo-boo (*informal*), barry *or* Barry Crocker (*Austral slang*) 2 OVERSIGHT, error, slip, inaccuracy, fault, slip-up (*informal*), howler (*informal*), goof, solecism, erratum, barry *or* Barry Crocker (*Austral slang*) ▷ *verb* MISUNDERSTAND, misinterpret, misjudge, misread, misconstrue, get wrong, misapprehend, misconceive ▷▷ **mistake something** *or* **someone for something** *or* **someone** CONFUSE WITH, accept as, take for, mix up with, misinterpret as, confound with

mistaken *adjective* 1 WRONG, incorrect, misled, in the wrong, misguided, off the mark, off target, wide of the mark, misinformed, off base (*US & Canad informal*), barking up the wrong tree (*informal*), off beam (*informal*), getting the wrong end of the stick (*informal*), way off beam (*informal*), labouring under a misapprehension << ANTONYM correct 2 INACCURATE, false, inappropriate, faulty, unfounded, erroneous, unsound, fallacious << ANTONYM accurate

mistakenly *adverb* INCORRECTLY, wrongly, falsely, by mistake, inappropriately, erroneously, in error, inaccurately, misguidedly, fallaciously

mistimed *adjective* INOPPORTUNE, badly timed, inconvenient, untimely, ill-timed, unseasonable, unsynchronized

mistreat *verb* ABUSE, injure, harm, molest, misuse, maul, manhandle, wrong, rough up, ill-treat, brutalize, maltreat, ill-use, handle roughly, knock about *or* around

mistreatment *noun* ABUSE, ill-treatment, maltreatment, injury, harm, misuse, mauling, manhandling, roughing up, molestation, unkindness, rough handling, brutalization, ill-usage

mistress *noun* LOVER, girlfriend, concubine, kept woman, paramour, floozy (*slang*), fancy woman (*slang*), inamorata, doxy (*archaic*), fancy bit (*slang*), ladylove (*rare*)

mistrust *noun* SUSPICION, scepticism, distrust, doubt, uncertainty, apprehension, misgiving, wariness, dubiety ▷ *verb* BE WARY OF, suspect, beware, distrust, apprehend, have doubts about

misty *adjective* FOGGY, unclear, murky, fuzzy, obscure, blurred, vague, dim, opaque, cloudy, hazy, overcast, bleary, nebulous, indistinct << ANTONYM clear

misunderstand *verb* 1 MISINTERPRET, misread, get the wrong idea (about), mistake, misjudge, misconstrue, mishear, misapprehend, be at cross-purposes with, misconceive 2 MISS THE POINT, get the wrong end of the stick, get your wires crossed, get your lines crossed

misunderstanding *noun* 1 MISTAKE, error, mix-up, misconception, misreading, misapprehension, false impression, misinterpretation, misjudgment, wrong idea, misconstruction 2 DISAGREEMENT, difference, conflict, argument, difficulty, breach, falling-out (*informal*), quarrel, rift, squabble, rupture, variance, discord, dissension

misunderstood *adjective* MISJUDGED, misinterpreted, misread, misconstrued, unrecognized, misheard, unappreciated

misuse *noun* 1 WASTE, embezzlement, squandering, dissipation, fraudulent use, misemployment, misusage 2 ABUSE, corruption, exploitation 3 ILLEGAL USE, abuse, misapplication, wrong use 4 PERVERSION, distortion, desecration, profanation 5 MISAPPLICATION, solecism, malapropism, catachresis 6 MISTREATMENT, abuse, harm, exploitation, injury, manhandling, ill-treatment, maltreatment, rough handling, inhumane treatment, cruel treatment, ill-usage ▷ *verb* 1 ABUSE, misapply, misemploy, prostitute 2 WASTE, squander, dissipate, embezzle, misappropriate 3 MISTREAT, abuse, injure, harm, exploit, wrong, molest, manhandle, ill-treat, brutalize, maltreat, ill-use, handle roughly << ANTONYM cherish 4 PROFANE, corrupt, desecrate, pervert

mitigate *verb* EASE, moderate, soften, check, quiet, calm, weaken, dull, diminish, temper,

blunt, soothe, subdue, lessen, appease, lighten, remit, allay, placate, abate, tone down, assuage, pacify, mollify, take the edge off, extenuate, tranquillize, palliate, reduce the force of << ANTONYM intensify

mitigation *noun* 1 EXTENUATION, explanation, excuse 2 RELIEF, moderation, allaying, remission, diminution, abatement, alleviation, easement, extenuation, mollification, palliation, assuagement

mix *verb* 1 BLEND, combine, merge, unite, join, cross, compound, incorporate, put together, fuse, mingle, jumble, alloy, amalgamate, interweave, coalesce, intermingle, meld, commingle, commix 2 SOCIALIZE, associate, hang out (*informal*), mingle, circulate, come together, consort, hobnob, fraternize, rub elbows (*informal*) 3 *often with* **up** COMBINE, marry, blend, integrate, amalgamate, coalesce, meld, commix ▷ *noun* MIXTURE, combination, blend, fusion, compound, jumble, assortment, alloy, medley, concoction, amalgam, mixed bag (*informal*), meld, melange, miscellany ▷▷ **mix someone up** BEWILDER, upset, confuse, disturb, puzzle, muddle, perplex, unnerve, fluster, throw into confusion ▷▷ **mix someone up in something** *usually passive* ENTANGLE, involve, implicate, embroil, rope in ▷▷ **mix something up** 1 CONFUSE, scramble, muddle, confound 2 BLEND, beat, mix, stir, fold

mixed *adjective* 1 UNCERTAIN, conflicting, confused, doubtful, unsure, muddled, contradictory, ambivalent, indecisive, equivocal 2 VARIED, diverse, different, differing, diversified, cosmopolitan, assorted, jumbled, disparate, miscellaneous, motley, haphazard, manifold, heterogeneous << ANTONYM homogeneous 3 COMBINED, blended, fused, alloyed, united, compound, incorporated, composite, mingled, amalgamated << ANTONYM pure

mixed-up *adjective* CONFUSED, disturbed, puzzled, bewildered, at sea, upset, distraught, muddled, perplexed, maladjusted

mixture *noun* 1 BLEND, mix, variety, fusion, assortment, combine, brew, jumble, medley, concoction, amalgam, amalgamation, mixed bag (*informal*), meld, potpourri, mélange (*French*), miscellany, conglomeration, hotchpotch, admixture, salmagundi 2 COMPOSITE, union, compound, alloy 3 CROSS, combination, blend, association 4 CONCOCTION, union, compound, blend, brew, composite, amalgam, conglomeration

mix-up *noun* CONFUSION, mistake, misunderstanding, mess, tangle, muddle, jumble, fankle (*Scot*)

moan *verb* **1** GROAN, sigh, sob, whine, keen, lament, deplore, bemoan, bewail **2** (*informal*) GRUMBLE, complain, groan, whine, beef (*slang*), carp, bitch (*slang*), grouse, gripe (*informal*), whinge (*informal*), bleat, moan and groan, grouch (*informal*) ▷ *noun* **1** GROAN, sigh, sob, lament, wail, grunt, whine, lamentation **2** (*informal*) COMPLAINT, protest, grumble, beef (*slang*), bitch (*slang*), whine, grouse, gripe (*informal*), grouch (*informal*), kvetch (*US slang*)

mob *noun* **1** CROWD, pack, collection, mass, body, press, host, gathering, drove, gang, flock, herd, swarm, horde, multitude, throng, assemblage **2** MASSES, rabble, hoi polloi, scum, great unwashed (*informal* or *derogatory*), riffraff, canaille (*French*), commonalty **3** GANG, company, group, set, lot, troop, crew (*informal*) ▷ *verb* **1** SURROUND, besiege, overrun, jostle, fall on, set upon, crowd around, swarm around **2** CROWD INTO, fill, crowd, pack, jam, cram into, fill to overflowing

mobile *adjective* **1** MOVABLE, moving, travelling, wandering, portable, locomotive, itinerant, peripatetic, ambulatory, motile **2** CHANGEABLE, meaning, animated, expressive, eloquent, suggestive, ever-changing

mobilize *verb* **1** RALLY, organize, stimulate, excite, prompt, marshal, activate, awaken, animate, muster, foment, put in motion **2** DEPLOY, prepare, ready, rally, assemble, call up, marshal, muster, call to arms, get *or* make ready

mock *verb* LAUGH AT, insult, tease, ridicule, taunt, scorn, sneer, scoff, deride, flout, make fun of, wind someone up (*Brit slang*), poke fun at, chaff, take the mickey out of (*informal*), jeer at, show contempt for, make a monkey out of, laugh to scorn << ANTONYM respect ▷ *adjective* IMITATION, pretended, artificial, forged, fake, false, faked, dummy, bogus, sham, fraudulent, pseudo (*informal*), counterfeit, feigned, spurious, ersatz, phoney *or* phony (*informal*) << ANTONYM genuine ▷ *noun* LAUGHING STOCK, fool, dupe, sport, travesty, jest, Aunt Sally (*Brit*)

mockery *noun* **1** DERISION, contempt, ridicule, scorn, jeering, disdain, scoffing, disrespect, gibes, contumely **2** FARCE, laughing stock, joke, apology (*informal*), letdown

mocking *adjective* SCORNFUL, insulting, taunting, scoffing, satirical, contemptuous, irreverent, sarcastic, sardonic, derisory, disrespectful, disdainful, derisive, satiric, contumelious

mode *noun* **1** METHOD, way, plan, course, system, form, state, process, condition, style, approach, quality, practice, fashion, technique, manner, procedure, custom, vein **2** FASHION, style, trend, rage, vogue, look, craze

model *noun* **1** REPRESENTATION, image, copy, miniature, dummy, replica, imitation, duplicate, lookalike, facsimile, mock-up **2** PATTERN, example, design, standard, type, original, ideal, mould, norm, gauge, prototype, paradigm, archetype, exemplar, lodestar **3** VERSION, form, kind, design, style, type, variety, stamp, mode, configuration **4** SITTER, subject, poser **5** MANNEQUIN, supermodel, fashion model, clothes horse (*informal*) ▷ *modifier* **1** IMITATION, copy, toy, miniature, dummy, duplicate, facsimile **2** IDEAL, perfect, impeccable, exemplary, consummate, flawless, faultless << ANTONYM imperfect **3** ARCHETYPAL, standard, typical, illustrative, paradigmatic ▷ *verb* **1** BASE, shape, plan, found, pattern, mould **2** SHOW OFF (*informal*), wear, display, sport **3** SHAPE, form, design, fashion, cast, stamp, carve, mould, sculpt

moderate *adjective* **1** MILD, reasonable, controlled, limited, cool, calm, steady, modest, restrained, deliberate, sober, middle-of-the-road, temperate, judicious, peaceable, equable << ANTONYM extreme **2** AVERAGE, middling, medium, fair, ordinary, indifferent, mediocre, so-so (*informal*), passable, unexceptional, fairish, half-pie (*NZ informal*), fair to middling (*informal*) ▷ *verb* **1** SOFTEN, control, calm, temper, regulate, quiet, diminish, decrease, curb, restrain, tame, subdue, play down, lessen, repress, mitigate, tone down, pacify, modulate, soft-pedal (*informal*) **2** LESSEN, relax, ease, wane, abate << ANTONYM intensify **3** ARBITRATE, judge, chair, referee, preside, mediate, take the chair

moderation *noun* RESTRAINT, justice, fairness, composure, coolness, temperance, calmness, equanimity, reasonableness, mildness, justness, judiciousness, sedateness, moderateness ▷▷ **in moderation** MODERATELY, within reason, within limits, within bounds, in moderate quantities

modern *adjective* **1** CURRENT, present, contemporary, recent, late, present-day, latter-day **2** UP-TO-DATE, latest, fresh, new, novel, with it (*informal*), up-to-the-minute, newfangled, neoteric (*rare*) << ANTONYM old-fashioned

modernity *noun* NOVELTY, currency, innovation, freshness, newness, contemporaneity, recentness

modernize *verb* UPDATE, renew, revamp, remake, renovate, remodel, rejuvenate, make over, face-lift, bring up to date, rebrand

modest *adjective* **1** MODERATE, small, limited, fair, ordinary, middling, meagre, frugal, scanty, unexceptional **2** UNPRETENTIOUS, simple, reserved, retiring, quiet, shy, humble, discreet, blushing, self-conscious, coy, meek, reticent, unassuming, self-effacing, demure, diffident, bashful

modesty *noun* RESERVE, decency, humility, shyness, propriety, reticence, timidity, diffidence, quietness, coyness, self-effacement, meekness, lack of pretension, bashfulness, humbleness, unpretentiousness, demureness, unobtrusiveness, discreetness << ANTONYM conceit

modicum *noun* LITTLE, bit, drop, touch, inch, scrap, dash, grain, particle, fragment, atom, pinch, ounce, shred, small amount, crumb, tinge, mite, tad (*informal, chiefly US*), speck, iota

modification *noun* CHANGE, restriction, variation, qualification, adjustment, revision, alteration, mutation, reformation, refinement, modulation

modify *verb* **1** CHANGE, reform, vary, convert, transform, alter, adjust, adapt, revise, remodel, rework, tweak (*informal*), reorganize, recast, reshape, redo, refashion **2** TONE DOWN, limit, reduce, lower, qualify, relax, ease, restrict, moderate, temper, soften, restrain, lessen, abate

modish *adjective* FASHIONABLE, current, smart, stylish, trendy (*Brit informal*), in, now (*informal*), with it (*informal*), contemporary, hip (*slang*), vogue, chic, all the rage, up-to-the-minute, à la mode, voguish, schmick (*Austral informal*)

modulate *verb* ADJUST, balance, vary, tone, tune, regulate, harmonize, inflect, attune

modus operandi *noun* PROCEDURE, way, system, process, operation, practice, method, technique, praxis

mogul *noun* TYCOON, lord, baron, notable, magnate, big gun (*informal*), big shot (*informal*), personage, nob (*slang, chiefly Brit*), potentate, big wheel (*slang*), big cheese (*slang or old-fashioned*), big noise (*informal*), big hitter (*informal*), heavy hitter (*informal*), nabob (*informal*), bashaw, V.I.P.

moist *adjective* DAMP, wet, dripping, rainy, soggy, humid, dank, clammy, dewy, not dry, drizzly, dampish, wettish

moisten *verb* DAMPEN, water, wet, soak, damp, moisturize, humidify, bedew

moisture *noun* DAMP, water, liquid, sweat, humidity, dew, perspiration, dampness, wetness, dankness, wateriness

molecule *noun* PARTICLE, atom, mite, jot, speck, mote, iota

molest *verb* **1** ABUSE, attack, hurt, injure, harm, interfere with, assail, accost, manhandle, ill-treat, maltreat **2** ANNOY, worry, upset, harry, bother, disturb, bug (*informal*), plague, irritate, tease, torment, harass, afflict, badger, persecute, beset, hector, pester, vex

mollify *verb* PACIFY, quiet, calm, compose, soothe, appease, quell, sweeten, placate, conciliate, propitiate

mom *noun* (*US & Canad*) MUM, mother, ma

moment *noun* **1** INSTANT, second, minute, flash, shake (*informal*), tick (*Brit informal*), no time, twinkling, split second, jiffy (*informal*), trice, two shakes (*informal*), two shakes of a lamb's tail (*informal*), bat of an eye (*informal*) **2** TIME, point, stage, instant, point in time, hour, juncture **3** IMPORTANCE, concern, value, worth, weight, import, consequence, substance, significance, gravity, seriousness, weightiness

momentarily *adverb* BRIEFLY, for a moment, temporarily, for a second, for a minute, for a short time, for an instant, for a little while, for a short while, for the nonce

momentary *adjective* SHORT-LIVED, short, brief, temporary, passing, quick, fleeting, hasty, transitory << ANTONYM lasting

momentous *adjective* SIGNIFICANT, important, serious, vital, critical, crucial, grave, historic, decisive, pivotal, fateful, weighty, consequential, of moment, earth-shaking (*informal*) << ANTONYM unimportant

momentum *noun* IMPETUS, force, power, drive, push, energy, strength, thrust, propulsion

monarch *noun* RULER, king *or* queen,

sovereign, tsar, potentate, crowned head, emperor or empress, prince or princess

monarchy noun 1 SOVEREIGNTY, despotism, autocracy, kingship, absolutism, royalism, monocracy 2 KINGDOM, empire, realm, principality

monastery noun ABBEY, house, convent, priory, cloister, religious community, nunnery, friary

monastic adjective MONKISH, secluded, cloistered, reclusive, withdrawn, austere, celibate, contemplative, ascetic, sequestered, hermit-like, conventual, cenobitic, coenobitic, cloistral, eremitic, monachal

monetary adjective FINANCIAL, money, economic, capital, cash, fiscal, budgetary, pecuniary

money noun CASH, funds, capital, currency, hard cash, green (slang), readies (informal), riches, necessary (informal), silver, bread (slang), coin, tin (slang), brass (N English dialect), loot (informal), dough (slang), the ready (informal), banknotes, dosh (Brit & Austral slang), lolly (Brit slang), the wherewithal, legal tender, megabucks (US & Canad slang), needful (informal), specie, shekels (informal), dibs (slang), filthy lucre (facetious), moolah (slang), ackers (slang), gelt (slang, chiefly US), spondulicks (slang), pelf (contemptuous), mazuma (slang, chiefly US), kembla (Austral slang) ▷▷ **in the money** (informal) RICH, wealthy, prosperous, affluent, rolling (slang), loaded (slang), flush (informal), well-off, well-heeled (informal), well-to-do, on Easy Street (informal), in clover (informal)

moneyed or **monied** adjective RICH, loaded (slang), wealthy, flush (informal), prosperous, affluent, well-off, well-heeled (informal), well-to-do

moneymaking adjective PROFITABLE, successful, lucrative, gainful, paying, thriving, remunerative

mongrel noun HYBRID, cross, half-breed, crossbreed, mixed breed, bigener (biology) ▷ adjective HALF-BREED, hybrid, crossbred, of mixed breed

monitor verb CHECK, follow, record, watch, survey, observe, scan, oversee, supervise, keep an eye on, keep track of, keep tabs on ▷ noun 1 GUIDE, observer, supervisor, overseer, invigilator 2 PREFECT (Brit), head girl, head boy, senior boy, senior girl

monk noun (Loosely) FRIAR, brother, religious, novice, monastic, oblate

monkey noun 1 SIMIAN, ape, primate, jackanapes (archaic) 2 RASCAL, horror, devil, rogue, imp, tyke, scallywag, mischief maker, scamp, nointer (Austral slang)

monolithic adjective HUGE, giant, massive, imposing, solid, substantial, gigantic, monumental, colossal, impenetrable, intractable, immovable

monologue noun SPEECH, lecture, sermon, harangue, soliloquy, oration, spiel (informal)

monopolize verb 1 CONTROL, corner, take over, dominate, exercise or have a monopoly of 2 KEEP TO YOURSELF, corner, hog (slang), engross

monotonous adjective 1 TEDIOUS, boring, dull, repetitive, uniform, all the same, plodding, tiresome, humdrum, unchanging, colourless, mind-numbing, soporific, ho-hum (informal), repetitious, wearisome, samey (informal), unvaried << ANTONYM interesting 2 TONELESS, flat, uniform, droning, unchanging, uninflected << ANTONYM animated

monotony noun TEDIUM, routine, boredom, dullness, sameness, uniformity, flatness, repetitiveness, tediousness, repetitiousness, colourlessness, tiresomeness

monster noun 1 GIANT, mammoth, titan, colossus, monstrosity, leviathan, behemoth 2 BRUTE, devil, savage, beast, demon, villain, barbarian, fiend, ogre, ghoul, bogeyman

monstrosity noun 1 FREAK, horror, monster, mutant, ogre, lusus naturae, miscreation, teratism 2 HIDEOUSNESS, horror, evil, atrocity, abnormality, obscenity, dreadfulness, frightfulness, heinousness, hellishness, loathsomeness

monstrous adjective 1 OUTRAGEOUS, shocking, evil, horrifying, vicious, foul, cruel, infamous, intolerable, disgraceful, scandalous, atrocious, inhuman, diabolical, heinous, odious, loathsome, devilish, egregious, fiendish, villainous << ANTONYM decent 2 HUGE, giant, massive, great, towering, vast, enormous, tremendous, immense, titanic, gigantic, mammoth, colossal, stellar (informal), prodigious, stupendous, gargantuan, elephantine, ginormous (informal), humongous or humungous (US slang) << ANTONYM tiny 3 UNNATURAL, terrible, horrible, dreadful, abnormal, obscene, horrendous, hideous, grotesque, gruesome, frightful, hellish, freakish, fiendish, miscreated << ANTONYM normal

month *noun* FOUR WEEKS, thirty days, moon

monument *noun* 1 MEMORIAL, cairn, statue, pillar, marker, shrine, tombstone, mausoleum, commemoration, headstone, gravestone, obelisk, cenotaph 2 TESTAMENT, record, witness, token, reminder, remembrance, memento

monumental *adjective* 1 IMPORTANT, classic, significant, outstanding, lasting, enormous, historic, enduring, memorable, awesome, majestic, immortal, unforgettable, prodigious, stupendous, awe-inspiring, epoch-making << ANTONYM unimportant 2 (*informal*) IMMENSE, great, massive, terrible, tremendous, horrible, staggering, catastrophic, gigantic, colossal, whopping (*informal*), indefensible, unforgivable, egregious << ANTONYM tiny 3 COMMEMORATIVE, memorial, monolithic, statuary, funerary

mood *noun* 1 STATE OF MIND, spirit, humour, temper, vein, tenor, disposition, frame of mind 2 DEPRESSION, sulk, bad temper, blues, dumps (*informal*), wax (*informal, chiefly Brit*), melancholy, doldrums, the hump (*Brit informal*), bate (*Brit slang*), fit of pique, low spirits, the sulks, grumps (*informal*), foulie (*Austral slang*) ▷▷ **in the mood** INCLINED, willing, interested, minded, keen, eager, disposed towards, in the (right) frame of mind, favourable towards

moody *adjective* 1 CHANGEABLE, volatile, unpredictable, unstable, erratic, fickle, temperamental, impulsive, mercurial, capricious, unsteady, fitful, flighty, faddish, inconstant << ANTONYM stable 2 SULKY, cross, wounded, angry, offended, irritable, crabbed, crusty, temperamental, touchy, curt, petulant, ill-tempered, irascible, cantankerous, tetchy, testy, chippy (*informal*), in a huff, short-tempered, waspish, piqued, crabby, huffy, splenetic, crotchety (*informal*), ill-humoured, huffish, tooshie (*Austral slang*) << ANTONYM cheerful 3 GLOOMY, sad, miserable, melancholy, frowning, dismal, dour, sullen, glum, introspective, in the doldrums, out of sorts (*informal*), downcast, morose, lugubrious, pensive, broody, crestfallen, doleful, down in the dumps (*informal*), saturnine, down in the mouth (*informal*), mopish, mopy << ANTONYM cheerful 4 SAD, gloomy, melancholy, sombre

moon *noun* SATELLITE ▷ *verb* IDLE, drift, loaf, languish, waste time, daydream, mope, mooch (*Brit slang*)

moor[1] *noun* MOORLAND, fell (*Brit*), heath, muir (*Scot*)

moor[2] *verb* TIE UP, fix, secure, anchor, dock, lash, berth, fasten, make fast

moot *verb* BRING UP, propose, suggest, introduce, put forward, ventilate, broach ▷ *adjective* DEBATABLE, open, controversial, doubtful, unsettled, unresolved, undecided, at issue, arguable, open to debate, contestable, disputable

mop *noun* 1 SQUEEGEE, sponge, swab 2 MANE, shock, mass, tangle, mat, thatch ▷ *verb* CLEAN, wash, wipe, sponge, swab, squeegee ▷▷ **mop something up** 1 CLEAN UP, wash, sponge, mop, soak up, swab, wipe up, sop up 2 (*military*) FINISH OFF, clear, account for, eliminate, round up, clean out, neutralize, pacify

mope *verb* BROOD, moon, pine, hang around, idle, fret, pout, languish, waste time, sulk, be gloomy, eat your heart out, be apathetic, be dejected, be down in the mouth (*informal*), have a long face, wear a long face, go about like a half-shut knife (*informal*)

moral *adjective* 1 ETHICAL, social, behavioural 2 PSYCHOLOGICAL, emotional, mental 3 GOOD, just, right, principled, pure, decent, innocent, proper, noble, ethical, upright, honourable, honest, righteous, virtuous, blameless, high-minded, chaste, upstanding, meritorious, incorruptible << ANTONYM immoral ▷ *noun* LESSON, meaning, point, message, teaching, import, significance, precept ▷ *plural noun* MORALITY, standards, conduct, principles, behaviour, manners, habits, ethics, integrity, mores, scruples

morale *noun* CONFIDENCE, heart, spirit, temper, self-esteem, team spirit, mettle, esprit de corps

morality *noun* 1 VIRTUE, justice, principles, morals, honour, integrity, goodness, honesty, decency, fair play, righteousness, good behaviour, propriety, chastity, probity, rectitude, rightness, uprightness 2 ETHICS, conduct, principles, ideals, morals, manners, habits, philosophy, mores, moral code 3 RIGHTS AND WRONGS, ethics, ethicality

morass *noun* 1 MESS, confusion, chaos, jam (*informal*), tangle, mix-up, muddle, quagmire 2 MARSH, swamp, bog, slough, fen, moss (*Scot & N English dialect*), quagmire, marshland, muskeg (*Canad*)

moratorium *noun* POSTPONEMENT, stay, freeze, halt, suspension, respite, standstill

morbid *adjective* 1 GRUESOME, sick, dreadful,

ghastly, hideous, unhealthy, grisly, macabre, horrid, ghoulish, unwholesome **2** GLOOMY, brooding, pessimistic, melancholy, sombre, grim, glum, lugubrious, funereal, low-spirited << ANTONYM cheerful **3** DISEASED, sick, infected, deadly, ailing, unhealthy, malignant, sickly, pathological, unsound << ANTONYM healthy

more *determiner* EXTRA, additional, spare, new, other, added, further, fresh, new-found, supplementary ▷ *adverb* **1** TO A GREATER EXTENT, longer, better, further, some more **2** MOREOVER, also, in addition, besides, furthermore, what's more, on top of that, to boot, into the bargain, over and above that ▷ see **most**

moreover *adverb* FURTHERMORE, also, further, in addition, too, as well, besides, likewise, what is more, to boot, additionally, into the bargain, withal (*literary*)

moribund *adjective* DECLINING, weak, waning, standing still, stagnant, stagnating, on the way out, at a standstill, obsolescent, on its last legs, forceless

morning *noun* **1** BEFORE NOON, forenoon, morn (*poetic*), a.m. **2** DAWN, sunrise, morrow (*archaic*), first light, daybreak, break of day

moron *noun* FOOL, idiot, dummy (*slang*), berk (*Brit slang*), charlie (*Brit informal*), tosser (*Brit slang*), dope (*informal*), jerk (*slang, chiefly US & Canad*), ass, plank (*Brit slang*), wally (*slang*), prat (*slang*), plonker (*slang*), coot, geek (*slang*), twit (*informal, chiefly Brit*), bonehead (*slang*), chump, dunce, imbecile, cretin, oaf, simpleton, airhead (*slang*), dimwit (*informal*), dipstick (*Brit slang*), gonzo (*slang*), schmuck (*US slang*), dork (*slang*), nitwit (*informal*), dolt, blockhead, divvy (*Brit slang*), pillock (*Brit slang*), halfwit, dweeb (*US slang*), putz (*US slang*), fathead (*informal*), weenie (*US informal*), eejit (*Scot & Irish*), dumb-ass (*slang*), dunderhead, numpty (*Scot informal*), doofus (*slang, chiefly US*), lamebrain (*informal*), mental defective, thickhead, muttonhead (*slang*), nerd *or* nurd (*slang*), numbskull *or* numskull, dorba *or* dorb (*Austral slang*), bogan (*Austral slang*)

moronic *adjective* IDIOTIC, simple, foolish, mindless, thick, stupid, daft (*informal*), retarded, gormless (*Brit informal*), brainless, cretinous, unintelligent, dimwitted (*informal*), asinine, imbecilic, braindead (*informal*), mentally defective, dumb-ass (*slang*), doltish, dead from the neck up (*informal*), halfwitted, muttonheaded (*slang*)

morose *adjective* SULLEN, miserable, moody, gloomy, down, low, cross, blue, depressed, sour, crabbed, pessimistic, perverse, melancholy, dour, crusty, glum, surly, mournful, gruff, churlish, sulky, taciturn, ill-tempered, in a bad mood, grouchy (*informal*), down in the dumps (*informal*), crabby, saturnine, ill-humoured, ill-natured << ANTONYM cheerful

morsel *noun* PIECE, bite, bit, slice, scrap, part, grain, taste, segment, fragment, fraction, snack, crumb, nibble, mouthful, tad (*informal, chiefly US*), titbit, soupçon (*French*)

mortal *adjective* **1** HUMAN, worldly, passing, earthly, fleshly, temporal, transient, ephemeral, perishable, corporeal, impermanent, sublunary **2** FATAL, killing, terminal, deadly, destructive, lethal, murderous, death-dealing **3** UNRELENTING, bitter, sworn, deadly, relentless, to the death, implacable, out-and-out, irreconcilable, remorseless **4** GREAT, serious, terrible, enormous, severe, extreme, grave, intense, awful, dire, agonizing ▷ *noun* HUMAN BEING, being, man, woman, body, person, human, individual, earthling

mortality *noun* **1** HUMANITY, transience, impermanence, ephemerality, temporality, corporeality, impermanency **2** DEATH, dying, fatality, loss of life

mortified *adjective* HUMILIATED, embarrassed, shamed, crushed, annoyed, humbled, horrified, put down, put out (*informal*), ashamed, confounded, deflated, vexed, affronted, displeased, chagrined, chastened, discomfited, abashed, put to shame, rendered speechless, made to eat humble pie (*informal*), given a showing-up (*informal*)

mortify *verb* **1** HUMILIATE, disappoint, embarrass, shame, crush, annoy, humble, deflate, vex, affront, displease, chagrin, discomfit, abase, put someone to shame, abash **2** DISCIPLINE, control, deny, subdue, chasten, abase

mortuary *noun* MORGUE, funeral home (*US*), funeral parlour

most *pronoun* NEARLY ALL, the majority, the mass, almost all, the bulk, the lion's share, the preponderance

mostly *adverb* **1** MAINLY, largely, chiefly, principally, primarily, above all, on the whole, predominantly, for the most part, almost entirely **2** GENERALLY, usually, on the whole, most often, as a rule, customarily

mote *noun* SPECK, spot, grain, particle,

fragment, atom, mite

mother *noun* FEMALE PARENT, mum (*Brit informal*), ma (*informal*), mater, dam, old woman (*US & Canad*), mom (*US & Canad*), mummy (*Brit informal*), old lady (*informal*), foster mother, birth mother, biological mother ▷ *verb* **1** GIVE BIRTH TO, produce, bear, bring forth, drop **2** NURTURE, raise, protect, tend, nurse, rear, care for, cherish ▷ *modifier* NATIVE, natural, innate, inborn, connate

motherly *adjective* MATERNAL, loving, kind, caring, warm, comforting, sheltering, gentle, tender, protective, fond, affectionate

motif *noun* **1** DESIGN, form, shape, decoration, ornament **2** THEME, idea, subject, concept, leitmotif

motion *noun* **1** MOVEMENT, action, mobility, passing, travel, progress, flow, passage, locomotion, motility, kinesics **2** GESTURE, sign, wave, signal, gesticulation **3** PROPOSAL, suggestion, recommendation, proposition, submission ▷ *verb* GESTURE, direct, wave, signal, nod, beckon, gesticulate ▷▷ **in motion 1** IN PROGRESS, going on, under way, afoot, on the go (*informal*) **2** MOVING, going, working, travelling, functioning, under way, operational, on the move (*informal*)

motionless *adjective* STILL, static, stationary, standing, fixed, frozen, calm, halted, paralysed, lifeless, inert, unmoved, transfixed, at rest, immobile, inanimate, at a standstill, unmoving, stock-still << ANTONYM moving

motivate *verb* **1** INSPIRE, drive, stimulate, provoke, lead, move, cause, prompt, stir, trigger, set off, induce, arouse, prod, get going, instigate, impel, actuate, give incentive to, inspirit **2** STIMULATE, drive, inspire, stir, arouse, get going, galvanize, incentivize

motivation *noun* **1** INCENTIVE, inspiration, motive, stimulus, reason, spur, impulse, persuasion, inducement, incitement, instigation, carrot and stick **2** INSPIRATION, drive, desire, ambition, hunger, interest

motive *noun* REASON, motivation, cause, ground(s), design, influence, purpose, object, intention, spur, incentive, inspiration, stimulus, rationale, inducement, incitement, mainspring, the why and wherefore ▷ *adjective* MOVING, driving, motivating, operative, activating, impelling

motley *adjective* MISCELLANEOUS, mixed, varied, diversified, mingled, unlike, assorted,

disparate, dissimilar, heterogeneous << ANTONYM homogeneous

mottled *adjective* BLOTCHY, spotted, pied, streaked, marbled, flecked, variegated, chequered, speckled, freckled, dappled, tabby, stippled, piebald, brindled

motto *noun* SAYING, slogan, maxim, rule, cry, formula, gnome, adage, proverb, dictum, precept, byword, watchword, tag-line

mould¹ *noun* **1** CAST, form, die, shape, pattern, stamp, matrix **2** DESIGN, line, style, fashion, build, form, cut, kind, shape, structure, pattern, brand, frame, construction, stamp, format, configuration **3** NATURE, character, sort, kind, quality, type, stamp, kidney, calibre, ilk ▷ *verb* **1** SHAPE, make, work, form, create, model, fashion, cast, stamp, construct, carve, forge, sculpt **2** INFLUENCE, make, form, control, direct, affect, shape

mould² *noun* FUNGUS, blight, mildew, mustiness, mouldiness

moulder *verb* DECAY, waste, break down, crumble, rot, disintegrate, perish, decompose

mouldy *adjective* STALE, spoiled, rotting, decaying, bad, rotten, blighted, musty, fusty, mildewed

mound *noun* **1** HEAP, bing (*Scot*), pile, drift, stack, rick **2** HILL, bank, rise, dune, embankment, knoll, hillock, kopje *or* koppie (*S African*) **3** (*Archaeology*) BARROW, tumulus **4** EARTHWORK, rampart, bulwark, motte (*history*)

mount *verb* **1** (*military*) LAUNCH, stage, prepare, deliver, set in motion **2** INCREASE, build, grow, swell, intensify, escalate, multiply << ANTONYM decrease **3** ACCUMULATE, increase, collect, gather, build up, pile up, amass, cumulate **4** ASCEND, scale, climb (up), go up, clamber up, make your way up << ANTONYM descend **5** GET (UP) ON, jump on, straddle, climb onto, climb up on, hop on to, bestride, get on the back of, get astride << ANTONYM get off **6** DISPLAY, set, frame, set off **7** FIT, place, set, position, set up, fix, secure, attach, install, erect, put in place, put in position, emplace **8** PRESENT, display, stage, prepare, put on, organize, get up (*informal*), exhibit, put on display ▷ *noun* **1** HORSE, steed (*literary*) **2** BACKING, setting, support, stand, base, mounting, frame, fixture, foil

mountain *noun* **1** PEAK, mount, height, ben (*Scot*), horn, ridge, fell (*Brit*), berg (*S African*), alp, pinnacle, elevation, Munro, eminence

2 HEAP, mass, masses, pile, a great deal, ton, stack, abundance, mound, profusion, shedload (*Brit informal*)

mountainous *adjective* **1** HIGH, towering, soaring, steep, rocky, highland, alpine, upland **2** HUGE, great, enormous, mighty, immense, daunting, gigantic, monumental, mammoth, prodigious, hulking, ponderous << ANTONYM tiny

mourn *verb* **1** *often with* **for** GRIEVE FOR, miss, lament, keen for, weep for, sorrow for, wail for, wear black for **2** BEMOAN, rue, deplore, bewail

mournful *adjective* **1** DISMAL, sad, unhappy, miserable, gloomy, grieving, melancholy, sombre, heartbroken, desolate, woeful, rueful, heavy, downcast, grief-stricken, lugubrious, disconsolate, joyless, funereal, heavy-hearted, down in the dumps (*informal*), cheerless, brokenhearted << ANTONYM happy **2** SAD, distressing, unhappy, tragic, painful, afflicting, melancholy, harrowing, grievous, woeful, deplorable, lamentable, plaintive, calamitous, sorrowful, piteous << ANTONYM cheerful

mourning *noun* **1** GRIEVING, grief, bereavement, weeping, woe, lamentation, keening **2** BLACK, weeds, sackcloth and ashes, widow's weeds

mouth *noun* **1** LIPS, trap (*slang*), chops (*slang*), jaws, gob (*slang, esp Brit*), maw, yap (*slang*), cakehole (*Brit slang*) **2** ENTRANCE, opening, gateway, cavity, door, aperture, crevice, orifice **3** OPENING, lip, rim **4** INLET, outlet, estuary, firth, outfall, debouchment **5** (*informal*) BOASTING, gas (*informal*), bragging, hot air (*slang*), braggadocio, idle talk, empty talk

mouthful *noun* TASTE, little, bite, bit, drop, sample, swallow, sip, sup, spoonful, morsel, forkful

mouthpiece *noun* **1** SPOKESPERSON, agent, representative, delegate, spokesman *or* spokeswoman **2** PUBLICATION, journal, organ, periodical

movable *adjective* PORTABLE, mobile, transferable, detachable, not fixed, transportable, portative

move *verb* **1** TRANSFER, change, carry, transport, switch, shift, transpose **2** GO, walk, march, advance, progress, shift, proceed, stir, budge, make a move, change position **3** RELOCATE, leave, remove, quit, go away, migrate, emigrate, move house, flit (*Scot & N English dialect*), decamp, up sticks (*Brit*

informal), pack your bags (*informal*), change residence **4** DRIVE, lead, cause, influence, persuade, push, shift, inspire, prompt, stimulate, motivate, induce, shove, activate, propel, rouse, prod, incite, impel, set going << ANTONYM discourage **5** TOUCH, affect, excite, impress, stir, agitate, disquiet, make an impression on, tug at your heartstrings (*often facetious*) **6** PROPOSE, suggest, urge, recommend, request, advocate, submit, put forward ▷ *noun* **1** ACTION, act, step, movement, shift, motion, manoeuvre, deed **2** PLOY, action, measure, step, initiative, stroke, tactic, manoeuvre, deed, tack, ruse, gambit, stratagem **3** TRANSFER, posting, shift, removal, migration, relocation, flit (*Scot & N English dialect*), flitting (*Scot & N English dialect*), change of address **4** TURN, go, play, chance, shot (*informal*), opportunity ▷▷ **get a move on** SPEED UP, hurry (up), get going, get moving, get cracking (*informal*), step on it (*informal*), make haste, shake a leg (*informal*), get your skates on (*informal*), stir yourself ▷▷ **on the move 1** IN TRANSIT, moving, travelling, journeying, on the road (*informal*), under way, voyaging, on the run, in motion, on the wing **2** ACTIVE, moving, developing, advancing, progressing, succeeding, stirring, going forward, astir

movement *noun* **1** GROUP, party, organization, grouping, front, camp, faction **2** CAMPAIGN, drive, push, crusade **3** MOVE, act, action, operation, motion, gesture, manoeuvre **4** ACTIVITY, moving, stirring, bustle, agitation **5** ADVANCE, progress, flow, progression **6** TRANSFER, transportation, displacement **7** TREND, flow, swing, current, tendency **8** DEVELOPMENT, change, shift, variation, fluctuation **9** PROGRESSION, advance, progress, breakthrough **10** (*music*) SECTION, part, division, passage

movie *noun* FILM, picture, feature, flick (*slang*), motion picture, moving picture (*US*) ▷▷ **the movies** THE CINEMA, a film, the pictures (*informal*), the flicks (*slang*), the silver screen (*informal*)

moving *adjective* **1** EMOTIONAL, touching, affecting, exciting, inspiring, stirring, arousing, poignant, emotive, impelling << ANTONYM unemotional **2** MOBILE, running, active, going, operational, in motion, driving, kinetic, movable, motile, unfixed << ANTONYM stationary **3** MOTIVATING, stimulating, dynamic, propelling, inspirational, impelling, stimulative

mow *verb* CUT, crop, trim, shear, scythe
▷▷ **mow something** *or* **someone down**
MASSACRE, butcher, slaughter, cut down, shoot down, blow away (*slang, chiefly US*), cut to pieces

much *adverb* **1** GREATLY, a lot, considerably, decidedly, exceedingly, appreciably
<< ANTONYM hardly **2** OFTEN, a lot, regularly, routinely, a great deal, frequently, many times, habitually, on many occasions, customarily ▷ *adjective* GREAT, a lot of, plenty of, considerable, substantial, piles of (*informal*), ample, abundant, copious, oodles of (*informal*), plenteous, sizable *or* sizeable amount, shedful (*slang*) << ANTONYM little ▷ *pronoun* A LOT, plenty, a great deal, lots (*informal*), masses (*informal*), loads (*informal*), tons (*informal*), heaps (*informal*), a good deal, an appreciable amount << ANTONYM little

muck *noun* **1** DIRT, mud, filth, crap (*taboo slang*), sewage, ooze, scum, sludge, mire, slime, slob (*Irish*), gunk (*informal*), gunge (*informal*), crud (*slang*), kak (*S African taboo*), grot (*slang*) **2** MANURE, crap (*taboo slang*), dung, ordure ▷▷ **muck something up** RUIN, bungle, botch, make a mess of, blow (*slang*), mar, spoil, muff, make a nonsense of, bodge (*informal*), make a pig's ear of (*informal*), flub (*US slang*), make a muck of (*slang*), mess something up, screw something up (*informal*), cock something up (*Brit slang*), crool *or* cruel (*Austral slang*)

mucky *adjective* DIRTY, soiled, muddy, filthy, messy, grimy, mud-caked, bespattered, begrimed, festy (*Austral slang*)

mud *noun* DIRT, clay, ooze, silt, sludge, mire, slime, slob (*Irish*), gloop (*informal*)

muddle *noun* CONFUSION, mess, disorder, chaos, plight, tangle, mix-up, clutter, disarray, daze, predicament, jumble, ravel, perplexity, disorganization, hotchpotch, hodgepodge (*US*), pig's breakfast (*informal*), fankle (*Scot*) ▷ *verb* **1** JUMBLE, confuse, disorder, scramble, tangle, mix up, make a mess of **2** CONFUSE, bewilder, daze, confound, perplex, disorient, stupefy, befuddle ▷▷ **muddle along** *or* **through** SCRAPE BY, make it, manage, cope, get along, get by (*informal*), manage somehow

muddled *adjective* **1** INCOHERENT, confused, loose, vague, unclear, woolly, muddleheaded << ANTONYM clear **2** BEWILDERED, confused, at sea, dazed, perplexed, disoriented, stupefied, befuddled **3** JUMBLED, confused,

disordered, scrambled, tangled, chaotic, messy, mixed-up, disorganized, higgledy-piggledy (*informal*), disarrayed << ANTONYM orderly

muddy *adjective* **1** BOGGY, swampy, marshy, miry, quaggy **2** DIRTY, soiled, grimy, mucky, mud-caked, bespattered, clarty (*Scot & N English dialect*) **3** DULL, flat, blurred, unclear, smoky, washed-out, dingy, lustreless **4** CLOUDY, dirty, foul, opaque, impure, turbid **5** CONFUSED, vague, unclear, muddled, fuzzy, woolly, hazy, indistinct ▷ *verb* SMEAR, soil, dirty, smirch, begrime, bespatter

muffle *verb* **1** DEADEN, suppress, gag, stifle, silence, dull, soften, hush, muzzle, quieten **2** *often with* **up** WRAP UP, cover, disguise, conceal, cloak, shroud, swathe, envelop, swaddle

muffled *adjective* INDISTINCT, suppressed, subdued, dull, faint, dim, muted, strangled, stifled

mug¹ *noun* CUP, pot, jug, beaker, tankard, stein, flagon, toby jug

mug² *noun* **1** (*slang*) FACE, features, countenance, visage, clock (*Brit slang*), kisser (*slang*), dial (*slang*), mush (*Brit slang*), puss (*slang*), phiz *or* phizog (*Brit slang*) **2** (*Brit*) FOOL, innocent, sucker (*slang*), charlie (*Brit informal*), gull (*archaic*), chump (*informal*), simpleton, putz (*US slang*), weenie (*US informal*), muggins (*Brit slang*), easy *or* soft touch (*slang*), dorba *or* dorb (*Austral slang*), bogan (*Austral slang*) ▷ *verb* (*informal*) ATTACK, assault, beat up, rob, steam (*informal*), hold up, do over (*Brit, Austral & NZ slang*), work over (*slang*), assail, lay into (*informal*), put the boot in (*slang*), duff up (*Brit slang*), set about *or* upon, beat *or* knock seven bells out of (*informal*) ▷▷ **mug up (on) something** STUDY, cram (*informal*), bone up on (*informal*), swot up on (*Brit informal*), get up (*informal*)

mull over *verb* PONDER, consider, study, think about, examine, review, weigh, contemplate, reflect on, think over, muse on, meditate on, ruminate on, deliberate on, turn something over in your mind

multiple *adjective* MANY, several, various, numerous, collective, sundry, manifold, multitudinous

multiplicity *noun* NUMBER, lot, host, mass, variety, load (*informal*), pile (*informal*), ton, stack, diversity, heap (*informal*), array, abundance, myriad, profusion

multiply *verb* **1** INCREASE, extend, expand, spread, build up, accumulate, augment,

proliferate << ANTONYM decrease
2 REPRODUCE, breed, propagate
multitude *noun* **1** GREAT NUMBER, lot, host,
collection, army, sea, mass, assembly, legion,
horde, myriad, concourse, assemblage
2 CROWD, host, mass, mob, congregation,
swarm, sea, horde, throng, great number
3 PUBLIC, mob, herd, populace, rabble,
proletariat, common people, hoi polloi,
commonally
mum *adjective* SILENT, quiet, dumb,
mute, secretive, uncommunicative,
unforthcoming, tight-lipped, closemouthed
mumbo jumbo *noun* **1** GIBBERISH, nonsense,
jargon, humbug, cant, Greek (*informal*),
claptrap (*informal*), gobbledegook (*informal*),
rigmarole, double talk **2** SUPERSTITION,
magic, ritual, hocus-pocus
munch *verb* CHEW, champ, crunch, chomp,
scrunch, masticate
mundane *adjective* **1** ORDINARY, routine,
commonplace, banal, everyday, day-to-day,
vanilla (*slang*), prosaic, humdrum, workaday
<< ANTONYM extraordinary **2** EARTHLY,
worldly, human, material, fleshly, secular,
mortal, terrestrial, temporal, sublunary
<< ANTONYM spiritual
municipal *adjective* CIVIC, city, public, local,
community, council, town, district, urban,
metropolitan, borough
municipality *noun* TOWN, city, district,
borough, township, burgh (*Scot*), urban
community, dorp (*S African*)
murder *noun* **1** KILLING, homicide, massacre,
assassination, slaying, bloodshed, carnage,
butchery **2** (*informal*) AGONY, misery, hell
(*informal*) ▷ *verb* **1** KILL, massacre, slaughter,
assassinate, hit (*slang*), destroy, waste
(*informal*), do in (*informal*), eliminate (*slang*),
take out (*slang*), butcher, dispatch, slay, blow
away (*slang, chiefly US*), bump off (*slang*), rub
out (*US slang*), take the life of, do to death
2 RUIN, destroy, mar, spoil, butcher, mangle
3 (*informal*) BEAT DECISIVELY, thrash, stuff
(*slang*), cream (*slang, chiefly US*), tank (*slang*),
hammer (*informal*), slaughter, lick (*informal*),
wipe the floor with (*informal*), make
mincemeat of (*informal*), blow someone out
of the water (*slang*), drub, defeat someone
utterly
murderer *noun* KILLER, assassin, slayer,
butcher, slaughterer, cut-throat, hit man
(*slang*)
murderous *adjective* **1** DEADLY, savage, brutal,
destructive, fell (*archaic*), bloody, devastating,

cruel, lethal, withering, ferocious, cut-throat,
bloodthirsty, barbarous, internecine, death-
dealing, sanguinary **2** (*informal*) UNPLEASANT,
difficult, dangerous, exhausting, sapping,
harrowing, strenuous, arduous, hellish
(*informal*), killing (*informal*)
murky *adjective* **1** DARK, gloomy, dismal,
grey, dull, obscure, dim, dreary, cloudy,
misty, impenetrable, foggy, overcast, dusky,
nebulous, cheerless << ANTONYM bright
2 OBSCURE, dark, cloudy, impenetrable
murmur *verb* MUMBLE, whisper, mutter,
drone, purr, babble, speak in an undertone
▷ *noun* **1** WHISPER, whispering, mutter,
mumble, drone, purr, babble, undertone
2 COMPLAINT, word, moan (*informal*),
grumble, beef (*slang*), grouse, gripe (*informal*)
muscle *noun* **1** TENDON, sinew, muscle tissue,
thew **2** STRENGTH, might, force, power,
weight, stamina, potency, brawn, sturdiness
▷▷ **muscle in** (*informal*) IMPOSE YOURSELF,
encroach, butt in, force your way in, elbow
your way in
muscular *adjective* STRONG, powerful, athletic,
strapping, robust, vigorous, sturdy, stalwart,
husky (*informal*), beefy (*informal*), lusty,
sinewy, muscle-bound, brawny, powerfully
built, thickset, well-knit
muse *verb* PONDER, consider, reflect,
contemplate, think, weigh up, deliberate,
speculate, brood, meditate, mull over, think
over, ruminate, cogitate, be lost in thought,
be in a brown study
mush *noun* **1** PULP, paste, mash, purée,
pap, slush, goo (*informal*) **2** (*informal*)
SENTIMENTALITY, corn (*informal*), slush
(*informal*), schmaltz (*slang*), mawkishness
mushroom *verb* EXPAND, increase, spread,
boom, flourish, sprout, burgeon, spring up,
shoot up, proliferate, luxuriate, grow rapidly
mushy *adjective* **1** SOFT, squidgy (*informal*),
slushy, squashy, squelchy, pulpy, doughy,
pappy, semi-liquid, paste-like, semi-solid
2 (*informal*) SENTIMENTAL, wet (*Brit informal*),
sloppy (*informal*), corny (*slang*), sugary,
maudlin, weepy, saccharine, syrupy, slushy
(*informal*), mawkish, schmaltzy (*slang*), icky
(*informal*), three-hankie (*informal*)
musical *adjective* MELODIOUS, lyrical,
harmonious, melodic, lilting, tuneful,
dulcet, sweet-sounding, euphonious,
euphonic << ANTONYM discordant
musing *noun* THINKING, reflection,
meditation, abstraction, contemplation,
introspection, reverie, dreaming, day-

dreaming, rumination, navel gazing (*slang*), absent-mindedness, cogitation, brown study, cerebration, woolgathering

muskeg *noun* (*Canad*) SWAMP, bog, marsh, quagmire, moss (*Scot & N English dialect*), slough, fen, mire, morass, everglade(s) (*US*), pakihi (*NZ*)

muss (*US & Canad*) *verb* MESS (UP), disarrange, dishevel, ruffle, rumple, make untidy, tumble

must¹ *noun* NECESSITY, essential, requirement, duty, fundamental, obligation, imperative, requisite, prerequisite, sine qua non (*Latin*), necessary thing, must-have

must² *noun* MOULD, rot, decay, mildew, mustiness, fustiness, fetor, mouldiness

muster *verb* 1 SUMMON UP, collect, call up, marshal 2 RALLY, group, gather, assemble, round up, marshal, mobilize, call together 3 ASSEMBLE, meet, come together, convene, congregate, convoke ▷ *noun* ASSEMBLY, meeting, collection, gathering, rally, convention, congregation, roundup, mobilization, hui (*NZ*), concourse, assemblage, convocation, runanga (*NZ*) ▷▷ **pass muster** BE ACCEPTABLE, qualify, measure up, make the grade, fill the bill (*informal*), be or come up to scratch

musty *adjective* STALE, stuffy, airless, decayed, smelly, dank, mouldy, fusty, mildewed, frowsty, mildewy

mutation *noun* 1 ANOMALY, variation, deviant, freak of nature 2 CHANGE, variation, evolution, transformation, modification, alteration, deviation, metamorphosis, transfiguration

mute *adjective* 1 CLOSE-MOUTHED, silent, taciturn, tongue-tied, tight-lipped, unspeaking 2 SILENT, dumb, unspoken, tacit, wordless, voiceless, unvoiced 3 DUMB, speechless, voiceless, unspeaking, aphasic, aphonic ▷ *verb* 1 TONE DOWN, lower, moderate, subdue, dampen, soft-pedal 2 MUFFLE, subdue, moderate, lower, turn down, soften, dampen, tone down, deaden

mutilate *verb* 1 MAIM, damage, injure, disable, butcher, cripple, hack, lame, cut up, mangle, mangulate (*Austral slang*), dismember, disfigure, lacerate, cut to pieces 2 DISTORT, cut, damage, mar, spoil, butcher, hack, censor, adulterate, expurgate, bowdlerize

mutiny *noun* REBELLION, revolt, uprising, insurrection, rising, strike, revolution, riot, resistance, disobedience, insubordination, refusal to obey orders ▷ *verb* REBEL, revolt,

rise up, disobey, strike, resist, defy authority, refuse to obey orders, be insubordinate

mutt *noun* (*slang*) 1 MONGREL, dog, hound, tyke, pooch (*informal*), cur 2 FOOL, idiot, berk (*Brit slang*), moron, charlie (*Brit informal*), jerk (*slang, chiefly US & Canad*), plank (*Brit slang*), wally (*slang*), prat (*slang*), plonker (*slang*), coot, geek (*slang*), twit (*informal, chiefly Brit*), imbecile (*informal*), ignoramus, dipstick (*Brit slang*), gonzo (*slang*), schmuck (*US slang*), dork (*slang*), dolt, divvy (*Brit slang*), pillock (*Brit slang*), dweeb (*US slang*), putz (*US slang*), weenie (*US informal*), eejit (*Scot & Irish*), dumb-ass (*slang*), dunderhead, numpty (*Scot informal*), doofus (*slang, chiefly US*), thickhead, nerd or nurd (*slang*), numbskull or numskull, dorba or dorb (*Austral slang*), bogan (*Austral slang*)

mutter *verb* GRUMBLE, complain, murmur, rumble, whine, mumble, grouse, bleat, grouch (*informal*), talk under your breath

mutual *adjective* SHARED, common, joint, interactive, returned, communal, reciprocal, interchangeable, reciprocated, correlative, requited

muzzle *noun* 1 JAWS, mouth, nose, snout 2 GAG, guard, restraint ▷ *verb* SUPPRESS, silence, curb, restrain, choke, gag, stifle, censor

myopic *adjective* 1 NARROW-MINDED, short-sighted, narrow, unimaginative, small-minded, unadventurous, near-sighted 2 SHORT-SIGHTED, near-sighted, as blind as a bat (*informal*)

myriad *noun* MULTITUDE, millions, scores, host, thousands, army, sea, mountain, flood, a million, a thousand, swarm, horde ▷ *adjective* INNUMERABLE, countless, untold, incalculable, immeasurable, a thousand and one, multitudinous

mysterious *adjective* 1 STRANGE, unknown, puzzling, curious, secret, hidden, weird, concealed, obscure, baffling, veiled, mystical, perplexing, uncanny, incomprehensible, mystifying, impenetrable, arcane, inexplicable, cryptic, insoluble, unfathomable, abstruse, recondite ≪ ANTONYM clear 2 SECRETIVE, enigmatic, evasive, discreet, covert, reticent, furtive, inscrutable, non-committal, surreptitious, cloak-and-dagger, sphinx-like

mystery *noun* 1 PUZZLE, problem, question, secret, riddle, enigma, conundrum, teaser, poser (*informal*), closed book 2 SECRECY, uncertainty, obscurity, mystique, darkness, ambiguity, ambiguousness

mystical *or* **mystic** *adjective* SUPERNATURAL, mysterious, transcendental, esoteric, occult, arcane, metaphysical, paranormal, inscrutable, otherworldly, abstruse, cabalistic, preternatural, nonrational

mystify *verb* PUZZLE, confuse, baffle, bewilder, beat (*slang*), escape, stump, elude, confound, perplex, bamboozle (*informal*), flummox, be all Greek to (*informal*), nonplus, befog

mystique *noun* FASCINATION, spell, magic, charm, glamour, awe, charisma

myth *noun* **1** LEGEND, story, tradition, fiction, saga, fable, parable, allegory, fairy story, folk tale, urban myth, urban legend **2** ILLUSION, story, fancy, fantasy, imagination, invention, delusion, superstition, fabrication, falsehood, figment, tall story, cock and bull story (*informal*)

mythical *adjective* **1** LEGENDARY, storied, fabulous, imaginary, fairy-tale, fabled, mythological, storybook, allegorical, folkloric, chimerical **2** IMAGINARY, made-up, fantasy, invented, pretended, untrue, unreal, fabricated, fanciful, fictitious, make-believe, nonexistent

mythological *adjective* LEGENDARY, fabulous, fabled, traditional, invented, heroic, imaginary, mythical, mythic, folkloric

mythology *noun* LEGEND, myths, folklore, stories, tradition, lore, folk tales, mythos

Nn

nab *verb* CATCH, arrest, apprehend, seize, lift (*slang*), nick (*slang, chiefly Brit*), grab, capture, nail (*informal*), collar (*informal*), snatch, catch in the act, feel your collar (*slang*)

nadir *noun* BOTTOM, depths, lowest point, rock bottom, all-time low << ANTONYM height

naff *adjective* (*Brit slang*) BAD, poor, inferior, worthless, pants (*slang*), duff (*Brit informal*), shabby, second-rate, shoddy, low-grade, low-quality, trashy, substandard, for the birds (*informal*), crappy (*slang*), valueless, rubbishy, poxy (*slang*), strictly for the birds (*informal*), twopenny-halfpenny, bodger *or* bodgie (*Austral slang*) << ANTONYM excellent

nag¹ *verb* SCOLD, harass, badger, pester, worry, harry, plague, hassle (*informal*), vex, berate, breathe down someone's neck, upbraid, chivvy, bend someone's ear (*informal*), be on your back (*slang*), henpeck ▷ *noun* SCOLD, complainer, grumbler, virago, shrew, tartar, moaner, harpy, harridan, termagant, fault-finder

nag² *noun* often derog HORSE, hack, jade, plug

nagging *adjective* **1** CONTINUOUS, persistent, continual, niggling, repeated, constant, endless, relentless, perpetual, never-ending, interminable, unrelenting, incessant, unremitting **2** SCOLDING, complaining, critical, sharp-tongued, shrewish

nail *noun* **1** TACK, spike, rivet, hobnail, brad (*technical*) **2** FINGERNAIL, toenail, talon, thumbnail, claw ▷ *verb* **1** FASTEN, fix, secure, attach, pin, hammer, tack **2** (*informal*) CATCH, arrest, capture, apprehend, lift (*slang*), trap, nab (*informal*), snare, ensnare, entrap, feel your collar (*slang*)

naive, naïve *or* **naïf** *adjective* GULLIBLE, trusting, credulous, unsuspicious, green, simple, innocent, childlike, callow,

unsophisticated, unworldly, artless, ingenuous, guileless, wet behind the ears (*informal*), jejune, as green as grass << ANTONYM worldly

naivety, naiveté *or* **naïveté** *noun* GULLIBILITY, innocence, simplicity, inexperience, credulity, ingenuousness, artlessness, guilelessness, callowness

naked *adjective* **1** NUDE, stripped, exposed, bare, uncovered, undressed, in the raw (*informal*), starkers (*informal*), stark-naked, unclothed, in the buff (*informal*), in the altogether (*informal*), buck naked (*slang*), undraped, in your birthday suit (*informal*), scuddy (*slang*), without a stitch on (*informal*), in the bare scud (*slang*), naked as the day you were born (*informal*) << ANTONYM dressed **2** UNDISGUISED, open, simple, plain, patent, evident, stark, manifest, blatant, overt, unmistakable, unqualified, unadorned, unvarnished, unconcealed << ANTONYM disguised

nakedness *noun* **1** NUDITY, undress, bareness, deshabille **2** STARKNESS, simplicity, openness, plainness

name *noun* **1** TITLE, nickname, designation, appellation, term, handle (*slang*), denomination, epithet, sobriquet, cognomen, moniker *or* monicker (*slang*) **2** REPUTATION, character, honour, fame, distinction, esteem, eminence, renown, repute, note ▷ *verb* **1** CALL, christen, baptize, dub, term, style, label, entitle, denominate **2** NOMINATE, choose, commission, mention, identify, select, appoint, specify, designate

named *adjective* **1** CALLED, christened, known as, dubbed, termed, styled, labelled, entitled, denominated, baptized **2** NOMINATED, chosen, picked, commissioned, mentioned, identified, selected, appointed, cited, specified, designated, singled out

nameless *adjective* 1 UNNAMED, unknown, obscure, anonymous, unheard-of, undistinguished, untitled 2 ANONYMOUS, unknown, unnamed, incognito 3 HORRIBLE, unspeakable, indescribable, abominable, ineffable, unutterable, inexpressible

namely *adverb* SPECIFICALLY, that is to say, to wit, i.e., viz.

nap¹ *verb* SLEEP, rest, nod, drop off (*informal*), doze, kip (*Brit slang*), snooze (*informal*), nod off (*informal*), catnap, drowse, zizz (*Brit informal*) ▷ *noun* SLEEP, rest, kip (*Brit slang*), siesta, catnap, forty winks (*informal*), shuteye (*slang*), zizz (*Brit informal*)

nap² *noun* PILE, down, fibre, weave, shag, grain

napkin *noun* SERVIETTE, cloth

narcissism *or* **narcism** *noun* EGOTISM, vanity, self-love, self-admiration

narcotic *noun* DRUG, anaesthetic, painkiller, sedative, opiate, tranquillizer, anodyne, analgesic ▷ *adjective* SEDATIVE, calming, dulling, numbing, hypnotic, analgesic, stupefying, soporific, painkilling

narrate *verb* TELL, recount, report, detail, describe, relate, unfold, chronicle, recite, set forth

narration *noun* 1 STORYTELLING, telling, reading, relation, explanation, description 2 ACCOUNT, explanation, description, recital, voice-over (*in film*)

narrative *noun* STORY, report, history, detail, account, statement, tale, chronicle

narrator *noun* STORYTELLER, writer, author, reporter, commentator, chronicler, reciter, raconteur

narrow *adjective* 1 THIN, fine, slim, pinched, slender, tapering, attenuated << ANTONYM broad 2 LIMITED, restricted, confined, tight, close, near, cramped, meagre, constricted, circumscribed, scanty, straitened, incapacious << ANTONYM wide 3 INSULAR, prejudiced, biased, partial, reactionary, puritan, bigoted, dogmatic, intolerant, narrow-minded, small-minded, illiberal << ANTONYM broad-minded 4 EXCLUSIVE, limited, select, restricted, confined ▷ *verb* 1 *often with* **down** RESTRICT, limit, reduce, diminish, constrict, circumscribe, straiten 2 GET NARROWER, taper, shrink, tighten, constrict

narrowly *adverb* 1 JUST, barely, only just, scarcely, by the skin of your teeth, by a whisker *or* hair's-breadth 2 CLOSELY,

keenly, carefully, intently, intensely, fixedly, searchingly

narrow-minded *adjective* INTOLERANT, conservative, prejudiced, biased, provincial, petty, reactionary, parochial, short-sighted, bigoted, insular, opinionated, small-minded, hidebound, illiberal, strait-laced << ANTONYM broad-minded

narrows *plural noun* CHANNEL, sound, gulf, passage, straits

nastiness *noun* 1 SPITE, malice, venom, unpleasantness, meanness, bitchiness (*slang*), offensiveness, spitefulness 2 OBSCENITY, porn (*informal*), pornography, indecency, licentiousness, ribaldry, smuttiness

nasty *adjective* 1 UNPLEASANT, ugly, disagreeable << ANTONYM pleasant 2 SPITEFUL, mean, offensive, annoying, vicious, unpleasant, abusive, vile, malicious, bad-tempered, despicable, disagreeable << ANTONYM pleasant 3 DISGUSTING, unpleasant, dirty, offensive, foul, horrible, polluted, filthy, sickening, vile, distasteful, repellent, obnoxious, objectionable, disagreeable, nauseating, odious, repugnant, loathsome, grotty (*slang*), malodorous, noisome, unappetizing, yucky *or* yukky (*slang*), festy (*Austral slang*), yucko (*Austral slang*) 4 SERIOUS, bad, dangerous, critical, severe, painful 5 OBSCENE, blue, gross, foul, indecent, pornographic, lewd, impure, lascivious, smutty, ribald, licentious << ANTONYM clean

nation *noun* 1 COUNTRY, state, commonwealth, realm 2 PUBLIC, people, community, society, population

national *adjective* 1 NATIONWIDE, state, public, civil, widespread, governmental, countrywide 2 ETHNIC, social ▷ *noun* CITIZEN, subject, resident, native, inhabitant

nationalism *noun* PATRIOTISM, loyalty to your country, chauvinism, jingoism, nationality, allegiance, fealty

nationalistic *adjective* PATRIOTIC, xenophobic, chauvinistic, jingoistic, loyal to your country

nationality *noun* 1 CITIZENSHIP, birth 2 RACE, nation, ethnic group

nationwide *adjective* NATIONAL, general, widespread, countrywide, overall

native *adjective* 1 INDIGENOUS, local, aboriginal (*often offensive*) 2 MOTHER, indigenous, vernacular 3 DOMESTIC, local, indigenous, home-made, home-grown, home ▷ *noun usually with* **of** INHABITANT, national, resident, citizen, countryman, aborigine (*often offensive*), dweller

Nativity *noun* BIRTH OF CHRIST, manger scene

natter (*Chiefly Brit informal*) *verb* GOSSIP, talk, rabbit (on) (*Brit informal*), jaw (*slang*), chatter, witter (*informal*), prattle, jabber, gabble, blather, blether, shoot the breeze (*informal*), run off at the mouth (*slang*), prate, talk idly, chew the fat or rag (*slang*), earbash (*Austral & NZ slang*) ▷ *noun* GOSSIP, talk, conversation, chat, jaw (*slang*), craic (*Irish informal*), gab (*informal*), prattle, jabber, gabble, palaver, blather, chitchat, blether, chinwag (*Brit informal*), gabfest (*informal, chiefly US & Canad*), confabulation

natty *adjective* SMART, sharp, dashing, elegant, trim, neat, fashionable, stylish, trendy (*Brit informal*), chic, spruce, well-dressed, dapper, snazzy (*informal*), well-turned-out, crucial (*slang*), schmick (*Austral informal*)

natural *adjective* 1 LOGICAL, reasonable, valid, legitimate 2 NORMAL, common, regular, usual, ordinary, typical, everyday << ANTONYM abnormal 3 INNATE, native, characteristic, indigenous, inherent, instinctive, intuitive, congenital, inborn, immanent, in your blood, essential 4 UNAFFECTED, open, frank, genuine, spontaneous, candid, unpretentious, unsophisticated, dinkum (*Austral & NZ informal*), artless, ingenuous, real, simple, unstudied << ANTONYM affected 5 PURE, plain, organic, whole, unrefined, unbleached, unpolished, unmixed << ANTONYM processed

naturalism *noun* REALISM, authenticity, plausibility, verisimilitude, factualism

naturalist *noun* BIOLOGIST, ecologist, botanist, zoologist

naturalistic *adjective* 1 REALISTIC, photographic, kitchen sink, representational, lifelike, warts and all (*informal*), true-to-life, vérité, factualistic 2 LIFELIKE, realistic, real-life, true-to-life

naturally *adverb* 1 OF COURSE, certainly, as a matter of course, as anticipated 2 TYPICALLY, simply, normally, spontaneously, customarily

nature *noun* 1 CREATION, world, earth, environment, universe, cosmos, natural world 2 FLORA AND FAUNA, country, landscape, countryside, scenery, natural history 3 QUALITY, character, make-up, constitution, attributes, essence, traits,

complexion, features 4 TEMPERAMENT, character, personality, disposition, outlook, mood, humour, temper 5 KIND, sort, style, type, variety, species, category, description

naughty *adjective* 1 DISOBEDIENT, bad, mischievous, badly behaved, wayward, playful, wicked, sinful, fractious, impish, roguish, refractory << ANTONYM good 2 OBSCENE, blue, vulgar, improper, lewd, risqué, X-rated (*informal*), bawdy, smutty, off-colour, ribald << ANTONYM clean

nausea *noun* 1 SICKNESS, vomiting, retching, squeamishness, queasiness, biliousness 2 DISGUST, loathing, aversion, revulsion, abhorrence, repugnance, odium

nauseate *verb* 1 SICKEN, turn your stomach 2 DISGUST, offend, horrify, revolt, repel, repulse, gross out (*US slang*)

nauseous *adjective* 1 SICK, crook (*Austral & NZ informal*) 2 SICKENING, offensive, disgusting, revolting, distasteful, repulsive, nauseating, repugnant, loathsome, abhorrent, detestable, yucky *or* yukky (*slang*), yucko (*Austral slang*)

nautical *adjective* MARITIME, marine, yachting, naval, seafaring, seagoing

naval *adjective* NAUTICAL, marine, maritime

navel *noun* 1 BELLYBUTTON (*informal*) 2 CENTRE, middle, hub, central point

navigate *verb* 1 STEER, drive, direct, guide, handle, pilot, sail, skipper, manoeuvre 2 MANOEUVRE, drive, direct, guide, handle, pilot 3 PLOT A COURSE, sail, find your way, plan a course 4 SAIL, cruise, manoeuvre, voyage

navigation *noun* SAILING, cruising, steering, voyaging, seamanship, helmsmanship

navigator *noun* HELMSMAN, pilot, seaman, mariner

navy *noun* FLEET, warships, flotilla, armada

near *adjective* 1 CLOSE, bordering, neighbouring, nearby, beside, adjacent, adjoining, close by, at close quarters, just round the corner, contiguous, proximate, within sniffing distance (*informal*), a hop, skip and a jump away (*informal*) << ANTONYM far 2 IMMINENT, forthcoming, approaching, looming, impending, upcoming, on the cards (*informal*), nigh, in the offing, near-at-hand, next << ANTONYM far-off 3 INTIMATE, close, related, allied, familiar, connected, attached, akin << ANTONYM distant 4 (*informal*) MEAN, stingy, parsimonious, miserly, niggardly, ungenerous, tightfisted, close-fisted

nearby *adjective* NEIGHBOURING, adjacent,

adjoining ▷ *adverb* CLOSE AT HAND, within reach, not far away, at close quarters, just round the corner, proximate, within sniffing distance (*informal*)

nearing *adjective* APPROACHING, coming, advancing, imminent, impending, upcoming

nearly *adverb* 1 PRACTICALLY, about, almost, virtually, all but, just about, not quite, as good as, well-nigh 2 ALMOST, about, approaching, roughly, just about, approximately

neat *adjective* 1 TIDY, nice, straight, trim, orderly, spruce, uncluttered, shipshape, spick-and-span << ANTONYM untidy 2 METHODICAL, tidy, systematic, fastidious << ANTONYM disorganized 3 SMART, trim, tidy, spruce, dapper, natty (*informal*), well-groomed, well-turned-out 4 GRACEFUL, elegant, adept, nimble, agile, adroit, efficient << ANTONYM clumsy 5 CLEVER, efficient, handy, apt, well-judged << ANTONYM inefficient 6 (*Chiefly US & Canad slang*) COOL, great (*informal*), excellent, brilliant, cracking (*Brit informal*), smashing (*informal*), superb, fantastic (*informal*), tremendous, ace (*informal*), fabulous (*informal*), marvellous, terrific, awesome (*slang*), mean (*slang*), super (*informal*), brill (*informal*), bodacious (*slang, chiefly US*), boffo (*slang*), chillin' (*US slang*), booshit (*Austral slang*), exo (*Austral slang*), sik (*Austral slang*), rad (*informal*), phat (*slang*), schmick (*Austral informal*) << ANTONYM terrible 7 (*of alcoholic drinks*) UNDILUTED, straight, pure, unmixed

neatly *adverb* 1 TIDILY, nicely, smartly, systematically, methodically, fastidiously 2 SMARTLY, elegantly, stylishly, tidily, nattily 3 GRACEFULLY, expertly, efficiently, adeptly, skilfully, nimbly, adroitly, dexterously, agilely 4 CLEVERLY, precisely, accurately, efficiently, aptly, elegantly

neatness *noun* 1 ORDER, organization, harmony, tidiness, orderliness 2 TIDINESS, niceness, orderliness, smartness, fastidiousness, trimness, spruceness 3 GRACE, skill, efficiency, expertise, precision, elegance, agility, dexterity, deftness, nimbleness, adroitness, adeptness, daintiness, gracefulness, preciseness, skilfulness 4 CLEVERNESS, efficiency, precision, elegance, aptness

nebulous *adjective* 1 VAGUE, confused, uncertain, obscure, unclear, ambiguous, indefinite, hazy, indeterminate, imprecise,

indistinct 2 (*rare*) OBSCURE, vague, dim, murky, shadowy, cloudy, misty, hazy, amorphous, indeterminate, shapeless, indistinct, unformed

necessarily *adverb* 1 AUTOMATICALLY, naturally, definitely, undoubtedly, accordingly, by definition, of course, certainly 2 INEVITABLY, of necessity, unavoidably, perforce, incontrovertibly, nolens volens (*Latin*)

necessary *adjective* 1 NEEDED, required, essential, vital, compulsory, mandatory, imperative, indispensable, obligatory, requisite, de rigueur (*French*), needful, must-have << ANTONYM unnecessary 2 INEVITABLE, certain, unavoidable, inescapable << ANTONYM avoidable

necessitate *verb* COMPEL, force, demand, require, call for, oblige, entail, constrain, impel, make necessary

necessity *noun* 1 NEED, demand, requirement, exigency, indispensability, needfulness 2 ESSENTIAL, need, necessary, requirement, fundamental, requisite, prerequisite, sine qua non (*Latin*), desideratum, want, must-have 3 INEVITABILITY, certainty 4 POVERTY, need, privation, penury, destitution, extremity, indigence 5 REQUIREMENT, essential, need, fundamental

necropolis *noun* CEMETERY, graveyard, churchyard, burial ground

need *verb* 1 WANT, miss, require, lack, have to have, demand 2 REQUIRE, want, demand, call for, entail, necessitate, have occasion to *or* for 3 HAVE TO, be obliged to ▷ *noun* 1 REQUIREMENT, demand, essential, necessity, requisite, desideratum, must-have 2 NECESSITY, call, demand, requirement, obligation 3 EMERGENCY, want, necessity, urgency, exigency 4 POVERTY, deprivation, destitution, neediness, distress, extremity, privation, penury, indigence, impecuniousness

needed *adjective* NECESSARY, wanted, required, lacked, called for, desired

needle *verb* IRRITATE, provoke, annoy, sting, bait, harass, taunt, nag, hassle (*informal*), aggravate (*informal*), prod, gall, ruffle, spur, prick, nettle, goad, irk, rile, get under your skin (*informal*), get on your nerves (*informal*), nark (*Brit, Austral & NZ slang*), hack you off (*informal*), get in your hair (*informal*)

needless *adjective* UNNECESSARY, excessive, pointless, gratuitous, useless, unwanted, redundant, superfluous, groundless, expendable, uncalled-for, dispensable, nonessential, undesired << ANTONYM essential

needlework *noun* EMBROIDERY, tailoring, stitching, sewing, needlecraft

needy *adjective* POOR, deprived, disadvantaged, impoverished, penniless, destitute, poverty-stricken, underprivileged, indigent, down at heel (*informal*), impecunious, dirt-poor, on the breadline (*informal*) << ANTONYM wealthy

negate *verb* 1 INVALIDATE, reverse, cancel, wipe out, void, repeal, revoke, retract, rescind, neutralize, annul, nullify, obviate, abrogate, countermand 2 DENY, oppose, contradict, refute, disallow, disprove, rebut, gainsay (*archaic* or *literary*) << ANTONYM confirm

negation *noun* 1 OPPOSITE, reverse, contrary, contradiction, converse, antithesis, inverse, antonym 2 DENIAL, refusal, rejection, contradiction, renunciation, repudiation, disavowal, veto

negative *adjective* 1 NEUTRALIZING, invalidating, annulling, nullifying, counteractive 2 PESSIMISTIC, cynical, unwilling, gloomy, antagonistic, jaundiced, uncooperative, contrary << ANTONYM optimistic 3 DISSENTING, contradictory, refusing, denying, rejecting, opposing, resisting, contrary << ANTONYM assenting ▷ *noun* DENIAL, no, refusal, rejection, contradiction

neglect *verb* 1 DISREGARD, ignore, leave alone, turn your back on, fail to look after << ANTONYM look after 2 SHIRK, forget, overlook, omit, evade, pass over, skimp, procrastinate over, let slide, be remiss in *or* about 3 FAIL, forget, omit ▷ *noun* 1 NEGLIGENCE, inattention, unconcern << ANTONYM care 2 SHIRKING, failure, oversight, carelessness, dereliction, forgetfulness, slackness, laxity, laxness, slovenliness, remissness

neglected *adjective* 1 UNCARED-FOR, abandoned, underestimated, disregarded, undervalued, unappreciated 2 RUN DOWN, derelict, overgrown, uncared-for

negligence *noun* CARELESSNESS, failure, neglect, disregard, shortcoming, omission, oversight, dereliction, forgetfulness, slackness, inattention, laxity, thoughtlessness, laxness, inadvertence, inattentiveness, heedlessness, remissness

negligent *adjective* CARELESS, slack,

thoughtless, unthinking, forgetful, slapdash, neglectful, heedless, slipshod, inattentive, remiss, unmindful, disregardful << ANTONYM careful

negligible *adjective* INSIGNIFICANT, small, minute, minor, petty, trivial, trifling, unimportant, inconsequential, imperceptible, nickel-and-dime (*US slang*) << ANTONYM significant

negotiable *adjective* 1 DEBATABLE, flexible, unsettled, undecided, open to discussion, discussable *or* discussible 2 VALID, transferable, transactional

negotiate *verb* 1 BARGAIN, deal, contract, discuss, debate, consult, confer, mediate, hold talks, arbitrate, cut a deal, conciliate, parley, discuss terms 2 ARRANGE, manage, settle, work out, bring about, transact 3 GET ROUND, clear, pass, cross, pass through, get over, get past, surmount

negotiation *noun* 1 BARGAINING, debate, discussion, transaction, dialogue, mediation, arbitration, wheeling and dealing (*informal*) 2 ARRANGEMENT, management, settlement, working out, transaction, bringing about

negotiator *noun* MEDIATOR, ambassador, diplomat, delegate, intermediary, arbitrator, moderator, honest broker

neighbourhood *or US* **neighborhood** *noun* 1 DISTRICT, community, quarter, region, surroundings, locality, locale 2 VICINITY, confines, proximity, precincts, environs, purlieus

neighbouring *or US* **neighboring** *adjective* NEARBY, next, near, bordering, surrounding, connecting, adjacent, adjoining, abutting, contiguous, nearest << ANTONYM remote

neighbourly *or US* **neighborly** *adjective* HELPFUL, kind, social, civil, friendly, obliging, harmonious, amiable, considerate, sociable, genial, hospitable, companionable, well-disposed

Nemesis *sometimes not cap. noun* RETRIBUTION, fate, destruction, destiny, vengeance

neophyte *noun* (*formal*) NOVICE, student, pupil, recruit, amateur, beginner, trainee, apprentice, disciple, learner, tyro, probationer, novitiate, proselyte, catechumen

nepotism *noun* FAVOURITISM, bias, patronage, preferential treatment, partiality

nerd *or* **nurd** *noun* (*slang*) 1 BORE, obsessive, anorak (*informal*), geek (*informal*), trainspotter (*informal*), dork (*slang*), wonk (*informal*) **2** FOOL, weed, drip (*informal*), sap (*slang*), wally (*slang*), sucker (*slang*), wimp (*informal*), booby, prat (*slang*), plonker (*slang*), twit (*informal, chiefly Brit*), simpleton, dipstick (*Brit slang*), schmuck (*US slang*), divvy (*Brit slang*), putz (*US slang*), wuss (*slang*), eejit (*Scot & Irish*), dumb-ass (*slang*), doofus (*slang, chiefly US*), dorba or dorb (*Austral slang*), bogan (*Austral slang*)

nerve *noun* **1** BRAVERY, courage, spirit, bottle (*Brit slang*), resolution, daring, determination, guts (*informal*), pluck, grit, fortitude, vigour, coolness, balls (*taboo slang*), mettle, firmness, spunk (*informal*), fearlessness, steadfastness, intrepidity, hardihood, gameness **2** (*informal*) IMPUDENCE, face (*informal*), front, neck (*informal*), sauce (*informal*), cheek (*informal*), brass (*informal*), gall, audacity, boldness, temerity, chutzpah (*US & Canad informal*), insolence, impertinence, effrontery, brass neck (*Brit informal*), brazenness, sassiness (*US slang*) ▷ *plural noun* (*informal*) TENSION, stress, strain, anxiety, butterflies (in your stomach) (*informal*), nervousness, cold feet (*informal*), heebie-jeebies (*slang*), worry ▷▷ **nerve yourself** BRACE YOURSELF, prepare yourself, steel yourself, fortify yourself, gear yourself up, gee yourself up

nerve-racking *or* **nerve-wracking** *adjective* TENSE, trying, difficult, worrying, frightening, distressing, daunting, harassing, stressful, harrowing, gut-wrenching

nervous *adjective often with of* APPREHENSIVE, anxious, uneasy, edgy, worried, wired (*slang*), tense, fearful, shaky, hysterical, neurotic, agitated, ruffled, timid, hyper (*informal*), jittery (*informal*), uptight (*informal*), flustered, on edge, excitable, nervy (*Brit informal*), jumpy, twitchy (*informal*), fidgety, timorous, highly strung, antsy (*informal*), toey (*Austral slang*), adrenalized << ANTONYM calm

nervous breakdown *noun* COLLAPSE, breakdown, crack-up (*informal*), neurasthenia (*obsolete*), nervous disorder

nervousness *noun* ANXIETY, stress, tension, strain, unease, disquiet, agitation, trepidation, timidity, excitability, perturbation, edginess, worry, jumpiness, antsiness (*informal*)

nervy *adjective* (*Brit informal*) ANXIOUS, nervous, tense, agitated, wired (*slang*), restless, jittery (*informal*), on edge, excitable, jumpy, twitchy (*informal*), fidgety,

adrenalized

nest *noun* **1** REFUGE, resort, retreat, haunt, den, hideaway **2** HOTBED, den, breeding-ground

nest egg *noun* SAVINGS, fund(s), store, reserve, deposit, fall-back, cache

nestle *verb often with* **up** *or* **down** SNUGGLE, cuddle, huddle, curl up, nuzzle

nestling *noun* CHICK, fledgling, baby bird

net¹ *noun* MESH, netting, network, web, lattice, lacework, openwork ▷ *verb* CATCH, bag, capture, trap, nab (*informal*), entangle, ensnare, enmesh

net² *or* **nett** *adjective* **1** AFTER TAXES, final, clear, take-home **2** FINAL, closing, ultimate, eventual, conclusive ▷ *verb* EARN, make, clear, gain, realize, bring in, accumulate, reap

nether *adjective* LOWER, bottom, beneath, underground, inferior, basal

nettle *verb* IRRITATE, provoke, annoy, gall, sting, aggravate (*informal*), incense, ruffle, exasperate, vex, goad, pique, get on your nerves (*informal*), nark (*Brit, Austral & NZ slang*), hack you off (*informal*)

network *noun* **1** WEB, system, arrangement, grid, mesh, lattice, circuitry, nexus, plexus, interconnection, net **2** MAZE, warren, labyrinth

neurosis *noun* OBSESSION, instability, mental illness, abnormality, phobia, derangement, mental disturbance, psychological *or* emotional disorder

neurotic *adjective* UNSTABLE, nervous, disturbed, anxious, abnormal, obsessive, compulsive, manic, unhealthy, hyper (*informal*), twitchy (*informal*), overwrought, maladjusted << ANTONYM rational

neuter *verb* CASTRATE, doctor (*informal*), emasculate, spay, dress, fix (*informal*), geld

neutral *adjective* **1** UNBIASED, impartial, disinterested, even-handed, dispassionate, sitting on the fence, uninvolved, noncommittal, nonpartisan, unprejudiced, nonaligned, unaligned, noncombatant, nonbelligerent << ANTONYM biased **2** EXPRESSIONLESS, dull, blank, deadpan, toneless **3** UNCONTROVERSIAL *or* NONCONTROVERSIAL, safe, inoffensive **4** COLOURLESS, achromatic

neutrality *noun* IMPARTIALITY, detachment, noninterference, nonpartisanship, noninvolvement, nonalignment, noninterventionism

neutralize *or* **neutralise** *verb* COUNTERACT, cancel, offset, undo, compensate for, negate, invalidate, counterbalance, nullify

never *adverb* **1** AT NO TIME, not once, not ever << ANTONYM always **2** UNDER NO CIRCUMSTANCES, no way, not at all, on no account, not on your life (*informal*), not on your nelly (*Brit slang*), not for love nor money (*informal*), not ever

never-never *noun* (*Brit informal*) HIRE-PURCHASE (*Brit*), H.P. (*Brit*)

nevertheless *adverb* EVEN SO, still, however, yet, regardless, nonetheless, notwithstanding, in spite of that, (even) though, but

new *adjective* **1** MODERN, recent, contemporary, up-to-date, latest, happening (*informal*), different, current, advanced, original, fresh, novel, topical, state-of-the-art, ground-breaking, modish, newfangled, modernistic, ultramodern, all-singing, all-dancing << ANTONYM old-fashioned **2** BRAND NEW, unused **3** EXTRA, more, added, new-found, supplementary **4** UNFAMILIAR, unaccustomed, strange, unknown **5** RENEWED, changed, improved, restored, altered, rejuvenated, revitalized

newcomer *noun* **1** NEW ARRIVAL, incomer, immigrant, stranger, foreigner, alien, settler **2** BEGINNER, stranger, outsider, novice, new arrival, parvenu, Johnny-come-lately (*informal*)

newly *adverb* RECENTLY, just, lately, freshly, anew, latterly

newness *noun* NOVELTY, innovation, originality, freshness, strangeness, unfamiliarity

news *noun* INFORMATION, latest (*informal*), report, word, story, release, account, statement, advice, exposé, intelligence, scandal, rumour, leak, revelation, buzz, gossip, dirt (*US slang*), goss (*informal*), disclosure, bulletin, dispatch, gen (*Brit informal*), communiqué, hearsay, tidings, news flash, scuttlebutt (*US slang*)

newsworthy *adjective* INTERESTING, important, arresting, significant, remarkable, notable, sensational, noteworthy

next *adjective* **1** FOLLOWING, later, succeeding, subsequent **2** ADJACENT, closest, nearest, neighbouring, adjoining ▷ *adverb* AFTERWARDS, then, later, following, subsequently, thereafter

nexus *noun* CONNECTION, link, tie, bond, junction, joining

nibble *verb often with* **at** BITE, eat, peck, pick at, nip, munch, gnaw ▷ *noun* SNACK, bite, taste, peck, crumb, morsel, titbit, soupçon (*French*)

nice *adjective* **1** PLEASANT, delightful, agreeable, good, attractive, charming, pleasurable, enjoyable << ANTONYM unpleasant **2** KIND, helpful, obliging, considerate << ANTONYM unkind **3** LIKABLE *or* LIKEABLE, friendly, engaging, charming, pleasant, agreeable, amiable, prepossessing **4** POLITE, cultured, refined, courteous, genteel, well-bred, well-mannered << ANTONYM vulgar **5** PRECISE, fine, careful, strict, accurate, exact, exacting, subtle, delicate, discriminating, rigorous, meticulous, scrupulous, fastidious << ANTONYM vague

nicely *adverb* **1** PLEASANTLY, well, delightfully, attractively, charmingly, agreeably, pleasingly, acceptably, pleasurably << ANTONYM unpleasantly **2** KINDLY, politely, thoughtfully, amiably, courteously **3** PRECISELY, exactly, accurately, finely, carefully, strictly, subtly, delicately, meticulously, rigorously, scrupulously << ANTONYM carelessly **4** SATISFACTORILY, well, adequately, acceptably, passably

nicety *noun* FINE POINT, distinction, subtlety, nuance, refinement, minutiae

niche *noun* **1** RECESS, opening, corner, hollow, nook, alcove **2** POSITION, calling, place, slot (*informal*), vocation, pigeonhole (*informal*)

nick *noun* CUT, mark, scratch, score, chip, scar, notch, dent, snick ▷ *verb* **1** (*slang, Chiefly Brit*) STEAL, pinch (*informal*), swipe (*slang*), pilfer, snitch (*slang*) **2** CUT, mark, score, damage, chip, scratch, scar, notch, dent, snick

nickname *noun* PET NAME, label, diminutive, epithet, sobriquet, familiar name, moniker *or* monicker (*slang*), handle (*slang*)

nifty *adjective* (*informal*) **1** SLICK, excellent, sharp, smart, clever, neat, stylish, schmick (*Austral informal*) **2** AGILE, quick, swift, skilful, deft

niggle *verb* **1** BOTHER, concern, worry, trouble, disturb, rankle **2** CRITICIZE, provoke, annoy, plague, irritate, hassle (*informal*), badger, find fault with, nag at, cavil, be on your back (*slang*) ▷ *noun* COMPLAINT, moan, grievance, grumble, beef (*slang*), bitch (*slang*), lament, grouse, gripe (*informal*), grouch (*informal*)

niggling *adjective* **1** IRRITATING, troubling, persistent, bothersome **2** PETTY, minor, trifling, insignificant, unimportant, fussy, quibbling, picky (*informal*), piddling (*informal*), nit-picking (*informal*), finicky, pettifogging

nigh *adverb* ALMOST, about, nearly, close to, practically, approximately ▷ *adjective* NEAR, next, close, imminent, impending, at hand, upcoming

night *noun* DARKNESS, dark, night-time, dead of night, night watches, hours of darkness

nightfall *noun* EVENING, sunset, twilight, dusk, sundown, eventide, gloaming (*Scot poetic*), eve (*archaic*), evo (*Austral slang*) << ANTONYM daybreak

nightly *adjective* NOCTURNAL, night-time ▷ *adverb* EVERY NIGHT, nights (*informal*), each night, night after night

nightmare *noun* 1 BAD DREAM, hallucination, night terror 2 ORDEAL, trial, hell, horror, torture, torment, tribulation, purgatory, hell on earth

nightmarish *adjective* TERRIFYING, frightening, disturbing, appalling, horrible, horrific, ghastly, hideous, harrowing, frightful

nihilism *noun* NEGATIVITY, rejection, denial, scepticism, cynicism, pessimism, renunciation, atheism, repudiation, agnosticism, unbelief, abnegation

nil *noun* 1 NOTHING, love, zero, zip (*US slang*) 2 ZERO, nothing, none, naught, zilch (*slang*), zip (*US slang*)

nimble *adjective* 1 AGILE, active, lively, deft, proficient, sprightly, nippy (*Brit informal*), spry, dexterous << ANTONYM clumsy 2 ALERT, ready, bright (*informal*), sharp, keen, active, smart, quick-witted

nimbus *noun* HALO, atmosphere, glow, aura, ambience, corona, irradiation, aureole

nip¹ *verb* 1 with **along, up, out** (*Brit informal*) POP, go, run, rush, dash 2 BITE, snap, nibble 3 PINCH, catch, grip, squeeze, clip, compress, tweak ▷▷ **nip something in the bud** THWART, check, frustrate

nip² *noun* DRAM, shot (*informal*), drop, taste, finger, swallow, portion, peg (*Brit*), sip, draught, sup, mouthful, snifter (*informal*), soupçon (*French*)

nipper *noun* 1 (*informal, Chiefly Brit & Austral*) CHILD, girl, boy, baby, kid (*informal*), infant, tot, little one, sprog (*slang*), munchkin (*informal, chiefly US*), rug rat (*slang*), littlie (*Austral informal*), ankle-biter (*Austral slang*), tacker (*Austral slang*) 2 PINCER, claw

nipple *noun* TEAT, breast, udder, tit, pap, papilla, mamilla

nippy *adjective* 1 CHILLY, biting, parky (*Brit informal*) 2 (*Brit informal*) FAST (*informal*),

quick, speedy 3 (*Brit informal*) AGILE, fast, quick, active, lively, nimble, sprightly, spry

nirvana *noun* (*Buddhism & Hinduism*) PARADISE, peace, joy, bliss, serenity, tranquillity

nitty-gritty *noun* (*informal*) BASICS, facts, reality, essentials, core, fundamentals, substance, essence, bottom line, crux, gist, nuts and bolts, heart of the matter, ins and outs, brass tacks (*informal*)

no *sentence substitute* NOT AT ALL, certainly not, of course not, absolutely not, never, no way, nay << ANTONYM yes ▷ *noun* 1 REFUSAL, rejection, denial, negation, veto << ANTONYM consent 2 OBJECTOR, protester, dissident, dissenter

nob *noun* (*slang, chiefly Brit*) ARISTOCRAT, fat cat (*slang, chiefly US*), toff (*Brit slang*), bigwig (*informal*), celeb (*informal*), big shot (*informal*), big hitter (*informal*), aristo (*informal*), heavy hitter (*informal*), nabob (*informal*), V.I.P.

nobble *verb* (*Brit slang*) 1 INFLUENCE, square, win over, pay off (*informal*), corrupt, intimidate, bribe, get at, buy off, suborn, grease the palm *or* hand of (*slang*) 2 DISABLE, handicap, weaken, incapacitate 3 THWART, check, defeat, frustrate, snooker, foil, baffle, balk, prevent

nobility *noun* 1 ARISTOCRACY, lords, elite, nobles, upper class, peerage, ruling class, patricians, high society 2 DIGNITY, majesty, greatness, grandeur, magnificence, stateliness, nobleness 3 INTEGRITY, honour, virtue, goodness, honesty, righteousness, probity, rectitude, worthiness, incorruptibility, uprightness

noble *adjective* 1 WORTHY, generous, upright, honourable, virtuous, magnanimous << ANTONYM despicable 2 DIGNIFIED, great, august, imposing, impressive, distinguished, magnificent, splendid, stately << ANTONYM lowly 3 ARISTOCRATIC, lordly, titled, gentle (*archaic*), patrician, blue-blooded, highborn << ANTONYM humble ▷ *noun* LORD, peer, aristocrat, nobleman, aristo (*informal*) << ANTONYM commoner

nobody *pronoun* NO-ONE ▷ *noun* NONENTITY, nothing (*informal*), lightweight (*informal*), zero, cipher << ANTONYM celebrity

nocturnal *adjective* NIGHTLY, night, of the night, night-time

nod *verb* 1 AGREE, concur, assent, show agreement 2 INCLINE, bob, bow, duck, dip 3 SIGNAL, indicate, motion, gesture 4 SALUTE, acknowledge ▷ *noun* 1 SIGNAL, sign, motion, gesture, indication **2** SALUTE, greeting, acknowledgment

node *noun* NODULE, growth, swelling, knot, lump, bump, bud, knob, protuberance

noise *noun* SOUND, talk, row, racket, outcry, clamour, din, clatter, uproar, babble, blare, fracas, commotion, pandemonium, rumpus, cry, tumult, hubbub << ANTONYM silence

noisy *adjective* **1** ROWDY, chattering, strident, boisterous, vociferous, riotous, uproarious, obstreperous, clamorous << ANTONYM quiet **2** LOUD, piercing, deafening, tumultuous, ear-splitting, cacophonous, clamorous << ANTONYM quiet

nomad *noun* WANDERER, migrant, rover, rambler, itinerant, drifter, vagabond

nomadic *adjective* WANDERING, travelling, roaming, migrant, roving, itinerant, migratory, vagrant, peripatetic

nomenclature *noun* TERMINOLOGY, vocabulary, classification, taxonomy, phraseology, locution

nominal *adjective* **1** TITULAR, formal, purported, in name only, supposed, so-called, pretended, theoretical, professed, ostensible **2** TOKEN, small, symbolic, minimal, trivial, trifling, insignificant, inconsiderable

nominate *verb* **1** PROPOSE, suggest, recommend, submit, put forward **2** APPOINT, name, choose, commission, select, elect, assign, designate, empower

nomination *noun* **1** PROPOSAL, suggestion, recommendation **2** APPOINTMENT, election, selection, designation, choice

nominee *noun* CANDIDATE, applicant, entrant, contestant, aspirant, runner

nonaligned *adjective* NEUTRAL, impartial, uninvolved, nonpartisan, noncombatant, nonbelligerent

nonchalance *noun* INDIFFERENCE, insouciance, detachment, unconcern, cool (*slang*), calm, apathy, composure, carelessness, equanimity, casualness, sang-froid, self-possession, dispassion, imperturbability

nonchalant *adjective* INDIFFERENT, cool, calm, casual, detached, careless, laid-back (*informal*), airy, unconcerned, apathetic, dispassionate, unfazed (*informal*), unperturbed, blasé, offhand, unemotional, insouciant, imperturbable << ANTONYM concerned

noncommittal *adjective* EVASIVE, politic, reserved, guarded, careful, cautious, neutral, vague, wary, discreet, tentative, ambiguous, indefinite, circumspect, tactful, equivocal, temporizing, unrevealing

nonconformist *noun* DISSENTER, rebel, radical, protester, eccentric, maverick, heretic, individualist, iconoclast, dissentient << ANTONYM traditionalist

nondescript *adjective* UNDISTINGUISHED, ordinary, dull, commonplace, unremarkable, run-of-the-mill, uninspiring, indeterminate, uninteresting, featureless, insipid, unexceptional, common or garden (*informal*), mousy, characterless, unmemorable, vanilla (*informal*), nothing to write home about << ANTONYM distinctive

none *pronoun* **1** NOT ANY, nothing, zero, not one, nil, no part, not a bit, zilch (*slang, chiefly US & Canad*), diddly (*US slang*) **2** NO-ONE, nobody, not one

nonentity *noun* NOBODY, lightweight (*informal*), mediocrity, cipher, small fry, unimportant person

nonetheless *sentence connector* NEVERTHELESS, however, yet, even so, despite that, in spite of that

nonevent *noun* FLOP (*informal*), failure, disappointment, fiasco, dud (*informal*), washout, clunker (*informal*)

nonexistent *adjective* IMAGINARY, imagined, fancied, fictional, mythical, unreal, hypothetical, illusory, insubstantial, hallucinatory << ANTONYM real

nonplussed *adjective* TAKEN ABACK, stunned, confused, embarrassed, puzzled, astonished, stumped, dismayed, baffled, bewildered, astounded, confounded, perplexed, disconcerted, mystified, fazed, dumbfounded, discomfited, flummoxed, discountenanced

nonsense *noun* **1** RUBBISH, hot air (*informal*), waffle (*informal, chiefly Brit*), twaddle, pants (*slang*), rot, crap (*slang*), garbage (*informal*), trash, bunk (*informal*), tosh (*slang, chiefly Brit*), rhubarb, pap, foolishness, bilge (*informal*), drivel, tripe (*informal*), gibberish, guff (*slang*), bombast, moonshine, claptrap (*informal*), hogwash, hokum (*slang, chiefly US & Canad*), blather, double Dutch (*Brit informal*), piffle (*informal*), poppycock (*informal*), balderdash, bosh (*informal*), eyewash (*informal*), stuff and nonsense, tommyrot, horsefeathers (*US slang*), bunkum *or* buncombe (*chiefly US*), bizzo (*Austral slang*), bull's wool (*Austral & NZ slang*) << ANTONYM sense **2** IDIOCY, folly, stupidity, absurdity, silliness, inanity, senselessness, ridiculousness, ludicrousness, fatuity

nonsensical *adjective* SENSELESS, crazy, silly, ridiculous, absurd, foolish, ludicrous, meaningless, irrational, incomprehensible, inane, asinine, cockamamie (*slang, chiefly US*)

nonstarter *noun* DEAD LOSS, dud (*informal*), washout (*informal*), no-hoper (*informal*), turkey (*informal*), lemon (*informal*), loser, waste of space *or* time

nonstop *adjective* CONTINUOUS, constant, relentless, uninterrupted, steady, endless, unbroken, interminable, incessant, unending, ceaseless, unremitting, unfaltering << ANTONYM occasional ▷ *adverb* CONTINUOUSLY, constantly, steadily, endlessly, relentlessly, perpetually, incessantly, without stopping, ceaselessly, interminably, unremittingly, uninterruptedly, unendingly, unfalteringly, unbrokenly

nook *noun* NICHE, corner, recess, cavity, crevice, alcove, cranny, inglenook (*Brit*), cubbyhole, opening

noon *noun* MIDDAY, high noon, noonday, noontime, twelve noon, noontide

norm *noun* STANDARD, rule, model, pattern, mean, type, measure, average, par, criterion, benchmark, yardstick

normal *adjective* 1 USUAL, common, standard, average, natural, regular, ordinary, acknowledged, typical, conventional, routine, accustomed, habitual, run-of-the-mill << ANTONYM unusual 2 SANE, reasonable, rational, lucid, well-adjusted, compos mentis (*Latin*), in your right mind, mentally sound, in possession of all your faculties

normality *or US* **normalcy** *noun* 1 REGULARITY, order, routine, ordinariness, naturalness, conventionality, usualness 2 SANITY, reason, balance, rationality, lucidity

normally *adverb* 1 USUALLY, generally, commonly, regularly, typically, ordinarily, as a rule, habitually 2 AS USUAL, naturally, properly, conventionally, in the usual way

normative *adjective* STANDARDIZING, controlling, regulating, prescriptive, normalizing, regularizing

north *adjective* NORTHERN, polar, arctic, boreal, northerly ▷ *adverb* NORTHWARD(s), in a northerly direction

North Star *noun* POLE STAR, Polaris, lodestar

nose *noun* SNOUT, bill, beak, hooter (*slang*), snitch (*slang*), conk (*slang*), neb (*archaic or dialect*), proboscis, schnozzle (*slang, chiefly US*) ▷ *verb* EASE FORWARD, push, edge, shove, nudge

nose dive *noun* 1 DROP, plunge, dive, plummet, sharp fall 2 (*informal*) SHARP FALL, plunge, drop, dive, plummet ▷ *verb* 1 DROP, plunge, dive, plummet, fall sharply 2 (*informal*) FALL SHARPLY, drop, plunge, dive, plummet

nosh (*slang*) *noun* 1 FOOD, eats (*slang*), fare, grub (*slang*), feed, tack (*informal*), scoff (*slang*), kai (*NZ informal*), chow (*informal*), sustenance, victuals, comestibles, nosebag (*slang*), vittles (*obsolete* or *dialect*), viands 2 MEAL, repast ▷ *verb* EAT, consume, scoff (*slang*), devour, feed on, munch, gobble, partake of, wolf down

nostalgia *noun* REMINISCENCE, longing, regret, pining, yearning, remembrance, homesickness, wistfulness

nostalgic *adjective* SENTIMENTAL, longing, emotional, homesick, wistful, maudlin, regretful

notable *adjective* 1 REMARKABLE, marked, striking, unusual, extraordinary, outstanding, evident, pronounced, memorable, noticeable, uncommon, conspicuous, salient, noteworthy << ANTONYM imperceptible 2 PROMINENT, famous, celebrated, distinguished, well-known, notorious, renowned, eminent, pre-eminent << ANTONYM unknown ▷ *noun* CELEBRITY, worthy, big name, dignitary, luminary, celeb (*informal*), personage, megastar (*informal*), notability, V.I.P.

notably *adverb* REMARKABLY, unusually, distinctly, extraordinarily, markedly, noticeably, strikingly, conspicuously, singularly, outstandingly, uncommonly, pre-eminently, signally

notation *noun* 1 SIGNS, system, characters, code, symbols, script 2 NOTE, record, noting, jotting

notch *noun* 1 (*informal*) LEVEL, step, degree, grade, cut (*informal*) 2 CUT, nick, incision, indentation, mark, score, cleft ▷ *verb* CUT, mark, score, nick, scratch, indent

note *noun* 1 MESSAGE, letter, communication, memo, memorandum, epistle 2 RECORD, reminder, memo, memorandum, jotting, minute 3 ANNOTATION, comment, remark, gloss 4 DOCUMENT, form, record, certificate 5 SYMBOL, mark, sign, indication, token 6 TONE, touch, trace, hint, sound ▷ *verb* 1 NOTICE, see, observe, perceive 2 BEAR IN MIND, be aware, take into account

3 MENTION, record, mark, indicate, register, remark **4** WRITE DOWN, record, scribble, take down, set down, jot down, put in writing, put down in black and white ▷▷ **of note 1** FAMOUS, prestigious, eminent, renowned, of standing, of character, of reputation, of consequence, celebrated **2** IMPORTANT, consequential, significant, of distinction ▷▷ **take note of something** *or* **someone** NOTICE, note, regard, observe, heed, pay attention to

notebook *noun* NOTEPAD, record book, exercise book, jotter, journal, diary, Filofax (*trademark*), memorandum book

noted *adjective* FAMOUS, celebrated, recognized, distinguished, well-known, prominent, notorious, acclaimed, notable, renowned, eminent, conspicuous, illustrious << ANTONYM unknown

noteworthy *adjective* REMARKABLE, interesting, important, significant, extraordinary, outstanding, exceptional, notable << ANTONYM ordinary

nothing *pronoun* **1** NOUGHT, zero, nil, naught, not a thing, zilch (*slang*), sod all (*slang*), damn all (*slang*), zip (*US slang*) **2** A TRIFLE, no big deal, a mere bagatelle **3** VOID, emptiness, nothingness, nullity, nonexistence ▷ *noun* (*informal*) NOBODY, cipher, nonentity

nothingness *noun* **1** OBLIVION, nullity, nonexistence, nonbeing **2** INSIGNIFICANCE, triviality, worthlessness, meaninglessness, unimportance

notice *noun* **1** SIGN, advertisement, poster, placard, warning, bill **2** NOTIFICATION, warning, advice, intimation, news, communication, intelligence, announcement, instruction, advance warning, wake-up call **3** REVIEW, comment, criticism, evaluation, critique, critical assessment **4** ATTENTION, interest, note, regard, consideration, observation, scrutiny, heed, cognizance << ANTONYM oversight **5** (*Chiefly Brit*) THE SACK (*informal*), dismissal, discharge, the boot (*slang*), the push (*slang*), marching orders (*informal*), the (old) heave-ho (*informal*), your books *or* cards (*informal*) ▷ *verb* OBSERVE, see, mind, note, spot, remark, distinguish, perceive, detect, heed, discern, behold (*archaic* or *literary*), mark, eyeball (*slang*) << ANTONYM overlook

noticeable *adjective* OBVIOUS, clear, striking, plain, bold, evident, distinct, manifest, conspicuous, unmistakable, salient, observable, perceptible, appreciable

notification *noun* ANNOUNCEMENT, declaration, notice, statement, telling, information, warning, message, advice, intelligence, publication, notifying

notify *verb* INFORM, tell, advise, alert to, announce, warn, acquaint with, make known to, apprise of

notion *noun* **1** IDEA, view, opinion, belief, concept, impression, judgment, sentiment, conception, apprehension, inkling, mental image *or* picture, picture **2** WHIM, wish, desire, fancy, impulse, inclination, caprice

notional *adjective* HYPOTHETICAL, ideal, abstract, theoretical, imaginary, speculative, conceptual, unreal, fanciful << ANTONYM actual

notoriety *noun* INFAMY, discredit, disrepute, dishonour, bad reputation, opprobrium, ill repute, obloquy

notorious *adjective* INFAMOUS, disreputable, opprobrious

notoriously *adverb* INFAMOUSLY, disreputably

notwithstanding *preposition* DESPITE, in spite of, regardless of ▷ *sentence connector* NEVERTHELESS, however, though, nonetheless

nought *or* (*archaic* or *literary*) **naught, ought** *or* **aught** *noun* **1** ZERO, nothing, nil **2** NOTHING, zip (*US slang*), slang, nothingness, nada, zilch, sod all (*slang*), damn all (*slang*)

nourish *verb* **1** FEED, supply, sustain, nurture **2** ENCOURAGE, support, maintain, promote, sustain, foster, cultivate

nourishing *adjective* NUTRITIOUS, beneficial, wholesome, healthful, health-giving, nutritive

nourishment *noun* FOOD, nutrition, sustenance, nutriment, tack (*informal*), kai (*NZ informal*), victuals, vittles (*obsolete* or *dialect*)

novel[1] *noun* STORY, tale, fiction, romance, narrative

novel[2] *adjective* NEW, different, original, fresh, unusual, innovative, uncommon, singular, ground-breaking, left-field (*informal*) << ANTONYM ordinary

novelist *noun* AUTHOR, writer

novelty *noun* **1** NEWNESS, originality, freshness, innovation, surprise, uniqueness, strangeness, unfamiliarity **2** CURIOSITY, marvel, rarity, oddity, wonder **3** TRINKET, souvenir, memento, bauble, bagatelle, gimcrack, trifle, gewgaw, knick-knack

novice *noun* BEGINNER, pupil, amateur, newcomer, trainee, apprentice, learner,

neophyte, tyro, probationer, proselyte
<< ANTONYM expert

now *adverb* **1** NOWADAYS, at the moment, these days **2** IMMEDIATELY, presently (*Scot & US*), promptly, instantly, at once, straightaway ▷▷ **now and then** *or* **again** OCCASIONALLY, sometimes, at times, from time to time, on and off, on occasion, once in a while, intermittently, infrequently, sporadically

nowadays *adverb* NOW, today, at the moment, these days, in this day and age

noxious *adjective* HARMFUL, deadly, poisonous, unhealthy, hurtful, pernicious, injurious, unwholesome, noisome, pestilential, insalubrious, foul << ANTONYM harmless

nuance *noun* SUBTLETY, degree, distinction, graduation, refinement, nicety, gradation

nub *noun* GIST, point, heart, core, essence, nucleus, kernel, crux, pith

nubile *adjective* ATTRACTIVE, sexy (*informal*), desirable, ripe (*informal*), marriageable

nucleus *noun* CENTRE, heart, focus, basis, core, pivot, kernel, nub

nude *adjective* NAKED, stripped, exposed, bare, uncovered, undressed, stark-naked, in the raw (*informal*), disrobed, starkers (*informal*), unclothed, in the buff (*informal*), au naturel (*French*), in the altogether (*informal*), buck naked (*slang*), unclad, undraped, in your birthday suit (*informal*), scuddy (*slang*), without a stitch on (*informal*), in the bare scud (*slang*), naked as the day you were born (*informal*) << ANTONYM dressed

nudge *verb* **1** PUSH, touch, dig, jog, prod, elbow, shove, poke **2** PROMPT, influence, urge, persuade, spur, prod, coax, prevail upon ▷ *noun* **1** PUSH, touch, dig, elbow, bump, shove, poke, jog, prod **2** PROMPTING, push, encouragement, prod

nudity *noun* NAKEDNESS, undress, nudism, bareness, deshabille

nugget *noun* LUMP, piece, mass, chunk, clump, hunk

nuisance *noun* TROUBLE, problem, trial, bore, drag (*informal*), bother, plague, pest, irritation, hassle (*informal*), inconvenience, annoyance, pain (*informal*), pain in the neck (*informal*), pain in the backside (*informal*), pain in the butt (*informal*) << ANTONYM benefit

null ▷▷ **null and void** INVALID, useless, void, worthless, ineffectual, valueless, inoperative

nullify *verb* **1** INVALIDATE, quash, revoke, render null and void, abolish, void, repeal,

rescind, annul, abrogate << ANTONYM validate **2** CANCEL OUT, counteract, negate, neutralize, obviate, countervail, bring to naught

numb *adjective* **1** UNFEELING, dead, frozen, paralysed, insensitive, deadened, immobilized, torpid, insensible << ANTONYM sensitive **2** STUPEFIED, deadened, unfeeling, insensible ▷ *verb* **1** STUN, knock out, paralyse, daze, stupefy **2** DEADEN, freeze, dull, paralyse, immobilize, benumb

number *noun* **1** NUMERAL, figure, character, digit, integer **2** AMOUNT, quantity, collection, total, count, sum, aggregate << ANTONYM shortage **3** CROWD, horde, multitude, throng **4** GROUP, company, set, band, crowd, gang, coterie **5** ISSUE, copy, edition, imprint, printing ▷ *verb* **1** AMOUNT TO, come to, total, add up to **2** CALCULATE, account, reckon, compute, enumerate << ANTONYM guess **3** INCLUDE, count

numbered *adjective* **1** RECKONED, totalled, counted **2** LIMITED, restricted, limited in number

numbness *noun* **1** DEADNESS, paralysis, insensitivity, dullness, torpor, insensibility **2** TORPOR, deadness, dullness, stupefaction

numeral *noun* NUMBER, figure, digit, character, symbol, cipher, integer

numerous *adjective* MANY, several, countless, lots, abundant, plentiful, innumerable, copious, manifold, umpteen (*informal*), profuse, thick on the ground << ANTONYM few

nuptial *adjective* MARITAL, wedding, wedded, bridal, matrimonial, conjugal, connubial, hymeneal (*poetic*)

nuptials *plural noun sometimes singular* WEDDING, marriage, matrimony, espousal (*archaic*)

nurse *verb* **1** LOOK AFTER, treat, tend, care for, take care of, minister to **2** HARBOUR, have, maintain, preserve, entertain, cherish, keep alive **3** BREAST-FEED, feed, nurture, nourish, suckle, wet-nurse

nursery *noun* CRÈCHE, kindergarten, playgroup, play-centre (*NZ*)

nurture *noun* UPBRINGING, training, education, instruction, rearing, development ▷ *verb* BRING UP, raise, look after, rear, care for, develop << ANTONYM neglect

nut *noun* **1** KERNEL, stone, seed, pip **2** (*slang*) MADMAN, eccentric, flake (*slang, chiefly US*), psycho (*slang*), crank (*informal*), lunatic, maniac, loony (*slang*), nutter (*Brit slang*), oddball (*informal*), crackpot (*informal*), wacko (*slang*), nutcase (*slang*), headcase (*informal*) **3** (*slang*) HEAD, skull, noggin

nutrition *noun* FOOD, nourishment, sustenance, nutriment

nutritious *adjective* NOURISHING, beneficial, wholesome, healthful, health-giving, nutritive

nuts *adjective* (*slang*) INSANE, mad, crazy (*informal*), bananas (*slang*), barking (*slang*), eccentric, batty (*slang*), psycho (*slang*), irrational, loony (*slang*), demented, nutty (*slang*), deranged, loopy (*informal*), out to lunch (*informal*), barking mad (*slang*), gonzo (*slang*), doolally (*slang*), off your trolley (*slang*), up the pole (*informal*), as daft as a brush (*informal, chiefly Brit*), not the full shilling (*informal*), wacko *or* whacko (*informal*), off the air (*Austral slang*) ▷▷ **nuts and bolts** (*informal*) ESSENTIALS, basics, fundamentals, nitty-gritty (*informal*), practicalities, ins and outs, details

nuzzle *verb* SNUGGLE, cuddle, nudge, burrow, nestle

nymph *noun* **1** (*mythology*) SYLPH, dryad, naiad, hamadryad, Oceanid (*Greek myth*), oread **2** (*chiefly poetic*) GIRL, lass, maiden, maid, damsel

oasis *noun* 1 WATERING HOLE 2 HAVEN, retreat, refuge, sanctuary, island, resting place, sanctum

oath *noun* 1 PROMISE, bond, pledge, vow, word, compact, covenant, affirmation, sworn statement, avowal, word of honour 2 SWEAR WORD, curse, obscenity, blasphemy, expletive, four-letter word, cuss (*informal*), profanity, strong language, imprecation, malediction

obedience *noun* COMPLIANCE, yielding, submission, respect, conformity, reverence, deference, observance, subservience, submissiveness, docility, complaisance, tractability, dutifulness, conformability << ANTONYM disobedience

obedient *adjective* SUBMISSIVE, yielding, compliant, under control, respectful, law-abiding, well-trained, amenable, docile, dutiful, subservient, deferential, tractable, acquiescent, biddable, accommodating, passive, meek, ingratiating, malleable, pliant, unresisting, bootlicking (*informal*), obeisant, duteous << ANTONYM disobedient

obese *adjective* FAT, overweight, heavy, solid, gross, plump, stout, fleshy, beefy (*informal*), tubby, portly, outsize, roly-poly, rotund, podgy, corpulent, elephantine, paunchy, well-upholstered (*informal*), Falstaffian << ANTONYM thin

obesity *or* **obeseness** *noun* FATNESS, flab, heaviness, a weight problem, grossness, corpulence, beef (*informal*), embonpoint (*French*), rotundity, fleshiness, stoutness, portliness, bulkiness, podginess, tubbiness << ANTONYM thinness

obey *verb* 1 SUBMIT TO, surrender (to), give way to, succumb to, bow to, give in to, yield to, serve, cave in to (*informal*), take orders from, do what you are told by << ANTONYM disobey 2 SUBMIT, yield, surrender, give in, give way, succumb, cave in, toe the line, knuckle under (*informal*), do what is expected, come to heel, get into line 3 CARRY OUT, follow, perform, respond to, implement, fulfil, execute, discharge, act upon, carry through << ANTONYM disregard 4 ABIDE BY, keep, follow, comply with, observe, mind, embrace, hold to, heed, conform to, keep to, adhere to, be ruled by

object¹ *noun* 1 THING, article, device, body, item, implement, entity, gadget, contrivance 2 PURPOSE, aim, end, point, plan, idea, reason, goal, design, target, principle, function, intention, objective, intent, motive, end in view, end purpose, the why and wherefore 3 TARGET, victim, focus, butt, recipient

object² *verb* 1 *often with* **to** PROTEST AGAINST, oppose, say no to, kick against (*informal*), argue against, draw the line at, take exception to, raise objections to, cry out against, complain against, take up the cudgels against, expostulate against << ANTONYM accept 2 DISAGREE, demur, remonstrate, expostulate, express disapproval << ANTONYM agree

objection *noun* PROTEST, opposition, complaint, doubt, exception, dissent, outcry, censure, disapproval, niggle (*informal*), protestation, scruple, demur, formal complaint, counter-argument, cavil, remonstrance, demurral << ANTONYM agreement

objectionable *adjective* OFFENSIVE, annoying, irritating, unacceptable, unpleasant, rude, intolerable, undesirable, distasteful, obnoxious, deplorable, displeasing, unseemly, disagreeable, repugnant, abhorrent, beyond the pale, insufferable, detestable, discourteous, uncivil, unmannerly, exceptionable, dislikable *or* dislikeable << ANTONYM pleasant

objective *adjective* 1 FACTUAL, real, circumstantial 2 UNBIASED, detached, just, fair, judicial, even-minded, equitable, impartial, impersonal, disinterested, even-handed, dispassionate, unemotional, uninvolved, unprejudiced, uncoloured << ANTONYM subjective ▷ *noun* PURPOSE, aim, goal, end, plan, hope, idea, design, target, wish, scheme, desire, object, intention, ambition, aspiration, Holy Grail (*informal*), end in view, why and wherefore

objectively *adverb* IMPARTIALLY, neutrally, fairly, justly, without prejudice, dispassionately, with an open mind, equitably, without fear or favour, even-handedly, without bias, disinterestedly, with objectivity *or* impartiality

objectivity *noun* IMPARTIALITY, detachment, neutrality, equity, fairness, disinterest, open-mindedness, even-handedness, impersonality, disinterestedness, dispassion, nonpartisanship, lack of bias, equitableness << ANTONYM subjectivity

obligation *noun* 1 DUTY, compulsion 2 TASK, job, duty, work, calling, business, charge, role, function, mission, province, assignment, pigeon (*informal*), chore 3 RESPONSIBILITY, duty, liability, accountability, culpability, answerability, accountableness

obligatory *adjective* 1 COMPULSORY, required, necessary, essential, binding, enforced, mandatory, imperative, unavoidable, requisite, coercive, de rigueur (*French*) << ANTONYM optional 2 CUSTOMARY, regular, usual, popular, normal, familiar, conventional, fashionable, bog-standard (*Brit & Irish slang*)

oblige *verb* 1 COMPEL, make, force, require, bind, railroad (*informal*), constrain, necessitate, coerce, impel, dragoon, obligate 2 HELP, assist, serve, benefit, please, favour, humour, accommodate, indulge, gratify, do someone a service, put yourself out for, do (someone) a favour *or* a kindness, meet the wants *or* needs of << ANTONYM bother

obliged *adjective* 1 FORCED, required, bound, compelled, obligated, duty-bound, under an obligation, under compulsion, without any option 2 GRATEFUL, in (someone's) debt, thankful, indebted, appreciative, beholden

obliging *adjective* ACCOMMODATING, kind,

helpful, willing, civil, friendly, polite, cooperative, agreeable, amiable, courteous, considerate, hospitable, unselfish, good-natured, eager to please, complaisant << ANTONYM unhelpful

oblique *adjective* 1 INDIRECT, implied, roundabout, backhanded, evasive, elliptical, circuitous, circumlocutory, inexplicit, periphrastic << ANTONYM direct 2 SLANTING, angled, sloped, sloping, inclined, tilted, tilting, slanted, diagonal, at an angle, asymmetrical, canted, aslant, slantwise, atilt, cater-cornered (*US informal*) 3 SIDELONG, sideways, covert, indirect, furtive, surreptitious

obliquely *adverb* 1 INDIRECTLY, evasively, not in so many words, circuitously, in a roundabout manner *or* way 2 AT AN ANGLE, sideways, diagonally, sidelong, aslant, slantwise, aslope

obliterate *verb* 1 DESTROY, eliminate, devastate, waste, wreck, wipe out, demolish, ravage, eradicate, desolate, annihilate, put paid to, raze, blow to bits, extirpate, blow sky-high, destroy root and branch, kennet (*Austral slang*), jeff (*Austral slang*), wipe from or off the face of the earth << ANTONYM create 2 ERADICATE, remove, eliminate, cancel, get rid of, wipe out, erase, excise, delete, extinguish, root out, efface, blot out, expunge, extirpate

oblivion *noun* NEGLECT, anonymity, insignificance, obscurity, limbo, nothingness, unimportance

oblivious *adjective usually with* **of** *or* **to** UNAWARE, unconscious, ignorant, regardless, careless, negligent, blind to, unaffected by, impervious to, forgetful, deaf to, unconcerned about, neglectful, heedless, inattentive, insensible, unmindful, unobservant, disregardful, incognizant << ANTONYM aware

obnoxious *adjective* LOATHSOME, offensive, nasty, foul, disgusting, unpleasant, revolting, obscene, sickening, vile, horrid, repellent, repulsive, objectionable, disagreeable, nauseating, odious, hateful, repugnant, reprehensible, abhorrent, abominable, insufferable, execrable, detestable, hateable, dislikable *or* dislikeable, yucky *or* yukky (*slang*), yucko (*Austral slang*) << ANTONYM pleasant

obscene *adjective* 1 INDECENT, dirty, offensive, gross, foul, coarse, filthy, vile, improper, immoral, pornographic, suggestive, blue, loose, shameless, lewd, depraved, X-rated (*informal*), bawdy, salacious, prurient, impure, lascivious, smutty, ribald, unwholesome, scabrous, immodest, licentious, indelicate, unchaste << ANTONYM decent 2 OFFENSIVE, shocking, evil, disgusting, outrageous, revolting, sickening, vile, wicked, repellent, atrocious, obnoxious, heinous, nauseating, odious, loathsome, abominable, detestable

obscenity *noun* 1 INDECENCY, pornography, impurity, impropriety, vulgarity, smut, prurience, coarseness, crudity, licentiousness, foulness, outrageousness, blueness, immodesty, suggestiveness, lewdness, dirtiness, grossness, vileness, filthiness, bawdiness, unseemliness, indelicacy, smuttiness, salacity << ANTONYM decency 2 SWEAR WORD, curse, oath, expletive, four-letter word, cuss (*informal*), profanity, vulgarism

obscure *adjective* 1 UNKNOWN, minor, little-known, humble, unfamiliar, out-of-the-way, unseen, lowly, unimportant, unheard-of, unsung, nameless, undistinguished, inconspicuous, unnoted, unhonoured, unrenowned << ANTONYM famous 2 ABSTRUSE, involved, complex, confusing, puzzling, subtle, mysterious, deep, vague, unclear, doubtful, mystical, intricate, ambiguous, enigmatic, esoteric, perplexing, occult, opaque, incomprehensible, arcane, cryptic, unfathomable, recondite, clear as mud (*informal*) << ANTONYM straightforward 3 UNCLEAR, hidden, uncertain, confused, mysterious, concealed, doubtful, indefinite, indeterminate << ANTONYM well-known 4 INDISTINCT, vague, blurred, dark, clouded, faint, dim, gloomy, veiled, murky, fuzzy, shadowy, cloudy, misty, hazy, indistinguishable, indeterminate, dusky, undefined, out of focus, ill-defined, obfuscated, indiscernible, tenebrous << ANTONYM clear ▷ *verb* 1 OBSTRUCT, hinder, block out 2 HIDE, cover (up), screen, mask, disguise, conceal, veil, cloak, shroud, camouflage, envelop, encase, enshroud << ANTONYM expose

obscurity *noun* 1 INSIGNIFICANCE, oblivion, unimportance, non-recognition, inconsequence, lowliness, inconspicuousness, namelessness, ingloriousness 2 VAGUENESS, complexity, ambiguity, intricacy, incomprehensibility, inexactitude, woolliness, abstruseness, impreciseness, impenetrableness, reconditeness, lack of preciseness << ANTONYM clarity 3 DARKNESS, dark, shadows, shade, gloom, haze, blackness, murk, dimness, murkiness, haziness, duskiness, shadiness, shadowiness, indistinctness

observable *adjective* NOTICEABLE, clear, obvious, open, striking, apparent, visible, patent, evident, distinct, manifest, blatant, conspicuous, unmistakable, discernible, salient, recognizable, detectable, perceptible, appreciable, perceivable

observance *noun* 1 *with of* CARRYING OUT OF, attention to, performance of, respect for, notice of, honouring of, observation of, compliance with, adherence to, fulfilment of, discharge of, obedience to, keeping of, heeding of, conformity to << ANTONYM disregard for 2 CEREMONY, rite, procedure, service, form, act, practice, tradition, celebration, custom, ritual, formality, ceremonial, ordinance, liturgy

observant *adjective* 1 ATTENTIVE, quick, alert, perceptive, concentrating, careful, vigilant, mindful, watchful, wide-awake, sharp-eyed, eagle-eyed, keen-eyed, on your toes, heedful << ANTONYM unobservant 2 DEVOUT, godly, holy, orthodox, pious, obedient, reverent

observation *noun* 1 WATCHING, study, survey, review, notice, investigation, monitoring, attention, consideration, examination, inspection, scrutiny, surveillance, contemplation, cognition, perusal 2 COMMENT, finding, thought, note, statement, opinion, remark, explanation, reflection, exposition, utterance, pronouncement, annotation, elucidation, obiter dictum 3 REMARK, thought, comment, statement, opinion, reflection, assertion, utterance, animadversion 4 *with of* OBSERVANCE OF, attention to, compliance with, notice of, honouring of, adherence to, fulfilment of, discharge of, heeding of, carrying out of

observe *verb* 1 WATCH, study, view, look at, note, check, regard, survey, monitor, contemplate, check out (*informal*), look on, keep an eye on (*informal*), gaze at, pay attention to, keep track of, scrutinize, keep tabs on (*informal*), recce (*slang*), keep under observation, watch like a hawk, take a dekko at (*Brit slang*) 2 NOTICE, see, note, mark, discover, spot, regard, witness, clock (*Brit slang*), distinguish, perceive, detect, discern, behold (*archaic* or *literary*), eye, eyeball (*slang*), peer at, espy, get a load of (*informal*) **3** REMARK, say, comment, state, note, reflect, mention, declare, opine, pass comment, animadvert **4** COMPLY WITH, keep, follow, mind, respect, perform, carry out, honour, fulfil, discharge, obey, heed, conform to, adhere to, abide by << ANTONYM disregard

observer *noun* **1** WITNESS, viewer, spectator, looker-on, watcher, onlooker, eyewitness, bystander, spotter, fly on the wall, beholder **2** COMMENTATOR, commenter, reporter, special correspondent **3** MONITOR, inspector, watchdog, supervisor, overseer, scrutineer

obsess *verb* PREOCCUPY, dominate, grip, absorb, possess, consume, rule, haunt, plague, hound, torment, bedevil, monopolize, be on your mind, engross, prey on your mind, be uppermost in your thoughts

obsessed *adjective often with* **with** *or* **by** ABSORBED, dominated, gripped, caught up, haunted, distracted, hung up (*slang*), preoccupied, immersed, beset, in the grip, infatuated, fixated, having a one-track mind << ANTONYM indifferent

obsession *noun* PREOCCUPATION, thing (*informal*), complex, enthusiasm, addiction, hang-up (*informal*), mania, phobia, fetish, fixation, infatuation, ruling passion, pet subject, hobbyhorse, idée fixe (*French*), bee in your bonnet (*informal*)

obsessive *adjective* COMPULSIVE, fixed, gripping, consuming, haunting, tormenting, irresistible, neurotic, besetting, uncontrollable, obsessional

obsolete *adjective* OUTDATED, old, passé, ancient, antique, old-fashioned, dated, discarded, extinct, past it, out of date, archaic, disused, out of fashion, out, antiquated, anachronistic, outmoded, musty, old hat, behind the times, superannuated, antediluvian, outworn, démodé (*French*), out of the ark (*informal*), vieux jeu (*French*) << ANTONYM up-to-date

obstacle *noun* **1** OBSTRUCTION, block, barrier, hurdle, hazard, snag, impediment, blockage, hindrance **2** HINDRANCE, check, bar, block, difficulty, barrier, handicap, hurdle, hitch, drawback, snag, deterrent, uphill (*S African*), obstruction, stumbling block, impediment << ANTONYM help

obstinacy *noun* STUBBORNNESS, persistence, tenacity, perseverance, resolution,

intransigence, firmness, single-mindedness, inflexibility, obduracy, doggedness, relentlessness, wilfulness, resoluteness, pig-headedness, pertinacity, tenaciousness, mulishness << ANTONYM flexibility

obstinate *adjective* STUBBORN, dogged, determined, persistent, firm, perverse, intractable, inflexible, wilful, tenacious, recalcitrant, steadfast, unyielding, opinionated, intransigent, immovable, headstrong, unmanageable, cussed, strong-minded, unbending, obdurate, stiff-necked, unshakable, self-willed, refractory, pig-headed, bull-headed, mulish, contumacious, pertinacious << ANTONYM flexible

obstruct *verb* **1** BLOCK, close, bar, cut off, plug, choke, clog, barricade, shut off, stop up, bung up (*informal*) **2** HOLD UP, stop, check, bar, block, prevent, arrest, restrict, interrupt, slow down, hamstring, interfere with, hamper, inhibit, clog, hinder, retard, impede, get in the way of, bring to a standstill, cumber **3** IMPEDE, prevent, frustrate, hold up, slow down, hamstring, interfere with, hamper, hold back, thwart, hinder, retard, get in the way of, trammel, cumber << ANTONYM help **4** OBSCURE, screen, cut off, cover, hide, mask, shield

obstruction *noun* **1** OBSTACLE, bar, block, difficulty, barrier, hazard, barricade, snag, impediment, hindrance **2** BLOCKAGE, stoppage, occlusion **3** HINDRANCE, stop, check, bar, block, difficulty, barrier, restriction, handicap, obstacle, restraint, deterrent, stumbling block, impediment, trammel << ANTONYM help

obstructive *adjective* UNHELPFUL, difficult, awkward, blocking, delaying, contrary, stalling, inhibiting, restrictive, hindering, uncooperative, disobliging, unaccommodating << ANTONYM helpful

obtain *verb* **1** GET, gain, acquire, land, net, pick up, bag, secure, get hold of, come by, procure, get your hands on, score (*slang*), come into possession of << ANTONYM lose **2** ACHIEVE, get, gain, realize, accomplish, attain **3** (*formal*) PREVAIL, hold, stand, exist, be the case, abound, predominate, be in force, be current, be prevalent

obtainable *adjective* **1** AVAILABLE, to be had, procurable **2** ATTAINABLE, accessible, achievable, at your fingertips, at your disposal, reachable, realizable, gettable, accomplishable

obtuse *adjective* STUPID, simple, slow, thick,

dull, dim, dense, dumb (*informal*), sluggish, retarded, simple-minded, dozy (*Brit informal*), witless, stolid, dopey (*informal*), moronic, brainless, uncomprehending, cretinous, unintelligent, half-witted, slow on the uptake (*informal*), braindead (*informal*), dumb-ass (*informal*), doltish, dead from the neck up (*informal*), boneheaded (*slang*), thickheaded, dull-witted, imperceptive, slow-witted, muttonheaded (*slang*), thick as mince (*Scot informal*), woodenheaded (*informal*) << ANTONYM clever

obviate *verb* (*formal*) AVERT, avoid, remove, prevent, counter, do away with, preclude, counteract, ward off, stave off, forestall, render unnecessary

obvious *adjective* CLEAR, open, plain, apparent, visible, bold, patent, evident, distinct, pronounced, straightforward, explicit, manifest, transparent, noticeable, blatant, conspicuous, overt, unmistakable, palpable, unequivocal, undeniable, salient, recognizable, unambiguous, self-evident, indisputable, perceptible, much in evidence, unquestionable, open-and-shut, cut-and-dried (*informal*), undisguised, incontrovertible, self-explanatory, unsubtle, unconcealed, clear as a bell, staring you in the face (*informal*), right under your nose (*informal*), sticking out a mile (*informal*), plain as the nose on your face (*informal*) << ANTONYM unclear

obviously *adverb* 1 CLEARLY, of course, certainly, needless to say, without doubt, assuredly 2 PLAINLY, patently, undoubtedly, evidently, manifestly, markedly, without doubt, unquestionably, undeniably, beyond doubt, palpably, indubitably, incontrovertibly, irrefutably, incontestably

occasion *noun* 1 TIME, moment, point, stage, incident, instance, occurrence, juncture 2 FUNCTION, event, affair, do (*informal*), happening, experience, gathering, celebration, occurrence, social occasion 3 OPPORTUNITY, chance, time, opening, window 4 REASON, cause, call, ground(s), basis, excuse, incentive, motive, warrant, justification, provocation, inducement ▷ *verb* (*formal*) CAUSE, begin, produce, create, effect, lead to, inspire, result in, generate, prompt, provoke, induce, bring about, originate, evoke, give rise to, precipitate, elicit, incite, engender

occasional *adjective* INFREQUENT, odd, rare, casual, irregular, sporadic, intermittent, few and far between, desultory, periodic << ANTONYM constant

occasionally *adverb* SOMETIMES, at times, from time to time, on and off, now and then, irregularly, on occasion, now and again, periodically, once in a while, every so often, at intervals, off and on, (every) now and then << ANTONYM constantly

occult *adjective* SUPERNATURAL, dark, magical, mysterious, psychic, mystical, mystic, unearthly, unnatural, esoteric, uncanny, arcane, paranormal, abstruse, recondite, preternatural, cabbalistic, supranatural ▷▷ **the occult** MAGIC, witchcraft, sorcery, wizardry, enchantment, occultism, black art, necromancy, theurgy

occultism *noun* BLACK MAGIC, magic, witchcraft, wizardry, sorcery, the black arts, necromancy, diabolism, theurgy, supernaturalism

occupancy *noun* OCCUPATION, use, residence, holding, term, possession, tenure, tenancy, habitation, inhabitancy

occupant *noun* OCCUPIER, resident, tenant, user, holder, inmate, inhabitant, incumbent, dweller, denizen, addressee, lessee, indweller

occupation *noun* 1 JOB, work, calling, business, line (of work), office, trade, position, post, career, situation, activity, employment, craft, profession, pursuit, vocation, livelihood, walk of life 2 HOBBY, pastime, diversion, relaxation, sideline, leisure pursuit, (leisure) activity 3 INVASION, seizure, conquest, incursion, subjugation, foreign rule 4 OCCUPANCY, use, residence, holding, control, possession, tenure, tenancy, habitation, inhabitancy

occupied *adjective* 1 IN USE, taken, full, engaged, unavailable 2 INHABITED, peopled, lived-in, settled, tenanted << ANTONYM uninhabited 3 BUSY, engaged, employed, working, active, tied up (*informal*), engrossed, hard at work, in harness, hard at it (*informal*), rushed off your feet

occupy *verb* 1 INHABIT, own, live in, stay in (*Scot*), be established in, dwell in, be in residence in, establish yourself in, ensconce yourself in, tenant, reside in, lodge in, take up residence in, make your home, abide in << ANTONYM vacate 2 INVADE, take over, capture, seize, conquer, keep, hold, garrison, overrun, annex, take possession of, colonize << ANTONYM withdraw 3 HOLD, control, dominate, possess 4 TAKE UP, consume, tie up, use up, monopolize, keep busy *or* occupied **5** *often passive* ENGAGE, interest, involve, employ, busy, entertain, absorb, amuse, divert, preoccupy, immerse, hold the attention of, engross, keep busy *or* occupied **6** FILL, take up, cover, fill up, utilize, pervade, permeate, extend over

occur *verb* **1** HAPPEN, take place, come about, follow, result, chance, arise, turn up (*informal*), come off (*informal*), ensue, crop up (*informal*), transpire (*informal*), befall, materialize, come to pass (*archaic*), betide, eventuate **2** EXIST, appear, be found, develop, obtain, turn up, be present, be met with, manifest itself, present itself, show itself ▷▷ **occur to someone** COME TO MIND, strike someone, dawn on someone, come to you, spring to mind, cross someone's mind, present itself to someone, enter someone's head, offer itself to someone, suggest itself to someone

occurrence *noun* **1** INCIDENT, happening, event, fact, matter, affair, proceeding, circumstance, episode, adventure, phenomenon, transaction **2** EXISTENCE, instance, appearance, manifestation, materialization

odd *adjective* **1** PECULIAR, strange, unusual, different, funny, extraordinary, bizarre, weird, exceptional, eccentric, abnormal, queer, rum (*Brit slang*), deviant, unconventional, far-out (*slang*), quaint, kinky (*informal*), off-the-wall (*slang*), outlandish, whimsical, oddball (*informal*), out of the ordinary, offbeat, left-field (*informal*), freakish, freaky (*slang*), wacko (*slang*), outré, daggy (*Austral & NZ informal*) **2** UNUSUAL, different, strange, rare, funny (*slang*), extraordinary, remarkable, bizarre, fantastic, curious, weird, exceptional, peculiar, abnormal, queer, irregular, uncommon, singular, uncanny, outlandish, out of the ordinary, freakish, atypical, freaky << ANTONYM normal **3** OCCASIONAL, various, varied, random, casual, seasonal, irregular, periodic, miscellaneous, sundry, incidental, intermittent, infrequent << ANTONYM regular **4** SPARE, remaining, extra, surplus, single, lone, solitary, uneven, leftover, unmatched, unpaired << ANTONYM matched ▷▷ **odd man** *or* **odd one out** MISFIT, exception, outsider, freak, eccentric, maverick, oddball (*informal*), nonconformist, fish out of water (*informal*), square peg in a round hole (*informal*)

oddity *noun* **1** MISFIT, eccentric, crank

(*informal*), nut (*slang*), maverick, flake (*slang, chiefly US*), oddball (*informal*), loose cannon, nonconformist, odd man out, wacko (*slang*), screwball (*slang, chiefly US & Canad*), card (*informal*), fish out of water, square peg (in a round hole) (*informal*), odd fish (*Brit informal*), odd bird (*informal*), rara avis, weirdo *or* weirdie (*informal*) **2** STRANGENESS, abnormality, peculiarity, eccentricity, weirdness, singularity, incongruity, oddness, unconventionality, queerness, unnaturalness, bizarreness, freakishness, extraordinariness, outlandishness **3** IRREGULARITY, phenomenon, anomaly, freak, abnormality, rarity, quirk, eccentricity, kink, peculiarity, idiosyncrasy, singularity, unorthodoxy, unconventionality

odds *plural noun* PROBABILITY, chances, likelihood ▷▷ **at odds 1** IN CONFLICT, arguing, quarrelling, in opposition to, at loggerheads, in disagreement, at daggers drawn, on bad terms **2** AT VARIANCE, conflicting, contrary to, at odds, out of line, out of step, at sixes and sevens (*informal*), not in keeping, out of harmony ▷▷ **odds and ends** SCRAPS, bits, pieces, remains, rubbish, fragments, litter, debris, shreds, remnants, bits and pieces, bric-a-brac, bits and bobs, oddments, odds and sods, leavings, miscellanea, sundry *or* miscellaneous items

odious *adjective* OFFENSIVE, nasty, foul, disgusting, horrible, unpleasant, revolting, obscene, sickening, vile, horrid, repellent, unsavoury, obnoxious, unpalatable, repulsive, disagreeable, nauseating, hateful, repugnant, loathsome, abhorrent, abominable, execrable, detestable, yucky *or* yukky (*slang*), yucko (*Austral slang*) << ANTONYM delightful

odour *or US* **odor** *noun* **1** SMELL, scent, perfume, fragrance, stink, bouquet, aroma, whiff, stench, pong (*Brit informal*), niff (*Brit slang*), redolence, malodour, fetor **2** ATMOSPHERE, feeling, air, quality, spirit, tone, climate, flavour, aura, vibe (*slang*)

Odyssey *noun often not cap.* JOURNEY, tour, trip, passage, quest, trek, expedition, voyage, crusade, excursion, pilgrimage, jaunt, peregrination

of *preposition* ABOUT, on, concerning, regarding, with respect to, as regards

off *adverb* **1** AWAY, out, apart, elsewhere, aside, hence, from here **2** ABSENT, gone, unavailable, not present, inoperative, nonattendant ▷ *adjective* **1** CANCELLED, abandoned, postponed, shelved **2** BAD, rotten, rancid, mouldy, high, turned, spoiled, sour, decayed, decomposed, putrid **3** UNACCEPTABLE, poor, unsatisfactory, disappointing, inadequate, second-rate, shoddy, displeasing, below par, mortifying, substandard, disheartening ▷▷ **off and on** OCCASIONALLY, sometimes, at times, from time to time, on and off, now and then, irregularly, on occasion, now and again, periodically, once in a while, every so often, intermittently, at intervals, sporadically, every once in a while, (every) now and again

offbeat *adjective* UNUSUAL, odd, strange, novel, extraordinary, bizarre, weird, way-out (*informal*), eccentric, queer, rum (*Brit slang*), uncommon, Bohemian, unconventional, far-out (*slang*), idiosyncratic, kinky (*informal*), off-the-wall (*slang*), unorthodox, oddball (*informal*), out of the ordinary, left-field (*informal*), freaky (*slang*), wacko (*slang*), outré, daggy (*Austral & NZ informal*) << ANTONYM conventional

offence *or US* **offense** *noun* **1** CRIME, wrong, sin, lapse, fault, violation, wrongdoing, trespass, felony, misdemeanour, delinquency, misdeed, transgression, peccadillo, unlawful act, breach of conduct **2** OUTRAGE, shock, anger, trouble, bother, grief (*informal*), resentment, irritation, hassle (*informal*), wrath, indignation, annoyance, ire (*literary*), displeasure, pique, aggravation, hard feelings, umbrage, vexation, wounded feelings **3** INSULT, injury, slight, hurt, harm, outrage, put-down (*slang*), injustice, snub, affront, indignity, displeasure, rudeness, slap in the face (*informal*), insolence ▷▷ **take offence** BE OFFENDED, resent, be upset, be outraged, be put out (*informal*), be miffed (*informal*), be displeased, take umbrage, be disgruntled, be affronted, be piqued, take the needle (*informal*), get riled, take the huff, go into a huff, be huffy

offend *verb* **1** DISTRESS, upset, outrage, pain, wound, slight, provoke, insult, annoy, irritate, put down, dismay, snub, aggravate (*informal*), gall, agitate, ruffle, disconcert, vex, affront, displease, rile, pique, give offence, hurt (someone's) feelings, nark (*Brit, Austral & NZ slang*), cut to the quick, miff (*informal*), tread on (someone's) toes (*informal*), put (someone's) nose out of joint, put (someone's) back up, disgruntle, get (someone's) goat (*slang*), hack you off (*informal*) << ANTONYM please **2** DISGUST,

revolt, turn (someone) off (*informal*), put off, sicken, repel, repulse, nauseate, gross out (*US slang*), make (someone) sick, turn your stomach, be disagreeable to, fill with loathing **3** BREAK THE LAW, sin, err, do wrong, fall, fall from grace, go astray

offended *adjective* UPSET, pained, hurt, bothered, disturbed, distressed, outraged, stung, put out (*informal*), grieved, disgruntled, agitated, ruffled, resentful, affronted, miffed (*informal*), displeased, in a huff, piqued, huffy, tooshie (*Austral slang*)

offender *noun* CRIMINAL, convict, con (*slang*), crook, lag (*slang*), villain, culprit, sinner, delinquent, felon, jailbird, wrongdoer, miscreant, malefactor, evildoer, transgressor, lawbreaker

offensive *adjective* **1** INSULTING, rude, abusive, embarrassing, slighting, annoying, irritating, degrading, affronting, contemptuous, disparaging, displeasing, objectionable, disrespectful, scurrilous, detestable, discourteous, uncivil, unmannerly << ANTONYM respectful **2** DISGUSTING, gross, nasty, foul, unpleasant, revolting, stinking, sickening, vile, repellent, unsavoury, obnoxious, unpalatable, objectionable, disagreeable, nauseating, odious, repugnant, loathsome, abominable, grotty (*slang*), detestable, noisome, yucky *or* yukky (*slang*), festy (*Austral slang*), yucko (*Austral slang*) << ANTONYM pleasant **3** ATTACKING, threatening, aggressive, striking, hostile, invading, combative << ANTONYM defensive ▷ *noun* ATTACK, charge, campaign, strike, push (*informal*), rush, assault, raid, drive, invasion, onslaught, foray, incursion

offer *verb* **1** PRESENT WITH, give, hand, hold out to **2** PROVIDE, present, furnish, make available, afford, place at (someone's) disposal << ANTONYM withhold **3** VOLUNTEER, come forward, offer your services, be at (someone's) service **4** PROPOSE, suggest, advance, extend, submit, put forward, put forth **5** GIVE, show, bring, provide, render, impart **6** PUT UP FOR SALE, sell, put on the market, put under the hammer **7** BID, submit, propose, extend, tender, proffer ▷ *noun* **1** PROPOSAL, suggestion, proposition, submission, attempt, endeavour, overture **2** BID, tender, bidding price

offering *noun* **1** CONTRIBUTION, gift, donation, present, subscription, hand-out, stipend, widow's mite **2** SACRIFICE, tribute, libation, burnt offering, oblation (*in religious contexts*)

offhand *adjective* CASUAL, informal, indifferent, careless, abrupt, cavalier, aloof, unconcerned, curt, uninterested, glib, cursory, couldn't-care-less, apathetic, perfunctory, blasé, brusque, take-it-or-leave-it (*informal*), nonchalant, lackadaisical, unceremonious, offhanded << ANTONYM attentive ▷ *adverb* OFF THE CUFF (*informal*), spontaneously, impromptu, just like that (*informal*), ad lib, extempore, off the top of your head (*informal*), without preparation, extemporaneously

office *noun* **1** PLACE OF WORK, workplace, base, workroom, place of business **2** BRANCH, department, division, section, wing, subdivision, subsection **3** POST, place, role, work, business, service, charge, situation, commission, station, responsibility, duty, function, employment, capacity, appointment, occupation ▷ *plural noun* SUPPORT, help, backing, aid, favour, assistance, intervention, recommendation, patronage, mediation, advocacy, auspices, aegis, moral support, intercession, espousal

officer *noun* **1** OFFICIAL, executive, agent, representative, bureaucrat, public servant, appointee, dignitary, functionary, office-holder, office bearer **2** POLICE OFFICER, detective, PC, police constable, police man, police woman

official *adjective* **1** AUTHORIZED, approved, formal, sanctioned, licensed, proper, endorsed, warranted, legitimate, authentic, ratified, certified, authoritative, accredited, bona fide, signed and sealed, ex officio, ex cathedra, straight from the horse's mouth (*informal*) << ANTONYM unofficial **2** FORMAL, prescribed, bureaucratic, ceremonial, solemn, ritualistic ▷ *noun* OFFICER, executive, agent, representative, bureaucrat, public servant, appointee, dignitary, functionary, office-holder, office bearer

officiate *verb* **1** PRESIDE, conduct, celebrate **2** SUPERINTEND, supervise, be in charge, run, control, serve, manage, direct, handle, chair, look after, overlook, oversee, preside, take charge, adjudicate, emcee (*informal*)

offing ▷▷ **in the offing** IMMINENT, coming, close, near, coming up, gathering, on the way, in the air, forthcoming, looming, brewing, hovering, impending, at hand, upcoming, on the cards, on the horizon, in the wings, in the pipeline, nigh (*archaic*), in prospect, close at hand, fast-approaching, in the immediate future, just round the corner

off-key *adjective* CACOPHONOUS, harsh, jarring, grating, shrill, jangling, discordant, dissonant, inharmonious, unmelodious

off-load *verb* GET RID OF, shift, dump, dispose of, unload, dispense with, jettison, foist, see the back of, palm off

off-putting *adjective* (*informal*) DISCOURAGING, upsetting, disturbing, frustrating, nasty, formidable, intimidating, dismaying, unsettling, daunting, dampening, unnerving, disconcerting, unfavourable, dispiriting, discomfiting

offset *verb* CANCEL OUT, balance, set off, make up for, compensate for, redeem, counteract, neutralize, counterbalance, nullify, obviate, balance out, counterpoise, countervail

offshoot *noun* BY-PRODUCT, development, product, branch, supplement, complement, spin-off, auxiliary, adjunct, appendage, outgrowth, appurtenance

offspring *noun* **1** CHILD, baby, kid (*informal*), youngster, infant, successor, babe, toddler, heir, issue, tot, descendant, wean (*Scot*), little one, brat, bairn (*Scot*), nipper (*informal*), chit, scion, babe in arms (*informal*), sprog (*slang*), munchkin (*informal, chiefly US*), rug rat (*slang*), littlie (*Austral informal*), ankle-biter (*Austral slang*), tacker (*Austral slang*) << ANTONYM parent **2** CHILDREN, kids (*informal*), young, family, issue, stock, seed (*chiefly biblical*), fry, successors, heirs, spawn, descendants, brood, posterity, lineage, progeny, scions

often *adverb* FREQUENTLY, much, generally, commonly, repeatedly, again and again, very often, oft (*archaic or poetic*), over and over again, time and again, habitually, time after time, customarily, oftentimes (*archaic*), not infrequently, many a time, ofttimes (*archaic*) << ANTONYM never

ogle *verb* LEER AT, stare at, eye up (*informal*), gawp at (*Brit slang*), give the once-over (*informal*), make sheep's eyes at (*informal*), give the glad eye (*informal*), lech or letch after (*informal*)

ogre *noun* **1** FIEND, monster, beast, villain, brute, bogeyman **2** MONSTER, giant, devil, beast, demon, bogey, spectre, fiend, ghoul, bogeyman, bugbear

oil *noun* **1** LUBRICANT, grease, lubrication, fuel oil **2** LOTION, cream, balm, salve, liniment, embrocation, solution ▷ *verb* LUBRICATE, grease, make slippery

oily *adjective* **1** GREASY, slick, slimy, fatty, slippery, oleaginous, smeary **2** SYCOPHANTIC, smooth, flattering, slick, plausible, hypocritical, fawning, grovelling, glib, ingratiating, fulsome, deferential, servile, unctuous, obsequious, smarmy (*Brit informal*), mealy-mouthed, toadying

ointment *noun* SALVE, dressing, cream, lotion, balm, lubricant, emollient, liniment, embrocation, unguent, cerate

O.K. *or* **okay** *sentence substitute* ALL RIGHT, right, yes, agreed, very good, roger, very well, ya (*S African*), righto (*Brit informal*), okey-dokey (*informal*), yebo (*S African informal*) ▷ *adjective* (*informal*) **1** ALL RIGHT, fine, fitting, fair, in order, correct, approved, permitted, suitable, acceptable, convenient, allowable << ANTONYM unacceptable **2** FINE, good, average, middling, fair, all right, acceptable, adequate, satisfactory, not bad (*informal*), so-so (*informal*), tolerable, up to scratch (*informal*), passable, unobjectionable << ANTONYM unsatisfactory **3** WELL, all right, safe, sound, healthy, hale, unharmed, uninjured, unimpaired ▷ *verb* APPROVE, allow, pass, agree to, permit, sanction, second, endorse, authorize, ratify, go along with, consent to, validate, countenance, give the go-ahead, rubber-stamp (*informal*), say yes to, give the green light, assent to, give the thumbs up (*informal*), concur in, give your consent to, give your blessing to ▷ *noun* AUTHORIZATION, agreement, sanction, licence, approval, go-ahead (*informal*), blessing, permission, consent, say-so (*informal*), confirmation, mandate, endorsement, green light, ratification, assent, seal of approval, approbation

old *adjective* **1** AGED, elderly, ancient, getting on, grey, mature, past it (*informal*), venerable, patriarchal, grey-haired, antiquated, over the hill (*informal*), senile, grizzled, decrepit, hoary, senescent, advanced in years, full of years, past your prime << ANTONYM young **2** TUMBLEDOWN, ruined, crumbling, decayed, shaky, disintegrating, worn-out, done, tottering, ramshackle, rickety, decrepit, falling to pieces **3** WORN, ragged, shabby, frayed, cast-off, tattered, tatty, threadbare **4** OUT OF DATE, old-fashioned, dated, passé, antique, outdated, obsolete, archaic, unfashionable, antiquated, outmoded, behind the times, superannuated, out of style, antediluvian, out of the ark (*informal*), démodé (*French*) << ANTONYM up-to-date **5** FORMER, earlier, past, previous, prior, one-time, erstwhile, late, quondam, whilom (*archaic*), ex- **6** LONG-STANDING, established, fixed, enduring, abiding, long-lasting, long-established, time-honoured **7** EARLY, ancient, original, remote, of old, antique, aboriginal, primitive, archaic, gone by, bygone, undeveloped, primordial, primeval, immemorial, of yore, olden (*archaic*), pristine **8** STALE, common, commonplace, worn-out, banal, threadbare, trite, old hat, insipid, hackneyed, overused, repetitious, unoriginal, platitudinous, cliché-ridden, timeworn **9** LONG-ESTABLISHED, seasoned, experienced, tried, tested, trained, professional, skilled, expert, master, qualified, familiar, capable, veteran, practised, accomplished, vintage, versed, hardened, competent, skilful, adept, knowledgeable, age-old, of long standing, well-versed **10** CUSTOMARY, established, traditional, conventional, historic, long-established, time-honoured, of long standing ▷ see **senile**

old-fashioned *adjective* **1** OUT OF DATE, ancient, dated, outdated, unfashionable, antiquated, outmoded, passé, old hat, behind the times, fusty, out of style, démodé (*French*), out of the ark (*informal*), not with it (*informal*), (old-)fogeyish << ANTONYM up-to-date **2** OLDFANGLED, square (*informal*), outdated, old, past, dead, past it (*informal*), obsolete, old-time, archaic, unfashionable, superannuated, obsolescent, out of the ark (*informal*)

old man *noun* **1** SENIOR CITIZEN, grandfather (*slang*), patriarch, old age pensioner, old person, old-timer (*US*), elder, elder statesman, wrinkly (*informal*), old codger (*informal*), old stager, greybeard, coffin-dodger (*slang*), oldster (*informal*), O.A.P. (*Brit*), koro (*NZ*) **2** (*informal*) FATHER, pop (*informal*), dad (*informal*), daddy (*informal*), pa (*informal*), old boy (*informal*), papa (*old-fashioned informal*), pater, paterfamilias **3** MANAGER, boss (*informal*), supervisor, governor (*informal*), ganger, superintendent, gaffer (*informal*), foreman, overseer, baas (*S African*) ▷ see **old person**

old person *noun* SENIOR CITIZEN, senior, retired person, old age pensioner, elder, pensioner (*slang*), coffin-dodger (*slang*), elderly person, O.A.P. (*Brit*)

old-time *adjective* OLD-FASHIONED, traditional, vintage, ancient, antique, old-style, bygone

old-world *adjective* TRADITIONAL, old-fashioned, picturesque, quaint, archaic, gentlemanly, courteous, gallant, courtly, chivalrous, ceremonious

Olympian *adjective* MAJESTIC, kingly, regal, royal, august, grand, princely, imperial, glorious, noble, splendid, elevated, awesome, dignified, regal, stately, sublime, lofty, pompous, grandiose, exalted, rarefied, godlike

omen *noun* PORTENT, sign, warning, threat, indication, foreshadowing, foreboding, harbinger, presage, forewarning, writing on the wall, prognostication, augury, prognostic, foretoken

ominous *adjective* THREATENING, menacing, sinister, dark, forbidding, grim, fateful, foreboding, unpromising, portentous, baleful, inauspicious, premonitory, unpropitious, minatory, bodeful
<< ANTONYM promising

omission *noun* **1** EXCLUSION, removal, leaving out, elimination, deletion, excision, noninclusion << ANTONYM inclusion
2 FAILURE, neglect, default, negligence, oversight, carelessness, dereliction, forgetfulness, slackness, laxity, laxness, slovenliness, neglectfulness, remissness
3 GAP, space, blank, exclusion, lacuna

omit *verb* **1** LEAVE OUT, miss (out), drop, exclude, eliminate, skip, give (something) a miss (*informal*) << ANTONYM include
2 FORGET, fail, overlook, neglect, pass over, lose sight of, leave (something) undone, let (something) slide

omnipotence *noun* SUPREMACY, sovereignty, dominance, domination, mastery, primacy, ascendancy, pre-eminence, predominance, invincibility, supreme power, absolute rule, undisputed sway << ANTONYM powerlessness

omnipotent *adjective* ALMIGHTY, supreme, invincible, all-powerful << ANTONYM powerless

once *adverb* **1** ON ONE OCCASION, one time, one single time **2** AT ONE TIME, in the past, previously, formerly, long ago, in the old days, once upon a time, in times past, in times gone by ▷ *conjunction* AS SOON AS, when, after, the moment, immediately, the instant ▷▷ **at once 1** IMMEDIATELY, now, right now, straight away, directly, promptly, instantly, right away, without delay, without hesitation, forthwith, this (very) minute, pronto (*informal*), this instant, straightway (*archaic*), posthaste, tout de suite (*French*) **2** SIMULTANEOUSLY, together, at the same time, all together, in concert, in unison, concurrently, in the same breath, in chorus, at *or* in one go (*informal*) ▷▷ **once and for all** FOR THE LAST TIME, finally, completely, for good, positively, permanently, for ever, decisively, inexorably, conclusively, irrevocably, for all time, inescapably, with finality, beyond the shadow of a doubt ▷▷ **once in a while** OCCASIONALLY, sometimes, at times, from time to time, on and off, irregularly, on occasion, now and again, periodically, every now and then, every so often, at intervals, off and on

oncoming *adjective* **1** APPROACHING, advancing, looming, onrushing
2 FORTHCOMING, coming, approaching, expected, threatening, advancing, gathering, imminent, impending, upcoming, fast-approaching

one-horse *adjective* (*informal*) (only used to describe *towns*) SMALL, slow, quiet, minor, obscure, sleepy, unimportant, small-time (*informal*), backwoods, tinpot (*Brit informal*)

onerous *adjective* TRYING, hard, taxing, demanding, difficult, heavy, responsible, grave, crushing, exhausting, exacting, formidable, troublesome, oppressive, weighty, laborious, burdensome, irksome, backbreaking, exigent << ANTONYM easy

one-sided *adjective* **1** UNEQUAL, unfair, uneven, unjust, unbalanced, lopsided, inequitable, ill-matched << ANTONYM equal
2 BIASED, prejudiced, weighted, twisted, coloured, unfair, partial, distorted, partisan, warped, slanted, unjust, discriminatory, lopsided << ANTONYM unbiased

one-time *adjective* FORMER, previous, prior, sometime, late, erstwhile, quondam, ci-devant (*French*), ex-

ongoing *adjective* IN PROGRESS, current, growing, developing, advancing, progressing, evolving, unfolding, unfinished, extant

onlooker *noun* SPECTATOR, witness, observer, viewer, looker-on, watcher, eyewitness, bystander

only *adjective* SOLE, one, single, individual, exclusive, unique, lone, solitary, one and only ▷ *adverb* **1** JUST, simply, purely, merely, no more than, nothing but, but, at most, at a push **2** HARDLY, just, barely, only just, scarcely, at most, at a push **3** EXCLUSIVELY, entirely, purely, solely

onset *noun* BEGINNING, start, rise, birth, kick-off (*informal*), outbreak, starting point, inception, commencement << ANTONYM end

onslaught *noun* ATTACK, charge, campaign, strike, rush, assault, raid, invasion, offensive, blitz, onset, foray, incursion, onrush, inroad << ANTONYM retreat

onus *noun* BURDEN, weight, responsibility, worry, task, stress, load, obligation, liability

onwards *or* **onward** *adverb* FORWARD, on, forwards, ahead, beyond, in front, forth

ooze¹ *verb* **1** SEEP, well, drop, escape, strain, leak, drain, sweat, filter, bleed, weep, drip, trickle, leach, dribble, percolate **2** EMIT, release, leak, sweat, bleed, discharge, drip, leach, give out, dribble, exude, give off, excrete, overflow with, pour forth **3** EXUDE, emit, radiate, display, exhibit, manifest, emanate, overflow with

ooze² *noun* MUD, clay, dirt, muck, silt, sludge, mire, slime, slob (*Irish*), gloop (*informal*), alluvium

opaque *adjective* **1** CLOUDY, clouded, dull, dim, muddied, muddy, murky, hazy, filmy, turbid, lustreless << ANTONYM clear **2** INCOMPREHENSIBLE, obscure, unclear, difficult, puzzling, baffling, enigmatic, perplexing, impenetrable, unintelligible, cryptic, unfathomable, abstruse, obfuscated, beyond comprehension << ANTONYM lucid

open *adjective* **1** UNCLOSED, unlocked, ajar, unfastened, yawning, gaping, unlatched, unbolted, partly open, unbarred, off the latch << ANTONYM closed **2** UNSEALED, unstoppered << ANTONYM unopened **3** EXTENDED, expanded, unfolded, stretched out, spread out, unfurled, straightened out, unrolled << ANTONYM shut **4** FRANK, direct, natural, plain, innocent, straightforward, sincere, transparent, honest, candid, truthful, upfront (*informal*), plain-spoken, above board, unreserved, artless, ingenuous, guileless, straight from the shoulder (*informal*) << ANTONYM sly **5** OBVIOUS, clear, frank, plain, apparent, visible, patent, evident, distinct, pronounced, manifest, transparent, noticeable, blatant, conspicuous, downright, overt, unmistakable, palpable, recognizable, avowed, flagrant, perceptible, much in evidence, undisguised, unsubtle, barefaced,

unconcealed << ANTONYM hidden **6** RECEPTIVE, welcoming, sympathetic, responsive, amenable **7** SUSCEPTIBLE, subject, exposed, vulnerable, in danger, disposed, liable, wide open, unprotected, at the mercy of, left open, laid bare, an easy target for, undefended, laid open, defenceless against, unfortified << ANTONYM defended **8** UNRESOLVED, unsettled, undecided, debatable, up in the air, moot, arguable, yet to be decided **9** CLEAR, free, passable, uncluttered, unhindered, unimpeded, navigable, unobstructed, unhampered << ANTONYM obstructed **10** UNENCLOSED, wide, rolling, sweeping, exposed, extensive, bare, spacious, wide-open, undeveloped, uncrowded, unfenced, not built-up, unsheltered << ANTONYM enclosed **11** UNDONE, gaping, unbuttoned, unzipped, agape, unfastened << ANTONYM fastened **12** AVAILABLE, to hand, accessible, handy, vacant, on hand, obtainable, attainable, at your fingertips, at your disposal **13** GENERAL, public, free, catholic, broad, universal, blanket, unconditional, across-the-board, unqualified, all-inclusive, unrestricted, overarching, free to all, nondiscriminatory, one-size-fits-all << ANTONYM restricted **14** VACANT, free, available, empty, up for grabs (*informal*), unoccupied, unfilled, unengaged **15** GENEROUS, kind, liberal, charitable, benevolent, prodigal, bountiful, open-handed, unstinting, beneficent, bounteous, munificent, ungrudging **16** GAPPY, loose, lacy, porous, honeycombed, spongy, filigree, fretted, holey, openwork ▷ *verb* **1** UNFASTEN, unlock, unclasp, throw wide, unbar, unclose << ANTONYM close **2** UNWRAP, uncover, undo, unravel, untie, unstrap, unseal, unlace << ANTONYM wrap **3** UNCORK, crack (open) **4** UNFOLD, spread (out), expand, stretch out, unfurl, unroll << ANTONYM fold **5** CLEAR, unblock << ANTONYM block **6** UNDO, loosen, unbutton, unfasten << ANTONYM fasten **7** BEGIN BUSINESS **8** START, begin, launch, trigger, kick off (*informal*), initiate, commence, get going, instigate, kick-start, inaugurate, set in motion, get (something) off the ground (*informal*), enter upon << ANTONYM end **9** BEGIN, start, commence << ANTONYM end

open-air *modifier* OUTDOOR, outside, out-of-door(s), alfresco

open-and-shut *adjective* STRAIGHTFORWARD, simple, obvious, routine, clear-cut, foregone, noncontroversial

opening *adjective* FIRST, early, earliest, beginning, premier, primary, initial, maiden, inaugural, commencing, introductory, initiatory ▷ *noun* **1** BEGINNING, start, launch, launching, birth, dawn, outset, starting point, onset, overture, initiation, inauguration, inception, commencement, kickoff (*informal*), opening move << ANTONYM ending **2** HOLE, break, space, tear, split, crack, gap, rent, breach, slot, outlet, vent, puncture, rupture, aperture, cleft, chink, fissure, orifice, perforation, interstice << ANTONYM blockage **3** OPPORTUNITY, chance, break (*informal*), time, place, moment, window, occasion, look-in (*informal*) **4** JOB, position, post, situation, opportunity, vacancy

openly *adverb* **1** FRANKLY, plainly, in public, honestly, face to face, overtly, candidly, unreservedly, unhesitatingly, forthrightly, straight from the shoulder (*informal*) << ANTONYM privately **2** BLATANTLY, publicly, brazenly, unashamedly, shamelessly, in full view, flagrantly, unabashedly, wantonly, undisguisedly, without pretence << ANTONYM secretly

open-minded *adjective* UNPREJUDICED, liberal, free, balanced, catholic, broad, objective, reasonable, enlightened, tolerant, impartial, receptive, unbiased, even-handed, dispassionate, fair-minded, broad-minded, undogmatic << ANTONYM narrow-minded

openness *noun* FRANKNESS, honesty, truthfulness, naturalness, bluntness, forthrightness, ingenuousness, artlessness, guilelessness, candidness, freeness, open-heartedness, absence of reserve, candour *or* (*U.S.*) candor, sincerity *or* sincereness, unreservedness

operate *verb* **1** MANAGE, run, direct, handle, govern, oversee, supervise, preside over, be in charge of, call the shots in, superintend, call the tune in **2** FUNCTION, work, act, be in business, be in action **3** RUN, work, use, control, drive, manoeuvre **4** WORK, go, run, perform, function << ANTONYM break down **5** PERFORM SURGERY, carry out surgery, put someone under the knife (*informal*)

operation *noun* **1** UNDERTAKING, process, affair, organization, proceeding, procedure, coordination **2** MANOEUVRE, campaign, movement, exercise, assault, deployment **3** BUSINESS, concern, firm, organization, corporation, venture, enterprise **4** SURGERY, surgical operation, surgical intervention **5** PERFORMANCE, working, running, action, movement, functioning, motion, manipulation **6** EFFECT, force, activity, agency, influence, impact, effectiveness, instrumentality ▷▷ **in operation** IN ACTION, current, effective, going, functioning, active, in effect, in business, operative, in force

operational *adjective* WORKING, going, running, ready, functioning, operative, viable, functional, up and running, workable, usable, in working order << ANTONYM inoperative

operative *adjective* **1** IN FORCE, current, effective, standing, functioning, active, efficient, in effect, in business, operational, functional, in operation, workable, serviceable << ANTONYM inoperative **2** RELEVANT, important, key, fitting, significant, appropriate, crucial, influential, apt, applicable, indicative, pertinent, apposite, germane ▷ *noun* **1** WORKER, hand, employee, mechanic, labourer, workman, artisan, machinist, working man *or* working woman **2** (*US & Canad*) SPY, secret agent, double agent, secret service agent, undercover agent, mole, foreign agent, fifth columnist, nark (*Brit, Austral & NZ slang*)

operator *noun* **1** WORKER, hand, driver, mechanic, operative, conductor, technician, handler, skilled employee **2** CONTRACTOR, dealer, trader, administrator **3** (*informal*) MANIPULATOR, worker, mover, Machiavellian, mover and shaker, machinator, wheeler-dealer (*informal*), wirepuller

opiate *noun* NARCOTIC, drug, downer (*slang*), painkiller, sedative, tranquillizer, bromide, anodyne, analgesic, soporific, pacifier, nepenthe

opine *verb* (*formal*) SUGGEST, say, think, believe, judge, suppose, declare, conclude, venture, volunteer, imply, intimate, presume, conjecture, surmise, ween (*poetic*), give as your opinion

opinion *noun* **1** BELIEF, feeling, view, idea, theory, notion, conviction, point of view, sentiment, viewpoint, persuasion, conjecture **2** ESTIMATION, view, impression, assessment, judgment, evaluation, conception, appraisal, considered opinion ▷▷ **be of the opinion** BELIEVE, think, hold, consider, judge, suppose, maintain, imagine, guess (*informal, chiefly US & Canad*), reckon, conclude, be convinced, speculate, presume, conjecture, postulate, surmise, be under the impression ▷▷ **matter of opinion** DEBATABLE POINT, debatable, open question, open to question, moot point, open for discussion, matter of judgment

opinionated *adjective* DOGMATIC, prejudiced, biased, arrogant, adamant, stubborn, assertive, uncompromising, single-minded, inflexible, bigoted, dictatorial, imperious, overbearing, obstinate, doctrinaire, obdurate, cocksure, pig-headed, self-assertive, bull-headed << ANTONYM open-minded

opponent *noun* 1 ADVERSARY, rival, enemy, the opposition, competitor, challenger, foe, contestant, antagonist << ANTONYM ally 2 OPPOSER, dissident, objector, dissentient, disputant << ANTONYM supporter

opportune *adjective* (*formal*) TIMELY, fitting, fit, welcome, lucky, appropriate, suitable, happy, proper, convenient, fortunate, favourable, apt, advantageous, auspicious, fortuitous, well-timed, propitious, heaven-sent, felicitous, providential, seasonable, falling into your lap << ANTONYM inopportune

opportunism *noun* EXPEDIENCY, convenience, exploitation, realism, manipulation, pragmatism, capitalization, realpolitik, utilitarianism, making hay while the sun shines (*informal*), striking while the iron is hot (*informal*), unscrupulousness, Machiavellianism

opportunity *noun* CHANCE, opening, time, turn, hour, break (*informal*), moment, window, possibility, occasion, slot, scope, look-in (*informal*)

oppose *verb* BE AGAINST, fight (against), check, bar, block, prevent, take on, counter, contest, resist, confront, face, combat, defy, thwart, contradict, withstand, stand up to, hinder, struggle against, obstruct, fly in the face of, take issue with, be hostile to, counterattack, speak (out) against, be in opposition to, be in defiance of, strive against, set your face against, take *or* make a stand against << ANTONYM support

opposed *adjective* 1 *with* to AGAINST, anti (*informal*), hostile, adverse, contra (*informal*), in opposition, averse, antagonistic, inimical, (dead) set against 2 CONTRARY, opposite, conflicting, opposing, clashing, counter, adverse, contradictory, in opposition, incompatible, antithetical, antipathetic, dissentient

opposing *adjective* 1 CONFLICTING, different, opposed, contrasting, opposite, differing, contrary, contradictory, incompatible, irreconcilable 2 RIVAL, warring, conflicting, clashing, competing, enemy, opposite, hostile, combatant, antagonistic, antipathetic

opposite *adjective* 1 FACING, other, opposing 2 DIFFERENT, conflicting, opposed, contrasted, contrasting, unlike, differing, contrary, diverse, adverse, at odds, contradictory, inconsistent, dissimilar, divergent, irreconcilable, at variance, poles apart, diametrically opposed, antithetical, streets apart << ANTONYM alike 3 RIVAL, conflicting, opposed, opposing, competing, hostile, antagonistic, inimical ▷ *preposition* often *with* to FACING, face to face with, across from, eyeball to eyeball with (*informal*) ▷ *noun* REVERSE, contrary, converse, antithesis, the other extreme, contradiction, inverse, the other side of the coin (*informal*), obverse

opposition *noun* 1 HOSTILITY, resistance, resentment, disapproval, obstruction, animosity, aversion, antagonism, antipathy, obstructiveness, counteraction, contrariety << ANTONYM support 2 OPPONENT(s), competition, rival(s), enemy, competitor(s), other side, challenger(s), foe, contestant(s), antagonist(s)

oppress *verb* 1 SUBJUGATE, abuse, suppress, wrong, master, overcome, crush, overwhelm, put down, subdue, overpower, persecute, rule over, enslave, maltreat, hold sway over, trample underfoot, bring someone to heel, tyrannize over, rule with an iron hand, bring someone under the yoke << ANTONYM liberate 2 DEPRESS, burden, discourage, torment, daunt, harass, afflict, sadden, vex, weigh down, dishearten, cast someone down, dispirit, take the heart out of, deject, lie *or* weigh heavy upon, make someone despondent

oppressed *adjective* DOWNTRODDEN, abused, exploited, subject, burdened, distressed, slave, disadvantaged, helpless, misused, enslaved, prostrate, underprivileged, subservient, subjugated, browbeaten, maltreated, tyrannized, henpecked << ANTONYM liberated

oppression *noun* PERSECUTION, control, suffering, abuse, injury, injustice, cruelty, domination, repression, brutality, suppression, severity, tyranny, authoritarianism, harshness, despotism, ill-treatment, subjugation, subjection, maltreatment << ANTONYM justice

oppressive *adjective* **1** TYRANNICAL, severe, harsh, heavy, overwhelming, cruel, brutal, authoritarian, unjust, repressive, Draconian, autocratic, inhuman, dictatorial, coercive, imperious, domineering, overbearing, burdensome, despotic, high-handed, peremptory, overweening, tyrannous << ANTONYM merciful **2** STIFLING, close, heavy, sticky, overpowering, suffocating, stuffy, humid, torrid, sultry, airless, muggy

oppressor *noun* PERSECUTOR, tyrant, bully, scourge, tormentor, despot, autocrat, taskmaster, iron hand, slave-driver, harrier, intimidator, subjugator

opt *verb* CHOOSE, decide, prefer, select, elect, see fit, make a selection << ANTONYM reject
▷▷ **opt for something** *or* **someone** CHOOSE, pick, select, take, adopt, go for, designate, decide on, single out, espouse, fix on, plump for, settle upon, exercise your discretion in favour of

optimistic *adjective* **1** HOPEFUL, positive, confident, encouraged, can-do (*informal*), bright, assured, cheerful, rosy, buoyant, idealistic, Utopian, sanguine, expectant, looking on the bright side, buoyed up, disposed to take a favourable view, seeing through rose-coloured spectacles << ANTONYM pessimistic **2** ENCOURAGING, promising, bright, good, cheering, reassuring, satisfactory, rosy, heartening, auspicious, propitious << ANTONYM discouraging

optimum *adjective* IDEAL, best, highest, finest, choicest, perfect, supreme, peak, outstanding, first-class, foremost, first-rate, flawless, superlative, pre-eminent, most excellent, A1 *or* A-one (*informal*), most favourable *or* advantageous << ANTONYM worst

option *noun* CHOICE, alternative, selection, preference, freedom of choice, power to choose, election

optional *adjective* VOLUNTARY, open, discretionary, possible, extra, elective, up to the individual, noncompulsory << ANTONYM compulsory

opulence *or* **opulency** *noun* **1** LUXURY, riches, wealth, splendour, prosperity, richness, affluence, voluptuousness, lavishness, sumptuousness, luxuriance

2 WEALTH, means, riches (*informal*), capital, resources, assets, fortune, substance, prosperity, affluence, easy circumstances, prosperousness << ANTONYM poverty

opulent *adjective* **1** LUXURIOUS, expensive, magnificent, costly, splendid, lavish, sumptuous, plush (*informal*), ritzy (*slang*), de luxe, well-appointed **2** RICH, wealthy, prosperous, propertied, loaded (*slang*), flush (*informal*), affluent, well-off, well-heeled (*informal*), well-to-do, moneyed, filthy rich, stinking rich (*informal*), made of money (*informal*) << ANTONYM poor

opus *noun* WORK, piece, production, creation, composition, work of art, brainchild, oeuvre (*French*)

oracle *noun* **1** PROPHET, diviner, sage, seer, clairvoyant, augur, soothsayer, sibyl, prophesier **2** PROPHECY, vision, revelation, forecast, prediction, divination, prognostication, augury, divine utterance

oral *adjective* SPOKEN, vocal, verbal, unwritten, viva voce

oration *noun* SPEECH, talk, address, lecture, discourse, harangue, homily, spiel (*informal*), disquisition, declamation, whaikorero (*NZ*)

orator *noun* PUBLIC SPEAKER, speaker, lecturer, spokesperson, declaimer, rhetorician, Cicero, spieler (*informal*), word-spinner, spokesman *or* spokeswoman

oratory *noun* RHETORIC, eloquence, public speaking, speech-making, expressiveness, fluency, a way with words, declamation, speechifying, grandiloquence, spieling (*informal*), whaikorero (*NZ*)

orb *noun* SPHERE, ball, circle, globe, round

orbit *noun* **1** PATH, course, track, cycle, circle, revolution, passage, rotation, trajectory, sweep, ellipse, circumgyration **2** SPHERE OF INFLUENCE, reach, range, influence, province, scope, sphere, domain, compass, ambit ▷ *verb* CIRCLE, ring, go round, compass, revolve around, encircle, circumscribe, gird, circumnavigate

orchestrate *verb* **1** ORGANIZE, plan, run, set up, arrange, be responsible for, put together, see to (*informal*), marshal, coordinate, concert, stage-manage **2** SCORE, set, arrange, adapt

ordain *verb* **1** APPOINT, call, name, commission, select, elect, invest, install, nominate, anoint, consecrate, frock **2** (*formal*) ORDER, will, rule, demand, require, direct, establish, command, dictate, prescribe, pronounce, lay down, decree, instruct, enact, legislate, enjoin **3** PREDESTINE, fate, intend, mark out, predetermine, foreordain, destine, preordain

ordeal *noun* HARDSHIP, trial, difficulty, test, labour, suffering, trouble(s), nightmare, burden, torture, misery, agony, torment, anguish, toil, affliction, tribulation(s), baptism of fire << ANTONYM pleasure

order *verb* **1** COMMAND, instruct, direct, charge, demand, require, bid, compel, enjoin, adjure << ANTONYM forbid **2** DECREE, rule, demand, establish, prescribe, pronounce, ordain << ANTONYM ban **3** REQUEST, ask (for), book, demand, seek, call for, reserve, engage, apply for, contract for, solicit, requisition, put in for, send away for **4** ARRANGE, group, sort, class, position, range, file, rank, line up, organize, set out, sequence, catalogue, sort out, classify, array, dispose, tidy, marshal, lay out, tabulate, systematize, neaten, put in order, set in order, put to rights << ANTONYM disarrange ▷ *noun* **1** INSTRUCTION, ruling, demand, direction, command, say-so (*informal*), dictate, decree, mandate, directive, injunction, behest, stipulation **2** REQUEST, booking, demand, commission, application, reservation, requisition **3** SEQUENCE, grouping, ordering, line, series, structure, chain, arrangement, line-up, succession, disposal, array, placement, classification, layout, progression, disposition, setup (*informal*), categorization, codification **4** ORGANIZATION, system, method, plan, pattern, arrangement, harmony, symmetry, regularity, propriety, neatness, tidiness, orderliness << ANTONYM chaos **5** PEACE, control, law, quiet, calm, discipline, law and order, tranquillity, peacefulness, lawfulness **6** SOCIETY, company, group, club, union, community, league, association, institute, organization, circle, corporation, lodge, guild, sect, fellowship, fraternity, brotherhood, sisterhood, sodality **7** CLASS, set, rank, degree, grade, sphere, caste **8** (*biology*) KIND, group, class, family, form, sort, type, variety, cast, species, breed, strain, category, tribe, genre, classification, genus, ilk, subdivision, subclass, taxonomic group ▷▷ **in order 1** TIDY, ordered, neat, arranged, trim, orderly, spruce, well-kept, well-ordered, shipshape, spick-and-span, trig (*archaic* or *dialect*), in apple-pie order (*informal*) **2** APPROPRIATE, right, fitting, seemly, called for, correct, suitable, acceptable, proper, to the point, apt,

applicable, pertinent, befitting, well-suited, well-timed, apposite, germane, to the purpose, meet (*archaic*), O.K. *or* okay (*informal*) ▷▷ **out of order 1** NOT WORKING, broken, broken-down, ruined, bust (*informal*), defective, wonky (*Brit slang*), not functioning, out of commission, on the blink (*slang*), on its last legs, inoperative, kaput (*informal*), in disrepair, gone haywire (*informal*), nonfunctional, on the fritz (*US slang*), gone phut (*informal*), US(*informal*) **2** IMPROPER, wrong, unsuitable, not done, not on (*informal*), unfitting, vulgar, out of place, unseemly, untoward, unbecoming, impolite, off-colour, out of turn, uncalled-for, not cricket (*informal*), indelicate, indecorous

orderly *adjective* **1** WELL-BEHAVED, controlled, disciplined, quiet, restrained, law-abiding, nonviolent, peaceable, decorous << ANTONYM disorderly **2** WELL-ORGANIZED, ordered, regular, in order, organized, trim, precise, neat, tidy, systematic, businesslike, methodical, well-kept, shipshape, systematized, well-regulated, in apple-pie order (*informal*) << ANTONYM disorganized

ordinance *noun* RULE, order, law, ruling, standard, guide, direction, principle, command, regulation, guideline, criterion, decree, canon, statute, fiat, edict, dictum, precept

ordinarily *adverb* USUALLY, generally, normally, commonly, regularly, routinely, in general, as a rule, habitually, customarily, in the usual way, as is usual, as is the custom, in the general run (of things) << ANTONYM seldom

ordinary *adjective* **1** USUAL, standard, normal, common, established, settled, regular, familiar, household, typical, conventional, routine, stock, everyday, prevailing, accustomed, customary, habitual, quotidian, wonted **2** COMMONPLACE, plain, modest, humble, stereotyped, pedestrian, mundane, vanilla (*slang*), stale, banal, unremarkable, prosaic, run-of-the-mill, humdrum, homespun, uninteresting, workaday, common or garden (*informal*), unmemorable **3** AVERAGE, middling, fair, indifferent, not bad, mediocre, so-so (*informal*), unremarkable, tolerable, run-of-the-mill, passable, undistinguished, uninspired, unexceptional, bog-standard (*Brit & Irish slang*), no great shakes (*informal*), dime-a-dozen (*informal*) << ANTONYM extraordinary

▷▷ **out of the ordinary** UNUSUAL, different, odd, important, special, striking, surprising, significant, strange, exciting, rare, impressive, extraordinary, outstanding, remarkable, bizarre, distinguished, unexpected, curious, exceptional, notable, unfamiliar, abnormal, queer, uncommon, singular, unconventional, noteworthy, atypical

ordnance noun WEAPONS, arms, guns, artillery, cannon, firearms, weaponry, big guns, armaments, munitions, materiel, instruments of war

organ noun 1 BODY PART, part of the body, member, element, biological structure 2 NEWSPAPER, paper, medium, voice, agency, channel, vehicle, journal, publication, rag (*informal*), gazette, periodical, mouthpiece

organic adjective 1 NATURAL, biological, living, live, vital, animate, biotic 2 SYSTEMATIC, ordered, structured, organized, integrated, orderly, standardized, methodical, well-ordered, systematized 3 INTEGRAL, fundamental, constitutional, structural, inherent, innate, immanent

organism noun CREATURE, being, thing, body, animal, structure, beast, entity, living thing, critter (*US dialect*)

organization or **organisation** noun 1 GROUP, company, party, body, concern, league, association, band, institution, gathering, circle, corporation, federation, outfit (*informal*), faction, consortium, syndicate, combine, congregation, confederation 2 MANAGEMENT, running, planning, making, control, operation, handling, structuring, administration, direction, regulation, construction, organizing, supervision, governance, formulation, coordination, methodology, superintendence 3 STRUCTURE, grouping, plan, system, form, design, method, pattern, make-up, arrangement, construction, constitution, format, formation, framework, composition, chemistry, configuration, conformation, interrelation of parts

organize or **organise** verb 1 ARRANGE, run, plan, form, prepare, establish, set up, shape, schedule, frame, look after, be responsible for, construct, constitute, devise, put together, take care of, see to (*informal*), get together, marshal, contrive, get going, coordinate, fix up, straighten out, lay the foundations of, lick into shape, jack up (*NZ informal*) << ANTONYM disrupt 2 PUT

IN ORDER, arrange, group, list, file, index, catalogue, classify, codify, pigeonhole, tabulate, inventory, systematize, dispose << ANTONYM muddle

orgasm noun CLIMAX, coming (*taboo slang*), pleasure, the big O (*informal*), (sexual) satisfaction

orgy noun 1 PARTY, celebration, rave (*Brit slang*), revel, festivity, bender (*informal*), debauch, revelry, carouse, Saturnalia, bacchanal, rave-up (*Brit slang*), bacchanalia, carousal, hooley or hoolie (*chiefly Irish & NZ*) 2 SPREE, fit, spell, run, session, excess, bout, indulgence, binge (*informal*), splurge, surfeit, overindulgence

orient or **orientate** verb ADJUST, settle, adapt, tune, convert, alter, compose, accommodate, accustom, reconcile, align, harmonize, familiarize, acclimatize, find your feet (*informal*) ▷▷ **orient yourself** GET YOUR BEARINGS, get the lie of the land, establish your location

orientation noun 1 INCLINATION, tendency, bias, leaning, bent, disposition, predisposition, predilection, proclivity, partiality, turn of mind 2 INDUCTION, introduction, breaking in, adjustment, settling in, adaptation, initiation, assimilation, familiarization, acclimatization 3 POSITION, situation, location, site, bearings, direction, arrangement, whereabouts, disposition, coordination

orifice noun OPENING, space, hole, split, mouth, gap, rent, breach, vent, pore, rupture, aperture, cleft, chink, fissure, perforation, interstice

origin noun 1 BEGINNING, start, birth, source, launch, foundation, creation, dawning, early stages, emergence, outset, starting point, onset, genesis, initiation, inauguration, inception, font (*poetic*), commencement, fountain, fount, origination, fountainhead, mainspring << ANTONYM end 2 ROOT, source, basis, beginnings, base, cause, spring, roots, seed, foundation, nucleus, germ, provenance, derivation, wellspring, fons et origo (*Latin*) 3 ANCESTRY, family, race, beginnings, stock, blood, birth, heritage, ancestors, descent, pedigree, extraction, lineage, forebears, antecedents, parentage, forefathers, genealogy, derivation, progenitors, stirps

original adjective 1 FIRST, earliest, early, initial, aboriginal, primitive, pristine, primordial, primeval, autochthonous 2 INITIAL, first, starting, opening, primary, inaugural, commencing, introductory << ANTONYM final **3** AUTHENTIC, real, actual, genuine, legitimate, first generation, bona fide, the real McCoy << ANTONYM copied **4** NEW, fresh, novel, different, unusual, unknown, unprecedented, innovative, unfamiliar, unconventional, seminal, ground-breaking, untried, innovatory, newfangled << ANTONYM unoriginal **5** CREATIVE, inspired, imaginative, artistic, fertile, ingenious, visionary, inventive, resourceful ▷ *noun* **1** PROTOTYPE, master, pattern << ANTONYM copy **2** CHARACTER, eccentric, case (*informal*), card (*informal*), nut (*slang*), flake (*slang, chiefly US*), anomaly, oddity, oddball (*informal*), nonconformist, wacko (*slang*), odd bod (*informal*), queer fish (*Brit informal*), weirdo or weirdie (*informal*)

originality *noun* NOVELTY, imagination, creativity, innovation, new ideas, individuality, ingenuity, freshness, uniqueness, boldness, inventiveness, cleverness, resourcefulness, break with tradition, newness, unfamiliarity, creative spirit, unorthodoxy, unconventionality, creativeness, innovativeness, imaginativeness << ANTONYM conventionality

originally *adverb* INITIALLY, first, firstly, at first, primarily, at the start, in the first place, to begin with, at the outset, in the beginning, in the early stages

originate *verb* **1** BEGIN, start, emerge, come, issue, happen, rise, appear, spring, flow, be born, proceed, arise, dawn, stem, derive, commence, emanate, crop up (*informal*), come into being, come into existence << ANTONYM end **2** INVENT, produce, create, form, develop, design, launch, set up, introduce, imagine, institute, generate, come up with (*informal*), pioneer, evolve, devise, initiate, conceive, bring about, formulate, give birth to, contrive, improvise, dream up (*informal*), inaugurate, think up, set in motion

originator *noun* CREATOR, father *or* mother, founder, author, maker, framer, designer, architect, pioneer, generator, inventor, innovator, prime mover, initiator, begetter

ornament *noun* **1** DECORATION, trimming, accessory, garnish, frill, festoon, trinket, bauble, flounce, gewgaw, knick-knack, furbelow, falderal **2** EMBELLISHMENT, trimming, decoration, embroidery, elaboration, adornment, ornamentation ▷ *verb* DECORATE, trim, adorn, enhance, deck, array, dress up, enrich, brighten, garnish, gild, do up (*informal*), embellish, emblazon, festoon, bedeck, beautify, prettify, bedizen (*archaic*), engarland

ornamental *adjective* DECORATIVE, pretty, attractive, fancy, enhancing, for show, embellishing, showy, beautifying, nonfunctional

ornamentation *noun* DECORATION, trimming, frills, garnishing, embroidery, enrichment, elaboration, embellishment, adornment, beautification, ornateness

ornate *adjective* ELABORATE, fancy, decorated, detailed, beautiful, complex, busy, complicated, elegant, extravagant, baroque, ornamented, fussy, flowery, showy, ostentatious, rococo, florid, bedecked, overelaborate, high-wrought, aureate << ANTONYM plain

orthodox *adjective* **1** ESTABLISHED, official, accepted, received, common, popular, traditional, normal, regular, usual, ordinary, approved, familiar, acknowledged, conventional, routine, customary, well-established, kosher (*informal*) << ANTONYM unorthodox **2** CONFORMIST, conservative, traditional, strict, devout, observant, doctrinal << ANTONYM nonconformist

orthodoxy *noun* **1** DOCTRINE, teaching, opinion, principle, belief, convention, canon, creed, dogma, tenet, precept, article of faith **2** CONFORMITY, received wisdom, traditionalism, inflexibility, conformism, conventionality << ANTONYM nonconformity

oscillate *verb* **1** FLUCTUATE, swing, vary, sway, waver, veer, rise and fall, vibrate, undulate, go up and down, seesaw **2** WAVER, change, swing, shift, vary, sway, alternate, veer, ebb and flow, vacillate, seesaw << ANTONYM settle

oscillation *noun* **1** FLUCTUATION, swing, variation, instability, imbalance, wavering, volatility, variability, unpredictability, seesawing, disequilibrium, capriciousness, mutability, inconstancy, changeableness **2** WAVERING, swing, shift, swaying, alteration, veering, seesawing, vacillation

ostensible *adjective* APPARENT, seeming, supposed, alleged, so-called, pretended, exhibited, manifest, outward, superficial, professed, purported, avowed, specious

ostensibly *adverb* APPARENTLY, seemingly,

supposedly, outwardly, on the surface, on the face of it, superficially, to all intents and purposes, professedly, speciously, for the ostensible purpose of

ostentatious *adjective* PRETENTIOUS, extravagant, flamboyant, flash (*informal*), loud, dashing, inflated, conspicuous, vulgar, brash, high-flown, flashy, pompous, flaunted, flaunting, grandiose, crass, gaudy, showy, swanky (*informal*), snobbish, puffed up, specious, boastful, obtrusive, highfalutin (*informal*), arty-farty (*informal*), magniloquent << ANTONYM modest

ostracism *noun* EXCLUSION, boycott, isolation, exile, rejection, expulsion, avoidance, cold-shouldering, renunciation, banishment << ANTONYM acceptance

other *determiner* 1 ADDITIONAL, more, further, new, added, extra, fresh, spare, supplementary, auxiliary 2 DIFFERENT, alternative, contrasting, distinct, diverse, dissimilar, separate, alternative, substitute, alternate, unrelated, variant 3 REMAINING, left-over, residual, extant

otherwise *sentence connector* OR ELSE, or, if not, or then ▷ *adverb* 1 APART FROM THAT, in other ways, in (all) other respects 2 DIFFERENTLY, any other way, in another way, contrarily, contrastingly, in contrary fashion

ounce *noun* SHRED, bit, drop, trace, scrap, grain, particle, fragment, atom, crumb, snippet, speck, whit, iota

oust *verb* EXPEL, turn out, dismiss, exclude, exile, discharge, throw out, relegate, displace, topple, banish, eject, depose, evict, dislodge, unseat, dispossess, send packing, turf out (*informal*), disinherit, drum out, show someone the door, give someone the bum's rush (*slang*), throw out on your ear (*informal*)

out *adjective* 1 NOT IN, away, elsewhere, outside, gone, abroad, from home, absent, not here, not there, not at home 2 EXTINGUISHED, ended, finished, dead, cold, exhausted, expired, used up, doused, at an end << ANTONYM alight 3 IN BLOOM, opening, open, flowering, blooming, in flower, in full bloom 4 AVAILABLE, on sale, in the shops, at hand, to be had, purchasable, procurable 5 NOT ALLOWED, banned, forbidden, ruled out, vetoed, not on (*informal*), unacceptable, prohibited, taboo, verboten (*German*) << ANTONYM allowed 6 OUT OF DATE, dead, square (*informal*), old-fashioned, dated, outdated, unfashionable, antiquated, outmoded, passé, old hat, behind the times, out of style, démodé (*French*), not with it (*informal*) << ANTONYM fashionable 7 INACCURATE, wrong, incorrect, faulty, off the mark, erroneous, off target, wide of the mark << ANTONYM accurate 8 REVEALED, exposed, common knowledge, public knowledge, (out) in the open << ANTONYM kept secret ▷ *verb* EXPOSE, uncover, unmask

out-and-out *adjective* ABSOLUTE, complete, total, perfect, sheer, utter, outright, thorough, downright, consummate, unqualified, unmitigated, dyed-in-the-wool, thoroughgoing, unalloyed, arrant, deep-dyed (*usually derogatory*)

outbreak *noun* 1 ERUPTION, burst, explosion, epidemic, rash, outburst, flare-up, flash, spasm, upsurge 2 ONSET, beginning, outset, opening, dawn, commencement

outburst *noun* 1 EXPLOSION, surge, outbreak, eruption, flare-up 2 FIT, storm, attack, gush, flare-up, eruption, spasm, outpouring, paroxysm

outcast *noun* PARIAH, exile, outlaw, undesirable, untouchable, leper, vagabond, wretch, persona non grata (*Latin*)

outclass *verb* SURPASS, top, beat, cap (*informal*), exceed, eclipse, overshadow, excel, transcend, outstrip, outdo, outshine, leave standing (*informal*), tower above, go one better than (*informal*), be a cut above (*informal*), run rings around (*informal*), outdistance, outrank, put in the shade, leave in the shade

outcome *noun* RESULT, end, consequence, conclusion, end result, payoff (*informal*), upshot

outcry *noun* PROTEST, complaint, objection, cry, dissent, outburst, disapproval, clamour, uproar, commotion, protestation, exclamation, formal complaint, hue and cry, hullaballoo, demurral

outdated *adjective* OLD-FASHIONED, dated, obsolete, out of date, passé, antique, archaic, unfashionable, antiquated, outmoded, behind the times, out of style, obsolescent, démodé (*French*), out of the ark (*informal*), oldfangled << ANTONYM modern

outdo *verb* SURPASS, best, top, beat, overcome, exceed, eclipse, overshadow, excel, transcend, outstrip, get the better of, outclass, outshine, tower above, outsmart (*informal*), outmanoeuvre, go one better than (*informal*), run rings around (*informal*), outfox, outdistance, be one up on, score points off, put in the shade, outjockey

outdoor *adjective* OPEN-AIR, outside, out-of-door(s), alfresco << ANTONYM indoor

outer *adjective* 1 EXTERNAL, outside, outward, exterior, exposed, outermost << ANTONYM inner 2 SURFACE, external, outward, exterior, superficial 3 OUTLYING, remote, distant, provincial, out-of-the-way, peripheral, far-flung << ANTONYM central

outfit *noun* 1 COSTUME, dress, clothes, clothing, suit, gear (*informal*), get-up (*informal*), kit, ensemble, apparel, attire, garb, togs (*informal*), threads (*slang*), schmutter (*slang*), rigout (*informal*) 2 (*informal*) GROUP, company, team, set, party, firm, association, unit, crowd, squad, organization, crew, gang, corps, setup (*informal*), galère (*French*) ▷ *verb* 1 EQUIP, stock, supply, turn out, appoint, provision, furnish, fit out, deck out, kit out, fit up, accoutre 2 DRESS, clothe, attire, deck out, kit out, rig out

outfitter *noun* (*old-fashioned*) CLOTHIER, tailor, couturier, dressmaker, seamstress, haberdasher (*US*), costumier, garment maker, modiste

outflow *noun* 1 STREAM, issue, flow, rush, emergence, spate, deluge, outpouring, effusion, emanation, efflux 2 DISCHARGE, flow, jet, cascade, ebb, gush, drainage, torrent, deluge, spurt, spout, outpouring, outfall, efflux, effluence, debouchment

outgoing *adjective* 1 LEAVING, last, former, past, previous, retiring, withdrawing, prior, departing, erstwhile, late, ex- << ANTONYM incoming 2 SOCIABLE, open, social, warm, friendly, accessible, expansive, cordial, genial, affable, extrovert, approachable, gregarious, communicative, convivial, demonstrative, unreserved, companionable << ANTONYM reserved

outgoings *plural noun* EXPENSES, costs, payments, expenditure, overheads, outlay

outgrowth *noun* 1 PRODUCT, result, development, fruit, consequence, outcome, legacy, emergence, derivative, spin-off, by-product, end result, offshoot, upshot 2 OFFSHOOT, shoot, branch, limb, projection, sprout, node, outcrop, appendage, scion, protuberance, excrescence

outing *noun* JOURNEY, run, trip, tour, expedition, excursion, spin (*informal*), ramble, jaunt, pleasure trip

outlandish *adjective* STRANGE, odd, extraordinary, wonderful, funny, bizarre, fantastic, astonishing, curious, weird, foreign, alien, exotic, exceptional, peculiar, eccentric, abnormal, out-of-the-way, queer, irregular, singular, grotesque, far-out (*slang*), unheard-of, preposterous, off-the-wall (*slang*), left-field (*informal*), freakish, barbarous, outré, daggy (*Austral & NZ informal*) << ANTONYM normal

outlast *verb* OUTLIVE, survive, live after, outstay, live on after, endure beyond, outwear, remain alive after

outlaw *noun* BANDIT, criminal, thief, crook, robber, fugitive, outcast, delinquent, felon, highwayman, desperado, marauder, brigand, lawbreaker, footpad (*archaic*) ▷ *verb* 1 BAN, bar, veto, forbid, condemn, exclude, embargo, suppress, prohibit, banish, disallow, proscribe, make illegal, interdict << ANTONYM legalise 2 BANISH, excommunicate, ostracize, put a price on (someone's) head

outlay *noun* EXPENDITURE, cost, spending, charge, investment, payment, expense(s), outgoings, disbursement

outlet *noun* 1 SHOP, store, supermarket, market, mart, boutique, emporium, hypermarket 2 CHANNEL, release, medium, avenue, vent, conduit, safety valve, means of expression 3 PIPE, opening, channel, passage, tube, exit, canal, way out, funnel, conduit, duct, orifice, egress

outline *noun* 1 SUMMARY, review, résumé, abstract, summing-up, digest, rundown, compendium, main features, synopsis, rough idea, précis, bare facts, thumbnail sketch, recapitulation, abridgment 2 DRAFT, plan, drawing, frame, tracing, rough, framework, sketch, skeleton, layout, delineation, preliminary form 3 SHAPE, lines, form, figure, profile, silhouette, configuration, contour(s), delineation, lineament(s) ▷ *verb* 1 SUMMARIZE, review, draft, plan, trace, sketch (in), sum up, encapsulate, delineate, rough out, adumbrate 2 SILHOUETTE, etch, delineate

outlive *verb* SURVIVE, outlast, live on after, endure beyond, remain alive after

outlook *noun* 1 ATTITUDE, views, opinion, position, approach, mood, perspective, point of view, stance, viewpoint, disposition, standpoint, frame of mind 2 PROSPECT(S), future, expectations, forecast, prediction, projection, probability, prognosis 3 VIEW, prospect, scene, aspect, perspective, panorama, vista

outlying *adjective* REMOTE, isolated, distant, outer, provincial, out-of-the-way, peripheral, far-off, secluded, far-flung, faraway, in the middle of nowhere, off the beaten track, backwoods, godforsaken

outmanoeuvre *or US* **outmaneuver** *verb* OUTWIT, outdo, get the better of, circumvent, outflank, outsmart (*informal*), steal a march on (*informal*), put one over on (*informal*), outfox, run rings round (*informal*), outthink, outgeneral, outjockey

outmoded *adjective* OLD-FASHIONED, passé, dated, out, dead, square (*informal*), ancient, antique, outdated, obsolete, out-of-date, old-time, archaic, unfashionable, superseded, bygone, antiquated, anachronistic, olden (*archaic*), behind the times, superannuated, fossilized, out of style, antediluvian, outworn, obsolescent, démodé (*French*), out of the ark (*informal*), not with it (*informal*), oldfangled << ANTONYM modern

out of date *adjective* **1** OLD-FASHIONED, ancient, dated, discarded, extinct, outdated, stale, obsolete, démodé (*French*), archaic, unfashionable, superseded, antiquated, outmoded, passé, old hat, behind the times, superannuated, out of style, outworn, obsolescent, out of the ark (*informal*), oldfangled << ANTONYM modern **2** INVALID, expired, lapsed, void, superseded, elapsed, null and void

out of the way *adjective* **1** REMOTE, far, distant, isolated, lonely, obscure, far-off, secluded, inaccessible, far-flung, faraway, outlying, in the middle of nowhere, off the beaten track, backwoods, godforsaken, unfrequented << ANTONYM nearby **2** UNUSUAL, surprising, odd, strange, extraordinary, remarkable, bizarre, unexpected, curious, exceptional, notable, peculiar, abnormal, queer, uncommon, singular, unconventional, outlandish, out of the ordinary, left-field (*informal*), atypical

outpouring *noun* OUTBURST, storm, stream, explosion, surge, outbreak, deluge, eruption, spasm, paroxysm, effusion, issue

output *noun* PRODUCTION, manufacture, manufacturing, yield, productivity, outturn (*rare*)

outrage *noun* **1** INDIGNATION, shock, anger, rage, fury, hurt, resentment, scorn, wrath, ire (*literary*), exasperation, umbrage, righteous anger **2** ATROCITY, crime, horror, evil, cruelty, brutality, enormity, barbarism, inhumanity, abomination, barbarity, villainy, act of cruelty ▷ *verb* OFFEND, shock, upset, pain, wound, provoke, insult, infuriate, incense, gall, madden, vex, affront, displease, rile, scandalize, give offence, nark (*Brit, Austral & NZ slang*), cut to the quick, make your blood boil, put your nose out of joint, put your back up, disgruntle

outrageous *adjective* **1** ATROCIOUS, shocking, terrible, violent, offensive, appalling, cruel, savage, horrible, beastly, horrifying, vicious, ruthless, infamous, disgraceful, scandalous, wicked, barbaric, unspeakable, inhuman, diabolical, heinous, flagrant, egregious, abominable, infernal, fiendish, villainous, nefarious, iniquitous, execrable, godawful (*slang*), hellacious (*US slang*) << ANTONYM mild **2** UNREASONABLE, unfair, excessive, steep (*informal*), shocking, over the top (*slang*), extravagant, too great, scandalous, preposterous, unwarranted, exorbitant, extortionate, immoderate, O.T.T. (*slang*) << ANTONYM reasonable

outright *adjective* **1** ABSOLUTE, complete, total, direct, perfect, pure, sheer, utter, thorough, wholesale, unconditional, downright, consummate, unqualified, undeniable, out-and-out, unadulterated, unmitigated, thoroughgoing, unalloyed, arrant, deep-dyed (*usually derogatory*) **2** DEFINITE, clear, certain, straight, flat, absolute, black-and-white, decisive, straightforward, clear-cut, unmistakable, unequivocal, unqualified, unambiguous, cut-and-dried (*informal*), incontrovertible, uncontestable ▷ *adverb* **1** OPENLY, frankly, plainly, face to face, explicitly, overtly, candidly, unreservedly, unhesitatingly, forthrightly, straight from the shoulder (*informal*) **2** ABSOLUTELY, completely, totally, fully, entirely, thoroughly, wholly, utterly, to the full, without hesitation, to the hilt, one hundred per cent, straightforwardly, without restraint, unmitigatedly, lock, stock and barrel **3** INSTANTLY, immediately, at once, straight away, cleanly, on the spot, right away, there and then, instantaneously

outset *noun* BEGINNING, start, opening, early days, starting point, onset, inauguration, inception, commencement, kickoff (*informal*) << ANTONYM finish

outside *adjective* **1** EXTERNAL, outer, exterior, surface, extreme, outdoor, outward, superficial, extraneous, outermost, extramural << ANTONYM inner **2** REMOTE, small, unlikely, slight, slim, poor, distant, faint, marginal, doubtful, dubious, slender, meagre, negligible, inconsiderable ▷ *adverb* OUTDOORS, out, out of the house, out-of-doors ▷ *noun* EXTERIOR, face, front, covering, skin, surface, shell, coating, finish, façade, topside

outsider *noun* STRANGER, incomer, visitor, foreigner, alien, newcomer, intruder, new arrival, unknown, interloper, odd one out, nonmember, outlander

outsize *adjective* 1 HUGE, great, large, giant, massive, enormous, monster, immense, mega (*slang*), jumbo (*informal*), gigantic, monumental, mammoth, bulky, colossal, mountainous, oversized, stupendous, gargantuan, elephantine, ginormous (*informal*), Brobdingnagian, humongous *or* humungous (*US slang*) << ANTONYM tiny 2 EXTRA-LARGE, large, generous, ample, roomy

outskirts *plural noun* EDGE, borders, boundary, suburbs, fringe, perimeter, vicinity, periphery, suburbia, environs, purlieus, faubourgs

outsmart *verb* (*informal*) OUTWIT, trick, take in (*informal*), cheat, deceive, defraud, dupe, gull (*archaic*), get the better of, swindle, circumvent, outperform, make a fool of (*informal*), outmanoeuvre, go one better than (*informal*), put one over on (*informal*), outfox, run rings round (*informal*), pull a fast one on (*informal*), outthink, outjockey

outspan *verb* (*S African*) RELAX, chill out (*slang, chiefly US*), take it easy, loosen up, laze, lighten up (*slang*), put your feet up, hang loose (*slang*), let yourself go (*informal*), let your hair down (*informal*), mellow out (*informal*), make yourself at home

outspoken *adjective* FORTHRIGHT, open, free, direct, frank, straightforward, blunt, explicit, downright, candid, upfront (*informal*), unequivocal, undisguised, plain-spoken, unreserved, unconcealed, unceremonious, free-spoken, straight from the shoulder (*informal*), undissembling << ANTONYM reserved

outstanding *adjective* 1 EXCELLENT, good, great, important, special, fine, noted, champion, celebrated, brilliant, impressive, superb, distinguished, well-known, prominent, superior, first-class, exceptional, notable, world-class, exquisite, admirable, eminent, exemplary, first-rate, stellar (*informal*), superlative, top-notch (*informal*),

mean (*slang*), pre-eminent, meritorious, estimable, tiptop, A1 *or* A-one (*informal*), booshit (*Austral slang*), exo (*Austral slang*), sik (*Austral slang*), rad (*informal*), phat (*slang*), schmick (*Austral informal*) << ANTONYM mediocre 2 CONSPICUOUS, marked, striking, arresting, signal, remarkable, memorable, notable, eye-catching, salient, noteworthy 3 UNPAID, remaining, due, owing, ongoing, pending, payable, unsettled, unresolved, uncollected 4 UNDONE, left, not done, omitted, unfinished, incomplete, passed over, unfulfilled, not completed, unperformed, unattended to

outstrip *verb* 1 EXCEED, eclipse, overtake, top, cap (*informal*), go beyond, surpass, outdo 2 SURPASS (*informal*), beat, leave behind, eclipse, overtake, best, top, better, overshadow, outdo, outclass, outperform, outshine, leave standing (*informal*), tower above, get ahead of, go one better than (*informal*), run rings around, knock spots off (*informal*), put in the shade 3 OUTDISTANCE, shake off, outrun, outpace

outward *adjective* APPARENT, seeming, outside, surface, external, outer, superficial, ostensible << ANTONYM inward

outwardly *adverb* APPARENTLY, externally, seemingly, it seems that, on the surface, it appears that, ostensibly, on the face of it, superficially, to the eye, to all intents and purposes, to all appearances, as far as you can see, professedly

outweigh *verb* OVERRIDE, cancel (out), eclipse, offset, make up for, compensate for, redeem, supersede, neutralize, counterbalance, nullify, take precedence over, prevail over, obviate, balance out, preponderate, outbalance

outwit *verb* OUTSMART (*informal*), get the better of, circumvent, outperform, outmanoeuvre, go one better than (*informal*), put one over on (*informal*), outfox, run rings round (*informal*), pull a fast one on (*informal*), outthink, outjockey

oval *adjective* ELLIPTICAL, egg-shaped, ovoid, ovate, ellipsoidal, oviform

ovation *noun* APPLAUSE, hand, cheering, cheers, praise, tribute, acclaim, clapping, accolade, plaudits, big hand, commendation, hand-clapping, acclamation, laudation << ANTONYM derision

over *preposition* 1 ABOVE, on top of, atop 2 ON TOP OF, on, across, upon 3 ACROSS, past, (looking) onto 4 MORE THAN, above, exceeding, in excess of, upwards of **5** ABOUT, regarding, relating to, with respect to, re, concerning, apropos of, anent (*Scot*) ▷ *adverb* **1** ABOVE, overhead, in the sky, on high, aloft, up above **2** EXTRA, more, other, further, beyond, additional, in addition, surplus, in excess, left over, unused, supplementary, auxiliary ▷ *adjective* FINISHED, by, done (with), through, ended, closed, past, completed, complete, gone, in the past, settled, concluded, accomplished, wrapped up (*informal*), bygone, at an end, ancient history (*informal*), over and done with ▷▷ **over and above** IN ADDITION TO, added to, on top of, besides, plus, let alone, not to mention, as well as, over and beyond ▷▷ **over and over (again)** REPEATEDLY, frequently, again and again, often, many times, time and (time) again, time after time, ad nauseam

overall *adjective* TOTAL, full, whole, general, complete, long-term, entire, global, comprehensive, gross, blanket, umbrella, long-range, inclusive, all-embracing, overarching ▷ *adverb* IN GENERAL, generally, mostly, all things considered, on average, in (the) large, on the whole, predominantly, in the main, in the long term, by and large, all in all, on balance, generally speaking, taking everything into consideration

overawed *adjective* INTIMIDATED, threatened, alarmed, frightened, scared, terrified, cowed, put off, daunted, unnerved

overbearing *adjective* DOMINEERING, lordly, superior, arrogant, authoritarian, oppressive, autocratic, masterful, dictatorial, coercive, bossy (*informal*), imperious, haughty, tyrannical, magisterial, despotic, high-handed, peremptory, supercilious, officious, overweening, iron-handed << ANTONYM submissive

overblown *adjective* **1** EXCESSIVE, exaggerated, over the top (*slang*), too much, inflated, extravagant, overdone, disproportionate, undue, fulsome, intemperate, immoderate, O.T.T. (*slang*) **2** INFLATED, rhetorical, high-flown, pompous, pretentious, flowery, florid, turgid, bombastic, windy, grandiloquent, fustian, magniloquent, aureate, euphuistic

overcast *adjective* CLOUDY, grey, dull, threatening, dark, clouded, dim, gloomy, dismal, murky, dreary, leaden, clouded over, sunless, louring *or* lowering << ANTONYM bright

overcharge *verb* CHEAT, con (*informal*), do (*slang*), skin (*slang*), stiff (*slang*), sting

(*informal*), rip off (*slang*), fleece, defraud, surcharge, swindle, stitch up (*slang*), rook (*slang*), short-change, diddle (*informal*), take for a ride (*informal*), cozen

overcome *verb* **1** DEFEAT, beat, conquer, master, tank (*slang*), crush, overwhelm, overthrow, lick (*informal*), undo, subdue, rout, overpower, quell, triumph over, best, get the better of, trounce, worst, clobber (*slang*), stuff (*slang*), vanquish, surmount, subjugate, prevail over, wipe the floor with (*informal*), make mincemeat of (*informal*), blow (someone) out of the water (*slang*), come out on top of (*informal*), bring (someone) to their knees (*informal*), render incapable, render powerless, be victorious over, render helpless **2** CONQUER, beat, master, survive, weather, curb, suppress, subdue, rise above, quell, triumph over, get the better of, vanquish

overdo *verb* EXAGGERATE, overstate, overuse, overplay, do to death (*informal*), belabour, carry *or* take too far, make a production (out) of (*informal*), lay (something) on thick (*informal*) << ANTONYM minimize ▷▷ **overdo it** OVERWORK, go too far, go overboard, strain *or* overstrain yourself, burn the midnight oil, burn the candle at both ends (*informal*), wear yourself out, bite off more than you can chew, have too many irons in the fire, overtire yourself, drive yourself too far, overburden yourself, overload yourself, overtax your strength, work your fingers to the bone

overdone *adjective* **1** OVERCOOKED, burnt, spoiled, dried up, charred, burnt to a crisp *or* cinder **2** EXCESSIVE, too much, unfair, unnecessary, exaggerated, over the top (*slang*), needless, unreasonable, disproportionate, undue, hyped, preposterous, inordinate, fulsome, immoderate, overelaborate, beyond all bounds, O.T.T. (*slang*) << ANTONYM minimized

overdue *adjective* **1** DELAYED, belated, late, late in the day, long delayed, behind schedule, tardy, not before time (*informal*), behind time, unpunctual, behindhand << ANTONYM early **2** UNPAID, owing

overflow *verb* **1** SPILL OVER, discharge, well over, run over, pour over, pour out, bubble over, brim over, surge over, slop over, teem over **2** FLOOD, swamp, submerge, cover, drown, soak, immerse, inundate, deluge, pour over ▷ *noun* **1** FLOOD, flooding, spill, discharge, spilling over, inundation **2** SURPLUS, extra, excess, overspill, inundation, overabundance, additional people *or* things

overflowing *adjective* FULL, abounding, swarming, rife, plentiful, thronged, teeming, copious, bountiful, profuse, brimful, overfull, superabundant << ANTONYM deficient

overhang *verb* PROJECT (OVER), extend (over), loom (over), stand out (over), bulge (over), stick out (over), protrude (over), jut (over), impend (over)

overhaul *verb* **1** CHECK, service, maintain, examine, restore, tune (up), repair, go over, inspect, fine tune, do up (*informal*), re-examine, recondition **2** OVERTAKE, pass, leave behind, catch up with, get past, outstrip, get ahead of, draw level with, outdistance ▷ *noun* CHECK, service, examination, going-over (*informal*), inspection, once-over (*informal*), checkup, reconditioning

overhead *adjective* RAISED, suspended, elevated, aerial, overhanging ▷ *adverb* ABOVE, in the sky, on high, aloft, up above << ANTONYM underneath

overheads *plural noun* RUNNING COSTS, expenses, outgoings, operating costs, oncosts

overjoyed *adjective* DELIGHTED, happy, pleased, thrilled, ecstatic, jubilant, joyous, joyful, elated, over the moon (*informal*), euphoric, rapturous, rapt, only too happy, gladdened, on cloud nine (*informal*), transported, cock-a-hoop, blissed out, in raptures, tickled pink (*informal*), deliriously happy, in seventh heaven, floating on air, stoked (*Austral & NZ informal*) << ANTONYM heartbroken

overlay *verb* COVER, coat, blanket, adorn, mantle, ornament, envelop, veneer, encase, inlay, superimpose, laminate, overspread ▷ *noun* COVERING, casing, wrapping, decoration, veneer, adornment, ornamentation, appliqué

overlook *verb* **1** LOOK OVER *or* OUT ON, have a view of, command a view of, front on to, give upon, afford a view of **2** MISS, forget, neglect, omit, disregard, pass over, fail to notice, leave undone, slip up on, leave out of consideration << ANTONYM notice **3** IGNORE, excuse, forgive, pardon, disregard, condone, turn a blind eye to, wink at, blink at, make allowances for, let someone off

with, let pass, let ride, discount, pass over, take no notice of, be oblivious to, pay no attention to, turn a deaf ear to, shut your eyes to

overly *adverb* TOO, very, extremely, exceedingly, unduly, excessively, unreasonably, inordinately, immoderately, over-

overpower *verb* **1** OVERCOME, master, overwhelm, overthrow, subdue, quell, get the better of, subjugate, prevail over, immobilize, bring (someone) to their knees (*informal*), render incapable, render powerless, render helpless, get the upper hand over **2** BEAT, defeat, tank (*slang*), crush, lick (*informal*), triumph over, best, clobber (*slang*), stuff (*slang*), vanquish, be victorious (over), wipe the floor with (*informal*), make mincemeat of (*informal*), worst **3** OVERWHELM, overcome, bowl over (*informal*), stagger

overpowering *adjective* **1** OVERWHELMING, powerful, extreme, compelling, irresistible, breathtaking, compulsive, invincible, uncontrollable **2** STRONG, marked, powerful, distinct, sickening, unbearable, suffocating, unmistakable, nauseating **3** FORCEFUL, powerful, overwhelming, dynamic, compelling, persuasive, overbearing

overrate *verb* OVERESTIMATE, glorify, overvalue, oversell, make too much of, rate too highly, assess too highly, overpraise, exaggerate the worth of, overprize, think *or* expect too much of, think too highly of, attach too much importance to

override *verb* **1** OUTWEIGH, overcome, eclipse, supersede, take precedence over, prevail over, outbalance **2** OVERRULE, reverse, cancel, overturn, set aside, repeal, quash, revoke, disallow, rescind, upset, rule against, invalidate, annul, nullify, ride roughshod over, outvote, countermand, trample underfoot, make null and void **3** IGNORE, reject, discount, overlook, set aside, disregard, pass over, take no notice of, take no account of, pay no attention to, turn a deaf ear to

overriding *adjective* MAJOR, chief, main, prime, predominant, leading, controlling, final, ruling, determining, primary, supreme, principal, ultimate, dominant, compelling, prevailing, cardinal, sovereign, paramount, prevalent, pivotal, top-priority, overruling, preponderant, number one << ANTONYM minor

overrule *verb* REVERSE, alter, cancel, recall, discount, overturn, set aside, override, repeal, quash, revoke, disallow, rescind, rule against, invalidate, annul, nullify, outvote, countermand, make null and void << ANTONYM approve

overrun *verb* **1** OVERWHELM, attack, assault, occupy, raid, invade, penetrate, swamp, rout, assail, descend upon, run riot over **2** SPREAD OVER, overwhelm, choke, swamp, overflow, infest, inundate, permeate, spread like wildfire, swarm over, surge over, overgrow **3** EXCEED, go beyond, surpass, overshoot, outrun, run over *or* on

overseer *noun* SUPERVISOR, manager, chief, boss (*informal*), master, inspector, superior, administrator, steward, superintendent, gaffer (*informal, chiefly Brit*), foreman, super (*informal*), baas (*S African*)

overshadow *verb* **1** SPOIL, ruin, mar, wreck, scar, blight, crool *or* cruel (*Austral slang*), mess up, take the edge off, put a damper on, cast a gloom upon, take the pleasure *or* enjoyment out of **2** OUTSHINE, eclipse, surpass, dwarf, rise above, take precedence over, tower above, steal the limelight from, leave *or* put in the shade, render insignificant by comparison, throw into the shade **3** SHADE, cloud, eclipse, darken, overcast, adumbrate

oversight *noun* **1** MISTAKE, error, slip, fault, misunderstanding, blunder, lapse, omission, boob (*Brit slang*), gaffe, slip-up (*informal*), delinquency, inaccuracy, carelessness, howler (*informal*), goof (*informal*), bloomer (*Brit informal*), clanger (*informal*), miscalculation, error of judgment, faux pas, inattention, laxity, boo-boo (*informal*), erratum, barry *or* Barry Crocker (*Austral slang*) **2** SUPERVISION, keeping, control, charge, care, management, handling, administration, direction, custody, stewardship, superintendence

overt *adjective* OPEN, obvious, plain, public, clear, apparent, visible, patent, evident, manifest, noticeable, blatant, downright, avowed, flagrant, observable, undisguised, barefaced, unconcealed << ANTONYM hidden

overtake *verb* **1** PASS, leave behind, overhaul, catch up with, get past, draw level with, outdistance, go by *or* past **2** OUTDO, top, exceed, eclipse, surpass, outstrip, get the better of, outclass, outshine, best, go one better than (*informal*), outdistance, be one up

on **3** BEFALL, hit, happen to, come upon, take by surprise, catch off guard, catch unawares, catch unprepared **4** ENGULF, overwhelm, hit, strike, consume, swamp, envelop, swallow up

overthrow *verb* DEFEAT, beat, master, overcome, crush, overwhelm, conquer, bring down, oust, lick (*informal*), topple, subdue, rout, overpower, do away with, depose, trounce, unseat, vanquish, subjugate, dethrone << ANTONYM uphold ▷ *noun* DOWNFALL, end, fall, defeat, collapse, ruin, destruction, breakdown, ousting, undoing, rout, suppression, displacement, subversion, deposition, unseating, subjugation, dispossession, disestablishment, dethronement << ANTONYM preservation

overtone *noun often plural* CONNOTATION, association, suggestion, sense, hint, flavour, implication, significance, nuance, colouring, innuendo, undercurrent, intimation

overture *noun* (*music*) PRELUDE, opening, introduction, introductory movement << ANTONYM finale

overtures *plural noun* APPROACH, offer, advance, proposal, appeal, invitation, tender, proposition, opening move, conciliatory move << ANTONYM rejection

overturn *verb* **1** TIP OVER, spill, topple, upturn, capsize, upend, keel over, overbalance **2** KNOCK OVER *or* DOWN, upset, upturn, tip over, upend **3** REVERSE, change, alter, cancel, abolish, overthrow, set aside, repeal, quash, revoke, overrule, override, negate, rescind, invalidate, annul, nullify, obviate, countermand, declare null and void, overset **4** OVERTHROW, defeat, destroy, overcome, crush, bring down, oust, topple, do away with, depose, unseat, dethrone

overweight *adjective* FAT, heavy, stout, huge, massive, solid, gross, hefty, ample, plump, bulky, chunky, obese, fleshy, beefy (*informal*), tubby (*informal*), portly, outsize, buxom, roly-poly, rotund, podgy, corpulent, elephantine, well-padded (*informal*), well-upholstered (*informal*), broad in the beam (*informal*), on the plump side << ANTONYM underweight

overwhelm *verb* **1** OVERCOME, overpower, devastate, stagger, get the better of, bowl (someone) over (*informal*), prostrate, knock (someone) for six (*informal*), render (someone) speechless, render (someone) incapable, render (someone) powerless, render (someone) helpless, sweep (someone) off his *or* her feet, take (someone's) breath away **2** DESTROY, beat, defeat, overcome, smash, crush, massacre, conquer, wipe out, overthrow, knock out, lick (*informal*), subdue, rout, eradicate, overpower, quell, annihilate, put paid to, vanquish, subjugate, immobilize, make mincemeat of (*informal*), cut to pieces **3** SWAMP, bury, flood, crush, engulf, submerge, beset, inundate, deluge, snow under

overwhelming *adjective* **1** OVERPOWERING, strong, powerful, towering, vast, stunning, extreme, crushing, devastating, shattering, compelling, irresistible, breathtaking, compulsive, forceful, unbearable, uncontrollable << ANTONYM negligible **2** VAST, huge, massive, enormous, tremendous, immense, very large, astronomic, humongous *or* humungous (*US slang*) << ANTONYM insignificant

overwork *verb* **1** WEAR YOURSELF OUT, burn the midnight oil, burn the candle at both ends, bite off more than you can chew, strain yourself, overstrain yourself, work your fingers to the bone, overtire yourself, drive yourself too far, overburden yourself, overload yourself, overtax yourself **2** EXPLOIT, exhaust, fatigue, weary, oppress, wear out, prostrate, overtax, drive into the ground, be a slave-driver *or* hard taskmaster to

overwrought *adjective* **1** DISTRAUGHT, upset, excited, desperate, wired (*slang*), anxious, distressed, tense, distracted, frantic, in a state, hysterical, wound up (*informal*), worked up (*informal*), agitated, uptight (*informal*), on edge, strung out (*informal*), out of your mind, keyed up, overexcited, in a tizzy (*informal*), at the end of your tether, wrought-up, beside

yourself, in a twitter (*informal*), tooshie (*Austral slang*), adrenalized << ANTONYM calm **2** OVERELABORATE, contrived, overdone, flamboyant, baroque, high-flown, ornate, fussy, flowery, busy, rococo, florid, grandiloquent, euphuistic, overembellished, overornate

owe *verb* BE IN DEBT (TO), be in arrears (to), be overdrawn (by), be beholden to, be under an obligation to, be obligated *or* indebted (to)

owing *adjective* UNPAID, due, outstanding, owed, payable, unsettled, overdue ▷▷ **owing to** BECAUSE OF, thanks to, as a result of, on account of, by reason of

own *determiner* PERSONAL, special, private, individual, particular, exclusive ▷ *verb* POSSESS, have, keep, hold, enjoy, retain, be responsible for, be in possession of, have to your name ▷▷ **hold your own** KEEP GOING, compete, get on, get along, stand your ground, keep your head above water, keep your end up, maintain your position ▷▷ **on your own 1** ALONE, by yourself, all alone, unaccompanied, on your tod (*Brit slang*) **2** INDEPENDENTLY, alone, singly, single-handedly, by yourself, unaided, without help, unassisted, left to your own devices, under your own steam, off your own bat, by your own efforts, (standing) on your own two feet

owner *noun* POSSESSOR, holder, proprietor, freeholder, titleholder, proprietress, proprietrix, landlord *or* landlady, master *or* mistress, deed holder

ownership *noun* POSSESSION, occupation, tenure, dominion, occupancy, proprietorship, proprietary rights, right of possession

pace *noun* 1 SPEED, rate, momentum, tempo, progress, motion, clip (*informal*), lick (*informal*), velocity 2 STEP, walk, stride, tread, gait 3 FOOTSTEP, step, stride ▷ *verb* STRIDE, walk, pound, patrol, walk up and down, march up and down, walk back and forth

pacific *adjective* 1 NONAGGRESSIVE, pacifist, nonviolent, friendly, gentle, mild, peace-loving, peaceable, dovish, nonbelligerent, dovelike << ANTONYM aggressive 2 PEACEMAKING, diplomatic, appeasing, conciliatory, placatory, propitiatory, irenic, pacificatory

pacifist *noun* PEACE LOVER, dove, conscientious objector, peacenik (*informal*), conchie (*informal*), peacemonger, satyagrahi (*rare*), passive resister

pacify *verb* CALM (DOWN), appease, placate, still, content, quiet, moderate, compose, soften, soothe, allay, assuage, make peace with, mollify, ameliorate, conciliate, propitiate, tranquillize, smooth someone's ruffled feathers, clear the air with, restore harmony to

pack *verb* 1 PACKAGE, load, store, bundle, batch, stow 2 CRAM, charge, crowd, press, fill, stuff, jam, compact, mob, ram, wedge, compress, throng, tamp ▷ *noun* 1 PACKET, box, package, carton 2 BUNDLE, kit, parcel, load, burden, bale, rucksack, truss, knapsack, back pack, kitbag, fardel (*archaic*) 3 GROUP, crowd, collection, company, set, lot, band, troop, crew, drove, gang, deck, bunch, mob, flock, herd, assemblage ▷▷ **pack someone off** SEND AWAY, dismiss, send packing (*informal*), bundle out, hustle out ▷▷ **pack something in** 1 (*Brit & NZ informal*) RESIGN FROM, leave, give up, quit (*informal*), chuck (*informal*), jack in (*informal*) 2 STOP, give up, kick (*informal*), cease, chuck (*informal*), leave off, jack in,

desist from ▷▷ **pack something up** 1 PUT AWAY, store, tidy up 2 (*informal*) STOP, finish, give up, pack in (*Brit informal*), call it a day (*informal*), call it a night (*informal*) ▷▷ **pack up** BREAK DOWN, stop, fail, stall, give out, conk out (*informal*) ▷▷ **send someone packing** (*informal*) SEND SOMEONE AWAY, dismiss, discharge, give someone the bird (*informal*), give someone the brushoff (*slang*), send someone about his *or* her business, send someone away with a flea in his *or* her ear (*informal*)

package *noun* 1 PARCEL, box, container, packet, carton 2 COLLECTION, lot, unit, combination, compilation ▷ *verb* PACK, box, wrap up, parcel (up), batch

packaging *noun* WRAPPING, casing, covering, cover, box, packing, wrapper

packed *adjective* FILLED, full, crowded, jammed, crammed, swarming, overflowing, overloaded, seething, congested, jam-packed, chock-full, bursting at the seams, cram-full, brimful, chock-a-block, packed like sardines, hoatching (*Scot*), loaded *or* full to the gunwales << ANTONYM empty

packet *noun* 1 CONTAINER, box, package, wrapping, poke (*dialect*), carton, wrapper 2 PACKAGE, parcel 3 (*slang*) A FORTUNE, lot(s), pot(s) (*informal*), a bomb (*Brit slang*), a pile (*informal*), big money, a bundle (*slang*), big bucks (*informal, chiefly US*), a small fortune, a mint, a wad (*US & Canad slang*), megabucks (*US & Canad slang*), an arm and a leg (*informal*), a bob or two (*Brit informal*), a tidy sum (*informal*), a king's ransom (*informal*), a pretty penny (*informal*), top whack (*informal*)

pact *noun* AGREEMENT, contract, alliance, treaty, deal, understanding, league, bond, arrangement, bargain, convention, compact, protocol, covenant, concord, concordat

pad¹ *noun* 1 WAD, dressing, pack, padding, compress, wadding 2 CUSHION, filling, stuffing, pillow, bolster, upholstery 3 NOTEPAD, block, tablet, notebook, jotter, writing pad 4 (*slang*) HOME, flat, apartment, place, room, quarters, hang-out (*informal*), bachelor apartment (*Canad*) 5 PAW, foot, sole ▷ *verb* PACK, line, fill, protect, shape, stuff, cushion ▷▷ **pad something out** LENGTHEN, stretch, elaborate, inflate, fill out, amplify, augment, spin out, flesh out, eke out, protract

pad² *verb* SNEAK, creep, steal, pussyfoot (*informal*), go barefoot

padding *noun* 1 FILLING, stuffing, packing, wadding 2 WAFFLE (*informal, chiefly Brit*), hot air (*informal*), verbiage, wordiness, verbosity, prolixity

paddle¹ *noun* OAR, sweep, scull ▷ *verb* ROW, pull, scull

paddle² *verb* WADE, splash (about), slop, plash

paddy *noun* (*Brit slang*) TEMPER, tantrum, bad mood, passion, rage, pet, fit of pique, fit of temper, foulie (*Austral slang*), hissy fit (*informal*)

paean *or* (*sometimes*) *US* **pean** *noun* (*literary*) EULOGY, tribute, panegyric, hymn of praise, encomium

pagan *noun* HEATHEN, infidel, unbeliever, polytheist, idolater ▷ *adjective* HEATHEN, infidel, irreligious, polytheistic, idolatrous, heathenish

page¹ *noun* 1 FOLIO, side, leaf, sheet 2 PERIOD, chapter, phase, era, episode, time, point, event, stage, incident, epoch

page² *noun* 1 ATTENDANT, bellboy (*US*), pageboy, footboy 2 SERVANT, attendant, squire, pageboy, footboy ▷ *verb* CALL, seek, summon, call out for, send for

pageant *noun* SHOW, display, parade, ritual, spectacle, procession, extravaganza, tableau

pageantry *noun* SPECTACLE, show, display, drama, parade, splash (*informal*), state, glitter, glamour, grandeur, splendour, extravagance, pomp, magnificence, theatricality, showiness

pain *noun* 1 SUFFERING, discomfort, trouble, hurt, irritation, tenderness, soreness 2 ACHE, smarting, stinging, aching, cramp, cramp, throb, throbbing, spasm, pang, twinge, shooting pain 3 SORROW, suffering, torture, distress, despair, grief, misery, agony, sadness, torment, hardship, bitterness, woe, anguish, heartache, affliction, tribulation, desolation, wretchedness ▷ *plural noun* TROUBLE, labour, effort, industry, care, bother, diligence, special attention, assiduousness ▷ *verb* 1 DISTRESS, worry, hurt, wound, torture, grieve, torment, afflict, sadden, disquiet, vex, agonize, cut to the quick, aggrieve 2 HURT, chafe, cause pain to, cause discomfort to

pained *adjective* DISTRESSED, worried, hurt, injured, wounded, upset, unhappy, stung, offended, aggrieved, anguished, miffed (*informal*), reproachful

painful *adjective* 1 SORE, hurting, smarting, aching, raw, tender, throbbing, inflamed, excruciating << ANTONYM painless 2 DISTRESSING, unpleasant, harrowing, saddening, grievous, distasteful, agonizing, disagreeable, afflictive << ANTONYM pleasant 3 DIFFICULT, arduous, trying, hard, severe, troublesome, laborious, vexatious << ANTONYM easy 4 (*informal*) TERRIBLE, awful, dreadful, dire, excruciating, abysmal, gut-wrenching, godawful, extremely bad

painfully *adverb* DISTRESSINGLY, clearly, sadly, unfortunately, markedly, excessively, alarmingly, woefully, dreadfully, deplorably

painkiller *noun* ANALGESIC, drug, remedy, anaesthetic, sedative, palliative, anodyne

painless *adjective* 1 PAIN-FREE, without pain 2 SIMPLE, easy, fast, quick, no trouble, effortless, trouble-free

painstaking *adjective* THOROUGH, careful, meticulous, earnest, exacting, strenuous, conscientious, persevering, diligent, scrupulous, industrious, assiduous, thoroughgoing, punctilious, sedulous << ANTONYM careless

paint *noun* COLOURING, colour, stain, dye, tint, pigment, emulsion ▷ *verb* 1 COLOUR, cover, coat, decorate, stain, whitewash, daub, distemper, apply paint to 2 DEPICT, draw, portray, figure, picture, represent, sketch, delineate, catch a likeness 3 DESCRIBE, capture, portray, depict, evoke, recount, bring to life, make you see, conjure up a vision, put graphically, tell vividly ▷▷ **paint the town red** (*informal*) CELEBRATE, revel, carouse, live it up (*informal*), make merry, make whoopee (*informal*), go on a binge (*informal*), go on a spree, go on the town

pair *noun* 1 SET, match, combination, doublet, matched set, two of a kind 2 COUPLE, brace, duo, twosome ▷ *verb often with* **off** TEAM, match (up), join, couple, marry, wed, twin, put together, bracket, yoke, pair off

pal *noun* (*informal*) FRIEND, companion, mate

(*informal*), buddy (*informal*), comrade, chum (*informal*), crony, cock (*Brit informal*), main man (*slang, chiefly US*), homeboy (*slang, chiefly US*), cobber (*Austral & NZ old-fashioned informal*), boon companion, E hoa (*NZ*)

palatable *adjective* **1** DELICIOUS, tasty, luscious, savoury, delectable, mouthwatering, appetizing, toothsome, yummo (*Austral slang*) << ANTONYM unpalatable **2** ACCEPTABLE, pleasant, agreeable, fair, attractive, satisfactory, enjoyable

palate *noun* TASTE, heart, stomach, appetite

palatial *adjective* MAGNIFICENT, grand, imposing, splendid, gorgeous, luxurious, spacious, majestic, regal, stately, sumptuous, plush (*informal*), illustrious, grandiose, opulent, de luxe, splendiferous (*facetious*)

pale¹ *adjective* **1** LIGHT, soft, faded, subtle, muted, bleached, pastel, light-coloured **2** DIM, weak, faint, feeble, thin, wan, watery **3** WHITE, pasty, bleached, washed-out, wan, bloodless, colourless, pallid, anaemic, ashen, sallow, whitish, ashy, like death warmed up (*informal*) << ANTONYM rosy-cheeked **4** POOR, weak, inadequate, pathetic, feeble ▷ *verb* **1** FADE, dull, diminish, decrease, dim, lessen, grow dull, lose lustre **2** BECOME PALE, blanch, whiten, go white, lose colour

pale² *noun* POST, stake, paling, upright, picket, slat, palisade ▷▷ **beyond the pale** UNACCEPTABLE, not done, forbidden, irregular, indecent, unsuitable, improper, barbaric, unspeakable, out of line, unseemly, inadmissible

pall¹ *noun* **1** CLOUD, shadow, veil, mantle, shroud **2** GLOOM, damp, dismay, melancholy, damper, check

pall² *verb often with* **on** BECOME BORING, become dull, become tedious, become tiresome, jade, cloy, become wearisome

pallid *adjective* PALE, wan, pasty, colourless, anaemic, ashen, sallow, whitish, cadaverous, waxen, ashy, like death warmed up (*informal*), wheyfaced

pallor *noun* PALENESS, whiteness, lack of colour, wanness, bloodlessness, ashen hue, pallidness

palm *noun* HAND, hook, paw (*informal*), mitt (*slang*), meathook (*slang*) ▷▷ **in the palm of your hand** IN YOUR POWER, in your control, in your clutches, at your mercy ▷▷ **palm someone off** FOB OFF, dismiss, disregard, pooh-pooh (*informal*) ▷▷ **palm something off on someone** FOIST ON, force upon, impose upon, pass off, thrust upon, unload upon

palpable *adjective* OBVIOUS, apparent, patent, clear, plain, visible, evident, manifest, open, blatant, conspicuous, unmistakable, salient

paltry *adjective* **1** MEAGRE, petty, trivial, trifling, beggarly, derisory, measly, piddling (*informal*), inconsiderable << ANTONYM considerable **2** INSIGNIFICANT, trivial, worthless, unimportant, small, low, base, minor, slight, petty, trifling, Mickey Mouse (*slang*), piddling (*informal*), toytown (*slang*), poxy (*slang*), nickel-and-dime (*US slang*), picayune (*US*), twopenny-halfpenny (*Brit informal*) << ANTONYM important

pamper *verb* SPOIL, indulge, gratify, baby, pet, humour, pander to, fondle, cosset, coddle, mollycoddle, wait on (someone) hand and foot, cater to someone's every whim

pamphlet *noun* BOOKLET, leaflet, brochure, circular, tract, folder

pan¹ *noun* POT, vessel, container, saucepan ▷ *verb* **1** (*informal*) CRITICIZE, knock, blast, hammer (*Brit informal*), slam (*slang*), rubbish (*informal*), roast (*informal*), put down, slate (*informal*), censure, slag (off) (*slang*), tear into (*informal*), flay, lambast(e), throw brickbats at (*informal*) **2** SIFT OUT, look for, wash, search for ▷▷ **pan out** (*informal*) WORK OUT, happen, result, come out, turn out, culminate, come to pass (*archaic*), eventuate

pan² *verb* MOVE ALONG *or* ACROSS, follow, track, sweep, scan, traverse, swing across

panacea *noun* CURE-ALL, elixir, nostrum, heal-all, sovereign remedy, universal cure

panache *noun* STYLE, spirit, dash, flair, verve, swagger, flourish, élan, flamboyance, brio

pandemonium *noun* UPROAR, confusion, chaos, turmoil, racket, clamour, din, commotion, rumpus, bedlam, babel, tumult, hubbub, ruction (*informal*), hullabaloo, hue and cry, ruckus (*informal*) << ANTONYM order

pander ▷▷ **pander to something** *or* **someone** INDULGE, please, satisfy, gratify, cater to, play up to (*informal*), fawn on

pang *noun* **1** PAIN, stab, sting, stitch, ache, wrench, prick, spasm, twinge, throe (*rare*) **2** TWINGE, stab, prick, spasm, qualm, gnawing

panic *noun* FEAR, alarm, horror, terror, anxiety, dismay, hysteria, fright, agitation, consternation, trepidation, a flap (*informal*) ▷ *verb* **1** GO TO PIECES, overreact, become hysterical, have kittens (*informal*), lose your nerve, be terror-stricken, lose your bottle (*Brit slang*) **2** ALARM, scare, terrify, startle, unnerve

panicky *adjective* FRIGHTENED, worried, afraid, nervous, distressed, fearful, frantic, frenzied, hysterical, worked up, windy (*slang*), agitated, jittery (*informal*), in a flap (*informal*), antsy (*informal*), in a tizzy (*informal*) << ANTONYM calm

panic-stricken *or* **panic-struck** *adjective* FRIGHTENED, alarmed, scared, terrified, startled, horrified, fearful, frenzied, hysterical, agitated, unnerved, petrified, aghast, panicky, scared stiff, in a cold sweat (*informal*), frightened to death, terror-stricken, horror-stricken, frightened out of your wits

panoply *noun* 1 ARRAY, range, display, collection 2 TRAPPINGS, show, dress, get-up (*informal*), turnout, attire, garb, insignia, regalia, raiment (*archaic or poetic*)

panorama *noun* 1 VIEW, prospect, scenery, vista, bird's-eye view, scenic view 2 SURVEY, perspective, overview, overall picture

panoramic *adjective* 1 WIDE, overall, extensive, scenic, bird's-eye 2 COMPREHENSIVE, general, extensive, sweeping, inclusive, far-reaching, all-embracing

pant *verb* PUFF, blow, breathe, gasp, throb, wheeze, huff, heave, palpitate ▷ *noun* GASP, puff, wheeze, huff ▷▷ **pant for something** LONG FOR, want, desire, crave for, covet, yearn for, thirst for, hunger for, pine for, hanker after, ache for, sigh for, set your heart on, eat your heart out over, suspire for (*archaic or poetic*)

panting *adjective* 1 OUT OF BREATH, winded, gasping, puffed, puffing, breathless, puffed out, short of breath, out of puff, out of whack (*informal*) 2 EAGER, raring, anxious, impatient, champing at the bit (*informal*), all agog

pants *plural noun* 1 (*Brit*) UNDERPANTS, briefs, drawers, knickers, panties, boxer shorts, Y-fronts (*trademark*), broekies (*S African*), underdaks (*Austral slang*) 2 (*US*) TROUSERS, slacks

pap *noun* RUBBISH, trash, trivia, drivel

paper *noun* 1 NEWSPAPER, news, daily, journal, organ, rag (*informal*), tabloid, gazette, broadsheet 2 ESSAY, study, article, analysis, script, composition, assignment, thesis, critique, treatise, dissertation, monograph 3 EXAMINATION, test, exam 4 REPORT, study, survey, inquiry ▷ *plural noun* LETTERS, records, documents, file, diaries, archive, paperwork, dossier 2 DOCUMENTS, records,

certificates, identification, deeds, identity papers, I.D. (*informal*) ▷ *verb* WALLPAPER, line, hang, paste up, cover with paper ▷▷ **on paper** 1 IN WRITING, written down, on (the) record, in print, in black and white 2 IN THEORY, ideally, theoretically, in the abstract

parable *noun* LESSON, story, fable, allegory, moral tale, exemplum

parade *noun* 1 PROCESSION, march, ceremony, pageant, train, review, column, spectacle, tattoo, motorcade, cavalcade, cortège 2 SHOW, display, exhibition, spectacle, array ▷ *verb* 1 MARCH, process, file, promenade 2 FLAUNT, show, display, exhibit, show off (*informal*), air, draw attention to, brandish, vaunt, make a show of 3 STRUT, show off (*informal*), swagger, swank

paradigm *noun* MODEL, example, original, pattern, ideal, norm, prototype, archetype, exemplar

paradise *noun* 1 HEAVEN, Promised Land, Zion (*Christianity*), Happy Valley (*Islam*), City of God, Elysian fields, garden of delights, divine abode, heavenly kingdom 2 GARDEN OF EDEN, Eden 3 BLISS, delight, heaven, felicity, utopia, seventh heaven

paradox *noun* CONTRADICTION, mystery, puzzle, ambiguity, anomaly, inconsistency, enigma, oddity, absurdity

paradoxical *adjective* CONTRADICTORY, inconsistent, impossible, puzzling, absurd, baffling, riddling, ambiguous, improbable, confounding, enigmatic, illogical, equivocal, oracular

paragon *noun* MODEL, standard, pattern, ideal, criterion, norm, jewel, masterpiece, prototype, paradigm, archetype, epitome, exemplar, apotheosis, quintessence, nonesuch (*archaic*), nonpareil, best *or* greatest thing since sliced bread (*informal*), cynosure

paragraph *noun* SECTION, part, notice, item, passage, clause, portion, subdivision

parallel *noun* 1 EQUIVALENT, counterpart, match, equal, twin, complement, duplicate, analogue, likeness, corollary << ANTONYM opposite 2 SIMILARITY, correspondence, correlation, comparison, analogy, resemblance, likeness, parallelism << ANTONYM difference ▷ *verb* 1 CORRESPOND TO, compare with, agree with, complement, conform to, be alike, chime with, correlate to << ANTONYM differ from 2 MATCH, equal, duplicate, keep pace (with), measure up to ▷ *adjective* 1 MATCHING, correspondent, corresponding, like, similar, uniform, resembling, complementary, akin, analogous << ANTONYM different **2** EQUIDISTANT, alongside, aligned, side by side, coextensive << ANTONYM divergent

paralyse *verb* **1** DISABLE, cripple, lame, debilitate, incapacitate **2** FREEZE, stun, numb, petrify, transfix, stupefy, halt, stop dead, immobilize, anaesthetize, benumb **3** IMMOBILIZE, freeze, halt, disable, cripple, arrest, incapacitate, bring to a standstill

paralysis *noun* **1** IMMOBILITY, palsy, paresis (*pathology*) **2** STANDSTILL, breakdown, stoppage, shutdown, halt, stagnation, inactivity

parameter *noun usually plural (informal)* LIMIT, constant, restriction, guideline, criterion, framework, limitation, specification

paramount *adjective* PRINCIPAL, prime, first, chief, main, capital, primary, supreme, outstanding, superior, dominant, cardinal, foremost, eminent, predominant, pre-eminent << ANTONYM secondary

paranoid *adjective* **1** (*informal*) SUSPICIOUS, worried, nervous, fearful, apprehensive, antsy (*informal*) **2** OBSESSIVE, disturbed, unstable, manic, neurotic, mentally ill, psychotic, deluded, paranoiac

paraphernalia *noun* EQUIPMENT, things, effects, material, stuff, tackle, gear, baggage, apparatus, belongings, clobber (*Brit slang*), accoutrements, impedimenta, appurtenances, equipage

paraphrase *verb* REWORD, interpret, render, restate, rehash, rephrase, express in other words *or* your own words ▷ *noun* REWORDING, version, interpretation, rendering, translation, rendition, rehash, restatement, rephrasing

parasite *noun* SPONGER (*informal*), sponge (*informal*), drone (*Brit*), leech, hanger-on, scrounger (*informal*), bloodsucker (*informal*), cadger, quandong (*Austral slang*)

parasitic *or* **parasitical** *adjective* SCROUNGING (*informal*), sponging (*informal*), cadging, bloodsucking (*informal*), leechlike

parcel *noun* **1** PACKAGE, case, box, pack, packet, bundle, carton **2** PLOT, area, property, section, patch, tract, allotment, piece of land **3** GROUP, crowd, pack, company, lot, band, collection, crew, gang, bunch, batch ▷ *verb often with* **up** WRAP, pack, package, tie up, do up, gift-wrap, box up, fasten together ▷▷ **parcel something out** DISTRIBUTE, divide, portion, allocate, split up, dispense, allot,

carve up, mete out, dole out, share out, apportion, deal out

parched *adjective* **1** DRIED OUT *or* UP, dry, withered, scorched, arid, torrid, shrivelled, dehydrated, waterless **2** THIRSTY, dry, dehydrated, drouthy (*Scot*)

pardon *verb* ACQUIT, free, release, liberate, reprieve, remit, amnesty, let off (*informal*), exonerate, absolve, exculpate << ANTONYM punish ▷ *noun* **1** FORGIVENESS, mercy, indulgence, absolution, grace << ANTONYM condemnation **2** ACQUITTAL, release, discharge, amnesty, reprieve, remission, exoneration << ANTONYM punishment ▷▷ **pardon me** FORGIVE ME, excuse me

pare *verb* **1** PEEL, cut, skin, trim, clip, shave **2** CUT BACK, cut, reduce, crop, decrease, dock, prune, shear, lop, retrench

parent *noun* **1** FATHER *or* MOTHER, sire, progenitor, begetter, procreator, old (*Austral & NZ informal*), oldie (*Austral informal*), patriarch **2** SOURCE, cause, author, root, origin, architect, creator, prototype, forerunner, originator, wellspring

parentage *noun* FAMILY, birth, origin, descent, line, race, stock, pedigree, extraction, ancestry, lineage, paternity, derivation

parenthood *noun* FATHERHOOD *or* MOTHERHOOD, parenting, rearing, bringing up, nurturing, upbringing, child rearing, baby *or* child care, fathering *or* mothering

pariah *noun* OUTCAST, exile, outlaw, undesirable, untouchable, leper, unperson

parings *plural noun* PEELINGS, skins, slices, clippings, peel, fragments, shavings, shreds, flakes, rind, snippets, slivers

parish *noun* **1** DISTRICT, community **2** COMMUNITY, fold, flock, church, congregation, parishioners, churchgoers

parity *noun* EQUALITY, correspondence, consistency, equivalence, quits (*informal*), par, unity, similarity, likeness, uniformity, equal terms, sameness, parallelism, congruity

park *noun* **1** RECREATION GROUND, garden, playground, pleasure garden, playpark, domain (*NZ*), forest park (*NZ*) **2** PARKLAND, grounds, estate, lawns, woodland, grassland **3** FIELD, pitch, playing field ▷ *verb* **1** LEAVE, stop, station, position **2** PUT (DOWN), leave, place, stick, deposit, dump, shove, plonk (*informal*)

parlance *noun* LANGUAGE, talk, speech, tongue, jargon, idiom, lingo (*informal*), phraseology, manner of speaking

parliament *noun* **1** ASSEMBLY, council, congress, senate, convention, legislature, talking shop (*informal*), convocation **2** SITTING, diet **3** *with cap.* HOUSES OF PARLIAMENT, the House, Westminster, Mother of Parliaments, the House of Commons and the House of Lords, House of Representatives (*NZ*)

parliamentary *adjective* GOVERNMENTAL, congressional, legislative, law-making, law-giving, deliberative

parlour *or US* **parlor** *noun* **1** (*old-fashioned*) SITTING ROOM, lounge, living room, drawing room, front room, reception room, best room **2** ESTABLISHMENT, shop, store, salon

parlous *adjective* (*archaic or humorous*) DANGEROUS, difficult, desperate, risky, dire, hazardous, hairy (*slang*), perilous, chancy (*informal*)

parochial *adjective* PROVINCIAL, narrow, insular, limited, restricted, petty, narrow-minded, inward-looking, small-minded, parish-pump << ANTONYM cosmopolitan

parody *noun* **1** TAKEOFF (*informal*), imitation, satire, caricature, send-up (*Brit informal*), spoof (*informal*), lampoon, skit, burlesque **2** TRAVESTY, farce, caricature, mockery, apology for ▷ *verb* TAKE OFF (*informal*), mimic, caricature, send up (*Brit informal*), spoof (*informal*), travesty, lampoon, poke fun at, burlesque, satirize, do a takeoff of (*informal*)

paroxysm *noun* OUTBURST, attack, fit, seizure, flare-up (*informal*), eruption, spasm, convulsion

parrot *verb* REPEAT, echo, imitate, copy, reiterate, mimic

parry *verb* **1** EVADE, avoid, fence off, dodge, duck (*informal*), shun, sidestep, circumvent, fight shy of **2** WARD OFF, block, deflect, repel, rebuff, fend off, stave off, repulse, hold at bay

parsimonious *adjective* MEAN, stingy, penny-pinching (*informal*), miserly, near (*informal*), saving, sparing, grasping, miserable, stinting, frugal, niggardly, penurious, tightfisted, close-fisted, mingy (*Brit informal*), cheeseparing, skinflinty, snoep (*S African informal*) << ANTONYM extravagant

parson *noun* CLERGYMAN, minister, priest, vicar, divine, incumbent, reverend (*informal*), preacher, pastor, cleric, rector, curate, churchman, man of God, man of the cloth, ecclesiastic

part *noun* **1** PIECE, share, proportion, percentage, lot, bit, section, sector, slice, scrap, particle, segment, portion, fragment, lump, fraction, chunk, wedge << ANTONYM entirety **2** *often plural* REGION, area, district, territory, neighbourhood, quarter, vicinity, neck of the woods (*informal*), airt (*Scot*) **3** COMPONENT, bit, piece, unit, element, ingredient, constituent, module **4** BRANCH, department, division, office, section, wing, subdivision, subsection **5** ORGAN, member, limb **6** (*theatre*) ROLE, representation, persona, portrayal, depiction, character part **7** (*theatre*) LINES, words, script, dialogue **8** DUTY, say, place, work, role, hand, business, share, charge, responsibility, task, function, capacity, involvement, participation **9** SIDE, behalf ▷ *verb* **1** DIVIDE, separate, break, tear, split, rend, detach, sever, disconnect, cleave, come apart, disunite, disjoin << ANTONYM join **2** PART COMPANY, separate, break up, split up, say goodbye, go (their) separate ways << ANTONYM meet ▷▷ **for the most part** MAINLY, largely, generally, chiefly, mostly, principally, on the whole, in the main ▷▷ **in good part** GOOD-NATUREDLY, well, cheerfully, cordially, without offence ▷▷ **in part** PARTLY, a little, somewhat, slightly, partially, to some degree, to a certain extent, in some measure ▷▷ **on the part of** BY, in, from, made by, carried out by ▷▷ **part with something** GIVE UP, abandon, yield, sacrifice, surrender, discard, relinquish, renounce, let go of, forgo ▷▷ **take part in** PARTICIPATE IN, be involved in, join in, play a part in, be instrumental in, have a hand in, partake in, take a hand in, associate yourself with, put your twopence-worth in

partake ▷▷ **partake in something** PARTICIPATE IN, share in, take part in, engage in, enter into ▷▷ **partake of something 1** CONSUME, take, share, receive, eat **2** DISPLAY, exhibit, evoke, hint at, be characterized by

partial *adjective* **1** INCOMPLETE, limited, unfinished, imperfect, fragmentary, uncompleted << ANTONYM complete **2** BIASED, prejudiced, discriminatory, partisan, influenced, unfair, one-sided, unjust, predisposed, tendentious << ANTONYM unbiased

partially *adverb* PARTLY, somewhat, moderately, in part, halfway, piecemeal, not wholly, fractionally, incompletely, to a certain extent *or* degree ▷ *see* **partly**

participant *noun* PARTICIPATOR, party, member, player, associate, shareholder,

contributor, stakeholder, partaker
participate *verb* TAKE PART, be involved,
engage, perform, join, enter, partake, have
a hand, get in on the act, be a party to, be a
participant << ANTONYM refrain from
participation *noun* TAKING PART,
contribution, partnership, involvement,
assistance, sharing in, joining in, partaking
particle *noun* BIT, piece, scrap, grain,
molecule, atom, shred, crumb, mite, jot,
speck, mote, whit, tittle, iota
particular *adjective* **1** SPECIFIC, special,
express, exact, precise, distinct, peculiar
<< ANTONYM general **2** SPECIAL,
exceptional, notable, uncommon, marked,
unusual, remarkable, singular, noteworthy,
especial **3** FUSSY, demanding, critical,
exacting, discriminating, meticulous,
fastidious, dainty, choosy (*informal*), picky
(*informal*), finicky, pernickety (*informal*),
overnice << ANTONYM indiscriminate
4 DETAILED, minute, precise, thorough,
selective, painstaking, circumstantial,
itemized, blow-by-blow ▷ *noun usually plural*
DETAIL, fact, feature, item, circumstance,
specification ▷▷ **in particular** ESPECIALLY,
particularly, expressly, specifically, exactly,
distinctly
particularly *adverb* **1** SPECIFICALLY, expressly,
explicitly, especially, in particular,
distinctly **2** ESPECIALLY, surprisingly,
notably, unusually, exceptionally,
decidedly, markedly, peculiarly, singularly,
outstandingly, uncommonly
parting *noun* **1** FAREWELL, departure, goodbye,
leave-taking, adieu, valediction **2** DIVISION,
breaking, split, separation, rift, partition,
detachment, rupture, divergence ▷ *modifier*
FAREWELL, last, final, departing, valedictory
partisan *adjective* **1** PREJUDICED, one-
sided, biased, partial, sectarian, factional,
tendentious << ANTONYM unbiased
2 UNDERGROUND, resistance, guerrilla,
irregular ▷ *noun* **1** SUPPORTER, champion,
follower, backer, disciple, stalwart, devotee,
adherent, upholder, votary << ANTONYM
opponent **2** UNDERGROUND FIGHTER,
guerrilla, irregular, freedom fighter,
resistance fighter
partition *noun* **1** SCREEN, wall, barrier, divider,
room divider **2** DIVISION, splitting, dividing,
separation, segregation, severance ▷ *verb*
1 SEPARATE, screen, divide, fence off, wall
off **2** DIVIDE, separate, segment, split up,
share, section, portion, cut up, apportion,

subdivide, parcel out
partly *adverb* PARTIALLY, relatively, somewhat,
slightly, in part, halfway, not fully, in some
measure, incompletely, up to a certain point,
to a certain degree *or* extent << ANTONYM
completely
partner *noun* **1** SPOUSE, consort, bedfellow,
significant other (*US informal*), mate, better
half (*Brit informal*), helpmate, husband *or*
wife **2** COMPANION, collaborator, accomplice,
ally, colleague, associate, mate, team-
mate, participant, comrade, confederate,
bedfellow, copartner **3** ASSOCIATE, colleague,
collaborator, copartner
partnership *noun* **1** COOPERATION, association,
alliance, sharing, union, connection,
participation, copartnership **2** COMPANY,
firm, corporation, house, interest, society,
conglomerate, cooperative
party *noun* **1** FACTION, association,
alliance, grouping, set, side, league, camp,
combination, coalition, clique, coterie,
schism, confederacy, cabal **2** GET-TOGETHER
(*informal*), celebration, do (*informal*), social,
at-home, gathering, function, reception,
bash (*informal*), rave (*Brit slang*), festivity,
knees-up (*Brit informal*), beano (*Brit slang*),
social gathering, shindig (*informal*), soirée,
rave-up (*Brit slang*), hooley *or* hoolie (*chiefly
Irish* & *NZ*) **3** GROUP, team, band, company,
body, unit, squad, gathering, crew, gang,
bunch (*informal*), detachment (*military*)
4 (*law*) LITIGANT, defendant, participant,
contractor (*law*), plaintiff
pass *verb* **1** GO BY *or* PAST, overtake, drive
past, lap, leave behind, pull ahead of
<< ANTONYM stop **2** GO, move, travel, roll,
progress, flow, proceed, move onwards
3 RUN, move, stroke **4** GIVE, hand, send,
throw, exchange, transfer, deliver, toss,
transmit, convey, chuck (*informal*), let
someone have **5** BE LEFT, come, be
bequeathed, be inherited by **6** KICK, hit,
loft, head, lob **7** ELAPSE, progress, go by,
lapse, wear on, go past, tick by **8** END, go,
die, disappear, fade, cease, vanish, dissolve,
expire, terminate, dwindle, evaporate,
wane, ebb, melt away, blow over **9** SPEND,
use (up), kill, fill, waste, employ, occupy,
devote, beguile, while away **10** EXCEED,
beat, overtake, go beyond, excel, surpass,
transcend, outstrip, outdo, surmount
11 BE SUCCESSFUL (IN), qualify (in), succeed
(in), graduate (in), get through, do, pass
muster (in), come up to scratch (in)

(*informal*), gain a pass (in) << ANTONYM
fail **12** APPROVE, accept, establish, adopt,
sanction, decree, enact, authorize, ratify,
ordain, validate, legislate (for) << ANTONYM
ban **13** PRONOUNCE, deliver, issue, set
forth **14** UTTER, speak, voice, express,
declare **15** DISCHARGE, release, expel,
evacuate, emit, let out, eliminate (*rare*) ▷
noun **1** LICENCE, ticket, permit, permission,
passport, warrant, identification, identity
card, authorization **2** GAP, route, canyon,
col, gorge, ravine, defile **3** PREDICAMENT,
condition, situation, state, stage, pinch,
plight, straits, state of affairs, juncture
▷▷ **make a pass at someone** MAKE ADVANCES
TO, proposition, hit on (*US & Canad slang*),
come on to (*informal*), make a play for
(*informal*), make an approach to, make sexual
overtures to ▷▷ **pass as** or **for something** or
someone BE MISTAKEN FOR, be taken for,
impersonate, be accepted as, be regarded
as ▷▷ **pass away** or **on** (*euphemistic*) DIE,
pass on, depart (this life), buy it (*US slang*),
expire, check out (*US slang*), pass over, kick
it (*slang*), croak (*slang*), go belly-up (*slang*),
snuff it (*informal*), peg out (*informal*), kick
the bucket (*slang*), buy the farm (*US slang*),
peg it (*informal*), decease, shuffle off this
mortal coil, cark it (*Austral & NZ informal*),
pop your clogs (*informal*) ▷▷ **pass off 1** TAKE
PLACE, happen, occur, turn out, go down
(*US & Canad*), be completed, go off, fall
out, be finished, pan out **2** COME TO AN
END, disappear, vanish, die away, fade out
or away ▷▷ **pass out** (*informal*) FAINT, drop,
black out (*informal*), swoon (*literary*), lose
consciousness, keel over (*informal*), flake
out (*informal*), become unconscious ▷▷ **pass
someone over** OVERLOOK, ignore, discount,
pass by, disregard, not consider, take no
notice of, not take into consideration, pay
no attention to ▷▷ **pass something out** HAND
OUT, distribute, dole out, deal out ▷▷ **pass
something over** DISREGARD, forget, ignore,
skip, omit, pass by, not dwell on ▷▷ **pass
something** or **someone off as something** or
someone MISREPRESENT, palm something
or someone off, falsely represent, disguise
something or someone, dress something or
someone up ▷▷ **pass something up** (*informal*)
MISS, ignore, let slip, refuse, decline, reject,
neglect, forgo, abstain from, let (something)
go by, give (something) a miss (*informal*)
passable *adjective* **1** ADEQUATE, middling,
average, fair, all right, ordinary, acceptable,

moderate, fair enough, mediocre, so-so
(*informal*), tolerable, not too bad, allowable,
presentable, admissible, unexceptional,
half-pie (*NZ informal*) << ANTONYM
unsatisfactory **2** CLEAR, open, navigable,
unobstructed, traversable, crossable
<< ANTONYM impassable
passage *noun* **1** CORRIDOR, hallway,
passageway, hall, lobby, entrance, exit,
doorway, aisle, entrance hall, vestibule
2 ALLEY, way, opening, close (*Brit*), course,
road, channel, route, path, lane, avenue,
thoroughfare **3** EXTRACT, reading, piece,
section, sentence, text, clause, excerpt,
paragraph, verse, quotation **4** MOVEMENT,
passing, advance, progress, flow, motion,
transit, progression **5** TRANSITION, change,
move, development, progress, shift,
conversion, progression, metamorphosis
6 ESTABLISHMENT, passing, legislation,
sanction, approval, acceptance, adoption,
ratification, enactment, authorization,
validation, legalization **7** JOURNEY, crossing,
tour, trip, trek, voyage **8** SAFE-CONDUCT,
right to travel, freedom to travel, permission
to travel, authorization to travel
passageway *noun* CORRIDOR, passage, hallway,
hall, lane, lobby, entrance, exit, alley, aisle,
wynd (*Scot*)
passé *adjective* OUT-OF-DATE, old-fashioned,
dated, outdated, obsolete, unfashionable,
antiquated, outmoded, old hat, outworn,
démodé (*French*)
passenger *noun* TRAVELLER, rider, fare,
commuter, hitchhiker, pillion rider, fare
payer
passer-by *noun* BYSTANDER, witness, observer,
viewer, spectator, looker-on, watcher,
onlooker, eyewitness
passing *adjective* **1** MOMENTARY, fleeting,
short-lived, transient, ephemeral, short,
brief, temporary, transitory, evanescent,
fugacious (*rare*) **2** SUPERFICIAL, short, quick,
slight, glancing, casual, summary, shallow,
hasty, cursory, perfunctory, desultory ▷ *noun*
1 END, finish, loss, vanishing, disappearance,
termination, dying out, expiry, expiration
2 DEATH, demise, decease, passing on or
away ▷▷ **in passing** INCIDENTALLY, on the
way, by the way, accidentally, en passant, by
the bye
passion *noun* **1** LOVE, desire, affection, lust,
the hots (*slang*), attachment, itch, fondness,
adoration, infatuation, ardour, keenness,
concupiscence **2** EMOTION, feeling, fire,

heat, spirit, transport, joy, excitement, intensity, warmth, animation, zeal, zest, fervour, eagerness, rapture, ardour << ANTONYM indifference **3** MANIA, fancy, enthusiasm, obsession, bug (*informal*), craving, fascination, craze, infatuation **4** RAGE, fit, storm, anger, fury, resentment, outburst, frenzy, wrath, indignation, flare-up (*informal*), ire, vehemence, paroxysm

passionate *adjective* **1** EMOTIONAL, excited, eager, enthusiastic, animated, strong, warm, wild, intense, flaming, fierce, frenzied, ardent, fervent, heartfelt, impassioned, zealous, impulsive, vehement, impetuous, fervid << ANTONYM unemotional **2** LOVING, erotic, hot, sexy (*informal*), aroused, sensual, ardent, steamy (*informal*), wanton, amorous, lustful, desirous << ANTONYM cold

passionately *adverb* **1** EMOTIONALLY, eagerly, enthusiastically, vehemently, excitedly, strongly, warmly, wildly, fiercely, intensely, fervently, impulsively, ardently, zealously, animatedly, with all your heart, frenziedly, impetuously, fervidly << ANTONYM unemotionally **2** LOVINGLY, with passion, erotically, ardently, sexily (*informal*), sensually, lustfully, amorously, steamily (*informal*), libidinously, desirously << ANTONYM coldly

passive *adjective* **1** SUBMISSIVE, resigned, compliant, receptive, lifeless, docile, nonviolent, quiescent, acquiescent, unassertive, unresisting << ANTONYM spirited **2** INACTIVE, inert, uninvolved, non-participating << ANTONYM active

password *noun* WATCHWORD, key word, magic word (*informal*), open sesame

past *noun* **1** FORMER TIMES, history, long ago, antiquity, the good old days, yesteryear (*literary*), times past, the old times, days gone by, the olden days, days of yore << ANTONYM future **2** BACKGROUND, life, experience, history, past life, life story, career to date ▷ *adjective* **1** FORMER, late, early, recent, previous, ancient, prior, long-ago, preceding, foregoing, erstwhile, bygone, olden << ANTONYM future **2** PREVIOUS, former, one-time, sometime, erstwhile, quondam, ex- **3** LAST, recent, previous, preceding **4** OVER, done, ended, spent, finished, completed, gone, forgotten, accomplished, extinct, elapsed, over and done with ▷ *preposition* **1** AFTER, beyond, later than, over, outside, farther than, in excess of, subsequent to **2** BY, across, in front of ▷

adverb ON, by, along

paste *noun* **1** ADHESIVE, glue, cement, gum, mucilage **2** PURÉE, pâté, spread ▷ *verb* STICK, fix, glue, cement, gum, fasten

pastel *adjective* PALE, light, soft, delicate, muted, soft-hued << ANTONYM bright

pastiche *noun* **1** MEDLEY, mixture, blend, motley, mélange (*French*), miscellany, farrago, hotchpotch, gallimaufry **2** PARODY, take-off, imitation

pastime *noun* ACTIVITY, game, sport, entertainment, leisure, hobby, relaxation, recreation, distraction, amusement, diversion

pastor *noun* CLERGYMAN, minister, priest, vicar, divine, parson, rector, curate, churchman, ecclesiastic

pastoral *adjective* **1** ECCLESIASTICAL, priestly, ministerial, clerical **2** RUSTIC, country, simple, rural, idyllic, bucolic, Arcadian, georgic (*literary*), agrestic

pasture *noun* GRASSLAND, grass, meadow, grazing, lea (*poetic*), grazing land, pasturage, shieling (*Scot*)

pasty *adjective* PALE, unhealthy, wan, sickly, pallid, anaemic, sallow, like death warmed up (*informal*), wheyfaced

pat¹ *verb* STROKE, touch, tap, pet, slap, dab, caress, fondle ▷ *noun* **1** TAP, stroke, slap, clap, dab, light blow **2** LUMP, cake, portion, dab, small piece

pat² *adjective* GLIB, easy, ready, smooth, automatic, slick, simplistic, facile ▷▷ **off pat** PERFECTLY, precisely, exactly, flawlessly, faultlessly

patch *noun* **1** SPOT, bit, stretch, scrap, shred, small piece **2** PLOT, area, ground, land, tract **3** REINFORCEMENT, piece of fabric, piece of cloth, piece of material, piece sewn on ▷ *verb* **1** *often with* **up** SEW (UP), mend, repair, reinforce, stitch (up) **2** *often with* **up** MEND, cover, fix, reinforce ▷▷ **patch things up** SETTLE, make friends, placate, bury the hatchet, conciliate, settle differences, smooth something over

patchwork *noun* MIXTURE, confusion, jumble, medley, hash, pastiche, mishmash, hotchpotch

patchy *adjective* **1** UNEVEN, irregular, variegated, spotty, mottled, dappled << ANTONYM even **2** IRREGULAR, varying, variable, random, erratic, uneven, sketchy, fitful, bitty, inconstant, scattershot << ANTONYM constant

patent *noun* COPYRIGHT, licence, franchise,

registered trademark ▷ *adjective* OBVIOUS, apparent, evident, blatant, open, clear, glaring, manifest, transparent, conspicuous, downright, unmistakable, palpable, unequivocal, flagrant, indisputable, unconcealed

paternal *adjective* **1** FATHERLY, concerned, protective, benevolent, vigilant, solicitous, fatherlike **2** PATRILINEAL, patrimonial

paternity *noun* FATHERHOOD, fathership (*rare*)

path *noun* **1** WAY, road, walk, track, trail, avenue, pathway, footpath, walkway (*chiefly US*), towpath, footway, berm (*NZ*) **2** ROUTE, way, course, direction, passage **3** COURSE, way, road, track, route, procedure

pathetic *adjective* **1** SAD, moving, touching, affecting, distressing, tender, melting, poignant, harrowing, heartbreaking, plaintive, heart-rending, gut-wrenching, pitiable << ANTONYM funny **2** INADEQUATE, useless, feeble, poor, sorry, wet (*Brit informal*), pants (*informal*), miserable, petty, worthless, meagre, pitiful, woeful, deplorable, lamentable, trashy, measly, crummy (*slang*), crappy (*slang*), rubbishy, poxy (*slang*)

pathfinder *noun* PIONEER, guide, scout, explorer, discoverer, trailblazer

pathos *noun* SADNESS, poignancy, plaintiveness, pitifulness, pitiableness

patience *noun* **1** FORBEARANCE, tolerance, composure, serenity, cool (*slang*), restraint, calmness, equanimity, toleration, sufferance, even temper, imperturbability << ANTONYM impatience **2** ENDURANCE, resignation, submission, fortitude, persistence, long-suffering, perseverance, stoicism, constancy

patient *noun* SICK PERSON, case, sufferer, invalid ▷ *adjective* **1** FORBEARING, understanding, forgiving, mild, accommodating, tolerant, indulgent, lenient, even-tempered << ANTONYM impatient **2** LONG-SUFFERING, resigned, calm, enduring, quiet, composed, persistent, philosophical, serene, persevering, stoical, submissive, self-possessed, uncomplaining, untiring

patois *noun* **1** DIALECT, vernacular **2** JARGON, slang, vernacular, patter, cant, lingo (*informal*), argot

patriarch *noun* FATHER, old man, elder, grandfather, sire, paterfamilias, greybeard

patrician *noun* ARISTOCRAT, peer, noble, nobleman, aristo (*informal*) ▷ *adjective* ARISTOCRATIC, noble, lordly, high-class, blue-blooded, highborn

patriot *noun* NATIONALIST, loyalist, chauvinist, flag-waver (*informal*), lover of your country

patriotic *adjective* NATIONALISTIC, loyal, flag-waving (*informal*), chauvinistic, jingoistic

patriotism *noun* NATIONALISM, loyalty, flag-waving (*informal*), jingoism, love of your country

patrol *verb* POLICE, guard, keep watch (on), pound, range (over), cruise, inspect, safeguard, make the rounds (of), keep guard (on), walk *or* pound the beat (of) ▷ *noun* GUARD, watch, garrison, watchman, sentinel, patrolman

patron *noun* **1** SUPPORTER, friend, champion, defender, sponsor, guardian, angel (*informal*), advocate, backer, helper, protagonist, protector, benefactor, philanthropist **2** CUSTOMER, client, buyer, frequenter, shopper, habitué

patronage *noun* SUPPORT, promotion, sponsorship, backing, help, aid, championship, assistance, encouragement, espousal, benefaction

patronize *verb* **1** TALK DOWN TO, look down on, treat as inferior, treat like a child, be lofty with, treat condescendingly **2** SUPPORT, promote, sponsor, back, help, fund, maintain, foster, assist, subscribe to, befriend **3** BE A CUSTOMER *or* CLIENT OF, deal with, frequent, buy from, trade with, shop at, do business with

patronizing *adjective* CONDESCENDING, superior, stooping, lofty, gracious, contemptuous, haughty, snobbish, disdainful, supercilious, toffee-nosed (*slang, chiefly Brit*) << ANTONYM respectful

patter¹ *verb* TAP, beat, pat, pelt, spatter, rat-a-tat, pitter-patter, pitapat ▷ *noun* TAPPING, pattering, pitter-patter, pitapat

patter² *noun* **1** SPIEL (*informal*), line, pitch, monologue **2** CHATTER, prattle, nattering, jabber, gabble, yak (*slang*) **3** JARGON, slang, vernacular, cant, lingo (*informal*), patois, argot

pattern *noun* **1** ORDER, plan, system, method, arrangement, sequence, orderliness **2** DESIGN, arrangement, motif, figure, device, decoration, ornament, decorative design **3** PLAN, design, original, guide, instructions, diagram, stencil, template **4** MODEL, example, standard, original, guide, par, criterion, norm, prototype, paradigm, archetype, paragon, exemplar, cynosure

paucity *noun* (*formal*) SCARCITY, lack, poverty, shortage, deficiency, rarity, dearth, smallness, insufficiency, slenderness, sparseness, slightness, sparsity, meagreness, paltriness, scantiness

paunch *noun* BELLY, beer-belly (*informal*), spread (*informal*), corporation (*informal*), pot, spare tyre (*Brit slang*), middle-age spread (*informal*), potbelly, large abdomen, puku (*NZ*)

pauper *noun* DOWN-AND-OUT, have-not, bankrupt, beggar, insolvent, indigent, poor person, mendicant

pause *verb* STOP BRIEFLY, delay, hesitate, break, wait, rest, halt, cease, interrupt, deliberate, waver, take a break, discontinue, desist, have a breather (*informal*) << ANTONYM continue ▷ *noun* STOP, break, delay, interval, hesitation, stay, wait, rest, gap, halt, interruption, respite, lull, stoppage, interlude, cessation, let-up (*informal*), breathing space, breather (*informal*), intermission, discontinuance, entr'acte, caesura << ANTONYM continuance

pave *verb* COVER, floor, surface, flag, concrete, tile, tar, asphalt, macadamize

paw *verb* (*informal*) MANHANDLE, grab, maul, molest, handle roughly

pawn[1] *verb* HOCK (*informal, chiefly US*), pop (*Brit informal*), stake, mortgage, deposit, pledge, hazard, wager

pawn[2] *noun* TOOL, instrument, toy, creature, puppet, dupe, stooge (*slang*), plaything, cat's-paw

pay *verb* 1 REWARD, compensate, reimburse, recompense, requite, remunerate 2 SPEND, offer, give, fork out (*informal*), remit, cough up (*informal*), shell out (*informal*) 3 SETTLE, meet, clear, foot, honour, discharge, liquidate, square up 4 BRING IN, earn, return, net, yield 5 BE PROFITABLE, make money, make a return, provide a living, be remunerative 6 BENEFIT, serve, repay, be worthwhile, be advantageous 7 GIVE, extend, present with, grant, render, hand out, bestow, proffer ▷ *noun* WAGES, income, payment, earnings, fee, reward, hire, salary, compensation, allowance, remuneration, takings, reimbursement, hand-outs, recompense, stipend, emolument, meed (*archaic*) ▷▷ **pay off** SUCCEED, work, be successful, be effective, be profitable ▷▷ **pay someone back** GET EVEN WITH (*informal*), punish, repay, retaliate, hit back at, reciprocate, recompense, get revenge on, settle a score with, get your own back on, revenge yourself on, avenge yourself

for ▷▷ **pay someone off** 1 (*informal*) BRIBE, corrupt, oil (*informal*), get at, buy off, suborn, grease the palm of (*slang*) 2 DISMISS, fire, sack (*informal*), discharge, let go, lay off, kennet (*Austral slang*), jeff (*Austral slang*) ▷▷ **pay something back** REPAY, return, square, refund, reimburse, settle up ▷▷ **pay something off** SETTLE, clear, square, discharge, liquidate, pay in full ▷▷ **pay something out** SPEND, lay out (*informal*), expend, cough up (*informal*), shell out (*informal*), disburse, fork out *or* over *or* up (*slang*) ▷▷ **pay up** PAY, fork out (*informal*), stump up (*Brit informal*), make payment, pay in full, settle up, come up with the money

payable *adjective* DUE, outstanding, owed, owing, mature, to be paid, obligatory, receivable

payment *noun* 1 REMITTANCE, advance, deposit, premium, portion, instalment 2 SETTLEMENT, paying, discharge, outlay, remittance, defrayal 3 WAGES, fee, reward, hire, remuneration

payoff *noun* 1 BRIBE, incentive, cut (*informal*), payment, sweetener (*informal*), bung (*Brit informal*), inducement, kick-back (*informal*), backhander (*informal*), hush money (*informal*) 2 SETTLEMENT, payment, reward, payout, recompense 3 (*informal*) OUTCOME, result, consequence, conclusion, climax, finale, culmination, the crunch (*informal*), upshot, moment of truth, clincher (*informal*), punch line

peace *noun* 1 TRUCE, ceasefire, treaty, armistice, pacification, conciliation, cessation of hostilities << ANTONYM war 2 STILLNESS, rest, quiet, silence, hush, tranquillity, seclusion, repose, calmness, peacefulness, quietude, restfulness 3 SERENITY, calm, relaxation, composure, contentment, repose, equanimity, peacefulness, placidity, harmoniousness 4 HARMONY, accord, agreement, concord, amity

peaceable *adjective* PEACE-LOVING, friendly, gentle, peaceful, mild, conciliatory, amiable, pacific, amicable, placid, inoffensive, dovish, unwarlike, nonbelligerent

peaceful *adjective* 1 AT PEACE, friendly, harmonious, amicable, cordial, nonviolent, without hostility, free from strife, on friendly *or* good terms << ANTONYM hostile 2 PEACE-LOVING, conciliatory, peaceable, placatory, irenic, pacific, unwarlike << ANTONYM belligerent 3 CALM, still, quiet, gentle, pleasant, soothing, tranquil, placid, restful << ANTONYM agitated **4** SERENE, placid, undisturbed, untroubled, unruffled

peacemaker *noun* MEDIATOR, appeaser, arbitrator, conciliator, pacifier, peacemonger

peak *noun* **1** HIGH POINT, crown, climax, culmination, zenith, maximum point, apogee, acme, ne plus ultra (*Latin*) **2** POINT, top, tip, summit, brow, crest, pinnacle, apex, aiguille ▷ *verb* CULMINATE, climax, come to a head, be at its height, reach its highest point, reach the zenith

peal *verb* RING, sound, toll, resound, chime, resonate, tintinnabulate ▷ *noun* **1** RING, sound, ringing, clamour, chime, clang, carillon, tintinnabulation **2** CLAP, sound, crash, blast, roar, rumble, resounding, reverberation **3** ROAR, fit, shout, scream, gale, howl, shriek, hoot

pearly *adjective* **1** IRIDESCENT, mother-of-pearl, opalescent, nacreous, margaric, margaritic **2** IVORY, creamy, milky, silvery

peasant *noun* **1** RUSTIC, countryman, hind (*obsolete*), swain (*archaic*), son of the soil, churl (*archaic*) **2** (*informal*) BOOR, provincial, hick (*informal, chiefly US & Canad*), lout, yokel, country bumpkin, hayseed (*US & Canad informal*), churl

peck *verb* **1** PICK, bite, hit, strike, tap, poke, jab, prick, nibble **2** KISS, plant a kiss on, give someone a smacker, give someone a peck *or* kiss ▷ *noun* KISS, smacker, osculation (*rare*)

peculiar *adjective* **1** ODD, strange, unusual, bizarre, funny, extraordinary, curious, weird, exceptional, eccentric, abnormal, out-of-the-way, queer, uncommon, singular, unconventional, far-out (*slang*), quaint, off-the-wall (*slang*), outlandish, offbeat, freakish, wacko (*slang*), outré, daggy (*Austral & NZ informal*) << ANTONYM ordinary **2** SPECIAL, private, individual, personal, particular, unique, characteristic, distinguishing, distinct, idiosyncratic << ANTONYM common **3** *with* **to** SPECIFIC TO, restricted to, appropriate to, endemic to

peculiarity *noun* **1** ODDITY, abnormality, eccentricity, weirdness, queerness, bizarreness, freakishness **2** QUIRK, caprice, mannerism, whimsy, foible, idiosyncrasy, odd trait **3** CHARACTERISTIC, mark, feature, quality, property, attribute, trait, speciality, singularity, distinctiveness, particularity

pecuniary *adjective* MONETARY, economic, financial, capital, commercial, fiscal, budgetary

pedantic *adjective* **1** HAIRSPLITTING, particular, formal, precise, fussy, picky (*informal*), nit-picking (*informal*), punctilious, priggish, pedagogic, overnice **2** ACADEMIC, pompous, schoolmasterly, stilted, erudite, scholastic, didactic, bookish, abstruse, donnish, sententious

peddle *verb* SELL, trade, push (*informal*), market, hawk, flog (*slang*), vend, huckster, sell door to door

peddler *or* **pedlar** *noun* SELLER, vendor, hawker, duffer (*dialect*), huckster, door-to-door salesman, cheap-jack (*informal*), colporteur

pedestal *noun* SUPPORT, stand, base, foot, mounting, foundation, pier, plinth, dado (*architecture*) ▷▷ **put someone on a pedestal** WORSHIP, dignify, glorify, exalt, idealize, ennoble, deify, apotheosize

pedestrian *noun* WALKER, foot-traveller, footslogger << ANTONYM driver ▷ *adjective* DULL, flat, ordinary, boring, commonplace, mundane, mediocre, plodding, banal, prosaic, run-of-the-mill, humdrum, unimaginative, uninteresting, uninspired, ho-hum (*informal*), no great shakes (*informal*), half-pie (*NZ informal*) << ANTONYM exciting

pedigree *modifier* PUREBRED, thoroughbred, full-blooded ▷ *noun* LINEAGE, family, line, race, stock, blood, breed, heritage, descent, extraction, ancestry, family tree, genealogy, derivation

pedlar ▷ see **peddler**

peek *verb* GLANCE, look, peer, spy, take a look, peep, eyeball (*slang*), sneak a look, keek (*Scot*), snatch a glimpse, take *or* have a gander (*informal*) ▷ *noun* GLANCE, look, glimpse, blink, peep, butcher's (*Brit slang*), gander (*informal*), look-see (*slang*), shufti (*Brit slang*), keek (*Scot*)

peel *noun* RIND, skin, peeling, epicarp, exocarp ▷ *verb* SKIN, scale, strip, pare, shuck, flake off, decorticate (*rare*), take the skin *or* rind off

peep *verb* **1** PEEK, look, peer, spy, eyeball (*slang*), sneak a look, steal a look, keek (*Scot*), look surreptitiously, look from hiding **2** APPEAR BRIEFLY, emerge, pop up, spring up, issue from, peer out, peek from, show partially ▷ *noun* LOOK, glimpse, peek, butcher's (*Brit slang*), gander (*informal*), look-see (*slang*), shufti (*Brit slang*), keek (*Scot*)

peer[1] *noun* **1** NOBLE, lord, count, duke, earl, baron, aristocrat, viscount, marquess, marquis, nobleman, aristo (*informal*)

2 EQUAL, like, match, fellow, contemporary, coequal, compeer

peer² *verb* SQUINT, look, spy, gaze, scan, inspect, peep, peek, snoop, scrutinize, look closely

peerage *noun* ARISTOCRACY, peers, nobility, lords and ladies, titled classes

peerless *adjective* UNEQUALLED, excellent, unique, outstanding, unparalleled, superlative, unrivalled, second to none, incomparable, unmatched, unsurpassed, matchless, beyond compare, nonpareil << ANTONYM mediocre

peeved *adjective* IRRITATED, upset, annoyed, put out, hacked off (*US slang*), sore, galled, exasperated, nettled, vexed, irked, riled, piqued, tooshie (*Austral slang*)

peg *noun* PIN, spike, rivet, skewer, dowel, spigot ▷ *verb* 1 FASTEN, join, fix, secure, attach, make fast 2 FIX, set, control, limit, freeze

pejorative *adjective* DEROGATORY, negative, slighting, unpleasant, belittling, disparaging, debasing, deprecatory, uncomplimentary, depreciatory, detractive, detractory

pelt¹ *verb* 1 SHOWER, beat, strike, pepper, batter, thrash, bombard, wallop (*informal*), assail, pummel, hurl at, cast at, belabour, sling at 2 POUR, teem, rain hard, bucket down (*informal*), rain cats and dogs (*informal*) 3 RUSH, charge, shoot, career, speed, tear, belt (*slang*), dash, hurry, barrel (along) (*informal, chiefly US & Canad*), whizz (*informal*), stampede, run fast, burn rubber (*informal*)

pelt² *noun* COAT, fell, skin, hide

pen¹ *verb* WRITE (DOWN), draft, compose, pencil, draw up, scribble, take down, inscribe, scrawl, jot down, dash off, commit to paper

pen² *noun* ENCLOSURE, pound, fold, cage, coop, hutch, corral (*chiefly US & Canad*), sty ▷ *verb* ENCLOSE, confine, cage, pound, mew (up), fence in, impound, hem in, coop up, hedge in, shut up *or* in

penal *adjective* DISCIPLINARY, punitive, corrective, penalizing, retributive

penalize *verb* 1 PUNISH, discipline, correct, handicap, award a penalty against (*sport*), impose a penalty on 2 PUT AT A DISADVANTAGE, handicap, cause to suffer, unfairly disadvantage, inflict a handicap on

penalty *noun* PUNISHMENT, price, fine, handicap, forfeit, retribution, forfeiture

penance *noun* ATONEMENT, punishment, penalty, reparation, expiation, sackcloth and ashes, self-punishment, self-mortification

penchant *noun* LIKING, taste, tendency, turn, leaning, bent, bias, inclination, affinity, disposition, fondness, propensity, predisposition, predilection, proclivity, partiality, proneness

pending *adjective* 1 UNDECIDED, unsettled, in the balance, up in the air, undetermined 2 FORTHCOMING, imminent, prospective, impending, in the wind, in the offing ▷ *preposition* AWAITING, until, waiting for, till

penetrate *verb* 1 PIERCE, enter, go through, bore, probe, stab, prick, perforate, impale 2 PERVADE, enter, permeate, filter through, suffuse, seep through, get in through, percolate through 3 INFILTRATE, enter, get in to, make inroads into, sneak in to (*informal*), work *or* worm your way into 4 GRASP, understand, work out, figure out (*informal*), unravel, discern, comprehend, fathom, decipher, suss (out) (*slang*), get to the bottom of

penetrating *adjective* 1 SHARP, harsh, piercing, carrying, piping, loud, intrusive, strident, shrill, high-pitched, ear-splitting << ANTONYM sweet 2 PUNGENT, biting, strong, powerful, sharp, heady, pervasive, aromatic 3 PIERCING, cutting, biting, sharp, freezing, fierce, stinging, frosty, bitterly cold, artic 4 INTELLIGENT, quick, sharp, keen, critical, acute, profound, discriminating, shrewd, discerning, astute, perceptive, incisive, sharp-witted, perspicacious, sagacious << ANTONYM dull 5 PERCEPTIVE, searching, sharp, keen, alert, probing, discerning << ANTONYM unperceptive

penetration *noun* 1 PIERCING, entry, entrance, invasion, puncturing, incision, perforation 2 ENTRY, entrance, inroad

pennant *noun* FLAG, jack, banner, ensign, streamer, burgee (*nautical*), pennon, banderole

penniless *adjective* POOR, broke (*informal*), bankrupt, impoverished, short, ruined, strapped (*slang*), needy, cleaned out (*slang*), destitute, poverty-stricken, down and out, skint (*Brit slang*), indigent, down at heel, impecunious, dirt-poor (*informal*), on the breadline, flat broke (*informal*), penurious, on your uppers, stony-broke (*Brit slang*), necessitous, in queer street, moneyless, without two pennies to rub together (*informal*), without a penny to your name

<< ANTONYM rich

penny-pinching *adjective* MEAN, close, near
(*informal*), frugal, stingy, scrimping, miserly,
niggardly, tightfisted, Scrooge-like, mingy
(*Brit informal*), cheeseparing, snoep (*S African
informal*) << ANTONYM generous

pension *noun* ALLOWANCE, benefit, welfare,
annuity, superannuation

pensioner *noun* SENIOR CITIZEN, retired
person, retiree (*US*), old-age pensioner,
O.A.P.

pensive *adjective* THOUGHTFUL, serious,
sad, blue (*informal*), grave, sober, musing,
preoccupied, melancholy, solemn, reflective,
dreamy, wistful, mournful, contemplative,
meditative, sorrowful, ruminative, in
a brown study (*informal*), cogitative
<< ANTONYM carefree

pent-up *adjective* SUPPRESSED, checked,
curbed, inhibited, held back, stifled,
repressed, smothered, constrained, bridled,
bottled up

penury *noun* POVERTY, want, need, privation,
destitution, straitened circumstances,
beggary, indigence, pauperism

people *plural noun* 1 PERSONS, humans,
individuals, folk (*informal*), men and women,
human beings, humanity, mankind,
mortals, the human race, Homo sapiens
2 THE PUBLIC, the crowd, the masses, the
general public, the mob, the herd, the grass
roots, the rank and file, the multitude, the
populace, the proletariat, the rabble, the
plebs, the proles (*derogatory slang, chiefly Brit*),
the commonalty, (the) hoi polloi 3 NATION,
public, community, subjects, population,
residents, citizens, folk, inhabitants, electors,
populace, tax payers, citizenry, (general)
public 4 RACE, tribe, ethnic group 5 FAMILY,
parents, relations, relatives, folk, folks
(*informal*), clan, kin, next of kin, kinsmen,
nearest and dearest, kith and kin, your own
flesh and blood, rellies (*Austral slang*) ▷ *verb*
INHABIT, occupy, settle, populate, colonize

pep *noun* ENERGY, life, spirit, zip (*informal*),
vitality, animation, vigour, verve, high
spirits, gusto, get-up-and-go (*informal*),
brio, vivacity, liveliness, vim (*slang*) ▷▷ **pep
something** or **someone up** ENLIVEN, inspire,
stimulate, animate, exhilarate, quicken,
invigorate, jazz up (*informal*), vitalize, vivify

pepper *noun* SEASONING, flavour, spice ▷ *verb*
1 PELT, hit, shower, scatter, blitz, riddle,
rake, bombard, assail, strafe, rain down on
2 SPRINKLE, spot, scatter, dot, stud, fleck,
intersperse, speck, spatter, freckle, stipple,
bespatter

peppery *adjective* HOT, fiery, spicy, pungent,
highly seasoned, piquant << ANTONYM mild

perceive *verb* 1 SEE, notice, note, identify,
discover, spot, observe, remark, recognize,
distinguish, glimpse, make out, pick
out, discern, behold, catch sight of, espy,
descry 2 UNDERSTAND, sense, gather, get
(*informal*), know, see, feel, learn, realize,
conclude, appreciate, grasp, comprehend,
get the message about, deduce, apprehend,
suss (out) (*slang*), get the picture about
3 CONSIDER, believe, judge, suppose, rate,
deem, adjudge

perceptible *adjective* NOTICEABLE, clear,
obvious, apparent, visible, evident, distinct,
tangible, blatant, conspicuous, palpable,
discernible, recognizable, detectable,
observable, appreciable, perceivable
<< ANTONYM imperceptible

perception *noun* 1 AWARENESS,
understanding, sense, impression, feeling,
idea, taste, notion, recognition, observation,
consciousness, grasp, sensation, conception,
apprehension 2 UNDERSTANDING,
intelligence, observation, discrimination,
insight, sharpness, cleverness, keenness,
shrewdness, acuity, discernment,
perspicacity, astuteness, incisiveness,
perceptiveness, quick-wittedness,
perspicuity

perceptive *adjective* OBSERVANT, acute,
intelligent, discerning, quick, aware, sharp,
sensitive, alert, penetrating, discriminating,
shrewd, responsive, astute, intuitive,
insightful, percipient, perspicacious
<< ANTONYM obtuse

perch *verb* 1 SIT, rest, balance, settle 2 PLACE,
put, rest, balance 3 LAND, alight, roost ▷ *noun*
RESTING PLACE, post, branch, pole, roost

percolate *verb* 1 PENETRATE, filter, seep,
pervade, permeate, transfuse 2 FILTER,
brew, perk (*informal*) 3 SEEP, strain, drain,
filter, penetrate, drip, leach, ooze, pervade,
permeate, filtrate

perennial *adjective* CONTINUAL, lasting,
continuing, permanent, constant, enduring,
chronic, persistent, abiding, lifelong,
perpetual, recurrent, never-ending,
incessant, unchanging, inveterate

perfect *adjective* 1 FAULTLESS, correct, pure,
accurate, faithful, impeccable, exemplary,
flawless, foolproof, blameless << ANTONYM
deficient 2 EXCELLENT, ideal, supreme,

superb, splendid, sublime, superlative
3 IMMACULATE, impeccable, flawless, spotless, unblemished, untarnished, unmarred << ANTONYM flawed **4** COMPLETE, absolute, sheer, utter, consummate, out-and-out, unadulterated, unmitigated, unalloyed << ANTONYM partial **5** EXACT, true, accurate, precise, right, close, correct, strict, faithful, spot-on (*Brit informal*), on the money (*US*), unerring ▷ *verb* IMPROVE, develop, polish, elaborate, refine, cultivate, hone << ANTONYM mar

perfection *noun* **1** EXCELLENCE, integrity, superiority, purity, wholeness, sublimity, exquisiteness, faultlessness, flawlessness, perfectness, immaculateness **2** THE IDEAL, the crown, the last word, one in a million (*informal*), a paragon, the crème de la crème, the acme, a nonpareil, the beau idéal **3** ACCOMPLISHMENT, achieving, achievement, polishing, evolution, refining, completion, realization, fulfilment, consummation

perfectionist *noun* STICKLER, purist, formalist, precisionist, precisian

perfectly *adverb* **1** COMPLETELY, totally, entirely, absolutely, quite, fully, altogether, thoroughly, wholly, utterly, consummately, every inch << ANTONYM partially
2 FLAWLESSLY, ideally, wonderfully, superbly, admirably, supremely, to perfection, exquisitely, superlatively, impeccably, like a dream, faultlessly << ANTONYM badly

perforate *verb* PIERCE, hole, bore, punch, drill, penetrate, puncture, honeycomb

perform *verb* **1** DO, achieve, carry out, effect, complete, satisfy, observe, fulfil, accomplish, execute, bring about, pull off, act out, transact **2** FULFIL, carry out, execute, discharge **3** PRESENT, act (out), stage, play, produce, represent, put on, render, depict, enact, appear as **4** APPEAR ON STAGE, act

performance *noun* **1** PRESENTATION, playing, acting (out), staging, production, exhibition, interpretation, representation, rendering, portrayal, rendition **2** SHOW, appearance, concert, gig (*informal*), recital **3** WORK, acts, conduct, exploits, feats **4** FUNCTIONING, running, operation, working, action, behaviour, capacity, efficiency, capabilities **5** CARRYING OUT, practice, achievement, discharge, execution, completion, accomplishment, fulfilment, consummation **6** (*informal*) CARRY-ON (*informal, chiefly Brit*), business, to-do, act, scene, display, bother, fuss, pantomime (*informal, chiefly Brit*), song and dance (*informal*), palaver, rigmarole, pother

performer *noun* ARTISTE, player, Thespian, trouper, play-actor, actor *or* actress

perfume *noun* **1** FRAGRANCE, scent, essence, incense, cologne, eau de toilette, eau de cologne, attar **2** SCENT, smell, fragrance, bouquet, aroma, odour, sweetness, niff (*Brit slang*), redolence, balminess

perfunctory *adjective* OFFHAND, routine, wooden, automatic, stereotyped, mechanical, indifferent, careless, superficial, negligent, sketchy, unconcerned, cursory, unthinking, slovenly, heedless, slipshod, inattentive << ANTONYM thorough

perhaps *adverb* MAYBE, possibly, it may be, it is possible (that), conceivably, as the case may be, perchance (*archaic*), feasibly, for all you know, happen (*N English dialect*)

peril *noun* **1** DANGER, risk, threat, hazard, menace, jeopardy, perilousness **2** *often plural* PITFALL, problem, risk, hazard << ANTONYM safety

perilous *adjective* DANGEROUS, threatening, exposed, vulnerable, risky, unsure, hazardous, hairy (*slang*), unsafe, precarious, parlous (*archaic*), fraught with danger, chancy (*informal*)

perimeter *noun* BOUNDARY, edge, border, bounds, limit, margin, confines, periphery, borderline, circumference, ambit << ANTONYM centre

period *noun* **1** TIME, term, season, space, run, stretch, spell, phase, patch (*Brit informal*), interval, span **2** AGE, generation, years, time, days, term, stage, date, cycle, era, epoch, aeon

periodic *adjective* RECURRENT, regular, repeated, occasional, periodical, seasonal, cyclical, sporadic, intermittent, every so often, infrequent, cyclic, every once in a while, spasmodic, at fixed intervals

periodical *noun* PUBLICATION, paper, review, magazine, journal, weekly, monthly, organ, serial, quarterly, zine (*informal*) ▷ *adjective* RECURRENT, regular, repeated, occasional, seasonal, cyclical, sporadic, intermittent, every so often, infrequent, cyclic, every once in a while, spasmodic, at fixed intervals

peripheral *adjective* **1** SECONDARY, beside the point, minor, marginal, irrelevant, superficial, unimportant, incidental, tangential, inessential **2** OUTERMOST, outside, external, outer, exterior, borderline, perimetric

periphery *noun* BOUNDARY, edge, border, skirt, fringe, verge, brink, outskirts, rim, hem, brim, perimeter, circumference, outer edge, ambit

perish *verb* 1 DIE, be killed, be lost, expire, pass away, lose your life, decease, cark it (*Austral & NZ slang*) 2 BE DESTROYED, fall, decline, collapse, disappear, vanish, go under 3 ROT, waste away, break down, decay, wither, disintegrate, decompose, moulder

perishable *adjective* SHORT-LIVED, biodegradable, easily spoilt, decomposable, liable to rot << ANTONYM non-perishable

perjury *noun* LYING UNDER OATH, false statement, forswearing, bearing false witness, giving false testimony, false oath, oath breaking, false swearing, violation of an oath, wilful falsehood

perk *noun* (*Brit informal*) BONUS, benefit, extra, plus, dividend, icing on the cake, fringe benefit, perquisite

perk up *verb* CHEER UP, recover, rally, revive, look up, brighten, take heart, recuperate, buck up (*informal*) ▷▷ **perk something or someone up** LIVEN UP, revive, cheer up, pep up

perky *adjective* LIVELY, spirited, bright, sunny, cheerful, animated, upbeat (*informal*), buoyant, bubbly, cheery, bouncy, genial, jaunty, chirpy (*informal*), sprightly, vivacious, in fine fettle, full of beans (*informal*), gay, bright-eyed and bushy-tailed (*informal*)

permanence *noun* CONTINUITY, survival, stability, duration, endurance, immortality, durability, finality, perpetuity, constancy, continuance, dependability, permanency, fixity, indestructibility, fixedness, lastingness, perdurability (*rare*)

permanent *adjective* 1 LASTING, fixed, constant, enduring, persistent, eternal, abiding, perennial, durable, perpetual, everlasting, unchanging, immutable, indestructible, immovable, invariable, imperishable, unfading << ANTONYM temporary 2 LONG-TERM, established, secure, stable, steady, long-lasting << ANTONYM temporary

permanently *adverb* FOR EVER, constantly, continually, always, invariably, perennially, persistently, eternally, perpetually, steadfastly, indelibly, in perpetuity, enduringly, unwaveringly, immutably, lastingly, immovably, abidingly, unchangingly, unfadingly << ANTONYM temporarily

permeable *adjective* PENETRABLE, porous, absorbent, spongy, absorptive, pervious

permeate *verb* 1 INFILTRATE, fill, pass through, pervade, filter through, spread through, diffuse throughout 2 PERVADE, saturate, charge, fill, pass through, penetrate, infiltrate, imbue, filter through, spread through, impregnate, seep through, percolate, soak through, diffuse throughout

permissible *adjective* PERMITTED, acceptable, legitimate, legal, all right, sanctioned, proper, authorized, lawful, allowable, kosher (*informal*), admissible, legit (*slang*), licit, O.K. or okay (*informal*) << ANTONYM forbidden

permission *noun* AUTHORIZATION, sanction, licence, approval, leave, freedom, permit, go-ahead (*informal*), liberty, consent, allowance, tolerance, green light, assent, dispensation, carte blanche, blank cheque, sufferance << ANTONYM prohibition

permissive *adjective* TOLERANT, liberal, open-minded, indulgent, easy-going, free, lax, lenient, forbearing, acquiescent, latitudinarian, easy-oasy (*slang*) << ANTONYM strict

permit *verb* 1 ALLOW, admit, grant, sanction, let, suffer, agree to, entitle, endure, license, endorse, warrant, tolerate, authorize, empower, consent to, give the green light to, give leave or permission << ANTONYM forbid 2 ENABLE, let, allow, cause ▷ *noun* LICENCE, pass, document, certificate, passport, visa, warrant, authorization << ANTONYM prohibition

permutation *noun* TRANSFORMATION, change, shift, variation, modification, alteration, mutation, transmutation, transposition

pernicious *adjective* (*formal*) WICKED, bad, damaging, dangerous, evil, offensive, fatal, deadly, destructive, harmful, poisonous, malicious, malign, malignant, detrimental, hurtful, malevolent, noxious, venomous, ruinous, baleful, deleterious, injurious, noisome, baneful (*archaic*), pestilent, maleficent

perpendicular *adjective* 1 UPRIGHT, straight, vertical, plumb, on end 2 AT RIGHT ANGLES, at 90 degrees

perpetrate *verb* COMMIT, do, perform, carry out, effect, be responsible for, execute, inflict, bring about, enact, wreak

perpetual *adjective* 1 EVERLASTING, permanent, endless, eternal, lasting, enduring, abiding, perennial, infinite, immortal, never-ending, unending,

unchanging, undying, sempiternal (*literary*)
<< ANTONYM temporary **2** CONTINUAL,
repeated, constant, endless, continuous,
persistent, perennial, recurrent, never-
ending, uninterrupted, interminable,
incessant, ceaseless, unremitting, unfailing,
unceasing << ANTONYM brief

perpetuate *verb* MAINTAIN, preserve, sustain,
keep up, keep going, continue, keep alive,
immortalize, eternalize << ANTONYM end
▷ see **perpetrate**

perplex *verb* PUZZLE, confuse, stump,
baffle, bewilder, muddle, confound, beset,
mystify, faze, befuddle, flummox, bemuse,
dumbfound, nonplus, mix you up

perplexing *adjective* PUZZLING, complex,
confusing, complicated, involved, hard,
taxing, difficult, strange, weird, mysterious,
baffling, bewildering, intricate, enigmatic,
mystifying, inexplicable, thorny, paradoxical,
unaccountable, knotty, labyrinthine

perplexity *noun* **1** PUZZLEMENT, confusion,
bewilderment, incomprehension,
bafflement, mystification, stupefaction
2 *usually plural* COMPLEXITY, difficulty,
mystery, involvement, puzzle, paradox,
obscurity, enigma, intricacy, inextricability

per se *adverb* IN ITSELF, essentially, as such,
in essence, by itself, of itself, by definition,
intrinsically, by its very nature

persecute *verb* **1** VICTIMIZE, hunt, injure,
pursue, torture, hound, torment, martyr,
oppress, pick on, molest, ill-treat, maltreat
<< ANTONYM mollycoddle **2** HARASS, bother,
annoy, bait, tease, worry, hassle (*informal*),
badger, pester, vex, be on your back (*slang*)
<< ANTONYM leave alone

perseverance *noun* PERSISTENCE, resolution,
determination, dedication, stamina,
endurance, tenacity, diligence, constancy,
steadfastness, doggedness, purposefulness,
pertinacity, indefatigability, sedulity

persevere *verb* KEEP GOING, continue, go on,
carry on, endure, hold on (*informal*), hang on,
persist, stand firm, plug away (*informal*), hold
fast, remain firm, stay the course, keep your
hand in, pursue your goal, be determined
or resolved, keep on *or* at, stick at *or* to
<< ANTONYM give up

persist *verb* **1** CONTINUE, last, remain,
carry on, endure, keep up, linger, abide
2 PERSEVERE, continue, go on, carry on, hold
on (*informal*), keep on, keep going, press on,
not give up, stand firm, soldier on (*informal*),
stay the course, plough on, be resolute, stick

to your guns (*informal*), show determination

persistence *noun* DETERMINATION,
resolution, pluck, stamina, grit, endurance,
tenacity, diligence, perseverance, constancy,
steadfastness, doggedness, pertinacity,
indefatigability, tirelessness

persistent *adjective* **1** CONTINUOUS, constant,
relentless, lasting, repeated, endless,
perpetual, continual, never-ending,
interminable, unrelenting, incessant,
unremitting << ANTONYM occasional
2 DETERMINED, dogged, fixed, steady,
enduring, stubborn, persevering, resolute,
tireless, tenacious, steadfast, obstinate,
indefatigable, immovable, assiduous,
obdurate, stiff-necked, unflagging,
pertinacious << ANTONYM irresolute

person *noun* INDIVIDUAL, being, body,
human, soul, creature, human being, mortal,
living soul, man *or* woman ▷▷ **in person**
1 PERSONALLY, yourself **2** IN THE FLESH,
actually, physically, bodily

persona *noun* PERSONALITY, part, face, front,
role, character, mask, façade, public face,
assumed role

personable *adjective* PLEASANT, pleasing,
nice, attractive, charming, handsome,
good-looking, winning, agreeable, amiable,
affable, presentable, likable *or* likeable
<< ANTONYM unpleasant

personage *noun* PERSONALITY, celebrity, big
name, somebody, worthy, notable, public
figure, dignitary, luminary, celeb (*informal*),
big shot (*informal*), megastar (*informal*), big
noise (*informal*), well-known person, V.I.P.

personal *adjective* **1** OWN, special, private,
individual, particular, peculiar, privy
2 INDIVIDUAL, special, particular,
exclusive **3** PRIVATE, intimate, confidential
4 OFFENSIVE, critical, slighting, nasty,
insulting, rude, belittling, disparaging,
derogatory, disrespectful, pejorative
5 PHYSICAL, intimate, bodily, corporal,
corporeal

personality *noun* **1** NATURE, character, make-
up, identity, temper, traits, temperament,
psyche, disposition, individuality
2 CHARACTER, charm, attraction, charisma,
attractiveness, dynamism, magnetism,
pleasantness, likableness *or* likeableness
3 CELEBRITY, star, big name, notable,
household name, famous name, celeb
(*informal*), personage, megastar (*informal*),
well-known face, well-known person

personalized *adjective* CUSTOMIZED, special,

private, individual, distinctive, tailor-made, individualized, monogrammed

personally *adverb* **1** IN YOUR OPINION, for yourself, in your book, for your part, from your own viewpoint, in your own view **2** BY YOURSELF, alone, independently, solely, on your own, in person, in the flesh **3** INDIVIDUALLY, specially, subjectively, individualistically **4** PRIVATELY, in private, off the record

personification *noun* EMBODIMENT, image, representation, recreation, portrayal, incarnation, likeness, semblance, epitome

personify *verb* EMBODY, represent, express, mirror, exemplify, symbolize, typify, incarnate, image (*rare*), epitomize, body forth

personnel *noun* EMPLOYEES, people, members, staff, workers, men and women, workforce, human resources, helpers, liveware

perspective *noun* **1** OUTLOOK, attitude, context, angle, overview, way of looking, frame of reference, broad view **2** OBJECTIVITY, proportion, relation, relativity, relative importance **3** VIEW, scene, prospect, outlook, panorama, vista

perspiration *noun* SWEAT, moisture, wetness, exudation

perspire *verb* SWEAT, glow, swelter, drip with sweat, break out in a sweat, pour with sweat, secrete sweat, be damp *or* wet *or* soaked with sweat, exude sweat

persuade *verb* **1** TALK (SOMEONE) INTO, urge, advise, prompt, influence, counsel, win (someone) over, induce, sway, entice, coax, incite, prevail upon, inveigle, bring (someone) round (*informal*), twist (someone's) arm, argue (someone) into << ANTONYM dissuade **2** CAUSE, prompt, lead, move, influence, motivate, induce, incline, dispose, impel, actuate **3** CONVINCE, satisfy, assure, prove to, convert to, cause to believe

persuasion *noun* **1** URGING, influencing, conversion, inducement, exhortation, wheedling, enticement, cajolery, blandishment, inveiglement **2** BELIEF, views, opinion, party, school, side, camp, faith, conviction, faction, cult, sect, creed, denomination, tenet, school of thought, credo, firm belief, certitude, fixed opinion

persuasive *adjective* CONVINCING, telling, effective, winning, moving, sound, touching, impressive, compelling, influential, valid, inducing, logical, credible, plausible, forceful, eloquent, weighty, impelling,

cogent << ANTONYM unconvincing

pertain to *verb* RELATE TO, concern, refer to, regard, be part of, belong to, apply to, bear on, befit, be relevant to, be appropriate to, appertain to

pertinent *adjective* RELEVANT, fitting, fit, material, appropriate, pat, suitable, proper, to the point, apt, applicable, apposite, apropos, admissible, germane, to the purpose, ad rem (*Latin*) << ANTONYM irrelevant

perturb *verb* DISTURB, worry, trouble, upset, alarm, bother, unsettle, agitate, ruffle, unnerve, disconcert, disquiet, vex, fluster, faze, discountenance, discompose

perturbed *adjective* DISTURBED, worried, troubled, shaken, upset, alarmed, nervous, anxious, uncomfortable, uneasy, fearful, restless, flurried, agitated, disconcerted, disquieted, flustered, ill at ease, antsy (*informal*) << ANTONYM relaxed

peruse *verb* READ, study, scan, check, examine, inspect, browse, look through, eyeball (*slang*), work over, scrutinize, run your eye over, surf (*computing*)

pervade *verb* SPREAD THROUGH, fill, affect, penetrate, infuse, permeate, imbue, suffuse, percolate, extend through, diffuse through, overspread

pervasive *adjective* WIDESPREAD, general, common, extensive, universal, prevalent, ubiquitous, rife, pervading, permeating, inescapable, omnipresent

perverse *adjective* **1** STUBBORN, contrary, unreasonable, dogged, contradictory, troublesome, rebellious, wayward, delinquent, intractable, wilful, unyielding, obstinate, intransigent, headstrong, unmanageable, cussed (*informal*), obdurate, stiff-necked, disobedient, wrong-headed, refractory, pig-headed, miscreant, mulish, cross-grained, contumacious << ANTONYM cooperative **2** ILL-NATURED, cross, surly, petulant, crabbed, fractious, spiteful, churlish, ill-tempered, stroppy (*Brit slang*), cantankerous, peevish, shrewish << ANTONYM good-natured **3** ABNORMAL, incorrect, unhealthy, improper, deviant, depraved

perversion *noun* **1** DEVIATION, vice, abnormality, aberration, kink (*Brit informal*), wickedness, depravity, immorality, debauchery, unnaturalness, kinkiness (*slang*), vitiation **2** DISTORTION, twisting, corruption, misuse, misrepresentation, misinterpretation, falsification

perversity noun CONTRARINESS, intransigence, obduracy, waywardness, contradictoriness, wrong-headedness, refractoriness, contumacy, contradictiveness, frowardness (archaic)

pervert verb 1 DISTORT, abuse, twist, misuse, warp, misinterpret, misrepresent, falsify, misconstrue 2 CORRUPT, degrade, subvert, deprave, debase, desecrate, debauch, lead astray ▷ noun DEVIANT, degenerate, sicko (informal), sleazeball (slang), debauchee, weirdo or weirdie (informal)

perverted adjective UNNATURAL, sick, corrupt, distorted, abnormal, evil, twisted, impaired, warped, misguided, unhealthy, immoral, deviant, wicked, kinky (slang), depraved, debased, debauched, aberrant, vitiated, pervy (slang), sicko (slang)

pessimism noun GLOOMINESS, depression, despair, gloom, cynicism, melancholy, hopelessness, despondency, dejection, glumness

pessimist noun DEFEATIST, cynic, melancholic, worrier, killjoy, prophet of doom, misanthrope, wet blanket (informal), gloom merchant (informal), doomster

pessimistic adjective GLOOMY, dark, despairing, bleak, resigned, sad, depressed, cynical, hopeless, melancholy, glum, dejected, foreboding, despondent, morose, fatalistic, distrustful, downhearted, misanthropic << ANTONYM optimistic

pest noun 1 INFECTION, bug, insect, plague, epidemic, blight, scourge, bane, pestilence, gogga (S African informal) 2 NUISANCE, bore, trial, pain (informal), drag (informal), bother, irritation, gall, annoyance, bane, pain in the neck (informal), vexation, thorn in your flesh

pester verb ANNOY, worry, bother, disturb, bug (informal), plague, torment, get at, harass, nag, hassle (informal), harry, aggravate (informal), fret, badger, pick on, irk, bedevil, chivvy, get on your nerves (informal), bend someone's ear (informal), drive you up the wall (slang), be on your back (slang), get in your hair (informal)

pestilence noun PLAGUE, epidemic, visitation, pandemic

pet adjective 1 FAVOURITE, chosen, special, personal, particular, prized, preferred, favoured, dearest, cherished, fave (informal), dear to your heart 2 TAME, trained, domestic, house, domesticated, house-trained (Brit), house-broken ▷ noun FAVOURITE, treasure, darling, jewel, idol, fave (informal), apple of your eye, blue-eyed boy or girl (Brit informal) ▷ verb 1 FONDLE, pat, stroke, caress 2 PAMPER, spoil, indulge, cosset, baby, dote on, coddle, mollycoddle, wrap in cotton wool 3 (informal) CUDDLE, kiss, snog (Brit slang), smooch (informal), neck (informal), canoodle (slang)

peter out verb DIE OUT, stop, fail, run out, fade, dwindle, evaporate, wane, give out, ebb, come to nothing, run dry, taper off

petite adjective SMALL, little, slight, delicate, dainty, dinky (Brit informal), elfin

petition noun 1 APPEAL, round robin, list of signatures 2 ENTREATY, appeal, address, suit, application, request, prayer, plea, invocation, solicitation, supplication ▷ verb APPEAL, press, plead, call (upon), ask, urge, sue, pray, beg, crave, solicit, beseech, entreat, adjure, supplicate

petrified adjective 1 TERRIFIED, horrified, shocked, frozen, stunned, appalled, numb, dazed, speechless, aghast, dumbfounded, stupefied, scared stiff, terror-stricken 2 FOSSILIZED, ossified, rocklike

petrify verb 1 TERRIFY, horrify, amaze, astonish, stun, appal, paralyse, astound, confound, transfix, stupefy, immobilize, dumbfound 2 FOSSILIZE, set, harden, solidify, ossify, turn to stone, calcify

petty adjective 1 TRIVIAL, inferior, insignificant, little, small, slight, trifling, negligible, unimportant, paltry, measly (informal), contemptible, piddling (informal), inconsiderable, inessential, nickel-and-dime (US slang) << ANTONYM important 2 SMALL-MINDED, mean, cheap, grudging, shabby, spiteful, stingy, ungenerous, mean-minded << ANTONYM broad-minded 3 MINOR, lower, junior, secondary, lesser, subordinate, inferior

petulance noun SULKINESS, bad temper, irritability, spleen, pique, sullenness, ill-humour, peevishness, querulousness, crabbiness, waspishness, pettishness

petulant adjective SULKY, cross, moody, sour, crabbed, impatient, pouting, perverse, irritable, crusty, sullen, bad-tempered, ratty (Brit & NZ informal), fretful, waspish, querulous, peevish, ungracious, cavilling, huffy, fault-finding, snappish, ill-humoured, captious << ANTONYM good-natured

phantom noun SPECTRE, ghost, spirit, shade (literary), spook (informal), apparition, wraith, revenant, phantasm

phase *noun* STAGE, time, state, point, position, step, development, condition, period, chapter, aspect, juncture ▷▷ **phase something in** INTRODUCE, incorporate, ease in, start ▷▷ **phase something out** ELIMINATE, close, pull, remove, replace, withdraw, pull out, axe (*informal*), wind up, run down, terminate, wind down, ease off, taper off, deactivate, dispose of gradually

phenomenal *adjective* EXTRAORDINARY, outstanding, remarkable, fantastic, unique, unusual, marvellous, exceptional, notable, sensational, uncommon, singular, miraculous, stellar (*informal*), prodigious, unparalleled, wondrous (*archaic or literary*) << ANTONYM unremarkable

phenomenon *noun* 1 OCCURRENCE, happening, fact, event, incident, circumstance, episode 2 WONDER, sensation, spectacle, sight, exception, miracle, marvel, prodigy, rarity, nonpareil

philanthropic *adjective* HUMANITARIAN, generous, charitable, benevolent, kind, humane, gracious, altruistic, public-spirited, beneficent, kind-hearted, munificent, almsgiving, benignant << ANTONYM selfish

philanthropist *noun* HUMANITARIAN, patron, benefactor, giver, donor, contributor, altruist, almsgiver

philanthropy *noun* HUMANITARIANISM, charity, generosity, patronage, bounty, altruism, benevolence, munificence, beneficence, liberality, public-spiritedness, benignity, almsgiving, brotherly love, charitableness, kind-heartedness, generousness, open-handedness, largesse *or* largess

Philistine *sometimes not cap noun* BOOR, barbarian, yahoo, lout, bourgeois, hoon (*Austral & NZ*), ignoramus, lowbrow, vulgarian, cougan (*Austral slang*), scozza (*Austral slang*), bogan (*Austral slang*) ▷ *adjective* UNCULTURED, ignorant, crass, tasteless, bourgeois, uneducated, boorish, unrefined, uncultivated, anti-intellectual, lowbrow, inartistic

philosopher *noun* THINKER, theorist, sage, wise man, logician, metaphysician, dialectician, seeker after truth

philosophical *or* **philosophic** *adjective* 1 THEORETICAL, abstract, learned, wise, rational, logical, thoughtful, erudite, sagacious << ANTONYM practical 2 STOICAL, calm, composed, patient, cool, collected, resigned, serene, tranquil, sedate, impassive,

unruffled, imperturbable << ANTONYM emotional

philosophy *noun* 1 THOUGHT, reason, knowledge, thinking, reasoning, wisdom, logic, metaphysics 2 OUTLOOK, values, principles, convictions, thinking, beliefs, doctrine, ideology, viewpoint, tenets, world view, basic idea, attitude to life, Weltanschauung (*German*)

phlegmatic *adjective* UNEMOTIONAL, indifferent, cold, heavy, dull, sluggish, matter-of-fact, placid, stoical, lethargic, bovine, apathetic, frigid, lymphatic, listless, impassive, stolid, unfeeling, undemonstrative << ANTONYM emotional

phobia *noun* FEAR, horror, terror, thing (*informal*), obsession, dislike, dread, hatred, loathing, distaste, revulsion, aversion, repulsion, irrational fear, detestation, overwhelming anxiety << ANTONYM liking

phone *noun* 1 TELEPHONE, blower (*informal*), dog and bone (*slang*) 2 CALL, ring (*informal, chiefly Brit*), bell (*Brit slang*), buzz (*informal*), tinkle (*Brit informal*) ▷ *verb* CALL, telephone, ring (up) (*informal, chiefly Brit*), give someone a call, give someone a ring (*informal, chiefly Brit*), make a call, give someone a buzz (*informal*), give someone a bell (*Brit slang*), give someone a tinkle (*Brit informal*), get on the blower (*informal*)

phoney (*informal*) *adjective* 1 FAKE, affected, assumed, trick, put-on, false, forged, imitation, sham, pseudo (*informal*), counterfeit, feigned, spurious << ANTONYM genuine 2 BOGUS, false, fake, pseudo (*informal*), ersatz ▷ *noun* 1 FAKER, fraud, fake, pretender, humbug, impostor, pseud (*informal*) 2 FAKE, sham, forgery, counterfeit

photograph *noun* PICTURE, photo (*informal*), shot, image, print, slide, snap (*informal*), snapshot, transparency, likeness ▷ *verb* TAKE A PICTURE OF, record, film, shoot, snap (*informal*), take (someone's) picture, capture on film, get a shot of

photographic *adjective* 1 PICTORIAL, visual, graphic, cinematic, filmic 2 ACCURATE, minute, detailed, exact, precise, faithful, retentive

phrase *noun* EXPRESSION, saying, remark, motto, construction, tag, quotation, maxim, idiom, utterance, adage, dictum, way of speaking, group of words, locution ▷ *verb* EXPRESS, say, word, put, term, present, voice, frame, communicate, convey, utter, couch, formulate, put into words

physical *adjective* 1 CORPORAL, fleshly, bodily, carnal, somatic, corporeal 2 EARTHLY, fleshly, mortal, incarnate, unspiritual 3 MATERIAL, real, substantial, natural, solid, visible, sensible, tangible, palpable

physician *noun* DOCTOR, specialist, doc (*informal*), healer, medic (*informal*), general practitioner, medical practitioner, medico (*informal*), doctor of medicine, sawbones (*slang*), G.P., M.D.

physique *noun* BUILD, form, body, figure, shape, structure, make-up, frame, constitution

pick *verb* 1 SELECT, choose, identify, elect, nominate, sort out, specify, opt for, single out, mark out, plump for, hand-pick, decide upon, cherry-pick, fix upon, settle on or upon, sift out << ANTONYM reject 2 GATHER, cut, pull, collect, take in, harvest, pluck, garner, cull 3 PROVOKE, start, cause, stir up, incite, instigate, foment 4 OPEN, force, crack (*informal*), break into, break open, prise open, jemmy (*informal*) ▷ *noun* 1 CHOICE, decision, choosing, option, selection, preference 2 BEST, prime, finest, tops (*slang*), choicest, flower, prize, elect, elite, cream, jewel in the crown, crème de la crème (*French*) ▷▷ **pick at something** NIBBLE (AT), peck at, have no appetite for, play or toy with, push round the plate, eat listlessly ▷▷ **pick on someone** 1 TORMENT, bully, bait, tease, get at (*informal*), badger, persecute, hector, goad, victimize, have it in for (*informal*), tyrannize, have a down on (*informal*) 2 CHOOSE, select, prefer, elect, single out, fix on, settle upon ▷▷ **pick someone up** ARREST, nick (*slang, chiefly Brit*), bust (*informal*), do (*slang*), lift (*slang*), run in (*slang*), nail (*informal*), collar (*informal*), pinch (*informal*), pull in (*Brit slang*), nab (*informal*), apprehend, take someone into custody, feel your collar (*slang*) ▷▷ **pick something up** 1 LEARN, master, acquire, get the hang of (*informal*), become proficient in 2 OBTAIN, get, find, buy, score (*slang*), discover, purchase, acquire, locate, come across, come by, unearth, garner, stumble across, chance upon, happen upon ▷▷ **pick something or someone out** 1 IDENTIFY, notice, recognize, distinguish, perceive, discriminate, make something or someone out, tell something or someone apart, single something or someone out 2 SELECT, choose, decide on, take, sort out, opt for, cull, plump for, hand-pick ▷▷ **pick something or someone up** 1 LIFT, raise, gather, take up,

grasp, uplift, hoist 2 COLLECT, get, call for, go for, go to get, fetch, uplift (*Scot*), go and get, give someone a lift or a ride ▷▷ **pick up** 1 IMPROVE, recover, rally, get better, bounce back, make progress, make a comeback (*informal*), perk up, turn the corner, gain ground, take a turn for the better, be on the road to recovery 2 RECOVER, improve, rally, get better, mend, perk up, turn the corner, be on the mend, take a turn for the better ▷▷ **pick your way** TREAD CAREFULLY, work through, move cautiously, walk tentatively, find or make your way

picket *verb* BLOCKADE, boycott, demonstrate outside ▷ *noun* 1 DEMONSTRATION, strike, blockade 2 PROTESTER, demonstrator, picketer, flying picket 3 LOOKOUT, watch, guard, patrol, scout, spotter, sentry, sentinel, vedette (*military*) 4 STAKE, post, pale, paling, peg, upright, palisade, stanchion

pickings *plural noun* PROFITS, returns, rewards, earnings, yield, proceeds, spoils, loot, plunder, gravy (*slang*), booty, ill-gotten gains

pickle *verb* PRESERVE, marinade, keep, cure, steep ▷ *noun* 1 CHUTNEY, relish, piccalilli 2 (*informal*) PREDICAMENT, spot (*informal*), fix (*informal*), difficulty, bind (*informal*), jam (*informal*), dilemma, scrape (*informal*), hot water (*informal*), uphill (*S African*), quandary, tight spot

pick-me-up *noun* (*informal*) TONIC, drink, pick-up (*slang*), bracer (*informal*), refreshment, stimulant, shot in the arm (*informal*), restorative

pick-up *noun* IMPROVEMENT, recovery, rise, gain, rally, strengthening, revival, upturn, change for the better, upswing

picky *adjective* (*informal*) FUSSY, particular, critical, carping, fastidious, dainty, choosy, finicky, cavilling, pernickety (*informal*), fault-finding, captious

picnic *noun* 1 EXCURSION, fête champêtre (*French*), barbecue, barbie (*informal*), cookout (*US & Canad*), alfresco meal, déjèuner sur l'herbe (*French*), clambake (*US & Canad*), outdoor meal, outing 2 (*informal*) (In this sense, the construction is always negative) WALKOVER (*informal*), breeze (*US & Canad informal*), pushover (*slang*), snap (*informal*), child's play (*informal*), piece of cake (*Brit informal*), cinch (*slang*), cakewalk (*informal*), duck soup (*US slang*)

pictorial *adjective* GRAPHIC, striking, illustrated, vivid, picturesque, expressive, scenic, representational

picture noun 1 REPRESENTATION, drawing, painting, portrait, image, print, illustration, sketch, portrayal, engraving, likeness, effigy, delineation, similitude 2 PHOTOGRAPH, photo, still, shot, image, print, frame, slide, snap, exposure, portrait, snapshot, transparency, enlargement 3 FILM, movie (*US informal*), flick (*slang*), feature film, motion picture 4 IDEA, vision, concept, impression, notion, visualization, mental picture, mental image 5 DESCRIPTION, impression, explanation, report, account, image, sketch, depiction, re-creation 6 PERSONIFICATION, model, embodiment, soul, essence, archetype, epitome, perfect example, exemplar, quintessence, living example ▷ *verb* 1 IMAGINE, see, envision, visualize, conceive of, fantasize about, conjure up an image of, see in the mind's eye 2 REPRESENT, show, describe, draw, paint, illustrate, portray, sketch, render, depict, delineate 3 SHOW, photograph, capture on film

picturesque adjective 1 INTERESTING, pretty, beautiful, attractive, charming, scenic, quaint << ANTONYM unattractive 2 VIVID, striking, graphic, colourful, memorable << ANTONYM dull

piddling adjective (*informal*) TRIVIAL, little, petty, worthless, insignificant, pants (*informal*), useless, fiddling, trifling, unimportant, paltry, Mickey Mouse (*slang*), puny, derisory, measly (*informal*), crappy (*slang*), toytown (*slang*), piffling, poxy (*slang*), nickel-and-dime (*US slang*) << ANTONYM significant

piece noun 1 BIT, section, slice, part, share, division, block, length, quantity, scrap, segment, portion, fragment, fraction, chunk, wedge, shred, slab, mouthful, morsel, wodge (*Brit informal*) 2 COMPONENT, part, section, bit, unit, segment, constituent, module 3 INSTANCE, case, example, sample, specimen, occurrence 4 ITEM, report, story, bit (*informal*), study, production, review, article 5 COMPOSITION, work, production, opus 6 WORK OF ART, work, creation 7 SHARE, cut (*informal*), slice, percentage, quantity, portion, quota, fraction, allotment, subdivision ▷▷ **go** *or* **fall to pieces** BREAK DOWN, fall apart, disintegrate, lose control, crumple, crack up (*informal*), have a breakdown, lose your head ▷▷ **of a piece (with)** LIKE, the same (as), similar (to),

consistent (with), identical (to), analogous (to), of the same kind (as)

piecemeal adjective UNSYSTEMATIC, interrupted, partial, patchy, intermittent, spotty, fragmentary ▷ *adverb* BIT BY BIT, slowly, gradually, partially, intermittently, at intervals, little by little, fitfully, by degrees, by fits and starts

pied adjective VARIEGATED, spotted, streaked, irregular, flecked, motley, mottled, dappled, multicoloured, piebald, parti-coloured, varicoloured

pier noun 1 JETTY, wharf, quay, promenade, landing place 2 PILLAR, support, post, column, pile, piling, upright, buttress

pierce verb 1 PENETRATE, stab, spike, enter, bore, probe, drill, run through, lance, puncture, prick, transfix, stick into, perforate, impale 2 HURT, cut, wound, strike, touch, affect, pain, move, excite, stir, thrill, sting, rouse, cut to the quick

piercing adjective 1 (*of sound*) PENETRATING, sharp, loud, shattering, shrill, high-pitched, ear-splitting << ANTONYM low 2 PERCEPTIVE, searching, aware, bright (*informal*), sharp, keen, alert, probing, penetrating, shrewd, perspicacious, quick-witted << ANTONYM unperceptive 3 SHARP, shooting, powerful, acute, severe, intense, painful, stabbing, fierce, racking, exquisite, excruciating, agonizing 4 (*of weather*) COLD, biting, keen, freezing, bitter, raw, arctic, nipping, numbing, frosty, wintry, nippy

piety noun HOLINESS, duty, faith, religion, grace, devotion, reverence, sanctity, veneration, godliness, devoutness, dutifulness, piousness

pig noun 1 HOG, sow, boar, piggy, swine, grunter, piglet, porker, shoat 2 (*informal*) SLOB, hog (*informal*), guzzler (*slang*), glutton, gannet (*informal*), sloven, greedy guts (*slang*) 3 (*informal*) BRUTE, monster, scoundrel, animal, beast, rogue, swine, rotter, boor

pigeon noun SQUAB, bird, dove, culver (*archaic*)

pigment noun COLOUR, colouring, paint, stain, dye, tint, tincture, colouring matter, colorant, dyestuff

piker noun (*Austral & NZ slang*) SLACKER, shirker, skiver (*Brit slang*), loafer, layabout, idler, passenger, do-nothing, dodger, good-for-nothing, bludger (*Austral & NZ informal*), gold brick (*US slang*), scrimshanker (*Brit military slang*)

pile[1] noun 1 HEAP, collection, mountain, mass, stack, rick, mound, accumulation, stockpile, hoard, assortment, assemblage **2** (*informal*) *often plural* LOT(s), mountain(s), load(s) (*informal*), oceans, wealth, great deal, stack(s), abundance, large quantity, oodles (*informal*), shedload (*Brit informal*) **3** MANSION, building, residence, manor, country house, seat, big house, stately home, manor house **4** (*informal*) FORTUNE, bomb (*Brit slang*), pot, packet (*slang*), mint, big money, wad (*US & Canad slang*), big bucks (*informal, chiefly US*), megabucks (*US & Canad slang*), tidy sum (*informal*), pretty penny (*informal*), top whack (*informal*) ▷ *verb* **1** LOAD, stuff, pack, stack, charge, heap, cram, lade **2** CROWD, pack, charge, rush, climb, flood, stream, crush, squeeze, jam, flock, shove ▷▷ **pile something up 1** GATHER (UP), collect, assemble, stack (up), mass, heap (up), load up **2** COLLECT, accumulate, gather in, pull in, amass, hoard, stack up, store up, heap up ▷▷ **pile up** ACCUMULATE, collect, gather (up), build up, amass

pile² *noun* FOUNDATION, support, post, column, piling, beam, upright, pier, pillar

pile³ *noun* NAP, fibre, down, hair, surface, fur, plush, shag, filament

piles *plural noun* HAEMORRHOIDS

pile-up *noun* (*informal*) COLLISION, crash, accident, smash, smash-up (*informal*), multiple collision

pilfer *verb* STEAL, take, rob, lift (*informal*), nick (*slang, chiefly Brit*), appropriate, rifle, pinch (*informal*), swipe (*slang*), embezzle, blag (*slang*), walk off with, snitch (*slang*), purloin, filch, snaffle (*Brit informal*), thieve

pilgrim *noun* TRAVELLER, crusader, wanderer, devotee, palmer, haji (*Islam*), wayfarer

pilgrimage *noun* JOURNEY, tour, trip, mission, expedition, crusade, excursion, hajj (*Islam*)

pill *noun* TABLET, capsule, pellet, bolus, pilule ▷▷ **a bitter pill (to swallow)** TRIAL, pain (*informal*), bore, drag (*informal*), pest, nuisance, pain in the neck (*informal*)

pillage *verb* PLUNDER, strip, sack, rob, raid, spoil (*archaic*), rifle, loot, ravage, ransack, despoil, maraud, reive (*dialect*), depredate (*rare*), freeboot, spoliate ▷ *noun* PLUNDERING, sacking, robbery, plunder, sack, devastation, marauding, depredation, rapine, spoliation

pillar *noun* **1** SUPPORT, post, column, piling, prop, shaft, upright, pier, obelisk, stanchion, pilaster **2** SUPPORTER, leader, rock, worthy, mainstay, leading light (*informal*), tower of strength, upholder, torchbearer

pillory *verb* RIDICULE, denounce, stigmatize,

brand, lash, show someone up, expose someone to ridicule, cast a slur on, heap or pour scorn on, hold someone up to shame

pilot *noun* **1** AIRMAN, captain, flyer, aviator, aeronaut **2** HELMSMAN, guide, navigator, leader, director, conductor, coxswain, steersman ▷ *verb* **1** FLY, control, operate, be at the controls of **2** NAVIGATE, drive, manage, direct, guide, handle, conduct, steer **3** DIRECT, lead, manage, conduct, steer ▷ *modifier* TRIAL, test, model, sample, experimental

pimp *noun* PROCURER, go-between, bawd (*archaic*), white-slaver, pander, panderer, whoremaster (*archaic*) ▷ *verb* PROCURE, sell, tout, solicit, live off immoral earnings

pimple *noun* SPOT, boil, swelling, pustule, zit (*slang*), papule (*pathology*), plook (*Scot*)

pin *noun* **1** TACK, nail, needle, safety pin **2** PEG, rod, brace, bolt ▷ *verb* **1** FASTEN, stick, attach, join, fix, secure, nail, clip, staple, tack, affix **2** HOLD FAST, hold down, press, restrain, constrain, immobilize, pinion ▷▷ **pin someone down** FORCE, pressure, compel, put pressure on, pressurize, nail someone down, make someone commit themselves ▷▷ **pin something down 1** DETERMINE, identify, locate, name, specify, designate, pinpoint, home in on **2** TRAP, confine, constrain, bind, squash, tie down, nail down, immobilize

pinch *verb* **1** NIP, press, squeeze, grasp, compress, tweak **2** HURT, crush, squeeze, pain, confine, cramp, chafe **3** (*Brit informal*) STEAL, rob, snatch, lift (*informal*), nick (*slang, chiefly Brit*), swipe (*slang*), knock off (*slang*), blag (*slang*), pilfer, snitch (*slang*), purloin, filch, snaffle (*Brit informal*) ▷ *noun* **1** NIP, squeeze, tweak **2** DASH, bit, taste, mite, jot, speck, small quantity, smidgen (*informal*), soupçon (*French*) **3** EMERGENCY, crisis, difficulty, plight, scrape (*informal*), strait, uphill (*S African*), predicament, extremity, hardship

pinched *adjective* THIN, starved, worn, drawn, gaunt, haggard, careworn, peaky << ANTONYM plump

pine *verb* WASTE, decline, weaken, sicken, sink, flag, fade, decay, dwindle, wither, wilt, languish, droop ▷▷ **pine for something or someone 1** LONG FOR, ache for, crave, yearn for, sigh for, carry a torch for, eat your heart out over, suspire for (*archaic or poetic*) **2** HANKER AFTER, crave, covet, wish for, yearn for, thirst for, hunger for, lust after

pink *adjective* ROSY, rose, salmon, flushed,

reddish, flesh coloured, roseate

pinnacle noun **1** SUMMIT, top, height, peak, eminence **2** HEIGHT, top, crown, crest, meridian, zenith, apex, apogee, acme, vertex

pinpoint verb **1** IDENTIFY, discover, spot, define, distinguish, put your finger on **2** LOCATE, find, spot, identify, home in on, zero in on, get a fix on

pint noun (Brit informal) BEER, jar (Brit informal), jug (Brit informal), ale

pint-sized adjective (informal) SMALL, little, tiny, wee, pocket-sized, miniature, diminutive, midget, teeny-weeny, teensy-weensy, pygmy or pigmy

pioneer noun **1** FOUNDER, leader, developer, innovator, founding father, trailblazer **2** SETTLER, explorer, colonist, colonizer, frontiersman ▷ verb DEVELOP, create, launch, establish, start, prepare, discover, institute, invent, open up, initiate, originate, take the lead on, instigate, map out, show the way on, lay the groundwork on

pious adjective **1** RELIGIOUS, godly, devoted, spiritual, holy, dedicated, righteous, devout, saintly, God-fearing, reverent << ANTONYM irreligious **2** SELF-RIGHTEOUS, hypocritical, sanctimonious, goody-goody, unctuous, holier-than-thou, pietistic, religiose << ANTONYM humble

pipe noun **1** TUBE, drain, canal, pipeline, line, main, passage, cylinder, hose, conduit, duct, conveyor **2** CLAY (PIPE), briar, calabash (rare), meerschaum, hookah (rare) **3** WHISTLE, horn, recorder, fife, flute, wind instrument, penny whistle ▷ verb CONVEY, channel, supply, conduct, bring in, transmit, siphon ▷▷ **pipe down** (informal) BE QUIET, shut up (informal), hush, stop talking, quieten down, shush, button it (slang), belt up (slang), shut your mouth, hold your tongue, put a sock in it (Brit slang), button your lip (slang) ▷▷ **pipe up** SPEAK, volunteer, speak up, have your say, raise your voice, make yourself heard, put your oar in

pipe dream noun DAYDREAM, dream, notion, fantasy, delusion, vagary, reverie, chimera, castle in the air

pipeline noun TUBE, passage, pipe, line, conduit, duct, conveyor ▷▷ **in the pipeline** ON THE WAY, expected, coming, close, near, being prepared, anticipated, forthcoming, under way, brewing, imminent, in preparation, in production, in process, in the offing

piquant adjective **1** SPICY, biting, sharp, stinging, tart, savoury, pungent, tangy, highly-seasoned, peppery, zesty, with a kick (informal), acerb << ANTONYM mild **2** INTERESTING, spirited, stimulating, lively, sparkling, provocative, salty, racy, scintillating << ANTONYM dull

pique noun RESENTMENT, offence, irritation, annoyance, huff, displeasure, umbrage, hurt feelings, vexation, wounded pride ▷ verb **1** AROUSE, excite, stir, spur, stimulate, provoke, rouse, goad, whet, kindle, galvanize **2** DISPLEASE, wound, provoke, annoy, get (informal), sting, offend, irritate, put out, incense, gall, nettle, vex, affront, mortify, irk, rile, peeve (informal), nark (Brit, Austral & NZ slang), put someone's nose out of joint (informal), miff (informal), hack off (informal)

piracy noun **1** ROBBERY, stealing, theft, hijacking, infringement, buccaneering, rapine, freebooting **2** ILLEGAL COPYING, bootlegging, plagiarism, copyright infringement, illegal reproduction

pirate noun BUCCANEER, raider, rover, filibuster, marauder, corsair, sea wolf, freebooter, sea robber, sea rover ▷ verb COPY, steal, reproduce, bootleg, lift (informal), appropriate, borrow, poach, crib (informal), plagiarize

pirouette noun SPIN, turn, whirl, pivot, twirl ▷ verb SPIN, turn, whirl, pivot, twirl

pit noun **1** COAL MINE, mine, shaft, colliery, mine shaft **2** HOLE, gulf, depression, hollow, trench, crater, trough, cavity, abyss, chasm, excavation, pothole ▷ verb SCAR, mark, hole, nick, notch, dent, gouge, indent, dint, pockmark ▷▷ **pit something or someone against something or someone** SET AGAINST, oppose, match against, measure against, put in competition with, put in opposition to

pitch noun **1** SPORTS FIELD, ground, stadium, arena, park, field of play **2** TONE, sound, key, frequency, timbre, modulation **3** LEVEL, point, degree, summit, extent, height, intensity, high point **4** TALK, line, patter, spiel (informal) ▷ verb **1** THROW, launch, cast, toss, hurl, fling, chuck (informal), sling, lob (informal), bung (Brit slang), heave **2** FALL, drop, plunge, dive, stagger, tumble, topple, plummet, fall headlong, (take a) nosedive **3** SET UP, place, station, locate, raise, plant, settle, fix, put up, erect **4** TOSS (ABOUT), roll, plunge, flounder, lurch, wallow, welter, make heavy weather ▷▷ **pitch in** HELP, contribute, participate, join in, cooperate, chip in (informal), get stuck in (Brit informal), lend a hand, muck in (*Brit informal*), do your bit, lend a helping hand

pitch-black *or* **pitch-dark** *adjective* DARK, black, jet, raven, ebony, sable, unlit, jet-black, inky, Stygian, pitchy, unilluminated

pitfall *noun usually plural* DANGER, difficulty, peril, catch, trap, hazard, drawback, snag, uphill (*S African*), banana skin (*informal*)

pithy *adjective* SUCCINCT, pointed, short, brief, to the point, compact, meaningful, forceful, expressive, concise, terse, laconic, trenchant, cogent, epigrammatic, finely honed << ANTONYM long-winded

pitiful *adjective* 1 PATHETIC, distressing, miserable, harrowing, heartbreaking, grievous, sad, woeful, deplorable, lamentable, heart-rending, gut-wrenching, wretched, pitiable, piteous << ANTONYM funny 2 INADEQUATE, mean, low, miserable, dismal, beggarly, shabby, insignificant, paltry, despicable, measly, contemptible << ANTONYM adequate 3 WORTHLESS, base, sorry, vile, abject, scurvy << ANTONYM admirable

pitiless *adjective* MERCILESS, ruthless, heartless, harsh, cruel, brutal, relentless, callous, inhuman, inexorable, implacable, unsympathetic, cold-blooded, uncaring, unfeeling, cold-hearted, unmerciful, hardhearted << ANTONYM merciful

pittance *noun* PEANUTS (*slang*), trifle, modicum, drop, mite, chicken feed (*slang*), slave wages, small allowance

pitted *adjective* SCARRED, marked, rough, scratched, dented, riddled, blemished, potholed, indented, eaten away, holey, pockmarked, rutty

pity *noun* 1 COMPASSION, understanding, charity, sympathy, distress, sadness, sorrow, kindness, tenderness, condolence, commiseration, fellow feeling << ANTONYM mercilessness 2 SHAME, crime (*informal*), sin (*informal*), misfortune, bad luck, sad thing, bummer (*slang*), crying shame, source of regret 3 MERCY, kindness, clemency, leniency, forbearance, quarter ▷ *verb* FEEL SORRY FOR, feel for, sympathize with, grieve for, weep for, take pity on, empathize with, bleed for, commiserate with, have compassion for, condole with ▷▷ **take pity on something** *or* **someone** HAVE MERCY ON, spare, forgive, pity, pardon, reprieve, show mercy to, feel compassion for, put out of your misery, relent against

pivot *noun* 1 HUB, centre, heart, hinge, focal point, kingpin 2 AXIS, swivel, axle, spindle, fulcrum ▷ *verb* TURN, spin, revolve, rotate, swivel, twirl

pivotal *adjective* CRUCIAL, central, determining, vital, critical, decisive, focal, climactic

pixie *noun* ELF, fairy, brownie, sprite, peri

placard *noun* NOTICE, bill, advertisement, poster, sticker, public notice, affiche (*French*)

placate *verb* CALM, satisfy, humour, soothe, appease, assuage, pacify, mollify, win someone over, conciliate, propitiate

place *noun* 1 SPOT, point, position, site, area, situation, station, location, venue, whereabouts, locus 2 REGION, city, town, quarter, village, district, neighbourhood, hamlet, vicinity, locality, locale, dorp (*S African*) 3 POSITION, point, spot, location 4 SPACE, position, seat, chair 5 SITUATION, position, circumstances, shoes (*informal*) 6 JOB, position, post, situation, office, employment, appointment, berth (*informal*), billet (*informal*) 7 HOME, house, room, property, seat, flat, apartment, accommodation, pad (*slang*), residence, mansion, dwelling, manor, abode, domicile, bachelor apartment (*Canad*) 8 (In this context, the construction is always negative) DUTY, right, job, charge, concern, role, affair, responsibility, task, function, prerogative ▷ *verb* 1 LAY (DOWN), leave, put (down), set (down), stand, sit, position, rest, plant, station, establish, stick (*informal*), settle, fix, arrange, lean, deposit, locate, set out, install, prop, dispose, situate, stow, bung (*Brit slang*), plonk (*informal*), array 2 PUT, lay, set, invest, pin 3 CLASSIFY, class, group, put, order, sort, rank, arrange, grade, assign, categorize 4 ENTRUST TO, give to, assign to, appoint to, allocate to, find a home for 5 IDENTIFY, remember, recognize, pin someone down, put your finger on, put a name to, set someone in context ▷▷ **in place of** INSTEAD OF, rather than, in exchange for, as an alternative to, taking the place of, in lieu of, as a substitute for, as a replacement for ▷▷ **know your place** KNOW YOUR RANK, know your standing, know your position, know your footing, know your station, know your status, know your grade, know your niche ▷▷ **put someone in their place** HUMBLE, humiliate, deflate, crush, mortify, take the wind out of someone's sails, cut someone down to size (*informal*), take someone down a peg (*informal*), make someone eat humble pie, bring someone down to size (*informal*), make someone swallow their pride, settle someone's hash (*informal*) ▷▷ **take place** HAPPEN, occur, go on, go down (*US & Canad*), arise, come about, crop up, transpire (*informal*), befall, materialize, come to pass (*archaic*), betide

placement *noun* **1** POSITIONING, stationing, arrangement, location, ordering, distribution, locating, installation, deployment, disposition, emplacement **2** APPOINTMENT, employment, engagement, assignment

placid *adjective* **1** CALM, cool, quiet, peaceful, even, collected, gentle, mild, composed, serene, tranquil, undisturbed, unmoved, untroubled, unfazed (*informal*), unruffled, self-possessed, imperturbable, equable, even-tempered, unexcitable << ANTONYM excitable **2** STILL, quiet, calm, peaceful, serene, tranquil, undisturbed, halcyon, unruffled << ANTONYM rough

plagiarism *noun* COPYING, borrowing, theft, appropriation, infringement, piracy, lifting (*informal*), cribbing (*informal*)

plague *noun* **1** DISEASE, infection, epidemic, contagion, pandemic, pestilence, lurgy (*informal*) **2** INFESTATION, invasion, epidemic, influx, host, swarm, multitude **3** (*informal*) BANE, trial, cancer, evil, curse, torment, blight, calamity, scourge, affliction **4** (*informal*) NUISANCE, problem, pain (*informal*), bother, pest, hassle (*informal*), annoyance, irritant, aggravation (*informal*), vexation, thorn in your flesh ▷ *verb* **1** TORMENT, trouble, pain, torture, haunt, afflict **2** PESTER, trouble, bother, disturb, annoy, tease, harry, harass, hassle, fret, badger, persecute, molest, vex, bedevil, get on your nerves (*informal*), give someone grief (*Brit & S African*), be on your back (*slang*), get in your hair (*informal*)

plain *adjective* **1** UNADORNED, simple, basic, severe, pure, bare, modest, stark, restrained, muted, discreet, austere, spartan, unfussy, unvarnished, unembellished, unornamented, unpatterned << ANTONYM ornate **2** CLEAR, obvious, patent, evident, apparent, visible, distinct, understandable, manifest, transparent, overt, unmistakable, lucid, unambiguous, comprehensible, legible << ANTONYM hidden **3** STRAIGHTFORWARD, open, direct, frank, bold, blunt, sincere, outspoken, honest, downright, candid, forthright,

upfront (*informal*), artless, ingenuous, guileless << ANTONYM roundabout **4** UGLY, ordinary, unattractive, homely (*US & Canad*), not striking, unlovely, unprepossessing, not beautiful, no oil painting (*informal*), ill-favoured, unalluring << ANTONYM attractive **5** ORDINARY, homely, common, simple, modest, everyday, commonplace, lowly, unaffected, unpretentious, frugal, workaday << ANTONYM sophisticated ▷ *noun* FLATLAND, plateau, prairie, grassland, mesa, lowland, steppe, open country, pampas, tableland, veld, llano

plain-spoken *adjective* BLUNT, direct, frank, straightforward, open, explicit, outright, outspoken, downright, candid, forthright, upfront (*informal*), unequivocal << ANTONYM tactful

plaintive *adjective* SORROWFUL, sad, pathetic, melancholy, grievous, pitiful, woeful, wistful, mournful, heart-rending, rueful, grief-stricken, disconsolate, doleful, woebegone, piteous

plan *noun* **1** SCHEME, system, design, idea, programme, project, proposal, strategy, method, suggestion, procedure, plot, device, scenario, proposition, contrivance **2** DIAGRAM, map, drawing, chart, illustration, representation, sketch, blueprint, layout, delineation, scale drawing ▷ *verb* **1** DEVISE, arrange, prepare, scheme, frame, plot, draft, organize, outline, invent, formulate, contrive, think out, concoct **2** INTEND, aim, mean, propose, purpose, contemplate, envisage, foresee **3** DESIGN, outline, draw up a plan of

plane *noun* **1** AEROPLANE, aircraft, jet, airliner, jumbo jet **2** FLAT SURFACE, the flat, horizontal, level surface **3** LEVEL, position, stage, footing, condition, standard, degree, rung, stratum, echelon ▷ *adjective* LEVEL, even, flat, regular, plain, smooth, uniform, flush, horizontal ▷ *verb* SKIM, sail, skate, glide

plant¹ *noun* FLOWER, bush, vegetable, herb, weed, shrub ▷ *verb* **1** SOW, scatter, set out, transplant, implant, put in the ground **2** SEED, sow, implant **3** PLACE, put, set, settle, fix **4** HIDE, put, place, conceal **5** PUT, place, establish, found, fix, institute, root, lodge, insert, sow the seeds of, imbed

plant² *noun* **1** FACTORY, works, shop, yard, mill, foundry **2** MACHINERY, equipment, gear, apparatus

plaque *noun* PLATE, panel, medal, tablet,

badge, slab, brooch, medallion, cartouch(e)

plaster *noun* **1** MORTAR, stucco, gypsum, plaster of Paris, gesso **2** BANDAGE, dressing, sticking plaster, Elastoplast (*trademark*), adhesive plaster ▷ *verb* COVER, spread, coat, smear, overlay, daub, besmear, bedaub

plastic *adjective* **1** (*slang*) FALSE, artificial, synthetic, superficial, sham, pseudo (*informal*), spurious, specious, meretricious, phoney or phony (*informal*) << ANTONYM natural **2** PLIANT, soft, flexible, supple, pliable, tensile, ductile, mouldable, fictile << ANTONYM rigid

plate *noun* **1** PLATTER, dish, dinner plate, salver, trencher (*archaic*) **2** HELPING, course, serving, dish, portion, platter, plateful **3** LAYER, panel, sheet, slab **4** ILLUSTRATION, picture, photograph, print, engraving, lithograph ▷ *verb* COAT, gild, laminate, face, cover, silver, nickel, overlay, electroplate, anodize, platinize

plateau *noun* **1** UPLAND, table, highland, mesa, tableland **2** LEVELLING OFF, level, stage, stability

platform *noun* **1** STAGE, stand, podium, rostrum, dais, soapbox **2** POLICY, programme, principle, objective(s), manifesto, tenet(s), party line

platitude *noun* CLICHÉ, stereotype, commonplace, banality, truism, bromide, verbiage, inanity, trite remark, hackneyed saying

Platonic *adjective often not cap* NONPHYSICAL, ideal, intellectual, spiritual, idealistic, transcendent

platoon *noun* SQUAD, company, group, team, outfit (*informal*), patrol, squadron

platter *noun* PLATE, dish, tray, charger, salver, trencher (*archaic*)

plaudits *plural noun* APPROVAL, acclaim, applause, praise, clapping, ovation, kudos, congratulation, round of applause, commendation, approbation, acclamation

plausible *adjective* **1** BELIEVABLE, possible, likely, reasonable, credible, probable, persuasive, conceivable, tenable, colourable, verisimilar << ANTONYM unbelievable **2** GLIB, smooth, specious, smooth-talking, smooth-tongued, fair-spoken

play *verb* **1** AMUSE YOURSELF, have fun, frolic, sport, fool, romp, revel, trifle, caper, frisk, gambol, entertain yourself, engage in games **2** TAKE PART IN, be involved in, engage in, participate in, compete in, be in a team for **3** COMPETE AGAINST, challenge,

take on, rival, oppose, vie with, contend against **4** PERFORM, carry out, execute **5** ACT, portray, represent, perform, impersonate, act the part of, take the part of, personate **6** PERFORM ON, strum, make music on **7** *often with* **about** *or* **around** FOOL AROUND, toy, fiddle, trifle, mess around, take something lightly ▷ *noun* **1** AMUSEMENT, pleasure, leisure, games, sport, fun, entertainment, relaxation, a good time, recreation, enjoyment, romping, larks, capering, frolicking, junketing, fun and games, revelry, skylarking, living it up (*informal*), gambolling, horseplay, merrymaking, me-time **2** DRAMA, show, performance, piece, comedy, entertainment, tragedy, farce, soap opera, soapie or soapie (*Austral slang*), pantomime, stage show, television drama, radio play, masque, dramatic piece ▷▷ **in play** IN or FOR FUN, for sport, for a joke, for a lark (*informal*), as a prank, for a jest ▷▷ **play around** PHILANDER, have an affair, carry on (*informal*), fool around, dally, sleep around (*informal*), womanize, play away from home (*informal*) ▷▷ **play at something** PRETEND TO BE, pose as, impersonate, make like (*US & Canad informal*), profess to be, assume the role of, give the appearance of, masquerade as, pass yourself off as ▷▷ **play on** or **upon something** TAKE ADVANTAGE OF, abuse, exploit, impose on, trade on, misuse, milk, make use of, utilize, profit by, capitalize on, turn to your account ▷▷ **play something down** MINIMIZE, make light of, gloss over, talk down, underrate, underplay, pooh-pooh (*informal*), soft-pedal (*informal*), make little of, set no store by ▷▷ **play something up** EMPHASIZE, highlight, underline, magnify, stress, accentuate, point up, call attention to, turn the spotlight on, bring to the fore ▷▷ **play up** (*Brit informal*) **1** HURT, be painful, bother you, trouble you, be sore, pain you, give you trouble, give you gyp (*Brit & NZ slang*) **2** MALFUNCTION, not work properly, be on the blink (*slang*), be wonky (*Brit slang*) **3** BE AWKWARD, misbehave, give trouble, be disobedient, give someone grief (*Brit & S African*), be stroppy (*Brit slang*), be bolshie (*Brit informal*) ▷▷ **play up to someone** (*informal*) BUTTER UP, flatter, pander to, crawl to, get in with, suck up to (*informal*), curry favour with, toady, fawn over, keep someone sweet, bootlick (*informal*), ingratiate yourself to

playboy *noun* WOMANIZER, philanderer, rake,

socialite, man about town, pleasure seeker, lady-killer (*informal*), roué, lover boy (*slang*), ladies' man

player *noun* **1** SPORTSMAN *or* SPORTSWOMAN, competitor, participant, contestant, team member **2** MUSICIAN, artist, performer, virtuoso, instrumentalist, music maker **3** PERFORMER, entertainer, Thespian, trouper, actor *or* actress

playful *adjective* **1** JOKING, humorous, jokey, arch, teasing, coy, tongue-in-cheek, jesting, flirtatious, good-natured, roguish, waggish **2** LIVELY, spirited, cheerful, merry, mischievous, joyous, sprightly, vivacious, rollicking, impish, frisky, puckish, coltish, kittenish, frolicsome, ludic (*literary*), sportive, gay, larkish (*informal*) << ANTONYM sedate

playmate *noun* FRIEND, companion, comrade, chum (*informal*), pal (*informal*), cobber (*Austral & NZ old-fashioned informal*), playfellow

plaything *noun* TOY, amusement, game, pastime, trifle, trinket, bauble, gimcrack, gewgaw

playwright *noun* DRAMATIST, scriptwriter, tragedian, dramaturge, dramaturgist

plea *noun* **1** APPEAL, request, suit, prayer, begging, petition, overture, entreaty, intercession, supplication **2** (*law*) SUIT, cause, action, allegation **3** EXCUSE, claim, defence, explanation, justification, pretext, vindication, extenuation

plead *verb* **1** APPEAL, ask, request, beg, petition, crave, solicit, implore, beseech, entreat, importune, supplicate **2** ALLEGE, claim, argue, maintain, assert, put forward, adduce, use as an excuse

pleasant *adjective* **1** PLEASING, nice, welcome, satisfying, fine, lovely, acceptable, amusing, refreshing, delightful, enjoyable, gratifying, agreeable, pleasurable, delectable, lekker (*S African slang*) << ANTONYM horrible **2** FRIENDLY, nice, agreeable, likable *or* likeable, engaging, charming, cheerful, cheery, good-humoured, amiable, genial, affable, congenial << ANTONYM disagreeable

pleasantry *noun usually plural* COMMENT, remark, casual remark, polite remark

please *verb* DELIGHT, entertain, humour, amuse, suit, content, satisfy, charm, cheer, indulge, tickle, gratify, gladden, give pleasure to, tickle someone pink (*informal*) << ANTONYM annoy

pleased *adjective* HAPPY, delighted, contented, satisfied, thrilled, glad, tickled, gratified, over the moon (*informal*), chuffed (*Brit slang*), euphoric, rapt, in high spirits, tickled pink (*informal*), pleased as punch (*informal*)

pleasing *adjective* **1** ENJOYABLE, satisfying, attractive, charming, entertaining, delightful, gratifying, agreeable, pleasurable << ANTONYM unpleasant **2** LIKABLE *or* LIKEABLE, attractive, engaging, charming, winning, entertaining, amusing, delightful, polite, agreeable, amiable << ANTONYM disagreeable

pleasurable *adjective* ENJOYABLE, pleasant, diverting, good, nice, welcome, fun, lovely, entertaining, delightful, gratifying, agreeable, congenial

pleasure *noun* **1** HAPPINESS, delight, satisfaction, enjoyment, bliss, gratification, contentment, gladness, delectation << ANTONYM displeasure **2** AMUSEMENT, joy, recreation, diversion, solace, jollies (*slang*), beer and skittles (*informal*) << ANTONYM duty **3** WISH, choice, desire, will, mind, option, preference, inclination

pledge *noun* **1** PROMISE, vow, assurance, word, undertaking, warrant, oath, covenant, word of honour **2** GUARANTEE, security, deposit, bail, bond, collateral, earnest, pawn, gage, surety ▷ *verb* **1** PROMISE, vow, vouch, swear, contract, engage, undertake, give your word, give your word of honour, give your oath **2** BIND, guarantee, mortgage, engage, gage (*archaic*)

plenary *adjective* **1** (*of assemblies, councils, etc*) FULL, open, general, whole, complete, entire **2** COMPLETE, full, sweeping, absolute, thorough, unlimited, unconditional, unqualified, unrestricted

plentiful *adjective* **1** ABUNDANT, liberal, generous, lavish, complete, ample, infinite, overflowing, copious, inexhaustible, bountiful, profuse, thick on the ground, bounteous (*literary*), plenteous << ANTONYM scarce **2** PRODUCTIVE, bumper, fertile, prolific, fruitful, luxuriant, plenteous

plenty *noun* **1** ABUNDANCE, wealth, luxury, prosperity, fertility, profusion, affluence, opulence, plenitude, fruitfulness, copiousness, plenteousness, plentifulness **2** *usually with* **of** LOTS OF (*informal*), enough, a great deal of, masses of, quantities of, piles of (*informal*), mountains of, a good deal of, stacks of, heaps of (*informal*), a mass of, a volume of, an abundance of, a plethora of, a quantity of, a fund of, oodles of (*informal*), a store of, a mine of, a sufficiency of

plethora noun EXCESS, surplus, glut, profusion, surfeit, overabundance, superabundance, superfluity << ANTONYM shortage

pliable adjective **1** FLEXIBLE, plastic, supple, lithe, limber, malleable, pliant, tensile, bendy, ductile, bendable << ANTONYM rigid **2** COMPLIANT, susceptible, responsive, manageable, receptive, yielding, adaptable, docile, impressionable, easily led, pliant, tractable, persuadable, influenceable, like putty in your hands << ANTONYM stubborn

plight noun DIFFICULTY, condition, state, situation, trouble, circumstances, dilemma, straits, predicament, extremity, perplexity

plod verb **1** TRUDGE, drag, tread, clump, lumber, tramp, stomp (informal), slog **2** SLOG AWAY, labour, grind away (informal), toil, grub, persevere, soldier on, plough through, plug away (informal), drudge, peg away

plot¹ noun **1** PLAN, scheme, intrigue, conspiracy, cabal, stratagem, machination, covin (law) **2** STORY, action, subject, theme, outline, scenario, narrative, thread, story line ▷ verb **1** PLAN, scheme, conspire, intrigue, manoeuvre, contrive, collude, cabal, hatch a plot, machinate **2** DEVISE, design, project, lay, imagine, frame, conceive, brew, hatch, contrive, concoct, cook up (informal) **3** CHART, mark, draw, map, draft, locate, calculate, outline, compute

plot² noun PATCH, lot, area, ground, parcel, tract, allotment

plotter noun CONSPIRATOR, architect, intriguer, planner, conspirer, strategist, conniver, Machiavellian, schemer, cabalist

plough verb TURN OVER, dig, till, ridge, cultivate, furrow, break ground ▷▷ **plough into something** or **someone** PLUNGE INTO, crash into, smash into, career into, shove into, hurtle into, bulldoze into ▷▷ **plough through something** FORGE, cut, drive, press, push, plunge, surge, stagger, wade, flounder, trudge, plod

ploy noun TACTIC, move, trick, device, game, scheme, manoeuvre, dodge, ruse, gambit, subterfuge, stratagem, contrivance, wile

pluck verb **1** PULL OUT or OFF, pick, draw, collect, gather, harvest **2** TUG, catch, snatch, clutch, jerk, yank, tweak, pull at **3** STRUM, pick, finger, twang, thrum, plunk ▷ noun COURAGE, nerve, heart, spirit, bottle (Brit slang), resolution, determination, guts (informal), grit, bravery, backbone, mettle,

boldness, spunk (informal), intrepidity, hardihood

plucky adjective COURAGEOUS, spirited, brave, daring, bold, game, hardy, heroic, gritty, feisty (informal, chiefly US & Canad), gutsy (slang), intrepid, valiant, doughty, undaunted, unflinching, spunky (informal), ballsy (taboo slang), mettlesome, (as) game as Ned Kelly (Austral slang) << ANTONYM cowardly

plug noun **1** STOPPER, cork, bung, spigot, stopple **2** (informal) MENTION, advertisement, advert (Brit informal), push, promotion, publicity, puff, hype, good word ▷ verb **1** SEAL, close, stop, fill, cover, block, stuff, pack, cork, choke, stopper, bung, stop up, stopple **2** (informal) MENTION, push, promote, publicize, advertise, build up, puff, hype, write up ▷▷ **plug away** (informal) SLOG AWAY, labour, toil away, grind away (informal), peg away, plod away, drudge away

plum modifier CHOICE, prize, first-class

plumb verb DELVE INTO, measure, explore, probe, sound out, search, go into, penetrate, gauge, unravel, fathom ▷ adverb EXACTLY, precisely, bang, slap, spot-on (Brit informal)

plume noun FEATHER, crest, quill, pinion, aigrette

plummet verb **1** DROP, fall, crash, nose-dive, descend rapidly **2** PLUNGE, fall, drop, crash, tumble, swoop, stoop, nose-dive, descend rapidly

plummy adjective (of a voice) DEEP, posh (informal, chiefly Brit), refined, upper-class, fruity, resonant

plump¹ adjective CHUBBY, fat, stout, full, round, burly, obese, fleshy, beefy (informal), tubby, portly, buxom, dumpy, roly-poly, well-covered, rotund, podgy, corpulent, well-upholstered (informal) << ANTONYM scrawny

plump² verb FLOP, fall, drop, sink, dump, slump ▷▷ **plump for something** or **someone** CHOOSE, favour, go for, back, support, opt for, side with, come down in favour of

plunder verb **1** LOOT, strip, sack, rob, raid, devastate, spoil, rifle, ravage, ransack, pillage, despoil **2** STEAL, rob, take, nick (informal), pinch (informal), embezzle, pilfer, thieve ▷ noun **1** PILLAGE, sacking, robbery, marauding, rapine, spoliation **2** LOOT, spoils, prey, booty, swag (slang), ill-gotten gains

plunge verb **1** DESCEND, fall, drop, crash, pitch, sink, go down, dive, tumble, plummet, nose-dive **2** HURTLE, charge, career, jump, tear, rush, dive, dash, swoop, lurch **3** SUBMERGE,

sink, duck, dip, immerse, douse, dunk
4 THROW, cast, pitch, propel 5 FALL STEEPLY,
drop, crash (*informal*), go down, slump,
plummet, take a nosedive (*informal*) ▷
noun 1 FALL, crash (*informal*), slump, drop,
tumble 2 DIVE, jump, duck, swoop, descent,
immersion, submersion

plurality *noun* MULTIPLICITY, variety,
diversity, profusion, numerousness

plus *preposition* AND, with, added to, coupled
with, with the addition of ▷ *noun* (*informal*)
ADVANTAGE, benefit, asset, gain, extra, bonus,
perk (*Brit informal*), good point, icing on the
cake ▷ *adjective* ADDITIONAL, added, extra,
positive, supplementary, add-on

plush *adjective* LUXURIOUS, luxury, costly,
lavish, rich, sumptuous, opulent, palatial,
ritzy (*slang*), de luxe << ANTONYM cheap

ply¹ *verb* 1 PROVIDE, supply, shower, lavish,
regale 2 BOMBARD, press, harass, besiege,
beset, assail, importune 3 WORK AT, follow,
exercise, pursue, carry on, practise 4 TRAVEL,
go, ferry, shuttle 5 USE, handle, employ,
swing, manipulate, wield, utilize

ply² *noun* THICKNESS, leaf, sheet, layer, fold,
strand

poach *verb* 1 STEAL, rob, plunder, hunt *or* fish
illegally 2 TAKE, steal, appropriate, snatch
(*informal*), nab (*informal*), purloin

pocket *noun* POUCH, bag, sack, hollow,
compartment, receptacle ▷ *modifier* SMALL,
compact, miniature, portable, little, potted
(*informal*), concise, pint-size(d) (*informal*),
abridged ▷ *verb* STEAL, take, lift (*informal*),
appropriate, pilfer, purloin, filch, help
yourself to, snaffle (*Brit informal*)

pod *noun* SHELL, case, hull, husk, shuck

podium *noun* PLATFORM, stand, stage,
rostrum, dais

poem *noun* VERSE, song, lyric, rhyme, sonnet,
ode, verse composition

poet *noun* BARD, rhymer, lyricist, lyric poet,
versifier, maker (*archaic*), elegist

poetic *adjective* 1 FIGURATIVE, creative, lyric,
symbolic, lyrical, rhythmic, rhythmical,
songlike 2 LYRICAL, lyric, rhythmic, elegiac,
rhythmical, metrical

poetry *noun* VERSE, poems, rhyme, rhyming,
poesy (*archaic*), verse composition, metrical
composition

po-faced *adjective* HUMOURLESS,
disapproving, solemn, prim, puritanical,
narrow-minded, stolid, prudish, strait-laced

pogey *noun* (*Canad*) BENEFITS, the dole
(*Brit & Austral*), welfare, social security,

unemployment benefit, state benefit,
allowance

poignancy *noun* SADNESS, emotion,
sentiment, intensity, feeling, tenderness,
pathos, emotionalism, plaintiveness,
evocativeness, piteousness

poignant *adjective* MOVING, touching,
affecting, upsetting, sad, bitter, intense,
painful, distressing, pathetic, harrowing,
heartbreaking, agonizing, heart-rending,
gut-wrenching

point *noun* 1 ESSENCE, meaning, subject,
question, matter, heart, theme, import, text,
core, burden, drift, thrust, proposition,
marrow, crux, gist, main idea, nub, pith
2 PURPOSE, aim, object, use, end, reason,
goal, design, intention, objective, utility,
intent, motive, usefulness 3 ASPECT, detail,
feature, side, quality, property, particular,
respect, item, instance, characteristic, topic,
attribute, trait, facet, peculiarity, nicety
4 PLACE, area, position, station, site, spot,
location, locality, locale 5 MOMENT, time,
stage, period, phase, instant, juncture,
moment in time, very minute 6 STAGE,
level, position, condition, degree, pitch,
circumstance, extent 7 END, tip, sharp
end, top, spur, spike, apex, nib, tine, prong
8 SCORE, tally, mark 9 HEADLAND, head,
bill, cape, ness (*archaic*), promontory,
foreland 10 PINPOINT, mark, spot, dot,
fleck, speck ▷ *verb* 1 *usually followed by* at
or to AIM, level, train, direct 2 FACE, look,
direct ▷▷ **beside the point** IRRELEVANT,
inappropriate, pointless, peripheral,
unimportant, incidental, unconnected,
immaterial, inconsequential, nothing to
do with it, extraneous, neither here nor
there, off the subject, inapplicable, not to
the point, inapposite, without connection,
inconsequent, not pertinent, not germane,
not to the purpose ▷▷ **point at** *or* **to**
something *or* **someone** INDICATE, show,
signal, point to, point out, specify, designate,
gesture towards ▷▷ **point of view** 1 OPINION,
view, attitude, belief, feeling, thought, idea,
approach, judgment, sentiment, viewpoint,
way of thinking, way of looking at it
2 PERSPECTIVE, side, position, stance, stand,
angle, outlook, orientation, viewpoint, slant,
standpoint, frame of reference ▷▷ **point**
something up EMPHASIZE, stress, highlight,
underline, make clear, accent, spotlight,
draw attention to, underscore, play up,
accentuate, foreground, focus attention on,

give prominence to, turn the spotlight on, bring to the fore, put emphasis on ▷▷ **point something** *or* **someone out 1** IDENTIFY, show, point to, indicate, finger (*informal, chiefly US*), single out, call attention to, draw attention to **2** ALLUDE TO, reveal, mention, identify, indicate, bring up, specify, call attention to, draw attention to ▷▷ **point to something 1** DENOTE, reveal, indicate, show, suggest, evidence, signal, signify, be evidence of, bespeak (*literary*) **2** REFER TO, mention, indicate, specify, single out, touch on, call attention to ▷▷ **to the point** RELEVANT, appropriate, apt, pointed, short, fitting, material, related, brief, suitable, applicable, pertinent, terse, pithy, apposite, apropos, germane

point-blank *adjective* DIRECT, plain, blunt, explicit, abrupt, express, downright, categorical, unreserved, straight-from-the-shoulder ▷ *adverb* DIRECTLY, openly, straight, frankly, plainly, bluntly, explicitly, overtly, candidly, brusquely, straightforwardly, forthrightly

pointed *adjective* **1** SHARP, edged, acute, barbed **2** CUTTING, telling, biting, sharp, keen, acute, accurate, penetrating, pertinent, incisive, trenchant

pointer *noun* **1** HINT, tip, suggestion, warning, recommendation, caution, piece of information, piece of advice **2** INDICATOR, hand, guide, needle, arrow

pointless *adjective* SENSELESS, meaningless, futile, fruitless, unproductive, stupid, silly, useless, absurd, irrelevant, in vain, worthless, ineffectual, unprofitable, nonsensical, aimless, inane, unavailing, without rhyme or reason << ANTONYM worthwhile

poise *noun* **1** COMPOSURE, cool (*slang*), presence, assurance, dignity, equilibrium, serenity, coolness, aplomb, calmness, equanimity, presence of mind, sang-froid, savoir-faire, self-possession **2** GRACE, balance, equilibrium, elegance

poised *adjective* **1** READY, waiting, prepared, standing by, on the brink, in the wings, all set **2** COMPOSED, calm, together (*informal*), collected, dignified, graceful, serene, suave, urbane, self-confident, unfazed (*informal*), debonair, unruffled, nonchalant, self-possessed << ANTONYM agitated

poison *noun* **1** TOXIN, venom, bane (*archaic*) **2** CONTAMINATION, corruption, contagion, cancer, virus, blight, bane, malignancy, miasma, canker ▷ *verb* **1** MURDER, kill, give

someone poison, administer poison to **2** CONTAMINATE, foul, infect, spoil, pollute, blight, taint, adulterate, envenom, befoul **3** CORRUPT, colour, undermine, bias, sour, pervert, warp, taint, subvert, embitter, deprave, defile, jaundice, vitiate, envenom

poisonous *adjective* **1** TOXIC, fatal, deadly, lethal, mortal, virulent, noxious, venomous, baneful (*archaic*), mephitic **2** EVIL, vicious, malicious, corrupting, pernicious, baleful, baneful (*archaic*), pestiferous

poke *verb* **1** JAB, hit, push, stick, dig, punch, stab, thrust, butt, elbow, shove, nudge, prod **2** PROTRUDE, stick, thrust, jut ▷ *noun* JAB, hit, dig, punch, thrust, butt, nudge, prod

polar *adjective* OPPOSITE, opposed, contrary, contradictory, antagonistic, antithetical, diametric, antipodal

polarity *noun* OPPOSITION, contradiction, paradox, ambivalence, dichotomy, duality, contrariety

pole[1] *noun* ROD, post, support, staff, standard, bar, stick, stake, paling, shaft, upright, pillar, mast, picket, spar, stave

pole[2] *noun* EXTREMITY, limit, terminus, antipode ▷▷ **poles apart** AT OPPOSITE EXTREMES, incompatible, irreconcilable, worlds apart, miles apart, like chalk and cheese (*Brit*), like night and day, widely separated, completely different, at opposite ends of the earth

polemic *noun* ARGUMENT, attack, debate, dispute, controversy, rant, tirade, diatribe, invective, philippic (*rare*)

polemics *noun* DISPUTE, debate, argument, discussion, controversy, contention, wrangling, disputation, argumentation

police *noun* THE LAW (*informal*), police force, constabulary, fuzz (*slang*), law enforcement agency, boys in blue (*informal*), the Old Bill (*slang*), rozzers (*slang*) ▷ *verb* **1** CONTROL, patrol, guard, watch, protect, regulate, keep the peace, keep in order **2** MONITOR, check, observe, oversee, supervise

police officer *noun* COP (*slang*), officer, pig (*offensive slang*), bobby (*informal*), copper (*slang*), constable, peeler (*Irish & Brit obsolete slang*), gendarme (*slang*), fuzz (*slang*), woodentop (*slang*), bizzy (*informal*), flatfoot (*slang*), rozzer (*slang*), policeman *or* policewoman

policy *noun* **1** PROCEDURE, plan, action, programme, practice, scheme, theory, code, custom, stratagem **2** LINE, rules, approach, guideline, protocol

polish *noun* **1** VARNISH, wax, glaze, lacquer, japan **2** SHEEN, finish, sparkle, glaze, gloss, brilliance, brightness, veneer, lustre, smoothness **3** STYLE, class (*informal*), finish, breeding, grace, elegance, refinement, finesse, urbanity, suavity, politesse ▷ *verb* **1** SHINE, wax, clean, smooth, rub, buff, brighten, burnish, furbish **2** *often with up* PERFECT, improve, enhance, refine, finish, correct, cultivate, brush up, touch up, emend ▷▷ **polish someone off** ELIMINATE, take out (*slang*), get rid of, dispose of, do away with, blow away (*slang, chiefly US*), beat someone once and for all ▷▷ **polish something off** (*informal*) FINISH, down, shift (*informal*), wolf, consume, put away, eat up, swill

polished *adjective* **1** ELEGANT, sophisticated, refined, polite, cultivated, civilized, genteel, suave, finished, urbane, courtly, well-bred << ANTONYM unsophisticated **2** ACCOMPLISHED, professional, masterly, fine, expert, outstanding, skilful, adept, impeccable, flawless, superlative, faultless << ANTONYM amateurish **3** SHINING, bright, smooth, gleaming, glossy, slippery, burnished, glassy, furbished << ANTONYM dull

polite *adjective* **1** MANNERLY, civil, courteous, affable, obliging, gracious, respectful, well-behaved, deferential, complaisant, well-mannered << ANTONYM rude **2** REFINED, cultured, civilized, polished, sophisticated, elegant, genteel, urbane, courtly, well-bred << ANTONYM uncultured

politeness *noun* COURTESY, decency, correctness, etiquette, deference, grace, civility, graciousness, common courtesy, complaisance, courteousness, respectfulness, mannerliness, obligingness

politic *adjective* WISE, diplomatic, sensible, discreet, prudent, advisable, expedient, judicious, tactful, sagacious, in your best interests

political *adjective* **1** GOVERNMENTAL, government, state, parliamentary, constitutional, administrative, legislative, civic, ministerial, policy-making, party political **2** FACTIONAL, party, militant, partisan

politician *noun* STATESMAN *or* STATESWOMAN, representative, senator (*US*), congressman (*US*), Member of Parliament, legislator, public servant, congresswoman (*US*), politico (*informal, chiefly US*), lawmaker, office bearer, M.P., elected offical

politics *noun* **1** AFFAIRS OF STATE, government, government policy, public affairs, civics **2** POLITICAL BELIEFS, party politics, political allegiances, political leanings, political sympathies **3** POLITICAL SCIENCE, polity, statesmanship, civics, statecraft **4** POWER STRUGGLE, machinations, opportunism, realpolitik, Machiavellianism

poll *noun* **1** SURVEY, figures, count, sampling, returns, ballot, tally, census, canvass, Gallup Poll, (public) opinion poll **2** ELECTION, vote, voting, referendum, ballot, plebiscite ▷ *verb* **1** QUESTION, interview, survey, sample, ballot, canvass **2** GAIN, return, record, register, tally

pollute *verb* **1** CONTAMINATE, dirty, mar, poison, soil, foul, infect, spoil, stain, taint, adulterate, make filthy, smirch, befoul << ANTONYM decontaminate **2** DEFILE, violate, corrupt, sully, deprave, debase, profane, desecrate, dishonour, debauch, besmirch << ANTONYM honour

pollution *noun* **1** CONTAMINATION, dirtying, corruption, taint, adulteration, foulness, defilement, uncleanness, vitiation **2** WASTE, poisons, dirt, impurities

pomp *noun* **1** CEREMONY, grandeur, splendour, state, show, display, parade, flourish, pageant, magnificence, solemnity, pageantry, ostentation, éclat **2** SHOW, pomposity, grandiosity, vainglory

pompous *adjective* **1** SELF-IMPORTANT, affected, arrogant, pretentious, bloated, grandiose, imperious, showy, overbearing, ostentatious, puffed up, portentous, magisterial, supercilious, pontifical, vainglorious << ANTONYM unpretentious **2** GRANDILOQUENT, high-flown, inflated, windy, overblown, turgid, bombastic, boastful, flatulent, arty-farty (*informal*), fustian, orotund, magniloquent << ANTONYM simple

pond *noun* POOL, tarn, small lake, fish pond, duck pond, millpond, lochan (*Scot*), dew pond

ponder *verb* THINK ABOUT, consider, study, reflect on, examine, weigh up, contemplate, deliberate about, muse on, brood on, meditate on, mull over, puzzle over, ruminate on, give thought to, cogitate on, rack your brains about, excogitate

ponderous *adjective* **1** DULL, laboured, pedestrian, dreary, heavy, tedious, plodding, tiresome, lifeless, stilted, stodgy, pedantic, long-winded, verbose, prolix **2** CLUMSY, awkward, lumbering, laborious, graceless, elephantine, heavy-footed, unco (*Austral slang*) << ANTONYM graceful

pontificate *verb* EXPOUND, preach, sound off, pronounce, declaim, lay down the law, hold forth, dogmatize, pontify

pool¹ *noun* **1** SWIMMING POOL, lido, swimming bath(s) (*Brit*), bathing pool (*archaic*) **2** POND, lake, mere, tarn **3** PUDDLE, drop, patch, splash

pool² *noun* **1** SUPPLY, reserve, fall-back **2** KITTY, bank, fund, stock, store, pot, jackpot, stockpile, hoard, cache ▷ *verb* COMBINE, share, merge, put together, amalgamate, lump together, join forces on

poor *adjective* **1** IMPOVERISHED, broke (*informal*), badly off, hard up (*informal*), short, in need, needy, on the rocks, penniless, destitute, poverty-stricken, down and out, skint (*Brit slang*), in want, indigent, down at heel, impecunious, dirt-poor (*informal*), on the breadline, flat broke (*informal*), penurious, on your uppers, stony-broke (*Brit slang*), necessitous, in queer street, without two pennies to rub together (*informal*), on your beam-ends << ANTONYM rich **2** UNFORTUNATE, pathetic, miserable, unlucky, hapless, pitiful, luckless, wretched, ill-starred, pitiable, ill-fated << ANTONYM fortunate **3** INFERIOR, unsatisfactory, mediocre, second-rate, sorry, weak, pants (*informal*), rotten (*informal*), faulty, feeble, worthless, shabby, shoddy, low-grade, below par, substandard, low-rent (*informal*), crappy (*slang*), valueless, no great shakes (*informal*), rubbishy, poxy (*slang*), not much cop (*Brit slang*), half-pie (*NZ informal*), bodger *or* bodgie (*Austral slang*) << ANTONYM excellent **4** MEAGRE, inadequate, insufficient, reduced, lacking, slight, miserable, pathetic, incomplete, scant, sparse, deficient, skimpy, measly, scanty, pitiable, niggardly, straitened, exiguous << ANTONYM ample **5** UNPRODUCTIVE, barren, fruitless, bad, bare, exhausted, depleted, impoverished, sterile, infertile, unfruitful << ANTONYM productive

poorly *adverb* BADLY, incompetently, inadequately, crudely, inferiorly, unsuccessfully, insufficiently, shabbily, unsatisfactorily, inexpertly << ANTONYM well ▷ *adjective* (*informal*) ILL, sick, ailing, unwell, crook (*Austral & NZ informal*), seedy (*informal*), below par, out of sorts, off colour,

under the weather (*informal*), indisposed, feeling rotten (*informal*) << ANTONYM healthy

pop *noun* **1** (*informal*) SOFT DRINK, ginger (*Scot*), soda (*US & Canad*), fizzy drink, cool drink (*S African*) **2** BANG, report, crack, noise, burst, explosion ▷ *verb* **1** BURST, crack, snap, bang, explode, report, go off (with a bang) **2** PROTRUDE, bulge, stick out **3** PUT, insert, push, stick, slip, thrust, tuck, shove **4** (*informal*) *often with* **in, out,** *etc.* CALL, visit, appear, drop in (*informal*), leave quickly, come *or* go suddenly, nip in *or* out (*Brit informal*)

pope *noun* HOLY FATHER, pontiff, His Holiness, Bishop of Rome, Vicar of Christ

populace *noun* PEOPLE, crowd, masses, mob, inhabitants, general public, multitude, throng, rabble, hoi polloi, Joe Public (*slang*), Joe Six-Pack (*US slang*), commonalty

popular *adjective* **1** WELL-LIKED, liked, favoured, celebrated, in, accepted, favourite, famous, approved, in favour, fashionable, in demand, sought-after, fave (*informal*) << ANTONYM unpopular **2** COMMON, general, standard, widespread, prevailing, stock, current, public, conventional, universal, prevalent, ubiquitous << ANTONYM rare

popularity *noun* **1** FAVOUR, fame, esteem, acclaim, regard, reputation, approval, recognition, celebrity, vogue, adoration, renown, repute, idolization, lionization **2** CURRENCY, acceptance, circulation, vogue, prevalence

popularize *verb* **1** MAKE SOMETHING POPULAR, spread the word about, disseminate, universalize, give mass appeal to **2** SIMPLIFY, make available to all, give currency to, give mass appeal to

popularly *adverb* GENERALLY, commonly, widely, usually, regularly, universally, traditionally, ordinarily, conventionally, customarily

populate *verb* **1** INHABIT, people, live in, occupy, reside in, dwell in (*formal*) **2** SETTLE, people, occupy, pioneer, colonize

population *noun* INHABITANTS, people, community, society, residents, natives, folk, occupants, populace, denizens, citizenry

populous *adjective* POPULATED, crowded, packed, swarming, thronged, teeming, heavily populated, overpopulated

pore¹ *noun* OPENING, hole, outlet, orifice, stoma

pore² *verb* **1** *followed by* **over** STUDY, read, examine, go over, scrutinize, peruse **2** *followed by* **over, on** *or* **upon** CONTEMPLATE, ponder, brood, dwell on, work over▷ see **pour**

pornographic *adjective* OBSCENE, erotic, indecent, blue, dirty, offensive, rude, sexy, filthy, lewd, risqué, X-rated (*informal*), salacious, prurient, smutty

pornography *noun* OBSCENITY, porn (*informal*), erotica, dirt, filth, indecency, porno (*informal*), smut

porous *adjective* PERMEABLE, absorbent, spongy, absorptive, penetrable, pervious << ANTONYM impermeable

port *noun* HARBOUR, haven, anchorage, seaport, roadstead

portable *adjective* LIGHT, compact, convenient, handy, lightweight, manageable, movable, easily carried, portative

portal *noun* (*literary*) DOORWAY, door, entry, way in, entrance, gateway, entrance way

portent *noun* OMEN, sign, warning, threat, indication, premonition, foreshadowing, foreboding, harbinger, presage, forewarning, prognostication, augury, presentiment, prognostic

portentous *adjective* **1** POMPOUS, solemn, ponderous, self-important, pontifical **2** SIGNIFICANT, alarming, sinister, ominous, important, threatening, crucial, forbidding, menacing, momentous, fateful, minatory, bodeful

porter¹ *noun* BAGGAGE ATTENDANT, carrier, bearer, baggage-carrier

porter² *noun* (*Chiefly Brit*) DOORMAN, caretaker, janitor, concierge, gatekeeper

portion *noun* **1** PART, bit, piece, section, scrap, segment, fragment, fraction, chunk, wedge, hunk, morsel **2** HELPING, serving, piece, plateful **3** SHARE, division, allowance, lot, measure, quantity, quota, ration, allocation, allotment

portly *adjective* STOUT, fat, overweight, plump, large, heavy, ample, bulky, burly, obese, fleshy, beefy (*informal*), tubby (*informal*), rotund, corpulent

portrait *noun* **1** PICTURE, painting, image, photograph, representation, sketch, likeness, portraiture **2** DESCRIPTION, account, profile, biography, portrayal, depiction, vignette, characterization, thumbnail sketch

portray *verb* **1** PLAY, take the role of, act the part of, represent, personate (*rare*) **2** DESCRIBE, present, depict, evoke, delineate,

put in words **3** REPRESENT, draw, paint, illustrate, sketch, figure, picture, render, depict, delineate **4** CHARACTERIZE, describe, represent, depict, paint a mental picture of

portrayal *noun* **1** PERFORMANCE, interpretation, enacting, take (*informal, chiefly US*), acting, impersonation, performance as, characterization, personation (*rare*) **2** DEPICTION, picture, representation, sketch, rendering, delineation **3** DESCRIPTION, account, representation **4** CHARACTERIZATION, representation, depiction

pose *verb* **1** PRESENT, cause, produce, create, lead to, result in, constitute, give rise to **2** ASK, state, advance, put, set, submit, put forward, posit, propound **3** POSITION YOURSELF, sit, model, strike a pose, arrange yourself **4** PUT ON AIRS, affect, posture, show off (*informal*), strike an attitude, attitudinize ▷ *noun* **1** POSTURE, position, bearing, attitude, stance, mien (*literary*) **2** ACT, role, façade, air, front, posturing, pretence, masquerade, mannerism, affectation, attitudinizing ▷▷ **pose as something** *or* **someone** IMPERSONATE, pretend to be, sham, feign, profess to be, masquerade as, pass yourself off as

poser¹ *noun* PUZZLE, problem, question, riddle, enigma, conundrum, teaser, tough one, vexed question, brain-teaser (*informal*), knotty point

poser² *noun* SHOW-OFF (*informal*), poseur, posturer, masquerader, hot dog (*chiefly US*), impostor, exhibitionist, self-publicist, mannerist, attitudinizer

posh *adjective* (*informal, chiefly Brit*) **1** SMART, grand, exclusive, luxury, elegant, fashionable, stylish, luxurious, classy (*slang*), swish (*informal, chiefly Brit*), up-market, swanky (*informal*), ritzy (*slang*), schmick (*Austral informal*) **2** UPPER-CLASS, high-class, top-drawer, plummy, high-toned, la-di-da (*informal*)

posit *verb* PUT FORWARD, advance, submit, state, assume, assert, presume, predicate, postulate, propound

position *noun* **1** LOCATION, place, point, area, post, situation, station, site, spot, bearings, reference, orientation, whereabouts, locality, locale **2** POSTURE, attitude, arrangement, pose, stance, disposition **3** STATUS, place, standing, class, footing, station, rank, reputation, importance, consequence, prestige, caste, stature, eminence, repute

4 JOB, place, post, opening, office, role, situation, duty, function, employment, capacity, occupation, berth (*informal*), billet (*informal*) **5** PLACE, standing, rank, status **6** SITUATION, state, condition, set of circumstances, plight, strait(s), predicament **7** ATTITUDE, view, perspective, point of view, standing, opinion, belief, angle, stance, outlook, posture, viewpoint, slant, way of thinking, standpoint ▷ *verb* PLACE, put, set, stand, stick (*informal*), settle, fix, arrange, locate, sequence, array, dispose, lay out

positive *adjective* **1** BENEFICIAL, effective, useful, practical, helpful, progressive, productive, worthwhile, constructive, pragmatic, efficacious << ANTONYM harmful **2** CERTAIN, sure, convinced, confident, satisfied, assured, free from doubt << ANTONYM uncertain **3** DEFINITE, real, clear, firm, certain, direct, express, actual, absolute, concrete, decisive, explicit, affirmative, clear-cut, unmistakable, conclusive, unequivocal, indisputable, categorical, incontrovertible, nailed-on (*slang*) << ANTONYM inconclusive **4** (*informal*) ABSOLUTE, complete, perfect, right (*Brit informal*), real, total, rank, sheer, utter, thorough, downright, consummate, veritable, unqualified, out-and-out, unmitigated, thoroughgoing, unalloyed

positively *adverb* **1** DEFINITELY, surely, firmly, certainly, absolutely, emphatically, unquestionably, undeniably, categorically, unequivocally, unmistakably, with certainty, assuredly, without qualification **2** REALLY, completely, simply, plain (*informal*), absolutely, thoroughly, utterly, downright

possess *verb* **1** OWN, have, hold, be in possession of, be the owner of, have in your possession, have to your name **2** BE ENDOWED WITH, have, enjoy, benefit from, be born with, be blessed with, be possessed of, be gifted with **3** CONTROL, influence, dominate, consume, obsess, bedevil, mesmerize, eat someone up, fixate, put under a spell **4** SEIZE, hold, control, dominate, occupy, haunt, take someone over, bewitch, take possession of, have power over, have mastery over

possessed *adjective* CRAZED, haunted, cursed, obsessed, raving, frenzied, consumed, enchanted, maddened, demented, frenetic, berserk, bewitched, bedevilled, under a spell, hag-ridden

possession *noun* **1** OWNERSHIP, control, custody, hold, hands, tenure, occupancy, proprietorship **2** PROVINCE, territory, colony, dominion, protectorate ▷ *plural noun* PROPERTY, things, effects, estate, assets, wealth, belongings, chattels, goods and chattels

possessive *adjective* **1** JEALOUS, controlling, dominating, domineering, proprietorial, overprotective **2** SELFISH, grasping, acquisitive

possibility *noun* **1** FEASIBILITY, likelihood, plausibility, potentiality, practicability, workableness **2** LIKELIHOOD, chance, risk, odds, prospect, liability, hazard, probability **3** *often plural* POTENTIAL, promise, prospects, talent, capabilities, potentiality

possible *adjective* **1** FEASIBLE, viable, workable, achievable, within reach, on (*informal*), practicable, attainable, doable, realizable << ANTONYM unfeasible **2** LIKELY, potential, anticipated, probable, odds-on, on the cards << ANTONYM improbable **3** CONCEIVABLE, likely, credible, plausible, hypothetical, imaginable, believable, thinkable << ANTONYM inconceivable **4** ASPIRING, would-be, promising, hopeful, prospective, wannabe (*informal*)

possibly *adverb* **1** PERHAPS, maybe, God willing, perchance (*archaic*), mayhap (*archaic*), peradventure (*archaic*), haply (*archaic*) **2** AT ALL, in any way, conceivably, by any means, under any circumstances, by any chance

post[1] *noun* SUPPORT, stake, pole, stock, standard, column, pale, shaft, upright, pillar, picket, palisade, newel ▷ *verb* PUT UP, announce, publish, display, advertise, proclaim, publicize, promulgate, affix, stick something up, make something known, pin something up

post[2] *noun* **1** JOB, place, office, position, situation, employment, appointment, assignment, berth (*informal*), billet (*informal*) **2** POSITION, place, base, beat, station ▷ *verb* STATION, assign, put, place, position, establish, locate, situate, put on duty

post[3] *noun* **1** MAIL, collection, delivery, postal service, snail mail (*informal*) **2** CORRESPONDENCE, letters, cards, mail ▷ *verb* SEND (OFF), forward, mail, get off, transmit, dispatch, consign ▷▷ **keep someone posted** NOTIFY, brief, advise, inform, report to, keep someone informed, keep someone up to date, apprise, fill someone in on (*informal*)

poster *noun* NOTICE, bill, announcement,

advertisement, sticker, placard, public notice, affiche (*French*)

posterior *noun* BOTTOM, behind (*informal*), bum (*Brit slang*), seat, rear, tail (*informal*), butt (*US & Canad informal*), buns (*US slang*), buttocks, backside, rump, rear end, derrière (*euphemistic*), tush (*US slang*), fundament, jacksy (*Brit slang*) ▷ *adjective* REAR, back, hinder, hind

posterity *noun* THE FUTURE, future generations, succeeding generations

postpone *verb* PUT OFF, delay, suspend, adjourn, table, shelve, defer, put back, hold over, put on ice (*informal*), put on the back burner (*informal*), take a rain check on (*US & Canad informal*) << ANTONYM go ahead with

postponement *noun* DELAY, stay, suspension, moratorium, respite, adjournment, deferment, deferral

postscript *noun* P.S., addition, supplement, appendix, afterthought, afterword

postulate *verb* (*formal*) PRESUPPOSE, suppose, advance, propose, assume, put forward, take for granted, predicate, theorize, posit, hypothesize

posture *noun* 1 BEARING, set, position, attitude, pose, stance, carriage, disposition, mien (*literary*) 2 ATTITUDE, feeling, mood, point of view, stance, outlook, inclination, disposition, standpoint, frame of mind ▷ *verb* SHOW OFF (*informal*), pose, affect, hot-dog (*chiefly US*), make a show, put on airs, try to attract attention, attitudinize, do something for effect

posy *noun* BOUQUET, spray, buttonhole, corsage, nosegay, boutonniere

pot *noun* 1 CONTAINER, bowl, pan, vessel, basin, vase, jug, cauldron, urn, utensil, crock, skillet 2 JACKPOT, bank, prize, stakes, purse 3 KITTY, funds, pool 4 PAUNCH, beer belly or gut (*informal*), spread (*informal*), corporation (*informal*), gut, bulge, spare tyre (*Brit slang*), potbelly

pot-bellied *adjective* FAT, overweight, bloated, obese, distended, corpulent, paunchy

pot belly *noun* PAUNCH, beer belly or gut (*informal*), spread (*informal*), corporation (*informal*), pot, gut, spare tyre (*Brit slang*), middle-age spread (*informal*), puku (*NZ*)

potency *noun* 1 INFLUENCE, might, force, control, authority, energy, potential, strength, capacity, mana (*NZ*) 2 PERSUASIVENESS, force, strength, muscle, effectiveness, sway, forcefulness, cogency, impressiveness 3 POWER, force, strength, effectiveness, efficacy 4 VIGOUR, puissance

potent *adjective* 1 POWERFUL, commanding, dynamic, dominant, influential, authoritative 2 PERSUASIVE, telling, convincing, effective, impressive, compelling, forceful, cogent << ANTONYM unconvincing 3 STRONG, powerful, mighty, vigorous, forceful, efficacious, puissant << ANTONYM weak

potentate *noun* RULER, king, prince, emperor, monarch, sovereign, mogul, overlord

potential *adjective* 1 POSSIBLE, future, likely, promising, budding, embryonic, undeveloped, unrealized, probable 2 HIDDEN, possible, inherent, dormant, latent ▷ *noun* ABILITY, possibilities, capacity, capability, the makings, what it takes (*informal*), aptitude, wherewithal, potentiality

potion *noun* CONCOCTION, mixture, brew, tonic, cup, dose, draught, elixir, philtre

potter *verb usually with* **around** *or* **about** MESS ABOUT, fiddle (*informal*), tinker, dabble, fritter, footle (*informal*), poke along, fribble

pottery *noun* CERAMICS, terracotta, crockery, earthenware, stoneware

potty *adjective* (*Brit informal*) CRAZY, eccentric, crackers (*Brit slang*), barmy (*slang*), touched, soft (*informal*), silly, foolish, daft (*informal*), off-the-wall (*slang*), oddball (*informal*), off the rails, dotty (*slang, chiefly Brit*), loopy (*informal*), crackpot (*informal*), out to lunch (*informal*), dippy (*slang*), gonzo (*slang*), doolally (*slang*), off your trolley (*slang*), up the pole (*informal*), off your chump (*slang*), wacko or whacko (*informal*), off the air (*Austral slang*), porangi (*NZ*), daggy (*Austral & NZ informal*)

pouch *noun* BAG, pocket, sack, container, purse, poke (*dialect*)

pounce *verb often followed by* **on** *or* **upon** ATTACK, strike, jump, leap, swoop

pound[1] *noun* ENCLOSURE, yard, pen, compound, kennels, corral (*chiefly US & Canad*)

pound[2] *verb* 1 *sometimes with* **on** BEAT, strike, hammer, batter, thrash, thump, pelt, clobber (*slang*), pummel, belabour, beat or knock seven bells out of (*informal*), beat the living daylights out of 2 CRUSH, powder, bruise, bray (*dialect*), pulverize 3 PULSATE, beat, pulse, throb, palpitate, pitapat 4 *often with* **out** THUMP, beat, hammer, bang 5 STOMP, tramp, march, thunder (*informal*), clomp

pour *verb* 1 LET FLOW, spill, splash, dribble, drizzle, slop (*informal*), slosh (*informal*), decant 2 FLOW, stream, run, course, rush,

emit, cascade, gush, spout, spew **3** RAIN,
sheet, pelt (down), teem, bucket down
(*informal*), rain cats and dogs (*informal*),
come down in torrents, rain hard *or* heavily
4 STREAM, crowd, flood, swarm, gush,
throng, teem

pout *verb* SULK, glower, mope, look sullen,
purse your lips, look petulant, pull a long
face, lour *or* lower, make a moue, turn down
the corners of your mouth ▷ *noun* SULLEN
LOOK, glower, long face, moue (*French*)

poverty *noun* **1** PENNILESSNESS, want, need,
distress, necessity, hardship, insolvency,
privation, penury, destitution, hand-to-
mouth existence, beggary, indigence,
pauperism, necessitousness << ANTONYM
wealth **2** SCARCITY, lack, absence, want,
deficit, shortage, deficiency, inadequacy,
dearth, paucity, insufficiency, sparsity
<< ANTONYM abundance **3** BARRENNESS,
deficiency, infertility, sterility, aridity,
bareness, poorness, meagreness,
unfruitfulness << ANTONYM fertility

poverty-stricken *adjective* PENNILESS, broke
(*informal*), bankrupt, impoverished, short,
poor, distressed, beggared, needy, destitute,
down and out, skint (*Brit slang*), indigent,
down at heel, impecunious, dirt-poor
(*informal*), on the breadline, flat broke
(*informal*), penurious, on your uppers, stony-
broke (*Brit slang*), in queer street, without
two pennies to rub together (*informal*), on
your beam-ends

powder *noun* DUST, pounce (*rare*), talc, fine
grains, loose particles ▷ *verb* **1** DUST, cover,
scatter, sprinkle, strew, dredge **2** GRIND,
crush, pound, pestle, pulverize, granulate

powdery *adjective* FINE, dry, sandy, dusty,
loose, crumbling, grainy, chalky, crumbly,
granular, pulverized, friable

power *noun* **1** CONTROL, authority, influence,
command, sovereignty, sway, dominance,
domination, supremacy, mastery, dominion,
ascendancy, mana (*NZ*) **2** ABILITY,
capacity, faculty, property, potential,
capability, competence, competency
<< ANTONYM inability **3** AUTHORITY, right,
licence, privilege, warrant, prerogative,
authorization **4** STRENGTH, might, energy,
weight, muscle, vigour, potency, brawn
<< ANTONYM weakness **5** FORCEFULNESS,
force, strength, punch (*informal*), intensity,
potency, eloquence, persuasiveness, cogency,
powerfulness

powerful *adjective* **1** INFLUENTIAL, dominant,

controlling, commanding, supreme,
prevailing, sovereign, authoritative,
puissant, skookum (*Canad*) << ANTONYM
powerless **2** STRONG, strapping, mighty,
robust, vigorous, potent, energetic, sturdy,
stalwart << ANTONYM weak **3** PERSUASIVE,
convincing, effective, telling, moving,
striking, storming, dramatic, impressive,
compelling, authoritative, forceful, weighty,
forcible, cogent, effectual

powerfully *adverb* STRONGLY, hard, vigorously,
forcibly, forcefully, mightily, with might
and main

powerless *adjective* **1** DEFENCELESS,
vulnerable, dependent, subject, tied,
ineffective, unarmed, disenfranchised, over
a barrel (*informal*), disfranchised **2** WEAK,
disabled, helpless, incapable, paralysed, frail,
feeble, debilitated, impotent, ineffectual,
incapacitated, prostrate, infirm, etiolated
<< ANTONYM strong

practicable *adjective* FEASIBLE, possible, viable,
workable, achievable, attainable, doable,
within the realm of possibility, performable
<< ANTONYM unfeasible ▷ see **practical**

practical *adjective* **1** FUNCTIONAL, efficient,
realistic, pragmatic << ANTONYM
impractical **2** EMPIRICAL, real, applied,
actual, hands-on, in the field, experimental,
factual << ANTONYM theoretical **3** SENSIBLE,
ordinary, realistic, down-to-earth, mundane,
matter-of-fact, no-nonsense, businesslike,
hard-headed, workaday << ANTONYM
impractical **4** FEASIBLE, possible, sound,
viable, constructive, workable, practicable,
doable << ANTONYM impractical **5** USEFUL,
ordinary, appropriate, sensible, everyday,
functional, utilitarian, serviceable **6** SKILLED,
working, seasoned, trained, experienced,
qualified, veteran, efficient, accomplished,
proficient << ANTONYM inexperienced

practically *adverb* **1** ALMOST, nearly,
close to, essentially, virtually, basically,
fundamentally, all but, just about, in effect,
very nearly, to all intents and purposes,
well-nigh **2** SENSIBLY, reasonably, matter-of-
factly, realistically, rationally, pragmatically,
with common sense, unsentimentally

practice *noun* **1** CUSTOM, use, way, system,
rule, method, tradition, habit, routine,
mode, usage, wont, praxis, usual procedure,
tikanga (*NZ*) **2** TRAINING, study, exercise,
work-out, discipline, preparation, drill,
rehearsal, repetition **3** PROFESSION, work,
business, career, occupation, pursuit,

vocation **4** BUSINESS, company, office, firm, enterprise, partnership, outfit (*informal*) **5** USE, experience, action, effect, operation, application, enactment

practise *verb* **1** REHEARSE, study, prepare, perfect, repeat, go through, polish, go over, refine, run through **2** DO, train, exercise, work out, drill, warm up, keep your hand in **3** CARRY OUT, follow, apply, perform, observe, engage in, live up to, put into practice **4** WORK AT, pursue, carry on, undertake, specialize in, ply your trade

practised *adjective* SKILLED, trained, experienced, seasoned, able, expert, qualified, accomplished, versed, proficient << ANTONYM inexperienced

pragmatic *adjective* PRACTICAL, efficient, sensible, realistic, down-to-earth, matter-of-fact, utilitarian, businesslike, hard-headed << ANTONYM idealistic

praise *verb* **1** ACCLAIM, approve of, honour, cheer, admire, applaud, compliment, congratulate, pay tribute to, laud, extol, sing the praises of, pat someone on the back, cry someone up, big someone up (*slang, chiefly Caribbean*), eulogize, take your hat off to, crack someone up (*informal*) << ANTONYM criticize **2** GIVE THANKS TO, bless, worship, adore, magnify (*archaic*), glorify, exalt, pay homage to ▷ *noun* **1** APPROVAL, acclaim, applause, cheering, tribute, compliment, congratulations, ovation, accolade, good word, kudos, eulogy, commendation, approbation, acclamation, panegyric, encomium, plaudit, laudation << ANTONYM criticism **2** THANKS, glory, worship, devotion, homage, adoration

prance *verb* **1** DANCE, bound, leap, trip, spring, jump, skip, romp, caper, cavort, frisk, gambol, cut a rug (*informal*) **2** STRUT, parade, stalk, show off (*informal*), swagger, swank (*informal*)

prank *noun* TRICK, lark (*informal*), caper, frolic, escapade, practical joke, skylarking (*informal*), antic, jape

prattle *verb* CHATTER, babble, waffle (*informal, chiefly Brit*), run on, rabbit on (*Brit informal*), witter on (*informal*), patter, drivel, clack, twitter, jabber, gabble, rattle on, blather, blether, run off at the mouth (*slang*), earbash (*Austral & NZ slang*) ▷ *noun* CHATTER, talk, babble, waffle (*informal*), rambling, wittering (*informal*), prating, drivel, jabber, gabble, blather, blether

pray *verb* **1** SAY YOUR PRAYERS, offer a prayer,

recite the rosary **2** BEG, ask, plead, petition, urge, request, sue, crave, invoke, call upon, cry, solicit, implore, beseech, entreat, importune, adjure, supplicate

prayer *noun* **1** SUPPLICATION, devotion, communion **2** ORISON, litany, invocation, intercession **3** PLEA, appeal, suit, request, petition, entreaty, supplication

preach *verb* **1** *often with* **to** DELIVER A SERMON, address, exhort, evangelize, preach a sermon, orate **2** URGE, teach, champion, recommend, advise, counsel, advocate, exhort

preacher *noun* CLERGYMAN, minister, parson, missionary, evangelist, revivalist

preamble *noun* INTRODUCTION, prelude, preface, foreword, overture, opening move, proem, prolegomenon, exordium, opening statement *or* remarks

precarious *adjective* **1** INSECURE, dangerous, uncertain, tricky, risky, doubtful, dubious, unsettled, dodgy (*Brit, Austral & NZ informal*), unstable, unsure, hazardous, shaky, hairy (*slang*), perilous, touch and go, dicey (*informal, chiefly Brit*), chancy (*informal*), built on sand, shonky (*Austral & NZ informal*) << ANTONYM secure **2** DANGEROUS, unstable, shaky, slippery, insecure, unsafe, unreliable, unsteady << ANTONYM stable

precaution *noun* SAFEGUARD, insurance, protection, provision, safety measure, preventative measure, belt and braces (*informal*)

precede *verb* **1** GO BEFORE, introduce, herald, pave the way for, usher in, antedate, antecede, forerun **2** GO AHEAD OF, lead, head, go before, take precedence **3** PREFACE, introduce, go before, launch, prefix

precedence *noun* PRIORITY, lead, rank, preference, superiority, supremacy, seniority, primacy, pre-eminence, antecedence

precedent *noun* INSTANCE, example, authority, standard, model, pattern, criterion, prototype, paradigm, antecedent, exemplar, previous example

preceding *adjective* **1** PREVIOUS, earlier, former, above, foregoing, aforementioned, anterior, aforesaid **2** PAST, earlier, former, prior, foregoing

precept *noun* **1** RULE, order, law, direction, principle, command, regulation, instruction, decree, mandate, canon, statute, ordinance, commandment, behest, dictum **2** MAXIM, saying, rule, principle, guideline, motto, dictum, axiom, byword

precinct *noun* AREA, quarter, section, sector, district, zone ▷ *plural noun* DISTRICT, limits, region, borders, bounds, boundaries, confines, neighbourhood, milieu, surrounding area, environs, purlieus

precious *adjective* **1** VALUABLE, expensive, rare, fine, choice, prized, dear, costly, high-priced, exquisite, invaluable, priceless, recherché, inestimable << ANTONYM worthless **2** LOVED, valued, favourite, prized, dear, dearest, treasured, darling, beloved, adored, cherished, fave (*informal*), idolized, worth your *or* its weight in gold **3** AFFECTED, artificial, fastidious, twee (*Brit informal*), chichi, overrefined, overnice

precipice *noun* CLIFF, crag, rock face, cliff face, height, brink, bluff, sheer drop, steep cliff, scarp

precipitate *verb* **1** QUICKEN, trigger, accelerate, further, press, advance, hurry, dispatch, speed up, bring on, hasten, push forward, expedite **2** THROW, launch, cast, discharge, hurl, fling, let fly, send forth ▷ *adjective* **1** HASTY, hurried, frantic, rash, reckless, impulsive, madcap, ill-advised, precipitous, impetuous, indiscreet, heedless, harum-scarum **2** SUDDEN, quick, brief, rushing, violent, plunging, rapid, unexpected, swift, abrupt, without warning, headlong, breakneck

precipitous *adjective* **1** SHEER, high, steep, dizzy, abrupt, perpendicular, falling sharply **2** HASTY, sudden, hurried, precipitate, abrupt, harum-scarum

precise *adjective* **1** EXACT, specific, actual, particular, express, fixed, correct, absolute, accurate, explicit, definite, clear-cut, literal, unequivocal << ANTONYM vague **2** STRICT, particular, exact, nice, formal, careful, stiff, rigid, meticulous, inflexible, scrupulous, fastidious, prim, puritanical, finicky, punctilious, ceremonious << ANTONYM inexact

precisely *adverb* **1** EXACTLY, bang on, squarely, correctly, absolutely, strictly, accurately, plumb (*informal*), slap on (*informal*), square on, on the dot, smack on (*informal*) **2** JUST SO, yes, absolutely, exactly, quite so, you bet (*informal*), without a doubt, on the button (*informal*), indubitably **3** JUST, entirely, absolutely, altogether, exactly, in all respects **4** WORD FOR WORD, literally, exactly, to the letter, neither more nor less

precision *noun* EXACTNESS, care, accuracy, fidelity, correctness, rigour, nicety, particularity, exactitude, meticulousness, definiteness, dotting the i's and crossing the t's, preciseness

preclude *verb* **1** RULE OUT, put a stop to, obviate, make impossible, make impracticable **2** PREVENT, stop, check, exclude, restrain, prohibit, inhibit, hinder, forestall, debar

precocious *adjective* ADVANCED, developed, forward, quick, bright, smart << ANTONYM backward

preconceived *adjective* PRESUMED, premature, predetermined, presupposed, prejudged, forejudged

preconception *noun* PRECONCEIVED IDEA *or* NOTION, notion, prejudice, bias, presumption, predisposition, presupposition, prepossession

precondition *noun* NECESSITY, essential, requirement, prerequisite, must, sine qua non (*Latin*), must-have

precursor *noun* **1** FORERUNNER, pioneer, predecessor, forebear, antecedent, originator **2** HERALD, usher, messenger, vanguard, forerunner, harbinger

predatory *adjective* **1** HUNTING, ravening, carnivorous, rapacious, raptorial, predacious **2** PLUNDERING, ravaging, pillaging, marauding, thieving, despoiling **3** RAPACIOUS, greedy, voracious, vulturous, vulturine

predecessor *noun* **1** PREVIOUS JOB HOLDER, precursor, forerunner, antecedent, former job holder, prior job holder **2** ANCESTOR, forebear, antecedent, forefather, tupuna *or* tipuna (*NZ*)

predetermined *adjective* **1** FATED, predestined, preordained, meant, doomed, foreordained, pre-elected, predestinated **2** PREARRANGED, set, agreed, set up, settled, fixed, cut and dried (*informal*), preplanned, decided beforehand, arranged in advance

predicament *noun* FIX (*informal*), state, situation, spot (*informal*), corner, hole (*slang*), emergency, mess, jam (*informal*), dilemma, pinch, plight, scrape (*informal*), hot water (*informal*), pickle (*informal*), how-do-you-do (*informal*), quandary, tight spot

predict *verb* FORETELL, forecast, divine, foresee, prophesy, call, augur, presage, portend, prognosticate, forebode, soothsay, vaticinate (*rare*)

predictable *adjective* LIKELY, expected, sure, certain, anticipated, reliable, foreseen, on the cards, foreseeable, sure-fire (*informal*), calculable << ANTONYM unpredictable

prediction *noun* PROPHECY, forecast, prognosis, divination, prognostication, augury, soothsaying, sortilege

predilection *noun* LIKING, love, taste, weakness, fancy, leaning, tendency, preference, bias, inclination, penchant, fondness, propensity, predisposition, proclivity, partiality, proneness

predispose *verb* INCLINE, influence, prepare, prompt, lead, prime, affect, prejudice, bias, induce, dispose, sway, make you of a mind to

predisposed *adjective* 1 INCLINED, willing, given, minded, ready, agreeable, amenable 2 SUSCEPTIBLE, subject, prone, liable

predisposition *noun* 1 INCLINATION, tendency, disposition, bent, bias, willingness, likelihood, penchant, propensity, predilection, proclivity, potentiality, proneness 2 SUSCEPTIBILITY, tendency, proneness

predominance *noun* 1 PREVALENCE, weight, preponderance, greater number 2 DOMINANCE, hold, control, edge, leadership, sway, supremacy, mastery, dominion, upper hand, ascendancy, paramountcy

predominant *adjective* 1 MAIN, chief, prevailing, notable, paramount, prevalent, preponderant 2 PRINCIPAL, leading, important, prime, controlling, ruling, chief, capital, primary, supreme, prominent, superior, dominant, sovereign, top-priority, ascendant << ANTONYM minor

predominantly *adverb* MAINLY, largely, chiefly, mostly, generally, principally, primarily, on the whole, in the main, for the most part, to a great extent, preponderantly

predominate *verb* 1 BE IN THE MAJORITY, dominate, prevail, stand out, be predominant, be most noticeable, preponderate 2 PREVAIL, rule, reign, hold sway, get the upper hand, carry weight

pre-eminence *noun* SUPERIORITY, distinction, excellence, supremacy, prestige, prominence, transcendence, renown, predominance, paramountcy

pre-eminent *adjective* OUTSTANDING, supreme, paramount, chief, excellent, distinguished, superior, renowned, foremost, consummate, predominant, transcendent, unrivalled, incomparable, peerless, unsurpassed, unequalled, matchless

preen *verb* 1 *often reflexive* SMARTEN, admire, dress up, doll up (*slang*), trim, array, deck out, spruce up, prettify, primp, trig (*archaic* or *dialect*), titivate, prink 2 (*of birds*) CLEAN, smooth, groom, tidy, plume ▷▷ **preen yourself** PRIDE YOURSELF, congratulate yourself, give yourself a pat on the back, pique yourself, plume yourself

preface *noun* INTRODUCTION, preliminary, prelude, preamble, foreword, prologue, proem, prolegomenon, exordium ▷ *verb* INTRODUCE, precede, open, begin, launch, lead up to, prefix

prefer *verb* 1 LIKE BETTER, favour, go for, pick, select, adopt, fancy, opt for, single out, plump for, incline towards, be partial to 2 CHOOSE, elect, opt for, pick, wish, desire, would rather, would sooner, incline towards

preferable *adjective* BETTER, best, chosen, choice, preferred, recommended, favoured, superior, worthier, more suitable, more desirable, more eligible << ANTONYM undesirable ▷ see **prefer**

preferably *adverb* IDEALLY, if possible, rather, sooner, much rather, by choice, much sooner, as a matter of choice, in *or* for preference

preference *noun* 1 LIKING, wish, taste, desire, bag (*slang*), leaning, bent, bias, cup of tea (*informal*), inclination, penchant, fondness, predisposition, predilection, proclivity, partiality 2 FIRST CHOICE, choice, favourite, election, pick, option, selection, top of the list, fave (*informal*) 3 PRIORITY, first place, precedence, advantage, favouritism, pride of place, favoured treatment

preferential *adjective* PRIVILEGED, favoured, superior, better, special, partial, partisan, advantageous

prefigure *verb* FORESHADOW, suggest, indicate, intimate, presage, portend, shadow forth, adumbrate, foretoken

pregnancy *noun* GESTATION, gravidity

pregnant *adjective* 1 EXPECTANT, expecting (*informal*), with child, in the club (*Brit slang*), in the family way (*informal*), gravid, preggers (*Brit informal*), enceinte, in the pudding club (*slang*), big *or* heavy with child 2 MEANINGFUL, pointed, charged, significant, telling, loaded, expressive, eloquent, weighty, suggestive 3 *with* **with** FULL OF, rich in, fraught with, teeming with, replete with, abounding in, abundant in, fecund with

prehistoric *adjective* EARLIEST, early, primitive, primordial, primeval

prejudice *noun* **1** DISCRIMINATION, racism, injustice, sexism, intolerance, bigotry, unfairness, chauvinism, narrow-mindedness **2** BIAS, preconception, partiality, preconceived notion, warp, jaundiced eye, prejudgment **3** HARM, damage, hurt, disadvantage, loss, mischief, detriment, impairment ▷ *verb* **1** BIAS, influence, colour, poison, distort, sway, warp, slant, predispose, jaundice, prepossess **2** HARM, damage, hurt, injure, mar, undermine, spoil, impair, hinder, crool *or* cruel (*Austral slang*)

prejudiced *adjective* BIASED, influenced, unfair, one-sided, conditioned, partial, partisan, discriminatory, bigoted, intolerant, opinionated, narrow-minded, jaundiced, prepossessed << ANTONYM unbiased

prejudicial *adjective* HARMFUL, damaging, undermining, detrimental, hurtful, unfavourable, counterproductive, deleterious, injurious, inimical, disadvantageous

preliminary *adjective* **1** FIRST, opening, trial, initial, test, pilot, prior, introductory, preparatory, exploratory, initiatory, prefatory, precursory **2** QUALIFYING, eliminating ▷ *noun* INTRODUCTION, opening, beginning, foundation, start, preparation, first round, prelude, preface, overture, initiation, preamble, groundwork, prelims

prelude *noun* **1** INTRODUCTION, beginning, preparation, preliminary, start, commencement, curtain-raiser **2** OVERTURE, opening, introduction, introductory movement

premature *adjective* **1** EARLY, untimely, before time, unseasonable **2** HASTY, rash, too soon, precipitate, impulsive, untimely, ill-considered, jumping the gun, ill-timed, inopportune, overhasty **3** PRETERM, prem (*informal*), preemie (*US & Canad informal*)

prematurely *adverb* **1** TOO EARLY, too soon, before your time, preterm **2** OVERHASTILY, rashly, too soon, precipitately, too hastily, half-cocked, at half-cock

premeditated *adjective* PLANNED, calculated, deliberate, considered, studied, intended, conscious, contrived, intentional, wilful, aforethought, prepense << ANTONYM unplanned

premier *noun* HEAD OF GOVERNMENT, prime minister, chancellor, chief minister, P.M. ▷ *adjective* CHIEF, leading, top, first, highest, head, main, prime, primary, principal, arch, foremost

premiere *noun* FIRST NIGHT, opening, debut, first showing, first performance

premise *noun* ASSUMPTION, proposition, thesis, ground, argument, hypothesis, assertion, postulate, supposition, presupposition, postulation

premises *plural noun* BUILDING(s), place, office, property, site, establishment

premium *noun* **1** FEE, charge, payment, instalment **2** SURCHARGE, extra charge, additional fee *or* charge **3** BONUS, reward, prize, percentage (*informal*), perk (*Brit informal*), boon, bounty, remuneration, recompense, perquisite ▷▷ **at a premium** IN GREAT DEMAND, valuable, expensive, rare, costly, scarce, in short supply, hard to come by, like gold dust, beyond your means, not to be had for love or money

premonition *noun* FEELING, idea, intuition, suspicion, hunch, apprehension, misgiving, foreboding, funny feeling (*informal*), presentiment, feeling in your bones

preoccupation *noun* **1** OBSESSION, concern, hang-up (*informal*), fixation, pet subject, hobbyhorse, idée fixe (*French*), bee in your bonnet **2** ABSORPTION, musing, oblivion, abstraction, daydreaming, immersion, reverie, absent-mindedness, brown study, inattentiveness, absence of mind, pensiveness, engrossment, prepossession, woolgathering

preoccupied *adjective* **1** ABSORBED, taken up, caught up, lost, intent, wrapped up, immersed, engrossed, rapt **2** LOST IN THOUGHT, abstracted, distracted, unaware, oblivious, faraway, absent-minded, heedless, distrait, in a brown study

preparation *noun* **1** GROUNDWORK, development, preparing, arranging, devising, getting ready, thinking-up, putting in order **2** READINESS, expectation, provision, safeguard, precaution, anticipation, foresight, preparedness, alertness **3** *usually plural* ARRANGEMENT, plan, measure, provision **4** MIXTURE, cream, medicine, compound, composition, lotion, concoction, amalgam, ointment, tincture

preparatory *adjective* INTRODUCTORY, preliminary, opening, basic, primary, elementary, prefatory, preparative ▷▷ **preparatory to** BEFORE, prior to, in preparation for, in advance of, in anticipation of

prepare verb 1 MAKE or GET READY, arrange, draw up, form, fashion, get up (informal), construct, assemble, contrive, put together, make provision, put in order, jack up (NZ informal) 2 EQUIP, fit, adapt, adjust, outfit, furnish, fit out, accoutre 3 TRAIN, guide, prime, direct, coach, brief, discipline, groom, put someone in the picture 4 MAKE, cook, put together, get, produce, assemble, muster, concoct, fix up, dish up, rustle up (informal) 5 GET READY, plan, anticipate, make provision, lay the groundwork, make preparations, arrange things, get everything set 6 PRACTISE, get ready, train, exercise, warm up, get into shape

prepared adjective 1 WILLING, minded, able, ready, inclined, disposed, in the mood, predisposed, of a mind 2 READY, set, all set 3 FIT, primed, in order, arranged, in readiness, all systems go (informal)

preparedness noun READINESS, order, preparation, fitness, alertness

preponderance noun 1 PREDOMINANCE, instance, dominance, prevalence 2 GREATER PART, mass, bulk, weight, lion's share, greater numbers, extensiveness 3 DOMINATION, power, sway, superiority, supremacy, dominion, ascendancy

preposterous adjective RIDICULOUS, bizarre, incredible, outrageous, shocking, impossible, extreme, crazy, excessive, absurd, foolish, ludicrous, extravagant, unthinkable, unreasonable, insane, irrational, monstrous, senseless, out of the question, laughable, exorbitant, nonsensical, risible, asinine, cockamamie (slang, chiefly US)

prerequisite noun REQUIREMENT, must, essential, necessity, condition, qualification, imperative, precondition, requisite, sine qua non (Latin), must-have ▷ adjective REQUIRED, necessary, essential, called for, vital, mandatory, imperative, indispensable, obligatory, requisite, of the essence, needful

prerogative noun RIGHT, choice, claim, authority, title, due, advantage, sanction, liberty, privilege, immunity, exemption, birthright, droit, perquisite

presage verb PORTEND, point to, warn of, signify, omen, bode, foreshadow, augur, betoken, adumbrate, forebode, foretoken ▷ noun OMEN, sign, warning, forecast, prediction, prophecy, portent, harbinger, intimation, forewarning, prognostication, augury, prognostic, auspice

prescient adjective FORESIGHTED, psychic, prophetic, divining, discerning, perceptive, clairvoyant, far-sighted, divinatory, mantic

prescribe verb 1 SPECIFY, order, direct, stipulate, write a prescription for 2 ORDAIN, set, order, establish, rule, require, fix, recommend, impose, appoint, command, define, dictate, assign, lay down, decree, stipulate, enjoin

prescription noun 1 INSTRUCTION, direction, formula, script (informal), recipe 2 MEDICINE, drug, treatment, preparation, cure, mixture, dose, remedy

prescriptive adjective DICTATORIAL, rigid, authoritarian, legislating, dogmatic, didactic, preceptive

presence noun 1 BEING, existence, company, residence, attendance, showing up, companionship, occupancy, habitation, inhabitance 2 PROXIMITY, closeness, vicinity, nearness, neighbourhood, immediate circle, propinquity 3 PERSONALITY, bearing, appearance, aspect, air, ease, carriage, aura, poise, demeanour, self-assurance, mien (literary), comportment 4 SPIRIT, ghost, manifestation, spectre, apparition, shade (literary), wraith, supernatural being, revenant, eidolon, atua (NZ), wairua (NZ)
▷▷ **presence of mind** LEVEL-HEADEDNESS, assurance, composure, poise, cool (slang), wits, countenance, coolness, aplomb, alertness, calmness, equanimity, self-assurance, phlegm, quickness, sang-froid, self-possession, unflappability (informal), imperturbability, quick-wittedness, self-command, collectedness

present¹ adjective 1 CURRENT, existing, immediate, contemporary, instant, present-day, existent, extant 2 HERE, there, near, available, ready, nearby, accounted for, to hand, at hand, in attendance << ANTONYM absent 3 IN EXISTENCE, existing, existent, extant ▷▷ **at present** JUST NOW, now, presently, currently, at the moment, right now, nowadays, at this time, at the present time, in this day and age ▷▷ **for the present** FOR NOW, for a while, in the meantime, temporarily, for the moment, for the time being, provisionally, not for long, for the nonce ▷▷ **the present** NOW, today, the time being, here and now, this day and age, the present moment

present² noun GIFT, offering, grant, favour, donation, hand-out, endowment, boon, bounty, gratuity, prezzie (informal), benefaction, bonsela (S African), koha (NZ),

largesse or largess ▷ verb 1 GIVE, award,
hand over, offer, grant, donate, hand out,
furnish, confer, bestow, entrust, proffer, put
at someone's disposal 2 PUT FORWARD, offer,
suggest, raise, state, produce, introduce,
advance, relate, declare, extend, pose,
submit, tender, hold out, recount, expound,
proffer, adduce 3 PUT ON, stage, perform,
give, show, mount, render, put before the
public 4 LAUNCH, display, demonstrate,
parade, exhibit, unveil 5 INTRODUCE, make
known, acquaint someone with

presentable adjective 1 TIDY, elegant,
well groomed, becoming, trim, spruce,
dapper, natty (informal), smartly dressed,
fit to be seen << ANTONYM unpresentable
2 SATISFACTORY, suitable, decent, acceptable,
proper, good enough, respectable, not bad
(informal), tolerable, passable, O.K. or okay
(informal) << ANTONYM unsatisfactory

presentation noun 1 GIVING, award,
offering, donation, investiture, bestowal,
conferral 2 APPEARANCE, look, display,
packaging, arrangement, layout delivery
3 PERFORMANCE, staging, production, show,
arrangement, representation, portrayal,
rendition

present-day adjective CURRENT, modern,
present, recent, contemporary, up-to-date,
latter-day, newfangled

presently adverb 1 AT PRESENT, currently, now,
today, these days, nowadays, at the present
time, in this day and age, at the minute
(Brit informal) 2 SOON, shortly, directly,
before long, momentarily (US & Canad), in a
moment, in a minute, pretty soon (informal),
anon (archaic), by and by, in a short while, in
a jiffy (informal), erelong (archaic or poetic)

preservation noun 1 UPHOLDING, keeping,
support, security, defence, maintenance,
perpetuation 2 PROTECTION, safety,
maintenance, conservation, salvation,
safeguarding, safekeeping 3 STORAGE,
smoking, drying, bottling, freezing, curing,
chilling, candying, pickling, conserving,
tinning

preserve verb 1 MAINTAIN, keep, continue,
retain, sustain, keep up, prolong,
uphold, conserve, perpetuate, keep alive
<< ANTONYM end 2 PROTECT, keep, save,
maintain, guard, defend, secure, shelter,
shield, care for, safeguard, conserve
<< ANTONYM attack 3 KEEP, save, store,
can, dry, bottle, salt, cure, candy, pickle,
conserve ▷ noun 1 often plural JAM, jelly,

conserve, marmalade, confection,
sweetmeat, confiture 2 AREA, department,
field, territory, province, arena, orbit, sphere,
realm, domain, specialism 3 RESERVE,
reservation, sanctuary, game reserve

preside verb OFFICIATE, chair, moderate, be
chairperson ▷▷ **preside over something** or
someone RUN, lead, head, control, manage,
direct, conduct, govern, administer,
supervise, be at the head of, be in authority

press verb 1 PUSH (DOWN), depress, lean
on, bear down, press down, force down
2 PUSH, squeeze, jam, thrust, ram, wedge,
shove 3 HUG, squeeze, embrace, clasp,
crush, encircle, enfold, hold close, fold
in your arms 4 URGE, force, beg, petition,
sue, enforce, insist on, compel, constrain,
exhort, implore, enjoin, pressurize, entreat,
importune, supplicate 5 PLEAD, present,
lodge, submit, tender, advance insistently
6 IRON, finish, steam, smooth, flatten, put
the creases in 7 COMPRESS, grind, reduce,
mill, crush, pound, squeeze, tread, pulp,
mash, trample, condense, pulverize, tamp,
macerate 8 CROWD, push, gather, rush,
surge, mill, hurry, cluster, flock, herd,
swarm, hasten, seethe, throng ▷▷ **the press**
1 NEWSPAPERS, the papers, journalism,
news media, Fleet Street, fourth estate
2 JOURNALISTS, correspondents, reporters,
photographers, columnists, pressmen,
newsmen, journos (slang), gentlemen of the
press

pressing adjective URGENT, serious, burning,
vital, crucial, imperative, important,
constraining, high-priority, now or never,
importunate, exigent << ANTONYM
unimportant

pressure noun 1 FORCE, crushing, squeezing,
compressing, weight, compression,
heaviness 2 POWER, influence, force,
obligation, constraint, sway, compulsion,
coercion 3 STRESS, demands, difficulty,
strain, press, heat, load, burden, distress,
hurry, urgency, hassle (informal), uphill (S
African), adversity, affliction, exigency

pressurize verb FORCE, drive, compel,
intimidate, coerce, dragoon, breathe down
someone's neck, browbeat, press-gang, twist
someone's arm (informal), turn on the heat
(informal), put the screws on (slang)

prestige noun STATUS, standing, authority,
influence, credit, regard, weight, reputation,
honour, importance, fame, celebrity,
distinction, esteem, stature, eminence,

kudos, cachet, renown, Brownie points, mana (NZ)

prestigious *adjective* CELEBRATED, respected, prominent, great, important, imposing, impressive, influential, esteemed, notable, renowned, eminent, illustrious, reputable, exalted << ANTONYM unknown

presumably *adverb* IT WOULD SEEM, probably, likely, apparently, most likely, seemingly, doubtless, on the face of it, in all probability, in all likelihood, doubtlessly

presume *verb* 1 BELIEVE, think, suppose, assume, guess (*informal, chiefly US & Canad*), take it, take for granted, infer, conjecture, postulate, surmise, posit, presuppose 2 DARE, venture, undertake, go so far as, have the audacity, take the liberty, make bold, make so bold as ▷▷ **presume on something** *or* **someone** DEPEND ON, rely on, exploit, take advantage of, count on, bank on, take liberties with, trust in or to

presumption *noun* 1 ASSUMPTION, opinion, belief, guess, hypothesis, anticipation, conjecture, surmise, supposition, presupposition, premiss 2 CHEEK (*informal*), front, neck (*informal*), nerve (*informal*), assurance, brass (*informal*), gall (*informal*), audacity, boldness, temerity, chutzpah (*US & Canad informal*), insolence, impudence, effrontery, brass neck (*Brit informal*), sassiness (*US informal*), presumptuousness, forwardness

presumptuous *adjective* PUSHY (*informal*), forward, bold, arrogant, presuming, rash, audacious, conceited, foolhardy, insolent, overweening, overconfident, overfamiliar, bigheaded (*informal*), uppish (*Brit informal*), too big for your boots << ANTONYM shy

presuppose *verb* PRESUME, consider, accept, suppose, assume, take it, imply, take for granted, postulate, posit, take as read

presupposition *noun* ASSUMPTION, theory, belief, premise, hypothesis, presumption, preconception, supposition, preconceived idea

pretence *noun* 1 DECEPTION, invention, sham, fabrication, acting, faking, simulation, deceit, feigning, charade, make-believe, trickery, falsehood, subterfuge, fakery << ANTONYM candour 2 SHOW, posturing, artifice, affectation, display, appearance, posing, façade, veneer, pretentiousness, hokum (*slang, chiefly US & Canad*) << ANTONYM reality 3 PRETEXT, claim, excuse, show, cover, mask, veil, cloak, guise, façade, masquerade, semblance, ruse, garb, wile

pretend *verb* 1 FEIGN, affect, assume, allege, put on, fake, make out, simulate, profess, sham, counterfeit, falsify, impersonate, dissemble, dissimulate, pass yourself off as 2 MAKE BELIEVE, suppose, imagine, play, act, make up, play the part of 3 LAY CLAIM, claim, allege, aspire, profess, purport

pretended *adjective* FEIGNED, alleged, so-called, phoney *or* phony (*informal*), false, pretend (*informal*), fake, imaginary, bogus, professed, sham, purported, pseudo (*informal*), counterfeit, spurious, fictitious, avowed, ostensible

pretender *noun* CLAIMANT, claimer, aspirant

pretension *noun* 1 AFFECTATION, hypocrisy, conceit, show, airs, vanity, snobbery, pomposity, self-importance, ostentation, pretentiousness, snobbishness, vainglory, showiness 2 *usually plural* ASPIRATION, claim, demand, profession, assumption, assertion, pretence

pretentious *adjective* AFFECTED, mannered, exaggerated, pompous, assuming, hollow, inflated, extravagant, high-flown, flaunting, grandiose, conceited, showy, ostentatious, snobbish, puffed up, bombastic, specious, grandiloquent, vainglorious, high-sounding, highfalutin (*informal*), overambitious, arty-farty (*informal*), magniloquent << ANTONYM unpretentious

pretext *noun* GUISE, excuse, veil, show, cover, appearance, device, mask, ploy, cloak, simulation, pretence, semblance, ruse, red herring, alleged reason

pretty *adjective* 1 ATTRACTIVE, appealing, beautiful, sweet, lovely, charming, fair, fetching, good-looking, cute, graceful, bonny, personable, comely, prepossessing << ANTONYM plain 2 PLEASANT, fine, pleasing, nice, elegant, trim, delicate, neat, tasteful, dainty, bijou ▷ *adverb* (*informal*) FAIRLY, rather, quite, kind of (*informal*), somewhat, moderately, reasonably

prevail *verb* 1 WIN, succeed, triumph, overcome, overrule, be victorious, carry the day, prove superior, gain mastery 2 BE WIDESPREAD, abound, predominate, be current, be prevalent, preponderate, exist generally ▷▷ **prevail on** *or* **upon someone** PERSUADE, influence, convince, prompt, win over, induce, incline, dispose, sway, talk into, bring round

prevailing *adjective* 1 WIDESPREAD, general,

established, popular, common, set, current, usual, ordinary, fashionable, in style, customary, prevalent, in vogue **2** PREDOMINATING, ruling, main, existing, principal

prevalence *noun* COMMONNESS, frequency, regularity, currency, universality, ubiquity, common occurrence, pervasiveness, extensiveness, widespread presence, rampancy, rifeness

prevalent *adjective* COMMON, accepted, established, popular, general, current, usual, widespread, extensive, universal, frequent, everyday, rampant, customary, commonplace, ubiquitous, rife, habitual << ANTONYM rare

prevent *verb* STOP, avoid, frustrate, restrain, check, bar, block, anticipate, hamper, foil, inhibit, head off, avert, thwart, intercept, hinder, obstruct, preclude, impede, counteract, ward off, balk, stave off, forestall, defend against, obviate, nip in the bud << ANTONYM help

prevention *noun* ELIMINATION, safeguard, precaution, anticipation, thwarting, avoidance, deterrence, forestalling, prophylaxis, preclusion, obviation

preventive *or* **preventative** *adjective* **1** PRECAUTIONARY, protective, hampering, hindering, deterrent, impeding, pre-emptive, obstructive, inhibitory **2** PROPHYLACTIC, protective, precautionary, counteractive

preview *noun* SAMPLE, sneak preview, trailer, sampler, taster, foretaste, advance showing ▷ *verb* SAMPLE, taste, give a foretaste of

previous *adjective* **1** EARLIER, former, past, prior, one-time, preceding, sometime, erstwhile, antecedent, anterior, quondam, ex- << ANTONYM later **2** PRECEDING, past, prior, foregoing

previously *adverb* BEFORE, earlier, once, in the past, formerly, back then, until now, at one time, hitherto, beforehand, a while ago, heretofore, in days *or* years gone by

prey *noun* **1** QUARRY, game, kill **2** VICTIM, target, mark, mug (*Brit slang*), dupe, fall guy (*informal*) ▷▷ **prey on something** *or* **someone 1** HUNT, live off, eat, seize, devour, feed upon **2** VICTIMIZE, bully, intimidate, exploit, take advantage of, bleed (*informal*), blackmail, terrorize **3** WORRY, trouble, burden, distress, haunt, hang over, oppress, weigh down, weigh heavily

price *noun* **1** COST, value, rate, charge,

bill, figure, worth, damage (*informal*), amount, estimate, fee, payment, expense, assessment, expenditure, valuation, face value, outlay, asking price **2** CONSEQUENCES, penalty, cost, result, sacrifice, toll, forfeit **3** REWARD, bounty, compensation, premium, recompense ▷ *verb* EVALUATE, value, estimate, rate, cost, assess, put a price on ▷▷ **at any price** WHATEVER THE COST, regardless, no matter what the cost, anyhow, cost what it may, expense no object

priceless *adjective* VALUABLE, expensive, precious, invaluable, rich, prized, dear, rare, treasured, costly, cherished, incomparable, irreplaceable, incalculable, inestimable, beyond price, worth a king's ransom, worth your *or* its weight in gold << ANTONYM worthless

pricey *or* **pricy** *adjective* EXPENSIVE, dear, steep (*informal*), costly, high-priced, exorbitant, over the odds (*Brit informal*), extortionate

prick *verb* **1** PIERCE, stab, puncture, bore, pink, punch, lance, jab, perforate, impale **2** MOVE, trouble, touch, pain, wound, distress, grieve ▷ *noun* **1** PANG, smart, sting, spasm, gnawing, twinge, prickle **2** PUNCTURE, cut, hole, wound, gash, perforation, pinhole ▷▷ **prick up** RAISE, point, rise, stand erect

prickle *verb* **1** TINGLE, smart, sting, twitch, itch **2** PRICK, stick into, nick, jab ▷ *noun* **1** TINGLING, smart, chill, tickle, tingle, pins and needles (*informal*), goose bumps, goose flesh **2** SPIKE, point, spur, needle, spine, thorn, barb

prickly *adjective* **1** SPINY, barbed, thorny, bristly, brambly, briery **2** ITCHY, sharp, smarting, stinging, crawling, pricking, tingling, scratchy, prickling **3** IRRITABLE, edgy, grumpy, touchy, bad-tempered, fractious, petulant, stroppy (*Brit slang*), cantankerous, tetchy, ratty (*Brit & NZ informal*), chippy (*informal*), waspish, shirty (*slang, chiefly Brit*), peevish, snappish, liverish, pettish **4** DIFFICULT, complicated, tricky, trying, involved, intricate, troublesome, thorny, knotty, ticklish

pride *noun* **1** SATISFACTION, achievement, fulfilment, delight, content, pleasure, joy, gratification **2** SELF-RESPECT, honour, ego, dignity, self-esteem, self-image, self-worth, amour-propre (*French*) **3** CONCEIT, vanity, arrogance, pretension, presumption, snobbery, morgue (*French*), hubris, smugness, self-importance, egotism, self-love, hauteur, pretentiousness, haughtiness, loftiness, vainglory, superciliousness, bigheadedness (*informal*) << ANTONYM humility **4** ELITE, pick, best, choice, flower, prize, cream, glory, boast, treasure, jewel, gem, pride and joy ▷▷ **pride yourself on something** BE PROUD OF, revel in, boast of, glory in, vaunt, take pride in, brag about, crow about, exult in, congratulate yourself on, flatter yourself that, pique yourself on, plume yourself on

priest *noun* CLERGYMAN, minister, father, divine, vicar, pastor, cleric, curate, churchman, padre (*informal*), holy man, man of God, man of the cloth, ecclesiastic, father confessor

priestly *adjective* ECCLESIASTIC, pastoral, clerical, canonical, hieratic, sacerdotal, priestlike

prim *adjective* PRUDISH, particular, formal, proper, precise, stiff, fussy, fastidious, puritanical, demure, starchy (*informal*), prissy (*informal*), strait-laced, priggish, schoolmarmish (*Brit informal*), old-maidish (*informal*), niminy-piminy << ANTONYM liberal

primacy *noun* SUPREMACY, leadership, command, dominance, superiority, dominion, ascendancy, pre-eminence

prima donna *noun* DIVA, star, leading lady, female lead

primal *adjective* **1** BASIC, prime, central, first, highest, greatest, major, chief, main, most important, principal, paramount **2** EARLIEST, prime, original, primary, first, initial, primitive, pristine, primordial

primarily *adverb* **1** CHIEFLY, largely, generally, mainly, especially, essentially, mostly, basically, principally, fundamentally, above all, on the whole, for the most part **2** AT FIRST, originally, initially, in the first place, in the beginning, first and foremost, at or from the start

primary *adjective* **1** CHIEF, leading, main, best, first, highest, greatest, top, prime, capital, principal, dominant, cardinal, paramount << ANTONYM subordinate **2** BASIC, essential, radical, fundamental, ultimate, underlying, elemental, bog-standard (*informal*) << ANTONYM secondary

prime *adjective* **1** MAIN, leading, chief, central, major, ruling, key, senior, primary, supreme, principal, ultimate, cardinal, paramount, overriding, foremost, predominant, pre-eminent, number-one (*informal*) **2** BEST, top, select, highest, capital, quality, choice,

selected, excellent, superior, first-class, first-rate, grade-A **3** FUNDAMENTAL, original, basic, primary, underlying ▷ *noun* PEAK, flower, bloom, maturity, height, perfection, best days, heyday, zenith, full flowering ▷ *verb* **1** INFORM, tell, train, coach, brief, fill in (*informal*), groom (*informal*), notify, clue in (*informal*), gen up (*Brit informal*), give someone the lowdown, clue up (*informal*) **2** PREPARE, set up, load, equip, get ready, make ready

primeval *or* **primaeval** *adjective* **1** EARLIEST, old, original, ancient, primitive, first, early, pristine, primal, prehistoric, primordial **2** PRIMAL, primitive, natural, basic, inherited, inherent, hereditary, instinctive, innate, congenital, primordial, inborn, inbred

primitive *adjective* **1** UNCIVILIZED, savage, barbarian, barbaric, undeveloped, uncultivated << ANTONYM civilized **2** EARLY, first, earliest, original, primary, elementary, pristine, primordial, primeval << ANTONYM modern **3** SIMPLE, naive, childlike, untrained, undeveloped, unsophisticated, untutored << ANTONYM sophisticated **4** CRUDE, simple, rough, rude, rudimentary, unrefined << ANTONYM elaborate

primordial *adjective* **1** PRIMEVAL, primitive, first, earliest, pristine, primal, prehistoric **2** FUNDAMENTAL, original, basic, radical, elemental

prince *noun* RULER, lord, monarch, sovereign, crown prince, liege, potentate, prince regent, crowned head, dynast

princely *adjective* **1** SUBSTANTIAL, considerable, goodly, large, huge, massive, enormous, tidy (*informal*), whopping (great) (*informal*), sizable *or* sizeable **2** REGAL, royal, imposing, magnificent, august, grand, imperial, noble, sovereign, majestic, dignified, stately, lofty, high-born

princess *noun* RULER, lady, monarch, sovereign, liege, crowned head, crowned princess, dynast, princess regent

principal *adjective* MAIN, leading, chief, prime, first, highest, controlling, strongest, capital, key, essential, primary, most important, dominant, arch, cardinal, paramount, foremost, pre-eminent << ANTONYM minor ▷ *noun* **1** HEADMASTER *or* HEADMISTRESS, head (*informal*), director, dean, head teacher, rector, master *or* mistress **2** BOSS, head, leader, director, chief (*informal*), master, ruler, superintendent, baas (*S African*), sherang (*Austral & NZ*) **3** STAR, lead, leader, prima ballerina, first violin, leading man *or* lady, coryphée **4** CAPITAL, money, assets, working capital, capital funds ▷ see **principle**

principally *adverb* MAINLY, largely, chiefly, especially, particularly, mostly, primarily, above all, predominantly, in the main, for the most part, first and foremost

principle *noun* **1** MORALS, standards, ideals, honour, virtue, ethics, integrity, conscience, morality, decency, scruples, probity, rectitude, moral standards, sense of duty, moral law, sense of honour, uprightness, kaupapa (*NZ*) **2** BELIEF, rule, standard, attitude, code, notion, criterion, ethic, doctrine, canon, creed, maxim, dogma, tenet, dictum, credo, axiom **3** RULE, idea, law, theory, basis, truth, concept, formula, fundamental, assumption, essence, proposition, verity, golden rule, precept ▷▷ **in principle 1** IN GENERAL, generally, all things considered, on the whole, in the main, by and large, in essence, all in all, on balance **2** IN THEORY, ideally, on paper, theoretically, in an ideal world, en principe (*French*)

principled *adjective* MORAL, ethical, upright, honourable, just, correct, decent, righteous, conscientious, virtuous, scrupulous, right-minded, high-minded

print *verb* **1** RUN OFF, publish, copy, reproduce, issue, engrave, go to press, put to bed (*informal*) **2** PUBLISH, release, circulate, issue, disseminate **3** MARK, impress, stamp, imprint ▷ *noun* **1** PHOTOGRAPH, photo, snap **2** PICTURE, plate, etching, engraving, lithograph, woodcut, linocut **3** COPY, photo (*informal*), picture, reproduction, replica **4** TYPE, lettering, letters, characters, face, font (*chiefly US*), fount, typeface ▷▷ **in print 1** PUBLISHED, printed, on the streets, on paper, in black and white, out **2** AVAILABLE, current, on the market, in the shops, on the shelves, obtainable ▷▷ **out of print** UNAVAILABLE, unobtainable, no longer published, o.p.

prior *adjective* EARLIER, previous, former, preceding, foregoing, antecedent, aforementioned, pre-existing, anterior, pre-existent ▷▷ **prior to** BEFORE, preceding, earlier than, in advance of, previous to

priority *noun* **1** PRIME CONCERN, first concern, primary issue, most pressing matter **2** PRECEDENCE, preference, greater importance, primacy, predominance

3 SUPREMACY, rank, the lead, superiority, precedence, prerogative, seniority, right of way, pre-eminence

priory *noun* MONASTERY, abbey, convent, cloister, nunnery, religious house

prise ▷ see **prize**3

prison *noun* JAIL, confinement, can (*slang*), pound, nick (*Brit slang*), stir (*slang*), cooler (*slang*), jug (*slang*), dungeon, clink (*slang*), glasshouse (*military informal*), gaol, penitentiary (*US*), slammer (*slang*), lockup, quod (*slang*), penal institution, calaboose (*US informal*), choky (*slang*), poky *or* pokey (*US & Canad slang*), boob (*Austral slang*)

prisoner *noun* **1** CONVICT, con (*slang*), lag (*slang*), jailbird **2** CAPTIVE, hostage, detainee, internee

prissy *adjective* PRIM, precious, fussy, fastidious, squeamish, prudish, finicky, strait-laced, schoolmarmish (*Brit informal*), old-maidish (*informal*), niminy-piminy, overnice, prim and proper

pristine *adjective* NEW, pure, virgin, immaculate, untouched, unspoiled, virginal, unsullied, uncorrupted, undefiled

privacy *noun* SECLUSION, isolation, solitude, retirement, retreat, separateness, sequestration, privateness

private *adjective* **1** NONPUBLIC, independent, commercial, privatised, private-enterprise, denationalized **2** EXCLUSIVE, individual, privately owned, own, special, particular, reserved << ANTONYM public **3** SECRET, confidential, covert, inside, closet, unofficial, privy (*archaic*), clandestine, off the record, hush-hush (*informal*), in camera << ANTONYM public **4** PERSONAL, individual, secret, intimate, undisclosed, unspoken, innermost, unvoiced **5** SECLUDED, secret, separate, isolated, concealed, retired, sequestered, not overlooked << ANTONYM busy **6** SOLITARY, reserved, retiring, withdrawn, discreet, secretive, self-contained, reclusive, reticent, insular, introvert, uncommunicative << ANTONYM sociable ▷ *noun* ENLISTED MAN (*US*), tommy (*Brit informal*), private soldier, Tommy Atkins (*Brit informal*), squaddie *or* squaddy (*Brit slang*) ▷▷ **in private** IN SECRET, privately, personally, behind closed doors, in camera, between ourselves, confidentially

privation *noun* (*formal*) WANT, poverty, need, suffering, loss, lack, distress, misery, necessity, hardship, penury, destitution, neediness, indigence

privilege *noun* RIGHT, benefit, due, advantage, claim, freedom, sanction, liberty, concession, franchise, entitlement, prerogative, birthright

privileged *adjective* 1 SPECIAL, powerful, advantaged, favoured, ruling, honoured, entitled, elite, indulged 2 CONFIDENTIAL, special, inside, exceptional, privy, off the record, not for publication

privy *noun* (*obsolete*) LAVATORY, closet, bog (*slang*), latrine, outside toilet, earth closet, pissoir (*French*), bogger (*Austral slang*), brasco (*Austral slang*) ▷ *adjective* **with to** INFORMED OF, aware of, in on, wise to (*slang*), hip to (*slang*), in the loop, apprised of, cognizant of, in the know about (*informal*)

prize¹ *noun* 1 REWARD, cup, award, honour, premium, medal, trophy, accolade 2 WINNINGS, haul, jackpot, stakes, purse, windfall 3 GOAL, hope, gain, aim, desire, ambition, conquest, Holy Grail (*informal*) ▷ *modifier* CHAMPION, best, winning, top, outstanding, award-winning, first-rate, top-notch (*informal*)

prize² *verb* VALUE, appreciate, treasure, esteem, cherish, hold dear, regard highly, set store by

prize³ *or* **prise** *verb* 1 FORCE, pull, lever 2 DRAG, force, draw, wring, extort

probability *noun* 1 LIKELIHOOD, prospect, chance, odds, expectation, liability, presumption, likeliness 2 CHANCE, odds, possibility, likelihood

probable *adjective* LIKELY, possible, apparent, reasonable to think, most likely, presumed, credible, plausible, feasible, odds-on, on the cards, presumable << ANTONYM unlikely

probably *adverb* LIKELY, perhaps, maybe, possibly, presumably, most likely, doubtless, in all probability, in all likelihood, perchance (*archaic*), as likely as not

probation *noun* TRIAL PERIOD, test, trial, examination, apprenticeship, initiation, novitiate

probe *verb* 1 *often with* **into** EXAMINE, research, go into, investigate, explore, test, sound, search, look into, query, verify, sift, analyze, dissect, delve into, work over, scrutinize 2 EXPLORE, examine, poke, prod, feel around ▷ *noun* INVESTIGATION, study, research, inquiry, analysis, examination, exploration, scrutiny, inquest, scrutinization

probity *noun* (*formal*) INTEGRITY, worth, justice, honour, equity, virtue, goodness, morality, honesty, fairness, fidelity, sincerity,

righteousness, rectitude, truthfulness, trustworthiness, uprightness

problem *noun* 1 DIFFICULTY, trouble, dispute, plight, obstacle, dilemma, headache (*informal*), disagreement, complication, predicament, quandary 2 PUZZLE, question, riddle, enigma, conundrum, teaser, poser, brain-teaser (*informal*) ▷ *modifier* DIFFICULT, disturbed, troublesome, unruly, delinquent, uncontrollable, intractable, recalcitrant, intransigent, unmanageable, disobedient, ungovernable, refractory, maladjusted

problematic *adjective* TRICKY, puzzling, uncertain, doubtful, dubious, unsettled, questionable, enigmatic, debatable, moot, problematical, chancy (*informal*), open to doubt << ANTONYM clear

procedure *noun* METHOD, policy, process, course, system, form, action, step, performance, operation, practice, scheme, strategy, conduct, formula, custom, routine, transaction, plan of action, modus operandi

proceed *verb* 1 BEGIN, go ahead, get going, make a start, get under way, set something in motion 2 CONTINUE, go on, progress, carry on, go ahead, get on, press on << ANTONYM discontinue 3 GO ON, continue, advance, progress, carry on, go ahead, move on, move forward, press on, push on, make your way << ANTONYM stop 4 ARISE, come, follow, issue, result, spring, flow, stem, derive, originate, ensue, emanate

proceeding *noun* ACTION, process, procedure, move, act, step, measure, venture, undertaking, deed, occurrence, course of action

proceeds *plural noun* INCOME, profit, revenue, returns, produce, products, gain, earnings, yield, receipts, takings

process *noun* 1 PROCEDURE, means, course, system, action, performance, operation, measure, proceeding, manner, transaction, mode, course of action 2 DEVELOPMENT, growth, progress, course, stage, step, movement, advance, formation, evolution, unfolding, progression 3 METHOD, system, practice, technique, procedure 4 (*law*) ACTION, case, trial, suit ▷ *verb* 1 PREPARE, treat, convert, transform, alter, refine 2 HANDLE, manage, action, deal with, fulfil, take care of, dispose of

procession *noun* PARADE, train, march, file, column, motorcade, cavalcade, cortege

proclaim *verb* 1 ANNOUNCE, declare, advertise, show, publish, indicate, blaze (abroad), herald, circulate, trumpet, affirm, give out, profess, promulgate, make known, enunciate, blazon (abroad), shout from the housetops (*informal*) << ANTONYM keep secret **2** PRONOUNCE, announce, declare

proclamation *noun* **1** DECLARATION, notice, announcement, decree, manifesto, edict, pronouncement, pronunciamento **2** PUBLISHING, broadcasting, announcement, publication, declaration, notification, pronouncement, promulgation

proclivity *noun* (*formal*) TENDENCY, liking, leaning, inclination, bent, weakness, bias, disposition, penchant, propensity, kink, predisposition, predilection, partiality, proneness, liableness

procrastinate *verb* DELAY, stall, postpone, prolong, put off, defer, adjourn, retard, dally, play for time, gain time, temporize, play a waiting game, protract, drag your feet (*informal*), be dilatory << ANTONYM hurry (up)

procrastination *noun* DELAY, hesitation, slowness, slackness, dilatoriness, temporization *or* temporisation

procure *verb* OBTAIN, get, find, buy, win, land, score (*slang*), gain, earn, pick up, purchase, secure, appropriate, acquire, manage to get, get hold of, come by, lay hands on

prod *verb* **1** POKE, push, dig, shove, propel, nudge, jab, prick **2** PROMPT, move, urge, motivate, spur, stimulate, rouse, stir up, incite, egg on, goad, impel, put a bomb under (*informal*) ▷ *noun* **1** POKE, push, boost, dig, elbow, shove, nudge, jab **2** PROMPT, boost, signal, cue, reminder, stimulus **3** GOAD, stick, spur, poker

prodigal *adjective* **1** EXTRAVAGANT, excessive, reckless, squandering, wasteful, wanton, profligate, spendthrift, intemperate, immoderate, improvident << ANTONYM thrifty **2** *often with* **of** LAVISH, bountiful, unstinting, unsparing, bounteous, profuse << ANTONYM generous

prodigious *adjective* **1** HUGE, giant, massive, vast, enormous, tremendous, immense, gigantic, monumental, monstrous, mammoth, colossal, stellar (*informal*), stupendous, inordinate, immeasurable << ANTONYM tiny **2** WONDERFUL, striking, amazing, unusual, dramatic, impressive, extraordinary, remarkable, fantastic (*informal*), fabulous, staggering, marvellous, startling, exceptional, abnormal, phenomenal, astounding, miraculous,

stupendous, flabbergasting (*informal*) << ANTONYM ordinary

prodigy *noun* GENIUS, talent, wizard, mastermind, whizz (*informal*), whizz kid (*informal*), wunderkind, brainbox, child genius, wonder child, up-and-comer (*informal*)

produce *verb* **1** CAUSE, lead to, result in, effect, occasion, generate, trigger, make for, provoke, set off, induce, bring about, give rise to, engender **2** MAKE, build, create, develop, turn out, manufacture, construct, invent, assemble, put together, originate, fabricate, mass-produce **3** CREATE, develop, write, turn out, compose, originate, churn out (*informal*) **4** YIELD, provide, grow, bear, give, supply, afford, render, furnish **5** BRING FORTH, bear, deliver, breed, give birth to, beget, bring into the world **6** SHOW, provide, present, advance, demonstrate, offer, come up with, exhibit, put forward, furnish, bring forward, set forth, bring to light **7** DISPLAY, show, present, proffer **8** PRESENT, stage, direct, put on, do, show, mount, exhibit, put before the public ▷ *noun* FRUIT AND VEGETABLES, goods, food, products, crops, yield, harvest, greengrocery (*Brit*)

producer *noun* **1** DIRECTOR, promoter, impresario, régisseur (*French*) **2** MAKER, manufacturer, builder, creator, fabricator **3** GROWER, farmer

product *noun* **1** GOODS, produce, production, creation, commodity, invention, merchandise, artefact, concoction **2** RESULT, fruit, consequence, yield, returns, issue, effect, outcome, legacy, spin-off, end result, offshoot, upshot

production *noun* **1** PRODUCING, making, manufacture, manufacturing, construction, assembly, preparation, formation, fabrication, origination **2** CREATION, development, fashioning, composition, origination **3** MANAGEMENT, administration, direction **4** PRESENTATION, staging, mounting

productive *adjective* **1** FERTILE, rich, producing, prolific, plentiful, fruitful, teeming, generative, fecund << ANTONYM barren **2** CREATIVE, dynamic, vigorous, energetic, inventive **3** USEFUL, rewarding, valuable, profitable, effective, worthwhile, beneficial, constructive, gratifying, fruitful, advantageous, gainful << ANTONYM useless

productivity *noun* OUTPUT, production, capacity, yield, efficiency, mass production, work rate, productive capacity, productiveness

profane *adjective* 1 SACRILEGIOUS, wicked, irreverent, sinful, disrespectful, heathen, impure, godless, ungodly, irreligious, impious, idolatrous << ANTONYM religious 2 CRUDE, foul, obscene, abusive, coarse, filthy, vulgar, blasphemous 3 SECULAR, lay, temporal, unholy, worldly, unconsecrated, unhallowed, unsanctified ▷ *verb* DESECRATE, violate, abuse, prostitute, contaminate, pollute, pervert, misuse, debase, defile, vitiate, commit sacrilege

profess *verb* 1 CLAIM, allege, pretend, fake, make out, sham, purport, feign, act as if, let on, dissemble 2 STATE, admit, announce, maintain, own, confirm, declare, acknowledge, confess, assert, proclaim, affirm, certify, avow, vouch, aver, asseverate

professed *adjective* 1 SUPPOSED, would-be, alleged, so-called, apparent, pretended, purported, self-styled, ostensible, soi-disant (*French*) 2 DECLARED, confirmed, confessed, proclaimed, certified, self-confessed, avowed, self-acknowledged

profession *noun* OCCUPATION, calling, business, career, employment, line, office, position, sphere, vocation, walk of life, line of work, métier

professional *adjective* 1 QUALIFIED, trained, skilled, white-collar 2 EXPERT, experienced, finished, skilled, masterly, efficient, crack (*slang*), polished, practised, ace (*informal*), accomplished, slick, competent, adept, proficient << ANTONYM amateurish ▷ *noun* EXPERT, authority, master, pro (*informal*), specialist, guru, buff (*informal*), wizard, adept, whizz (*informal*), maestro, virtuoso, hotshot (*informal*), past master, dab hand (*Brit informal*), wonk (*informal*), maven (*US*), fundi (*S African*)

professor *noun* DON (*Brit*), fellow (*Brit*), prof (*informal*), head of faculty

proffer *verb* 1 OFFER, hand over, present, extend, hold out 2 SUGGEST, propose, volunteer, submit, tender, propound

proficiency *noun* SKILL, ability, know-how (*informal*), talent, facility, craft, expertise, competence, accomplishment, mastery, knack, aptitude, dexterity, expertness, skilfulness

proficient *adjective* SKILLED, trained, experienced, qualified, able, expert, masterly, talented, gifted, capable, efficient, clever, accomplished, versed, competent, apt,

skilful, adept, conversant << ANTONYM unskilled

profile *noun* 1 OUTLINE, lines, form, figure, shape, silhouette, contour, side view 2 BIOGRAPHY, sketch, vignette, characterization, thumbnail sketch, character sketch 3 ANALYSIS, study, table, review, survey, chart, examination, diagram, graph

profit *noun* 1 *often plural* EARNINGS, winnings, return, revenue, gain, boot (*dialect*), yield, proceeds, percentage (*informal*), surplus, receipts, bottom line, takings, emoluments << ANTONYM loss 2 BENEFIT, good, use, interest, value, gain, advantage, advancement, mileage (*informal*), avail << ANTONYM disadvantage ▷ *verb* 1 MAKE MONEY, clear up, gain, earn, clean up (*informal*), rake in (*informal*), make a killing (*informal*), make a good thing of (*informal*) 2 BENEFIT, help, serve, aid, gain, promote, contribute to, avail, be of advantage to

profitable *adjective* 1 MONEY-MAKING, lucrative, paying, commercial, rewarding, worthwhile, cost-effective, fruitful, gainful, remunerative 2 BENEFICIAL, useful, rewarding, valuable, productive, worthwhile, fruitful, advantageous, expedient, serviceable << ANTONYM useless

profligacy *noun* EXTRAVAGANCE, excess, squandering, waste, recklessness, wastefulness, lavishness, prodigality, improvidence

profligate *adjective* EXTRAVAGANT, reckless, squandering, wasteful, prodigal, spendthrift, immoderate, improvident

profound *adjective* 1 SINCERE, acute, intense, great, keen, extreme, hearty, heartfelt, abject, deeply felt, heartrending << ANTONYM insincere 2 WISE, learned, serious, deep, skilled, subtle, penetrating, philosophical, thoughtful, sage, discerning, weighty, insightful, erudite, abstruse, recondite, sagacious << ANTONYM uninformed 3 COMPLETE, intense, absolute, serious (*informal*), total, extreme, pronounced, utter, consummate, unqualified, out-and-out << ANTONYM slight 4 RADICAL, extensive, thorough, far-reaching, exhaustive, thoroughgoing

profoundly *adverb* GREATLY, very, deeply, seriously, keenly, extremely, thoroughly, sincerely, intensely, acutely, heartily, to the core, abjectly, to the nth degree, from the bottom of your heart

profundity *noun* INSIGHT, intelligence, depth, wisdom, learning, penetration, acumen, erudition, acuity, perspicacity, sagacity, perceptiveness, perspicuity

profuse *adjective* **1** PLENTIFUL, ample, prolific, abundant, overflowing, teeming, copious, bountiful, luxuriant << ANTONYM sparse **2** EXTRAVAGANT, liberal, generous, excessive, lavish, exuberant, prodigal, fulsome, open-handed, unstinting, immoderate << ANTONYM moderate

profusion *noun* ABUNDANCE, wealth, excess, quantity, surplus, riot, multitude, bounty, plethora, exuberance, glut, extravagance, cornucopia, oversupply, plenitude, superabundance, superfluity, lavishness, luxuriance, prodigality, copiousness

progenitor *noun* **1** ANCESTOR, parent, forebear, forefather, begetter, procreator, primogenitor **2** ORIGINATOR, source, predecessor, precursor, forerunner, antecedent, instigator

progeny *noun* **1** CHILDREN, family, young, issue, offspring, descendants **2** RACE, stock, breed, posterity (*archaic*), seed (*chiefly biblical*), lineage, scions

prognosis *noun* FORECAST, prediction, diagnosis, expectation, speculation, projection, surmise, prognostication

programme *noun* **1** PLAN, scheme, strategy, procedure, project, plan of action **2** SCHEDULE, plan, agenda, timetable, listing, list, line-up, calendar, order **3** COURSE, curriculum, syllabus **4** SHOW, performance, production, broadcast, episode, presentation, transmission, telecast ▷ *verb* **1** SCHEDULE, plan, timetable, book, bill, list, design, arrange, work out, line up, organize, lay on, formulate, map out, itemize, prearrange **2** SET, fix

progress *noun* **1** DEVELOPMENT, increase, growth, advance, gain, improvement, promotion, breakthrough, step forward, advancement, progression, headway, betterment, amelioration << ANTONYM regression **2** MOVEMENT FORWARD, passage, advancement, progression, course, advance, headway, onward movement << ANTONYM movement backward ▷ *verb* **1** MOVE ON, continue, travel, advance, proceed, go forward, gain ground, forge ahead, make inroads (into), make headway, make your way, cover ground, make strides, gather way << ANTONYM move back **2** DEVELOP, improve, advance, better, increase, grow,

gain, get on, come on, mature, blossom, ameliorate << ANTONYM get behind ▷▷ **in progress** GOING ON, happening, continuing, being done, occurring, taking place, proceeding, under way, ongoing, being performed, in operation

progression *noun* **1** PROGRESS, advance, advancement, gain, headway, furtherance, movement forward **2** SEQUENCE, course, order, series, chain, cycle, string, succession

progressive *adjective* **1** ENLIGHTENED, liberal, modern, advanced, radical, enterprising, go-ahead, revolutionary, dynamic, avant-garde, reformist, up-and-coming, forward-looking **2** GROWING, continuing, increasing, developing, advancing, accelerating, ongoing, continuous, intensifying, escalating

prohibit *verb* **1** FORBID, ban, rule out, veto, outlaw, disallow, proscribe, debar, interdict << ANTONYM permit **2** PREVENT, restrict, rule out, stop, hamper, hinder, constrain, obstruct, preclude, impede, make impossible << ANTONYM allow

prohibited *adjective* FORBIDDEN, barred, banned, illegal, not allowed, vetoed, taboo, off limits, proscribed, verboten (*German*)

prohibition *noun* BAN, boycott, embargo, bar, veto, prevention, exclusion, injunction, disqualification, interdiction, interdict, proscription, disallowance, forbiddance, restraining order (*US law*)

prohibitive *adjective* **1** EXORBITANT, excessive, steep (*informal*), high-priced, preposterous, sky-high, extortionate, beyond your means **2** PROHIBITING, forbidding, restraining, restrictive, repressive, suppressive, proscriptive

project *noun* **1** SCHEME, plan, job, idea, design, programme, campaign, operation, activity, proposal, venture, enterprise, undertaking, occupation, proposition, plan of action **2** ASSIGNMENT, task, homework, piece of research ▷ *verb* **1** FORECAST, expect, estimate, predict, reckon, calculate, gauge, extrapolate, predetermine **2** PLAN, propose, design, scheme, purpose, frame, draft, outline, devise, contemplate, contrive, map out **3** LAUNCH, shoot, throw, cast, transmit, discharge, hurl, fling, propel **4** STICK OUT, extend, stand out, bulge, beetle, protrude, overhang, jut

projectile *noun* MISSILE, shell, bullet, rocket

projection *noun* FORECAST, estimate, reckoning, prediction, calculation, estimation, computation, extrapolation

proletarian *adjective* WORKING-CLASS, common, cloth-cap (*informal*), plebeian, blue-singlet (*Austral slang*) ▷ *noun* WORKER, commoner, Joe Bloggs (*Brit informal*), pleb, plebeian, prole (*derogatory slang, chiefly Brit*)

proletariat *noun* WORKING CLASS, the masses, lower classes, commoners, the herd, wage-earners, lower orders, the common people, hoi polloi, plebs, the rabble, the great unwashed (*derogatory*), labouring classes, proles (*derogatory slang, chiefly Brit*), commonalty << ANTONYM ruling class

proliferate *verb* INCREASE, expand, breed, mushroom, escalate, multiply, burgeon, snowball, run riot, grow rapidly

proliferation *noun* MULTIPLICATION, increase, spread, build-up, concentration, expansion, extension, step-up (*informal*), escalation, intensification

prolific *adjective* 1 PRODUCTIVE, creative, fertile, inventive, copious 2 FRUITFUL, fertile, abundant, rich, rank, teeming, bountiful, luxuriant, generative, profuse, fecund << ANTONYM unproductive

prologue *noun* INTRODUCTION, preliminary, prelude, preface, preamble, foreword, proem, exordium

prolong *verb* LENGTHEN, continue, perpetuate, draw out, extend, delay, stretch out, carry on, spin out, drag out, make longer, protract << ANTONYM shorten

promenade *noun* 1 WALKWAY, parade, boulevard, prom, esplanade, public walk 2 STROLL, walk, turn, airing, constitutional, saunter ▷ *verb* 1 STROLL, walk, saunter, take a walk, perambulate, stretch your legs 2 PARADE, strut, swagger, flaunt

prominence *noun* 1 FAME, name, standing, rank, reputation, importance, celebrity, distinction, prestige, greatness, eminence, pre-eminence, notability, outstandingness 2 CONSPICUOUSNESS, weight, precedence, top billing, specialness, salience, markedness 3 PROTRUSION, swelling, projection, bulge, jutting, protuberance

prominent *adjective* 1 FAMOUS, leading, top, chief, important, main, noted, popular, respected, celebrated, outstanding, distinguished, well-known, notable, renowned, big-time (*informal*), foremost, eminent, major league (*informal*), pre-eminent, well-thought-of << ANTONYM unknown 2 NOTICEABLE, striking, obvious, outstanding, remarkable, pronounced,

blatant, conspicuous, to the fore, unmistakable, eye-catching, salient, in the foreground, easily seen, obtrusive << ANTONYM inconspicuous 3 JUTTING, projecting, standing out, bulging, hanging over, protruding, protuberant, protrusive << ANTONYM indented

promiscuity *noun* LICENTIOUSNESS, profligacy, sleeping around (*informal*), permissiveness, abandon, incontinence, depravity, immorality, debauchery, laxity, dissipation, looseness, amorality, lechery, laxness, wantonness, libertinism, promiscuousness

promiscuous *adjective* LICENTIOUS, wanton, profligate, debauched, fast, wild, abandoned, loose, immoral, lax, dissipated, unbridled, dissolute, libertine, of easy virtue, unchaste << ANTONYM chaste

promise *verb* 1 GUARANTEE, pledge, vow, swear, contract, assure, undertake, warrant, plight, stipulate, vouch, take an oath, give an undertaking, cross your heart, give your word 2 SEEM LIKELY, look like, hint at, show signs of, bespeak, augur, betoken, lead you to expect, hold out hopes of, give hope of, bid fair, hold a probability of ▷ *noun* 1 GUARANTEE, word, bond, vow, commitment, pledge, undertaking, assurance, engagement, compact, oath, covenant, word of honour 2 POTENTIAL, ability, talent, capacity, capability, flair, aptitude

promising *adjective* 1 ENCOURAGING, likely, bright, reassuring, hopeful, favourable, rosy, auspicious, propitious, full of promise << ANTONYM unpromising 2 TALENTED, able, gifted, rising, likely, up-and-coming

promontory *noun* POINT, cape, head, spur, ness (*archaic*), headland, foreland

promote *verb* 1 HELP, back, support, further, develop, aid, forward, champion, encourage, advance, work for, urge, boost, recommend, sponsor, foster, contribute to, assist, advocate, stimulate, endorse, prescribe, speak for, nurture, push for, espouse, popularize, gee up << ANTONYM impede 2 ADVERTISE, sell, hype, publicize, push, plug (*informal*), puff, call attention to, beat the drum for (*informal*) 3 RAISE, upgrade, elevate, honour, dignify, exalt, kick upstairs (*informal*), aggrandize << ANTONYM demote

promoter *noun* 1 ORGANIZER, arranger, entrepreneur, impresario 2 SUPPORTER, champion, advocate, campaigner, helper, proponent, stalwart, mainstay, upholder

promotion *noun* **1** RISE, upgrading, move up, advancement, elevation, exaltation, preferment, aggrandizement, ennoblement **2** PUBLICITY, advertising, hype, pushing, plugging (*informal*), propaganda, advertising campaign, hard sell, media hype, ballyhoo (*informal*), puffery (*informal*), boosterism **3** ENCOURAGEMENT, backing, support, development, progress, boosting, advancement, advocacy, cultivation, espousal, furtherance, boosterism

prompt *verb* **1** CAUSE, move, inspire, stimulate, occasion, urge, spur, provoke, motivate, induce, evoke, give rise to, elicit, incite, instigate, impel, call forth << ANTONYM discourage **2** REMIND, assist, cue, help out, prod, jog the memory, refresh the memory ▷ *adjective* **1** IMMEDIATE, quick, rapid, instant, timely, early, swift, on time, speedy, instantaneous, punctual, pdq (*slang*), unhesitating << ANTONYM slow **2** QUICK, ready, efficient, eager, willing, smart, alert, brisk, responsive, expeditious << ANTONYM inefficient ▷ *adverb* (*informal*) EXACTLY, sharp, promptly, on the dot, punctually ▷ *noun* REMINDER, hint, cue, help, spur, stimulus, jog, prod, jolt

promptly *adverb* **1** IMMEDIATELY, instantly, swiftly, directly, quickly, at once, speedily, by return, pronto (*informal*), unhesitatingly, hotfoot, pdq (*slang*), posthaste **2** PUNCTUALLY, on time, spot on (*informal*), bang on (*informal*), on the dot, on the button (*US*), on the nail

promulgate *verb* **1** MAKE KNOWN, issue, announce, publish, spread, promote, advertise, broadcast, communicate, proclaim, circulate, notify, make public, disseminate **2** MAKE OFFICIAL, pass, declare, decree

prone *adjective* **1** LIABLE, given, subject, inclined, tending, bent, disposed, susceptible, apt, predisposed << ANTONYM disinclined **2** FACE DOWN, flat, lying down, horizontal, prostrate, recumbent, procumbent << ANTONYM face up

pronounce *verb* **1** SAY, speak, voice, stress, sound, utter, articulate, enunciate, vocalize **2** DECLARE, announce, judge, deliver, assert, proclaim, decree, affirm

pronounced *adjective* NOTICEABLE, clear, decided, strong, marked, striking, obvious, broad, evident, distinct, definite, conspicuous, unmistakable, salient

<< ANTONYM imperceptible

pronouncement *noun* ANNOUNCEMENT, statement, declaration, judgment, decree, manifesto, proclamation, notification, edict, dictum, promulgation, pronunciamento

pronunciation *noun* INTONATION, accent, speech, stress, articulation, inflection, diction, elocution, enunciation, accentuation

proof *noun* **1** EVIDENCE, demonstration, testimony, confirmation, verification, certification, corroboration, authentication, substantiation, attestation **2** (*printing*) TRIAL PRINT, pull, slip, galley, page proof, galley proof, trial impression ▷ *adjective* IMPERVIOUS, strong, tight, resistant, impenetrable, repellent

prop *verb* **1** LEAN, place, set, stand, position, rest, lay, balance, steady **2** *often with* **up** SUPPORT, maintain, sustain, shore, hold up, brace, uphold, bolster, truss, buttress ▷ *noun* **1** SUPPORT, stay, brace, mainstay, truss, buttress, stanchion **2** MAINSTAY, support, sustainer, anchor, backbone, cornerstone, upholder **3** SUBSIDIZE, support, fund, finance, maintain, underwrite, shore up, buttress, bolster up

propaganda *noun* INFORMATION, advertising, promotion, publicity, hype, brainwashing, disinformation, ballyhoo (*informal*), agitprop, newspeak, boosterism

propagandist *noun* PUBLICIST, advocate, promoter, proponent, evangelist, proselytizer, pamphleteer, indoctrinator

propagate *verb* **1** SPREAD, publish, promote, broadcast, proclaim, transmit, circulate, diffuse, publicize, disseminate, promulgate, make known << ANTONYM suppress **2** PRODUCE, generate, engender, increase **3** REPRODUCE, breed, multiply, proliferate, beget, procreate

propagation *noun* **1** SPREADING, spread, promotion, communication, distribution, circulation, transmission, diffusion, dissemination, promulgation **2** REPRODUCTION, generation, breeding, increase, proliferation, multiplication, procreation

propel *verb* **1** DRIVE, launch, start, force, send, shoot, push, thrust, shove, set in motion << ANTONYM stop **2** IMPEL, drive, push, prompt, spur, motivate << ANTONYM hold back

propensity *noun* TENDENCY, leaning, weakness, inclination, bent, liability, bias, disposition, penchant, susceptibility, predisposition, proclivity, proneness, aptness

proper *adjective* **1** REAL, actual, genuine, true, bona fide, kosher (*informal*), dinkum (*Austral & NZ informal*) **2** CORRECT, accepted, established, appropriate, right, formal, conventional, accurate, exact, precise, legitimate, orthodox, apt << ANTONYM improper **3** POLITE, right, becoming, seemly, fitting, fit, mannerly, suitable, decent, gentlemanly, refined, respectable, befitting, genteel, de rigueur (*French*), ladylike, meet (*archaic*), decorous, punctilious, comme il faut (*French*) << ANTONYM unseemly **4** CHARACTERISTIC, own, special, individual, personal, particular, specific, peculiar, respective

properly *adverb* **1** CORRECTLY, rightly, fittingly, appropriately, legitimately, accurately, suitably, aptly, deservedly, as intended, in the true sense, in the accepted *or* approved manner << ANTONYM incorrectly **2** POLITELY, respectfully, ethically, decently, respectably, decorously, punctiliously << ANTONYM badly

property *noun* **1** POSSESSIONS, goods, means, effects, holdings, capital, riches, resources, estate, assets, wealth, belongings, chattels **2** LAND, holding, title, estate, acres, real estate, freehold, realty, real property **3** QUALITY, feature, characteristic, mark, ability, attribute, virtue, trait, hallmark, peculiarity, idiosyncrasy

prophecy *noun* **1** PREDICTION, forecast, revelation, prognosis, foretelling, prognostication, augury, sortilege, vaticination (*rare*) **2** SECOND SIGHT, divination, augury, telling the future, soothsaying

prophesy *verb* PREDICT, forecast, divine, foresee, augur, presage, foretell, forewarn, prognosticate, soothsay, vaticinate (*rare*)

prophet *or* **prophetess** *noun* SOOTHSAYER, forecaster, diviner, oracle, seer, clairvoyant, augur, sibyl, prognosticator, prophesier

prophetic *adjective* PREDICTIVE, foreshadowing, presaging, prescient, divinatory, oracular, sibylline, prognostic, mantic, vatic (*rare*), augural, fatidic (*rare*)

propitious *adjective* FAVOURABLE, timely, promising, encouraging, bright, lucky, fortunate, prosperous, rosy, advantageous, auspicious, opportune, full of promise

proponent *noun* SUPPORTER, friend, champion, defender, advocate, patron, enthusiast, subscriber, backer, partisan, exponent, apologist, upholder, vindicator, spokesman *or* spokeswoman

proportion *noun* **1** PART, share, cut (*informal*), amount, measure, division, percentage, segment, quota, fraction **2** RELATIVE AMOUNT, relationship, distribution, ratio **3** BALANCE, agreement, harmony, correspondence, symmetry, concord, congruity ▷ *plural noun* DIMENSIONS, size, volume, capacity, extent, range, bulk, scope, measurements, magnitude, breadth, expanse, amplitude

proportional *or* **proportionate** *adjective* CORRESPONDENT, equivalent, corresponding, even, balanced, consistent, comparable, compatible, equitable, in proportion, analogous, commensurate << ANTONYM disproportionate

proposal *noun* SUGGESTION, plan, programme, scheme, offer, terms, design, project, bid, motion, recommendation, tender, presentation, proposition, overture

propose *verb* **1** PUT FORWARD, present, suggest, advance, come up with, submit, tender, proffer, propound **2** INTEND, mean, plan, aim, design, scheme, purpose, have in mind, have every intention **3** NOMINATE, name, present, introduce, invite, recommend, put up **4** OFFER MARRIAGE, pop the question (*informal*), ask for someone's hand (in marriage), pay suit

proposition *noun* **1** TASK, problem, activity, job, affair, venture, undertaking **2** THEORY, idea, argument, concept, thesis, hypothesis, theorem, premiss, postulation **3** PROPOSAL, plan, suggestion, scheme, bid, motion, recommendation **4** ADVANCE, pass (*informal*), proposal, overture, improper suggestion, come-on (*informal*) ▷ *verb* MAKE A PASS AT, solicit, accost, make an indecent proposal to, make an improper suggestion to

propound *verb* PUT FORWARD, present, advance, propose, advocate, submit, suggest, lay down, contend, postulate, set forth

proprietor *or* **proprietress** *noun* OWNER, landowner, freeholder, possessor, titleholder, deed holder, landlord *or* landlady

propriety *noun* **1** DECORUM, manners, courtesy, protocol, good form, decency, breeding, delicacy, modesty, respectability, etiquette, refinement, politeness, good manners, rectitude, punctilio, seemliness

<< ANTONYM indecorum **2** CORRECTNESS, fitness, appropriateness, rightness, aptness, seemliness, suitableness >> **the proprieties** ETIQUETTE, the niceties, the civilities, the amenities, the done thing, the social graces, the rules of conduct, the social conventions, social code, accepted conduct, kawa (*NZ*), tikanga (*NZ*)

propulsion noun POWER, pressure, push, thrust, momentum, impulse, impetus, motive power, impulsion, propelling force

prosaic *adjective* DULL, ordinary, boring, routine, flat, dry, everyday, tame, pedestrian, commonplace, mundane, matter-of-fact, stale, banal, uninspiring, humdrum, trite, unimaginative, hackneyed, workaday, vapid << ANTONYM exciting

proscribe *verb* **1** PROHIBIT, ban, forbid, boycott, embargo, interdict << ANTONYM permit **2** CONDEMN, reject, damn, denounce, censure **3** OUTLAW, exclude, exile, expel, banish, deport, expatriate, excommunicate, ostracize, blackball, attaint (*archaic*)

prosecute *verb* **1** (*law*) TAKE SOMEONE TO COURT, try, sue, summon, indict, do (*slang*), arraign, seek redress, put someone on trial, litigate, bring suit against, bring someone to trial, put someone in the dock, bring action against, prefer charges against **2** CONDUCT, continue, manage, direct, pursue, work at, carry on, practise, engage in, discharge, persist in, see through, follow through, persevere, carry through

prospect noun **1** LIKELIHOOD, chance, possibility, plan, hope, promise, proposal, odds, expectation, probability, anticipation, presumption **2** IDEA, thought, outlook, contemplation **3** VIEW, perspective, landscape, scene, sight, vision, outlook, spectacle, panorama, vista ▷ *plural noun* POSSIBILITIES, openings, chances, future, potential, expectations, outlook, scope ▷ *verb* LOOK, search, seek, survey, explore, drill, go after, dowse

prospective *adjective* **1** POTENTIAL, possible, to come, about to be, upcoming, soon-to-be **2** EXPECTED, coming, future, approaching, likely, looked-for, intended, awaited, hoped-for, anticipated, forthcoming, imminent, destined, eventual, on the cards

prospectus noun CATALOGUE, plan, list, programme, announcement, outline, brochure, handbook, syllabus, synopsis, conspectus

prosper *verb* SUCCEED, advance, progress, thrive, make it (*informal*), flower, get on, do well, flourish, bloom, make good, be fortunate, grow rich, fare well

prosperity noun SUCCESS, riches, plenty, ease, fortune, wealth, boom, luxury, well-being, good times, good fortune, the good life, affluence, life of luxury, life of Riley (*informal*), prosperousness << ANTONYM poverty

prosperous *adjective* **1** WEALTHY, rich, affluent, well-off, in the money (*informal*), blooming, opulent, well-heeled (*informal*), well-to-do, moneyed, in clover (*informal*) << ANTONYM poor **2** SUCCESSFUL, booming, thriving, flourishing, doing well, prospering, on a roll, on the up and up (*Brit*), palmy << ANTONYM unsuccessful

prostitute noun WHORE, hooker (*US slang*), pro (*slang*), brass (*slang*), tart (*informal*), hustler (*US & Canad slang*), moll (*slang*), call girl, courtesan, working girl (*facetious slang*), harlot, streetwalker, camp follower, loose woman, fallen woman, scrubber (*Brit & Austral slang*), strumpet, trollop, white slave, bawd (*archaic*), cocotte, fille de joie (*French*) ▷ *verb* CHEAPEN, sell out, pervert, degrade, devalue, squander, demean, debase, profane, misapply

prostitution noun HARLOTRY, the game (*slang*), vice, the oldest profession, whoredom, streetwalking, harlot's trade, Mrs. Warren's profession

prostrate *adjective* **1** PRONE, fallen, flat, horizontal, abject, bowed low, kowtowing, procumbent **2** EXHAUSTED, overcome, depressed, drained, spent, worn out, desolate, dejected, inconsolable, at a low ebb, fagged out (*informal*) **3** HELPLESS, overwhelmed, disarmed, paralysed, powerless, reduced, impotent, defenceless, brought to your knees ▷ *verb* EXHAUST, tire, drain, fatigue, weary, sap, wear out, fag out (*informal*) >> **prostrate yourself** BOW DOWN, submit, kneel, cringe, grovel, fall at someone's feet, bow, kowtow, bend the knee, abase yourself, cast yourself, fall on your knees

protagonist noun **1** SUPPORTER, leader, champion, advocate, exponent, mainstay, prime mover, standard-bearer, moving spirit, torchbearer **2** LEADING CHARACTER, lead, principal, central character, hero *or* heroine

protean *adjective* CHANGEABLE, variable, volatile, versatile, temperamental, ever-changing, mercurial, many-sided, mutable, polymorphous, multiform

protect *verb* KEEP SOMEONE SAFE, defend, keep, support, save, guard, secure, preserve, look after, foster, shelter, screen, barrier, shield, care for, harbour, safeguard, watch over, stick up for (*informal*), cover up for, chaperon, give someone sanctuary, take someone under your wing, mount *or* stand guard over << ANTONYM endanger

protection *noun* 1 SAFETY, charge, care, defence, protecting, security, guarding, custody, safeguard, preservation, aegis, guardianship, safekeeping 2 SAFEGUARD, cover, guard, shelter, screen, barrier, shield, refuge, buffer, bulwark 3 ARMOUR, cover, screen, barrier, shelter, shield, bulwark

protective *adjective* 1 PROTECTING, covering, sheltering, shielding, safeguarding, insulating 2 CARING, defensive, motherly, fatherly, warm, careful, maternal, vigilant, watchful, paternal, possessive

protector *noun* 1 DEFENDER, champion, guard, guardian, counsel, advocate, patron, safeguard, bodyguard, benefactor, guardian angel, tower of strength, knight in shining armour 2 GUARD, screen, protection, shield, pad, cushion, buffer

protégé *or* **protégée** *noun* CHARGE, student, pupil, ward, discovery, dependant

protest *verb* 1 OBJECT, demonstrate, oppose, complain, disagree, cry out, disapprove, say no to, demur, take exception, remonstrate, kick against (*informal*), expostulate, take up the cudgels, express disapproval 2 ASSERT, argue, insist, maintain, declare, vow, testify, contend, affirm, profess, attest, avow, asseverate ▷ *noun* 1 DEMONSTRATION, march, rally, sit-in, demo (*informal*), hikoi (*NZ*) 2 OBJECTION, complaint, declaration, dissent, outcry, disapproval, protestation, demur, formal complaint, remonstrance, demurral

protestation *noun* (*formal*) DECLARATION, pledge, vow, oath, profession, affirmation, avowal, asseveration

protester *noun* 1 DEMONSTRATOR, rebel, dissident, dissenter, agitator, picketers, protest marcher 2 OBJECTOR, opposer, complainer, opponent, dissident, dissenter

protocol *noun* 1 CODE OF BEHAVIOUR, manners, courtesies, conventions, customs, formalities, good form, etiquette, propriety, decorum, rules of conduct, politesse, p's and q's 2 AGREEMENT, contract, treaty, convention, pact, compact, covenant, concordat

prototype *noun* ORIGINAL, model, precedent, first, example, standard, paradigm, archetype, mock-up

protracted *adjective* EXTENDED, long, prolonged, lengthy, time-consuming, never-ending, drawn-out, interminable, spun out, dragged out, long-drawn-out, overlong

protrude *verb* STICK OUT (from), point, project, pop (*of eyes*), extend, come through, stand out, bulge, shoot out, jut, stick out like a sore thumb, obtrude

proud *adjective* 1 SATISFIED, pleased, content, contented, honoured, thrilled, glad, gratified, joyful, appreciative, well-pleased << ANTONYM dissatisfied 2 GLORIOUS, rewarding, memorable, pleasing, satisfying, illustrious, gratifying, exalted, red-letter 3 DISTINGUISHED, great, grand, imposing, magnificent, noble, august, splendid, eminent, majestic, stately, illustrious << ANTONYM lowly 4 CONCEITED, vain, arrogant, stuck-up (*informal*), lordly, imperious, narcissistic, overbearing, snooty (*informal*), haughty, snobbish, egotistical, self-satisfied, disdainful, self-important, presumptuous, boastful, supercilious, high and mighty (*informal*), toffee-nosed (*slang, chiefly Brit*), too big for your boots *or* breeches << ANTONYM humble

prove *verb* 1 TURN OUT, come out, end up, be found to be 2 VERIFY, establish, determine, show, evidence, confirm, demonstrate, justify, ascertain, bear out, attest, substantiate, corroborate, authenticate, evince, show clearly << ANTONYM disprove

proven *adjective* ESTABLISHED, accepted, proved, confirmed, tried, tested, checked, reliable, valid, definite, authentic, certified, verified, attested, undoubted, dependable, trustworthy

provenance *noun* ORIGIN, source, birthplace, derivation

proverb *noun* SAYING, saw, maxim, gnome, adage, dictum, aphorism, byword, apophthegm

proverbial *adjective* CONVENTIONAL, accepted, traditional, famous, acknowledged, typical, well-known, legendary, notorious, customary, famed, archetypal, time-honoured, self-evident, unquestioned, axiomatic

provide *verb* 1 SUPPLY, give, contribute, provision, distribute, outfit, equip, accommodate, donate, furnish, dispense, part with, fork out (*informal*), stock up, cater to, purvey << ANTONYM withhold **2** GIVE, bring, add, produce, present, serve, afford, yield, lend, render, impart **3** STIPULATE, state, require, determine, specify, lay down ▷▷ **provide for someone** SUPPORT, look after, care for, keep, maintain, sustain, take care of, fend for ▷▷ **provide for something** TAKE PRECAUTIONS AGAINST, plan for, prepare for, anticipate, arrange for, get ready for, make plans for, make arrangements for, plan ahead for, take measures against, forearm for

providence *noun* FATE, fortune, destiny, God's will, divine intervention, predestination

provider *noun* **1** SUPPLIER, giver, source, donor, benefactor **2** BREADWINNER, supporter, earner, mainstay, wage earner

providing *or* **provided** *conjunction often with* **that** ON CONDITION THAT, if, subject to, given that, on the assumption that, in the event that, with the proviso that, contingent upon, with the understanding that, as long as, if and only if, upon these terms

province *noun* **1** REGION, section, county, district, territory, zone, patch, colony, domain, dependency, tract **2** AREA, business, concern, responsibility, part, line, charge, role, post, department, field, duty, function, employment, capacity, orbit, sphere, turf (*US slang*), pigeon (*Brit informal*)

provincial *adjective* **1** REGIONAL, state, local, county, district, territorial, parochial **2** RURAL, country, local, home-grown, rustic, homespun, hick (*informal, chiefly US & Canad*), backwoods << ANTONYM urban **3** PAROCHIAL, insular, narrow-minded, unsophisticated, limited, narrow, small-town (*chiefly US*), uninformed, inward-looking, small-minded, parish-pump, upcountry << ANTONYM cosmopolitan ▷ *noun* YOKEL, hick (*informal, chiefly US & Canad*), rustic, country cousin, hayseed (*US & Canad informal*)

provision *noun* **1** SUPPLYING, giving, providing, supply, delivery, distribution, catering, presentation, equipping, furnishing, allocation, fitting out, purveying, accoutrement **2** ARRANGEMENT, plan, planning, preparation, precaution, contingency, prearrangement **3** FACILITIES, services, funds, resources, means, opportunities, arrangements, assistance, concession(s), allowance(s),

amenities **4** CONDITION, term, agreement, requirement, demand, rider, restriction, qualification, clause, reservation, specification, caveat, proviso, stipulation ▷ *plural noun* FOOD, supplies, stores, feed, fare, rations, eats (*slang*), groceries, tack (*informal*), grub (*slang*), foodstuff, kai (*NZ informal*), sustenance, victuals, edibles, comestibles, provender, nosebag (*slang*), vittles (*obsolete or dialect*), viands, eatables

provisional *adjective* **1** TEMPORARY, interim, transitional, stopgap, pro tem << ANTONYM permanent **2** CONDITIONAL, limited, qualified, contingent, tentative, provisory << ANTONYM definite

proviso *noun* CONDITION, requirement, provision, strings, rider, restriction, qualification, clause, reservation, limitation, stipulation

provocation *noun* **1** CAUSE, reason, grounds, motivation, justification, stimulus, inducement, incitement, instigation, casus belli (*Latin*) **2** OFFENCE, challenge, insult, taunt, injury, dare, grievance, annoyance, affront, indignity, red rag, vexation

provocative *adjective* **1** OFFENSIVE, provoking, insulting, challenging, disturbing, stimulating, annoying, outrageous, aggravating (*informal*), incensing, galling, goading **2** SUGGESTIVE, tempting, stimulating, exciting, inviting, sexy (*informal*), arousing, erotic, seductive, alluring, tantalizing

provoke *verb* **1** ANGER, insult, annoy, offend, irritate, infuriate, hassle (*informal*), aggravate (*informal*), incense, enrage, gall, put someone out, madden, exasperate, vex, affront, chafe, irk, rile, pique, get on someone's nerves (*informal*), get someone's back up, put someone's back up, try someone's patience, nark (*Brit, Austral & NZ slang*), make someone's blood boil, get in someone's hair (*informal*), rub someone up the wrong way, hack someone off (*informal*) << ANTONYM pacify **2** ROUSE, cause, produce, lead to, move, fire, promote, occasion, excite, inspire, generate, prompt, stir, stimulate, motivate, induce, bring about, evoke, give rise to, precipitate, elicit, inflame, incite, instigate, kindle, foment, call forth, draw forth, bring on *or* down << ANTONYM curb

prowess *noun* **1** SKILL, ability, talent, expertise, facility, command, genius, excellence, accomplishment, mastery, attainment, aptitude, dexterity, adroitness,

adeptness, expertness << ANTONYM
inability **2** BRAVERY, daring, courage,
heroism, mettle, boldness, gallantry,
valour, fearlessness, intrepidity, hardihood,
valiance, dauntlessness, doughtiness
<< ANTONYM cowardice

prowl *verb* MOVE STEALTHILY, hunt, patrol,
range, steal, cruise, stalk, sneak, lurk, roam,
rove, scavenge, slink, skulk, nose around

proximity *noun* NEARNESS, closeness, vicinity,
neighbourhood, juxtaposition, contiguity,
propinquity, adjacency

proxy *noun* REPRESENTATIVE, agent, deputy,
substitute, factor, attorney, delegate,
surrogate

prudence *noun* **1** CAUTION, care, discretion,
vigilance, wariness, circumspection,
canniness, heedfulness **2** WISDOM, common
sense, good sense, good judgment, sagacity,
judiciousness **3** THRIFT, economy, planning,
saving, precaution, foresight, providence,
preparedness, good management,
husbandry, frugality, forethought,
economizing, far-sightedness, careful
budgeting

prudent *adjective* **1** CAUTIOUS, careful, wary,
discreet, canny, vigilant, circumspect
<< ANTONYM careless **2** WISE, politic,
sensible, sage, shrewd, discerning, judicious,
sagacious << ANTONYM unwise **3** THRIFTY,
economical, sparing, careful, canny,
provident, frugal, far-sighted << ANTONYM
extravagant

prudish *adjective* PRIM, formal, proper,
stuffy, puritanical, demure, squeamish,
narrow-minded, starchy (*informal*), prissy
(*informal*), strait-laced, Victorian, priggish,
schoolmarmish (*Brit informal*), old-maidish
(*informal*), niminy-piminy, overmodest,
overnice << ANTONYM broad-minded

prune *verb* **1** CUT, trim, clip, dock, shape,
cut back, shorten, snip, lop, pare down
2 REDUCE, cut, cut back, trim, cut down, pare
down, make reductions in

prurient *adjective* **1** LECHEROUS, longing, lewd,
salacious, lascivious, itching, hankering,
voyeuristic, lustful, libidinous, desirous,
concupiscent **2** INDECENT, dirty, erotic,
obscene, steamy (*informal*), pornographic,
X-rated (*informal*), salacious, smutty

pry *verb* BE INQUISITIVE, peer, interfere, poke,
peep, meddle, intrude, snoop (*informal*), nose
into, be nosy (*informal*), be a busybody, ferret
about, poke your nose in *or* into (*informal*)

prying *adjective* INQUISITIVE, spying,

curious, interfering, meddling, intrusive,
eavesdropping, snooping (*informal*), snoopy
(*informal*), impertinent, nosy (*informal*),
meddlesome

psalm *noun* HYMN, carol, chant, paean, song
of praise

pseudonym *noun* FALSE NAME, alias,
incognito, stage name, pen name, assumed
name, nom de guerre, nom de plume,
professional name

psyche *noun* SOUL, mind, self, spirit,
personality, individuality, subconscious,
true being, anima, essential nature, pneuma
(*philosophy*), innermost self, inner man,
wairua (*NZ*)

psychedelic *adjective* **1** HALLUCINOGENIC,
mind-blowing (*informal*), psychoactive,
hallucinatory, mind-bending (*informal*),
psychotropic, mind-expanding,
consciousness-expanding, psychotomimetic
2 MULTICOLOURED, wild, crazy, freaky (*slang*),
kaleidoscopic

psychiatrist *noun* PSYCHOTHERAPIST, analyst,
therapist, psychologist, shrink (*slang*),
psychoanalyst, psychoanalyser, headshrinker
(*slang*)

psychic *adjective* **1** SUPERNATURAL,
mystic, occult, clairvoyant, telepathic,
extrasensory, preternatural, telekinetic
2 MYSTICAL, spiritual, magical, otherworldly, paranormal, preternatural
3 PSYCHOLOGICAL, emotional, mental,
spiritual, inner, psychiatric, cognitive,
psychogenic ▷ *noun* CLAIRVOYANT, fortune
teller

psychological *adjective* **1** MENTAL, emotional,
intellectual, inner, cognitive, cerebral
2 IMAGINARY, psychosomatic, unconscious,
subconscious, subjective, irrational, unreal,
all in the mind

psychology *noun* **1** BEHAVIOURISM, study of
personality, science of mind **2** (*informal*)
WAY OF THINKING, attitude, behaviour,
temperament, mentality, thought processes,
mental processes, what makes you tick,
mental make-up

psychopath *noun* MADMAN, lunatic, maniac,
psychotic, nutter (*Brit slang*), nutcase (*slang*),
sociopath, headcase (*informal*), mental case
(*slang*), headbanger (*informal*), insane person
▷ see **mad**

psychotic *adjective* MAD, mental (*slang*),
insane, lunatic, demented, unbalanced,
deranged, psychopathic, round the bend
(*Brit slang*), certifiable, off your head (*slang*),

off your trolley (*slang*), not right in the head, non compos mentis (*Latin*), off your rocker (*slang*), off your chump ▷ *noun* LUNATIC, maniac, psychopath, nut (*slang*), psycho (*slang*), loony (*slang*), nutter (*Brit slang*), nutcase (*slang*), headcase (*informal*), mental case (*slang*), headbanger (*informal*) ▷ see **mad**

pub *or* **public house** *noun* TAVERN, bar, inn, local (*Brit informal*), saloon, watering hole (*facetious slang*), boozer (*Brit, Austral & NZ informal*), beer parlour (*Canad*), beverage room (*Canad*), roadhouse, hostelry (*archaic or facetious*), alehouse (*archaic*), taproom

puberty *noun* ADOLESCENCE, teenage, teens, young adulthood, pubescence, awkward age, juvenescence

public *noun* PEOPLE, society, country, population, masses, community, nation, everyone, citizens, voters, electorate, multitude, populace, hoi polloi, Joe Public (*slang*), Joe Six-Pack (*US slang*), commonalty ▷ *adjective* **1** CIVIC, government, state, national, local, official, community, social, federal, civil, constitutional, municipal **2** GENERAL, popular, national, shared, common, widespread, universal, collective **3** OPEN, community, accessible, communal, open to the public, unrestricted, free to all, not private << ANTONYM private **4** WELL-KNOWN, leading, important, respected, famous, celebrated, recognized, distinguished, prominent, influential, notable, renowned, eminent, famed, noteworthy, in the public eye **5** KNOWN, published, exposed, open, obvious, acknowledged, recognized, plain, patent, notorious, overt, in circulation << ANTONYM secret

publication *noun* **1** PAMPHLET, book, newspaper, magazine, issue, title, leaflet, brochure, booklet, paperback, hardback, periodical, zine (*informal*), handbill **2** ANNOUNCEMENT, publishing, broadcasting, reporting, airing, appearance, declaration, advertisement, disclosure, proclamation, notification, dissemination, promulgation

publicity *noun* **1** ADVERTISING, press, promotion, hype, boost, build-up, plug (*informal*), puff, ballyhoo (*informal*), puffery (*informal*), boosterism **2** ATTENTION, exposure, fame, celebrity, fuss, public interest, limelight, notoriety, media attention, renown, public notice

publicize *verb* **1** ADVERTISE, promote, plug

(*informal*), hype, push, spotlight, puff, play up, write up, spread about, beat the drum for (*informal*), give publicity to, bring to public notice **2** MAKE KNOWN, report, reveal, publish, broadcast, leak, disclose, proclaim, circulate, make public, divulge << ANTONYM keep secret

public-spirited *adjective* ALTRUISTIC, generous, humanitarian, charitable, philanthropic, unselfish, community-minded

publish *verb* **1** PUT OUT, issue, produce, print, bring out **2** ANNOUNCE, reveal, declare, spread, advertise, broadcast, leak, distribute, communicate, disclose, proclaim, circulate, impart, publicize, divulge, promulgate, shout from the rooftops (*informal*), blow wide open (*slang*)

pucker *verb* WRINKLE, tighten, purse, pout, contract, gather, knit, crease, compress, crumple, ruffle, furrow, screw up, crinkle, draw together, ruck up, ruckle ▷ *noun* WRINKLE, fold, crease, crumple, ruck, crinkle, ruckle

pudding *noun* DESSERT, afters (*Brit informal*), sweet, pud (*informal*), second course, last course

puerile *adjective* CHILDISH, juvenile, naive, weak, silly, ridiculous, foolish, petty, trivial, irresponsible, immature, infantile, inane, babyish, jejune << ANTONYM mature

puff *verb* **1** SMOKE, draw, drag (*slang*), suck, inhale, pull at *or* on **2** BREATHE HEAVILY, pant, exhale, blow, gasp, gulp, wheeze, fight for breath, puff and pant **3** PROMOTE, push, plug (*informal*), hype, publicize, advertise, praise, crack up (*informal*), big up (*slang, chiefly Caribbean*), overpraise ▷ *noun* **1** DRAG (*slang*), pull, smoke **2** BLAST, breath, flurry, whiff, draught, gust, emanation **3** ADVERTISEMENT, ad (*informal*), promotion, plug (*informal*), good word, commendation, sales talk, favourable mention, piece of publicity ▷▷ **puff out** *or* **up** SWELL, expand, enlarge, inflate, dilate, distend, bloat

puffy *adjective* SWOLLEN, enlarged, inflated, inflamed, bloated, puffed up, distended

pugnacious *adjective* AGGRESSIVE, contentious, irritable, belligerent, combative, petulant, antagonistic, argumentative, bellicose, irascible, quarrelsome, hot-tempered, choleric, disputatious, aggers (*Austral slang*), biffo (*Austral slang*) << ANTONYM peaceful

puke *verb* (*slang*) VOMIT, be sick, throw up

(*informal*), spew, heave, regurgitate, disgorge, retch, be nauseated, chuck (*Austral & NZ informal*), barf (*US slang*), chunder (*slang, chiefly Austral*), upchuck (*US slang*), do a technicolour yawn (*slang*), toss your cookies (*US slang*)

pull *verb* **1** DRAW, haul, drag, trail, tow, tug, jerk, yank, prise, wrench, lug, wrest << ANTONYM push **2** EXTRACT, pick, remove, gather, take out, weed, pluck, cull, uproot, draw out << ANTONYM insert **3** (*informal*) ATTRACT, draw, bring in, tempt, lure, interest, entice, pull in, magnetize << ANTONYM repel **4** STRAIN, tear, stretch, rend, rip, wrench, dislocate, sprain ▷ *noun* **1** TUG, jerk, yank, twitch, heave << ANTONYM shove **2** ATTRACTION, appeal, lure, fascination, force, draw, influence, magnetism, enchantment, drawing power, enticement, allurement **3** FORCE, exertion, magnetism, forcefulness **4** PUFF, drag (*slang*), inhalation **5** (*informal*) INFLUENCE, power, authority, say, standing, weight, advantage, muscle, sway, prestige, clout (*informal*), leverage, kai (*NZ informal*) ▷▷ **pull a fast one on someone** (*informal*) TRICK, cheat, con (*informal*), take advantage of, deceive, defraud, swindle, bamboozle (*informal*), hoodwink, take for a ride (*informal*), put one over on (*informal*) ▷▷ **pull in** DRAW IN, stop, park, arrive, come in, halt, draw up, pull over, come to a halt ▷▷ **pull out (of)** **1** WITHDRAW, retire from, abandon, quit, step down from, back out, bow out, stop participating in **2** LEAVE, abandon, get out, quit, retreat from, depart, evacuate ▷▷ **pull someone in** (*Brit slang*) ARREST, nail (*informal*), bust (*informal*), lift (*slang*), run in (*slang*), collar (*informal*), pinch (*informal*), nab (*informal*), take someone into custody, feel someone's collar (*slang*) ▷▷ **pull someone up** REPRIMAND, lecture, rebuke, reproach, carpet (*informal*), censure, scold, berate, castigate, admonish, chastise, tear into (*informal*), read the riot act to, tell someone off (*informal*), reprove, upbraid, take someone to task, tick someone off (*informal*), read someone the riot act, bawl someone out (*informal*), dress someone down (*informal*), lambaste, give someone an earful, chew someone out (*US & Canad informal*), tear someone off a strip (*Brit informal*), haul someone over the coals, give someone a dressing down, give someone a rocket (*Brit & NZ informal*), slap someone on the wrist,

rap someone over the knuckles ▷▷ **pull something apart** *or* **to pieces** **1** DISMANTLE, strip down, disassemble, take something apart, break something up, take something to bits **2** CRITICIZE, attack, blast, pan (*informal*), slam (*slang*), put down, run down, slate (*informal*), tear into (*informal*), lay into (*informal*), flay, diss (*slang, chiefly US*), find fault with, lambast(e), pick holes in ▷▷ **pull something down** DEMOLISH, level, destroy, dismantle, remove, flatten, knock down, take down, tear down, bulldoze, raze, lay waste, raze to the ground, kennet (*Austral slang*), jeff (*Austral slang*) ▷▷ **pull something in** **1** ATTRACT, draw, pull, bring in, lure **2** EARN, make, clear, gain, net, collect, be paid, pocket, bring in, gross, take home, rake in ▷▷ **pull something off** **1** (*informal*) SUCCEED IN, manage, establish, effect, complete, achieve, engineer, carry out, crack (*informal*), fulfil, accomplish, execute, discharge, clinch, bring about, carry off, perpetrate, bring off **2** REMOVE, detach, rip off, tear off, doff, wrench off ▷▷ **pull something out** PRODUCE, draw, bring out, draw out ▷▷ **pull something up** UPROOT, raise, lift, weed, dig up, dig out, rip up ▷▷ **pull through** SURVIVE, improve, recover, rally, come through, get better, be all right, recuperate, turn the corner, pull round, get well again ▷▷ **pull up** STOP, park, halt, arrive, brake, draw up, come to a halt, reach a standstill ▷▷ **pull yourself together** (*informal*) GET A GRIP ON YOURSELF, recover, get over it, buck up (*informal*), snap out of it (*informal*), get your act together, regain your composure

pulp *noun* **1** PASTE, mash, pap, mush, semisolid, pomace, semiliquid **2** FLESH, meat, marrow, soft part ▷ *modifier* CHEAP, sensational, lurid, mushy (*informal*), trashy, rubbishy ▷ *verb* CRUSH, squash, mash, pulverize

pulsate *verb* THROB, pound, beat, hammer, pulse, tick, thump, quiver, vibrate, thud, palpitate

pulse *noun* BEAT, rhythm, vibration, beating, stroke, throb, throbbing, oscillation, pulsation ▷ *verb* BEAT, tick, throb, vibrate, pulsate

pummel *verb* BEAT, punch, pound, strike, knock, belt (*informal*), hammer, bang, batter, thump, clobber (*slang*), lambast(e), beat the living daylights out of, rain blows upon, beat *or* knock seven bells out of (*informal*)

pump *verb* **1** DRIVE OUT, empty, drain, force

out, bail out, siphon, draw off **2** SUPPLY,
send, pour, inject **3** INTERROGATE, probe,
quiz, cross-examine, grill (*informal*), worm
out of, give someone the third degree,
question closely ▷▷ **pump something up**
INFLATE, blow up, fill up, dilate, puff up,
aerate

pun *noun* PLAY ON WORDS, quip, double
entendre, witticism, paronomasia (*rhetoric*),
equivoque

punch¹ *verb* HIT, strike, box, smash, belt
(*informal*), slam, plug (*slang*), bash (*informal*),
sock (*slang*), clout (*informal*), slug, swipe
(*informal*), biff (*slang*), bop (*informal*), wallop
(*informal*), pummel ▷ *noun* **1** BLOW, hit,
knock, bash (*informal*), plug (*slang*), sock
(*slang*), thump, clout (*informal*), jab, swipe
(*informal*), biff (*slang*), bop (*informal*), wallop
(*informal*) **2** (*informal*) EFFECTIVENESS, force,
bite, impact, point, drive, vigour, verve,
forcefulness

punch² *verb* PIERCE, cut, bore, drill, pink,
stamp, puncture, prick, perforate

punch-up *noun* (*Brit informal*) FIGHT, row,
argument, set-to (*informal*), scrap (*informal*),
brawl, free-for-all (*informal*), dust-up
(*informal*), shindig (*informal*), battle royal,
stand-up fight (*informal*), dingdong, shindy
(*informal*), bagarre (*French*), biffo (*Austral
slang*)

punchy *adjective* (*informal*) EFFECTIVE,
spirited, dynamic, lively, storming (*informal*),
aggressive, vigorous, forceful, incisive, in-
your-face (*slang*)

punctual *adjective* ON TIME, timely, early,
prompt, strict, exact, precise, in good time,
on the dot, seasonable << ANTONYM late

punctuality *noun* PROMPTNESS, readiness,
regularity, promptitude

punctuate *verb* INTERRUPT, break, pepper,
sprinkle, intersperse, interject

puncture *noun* **1** FLAT TYRE, flat, flattie (*NZ*)
2 HOLE, opening, break, cut, nick, leak, slit,
rupture, perforation ▷ *verb* **1** PIERCE, cut,
nick, penetrate, prick, rupture, perforate,
impale, bore a hole **2** DEFLATE, go down,
go flat **3** HUMBLE, discourage, disillusion,
flatten, deflate, take down a peg (*informal*)

pundit *noun* EXPERT, guru, maestro, buff
(*informal*), wonk (*informal*), fundi (*S African*),
one of the cognoscenti, (self-appointed)
expert or authority

pungent *adjective* **1** STRONG, hot, spicy,
seasoned, sharp, acid, bitter, stinging, sour,
tart, aromatic, tangy, acrid, peppery, piquant,

highly flavoured, acerb << ANTONYM mild
2 CUTTING, pointed, biting, acute, telling,
sharp, keen, stinging, piercing, penetrating,
poignant, stringent, scathing, acrimonious,
barbed, incisive, sarcastic, caustic,
vitriolic, trenchant, mordant, mordacious
<< ANTONYM dull

punish *verb* DISCIPLINE, correct, castigate,
chastise, beat, sentence, whip, lash, cane,
flog, scourge, chasten, penalize, bring
someone to book, slap someone's wrist,
throw the book at, rap someone's knuckles,
give someone the works (*slang*), give a lesson
to

punishable *adjective* CULPABLE, criminal,
chargeable, indictable, blameworthy,
convictable

punishing *adjective* HARD, taxing, demanding,
grinding, wearing, tiring, exhausting, uphill,
gruelling, strenuous, arduous, burdensome,
backbreaking << ANTONYM easy

punishment *noun* **1** PENALIZING, discipline,
correction, retribution, what for (*informal*),
chastening, just deserts, chastisement,
punitive measures **2** PENALTY, reward,
sanction, penance, comeuppance (*slang*)
3 (*informal*) BEATING, abuse, torture, pain,
victimization, manhandling, maltreatment,
rough treatment **4** ROUGH TREATMENT,
abuse, maltreatment

punitive *adjective* RETALIATORY, in retaliation,
vindictive, in reprisal, revengeful, retaliative,
punitory

punt *verb* BET, back, stake, gamble, lay, wager
▷ *noun* BET, stake, gamble, wager

punter *noun* **1** GAMBLER, better, backer, punt
(*chiefly Brit*) **2** (*informal*) CUSTOMER, guest,
client, patron, member of the audience
3 (*informal*) PERSON, guy (*informal*), fellow,
bloke (*Brit informal*), man in the street

puny *adjective* **1** FEEBLE, weak, frail, little,
tiny, weakly, stunted, diminutive, sickly,
undeveloped, pint-sized (*informal*),
undersized, underfed, dwarfish,
pygmy *or* pigmy << ANTONYM strong
2 INSIGNIFICANT, minor, petty, inferior,
trivial, worthless, trifling, paltry,
inconsequential, piddling (*informal*)

pup *or* **puppy** *noun* WHIPPERSNAPPER,
braggart, whelp, jackanapes, popinjay

pupil *noun* **1** STUDENT, scholar, schoolboy
or schoolgirl, schoolchild << ANTONYM
teacher **2** LEARNER, student, follower,
trainee, novice, beginner, apprentice,
disciple, protégé, neophyte, tyro,

catechumen << ANTONYM instructor

puppet *noun* 1 MARIONETTE, doll, glove puppet, finger puppet 2 PAWN, tool, instrument, creature, dupe, gull (*archaic*), figurehead, mouthpiece, stooge, cat's-paw

purchase *verb* BUY, pay for, obtain, get, score (*slang*), gain, pick up, secure, acquire, invest in, shop for, get hold of, come by, procure, make a purchase of << ANTONYM sell ▷ *noun* 1 ACQUISITION, buy, investment, property, gain, asset, possession 2 GRIP, hold, support, footing, influence, edge, advantage, grasp, lever, leverage, foothold, toehold

purchaser *noun* BUYER, customer, consumer, vendee (*law*) << ANTONYM seller

pure *adjective* 1 UNMIXED, real, clear, true, simple, natural, straight, perfect, genuine, neat, authentic, flawless, unalloyed << ANTONYM adulterated 2 CLEAN, immaculate, sterile, wholesome, sanitary, spotless, sterilized, squeaky-clean, unblemished, unadulterated, untainted, disinfected, uncontaminated, unpolluted, pasteurized, germ-free << ANTONYM contaminated 3 THEORETICAL, abstract, philosophical, speculative, academic, conceptual, hypothetical, conjectural, non-practical << ANTONYM practical 4 COMPLETE, total, perfect, absolute, mere, sheer, patent, utter, outright, thorough, downright, palpable, unqualified, out-and-out, unmitigated << ANTONYM qualified 5 INNOCENT, virgin, modest, good, true, moral, maidenly, upright, honest, immaculate, impeccable, righteous, virtuous, squeaky-clean, blameless, chaste, virginal, unsullied, guileless, uncorrupted, unstained, undefiled, unspotted << ANTONYM corrupt

purely *adverb* ABSOLUTELY, just, only, completely, simply, totally, entirely, exclusively, plainly, merely, solely, wholly

purgatory *noun* TORMENT, agony, murder (*informal*), hell (*informal*), torture, misery, hell on earth

purge *verb* 1 RID, clear, cleanse, strip, empty, void 2 GET RID OF, kill, remove, dismiss, axe (*informal*), expel, wipe out, oust, eradicate, eject, do away with, liquidate, exterminate, sweep out, rout out, wipe from the face of the earth, rid somewhere of 3 CLEANSE, clear, purify, wash, clean out, expiate ▷ *noun* REMOVAL, elimination, crushing, expulsion, suppression, liquidation, cleanup, witch hunt, eradication, ejection

purify *verb* 1 CLEAN, filter, cleanse, refine, clarify,

disinfect, fumigate, decontaminate, sanitize << ANTONYM contaminate 2 ABSOLVE, cleanse, redeem, exonerate, sanctify, exculpate, shrive, lustrate << ANTONYM sully

purist *noun* STICKLER, traditionalist, perfectionist, classicist, pedant, formalist, literalist

puritan *noun* MORALIST, fanatic, zealot, prude, pietist, rigorist ▷ *adjective* STRICT, austere, puritanical, narrow, severe, intolerant, ascetic, narrow-minded, moralistic, prudish, hidebound, strait-laced

puritanical *adjective* STRICT, forbidding, puritan, stuffy, narrow, severe, proper, stiff, rigid, disapproving, austere, fanatical, bigoted, prim, ascetic, narrow-minded, prudish, strait-laced << ANTONYM liberal

puritanism *noun* STRICTNESS, austerity, severity, zeal, piety, rigidity, fanaticism, narrowness, asceticism, moralism, prudishness, rigorism, piousness

purity *noun* 1 CLEANNESS, clarity, cleanliness, brilliance, genuineness, wholesomeness, fineness, clearness, pureness, faultlessness, immaculateness, untaintedness << ANTONYM impurity 2 INNOCENCE, virtue, integrity, honesty, decency, sincerity, virginity, piety, chastity, rectitude, guilelessness, virtuousness, chasteness, blamelessness << ANTONYM immorality

purport *verb* CLAIM, allege, proclaim, maintain, declare, pretend, assert, pose as, profess

purpose *noun* 1 REASON, point, idea, goal, grounds, design, aim, basis, principle, function, object, intention, objective, motive, motivation, justification, impetus, the why and wherefore 2 AIM, end, plan, hope, view, goal, design, project, target, wish, scheme, desire, object, intention, objective, ambition, aspiration, Holy Grail (*informal*) 3 DETERMINATION, commitment, resolve, will, resolution, initiative, enterprise, ambition, conviction, motivation, persistence, tenacity, firmness, constancy, single-mindedness, steadfastness 4 USE, good, return, result, effect, value, benefit, profit, worth, gain, advantage, outcome, utility, merit, mileage (*informal*), avail, behoof (*archaic*) ▷▷ **on purpose** DELIBERATELY, purposely, consciously, intentionally, knowingly, wilfully, by design, wittingly, calculatedly, designedly

purposeful *adjective* DETERMINED, resolved,

resolute, decided, firm, settled, positive, fixed, deliberate, single-minded, tenacious, strong-willed, steadfast, immovable, unfaltering << ANTONYM undecided ▷ see **purpose**

purposely *adverb* DELIBERATELY, expressly, consciously, intentionally, knowingly, with intent, on purpose, wilfully, by design, calculatedly, designedly << ANTONYM accidentally ▷ see **purpose**

purse *noun* 1 POUCH, wallet, money-bag 2 (*US*) HANDBAG, bag, shoulder bag, pocket book, clutch bag 3 FUNDS, means, money, resources, treasury, wealth, exchequer, coffers, wherewithal 4 PRIZE, winnings, award, gift, reward ▷ *verb* PUCKER, close, contract, tighten, knit, wrinkle, pout, press together

pursue *verb* 1 ENGAGE IN, follow, perform, conduct, wage, tackle, take up, work at, carry on, practise, participate in, prosecute, ply, go in for, apply yourself to 2 TRY FOR, seek, desire, search for, aim for, aspire to, work towards, strive for, have as a goal 3 CONTINUE, maintain, carry on, keep on, hold to, see through, adhere to, persist in, proceed in, persevere in 4 FOLLOW, track, hunt, chase, dog, attend, shadow, accompany, harry, tail (*informal*), haunt, plague, hound, stalk, harass, go after, run after, hunt down, give chase to << ANTONYM flee 5 COURT, woo, pay attention to, make up to (*informal*), chase after, pay court to, set your cap at << ANTONYM fight shy of

pursuit *noun* 1 QUEST, seeking, search, aim of, aspiration for, striving towards 2 PURSUING, seeking, tracking, search, hunt, hunting, chase, trail, trailing 3 OCCUPATION, activity, interest, line, pleasure, hobby, pastime, vocation

push *verb* 1 SHOVE, force, press, thrust, drive, knock, sweep, plunge, elbow, bump, ram, poke, propel, nudge, prod, jostle, hustle, bulldoze, impel, manhandle << ANTONYM pull 2 PRESS, operate, depress, squeeze, activate, hold down 3 MAKE *or* FORCE YOUR WAY, move, shoulder, inch, squeeze, thrust, elbow, shove, jostle, work your way, thread your way 4 URGE, encourage, persuade, spur, drive, press, influence, prod, constrain, incite, coerce, egg on, impel, browbeat, exert influence on << ANTONYM discourage 5 PROMOTE, advertise, hype, publicize, boost, plug (*informal*), puff, make known, propagandize, cry up ▷ *noun*

1 SHOVE, thrust, butt, elbow, poke, nudge, prod, jolt << ANTONYM pull 2 (*informal*) EFFORT, charge, attack, campaign, advance, assault, raid, offensive, sally, thrust, blitz, onset 3 (*informal*) DRIVE, go (*informal*), energy, initiative, enterprise, ambition, determination, pep, vitality, vigour, dynamism, get-up-and-go (*informal*), gumption (*informal*) ▷▷ **push off** (*informal*) GO AWAY, leave, get lost (*informal*), clear off (*informal*), depart, beat it (*slang*), light out (*informal*), hit the road (*slang*), hook it (*slang*), slope off, pack your bags (*informal*), make tracks, buzz off (*informal*), hop it (*informal*), shove off (*informal*), skedaddle (*informal*), naff off (*informal*), be off with you, sling your hook (*informal*), make yourself scarce (*informal*), voetsek (*S African offensive*), rack off (*Austral & NZ slang*) ▷▷ **the push** (*informal, chiefly Brit*) DISMISSAL, the sack (*informal*), discharge, the boot (*slang*), your cards (*informal*), your books (*informal*), marching orders (*informal*), the kiss-off (*slang, chiefly US & Canad*), the (old) heave-ho (*informal*), the order of the boot (*slang*)

pushed *adjective often with* **for** (*informal*) SHORT OF, pressed, rushed, tight, hurried, under pressure, in difficulty, up against it (*informal*)

pushover *noun* 1 SUCKER (*slang*), mug (*Brit slang*), stooge (*slang*), soft touch (*slang*), chump (*informal*), walkover (*informal*), easy game (*informal*), easy *or* soft mark (*informal*) 2 (*informal*) PIECE OF CAKE (*Brit informal*), breeze (*US & Canad informal*), picnic (*informal*), child's play (*informal*), plain sailing, doddle (*Brit slang*), walkover (*informal*), cinch (*slang*), cakewalk (*informal*), duck soup (*US slang*) << ANTONYM challenge

pushy *adjective* FORCEFUL, aggressive, assertive, brash, loud, offensive, ambitious, bold, obnoxious, presumptuous, obtrusive, officious, bumptious, self-assertive << ANTONYM shy

put *verb* 1 PLACE, leave, set, position, rest, park (*informal*), plant, establish, lay, stick (*informal*), settle, fix, lean, deposit, dump (*informal*), prop, lay down, put down, situate, set down, stow, bung (*informal*), plonk (*informal*) 2 CONSIGN TO, place, commit to, doom to, condemn to 3 IMPOSE, subject, levy, inflict 4 EXPRESS, state, word, phrase, set, pose, utter 5 PRESENT, suggest, advance,

propose, offer, forward, submit, tender, bring forward, proffer, posit, set before, lay before ▷▷ **put someone away** (*informal*) COMMIT, confine, cage (*informal*), imprison, certify, institutionalize, incarcerate, put in prison, put behind bars, lock up *or* away ▷▷ **put someone down** (*slang*) HUMILIATE, shame, crush, show up, reject, dismiss, condemn, slight, criticize, snub, have a go at (*informal*), deflate, denigrate, belittle, disparage, deprecate, mortify, diss (*slang, chiefly US*) ▷▷ **put someone off**
1 DISCOURAGE, intimidate, deter, daunt, dissuade, demoralize, scare off, dishearten 2 DISCONCERT, confuse, unsettle, throw (*informal*), distress, rattle (*informal*), dismay, perturb, faze, discomfit, take the wind out of someone's sails, nonplus, abash ▷▷ **put someone out 1** INCONVENIENCE, trouble, upset, bother, disturb, impose upon, discomfit, discommode, incommode 2 ANNOY, anger, provoke, irritate, disturb, harass, confound, exasperate, disconcert, nettle, vex, perturb, irk, put on the spot, take the wind out of someone's sails, discountenance, discompose ▷▷ **put someone up 1** ACCOMMODATE, house, board, lodge, quarter, entertain, take someone in, billet, give someone lodging 2 NOMINATE, put forward, offer, present, propose, recommend, float, submit ▷▷ **put someone up to something** ENCOURAGE, urge, persuade, prompt, incite, egg on, goad, put the idea into someone's head ▷▷ **put something across** *or* **over** COMMUNICATE, explain, clarify, express, get through, convey, make clear, spell out, get across, make yourself understood ▷▷ **put something aside** *or* **by 1** SAVE, store, stockpile, deposit, hoard, cache, lay by, stow away, salt away, keep in reserve, squirrel away 2 DISREGARD, forget, ignore, bury, discount, set aside, pay no heed to ▷▷ **put something away 1** STORE AWAY, replace, put back, tidy up, clear away, tidy away, return to its place 2 SAVE, set aside, put aside, keep, deposit, put by, stash away, store away 3 (*informal*) CONSUME, devour, eat up, demolish (*informal*), gobble, guzzle, polish off (*informal*), gulp down, wolf down, pig out on (*informal*) ▷▷ **put something down**
1 RECORD, write down, list, enter, log, take down, inscribe, set down, transcribe, put in black and white 2 REPRESS, crush, suppress, check, silence, overthrow, squash, subdue, quash, quell, stamp out 3 PUT TO SLEEP,

kill, destroy, do away with, put away, put out of its misery ▷▷ **put something down to something** ATTRIBUTE, blame, ascribe, set down, impute, chalk up ▷▷ **put something forward** RECOMMEND, present, suggest, introduce, advance, propose, press, submit, tender, nominate, prescribe, move for, proffer ▷▷ **put something off** POSTPONE, delay, defer, adjourn, put back, hold over, reschedule, put on ice, put on the back burner (*informal*), take a rain check on (*US & Canad informal*) ▷▷ **put something on**
1 DON, dress in, slip into, pull on, climb into, change into, throw on, get dressed in, fling on, pour yourself into, doll yourself up in 2 PRESENT, stage, perform, do, show, produce, mount 3 ADD, gain, increase by 4 BET, back, place, chance, risk, lay, stake, hazard, wager 5 FAKE, affect, assume, simulate, feign, make believe, play-act ▷▷ **put something out 1** ISSUE, release, publish, broadcast, bring out, circulate, make public, make known *verb* 2 EXTINGUISH, smother, blow out, stamp out, douse, snuff out, quench ▷▷ **put something up 1** BUILD, raise, set up, construct, erect, fabricate 2 OFFER, present, mount, put forward 3 PROVIDE, advance, invest, contribute, give, pay up, supply, come up with, pledge, donate, furnish, fork out (*informal*), cough up (*informal*), shell out (*informal*) ▷▷ **put up with something** *or* **someone** (*informal*) STAND, suffer, bear, take, wear (*Brit informal*), stomach, endure, swallow, brook, stand for, lump (*informal*), tolerate, hack (*slang*), abide, countenance ▷▷ **put upon someone** TAKE ADVANTAGE OF, trouble, abuse, harry, exploit, saddle, take for granted, put someone out, inconvenience, beset, overwork, impose upon, take for a fool

putative *adjective* (*formal*) SUPPOSED, reported, assumed, alleged, presumed, reputed, imputed, presumptive, commonly believed
put-down *noun* HUMILIATION, slight, snub, knock (*informal*), dig, sneer, rebuff, barb, sarcasm, kick in the teeth (*slang*), gibe, disparagement, one in the eye (*informal*)
puzzle *verb* PERPLEX, beat (*slang*), confuse, baffle, stump, bewilder, confound, mystify, faze, flummox, bemuse, nonplus ▷ *noun*
1 PROBLEM, riddle, maze, labyrinth, question, conundrum, teaser, poser, brain-teaser (*informal*) 2 MYSTERY, problem, paradox, enigma, conundrum ▷▷ **puzzle over something** THINK ABOUT, study, wonder

about, mull over, muse on, think hard about, ponder on, brood over, ask yourself about, cudgel *or* rack your brains ▷▷ **puzzle something out** SOLVE, work out, figure out, unravel, see, get, crack, resolve, sort out, clear up, decipher, think through, suss (out) (*slang*), get the answer of, find the key to, crack the code of

puzzled *adjective* PERPLEXED, beaten, confused, baffled, lost, stuck, stumped, doubtful, at sea, bewildered, mixed up, at a loss, mystified, clueless, nonplussed, flummoxed, in a fog, without a clue

puzzlement *noun* PERPLEXITY, questioning, surprise, doubt, wonder, confusion, uncertainty, bewilderment, disorientation, bafflement, mystification, doubtfulness

puzzling *adjective* PERPLEXING, baffling, bewildering, hard, involved, misleading, unclear, ambiguous, enigmatic, incomprehensible, mystifying, inexplicable, unaccountable, knotty, unfathomable, labyrinthine, full of surprises, abstruse, beyond you, oracular << ANTONYM simple

pygmy *or* **pigmy** *modifier* SMALL, miniature, dwarf, tiny, wee, stunted, diminutive, minuscule, midget, elfin, undersized, teeny-weeny, Lilliputian, dwarfish, teensy-weensy, pygmean ▷ *noun* 1 MIDGET, dwarf, shrimp (*informal*), Lilliputian, Tom Thumb, munchkin (*informal, chiefly US*), homunculus, manikin 2 NONENTITY, nobody, lightweight (*informal*), mediocrity, cipher, small fry, pipsqueak (*informal*)

quack *noun* CHARLATAN, fraud, fake, pretender, humbug, impostor, mountebank, phoney *or* phony (*informal*) ▷ *modifier* FAKE, fraudulent, phoney *or* phony (*informal*), pretended, sham, counterfeit

quaff *verb* DRINK, gulp, swig (*informal*), have, down, swallow, slug, guzzle, imbibe, partake of

quagmire *noun* **1** PREDICAMENT, difficulty, quandary, pass, fix (*informal*), jam (*informal*), dilemma, pinch, plight, scrape (*informal*), muddle, pickle (*informal*), impasse, entanglement, imbroglio **2** BOG, marsh, swamp, slough, fen, mire, morass, quicksand, muskeg (*Canad*)

quail *verb* SHRINK, cringe, flinch, shake, faint, tremble, quake, shudder, falter, droop, blanch, recoil, cower, blench, have cold feet (*informal*)

quaint *adjective* **1** UNUSUAL, odd, curious, original, strange, bizarre, fantastic, old-fashioned, peculiar, eccentric, queer, rum (*Brit slang*), singular, fanciful, whimsical, droll << ANTONYM ordinary **2** OLD-FASHIONED, charming, picturesque, antique, gothic, old-world, antiquated << ANTONYM modern

quake *verb* SHAKE, tremble, quiver, move, rock, shiver, throb, shudder, wobble, waver, vibrate, pulsate, quail, totter, convulse

qualification *noun* **1** ELIGIBILITY, quality, ability, skill, capacity, fitness, attribute, capability, endowment(s), accomplishment, achievement, aptitude, suitability, suitableness **2** CONDITION, restriction, proviso, requirement, rider, exception, criterion, reservation, allowance, objection, limitation, modification, exemption, prerequisite, caveat, stipulation

qualified *adjective* **1** CAPABLE, trained, experienced, seasoned, able, fit, expert, talented, chartered, efficient, practised, licensed, certificated, equipped, accomplished, eligible, competent, skilful, adept, knowledgeable, proficient << ANTONYM untrained **2** RESTRICTED, limited, provisional, conditional, reserved, guarded, bounded, adjusted, moderated, adapted, confined, modified, tempered, cautious, refined, amended, contingent, tentative, hesitant, circumscribed, equivocal << ANTONYM unconditional

qualify *verb* **1** CERTIFY, equip, empower, train, ground, condition, prepare, fit, commission, ready, permit, sanction, endow, capacitate << ANTONYM disqualify **2** BE DESCRIBED, count, be considered as, be named, be counted, be eligible, be characterized, be designated, be distinguished **3** RESTRICT, limit, reduce, vary, ease, moderate, adapt, modify, regulate, diminish, temper, soften, restrain, lessen, mitigate, abate, tone down, assuage, modulate, circumscribe

quality *noun* **1** STANDARD, standing, class, condition, value, rank, grade, merit, classification, calibre **2** EXCELLENCE, status, merit, position, value, worth, distinction, virtue, superiority, calibre, eminence, pre-eminence **3** CHARACTERISTIC, feature, attribute, point, side, mark, property, aspect, streak, trait, facet, quirk, peculiarity, idiosyncrasy **4** NATURE, character, constitution, make, sort, kind, worth, description, essence

qualm *noun* MISGIVING, doubt, uneasiness, regret, anxiety, uncertainty, reluctance, hesitation, remorse, apprehension, disquiet, scruple, compunction, twinge *or* pang of conscience

quandary *noun* DIFFICULTY, dilemma,

predicament, puzzle, uncertainty, embarrassment, plight, strait, impasse, bewilderment, perplexity, delicate situation, cleft stick

quantity noun **1** AMOUNT, lot, total, sum, part, portion, quota, aggregate, number, allotment **2** SIZE, measure, mass, volume, length, capacity, extent, bulk, magnitude, greatness, expanse

quarrel noun DISAGREEMENT, fight, row, difference (of opinion), argument, dispute, controversy, breach, scrap (*informal*), disturbance, misunderstanding, contention, feud, fray, brawl, spat, squabble, strife, wrangle, skirmish, vendetta, discord, fracas, commotion, tiff, altercation, broil, tumult, dissension, affray, shindig (*informal*), disputation, dissidence, shindy (*informal*), bagarre (*French*), biffo (*Austral slang*) << ANTONYM accord ▷ verb DISAGREE, fight, argue, row, clash, dispute, scrap (*informal*), differ, fall out (*informal*), brawl, squabble, spar, wrangle, bicker, be at odds, lock horns, cross swords, fight like cat and dog, go at it hammer and tongs, altercate << ANTONYM get on or along (with)

quarrelsome adjective ARGUMENTATIVE, belligerent, pugnacious, cross, contentious, irritable, combative, fractious, petulant, ill-tempered, irascible, cantankerous, litigious, querulous, peevish, choleric, disputatious << ANTONYM easy-going

quarry noun PREY, victim, game, goal, aim, prize, objective

quarter noun **1** DISTRICT, region, neighbourhood, place, point, part, side, area, position, station, spot, territory, zone, location, province, colony, locality **2** MERCY, pity, compassion, favour, charity, sympathy, tolerance, kindness, forgiveness, indulgence, clemency, leniency, forbearance, lenity ▷ verb ACCOMMODATE, house, lodge, place, board, post, station, install, put up, billet, give accommodation, provide with accommodation

quarters plural noun LODGINGS, rooms, accommodation, post, station, chambers, digs (*Brit informal*), shelter, lodging, residence, dwelling, barracks, abode, habitation, billet, domicile, cantonment (*military*)

quash verb **1** ANNUL, overturn, reverse, cancel, overthrow, set aside, void, revoke, overrule, rescind, invalidate, nullify, declare null and void **2** SUPPRESS, crush, put down, beat,

destroy, overthrow, squash, subdue, repress, quell, extinguish, quench, extirpate

quaver verb TREMBLE, shake, quiver, thrill, quake, shudder, flicker, flutter, waver, vibrate, pulsate, oscillate, trill, twitter

queasy adjective **1** SICK, ill, nauseous, squeamish, upset, uncomfortable, crook (*Austral & NZ informal*), queer, unwell, giddy, nauseated, groggy (*informal*), off colour, bilious, indisposed, green around the gills (*informal*), sickish **2** UNEASY, concerned, worried, troubled, disturbed, anxious, uncertain, restless, ill at ease, fidgety

queen noun **1** SOVEREIGN, ruler, monarch, leader, Crown, princess, majesty, head of state, Her Majesty, empress, crowned head **2** LEADING LIGHT, star, favourite, celebrity, darling, mistress, idol, big name, doyenne

queer adjective **1** STRANGE, odd, funny, unusual, extraordinary, remarkable, curious, weird, peculiar, abnormal, rum (*Brit slang*), uncommon, erratic, singular, eerie, unnatural, unconventional, uncanny, disquieting, unorthodox, outlandish, left-field (*informal*), anomalous, droll, atypical, outré << ANTONYM normal **2** FAINT, dizzy, giddy, queasy, light-headed, reeling

quell verb **1** SUPPRESS, crush, put down, defeat, overcome, conquer, subdue, stifle, overpower, quash, extinguish, stamp out, vanquish, squelch **2** CALM, quiet, silence, moderate, dull, soothe, alleviate, appease, allay, mitigate, assuage, pacify, mollify, deaden

quench verb **1** SATISFY, appease, allay, satiate, slake, sate **2** PUT OUT, extinguish, douse, end, check, destroy, crush, suppress, stifle, smother, snuff out, squelch

query noun **1** QUESTION, inquiry, problem, demand **2** DOUBT, suspicion, reservation, objection, hesitation, scepticism ▷ verb **1** QUESTION, challenge, doubt, suspect, dispute, object to, distrust, mistrust, call into question, disbelieve, feel uneasy about, throw doubt on, harbour reservations about **2** ASK, inquire or enquire, question

quest noun **1** SEARCH, hunt, mission, enterprise, undertaking, exploration, crusade **2** EXPEDITION, journey, adventure, voyage, pilgrimage

question noun **1** INQUIRY, enquiry, query, investigation, examination, interrogation << ANTONYM answer **2** DIFFICULTY, problem, doubt, debate, argument, dispute, controversy, confusion, uncertainty, query, contention, misgiving, can of worms (*informal*), dubiety **3** ISSUE, point, matter, subject, problem, debate, proposal, theme, motion, topic, proposition, bone of contention, point at issue ▷ *verb* **1** INTERROGATE, cross-examine, interview, examine, investigate, pump (*informal*), probe, grill (*informal*), quiz, ask questions, sound out, catechize **2** DISPUTE, challenge, doubt, suspect, oppose, query, distrust, mistrust, call in question, disbelieve, impugn, cast aspersions on, cast doubt upon, controvert << ANTONYM accept ▷▷ **in question** UNDER DISCUSSION, at issue, under consideration, in doubt, on the agenda, to be discussed, for debate, open to debate ▷▷ **out of the question** IMPOSSIBLE, unthinkable, inconceivable, not on (*informal*), hopeless, unimaginable, unworkable, unattainable, unobtainable, not feasible, impracticable, unachievable, unrealizable, not worth considering, not to be thought of

questionable *adjective* DUBIOUS, suspect, doubtful, controversial, uncertain, suspicious, dodgy (*Brit, Austral & NZ informal*), unreliable, shady (*informal*), debatable, unproven, fishy (*informal*), moot, arguable, iffy (*informal*), equivocal, problematical, disputable, controvertible, dubitable, shonky (*Austral & NZ informal*) << ANTONYM indisputable

queue *noun* LINE, row, file, train, series, chain, string, column, sequence, succession, procession, crocodile (*Brit informal*), progression, cavalcade, concatenation

quibble *verb* SPLIT HAIRS, carp, cavil, prevaricate, beat about the bush, equivocate ▷ *noun* OBJECTION, complaint, niggle, protest, criticism, nicety, equivocation, prevarication, cavil, quiddity, sophism

quick *adjective* **1** FAST, swift, speedy, express, active, cracking (*Brit informal*), smart, rapid, fleet, brisk, hasty, headlong, nippy (*informal*), pdq (*slang*) << ANTONYM slow **2** BRIEF, passing, hurried, flying, fleeting, summary, lightning, short-lived, hasty, cursory, perfunctory << ANTONYM long **3** IMMEDIATE, instant, prompt, sudden, abrupt, instantaneous, expeditious **4** EXCITABLE, passionate, impatient, abrupt, hasty, irritable, touchy, curt, petulant, irascible, testy << ANTONYM calm **5** INTELLIGENT, bright (*informal*), alert, sharp, acute, smart, clever, all there

(*informal*), shrewd, discerning, astute, receptive, perceptive, quick-witted, quick on the uptake (*informal*), nimble-witted << ANTONYM stupid

quicken *verb* **1** SPEED UP, hurry, accelerate, hasten, gee up **2** STIMULATE, inspire, arouse, excite, strengthen, revive, refresh, activate, animate, rouse, incite, resuscitate, energize, revitalize, kindle, galvanize, invigorate, reinvigorate, vitalize, vivify

quickly *adverb* **1** SWIFTLY, rapidly, hurriedly, speedily, fast, quick, hastily, briskly, at high speed, apace, at full speed, hell for leather (*informal*), like lightning, at the speed of light, at full tilt, hotfoot, at a rate of knots (*informal*), like the clappers (*Brit informal*), pdq (*slang*), like nobody's business (*informal*), with all speed, posthaste, lickety-split (*US informal*), like greased lightning (*informal*), at *or* on the double << ANTONYM slowly **2** SOON, speedily, as soon as possible, momentarily (*US*), instantaneously, pronto (*informal*), a.s.a.p. (*informal*) **3** IMMEDIATELY, instantly, at once, directly, promptly, abruptly, without delay, expeditiously

quick-witted *adjective* CLEVER, bright (*informal*), sharp, keen, smart, alert, shrewd, astute, perceptive << ANTONYM slow

quid pro quo *noun* EXCHANGE, interchange, tit for tat, equivalent, compensation, retaliation, reprisal, substitution

quiet *adjective* **1** SOFT, low, muted, lowered, whispered, faint, suppressed, stifled, hushed, muffled, inaudible, indistinct, low-pitched << ANTONYM loud **2** PEACEFUL, silent, hushed, soundless, noiseless << ANTONYM noisy **3** CALM, peaceful, tranquil, contented, gentle, mild, serene, pacific, placid, restful, untroubled << ANTONYM exciting **4** STILL, motionless, calm, peaceful, tranquil, untroubled << ANTONYM troubled **5** UNDISTURBED, isolated, secluded, private, secret, retired, sequestered, unfrequented << ANTONYM crowded **6** SILENT, dumb **7** RESERVED, retiring, shy, collected, gentle, mild, composed, serene, sedate, meek, placid, docile, unflappable (*informal*), phlegmatic, peaceable, imperturbable, equable, even-tempered, unexcitable << ANTONYM excitable **8** SUBDUED, conservative, plain, sober, simple, modest, restrained, unassuming, unpretentious, unobtrusive << ANTONYM bright ▷ *noun* PEACE, rest, tranquillity, ease, silence, solitude, serenity, stillness, repose, calmness,

quietness, peacefulness, restfulness
<< ANTONYM noise

quieten *verb* 1 SILENCE, subdue, stifle, still, stop, quiet, mute, hush, quell, muffle, shush (*informal*) 2 SOOTHE, calm, allay, dull, blunt, alleviate, appease, lull, mitigate, assuage, mollify, deaden, tranquillize, palliate
<< ANTONYM provoke

quietly *adverb* 1 NOISELESSLY, silently 2 SOFTLY, in hushed tones, in a low voice *or* whisper, inaudibly, in an undertone, under your breath 3 PRIVATELY, secretly, confidentially 4 CALMLY, serenely, placidly, patiently, mildly, meekly, contentedly, dispassionately, undemonstratively 5 SILENTLY, in silence, mutely, without talking, dumbly 6 MODESTLY, humbly, unobtrusively, diffidently, unpretentiously, unassumingly, unostentatiously

quilt *noun* BEDSPREAD, duvet, comforter (*US*), downie (*informal*), coverlet, eiderdown, counterpane, doona (*Austral*), continental quilt

quintessential *adjective* ULTIMATE, essential, typical, fundamental, definitive, archetypal, prototypical

quip *noun* JOKE, sally, jest, riposte, wisecrack (*informal*), retort, counterattack, pleasantry, repartee, gibe, witticism, bon mot, badinage

quirk *noun* PECULIARITY, eccentricity, mannerism, foible, idiosyncrasy, habit, fancy, characteristic, trait, whim, oddity, caprice, fetish, aberration, kink, vagary, singularity, idée fixe (*French*)

quirky *adjective* ODD, unusual, eccentric, idiosyncratic, curious, peculiar, unpredictable, rum (*Brit slang*), singular, fanciful, whimsical, capricious, offbeat

quit *verb* 1 RESIGN (FROM), leave, retire (from), pull out (of), surrender, chuck (*informal*), step down (from) (*informal*), relinquish, renounce, pack in (*informal*), abdicate 2 STOP, give up, cease, end, drop, abandon, suspend, halt, discontinue, belay (*nautical*)
<< ANTONYM continue 3 LEAVE, depart from, go out of, abandon, desert, exit, withdraw from, forsake, go away from, pull out from, decamp from

quite *adverb* 1 SOMEWHAT, rather, fairly, reasonably, kind of (*informal*), pretty (*informal*), relatively, moderately, to some extent, comparatively, to some degree, to a certain extent 2 ABSOLUTELY, perfectly, completely, totally, fully, entirely, precisely, considerably, wholly, in all respects, without reservation

quiver *verb* SHAKE, tremble, shiver, quake, shudder, agitate, vibrate, pulsate, quaver, convulse, palpitate ▷ *noun* SHAKE, tremble, shiver, throb, shudder, tremor, spasm, vibration, tic, convulsion, palpitation, pulsation

quixotic *adjective* UNREALISTIC, idealistic, romantic, absurd, imaginary, visionary, fanciful, impractical, dreamy, Utopian, impulsive, fantastical, impracticable, chivalrous, unworldly, chimerical

quiz *noun* EXAMINATION, questioning, interrogation, interview, investigation, grilling (*informal*), cross-examination, cross-questioning, the third degree (*informal*) ▷ *verb* QUESTION, ask, interrogate, examine, investigate, pump (*informal*), grill (*informal*), catechize

quizzical *adjective* MOCKING, questioning, inquiring, curious, arch, teasing, bantering, sardonic, derisive, supercilious

quota *noun* SHARE, allowance, ration, allocation, part, cut (*informal*), limit, proportion, slice, quantity, portion, assignment, whack (*informal*), dispensation

quotation *noun* 1 PASSAGE, quote (*informal*), excerpt, cutting, selection, reference, extract, citation 2 (*commerce*) ESTIMATE, price, tender, rate, cost, charge, figure, quote (*informal*), bid price

quote *verb* 1 REPEAT, recite, reproduce, recall, echo, extract, excerpt, proclaim, parrot, paraphrase, retell 2 REFER TO, cite, give, name, detail, relate, mention, instance, specify, spell out, recount, recollect, make reference to, adduce

rabble *noun* **1** MOB, crowd, herd, swarm, horde, throng, canaille **2** (*contemptuous*) COMMONERS, proletariat, common people, riffraff, crowd, masses, trash (*chiefly US & Canad*), scum, lower classes, populace, peasantry, dregs, hoi polloi, the great unwashed (*derogatory*), canaille, lumpenproletariat, commonalty << ANTONYM upper classes

rabid *adjective* **1** FANATICAL, extreme, irrational, fervent, zealous, bigoted, intolerant, narrow-minded, intemperate << ANTONYM moderate **2** CRAZED, wild, violent, mad, raging, furious, frantic, frenzied, infuriated, berserk, maniacal, berko (*Austral slang*)

race¹ *noun* **1** COMPETITION, contest, chase, dash, pursuit, contention **2** CONTEST, competition, rivalry, contention ▷ *verb* **1** COMPETE AGAINST, run against **2** COMPETE, run, contend, take part in a race **3** RUN, fly, career, speed, tear, dash, hurry, barrel (along) (*informal, chiefly US & Canad*), dart, gallop, zoom, hare (*Brit informal*), hasten, burn rubber (*informal*), go like a bomb (*Brit & NZ informal*), run like mad (*informal*)

race² *noun* PEOPLE, ethnic group, nation, blood, house, family, line, issue, stock, type, seed (*chiefly biblical*), breed, folk, tribe, offspring, clan, kin, lineage, progeny, kindred

racial *adjective* ETHNIC, ethnological, national, folk, genetic, tribal, genealogical

rack *noun* FRAME, stand, structure, framework ▷ *verb* TORTURE, distress, torment, harass, afflict, oppress, harrow, crucify, agonize, pain, excruciate

racket *noun* **1** NOISE, row, shouting, fuss, disturbance, outcry, clamour, din, uproar, commotion, pandemonium, rumpus,

babel, tumult, hubbub, hullabaloo, ballyhoo (*informal*) **2** FRAUD, scheme, criminal activity, illegal enterprise

racy *adjective* **1** RISQUÉ, naughty, indecent, bawdy, blue, broad, spicy (*informal*), suggestive, smutty, off colour, immodest, indelicate, near the knuckle (*informal*) **2** LIVELY, spirited, exciting, dramatic, entertaining, stimulating, sexy (*informal*), sparkling, vigorous, energetic, animated, heady, buoyant, exhilarating, zestful

radiance *noun* **1** HAPPINESS, delight, pleasure, joy, warmth, rapture, gaiety **2** BRIGHTNESS, light, shine, glow, glitter, glare, gleam, brilliance, lustre, luminosity, incandescence, resplendence, effulgence

radiant *adjective* **1** HAPPY, glowing, ecstatic, joyful, sent (*informal*), gay, delighted, beaming, joyous, blissful, rapturous, rapt, on cloud nine (*informal*), beatific, blissed out (*informal*), floating on air << ANTONYM miserable **2** BRIGHT, brilliant, shining, glorious, beaming, glowing, sparkling, sunny, glittering, gleaming, luminous, resplendent, incandescent, lustrous, effulgent << ANTONYM dull

radiate *verb* **1** EMIT, spread, send out, disseminate, pour, shed, scatter, glitter, gleam **2** SHINE, emanate, be diffused **3** SHOW, display, demonstrate, exhibit, emanate, give off *or* out **4** SPREAD OUT, diverge, branch out

radiation *noun* EMISSION, rays, emanation

radical *adjective* **1** EXTREME, complete, entire, sweeping, violent, severe, excessive, thorough, drastic **2** REVOLUTIONARY, extremist, fanatical **3** FUNDAMENTAL, natural, basic, essential, native, constitutional, organic, profound, innate, deep-seated, thoroughgoing << ANTONYM superficial ▷ *noun* EXTREMIST, revolutionary, militant, fanatic << ANTONYM conservative

raffle *noun* DRAW, lottery, sweepstake, sweep

rage *noun* **1** FURY, temper, frenzy, rampage, tantrum, foulie (*Austral slang*), hissy fit (*informal*) << ANTONYM calmness **2** ANGER, violence, passion, obsession, madness, raving, wrath, mania, agitation, ire, vehemence, high dudgeon **3** CRAZE, fashion, enthusiasm, vogue, fad (*informal*), latest thing ▷ *verb* **1** BE AT ITS HEIGHT, surge, rampage, be uncontrollable, storm **2** BE FURIOUS, rave, blow up (*informal*), fume, lose it (*informal*), fret, seethe, crack up (*informal*), see red (*informal*), lose the plot (*informal*), go ballistic (*slang, chiefly US*), rant and rave, foam at the mouth, lose your temper, blow a fuse (*slang, chiefly US*), fly off the handle (*informal*), be incandescent, go off the deep end (*informal*), throw a fit (*informal*), wig out (*slang*), go up the wall (*slang*), blow your top, lose your rag (*slang*), be beside yourself, flip your lid (*slang*) << ANTONYM stay calm

ragged *adjective* **1** TATTY, worn, poor, torn, rent, faded, neglected, run-down, frayed, shabby, worn-out, seedy, scruffy, in tatters, dilapidated, tattered, threadbare, unkempt, in rags, down at heel, the worse for wear, in holes, having seen better days, scraggy << ANTONYM smart **2** ROUGH, fragmented, crude, rugged, notched, irregular, unfinished, uneven, jagged, serrated

raging *adjective* FURIOUS, mad, raving, fuming, frenzied, infuriated, incensed, enraged, seething, fizzing (*Scot*), incandescent, foaming at the mouth, fit to be tied (*slang*), boiling mad (*informal*), beside yourself, doing your nut (*Brit slang*), off the air (*Austral slang*)

raid *verb* **1** STEAL FROM, break into, plunder, pillage, sack **2** ATTACK, invade, assault, rifle, forage (*military*), fall upon, swoop down upon, reive (*dialect*) **3** MAKE A SEARCH OF, search, bust (*informal*), descend on, make a raid on, make a swoop on ▷ *noun* **1** ATTACK, invasion, seizure, onset, foray, sortie, incursion, surprise attack, hit-and-run attack, sally, inroad, irruption **2** BUST (*informal*), swoop, descent, surprise search

raider *noun* ATTACKER, thief, robber, plunderer, invader, forager (*military*), marauder, reiver (*dialect*)

rail *verb* COMPLAIN, attack, abuse, blast, put down, criticize, censure, scold, castigate, revile, tear into (*informal*), fulminate, inveigh, upbraid, lambast(e), vituperate, vociferate

railing *noun* FENCE, rails, barrier, paling, balustrade

rain *noun* **1** RAINFALL, fall, showers, deluge, drizzle, downpour, precipitation, raindrops, cloudburst **2** SHOWER, flood, stream, hail, volley, spate, torrent, deluge ▷ *verb* **1** POUR, pelt (down), teem, bucket down (*informal*), fall, shower, drizzle, rain cats and dogs (*informal*), come down in buckets (*informal*) **2** FALL, shower, be dropped, sprinkle, be deposited **3** BESTOW, pour, shower, lavish

rainy *adjective* WET, damp, drizzly, showery << ANTONYM dry

raise *verb* **1** LIFT, move up, elevate, uplift, heave **2** SET UPRIGHT, lift, elevate **3** INCREASE, reinforce, intensify, heighten, advance, boost, strengthen, enhance, put up, exaggerate, hike (up) (*informal*), enlarge, escalate, inflate, aggravate, magnify, amplify, augment, jack up << ANTONYM reduce **4** MAKE LOUDER, heighten, amplify, louden **5** COLLECT, get, gather, obtain **6** MOBILIZE, form, mass, rally, recruit, assemble, levy, muster **7** CAUSE, start, produce, create, occasion, provoke, bring about, originate, give rise to, engender **8** PUT FORWARD, suggest, introduce, advance, bring up, broach, moot **9** BRING UP, develop, rear, nurture **10** GROW, produce, rear, cultivate, propagate **11** BREED, keep **12** BUILD, construct, put up, erect << ANTONYM demolish **13** PROMOTE, upgrade, elevate, advance, prefer, exalt, aggrandize << ANTONYM demote

rake[1] *verb* **1** SCRAPE, break up, scratch, scour, harrow, hoe **2** GATHER, collect, scrape together, scrape up, remove **3** STRAFE, pepper, enfilade **4** GRAZE, scratch, scrape **5** *with* **through** SEARCH, hunt, examine, scan, comb, scour, ransack, forage, scrutinize, fossick (*Austral & NZ*)

rake[2] *noun* LIBERTINE, playboy, swinger (*slang*), profligate, lecher, roué, sensualist, voluptuary, debauchee, rakehell (*archaic*), dissolute man, lech *or* letch (*informal*) << ANTONYM puritan

rakish *adjective* DASHING, smart, sporty, flashy, breezy, jaunty, dapper, natty (*informal*), debonair, snazzy (*informal*), raffish, devil-may-care

rally *noun* **1** GATHERING, mass meeting, convention, convocation, meeting, conference, congress, assembly, congregation, muster, hui (*NZ*) **2** RECOVERY, improvement, comeback (*informal*), revival, renewal, resurgence, recuperation, turn for the better << ANTONYM relapse ▷ *verb* **1** GATHER TOGETHER, unite, bring together, regroup, reorganize, reassemble, re-form **2** RECOVER, improve, pick up, revive, get better, come round, perk up, recuperate, turn the corner, pull through, take a turn for the better, regain your strength, get your second wind << ANTONYM get worse

ram *verb* **1** HIT, force, drive into, strike, crash, impact, smash, slam, dash, run into, butt, collide with **2** CRAM, pound, force, stuff, pack, hammer, jam, thrust, tamp

ramble *noun* WALK, tour, trip, stroll, hike, roaming, excursion, roving, saunter, traipse (*informal*), peregrination, perambulation ▷ *verb* **1** WALK, range, drift, wander, stroll, stray, roam, rove, amble, saunter, straggle, traipse (*informal*), go walkabout (*Austral*), perambulate, stravaig (*Scot & N English dialect*), peregrinate **2** *often with* **on** BABBLE, wander, rabbit (on) (*Brit informal*), chatter, waffle (*informal, chiefly Brit*), digress, rattle on, maunder, witter on (*informal*), expatiate, run off at the mouth (*slang*)

rambler *noun* WALKER, roamer, wanderer, rover, hiker, drifter, stroller, wayfarer

rambling *adjective* **1** SPRAWLING, spreading, trailing, irregular, straggling **2** LONG-WINDED, incoherent, disjointed, prolix, irregular, diffuse, disconnected, desultory, wordy, circuitous, discursive, digressive, periphrastic << ANTONYM concise

ramification *noun usually plural* CONSEQUENCES, results, developments, complications, sequel, upshot

ramp *noun* SLOPE, grade, incline, gradient, inclined plane, rise

rampage *verb* GO BERSERK, tear, storm, rage, run riot, run amok, run wild, go ballistic (*slang*), go ape (*slang*) ▷▷ **on the rampage** BERSERK, wild, violent, raging, destructive, out of control, rampant, amok, riotous, berko (*Austral slang*)

rampant *adjective* **1** WIDESPREAD, rank, epidemic, prevalent, rife, exuberant, uncontrolled, unchecked, unrestrained, luxuriant, profuse, spreading like wildfire **2** UNRESTRAINED, wild, violent, raging, aggressive, dominant, excessive, outrageous, out of control, rampaging, out of hand, uncontrollable, flagrant, unbridled, vehement, wanton, riotous, on the rampage,

ungovernable **3** (*heraldry*) UPRIGHT, standing, rearing, erect

rampart *noun* DEFENCE, wall, parapet, fortification, security, guard, fence, fort, barricade, stronghold, bastion, embankment, bulwark, earthwork, breastwork

ramshackle *adjective* RICKETY, broken-down, crumbling, shaky, unsafe, derelict, flimsy, tottering, dilapidated, decrepit, unsteady, tumbledown, jerry-built << ANTONYM stable

rancid *adjective* ROTTEN, sour, foul, bad, off, rank, tainted, stale, musty, fetid, putrid, fusty, strong-smelling, frowsty << ANTONYM fresh

rancour *noun* HATRED, hate, spite, hostility, resentment, bitterness, grudge, malice, animosity, venom, antipathy, spleen, enmity, ill feeling, bad blood, ill will, animus, malevolence, malignity, chip on your shoulder (*informal*), resentfulness

random *adjective* **1** CHANCE, spot, casual, stray, accidental, arbitrary, incidental, indiscriminate, haphazard, unplanned, fortuitous, aimless, desultory, hit or miss, purposeless, unpremeditated, adventitious << ANTONYM planned **2** CASUAL, arbitrary, indiscriminate, unplanned, aimless, purposeless, unpremeditated ▷▷ **at random** HAPHAZARDLY, randomly, arbitrarily, casually, accidentally, irregularly, by chance, indiscriminately, aimlessly, willy-nilly, unsystematically, purposelessly, adventitiously

randy *adjective* (*informal*) LUSTFUL, hot, sexy (*informal*), turned-on (*slang*), aroused, raunchy (*slang*), horny (*slang*), amorous, lascivious, lecherous, sexually excited, concupiscent, satyric

range *noun* **1** SERIES, variety, selection, assortment, lot, collection, gamut **2** LIMITS, reach, distance, sweep, extent, pale, confines, parameters (*informal*), ambit **3** SCOPE, area, field, bounds, province, orbit, span, domain, compass, latitude, radius, amplitude, purview, sphere **4** ROW, series, line, file, rank, chain, string, sequence, tier ▷ *verb* **1** VARY, run, reach, extend, go, stretch, fluctuate **2** ARRANGE, order, line up, sequence, array, dispose, draw up, align **3** ROAM, explore, wander, rove, sweep, cruise, stroll, ramble, traverse **4** GROUP, class, file, rank, arrange, grade, catalogue, classify, bracket, categorize, pigeonhole

rank¹ *noun* **1** STATUS, level, position, grade,

order, standing, sort, quality, type, station, division, degree, classification, echelon **2** CLASS, dignity, caste, nobility, stratum **3** ROW, line, file, column, group, range, series, formation, tier ▷ *verb* **1** ORDER, class, grade, classify, dispose **2** ARRANGE, sort, position, range, line up, locate, sequence, array, marshal, align ▷▷ **rank and file 1** GENERAL PUBLIC, body, majority, mass, masses, Joe (and Eileen) Public (*slang*), Joe Six-Pack (*US slang*) **2** LOWER RANKS, men, troops, soldiers, other ranks, private soldiers

rank² *adjective* **1** ABSOLUTE, complete, total, gross, sheer, excessive, utter, glaring, thorough, extravagant, rampant, blatant, downright, flagrant, egregious, unmitigated, undisguised, arrant **2** FOUL, off, bad, offensive, disgusting, revolting, stinking, stale, pungent, noxious, disagreeable, musty, rancid, fetid, putrid, fusty, strong-smelling, gamey, noisome, mephitic, olid, yucky or yukky (*slang*), festy (*Austral slang*) **3** ABUNDANT, flourishing, lush, luxuriant, productive, vigorous, dense, exuberant, profuse, strong-growing

rankle *verb* ANNOY, anger, irritate, gall, fester, embitter, chafe, irk, rile, get on your nerves (*informal*), get your goat (*slang*), hack you off (*informal*)

ransack *verb* **1** SEARCH, go through, rummage through, rake through, explore, comb, scour, forage, turn inside out, fossick (*Austral & NZ*) **2** PLUNDER, raid, loot, pillage, strip, sack, gut, rifle, ravage, despoil

ransom *noun* **1** PAYMENT, money, price, payoff **2** RELEASE, rescue, liberation, redemption, deliverance ▷ *verb* BUY THE FREEDOM OF, release, deliver, rescue, liberate, buy (someone) out (*informal*), redeem, set free, obtain or pay for the release of

rant *verb* SHOUT, roar, yell, rave, bellow, cry, spout (*informal*), bluster, declaim, vociferate ▷ *noun* TIRADE, rhetoric, bluster, diatribe, harangue, bombast, philippic, vociferation, fanfaronade (*rare*)

rap *verb* **1** HIT, strike, knock, crack, tap **2** REPRIMAND, knock (*informal*), blast, pan (*informal*), carpet (*informal*), criticize, censure, scold, tick off (*informal*), castigate, diss (*slang, chiefly US*), read the riot act, lambast(e), chew out (*US & Canad informal*), give a rocket (*Brit & NZ informal*) **3** (*slang*) TALK, chat, discourse, converse, shoot the breeze (*slang, chiefly US*), confabulate ▷ *noun* **1** BLOW, knock, crack, tap, clout (*informal*) **2** (*slang*) REBUKE, sentence,

blame, responsibility, punishment, censure, chiding

rapacious *adjective* GREEDY, grasping, insatiable, ravenous, preying, plundering, predatory, voracious, marauding, extortionate, avaricious, wolfish, usurious

rape *verb* SEXUALLY ASSAULT, violate, abuse, ravish, force, outrage ▷ *noun* **1** SEXUAL ASSAULT, violation, ravishment, outrage **2** PLUNDERING, pillage, depredation, despoliation, rapine, spoliation, despoilment, sack

rapid *adjective* **1** SUDDEN, prompt, speedy, precipitate, express, fleet, swift, quickie (*informal*), expeditious << ANTONYM gradual **2** QUICK, fast, hurried, swift, brisk, hasty, flying, pdq (*slang*) << ANTONYM slow

rapidity *noun* SPEED, swiftness, promptness, speediness, rush, hurry, expedition, dispatch, velocity, haste, alacrity, quickness, briskness, fleetness, celerity, promptitude, precipitateness

rapidly *adverb* QUICKLY, fast, swiftly, briskly, promptly, hastily, precipitately, in a hurry, at speed, hurriedly, speedily, apace, in a rush, in haste, like a shot, pronto (*informal*), hell for leather, like lightning, expeditiously, hotfoot, like the clappers (*Brit informal*), pdq (*slang*), like nobody's business (*informal*), posthaste, with dispatch, like greased lightning (*informal*)

rapport *noun* BOND, understanding, relationship, link, tie, sympathy, harmony, affinity, empathy, interrelationship

rapprochement *noun* RECONCILIATION, softening, reunion, détente, reconcilement, restoration of harmony << ANTONYM dissension

rapt *adjective* **1** SPELLBOUND, entranced, enthralled, engrossed, held, gripped, fascinated, absorbed, intent, preoccupied, carried away << ANTONYM uninterested **2** RAPTUROUS, enchanted, captivated, bewitched, sent, transported, delighted, charmed, ecstatic, blissful, ravished, enraptured, blissed out

rapture *noun* ECSTASY, delight, enthusiasm, joy, transport, spell, happiness, bliss, euphoria, felicity, rhapsody, exaltation, cloud nine (*informal*), seventh heaven, delectation, beatitude, ravishment

rapturous *adjective* ECSTATIC, delighted, enthusiastic, rapt, sent (*informal*), happy, transported, joyous, exalted, joyful, over the moon (*informal*), overjoyed, blissful, ravished, euphoric, on cloud nine (*informal*), blissed out (*informal*), rhapsodic, in seventh heaven, floating on air

rare¹ *adjective* **1** PRICELESS, rich, precious, invaluable **2** UNCOMMON, unusual, exceptional, out of the ordinary, few, strange, scarce, singular, sporadic, sparse, infrequent, thin on the ground, recherché << ANTONYM common **3** SUPERB, great, fine, excellent, extreme, exquisite, admirable, superlative, choice, incomparable, peerless

rare² *adjective* UNDERDONE, bloody, undercooked, half-cooked, half-raw

rarefied *adjective* EXCLUSIVE, select, esoteric, cliquish, private, occult, clannish

rarely *adverb* SELDOM, hardly, almost never, hardly ever, little, once in a while, infrequently, on rare occasions, once in a blue moon, only now and then, scarcely ever << ANTONYM often

raring *adjective* (in construction *raring to do something*) EAGER, impatient, longing, yearning, willing, ready, keen, desperate, enthusiastic, avid, champing at the bit (*informal*), keen as mustard, athirst

rarity *noun* **1** CURIO, find, treasure, pearl, one-off, curiosity, gem, collector's item **2** UNCOMMONNESS, scarcity, infrequency, unusualness, shortage, strangeness, singularity, sparseness

rascal *noun* ROGUE, devil, villain, scoundrel, disgrace, rake, pickle (*Brit informal*), imp, scally (*Northwest English dialect*), wretch, knave (*archaic*), ne'er-do-well, reprobate, scallywag (*informal*), good-for-nothing, miscreant, scamp, wastrel, bad egg (*old-fashioned informal*), blackguard, varmint (*informal*), rapscallion, caitiff (*archaic*), wrong 'un (*Austral slang*), nointer (*Austral slang*)

rash¹ *adjective* RECKLESS, hasty, impulsive, imprudent, premature, adventurous, careless, precipitate, brash, audacious, headlong, madcap, ill-advised, foolhardy, unwary, thoughtless, unguarded, headstrong, impetuous, indiscreet, unthinking, helter-skelter, ill-considered, hot-headed, heedless, injudicious, incautious, venturesome, harebrained, harum-scarum << ANTONYM cautious

rash² *noun* **1** OUTBREAK OF SPOTS, (skin) eruption **2** SPATE, series, wave, flood, succession, plague, outbreak, epidemic

rasp *verb* SCRAPE, grind, rub, scour, excoriate, abrade ▷ *noun* GRATING, grinding, scratch, scrape

rasping *or* **raspy** *adjective* HARSH, rough, hoarse, gravelly, jarring, grating, creaking, husky, croaking, gruff, croaky

rat (*informal*) *noun* **1** TRAITOR, grass (*Brit informal*), betrayer, deceiver, informer, defector, deserter, double-crosser, quisling, stool pigeon, nark (*Brit, Austral & NZ slang*), snake in the grass, two-timer (*informal*), fizgig (*Austral slang*) **2** ROGUE, scoundrel, heel (*slang*), cad (*old-fashioned informal, Brit*), bounder (*old-fashioned slang, Brit*), rotter (*slang, chiefly Brit*), bad lot, shyster (*informal, chiefly US*), ratfink (*slang, chiefly US & Canad*), wrong 'un (*Austral slang*) ▷▷ **rat on someone** BETRAY, denounce, tell on, shop (*slang, chiefly Brit*), grass (*Brit slang*), peach (*slang*), squeal (*slang*), incriminate (*informal*), blow the whistle on (*informal*), spill the beans (*informal*), snitch (*slang*), blab, let the cat out of the bag, blow the gaff (*Brit slang*), nark (*Brit, Austral & NZ slang*), put the finger on (*informal*), spill your guts (*slang*), inculpate, clype (*Scot*), dob in (*Austral slang*)

rate *noun* **1** SPEED, pace, tempo, velocity, time, measure, gait, frequency **2** DEGREE, standard, scale, proportion, percentage, ratio **3** CHARGE, price, cost, fee, tax, figure, dues, duty, hire, toll, tariff ▷ *verb* **1** EVALUATE, consider, rank, reckon, class, value, measure, regard, estimate, count, grade, assess, weigh, esteem, classify, appraise, adjudge **2** DESERVE, merit, be entitled to, be worthy of ▷▷ **at any rate** IN ANY CASE, anyway, nevertheless, anyhow, at all events

rather *adverb* **1** PREFERABLY, sooner, instead, more readily, more willingly **2** TO SOME EXTENT, quite, sort of (*informal*), kind of (*informal*), a little, a bit, pretty (*informal*), fairly, relatively, somewhat, slightly, moderately, to some degree

ratify *verb* APPROVE, sign, establish, confirm, bind, sanction, endorse, uphold, authorize, affirm, certify, consent to, validate, bear out, corroborate, authenticate << ANTONYM annul

rating *noun* POSITION, evaluation, classification, placing, rate, order, standing, class, degree, estimate, rank, status, grade, designation

ratio *noun* PROPORTION, rate, relationship, relation, arrangement, percentage, equation, fraction, correspondence, correlation

ration *noun* ALLOWANCE, quota, allotment, provision, helping, part, share, measure, dole, portion ▷ *verb* **1** LIMIT, control, restrict,

save, budget, conserve **2** DISTRIBUTE, issue,
deal, dole, allocate, give out, allot, mete,
apportion, measure out, parcel out

rational *adjective* **1** SENSIBLE, sound, wise,
reasonable, intelligent, realistic, logical,
enlightened, sane, lucid, judicious, sagacious
2 REASONING, thinking, cognitive, cerebral,
ratiocinative **3** SANE, balanced, normal,
all there (*informal*), lucid, of sound mind,
compos mentis (*Latin*), in your right mind
<< ANTONYM insane

rationale *noun* REASON, grounds, theory,
principle, philosophy, logic, motivation,
exposition, raison d'être (*French*)

rationalize *verb* **1** JUSTIFY, excuse, account for,
vindicate, explain away, make allowances for,
make excuses for, extenuate **2** REASON OUT,
resolve, think through, elucidate, apply logic
to **3** STREAMLINE, trim, make more efficient,
make cuts in

rattle *verb* **1** CLATTER, bang, jangle **2** SHAKE,
jiggle, jolt, vibrate, bounce, jar, jounce
3 (*informal*) FLUSTER, shake, upset, frighten,
scare, disturb, disconcert, perturb, faze,
discomfit, discountenance, put (someone)
off his stride, discompose, put (someone)
out of countenance ▷▷ **rattle on** PRATTLE,
rabbit (on) (*Brit informal*), chatter, witter
(*informal*), cackle, yak (away) (*slang*), gibber,
jabber, gabble, blether, prate, run on,
earbash (*Austral & NZ slang*) ▷▷ **rattle
something off** RECITE, list, run through,
rehearse, reel off, spiel off (*informal*)

ratty *adjective* IRRITABLE, cross, angry,
annoyed, crabbed, impatient, snappy,
touchy, tetchy, testy, short-tempered, tooshie
(*Austral slang*)

raucous *adjective* HARSH, rough, loud, noisy,
grating, strident, rasping, husky, hoarse
<< ANTONYM quiet

raunchy *adjective* (*slang*) SEXY, sexual, steamy
(*informal*), earthy, suggestive, lewd, lusty,
bawdy, salacious, smutty, lustful, lecherous,
ribald, coarse

ravage *verb* DESTROY, ruin, devastate,
wreck, shatter, gut, spoil, loot, demolish,
plunder, desolate, sack, ransack, pillage,
raze, lay waste, wreak havoc on, despoil,
leave in ruins ▷ *noun often plural* DAMAGE,
destruction, devastation, desolation, waste,
ruin, havoc, demolition, plunder, pillage,
depredation, ruination, rapine, spoliation

rave *verb* **1** RANT, rage, roar, thunder, fume,
go mad (*informal*), babble, splutter, storm,
be delirious, talk wildly **2** *usually with*

about (*informal*) ENTHUSE, praise, gush, be
delighted by, be mad about (*informal*), big
up (*slang, chiefly Caribbean*), rhapsodize,
be wild about (*informal*), cry up ▷ *noun*
PARTY, rave-up (*Brit slang*), do (*informal*),
affair, celebration, bash (*informal*), blow-out
(*slang*), beano (*Brit slang*), hooley *or* hoolie
(*chiefly Irish & NZ*) ▷ *modifier* (*informal*)
ENTHUSIASTIC, excellent, favourable,
ecstatic, laudatory

ravenous *adjective* **1** STARVING, starved, very
hungry, famished, esurient << ANTONYM
sated **2** GREEDY, insatiable, avaricious,
covetous, grasping, insatiate

ravine *noun* CANYON, pass, gap (*US*), gorge,
clough (*dialect*), gully, defile, linn (*Scot*), gulch
(*US & Canad*), flume

raving *adjective* MAD, wild, raging, crazy,
furious, frantic, frenzied, hysterical, insane,
irrational, crazed, berserk, delirious, rabid,
out of your mind, gonzo (*slang*), berko
(*Austral slang*), off the air (*Austral slang*)

ravish *verb* **1** (*literary*) RAPE, sexually assault,
violate, abuse, force, outrage **2** ENCHANT,
transport, delight, charm, fascinate,
entrance, captivate, enrapture, spellbind,
overjoy

ravishing *adjective* ENCHANTING, beautiful,
lovely, stunning (*informal*), charming,
entrancing, gorgeous, dazzling, delightful,
radiant, drop-dead (*slang*), bewitching

raw *adjective* **1** UNREFINED, natural, crude,
unprocessed, basic, rough, organic, coarse,
unfinished, untreated, unripe << ANTONYM
refined **2** UNCOOKED, natural, fresh,
bloody (*of meat*), undressed, unprepared
<< ANTONYM cooked **3** SORE, open, skinned,
sensitive, tender, scratched, grazed, chafed,
abraded **4** FRANK, plain, bare, naked,
realistic, brutal, blunt, candid, unvarnished,
unembellished << ANTONYM embellished
5 INEXPERIENCED, new, green, ignorant,
immature, unskilled, callow, untrained,
untried, undisciplined, unseasoned,
unpractised << ANTONYM experienced
6 CHILLY, biting, cold, freezing, bitter, wet,
chill, harsh, piercing, damp, unpleasant,
bleak, parky (*Brit informal*)

ray *noun* **1** BEAM, bar, flash, shaft, gleam
2 TRACE, spark, flicker, glimmer, hint,
indication, scintilla

raze *verb* DESTROY, level, remove, ruin,
demolish, flatten, knock down, pull down,
tear down, throw down, bulldoze, kennet
(*Austral slang*), jeff (*Austral slang*)

re *preposition* CONCERNING, about, regarding, respecting, with regard to, on the subject of, in respect of, with reference to, apropos, anent (*Scot*)

reach *verb* 1 ARRIVE AT, get to, get as far as, make, attain, land at 2 ATTAIN, get to, amount to 3 TOUCH, grasp, extend to, get (a) hold of, stretch to, go as far as, contact 4 CONTACT, get in touch with, get through to, make contact with, get, find, communicate with, get hold of, establish contact with 5 COME TO, move to, rise to, fall to, drop to, sink to 6 ACHIEVE, come to, arrive at ▷ *noun* 1 GRASP, range, distance, stretch, sweep, capacity, extent, extension, scope 2 JURISDICTION, power, influence, command, compass, mastery, ambit

react *verb* RESPOND, act, proceed, behave, conduct yourself

reaction *noun* 1 RESPONSE, acknowledgment, feedback, answer, reply 2 COUNTERACTION, compensation, backlash, recoil, counterbalance, counterpoise 3 CONSERVATISM, the right, counter-revolution, obscurantism

reactionary *adjective* CONSERVATIVE, right-wing, counter-revolutionary, obscurantist, blimpish << ANTONYM radical ▷ *noun* CONSERVATIVE, die-hard, right-winger, rightist, counter-revolutionary, obscurantist, Colonel Blimp << ANTONYM radical

read *verb* 1 SCAN, study, look at, refer to, glance at, pore over, peruse, run your eye over 2 RECITE, deliver, utter, declaim, speak, announce 3 UNDERSTAND, interpret, comprehend, construe, decipher, perceive the meaning of, see, discover 4 REGISTER, show, record, display, indicate

readable *adjective* 1 ENJOYABLE, interesting, gripping, entertaining, pleasant, enthralling, easy to read, worth reading << ANTONYM dull 2 LEGIBLE, clear, plain, understandable, comprehensible, intelligible, decipherable << ANTONYM illegible

readily *adverb* 1 WILLINGLY, freely, quickly, gladly, eagerly, voluntarily, cheerfully, with pleasure, with good grace, lief (*rare*) << ANTONYM reluctantly 2 PROMPTLY, quickly, easily, smoothly, at once, straight away, right away, effortlessly, in no time, speedily, without delay, without hesitation, without difficulty, unhesitatingly, hotfoot, without demur, pdq (*slang*) << ANTONYM with difficulty

readiness *noun* 1 WILLINGNESS, inclination, eagerness, keenness, aptness, gameness (*informal*) 2 PREPAREDNESS, preparation, fitness, maturity, ripeness 3 PROMPTNESS, facility, ease, skill, dexterity, rapidity, quickness, adroitness, handiness, promptitude ▷▷ **in readiness** PREPARED, set, waiting, primed, ready, all set, waiting in the wings, at the ready, at *or* on hand, fit

reading *noun* 1 PERUSAL, study, review, examination, inspection, scrutiny 2 LEARNING, education, knowledge, scholarship, erudition, edification, book-learning 3 RECITAL, performance, rendering, rendition, lesson, lecture, sermon, homily 4 INTERPRETATION, take (*informal, chiefly US*), understanding, treatment, version, construction, impression, grasp, conception

ready *adjective* 1 PREPARED, set, primed, organized, all set, in readiness << ANTONYM unprepared 2 COMPLETED, arranged 3 MATURE, ripe, mellow, ripened, fully developed, fully grown, seasoned 4 WILLING, happy, glad, disposed, game (*informal*), minded, keen, eager, inclined, prone, have-a-go (*informal*), apt, agreeable, predisposed << ANTONYM reluctant 5 PROMPT, smart, quick, bright, sharp, keen, acute, rapid, alert, clever, intelligent, handy, apt, skilful, astute, perceptive, expert, deft, resourceful, adroit, quick-witted, dexterous << ANTONYM slow 6 AVAILABLE, handy, at the ready, at your fingertips, present, near, accessible, convenient, on call, on tap (*informal*), close to hand, at *or* on hand << ANTONYM unavailable 7 *with* **to** ON THE POINT OF, close to, about to, on the verge of, likely to, in danger of, liable to, on the brink of ▷ *verb* PREPARE, get set, organize, get ready, order, arrange, equip, fit out, make ready, jack up (*NZ informal*)

real *adjective* 1 TRUE, genuine, sincere, honest, factual, existent, dinkum (*Austral & NZ informal*), unfeigned 2 GENUINE, authentic, bona fide, dinkum (*Austral & NZ informal*) << ANTONYM fake 3 PROPER, true, valid, legitimate 4 ACTUAL, true 5 TYPICAL, true, genuine, sincere, unaffected, dinkum (*Austral & NZ informal*), unfeigned 6 COMPLETE, right, total, perfect, positive, absolute, utter, thorough, veritable, out-and-out

realistic *adjective* 1 PRACTICAL, real, sensible, rational, common-sense, sober, pragmatic, down-to-earth, matter-of-fact, businesslike, level-headed, hard-headed,

unsentimental, unromantic << ANTONYM
impractical **2** ATTAINABLE, reasonable,
sensible **3** LIFELIKE, true to life, authentic,
naturalistic, true, natural, genuine, graphic,
faithful, truthful, representational, vérité

reality *noun* **1** FACT, truth, certainty, realism,
validity, authenticity, verity, actuality,
materiality, genuineness, verisimilitude,
corporeality **2** TRUTH, fact, actuality ▷▷ **in
reality** IN FACT, really, actually, in truth, as a
matter of fact, in actuality, in point of fact

realization *noun* **1** AWARENESS, understanding,
recognition, perception, imagination,
consciousness, grasp, appreciation,
conception, comprehension, apprehension,
cognizance, aha moment, light bulb
moment (*informal*) **2** ACHIEVEMENT,
carrying-out, completion, accomplishment,
fulfilment, consummation, effectuation

realize *verb* **1** BECOME AWARE OF, understand,
recognize, appreciate, take in, grasp,
conceive, catch on (*informal*), comprehend,
twig (*Brit informal*), get the message,
apprehend, become conscious of, be
cognizant of **2** FULFIL, achieve, accomplish,
make real **3** ACHIEVE, do, effect, complete,
perform, fulfil, accomplish, bring about,
consummate, incarnate, bring off, make
concrete, bring to fruition, actualize,
make happen, effectuate, reify, carry out *or*
through **4** SELL FOR, go for, bring *or* take in,
make, get, clear, produce, gain, net, earn,
obtain, acquire

really *adverb* **1** CERTAINLY, absolutely,
undoubtedly, genuinely, positively,
categorically, without a doubt, assuredly,
verily, surely **2** TRULY, actually, in fact,
indeed, in reality, in actuality

realm *noun* **1** FIELD, world, area, province,
sphere, department, region, branch,
territory, zone, patch, orbit, turf (*US
slang*) **2** KINGDOM, state, country, empire,
monarchy, land, province, domain,
dominion, principality

reap *verb* **1** GET, win, gain, obtain, acquire,
derive **2** COLLECT, gather, bring in, harvest,
garner, cut

rear¹ *noun* **1** BACK PART, back << ANTONYM
front **2** BACK, end, tail, rearguard, tail
end, back end ▷ *modifier* BACK, aft, hind,
hindmost, after (*nautical*), last, following,
trailing << ANTONYM front

rear² *verb* **1** BRING UP, raise, educate, care for,
train, nurse, foster, nurture **2** BREED, keep
3 *often with* **up** *or* **over** RISE, tower, soar, loom

reason *noun* **1** CAUSE, grounds, purpose,
motive, end, goal, design, target, aim, basis,
occasion, object, intention, incentive,
warrant, impetus, inducement, why and
wherefore (*informal*) **2** JUSTIFICATION, case,
grounds, defence, argument, explanation,
excuse, apology, rationale, exposition,
vindication, apologia **3** SENSE, mind,
reasoning, understanding, brains, judgment,
logic, mentality, intellect, comprehension,
apprehension, sanity, rationality, soundness,
sound mind, ratiocination << ANTONYM
emotion ▷ *verb* DEDUCE, conclude, work
out, solve, resolve, make out, infer, draw
conclusions, think, ratiocinate, syllogize
▷▷ **in** *or* **within reason** WITHIN LIMITS,
within reasonable limits, within bounds
▷▷ **reason with someone** PERSUADE, debate
with, remonstrate with, bring round, urge,
win over, argue with, dispute with, dissuade,
prevail upon (*informal*), expostulate with,
show (someone) the error of his ways, talk
into *or* out of

reasonable *adjective* **1** SENSIBLE, reasoned,
sound, practical, wise, intelligent, rational,
logical, sober, credible, plausible, sane,
judicious << ANTONYM irrational **2** FAIR,
just, right, acceptable, moderate, equitable,
justifiable, well-advised, well-thought-out,
tenable << ANTONYM unfair **3** WITHIN
REASON, fit, proper << ANTONYM impossible
4 LOW, cheap, competitive, moderate,
modest, inexpensive, tolerable **5** AVERAGE,
fair, moderate, modest, tolerable, O.K. *or*
okay (*informal*)

reasoned *adjective* SENSIBLE, clear, logical,
systematic, judicious, well-thought-out,
well-presented, well-expressed

reasoning *noun* **1** THINKING, thought, reason,
analysis, logic, deduction, cogitation,
ratiocination **2** CASE, argument, proof,
interpretation, hypothesis, exposition, train
of thought

reassure *verb* ENCOURAGE, comfort, bolster,
hearten, cheer up, buoy up, gee up, restore
confidence to, inspirit, relieve (someone) of
anxiety, put *or* set your mind at rest

rebate *noun* REFUND, discount, reduction,
bonus, allowance, deduction

rebel *noun* **1** REVOLUTIONARY, resistance
fighter, insurgent, secessionist,
mutineer, insurrectionary, revolutionist
2 NONCONFORMIST, dissenter, heretic,
apostate, schismatic ▷ *verb* **1** REVOLT, resist,
rise up, mutiny, take to the streets, take up

arms, man the barricades **2** DEFY, dissent, disobey, come out against, refuse to obey, dig your heels in (*informal*) **3** RECOIL, shrink, shy away, flinch, show repugnance ▷ *modifier* REBELLIOUS, revolutionary, insurgent, mutinous, insubordinate, insurrectionary

rebellion *noun* **1** RESISTANCE, rising, revolution, revolt, uprising, mutiny, insurrection, insurgency, insurgence **2** NONCONFORMITY, dissent, defiance, heresy, disobedience, schism, insubordination, apostasy

rebellious *adjective* **1** DEFIANT, difficult, resistant, intractable, recalcitrant, obstinate, unmanageable, incorrigible, refractory, contumacious << ANTONYM obedient **2** REVOLUTIONARY, rebel, disorderly, unruly, turbulent, disaffected, insurgent, recalcitrant, disloyal, seditious, mutinous, disobedient, ungovernable, insubordinate, insurrectionary << ANTONYM obedient

rebirth *noun* REVIVAL, restoration, renaissance, renewal, resurrection, reincarnation, regeneration, resurgence, new beginning, revitalization, renascence

rebound *verb* **1** BOUNCE, ricochet, spring back, return, resound, recoil **2** MISFIRE, backfire, recoil, boomerang

rebuff *verb* REJECT, decline, refuse, turn down, cut, check, deny, resist, slight, discourage, put off, snub, spurn, knock back (*slang*), brush off (*slang*), repulse, cold-shoulder << ANTONYM encourage ▷ *noun* REJECTION, defeat, snub, knock-back, check, opposition, slight, refusal, denial, brush-off (*slang*), repulse, thumbs down, cold shoulder, slap in the face (*informal*), kick in the teeth (*slang*), discouragement << ANTONYM encouragement

rebuke *verb* SCOLD, censure, reprimand, reproach, blame, lecture, carpet (*informal*), berate, tick off (*informal*), castigate, chide, dress down (*informal*), admonish, tear into (*informal*), tell off (*informal*), take to task, read the riot act, reprove, upbraid, bawl out (*informal*), haul (someone) over the coals (*informal*), chew out (*US & Canad informal*), tear (someone) off a strip (*informal*), give a rocket (*Brit & NZ informal*), reprehend << ANTONYM praise ▷ *noun* SCOLDING, censure, reprimand, reproach, blame, row, lecture, wigging (*Brit slang*), ticking-off (*informal*), dressing down (*informal*), telling-off (*informal*), admonition, tongue-lashing, reproof, castigation, reproval << ANTONYM

praise

rebut *verb* DISPROVE, defeat, overturn, quash, refute, negate, invalidate, prove wrong, confute

rebuttal *noun* DISPROOF, negation, refutation, invalidation, confutation, defeat

recalcitrant *adjective* DISOBEDIENT, contrary, unwilling, defiant, stubborn, wayward, unruly, uncontrollable, intractable, wilful, obstinate, unmanageable, ungovernable, refractory, insubordinate, contumacious << ANTONYM obedient

recall *verb* **1** RECOLLECT, remember, call up, evoke, reminisce about, call to mind, look *or* think back to, mind (*dialect*) **2** CALL BACK **3** ANNUL, withdraw, call in, take back, cancel, repeal, call back, revoke, retract, rescind, nullify, countermand, abjure ▷ *noun* **1** RECOLLECTION, memory, remembrance **2** ANNULMENT, withdrawal, repeal, cancellation, retraction, revocation, nullification, rescission, rescindment

recant *verb* WITHDRAW, take back, retract, disclaim, deny, recall, renounce, revoke, repudiate, renege, disown, disavow, forswear, abjure, unsay, apostatize << ANTONYM maintain

recede *verb* **1** FALL BACK, withdraw, retreat, draw back, return, go back, retire, back off, regress, retrogress, retrocede **2** LESSEN, decline, subside, abate, sink, fade, shrink, diminish, dwindle, wane, ebb

receipt *noun* **1** SALES SLIP, proof of purchase, voucher, stub, acknowledgment, counterfoil **2** RECEIVING, delivery, reception, acceptance, recipience ▷ *plural noun* TAKINGS, return, profits, gains, income, gate, proceeds

receive *verb* **1** GET, accept, be given, pick up, collect, obtain, acquire, take, derive, be in receipt of, accept delivery of **2** EXPERIENCE, suffer, bear, go through, encounter, meet with, sustain, undergo, be subjected to **3** GREET, meet, admit, welcome, entertain, take in, accommodate, be at home to

recent *adjective* NEW, modern, contemporary, up-to-date, late, young, happening (*informal*), current, fresh, novel, latter, present-day, latter-day << ANTONYM old

recently *adverb* NOT LONG AGO, newly, lately, currently, freshly, of late, latterly

receptacle *noun* CONTAINER, holder, repository

reception *noun* **1** PARTY, gathering, get-together, social gathering, do (*informal*), social, function, entertainment, celebration, bash (*informal*), festivity, knees-up (*Brit informal*), shindig (*informal*), soirée, levee, rave-up (*Brit slang*) **2** RESPONSE, reaction, acknowledgment, recognition, treatment, welcome, greeting **3** RECEIVING, admission, acceptance, receipt, recipience

receptive *adjective* OPEN, sympathetic, favourable, amenable, interested, welcoming, friendly, accessible, susceptible, open-minded, hospitable, approachable, open to suggestions << ANTONYM narrow-minded

recess *noun* **1** BREAK, rest, holiday, closure, interval, vacation, respite, intermission, cessation of business, schoolie (*Austral*) **2** ALCOVE, corner, bay, depression, hollow, niche, cavity, nook, oriel, indentation **3** *often plural* DEPTHS, reaches, heart, retreats, bowels, innards (*informal*), secret places, innermost parts, penetralia

recession *noun* DEPRESSION, drop, decline, slump, downturn << ANTONYM boom

recherché *adjective* REFINED, rare, exotic, esoteric, arcane, far-fetched, choice

recipe *noun* DIRECTIONS, instructions, ingredients, receipt (*obsolete*) ▷▷ **a recipe for something** METHOD, formula, prescription, process, programme, technique, procedure, modus operandi

reciprocal *adjective* MUTUAL, corresponding, reciprocative, reciprocatory, exchanged, equivalent, alternate, complementary, interchangeable, give-and-take, interdependent, correlative << ANTONYM unilateral

reciprocate *verb* RETURN, requite, feel in return, match, respond, equal, return the compliment

recital *noun* **1** PERFORMANCE, rendering, rehearsal, reading **2** ACCOUNT, telling, story, detailing, statement, relation, tale, description, narrative, narration, enumeration, recapitulation **3** RECITATION, repetition

recitation *noun* RECITAL, reading, performance, piece, passage, lecture, rendering, narration, telling

recite *verb* PERFORM, relate, deliver, repeat, rehearse, declaim, recapitulate, do your party piece (*informal*)

reckless *adjective* CARELESS, wild, rash, irresponsible, precipitate, hasty, mindless, negligent, headlong, madcap, ill-advised, regardless, foolhardy, daredevil, thoughtless, indiscreet, imprudent, heedless, devil-may-care, inattentive, incautious, harebrained, harum-scarum, overventuresome << ANTONYM cautious

reckon *verb* **1** (*informal*) THINK, believe, suppose, imagine, assume, guess (*informal, chiefly US & Canad*), fancy, conjecture, surmise, be of the opinion **2** CONSIDER, hold, rate, account, judge, think of, regard, estimate, count, evaluate, esteem, deem, gauge, look upon, appraise **3** COUNT, figure, total, calculate, compute, add up, tally, number, enumerate ▷▷ **reckon on** *or* **upon something** RELY ON, count on, bank on, depend on, hope for, calculate, trust in, take for granted ▷▷ **reckon with something** *or* **someone** (*usually in negative construction*) TAKE INTO ACCOUNT, expect, plan for, anticipate, be prepared for, bear in mind, foresee, bargain for, take cognizance of ▷▷ **to be reckoned with** POWERFUL, important, strong, significant, considerable, influential, weighty, consequential, skookum (*Canad*)

reckoning *noun* **1** COUNT, working, estimate, calculation, adding, counting, addition, computation, summation **2** DAY OF RETRIBUTION, doom, judgment day, last judgment

reclaim *verb* **1** RETRIEVE, get *or* take back, rescue, regain, reinstate **2** REGAIN, restore, salvage, recapture, regenerate **3** RESCUE, reform, redeem

recline *verb* LEAN, lie (down), stretch out, rest, lounge, sprawl, loll, repose, be recumbent << ANTONYM stand up

recluse *noun* HERMIT, solitary, ascetic, anchoress, monk, anchorite, eremite

reclusive *adjective* SOLITARY, retiring, withdrawn, isolated, secluded, cloistered, monastic, recluse, ascetic, sequestered, hermit-like, hermitic, eremitic << ANTONYM sociable

recognition *noun* **1** IDENTIFICATION, recall, recollection, discovery, detection, remembrance **2** ACCEPTANCE, acknowledgement, understanding, admission, perception, awareness, concession, allowance, confession, realization, avowal **3** ACKNOWLEDGMENT, approval **4** APPROVAL, honour, appreciation, salute, gratitude, acknowledgment

recognize *verb* **1** IDENTIFY, know, place, remember, spot, notice, recall, make out, recollect, know again, put your finger on **2** ACKNOWLEDGE, see, allow, understand, accept, admit, grant, realize, concede, perceive, confess, be aware of, take on board, avow << ANTONYM ignore **3** APPROVE, acknowledge, appreciate, greet, honour **4** APPRECIATE, respect, notice, salute

recoil verb **1** JERK BACK, kick, react, rebound, spring back, resile **2** DRAW BACK, shrink, falter, shy away, flinch, quail, balk at ▷ noun **1** JERKING BACK, reaction, springing back **2** KICKBACK, kick

recollect verb REMEMBER, mind (dialect), recall, reminisce, summon up, call to mind, place

recollection noun MEMORY, recall, impression, remembrance, reminiscence, mental image

recommend verb **1** ADVOCATE, suggest, propose, approve, endorse, commend << ANTONYM disapprove of **2** PUT FORWARD, approve, endorse, commend, vouch for, praise, big up (slang, chiefly Caribbean), speak well of, put in a good word for **3** ADVISE, suggest, advance, propose, urge, counsel, advocate, prescribe, put forward, exhort, enjoin **4** MAKE ATTRACTIVE, make interesting, make appealing, make acceptable

recommendation noun **1** ADVICE, proposal, suggestion, counsel, urging **2** COMMENDATION, reference, praise, sanction, approval, blessing, plug (informal), endorsement, advocacy, testimonial, good word, approbation, favourable mention

recompense noun COMPENSATION, pay, payment, satisfaction, amends, repayment, remuneration, reparation, indemnity, restitution, damages, emolument, indemnification, requital ▷ verb COMPENSATE, reimburse, redress, repay, pay for, satisfy, make good, make up for, make amends for, indemnify, requite, make restitution for

reconcile verb **1** RESOLVE, settle, square, adjust, compose, rectify, patch up, harmonize, put to rights **2** REUNITE, bring back together, make peace between, pacify, conciliate **3** MAKE PEACE BETWEEN, reunite, propitiate, bring to terms, restore harmony between, re-establish friendly relations between ▷▷ **reconcile yourself to something** often passive ACCEPT, resign yourself to, get used to, put up with (informal), submit to, yield to, make the best of, accommodate yourself to

reconciliation noun **1** REUNION, conciliation, rapprochement (French), appeasement, détente, pacification, propitiation,

understanding, reconcilement << ANTONYM separation **2** ACCOMMODATION, settlement, compromise

reconnaissance noun INSPECTION, survey, investigation, observation, patrol, scan, exploration, scouting, scrutiny, recce (slang), reconnoitring

reconsider verb RETHINK, review, revise, think again, think twice, reassess, re-examine, have second thoughts, change your mind, re-evaluate, think over, think better of, take another look at

reconstruct verb **1** REBUILD, reform, restore, recreate, remake, renovate, remodel, re-establish, regenerate, reorganize, reassemble **2** BUILD UP A PICTURE OF, build up, piece together, deduce

record noun **1** DOCUMENT, file, register, log, report, minute, account, entry, journal, diary, memorial, archives, memoir, chronicle, memorandum, annals **2** EVIDENCE, trace, documentation, testimony, witness, memorial, remembrance **3** DISC, recording, single, release, album, waxing (informal), LP, vinyl, EP, forty-five, platter (US slang), seventy-eight, gramophone record, black disc **4** BACKGROUND, history, performance, career, track record (informal), curriculum vitae ▷ verb **1** SET DOWN, report, minute, note, enter, document, register, preserve, log, put down, chronicle, write down, enrol, take down, inscribe, transcribe, chalk up (informal), put on record, put on file **2** MAKE A RECORDING OF, cut, video, tape, lay down (slang), wax (informal), video-tape, tape-record, put on wax (informal) **3** REGISTER, show, read, contain, indicate, give evidence of ▷▷ **off the record 1** CONFIDENTIALLY, in private, in confidence, unofficially, sub rosa, under the rose **2** CONFIDENTIAL, private, unofficial, not for publication

recorder noun CHRONICLER, archivist, historian, scorer, clerk, registrar, scribe, diarist, scorekeeper, annalist

recording noun RECORD, video, tape, disc, gramophone record, cut (informal)

recount verb TELL, report, detail, describe, relate, repeat, portray, depict, rehearse, recite, tell the story of, narrate, delineate, enumerate, give an account of

recoup verb REGAIN, recover, make good, retrieve, redeem, win back

recourse noun OPTION, choice, alternative, resort, appeal, resource, remedy, way out, refuge, expedient

recover *verb* 1 GET BETTER, improve, get well, recuperate, pick up, heal, revive, come round, bounce back, mend, turn the corner, pull through, convalesce, be on the mend, take a turn for the better, get back on your feet, feel yourself again, regain your health *or* strength << ANTONYM relapse 2 RALLY 3 SAVE, rescue, retrieve, salvage, reclaim << ANTONYM abandon 4 RECOUP, restore, repair, get back, regain, make good, retrieve, reclaim, redeem, recapture, win back, take back, repossess, retake, find again << ANTONYM lose

recovery *noun* 1 IMPROVEMENT, return to health, rally, healing, revival, mending, recuperation, convalescence, turn for the better 2 REVIVAL, improvement, rally, restoration, rehabilitation, upturn, betterment, amelioration 3 RETRIEVAL, repossession, reclamation, restoration, repair, redemption, recapture

recreation *noun* LEISURE, play, sport, exercise, fun, relief, pleasure, entertainment, relaxation, enjoyment, distraction, amusement, diversion, refreshment, beer and skittles (*informal*), me-time

recrimination *noun* BICKERING, retaliation, counterattack, mutual accusation, retort, quarrel, squabbling, name-calling, countercharge

recruit *verb* 1 GATHER, take on, obtain, engage, round up, enrol, procure, proselytize 2 ASSEMBLE, raise, levy, muster, mobilize 3 ENLIST, draft, impress, enrol << ANTONYM dismiss ▷ *noun* BEGINNER, trainee, apprentice, novice, convert, initiate, rookie (*informal*), helper, learner, neophyte, tyro, greenhorn (*informal*), proselyte

rectify *verb* CORRECT, right, improve, reform, square, fix, repair, adjust, remedy, amend, make good, mend, redress, put right, set the record straight

rectitude *noun* 1 MORALITY, principle, honour, virtue, decency, justice, equity, integrity, goodness, honesty, correctness, righteousness, probity, incorruptibility, scrupulousness, uprightness << ANTONYM immorality 2 CORRECTNESS, justice, accuracy, precision, verity, rightness, soundness, exactness

recuperate *verb* RECOVER, improve, pick up, get better, mend, turn the corner, convalesce, be on the mend, get back on your feet, regain your health

recur *verb* HAPPEN AGAIN, return, come back, repeat, persist, revert, reappear, come and go, come again

recurrent *adjective* PERIODIC, continued, regular, repeated, frequent, recurring, repetitive, cyclical, habitual << ANTONYM one-off

recycle *verb* REPROCESS, reuse, salvage, reclaim, save

red *noun* CRIMSON, scarlet, ruby, vermilion, rose, wine, pink, cherry, cardinal, coral, maroon, claret, carmine ▷ *adjective* 1 CRIMSON, scarlet, ruby, vermilion, rose, wine, pink, cherry, cardinal, coral, maroon, claret, carmine 2 FLUSHED, embarrassed, blushing, suffused, florid, shamefaced, rubicund 3 (*of hair*) CHESTNUT, flaming, reddish, flame-coloured, bay, sandy, foxy, Titian, carroty 4 BLOODSHOT, inflamed, red-rimmed 5 ROSY, healthy, glowing, blooming, ruddy, roseate ▷▷ **in the red** (*informal*) IN DEBT, bankrupt, on the rocks, insolvent, in arrears, overdrawn, owing money, in deficit, showing a loss, in debit ▷▷ **see red** (*informal*) LOSE YOUR TEMPER, boil, lose it (*informal*), seethe, go mad (*informal*), crack up (*informal*), lose the plot (*informal*), go ballistic (*slang, chiefly US*), blow a fuse (*slang, chiefly US*), fly off the handle (*informal*), become enraged, go off the deep end (*informal*), wig out (*slang*), go up the wall (*slang*), blow your top, lose your rag (*slang*), be beside yourself with rage (*informal*), be *or* get very angry, go off your head (*slang*)

red-blooded *adjective* (*informal*) VIGOROUS, manly, lusty, virile, strong, vital, robust, hearty

redden *verb* FLUSH, colour (up), blush, crimson, suffuse, go red, go beetroot (*informal*)

redeem *verb* 1 REINSTATE, absolve, restore to favour, rehabilitate 2 MAKE UP FOR, offset, make good, compensate for, outweigh, redress, atone for, make amends for, defray 3 TRADE IN, cash (in), exchange, change 4 BUY BACK, recover, regain, retrieve, reclaim, win back, repossess, repurchase, recover possession of 5 SAVE, free, deliver, rescue, liberate, ransom, set free, extricate, emancipate, buy the freedom of, pay the ransom of 6 FULFIL, meet, keep, carry out, satisfy, discharge, make good, hold to, acquit, adhere to, abide by, keep faith with, be faithful to, perform

redemption *noun* 1 COMPENSATION, amends, reparation, atonement, expiation

2 SALVATION, release, rescue, liberation, ransom, emancipation, deliverance **3** PAYING-OFF, paying back **4** TRADE-IN, recovery, retrieval, repurchase, repossession, reclamation, quid pro quo

red-handed *adjective* IN THE ACT, with your pants down (*US slang*), (in) flagrante delicto, with your fingers *or* hand in the till (*informal*), bang to rights (*slang*)

redolent *adjective* **1** REMINISCENT, evocative, suggestive, remindful **2** SCENTED, perfumed, fragrant, aromatic, sweet-smelling, odorous

redoubtable *adjective* FORMIDABLE, strong, powerful, terrible, awful, mighty, dreadful, fearful, fearsome, resolute, valiant, doughty

redress *verb* **1** MAKE AMENDS FOR, pay for, make up for, compensate for, put right, recompense for, make reparation for, make restitution for **2** PUT RIGHT, reform, balance, square, correct, ease, repair, relieve, adjust, regulate, remedy, amend, mend, rectify, even up, restore the balance ▷ *noun* AMENDS, payment, compensation, reparation, restitution, atonement, recompense, requital, quittance

reduce *verb* **1** LESSEN, cut, contract, lower, depress, moderate, weaken, diminish, turn down, decrease, slow down, cut down, shorten, dilute, impair, curtail, wind down, abate, tone down, debase, truncate, abridge, downsize, kennet (*Austral slang*), jeff (*Austral slang*) << ANTONYM increase **2** DEGRADE, downgrade, demote, lower in rank, break, humble, humiliate, bring low, take down a peg (*informal*), lower the status of << ANTONYM promote **3** DRIVE, force, bring, bring to the point of **4** CHEAPEN, cut, lower, discount, slash, mark down, bring down the price of **5** IMPOVERISH, ruin, bankrupt, pauperize ▷▷ **in reduced circumstances** IMPOVERISHED, broke (*informal*), badly off, hard up (*informal*), short, in need, needy, on the rocks, penniless, destitute, poverty-stricken, down and out, skint (*Brit slang*), in want, indigent, down at heel, impecunious, dirt-poor (*informal*), on the breadline, flat broke (*informal*), penurious, on your uppers, stony-broke (*Brit slang*), necessitous, in queer street, without two pennies to rub together (*informal*), on your beam-ends

redundancy *noun* **1** LAYOFF, sacking, dismissal **2** UNEMPLOYMENT, the sack (*informal*), the axe (*informal*), joblessness **3** SUPERFLUITY, surplus, surfeit, superabundance

redundant *adjective* **1** SUPERFLUOUS, extra, surplus, excessive, unnecessary, unwanted, inordinate, inessential, supernumerary, de trop (*French*), supererogatory << ANTONYM essential **2** TAUTOLOGICAL, wordy, repetitious, verbose, padded, diffuse, prolix, iterative, periphrastic, pleonastic

reek *verb* **1** STINK, smell, pong (*Brit informal*), smell to high heaven, hum (*slang*) **2** *with of* BE REDOLENT OF, suggest, smack of, testify to, be characterized by, bear the stamp of, be permeated by, be suggestive *or* indicative of ▷ *noun* STINK, smell, odour, stench, pong (*Brit informal*), effluvium, niff (*Brit slang*), malodour, mephitis, fetor

reel *verb* **1** STAGGER, rock, roll, pitch, stumble, sway, falter, lurch, wobble, waver, totter **2** WHIRL, swim, spin, revolve, swirl, twirl, go round and round

refer *verb* **1** PASS ON, transfer, deliver, commit, hand over, submit, turn over, consign **2** DIRECT, point, send, guide, recommend ▷▷ **refer to something** *or* **someone 1** ALLUDE TO, mention, cite, speak of, bring up, invoke, hint at, touch on, make reference to, make mention of **2** RELATE TO, concern, apply to, pertain to, be relevant to **3** CONSULT, go, apply, turn to, look up, have recourse to, seek information from

referee *noun* UMPIRE, umpie (*Austral slang*), judge, ref (*informal*), arbiter, arbitrator, adjudicator ▷ *verb* UMPIRE, judge, mediate, adjudicate, arbitrate

reference *noun* **1** ALLUSION, note, mention, remark, quotation **2** CITATION **3** TESTIMONIAL, recommendation, credentials, endorsement, certification, good word, character reference

referendum *noun* PUBLIC VOTE, popular vote, plebiscite

refine *verb* **1** PURIFY, process, filter, cleanse, clarify, distil, rarefy **2** IMPROVE, perfect, polish, temper, elevate, hone

refined *adjective* **1** PURIFIED, processed, pure, filtered, clean, clarified, distilled << ANTONYM unrefined **2** CULTURED, civil, polished, sophisticated, gentlemanly, elegant, polite, cultivated, gracious, civilized, genteel, urbane, courtly, well-bred, ladylike, well-mannered << ANTONYM coarse **3** DISCERNING, fine, nice, sensitive, exact, subtle, delicate, precise, discriminating, sublime, fastidious, punctilious

refinement *noun* **1** SUBTLETY, nuance, nicety, fine point **2** SOPHISTICATION, finish, style, culture, taste, breeding, polish, grace, discrimination, courtesy, civilization, precision, elegance, delicacy, cultivation, finesse, politeness, good manners, civility, gentility, good breeding, graciousness, urbanity, fastidiousness, fineness, courtliness, politesse **3** PURIFICATION, processing, filtering, cleansing, clarification, distillation, rectification, rarefaction

reflect *verb* **1** SHOW, reveal, express, display, indicate, demonstrate, exhibit, communicate, manifest, bear out, bespeak, evince **2** THROW BACK, return, mirror, echo, reproduce, imitate, give back **3** *usually followed by* **on** CONSIDER, think, contemplate, deliberate, muse, ponder, meditate, mull over, ruminate, cogitate, wonder

reflection *noun* **1** IMAGE, echo, counterpart, mirror image **2** CRITICISM, censure, slur, reproach, imputation, derogation, aspersion **3** CONSIDERATION, thinking, pondering, deliberation, thought, idea, view, study, opinion, impression, observation, musing, meditation, contemplation, rumination, perusal, cogitation, cerebration

reflective *adjective* THOUGHTFUL, contemplative, meditative, pensive, reasoning, pondering, deliberative, ruminative, cogitating

reform *noun* IMPROVEMENT, amendment, correction, rehabilitation, renovation, betterment, rectification, amelioration ▷ *verb* **1** IMPROVE, better, correct, restore, repair, rebuild, amend, reclaim, mend, renovate, reconstruct, remodel, rectify, rehabilitate, regenerate, reorganize, reconstitute, revolutionize, ameliorate, emend **2** MEND YOUR WAYS, go straight (*informal*), shape up (*informal*), get it together (*informal*), turn over a new leaf, get your act together (*informal*), clean up your act (*informal*), pull your socks up (*Brit informal*), get back on the straight and narrow (*informal*)

refrain¹ *verb* STOP, avoid, give up, cease, do without, renounce, abstain, eschew, leave off, desist, forbear, kick (*informal*)

refrain² *noun* CHORUS, song, tune, melody

refresh *verb* **1** REVIVE, cool, freshen, revitalize, cheer, stimulate, brace, rejuvenate, kick-start (*informal*), enliven, breathe new life into, invigorate, revivify, reanimate, inspirit **2** REPLENISH, restore, repair, renew, top up, renovate **3** STIMULATE, prompt, renew, jog, prod, brush up (*informal*)

refreshing *adjective* **1** NEW, different, original, novel **2** STIMULATING, fresh, cooling, bracing, invigorating, revivifying, thirst-quenching, inspiriting << ANTONYM tiring

refreshment *noun* **1** REVIVAL, restoration, renewal, stimulation, renovation, freshening, reanimation, enlivenment, repair **2** *plural* FOOD AND DRINK, drinks, snacks, titbits, kai (*NZ informal*)

refrigerate *verb* COOL, freeze, chill, keep cold

refuge *noun* **1** PROTECTION, security, shelter, harbour, asylum **2** HAVEN, resort, retreat, sanctuary, hide-out, bolt hole

refugee *noun* EXILE, émigré, displaced person, runaway, fugitive, escapee

refund *noun* REPAYMENT, reimbursement, return ▷ *verb* REPAY, return, restore, make good, pay back, reimburse, give back

refurbish *verb* RENOVATE, restore, repair, clean up, overhaul, revamp, mend, remodel, do up (*informal*), refit, fix up (*informal, chiefly US & Canad*), spruce up, re-equip, set to rights

refusal *noun* REJECTION, denial, defiance, rebuff, knock-back (*slang*), thumbs down, repudiation, kick in the teeth (*slang*), negation, no ▷▷ **first refusal** OPTION, choice, opportunity, consideration

refuse¹ *verb* **1** DECLINE, reject, turn down, say no to, repudiate **2** DENY, decline, withhold << ANTONYM allow

refuse² *noun* RUBBISH, waste, sweepings, junk (*informal*), litter, garbage, trash, sediment, scum, dross, dregs, leavings, dreck (*slang, chiefly US*), offscourings, lees

refute *verb* DISPROVE, counter, discredit, prove false, silence, overthrow, negate, rebut, give the lie to, blow out of the water (*slang*), confute << ANTONYM prove

regain *verb* **1** RECOVER, get back, retrieve, redeem, recapture, win back, take back, recoup, repossess, retake **2** GET BACK TO, return to, reach again, reattain

regal *adjective* ROYAL, majestic, kingly *or* queenly, noble, princely, proud, magnificent, sovereign, fit for a king *or* queen

regale *verb* **1** ENTERTAIN, delight, amuse, divert, gratify **2** SERVE, refresh, ply

regalia *plural noun* TRAPPINGS, gear, decorations, finery, apparatus, emblems, paraphernalia, garb, accoutrements, rigout (*informal*)

regard *verb* **1** CONSIDER, see, hold, rate, view, value, account, judge, treat, think of, esteem, deem, look upon, adjudge **2** LOOK AT, view, eye, watch, observe, check, notice, clock (*Brit slang*), remark, check out (*informal*), gaze at, behold, eyeball (*US slang*), scrutinize, get a load of (*informal*), take a dekko at (*Brit slang*) ▷ *noun* **1** RESPECT, esteem, deference, store, thought, love, concern, care, account, note, reputation, honour, consideration, sympathy, affection, attachment, repute **2** LOOK, gaze, scrutiny, stare, glance **3** *plural* GOOD WISHES, respects, greetings, compliments, best wishes, salutations, devoirs ▷▷ **as regards** CONCERNING, regarding, relating to, pertaining to ▷▷ **in this regard** ON THIS POINT, on this matter, on this detail, in this respect ▷▷ **with regard to** CONCERNING, regarding, relating to, with respect to, as regards

regarding *preposition* CONCERNING, about, as to, on the subject of, re, respecting, in respect of, as regards, with reference to, in re, in the matter of, apropos, in *or* with regard to

regardless *adverb* IN SPITE OF EVERYTHING, anyway, nevertheless, nonetheless, in any case, no matter what, for all that, rain or shine, despite everything, come what may ▷ *adjective with* **of** IRRESPECTIVE OF, disregarding, unconcerned about, heedless of, unmindful of

regenerate *verb* RENEW, restore, revive, renovate, change, reproduce, uplift, reconstruct, re-establish, rejuvenate, kick-start (*informal*), breathe new life into, invigorate, reinvigorate, reawaken, revivify, give a shot in the arm, inspirit << ANTONYM degenerate

regime *noun* **1** GOVERNMENT, rule, management, administration, leadership, establishment, reign **2** PLAN, course, system, policy, programme, scheme, regimen

region *noun* AREA, country, place, part, land, quarter, division, section, sector, district, territory, zone, province, patch, turf (*US slang*), tract, expanse, locality

regional *adjective* LOCAL, district, provincial, parochial, sectional, zonal

register *noun* LIST, record, roll, file, schedule, diary, catalogue, log, archives, chronicle, memorandum, roster, ledger, annals ▷ *verb* **1** ENROL, sign on *or* up, enlist, list, note, enter, check in, inscribe, set down **2** RECORD, catalogue, chronicle, take down **3** INDICATE, show, record, read **4** SHOW, mark, record, reflect, indicate, betray, manifest, bespeak **5** EXPRESS, say, show, reveal, display, exhibit **6** (*informal*) HAVE AN EFFECT, get through, sink in, make an impression, tell, impress, come home, dawn on

regress *verb* REVERT, deteriorate, return, go back, retreat, lapse, fall back, wane, recede, ebb, degenerate, relapse, lose ground, turn the clock back, backslide, retrogress, retrocede, fall away *or* off << ANTONYM progress

regret *verb* **1** BE *or* FEEL SORRY ABOUT, feel remorse about, be upset about, rue, deplore, bemoan, repent (of), weep over, bewail, cry over spilt milk << ANTONYM be satisfied with **2** MOURN, miss, grieve for *or* over ▷ *noun* **1** REMORSE, compunction, self-reproach, pang of conscience, bitterness, repentance, contrition, penitence, ruefulness **2** SORROW, disappointment, grief, lamentation << ANTONYM satisfaction

regretful *adjective* SORRY, disappointed, sad, ashamed, apologetic, mournful, rueful, contrite, sorrowful, repentant, remorseful, penitent

regrettable *adjective* UNFORTUNATE, wrong, disappointing, sad, distressing, unhappy, shameful, woeful, deplorable, ill-advised, lamentable, pitiable ▷ see **regretful**

regular *adjective* **1** FREQUENT, daily **2** NORMAL, common, established, usual, ordinary, typical, routine, everyday, customary, commonplace, habitual, unvarying << ANTONYM infrequent **3** STEADY, consistent **4** EVEN, level, balanced, straight, flat, fixed, smooth, uniform, symmetrical << ANTONYM uneven **5** METHODICAL, set, ordered, formal, steady, efficient, systematic, orderly, standardized, dependable, consistent << ANTONYM inconsistent **6** OFFICIAL, standard, established, traditional, classic, correct, approved, formal, sanctioned, proper, prevailing, orthodox, time-honoured, bona fide

regulate *verb* **1** CONTROL, run, order, rule, manage, direct, guide, handle, conduct, arrange, monitor, organize, govern, administer, oversee, supervise, systematize, superintend **2** MODERATE, control, modulate, settle, fit, balance, tune, adjust

regulation *noun* **1** RULE, order, law, direction, procedure, requirement, dictate, decree, canon, statute, ordinance, commandment, edict, precept, standing order **2** CONTROL, government, management, administration, direction, arrangement, supervision, governance, rule ▷ *modifier* CONVENTIONAL, official, standard, required, normal, usual, prescribed, mandatory, customary

regurgitate *verb* DISGORGE, throw up

(*informal*), chuck up (*slang, chiefly US*), puke up (*slang*), sick up (*informal*), spew out *or* up

rehabilitate *verb* 1 REINTEGRATE 2 RESTORE, convert, renew, adjust, rebuild, make good, mend, renovate, reconstruct, reinstate, re-establish, fix up (*informal, chiefly US & Canad*), reconstitute, recondition, reinvigorate

rehash *noun* REWORKING, rewrite, new version, rearrangement ▷ *verb* REWORK, rewrite, rearrange, change, alter, reshuffle, make over, reuse, rejig (*informal*), refashion

rehearsal *noun* PRACTICE, rehearsing, practice session, run-through, reading, preparation, drill, going-over (*informal*)

rehearse *verb* 1 PRACTISE, prepare, run through, go over, train, act, study, ready, repeat, drill, try out, recite 2 RECITE, practice, go over, run through, tell, list, detail, describe, review, relate, depict, spell out, recount, narrate, trot out (*informal*), delineate, enumerate

reign *verb* 1 BE SUPREME, prevail, predominate, hold sway, be rife, be rampant 2 RULE, govern, be in power, occupy *or* sit on the throne, influence, command, administer, hold sway, wear the crown, wield the sceptre ▷ *noun* RULE, sovereignty, supremacy, power, control, influence, command, empire, monarchy, sway, dominion, hegemony, ascendancy

reimburse *verb* PAY BACK, refund, repay, recompense, return, restore, compensate, indemnify, remunerate

rein *noun* CONTROL, harness, bridle, hold, check, restriction, brake, curb, restraint ▷▷ **give (a) free rein to something** *or* **someone** GIVE A FREE HAND (TO), give carte blanche (to), give a blank cheque (to), remove restraints (from), indulge, let go, give way to, give (someone) his *or* her head ▷▷ **rein something in** *or* **back** CHECK, control, limit, contain, master, curb, restrain, hold back, constrain, bridle, keep in check ▷ see **reign**

reincarnation *noun* REBIRTH, metempsychosis, transmigration of souls

reinforce *verb* 1 SUPPORT, strengthen, fortify, toughen, stress, prop, supplement, emphasize, underline, harden, bolster, stiffen, shore up, buttress 2 INCREASE, extend, add to, strengthen, supplement, augment

reinforcement *noun* 1 STRENGTHENING, increase, supplement, enlargement, fortification, amplification, augmentation 2 SUPPORT, stay, shore, prop, brace, buttress

3 *plural* RESERVES, support, auxiliaries, additional *or* fresh troops

reinstate *verb* RESTORE, recall, bring back, re-establish, return, rehabilitate

reiterate *verb* (*formal*) REPEAT, restate, say again, retell, do again, recapitulate, iterate

reject *verb* 1 REBUFF, drop, jilt, desert, turn down, ditch (*slang*), break with, spurn, refuse, say no to, repulse, throw over << ANTONYM accept 2 DENY, decline, abandon, exclude, veto, discard, relinquish, renounce, spurn, eschew, leave off, throw off, disallow, forsake, retract, repudiate, cast off, disown, forgo, disclaim, forswear, swear off, wash your hands of << ANTONYM approve 3 DISCARD, decline, eliminate, scrap, bin, jettison, cast aside, throw away *or* out << ANTONYM accept ▷ *noun* 1 CASTOFF, second, discard, flotsam, clunker (*informal*) << ANTONYM treasure 2 FAILURE, loser, flop

rejection *noun* 1 DENIAL, veto, dismissal, exclusion, abandonment, spurning, casting off, disowning, thumbs down, renunciation, repudiation, eschewal << ANTONYM approval 2 REBUFF, refusal, knock-back (*slang*), kick in the teeth (*slang*), bum's rush (*slang*), the (old) heave-ho (*informal*), brushoff (*slang*) << ANTONYM acceptance

rejoice *verb* BE GLAD, celebrate, delight, be happy, joy, triumph, glory, revel, be overjoyed, exult, jump for joy, make merry << ANTONYM lament

rejoicing *noun* HAPPINESS, delight, joy, triumph, celebration, cheer, festivity, elation, gaiety, jubilation, revelry, exultation, gladness, merrymaking

rejoin *verb* REPLY, answer, respond, retort, come back with, riposte, return

rejuvenate *verb* REVITALIZE, restore, renew, refresh, regenerate, breathe new life into, reinvigorate, revivify, give new life to, reanimate, make young again, restore vitality to

relapse *verb* 1 LAPSE, revert, degenerate, slip back, fail, weaken, fall back, regress, backslide, retrogress 2 WORSEN, deteriorate, sicken, weaken, fail, sink, fade << ANTONYM recover ▷ *noun* 1 LAPSE, regression, fall from grace, reversion, backsliding, recidivism, retrogression 2 WORSENING, setback, deterioration, recurrence, turn for the worse, weakening << ANTONYM recovery

relate *verb* 1 TELL, recount, report, present, detail, describe, chronicle, rehearse, recite, impart, narrate, set forth, give an account

of ▷▷ **relate to something** or **someone**
1 CONCERN, refer to, apply to, have to do
with, pertain to, be relevant to, bear upon,
appertain to, have reference to 2 CONNECT
WITH, associate with, link with, couple with,
join with, ally with, correlate to, coordinate
with

related adjective 1 ASSOCIATED, linked,
allied, joint, accompanying, connected,
affiliated, akin, correlated, interconnected,
concomitant, cognate, agnate << ANTONYM
unconnected 2 AKIN, kin, kindred, cognate,
consanguineous, agnate << ANTONYM
unrelated

relation noun 1 SIMILARITY, link, bearing,
bond, application, comparison, tie-in,
correlation, interdependence, pertinence,
connection 2 RELATIVE, kin, kinsman or
kinswoman, rellie (Austral slang) ▷ plural
noun 1 DEALINGS, relationship, rapport,
communications, meetings, terms,
associations, affairs, contact, connections,
interaction, intercourse, liaison 2 FAMILY,
relatives, tribe, clan, kin, kindred, kinsmen,
kinsfolk, ainga (NZ), rellie (Austral slang)

relationship noun 1 ASSOCIATION, bond,
communications, connection, conjunction,
affinity, rapport, kinship 2 AFFAIR, romance,
liaison, amour, intrigue 3 CONNECTION, link,
proportion, parallel, ratio, similarity, tie-up,
correlation

relative noun RELATION, connection,
kinsman or kinswoman, member of
your or the family, rellie (Austral slang) ▷
adjective 1 COMPARATIVE 2 CORRESPONDING,
respective, reciprocal 3 with **to** IN
PROPORTION TO, corresponding to,
proportionate to, proportional to

relatively adverb COMPARATIVELY, rather,
somewhat, to some extent, in or by
comparison

relax verb 1 BE or FEEL AT EASE, chill out
(slang, chiefly US), take it easy, loosen up,
laze, lighten up (slang), put your feet up,
hang loose (slang), let yourself go (informal),
let your hair down (informal), mellow out
(informal), make yourself at home, outspan
(S African), take your ease << ANTONYM
be alarmed 2 CALM DOWN, calm, unwind,
loosen up, tranquillize 3 MAKE LESS TENSE,
soften, loosen up, unbend, rest 4 LESSEN,
reduce, ease, relieve, weaken, loosen, let up,
slacken << ANTONYM tighten 5 MODERATE,
ease, relieve, weaken, diminish, mitigate,
slacken << ANTONYM tighten up

relaxation noun 1 LEISURE, rest, fun, pleasure,
entertainment, recreation, enjoyment,
amusement, refreshment, beer and
skittles (informal), me-time 2 LESSENING,
easing, reduction, weakening, moderation,
let-up (informal), slackening, diminution,
abatement

relaxed adjective 1 EASY-GOING, easy, casual,
informal, laid-back (informal), mellow,
leisurely, downbeat (informal), unhurried,
nonchalant, free and easy, mild, insouciant,
untaxing 2 COMFORTABLE, easy-going,
casual, laid-back (informal), informal

relay verb BROADCAST, carry, spread,
communicate, transmit, send out

release verb 1 SET FREE, free, discharge,
liberate, drop, deliver, loose, let go, undo, let
out, extricate, untie, disengage, emancipate,
unchain, unfasten, turn loose, unshackle,
unloose, unfetter, unbridle, manumit
<< ANTONYM imprison 2 ACQUIT, excuse,
exempt, let go, dispense, let off, exonerate,
absolve 3 ISSUE, publish, make public, make
known, break, present, launch, distribute,
unveil, put out, circulate, disseminate
<< ANTONYM withhold ▷ noun 1 LIBERATION,
freedom, delivery, liberty, discharge,
emancipation, deliverance, manumission,
relief << ANTONYM imprisonment
2 ACQUITTAL, exemption, let-off (informal),
dispensation, absolution, exoneration,
acquittance 3 ISSUE, announcement,
publication, proclamation, offering

relegate verb 1 DEMOTE, degrade, downgrade,
declass 2 BANISH, exile, expel, throw out,
oust, deport, eject, expatriate

relent verb 1 BE MERCIFUL, yield, give in,
soften, give way, come round, capitulate,
acquiesce, change your mind, unbend,
forbear, show mercy, have pity, melt, give
quarter << ANTONYM show no mercy 2 EASE,
die down, let up, fall, drop, slow, relax,
weaken, slacken << ANTONYM intensify

relentless adjective 1 MERCILESS, hard,
fierce, harsh, cruel, grim, ruthless,
uncompromising, unstoppable, inflexible,
unrelenting, unforgiving, inexorable,
implacable, unyielding, remorseless,
pitiless, undeviating << ANTONYM merciful
2 UNREMITTING, sustained, punishing,
persistent, unstoppable, unbroken,
unrelenting, incessant, unabated, nonstop,
unrelieved, unflagging, unfaltering

relevant adjective SIGNIFICANT, appropriate,
proper, related, fitting, material, suited,

relative, to the point, apt, applicable, pertinent, apposite, admissible, germane, to the purpose, appurtenant, ad rem (*Latin*) << ANTONYM irrelevant

reliable *adjective* **1** DEPENDABLE, trustworthy, honest, responsible, sure, sound, true, certain, regular, stable, faithful, predictable, upright, staunch, reputable, trusty, unfailing, tried and true << ANTONYM unreliable **2** SAFE, dependable **3** DEFINITIVE, sound, dependable, trustworthy

reliance *noun* **1** DEPENDENCY, dependence **2** TRUST, confidence, belief, faith, assurance, credence, credit

relic *noun* REMNANT, vestige, memento, trace, survival, scrap, token, fragment, souvenir, remembrance, keepsake

relief *noun* **1** EASE, release, comfort, cure, remedy, solace, balm, deliverance, mitigation, abatement, alleviation, easement, palliation, assuagement **2** REST, respite, let-up, relaxation, break, diversion, refreshment (*informal*), remission, breather (*informal*) **3** AID, help, support, assistance, sustenance, succour

relieve *verb* **1** EASE, soothe, alleviate, allay, relax, comfort, calm, cure, dull, diminish, soften, console, appease, solace, mitigate, abate, assuage, mollify, salve, palliate << ANTONYM intensify **2** FREE, release, deliver, discharge, exempt, unburden, disembarrass, disencumber **3** TAKE OVER FROM, substitute for, stand in for, take the place of, give (someone) a break *or* rest **4** HELP, support, aid, sustain, assist, succour, bring aid to

religion *noun* BELIEF, faith, theology, creed

religious *adjective* **1** SPIRITUAL, holy, sacred, divine, theological, righteous, sectarian, doctrinal, devotional, scriptural **2** CONSCIENTIOUS, exact, faithful, rigid, rigorous, meticulous, scrupulous, fastidious, unerring, unswerving, punctilious

relinquish *verb* (*formal*) GIVE UP, leave, release, drop, abandon, resign, desert, quit, yield, hand over, surrender, withdraw from, let go, retire from, renounce, waive, vacate, say goodbye to, forsake, cede, repudiate, cast off, forgo, abdicate, kiss (something) goodbye, lay aside

relish *verb* **1** ENJOY, like, prefer, taste, appreciate, savour, revel in, luxuriate in << ANTONYM dislike **2** LOOK FORWARD TO, fancy, delight in, lick your lips over ▷ *noun* **1** ENJOYMENT, liking, love, taste, fancy,

stomach, appetite, appreciation, penchant, zest, fondness, gusto, predilection, zing (*informal*), partiality << ANTONYM distaste **2** CONDIMENT, seasoning, sauce, appetizer

reluctance *noun* UNWILLINGNESS, dislike, loathing, distaste, aversion, backwardness, hesitancy, disinclination, repugnance, indisposition, disrelish

reluctant *adjective* UNWILLING, slow, backward, grudging, hesitant, averse, recalcitrant, loath, disinclined, unenthusiastic, indisposed << ANTONYM willing

rely on *verb* **1** DEPEND ON, lean on **2** BE CONFIDENT OF, bank on, trust, count on, bet on, reckon on, lean on, be sure of, have confidence in, swear by, repose trust in

remain *verb* **1** STAY, continue, go on, stand, dwell, bide **2** STAY BEHIND, wait, delay, stay put (*informal*), tarry << ANTONYM go **3** CONTINUE, be left, endure, persist, linger, hang in the air, stay

remainder *noun* REST, remains, balance, trace, excess, surplus, butt, remnant, relic, residue, stub, vestige(s), tail end, dregs, oddment, leavings, residuum

remaining *adjective* **1** LEFT-OVER, surviving, outstanding, lingering, unfinished, residual **2** SURVIVING, lasting, persisting, abiding, extant

remains *plural noun* **1** REMNANTS, leftovers, remainder, scraps, rest, pieces, balance, traces, fragments, debris, residue, crumbs, vestiges, detritus, dregs, odds and ends, oddments, leavings **2** RELICS **3** CORPSE, body, carcass, cadaver

remark *verb* **1** COMMENT, say, state, reflect, mention, declare, observe, pass comment, animadvert **2** NOTICE, note, observe, perceive, see, mark, regard, make out, heed, espy, take note *or* notice of ▷ *noun* **1** COMMENT, observation, reflection, statement, thought, word, opinion, declaration, assertion, utterance **2** NOTICE, thought, comment, attention, regard, mention, recognition, consideration, observation, heed, acknowledgment

remarkable *adjective* EXTRAORDINARY, striking, outstanding, famous, odd, strange, wonderful, signal, rare, unusual, impressive, surprising, distinguished, prominent, notable, phenomenal, uncommon, conspicuous, singular, miraculous, noteworthy, pre-eminent << ANTONYM ordinary

remedy *noun* **1** SOLUTION, relief, redress, antidote, corrective, panacea, countermeasure **2** CURE, treatment, specific, medicine, therapy, antidote, panacea, restorative, relief, nostrum, physic (*rare*), medicament, counteractive ▷ *verb* **1** PUT RIGHT, redress, rectify, reform, fix, correct, solve, repair, relieve, ameliorate, set to rights **2** CURE, treat, heal, help, control, ease, restore, relieve, soothe, alleviate, mitigate, assuage, palliate

remember *verb* **1** RECALL, think back to, recollect, reminisce about, retain, recognize, call up, summon up, call to mind << ANTONYM forget **2** BEAR IN MIND, keep in mind **3** LOOK BACK (ON), commemorate

remembrance *noun* **1** COMMEMORATION, memorial, testimonial **2** SOUVENIR, token, reminder, monument, relic, remembrancer (*archaic*), memento, keepsake **3** MEMORY, recollection, thought, recall, recognition, retrospect, reminiscence, anamnesis

remind *verb* JOG YOUR MEMORY, prompt, refresh your memory, make you remember ▷▷ **remind someone of something** *or* **someone** BRING TO MIND, call to mind, put in mind, awaken memories of, call up, bring back to

reminisce *verb* RECALL, remember, look back, hark back, review, think back, recollect, live in the past, go over in the memory

reminiscence *plural noun* RECOLLECTIONS, memories, reflections, retrospections, reviews, recalls, memoirs, anecdotes, remembrances

reminiscent *adjective* SUGGESTIVE, evocative, redolent, remindful, similar

remission *noun* **1** LESSENING, abatement, abeyance, lull, relaxation, ebb, respite, moderation, let-up (*informal*), alleviation, amelioration **2** REDUCTION, lessening, suspension, decrease, diminution **3** PARDON, release, discharge, amnesty, forgiveness, indulgence, exemption, reprieve, acquittal, absolution, exoneration, excuse

remit *noun* INSTRUCTIONS, brief, guidelines, authorization, terms of reference, orders ▷ *verb* **1** SEND, post, forward, mail, transmit, dispatch **2** CANCEL, stop, halt, repeal, rescind, desist, forbear **3** LESSEN, diminish, abate, ease up, reduce, relax, moderate, weaken, decrease, soften, dwindle, alleviate, wane, fall away, mitigate, slacken

remittance *noun* PAYMENT, fee, consideration, allowance

remnant *noun* REMAINDER, remains, trace, fragment, end, bit, rest, piece, balance, survival, scrap, butt, shred, hangover, residue, rump, leftovers, stub, vestige, tail end, oddment, residuum

remonstrate *verb* (*formal*) PROTEST, challenge, argue, take issue, object, complain, dispute, dissent, take exception, expostulate

remorse *noun* REGRET, shame, guilt, pity, grief, compassion, sorrow, anguish, repentance, contrition, compunction, penitence, self-reproach, pangs of conscience, ruefulness, bad *or* guilty conscience

remorseless *adjective* PITILESS, hard, harsh, cruel, savage, ruthless, callous, merciless, unforgiving, implacable, inhumane, unmerciful, hardhearted, uncompassionate

remote *adjective* **1** DISTANT, far, isolated, lonely, out-of-the-way, far-off, secluded, inaccessible, faraway, outlying, in the middle of nowhere, off the beaten track, backwoods, godforsaken << ANTONYM nearby **2** FAR, distant, obscure, far-off << ANTONYM relevant **3** SLIGHT, small, outside, poor, unlikely, slim, faint, doubtful, dubious, slender, meagre, negligible, implausible, inconsiderable << ANTONYM strong **4** ALOOF, cold, removed, reserved, withdrawn, distant, abstracted, detached, indifferent, faraway, introspective, uninterested, introverted, uninvolved, unapproachable, uncommunicative, standoffish << ANTONYM outgoing

removal *noun* **1** EXTRACTION, stripping, withdrawal, purging, abstraction, uprooting, displacement, eradication, erasure, subtraction, dislodgment, expunction, taking away *or* off *or* out **2** DISMISSAL, expulsion, elimination, ejection, dispossession **3** MOVE, transfer, departure, relocation, flitting (*Scot & N English dialect*)

remove *verb* **1** TAKE OUT, withdraw, extract, abstract << ANTONYM insert **2** TAKE OFF, doff << ANTONYM put on **3** ERASE, eliminate, take out **4** DISMISS, eliminate, get rid of, discharge, abolish, expel, throw out, oust, relegate, purge, eject, do away with, depose, unseat, see the back of, dethrone, show someone the door, give the bum's rush (*slang*), throw out on your ear (*informal*) << ANTONYM appoint **5** GET RID OF, wipe out, erase, eradicate, blow away (*slang, chiefly US*), blot out, expunge **6** TAKE AWAY, move, pull, transfer, detach, displace, do away with, dislodge, cart off (*slang*), carry off *or* away << ANTONYM put back **7** DELETE, shed, get rid of, erase, excise, strike out, efface, expunge << ANTONYM join **8** MOVE, transfer, transport, shift, quit, depart, move away, relocate, vacate, flit (*Scot & N English dialect*) **9** KILL, murder, do in (*slang*), eliminate, take out (*slang*), get rid of, execute, wipe out, dispose of, assassinate, do away with, liquidate, bump off (*slang*), wipe from the face of the earth

remuneration *noun* PAYMENT, income, earnings, salary, pay, return, profit, fee, wages, reward, compensation, repayment, reparation, indemnity, retainer, reimbursement, recompense, stipend, emolument, meed (*archaic*)

renaissance *or* **renascence** *noun* REBIRTH, revival, restoration, renewal, awakening, resurrection, regeneration, resurgence, reappearance, new dawn, re-emergence, reawakening, new birth

rend *verb* (*literary*) TEAR, break, split, rip, pull, separate, divide, crack, burst, smash, disturb, shatter, pierce, fracture, sever, wrench, splinter, rupture, cleave, lacerate, rive, tear to pieces, sunder (*literary*), dissever

render *verb* **1** MAKE, cause to become, leave **2** PROVIDE, give, show, pay, present, supply, deliver, contribute, yield, submit, tender, hand out, furnish, turn over, make available **3** DELIVER, give, return, announce, pronounce **4** TRANSLATE, put, explain, interpret, reproduce, transcribe, construe, restate **5** *sometimes followed by* **up** GIVE UP, give, deliver, yield, hand over, surrender, turn over, relinquish, cede **6** REPRESENT, interpret, portray, depict, do, give, play, act, present, perform

rendezvous *noun* **1** APPOINTMENT, meeting, date, engagement, tryst (*archaic*), assignation **2** MEETING PLACE, venue, gathering point, place of assignation, trysting-place (*archaic*) ▷ *verb* MEET, assemble, get together, come together, collect, gather, rally, muster, converge, join up, be reunited

rendition *noun* (*formal*) **1** PERFORMANCE, arrangement, interpretation, rendering, take (*informal, chiefly US*), reading, version, delivery, presentation, execution, portrayal, depiction **2** TRANSLATION, reading, version, construction, explanation, interpretation, transcription

renegade *noun* DESERTER, rebel, betrayer, dissident, outlaw, runaway, traitor, defector,

mutineer, turncoat, apostate, backslider, recreant (*archaic*) ▷ *modifier* TRAITOROUS, rebel, dissident, outlaw, runaway, rebellious, unfaithful, disloyal, backsliding, mutinous, apostate, recreant (*archaic*)

renege *verb* BREAK YOUR WORD, go back, welsh (*slang*), default, back out, repudiate, break a promise

renew *verb* **1** RECOMMENCE, continue, extend, repeat, resume, prolong, reopen, recreate, reaffirm, re-establish, rejuvenate, regenerate, restate, begin again, revitalize, bring up to date **2** REAFFIRM, resume, breathe new life into, recommence **3** REPLACE, refresh, replenish, restock **4** RESTORE, repair, transform, overhaul, mend, refurbish, renovate, refit, fix up (*informal, chiefly US & Canad*), modernize

renounce *verb* **1** DISOWN, reject, abandon, quit, discard, spurn, eschew, leave off, throw off, forsake, retract, repudiate, cast off, abstain from, recant, forswear, abjure, swear off, wash your hands of **2** DISCLAIM, deny, decline, give up, resign, relinquish, waive, renege, forgo, abdicate, abjure, abnegate << ANTONYM assert

renovate *verb* RESTORE, repair, refurbish, do up (*informal*), reform, renew, overhaul, revamp, recreate, remodel, rehabilitate, refit, fix up (*informal, chiefly US & Canad*), modernize, reconstitute, recondition

renown *noun* FAME, note, distinction, repute, mark, reputation, honour, glory, celebrity, acclaim, stardom, eminence, lustre, illustriousness

renowned *adjective* FAMOUS, noted, celebrated, well-known, distinguished, esteemed, acclaimed, notable, eminent, famed, illustrious << ANTONYM unknown

rent[1] *verb* **1** HIRE, lease **2** LET, lease ▷ *noun* HIRE, rental, lease, tariff, fee, payment

rent[2] *noun* **1** TEAR, split, rip, slash, slit, gash, perforation, hole **2** OPENING, break, hole, crack, breach, flaw, chink

renunciation *noun* **1** REJECTION, giving up, denial, abandonment, spurning, abstention, repudiation, forswearing, disavowal, abnegation, eschewal, abjuration **2** GIVING UP, resignation, surrender, waiver, disclaimer, abdication, relinquishment, abjuration

repair[1] *verb* **1** MEND, fix, recover, restore, heal, renew, patch, make good, renovate, patch up, put back together, restore to working order << ANTONYM damage **2** PUT RIGHT, make up for, compensate for, rectify, square, retrieve, redress ▷ *noun* **1** MEND, restoration, overhaul, adjustment **2** DARN, mend, patch **3** CONDITION, state, form, shape (*informal*), nick (*informal*), fettle

repair² *verb* GO, retire, withdraw, head for, move, remove, leave for, set off for, betake yourself

reparation *noun* COMPENSATION, damages, repair, satisfaction, amends, renewal, redress, indemnity, restitution, atonement, recompense, propitiation, requital

repay *verb* **1** PAY BACK, refund, settle up, return, square, restore, compensate, reimburse, recompense, requite, remunerate **2** REWARD, make restitution

repeal *verb* ABOLISH, reverse, revoke, annul, recall, withdraw, cancel, set aside, rescind, invalidate, nullify, obviate, abrogate, countermand, declare null and void << ANTONYM pass ▷ *noun* ABOLITION, withdrawal, cancellation, rescinding, annulment, revocation, nullification, abrogation, rescission, invalidation, rescindment << ANTONYM passing

repeat *verb* **1** REITERATE, restate, recapitulate, iterate **2** RETELL, relate, quote, renew, echo, replay, reproduce, rehearse, recite, duplicate, redo, rerun, reshow ▷ *noun* **1** REPETITION, echo, duplicate, reiteration, recapitulation **2** RERUN, replay, reproduction, reshowing

repeatedly *adverb* OVER AND OVER, often, frequently, many times, again and again, time and (time) again, time after time, many a time and oft (*archaic* or *poetic*)

repel *verb* **1** DRIVE OFF, fight, refuse, check, decline, reject, oppose, resist, confront, parry, hold off, rebuff, ward off, beat off, repulse, keep at arm's length, put to flight << ANTONYM submit to **2** DISGUST, offend, revolt, sicken, nauseate, put you off, make you sick, gross out (*US slang*), turn you off (*informal*), make you shudder, turn your stomach, give you the creeps (*informal*) << ANTONYM delight ▷ see **repulse**

repellent *adjective* **1** DISGUSTING, offensive, revolting, obscene, sickening, distasteful, horrid, obnoxious, repulsive, noxious, nauseating, odious, hateful, repugnant, off-putting (*Brit informal*), loathsome, abhorrent, abominable, cringe-making (*Brit informal*), yucky *or* yukky (*slang*), yucko (*Austral slang*), discouraging **2** PROOF, resistant, repelling, impermeable

repent *verb* REGRET, lament, rue, sorrow, be

sorry about, deplore, be ashamed of, relent, atone for, be contrite about, feel remorse about, reproach yourself for, see the error of your ways, show penitence

repentance *noun* REGRET, guilt, grief, sorrow, remorse, contrition, compunction, penitence, self-reproach, sackcloth and ashes, sorriness

repercussion *noun* *often plural* CONSEQUENCES, result, side effects, backlash, sequel

repertoire *noun* RANGE, list, stock, supply, store, collection, repertory, repository

repertory *noun* REPERTOIRE, list, range, stock, supply, store, collection, repository

repetition *noun* **1** RECURRENCE, repeating, reappearance, duplication, echo **2** REPEATING, redundancy, replication, duplication, restatement, iteration, reiteration, tautology, recapitulation, repetitiousness

repetitive *adjective* MONOTONOUS, boring, dull, mechanical, tedious, recurrent, unchanging, samey (*informal*), unvaried

replace *verb* **1** TAKE THE PLACE OF, follow, succeed, oust, take over from, supersede, supplant, stand in lieu of, fill (someone's) shoes *or* boots, step into (someone's) shoes *or* boots **2** SUBSTITUTE, change, exchange, switch, swap, commute **3** PUT BACK, restore

replacement *noun* **1** REPLACING **2** SUCCESSOR, double, substitute, stand-in, fill-in, proxy, surrogate, understudy

replenish *verb* **1** FILL, top up, refill, replace, renew, furnish << ANTONYM empty **2** REFILL, provide, stock, supply, fill, make up, restore, top up, reload, restock

replete *adjective* **1** FILLED, stuffed, jammed, crammed, abounding, brimming, teeming, glutted, well-stocked, jam-packed, well-provided, chock-full, brimful, full to bursting, charged << ANTONYM empty **2** SATED, full, gorged, full up, satiated << ANTONYM hungry

replica *noun* **1** REPRODUCTION, model, copy, imitation, facsimile, carbon copy << ANTONYM original **2** DUPLICATE, copy, carbon copy

replicate *verb* COPY, follow, repeat, reproduce, recreate, ape, mimic, duplicate, reduplicate

reply *verb* ANSWER, respond, retort, return, come back, counter, acknowledge, react, echo, rejoin, retaliate, write back, reciprocate, riposte, make answer ▷ *noun* ANSWER, response, reaction, counter, echo, comeback (*informal*), retort, retaliation, acknowledgment, riposte, counterattack, return, rejoinder, reciprocation

report *verb* **1** INFORM OF, communicate, announce, mention, declare, recount, give an account of, bring word on **2** *often with* **on** COMMUNICATE, publish, record, announce, tell, state, air, detail, describe, note, cover, document, give an account of, relate, broadcast, pass on, proclaim, circulate, relay, recite, narrate, write up **3** PRESENT YOURSELF, come, appear, arrive, turn up, be present, show up (*informal*), clock in *or* on ▷ *noun* **1** ARTICLE, story, dispatch, piece, message, communiqué, write-up **2** ACCOUNT, record, detail, note, statement, relation, version, communication, tale, description, declaration, narrative, summary, recital **3** *often plural* NEWS, word, information, announcement, tidings **4** BANG, sound, crash, crack, noise, blast, boom, explosion, discharge, detonation, reverberation **5** RUMOUR, talk, buzz, gossip, goss (*informal*), hearsay, scuttlebutt (*US slang*) **6** REPUTE, character, regard, reputation, fame, esteem, eminence

reporter *noun* JOURNALIST, writer, correspondent, newscaster, hack (*derogatory*), announcer, pressman, journo (*slang*), newshound (*informal*), newspaperman *or* newspaperwoman

repose[1] *noun* **1** REST, relaxation, inactivity, restfulness **2** PEACE, rest, quiet, ease, relaxation, respite, tranquillity, stillness, inactivity, quietness, quietude, restfulness **3** COMPOSURE, dignity, peace of mind, poise, serenity, tranquillity, aplomb, calmness, equanimity, self-possession ▷ *verb* LIE, rest, sleep, relax, lie down, recline, take it easy, slumber, rest upon, lie upon, drowse, outspan (*S African*), take your ease

repose[2] *verb* PLACE, put, store, invest, deposit, lodge, confide, entrust

repository *noun* STORE, archive, storehouse, depository, magazine, treasury, warehouse, vault, depot, emporium, receptacle

reprehensible *adjective* BLAMEWORTHY, bad, disgraceful, shameful, delinquent, errant, unworthy, objectionable, culpable, ignoble, discreditable, remiss, erring, opprobrious, condemnable, censurable << ANTONYM praiseworthy

represent *verb* **1** ACT FOR, speak for **2** STAND FOR, substitute for, play the part of, assume the role of, serve as **3** EXPRESS, equal, correspond to, symbolize, equate with,

mean, betoken **4** EXEMPLIFY, embody, symbolize, typify, personify, epitomize **5** DEPICT, show, describe, picture, express, illustrate, outline, portray, sketch, render, designate, reproduce, evoke, denote, delineate ▷▷ **represent someone as something** *or* **someone** MAKE OUT TO BE, describe as

representation *noun* **1** BODY OF REPRESENTATIVES, committee, embassy, delegates, delegation **2** PICTURE, model, image, portrait, illustration, sketch, resemblance, likeness **3** PORTRAYAL, depiction, account, relation, description, narrative, narration, delineation **4** *often plural* STATEMENT, argument, explanation, exposition, remonstrance, expostulation, account

representative *noun* **1** DELEGATE, member, agent, deputy, commissioner, councillor, proxy, depute (*Scot*), spokesman *or* spokeswoman **2** MEMBER, congressman *or* congresswoman (*US*), member of parliament, Member of Congress (*US*), M.P. **3** AGENT, salesman, rep, traveller, commercial traveller ▷ *adjective* **1** CHOSEN, elected, delegated, elective **2** TYPICAL, characteristic, archetypal, exemplary, illustrative << ANTONYM uncharacteristic **3** SYMBOLIC, evocative, emblematic, typical

repress *verb* **1** CONTROL, suppress, hold back, bottle up, check, master, hold in, overcome, curb, restrain, inhibit, overpower, keep in check << ANTONYM release **2** HOLD BACK, suppress, stifle, smother, silence, swallow, muffle **3** SUBDUE, abuse, crush, quash, wrong, persecute, quell, subjugate, maltreat, trample underfoot, tyrannize over, rule with an iron hand << ANTONYM liberate

repression *noun* **1** SUBJUGATION, control, constraint, domination, censorship, tyranny, coercion, authoritarianism, despotism **2** SUPPRESSION, crushing, prohibition, quashing, dissolution **3** INHIBITION, control, holding in, restraint, suppression, bottling up

repressive *adjective* OPPRESSIVE, tough, severe, absolute, harsh, authoritarian, dictatorial, coercive, tyrannical, despotic << ANTONYM democratic

reprieve *verb* GRANT A STAY OF EXECUTION TO, pardon, let off the hook (*slang*), postpone *or* remit the punishment of ▷ *noun* STAY OF EXECUTION, suspension, amnesty, pardon, remission, abeyance, deferment, postponement of punishment

reprimand *verb* BLAME, censure, rebuke, reproach, check, lecture, carpet (*informal*), scold, tick off (*informal*), castigate, chide, dress down (*informal*), admonish, tear into (*informal*), tell off (*informal*), take to task, read the riot act, tongue-lash, reprove, upbraid, slap on the wrist (*informal*), bawl out (*informal*), rap over the knuckles, haul over the coals (*informal*), chew out (*US & Canad informal*), tear (someone) off a strip (*Brit informal*), give a rocket (*Brit & NZ informal*), reprehend, give (someone) a row (*informal*), send someone away with a flea in his *or* her ear (*informal*) << ANTONYM praise ▷ *noun* BLAME, talking-to (*informal*), row, lecture, wigging (*Brit slang*), censure, rebuke, reproach, ticking-off (*informal*), dressing-down (*informal*), telling-off (*informal*), admonition, tongue-lashing, reproof, castigation, reprehension, flea in your ear (*informal*) << ANTONYM praise

reprisal *noun* RETALIATION, revenge, vengeance, retribution, an eye for an eye, counterstroke, requital

reproach *verb* BLAME, criticize, rebuke, reprimand, abuse, blast, condemn, carpet (*informal*), discredit, censure, have a go at (*informal*), scold, disparage, chide, tear into (*informal*), diss (*slang, chiefly US*), defame, find fault with, take to task, read the riot act to, reprove, upbraid, lambast(e), bawl out (*informal*), chew out (*US & Canad informal*), tear (someone) off a strip (*Brit informal*), give a rocket (*Brit & NZ informal*), reprehend ▷ *noun* 1 REBUKE, lecture, wigging (*Brit slang*), censure, reprimand, scolding, ticking-off (*informal*), dressing down (*informal*), telling-off (*informal*), admonition, tongue-lashing, reproof, castigation, reproval 2 CENSURE, blame, abuse, contempt, condemnation, scorn, disapproval, opprobrium, odium, obloquy 3 DISGRACE, shame, slight, stain, discredit, stigma, slur, disrepute, blemish, indignity, ignominy, dishonour

reproduce *verb* 1 COPY, recreate, replicate, duplicate, match, represent, mirror, echo, parallel, imitate, emulate 2 PRINT, copy, transcribe 3 (*biology*) BREED, produce young, procreate, generate, multiply, spawn, propagate, proliferate

reproduction *noun* 1 COPY, picture, print, replica, imitation, duplicate, facsimile << ANTONYM original 2 (*biology*) BREEDING, procreation, propagation, increase,

generation, proliferation, multiplication

Republican *adjective* RIGHT-WING, Conservative ▷ *noun* RIGHT-WINGER, Conservative

repudiate *verb* 1 REJECT, renounce, retract, disown, abandon, desert, reverse, cut off, discard, revoke, forsake, cast off, rescind, disavow, turn your back on, abjure, wash your hands of << ANTONYM assert 2 DENY, oppose, disagree with, rebuff, refute, disprove, rebut, disclaim, gainsay (*archaic or literary*)

repugnant *adjective* 1 DISTASTEFUL, offensive, foul, disgusting, revolting, sickening, vile, horrid, repellent, obnoxious, objectionable, nauseating, odious, hateful, loathsome, abhorrent, abominable, yucky *or* yukky (*slang*), yucko (*Austral slang*) << ANTONYM pleasant 2 INCOMPATIBLE, opposed, hostile, adverse, contradictory, inconsistent, averse, antagonistic, inimical, antipathetic << ANTONYM compatible

repulse *verb* 1 DRIVE BACK, check, defeat, fight off, repel, rebuff, ward off, beat off, throw back 2 REJECT, refuse, turn down, snub, disregard, disdain, spurn, rebuff, give the cold shoulder to ▷ *noun* 1 DEFEAT, check 2 REJECTION, refusal, snub, spurning, rebuff, knock-back (*slang*), cold shoulder, kick in the teeth (*slang*), the (old) heave-ho (*informal*)

repulsive *adjective* DISGUSTING, offensive, foul, ugly, forbidding, unpleasant, revolting, obscene, sickening, hideous, vile, distasteful, horrid, repellent, obnoxious, objectionable, disagreeable, nauseating, odious, hateful, loathsome, abhorrent, abominable, yucky *or* yukky (*slang*), yucko (*Austral slang*) << ANTONYM delightful

reputable *adjective* RESPECTABLE, good, excellent, reliable, worthy, legitimate, upright, honourable, honoured, trustworthy, creditable, estimable, well-thought-of, of good repute << ANTONYM disreputable

reputation *noun* NAME, standing, credit, character, honour, fame, distinction, esteem, stature, eminence, renown, repute

repute *noun* 1 REPUTATION, standing, fame, celebrity, distinction, esteem, stature, eminence, estimation, renown 2 NAME, character, reputation

reputed *adjective* 1 SUPPOSED, said, seeming, held, believed, thought, considered, accounted, regarded, estimated, alleged, reckoned, rumoured, deemed 2 APPARENT, supposed, putative, ostensible

reputedly *adverb* SUPPOSEDLY, apparently, allegedly, seemingly, ostensibly

request *verb* 1 ASK FOR, apply for, appeal for, put in for, demand, desire, pray for, beg for, requisition, beseech 2 INVITE, call for, beg, petition, beseech, entreat, supplicate 3 SEEK, ask (for), sue for, solicit ▷ *noun* 1 APPEAL, call, demand, plea, desire, application, prayer, petition, requisition, solicitation, entreaty, supplication, suit 2 ASKING, plea, begging

require *verb* 1 NEED, crave, depend upon, have need of, want, miss, lack, wish, desire, stand in need of 2 DEMAND, take, involve, call for, entail, necessitate 3 ORDER, demand, direct, command, compel, exact, oblige, instruct, call upon, constrain, insist upon 4 ASK, enjoin

required *adjective* OBLIGATORY, prescribed, compulsory, mandatory, needed, set, demanded, necessary, called for, essential, recommended, vital, unavoidable, requisite, de rigueur (*French*) << ANTONYM optional

requirement *noun* NECESSITY, demand, specification, stipulation, want, need, must, essential, qualification, precondition, requisite, prerequisite, sine qua non (*Latin*), desideratum, must-have

requisite *adjective* NECESSARY, needed, required, called for, essential, vital, mandatory, indispensable, obligatory, prerequisite, needful ▷ *noun* NECESSITY, condition, requirement, precondition, need, must, essential, prerequisite, sine qua non (*Latin*), desideratum, must-have

requisition *verb* 1 TAKE OVER, appropriate, occupy, seize, commandeer, take possession of 2 DEMAND, call for, request, apply for, put in for ▷ *noun* 1 DEMAND, request, call, application, summons 2 TAKEOVER, occupation, seizure, appropriation, commandeering

rescind *verb* ANNUL, recall, reverse, cancel, overturn, set aside, void, repeal, quash, revoke, retract, invalidate, obviate, abrogate, countermand, declare null and void << ANTONYM confirm

rescue *verb* 1 SAVE, get out, save the life of, extricate, free, release, deliver, recover, liberate, set free, save (someone's) bacon (*Brit informal*) << ANTONYM desert 2 SALVAGE, deliver, redeem, come to the rescue of ▷ *noun* SAVING, salvage, deliverance, extrication, release, relief, recovery, liberation, salvation, redemption

research *noun* INVESTIGATION, study, inquiry, analysis, examination, probe, exploration, scrutiny, experimentation, delving, groundwork, fact-finding ▷ *verb* INVESTIGATE, study, examine, experiment, explore, probe, analyse, look into, work over, scrutinize, make inquiries, do tests, consult the archives

resemblance *noun* SIMILARITY, correspondence, conformity, semblance, image, comparison, parallel, counterpart, analogy, affinity, closeness, parity, likeness, kinship, facsimile, sameness, comparability, similitude << ANTONYM dissimilarity

resemble *verb* BE LIKE, look like, favour (*informal*), mirror, echo, parallel, be similar to, duplicate, take after, remind you of, bear a resemblance to, put you in mind of

resent *verb* BE BITTER ABOUT, dislike, object to, grudge, begrudge, take exception to, be offended by, be angry about, take offence at, take umbrage at, harbour a grudge against, take as an insult, bear a grudge about, be in a huff about, take amiss to, have hard feelings about << ANTONYM be content with

resentful *adjective* BITTER, hurt, wounded, angry, offended, put out, jealous, choked, incensed, grudging, exasperated, aggrieved, indignant, irate, miffed (*informal*), embittered, unforgiving, peeved (*informal*), in a huff, piqued, huffy, in high dudgeon, revengeful, huffish, tooshie (*Austral slang*) << ANTONYM content

resentment *noun* BITTERNESS, indignation, ill feeling, ill will, hurt, anger, rage, fury, irritation, grudge, wrath, malice, animosity, huff, ire, displeasure, pique, rancour, bad blood, umbrage, vexation, chip on your shoulder (*informal*)

reservation *noun* 1 *often plural* DOUBT, scepticism, scruples, demur, hesitancy 2 RESERVE, territory, preserve, homeland, sanctuary, tract, enclave

reserve *verb* 1 BOOK, prearrange, pre-engage, engage, bespeak 2 PUT BY, secure, retain 3 KEEP, hold, save, husband, store, retain, preserve, set aside, withhold, hang on to, conserve, stockpile, hoard, lay up, put by, keep back 4 DELAY, postpone, withhold, put off, defer, keep back ▷ *noun* 1 STORE, fund, savings, stock, capital, supply, reservoir, fall-back, stockpile, hoard, backlog, cache 2 PARK, reservation, preserve, sanctuary, tract, forest park (*NZ*) 3 SHYNESS, silence, restraint, constraint, reluctance, formality, modesty, reticence, coolness, aloofness, secretiveness, taciturnity **4** RESERVATION, doubt, delay, uncertainty, indecision, hesitancy, vacillation, irresolution, dubiety **5** SUBSTITUTE, extra, spare, alternative, fallback, auxiliary

reserved *adjective* **1** UNCOMMUNICATIVE, cold, cool, retiring, formal, silent, modest, shy, cautious, restrained, secretive, aloof, reticent, prim, demure, taciturn, unresponsive, unapproachable, unsociable, undemonstrative, standoffish, closemouthed, unforthcoming << ANTONYM uninhibited **2** SET ASIDE, taken, kept, held, booked, retained, engaged, restricted, spoken for

reservoir *noun* **1** LAKE, pond, basin **2** REPOSITORY, store, tank, holder, container, receptacle **3** STORE, stock, source, supply, reserves, fund, pool, accumulation, stockpile

reside *verb* **1** (*formal*) LIVE, lodge, dwell, have your home, remain, stay, settle, abide, hang out (*informal*), sojourn << ANTONYM visit **2** BE PRESENT, lie, exist, consist, dwell, abide, rest with, be intrinsic to, inhere, be vested

residence *noun* **1** HOME, house, household, dwelling, place, quarters, flat, lodging, pad (*slang*), abode, habitation, domicile **2** MANSION, seat, hall, palace, villa, manor **3** STAY, tenancy, occupancy, occupation, sojourn

resident *noun* **1** INHABITANT, citizen, denizen, indweller, local << ANTONYM nonresident **2** TENANT, occupant, lodger **3** GUEST, lodger ▷ *adjective* **1** INHABITING, living, settled, dwelling << ANTONYM nonresident **2** LOCAL, neighbourhood

residual *adjective* REMAINING, net, unused, leftover, vestigial, nett, unconsumed

residue *noun* REMAINDER, remains, remnant, leftovers, rest, extra, balance, excess, surplus, dregs, residuum

resign *verb* **1** QUIT, leave, step down (*informal*), vacate, abdicate, call it a day *or* night, give *or* hand in your notice **2** GIVE UP, abandon, yield, hand over, surrender, turn over, relinquish, renounce, forsake, cede, forgo ▷▷ **resign yourself to something** ACCEPT, reconcile yourself to, succumb to, submit to, bow to, give in to, yield to, acquiesce to

resignation *noun* **1** LEAVING, notice, retirement, departure, surrender, abandonment, abdication, renunciation, relinquishment **2** ACCEPTANCE, patience, submission, compliance, endurance, fortitude, passivity, acquiescence, forbearing,

sufferance, nonresistance << ANTONYM resistance

resigned *adjective* STOICAL, patient, subdued, long-suffering, compliant, submissive, acquiescent, unresisting, unprotesting

resilient *adjective* **1** FLEXIBLE, plastic, elastic, supple, bouncy, rubbery, pliable, springy, whippy << ANTONYM rigid **2** TOUGH, strong, hardy, buoyant, feisty (*informal, chiefly US & Canad*), bouncy, irrepressible, quick to recover << ANTONYM weak

resist *verb* **1** OPPOSE, fight, battle against, refuse, check, weather, dispute, confront, combat, defy, curb, thwart, stand up to, hinder, contend with, counteract, hold out against, put up a fight (against), countervail << ANTONYM accept **2** FIGHT AGAINST, fight, struggle against, put up a fight (against) **3** REFRAIN FROM, refuse, avoid, turn down, leave alone, keep from, forgo, abstain from, forbear, prevent yourself from << ANTONYM indulge in **4** WITHSTAND, repel, be proof against

resistance *noun* **1** OPPOSITION, hostility, aversion **2** FIGHTING, fight, battle, struggle, combat, contention, defiance, obstruction, impediment, intransigence, hindrance, counteraction

Resistance *noun* FREEDOM FIGHTERS, underground, guerrillas, partisans, irregulars, maquis

resistant *adjective* **1** OPPOSED, hostile, dissident, unwilling, defiant, intractable, combative, recalcitrant, antagonistic, intransigent **2** IMPERVIOUS, hard, strong, tough, unaffected, unyielding, insusceptible

resolute *adjective* DETERMINED, set, firm, dogged, fixed, constant, bold, relentless, stubborn, stalwart, staunch, persevering, inflexible, purposeful, tenacious, undaunted, strong-willed, steadfast, obstinate, unwavering, immovable, unflinching, unbending, unshakable, unshaken << ANTONYM irresolute

resolution *noun* **1** DECLARATION, motion, verdict, judgment **2** DECISION, resolve, intention, aim, purpose, determination, intent **3** DETERMINATION, energy, purpose, resolve, courage, dedication, fortitude, sincerity, tenacity, perseverance, willpower, boldness, firmness, staying power, stubbornness, constancy, earnestness, obstinacy, steadfastness, doggedness, relentlessness, resoluteness, staunchness **4** SOLUTION, end, settlement, outcome, finding, answer, working out, solving, sorting out, unravelling, upshot

resolve *verb* **1** WORK OUT, answer, solve, find the solution to, clear up, crack, fathom, suss (out) (*slang*), elucidate **2** DECIDE, determine, undertake, make up your mind, agree, design, settle, purpose, intend, fix, conclude **3** CHANGE, convert, transform, alter, metamorphose, transmute **4** DISPEL, explain, remove, clear up, banish ▷ *noun* **1** DETERMINATION, resolution, courage, willpower, boldness, firmness, earnestness, steadfastness, resoluteness << ANTONYM indecision **2** DECISION, resolution, undertaking, objective, design, project, purpose, conclusion, intention

resonant *adjective* **1** SONOROUS, full, rich, ringing, booming, vibrant **2** ECHOING, resounding, reverberating, reverberant

resort *noun* **1** HOLIDAY CENTRE, spot, retreat, haunt, refuge, tourist centre, watering place (*Brit*) **2** RECOURSE TO, reference to ▷▷ **resort to something** HAVE RECOURSE TO, turn to, fall back on, bring into play, use, exercise, employ, look to, make use of, utilize, avail yourself of

resound *verb* **1** ECHO, resonate, reverberate, fill the air, re-echo **2** RING

resounding *adjective* ECHOING, full, sounding, rich, ringing, powerful, booming, vibrant, reverberating, resonant, sonorous

resource *noun* **1** SUPPLY, source, reserve, stockpile, hoard **2** FACILITY **3** MEANS, course, resort, device, expedient ▷ *plural noun* **1** FUNDS, means, holdings, money, capital, wherewithal, riches, materials, assets, wealth, property **2** RESERVES, supplies, stocks

resourceful *adjective* INGENIOUS, able, bright, talented, sharp, capable, creative, clever, imaginative, inventive, quick-witted << ANTONYM unimaginative

respect *verb* **1** THINK HIGHLY OF, value, regard, honour, recognize, appreciate, admire, esteem, adore, revere, reverence, look up to, defer to, venerate, set store by, have a good *or* high opinion of **2** SHOW CONSIDERATION FOR, regard, notice, honour, observe, heed, attend to, pay attention to **3** ABIDE BY, follow, observe, comply with, obey, heed, keep to, adhere to << ANTONYM disregard ▷ *noun* **1** REGARD, honour, recognition, esteem, appreciation, admiration, reverence, estimation, veneration, approbation << ANTONYM contempt **2** CONSIDERATION, kindness,

deference, friendliness, tact, thoughtfulness, solicitude, kindliness, considerateness **3** PARTICULAR, way, point, matter, sense, detail, feature, aspect, characteristic, facet ▷ *plural noun* GREETINGS, regards, compliments, good wishes, salutations, devoirs ▷▷ **in respect of** *or* **with respect to** CONCERNING, in relation to, in connection with, with regard to, with reference to, apropos of

respectable *adjective* **1** HONOURABLE, good, respected, decent, proper, worthy, upright, admirable, honest, dignified, venerable, reputable, decorous, estimable << ANTONYM disreputable **2** DECENT, neat, tidy (*informal*), spruce **3** REASONABLE, considerable, substantial, fair, tidy (*informal*), ample, tolerable, presentable, appreciable, fairly good, sizable *or* sizeable, goodly << ANTONYM small

respectful *adjective* POLITE, civil, mannerly, humble, gracious, courteous, obedient, submissive, self-effacing, dutiful, courtly, deferential, reverential, solicitous, reverent, regardful, well-mannered

respective *adjective* SPECIFIC, own, several, individual, personal, particular, various, separate, relevant, corresponding

respite *noun* **1** PAUSE, break, rest, relief, halt, interval, relaxation, recess, interruption, lull, cessation, let-up (*informal*), breathing space, breather (*informal*), hiatus, intermission **2** REPRIEVE, stay, delay, suspension, moratorium, postponement, adjournment

resplendent *adjective* BRILLIANT, radiant, splendid, glorious, bright, shining, beaming, glittering, dazzling, gleaming, luminous, lustrous, refulgent (*literary*), effulgent, irradiant

respond *verb* **1** ANSWER, return, reply, come back, counter, acknowledge, retort, rejoin << ANTONYM remain silent **2** *often with* **to** REPLY TO, answer **3** REACT, retaliate, reciprocate, take the bait, rise to the bait, act in response

response *noun* ANSWER, return, reply, reaction, comeback (*informal*), feedback, retort, acknowledgment, riposte, counterattack, rejoinder, counterblast

responsibility *noun* **1** DUTY, business, job, role, task, accountability, answerability **2** FAULT, blame, liability, guilt, culpability, burden **3** OBLIGATION, duty, liability, charge, care **4** AUTHORITY, power, importance, mana (*NZ*) **5** JOB, task, function, role, pigeon (*informal*)

6 LEVEL-HEADEDNESS, stability, maturity, reliability, rationality, dependability, trustworthiness, conscientiousness, soberness, sensibleness

responsible *adjective* **1** TO BLAME, guilty, at fault, culpable **2** IN CHARGE, in control, at the helm, in authority, carrying the can (*informal*) **3** ACCOUNTABLE, subject, bound, liable, amenable, answerable, duty-bound, chargeable, under obligation << ANTONYM unaccountable **4** SENSIBLE, sound, adult, stable, mature, reliable, rational, sober, conscientious, dependable, trustworthy, level-headed << ANTONYM unreliable **5** AUTHORITATIVE, high, important, executive, decision-making

responsive *adjective* SENSITIVE, open, aware, sharp, alive, forthcoming, sympathetic, awake, susceptible, receptive, reactive, perceptive, impressionable, quick to react << ANTONYM unresponsive

rest¹ *verb* **1** RELAX, sleep, take it easy, lie down, idle, nap, be calm, doze, sit down, slumber, kip (*Brit slang*), snooze (*informal*), laze, lie still, be at ease, put your feet up, take a nap, drowse, mellow out (*informal*), have a snooze (*informal*), refresh yourself, outspan (*S African*), zizz (*Brit informal*), have forty winks (*informal*), take your ease << ANTONYM work **2** STOP, have a break, break off, take a breather (*informal*), stay, halt, cease, discontinue, knock off (*informal*), desist, come to a standstill << ANTONYM keep going **3** DEPEND, turn, lie, be founded, hang, be based, rely, hinge, reside **4** PLACE, lay, repose, stretch out, stand, sit, lean, prop **5** BE PLACED, sit, lie, be supported, recline ▷ *noun* **1** SLEEP, snooze (*informal*), lie-down, nap, doze, slumber, kip (*Brit slang*), siesta, forty winks (*informal*), zizz (*Brit informal*) **2** RELAXATION, repose, leisure, idleness, me-time << ANTONYM work **3** PAUSE, break, breather, time off, stop, holiday, halt, interval, vacation, respite, lull, interlude, cessation, breathing space (*informal*), intermission **4** REFRESHMENT, release, relief, ease, comfort, cure, remedy, solace, balm, deliverance, mitigation, abatement, alleviation, easement, palliation, assuagement **5** INACTIVITY, a halt, a stop, a standstill, motionlessness **6** SUPPORT, stand, base, holder, shelf, prop, trestle **7** CALM, tranquillity, stillness, somnolence ▷▷ **at rest 1** MOTIONLESS, still, stopped, at a standstill, unmoving **2** CALM, still, cool, quiet, pacific,

peaceful, composed, serene, tranquil, at peace, sedate, placid, undisturbed, restful, untroubled, unperturbed, unruffled, unexcited **3** ASLEEP, resting, sleeping, napping, dormant, crashed out (*slang*), dozing, slumbering, snoozing (*informal*), fast asleep, sound asleep, out for the count, dead to the world (*informal*)

rest² *noun* REMAINDER, remains, excess, remnants, others, balance, surplus, residue, rump, leftovers, residuum ▷ *verb* CONTINUE BEING, keep being, remain, stay, be left, go on being

restaurant *noun* CAFÉ, diner (*chiefly US & Canad*), bistro, cafeteria, trattoria, tearoom, eatery *or* eaterie

restful *adjective* RELAXING, quiet, relaxed, comfortable, pacific, calm, calming, peaceful, soothing, sleepy, serene, tranquil, placid, undisturbed, languid, unhurried, tranquillizing << ANTONYM busy

restitution *noun* **1** (*law*) COMPENSATION, satisfaction, amends, refund, repayment, redress, remuneration, reparation, indemnity, reimbursement, recompense, indemnification, requital **2** RETURN, replacement, restoration, reinstatement, re-establishment, reinstallation

restive *adjective* RESTLESS, nervous, uneasy, impatient, agitated, unruly, edgy, jittery (*informal*), recalcitrant, on edge, fractious, ill at ease, jumpy, fretful, fidgety, refractory, unquiet, antsy (*informal*) << ANTONYM calm

restless *adjective* **1** UNSETTLED, worried, troubled, nervous, disturbed, anxious, uneasy, agitated, unruly, edgy, fidgeting, on edge, ill at ease, restive, jumpy, fitful, fretful, fidgety, unquiet, antsy (*informal*) << ANTONYM relaxed **2** SLEEPLESS, disturbed, wakeful, unsleeping, insomniac, tossing and turning **3** MOVING, active, wandering, unsettled, unstable, bustling, turbulent, hurried, roving, transient, nomadic, unsteady, changeable, footloose, irresolute, inconstant, having itchy feet << ANTONYM settled

restlessness *noun* **1** MOVEMENT, activity, turmoil, unrest, instability, bustle, turbulence, hurry, transience, inconstancy, hurry-scurry, unsettledness **2** RESTIVENESS, anxiety, disturbance, nervousness, disquiet, agitation, insomnia, jitters (*informal*), uneasiness, edginess, heebie-jeebies (*slang*), jumpiness, fretfulness, ants in your pants (*slang*), fitfulness, inquietude, worriedness

restoration *noun* **1** REINSTATEMENT, return, revival, restitution, re-establishment, reinstallation, replacement << ANTONYM abolition **2** REPAIR, recovery, reconstruction, renewal, rehabilitation, refurbishing, refreshment, renovation, rejuvenation, revitalization << ANTONYM demolition

restore *verb* **1** REINSTATE, re-establish, reintroduce, reimpose, re-enforce, reconstitute << ANTONYM abolish **2** REVIVE, build up, strengthen, bring back, refresh, rejuvenate, revitalize, revivify, reanimate << ANTONYM make worse **3** RE-ESTABLISH, replace, reinstate, give back, reinstall, retrocede **4** REPAIR, refurbish, renovate, reconstruct, fix (up), recover, renew, rebuild, mend, rehabilitate, touch up, recondition, retouch, set to rights << ANTONYM demolish **5** RETURN, replace, recover, bring back, send back, hand back

restrain *verb* **1** HOLD BACK, hold, control, check, contain, prevent, restrict, handicap, confine, curb, hamper, rein, harness, subdue, hinder, constrain, curtail, bridle, debar, keep under control, have on a tight leash, straiten << ANTONYM encourage **2** CONTROL, keep in, limit, govern, suppress, inhibit, repress, muzzle, keep under control **3** IMPRISON, hold, arrest, jail, bind, chain, confine, detain, tie up, lock up, fetter, manacle, pinion << ANTONYM release

restrained *adjective* **1** CONTROLLED, reasonable, moderate, self-controlled, soft, calm, steady, mild, muted, reticent, temperate, undemonstrative << ANTONYM hot-headed **2** UNOBTRUSIVE, discreet, subdued, tasteful, quiet << ANTONYM garish

restraint *noun* **1** LIMITATION, limit, check, ban, boycott, embargo, curb, rein, taboo, bridle, disqualification, interdict, restraining order (*US law*) << ANTONYM freedom **2** SELF-CONTROL, self-discipline, self-restraint, self-possession, pulling your punches << ANTONYM self-indulgence **3** CONSTRAINT, limitation, inhibition, moderation, hold, control, restriction, prevention, suppression, hindrance, curtailment

restrict *verb* **1** LIMIT, fix, regulate, specify, curb, ration, keep within bounds *or* limits << ANTONYM widen **2** HAMPER, impede, handicap, restrain, cramp, inhibit, straiten

restriction *noun* **1** CONTROL, rule, condition, check, regulation, curb, restraint, constraint, confinement, containment, demarcation, stipulation **2** LIMITATION, handicap, inhibition

result *noun* **1** CONSEQUENCE, effect, outcome, end result, issue, event, development, product, reaction, fruit, sequel, upshot << ANTONYM cause **2** OUTCOME, conclusion, end, decision, termination ▷ *verb often followed by* **from** ARISE, follow, issue, happen, appear, develop, spring, flow, turn out, stem, derive, ensue, emanate, eventuate ▷▷ **result in something** END IN, bring about, cause, lead to, wind up, finish with, culminate in, terminate in

resume *verb* **1** BEGIN AGAIN, continue, go on with, proceed with, carry on, reopen, restart, recommence, reinstitute, take up or pick up where you left off << ANTONYM discontinue **2** TAKE UP AGAIN, assume again **3** OCCUPY AGAIN, take back, reoccupy

résumé *noun* **1** SUMMARY, synopsis, abstract, précis, review, digest, epitome, rundown, recapitulation **2** (*US*) CURRICULUM VITAE, CV, career history, details, biography

resumption *noun* CONTINUATION, carrying on, reopening, renewal, restart, resurgence, new beginning, re-establishment, fresh outbreak

resurgence *noun* REVIVAL, return, renaissance, resurrection, resumption, rebirth, re-emergence, recrudescence, renascence

resurrect *verb* **1** REVIVE, renew, bring back, kick-start (*informal*), reintroduce, breathe new life into **2** RESTORE TO LIFE, raise from the dead

resurrection *noun* **1** REVIVAL, restoration, renewal, resurgence, return, comeback (*informal*), renaissance, rebirth, reappearance, resuscitation, renascence << ANTONYM killing off **2** RAISING *or* RISING FROM THE DEAD, return from the dead << ANTONYM demise

resuscitate *verb* **1** GIVE ARTIFICIAL RESPIRATION TO, save, quicken, bring to life, bring round, give the kiss of life to **2** REVIVE, rescue, restore, renew, resurrect, revitalize, breathe new life into, revivify, reanimate

retain *verb* **1** MAINTAIN, keep, reserve, preserve, keep up, uphold, nurture, continue to have, hang *or* hold onto **2** KEEP, keep possession of, hang *or* hold onto, save << ANTONYM let go **3** REMEMBER, recall, bear in mind, keep in mind, memorize, recollect, impress on the memory << ANTONYM forget

retainer *noun* **1** FEE, advance, deposit **2** SERVANT, domestic, attendant, valet, supporter, dependant, henchman, footman, lackey, vassal, flunky

retaliate *verb* PAY SOMEONE BACK, hit back, strike back, reciprocate, take revenge, get back at someone, get even with (*informal*), even the score, get your own back (*informal*), wreak vengeance, exact retribution, give as good as you get (*informal*), take an eye for an eye, make reprisal, give (someone) a taste of his *or* her own medicine, give tit for tat, return like for like << ANTONYM turn the other cheek

retaliation *noun* REVENGE, repayment, vengeance, reprisal, retribution, tit for tat, an eye for an eye, reciprocation, counterstroke, requital, counterblow, a taste of your own medicine

retard *verb* SLOW DOWN, check, arrest, delay, handicap, stall, brake, detain, defer, clog, hinder, obstruct, impede, set back, encumber, decelerate, hold back *or* up << ANTONYM speed up

retch *verb* GAG, be sick, vomit, regurgitate, chuck (*Austral & NZ informal*), throw up (*informal*), spew, heave, puke (*slang*), disgorge, barf (*US slang*), chunder (*slang, chiefly Austral*), upchuck (*US slang*), do a technicolour yawn (*slang*), toss your cookies (*US slang*)

reticence *noun* SILENCE, reserve, restraint, quietness, secretiveness, taciturnity, uncommunicativeness, unforthcomingness

reticent *adjective* UNCOMMUNICATIVE, reserved, secretive, unforthcoming, quiet, silent, restrained, taciturn, tight-lipped, unspeaking, close-lipped, mum << ANTONYM communicative ▷ see **reluctant**

retinue *noun* ATTENDANTS, entourage, escort, servants, following, train, suite, aides, followers, cortege

retire *verb* **1** STOP WORKING, give up work, be pensioned off, (be) put out to grass (*informal*) **2** WITHDRAW, leave, remove, exit, go away, depart, absent yourself, betake yourself **3** GO TO BED, turn in (*informal*), go to sleep, hit the sack (*slang*), go to your room, kip down (*Brit slang*), hit the hay (*slang*) **4** RETREAT, withdraw, pull out, give way, recede, pull back, back off, decamp, give ground

retirement *noun* WITHDRAWAL, retreat, privacy, loneliness, obscurity, solitude, seclusion

retiring *adjective* SHY, reserved, quiet, modest, shrinking, humble, timid, coy, meek, reclusive, reticent, unassuming, self-effacing, demure, diffident, bashful, timorous, unassertive << ANTONYM outgoing

retort *verb* REPLY, return, answer, respond, counter, rejoin, retaliate, come back with, riposte, answer back ▷ *noun* REPLY, answer, response, comeback, riposte, rejoinder

retract *verb* **1** WITHDRAW, take back, revoke, disown, deny, recall, reverse, cancel, repeal, renounce, go back on, repudiate, rescind, renege on, back out of, disavow, recant, disclaim, abjure, eat your words, unsay **2** DRAW IN, pull in, pull back, reel in, sheathe

retreat *verb* WITHDRAW, retire, back off, draw back, leave, go back, shrink, depart, fall back, recede, pull back, back away, recoil, give ground, turn tail << ANTONYM advance ▷ *noun* **1** FLIGHT, retirement, departure, withdrawal, evacuation << ANTONYM advance **2** REFUGE, haven, resort, retirement, shelter, haunt, asylum, privacy, den, sanctuary, hideaway, seclusion

retrenchment *noun* CUTBACK, cuts, economy, reduction, pruning, contraction, cost-cutting, rundown, curtailment, tightening your belt << ANTONYM expansion

retribution *noun* PUNISHMENT, retaliation, reprisal, redress, justice, reward, reckoning, compensation, satisfaction, revenge, repayment, vengeance, Nemesis, recompense, an eye for an eye, requital

retrieve *verb* **1** GET BACK, regain, repossess, fetch back, recall, recover, restore, recapture **2** REDEEM, save, rescue, repair, salvage, win back, recoup

retro *adjective* OLD-TIME, old, former, past, period, antique, old-fashioned, nostalgia, old-world, bygone, of yesteryear

retrograde *adjective* DETERIORATING, backward, regressive, retrogressive, declining, negative, reverse, retreating, worsening, downward, waning, relapsing, inverse, degenerative

retrospect *noun* HINDSIGHT, review, afterthought, re-examination, survey, recollection, remembrance, reminiscence << ANTONYM foresight

return *verb* **1** COME BACK, go back, repair, retreat, turn back, revert, reappear << ANTONYM depart **2** PUT BACK, replace, restore, render, transmit, convey, send back, reinstate, take back, give back, carry back, retrocede << ANTONYM keep **3** GIVE

BACK, repay, refund, pay back, remit,
reimburse, recompense << ANTONYM keep
4 RECIPROCATE, requite, feel in return,
respond to **5** RECUR, come back, repeat,
persist, revert, happen again, reappear,
come and go, come again **6** ANNOUNCE,
report, come to, deliver, arrive at, bring
in, submit, render **7** EARN, make, net,
yield, bring in, repay << ANTONYM lose
8 ELECT, choose, pick, vote in ▷ *noun*
1 REAPPEARANCE << ANTONYM departure
2 RESTORATION, replacement, reinstatement,
re-establishment << ANTONYM removal
3 RECURRENCE, repetition, reappearance,
reversion, persistence **4** PROFIT, interest,
benefit, gain, income, advantage, revenue,
yield, proceeds, takings, boot (*dialect*)
5 REPAYMENT, reward, compensation,
reparation, reimbursement, recompense,
reciprocation, requital, retaliation, meed
(*archaic*) **6** STATEMENT, report, form, list,
account, summary

revamp *verb* RENOVATE, restore, overhaul,
refurbish, rehabilitate, do up (*informal*),
patch up, refit, repair, fix up (*informal, chiefly
US & Canad*), recondition, give a face-lift to

reveal *verb* **1** MAKE KNOWN, disclose, give
away, make public, tell, announce, publish,
broadcast, leak, communicate, proclaim,
betray, give out, let out, impart, divulge, let
slip, let on, take the wraps off (*informal*),
blow wide open (*slang*), get off your chest
(*informal*) << ANTONYM keep secret **2** SHOW,
display, bare, exhibit, unveil, uncover,
manifest, unearth, unmask, lay bare, bring
to light, expose to view << ANTONYM hide

revel *verb* CELEBRATE, rave (*Brit slang*),
carouse, live it up (*informal*), push the boat
out (*Brit informal*), whoop it up (*informal*),
make merry, paint the town red (*informal*),
go on a spree, roister ▷ *noun often plural*
MERRYMAKING, party, celebration, rave (*Brit
slang*), gala, spree, festivity, beano (*Brit slang*),
debauch, saturnalia, bacchanal, rave-up
(*Brit slang*), jollification, carousal, hooley *or*
hoolie (*chiefly Irish & NZ*), carouse ▷▷ **revel in
something** ENJOY, relish, indulge in, delight
in, savour, thrive on, bask in, wallow in, lap
up, take pleasure in, drool over, luxuriate
in, crow about, rejoice over, gloat about, rub
your hands about

revelation *noun* **1** DISCLOSURE, discovery,
news, broadcast, exposé, announcement,
publication, exposure, leak, uncovering,
confession, divulgence **2** EXHIBITION,

telling, communication, broadcasting,
discovery, publication, exposure, leaking,
unveiling, uncovering, manifestation,
unearthing, giveaway, proclamation,
exposition

reveller *noun* MERRYMAKER, carouser,
pleasure-seeker, partygoer, roisterer,
celebrator

revelry *noun* MERRYMAKING, partying, fun,
celebration, rave (*Brit slang*), spree, festivity,
beano (*Brit slang*), debauch, debauchery,
carouse, jollity, saturnalia, roistering, rave-
up (*Brit slang*), jollification, carousal, hooley
or hoolie (*chiefly Irish & NZ*)

revenge *noun* RETALIATION, satisfaction,
vengeance, reprisal, retribution,
vindictiveness, an eye for an eye, requital ▷
verb AVENGE, repay, vindicate, pay (someone)
back, take revenge for, requite, even the
score for, get your own back for (*informal*),
make reprisal for, take an eye for an eye for

revenue *noun* INCOME, interest, returns,
profits, gain, rewards, yield, proceeds,
receipts, takings << ANTONYM expenditure

reverberate *verb* ECHO, ring, resound, vibrate,
re-echo

reverberation *noun* ECHO, ringing, resonance,
resounding, vibration, re-echoing

revere *verb* BE IN AWE OF, respect, honour,
worship, adore, reverence, exalt, look up
to, defer to, venerate, have a high opinion
of, put on a pedestal, think highly of
<< ANTONYM despise

reverence *noun* RESPECT, honour, worship,
admiration, awe, devotion, homage,
deference, adoration, veneration, high
esteem << ANTONYM contempt ▷ *verb*
REVERE, respect, honour, admire, worship,
adore, pay homage to, venerate, be in awe of,
hold in awe

reverent *adjective* RESPECTFUL, awed, solemn,
deferential, loving, humble, adoring,
devout, pious, meek, submissive, reverential
<< ANTONYM disrespectful

reverie *noun* DAYDREAM, musing,
preoccupation, trance, abstraction,
daydreaming, inattention, absent-
mindedness, brown study, woolgathering,
castles in the air *or* Spain

reverse *verb* **1** (*law*) CHANGE, alter, cancel,
overturn, overthrow, set aside, undo,
repeal, quash, revoke, overrule, retract,
negate, rescind, invalidate, annul, obviate,
countermand, declare null and void,
overset, upset << ANTONYM implement

2 TURN ROUND, turn over, turn upside down, upend **3** TRANSPOSE, change, move, exchange, transfer, switch, shift, alter, swap, relocate, rearrange, invert, interchange, reorder **4** GO BACKWARDS, retreat, back up, turn back, backtrack, move backwards, back << ANTONYM go forward ▷ *noun* **1** OPPOSITE, contrary, converse, antithesis, inverse, contradiction **2** MISFORTUNE, check, defeat, blow, failure, disappointment, setback, hardship, reversal, adversity, mishap, affliction, repulse, trial, misadventure, vicissitude **3** BACK, rear, other side, wrong side, underside, flip side, verso << ANTONYM front ▷ *adjective* **1** OPPOSITE, contrary, converse, inverse **2** BACKWARD, inverted, back to front

revert *verb* **1** GO BACK, return, come back, resume, lapse, recur, relapse, regress, backslide, take up where you left off **2** RETURN

review *noun* **1** RE-EXAMINATION, revision, rethink, retrospect, another look, reassessment, fresh look, second look, reconsideration, re-evaluation, recapitulation **2** SURVEY, report, study, analysis, examination, scrutiny, perusal **3** CRITIQUE, commentary, evaluation, critical assessment, study, notice, criticism, judgment **4** INSPECTION, display, parade, procession, march past **5** MAGAZINE, journal, periodical, zine (*informal*) ▷ *verb* **1** RECONSIDER, revise, rethink, run over, reassess, re-examine, re-evaluate, think over, take another look at, recapitulate, look at again, go over again **2** ASSESS, write a critique of, study, judge, discuss, weigh, evaluate, criticize, read through, give your opinion of **3** INSPECT, check, survey, examine, vet, check out (*informal*), scrutinize, give (something or someone) the once-over (*informal*) **4** LOOK BACK ON, remember, recall, reflect on, summon up, recollect, call to mind

reviewer *noun* CRITIC, judge, commentator, connoisseur, arbiter, essayist

revile *verb* MALIGN, abuse, knock (*informal*), rubbish (*informal*), run down, smear, libel, scorn, slag (off) (*slang*), reproach, denigrate, vilify, slander, defame, bad-mouth (*slang, chiefly US & Canad*), traduce, calumniate, vituperate, asperse

revise *verb* **1** CHANGE, review, modify, reconsider, re-examine **2** EDIT, correct, alter, update, amend, rewrite, revamp, rework,

redo, emend **3** STUDY, go over, run through, cram (*informal*), memorize, reread, swot up on (*Brit informal*)

revision *noun* **1** EMENDATION, editing, updating, correction, rewriting **2** CHANGE, review, amendment, modification, alteration, re-examination **3** STUDYING, cramming (*informal*), memorizing, swotting (*Brit informal*), rereading, homework

revitalize *verb* REANIMATE, restore, renew, refresh, resurrect, rejuvenate, breathe new life into, bring back to life, revivify

revival *noun* **1** RESURGENCE << ANTONYM decline **2** REAWAKENING, restoration, renaissance, renewal, awakening, resurrection, refreshment, quickening, rebirth, resuscitation, revitalization, recrudescence, reanimation, renascence, revivification

revive *verb* **1** REVITALIZE, restore, rally, renew, renovate, rekindle, kick-start (*informal*), breathe new life into, invigorate, reanimate **2** BRING ROUND, awaken, animate, rouse, resuscitate, bring back to life **3** COME ROUND, recover, quicken, spring up again **4** REFRESH, restore, comfort, cheer, renew, resurrect, rejuvenate, revivify << ANTONYM exhaust

revoke *verb* CANCEL, recall, withdraw, reverse, abolish, set aside, repeal, renounce, quash, take back, call back, retract, repudiate, negate, renege, rescind, invalidate, annul, nullify, recant, obviate, disclaim, abrogate, countermand, declare null and void << ANTONYM endorse

revolt *noun* UPRISING, rising, revolution, rebellion, mutiny, defection, insurrection, insurgency, putsch, sedition ▷ *verb* **1** REBEL, rise up, resist, defect, mutiny, take to the streets, take up arms (against) **2** DISGUST, offend, turn off (*informal*), sicken, repel, repulse, nauseate, gross out (*US slang*), shock, turn your stomach, make your flesh creep, give you the creeps (*informal*)

revolting *adjective* DISGUSTING, shocking, offensive, appalling, nasty, foul, horrible, obscene, sickening, distasteful, horrid, repellent, obnoxious, repulsive, nauseating, repugnant, loathsome, abhorrent, abominable, nauseous, cringe-making (*Brit informal*), noisome, yucky or yukky (*slang*), yucko (*Austral slang*) << ANTONYM delightful

revolution *noun* **1** REVOLT, rising, coup, rebellion, uprising, mutiny, insurgency, coup d'état, putsch **2** TRANSFORMATION, shift, innovation, upheaval, reformation, metamorphosis, sea change, drastic *or* radical change **3** ROTATION, turn, cycle, circle, wheel, spin, lap, circuit, orbit, whirl, gyration, round

revolutionary *adjective* **1** REBEL, radical, extremist, subversive, insurgent, seditious, mutinous, insurrectionary << ANTONYM reactionary **2** INNOVATIVE, new, different, novel, radical, fundamental, progressive, experimental, drastic, avant-garde, ground-breaking, thoroughgoing << ANTONYM conventional ▷ *noun* REBEL, insurgent, mutineer, insurrectionary, revolutionist, insurrectionist << ANTONYM reactionary

revolutionize *verb* TRANSFORM, reform, revamp, modernize, metamorphose, break with the past

revolve *verb* **1** GO ROUND, circle, orbit, gyrate **2** ROTATE, turn, wheel, spin, twist, whirl **3** CONSIDER, study, reflect, think about, deliberate, ponder, turn over (in your mind), meditate, mull over, think over, ruminate

revulsion *noun* DISGUST, loathing, distaste, aversion, recoil, abomination, repulsion, abhorrence, repugnance, odium, detestation << ANTONYM liking

reward *noun* **1** PRIZE **2** PUNISHMENT, desert, retribution, comeuppance (*slang*), just deserts, requital **3** PAYMENT, return, benefit, profit, gain, prize, wages, honour, compensation, bonus, premium, merit, repayment, bounty, remuneration, recompense, meed (*archaic*), requital << ANTONYM penalty ▷ *verb* COMPENSATE, pay, honour, repay, recompense, requite, remunerate, make it worth your while << ANTONYM penalize

rewarding *adjective* SATISFYING, fulfilling, gratifying, edifying, economic, pleasing, valuable, profitable, productive, worthwhile, beneficial, enriching, fruitful, advantageous, gainful, remunerative << ANTONYM unrewarding

rewrite *verb* REVISE, correct, edit, recast, touch up, redraft, emend

rhetoric *noun* **1** HYPERBOLE, rant, hot air (*informal*), pomposity, bombast, wordiness, verbosity, fustian, grandiloquence, magniloquence **2** ORATORY, eloquence, public speaking, speech-making, elocution, declamation, speechifying, grandiloquence, spieling (*informal*), whaikorero (NZ)

rhetorical *adjective* **1** ORATORICAL, verbal, linguistic, stylistic **2** HIGH-FLOWN,

flamboyant, windy, flashy, pompous, pretentious, flowery, showy, florid, bombastic, hyperbolic, verbose, oratorical, grandiloquent, high-sounding, declamatory, arty-farty (*informal*), silver-tongued, magniloquent

rhyme *noun* POEM, song, verse, ode ▷▷ **rhyme or reason** (usually in negative construction) SENSE, meaning, plan, planning, system, method, pattern, logic

rhythm *noun* **1** BEAT, swing, accent, pulse, tempo, cadence, lilt **2** METRE, time, measure (*poetry*) **3** PATTERN, movement, flow, periodicity

rhythmic *or* **rhythmical** *adjective* CADENCED, throbbing, periodic, pulsating, flowing, musical, harmonious, lilting, melodious, metrical

rich *adjective* **1** WEALTHY, affluent, well-off, opulent, propertied, rolling (*slang*), loaded (*slang*), flush (*informal*), prosperous, well-heeled (*informal*), well-to-do, moneyed, filthy rich, stinking rich (*informal*), made of money (*informal*) << ANTONYM poor **2** WELL-STOCKED, full, productive, ample, abundant, plentiful, copious, well-provided, well-supplied, plenteous << ANTONYM scarce **3** FULL-BODIED, heavy, sweet, delicious, fatty, tasty, creamy, spicy, juicy, luscious, savoury, succulent, flavoursome, highly-flavoured << ANTONYM bland **4** FRUITFUL, productive, fertile, prolific, fecund << ANTONYM barren **5** ABOUNDING, full, luxurious, lush, abundant, exuberant, well-endowed **6** RESONANT, full, deep, mellow, mellifluous, dulcet << ANTONYM high-pitched **7** VIVID, strong, deep, warm, bright, intense, vibrant, gay << ANTONYM dull **8** COSTLY, fine, expensive, valuable, superb, elegant, precious, elaborate, splendid, gorgeous, lavish, exquisite, sumptuous, priceless, palatial, beyond price << ANTONYM cheap **9** FUNNY, amusing, ridiculous, hilarious, ludicrous, humorous, laughable, comical, risible, side-splitting

riches *plural noun* **1** WEALTH, money, property, gold, assets, plenty, fortune, substance, treasure, abundance, richness, affluence, opulence, top whack (*informal*) << ANTONYM poverty **2** RESOURCES, treasures

richly *adverb* **1** ELABORATELY, lavishly, elegantly, splendidly, exquisitely, expensively, luxuriously, gorgeously, sumptuously, opulently, palatially **2** FULLY, well, thoroughly, amply, appropriately, properly, suitably, in full measure

rickety *adjective* SHAKY, broken, weak, broken-down, frail, insecure, feeble, precarious, derelict, flimsy, wobbly, imperfect, tottering, ramshackle, dilapidated, decrepit, unsteady, unsound, infirm, jerry-built

rid *verb* FREE, clear, deliver, relieve, purge, lighten, unburden, disabuse, make free, disembarrass, disencumber, disburden
▷▷ **get rid of something** *or* **someone** DISPOSE OF, throw away *or* out, dispense with, dump, remove, eliminate, expel, unload, shake off, eject, do away with, jettison, weed out, see the back of, wipe from the face of the earth, give the bum's rush to (*slang*)

riddle¹ *noun* 1 PUZZLE, problem, conundrum, teaser, poser, rebus, brain-teaser (*informal*), Chinese puzzle 2 ENIGMA, question, secret, mystery, puzzle, conundrum, teaser, problem

riddle² *verb* 1 PIERCE, pepper, puncture, perforate, honeycomb 2 PERVADE, fill, spread through, mar, spoil, corrupt, impair, pervade, infest, permeate

ride *verb* 1 CONTROL, handle, sit on, manage 2 TRAVEL, be carried, be supported, be borne, go, move, sit, progress, journey ▷ *noun* JOURNEY, drive, trip, lift, spin (*informal*), outing, whirl (*informal*), jaunt

ridicule *verb* LAUGH AT, mock, make fun of, make a fool of, humiliate, taunt, sneer at, parody, caricature, jeer at, scoff at, deride, send up (*Brit informal*), lampoon, poke fun at, chaff, take the mickey out of (*informal*), satirize, pooh-pooh, laugh out of court, make a monkey out of, make someone a laughing stock, laugh to scorn ▷ *noun* MOCKERY, scorn, derision, laughter, irony, rib, taunting, sneer, satire, jeer, banter, sarcasm, chaff, gibe, raillery

ridiculous *adjective* LAUGHABLE, stupid, incredible, silly, outrageous, absurd, foolish, unbelievable, hilarious, ludicrous, preposterous, farcical, comical, zany, nonsensical, derisory, inane, risible, contemptible, cockamamie (*slang, chiefly US*) << ANTONYM sensible

rife *adjective* 1 WIDESPREAD, abundant, plentiful, rampant, general, common, current, raging, universal, frequent, prevailing, epidemic, prevalent, ubiquitous 2 *usually with* **with** ABOUNDING, seething, teeming

rifle *verb* 1 RUMMAGE, go, rake, fossick (*Austral & NZ*) 2 RANSACK, rob, burgle, loot, strip,

sack, gut, plunder, pillage, despoil

rift *noun* 1 BREACH, difference, division, split, separation, falling out (*informal*), disagreement, quarrel, alienation, schism, estrangement 2 SPLIT, opening, space, crack, gap, break, fault, breach, fracture, flaw, cleavage, cleft, chink, crevice, fissure, cranny

rig *verb* 1 FIX, doctor, engineer (*informal*), arrange, fake, manipulate, juggle, tamper with, fiddle with (*informal*), falsify, trump up, gerrymander 2 (*nautical*) EQUIP, fit out, kit out, outfit, supply, turn out, provision, furnish, accoutre ▷▷ **rig something up** *verb* SET UP, build, construct, put up, arrange, assemble, put together, erect, improvise, fix up, throw together, cobble together

right *adjective* 1 CORRECT, true, genuine, accurate, exact, precise, valid, authentic, satisfactory, spot-on (*Brit informal*), factual, on the money (*US*), unerring, admissible, dinkum (*Austral & NZ informal*), veracious, sound << ANTONYM wrong 2 PROPER, done, becoming, seemly, fitting, fit, appropriate, suitable, desirable, comme il faut (*French*) << ANTONYM inappropriate 3 FAVOURABLE, due, ideal, convenient, rightful, advantageous, opportune, propitious << ANTONYM disadvantageous 4 JUST, good, fair, moral, proper, ethical, upright, honourable, honest, equitable, righteous, virtuous, lawful << ANTONYM unfair 5 SANE, sound, balanced, normal, reasonable, rational, all there (*informal*), lucid, unimpaired, compos mentis (*Latin*) 6 HEALTHY, well, fine, fit, in good health, in the pink, up to par << ANTONYM unwell ▷ *adverb* 1 CORRECTLY, truly, precisely, exactly, genuinely, accurately, factually, aright << ANTONYM wrongly 2 SUITABLY, fittingly, appropriately, properly, aptly, satisfactorily, befittingly << ANTONYM improperly 3 EXACTLY, squarely, precisely, bang, slap-bang (*informal*) 4 DIRECTLY, straight, precisely, exactly, unswervingly, without deviation, by the shortest route, in a beeline 5 ALL THE WAY, completely, totally, perfectly, entirely, absolutely, altogether, thoroughly, wholly, utterly, quite 6 STRAIGHT, directly, immediately, quickly, promptly, instantly, straightaway, without delay << ANTONYM indirectly 7 PROPERLY, fittingly, fairly, morally, honestly, justly, ethically, honourably, righteously, virtuously 8 FAVOURABLY, well, fortunately, for the better, to advantage, beneficially,

advantageously << ANTONYM badly ▷ *noun*
1 PREROGATIVE, interest, business, power,
claim, authority, title, due, freedom, licence,
permission, liberty, privilege 2 JUSTICE,
good, reason, truth, honour, equity, virtue,
integrity, goodness, morality, fairness,
legality, righteousness, propriety, rectitude,
lawfulness, uprightness << ANTONYM
injustice ▷ *verb* RECTIFY, settle, fix, correct,
repair, sort out, compensate for, straighten,
redress, vindicate, put right ▷▷ **by rights**
IN FAIRNESS, properly, justly, equitably
▷▷ **put something to rights** ORDER, arrange,
straighten out

right away *adverb* IMMEDIATELY, now,
directly, promptly, instantly, at once, right
off, straightaway, without delay, without
hesitation, straight off (*informal*), forthwith,
pronto (*informal*), this instant, posthaste

righteous *adjective* VIRTUOUS, good, just, fair,
moral, pure, ethical, upright, honourable,
honest, equitable, law-abiding, squeaky-
clean, blameless << ANTONYM wicked

righteousness *noun* VIRTUE, justice, honour,
equity, integrity, goodness, morality,
honesty, purity, probity, rectitude,
faithfulness, uprightness, blamelessness,
ethicalness

rightful *adjective* LAWFUL, just, real, true, due,
legal, suitable, proper, valid, legitimate,
authorized, bona fide, de jure

right-wing *adjective* CONSERVATIVE, Tory,
reactionary << ANTONYM left-wing

rigid *adjective* 1 STRICT, set, fixed, exact,
rigorous, stringent, austere, severe
<< ANTONYM flexible 2 INFLEXIBLE,
harsh, stern, adamant, uncompromising,
unrelenting, unyielding, intransigent,
unbending, invariable, unalterable,
undeviating 3 STIFF, inflexible, inelastic
<< ANTONYM pliable

rigorous *adjective* 1 STRICT, hard, firm,
demanding, challenging, tough, severe,
exacting, harsh, stern, rigid, stringent,
austere, inflexible << ANTONYM soft
2 THOROUGH, meticulous, painstaking,
scrupulous, nice, accurate, exact, precise,
conscientious, punctilious << ANTONYM
careless

rigour *noun* 1 *often plural* ORDEAL, suffering,
trial, hardship, privation 2 STRICTNESS,
austerity, rigidity, firmness, hardness,
harshness, inflexibility, stringency,
asperity, sternness 3 THOROUGHNESS,
accuracy, precision, exactitude, exactness,

conscientiousness, meticulousness,
punctiliousness, preciseness

rile *verb* ANGER, upset, provoke, bug (*informal*),
annoy, irritate, aggravate (*informal*), gall,
nettle, vex, irk, pique, peeve (*informal*), get
under your skin (*informal*), get on your
nerves (*informal*), nark (*Brit, Austral & NZ
slang*), get your goat (*slang*), try your patience,
rub you up the wrong way, get or put your
back up, hack you off (*informal*)

rim *noun* 1 EDGE, lip, brim, flange 2 BORDER,
edge, trim, circumference 3 MARGIN, border,
verge, brink

rind *noun* 1 SKIN, peel, outer layer, epicarp
2 CRUST, husk, integument

ring¹ *verb* 1 PHONE, call, telephone, buzz
(*informal, chiefly Brit*) 2 CHIME, sound, toll,
resound, resonate, reverberate, clang, peal
3 REVERBERATE, resound, resonate ▷ *noun*
1 CALL, phone call, buzz (*informal, chiefly Brit*)
2 CHIME, knell, peal

ring² *noun* 1 CIRCLE, round, band, circuit,
loop, hoop, halo 2 ARENA, enclosure, circus,
rink 3 GANG, group, association, band,
cell, combine, organization, circle, crew
(*informal*), knot, mob, syndicate, cartel,
junta, clique, coterie, cabal ▷ *verb* ENCIRCLE,
surround, enclose, encompass, seal off,
girdle, circumscribe, hem in, gird

rinse *verb* WASH, clean, wet, dip, splash,
cleanse, bathe, wash out ▷ *noun* WASH,
wetting, dip, splash, bath

riot *noun* 1 DISTURBANCE, row, disorder,
confusion, turmoil, quarrel, upheaval, fray,
strife, uproar, turbulence, commotion,
lawlessness, street fighting, tumult,
donnybrook, mob violence 2 DISPLAY, show,
splash, flourish, extravaganza, profusion
3 LAUGH, joke, scream (*informal*), blast (*US
slang*), hoot (*informal*), lark ▷ *verb* RAMPAGE,
take to the streets, run riot, go on the
rampage, fight in the streets, raise an uproar
▷▷ **run riot** 1 RAMPAGE, go wild, be out of
control, raise hell, let yourself go, break or
cut loose, throw off all restraint 2 GROW
PROFUSELY, luxuriate, spread like wildfire,
grow like weeds

riotous *adjective* 1 RECKLESS, wild, outrageous,
lavish, rash, luxurious, extravagant, wanton,
unrestrained, intemperate, heedless,
immoderate 2 UNRESTRAINED, wild, loud,
noisy, boisterous, rollicking, uproarious,
orgiastic, side-splitting, rambunctious
(*informal*), saturnalian, roisterous 3 UNRULY,
violent, disorderly, rebellious, rowdy,

anarchic, tumultuous, lawless, mutinous, ungovernable, uproarious, refractory, insubordinate, rampageous << ANTONYM orderly

rip *verb* **1** TEAR, cut, score, split, burst, rend, slash, hack, claw, slit, gash, lacerate **2** BE TORN, tear, split, burst, be rent ▷ *noun* TEAR, cut, hole, split, rent, slash, slit, cleavage, gash, laceration ▷▷ **rip someone off** (*slang*) CHEAT, trick, rob, con (*informal*), skin (*slang*), stiff (*slang*), steal from, fleece, defraud, dupe, swindle, diddle (*informal*), do the dirty on (*Brit informal*), gyp (*slang*), cozen

ripe *adjective* **1** RIPENED, seasoned, ready, mature, mellow, fully developed, fully grown << ANTONYM unripe **2** RIGHT, suitable **3** MATURE **4** SUITABLE, timely, ideal, favourable, auspicious, opportune << ANTONYM unsuitable **5** *with* for READY FOR, prepared for, eager for, in readiness for

ripen *verb* MATURE, season, develop, get ready, burgeon, come of age, come to fruition, grow ripe, make ripe

rip-off *or* **ripoff** *noun* (*slang*) CHEAT, con (*informal*), scam (*slang*), con trick (*informal*), fraud, theft, sting (*informal*), robbery, exploitation, swindle, daylight robbery (*informal*)

riposte *noun* RETORT, return, answer, response, reply, sally, comeback (*informal*), counterattack, repartee, rejoinder ▷ *verb* RETORT, return, answer, reply, respond, come back, rejoin, reciprocate

ripple *noun* **1** WAVE, tremor, oscillation, undulation **2** FLUTTER, thrill, tremor, tingle, vibration, frisson

rise *verb* **1** GET UP, stand up, get to your feet **2** ARISE, surface, get out of bed, rise and shine **3** GO UP, climb, move up, ascend << ANTONYM descend **4** LOOM, tower **5** GET STEEPER, mount, climb, ascend, go uphill, slope upwards << ANTONYM drop **6** INCREASE, mount, soar << ANTONYM decrease **7** GROW, go up, intensify **8** REBEL, resist, revolt, mutiny, take up arms, mount the barricades **9** ADVANCE, progress, get on, be promoted, prosper, go places (*informal*), climb the ladder, work your way up ▷ *noun* **1** UPWARD SLOPE, incline, elevation, ascent, hillock, rising ground, acclivity, kopje *or* koppie (*S African*) **2** INCREASE, climb, upturn, upswing, advance, improvement, ascent, upsurge, upward turn << ANTONYM decrease **3** PAY INCREASE, raise (*US*), increment **4** ADVANCEMENT, progress, climb,

promotion, aggrandizement ▷▷ **give rise to something** CAUSE, produce, effect, result in, provoke, bring about, bring on

risible *adjective* (*formal*) RIDICULOUS, ludicrous, laughable, farcical, funny, amusing, absurd, hilarious, humorous, comical, droll, side-splitting, rib-tickling (*informal*)

risk *noun* **1** DANGER, chance, possibility, speculation, uncertainty, hazard **2** GAMBLE, chance, venture, speculation, leap in the dark **3** PERIL, jeopardy ▷ *verb* **1** STAND A CHANCE OF **2** DARE, endanger, jeopardize, imperil, venture, gamble, hazard, take a chance on, put in jeopardy, expose to danger

risky *adjective* DANGEROUS, hazardous, unsafe, perilous, uncertain, tricky, dodgy (*Brit, Austral & NZ informal*), precarious, touch-and-go, dicey (*informal, chiefly Brit*), fraught with danger, chancy (*informal*), shonky (*Austral & NZ informal*) << ANTONYM safe

risqué *adjective* SUGGESTIVE, blue, daring, naughty, improper, racy, bawdy, off colour, ribald, immodest, indelicate, near the knuckle (*informal*), Rabelaisian

rite *noun* CEREMONY, custom, ritual, act, service, form, practice, procedure, mystery, usage, formality, ceremonial, communion, ordinance, observance, sacrament, liturgy, solemnity

ritual *noun* **1** CEREMONY, rite, ceremonial, sacrament, service, mystery, communion, observance, liturgy, solemnity **2** CUSTOM, tradition, routine, convention, form, practice, procedure, habit, usage, protocol, formality, ordinance, tikanga (*NZ*) ▷ *adjective* CEREMONIAL, formal, conventional, routine, prescribed, stereotyped, customary, procedural, habitual, ceremonious

ritzy *adjective* (*slang*) LUXURIOUS, grand, luxury, elegant, glittering, glamorous, stylish, posh (*informal, chiefly Brit*), sumptuous, plush (*informal*), high-class, opulent, swanky (*informal*), de luxe, schmick (*Austral informal*)

rival *noun* **1** OPPONENT, competitor, contender, challenger, contestant, adversary, antagonist, emulator << ANTONYM supporter **2** EQUAL, match, fellow, equivalent, peer, compeer ▷ *verb* COMPETE WITH, match, equal, oppose, compare with, contend, come up to, emulate, vie with, measure up to, be a match for, bear comparison with, seek to displace ▷ *modifier* COMPETING, conflicting, opposed, opposing, competitive, emulating

rivalry *noun* COMPETITION, competitiveness, vying, opposition, struggle, conflict, contest, contention, duel, antagonism, emulation

river *noun* **1** STREAM, brook, creek, beck, waterway, tributary, rivulet, watercourse, burn (*Scot*) **2** FLOW, rush, flood, spate, torrent

riveting *adjective* ENTHRALLING, arresting, gripping, fascinating, absorbing, captivating, hypnotic, engrossing, spellbinding

road *noun* **1** ROADWAY, street, highway, motorway, track, direction, route, path, lane, avenue, pathway, thoroughfare, course **2** WAY, path

roam *verb* WANDER, walk, range, travel, drift, stroll, stray, ramble, prowl, meander, rove, stravaig (*Scot & N English dialect*), peregrinate

roar *verb* **1** THUNDER, crash, rumble **2** GUFFAW, laugh heartily, hoot, crack up (*informal*), bust a gut (*informal*), split your sides (*informal*) **3** CRY, shout, yell, howl, bellow, clamour, bawl, bay, vociferate ▷ *noun* **1** RUMBLE, thunder **2** GUFFAW, hoot, belly laugh (*informal*) **3** CRY, crash, shout, yell, howl, outcry, bellow, clamour

rob *verb* **1** STEAL FROM, hold up, rifle, mug (*informal*), stiff (*slang*) **2** RAID, hold up, sack, loot, plunder, burgle, ransack, pillage **3** DISPOSSESS, con (*informal*), rip off (*slang*), skin (*slang*), cheat, defraud, swindle, despoil, gyp (*slang*) **4** DEPRIVE, strip, do out of (*informal*)

robber *noun* THIEF, raider, burglar, looter, stealer, fraud, cheat, pirate, bandit, plunderer, mugger (*informal*), highwayman, con man (*informal*), fraudster, swindler, brigand, grifter (*slang, chiefly US & Canad*), footpad (*archaic*), rogue trader

robbery *noun* **1** BURGLARY, raid, hold-up, rip-off (*slang*), stick-up (*slang, chiefly US*), home invasion (*Austral & NZ*) **2** THEFT, stealing, fraud, steaming (*informal*), mugging (*informal*), plunder, swindle, pillage, embezzlement, larceny, depredation, filching, thievery, rapine, spoliation

robe *noun* **1** GOWN, costume, vestment, habit **2** DRESSING GOWN, wrapper, bathrobe, negligée, housecoat, peignoir

robot *noun* MACHINE, automaton, android, mechanical man

robust *adjective* **1** STRONG, tough, powerful, athletic, well, sound, fit, healthy, strapping, hardy, rude, vigorous, rugged, muscular, sturdy, hale, stout, staunch, hearty, husky (*informal*), in good health, lusty, alive

and kicking, fighting fit, sinewy, brawny, in fine fettle, thickset, fit as a fiddle (*informal*), able-bodied << ANTONYM weak **2** ROUGH, raw, rude, coarse, raunchy (*slang*), earthy, boisterous, rollicking, unsubtle, indecorous, roisterous << ANTONYM refined **3** STRAIGHTFORWARD, practical, sensible, realistic, pragmatic, down-to-earth, hard-headed, common-sensical

rock¹ *noun* **1** STONE, boulder **2** TOWER OF STRENGTH, foundation, cornerstone, mainstay, support, protection, anchor, bulwark

rock² *verb* **1** SWAY, pitch, swing, reel, toss, lurch, wobble, roll **2** SHOCK, surprise, shake, stun, astonish, stagger, jar, astound, daze, dumbfound, set you back on your heels (*informal*)

rocky¹ *adjective* ROUGH, rugged, stony, craggy, pebbly, boulder-strewn

rocky² *adjective* UNSTABLE, weak, uncertain, doubtful, shaky, unreliable, wobbly, rickety, unsteady, undependable

rod *noun* **1** STICK, bar, pole, shaft, switch, crook, cane, birch, dowel **2** STAFF, baton, mace, wand, sceptre

rogue *noun* **1** SCOUNDREL, crook (*informal*), villain, fraudster, sharper, fraud, cheat, devil, deceiver, charlatan, con man (*informal*), swindler, knave (*archaic*), ne'er-do-well, reprobate, scumbag (*slang*), blackguard, mountebank, grifter (*slang, chiefly US & Canad*), skelm (*S African*), rorter (*Austral slang*), wrong 'un (*Austral slang*) **2** SCAMP, rascal, scally (*Northwest English dialect*), rapscallion, nointer (*Austral slang*)

role *noun* **1** JOB, part, position, post, task, duty, function, capacity **2** PART, character, representation, portrayal, impersonation

roll *verb* **1** TURN, wheel, spin, reel, go round, revolve, rotate, whirl, swivel, pivot, twirl, gyrate **2** TRUNDLE, go, move **3** FLOW, run, course, slide, glide, purl **4** *often with* up WIND, bind, wrap, twist, curl, coil, swathe, envelop, entwine, furl, enfold **5** *often with* out LEVEL, even, press, spread, smooth, flatten **6** TOSS, rock, lurch, reel, tumble, sway, wallow, billow, swing, welter **7** RUMBLE, boom, echo, drum, roar, thunder, grumble, resound, reverberate **8** SWAY, reel, stagger, lurch, lumber, waddle, swagger **9** PASS, go past, elapse ▷ *noun* **1** REEL, ball, bobbin, cylinder **2** RUMBLE, boom, drumming, roar, thunder, grumble, resonance, growl, reverberation **3** REGISTER, record, list, table, schedule, index, catalogue, directory, inventory, census, chronicle, scroll, roster, annals **4** TOSSING, rocking, rolling, pitching, swell, lurching, wallowing **5** TURN, run, spin, rotation, cycle, wheel, revolution, reel, whirl, twirl, undulation, gyration

rollicking¹ *adjective* BOISTEROUS, spirited, lively, romping, merry, hearty, playful, exuberant, joyous, carefree, jaunty, cavorting, sprightly, jovial, swashbuckling, frisky, rip-roaring (*informal*), devil-may-care, full of beans (*informal*), frolicsome, sportive << ANTONYM sedate

rollicking² *noun* (*Brit informal*) SCOLDING, lecture, reprimand, telling-off, roasting (*informal*), wigging (*Brit slang*), ticking off (*informal*), dressing-down (*informal*), tongue-lashing (*informal*)

romance *noun* **1** LOVE AFFAIR, relationship, affair, intrigue, attachment, liaison, amour, affair of the heart, affaire (du coeur) (*French*) **2** LOVE **3** EXCITEMENT, colour, charm, mystery, adventure, sentiment, glamour, fascination, nostalgia, exoticness **4** STORY, novel, tale, fantasy, legend, fiction, fairy tale, love story, melodrama, idyll, tear-jerker (*informal*)

romantic *adjective* **1** LOVING, tender, passionate, fond, sentimental, sloppy (*informal*), amorous, mushy (*informal*), soppy (*Brit informal*), lovey-dovey, icky (*informal*) << ANTONYM unromantic **2** IDEALISTIC, unrealistic, visionary, high-flown, impractical, dreamy, utopian, whimsical, quixotic, starry-eyed << ANTONYM realistic **3** EXCITING, charming, fascinating, exotic, mysterious, colourful, glamorous, picturesque, nostalgic << ANTONYM unexciting **4** FICTITIOUS, made-up, fantastic, fabulous, legendary, exaggerated, imaginative, imaginary, extravagant, unrealistic, improbable, fairy-tale, idyllic, fanciful, wild, chimerical << ANTONYM realistic ▷ *noun* IDEALIST, romancer, visionary, dreamer, utopian, Don Quixote, sentimentalist

romp *verb* FROLIC, sport, skip, have fun, revel, caper, cavort, frisk, gambol, make merry, rollick, roister, cut capers ▷ *noun* FROLIC, lark (*informal*), caper ▷▷ **romp home** *or* **in** WIN EASILY, walk it (*informal*), win hands down, run away with it, win by a mile (*informal*)

room *noun* **1** CHAMBER, office, apartment **2** SPACE, area, territory, volume, capacity, extent, expanse, elbow room

3 OPPORTUNITY, scope, leeway, play, chance, range, occasion, margin, allowance, compass, latitude

roomy *adjective* SPACIOUS, large, wide, broad, extensive, generous, ample, capacious, commodious, sizable *or* sizeable << ANTONYM cramped

root¹ *noun* **1** STEM, tuber, rhizome, radix, radicle **2** SOURCE, cause, heart, bottom, beginnings, base, seat, occasion, seed, foundation, origin, core, fundamental, essence, nucleus, starting point, germ, crux, nub, derivation, fountainhead, mainspring ▷ *plural noun* SENSE OF BELONGING, origins, heritage, birthplace, home, family, cradle ▷▷ **root and branch 1** COMPLETE, total, entire, radical, thorough **2** COMPLETELY, finally, totally, entirely, radically, thoroughly, wholly, utterly, without exception, to the last man ▷▷ **root something** *or* **someone out 1** GET RID OF, remove, destroy, eliminate, abolish, cut out, erase, eradicate, do away with, uproot, weed out, efface, exterminate, extirpate, wipe from the face of the earth **2** DISCOVER, find, expose, turn up, uncover, unearth, bring to light, ferret out

root² *verb* DIG, hunt, nose, poke, burrow, delve, ferret, pry, rummage, forage, rootle

rooted *adjective* DEEP-SEATED, firm, deep, established, confirmed, fixed, radical, rigid, entrenched, ingrained, deeply felt

rootless *adjective* FOOTLOOSE, homeless, roving, transient, itinerant, vagabond

rope *noun* CORD, line, cable, strand, hawser ▷ *verb* TIE, bind, moor, lash, hitch, fasten, tether, pinion, lasso ▷▷ **know the ropes** BE EXPERIENCED, know the score (*informal*), be knowledgeable, know what's what, be an old hand, know your way around, know where it's at (*slang*), know all the ins and outs ▷▷ **rope someone in** *or* **into something** (*Brit*) PERSUADE, involve, engage, enlist, talk into, drag in, inveigle

roster *noun* ROTA, listing, list, table, roll, schedule, register, agenda, catalogue, inventory, scroll

rostrum *noun* STAGE, stand, platform, podium, dais

rosy *adjective* **1** GLOWING, fresh, blooming, flushed, blushing, radiant, reddish, ruddy, healthy-looking, roseate, rubicund << ANTONYM pale **2** PROMISING, encouraging, bright, reassuring, optimistic, hopeful, sunny, cheerful, favourable, auspicious, rose-coloured, roseate

<< ANTONYM gloomy **3** PINK, red, rose-coloured, roseate

rot *verb* **1** DECAY, break down, spoil, corrupt, deteriorate, taint, perish, degenerate, fester, decompose, corrode, moulder, go bad, putrefy **2** CRUMBLE, disintegrate, become rotten **3** DETERIORATE, decline, languish, degenerate, wither away, waste away ▷ *noun* **1** DECAY, disintegration, corrosion, decomposition, corruption, mould, blight, deterioration, canker, putrefaction, putrescence **2** (*informal*) NONSENSE, rubbish, drivel, twaddle, pants (*slang*), crap (*slang*), garbage (*chiefly US*), trash, bunk (*informal*), hot air (*informal*), tosh (*slang, chiefly Brit*), pap, bilge (*informal*), tripe (*informal*), guff (*slang*), moonshine, claptrap (*informal*), hogwash, hokum (*slang, chiefly US & Canad*), codswallop (*Brit slang*), piffle (*informal*), poppycock (*informal*), balderdash, bosh (*informal*), eyewash (*informal*), stuff and nonsense, flapdoodle (*slang*), tommyrot, horsefeathers (*US slang*), bunkum or buncombe (*chiefly US*), bizzo (*Austral slang*), bull's wool (*Austral & NZ slang*)

rotary *adjective* REVOLVING, turning, spinning, rotating, rotational, gyratory, rotatory

rotate *verb* **1** REVOLVE, turn, wheel, spin, reel, go round, swivel, pivot, gyrate, pirouette **2** FOLLOW IN SEQUENCE, switch, alternate, interchange, take turns

rotation *noun* **1** REVOLUTION, turning, turn, wheel, spin, spinning, reel, orbit, pirouette, gyration **2** SEQUENCE, switching, cycle, succession, interchanging, alternation

rotten *adjective* **1** DECAYING, bad, rank, foul, corrupt, sour, stinking, tainted, perished, festering, decomposed, decomposing, mouldy, mouldering, fetid, putrid, putrescent, festy (*Austral slang*) << ANTONYM fresh **2** CRUMBLING, decayed, disintegrating, perished, corroded, unsound **3** (*informal*) BAD, disappointing, unfortunate, unlucky, regrettable, deplorable **4** (*informal*) DESPICABLE, mean, base, dirty, nasty, unpleasant, filthy, vile, wicked, disagreeable, contemptible, scurrilous **5** (*informal*) UNWELL, poorly (*informal*), ill, sick, rough (*informal*), bad, crook (*Austral & NZ informal*), below par, off colour, under the weather (*informal*), ropey or ropy (*Brit informal*) **6** (*informal*) INFERIOR, poor, sorry, inadequate, unacceptable, punk, duff (*Brit informal*), unsatisfactory, lousy (*slang*), low-grade, substandard, ill-considered, crummy

(*slang*), ill-thought-out, poxy (*slang*), of a sort or of sorts, ropey or ropy (*Brit informal*), bodger or bodgie (*Austral slang*) **7** CORRUPT, immoral, deceitful, untrustworthy, bent (*slang*), crooked (*informal*), vicious, degenerate, mercenary, treacherous, dishonest, disloyal, faithless, venal, dishonourable, perfidious << ANTONYM honourable

rotund *adjective* **1** PLUMP, rounded, heavy, fat, stout, chubby, obese, fleshy, tubby, portly, roly-poly, podgy, corpulent << ANTONYM skinny **2** POMPOUS, orotund, magniloquent, full **3** ROUND, rounded, spherical, bulbous, globular, orbicular **4** SONOROUS, round, rich, resonant, orotund

rough *adjective* **1** UNEVEN, broken, rocky, rugged, irregular, jagged, bumpy, stony, craggy << ANTONYM even **2** COARSE, disordered, tangled, hairy, fuzzy, bushy, shaggy, dishevelled, uncut, unshaven, tousled, bristly, unshorn << ANTONYM smooth **3** BOISTEROUS, hard, tough, rugged, arduous **4** UNGRACIOUS, blunt, rude, coarse, bluff, curt, churlish, bearish, brusque, uncouth, unrefined, inconsiderate, impolite, loutish, untutored, discourteous, unpolished, indelicate, uncivil, uncultured, unceremonious, ill-bred, unmannerly, ill-mannered << ANTONYM refined **5** UNPLEASANT, hard, difficult, tough, uncomfortable, drastic, unjust << ANTONYM easy **6** (*informal*) UNWELL, poorly (*informal*), ill, upset, sick, crook (*Austral & NZ informal*), rotten (*informal*), below par, off colour, under the weather (*informal*), not a hundred per cent (*informal*), ropey or ropy (*Brit informal*) **7** APPROXIMATE, estimated << ANTONYM exact **8** VAGUE, general, sketchy, imprecise, hazy, foggy, amorphous, inexact **9** BASIC, quick, raw, crude, unfinished, incomplete, hasty, imperfect, rudimentary, sketchy, cursory, shapeless, rough-and-ready, unrefined, formless, rough-hewn, untutored, unpolished << ANTONYM complete **10** ROUGH-HEWN, crude, uncut, unpolished, raw, undressed, unprocessed, unhewn, unwrought **11** STORMY, wild, turbulent, agitated, choppy, tempestuous, inclement, squally << ANTONYM calm **12** GRATING, harsh, jarring, raucous, rasping, husky, discordant, gruff, cacophonous, unmusical, inharmonious << ANTONYM soft **13** HARSH, tough, sharp, severe, nasty, cruel, rowdy, curt, unfeeling << ANTONYM gentle ▷ *noun*

1 OUTLINE, draft, mock-up, preliminary sketch, suggestion **2** (*informal*) THUG, tough, casual, rowdy, hoon (*Austral & NZ*), bully boy, bruiser, ruffian, lager lout, roughneck (*slang*), ned (*slang*), cougan (*Austral slang*), scozza (*Austral slang*), bogan (*Austral slang*) ▷▷ **rough and ready 1** MAKESHIFT, adequate, crude, provisional, improvised, sketchy, thrown together, cobbled together, stopgap **2** UNREFINED, shabby, untidy, unkempt, unpolished, ungroomed, ill-groomed, daggy (*Austral & NZ informal*) ▷▷ **rough and tumble 1** FIGHT, struggle, scrap (*informal*), brawl, scuffle, punch-up (*Brit informal*), fracas, affray (*law*), dust-up (*informal*), shindig (*informal*), donnybrook, scrimmage, roughhouse (*slang*), shindy (*informal*), melee *or* mêlée, biffo (*Austral slang*) **2** DISORDERLY, rough, scrambled, scrambling, irregular, rowdy, boisterous, haphazard, indisciplined ▷▷ **rough someone up** (*informal*) BEAT UP, batter, thrash, do over (*Brit, Austral & NZ slang*), work over (*slang*), mistreat, manhandle, maltreat, bash up (*informal*), beat the living daylights out of (*informal*), knock about *or* around, beat *or* knock seven bells out of (*informal*) ▷▷ **rough something out** OUTLINE, plan, draft, sketch, suggest, block out, delineate, adumbrate

round *noun* **1** SERIES, session, cycle, sequence, succession, bout **2** STAGE, turn, level, period, division, session, lap **3** SPHERE, ball, band, ring, circle, disc, globe, orb **4** COURSE, turn, tour, circuit, beat, series, schedule, routine, compass, ambit **5** BULLET, shot, shell, discharge, cartridge ▷ *adjective* **1** SPHERICAL, rounded, bowed, curved, circular, cylindrical, bulbous, rotund, globular, curvilinear, ball-shaped, ring-shaped, disc-shaped, annular, discoid, orbicular **2** COMPLETE, full, whole, entire, solid, unbroken, undivided **3** PLUMP, full, rounded, ample, fleshy, roly-poly, rotund, full-fleshed ▷ *verb* GO ROUND, circle, skirt, flank, bypass, encircle, turn, circumnavigate ▷▷ **round on someone** ATTACK, abuse, turn on, retaliate against, have a go at (*Brit slang*), snap at, wade into, lose your temper with, bite (someone's) head off (*informal*) ▷▷ **round something off** COMPLETE, close, settle, crown, cap, conclude, finish off, put the finishing touch to, bring to a close ▷▷ **round something** *or* **someone up** GATHER, assemble, bring together, muster, group, drive, collect, rally, herd, marshal

roundabout *adjective* **1** INDIRECT, meandering, devious, tortuous, circuitous, evasive, discursive, circumlocutory << ANTONYM direct **2** OBLIQUE, implied, indirect, evasive, circuitous, circumlocutory, periphrastic

roundly *adverb* THOROUGHLY, sharply, severely, bitterly, fiercely, bluntly, intensely, violently, vehemently, rigorously, outspokenly, frankly

roundup *noun* **1** (*informal*) SUMMARY, survey, collation **2** MUSTER, collection, rally, assembly, herding

rouse *verb* **1** WAKE UP, call, wake, awaken **2** EXCITE, move, arouse, stir, disturb, provoke, anger, startle, animate, prod, exhilarate, get going, agitate, inflame, incite, whip up, galvanize, bestir **3** STIMULATE, provoke, arouse, incite, instigate

rousing *adjective* LIVELY, moving, spirited, exciting, inspiring, stirring, stimulating, vigorous, brisk, exhilarating, inflammatory, electrifying << ANTONYM dull

rout *verb* DEFEAT, beat, overthrow, thrash, stuff (*slang*), worst, destroy, chase, tank (*slang*), crush, scatter, conquer, lick (*informal*), dispel, drive off, overpower, clobber (*slang*), wipe the floor with (*informal*), cut to pieces, put to flight, drub, put to rout, throw back in confusion ▷ *noun* DEFEAT, beating, hiding (*informal*), ruin, overthrow, thrashing, licking (*informal*), pasting (*slang*), shambles, debacle, drubbing, overwhelming defeat, headlong flight, disorderly retreat ▷ see **route**

route *noun* **1** WAY, course, road, direction, path, journey, passage, avenue, itinerary **2** BEAT, run, round, circuit ▷ *verb* **1** DIRECT, lead, guide, steer, convey **2** SEND, forward, dispatch

routine *noun* **1** PROCEDURE, programme, way, order, practice, method, pattern, formula, custom, usage, wont **2** GRIND (*informal*), monotony, banality, groove, boredom, chore, the doldrums, dullness, sameness, ennui, drabness, deadness, dreariness, tediousness, lifelessness ▷ *adjective* **1** USUAL, standard, normal, customary, ordinary, familiar, typical, conventional, everyday, habitual, workaday, wonted << ANTONYM unusual **2** BORING, dull, predictable, tedious, tiresome, run-of-the-mill, humdrum, unimaginative, clichéd, uninspired, mind-numbing, hackneyed, unoriginal, shtick (*slang*)

rove *verb* WANDER, range, cruise, drift, stroll,

stray, roam, ramble, meander, traipse (*informal*), gallivant, gad about, stravaig (*Scot & N English dialect*)

rover *noun* WANDERER, traveller, gypsy, rolling stone, rambler, transient, nomad, itinerant, ranger, drifter, vagrant, stroller, bird of passage, gadabout (*informal*)

row[1] *noun* LINE, bank, range, series, file, rank, string, column, sequence, queue, tier ▷▷ **in a row** CONSECUTIVELY, running, in turn, one after the other, successively, in sequence

row[2] *noun* **1** QUARREL, dispute, argument, squabble, tiff, trouble, controversy, scrap (*informal*), fuss, falling-out (*informal*), fray, brawl, fracas, altercation, slanging match (*Brit*), shouting match (*informal*), shindig (*informal*), ruction (*informal*), ruckus (*informal*), shindy (*informal*), bagarre (*French*) **2** DISTURBANCE, noise, racket, uproar, commotion, rumpus, tumult **3** TELLING-OFF, talking-to (*informal*), lecture, reprimand, ticking-off (*informal*), dressing-down (*informal*), rollicking (*Brit informal*) (*informal*), tongue-lashing, reproof, castigation, flea in your ear (*informal*) ▷ *verb* QUARREL, fight, argue, dispute, scrap (*informal*), brawl, squabble, spar, wrangle, go at it hammer and tongs

rowdy *adjective* DISORDERLY, rough, loud, noisy, unruly, boisterous, loutish, wild, uproarious, obstreperous << ANTONYM orderly ▷ *noun* HOOLIGAN, tough, rough (*informal*), casual, ned (*Scot slang*), brawler, yahoo, lout, troublemaker, tearaway (*Brit*), ruffian, lager lout, yob *or* yobbo (*Brit slang*), cougan (*Austral slang*), scozza (*Austral slang*), bogan (*Austral slang*)

royal *adjective* **1** REGAL, kingly, queenly, princely, imperial, sovereign, monarchical, kinglike **2** SPLENDID, august, grand, impressive, superb, magnificent, superior, majestic, stately

rub *verb* **1** STROKE, smooth, massage, caress, knead **2** POLISH, clean, shine, wipe, scour **3** SPREAD, put, apply, smear **4** CHAFE, scrape, grate, abrade ▷ *noun* **1** MASSAGE, caress, kneading **2** POLISH, stroke, shine, wipe ▷▷ **rub something out** ERASE, remove, cancel, wipe out, excise, delete, obliterate, efface, expunge ▷▷ **the rub** DIFFICULTY, problem, catch, trouble, obstacle, hazard, hitch, drawback, snag, uphill (*S African*), impediment, hindrance

rubbish *noun* **1** WASTE, refuse, scrap, junk (*informal*), litter, debris, crap (*slang*), garbage (*chiefly US*), trash, lumber, offal, dross, dregs, flotsam and jetsam, grot (*slang*), dreck (*slang, chiefly US*), offscourings **2** NONSENSE, garbage (*chiefly US*), drivel, twaddle, pants (*slang*), rot, crap (*slang*), trash, hot air (*informal*), tosh (*slang, chiefly Brit*), pap, bilge (*informal*), tripe (*informal*), gibberish, guff (*slang*), havers (*Scot*), moonshine, claptrap (*informal*), hogwash, hokum (*slang, chiefly US & Canad*), codswallop (*Brit slang*), piffle (*informal*), poppycock (*informal*), balderdash, bosh (*informal*), wack (*US slang*), eyewash (*informal*), stuff and nonsense, flapdoodle (*slang*), tommyrot, horsefeathers (*US slang*), bunkum *or* buncombe (*chiefly US*), bizzo (*Austral slang*), bull's wool (*Austral & NZ slang*)

ruddy *adjective* **1** ROSY, red, fresh, healthy, glowing, blooming, flushed, blushing, radiant, reddish, sanguine, florid, sunburnt, rosy-cheeked, rubicund << ANTONYM pale **2** RED, pink, scarlet, ruby, crimson, reddish, roseate

rude *adjective* **1** IMPOLITE, insulting, cheeky, abrupt, short, blunt, abusive, curt, churlish, disrespectful, brusque, offhand, impertinent, insolent, inconsiderate, peremptory, impudent, discourteous, uncivil, unmannerly, ill-mannered << ANTONYM polite **2** UNCIVILIZED, low, rough, savage, ignorant, coarse, illiterate, uneducated, brutish, barbarous, scurrilous, boorish, uncouth, unrefined, loutish, untutored, graceless, ungracious, unpolished, oafish, uncultured **3** VULGAR, gross, crude << ANTONYM refined **4** UNPLEASANT, sharp, violent, sudden, harsh, startling, abrupt **5** ROUGHLY-MADE, simple, rough, raw, crude, primitive, makeshift, rough-hewn, artless, inelegant, inartistic << ANTONYM well-made

rudiment *noun often plural* BASICS, elements, essentials, fundamentals, beginnings, foundation, nuts and bolts, first principles

rudimentary *adjective* **1** PRIMITIVE, undeveloped **2** BASIC, fundamental, elementary, early, primary, initial, introductory **3** UNDEVELOPED, embryonic, vestigial << ANTONYM complete

rue *verb* (*literary*) REGRET, mourn, grieve, lament, deplore, bemoan, repent, be sorry for, weep over, sorrow for, bewail, kick yourself for, reproach yourself for

rueful *adjective* REGRETFUL, sad, dismal, melancholy, grievous, pitiful, woeful, sorry, mournful, plaintive, lugubrious, contrite,

sorrowful, repentant, doleful, remorseful,
penitent, pitiable, woebegone, conscience-
stricken, self-reproachful << ANTONYM
unrepentant

ruffle *verb* **1** DISARRANGE, disorder, wrinkle,
mess up, rumple, tousle, derange,
discompose, dishevel, muss (*US & Canad*)
2 ANNOY, worry, trouble, upset, confuse, stir,
disturb, rattle (*informal*), irritate, put out,
unsettle, shake up (*informal*), harass, hassle
(*informal*), agitate, unnerve, disconcert,
disquiet, nettle, vex, fluster, perturb,
faze, peeve (*informal*), hack off (*informal*)
<< ANTONYM calm

rugged *adjective* **1** ROCKY, broken, rough,
craggy, difficult, ragged, stark, irregular,
uneven, jagged, bumpy << ANTONYM
even **2** STRONG-FEATURED, lined, worn,
weathered, wrinkled, furrowed, leathery,
rough-hewn, weather-beaten << ANTONYM
delicate **3** WELL-BUILT, strong, tough, robust,
sturdy **4** (*chiefly US & Canad*) TOUGH, strong,
hardy, robust, vigorous, muscular, sturdy,
hale, burly, husky (*informal*), beefy (*informal*),
brawny << ANTONYM delicate **5** STERN, hard,
severe, rough, harsh, sour, rude, crabbed,
austere, dour, surly, gruff

ruin *verb* **1** DESTROY, devastate, wreck, trash
(*slang*), break, total (*slang*), defeat, smash,
crush, overwhelm, shatter, overturn,
overthrow, bring down, demolish, raze, lay
waste, lay in ruins, wreak havoc upon, bring
to ruin, bring to nothing, kennet (*Austral
slang*), jeff (*Austral slang*) << ANTONYM create
2 BANKRUPT, break, impoverish, beggar,
pauperize **3** SPOIL, damage, mar, mess up,
blow (*slang*), injure, undo, screw up (*informal*),
botch, mangle, cock up (*Brit slang*), disfigure,
make a mess of, bodge (*informal*), crool *or*
cruel (*Austral slang*) << ANTONYM improve ▷
noun **1** BANKRUPTCY, insolvency, destitution
2 DISREPAIR, decay, disintegration,
ruination, wreckage **3** DESTRUCTION, fall,
the end, breakdown, damage, defeat, failure,
crash, collapse, wreck, overthrow, undoing,
havoc, Waterloo, downfall, devastation,
dissolution, subversion, nemesis, crackup
(*informal*) << ANTONYM preservation

ruinous *adjective* **1** DESTRUCTIVE, devastating,
shattering, fatal, deadly, disastrous, dire,
withering, catastrophic, murderous,
pernicious, noxious, calamitous, baleful,
deleterious, injurious, baneful (*archaic*)
2 RUINED, broken-down, derelict,
ramshackle, dilapidated, in ruins, decrepit

rule *noun* **1** REGULATION, order, law, ruling,
guide, direction, guideline, decree,
ordinance, dictum **2** PRECEPT, principle,
criterion, canon, maxim, tenet, axiom
3 PROCEDURE, policy, standard, method,
way, course, formula **4** CUSTOM, procedure,
practice, routine, form, condition, tradition,
habit, convention, wont, order *or* way of
things **5** GOVERNMENT, power, control,
authority, influence, administration,
direction, leadership, command, regime,
empire, reign, sway, domination,
jurisdiction, supremacy, mastery, dominion,
ascendancy, mana (*NZ*) ▷ *verb* **1** GOVERN, lead,
control, manage, direct, guide, regulate,
administer, oversee, preside over, have
power over, reign over, command, have
charge of **2** REIGN, govern, be in power, hold
sway, wear the crown, be in authority, be
number one (*informal*) **3** CONTROL, dominate,
monopolize, tyrannize, be pre-eminent,
have the upper hand over **4** DECREE, find,
decide, judge, establish, determine, settle,
resolve, pronounce, lay down, adjudge **5** BE
PREVALENT, prevail, predominate, hold sway,
be customary, preponderate, obtain ▷▷ **as a
rule** USUALLY, generally, mainly, normally,
on the whole, for the most part, ordinarily,
customarily ▷▷ **rule someone out** EXCLUDE,
eliminate, disqualify, ban, prevent, reject,
dismiss, forbid, prohibit, leave out, preclude,
proscribe, obviate, debar ▷▷ **rule something
out** REJECT, exclude, eliminate

ruler *noun* **1** GOVERNOR, leader, lord,
commander, controller, monarch, sovereign,
head of state, potentate, crowned head,
emperor *or* empress, king *or* queen, prince
or princess **2** MEASURE, rule, yardstick,
straight edge

ruling *adjective* **1** GOVERNING, upper, reigning,
controlling, leading, commanding,
dominant, regnant **2** PREDOMINANT,
dominant, prevailing, preponderant, chief,
main, current, supreme, principal, prevalent,
pre-eminent, regnant << ANTONYM minor
▷ *noun* DECISION, finding, resolution,
verdict, judgment, decree, adjudication,
pronouncement

rum *adjective* (*Brit slang*) STRANGE, odd,
suspect, funny, unusual, curious, weird,
suspicious, peculiar, dodgy (*Brit, Austral &
NZ informal*), queer, singular, shonky (*Austral
& NZ informal*)

ruminate *verb* PONDER, think, consider,
reflect, contemplate, deliberate, muse,

brood, meditate, mull over things, chew over things, cogitate, rack your brains, turn over in your mind

rummage *verb* SEARCH, hunt, root, explore, delve, examine, ransack, forage, fossick (*Austral & NZ*), rootle

rumour *noun* STORY, news, report, talk, word, whisper, buzz, gossip, dirt (*US slang*), goss (*informal*), hearsay, canard, tidings, scuttlebutt (*US slang*), bush telegraph, bruit (*archaic*) ▷▷ **be rumoured** BE SAID, be told, be reported, be published, be circulated, be whispered, be passed around, be put about, be noised abroad

rump *noun* BUTTOCKS, bottom, rear, backside (*informal*), tail (*informal*), seat, butt (*US & Canad informal*), bum (*Brit slang*), buns (*US slang*), rear end, posterior, haunch, hindquarters, derrière (*euphemistic*), croup, jacksy (*Brit slang*)

rumple *verb* RUFFLE, crush, disorder, dishevel, wrinkle, crease, crumple, screw up, mess up, pucker, crinkle, scrunch, tousle, derange, muss (*US & Canad*)

rumpus *noun* COMMOTION, row, noise, confusion, fuss, disturbance, disruption, furore, uproar, tumult, brouhaha, shindig (*informal*), hue and cry, kerfuffle (*informal*), shindy (*informal*)

run *verb* 1 RACE, speed, rush, dash, hurry, career, barrel (along) (*informal, chiefly US & Canad*), sprint, scramble, bolt, dart, gallop, hare (*Brit informal*), jog, scud, hasten, scurry, stampede, scamper, leg it (*informal*), lope, hie, hotfoot << ANTONYM dawdle 2 FLEE, escape, take off (*informal*), depart, bolt, clear out, beat it (*slang*), leg it (*informal*), make off, abscond, decamp, take flight, do a runner (*slang*), scarper (*Brit slang*), slope off, cut and run (*informal*), make a run for it, fly the coop (*US & Canad informal*), beat a retreat, show a clean pair of heels, skedaddle (*informal*), take a powder (*US & Canad slang*), take it on the lam (*US & Canad slang*), take to your heels << ANTONYM stay 3 TAKE PART, compete 4 CONTINUE, go, stretch, last, reach, lie, range, extend, proceed << ANTONYM stop 5 (*Chiefly US & Canad*) COMPETE, stand, contend, be a candidate, put yourself up for, take part, challenge 6 MANAGE, lead, direct, be in charge of, own, head, control, boss (*informal*), operate, handle, conduct, look after, carry on, regulate, take care of, administer, oversee, supervise, mastermind, coordinate, superintend 7 GO, work, operate, perform, function, be in business, be in action, tick over 8 PERFORM, carry out 9 WORK, go, operate, function 10 DRIVE 11 OPERATE, go 12 GIVE A LIFT TO, drive, carry, transport, convey, bear, manoeuvre, propel 13 PASS, go, move, roll, slide, glide, skim 14 FLOW, pour, stream, cascade, go, move, issue, proceed, leak, spill, discharge, gush, spout, course 15 SPREAD, mix, bleed, be diffused, lose colour 16 CIRCULATE, spread, creep, go round 17 PUBLISH, feature, display, print 18 MELT, dissolve, liquefy, go soft, turn to liquid 19 UNRAVEL, tear, ladder, come apart, come undone 20 SMUGGLE, deal in, traffic in, bootleg, ship, sneak ▷ *noun* 1 RACE, rush, dash, sprint, gallop, jog, spurt 2 RIDE, drive, trip, lift, journey, spin (*informal*), outing, excursion, jaunt, joy ride (*informal*) 3 SEQUENCE, period, stretch, spell, course, season, round, series, chain, cycle, string, passage, streak 4 TYPE, sort, kind, class, variety, category, order 5 TEAR, rip, ladder, snag 6 ENCLOSURE, pen, coop 7 DIRECTION, way, course, current, movement, progress, flow, path, trend, motion, passage, stream, tendency, drift, tide, tenor 8 *with* **on** SUDDEN DEMAND FOR, pressure for, rush for ▷▷ **in the long run** IN THE END, eventually, in time, ultimately, at the end of the day, in the final analysis, when all is said and done, in the fullness of time ▷▷ **on the run** 1 ESCAPING, fugitive, in flight, at liberty, on the loose, on the lam (*US slang*) 2 IN RETREAT, defeated, fleeing, retreating, running away, falling back, in flight 3 HURRYING, hastily, in a hurry, at speed, hurriedly, in a rush, in haste ▷▷ **run across something** *or* **someone** MEET, encounter, meet with, come across, run into, bump into, come upon, chance upon ▷▷ **run away** *verb* FLEE, escape, take off, bolt, run off, clear out, beat it (*slang*), abscond, decamp, take flight, hook it (*slang*), do a runner (*slang*), scarper (*Brit slang*), cut and run (*informal*), make a run for it, turn tail, do a bunk (*Brit slang*), scram (*informal*), fly the coop (*US & Canad informal*), show a clean pair of heels, skedaddle (*informal*), take a powder (*US & Canad slang*), take it on the lam (*US & Canad slang*), take to your heels, do a Skase (*Austral informal*) ▷▷ **run away with something** *or* **someone** 1 ABSCOND WITH, run off with, elope with 2 WIN EASILY, walk it (*informal*), romp home, win hands down, win by a mile (*informal*) ▷▷ **run into someone** *verb* MEET, encounter, bump into, run across, chance upon, come across *or* upon ▷▷ **run into something 1** BE BESET BY, encounter, meet with, come across *or* upon, face, experience, be confronted by, happen on *or* upon **2** COLLIDE WITH, hit, strike, ram, bump into, crash into, dash against ▷▷ **run off** FLEE, escape, bolt, run away, clear out, make off, decamp, take flight, hook it (*slang*), do a runner (*slang*), scarper (*Brit slang*), cut and run (*informal*), turn tail, fly the coop (*US & Canad informal*), show a clean pair of heels, skedaddle (*informal*), take a powder (*US & Canad slang*), take it on the lam (*US & Canad slang*), take to your heels ▷▷ **run off with someone** RUN AWAY WITH, elope with, abscond with ▷▷ **run off with something** STEAL, take, lift (*informal*), nick (*slang, chiefly Brit*), pinch (*informal*), swipe (*slang*), run away with, make off with, embezzle, misappropriate, purloin, filch, walk *or* make off with ▷▷ **run out 1** BE USED UP, dry up, give out, peter out, fail, finish, cease, be exhausted **2** EXPIRE, end, terminate ▷▷ **run out of something** EXHAUST YOUR SUPPLY OF, be out of, be cleaned out, have no more, have none left, have no remaining ▷▷ **run out on someone** (*informal*) DESERT, abandon, strand, run away from, forsake, rat on (*informal*), leave high and dry, leave holding the baby, leave in the lurch ▷▷ **run over** OVERFLOW, spill over, brim over ▷▷ **run over something 1** EXCEED, overstep, go over the top of, go beyond the bounds of, go over the limit of **2** REVIEW, check, survey, examine, go through, go over, run through, rehearse, reiterate ▷▷ **run over something** *or* **someone** KNOCK DOWN, hit, strike, run down, knock over ▷▷ **run someone in** (*informal*) ARREST, apprehend, pull in (*Brit slang*), take into custody, lift (*slang*), pick up, jail, nail (*informal*), bust (*informal*), collar (*informal*), pinch (*informal*), nab (*informal*), throw in jail, take to jail, feel your collar (*slang*) ▷▷ **run something in** BREAK IN GENTLY, run gently ▷▷ **run something off** PRODUCE, print, duplicate, churn out (*informal*) ▷▷ **run something** *or* **someone down 1** CRITICIZE, denigrate, belittle, revile, knock (*informal*), rubbish (*informal*), put down, slag (off) (*slang*), disparage, decry, vilify, diss (*slang, chiefly US*), defame, bad-mouth (*slang, chiefly US & Canad*), speak ill of, asperse **2** DOWNSIZE, cut, drop, reduce, trim, decrease, cut back, curtail, pare down, kennet (*Austral slang*), jeff (*Austral slang*) **3** KNOCK DOWN, hit, strike, run

into, run over, knock over ▷▷ **run through something 1** REVIEW, check, survey, examine, go through, look over, run over **2** REHEARSE, read, practise, go over, run over **3** SQUANDER, waste, exhaust, throw away, dissipate, fritter away, spend like water, blow (*slang*)

runaway *adjective* **1** EASILY WON, easy, effortless **2** OUT OF CONTROL, uncontrolled **3** ESCAPED, wild, fleeing, loose, fugitive ▷ *noun* FUGITIVE, escaper, refugee, deserter, truant, escapee, absconder

run-down *or* **rundown** *adjective* **1** EXHAUSTED, weak, tired, drained, fatigued, weary, unhealthy, worn-out, debilitated, below par, under the weather (*informal*), enervated, out of condition, peaky << ANTONYM fit **2** DILAPIDATED, broken-down, shabby, worn-out, seedy, ramshackle, dingy, decrepit, tumbledown ▷ *noun* SUMMARY, review, briefing, résumé, outline, sketch, run-through, synopsis, recap (*informal*), précis

run-in *noun* (*informal*) FIGHT, row, argument, dispute, set-to (*informal*), encounter, brush, confrontation, quarrel, skirmish, tussle, altercation, face-off (*slang*), dust-up (*informal*), contretemps, biffo (*Austral slang*)

runner *noun* **1** ATHLETE, miler, sprinter, harrier, jogger **2** MESSENGER, courier, errand boy, dispatch bearer **3** (*botany*) STEM, shoot, sprout, sprig, offshoot, tendril, stolon (*botany*)

running *noun* **1** MANAGEMENT, control, administration, direction, conduct, charge, leadership, organization, regulation, supervision, coordination, superintendency **2** WORKING, performance, operation, functioning, maintenance ▷ *adjective* **1** CONTINUOUS, constant, perpetual, uninterrupted, incessant, unceasing **2** IN SUCCESSION, together, unbroken, on the trot (*informal*) **3** FLOWING, moving, streaming, coursing

runny *adjective* FLOWING, liquid, melted, fluid, diluted, watery, streaming, liquefied

run-of-the-mill *adjective* ORDINARY, middling, average, fair, modest, commonplace, common, vanilla (*informal*), mediocre, banal, tolerable, passable, undistinguished, unimpressive, unexciting, unexceptional, bog-standard (*Brit & Irish slang*), no great shakes (*informal*), dime-a-dozen (*informal*) << ANTONYM exceptional

run-up *noun* TIME LEADING UP TO, approach, build-up, preliminaries

rupture *noun* **1** HERNIA (*medical*) **2** BREACH,

split, hostility, falling-out (*informal*), disagreement, contention, feud, disruption, quarrel, rift, break, bust-up (*informal*), dissolution, altercation, schism, estrangement **3** BREAK, tear, split, crack, rent, burst, breach, fracture, cleavage, cleft, fissure ▷ *verb* **1** BREAK, separate, tear, split, crack, burst, rend, fracture, sever, puncture, cleave **2** CAUSE A BREACH, split, divide, disrupt, break off, come between, dissever

rural *adjective* **1** AGRICULTURAL, country, agrarian, upcountry, agrestic **2** RUSTIC, country, hick (*informal, chiefly US & Canad*), pastoral, bucolic, sylvan, Arcadian, countrified << ANTONYM urban

ruse *noun* TRICK, deception, ploy, hoax, device, manoeuvre, dodge, sham, artifice, blind, subterfuge, stratagem, wile, imposture

rush *verb* **1** HURRY, run, race, shoot, fly, career, speed, tear, dash, sprint, scramble, bolt, dart, hasten, scurry, stampede, lose no time, make short work of, burn rubber (*informal*), make haste, hotfoot << ANTONYM dawdle **2** PUSH, hurry, accelerate, dispatch, speed up, quicken, press, hustle, expedite **3** ATTACK, storm, capture, overcome, charge at, take by storm ▷ *noun* **1** DASH, charge, race, scramble, stampede, expedition, speed, dispatch **2** HURRY, urgency, bustle, haste, hustle, helter-skelter, hastiness **3** SURGE, flow, gush **4** ATTACK, charge, push, storm, assault, surge, onslaught ▷ *adjective* HASTY, fast, quick, hurried, emergency, prompt, rapid, urgent, swift, brisk, cursory, expeditious << ANTONYM leisurely

rust *noun* **1** CORROSION, oxidation **2** MILDEW, must, mould, rot, blight ▷ *verb* **1** CORRODE,

tarnish, oxidize **2** DETERIORATE, decline, decay, stagnate, atrophy, go stale

rustic *adjective* **1** RURAL, country, pastoral, bucolic, sylvan, Arcadian, countrified, upcountry, agrestic << ANTONYM urban **2** SIMPLE, homely, plain, homespun, unsophisticated, unrefined, artless, unpolished << ANTONYM grand ▷ *noun* YOKEL, peasant, hick (*informal, chiefly US & Canad*), bumpkin, swain (*archaic*), hillbilly, country boy, clod, boor, country cousin, hayseed (*US & Canad informal*), clodhopper (*informal*), son of the soil, clown, countryman *or* countrywoman << ANTONYM sophisticate

rustle *verb* CRACKLE, whisper, swish, whoosh, crinkle, whish, crepitate, susurrate (*literary*) ▷ *noun* CRACKLE, whisper, rustling, crinkling, crepitation, susurration *or* susurrus (*literary*)

rusty *adjective* **1** CORRODED, rusted, oxidized, rust-covered **2** OUT OF PRACTICE, weak, impaired, sluggish, stale, deficient, not what it was, unpractised **3** REDDISH-BROWN, chestnut, reddish, russet, coppery, rust-coloured **4** CROAKING, cracked, creaking, hoarse, croaky

rut *noun* **1** HABIT, routine, dead end, humdrum existence, system, pattern, groove **2** GROOVE, score, track, trough, furrow, gouge, pothole, indentation, wheel mark

ruthless *adjective* MERCILESS, hard, severe, fierce, harsh, cruel, savage, brutal, stern, relentless, adamant, ferocious, callous, heartless, unrelenting, inhuman, inexorable, remorseless, barbarous, pitiless, unfeeling, hard-hearted, without pity, unmerciful, unpitying << ANTONYM merciful

rutted *adjective* GROOVED, cut, marked, scored, holed, furrowed, gouged, indented

Ss

sable *adjective* **1** BLACK, jet, raven, jetty, ebony, ebon (*poetic*) **2** DARK, black, dim, gloomy, dismal, dreary, sombre, shadowy

sabotage *verb* **1** DAMAGE, destroy, wreck, undermine, disable, disrupt, cripple, subvert, incapacitate, vandalize, throw a spanner in the works (*Brit informal*) **2** DISRUPT, ruin, wreck, spoil, interrupt, interfere with, obstruct, intrude, crool *or* cruel (*Austral slang*) ▷ *noun* **1** DAMAGE, destruction, wrecking, vandalism, deliberate damage **2** DISRUPTION, ruining, wrecking, spoiling, interference, intrusion, interruption, obstruction

saboteur *noun* DEMONSTRATOR, rebel, dissident, hooligan, vandal, delinquent, dissenter, agitator, protest marcher

sac *noun* POUCH, bag, pocket, bladder, pod, cyst, vesicle

saccharine *adjective* SICKLY, honeyed, sentimental, sugary, nauseating, soppy (*Brit informal*), cloying, maudlin, syrupy (*informal*), mawkish, icky (*informal*), treacly, oversweet

sack¹ *noun* BAG, pocket, poke (*Scot*), sac, pouch, receptacle ▷ *verb* (*informal*) DISMISS, fire (*informal*), axe (*informal*), discharge, kick out (*informal*), give (someone) the boot (*slang*), give (someone) his marching orders, kiss off (*slang, chiefly US & Canad*), give (someone) the push (*informal*), give (someone) the bullet (*Brit slang*), give (someone) his books (*informal*), give (someone) the elbow, give (someone) his cards, kennet (*Austral slang*), jeff (*Austral slang*) ▷▷ **hit the sack** (*slang*) GO TO BED, retire, turn in (*informal*), bed down, hit the hay (*slang*) ▷▷ **the sack** (*informal*) DISMISSAL, discharge, the boot (*slang*), the axe (*informal*), the chop (*Brit slang*), the push (*slang*), the (old) heave-ho (*informal*), termination of employment, the order of the boot (*slang*)

sack² *verb* PLUNDER, loot, pillage, destroy, strip, rob, raid, ruin, devastate, spoil, rifle, demolish, ravage, lay waste, despoil, maraud, depredate (*rare*) ▷ *noun* PLUNDERING, looting, pillage, waste, rape, ruin, destruction, ravage, plunder, devastation, depredation, despoliation, rapine

sacred *adjective* **1** HOLY, hallowed, consecrated, blessed, divine, revered, venerable, sanctified << ANTONYM secular **2** RELIGIOUS, holy, ecclesiastical, hallowed, venerated << ANTONYM unconsecrated **3** INVIOLABLE, protected, sacrosanct, secure, hallowed, inalienable, invulnerable, inviolate, unalterable

sacrifice *verb* **1** OFFER, offer up, immolate **2** GIVE UP, abandon, relinquish, lose, surrender, let go, do without, renounce, forfeit, forego, say goodbye to ▷ *noun* **1** OFFERING, immolation, oblation, hecatomb **2** SURRENDER, loss, giving up, resignation, rejection, waiver, abdication, renunciation, repudiation, forswearing, relinquishment, eschewal, self-denial

sacrificial *adjective* PROPITIATORY, atoning, reparative, expiatory, oblatory

sacrilege *noun* DESECRATION, violation, blasphemy, mockery, heresy, irreverence, profanity, impiety, profanation, profaneness << ANTONYM reverence

sacrosanct *adjective* INVIOLABLE, sacred, inviolate, untouchable, hallowed, sanctified, set apart

sad *adjective* **1** UNHAPPY, down, low, blue, depressed, gloomy, grieved, dismal, melancholy, sombre, glum, wistful, mournful, dejected, downcast, grief-stricken, tearful, lugubrious, pensive, disconsolate, doleful, heavy-hearted, down in the dumps (*informal*), cheerless, lachrymose, woebegone, down in the mouth (*informal*), low-spirited, triste (*archaic*), sick at heart << ANTONYM happy **2** TRAGIC, moving, upsetting, dark, sorry, depressing, disastrous, dismal, pathetic, poignant, harrowing, grievous, pitiful, calamitous, heart-rending, pitiable **3** DEPLORABLE, bad, sorry, terrible, distressing, unfortunate, miserable, dismal, shabby, heartbreaking, regrettable, lamentable, wretched, to be deplored << ANTONYM good **4** REGRETTABLE, disappointing, distressing, unhappy, unfortunate, unsatisfactory, woeful, deplorable, lamentable << ANTONYM fortunate

sadden *verb* UPSET, depress, distress, grieve, desolate, cast down, bring tears to your eyes, make sad, dispirit, make your heart bleed, aggrieve, deject, cast a gloom upon

saddle *verb* BURDEN, load, lumber (*Brit informal*), charge, tax, task, encumber

sadism *noun* CRUELTY, savagery, brutality, severity, ferocity, spite, ruthlessness, depravity, harshness, inhumanity, barbarity, callousness, viciousness, bestiality, heartlessness, brutishness, spitefulness, bloodthirstiness, murderousness, mercilessness, fiendishness, hardheartedness

sadistic *adjective* CRUEL, savage, brutal, beastly, vicious, ruthless, perverted, perverse, inhuman, barbarous, fiendish

sadness *noun* UNHAPPINESS, sorrow, grief, tragedy, depression, the blues, misery, melancholy, poignancy, despondency, bleakness, heavy heart, dejection, wretchedness, gloominess, mournfulness, dolour (*poetic*), dolefulness, cheerlessness, sorrowfulness << ANTONYM happiness

safe *adjective* **1** PROTECTED, secure, in safety, impregnable, out of danger, safe and sound, in safe hands, out of harm's way, free from harm << ANTONYM endangered **2** ALL RIGHT, fine, intact, unscathed, unhurt, unharmed, undamaged, out of the woods, O.K. or okay (*informal*) **3** CAUTIOUS, prudent, sure, conservative, reliable, realistic, discreet, dependable, trustworthy, circumspect, on the safe side, unadventurous, tried and true << ANTONYM risky **4** RISK-FREE, sound, secure, certain, impregnable, riskless **5** HARMLESS, wholesome, innocuous, pure, tame, unpolluted, nontoxic, nonpoisonous << ANTONYM dangerous ▷ *noun* STRONGBOX,

vault, coffer, repository, deposit box, safe-deposit box

safeguard *verb* PROTECT, guard, defend, save, screen, secure, preserve, look after, shield, watch over, keep safe ▷ *noun* PROTECTION, security, defence, guard, shield, armour, aegis, bulwark, surety

safely *adverb* IN SAFETY, securely, with impunity, without risk, with safety, safe and sound

safety *noun* **1** SECURITY, protection, safeguards, assurance, precautions, immunity, safety measures, impregnability << ANTONYM risk **2** SHELTER, haven, protection, cover, retreat, asylum, refuge, sanctuary

sag *verb* **1** SINK, bag, droop, fall, drop, seat (*of skirts, etc*), settle, slump, dip, give way, bulge, swag, hang loosely, fall unevenly **2** DROP, sink, slump, flop, droop, loll **3** DECLINE, fall, slip, tire, slide, flag, slump, weaken, wilt, wane, cave in, droop

saga *noun* **1** CARRY-ON (*informal*), to-do, performance (*informal*), rigmarole, soap opera, pantomime (*informal*) **2** EPIC, story, tale, legend, adventure, romance, narrative, chronicle, yarn, fairy tale, folk tale, roman-fleuve (*French*)

sage *noun* WISE MAN, philosopher, guru, authority, expert, master, elder, pundit, Solomon, mahatma, Nestor, savant, Solon, man of learning, tohunga (*NZ*) ▷ *adjective* WISE, learned, intelligent, sensible, politic, acute, discerning, prudent, canny, judicious, perspicacious, sagacious, sapient

sail *noun* SHEET, canvas ▷ *verb* **1** GO BY WATER, cruise, voyage, ride the waves, go by sea **2** SET SAIL, embark, get under way, put to sea, put off, leave port, hoist sail, cast *or* weigh anchor **3** PILOT, steer, navigate, captain, skipper **4** GLIDE, sweep, float, shoot, fly, wing, soar, drift, skim, scud, skirr ▷▷ **sail through something** CRUISE THROUGH, walk through, romp through, pass easily, succeed easily at ▷▷ **set sail** PUT TO SEA, embark, get under way, put off, leave port, hoist sail, cast *or* weigh anchor

sailor *noun* MARINER, marine, seaman, salt, tar (*informal*), hearty (*informal*), navigator, sea dog, seafarer, matelot (*slang, chiefly Brit*), Jack Tar, seafaring man, lascar, leatherneck (*slang*)

saintly *adjective* VIRTUOUS, godly, holy, religious, sainted, blessed, worthy, righteous, devout, pious, angelic, blameless, god-fearing, beatific, sinless, saintlike, full of good works

sake *noun* PURPOSE, interest, cause, reason, end, aim, principle, objective, motive ▷▷ **for someone's sake** IN SOMEONE'S INTERESTS, to someone's advantage, on someone's account, for the benefit of, for the good of, for the welfare of, out of respect for, out of consideration for, out of regard for

salacious *adjective* OBSCENE, indecent, pornographic, blue, erotic, steamy (*informal*), lewd, X-rated (*informal*), bawdy, smutty, lustful, ribald, ruttish

salary *noun* PAY, income, wage, fee, payment, wages, earnings, allowance, remuneration, recompense, stipend, emolument

sale *noun* 1 SELLING, marketing, dealing, trading, transaction, disposal, vending 2 AUCTION, fair, mart, bazaar

salient *adjective* PROMINENT, outstanding, important, marked, striking, arresting, signal, remarkable, pronounced, noticeable, conspicuous

saliva *noun* SPIT, dribble, drool, slaver, spittle, sputum

sallow *adjective* WAN, pale, sickly, pasty, pallid, unhealthy, yellowish, anaemic, bilious, jaundiced-looking, peely-wally (*Scot*) << ANTONYM rosy

sally *noun* WITTICISM, joke, quip, crack (*informal*), retort, jest, riposte, wisecrack (*informal*), bon mot, smart remark ▷ *verb* GO FORTH, set out, rush, issue, surge, erupt

salon *noun* 1 SHOP, store, establishment, parlour, boutique 2 SITTING ROOM, lounge, living room, parlour, drawing room, front room, reception room, morning room

salt *noun* 1 SEASONING, sodium chloride, table salt, rock salt 2 SAILOR, marine, seaman, mariner, tar (*informal*), hearty (*informal*), navigator, sea dog, seafarer, matelot (*slang, chiefly Brit*), Jack Tar, seafaring man, lascar, leatherneck (*slang*) ▷ *adjective* SALTY, salted, saline, brackish, briny ▷▷ **rub salt into the wound** MAKE SOMETHING WORSE, add insult to injury, fan the flames, aggravate matters, magnify a problem ▷▷ **with a grain or pinch of salt** SCEPTICALLY, suspiciously, cynically, doubtfully, with reservations, disbelievingly, mistrustfully

salty *adjective* SALT, salted, saline, brackish, briny, over-salted, brak (*S African*)

salubrious *adjective* HEALTHY, beneficial, good for you, wholesome, invigorating, salutary, healthful, health-giving

salutary *adjective* BENEFICIAL, useful, valuable, helpful, profitable, good, practical, good for you, advantageous

salute *verb* 1 GREET, welcome, acknowledge, address, kiss, hail, salaam, accost, pay your respects to, doff your cap to, mihi (*NZ*) 2 HONOUR, acknowledge, recognize, take your hat off to (*informal*), pay tribute *or* homage to ▷ *noun* GREETING, recognition, salutation, address, kiss, salaam, obeisance

salvage *verb* SAVE, recover, rescue, restore, repair, get back, retrieve, redeem, glean, repossess, fetch back ▷ *noun* 1 RESCUE, saving, recovery, release, relief, liberation, salvation, deliverance, extrication 2 SCRAP, remains, waste, junk, offcuts

salvation *noun* 1 SAVING, rescue, recovery, restoration, salvage, redemption, deliverance << ANTONYM ruin 2 LIFELINE, escape, relief, preservation

salve *verb* EASE, soothe, appease, still, allay, pacify, mollify, tranquillize, palliate ▷ *noun* BALM, cream, medication, lotion, lubricant, ointment, emollient, liniment, dressing, unguent

salvo *noun* BARRAGE, storm, bombardment, strafe, cannonade

same *adjective* 1 IDENTICAL, similar, alike, equal, twin, equivalent, corresponding, comparable, duplicate, indistinguishable, interchangeable << ANTONYM different 2 THE VERY SAME, very, one and the same, selfsame 3 AFOREMENTIONED, aforesaid, selfsame 4 UNCHANGED, consistent, constant, uniform, unaltered, unfailing, invariable, unvarying, changeless << ANTONYM altered ▷▷ **all the same** 1 NEVERTHELESS, still, regardless, nonetheless, after all, in any case, for all that, notwithstanding, in any event, anyhow, just the same, be that as it may 2 UNIMPORTANT, insignificant, immaterial, inconsequential, of no consequence, of little account, not worth mentioning

sameness *noun* SIMILARITY, resemblance, uniformity, likeness, oneness, standardization, indistinguishability, identicalness

sample *noun* 1 SPECIMEN, example, model, pattern, instance, representative, indication, illustration, exemplification 2 CROSS SECTION, test, sampling ▷ *verb* TEST, try, check out (*informal*), experience, taste, examine, evaluate, inspect, experiment with, appraise, partake of

sanctify *verb* 1 CONSECRATE, bless, anoint,

set apart, hallow, make sacred **2** CLEANSE, redeem, purify, absolve

sanctimonious *adjective* PIOUS, smug, hypocritical, pi (*Brit slang*), too good to be true, self-righteous, self-satisfied, goody-goody (*informal*), unctuous, holier-than-thou, priggish, pietistic, canting, pharisaical

sanction *verb* PERMIT, back, support, allow, approve, entitle, endorse, authorize, countenance, vouch for, lend your name to << ANTONYM forbid ▷ *noun* **1** *often plural* BAN, restriction, boycott, embargo, exclusion, penalty, deterrent, prohibition, coercive measures << ANTONYM permission **2** PERMISSION, backing, support, authority, approval, allowance, confirmation, endorsement, countenance, ratification, authorization, approbation, O.K. *or* okay (*informal*), stamp *or* seal of approval << ANTONYM ban

sanctity *noun* SACREDNESS, inviolability, inalienability, hallowedness, sacrosanctness

sanctuary *noun* **1** PROTECTION, shelter, refuge, haven, retreat, asylum **2** RESERVE, park, preserve, reservation, national park, tract, nature reserve, conservation area

sanctum *noun* **1** REFUGE, retreat, den, private room **2** SANCTUARY, shrine, altar, holy place, Holy of Holies

sands *plural noun* BEACH, shore, strand (*literary*), dunes

sane *adjective* **1** RATIONAL, normal, all there (*informal*), lucid, of sound mind, compos mentis (*Latin*), in your right mind, mentally sound, in possession of all your faculties << ANTONYM insane **2** SENSIBLE, sound, reasonable, balanced, moderate, sober, judicious, level-headed << ANTONYM foolish

sanguine *adjective* CHEERFUL, confident, optimistic, assured, hopeful, buoyant, in good heart << ANTONYM gloomy

sanitary *adjective* HYGIENIC, clean, healthy, wholesome, salubrious, unpolluted, germ-free

sanitation *noun* HYGIENE, cleanliness, sewerage

sanity *noun* **1** MENTAL HEALTH, reason, rationality, stability, normality, right mind (*informal*), saneness << ANTONYM insanity **2** COMMON SENSE, sense, good sense, rationality, level-headedness, judiciousness, soundness of judgment << ANTONYM stupidity

sap¹ *noun* **1** JUICE, essence, vital fluid,

secretion, lifeblood, plant fluid **2** (*slang*) FOOL, jerk (*slang, chiefly US & Canad*), idiot, noodle, wally (*slang*), wet (*Brit informal*), charlie (*Brit informal*), drip (*informal*), gull (*archaic*), prat (*slang*), plonker (*slang*), noddy, twit (*informal*), chump (*informal*), oaf, simpleton, nitwit (*informal*), ninny, nincompoop, dweeb (*US slang*), wuss (*slang*), Simple Simon, weenie (*US informal*), muggins (*Brit slang*), eejit (*Scot & Irish*), dumb-ass (*slang*), numpty (*Scot informal*), doofus (*slang, chiefly US*), nerd *or* nurd (*slang*), numskull *or* numbskull, dorba *or* dorb (*Austral slang*), bogan (*Austral slang*)

sap² *verb* WEAKEN, drain, undermine, rob, exhaust, bleed, erode, deplete, wear down, enervate, devitalize

sarcasm *noun* IRONY, satire, cynicism, contempt, ridicule, bitterness, scorn, sneering, mockery, venom, derision, vitriol, mordancy, causticness

sarcastic *adjective* IRONICAL, cynical, satirical, cutting, biting, sharp, acid, mocking, taunting, sneering, acrimonious, backhanded, contemptuous, disparaging, sardonic, caustic, bitchy (*informal*), vitriolic, acerbic, derisive, ironic, mordant, sarky (*Brit informal*), mordacious, acerb

sardonic *adjective* MOCKING, cynical, dry, bitter, sneering, jeering, malicious, wry, sarcastic, derisive, ironical, mordant, mordacious

sash *noun* BELT, girdle, waistband, cummerbund

Satan *noun* THE DEVIL, Lucifer, Prince of Darkness, Lord of the Flies, Mephistopheles, Beelzebub, Old Nick (*informal*), The Evil One, Apollyon, Old Scratch (*informal*)

satanic *adjective* EVIL, demonic, hellish, black, malignant, wicked, inhuman, malevolent, devilish, infernal, fiendish, accursed, iniquitous, diabolic, demoniac, demoniacal << ANTONYM godly

sate *verb* SATISFY, satiate, slake, indulge to the full

satellite *noun* **1** SPACECRAFT, communications satellite, sputnik, space capsule **2** MOON, secondary planet

satire *noun* **1** MOCKERY, wit, irony, ridicule, sarcasm **2** PARODY, mockery, caricature, send-up (*Brit informal*), spoof (*informal*), travesty, takeoff (*informal*), lampoon, skit, burlesque

satirical *or* **satiric** *adjective* MOCKING, ironical, cynical, cutting, biting, bitter, taunting, pungent, incisive, sarcastic, sardonic, caustic, vitriolic, burlesque, mordant, Rabelaisian, mordacious

satisfaction *noun* **1** FULFILMENT, pleasure, achievement, joy, relish, glee, gratification, pride, complacency << ANTONYM dissatisfaction **2** COMPENSATION, damages, justice, amends, settlement, redress, remuneration, reparation, vindication, restitution, reimbursement, atonement, recompense, indemnification, requital << ANTONYM injury **3** CONTENTMENT, content, comfort, ease, pleasure, well-being, happiness, enjoyment, peace of mind, gratification, satiety, repletion, contentedness << ANTONYM discontent

satisfactory *adjective* ADEQUATE, acceptable, good enough, average, fair, all right, suitable, sufficient, competent, up to scratch, passable, up to standard, up to the mark << ANTONYM unsatisfactory

satisfied *adjective* **1** CONTENTED, happy, content, pacified, pleased << ANTONYM dissatisfied **2** SURE, smug, convinced, positive, easy in your mind

satisfy *verb* **1** CONTENT, please, indulge, fill, feed, appease, gratify, pander to, assuage, pacify, quench, mollify, surfeit, satiate, slake, sate << ANTONYM dissatisfy **2** CONVINCE, persuade, assure, reassure, dispel (someone's) doubts, put (someone's) mind at rest << ANTONYM dissuade **3** COMPLY WITH, meet, fulfil, answer, serve, fill, observe, obey, conform to << ANTONYM fail to meet

satisfying *adjective* SATISFACTORY, pleasing, gratifying, pleasurable, cheering

saturate *verb* **1** FLOOD, overwhelm, swamp, overrun, deluge, glut **2** SOAK, steep, drench, seep, imbue, douse, impregnate, suffuse, ret (*used of flax, etc*), wet through, waterlog, souse, drouk (*Scot*)

saturated *adjective* SOAKED, soaking (wet), drenched, sodden, dripping, waterlogged, sopping (wet), wet through, soaked to the skin, wringing wet, droukit *or* drookit (*Scot*)

sauce *noun* DRESSING, dip, relish, condiment

saucy *adjective* IMPUDENT, cheeky (*informal*), impertinent, forward, fresh (*informal*), flip (*informal*), rude, sassy (*US informal*), pert, disrespectful, flippant, presumptuous, insolent, lippy (*US & Canad slang*), smart-alecky (*informal*)

saunter *verb* STROLL, wander, amble, roam, ramble, meander, rove, take a stroll, mosey (*informal*), stravaig (*Scot & N English*

dialect) ▷ *noun* STROLL, walk, amble, turn, airing, constitutional, ramble, promenade, breather, perambulation

savage *adjective* **1** CRUEL, brutal, vicious, bloody, fierce, harsh, beastly, ruthless, ferocious, murderous, ravening, sadistic, inhuman, merciless, diabolical, brutish, devilish, bloodthirsty, barbarous, pitiless, bestial << ANTONYM gentle **2** WILD, fierce, ferocious, unbroken, feral, untamed, undomesticated << ANTONYM tame **3** PRIMITIVE, undeveloped, uncultivated, uncivilized, in a state of nature, nonliterate **4** UNCULTIVATED, rugged, unspoilt, uninhabited, waste, rough, uncivilized, unfrequented << ANTONYM cultivated ▷ *noun* **1** NATIVE, barbarian, heathen, indigene, primitive person, autochthon **2** LOUT, yob (*Brit slang*), brute, bear, monster, beast, barbarian, fiend, yahoo, hoon (*Austral & NZ*), yobbo (*Brit slang*), roughneck (*slang*), boor, cougan (*Austral slang*), scozza (*Austral slang*), bogan (*Austral slang*) ▷ *verb* **1** MAUL, tear, claw, attack, mangle, lacerate, mangulate (*Austral slang*) **2** CRITICIZE, attack, knock (*informal*), blast, pan (*informal*), slam (*slang*), put down, slate (*informal*), have a go (at) (*informal*), disparage, tear into (*informal*), find fault with, lambast(e), pick holes in, pick to pieces, give (someone *or* something) a bad press << ANTONYM praise

savagery *noun* CRUELTY, brutality, ferocity, ruthlessness, sadism, inhumanity, barbarity, viciousness, bestiality, fierceness, bloodthirstiness

save *verb* **1** RESCUE, free, release, deliver, recover, get out, liberate, salvage, redeem, bail out, come to someone's rescue, set free, save the life of, extricate, save someone's bacon (*Brit informal*) << ANTONYM endanger **2** KEEP, reserve, set aside, store, collect, gather, hold, hoard, hide away, lay by, put by, salt away, treasure up, keep up your sleeve (*informal*), put aside for a rainy day << ANTONYM spend **3** PROTECT, keep, guard, preserve, look after, take care of, safeguard, salvage, conserve, keep safe **4** BUDGET, be economical, economize, scrimp and save, retrench, be frugal, make economies, be thrifty, tighten your belt (*informal*) **5** PUT ASIDE, keep, reserve, collect, retain, set aside, amass, put by **6** PREVENT, avoid, spare, rule out, avert, obviate

saving *noun* ECONOMY, discount, reduction, bargain, cut ▷ *plural noun* NEST EGG, fund, store, reserves, resources, fall-back, provision for a rainy day

saviour *noun* RESCUER, deliverer, defender, guardian, salvation, protector, liberator, Good Samaritan, redeemer, preserver, knight in shining armour, friend in need

Saviour *noun* CHRIST, Jesus, the Messiah, the Redeemer

savour *verb* 1 RELISH, like, delight in, revel in, luxuriate in, gloat over 2 ENJOY, appreciate, relish, delight in, revel in, partake of, drool over, luxuriate in, enjoy to the full, smack your lips over ▷ *noun* 1 FLAVOUR, taste, smell, relish, smack, zest, tang, zing (*informal*), piquancy 2 ZEST, interest, spice, excitement, salt, flavour

savoury *adjective* 1 SPICY, rich, delicious, tasty, luscious, palatable, tangy, dainty, delectable, mouthwatering, piquant, full-flavoured, scrumptious (*informal*), appetizing, toothsome, yummo (*Austral slang*) << ANTONYM tasteless 2 WHOLESOME, decent, respectable, honest, reputable, apple-pie (*informal*) << ANTONYM disreputable ▷ *plural noun* APPETIZERS, nibbles, apéritifs, canapés, titbits, hors d'oeuvres

savvy (*slang*) *noun* UNDERSTANDING, perception, grasp, ken, comprehension, apprehension ▷ *adjective* SHREWD, sharp, astute, knowing, fly (*slang*), keen, smart, clever, intelligent, discriminating, discerning, canny, perceptive, artful, far-sighted, far-seeing, long-headed, perspicacious, sagacious

say *verb* 1 STATE, declare, remark, add, announce, maintain, mention, assert, affirm, asseverate 2 SPEAK, utter, voice, express, pronounce, come out with (*informal*), put into words, give voice *or* utterance to 3 MAKE KNOWN, reveal, disclose, divulge, answer, reply, respond, give as your opinion 4 SUGGEST, express, imply, communicate, disclose, give away, convey, divulge 5 SUPPOSE, supposing, imagine, assume, presume 6 ESTIMATE, suppose, guess, conjecture, surmise, dare say, hazard a guess 7 RECITE, perform, deliver, do, read, repeat, render, rehearse, orate 8 ALLEGE, report, claim, hold, suggest, insist, maintain, rumour, assert, uphold, profess, put about that ▷ *noun* 1 INFLUENCE, power, control, authority, weight, sway, clout (*informal*), predominance, mana (*NZ*) 2 CHANCE TO SPEAK, vote, voice, crack (*informal*),

opportunity to speak, turn to speak ▷▷ **to say the least** AT THE VERY LEAST, without any exaggeration, to put it mildly

saying *noun* PROVERB, maxim, adage, saw, slogan, gnome, dictum, axiom, aphorism, byword, apophthegm ▷▷ **go without saying** BE OBVIOUS, be understood, be taken for granted, be accepted, be self-evident, be taken as read, be a matter of course

say-so *noun* (*informal*) ASSERTION, authority, agreement, word, guarantee, sanction, permission, consent, assurance, assent, authorization, dictum, asseveration, O.K. *or* okay (*informal*)

scalding *adjective* BURNING, boiling, searing, blistering, piping hot

scale[1] *noun* FLAKE, plate, layer, lamina

scale[2] *noun* 1 DEGREE, size, range, spread, extent, dimensions, scope, magnitude, breadth 2 SYSTEM OF MEASUREMENT, register, measuring system, graduated system, calibration, calibrated system 3 RANKING, ladder, spectrum, hierarchy, series, sequence, progression, pecking order (*informal*) 4 RATIO, proportion, relative size ▷ *verb* CLIMB UP, mount, go up, ascend, surmount, scramble up, clamber up, escalade ▷▷ **scale something down** REDUCE, cut, moderate, slow down, cut down, wind down, tone down, downsize, kennet (*Austral slang*), jeff (*Austral slang*) ▷▷ **scale something up** EXPAND, extend, blow up, enlarge, lengthen, magnify, amplify, augment

scaly *adjective* 1 SQUAMOUS, squamate, lamellose, lamelliform 2 FLAKY, scabrous, scurfy, furfuraceous (*medical*), squamous *or* squamose (*biology*), squamulose

scamper *verb* RUN, dash, dart, fly, hurry, sprint, romp, beetle, hasten, scuttle, scurry, scoot

scan *verb* 1 GLANCE OVER, skim, look over, eye, check, clock (*Brit slang*), examine, check out (*informal*), run over, eyeball (*slang*), size up (*informal*), get a load of (*informal*), look someone up and down, run your eye over, take a dekko at (*Brit slang*), surf (*computing*) 2 SURVEY, search, investigate, sweep, con (*archaic*), scour, scrutinize, take stock of, recce (*slang*) ▷ *noun* 1 LOOK, glance, skim, browse, flick, squint, butcher's (*Brit slang*), brief look, dekko (*Brit slang*), shufti (*Brit slang*) 2 EXAMINATION, scanning, ultrasound

scandal *noun* 1 DISGRACE, crime, offence, sin, embarrassment, wrongdoing, skeleton in the cupboard, dishonourable behaviour, discreditable behaviour 2 GOSSIP, goss (*informal*), talk, rumours, dirt, slander, tattle, dirty linen (*informal*), calumny, backbiting, aspersion 3 SHAME, offence, disgrace, stigma, infamy, opprobrium, obloquy 4 OUTRAGE, shame, insult, disgrace, injustice, crying shame

scandalous *adjective* 1 SHOCKING, disgraceful, outrageous, offensive, appalling, foul, dreadful, horrifying, obscene, monstrous, unspeakable, atrocious, frightful, abominable << ANTONYM decent 2 SLANDEROUS, gossiping, scurrilous, untrue, defamatory, libellous << ANTONYM laudatory 3 OUTRAGEOUS, shocking, infamous, disgraceful, monstrous, shameful, atrocious, unseemly, odious, disreputable, opprobrious, highly improper << ANTONYM proper

scant *adjective* 1 INADEQUATE, insufficient, meagre, sparse, little, limited, bare, minimal, deficient, barely sufficient << ANTONYM adequate 2 SMALL, limited, inadequate, insufficient, meagre, measly, scanty, inconsiderable

scanty *adjective* 1 MEAGRE, sparse, poor, thin, narrow, sparing, restricted, bare, inadequate, pathetic, insufficient, slender, scant, deficient, exiguous 2 SKIMPY, short, brief, tight, thin

scapegoat *noun* FALL GUY, whipping boy

scar *noun* 1 MARK, injury, wound, trauma (*pathology*), blemish, cicatrix 2 TRAUMA, suffering, pain, strain, torture, disturbance, anguish ▷ *verb* MARK, disfigure, damage, brand, mar, mutilate, maim, blemish, deface, traumatize, disfeature

scarce *adjective* 1 IN SHORT SUPPLY, wanting, insufficient, deficient, at a premium, thin on the ground << ANTONYM plentiful 2 RARE, few, unusual, uncommon, few and far between, infrequent, thin on the ground << ANTONYM common

scarcely *adverb* 1 HARDLY, barely, only just, scarce (*archaic*) 2 (*often used ironically*) BY NO MEANS, hardly, not at all, definitely not, under no circumstances, on no account

scarcity *noun* SHORTAGE, lack, deficiency, poverty, want, dearth, paucity, insufficiency, infrequency, undersupply, rareness << ANTONYM abundance

scare *verb* FRIGHTEN, alarm, terrify, panic, shock, startle, intimidate, dismay, daunt, terrorize, put the wind up (someone) (*informal*), give (someone) a fright, give

(someone) a turn (*informal*), affright (*archaic*) ▷ *noun* 1 FRIGHT, shock, start 2 PANIC, hysteria 3 ALERT, warning, alarm

scared *adjective* AFRAID, alarmed, frightened, terrified, shaken, cowed, startled, fearful, unnerved, petrified, panicky, terrorized, panic-stricken, scared stiff, terror-stricken

scarf *noun* MUFFLER, stole, headscarf, comforter, cravat, neckerchief, headsquare

scary *adjective* (*informal*) FRIGHTENING, alarming, terrifying, shocking, chilling, horrifying, intimidating, horrendous, hairy (*slang*), unnerving, spooky (*informal*), creepy (*informal*), hair-raising, spine-chilling, bloodcurdling

scathing *adjective* CRITICAL, cutting, biting, harsh, savage, brutal, searing, withering, belittling, sarcastic, caustic, scornful, vitriolic, trenchant, mordant, mordacious

scatter *verb* 1 THROW ABOUT, spread, sprinkle, strew, broadcast, shower, fling, litter, sow, diffuse, disseminate << ANTONYM gather 2 DISPERSE, separate, break up, dispel, disband, dissipate, disunite, put to flight << ANTONYM assemble

scattering *noun* SPRINKLING, few, handful, scatter, smattering, smatter

scavenge *verb* SEARCH, hunt, forage, rummage, root about, fossick (*Austral & NZ*), scratch about

scenario *noun* 1 SITUATION, sequence of events, chain of events, course of events, series of developments 2 STORY LINE, résumé, outline, sketch, summary, rundown, synopsis

scene *noun* 1 ACT, part, division, episode 2 SETTING, set, background, location, backdrop, mise en scène (*French*) 3 INCIDENT, happening, event, episode 4 SITE, place, setting, area, position, stage, situation, spot, whereabouts, locality 5 (*informal*) WORLD, business, environment, preserve, arena, realm, domain, milieu, thing, field of interest 6 VIEW, prospect, panorama, vista, landscape, tableau, outlook 7 FUSS, to-do, row, performance, upset, drama, exhibition, carry-on (*informal, chiefly Brit*), confrontation, tantrum, commotion, hue and cry, display of emotion, hissy fit (*informal*) 8 SECTION, part, sequence, segment, clip

scenery *noun* 1 LANDSCAPE, view, surroundings, terrain, vista 2 (*theatre*) SET, setting, backdrop, flats, décor, stage set

scenic *adjective* PICTURESQUE, beautiful, spectacular, striking, grand, impressive, breathtaking, panoramic

scent *noun* 1 FRAGRANCE, smell, perfume, bouquet, aroma, odour, niff (*Brit slang*), redolence 2 TRAIL, track, spoor 3 PERFUME, fragrance, cologne, eau de toilette (*French*), eau de cologne (*French*), toilet water ▷ *verb* SMELL, sense, recognize, detect, sniff, discern, sniff out, nose out, get wind of (*informal*), be on the track *or* trail of

scented *adjective* FRAGRANT, perfumed, aromatic, sweet-smelling, redolent, ambrosial, odoriferous

sceptic *noun* 1 DOUBTER, cynic, scoffer, disbeliever, Pyrrhonist 2 AGNOSTIC, doubter, unbeliever, doubting Thomas

sceptical *adjective* DOUBTFUL, cynical, dubious, questioning, doubting, hesitating, scoffing, unconvinced, disbelieving, incredulous, quizzical, mistrustful, unbelieving << ANTONYM convinced

scepticism *noun* DOUBT, suspicion, disbelief, cynicism, incredulity

schedule *noun* 1 PLAN, programme, agenda, calendar, timetable, itinerary, list of appointments 2 LIST, catalogue, inventory, syllabus ▷ *verb* PLAN, set up, book, programme, arrange, organize, timetable

schematic *adjective* GRAPHIC, representational, illustrative, diagrammatic, diagrammatical

scheme *noun* 1 PLAN, programme, strategy, system, design, project, theory, proposal, device, tactics, course of action, contrivance 2 PLOT, dodge, ploy, ruse, game (*informal*), shift, intrigue, conspiracy, manoeuvre, machinations, subterfuge, stratagem ▷ *verb* PLOT, plan, intrigue, manoeuvre, conspire, contrive, collude, wheel and deal, machinate

scheming *adjective* CALCULATING, cunning, sly, designing, tricky, slippery, wily, artful, conniving, Machiavellian, foxy, deceitful, underhand, duplicitous << ANTONYM straightforward

schism *noun* DIVISION, break, split, breach, separation, rift, splintering, rupture, discord, disunion

schmick *adjective* (*Austral slang*) 1 EXCELLENT, outstanding, good, great, fine, prime, capital, noted, choice, champion, cool (*informal*), select, brilliant, very good, cracking (*Brit informal*), crucial (*slang*), mean (*slang*), superb, distinguished, fantastic, magnificent, superior, sterling, worthy, first-class, marvellous, exceptional, terrific, splendid, notable, mega (*slang*), topping (*Brit* *slang*), sovereign, dope (*slang*), world-class, exquisite, admirable, exemplary, wicked (*slang*), first-rate, def (*slang*), superlative, top-notch (*informal*), brill (*informal*), pre-eminent, meritorious, estimable, tiptop, bodacious (*slang, chiefly US*), boffo (*slang*), jim-dandy (*slang*), A1 *or* A-one (*informal*), bitchin' (*US slang*), chillin' (*US slang*), booshit (*Austral slang*), exo (*Austral slang*), sik (*Austral slang*), rad (*informal*), phat (*slang*) << ANTONYM terrible 2 STYLISH, smart, chic, polished, fashionable, trendy (*Brit informal*), classy (*slang*), in fashion, snappy, in vogue, dapper, natty (*informal*), snazzy (*informal*), modish, well turned-out, dressy (*informal*), à la mode, voguish << ANTONYM scruffy

scholar *noun* 1 INTELLECTUAL, academic, man of letters, bookworm, egghead (*informal*), savant, bluestocking (*usually disparaging*), acca (*Austral slang*) 2 STUDENT, pupil, learner, schoolboy *or* schoolgirl

scholarly *adjective* LEARNED, academic, intellectual, lettered, erudite, scholastic, well-read, studious, bookish, swotty (*Brit informal*) << ANTONYM uneducated

scholarship *noun* 1 GRANT, award, payment, exhibition, endowment, fellowship, bursary 2 LEARNING, education, culture, knowledge, wisdom, accomplishments, attainments, lore, erudition, academic study, book-learning

scholastic *adjective* LEARNED, academic, scholarly, lettered, literary, bookish

school *noun* 1 ACADEMY, college, institution, institute, discipline, seminary, educational institution, centre of learning, alma mater 2 GROUP, set, circle, following, class, faction, followers, disciples, sect, devotees, denomination, clique, adherents, schism 3 WAY OF LIFE, creed, faith, outlook, persuasion, school of thought ▷ *verb* TRAIN, prime, coach, prepare, discipline, educate, drill, tutor, instruct, verse, indoctrinate

schooling *noun* 1 TEACHING, education, tuition, formal education, book-learning 2 TRAINING, coaching, instruction, grounding, preparation, drill, guidance

schoolteacher *noun* SCHOOLMASTER *or* SCHOOLMISTRESS, instructor, pedagogue, schoolmarm (*informal*), dominie (*Scot*)

science *noun* DISCIPLINE, body of knowledge, branch of knowledge

scientific *adjective* 1 TECHNOLOGICAL, technical, chemical, biological, empirical, factual 2 SYSTEMATIC, accurate, exact, precise, controlled, mathematical

scientist *noun* RESEARCHER, inventor, boffin (*informal*), technophile

scintillating *adjective* BRILLIANT, exciting, stimulating, lively, sparkling, bright, glittering, dazzling, witty, animated

scion *noun* DESCENDANT, child, offspring, successor, heir

scoff¹ *verb* SCORN, mock, laugh at, ridicule, knock (*informal*), taunt, despise, sneer, jeer, deride, slag (off) (*slang*), flout, belittle, revile, make light of, poke fun at, twit, gibe, pooh-pooh, make sport of

scoff² *verb* GOBBLE (UP), wolf, devour, bolt, cram, put away, guzzle, gulp down, gorge yourself on, gollop, stuff yourself with, cram yourself on, make a pig of yourself on (*informal*)

scold *verb* REPRIMAND, censure, rebuke, rate, blame, lecture, carpet (*informal*), slate (*informal, chiefly Brit*), nag, go on at, reproach, berate, tick off (*informal*), castigate, chide, tear into (*informal*), tell off (*informal*), find fault with, remonstrate with, bring (someone) to book, take (someone) to task, read the riot act, reprove, upbraid, bawl out (*informal*), give (someone) a talking-to (*informal*), haul (someone) over the coals (*informal*), chew out (*US & Canad informal*), give (someone) a dressing-down, tear (someone) off a strip (*Brit informal*), give a rocket (*Brit & NZ informal*), vituperate, give (someone) a row, have (someone) on the carpet (*informal*) << ANTONYM praise

scolding *noun* TICKING-OFF, row, lecture, wigging (*Brit slang*), rebuke (*informal*), dressing-down (*informal*), telling-off (*informal*), tongue-lashing, piece of your mind, (good) talking-to (*informal*)

scoop *verb* WIN, get, receive, land, gain, achieve, net, earn, pick up, bag (*informal*), secure, collect, obtain, procure, come away with ▷ *noun* **1** LADLE, spoon, dipper **2** SPOONFUL, lump, dollop (*informal*), ball, ladleful **3** EXCLUSIVE, exposé, coup, revelation, sensation, inside story ▷▷ **scoop something out** **1** TAKE OUT, empty, dig out, scrape out, spoon out, bail or bale out **2** DIG, shovel, excavate, gouge, hollow out ▷▷ **scoop something** or **someone up** GATHER UP, lift, pick up, take up, sweep up or away

scoot *verb* DASH, run, dart, sprint, bolt, zip, scuttle, scurry, scamper, skitter, skedaddle (*informal*), skirr

scope *noun* **1** OPPORTUNITY, room, freedom, space, liberty, latitude, elbowroom, leeway **2** RANGE, capacity, reach, area, extent, outlook, orbit, span, sphere, ambit, purview, field of reference

scorch *verb* BURN, sear, char, roast, blister, wither, blacken, shrivel, parch, singe

scorching *adjective* BURNING, boiling, baking, flaming, tropical, roasting, searing, fiery, sizzling, red-hot, torrid, sweltering, broiling, unbearably hot

score *verb* **1** GAIN, win, achieve, make, get, net, bag, obtain, bring in, attain, amass, notch up (*informal*), chalk up (*informal*) **2** GO DOWN WELL WITH (SOMEONE), impress, triumph, make a hit (*informal*), make a point, gain an advantage, put yourself across, make an impact or impression **3** (*music*) ARRANGE, set, orchestrate, adapt **4** CUT, scratch, nick, mark, mar, slash, scrape, notch, graze, gouge, deface, indent, crosshatch ▷ *noun* **1** RATING, mark, grade, percentage **2** POINTS, result, total, outcome **3** COMPOSITION, soundtrack, arrangement, orchestration **4** GRIEVANCE, wrong, injury, injustice, grudge, bone of contention, bone to pick **5** CHARGE, bill, account, total, debt, reckoning, tab (*US informal*), tally, amount due ▷ *plural noun* LOTS, loads, many, millions, gazillions (*informal*), hundreds, hosts, crowds, masses, droves, an army, legions, swarms, multitudes, myriads, very many, a flock, a throng, a great number ▷▷ **score something out** or **through** CROSS OUT, delete, strike out, cancel, obliterate, put a line through

scorn *noun* CONTEMPT, disdain, mockery, derision, despite, slight, sneer, sarcasm, disparagement, contumely, contemptuousness, scornfulness << ANTONYM respect ▷ *verb* DESPISE, reject, disdain, slight, snub, shun, be above, spurn, rebuff, deride, flout, look down on, scoff at, make fun of, sneer at, hold in contempt, turn up your nose at (*informal*), contemn, curl your lip at, consider beneath you << ANTONYM respect

scornful *adjective* CONTEMPTUOUS, insulting, mocking, defiant, withering, sneering, slighting, jeering, scoffing, scathing, sarcastic, sardonic, haughty, disdainful, insolent, derisive, supercilious, contumelious

scornfully *adverb* CONTEMPTUOUSLY, with contempt, dismissively, disdainfully, with disdain, scathingly, witheringly, with a sneer, slightingly, with lip curled

scotch *verb* PUT AN END TO, destroy, smash, devastate, wreck, thwart, scupper, extinguish, put paid to, nip in the bud, bring to an end, put the lid on, put the kibosh on

scoundrel *noun* (*old-fashioned*) ROGUE, villain, heel (*slang*), cheat, swine, rascal, son-of-a-bitch (*slang, chiefly US & Canad*), scally (*Northwest English dialect*), wretch, incorrigible, knave (*archaic*), rotter (*slang, chiefly Brit*), ne'er-do-well, reprobate, scumbag (*slang*), good-for-nothing, miscreant, scamp, bad egg (*old-fashioned informal*), blackguard, scapegrace, caitiff (*archaic*), dastard (*archaic*), skelm (*S African*), wrong 'un (*Austral slang*)

scour¹ *verb* SCRUB, clean, polish, rub, cleanse, buff, burnish, whiten, furbish, abrade

scour² *verb* SEARCH, hunt, comb, ransack, forage, look high and low, go over with a fine-tooth comb

scourge *noun* **1** AFFLICTION, plague, curse, terror, pest, torment, misfortune, visitation, bane, infliction << ANTONYM benefit **2** WHIP, lash, thong, switch, strap, cat-o'-nine-tails ▷ *verb* **1** AFFLICT, plague, curse, torment, harass, terrorize, excoriate **2** WHIP, beat, lash, thrash, discipline, belt (*informal*), leather, punish, whale, cane, flog, trounce, castigate, wallop (*informal*), chastise, lather (*informal*), horsewhip, tan (someone's) hide (*slang*), take a strap to

scout *noun* VANGUARD, lookout, precursor, outrider, reconnoitrer, advance guard ▷ *verb* RECONNOITRE, investigate, check out, case (*slang*), watch, survey, observe, spy, probe, recce (*slang*), spy out, make a reconnaissance, see how the land lies ▷▷ **scout around** *or* **round** SEARCH, look for, hunt for, fossick (*Austral & NZ*), cast about *or* around, ferret about *or* around

scowl *verb* GLOWER, frown, look daggers, grimace, lour *or* lower ▷ *noun* GLOWER, frown, dirty look, black look, grimace

scrabble *verb* SCRAPE, scratch, scramble, dig, claw, paw, grope, clamber

scramble *verb* **1** STRUGGLE, climb, clamber, push, crawl, swarm, scrabble, move with difficulty **2** STRIVE, rush, contend, vie, run, push, hasten, jostle, jockey for position, make haste **3** JUMBLE, mix up, muddle, shuffle, entangle, disarrange ▷ *noun* **1** CLAMBER, ascent **2** RACE, competition, struggle, rush, confusion, hustle, free-for-all (*informal*), commotion, melee *or* mêlée

scrap¹ *noun* **1** PIECE, fragment, bit, trace, grain, particle, portion, snatch, part, atom, remnant, crumb, mite, bite, mouthful, snippet, sliver, morsel, modicum, iota **2** WASTE, junk, off cuts ▷ *plural noun* LEFTOVERS, remains, bits, scrapings, leavings ▷ *verb* GET RID OF, drop, abandon, shed, break up, ditch (*slang*), junk (*informal*), chuck (*informal*), discard, write off, demolish, trash (*slang*), dispense with, jettison, toss out, throw on the scrapheap, throw away *or* out << ANTONYM bring back

scrap² (*informal*) *noun* FIGHT, battle, row, argument, dispute, set-to (*informal*), disagreement, quarrel, brawl, squabble, wrangle, scuffle, tiff, dust-up (*informal*), shindig (*informal*), scrimmage, shindy (*informal*), bagarre (*French*), biffo (*Austral slang*) ▷ *verb* FIGHT, argue, row, fall out (*informal*), barney (*informal*), squabble, spar, wrangle, bicker, have words, come to blows, have a shouting match (*informal*)

scrape *verb* **1** RAKE, sweep, drag, brush **2** GRATE, grind, scratch, screech, squeak, rasp **3** GRAZE, skin, scratch, bark, scuff, rub, abrade **4** CLEAN, remove, scour ▷ *noun* (*informal*) PREDICAMENT, trouble, difficulty, spot (*informal*), fix (*informal*), mess, distress, dilemma, plight, tight spot, awkward situation, pretty pickle (*informal*) ▷▷ **scrape something together** COLLECT, save, muster, get hold of, amass, hoard, glean, dredge up, rake up *or* together

scrapheap *noun* ▷▷ **on the scrapheap** DISCARDED, ditched (*slang*), redundant, written off, jettisoned, put out to grass (*informal*)

scrappy *adjective* INCOMPLETE, sketchy, piecemeal, disjointed, perfunctory, thrown together, fragmentary, bitty

scratch *verb* **1** RUB, scrape, claw at **2** MARK, cut, score, damage, grate, graze, etch, lacerate, incise, make a mark on ▷ *noun* MARK, scrape, graze, blemish, gash, laceration, claw mark ▷▷ **scratch something out** ERASE, eliminate, delete, cancel, strike off, annul, cross out ▷▷ **not up to scratch** (*informal*) INADEQUATE, unacceptable, unsatisfactory, incapable, insufficient, incompetent, not up to standard, not up to snuff (*informal*)

scrawl *verb* SCRIBBLE, doodle, squiggle ▷ *noun* SCRIBBLE, doodle, squiggle

scrawny *adjective* THIN, lean, skinny, angular, gaunt, skeletal, bony, lanky, undernourished, skin-and-bones (*informal*), scraggy, rawboned, macilent (*rare*)

scream *verb* CRY, yell, shriek, screech, squeal, shrill, bawl, howl, holler (*informal*), sing out ▷ *noun* **1** CRY, yell, howl, wail, outcry, shriek, screech, yelp **2** (*informal*) LAUGH, card (*informal*), riot (*slang*), comic, character (*informal*), caution (*informal*), sensation, wit, comedian, entertainer, wag, joker, hoot (*informal*)

screech *verb* SHRIEK, scream, yell, howl, wail, squeal, holler ▷ *noun* CRY, scream, shriek, squeal, squawk, yelp

screen *noun* COVER, guard, shade, shelter, shield, hedge, partition, cloak, mantle, shroud, canopy, awning, concealment, room divider ▷ *verb* **1** BROADCAST, show, put on, present, air, cable, beam, transmit, relay, televise, put on the air **2** COVER, hide, conceal, shade, mask, veil, cloak, shroud, shut out **3** INVESTIGATE, test, check, examine, scan **4** PROCESS, sort, examine, grade, filter, scan, evaluate, gauge, sift **5** PROTECT, guard, shield, defend, shelter, safeguard

screw *noun* NAIL, pin, tack, rivet, fastener, spike ▷ *verb* **1** FASTEN, fix, attach, bolt, clamp, rivet **2** TURN, twist, tighten, work in **3** (*informal*) CONTORT, twist, distort, contract, wrinkle, warp, crumple, deform, pucker **4** (*informal*) CHEAT, do (*slang*), rip (someone) off (*slang*), skin (*slang*), trick, con, stiff (*slang*), sting (*informal*), deceive, fleece, dupe, overcharge, rook (*slang*), bamboozle (*informal*), diddle (*informal*), take (someone) for a ride (*informal*), put one over on (someone) (*informal*), pull a fast one (on someone) (*informal*), take to the cleaners (*informal*), sell a pup (to) (*slang*), hornswoggle (*slang*) **5** (*informal*) *often with* **out of** SQUEEZE, wring, extract, wrest, bleed someone of something ▷▷ **put the screws on someone** (*slang*) COERCE, force, compel, drive, squeeze, intimidate, constrain, oppress, pressurize, browbeat, press-gang, bring pressure to bear on, hold a knife to someone's throat ▷▷ **screw something up 1** CONTORT, contract, wrinkle, knot, knit, distort, crumple, pucker **2** (*informal*) BUNGLE, botch, mess up, spoil, bitch (up) (*slang*), queer (*informal*), cock up (*Brit slang*), mishandle, make a mess of (*slang*), mismanage, make a hash of (*informal*), make a nonsense of, bodge (*informal*), flub (*US slang*), louse up (*slang*), crool *or* cruel (*Austral slang*)

scribble *verb* SCRAWL, write, jot, pen, scratch, doodle, dash off

scribe *noun* SECRETARY, clerk, scrivener (*archaic*), notary (*archaic*), amanuensis, copyist

script *noun* **1** TEXT, lines, words, book, copy, dialogue, manuscript, libretto **2** HANDWRITING, writing, hand, letters, calligraphy, longhand, penmanship ▷ *verb* WRITE, draft, compose, author

scripture *noun* THE BIBLE, The Word, The Gospels, The Scriptures, The Word of God, The Good Book, Holy Scripture, Holy Writ, Holy Bible, The Book of Books

Scrooge *noun* MISER, penny-pincher (*informal*), skinflint, cheapskate (*informal*), tightwad (*US & Canad slang*), niggard, money-grubber (*informal*), meanie *or* meany (*informal, chiefly Brit*)

scrounge *verb* (*informal*) CADGE, beg, sponge (*informal*), bum (*informal*), touch (someone) for (*slang*), blag (*slang*), wheedle, mooch (*slang*), forage for, hunt around (for), sorn (*Scot*), freeload (*slang*), bludge (*Austral & NZ informal*)

scrounger *noun* PARASITE, freeloader (*slang*), sponger (*informal*), bum (*informal*), cadger, bludger (*Austral & NZ informal*), sorner (*Scot*), quandong (*Austral slang*)

scrub *verb* **1** SCOUR, clean, polish, rub, wash, cleanse, buff **2** (*informal*) CANCEL, drop, give up, abandon, abolish, forget about, call off, delete, do away with, discontinue

scruff *noun* NAPE, scrag (*informal*)

scruffy *adjective* SHABBY, untidy, ragged, run-down, messy, sloppy (*informal*), seedy, squalid, tattered, tatty, unkempt, disreputable, scrubby (*Brit informal*), grungy, slovenly, mangy, sluttish, slatternly, ungroomed, frowzy, ill-groomed, draggletailed (*archaic*), daggy (*Austral & NZ informal*) << ANTONYM neat

scrumptious *adjective* (*informal*) DELICIOUS, delectable, inviting, magnificent, exquisite, luscious, succulent, mouthwatering, yummy (*slang*), appetizing, moreish (*informal*), yummo (*Austral slang*)

scrunch *verb* CRUMPLE, crush, squash, crunch, mash, ruck up

scruple *noun* MISGIVING, hesitation, qualm, doubt, difficulty, caution, reluctance, second thoughts, uneasiness, perplexity, compunction, squeamishness, twinge of conscience

scrupulous *adjective* **1** MORAL, principled, upright, honourable, conscientious << ANTONYM unscrupulous **2** CAREFUL, strict, precise, minute, nice, exact, rigorous, meticulous, painstaking, fastidious, punctilious << ANTONYM careless

scrutinize *verb* EXAMINE, study, inspect, research, search, investigate, explore, probe, analyse, scan, sift, dissect, work over, pore over, peruse, inquire into, go over with a fine-tooth comb

scrutiny *noun* EXAMINATION, study, investigation, search, inquiry, analysis, inspection, exploration, sifting, once-over (*informal*), perusal, close study

scud *verb* FLY, race, speed, shoot, blow, sail, skim

scuffle *noun* FIGHT, set-to (*informal*), scrap (*informal*), disturbance, fray, brawl, barney (*informal*), ruck (*slang*), skirmish, tussle, commotion, rumpus, affray (*law*), shindig (*informal*), ruction (*informal*), ruckus (*informal*), scrimmage, shindy (*informal*), bagarre (*French*), biffo (*Austral slang*) ▷ *verb* FIGHT, struggle, clash, contend, grapple, jostle, tussle, come to blows, exchange blows

sculpture *noun* STATUE, figure, model, bust, effigy, figurine, statuette ▷ *verb* CARVE, form, cut, model, fashion, shape, mould, sculpt, chisel, hew, sculp

scum *noun* 1 RABBLE, trash (*chiefly US & Canad*), riffraff, rubbish, dross, lowest of the low, dregs of society, canaille (*French*), ragtag and bobtail 2 IMPURITIES, film, crust, froth, scruff, dross, offscourings

scungy *adjective* (*Austral & NZ slang*) SORDID, seedy, sleazy, squalid, mean, dirty, foul, filthy, unclean, wretched, seamy, slovenly, skanky (*slang*), slummy, festy (*Austral slang*)

scupper *verb* (*Brit slang*) DESTROY, ruin, wreck, defeat, overwhelm, disable, overthrow, demolish, undo, torpedo, put paid to, discomfit

scurrilous *adjective* SLANDEROUS, scandalous, defamatory, low, offensive, gross, foul, insulting, infamous, obscene, abusive, coarse, indecent, vulgar, foul-mouthed, salacious, ribald, vituperative, scabrous, Rabelaisian

scurry *verb* HURRY, race, dash, fly, sprint, dart, whisk, skim, beetle, scud, scuttle, scoot, scamper << ANTONYM amble ▷ *noun* FLURRY, race, bustle, whirl, scampering

scuttle *verb* RUN, scurry, scamper, rush, hurry, scramble, hare (*Brit informal*), bustle, beetle, scud, hasten, scoot, scutter (*Brit informal*)

sea *noun* 1 OCEAN, the deep, the waves, the drink (*informal*), the briny (*informal*), main 2 MASS, lot, lots (*informal*), army, host, crowd, collection, sheet, assembly, mob, congregation, legion, abundance, swarm, horde, multitude, myriad, throng, expanse, plethora, profusion, concourse, assemblage, vast number, great number ▷ *modifier* MARINE, ocean, maritime, aquatic, oceanic, saltwater, ocean-going, seagoing, pelagic, briny, salt ▷▷ **at sea** BEWILDERED, lost, confused, puzzled, uncertain, baffled, adrift, perplexed, disconcerted, at a loss, mystified, disoriented, bamboozled (*informal*), flummoxed, at sixes and sevens

seafaring *adjective* NAUTICAL, marine, naval, maritime, oceanic

seal *verb* SETTLE, clinch, conclude, consummate, finalize, shake hands on (*informal*) ▷ *noun* 1 SEALANT, sealer, adhesive 2 AUTHENTICATION, stamp, confirmation, assurance, ratification, notification, insignia, imprimatur, attestation ▷▷ **set the seal on something** CONFIRM, establish, assure, stamp, ratify, validate, attest, authenticate

seam *noun* 1 JOINT, closure, suture (*surgery*) 2 LAYER, vein, stratum, lode

sear *verb* WITHER, burn, blight, brand, scorch, sizzle, shrivel, cauterize, desiccate, dry up *or* out

search *verb* EXAMINE, check, investigate, explore, probe, inspect, comb, inquire, sift, scour, ferret, pry, ransack, forage, scrutinize, turn upside down, rummage through, frisk (*informal*), cast around, rifle through, leave no stone unturned, turn inside out, fossick (*Austral & NZ*), go over with a fine-tooth comb ▷ *noun* HUNT, look, inquiry, investigation, examination, pursuit, quest, going-over (*informal*), inspection, exploration, scrutiny, rummage ▷▷ **search for something** *or* **someone** LOOK FOR, seek, hunt for, pursue, go in search of, cast around for, go in pursuit of, go in quest of, ferret around for, look high and low for

searching *adjective* KEEN, sharp, probing, close, severe, intent, piercing, penetrating, thorough, quizzical << ANTONYM superficial

searing *adjective* 1 ACUTE, sharp, intense, shooting, violent, severe, painful, distressing, stabbing, fierce, stinging, piercing, sore, excruciating, gut-wrenching 2 CUTTING, biting, severe, bitter, harsh, scathing, acrimonious, barbed, hurtful, sarcastic, sardonic, caustic, vitriolic, trenchant, mordant, mordacious, acerb

season *noun* PERIOD, time, term, spell, time of year ▷ *verb* 1 FLAVOUR, salt, spice, lace,

salt and pepper, enliven, pep up, leaven
2 MATURE, age, condition, prime, prepare,
temper, mellow, ripen, acclimatize **3** MAKE
EXPERIENCED, train, mature, prepare,
discipline, harden, accustom, toughen,
inure, habituate, acclimatize, anneal

seasoned *adjective* EXPERIENCED, veteran,
mature, practised, old, weathered, hardened,
long-serving, battle-scarred, time-served,
well-versed << ANTONYM inexperienced

seasoning *noun* FLAVOURING, spice, salt and
pepper, condiment

seat *noun* **1** CHAIR, bench, stall, throne,
stool, pew, settle **2** MEMBERSHIP, place,
constituency, chair, incumbency **3** CENTRE,
place, site, heart, capital, situation, source,
station, location, headquarters, axis, cradle,
hub **4** MANSION, house, residence, abode,
ancestral hall ▷ *verb* **1** SIT, place, settle, set,
fix, deposit, locate, install **2** HOLD, take,
accommodate, sit, contain, cater for, have
room *or* capacity for

seating *noun* ACCOMMODATION, room, places,
seats, chairs

secede *verb* WITHDRAW, leave, resign,
separate, retire, quit, pull out, break with,
split from, disaffiliate, apostatize

secession *noun* WITHDRAWAL, break, split,
defection, seceding, apostasy, disaffiliation

secluded *adjective* PRIVATE, sheltered,
isolated, remote, lonely, cut off, solitary,
out-of-the-way, tucked away, cloistered,
sequestered, off the beaten track,
unfrequented << ANTONYM public

seclusion *noun* PRIVACY, isolation, solitude,
hiding, retirement, shelter, retreat,
remoteness, ivory tower, concealment,
purdah

second¹ *adjective* **1** NEXT, following,
succeeding, subsequent **2** ADDITIONAL,
other, further, extra, alternative, repeated
3 SPARE, duplicate, alternative, additional,
back-up **4** INFERIOR, secondary, subordinate,
supporting, lower, lesser ▷ *noun* SUPPORTER,
assistant, aide, partner, colleague, associate,
backer, helper, collaborator, henchman,
right-hand man, cooperator ▷ *verb* SUPPORT,
back, endorse, forward, promote, approve,
go along with, commend, give moral
support to

second² *noun* MOMENT, minute, instant,
flash, tick (*Brit informal*), sec (*informal*),
twinkling, split second, jiffy (*informal*), trice,
twinkling of an eye, two shakes of a lamb's
tail (*informal*), bat of an eye (*informal*)

secondary *adjective* **1** SUBORDINATE, minor,
lesser, lower, inferior, unimportant, second-
rate << ANTONYM main **2** RESULTANT,
resulting, contingent, derived, derivative,
indirect, second-hand, consequential
<< ANTONYM original

second-class *adjective* **1** INFERIOR, lesser,
second-best, unimportant, second-rate,
low-class **2** MEDIOCRE, second-rate, mean,
middling, ordinary, inferior, indifferent,
commonplace, insignificant, so-so (*informal*),
outclassed, uninspiring, undistinguished,
uninspired, bog-standard (*Brit & Irish slang*),
no great shakes (*informal*), déclassé, half-pie
(*NZ informal*), fair to middling (*informal*)

second-hand *adjective* USED, old, handed
down, hand-me-down (*informal*), nearly new,
reach-me-down (*informal*), preloved (*Austral
slang*)

secondly *adverb* NEXT, second, moreover,
furthermore, also, in the second place

second-rate *adjective* INFERIOR, mediocre,
poor, cheap, pants (*slang*), commonplace,
tacky (*informal*), shoddy, low-grade, tawdry,
low-quality, substandard, low-rent (*informal,
chiefly US*), for the birds (*informal*), two-bit
(*US & Canad slang*), end-of-the-pier (*Brit
informal*), no great shakes (*informal*), cheap
and nasty (*informal*), rubbishy, dime-a-
dozen (*informal*), bush-league (*Austral &
NZ informal*), not much cop (*Brit slang*),
tinhorn (*US slang*), strictly for the birds
(*informal*), bodger *or* bodgie (*Austral slang*)
<< ANTONYM first-rate

secrecy *noun* **1** MYSTERY, stealth, concealment,
furtiveness, cloak and dagger, secretiveness,
huggermugger (*rare*), clandestineness,
covertness **2** CONFIDENTIALITY, privacy
3 PRIVACY, silence, retirement, solitude,
seclusion

secret *adjective* **1** UNDISCLOSED, unknown,
confidential, underground, undercover,
unpublished, under wraps, unrevealed
2 CONCEALED, hidden, disguised, covered,
camouflaged, unseen << ANTONYM
unconcealed **3** UNDERCOVER, covert,
furtive, shrouded, behind someone's
back, conspiratorial, hush-hush (*informal*),
surreptitious, cloak-and-dagger, backstairs
<< ANTONYM open **4** SECRETIVE, reserved,
withdrawn, close, deep, discreet, enigmatic,
reticent, cagey (*informal*), unforthcoming
<< ANTONYM frank **5** MYSTERIOUS, cryptic,
abstruse, classified, esoteric, occult,
clandestine, arcane, recondite, cabbalistic

<< ANTONYM straightforward ▷ *noun*
1 PRIVATE AFFAIR, confidence, skeleton in
the cupboard **2** KEY, answer, formula, recipe
▷▷ **in secret** SECRETLY, surreptitiously, slyly,
behind closed doors, incognito, by stealth,
in camera, huggermugger (*archaic*)

secret agent *noun* SPY, undercover agent,
spook (*US & Canad informal*), nark (*Brit,
Austral & NZ slang*), cloak-and-dagger man

secrete[1] *verb* GIVE OFF, emit, emanate, exude,
extrude

secrete[2] *verb* HIDE, conceal, stash (*informal*),
cover, screen, secure, bury, harbour,
disguise, veil, shroud, stow, cache, stash
away (*informal*) << ANTONYM display

secretion *noun* DISCHARGE, emission,
excretion, exudation, extravasation (*medical*)

secretive *adjective* RETICENT, reserved,
withdrawn, close, deep, enigmatic, cryptic,
cagey (*informal*), uncommunicative,
unforthcoming, tight-lipped, playing
your cards close to your chest, clamlike
<< ANTONYM open

secretly *adverb* IN SECRET, privately,
surreptitiously, quietly, covertly, behind
closed doors, in confidence, in your heart,
furtively, in camera, confidentially, on
the fly (*slang, chiefly Brit*), stealthily, under
the counter, clandestinely, unobserved,
on the sly, in your heart of hearts, behind
(someone's) back, in your innermost
thoughts, on the q.t. (*informal*)

sect *noun* GROUP, division, faction, party,
school, camp, wing, denomination, school
of thought, schism, splinter group

sectarian *adjective* NARROW-MINDED, partisan,
fanatic, fanatical, limited, exclusive, rigid,
parochial, factional, bigoted, dogmatic,
insular, doctrinaire, hidebound, clannish,
cliquish << ANTONYM tolerant ▷ *noun*
BIGOT, extremist, partisan, disciple, fanatic,
adherent, zealot, true believer, dogmatist

section *noun* **1** PART, piece, portion, division,
sample, slice, passage, component, segment,
fragment, fraction, instalment, cross
section, subdivision **2** DISTRICT, area,
region, sector, zone

sectional *adjective* REGIONAL, local, separate,
divided, exclusive, partial, separatist,
factional, localized

sector *noun* **1** PART, division, category,
stratum, subdivision **2** AREA, part, region,
district, zone, quarter

secular *adjective* WORLDLY, state, lay, earthly,
civil, temporal, profane, laic, nonspiritual,

laical << ANTONYM religious

secure *verb* **1** OBTAIN, get, acquire, land
(*informal*), score (*slang*), gain, pick up, get
hold of, come by, procure, make sure of, win
possession of << ANTONYM lose **2** ATTACH,
stick, fix, bind, pin, lash, glue, fasten,
rivet << ANTONYM detach **3** GUARANTEE,
insure, ensure, assure << ANTONYM
endanger ▷ *adjective* **1** SAFE, protected,
shielded, sheltered, immune, unassailable,
impregnable << ANTONYM unprotected
2 FAST, firm, fixed, tight, stable, steady,
fortified, fastened, dependable, immovable
<< ANTONYM insecure **3** RELIABLE, definite,
solid, absolute, conclusive, in the bag
(*informal*) **4** CONFIDENT, sure, easy, certain,
assured, reassured << ANTONYM uneasy

security *noun* **1** PRECAUTIONS, defence,
safeguards, guards, protection, surveillance,
safety measures **2** ASSURANCE, confidence,
conviction, certainty, reliance, sureness,
positiveness, ease of mind, freedom from
doubt << ANTONYM insecurity **3** PLEDGE,
insurance, guarantee, hostage, collateral,
pawn, gage, surety **4** PROTECTION, cover,
safety, retreat, asylum, custody, refuge,
sanctuary, immunity, preservation,
safekeeping << ANTONYM vulnerability

sedate *adjective* **1** CALM, collected, quiet,
seemly, serious, earnest, cool, grave, proper,
middle-aged, composed, sober, dignified,
solemn, serene, tranquil, placid, staid,
demure, unflappable (*informal*), unruffled,
decorous, imperturbable << ANTONYM wild
2 UNHURRIED, easy, relaxed, comfortable,
steady, gentle, deliberate, leisurely, slow-
moving

sedative *adjective* CALMING, relaxing,
soothing, allaying, anodyne, soporific, sleep-
inducing, tranquillizing, calmative, lenitive
▷ *noun* TRANQUILLIZER, narcotic, sleeping
pill, opiate, anodyne, calmative, downer *or*
down (*slang*)

sedentary *adjective* INACTIVE, sitting, seated,
desk, motionless, torpid, desk-bound
<< ANTONYM active

sediment *noun* DREGS, grounds, residue, lees,
deposit, precipitate, settlings

sedition *noun* RABBLE-ROUSING, treason,
subversion, agitation, disloyalty, incitement
to riot

seduce *verb* **1** TEMPT, attract, lure, entice,
mislead, deceive, beguile, allure, decoy,
ensnare, lead astray, inveigle **2** CORRUPT,
ruin (*archaic*), betray, deprave, dishonour,

debauch, deflower

seduction noun **1** TEMPTATION, lure, snare, allure, enticement **2** CORRUPTION, ruin (archaic), defloration

seductive adjective TEMPTING, inviting, attractive, sexy (informal), irresistible, siren, enticing, provocative, captivating, beguiling, alluring, bewitching, ravishing, flirtatious, come-to-bed (informal), come-hither (informal)

see verb **1** PERCEIVE, note, spot, notice, mark, view, eye, check, regard, identify, sight, witness, clock (Brit slang), observe, recognize, distinguish, glimpse, check out (informal), make out, heed, discern, behold, eyeball (slang), catch a glimpse of, catch sight of, espy, get a load of (slang), descry, take a dekko at (Brit slang), lay or clap eyes on (informal) **2** UNDERSTAND, get, follow, realize, know, appreciate, take in, grasp, make out, catch on (informal), comprehend, fathom, get the hang of (informal), get the drift of **3** FORESEE, picture, imagine, anticipate, divine, envisage, visualize, foretell **4** FIND OUT, learn, discover, determine, investigate, verify, ascertain, make inquiries **5** CONSIDER, decide, judge, reflect, deliberate, mull over, think over, make up your mind, give some thought to **6** MAKE SURE, mind, ensure, guarantee, take care, make certain, see to it **7** ACCOMPANY, show, escort, lead, walk, attend, usher **8** SPEAK TO, receive, interview, consult, confer with **9** MEET, encounter, come across, run into, happen on, bump into, run across, chance on **10** GO OUT WITH, court, date (informal, chiefly US), walk out with (obsolete), keep company with, go steady with (informal), consort or associate with ▷▷ **see about something** TAKE CARE OF, deal with, look after, see to, attend to ▷▷ **see something through** PERSEVERE (WITH), keep at, persist, stick out (informal), see out, stay to the bitter end ▷▷ **see through something or someone** BE UNDECEIVED BY, penetrate, be wise to (informal), fathom, get to the bottom of, not fall for, have (someone's) number (informal), read (someone) like a book ▷▷ **see to something or someone** TAKE CARE OF, manage, arrange, look after, organize, be responsible for, sort out, attend to, take charge of, do ▷▷ **seeing as** SINCE, as, in view of the fact that, inasmuch as

seed noun **1** GRAIN, pip, germ, kernel, egg, embryo, spore, ovum, egg cell, ovule **2** BEGINNING, start, suspicion, germ, inkling **3** ORIGIN, source, nucleus **4** (Chiefly Bible) OFFSPRING, children, descendants, issue, race, successors, heirs, spawn, progeny, scions ▷▷ **go or run to seed** DECLINE, deteriorate, degenerate, go downhill (informal), go to waste, go to pieces, let yourself go, go to pot, go to rack and ruin, retrogress

seedy adjective **1** SHABBY, run-down, scruffy, old, worn, faded, decaying, grubby, dilapidated, tatty, unkempt, grotty (slang), crummy (slang), down at heel, slovenly, mangy, manky (Scot dialect), scungy (Austral & NZ) << ANTONYM smart **2** (informal) UNWELL, ill, poorly (informal), crook (Austral & NZ informal), ailing, sickly, out of sorts, off colour, under the weather (informal), peely-wally (Scot)

seek verb **1** LOOK FOR, pursue, search for, be after, hunt, go in search of, go in pursuit of, go gunning for, go in quest of **2** REQUEST, invite, ask for, petition, plead for, solicit, beg for, petition for **3** TRY, attempt, aim, strive, endeavour, essay, aspire to, have a go at (informal)

seem verb APPEAR, give the impression of being, look, look to be, sound as if you are, look as if you are, look like you are, strike you as being, have the or every appearance of being

seeming adjective APPARENT, appearing, outward, surface, illusory, ostensible, specious, quasi-

seemingly adverb APPARENTLY, outwardly, on the surface, ostensibly, on the face of it, to all intents and purposes, to all appearances, as far as anyone could tell

seep verb OOZE, well, leak, soak, bleed, weep, trickle, leach, exude, permeate, percolate

seer noun PROPHET, augur, predictor, soothsayer, sibyl

seesaw verb ALTERNATE, swing, fluctuate, teeter, oscillate, go from one extreme to the other

seethe verb **1** BE FURIOUS, storm, rage, fume, simmer, be in a state (informal), see red (informal), be incensed, be livid, go ballistic (slang, chiefly US), foam at the mouth, be incandescent, get hot under the collar (informal), wig out (slang), breathe fire and slaughter **2** BOIL, bubble, foam, churn, fizz, ferment, froth

segment noun SECTION, part, piece, division, slice, portion, wedge, compartment

segregate verb SET APART, divide, separate,

isolate, single out, discriminate against, dissociate << ANTONYM unite

segregation *noun* SEPARATION, discrimination, apartheid, isolation

seize *verb* 1 GRAB, grip, grasp, take, snatch, clutch, snap up, pluck, fasten, latch on to, lay hands on, catch *or* take hold of << ANTONYM let go 2 TAKE BY STORM, take over, acquire, occupy, conquer, annex, usurp 3 CONFISCATE, appropriate, commandeer, impound, take possession of, requisition, sequester, expropriate, sequestrate << ANTONYM hand back 4 CAPTURE, catch, arrest, get, nail (*informal*), grasp, collar (*informal*), hijack, abduct, nab (*informal*), apprehend, take captive << ANTONYM release

seizure *noun* 1 ATTACK, fit, spasm, convulsion, paroxysm 2 TAKING, grabbing, annexation, confiscation, commandeering 3 CAPTURE, arrest, apprehension, abduction

seldom *adverb* RARELY, occasionally, not often, infrequently, once in a blue moon (*informal*), hardly ever, scarcely ever << ANTONYM often

select *verb* CHOOSE, take, pick, prefer, opt for, decide on, single out, adopt, single out, fix on, cherry-pick, settle upon << ANTONYM reject ▷ *adjective* 1 CHOICE, special, prime, picked, selected, excellent, rare, superior, first-class, posh (*informal, chiefly Brit*), first-rate, hand-picked, top-notch (*informal*), recherché << ANTONYM ordinary 2 EXCLUSIVE, elite, privileged, limited, cliquish << ANTONYM indiscriminate

selection *noun* 1 CHOICE, choosing, pick, option, preference 2 ANTHOLOGY, collection, medley, choice, line-up, mixed bag (*informal*), potpourri, miscellany

selective *adjective* PARTICULAR, discriminating, critical, careful, discerning, astute, discriminatory, tasteful, fastidious << ANTONYM indiscriminate

self-assurance *noun* CONFIDENCE, self-confidence, poise, nerve, assertiveness, self-possession, positiveness

self-centred *adjective* SELFISH, narcissistic, self-absorbed, inward looking, self-seeking, egotistic, wrapped up in yourself

self-confidence *noun* SELF-ASSURANCE, confidence, poise, nerve, self-respect, aplomb, self-reliance, high morale

self-confident *adjective* SELF-ASSURED, confident, assured, secure, poised, fearless, self-reliant, sure of yourself

self-conscious *adjective* EMBARRASSED, nervous, uncomfortable, awkward, insecure, diffident, ill at ease, sheepish, bashful, shamefaced, like a fish out of water, out of countenance

self-control *noun* WILLPOWER, restraint, self-discipline, cool, coolness, calmness, self-restraint, self-mastery, strength of mind *or* will

self-denial *noun* SELF-SACRIFICE, renunciation, asceticism, abstemiousness, selflessness, unselfishness, self-abnegation

self-esteem *noun* SELF-RESPECT, confidence, courage, vanity, boldness, self-reliance, self-assurance, self-regard, self-possession, amour-propre (*French*), faith in yourself, pride in yourself

self-evident *adjective* OBVIOUS, clear, undeniable, inescapable, written all over (something), cut-and-dried (*informal*), incontrovertible, axiomatic, manifestly *or* patently true

self-government *noun* INDEPENDENCE, democracy, sovereignty, autonomy, devolution, self-determination, self-rule, home rule

self-important *adjective* CONCEITED, arrogant, pompous, strutting, swaggering, cocky, pushy (*informal*), overbearing, presumptuous, bumptious, swollen-headed, bigheaded, full of yourself

self-indulgence *noun* EXTRAVAGANCE, excess, incontinence, dissipation, self-gratification, intemperance, sensualism

selfish *adjective* SELF-CENTRED, self-interested, greedy, mercenary, self-seeking, ungenerous, egoistic *or* egoistical, egotistic *or* egotistical, looking out for number one (*informal*) << ANTONYM unselfish

selfless *adjective* UNSELFISH, generous, altruistic, self-sacrificing, magnanimous, self-denying, ungrudging

self-reliant *adjective* INDEPENDENT, capable, self-sufficient, self-supporting, able to stand on your own two feet (*informal*) << ANTONYM dependent

self-respect *noun* PRIDE, dignity, self-esteem, morale, amour-propre (*French*), faith in yourself

self-restraint *noun* SELF-CONTROL, self-discipline, willpower, patience, forbearance, abstemiousness, self-command

self-righteous *adjective* SANCTIMONIOUS, smug, pious, superior, complacent, hypocritical, pi (*Brit slang*), too good to be true, self-satisfied, goody-goody (*informal*), holier-than-thou, priggish, pietistic, pharisaic

self-sacrifice *noun* SELFLESSNESS, altruism, self-denial, generosity, self-abnegation

self-satisfied *adjective* SMUG, complacent, proud of yourself, well-pleased, puffed up, self-congratulatory, flushed with success, pleased with yourself, like a cat that has swallowed the canary, too big for your boots *or* breeches

self-styled *adjective* SO-CALLED, would-be, professed, self-appointed, soi-disant (*French*), quasi-

sell *verb* **1** TRADE, dispose of, exchange, barter, put up for sale << ANTONYM buy **2** DEAL IN, market, trade in, stock, handle, retail, hawk, merchandise, peddle, traffic in, vend, be in the business of << ANTONYM buy **3** PROMOTE, put across, gain acceptance for ▷▷ **sell out of something** RUN OUT OF, be out of stock of

seller *noun* DEALER, merchant, vendor, agent, representative, rep, retailer, traveller, supplier, shopkeeper, purveyor, tradesman, salesman *or* saleswoman

semblance *noun* APPEARANCE, show, form, air, figure, front, image, bearing, aspect, mask, similarity, resemblance, guise, façade, pretence, veneer, likeness, mien

semen *noun* SPERM, seed (*archaic or dialect*), scum (*US slang*), seminal fluid, spermatic fluid

seminal *adjective* INFLUENTIAL, important, ground-breaking, original, creative, productive, innovative, imaginative, formative

send *verb* **1** DISPATCH, forward, direct, convey, consign, remit **2** TRANSMIT, broadcast, communicate **3** PROPEL, hurl, fling, shoot, fire, deliver, cast, let fly ▷▷ **send something** *or* **someone up** (*Brit informal*) MOCK, mimic, parody, spoof (*informal*), imitate, take off (*informal*), make fun of, lampoon, burlesque, take the mickey out of (*informal*), satirize

sendoff *noun* FAREWELL, departure, leave-taking, valediction, going-away party

send-up *noun* (*Brit informal*) PARODY, take-off (*informal*), satire, mockery, spoof (*informal*), imitation, skit, mickey-take (*informal*)

senile *adjective* DODDERING, doting, decrepit, failing, imbecile, gaga (*informal*), in your dotage, in your second childhood

senility *noun* DOTAGE, Alzheimer's disease, infirmity, senile dementia, decrepitude,

senescence, second childhood, caducity, loss of your faculties

senior *adjective* **1** HIGHER RANKING, superior << ANTONYM subordinate **2** THE ELDER, major (*Brit*) << ANTONYM junior

senior citizen *noun* PENSIONER, retired person, old age pensioner, O.A.P., elder, old *or* elderly person

seniority *noun* SUPERIORITY, rank, priority, precedence, longer service

sensation *noun* **1** FEELING, sense, impression, perception, awareness, consciousness **2** EXCITEMENT, surprise, thrill, stir, scandal, furore, agitation, commotion **3** HIT, wow (*slang, chiefly US*), crowd puller (*informal*)

sensational *adjective* **1** AMAZING, dramatic, thrilling, revealing, spectacular, staggering, startling, horrifying, breathtaking, astounding, lurid, electrifying, hair-raising << ANTONYM dull **2** SHOCKING, scandalous, exciting, yellow (*of the press*), melodramatic, shock-horror (*facetious*), sensationalistic << ANTONYM unexciting **3** (*informal*) EXCELLENT, brilliant, superb, mean (*slang*), topping (*Brit slang*), cracking (*Brit informal*), crucial (*slang*), impressive, smashing (*informal*), fabulous (*informal*), first class, marvellous, exceptional, mega (*slang*), sovereign, awesome (*slang*), def (*slang*), brill (*informal*), out of this world (*informal*), mind-blowing (*informal*), bodacious (*slang, chiefly US*), boffo (*slang*), jim-dandy (*slang*), chillin' (*US slang*), booshit (*Austral slang*), exo (*Austral slang*), sik (*Austral slang*), rad (*informal*), phat (*slang*), schmick (*Austral informal*) << ANTONYM ordinary

sense *noun* **1** FACULTY, sensibility **2** FEELING, impression, perception, awareness, consciousness, atmosphere, aura, intuition, premonition, presentiment **3** UNDERSTANDING, awareness, appreciation **4** *sometimes plural* INTELLIGENCE, reason, understanding, brains (*informal*), smarts (*slang, chiefly US*), judgment, discrimination, wisdom, wit(s), common sense, sanity, sharpness, tact, nous (*Brit slang*), cleverness, quickness, discernment, gumption (*Brit informal*), sagacity, clear-headedness, mother wit << ANTONYM foolishness **5** POINT, good, use, reason, value, worth, advantage, purpose, logic **6** MEANING, definition, interpretation, significance, message, import, substance, implication, drift, purport, nuance, gist, signification, denotation ▷ *verb* PERCEIVE, feel, understand, notice, pick up, suspect, realize, observe, appreciate, grasp, be aware of, divine, discern, just know, have a (funny) feeling (*informal*), get the impression, apprehend, have a hunch << ANTONYM be unaware of

senseless *adjective* **1** POINTLESS, mad, crazy, stupid, silly, ridiculous, absurd, foolish, daft (*informal*), ludicrous, meaningless, unreasonable, irrational, inconsistent, unwise, mindless, illogical, incongruous, idiotic, nonsensical, inane, fatuous, moronic, unintelligent, asinine, imbecilic, dumb-ass (*slang*), without rhyme or reason, halfwitted << ANTONYM sensible **2** UNCONSCIOUS, stunned, insensible, out, cold, numb, numbed, deadened, unfeeling, out cold, anaesthetized, insensate << ANTONYM conscious

sensibility *noun* **1** AWARENESS, insight, intuition, taste, appreciation, delicacy, discernment, perceptiveness << ANTONYM lack of awareness **2** *often plural* FEELINGS, emotions, sentiments, susceptibilities, moral sense

sensible *adjective* **1** WISE, practical, prudent, shrewd, well-informed, judicious, well-advised << ANTONYM foolish **2** INTELLIGENT, practical, reasonable, rational, sound, realistic, sober, discriminating, discreet, sage, shrewd, down-to-earth, matter-of-fact, prudent, sane, canny, judicious, far-sighted, sagacious << ANTONYM senseless

sensitive *adjective* **1** THOUGHTFUL, kind, kindly, concerned, patient, attentive, tactful, unselfish **2** DELICATE, tender **3** SUSCEPTIBLE, responsive, reactive, easily affected **4** TOUCHY, oversensitive, easily upset, easily offended, easily hurt, umbrageous (*rare*) << ANTONYM insensitive **5** PRECISE, fine, acute, keen, responsive, perceptive << ANTONYM imprecise

sensitivity *noun* **1** SUSCEPTIBILITY, responsiveness, reactivity, receptiveness, sensitiveness, reactiveness **2** CONSIDERATION, patience, thoughtfulness **3** TOUCHINESS, oversensitivity **4** RESPONSIVENESS, precision, keenness, acuteness

sensual *adjective* **1** SEXUAL, sexy (*informal*), erotic, randy (*informal, chiefly Brit*), steamy (*informal*), raunchy (*slang*), lewd, lascivious, lustful, lecherous, libidinous, licentious, unchaste **2** PHYSICAL, bodily, voluptuous, animal, luxurious, fleshly, carnal, epicurean,

unspiritual

sensuality *noun* EROTICISM, sexiness (*informal*), voluptuousness, prurience, licentiousness, carnality, lewdness, salaciousness, lasciviousness, animalism, libidinousness, lecherousness

sensuous *adjective* PLEASURABLE, pleasing, sensory, gratifying

sentence *noun* **1** PUNISHMENT, prison term, condemnation **2** VERDICT, order, ruling, decision, judgment, decree, pronouncement ▷ *verb* **1** CONDEMN, doom **2** CONVICT, condemn, penalize, pass judgment on, mete out justice to

sentient *adjective* FEELING, living, conscious, live, sensitive, reactive

sentiment *noun* **1** FEELING, thought, idea, view, opinion, attitude, belief, judgment, persuasion, way of thinking **2** SENTIMENTALITY, emotion, tenderness, romanticism, sensibility, slush (*informal*), emotionalism, tender feeling, mawkishness, soft-heartedness, overemotionalism

sentimental *adjective* ROMANTIC, touching, emotional, tender, pathetic, nostalgic, sloppy (*informal*), tearful, corny (*slang*), impressionable, mushy (*informal*), maudlin, simpering, weepy (*informal*), slushy (*informal*), mawkish, tear-jerking (*informal*), drippy (*informal*), schmaltzy (*slang*), icky (*informal*), gushy (*informal*), soft-hearted, overemotional, dewy-eyed, three-hankie (*informal*) << ANTONYM unsentimental

sentimentality *noun* ROMANTICISM, nostalgia, tenderness, gush (*informal*), pathos, slush (*informal*), mush (*informal*), schmaltz (*slang*), sloppiness (*informal*), emotionalism, bathos, mawkishness, corniness (*slang*), play on the emotions, sob stuff (*informal*)

sentinel *noun* GUARD, watch, lookout, sentry, picket, watchman

separate *adjective* **1** UNCONNECTED, individual, particular, divided, divorced, isolated, detached, disconnected, discrete, unattached, disjointed << ANTONYM connected **2** INDIVIDUAL, independent, apart, distinct, autonomous << ANTONYM joined ▷ *verb* **1** DIVIDE, detach, disconnect, come between, disentangle, keep apart, disjoin << ANTONYM combine **2** COME APART, split, break off, come away << ANTONYM connect **3** SEVER, disconnect, break apart, split in two, divide in two, uncouple, bifurcate << ANTONYM join **4** SPLIT UP, part, divorce, break up, part company, get divorced, be estranged, go different ways **5** DISTINGUISH, mark, single out, set apart, make distinctive, set at variance *or* at odds << ANTONYM link

separated *adjective* **1** ESTRANGED, parted, split up, separate, apart, broken up, disunited, living apart *or* separately **2** DISCONNECTED, parted, divided, separate, disassociated, disunited, put asunder

separately *adverb* **1** ALONE, independently, apart, personally, not together, severally << ANTONYM together **2** INDIVIDUALLY, singly, one by one, one at a time

separation *noun* **1** DIVISION, break, segregation, detachment, severance, disengagement, dissociation, disconnection, disjunction, disunion **2** SPLIT-UP, parting, split, divorce, break-up, farewell, rift, estrangement, leave-taking

septic *adjective* INFECTED, poisoned, toxic, festering, pussy, putrid, putrefying, suppurating, putrefactive

sequel *noun* **1** FOLLOW-UP, continuation, development **2** CONSEQUENCE, result, outcome, conclusion, end, issue, payoff (*informal*), upshot

sequence *noun* **1** SUCCESSION, course, series, order, chain, cycle, arrangement, procession, progression **2** ORDER, structure, arrangement, ordering, placement, layout, progression

serene *adjective* CALM, peaceful, tranquil, composed, sedate, placid, undisturbed, untroubled, unruffled, imperturbable << ANTONYM troubled

serenity *noun* CALM, peace, tranquillity, composure, peace of mind, stillness, calmness, quietness, peacefulness, quietude, placidity

serf *noun* VASSAL, servant, slave, thrall, bondsman, varlet (*archaic*), helot, villein, liegeman

series *noun* **1** SEQUENCE, course, chain, succession, run, set, line, order, train, arrangement, string, progression **2** DRAMA, serial, soap (*informal*), sitcom (*informal*), soap opera, soapie *or* soapie (*Austral slang*), situation comedy

serious *adjective* **1** GRAVE, bad, critical, worrying, dangerous, acute, alarming, severe, extreme, grievous **2** IMPORTANT, crucial, urgent, pressing, difficult, worrying, deep, significant, grim, far-reaching, momentous, fateful, weighty, no laughing matter, of moment *or* consequence

<< ANTONYM unimportant **3** THOUGHTFUL, detailed, careful, deep, profound, in-depth **4** DEEP, sophisticated, highbrowed **5** SOLEMN, earnest, grave, stern, sober, thoughtful, sedate, glum, staid, humourless, long-faced, pensive, unsmiling << ANTONYM light-hearted **6** SINCERE, determined, earnest, resolved, genuine, deliberate, honest, resolute, in earnest << ANTONYM insincere

seriously *adverb* **1** TRULY, no joking (*informal*), in earnest, all joking aside **2** BADLY, severely, gravely, critically, acutely, sorely, dangerously, distressingly, grievously

seriousness *noun* **1** IMPORTANCE, gravity, urgency, moment, weight, danger, significance **2** SOLEMNITY, gravity, earnestness, sobriety, gravitas, sternness, humourlessness, staidness, sedateness

sermon *noun* HOMILY, address, exhortation

serpentine *adjective* TWISTING, winding, snaking, crooked, coiling, meandering, tortuous, sinuous, twisty, snaky

serrated *adjective* NOTCHED, toothed, sawtoothed, serrate, serrulate, sawlike, serriform (*biology*)

servant *noun* ATTENDANT, domestic, slave, maid, help, helper, retainer, menial, drudge, lackey, vassal, skivvy (*chiefly Brit*), servitor (*archaic*), varlet (*archaic*), liegeman

serve *verb* **1** WORK FOR, help, aid, assist, be in the service of **2** PERFORM, do, complete, go through, fulfil, pass, discharge **3** BE ADEQUATE, do, suffice, answer, suit, content, satisfy, be good enough, be acceptable, fill the bill (*informal*), answer the purpose **4** PRESENT, provide, supply, deliver, arrange, set out, distribute, dish up, purvey ▷▷ **serve as something** *or* **someone** ACT AS, function as, do the work of, do duty as

service *noun* **1** FACILITY, system, resource, utility, amenity **2** CEREMONY, worship, rite, function, observance **3** WORK, labour, employment, business, office, duty, employ **4** CHECK, servicing, maintenance check ▷ *verb* OVERHAUL, check, maintain, tune (up), repair, go over, fine tune, recondition

serviceable *adjective* USEFUL, practical, efficient, helpful, profitable, convenient, operative, beneficial, functional, durable, usable, dependable, advantageous, utilitarian, hard-wearing << ANTONYM useless

servile *adjective* SUBSERVIENT, cringing, grovelling, mean, low, base, humble, craven, fawning, abject, submissive, menial, sycophantic, slavish, unctuous, obsequious, toadying, bootlicking (*informal*), toadyish

serving noun PORTION, helping, plateful

servitude noun SLAVERY, bondage, enslavement, bonds, chains, obedience, thrall, subjugation, serfdom, vassalage, thraldom

session noun MEETING, hearing, sitting, term, period, conference, congress, discussion, assembly, seminar, get-together (*informal*)

set¹ verb 1 PUT, place, lay, park (*informal*), position, rest, plant, station, stick, deposit, locate, lodge, situate, plump, plonk 2 SWITCH ON, turn on, activate, programme 3 ADJUST, regulate, coordinate, rectify, synchronize 4 EMBED, fix, mount, install, fasten 5 ARRANGE, decide (upon), settle, name, establish, determine, fix, schedule, appoint, specify, allocate, designate, ordain, fix up, agree upon 6 ASSIGN, give, allot, prescribe 7 HARDEN, stiffen, condense, solidify, cake, thicken, crystallize, congeal, jell, gelatinize 8 GO DOWN, sink, dip, decline, disappear, vanish, subside 9 PREPARE, lay, spread, arrange, make ready ▷ *adjective* 1 ESTABLISHED, planned, decided, agreed, usual, arranged, rigid, definite, inflexible, hard and fast, immovable 2 STRICT, firm, rigid, hardened, stubborn, entrenched, inflexible, hidebound << ANTONYM flexible 3 CONVENTIONAL, stock, standard, traditional, formal, routine, artificial, stereotyped, rehearsed, hackneyed, unspontaneous ▷ *noun* 1 SCENERY, setting, scene, stage setting, stage set, mise-en-scène (*French*) 2 POSITION, bearing, attitude, carriage, turn, fit, hang, posture ▷▷ **set about someone** ASSAULT, attack, mug (*informal*), assail, sail into (*informal*), lambast(e), belabour ▷▷ **set about something** BEGIN, start, get down to, attack, tackle, set to, get to work, sail into (*informal*), take the first step, wade into, get cracking (*informal*), make a start on, roll up your sleeves, get weaving (*informal*), address yourself to, put your shoulder to the wheel (*informal*) ▷▷ **set off** LEAVE, set out, depart, embark, start out, sally forth ▷▷ **set on** *or* **upon someone** ATTACK, beat up, assault, turn on, mug (*informal*), set about, ambush, go for, sic, pounce on, fly at, work over (*slang*), assail, sail into (*informal*), fall upon, lay into (*informal*), put the boot in (*slang*), pitch into (*informal*), let fly at, beat *or* knock seven bells out of (*informal*) ▷▷ **set on** *or* **upon something** DETERMINED TO, intent on, bent on, resolute about ▷▷ **set out** EMBARK, set off, start out, begin, get under way, hit the road (*slang*), take to the road, sally forth ▷▷ **set someone against someone** ALIENATE, oppose, divide, drive a wedge between, disunite, estrange, set at odds, make bad blood between, make mischief between, set at cross purposes, set by the ears (*informal*), sow dissension amongst ▷▷ **set someone up** 1 FINANCE, back, fund, establish, promote, build up, subsidize 2 PREPARE, prime, warm up, dispose, make ready, put in order, put in a good position ▷▷ **set something against something** BALANCE, compare, contrast, weigh, juxtapose ▷▷ **set something aside** 1 RESERVE, keep, save, separate, select, single out, earmark, keep back, set apart, put on one side 2 REJECT, dismiss, reverse, cancel, overturn, discard, quash, overrule, repudiate, annul, nullify, abrogate, render null and void ▷▷ **set something back** HOLD UP, slow, delay, hold back, hinder, obstruct, retard, impede, slow up ▷▷ **set something off** 1 DETONATE, trigger (off), explode, ignite, light, set in motion, touch off 2 CAUSE, start, produce, generate, prompt, trigger (off), provoke, bring about, give rise to, spark off, set in motion 3 ENHANCE, show off, throw into relief, bring out the highlights in ▷▷ **set something out** 1 ARRANGE, present, display, lay out, exhibit, array, dispose, set forth, expose to view 2 EXPLAIN, list, describe, detail, elaborate, recount, enumerate, elucidate, itemize, particularize ▷▷ **set something up** 1 ARRANGE, organize, prepare, make provision for, prearrange 2 ESTABLISH, begin, found, institute, install, initiate 3 BUILD, raise, construct, put up, assemble, put together, erect, elevate 4 ASSEMBLE, put up

set² noun 1 SERIES, collection, assortment, kit, outfit, batch, compendium, assemblage, coordinated group, ensemble 2 GROUP, company, crowd, circle, class, band, crew (*informal*), gang, outfit, faction, sect, posse (*informal*), clique, coterie, schism

setback noun HOLD-UP, check, defeat, blow, upset, reverse, disappointment, hitch, misfortune, rebuff, whammy (*informal, chiefly US*), bummer (*slang*), bit of trouble

setting noun SURROUNDINGS, site, location, set, scene, surround, background, frame, context, perspective, backdrop, scenery, locale, mise en scène (*French*)

settle *verb* 1 RESOLVE, work out, put an end to, straighten out, set to rights 2 PAY, clear, square (up), discharge 3 MOVE TO, take up residence in, live in, dwell in, inhabit, reside in, set up home in, put down roots in, make your home in 4 COLONIZE, populate, people, pioneer 5 MAKE COMFORTABLE, bed down 6 SUBSIDE, fall, sink, decline 7 LAND, alight, descend, light, come to rest 8 CALM, quiet, relax, relieve, reassure, compose, soothe, lull, quell, allay, sedate, pacify, quieten, tranquillize << ANTONYM disturb >> **settle on** *or* **upon something** *or* **someone** DECIDE ON, choose, pick, select, adopt, agree on, opt for, fix on, elect for

settlement *noun* 1 AGREEMENT, arrangement, resolution, working out, conclusion, establishment, adjustment, confirmation, completion, disposition, termination 2 PAYMENT, clearing, discharge, clearance, defrayal 3 COLONY, community, outpost, peopling, hamlet, encampment, colonization, kainga *or* kaika (*NZ*)

settler *noun* COLONIST, immigrant, pioneer, colonizer, frontiersman

setup *noun* (*informal*) ARRANGEMENT, system, structure, organization, conditions, circumstances, regime

sever *verb* 1 CUT, separate, split, part, divide, rend, detach, disconnect, cleave, bisect, disunite, cut in two, sunder, disjoin << ANTONYM join 2 DISCONTINUE, terminate, break off, abandon, dissolve, put an end to, dissociate << ANTONYM continue

several *adjective* VARIOUS, different, diverse, divers (*archaic*), assorted, disparate, indefinite, sundry

severe *adjective* 1 SERIOUS, critical, terrible, desperate, alarming, extreme, awful, distressing, appalling, drastic, catastrophic, woeful, ruinous 2 ACUTE, extreme, intense, burning, violent, piercing, racking, searing, tormenting, exquisite, harrowing, unbearable, agonizing, insufferable, torturous, unendurable 3 TOUGH, hard, difficult, taxing, demanding, fierce, punishing, exacting, rigorous, stringent, arduous, unrelenting << ANTONYM easy 4 STRICT, hard, harsh, cruel, rigid, relentless, drastic, oppressive, austere, Draconian, unrelenting, inexorable, pitiless, unbending, iron-handed << ANTONYM lenient 5 GRIM, serious, grave, cold, forbidding, stern, sober, disapproving, dour, unsmiling, flinty, strait-laced, tight-lipped << ANTONYM genial 6 PLAIN, simple, austere, classic, restrained, functional, Spartan, ascetic, unadorned, unfussy, unembellished << ANTONYM fancy 7 HARSH, cutting, biting, scathing, satirical, caustic, astringent, vitriolic, mordant, unsparing, mordacious << ANTONYM kind

severely *adverb* 1 SERIOUSLY, badly, extremely, gravely, hard, sorely, dangerously, critically, acutely 2 STRICTLY, harshly, sternly, rigorously, sharply, like a ton of bricks (*informal*), with an iron hand, with a rod of iron

severity *noun* STRICTNESS, seriousness, harshness, austerity, rigour, toughness, hardness, stringency, sternness, severeness

sew *verb* STITCH, tack, seam, hem

sex *noun* 1 GENDER 2 FACTS OF LIFE, sexuality, reproduction, the birds and the bees (*informal*) 3 (*informal*) LOVEMAKING, sexual relations, copulation, the other (*informal*), screwing (*taboo slang*), intimacy, going to bed (with someone), shagging (*Brit taboo slang*), nookie (*slang*), fornication, coitus, rumpy-pumpy (*slang*), legover (*slang*), coition, rumpo (*slang*)

sex appeal *noun* DESIRABILITY, attractiveness, allure, glamour, sensuality, magnetism, sexiness (*informal*), oomph (*informal*), it (*informal*), voluptuousness, seductiveness

sexual *adjective* 1 CARNAL, erotic, intimate, of the flesh, coital 2 SEXY, erotic, sensual, inviting, bedroom, provoking, arousing, naughty, provocative, seductive, sensuous, suggestive, voluptuous, slinky, titillating, flirtatious, come-hither (*informal*), kissable, beddable

sexual intercourse *noun* COPULATION, sex (*informal*), the other (*informal*), union, coupling, congress, mating, commerce (*archaic*), screwing (*taboo slang*), intimacy, penetration, shagging (*Brit taboo slang*), nookie (*slang*), consummation, bonking (*informal*), coitus, carnal knowledge, rumpy-pumpy (*slang*), legover (*slang*), coition

sexuality *noun* DESIRE, lust, eroticism, sensuality, virility, sexiness (*informal*), voluptuousness, carnality, bodily appetites

sexy *adjective* EROTIC, sensual, seductive, inviting, bedroom, provoking, arousing, naughty, provocative, sensuous, suggestive, voluptuous, slinky, titillating, flirtatious, come-hither (*informal*), kissable, beddable

shabby *adjective* 1 TATTY, worn, ragged, scruffy, faded, frayed, worn-out, tattered,

threadbare, down at heel, the worse for
wear, having seen better days << ANTONYM
smart **2** RUN-DOWN, seedy, mean, neglected,
dilapidated **3** MEAN, low, rotten (*informal*),
cheap, dirty, shameful, low-down (*informal*),
shoddy, unworthy, despicable, contemptible,
scurvy, dishonourable, ignoble,
ungentlemanly << ANTONYM fair

shack *noun* HUT, cabin, shanty, lean-to, dump
(*informal*), hovel, shiel (*Scot*), shieling (*Scot*),
whare (*NZ*)

shackle *verb* **1** HAMPER, limit, restrict,
restrain, hamstring, inhibit, constrain,
obstruct, impede, encumber, tie (someone's)
hands **2** FETTER, chain, handcuff, secure,
bind, hobble, manacle, trammel, put in
irons ▷ *noun often plural* FETTER, chain, iron,
bond, handcuff, hobble, manacle, leg-iron,
gyve (*archaic*)

shade *noun* **1** HUE, tone, colour, tint
2 SHADOW, screen, shadows, coolness,
shadiness **3** DASH, trace, hint, suggestion,
suspicion, small amount, semblance
4 NUANCE, difference, degree, graduation,
subtlety **5** SCREEN, covering, cover, blind,
curtain, shield, veil, canopy **6** (*literary*)
GHOST, spirit, shadow, phantom, spectre,
manes, apparition, eidolon, kehua (*NZ*) ▷
verb **1** DARKEN, shadow, cloud, dim, cast a
shadow over, shut out the light **2** COVER,
protect, screen, hide, shield, conceal,
obscure, veil, mute

shadow *noun* **1** SILHOUETTE, shape, outline,
profile **2** SHADE, dimness, darkness, gloom,
cover, protection, shelter, dusk, obscurity,
gloaming (*Scot poetic*), gathering darkness
▷ *verb* **1** SHADE, screen, shield, darken,
overhang, cast a shadow over **2** FOLLOW, dog,
tail (*informal*), trail, stalk, spy on

shadowy *adjective* **1** DARK, shaded, dim,
gloomy, shady, obscure, murky, dusky,
funereal, crepuscular, tenebrous, tenebrious
2 VAGUE, indistinct, faint, ghostly,
obscure, dim, phantom, imaginary, unreal,
intangible, illusory, spectral, undefined,
nebulous, dreamlike, impalpable,
unsubstantial, wraithlike

shady *adjective* **1** SHADED, cool, shadowy, dim,
leafy, bowery, bosky (*literary*), umbrageous
<< ANTONYM sunny **2** (*informal*) CROOKED,
dodgy (*Brit, Austral & NZ informal*), unethical,
suspect, suspicious, dubious, slippery,
questionable, unscrupulous, fishy (*informal*),
shifty, disreputable, untrustworthy, shonky
(*Austral & NZ informal*) << ANTONYM honest

shaft *noun* **1** TUNNEL, hole, passage, burrow,
passageway, channel **2** HANDLE, staff, pole,
rod, stem, upright, baton, shank **3** RAY,
beam, gleam, streak

shaggy *adjective* UNKEMPT, rough, tousled,
hairy, long-haired, hirsute, unshorn
<< ANTONYM smooth

shake *verb* **1** JIGGLE, agitate, joggle **2** TREMBLE,
shiver, quake, shudder, quiver **3** ROCK, sway,
shudder, wobble, waver, totter, oscillate
4 WAVE, wield, flourish, brandish **5** UPSET,
shock, frighten, disturb, distress, move,
rattle (*informal*), intimidate, unnerve,
discompose, traumatize **6** UNDERMINE,
threaten, disable, weaken, impair, sap,
debilitate, subvert, pull the rug out
from under (*informal*) ▷ *noun* VIBRATION,
trembling, quaking, shock, jar, disturbance,
jerk, shiver, shudder, jolt, tremor, agitation,
convulsion, pulsation, jounce ▷▷ **shake**
someone off LEAVE BEHIND, lose, get rid of,
get away from, elude, get rid of, throw off,
get shot of (*slang*), rid yourself of, give the
slip ▷▷ **shake someone up** (*informal*) UPSET,
shock, frighten, disturb, distress, rattle
(*informal*), unsettle, unnerve, discompose
▷▷ **shake something off** GET RID OF, lose,
recuperate from ▷▷ **shake something up**
RESTRUCTURE, reorganize, mix, overturn,
churn (up), turn upside down

shaky *adjective* **1** UNSTABLE, weak, precarious,
tottering, rickety << ANTONYM stable
2 UNSTEADY, faint, trembling, faltering,
wobbly, tremulous, quivery, all of a quiver
(*informal*) **3** UNCERTAIN, suspect, dubious,
questionable, unreliable, unsound, iffy
(*informal*), unsupported, undependable
<< ANTONYM reliable

shallow *adjective* SUPERFICIAL, surface, empty,
slight, foolish, idle, trivial, meaningless,
flimsy, frivolous, skin-deep << ANTONYM
deep

sham *noun* FRAUD, imitation, hoax, pretence,
forgery, counterfeit, pretender, humbug,
impostor, feint, pseud (*informal*), wolf in
sheep's clothing, imposture, phoney *or*
phony (*informal*) << ANTONYM the real thing
▷ *adjective* FALSE, artificial, bogus, pretended,
mock, synthetic, imitation, simulated,
pseudo (*informal*), counterfeit, feigned,
spurious, ersatz, pseud (*informal*), phoney *or*
phony (*informal*) << ANTONYM real

shambles *noun* **1** CHAOS, mess, disorder,
confusion, muddle, havoc, anarchy, disarray,
madhouse, disorganization **2** MESS, state,

jumble, untidiness

shambling *adjective* CLUMSY, awkward, shuffling, lurching, lumbering, unsteady, ungainly, unco (*Austral slang*)

shambolic *adjective* (*informal*) DISORGANIZED, disordered, chaotic, confused, muddled, inefficient, anarchic, topsy-turvy, at sixes and sevens, in total disarray, unsystematic

shame *noun* **1** EMBARRASSMENT, humiliation, chagrin, ignominy, compunction, mortification, loss of face, abashment << ANTONYM shamelessness **2** DISGRACE, scandal, discredit, contempt, smear, degradation, disrepute, reproach, derision, dishonour, infamy, opprobrium, odium, ill repute, obloquy << ANTONYM honour ▷ *verb* **1** EMBARRASS, disgrace, humiliate, humble, disconcert, mortify, take (someone) down a peg (*informal*), abash << ANTONYM make proud **2** DISHONOUR, discredit, degrade, stain, smear, blot, debase, defile << ANTONYM honour ▷▷ **put something or someone to shame** SHOW UP, disgrace, eclipse, surpass, outstrip, outclass

shameful *adjective* DISGRACEFUL, outrageous, scandalous, mean, low, base, infamous, indecent, degrading, vile, wicked, atrocious, unworthy, reprehensible, ignominious, dastardly, unbecoming, dishonourable << ANTONYM admirable

shameless *adjective* BRAZEN, audacious, flagrant, abandoned, corrupt, hardened, indecent, brash, improper, depraved, wanton, unabashed, profligate, unashamed, incorrigible, insolent, unprincipled, impudent, dissolute, reprobate, immodest, barefaced, unblushing

shanty *noun* SHACK, shed, cabin, hut, lean-to, hovel, shiel (*Scot*), bothy (*Scot*), shieling (*Scot*)

shape *noun* **1** APPEARANCE, form, aspect, guise, likeness, semblance **2** FORM, profile, outline, lines, build, cut, figure, silhouette, configuration, contours **3** PATTERN, model, frame, mould **4** CONDITION, state, health, trim, kilter, fettle ▷ *verb* **1** FORM, make, produce, create, model, fashion, mould **2** MOULD, form, make, fashion, model, frame

shapeless *adjective* FORMLESS, irregular, amorphous, unstructured, misshapen, asymmetrical << ANTONYM well-formed

shapely *adjective* WELL-FORMED, elegant, trim, neat, graceful, well-turned, curvaceous, sightly, comely, well-proportioned

share *noun* PART, portion, quota, ration, lot, cut (*informal*), due, division, contribution, proportion, allowance, whack (*informal*), allotment ▷ *verb* **1** DIVIDE, split, distribute, assign, apportion, parcel out, divvy up (*informal*) **2** GO HALVES ON, go fifty-fifty on (*informal*), go Dutch on (*informal*)

sharp *adjective* **1** KEEN, cutting, sharpened, honed, jagged, knife-edged, razor-sharp, serrated, knifelike << ANTONYM blunt **2** QUICK-WITTED, clever, astute, knowing, ready, quick, bright, alert, subtle, penetrating, apt, discerning, on the ball (*informal*), perceptive, observant, long-headed << ANTONYM dim **3** CUTTING, biting, severe, bitter, harsh, scathing, acrimonious, barbed, hurtful, sarcastic, sardonic, caustic, vitriolic, trenchant, mordant, mordacious, acerb << ANTONYM gentle **4** SUDDEN, marked, abrupt, extreme, distinct << ANTONYM gradual **5** CLEAR, distinct, clear-cut, well-defined, crisp << ANTONYM indistinct **6** SOUR, tart, pungent, hot, burning, acid, acerbic, acrid, piquant, acetic, vinegary, acerb << ANTONYM bland **7** (*informal*) STYLISH, smart, fashionable, trendy (*informal*), chic, classy (*slang*), snappy, natty (*informal*), dressy, schmick (*Austral informal*) **8** ACUTE, violent, severe, intense, painful, shooting, distressing, stabbing, fierce, stinging, piercing, sore, excruciating, gut-wrenching ▷ *adverb* PROMPTLY, precisely, exactly, on time, on the dot, punctually << ANTONYM approximately **sharpen** *verb* MAKE SHARP, hone, whet, grind, edge, strop, put an edge on

shatter *verb* **1** SMASH, break, burst, split, crack, crush, explode, demolish, shiver, implode, pulverize, crush to smithereens **2** DESTROY, ruin, wreck, blast, disable, overturn, demolish, impair, blight, torpedo, bring to nought **3** DEVASTATE, shock, stun, crush, overwhelm, upset, break (someone's) heart, knock the stuffing out of (someone) (*informal*), traumatize

shattered *adjective* **1** DEVASTATED, crushed, upset, gutted (*slang*) **2** (*informal*) EXHAUSTED, drained, worn out, spent, done in (*informal*), all in (*slang*), wiped out (*informal*), weary, knackered (*slang*), clapped out (*Brit, Austral & NZ informal*), tired out, ready to drop, dog-tired (*informal*), zonked (*slang*), dead tired (*informal*), dead beat (*informal*), shagged out (*Brit slang*), jiggered (*informal*)

shattering *adjective* DEVASTATING, stunning, severe, crushing, overwhelming, paralysing shave *verb* 1 TRIM, crop 2 SCRAPE, plane, trim, shear, pare 3 BRUSH PAST, touch, graze

shed¹ *noun* HUT, shack, lean-to, outhouse, lockup, bothy (*chiefly Scot*), whare (*NZ*)

shed² *verb* 1 DROP, spill, scatter 2 CAST OFF, discard, moult, slough off, exuviate 3 GIVE OUT, cast, emit, give, throw, afford, radiate, diffuse, pour forth

sheen *noun* SHINE, gleam, gloss, polish, brightness, lustre, burnish, patina, shininess

sheepish *adjective* EMBARRASSED, uncomfortable, ashamed, silly, foolish, self-conscious, chagrined, mortified, abashed, shamefaced << ANTONYM unembarrassed

sheer *adjective* 1 TOTAL, complete, absolute, utter, rank, pure, downright, unqualified, out-and-out, unadulterated, unmitigated, thoroughgoing, unalloyed, arrant << ANTONYM moderate 2 STEEP, abrupt, perpendicular, precipitous << ANTONYM gradual 3 FINE, thin, transparent, see-through, gossamer, diaphanous, gauzy << ANTONYM thick

sheet *noun* 1 PAGE, leaf, folio, piece of paper 2 PLATE, piece, panel, slab, pane 3 COAT, film, layer, membrane, surface, stratum, veneer, overlay, lamina 4 EXPANSE, area, stretch, sweep, covering, blanket

shell *noun* 1 HUSK, case, pod, shuck 2 CARAPACE, armour 3 FRAME, structure, hull, framework, skeleton, chassis ▷ *verb* 1 REMOVE THE SHELLS FROM, husk, shuck (*US*) 2 BOMB, barrage, bombard, attack, strike, blitz, strafe ▷▷ shell something out (*informal*) PAY OUT, fork out (*slang*), expend, give, hand over, lay out (*informal*), disburse, ante up (*informal, chiefly US*)

shelter *noun* 1 COVER, screen, awning, shiel (*Scot*) 2 PROTECTION, safety, refuge, cover, security, defence, sanctuary 3 REFUGE, haven, sanctuary, retreat, asylum ▷ *verb* 1 TAKE SHELTER, hide, seek refuge, take cover 2 PROTECT, shield, harbour, safeguard, cover, hide, guard, defend, take in << ANTONYM endanger

sheltered *adjective* 1 SCREENED, covered, protected, shielded, secluded << ANTONYM exposed 2 PROTECTED, screened, shielded, quiet, withdrawn, isolated, secluded, cloistered, reclusive, ensconced, hermitic, conventual

shelve *verb* POSTPONE, put off, defer, table (*US*), dismiss, freeze, suspend, put aside, hold over, mothball, pigeonhole, lay aside, put on ice, put on the back burner (*informal*),

hold in abeyance, take a rain check on (*US & Canad informal*)

shepherd *noun* DROVER, stockman, herdsman, grazier ▷ *verb* GUIDE, conduct, steer, convoy, herd, marshal, usher

sherang *noun* (*Austral & NZ*) BOSS, manager, head, leader, director, chief, executive, owner, master, governor (*informal*), employer, administrator, supervisor, superintendent, gaffer (*informal, chiefly Brit*), foreman, overseer, kingpin, big cheese (*old-fashioned slang*), baas (*S African*), numero uno (*informal*), Mister Big (*slang, chiefly US*)

shield *noun* 1 PROTECTION, cover, defence, screen, guard, ward (*archaic*), shelter, safeguard, aegis, rampart, bulwark 2 BUCKLER, escutcheon (*heraldry*), targe (*archaic*) ▷ *verb* PROTECT, cover, screen, guard, defend, shelter, safeguard

shift *verb* 1 MOVE, drift, move around, veer, budge, swerve, change position 2 REMOVE, move, transfer, displace, relocate, rearrange, transpose, reposition ▷ *noun* 1 CHANGE, switch, shifting, modification, alteration, displacement, about-turn, permutation, fluctuation 2 MOVE, transfer, removal, veering, rearrangement

shifty *adjective* (*informal*) UNTRUSTWORTHY, sly, devious, scheming, tricky, slippery, contriving, wily, crafty, evasive, furtive, deceitful, underhand, unprincipled, duplicitous, fly-by-night (*informal*) << ANTONYM honest

shimmer *verb* GLEAM, twinkle, glimmer, dance, glisten, scintillate ▷ *noun* GLEAM, glimmer, iridescence, unsteady light

shine *verb* 1 GLEAM, flash, beam, glow, sparkle, glitter, glare, shimmer, radiate, twinkle, glimmer, glisten, emit light, give off light, scintillate 2 POLISH, buff, burnish, brush, rub up 3 BE OUTSTANDING, stand out, excel, star, be distinguished, steal the show, be conspicuous, be pre-eminent, stand out in a crowd ▷ *noun* 1 POLISH, gloss, sheen, glaze, lustre, patina 2 BRIGHTNESS, light, sparkle, radiance

shining *adjective* 1 OUTSTANDING, glorious, splendid, leading, celebrated, brilliant, distinguished, eminent, conspicuous, illustrious 2 BRIGHT, brilliant, gleaming, beaming, sparkling, glittering, shimmering, radiant, luminous, glistening, resplendent, aglow, effulgent, incandescent

shiny *adjective* BRIGHT, gleaming, glossy, glistening, polished, burnished, lustrous, satiny, sheeny, agleam

ship *noun* VESSEL, boat, craft

shirk *verb* **1** DODGE, avoid, evade, get out of, duck (out of) (*informal*), shun, sidestep, body-swerve (*Scot*), bob off (*Brit slang*), scrimshank (*Brit military slang*) **2** SKIVE (*Brit slang*), slack, idle, malinger, swing the lead, gold-brick (*US slang*), bob off (*Brit slang*), bludge (*Austral & NZ informal*), scrimshank (*Brit military slang*)

shiver *verb* SHUDDER, shake, tremble, quake, quiver, palpitate ▷ *noun* TREMBLE, shudder, quiver, thrill, trembling, flutter, tremor, frisson (*French*) ▷▷ **the shivers** THE SHAKES, a chill (*informal*), goose pimples, goose flesh, chattering teeth

shock *noun* **1** UPSET, blow, trauma, bombshell, turn (*informal*), distress, disturbance, consternation, whammy (*informal, chiefly US*), state of shock, rude awakening, bolt from the blue, prostration **2** IMPACT, blow, jolt, clash, encounter, jarring, collision **3** START, scare, fright, turn, jolt ▷ *verb* **1** SHAKE, stun, stagger, jar, shake up (*informal*), paralyse, numb, jolt, stupefy, shake out of your complacency **2** HORRIFY, appal, disgust, outrage, offend, revolt, unsettle, sicken, agitate, disquiet, nauseate, raise someone's eyebrows, scandalize, gross out (*US slang*), traumatize, give (someone) a turn (*informal*)

shocking *adjective* **1** (*informal*) TERRIBLE, appalling, dreadful, bad, fearful, dire, horrendous, ghastly, from hell (*informal*), deplorable, abysmal, frightful, godawful (*slang*) **2** APPALLING, outrageous, disgraceful, offensive, distressing, disgusting, horrible, dreadful, horrifying, revolting, obscene, sickening, ghastly, hideous, monstrous, scandalous, disquieting, unspeakable, atrocious, repulsive, nauseating, odious, loathsome, abominable, stupefying, hellacious (*US slang*) << ANTONYM wonderful

shoddy *adjective* INFERIOR, poor, second-rate, cheap, tacky (*informal*), tawdry, tatty, trashy, low-rent (*informal, chiefly US*), slipshod, cheapo (*informal*), rubbishy, junky (*informal*), cheap-jack (*informal*), bodger *or* bodgie (*Austral slang*) << ANTONYM excellent

shoemaker *noun* COBBLER, bootmaker, souter (*Scot*)

shoot *verb* **1** OPEN FIRE ON, blast (*slang*), hit, kill, bag, plug (*slang*), bring down, blow away (*slang, chiefly US*), zap (*slang*), pick off, pump full of lead (*slang*) **2** FIRE, launch,

discharge, project, hurl, fling, propel, emit, let fly **3** SPEED, race, rush, charge, fly, spring, tear, flash, dash, barrel (along) (*informal, chiefly US & Canad*), bolt, streak, dart, whisk, whizz (*informal*), hurtle, scoot, burn rubber (*informal*) ▷ *noun* SPROUT, branch, bud, twig, sprig, offshoot, scion, slip

shop *noun* STORE, market, supermarket, mart, boutique, emporium, hypermarket, dairy (*NZ*)

shore *noun* BEACH, coast, sands, strand (*poetic*), lakeside, waterside, seaboard (*chiefly US*), foreshore, seashore

shore up *verb* SUPPORT, strengthen, reinforce, prop, brace, underpin, augment, buttress

short *adjective* **1** BRIEF, fleeting, short-term, short-lived, momentary << ANTONYM long **2** CONCISE, brief, succinct, clipped, summary, compressed, curtailed, terse, laconic, pithy, abridged, compendious, sententious << ANTONYM lengthy **3** SMALL, little, wee, squat, diminutive, petite, dumpy, knee high to a grasshopper, fubsy (*archaic or dialect*), knee high to a gnat << ANTONYM tall **4** ABRUPT, sharp, terse, curt, blunt, crusty, gruff, brusque, offhand, testy, impolite, discourteous, uncivil << ANTONYM polite **5** (*of pastry*) CRUMBLY, crisp, brittle, friable **6** SCARCE, wanting, low, missing, limited, lacking, tight, slim, inadequate, insufficient, slender, scant, meagre, sparse, deficient, scanty << ANTONYM plentiful ▷ *adverb* ABRUPTLY, suddenly, unaware, by surprise, without warning << ANTONYM gradually

shortage *noun* DEFICIENCY, want, lack, failure, deficit, poverty, shortfall, inadequacy, scarcity, dearth, paucity, insufficiency << ANTONYM abundance

shortcoming *noun* FAILING, fault, weakness, defect, flaw, drawback, imperfection, frailty, foible, weak point

shorten *verb* **1** CUT, reduce, decrease, cut down, trim, diminish, dock, cut back, prune, lessen, curtail, abbreviate, truncate, abridge, downsize << ANTONYM increase **2** TURN UP, trim

short-lived *adjective* BRIEF, short, temporary, fleeting, passing, transient, ephemeral, transitory, impermanent

shortly *adverb* **1** SOON, presently, before long, anon (*archaic*), in a little while, any minute now, erelong (*archaic or poetic*) **2** CURTLY, sharply, abruptly, tartly, tersely, succinctly, briefly, concisely, in a few words

short-sighted *adjective* **1** NEAR-SIGHTED, myopic, blind as a bat **2** IMPRUDENT, injudicious, ill-advised, unthinking, careless, impractical, ill-considered, improvident, impolitic, seeing no further than (the end of) your nose

shot *noun* **1** DISCHARGE, report, gunfire, crack, blast, explosion, bang **2** AMMUNITION, bullet, slug, pellet, projectile, lead, ball **3** MARKSMAN, shooter, markswoman **4** STRIKE, throw, lob **5** (*informal*) ATTEMPT, go (*informal*), try, turn, chance, effort, opportunity, crack (*informal*), essay, stab (*informal*), endeavour ▷▷ **a shot in the arm** (*informal*) BOOST, lift, encouragement, stimulus, impetus, fillip, geeing-up ▷▷ **have a shot** (*informal*) MAKE AN ATTEMPT, have a go, try, have a crack (*informal*), try your luck, have a stab (*informal*), have a bash (*informal*), tackle ▷▷ **like a shot** AT ONCE, immediately, in a flash, quickly, eagerly, unhesitatingly, like a bat out of hell (*slang*)

shoulder *verb* **1** BEAR, carry, take on, accept, assume, be responsible for, take upon yourself **2** PUSH, thrust, elbow, shove, jostle, press ▷▷ **give someone the cold shoulder** (*informal*) SNUB, ignore, blank (*slang*), put down, shun, rebuff, kick in the teeth (*slang*), ostracize, send someone to Coventry, cut (*informal*) ▷▷ **rub shoulders with someone** (*informal*) MIX WITH, associate with, consort with, hobnob with, socialize with, fraternize with ▷▷ **shoulder to shoulder 1** SIDE BY SIDE, abreast, next to each other **2** TOGETHER, united, jointly, as one, in partnership, in cooperation, in unity

shout *verb* CRY (OUT), call (out), yell, scream, roar, shriek, bellow, bawl, holler (*informal*), raise your voice ▷ *noun* CRY, call, yell, scream, roar, shriek, bellow ▷▷ **shout someone down** DROWN OUT, overwhelm, drown, silence

shove *verb* PUSH, shoulder, thrust, elbow, drive, press, crowd, propel, jostle, impel ▷ *noun* PUSH, knock, thrust, elbow, bump, nudge, jostle ▷▷ **shove off** (*informal*) GO AWAY, leave, clear off (*informal*), depart, go to hell (*informal*), push off (*informal*), slope off, pack your bags (*informal*), scram (*informal*), get on your bike (*Brit slang*), take yourself off, vamoose (*slang, chiefly US*), sling your hook (*Brit slang*), rack off (*Austral & NZ slang*)

shovel *noun* SPADE, scoop ▷ *verb* **1** MOVE, scoop, dredge, shift, load, heap **2** STUFF, spoon, ladle

show *verb* **1** INDICATE, demonstrate, prove, reveal, display, evidence, point out, manifest, testify to, evince << ANTONYM disprove **2** DISPLAY, exhibit, put on display, present, put on show, put before the public **3** GUIDE, lead, conduct, accompany, direct, steer, escort **4** DEMONSTRATE, describe, explain, teach, illustrate, instruct **5** BE VISIBLE << ANTONYM be invisible **6** EXPRESS, display, reveal, indicate, register, demonstrate, disclose, manifest, divulge, make known, evince << ANTONYM hide **7** (*informal*) TURN UP, come, appear, arrive, attend, show up (*informal*), put in *or* make an appearance **8** BROADCAST, transmit, air, beam, relay, televise, put on the air ▷ *noun* **1** DISPLAY, view, sight, spectacle, array **2** EXHIBITION, fair, display, parade, expo (*informal*), exposition, pageant, pageantry **3** APPEARANCE, display, pose, profession, parade, ostentation **4** PRETENCE, appearance, semblance, illusion, pretext, likeness, affectation **5** PROGRAMME, broadcast, presentation, production **6** ENTERTAINMENT, performance, play, production, drama, musical, presentation, theatrical performance ▷▷ **show off** (*informal*) BOAST, brag, blow your own trumpet, swagger, hot-dog (*chiefly US*), strut your stuff (*chiefly US*), make a spectacle of yourself ▷▷ **show someone up** (*informal*) EMBARRASS, shame, let down, mortify, put to shame, show in a bad light ▷▷ **show something off** EXHIBIT, display, parade, advertise, demonstrate, spread out, flaunt ▷▷ **show something up** REVEAL, expose, highlight, pinpoint, unmask, lay bare, put the spotlight on

showdown *noun* (*informal*) CONFRONTATION, crisis, clash, moment of truth, face-off (*slang*)

shower *noun* **1** DELUGE, downpour **2** PROFUSION, plethora ▷ *verb* **1** COVER, dust, spray, sprinkle **2** INUNDATE, load, heap, lavish, pour, deluge

showing *noun* **1** DISPLAY, staging, presentation, exhibition, demonstration **2** PERFORMANCE, demonstration, track record, show, appearance, impression, account of yourself

showman *noun* PERFORMER, entertainer, artiste, player, Thespian, trouper, play-actor, actor *or* actress

show-off *noun* (*informal*) EXHIBITIONIST, boaster, swaggerer, hot dog (*chiefly US*), poseur, egotist, braggart, braggadocio, peacock, figjam (*Austral slang*)

showy *adjective* OSTENTATIOUS, flamboyant, flashy, flash (*informal*), loud, over the top (*informal*), brash, pompous, pretentious, gaudy, garish, tawdry, splashy (*informal*), tinselly << ANTONYM tasteful

shred *noun* **1** STRIP, bit, piece, scrap, fragment, rag, ribbon, snippet, sliver, tatter **2** PARTICLE, trace, scrap, grain, atom, jot, whit, iota

shrew *noun* NAG, fury, dragon (*informal*), spitfire, virago, vixen, harpy, harridan, termagant (*rare*), scold, Xanthippe

shrewd *adjective* ASTUTE, clever, sharp, knowing, fly (*slang*), keen, acute, smart, calculated, calculating, intelligent, discriminating, cunning, discerning, sly, canny, perceptive, wily, crafty, artful, far-sighted, far-seeing, long-headed, perspicacious, sagacious << ANTONYM naive

shrewdly *adverb* ASTUTELY, perceptively, cleverly, knowingly, artfully, cannily, with consummate skill, sagaciously, far-sightedly, perspicaciously, with all your wits about you

shriek *verb* SCREAM, cry, yell, howl, wail, whoop, screech, squeal, holler ▷ *noun* SCREAM, cry, yell, howl, wail, whoop, screech, squeal, holler

shrill *adjective* PIERCING, high, sharp, acute, piping, penetrating, screeching, high-pitched, ear-splitting, ear-piercing << ANTONYM deep

shrink *verb* DECREASE, dwindle, lessen, grow or get smaller, contract, narrow, diminish, fall off, shorten, wrinkle, wither, drop off, deflate, shrivel, downsize << ANTONYM grow

shrivel *verb* WITHER, dry (up), wilt, shrink, wrinkle, dwindle, dehydrate, desiccate, wizen

shrivelled *adjective* WITHERED, dry, dried up, wrinkled, shrunken, wizened, desiccated, sere (*archaic*)

shroud *noun* **1** WINDING SHEET, grave clothes, cerecloth, cerement **2** COVERING, veil, mantle, screen, cloud, pall ▷ *verb* CONCEAL, cover, screen, hide, blanket, veil, cloak, swathe, envelop

shudder *verb* SHIVER, shake, tremble, quake, quiver, convulse ▷ *noun* SHIVER, trembling, tremor, quiver, spasm, convulsion

shuffle *verb* **1** SHAMBLE, stagger, stumble, dodder **2** SCUFFLE, drag, scrape, scuff **3** REARRANGE, jumble, mix, shift, disorder, disarrange, intermix

shun *verb* AVOID, steer clear of, keep away from, evade, eschew, shy away from, cold-shoulder, have no part in, fight shy of, give

(someone *or* something) a wide berth, body-swerve (*Scot*)

shut *verb* CLOSE, secure, fasten, bar, seal, slam, push to, draw to << ANTONYM open ▷ *adjective* CLOSED, fastened, sealed, locked << ANTONYM open ▷▷ **shut down** STOP WORK, halt work, cease operating, close down, cease trading, discontinue ▷▷ **shut someone out** EXCLUDE, bar, keep out, black, lock out, ostracize, debar, blackball ▷▷ **shut someone up 1** (*informal*) SILENCE, gag, hush, muzzle, fall silent, button it (*slang*), pipe down (*slang*), hold your tongue, put a sock in it (*Brit slang*), keep your trap shut (*slang*), cut the cackle (*informal*), button your lip (*slang*) **2** CONFINE, cage, imprison, keep in, box in, intern, incarcerate, coop up, immure ▷▷ **shut something in** CONFINE, cage, enclose, imprison, impound, pound, wall off *or* up ▷▷ **shut something out** BLOCK OUT, screen, hide, cover, mask, veil

shuttle *verb* GO BACK AND FORTH, commute, go to and fro, alternate, ply, shunt, seesaw

shy *adjective* **1** TIMID, self-conscious, bashful, reserved, retiring, nervous, modest, shrinking, backward, coy, reticent, self-effacing, diffident, mousy << ANTONYM confident **2** CAUTIOUS, wary, hesitant, suspicious, reticent, distrustful, chary << ANTONYM reckless ▷ *verb sometimes with* **off** *or* **away** RECOIL, flinch, draw back, start, rear, buck, wince, swerve, balk, quail, take fright

shyness *noun* TIMIDITY, self-consciousness, bashfulness, modesty, nervousness, lack of confidence, reticence, diffidence, timorousness, mousiness, timidness

sick *adjective* **1** UNWELL, ill, poorly (*informal*), diseased, weak, crook (*Austral & NZ informal*), under par (*informal*), ailing, feeble, laid up (*informal*), under the weather, indisposed, on the sick list (*informal*) << ANTONYM well **2** NAUSEOUS, ill, queasy, nauseated, green about the gills (*informal*), qualmish **3** (*informal*) TIRED, bored, fed up, weary, jaded, blasé, satiated **4** (*informal*) MORBID, cruel, sadistic, black, macabre, ghoulish

sicken *verb* **1** DISGUST, revolt, nauseate, repel, gross out (*US slang*), turn your stomach, make your gorge rise **2** FALL ILL, take sick, ail, go down with something, contract something, be stricken by something

sickening *adjective* DISGUSTING, revolting, vile, offensive, foul, distasteful, repulsive, nauseating, loathsome, nauseous, gut-wrenching, putrid, stomach-turning (*informal*), cringe-making (*Brit informal*), noisome, yucky *or* yukky (*slang*), yucko (*Austral slang*) << ANTONYM delightful

sickly *adjective* 1 UNHEALTHY, weak, delicate, ailing, feeble, infirm, in poor health, indisposed 2 PALE, wan, pasty, bloodless, pallid, sallow, ashen-faced, waxen, peaky 3 NAUSEATING, revolting (*informal*), cloying, icky (*informal*) 4 SENTIMENTAL, romantic, sloppy (*informal*), corny (*slang*), mushy (*informal*), weepy (*informal*), slushy (*informal*), mawkish, tear-jerking (*informal*), schmaltzy (*slang*), gushy (*informal*)

sickness *noun* 1 ILLNESS, disorder, ailment, disease, complaint, bug (*informal*), affliction, malady, infirmity, indisposition, lurgy (*informal*) 2 NAUSEA, queasiness 3 VOMITING, nausea, upset stomach, throwing up, puking (*slang*), retching, barfing (*US slang*)

side *noun* 1 BORDER, margin, boundary, verge, flank, rim, perimeter, periphery, edge << ANTONYM middle 2 FACE, surface, facet 3 HALF, part 4 DISTRICT, area, region, quarter, sector, neighbourhood, vicinity, locality, locale, neck of the woods (*informal*) 5 PARTY, camp, faction, cause 6 POINT OF VIEW, viewpoint, position, opinion, angle, slant, standpoint 7 TEAM, squad, crew, line-up 8 ASPECT, feature, angle, facet ▷ *adjective* SUBORDINATE, minor, secondary, subsidiary, lesser, marginal, indirect, incidental, ancillary << ANTONYM main ▷▷ **side with someone** SUPPORT, back, champion, agree with, stand up for, second, favour, defend, team up with (*informal*), go along with, befriend, join with, sympathize with, be loyal to, take the part of, associate yourself with, ally yourself with

sidestep *verb* AVOID, dodge, evade, duck (*informal*), skirt, skip, bypass, elude, circumvent, find a way round, body-swerve (*Scot*)

sidetrack *verb* DISTRACT, divert, lead off the subject, deflect

sidewalk *noun* (*US & Canad*) PAVEMENT, footpath (*Austral & NZ*)

sideways *adverb* 1 INDIRECTLY, obliquely 2 TO THE SIDE, laterally, crabwise ▷ *adjective* SIDELONG, side, slanted, oblique

sidle *verb* EDGE, steal, slink, inch, creep, sneak

siesta *noun* NAP, rest, sleep, doze, kip (*Brit slang*), snooze (*informal*), catnap, forty winks (*informal*), zizz (*Brit informal*)

sieve *noun* STRAINER, sifter, colander, screen, riddle, tammy cloth ▷ *verb* SIFT, filter, strain, separate, pan, bolt, riddle

sift *verb* 1 PART, filter, strain, separate, pan, bolt, riddle, sieve 2 EXAMINE, investigate, go through, research, screen, probe, analyse, work over, pore over, scrutinize

sigh *verb* 1 BREATHE OUT, exhale, moan, suspire (*archaic*) 2 MOAN, complain, groan, grieve, lament, sorrow ▷▷ **sigh for something** *or* **someone** LONG FOR, yearn for, pine for, mourn for, languish over, eat your heart out over

sight *noun* 1 VISION, eyes, eyesight, seeing, eye 2 SPECTACLE, show, scene, display, exhibition, vista, pageant 3 VIEW, field of vision, range of vision, eyeshot, viewing, ken, visibility 4 (*informal*) EYESORE, mess, spectacle, fright (*informal*), monstrosity, blot on the landscape (*informal*) ▷ *verb* SPOT, see, observe, distinguish, perceive, make out, discern, behold

sign *noun* 1 SYMBOL, mark, character, figure, device, representation, logo, badge, emblem, ensign, cipher 2 FIGURE, form, shape, outline 3 GESTURE, signal, motion, indication, cue, gesticulation 4 NOTICE, board, warning, signpost, placard 5 INDICATION, evidence, trace, mark, note, signal, suggestion, symptom, hint, proof, gesture, clue, token, manifestation, giveaway, vestige, spoor 6 OMEN, warning, portent, foreboding, presage, forewarning, writing on the wall, augury, auspice, wake-up call ▷ *verb* 1 GESTURE, indicate, signal, wave, beckon, gesticulate, use sign language 2 AUTOGRAPH, initial, inscribe, subscribe, set your hand to ▷▷ **sign someone up** ENGAGE, recruit, employ, take on, hire, contract, take on board (*informal*), put on the payroll, take into service ▷▷ **sign something away** GIVE UP, relinquish, renounce, lose, transfer, abandon, surrender, dispose of, waive, forgo ▷▷ **sign up** ENLIST, join, volunteer, register, enrol, join up

signal *noun* 1 FLARE, rocket, beam, beacon, smoke signal, signal fire 2 CUE, sign, nod, prompting, go-ahead (*informal*), reminder, green light 3 SIGN, gesture, indication, mark, note, evidence, expression, proof, token, indicator, manifestation ▷ *verb* GESTURE, sign, wave, indicate, nod, motion, beckon, gesticulate, give a sign to

significance *noun* IMPORTANCE, import, consequence, matter, moment, weight, consideration, gravity, relevance, magnitude, impressiveness

significant *adjective* **1** IMPORTANT, notable, serious, material, vital, critical, considerable, momentous, weighty, noteworthy << ANTONYM insignificant **2** MEANINGFUL, expressive, eloquent, knowing, meaning, expressing, pregnant, indicative, suggestive << ANTONYM meaningless

signify *verb* INDICATE, show, mean, matter, suggest, announce, evidence, represent, express, imply, exhibit, communicate, intimate, stand for, proclaim, convey, be a sign of, symbolize, denote, connote, portend, betoken

silence *noun* **1** QUIET, peace, calm, hush, lull, stillness, quiescence, noiselessness << ANTONYM noise **2** RETICENCE, dumbness, taciturnity, speechlessness, muteness, uncommunicativeness << ANTONYM speech ▷ *verb* QUIETEN, still, quiet, cut off, subdue, stifle, cut short, quell, muffle, deaden, strike dumb << ANTONYM make louder

silent *adjective* **1** MUTE, dumb, speechless, wordless, mum, struck dumb, voiceless, unspeaking << ANTONYM noisy **2** UNCOMMUNICATIVE, quiet, taciturn, tongue-tied, unspeaking, nonvocal, not talkative **3** QUIET, still, hushed, soundless, noiseless, muted, stilly (*poetic*) << ANTONYM loud **4** UNSPOKEN, implied, implicit, tacit, understood, unexpressed

silently *adverb* **1** QUIETLY, in silence, soundlessly, noiselessly, inaudibly, without a sound **2** MUTELY, dumbly, in silence, wordlessly, speechlessly

silhouette *noun* OUTLINE, form, shape, profile, delineation ▷ *verb* OUTLINE, delineate, etch

silky *adjective* SMOOTH, soft, sleek, velvety, silken

silly *adjective* **1** STUPID, ridiculous, absurd, daft, inane, childish, immature, senseless, frivolous, preposterous, giddy, goofy (*informal*), idiotic, dozy (*Brit informal*), fatuous, witless, puerile, brainless, asinine, dumb-ass (*slang*), dopy (*slang*) << ANTONYM clever **2** FOOLISH, stupid, unwise, inappropriate, rash, irresponsible, reckless, foolhardy, idiotic, thoughtless, imprudent, inadvisable << ANTONYM sensible ▷ *noun* (*informal*) FOOL, twit (*informal*), goose (*informal*), clot (*Brit informal*), wally (*slang*), prat (*slang*), plonker (*slang*), duffer (*informal*), simpleton, ignoramus, nitwit (*informal*), ninny, silly-billy (*informal*), dweeb (*US slang*),

putz (*US slang*), eejit (*Scot & Irish*), doofus (*slang, chiefly US*), nerd *or* nurd (*slang*), dorba *or* dorb (*Austral slang*), bogan (*Austral slang*)

silt *noun* SEDIMENT, deposit, residue, ooze, sludge, alluvium ▷▷ **silt something up** CLOG UP, block up, choke up, obstruct, stop up, jam up, dam up, bung up, occlude, congest

silver *noun* SILVERWARE, silver plate ▷ *adjective* SNOWY, white, grey, silvery, greyish-white, whitish-grey

similar *adjective* **1** ALIKE, uniform, resembling, corresponding, comparable, much the same, homogeneous, of a piece, homogenous, cut from the same cloth, congruous << ANTONYM different **2** *with* **to** LIKE, much the same as, comparable to, analogous to, close to, cut from the same cloth as

similarity *noun* RESEMBLANCE, likeness, sameness, agreement, relation, correspondence, analogy, affinity, closeness, concordance, congruence, comparability, point of comparison, similitude << ANTONYM difference

similarly *adverb* **1** IN THE SAME WAY, the same, identically, in a similar fashion, uniformly, homogeneously, undistinguishably **2** LIKEWISE, in the same way, by the same token, correspondingly, in like manner

simmer *verb* **1** BUBBLE, stew, boil gently, seethe, cook gently **2** FUME, seethe, smoulder, burn, smart, rage, boil, be angry, see red (*informal*), be tense, be agitated, be uptight (*informal*) ▷▷ **simmer down** (*informal*) CALM DOWN, grow quieter, control yourself, unwind (*informal*), contain yourself, collect yourself, cool off *or* down, get down off your high horse (*informal*)

simper *verb* SMILE COYLY, smirk, smile self-consciously, smile affectedly

simpering *adjective* COY, affected, flirtatious, coquettish, kittenish

simple *adjective* **1** UNCOMPLICATED, clear, plain, understandable, coherent, lucid, recognizable, unambiguous, comprehensible, intelligible, uninvolved << ANTONYM complicated **2** EASY, straightforward, not difficult, light, elementary, manageable, effortless, painless, uncomplicated, undemanding, easy-peasy (*slang*) **3** PLAIN, natural, basic, classic, severe, Spartan, uncluttered, unadorned, unfussy, unembellished << ANTONYM elaborate **4** PURE, mere, sheer, unalloyed **5** ARTLESS, innocent, naive, natural, frank, green, sincere, simplistic, unaffected, childlike, unpretentious, unsophisticated, ingenuous, guileless << ANTONYM sophisticated **6** UNPRETENTIOUS, modest, humble, homely, lowly, rustic, uncluttered, unfussy, unembellished << ANTONYM fancy

simple-minded *adjective* STUPID, simple, foolish, backward, idiot, retarded, idiotic, moronic, brainless, feeble-minded, addle-brained, dead from the neck up (*informal*), a bit lacking (*informal*), dim-witted

simplicity *noun* **1** STRAIGHTFORWARDNESS, ease, clarity, obviousness, easiness, clearness, absence of complications, elementariness << ANTONYM complexity **2** PLAINNESS, restraint, purity, clean lines, naturalness, lack of adornment << ANTONYM elaborateness

simplify *verb* MAKE SIMPLER, facilitate, streamline, disentangle, dumb down, make intelligible, reduce to essentials, declutter

simplistic *adjective* OVERSIMPLIFIED, shallow, facile, naive, oversimple

simply *adverb* **1** JUST, only, merely, purely, solely **2** TOTALLY, really, completely, absolutely, altogether, wholly, utterly, unreservedly **3** CLEARLY, straightforwardly, directly, plainly, intelligibly, unaffectedly **4** PLAINLY, naturally, modestly, with restraint, unpretentiously, without any elaboration **5** WITHOUT DOUBT, surely, certainly, definitely, unquestionably, undeniably, unmistakably, beyond question, beyond a shadow of (a) doubt

simulate *verb* PRETEND, act, feign, affect, assume, put on, reproduce, imitate, sham, fabricate, counterfeit, make believe

simulated *adjective* **1** PRETENDED, put-on, feigned, assumed, artificial, make-believe, insincere, phoney *or* phony (*informal*) **2** SYNTHETIC, artificial, fake, substitute, mock, imitation, man-made, sham, pseudo (*informal*)

simultaneous *adjective* COINCIDING, concurrent, contemporaneous, coincident, synchronous, happening at the same time

simultaneously *adverb* AT THE SAME TIME, together, all together, in concert, in unison, concurrently, in the same breath, in chorus

sin *noun* **1** WICKEDNESS, wrong, evil, crime, error, trespass, immorality, transgression, iniquity, sinfulness, unrighteousness, ungodliness **2** CRIME, offence, misdemeanour, error, wrongdoing, misdeed, transgression, act of evil, guilt ▷ *verb* TRANSGRESS, offend, lapse, err, trespass

(*archaic*), fall from grace, go astray, commit a sin, do wrong

sincere *adjective* HONEST, genuine, real, true, serious, natural, earnest, frank, open, straightforward, candid, no-nonsense, heartfelt, upfront (*informal*), bona fide, wholehearted, dinkum (*Austral & NZ informal*), artless, guileless, unfeigned << ANTONYM false

sincerely *adverb* HONESTLY, really, truly, genuinely, seriously, earnestly, wholeheartedly, in good faith, in earnest, in all sincerity, from the bottom of your heart

sincerity *noun* HONESTY, truth, candour, frankness, seriousness, good faith, probity, bona fides, genuineness, straightforwardness, artlessness, guilelessness, wholeheartedness

sinewy *adjective* MUSCULAR, strong, powerful, athletic, robust, wiry, brawny

sinful *adjective* WICKED, bad, criminal, guilty, corrupt, immoral, erring, unholy, depraved, iniquitous, ungodly, irreligious, unrighteous, morally wrong << ANTONYM virtuous

sing *verb* **1** CROON, carol, chant, warble, yodel, pipe, vocalize **2** TRILL, chirp, warble, make melody ▷▷ **sing out** CALL (OUT), cry (out), shout, yell, holler (*informal*), halloo

singe *verb* BURN, sear, scorch, char

singer *noun* VOCALIST, crooner, minstrel, soloist, cantor, troubadour, chorister, chanteuse (*fem*), balladeer, songster *or* songstress

single *adjective* **1** ONE, sole, lone, solitary, only, only one, unique, singular **2** INDIVIDUAL, particular, separate, distinct **3** UNMARRIED, free, unattached, a bachelor, unwed, a spinster **4** SEPARATE, individual, exclusive, undivided, unshared **5** SIMPLE, unmixed, unblended, uncompounded ▷▷ **single something** *or* **someone out** PICK, choose, select, separate, distinguish, fix on, set apart, winnow, put on one side, pick on *or* out

single-handed *adverb* UNAIDED, on your own, by yourself, alone, independently, solo, without help, unassisted, under your own steam

single-minded *adjective* DETERMINED, dogged, fixed, dedicated, stubborn, tireless, steadfast, unwavering, unswerving, hellbent (*informal*), undeviating, monomaniacal

singly *adverb* ONE BY ONE, individually, one at a time, separately, one after the other

singular *adjective* **1** SINGLE, individual

2 REMARKABLE, unique, extraordinary, outstanding, exceptional, rare, notable, eminent, uncommon, conspicuous, prodigious, unparalleled, noteworthy << ANTONYM ordinary **3** UNUSUAL, odd, strange, extraordinary, puzzling, curious, peculiar, eccentric, out-of-the-way, queer, oddball (*informal*), atypical, wacko (*slang*), outré, daggy (*Austral & NZ informal*) << ANTONYM conventional

singularity *noun* ODDITY, abnormality, eccentricity, peculiarity, strangeness, idiosyncrasy, irregularity, particularity, oddness, queerness, extraordinariness, curiousness

singularly *adverb* REMARKABLY, particularly, exceptionally, especially, seriously (*informal*), surprisingly, notably, unusually, extraordinarily, conspicuously, outstandingly, uncommonly, prodigiously

sinister *adjective* THREATENING, evil, menacing, forbidding, dire, ominous, malign, disquieting, malignant, malevolent, baleful, injurious, bodeful << ANTONYM reassuring

sink *noun* BASIN, washbasin, hand basin, wash-hand basin ▷ *verb* **1** SCUPPER, scuttle **2** GO DOWN, founder, go under, submerge, capsize **3** SLUMP, drop, flop, collapse, droop **4** FALL, drop, decline, slip, plunge, plummet, subside, relapse, abate, retrogress **5** DROP, fall **6** STOOP, descend, be reduced to, succumb, lower yourself, debase yourself, demean yourself **7** DECLINE, die, fade, fail, flag, weaken, diminish, decrease, deteriorate, decay, worsen, dwindle, lessen, degenerate, depreciate, go downhill (*informal*) << ANTONYM improve **8** DIG, bore, drill, drive, lay, put down, excavate

sinner *noun* WRONGDOER, offender, evildoer, trespasser (*archaic*), reprobate, miscreant, malefactor, transgressor

sinuous *adjective* CURVING, winding, meandering, crooked, coiling, tortuous, undulating, serpentine, curvy, lithe, twisty, mazy

sip *verb* DRINK, taste, sample, sup ▷ *noun* SWALLOW, mouthful, swig, drop, taste, thimbleful

siren *noun* **1** ALERT, warning, signal, alarm **2** SEDUCTRESS, vamp (*informal*), femme fatale (*French*), witch, charmer, temptress, Lorelei, Circe

sissy *or* **cissy** *noun* WIMP, softie (*informal*), weakling, baby, wet (*Brit informal*), coward (*informal*), jessie (*Scot slang*), pansy, pussy (*slang, chiefly US*), mummy's boy, mollycoddle, namby-pamby, wuss (*slang*), milksop, milquetoast (*US*), sisspot (*informal*) ▷ *adjective* WIMPISH *or* WIMPY (*informal*), soft (*informal*), weak, wet (*Brit informal*), cowardly, feeble, unmanly, effeminate, namby-pamby, wussy (*slang*), sissified (*informal*)

sit *verb* **1** TAKE A SEAT, perch, settle down, be seated, take the weight off your feet **2** PLACE, set, put, position, rest, lay, settle, deposit, situate **3** BE A MEMBER OF, serve on, have a seat on, preside on **4** CONVENE, meet, assemble, officiate, be in session

site *noun* **1** AREA, ground, plot, patch, tract **2** LOCATION, place, setting, point, position, situation, spot, whereabouts, locus ▷ *verb* LOCATE, put, place, set, position, establish, install, situate

sitting *noun* **1** SESSION, period **2** MEETING, hearing, session, congress, consultation, get-together (*informal*)

situation *noun* **1** POSITION, state, case, condition, circumstances, equation, plight, status quo, state of affairs, ball game (*informal*), kettle of fish (*informal*) **2** SCENARIO, the picture (*informal*), the score (*informal*), state of affairs, lie of the land **3** LOCATION, place, setting, position, seat, site, spot, locality, locale

sixth sense *noun* INTUITION, second sight, clairvoyance

size *noun* DIMENSIONS, extent, measurement(s), range, amount, mass, length, volume, capacity, proportions, bulk, width, magnitude, greatness, vastness, immensity, bigness, largeness, hugeness ▷▷ **size something** *or* **someone up** (*informal*) ASSESS, evaluate, appraise, take stock of, eye up, get the measure of, get (something) taped (*Brit informal*)

sizeable *or* **sizable** *adjective* LARGE, considerable, substantial, goodly, decent, respectable, tidy (*informal*), decent-sized, largish

sizzle *verb* HISS, spit, crackle, sputter, fry, frizzle

skeletal *adjective* EMACIATED, wasted, gaunt, skin-and-bone (*informal*), cadaverous, hollow-cheeked, lantern-jawed, fleshless, worn to a shadow

skeleton *noun* **1** BONES, bare bones **2** FRAME, shell, framework, basic structure **3** PLAN, structure, frame, draft, outline, framework, sketch, abstract, blueprint, main points

▷ *modifier* MINIMUM, reduced, minimal, essential

sketch *noun* **1** DRAWING, design, draft, delineation **2** DRAFT, outline, framework, plan, frame, rough, skeleton, layout, lineament(s) **3** SKIT, piece, scene, turn, act, performance, item, routine, number ▷ *verb* DRAW, paint, outline, represent, draft, portray, depict, delineate, rough out

sketchy *adjective* INCOMPLETE, rough, vague, slight, outline, inadequate, crude, superficial, unfinished, skimpy, scrappy, cursory, perfunctory, cobbled together, bitty << ANTONYM complete

skid *verb* SLIDE, slip, slither, coast, glide, skim, veer, toboggan

skilful *adjective* EXPERT, skilled, masterly, trained, experienced, able, professional, quick, clever, practised, accomplished, handy, competent, apt, adept, proficient, adroit, dexterous << ANTONYM clumsy

skill *noun* EXPERTISE, ability, proficiency, experience, art, technique, facility, talent, intelligence, craft, competence, readiness, accomplishment, knack, ingenuity, finesse, aptitude, dexterity, cleverness, quickness, adroitness, expertness, handiness, skilfulness << ANTONYM clumsiness

skilled *adjective* EXPERT, professional, accomplished, trained, experienced, able, masterly, practised, skilful, proficient, a dab hand at (*Brit informal*) << ANTONYM unskilled

skim *verb* **1** REMOVE, separate, cream, take off **2** GLIDE, fly, coast, sail, float, brush, dart **3** *usually with* **over** *or* **through** SCAN, glance, run your eye over, thumb or leaf through

skimp *verb* STINT, scrimp, be sparing with, pinch, withhold, scant, cut corners, scamp, be mean with, be niggardly, tighten your belt << ANTONYM be extravagant

skimpy *adjective* INADEQUATE, insufficient, scant, meagre, short, tight, thin, sparse, scanty, miserly, niggardly, exiguous

skin *noun* **1** COMPLEXION, colouring, skin tone **2** HIDE, fleece, pelt, fell, integument, tegument **3** PEEL, rind, husk, casing, outside, crust **4** FILM, coating, coat, membrane ▷ *verb* **1** PEEL, pare, hull **2** SCRAPE, graze, bark, flay, excoriate, abrade ▷▷ **by the skin of your teeth** NARROWLY, only just, by a whisker (*informal*), by a narrow margin, by a hair's-breadth ▷▷ **get under your skin** (*informal*) ANNOY, irritate, aggravate (*informal*), needle (*informal*), nettle, irk, grate on, get on your

nerves (*informal*), get in your hair (*informal*), rub you up the wrong way, hack you off (*informal*)

skin-deep *adjective* SUPERFICIAL, surface, external, artificial, shallow, on the surface, meaningless

skinny *adjective* THIN, lean, scrawny, skeletal, emaciated, twiggy, undernourished, skin-and-bone (*informal*), scraggy << ANTONYM fat

skip *verb* **1** HOP, dance, bob, trip, bounce, caper, prance, cavort, frisk, gambol **2** MISS OUT, omit, leave out, overlook, pass over, eschew, forego, skim over, give (something) a miss **3** (*informal*) MISS, cut (*informal*), bunk off (*slang*), play truant from, wag (*dialect*), dog it or dog off (*dialect*)

skirmish *noun* FIGHT, battle, conflict, incident, clash, contest, set-to (*informal*), encounter, brush, combat, scrap (*informal*), engagement, spat, tussle, fracas, affray (*law*), dust-up (*informal*), scrimmage, biffo (*Austral slang*), boilover (*Austral*) ▷ *verb* FIGHT, clash, come to blows, scrap (*informal*), collide, grapple, wrangle, tussle, lock horns, cross swords

skirt *verb* **1** BORDER, edge, lie alongside, line, fringe, flank **2** *often with* **around** *or* **round** GO ROUND, bypass, walk round, circumvent **3** *often with* **around** *or* **round** AVOID, evade, steer clear of, sidestep, circumvent, detour, body-swerve (*Scot*) ▷ *noun often plural* BORDER, edge, margin, fringe, outskirts, rim, hem, periphery, purlieus

skit *noun* PARODY, spoof (*informal*), travesty, takeoff (*informal*), burlesque, turn, sketch

skittish *adjective* NERVOUS, lively, excitable, jumpy, restive, fidgety, highly strung, antsy (*informal*) << ANTONYM calm

skookum *adjective* (*Canad*) POWERFUL, influential, big, dominant, controlling, commanding, supreme, prevailing, sovereign, authoritative, puissant

skulduggery *noun* (*informal*) TRICKERY, swindling, machinations, duplicity, double-dealing, fraudulence, shenanigan(s) (*informal*), unscrupulousness, underhandedness

skulk *verb* **1** CREEP, sneak, slink, pad, prowl **2** LURK, hide, lie in wait, loiter

sky *noun* HEAVENS, firmament, upper atmosphere, azure (*poetic*), welkin (*archaic*), vault of heaven, rangi (*NZ*)

slab *noun* PIECE, slice, lump, chunk, wedge, hunk, portion, nugget, wodge (*Brit informal*)

slack *adjective* **1** LIMP, relaxed, loose, lax, flaccid, not taut **2** LOOSE, hanging, flapping, baggy << ANTONYM taut **3** SLOW, quiet, inactive, dull, sluggish, slow-moving << ANTONYM busy **4** NEGLIGENT, lazy, lax, idle, easy-going, inactive, tardy, slapdash, neglectful, slipshod, inattentive, remiss, asleep on the job (*informal*) << ANTONYM strict ▷ *noun* **1** SURPLUS, excess, overflow, leftover, glut, surfeit, overabundance, superabundance, superfluity **2** ROOM, excess, leeway, give (*informal*), play, looseness ▷ *verb* SHIRK, idle, relax, flag, neglect, dodge, skive (*Brit slang*), bob off (*Brit slang*), bludge (*Austral & NZ slang*)

slacken *verb often with* **off** LESSEN, reduce, decrease, ease (off), moderate, diminish, slow down, drop off, abate, let up, slack off

slacker *noun* LAYABOUT, shirker, loafer, skiver (*Brit slang*), idler, passenger, do-nothing, piker (*Austral & NZ slang*), dodger, good-for-nothing, bludger (*Austral & NZ informal*), gold brick (*US slang*), scrimshanker (*Brit military slang*)

slag *noun* (*Brit slang*) TART (*informal*), scrubber (*Brit & Austral slang*), whore, pro (*slang*), brass (*slang*), prostitute, hooker (*US slang*), hustler (*US & Canad slang*), moll (*slang*), call girl, courtesan, working girl (*facetious slang*), harlot, slapper (*Brit informal*), streetwalker, camp follower, loose woman, fallen woman, strumpet, trollop, white slave, bawd (*archaic*), cocotte, fille de joie (*French*) ▷▷ **slag something** *or* **someone off** (*slang*) CRITICIZE, abuse, malign, slam, insult, mock, slate, slang, deride, berate, slander, diss (*slang, chiefly US*), lambast(e), flame (*informal*)

slam *verb* **1** BANG, crash, smash, thump, shut with a bang, shut noisily **2** THROW, dash, hurl, fling **3** (*slang*) CRITICIZE, attack, blast, pan (*informal*), damn, slate (*informal*), shoot down (*informal*), castigate, vilify, pillory, tear into (*informal*), diss (*slang, chiefly US*), lambast(e), excoriate

slander *noun* DEFAMATION, smear, libel, scandal, misrepresentation, calumny, backbiting, muckraking, obloquy, aspersion, detraction << ANTONYM praise ▷ *verb* DEFAME, smear, libel, slur, malign, detract, disparage, decry, vilify, traduce, backbite, blacken (someone's) name, calumniate, muckrake << ANTONYM praise

slang *noun* COLLOQUIALISMS, jargon, idioms, argot, informal language

slant *verb* **1** SLOPE, incline, tilt, list, bend, lean, heel, shelve, skew, cant, bevel, angle off **2** BIAS, colour, weight, twist, angle, distort ▷ *noun* **1** SLOPE, incline, tilt, gradient, pitch, ramp, diagonal, camber, declination **2** BIAS, emphasis, prejudice, angle, leaning, point of view, viewpoint, one-sidedness

slanting *adjective* SLOPING, angled, inclined, tilted, tilting, sideways, slanted, bent, diagonal, oblique, at an angle, canted, on the bias, aslant, slantwise, atilt, cater-cornered (*US informal*)

slap *verb* **1** SMACK, hit, strike, beat, bang, clap, clout (*informal*), cuff, whack, swipe, spank, clobber (*slang*), wallop (*informal*), lay one on (*slang*) **2** (*informal, chiefly Brit*) PLASTER, apply, spread, daub ▷ *noun* SMACK, blow, whack, wallop (*informal*), bang, clout (*informal*), cuff, swipe, spank ▷▷ **a slap in the face** INSULT, humiliation, snub, affront, blow, rejection, put-down, rebuke, rebuff, repulse

slapstick *noun* FARCE, horseplay, buffoonery, knockabout comedy

slap-up *adjective* (*Brit informal*) LUXURIOUS, lavish, sumptuous, princely, excellent, superb, magnificent, elaborate, splendid, first-rate, no-expense-spared, fit for a king

slash *verb* **1** CUT, slit, gash, lacerate, score, rend, rip, hack **2** REDUCE, cut, decrease, drop, lower, moderate, cut down, lessen, curtail ▷ *noun* CUT, slit, gash, rent, rip, incision, laceration

slate *verb* (*informal, chiefly Brit*) CRITICIZE, blast, pan (*informal*), slam (*slang*), blame, roast (*informal*), censure, rebuke, slang, scold, berate, castigate, rail against, tear into (*informal*), lay into (*informal*), pitch into (*informal*), take to task, lambast(e), flame (*informal*), excoriate, haul over the coals (*informal*), tear (someone) off a strip (*informal*), rap (someone's) knuckles

slaughter *verb* **1** KILL, murder, massacre, destroy, do in (*slang*), execute, dispatch, assassinate, blow away (*slang, chiefly US*), annihilate, bump off (*slang*) **2** BUTCHER, kill, slay, destroy, massacre, exterminate **3** DEFEAT, thrash, vanquish, stuff (*slang*), tank (*slang*), hammer (*informal*), crush, overwhelm, lick (*informal*), undo, rout, trounce, wipe the floor with (*informal*), blow out of the water (*slang*) ▷ *noun* SLAYING, killing, murder, massacre, holocaust, bloodshed, carnage, liquidation, extermination, butchery, blood bath

slaughterhouse *noun* ABATTOIR, butchery, shambles

slave *noun* **1** SERVANT, serf, vassal, bondsman, slavey (*Brit informal*), varlet (*archaic*), villein, bondservant **2** DRUDGE, skivvy (*chiefly Brit*), scullion (*archaic*) ▷ *verb* TOIL, labour, grind (*informal*), drudge, sweat, graft, slog, skivvy (*Brit*), work your fingers to the bone

slaver *verb* DRIBBLE, drool, salivate, slobber

slavery *noun* ENSLAVEMENT, servitude, subjugation, captivity, bondage, thrall, serfdom, vassalage, thraldom << ANTONYM freedom

slavish *adjective* **1** IMITATIVE, unimaginative, unoriginal, conventional, second-hand, uninspired << ANTONYM original **2** SERVILE, cringing, abject, submissive, grovelling, mean, low, base, fawning, despicable, menial, sycophantic, obsequious << ANTONYM rebellious

slay *verb* **1** (*archaic or literary*) KILL, destroy, slaughter, eliminate, massacre, butcher, dispatch, annihilate, exterminate **2** MURDER, kill, assassinate, do in (*slang*), eliminate, massacre, slaughter, do away with, exterminate, mow down, rub out (*US slang*)

sleaze *noun* (*informal*) CORRUPTION, fraud, dishonesty, fiddling (*informal*), bribery, extortion, venality, shady dealings (*informal*), crookedness (*informal*), unscrupulousness

sleazy *adjective* SQUALID, seedy, sordid, low, run-down, tacky (*informal*), disreputable, crummy, scungy (*Austral & NZ*)

sleek *adjective* GLOSSY, shiny, lustrous, smooth, silky, velvety, well-groomed << ANTONYM shaggy

sleep *noun* SLUMBER(s), rest, nap, doze, kip (*Brit slang*), snooze (*informal*), repose, hibernation, siesta, dormancy, beauty sleep (*informal*), forty winks (*informal*), shuteye (*slang*), zizz (*Brit informal*) ▷ *verb* SLUMBER, drop off (*informal*), doze, kip (*Brit slang*), snooze (*informal*), snore, hibernate, nod off (*informal*), take a nap, catnap, drowse, go out like a light, take forty winks (*informal*), zizz (*Brit informal*), be in the land of Nod, rest in the arms of Morpheus

sleepless *adjective* **1** WAKEFUL, disturbed, restless, insomniac, unsleeping **2** ALERT, vigilant, watchful, wide awake, unsleeping

sleepwalking *noun* SOMNAMBULISM, noctambulation, noctambulism, somnambulation

sleepy *adjective* **1** DROWSY, sluggish, lethargic, heavy, dull, inactive, somnolent, torpid << ANTONYM wide-awake **2** SOPORIFIC, hypnotic, somnolent, sleep-inducing,

slumberous **3** QUIET, peaceful, dull, tranquil, inactive << ANTONYM busy

slender *adjective* **1** SLIM, narrow, slight, lean, svelte, willowy, sylphlike << ANTONYM chubby **2** FAINT, slight, remote, slim, thin, weak, fragile, feeble, flimsy, tenuous << ANTONYM strong **3** MEAGRE, little, small, inadequate, insufficient, scant, scanty, inconsiderable << ANTONYM large

sleuth *noun* (*informal*) DETECTIVE, private eye (*informal*), (private) investigator, tail (*informal*), dick (*slang, chiefly US*), gumshoe (*US slang*), sleuthhound (*informal*)

slice *noun* PIECE, segment, portion, wedge, sliver, helping, share, cut ▷ *verb* DIVIDE, carve, segment, sever, dissect, cleave, bisect

slick *adjective* **1** EFFICIENT, professional, smart, smooth, streamlined, masterly, sharp, deft, well-organized, adroit **2** SKILFUL, deft, adroit, dextrous, dexterous, professional, polished << ANTONYM clumsy **3** GLIB, smooth, sophisticated, plausible, polished, specious, meretricious ▷ *verb* SMOOTH, oil, grease, sleek, plaster down, make glossy, smarm down (*Brit informal*)

slide *verb* SLIP, slither, glide, skim, coast, toboggan, glissade ▷▷ **let something slide** NEGLECT, forget, ignore, pass over, turn a blind eye to, gloss over, push to the back of your mind, let ride

slight *adjective* **1** SMALL, minor, insignificant, negligible, weak, modest, trivial, superficial, feeble, trifling, meagre, unimportant, paltry, measly, insubstantial, scanty, inconsiderable << ANTONYM large **2** SLIM, small, delicate, spare, fragile, lightly-built << ANTONYM sturdy ▷ *verb* SNUB, insult, ignore, rebuff, affront, neglect, put down, despise, scorn, disdain, disparage, cold-shoulder, treat with contempt, show disrespect for, give offence *or* umbrage to << ANTONYM compliment ▷ *noun* INSULT, snub, affront, contempt, disregard, indifference, disdain, rebuff, disrespect, slap in the face (*informal*), inattention, discourtesy, (the) cold shoulder << ANTONYM compliment

slightly *adverb* A LITTLE, a bit, somewhat, moderately, marginally, a shade, to some degree, on a small scale, to some extent *or* degree

slim *adjective* **1** SLENDER, slight, trim, thin, narrow, lean, svelte, willowy, sylphlike << ANTONYM chubby **2** SLIGHT, remote, faint, distant, slender << ANTONYM strong ▷ *verb* LOSE WEIGHT, diet, get thinner, get into

shape, slenderize (*chiefly US*) << ANTONYM
put on weight

slimy *adjective* **1** VISCOUS, clammy, glutinous,
muddy, mucous, gloopy (*informal*), oozy, miry
2 (*Chiefly Brit*) OBSEQUIOUS, creepy, unctuous,
smarmy (*Brit informal*), oily, grovelling, soapy
(*slang*), sycophantic, servile, toadying

sling *verb* **1** (*informal*) THROW, cast, toss, hurl,
fling, chuck (*informal*), lob (*informal*), heave,
shy **2** HANG, swing, suspend, string, drape,
dangle ▷ *noun* HARNESS, support, bandage,
strap

slink *verb* CREEP, steal, sneak, slip, prowl,
skulk, pussyfoot (*informal*)

slinky *adjective* FIGURE-HUGGING, clinging,
sleek, close-fitting, skintight

slip¹ *verb* **1** FALL, trip (over), slide, skid, lose
your balance, miss *or* lose your footing
2 SLIDE, fall, drop, slither **3** SNEAK, creep,
steal, insinuate yourself ▷ *noun* MISTAKE,
failure, error, blunder, lapse, omission, boob
(*Brit slang*), oversight, slip-up (*informal*),
indiscretion, bloomer (*Brit informal*), faux
pas, slip of the tongue, imprudence, barry
or Barry Crocker (*Austral slang*) ▷▷ **give
someone the slip** ESCAPE FROM, get away
from, evade, shake (someone) off, elude, lose
(someone), flee, dodge, outwit, slip through
someone's fingers ▷▷ **let something slip**
GIVE AWAY, reveal, disclose, divulge, leak,
come out with (*informal*), let out (*informal*),
blurt out, let the cat out of the bag ▷▷ **slip
away** GET AWAY, escape, disappear, break
away, break free, get clear of, take French
leave ▷▷ **slip up** MAKE A MISTAKE, go wrong,
blunder, mistake, boob (*Brit slang*), err,
misjudge, miscalculate, drop a brick *or*
clanger (*informal*)

slip² *noun* STRIP, piece, sliver

slippery *adjective* **1** SMOOTH, icy, greasy, glassy,
slippy (*informal or dialect*), unsafe, lubricious
(*rare*), skiddy (*informal*) **2** UNTRUSTWORTHY,
tricky, cunning, false, treacherous,
dishonest, devious, crafty, evasive, sneaky,
two-faced, shifty, foxy, duplicitous

slit *verb* CUT (OPEN), rip, slash, knife, pierce,
lance, gash, split open ▷ *noun* **1** CUT, gash,
incision, tear, rent, fissure **2** OPENING, split,
crack, aperture, chink, space

slither *verb* SLIDE, slip, glide, snake, undulate,
slink, skitter

sliver *noun* SHRED, fragment, splinter, slip,
shaving, flake, paring

slob *noun* (*informal*) LAYABOUT, lounger, loafer,
couch potato (*slang*), idler, good-for-nothing

slog *verb* **1** WORK, labour, toil, slave, plod,
persevere, plough through, sweat blood
(*informal*), apply yourself to, work your
fingers to the bone, peg away at, keep your
nose to the grindstone **2** TRUDGE, tramp,
plod, trek, hike, traipse (*informal*), yomp,
walk heavily, footslog ▷ *noun* **1** WORK,
labour, toil, industry, grind (*informal*), effort,
struggle, pains, sweat (*informal*), painstaking,
exertion, donkey-work, blood, sweat, and
tears (*informal*) **2** TRUDGE, tramp, trek, hike,
traipse (*informal*), yomp, footslog

slogan *noun* CATCH PHRASE, motto, jingle,
rallying cry, tag-line, catchword, catchcry
(*Austral*)

slop *verb* SPILL, splash, overflow, splatter,
spatter, slosh (*informal*)

slope *noun* INCLINATION, rise, incline, tilt,
descent, downgrade (*chiefly US*), slant, ramp,
gradient, brae (*Scot*), scarp, declination,
declivity ▷ *verb* SLANT, incline, drop away,
fall, rise, pitch, lean, tilt ▷▷ **slope off** SLINK
AWAY, slip away, steal away, skulk, creep
away, make yourself scarce

sloping *adjective* SLANTING, leaning, inclined,
inclining, oblique, atilt

sloppy *adjective* **1** (*informal*) CARELESS, slovenly,
slipshod, messy, clumsy, untidy, amateurish,
hit-or-miss (*informal*), inattentive **2** (*informal*)
SENTIMENTAL, mushy (*informal*), soppy
(*Brit informal*), slushy (*informal*), wet (*Brit
informal*), gushing, banal, trite, mawkish,
icky (*informal*), overemotional, three-hankie
(*informal*) **3** WET, watery, slushy, splashy,
sludgy

slosh *verb* **1** SPLASH, wash, slop, break, plash
2 WADE, splash, flounder, paddle, dabble,
wallow, swash

slot *noun* **1** OPENING, hole, groove, vent, slit,
aperture, channel **2** (*informal*) PLACE, time,
space, spot, opening, position, window,
vacancy, niche ▷ *verb* FIT, slide, insert, put,
place

sloth *noun* LAZINESS, inactivity, idleness,
inertia, torpor, sluggishness, slackness,
indolence

slouch *verb* LOUNGE, slump, flop, sprawl,
stoop, droop, loll, lean

slouching *adjective* SHAMBLING, lumbering,
ungainly, awkward, uncouth, loutish

slow *adjective* **1** UNHURRIED, sluggish,
leisurely, easy, measured, creeping,
deliberate, lagging, lazy, plodding,
slow-moving, loitering, ponderous,
leaden, dawdling, laggard, lackadaisical,

tortoise-like, sluggardly << ANTONYM quick **2** PROLONGED, time-consuming, protracted, long-drawn-out, lingering, gradual **3** UNWILLING, reluctant, loath, averse, hesitant, disinclined, indisposed **4** LATE, unpunctual, behindhand, behind, tardy **5** STUPID, dim, dense, thick, dull, dumb (*informal*), retarded, bovine, dozy (*Brit informal*), unresponsive, obtuse, slow on the uptake (*informal*), braindead (*informal*), dull-witted, blockish, slow-witted, intellectually handicapped (*Austral*) << ANTONYM bright **6** DULL, quiet, boring, dead, tame, slack, sleepy, sluggish, tedious, stagnant, unproductive, inactive, one-horse (*informal*), uneventful, uninteresting, wearisome, dead-and-alive (*Brit*), unprogressive << ANTONYM exciting ▷ *verb* **1** *often with* **down** DECELERATE, brake, lag **2** *often with* **down** DELAY, hold up, hinder, check, restrict, handicap, detain, curb, retard, rein in << ANTONYM speed up

slowly *adverb* GRADUALLY, steadily, by degrees, unhurriedly, taking your time, at your leisure, at a snail's pace, in your own (good) time, ploddingly, inchmeal << ANTONYM quickly

sludge *noun* SEDIMENT, ooze, silt, mud, muck, residue, slop, mire, slime, slush, slob (*Irish*), dregs, gloop (*informal*)

sluggish *adjective* INACTIVE, slow, lethargic, listless, heavy, dull, lifeless, inert, slow-moving, unresponsive, phlegmatic, indolent, torpid, slothful << ANTONYM energetic

sluice *verb* DRAIN, cleanse, flush, drench, wash out, wash down

slum *noun* HOVEL, ghetto, shanty

slumber *noun* SLEEP, nap, doze, rest, kip (*Brit informal*), snooze (*informal*), siesta, catnap, forty winks (*informal*) ▷ *verb* SLEEP, nap, doze, kip (*Brit slang*), snooze (*informal*), lie dormant, drowse, zizz (*Brit informal*)

slump *verb* **1** FALL, decline, sink, plunge, crash, collapse, slip, deteriorate, fall off, plummet, go downhill (*informal*) << ANTONYM increase **2** SAG, bend, hunch, droop, slouch, loll ▷ *noun* **1** FALL, drop, decline, crash, collapse, reverse, lapse, falling-off, downturn, depreciation, trough, meltdown (*informal*) << ANTONYM increase **2** RECESSION, depression, stagnation, inactivity, hard *or* bad times

slur *noun* INSULT, stain, smear, stigma, disgrace, discredit, blot, affront, innuendo, calumny, insinuation, aspersion ▷ *verb*

MUMBLE, stammer, stutter, stumble over, falter, mispronounce, garble, speak unclearly

slut *noun* TART, slag (*Brit slang*), slapper (*Brit slang*), scrubber (*Brit & Austral slang*), trollop, drab (*archaic*), sloven, slattern, hornbag (*Austral slang*)

sly *adjective* **1** ROGUISH, knowing, arch, mischievous, impish **2** CUNNING, scheming, devious, secret, clever, subtle, tricky, covert, astute, wily, insidious, crafty, artful, furtive, conniving, Machiavellian, shifty, foxy, underhand, stealthy, guileful << ANTONYM open **3** SECRET, furtive, surreptitious, stealthy, sneaking, covert, clandestine ▷▷ **on the sly** SECRETLY, privately, covertly, surreptitiously, under the counter (*informal*), on the quiet, behind (someone's) back, like a thief in the night, underhandedly, on the q.t. (*informal*)

smack *verb* **1** SLAP, hit, strike, pat, tap, sock (*slang*), clap, cuff, swipe, box, spank **2** DRIVE, hit, strike, thrust, impel ▷ *noun* SLAP, blow, whack, clout (*informal*), cuff, crack, swipe, spank, wallop (*informal*) ▷ *adverb* (*informal*) DIRECTLY, right, straight, squarely, precisely, exactly, slap (*informal*), plumb, point-blank ▷▷ **smack of something** BE SUGGESTIVE *or* INDICATIVE OF, suggest, smell of, testify to, reek of, have all the hallmarks of, betoken, be redolent of, bear the stamp of

small *adjective* **1** LITTLE, minute, tiny, slight, mini, miniature, minuscule, diminutive, petite, teeny, puny, pint-sized (*informal*), pocket-sized, undersized, teeny-weeny, Lilliputian, teensy-weensy, pygmy *or* pigmy << ANTONYM big **2** INTIMATE, close, private **3** YOUNG, little, growing up, junior, wee, juvenile, youthful, immature, unfledged, in the springtime of life **4** UNIMPORTANT, minor, trivial, insignificant, little, lesser, petty, trifling, negligible, paltry, piddling (*informal*) << ANTONYM important **5** MODEST, small-scale, humble, unpretentious << ANTONYM grand **6** SOFT, low, inaudible, low-pitched, noiseless **7** MEAGRE, inadequate, insufficient, scant, measly, scanty, limited, inconsiderable << ANTONYM ample

small-minded *adjective* PETTY, mean, rigid, grudging, envious, bigoted, intolerant, narrow-minded, hidebound, ungenerous << ANTONYM broad-minded

small-time *adjective* (*informal*) MINOR, insignificant, unimportant, petty, no-account (*US informal*), piddling (*informal*), of no consequence, of no account

smart *adjective* **1** CHIC, trim, neat, fashionable, stylish, fine, elegant, trendy (*Brit informal*), spruce, snappy, natty (*informal*), modish, well turned-out, schmick (*Austral informal*) << ANTONYM scruffy **2** CLEVER, bright, intelligent, quick, sharp, keen, acute, shrewd, apt, ingenious, astute, canny, quick-witted << ANTONYM stupid **3** FASHIONABLE, stylish, chic, genteel, in vogue, voguish (*informal*) **4** BRISK, quick, lively, vigorous, spirited, cracking (*informal*), spanking, jaunty ▷ *verb* STING, burn, tingle, pain, hurt, throb

smarten *verb often with* **up** TIDY, spruce up, groom, beautify, put in order, put to rights, gussy up (*slang, chiefly US*)

smash *verb* **1** BREAK, crush, shatter, crack, demolish, shiver, disintegrate, pulverize, crush to smithereens **2** SHATTER, break, disintegrate, split, crack, explode, splinter **3** COLLIDE, crash, meet head-on, clash, come into collision **4** DESTROY, ruin, wreck, total (*slang*), defeat, overthrow, trash (*slang*), lay waste ▷ *noun* **1** (*informal*) SUCCESS, hit, winner, triumph (*informal*), belter (*slang*), sensation, smash hit, sellout **2** COLLISION, crash, accident, pile-up (*informal*), smash-up (*informal*) **3** CRASH, smashing, clatter, clash, bang, thunder, racket, din, clattering, clang

smashing *adjective* (*informal, chiefly Brit*) EXCELLENT, mean (*slang*), great (*informal*), wonderful, topping (*Brit slang*), brilliant (*informal*), cracking (*Brit informal*), crucial (*slang*), superb, fantastic (*informal*), magnificent, fabulous (*informal*), first-class, marvellous, terrific (*informal*), sensational (*informal*), mega (*slang*), sovereign, awesome (*slang*), world-class, exhilarating, fab (*informal, chiefly Brit*), super (*informal*), first-rate, def (*slang*), superlative, brill (*informal*), stupendous, out of this world (*informal*), bodacious (*slang, chiefly US*), boffo (*slang*), jim-dandy (*slang*), chillin' (*US slang*), booshit (*Austral slang*), exo (*Austral slang*), sik (*Austral slang*), rad (*informal*), phat (*slang*), schmick (*Austral informal*) << ANTONYM awful

smattering *noun* MODICUM, dash, rudiments, bit, elements, sprinkling, passing acquaintance, nodding acquaintance, smatter

smear *verb* **1** SPREAD OVER, daub, rub on, cover, coat, plaster, bedaub **2** SLANDER, tarnish, malign, vilify, blacken, sully, besmirch, traduce, calumniate, asperse,

drag (someone's) name through the mud **3** SMUDGE, soil, dirty, stain, sully, besmirch, smirch ▷ *noun* **1** SMUDGE, daub, streak, blot, blotch, splotch, smirch **2** SLANDER, libel, defamation, vilification, whispering campaign, calumny, mudslinging

smell *noun* **1** ODOUR, scent, fragrance, perfume, bouquet, aroma, whiff, niff (*Brit slang*), redolence **2** STINK, stench, reek, pong (*Brit informal*), niff (*Brit slang*), malodour, fetor ▷ *verb* **1** STINK, reek, pong (*Brit informal*), hum (*slang*), whiff (*Brit slang*), stink to high heaven (*informal*), niff (*Brit slang*), be malodorous **2** SNIFF, scent, get a whiff of, nose

smelly *adjective* STINKING, reeking, fetid, foul-smelling, high, strong, foul, putrid, strong-smelling, stinky (*informal*), malodorous, evil-smelling, noisome, whiffy (*Brit slang*), pongy (*Brit informal*), mephitic, niffy (*Brit slang*), olid, festy (*Austral slang*) << ANTONYM fragrant

smile *verb* GRIN, beam, smirk, twinkle, grin from ear to ear ▷ *noun* GRIN, beam, smirk

smirk *noun* SMUG SMILE, grin, simper ▷ *verb* GIVE A SMUG LOOK, grin, simper

smitten *adjective* **1** INFATUATED, charmed, captivated, beguiled, bewitched, bowled over (*informal*), enamoured, swept off your feet **2** AFFLICTED, struck, beset, laid low, plagued

smoky *adjective* THICK, murky, hazy

smooth *adjective* **1** EVEN, level, flat, plane, plain, flush, horizontal, unwrinkled << ANTONYM uneven **2** SLEEK, polished, shiny, glossy, silky, velvety, glassy, mirror-like << ANTONYM rough **3** MELLOW, pleasant, mild, soothing, bland, agreeable **4** FLOWING, steady, fluent, regular, uniform, rhythmic **5** CALM, peaceful, serene, tranquil, undisturbed, unruffled, equable << ANTONYM troubled **6** EASY, effortless, untroubled, well-ordered **7** SUAVE, slick, persuasive, urbane, silky, glib, facile, ingratiating, debonair, unctuous, smarmy (*Brit informal*) ▷ *verb* **1** FLATTEN, level, press, plane, iron **2** EASE, aid, assist, facilitate, pave the way, make easier, help along, iron out the difficulties of << ANTONYM hinder

smoothness *noun* **1** EVENNESS, regularity, levelness, flushness, unbrokenness **2** FLUENCY, finish, flow, ease, polish, rhythm, efficiency, felicity, smooth running, slickness, effortlessness **3** SLEEKNESS, softness, smooth texture, silkiness, velvetiness **4** SUAVITY, urbanity, oiliness, glibness, smarminess (*Brit informal*)

smother *verb* 1 EXTINGUISH, put out, stifle, snuff 2 SUFFOCATE, choke, strangle, stifle 3 SUPPRESS, stifle, repress, hide, conceal, muffle, keep back 4 OVERWHELM, cover, shower, surround, heap, shroud, inundate, envelop, cocoon 5 STIFLE, suppress, hold in, restrain, hold back, repress, muffle, bottle up, keep in check 6 SMEAR, cover, spread

smoulder *verb* 1 SMOKE, burn slowly 2 SEETHE, rage, fume, burn, boil, simmer, fester, be resentful, smart

smudge *noun* SMEAR, blot, smut, smutch ▷ *verb* 1 SMEAR, blur, blot 2 MARK, soil, dirty, daub, smirch

smug *adjective* SELF-SATISFIED, superior, complacent, conceited, self-righteous, holier-than-thou, priggish, self-opinionated

smuggler *noun* TRAFFICKER, runner, bootlegger, moonshiner (*US*), rum-runner, contrabandist

snack *noun* LIGHT MEAL, bite, refreshment(s), nibble, titbit, bite to eat, elevenses (*Brit informal*)

snag *noun* DIFFICULTY, hitch, problem, obstacle, catch, hazard, disadvantage, complication, drawback, inconvenience, downside, stumbling block, the rub ▷ *verb* CATCH, tear, rip, hole

snake *noun* SERPENT ▷ *verb* WIND, twist, curve, turn, bend, ramble, meander, deviate, zigzag

snap *verb* 1 BREAK, split, crack, separate, fracture, give way, come apart 2 POP, click, crackle 3 SPEAK SHARPLY, bark, lash out at, flash, retort, snarl, growl, fly off the handle at (*informal*), jump down (someone's) throat (*informal*) 4 BITE AT, bite, nip ▷ *noun* 1 CRACK, pop, crash, report, burst, explosion, clap 2 POP, crack, smack, whack ▷ *modifier* INSTANT, immediate, sudden, abrupt, spur-of-the-moment, unpremeditated ▷▷ **snap out of it** (*informal*) GET OVER IT, recover, cheer up, perk up, liven up, pull yourself together (*informal*), get a grip on yourself ▷▷ **snap something up** GRAB, seize, take advantage of, swoop down on, pounce upon, avail yourself of

snappy *adjective* 1 SMART, fashionable, stylish, trendy (*Brit informal*), chic, dapper, up-to-the-minute, natty (*informal*), modish, voguish, schmick (*Austral informal*) 2 IRRITABLE, cross, bad-tempered, tart, impatient, edgy, touchy, tetchy, ratty (*Brit & NZ informal*), testy, waspish, quick-tempered, snappish, like a bear with a sore head

(*informal*), apt to fly off the handle (*informal*) ▷▷ **make it snappy** (*slang*) HURRY (UP), be quick, get a move on (*informal*), buck up (*informal*), make haste, look lively, get your skates on

snare *noun* TRAP, net, wire, gin, pitfall, noose, springe ▷ *verb* TRAP, catch, net, wire, seize, entrap, springe

snarl[1] *verb* 1 GROWL, show your teeth (*of an animal*) 2 SNAP, bark, lash out, speak angrily, jump down someone's throat, speak roughly

snarl[2] ▷▷ **snarl something up** TANGLE, complicate, muddle, embroil, entangle, entwine, ravel, enmesh

snatch *verb* 1 GRAB, seize, wrench, wrest, take, grip, grasp, clutch, take hold of 2 STEAL, take, nick (*slang, chiefly Brit*), pinch (*informal*), swipe (*slang*), lift (*informal*), pilfer, filch, shoplift, thieve, walk or make off with 3 WIN, take, score, gain, secure, obtain 4 SAVE, free, rescue, pull, recover, get out, salvage, extricate ▷ *noun* BIT, part, fragment, piece, spell, snippet, smattering

snazzy *adjective* (*informal*) STYLISH, smart, dashing, with it (*informal*), attractive, sophisticated, flamboyant, sporty, flashy, jazzy (*informal*), showy, ritzy (*slang*), raffish, schmick (*Austral informal*)

sneak *verb* 1 SLINK, slip, steal, pad, sidle, skulk 2 SLIP, smuggle, spirit ▷ *noun* INFORMER, grass (*Brit slang*), betrayer, telltale, squealer (*slang*), Judas, accuser, stool pigeon, snake in the grass, nark (*Brit, Austral & NZ slang*), fizgig (*Austral slang*) ▷ *modifier* SECRET, quick, clandestine, furtive, stealthy

sneaking *adjective* 1 NAGGING, worrying, persistent, niggling, uncomfortable 2 SECRET, private, hidden, suppressed, unexpressed, unvoiced, unavowed, unconfessed, undivulged

sneaky *adjective* SLY, dishonest, devious, mean, low, base, nasty, cowardly, slippery, unreliable, malicious, unscrupulous, furtive, disingenuous, shifty, snide, deceitful, contemptible, untrustworthy, double-dealing

sneer *verb* 1 SCORN, mock, ridicule, laugh, jeer, disdain, scoff, deride, look down on, snigger, sniff at, gibe, hold in contempt, hold up to ridicule, turn up your nose (*informal*) 2 SAY CONTEMPTUOUSLY, snigger ▷ *noun* 1 SCORN, ridicule, mockery, derision, jeer, disdain, snigger, gibe, snidery 2 CONTEMPTUOUS SMILE, snigger, curl of the lip

snide *or* **snidey** *adjective* NASTY, sneering,

malicious, mean, cynical, unkind, hurtful, sarcastic, disparaging, spiteful, insinuating, scornful, shrewish, ill-natured, snarky (*informal*)

sniff *verb* 1 BREATHE IN, inhale, snuffle, snuff 2 SMELL, nose, breathe in, scent, get a whiff of 3 INHALE, breathe in, suck in, draw in

sniffy *adjective* (*informal*) CONTEMPTUOUS, superior, condescending, haughty, scornful, disdainful, supercilious

snigger *verb* LAUGH, giggle, sneer, snicker, titter ▷ *noun* LAUGH, giggle, sneer, snicker, titter

snip *verb* CUT, nick, clip, crop, trim, dock, notch, nip off ▷ *noun* (*informal, chiefly Brit*) BARGAIN, steal (*informal*), good buy, giveaway

snipe *verb* CRITICIZE, knock (*informal*), put down, carp, bitch, have a go (at) (*informal*), jeer, denigrate, disparage

snippet *noun* PIECE, scrap, fragment, part, particle, snatch, shred

snob *noun* ELITIST, highbrow, social climber

snobbery *noun* ARROGANCE, airs, pride, pretension, condescension, snobbishness, snootiness (*informal*), side (*Brit slang*), uppishness (*Brit informal*)

snobbish *adjective* SUPERIOR, arrogant, stuck-up (*informal*), patronizing, condescending, snooty (*informal*), pretentious, uppity, high and mighty (*informal*), toffee-nosed (*slang, chiefly Brit*), hoity-toity (*informal*), high-hat (*informal, chiefly US*), uppish (*Brit informal*) << ANTONYM humble

snoop *verb* 1 INVESTIGATE, explore, have a good look at, prowl around, nose around, peer into 2 SPY, poke your nose in, nose, interfere, pry (*informal*) ▷ *noun* LOOK, search, nose, prowl, investigation

snooty *adjective* (*informal*) SNOBBISH, superior, aloof, pretentious, stuck-up (*informal*), condescending, proud, haughty, disdainful, snotty, uppity, supercilious, high and mighty (*informal*), toffee-nosed (*slang, chiefly Brit*), hoity-toity (*informal*), high-hat (*informal, chiefly US*), uppish (*Brit informal*), toplofty (*informal*) << ANTONYM humble

snooze (*informal*) *noun* DOZE, nap, kip (*Brit slang*), siesta, catnap, forty winks (*informal*) ▷ *verb* DOZE, drop off (*informal*), nap, kip (*Brit slang*), nod off (*informal*), catnap, drowse, take forty winks (*informal*)

snub *verb* INSULT, slight, put down, humiliate, cut (*informal*), shame, humble, rebuff, mortify, cold-shoulder, kick in the teeth (*slang*), give (someone) the cold shoulder, give (someone) the brush-off (*slang*), cut dead (*informal*) ▷ *noun* INSULT, put-down, humiliation, affront, slap in the face, brush-off (*slang*)

snug *adjective* 1 COSY, warm, comfortable, homely, sheltered, intimate, comfy (*informal*) 2 TIGHT, close, trim, neat

snuggle *verb* NESTLE, cuddle up

so *sentence connector* THEREFORE, thus, hence, consequently, then, as a result, accordingly, for that reason, whence, thence, ergo

soak *verb* 1 STEEP, immerse, submerge, infuse, marinate (*cookery*), dunk, submerse 2 WET, damp, saturate, drench, douse, moisten, suffuse, wet through, waterlog, souse, drouk (*Scot*) 3 PENETRATE, pervade, permeate, enter, get in, infiltrate, diffuse, seep, suffuse, make inroads (into) ▷▷ **soak something up** ABSORB, suck up, take in *or* up, drink in, assimilate

soaking *adjective* SOAKED, dripping, saturated, drenched, sodden, waterlogged, streaming, sopping, wet through, soaked to the skin, wringing wet, like a drowned rat, droukit *or* drookit (*Scot*)

soar *verb* 1 RISE, increase, grow, mount, climb, go up, rocket, swell, escalate, shoot up 2 FLY, rise, wing, climb, ascend, fly up << ANTONYM plunge 3 TOWER, rise, climb, go up

sob *verb* CRY, weep, blubber, greet (*Scot archaic*), howl, bawl, snivel, shed tears, boohoo ▷ *noun* CRY, whimper, howl

sober *adjective* 1 ABSTINENT, temperate, abstemious, moderate, on the wagon (*informal*) << ANTONYM drunk 2 SERIOUS, practical, realistic, sound, cool, calm, grave, reasonable, steady, composed, rational, solemn, lucid, sedate, staid, level-headed, dispassionate, unruffled, clear-headed, unexcited << ANTONYM frivolous 3 PLAIN, dark, sombre, quiet, severe, subdued, drab << ANTONYM bright ▷ *verb* 1 *usually with* up COME TO YOUR SENSES << ANTONYM get drunk 2 *usually with* up CLEAR YOUR HEAD

sobriety *noun* 1 ABSTINENCE, temperance, abstemiousness, moderation, self-restraint, soberness, nonindulgence 2 SERIOUSNESS, gravity, steadiness, restraint, composure, coolness, calmness, solemnity, reasonableness, level-headedness, staidness, sedateness

so-called *adjective* ALLEGED, supposed, professed, pretended, self-styled, ostensible, soi-disant (*French*)

sociability *noun* FRIENDLINESS, conviviality,

cordiality, congeniality, neighbourliness, affability, gregariousness, companionability

sociable *adjective* FRIENDLY, social, outgoing, warm, neighbourly, accessible, cordial, genial, affable, approachable, gregarious, convivial, companionable, conversable << ANTONYM unsociable

social *adjective* 1 COMMUNAL, community, collective, group, public, general, common, societal 2 SOCIABLE, friendly, companionable, neighbourly 3 ORGANIZED, gregarious ▷ *noun* GET-TOGETHER (*informal*), party, gathering, function, do (*informal*), reception, bash (*informal*), social gathering

socialize *verb* MIX, interact, mingle, be sociable, meet, go out, entertain, get together, fraternize, be a good mixer, get about *or* around

society *noun* 1 THE COMMUNITY, social order, people, the public, the population, humanity, civilization, mankind, the general public, the world at large 2 CULTURE, community, population 3 ORGANIZATION, group, club, union, league, association, institute, circle, corporation, guild, fellowship, fraternity, brotherhood *or* sisterhood 4 UPPER CLASSES, gentry, upper crust (*informal*), elite, the swells (*informal*), high society, the top drawer, polite society, the toffs (*Brit slang*), the smart set, beau monde, the nobs (*slang*), the country set, haut monde (*French*) 5 (*old-fashioned*) COMPANIONSHIP, company, fellowship, friendship, camaraderie

sodden *adjective* SOAKED, saturated, sopping, drenched, soggy, waterlogged, marshy, boggy, miry, droukit *or* drookit (*Scot*)

sodomy *noun* ANAL INTERCOURSE, anal sex, buggery

sofa *noun* COUCH, settee, divan, chaise longue, chesterfield, ottoman

soft *adjective* 1 VELVETY, smooth, silky, furry, feathery, downy, fleecy, like a baby's bottom (*informal*) << ANTONYM rough 2 YIELDING, flexible, pliable, cushioned, elastic, malleable, spongy, springy, cushiony << ANTONYM hard 3 SOGGY, swampy, marshy, boggy, squelchy, quaggy 4 SQUASHY, sloppy, mushy, spongy, squidgy (*Brit informal*), squishy, gelatinous, squelchy, pulpy, doughy 5 PLIABLE, flexible, supple, malleable, plastic, elastic, tensile, ductile (*of metals*), bendable, mouldable, impressible 6 QUIET, low, gentle, sweet, whispered, soothing, murmured, muted,

subdued, mellow, understated, melodious, mellifluous, dulcet, soft-toned << ANTONYM loud 7 LENIENT, easy-going, lax, liberal, weak, indulgent, permissive, spineless, boneless, overindulgent << ANTONYM harsh 8 KIND, tender, sentimental, compassionate, sensitive, gentle, pitying, sympathetic, tenderhearted, touchy-feely (*informal*) 9 (*informal*) EASY, comfortable, undemanding, cushy (*informal*), easy-peasy (*slang*) 10 PALE, light, subdued, pastel, pleasing, bland, mellow << ANTONYM bright 11 DIM, faint, dimmed << ANTONYM bright 12 MILD, delicate, caressing, temperate, balmy 13 (*informal*) FEEBLE-MINDED, simple, silly, foolish, daft (*informal*), soft in the head (*informal*), a bit lacking (*informal*)

soften *verb* 1 MELT, tenderize 2 LESSEN, moderate, diminish, temper, lower, relax, ease, calm, modify, cushion, soothe, subdue, alleviate, lighten, quell, muffle, allay, mitigate, abate, tone down, assuage

soggy *adjective* SODDEN, saturated, moist, heavy, soaked, dripping, waterlogged, sopping, mushy, spongy, pulpy

soil¹ *noun* 1 EARTH, ground, clay, dust, dirt, loam 2 TERRITORY, country, land, region, turf (*US slang*), terrain

soil² *verb* DIRTY, foul, stain, smear, muddy, pollute, tarnish, spatter, sully, defile, besmirch, smirch, bedraggle, befoul, begrime << ANTONYM clean

sojourn (*literary*) *noun* STAY, visit, stop, rest, stopover

solace *noun* COMFORT, consolation, help, support, relief, succour, alleviation, assuagement ▷ *verb* COMFORT, console, soothe

soldier *noun* FIGHTER, serviceman, trooper, warrior, Tommy (*Brit informal*), GI (*US informal*), military man, redcoat, enlisted man (*US*), man-at-arms, squaddie *or* squaddy (*Brit slang*)

sole *adjective* ONLY, one, single, individual, alone, exclusive, solitary, singular, one and only

solely *adverb* ONLY, completely, entirely, exclusively, alone, singly, merely, single-handedly

solemn *adjective* 1 SERIOUS, earnest, grave, sober, thoughtful, sedate, glum, staid, portentous << ANTONYM cheerful 2 FORMAL, august, grand, imposing, impressive, grave, majestic, dignified, ceremonial, stately, momentous, awe-inspiring, ceremonious << ᴀɴᴛᴏɴʏᴍ informal **3** ꜱᴀᴄʀᴇᴅ, religious, holy, ritual, venerable, hallowed, sanctified, devotional, reverential << ᴀɴᴛᴏɴʏᴍ irreligious

solemnity *noun* **1** ꜱᴇʀɪᴏᴜꜱɴᴇꜱꜱ, gravity, formality, grandeur, gravitas, earnestness, portentousness, momentousness, impressiveness **2** *often plural* ʀɪᴛᴜᴀʟ, proceedings, ceremony, rite, formalities, ceremonial, observance, celebration

solicit *verb* **1** ʀᴇQᴜᴇꜱᴛ, seek, ask for, petition, crave, pray for, plead for, canvass, beg for **2** ᴀᴘᴘᴇᴀʟ ᴛᴏ, ask, call on, lobby, press, beg, petition, plead with, implore, beseech, entreat, importune, supplicate

solicitous *adjective* ᴄᴏɴᴄᴇʀɴᴇᴅ, caring, attentive, careful

solid *adjective* **1** ꜰɪʀᴍ, hard, compact, dense, massed, concrete << ᴀɴᴛᴏɴʏᴍ unsubstantial **2** ꜱᴛʀᴏɴɢ, stable, sturdy, sound, substantial, unshakable << ᴀɴᴛᴏɴʏᴍ unstable **3** ᴘᴜʀᴇ, unalloyed, unmixed, complete **4** ᴄᴏɴᴛɪɴᴜᴏᴜꜱ, unbroken, uninterrupted **5** ʀᴇʟɪᴀʙʟᴇ, decent, dependable, upstanding, serious, constant, sensible, worthy, upright, sober, law-abiding, trusty, level-headed, estimable << ᴀɴᴛᴏɴʏᴍ unreliable **6** ꜱᴏᴜɴᴅ, real, reliable, good, genuine, dinkum (*Austral & NZ informal*) << ᴀɴᴛᴏɴʏᴍ unsound

solidarity *noun* ᴜɴɪᴛʏ, harmony, unification, accord, stability, cohesion, team spirit, camaraderie, unanimity, soundness, concordance, esprit de corps, community of interest, singleness of purpose, like-mindedness, kotahitanga (*NZ*)

solidify *verb* ʜᴀʀᴅᴇɴ, set, congeal, cake, jell, coagulate, cohere

soliloquy *noun* ᴍᴏɴᴏʟᴏɢᴜᴇ, address, speech, aside, oration, dramatic monologue

solitary *adjective* **1** ᴜɴꜱᴏᴄɪᴀʙʟᴇ, retiring, reclusive, unsocial, isolated, lonely, cloistered, lonesome, friendless, companionless << ᴀɴᴛᴏɴʏᴍ sociable **2** ʟᴏɴᴇ, alone **3** ɪꜱᴏʟᴀᴛᴇᴅ, remote, out-of-the-way, desolate, hidden, sequestered, unvisited, unfrequented << ᴀɴᴛᴏɴʏᴍ busy

solitude *noun* **1** ɪꜱᴏʟᴀᴛɪᴏɴ, privacy, seclusion, retirement, loneliness, ivory tower, reclusiveness **2** (*poetic*) ᴡɪʟᴅᴇʀɴᴇꜱꜱ, waste, desert, emptiness, wasteland

solution *noun* **1** ᴀɴꜱᴡᴇʀ, resolution, key, result, solving, explanation, unfolding, unravelling, clarification, explication, elucidation **2** (*chemistry*) ᴍɪxᴛᴜʀᴇ, mix,

compound, blend, suspension, solvent, emulsion

solve *verb* ᴀɴꜱᴡᴇʀ, work out, resolve, explain, crack, interpret, unfold, clarify, clear up, unravel, decipher, expound, suss (out) (*slang*), get to the bottom of, disentangle, elucidate

solvent *adjective* ꜰɪɴᴀɴᴄɪᴀʟʟʏ ꜱᴏᴜɴᴅ, secure, in the black, solid, profit-making, in credit, debt-free, unindebted

sombre *adjective* **1** ɢʟᴏᴏᴍʏ, sad, sober, grave, dismal, melancholy, mournful, lugubrious, joyless, funereal, doleful, sepulchral << ᴀɴᴛᴏɴʏᴍ cheerful **2** ᴅᴀʀᴋ, dull, gloomy, sober, drab << ᴀɴᴛᴏɴʏᴍ bright

somebody *noun* ᴄᴇʟᴇʙʀɪᴛʏ, big name, public figure, name, star, heavyweight (*informal*), notable, superstar, household name, dignitary, luminary, bigwig (*informal*), celeb (*informal*), big shot (*informal*), personage, megastar (*informal*), big wheel (*slang*), big noise (*informal*), big hitter (*informal*), heavy hitter (*informal*), person of note, V.I.P., someone << ᴀɴᴛᴏɴʏᴍ nobody

someday *adverb* ᴏɴᴇ ᴅᴀʏ, eventually, ultimately, sooner or later, one of these (fine) days, in the fullness of time

somehow *adverb* ᴏɴᴇ ᴡᴀʏ ᴏʀ ᴀɴᴏᴛʜᴇʀ, come what may, come hell or high water (*informal*), by fair means or foul, by hook or (by) crook, by some means or other

sometime *adverb* ꜱᴏᴍᴇ ᴅᴀʏ, one day, at some point in the future, sooner or later, one of these days, by and by ▷ *adjective* ꜰᴏʀᴍᴇʀ, one-time, erstwhile, ex-, late, past, previous

sometimes *adverb* ᴏᴄᴄᴀꜱɪᴏɴᴀʟʟʏ, at times, now and then, from time to time, on occasion, now and again, once in a while, every now and then, every so often, off and on << ᴀɴᴛᴏɴʏᴍ always

son *noun* ᴍᴀʟᴇ ᴄʜɪʟᴅ, boy, lad (*informal*), descendant, son and heir

song *noun* ʙᴀʟʟᴀᴅ, air, tune, lay, strain, carol, lyric, chant, chorus, melody, anthem, number, hymn, psalm, shanty, pop song, ditty, canticle, canzonet, waiata (*NZ*)

song and dance *noun* (*Brit informal*) ꜰᴜꜱꜱ, to-do, flap (*informal*), performance (*informal*), stir, pantomime (*informal*), commotion, ado, shindig (*informal*), kerfuffle (*informal*), hoo-ha, pother, shindy (*informal*)

soon *adverb* ʙᴇꜰᴏʀᴇ ʟᴏɴɢ, shortly, in the near future, in a minute, anon (*archaic*), in a short time, in a little while, any minute now, betimes (*archaic*), in two shakes of a lamb's tail, erelong (*archaic or poetic*), in a couple of shakes

sooner *adverb* **1** EARLIER, before, already, beforehand, ahead of time **2** RATHER, more readily, by preference, more willingly

soothe *verb* **1** CALM, still, quiet, hush, settle, calm down, appease, lull, mitigate, pacify, mollify, smooth down, tranquillize << ANTONYM upset **2** RELIEVE, ease, alleviate, dull, diminish, assuage << ANTONYM irritate

soothing *adjective* **1** CALMING, relaxing, peaceful, quiet, calm, restful **2** EMOLLIENT, palliative, balsamic, demulcent, easeful, lenitive

sophisticated *adjective* **1** COMPLEX, advanced, complicated, subtle, delicate, elaborate, refined, intricate, multifaceted, highly-developed << ANTONYM simple **2** CULTURED, refined, cultivated, worldly, cosmopolitan, urbane, jet-set, world-weary, citified, worldly-wise << ANTONYM unsophisticated

sophistication *noun* POISE, worldliness, savoir-faire, urbanity, finesse, savoir-vivre (*French*), worldly wisdom

soporific *adjective* SLEEP-INDUCING, hypnotic, sedative, sleepy, somnolent, tranquillizing, somniferous (*rare*)

soppy *adjective* (*Brit informal*) SENTIMENTAL, corny (*slang*), slushy (*informal*), soft (*informal*), silly, daft (*informal*), weepy (*informal*), mawkish, drippy (*informal*), lovey-dovey, schmaltzy (*slang*), icky (*informal*), gushy (*informal*), overemotional, three-hankie (*informal*)

sorcerer *or* **sorceress** *noun* MAGICIAN, witch, wizard, magus, warlock, mage (*archaic*), enchanter, necromancer

sorcery *noun* BLACK MAGIC, witchcraft, black art, necromancy, spell, magic, charm, wizardry, enchantment, divination, incantation, witchery

sordid *adjective* **1** BASE, degraded, shameful, low, vicious, shabby, vile, degenerate, despicable, disreputable, debauched << ANTONYM honourable **2** DIRTY, seedy, sleazy, squalid, mean, foul, filthy, unclean, wretched, seamy, slovenly, slummy, scungy (*Austral & NZ*), festy (*Austral slang*) << ANTONYM clean

sore *adjective* **1** PAINFUL, smarting, raw, tender, burning, angry, sensitive, irritated, inflamed, chafed, reddened **2** ANNOYED, cross, angry, pained, hurt, upset, stung, irritated, grieved, resentful, aggrieved, vexed, irked, peeved (*informal*), tooshie (*Austral slang*), hoha (*NZ*) **3** ANNOYING, distressing, troublesome, harrowing, grievous **4** URGENT, desperate, extreme, dire, pressing, critical, acute ▷ *noun* ABSCESS, boil, ulcer, inflammation, gathering

sorrow *noun* **1** GRIEF, sadness, woe, regret, distress, misery, mourning, anguish, unhappiness, heartache, heartbreak, affliction << ANTONYM joy **2** HARDSHIP, trial, tribulation, affliction, worry, trouble, blow, woe, misfortune, bummer (*slang*) << ANTONYM good fortune ▷ *verb* GRIEVE, mourn, lament, weep, moan, be sad, bemoan, agonize, eat your heart out, bewail << ANTONYM rejoice

sorrowful *adjective* SAD, unhappy, miserable, sorry, depressed, painful, distressed, grieving, dismal, afflicted, melancholy, tearful, heartbroken, woeful, mournful, dejected, rueful, lugubrious, wretched, disconsolate, doleful, heavy-hearted, down in the dumps (*informal*), woebegone, piteous, sick at heart

sorry *adjective* **1** REGRETFUL, apologetic, contrite, repentant, guilt-ridden, remorseful, penitent, shamefaced, conscience-stricken, in sackcloth and ashes, self-reproachful << ANTONYM unapologetic **2** SYMPATHETIC, moved, full of pity, pitying, compassionate, commiserative << ANTONYM unsympathetic **3** SAD, distressed, unhappy, grieved, melancholy, mournful, sorrowful, disconsolate << ANTONYM happy **4** WRETCHED, miserable, pathetic, mean, base, poor, sad, distressing, dismal, shabby, vile, paltry, pitiful, abject, deplorable, pitiable, piteous

sort *noun* KIND, type, class, make, group, family, order, race, style, quality, character, nature, variety, brand, species, breed, category, stamp, description, denomination, genus, ilk ▷ *verb* ARRANGE, group, order, class, separate, file, rank, divide, grade, distribute, catalogue, classify, categorize, tabulate, systematize, put in order ▷▷ **out of sorts 1** IRRITABLE, cross, edgy, tense, crabbed, snarling, prickly, snappy, touchy, bad-tempered, petulant, ill-tempered, irascible, cantankerous, tetchy, ratty (*Brit & NZ informal*), testy, fretful, grouchy (*informal*), peevish, crabby, dyspeptic, choleric, crotchety, oversensitive, snappish, ill-humoured, narky (*Brit slang*), out of humour **2** DEPRESSED, miserable, in low spirits, down, low, blue, sad, unhappy, gloomy, melancholy, mournful, dejected, despondent, dispirited, downcast, long-faced, sorrowful, disconsolate, crestfallen, down in the dumps (*informal*), down in the mouth (*informal*), mopy **3** UNWELL, ill, sick, poorly (*informal*), funny (*informal*), crook (*Austral & NZ informal*), ailing, queer, unhealthy, seedy (*informal*), laid up (*informal*), queasy, infirm, dicky (*Brit informal*), off colour, under the weather (*informal*), at death's door, indisposed, on the sick list (*informal*), not up to par, valetudinarian, green about the gills, not up to snuff (*informal*) ▷▷ **sort of** RATHER, somewhat, as it were, slightly, moderately, in part, reasonably

so-so *adjective* (*informal*) AVERAGE, middling, fair, ordinary, moderate, adequate, respectable, indifferent, not bad (*informal*), tolerable, run-of-the-mill, passable, undistinguished, fair to middling (*informal*), O.K. *or* okay (*informal*)

soul *noun* **1** SPIRIT, essence, psyche, life, mind, reason, intellect, vital force, animating principle, wairua (*NZ*) **2** EMBODIMENT, essence, incarnation, epitome, personification, quintessence, type **3** PERSON, being, human, individual, body, creature, mortal, man *or* woman **4** FEELING, force, energy, vitality, animation, fervour, ardour, vivacity

soulful *adjective* EXPRESSIVE, sensitive, eloquent, moving, profound, meaningful, heartfelt, mournful

soulless *adjective* **1** CHARACTERLESS, dull, bland, mundane, ordinary, grey, commonplace, dreary, mediocre, drab, uninspiring, colourless, featureless, unexceptional **2** UNFEELING, dead, cold, lifeless, inhuman, harsh, cruel, callous, unkind, unsympathetic, spiritless

sound¹ *noun* **1** NOISE, racket, din, report, tone, resonance, hubbub, reverberation **2** IDEA, impression, implication(s), drift **3** CRY, noise, peep, squeak **4** TONE, music, note, chord **5** EARSHOT, hearing, hearing distance ▷ *verb* **1** TOLL, set off **2** RESOUND, echo, go off, toll, set off, chime, resonate, reverberate, clang, peal **3** SEEM, seem to be, appear to be, give the impression of being, strike you as being

sound² *adjective* **1** FIT, healthy, robust, firm, perfect, intact, vigorous, hale, unhurt, undamaged, uninjured, unimpaired, hale and hearty << ANTONYM frail **2** STURDY, strong, solid, stable, substantial, durable, stout, well-constructed **3** SAFE, secure, reliable, proven, established, recognized, solid, stable, solvent, reputable, tried-and-true << ANTONYM unreliable **4** SENSIBLE, wise, reasonable, right, true, responsible, correct, proper, reliable, valid, orthodox, rational, logical, prudent, trustworthy, well-founded, level-headed, right-thinking, well-grounded << ANTONYM irresponsible **5** DEEP, peaceful, unbroken, undisturbed, untroubled << ANTONYM troubled

sound³ ▷▷ **sound someone out** QUESTION, interview, survey, poll, examine, investigate, pump (*informal*), inspect, canvass, test the opinion of ▷▷ **sound something out** INVESTIGATE, research, examine, probe, look into, test the water, put out feelers to, see how the land lies, carry out an investigation of

sound⁴ *noun* CHANNEL, passage, strait, inlet, fjord, voe, arm of the sea

sour *adjective* **1** SHARP, acid, tart, bitter, unpleasant, pungent, acetic, acidulated, acerb << ANTONYM sweet **2** RANCID, turned, gone off, fermented, unsavoury, curdled, unwholesome, gone bad, off << ANTONYM fresh **3** BITTER, cynical, crabbed, tart, discontented, grudging, acrimonious, embittered, disagreeable, churlish, ill-tempered, jaundiced, waspish, grouchy (*informal*), ungenerous, peevish, ill-natured << ANTONYM good-natured ▷ *verb* EMBITTER, disenchant, alienate, envenom

source *noun* **1** CAUSE, origin, derivation, beginning, author **2** INFORMANT, authority, documentation **3** ORIGIN, spring, fount, fountainhead, wellspring, rise

souvenir *noun* KEEPSAKE, token, reminder, relic, remembrancer (*archaic*), memento

sovereign *adjective* **1** SUPREME, ruling, absolute, chief, royal, principal, dominant, imperial, unlimited, paramount, regal, predominant, monarchal, kingly *or* queenly **2** EXCELLENT, efficient, efficacious, effectual ▷ *noun* MONARCH, ruler, king *or* queen, chief, shah, potentate, supreme ruler, emperor *or* empress, prince *or* princess, tsar *or* tsarina

sovereignty *noun* SUPREME POWER, domination, supremacy, primacy, sway, ascendancy, kingship, suzerainty, rangatiratanga (*NZ*)

sow *verb* SCATTER, plant, seed, lodge, implant, disseminate, broadcast, inseminate

space *noun* **1** ROOM, volume, capacity, extent, margin, extension, scope, play, expanse, leeway, amplitude, spaciousness, elbowroom **2** GAP, opening, interval, gulf, cavity, aperture **3** PERIOD, interval, time, while, span, duration, time frame, timeline **4** OUTER SPACE, the universe, the galaxy, the solar system, the cosmos **5** BLANK, gap, interval

spaceman *or* **spacewoman** *noun* ASTRONAUT, cosmonaut, space cadet, space traveller

spacious *adjective* ROOMY, large, huge, broad, vast, extensive, ample, expansive, capacious, uncrowded, commodious, comfortable, sizable *or* sizeable << ANTONYM limited

span *noun* **1** PERIOD, term, duration, spell **2** EXTENT, reach, spread, length, distance, stretch ▷ *verb* EXTEND ACROSS, cross, bridge, cover, link, vault, traverse, range over, arch across

spank *verb* SMACK, slap, whack, belt (*informal*), tan (*slang*), slipper (*informal*), cuff, wallop (*informal*), give (someone) a hiding (*informal*), put (someone) over your knee

spanking *noun* SMACKING, hiding (*informal*), whacking, slapping, walloping (*informal*)

spanking *adjective* **1** (*informal*) SMART, brand-new, fine, gleaming **2** FAST, quick, brisk, lively, smart, vigorous, energetic, snappy

spar *verb* ARGUE, row, squabble, dispute, scrap (*informal*), fall out (*informal*), spat (*US*), wrangle, skirmish, bicker, have a tiff

spare *adjective* **1** BACK-UP, reserve, second, extra, relief, emergency, additional, substitute, fall-back, auxiliary, in reserve **2** EXTRA, surplus, leftover, over, free, odd, unwanted, in excess, unused, superfluous, supernumerary << ANTONYM necessary **3** FREE, leisure, unoccupied **4** THIN, lean, slim, slender, slight, meagre, gaunt, wiry, lank << ANTONYM plump **5** MEAGRE, sparing, modest, economical, frugal, scanty ▷ *verb* **1** AFFORD, give, grant, do without, relinquish, part with, allow, bestow, dispense with, manage without, let someone have **2** HAVE MERCY ON, pardon, have pity on, leave, release, excuse, let off (*informal*), go easy on (*informal*), be merciful to, grant pardon to, deal leniently with, refrain from hurting, save (from harm) << ANTONYM show no mercy to

sparing *adjective* ECONOMICAL, frugal, thrifty, saving, careful, prudent, cost-conscious, chary, money-conscious << ANTONYM lavish

spark *noun* **1** FLICKER, flash, gleam, glint, spit, flare, scintillation **2** TRACE, hint, scrap, atom, jot, vestige, scintilla ▷ *verb often with*

off START, stimulate, provoke, excite, inspire, stir, trigger (off), set off, animate, rouse, prod, precipitate, kick-start, set in motion, kindle, touch off

sparkle *verb* GLITTER, flash, spark, shine, beam, glow, gleam, wink, shimmer, twinkle, dance, glint, glisten, glister (*archaic*), scintillate ▷ *noun* **1** GLITTER, flash, gleam, spark, dazzle, flicker, brilliance, twinkle, glint, radiance **2** VIVACITY, life, spirit, dash, zip (*informal*), vitality, animation, panache, gaiety, élan, brio, liveliness, vim (*slang*)

sparse *adjective* SCATTERED, scarce, meagre, sporadic, few and far between, scanty << ANTONYM thick

Spartan *adjective* AUSTERE, severe, frugal, ascetic, plain, disciplined, extreme, strict, stern, bleak, rigorous, stringent, abstemious, self-denying

spasm *noun* **1** CONVULSION, contraction, paroxysm, twitch, throe (*rare*) **2** BURST, fit, outburst, seizure, frenzy, eruption, access

spasmodic *adjective* SPORADIC, irregular, erratic, intermittent, jerky, fitful, convulsive

spat *noun* QUARREL, dispute, squabble, controversy, contention, bickering, tiff, altercation

spate *noun* **1** FLOOD, flow, torrent, rush, deluge, outpouring **2** SERIES, sequence, course, chain, succession, run, train, string

spatter *verb* SPLASH, spray, sprinkle, soil, dirty, scatter, daub, speckle, splodge, bespatter, bestrew

spawn *verb* GENERATE, produce, give rise to, start, prompt, provoke, set off, bring about, spark off, set in motion

speak *verb* **1** TALK, say something **2** ARTICULATE, say, voice, pronounce, utter, tell, state, talk, express, communicate, make known, enunciate **3** CONVERSE, talk, chat, discourse, confer, commune, exchange views, shoot the breeze (*slang, chiefly US & Canad*) **4** LECTURE, talk, discourse, spout (*informal*), make a speech, pontificate, give a speech, declaim, hold forth, spiel (*informal*), address an audience, deliver an address, speechify ▷▷ **speak for something** *or* **someone 1** REPRESENT, act for *or* on behalf of, appear for, hold a brief for, hold a mandate for **2** SUPPORT, back, champion, defend, promote, advocate, fight for, uphold, commend, espouse, stick up for (*informal*)

speaker *noun* ORATOR, public speaker, lecturer, spokesperson, mouthpiece, spieler (*informal*), word-spinner, spokesman *or* spokeswoman

spearhead *verb* LEAD, head, pioneer, launch, set off, initiate, lead the way, set in motion, blaze the trail, be in the van, lay the first stone

special *adjective* **1** EXCEPTIONAL, important, significant, particular, unique, unusual, extraordinary, distinguished, memorable, gala, festive, uncommon, momentous, out of the ordinary, one in a million, red-letter, especial << ANTONYM ordinary **2** MAJOR, chief, main, primary **3** SPECIFIC, particular, distinctive, certain, individual, appropriate, characteristic, precise, peculiar, specialized, especial << ANTONYM general

specialist *noun* EXPERT, authority, professional, master, consultant, guru, buff (*informal*), whizz (*informal*), connoisseur, boffin (*Brit informal*), hotshot (*informal*), wonk (*informal*), maven (*US*), fundi (*S African*)

speciality *noun* **1** FORTE, strength, special talent, métier, specialty, bag (*slang*), claim to fame, pièce de résistance (*French*), distinctive *or* distinguishing feature **2** SPECIAL SUBJECT, specialty, field of study, branch of knowledge, area of specialization

species *noun* KIND, sort, type, group, class, variety, breed, category, description, genus

specific *adjective* **1** PARTICULAR, special, characteristic, distinguishing, peculiar, definite, especial << ANTONYM general **2** PRECISE, exact, explicit, definite, limited, express, clear-cut, unequivocal, unambiguous << ANTONYM vague **3** PECULIAR, appropriate, individual, particular, personal, unique, restricted, idiosyncratic, endemic

specification *noun* REQUIREMENT, detail, particular, stipulation, condition, qualification

specify *verb* STATE, designate, spell out, stipulate, name, detail, mention, indicate, define, cite, individualize, enumerate, itemize, be specific about, particularize

specimen *noun* **1** SAMPLE, example, individual, model, type, pattern, instance, representative, exemplar, exemplification **2** EXAMPLE, model, exhibit, embodiment, type

specious *adjective* FALLACIOUS, misleading, deceptive, plausible, unsound, sophistic, sophistical, casuistic

speck *noun* **1** MARK, spot, dot, stain, blot, fleck, speckle, mote **2** PARTICLE, bit, grain, dot, atom, shred, mite, jot, modicum, whit,

tittle, iota

speckled *adjective* FLECKED, spotted, dotted, sprinkled, spotty, freckled, mottled, dappled, stippled, brindled, speckledy

spectacle *noun* **1** SHOW, display, exhibition, event, performance, sight, parade, extravaganza, pageant **2** SIGHT, wonder, scene, phenomenon, curiosity, marvel, laughing stock

spectacles *plural noun* GLASSES, specs (*informal*), eyeglasses (*US*), eyewear

spectacular *adjective* IMPRESSIVE, striking, dramatic, stunning (*informal*), marked, grand, remarkable, fantastic (*informal*), magnificent, staggering, splendid, dazzling, sensational, breathtaking, eye-catching << ANTONYM unimpressive ▷ *noun* SHOW, display, spectacle, extravaganza

spectator *noun* ONLOOKER, observer, viewer, witness, looker-on, watcher, eyewitness, bystander, beholder << ANTONYM participant

spectral *adjective* GHOSTLY, unearthly, eerie, supernatural, weird, phantom, shadowy, uncanny, spooky (*informal*), insubstantial, incorporeal, wraithlike

spectre *noun* GHOST, spirit, phantom, presence, vision, shadow, shade (*literary*), apparition, wraith, kehua (*NZ*)

speculate *verb* **1** CONJECTURE, consider, wonder, guess, contemplate, deliberate, muse, meditate, surmise, theorize, hypothesize, cogitate **2** GAMBLE, risk, venture, hazard, have a flutter (*informal*), take a chance with, play the market

speculation *noun* **1** THEORY, opinion, hypothesis, conjecture, guess, consideration, deliberation, contemplation, surmise, guesswork, supposition **2** GAMBLE, risk, gambling, hazard

speculative *adjective* **1** HYPOTHETICAL, academic, theoretical, abstract, tentative, notional, conjectural, suppositional **2** RISKY, uncertain, hazardous, unpredictable, dicey (*informal, chiefly Brit*), chancy (*informal*)

speech *noun* **1** COMMUNICATION, talk, conversation, articulation, discussion, dialogue, intercourse **2** DICTION, pronunciation, articulation, delivery, fluency, inflection, intonation, elocution, enunciation **3** LANGUAGE, tongue, utterance, jargon, dialect, idiom, parlance, articulation, diction, lingo (*informal*), enunciation **4** TALK, address, lecture, discourse, harangue, homily, oration, spiel (*informal*), disquisition, whaikorero (*NZ*)

speechless *adjective* DUMB, dumbfounded, lost for words, dumbstruck, astounded, shocked, mum, amazed, silent, mute, dazed, aghast, inarticulate, tongue-tied, wordless, thunderstruck, unable to get a word out (*informal*)

speed *noun* **1** RATE, pace, momentum, tempo, velocity **2** VELOCITY, swiftness, acceleration, precipitation, rapidity, quickness, fastness, briskness, speediness, precipitateness **3** SWIFTNESS, rush, hurry, expedition, haste, rapidity, quickness, fleetness, celerity << ANTONYM slowness ▷ *verb* **1** RACE, rush, hurry, zoom, career, bomb (along), tear, flash, belt (along) (*slang*), barrel (along) (*informal, chiefly US & Canad*), sprint, gallop, hasten, press on, quicken, lose no time, get a move on (*informal*), burn rubber (*informal*), bowl along, put your foot down (*informal*), step on it (*informal*), make haste, go hell for leather (*informal*), exceed the speed limit, go like a bomb (*Brit & NZ informal*), go like the wind, go like a bat out of hell << ANTONYM crawl **2** HELP, further, advance, aid, promote, boost, assist, facilitate, impel, expedite << ANTONYM hinder ▷▷ **speed something up** ACCELERATE, promote, hasten, help along, further, forward, advance

speedy *adjective* QUICK, fast, rapid, swift, express, winged, immediate, prompt, fleet, hurried, summary, precipitate, hasty, headlong, quickie (*informal*), expeditious, fleet of foot, pdq (*slang*) << ANTONYM slow

spell[1] *verb* INDICATE, mean, signify, suggest, promise, point to, imply, amount to, herald, augur, presage, portend ▷▷ **spell something out** MAKE CLEAR or PLAIN, specify, make explicit, clarify, elucidate, explicate

spell[2] *noun* **1** INCANTATION, charm, sorcery, exorcism, abracadabra, witchery, conjuration, makutu (*NZ*) **2** ENCHANTMENT, magic, fascination, glamour, allure, bewitchment

spell[3] *noun* PERIOD, time, term, stretch, turn, course, season, patch, interval, bout, stint

spellbound *adjective* ENTRANCED, gripped, fascinated, transported, charmed, hooked, possessed, bemused, captivated, enthralled, bewitched, transfixed, rapt, mesmerized, under a spell

spelling *noun* ORTHOGRAPHY

spend *verb* **1** PAY OUT, fork out (*slang*), expend, lay out, splash out (*Brit informal*), shell out (*informal*), disburse << ANTONYM save **2** APPLY, use, employ, concentrate, invest, put in, devote, lavish, exert, bestow **3** PASS, fill, occupy, while away **4** USE UP, waste, squander, blow (*slang*), empty, drain, exhaust, consume, run through, deplete, dissipate, fritter away << ANTONYM save

spendthrift *noun* SQUANDERER, spender, profligate, prodigal, big spender, waster, wastrel << ANTONYM miser ▷ *adjective* WASTEFUL, extravagant, prodigal, profligate, improvident << ANTONYM economical

spent *adjective* **1** USED UP, finished, gone, consumed, expended **2** EXHAUSTED, drained, worn out, bushed (*informal*), all in (*slang*), shattered (*informal*), weakened, wiped out (*informal*), wearied, weary, played out (*informal*), burnt out, fagged (out) (*informal*), whacked (*Brit informal*), debilitated, knackered (*slang*), prostrate, clapped out (*Brit, Austral & NZ informal*), tired out, ready to drop (*informal*), dog-tired (*informal*), zonked (*informal*), dead beat (*informal*), shagged out (*Brit slang*), done in or up (*informal*)

sperm *noun* **1** SPERMATOZOON, reproductive cell, male gamete **2** SEMEN, seed (*archaic or dialect*), spermatozoa, scum (*US slang*), come or cum (*taboo*), jism or jissom (*taboo*)

spew *verb* **1** SHED, discharge, send out, issue, throw out, eject, diffuse, emanate, exude, cast out **2** VOMIT, throw up (*informal*), puke (*slang*), chuck (*Austral & NZ informal*), spit out, regurgitate, disgorge, barf (*US slang*), chunder (*slang, chiefly Austral*), belch forth, upchuck (*US slang*), do a technicolour yawn (*slang*), toss your cookies (*US slang*)

sphere *noun* **1** BALL, globe, orb, globule, circle **2** FIELD, range, area, department, function, territory, capacity, province, patch, scope, turf (*US slang*), realm, domain, compass, walk of life **3** RANK, class, station, status, stratum

spherical *adjective* ROUND, globular, globe-shaped, rotund, orbicular

spice *noun* **1** SEASONING, condiment **2** EXCITEMENT, kick (*informal*), zest, colour, pep, zip (*informal*), tang, zap (*slang*), gusto, zing (*informal*), piquancy

spicy *adjective* **1** HOT, seasoned, pungent, aromatic, savoury, tangy, piquant, flavoursome **2** (*informal*) RISQUÉ, racy, off-colour, ribald, hot (*informal*), broad, improper, suggestive, unseemly, titillating, indelicate, indecorous

spiel *noun* PATTER, speech, pitch, recital,

harangue, sales talk, sales patter

spike *noun* POINT, stake, spur, pin, nail, spine, barb, tine, prong ▷ *verb* 1 DRUG, lace, dope, cut, contaminate, adulterate 2 IMPALE, spit, spear, stick

spill *verb* 1 TIP OVER, upset, overturn, capsize, knock over, topple over 2 SHED, scatter, discharge, throw off, disgorge, spill *or* run over 3 SLOP, flow, pour, run, overflow, slosh, splosh 4 EMERGE, flood, pour, mill, stream, surge, swarm, crowd, teem ▷ *noun* SPILLAGE, flood, leak, leakage, overspill

spin *verb* 1 REVOLVE, turn, rotate, wheel, twist, reel, whirl, twirl, gyrate, pirouette, birl (*Scot*) 2 REEL, swim, whirl, be giddy, be in a whirl, grow dizzy 3 (*informal*) TELL, relate, recount, develop, invent, unfold, concoct, narrate ▷ *noun* 1 (*informal*) DRIVE, ride, turn, hurl (*Scot*), whirl, joy ride (*informal*) 2 REVOLUTION, roll, whirl, twist, gyration ▷▷ **spin something out** PROLONG, extend, lengthen, draw out, drag out, delay, amplify, pad out, protract, prolongate

spindly *adjective* LANKY, gangly, spidery, leggy, twiggy, attenuated, gangling, spindle-shanked

spine *noun* 1 BACKBONE, vertebrae, spinal column, vertebral column 2 BARB, spur, needle, spike, ray, quill 3 DETERMINATION, resolution, backbone, resolve, drive, conviction, fortitude, persistence, tenacity, perseverance, willpower, firmness, constancy, single-mindedness, steadfastness, doggedness, resoluteness, indomitability

spineless *adjective* WEAK, soft, cowardly, ineffective, feeble, yellow (*informal*), inadequate, pathetic, submissive, squeamish, vacillating, boneless, gutless (*informal*), weak-willed, weak-kneed (*informal*), faint-hearted, irresolute, spiritless, lily-livered, without a will of your own << ANTONYM brave

spiral *adjective* COILED, winding, corkscrew, circular, scrolled, whorled, helical, cochlear, voluted, cochleate (*biology*) ▷ *noun* COIL, helix, corkscrew, whorl, screw, curlicue

spirit *noun* 1 SOUL, life, psyche, essential being 2 LIFE FORCE, vital spark, breath, mauri (*NZ*) 3 GHOST, phantom, spectre, vision, shadow, shade (*literary*), spook (*informal*), apparition, sprite, atua (*NZ*), kehua (*NZ*) 4 COURAGE, guts (*informal*), grit, balls (*taboo slang*), backbone, spunk (*informal*), gameness, ballsiness (*taboo slang*), dauntlessness, stoutheartedness 5 LIVELINESS, energy, vigour, life, force, fire, resolution, enterprise, enthusiasm,

sparkle, warmth, animation, zest, mettle, ardour, earnestness, brio 6 ATTITUDE, character, quality, humour, temper, outlook, temperament, complexion, disposition 7 HEART, sense, nature, soul, core, substance, essence, lifeblood, quintessence, fundamental nature 8 INTENTION, meaning, purpose, substance, intent, essence, purport, gist 9 FEELING, atmosphere, character, feel, quality, tone, mood, flavour, tenor, ambience, vibes (*slang*) 10 RESOLVE, will, drive, resolution, conviction, motivation, dedication, backbone, fortitude, persistence, tenacity, perseverance, willpower, firmness, constancy, single-mindedness, steadfastness, doggedness, resoluteness, indomitability 11 *plural* MOOD, feelings, morale, humour, temper, tenor, disposition, state of mind, frame of mind

spirited *adjective* LIVELY, vigorous, energetic, animated, game, active, bold, sparkling, have-a-go (*informal*), courageous, ardent, feisty (*informal, chiefly US & Canad*), plucky, high-spirited, sprightly, vivacious, spunky (*informal*), mettlesome, (as) game as Ned Kelly (*Austral slang*) << ANTONYM lifeless

spirits *plural noun* STRONG ALCOHOL, liquor, the hard stuff (*informal*), firewater, strong liquor

spiritual *adjective* 1 NONMATERIAL, immaterial, incorporeal << ANTONYM material 2 SACRED, religious, holy, divine, ethereal, devotional, otherworldly

spit *verb* 1 EXPECTORATE, sputter 2 EJECT, discharge, throw out ▷ *noun* SALIVA, dribble, spittle, drool, slaver, sputum

spite *noun* MALICE, malevolence, ill will, hate, hatred, gall, animosity, venom, spleen, pique, rancour, bitchiness (*slang*), malignity, spitefulness << ANTONYM kindness ▷ *verb* ANNOY, hurt, injure, harm, provoke, offend, needle (*informal*), put out, gall, nettle, vex, pique, discomfit, put someone's nose out of joint (*informal*), hack someone off (*informal*) << ANTONYM benefit ▷▷ **in spite of** DESPITE, regardless of, notwithstanding, in defiance of, (even) though

spiteful *adjective* MALICIOUS, nasty, vindictive, cruel, malignant, barbed, malevolent, venomous, bitchy (*informal*), snide, rancorous, catty (*informal*), splenetic, shrewish, ill-disposed, ill-natured

spitting image *noun* DOUBLE, lookalike, (dead) ringer (*slang*), picture, spit (*informal, chiefly Brit*), clone, replica, likeness, living image, spit and image (*informal*)

splash *verb* **1** PADDLE, plunge, bathe, dabble, wade, wallow **2** SCATTER, shower, spray, sprinkle, spread, wet, strew, squirt, spatter, slop, slosh (*informal*) **3** SPATTER, mark, stain, smear, speck, speckle, blotch, splodge, bespatter **4** DASH, break, strike, wash, batter, surge, smack, buffet, plop, plash ▷ *noun* **1** SPLASHING, dashing, plash, beating, battering, swashing **2** DASH, touch, spattering, splodge **3** SPOT, burst, patch, stretch, spurt **4** BLOB, spot, smudge, stain, smear, fleck, speck ▷▷ **make a splash** (*informal*) CAUSE A STIR, make an impact, cause a sensation, cut a dash, be ostentatious

spleen *noun* SPITE, anger, bitterness, hostility, hatred, resentment, wrath, gall, malice, animosity, venom, bile, bad temper, acrimony, pique, rancour, ill will, animus, malevolence, vindictiveness, malignity, spitefulness, ill humour, peevishness

splendid *adjective* **1** EXCELLENT, wonderful, marvellous, mean (*slang*), great (*informal*), topping (*Brit slang*), fine, cracking (*Brit informal*), crucial (*slang*), fantastic (*informal*), first-class, glorious, mega (*slang*), sovereign, awesome (*slang*), def (*slang*), brill (*informal*), bodacious (*slang, chiefly US*), boffo (*slang*), chillin' (*US slang*), booshit (*Austral slang*), exo (*Austral slang*), sik (*Austral slang*), rad (*informal*), phat (*slang*), schmick (*Austral informal*) << ANTONYM poor **2** MAGNIFICENT, grand, imposing, impressive, rich, superb, costly, gorgeous, dazzling, lavish, luxurious, sumptuous, ornate, resplendent, splendiferous (*facetious*) << ANTONYM squalid **3** GLORIOUS, superb, magnificent, grand, brilliant, rare, supreme, outstanding, remarkable, sterling, exceptional, renowned, admirable, sublime, illustrious << ANTONYM ignoble

splendour *noun* MAGNIFICENCE, glory, grandeur, show, display, ceremony, luxury, spectacle, majesty, richness, nobility, pomp, opulence, solemnity, éclat, gorgeousness, sumptuousness, stateliness, resplendence, luxuriousness << ANTONYM squalor

splice *verb* JOIN, unite, graft, marry, wed, knit, mesh, braid, intertwine, interweave, yoke, plait, entwine, interlace, intertwist

splinter *noun* SLIVER, fragment, chip, needle, shaving, flake, paring ▷ *verb* SHATTER, split, fracture, shiver, disintegrate, break into fragments

split *verb* **1** BREAK, crack, burst, snap, break up, open, give way, splinter, gape, come apart, come undone **2** CUT, break, crack, snap, chop, cleave, hew **3** DIVIDE, separate, disunite, disrupt, disband, cleave, pull apart, set at odds, set at variance **4** DIVERGE, separate, branch, fork, part, go separate ways **5** TEAR, rend, rip, slash, slit **6** SHARE OUT, divide, distribute, halve, allocate, partition, allot, carve up, dole out, apportion, slice up, parcel out, divvy up (*informal*) ▷ *noun* **1** DIVISION, break, breach, rift, difference, disruption, rupture, discord, divergence, schism, estrangement, dissension, disunion **2** SEPARATION, break, divorce, break-up, split-up, disunion **3** CRACK, tear, rip, damage, gap, rent, breach, slash, slit, fissure ▷ *adjective* **1** DIVIDED, ambivalent, bisected **2** BROKEN, cracked, snapped, fractured, splintered, ruptured, cleft ▷▷ **split on someone** (*slang*) BETRAY, tell on, shop (*slang, chiefly Brit*), sing (*slang, chiefly US*), grass (*Brit slang*), give away, squeal (*slang*), inform on, spill your guts (*slang*), dob in (*Austral slang*) ▷▷ **split up** BREAK UP, part, separate, divorce, disband, part company, go separate ways

spoil *verb* **1** RUIN, destroy, wreck, damage, total (*slang*), blow (*slang*), injure, upset, harm, mar, scar, undo, trash (*slang*), impair, mess up, blemish, disfigure, debase, deface, put a damper on, crool *or* cruel (*Austral slang*) << ANTONYM improve **2** OVERINDULGE, indulge, pamper, baby, cosset, coddle, spoon-feed, mollycoddle, kill with kindness << ANTONYM deprive **3** INDULGE, treat, pamper, satisfy, gratify, pander to, regale **4** GO BAD, turn, go off (*Brit informal*), rot, decay, decompose, curdle, mildew, addle, putrefy, become tainted

spoils *plural noun* BOOTY, loot, plunder, gain, prizes, prey, pickings, pillage, swag (*slang*), boodle (*slang, chiefly US*), rapine

spoken *adjective* VERBAL, voiced, expressed, uttered, oral, said, told, unwritten, phonetic, by word of mouth, put into words, viva voce ▷▷ **spoken for 1** RESERVED, booked, claimed, chosen, selected, set aside **2** ENGAGED, taken, going out with someone, betrothed (*archaic*), going steady

spokesperson *noun* SPEAKER, official, spokesman *or* spokeswoman, voice, spin doctor (*informal*), mouthpiece

spongy *adjective* POROUS, light, absorbent, springy, cushioned, elastic, cushiony

sponsor *verb* BACK, fund, finance, promote, subsidize, patronize, put up the money for, lend your name to ▷ *noun* BACKER, patron, promoter, angel (*informal*), guarantor

spontaneous *adjective* UNPLANNED, impromptu, unprompted, willing, free, natural, voluntary, instinctive, impulsive, unforced, unbidden, unconstrained, unpremeditated, extempore, uncompelled << ANTONYM planned

spontaneously *adverb* VOLUNTARILY, freely, instinctively, impromptu, off the cuff (*informal*), on impulse, impulsively, in the heat of the moment, extempore, off your own bat, of your own accord, quite unprompted

spoof *noun* (*informal*) PARODY, take-off (*informal*), satire, caricature, mockery, send-up (*Brit informal*), travesty, lampoon, burlesque

spook (*informal*) *noun* GHOST, spirit, phantom, spectre, soul, shade (*literary*), manes, apparition, wraith, revenant, phantasm, eidolon, kehua (*NZ*) ▷ *verb* FRIGHTEN, alarm, scare, terrify, startle, intimidate, daunt, unnerve, petrify, scare (someone) stiff, put the wind up (someone) (*informal*), scare the living daylights out of (someone) (*informal*), make your hair stand on end (*informal*), get the wind up, make your blood run cold, throw into a panic, scare the bejesus out of (*informal*), affright (*archaic*), freeze your blood, make (someone) jump out of his skin (*informal*), throw into a fright

spooky *adjective* EERIE, frightening, chilling, ghostly, weird, mysterious, scary (*informal*), unearthly, supernatural, uncanny, creepy (*informal*), spine-chilling

sporadic *adjective* INTERMITTENT, occasional, scattered, isolated, random, on and off, irregular, infrequent, spasmodic, scattershot << ANTONYM steady

sport *noun* 1 GAME, exercise, recreation, play, entertainment, amusement, diversion, pastime, physical activity 2 FUN, kidding (*informal*), joking, teasing, ridicule, joshing (*slang, chiefly US & Canad*), banter, frolic, jest, mirth, merriment, badinage, raillery ▷ *verb* (*informal*) WEAR, display, flaunt, boast, exhibit, flourish, show off, vaunt

sporting *adjective* FAIR, sportsmanlike, game (*informal*), gentlemanly << ANTONYM unfair

sporty *adjective* 1 ATHLETIC, outdoor, energetic, hearty 2 CASUAL, stylish, jazzy (*informal*), loud, informal, trendy (*Brit informal*), flashy, jaunty, showy, snazzy (*informal*), raffish, rakish, gay, schmick

(*Austral informal*)

spot *noun* 1 MARK, stain, speck, scar, flaw, taint, blot, smudge, blemish, daub, speckle, blotch, discoloration 2 PIMPLE, blackhead, pustule, zit (*slang*), plook (*Scot*), acne 3 (*informal, chiefly Brit*) BIT, little, drop, bite, splash, small amount, tad, morsel 4 PLACE, situation, site, point, position, scene, location, locality 5 (*informal*) PREDICAMENT, trouble, difficulty, mess, plight, hot water (*informal*), quandary, tight spot ▷ *verb* 1 SEE, observe, catch sight of, identify, sight, recognize, detect, make out, pick out, discern, behold (*archaic or literary*), espy, descry 2 MARK, stain, dot, soil, dirty, scar, taint, tarnish, blot, fleck, spatter, sully, speckle, besmirch, splodge, splotch, mottle, smirch

spotless *adjective* 1 CLEAN, immaculate, impeccable, white, pure, virgin, shining, gleaming, snowy, flawless, faultless, unblemished, virginal, unsullied, untarnished, unstained << ANTONYM dirty 2 BLAMELESS, squeaky-clean, unimpeachable, innocent, chaste, irreproachable, above reproach << ANTONYM reprehensible

spotlight *noun* 1 SEARCH LIGHT, headlight, floodlight, headlamp, foglamp 2 ATTENTION, limelight, public eye, interest, fame, notoriety, public attention ▷ *verb* HIGHLIGHT, feature, draw attention to, focus attention on, accentuate, point up, give prominence to, throw into relief

spot-on *adjective* (*Brit informal*) ACCURATE, exact, precise, right, correct, on the money (*US*), unerring, punctual (to the minute), hitting the nail on the head (*informal*), on the bull's-eye (*informal*)

spotted *adjective* SPECKLED, dotted, flecked, pied, specked, mottled, dappled, polka-dot

spotty *adjective* 1 PIMPLY, pimpled, blotchy, poor-complexioned, plooky-faced (*Scot*) 2 INCONSISTENT, irregular, erratic, uneven, fluctuating, patchy, sporadic

spouse *noun* PARTNER, mate, husband *or* wife, companion, consort, significant other (*US informal*), better half (*humorous*), her indoors (*Brit slang*), helpmate

spout *verb* 1 STREAM, shoot, gush, spurt, jet, spray, surge, discharge, erupt, emit, squirt 2 (*informal*) HOLD FORTH, talk, rant, go on (*informal*), rabbit (on) (*Brit informal*), ramble (on), pontificate, declaim, spiel (*informal*), expatiate, orate, speechify

sprawl *verb* LOLL, slump, lounge, flop, slouch

spray¹ *noun* **1** DROPLETS, moisture, fine mist, drizzle, spindrift, spoondrift **2** AEROSOL, sprinkler, atomizer ▷ *verb* SCATTER, shower, sprinkle, diffuse

spray² *noun* SPRIG, floral arrangement, branch, bough, shoot, corsage

spread *verb* **1** OPEN (OUT), extend, stretch, unfold, sprawl, unfurl, fan out, unroll **2** EXTEND, open, stretch **3** COAT, cover, smear, smother **4** SMEAR, apply, rub, put, smooth, plaster, daub **5** GROW, increase, develop, expand, widen, mushroom, escalate, proliferate, multiply, broaden **6** SPACE OUT, stagger **7** CIRCULATE, publish, broadcast, advertise, distribute, scatter, proclaim, transmit, make public, publicize, propagate, disseminate, promulgate, make known, blazon, bruit << ANTONYM suppress **8** DIFFUSE, cast, shed, radiate ▷ *noun* **1** INCREASE, development, advance, spreading, expansion, transmission, proliferation, advancement, escalation, diffusion, dissemination, dispersal, suffusion **2** EXTENT, reach, span, stretch, sweep, compass **3** (*informal*) FEAST, banquet, blowout (*slang*), repast, array

spree *noun* **1** FLING, binge (*informal*), orgy, splurge **2** BINGE, bender (*informal*), orgy, revel (*informal*), jag (*slang*), junketing, beano (*Brit slang*), debauch, carouse, bacchanalia, carousal

sprightly *adjective* LIVELY, spirited, active, energetic, animated, brisk, nimble, agile, jaunty, gay, perky, vivacious, spry, bright-eyed and bushy-tailed << ANTONYM inactive

spring *noun* **1** SPRINGTIME, springtide (*literary*) **2** SOURCE, root, origin, well, beginning, cause, fount, fountainhead, wellspring **3** FLEXIBILITY, give (*informal*), bounce, resilience, elasticity, recoil, buoyancy, springiness, bounciness ▷ *verb* **1** JUMP, bound, leap, bounce, hop, rebound, vault, recoil **2** *usually followed by* **from** ORIGINATE, come, derive, start, issue, grow, emerge, proceed, arise, stem, descend, be derived, emanate, be descended ▷ *modifier* VERNAL, springlike

springy *adjective* FLEXIBLE, elastic, resilient, bouncy, rubbery, spongy

sprinkle *verb* SCATTER, dust, strew, pepper, shower, spray, powder, dredge

sprinkling *noun* SCATTERING, dusting, scatter, few, dash, handful, sprinkle, smattering, admixture

sprint *verb* RUN, race, shoot, tear, dash, barrel (along) (*informal, chiefly US & Canad*), dart, hare (*Brit informal*), whizz (*informal*), scamper, hotfoot, go like a bomb (*Brit & NZ informal*), put on a burst of speed, go at top speed

sprite *noun* SPIRIT, fairy, elf, nymph, brownie, pixie, apparition, imp, goblin, leprechaun, peri, dryad, naiad, sylph, Oceanid (*Greek myth*), atua (*NZ*)

sprout *verb* **1** GERMINATE, bud, shoot, push, spring, vegetate **2** GROW, develop, blossom, ripen

spruce *adjective* SMART, trim, neat, elegant, dainty, dapper, natty (*informal*), well-groomed, well turned out, trig (*archaic or dialect*), as if you had just stepped out of a bandbox, soigné *or* soignée << ANTONYM untidy

spry *adjective* ACTIVE, sprightly, quick, brisk, supple, nimble, agile, nippy (*Brit informal*) << ANTONYM inactive

spur *verb* INCITE, drive, prompt, press, urge, stimulate, animate, prod, prick, goad, impel ▷ *noun* STIMULUS, incentive, impetus, motive, impulse, inducement, incitement, kick up the backside (*informal*) ▷▷ **on the spur of the moment** ON IMPULSE, without thinking, impulsively, on the spot, impromptu, unthinkingly, without planning, impetuously, unpremeditatedly

spurious *adjective* FALSE, bogus, sham, pretended, artificial, forged, fake, mock, imitation, simulated, contrived, pseudo (*informal*), counterfeit, feigned, ersatz, specious, unauthentic, phoney *or* phony (*informal*) << ANTONYM genuine

spurn *verb* REJECT, slight, scorn, rebuff, put down, snub, disregard, despise, disdain, repulse, cold-shoulder, kick in the teeth (*slang*), turn your nose up at (*informal*), contemn (*formal*) << ANTONYM accept

spurt *verb* GUSH, shoot, burst, jet, surge, erupt, spew, squirt ▷ *noun* **1** GUSH, jet, burst, spray, surge, eruption, squirt **2** BURST, rush, surge, fit, access, spate

spy *noun* UNDERCOVER AGENT, secret agent, double agent, secret service agent, foreign agent, mole, fifth columnist, nark (*Brit, Austral & NZ slang*) ▷ *verb* **1** BE A SPY, snoop (*informal*), gather intelligence **2** *usually followed by* **on** WATCH, follow, shadow, tail (*informal*), trail, keep watch on, keep under surveillance **3** CATCH SIGHT OF, see, spot, notice, sight, observe, glimpse, behold (*archaic or literary*), set eyes on, espy, descry

spying *noun* ESPIONAGE, reconnaissance,

665

infiltration, undercover work

squabble *verb* QUARREL, fight, argue, row, clash, dispute, scrap (*informal*), fall out (*informal*), brawl, spar, wrangle, bicker, have words, fight like cat and dog, go at it hammer and tongs ▷ *noun* QUARREL, fight, row, argument, dispute, set-to (*informal*), scrap (*informal*), disagreement, barney (*informal*), spat, difference of opinion, tiff, bagarre (*French*)

squad *noun* TEAM, group, band, company, force, troop, crew, gang

squalid *adjective* 1 DIRTY, filthy, seedy, sleazy, sordid, low, nasty, foul, disgusting, run-down, decayed, repulsive, poverty-stricken, unclean, fetid, slovenly, skanky (*slang*), slummy, yucky or yukky (*slang*), yucko (*Austral slang*), festy (*Austral slang*) << ANTONYM hygienic 2 UNSEEMLY, sordid, inappropriate, unsuitable, out of place, improper, undignified, disreputable, unbecoming, unrefined, out of keeping, discreditable, indelicate, in poor taste, indecorous, unbefitting

squalor *noun* FILTH, wretchedness, sleaziness, decay, foulness, slumminess, squalidness, meanness << ANTONYM luxury

squander *verb* WASTE, spend, fritter away, blow (*slang*), consume, scatter, run through, lavish, throw away, misuse, dissipate, expend, misspend, be prodigal with, frivol away, spend like water << ANTONYM save

square *noun* 1 TOWN SQUARE, close, quad, market square, quadrangle, village square 2 (*informal*) CONSERVATIVE, dinosaur, traditionalist, die-hard, stick-in-the-mud (*informal*), fuddy-duddy (*informal*), old buffer (*Brit informal*), antediluvian, back number (*informal*), (old) fogey ▷ *adjective* 1 FAIR, just, straight, genuine, decent, ethical, straightforward, upright, honest, equitable, upfront (*informal*), on the level (*informal*), kosher (*informal*), dinkum (*Austral & NZ informal*), above board, fair and square, on the up and up 2 (*informal*) OLD-FASHIONED, straight (*slang*), conservative, conventional, dated, bourgeois, out of date, stuffy, behind the times, strait-laced, out of the ark (*informal*), Pooterish << ANTONYM fashionable ▷ *verb often followed by* **with** AGREE, match, fit, accord, correspond, tally, conform, reconcile, harmonize

squash *verb* 1 CRUSH, press, flatten, mash, pound, smash, distort, pulp, compress, stamp on, trample down 2 SUPPRESS, put

down (*slang*), quell, silence, sit on (*informal*), crush, quash, annihilate 3 EMBARRASS, put down, humiliate, shame, disgrace, degrade, mortify, debase, discomfit, take the wind out of someone's sails, put (someone) in his (or her) place, take down a peg (*informal*)

squawk *verb* 1 CRY, crow, screech, hoot, yelp, cackle 2 (*informal*) COMPLAIN, protest, squeal (*informal, chiefly Brit*), kick up a fuss (*informal*), raise Cain (*slang*) ▷ *noun* 1 CRY, crow, screech, hoot, yelp, cackle 2 SCREAM, cry, yell, wail, shriek, screech, squeal, yelp, yowl

squeak *verb* SQUEAL, pipe, peep, shrill, whine, yelp

squeal *verb* 1 SCREAM, yell, shriek, screech, yelp, wail, yowl 2 (*informal, chiefly Brit*) COMPLAIN, protest, moan, squawk (*informal*), kick up a fuss (*informal*) 3 (*slang*) INFORM ON, grass (*Brit slang*), betray, shop (*slang, chiefly Brit*), sing (*slang, chiefly US*), peach (*slang*), tell all, spill the beans (*informal*), snitch (*slang*), blab, rat on (*informal*), sell (someone) down the river (*informal*), blow the gaff (*Brit slang*), spill your guts (*slang*), dob in (*Austral slang*) ▷ *noun* SCREAM, shriek, screech, yell, shriek, wail, yelp, yowl

squeamish *adjective* 1 QUEASY, sick, nauseous, queer, sickish, qualmish << ANTONYM strong-stomached 2 FASTIDIOUS, particular, delicate, nice (*rare*), scrupulous, prudish, prissy (*informal*), finicky, strait-laced, punctilious << ANTONYM coarse

squeeze *verb* 1 PRESS, crush, squash, pinch 2 CLUTCH, press, grip, crush, pinch, squash, nip, compress, wring 3 EXTRACT, force, press, express 4 CRAM, press, crowd, force, stuff, pack, jam, thrust, ram, wedge, jostle 5 PRESSURIZE, lean on (*informal*), bring pressure to bear on, milk, bleed (*informal*), oppress, wrest, extort, put the squeeze on (*informal*), put the screws on (*informal*) 6 HUG, embrace, cuddle, clasp, enfold, hold tight ▷ *noun* 1 PRESS, grip, clasp, crush, pinch, squash, nip, wring 2 CRUSH, jam, squash, press, crowd, congestion 3 HUG, embrace, cuddle, hold, clasp, handclasp

squint *verb* PEER, screw up your eyes, narrow your eyes, look through narrowed eyes ▷ *noun* CROSS EYES, strabismus

squirm *verb* WRIGGLE, twist, writhe, shift, flounder, wiggle, fidget

squirt *verb* SPURT, shoot, gush, burst, jet, surge, erupt, spew ▷ *noun* SPURT, jet, burst, gush, surge, eruption

stab *verb* PIERCE, cut, gore, run through,

stick, injure, wound, knife, thrust, spear, jab, puncture, bayonet, transfix, impale, spill blood ▷ *noun* **1** (*informal*) ATTEMPT, go, try, shot (*informal*), crack (*informal*), essay (*informal*), endeavour **2** TWINGE, prick, pang, ache ▷▷ **stab someone in the back** BETRAY, double-cross (*informal*), sell out (*informal*), sell, let down, inform on, do the dirty on (*Brit slang*), break faith with, play false, give the Judas kiss to, dob in (*Austral slang*)

stability *noun* FIRMNESS, strength, soundness, durability, permanence, solidity, constancy, steadiness, steadfastness << ANTONYM instability

stable *adjective* **1** SECURE, lasting, strong, sound, fast, sure, established, permanent, constant, steady, enduring, reliable, abiding, durable, deep-rooted, well-founded, steadfast, immutable, unwavering, invariable, unalterable, unchangeable << ANTONYM insecure **2** WELL-BALANCED, balanced, sensible, reasonable, rational, mentally sound **3** SOLID, firm, secure, fixed, substantial, sturdy, durable, well-made, well-built, immovable, built to last << ANTONYM unstable

stack *noun* **1** PILE, heap, mountain, mass, load, cock, rick, clamp (*Brit agriculture*), mound **2** LOT, mass, load (*informal*), ton (*informal*), heap (*informal*), large quantity, great amount ▷ *verb* PILE, heap up, load, assemble, accumulate, amass, stockpile, bank up

staff *noun* **1** WORKERS, employees, personnel, workforce, team, organization **2** STICK, pole, rod, prop, crook, cane, stave, wand, sceptre

stage *noun* STEP, leg, phase, point, level, period, division, length, lap, juncture ▷ *verb* **1** PRESENT, produce, perform, put on, do, give, play **2** ORGANIZE, mount, arrange, lay on, orchestrate, engineer

stagger *verb* **1** TOTTER, reel, sway, falter, lurch, wobble, waver, teeter **2** ASTOUND, amaze, stun, surprise, shock, shake, overwhelm, astonish, confound, take (someone) aback, bowl (someone) over (*informal*), stupefy, strike (someone) dumb, throw (someone) off balance, give (someone) a shock, dumbfound, nonplus, flabbergast, take (someone's) breath away

stagnant *adjective* **1** STALE, still, standing, quiet, sluggish, motionless, brackish << ANTONYM flowing **2** INACTIVE, declining, stagnating, slow, depressed, sluggish, slow-moving

stagnate *verb* VEGETATE, decline, deteriorate, rot, decay, idle, rust, languish, stand still, fester, go to seed, lie fallow

staid *adjective* SEDATE, serious, sober, quiet, calm, grave, steady, composed, solemn, demure, decorous, self-restrained, set in your ways << ANTONYM wild

stain *noun* **1** MARK, spot, blot, blemish, discoloration, smirch **2** STIGMA, shame, disgrace, slur, reproach, blemish, dishonour, infamy, blot on the escutcheon **3** DYE, colour, tint ▷ *verb* **1** MARK, soil, discolour, dirty, tarnish, tinge, spot, blot, blemish, smirch **2** DYE, colour, tint **3** DISGRACE, taint, blacken, sully, corrupt, contaminate, deprave, defile, besmirch, drag through the mud

stake¹ *noun* POLE, post, spike, stick, pale, paling, picket, stave, palisade ▷ *verb* SUPPORT, secure, prop, brace, tie up, tether ▷▷ **stake something out** LAY CLAIM TO, define, outline, mark out, demarcate, delimit

stake² *noun* **1** BET, ante, wager, chance, risk, venture, hazard **2** INTEREST, share, involvement, claim, concern, investment ▷ *verb* BET, gamble, wager, chance, risk, venture, hazard, jeopardize, imperil, put on the line ▷▷ **at stake** TO LOSE, at risk, being risked

stale *adjective* **1** OLD, hard, dry, decayed, fetid << ANTONYM fresh **2** MUSTY, stagnant, fusty **3** TASTELESS, flat, sour, insipid **4** UNORIGINAL, banal, trite, common, flat, stereotyped, commonplace, worn-out, antiquated, threadbare, old hat, insipid, hackneyed, overused, repetitious, platitudinous, cliché-ridden << ANTONYM original

stalemate *noun* DEADLOCK, draw, tie, impasse, standstill

stalk *verb* **1** PURSUE, follow, track, hunt, shadow, tail (*informal*), haunt, creep up on **2** MARCH, pace, stride, strut, flounce

stall¹ *verb* STOP DEAD, jam, seize up, catch, stick, stop short ▷ *noun* **1** STAND, table, counter, booth, kiosk **2** ENCLOSURE, pen, coop, corral, sty

stall² *verb* **1** HINDER, obstruct, impede, block, check, arrest, halt, slow down, hamper, thwart, sabotage **2** PLAY FOR TIME, delay, hedge, procrastinate, stonewall, beat about the bush (*informal*), temporize, drag your feet **3** HOLD UP, delay, detain, divert, distract

stalwart *adjective* **1** LOYAL, faithful, strong, firm, true, constant, resolute, dependable, steadfast, true-blue, tried and true **2** STRONG, strapping, robust, athletic, vigorous, rugged, manly, hefty (*informal*), muscular, sturdy, stout, husky (*informal*), beefy (*informal*), lusty, sinewy, brawny << ANTONYM puny

stamina *noun* STAYING POWER, endurance, resilience, force, power, energy, strength, resistance, grit, vigour, tenacity, power of endurance, indefatigability, lustiness

stammer *verb* STUTTER, falter, splutter, pause, hesitate, hem and haw, stumble over your words ▷ *noun* SPEECH IMPEDIMENT, stutter, speech defect

stamp *noun* **1** IMPRINT, mark, brand, cast, mould, signature, earmark, hallmark **2** STOMP, stump, clump, tramp, clomp **3** TYPE, sort, kind, form, cut, character, fashion, cast, breed, description ▷ *verb* **1** PRINT, mark, fix, impress, mould, imprint, engrave, inscribe **2** STOMP, stump, clump, tramp, clomp **3** TRAMPLE, step, tread, crush **4** IDENTIFY, mark, brand, label, reveal, exhibit, betray, pronounce, show to be, categorize, typecast ▷▷ **stamp something out** ELIMINATE, destroy, eradicate, crush, suppress, put down, put out, scotch, quell, extinguish, quench, extirpate

stampede *noun* RUSH, charge, flight, scattering, rout ▷ *verb* BOLT, run, charge, race, career, rush, dash

stance *noun* **1** ATTITUDE, stand, position, viewpoint, standpoint **2** POSTURE, carriage, bearing, deportment

stand *verb* **1** BE UPRIGHT, be erect, be vertical **2** GET TO YOUR FEET, rise, stand up, straighten up **3** BE LOCATED, be, sit, perch, nestle, be positioned, be sited, be perched, be situated *or* located **4** BE VALID, be in force, continue, stay, exist, prevail, remain valid **5** PUT, place, position, set, mount **6** SIT, rest, mellow, maturate **7** RESIST, endure, withstand, wear (*Brit slang*), weather, undergo, defy, tolerate, stand up to, hold out against, stand firm against **8** TOLERATE, bear, abide, suffer, stomach, endure, brook, hack (*slang*), submit to, thole (*dialect*) **9** TAKE, bear, handle, cope with, experience, sustain, endure, undergo, put up with (*informal*), withstand, countenance ▷ *noun* **1** POSITION, attitude, stance, opinion, determination, standpoint, firm stand **2** STALL, booth, kiosk, table **3** GRANDSTAND **4** SUPPORT, base, platform, place, stage, frame, rack, bracket, tripod, dais, trivet ▷▷ **stand by 1** BE PREPARED, wait, stand ready, prepare yourself, wait in the wings

2 LOOK ON, watch, not lift a finger, wait, turn a blind eye ▷▷ **stand by something** SUPPORT, maintain, defend, champion, justify, sustain, endorse, assert, uphold, vindicate, stand up for, espouse, speak up for, stick up for (*informal*) ▷▷ **stand by someone** SUPPORT, back, champion, defend, take (someone's) part, uphold, befriend, be loyal to, stick up for (*informal*) ▷▷ **stand for something 1** REPRESENT, mean, signify, denote, indicate, exemplify, symbolize, betoken *verb* **2** (*informal*) TOLERATE, suffer, bear, endure, put up with, wear (*Brit informal*), brook, lie down under (*informal*) ▷▷ **stand in for someone** BE A SUBSTITUTE FOR, represent, cover for, take the place of, replace, understudy, hold the fort for, do duty for, deputize for ▷▷ **stand out 1** BE CONSPICUOUS, be striking, be prominent, be obvious, be highlighted, attract attention, catch the eye, be distinct, stick out like a sore thumb (*informal*), stare you in the face (*informal*), be thrown into relief, bulk large, stick out a mile (*informal*), leap to the eye **2** PROJECT, protrude, bristle ▷▷ **stand up for something** *or* **someone** SUPPORT, champion, defend, uphold, side with, stick up for (*informal*), come to the defence of ▷▷ **stand up to something** *or* **someone 1** WITHSTAND, take, bear, weather, cope with, resist, endure, tolerate, hold out against, stand firm against *verb* **2** RESIST, oppose, confront, tackle, brave, defy

standard *noun* **1** LEVEL, grade **2** CRITERION, measure, guideline, example, model, average, guide, pattern, sample, par, norm, gauge, benchmark, yardstick, touchstone **3** *often plural* PRINCIPLES, ideals, morals, rule, ethics, canon, moral principles, code of honour **4** FLAG, banner, pennant, colours, ensign, pennon ▷ *adjective* **1** USUAL, normal, customary, set, stock, average, popular, basic, regular, typical, prevailing, orthodox, staple, one-size-fits-all << ANTONYM unusual **2** ACCEPTED, official, established, classic, approved, recognized, definitive, authoritative << ANTONYM unofficial

standardize *verb* BRING INTO LINE, stereotype, regiment, assimilate, mass-produce, institutionalize

stand-in *noun* SUBSTITUTE, deputy, replacement, reserve, surrogate, understudy, locum, stopgap

standing *noun* **1** STATUS, position, station, footing, condition, credit, rank, reputation, eminence, estimation, repute **2** DURATION, existence, experience, continuance ▷ *adjective* **1** PERMANENT, lasting, fixed, regular, repeated, perpetual **2** UPRIGHT, erect, vertical, rampant (*heraldry*), perpendicular, upended

standpoint *noun* POINT OF VIEW, position, angle, viewpoint, stance, vantage point

staple *adjective* PRINCIPAL, chief, main, key, basic, essential, primary, fundamental, predominant

star *noun* **1** HEAVENLY BODY, sun, celestial body **2** CELEBRITY, big name, celeb (*informal*), megastar (*informal*), name, draw, idol, luminary, leading man *or* lady, lead, hero *or* heroine, principal, main attraction ▷ *plural noun* HOROSCOPE, forecast, astrological chart ▷ *verb* PLAY THE LEAD, appear, feature, perform

starchy *adjective* FORMAL, stiff, stuffy, conventional, precise, prim, punctilious, ceremonious

stare *verb* GAZE, look, goggle, watch, gape, eyeball (*slang*), ogle, gawp (*Brit slang*), gawk, rubberneck (*slang*)

stark *adjective* **1** PLAIN, simple, harsh, basic, bare, grim, straightforward, blunt, bald **2** SHARP, clear, striking, distinct, clear-cut **3** AUSTERE, severe, plain, bare, harsh, unadorned **4** BLEAK, grim, barren, hard, cold, depressing, dreary, desolate, forsaken, godforsaken, drear (*literary*) **5** ABSOLUTE, pure, sheer, utter, downright, patent, consummate, palpable, out-and-out, flagrant, unmitigated, unalloyed, arrant ▷ *adverb* ABSOLUTELY, quite, completely, clean, entirely, altogether, wholly, utterly

start *verb* **1** SET ABOUT, begin, proceed, embark upon, take the plunge (*informal*), take the first step, make a beginning, put your hand to the plough (*informal*) << ANTONYM stop **2** BEGIN, arise, originate, issue, appear, commence, get under way, come into being, come into existence, first see the light of day << ANTONYM end **3** SET IN MOTION, initiate, instigate, open, trigger, kick off (*informal*), originate, get going, engender, kick-start, get (something) off the ground (*informal*), enter upon, get *or* set *or* start the ball rolling << ANTONYM stop **4** ESTABLISH, begin, found, father, create, launch, set up, introduce, institute, pioneer, initiate, inaugurate, lay the foundations of << ANTONYM terminate **5** START UP, activate, get something going << ANTONYM

turn off **6** JUMP, shy, jerk, twitch, flinch, recoil ▷ *noun* **1** BEGINNING, outset, opening, birth, foundation, dawn, first step(s), onset, initiation, inauguration, inception, commencement, kickoff (*informal*), opening move << ANTONYM end **2** JUMP, jerk, twitch, spasm, convulsion

startle *verb* SURPRISE, shock, alarm, frighten, scare, agitate, take (someone) aback, make (someone) jump, give (someone) a turn (*informal*)

startling *adjective* SURPRISING, shocking, alarming, extraordinary, sudden, unexpected, staggering, unforeseen, jaw-dropping

starving *adjective* HUNGRY, starved, ravenous, famished, hungering, sharp-set, esurient, faint from lack of food, ready to eat a horse (*informal*)

stash (*informal*) *verb* STORE, stockpile, save up, hoard, hide, secrete, stow, cache, lay up, salt away, put aside for a rainy day ▷ *noun* HOARD, supply, store, stockpile, cache, collection

state *noun* **1** COUNTRY, nation, land, republic, territory, federation, commonwealth, kingdom, body politic **2** PROVINCE, region, district, area, territory, federal state **3** GOVERNMENT, ministry, administration, executive, regime, powers-that-be **4** CONDITION, shape, state of affairs **5** FRAME OF MIND, condition, spirits, attitude, mood, humour **6** CEREMONY, glory, grandeur, splendour, dignity, majesty, pomp **7** CIRCUMSTANCES, situation, position, case, pass, mode, plight, predicament ▷ *verb* SAY, report, declare, specify, put, present, explain, voice, express, assert, utter, articulate, affirm, expound, enumerate, propound, aver, assevcrate ▷▷ **in a state** (*informal*) **1** DISTRESSED, upset, agitated, disturbed, anxious, ruffled, uptight (*informal*), flustered, panic-stricken, het up, all steamed up (*slang*) **2** UNTIDY, disordered, messy, muddled, cluttered, jumbled, in disarray, topsy-turvy, higgledy-piggledy (*informal*)

stately *adjective* GRAND, majestic, dignified, royal, august, imposing, impressive, elegant, imperial, noble, regal, solemn, lofty, pompous, ceremonious << ANTONYM lowly

statement *noun* **1** ANNOUNCEMENT, declaration, communication, explanation, communiqué, proclamation, utterance **2** ACCOUNT, report, testimony, evidence

state-of-the-art *adjective* LATEST, newest, up-to-date, up-to-the-minute << ANTONYM old-fashioned

static *adjective* STATIONARY, still, motionless, fixed, constant, stagnant, inert, immobile, unmoving, stock-still, unvarying, changeless << ANTONYM moving

station *noun* **1** RAILWAY STATION, stop, stage, halt, terminal, train station, terminus **2** HEADQUARTERS, base, depot **3** CHANNEL, wavelength, broadcasting company **4** POSITION, rank, status, standing, post, situation, grade, sphere **5** POST, place, location, position, situation, seat ▷ *verb* ASSIGN, post, locate, set, establish, fix, install, garrison

stationary *adjective* MOTIONLESS, standing, at a standstill, parked, fixed, moored, static, inert, unmoving, stock-still << ANTONYM moving

statuesque *adjective* WELL-PROPORTIONED, stately, Junoesque, imposing, majestic, dignified, regal

stature *noun* **1** HEIGHT, build, size **2** IMPORTANCE, standing, prestige, size, rank, consequence, prominence, eminence, high station

status *noun* **1** POSITION, rank, grade, degree **2** PRESTIGE, standing, authority, influence, weight, reputation, honour, importance, consequence, fame, distinction, eminence, renown, mana (NZ) **3** STATE OF PLAY, development, progress, condition, evolution, progression

statute *noun* LAW, act, rule, regulation, decree, ordinance, enactment, edict

staunch *adjective* LOYAL, faithful, stalwart, sure, strong, firm, sound, true, constant, reliable, stout, resolute, dependable, trustworthy, trusty, steadfast, true-blue, immovable, tried and true

stay *verb* **1** REMAIN, continue to be, linger, stand, stop, wait, settle, delay, halt, pause, hover, abide, hang around (*informal*), reside, stay put, bide, loiter, hang in the air, tarry, put down roots, establish yourself << ANTONYM go **2** *often with* at LODGE, visit, sojourn, put up at, be accommodated at **3** CONTINUE, remain, go on, survive, endure **4** SUSPEND, put off, defer, adjourn, hold over, hold in abeyance, prorogue ▷ *noun* **1** VISIT, stop, holiday, stopover, sojourn **2** POSTPONEMENT, delay, suspension, stopping, halt, pause, reprieve, remission, deferment

staying power *noun* ENDURANCE, strength, stamina, toughness

steadfast *adjective* **1** LOYAL, faithful, stalwart, staunch, constant, steady, dedicated, reliable, persevering, dependable << ANTONYM undependable **2** RESOLUTE, firm, fast, fixed, stable, intent, single-minded, unwavering, immovable, unflinching, unswerving, unfaltering << ANTONYM irresolute

steady *adjective* **1** CONTINUOUS, even, regular, constant, consistent, persistent, rhythmic, unbroken, habitual, uninterrupted, incessant, ceaseless, unremitting, unwavering, nonstop, unvarying, unfaltering, unfluctuating << ANTONYM irregular **2** STABLE, fixed, secure, firm, safe, immovable, on an even keel << ANTONYM unstable **3** REGULAR, established **4** DEPENDABLE, sensible, reliable, balanced, settled, secure, calm, supportive, sober, staunch, serene, sedate, staid, steadfast, level-headed, serious-minded, imperturbable, equable, unchangeable, having both feet on the ground << ANTONYM undependable

steal *verb* **1** TAKE, nick (*slang, chiefly Brit*), pinch (*informal*), lift (*informal*), cabbage (*Brit slang*), swipe (*slang*), half-inch (*old-fashioned slang*), heist (*US slang*), embezzle, blag (*slang*), pilfer, misappropriate, snitch (*slang*), purloin, filch, prig (*Brit slang*), shoplift, thieve, be light-fingered, peculate, walk or make off with **2** COPY, take, plagiarize, appropriate, pinch (*informal*), pirate, poach **3** SNEAK, slip, creep, flit, tiptoe, slink, insinuate yourself

stealth *noun* SECRECY, furtiveness, slyness, sneakiness, unobtrusiveness, stealthiness, surreptitiousness

stealthy *adjective* SECRET, secretive, furtive, sneaking, covert, sly, clandestine, sneaky, skulking, underhand, surreptitious

steamy *adjective* **1** (*informal*) EROTIC, hot (*slang*), sexy (*informal*), sensual, raunchy (*slang*), lewd, carnal, titillating, prurient, lascivious, lustful, lubricious (*formal or literary*) **2** MUGGY, damp, humid, sweaty, like a sauna

steep[1] *adjective* **1** SHEER, precipitous, perpendicular, abrupt, headlong, vertical << ANTONYM gradual **2** SHARP, sudden, abrupt, marked, extreme, distinct **3** (*informal*) HIGH, excessive, exorbitant, extreme, stiff, unreasonable, overpriced, extortionate, uncalled-for << ANTONYM reasonable

steep[2] *verb* SOAK, immerse, marinate (*cookery*), damp, submerge, drench, moisten, macerate, souse, imbrue (*rare*)

steeped *adjective* SATURATED, pervaded, permeated, filled, infused, imbued, suffused

steer *verb* 1 DRIVE, control, direct, handle, conduct, pilot, govern, be in the driver's seat 2 DIRECT, lead, guide, conduct, escort, show in *or* out ▷▷ **steer clear of something** *or* **someone** AVOID, evade, fight shy of, shun, eschew, circumvent, body-swerve (*Scot*), give a wide berth to, sheer off

stem[1] *noun* STALK, branch, trunk, shoot, stock, axis, peduncle ▷▷ **stem from something** ORIGINATE FROM, be caused by, derive from, arise from, flow from, emanate from, develop from, be generated by, be brought about by, be bred by, issue forth from

stem[2] *verb* STOP, hold back, staunch, stay (*archaic*), check, contain, dam, curb, restrain, bring to a standstill, stanch

stench *noun* STINK, whiff (*Brit slang*), reek, pong (*Brit informal*), foul smell, niff (*Brit slang*), malodour, mephitis, noisomeness

step *noun* 1 PACE, stride, footstep 2 FOOTFALL 3 STAIR, tread, rung 4 MOVE, measure, action, means, act, proceeding, procedure, manoeuvre, deed, expedient 5 STAGE, point, phase 6 GAIT, walk 7 LEVEL, rank, remove, degree ▷ *verb* WALK, pace, tread, move ▷▷ **in step** (*informal*) IN AGREEMENT, in harmony, in unison, in line, coinciding, conforming, in conformity ▷▷ **mind** *or* **watch your step** (*informal*) BE CAREFUL, take care, look out, be cautious, be discreet, take heed, tread carefully, be canny, be on your guard, mind how you go, have your wits about you, mind your p's and q's ▷▷ **out of step** (*informal*) IN DISAGREEMENT, out of line, out of phase, out of harmony, incongruous, pulling different ways ▷▷ **step down** *or* **aside** (*informal*) RESIGN, retire, quit, leave, give up, pull out, bow out, abdicate ▷▷ **step in** (*informal*) INTERVENE, take action, become involved, chip in (*informal*), intercede, take a hand ▷▷ **step something up** INCREASE, boost, intensify, up, raise, accelerate, speed up, escalate, augment ▷▷ **take steps** TAKE ACTION, act, intervene, move in, take the initiative, take measures

stereotype *noun* FORMULA, cliché, pattern, mould, received idea ▷ *verb* CATEGORIZE, typecast, pigeonhole, dub, standardize, take to be, ghettoize, conventionalize

stereotyped *adjective* UNORIGINAL, stock, standard, tired, conventional, played out, stale, banal, standardized, mass-produced, corny (*slang*), threadbare, trite, hackneyed, overused, platitudinous, cliché-ridden

sterile *adjective* 1 GERM-FREE, antiseptic, sterilized, disinfected, aseptic << ANTONYM unhygienic 2 BARREN, infertile, unproductive, childless, infecund << ANTONYM fertile

sterilize *verb* DISINFECT, purify, fumigate, decontaminate, autoclave, sanitize

sterling *adjective* EXCELLENT, sound, fine, first-class, superlative

stern *adjective* 1 STRICT, harsh, rigorous, hard, cruel, grim, rigid, relentless, drastic, authoritarian, austere, inflexible, unrelenting, unyielding, unsparing << ANTONYM lenient 2 SEVERE, serious, forbidding, steely, flinty << ANTONYM friendly

stew *noun* HASH, goulash, ragout, olla, olio, olla podrida ▷ *verb* BRAISE, boil, simmer, casserole ▷▷ **in a stew** (*informal*) TROUBLED, concerned, anxious, worried, fretting, in a panic, in a lather (*informal*)

stick[1] *noun* 1 TWIG, branch, birch, offshoot 2 CANE, staff, pole, rod, stake, switch, crook, baton, wand, sceptre 3 (*slang*) ABUSE, criticism, flak (*informal*), blame, knocking (*informal*), hostility, slagging (*slang*), denigration, critical remarks, fault-finding

stick[2] *verb* 1 (*informal*) PUT, place, set, position, drop, plant, store, lay, stuff, fix, deposit, install, plonk 2 POKE, dig, stab, insert, thrust, pierce, penetrate, spear, prod, jab, transfix 3 FASTEN, fix, bind, hold, bond, attach, hold on, glue, fuse, paste, adhere, affix 4 ADHERE, cling, cleave, become joined, become cemented, become welded 5 STAY, remain, linger, persist 6 CATCH, lodge, jam, stop, clog, snag, be embedded, be bogged down, come to a standstill, become immobilized 7 (*slang*) TOLERATE, take, stand, stomach, endure, hack (*slang*), abide, bear up under ▷▷ **stick out** PROTRUDE, stand out, jut out, show, project, bulge, obtrude ▷▷ **stick something out** 1 OFFER, present, extend, hold out, advance, reach out, stretch out, proffer 2 (*informal*) ENDURE, bear, put up with (*informal*), weather, take it (*informal*), see through, soldier on, last out, grin and bear it (*informal*) ▷▷ **stick to something** 1 KEEP TO, persevere in, cleave to 2 ADHERE TO, honour, hold to, keep to, abide by, stand by ▷▷ **stick up for someone** (*informal*) DEFEND, support, champion, uphold, stand up for, take the part *or* side of

stickler noun FANATIC, nut (*slang*), maniac (*informal*), purist, perfectionist, pedant, martinet, hard taskmaster, fusspot (*Brit informal*)

sticky *adjective* 1 ADHESIVE, gummed, adherent 2 GOOEY, tacky (*informal*), syrupy, viscous, glutinous, gummy, icky (*informal*), gluey, clinging, claggy (*dialect*), viscid 3 (*informal*) DIFFICULT, awkward, tricky, embarrassing, painful, nasty, delicate, unpleasant, discomforting, hairy (*slang*), thorny, barro (*Austral slang*) 4 HUMID, close, sultry, oppressive, sweltering, clammy, muggy

stiff *adjective* 1 INFLEXIBLE, rigid, unyielding, hard, firm, tight, solid, tense, hardened, brittle, taut, solidified, unbending, inelastic << ANTONYM flexible 2 UNSUPPLE, arthritic, creaky (*informal*), rheumaticky << ANTONYM supple 3 FORMAL, constrained, forced, laboured, cold, mannered, wooden, artificial, uneasy, chilly, unnatural, austere, pompous, prim, stilted, starchy (*informal*), punctilious, priggish, standoffish, ceremonious, unrelaxed << ANTONYM informal 4 VIGOROUS, great, strong 5 SEVERE, strict, harsh, hard, heavy, sharp, extreme, cruel, drastic, rigorous, stringent, oppressive, austere, inexorable, pitiless 6 STRONG, fresh, powerful, vigorous, brisk 7 DIFFICULT, hard, tough, exacting, formidable, trying, fatiguing, uphill, arduous, laborious

stifle *verb* 1 SUPPRESS, repress, prevent, stop, check, silence, curb, restrain, cover up, gag, hush, smother, extinguish, muffle, choke back 2 RESTRAIN, suppress, repress, smother

stigma noun DISGRACE, shame, dishonour, mark, spot, brand, stain, slur, blot, reproach, imputation, smirch

stigmatize *verb* BRAND, label, denounce, mark, discredit, pillory, defame, cast a slur upon

still *adjective* 1 MOTIONLESS, stationary, at rest, calm, smooth, peaceful, serene, tranquil, lifeless, placid, undisturbed, inert, restful, unruffled, unstirring << ANTONYM moving 2 SILENT, quiet, hushed, noiseless, stilly (*poetic*) << ANTONYM noisy ▷ *verb* QUIETEN, calm, subdue, settle, quiet, silence, soothe, hush, alleviate, lull, tranquillize << ANTONYM get louder ▷ *noun* (*poetic*) STILLNESS, peace, quiet, silence, hush, tranquillity << ANTONYM noise ▷ *adverb* YET, even now, up until now, up to this time ▷ *sentence connector* HOWEVER, but, yet, nevertheless, for all that, notwithstanding

stilted *adjective* STIFF, forced, wooden, laboured, artificial, inflated, constrained, unnatural, high-flown, pompous, pretentious, pedantic, bombastic, grandiloquent, high-sounding, arty-farty (*informal*), fustian << ANTONYM natural

stimulant noun PICK-ME-UP, tonic, restorative, upper (*slang*), reviver, bracer (*informal* or *informal*), energizer, pep pill (*informal*), excitant, analeptic << ANTONYM sedative

stimulate *verb* ENCOURAGE, inspire, prompt, fire, fan, urge, spur, provoke, turn on (*slang*), arouse, animate, rouse, prod, quicken, inflame, incite, instigate, goad, whet, impel, foment, gee up

stimulating *adjective* EXCITING, inspiring, stirring, provoking, intriguing, rousing, provocative, exhilarating, thought-provoking, galvanic << ANTONYM boring

stimulus noun INCENTIVE, spur, encouragement, impetus, provocation, inducement, goad, incitement, fillip, shot in the arm (*informal*), clarion call, geeing-up

sting *verb* 1 HURT, burn, wound 2 SMART, burn, pain, hurt, tingle 3 ANGER, provoke, infuriate, incense, gall, inflame, nettle, rile, pique ▷ *noun* SMARTING, pain, stinging, pricking, soreness, prickling

stingy *adjective* 1 MEAN, penny-pinching (*informal*), miserly, near, parsimonious, scrimping, illiberal, avaricious, niggardly, ungenerous, penurious, tightfisted, close-fisted, mingy (*Brit informal*), cheeseparing, snoep (*S African informal*) 2 INSUFFICIENT, inadequate, meagre, small, pathetic, scant, skimpy, measly (*informal*), scanty, on the small side

stink *verb* 1 REEK, pong (*Brit informal*), whiff (*Brit slang*), stink to high heaven (*informal*), offend the nostrils 2 (*slang*) BE BAD, be no good, be rotten, be offensive, be abhorrent, have a bad name, be detestable, be held in disrepute ▷ *noun* 1 STENCH, pong (*Brit informal*), foul smell, foulness, malodour, fetor, noisomeness 2 (*slang*) FUSS, to-do, row, upset, scandal, stir, disturbance, uproar, commotion, rumpus, hubbub, brouhaha, deal of trouble (*informal*)

stinker noun (*slang*) SCOUNDREL, heel, sod (*slang*), cad (*Brit informal*), swine, bounder (*Brit old-fashioned slang*), cur, rotter (*slang, chiefly Brit*), nasty piece of work (*informal*), dastard (*archaic*), wrong 'un (*Austral slang*)

stinking *adjective* 1 (*informal*) ROTTEN,

disgusting, unpleasant, vile, contemptible, wretched **2** FOUL-SMELLING, smelly, reeking, fetid, malodorous, noisome, whiffy (*Brit slang*), pongy (*Brit informal*), mephitic, ill-smelling, niffy (*Brit slang*), olid, festy (*Austral slang*), yucko (*Austral slang*)

stint *noun* TERM, time, turn, bit, period, share, tour, shift, stretch, spell, quota, assignment ▷ *verb* BE MEAN, hold back, be sparing, scrimp, skimp on, save, withhold, begrudge, economize, be frugal, be parsimonious, be mingy (*Brit informal*), spoil the ship for a ha'porth of tar

stipulate *verb* SPECIFY, agree, require, promise, contract, settle, guarantee, engage, pledge, lay down, covenant, postulate, insist upon, lay down *or* impose conditions

stipulation *noun* CONDITION, requirement, provision, term, contract, agreement, settlement, rider, restriction, qualification, clause, engagement, specification, precondition, prerequisite, proviso, sine qua non (*Latin*)

stir *verb* **1** MIX, beat, agitate **2** MOVE, change position **3** GET MOVING, move, get a move on (*informal*), hasten, budge, make an effort, be up and about (*informal*), look lively (*informal*), shake a leg (*informal*), exert yourself, bestir yourself **4** STIMULATE, move, excite, fire, raise, touch, affect, urge, inspire, prompt, spur, thrill, provoke, arouse, awaken, animate, rouse, prod, quicken, inflame, incite, instigate, electrify, kindle << ANTONYM inhibit **5** SPUR, drive, prompt, stimulate, prod, press, urge, animate, prick, incite, goad, impel ▷ *noun* COMMOTION, to-do, excitement, activity, movement, disorder, fuss, disturbance, bustle, flurry, uproar, ferment, agitation, ado, tumult

stirring *adjective* EXCITING, dramatic, thrilling, moving, spirited, inspiring, stimulating, lively, animating, rousing, heady, exhilarating, impassioned, emotive, intoxicating

stock *noun* **1** SHARES, holdings, securities, investments, bonds, equities **2** PROPERTY, capital, assets, funds **3** GOODS, merchandise, wares, range, choice, variety, selection, commodities, array, assortment **4** SUPPLY, store, reserve, fund, reservoir, stockpile, hoard, cache **5** LINEAGE, descent, extraction, ancestry, house, family, line, race, type, variety, background, breed, strain, pedigree, forebears, parentage, line of descent **6** LIVESTOCK, cattle, beasts, domestic

animals ▷ *verb* **1** SELL, supply, handle, keep, trade in, deal in **2** FILL, supply, provide with, provision, equip, furnish, fit out, kit out ▷ *adjective* **1** HACKNEYED, standard, usual, set, routine, stereotyped, staple, commonplace, worn-out, banal, run-of-the-mill, trite, overused **2** REGULAR, traditional, usual, basic, ordinary, conventional, staple, customary ▷▷ **stock up with something** STORE (UP), lay in, hoard, save, gather, accumulate, amass, buy up, put away, replenish supplies of ▷▷ **take stock** REVIEW THE SITUATION, weigh up, appraise, estimate, size up (*informal*), see how the land lies

stocky *adjective* THICKSET, solid, sturdy, chunky, stubby, dumpy, stumpy, mesomorphic

stodgy *adjective* **1** HEAVY, filling, substantial, leaden, starchy << ANTONYM light **2** DULL, boring, stuffy, formal, tedious, tiresome, staid, unimaginative, turgid, uninspired, unexciting, ho-hum, heavy going, fuddy-duddy (*informal*), dull as ditchwater << ANTONYM exciting

stoical *adjective* RESIGNED, long-suffering, phlegmatic, philosophic, cool, calm, indifferent, stoic, dispassionate, impassive, stolid, imperturbable

stoicism *noun* RESIGNATION, acceptance, patience, indifference, fortitude, long-suffering, calmness, fatalism, forbearance, stolidity, dispassion, impassivity, imperturbability

stolen *adjective* HOT (*slang*), bent (*slang*), hooky (*slang*)

stolid *adjective* APATHETIC, unemotional, dull, heavy, slow, wooden, stupid, bovine, dozy (*Brit informal*), obtuse, lumpish, doltish << ANTONYM lively

stomach *noun* **1** BELLY, inside(s) (*informal*), gut (*informal*), abdomen, tummy (*informal*), puku (*NZ*) **2** TUMMY, pot, spare tyre (*informal*), paunch, breadbasket (*slang*), potbelly **3** INCLINATION, taste, desire, appetite, relish, mind ▷ *verb* BEAR, take, tolerate, suffer, endure, swallow, hack (*slang*), abide, put up with (*informal*), submit to, reconcile *or* resign yourself

stone *noun* **1** MASONRY, rock **2** ROCK, pebble **3** PIP, seed, pit, kernel

stony *adjective* **1** ROCKY, rough, gritty, gravelly, rock-strewn, pebble **2** COLD, icy, hostile, hard, harsh, blank, adamant, indifferent, chilly, callous, heartless, merciless, unforgiving, inexorable, frigid, expressionless, unresponsive, pitiless, unfeeling, obdurate

stooge *noun* (*slang*) PAWN, puppet, fall guy (*informal*), butt, foil, patsy (*slang, chiefly US & Canad*), dupe, henchman, lackey

stoop *verb* 1 HUNCH, be bowed *or* round-shouldered 2 BEND, lean, bow, duck, descend, incline, kneel, crouch, squat ▷ *noun* SLOUCH, slump, droop, sag, bad posture, round-shoulderedness ▷▷ **stoop to something** RESORT TO, sink to, descend to, deign to, condescend to, demean yourself by, lower yourself by

stop *verb* 1 QUIT, cease, refrain, break off, put an end to, pack in (*Brit informal*), discontinue, leave off, call it a day (*informal*), desist, belay (*nautical*), bring *or* come to a halt *or* standstill << ANTONYM start 2 PREVENT, suspend, cut short, close, break, check, bar, arrest, silence, frustrate, axe (*informal*), interrupt, restrain, hold back, intercept, hinder, repress, impede, rein in, forestall, nip (something) in the bud << ANTONYM facilitate 3 END, conclude, finish, be over, cut out (*informal*), terminate, come to an end, peter out << ANTONYM continue 4 CEASE, shut down, discontinue, desist << ANTONYM continue 5 HALT, pause, stall, draw up, pull up << ANTONYM keep going 6 PAUSE, wait, rest, hesitate, deliberate, take a break, have a breather (*informal*), stop briefly 7 STAY, rest, put up, lodge, sojourn, tarry, break your journey ▷ *noun* 1 HALT, standstill 2 STATION, stage, halt, destination, depot, termination, terminus 3 STAY, break, visit, rest, stopover, sojourn

stopgap *noun* MAKESHIFT, improvisation, temporary expedient, shift, resort, substitute ▷ *modifier* MAKESHIFT, emergency, temporary, provisional, improvised, impromptu, rough-and-ready

stoppage *noun* 1 STOPPING, halt, standstill, close, arrest, lay-off, shutdown, cutoff, abeyance, discontinuance 2 BLOCKAGE, obstruction, stopping up, occlusion

store *noun* 1 SHOP, outlet, department store, market, supermarket, mart, emporium, chain store, hypermarket 2 SUPPLY, stock, reserve, lot, fund, mine, plenty, provision, wealth, quantity, reservoir, abundance, accumulation, stockpile, hoard, plethora, cache 3 REPOSITORY, warehouse, depot, storehouse, depository, storeroom ▷ *verb* 1 *often with* **away** *or* **up** PUT BY, save, hoard, keep, stock, husband, reserve, deposit,

accumulate, garner, stockpile, put aside, stash (*informal*), salt away, keep in reserve, put aside for a rainy day, lay by *or* in 2 PUT AWAY, put in storage, put in store, lock away 3 KEEP, hold, preserve, maintain, retain, conserve ▷▷ **set great store by something** VALUE, prize, esteem, appreciate, hold in high regard, think highly of

storm *noun* 1 TEMPEST, blast, hurricane, gale, tornado, cyclone, blizzard, whirlwind, gust, squall 2 OUTBURST, row, stir, outcry, furore, violence, anger, passion, outbreak, turmoil, disturbance, strife, clamour, agitation, commotion, rumpus, tumult, hubbub 3 ROAR, thunder, clamour, din 4 BARRAGE, volley, salvo, rain, shower, spray, discharge, fusillade ▷ *verb* 1 RUSH, stamp, flounce, fly, stalk, stomp (*informal*) 2 RAGE, fume, rant, complain, thunder, rave, scold, bluster, go ballistic (*slang, chiefly US*), fly off the handle (*informal*), wig out (*slang*) 3 ATTACK, charge, rush, assault, beset, assail, take by storm

stormy *adjective* 1 WILD, rough, tempestuous, raging, dirty, foul, turbulent, windy, blustering, blustery, gusty, inclement, squally 2 ROUGH, wild, turbulent, tempestuous, raging 3 ANGRY, heated, fierce, passionate, fiery, impassioned, tumultuous

story *noun* 1 TALE, romance, narrative, record, history, version, novel, legend, chronicle, yarn, recital, narration, urban myth, urban legend, fictional account 2 ANECDOTE, account, tale, report, detail, relation 3 (*informal*) LIE, falsehood, fib, fiction, untruth, porky (*Brit slang*), pork pie (*Brit slang*), white lie 4 REPORT, news, article, feature, scoop, news item

storyteller *noun* RACONTEUR, author, narrator, romancer, novelist, chronicler, bard, fabulist, spinner of yarns, anecdotist

stout *adjective* 1 FAT, big, heavy, overweight, plump, bulky, substantial, burly, obese, fleshy, tubby, portly, rotund, corpulent, on the large *or* heavy side << ANTONYM slim 2 STRONG, strapping, muscular, tough, substantial, athletic, hardy, robust, vigorous, sturdy, stalwart, husky (*informal*), hulking, beefy (*informal*), lusty, brawny, thickset, able-bodied << ANTONYM puny 3 BRAVE, bold, courageous, fearless, resolute, gallant, intrepid, valiant, plucky, doughty, indomitable, dauntless, lion-hearted, valorous << ANTONYM timid

stow *verb* PACK, load, put away, store, stuff, deposit, jam, tuck, bundle, cram, stash (*informal*), secrete

straggle *verb* TRAIL, drift, wander, range, lag, stray, roam, ramble, rove, loiter, string out

straggly *adjective* SPREAD OUT, spreading, rambling, untidy, loose, drifting, random, straying, irregular, aimless, disorganized, straggling

straight *adjective* 1 DIRECT, unswerving, undeviating << ANTONYM indirect 2 LEVEL, even, right, square, true, smooth, in line, aligned, horizontal << ANTONYM crooked 3 FRANK, plain, straightforward, blunt, outright, honest, downright, candid, forthright, bold, point-blank, upfront (*informal*), unqualified << ANTONYM evasive 4 SUCCESSIVE, consecutive, continuous, through, running, solid, sustained, uninterrupted, nonstop, unrelieved << ANTONYM discontinuous 5 (*slang*) CONVENTIONAL, conservative, orthodox, traditional, square (*informal*), bourgeois, Pooterish << ANTONYM fashionable 6 HONEST, just, fair, decent, reliable, respectable, upright, honourable, equitable, law-abiding, trustworthy, above board, fair and square << ANTONYM dishonest 7 UNDILUTED, pure, neat, unadulterated, unmixed 8 IN ORDER, organized, arranged, sorted out, neat, tidy, orderly, shipshape, put to rights << ANTONYM untidy ▷ *adverb* 1 DIRECTLY, precisely, exactly, as the crow flies, unswervingly, by the shortest route, in a beeline 2 IMMEDIATELY, directly, promptly, instantly, at once, straight away, without delay, without hesitation, forthwith, unhesitatingly, before you could say Jack Robinson (*informal*) 3 FRANKLY, honestly, point-blank, candidly, pulling no punches (*informal*), in plain English, with no holds barred

straightaway *adverb* IMMEDIATELY, now, at once, directly, instantly, on the spot, right away, there and then, this minute, straightway (*archaic*), without more ado, without any delay

straighten *verb* NEATEN, arrange, tidy (up), order, spruce up, smarten up, put in order, set *or* put to rights ▷▷ **straighten something out** SORT OUT, resolve, put right, settle, correct, work out, clear up, rectify, disentangle, unsnarl

straightforward *adjective* 1 (*Chiefly Brit*) SIMPLE, easy, uncomplicated, routine, elementary, clear-cut, undemanding, easy-peasy (*slang*) << ANTONYM complicated

2 HONEST, open, direct, genuine, sincere, candid, truthful, forthright, upfront (*informal*), dinkum (*Austral & NZ informal*), above board, guileless << ANTONYM devious

strain[1] *noun* 1 PRESSURE, stress, difficulty, demands, burden, adversity 2 STRESS, pressure, anxiety, difficulty, distress, nervous tension 3 WORRY, effort, struggle, tension, hassle << ANTONYM ease 4 BURDEN, tension 5 INJURY, wrench, sprain, pull, tension, tautness, tensity (*rare*) 6 TUNE, air, melody, measure (*poetic*), lay, song, theme ▷ *verb* 1 STRETCH, test, tax, overtax, push to the limit 2 INJURE, wrench, sprain, damage, pull, tear, hurt, twist, rick 3 STRIVE, struggle, endeavour, labour, go for it (*informal*), bend over backwards (*informal*), go for broke (*slang*), go all out for (*informal*), bust a gut (*informal*), give it your best shot (*informal*), make an all-out effort (*informal*), knock yourself out (*informal*), do your damnedest (*informal*), give it your all (*informal*), break your back *or* neck (*informal*), rupture yourself (*informal*) << ANTONYM relax 4 SIEVE, filter, sift, screen, separate, riddle, purify

strain[2] *noun* 1 TRACE, suggestion, suspicion, tendency, streak, trait 2 BREED, type, stock, family, race, blood, descent, pedigree, extraction, ancestry, lineage

strained *adjective* 1 TENSE, difficult, uncomfortable, awkward, embarrassed, stiff, uneasy, constrained, self-conscious, unrelaxed << ANTONYM relaxed 2 FORCED, put on, false, artificial, unnatural, laboured << ANTONYM natural

strait *noun often plural* CHANNEL, sound, narrows, stretch of water, sea passage ▷ *plural noun* DIFFICULTY, crisis, mess, pass, hole (*slang*), emergency, distress, dilemma, embarrassment, plight, hardship, uphill (*S African*), predicament, extremity, perplexity, panic stations (*informal*), pretty *or* fine kettle of fish (*informal*)

strand *noun* FILAMENT, fibre, thread, length, lock, string, twist, rope, wisp, tress

stranded *adjective* 1 BEACHED, grounded, marooned, ashore, shipwrecked, aground, cast away 2 HELPLESS, abandoned, high and dry, left in the lurch

strange *adjective* 1 ODD, unusual, curious, weird, wonderful, rare, funny, extraordinary, remarkable, bizarre, fantastic, astonishing, marvellous, exceptional, peculiar, eccentric, abnormal, out-of-the-way, queer, irregular, rum (*Brit slang*), uncommon, singular, perplexing, uncanny, mystifying, unheard-of, off-the-wall (*slang*), oddball (*informal*), unaccountable, left-field (*informal*), outré, curiouser and curiouser, daggy (*Austral & NZ informal*) << ANTONYM ordinary **2** OUT OF PLACE, lost, uncomfortable, awkward, bewildered, disoriented, ill at ease, like a fish out of water << ANTONYM comfortable **3** UNFAMILIAR, new, unknown, foreign, novel, alien, exotic, untried, unexplored, outside your experience << ANTONYM familiar

stranger *noun* **1** UNKNOWN PERSON **2** NEWCOMER, incomer, foreigner, guest, visitor, unknown, alien, new arrival, outlander ▷▷ **a stranger to something** UNACCUSTOMED TO, new to, unused to, ignorant of, inexperienced in, unversed in, unpractised in, unseasoned in

strangle *verb* **1** THROTTLE, choke, asphyxiate, garrotte, strangulate, smother, suffocate **2** SUPPRESS, inhibit, subdue, stifle, gag, repress, overpower, quash, quell, quench

strap *noun* TIE, thong, leash, belt ▷ *verb* FASTEN, tie, secure, bind, lash, buckle, truss

strapping *adjective* WELL-BUILT, big, powerful, robust, hefty (*informal*), sturdy, stalwart, burly, husky (*informal*), hulking, beefy (*informal*), brawny, well set-up

stratagem *noun* TRICK, scheme, manoeuvre, plan, plot, device, intrigue, dodge, ploy, ruse, artifice, subterfuge, feint, wile

strategic *adjective* **1** TACTICAL, calculated, deliberate, planned, politic, diplomatic **2** CRUCIAL, important, key, vital, critical, decisive, cardinal

strategy *noun* **1** POLICY, procedure, planning, programme, approach, scheme, manoeuvring, grand design **2** PLAN, approach, scheme, manoeuvring, grand design

stratum *noun* **1** CLASS, group, level, station, estate, rank, grade, category, bracket, caste **2** LAYER, level, seam, table, bed, vein, tier, stratification, lode

stray *verb* **1** WANDER, roam, go astray, range, drift, meander, rove, straggle, lose your way, be abandoned *or* lost **2** DRIFT, wander, roam, meander, rove **3** DIGRESS, diverge, deviate, ramble, get sidetracked, go off at a tangent, get off the point ▷ *adjective* **1** LOST, abandoned, homeless, roaming, vagrant **2** RANDOM, chance, freak, accidental, odd, scattered, erratic, scattershot

streak *noun* **1** BAND, line, strip, stroke, layer, slash, vein, stripe, smear **2** TRACE, touch, element, strain, dash, vein ▷ *verb* **1** FLECK, smear, daub, band, slash, stripe, striate **2** SPEED, fly, tear, sweep, flash, barrel (along) (*informal, chiefly US & Canad*), whistle, sprint, dart, zoom, whizz (*informal*), hurtle, burn rubber (*informal*), move like greased lightning (*informal*)

stream *noun* **1** RIVER, brook, creek (*US*), burn (*Scot*), beck, tributary, bayou, rivulet, rill, freshet **2** FLOW, current, rush, run, course, drift, surge, tide, torrent, outpouring, tideway **3** SUCCESSION, series, flood, chain, battery, volley, avalanche, barrage, torrent ▷ *verb* **1** FLOW, run, pour, course, issue, flood, shed, spill, emit, glide, cascade, gush, spout **2** RUSH, fly, speed, tear, flood, pour

streamer *noun* BANNER, flag, pennant, standard, colours, ribbon, ensign, pennon

streamlined *adjective* EFFICIENT, organized, modernized, rationalized, smooth, slick, sleek, well-run, time-saving, smooth-running

street *noun* ROAD, lane, avenue, terrace, row, boulevard, roadway, thoroughfare ▷▷ **up one's street** (*informal*) TO ONE'S LIKING, to one's taste, one's cup of tea (*informal*), pleasing, familiar, suitable, acceptable, compatible, congenial

strength *noun* **1** MIGHT, muscle, brawn, sinew, brawniness << ANTONYM weakness **2** WILL, spirit, resolution, resolve, courage, character, nerve, determination, pluck, stamina, grit, backbone, fortitude, toughness, tenacity, willpower, mettle, firmness, strength of character, steadfastness, moral fibre **3** HEALTH, fitness, vigour, lustiness **4** MAINSTAY, anchor, tower of strength, security, succour **5** TOUGHNESS, soundness, robustness, sturdiness, stoutness **6** FORCE, power, intensity, energy, vehemence, intenseness << ANTONYM weakness **7** POTENCY, effectiveness, concentration, efficacy **8** STRONG POINT, skill, asset, advantage, talent, forte, speciality, aptitude << ANTONYM failing

strengthen *verb* **1** FORTIFY, encourage, harden, toughen, consolidate, stiffen, hearten, gee up, brace up, give new energy to << ANTONYM weaken **2** REINFORCE, support, confirm, establish, justify, enhance, intensify, bolster, substantiate, buttress, corroborate, give a boost to **3** BOLSTER, harden, reinforce, give a boost to **4** HEIGHTEN, intensify **5** MAKE STRONGER, build up, invigorate, restore, nourish, rejuvenate, give strength to **6** SUPPORT, brace, steel, reinforce, consolidate, harden, bolster, augment, buttress **7** BECOME STRONGER, intensify, heighten, gain strength

strenuous *adjective* **1** DEMANDING, hard, tough, exhausting, taxing, uphill, arduous, laborious, Herculean, tough going, toilsome, unrelaxing << ANTONYM easy **2** TIRELESS, determined, zealous, strong, earnest, spirited, active, eager, bold, persistent, vigorous, energetic, resolute

stress *verb* **1** EMPHASIZE, highlight, underline, repeat, draw attention to, dwell on, underscore, accentuate, point up, rub in, harp on, belabour **2** PLACE THE EMPHASIS ON, emphasize, give emphasis to, place the accent on, lay emphasis upon ▷ *noun* **1** EMPHASIS, importance, significance, force, weight, urgency **2** STRAIN, pressure, worry, tension, burden, anxiety, trauma, oppression, hassle (*informal*), nervous tension **3** ACCENT, beat, emphasis, accentuation, ictus

stressful *adjective* WORRYING, anxious, tense, taxing, demanding, tough, draining, exhausting, exacting, traumatic, agitating, nerve-racking

stretch *verb* **1** EXTEND, cover, spread, reach, unfold, put forth, unroll **2** LAST, continue, go on, extend, carry on, reach **3** EXPAND, lengthen, be elastic, be stretchy **4** PULL, distend, pull out of shape, strain, swell, tighten, rack, inflate, lengthen, draw out, elongate **5** HOLD OUT, offer, present, extend, proffer ▷ *noun* **1** EXPANSE, area, tract, spread, distance, sweep, extent **2** PERIOD, time, spell, stint, run, term, bit, space

strew *verb* SCATTER, spread, litter, toss, sprinkle, disperse, bestrew

stricken *adjective* AFFECTED, hit, afflicted, struck, injured, struck down, smitten, laid low

strict *adjective* **1** SEVERE, harsh, stern, firm, rigid, rigorous, stringent, austere << ANTONYM easy-going **2** STERN, firm, severe, harsh, authoritarian, austere, no-nonsense **3** EXACT, accurate, precise, close, true, particular, religious, faithful, meticulous, scrupulous **4** DEVOUT, religious, orthodox, pious, pure, reverent, prayerful **5** ABSOLUTE, complete, total, perfect, utter

stricture *noun* CRITICISM, censure, stick (*slang*), blame, rebuke, flak (*informal*), bad press, animadversion

strident *adjective* HARSH, jarring, grating, clashing, screeching, raucous, shrill, rasping, jangling, discordant, clamorous, unmusical, stridulant, stridulous << ANTONYM soft

strife *noun* CONFLICT, battle, struggle, row, clash, clashes, contest, controversy, combat, warfare, rivalry, contention, quarrel, friction, squabbling, wrangling, bickering, animosity, discord, dissension

strike *noun* WALKOUT, industrial action, mutiny, revolt ▷ *verb* **1** WALK OUT, take industrial action, down tools, revolt, mutiny **2** HIT, smack, thump, pound, beat, box, knock, punch, hammer, deck (*slang*), slap, sock (*slang*), chin (*slang*), buffet, clout (*informal*), cuff, clump (*slang*), swipe, clobber (*slang*), smite, wallop (*informal*), lambast(e), lay a finger on (*informal*), lay one on (*slang*), beat *or* knock seven bells out of (*informal*) **3** DRIVE, propel, force, hit, smack, wallop (*informal*) **4** COLLIDE WITH, hit, run into, bump into, touch, smash into, come into contact with, knock into, be in collision with **5** KNOCK, bang, smack, thump, beat, smite **6** AFFECT, move, hit, touch, devastate, overwhelm, leave a mark on, make an impact *or* impression on **7** ATTACK, assault someone, fall upon someone, set upon someone, lay into someone (*informal*) **8** OCCUR TO, hit, come to, register (*informal*), come to the mind of, dawn on *or* upon **9** SEEM TO, appear to, look to, give the impression to **10** MOVE, touch, impress, hit, affect, overcome, stir, disturb, perturb, make an impact on **11** ACHIEVE, arrive at, attain, reach, effect, arrange **12** *sometimes with* **upon** DISCOVER, find, come upon *or* across, reach, encounter, turn up, uncover, unearth, hit upon, light upon, happen *or* chance upon, stumble upon *or* across ▷▷ **strike out** SET OUT, set off, start out, sally forth ▷▷ **strike someone down** KILL, destroy, slay, ruin, afflict, smite, bring low, deal a deathblow to ▷▷ **strike something out, off** *or* **through** SCORE OUT, delete, cross out, remove, cancel, erase, excise, efface, expunge

striking *adjective* **1** DISTINCT, noticeable, conspicuous, clear, obvious, evident, manifest, unmistakable, observable, perceptible, appreciable **2** IMPRESSIVE, dramatic, stunning (*informal*), wonderful, extraordinary, outstanding, astonishing, memorable, dazzling, noticeable, conspicuous, drop-dead (*slang*), out of the ordinary, forcible, jaw-dropping

<< ANTONYM unimpressive

string *noun* 1 CORD, yarn, twine, strand, fibre, thread 2 SERIES, line, row, file, sequence, queue, succession, procession 3 SEQUENCE, run, series, chain, succession, streak ▷ *plural noun* 1 STRINGED INSTRUMENTS 2 CONDITIONS, catches (*informal*), provisos, stipulations, requirements, riders, obligations, qualifications, complications, prerequisites ▷ *verb* HANG, stretch, suspend, sling, thread, loop, festoon ▷▷ **string along with someone** ACCOMPANY, go with, go along with, chaperon ▷▷ **string someone along** DECEIVE, fool, take (someone) for a ride (*informal*), kid (*informal*), bluff, hoax, dupe, put one over on (someone) (*informal*), play fast and loose with (someone) (*informal*), play (someone) false

stringent *adjective* STRICT, tough, rigorous, demanding, binding, tight, severe, exacting, rigid, inflexible << ANTONYM lax

stringy *adjective* FIBROUS, tough, chewy, sinewy, gristly, wiry

strip[1] *verb* 1 UNDRESS, disrobe, unclothe, uncover yourself 2 PLUNDER, rob, loot, empty, sack, deprive, ransack, pillage, divest, denude

strip[2] *noun* 1 PIECE, shred, bit, band, slip, belt, tongue, ribbon, fillet, swathe 2 STRETCH, area, tract, expanse, extent

striped *adjective* BANDED, stripy, barred, striated

stripy *or* **stripey** *adjective* BANDED, striped, streaky

strive *verb* TRY, labour, struggle, fight, attempt, compete, strain, contend, endeavour, go for it (*informal*), try hard, toil, make every effort, go all out (*informal*), bend over backwards (*informal*), do your best, go for broke (*slang*), leave no stone unturned, bust a gut (*informal*), do all you can, give it your best shot (*informal*), jump through hoops (*informal*), break your neck (*informal*), exert yourself, make an all-out effort (*informal*), knock yourself out (*informal*), do your utmost, do your damnedest (*informal*), give it your all (*informal*), rupture yourself (*informal*)

stroke *verb* CARESS, rub, fondle, pat, pet ▷ *noun* 1 APOPLEXY, fit, seizure, attack, shock, collapse 2 MARK, line, slash 3 MOVEMENT, action, motion 4 BLOW, hit, knock, pat, rap, thump, swipe 5 FEAT, move, achievement, accomplishment, movement

stroll *verb* WALK, ramble, amble, wander, promenade, saunter, stooge (*slang*), take a turn, toddle, make your way, mooch (*slang*), mosey (*informal*), stretch your legs ▷ *noun* WALK, promenade, turn, airing, run, constitutional, excursion, ramble, breath of air

strong *adjective* 1 POWERFUL, muscular, tough, capable, athletic, strapping, hardy, sturdy, stout, stalwart, burly, beefy (*informal*), virile, Herculean, sinewy, brawny << ANTONYM weak 2 FIT, sound, healthy, robust, hale, in good shape, in good condition, lusty, fighting fit, fit as a fiddle 3 SELF-CONFIDENT, determined, tough, brave, aggressive, courageous, high-powered, forceful, resilient, feisty (*informal, chiefly US & Canad*), resolute, resourceful, tenacious, plucky, hard-nosed (*informal*), steadfast, unyielding, hard as nails, self-assertive, stouthearted, firm in spirit << ANTONYM timid 4 DURABLE, substantial, sturdy, reinforced, heavy-duty, well-built, well-armed, hard-wearing, well-protected, on a firm foundation << ANTONYM flimsy 5 FORCEFUL, powerful, intense, vigorous 6 EXTREME, radical, drastic, strict, harsh, rigid, forceful, uncompromising, Draconian, unbending 7 DECISIVE, firm, forceful, decided, determined, severe, resolute, incisive 8 PERSUASIVE, convincing, compelling, telling, great, clear, sound, effective, urgent, formidable, potent, well-established, clear-cut, overpowering, weighty, well-founded, redoubtable, trenchant, cogent 9 PUNGENT, powerful, concentrated, pure, undiluted << ANTONYM bland 10 HIGHLY-FLAVOURED, hot, spicy, piquant, biting, sharp, heady, overpowering, intoxicating, highly-seasoned 11 KEEN, deep, acute, eager, fervent, zealous, vehement 12 INTENSE, deep, passionate, ardent, fierce, profound, forceful, fervent, deep-rooted, vehement, fervid 13 STAUNCH, firm, keen, dedicated, fierce, ardent, eager, enthusiastic, passionate, fervent 14 DISTINCT, marked, clear, unmistakable << ANTONYM slight 15 BRIGHT, brilliant, dazzling, loud, bold, stark, glaring << ANTONYM dull

strong-arm *modifier* (*informal*) BULLYING, threatening, aggressive, violent, terror, forceful, high-pressure, coercive, terrorizing, thuggish

stronghold *noun* 1 BASTION, fortress, bulwark, fastness 2 REFUGE, haven, retreat, sanctuary, hide-out, bolt hole

strong-minded *adjective* DETERMINED, resolute, strong-willed, firm, independent, uncompromising, iron-willed, unbending

strong point *noun* FORTE, strength, speciality, advantage, asset, strong suit, métier, long suit (*informal*)

stroppy *adjective* (*Brit informal*) AWKWARD, difficult, obstreperous, destructive, perverse, unhelpful, cantankerous, bloody-minded (*Brit informal*), quarrelsome, litigious, uncooperative

structure *noun* 1 ARRANGEMENT, form, make-up, make, design, organization, construction, fabric, formation, configuration, conformation, interrelation of parts 2 BUILDING, construction, erection, edifice, pile ▷ *verb* ARRANGE, organize, design, shape, build up, assemble, put together

struggle *verb* 1 STRIVE, labour, toil, work, strain, go for it (*informal*), make every effort, go all out (*informal*), bend over backwards (*informal*), go for broke (*slang*), bust a gut (*informal*), give it your best shot (*informal*), break your neck (*informal*), exert yourself, make an all-out effort (*informal*), work like a Trojan, knock yourself out (*informal*), do your damnedest (*informal*), give it your all (*informal*), rupture yourself (*informal*) 2 FIGHT, battle, wrestle, grapple, compete, contend, scuffle, lock horns 3 HAVE TROUBLE, have problems, have difficulties, fight, come unstuck ▷ *noun* 1 PROBLEM, battle, effort, trial, strain 2 EFFORT, labour, toil, work, grind (*informal*), pains, scramble, long haul, exertion 3 FIGHT, battle, conflict, clash, contest, encounter, brush, combat, hostilities, strife, skirmish, tussle, biffo (*Austral slang*)

strut *verb* SWAGGER, parade, stalk, peacock, prance

stub *noun* 1 BUTT, end, stump, tail, remnant, tail end, fag end (*informal*), dog-end (*informal*) 2 COUNTERFOIL

stubborn *adjective* OBSTINATE, dogged, inflexible, fixed, persistent, intractable, wilful, tenacious, recalcitrant, unyielding, headstrong, unmanageable, unbending, obdurate, stiff-necked, unshakeable, self-willed, refractory, pig-headed, bull-headed, mulish, cross-grained, contumacious << ANTONYM compliant

stubby *adjective* STUMPY, short, squat, stocky, chunky, dumpy, thickset, fubsy (*archaic or dialect*)

stuck *adjective* 1 FASTENED, fast, fixed, joined, glued, cemented 2 TRAPPED, caught, ensnared 3 BURDENED, saddled, lumbered, landed, loaded, encumbered 4 (*informal*) BAFFLED, stumped, at a loss, beaten, nonplussed, at a standstill, bereft of ideas, up against a brick wall (*informal*), at your wits' end ▷▷ **stuck on something** *or* **someone** (*slang*) INFATUATED WITH, obsessed with, keen on, enthusiastic about, mad about, wild about (*informal*), hung up on (*slang*), crazy about, for, *or* over (*informal*) ▷▷ **get stuck into something** (*informal*) SET ABOUT, tackle, get down to, make a start on, take the bit between your teeth

stuck-up *adjective* (*informal*) SNOBBISH, arrogant, conceited, proud, patronizing, condescending, snooty (*informal*), haughty, uppity (*informal*), high and mighty (*informal*), toffee-nosed (*slang, chiefly Brit*), hoity-toity (*informal*), swollen-headed, bigheaded (*informal*), uppish (*Brit informal*)

student *noun* 1 UNDERGRADUATE, scholar 2 PUPIL, scholar, schoolchild, schoolboy *or* schoolgirl 3 LEARNER, observer, trainee, apprentice, disciple

studied *adjective* PLANNED, calculated, deliberate, conscious, intentional, wilful, purposeful, premeditated, well-considered << ANTONYM unplanned

studio *noun* WORKSHOP, shop, workroom, atelier

studious *adjective* 1 SCHOLARLY, academic, intellectual, serious, earnest, hard-working, thoughtful, reflective, diligent, meditative, bookish, assiduous, sedulous << ANTONYM unacademic 2 INTENT, attentive, watchful, listening, concentrating, careful, regardful << ANTONYM careless 3 DELIBERATE, planned, conscious, calculated, considered, studied, designed, thoughtful, intentional, wilful, purposeful, premeditated, prearranged

study *verb* 1 LEARN, cram (*informal*), swot (up) (*Brit informal*), read up, hammer away at, bone up on (*informal*), burn the midnight oil, mug up (*Brit slang*) 2 EXAMINE, survey, look at, scrutinize, peruse 3 CONTEMPLATE, read, examine, consider, go into, con (*archaic*), pore over, apply yourself (to) ▷ *noun* 1 EXAMINATION, investigation, analysis, consideration, inspection, scrutiny, contemplation, perusal, cogitation 2 PIECE OF RESEARCH, survey, report, paper, review, article, inquiry, investigation 3 LEARNING, lessons, school work, academic work, reading, research, cramming (*informal*), swotting (*Brit informal*), book work **4** OFFICE, room, studio, workplace, den, place of work, workroom

stuff *noun* **1** THINGS, gear, possessions, effects, materials, equipment, objects, tackle, kit, junk, luggage, belongings, trappings, bits and pieces, paraphernalia, clobber (*Brit slang*), impedimenta, goods and chattels **2** NONSENSE, rubbish, rot, trash, bunk (*informal*), foolishness, humbug, twaddle, tripe (*informal*), baloney (*informal*), verbiage, claptrap (*informal*), bunkum, poppycock (*informal*), balderdash, pants (*slang*), bosh (*informal*), stuff and nonsense, tommyrot, bizzo (*Austral slang*), bull's wool (*Austral & NZ slang*) **3** SUBSTANCE, material, essence, matter, staple, pith, quintessence ▷ *verb* **1** SHOVE, force, push, squeeze, jam, ram, wedge, compress, stow **2** CRAM, fill, pack, load, crowd

stuffing *noun* **1** FILLING, forcemeat **2** WADDING, filling, packing, quilting, kapok

stuffy *adjective* **1** STAID, conventional, dull, old-fashioned, deadly, dreary, pompous, formal, prim, stilted, musty, stodgy, uninteresting, humourless, fusty, strait-laced, priggish, as dry as dust, old-fogeyish, niminy-piminy, prim and proper **2** AIRLESS, stifling, oppressive, close, heavy, stale, suffocating, sultry, fetid, muggy, unventilated, fuggy, frowsty << ANTONYM airy

stumble *verb* **1** TRIP, fall, slip, reel, stagger, falter, flounder, lurch, come a cropper (*informal*), lose your balance, blunder about **2** TOTTER, reel, stagger, blunder, falter, lurch, wobble, teeter **3** FALTER, hesitate, stammer, stutter, fluff (*informal*) ▷▷ **stumble across, on** *or* **upon something** *or* **someone** DISCOVER, find, come across, encounter, run across, chance upon, happen upon, light upon, blunder upon

stumbling block *noun* OBSTACLE, difficulty, bar, barrier, hurdle, hazard, snag, uphill (*S African*), obstruction, impediment, hindrance

stump *noun* TAIL END, end, remnant, remainder ▷ *verb* **1** BAFFLE, confuse, puzzle, snooker, foil, bewilder, confound, perplex, mystify, outwit, stymie, flummox, bring (someone) up short, dumbfound, nonplus **2** STAMP, clump, stomp (*informal*), trudge, plod, clomp ▷▷ **stump something up** (*Brit informal*) (with money or a sum of money as object) PAY, fork out (*slang*), shell out (*informal*), contribute, hand over, donate, chip in (*informal*), cough up (*informal*), come across with (*informal*)

stumped *adjective* BAFFLED, perplexed, at a loss, floored (*informal*), at sea, stymied, nonplussed, flummoxed, brought to a standstill, uncertain which way to turn, at your wits' end

stun *verb* **1** OVERCOME, shock, amaze, confuse, astonish, stagger, bewilder, astound, overpower, confound, stupefy, strike (someone) dumb, knock (someone) for six (*informal*), dumbfound, flabbergast (*informal*), hit (someone) like a ton of bricks (*informal*), take (someone's) breath away **2** DAZE, knock out, stupefy, numb, benumb

stung *adjective* HURT, wounded, angered, roused, incensed, exasperated, resentful, nettled, goaded, piqued

stunned *adjective* STAGGERED, shocked, devastated, numb, astounded, bowled over (*informal*), gobsmacked (*Brit slang*), dumbfounded, flabbergasted (*informal*), struck dumb, at a loss for words

stunner *noun* (*informal*) BEAUTY, looker (*informal, chiefly US*), lovely (*slang*), dish (*informal*), sensation, honey (*informal*), good-looker, dazzler, peach (*informal*), wow (*slang, chiefly US*), dolly (*slang*), knockout (*informal*), heart-throb, charmer, eyeful (*informal*), smasher (*informal*), humdinger (*slang*), glamour puss, beaut (*Austral & NZ slang*)

stunning *adjective* (*informal*) WONDERFUL, beautiful, impressive, great (*informal*), striking, brilliant, dramatic, lovely, remarkable, smashing (*informal*), heavenly, devastating (*informal*), spectacular, marvellous, splendid, gorgeous, dazzling, sensational (*informal*), drop-dead (*slang*), ravishing, out of this world (*informal*), jaw-dropping << ANTONYM unimpressive

stunt *noun* FEAT, act, trick, exploit, deed, tour de force (*French*)

stunted *adjective* UNDERSIZED, dwarfed, little, small, tiny, diminutive, dwarfish

stupefy *verb* ASTOUND, shock, amaze, stun, stagger, bewilder, numb, daze, confound, knock senseless, dumbfound

stupendous *adjective* **1** WONDERFUL, brilliant, amazing, stunning (*informal*), superb, overwhelming, fantastic (*informal*), tremendous (*informal*), fabulous (*informal*), surprising, staggering, marvellous, sensational (*informal*), breathtaking, phenomenal, astounding, prodigious, wondrous (*archaic* or *literary*), mind-boggling (*informal*), out of this world (*informal*), mind-blowing (*informal*), jaw-dropping, surpassing belief << ANTONYM unremarkable **2** HUGE, vast, enormous, mega (*slang*), gigantic, colossal << ANTONYM tiny

stupid *adjective* **1** UNINTELLIGENT, thick, dumb (*informal*), simple, slow, dull, dim, dense, sluggish, deficient, crass, gullible, simple-minded, dozy (*Brit informal*), witless, stolid, dopey (*informal*), moronic, obtuse, brainless, cretinous, half-witted, slow on the uptake (*informal*), braindead (*informal*), dumb-ass (*slang*), doltish, dead from the neck up, thickheaded, slow-witted, Boeotian, thick as mince (*Scot informal*), woodenheaded (*informal*) << ANTONYM intelligent **2** SILLY, foolish, daft (*informal*), rash, trivial, ludicrous, meaningless, irresponsible, pointless, futile, senseless, mindless, laughable, short-sighted, ill-advised, idiotic, fatuous, nonsensical, half-baked (*informal*), inane, crackpot (*informal*), unthinking, puerile, unintelligent, asinine, imbecilic, crackbrained << ANTONYM sensible **3** SENSELESS, dazed, groggy, punch-drunk, insensate, semiconscious, into a daze

stupidity *noun* **1** LACK OF INTELLIGENCE, imbecility, obtuseness, simplicity, thickness, slowness, dullness, dimness, dumbness (*informal*), feeble-mindedness, lack of brain, denseness, brainlessness, doziness (*Brit informal*), asininity, dopiness (*slang*), thickheadedness **2** SILLINESS, folly, foolishness, idiocy, madness, absurdity, futility, lunacy, irresponsibility, pointlessness, inanity, rashness, impracticality, foolhardiness, senselessness, bêtise (*rare*), ludicrousness, puerility, fatuousness, fatuity

stupor *noun* DAZE, numbness, unconsciousness, trance, coma, inertia, lethargy, torpor, stupefaction, insensibility

sturdy *adjective* **1** ROBUST, hardy, vigorous, powerful, athletic, muscular, stalwart, staunch, hearty, lusty, brawny, thickset << ANTONYM puny **2** SUBSTANTIAL, secure, solid, durable, well-made, well-built, built to last << ANTONYM flimsy

stutter *noun* STAMMER, faltering, speech impediment, speech defect, hesitance ▷ *verb* STAMMER, stumble, falter, hesitate, splutter, speak haltingly

style *noun* **1** MANNER, way, method, approach, technique, custom, mode **2** ELEGANCE, taste, chic, flair, polish, grace, dash, sophistication, refinement, panache, élan, cosmopolitanism, savoir-faire, smartness, urbanity, stylishness, bon ton (*French*), fashionableness, dressiness (*informal*) **3** DESIGN, form, cut **4** TYPE, sort, kind, spirit, pattern, variety, appearance, tone, strain, category, characteristic, genre, tenor **5** FASHION, trend, mode, vogue, rage **6** LUXURY, ease, comfort, elegance, grandeur, affluence, gracious living **7** MODE OF EXPRESSION, phrasing, turn of phrase, wording, treatment, expression, vein, diction, phraseology ▷ *verb* **1** DESIGN, cut, tailor, fashion, shape, arrange, adapt **2** CALL, name, term, address, label, entitle, dub, designate, christen, denominate

stylish *adjective* SMART, chic, polished, fashionable, trendy (*Brit informal*), classy (*slang*), in fashion, snappy, in vogue, dapper, natty (*informal*), snazzy (*informal*), modish, well turned-out, dressy (*informal*), à la mode, voguish, schmick (*Austral informal*) << ANTONYM scruffy

stymie *verb* FRUSTRATE, defeat, foil, thwart, puzzle, stump, snooker, hinder, confound, mystify, balk, flummox, throw a spanner in the works (*Brit informal*), nonplus, spike (someone's) guns

suave *adjective* SMOOTH, charming, urbane, debonair, worldly, cool (*informal*), sophisticated, polite, gracious, agreeable, courteous, affable, smooth-tongued ▷

subconscious *noun* MIND, psyche ▷ *adjective* HIDDEN, inner, suppressed, repressed, intuitive, latent, innermost, subliminal << ANTONYM conscious

subdue *verb* **1** OVERCOME, defeat, master, break, control, discipline, crush, humble, put down, conquer, tame, overpower, overrun, trample, quell, triumph over, get the better of, vanquish, beat down, get under control, get the upper hand over, gain ascendancy over **2** MODERATE, control, check, suppress, soften, repress, mellow, tone down, quieten down << ANTONYM arouse

subdued *adjective* **1** QUIET, serious, sober, sad, grave, restrained, repressed, solemn, chastened, dejected, downcast, crestfallen, repentant, down in the mouth, sadder and wiser, out of spirits << ANTONYM lively **2** HUSHED, soft, quiet, whispered,

murmured, muted << ANTONYM loud
3 DIM, soft, subtle, muted, shaded, low-key,
understated, toned down, unobtrusive
<< ANTONYM bright

subject noun 1 TOPIC, question, issue, matter,
point, business, affair, object, theme,
substance, subject matter, field of inquiry
or reference 2 BRANCH OF STUDY, area, field,
discipline, speciality, branch of knowledge
3 PARTICIPANT, case, patient, victim, client,
guinea pig (informal) 4 CITIZEN, resident,
native, inhabitant, national 5 DEPENDANT,
subordinate, vassal, liegeman ▷ adjective
SUBORDINATE, dependent, satellite,
inferior, captive, obedient, enslaved,
submissive, subservient, subjugated ▷ verb
PUT THROUGH, expose, submit, lay open,
make liable ▷▷ **subject to 1** LIABLE TO,
open to, exposed to, vulnerable to, prone
to, susceptible to, disposed to 2 BOUND
BY, under the control of, constrained by
3 DEPENDENT ON, contingent on, controlled
by, conditional on

subjective adjective PERSONAL, emotional,
prejudiced, biased, instinctive, intuitive,
idiosyncratic, nonobjective << ANTONYM
objective

subjugate verb CONQUER, master, overcome,
defeat, crush, suppress, put down,
overthrow, tame, lick (informal), subdue,
overpower, quell, rule over, enslave,
vanquish, hold sway over, bring to heel,
bring (someone) to his knees, bring under
the yoke

sublimate verb CHANNEL, transfer, divert,
redirect, turn

sublime adjective NOBLE, magnificent,
glorious, high, great, grand, imposing,
elevated, eminent, majestic, lofty, exalted,
transcendent << ANTONYM lowly

subliminal adjective SUBCONSCIOUS,
unconscious

submerge verb 1 FLOOD, swamp, engulf,
drown, overflow, inundate, deluge
2 IMMERSE, plunge, dip, duck, dunk 3 SINK,
plunge, go under water 4 OVERWHELM,
swamp, engulf, overload, inundate, deluge,
snow under, overburden

submerged adjective IMMERSED, sunk,
underwater, drowned, submarine, sunken,
undersea, subaqueous, submersed,
subaquatic

submission noun 1 SURRENDER, yielding,
giving in, cave-in (informal), capitulation,
acquiescence 2 PRESENTATION, submitting,

handing in, entry, tendering 3 PROPOSAL,
argument, contention 4 COMPLIANCE,
obedience, submissiveness, meekness,
resignation, deference, passivity, docility,
tractability, unassertiveness

submissive adjective MEEK, passive, obedient,
compliant, patient, resigned, yielding,
accommodating, humble, subdued,
lowly, abject, amenable, docile, dutiful,
ingratiating, malleable, deferential, pliant,
obsequious, uncomplaining, tractable,
acquiescent, biddable, unresisting,
bootlicking (informal), obeisant << ANTONYM
obstinate

submit verb 1 SURRENDER, yield, give in, agree,
bend, bow, endure, tolerate, comply, put up
with (informal), succumb, defer, stoop, cave
in (informal), capitulate, accede, acquiesce,
toe the line, knuckle under, resign yourself,
lay down arms, hoist the white flag, throw
in the sponge 2 PRESENT, hand in, tender,
put forward, table, commit, refer, proffer
3 SUGGEST, claim, argue, propose, state, put,
move, advance, volunteer, assert, contend,
propound

subordinate noun INFERIOR, junior, assistant,
aide, second, attendant, dependant,
underling, subaltern << ANTONYM superior
▷ adjective 1 INFERIOR, lesser, lower, junior,
subject, minor, secondary, dependent,
subservient << ANTONYM superior
2 SUBSIDIARY, supplementary, auxiliary,
ancillary

subordination noun INFERIORITY, servitude,
subjection, inferior or secondary status

subscribe to verb 1 SUPPORT, agree with,
advocate, consent to, endorse, countenance,
acquiesce with 2 CONTRIBUTE TO, give to,
donate to, chip in to (informal)

subscription noun (Chiefly Brit) MEMBERSHIP
FEE, charge, dues, annual payment

subsequent adjective FOLLOWING, later,
succeeding, after, successive, ensuing,
consequent << ANTONYM previous

subsequently adverb LATER, afterwards, in the
end, consequently, in the aftermath (of), at
a later date

subservient adjective 1 SERVILE, submissive,
deferential, subject, inferior, abject,
sycophantic, slavish, obsequious, truckling,
bootlicking (informal) << ANTONYM
domineering 2 SUBORDINATE, subsidiary,
accessory, auxiliary, conducive, ancillary

subside verb 1 DECREASE, diminish, lessen,
ease, moderate, dwindle, wane, recede, ebb,

abate, let up, peter out, slacken, melt away, quieten, level off, de-escalate << ANTONYM increase **2** COLLAPSE, sink, cave in, drop, lower, settle **3** DROP, fall, decline, ebb, descend

subsidence *noun* SINKING, settling, collapse, settlement

subsidiary *noun* BRANCH, division, section, office, department, wing, subdivision, subsection, local office ▷ *adjective* SECONDARY, lesser, subordinate, minor, supplementary, auxiliary, supplemental, contributory, ancillary, subservient << ANTONYM main

subsidize *verb* FUND, finance, support, promote, sponsor, underwrite, put up the money for

subsidy *noun* AID, help, support, grant, contribution, assistance, allowance, financial aid, stipend, subvention

subsist *verb* STAY ALIVE, survive, keep going, make ends meet, last, live, continue, exist, endure, eke out an existence, keep your head above water, sustain yourself

subsistence *noun* LIVING, maintenance, upkeep, keep, support, existence, survival, livelihood

substance *noun* **1** MATERIAL, body, stuff, element, fabric, texture **2** IMPORTANCE, significance, concreteness **3** MEANING, main point, gist, matter, subject, theme, import, significance, essence, pith, burden, sum and substance **4** TRUTH, fact, reality, certainty, validity, authenticity, verity, verisimilitude **5** WEALTH, means, property, assets, resources, estate, affluence

substandard *adjective* INFERIOR, inadequate, unacceptable, damaged, imperfect, second-rate, shoddy

substantial *adjective* **1** BIG, significant, considerable, goodly, large, important, generous, worthwhile, tidy (*informal*), ample, sizable *or* sizeable << ANTONYM small **2** SOLID, sound, sturdy, strong, firm, massive, hefty, durable, bulky, well-built << ANTONYM insubstantial

substantially *adverb* **1** CONSIDERABLY, significantly, very much, greatly, seriously (*informal*), remarkably, markedly, noticeably, appreciably **2** ESSENTIALLY, largely, mainly, materially, in the main, in essence, to a large extent, in substance, in essentials

substantiate *verb* SUPPORT, prove, confirm, establish, affirm, verify, validate, bear out, corroborate, attest to, authenticate

<< ANTONYM disprove

substitute *verb* **1** REPLACE, exchange, swap, change, switch, commute, interchange **2** *with* **for** STAND IN FOR, cover for, take over from, relieve, act for, double for, fill in for, hold the fort for, be in place of, deputize for ▷ *noun* REPLACEMENT, reserve, equivalent, surrogate, deputy, relief, representative, sub, temporary, stand-by, makeshift, proxy, temp (*informal*), expedient, locum, depute (*Scot*), stopgap, locum tenens

substitution *noun* REPLACEMENT, exchange, switch, swap, change, interchange

subterfuge *noun* TRICK, dodge, ploy, shift, manoeuvre, deception, evasion, pretence, pretext, ruse, artifice, duplicity, stratagem, deviousness, machination

subtle *adjective* **1** FAINT, slight, implied, delicate, indirect, understated, insinuated << ANTONYM obvious **2** CRAFTY, cunning, sly, designing, scheming, intriguing, shrewd, ingenious, astute, devious, wily, artful, Machiavellian << ANTONYM straightforward **3** MUTED, soft, subdued, low-key, toned down **4** FINE, minute, narrow, tenuous, hair-splitting

subtlety *noun* **1** FINE POINT, refinement, nicety, sophistication, delicacy, intricacy, discernment **2** SKILL, acumen, astuteness, ingenuity, guile, cleverness, deviousness, sagacity, acuteness, craftiness, artfulness, slyness, wiliness **3** SENSITIVITY, diplomacy, discretion, delicacy, understanding, skill, consideration, judgment, perception, finesse, thoughtfulness, discernment, savoir-faire, adroitness

subtract *verb* TAKE AWAY, take off, deduct, remove, withdraw, diminish, take from, detract << ANTONYM add

suburb *noun* RESIDENTIAL AREA, neighbourhood, outskirts, precincts, suburbia, environs, purlieus, dormitory area (*Brit*), faubourgs

subversive *adjective* SEDITIOUS, inflammatory, incendiary, underground, undermining, destructive, overthrowing, riotous, insurrectionary, treasonous, perversive ▷ *noun* DISSIDENT, terrorist, saboteur, insurrectionist, quisling, fifth columnist, deviationist, seditionary, seditionist

subvert *verb* **1** OVERTURN, destroy, undermine, upset, ruin, wreck, demolish, sabotage **2** CORRUPT, pervert, deprave, poison, contaminate, confound, debase, demoralize, vitiate

succeed *verb* **1** TRIUMPH, win, prevail **2** WORK OUT, work, be successful, come off (*informal*), do the trick (*informal*), turn out well, go like a bomb (*Brit & NZ informal*), go down a bomb (*informal, chiefly Brit*), do the business (*informal*) **3** MAKE IT (*informal*), do well, be successful, arrive (*informal*), triumph, thrive, flourish, make good, prosper, cut it (*informal*), make the grade (*informal*), get to the top, crack it (*informal*), hit the jackpot (*informal*), bring home the bacon (*informal*), make your mark (*informal*), gain your end, carry all before you, do all right for yourself << ANTONYM fail **4** TAKE OVER FROM, replace, assume the office of, fill (someone's) boots, step into (someone's) boots **5** *with* **to** TAKE OVER, assume, attain, acquire, come into, inherit, accede to, come into possession of **6** FOLLOW, come after, follow after, replace, be subsequent to, supervene << ANTONYM precede

success *noun* **1** VICTORY, triumph, positive result, favourable outcome << ANTONYM failure **2** PROSPERITY, fortune, luck, fame, eminence, ascendancy **3** HIT (*informal*), winner, smash (*informal*), triumph, sensation, wow (*slang*), best seller, market leader, smash hit (*informal*) << ANTONYM flop (*informal*) **4** BIG NAME, star, hit (*informal*), somebody, celebrity, sensation, megastar (*informal*), V.I.P. << ANTONYM nobody

successful *adjective* **1** TRIUMPHANT, victorious, lucky, fortunate **2** THRIVING, profitable, productive, paying, effective, rewarding, booming, efficient, flourishing, unbeaten, lucrative, favourable, fruitful, efficacious, moneymaking << ANTONYM unprofitable **3** TOP, prosperous, acknowledged, wealthy, out in front (*informal*), going places, at the top of the tree

successfully *adverb* WELL, favourably, in triumph, with flying colours, famously (*informal*), swimmingly, victoriously

succession *noun* **1** SERIES, run, sequence, course, order, train, flow, chain, cycle, procession, continuation, progression **2** TAKING OVER, assumption, inheritance, elevation, accession, entering upon ▷▷ **in succession** ONE AFTER THE OTHER, running, successively, consecutively, on the trot (*informal*), one behind the other

successive *adjective* CONSECUTIVE, following, succeeding, in a row, in succession, sequent

succinct *adjective* BRIEF, to the point, concise, compact, summary, condensed, terse,

laconic, pithy, gnomic, compendious, in a few well-chosen words << ANTONYM rambling

succour *noun* HELP, support, aid, relief, comfort, assistance ▷ *verb* HELP, support, aid, encourage, nurse, comfort, foster, assist, relieve, minister to, befriend, render assistance to, give aid and encouragement to

succulent *adjective* JUICY, moist, luscious, rich, lush, mellow, mouthwatering

succumb *verb* **1** *often with* **to** SURRENDER (TO), yield (to), submit (to), give in (to), give way (to), go under (to), cave in (to) (*informal*), capitulate (to), knuckle under (to) << ANTONYM beat **2** *with* **to** (with an illness as object) CATCH, fall victim to, fall ill with

suck *verb* **1** DRINK, sip, draw **2** TAKE, draw, pull, extract ▷▷ **suck up to someone** (*informal*) INGRATIATE YOURSELF WITH, play up to (*informal*), curry favour with, flatter, pander to, toady, butter up, keep in with (*informal*), fawn on, truckle, lick someone's boots, dance attendance on, get on the right side of, worm yourself into (someone's) favour

sucker *noun* (*slang*) FOOL, mug (*Brit slang*), dupe, victim, butt, sap (*slang*), pushover (*slang*), sitting duck (*informal*), sitting target, putz (*US slang*), cat's paw, easy game or mark (*informal*), nerd or nurd (*slang*), dorba or dorb (*Austral slang*), bogan (*Austral slang*)

sudden *adjective* QUICK, rapid, unexpected, swift, hurried, abrupt, hasty, impulsive, unforeseen << ANTONYM gradual

suddenly *adverb* ABRUPTLY, all of a sudden, all at once, unexpectedly, out of the blue (*informal*), without warning, on the spur of the moment

sue *verb* **1** (*law*) TAKE (SOMEONE) TO COURT, prosecute, bring an action against (someone), charge, summon, indict, have the law on (someone) (*informal*), prefer charges against (someone), institute legal proceedings against (someone) **2** APPEAL FOR, plead, beg, petition, solicit, beseech, entreat, supplicate

suffer *verb* **1** BE IN PAIN, hurt, ache, be racked, have a bad time, go through a lot (*informal*), go through the mill (*informal*), feel wretched **2** BE AFFECTED, have trouble with, be afflicted, be troubled with **3** UNDERGO, experience, sustain, feel, bear, go through, endure **4** DETERIORATE, decline, get worse, fall off, be impaired **5** TOLERATE, stand, put up with (*informal*), support, bear, endure, hack (*Brit informal*), abide

suffering *noun* PAIN, torture, distress, agony, misery, ordeal, discomfort, torment, hardship, anguish, affliction, martyrdom

suffice *verb* BE ENOUGH, do, be sufficient, be adequate, answer, serve, content, satisfy, fill the bill (*informal*), meet requirements

sufficient *adjective* ADEQUATE, enough, ample, satisfactory, enow (*archaic*) << ANTONYM insufficient

suffocate *verb* 1 CHOKE, stifle, smother, asphyxiate 2 BE CHOKED, be stifled, be smothered, be asphyxiated

suffuse *verb* SPREAD THROUGH *or* OVER, flood, infuse, steep, bathe, mantle, pervade, permeate, imbue, overspread, transfuse

suggest *verb* 1 RECOMMEND, propose, advise, move, advocate, prescribe, put forward, offer a suggestion 2 INDICATE, lead you to believe 3 HINT AT, imply, insinuate, intimate, get at, drive at (*informal*) 4 BRING TO MIND, evoke, remind you of, connote, make you think of, put you in mind of

suggestion *noun* 1 RECOMMENDATION, proposal, proposition, plan, motion 2 HINT, implication, insinuation, intimation 3 TRACE, touch, hint, breath, indication, whisper, suspicion, intimation

suggestive *adjective* SMUTTY, rude, indecent, improper, blue, provocative, spicy (*informal*), racy, unseemly, titillating, risqué, bawdy, prurient, off colour, ribald, immodest, indelicate ▷▷ **suggestive of** REMINISCENT OF, indicative of, redolent of, evocative of

suit *noun* 1 OUTFIT, costume, ensemble, dress, clothing, habit 2 LAWSUIT, case, trial, proceeding, cause, action, prosecution, industrial tribunal ▷ *verb* 1 BE ACCEPTABLE TO, please, satisfy, do, answer, gratify 2 AGREE WITH, become, match, go with, correspond with, conform to, befit, harmonize with ▷▷ **follow suit** COPY SOMEONE, emulate someone, accord with someone, take your cue from someone, run with the herd

suitability *noun* APPROPRIATENESS, fitness, rightness, aptness

suitable *adjective* 1 APPROPRIATE, right, fitting, fit, suited, acceptable, becoming, satisfactory, apt, befitting << ANTONYM inappropriate 2 SEEMLY, fitting, becoming, due, proper, correct << ANTONYM unseemly 3 SUITED, appropriate, in keeping with, in character, cut out for << ANTONYM out of keeping 4 PERTINENT, relevant, applicable, fitting, appropriate, to the point, apt,

apposite, germane << ANTONYM irrelevant 5 CONVENIENT, timely, appropriate, well-timed, opportune, commodious << ANTONYM inopportune

suite *noun* 1 ROOMS, apartment, set of rooms, living quarters 2 SET, series, collection 3 ATTENDANTS, escorts, entourage, train, followers, retainers, retinue

suitor *noun* ADMIRER, young man, beau, follower (*obsolete*), swain (*archaic*), wooer

sulk *verb* BE SULLEN, brood, be in a huff, pout, be put out, have the hump (*Brit informal*)

sulky *adjective* HUFFY, sullen, petulant, cross, put out, moody, perverse, disgruntled, aloof, resentful, vexed, churlish, morose, querulous, ill-humoured, in the sulks

sullen *adjective* MOROSE, cross, moody, sour, gloomy, brooding, dour, surly, glowering, sulky, unsociable, out of humour << ANTONYM cheerful

sully *verb* 1 DISHONOUR, ruin, disgrace, besmirch, smirch 2 DEFILE, dirty, stain, spot, spoil, contaminate, pollute, taint, tarnish, blemish, befoul

sultry *adjective* 1 HUMID, close, hot, sticky, stifling, oppressive, stuffy, sweltering, muggy << ANTONYM cool 2 SEDUCTIVE, sexy (*informal*), sensual, voluptuous, passionate, erotic, provocative, amorous, come-hither (*informal*)

sum *noun* 1 AMOUNT, quantity, volume 2 CALCULATION, figures, arithmetic, problem, numbers, reckonings, mathematics, maths (*Brit informal*), tally, math (*US informal*), arithmetical problem 3 TOTAL, aggregate, entirety, sum total 4 TOTALITY, whole ▷▷ **sum something** *or* **someone up** SIZE UP, estimate (*informal*), get the measure of, form an opinion of

summarily *adverb* IMMEDIATELY, promptly, swiftly, on the spot, speedily, without delay, arbitrarily, at short notice, forthwith, expeditiously, peremptorily, without wasting words

summarize *verb* SUM UP, recap, review, outline, condense, encapsulate, epitomize, abridge, précis, recapitulate, give a rundown of, put in a nutshell, give the main points of

summary *noun* SYNOPSIS, résumé, précis, recapitulation, review, outline, extract, essence, abstract, summing-up, digest, epitome, rundown, compendium, abridgment ▷ *adjective* 1 HASTY, cursory, perfunctory, arbitrary 2 CONCISE, brief, compact, condensed, laconic, succinct, pithy, compendious

summit *noun* 1 MEETING, talks, conference, discussion, negotiation, dialogue 2 PEAK, top, tip, pinnacle, apex, head, crown, crest << ANTONYM base 3 HEIGHT, pinnacle, culmination, peak, high point, zenith, acme, crowning point << ANTONYM depths

summon *verb* 1 SEND FOR, call, bid, invite, rally, assemble, convene, call together, convoke 2 *often with* **up** GATHER, muster, draw on, invoke, mobilize, call into action

sumptuous *adjective* LUXURIOUS, rich, grand, expensive, superb, magnificent, costly, splendid, posh (*informal, chiefly Brit*), gorgeous, lavish, extravagant, plush (*informal*), opulent, palatial, ritzy (*slang*), de luxe, splendiferous (*facetious*) << ANTONYM plain

sun *noun* SOL (*Roman myth*), Helios (*Greek myth*), Phoebus (*Greek myth*), daystar (*poetic*), eye of heaven, Phoebus Apollo (*Greek myth*)
▷▷ **sun yourself** SUNBATHE, tan, bask

sundry *determiner* VARIOUS, several, varied, assorted, some, different, divers (*archaic*), miscellaneous

sunk *adjective* RUINED, lost, finished, done for (*informal*), on the rocks, all washed up (*informal*), up the creek without a paddle (*informal*)

sunken *adjective* 1 SUBMERGED, immersed, submersed 2 LOWERED, buried, depressed, recessed, below ground, at a lower level 3 HOLLOW, drawn, haggard, hollowed, concave

sunny *adjective* 1 BRIGHT, clear, fine, brilliant, radiant, luminous, sunlit, summery, unclouded, sunshiny, without a cloud in the sky << ANTONYM dull 2 CHEERFUL, happy, cheery, smiling, beaming, pleasant, optimistic, buoyant, joyful, genial, chirpy (*informal*), blithe, light-hearted << ANTONYM gloomy

sunrise *noun* DAWN, daybreak, break of day, daylight, aurora (*poetic*), sunup, cockcrow, dayspring (*poetic*)

sunset *noun* NIGHTFALL, dusk, sundown, eventide, gloaming (*Scot poetic*), close of (the) day

super *adjective* (*informal*) EXCELLENT, wonderful, marvellous, mean (*slang*), topping (*Brit slang*), cracking (*Brit informal*), crucial (*slang*), outstanding, smashing (*informal*), superb, magnificent, glorious, terrific (*informal*), sensational (*informal*), mega (*slang*), sovereign, awesome (*slang*), def (*slang*), top-notch (*informal*), brill (*informal*), incomparable, out of this world (*informal*), peerless, matchless, boffo (*slang*), jim-dandy (*slang*), chillin' (*US slang*), booshit (*Austral slang*), exo (*Austral slang*), sik (*Austral slang*), rad (*informal*), phat (*slang*), schmick (*Austral informal*)

superb *adjective* 1 SPLENDID, excellent, magnificent, topping (*Brit slang*), fine, choice, grand, superior, divine, marvellous, gorgeous, mega (*slang*), awesome (*slang*), world-class, exquisite, breathtaking, first-rate, superlative, unrivalled, brill (*informal*), bodacious (*slang, chiefly US*), boffo (*slang*), splendiferous (*facetious*), of the first water, chillin' (*US slang*), booshit (*Austral slang*), exo (*Austral slang*), sik (*Austral slang*), rad (*informal*), phat (*slang*), schmick (*Austral informal*) << ANTONYM inferior 2 MAGNIFICENT, superior, marvellous, exquisite, breathtaking, admirable, superlative, unrivalled, splendiferous (*facetious*) << ANTONYM terrible

superficial *adjective* 1 SHALLOW, frivolous, empty-headed, empty, silly, lightweight, trivial << ANTONYM serious 2 HASTY, cursory, perfunctory, passing, nodding, hurried, casual, sketchy, facile, desultory, slapdash, inattentive << ANTONYM thorough 3 SLIGHT, surface, external, cosmetic, on the surface, exterior, peripheral, skin-deep << ANTONYM profound

superficially *adverb* AT FIRST GLANCE, apparently, on the surface, ostensibly, externally, at face value, to the casual eye

superfluous *adjective* EXCESS, surplus, redundant, remaining, extra, spare, excessive, unnecessary, in excess, needless, left over, on your hands, surplus to requirements, uncalled-for, unneeded, residuary, supernumerary, superabundant, pleonastic (*rhetoric*), unrequired, supererogatory << ANTONYM necessary

superhuman *adjective* HEROIC, phenomenal, prodigious, stupendous, herculean

superintend *verb* SUPERVISE, run, oversee, control, manage, direct, handle, look after, overlook, administer, inspect

superintendent *noun* 1 SUPERVISOR, director, manager, chief, governor, inspector, administrator, conductor, controller, overseer 2 (*US*) WARDEN, caretaker, curator, keeper, porter, custodian, watchman, janitor, concierge

superior *adjective* **1** BETTER, higher, greater, grander, preferred, prevailing, paramount, surpassing, more advanced, predominant, unrivalled, more extensive, more skilful, more expert, a cut above (*informal*), streets ahead (*informal*), running rings around (*informal*) << ANTONYM inferior **2** FIRST-CLASS, excellent, first-rate, good, fine, choice, exclusive, distinguished, exceptional, world-class, good quality, admirable, high-class, high calibre, de luxe, of the first order, booshit (*Austral slang*), exo (*Austral slang*), sik (*Austral slang*), rad (*informal*), phat (*slang*), schmick (*Austral informal*) << ANTONYM average **3** HIGHER-RANKING, senior, higher-level, upper-level **4** SUPERCILIOUS, patronizing, condescending, haughty, disdainful, lordly, lofty, airy, pretentious, stuck-up (*informal*), snobbish, on your high horse (*informal*) ▷ *noun* BOSS, senior, director, manager, chief (*informal*), principal, supervisor, baas (*S African*), sherang (*Austral & NZ*) << ANTONYM subordinate

superiority *noun* SUPREMACY, lead, advantage, excellence, prevalence, ascendancy, pre-eminence, preponderance, predominance

superlative *adjective* SUPREME, excellent, outstanding, highest, greatest, crack (*slang*), magnificent, surpassing, consummate, stellar (*informal*), unparalleled, transcendent, unrivalled, peerless, unsurpassed, matchless, of the highest order, of the first water << ANTONYM average

supernatural *adjective* PARANORMAL, mysterious, unearthly, uncanny, dark, hidden, ghostly, psychic, phantom, abnormal, mystic, miraculous, unnatural, occult, spectral, preternatural, supranatural

supersede *verb* REPLACE, displace, usurp, supplant, remove, take over, oust, take the place of, fill or step into (someone's) boots

supervise *verb* **1** OBSERVE, guide, monitor, oversee, keep an eye on **2** OVERSEE, run, manage, control, direct, handle, conduct, look after, be responsible for, administer, inspect, preside over, keep an eye on, be on duty at, superintend, have or be in charge of

supervision *noun* SUPERINTENDENCE, direction, instruction, control, charge, care, management, administration, guidance, surveillance, oversight, auspices, stewardship

supervisor *noun* BOSS (*informal*), manager, superintendent, chief, inspector, administrator, steward, gaffer (*informal*,

chiefly *Brit*), foreman, overseer, baas (*S African*)

supervisory *adjective* MANAGERIAL, administrative, overseeing, superintendent, executive

supine *adjective* **1** FLAT ON YOUR BACK, flat, horizontal, recumbent << ANTONYM prone **2** LETHARGIC, passive, lazy, idle, indifferent, careless, sluggish, negligent, inert, languid, uninterested, apathetic, lymphatic, listless, indolent, heedless, torpid, slothful, spiritless

supplant *verb* REPLACE, oust, displace, supersede, remove, take over, undermine, overthrow, unseat, take the place of

supple *adjective* **1** PLIANT, flexible, pliable, plastic, bending, elastic << ANTONYM rigid **2** FLEXIBLE, lithe, limber, lissom(e), loose-limbed << ANTONYM stiff

supplement *verb* ADD TO, reinforce, complement, augment, extend, top up, fill out ▷ *noun* **1** PULL-OUT, insert, magazine section, added feature **2** APPENDIX, sequel, add-on, complement, postscript, addendum, codicil **3** ADDITION, extra, surcharge

supplementary *adjective* ADDITIONAL, extra, complementary, accompanying, secondary, auxiliary, add-on, supplemental, ancillary

supply *verb* **1** PROVIDE, give, furnish, produce, stock, store, grant, afford, contribute, yield, come up with, outfit, endow, purvey, victual **2** FURNISH, provide, equip, endow **3** MEET, provide for, fill, satisfy, fulfil, be adequate for, cater to or for ▷ *noun* STORE, fund, stock, source, reserve, quantity, reservoir, stockpile, hoard, cache ▷ *plural noun* PROVISIONS, necessities, stores, food, materials, items, equipment, rations, foodstuff, provender

support *verb* **1** HELP, back, champion, second, aid, forward, encourage, defend, promote, take (someone's) part, strengthen, assist, advocate, uphold, side with, go along with, stand up for, espouse, stand behind, hold (someone's) hand, stick up for (*informal*), succour, buoy up, boost (someone's) morale, take up the cudgels for, be a source of strength to << ANTONYM oppose **2** PROVIDE FOR, maintain, look after, keep, fund, finance, sustain, foster, take care of, subsidize << ANTONYM live off **3** BEAR OUT, confirm, verify, substantiate, corroborate, document, endorse, attest to, authenticate, lend credence to << ANTONYM refute **4** BEAR, hold up, carry, sustain, prop (up), reinforce, hold, brace, uphold, bolster, underpin, shore up, buttress ▷ *noun* **1** FURTHERANCE, backing,

promotion, championship, approval,
assistance, encouragement, espousal **2** HELP,
protection, comfort, friendship, assistance,
blessing, loyalty, patronage, moral support,
succour << ANTONYM opposition **3** AID,
help, benefits, relief, assistance **4** PROP,
post, foundation, back, lining, stay, shore,
brace, pillar, underpinning, stanchion,
stiffener, abutment **5** SUPPORTER, prop,
mainstay, tower of strength, second, stay,
backer, backbone, comforter << ANTONYM
antagonist **6** UPKEEP, maintenance, keep,
livelihood, subsistence, sustenance

supporter *noun* FOLLOWER, fan, advocate,
friend, champion, ally, defender, sponsor,
patron, helper, protagonist, adherent,
henchman, apologist, upholder, well-wisher
<< ANTONYM opponent

supportive *adjective* HELPFUL, caring,
encouraging, understanding, reassuring,
sympathetic

suppose *verb* **1** IMAGINE, believe, consider,
conclude, fancy, conceive, conjecture,
postulate, hypothesize **2** THINK, imagine,
expect, judge, assume, guess (*informal, chiefly
US & Canad*) calculate (*US dialect*), presume,
take for granted, infer, conjecture, surmise,
dare say, opine, presuppose, take as read

supposed *adjective* **1** *usually with* **to** MEANT,
expected, required, obliged **2** PRESUMED,
alleged, professed, reputed, accepted,
assumed, rumoured, hypothetical, putative,
presupposed

supposedly *adverb* PRESUMABLY, allegedly,
ostensibly, theoretically, by all accounts,
purportedly, avowedly, hypothetically, at a
guess, professedly << ANTONYM actually

supposition *noun* BELIEF, idea, notion, view,
theory, speculation, assumption, hypothesis,
presumption, conjecture, surmise,
guesswork

suppress *verb* **1** STAMP OUT, stop, check,
crush, conquer, overthrow, subdue, put an
end to, overpower, quash, crack down on,
quell, extinguish, clamp down on, snuff
out, quench, beat down, trample on, drive
underground << ANTONYM encourage
2 CHECK, inhibit, subdue, stop, quell,
quench **3** RESTRAIN, cover up, withhold,
stifle, contain, silence, conceal, curb, repress,
smother, keep secret, muffle, muzzle, hold
in check, hold in *or* back **4** CONCEAL, hide,
keep secret, hush up, stonewall, sweep
under the carpet, draw a veil over, keep
silent about, keep dark, keep under your hat

(*informal*)

suppression *noun* **1** ELIMINATION,
crushing, crackdown, check, extinction,
prohibition, quashing, dissolution,
termination, clampdown **2** INHIBITION,
blocking, restriction, restraint, smothering
3 CONCEALMENT, covering, hiding,
disguising, camouflage **4** HIDING, hushing
up, stonewalling

supremacy *noun* DOMINATION, dominance,
ascendancy, sovereignty, sway, lordship,
mastery, dominion, primacy, pre-eminence,
predominance, supreme power, absolute
rule, paramountcy

supreme *adjective* **1** PARAMOUNT, surpassing,
superlative, prevailing, sovereign,
predominant, incomparable, mother of
all (*informal*), unsurpassed, matchless
<< ANTONYM least **2** CHIEF, leading,
principal, first, highest, head, top, prime,
cardinal, foremost, pre-eminent, peerless
<< ANTONYM lowest **3** ULTIMATE, highest,
greatest, utmost, final, crowning, extreme,
culminating

supremo *noun* (*Brit informal*) HEAD, leader,
boss (*informal*), director, master, governor,
commander, principal, ruler, baas (*S African*)

sure *adjective* **1** CERTAIN, positive, clear,
decided, convinced, persuaded, confident,
satisfied, assured, definite, free from doubt
<< ANTONYM uncertain **2** INEVITABLE,
guaranteed, bound, assured, in the bag
(*slang*), inescapable, irrevocable, ineluctable,
nailed-on (*slang*) << ANTONYM unsure
3 RELIABLE, accurate, dependable, effective,
precise, honest, unmistakable, undoubted,
undeniable, trustworthy, never-failing,
trusty, foolproof, infallible, indisputable,
sure-fire (*informal*), unerring, well-proven,
unfailing, tried and true << ANTONYM
unreliable **4** SECURE, firm, steady, fast, safe,
solid, stable

surely *adverb* **1** IT MUST BE THE CASE THAT,
assuredly **2** UNDOUBTEDLY, certainly,
definitely, inevitably, doubtless, for certain,
without doubt, unquestionably, inexorably,
come what may, without fail, indubitably,
doubtlessly, beyond the shadow of a doubt

surety *noun* **1** SECURITY, guarantee, deposit,
insurance, bond, safety, pledge, bail,
warranty, indemnity **2** GUARANTOR, sponsor,
hostage, bondsman, mortgagor

surface *noun* **1** COVERING, face, exterior, side,
top, skin, plane, facet, veneer **2** FAÇADE,
outward appearance ▷ *modifier* SUPERFICIAL,

external, outward, exterior ▷ *verb* **1** EMERGE, come up, come to the surface **2** APPEAR, emerge, arise, come to light, crop up (*informal*), transpire, materialize ▷▷ **on the surface** AT FIRST GLANCE, apparently, outwardly, seemingly, ostensibly, superficially, to all appearances, to the casual eye

surfeit *noun* EXCESS, plethora, glut, satiety, overindulgence, superabundance, superfluity << ANTONYM shortage

surge *noun* **1** RUSH, flood, upsurge, sudden increase, uprush **2** FLOW, wave, rush, roller, breaker, gush, upsurge, outpouring, uprush **3** TIDE, roll, rolling, swell, swirling, billowing **4** WAVE, rush, storm, outburst, torrent, eruption ▷ *verb* **1** RUSH, pour, stream, rise, swell, spill, swarm, seethe, gush, well forth **2** ROLL, rush, billow, heave, swirl, eddy, undulate **3** SWEEP, rush, storm

surly *adjective* ILL-TEMPERED, cross, churlish, crabbed, perverse, crusty, sullen, gruff, bearish, sulky, morose, brusque, testy, grouchy (*informal*), curmudgeonly, ungracious, uncivil, shrewish << ANTONYM cheerful

surmise *verb* GUESS, suppose, imagine, presume, consider, suspect, conclude, fancy, speculate, infer, deduce, come to the conclusion, conjecture, opine, hazard a guess ▷ *noun* GUESS, speculation, assumption, thought, idea, conclusion, notion, suspicion, hypothesis, deduction, inference, presumption, conjecture, supposition

surmount *verb* OVERCOME, master, conquer, pass, exceed, surpass, overpower, triumph over, vanquish, prevail over

surpass *verb* OUTDO, top, beat, best, cap (*informal*), exceed, eclipse, overshadow, excel, transcend, outstrip, outshine, tower above, go one better than (*informal*), put in the shade

surpassing *adjective* SUPREME, extraordinary, outstanding, exceptional, rare, phenomenal, stellar (*informal*), transcendent, unrivalled, incomparable, matchless

surplus *noun* EXCESS, surfeit, superabundance, superfluity << ANTONYM shortage ▷ *adjective* EXTRA, spare, excess, remaining, odd, in excess, left over, unused, superfluous << ANTONYM insufficient

surprise *noun* **1** SHOCK, start (*informal*), revelation, jolt, bombshell, eye-opener (*informal*), bolt from the blue, turn-up

for the books (*informal*) **2** AMAZEMENT, astonishment, wonder, incredulity, stupefaction ▷ *verb* **1** AMAZE, astonish, astound, stun, startle, stagger, disconcert, take aback, bowl over (*informal*), leave open-mouthed, nonplus, flabbergast (*informal*), take (someone's) breath away **2** CATCH UNAWARES *or* OFF-GUARD, catch napping, catch on the hop (*informal*), burst in on, spring upon, catch in the act *or* red-handed, come down on like a bolt from the blue

surprised *adjective* AMAZED, astonished, startled, disconcerted, at a loss, taken aback, speechless, incredulous, open-mouthed, nonplussed, thunderstruck, unable to believe your eyes

surprising *adjective* AMAZING, remarkable, incredible, astonishing, wonderful, unusual, extraordinary, unexpected, staggering, marvellous, startling, astounding, jaw-dropping, unlooked-for

surrender *verb* **1** GIVE IN, yield, submit, give way, quit, succumb, cave in (*informal*), capitulate, throw in the towel, lay down arms, give yourself up, show the white flag << ANTONYM resist **2** GIVE UP, abandon, relinquish, resign, yield, concede, part with, renounce, waive, forego, cede, deliver up ▷ *noun* SUBMISSION, yielding, cave-in (*informal*), capitulation, resignation, renunciation, relinquishment

surreptitious *adjective* SECRET, clandestine, furtive, sneaking, veiled, covert, sly, fraudulent, unauthorized, underhand, stealthy << ANTONYM open

surrogate *noun* SUBSTITUTE, deputy, representative, stand-in, proxy

surround *verb* **1** ENCLOSE, ring, encircle, encompass, envelop, close in on, fence in, girdle, hem in, environ, enwreath **2** BESIEGE, beset, lay siege to, invest (*rare*)

surrounding *adjective* NEARBY, neighbouring

surroundings *plural noun* ENVIRONMENT, setting, background, location, neighbourhood, milieu, environs

surveillance *noun* OBSERVATION, watch, scrutiny, supervision, control, care, direction, inspection, vigilance, superintendence

survey *noun* **1** POLL, study, research, review, inquiry, investigation, opinion poll, questionnaire, census **2** EXAMINATION, inspection, scrutiny, overview, once-over (*informal*), perusal **3** VALUATION, estimate, assessment, appraisal ▷ *verb* **1** INTERVIEW, question, poll, study, research, investigate, sample, canvass **2** LOOK OVER, view, scan, examine, observe, contemplate, supervise, inspect, eyeball (*slang*), scrutinize, size up, take stock of, eye up, recce (*slang*), reconnoitre **3** MEASURE, estimate, prospect, assess, appraise, triangulate

survive *verb* **1** REMAIN ALIVE, live, pull through, last, exist, live on, endure, hold out, subsist, keep body and soul together (*informal*), be extant, fight for your life, keep your head above water **2** CONTINUE, last, live on, pull through **3** LIVE LONGER THAN, outlive, outlast

susceptibility *noun* VULNERABILITY, weakness, liability, propensity, predisposition, proneness

susceptible *adjective* **1** RESPONSIVE, sensitive, receptive, alive to, impressionable, easily moved, suggestible << ANTONYM unresponsive **2** *usually with* **to** LIABLE, inclined, prone, given, open, subject, vulnerable, disposed, predisposed << ANTONYM resistant

suspect *verb* **1** BELIEVE, feel, guess, consider, suppose, conclude, fancy, speculate, conjecture, surmise, hazard a guess, have a sneaking suspicion, think probable << ANTONYM know **2** DISTRUST, doubt, mistrust, smell a rat (*informal*), harbour suspicions about, have your doubts about << ANTONYM trust ▷ *adjective* DUBIOUS, doubtful, dodgy (*Brit, Austral & NZ informal*), questionable, fishy (*informal*), iffy (*informal*), open to suspicion, shonky (*Austral & NZ informal*) << ANTONYM innocent

suspend *verb* **1** POSTPONE, delay, put off, arrest, cease, interrupt, shelve, withhold, defer, adjourn, hold off, cut short, discontinue, lay aside, put in cold storage << ANTONYM continue **2** REMOVE, expel, eject, debar << ANTONYM reinstate **3** HANG, attach, dangle, swing, append

suspense *noun* UNCERTAINTY, doubt, tension, anticipation, expectation, anxiety, insecurity, expectancy, apprehension

suspension *noun* POSTPONEMENT, delay, break, stay, breaking off, interruption, moratorium, respite, remission, adjournment, abeyance, deferment, discontinuation, disbarment

suspicion *noun* **1** FEELING, theory, impression, intuition, conjecture, surmise, funny feeling (*informal*), presentiment **2** DISTRUST, scepticism, mistrust, doubt,

misgiving, qualm, lack of confidence, wariness, bad vibes (*slang*), dubiety, chariness **3** IDEA, notion, hunch, guess, impression, conjecture, surmise, gut feeling (*informal*), supposition **4** TRACE, touch, hint, shadow, suggestion, strain, shade, streak, tinge, glimmer, soupçon (*French*) ▷▷ **above suspicion** BLAMELESS, unimpeachable, above reproach, pure, honourable, virtuous, sinless, like Caesar's wife

suspicious *adjective* **1** DISTRUSTFUL, suspecting, sceptical, doubtful, apprehensive, leery (*slang*), mistrustful, unbelieving, wary << ANTONYM trusting **2** SUSPECT, dubious, questionable, funny, doubtful, dodgy (*Brit, Austral & NZ informal*), queer, irregular, shady (*informal*), fishy (*informal*), of doubtful honesty, open to doubt *or* misconstruction, shonky (*Austral & NZ informal*) << ANTONYM beyond suspicion **3** ODD, strange, mysterious, dark, dubious, irregular, questionable, murky (*informal*), shady (*informal*), fishy

sustain *verb* **1** MAINTAIN, continue, keep up, prolong, keep going, keep alive, protract **2** SUFFER, experience, undergo, feel, bear, endure, withstand, bear up under **3** HELP, aid, comfort, foster, assist, relieve, nurture **4** KEEP ALIVE, nourish, provide for **5** SUPPORT, carry, bear, keep up, uphold, keep from falling **6** UPHOLD, confirm, endorse, approve, ratify, verify, validate

sustained *adjective* CONTINUOUS, constant, steady, prolonged, perpetual, unremitting, nonstop << ANTONYM periodic

sustenance *noun* **1** NOURISHMENT, food, provisions, rations, refreshments, kai (*NZ informal*), daily bread, victuals, edibles, comestibles, provender, aliment, eatables, refection **2** SUPPORT, maintenance, livelihood, subsistence

svelte *adjective* SLENDER, lithe, willowy, graceful, slinky, lissom(e), sylphlike

swagger *verb* **1** STRIDE, parade, strut, prance **2** SHOW OFF, boast, brag, hot-dog (*chiefly US*), bluster, swank (*informal*), gasconade (*rare*) ▷ *noun* **1** STRUT **2** OSTENTATION, show, display, showing off (*informal*), bluster, swashbuckling, swank (*informal*), braggadocio, gasconade (*rare*)

swallow *verb* **1** EAT, down (*informal*), consume, devour, absorb, swig (*informal*), swill, wash down, ingest **2** GULP, drink **3** (*informal*) BELIEVE, accept, buy (*slang*), fall for, take (something) as gospel **4** SUPPRESS, hold in, restrain, contain, hold back, stifle, repress, bottle up, bite back, choke back ▷▷ **swallow something** or **someone up 1** ENGULF, overwhelmed, overrun, consume **2** ABSORB, assimilate, envelop

swamp *noun* BOG, marsh, quagmire, moss (*Scot & N English dialect*), slough, fen, mire, morass, everglade(s) (*US*), pakihi (*NZ*), muskeg (*Canad*) ▷ *verb* **1** FLOOD, engulf, submerge, inundate, deluge **2** OVERLOAD, overwhelm, inundate, besiege, beset, snow under

swampy *adjective* BOGGY, waterlogged, marshy, wet, fenny, miry, quaggy, marish (*obsolete*)

swank (*informal*) *verb* SHOW OFF, swagger, give yourself airs, posture (*informal*), hot-dog (*chiefly US*), put on side (*Brit slang*) ▷ *noun* BOASTFULNESS, show, ostentation, display, swagger, vainglory

swanky *adjective* (*informal*) OSTENTATIOUS, grand, posh (*informal, chiefly Brit*), rich, expensive, exclusive, smart, fancy, flash, fashionable, glamorous, stylish, gorgeous, lavish, luxurious, sumptuous, plush (*informal*), flashy, swish (*informal, chiefly Brit*), glitzy (*slang*), showy, ritzy (*slang*), de luxe, swank (*informal*), plushy (*informal*), schmick (*Austral informal*) << ANTONYM modest

swap or **swop** *verb* EXCHANGE, trade, switch, traffic, interchange, barter

swarm *noun* MULTITUDE, crowd, mass, army, host, drove, flock, herd, horde, myriad, throng, shoal, concourse, bevy ▷ *verb* **1** CROWD, flock, throng, mass, stream, congregate **2** TEEM, crawl, be alive, abound, bristle, be overrun, be infested

swarthy *adjective* DARK-SKINNED, black, brown, dark, tawny, dusky, swart (*archaic*), dark-complexioned

swashbuckling *adjective* DASHING, spirited, bold, flamboyant, swaggering, gallant, daredevil, mettlesome, roisterous

swastika *noun* CROOKED CROSS, fylfot

swath or **swathe** *noun* AREA, section, stretch, patch, tract

swathe *verb* WRAP, drape, envelop, bind, lap, fold, bandage, cloak, shroud, swaddle, furl, sheathe, enfold, bundle up, muffle up, enwrap

sway *verb* **1** MOVE FROM SIDE TO SIDE, rock, wave, roll, swing, bend, lean, incline, lurch, oscillate, move to and fro **2** INFLUENCE, control, direct, affect, guide, dominate, persuade, govern, win over, induce, prevail

on ▷ *noun* POWER, control, influence, government, rule, authority, command, sovereignty, jurisdiction, clout (*informal*), dominion, predominance, ascendency ▷▷ **hold sway** PREVAIL, rule, predominate, reign

swear *verb* **1** CURSE, cuss (*informal*), blaspheme, turn the air blue (*informal*), be foul-mouthed, take the Lord's name in vain, utter profanities, imprecate **2** VOW, promise, take an oath, warrant, testify, depose, attest, avow, give your word, state under oath, pledge yourself **3** DECLARE, assert, affirm, swear blind, asseverate ▷▷ **swear by something** BELIEVE IN, trust, depend on, rely on, have confidence in

swearing *noun* BAD LANGUAGE, cursing, profanity, blasphemy, cussing (*informal*), foul language, imprecations, malediction

swearword *noun* OATH, curse, obscenity, expletive, four-letter word, cuss (*informal*), profanity

sweat *noun* **1** PERSPIRATION, moisture, dampness **2** (*informal*) PANIC, anxiety, state (*informal*), worry, distress, flap (*informal*), agitation, fluster, lather (*informal*), tizzy (*informal*), state of anxiety ▷ *verb* **1** PERSPIRE, swelter, break out in a sweat, exude moisture, glow **2** (*informal*) WORRY, fret, agonize, lose sleep over, be on tenterhooks, torture yourself, be on pins and needles (*informal*) ▷▷ **sweat something out** (*informal*) ENDURE, see (something) through, stick it out (*informal*), stay the course

sweaty *adjective* PERSPIRING, sweating, sticky, clammy, bathed or drenched or soaked in perspiration, glowing

sweep *verb* **1** BRUSH, clean **2** CLEAR, remove, brush, clean **3** SAIL, pass, fly, tear, zoom, glide, skim, scud, hurtle **4** SWAGGER, sail, breeze, stride, stroll, glide, flounce ▷ *noun* **1** MOVEMENT, move, swing, stroke, gesture **2** ARC, bend, curve **3** EXTENT, range, span, stretch, scope, compass

sweeping *adjective* **1** INDISCRIMINATE, blanket, across-the-board, wholesale, exaggerated, overstated, overdrawn **2** WIDE-RANGING, global, comprehensive, wide, broad, radical, extensive, all-inclusive, all-embracing, overarching, thoroughgoing << ANTONYM limited

sweet *adjective* **1** SUGARY, sweetened, cloying, honeyed, saccharine, syrupy, icky (*informal*), treacly << ANTONYM sour **2** FRAGRANT, perfumed, aromatic, redolent, sweet-smelling << ANTONYM stinking **3** FRESH, clean, pure, wholesome **4** MELODIOUS, musical, harmonious, soft, mellow, silvery, tuneful, dulcet, sweet-sounding, euphonious, silver-toned, euphonic << ANTONYM harsh **5** CHARMING, kind, gentle, tender, affectionate, agreeable, amiable, sweet-tempered << ANTONYM nasty **6** DELIGHTFUL, appealing, cute, taking, winning, fair, beautiful, attractive, engaging, lovable, winsome, cutesy (*informal, chiefly US*), likable *or* likeable << ANTONYM unpleasant **7** (*archaic*) BELOVED, dear, darling, dearest, pet, treasured, precious, cherished ▷ *noun* **1** *usually plural* (*Brit*) CONFECTIONERY, candy (*US*), sweetie, lolly (*Austral & NZ*), sweetmeat, bonbon **2** (*Brit*) DESSERT, pudding, afters (*Brit informal*), sweet course ▷▷ **sweet on** IN LOVE WITH, keen on, infatuated with, gone on (*slang*), fond of, taken with, enamoured of, head over heels in love with, obsessed *or* bewitched by, wild *or* mad about (*informal*)

sweeten *verb* **1** SUGAR **2** SOFTEN, ease, alleviate, relieve, temper, cushion, mellow, make less painful **3** MOLLIFY, appease, soothe, pacify, soften up, sugar the pill

sweetheart *noun* **1** DEAREST, beloved, sweet, angel, treasure, honey, dear, sweetie (*informal*) **2** LOVE, boyfriend *or* girlfriend, beloved, lover, steady (*informal*), flame (*informal*), darling, follower (*obsolete*), valentine, admirer, suitor, beau, swain (*archaic*), truelove, leman (*archaic*), inamorata *or* inamorato

swell *verb* **1** INCREASE, rise, grow, mount, expand, accelerate, escalate, multiply, grow larger << ANTONYM decrease **2** EXPAND, increase, grow, rise, extend, balloon, belly, enlarge, bulge, protrude, well up, billow, fatten, dilate, puff up, round out, be inflated, become larger, distend, bloat, tumefy, become bloated *or* distended << ANTONYM shrink ▷ *noun* WAVE, rise, surge, billow

swelling *noun* ENLARGEMENT, lump, puffiness, bump, blister, bulge, inflammation, dilation, protuberance, distension, tumescence

sweltering *adjective* HOT, burning, boiling, steaming, baking, roasting, stifling, scorching, oppressive, humid, torrid, sultry, airless

swerve *verb* VEER, turn, swing, shift, bend, incline, deflect, depart from, skew, diverge, deviate, turn aside, sheer off

swift *adjective* **1** QUICK, immediate, prompt,

rapid, instant, abrupt, ready, expeditious **2** FAST, quick, rapid, flying, express, winged, sudden, fleet, hurried, speedy, spanking, nimble, quickie (*informal*), nippy (*Brit informal*), fleet-footed, pdq (*slang*) << ANTONYM slow

swiftly *adverb* **1** QUICKLY, rapidly, speedily, without losing time **2** FAST, promptly, hurriedly, apace, pronto (*informal*), double-quick, hell for leather, like lightning, hotfoot, like the clappers (*Brit informal*), posthaste, like greased lightning (*informal*), nippily (*Brit informal*), in less than no time, as fast as your legs can carry you, (at) full tilt

swill *verb* **1** DRINK, gulp, swig (*informal*), guzzle, drain, consume, swallow, imbibe, quaff, bevvy (*dialect*), toss off, bend the elbow (*informal*), pour down your gullet **2** (*Chiefly Brit*) *often with* **out** RINSE, wash out, sluice, flush, drench, wash down ▷ *noun* WASTE, slops, mash, mush, hogwash, pigswill, scourings

swindle *verb* CHEAT, do (*slang*), con, skin (*slang*), trick, stiff (*slang*), sting (*informal*), rip (someone) off (*slang*), deceive, fleece, defraud, dupe, overcharge, rook (*slang*), bamboozle (*informal*), diddle (*informal*), take (someone) for a ride (*informal*), put one over on (someone) (*informal*), pull a fast one (on someone) (*informal*), bilk (of), take to the cleaners (*informal*), sell a pup (to) (*slang*), cozen, hornswoggle (*slang*) ▷ *noun* FRAUD, fiddle (*Brit informal*), rip-off (*slang*), racket, scam (*slang*), sting (*informal*), deception, imposition, deceit, trickery, double-dealing, con trick (*informal*), sharp practice, swizzle (*Brit informal*), knavery, swizz (*Brit informal*), roguery, fastie (*Austral slang*)

swing *verb* **1** BRANDISH, wave, shake, flourish, wield, dangle **2** SWAY, rock, wave, veer, vibrate, oscillate, move back and forth, move to and fro **3** *usually with* **round** TURN, veer, swivel, twist, curve, rotate, pivot, turn on your heel **4** HIT OUT, strike, swipe, lash out at, slap **5** HANG, dangle, be suspended, suspend, move back and forth ▷ *noun* **1** SWAYING, sway **2** FLUCTUATION, change, shift, switch, variation ▷▷ **in full swing** AT ITS HEIGHT, under way, on the go (*informal*)

swingeing *adjective* (*Chiefly Brit*) SEVERE, heavy, drastic, huge, punishing, harsh, excessive, daunting, stringent, oppressive, Draconian, exorbitant

swipe *verb* **1** (*informal*) HIT OUT, strike, slap, lash out at **2** (*slang*) STEAL, nick (*slang*, chiefly *Brit*), pinch (*informal*), lift (*informal*), appropriate, cabbage (*Brit slang*), make off with, pilfer, purloin, filch, snaffle (*Brit informal*), thump, clout (*informal*), cuff, clump (*slang*), wallop (*informal*)

swirl *verb* WHIRL, churn, spin, twist, boil, surge, agitate, eddy, twirl

swish *adjective* (*informal, chiefly Brit*) SMART, grand, posh (*informal, chiefly Brit*), exclusive, elegant, swell (*informal*), fashionable, sumptuous, ritzy (*slang*), de luxe, plush *or* plushy (*informal*)

switch *noun* 1 CONTROL, button, lever, on/off device 2 CHANGE, shift, transition, conversion, reversal, alteration, about-turn, change of direction ▷ *verb* 1 CHANGE, shift, convert, divert, deviate, change course 2 EXCHANGE, trade, swap, replace, substitute, rearrange, interchange ▷▷ **switch something off** TURN OFF, shut off, deactivate, cut ▷▷ **switch something on** TURN ON, put on, set off, activate, set in motion

swivel *verb* TURN, spin, revolve, rotate, pivot, pirouette, swing round

swollen *adjective* ENLARGED, bloated, puffy, inflamed, puffed up, distended, tumescent, oedematous, dropsical, tumid, edematous

swoop *verb* 1 POUNCE, attack, charge, rush, descend 2 DROP, plunge, dive, sweep, descend, plummet, pounce, stoop ▷ *noun* RAID, attack, assault, surprise search

swop ▷ see **swap**

sword *noun* BLADE, brand (*archaic*), trusty steel

swot *verb* (*informal*) STUDY, revise, cram (*informal*), work, get up (*informal*), pore over, bone up on (*informal*), burn the midnight oil, mug up (*Brit slang*), toil over, apply yourself to, lucubrate (*rare*)

sycophant *noun* CRAWLER, yes man, toady, slave, parasite, cringer, fawner, hanger-on, sponger, flatterer, truckler, lickspittle, apple polisher (*US slang*), bootlicker (*informal*), toadeater (*rare*)

sycophantic *adjective* OBSEQUIOUS, grovelling, ingratiating, servile, crawling, flattering, cringing, fawning, slimy, slavish, unctuous, smarmy (*Brit informal*), toadying, parasitical, bootlicking (*informal*), timeserving

syllabus *noun* COURSE OF STUDY, curriculum

symbol *noun* 1 METAPHOR, image, sign, representation, token 2 REPRESENTATION, sign, figure, mark, type, image, token, logo, badge, emblem, glyph

symbolic *adjective* 1 REPRESENTATIVE, token,

emblematic, allegorical 2 FIGURATIVE, representative

symbolize *verb* REPRESENT, signify, stand for, mean, exemplify, denote, typify, personify, connote, betoken, body forth

symmetrical *adjective* BALANCED, regular, proportional, in proportion, well-proportioned << ANTONYM unbalanced

symmetry *noun* BALANCE, proportion, regularity, form, order, harmony, correspondence, evenness

sympathetic *adjective* 1 CARING, kind, understanding, concerned, feeling, interested, kindly, warm, tender, pitying, supportive, responsive, affectionate, compassionate, commiserating, warm-hearted, condoling << ANTONYM uncaring 2 SUPPORTIVE, encouraging, pro, approving of, friendly to, in sympathy with, well-disposed towards, favourably disposed towards 3 LIKE-MINDED, compatible, agreeable, friendly, responsive, appreciative, congenial, companionable, well-intentioned << ANTONYM uncongenial

sympathetically *adverb* FEELINGLY, kindly, understandingly, warmly, with interest, with feeling, sensitively, with compassion, appreciatively, perceptively, responsively, warm-heartedly

sympathize with *verb* 1 FEEL FOR, pity, empathize with, commiserate with, bleed for, have compassion for, grieve with, offer consolation for, condole with, share another's sorrow, feel your heart go out to << ANTONYM have no feelings for 2 AGREE WITH, support, side with, understand, identify with, go along with, be in accord with, be in sympathy with << ANTONYM disagree with

sympathizer *noun* SUPPORTER, partisan, protagonist, fellow traveller, well-wisher

sympathy *noun* 1 COMPASSION, understanding, pity, empathy, tenderness, condolence(s), thoughtfulness, commiseration, aroha (*NZ*) << ANTONYM indifference 2 AFFINITY, agreement, rapport, union, harmony, warmth, correspondence, fellow feeling, congeniality << ANTONYM opposition

symptom *noun* 1 SIGN, mark, indication, warning 2 MANIFESTATION, sign, indication, mark, evidence, expression, proof, token

symptomatic *adjective* INDICATIVE, characteristic, suggestive

synonymous with *adjective* EQUIVALENT

TO, the same as, identical to, similar to, identified with, equal to, tantamount to, interchangeable with, one and the same as

synopsis *noun* SUMMARY, review, résumé, outline, abstract, digest, epitome, rundown, condensation, compendium, précis, aperçu (*French*), abridgment, conspectus, outline sketch

synthesis *noun* COMBINING, integration, amalgamation, unification, welding, coalescence

synthetic *adjective* ARTIFICIAL, manufactured, fake, man-made, mock, simulated, sham, pseudo (*informal*), ersatz << ANTONYM real

system *noun* 1 ARRANGEMENT, structure, organization, scheme, combination, classification, coordination, setup (*informal*) 2 NETWORK, organization, web, grid, set of channels 3 METHOD, practice, technique, procedure, routine, theory, usage, methodology, frame of reference, modus operandi, fixed order

systematic *adjective* METHODICAL, organized, efficient, precise, orderly, standardized, businesslike, well-ordered, systematized << ANTONYM unmethodical

tab *noun* FLAP, tag, label, ticket, flag, marker, sticker

table *noun* **1** COUNTER, bench, stand, board, surface, slab, work surface **2** LIST, chart, tabulation, record, roll, index, register, digest, diagram, inventory, graph, synopsis, itemization **3** (*formal*) FOOD, spread (*informal*), board, diet, fare, kai (*NZ informal*), victuals ▷ *verb* (*Brit*) SUBMIT, propose, put forward, move, suggest, enter, file, lodge, moot

tableau *noun* PICTURE, scene, representation, arrangement, spectacle

taboo *or* **tabu** *adjective* FORBIDDEN, banned, prohibited, ruled out, not allowed, unacceptable, outlawed, unthinkable, not permitted, disapproved of, anathema, off limits, frowned on, proscribed, beyond the pale, unmentionable << ANTONYM permitted ▷ *noun* PROHIBITION, ban, restriction, disapproval, anathema, interdict, proscription, tapu (*NZ*)

tacit *adjective* IMPLIED, understood, implicit, silent, taken for granted, unspoken, inferred, undeclared, wordless, unstated, unexpressed << ANTONYM stated

taciturn *adjective* UNCOMMUNICATIVE, reserved, reticent, unforthcoming, quiet, withdrawn, silent, distant, dumb, mute, aloof, antisocial, tight-lipped, close-lipped << ANTONYM communicative

tack *noun* NAIL, pin, stud, staple, rivet, drawing pin, thumbtack (*US*), tintack ▷ *verb* **1** FASTEN, fix, attach, pin, nail, staple, affix **2** (*Brit*) STITCH, sew, hem, bind, baste ▷▷ **tack something on to something** APPEND, add, attach, tag, annex

tackle *noun* **1** (*sport*) BLOCK, stop, challenge **2** RIG, rigging, apparatus ▷ *verb* **1** DEAL WITH, take on, set about, wade into, get stuck into (*informal*), sink your teeth into, apply yourself to, come *or* get to grips with **2** UNDERTAKE, deal with, attempt, try, begin, essay, engage in, embark upon, get stuck into (*informal*), turn your hand to, have a go or stab at (*informal*) **3** (*sport*) INTERCEPT, block, bring down, stop, challenge

tacky¹ *adjective* STICKY, wet, adhesive, gummy, icky (*informal*), gluey

tacky² *adjective* (*informal*) **1** VULGAR, cheap, tasteless, nasty, sleazy, naff (*Brit slang*) **2** SEEDY, shabby, shoddy

tact *noun* DIPLOMACY, understanding, consideration, sensitivity, delicacy, skill, judgment, perception, discretion, finesse, thoughtfulness, savoir-faire, adroitness << ANTONYM tactlessness

tactful *adjective* DIPLOMATIC, politic, discreet, prudent, understanding, sensitive, polished, careful, subtle, delicate, polite, thoughtful, perceptive, considerate, judicious << ANTONYM tactless

tactic *noun* POLICY, approach, course, way, means, move, line, scheme, plans, method, trick, device, manoeuvre, tack, ploy, stratagem

tactical *adjective* STRATEGIC, politic, shrewd, smart, diplomatic, clever, cunning, skilful, artful, foxy, adroit << ANTONYM impolitic

tactician *noun* STRATEGIST, campaigner, planner, mastermind, general, director, brain (*informal*), coordinator, schemer

tactics *plural noun* STRATEGY, campaigning, manoeuvres, generalship

tag *noun* LABEL, tab, sticker, note, ticket, slip, flag, identification, marker, flap, docket ▷ *verb* **1** LABEL, mark, flag, ticket, identify, earmark **2** NAME, call, label, term, style, dub, nickname, christen

tail *noun* **1** EXTREMITY, appendage, brush, rear end, hindquarters, hind part, empennage

2 (*astronomy*) TRAIN, end, trail, tailpiece **3** (*informal*) BUTTOCKS, behind (*informal*), bottom, butt (*US & Canad informal*), bum (*Brit slang*), rear (*informal*), buns (*US slang*), backside (*informal*), rump, rear end, posterior, derrière (*euphemistic*), jacksy (*Brit slang*) **4** (*used of hair*) PONYTAIL, braid, plait, tress, pigtail ▷ *verb* (*informal*) FOLLOW, track, shadow, trail, stalk, keep an eye on, dog the footsteps of ▷▷ **turn tail** RUN AWAY, flee, run off, escape, take off (*informal*), retreat, make off, hook it (*slang*), run for it (*informal*), scarper (*Brit slang*), cut and run, show a clean pair of heels, skedaddle (*informal*), take to your heels

tailor *noun* OUTFITTER, couturier, dressmaker, seamstress, clothier, costumier, garment maker ▷ *verb* ADAPT, adjust, modify, cut, style, fit, fashion, shape, suit, convert, alter, accommodate, mould, customize

tailor-made *adjective* **1** PERFECT, right, ideal, suitable, just right, right up your street (*informal*), up your alley **2** MADE-TO-MEASURE, fitted, cut to fit, made to order

taint *verb* **1** DISGRACE, shame, dishonour, brand, ruin, blacken, stigmatize **2** SPOIL, ruin, contaminate, damage, soil, dirty, poison, foul, infect, stain, corrupt, smear, muddy, pollute, blight, tarnish, blot, blemish, sully, defile, adulterate, besmirch, vitiate, smirch << ANTONYM purify

take *verb* **1** GRIP, grab, seize, catch, grasp, clutch, get hold of, clasp, take hold of, lay hold of **2** CARRY, bring, bear, transport, ferry, haul, convey, fetch, cart, tote (*informal*) << ANTONYM send **3** ACCOMPANY, lead, bring, guide, conduct, escort, convoy, usher **4** REMOVE, draw, pull, fish, withdraw, extract, abstract **5** STEAL, nick (*slang, chiefly Brit*), appropriate, pocket, pinch (*informal*), carry off, swipe (*slang*), run off with, blag (*slang*), walk off with, misappropriate, cart off (*slang*), purloin, filch, help yourself to, gain possession of << ANTONYM return **6** CAPTURE, arrest, seize, abduct, take into custody, ensnare, entrap, lay hold of << ANTONYM release **7** TOLERATE, stand, bear, suffer, weather, go through, brave, stomach, endure, undergo, swallow, brook, hack (*slang*), abide, put up with (*informal*), withstand, submit to, countenance, pocket, thole (*Scot*) << ANTONYM avoid **8** REQUIRE, need, involve, demand, call for, entail, necessitate **9** ACCEPT, assume, take on, undertake, adopt, take up, enter upon

<< ANTONYM reject **10** UNDERSTAND, follow, comprehend, get, see, grasp, apprehend **11** HIRE, book, rent, lease, reserve, pay for, engage, make a reservation for **12** PERFORM, have, do, make, effect, accomplish, execute **13** INGEST, consume, swallow, inhale **14** CONSUME, have, drink, eat, imbibe **15** HAVE ROOM FOR, hold, contain, accommodate, accept **16** WORK, succeed, do the trick (*informal*), have effect, be efficacious << ANTONYM fail ▷ *noun* (*informal, chiefly US*) TAKINGS, profits, revenue, return, gate, yield, proceeds, haul, receipts ▷▷ **take it** ASSUME, suppose, presume, expect, imagine, guess (*informal, chiefly US & Canad*) ▷▷ **take off 1** LIFT OFF, leave the ground, take to the air, become airborne **2** (*informal*) DEPART, go, leave, split (*slang*), disappear, set out, strike out, beat it (*slang*), hit the road (*slang*), abscond, decamp, hook it (*slang*), slope off, pack your bags (*informal*) ▷▷ **take on** (*informal*) GET UPSET, get excited, make a fuss, break down, give way ▷▷ **take someone for something** (*informal*) REGARD AS, see as, believe to be, consider to be, think of as, deem to be, perceive to be, hold to be, judge to be, reckon to be, presume to be, look on as ▷▷ **take someone in 1** LET IN, receive, admit, board, welcome, harbour, accommodate, take care of, put up, billet **2** (*informal*) DECEIVE, fool, con (*informal*), do (*slang*), trick, cheat, mislead, dupe, gull (*archaic*), swindle, hoodwink, pull the wool over someone's eyes (*informal*), bilk, cozen ▷▷ **take someone off** (*informal*) PARODY, imitate, mimic, mock, ridicule, ape, caricature, send up (*Brit informal*), spoof (*informal*), travesty, impersonate, lampoon, burlesque, satirize ▷▷ **take someone on 1** COMPETE AGAINST, face, contend with, fight, oppose, vie with, pit yourself against, enter the lists against, match yourself against **2** ENGAGE, employ, hire, retain, enlist, enrol ▷▷ **take something back 1** RETURN, bring back, send back, hand back **2** RETRACT, withdraw, renounce, renege on, disavow, recant, disclaim, unsay **3** REGAIN, get back, reclaim, recapture, repossess, retake, reconquer ▷▷ **take something down 1** REMOVE, take off, extract **2** DISMANTLE, demolish, take apart, disassemble, level, tear down, raze, take to pieces **3** MAKE A NOTE OF, record, write down, minute, note, set down, transcribe, put on record ▷▷ **take something in 1** UNDERSTAND, absorb, grasp,

digest, comprehend, assimilate, get the hang of (*informal*) **2** INCLUDE, contain, comprise, cover, embrace, encompass ▷▷ **take something off** REMOVE, discard, strip off, drop, peel off, doff, divest yourself of ▷▷ **take something on 1** ACCEPT, tackle, undertake, shoulder, have a go at (*informal*), agree to do, address yourself to **2** (with a quality or identity as object) ACQUIRE, assume, come to have ▷▷ **take something over** GAIN CONTROL OF, take command of, assume control of, come to power in, become leader of ▷▷ **take something up 1** START, begin, engage in, assume, adopt, become involved in **2** OCCUPY, absorb, consume, use up, cover, fill, waste, squander, extend over **3** RESUME, continue, go on with, pick up, proceed with, restart, carry on with, recommence, follow on with, begin something again ▷▷ **take to someone** LIKE, get on with, warm to, be taken with, be pleased by, become friendly with, conceive an affection for ▷▷ **take to something 1** START, resort to, make a habit of, have recourse to **2** HEAD FOR, make for, run for, flee to

takeoff *noun* **1** DEPARTURE, launch, liftoff **2** (*informal*) PARODY, imitation, send-up (*Brit informal*), mocking, satire, caricature, spoof (*informal*), travesty, lampoon

takeover *noun* MERGER, coup, change of leadership, incorporation

tale *noun* **1** STORY, narrative, anecdote, account, relation, novel, legend, fiction, romance, saga, short story, yarn (*informal*), fable, narration, conte (*French*), spiel (*informal*), urban myth, urban legend **2** LIE, fabrication, falsehood, fib, untruth, spiel (*informal*), tall story (*informal*), rigmarole, cock-and-bull story (*informal*)

talent *noun* ABILITY, gift, aptitude, power, skill, facility, capacity, bent, genius, expertise, faculty, endowment, forte, flair, knack

talented *adjective* GIFTED, able, expert, master, masterly, brilliant, ace (*informal*), artistic, consummate, first-rate, top-notch (*informal*), adroit

talisman *noun* CHARM, mascot, amulet, lucky charm, fetish, juju

talk *verb* **1** SPEAK, chat, chatter, converse, communicate, rap (*slang*), articulate, witter (*informal*), gab (*informal*), express yourself, prattle, natter, shoot the breeze (*US slang*), prate, run off at the mouth (*slang*), earbash (*Austral & NZ slang*) **2** DISCUSS, confer, hold

discussions, negotiate, palaver, parley, confabulate, have a confab (*informal*), chew the rag *or* fat (*slang*) **3** INFORM, shop (*slang, chiefly Brit*), grass (*Brit slang*), sing (*slang, chiefly US*), squeal (*slang*), squeak (*informal*), tell all, spill the beans (*informal*), give the game away, blab, let the cat out of the bag, reveal information, spill your guts (*slang*) ▷ *noun* **1** SPEECH, lecture, presentation, report, address, seminar, discourse, sermon, symposium, dissertation, harangue, oration, disquisition, whaikorero (*NZ*) **2** DISCUSSION, tête-à-tête, conference, dialogue, consultation, heart-to-heart, confabulation, confab (*informal*), powwow **3** CONVERSATION, chat, natter, crack (*Scot & Irish*), rap (*slang*), jaw (*slang*), chatter, gab (*informal*), chitchat, blether, blather **4** GOSSIP, rumour, hearsay, tittle-tattle, goss (*informal*) **5** LANGUAGE, words, speech, jargon, slang, dialect, lingo (*informal*), patois, argot **6** *often plural* MEETING, conference, discussions, negotiations, congress, summit, mediation, arbitration, conciliation, conclave, palaver, parley, hui (*NZ*) ▷▷ **talk big** BOAST, exaggerate, brag, crow, vaunt, bluster, blow your own trumpet ▷▷ **talk someone into something** PERSUADE, convince, win someone over, sway, bring round (*informal*), sweet-talk someone into, prevail on *or* upon

talkative *adjective* LOQUACIOUS, chatty, garrulous, long-winded, big-mouthed (*slang*), wordy, effusive, gabby (*informal*), voluble, gossipy, verbose, mouthy, prolix << ANTONYM reserved

talker *noun* SPEAKER, lecturer, orator, conversationalist, chatterbox, speechmaker

talking-to *noun* (*informal*) REPRIMAND, lecture, rebuke, scolding, row, criticism, wigging (*Brit slang*), slating (*informal*), reproach, ticking-off (*informal*), dressing-down (*informal*), telling-off (*informal*), reproof, rap on the knuckles << ANTONYM praise

tall *adjective* **1** LOFTY, big, giant, long-legged, lanky, leggy **2** HIGH, towering, soaring, steep, elevated, lofty << ANTONYM short

tally *verb* **1** AGREE, match, accord, fit, suit, square, parallel, coincide, correspond, conform, concur, harmonize << ANTONYM disagree **2** COUNT UP, total, compute, keep score ▷ *noun* RECORD, score, total, count, reckoning, running total

tame *adjective* **1** DOMESTICATED, unafraid, docile, broken, gentle, fearless, obedient, amenable, tractable, used to human contact

<< ANTONYM wild **2** SUBMISSIVE, meek, compliant, subdued, manageable, obedient, docile, spiritless, unresisting << ANTONYM stubborn **3** UNEXCITING, boring, dull, bland, tedious, flat, tiresome, lifeless, prosaic, uninspiring, humdrum, uninteresting, insipid, vapid, wearisome << ANTONYM exciting ▷ *verb* **1** DOMESTICATE, train, break in, gentle, pacify, house-train, make tame << ANTONYM make fiercer **2** SUBDUE, suppress, master, discipline, curb, humble, conquer, repress, bridle, enslave, subjugate, bring to heel, break the spirit of << ANTONYM arouse

tamper *verb usually with* **with 1** INTERFERE WITH, tinker with, meddle with, alter, fiddle with (*informal*), mess about with, muck about with (*Brit slang*), monkey around with, fool about with (*informal*) **2** INFLUENCE, fix (*informal*), rig, corrupt, manipulate

tang *noun* **1** SCENT, smell, odour, perfume, fragrance, aroma, reek, redolence **2** TASTE, bite, flavour, edge, relish, smack, savour, zest, sharpness, piquancy, spiciness, zestiness **3** TRACE, touch, tinge, suggestion, hint, whiff, smattering

tangible *adjective* DEFINITE, real, positive, solid, material, physical, actual, substantial, objective, concrete, evident, manifest, palpable, discernible, tactile, perceptible, corporeal, touchable << ANTONYM intangible

tangle *noun* **1** KNOT, mass, twist, web, jungle, mat, coil, snarl, mesh, ravel, entanglement **2** MESS, jam, fix (*informal*), confusion, complication, maze, mix-up, shambles, labyrinth, entanglement, imbroglio ▷ *verb* **1** TWIST, knot, mat, coil, snarl, mesh, entangle, interlock, kink, interweave, ravel, interlace, enmesh, intertwist << ANTONYM disentangle **2** *sometimes with* **up** ENTANGLE, catch, ensnare, entrap **3** CONFUSE, mix up, muddle, jumble, scramble ▷▷ **tangle with someone** COME INTO CONFLICT WITH, come up against, cross swords with, dispute with, contend with, contest with, lock horns with

tangled *adjective* **1** KNOTTED, twisted, matted, messy, snarled, jumbled, entangled, knotty, tousled **2** COMPLICATED, involved, complex, confused, messy, mixed-up, convoluted, knotty

tangy *adjective* SHARP, tart, piquant, biting, fresh, spicy, pungent, briny, acerb

tantalize *or* **tantalise** *verb* TORMENT, tease, taunt, torture, provoke, entice, lead on, titillate, make someone's mouth water, keep someone hanging on

tantamount ▷▷ **tantamount to** EQUIVALENT TO, equal to, as good as, synonymous with, the same as, commensurate with

tantrum *noun* OUTBURST, temper, hysterics, fit, storm, paddy (*Brit informal*), wax (*informal, chiefly Brit*), flare-up, paroxysm, bate (*Brit slang*), ill humour, foulie (*Austral slang*), hissy fit (*informal*)

tap[1] *verb* KNOCK, strike, pat, rap, beat, touch, drum ▷ *noun* KNOCK, pat, rap, beat, touch, drumming, light blow

tap[2] *noun* **1** VALVE, spout, faucet (*US & Canad*), spigot, stopcock **2** BUG (*informal*), listening device, wiretap, bugging device, hidden microphone ▷ *verb* LISTEN IN ON, monitor, bug (*informal*), spy on, eavesdrop on, wiretap ▷▷ **on tap 1** (*informal*) AVAILABLE, ready, standing by, to hand, on hand, at hand, in reserve **2** ON DRAUGHT, cask-conditioned, from barrels, not bottled *or* canned

tape *noun* BINDING, strip, band, string, ribbon ▷ *verb* **1** RECORD, video, tape-record, make a recording of **2** *sometimes with* **up** BIND, secure, stick, seal, wrap

taper *verb* NARROW, thin, attenuate, come to a point, become thinner, become narrow ▷▷ **taper off** DECREASE, dwindle, lessen, reduce, fade, weaken, wane, subside, wind down, die out, die away, thin out << ANTONYM widen

tardy *adjective* **1** LATE, overdue, unpunctual, belated, dilatory, behindhand **2** SLOW, belated, delayed

target *noun* **1** MARK, goal, bull's-eye **2** GOAL, aim, objective, end, mark, object, intention, ambition, Holy Grail (*informal*) **3** VICTIM, butt, prey, quarry, scapegoat

tariff *noun* **1** TAX, rate, duty, toll, levy, excise, impost, assessment **2** PRICE LIST, charges, schedule

tarnish *verb* **1** STAIN, dull, discolour, spot, soil, dim, rust, darken, blot, blemish, befoul, lose lustre *or* shine << ANTONYM brighten **2** DAMAGE, taint, blacken, sully, drag through the mud, smirch << ANTONYM enhance ▷ *noun* STAIN, taint, discoloration, spot, rust, blot, blemish

tarry *verb* LINGER, remain, loiter, wait, delay, pause, hang around (*informal*), lose time, bide, dally, take your time, dawdle, drag your feet *or* heels << ANTONYM hurry

tart[1] *noun* PIE, pastry, pasty, tartlet, patty

tart[2] *adjective* **1** SHARP, acid, sour, bitter,

pungent, tangy, astringent, piquant, vinegary, acidulous, acerb << ANTONYM sweet **2** CUTTING, biting, sharp, short, wounding, nasty, harsh, scathing, acrimonious, barbed, hurtful, caustic, astringent, vitriolic, trenchant, testy, mordant, snappish, mordacious << ANTONYM kind

tart³ noun (informal) SLUT, prostitute, hooker (US slang), whore, slag (Brit slang), call girl, working girl (facetious slang), harlot, streetwalker, loose woman, fallen woman, scrubber (Brit & Austral slang), strumpet, trollop, floozy (slang), woman of easy virtue, fille de joie (French), hornbag (Austral slang)

task noun JOB, duty, assignment, work, business, charge, labour, exercise, mission, employment, enterprise, undertaking, occupation, chore, toil ▷ verb CHARGE, assign to, entrust ▷▷ **take someone to task** CRITICIZE, blame, blast, lecture, carpet (informal), censure, rebuke, reprimand, reproach, scold, tear into (informal), tell off (informal), diss (slang, chiefly US), read the riot act, reprove, upbraid, lambast(e), bawl out (informal), chew out (US & Canad informal), tear (someone) off a strip (Brit informal), give a rocket (Brit & NZ informal)

taste noun **1** FLAVOUR, savour, relish, smack, tang << ANTONYM blandness **2** BIT, bite, drop, swallow, sip, mouthful, touch, sample, dash, nip, spoonful, morsel, titbit, soupçon (French) **3** LIKING, preference, penchant, fondness, partiality, desire, fancy, leaning, bent, appetite, relish, inclination, palate, predilection << ANTONYM dislike **4** REFINEMENT, style, judgment, culture, polish, grace, discrimination, perception, appreciation, elegance, sophistication, cultivation, discernment << ANTONYM lack of judgment **5** PROPRIETY, discretion, correctness, delicacy, tact, politeness, nicety, decorum, tactfulness << ANTONYM impropriety ▷ verb **1** often with **of** HAVE A FLAVOUR OF, smack of, savour of **2** SAMPLE, try, test, relish, sip, savour, nibble **3** DISTINGUISH, perceive, discern, differentiate **4** EXPERIENCE, know, undergo, partake of, feel, encounter, meet with, come up against, have knowledge of << ANTONYM miss

tasteful adjective REFINED, stylish, elegant, cultured, beautiful, smart, charming, polished, delicate, artistic, handsome, cultivated, discriminating, exquisite, graceful, harmonious, urbane, fastidious, aesthetically pleasing, in good taste << ANTONYM tasteless

tasteless adjective **1** GAUDY, cheap, vulgar, tacky (informal), flashy, naff (Brit slang), garish, inelegant, tawdry << ANTONYM tasteful **2** VULGAR, crude, improper, low, gross, rude, coarse, crass, unseemly, indiscreet, tactless, uncouth, impolite, graceless, indelicate, indecorous **3** INSIPID, bland, flat, boring, thin, weak, dull, mild, tame, watered-down, uninteresting, uninspired, vapid, flavourless << ANTONYM tasty

tasty adjective DELICIOUS, luscious, palatable, delectable, good-tasting, savoury, full-flavoured, yummy (slang), flavoursome, scrumptious (informal), appetizing, toothsome, flavourful, sapid, lekker (S African slang), yummo (Austral slang) << ANTONYM bland

tattletale noun (chiefly US & Canad) GOSSIP, busybody, babbler, prattler, chatterbox (informal), blether, chatterer, bigmouth (slang), scandalmonger, gossipmonger

tatty adjective (Chiefly Brit) SHABBY, seedy, scruffy, worn, poor, neglected, ragged, run-down, frayed, worn out, dilapidated, tattered, tawdry, threadbare, rumpled, bedraggled, unkempt, down at heel, the worse for wear, having seen better days << ANTONYM smart

taunt verb JEER, mock, tease, ridicule, provoke, insult, torment, sneer, deride, revile, twit, guy (informal), gibe ▷ noun JEER, dig, insult, ridicule, cut, teasing, provocation, barb, derision, sarcasm, gibe

taut adjective **1** TENSE, rigid, tight, stressed, stretched, strained, flexed << ANTONYM relaxed **2** TIGHT, stretched, rigid, tightly stretched << ANTONYM slack

tavern noun INN, bar, pub (informal, chiefly Brit), public house, watering hole (facetious slang), boozer (Brit, Austral & NZ informal), beer parlour (Canad), beverage room (Canad), hostelry, alehouse (archaic), taproom

tawdry adjective VULGAR, cheap, tacky (informal), flashy, tasteless, plastic (slang), glittering, naff (Brit slang), gaudy, tatty, showy, tinsel, raffish, gimcrack, meretricious, tinselly, cheap-jack (informal) << ANTONYM stylish

tax noun **1** CHARGE, rate, duty, toll, levy, tariff, excise, contribution, assessment, customs, tribute, imposition, tithe, impost **2** STRAIN, demand, burden, pressure, weight, load, drain ▷ *verb* 1 CHARGE, impose a tax on, levy a tax on, rate, demand, assess, extract, exact, tithe 2 STRAIN, push, stretch, try, test, task, load, burden, drain, exhaust, weaken, weary, put pressure on, sap, wear out, weigh heavily on, overburden, make heavy demands on, enervate 3 ACCUSE, charge, blame, confront, impeach, incriminate, arraign, impugn, lay at your door << ANTONYM acquit

taxing *adjective* DEMANDING, trying, wearing, heavy, tough, tiring, punishing, exacting, stressful, sapping, onerous, burdensome, wearisome, enervating << ANTONYM easy

teach *verb* 1 INSTRUCT, train, coach, school, direct, advise, inform, discipline, educate, drill, tutor, enlighten, impart, instil, inculcate, edify, give lessons in 2 *often with* **how** SHOW, train, demonstrate

teacher *noun* INSTRUCTOR, coach, tutor, don, guide, professor, trainer, lecturer, guru, mentor, educator, handler, schoolteacher, pedagogue, dominie (*Scot*), master *or* mistress, schoolmaster *or* schoolmistress

team *noun* 1 SIDE, squad, troupe 2 GROUP, company, set, body, band, crew, gang, line-up, bunch, posse (*informal*) 3 PAIR, span, yoke ▷▷ **team up** JOIN, unite, work together, cooperate, couple, link up, get together, yoke, band together, collaborate, join forces ▷ *see* **family**

teamwork *noun* COOPERATION, collaboration, unity, concert, harmony, fellowship, coordination, joint action, esprit de corps

tear *verb* 1 RIP, split, rend, shred, rupture, sunder 2 RUN, rip, ladder, snag 3 SCRATCH, cut (open), gash, lacerate, injure, mangle, cut to pieces, cut to ribbons, mangulate (*Austral slang*) 4 PULL APART, claw, lacerate, sever, mutilate, mangle, mangulate (*Austral slang*) 5 RUSH, run, charge, race, shoot, fly, career, speed, belt (*slang*), dash, hurry, barrel (along) (*informal, chiefly US & Canad*), sprint, bolt, dart, gallop, zoom, burn rubber (*informal*) 6 *often with* **away** *or* **from** PULL, seize, rip, grab, snatch, pluck, yank, wrench, wrest ▷ *noun* HOLE, split, rip, run, rent, snag, rupture

tearaway *noun* (*Brit*) HOOLIGAN, delinquent, tough, rough (*informal*), rowdy, ruffian, roughneck (*slang*), good-for-nothing

tearful *adjective* 1 WEEPING, crying, sobbing, in tears, whimpering, blubbering, weepy (*informal*), lachrymose 2 SAD, pathetic, poignant, upsetting, distressing, harrowing, pitiful, woeful, mournful, lamentable,

sorrowful, pitiable, dolorous

tears *plural noun* CRYING, weeping, sobbing, wailing, whimpering, blubbering, lamentation ▷▷ **in tears** WEEPING, crying, sobbing, whimpering, blubbering, visibly moved

tease *verb* 1 MOCK, bait, wind up (*Brit slang*), worry, bother, provoke, annoy, needle (*informal*), plague (*informal*), rag, rib (*informal*), torment, ridicule, taunt, aggravate (*informal*), badger, pester, vex, goad, bedevil, take the mickey out of (*informal*), twit, chaff, guy (*informal*), gibe, pull someone's leg (*informal*), make fun of 2 TANTALIZE, lead on, flirt with, titillate

technical *adjective* SCIENTIFIC, technological, skilled, specialist, specialized, hi-tech *or* high-tech

technique *noun* 1 METHOD, way, system, approach, means, course, style, fashion, manner, procedure, mode, MO, modus operandi 2 SKILL, art, performance, craft, touch, know-how (*informal*), facility, delivery, execution, knack, artistry, craftsmanship, proficiency, adroitness

tedious *adjective* BORING, dull, dreary, monotonous, tiring, annoying, fatiguing, drab, banal, tiresome, lifeless, prosaic, laborious, humdrum, uninteresting, long-drawn-out, mind-numbing, irksome, unexciting, soporific, ho-hum (*informal*), vapid, wearisome, deadly dull, prosy, dreich (*Scot*) << ANTONYM exciting

tedium *noun* BOREDOM, monotony, dullness, routine, the doldrums, banality, sameness, ennui, drabness, deadness, dreariness, tediousness, lifelessness << ANTONYM excitement

teem[1] *verb* BE FULL OF, abound, swarm, bristle, brim, overflow, be abundant, burst at the seams, be prolific, be crawling, pullulate

teem[2] *verb often with* **down** *or with* **rain** POUR, lash, pelt (down), sheet, stream, belt (*slang*), bucket down (*informal*), rain cats and dogs (*informal*)

teeming[1] *adjective* FULL, packed, crowded, alive, thick, bursting, numerous, crawling, swarming, abundant, bristling, brimming, overflowing, fruitful, replete, chock-full, brimful, chock-a-block << ANTONYM lacking

teeming[2] *adjective* POURING, lashing, pelting, sheeting, streaming, belting (*slang*), bucketing down (*informal*)

teenage *adjective* YOUTHFUL, adolescent,

juvenile, immature

teenager *noun* YOUTH, minor, adolescent, juvenile, girl, boy

teeny *adjective* (*informal*) TINY, minute, wee, miniature, microscopic, diminutive, minuscule, teeny-weeny, teensy-weensy

teeter *verb* WOBBLE, rock, totter, balance, stagger, sway, tremble, waver, pivot, seesaw

telegram *noun* CABLE, wire (*informal*), telegraph, telex, radiogram

telegraph *verb* CABLE, wire (*informal*), transmit, telex, send

telepathy *noun* MIND-READING, ESP, sixth sense, clairvoyance, extra sensory perception, psychometry, thought transference

telephone *noun* PHONE, blower (*informal*), mobile (phone), handset, dog and bone (*slang*) ▷ *verb* CALL, phone, ring (*chiefly Brit*), buzz (*informal*), dial, call up, give someone a call, give someone a ring (*informal, chiefly Brit*), give someone a buzz (*informal*), give someone a bell (*Brit slang*), put a call through to, give someone a tinkle (*Brit informal*), get on the blower to (*informal*)

telescope *noun* GLASS, scope (*informal*), spyglass ▷ *verb* SHORTEN, contract, compress, cut, trim, shrink, tighten, condense, abbreviate, abridge, capsulize << ANTONYM lengthen

television *noun* TV, telly (*Brit informal*), small screen (*informal*), the box (*Brit informal*), receiver, the tube (*slang*), TV set, gogglebox (*Brit slang*), idiot box (*slang*)

tell *verb* 1 INFORM, notify, make aware, say to, state to, warn, reveal to, express to, brief, advise, disclose to, proclaim to, fill in, speak about to, confess to, impart, alert to, divulge, announce to, acquaint with, communicate to, mention to, make known to, apprise, utter to, get off your chest (*informal*), let know 2 DESCRIBE, relate, recount, report, portray, depict, chronicle, rehearse, narrate, give an account of 3 INSTRUCT, order, command, direct, bid, enjoin 4 SEE, make out, discern, understand, discover, be certain, comprehend 5 DISTINGUISH, discriminate, discern, differentiate, identify 6 HAVE *or* TAKE EFFECT, register, weigh, have force, count, take its toll, carry weight, make its presence felt ▷▷ **tell someone off** REPRIMAND, rebuke, scold, lecture, carpet (*informal*), censure, reproach, berate, chide, tear into (*informal*), read the riot act, reprove, upbraid, take to task, tick off (*informal*),

bawl out (*informal*), chew out (*US & Canad informal*), tear off a strip (*Brit informal*), give a piece of your mind to, haul over the coals (*informal*), give a rocket to (*Brit & NZ informal*)

telling *adjective* EFFECTIVE, significant, considerable, marked, striking, powerful, solid, impressive, influential, decisive, potent, forceful, weighty, forcible, trenchant, effectual << ANTONYM unimportant

temerity *noun* AUDACITY, nerve (*informal*), cheek, gall (*informal*), front, assurance, pluck, boldness, recklessness, chutzpah (*US & Canad informal*), impudence, effrontery, impulsiveness, rashness, brass neck (*Brit informal*), foolhardiness, sassiness (*US informal*), forwardness, heedlessness

temper *noun* 1 IRRITABILITY, anger, irascibility, passion, resentment, irritation, annoyance, petulance, surliness, ill humour, peevishness, hot-headedness << ANTONYM good humour 2 FRAME OF MIND, character, nature, attitude, mind, mood, constitution, humour, vein, temperament, tenor, disposition 3 RAGE, fury, bad mood, passion, paddy (*Brit informal*), wax (*informal, chiefly Brit*), tantrum, bate (*Brit slang*), fit of pique, foulie (*Austral slang*), hissy fit (*informal*) 4 SELF-CONTROL, composure, cool (*slang*), calm, good humour, tranquillity, coolness, calmness, equanimity << ANTONYM anger ▷ *verb* 1 MODERATE, restrain, tone down, calm, soften, soothe, lessen, allay, mitigate, abate, assuage, mollify, soft-pedal (*informal*), palliate, admix << ANTONYM intensify 2 STRENGTHEN, harden, toughen, anneal << ANTONYM soften

temperament *noun* NATURE, character, personality, quality, spirit, make-up, soul, constitution, bent, stamp, humour, tendencies, tendency, temper, outlook, complexion, disposition, frame of mind, mettle, cast of mind

temperamental *adjective* 1 MOODY, emotional, touchy, sensitive, explosive, passionate, volatile, fiery, impatient, erratic, neurotic, irritable, mercurial, excitable, capricious, petulant, hot-headed, hypersensitive, highly strung, easily upset, unstable << ANTONYM even-tempered 2 (*informal*) UNRELIABLE, unpredictable, undependable, inconsistent, erratic, inconstant, unstable << ANTONYM reliable 3 NATURAL, inherent, innate, constitutional, ingrained, congenital, inborn

temperance *noun* 1 TEETOTALISM, abstinence,

sobriety, abstemiousness **2** MODERATION, restraint, self-control, self-discipline, continence, self-restraint, forbearance << ANTONYM excess

temperate *adjective* **1** MILD, moderate, balmy, fair, cool, soft, calm, gentle, pleasant, clement, agreeable << ANTONYM extreme **2** MODERATE, dispassionate, self-controlled, calm, stable, reasonable, sensible, mild, composed, equable, even-tempered, self-restrained << ANTONYM unrestrained

tempest *noun* **1** (*literary*) STORM, hurricane, gale, tornado, cyclone, typhoon, squall **2** UPROAR, storm, furore, disturbance, upheaval, ferment, commotion, tumult << ANTONYM calm

tempestuous *adjective* **1** PASSIONATE, intense, turbulent, heated, wild, excited, emotional, violent, flaming, hysterical, stormy, impassioned, uncontrolled, boisterous, feverish << ANTONYM peaceful **2** STORMY, turbulent, inclement, raging, windy, boisterous, blustery, gusty, squally

temple *noun* SHRINE, church, sanctuary, holy place, place of worship, house of God

tempo *noun* PACE, time, rate, beat, measure (*poetry*), speed, metre, rhythm, cadence, pulse

temporal *adjective* **1** SECULAR, worldly, lay, earthly, mundane, material, civil, fleshly, mortal, terrestrial, carnal, profane, sublunary **2** TEMPORARY, passing, transitory, fleeting, short-lived, fugitive, transient, momentary, evanescent, impermanent, fugacious

temporarily *adverb* BRIEFLY, for the moment, for the time being, momentarily, for a moment, for a short time, for a little while, fleetingly, for a short while, pro tem, for the nonce

temporary *adjective* **1** IMPERMANENT, passing, transitory, brief, fleeting, interim, short-lived, fugitive, transient, momentary, ephemeral, evanescent, pro tem, here today and gone tomorrow, pro tempore (*Latin*), fugacious << ANTONYM permanent **2** SHORT-TERM, acting, interim, supply, stand-in, fill-in, caretaker, provisional, stopgap

tempt *verb* **1** ATTRACT, draw, appeal to, allure, whet the appetite of, make your mouth water **2** ENTICE, lure, lead on, invite, woo, seduce, coax, decoy, inveigle << ANTONYM discourage **3** PROVOKE, try, test, risk, dare, bait, fly in the face of

temptation *noun* **1** ENTICEMENT, lure,

inducement, pull, come-on (*informal*), invitation, bait, coaxing, snare, seduction, decoy, allurement, tantalization **2** APPEAL, draw, attraction, attractiveness

tempting *adjective* INVITING, enticing, seductive, alluring, attractive, mouthwatering, appetizing << ANTONYM uninviting

tenacious *adjective* **1** STUBBORN, dogged, determined, persistent, sure, firm, adamant, staunch, resolute, inflexible, strong-willed, steadfast, unyielding, obstinate, intransigent, immovable, unswerving, obdurate, stiff-necked, pertinacious << ANTONYM irresolute **2** FIRM, dogged, persistent, unyielding, unswerving **3** STRONG, firm, fast, iron, tight, clinging, forceful, immovable, unshakeable **4** RETENTIVE, good, photographic, unforgetful **5** ADHESIVE, clinging, sticky, glutinous, gluey, mucilaginous

tenacity *noun* PERSEVERANCE, resolution, determination, application, resolve, persistence, diligence, intransigence, firmness, stubbornness, inflexibility, obstinacy, steadfastness, obduracy, doggedness, strength of will, strength of purpose, resoluteness, pertinacity, staunchness

tenancy *noun* **1** LEASE, residence, occupancy, holding, renting, possession, occupation **2** PERIOD OF OFFICE, tenure, incumbency, time in office

tenant *noun* LEASEHOLDER, resident, renter, occupant, holder, inhabitant, occupier, lodger, boarder, lessee

tend[1] *verb* BE INCLINED, be likely, be liable, have a tendency, be apt, be prone, trend, lean, incline, be biased, be disposed, gravitate, have a leaning, have an inclination

tend[2] *verb* **1** TAKE CARE OF, look after, care for, keep, watch, serve, protect, feed, handle, attend, guard, nurse, see to, nurture, minister to, cater for, keep an eye on, wait on, watch over << ANTONYM neglect **2** MAINTAIN, take care of, nurture, cultivate, manage << ANTONYM neglect

tendency *noun* **1** TREND, drift, movement, turning, heading, course, drive, bearing, direction, bias **2** INCLINATION, leaning, bent, liability, readiness, disposition, penchant, propensity, susceptibility, predisposition, predilection, proclivity, partiality, proneness

tender[1] *adjective* **1** GENTLE, loving, kind, caring, warm, sympathetic, fond, sentimental, humane, affectionate, compassionate, benevolent, considerate, merciful, amorous, warm-hearted, tenderhearted, softhearted, touchy-feely (*informal*) << ANTONYM harsh **2** ROMANTIC, moving, touching, emotional, sentimental, poignant, evocative, soppy (*Brit informal*) **3** VULNERABLE, young, sensitive, new, green, raw, youthful, inexperienced, immature, callow, impressionable, unripe, wet behind the ears (*informal*) << ANTONYM experienced **4** SENSITIVE, painful, sore, smarting, raw, bruised, irritated, aching, inflamed **5** FRAGILE, delicate, frail, soft, weak, feeble, breakable **6** DIFFICULT, sensitive, tricky, dangerous, complicated, risky, touchy, ticklish

tender² *verb* OFFER, present, submit, give, suggest, propose, extend, volunteer, hand in, put forward, proffer ▷ *noun* OFFER, bid, estimate, proposal, suggestion, submission, proffer

tenderness *noun* **1** GENTLENESS, love, affection, liking, care, consideration, sympathy, pity, humanity, warmth, mercy, attachment, compassion, devotion, kindness, fondness, sentimentality, benevolence, humaneness, amorousness, warm-heartedness, softheartedness, tenderheartedness << ANTONYM harshness **2** SORENESS, pain, sensitivity, smart, bruising, ache, aching, irritation, inflammation, rawness, sensitiveness, painfulness **3** FRAGILITY, vulnerability, weakness, sensitivity, softness, feebleness, sensitiveness, frailness, delicateness

tenet *noun* PRINCIPLE, rule, doctrine, creed, view, teaching, opinion, belief, conviction, canon, thesis, maxim, dogma, precept, article of faith, kaupapa (*NZ*)

tenor *noun* MEANING, trend, drift, way, course, sense, aim, purpose, direction, path, theme, substance, burden, tendency, intent, purport

tense *adjective* **1** STRAINED, uneasy, stressful, fraught, charged, difficult, worrying, exciting, uncomfortable, knife-edge, nail-biting, nerve-racking **2** NERVOUS, wound up (*informal*), edgy, strained, wired (*slang*), anxious, under pressure, restless, apprehensive, jittery (*informal*), uptight (*informal*), on edge, jumpy, twitchy (*informal*), overwrought, strung up (*informal*), on tenterhooks, fidgety, keyed up, antsy (*informal*), wrought up, adrenalized << ANTONYM calm **3** RIGID, strained, taut,

stretched, tight << ANTONYM relaxed ▷ *verb* TIGHTEN, strain, brace, tauten, stretch, flex, stiffen << ANTONYM relax

tension *noun* **1** STRAIN, stress, nervousness, pressure, anxiety, unease, apprehension, suspense, restlessness, the jitters (*informal*), edginess << ANTONYM calmness **2** FRICTION, hostility, unease, antagonism, antipathy, enmity, ill feeling **3** RIGIDITY, tightness, stiffness, pressure, stress, stretching, straining, tautness

tentative *adjective* **1** UNCONFIRMED, provisional, indefinite, test, trial, pilot, preliminary, experimental, unsettled, speculative, pencilled in, exploratory, to be confirmed, TBC, conjectural << ANTONYM confirmed **2** HESITANT, cautious, uncertain, doubtful, backward, faltering, unsure, timid, undecided, diffident, iffy (*informal*) << ANTONYM confident

tenuous *adjective* **1** SLIGHT, weak, dubious, shaky, doubtful, questionable, insignificant, flimsy, sketchy, insubstantial, nebulous << ANTONYM strong **2** FINE, slim, delicate, attenuated, gossamer

tenure *noun* **1** OCCUPANCY, holding, occupation, residence, tenancy, possession, proprietorship **2** TERM OF OFFICE, term, incumbency, period in office, time

tepid *adjective* **1** LUKEWARM, warmish, slightly warm **2** UNENTHUSIASTIC, half-hearted, indifferent, cool, lukewarm, apathetic << ANTONYM enthusiastic

term *noun* **1** WORD, name, expression, title, label, phrase, denomination, designation, appellation, locution **2** SESSION, course, quarter (*US*), semester, trimester (*US*) **3** PERIOD, time, spell, while, season, space, interval, span, duration, incumbency **4** CONCLUSION, end, close, finish, culmination, fruition ▷ *verb* CALL, name, label, style, entitle, tag, dub, designate, describe as, denominate

terminal *adjective* **1** FATAL, deadly, lethal, killing, mortal, incurable, inoperable, untreatable **2** FINAL, last, closing, finishing, concluding, ultimate, terminating << ANTONYM initial ▷ *noun* TERMINUS, station, depot, end of the line

terminate *verb* **1** END, stop, conclude, finish, complete, axe (*informal*), cut off, wind up, put an end to, discontinue, pull the plug on (*informal*), belay (*nautical*), bring to an end << ANTONYM begin **2** CEASE, end, close, finish, run out, expire, lapse, come to an end

3 ABORT, end

termination *noun* 1 ENDING, end, close, finish, conclusion, wind-up, completion, cessation, expiry, cut-off point, finis, discontinuation << ANTONYM beginning 2 ABORTION, ending, discontinuation

terminology *noun* LANGUAGE, terms, vocabulary, jargon, cant, lingo (*informal*), nomenclature, patois, phraseology, argot

terminus *noun* END OF THE LINE, terminal, station, depot, last stop, garage

terms *plural noun* 1 LANGUAGE, terminology, phraseology, manner of speaking 2 CONDITIONS, particulars, provisions, provisos, stipulations, qualifications, premises (*law*), specifications 3 RELATIONSHIP, standing, footing, relations, position, status 4 PRICE, rates, charges, fee, payment ▷▷ **come to terms** COME TO AN AGREEMENT, reach agreement, come to an understanding, conclude agreement ▷▷ **come to terms with something** LEARN TO LIVE WITH, come to accept, be reconciled to, reach acceptance of

terrain *noun* GROUND, country, land, landscape, topography, going

terrestrial *adjective* EARTHLY, worldly, global, mundane, sublunary, tellurian, terrene

terrible *adjective* 1 AWFUL, shocking, appalling, terrifying, horrible, dreadful, horrifying, dread, dreaded, fearful, horrendous, monstrous, harrowing, gruesome, horrid, unspeakable, frightful, hellacious (*US slang*) 2 (*informal*) BAD, awful, dreadful, beastly (*informal*), dire, abysmal, abhorrent, poor, offensive, foul, unpleasant, revolting, rotten (*informal*), obscene, hideous, vile, from hell (*informal*), obnoxious, repulsive, frightful, odious, hateful, loathsome, godawful (*slang*) << ANTONYM wonderful 3 SERIOUS, desperate, severe, extreme, bad, dangerous, insufferable << ANTONYM mild

terribly *adverb* 1 VERY MUCH, greatly, very, much, dreadfully, seriously, extremely, gravely, desperately, thoroughly, decidedly, awfully (*informal*), exceedingly 2 EXTREMELY, very, much, greatly, dreadfully, seriously, desperately, thoroughly, decidedly, awfully (*informal*), exceedingly

terrific *adjective* 1 (*informal*) EXCELLENT, great (*informal*), wonderful, mean (*slang*), topping (*Brit slang*), fine, brilliant, very good, cracking (*Brit informal*), amazing, outstanding, smashing (*informal*), superb, fantastic (*informal*), ace (*informal*), magnificent, fabulous (*informal*), marvellous, sensational (*informal*), sovereign, awesome (*slang*), breathtaking, super (*informal*), brill (*informal*), stupendous, bodacious (*slang, chiefly US*), boffo (*slang*), jim-dandy (*slang*), chillin' (*US slang*), booshit (*Austral slang*), exo (*Austral slang*), sik (*Austral slang*), ka pai (*NZ*), rad (*informal*), phat (*slang*), schmick (*Austral informal*) << ANTONYM awful 2 INTENSE, great, huge, terrible, enormous, severe, extreme, awful, tremendous, fierce, harsh, excessive, dreadful, horrific, fearful, awesome, gigantic, monstrous

terrified *adjective* FRIGHTENED, scared, petrified, alarmed, intimidated, awed, panic-stricken, scared to death, scared stiff, terror-stricken, horror-struck, frightened out of your wits

terrify *verb* FRIGHTEN, scare, petrify, alarm, intimidate, terrorize, scare to death, put the fear of God into, make your hair stand on end, fill with terror, make your flesh creep, make your blood run cold, frighten out of your wits

territory *noun* DISTRICT, area, land, region, state, country, sector, zone, province, patch, turf (*US slang*), domain, terrain, tract, bailiwick

terror *noun* 1 FEAR, alarm, dread, fright, panic, anxiety, intimidation, fear and trembling 2 NIGHTMARE, monster, bogeyman, devil, fiend, bugbear, scourge

terrorize *or* **terrorise** *verb* 1 BULLY, menace, intimidate, threaten, oppress, coerce, strong-arm (*informal*), browbeat 2 TERRIFY, alarm, frighten, scare, intimidate, petrify, scare to death, strike terror into, put the fear of God into, fill with terror, frighten out of your wits, inspire panic in

terse *adjective* 1 CURT, abrupt, brusque, short, rude, tart, snappy, gruff << ANTONYM polite 2 CONCISE, short, brief, clipped, neat, to the point, crisp, compact, summary, condensed, incisive, elliptical, laconic, succinct, pithy, monosyllabic, gnomic, epigrammatic, aphoristic, sententious << ANTONYM lengthy

test *verb* 1 CHECK, try, investigate, assess, research, prove, analyse, experiment with, try out, verify, assay, put something to the proof, put something to the test 2 EXAMINE, put someone to the test, put someone through their paces ▷ *noun* 1 TRIAL, research, check, investigation, attempt, analysis, assessment, proof, examination, evaluation, acid test **2** EXAMINATION, paper, assessment, evaluation

testament *noun* **1** PROOF, evidence, testimony, witness, demonstration, tribute, attestation, exemplification **2** (*law*) WILL, last wishes

testify *verb* BEAR WITNESS, state, swear, certify, declare, witness, assert, affirm, depose (*law*), attest, corroborate, vouch, evince, give testimony, asseverate << ANTONYM disprove

testimonial *noun* REFERENCE, recommendation, credential, character, tribute, certificate, endorsement, commendation

testimony *noun* **1** (*law*) EVIDENCE, information, statement, witness, profession, declaration, confirmation, submission, affirmation, affidavit, deposition, corroboration, avowal, attestation **2** PROOF, evidence, demonstration, indication, support, manifestation, verification, corroboration ▷ see **testimonial**

testing *adjective* DIFFICULT, trying, demanding, taxing, challenging, searching, tough, exacting, formidable, rigorous, strenuous, arduous << ANTONYM undemanding

testy *adjective* IRRITABLE, cross, grumpy, crabbed, impatient, snappy, sullen, touchy, bad-tempered, petulant, irascible, cantankerous, peppery, tetchy, ratty (*Brit & NZ informal*), quarrelsome, fretful, short-tempered, waspish, peevish, quick-tempered, splenetic, snappish, liverish, captious

tetchy *adjective* IRRITABLE, cross, grumpy, crabbed, impatient, snappy, sullen, touchy, bad-tempered, petulant, irascible, cantankerous, peppery, ratty (*Brit & NZ informal*), testy, quarrelsome, fretful, short-tempered, waspish, peevish, quick-tempered, splenetic, snappish, liverish, captious

tether *noun* LEASH, rope, lead, bond, chain, restraint, fastening, shackle, fetter, halter ▷ *verb* TIE, secure, bind, chain, rope, restrain, fasten, shackle, leash, fetter, manacle ▷▷ **at the end of your tether** EXASPERATED, exhausted, at your wits' end, finished, out of patience, at the limit of your endurance

text *noun* **1** CONTENTS, words, content, wording, body, matter, subject matter, main body **2** WORDS, wording **3** TRANSCRIPT, script **4** REFERENCE BOOK, textbook, source, reader **5** PASSAGE, extract, line, sentence, paragraph, verse **6** SUBJECT, matter, topic, argument, theme, thesis, motif

texture *noun* FEEL, quality, character, consistency, structure, surface, constitution, fabric, tissue, grain, weave, composition

thank *verb* SAY THANK YOU TO, express gratitude to, show gratitude to, show your appreciation to

thankful *adjective* GRATEFUL, pleased, relieved, obliged, in (someone's) debt, indebted, appreciative, beholden << ANTONYM ungrateful

thankless *adjective* UNREWARDING, unappreciated << ANTONYM rewarding

thanks *plural noun* GRATITUDE, appreciation, thanksgiving, credit, recognition, acknowledgment, gratefulness ▷▷ **thanks to** BECAUSE OF, through, due to, as a result of, owing to, by reason of

thaw *verb* MELT, dissolve, soften, defrost, warm, liquefy, unfreeze << ANTONYM freeze

theatrical *adjective* **1** DRAMATIC, stage, Thespian, dramaturgical **2** EXAGGERATED, dramatic, melodramatic, histrionic, affected, camp (*informal*), mannered, artificial, overdone, unreal, pompous, stilted, showy, ostentatious, hammy (*informal*), ceremonious, stagy, actorly or actressy << ANTONYM natural

theft *noun* STEALING, robbery, thieving, fraud, rip-off (*slang*), swindling, embezzlement, pilfering, larceny, purloining, thievery

theme *noun* **1** MOTIF, leitmotif, recurrent image, unifying idea **2** SUBJECT, idea, topic, matter, argument, text, burden, essence, thesis, subject matter, keynote, gist

theological *adjective* RELIGIOUS, ecclesiastical, doctrinal, divine

theorem *noun* PROPOSITION, statement, formula, rule, principle, thesis, hypothesis, deduction, dictum

theoretical *or* **theoretic** *adjective* **1** ABSTRACT, pure, speculative, ideal, impractical << ANTONYM practical **2** HYPOTHETICAL, academic, notional, unproven, conjectural, postulatory

theorize *or* **theorise** *verb* SPECULATE, conjecture, hypothesize, project, suppose, guess, formulate, propound

theory *noun* **1** HYPOTHESIS, philosophy, system of ideas, plan, system, science, scheme, proposal, principles, ideology, thesis << ANTONYM fact **2** BELIEF, feeling, speculation, assumption, guess, hunch, presumption, conjecture, surmise, supposition

therapeutic *adjective* BENEFICIAL, healing, restorative, good, corrective, remedial, salutary, curative, salubrious, ameliorative, analeptic, sanative << ANTONYM harmful

therapist *noun* PSYCHOLOGIST, analyst, psychiatrist, shrink (*informal*), counsellor, healer, psychotherapist, psychoanalyst, trick cyclist (*informal*)

therapy *noun* REMEDY, treatment, cure, healing, method of healing, remedial treatment

therefore *adverb* CONSEQUENTLY, so, thus, as a result, hence, accordingly, for that reason, whence, thence, ergo

thesaurus *noun* WORDBOOK, wordfinder

thesis *noun* 1 PROPOSITION, theory, hypothesis, idea, view, opinion, proposal, contention, line of argument 2 DISSERTATION, paper, treatise, essay, composition, monograph, disquisition 3 PREMISE, subject, statement, proposition, theme, topic, assumption, postulate, surmise, supposition

thick *adjective* 1 BULKY, broad, big, large, fat, solid, substantial, hefty, plump, sturdy, stout, chunky, stocky, meaty, beefy, thickset << ANTONYM thin 2 WIDE, across, deep, broad, in extent *or* diameter 3 DENSE, close, heavy, deep, compact, impenetrable, lush 4 HEAVY, heavyweight, dense, chunky, bulky, woolly 5 OPAQUE, heavy, dense, impenetrable 6 VISCOUS, concentrated, stiff, condensed, clotted, coagulated, gelatinous, semi-solid, viscid << ANTONYM runny 7 CROWDED, full, packed, covered, filled, bursting, jammed, crawling, choked, crammed, swarming, abundant, bristling, brimming, overflowing, seething, thronged, teeming, congested, replete, chock-full, bursting at the seams, chock-a-block << ANTONYM empty 8 HUSKY, rough, hoarse, distorted, muffled, croaking, inarticulate, throaty, indistinct, gravelly, guttural, raspy, croaky << ANTONYM clear 9 STRONG, marked, broad, decided, rich, distinct, pronounced << ANTONYM slight 10 STUPID, slow, dull, dense, insensitive, dozy (*Brit informal*), dopey (*informal*), moronic, obtuse, brainless, blockheaded, braindead (*informal*), dumb-ass (*informal*), thickheaded, dim-witted (*informal*), slow-witted << ANTONYM clever 11 (*informal*) FRIENDLY, close, intimate, familiar, pally (*informal*), devoted, well in (*informal*), confidential, inseparable, on good terms, chummy (*informal*), hand in glove, buddy-buddy (*slang, chiefly US & Canad*), palsy-walsy (*informal*), matey *or* maty (*Brit informal*) << ANTONYM unfriendly ▷ *noun* MIDDLE, centre, heart, focus, core, midst, hub

thicken *verb* SET, condense, congeal, cake, gel, clot, jell, coagulate, inspissate (*archaic*) << ANTONYM thin

thicket *noun* WOOD, grove, woodland, brake, clump, covert, hurst (*archaic*), copse, coppice, spinney (*Brit*)

thick-skinned *adjective* INSENSITIVE, tough, callous, hardened, hard-boiled (*informal*), impervious, stolid, unfeeling, case-hardened, unsusceptible << ANTONYM sensitive

thief *noun* ROBBER, crook (*informal*), burglar, stealer, bandit, plunderer, mugger (*informal*), shoplifter, embezzler, pickpocket, pilferer, swindler, purloiner, housebreaker, footpad (*archaic*), cracksman (*slang*), larcenist

thin *adjective* 1 NARROW, fine, attenuate, attenuated, threadlike << ANTONYM thick 2 SLIM, spare, lean, slight, slender, skinny, light, meagre, skeletal, bony, lanky, emaciated, spindly, underweight, scrawny, lank, undernourished, skin and bone, scraggy, thin as a rake << ANTONYM fat 3 WATERY, weak, diluted, dilute, runny, rarefied, wishy-washy (*informal*) << ANTONYM viscous 4 MEAGRE, sparse, scanty, poor, scattered, inadequate, insufficient, deficient, paltry << ANTONYM plentiful 5 FINE, delicate, flimsy, sheer, transparent, see-through, translucent, skimpy, gossamer, diaphanous, filmy, unsubstantial << ANTONYM thick 6 UNCONVINCING, inadequate, feeble, poor, weak, slight, shallow, insufficient, superficial, lame, scant, flimsy, scanty, unsubstantial << ANTONYM convincing 7 WISPY, thinning, sparse, scarce, scanty ▷ *verb* 1 PRUNE, trim, cut back, weed out 2 DILUTE, water down, weaken, attenuate

thing *noun* 1 OBJECT, article, implement, machine, device, tool, instrument, mechanism, apparatus, gadget, gizmo (*informal*), contrivance, whatsit (*informal*), doo-dah (*informal*), thingummy (*informal*), thingummyjig (*informal*) 2 SUBSTANCE, stuff, element, being, body, material, fabric, texture, entity 3 CONCEPT, idea, notion, conception 4 MATTER, issue, subject, thought, concern, worry, topic, preoccupation 5 AFFAIR, situation, state of affairs, state, circumstance, scenario

6 FACT, detail, particular, point, factor, piece of information **7** FEATURE, point, detail, something, particular, factor, item, aspect, facet **8** HAPPENING, event, incident, proceeding, phenomenon, occurrence, eventuality **9** (*informal*) PHOBIA, fear, complex, horror, terror, hang-up (*informal*), aversion, neurosis, bee in your bonnet (*informal*) **10** (*informal*) OBSESSION, liking, preoccupation, mania, quirk, fetish, fixation, soft spot, predilection, idée fixe (*French*) **11** REMARK, comment, statement, observation, declaration, utterance, pronouncement ▷ *plural noun* **1** POSSESSIONS, stuff, gear, belongings, goods, effects, clothes, luggage, baggage, bits and pieces, paraphernalia, clobber (*Brit slang*), odds and ends, chattels, impedimenta **2** EQUIPMENT, gear, tool, stuff, tackle, implement, kit, apparatus, utensil, accoutrement **3** CIRCUMSTANCES, the situation, the state of affairs, matters, life, affairs

think *verb* **1** BELIEVE, hold that, be of the opinion, conclude, esteem, conceive, be of the view **2** ANTICIPATE, expect, figure (*US informal*), suppose, imagine, guess (*informal, chiefly US & Canad*), reckon (*informal*), presume, envisage, foresee, surmise **3** JUDGE, consider, estimate, reckon, deem, regard as **4** PONDER, reflect, contemplate, deliberate, brood, meditate, ruminate, cogitate, rack your brains, be lost in thought, cerebrate **5** REMEMBER, recall, recollect, review, think back to, bring to mind, call to mind ▷ *noun* (*informal*) PONDER, consideration, muse, assessment, reflection, deliberation, contemplation ▷▷ **think something over** CONSIDER, contemplate, ponder, reflect upon, give thought to, consider the pros and cons of, weigh up, rack your brains about, chew over (*informal*), mull over, turn over in your mind ▷▷ **think something up** DEVISE, create, imagine, manufacture, come up with, invent, contrive, improvise, visualize, concoct, dream up, trump up

thinker *noun* PHILOSOPHER, intellect (*informal*), wise man, sage, brain (*informal*), theorist, mastermind, mahatma

thinking *noun* REASONING, thoughts, philosophy, idea, view, position, theory, opinion, conclusions, assessment, judgment, outlook, conjecture ▷ *adjective* THOUGHTFUL, intelligent, cultured, reasoning, sophisticated, rational, philosophical, reflective, contemplative, meditative, ratiocinative

third-rate *adjective* MEDIOCRE, bad, inferior, indifferent, poor, duff (*Brit informal*), shoddy, poor-quality, low-grade, no great shakes (*informal*), not much cop (*informal*), cheap-jack, half-pie (*NZ informal*), of a sort or of sorts, ropey *or* ropy (*Brit informal*), bodger *or* bodgie (*Austral slang*)

thirst *noun* **1** DRYNESS, thirstiness, drought, craving to drink **2** CRAVING, hunger, appetite, longing, desire, passion, yen (*informal*), ache, lust, yearning, eagerness, hankering, keenness << ANTONYM aversion

thirsty *adjective* **1** PARCHED, dry, dehydrated **2** *with* **for** EAGER FOR, longing for, hungry for, dying for, yearning for, lusting for, craving for, thirsting for, burning for, hankering for, itching for, greedy for, desirous of, avid for, athirst for

thorn *noun* PRICKLE, spike, spine, barb ▷▷ **thorn in your side** IRRITATION, nuisance, annoyance, trouble, bother, torture, plague, curse, pest, torment, hassle (*informal*), scourge, affliction, irritant, bane

thorny *adjective* **1** PRICKLY, spiky, spiny, pointed, sharp, barbed, bristly, spinous, bristling with thorns **2** TROUBLESOME, difficult, problematic(al), trying, hard, worrying, tough, upsetting, awkward, unpleasant, sticky (*informal*), harassing, irksome, ticklish, vexatious

thorough *adjective* **1** COMPREHENSIVE, full, complete, sweeping, intensive, in-depth, exhaustive, all-inclusive, all-embracing, leaving no stone unturned << ANTONYM cursory **2** CAREFUL, conscientious, painstaking, efficient, meticulous, exhaustive, scrupulous, assiduous << ANTONYM careless **3** COMPLETE, total, absolute, utter, perfect, entire, pure, sheer, outright, downright, unqualified, out-and-out, unmitigated, arrant, deep-dyed (*usually derogatory*) << ANTONYM partial

thoroughbred *adjective* PUREBRED, pedigree, pure-blooded, blood, full-blooded, of unmixed stock << ANTONYM mongrel

thoroughfare *noun* **1** ROAD, way, street, highway, roadway, passageway, avenue **2** ACCESS, way, passage

thoroughly *adverb* **1** CAREFULLY, completely, fully, comprehensively, sweepingly, efficiently, inside out, meticulously, painstakingly, scrupulously, assiduously, intensively, from top to bottom, conscientiously, exhaustively, leaving no

stone unturned << ANTONYM carelessly
2 FULLY, completely, throughout, inside out,
through and through **3** COMPLETELY, quite,
totally, perfectly, entirely, absolutely, utterly,
to the full, downright, to the hilt, without
reservation << ANTONYM partly

though *conjunction* ALTHOUGH, while, even
if, despite the fact that, allowing, granted,
even though, albeit, notwithstanding,
even supposing, tho' (*US poetic*) ▷ *adverb*
NEVERTHELESS, still, however, yet,
nonetheless, all the same, for all that,
notwithstanding

thought *noun* **1** THINKING, consideration,
reflection, deliberation, regard, musing,
meditation, contemplation, introspection,
rumination, navel-gazing (*slang*), cogitation,
brainwork, cerebration **2** OPINION, view,
belief, idea, thinking, concept, conclusion,
assessment, notion, conviction, judgment,
conception, conjecture, estimation
3 CONSIDERATION, study, attention, care,
regard, scrutiny, heed **4** INTENTION, plan,
idea, design, aim, purpose, object, notion
5 HOPE, expectation, dream, prospect,
aspiration, anticipation **6** CONCERN, care,
regard, anxiety, sympathy, compassion,
thoughtfulness, solicitude, attentiveness

thoughtful *adjective* **1** REFLECTIVE, pensive,
contemplative, meditative, thinking,
serious, musing, wistful, introspective,
rapt, studious, lost in thought, deliberative,
ruminative, in a brown study << ANTONYM
shallow **2** CONSIDERATE, kind, caring, kindly,
helpful, attentive, unselfish, solicitous
<< ANTONYM inconsiderate

thoughtless *adjective* **1** INCONSIDERATE,
rude, selfish, insensitive, unkind, uncaring,
indiscreet, tactless, impolite, undiplomatic
<< ANTONYM considerate **2** UNTHINKING,
stupid, silly, careless, regardless, foolish,
rash, reckless, mindless, negligent,
inadvertent, ill-considered, tactless, absent-
minded, imprudent, slapdash, neglectful,
heedless, slipshod, inattentive, injudicious,
remiss, unmindful, unobservant, ditzy *or*
ditzy (*slang*) << ANTONYM wise

thrall *noun* SLAVERY, bondage, servitude,
enslavement, subjugation, serfdom,
subjection, vassalage, thraldom

thrash *verb* **1** DEFEAT, beat, hammer (*informal*),
stuff (*slang*), tank (*slang*), crush, overwhelm,
slaughter (*informal*), lick (*informal*), paste
(*slang*), rout, maul, trounce, clobber (*slang*),
run rings around (*informal*), wipe the

floor with (*informal*), make mincemeat
of (*informal*), blow someone out of the
water (*slang*), drub, beat someone hollow
(*Brit informal*) **2** BEAT, wallop, whip, hide
(*informal*), belt (*informal*), leather, tan (*slang*),
cane, lick (*informal*), paste (*slang*), birch, flog,
scourge, spank, clobber (*slang*), lambast(e),
flagellate, horsewhip, give someone a (good)
hiding (*informal*), drub, take a stick to, beat *or*
knock seven bells out of (*informal*) **3** THRESH,
flail, jerk, plunge, toss, squirm, writhe,
heave, toss and turn ▷▷ **thrash something out**
SETTLE, resolve, discuss, debate, solve, argue
out, have out, talk over

thrashing *noun* **1** DEFEAT, beating,
hammering (*informal*), hiding (*informal*),
pasting (*slang*), rout, mauling, trouncing,
drubbing **2** BEATING, hiding (*informal*),
belting (*informal*), whipping, tanning (*slang*),
lashing, caning, pasting (*slang*), flogging,
drubbing, chastisement

thread *noun* **1** STRAND, fibre, yarn, filament,
line, string, cotton, twine **2** THEME, motif,
train of thought, course, direction, strain,
plot, drift, tenor, story line ▷ *verb* MOVE,
pass, inch, ease, thrust, meander, squeeze
through, pick your way

threadbare *adjective* **1** SHABBY, worn, frayed,
old, ragged, worn-out, scruffy, tattered,
tatty, down at heel << ANTONYM new
2 HACKNEYED, common, tired, stale, corny
(*slang*), stock, familiar, conventional,
stereotyped, commonplace, well-worn,
trite, clichéd, overused, cliché-ridden
<< ANTONYM original

threat *noun* **1** DANGER, risk, hazard, menace,
peril **2** THREATENING REMARK, menace,
commination, intimidatory remark
3 WARNING, foreshadowing, foreboding

threaten *verb* **1** INTIMIDATE, bully, menace,
terrorize, warn, cow, lean on (*slang*),
pressurize, browbeat, make threats
to << ANTONYM defend **2** ENDANGER,
jeopardize, put at risk, imperil, put in
jeopardy, put on the line << ANTONYM
protect **3** BE IMMINENT, hang over, be in
the air, loom, be in the offing, hang over
someone's head, impend

threatening *adjective* **1** MENACING, bullying,
intimidatory, terrorizing, minatory,
comminatory **2** OMINOUS, sinister,
forbidding, grim, baleful, inauspicious,
bodeful << ANTONYM promising

threesome *noun* TRIO, trinity, trilogy, triplet,
triad, triumvirate, troika, triptych, triplex,

trine, triune

threshold *noun* 1 ENTRANCE, doorway, door, doorstep, sill, doorsill 2 START, beginning, opening, dawn, verge, brink, outset, starting point, inception << ANTONYM end 3 LIMIT, margin, starting point, minimum

thrift *noun* ECONOMY, prudence, frugality, saving, parsimony, carefulness, good husbandry, thriftiness << ANTONYM extravagance

thrifty *adjective* ECONOMICAL, prudent, provident, frugal, saving, sparing, careful, parsimonious << ANTONYM extravagant

thrill *noun* 1 PLEASURE, charge (*slang*), kick (*informal*), glow, sensation, buzz (*slang*), high, stimulation, tingle, titillation, flush of excitement << ANTONYM tedium 2 TREMBLING, throb, shudder, flutter, fluttering, tremor, quiver, vibration ▷ *verb* EXCITE, stimulate, arouse, move, send (*slang*), stir, flush, tingle, electrify, titillate, give someone a kick

thrilling *adjective* EXCITING, gripping, stimulating, stirring, sensational, rousing, riveting, electrifying, hair-raising, rip-roaring (*informal*) << ANTONYM boring

thrive *verb* PROSPER, do well, flourish, increase, grow, develop, advance, succeed, get on, boom, bloom, wax, burgeon, grow rich << ANTONYM decline

thriving *adjective* SUCCESSFUL, doing well, flourishing, growing, developing, healthy, booming, wealthy, blooming, prosperous, burgeoning, going strong << ANTONYM unsuccessful

throaty *adjective* HOARSE, husky, gruff, low, deep, thick, guttural

throb *verb* 1 PULSATE, pound, beat, pulse, thump, palpitate 2 VIBRATE, pulse, resonate, pulsate, reverberate, shake, judder (*informal*) ▷ *noun* 1 PULSE, pounding, beat, thump, thumping, pulsating, palpitation 2 VIBRATION, pulse, throbbing, resonance, reverberation, judder (*informal*), pulsation

throes *plural noun* PAINS, spasms, pangs, fit, stabs, convulsions, paroxysm ▷▷ **in the throes of something** IN THE MIDST OF, in the process of, suffering from, struggling with, wrestling with, toiling with, anguished by, agonized by, in the pangs of

throng *noun* CROWD, mob, horde, press, host, pack, mass, crush, jam, congregation, swarm, multitude, concourse, assemblage ▷ *verb* 1 CROWD, flock, congregate, troop, bunch, herd, cram, converge, hem in, mill around,

swarm around << ANTONYM disperse 2 PACK, fill, crowd, press, jam

throttle *verb* 1 STRANGLE, choke, garrotte, strangulate 2 SUPPRESS, inhibit, stifle, control, silence, gag

through *preposition* 1 VIA, by way of, by, between, past, in and out of, from end to end of, from one side to the other of 2 BECAUSE OF, by way of, by means of, by virtue of, with the assistance of, as a consequence or result of 3 USING, via, by way of, by means of, by virtue of, with the assistance of 4 DURING, throughout, in the middle of, for the duration of, in ▷ *adjective* 1 *with* **with** FINISHED WITH, done with, having had enough of 2 COMPLETED, done, finished, ended, terminated ▷▷ **through and through** COMPLETELY, totally, fully, thoroughly, entirely, altogether, wholly, utterly, to the core, unreservedly

throughout *preposition* 1 RIGHT THROUGH, all through, everywhere in, for the duration of, during the whole of, through the whole of, from end to end of 2 ALL OVER, all through, everywhere in, through the whole of, over the length and breadth of ▷ *adverb* 1 FROM START TO FINISH, right through, the whole time, all the time, from the start, all through, from beginning to end 2 ALL THROUGH, right through, in every nook and cranny

throw *verb* 1 HURL, toss, fling, send, project, launch, cast, pitch, shy, chuck (*informal*), propel, sling, lob (*informal*), heave, put 2 TOSS, fling, chuck (*informal*), cast, hurl, sling, heave, put 3 DISLODGE, unseat, upset, overturn, hurl to the ground 4 (*informal*) CONFUSE, baffle, faze, astonish, confound, unnerve, disconcert, perturb, throw you out, throw you off, dumbfound, discompose, put your off your stroke, throw you off your stride, unsettle ▷ *noun* TOSS, pitch, fling, put, cast, shy, sling, lob (*informal*), heave ▷▷ **throw someone off** 1 DISCONCERT, unsettle, faze, throw (*informal*), upset, confuse, disturb, put you off your stroke, throw you off your stride 2 ESCAPE FROM, lose, leave behind, get away from, evade, shake off, elude, outrun, outdistance, give someone the slip, show a clean pair of heels to ▷▷ **throw someone out** EXPEL, eject, evict, dismiss, get rid of, oust, kick out (*informal*), show the door to, turf out (*Brit informal*), give the bum's rush to (*slang*), kiss off (*slang, chiefly US & Canad*) ▷▷ **throw something away** 1 DISCARD, dump (*informal*), get rid of, reject, scrap, axe (*informal*), bin (*informal*), ditch (*slang*), junk (*informal*), chuck (*informal*), throw out, dispose of, dispense with, jettison, cast off **2** WASTE, lose, blow (*slang*), squander, fritter away, fail to make use of, make poor use of ▷▷ **throw something off** CAST OFF, shake off, rid yourself of, free yourself of, drop, abandon, discard ▷▷ **throw something out 1** DISCARD, dump (*informal*), get rid of, reject, scrap, bin (*informal*), ditch (*slang*), junk (*informal*), chuck (*informal*), throw away, dispose of, dispense with, jettison, cast off **2** EMIT, radiate, give off, diffuse, disseminate, put forth ▷▷ **throw something up 1** THROW TOGETHER, jerry-build, run up, slap together *verb* **2** PRODUCE, reveal, bring to light, bring forward, bring to the surface, bring to notice **3** GIVE UP, leave, abandon, quit, chuck (*informal*), resign from, relinquish, renounce, step down from (*informal*), jack in ▷▷ **throw up** (*informal*) VOMIT, be sick, spew, puke (*slang*), chuck (*Austral & NZ informal*), heave, regurgitate, disgorge, retch, barf (*US slang*), chunder (*slang, chiefly Austral*), upchuck (*US slang*), do a technicolour yawn (*slang*), toss your cookies (*US slang*)

throwaway *adjective* (*Chiefly Brit*) CASUAL, passing, offhand, careless, understated, unthinking, ill-considered

thrust *verb* **1** PUSH, force, shove, drive, press, plunge, jam, butt, ram, poke, propel, prod, impel **2** SHOVE, push, shoulder, lunge, jostle, elbow *or* shoulder your way **3** *often with* **through** *or* **into** STAB, stick, jab, pierce ▷ *noun* **1** STAB, pierce, lunge **2** PUSH, shove, poke, prod **3** MOMENTUM, impetus, drive, motive power, motive force, propulsive force

thud *noun* THUMP, crash, knock, smack, clump, wallop (*informal*), clunk, clonk ▷ *verb* THUMP, crash, knock, smack, clump, wallop (*informal*), clunk, clonk

thug *noun* RUFFIAN, hooligan, tough, heavy (*slang*), killer, murderer, robber, gangster, assassin, bandit, mugger (*informal*), cut-throat, bully boy, bruiser (*informal*), tsotsi (*S African*)

thumb *noun* DIGIT ▷ *verb* **1** HANDLE, finger, mark, soil, maul, mess up, dog-ear **2** HITCH, request (*informal*), signal for, hitchhike ▷▷ **all thumbs** CLUMSY, inept, cack-handed (*informal*), maladroit, butterfingered (*informal*), ham-fisted (*informal*), unco (*Austral slang*) ▷▷ **thumb through something** FLICK THROUGH, browse through, leaf through,

glance at, turn over, flip through, skim through, riffle through, scan the pages of, run your eye over ▷▷ **thumbs down** DISAPPROVAL, refusal, rejection, no, rebuff, negation ▷▷ **thumbs up** APPROVAL, go-ahead (*informal*), acceptance, yes, encouragement, green light, affirmation, O.K. *or* okay (*informal*)

thumbnail *adjective* BRIEF, short, concise, quick, compact, succinct, pithy

thump *noun* **1** BLOW, knock, punch, rap, smack, clout (*informal*), whack, swipe, wallop (*informal*) **2** THUD, crash, bang, clunk, thwack ▷ *verb* **1** STRIKE, hit, punch, pound, beat, knock, deck (*slang*), batter, rap, chin (*slang*), smack, thrash, clout (*informal*), whack, swipe, clobber (*slang*), wallop (*informal*), lambast(e), belabour, lay one on (*slang*), beat *or* knock seven bells out of (*informal*) **2** THUD, crash, bang, thwack **3** THROB, pound, beat, pulse, pulsate, palpitate

thumping *adjective* (*slang*) HUGE, massive, enormous, great, impressive, tremendous, excessive, terrific, thundering (*slang*), titanic, gigantic, monumental, mammoth, colossal, whopping (*informal*), stellar (*informal*), exorbitant, gargantuan, elephantine, humongous *or* humungous (*US slang*) << ANTONYM insignificant

thunder *noun* RUMBLE, crash, crashing, boom, booming, explosion, rumbling, pealing, detonation, cracking ▷ *verb* **1** RUMBLE, crash, blast, boom, explode, roar, clap, resound, detonate, reverberate, crack, peal **2** SHOUT, roar, yell, bark, bellow, declaim **3** RAIL, curse, fulminate

thunderous *adjective* LOUD, noisy, deafening, booming, roaring, resounding, tumultuous, ear-splitting

thus *adverb* **1** IN THIS WAY, so, like this, as follows, like so, in this manner, in this fashion, to such a degree **2** THEREFORE, so, hence, consequently, accordingly, for this reason, ergo, on that account

thwart *verb* FRUSTRATE, stop, foil, check, defeat, prevent, oppose, snooker, baffle, hinder, obstruct, impede, balk, outwit, stymie, cook someone's goose (*informal*), put a spoke in someone's wheel (*informal*) << ANTONYM assist

tic *noun* TWITCH, jerk, spasm

tick *noun* **1** CHECK MARK, mark, line, stroke, dash **2** CLICK, tap, tapping, clicking, clack, ticktock **3** (*Brit informal*) MOMENT, second, minute, shake (*informal*), flash, instant, sec (*informal*), twinkling, split second, jiffy (*informal*), trice, half a mo (*Brit informal*), two shakes of a lamb's tail (*informal*), bat of an eye (*informal*) ▷ *verb* 1 MARK, indicate, mark off, check off, choose, select 2 CLICK, tap, clack, ticktock ▷▷ **tick someone off** (*informal, chiefly Brit*) SCOLD, rebuke, tell off (*informal*), lecture, carpet (*informal*), censure, reprimand, reproach, berate, chide, tear into (*informal*), reprove, upbraid, take to task, read the riot act to, bawl out (*informal*), chew out (*US & Canad informal*), tear off a strip (*Brit informal*), haul over the coals (*informal*), give a rocket (*Brit & NZ informal*) ▷▷ **tick something off** MARK OFF, check off, put a tick at

ticket *noun* 1 VOUCHER, pass, coupon, card, slip, certificate, token, chit 2 LABEL, tag, marker, sticker, card, slip, tab, docket

tickle *verb* AMUSE, delight, entertain, please, divert, gratify, titillate << ANTONYM bore

tide *noun* 1 CURRENT, flow, stream, course, ebb, undertow, tideway 2 COURSE, direction, trend, current, movement, tendency, drift ▷▷ **tide someone over** KEEP YOU GOING, see you through, keep the wolf from the door, keep your head above water, bridge the gap for

tidings *plural noun* NEWS, report, word, message, latest (*informal*), information, communication, intelligence, bulletin, gen (*Brit informal*)

tidy *adjective* 1 NEAT, orderly, ordered, clean, trim, systematic, spruce, businesslike, well-kept, well-ordered, shipshape, spick-and-span, trig (*archaic or dialect*), in apple-pie order (*informal*) << ANTONYM untidy 2 ORGANIZED, neat, fastidious, methodical, smart, efficient, spruce, businesslike, well-groomed, well turned out 3 (*informal*) CONSIDERABLE, large, substantial, good, goodly, fair, healthy, generous, handsome, respectable, ample, largish, sizable *or* sizeable << ANTONYM small ▷ *verb* NEATEN, straighten, put in order, order, clean, groom, spruce up, put to rights, put in trim << ANTONYM disorder

tie *verb* 1 FASTEN, bind, join, unite, link, connect, attach, knot, truss, interlace << ANTONYM unfasten 2 TETHER, secure, rope, moor, lash, make fast 3 RESTRICT, limit, confine, hold, bind, restrain, hamper, hinder << ANTONYM free 4 DRAW, be even, be level, be neck and neck, match, equal ▷ *noun* 1 FASTENING, binding, link, band, bond, joint, connection, string, rope, knot,

cord, fetter, ligature 2 BOND, relationship, connection, duty, commitment, obligation, liaison, allegiance, affinity, affiliation, kinship 3 DRAW, dead heat, deadlock, stalemate 4 (*Brit sport*) MATCH, game, contest, fixture, meeting, event, trial, bout 5 ENCUMBRANCE, restriction, limitation, check, handicap, restraint, hindrance, bind (*informal*) ▷▷ **tie in with something** 1 LINK, relate to, connect, be relevant to, come in to, have a bearing on 2 FIT IN WITH, coincide with, coordinate with, harmonize with, occur simultaneously with ▷▷ **tie something up** 1 SECURE, lash, tether, make fast, moor, attach, rope 2 CONCLUDE, settle, wrap up (*informal*), end, wind up, terminate, finish off, bring to a close ▷▷ **tie something** *or* **someone up** BIND, restrain, pinion, truss up

tie in *or* **tie-in** *noun* LINK, connection, relation, relationship, association, tie-up, liaison, coordination, hook-up

tier *noun* ROW, bank, layer, line, order, level, series, file, rank, storey, stratum, echelon

tie-up *noun* LINK, association, connection, relationship, relation, liaison, tie-in, coordination, hook-up, linkup

tiff *noun* QUARREL, row, disagreement, words, difference, dispute, scrap (*informal*), falling-out (*informal*), squabble, petty quarrel

tight *adjective* 1 CLOSE-FITTING, narrow, cramped, snug, constricted, close << ANTONYM loose 2 SECURE, firm, fast, fixed 3 TAUT, stretched, tense, rigid, stiff << ANTONYM slack 4 STRICT, stringent, severe, tough, harsh, stern, rigid, rigorous, uncompromising, inflexible, unyielding << ANTONYM easy-going 5 SEALED, watertight, impervious, sound, proof, hermetic << ANTONYM open 6 CLOSE, even, well-matched, near, hard-fought, evenly-balanced << ANTONYM uneven 7 (*informal*) MISERLY, mean, stingy, close, sparing, grasping, parsimonious, niggardly, penurious, tightfisted << ANTONYM generous 8 DIFFICULT, tough, dangerous, tricky, sticky (*informal*), hazardous, troublesome, problematic, precarious, perilous, worrisome, ticklish 9 (*informal*) DRUNK, intoxicated, flying (*slang*), bombed (*slang*), stoned (*slang*), wasted (*slang*), smashed (*slang*), steaming (*slang*), wrecked (*slang*), out of it (*slang*), plastered (*slang*), blitzed (*slang*), lit up (*slang*), stewed (*slang*), pickled (*informal*), bladdered (*slang*), under the influence (*informal*), tipsy, legless

tighten

(*informal*), paralytic (*informal*), sozzled (*informal*), steamboats (*Scot slang*), tiddly (*slang, chiefly Brit*), half cut (*Brit slang*), zonked (*slang*), blotto (*slang*), inebriated, out to it (*Austral & NZ slang*), three sheets to the wind (*slang*), in your cups, half seas over (*Brit informal*), bevvied (*dialect*), pie-eyed (*slang*) << ANTONYM sober

tighten *verb* 1 CLOSE, narrow, strengthen, squeeze, harden, constrict << ANTONYM slacken 2 STRETCH, strain, tense, tauten, stiffen, rigidify << ANTONYM slacken 3 FASTEN, secure, screw, fix << ANTONYM unfasten

tight-lipped *adjective* SECRETIVE, reticent, uncommunicative, reserved, quiet, silent, mute, taciturn, close-mouthed, unforthcoming, close-lipped

till¹ *verb* CULTIVATE, dig, plough, work, turn over

till² *noun* CASH REGISTER, cash box, cash drawer

tilt *verb* SLANT, tip, slope, list, lean, heel, incline, cant ▷ *noun* 1 SLOPE, angle, inclination, list, pitch, incline, slant, cant, camber, gradient 2 (*medieval history*) JOUST, fight, tournament, lists, clash, set-to (*informal*), encounter, combat, duel, tourney

timber *noun* 1 BEAMS, boards, planks 2 WOOD, logs

timbre *noun* TONE, sound, ring, resonance, colour, tonality, tone colour, quality of sound

time *noun* 1 PERIOD, while, term, season, space, stretch, spell, phase, interval, span, period of time, stint, duration, length of time, time frame, timeline 2 OCCASION, point, moment, stage, instance, point in time, juncture 3 AGE, days, era, year, date, generation, duration, epoch, chronology, aeon 4 TEMPO, beat, rhythm, measure, metre 5 LIFETIME, day, life, season, duration, life span, allotted span 6 HEYDAY, prime, peak, hour, springtime, salad days, best years *or* days ▷ *verb* 1 MEASURE, judge, clock, count 2 SCHEDULE, set, plan, book, programme, set up, fix, arrange, line up, organize, timetable, slate (*US*), fix up, prearrange 3 REGULATE, control, calculate ▷▷ **at one time** ONCE, previously, formerly, for a while, hitherto, once upon a time ▷▷ **at times** SOMETIMES, occasionally, from time to time, now and then, on occasion, once in a while, every now and then, every so often ▷▷ **for the time being** FOR NOW, meanwhile, meantime,

in the meantime, temporarily, for the moment, for the present, pro tem, for the nonce ▷▷ **from time to time** OCCASIONALLY, sometimes, now and then, at times, on occasion, once in a while, every now and then, every so often ▷▷ **in good time** 1 ON TIME, early, ahead of schedule, ahead of time, with time to spare 2 PROMPTLY, quickly, rapidly, swiftly, speedily, with dispatch ▷▷ **in no time** QUICKLY, rapidly, swiftly, in a moment, in a flash, speedily, in an instant, apace, before you know it, in a trice, in a jiffy (*informal*), in two shakes of a lamb's tail (*informal*), before you can say Jack Robinson ▷▷ **in time** 1 ON TIME, on schedule, in good time, at the appointed time, early, with time to spare 2 EVENTUALLY, one day, ultimately, sooner or later, someday, in the fullness of time, by and by ▷▷ **on time** PUNCTUAL(LY), prompt(ly), on schedule, in good time, on the dot ▷▷ **time and again** OVER AND OVER AGAIN, repeatedly, time after time

time-honoured *adjective* LONG-ESTABLISHED, traditional, customary, old, established, fixed, usual, ancient, conventional, venerable, age-old

timeless *adjective* ETERNAL, lasting, permanent, enduring, abiding, immortal, everlasting, ceaseless, immutable, indestructible, undying, ageless, imperishable, deathless, changeless << ANTONYM temporary

timely *adjective* OPPORTUNE, appropriate, well-timed, prompt, suitable, convenient, at the right time, judicious, punctual, propitious, seasonable << ANTONYM untimely

timetable *noun* 1 SCHEDULE, programme, agenda, list, diary, calendar, order of the day 2 SYLLABUS, course, curriculum, programme, teaching programme

timid *adjective* NERVOUS, shy, retiring, modest, shrinking, fearful, cowardly, apprehensive, coy, diffident, bashful, mousy, timorous, pusillanimous, faint-hearted, irresolute << ANTONYM bold

tincture *noun* TINGE, trace, hint, colour, touch, suggestion, shade, flavour, dash, stain, smack, aroma, tint, hue, soupçon (*French*)

tinge *noun* 1 TINT, colour, shade, cast, wash, stain, dye, tincture 2 TRACE, bit, drop, touch, suggestion, dash, pinch, smack, sprinkling, smattering, soupçon (*French*) ▷ *verb* TINT, colour, shade, stain, dye

tingle *verb* PRICKLE, sting, itch, tickle, have

goose pimples ▷ *noun* PRICKLING, stinging, itch, itching, tickle, tickling, pins and needles (*informal*)

tinker *verb* MEDDLE, play, toy, monkey, potter, fiddle (*informal*), dabble, mess about, muck about (*Brit slang*)

tinsel *adjective* SHOWY, flashy, gaudy, cheap, plastic (*slang*), superficial, sham, tawdry, ostentatious, trashy, specious, gimcrack, meretricious, pinchbeck

tint *noun* 1 SHADE, colour, tone, hue, cast 2 DYE, wash, stain, rinse, tinge, tincture 3 HINT, touch, trace, suggestion, shade, tinge ▷ *verb* DYE, colour, stain, rinse, tinge, tincture

tiny *adjective* SMALL, little, minute, slight, mini, wee, miniature, trifling, insignificant, negligible, microscopic, diminutive, petite, puny, pint-sized (*informal*), infinitesimal, teeny-weeny, Lilliputian, dwarfish, teensy-weensy, pygmy *or* pigmy << ANTONYM huge

tip¹ *noun* 1 END, point, head, extremity, sharp end, nib, prong 2 PEAK, top, summit, pinnacle, crown, cap, zenith, apex, spire, acme, vertex ▷ *verb* CAP, top, crown, surmount, finish

tip² *noun* 1 GRATUITY, gift, reward, present, sweetener (*informal*), perquisite, baksheesh, pourboire (*French*) 2 HINT, suggestion, piece of information, piece of advice, gen (*Brit informal*), pointer, piece of inside information ▷ *verb* 1 REWARD, remunerate, give a tip to, sweeten (*informal*) 2 PREDICT, back, recommend, think of

tip³ *verb* 1 POUR, drop, empty, dump, drain, spill, discharge, unload, jettison, offload, slop (*informal*), slosh (*informal*), decant 2 (*Brit*) DUMP, empty, ditch (*slang*), unload, pour out ▷ *noun* (*Brit*) DUMP, midden, rubbish heap, refuse heap ▷▷ **tip off** ADVISE, warn, caution, forewarn, give a clue to, give a hint to, tip someone the wink (*Brit informal*)

tip-off *noun* HINT, word, information, warning, suggestion, clue, pointer, inside information, word of advice

tipple *verb* DRINK, imbibe, tope, indulge (*informal*), swig, quaff, take a drink, bevvy (*dialect*), bend the elbow (*informal*) ▷ *noun* ALCOHOL, drink, booze (*informal*), poison (*informal*), liquor, John Barleycorn

tipsy *adjective* TIDDLY (*slang, chiefly Brit*), fuddled, slightly drunk, happy (*informal*), merry (*Brit informal*), mellow, woozy (*slang, chiefly Brit*)

tirade *noun* OUTBURST, diatribe, harangue, abuse, lecture, denunciation, invective,

fulmination, philippic

tire *verb* 1 EXHAUST, drain, fatigue, weary, fag (*informal*), whack (*Brit informal*), wear out, wear down, take it out of (*informal*), knacker (*slang*), enervate << ANTONYM refresh 2 FLAG, become tired, fail, droop

tired *adjective* 1 EXHAUSTED, fatigued, weary, spent, done in (*informal*), flagging, all in (*slang*), drained, sleepy, fagged (*informal*), whacked (*Brit informal*), worn out, drooping, knackered (*slang*), drowsy, clapped out (*Brit, Austral & NZ informal*), enervated, ready to drop, dog-tired (*informal*), zonked (*slang*), dead beat (*informal*), tuckered out (*Austral & NZ informal*), asleep *or* dead on your feet (*informal*) << ANTONYM energetic 2 BORED, fed up, weary, sick, annoyed, irritated, exasperated, irked, hoha (*NZ*) << ANTONYM enthusiastic about 3 HACKNEYED, stale, well-worn, old, stock, familiar, conventional, corny (*slang*), threadbare, trite, clichéd, outworn << ANTONYM original

tireless *adjective* ENERGETIC, vigorous, industrious, determined, resolute, indefatigable, unflagging, untiring, unwearied << ANTONYM exhausted

tiresome *adjective* BORING, annoying, irritating, trying, wearing, dull, tedious, exasperating, monotonous, laborious, uninteresting, irksome, wearisome, vexatious << ANTONYM interesting

tiring *adjective* EXHAUSTING, demanding, wearing, tough, exacting, fatiguing, wearying, strenuous, arduous, laborious, enervative

tissue *noun* 1 MATTER, material, substance, stuff, structure 2 PAPER, wipe, paper handkerchief, wrapping paper 3 SERIES, pack, collection, mass, network, chain, combination, web, accumulation, fabrication, conglomeration, concatenation

titan *noun* GIANT, superman, colossus, leviathan

titanic *adjective* GIGANTIC, huge, giant, massive, towering, vast, enormous, mighty, immense, jumbo (*informal*), monstrous, mammoth, colossal, mountainous, stellar (*informal*), prodigious, stupendous, herculean, elephantine, humongous *or* humungous (*US slang*)

titbit *or esp US* **tidbit** *noun* DELICACY, goody, dainty, morsel, treat, snack, choice item, juicy bit, bonne bouche (*French*)

tit for tat *noun* RETALIATION, like for like, measure for measure, an eye for an eye, a tooth for a tooth, blow for blow, as good as you get

tithe *noun* TAX, levy, duty, assessment, tribute, toll, tariff, tenth, impost

titillate *verb* EXCITE, stimulate, arouse, interest, thrill, provoke, turn on (*slang*), tease, tickle, tantalize

titillating *adjective* EXCITING, stimulating, interesting, thrilling, arousing, sensational, teasing, provocative, lurid, suggestive, lewd

title *noun* 1 HEADING, name, caption, label, legend, inscription 2 NAME, designation, epithet, term, handle (*slang*), nickname, denomination, pseudonym, appellation, sobriquet, nom de plume, moniker *or* monicker (*slang*) 3 (*sport*) CHAMPIONSHIP, trophy, laurels, bays, crown, honour 4 (*law*) OWNERSHIP, right, claim, privilege, entitlement, tenure, prerogative, freehold ▷ *verb* NAME, call, term, style, label, tag, designate

titter *verb* SNIGGER, laugh, giggle, chuckle, chortle (*informal*), tee-hee, te-hee

toast[1] *verb* 1 BROWN, grill, crisp, roast 2 WARM (UP), heat (up), thaw, bring back to life

toast[2] *noun* 1 TRIBUTE, drink, compliment, salute, health, pledge, salutation 2 FAVOURITE, celebrity, darling, talk, pet, focus of attention, hero *or* heroine, blue-eyed boy *or* girl (*Brit informal*) ▷ *verb* DRINK TO, honour, pledge to, salute, drink (to) the health of

to-do *noun* FUSS, performance (*informal*), disturbance, bother, stir, turmoil, unrest, flap (*informal*), quarrel, upheaval, bustle, furore, uproar, agitation, commotion, rumpus, tumult, brouhaha, ruction (*informal*), hue and cry, hoo-ha

together *adverb* 1 COLLECTIVELY, jointly, closely, as one, with each other, in conjunction, side by side, mutually, hand in hand, as a group, in partnership, in concert, in unison, shoulder to shoulder, cheek by jowl, in cooperation, in a body, hand in glove << ANTONYM separately 2 AT THE SAME TIME, simultaneously, in unison, as one, (all) at once, en masse, concurrently, contemporaneously, with one accord, at one fell swoop ▷ *adjective* (*informal*) SELF-POSSESSED, calm, composed, well-balanced, cool, stable, well-organized, well-adjusted

toil *noun* HARD WORK, industry, labour, effort, pains, application, sweat, graft (*informal*), slog, exertion, drudgery, travail, donkey-work, elbow grease (*informal*), blood, sweat,

and tears (*informal*) << ANTONYM idleness ▷ *verb* 1 LABOUR, work, struggle, strive, grind (*informal*), sweat (*informal*), slave, graft (*informal*), go for it (*informal*), slog, grub, bend over backwards (*informal*), drudge, go for broke (*slang*), push yourself, bust a gut (*informal*), give it your best shot (*informal*), break your neck (*informal*), work like a dog, make an all-out effort (*informal*), work like a Trojan, knock yourself out (*informal*), do your damnedest (*informal*), give it your all (*informal*), work your fingers to the bone, rupture yourself (*informal*) 2 STRUGGLE, trek, slog, trudge, push yourself, fight your way, drag yourself, footslog

toilet *noun* 1 LAVATORY, bathroom, loo (*Brit informal*), bog (*slang*), gents *or* ladies, can (*US & Canad slang*), john (*slang, chiefly US & Canad*), head(s) (*nautical slang*), throne (*informal*), closet, privy, cloakroom (*Brit*), urinal, latrine, washroom, powder room, ablutions (*military informal*), dunny (*Austral & NZ old-fashioned informal*), water closet, khazi (*slang*), pissoir (*French*), little boy's room *or* little girl's room (*informal*), (public) convenience, W.C., bogger (*Austral slang*), brasco (*Austral slang*) 2 BATHROOM, washroom, gents *or* ladies (*Brit informal*), privy, outhouse, latrine, powder room, water closet, pissoir (*French*), ladies' room, little boy's *or* little girl's room, W.C.

token *noun* SYMBOL, mark, sign, note, evidence, earnest, index, expression, demonstration, proof, indication, clue, representation, badge, manifestation ▷ *adjective* NOMINAL, symbolic, minimal, hollow, superficial, perfunctory

tolerable *adjective* 1 BEARABLE, acceptable, allowable, supportable, endurable, sufferable << ANTONYM intolerable 2 (*informal*) FAIR, O.K. *or* okay (*informal*), middling, average, all right, ordinary, acceptable, reasonable, good enough, adequate, indifferent, not bad (*informal*), mediocre, so-so (*informal*), run-of-the-mill, passable, unexceptional, fairly good, fair to middling << ANTONYM dreadful

tolerance *noun* 1 BROAD-MINDEDNESS, charity, sympathy, patience, indulgence, forbearance, permissiveness, magnanimity, open-mindedness, sufferance, lenity << ANTONYM intolerance 2 ENDURANCE, resistance, stamina, fortitude, resilience, toughness, staying power, hardness, hardiness 3 RESISTANCE, immunity, resilience, nonsusceptibility

tolerant *adjective* BROAD-MINDED, understanding, sympathetic, open-minded, patient, fair, soft, catholic, charitable, indulgent, easy-going, long-suffering, lax, lenient, permissive, magnanimous, free and easy, forbearing, kind-hearted, unprejudiced, complaisant, latitudinarian, unbigoted, easy-oasy (*slang*) << ANTONYM intolerant

tolerate *verb* 1 ENDURE, stand, suffer, bear, take, stomach, undergo, swallow, hack (*slang*), abide, put up with (*informal*), submit to, thole (*Scot*) 2 ALLOW, accept, permit, sanction, take, receive, admit, brook, indulge, put up with (*informal*), condone, countenance, turn a blind eye to, wink at << ANTONYM forbid

toleration *noun* 1 ACCEPTANCE, endurance, indulgence, sanction, allowance, permissiveness, sufferance, condonation 2 RELIGIOUS FREEDOM, freedom of conscience, freedom of worship

toll¹ *verb* 1 RING, sound, strike, chime, knell, clang, peal 2 ANNOUNCE, call, signal, warn of ▷ *noun* RINGING, ring, tolling, chime, knell, clang, peal

toll² *noun* 1 CHARGE, tax, fee, duty, rate, demand, payment, assessment, customs, tribute, levy, tariff, impost 2 DAMAGE, cost, loss, roll, penalty, sum, number, roster, inroad 3 ADVERSE EFFECTS, price, cost, suffering, damage, penalty, harm

tomb *noun* GRAVE, vault, crypt, mausoleum, sarcophagus, catacomb, sepulchre, burial chamber

tombstone *noun* GRAVESTONE, memorial, monument, marker, headstone

tome *noun* BOOK, work, title, volume, opus, publication

tone *noun* 1 PITCH, stress, volume, accent, force, strength, emphasis, inflection, intonation, timbre, modulation, tonality 2 VOLUME, timbre, tonality 3 CHARACTER, style, approach, feel, air, effect, note, quality, spirit, attitude, aspect, frame, manner, mood, drift, grain, temper, vein, tenor 4 COLOUR, cast, shade, tint, tinge, hue ▷ *verb* 1 HARMONIZE, match, blend, suit, go well with ▷▷ **tone something down** 1 MODERATE, temper, soften, restrain, subdue, play down, dampen, mitigate, modulate, soft-pedal (*informal*) 2 REDUCE, moderate, soften, lessen ▷▷ **tone something up** GET INTO CONDITION, trim, shape up, freshen, tune up, sharpen

up, limber up, invigorate, get in shape

tongue *noun* 1 LANGUAGE, speech, vernacular, talk, dialect, idiom, parlance, lingo (*informal*), patois, argot 2 UTTERANCE, voice, speech, articulation, verbal expression

tongue-tied *adjective* SPEECHLESS, dumb, mute, inarticulate, dumbstruck, struck dumb, at a loss for words << ANTONYM talkative

tonic *noun* STIMULANT, boost, bracer (*informal*), refresher, cordial, pick-me-up (*informal*), fillip, shot in the arm (*informal*), restorative, livener, analeptic, roborant

too *adverb* 1 ALSO, as well, further, in addition, moreover, besides, likewise, to boot, into the bargain 2 EXCESSIVELY, very, extremely, overly, unduly, unreasonably, inordinately, exorbitantly, immoderately, over- ▷ see **very**

tool *noun* 1 IMPLEMENT, device, appliance, apparatus, machine, instrument, gadget, utensil, contraption, contrivance 2 MEANS, agency, vehicle, medium, agent, intermediary, wherewithal 3 PUPPET, creature, pawn, dupe, stooge (*slang*), jackal, minion, lackey, flunkey, hireling, cat's-paw ▷ *verb* MAKE, work, cut, shape, chase, decorate, ornament

top *noun* 1 PEAK, summit, head, crown, height, ridge, brow, crest, high point, pinnacle, culmination, meridian, zenith, apex, apogee, acme, vertex << ANTONYM bottom 2 LID, cover, cap, cork, plug, stopper, bung 3 FIRST PLACE, head, peak, lead, highest rank, high point ▷ *adjective* 1 HIGHEST, upper, loftiest, furthest up, uppermost, topmost 2 LEADING, best, first, highest, greatest, lead, head, prime, finest, crowning, crack (*informal*), elite, superior, dominant, foremost, pre-eminent << ANTONYM lowest 3 CHIEF, most important, principal, most powerful, highest, lead, head, ruling, leading, main, commanding, prominent, notable, sovereign, eminent, high-ranking, illustrious 4 PRIME, best, select, first-class, capital, quality, choice, excellent, premier, superb, elite, superior, top-class, A1 (*informal*), top-quality, first-rate, top-notch (*informal*), grade A, top-grade ▷ *verb* 1 LEAD, head, command, be at the top of, be first in 2 COVER, coat, garnish, finish, crown, cap, overspread 3 SURPASS, better, beat, improve on, cap, exceed, best, eclipse, go beyond, excel, transcend, outstrip, outdo, outshine << ANTONYM not be as good as 4 REACH THE TOP OF, scale, mount, climb, conquer, crest, ascend, surmount ▷▷ **over the top** EXCESSIVE, too much, going too far, inordinate, over the limit, a bit much (*informal*), uncalled-for, immoderate ▷▷ **top something up 1** FILL (UP), refresh, recharge, refill, replenish, freshen **2** SUPPLEMENT, boost, add to, enhance, augment

topic *noun* SUBJECT, point, question, issue, matter, theme, text, thesis, subject matter

topical *adjective* CURRENT, popular, contemporary, up-to-date, up-to-the-minute, newsworthy

topple *verb* **1** FALL OVER, fall, collapse, tumble, overturn, capsize, totter, tip over, keel over, overbalance, fall headlong **2** KNOCK OVER, upset, knock down, tip over **3** OVERTHROW, overturn, bring down, oust, unseat, bring low

topsy-turvy *adjective* CONFUSED, upside-down, disorderly, chaotic, messy, mixed-up, jumbled, inside-out, untidy, disorganized, disarranged << ANTONYM orderly

torment *verb* **1** TORTURE, pain, distress, afflict, rack, harrow, crucify, agonize, excruciate << ANTONYM comfort **2** TEASE, annoy, worry, trouble, bother, provoke, devil (*informal*), harry, plague, irritate, hound, harass, hassle (*informal*), aggravate (*informal*), persecute, pester, vex, bedevil, chivvy, give someone grief (*Brit & S African*), lead someone a merry dance (*Brit informal*) ▷ *noun* **1** SUFFERING, distress, misery, pain, hell, torture, agony, anguish << ANTONYM bliss **2** TROUBLE, worry, bother, plague, irritation, hassle (*informal*), nuisance, annoyance, bane, pain in the neck (*informal*)

torn *adjective* **1** CUT, split, rent, ripped, ragged, slit, lacerated **2** UNDECIDED, divided, uncertain, split, unsure, wavering, vacillating, in two minds (*informal*), irresolute

tornado *noun* WHIRLWIND, storm, hurricane, gale, cyclone, typhoon, tempest, squall, twister (*US informal*), windstorm

torpor *noun* INACTIVITY, apathy, inertia, lethargy, passivity, laziness, numbness, sloth, stupor, drowsiness, dullness, sluggishness, indolence, languor, listlessness, somnolence, inertness, stagnancy, accidie (*theology*), inanition, torpidity << ANTONYM vigour

torrent *noun* **1** STREAM, flow, rush, flood, tide, spate, cascade, gush, effusion, inundation **2** DOWNPOUR, flood, shower, deluge, rainstorm **3** OUTBURST, stream, barrage, hail, spate, outpouring, effusion

torrid *adjective* **1** HOT, tropical, burning, dry, boiling, flaming, blistering, stifling, fiery, scorched, scorching, sizzling, arid, sultry, sweltering, parched, parching, broiling **2** PASSIONATE, intense, sexy (*informal*), hot, flaming, erotic, ardent, steamy (*informal*), fervent

tortuous *adjective* **1** WINDING, twisting, meandering, bent, twisted, curved, crooked, indirect, convoluted, serpentine, zigzag, sinuous, circuitous, twisty, mazy **2** COMPLICATED, involved, misleading, tricky, indirect, ambiguous, roundabout, deceptive, devious, convoluted, mazy << ANTONYM straightforward

torture *verb* **1** TORMENT, abuse, persecute, afflict, martyr, scourge, molest, crucify, mistreat, ill-treat, maltreat, put on the rack << ANTONYM comfort **2** DISTRESS, torment, worry, trouble, pain, rack, afflict, harrow, agonize, give someone grief (*Brit & S African*), inflict anguish on ▷ *noun* **1** ILL-TREATMENT, abuse, torment, persecution, martyrdom, maltreatment, harsh treatment **2** AGONY, suffering, misery, anguish, hell, distress, torment, heartbreak << ANTONYM bliss

toss *verb* **1** THROW, pitch, hurl, fling, project, launch, cast, shy, chuck (*informal*), flip, propel, sling, lob (*informal*) **2** SHAKE, turn, mix, stir, tumble, agitate, jiggle **3** HEAVE, labour, rock, roll, pitch, lurch, jolt, wallow **4** THRASH (ABOUT), twitch, wriggle, squirm, writhe ▷ *noun* THROW, cast, pitch, shy, fling, lob (*informal*)

tot *noun* **1** INFANT, child, baby, toddler, mite, wean (*Scot*), little one, sprog (*slang*), munchkin (*informal, chiefly US*), rug rat (*slang*), littlie (*Austral informal*), ankle-biter (*Austral slang*), tacker (*Austral slang*) **2** MEASURE, shot (*informal*), finger, nip, slug, dram, snifter (*informal*), toothful ▷▷ **tot something up** (*Chiefly Brit*) ADD UP, calculate, sum (up), total, reckon, compute, tally, enumerate, count up

total *noun* SUM, mass, entirety, grand total, whole, amount, aggregate, totality, full amount, sum total << ANTONYM part ▷ *adjective* COMPLETE, absolute, utter, whole, perfect, entire, sheer, outright, all-out, thorough, unconditional, downright, undisputed, consummate, unqualified, out-and-out, overarching, unmitigated, thoroughgoing, arrant, deep-dyed (*usually derogatory*) << ANTONYM partial ▷ *verb* **1** AMOUNT TO, make, come to, reach, equal, run to, number, add up to, correspond to, work out as, mount up to, tot up to **2** ADD UP, work out, sum up, compute, reckon, tot up << ANTONYM subtract

totalitarian *adjective* DICTATORIAL, authoritarian, one-party, oppressive, undemocratic, monolithic, despotic, tyrannous << ANTONYM democratic

totality *noun* **1** ENTIRETY, unity, fullness, wholeness, completeness, entireness **2** AGGREGATE, whole, entirety, all, total, sum, sum total

totally *adverb* COMPLETELY, entirely, absolutely, quite, perfectly, fully, comprehensively, thoroughly, wholly, utterly, consummately, wholeheartedly, unconditionally, to the hilt, one hundred per cent, unmitigatedly << ANTONYM partly

totter *verb* **1** STAGGER, stumble, reel, sway, falter, lurch, wobble, walk unsteadily **2** SHAKE, sway, rock, tremble, quake, shudder, lurch, waver, quiver, vibrate, teeter, judder

touch *verb* **1** FEEL, handle, finger, stroke, brush, make contact with, graze, caress, fondle, lay a finger on, palpate **2** COME INTO CONTACT, meet, contact, border, brush, come together, graze, adjoin, converge, be in contact, abut, impinge upon **3** TAP, hit, strike, push, pat **4** AFFECT, mark, involve, strike, get to (*informal*), influence, inspire, impress, get through to, have an effect on, make an impression on **5** CONSUME, take, drink, eat, partake of **6** MOVE, upset, stir, disturb, melt, soften, tug at someone's heartstrings (*often facetious*), leave an impression on **7** MATCH, rival, equal, compare with, parallel, come up to, come near, be on a par with, be a match for, hold a candle to (*informal*), be in the same league as **8** GET INVOLVED IN, use, deal with, handle, have to do with, be a party to, concern yourself with **9** REACH, hit (*informal*), come to, rise to, arrive at, attain, get up to ▷ *noun* **1** CONTACT, push, stroke, brush, press, tap, poke, nudge, prod, caress, fondling **2** FEELING, feel, handling, physical contact, palpation, tactility **3** BIT, spot, trace, drop, taste, suggestion, hint, dash, suspicion, pinch, smack, small amount, tinge, whiff, jot, speck, smattering, intimation, tincture **4** STYLE, approach, method, technique, way, manner, characteristic, trademark, handiwork **5** AWARENESS, understanding, acquaintance,

familiarity **6** COMMUNICATION, contact, association, connection, correspondence **7** SKILL, ability, flair, art, facility, command, craft, mastery, knack, artistry, virtuosity, deftness, adroitness **8** INFLUENCE, hand, effect, management, direction ▷▷ **touch and go** RISKY, close, near, dangerous, critical, tricky, sticky (*informal*), hazardous, hairy (*slang*), precarious, perilous, nerve-racking, parlous ▷▷ **touch on** *or* **upon something** REFER TO, cover, raise, deal with, mention, bring in, speak of, hint at, allude to, broach, make allusions to ▷▷ **touch something off** **1** TRIGGER (OFF), start, begin, cause, provoke, set off, initiate, arouse, give rise to, ignite, stir up, instigate, spark off, set in motion, foment **2** IGNITE, light, fire, set off, detonate, put a match to ▷▷ **touch something up** **1** ENHANCE, revamp, renovate, patch up, brush up, gloss over, polish up, retouch, titivate, give a face-lift to **2** IMPROVE, perfect, round off, enhance, dress up, finish off, embellish, put the finishing touches to

touched *adjective* **1** MOVED, affected, upset, impressed, stirred, disturbed, melted, softened, swayed **2** MAD, crazy, nuts (*slang*), daft (*informal*), batty (*slang*), cuckoo (*informal*), barmy (*slang*), nutty (*slang*), bonkers (*slang, chiefly Brit*), loopy (*informal*), crackpot (*informal*), out to lunch (*informal*), gonzo (*slang*), not all there, doolally (*slang*), off your trolley (*slang*), up the pole (*informal*), soft in the head (*informal*), not right in the head, off your rocker (*slang*), nutty as a fruitcake (*slang*), wacko *or* whacko (*informal*), off the air (*Austral slang*)

touching *adjective* MOVING, affecting, sad, stirring, tender, melting, pathetic, poignant, heartbreaking, emotive, pitiful, pitiable, piteous

touchstone *noun* STANDARD, measure, par, criterion, norm, gauge, yardstick

touchy *adjective* **1** OVERSENSITIVE, irritable, bad-tempered, cross, crabbed, grumpy, surly, petulant, irascible, tetchy, ratty (*Brit & NZ informal*), testy, thin-skinned, grouchy (*informal*), querulous, peevish, quick-tempered, splenetic, easily offended, captious, pettish, toey (*NZ slang*) << ANTONYM thick-skinned **2** DELICATE, sensitive, tricky, risky, sticky (*informal*), thorny, knotty, ticklish

tough *adjective* **1** STRONG, determined, aggressive, high-powered, feisty (*informal, chiefly US & Canad*), hard-nosed (*informal*), self-confident, unyielding, hard as nails, self-assertive, badass (*slang, chiefly US*) << ANTONYM weak **2** HARDY, strong, seasoned, fit, strapping, hardened, vigorous, sturdy, stout, stalwart, resilient, brawny, hard as nails **3** VIOLENT, rough, vicious, ruthless, pugnacious, hard-bitten, ruffianly **4** STRICT, severe, stern, hard, firm, exacting, adamant, resolute, draconian, intractable, inflexible, merciless, unforgiving, unyielding, unbending << ANTONYM lenient **5** HARD, difficult, exhausting, troublesome, uphill, strenuous, arduous, thorny, laborious, irksome **6** RESILIENT, hard, resistant, durable, strong, firm, solid, stiff, rigid, rugged, sturdy, inflexible, cohesive, tenacious, leathery, hard-wearing, robust << ANTONYM fragile ▷ *noun* RUFFIAN, heavy (*slang*), rough (*informal*), bully, thug, hooligan, brute, rowdy, bravo, bully boy, bruiser (*informal*), roughneck (*slang*), tsotsi (*S African*)

tour *noun* **1** CIRCUIT, course, round **2** JOURNEY, expedition, excursion, trip, progress, outing, jaunt, junket, peregrination ▷ *verb* **1** TRAVEL ROUND, holiday in, travel through, journey round, trek round, go on a trip through **2** VISIT, explore, go round, inspect, walk round, drive round, sightsee

tourist *noun* TRAVELLER, journeyer, voyager, tripper, globetrotter, holiday-maker, sightseer, excursionist

tournament *noun* **1** COMPETITION, meeting, match, event, series, contest **2** (*medieval history*) JOUST, the lists, tourney

tousled *adjective* DISHEVELLED, disordered, tangled, ruffled, messed up, rumpled, disarranged, disarrayed

tout *verb* **1** (*informal*) RECOMMEND, promote, endorse, support, tip, urge, approve, praise, commend, speak well of **2** SOLICIT, canvass, drum up, bark (*US informal*), spiel ▷ *noun* SELLER, solicitor, barker, canvasser, spieler

tow *verb* DRAG, draw, pull, trail, haul, tug, yank, hale, trawl, lug

towards *preposition* **1** IN THE DIRECTION OF, to, for, on the way to, on the road to, en route for **2** REGARDING, about, concerning, respecting, in relation to, with regard to, with respect to, apropos **3** JUST BEFORE, nearing, close to, coming up to, almost at, getting on for, shortly before

tower *noun* **1** COLUMN, pillar, turret, belfry, steeple, obelisk **2** STRONGHOLD, castle, fort, refuge, keep, fortress, citadel, fortification ▷ *verb often with* **over** RISE, dominate, loom, top, mount, rear, soar, overlook, surpass, transcend, ascend, be head and shoulders above, overtop

towering *adjective* **1** TALL, high, great, soaring, elevated, gigantic, lofty, colossal **2** IMPRESSIVE, imposing, supreme, striking, extraordinary, outstanding, magnificent, superior, paramount, surpassing, sublime, stellar (*informal*), prodigious, transcendent **3** INTENSE, violent, extreme, excessive, burning, passionate, mighty, fiery, vehement, inordinate, intemperate, immoderate

toxic *adjective* POISONOUS, deadly, lethal, harmful, pernicious, noxious, septic, pestilential, baneful (*archaic*) << ANTONYM harmless

toy *noun* PLAYTHING, game, doll ▷▷ **toy with something** PLAY WITH, consider, trifle with, flirt with, dally with, entertain the possibility of, amuse yourself with, think idly of

trace *noun* **1** BIT, drop, touch, shadow, suggestion, hint, dash, suspicion, tinge, trifle, whiff, jot, tincture, iota **2** REMNANT, remains, sign, record, mark, evidence, indication, token, relic, vestige **3** TRACK, trail, footstep, path, slot, footprint, spoor, footmark ▷ *verb* **1** SEARCH FOR, follow, seek out, track, determine, pursue, unearth, ascertain, hunt down **2** FIND, track (down), discover, trail, detect, unearth, hunt down, ferret out, locate **3** OUTLINE, chart, sketch, draw, map out, depict, mark out, delineate **4** COPY, map, draft, outline, sketch, reproduce, draw over

track *noun* **1** PATH, way, road, route, trail, pathway, footpath **2** COURSE, line, path, orbit, trajectory, flight path **3** LINE, rail, tramline ▷ *verb* FOLLOW, pursue, chase, trace, tail (*informal*), dog, shadow, trail, stalk, hunt down, follow the trail of ▷▷ **keep track of something** *or* **someone** KEEP UP WITH, follow, monitor, watch, keep an eye on, keep in touch with, keep up to date with ▷▷ **lose track of something** *or* **someone** LOSE, lose sight of, misplace ▷▷ **track something** *or* **someone down** FIND, catch, capture, apprehend, discover, expose, trace, unearth, dig up, hunt down, sniff out, bring to light, ferret out, run to earth *or* ground

tracks *plural noun* TRAIL, marks, impressions, traces, imprints, prints

tract[1] *noun* AREA, lot, region, estate, district, stretch, quarter, territory, extent, zone, plot, expanse

tract[2] *noun* TREATISE, essay, leaflet, brochure, booklet, pamphlet, dissertation, monograph, homily, disquisition, tractate

traction *noun* GRIP, resistance, friction, adhesion, purchase

trade *noun* 1 COMMERCE, business, transactions, buying and selling, dealing, exchange, traffic, truck, barter 2 JOB, employment, calling, business, line, skill, craft, profession, occupation, pursuit, line of work, métier, avocation 3 EXCHANGE, deal, swap, interchange ▷ *verb* 1 DEAL, do business, buy and sell, exchange, traffic, truck, bargain, peddle, barter, transact, cut a deal, have dealings 2 EXCHANGE, switch, swap, barter 3 OPERATE, run, deal, do business

trader *noun* DEALER, marketer, buyer, broker, supplier, merchant, seller, purveyor, merchandiser

tradesman *noun* CRAFTSMAN, workman, artisan, journeyman, skilled worker

tradition *noun* 1 CUSTOMS, institution, ritual, folklore, lore, praxis, tikanga (NZ) 2 ESTABLISHED PRACTICE, custom, convention, habit, ritual, unwritten law

traditional *adjective* 1 OLD-FASHIONED, old, established, conventional, fixed, usual, transmitted, accustomed, customary, ancestral, long-established, unwritten, time-honoured << ANTONYM revolutionary 2 FOLK, old, historical

traffic *noun* 1 TRANSPORT, movement, vehicles, transportation, freight, coming and going 2 TRADE, dealing, commerce, buying and selling, business, exchange, truck, dealings, peddling, barter, doings ▷ *verb often with* in TRADE, market, deal, exchange, truck, bargain, do business, buy and sell, peddle, barter, cut a deal, have dealings, have transactions

tragedy *noun* DISASTER, catastrophe, misfortune, adversity, calamity, affliction, whammy (*informal, chiefly US*), bummer (*slang*), grievous blow << ANTONYM fortune

tragic *or* **tragical** *adjective* 1 DISTRESSING, shocking, sad, awful, appalling, fatal, deadly, unfortunate, disastrous, dreadful, dire, catastrophic, grievous, woeful, lamentable, ruinous, calamitous, wretched, ill-starred, ill-fated << ANTONYM fortunate 2 SAD, miserable, dismal, pathetic, heartbreaking, anguished, mournful, heart-rending, sorrowful, doleful, pitiable << ANTONYM happy

trail *noun* 1 PATH, track, route, way, course, road, pathway, footpath, beaten track 2 TRACKS, path, mark, marks, wake, trace, scent, footsteps, footprints, spoor 3 WAKE, stream, tail, slipstream ▷ *verb* 1 FOLLOW, track, chase, pursue, dog, hunt, shadow, trace, tail (*informal*), hound, stalk, keep an eye on, keep tabs on (*informal*), run to ground 2 DRAG, draw, pull, sweep, stream, haul, tow, dangle, droop 3 LAG, follow, drift, wander, linger, trudge, fall behind, plod, meander, amble, loiter, straggle, traipse (*informal*), dawdle, hang back, tag along (*informal*), bring up the rear, drag yourself ▷▷ **trail away** *or* **off** FADE AWAY *or* OUT, sink, weaken, diminish, decrease, dwindle, shrink, lessen, subside, fall away, peter out, die away, tail off, taper off, grow weak, grow faint

train *verb* 1 INSTRUCT, school, prepare, improve, coach, teach, guide, discipline, rear, educate, drill, tutor, rehearse 2 EXERCISE, prepare, work out, practise, do exercise, get into shape 3 AIM, point, level, position, direct, focus, sight, line up, turn on, fix on, zero in, bring to bear ▷ *noun* 1 CONVOY, file, rank, string, column, queue, succession, caravan, procession, progression, cavalcade 2 SEQUENCE, series, chain, string, set, course, order, cycle, trail, succession, progression, concatenation 3 TAIL, trail, appendage 4 RETINUE, following, entourage, court, staff, household, suite, cortège

trainer *noun* COACH, manager, guide, adviser, tutor, instructor, counsellor, guru, handler

training *noun* INSTRUCTION, practice, schooling, grounding, education, preparation, exercise, working out, body building, tutelage

traipse *or* **trapse** *verb* (*informal*) TRUDGE, trail, tramp, slouch, drag yourself, footslog ▷ *noun* TRUDGE, trek, tramp, slog, long walk

trait *noun* CHARACTERISTIC, feature, quality, attribute, quirk, peculiarity, mannerism, idiosyncrasy, lineament

traitor *noun* BETRAYER, deserter, turncoat, deceiver, informer, renegade, defector, Judas, double-crosser (*informal*), quisling, apostate, miscreant, fifth columnist, snake in the grass (*informal*), back-stabber, fizgig (*Austral slang*) << ANTONYM loyalist

trajectory *noun* PATH, line, course, track, flight, route, flight path

tramp *verb* 1 TRUDGE, march, stamp, stump,

toil, plod, traipse (*informal*), walk heavily
2 HIKE, walk, trek, roam, march, range,
ramble, slog, rove, yomp, footslog ▷ *noun*
1 VAGRANT, bum (*informal*), derelict, drifter,
down-and-out, hobo (*chiefly US*), vagabond,
bag lady (*chiefly US*), dosser (*Brit slang*), derro
(*Austral slang*) **2** TREAD, stamp, footstep,
footfall **3** HIKE, march, trek, ramble, slog

trample *verb often with* **on**, **upon** *or* **over**
STAMP, crush, squash, tread, flatten, run
over, walk over

trance *noun* DAZE, dream, spell, ecstasy,
muse, abstraction, rapture, reverie, stupor,
unconsciousness, hypnotic state

tranquil *adjective* **1** PEACEFUL, quiet, calm,
serene, still, cool, pacific, composed, at
peace, sedate, placid, undisturbed, restful,
untroubled, unperturbed, unruffled,
unexcited **2** CALM, quiet, peaceful, serene,
still, cool, pacific, composed, sedate,
placid, undisturbed, restful, untroubled,
unperturbed, unruffled, unexcited
<< ANTONYM troubled

tranquillity *or* (*sometimes*) *US* **tranquility**
noun **1** PEACE, calm, quiet, hush,
composure, serenity, stillness, coolness,
repose, rest, calmness, equanimity,
quietness, peacefulness, quietude,
placidity, restfulness, sedateness **2** CALM,
peace, composure, serenity, stillness,
coolness, repose, calmness, equanimity,
quietness, peacefulness, quietude, placidity,
imperturbability, restfulness, sedateness
<< ANTONYM agitation

tranquillizer, tranquilliser *or* *US* **tranquilizer**
noun SEDATIVE, opiate, barbiturate, downer
(*slang*), red (*slang*), bromide

transact *verb* CARRY OUT, handle, conduct, do,
manage, perform, settle, conclude, negotiate,
carry on, accomplish, execute, take care of,
discharge, see to, prosecute, enact

transaction *noun* **1** DEAL, matter, affair,
negotiation, business, action, event,
proceeding, enterprise, bargain, coup,
undertaking, deed, occurrence **2** *plural*
RECORDS, minutes, affairs, proceedings,
goings-on (*informal*), annals, doings

transcend *verb* SURPASS, exceed, go beyond,
rise above, leave behind, eclipse, excel,
outstrip, outdo, outshine, overstep, go above,
leave in the shade (*informal*), outrival, outvie

transcendence *or* **transcendency** *noun*
GREATNESS, excellence, superiority,
supremacy, ascendancy, pre-eminence,
sublimity, paramountcy, incomparability,
matchlessness

transcendent *adjective* UNPARALLELED,
unique, extraordinary, superior, exceeding,
sublime, consummate, unrivalled, second
to none, pre-eminent, transcendental,
incomparable, peerless, unequalled,
matchless

transcribe *verb* **1** WRITE OUT, reproduce,
take down, copy out, note, transfer, set
out, rewrite **2** (*music*) TRANSLATE, interpret,
render, transliterate

transcript *noun* COPY, record, note, summary,
notes, version, carbon, log, translation,
manuscript, reproduction, duplicate,
transcription, carbon copy, transliteration,
written version

transfer *verb* MOVE, carry, remove, transport,
shift, transplant, displace, relocate,
transpose, change ▷ *noun* TRANSFERENCE,
move, removal, handover, change, shift,
transmission, translation, displacement,
relocation, transposition

transfix *verb* STUN, hold, fascinate, paralyse,
petrify, mesmerize, hypnotize, stop dead,
root to the spot, engross, rivet the attention
of, spellbind, halt *or* stop in your tracks
<< ANTONYM bore

transform *verb* **1** CHANGE, convert, alter,
translate, reconstruct, metamorphose,
transmute, renew, transmogrify (*jocular*)
2 MAKE OVER, overhaul, revamp, remake,
renovate, remodel, revolutionize, redo,
transfigure, restyle

transformation *noun* **1** CHANGE, conversion,
alteration, metamorphosis, transmutation,
renewal, transmogrification (*jocular*)
2 REVOLUTION, radical change, sea change,
revolutionary change, transfiguration

transgress *verb* **1** MISBEHAVE, sin, offend,
break the law, err, lapse, fall from grace, go
astray, be out of order, do *or* go wrong **2** GO
BEYOND, exceed, infringe, overstep, break,
defy, violate, trespass, contravene, disobey,
encroach upon

transgression *noun* CRIME, wrong, fault,
error, offence, breach, sin, lapse, violation,
wrongdoing, infringement, trespass,
misdemeanour, misdeed, encroachment,
misbehaviour, contravention, iniquity,
peccadillo, infraction

transient *adjective* BRIEF, passing, short-term,
temporary, short, flying, fleeting, short-lived,
fugitive, momentary, ephemeral, transitory,
evanescent, impermanent, here today and
gone tomorrow, fugacious << ANTONYM

lasting

transit *noun* MOVEMENT, transfer, transport, passage, travel, crossing, motion, transportation, carriage, shipment, traverse, conveyance, portage ▷ *verb* PASS, travel, cross, journey, traverse, move ▷▷ **in transit** EN ROUTE, on the way, on the road, on the move, in motion, on the go (*informal*), on the journey, while travelling, during transport, during passage

transition *noun* CHANGE, passing, development, shift, passage, conversion, evolution, transit, upheaval, alteration, progression, flux, metamorphosis, changeover, transmutation, metastasis

transitional *adjective* 1 CHANGING, passing, fluid, intermediate, unsettled, developmental, transitionary 2 TEMPORARY, working, acting, short-term, interim, fill-in, caretaker, provisional, makeshift, make-do, stopgap, pro tem

transitory *adjective* SHORT-LIVED, short, passing, brief, short-term, temporary, fleeting, transient, flying, momentary, ephemeral, evanescent, impermanent, here today and gone tomorrow, fugacious << ANTONYM lasting

translate *verb* 1 RENDER, put, change, convert, interpret, decode, transcribe, construe, paraphrase, decipher, transliterate 2 PUT IN PLAIN ENGLISH, explain, make clear, clarify, spell out, simplify, gloss, unravel, decode, paraphrase, decipher, elucidate, rephrase, reword, state in layman's language 3 CONVERT, change, turn, transform, alter, render, metamorphose, transmute, transfigure 4 TRANSFER, move, send, relocate, carry, remove, transport, shift, convey, transplant, transpose

translation *noun* 1 INTERPRETATION, version, rendering, gloss, rendition, decoding, transcription, paraphrase, transliteration 2 CONVERSION, change, rendering, transformation, alteration, metamorphosis, transfiguration, transmutation

translator *noun* INTERPRETER, transcriber, paraphraser, decipherer, linguist, metaphrast, paraphrast, transliterator

translucent *adjective* SEMITRANSPARENT, clear, limpid, lucent, diaphanous, pellucid

transmission *noun* 1 TRANSFER, spread, spreading, communication, passing on, circulation, dispatch, relaying, mediation, imparting, diffusion, transference, dissemination, conveyance, channeling

2 BROADCASTING, showing, putting out, relaying, sending 3 PROGRAMME, broadcast, show, production, telecast

transmit *verb* 1 BROADCAST, put on the air, televise, relay, send, air, radio, send out, disseminate, beam out 2 PASS ON, carry, spread, communicate, take, send, forward, bear, transfer, transport, hand on, convey, dispatch, hand down, diffuse, remit, impart, disseminate

transmute *verb* TRANSFORM, change, convert, alter, metamorphose, transfigure, alchemize

transparency *noun* 1 PHOTOGRAPH, slide, exposure, photo, picture, image, print, plate, still 2 CLARITY, translucency, translucence, clearness, limpidity, transparence, diaphaneity, filminess, diaphanousness, gauziness, limpidness, pellucidity, pellucidness, sheerness << ANTONYM opacity 3 FRANKNESS, openness, candour, directness, forthrightness, straightforwardness << ANTONYM ambiguity

transparent *adjective* 1 CLEAR, sheer, see-through, lucid, translucent, crystal clear, crystalline, limpid, lucent, diaphanous, gauzy, filmy, pellucid << ANTONYM opaque 2 FRANK, open, direct, straight, straightforward, candid, forthright, unequivocal, unambiguous, plain-spoken << ANTONYM unclear 3 OBVIOUS, plain, apparent, visible, bold, patent, evident, distinct, explicit, easy, understandable, manifest, recognizable, unambiguous, undisguised, as plain as the nose on your face (*informal*), perspicuous << ANTONYM uncertain

transpire *verb* 1 BECOME KNOWN, emerge, come out, be discovered, come to light, be disclosed, be made public 2 (*informal*) HAPPEN, occur, take place, arise, turn up, come about, come to pass (*archaic*)

transplant *verb* 1 (*surgery*) IMPLANT, transfer, graft 2 TRANSFER, take, bring, carry, remove, transport, shift, convey, fetch, displace, relocate, uproot

transport *verb* 1 CONVEY, take, run, move, bring, send, carry, bear, remove, ship, transfer, deliver, conduct, shift, ferry, haul, fetch 2 ENRAPTURE, move, delight, entrance, enchant, carry away, captivate, electrify, ravish, spellbind 3 EXILE, banish, deport, sentence to transportation ▷ *noun* 1 VEHICLE, wheels (*informal*), transportation, conveyance 2 TRANSFERENCE, carrying, shipping, delivery, distribution, removal, transportation, carriage, shipment, freight, haulage, conveyance, freightage **3** *often plural* ECSTASY, delight, heaven, happiness, bliss, euphoria, rapture, enchantment, cloud nine (*informal*), seventh heaven, ravishment << ANTONYM despondency

transpose *verb* **1** TRANSPLANT, move, transfer, shift, displace, relocate, reposition **2** INTERCHANGE, switch, swap, reorder, change, move, exchange, substitute, alter, rearrange

transverse *adjective* CROSSWAYS, diagonal, oblique, crosswise, athwart

trap *noun* **1** SNARE, net, booby trap, gin, toils (*old-fashioned*), pitfall, noose, springe **2** AMBUSH, set-up (*informal*), device, lure, bait, honey trap, ambuscade (*old-fashioned*) **3** TRICK, set-up (*informal*), deception, ploy, ruse, artifice, trickery, subterfuge, stratagem, wile, device ▷ *verb* **1** CATCH, snare, ensnare, entrap, take, corner, bag, lay hold of, enmesh, lay a trap for, run to earth *or* ground **2** TRICK, fool, cheat, lure, seduce, deceive, dupe, beguile, gull, cajole, ensnare, hoodwink, wheedle, inveigle **3** CAPTURE, catch, arrest, seize, take, lift (*slang*), secure, nail (*informal*), collar (*informal*), nab (*informal*), apprehend, take prisoner, take into custody

trapped *adjective* CAUGHT, cornered, snared, ensnared, stuck (*informal*), netted, surrounded, cut off, at bay, in a tight corner, in a tight spot, with your back to the wall

trappings *plural noun* ACCESSORIES, trimmings, paraphernalia, finery, things, fittings, dress, equipment, gear, fixtures, decorations, furnishings, ornaments, livery, adornments, panoply, accoutrements, fripperies, bells and whistles, raiment (*archaic or poetic*)

trash *noun* **1** NONSENSE, rubbish, garbage (*informal*), rot, pants (*slang*), crap (*slang*), hot air (*informal*), tosh (*slang, chiefly Brit*), pap, bilge (*informal*), drivel, twaddle, tripe (*informal*), guff (*slang*), moonshine, hogwash, hokum (*slang, chiefly US & Canad*), piffle (*informal*), poppycock (*informal*), inanity, balderdash, bosh (*informal*), eyewash (*informal*), kak (*S African taboo slang*), trumpery, tommyrot, foolish talk, horsefeathers (*US slang*), bunkum *or* buncombe (*chiefly US*), bizzo (*Austral slang*), bull's wool (*Austral & NZ slang*) << ANTONYM sense 2 (*Chiefly US & Canad*) LITTER, refuse, waste, rubbish, sweepings, junk (*informal*),

garbage, dross, dregs, dreck (*slang, chiefly US*), offscourings

trashy *adjective* WORTHLESS, cheap, inferior, shabby, flimsy, shoddy, tawdry, tinsel, thrown together, crappy (*slang*), meretricious, rubbishy, poxy (*slang*), catchpenny, cheap-jack (*informal*), of a sort *or* of sorts << ANTONYM excellent

trauma *noun* **1** SHOCK, suffering, worry, pain, stress, upset, strain, torture, distress, misery, disturbance, ordeal, anguish, upheaval, jolt **2** (*pathology*) INJURY, damage, hurt, wound, agony

traumatic *adjective* SHOCKING, upsetting, alarming, awful, disturbing, devastating, painful, distressing, terrifying, scarring, harrowing << ANTONYM calming

travel *verb* **1** GO, journey, proceed, make a journey, move, walk, cross, tour, progress, wander, trek, voyage, roam, ramble, traverse, rove, take a trip, make your way, wend your way **2** BE TRANSMITTED, move, advance, proceed, get through ▷ *noun usually plural* JOURNEY, wandering, expedition, globetrotting, walk, tour, touring, movement, trip, passage, voyage, excursion, ramble, peregrination

traveller *noun* **1** VOYAGER, tourist, passenger, journeyer, explorer, hiker, tripper, globetrotter, holiday-maker, wayfarer, excursionist **2** TRAVELLING SALESMAN, representative, rep, salesman, sales rep, commercial traveller, agent

travelling *adjective* ITINERANT, moving, touring, mobile, wandering, unsettled, roaming, migrant, restless, roving, nomadic, migratory, peripatetic, wayfaring

traverse *verb* **1** CROSS, go across, travel over, make your way across, cover, range, bridge, negotiate, wander, go over, span, roam, ply **2** CUT ACROSS, pass over, stretch across, extend across, lie across

travesty *noun* MOCKERY, distortion, parody, caricature, sham, send-up (*Brit informal*), spoof (*informal*), perversion, takeoff (*informal*), lampoon, burlesque

treacherous *adjective* **1** DISLOYAL, deceitful, untrustworthy, duplicitous, false, untrue, unreliable, unfaithful, faithless, double-crossing (*informal*), double-dealing, perfidious, traitorous, treasonable, recreant (*archaic*) << ANTONYM loyal **2** DANGEROUS, tricky, risky, unstable, hazardous, icy, slippery, unsafe, unreliable, precarious, deceptive, perilous, slippy (*informal or* *dialect*) << ANTONYM safe

treachery *noun* BETRAYAL, infidelity, treason, duplicity, disloyalty, double-cross (*informal*), double-dealing, stab in the back, perfidy, faithlessness, perfidiousness << ANTONYM loyalty

tread *verb* STEP, walk, march, pace, stamp, stride, hike, tramp, trudge, plod ▷ *noun* STEP, walk, pace, stride, footstep, gait, footfall ▷▷ **tread on something 1** CRUSH UNDERFOOT, step on, stamp on, trample (on), stomp on, squash, flatten **2** REPRESS, crush, suppress, subdue, oppress, quell, bear down on, subjugate, ride roughshod over

treason *noun* DISLOYALTY, mutiny, treachery, subversion, disaffection, duplicity, sedition, perfidy, lese-majesty, traitorousness << ANTONYM loyalty

treasure *noun* **1** RICHES, money, gold, fortune, wealth, valuables, jewels, funds, cash **2** ANGEL, darling, find, star (*informal*), prize, pearl, something else (*informal*), jewel, gem, paragon, one in a million (*informal*), one of a kind (*informal*), nonpareil ▷ *verb* PRIZE, value, worship, esteem, adore, cherish, revere, venerate, hold dear, love, idolize, set great store by, dote upon, place great value on

treasury *noun* **1** FUNDS, money, capital, finances, resources, assets, revenues, exchequer, coffers **2** STOREHOUSE, bank, store, vault, hoard, cache, repository

treat *verb* **1** BEHAVE TOWARDS, deal with, handle, act towards, use, consider, serve, manage, regard, look upon **2** TAKE CARE OF, minister to, attend to, give medical treatment to, doctor (*informal*), nurse, care for, medicate, prescribe medicine for, apply treatment to **3** *often with* **to** PROVIDE, give, buy, stand (*informal*), pay for, entertain, feast, lay on, regale, wine and dine, take out for, foot *or* pay the bill **4** NEGOTIATE, bargain, consult, have talks, confer, come to terms, parley, make a bargain, make terms ▷ *noun* **1** ENTERTAINMENT, party, surprise, gift, celebration, feast, outing, excursion, banquet, refreshment **2** PLEASURE, delight, joy, thrill, satisfaction, enjoyment, gratification, source of pleasure, fun ▷▷ **treat of something** DEAL WITH, discuss, go into, be concerned with, touch upon, discourse upon

treatise *noun* PAPER, work, writing, study, essay, thesis, tract, pamphlet, exposition, dissertation, monograph, disquisition

treatment *noun* **1** CARE, medical care, nursing, medicine, surgery, therapy, healing, medication, therapeutics, ministrations **2** CURE, remedy, medication, medicine **3** *often with* **of** HANDLING, dealings with, behaviour towards, conduct towards, management, reception, usage, manipulation, action towards

treaty *noun* AGREEMENT, pact, contract, bond, alliance, bargain, convention, compact, covenant, entente, concordat

trek *noun* **1** SLOG, tramp, long haul, footslog **2** JOURNEY, hike, expedition, safari, march, odyssey ▷ *verb* **1** JOURNEY, march, range, hike, roam, tramp, rove, go walkabout (*Austral*) **2** TRUDGE, plod, traipse (*informal*), footslog, slog

tremble *verb* **1** SHAKE, shiver, quake, shudder, quiver, teeter, totter, quake in your boots, shake in your boots *or* shoes **2** VIBRATE, rock, shake, quake, wobble, oscillate ▷ *noun* SHAKE, shiver, quake, shudder, wobble, tremor, quiver, vibration, oscillation

tremendous *adjective* **1** HUGE, great, towering, vast, enormous, terrific, formidable, immense, awesome, titanic, gigantic, monstrous, mammoth, colossal, whopping (*informal*), stellar (*informal*), prodigious, stupendous, gargantuan << ANTONYM tiny **2** (*informal*) EXCELLENT, great, wonderful, brilliant, mean (*slang*), topping (*Brit slang*), cracking (*Brit informal*), amazing, extraordinary, fantastic (*informal*), ace (*informal*), incredible, fabulous (*informal*), marvellous, exceptional, terrific (*informal*), sensational (*informal*), sovereign, awesome (*slang*), super (*informal*), brill (*informal*), bodacious (*slang, chiefly US*), boffo (*slang*), jim-dandy (*slang*), chillin' (*US slang*), booshit (*Austral slang*), exo (*Austral slang*), sik (*Austral slang*), rad (*informal*), phat (*slang*), schmick (*Austral informal*) << ANTONYM terrible

tremor *noun* **1** SHAKE, shaking, tremble, trembling, shiver, quaking, wobble, quiver, quivering, agitation, vibration, quaver **2** EARTHQUAKE, shock, quake (*informal*), tremblor (*US informal*)

trench *noun* DITCH, cut, channel, drain, pit, waterway, gutter, trough, furrow, excavation, earthwork, fosse, entrenchment

trenchant *adjective* **1** SCATHING, pointed, cutting, biting, sharp, keen, acute, severe, acid, penetrating, tart, pungent, incisive, hurtful, sarcastic, caustic, astringent, vitriolic, acerbic, piquant, mordant, acidulous, mordacious << ANTONYM kind

2 CLEAR, driving, strong, powerful, effective, distinct, crisp, explicit, vigorous, potent, energetic, clear-cut, forceful, emphatic, unequivocal, salient, well-defined, effectual, distinctly defined << ANTONYM vague

trend *noun* **1** TENDENCY, swing, drift, inclination, current, direction, flow, leaning, bias **2** FASHION, craze, fad (*informal*), mode, look, thing, style, rage, vogue, mania ▷ *verb* TEND, turn, head, swing, flow, bend, lean, incline, veer, run

trendy (*Brit informal*) *adjective* FASHIONABLE, in (*slang*), now (*informal*), latest, with it (*informal*), flash (*informal*), stylish, in fashion, in vogue, up to the minute, modish, voguish, schmick (*Austral informal*) ▷ *noun* POSER (*informal*), pseud (*informal*)

trepidation *noun* (*formal*) ANXIETY, fear, worry, alarm, emotion, excitement, dread, butterflies (*informal*), shaking, disturbance, dismay, trembling, fright, apprehension, tremor, quivering, nervousness, disquiet, agitation, consternation, jitters (*informal*), cold feet (*informal*), uneasiness, palpitation, cold sweat (*informal*), perturbation, the heebie-jeebies (*slang*) << ANTONYM composure

trespass *verb* **1** INTRUDE, infringe, encroach, enter without permission, invade, poach, obtrude **2** *often with* **against** (*archaic*) SIN, offend, transgress, commit a sin ▷ *noun* **1** INTRUSION, infringement, encroachment, unlawful entry, invasion, poaching, wrongful entry **2** SIN, crime, fault, error, offence, breach, misconduct, wrongdoing, misdemeanour, delinquency, misdeed, transgression, misbehaviour, iniquity, infraction, evildoing, injury

tress *noun often plural* HAIR, lock, curl, braid, plait, pigtail, ringlet

triad *noun* THREESOME, triple, trio, trinity, trilogy, triplet, triumvirate, triptych, trine, triune

trial *noun* **1** (*law*) HEARING, case, court case, inquiry, contest, tribunal, lawsuit, appeal, litigation, industrial tribunal, court martial, legal proceedings, judicial proceedings, judicial examination **2** TEST, testing, experiment, evaluation, check, examination, audition, assay, dry run (*informal*), assessment, proof, probation, appraisal, try-out, test-run, pilot study, dummy run **3** HARDSHIP, suffering, trouble, pain, load, burden, distress, grief, misery, ordeal, hard times, woe, unhappiness, adversity,

affliction, tribulation, wretchedness, vexation, cross to bear **4** NUISANCE, drag (*informal*), bother, plague (*informal*), pest, irritation, hassle (*informal*), bane, pain in the neck (*informal*), vexation, thorn in your flesh *or* side ▷ *adjective* EXPERIMENTAL, probationary, testing, pilot, provisional, exploratory

tribe *noun* RACE, ethnic group, people, family, class, stock, house, division, blood, seed (*chiefly biblical*), sept, gens, clan, caste, dynasty, hapu (*NZ*), iwi (*NZ*)

tribulation *noun* TROUBLE, care, suffering, worry, trial, blow, pain, burden, distress, grief, misery, curse, ordeal, hardship, sorrow, woe, hassle (*informal*), misfortune, bad luck, unhappiness, heartache, adversity, affliction, bummer (*slang*), wretchedness, vexation, ill fortune, cross to bear << ANTONYM joy

tribunal *noun* HEARING, court, trial, bar, bench, industrial tribunal, judgment seat, judicial examination

tribute *noun* ACCOLADE, testimonial, eulogy, recognition, respect, gift, honour, praise, esteem, applause, compliment, gratitude, acknowledgment, commendation, panegyric, encomium, laudation << ANTONYM criticism

trick *noun* **1** JOKE, put-on (*slang*), gag (*informal*), stunt, spoof (*informal*), caper, prank, frolic, practical joke, antic, jape, leg-pull (*Brit informal*), cantrip (*Scot*) **2** DECEPTION, trap, fraud, con (*slang*), sting (*informal*), manoeuvre, dodge, ploy, scam (*slang*), imposition, gimmick, device, hoax, deceit, swindle, ruse, artifice, subterfuge, canard, feint, stratagem, wile, imposture, fastie (*Austral slang*) **3** SLEIGHT OF HAND, device, feat, stunt, juggle, legerdemain **4** SECRET, skill, device, knack, art, hang (*informal*), technique, know-how (*informal*), gift, command, craft, expertise **5** MANNERISM, habit, characteristic, trait, quirk, peculiarity, foible, idiosyncrasy, practice, crotchet ▷ *verb* DECEIVE, trap, have someone on, take someone in (*informal*), fool, cheat, con (*informal*), kid (*informal*), stiff (*slang*), sting (*informal*), mislead, hoax, defraud, dupe, gull (*archaic*), delude, swindle, impose upon, bamboozle (*informal*), hoodwink, put one over on (*informal*), pull the wool over someone's eyes, pull a fast one on (*informal*) ▷▷ **do the trick** (*informal*) WORK, fit the bill, have effect, achieve the desired result, produce the desired result, take care of the problem, be effective *or* effectual, do the business (*informal*)

trickery *noun* DECEPTION, fraud, cheating, con (*informal*), hoax, pretence, deceit, dishonesty, swindling, guile, double-dealing, skulduggery (*informal*), chicanery, hanky-panky (*informal*), hokum (*slang, chiefly US & Canad*), monkey business (*informal*), funny business, jiggery-pokery (*informal, chiefly Brit*), imposture << ANTONYM honesty

trickle *verb* DRIBBLE, run, drop, stream, creep, crawl, drip, ooze, seep, exude, percolate ▷ *noun* DRIBBLE, drip, seepage, thin stream

trickster *noun* DECEIVER, fraud, cheat, joker, hoaxer, pretender, hustler (*US informal*), con man (*informal*), impostor, fraudster, swindler, practical joker, grifter (*slang, chiefly US & Canad*), chiseller (*informal*), rorter (*Austral slang*), rogue trader

tricky *adjective* 1 DIFFICULT, sensitive, complicated, delicate, risky, sticky (*informal*), hairy (*informal*), problematic, thorny, touch-and-go, knotty, dicey (*informal*), ticklish << ANTONYM simple 2 CRAFTY, scheming, subtle, cunning, slippery, sly, deceptive, devious, wily, artful, foxy, deceitful << ANTONYM open

trifle *noun* KNICK-KNACK, nothing, toy, plaything, bauble, triviality, bagatelle, gewgaw ▷▷ **a trifle** SLIGHTLY, a little, a bit, somewhat, rather, moderately, marginally, a shade, to some degree, on a small scale, to some extent

trifling *adjective* INSIGNIFICANT, small, tiny, empty, slight, silly, shallow, petty, idle, trivial, worthless, negligible, unimportant, frivolous, paltry, minuscule, puny, measly, piddling (*informal*), inconsiderable, valueless, nickel-and-dime (*US slang*), footling (*informal*) << ANTONYM significant

trigger *verb* BRING ABOUT, start, cause, produce, generate, prompt, provoke, set off, activate, give rise to, elicit, spark off, set in motion << ANTONYM prevent

trim *adjective* 1 NEAT, nice, smart, compact, tidy, orderly, spruce, dapper, natty (*informal*), well-groomed, well-ordered, well turned-out, shipshape, spick-and-span, trig (*archaic or dialect*), soigné *or* soignée << ANTONYM untidy 2 SLENDER, fit, slim, sleek, streamlined, shapely, svelte, willowy, lissom ▷ *verb* 1 CUT, crop, clip, dock, shave, barber, tidy, prune, shear, pare, lop, even up, neaten 2 DECORATE, dress, array, adorn, embroider, garnish, ornament,

embellish, deck out, bedeck, beautify, trick out ▷ *noun* 1 DECORATION, edging, border, piping, trimming, fringe, garnish, frill, embellishment, adornment, ornamentation 2 CONDITION, form, health, shape (*informal*), repair, fitness, wellness, order, fettle 3 CUT, crop, trimming, clipping, shave, pruning, shearing, tidying up

trimming *noun* DECORATION, edging, border, piping, fringe, garnish, braid, frill, festoon, embellishment, adornment, ornamentation ▷ *plural noun* 1 EXTRAS, accessories, garnish, ornaments, accompaniments, frills, trappings, paraphernalia, appurtenances 2 CLIPPINGS, ends, cuttings, shavings, brash, parings

trinity *noun* THREESOME, triple, trio, trilogy, triplet, triad, triumvirate, triptych, trine, triune

trinket *noun* ORNAMENT, bauble, knick-knack, piece of bric-a-brac, nothing, toy, trifle, bagatelle, gimcrack, gewgaw, bibelot, kickshaw

trio *noun* THREESOME, triple, trinity, trilogy, triplet, triad, triumvirate, triptych, trine, triune

trip *noun* 1 JOURNEY, outing, excursion, day out, run, drive, travel, tour, spin (*informal*), expedition, voyage, ramble, foray, jaunt, errand, junket (*informal*) 2 STUMBLE, fall, slip, blunder, false move, misstep, false step ▷ *verb* 1 *often with* up STUMBLE, fall, fall over, slip, tumble, topple, stagger, misstep, lose your balance, make a false move, lose your footing, take a spill 2 SKIP, dance, spring, hop, caper, flit, frisk, gambol, tread lightly 3 (*informal*) TAKE DRUGS, get high (*informal*), get stoned (*slang*), turn on (*slang*) 4 ACTIVATE, turn on, flip, release, pull, throw, engage, set off, switch on ▷▷ **trip someone up** CATCH OUT, trap, confuse, unsettle, disconcert, throw you off, wrongfoot, put you off your stride

tripe *noun* (*informal*) NONSENSE, rot, trash, twaddle, rubbish, pants (*slang*), crap (*slang*), garbage (*informal*), hot air (*informal*), tosh (*slang, chiefly Brit*), pap, bilge (*informal*), drivel, guff (*slang*), moonshine, claptrap (*informal*), hogwash, hokum (*slang, chiefly US & Canad*), piffle (*informal*), poppycock (*informal*), inanity, balderdash, bosh (*informal*), eyewash (*informal*), trumpery, tommyrot, foolish talk, horsefeathers (*US slang*), bunkum *or* buncombe (*chiefly US*), bizzo (*Austral slang*), bull's wool (*Austral & NZ slang*)

triple *adjective* **1** TREBLE, three times, three times as much as **2** THREE-WAY, threefold, tripartite ▷ *verb* TREBLE, triplicate, increase threefold

triplet *noun* THREESOME, triple, trio, trinity, trilogy, triad, triumvirate, trine, triune

tripper *noun* (*Chiefly Brit*) TOURIST, holiday-maker, sightseer, excursionist, journeyer, voyager

trite *adjective* UNORIGINAL, worn, common, stock, ordinary, tired, routine, dull, stereotyped, hack, pedestrian, commonplace, stale, banal, corny (*slang*), run-of-the-mill, threadbare, clichéd, uninspired, hackneyed, bromidic << ANTONYM original

triumph *noun* **1** SUCCESS, victory, accomplishment, mastery, hit (*informal*), achievement, smash (*informal*), coup, sensation, feat, conquest, attainment, smash hit (*informal*), tour de force (*French*), walkover (*informal*), feather in your cap, smasheroo (*slang*) << ANTONYM failure **2** JOY, pride, happiness, rejoicing, elation, jubilation, exultation ▷ *verb* **1** *often with* **over** SUCCEED, win, overcome, prevail, best, dominate, overwhelm, thrive, flourish, subdue, prosper, get the better of, vanquish, come out on top (*informal*), carry the day, take the honours << ANTONYM fail **2** REJOICE, celebrate, glory, revel, swagger, drool, gloat, exult, jubilate, crow

triumphant *adjective* **1** VICTORIOUS, winning, successful, dominant, conquering, undefeated << ANTONYM defeated **2** CELEBRATORY, rejoicing, jubilant, triumphal, proud, glorious, swaggering, elated, exultant, boastful, cock-a-hoop

trivia *noun* MINUTIAE, details, trifles, trivialities, petty details << ANTONYM essentials

trivial *adjective* UNIMPORTANT, little, small, minor, slight, everyday, petty, meaningless, commonplace, worthless, trifling, insignificant, negligible, frivolous, paltry, incidental, puny, inconsequential, trite, inconsiderable, valueless, nickel-and-dime (*US slang*) << ANTONYM important

triviality *noun* **1** INSIGNIFICANCE, frivolity, smallness, pettiness, worthlessness, meaninglessness, unimportance, littleness, slightness, triteness, paltriness, inconsequentiality, valuelessness, negligibility, much ado about nothing << ANTONYM importance **2** TRIFLE, nothing, detail, technicality, petty detail, no big thing, no great matter << ANTONYM essential

troop *noun* **1** GROUP, company, team, body, unit, band, crowd, pack, squad, gathering, crew (*informal*), drove, gang, bunch (*informal*), flock, herd, contingent, swarm, horde, multitude, throng, posse (*informal*), bevy, assemblage **2** *plural* SOLDIERS, men, armed forces, servicemen, fighting men, military, army, soldiery ▷ *verb* FLOCK, march, crowd, stream, parade, swarm, throng, traipse (*informal*)

trophy *noun* **1** PRIZE, cup, award, bays, laurels **2** SOUVENIR, spoils, relic, memento, booty, keepsake

tropical *adjective* HOT, stifling, lush, steamy, humid, torrid, sultry, sweltering << ANTONYM cold

trot *verb* RUN, jog, scamper, lope, go briskly, canter ▷ *noun* RUN, jog, lope, brisk pace, canter ▷▷ **on the trot** (*informal*) ONE AFTER THE OTHER, in a row, in succession, without break, without interruption, consecutively ▷▷ **trot something out** (*informal*) REPEAT, relate, exhibit, bring up, reiterate, recite, come out with, bring forward, drag up

troubadour *noun* MINSTREL, singer, poet, balladeer, lyric poet, jongleur

trouble *noun* **1** BOTHER, problems, concern, worry, stress, difficulty (*informal*), anxiety, distress, grief (*Brit & S African*), irritation, hassle (*informal*), strife, inconvenience, unease, disquiet, annoyance, agitation, commotion, unpleasantness, vexation **2** *often plural* DISTRESS, problem, suffering, worry, pain, anxiety, grief, torment, hardship, sorrow, woe, irritation, hassle (*informal*), misfortune, heartache, disquiet, annoyance, agitation, tribulation, bummer (*slang*), vexation << ANTONYM pleasure **3** AILMENT, disease, failure, complaint, upset, illness, disorder, disability, defect, malfunction **4** DISORDER, fighting, row, conflict, bother, grief (*Brit & S African*), unrest, disturbance, to-do (*informal*), discontent, dissatisfaction, furore, uproar, scuffling, discord, fracas, commotion, rumpus, breach of the peace, tumult, affray (*law*), brouhaha, ructions, hullabaloo (*informal*), kerfuffle (*Brit informal*), hoo-ha (*informal*), biffo (*Austral slang*), boilover (*Austral*) << ANTONYM peace **5** PROBLEM, bother, concern, pest, irritation, hassle (*informal*), nuisance, inconvenience, irritant, cause of annoyance **6** EFFORT, work, thought, care, labour, struggle, pains, bother, grief (*Brit & S African*), hassle (*informal*), inconvenience, exertion << ANTONYM convenience **7** DIFFICULTY, hot water (*informal*), predicament, deep water (*informal*), spot (*informal*), danger, mess, dilemma, scrape (*informal*), pickle (*informal*), dire straits, tight spot ▷ *verb* **1** BOTHER, worry, upset, disturb, distress, annoy, plague, grieve, torment, harass, hassle (*informal*), afflict, pain, fret, agitate, sadden, perplex, disconcert, disquiet, pester, vex, perturb, faze, give someone grief (*Brit & S African*), discompose, put *or* get someone's back up, hack you off (*informal*) << ANTONYM please **2** AFFLICT, hurt, bother, cause discomfort to, cause discomfort to, pain, grieve **3** INCONVENIENCE, disturb, burden, put out, impose upon, discommode, incommode << ANTONYM relieve **4** TAKE PAINS, take the time, make an effort, go to the effort of, exert yourself << ANTONYM avoid

troublemaker *noun* MISCHIEF-MAKER, firebrand, instigator, agitator, bad apple (*US informal*), rabble-rouser, agent provocateur (*French*), stirrer (*informal*), incendiary, rotten apple (*Brit informal*), meddler, stormy petrel << ANTONYM peace-maker

troublesome *adjective* **1** BOTHERSOME, trying, taxing, demanding, difficult, worrying, upsetting, annoying, irritating, tricky, harassing, oppressive, arduous, tiresome, inconvenient, laborious, burdensome, hard, worrisome, irksome, wearisome, vexatious, importunate, pestilential, plaguy (*informal*) << ANTONYM simple **2** DISORDERLY, violent, turbulent, rebellious, unruly, rowdy, recalcitrant, undisciplined, uncooperative, refractory, insubordinate << ANTONYM well-behaved

trough *noun* MANGER, crib, water trough

trounce *verb* DEFEAT SOMEONE HEAVILY *or* UTTERLY, beat, thrash, slaughter (*informal*), stuff (*slang*), tank (*slang*), hammer (*informal*), crush, overwhelm, lick (*informal*), paste (*slang*), rout, walk over (*informal*), clobber (*slang*), run rings around (*informal*), wipe the floor with (*informal*), make mincemeat of, blow someone out of the water (*slang*), give someone a hiding (*informal*), drub, beat someone hollow (*Brit informal*), give someone a pasting (*slang*)

troupe *noun* COMPANY, group, band, cast, ensemble

truancy *noun* ABSENCE, shirking, skiving (*Brit slang*), malingering, absence without leave

truant *noun* ABSENTEE, skiver (*Brit slang*), shirker, dodger, runaway, delinquent, deserter, straggler, malingerer ▷ *adjective* ABSENT, missing, skiving (*Brit slang*), absent without leave, A.W.O.L. ▷ *verb* ABSENT YOURSELF, play truant, skive (*Brit slang*), bunk off (*slang*), desert, run away, dodge, wag (*dialect*), go missing, shirk, malinger, bob off (*Brit slang*)

truce *noun* CEASEFIRE, break, stay, rest, peace, treaty, interval, moratorium, respite, lull, cessation, let-up (*informal*), armistice, intermission, cessation of hostilities

truculent *adjective* HOSTILE, defiant, belligerent, bad-tempered, cross, violent, aggressive, fierce, contentious, combative, sullen, scrappy (*informal*), antagonistic, pugnacious, ill-tempered, bellicose, obstreperous, itching *or* spoiling for a fight (*informal*), aggers (*Austral slang*) << ANTONYM amiable

trudge *verb* PLOD, trek, tramp, traipse (*informal*), march, stump, hike, clump, lumber, slog, drag yourself, yomp, walk heavily, footslog ▷ *noun* TRAMP, march, haul, trek, hike, slog, traipse (*informal*), yomp, footslog

true *adjective* **1** CORRECT, right, accurate, exact, precise, valid, legitimate, factual, truthful, veritable, bona fide, veracious << ANTONYM false **2** ACTUAL, real, natural, pure, genuine, proper, authentic, dinkum (*Austral & NZ informal*) **3** FAITHFUL, loyal, devoted, dedicated, firm, fast, constant, pure, steady, reliable, upright, sincere, honourable, honest, staunch, trustworthy, trusty, dutiful, true-blue, unswerving << ANTONYM unfaithful **4** EXACT, perfect, correct, accurate, proper, precise, spot-on (*Brit informal*), on target, unerring << ANTONYM inaccurate ▷ *adverb* **1** TRUTHFULLY, honestly, veritably, veraciously, rightly **2** PRECISELY, accurately, on target, perfectly, correctly, properly, unerringly

true-blue *adjective* STAUNCH, confirmed, constant, devoted, dedicated, loyal, faithful, orthodox, uncompromising, trusty, unwavering, dyed-in-the-wool

truism *noun* CLICHÉ, commonplace, platitude, axiom, stock phrase, trite saying

truly *adverb* **1** GENUINELY, really, correctly, truthfully, rightly, in fact, precisely, exactly, legitimately, accurately, in reality, in truth, beyond doubt, without a doubt, authentically, beyond question, factually, in

actuality, veritably, veraciously << ANTONYM
falsely **2** REALLY, very, greatly, indeed,
seriously (*informal*), extremely, to be sure,
exceptionally, verily **3** FAITHFULLY, firmly,
constantly, steadily, honestly, sincerely,
staunchly, dutifully, loyally, honourably,
devotedly, with all your heart, with
dedication, with devotion, confirmedly

trump *verb* OUTDO, top, cap, surpass, score
points off, excel ▷▷ **trump something up**
INVENT, create, make up, manufacture,
fake, contrive, fabricate, concoct, cook up
(*informal*)

trumped up *adjective* INVENTED, made-up,
manufactured, false, fake, contrived, untrue,
fabricated, concocted, falsified, cooked-
up (*informal*), phoney *or* phony (*informal*)
<< ANTONYM genuine

trumpet *noun* HORN, clarion, bugle ▷ *verb*
1 PROCLAIM, advertise, extol, tout (*informal*),
announce, publish, broadcast, crack up
(*informal*), sound loudly, shout from the
rooftops, noise abroad << ANTONYM keep
secret **2** ROAR, call, cry, bay, bellow ▷▷ **blow
your own trumpet** BOAST, crow, brag, vaunt,
sing your own praises, big yourself up (*slang,
chiefly Caribbean*)

truncate *verb* SHORTEN, cut, crop, trim, clip,
dock, prune, curtail, cut short, pare, lop,
abbreviate << ANTONYM lengthen

truncheon *noun* (*Chiefly Brit*) CLUB, staff, stick,
baton, cudgel, mere (*NZ*), patu (*NZ*)

trunk *noun* **1** STEM, stock, stalk, bole **2** CHEST,
case, box, crate, bin, suitcase, locker,
coffer, casket, portmanteau, kist (*Scot & N
English dialect*) **3** BODY, torso **4** SNOUT, nose,
proboscis

truss *verb often with up* TIE, secure, bind,
strap, fasten, tether, pinion, make fast ▷ *noun*
1 (*medical*) SUPPORT, pad, bandage **2** JOIST,
support, stay, shore, beam, prop, brace, strut,
buttress, stanchion

trust *noun* **1** CONFIDENCE, credit, belief, faith,
expectation, conviction, assurance, certainty,
reliance, credence, certitude << ANTONYM
distrust **2** RESPONSIBILITY, duty, obligation
3 CUSTODY, care, guard, protection,
guardianship, safekeeping, trusteeship ▷
verb **1** BELIEVE IN, have faith in, depend
on, count on, bank on, lean on, rely upon,
swear by, take at face value, take as gospel,
place reliance on, place your trust in, pin
your faith on, place *or* have confidence in
<< ANTONYM distrust **2** ENTRUST, commit,
assign, confide, consign, put into the hands

of, allow to look after, hand over, turn over,
sign over, delegate **3** EXPECT, believe, hope,
suppose, assume, guess (*informal*), take it,
presume, surmise, think likely

trustful *or* **trusting** *adjective* UNSUSPECTING,
simple, innocent, optimistic, naive,
confiding, gullible, unwary, unguarded,
credulous, unsuspicious << ANTONYM
suspicious

trustworthy *adjective* DEPENDABLE,
responsible, principled, mature, sensible,
reliable, ethical, upright, true, honourable,
honest, staunch, righteous, reputable,
truthful, trusty, steadfast, level-headed, to be
trusted << ANTONYM untrustworthy

trusty *adjective* RELIABLE, dependable,
trustworthy, responsible, solid, strong,
firm, true, steady, faithful, straightforward,
upright, honest, staunch << ANTONYM
unreliable

truth *noun* **1** REALITY, fact(s), real life,
actuality << ANTONYM unreality
2 TRUTHFULNESS, fact, accuracy, honesty,
precision, validity, legitimacy, authenticity,
correctness, sincerity, verity, candour,
veracity, rightness, genuineness, exactness,
factuality, factualness << ANTONYM
inaccuracy **3** FACT, law, reality, certainty,
maxim, verity, axiom, truism, proven
principle **4** HONESTY, principle, honour,
virtue, integrity, goodness, righteousness,
candour, frankness, probity, rectitude,
incorruptibility, uprightness << ANTONYM
dishonesty

truthful *adjective* **1** HONEST, frank, candid,
upfront (*informal*), true, straight, reliable,
faithful, straightforward, sincere, forthright,
trustworthy, plain-spoken, veracious
<< ANTONYM dishonest **2** TRUE, correct,
accurate, exact, realistic, precise, literal,
veritable, naturalistic << ANTONYM untrue

try *verb* **1** ATTEMPT, seek, aim, undertake,
essay, strive, struggle, endeavour, have a go,
go for it (*informal*), make an effort, have a
shot (*informal*), have a crack (*informal*), bend
over backwards (*informal*), do your best, go
for broke (*slang*), make an attempt, move
heaven and earth, bust a gut (*informal*),
give it your best shot (*informal*), have a stab
(*informal*), break your neck (*informal*), exert
yourself, make an all-out effort (*informal*),
knock yourself out (*informal*), have a whack
(*informal*), do your damnedest (*informal*),
give it your all (*informal*), rupture yourself
(*informal*) **2** EXPERIMENT WITH, try out, put

to the test, test, taste, examine, investigate, sample, evaluate, check out, inspect, appraise **3** JUDGE, hear, consider, examine, adjudicate, adjudge, pass judgement on **4** TAX, test, trouble, pain, stress, upset, tire, strain, drain, exhaust, annoy, plague, irritate, weary, afflict, sap, inconvenience, wear out, vex, irk, make demands on, give someone grief (*Brit & S African*) ▷ *noun* ATTEMPT, go (*informal*), shot (*informal*), effort, crack (*informal*), essay, stab (*informal*), bash (*informal*), endeavour, whack (*informal*) ▷▷ **try something out** TEST, experiment with, appraise, put to the test, taste, sample, evaluate, check out, inspect, put into practice

trying *adjective* ANNOYING, hard, taxing, difficult, tough, upsetting, irritating, fatiguing, stressful, aggravating (*informal*), troublesome, exasperating, arduous, tiresome, vexing, irksome, wearisome, bothersome << ANTONYM straightforward

tsar *or* **czar** *noun* (*informal*) HEAD, chief, boss, big cheese (*informal*), baas (*S African*), head honcho (*informal*), sherang (*Austral & NZ*)

tubby *adjective* FAT, overweight, plump, stout, chubby, obese, portly, roly-poly, podgy, corpulent, paunchy

tuck *verb* PUSH, stick, stuff, slip, ease, insert, pop (*informal*) ▷ *noun* **1** (*Brit informal*) FOOD, eats (*slang*), tack (*informal*), scoff (*slang*), grub (*slang*), kai (*NZ informal*), nosh (*slang*), victuals, comestibles, nosebag (*slang*), vittles (*obsolete or dialect*) **2** FOLD, gather, pleat, pinch ▷▷ **tuck in** (*informal*) EAT UP, get stuck in (*informal*), eat heartily, fall to, chow down (*slang*) ▷▷ **tuck someone in** MAKE SNUG, wrap up, put to bed, bed down, swaddle

tuft *noun* CLUMP, bunch, shock, collection, knot, cluster, tussock, topknot

tug *verb* **1** PULL, drag, pluck, jerk, yank, wrench, lug **2** DRAG, pull, haul, tow, lug, heave, draw ▷ *noun* PULL, jerk, yank, wrench, drag, haul, tow, traction, heave

tuition *noun* TRAINING, schooling, education, teaching, lessons, instruction, tutoring, tutelage

tumble *verb* FALL, drop, topple, plummet, roll, pitch, toss, stumble, flop, trip up, fall head over heels, fall headlong, fall end over end ▷ *noun* FALL, drop, roll, trip, collapse, plunge, spill, toss, stumble, flop, headlong fall

tummy *noun* (*informal*) STOMACH, belly, abdomen, corporation (*informal*), pot, gut (*informal*), paunch, tum (*informal*), spare tyre (*informal*), breadbasket (*slang*), potbelly

tumour *or US* **tumor** *noun* GROWTH, cancer, swelling, lump, carcinoma (*pathology*), sarcoma (*medical*), neoplasm (*medical*)

tumult *noun* **1** DISTURBANCE, trouble, chaos, turmoil, storms, upset, stir, disorder, excitement, unrest, upheaval, havoc, mayhem, strife, disarray, turbulence, ferment, agitation, convulsions, bedlam **2** CLAMOUR, row, outbreak, racket, din, uproar, fracas, commotion, pandemonium, babel, hubbub, hullaballoo << ANTONYM silence

tumultuous *adjective* **1** TURBULENT, exciting, confused, disturbed, hectic, stormy, agitated << ANTONYM quiet **2** WILD, excited, riotous, unrestrained, violent, raging, disorderly, fierce, passionate, noisy, restless, unruly, rowdy, boisterous, full-on (*informal*), lawless, vociferous, rumbustious, uproarious, obstreperous, clamorous

tune *noun* **1** MELODY, air, song, theme, strain(s), motif, jingle, ditty, melody line **2** HARMONY, pitch, euphony ▷ *verb* **1** TUNE UP, adjust, bring into harmony **2** REGULATE, adapt, modulate, harmonize, attune, pitch

tuneful *adjective* MELODIOUS, musical, pleasant, harmonious, melodic, catchy, consonant (*music*), symphonic, mellifluous, easy on the ear (*informal*), euphonious, euphonic << ANTONYM discordant

tunnel *noun* PASSAGE, underpass, passageway, subway, channel, hole, shaft ▷ *verb* DIG, dig your way, burrow, mine, bore, drill, excavate

turbulence *noun* CONFUSION, turmoil, unrest, instability, storm, boiling, disorder, upheaval, agitation, commotion, pandemonium, tumult, roughness << ANTONYM peace

turbulent *adjective* **1** WILD, violent, disorderly, agitated, rebellious, unruly, rowdy, boisterous, anarchic, tumultuous, lawless, unbridled, riotous, undisciplined, seditious, mutinous, ungovernable, uproarious, refractory, obstreperous, insubordinate **2** STORMY, rough, raging, tempestuous, boiling, disordered, furious, unsettled, foaming, unstable, agitated, tumultuous, choppy, blustery << ANTONYM calm

turf *noun* **1** GRASS, green, sward **2** SOD, divot, clod ▷▷ **the turf** HORSE-RACING, the flat, racecourse, racetrack, racing ▷▷ **turf someone out** (*Brit informal*) THROW OUT, evict, cast out, kick out (*informal*), fire (*informal*), dismiss, sack (*informal*), bounce (*slang*), discharge, expel, oust, relegate, banish, eject, dispossess, chuck out (*informal*), fling out, kiss off (*slang, chiefly US & Canad*), show someone the door, give someone the sack (*informal*), give someone the bum's rush (*slang*), kennel (*Austral slang*), jeff (*Austral slang*)

turgid *adjective* POMPOUS, inflated, windy, high-flown, pretentious, grandiose, flowery, overblown, stilted, ostentatious, fulsome, bombastic, grandiloquent, arty-farty (*informal*), fustian, orotund, magniloquent, sesquipedalian, tumid

turmoil *noun* CONFUSION, trouble, violence, row, noise, stir, disorder, chaos, disturbance, upheaval, bustle, flurry, strife, disarray, uproar, turbulence, ferment, agitation, commotion, pandemonium, bedlam, tumult, hubbub, brouhaha << ANTONYM peace

turn *verb* 1 *sometimes with* **round** CHANGE COURSE, swing round, wheel round, veer, move, return, go back, switch, shift, reverse, swerve, change position 2 ROTATE, spin, go round (and round), revolve, roll, circle, wheel, twist, spiral, whirl, swivel, pivot, twirl, gyrate, go round in circles, move in a circle 3 GO ROUND, come round, negotiate, pass, corner, pass around, take a bend 4 *with* **into** CHANGE, transform, fashion, shape, convert, alter, adapt, mould, remodel, form, mutate, refit, metamorphose, transmute, transfigure 5 SHAPE, form, fashion, cast, frame, construct, execute, mould, make 6 SICKEN, upset, nauseate 7 GO BAD, go off (*Brit informal*), curdle, go sour, become rancid 8 MAKE RANCID, spoil, sour, taint ▷ *noun* 1 ROTATION, turning, cycle, circle, revolution, spin, twist, reversal, whirl, swivel, pivot, gyration 2 CHANGE OF DIRECTION, bend, curve, change of course, shift, departure, deviation 3 DIRECTION, course, tack, swing, tendency, drift, bias 4 OPPORTUNITY, go, spell, shot (*informal*), time, try, round, chance, period, shift, crack (*informal*), succession, fling, stint, whack (*informal*) 5 STROLL, airing, walk, drive, ride, spin (*informal*), circuit, constitutional, outing, excursion, promenade, jaunt, saunter 6 DEED, service, act, action, favour, gesture 7 (*informal*) SHOCK, start, surprise, scare, jolt, fright 8 INCLINATION, talent, gift, leaning, bent, bias, flair, affinity, knack, propensity, aptitude ▷▷ **by turns** ALTERNATELY, in succession, turn and turn

about, reciprocally ▷▷ **to a turn** (*informal*) PERFECTLY, correctly, precisely, exactly, just right ▷▷ **turn off** BRANCH OFF, leave, quit, depart from, deviate, change direction, take a side road, take another road ▷▷ **turn on someone** ATTACK, assault, fall on, round on, lash out at, assail, lay into (*informal*), let fly at, lose your temper with ▷▷ **turn on something** DEPEND ON, hang on, rest on, hinge on, be decided by, balance on, be contingent on, pivot on ▷▷ **turn out** 1 PROVE TO BE, transpire, become apparent, happen, emerge, become known, develop, come to light, crop up (*informal*) 2 END UP, happen, result, work out, evolve, come to be, come about, transpire, pan out (*informal*), eventuate 3 COME, be present, turn up, show up (*informal*), go, appear, attend, gather, assemble, put in an appearance ▷▷ **turn over** OVERTURN, tip over, flip over, upend, be upset, reverse, capsize, keel over ▷▷ **turn someone off** (*informal*) REPEL, bore, put someone off, disgust, offend, irritate, alienate, sicken, displease, nauseate, gross someone out (*US slang*), disenchant, lose your interest ▷▷ **turn someone on** (*slang*) AROUSE, attract, excite, thrill, stimulate, please, press someone's buttons (*slang*), work someone up, titillate, ring someone's bell (*US slang*), arouse someone's desire ▷▷ **turn someone out** EXPEL, drive out, evict, throw out, fire (*informal*), dismiss, sack (*informal*), axe (*informal*), discharge, oust, relegate, banish, deport, put out, cashier, unseat, dispossess, kick out (*informal*), cast out, drum out, show the door, turf out (*Brit informal*), give someone the sack (*informal*), give someone the bum's rush (*slang*), kiss off (*slang, chiefly US & Canad*), kennel (*Austral slang*), jeff (*Austral slang*) ▷▷ **turn something down** 1 REFUSE, decline, reject, spurn, rebuff, say no to, repudiate, abstain from, throw something out 2 LOWER, soften, reduce the volume of, mute, lessen, muffle, quieten, diminish ▷▷ **turn something in** HAND IN, return, deliver, give back, give up, hand over, submit, surrender, tender ▷▷ **turn something off** SWITCH OFF, turn out, put out, stop, kill, cut out, shut down, unplug, flick off ▷▷ **turn something on** SWITCH ON, put on, activate, start, start up, ignite, kick-start, set in motion, energize ▷▷ **turn something out** 1 TURN OFF, put out, switch off, extinguish, disconnect, unplug, flick off 2 PRODUCE, make, process, finish, manufacture, assemble, put together, put out, bring out, fabricate, churn out ▷▷ **turn something over 1** FLIP OVER, flick through, leaf through **2** CONSIDER, think about, contemplate, ponder, reflect on, wonder about, mull over, think over, deliberate on, give thought to, ruminate about, revolve **3** HAND OVER, transfer, deliver, commit, give up, yield, surrender, pass on, render, assign, commend, give over **4** START UP, warm up, activate, switch on, crank, set something in motion, set something going, switch on the ignition of ▷▷ **turn something up 1** FIND, reveal, discover, expose, come up with, disclose, unearth, dig up, bring to light **2** INCREASE, raise, boost, enhance, intensify, amplify, increase the volume of, make louder ▷▷ **turn up 1** ARRIVE, come, appear, show up (*informal*), show (*informal*), attend, put in an appearance, show your face **2** COME TO LIGHT, be found, show up, pop up, materialize, appear

turning *noun* **1** TURN-OFF, turn, junction, crossroads, side road, exit **2** BEND, turn, curve

turning point *noun* CROSSROADS, critical moment, decisive moment, change, crisis, crux, moment of truth, point of no return, moment of decision, climacteric, tipping point

turn-off *noun* TURNING, turn, branch, exit, side road

turnout *noun* ATTENDANCE, crowd, audience, gate, assembly, congregation, number, throng, assemblage

turnover *noun* **1** OUTPUT, business, production, flow, volume, yield, productivity, outturn (*rare*) **2** MOVEMENT, replacement, coming and going, change

tussle *verb* FIGHT, battle, struggle, scrap (*informal*), contend, wrestle, vie, brawl, grapple, scuffle ▷ *noun* FIGHT, scrap (*informal*), brawl, scuffle, battle, competition, struggle, conflict, contest, set-to (*informal*), bout, contention, fray, punch-up (*Brit informal*), fracas, shindig (*informal*), scrimmage, shindy (*informal*), bagarre (*French*), biffo (*Austral slang*)

tutelage *noun* (*formal*) GUIDANCE, education, instruction, preparation, schooling, charge, care, teaching, protection, custody, tuition, dependence, patronage, guardianship, wardship

tutor *noun* TEACHER, coach, instructor, educator, guide, governor, guardian,

lecturer, guru, mentor, preceptor, master *or* mistress, schoolmaster *or* schoolmistress ▷ *verb* TEACH, educate, school, train, coach, guide, discipline, lecture, drill, instruct, edify, direct

tutorial *noun* SEMINAR, lesson, individual instruction ▷ *adjective* TEACHING, coaching, guiding, instructional

TV *noun* TELEVISION, telly (*Brit informal*), the box (*Brit informal*), receiver, the tube (*slang*), television set, TV set, small screen (*informal*), gogglebox (*Brit slang*), idiot box (*slang*)

twaddle *noun* NONSENSE, rubbish, rot, garbage (*informal*), pants (*slang*), gossip, crap (*slang*), trash, hot air (*informal*), tosh (*slang, chiefly Brit*), waffle (*informal, chiefly Brit*), pap, bilge (*informal*), drivel, tripe (*informal*), guff (*slang*), tattle, moonshine, verbiage, gabble, claptrap (*informal*), gobbledegook (*informal*), hogwash, hokum (*slang, chiefly US & Canad*), rigmarole, blather, piffle (*informal*), poppycock (*informal*), inanity, balderdash, bosh (*informal*), eyewash (*informal*), trumpery, tommyrot, foolish talk, horsefeathers (*US slang*), bunkum *or* buncombe (*chiefly US*), bizzo (*Austral slang*), bull's wool (*Austral & NZ slang*)

tweak *verb* TWIST, pull, pinch, jerk, squeeze, nip, twitch ▷ *noun* TWIST, pull, squeeze, pinch, jerk, nip, twitch

twee *adjective* (*Brit*) **1** SWEET, pretty, cute, sentimental, quaint, dainty, cutesy (*informal, chiefly US*), bijou, precious **2** SENTIMENTAL, over-sentimental, soppy (*Brit informal*), mawkish, affected, precious

twiddle *verb* FIDDLE WITH, adjust, finger, play with, juggle, wiggle (*informal*), twirl, jiggle, monkey with (*informal*)

twig¹ *noun* BRANCH, stick, sprig, offshoot, shoot, spray, withe

twig² *verb* (*Brit informal*) UNDERSTAND, get, see, find out, grasp, make out, rumble (*Brit informal*), catch on (*informal*), comprehend, fathom, tumble to (*informal*)

twilight *noun* **1** DUSK, evening, sunset, early evening, nightfall, sundown, gloaming (*Scot poetic*), close of day, evo (*Austral slang*) << ANTONYM dawn **2** HALF-LIGHT, gloom, dimness, semi-darkness **3** DECLINE, last years, final years, closing years, autumn, downturn, ebb, last phase << ANTONYM height ▷ *adjective* **1** EVENING, dim, darkening, evo (*Austral slang*) **2** DECLINING, last, final, dying, ebbing

twin *noun* DOUBLE, counterpart, mate, match,

fellow, clone, duplicate, lookalike, likeness, ringer (*slang*), corollary ▷ *verb* PAIR, match, join, couple, link, yoke ▷ *adjective* IDENTICAL, matched, matching, double, paired, parallel, corresponding, dual, duplicate, twofold, geminate

twine *noun* STRING, cord, yarn, strong thread ▷ *verb* **1** TWIST TOGETHER, weave, knit, braid, splice, interweave, plait, entwine, interlace, twist **2** COIL, wind, surround, bend, wrap, twist, curl, loop, spiral, meander, encircle, wreathe

twinge *noun* **1** PANG, twitch, tweak, throe (*rare*), twist **2** PAIN, sharp pain, gripe, stab, bite, twist, stitch, pinch, throb, twitch, prick, spasm, tweak, tic

twinkle *verb* SPARKLE, flash, shine, glitter, gleam, blink, flicker, wink, shimmer, glint, glisten, scintillate, coruscate ▷ *noun* **1** SPARKLE, light, flash, spark, shine, glittering, gleam, blink, flicker, wink, shimmer, glimmer, glistening, scintillation, coruscation **2** MOMENT, second, shake (*informal*), flash, instant, tick (*Brit informal*), twinkling, split second, jiffy (*informal*), trice, two shakes of a lamb's tail (*informal*)

twinkling *or* **twink** *noun* MOMENT, second, flash, instant, tick (*Brit informal*), twinkle, split second, jiffy (*informal*), trice, two shakes of a lamb's tail (*informal*), shake (*informal*), bat of an eye (*informal*)

twirl *verb* **1** TWIDDLE, turn, rotate, wind, spin, twist, revolve, whirl **2** TURN, whirl, wheel, spin, twist, pivot, gyrate, pirouette, turn on your heel ▷ *noun* TURN, spin, rotation, whirl, wheel, revolution, twist, pirouette, gyration

twist *verb* **1** COIL, curl, wind, plait, wrap, screw, twirl **2** INTERTWINE, wind, weave, braid, interweave, plait, entwine, twine, wreathe, interlace **3** DISTORT, screw up, contort, mangle, mangulate (*Austral slang*) << ANTONYM straighten **4** SPRAIN, turn, rick, wrench **5** MISREPRESENT, distort, misquote, alter, change, pervert, warp, falsify, garble **6** SQUIRM, wriggle, writhe ▷ *noun* **1** SURPRISE, change, turn, development, revelation **2** DEVELOPMENT, emphasis, variation, slant **3** WIND, turn, spin, swivel, twirl **4** COIL, roll, curl, hank, twine **5** CURVE, turn, bend, loop, arc, kink, zigzag, convolution, dog-leg, undulation **6** TRAIT, fault, defect, peculiarity, bent, characteristic, flaw, deviation, quirk, eccentricity, oddity, aberration, imperfection, kink, foible,

idiosyncrasy, proclivity, crotchet **7** SPRAIN, turn, pull, jerk, wrench

twit *noun* (*informal, chiefly Brit*) FOOL, idiot, jerk (*slang, chiefly US & Canad*), charlie (*Brit informal*), dope (*informal*), clown, ass, plank (*Brit slang*), berk (*Brit slang*), wally (*slang*), prat (*slang*), plonker (*slang*), geek (*slang*), chump (*informal*), oaf, simpleton, airhead (*slang*), dipstick (*Brit slang*), gonzo (*slang*), schmuck (*US slang*), dork (*slang*), nitwit (*informal*), blockhead, ninny, divvy (*Brit slang*), pillock (*Brit slang*), halfwit, silly-billy (*informal*), nincompoop, dweeb (*US slang*), putz (*US slang*), weenie (*US informal*), eejit (*Scot & Irish*), dumb-ass (*slang*), numpty (*Scot informal*), doofus (*slang, chiefly US*), juggins (*Brit informal*), dickwit (*slang*), nerd *or* nurd (*slang*), numbskull *or* numskull, twerp *or* twirp (*informal*), dorba *or* dorb (*Austral slang*), bogan (*Austral slang*)

twitch *verb* **1** JERK, blink, flutter, jump, squirm **2** PULL (AT), snatch (at), tug (at), pluck (at), yank (at) ▷ *noun* JERK, tic, spasm, twinge, jump, blink, flutter, tremor

twitter *verb* **1** CHIRRUP, whistle, chatter, trill, chirp, warble, cheep, tweet **2** CHATTER, chat, rabbit (on) (*Brit informal*), gossip, babble, gab (*informal*), prattle, natter, jabber, blather, prate ▷ *noun* CHIRRUP, call, song, cry, whistle, chatter, trill, chirp, warble, cheep, tweet

two-faced *adjective* HYPOCRITICAL, false, deceiving, treacherous, deceitful, untrustworthy, insincere, double-dealing, duplicitous, dissembling, perfidious, Janus-faced << ANTONYM honest

tycoon *noun* MAGNATE, capitalist, baron, industrialist, financier, fat cat (*slang, chiefly US*), mogul, captain of industry, potentate, wealthy businessman, big cheese (*slang or old-fashioned*), plutocrat, big noise (*informal*), merchant prince

type *noun* **1** KIND, sort, class, variety, group, form, order, style, species, breed, strain, category, stamp, kidney, genre, classification, ilk, subdivision **2** PRINT, printing, face, case, characters, font, fount

typhoon *noun* STORM, tornado, cyclone, tempest, squall, tropical storm

typical *adjective* **1** ARCHETYPAL, standard, model, normal, classic, stock, essential, representative, usual, conventional, regular, characteristic, orthodox, indicative, illustrative, archetypical, stereotypical << ANTONYM unusual **2** CHARACTERISTIC, in keeping, in character, true to type

3 AVERAGE, normal, usual, conventional, routine, regular, orthodox, predictable, run-of-the-mill, bog-standard (*Brit & Irish slang*)

typify *verb* REPRESENT, illustrate, sum up, characterize, embody, exemplify, personify, incarnate, epitomize

tyrannical *or* **tyrannic** *adjective* OPPRESSIVE, cruel, authoritarian, dictatorial, severe, absolute, unreasonable, arbitrary, unjust, autocratic, inhuman, coercive, imperious, domineering, overbearing, magisterial, despotic, high-handed, peremptory, overweening, tyrannous << ANTONYM liberal

tyranny *noun* OPPRESSION, cruelty, dictatorship, authoritarianism, reign of terror, despotism, autocracy, absolutism, coercion, high-handedness, harsh discipline, unreasonableness, imperiousness, peremptoriness << ANTONYM liberality

tyrant *noun* DICTATOR, bully, authoritarian, oppressor, despot, autocrat, absolutist, martinet, slave-driver, Hitler

tyro *or* **tiro** *noun* BEGINNER, novice, apprentice, learner, neophyte, rookie (*informal*), greenhorn (*informal*), catechumen

ubiquitous *adjective* EVER-PRESENT, pervasive, omnipresent, all-over, everywhere, universal

ugly *adjective* 1 UNATTRACTIVE, homely (*chiefly US*), plain, unsightly, unlovely, unprepossessing, not much to look at, no oil painting (*informal*), ill-favoured, hard-featured, hard-favoured << ANTONYM beautiful 2 UNPLEASANT, shocking, terrible, offensive, nasty, disgusting, revolting, obscene, hideous, monstrous, vile, distasteful, horrid, repulsive, frightful, objectionable, disagreeable, repugnant << ANTONYM pleasant 3 BAD-TEMPERED, nasty, sullen, surly, threatening, dangerous, angry, forbidding, menacing, sinister, ominous, malevolent, spiteful, baleful, bodeful << ANTONYM good-natured

ulcer *noun* SORE, abscess, gathering, peptic ulcer, gumboil

ulterior *adjective* HIDDEN, secret, concealed, personal, secondary, selfish, covert, undisclosed, unexpressed << ANTONYM obvious

ultimate *adjective* 1 FINAL, eventual, conclusive, last, end, furthest, extreme, terminal, decisive 2 FUNDAMENTAL, basic, primary, radical, elemental 3 SUPREME, highest, greatest, maximum, paramount, most significant, superlative, topmost 4 WORST, greatest, utmost, extreme 5 BEST, greatest, supreme, optimum, quintessential ▷ *noun* EPITOME, height, greatest, summit, peak, extreme, perfection, the last word

ultimately *adverb* 1 FINALLY, eventually, in the end, after all, at last, at the end of the day, sooner or later, in the fullness of time, in due time 2 FUNDAMENTALLY, essentially, basically, primarily, at heart, deep down

ultra-modern *adjective* ADVANCED, progressive, avant-garde, futuristic, ahead of its time, modernistic, neoteric (*rare*)

umbrella *noun* 1 BROLLY (*Brit informal*), parasol, sunshade, gamp 2 COVER, protection, guardianship, backing, support, charge, care, agency, responsibility, guidance, patronage, auspices, aegis, safe keeping, protectorship

umpire *noun* REFEREE, judge, ref (*informal*), arbiter, arbitrator, moderator, adjudicator, umpie (*Austral slang*) ▷ *verb* REFEREE, judge, adjudicate, arbitrate, call (*sport*), moderate, mediate

umpteen *adjective* (*informal*) VERY MANY, numerous, countless, millions, gazillions (*informal*), considerable, a good many, a thousand and one, ever so many

unable *adjective with* to INCAPABLE, inadequate, powerless, unfit, unfitted, not able, impotent, not up to, unqualified, ineffectual, not equal to << ANTONYM able

unaccountable *adjective* 1 INEXPLICABLE, mysterious, baffling, odd, strange, puzzling, peculiar, incomprehensible, inscrutable, unfathomable, unexplainable << ANTONYM understandable 2 NOT ANSWERABLE, exempt, not responsible, free, unliable

unaccustomed *adjective* 1 UNFAMILIAR, unusual, unexpected, new, special, surprising, strange, remarkable, unprecedented, uncommon, out of the ordinary, unwonted << ANTONYM familiar 2 *with* to NOT USED TO, unfamiliar with, unused to, not given to, a newcomer to, a novice at, inexperienced at, unversed in, unpractised in << ANTONYM used to

unaffected¹ *adjective* NATURAL, genuine, unpretentious, simple, plain, straightforward, naive, sincere, honest, unassuming, unspoilt, unsophisticated, dinkum (*Austral & NZ informal*), artless,

ingenuous, without airs, unstudied
<< ANTONYM pretentious

unaffected² *adjective often with* **by** IMPERVIOUS
TO, unchanged, untouched, unimpressed,
unmoved, unaltered, not influenced,
unresponsive to, unstirred << ANTONYM
affected

unanimity *noun* AGREEMENT, accord,
consensus, concert, unity, harmony,
chorus, unison, assent, concord, one mind,
concurrence, like-mindedness << ANTONYM
disagreement

unanimous *adjective* **1** AGREED, united, in
agreement, agreeing, at one, harmonious,
like-minded, concordant, of one mind,
of the same mind, in complete accord
<< ANTONYM divided **2** UNITED, common,
concerted, solid, consistent, harmonious,
undivided, congruent, concordant,
unopposed << ANTONYM split

unanimously *adverb* WITHOUT EXCEPTION, by
common consent, without opposition, with
one accord, unitedly, nem. con.

unarmed *adjective* DEFENCELESS, helpless,
unprotected, without arms, unarmoured,
weaponless << ANTONYM armed

unassailable *adjective* UNDENIABLE,
indisputable, irrefutable, sound,
proven, positive, absolute, conclusive,
incontrovertible, incontestable
<< ANTONYM doubtful

unassuming *adjective* MODEST, quiet,
humble, meek, simple, reserved, retiring,
unpretentious, unobtrusive, self-effacing,
diffident, unassertive, unostentatious
<< ANTONYM conceited

unattached *adjective* **1** SINGLE, available,
unmarried, on your own, by yourself, a
free agent, not spoken for, left on the
shelf, footloose and fancy-free, unengaged
2 *often with* **to** INDEPENDENT (FROM),
unaffiliated (to), nonaligned (to), free (from),
autonomous (from), uncommitted (to)
<< ANTONYM attached (to)

unavoidable *adjective* INEVITABLE,
inescapable, inexorable, sure, certain,
necessary, fated, compulsory, obligatory,
bound to happen, ineluctable

unaware *adjective* IGNORANT, unconscious,
oblivious, in the dark (*informal*),
unsuspecting, uninformed, unknowing,
heedless, unenlightened, unmindful,
not in the loop (*informal*), incognizant
<< ANTONYM aware

unawares *adverb* **1** BY SURPRISE, unprepared,

off guard, suddenly, unexpectedly, abruptly,
aback, without warning, on the hop (*Brit
informal*), caught napping << ANTONYM
prepared **2** UNKNOWINGLY, unwittingly,
unconsciously << ANTONYM knowingly

unbalanced *adjective* **1** DERANGED, disturbed,
unstable, touched, mad, crazy, barking
(*slang*), eccentric, insane, irrational, erratic,
lunatic, demented, unsound, unhinged,
loopy (*informal*), out to lunch (*informal*),
barking mad (*slang*), gonzo (*slang*), not
all there, doolally (*slang*), off your trolley
(*slang*), up the pole (*informal*), non compos
mentis (*Latin*), not the full shilling
(*informal*), wacko *or* whacko (*informal*), off
the air (*Austral slang*), daggy (*Austral & NZ
informal*) **2** BIASED, one-sided, prejudiced,
unfair, partial, partisan, unjust, inequitable
3 IRREGULAR, not balanced, lacking **4** SHAKY,
unstable, wobbly << ANTONYM stable

unbearable *adjective* INTOLERABLE,
insufferable, unendurable, too much
(*informal*), unacceptable, oppressive,
insupportable << ANTONYM tolerable

unbeatable *adjective* **1** UNSURPASSED,
matchless, unsurpassable **2** INVINCIBLE,
unstoppable, indomitable, unconquerable

unbeaten *adjective* UNDEFEATED, winning,
triumphant, victorious, unsurpassed,
unbowed, unvanquished, unsubdued

unbelievable *adjective* **1** WONDERFUL,
excellent, superb, fantastic (*informal*), mean
(*slang*), great (*informal*), topping (*Brit slang*),
bad (*slang*), cracking (*Brit informal*), crucial
(*slang*), smashing (*informal*), magnificent,
fabulous (*informal*), divine (*informal*),
glorious, terrific (*informal*), splendid,
sensational (*informal*), mega (*slang*),
sovereign, awesome (*slang*), colossal, super
(*informal*), wicked (*informal*), def (*slang*),
brill (*informal*), stupendous, bodacious
(*slang, chiefly US*), boffo (*slang*), jim-dandy
(*slang*), chillin' (*US slang*), booshit (*Austral
slang*), exo (*Austral slang*), sik (*Austral
slang*), rad (*informal*), phat (*slang*), schmick
(*Austral informal*) << ANTONYM terrible
2 INCREDIBLE, impossible, unthinkable,
astonishing, staggering, questionable,
improbable, inconceivable, preposterous,
unconvincing, unimaginable, outlandish,
far-fetched, implausible, beyond belief,
jaw-dropping, cock-and-bull (*informal*)
<< ANTONYM believable

unbeliever *noun* ATHEIST, sceptic, disbeliever,
agnostic, infidel, doubting Thomas

unborn *adjective* EXPECTED, awaited, embryonic, in utero (*Latin*)

unbridled *adjective* UNRESTRAINED, uncontrolled, unchecked, violent, excessive, rampant, unruly, full-on (*informal*), wanton, riotous, intemperate, ungovernable, unconstrained, licentious, ungoverned, uncurbed

unbroken *adjective* 1 INTACT, whole, undamaged, complete, total, entire, solid, untouched, unscathed, unspoiled, unimpaired << ANTONYM broken 2 CONTINUOUS, uninterrupted, constant, successive, endless, progressive, incessant, ceaseless, unremitting << ANTONYM interrupted 3 UNDISTURBED, uninterrupted, sound, fast, deep, profound, untroubled, unruffled 4 UNTAMED, wild, undomesticated

unburden *verb* 1 REVEAL, confide, disclose, lay bare, unbosom 2 UNLOAD, relieve, discharge, lighten, disencumber, disburden, ease the load of ▷▷ **unburden yourself** CONFESS, come clean about (*informal*), get something off your chest (*informal*), tell all about, empty yourself, spill your guts about (*slang*), make a clean breast of something

uncanny *adjective* 1 WEIRD, strange, mysterious, queer, unearthly, eerie, supernatural, unnatural, spooky (*informal*), creepy (*informal*), eldritch (*poetic*), preternatural 2 EXTRAORDINARY, remarkable, incredible, unusual, fantastic, astonishing, exceptional, astounding, singular, miraculous, unheard-of, prodigious

uncertain *adjective* 1 UNSURE, undecided, at a loss, vague, unclear, doubtful, dubious, ambivalent, hazy, hesitant, vacillating, in two minds, undetermined, irresolute << ANTONYM sure 2 DOUBTFUL, undetermined, unpredictable, insecure, questionable, ambiguous, unreliable, precarious, indefinite, indeterminate, incalculable, iffy (*informal*), changeable, indistinct, chancy, unforeseeable, unsettled, unresolved, in the balance, unconfirmed, up in the air, unfixed, conjectural << ANTONYM decided

uncertainty *noun* 1 UNPREDICTABILITY, precariousness, state of suspense, ambiguity, unreliability, fickleness, inconclusiveness, chanciness, changeableness << ANTONYM predictability 2 DOUBT, confusion, dilemma, misgiving, qualm, bewilderment, quandary, puzzlement, perplexity, mystification

<< ANTONYM confidence 3 HESITANCY, hesitation, indecision, lack of confidence, vagueness, irresolution

uncharted *adjective* UNEXPLORED, unknown, undiscovered, strange, virgin, unfamiliar, unplumbed, not mapped

unclean *adjective* 1 DIRTY, soiled, foul, contaminated, polluted, nasty, filthy, defiled, impure, scuzzy (*slang, chiefly US*) << ANTONYM clean 2 IMMORAL, corrupt, impure, evil, dirty, nasty, foul, polluted, filthy, scuzzy (*slang, chiefly US*)

uncomfortable *adjective* 1 UNEASY, troubled, disturbed, embarrassed, distressed, awkward, out of place, self-conscious, disquieted, ill at ease, discomfited, like a fish out of water << ANTONYM comfortable 2 PAINFUL, awkward, irritating, hard, rough, troublesome, disagreeable, causing discomfort

uncommitted *adjective* UNDECIDED, uninvolved, nonpartisan, nonaligned, free, floating, neutral, not involved, unattached, free-floating, (sitting) on the fence

uncommon *adjective* 1 RARE, unusual, odd, novel, strange, bizarre, curious, peculiar, unfamiliar, scarce, queer, singular, few and far between, out of the ordinary, infrequent, thin on the ground << ANTONYM common 2 EXTRAORDINARY, rare, remarkable, special, outstanding, superior, distinctive, exceptional, unprecedented, notable, singular, unparalleled, noteworthy, inimitable, incomparable << ANTONYM ordinary

uncommonly *adverb* 1 EXCEPTIONALLY, very, extremely, remarkably, particularly, strangely, seriously (*informal*), unusually, peculiarly, to the nth degree 2 (always used in a negative construction) RARELY, occasionally, seldom, not often, infrequently, hardly ever, only now and then, scarcely ever

uncompromising *adjective* INFLEXIBLE, strict, rigid, decided, firm, tough, stubborn, hardline, die-hard, inexorable, steadfast, unyielding, obstinate, intransigent, unbending, obdurate, stiff-necked

unconcerned *adjective* UNTROUBLED, relaxed, unperturbed, nonchalant, easy, careless, not bothered, serene, callous, carefree, unruffled, blithe, insouciant, unworried, not giving a toss (*informal*) << ANTONYM concerned

unconditional *adjective* ABSOLUTE, full, complete, total, positive, entire, utter, explicit, outright, unlimited, downright, unqualified, unrestricted, out-and-out, plenary, categorical, unreserved << ANTONYM qualified

unconscious *adjective* 1 SENSELESS, knocked out, out cold (*informal*), out, stunned, numb, dazed, blacked out (*informal*), in a coma, comatose, stupefied, asleep, out for the count (*informal*), insensible, dead to the world (*informal*) << ANTONYM awake 2 UNAWARE, ignorant, oblivious, unsuspecting, lost to, blind to, in ignorance, unknowing << ANTONYM aware 3 UNINTENTIONAL, unwitting, unintended, inadvertent, accidental, unpremeditated << ANTONYM intentional 4 SUBCONSCIOUS, automatic, suppressed, repressed, inherent, reflex, instinctive, innate, involuntary, latent, subliminal, unrealized, gut (*informal*)

unconventional *adjective* 1 UNUSUAL, unorthodox, odd, eccentric, different, individual, original, bizarre, way-out (*informal*), informal, irregular, bohemian, far-out (*slang*), idiosyncratic, off-the-wall (*slang*), oddball (*informal*), individualistic, out of the ordinary, offbeat, left-field (*informal*), freakish, atypical, nonconformist, wacko (*slang*), outré, uncustomary, daggy (*Austral & NZ informal*) << ANTONYM conventional 2 UNORTHODOX, original, unusual, irregular, atypical, different, uncustomary << ANTONYM normal

uncover *verb* 1 REVEAL, find, discover, expose, encounter, turn up, detect, disclose, unveil, come across, unearth, dig up, divulge, chance on, root out, unmask, lay bare, make known, blow the whistle on (*informal*), bring to light, smoke out, take the wraps off, blow wide open (*slang*), stumble on or across << ANTONYM conceal 2 OPEN, unveil, unwrap, show, strip, expose, bare, lay bare, lift the lid, lay open

undaunted *adjective* UNDETERRED, unflinching, not discouraged, not put off, brave, bold, courageous, gritty, fearless, resolute, gallant, intrepid, steadfast, indomitable, dauntless, undismayed, unfaltering, nothing daunted, undiscouraged, unshrinking

undecided *adjective* 1 UNSURE, uncertain, uncommitted, torn, doubtful, dubious, wavering, hesitant, ambivalent, dithering (*chiefly Brit*), in two minds, irresolute, swithering (*Scot*) << ANTONYM sure 2 UNSETTLED, open, undetermined, vague, pending, tentative, in the balance, indefinite,

debatable, up in the air, moot, iffy (*informal*), unconcluded << ANTONYM settled

undeniable *adjective* CERTAIN, evident, undoubted, incontrovertible, clear, sure, sound, proven, obvious, patent, manifest, beyond (a) doubt, unassailable, indisputable, irrefutable, unquestionable, beyond question, incontestable, indubitable << ANTONYM doubtful

under *preposition* 1 BELOW, beneath, underneath, on the bottom of << ANTONYM over 2 SUBORDINATE TO, subject to, reporting to, directed by, governed by, inferior to, secondary to, subservient to, junior to 3 INCLUDED IN, belonging to, subsumed under, comprised in ▷ *adverb* BELOW, down, beneath, downward, to the bottom << ANTONYM up

undercover *adjective* SECRET, covert, clandestine, private, hidden, intelligence, underground, spy, concealed, confidential, hush-hush (*informal*), surreptitious << ANTONYM open

undercurrent *noun* 1 UNDERTONE, feeling, atmosphere, sense, suggestion, trend, hint, flavour, tendency, drift, murmur, tenor, aura, tinge, vibes (*slang*), vibrations, overtone, hidden feeling 2 UNDERTOW, tideway, riptide, rip, rip current, crosscurrent, underflow

undercut *verb* UNDERPRICE, sell cheaply, sell at a loss, undersell, sacrifice, undercharge

underdog *noun* WEAKER PARTY, victim, loser, little fellow (*informal*), outsider, fall guy (*informal*)

underestimate *verb* 1 UNDERVALUE, understate, underrate, diminish, play down, minimize, downgrade, miscalculate, trivialize, rate too low, underemphasize, hold cheap, misprize << ANTONYM overestimate 2 UNDERRATE, undervalue, belittle, sell short (*informal*), not do justice to, rate too low, set no store by, hold cheap, think too little of << ANTONYM overrate

undergo *verb* EXPERIENCE, go through, be subjected to, stand, suffer, bear, weather, sustain, endure, withstand, submit to

underground *adjective* 1 SUBTERRANEAN, basement, lower-level, sunken, covered, buried, below the surface, below ground, subterrestrial 2 SECRET, undercover, covert, hidden, guerrilla, revolutionary, concealed, confidential, dissident, closet, subversive, clandestine, renegade, insurgent, hush-hush (*informal*), surreptitious, cloak-and-dagger, hugger-mugger, insurrectionist, hole-and-corner, radical ▷▷ **the underground 1** THE TUBE (*Brit*), the subway, the metro **2** THE RESISTANCE, partisans, freedom fighters, the Maquis

undergrowth *noun* SCRUB, brush, underwood, bracken, brambles, briars, underbrush, brushwood, underbush

underhand *adjective* SLY, secret, crooked (*informal*), devious, sneaky, secretive, fraudulent, treacherous, dishonest, deceptive, clandestine, unscrupulous, crafty, unethical, furtive, deceitful, surreptitious, stealthy, dishonourable, below the belt (*informal*), underhanded << ANTONYM honest

underline *verb* **1** EMPHASIZE, stress, highlight, bring home, accentuate, point up, give emphasis to, call *or* draw attention to << ANTONYM minimize **2** UNDERSCORE, mark, italicize, rule a line under

underling *noun* (*derogatory*) SUBORDINATE, inferior, minion, servant, slave, cohort (*chiefly US*), retainer, menial, nonentity, lackey, hireling, flunky, understrapper

underlying *adjective* **1** FUNDAMENTAL, basic, essential, root, prime, primary, radical, elementary, intrinsic, basal **2** HIDDEN, concealed, lurking, veiled, latent

undermine *verb* WEAKEN, sabotage, subvert, compromise, disable, debilitate << ANTONYM reinforce

underpinning *noun* SUPPORT, base, foundation, footing, groundwork, substructure

underprivileged *adjective* DISADVANTAGED, poor, deprived, in need, impoverished, needy, badly off, destitute, in want, on the breadline

underrate *verb* UNDERESTIMATE, discount, undervalue, belittle, disparage, fail to appreciate, not do justice to, set (too) little store by, misprize << ANTONYM overestimate

understand *verb* **1** COMPREHEND, get, take in, perceive, grasp, know, see, follow, realize, recognize, appreciate, be aware of, penetrate, make out, discern, twig (*Brit informal*), fathom, savvy (*slang*), apprehend, conceive of, suss (*Brit informal*), get to the bottom of, get the hang of (*informal*), tumble to (*informal*), catch on to (*informal*), cotton on to (*informal*), make head or tail of (*informal*), get your head round **2** SYMPATHIZE WITH, appreciate, be aware of, be able to see, take on board

(*informal*), empathize with, commiserate with, show compassion for **3** BELIEVE, hear, learn, gather, think, see, suppose, notice, assume, take it, conclude, fancy, presume, be informed, infer, surmise, hear tell, draw the inference

understandable *adjective* REASONABLE, natural, normal, justified, expected, inevitable, legitimate, logical, predictable, accountable, on the cards (*informal*), foreseeable, to be expected, justifiable, unsurprising, excusable, pardonable

understanding *noun* **1** PERCEPTION, knowledge, grasp, sense, know-how (*informal*), intelligence, judgment, awareness, appreciation, insight, skill, penetration, mastery, comprehension, familiarity with, discernment, proficiency << ANTONYM ignorance **2** AGREEMENT, deal, promise, arrangement, accord, contract, bond, pledge, bargain, pact, compact, concord, gentlemen's agreement << ANTONYM disagreement **3** BELIEF, view, opinion, impression, interpretation, feeling, idea, conclusion, notion, conviction, judgment, assumption, point of view, perception, suspicion, viewpoint, hunch, way of thinking, estimation, supposition, sneaking suspicion, funny feeling ▷ *adjective* SYMPATHETIC, kind, compassionate, considerate, kindly, accepting, patient, sensitive, forgiving, discerning, tolerant, responsive, perceptive, forbearing << ANTONYM unsympathetic

understood *adjective* **1** ASSUMED, presumed, accepted, taken for granted **2** IMPLIED, implicit, unspoken, inferred, tacit, unstated

understudy *noun* STAND-IN, reserve, substitute, double, sub, replacement, fill-in

undertake *verb* **1** TAKE ON, embark on, set about, commence, try, begin, attempt, tackle, enter upon, endeavour to do **2** AGREE, promise, contract, guarantee, engage, pledge, covenant, commit yourself, take upon yourself

undertaker *noun* FUNERAL DIRECTOR, mortician (*US*)

undertaking *noun* **1** TASK, business, operation, project, game, attempt, effort, affair, venture, enterprise, endeavour **2** PROMISE, commitment, pledge, word, vow, assurance, word of honour, solemn word

undertone *noun* **1** MURMUR, whisper, low tone, subdued voice **2** UNDERCURRENT, suggestion, trace, hint, feeling, touch, atmosphere, flavour, tinge, vibes (*slang*)

undervalue *verb* UNDERRATE, underestimate, minimize, look down on, misjudge, depreciate, make light of, set no store by, hold cheap, misprize << ANTONYM overrate

underwater *adjective* SUBMERGED, submarine, immersed, sunken, undersea, subaqueous, subaquatic

under way *adjective* IN PROGRESS, going on, started, begun, in business, in motion, in operation, afoot

underwear *noun* UNDERCLOTHES, lingerie, undies (*informal*), smalls (*informal*), undergarments, unmentionables (*humorous*), underclothing, underthings, underlinen, broekies (*S African informal*), underdaks (*Austral slang*)

underweight *adjective* SKINNY, puny, emaciated, undernourished, skin and bone (*informal*), undersized, half-starved, underfed

underworld *noun* **1** CRIMINALS, gangsters, organized crime, gangland (*informal*), criminal element **2** NETHER WORLD, hell, Hades, the inferno, nether regions, infernal region, abode of the dead

underwrite *verb* FINANCE, back, fund, guarantee, sponsor, insure, ratify, subsidize, bankroll (*US informal*), provide security, provide capital for

undesirable *adjective* UNWANTED, unwelcome, disagreeable, objectionable, offensive, disliked, unacceptable, dreaded, unpopular, unsuitable, out of place, unattractive, distasteful, unsavoury, obnoxious, repugnant, unpleasing, unwished-for << ANTONYM desirable

undo *verb* **1** OPEN, unfasten, loose, loosen, unlock, unwrap, untie, disengage, unbutton, disentangle, unstrap, unclasp **2** REVERSE, cancel, offset, wipe out, neutralize, invalidate, annul, nullify **3** RUIN, defeat, destroy, wreck, shatter, upset, mar, undermine, overturn, quash, subvert, bring to naught

undoing *noun* DOWNFALL, weakness, curse, trouble, trial, misfortune, blight, affliction, the last straw, fatal flaw

undone¹ *adjective* UNFINISHED, left, outstanding, not done, neglected, omitted, incomplete, passed over, unfulfilled, not completed, unperformed, unattended to << ANTONYM finished

undone² *adjective* (*literary*) RUINED, destroyed, overcome, hapless, forlorn, prostrate, wretched

undoubted *adjective* CERTAIN, sure, definite, confirmed, positive, obvious, acknowledged, patent, evident, manifest, transparent, clear-cut, undisputed, indisputable, unquestioned, unquestionable, incontrovertible, indubitable, nailed-on (*slang*)

undoubtedly *adverb* CERTAINLY, definitely, undeniably, surely, of course, doubtless, without doubt, unquestionably, unmistakably, assuredly, beyond question, beyond a shadow of (a) doubt

undress *verb* STRIP, strip naked, disrobe, take off your clothes, peel off, doff your clothes ▷ *noun* NAKEDNESS, nudity, disarray, deshabille

undue *adjective* EXCESSIVE, too much, inappropriate, extreme, unnecessary, extravagant, needless, unsuitable, improper, too great, disproportionate, unjustified, unwarranted, unseemly, inordinate, undeserved, intemperate, uncalled-for, overmuch, immoderate << ANTONYM appropriate

undulate *verb* WAVE, roll, surge, swell, ripple, rise and fall, billow, heave

unduly *adverb* EXCESSIVELY, overly, too much, unnecessarily, disproportionately, improperly, unreasonably, extravagantly, out of all proportion, inordinately, unjustifiably, overmuch, immoderately << ANTONYM reasonably

undying *adjective* ETERNAL, everlasting, perpetual, continuing, permanent, constant, perennial, infinite, unending, indestructible, undiminished, imperishable, deathless, inextinguishable, unfading, sempiternal (*literary*) << ANTONYM short-lived

unearth *verb* **1** DISCOVER, find, reveal, expose, turn up, uncover, bring to light, ferret out, root up **2** DIG UP, excavate, exhume, dredge up, disinter

unearthly *adjective* **1** EERIE, strange, supernatural, ghostly, weird, phantom, uncanny, spooky (*informal*), nightmarish, spectral, eldritch (*poetic*), preternatural **2** UNREASONABLE, ridiculous, absurd, strange, extraordinary, abnormal, unholy (*informal*), ungodly (*informal*)

uneasiness *noun* ANXIETY, apprehension, misgiving, worry, doubt, alarm, suspicion, nervousness, disquiet, agitation, qualms, trepidation, perturbation, apprehensiveness, dubiety << ANTONYM ease

uneasy *adjective* **1** ANXIOUS, worried, troubled, upset, wired (*slang*), nervous, disturbed, uncomfortable, unsettled, impatient, restless, agitated, apprehensive, edgy, jittery (*informal*), perturbed, on edge, ill at ease, restive, twitchy (*informal*), like a fish out of water, antsy (*informal*), discomposed << ANTONYM relaxed **2** PRECARIOUS, strained, uncomfortable, tense, awkward, unstable, shaky, insecure, constrained **3** DISTURBING, upsetting, disquieting, worrying, troubling, bothering, dismaying

uneconomic *adjective* UNPROFITABLE, loss-making, non-profit-making, nonpaying, nonviable << ANTONYM profitable

unemployed *adjective* OUT OF WORK, redundant, laid off, jobless, idle, on the dole (*Brit informal*), out of a job, workless, resting (*of an actor*) << ANTONYM working

unequal *adjective* **1** DISPROPORTIONATE, uneven, unbalanced, unfair, irregular, unjust, inequitable, ill-matched **2** DIFFERENT, differing, dissimilar, unlike, varying, variable, disparate, unmatched, not uniform << ANTONYM identical **3** *with* **to** NOT UP TO, not qualified for, inadequate for, insufficient for, found wanting in, not cut out for (*informal*), incompetent at

unequalled *or US* **unequaled** *adjective* INCOMPARABLE, supreme, unparalleled, paramount, transcendent, unrivalled, second to none, pre-eminent, inimitable, unmatched, peerless, unsurpassed, matchless, beyond compare, without equal, nonpareil

unequivocal *adjective* CLEAR, absolute, definite, certain, direct, straight, positive, plain, evident, black-and-white, decisive, explicit, manifest, clear-cut, unmistakable, unambiguous, cut-and-dried (*informal*), incontrovertible, indubitable, uncontestable, nailed-on (*slang*) << ANTONYM vague

unerring *adjective* ACCURATE, sure, certain, perfect, exact, impeccable, faultless, infallible, unfailing

uneven *adjective* **1** ROUGH, bumpy, not flat, not level, not smooth << ANTONYM level **2** IRREGULAR, unsteady, fitful, variable, broken, fluctuating, patchy, intermittent, jerky, changeable, spasmodic, inconsistent **3** UNEQUAL, unfair, one-sided, ill-matched **4** LOPSIDED, unbalanced, asymmetrical, odd, out of true, not parallel

uneventful *adjective* HUMDRUM, ordinary, routine, quiet, boring, dull, commonplace, tedious, monotonous, unremarkable, uninteresting, unexciting, unexceptional,

ho-hum (*informal*), unmemorable, unvaried << ANTONYM exciting

unexpected *adjective* UNFORESEEN, surprising, unanticipated, chance, sudden, astonishing, startling, unpredictable, accidental, abrupt, out of the blue, unannounced, fortuitous, unheralded, unlooked-for, not bargained for << ANTONYM expected

unfailing *adjective* **1** CONTINUOUS, endless, persistent, unlimited, continual, never-failing, boundless, bottomless, ceaseless, inexhaustible, unflagging **2** RELIABLE, constant, dependable, sure, true, certain, loyal, faithful, staunch, infallible, steadfast, tried and true << ANTONYM unreliable

unfair *adjective* **1** BIASED, prejudiced, unjust, one-sided, partial, partisan, arbitrary, discriminatory, bigoted, inequitable **2** UNSCRUPULOUS, crooked (*informal*), dishonest, unethical, wrongful, unprincipled, dishonourable, unsporting << ANTONYM ethical

unfaithful *adjective* **1** FAITHLESS, untrue, two-timing (*informal*), adulterous, fickle, inconstant, unchaste << ANTONYM faithful **2** DISLOYAL, false, treacherous, deceitful, faithless, perfidious, traitorous, treasonable, false-hearted, recreant (*archaic*) << ANTONYM loyal

unfamiliar *adjective* **1** STRANGE, new, unknown, different, novel, unusual, curious, alien, out-of-the-way, uncommon, little known, unaccustomed, beyond your ken << ANTONYM familiar **2** *with* **with** UNACQUAINTED WITH, a stranger to, unaccustomed to, inexperienced in, uninformed about, unversed in, uninitiated in, unskilled at, unpractised in, unconversant with << ANTONYM acquainted with

unfathomable *adjective* **1** BAFFLING, incomprehensible, inexplicable, deep, profound, esoteric, impenetrable, unknowable, abstruse, indecipherable **2** IMMEASURABLE, bottomless, unmeasured, unplumbed, unsounded

unfavourable *or US* **unfavorable** *adjective* ADVERSE, bad, unfortunate, disadvantageous, threatening, contrary, unlucky, ominous, untimely, untoward, unpromising, unsuited, inauspicious, ill-suited, inopportune, unseasonable, unpropitious, infelicitous << ANTONYM positive

unfinished *adjective* **1** INCOMPLETE, uncompleted, half-done, lacking, undone, in the making, imperfect, unfulfilled, unaccomplished **2** NATURAL, rough, raw, bare, crude, unrefined, unvarnished, unpolished << ANTONYM polished

unfit *adjective* **1** OUT OF SHAPE, feeble, unhealthy, debilitated, flabby, decrepit, in poor condition, out of trim, out of kilter << ANTONYM healthy **2** INCAPABLE, inadequate, incompetent, no good, useless, not up to, unprepared, ineligible, unqualified, untrained, ill-equipped, not equal, not cut out << ANTONYM capable **3** UNSUITABLE, inadequate, inappropriate, useless, not fit, not designed, unsuited, ill-adapted << ANTONYM suitable

unflappable *adjective (informal)* IMPERTURBABLE, cool, collected, calm, composed, level-headed, unfazed (*informal*), impassive, unruffled, self-possessed, not given to worry << ANTONYM excitable

unflinching *adjective* DETERMINED, firm, steady, constant, bold, stalwart, staunch, resolute, steadfast, unwavering, immovable, unswerving, unshaken, unfaltering, unshrinking << ANTONYM wavering

unfold *verb* **1** DEVELOP, happen, progress, grow, emerge, occur, take place, expand, work out, mature, evolve, blossom, transpire, bear fruit **2** REVEAL, tell, present, show, describe, explain, illustrate, disclose, uncover, clarify, divulge, narrate, make known **3** OPEN, spread out, undo, expand, flatten, straighten, stretch out, unfurl, unwrap, unroll

unfortunate *adjective* **1** DISASTROUS, calamitous, inopportune, adverse, untimely, unfavourable, untoward, ruinous, ill-starred, infelicitous, ill-fated << ANTONYM opportune **2** REGRETTABLE, deplorable, lamentable, inappropriate, unsuitable, ill-advised, unbecoming << ANTONYM becoming **3** UNLUCKY, poor, unhappy, doomed, cursed, hopeless, unsuccessful, hapless, luckless, out of luck, wretched, star-crossed, unprosperous << ANTONYM fortunate

unfounded *adjective* GROUNDLESS, false, unjustified, unproven, unsubstantiated, idle, fabricated, spurious, trumped up, baseless, without foundation, without basis << ANTONYM justified

unfriendly *adjective* **1** HOSTILE, cold, distant, sour, chilly, aloof, surly, antagonistic, disagreeable, quarrelsome, unsociable, ill-disposed, unneighbourly << ANTONYM

friendly **2** UNFAVOURABLE, hostile, inhospitable, alien, inauspicious, inimical, uncongenial, unpropitious, unkind << ANTONYM congenial

ungainly *adjective* AWKWARD, clumsy, inelegant, lumbering, slouching, gawky, uncouth, gangling, loutish, uncoordinated, ungraceful, lubberly, unco (*Austral slang*) << ANTONYM graceful

unguarded *adjective* **1** UNPROTECTED, vulnerable, defenceless, undefended, open to attack, unpatrolled **2** CARELESS, rash, unwary, foolhardy, thoughtless, indiscreet, unthinking, ill-considered, imprudent, heedless, incautious, undiplomatic, impolitic, uncircumspect << ANTONYM cautious

unhappiness *noun* SADNESS, depression, misery, gloom, sorrow, melancholy, heartache, despondency, blues, dejection, wretchedness, low spirits

unhappy *adjective* **1** SAD, depressed, miserable, down, low, blue, gloomy, melancholy, mournful, dejected, despondent, dispirited, downcast, long-faced, sorrowful, disconsolate, crestfallen, down in the dumps (*informal*) << ANTONYM happy **2** UNLUCKY, unfortunate, hapless, luckless, cursed, wretched, ill-omened, ill-fated << ANTONYM fortunate **3** INAPPROPRIATE, awkward, clumsy, unsuitable, inept, ill-advised, tactless, ill-timed, injudicious, infelicitous, malapropos, untactful << ANTONYM apt

unhealthy *adjective* **1** HARMFUL, detrimental, unwholesome, noxious, deleterious, insanitary, noisome, insalubrious << ANTONYM beneficial **2** SICK, sickly, unwell, poorly (*informal*), weak, delicate, crook (*Austral & NZ informal*), ailing, frail, feeble, invalid, unsound, infirm, in poor health << ANTONYM well **3** WEAK, unsound, ailing << ANTONYM strong **4** UNWHOLESOME, morbid, bad, negative, corrupt, corrupting, degrading, undesirable, demoralizing, baneful (*archaic*) << ANTONYM wholesome

unheard-of *adjective* **1** UNPRECEDENTED, inconceivable, undreamed-of, new, novel, unique, unusual, unbelievable, singular, ground-breaking, never before encountered, unexampled **2** SHOCKING, extreme, outrageous, offensive, unacceptable, unthinkable, disgraceful, preposterous, outlandish **3** OBSCURE, unknown, undiscovered, unfamiliar, little known, unsung, unremarked, unregarded

unhinge *verb* UNBALANCE, confuse, derange, disorder, unsettle, madden, craze, confound, distemper (*archaic*), dement, drive you out of your mind

unholy *adjective* 1 (*informal*) SHOCKING, awful, appalling, dreadful, outrageous, horrendous, unearthly, ungodly (*informal*) 2 EVIL, vile, wicked, base, corrupt, immoral, dishonest, sinful, heinous, depraved, profane, iniquitous, ungodly, irreligious << ANTONYM holy

unification *noun* UNION, uniting, alliance, combination, coalition, merger, federation, confederation, fusion, amalgamation, coalescence

uniform *noun* 1 REGALIA, suit, livery, colours, habit, regimentals 2 OUTFIT, dress, costume, attire, gear (*informal*), get-up (*informal*), ensemble, garb ▷ *adjective* 1 CONSISTENT, unvarying, similar, even, same, matching, regular, constant, equivalent, identical, homogeneous, unchanging, equable, undeviating << ANTONYM varying 2 ALIKE, similar, identical, like, same, equal, selfsame

uniformity *noun* 1 REGULARITY, similarity, sameness, constancy, homogeneity, evenness, invariability 2 MONOTONY, sameness, tedium, dullness, flatness, drabness, lack of diversity

unify *verb* UNITE, join, combine, merge, consolidate, bring together, fuse, confederate, amalgamate, federate << ANTONYM divide

uninterested *adjective* INDIFFERENT, unconcerned, apathetic, bored, distant, listless, impassive, blasé, unresponsive, uninvolved, incurious << ANTONYM concerned ▷ see **disinterested**

union *noun* 1 JOINING, uniting, unification, combination, coalition, merger, mixture, blend, merging, integration, conjunction, fusion, synthesis, amalgamating, amalgam, amalgamation 2 ALLIANCE, league, association, coalition, federation, confederation, confederacy, Bund 3 MARRIAGE, match, wedlock, matrimony 4 INTERCOURSE, coupling, copulation, the other (*informal*), nookie (*slang*), coitus, rumpy-pumpy (*slang*), coition

unique *adjective* 1 DISTINCT, special, exclusive, peculiar, only, single, lone, solitary, one and only, sui generis 2 UNPARALLELED, unrivalled, incomparable, inimitable, unmatched, peerless, unequalled, matchless,

without equal, nonpareil, unexampled

unit *noun* 1 ENTITY, whole, item, feature, piece, portion, module 2 SECTION, company, group, force, detail, division, cell, squad, crew, outfit, faction, corps, brigade, regiment, battalion, legion, contingent, squadron, garrison, detachment, platoon 3 MEASURE, quantity, measurement 4 PART, section, segment, class, element, component, constituent, tutorial

unite *verb* 1 JOIN, link, combine, couple, marry, wed, blend, incorporate, merge, consolidate, unify, fuse, amalgamate, coalesce, meld << ANTONYM separate 2 COOPERATE, ally, join forces, league, band, associate, pool, collaborate, confederate, pull together, join together, close ranks, club together << ANTONYM split

united *adjective* 1 IN AGREEMENT, agreed, unanimous, one, like-minded, in accord, of like mind, of one mind, of the same opinion 2 COMBINED, leagued, allied, unified, pooled, concerted, collective, affiliated, in partnership, banded together

unity *noun* 1 UNION, unification, coalition, federation, integration, confederation, amalgamation 2 WHOLENESS, integrity, oneness, union, unification, entity, singleness, undividedness << ANTONYM disunity 3 AGREEMENT, accord, consensus, peace, harmony, solidarity, unison, assent, unanimity, concord, concurrence << ANTONYM disagreement

universal *adjective* 1 WIDESPREAD, general, common, whole, total, entire, catholic, unlimited, ecumenical, omnipresent, all-embracing, overarching, one-size-fits-all 2 GLOBAL, worldwide, international, pandemic

universality *noun* COMPREHENSIVENESS, generalization, generality, totality, completeness, ubiquity, all-inclusiveness

universally *adverb* WITHOUT EXCEPTION, uniformly, everywhere, always, invariably, across the board, in all cases, in every instance

universe *noun* COSMOS, space, creation, everything, nature, heavens, the natural world, macrocosm, all existence

unjust *adjective* UNFAIR, prejudiced, biased, wrong, one-sided, partial, partisan, unjustified, wrongful, undeserved, inequitable, unmerited << ANTONYM fair

unkempt *adjective* 1 UNCOMBED, tousled, shaggy, ungroomed 2 UNTIDY, scruffy, dishevelled, disordered, messy, sloppy (*informal*), shabby, rumpled, bedraggled, slovenly, blowsy, sluttish, slatternly, disarranged, ungroomed, disarrayed, frowzy, daggy (*Austral & NZ informal*) << ANTONYM tidy

unkind *adjective* CRUEL, mean, nasty, spiteful, harsh, malicious, insensitive, unfriendly, inhuman, unsympathetic, uncaring, thoughtless, unfeeling, inconsiderate, uncharitable, unchristian, hardhearted << ANTONYM kind

unknown *adjective* 1 STRANGE, new, undiscovered, uncharted, unexplored, virgin, remote, alien, exotic, outlandish, unmapped, untravelled, beyond your ken 2 UNIDENTIFIED, mysterious, anonymous, unnamed, nameless, incognito 3 OBSCURE, little known, minor, humble, unfamiliar, insignificant, lowly, unimportant, unheard-of, unsung, inconsequential, undistinguished, unrenowned << ANTONYM famous

unleash *verb* RELEASE, let go, let loose, free, untie, unloose, unbridle

unlike *preposition* 1 DIFFERENT FROM, dissimilar to, not resembling, far from, not like, distinct from, incompatible with, unrelated to, distant from, unequal to, far apart from, divergent from, not similar to, as different as chalk and cheese from (*informal*) << ANTONYM similar to 2 CONTRASTED WITH, not like, in contradiction to, in contrast with *or* to, as opposed to, differently from, opposite to

unlikely *adjective* 1 IMPROBABLE, doubtful, remote, slight, faint, not likely, unimaginable << ANTONYM probable 2 UNBELIEVABLE, incredible, unconvincing, implausible, questionable, cock-and-bull (*informal*) << ANTONYM believable

unlimited *adjective* 1 INFINITE, endless, countless, great, vast, extensive, immense, stellar (*informal*), limitless, boundless, incalculable, immeasurable, unbounded, illimitable << ANTONYM finite 2 TOTAL, full, complete, absolute, unconditional, unqualified, unfettered, unrestricted, all-encompassing, unconstrained << ANTONYM restricted

unload *verb* 1 EMPTY, clear, unpack, dump, discharge, off-load, disburden, unlade 2 UNBURDEN, relieve, lighten, disburden

unlock *verb* OPEN, undo, unfasten, release, unbolt, unlatch, unbar

unlucky *adjective* 1 UNFORTUNATE, unhappy, disastrous << ANTONYM fortunate 2 ILL-FATED, doomed, inauspicious, ominous, untimely, unfavourable, cursed, ill-starred, ill-omened

unmask *verb* REVEAL, expose, uncover, discover, disclose, unveil, show up, lay bare, bring to light, uncloak

unmistakable *adjective* CLEAR, certain, positive, decided, sure, obvious, plain, patent, evident, distinct, pronounced, glaring, manifest, blatant, conspicuous, palpable, unequivocal, unambiguous, indisputable << ANTONYM doubtful

unmitigated *adjective* 1 UNRELIEVED, relentless, unalleviated, intense, harsh, grim, persistent, oppressive, unbroken, unqualified, unabated, undiminished, unmodified, unredeemed 2 COMPLETE, absolute, utter, perfect, rank, sheer, total, outright, thorough, downright, consummate, out-and-out, thoroughgoing, arrant, deep-dyed (*usually derogatory*)

unnatural *adjective* 1 ABNORMAL, odd, strange, unusual, extraordinary, bizarre, perverted, queer, irregular, perverse, supernatural, uncanny, outlandish, unaccountable, anomalous, freakish, aberrant << ANTONYM normal 2 FALSE, forced, artificial, studied, laboured, affected, assumed, mannered, strained, stiff, theatrical, contrived, self-conscious, feigned, stilted, insincere, factitious, stagy, phoney *or* phony (*informal*) << ANTONYM genuine 3 INHUMAN, evil, monstrous, wicked, savage, brutal, ruthless, callous, heartless, cold-blooded, fiendish, unfeeling << ANTONYM humane

unnecessary *adjective* NEEDLESS, excessive, unwarranted, useless, pointless, not needed, redundant, wasteful, gratuitous, superfluous, wanton, expendable, surplus to requirements, uncalled-for, dispensable, unneeded, nonessential, inessential, unmerited, to no purpose, unrequired, supererogatory << ANTONYM essential

unnerve *verb* SHAKE, upset, disconcert, disturb, intimidate, frighten, rattle (*informal*), discourage, dismay, daunt, disarm, confound, fluster, faze, unman, demoralize, unhinge, psych out (*informal*), throw off balance, dishearten, dispirit << ANTONYM strengthen

unoccupied *adjective* 1 EMPTY, vacant, uninhabited, untenanted, tenantless 2 IDLE, unemployed, inactive, disengaged, at leisure, at a loose end

unofficial *adjective* **1** UNCONFIRMED, off the record, unsubstantiated, private, personal, unauthorized, undocumented, uncorroborated **2** UNAUTHORIZED, informal, unsanctioned, casual, wildcat

unparalleled *adjective* UNEQUALLED, exceptional, unprecedented, rare, unique, singular, consummate, superlative, unrivalled, incomparable, unmatched, peerless, unsurpassed, matchless, beyond compare, without equal

unpleasant *adjective* **1** NASTY, bad, horrid, distressing, annoying, irritating, miserable, troublesome, distasteful, obnoxious, unpalatable, displeasing, repulsive, objectionable, disagreeable, abhorrent, irksome, unlovely, execrable << ANTONYM nice **2** OBNOXIOUS, disagreeable, vicious, malicious, rude, mean, cruel, poisonous, unattractive, unfriendly, vindictive, venomous, mean-spirited, inconsiderate, impolite, unloveable, ill-natured, unlikable *or* unlikeable << ANTONYM likable *or* likeable

unpleasantness *noun* **1** HOSTILITY, animosity, antagonism, bad feeling, malice, rudeness, offensiveness, abrasiveness, argumentativeness, unfriendliness, quarrelsomeness, ill humour *or* will << ANTONYM friendliness **2** NASTINESS, awfulness, grimness, trouble, misery, woe, ugliness, unacceptability, dreadfulness, disagreeableness, horridness << ANTONYM pleasantness

unpopular *adjective* DISLIKED, rejected, unwanted, avoided, shunned, unwelcome, undesirable, unattractive, detested, out of favour, unloved, out in the cold, cold-shouldered, not sought out, sent to Coventry (*Brit*) << ANTONYM popular

unprecedented *adjective* **1** UNPARALLELED, unheard-of, exceptional, new, original, novel, unusual, abnormal, singular, ground-breaking, unrivalled, freakish, unexampled **2** EXTRAORDINARY, amazing, remarkable, outstanding, fantastic, marvellous, exceptional, phenomenal, uncommon

unprofessional *adjective* **1** UNETHICAL, unfitting, improper, lax, negligent, unworthy, unseemly, unprincipled **2** AMATEURISH, amateur, incompetent, inefficient, cowboy (*informal*), inexperienced, untrained, slapdash, slipshod, inexpert << ANTONYM skilful

unqualified *adjective* **1** UNFIT, incapable, incompetent, not up to, unprepared, ineligible, ill-equipped, not equal to **2** UNCONDITIONAL, complete, total, absolute, utter, outright, thorough, downright, consummate, unrestricted, out-and-out, categorical, unmitigated, unreserved, thoroughgoing, without reservation, arrant, deep-dyed (*usually derogatory*)

unquestionable *adjective* CERTAIN, undeniable, indisputable, clear, sure, perfect, absolute, patent, definite, manifest, unmistakable, conclusive, flawless, unequivocal, faultless, self-evident, irrefutable, incontrovertible, incontestable, indubitable, beyond a shadow of doubt, nailed-on (*slang*) << ANTONYM doubtful

unravel *verb* **1** SOLVE, explain, work out, resolve, interpret, figure out (*informal*), make out, clear up, suss (out) (*slang*), get to the bottom of, get straight, puzzle out **2** UNDO, separate, disentangle, free, unwind, extricate, straighten out, untangle, unknot

unreadable *adjective* **1** TURGID, heavy going, badly written, dry as dust **2** ILLEGIBLE, undecipherable, crabbed

unreal *adjective* IMAGINARY, make-believe, illusory, fabulous, visionary, mythical, fanciful, fictitious, intangible, immaterial, storybook, insubstantial, nebulous, dreamlike, impalpable, chimerical, phantasmagoric

unreasonable *adjective* **1** BIASED, arbitrary, irrational, illogical, blinkered, opinionated, headstrong << ANTONYM open-minded **2** EXCESSIVE, steep (*informal*), exorbitant, unfair, absurd, extravagant, unjust, too great, undue, preposterous, unwarranted, far-fetched, extortionate, uncalled-for, immoderate << ANTONYM moderate

unrelenting *adjective* **1** MERCILESS, tough, ruthless, relentless, cruel, stern, inexorable, implacable, intransigent, remorseless, pitiless, unsparing **2** STEADY, constant, continuous, endless, perpetual, continual, unbroken, incessant, unabated, ceaseless, unremitting, unwavering

unremitting *adjective* CONSTANT, continuous, relentless, perpetual, continual, unbroken, incessant, diligent, unabated, unwavering, indefatigable, remorseless, assiduous, unceasing, sedulous, unwearied

unrest *noun* DISCONTENT, rebellion, dissatisfaction, protest, turmoil, upheaval, strife, agitation, discord, disaffection, sedition, tumult, dissension << ANTONYM peace

unrivalled *adjective* UNPARALLELED, incomparable, unsurpassed, supreme, unmatched, peerless, unequalled, matchless, beyond compare, without equal, nonpareil, unexcelled

unruffled *adjective* **1** CALM, cool, collected, peaceful, composed, serene, tranquil, sedate, placid, undisturbed, unmoved, unfazed (*informal*), unperturbed, unflustered **2** SMOOTH, even, level, flat, unbroken

unruly *adjective* UNCONTROLLABLE, wild, unmanageable, disorderly, turbulent, rebellious, wayward, rowdy, intractable, wilful, lawless, fractious, riotous, headstrong, mutinous, disobedient, ungovernable, refractory, obstreperous, insubordinate << ANTONYM manageable

unsafe *adjective* DANGEROUS, risky, hazardous, threatening, uncertain, unstable, insecure, unreliable, precarious, treacherous, perilous, unsound << ANTONYM safe

unsavoury *adjective* **1** UNPLEASANT, nasty, obnoxious, offensive, revolting, distasteful, repellent, repulsive, objectionable, repugnant **2** UNAPPETIZING, unpalatable, distasteful, sickening, disagreeable, nauseating << ANTONYM appetizing

unscathed *adjective* UNHARMED, unhurt, uninjured, whole, sound, safe, untouched, unmarked, in one piece, unscarred, unscratched

unscrupulous *adjective* UNPRINCIPLED, corrupt, crooked (*informal*), ruthless, improper, immoral, dishonest, unethical, exploitative, dishonourable, roguish, unconscionable, knavish, conscienceless, unconscientious << ANTONYM honourable

unseat *verb* **1** DEPOSE, overthrow, oust, remove, dismiss, discharge, displace, dethrone **2** THROW, unsaddle, unhorse

unseemly *adjective* IMPROPER, inappropriate, unsuitable, out of place, undignified, disreputable, unbecoming, unrefined, out of keeping, discreditable, indelicate, in poor taste, indecorous, unbefitting << ANTONYM proper

unseen *adjective* **1** UNOBSERVED, undetected, unperceived, lurking, unnoticed, unobtrusive **2** HIDDEN, concealed, invisible, veiled, obscure

unselfish *adjective* GENEROUS, selfless, noble, kind, liberal, devoted, humanitarian, charitable, disinterested, altruistic, self-sacrificing, magnanimous, self-denying

unsettle *verb* DISTURB, trouble, upset, throw (*informal*), bother, confuse, disorder, rattle (*informal*), agitate, ruffle, unnerve, disconcert, unbalance, fluster, perturb, faze, throw into confusion, throw off balance, discompose, throw into disorder, throw into uproar

unsettled *adjective* **1** UNSTABLE, shaky, insecure, disorderly, unsteady **2** RESTLESS, tense, uneasy, troubled, shaken, confused, wired (*slang*), disturbed, anxious, agitated, unnerved, flustered, perturbed, on edge, restive, adrenalized **3** UNRESOLVED, undecided, undetermined, open, doubtful, debatable, up in the air, moot **4** INCONSTANT, changing, unpredictable, variable, uncertain, changeable **5** OWING, due, outstanding, pending, payable, in arrears

unsightly *adjective* UGLY, unattractive, repulsive, unpleasant, revolting (*informal*), hideous, horrid, disagreeable, unprepossessing << ANTONYM attractive

unskilled *adjective* UNPROFESSIONAL, inexperienced, unqualified, untrained, uneducated, amateurish, cowboy (*informal*), untalented << ANTONYM skilled

unsophisticated *adjective* **1** SIMPLE, plain, uncomplicated, straightforward, unrefined, uninvolved, unspecialized, uncomplex << ANTONYM advanced **2** NAIVE, innocent, inexperienced, unworldly, unaffected, childlike, natural, artless, ingenuous, guileless

unsound *adjective* **1** FLAWED, faulty, weak, false, shaky, unreliable, invalid, defective, illogical, erroneous, specious, fallacious, ill-founded **2** UNSTABLE, shaky, insecure, unsafe, unreliable, flimsy, wobbly, tottering, rickety, unsteady, not solid << ANTONYM stable **3** UNHEALTHY, unstable, unbalanced, diseased, ill, weak, delicate, ailing, frail, defective, unwell, deranged, unhinged

unspeakable *adjective* DREADFUL, shocking, appalling, evil, awful, overwhelming, horrible, unbelievable, monstrous, from hell (*informal*), inconceivable, unimaginable, repellent, abysmal, frightful, heinous, odious, indescribable, loathsome, abominable, ineffable, beyond words, execrable, unutterable, inexpressible, beyond description, hellacious (*US slang*), too horrible for words

unstable *adjective* **1** CHANGEABLE, volatile, unpredictable, variable, fluctuating,

745

unsteady, fitful, inconstant << ANTONYM
constant 2 INSECURE, shaky, precarious,
unsettled, wobbly, tottering, rickety,
unsteady, not fixed 3 UNPREDICTABLE,
irrational, erratic, inconsistent, unreliable,
temperamental, capricious, changeable,
untrustworthy, vacillating << ANTONYM
level-headed

unsteady *adjective* 1 UNSTABLE, shaky,
insecure, unsafe, precarious, treacherous,
rickety, infirm 2 REELING, wobbly, tottering
3 ERRATIC, unpredictable, volatile, unsettled,
wavering, unreliable, temperamental,
changeable, vacillating, flighty, inconstant

unsung *adjective* UNACKNOWLEDGED,
unrecognized, unappreciated, unknown,
neglected, anonymous, disregarded,
unnamed, uncelebrated, unhonoured,
unacclaimed, unhailed

unswerving *adjective* FIRM, staunch,
steadfast, constant, true, direct, devoted,
steady, dedicated, resolute, single-minded,
unwavering, unflagging, untiring,
unfaltering, undeviating

untangle *verb* 1 DISENTANGLE, unravel, sort
out, extricate, straighten out, untwist,
unsnarl << ANTONYM entangle 2 SOLVE,
clear up, straighten out, understand,
explain, figure out (*informal*), clarify, unravel,
fathom, get to the bottom of, elucidate,
suss out (*informal*), puzzle out << ANTONYM
complicate

untenable *adjective* UNSUSTAINABLE,
indefensible, unsound, groundless, weak,
flawed, shaky, unreasonable, illogical,
fallacious, insupportable << ANTONYM
justified

unthinkable *adjective* 1 IMPOSSIBLE, out of
the question, inconceivable, unlikely, not on
(*informal*), absurd, unreasonable, improbable,
preposterous, illogical 2 INCONCEIVABLE,
incredible, unbelievable, unimaginable,
beyond belief, beyond the bounds of
possibility

unthinking *adjective* 1 THOUGHTLESS,
insensitive, tactless, rude, blundering,
inconsiderate, undiplomatic 2 IMPULSIVE,
senseless, unconscious, mechanical, rash,
careless, instinctive, oblivious, negligent,
unwitting, witless, inadvertent, heedless,
unmindful << ANTONYM deliberate

untidy *adjective* 1 MESSY, disordered, chaotic,
littered, muddled, cluttered, jumbled,
rumpled, shambolic, bedraggled, unkempt,
topsy-turvy, higgledy-piggledy (*informal*),

mussy (*US informal*), muddly, disarrayed
<< ANTONYM neat 2 UNKEMPT, dishevelled,
tousled, disordered, messy, ruffled, scruffy,
rumpled, bedraggled, ratty (*informal*),
straggly, windblown, disarranged, mussed
up (*informal*), daggy (*Austral & NZ informal*)
3 SLOPPY, messy (*informal*), slovenly, slipshod,
slatternly << ANTONYM methodical

untie *verb* UNDO, free, release, loosen,
unfasten, unbind, unstrap, unclasp, unlace,
unknot, unmoor, unbridle

untimely *adjective* 1 EARLY, premature,
before time, unseasonable << ANTONYM
timely 2 ILL-TIMED, inappropriate, badly
timed, inopportune, unfortunate, awkward,
unsuitable, inconvenient, mistimed,
inauspicious << ANTONYM well-timed

untold *adjective* 1 INDESCRIBABLE,
unthinkable, unimaginable, unspeakable,
undreamed of, unutterable, inexpressible
2 COUNTLESS, incalculable, innumerable,
myriad, numberless, uncounted,
uncountable, unnumbered, measureless
3 UNDISCLOSED, unknown, unrevealed,
private, secret, hidden, unrelated,
unpublished, unrecounted

untoward *adjective* UNFAVOURABLE,
unfortunate, disastrous, adverse, contrary,
annoying, awkward, irritating, unlucky,
inconvenient, untimely, inauspicious,
inimical, ill-timed, vexatious, inopportune

untrue *adjective* 1 FALSE, lying, wrong,
mistaken, misleading, incorrect,
inaccurate, sham, dishonest, deceptive,
spurious, erroneous, fallacious, untruthful
<< ANTONYM true 2 UNFAITHFUL, disloyal,
deceitful, treacherous, two-faced, faithless,
false, untrustworthy, perfidious, forsworn,
traitorous, inconstant << ANTONYM faithful

untruth *noun* LIE, fabrication, falsehood, fib,
story, tale, fiction, deceit, whopper (*informal*),
porky (*Brit slang*), pork pie (*Brit slang*),
falsification, prevarication

unused *adjective* 1 NEW, untouched,
remaining, fresh, intact, immaculate,
pristine 2 REMAINING, leftover,
unconsumed, left, available, extra,
unutilized 3 *with* **to** UNACCUSTOMED TO,
new to, unfamiliar with, not up to, not
ready for, a stranger to, inexperienced in,
unhabituated to

unusual *adjective* 1 RARE, odd, strange,
extraordinary, different, surprising,
novel, bizarre, unexpected, curious, weird
(*informal*), unfamiliar, abnormal, queer,

phenomenal, uncommon, out of the ordinary, left-field (*informal*), unwonted << ANTONYM common **2** EXTRAORDINARY, unique, remarkable, exceptional, notable, phenomenal, uncommon, singular, unconventional, out of the ordinary, atypical << ANTONYM average

unveil *verb* REVEAL, publish, launch, introduce, release, display, broadcast, demonstrate, expose, bare, parade, exhibit, disclose, uncover, bring out, make public, flaunt, divulge, lay bare, make known, bring to light, put on display, lay open, put on show, put on view << ANTONYM conceal

unwarranted *adjective* UNNECESSARY, unjustified, indefensible, wrong, unreasonable, unjust, gratuitous, unprovoked, inexcusable, groundless, uncalled-for

unwary *adjective* CARELESS, rash, reckless, hasty, thoughtless, unguarded, indiscreet, imprudent, heedless, incautious, uncircumspect, unwatchful << ANTONYM cautious

unwell *adjective* ILL, poorly (*informal*), sick, crook (*Austral & NZ informal*), ailing, unhealthy, sickly, out of sorts, off colour, under the weather (*informal*), in poor health, at death's door, indisposed, green about the gills << ANTONYM well

unwieldy *adjective* **1** BULKY, massive, hefty, clumsy, weighty, ponderous, ungainly, clunky (*informal*) **2** AWKWARD, cumbersome, inconvenient, burdensome, unmanageable, unhandy

unwilling *adjective* **1** DISINCLINED, reluctant, averse, loath, slow, opposed, resistant, not about, not in the mood, indisposed << ANTONYM willing **2** RELUCTANT, grudging, unenthusiastic, resistant, involuntary, averse, demurring, laggard (*rare*) << ANTONYM eager

unwind *verb* **1** RELAX, wind down, take it easy, slow down, sit back, calm down, take a break, loosen up, quieten down, let yourself go, mellow out (*informal*), make yourself at home, outspan (*S African*) **2** UNRAVEL, undo, uncoil, slacken, disentangle, unroll, unreel, untwist, untwine

unwise *adjective* FOOLISH, stupid, silly, rash, irresponsible, reckless, senseless, short-sighted, ill-advised, foolhardy, inane, indiscreet, ill-judged, ill-considered, imprudent, inadvisable, asinine, injudicious, improvident, impolitic << ANTONYM wise

unwitting *adjective* **1** UNINTENTIONAL, involuntary, inadvertent, chance, accidental, unintended, unplanned, undesigned, unmeant << ANTONYM deliberate **2** UNKNOWING, innocent, unsuspecting, unconscious, unaware, ignorant << ANTONYM knowing

unworthy *adjective* **1** UNDESERVING, not good enough, not fit, not worth, ineligible, not deserving << ANTONYM deserving **2** DISHONOURABLE, base, contemptible, degrading, disgraceful, shameful, disreputable, ignoble, discreditable << ANTONYM commendable **3** *with* **of** UNBEFITTING, beneath, unfitting to, unsuitable for, inappropriate to, improper to, out of character with, out of place with, unbecoming to

unwritten *adjective* **1** ORAL, word-of-mouth, unrecorded, vocal **2** UNDERSTOOD, accepted, tacit, traditional, conventional, silent, customary, implicit, unformulated

up ▷▷ **ups and downs** FLUCTUATIONS, changes, vicissitudes, moods, ebb and flow

up-and-coming *adjective* PROMISING, ambitious, go-getting (*informal*), pushing, eager

upbeat *adjective* (*informal*) CHEERFUL, positive, optimistic, promising, encouraging, looking up, hopeful, favourable, rosy, buoyant, heartening, cheery, forward-looking

upbringing *noun* EDUCATION, training, breeding, rearing, care, raising, tending, bringing-up, nurture, cultivation

update *verb* BRING UP TO DATE, improve, correct, renew, revise, upgrade, amend, overhaul, streamline, modernize, rebrand

upgrade *verb* **1** IMPROVE, better, update, reform, add to, enhance, refurbish, renovate, remodel, make better, modernize, spruce up, ameliorate **2** PROMOTE, raise, advance, boost, move up, elevate, kick upstairs (*informal*), give promotion to << ANTONYM demote

upheaval *noun* DISTURBANCE, revolution, disorder, turmoil, overthrow, disruption, eruption, cataclysm, violent change

uphill *adjective* **1** ASCENDING, rising, upward, mounting, climbing << ANTONYM descending **2** ARDUOUS, hard, taxing, difficult, tough, exhausting, punishing, gruelling, strenuous, laborious, wearisome, Sisyphean

uphold *verb* **1** SUPPORT, back, defend, aid, champion, encourage, maintain, promote, sustain, advocate, stand by, stick up for (*informal*) **2** CONFIRM, support, sustain, endorse, approve, justify, hold to, ratify, vindicate, validate

upkeep *noun* **1** MAINTENANCE, running, keep, subsistence, support, repair, conservation, preservation, sustenance **2** RUNNING COSTS, expenses, overheads, expenditure, outlay, operating costs, oncosts (*Brit*)

uplift *verb* IMPROVE, better, raise, advance, inspire, upgrade, refine, cultivate, civilize, ameliorate, edify ▷ *noun* IMPROVEMENT, enlightenment, advancement, cultivation, refinement, enhancement, enrichment, betterment, edification

upper *adjective* **1** TOPMOST, top << ANTONYM bottom **2** HIGHER, high << ANTONYM lower **3** SUPERIOR, senior, higher-level, greater, top, important, chief, most important, elevated, eminent, higher-ranking << ANTONYM inferior

upper class *adjective* ARISTOCRATIC, upper-class, noble, high-class, patrician, top-drawer, blue-blooded, highborn

uppermost *adjective* **1** TOP, highest, topmost, upmost, loftiest, most elevated << ANTONYM bottom **2** SUPREME, greatest, chief, leading, main, primary, principal, dominant, paramount, foremost, predominant, pre-eminent << ANTONYM least

upright *adjective* **1** VERTICAL, straight, standing up, erect, on end, perpendicular, bolt upright << ANTONYM horizontal **2** HONEST, good, principled, just, true, faithful, ethical, straightforward, honourable, righteous, conscientious, virtuous, trustworthy, high-minded, above board, incorruptible, unimpeachable << ANTONYM dishonourable

uprising *noun* REBELLION, rising, revolution, outbreak, revolt, disturbance, upheaval, mutiny, insurrection, putsch, insurgence

uproar *noun* **1** COMMOTION, noise, racket, riot, confusion, turmoil, brawl, mayhem, clamour, din, turbulence, pandemonium, rumpus, hubbub, hurly-burly, brouhaha, ruction (*informal*), hullabaloo, ruckus (*informal*), bagarre (*French*) **2** PROTEST, outrage, complaint, objection, fuss, stink (*informal*), outcry, furore, hue and cry

uproot *verb* **1** DISPLACE, remove, exile, disorient, deracinate **2** PULL UP, dig up, root out, weed out, rip up, grub up, extirpate, deracinate, pull out by the roots

upset *adjective* **1** DISTRESSED, shaken, disturbed, worried, troubled, hurt, bothered,

confused, unhappy, gutted (*Brit informal*), put out, dismayed, choked (*informal*), grieved, frantic, hassled (*informal*), agitated, ruffled, cut up (*informal*), disconcerted, disquieted, overwrought, discomposed **2** SICK, queasy, bad, poorly (*informal*), ill, gippy (*slang*) ▷ *verb* **1** DISTRESS, trouble, disturb, worry, alarm, bother, dismay, grieve, hassle (*informal*), agitate, ruffle, unnerve, disconcert, disquiet, fluster, perturb, faze, throw someone off balance, give someone grief (*Brit & S African*), discompose **2** TIP OVER, overturn, capsize, knock over, spill, topple over **3** MESS UP, spoil, disturb, change, confuse, disorder, unsettle, mix up, disorganize, turn topsy-turvy, put out of order, throw into disorder ▷ *noun* **1** DISTRESS, worry, trouble, shock, bother, disturbance, hassle (*informal*), disquiet, agitation, discomposure **2** REVERSAL, surprise, shake-up (*informal*), defeat, sudden change **3** ILLNESS, complaint, disorder, bug (*informal*), disturbance, sickness, malady, queasiness, indisposition

upshot *noun* RESULT, consequence, outcome, end, issue, event, conclusion, sequel, finale, culmination, end result, payoff (*informal*)

upside down *or* **upside-down** *adverb* WRONG SIDE UP, bottom up, on its head ▷ *adjective* **1** INVERTED, overturned, upturned, on its head, bottom up, wrong side up **2** (*informal*) CONFUSED, disordered, chaotic, muddled, jumbled, in disarray, in chaos, topsy-turvy, in confusion, higgledy-piggledy (*informal*), in disorder

upstanding *adjective* HONEST, principled, upright, honourable, good, moral, ethical, trustworthy, incorruptible, true << ANTONYM immoral

upstart *noun* SOCIAL CLIMBER, nobody, nouveau riche (*French*), parvenu, arriviste, status seeker

uptight *adjective* (*informal*) TENSE, wired (*slang*), anxious, neurotic, uneasy, prickly, edgy, on the defensive, on edge, nervy (*Brit informal*), adrenalized

up-to-date *adjective* MODERN, fashionable, trendy (*Brit informal*), in, newest, now (*informal*), happening (*informal*), current, with it (*informal*), stylish, in vogue, all the rage, up-to-the-minute, having your finger on the pulse << ANTONYM out of date

upturn *noun* RISE, increase, boost, improvement, recovery, revival, advancement, upsurge, upswing

urban *adjective* CIVIC, city, town, metropolitan,

municipal, dorp (*S African*), inner-city

urbane *adjective* SOPHISTICATED, cultured, polished, civil, mannerly, smooth, elegant, refined, cultivated, cosmopolitan, civilized, courteous, suave, well-bred, debonair, well-mannered << ANTONYM boorish

urchin *noun* (*old-fashioned*) RAGAMUFFIN, waif, guttersnipe, brat, mudlark (*slang*), gamin, street Arab (*offensive*), young rogue

urge *verb* 1 BEG, appeal to, exhort, press, prompt, plead, put pressure on, lean on, solicit, goad, implore, enjoin, beseech, pressurize, entreat, twist someone's arm (*informal*), put the heat on (*informal*), put the screws on (*informal*) 2 ADVOCATE, suggest, recommend, advise, back, support, champion, counsel, insist on, endorse, push for << ANTONYM discourage ▷ *noun* IMPULSE, longing, wish, desire, fancy, drive, yen (*informal*), hunger, appetite, craving, yearning, itch (*informal*), thirst, compulsion, hankering << ANTONYM reluctance ▷▷ **urge someone on** DRIVE ON, push, encourage, force, press, prompt, stimulate, compel, induce, propel, hasten, constrain, incite, egg on, goad, spur on, impel, gee up

urgency *noun* IMPORTANCE, need, necessity, gravity, pressure, hurry, seriousness, extremity, exigency, imperativeness

urgent *adjective* 1 CRUCIAL, desperate, pressing, great, important, crying, critical, immediate, acute, grave, instant, compelling, imperative, top-priority, now or never, exigent, not to be delayed << ANTONYM unimportant 2 INSISTENT, earnest, determined, intense, persistent, persuasive, resolute, clamorous, importunate << ANTONYM casual

urinate *verb* PEE, wee, leak (*slang or slang*), tinkle (*Brit informal*), piddle (*informal*), spend a penny (*Brit informal*), make water, pass water, wee-wee (*informal*), micturate, take a whizz (*slang, chiefly US*)

usable *adjective* SERVICEABLE, working, functional, available, current, practical, valid, at your disposal, ready for use, in running order, fit for use, utilizable

usage *noun* 1 USE, operation, employment, running, control, management, treatment, handling 2 PRACTICE, method, procedure, form, rule, tradition, habit, regime, custom, routine, convention, mode, matter of course, wont

use *verb* 1 EMPLOY, utilize, make use of, work, apply, operate, exercise, practise, resort

to, exert, wield, ply, put to use, bring into play, find a use for, avail yourself of, turn to account 2 *sometimes with* **up** CONSUME, go through, exhaust, spend, waste, get through, run through, deplete, dissipate, expend, fritter away 3 TAKE ADVANTAGE OF, exploit, manipulate, abuse, milk, profit from, impose on, misuse, make use of, cash in on (*informal*), walk all over (*informal*), take liberties with ▷ *noun* 1 USAGE, employment, utilization, operation, application 2 SERVICE, handling, wear and tear, treatment, practice, exercise 3 PURPOSE, call, need, end, point, cause, reason, occasion, object, necessity 4 GOOD, point, help, service, value, benefit, profit, worth, advantage, utility, mileage (*informal*), avail, usefulness ▷▷ **use something up** CONSUME, drain, exhaust, finish, waste, absorb, run through, deplete, squander, devour, swallow up, burn up, fritter away

used *adjective* SECOND-HAND, worn, not new, cast-off, hand-me-down (*informal*), nearly new, shopsoiled, reach-me-down (*informal*), preloved (*Austral slang*) << ANTONYM new

used to *adjective* ACCUSTOMED TO, familiar with, in the habit of, given to, at home in, attuned to, tolerant of, wont to, inured to, hardened to, habituated to

useful *adjective* HELPFUL, effective, valuable, practical, of use, profitable, of service, worthwhile, beneficial, of help, fruitful, advantageous, all-purpose, salutary, general-purpose, serviceable << ANTONYM useless

usefulness *noun* HELPFULNESS, value, worth, use, help, service, benefit, profit, utility, effectiveness, convenience, practicality, efficacy

useless *adjective* 1 WORTHLESS, of no use, valueless, pants (*slang*), ineffective, impractical, fruitless, unproductive, ineffectual, unworkable, disadvantageous, unavailing, bootless, unsuitable << ANTONYM useful 2 POINTLESS, hopeless, futile, vain, idle, profitless << ANTONYM worthwhile 3 (*informal*) INEPT, no good, hopeless, weak, stupid, pants (*slang*), incompetent, ineffectual

usher *verb* ESCORT, lead, direct, guide, conduct, pilot, steer, show ▷ *noun* ATTENDANT, guide, doorman, usherette, escort, doorkeeper ▷▷ **usher something in** INTRODUCE, launch, bring in, precede, initiate, herald, pave the way for, ring in, open the door to, inaugurate

usual *adjective* NORMAL, customary, regular,

expected, general, common, stock, standard, fixed, ordinary, familiar, typical, constant, routine, everyday, accustomed, habitual, bog-standard (*Brit & Irish slang*), wonted
<< ANTONYM unusual

usually *adverb* NORMALLY, generally, mainly, commonly, regularly, mostly, routinely, on the whole, in the main, for the most part, by and large, most often, ordinarily, as a rule, habitually, as is usual, as is the custom

usurp *verb* SEIZE, take over, assume, take, appropriate, wrest, commandeer, arrogate, infringe upon, lay hold of

utility *noun* USEFULNESS, use, point, benefit, service, profit, fitness, convenience, mileage (*informal*), avail, practicality, efficacy, advantageousness, serviceableness

utilize *verb* USE, employ, deploy, take advantage of, resort to, make the most of, make use of, put to use, bring into play, have recourse to, avail yourself of, turn to account

utmost *adjective* 1 GREATEST, highest, maximum, supreme, extreme, paramount, pre-eminent 2 FARTHEST, extreme, last, final, outermost, uttermost, farthermost ▷ *noun* BEST, greatest, maximum, most, highest, hardest

utopia *noun* PARADISE, heaven, Eden, bliss, perfect place, Garden of Eden, Shangri-la, Happy Valley, seventh heaven, ideal life, Erewhon

utopian *adjective* PERFECT, ideal, romantic, dream, fantasy, imaginary, visionary, airy, idealistic, fanciful, impractical, illusory, chimerical ▷ *noun* DREAMER, visionary, idealist, Don Quixote, romanticist

utter[1] *verb* SAY, state, speak, voice, express, deliver, declare, mouth, breathe, pronounce, articulate, enunciate, put into words, verbalize, vocalize

utter[2] *adjective* ABSOLUTE, complete, total, perfect, positive, pure, sheer, stark, outright, all-out, thorough, downright, real, consummate, veritable, unqualified, out-and-out, unadulterated, unmitigated, thoroughgoing, arrant, deep-dyed (*usually derogatory*)

utterance *noun* 1 SPEECH, words, statement, comment, opinion, remark, expression, announcement, observation, declaration, reflection, pronouncement 2 SPEAKING, voicing, expression, breathing, delivery, ejaculation, articulation, enunciation, vocalization, verbalization, vociferation

utterly *adverb* TOTALLY, completely, absolutely, just, really, quite, perfectly, fully, entirely, extremely, altogether, thoroughly, wholly, downright, categorically, to the core, one hundred per cent, in all respects, to the nth degree, unqualifiedly

Vv

vacancy *noun* 1 OPENING, job, post, place, position, role, situation, opportunity, slot, berth (*informal*), niche, job opportunity, vacant position, situation vacant 2 ROOM, space, available accommodation, unoccupied room

vacant *adjective* 1 EMPTY, free, available, abandoned, deserted, to let, for sale, on the market, void, up for grabs, disengaged, uninhabited, unoccupied, not in use, unfilled, untenanted << ANTONYM occupied 2 UNFILLED, unoccupied << ANTONYM taken 3 BLANK, vague, dreamy, dreaming, empty, abstracted, idle, thoughtless, vacuous, inane, expressionless, unthinking, absent-minded, incurious, ditzy *or* ditsy (*slang*) << ANTONYM thoughtful

vacate *verb* 1 LEAVE, quit, move out of, give up, withdraw from, evacuate, depart from, go away from, leave empty, relinquish possession of 2 QUIT, leave, resign from, give up, withdraw from, chuck (*informal*), retire from, relinquish, renounce, walk out on, pack in (*informal*), abdicate, step down from (*informal*), stand down from

vacuous *adjective* VAPID, stupid, inane, blank, vacant, unintelligent

vacuum *noun* 1 GAP, lack, absence, space, deficiency, void 2 EMPTINESS, space, void, gap, empty space, nothingness, vacuity

vagabond *noun* TRAMP, bum (*informal*), drifter, vagrant, migrant, rolling stone, wanderer, beggar, outcast, rover, nomad, itinerant, down-and-out, hobo (*US*), bag lady (*chiefly US*), wayfarer, dosser (*Brit slang*), knight of the road, person of no fixed address, derro (*Austral slang*) ▷ *modifier* VAGRANT, drifting, wandering, homeless, journeying, unsettled, roaming, idle, roving, nomadic, destitute, itinerant, down and out, rootless, footloose,

fly-by-night (*informal*), shiftless

vagary *noun usually plural* WHIM, caprice, unpredictability, sport, urge, fancy, notion, humour, impulse, quirk, conceit, whimsy, crotchet, sudden notion

vagrant *noun* TRAMP, bum (*informal*), drifter, vagabond, rolling stone, wanderer, beggar, derelict, itinerant, down-and-out, hobo (*US*), bag lady (*chiefly US*), dosser (*Brit slang*), person of no fixed address, derro (*Austral slang*) ▷ *adjective* VAGABOND, drifting, wandering, homeless, journeying, unsettled, roaming, idle, roving, nomadic, destitute, itinerant, down and out, rootless, footloose, fly-by-night (*informal*), shiftless << ANTONYM settled

vague *adjective* 1 UNCLEAR, indefinite, hazy, confused, loose, uncertain, doubtful, unsure, superficial, incomplete, woolly, imperfect, sketchy, cursory << ANTONYM clear 2 IMPRECISE, unspecified, generalized, rough, loose, ambiguous, hazy, equivocal, ill-defined, non-specific, inexact, obfuscatory, inexplicit 3 ABSENT-MINDED, absorbed, abstracted, distracted, unaware, musing, vacant, preoccupied, bemused, oblivious, dreamy, daydreaming, faraway, unthinking, heedless, inattentive, unheeding 4 INDISTINCT, blurred, unclear, dim, fuzzy, unknown, obscure, faint, shadowy, indefinite, misty, hazy, indistinguishable, amorphous, indeterminate, bleary, nebulous, out of focus, ill-defined, indiscernible << ANTONYM distinct

vaguely *adverb* 1 SLIGHTLY, rather, sort of (*informal*), kind of (*informal*), a little, a bit, somewhat, moderately, faintly, dimly, to some extent, kinda (*informal*) 2 ABSENT-MINDEDLY, evasively, abstractedly, obscurely, vacantly, inattentively 3 ROUGHLY, loosely, indefinitely, carelessly, in a general way, imprecisely

vagueness *noun* **1** IMPRECISENESS, ambiguity, obscurity, looseness, inexactitude, woolliness, undecidedness, lack of preciseness << ANTONYM preciseness **2** ABSENT-MINDEDNESS, abstraction, forgetfulness, confusion, inattention, disorganization, giddiness, dreaminess, befuddlement, empty-headedness

vain *adjective* **1** FUTILE, useless, pointless, unsuccessful, empty, hollow, idle, trivial, worthless, trifling, senseless, unimportant, fruitless, unproductive, abortive, unprofitable, time-wasting, unavailing, nugatory << ANTONYM successful **2** CONCEITED, narcissistic, proud, arrogant, inflated, swaggering, stuck-up (*informal*), cocky, swanky (*informal*), ostentatious, egotistical, self-important, overweening, vainglorious, swollen-headed (*informal*), pleased with yourself, bigheaded (*informal*), peacockish << ANTONYM modest ▷▷ **in vain 1** USELESS, to no avail, unsuccessful, fruitless, wasted, vain, ineffectual, without success, to no purpose, bootless **2** USELESSLY, to no avail, unsuccessfully, fruitlessly, vainly, ineffectually, without success, to no purpose, bootlessly

valiant *adjective* BRAVE, heroic, courageous, bold, worthy, fearless, gallant, intrepid, plucky, doughty, indomitable, redoubtable, dauntless, lion-hearted, valorous, stouthearted << ANTONYM cowardly

valid *adjective* **1** SOUND, good, reasonable, just, telling, powerful, convincing, substantial, acceptable, sensible, rational, logical, viable, credible, sustainable, plausible, conclusive, weighty, well-founded, cogent, well-grounded << ANTONYM unfounded **2** LEGAL, official, legitimate, correct, genuine, proper, in effect, authentic, in force, lawful, bona fide, legally binding, signed and sealed << ANTONYM invalid

validate *verb* **1** CONFIRM, prove, certify, substantiate, corroborate **2** AUTHORIZE, endorse, ratify, legalize, authenticate, make legally binding, set your seal on *or* to

validity *noun* **1** SOUNDNESS, force, power, grounds, weight, strength, foundation, substance, point, cogency **2** LEGALITY, authority, legitimacy, right, lawfulness

valley *noun* HOLLOW, dale, glen, vale, depression, dell, dingle, strath (*Scot*), cwm (*Welsh*), coomb

valour *or US* **valor** *noun* BRAVERY, courage, heroism, spirit, boldness, gallantry, derring-do (*archaic*), fearlessness, intrepidity, doughtiness, lion-heartedness << ANTONYM cowardice

valuable *adjective* **1** USEFUL, important, profitable, worthwhile, beneficial, valued, helpful, worthy, of use, of help, invaluable, serviceable, worth its weight in gold << ANTONYM useless **2** TREASURED, esteemed, cherished, prized, precious, held dear, estimable, worth your weight in gold **3** PRECIOUS, expensive, costly, dear, high-priced, priceless, irreplaceable << ANTONYM worthless ▷ *plural noun* TREASURES, prized possessions, precious items, heirlooms, personal effects, costly article

value *noun* **1** IMPORTANCE, use, benefit, worth, merit, point, help, service, sense, profit, advantage, utility, significance, effectiveness, mileage (*informal*), practicality, usefulness, efficacy, desirability, serviceableness << ANTONYM worthlessness **2** COST, price, worth, rate, equivalent, market price, face value, asking price, selling price, monetary worth ▷ *plural noun* PRINCIPLES, morals, ethics, mores, standards of behaviour, code of behaviour, (moral) standards ▷ *verb* **1** APPRECIATE, rate, prize, regard highly, respect, admire, treasure, esteem, cherish, think much of, hold dear, have a high opinion of, set store by, hold in high regard *or* esteem << ANTONYM undervalue **2** *with* **at** EVALUATE, price, estimate, rate, cost, survey, assess, set at, appraise, put a price on

valued *adjective* APPRECIATED, prized, esteemed, highly regarded, loved, dear, treasured, cherished

vandal *noun* HOOLIGAN, ned (*Scot slang*), delinquent, rowdy, lager lout, graffiti artist, yob *or* yobbo (*Brit slang*), cougan (*Austral slang*), scozza (*Austral slang*), bogan (*Austral slang*)

vanguard *noun* FOREFRONT, front line, cutting edge, leaders, front, van, spearhead, forerunners, front rank, trailblazers, advance guard, trendsetters << ANTONYM rearguard

vanish *verb* **1** DISAPPEAR, become invisible, be lost to sight, dissolve, evaporate, fade away, melt away, disappear from sight, exit, evanesce << ANTONYM appear **2** DIE OUT, disappear, pass away, end, fade, dwindle, cease to exist, become extinct, disappear from the face of the earth

vanity *noun* **1** PRIDE, arrogance, conceit,

airs, showing off (*informal*), pretension,
narcissism, egotism, self-love, ostentation,
vainglory, self-admiration, affected ways,
bigheadedness (*informal*), conceitedness,
swollen-headedness (*informal*)
<< ANTONYM modesty **2** FUTILITY,
uselessness, worthlessness, emptiness,
frivolity, unreality, triviality, hollowness,
pointlessness, inanity, unproductiveness,
fruitlessness, unsubstantiality, profitlessness
<< ANTONYM value

vanquish *verb* (*literary*) DEFEAT, beat, conquer,
reduce, stuff (*slang*), master, tank (*slang*),
overcome, crush, overwhelm, put down,
lick (*informal*), undo, subdue, rout, repress,
overpower, quell, triumph over, clobber
(*slang*), subjugate, run rings around
(*informal*), wipe the floor with (*informal*), blow
out of the water (*slang*), put to flight, get the
upper hand over, put to rout

vapour or US **vapor** *noun* MIST, fog, haze,
smoke, breath, steam, fumes, dampness,
miasma, exhalation

variable *adjective* CHANGEABLE, unstable,
fluctuating, shifting, flexible, wavering,
uneven, fickle, temperamental, mercurial,
capricious, unsteady, protean, vacillating,
fitful, mutable, inconstant, chameleonic
<< ANTONYM constant

variance ▷▷ **at variance** IN DISAGREEMENT,
conflicting, at odds, in opposition, out of
line, at loggerheads, at sixes and sevens
(*informal*), out of harmony

variant *adjective* DIFFERENT, alternative,
modified, derived, exceptional, divergent
▷ *noun* VARIATION, form, version,
development, alternative, adaptation,
revision, modification, permutation,
transfiguration, aberration, derived form

variation *noun* **1** ALTERNATIVE, variety,
modification, departure, innovation, variant
2 VARIETY, change, deviation, difference,
diversity, diversion, novelty, alteration,
discrepancy, diversification, departure from
the norm, break in routine << ANTONYM
uniformity

varied *adjective* DIFFERENT, mixed, various,
diverse, assorted, miscellaneous, sundry,
motley, manifold, heterogeneous
<< ANTONYM unvarying

variegated *adjective* MOTTLED, pied, streaked,
motley, many-coloured, parti-coloured,
varicoloured

variety *noun* **1** DIVERSITY, change, variation,
difference, diversification, heterogeneity,

many-sidedness, multifariousness
<< ANTONYM uniformity **2** RANGE,
selection, assortment, mix, collection,
line-up, mixture, array, cross section,
medley, multiplicity, mixed bag (*informal*),
miscellany, motley collection, intermixture
3 TYPE, sort, kind, make, order, class, brand,
species, breed, strain, category

various *adjective* **1** DIFFERENT, assorted,
miscellaneous, varied, differing, distinct,
diverse, divers (*archaic*), diversified,
disparate, sundry, heterogeneous
<< ANTONYM similar **2** MANY, numerous,
countless, several, abundant, innumerable,
sundry, manifold, profuse

varnish *noun* LACQUER, polish, glaze, japan,
gloss, shellac ▷ *verb* **1** LACQUER, polish, glaze,
japan, gloss, shellac **2** POLISH, decorate,
glaze, adorn, gild, lacquer, embellish

vary *verb* **1** DIFFER, be different, be dissimilar,
disagree, diverge, be unlike **2** CHANGE, shift,
swing, transform, alter, fluctuate, oscillate,
see-saw **3** ALTERNATE, mix, diversify, reorder,
intermix, bring variety to, permutate,
variegate **4** MODIFY, change, alter, adjust

varying *adjective* **1** DIFFERENT, contrasting,
inconsistent, varied, distinct, diverse,
assorted, disparate, dissimilar,
distinguishable, discrepant, streets
apart **2** CHANGING, variable, irregular,
inconsistent, fluctuating << ANTONYM
unchanging

vassal *noun* SERF, slave, bondsman, subject,
retainer, thrall, varlet (*archaic*), bondservant,
liegeman

vast *adjective* HUGE, massive, enormous, great,
wide, sweeping, extensive, tremendous,
immense, mega (*slang*), unlimited,
gigantic, astronomical, monumental,
monstrous, mammoth, colossal, never-
ending, prodigious, limitless, boundless,
voluminous, immeasurable, unbounded,
elephantine, ginormous (*informal*),
vasty (*archaic*), measureless, illimitable,
humongous or humungous (*US slang*)
<< ANTONYM tiny

vault[1] *noun* **1** STRONGROOM, repository,
depository **2** CRYPT, tomb, catacomb, cellar,
mausoleum, charnel house, undercroft
3 ARCH, roof, ceiling, span

vault[2] *verb* JUMP, spring, leap, clear, bound,
hurdle

vaunted *adjective* BOASTED ABOUT, flaunted,
paraded, shown off, made much of, bragged
about, crowed about, exulted in, made a

display of, prated about

veer *verb* CHANGE DIRECTION, turn, swerve, shift, sheer, tack, be deflected, change course

vehemence *noun* FORCEFULNESS, force, violence, fire, energy, heat, passion, emphasis, enthusiasm, intensity, warmth, vigour, zeal, verve, fervour, eagerness, ardour, earnestness, keenness, fervency << ANTONYM indifference

vehement *adjective* STRONG, fierce, forceful, earnest, powerful, violent, intense, flaming, eager, enthusiastic, passionate, ardent, emphatic, fervent, impassioned, zealous, forcible, fervid << ANTONYM half-hearted

vehicle *noun* 1 CONVEYANCE, machine, motor vehicle, means of transport 2 MEDIUM, means, channel, mechanism, organ, apparatus, means of expression

veil *noun* 1 MASK, cover, shroud, film, shade, curtain, cloak 2 SCREEN, mask, disguise, blind 3 FILM, cover, curtain, cloak, shroud ▷ *verb* COVER, screen, hide, mask, shield, disguise, conceal, obscure, dim, cloak, mantle << ANTONYM reveal

veiled *adjective* DISGUISED, implied, hinted at, covert, masked, concealed, suppressed

vein *noun* 1 BLOOD VESSEL 2 MOOD, style, spirit, way, turn, note, key, character, attitude, atmosphere, tone, manner, bent, stamp, humour, tendency, mode, temper, temperament, tenor, inclination, disposition, frame of mind 3 STREAK, element, thread, suggestion, strain, trace, hint, dash, trait, sprinkling, nuance, smattering 4 SEAM, layer, stratum, course, current, bed, deposit, streak, stripe, lode

velocity *noun* SPEED, pace, rapidity, quickness, swiftness, fleetness, celerity

velvety *adjective* SOFT, smooth, downy, delicate, mossy, velvet-like

venal *adjective* CORRUPT, bent (*slang*), crooked (*informal*), prostituted, grafting (*informal*), mercenary, sordid, rapacious, unprincipled, dishonourable, corruptible, purchasable << ANTONYM honest

vendetta *noun* FEUD, dispute, quarrel, enmity, bad blood, blood feud

veneer *noun* 1 MASK, show, façade, front, appearance, guise, pretence, semblance, false front 2 LAYER, covering, finish, facing, film, gloss, patina, laminate, cladding, lamination

venerable *adjective* RESPECTED, august, sage, revered, honoured, wise, esteemed, reverenced

venerate *verb* RESPECT, honour, esteem, revere, worship, adore, reverence, look up to, hold in awe << ANTONYM scorn

veneration *noun* RESPECT, esteem, reverence, worship, awe, deference, adoration

vengeance *noun* REVENGE, retaliation, reprisal, retribution, avenging, an eye for an eye, settling of scores, requital, lex talionis << ANTONYM forgiveness ▷▷ **with a vengeance** TO THE UTMOST, greatly, extremely, to the full, and no mistake, to the nth degree, with no holds barred

vengeful *adjective* UNFORGIVING, relentless, avenging, vindictive, punitive, implacable, spiteful, retaliatory, rancorous, thirsting for revenge, revengeful

venom *noun* 1 MALICE, hate, spite, bitterness, grudge, gall, acidity, spleen, acrimony, rancour, ill will, malevolence, virulence, pungency, malignity, spitefulness, maliciousness << ANTONYM benevolence 2 POISON, toxin, bane

venomous *adjective* 1 MALICIOUS, vindictive, spiteful, hostile, savage, vicious, malignant, virulent, baleful, rancorous << ANTONYM benevolent 2 POISONOUS, poison, toxic, virulent, noxious, baneful (*archaic*), envenomed, mephitic << ANTONYM harmless

vent *noun* OUTLET, opening, hole, split, aperture, duct, orifice ▷ *verb* EXPRESS, release, voice, air, empty, discharge, utter, emit, come out with, pour out, give vent to, give expression to << ANTONYM hold back

ventilate *verb* 1 AERATE, fan, cool, refresh, air-condition, freshen, oxygenate 2 DISCUSS, air, bring out into the open, talk about, debate, examine, broadcast, sift, scrutinize, make known

venture *verb* 1 GO, travel, journey, set out, wander, stray, plunge into, rove, set forth 2 DARE, presume, have the courage to, be brave enough, hazard, go out on a limb (*informal*), take the liberty, stick your neck out (*informal*), go so far as, make so bold as, have the temerity *or* effrontery *or* nerve 3 PUT FORWARD, offer, suggest, present, air, table, advance, propose, volunteer, submit, bring up, postulate, proffer, broach, posit, moot, propound, dare to say ▷ *noun* UNDERTAKING, project, enterprise, chance, campaign, risk, operation, activity, scheme, task, mission, speculation, gamble, adventure, exploit, pursuit, fling, hazard, crusade, endeavour

veracity *noun* 1 ACCURACY, truth, credibility,

precision, exactitude **2** TRUTHFULNESS,
integrity, honesty, candour, frankness,
probity, rectitude, trustworthiness,
uprightness

verbal *adjective* **1** SPOKEN, oral, word-of-
mouth, unwritten **2** VERBATIM, literal

verbally *adverb* ORALLY, vocally, in words, in
speech, by word of mouth

verbatim *adverb* EXACTLY, to the letter,
word for word, closely, precisely, literally,
faithfully, rigorously, in every detail, letter
for letter ▷ *adjective* WORD FOR WORD, exact,
literal, close, precise, faithful, line by line,
unabridged, unvarnished, undeviating,
unembellished

verdant *adjective* (*literary*) GREEN, lush, leafy,
grassy, fresh, flourishing

verdict *noun* DECISION, finding, judgment,
opinion, sentence, conclusion, conviction,
adjudication, pronouncement

verge *noun* **1** BRINK, point, edge, threshold
2 (*Brit*) BORDER, edge, margin, limit, extreme,
lip, boundary, threshold, roadside, brim
▷▷ **verge on something** COME NEAR TO,
approach, border on, resemble, incline to,
be similar to, touch on, be more or less,
be tantamount to, tend towards, be not far
from, incline towards

verification *noun* PROOF, confirmation,
validation, corroboration, authentication,
substantiation

verify *verb* **1** CHECK, confirm, make sure,
examine, monitor, check out (*informal*),
inspect **2** CONFIRM, prove, substantiate,
support, validate, bear out, attest,
corroborate, attest to, authenticate
<< ANTONYM disprove

vernacular *noun* with the SPEECH, jargon,
idiom, parlance, cant, native language,
dialect, patois, argot, vulgar tongue ▷
adjective COLLOQUIAL, popular, informal,
local, common, native, indigenous, vulgar

versatile *adjective* **1** ADAPTABLE, flexible, all-
round, resourceful, protean, multifaceted,
many-sided, all-singing, all-dancing
<< ANTONYM unadaptable **2** ALL-PURPOSE,
handy, functional, variable, adjustable, all-
singing, all-dancing << ANTONYM limited

versed *adjective* with in KNOWLEDGEABLE,
experienced, skilled, seasoned, qualified,
familiar, practised, accomplished,
competent, acquainted, well-informed,
proficient, well up (*informal*), conversant
<< ANTONYM ignorant

version *noun* **1** FORM, variety, variant, sort,

kind, class, design, style, model, type, brand,
genre **2** ADAPTATION, edition, interpretation,
form, reading, copy, rendering, translation,
reproduction, portrayal **3** ACCOUNT, report,
side, description, record, reading, story, view,
understanding, history, statement, analysis,
take (*informal, chiefly US*), construction, tale,
impression, explanation, interpretation,
rendering, narrative, chronicle, rendition,
narration, construal

vertical *adjective* UPRIGHT, sheer,
perpendicular, straight (up and down), erect,
plumb, on end, precipitous, vertiginous, bolt
upright << ANTONYM horizontal

vertigo *noun* DIZZINESS, giddiness, light-
headedness, fear of heights, loss of balance,
acrophobia, loss of equilibrium, swimming
of the head

verve *noun* ENTHUSIASM, energy, spirit, life,
force, punch (*informal*), dash, pep, sparkle,
zip (*informal*), vitality, animation, vigour, zeal,
gusto, get-up-and-go (*informal*), élan, brio,
vivacity, liveliness, vim (*slang*) << ANTONYM
indifference

very *adverb* EXTREMELY, highly, greatly, really,
deeply, particularly, seriously (*informal*),
truly, absolutely, terribly, remarkably,
unusually, jolly (*Brit*), wonderfully,
profoundly, decidedly, awfully (*informal*),
acutely, exceedingly, excessively, noticeably,
eminently, superlatively, uncommonly,
surpassingly ▷ *adjective* **1** EXACT, actual,
precise, same, real, express, identical,
unqualified, selfsame **2** IDEAL, perfect, right,
fitting, appropriate, suitable, spot on (*Brit
informal*), apt, just the job (*Brit informal*)

vessel *noun* **1** SHIP, boat, craft, barque (*poetic*)
2 CONTAINER, receptacle, can, bowl, tank,
pot, drum, barrel, butt, vat, bin, jar, basin,
tub, jug, pitcher, urn, canister, repository,
cask

vest ▷▷ **vest in something** or **someone** *usually
passive* PLACE, invest, entrust, settle, lodge,
confer, endow, bestow, consign, put in the
hands of, be devolved upon ▷▷ **vest with
something** *usually passive* ENDOW WITH,
furnish with, entrust with, empower with,
authorize with

vestibule *noun* HALL, lobby, foyer, porch,
entrance hall, portico, anteroom

vestige *noun* TRACE, sign, hint, scrap,
evidence, indication, suspicion, glimmer

vet *verb* CHECK, examine, investigate, check
out, review, scan, look over, appraise,
scrutinize, size up (*informal*), give the once-

over (*informal*), pass under review

veteran *noun* OLD HAND, master, pro
(*informal*), old-timer, past master, trouper,
warhorse (*informal*), old stager << ANTONYM
novice ▷ *modifier* LONG-SERVING, seasoned,
experienced, old, established, expert,
qualified, mature, practised, hardened,
adept, proficient, well trained, battle-
scarred, worldly-wise

veto *noun* BAN, dismissal, rejection, vetoing,
boycott, embargo, prohibiting, prohibition,
suppression, knock-back (*informal*), interdict,
declination, preclusion, nonconsent
<< ANTONYM ratification ▷ *verb* BAN, block,
reject, rule out, kill (*informal*), negative, turn
down, forbid, boycott, prohibit, disallow, put
a stop to, refuse permission to, interdict,
give the thumbs down to, put the kibosh on
(*slang*) << ANTONYM pass

vex *verb* ANNOY, bother, irritate, worry,
trouble, upset, disturb, distress, provoke,
bug (*informal*), offend, needle (*informal*),
plague, put out, tease, torment, harass,
hassle (*informal*), aggravate (*informal*), afflict,
fret, gall, agitate, exasperate, nettle, pester,
displease, rile, pique, peeve (*informal*), grate
on, get on your nerves (*informal*), nark (*Brit,
Austral & NZ slang*), give someone grief (*Brit
& S African*), get your back up, put your back
up, hack you off (*informal*) << ANTONYM
soothe

vexed *adjective* **1** ANNOYED, upset, irritated,
worried, troubled, bothered, confused,
disturbed, distressed, provoked, put out,
fed up, tormented, harassed, aggravated
(*informal*), afflicted, agitated, ruffled,
exasperated, perplexed, nettled, miffed
(*informal*), displeased, riled, peeved
(*informal*), hacked off (*US slang*), out of
countenance, tooshie (*Austral slang*), hoha
(*NZ*) **2** CONTROVERSIAL, disputed, contested,
moot, much debated

viable *adjective* WORKABLE, practical,
feasible, suitable, realistic, operational,
applicable, usable, practicable, serviceable,
operable, within the bounds of possibility
<< ANTONYM unworkable

vibes *plural noun sometimes singular* (*slang*)
1 FEELINGS, emotions, response, reaction
2 ATMOSPHERE, aura, vibrations, feeling,
emanation

vibrant *adjective* **1** ENERGETIC, dynamic,
sparkling, vivid, spirited, storming, alive,
sensitive, colourful, vigorous, animated,
responsive, electrifying, vivacious, full of

pep (*informal*) **2** VIVID, bright, brilliant,
intense, clear, rich, glowing, colourful,
highly-coloured

vibrate *verb* **1** SHAKE, tremble, shiver,
fluctuate, quiver, oscillate, judder
(*informal*) **2** THROB, pulse, resonate, pulsate,
reverberate

vibration *noun* **1** SHAKING, shake, trembling,
quake, quaking, shudder, shuddering,
quiver, oscillation, judder (*informal*)
2 THROBBING, pulse, thumping, hum,
humming, throb, resonance, tremor, drone,
droning, reverberation, pulsation

vicarious *adjective* INDIRECT, substitute,
surrogate, by proxy, empathetic, at one
remove

vice *noun* **1** FAULT, failing, weakness,
limitation, defect, deficiency, flaw,
shortcoming, blemish, imperfection, frailty,
foible, weak point, infirmity << ANTONYM
good point **2** WICKEDNESS, evil, corruption,
sin, depravity, immorality, iniquity,
profligacy, degeneracy, venality, turpitude,
evildoing << ANTONYM virtue

vice versa *adverb* THE OTHER WAY ROUND,
conversely, in reverse, contrariwise

vicinity *noun* NEIGHBOURHOOD, area, district,
precincts, locality, environs, neck of the
woods (*informal*), purlieus

vicious *adjective* **1** SAVAGE, brutal, violent,
bad, dangerous, foul, cruel, ferocious,
monstrous, vile, atrocious, diabolical,
heinous, abhorrent, barbarous, fiendish
<< ANTONYM gentle **2** DEPRAVED, corrupt,
wicked, infamous, degraded, worthless,
degenerate, immoral, sinful, debased,
profligate, unprincipled << ANTONYM
virtuous **3** MALICIOUS, vindictive, spiteful,
mean, cruel, venomous, bitchy (*informal*),
defamatory, rancorous, backbiting,
slanderous << ANTONYM complimentary

vicissitude *noun often plural* VARIATION,
change, shift, change of fortune, life's ups
and downs (*informal*)

victim *noun* **1** CASUALTY, sufferer, injured
party, fatality << ANTONYM survivor **2** PREY,
patsy (*slang, chiefly US & Canad*), sucker
(*slang*), dupe, gull (*archaic*), stooge, sitting
duck (*informal*), sitting target, innocent
<< ANTONYM culprit **3** SCAPEGOAT, sacrifice,
martyr, fall guy (*informal*), whipping boy

victimize *or* **victimise** *verb* PERSECUTE, bully,
pick on, abuse, harass, discriminate against,
lean on, have it in for (*informal*), push
around, give a hard time, demonize, have a

down on (*informal*), have your knife into

victor *noun* WINNER, champion, conqueror, first, champ (*informal*), vanquisher, top dog (*informal*), prizewinner, conquering hero << ANTONYM loser

victorious *adjective* WINNING, successful, triumphant, first, champion, conquering, vanquishing, prizewinning << ANTONYM losing

victory *noun* WIN, success, triumph, the prize, superiority, conquest, laurels, mastery, walkover (*informal*) << ANTONYM defeat

vie *verb with* **with** *or* **for** COMPETE, struggle, contend, contest, strive, be rivals, match yourself against

view *noun* **1** *sometimes plural* OPINION, thought, idea, belief, thinking, feeling, attitude, reckoning, impression, notion, conviction, judgment, point of view, sentiment, viewpoint, persuasion, way of thinking, standpoint **2** SCENE, picture, sight, prospect, aspect, perspective, landscape, outlook, spectacle, panorama, vista **3** VISION, sight, visibility, perspective, eyeshot, range *or* field of vision **4** STUDY, review, survey, assessment, examination, scan, inspection, look, scrutiny, contemplation ▷ *verb* **1** REGARD, see, consider, judge, perceive, treat, estimate, reckon, deem, look on, adjudge, think about *or* of **2** LOOK AT, see, inspect, gaze at, eye, watch, check, regard, survey, witness, clock (*Brit slang*), examine, observe, explore, stare at, scan, contemplate, check out (*informal*), behold, eyeball (*slang*), gawp at, recce (*slang*), get a load of (*informal*), spectate, take a dekko at (*Brit slang*) ▷▷ **with a view to** WITH THE AIM *or* INTENTION OF, in order to, so as to, in the hope of

viewer *noun* WATCHER, observer, spectator, onlooker, couch potato (*informal*), TV watcher, one of an audience

viewpoint *noun* POINT OF VIEW, perspective, angle, position, attitude, stance, slant, belief, conviction, feeling, opinion, way of thinking, standpoint, vantage point, frame of reference

vigilance *noun* WATCHFULNESS, alertness, caution, observance, circumspection, attentiveness, carefulness

vigilant *adjective* WATCHFUL, alert, on the lookout, careful, cautious, attentive, circumspect, wide awake, on the alert, on your toes, wakeful, on your guard, on the watch, on the qui vive, keeping your eyes peeled *or* skinned (*informal*) << ANTONYM inattentive

vigorous *adjective* **1** STRENUOUS, energetic, arduous, hard, taxing, active, intense, exhausting, rigorous, brisk **2** SPIRITED, lively, energetic, active, intense, dynamic, sparkling, animated, forceful, feisty (*informal*), spanking, high-spirited, sprightly, vivacious, forcible, effervescent, full of energy, zippy (*informal*), spunky (*informal*) << ANTONYM lethargic **3** STRONG, powerful, robust, sound, healthy, vital, lively, flourishing, hardy, hale, hearty, lusty, virile, alive and kicking, red-blooded, fighting fit, full of energy, full of beans (*informal*), hale and hearty, fit as a fiddle (*informal*) << ANTONYM weak

vigorously *adverb* **1** ENERGETICALLY, hard, forcefully, strongly, all out, eagerly, with a vengeance, strenuously, like mad (*slang*), lustily, hammer and tongs, with might and main **2** FORCEFULLY, strongly, vehemently, strenuously

vigour *or US* **vigor** *noun* ENERGY, might, force, vitality, power, activity, spirit, strength, snap (*informal*), punch (*informal*), dash, pep, zip (*informal*), animation, verve, gusto, dynamism, oomph (*informal*), brio, robustness, liveliness, vim (*slang*), forcefulness << ANTONYM weakness

vile *adjective* **1** WICKED, base, evil, mean, bad, low, shocking, appalling, ugly, corrupt, miserable, vicious, humiliating, perverted, coarse, degrading, worthless, disgraceful, vulgar, degenerate, abject, sinful, despicable, depraved, debased, loathsome, contemptible, impure, wretched, nefarious, ignoble << ANTONYM honourable **2** DISGUSTING, foul, revolting, offensive, nasty, obscene, sickening, horrid, repellent, repulsive, noxious, nauseating, repugnant, loathsome, yucky *or* yukky (*slang*), yucko (*Austral slang*) << ANTONYM pleasant

vilification *noun* DENIGRATION, abuse, defamation, invective, calumny, mudslinging, disparagement, vituperation, contumely, aspersion, scurrility, calumniation

vilify *verb* MALIGN, abuse, denigrate, knock (*informal*), rubbish (*informal*), run down, smear, slag (off) (*slang*), berate, disparage, decry, revile, slander, dump on (*slang, chiefly US*), debase, defame, bad-mouth (*slang, chiefly US & Canad*), traduce, speak ill of, pull to pieces (*informal*), calumniate, vituperate, asperse << ANTONYM praise

villain *noun* **1** EVILDOER, criminal, rogue, profligate, scoundrel, wretch, libertine, knave (*archaic*), reprobate, miscreant, malefactor, blackguard, rapscallion, caitiff (*archaic*), wrong 'un (*Austral slang*) **2** BADDY (*informal*), antihero << ANTONYM hero

villainous *adjective* WICKED, evil, depraved, mean, bad, base, criminal, terrible, cruel, vicious, outrageous, infamous, vile, degenerate, atrocious, inhuman, sinful, diabolical, heinous, debased, hateful, scoundrelly, fiendish, ruffianly, nefarious, ignoble, detestable, blackguardly, thievish << ANTONYM virtuous

vindicate *verb* **1** CLEAR, acquit, exonerate, absolve, let off the hook, exculpate, free from blame << ANTONYM condemn **2** SUPPORT, uphold, ratify, defend, excuse, justify, substantiate

vindication *noun* **1** EXONERATION, pardon, acquittal, dismissal, discharge, amnesty, absolution, exculpating, exculpation **2** SUPPORT, defence, ratification, excuse, apology, justification, assertion, substantiation

vindictive *adjective* VENGEFUL, malicious, spiteful, relentless, resentful, malignant, unrelenting, unforgiving, implacable, venomous, rancorous, revengeful, full of spleen << ANTONYM merciful

vintage *noun* **1** (always used of wines) HARVEST, year, crop, yield **2** ERA, period, origin, sort, type, generation, stamp, epoch, ilk, time of origin ▷ *adjective* **1** (always used of wines) HIGH-QUALITY, best, prime, quality, choice, select, rare, superior **2** CLASSIC, old, veteran, historic, heritage, enduring, antique, timeless, old-world, age-old, ageless

violate *verb* **1** BREAK, infringe, disobey, transgress, ignore, defy, disregard, flout, rebel against, contravene, fly in the face of, overstep, not comply with, take no notice of, encroach upon, pay no heed to, infract << ANTONYM obey **2** INVADE, infringe on, disturb, upset, shatter, disrupt, impinge on, encroach on, intrude on, trespass on, obtrude on **3** DESECRATE, profane, defile, abuse, outrage, pollute, deface, dishonour, vandalize, treat with disrespect, befoul << ANTONYM honour **4** RAPE, molest, sexually assault, ravish, abuse, assault, interfere with, sexually abuse, indecently assault, force yourself on

violation *noun* **1** BREACH, abuse, infringement, contravention, abuse, trespass, transgression, infraction **2** INVASION, intrusion, trespass, breach, disturbance, disruption, interruption, encroachment **3** DESECRATION, sacrilege, defilement, profanation, spoliation **4** RAPE, sexual assault, molesting, ravishing (*old-fashioned*), abuse, sexual abuse, indecent assault, molestation

violence *noun* **1** BRUTALITY, bloodshed, savagery, fighting, terrorism, frenzy, thuggery, destructiveness, bestiality, strong-arm tactics (*informal*), rough handling, bloodthirstiness, murderousness **2** FORCE, power, strength, might, ferocity, brute force, fierceness, forcefulness, powerfulness **3** INTENSITY, passion, fury, force, cruelty, severity, fervour, sharpness, harshness, vehemence **4** POWER, turbulence, wildness, raging, tumult, roughness, boisterousness, storminess

violent *adjective* **1** BRUTAL, aggressive, savage, wild, rough, fierce, bullying, cruel, vicious, destructive, ruthless, murderous, maddened, berserk, merciless, bloodthirsty, homicidal, pitiless, hot-headed, thuggish, maniacal, hot-tempered << ANTONYM gentle **2** SHARP, hard, powerful, forceful, strong, fierce, fatal, savage, deadly, brutal, vicious, lethal, hefty, ferocious, death-dealing **3** INTENSE, acute, severe, biting, sharp, extreme, painful, harsh, excruciating, agonizing, inordinate **4** PASSIONATE, intense, extreme, strong, wild, consuming, uncontrollable, vehement, unrestrained, tempestuous, ungovernable **5** FIERY, raging, fierce, flaming, furious, passionate, peppery, ungovernable **6** POWERFUL, wild, devastating, strong, storming, raging, turbulent, tumultuous, tempestuous, gale force, blustery, ruinous, full of force << ANTONYM mild

VIP *noun* CELEBRITY, big name, public figure, star, somebody, lion, notable, luminary, bigwig (*informal*), leading light (*informal*), big shot (*informal*), personage, big noise (*informal*), big hitter (*informal*), heavy hitter (*informal*), man or woman of the hour

virago *noun* HARRIDAN, fury, shrew, vixen, scold, battle-axe (*informal*), termagant (*rare*)

virgin *noun* MAIDEN, maid (*archaic*), damsel (*archaic*), girl (*archaic*), celibate, vestal, virgo intacta ▷ *adjective* **1** UNTOUCHED, immaculate, fresh, new, pure, unused, pristine, flawless, unblemished, unadulterated, unsullied << ANTONYM spoiled 2 PURE, maidenly, chaste, immaculate, virginal, unsullied, vestal, uncorrupted, undefiled << ANTONYM corrupted

virginal *adjective* 1 CHASTE, pure, maidenly, virgin, immaculate, celibate, uncorrupted, undefiled 2 IMMACULATE, fresh, pristine, white, pure, untouched, snowy, undisturbed, spotless

virginity *noun* CHASTITY, maidenhead, maidenhood

virile *adjective* MANLY, masculine, macho, strong, male, robust, vigorous, potent, forceful, lusty, red-blooded, manlike << ANTONYM effeminate

virility *noun* MASCULINITY, manhood, potency, vigour, machismo << ANTONYM effeminacy

virtual *adjective* PRACTICAL, near, essential, implied, indirect, implicit, tacit, near enough, unacknowledged, in all but name

virtually *adverb* PRACTICALLY, almost, nearly, in effect, in essence, as good as, to all intents and purposes, in all but name, for all practical purposes, effectually

virtue *noun* 1 GOODNESS, honour, integrity, worth, dignity, excellence, morality, honesty, decency, respectability, nobility, righteousness, propriety, probity, rectitude, worthiness, high-mindedness, incorruptibility, uprightness, virtuousness, ethicalness << ANTONYM vice 2 MERIT, strength, asset, plus (*informal*), attribute, good quality, good point, strong point << ANTONYM failing 3 ADVANTAGE, benefit, merit, credit, usefulness, efficacy 4 CHASTITY, honour, virginity, innocence, purity, maidenhood, chasteness << ANTONYM unchastity >> **by virtue of** BECAUSE OF, in view of, on account of, based on, thanks to, as a result of, owing to, by reason of, by dint of

virtuosity *noun* MASTERY, skill, brilliance, polish, craft, expertise, flair, panache, éclat

virtuoso *noun* MASTER, artist, genius, maestro, magician, grandmaster, maven (*US*), master hand ▷ *modifier* MASTERLY, brilliant, dazzling, bravura (*music*)

virtuous *adjective* 1 GOOD, moral, ethical, upright, honourable, excellent, pure, worthy, honest, righteous, exemplary, squeaky-clean, blameless, praiseworthy, incorruptible, high-principled << ANTONYM corrupt 2 CHASTE, pure, innocent, celibate, spotless, virginal, clean-living << ANTONYM promiscuous

virulent *adjective* 1 VICIOUS, vindictive, bitter, hostile, malicious, resentful, acrimonious, malevolent, spiteful, venomous, rancorous, splenetic, envenomed << ANTONYM benign 2 DEADLY, lethal, toxic, poisonous, malignant, pernicious, venomous, septic, infective, injurious, baneful (*archaic*) << ANTONYM harmless

viscous *adjective* THICK, sticky, gooey (*informal*), adhesive, tenacious, clammy, syrupy, glutinous, gummy, gelatinous, icky (*informal*), gluey, treacly, mucilaginous, viscid

visible *adjective* PERCEPTIBLE, noticeable, observable, clear, obvious, plain, apparent, bold, patent, to be seen, evident, manifest, in sight, in view, conspicuous, unmistakable, palpable, discernible, salient, detectable, not hidden, distinguishable, unconcealed, perceivable, discoverable, anywhere to be seen << ANTONYM invisible

vision *noun* 1 IMAGE, idea, dream, plans, hopes, prospect, ideal, concept, fancy, fantasy, conception, delusion, daydream, reverie, flight of fancy, mental picture, pipe dream, imago (*psychoanalysis*), castle in the air, fanciful notion 2 HALLUCINATION, illusion, apparition, revelation, ghost, phantom, delusion, spectre, mirage, wraith, chimera, phantasm, eidolon 3 SIGHT, seeing, eyesight, view, eyes, perception 4 FORESIGHT, imagination, perception, insight, awareness, inspiration, innovation, creativity, intuition, penetration, inventiveness, shrewdness, discernment, prescience, perceptiveness, farsightedness, breadth of view 5 PICTURE, dream, sight, delight, beauty, joy, sensation, spectacle, knockout (*informal*), beautiful sight, perfect picture, feast for the eyes, sight for sore eyes, pearler (*Austral slang*), beaut (*Austral & NZ slang*)

visionary *adjective* 1 IDEALISTIC, romantic, unrealistic, utopian, dreaming, speculative, impractical, dreamy, unworkable, quixotic, starry-eyed, with your head in the clouds << ANTONYM realistic 2 PROPHETIC, mystical, divinatory, predictive, oracular, sibylline, mantic, vatic (*rare*), fatidic (*rare*) 3 IMAGINARY, fantastic, unreal, fanciful, ideal, idealized, illusory, imaginal (*psychoanalysis*), chimerical, delusory << ANTONYM real ▷ *noun* 1 IDEALIST, romantic, dreamer, daydreamer, utopian, enthusiast (*archaic*), theorist, zealot, Don Quixote << ANTONYM realist 2 PROPHET, diviner, mystic, seer, soothsayer, sibyl, scryer, spaewife (*Scot*)

visit *verb* **1** CALL ON, go to see, drop in on (*informal*), stop by, look up, call in on, pop in on (*informal*), pay a call on, go see (*US*) **2** STAY AT, stay with, spend time with, pay a visit to, be the guest of **3** STAY IN, see, tour, explore, take in (*informal*), holiday in, go to see, stop by, spend time in, vacation in (*US*), stop over in ▷ *noun* **1** CALL, social call **2** TRIP, stop, stay, break, tour, holiday, vacation (*informal*), stopover, sojourn

visitation *noun* **1** APPARITION, vision, manifestation, appearance, materialization **2** INSPECTION, survey, examination, visit, review, scrutiny

visitor *noun* GUEST, caller, company, visitant, manu(w)hiri (*NZ*)

vista *noun* VIEW, scene, prospect, landscape, panorama, perspective

visual *adjective* **1** OPTICAL, optic, ocular **2** OBSERVABLE, visible, perceptible, discernible << ANTONYM imperceptible

visualize or **visualise** *verb* PICTURE, imagine, think about, envisage, contemplate, conceive of, see in the mind's eye, conjure up a mental picture of

vital *adjective* **1** ESSENTIAL, important, necessary, key, basic, significant, critical, radical, crucial, fundamental, urgent, decisive, cardinal, imperative, indispensable, requisite, life-or-death, must-have << ANTONYM unnecessary **2** LIVELY, vigorous, energetic, spirited, dynamic, animated, vibrant, forceful, sparky, vivacious, full of beans (*informal*), zestful, full of the joy of living << ANTONYM lethargic

vitality *noun* ENERGY, vivacity, sparkle, go (*informal*), life, strength, pep, stamina, animation, vigour, exuberance, brio, robustness, liveliness, vim (*slang*), lustiness, vivaciousness << ANTONYM lethargy

vitriolic *adjective* VENOMOUS, scathing, malicious, acid, bitter, destructive, withering, virulent, sardonic, caustic, bitchy (*informal*), acerbic, envenomed, dripping with malice

vivacious *adjective* LIVELY, spirited, vital, gay, bubbling, sparkling, cheerful, jolly, animated, merry, upbeat (*informal*), high-spirited, ebullient, chirpy (*informal*), sparky, scintillating, sprightly, effervescent, full of life, full of beans (*informal*), frolicsome, sportive, light-hearted << ANTONYM dull

vivid *adjective* **1** CLEAR, detailed, realistic, telling, moving, strong, affecting, arresting, powerful, sharp, dramatic, stirring, stimulating, haunting, graphic, distinct, lively, memorable, unforgettable, evocative, lucid, lifelike, true to life, sharply-etched << ANTONYM vague **2** BRIGHT, brilliant, intense, clear, rich, glowing, colourful, highly-coloured << ANTONYM dull **3** LIVELY, strong, dynamic, striking, spirited, powerful, quick, storming, active, vigorous, energetic, animated, vibrant, fiery, flamboyant, expressive, vivacious, zestful << ANTONYM quiet

vixen *noun* SHREW, fury, spitfire, virago, harpy, scold, harridan, termagant (*rare*), hellcat

viz *adverb* NAMELY, that is to say, to wit, videlicet

vocabulary *noun* **1** LANGUAGE, words, lexicon, word stock, word hoard **2** WORDBOOK, dictionary, glossary, lexicon

vocal *adjective* **1** OUTSPOKEN, frank, blunt, forthright, strident, vociferous, noisy, articulate, expressive, eloquent, plain-spoken, clamorous, free-spoken << ANTONYM quiet **2** SPOKEN, voiced, uttered, oral, said, articulate, articulated, put into words

vocation *noun* PROFESSION, calling, job, business, office, trade, role, post, career, mission, employment, pursuit, life work, métier

vociferous *adjective* OUTSPOKEN, vocal, strident, noisy, shouting, loud, ranting, vehement, loudmouthed (*informal*), uproarious, obstreperous, clamorous << ANTONYM quiet

vogue *noun* FASHION, trend, craze, style, the latest, the thing (*informal*), mode, last word, the rage, passing fancy, dernier cri (*French*) ▷ *adjective* FASHIONABLE, trendy (*Brit informal*), in, now (*informal*), popular, with it (*informal*), prevalent, up-to-the-minute, modish, voguish ▷▷ **in vogue** POPULAR, big, fashionable, all the rage, happening, accepted, current, cool, in favour, stylish, up to date, in use, prevalent, up to the minute, modish, trendsetting, schmick (*Austral informal*)

voice *noun* **1** TONE, sound, language, articulation, power of speech **2** UTTERANCE, expression, words, airing, vocalization, verbalization **3** OPINION, will, feeling, wish, desire **4** SAY, part, view, decision, vote, comment, input **5** INSTRUMENT, medium, spokesman or spokeswoman, agency, channel, vehicle, organ, spokesperson,

intermediary, mouthpiece ▷ *verb* EXPRESS,
say, declare, air, raise, table, reveal, mention,
mouth, assert, pronounce, utter, articulate,
come out with (*informal*), divulge, ventilate,
enunciate, put into words, vocalize, give
expression *or* utterance to

void *adjective* 1 INVALID, null and void,
inoperative, useless, ineffective, worthless,
ineffectual, unenforceable, nonviable
2 *with* **of** DEVOID OF, without, lacking, free
from, wanting, bereft of, empty of, bare
of, destitute of, vacant of ▷ *noun* 1 GAP,
space, lack, want, hole, blank, emptiness
2 EMPTINESS, space, vacuum, oblivion,
blankness, nullity, vacuity ▷ *verb* INVALIDATE,
nullify, cancel, withdraw, reverse, undo,
repeal, quash, revoke, disallow, retract,
repudiate, negate, rescind, annul, abrogate,
countermand, render invalid, abnegate

volatile *adjective* 1 CHANGEABLE, shifting,
variable, unsettled, unstable, explosive,
unreliable, unsteady, inconstant
<< ANTONYM stable 2 TEMPERAMENTAL,
erratic, mercurial, up and down (*informal*),
fickle, whimsical, giddy, flighty, overemotional, inconstant << ANTONYM calm

volition *noun* FREE WILL, will, choice, election,
choosing, option, purpose, resolution,
determination, preference, discretion

volley *noun* BARRAGE, blast, burst, explosion,
shower, hail, discharge, bombardment, salvo,
fusillade, cannonade

voluble *adjective* TALKATIVE, garrulous,
loquacious, forthcoming, articulate, fluent,
glib, blessed with the gift of the gab
<< ANTONYM reticent

volume *noun* 1 AMOUNT, quantity, level, body,
total, measure, degree, mass, proportion,
bulk, aggregate 2 CAPACITY, size, mass,
extent, proportions, dimensions, bulk,
measurements, magnitude, compass,
largeness, cubic content 3 BOOK, work, title,
opus, publication, manual, tome, treatise,
almanac, compendium 4 LOUDNESS, sound,
amplification

voluminous *adjective* 1 LARGE, big, full,
massive, vast, ample, bulky, billowing,
roomy, cavernous, capacious << ANTONYM
small 2 COPIOUS, extensive, prolific,
abundant, plentiful, profuse << ANTONYM
scanty

voluntarily *adverb* WILLINGLY, freely, by
choice, without being asked, without
prompting, lief (*rare*), on your own initiative,
of your own free will, off your own bat, of

your own accord, of your own volition

voluntary *adjective* 1 INTENTIONAL, intended,
deliberate, planned, studied, purposed,
calculated, wilful, done on purpose
<< ANTONYM unintentional 2 OPTIONAL,
discretionary, up to the individual, open,
unforced, unconstrained, unenforced, at
your discretion, discretional, open to choice,
uncompelled << ANTONYM obligatory
3 UNPAID, volunteer, free, willing, honorary,
gratuitous, pro bono (*law*)

volunteer *verb* 1 OFFER, step forward, offer
your services, propose, let yourself in for
(*informal*), need no invitation, present your
services, proffer your services, put yourself
at someone's disposal << ANTONYM refuse
2 SUGGEST, advance, put forward, venture,
tender

voluptuous *adjective* 1 BUXOM, shapely,
curvaceous, erotic, ample, enticing,
provocative, seductive (*informal*), well-
stacked (*Brit slang*), full-bosomed
2 SENSUAL, luxurious, self-indulgent,
hedonistic, sybaritic, epicurean, licentious,
bacchanalian, pleasure-loving << ANTONYM
abstemious

vomit *verb* 1 BE SICK, throw up (*informal*),
spew, chuck (*Austral & NZ informal*), heave
(*slang*), puke (*slang*), retch, barf (*US slang*),
chunder (*slang, chiefly Austral*), belch forth,
upchuck (*US slang*), do a technicolour yawn,
toss your cookies (*US slang*) 2 *often with* **up**
BRING UP, throw up, regurgitate, chuck (up)
(*slang, chiefly US*), emit (*informal*), eject, puke
(*slang*), disgorge, sick up (*informal*), spew out
or up

voracious *adjective* 1 GLUTTONOUS, insatiable,
ravenous, hungry, greedy, ravening,
devouring 2 AVID, prodigious, insatiable,
uncontrolled, rapacious, unquenchable
<< ANTONYM moderate

vortex *noun* WHIRLPOOL, eddy, maelstrom,
gyre, countercurrent

vote *noun* 1 POLL, election, ballot,
referendum, popular vote, plebiscite,
straw poll, show of hands 2 RIGHT TO
VOTE, franchise, voting rights, suffrage,
say, voice, enfranchisement ▷ *verb* 1 CAST
YOUR VOTE, go to the polls, mark your
ballot paper 2 JUDGE, declare, pronounce,
decree, adjudge ▷▷ **vote someone in** ELECT,
choose, select, appoint, return, pick, opt for,
designate, decide on, settle on, fix on, plump
for, put in power

voucher *noun* TICKET, token, coupon, pass,

slip, chit, chitty (*Brit informal*), docket

vouch for *verb* **1** GUARANTEE, back, certify, answer for, swear to, stick up for (*informal*), stand witness, give assurance of, asseverate, go bail for **2** CONFIRM, support, affirm, attest to, assert, uphold

vow *noun* PROMISE, commitment, pledge, oath, profession, troth (*archaic*), avowal ▷ *verb* PROMISE, pledge, swear, commit, engage, affirm, avow, bind yourself, undertake solemnly

voyage *noun* JOURNEY, travels, trip, passage, expedition, crossing, sail, cruise, excursion ▷ *verb* TRAVEL, journey, tour, cruise, steam, take a trip, go on an expedition

vulgar *adjective* **1** TASTELESS, common, flashy, low, gross, nasty, gaudy, tawdry, cheap and nasty, common as muck << ANTONYM tasteful **2** CRUDE, dirty, rude, low, blue, nasty, naughty, coarse, indecent, improper, suggestive, tasteless, risqué, off colour, ribald, indelicate, indecorous **3** UNCOUTH, boorish, unrefined, impolite, ill-bred, unmannerly << ANTONYM refined **4** VERNACULAR, native, common, general, ordinary

vulgarity *noun* **1** TASTELESSNESS, bad taste, grossness, tawdriness, gaudiness, lack of refinement << ANTONYM tastefulness **2** CRUDENESS, rudeness, coarseness, crudity, ribaldry, suggestiveness, indelicacy, indecorum << ANTONYM decorum **3** COARSENESS, roughness, boorishness, rudeness, loutishness, oafishness, uncouthness << ANTONYM refinement

vulnerable *adjective* **1** SUSCEPTIBLE, helpless, unprotected, defenceless, exposed, weak, sensitive, tender, unguarded, thin-skinned << ANTONYM immune **2** (*military*) EXPOSED, open, unprotected, defenceless, accessible, wide open, open to attack, assailable << ANTONYM well-protected

wacky *adjective* UNUSUAL, odd, wild, strange, crazy, silly, weird, way-out (*informal*), eccentric, unpredictable, daft (*informal*), irrational, erratic, Bohemian, unconventional, far-out (*slang*), loony (*slang*), kinky (*informal*), off-the-wall (*slang*), unorthodox, nutty (*slang*), oddball, zany, goofy (*informal*), offbeat (*informal*), freaky (*slang*), outré, gonzo (*slang*), screwy (*informal*), wacko *or* whacko (*informal*), off the air (*Austral slang*)

wad *noun* 1 BUNDLE, roll, bankroll (*US & Canad*), pocketful 2 MASS, ball, lump, hunk, piece, block, plug, chunk

waddle *verb* SHUFFLE, shamble, totter, toddle, rock, stagger, sway, wobble

wade *verb* 1 PADDLE, splash, splash about, slop 2 WALK THROUGH, cross, ford, pass through, go across, travel across, make your way across ▷▷ **wade in** MOVE IN, pitch in, dive in (*informal*), set to work, advance, set to, get stuck in (*informal*), buckle down ▷▷ **wade into someone** LAUNCH YOURSELF AT, charge at, attack, rush, storm, tackle, go for, set about, strike at, assail, tear into (*informal*), fall upon, set upon, lay into (*informal*), light into (*informal*) ▷▷ **wade into something** GET INVOLVED IN, tackle, pitch in, interfere in, dive in, plunge in, get stuck into ▷▷ **wade through something** PLOUGH THROUGH, trawl through, labour at, work your way through, toil at, drudge at, peg away at

waffle *verb often followed by* **on** CHATTER, rabbit (on) (*Brit informal*), babble, drivel, prattle, jabber, gabble, rattle on, verbalize, blather, witter on (*informal*), blether, run off at the mouth (*slang*), prate, earbash (*Austral & NZ slang*) ▷ *noun* PRATTLE, nonsense, hot air (*informal*), twaddle, padding, prating, gibberish, jabber, verbiage, blather,

wordiness, verbosity, prolixity, bunkum *or* buncombe (*chiefly US*), bizzo (*Austral slang*), bull's wool (*Austral & NZ slang*)

waft *verb* 1 DRIFT, float, be carried, be transported, coast, flow, stray, glide, be borne, be conveyed 2 TRANSPORT, bring, carry, bear, guide, conduct, transmit, convey ▷ *noun* CURRENT, breath, puff, whiff, draught, breeze

wag[1] *verb* 1 WAVE, shake, swing, waggle, stir, sway, flutter, waver, quiver, vibrate, wiggle, oscillate 2 WAGGLE, wave, shake, flourish, brandish, wobble, wiggle 3 SHAKE, bob, nod ▷ *noun* 1 WAVE, shake, swing, toss, sway, flutter, waver, quiver, vibration, wiggle, oscillation, waggle 2 NOD, bob, shake

wag[2] *noun* JOKER, comic, wit, comedian, clown, card (*informal*), kidder (*informal*), jester, dag (*NZ informal*), prankster, buffoon, trickster, humorist, joculator *or (fem.)* joculatrix

wage *noun often plural* PAYMENT, pay, earnings, remuneration, fee, reward, compensation, income, allowance, recompense, stipend, emolument ▷ *verb* ENGAGE IN, conduct, pursue, carry on, undertake, practise, prosecute, proceed with

wager *verb* BET, chance, risk, stake, lay, venture, put on, pledge, gamble, hazard, speculate, punt (*chiefly Brit*) ▷ *noun* BET, stake, pledge, gamble, risk, flutter (*Brit informal*), ante, punt (*chiefly Brit*), long shot

waggle *verb* WAG, wiggle, wave, shake, flutter, wobble, oscillate

waif *noun* STRAY, orphan, outcast, urchin, foundling

wail *verb* CRY, weep, grieve, lament, keen, greet (*Scot archaic*), howl, whine, deplore, bemoan, bawl, bewail, yowl, ululate ▷ *noun* CRY, moan, sob, howl, keening, lament, bawl, lamentation, yowl, ululation

wait *verb* 1 STAY, remain, stop, pause, rest, delay, linger, hover, hang around (*informal*), dally, loiter, tarry << ANTONYM go 2 STAND BY, delay, hold on (*informal*), hold back, wait in the wings, mark time, hang fire, bide your time, kick your heels, cool your heels 3 BE POSTPONED, be suspended, be delayed, be put off, be put back, be deferred, be put on hold (*informal*), be shelved, be tabled, be held over, be put on ice (*informal*), be put on the back burner (*informal*) ▷ *noun* DELAY, gap, pause, interval, stay, rest, halt, hold-up, lull, stoppage, hindrance, hiatus, entr'acte ▷▷ **wait for** *or* **on something** *or* **someone** AWAIT, expect, look forward to, hope for, anticipate, look for ▷▷ **wait on** *or* **upon someone** SERVE, tend to, look after, take care of, minister to, attend to, cater to ▷▷ **wait up** STAY AWAKE, stay up, keep vigil

waiter *noun* ATTENDANT, server, flunkey, steward, servant

waitress *noun* ATTENDANT, server, stewardess, servant

waive *verb* 1 GIVE UP, relinquish, renounce, forsake, drop, abandon, resign, yield, surrender, set aside, dispense with, cede, forgo << ANTONYM claim 2 DISREGARD, ignore, discount, overlook, set aside, pass over, dispense with, brush aside, turn a blind eye to, forgo

waiver *noun* RENUNCIATION, surrender, remission, abdication, giving up, resignation, denial, setting aside, abandonment, disclaimer, disavowal, relinquishment, eschewal, abjuration

wake[1] *verb* 1 AWAKEN, stir, awaken, come to, arise, get up, rouse, get out of bed, waken, bestir, rouse from sleep, bestir yourself << ANTONYM fall asleep 2 AWAKEN, arouse, rouse, waken, rouse someone from sleep 3 EVOKE, recall, excite, renew, stimulate, revive, induce, arouse, call up, awaken, rouse, give rise to, conjure up, stir up, rekindle, summon up, reignite ▷ *noun* VIGIL, watch, funeral, deathwatch, tangi (*NZ*) ▷▷ **wake someone up** ACTIVATE, stimulate, enliven, galvanize, fire, excite, provoke, motivate, arouse, awaken, animate, rouse, mobilize, energize, kindle, switch someone on, stir someone up

wake[2] *noun* SLIPSTREAM, wash, trail, backwash, train, track, waves, path ▷▷ **in the wake of** IN THE AFTERMATH OF, following, because of, as a result of, on account of, as a consequence of

waken *verb* 1 AWAKEN, wake, stir, wake up, stimulate, revive, awake, arouse, activate, animate, rouse, enliven, galvanize 2 WAKE UP, come to, get up, awake, awaken, be roused, come awake << ANTONYM fall asleep ▷ see wake1

Wales *noun* CYMRU (*Welsh*), Cambria (*Latin*)

walk *verb* 1 STRIDE, wander, stroll, trudge, go, move, step, march, advance, pace, trek, hike, tread, ramble, tramp, promenade, amble, saunter, take a turn, traipse (*informal*), toddle, make your way, mosey (*informal*), plod on, perambulate, footslog 2 TRAVEL ON FOOT, go on foot, hoof it (*slang*), foot it, go by shanks's pony (*informal*) 3 ESCORT, take, see, show, partner, guide, conduct, accompany, shepherd, convoy, usher, chaperon ▷ *noun* 1 STROLL, hike, ramble, tramp, turn, march, constitutional, trek, outing, trudge, promenade, amble, saunter, traipse (*informal*), breath of air, perambulation 2 GAIT, manner of walking, step, bearing, pace, stride, carriage, tread 3 PATH, pathway, footpath, track, way, road, lane, trail, avenue, pavement, alley, aisle, sidewalk (*chiefly US*), walkway (*chiefly US*), promenade, towpath, esplanade, footway, berm (*NZ*) ▷▷ **walk of life** AREA, calling, business, line, course, trade, class, field, career, rank, employment, province, profession, occupation, arena, sphere, realm, domain, caste, vocation, line of work, métier ▷▷ **walk out** 1 LEAVE SUDDENLY, storm out, get up and go, flounce out, vote with your feet, make a sudden departure, take off (*informal*) 2 GO ON STRIKE, strike, revolt, mutiny, stop work, take industrial action, down tools, withdraw your labour ▷▷ **walk out on someone** ABANDON, leave, desert, strand, betray, chuck (*informal*), run away from, forsake, jilt, run out on (*informal*), throw over, leave high and dry, leave in the lurch

walker *noun* HIKER, rambler, backpacker, wayfarer, footslogger, pedestrian

walkout *noun* STRIKE, protest, revolt, stoppage, industrial action

wall *noun* 1 PARTITION, divider, room divider, screen, panel, barrier, enclosure 2 BARRICADE, rampart, fortification, bulwark, blockade, embankment, parapet, palisade, stockade, breastwork 3 BARRIER, obstacle, barricade, obstruction, check, bar, block, fence, impediment, hindrance ▷▷ **drive someone up the wall** (*informal*) INFURIATE,

madden, exasperate, get on your nerves
(*informal*), anger, provoke, annoy, irritate,
aggravate (*informal*), incense, enrage, gall,
rile, drive you crazy (*informal*), nark (*Brit,
Austral & NZ slang*), be like a red rag to a
bull, make your blood boil, get your goat
(*slang*), drive you insane, make your hackles
rise, raise your hackles, send you off your
head (*slang*), get your back up, make you see
red (*informal*), put your back up, hack you
off (*informal*) ▷▷ **go to the wall** (*informal*) FAIL,
close down, go under, go out of business,
fall, crash, collapse, fold (*informal*), be ruined,
go bust (*informal*), go bankrupt, go broke
(*informal*), go into receivership, become
insolvent

wallet *noun* PURSE, pocketbook, notecase,
pouch, case, holder, money-bag

wallop (*informal*) *verb* 1 HIT, beat, strike,
knock, belt (*informal*), deck (*slang*), bang,
batter, bash (*informal*), pound, chin (*slang*),
smack, thrash, thump, paste (*slang*), buffet,
clout (*informal*), slug, whack, swipe, clobber
(*slang*), pummel, tonk (*slang*), lambast(e),
lay one on (*slang*), beat or knock seven bells
out of (*informal*) 2 BEAT, defeat, slaughter,
thrash, best, stuff (*slang*), worst, tank,
hammer (*informal*), crush, overwhelm, lick
(*informal*), paste (*slang*), rout, walk over
(*informal*), trounce, clobber (*slang*), vanquish,
run rings around (*informal*), wipe the floor
with (*informal*), make mincemeat of, blow
out of the water (*slang*), drub, beat hollow
(*Brit informal*), defeat heavily or utterly ▷ *noun*
BLOW, strike, punch, thump, belt (*informal*),
bash, sock (*slang*), smack, clout (*informal*),
slug, whack, swipe, thwack, haymaker (*slang*)

wallow *verb* 1 REVEL, indulge, relish, savour,
delight, glory, thrive, bask, take pleasure,
luxuriate, indulge yourself << ANTONYM
refrain from 2 ROLL ABOUT, lie, tumble,
wade, slosh, welter, splash around

wan *adjective* 1 PALE, white, washed out, pasty,
faded, bleached, ghastly, sickly, bloodless,
colourless, pallid, anaemic, discoloured,
ashen, sallow, whitish, cadaverous, waxen,
like death warmed up (*informal*), wheyfaced
<< ANTONYM glowing 2 DIM, weak, pale,
faint, feeble

wand *noun* STICK, rod, cane, baton, stake,
switch, birch, twig, sprig, withe, withy

wander *verb* ROAM, walk, drift, stroll, range,
cruise, stray, ramble, prowl, meander, rove,
straggle, traipse (*informal*), mooch around
(*slang*), stravaig (*Scot & N English dialect*),

knock about or around, peregrinate ▷ *noun*
EXCURSION, turn, walk, stroll, cruise, ramble,
meander, promenade, traipse (*informal*),
mosey (*informal*), peregrination ▷▷ **wander
off** STRAY, roam, go astray, lose your way,
drift, depart, rove, straggle ▷▷ **wander off
something** DEVIATE, diverge, veer, swerve,
digress, go off at a tangent, go off course,
lapse

wanderer *noun* TRAVELLER, rover, nomad,
drifter, ranger, journeyer, gypsy, explorer,
migrant, rolling stone, rambler, voyager,
tripper, itinerant, globetrotter, vagrant,
stroller, vagabond, wayfarer, bird of passage

wandering *adjective* ITINERANT, travelling,
journeying, roving, drifting, homeless,
strolling, voyaging, unsettled, roaming,
rambling, nomadic, migratory, vagrant,
peripatetic, vagabond, rootless, wayfaring

wane *verb* 1 DECLINE, flag, weaken, diminish,
fall, fail, drop, sink, fade, decrease, dim,
dwindle, wither, lessen, subside, ebb, wind
down, die out, fade away, abate, draw to a
close, atrophy, taper off << ANTONYM grow
2 DIMINISH, decrease, dwindle << ANTONYM
wax ▷▷ **on the wane** DECLINING, dropping,
fading, weakening, dwindling, withering,
lessening, subsiding, ebbing, dying out, on
the way out, on the decline, tapering off,
obsolescent, on its last legs, at its lowest ebb

want *verb* 1 WISH FOR, desire, fancy, long
for, crave, covet, hope for, yearn for, thirst
for, hunger for, pine for, hanker after, set
your heart on, feel a need for, have a yen
for (*informal*), have a fancy for, eat your
heart out over, would give your eyeteeth
for << ANTONYM have 2 NEED, demand,
require, call for, have need of, stand in need
of 3 SHOULD, need, must, ought 4 DESIRE,
fancy, long for, crave, wish for, yearn for,
thirst for, hanker after, burn for 5 LACK,
need, require, be short of, miss, be deficient
in, be without, fall short in ▷ *noun* 1 LACK,
need, absence, shortage, deficiency, famine,
default, shortfall, inadequacy, scarcity,
dearth, paucity, shortness, insufficiency,
non-existence, scantiness << ANTONYM
abundance 2 POVERTY, need, hardship,
privation, penury, destitution, neediness,
hand-to-mouth existence, indigence,
pauperism, pennilessness, distress
<< ANTONYM wealth 3 WISH, will, need,
demand, desire, requirement, fancy, yen
(*informal*), longing, hunger, necessity,
appetite, craving, yearning, thirst, whim,

hankering

wanting *adjective* **1** DEFICIENT, poor, disappointing, inadequate, pathetic, inferior, insufficient, faulty, not good enough, defective, patchy, imperfect, sketchy, unsound, substandard, leaving much to be desired, not much cop (*Brit slang*), not up to par, not up to expectations, bodger *or* bodgie (*Austral slang*) << ANTONYM adequate **2** LACKING, missing, absent, incomplete, needing, short, shy << ANTONYM complete

wanton *adjective* **1** WILFUL, needless, senseless, unjustified, willed, evil, cruel, vicious, deliberate, arbitrary, malicious, wicked, purposeful, gratuitous, malevolent, spiteful, unprovoked, groundless, unjustifiable, uncalled-for, motiveless << ANTONYM justified **2** PROMISCUOUS, immoral, shameless, licentious, fast, wild, abandoned, loose, dissipated, lewd, profligate, debauched, lustful, lecherous, dissolute, libertine, libidinous, of easy virtue, unchaste << ANTONYM puritanical

war *noun* **1** CONFLICT, drive, attack, fighting, fight, operation, battle, movement, push, struggle, clash, combat, offensive, hostilities, hostility, warfare, expedition, crusade, strife, bloodshed, jihad, enmity, armed conflict << ANTONYM peace **2** CAMPAIGN, drive, attack, operation, movement, push, mission, offensive, crusade ▷ *verb* FIGHT, battle, clash, wage war, campaign, struggle, combat, contend, go to war, do battle, make war, take up arms, bear arms, cross swords, conduct a war, engage in hostilities, carry on hostilities << ANTONYM make peace

warble *verb* SING, trill, chirp, twitter, chirrup, make melody, pipe, quaver ▷ *noun* SONG, trill, quaver, twitter, call, cry, chirp, chirrup

ward *noun* **1** ROOM, department, unit, quarter, division, section, apartment, cubicle **2** DISTRICT, constituency, area, division, zone, parish, precinct **3** DEPENDANT, charge, pupil, minor, protégé ▷▷ **ward someone off** DRIVE OFF, resist, confront, fight off, block, oppose, thwart, hold off, repel, fend off, beat off, keep someone at bay, keep someone at arm's length ▷▷ **ward something off 1** AVERT, turn away, fend off, stave off, avoid, block, frustrate, deflect, repel, forestall **2** PARRY, avert, deflect, fend off, avoid, block, repel, turn aside

warden *noun* **1** STEWARD, guardian, administrator, superintendent, caretaker, curator, warder, custodian, watchman,

janitor **2** (*chiefly US & Canad*) JAILER, prison officer, guard, screw (*slang*), keeper, captor, turnkey (*archaic*), gaoler **3** (*Brit*) GOVERNOR, head, leader, director, manager, chief, executive, boss (*informal*), commander, ruler, controller, overseer, baas (*S African*) **4** RANGER, keeper, guardian, protector, custodian, official

warder *or* **wardress** *noun* (*Chiefly Brit*) JAILER, guard, screw (*slang*), warden, prison officer, keeper, captor, custodian, turnkey (*archaic*), gaoler

wardrobe *noun* **1** CLOTHES CUPBOARD, cupboard, closet (*US*), clothes-press, cabinet **2** CLOTHES, outfit, apparel, clobber (*Brit slang*), attire, collection of clothes

warehouse *noun* STORE, depot, storehouse, repository, depository, stockroom

wares *plural noun* GOODS, produce, stock, products, stuff, commodities, merchandise, lines

warfare *noun* WAR, fighting, campaigning, battle, struggle, conflict, combat, hostilities, strife, bloodshed, jihad, armed struggle, discord, enmity, armed conflict, clash of arms, passage of arms << ANTONYM peace

warily *adverb* **1** CAUTIOUSLY, carefully, discreetly, with care, tentatively, gingerly, guardedly, circumspectly, watchfully, vigilantly, cagily (*informal*), heedfully << ANTONYM carelessly **2** SUSPICIOUSLY, uneasily, guardedly, sceptically, cagily (*informal*), distrustfully, mistrustfully, charily

wariness *noun* **1** CAUTION, care, attention, prudence, discretion, deliberation, foresight, vigilance, alertness, forethought, circumspection, mindfulness, watchfulness, carefulness, caginess (*informal*), heedfulness << ANTONYM carelessness **2** SUSPICION, scepticism, distrust, mistrust

warlike *adjective* BELLIGERENT, military, aggressive, hostile, martial, combative, unfriendly, antagonistic, pugnacious, argumentative, bloodthirsty, hawkish, bellicose, quarrelsome, militaristic, inimical, sabre-rattling, jingoistic, warmongering, aggers (*Austral slang*), biffo (*Austral slang*) << ANTONYM peaceful

warm *adjective* **1** BALMY, mild, temperate, pleasant, fine, bright, sunny, agreeable, sultry, summery, moderately hot << ANTONYM cool **2** COSY, snug, toasty (*informal*), comfortable, homely, comfy (*informal*) **3** MODERATELY HOT, heated << ANTONYM cool **4** THERMAL, winter,

thick, chunky, woolly << ANTONYM cool
5 MELLOW, relaxing, pleasant, agreeable,
restful **6** AFFABLE, kindly, friendly,
affectionate, loving, happy, tender, pleasant,
cheerful, hearty, good-humoured, amiable,
amicable, cordial, sociable, genial, congenial,
hospitable, approachable, amorous, good-
natured, likable *or* likeable << ANTONYM
unfriendly **7** NEAR, close, hot, near to the
truth ▷ *verb* WARM UP, heat, thaw (out),
heat up << ANTONYM cool down ▷▷ **warm
something** *or* **someone up 1** HEAT, thaw,
heat up **2** ROUSE, stimulate, stir up, animate,
interest, excite, provoke, turn on (*slang*),
arouse, awaken, exhilarate, incite, whip up,
galvanize, put some life into, get something
or someone going, make something *or*
someone enthusiastic
warm-hearted *adjective* KINDLY, loving,
kind, warm, gentle, generous, tender,
pleasant, mild, sympathetic, affectionate,
compassionate, hearty, cordial, genial,
affable, good-natured, kind-hearted, tender-
hearted << ANTONYM cold-hearted
warmth *noun* **1** HEAT, snugness, warmness,
comfort, homeliness, hotness << ANTONYM
coolness **2** AFFECTION, feeling, love,
goodwill, kindness, tenderness, friendliness,
cheerfulness, amity, cordiality, affability,
kindliness, heartiness, amorousness,
hospitableness, fondness << ANTONYM
hostility
warn *verb* **1** NOTIFY, tell, remind, inform,
alert, tip off, give notice, make someone
aware, forewarn, apprise, give fair warning
2 ADVISE, urge, recommend, counsel,
caution, commend, exhort, admonish, put
someone on his *or* her guard
warning *noun* **1** CAUTION, information, advice,
injunction, notification, caveat, word to
the wise **2** NOTICE, notification, word, sign,
threat, tip, signal, alarm, announcement,
hint, alert, tip-off (*informal*) **3** OMEN, sign,
forecast, indication, token, prediction,
prophecy, premonition, foreboding,
portent, presage, augury, foretoken, rahui
(*NZ*) **4** REPRIMAND, talking-to (*informal*),
caution, censure, counsel, carpeting (*Brit
informal*), rebuke, reproach, scolding,
berating, ticking-off (*informal*), chiding,
dressing down (*informal*), telling-off
(*informal*), admonition, upbraiding, reproof,
remonstrance ▷ *adjective* CAUTIONARY,
threatening, ominous, premonitory,
admonitory, monitory, bodeful

warp *verb* **1** DISTORT, bend, twist, buckle,
deform, disfigure, contort, misshape,
malform **2** BECOME DISTORTED, bend,
twist, contort, become deformed, become
misshapen **3** PERVERT, twist, corrupt,
degrade, deprave, debase, desecrate,
debauch, lead astray ▷ *noun* TWIST, turn,
bend, defect, flaw, distortion, deviation,
quirk, imperfection, kink, contortion,
deformation
warrant *verb* CALL FOR, demand, require,
merit, rate, commission, earn, deserve,
permit, sanction, excuse, justify, license,
authorize, entail, necessitate, be worthy of,
give grounds for ▷ *noun* AUTHORIZATION,
permit, licence, permission, security,
authority, commission, sanction, pledge,
warranty, carte blanche
warranty *noun* GUARANTEE, promise, contract,
bond, pledge, certificate, assurance,
covenant
warring *adjective* HOSTILE, fighting,
conflicting, opposed, contending, at
war, embattled, belligerent, combatant,
antagonistic, warlike, bellicose, ill-disposed
warrior *noun* SOLDIER, combatant, fighter,
gladiator, champion, brave, trooper, military
man, fighting man, man-at-arms
wary *adjective* **1** SUSPICIOUS, sceptical,
mistrustful, suspecting, guarded,
apprehensive, cagey (*informal*), leery (*slang*),
distrustful, on your guard, chary, heedful
2 WATCHFUL, careful, alert, cautious,
prudent, attentive, vigilant, circumspect,
heedful << ANTONYM careless
wash *verb* **1** CLEAN, scrub, sponge, rinse, scour,
cleanse **2** LAUNDER, clean, wet, rinse, dry-
clean, moisten **3** RINSE, clean, scrub, lather
4 BATHE, bath, shower, take a bath *or* shower,
clean yourself, soak, sponge, douse, freshen
up, lave (*archaic*), soap, scrub yourself down
5 LAP, break, dash, roll, flow, surge, splash,
slap, ripple, swish, splosh **6** MOVE, overcome,
touch, upset, stir, disturb, perturb, surge
through, tug at someone's heartstrings (*often
facetious*) **7** (*informal*) (always used in negative
constructions) BE PLAUSIBLE, stand up, hold
up, pass muster, hold water, stick, carry
weight, be convincing, bear scrutiny ▷ *noun*
1 LAUNDERING, cleaning, clean, cleansing
2 BATHE, bath, shower, dip, soak, scrub,
shampoo, rinse, ablution **3** BACKWASH,
slipstream, path, trail, train, track, waves,
aftermath **4** SPLASH, roll, flow, sweep, surge,
swell, rise and fall, ebb and flow, undulation

5 COAT, film, covering, layer, screen, coating, stain, overlay, suffusion ▷▷ **wash something away** ERODE, corrode, eat into, wear something away, eat something away ▷▷ **wash something** *or* **someone away** SWEEP AWAY, carry off, bear away

washed out *adjective* **1** PALE, light, flat, mat, muted, drab, lacklustre, watery, lustreless **2** WAN, drawn, pale, pinched, blanched, haggard, bloodless, colourless, pallid, anaemic, ashen, chalky, peaky, deathly pale **3** FADED, bleached, blanched, colourless, stonewashed **4** EXHAUSTED, drained, worn-out, tired-out, spent, drawn, done in (*informal*), all in (*slang*), fatigued, wiped out (*informal*), weary, knackered (*slang*), clapped out (*Austral & NZ informal*), dog-tired (*informal*), zonked (*slang*), dead on your feet (*informal*) << ANTONYM lively

washout *noun* **1** FAILURE, disaster, disappointment, flop (*informal*), mess, fiasco, dud (*informal*), clunker (*informal*) << ANTONYM success **2** LOSER, failure, incompetent, no-hoper

waste *verb* **1** SQUANDER, throw away, blow (*slang*), run through, lavish, misuse, dissipate, fritter away, frivol away (*informal*) << ANTONYM save **2** *followed by* **away** WEAR OUT, wither, deplete, debilitate, drain, undermine, exhaust, disable, consume, gnaw, eat away, corrode, enfeeble, sap the strength of, emaciate ▷ *noun* **1** SQUANDERING, misuse, loss, expenditure, extravagance, frittering away, lost opportunity, dissipation, wastefulness, misapplication, prodigality, unthriftiness << ANTONYM saving **2** RUBBISH, refuse, debris, sweepings, scrap, litter, garbage, trash, leftovers, offal, dross, dregs, leavings, offscourings **3** *usually plural* DESERT, wilds, wilderness, void, solitude, wasteland ▷ *adjective* **1** UNWANTED, useless, worthless, unused, leftover, superfluous, unusable, supernumerary << ANTONYM necessary **2** UNCULTIVATED, wild, bare, barren, empty, devastated, dismal, dreary, desolate, unproductive, uninhabited << ANTONYM cultivated ▷▷ **lay something waste** DEVASTATE, destroy, ruin, spoil, total (*slang*), sack, undo, trash (*slang*), ravage, raze, kennet (*Austral slang*), jeff (*Austral slang*), despoil, wreak havoc upon, depredate (*rare*) ▷▷ **waste away** DECLINE, dwindle, wither, perish, sink, fade, crumble, decay, wane, ebb, wear out, atrophy

wasteful *adjective* EXTRAVAGANT, lavish,

prodigal, profligate, ruinous, spendthrift, uneconomical, improvident, unthrifty, thriftless << ANTONYM thrifty

wasteland *noun* WILDERNESS, waste, wild, desert, void

waster *noun* LAYABOUT, loser, good-for-nothing, shirker, piker (*Austral & NZ slang*), drone, loafer, skiver (*Brit slang*), idler, ne'er-do-well, wastrel, malingerer, bludger (*Austral & NZ informal*)

watch *verb* **1** LOOK AT, observe, regard, eye, see, mark, view, note, check, clock (*Brit slang*), stare at, contemplate, check out (*informal*), look on, gaze at, pay attention to, eyeball (*slang*), peer at, leer at, get a load of (*informal*), feast your eyes on, take a butcher's at (*Brit informal*), take a dekko at (*Brit slang*) **2** SPY ON, follow, track, monitor, keep an eye on, stake out, keep tabs on (*informal*), keep watch on, keep under observation, keep under surveillance **3** GUARD, keep, mind, protect, tend, look after, shelter, take care of, safeguard, superintend ▷ *noun* **1** WRISTWATCH, timepiece, pocket watch, clock, chronometer **2** GUARD, eye, attention, supervision, surveillance, notice, observation, inspection, vigil, lookout, vigilance ▷▷ **watch out for something** *or* **someone** KEEP A SHARP LOOKOUT FOR, look out for, be alert for, be on the alert for, keep your eyes open for, be on your guard for, be on (the) watch for, be vigilant for, keep a weather eye open for, be watchful for, keep your eyes peeled *or* skinned for (*informal*) ▷▷ **watch out** *or* **watch it** *or* **watch yourself** BE CAREFUL, look out, be wary, be alert, be on the lookout, be vigilant, take heed, have a care, be on the alert, watch yourself, keep your eyes open, be watchful, be on your guard, mind out, be on (the) watch, keep a sharp lookout, keep a weather eye open, keep your eyes peeled *or* skinned (*informal*), pay attention

watchdog *noun* **1** GUARDIAN, monitor, inspector, protector, custodian, scrutineer **2** GUARD DOG

watchful *adjective* ALERT, attentive, vigilant, observant, guarded, suspicious, wary, on the lookout, circumspect, wide awake, on your toes, on your guard, on the watch, on the qui vive, heedful << ANTONYM careless

watchman *noun* GUARD, security guard, security man, custodian, caretaker

watchword *noun* MOTTO, slogan, maxim, byword, rallying cry, battle cry, catch phrase, tag-line, catchword, catchcry (*Austral*)

water *noun* **1** LIQUID, aqua, Adam's ale *or* wine, H_2O, wai (*NZ*) **2** *often plural* SEA, main, waves, ocean, depths, briny ▷ *verb* **1** SPRINKLE, spray, soak, irrigate, damp, hose, dampen, drench, douse, moisten, souse, fertigate (*Austral*) **2** GET WET, cry, weep, become wet, exude water ▷▷ **hold water** BE SOUND, work, stand up, be convincing, hold up, make sense, be logical, ring true, be credible, pass the test, be plausible, be tenable, bear examination *or* scrutiny ▷▷ **water something down 1** DILUTE, add water to, put water in, weaken, water, doctor, thin, adulterate **2** MODERATE, weaken, temper, curb, soften, qualify, tame, mute, play down, mitigate, tone down, downplay, adulterate, soft-pedal

waterfall *noun* CASCADE, fall, cataract, chute, linn (*Scot*), force (*N English dialect*)

waterlogged *adjective* SOAKED, saturated, drenched, sodden, streaming, dripping, sopping, wet through, wringing wet, droukit *or* drookit (*Scot*)

watertight *adjective* **1** WATERPROOF, hermetically sealed, sealed, water-resistant, sound, coated, impermeable, weatherproof, water-repellent, damp-proof, rubberized << ANTONYM leaky **2** FOOLPROOF, firm, sound, perfect, conclusive, flawless, undeniable, unassailable, airtight, indisputable, impregnable, irrefutable, unquestionable, incontrovertible << ANTONYM weak

watery *adjective* **1** PALE, thin, weak, faint, feeble, washed-out, wan, colourless, anaemic, insipid, wishy-washy (*informal*) **2** DILUTED, thin, weak, dilute, watered-down, tasteless, runny, insipid, washy, adulterated, wishy-washy (*informal*), flavourless, waterish << ANTONYM concentrated **3** WET, damp, moist, soggy, humid, marshy, squelchy **4** LIQUID, fluid, aqueous, hydrous **5** TEARFUL, moist, weepy, lachrymose (*formal*), tear-filled, rheumy

wave *verb* **1** SIGNAL, sign, gesture, gesticulate **2** GUIDE, point, direct, indicate, signal, motion, gesture, nod, beckon, point in the direction **3** BRANDISH, swing, flourish, wield, wag, move something to and fro, shake **4** FLUTTER, flap, stir, waver, shake, swing, sway, ripple, wag, quiver, undulate, oscillate, move to and fro ▷ *noun* **1** GESTURE, sign, signal, indication, gesticulation **2** RIPPLE, breaker, sea surf, swell, ridge, roller, comber, billow **3** OUTBREAK, trend, rash, upsurge,

sweep, flood, tendency, surge, ground swell **4** STREAM, flood, surge, spate, current, movement, flow, rush, tide, torrent, deluge, upsurge

waver *verb* **1** HESITATE, dither (*chiefly Brit*), vacillate, be irresolute, falter, fluctuate, seesaw, blow hot and cold (*informal*), be indecisive, hum and haw, be unable to decide, shillyshally (*informal*), be unable to make up your mind, swither (*Scot*) << ANTONYM be decisive **2** FLICKER, wave, shake, vary, reel, weave, sway, tremble, wobble, fluctuate, quiver, undulate, totter

wax *verb* **1** INCREASE, rise, grow, develop, mount, expand, swell, enlarge, fill out, magnify, get bigger, dilate, become larger << ANTONYM wane **2** BECOME FULLER, become larger, enlarge, get bigger

way *noun* **1** METHOD, means, system, process, approach, practice, scheme, technique, manner, plan, procedure, mode, course of action **2** MANNER, style, fashion, mode **3** ASPECT, point, sense, detail, feature, particular, regard, respect, characteristic, facet **4** *often plural* CUSTOM, manner, habit, idiosyncrasy, style, practice, nature, conduct, personality, characteristic, trait, usage, wont, tikanga (*NZ*) **5** ROUTE, direction, course, road, path **6** ACCESS, street, road, track, channel, route, path, lane, trail, avenue, highway, pathway, thoroughfare **7** JOURNEY, approach, advance, progress, passage **8** ROOM, opening, space, elbowroom **9** DISTANCE, length, stretch, journey, trail **10** (*informal*) CONDITION, state, shape (*informal*), situation, status, circumstances, plight, predicament, fettle **11** WILL, demand, wish, desire, choice, aim, pleasure, ambition ▷▷ **by the way** INCIDENTALLY, in passing, in parenthesis, en passant, by the bye ▷▷ **give way 1** COLLAPSE, give, fall, crack, break down, subside, cave in, crumple, fall to pieces, go to pieces **2** CONCEDE, yield, back down, make concessions, accede, acquiesce, acknowledge defeat ▷▷ **give way to something** BE REPLACED BY, be succeeded by, be supplanted by ▷▷ **under way** IN PROGRESS, going, started, moving, begun, on the move, in motion, afoot, on the go (*informal*) ▷▷ **ways and means** CAPABILITY, methods, procedure, way, course, ability, resources, capacity, tools, wherewithal

way-out *adjective* OUTLANDISH, eccentric, unconventional, unorthodox, advanced, wild, crazy, bizarre, weird, progressive, experimental, avant-garde, far-out (*slang*), off-the-wall (*slang*), oddball (*informal*), offbeat, freaky (*slang*), outré, wacko *or* whacko (*informal*), off the air (*Austral slang*)

wayward *adjective* ERRATIC, unruly, wilful, unmanageable, disobedient, contrary, unpredictable, stubborn, perverse, rebellious, fickle, intractable, capricious, obstinate, headstrong, changeable, flighty, incorrigible, obdurate, ungovernable, self-willed, refractory, insubordinate, undependable, inconstant, mulish, cross-grained, contumacious, froward (*archaic*) << ANTONYM obedient

weak *adjective* 1 FEEBLE, exhausted, frail, debilitated, spent, wasted, weakly, tender, delicate, faint, fragile, shaky, sickly, languid, puny, decrepit, unsteady, infirm, anaemic, effete, enervated << ANTONYM strong 2 DEFICIENT, wanting, poor, lacking, inadequate, pathetic, faulty, substandard, under-strength << ANTONYM effective 3 INEFFECTUAL, pathetic, cowardly, powerless, soft, impotent, indecisive, infirm, spineless, boneless, timorous, weak-kneed (*informal*), namby-pamby, irresolute << ANTONYM firm 4 SLIGHT, faint, feeble, pathetic, shallow, hollow 5 FAINT, soft, quiet, slight, small, low, poor, distant, dull, muffled, imperceptible << ANTONYM loud 6 FRAGILE, brittle, flimsy, unsound, fine, delicate, frail, dainty, breakable 7 UNSAFE, exposed, vulnerable, helpless, wide open, unprotected, untenable, defenceless, unguarded << ANTONYM secure 8 UNCONVINCING, unsatisfactory, lame, invalid, flimsy, inconclusive, pathetic << ANTONYM convincing 9 TASTELESS, thin, diluted, watery, runny, insipid, wishy-washy (*informal*), under-strength, milk-and-water, waterish << ANTONYM strong

weaken *verb* 1 REDUCE, undermine, moderate, diminish, temper, impair, lessen, sap, mitigate, invalidate, soften up, take the edge off << ANTONYM boost 2 WANE, fail, diminish, dwindle, lower, flag, fade, give way, lessen, abate, droop, ease up << ANTONYM grow 3 SAP THE STRENGTH OF, tire, exhaust, debilitate, depress, disable, cripple, incapacitate, enfeeble, enervate << ANTONYM strengthen

weakness *noun* 1 FRAILTY, fatigue, exhaustion, fragility, infirmity, debility, feebleness, faintness, decrepitude, enervation << ANTONYM strength 2 LIKING, appetite,

penchant, soft spot, passion, inclination, fondness, predilection, proclivity, partiality, proneness << ANTONYM aversion 3 POWERLESSNESS, vulnerability, impotence, meekness, irresolution, spinelessness, ineffectuality, timorousness, cravenness, cowardliness 4 INADEQUACY, deficiency, transparency, lameness, hollowness, implausibility, flimsiness, unsoundness, tenuousness 5 FAILING, fault, defect, deficiency, flaw, shortcoming, blemish, imperfection, Achilles' heel, chink in your armour, lack << ANTONYM strong point

wealth *noun* 1 RICHES, fortune, prosperity, affluence, goods, means, money, funds, property, cash, resources, substance, possessions, big money, big bucks (*informal, chiefly US*), opulence, megabucks (*US & Canad slang*), lucre, pelf << ANTONYM poverty 2 PROPERTY, funds, capital, estate, assets, fortune, possessions 3 ABUNDANCE, store, plenty, richness, bounty, profusion, fullness, cornucopia, plenitude, copiousness << ANTONYM lack

wealthy *adjective* RICH, prosperous, affluent, well-off, loaded (*slang*), comfortable, flush (*informal*), in the money (*informal*), opulent, well-heeled (*informal*), well-to-do, moneyed, quids in (*slang*), filthy rich, rolling in it (*slang*), on Easy Street (*informal*), stinking rich (*slang*), made of money (*informal*) << ANTONYM poor

wear *verb* 1 BE DRESSED IN, have on, dress in, be clothed in, carry, sport (*informal*), bear, put on, clothe yourself in 2 SHOW, present, bear, display, assume, put on, exhibit 3 DETERIORATE, fray, wear thin, become threadbare 4 ACCEPT (*Brit informal*), take, allow, permit, stomach, swallow (*informal*), brook, stand for, fall for, put up with (*informal*), countenance ▷ *noun* 1 CLOTHES, things, dress, gear (*informal*), attire, habit, outfit, costume, threads (*slang*), garments, apparel, garb, raiments 2 USEFULNESS, use, service, employment, utility, mileage (*informal*) 3 DAMAGE, wear and tear, use, erosion, friction, deterioration, depreciation, attrition, corrosion, abrasion << ANTONYM repair ▷▷ **wear down** BE ERODED, erode, be consumed, wear away ▷▷ **wear off** 1 SUBSIDE, disappear, fade, weaken, diminish, decrease, dwindle, wane, ebb, abate, peter out, lose strength, lose effect 2 RUB AWAY, disappear, fade, abrade ▷▷ **wear out** DETERIORATE, become worn, become useless, wear

through, fray ▷▷ **wear someone down**
UNDERMINE, reduce, chip away at (*informal*),
fight a war of attrition against, overcome
gradually ▷▷ **wear someone out** (*informal*)
EXHAUST, tire, fatigue, weary, impair, sap,
prostrate, knacker (*slang*), frazzle (*informal*),
fag someone out (*informal*), enervate ▷▷ **wear
something down** ERODE, grind down,
consume, impair, corrode, grind down, rub
away, abrade ▷▷ **wear something out** ERODE,
go through, consume, use up, wear holes in,
make worn

weariness *noun* TIREDNESS, fatigue,
exhaustion, lethargy, drowsiness, lassitude,
languor, listlessness, prostration, enervation
<< ANTONYM energy

wearing *adjective* TIRESOME, trying, taxing,
tiring, exhausting, fatiguing, oppressive,
exasperating, irksome, wearisome
<< ANTONYM refreshing

weary *adjective* **1** TIRED, exhausted, drained,
worn out, spent, done in (*informal*),
flagging, all in (*slang*), fatigued, wearied,
sleepy, fagged (*informal*), whacked (*Brit
informal*), jaded, drooping, knackered
(*slang*), drowsy, clapped out (*Austral & NZ
informal*), enervated, ready to drop, dog-tired
(*informal*), zonked (*slang*), dead beat (*informal*),
asleep *or* dead on your feet (*informal*)
<< ANTONYM energetic **2** FED UP, bored,
sick (*informal*), discontented, impatient,
indifferent, jaded, sick and tired (*informal*),
browned-off (*informal*) << ANTONYM
excited **3** TIRING, taxing, wearing, arduous,
tiresome, laborious, irksome, wearisome,
enervative << ANTONYM refreshing ▷ *verb*
1 GROW TIRED, tire, sicken, have had enough,
become bored **2** BORE, annoy, plague, sicken,
jade, exasperate, vex, irk, try the patience
of, make discontented << ANTONYM excite
3 TIRE, tax, burden, drain, fatigue, fag
(*informal*), sap, wear out, debilitate, take it out
of (*informal*), tire out, enervate << ANTONYM
invigorate

weather *noun* CLIMATE, conditions,
temperature, forecast, outlook,
meteorological conditions, elements ▷
verb **1** TOUGHEN, season, wear, expose,
harden **2** WITHSTAND, stand, suffer,
survive, overcome, resist, brave, endure,
come through, get through, rise above,
live through, ride out, make it through
(*informal*), surmount, pull through, stick it
out (*informal*), bear up against << ANTONYM
surrender to ▷▷ **under the weather** ILL,

unwell, poorly (*informal*), sick, rough
(*informal*), crook (*Austral & NZ informal*),
ailing, not well, seedy (*informal*), below par,
queasy, out of sorts, nauseous, off-colour
(*Brit*), indisposed, peaky, ropy (*Brit informal*),
wabbit (*Scot informal*)

weave *verb* **1** KNIT, twist, intertwine, plait,
unite, introduce, blend, incorporate, merge,
mat, fuse, braid, entwine, intermingle,
interlace **2** ZIGZAG, wind, move in and out,
crisscross, weave your way **3** CREATE, tell,
recount, narrate, make, build, relate, make
up, spin, construct, invent, put together,
unfold, contrive, fabricate

web *noun* **1** COBWEB, spider's web **2** MESH,
net, netting, screen, webbing, weave, lattice,
latticework, interlacing, lacework **3** TANGLE,
series, network, mass, chain, knot, maze,
toils, nexus

wed *verb* **1** GET MARRIED TO, espouse, get
hitched to (*slang*), be united to, plight
your troth to (*old-fashioned*), get spliced
to (*informal*), take as your husband *or* wife
<< ANTONYM divorce **2** GET MARRIED,
marry, be united, tie the knot (*informal*),
take the plunge (*informal*), get hitched
(*slang*), get spliced (*informal*), become man
and wife, plight your troth (*old-fashioned*)
<< ANTONYM divorce **3** UNITE, combine,
bring together, amalgamate, join, link,
marry, ally, connect, blend, integrate, merge,
unify, make one, fuse, weld, interweave,
yoke, coalesce, commingle << ANTONYM
divide

wedding *noun* MARRIAGE, nuptials, wedding
ceremony, marriage ceremony, marriage
service, wedding service, nuptial rite,
espousals

wedge *verb* SQUEEZE, force, lodge, jam, crowd,
block, stuff, pack, thrust, ram, cram, stow ▷
noun BLOCK, segment, lump, chunk, triangle,
slab, hunk, chock, wodge (*Brit informal*)

wedlock *noun* MARRIAGE, matrimony, holy
matrimony, married state, conjugal bond

wee *adjective* LITTLE, small, minute, tiny,
miniature, insignificant, negligible,
microscopic, diminutive, minuscule, teeny,
itsy-bitsy (*informal*), teeny-weeny, titchy (*Brit
informal*), teensy-weensy, pygmy *or* pigmy

weedy *adjective* WEAK, thin, frail, skinny,
feeble, ineffectual, puny, undersized, weak-
kneed (*informal*), namby-pamby, nerdy *or*
nurdy (*slang*)

weekly *adjective* ONCE A WEEK, hebdomadal,
hebdomadary ▷ *adverb* EVERY WEEK, once a

week, by the week, hebdomadally

weep *verb* CRY, shed tears, sob, whimper, complain, keen, greet (*Scot archaic*), moan, mourn, grieve, lament, whinge (*informal*), blubber, snivel, ululate, blub (*slang*), boohoo << ANTONYM rejoice

weepy *adjective* TEARFUL, crying, weeping, sobbing, whimpering, close to tears, blubbering, lachrymose, on the verge of tears ▷ *noun* TEAR-JERKER (*informal*)

weigh *verb* 1 HAVE A WEIGHT OF, tip the scales at (*informal*) 2 MEASURE THE WEIGHT OF, put someone *or* something on the scales, measure how heavy someone *or* something is 3 CONSIDER, study, examine, contemplate, evaluate, ponder, mull over, think over, eye up, reflect upon, give thought to, meditate upon, deliberate upon 4 COMPARE, balance, contrast, juxtapose, place side by side 5 MATTER, carry weight, cut any ice (*informal*), impress, tell, count, have influence, be influential ▷▷ **weigh on someone** OPPRESS, burden, depress, distress, plague, prey, torment, hang over, bear down, gnaw at, cast down, take over ▷▷ **weigh someone down** 1 BURDEN, overload, encumber, overburden, tax, weight, strain, handicap, saddle, hamper 2 OPPRESS, worry, trouble, burden, depress, haunt, plague, get down, torment, take control of, hang over, beset, prey on, bear down, gnaw at, cast down, press down on, overburden, weigh upon, lie heavy on ▷▷ **weigh someone up** ASSESS, judge, gauge, appraise, eye someone up, size someone up (*informal*) ▷▷ **weigh something out** MEASURE, dole out, apportion, deal out

weight *noun* 1 HEAVINESS, mass, burden, poundage, pressure, load, gravity, tonnage, heft (*informal*), avoirdupois 2 LOAD, mass, ballast, heavy object 3 IMPORTANCE, force, power, moment, value, authority, influence, bottom, impact, import, muscle, consequence, substance, consideration, emphasis, significance, sway, clout (*informal*), leverage, efficacy, mana (*NZ*), persuasiveness 4 BURDEN, pressure, load, strain, oppression, albatross, millstone, encumbrance 5 PREPONDERANCE, mass, bulk, main body, most, majority, onus, lion's share, greatest force, main force, best *or* better part ▷ *verb* 1 *often with* **down** LOAD, ballast, make heavier 2 BIAS, load, slant, unbalance 3 BURDEN, handicap, oppress, impede, weigh down, encumber, overburden

weighty *adjective* 1 IMPORTANT, serious, significant, critical, crucial, considerable, substantial, grave, solemn, momentous, forcible, consequential, portentous << ANTONYM unimportant 2 HEAVY, massive, dense, hefty (*informal*), cumbersome, ponderous, burdensome 3 ONEROUS, taxing, demanding, difficult, worrying, crushing, exacting, oppressive, burdensome, worrisome, backbreaking

weird *adjective* 1 STRANGE, odd, unusual, bizarre, ghostly, mysterious, queer, unearthly, eerie, grotesque, supernatural, unnatural, far-out (*slang*), uncanny, spooky (*informal*), creepy (*informal*), eldritch (*poetic*) << ANTONYM normal 2 BIZARRE, odd, strange, unusual, queer, grotesque, unnatural, creepy (*informal*), outlandish, freakish << ANTONYM ordinary

weirdo *or* **weirdie** *noun* ECCENTRIC, nut (*slang*), freak (*informal*), crank (*informal*), loony (*slang*), nutter (*Brit slang*), oddball (*informal*), crackpot (*informal*), nutcase (*slang*), headcase (*informal*), headbanger (*informal*), queer fish (*Brit informal*)

welcome *verb* 1 GREET, meet, receive, embrace, hail, usher in, say hello to, roll out the red carpet for, offer hospitality to, receive with open arms, bid welcome, karanga (*NZ*), mihi (*NZ*) << ANTONYM reject 2 ACCEPT GLADLY, appreciate, embrace, approve of, be pleased by, give the thumbs up to (*informal*), be glad about, express pleasure *or* satisfaction at ▷ *noun* GREETING, welcoming, entertainment, reception, acceptance, hail, hospitality, salutation << ANTONYM rejection ▷ *adjective* 1 PLEASING, wanted, accepted, appreciated, acceptable, pleasant, desirable, refreshing, delightful, gratifying, agreeable, pleasurable, gladly received << ANTONYM unpleasant 2 WANTED, at home, invited << ANTONYM unwanted 3 FREE, invited

weld *verb* 1 JOIN, link, bond, bind, connect, cement, fuse, solder, braze 2 UNITE, combine, blend, consolidate, unify, fuse, meld ▷ *noun* JOINT, bond, seam, juncture

welfare *noun* 1 WELLBEING, good, interest, health, security, benefit, success, profit, safety, protection, fortune, comfort, happiness, prosperity, prosperousness 2 STATE BENEFIT, support, benefits, pensions, dole (*slang*), social security, unemployment benefit, state benefits, pogey (*Canad*)

well¹ *adverb* 1 SKILFULLY, expertly, adeptly, with skill, professionally, correctly, properly, effectively, efficiently, adequately, admirably, ably, conscientiously, proficiently << ANTONYM badly **2** SATISFACTORILY, nicely, smoothly, successfully, capitally, pleasantly, happily, famously (*informal*), splendidly, agreeably, like nobody's business (*informal*), in a satisfactory manner << ANTONYM badly **3** THOROUGHLY, completely, fully, carefully, effectively, efficiently, rigorously **4** INTIMATELY, closely, completely, deeply, fully, personally, profoundly << ANTONYM slightly **5** CAREFULLY, closely, minutely, fully, comprehensively, accurately, in detail, in depth, extensively, meticulously, painstakingly, rigorously, scrupulously, assiduously, intensively, from top to bottom, methodically, attentively, conscientiously, exhaustively **6** FAVOURABLY, highly, kindly, warmly, enthusiastically, graciously, approvingly, admiringly, with admiration, appreciatively, with praise, glowingly, with approbation << ANTONYM unfavourably **7** CONSIDERABLY, easily, very much, significantly, substantially, markedly **8** FULLY, highly, greatly, completely, amply, very much, thoroughly, considerably, sufficiently, substantially, heartily, abundantly **9** POSSIBLY, probably, certainly, reasonably, conceivably, justifiably **10** DECENTLY, right, kindly, fittingly, fairly, easily, correctly, properly, readily, politely, suitably, generously, justly, in all fairness, genially, civilly, hospitably << ANTONYM unfairly **11** PROSPEROUSLY, comfortably, splendidly, in comfort, in (the lap of) luxury, flourishingly, without hardship ▷ *adjective* **1** HEALTHY, strong, sound, fit, blooming, robust, hale, hearty, in good health, alive and kicking, fighting fit (*informal*), in fine fettle, up to par, fit as a fiddle, able-bodied, in good condition << ANTONYM ill **2** SATISFACTORY, good, right, fine, happy, fitting, pleasing, bright, useful, lucky, proper, thriving, flourishing, profitable, fortunate << ANTONYM unsatisfactory **3** ADVISABLE, useful, proper, prudent, agreeable << ANTONYM inadvisable ▷▷ **as well** ALSO, too, in addition, moreover, besides, to boot, into the bargain ▷▷ **as well as** INCLUDING, along with, in addition to, not to mention, at the same time as, over and above

well² *noun* **1** HOLE, bore, pit, shaft **2** WATERHOLE, source, spring, pool, fountain, fount **3** SOURCE, fund, mine, treasury,

reservoir, storehouse, repository, fount, wellspring ▷ *verb* **1** FLOW, trickle, seep, run, issue, spring, pour, jet, burst, stream, surge, discharge, trickle, gush, ooze, seep, exude, spurt, spout **2** RISE, increase, grow, mount, surge, swell, intensify

well-balanced *adjective* **1** SENSIBLE, rational, level-headed, well-adjusted, together (*slang*), sound, reasonable, sober, sane, judicious << ANTONYM unbalanced **2** WELL-PROPORTIONED, proportional, graceful, harmonious, symmetrical

well-bred *adjective* **1** POLITE, ladylike, well-brought-up, well-mannered, cultured, civil, mannerly, polished, sophisticated, gentlemanly, refined, cultivated, courteous, gallant, genteel, urbane, courtly << ANTONYM ill-bred **2** ARISTOCRATIC, gentle, noble, patrician, blue-blooded, well-born, highborn

well-groomed *adjective* SMART, trim, neat, tidy, spruce, well-dressed, dapper, well turned out, soigné *or* soignée

well-heeled *adjective* (*informal*) PROSPEROUS, rich, wealthy, affluent, loaded (*slang*), comfortable, flush (*informal*), well-off, in the money (*informal*), opulent, well-to-do, moneyed, well-situated, in clover (*informal*)

well-informed *adjective* EDUCATED, aware, informed, acquainted, knowledgeable *or* knowledgable, understanding, well-educated, in the know (*informal*), well-read, conversant, au fait (*French*), in the loop (*informal*), well-grounded, au courant (*French*), clued-up (*informal*), cognizant *or* cognisant, well-versed

well-known *adjective* **1** FAMOUS, important, celebrated, prominent, great, leading, noted, august, popular, familiar, distinguished, esteemed, acclaimed, notable, renowned, eminent, famed, illustrious, on the map, widely known **2** FAMILIAR, common, established, popular, everyday, widely known

well-mannered *adjective* POLITE, civil, mannerly, gentlemanly, gracious, respectful, courteous, genteel, well-bred, ladylike

well-nigh *adverb* ALMOST, nearly, virtually, practically, next to, all but, just about, more or less

well-off *adjective* **1** RICH, wealthy, comfortable, affluent, loaded (*slang*), flush (*informal*), prosperous, well-heeled (*informal*), well-to-do, moneyed << ANTONYM poor **2** FORTUNATE, lucky, comfortable, thriving, flourishing, successful

well-to-do *adjective* RICH, wealthy, affluent, well-off, loaded (*slang*), comfortable, flush (*informal*), prosperous, well-heeled (*informal*), moneyed << ANTONYM poor

well-worn *adjective* **1** STALE, tired, stereotyped, commonplace, banal, trite, hackneyed, overused, timeworn **2** SHABBY, worn, faded, ragged, frayed, worn-out, scruffy, tattered, tatty, threadbare

welter *noun* JUMBLE, confusion, muddle, hotchpotch, web, mess, tangle

wend ▷▷ **wend your way** GO, move, travel, progress, proceed, make for, direct your course

wet *adjective* **1** DAMP, soaked, soaking, dripping, saturated, moist, drenched, watery, soggy, sodden, waterlogged, moistened, dank, sopping, aqueous, wringing wet << ANTONYM dry **2** RAINY, damp, drizzly, showery, raining, pouring, drizzling, misty, teeming, humid, dank, clammy << ANTONYM sunny **3** (*informal*) FEEBLE, soft, weak, silly, foolish, ineffectual, weedy (*informal*), spineless, effete, boneless, timorous, namby-pamby, irresolute, wussy (*slang*), nerdy *or* nurdy (*slang*) ▷ *verb* MOISTEN, spray, damp, dampen, water, dip, splash, soak, steep, sprinkle, saturate, drench, douse, irrigate, humidify, fertigate (*Austral*) << ANTONYM dry ▷ *noun* **1** RAIN, rains, damp, drizzle, wet weather, rainy season, rainy weather, damp weather << ANTONYM fine weather **2** MOISTURE, water, liquid, damp, humidity, condensation, dampness, wetness, clamminess << ANTONYM dryness

whack (*informal*) *verb* STRIKE, hit, beat, box, belt (*informal*), deck (*slang*), bang, rap, slap, bash (*informal*), sock (*slang*), chin (*slang*), smack, thrash, thump, buffet, clout (*informal*), slug, cuff, swipe, clobber (*slang*), wallop (*informal*), thwack, lambast(e), lay one on (*slang*), beat *or* knock seven bells out of (*informal*) ▷ *noun* **1** BLOW, hit, box, stroke, belt (*informal*), bang, rap, slap, bash (*informal*), sock (*slang*), smack, thump, buffet, clout (*informal*), slug, cuff, swipe, wallop (*informal*), wham, thwack **2** SHARE, part, cut (*informal*), bit, portion, quota, allotment **3** ATTEMPT, go (*informal*), try, turn, shot (*informal*), crack (*informal*), stab (*informal*), bash (*informal*)

whacking *adjective* (*informal*) HUGE, big, large, giant, enormous, extraordinary, tremendous, gigantic, great, monstrous, mammoth, whopping (*informal*), prodigious, elephantine, humongous *or* humungous (*US slang*)

wharf *noun* DOCK, pier, berth, quay, jetty, landing stage

wheedle *verb* COAX, talk, court, draw, persuade, charm, worm, flatter, entice, cajole, inveigle

wheel *noun* DISC, ring, hoop ▷ *verb* **1** PUSH, trundle, roll **2** TURN, swing, spin, revolve, rotate, whirl, swivel **3** CIRCLE, orbit, go round, twirl, gyrate ▷▷ **at** *or* **behind the wheel** DRIVING, steering, in the driving seat, in the driver's seat

wheeze *verb* GASP, whistle, cough, hiss, rasp, catch your breath, breathe roughly ▷ *noun* **1** GASP, whistle, cough, hiss, rasp **2** (*Brit slang*) TRICK, plan, idea, scheme, stunt, ploy, expedient, ruse

whereabouts *plural noun* POSITION, situation, site, location

wherewithal *noun* RESOURCES, means, money, funds, capital, supplies, ready (*informal*), essentials, ready money

whet *verb* STIMULATE, increase, excite, stir, enhance, provoke, arouse, awaken, animate, rouse, quicken, incite, kindle, pique << ANTONYM suppress

whiff *noun* **1** SMELL, hint, scent, sniff, aroma, odour, draught, niff (*Brit slang*) **2** (*Brit slang*) STINK, stench, reek, pong (*Brit informal*), niff (*Brit slang*), malodour, hum (*slang*) **3** TRACE, suggestion, hint, suspicion, bit, drop, note, breath, whisper, shred, crumb, tinge, jot, smidgen (*informal*), soupçon **4** PUFF, breath, flurry, waft, rush, blast, draught, gust ▷ *verb* (*Brit slang*) STINK, stench, reek, pong (*Brit informal*), niff (*Brit slang*), hum (*slang*)

whim *noun* IMPULSE, sudden notion, caprice, fancy, sport, urge, notion, humour, freak, craze, fad (*informal*), quirk, conceit, vagary, whimsy, passing thought, crotchet

whimper *verb* CRY, moan, sob, weep, whine, whinge (*informal*), grizzle (*informal, chiefly Brit*), blubber, snivel, blub (*slang*), mewl ▷ *noun* SOB, moan, whine, snivel

whimsical *adjective* FANCIFUL, odd, funny, unusual, fantastic, curious, weird, peculiar, eccentric, queer, flaky (*slang, chiefly US*), singular, quaint, playful, mischievous, capricious, droll, freakish, fantastical, crotchety, chimerical, waggish

whine *verb* **1** CRY, sob, wail, whimper, sniffle, snivel, moan **2** COMPLAIN, grumble, gripe (*informal*), whinge (*informal*), moan, cry, beef (*slang*), carp, sob, wail, grouse, whimper, bleat, grizzle (*informal, chiefly Brit*), grouch (*informal*), bellyache (*slang*), kvetch (*US slang*) ▷ *noun* **1** CRY, moan, sob, wail, whimper, plaintive cry **2** DRONE, note, hum **3** COMPLAINT, moan, grumble, grouse, gripe (*informal*), whinge (*informal*), grouch (*informal*), beef (*slang*)

whinge (*informal*) *verb* COMPLAIN, moan, grumble, grouse, gripe (*informal*), beef (*slang*), carp, bleat, grizzle (*informal, chiefly Brit*), grouch (*informal*), bellyache (*slang*), kvetch (*US slang*) ▷ *noun* COMPLAINT, moan, grumble, whine, grouse, gripe (*informal*), grouch, beef (*slang*)

whip *noun* LASH, cane, birch, switch, crop, scourge, thong, rawhide, riding crop, horsewhip, bullwhip, knout, cat-o'-nine-tails ▷ *verb* **1** LASH, cane, flog, beat, switch, leather, punish, strap, tan (*slang*), thrash, lick (*informal*), birch, scourge, spank, castigate, lambast(e), flagellate, give a hiding (*informal*) **2** (*informal*) DASH, shoot, fly, tear, rush, dive, dart, whisk, flit **3** WHISK, beat, mix vigorously, stir vigorously **4** INCITE, drive, push, urge, stir, spur, provoke, compel, hound, prod, work up, get going, agitate, prick, inflame, instigate, goad, foment **5** (*informal*) BEAT, thrash, trounce, wipe the floor with (*informal*), best, defeat, stuff (*slang*), worst, overcome, hammer (*informal*), overwhelm, conquer, lick (*informal*), rout, overpower, outdo, clobber (*slang*), take apart (*slang*), run rings around (*informal*), blow out of the water (*slang*), make mincemeat out of (*informal*), drub ▷▷ **whip someone up** ROUSE, excite, provoke, arouse, stir up, work up, agitate, inflame ▷▷ **whip something out** PULL OUT, produce, remove, jerk out, show, flash, seize, whisk out, snatch out

whipping *noun* BEATING, lashing, thrashing, caning, hiding (*informal*), punishment, tanning (*slang*), birching, flogging, spanking, the strap, flagellation, castigation, leathering

whirl *verb* **1** SPIN, turn, circle, wheel, twist, reel, rotate, pivot, twirl **2** ROTATE, roll, twist, revolve, swirl, twirl, gyrate, pirouette **3** FEEL DIZZY, swim, spin, reel, go round ▷ *noun* **1** REVOLUTION, turn, roll, circle, wheel, spin, twist, reel, swirl, rotation, twirl, pirouette, gyration, birl (*Scot*) **2** BUSTLE, round, series, succession, flurry, merry-go-round **3** CONFUSION, daze, dither (*chiefly Brit*), giddiness **4** TUMULT, spin, stir, agitation, commotion, hurly-burly ▷▷ **give something a whirl** (*informal*) ATTEMPT, try, have a go at

(*informal*), have a crack at (*informal*), have a shot at (*informal*), have a stab at (*informal*), have a bash at, have a whack at (*informal*)

whirlwind *noun* **1** TORNADO, hurricane, cyclone, typhoon, twister (*US*), dust devil, waterspout **2** TURMOIL, chaos, swirl, mayhem, uproar, maelstrom, welter, bedlam, tumult, hurly-burly, madhouse ▷ *modifier* RAPID, short, quick, swift, lightning, rash, speedy, hasty, impulsive, headlong, impetuous << ANTONYM unhurried

whisk *verb* **1** RUSH, sweep, hurry **2** PULL, whip (*informal*), snatch, take **3** SPEED, race, shoot, fly, career, tear, rush, sweep, dash, hurry, barrel (along) (*informal, chiefly US & Canad*), sprint, dart, hasten, burn rubber (*informal*), go like the clappers (*Brit informal*), hightail it (*US informal*), wheech (*Scot informal*) **4** FLICK, whip, sweep, brush, wipe, twitch **5** BEAT, mix vigorously, stir vigorously, whip, fluff up ▷ *noun* **1** FLICK, sweep, brush, whip, wipe **2** BEATER, mixer, blender

whisky *noun* SCOTCH, malt, rye, bourbon, firewater, John Barleycorn, usquebaugh (*Gaelic*), barley-bree (*Scot*)

whisper *verb* **1** MURMUR, breathe, mutter, mumble, purr, speak in hushed tones, say softly, say sotto voce, utter under the breath << ANTONYM shout **2** GOSSIP, hint, intimate, murmur, insinuate, spread rumours **3** RUSTLE, sigh, moan, murmur, hiss, swish, sough, susurrate (*literary*) ▷ *noun* **1** MURMUR, mutter, mumble, undertone, low voice, soft voice, hushed tone **2** (*informal*) RUMOUR, report, word, story, hint, buzz, gossip, dirt (*US slang*), goss (*informal*), innuendo, insinuation, scuttlebutt (*US slang*) **3** RUSTLE, sigh, sighing, murmur, hiss, swish, soughing, susurration *or* susurrus (*literary*) **4** HINT, shadow, suggestion, trace, breath, suspicion, fraction, tinge, whiff

whit *noun* BIT, drop, piece, trace, scrap, dash, grain, particle, fragment, atom, pinch, shred, crumb, mite, jot, speck, modicum, least bit, iota

white *adjective* **1** PALE, grey, ghastly, wan, pasty, bloodless, pallid, ashen, waxen, like death warmed up (*informal*), wheyfaced **2** (only used of *hair*) SILVER, grey, snowy, grizzled, hoary

white-collar *adjective* CLERICAL, office, executive, professional, salaried, nonmanual

whiten *verb* **1** PALE, blanch, go white, turn pale, blench, fade, etiolate << ANTONYM darken **2** BLEACH, lighten << ANTONYM darken

whitewash *verb* COVER UP, conceal, suppress, camouflage, make light of, gloss over, extenuate << ANTONYM expose ▷ *noun* COVER-UP, deception, camouflage, concealment, extenuation

whittle *verb* CARVE, cut, hew, shape, trim, shave, pare ▷▷ **whittle something away** UNDERMINE, reduce, destroy, consume, erode, eat away, wear away, cut down, cut, decrease, prune, scale down

whole *noun* 1 TOTAL, all, lot, everything, aggregate, sum total, the entire amount 2 UNIT, body, piece, object, combination, unity, entity, ensemble, entirety, fullness, totality << ANTONYM part ▷ *adjective* 1 COMPLETE, full, total, entire, integral, uncut, undivided, unabridged, unexpurgated, uncondensed << ANTONYM partial 2 UNDAMAGED, intact, unscathed, unbroken, good, sound, perfect, mint, untouched, flawless, unhurt, faultless, unharmed, in one piece, uninjured, inviolate, unimpaired, unmutilated << ANTONYM damaged ▷ *adverb* IN ONE PIECE, in one ▷▷ **on the whole** 1 ALL IN ALL, altogether, all things considered, by and large, taking everything into consideration 2 GENERALLY, in general, for the most part, as a rule, chiefly, mainly, mostly, principally, on average, predominantly, in the main, to a large extent, as a general rule, generally speaking

wholehearted *adjective* SINCERE, complete, committed, genuine, real, true, determined, earnest, warm, devoted, dedicated, enthusiastic, emphatic, hearty, heartfelt, zealous, unqualified, unstinting, unreserved, unfeigned << ANTONYM half-hearted

wholesale *adjective* EXTENSIVE, total, mass, sweeping, broad, comprehensive, wide-ranging, blanket, outright, far-reaching, indiscriminate, all-inclusive << ANTONYM limited ▷ *adverb* EXTENSIVELY, comprehensively, across the board, all at once, indiscriminately, without exception, on a large scale

wholesome *adjective* 1 MORAL, nice, clean, pure, decent, innocent, worthy, ethical, respectable, honourable, uplifting, righteous, exemplary, virtuous, apple-pie (*informal*), squeaky-clean, edifying << ANTONYM corrupt 2 HEALTHY, good, strengthening, beneficial, nourishing, nutritious, sanitary, invigorating, salutary,

hygienic, healthful, health-giving << ANTONYM unhealthy

wholly *adverb* 1 COMPLETELY, totally, perfectly, fully, entirely, comprehensively, altogether, thoroughly, utterly, heart and soul, one hundred per cent (*informal*), in every respect << ANTONYM partly 2 SOLELY, only, exclusively, without exception, to the exclusion of everything else

whoop *verb* CRY, shout, scream, cheer, yell, shriek, hoot, holler (*informal*) ▷ *noun* CRY, shout, scream, cheer, yell, shriek, hoot, holler (*informal*), hurrah, halloo

whopper *noun* 1 BIG LIE, fabrication, falsehood, untruth, tall story (*informal*), fable 2 GIANT, monster, jumbo (*informal*), mammoth, colossus, leviathan, crackerjack (*informal*)

whopping *adjective* GIGANTIC, great, big, large, huge, giant, massive, enormous, extraordinary, tremendous, monstrous, whacking (*informal*), mammoth, prodigious, elephantine, humongous *or* humungous (*US slang*)

whore *noun* PROSTITUTE, hooker (*US slang*), tart (*informal*), streetwalker, tom (*Brit slang*), brass (*slang*), slag (*Brit slang*), hustler (*US & Canad slang*), call girl, courtesan, working girl (*facetious slang*), harlot, loose woman, fallen woman, scrubber (*Brit & Austral slang*), strumpet, trollop, lady of the night, cocotte, woman of easy virtue, demimondaine, woman of ill repute, fille de joie (*French*), demirep (*rare*) ▷ *verb* SLEEP AROUND, womanize, wanton (*informal*), wench (*archaic*), fornicate, lech *or* letch (*informal*)

whorl *noun* SWIRL, spiral, coil, twist, vortex, helix, corkscrew

wicked *adjective* 1 BAD, evil, corrupt, vile, guilty, abandoned, foul, vicious, worthless, shameful, immoral, scandalous, atrocious, sinful, heinous, depraved, debased, devilish, amoral, egregious, abominable, fiendish, villainous, unprincipled, nefarious, dissolute, iniquitous, irreligious, black-hearted, impious, unrighteous, maleficent, flagitious << ANTONYM virtuous 2 MISCHIEVOUS, playful, impish, devilish, arch, teasing, naughty, cheeky, rascally, incorrigible, raffish, roguish, rakish, tricksy, puckish, waggish << ANTONYM well-behaved 3 AGONIZING, terrible, acute, severe, intense, awful, painful, fierce, mighty, dreadful, fearful, gut-wrenching 4 HARMFUL, terrible, intense, mighty, crashing, dreadful,

destructive, injurious << ANTONYM
harmless 5 (slang) EXPERT, great (informal),
strong, powerful, masterly, wonderful,
outstanding, remarkable, ace (informal), first-
class, marvellous, mighty, dazzling, skilful,
A1 (informal), adept, deft, adroit

wide adjective 1 SPACIOUS, broad, extensive,
ample, roomy, commodious << ANTONYM
confined 2 BAGGY, full, loose, ample,
billowing, roomy, voluminous, capacious,
oversize, generously cut 3 EXPANDED,
dilated, fully open, distended << ANTONYM
shut 4 BROAD, comprehensive, extensive,
wide-ranging, large, catholic, expanded,
sweeping, vast, immense, ample, inclusive,
expansive, exhaustive, encyclopedic,
far-ranging, compendious << ANTONYM
restricted 5 EXTENSIVE, general, far-
reaching, overarching 6 LARGE, broad, vast,
immense 7 DISTANT, off, away, remote,
off course, off target ▷ adverb 1 FULLY,
completely, right out, as far as possible,
to the furthest extent << ANTONYM partly
2 OFF TARGET, nowhere near, astray, off
course, off the mark

wide-eyed adjective 1 NAIVE, green,
trusting, credulous, simple, innocent,
impressionable, unsophisticated,
ingenuous, wet behind the ears (informal),
unsuspicious, as green as grass 2 STARING,
spellbound, gobsmacked (Brit slang),
dumbfounded, agog, agape, thunderstruck,
goggle-eyed, awe-stricken

widen verb 1 BROADEN, expand, enlarge, dilate,
spread, extend, stretch, open wide, open out
or up << ANTONYM narrow 2 GET WIDER,
spread, extend, expand, broaden, open wide,
open out or up << ANTONYM narrow

wide open adjective 1 OUTSPREAD, spread,
outstretched, splayed, fully open, fully
extended, gaping 2 UNPROTECTED,
open, exposed, vulnerable, at risk, in
danger, susceptible, defenceless, in peril
3 UNCERTAIN, unsettled, unpredictable,
up for grabs (informal), indeterminate,
anybody's guess (informal)

widespread adjective COMMON, general,
popular, sweeping, broad, extensive,
universal, epidemic, wholesale, far-
reaching, prevalent, rife, pervasive, far-flung
<< ANTONYM limited

width noun BREADTH, extent, span, wideness,
reach, range, measure, scope, diameter,
compass, thickness, girth

wield verb 1 BRANDISH, flourish, manipulate,

swing, use, manage, handle, employ, ply
2 EXERT, hold, maintain, exercise, have,
control, manage, apply, command, possess,
make use of, utilize, put to use, be possessed
of, have at your disposal

wife noun SPOUSE, woman (informal), partner,
mate, bride, old woman (informal), old lady
(informal), little woman (informal), significant
other (US informal), better half (humorous),
her indoors (Brit slang), helpmate, helpmeet,
(the) missis or missus (informal), vrou (S
African), wahine (NZ), wifey (informal)

wiggle verb 1 JERK, shake, twitch, wag, jiggle,
waggle 2 SQUIRM, twitch, writhe, shimmy
▷ noun JERK, shake, twitch, wag, squirm,
writhe, jiggle, waggle, shimmy

wild adjective 1 UNTAMED, fierce, savage,
ferocious, unbroken, feral, undomesticated,
free, warrigal (Austral literary) << ANTONYM
tame 2 UNCULTIVATED, natural, native,
indigenous << ANTONYM cultivated
3 DESOLATE, empty, desert, deserted,
virgin, lonely, uninhabited, godforsaken,
uncultivated, uncivilized, trackless,
unpopulated << ANTONYM inhabited
4 STORMY, violent, rough, intense, raging,
furious, howling, choppy, tempestuous,
blustery 5 EXCITED, mad (informal), crazy
(informal), eager, nuts (slang), enthusiastic,
raving, frantic, daft (informal), frenzied,
hysterical, avid, potty (Brit informal),
delirious, agog << ANTONYM unenthusiastic
6 UNCONTROLLED, violent, rough, disorderly,
noisy, chaotic, turbulent, wayward, unruly,
rowdy, boisterous, lawless, unfettered,
unbridled, riotous, unrestrained,
unmanageable, impetuous, undisciplined,
ungovernable, self-willed, uproarious
<< ANTONYM calm 7 MAD (informal), furious,
fuming, infuriated, incensed, enraged,
very angry, irate, livid (informal), in a rage,
on the warpath (informal), hot under the
collar (informal), beside yourself, tooshie
(Austral slang), off the air (Austral slang)
8 OUTRAGEOUS, fantastic, foolish, rash,
extravagant, reckless, preposterous, giddy,
madcap, foolhardy, flighty, ill-considered,
imprudent, impracticable << ANTONYM
practical 9 DISHEVELLED, disordered, untidy,
unkempt, tousled, straggly, windblown,
daggy (Austral & NZ informal) 10 PASSIONATE,
mad (informal), ardent, fervent, zealous,
fervid 11 UNCIVILIZED, fierce, savage,
primitive, rude, ferocious, barbaric, brutish,
barbarous << ANTONYM civilized ▷▷ **the**

wilds WILDERNESS, desert, wasteland, middle of nowhere (*informal*), backwoods, back of beyond (*informal*), uninhabited area ▷▷ **run wild 1** GROW UNCHECKED, spread, ramble, straggle **2** GO ON THE RAMPAGE, stray, rampage, run riot, cut loose, run free, kick over the traces, be undisciplined, abandon all restraint

wilderness *noun* **1** WILDS, waste, desert, wasteland, uncultivated region **2** TANGLE, confusion, maze, muddle, clutter, jumble, welter, congeries, confused mass

wildlife *noun* FLORA AND FAUNA, animals, fauna

wile *noun* CUNNING, craft, fraud, cheating, guile, artifice, trickery, chicanery, craftiness, artfulness, slyness ▷ *plural noun* PLOYS, tricks, devices, lures, manoeuvres, dodges, ruses, artifices, subterfuges, stratagems, contrivances, impositions

wilful *or* **willful** *adjective* **1** INTENTIONAL, willed, intended, conscious, voluntary, deliberate, purposeful, volitional << ANTONYM unintentional **2** OBSTINATE, dogged, determined, persistent, adamant, stubborn, perverse, uncompromising, intractable, inflexible, unyielding, intransigent, headstrong, obdurate, stiff-necked, self-willed, refractory, pig-headed, bull-headed, mulish, froward (*archaic*) << ANTONYM obedient

will *noun* **1** DETERMINATION, drive, aim, purpose, commitment, resolution, resolve, intention, spine, backbone, tenacity, willpower, single-mindedness, doggedness, firmness of purpose **2** WISH, mind, desire, pleasure, intention, fancy, preference, inclination **3** CHOICE, decision, option, prerogative, volition **4** DECREE, wish, desire, command, dictate, ordinance **5** TESTAMENT, declaration, bequest(s), last wishes, last will and testament ▷ *verb* **1** DECREE, order, cause, effect, direct, determine, bid, intend, command, resolve, bring about, ordain **2** WISH, want, choose, prefer, desire, elect, opt, see fit **3** BEQUEATH, give, leave, transfer, gift, hand on, pass on, confer, hand down, settle on ▷▷ **at will** AS YOU PLEASE, at your discretion, as you think fit, at your pleasure, at your desire, at your whim, at your inclination, at your wish

willing *adjective* **1** INCLINED, prepared, happy, pleased, content, in favour, consenting, disposed, favourable, agreeable, in the mood, compliant, amenable, desirous, so minded, nothing loath << ANTONYM unwilling **2** READY, game (*informal*), eager, enthusiastic << ANTONYM reluctant

willingly *adverb* READILY, freely, gladly, happily, eagerly, voluntarily, cheerfully, with pleasure, without hesitation, by choice, with all your heart, lief (*rare*), of your own free will, of your own accord << ANTONYM unwillingly

willingness *noun* INCLINATION, will, agreement, wish, favour, desire, enthusiasm, consent, goodwill, disposition, volition, agreeableness << ANTONYM reluctance

willowy *adjective* SLENDER, slim, graceful, supple, lithe, limber, svelte, lissom(e), sylphlike

willpower *noun* SELF-CONTROL, drive, resolution, resolve, determination, grit, self-discipline, single-mindedness, fixity of purpose, firmness of purpose *or* will, force *or* strength of will << ANTONYM weakness

willy-nilly *adverb* **1** WHETHER YOU LIKE IT OR NOT, necessarily, of necessity, perforce, whether or no, whether desired or not, nolens volens (*Latin*) **2** HAPHAZARDLY, at random, randomly, without order, without method, without planning, any old how (*informal*)

wilt *verb* **1** DROOP, wither, sag, shrivel, become limp *or* flaccid **2** WEAKEN, sag, languish, droop **3** WANE, fail, sink, flag, fade, diminish, dwindle, wither, ebb, melt away, lose courage

wily *adjective* CUNNING, designing, scheming, sharp, intriguing, arch, tricky, crooked, shrewd, sly, astute, deceptive, crafty, artful, shifty, foxy, cagey (*informal*), deceitful, underhand, guileful, fly (*slang*) << ANTONYM straightforward

wimp *noun* (*informal*) WEAKLING, wet (*Brit slang*), mouse, drip (*informal*), coward, jessie (*Scot slang*), pussy (*slang, chiefly US*), jellyfish (*informal*), sissy, doormat (*slang*), wuss (*slang*), milksop, softy *or* softie

win *verb* **1** BE VICTORIOUS IN, succeed in, prevail in, come first in, finish first in, be the victor in, gain victory in, achieve first place in << ANTONYM lose **2** BE VICTORIOUS, succeed, triumph, overcome, prevail, conquer, come first, finish first, carry the day, sweep the board, take the prize, gain victory, achieve mastery, achieve first place, carry all before you << ANTONYM lose **3** GAIN, get, receive, land, catch, achieve, net, earn, pick up, bag (*informal*), secure, collect, obtain, acquire, accomplish, attain, procure,

come away with << ANTONYM forfeit ▷
noun VICTORY, success, triumph, conquest
<< ANTONYM defeat ▷▷ **win someone over**
or **round** CONVINCE, influence, attract,
persuade, convert, charm, sway, disarm,
allure, prevail upon, bring *or* talk round

wince *verb* FLINCH, start, shrink, cringe, quail,
recoil, cower, draw back, blench ▷ *noun*
FLINCH, start, cringe

wind¹ *noun* **1** AIR, blast, breath, hurricane,
breeze, draught, gust, zephyr, air-current,
current of air **2** FLATULENCE, gas, flatus
3 BREATH, puff, respiration **4** NONSENSE,
talk, boasting, hot air, babble, bluster,
humbug, twaddle (*informal*), gab (*informal*),
verbalizing, blather, codswallop (*informal*),
eyewash (*informal*), idle talk, empty talk,
bizzo (*Austral slang*), bull's wool (*Austral &*
NZ slang) ▷▷ **get wind of something** HEAR
ABOUT, learn of, find out about, become
aware of, be told about, be informed of, be
made aware of, hear tell of, have brought to
your notice, hear on the grapevine (*informal*)
▷▷ **in the wind** IMMINENT, coming, near,
approaching, on the way, looming, brewing,
impending, on the cards (*informal*), in the
offing, about to happen, close at hand ▷▷ **put**
the wind up someone (*informal*) SCARE, alarm,
frighten, panic, discourage, unnerve, scare
off, frighten off

wind² *verb* **1** MEANDER, turn, bend, twist,
curve, snake, ramble, twist and turn, deviate,
zigzag **2** WRAP, twist, reel, curl, loop, coil,
twine, furl, wreathe **3** COIL, curl, spiral,
encircle, twine ▷▷ **wind down 1** CALM DOWN,
unwind, take it easy, unbutton (*informal*), put
your feet up, de-stress (*informal*), outspan (*S*
African), cool down *or* off **2** SUBSIDE, decline,
diminish, come to an end, dwindle, tail off,
taper off, slacken off ▷▷ **wind someone up**
(*informal*) **1** IRRITATE, excite, anger, annoy,
exasperate, nettle, work someone up, pique,
make someone nervous, put someone
on edge, make someone tense, hack you
off (*informal*) **2** TEASE, kid (*informal*), have
someone on (*informal*), annoy, rag (*informal*),
rib (*informal*), josh (*informal*), vex, make fun
of, take the mickey out of (*informal*), send
someone up (*informal*), pull someone's
leg (*informal*), jerk *or* yank someone's
chain (*informal*) ▷▷ **wind something up**
1 END, finish, settle, conclude, tie up, wrap
up, finalize, bring to a close, tie up the
loose ends of (*informal*) **2** CLOSE DOWN,
close, dissolve, terminate, liquidate, put

something into liquidation ▷▷ **wind up** END
UP, be left, find yourself, finish up, fetch up
(*informal*), land up, end your days

winded *adjective* OUT OF BREATH, panting,
puffed, breathless, gasping for breath,
puffed out, out of puff, out of whack
(*informal*)

windfall *noun* GODSEND, find, jackpot,
bonanza, stroke of luck, manna from
heaven, pot of gold at the end of the
rainbow << ANTONYM misfortune

winding *adjective* TWISTING, turning,
bending, curving, crooked, spiral, indirect,
roundabout, meandering, tortuous,
convoluted, serpentine, sinuous, circuitous,
twisty, anfractuous, flexuous << ANTONYM
straight

windy *adjective* BREEZY, wild, stormy,
boisterous, blustering, windswept,
tempestuous, blustery, gusty, inclement,
squally, blowy << ANTONYM calm

wing *noun* **1** ORGAN OF FLIGHT, pinion (*poetic*),
pennon (*poetic*) **2** ANNEXE, part, side, section,
extension, adjunct, ell (*US*) **3** FACTION,
grouping, group, set, side, arm, section,
camp, branch, circle, lobby, segment, caucus,
clique, coterie, schism, cabal ▷ *verb* **1** FLY,
soar, glide, take wing **2** HURRY, fly, race,
speed, streak, zoom, hasten, hurtle **3** WOUND,
hit, nick, clip, graze

wink *verb* **1** BLINK, bat, flutter, nictate,
nictitate **2** TWINKLE, flash, shine, sparkle,
gleam, shimmer, glimmer ▷ *noun* **1** BLINK,
flutter, nictation, nictitation **2** TWINKLE,
flash, sparkle, gleam, blink, glimmering,
glimmer ▷▷ **wink at something** CONDONE,
allow, ignore, overlook, tolerate, put up with
(*informal*), disregard, turn a blind eye to,
blink at, connive at, pretend not to notice,
shut your eyes to

winner *noun* VICTOR, first, champion, master,
champ (*informal*), conqueror, vanquisher,
prizewinner, conquering hero << ANTONYM
loser

winning *adjective* **1** VICTORIOUS, first,
top, successful, unbeaten, conquering,
triumphant, undefeated, vanquishing,
top-scoring, unvanquished **2** CHARMING,
taking, pleasing, sweet, attractive, engaging,
lovely, fascinating, fetching, delightful,
cute, disarming, enchanting, endearing,
captivating, amiable, alluring, bewitching,
delectable, winsome, prepossessing, likable
or likeable << ANTONYM unpleasant ▷ *plural*
noun SPOILS, profits, gains, prize, proceeds,

takings, booty

winsome *adjective* CHARMING, taking, winning, pleasing, pretty, fair, sweet, attractive, engaging, fascinating, pleasant, fetching, cute, disarming, enchanting, endearing, captivating, agreeable, amiable, alluring, bewitching, delectable, comely, likable *or* likeable

wintry *adjective* **1** COLD, freezing, frozen, harsh, icy, chilly, snowy, frosty, hibernal << ANTONYM warm **2** UNFRIENDLY, cold, cool, remote, distant, bleak, chilly, frigid, cheerless

wipe *verb* **1** CLEAN, dry, polish, brush, dust, rub, sponge, mop, swab **2** ERASE, remove, take off, get rid of, take away, rub off, efface, clean off, sponge off ▷ *noun* RUB, clean, polish, brush, lick, sponge, mop, swab ▷▷ **wipe something** *or* **someone out** DESTROY, eliminate, take out (*slang*), massacre, slaughter, erase, eradicate, blow away (*slang, chiefly US*), obliterate, liquidate (*informal*), annihilate, efface, exterminate, expunge, extirpate, wipe from the face of the earth (*informal*), kill to the last man, kennet (*Austral slang*), jeff (*Austral slang*)

wiry *adjective* **1** LEAN, strong, tough, thin, spare, skinny, stringy, sinewy << ANTONYM flabby **2** STIFF, rough, coarse, curly, kinky, bristly

wisdom *noun* **1** UNDERSTANDING, learning, knowledge, intelligence, smarts (*slang, chiefly US*), judgment, insight, enlightenment, penetration, comprehension, foresight, erudition, discernment, sagacity, sound judgment, sapience << ANTONYM foolishness **2** PRUDENCE, reason, circumspection, judiciousness

wise *adjective* **1** SAGE, knowing, understanding, aware, informed, clever, intelligent, sensible, enlightened, shrewd, discerning, perceptive, well-informed, erudite, sagacious, sapient, clued-up (*informal*) << ANTONYM foolish **2** SENSIBLE, sound, politic, informed, reasonable, clever, intelligent, rational, logical, shrewd, prudent, judicious, well-advised << ANTONYM unwise

wisecrack *noun* JOKE, sally, gag (*informal*), quip, jibe, barb, jest, witticism, smart remark, pithy remark, sardonic remark

wish *noun* **1** DESIRE, liking, want, longing, hope, urge, intention, fancy (*informal*), ambition, yen (*informal*), hunger, aspiration, craving, lust, yearning, inclination,

itch (*informal*), thirst, whim, hankering << ANTONYM aversion **2** REQUEST, will, want, order, demand, desire, command, bidding, behest (*literary*) ▷ *verb* **1** WANT, feel, choose, please, desire, think fit **2** REQUIRE, ask, order, direct, bid, desire, command, instruct **3** BID, greet with ▷▷ **wish for** DESIRE, want, need, hope for, long for, crave, covet, aspire to, yearn for, thirst for, hunger for, hanker for, sigh for, set your heart on, desiderate

wisp *noun* PIECE, twist, strand, thread, shred, snippet

wispy *adjective* **1** STRAGGLY, fine, thin, frail, wisplike **2** THIN, light, fine, delicate, fragile, flimsy, ethereal, insubstantial, gossamer, diaphanous, wisplike

wistful *adjective* MELANCHOLY, longing, dreaming, sad, musing, yearning, thoughtful, reflective, dreamy, forlorn, mournful, contemplative, meditative, pensive, disconsolate

wit *noun* **1** HUMOUR, fun, quips, banter, puns, pleasantry, repartee, wordplay, levity, witticisms, badinage, jocularity, facetiousness, drollery, raillery, waggishness, wittiness << ANTONYM seriousness **2** HUMORIST, card (*informal*), comedian, wag, joker, dag (*NZ informal*), punster, epigrammatist **3** CLEVERNESS, mind, reason, understanding, sense, brains, smarts (*slang, chiefly US*), judgment, perception, wisdom, insight, common sense, intellect, comprehension, ingenuity, acumen, nous (*Brit slang*), discernment, practical intelligence << ANTONYM stupidity

witch *noun* ENCHANTRESS, magician, hag, crone, occultist, sorceress, Wiccan, necromancer

witchcraft *noun* MAGIC, spell, witching, voodoo, the occult, wizardry, black magic, enchantment, occultism, sorcery, incantation, Wicca, the black art, witchery, necromancy, sortilege, makutu (*NZ*)

withdraw *verb* **1** REMOVE, pull, take off, pull out, extract, take away, pull back, draw out, draw back **2** TAKE OUT, extract, draw out **3** RETREAT, go, leave (*informal*), retire, depart, pull out, fall back, pull back, back out, back off, cop out (*slang*), disengage from << ANTONYM advance **4** GO, leave, retire, retreat, depart, make yourself scarce, absent yourself **5** PULL OUT, leave, drop out, secede, disengage, detach yourself, absent yourself **6** RETRACT, recall, take back, revoke, rescind, disavow, recant, disclaim, abjure, unsay

withdrawal *noun* 1 REMOVAL, ending,
stopping, taking away, abolition,
elimination, cancellation, termination,
extraction, discontinuation 2 EXIT,
retirement, departure, pull-out, retreat,
exodus, evacuation, disengagement
3 DEPARTURE, retirement, exit, secession
4 RETRACTION, recall, disclaimer,
repudiation, revocation, disavowal,
recantation, rescission, abjuration

withdrawn *adjective* UNCOMMUNICATIVE,
reserved, retiring, quiet, silent, distant,
shy, shrinking, detached, aloof, taciturn,
introverted, timorous, unforthcoming
<< ANTONYM outgoing

wither *verb* 1 WILT, dry, decline, shrink, decay,
disintegrate, perish, languish, droop, shrivel,
desiccate << ANTONYM flourish 2 WASTE,
decline, shrink, shrivel, atrophy 3 FADE,
decline, wane, perish << ANTONYM increase
4 HUMILIATE, blast, shame, put down, snub,
mortify, abash

withering *adjective* SCORNFUL, blasting,
devastating, humiliating, snubbing,
blighting, hurtful, mortifying

withhold *verb* 1 KEEP SECRET, keep, refuse,
hide, reserve, retain, sit on (*informal*),
conceal, suppress, hold back, keep back
<< ANTONYM reveal 2 HOLD BACK, check,
resist, suppress, restrain, repress, keep back
<< ANTONYM release

withstand *verb* RESIST, take, face, suffer, bear,
weather, oppose, take on, cope with, brave,
confront, combat, endure, defy, tolerate, put
up with (*informal*), thwart, stand up to, hold
off, grapple with, hold out against, stand
firm against << ANTONYM give in to

witless *adjective* FOOLISH, crazy, stupid,
silly, dull, daft (*informal*), senseless, goofy
(*informal*), idiotic, dozy (*Brit informal*), inane,
loopy (*informal*), crackpot (*informal*), moronic,
obtuse, unintelligent, empty-headed,
asinine, imbecilic, braindead (*informal*),
dumb-ass (*slang*), halfwitted, rattlebrained
(*slang*)

witness *noun* 1 OBSERVER, viewer, spectator,
looker-on, watcher, onlooker, eyewitness,
bystander, beholder 2 TESTIFIER, deponent,
attestant ▷ *verb* 1 SEE, mark, view, watch,
note, notice, attend, observe, perceive, look
on, be present at, behold (*archaic* or *literary*)
2 COUNTERSIGN, sign, endorse, validate
▷▷ **bear witness** 1 CONFIRM, show, prove,
demonstrate, bear out, testify to, be evidence

of, corroborate, attest to, be proof of, vouch
for, evince, betoken, be a monument to,
constitute proof of 2 GIVE EVIDENCE, testify,
depose, give testimony, depone

witter *verb* CHATTER, chat, rabbit (on) (*Brit
informal*), babble, waffle (*informal, chiefly Brit*),
cackle, twaddle, clack, burble, gab (*informal*),
prattle, tattle, jabber, blab, gabble, blather,
blether, prate, earbash (*Austral & NZ slang*)

witty *adjective* HUMOROUS, gay, original,
brilliant, funny, clever, amusing, lively,
sparkling, ingenious, fanciful, whimsical,
droll, piquant, facetious, jocular,
epigrammatic, waggish << ANTONYM dull

wizard *noun* 1 MAGICIAN, witch, shaman,
sorcerer, occultist, magus, conjuror, warlock,
mage (*archaic*), enchanter, necromancer,
thaumaturge (*rare*), tohunga (*NZ*) 2 GENIUS,
star, expert, master, ace (*informal*), guru, buff
(*informal*), adept, whizz (*informal*), prodigy,
maestro, virtuoso, hotshot (*informal*), rocket
scientist (*informal, chiefly US*), wiz (*informal*),
whizz kid (*informal*), wonk (*informal*), maven
(*US*), fundi (*S African*), up-and-comer
(*informal*)

wizardry *noun* 1 EXPERTISE, skill, know-
how (*informal*), craft, mastery, cleverness,
expertness 2 MAGIC, witching, witchcraft,
voodoo, enchantment, occultism, sorcery,
the black art, witchery, necromancy,
conjuration, sortilege

wizened *adjective* WRINKLED, lined, worn,
withered, dried up, shrivelled, gnarled,
shrunken, sere (*archaic*) << ANTONYM
rounded

wobble *verb* 1 SHAKE, rock, sway, tremble,
quake, waver, teeter, totter, seesaw
2 TREMBLE, shake, vibrate 3 HESITATE, waver,
fluctuate, dither (*chiefly Brit*), be undecided,
vacillate, shillyshally (*informal*), be unable
to make up your mind, swither (*Scot*) ▷ *noun*
1 UNSTEADINESS, shake, tremble, quaking
2 SHAKE, unsteadiness, tremor, vibration

wobbly *adjective* 1 UNSTABLE, shaky, unsafe,
uneven, teetering, unbalanced, tottering,
rickety, unsteady, wonky (*Brit slang*)
2 UNSTEADY, weak, unstable, shaky, quivery,
all of a quiver (*informal*) 3 SHAKY, unsteady,
tremulous

woe *noun* 1 MISERY, suffering, trouble,
pain, disaster, depression, distress, grief,
agony, gloom, sadness, hardship, sorrow,
anguish, misfortune, unhappiness,
heartache, heartbreak, adversity, dejection,
wretchedness << ANTONYM happiness

2 PROBLEM, trouble, trial, burden, grief, misery, curse, hardship, sorrow, misfortune, heartache, heartbreak, affliction, tribulation

woeful *adjective* **1** WRETCHED, sad, unhappy, tragic, miserable, gloomy, grieving, dismal, pathetic, afflicted, pitiful, anguished, agonized, disconsolate, doleful, pitiable << ANTONYM happy **2** SAD, distressing, tragic, miserable, gloomy, dismal, pathetic, harrowing, heartbreaking, grievous, mournful, plaintive, heart-rending, sorrowful, doleful, piteous << ANTONYM happy **3** PITIFUL, mean, bad, poor, shocking, sorry, disappointing, terrible, awful, appalling, disastrous, inadequate, dreadful, miserable, hopeless, rotten (*informal*), pathetic, catastrophic, duff (*Brit informal*), feeble, disgraceful, lousy (*slang*), grievous, paltry, deplorable, abysmal, lamentable, calamitous, wretched, pitiable, godawful (*slang*), not much cop (*Brit slang*)

wolf *verb often with* **down** DEVOUR, stuff, bolt, cram, scoff (*slang*), gulp, gobble, pack away (*informal*), gorge on, gollop << ANTONYM nibble ▷ *noun* (*informal*) WOMANIZER, seducer, Don Juan, Casanova, philanderer, Lothario, lecher, lady-killer, lech *or* letch (*informal*)

woman *noun* **1** LADY, girl, miss, female, bird (*slang*), dame (*slang*), ho (*US derogatory slang*), sheila (*Austral & NZ informal*), vrou (*S African*), maiden (*archaic*), chick (*slang*), maid (*archaic*), gal (*slang*), lass, lassie (*informal*), wench (*facetious*), adult female, she, charlie (*Austral slang*), chook (*Austral slang*), wahine (*NZ*) << ANTONYM man **2** (*informal*) GIRLFRIEND, girl, wife, partner, mate, lover, bride, mistress, spouse, old lady (*informal*), sweetheart, significant other (*US informal*), ladylove, wifey (*informal*) **3** MAID, domestic, char (*informal*), housekeeper, lady-in-waiting, chambermaid, handmaiden, charwoman, maidservant, female servant

womanly *adjective* **1** FEMININE, motherly, female, warm, tender, matronly, ladylike **2** CURVACEOUS, ample, voluptuous, shapely, curvy (*informal*), busty (*informal*), buxom, full-figured, Rubenesque, Junoesque

wonder *verb* **1** THINK, question, doubt, puzzle, speculate, query, ponder, inquire, ask yourself, meditate, be curious, conjecture, be inquisitive **2** BE AMAZED, stare, marvel, be astonished, gape, boggle, be awed, be flabbergasted (*informal*), gawk, be dumbstruck, stand amazed ▷

noun **1** AMAZEMENT, surprise, curiosity, admiration, awe, fascination, astonishment, bewilderment, wonderment, stupefaction **2** PHENOMENON, sight, miracle, spectacle, curiosity, marvel, prodigy, rarity, portent, wonderment, nonpareil

wonderful *adjective* **1** EXCELLENT, mean (*slang*), great (*informal*), topping (*Brit slang*), brilliant, cracking (*Brit informal*), outstanding, smashing (*informal*), superb, fantastic (*informal*), tremendous, ace (*informal*), magnificent, fabulous (*informal*), marvellous, terrific, sensational (*informal*), sovereign, awesome (*slang*), admirable, super (*informal*), brill (*informal*), stupendous, out of this world (*informal*), tiptop, bodacious (*slang, chiefly US*), boffo (*slang*), jim-dandy (*slang*), chillin' (*US slang*), booshit (*Austral slang*), exo (*Austral slang*), sik (*Austral slang*), rad (*Austral slang*), phat (*slang*), schmick (*Austral informal*) << ANTONYM terrible **2** REMARKABLE, surprising, odd, strange, amazing, extraordinary, fantastic, incredible, astonishing, staggering, marvellous, startling, peculiar, awesome, phenomenal, astounding, miraculous, unheard-of, wondrous (*archaic or literary*), awe-inspiring, jaw-dropping << ANTONYM ordinary

wonky *adjective* **1** ASKEW, squint (*informal*), awry, out of alignment, skewwhiff (*Brit informal*) **2** SHAKY, weak, wobbly, unsteady, infirm

wont *adjective* ACCUSTOMED, used, given, in the habit of ▷ *noun* HABIT, use, way, rule, practice, custom

woo *verb* **1** SEEK, cultivate, try to attract, curry favour with, seek to win, solicit the goodwill of **2** COURT, chase, pursue, spark (*rare*), importune, seek to win, pay court to, seek the hand of, set your cap at (*old-fashioned*), pay your addresses to, pay suit to, press your suit with

wood *noun* **1** TIMBER, planks, planking, lumber (*US*) **2** Also woods WOODLAND, trees, forest, grove, hurst (*archaic*), thicket, copse, coppice, bushland **3** FIREWOOD, fuel, logs, kindling ▷▷ **out of the wood(s)** (usually used in a negative construction) SAFE, clear, secure, in the clear, out of danger, home and dry (*Brit slang*), safe and sound

wooded *adjective* TREE-COVERED, forested, timbered, woody, sylvan (*poetic*), tree-clad

wooden *adjective* **1** MADE OF WOOD, timber, woody, of wood, ligneous **2** AWKWARD, stiff, rigid, clumsy, lifeless, stilted, ungainly, gauche, gawky, inelegant, graceless, maladroit << ANTONYM graceful **3** EXPRESSIONLESS, empty, dull, blank, vacant, lifeless, deadpan, colourless, glassy, unresponsive, unemotional, emotionless, spiritless

wool *noun* **1** FLEECE, hair, coat **2** YARN ▷▷ **pull the wool over someone's eyes** DECEIVE, kid (*informal*), trick, fool, take in (*informal*), con (*slang*), dupe, delude, bamboozle (*informal*), hoodwink, put one over on (*slang*), pull a fast one on someone (*informal*), lead someone up the garden path (*informal*)

woolly *or* (*sometimes*) *US* **wooly** *adjective* **1** WOOLLEN, fleecy, made of wool **2** VAGUE, confused, clouded, blurred, unclear, muddled, fuzzy, indefinite, hazy, foggy, nebulous, ill-defined, indistinct << ANTONYM precise **3** DOWNY, hairy, shaggy, flocculent ▷ *noun* SWEATER, jersey, jumper, pullover

word *noun* **1** TERM, name, expression, designation, appellation (*formal*), locution, vocable **2** CHAT, tête-à-tête, talk, discussion, consultation, chitchat, brief conversation, colloquy, confabulation, confab (*informal*), heart-to-heart, powwow (*informal*) **3** COMMENT, remark, expression, declaration, utterance, brief statement **4** MESSAGE, news, latest (*informal*), report, information, account, notice, advice, communication, intelligence, bulletin, dispatch, gen (*Brit informal*), communiqué, intimation, tidings **5** PROMISE, guarantee, pledge, undertaking, vow, assurance, oath, parole, word of honour, solemn oath, solemn word **6** COMMAND, will, order, go-ahead (*informal*), decree, bidding, mandate, commandment, edict, ukase (*rare*) ▷ *verb* EXPRESS, say, state, put, phrase, utter, couch, formulate ▷▷ **in a word** BRIEFLY, in short, in a nutshell, to sum up, succinctly, concisely, not to put too fine a point on it, to put it briefly ▷▷ **the last word 1** FINAL SAY, ultimatum **2** SUMMATION, finis ▷▷ **the last word in something** EPITOME, newest, best, latest, crown, cream, rage, ultimate, vogue, perfection, mother of all (*informal*), quintessence, crème de la crème (*French*), ne plus ultra (*French*), dernier cri (*French*)

wording *noun* PHRASEOLOGY, words, language, phrasing, terminology, choice of words, mode of expression

wordy *adjective* LONG-WINDED, rambling, windy, diffuse, garrulous, discursive,

loquacious, verbose, prolix, pleonastic (*rare*) << ANTONYM brief

work *verb* **1** BE EMPLOYED, do business, have a job, earn a living, be in work, hold down a job **2** LABOUR, sweat, slave, toil, slog (away), drudge, peg away, exert yourself, break your back << ANTONYM relax **3** FUNCTION, go, run, operate, perform, be in working order << ANTONYM be out of order **4** SUCCEED, work out, pay off (*informal*), be successful, be effective, do the trick (*informal*), do the business (*informal*), get results, turn out well, have the desired result, go as planned **5** ACCOMPLISH, cause, create, effect, achieve, carry out, implement, execute, bring about, encompass, contrive **6** HANDLE, move, excite, manipulate, rouse, stir up, agitate, incite, whip up, galvanize **7** CULTIVATE, farm, dig, till, plough **8** OPERATE, use, move, control, drive, manage, direct, handle, manipulate, wield, ply **9** MANIPULATE, make, form, process, fashion, shape, handle, mould, knead **10** PROGRESS, move, force, manoeuvre, make your way **11** MOVE, twitch, writhe, convulse, be agitated **12** (*informal*) CONTRIVE, handle, fix (*informal*), swing (*informal*), arrange, exploit, manipulate, pull off, fiddle (*informal*), bring off ▷ *noun* **1** EMPLOYMENT, calling, business, job, line, office, trade, duty, craft, profession, occupation, pursuit, livelihood, métier << ANTONYM play **2** EFFORT, industry, labour, grind (*informal*), sweat, toil, slog, exertion, drudgery, travail (*literary*), elbow grease (*facetious*) << ANTONYM leisure **3** TASK, jobs, projects, commissions, duties, assignments, chores, yakka (*Austral & NZ informal*) **4** HANDIWORK, doing, act, feat, deed **5** CREATION, performance, piece, production, opus, achievement, composition, oeuvre (*French*), handiwork ▷▷ **work out 1** HAPPEN, go, result, develop, come out, turn out, evolve, pan out (*informal*) **2** SUCCEED, flourish, go well, be effective, prosper, go as planned, prove satisfactory, do the business (*informal*) **3** EXERCISE, train, practise, drill, warm up, do exercises ▷▷ **work out at something** AMOUNT TO, come to, reach, add up to, reach a total of ▷▷ **work someone up** *verb* EXCITE, move, spur, wind up (*informal*), arouse, animate, rouse, stir up, agitate, inflame, incite, instigate, get someone all steamed up (*slang*) ▷▷ **work something out 1** SOLVE, find out, resolve, calculate, figure out, clear up, suss (out) (*slang*), puzzle out **2** PLAN, form,

develop, arrange, construct, evolve, devise,
elaborate, put together, formulate, contrive
▷▷ **work something up** GENERATE, rouse,
instigate, foment, enkindle

workable *adjective* VIABLE, possible, practical,
feasible, practicable, doable << ANTONYM
unworkable

workaday *adjective* ORDINARY, common,
familiar, practical, routine, everyday,
commonplace, mundane, prosaic, run-of-
the-mill, humdrum, bog-standard (*Brit &
Irish slang*) << ANTONYM extraordinary

worker *noun* EMPLOYEE, hand, labourer,
workman, craftsman, artisan, tradesman,
wage earner, proletarian, working man *or*
working woman

working *adjective* 1 EMPLOYED, labouring,
in work, in a job 2 FUNCTIONING, going,
running, operating, active, operative,
operational, functional, usable, serviceable,
in working order 3 EFFECTIVE, useful,
practical, sufficient, adequate ▷ *noun*
OPERATION, running, action, method,
functioning, manner, mode of operation
▷ *plural noun* MINE, pit, shaft, quarry,
excavations, diggings

workman *noun* LABOURER, hand, worker,
employee, mechanic, operative, craftsman,
artisan, tradesman, journeyman, artificer
(*rare*)

workmanlike *adjective* EFFICIENT,
professional, skilled, expert, masterly,
careful, satisfactory, thorough, skilful,
adept, painstaking, proficient << ANTONYM
amateurish

workmanship *noun* SKILL, work, art,
technique, manufacture, craft, expertise,
execution, artistry, craftsmanship,
handiwork, handicraft

workout *noun* EXERCISE, training, drill,
warm-up, training session, practice session,
exercise session

works *plural noun* 1 FACTORY, shop, plant,
mill, workshop 2 WRITINGS, productions,
output, canon, oeuvre (*French*) 3 DEEDS, acts,
actions, doings 4 MECHANISM, workings,
parts, action, insides (*informal*), movement,
guts (*informal*), machinery, moving parts,
innards (*informal*)

workshop *noun* 1 SEMINAR, class, discussion
group, study group, masterclass 2 FACTORY,
works, shop, plant, mill 3 WORKROOM,
studio, atelier

world *noun* 1 EARTH, planet, globe, earthly
sphere 2 MANKIND, man, men, everyone,

the public, everybody, humanity, human
race, humankind, the race of man 3 SPHERE,
system, area, field, environment, province,
kingdom, realm, domain 4 LIFE, nature,
existence, creation, universe, cosmos
5 PLANET, star, orb, heavenly body 6 PERIOD,
times, days, age, era, epoch 7 (usually used in
phrase *a world of difference*) HUGE AMOUNT,
mountain, wealth, great deal, good deal,
abundance, enormous amount, vast amount
▷▷ **for all the world** EXACTLY, just like,
precisely, in every way, to all intents and
purposes, just as if, in every respect ▷▷ **on
top of the world** (*informal*) OVERJOYED, happy,
ecstatic, elated, over the moon (*informal*),
exultant, on cloud nine (*informal*), cock-a-
hoop, in raptures, beside yourself with joy,
stoked (*Austral & NZ informal*) ▷▷ **out of this
world** (*informal*) WONDERFUL, great (*informal*),
excellent, superb, fantastic (*informal*),
incredible, fabulous (*informal*), marvellous,
unbelievable, awesome (*slang*), indescribable,
bodacious (*slang, chiefly US*), booshit (*Austral
slang*), exo (*Austral slang*), sik (*Austral slang*),
rad (*informal*), phat (*slang*), schmick (*Austral
informal*)

worldly *adjective* 1 EARTHLY, lay, physical,
fleshly, secular, mundane, terrestrial,
temporal, carnal, profane, sublunary
<< ANTONYM spiritual 2 MATERIALISTIC,
grasping, selfish, greedy, avaricious,
covetous, worldly-minded << ANTONYM
nonmaterialistic 3 WORLDLY-WISE, knowing,
experienced, politic, sophisticated,
cosmopolitan, urbane, blasé, well versed in
the ways of the world << ANTONYM naive

worldwide *adjective* GLOBAL, general,
international, universal, ubiquitous,
omnipresent, pandemic << ANTONYM
limited

worn *adjective* 1 RAGGED, shiny, frayed, shabby,
tattered, tatty, threadbare, the worse for
wear 2 HAGGARD, lined, drawn, pinched,
wizened, careworn 3 EXHAUSTED, spent,
tired, fatigued, wearied, weary, played-out
(*informal*), worn-out, jaded, tired out

worn out *adjective* 1 WORN, done, used,
broken-down, ragged, useless, run-
down, frayed, used-up, shabby, tattered,
tatty, threadbare, decrepit, clapped out
(*Brit, Austral & NZ informal*), moth-eaten
2 EXHAUSTED, spent, done in (*informal*),
tired, all in (*slang*), fatigued, wiped out
(*informal*), weary, played-out, knackered
(*slang*), prostrate, clapped out (*Austral &*

NZ informal), tired out, dog-tired (*informal*), zonked (*slang*), shagged out (*Brit slang*), fit to drop, jiggered (*dialect*), dead *or* out on your feet (*informal*) << ANTONYM refreshed

worried *adjective* 1 ANXIOUS, concerned, troubled, upset, afraid, bothered, frightened, wired (*slang*), nervous, disturbed, distressed, tense, distracted, uneasy, fearful, tormented, distraught, apprehensive, perturbed, on edge, ill at ease, overwrought, fretful, hot and bothered, unquiet, antsy (*informal*) << ANTONYM unworried

worrisome *adjective* DISTURBING, worrying, upsetting, distressing, troublesome, disquieting, vexing, perturbing, irksome, bothersome

worry *verb* 1 BE ANXIOUS, be concerned, be worried, obsess, brood, fret, agonize, feel uneasy, get in a lather (*informal*), get in a sweat (*informal*), get in a tizzy (*informal*), get overwrought << ANTONYM be unconcerned 2 TROUBLE, upset, harry, bother, disturb, distress, annoy, plague, irritate, tease, unsettle, torment, harass, hassle (*informal*), badger, hector, disquiet, pester, vex, perturb, tantalize, importune, make anxious << ANTONYM soothe ▷ *noun* 1 ANXIETY, concern, care, fear, trouble, misery, disturbance, torment, woe, irritation, unease, apprehension, misgiving, annoyance, trepidation, perplexity, vexation << ANTONYM peace of mind 2 PROBLEM, care, trouble, trial, bother, plague, pest, torment, irritation, hassle (*informal*), annoyance, vexation

worsen *verb* 1 DETERIORATE, decline, sink, decay, get worse, degenerate, go downhill (*informal*), go from bad to worse, take a turn for the worse, retrogress << ANTONYM improve 2 AGGRAVATE, damage, exacerbate, make worse << ANTONYM improve

worship *verb* 1 REVERE, praise, respect, honour, adore, glorify, reverence, exalt, laud, pray to, venerate, deify, adulate << ANTONYM dishonour 2 LOVE, adore, idolize, put on a pedestal << ANTONYM despise ▷ *noun* REVERENCE, praise, love, regard, respect, honour, glory, prayer(s), devotion, homage, adulation, adoration, admiration, exaltation, glorification, deification, laudation

worth *noun* 1 VALUE, price, rate, cost, estimate, valuation << ANTONYM worthlessness 2 MERIT, value, quality, importance, desert(s), virtue, excellence, goodness, estimation, worthiness << ANTONYM unworthiness

3 USEFULNESS, value, benefit, quality, importance, utility, excellence, goodness << ANTONYM uselessness

worthless *adjective* 1 VALUELESS, poor, miserable, trivial, trifling, paltry, trashy, measly, wretched, two a penny (*informal*), rubbishy, poxy (*slang*), nickel-and-dime (*US slang*), wanky (*taboo slang*), a dime a dozen, nugatory, negligible << ANTONYM valuable 2 USELESS, meaningless, pointless, futile, no use, insignificant, unimportant, ineffectual, unusable, unavailing, not much cop (*Brit slang*), inutile, not worth a hill of beans (*chiefly US*), negligible, pants (*slang*) << ANTONYM useful 3 GOOD-FOR-NOTHING, base, abandoned, useless, vile, abject, despicable, depraved, contemptible, ignoble << ANTONYM honourable

worthwhile *adjective* USEFUL, good, valuable, helpful, worthy, profitable, productive, beneficial, meaningful, constructive, justifiable, expedient, gainful << ANTONYM useless

worthy *adjective* PRAISEWORTHY, good, excellent, deserving, valuable, decent, reliable, worthwhile, respectable, upright, admirable, honourable, honest, righteous, reputable, virtuous, dependable, commendable, creditable, laudable, meritorious, estimable << ANTONYM disreputable ▷ *noun* DIGNITARY, notable, luminary, bigwig (*informal*), big shot (*informal*), personage, big hitter (*informal*), heavy hitter (*informal*) << ANTONYM nobody

would-be *adjective* BUDDING, potential, so-called, professed, dormant, self-styled, latent, wannabe (*informal*), unfulfilled, undeveloped, self-appointed, unrealized, manqué, soi-disant (*French*), quasi-

wound *noun* 1 INJURY, cut, damage, hurt, harm, slash, trauma (*pathology*), gash, lesion, laceration 2 *often plural* TRAUMA, injury, shock, pain, offence, slight, torture, distress, insult, grief, torment, anguish, heartbreak, pang, sense of loss ▷ *verb* 1 INJURE, cut, hit, damage, wing, hurt, harm, slash, pierce, irritate, gash, lacerate 2 OFFEND, shock, pain, hurt, distress, annoy, sting, grieve, mortify, cut to the quick, hurt the feelings of, traumatize

wounding *adjective* HURTFUL, pointed, cutting, damaging, acid, bitter, slighting, offensive, distressing, insulting, cruel, savage, stinging, destructive, harmful, malicious, scathing, grievous, barbed,

unkind, pernicious, caustic, spiteful, vitriolic, trenchant, injurious, maleficent
wrangle *verb* ARGUE, fight, row, dispute, scrap, disagree, fall out (*informal*), contend, quarrel, brawl, squabble, spar, bicker, have words, altercate ▷ *noun* ARGUMENT, row, clash, dispute, contest, set-to (*informal*), controversy, falling-out (*informal*), quarrel, brawl, barney (*informal*), squabble, bickering, tiff, altercation, slanging match (*Brit*), angry exchange, argy-bargy (*Brit informal*), bagarre (*French*)
wrap *verb* 1 COVER, surround, fold, enclose, roll up, cloak, shroud, swathe, muffle, envelop, encase, sheathe, enfold, bundle up << ANTONYM uncover 2 PACK, package, parcel (up), tie up, gift-wrap << ANTONYM unpack 3 BIND, wind, fold, swathe << ANTONYM unwind ▷ *noun* CLOAK, cape, stole, mantle, shawl ▷▷ **wrap something up** 1 GIFTWRAP, pack, package, enclose, bundle up, enwrap 2 (*informal*) END, conclude, wind up, terminate, finish off, round off, tidy up, polish off, bring to a close ▷▷ **wrap up** DRESS WARMLY, muffle up, wear something warm, put warm clothes on
wrapper *noun* COVER, case, paper, packaging, wrapping, jacket, envelope, sleeve, sheath
wrath *noun* ANGER, passion, rage, temper, fury, resentment, irritation, indignation, ire, displeasure, exasperation, choler << ANTONYM satisfaction
wreak *verb* 1 CREATE, work, cause, visit, effect, exercise, carry out, execute, inflict, bring about 2 UNLEASH, express, indulge, vent, gratify, give vent to, give free rein to
wreath *noun* GARLAND, band, ring, crown, loop, festoon, coronet, chaplet
wreathe *verb* 1 SURROUND, envelop, encircle, enfold, coil around, writhe around, enwrap 2 FESTOON, wind, crown, wrap, twist, coil, adorn, intertwine, interweave, entwine, twine, engarland
wreck *verb* 1 DESTROY, break, total (*slang*), smash, ruin, devastate, mar, shatter, spoil, demolish, sabotage, trash (*slang*), ravage, dash to pieces, kennet (*Austral slang*), jeff (*Austral slang*) << ANTONYM build 2 SPOIL, blow (*slang*), ruin, devastate, shatter, undo, screw up (*informal*), cock up (*Brit slang*), play havoc with, crool *or* cruel (*Austral slang*) << ANTONYM save 3 RUN AGROUND, strand, shipwreck, run onto the rocks ▷ *noun* 1 SHIPWRECK, derelict, hulk, sunken vessel 2 RUIN, mess, destruction, overthrow,

undoing, disruption, devastation, desolation << ANTONYM preservation 3 Also wreckage REMAINS, pieces, ruin, fragments, debris, rubble, hulk, wrack 4 ACCIDENT, smash, pile-up
wrench *verb* 1 TWIST, force, pull, tear, rip, tug, jerk, yank, wring, wrest 2 SPRAIN, strain, rick, distort ▷ *noun* 1 TWIST, pull, rip, tug, jerk, yank 2 SPRAIN, strain, twist 3 BLOW, shock, pain, ache, upheaval, uprooting, pang 4 SPANNER, adjustable spanner, shifting spanner
wrest *verb* 1 SEIZE, take, win, extract 2 PULL, force, strain, seize, twist, extract, wrench, wring
wrestle *verb* FIGHT, battle, struggle, combat, contend, strive, grapple, tussle, scuffle
wretch *noun* 1 POOR THING, unfortunate, poor soul, poor devil (*informal*), miserable creature 2 SCOUNDREL, rat (*informal*), worm, villain, rogue, outcast, swine, rascal, son-of-a-bitch (*slang, chiefly US & Canad*), profligate, vagabond, ruffian, cur, rotter (*slang, chiefly Brit*), scumbag (*slang*), good-for-nothing, miscreant, bad egg (*old-fashioned informal*), blackguard, wrong 'un (*Austral slang*)
wretched *adjective* 1 UNFORTUNATE, poor, sorry, hapless, pitiful, luckless, star-crossed, pitiable << ANTONYM happy 2 WORTHLESS, poor, sorry, miserable, pathetic, inferior, paltry, deplorable << ANTONYM excellent 3 SHAMEFUL, mean, low, base, shabby, vile, low-down (*informal*), paltry, despicable, contemptible, scurvy, crappy (*slang*), poxy (*slang*) << ANTONYM admirable 4 ILL, poorly, sick, crook (*Austral & NZ informal*), sickly, unwell, off colour (*Brit informal*), under the weather (*informal*)
wriggle *verb* 1 JIGGLE, turn, twist, jerk, squirm, writhe 2 WIGGLE, jerk, wag, jiggle, waggle 3 CRAWL, snake, worm, twist and turn, zigzag, slink ▷ *noun* TWIST, turn, jerk, wag, squirm, wiggle, jiggle, waggle ▷▷ **wriggle out of something** AVOID, duck, dodge, extricate yourself from, talk your way out of, worm your way out of
wring *verb* TWIST, force, squeeze, extract, screw, wrench, coerce, wrest, extort
wrinkle *noun* 1 LINE, fold, crease, furrow, pucker, crow's-foot, corrugation 2 CREASE, gather, fold, crumple, furrow, rumple, pucker, crinkle, corrugation ▷ *verb* CREASE, line, gather, fold, crumple, ruck, furrow, rumple, pucker, crinkle, corrugate << ANTONYM smooth

writ *noun* SUMMONS, document, decree, indictment, court order, subpoena, arraignment

write *verb* **1** RECORD, copy, scribble, take down, inscribe, set down, transcribe, jot down, put in writing, commit to paper, indite, put down in black and white **2** COMPOSE, create, author, draft, pen, draw up **3** CORRESPOND, get in touch, keep in touch, write a letter, drop a line, drop a note ▷▷ **write something off 1** (*informal*) WRECK, total (*slang*), crash, destroy, trash (*slang*), smash up, damage beyond repair **2** (*accounting*) CANCEL, shelve, forget about, cross out, score out, give up for lost ▷▷ **write something or someone off** DISREGARD, ignore, dismiss, regard something *or* someone as finished, consider something *or* someone as unimportant

writer *noun* AUTHOR, novelist, hack, columnist, scribbler, scribe, essayist, penman, wordsmith, man of letters, penpusher, littérateur, penny-a-liner (*rare*)

writhe *verb* SQUIRM, struggle, twist, toss, distort, thrash, jerk, wriggle, wiggle, contort, convulse, thresh

writing *noun* **1** SCRIPT, hand, print, printing, fist (*informal*), scribble, handwriting, scrawl, calligraphy, longhand, penmanship, chirography **2** DOCUMENT, work, book, letter, title, opus, publication, literature, composition, belle-lettre

wrong *adjective* **1** AMISS, faulty, unsatisfactory, not right, defective, awry **2** INCORRECT, mistaken, false, faulty, inaccurate, untrue, erroneous, off target, unsound, in error, wide of the mark, fallacious, off base (*US & Canad informal*), off beam (*informal*), way off beam (*informal*) **3** INAPPROPRIATE, incorrect, unfitting, unsuitable, unhappy, not done, unacceptable, undesirable, improper, unconventional, incongruous, unseemly, unbecoming, indecorous, inapt, infelicitous, malapropos << ANTONYM correct **4** BAD, criminal, illegal, evil, unfair, crooked, unlawful, illicit, immoral, unjust, dishonest, wicked, sinful, unethical, wrongful, under-the-table, reprehensible, dishonourable, iniquitous, not cricket (*informal*), felonious, blameworthy << ANTONYM moral **5** DEFECTIVE, not working, faulty, out of order, awry, askew, out of commission **6** OPPOSITE, inside, reverse, inverse ▷ *adverb* **1** INCORRECTLY, badly, wrongly, mistakenly, erroneously, inaccurately << ANTONYM correctly **2** AMISS, astray, awry, askew ▷ *noun* **1** WICKEDNESS, injustice, unfairness, inequity, immorality, iniquity, sinfulness << ANTONYM morality **2** OFFENCE, injury, crime, abuse, error, sin, injustice, grievance, infringement, trespass, misdeed, transgression, infraction, bad *or* evil deed << ANTONYM good deed ▷ *verb* MISTREAT, abuse, hurt, injure, harm, cheat, take advantage of, discredit, oppress, malign, misrepresent, dump on (*slang, chiefly US*), impose upon, dishonour, ill-treat, maltreat, ill-use << ANTONYM treat well ▷▷ **go wrong 1** FAIL, flop (*informal*), fall through, come to nothing, miscarry, misfire, come to grief (*informal*), go pear-shaped (*informal*) **2** MAKE A MISTAKE, boob (*Brit slang*), err, slip up (*informal*), go astray **3** BREAK DOWN, fail, malfunction, misfire, cease to function, conk out (*informal*), go on the blink (*slang*), go kaput (*informal*), go phut (*informal*) **4** LAPSE, sin, err, fall from grace, go astray, go to the bad, go off the straight and narrow (*informal*)

wrongful *adjective* IMPROPER, illegal, unfair, inappropriate, unlawful, illicit, immoral, unjust, illegitimate, unethical, groundless << ANTONYM rightful

wry *adjective* **1** IRONIC, dry, mocking, sarcastic, sardonic, droll, pawky (*Scot*), mordacious **2** CONTORTED, twisted, crooked, distorted, warped, uneven, deformed, awry, askew, aslant, skewwhiff (*Brit informal*) << ANTONYM straight

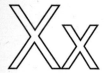

Xmas *noun* CHRISTMAS, Noel, festive season, Yule (*archaic*), Yuletide (*archaic*), Christmastime, Christmastide, Crimbo (*Brit informal*)

X-ray *noun* RADIOGRAPH, x-ray image, roentgen ray

yahoo *noun* PHILISTINE, savage, lout, beast, barbarian, brute, rowdy, hoon (*Austral & NZ*), roughneck (*slang*), boor, churl, yob *or* yobbo (*Brit slang*), cougan (*Austral slang*), scozza (*Austral slang*), bogan (*Austral slang*)

yak *verb* GOSSIP, go on, gab (*informal*), rabbit (on) (*Brit informal*), run on, jaw (*slang*), chatter, spout, waffle (*informal, chiefly Brit*), yap (*informal*), tattle, jabber, blather, chew the fat (*slang*), witter on (*informal*), run off at the mouth

yank *verb* PULL, tug, jerk, seize, snatch, pluck, hitch, wrench ▷ *noun* PULL, tug, jerk, snatch, hitch, wrench, tweak

yap *verb* **1** YELP, bark, woof, yip (*chiefly US*) **2** (*informal*) TALK, go on, rabbit (on) (*Brit informal*), gossip, jaw (*slang*), chatter, spout, babble, waffle (*informal, chiefly Brit*), prattle, jabber, blather, run off at the mouth (*slang*), earbash (*Austral & NZ slang*)

yardstick *noun* STANDARD, measure, criterion, gauge, benchmark, touchstone, par

yarn *noun* **1** THREAD, fibre, cotton, wool **2** (*informal*) STORY, tale, anecdote, account, narrative, fable, reminiscence, urban myth, tall story, urban legend, cock-and-bull story (*informal*)

yawning *adjective* GAPING, wide, huge, vast, wide-open, cavernous

yearly *adjective* ANNUAL, each year, every year, once a year ▷ *adverb* ANNUALLY, every year, by the year, once a year, per annum

yearn *verb often with* **for** LONG, desire, pine, pant, hunger, ache, lust, crave, covet, itch, languish, hanker after, have a yen for (*informal*), eat your heart out over, set your heart upon, suspire (*archaic or poetic*), would give your eyeteeth for

yell *verb* SCREAM, shout, cry out, howl, call out, wail, shriek, screech, squeal, bawl, holler (*informal*), yelp, call at the top of your voice << ANTONYM whisper ▷ *noun* SCREAM, cry, shout, roar, howl, shriek, whoop, screech, squeal, holler (*informal*), yelp, yowl << ANTONYM whisper

yellow *noun* LEMON, gold, amber

yelp *verb* BARK, howl, yap, yip (*chiefly US*), yowl ▷ *noun* CRY, squeal

yen *noun* LONGING, desire, craving, yearning, passion, hunger, ache, itch, thirst, hankering

yet *adverb* **1** SO FAR, until now, up to now, still, as yet, even now, thus far, up till now, up to the present time **2** NOW, right now, just now, so soon, already **3** STILL, further, in addition, as well, moreover, besides, to boot, additionally, over and above, into the bargain ▷ *conjunction* NEVERTHELESS, still, however, for all that, notwithstanding, just the same, be that as it may

yield *verb* **1** BOW, submit, give in, surrender, give way, succumb, cave in (*informal*), capitulate, knuckle under, resign yourself **2** RELINQUISH, resign, hand over, surrender, turn over, part with, make over, cede, give over, bequeath, abdicate, deliver up << ANTONYM retain **3** SURRENDER, give up, give in, concede defeat, cave in (*informal*), throw in the towel, admit defeat, accept defeat, give up the struggle, knuckle under, raise the white flag, lay down your arms, cry quits **4** PRODUCE, give, provide, pay, return, supply, bear, net, earn, afford, generate, bring in, furnish, bring forth << ANTONYM use up ▷ *noun* **1** PRODUCE, crop, harvest, output **2** PROFIT, return, income, revenue, earnings, takings << ANTONYM loss ▷▷ **yield to something** COMPLY WITH, agree to, concede, allow, grant, permit, go along with, bow to, consent to, accede to << ANTONYM resist

yielding *adjective* **1** SOFT, pliable, springy, elastic, resilient, supple, spongy, unresisting, quaggy **2** SUBMISSIVE, obedient, compliant, docile, easy, flexible, accommodating, pliant, tractable, acquiescent, biddable << ANTONYM obstinate

yob *or* **yobbo** *noun* THUG, hooligan, lout, heavy (*slang*), tough, rough (*informal*), rowdy, yahoo, hoon (*Austral & NZ slang*), hoodlum, ruffian, roughneck (*slang*), tsotsi (*S African*), cougan (*Austral slang*), scozza (*Austral slang*), bogan (*Austral slang*)

yoke *noun* **1** OPPRESSION, slavery, bondage, servitude, service, burden, enslavement, serfdom, servility, vassalage, thraldom **2** HARNESS, coupling, tackle, chain, collar, tack ▷ *verb* **1** UNITE, join, link, tie, bond, bind, connect **2** HARNESS, join, couple, link, tie, connect, bracket, hitch

young *adjective* **1** IMMATURE, juvenile, youthful, little, growing, green, junior, infant, adolescent, callow, unfledged, in the springtime of life << ANTONYM old **2** EARLY, new, undeveloped, fledgling, newish, not far advanced << ANTONYM advanced ▷ *noun*

OFFSPRING, baby, litter, family, issue, brood, little onesy, progeny << ANTONYM parent

youngster *noun* YOUTH, girl, boy, kid (*informal*), child, lad, teenager, juvenile, cub, young person, lass, young adult, pup (*informal, chiefly Brit*), urchin, teenybopper (*slang*), young shaver (*informal*), young 'un (*informal*)

youth *noun* **1** IMMATURITY, adolescence, early life, young days, boyhood *or* girlhood, salad days, juvenescence << ANTONYM old age **2** BOY, lad, youngster, kid (*informal*), teenager, young man, adolescent, teen (*informal*), stripling, young shaver (*informal*) << ANTONYM adult **3** YOUNG PEOPLE, the young, the younger generation, teenagers, the rising generation << ANTONYM old people

youthful *adjective* **1** YOUNG, juvenile, childish, immature, boyish, pubescent, girlish, puerile << ANTONYM elderly **2** VIGOROUS, fresh, active, young looking, young at heart, spry << ANTONYM tired

Zz

zany *adjective* COMICAL, crazy, nutty (*slang*), funny, eccentric, wacky (*slang*), loony (*slang*), oddball (*informal*), madcap, goofy (*informal*), kooky (*US informal*), clownish, wacko *or* whacko (*informal*), off the air (*Austral slang*)

zeal *noun* ENTHUSIASM, passion, zest, fire, spirit, warmth, devotion, verve, fervour, eagerness, gusto, militancy, fanaticism, ardour, earnestness, keenness, fervency << ANTONYM apathy

zealot *noun* FANATIC, enthusiast, extremist, militant, maniac, fiend (*informal*), bigot

zealous *adjective* ENTHUSIASTIC, passionate, earnest, burning, spirited, keen, devoted, eager, militant, ardent, fanatical, fervent, impassioned, rabid, fervid << ANTONYM apathetic

zenith *noun* HEIGHT, summit, peak, top, climax, crest, high point, pinnacle, meridian, apex, high noon, apogee, acme, vertex << ANTONYM lowest point

zero *noun* **1** NOUGHT, nothing, nil, naught, cipher **2** ROCK BOTTOM, the bottom, an all-time low, a nadir, as low as you can get, the lowest point *or* ebb ▷▷ **zero in on something 1** ZOOM IN ON, focus on, aim at, train on, home in on **2** FOCUS ON, concentrate on, home in on, pinpoint on, converge

zest *noun* **1** ENJOYMENT, love, appetite, relish, interest, joy, excitement, zeal, gusto, keenness, zing (*informal*), delectation << ANTONYM aversion **2** FLAVOUR, taste, savour, kick (*informal*), spice, relish, smack, tang, piquancy, pungency **3** RIND, skin, peel, outer layer

zip *verb* SPEED, shoot, fly, tear, rush, flash, dash, hurry, barrel (along) (*informal, chiefly US & Canad*), buzz, streak, hare (*Brit informal*), zoom, whizz (*informal*), hurtle, pelt, burn rubber (*informal*) ▷ *noun* (*informal*) ENERGY, go (*informal*), life, drive, spirit, punch (*informal*), pep, sparkle, vitality, vigour, verve, zest, gusto, get-up-and-go (*informal*), oomph (*informal*), brio, zing (*informal*), liveliness, vim (*slang*), pizzazz *or* pizazz (*informal*) << ANTONYM lethargy

zone *noun* AREA, region, section, sector, district, territory, belt, sphere, tract

zoom *verb* SPEED, shoot, fly, tear, rush, flash, dash, barrel (along) (*informal, chiefly US & Canad*), buzz, streak, hare (*Brit informal*), zip (*informal*), whizz (*informal*), hurtle, pelt, burn rubber (*informal*)

Supplement

Literally Speaking

Contents

The right word

The French novelist Gustave Flaubert was famous for his painstaking zeal in finding *le mot juste* – the right word – sometimes spending a day or more labouring over a single sentence. Few people have the time to mimic Flaubert's obsessive approach, but picking words with precision is an important skill for anyone who needs to communicate effectively. If you want to make a point, you will benefit from making it clearly and precisely, and your diction, or choice of words, is the key element in this. A clear and precise letter or memo is likely to achieve better results than one which is muddled and vague. This supplement is intended to help you achieve greater precision in your use of language – and improved results as a consequence.

English has a larger vocabulary than any other language, a result of its capacity to absorb words from other tongues. The wide range of possible sounds in English enables foreign words to be embraced by English speakers without being significantly anglicized, allowing an infinite expansion of the language – and bringing both advantages and challenges.

Denotation and connotation

One consequence of English having such a vast number of words is that there are almost always choices to be made, even when describing highly specific things. It is important, therefore, to pay attention to the subtle distinction between a word's *denotation* and its *connotation*. What a word denotes is what it actually means; what it connotes is what it suggests apart from the literal meaning. A good grasp of the connotations of certain words is essential for anyone who wants to be taken seriously when writing or speaking; using a word with an inappropriate connotation can lead to an unintentionally comic effect, or inadvertently cause offence. As an example, consider the word *crusade*. While the word can simply denote a campaign, and it is often used as such in both written and spoken English, it also recalls the Crusades of the Middle Ages, and as such, could cause offence to Muslim or Jewish audiences.

Connotations are the emotional overtones of a given word. They are thus somewhat intangible but extremely important. Denotations, on the other hand, are easy to come by – these are essentially dictionary definitions. In considering the connotation of a particular word, the first thing to do is see how it is labelled in this *Dictionary of Synonyms and Antonyms*. Is it *informal* or *archaic*? *Humorous* or *derogatory*? *Slang* or even *offensive*? This

3

information tells you the likely impact that a word will have. *Rubbish,* for instance, is more likely to offend than *poor-quality* when you are writing a product report. And you might want to refer to your *accountant* rather than your *bean counter* when completing a tax return.

Consider the following pairs of words or phrases, and the situations in which they would be appropriate or inappropriate. Sometimes the difference is simply one of formality against informality, but in other instances the distinction is more subtle.

apparel	clothes
ambitious	grandiose
disgraced	in the doghouse
exhausted	knackered
guru	teacher
idealistic	fanciful
inane	dumbass
luxury	posh
minimal	token
noise	sound
obscene	bawdy
postpone	shelve
shenanigans	misconduct
traipse	walk
tiny	dwarfish

Clichés

What is a cliché?

A *cliché* is a phrase that has been overused. Most clichés are similes or metaphors that were once fresh, original phrases but now have no linguistic impact.

The origin of the word *cliché* is interesting and instructive. Cliché comes from the French verb *clicher*, 'to stereotype' – in the printing sense of putting type together for printing. A cliché, originally, was a phrase that was used so often that the typesetters didn't bother to disassemble it into its constituent letters. Clichés, then and now, take little effort to use. But their use in speech – and especially in writing – is a bad habit. George Orwell gave good advice on the subject: 'Never use a metaphor, simile, or other figure of speech which you are used to seeing in print'. This is an invaluable rule to follow, especially in formal contexts.

Clichés are a problem for these reasons:

1. They are tired. Most clichés were once phrases that had novelty, wit, or humour in their favour. Now, however, people have heard them before – many times – and often look down on their use as a mark of laziness or even stupidity. Using a cliché can thus alienate your audience and cause them to lose respect for you – never a good thing!

2. They are often inexact. Clichés avoid the need to think, but the images they contain can be inappropriate or inadvertently amusing. It's much better to tailor the language you use to the situation in which you use it. This will make you appear much more relevant to your audience.

3. They waste words. Clichés tend to be flowery and take up space that could be used better elsewhere – or saved altogether. Remember the origin of the word *cliché* – a clump of several words bound together; usually there's one word that will do the same job much better.

How to spot a cliché

A good way of spotting a cliché is to see whether you know what's coming when you hear the first part of a phrase. When you hear *at this moment*, for instance, you can bet (but not *your bottom dollar!*) that the entirely redundant *in time* is on its way.

Test yourself with the following examples:

As cheap as ...

In this day ...

At the end ...

between a rock ...

by and ...

when all's said ...

no two ways ...

push the ...

singing from the ...

the fact of the ...

the mind ...

think outside the ...

Types of cliché:
While all clichés are tiresome and overused, we can distinguish different types – each objectionable in a different way.

1. Trite images
Many clichés consist of figurative speech – similes or metaphors – that lacks any wit or clarity. For example:

As cheap as a chips

This annoying phrase has stuck simply because of the assonance between *cheap* and *chips*. It's neither illuminating nor amusing – it simply wastes space.

2. Redundant words

Many clichés take many more words than necessary to get a simple point across. Consider one of the most infamous clichés of all:

At this moment in time

As *moment* is a word that refers exclusively to time, appending *in time* to it is entirely unnecessary – which is probably why this cliché particularly offends!

3. Meaningless phrases

Quite a few clichés – particularly those favoured by sports broadcasters – don't seem to mean anything at all! They simply spare the speaker the effort of thinking, as with the following (the most hated cliché in the UK, according to the Campaign for Plain English):

At the end of the day

You might argue that this means *really* or *ultimately,* but it's usually used just to give speakers time to think, or to lend their statements the illusion of gravity.

Clichés in business

Clichés are especially common in business contexts. Indeed, after sports commentators, managers and marketing people are probably the most flagrant spouters of cliché. Here are a few of the most tiresomely familiar business phrases:

value-added

a win-win situation

think outside the box

multitasking

to pursue other interests

cautiously optimistic

the ball's in your court

Tautology

An easy way to make your writing or speaking clearer and more precise is to avoid tautology. Tautology, in essence, is saying the same thing twice. This is often done by forgetting the full meaning of one of the words that you use, and including adjectives that don't add anything to this meaning. For example, if you say that something is *overly simplistic*, you are forgetting that *simplistic* means 'overly simple' in the first place. The *overly* is thus tautologous – that concept is already included in the word *simplistic*.

Here are some other glaring examples of tautology:

three-part trilogy (all trilogies have three parts)

ATM machine (an ATM is an Automated Telling *Machine*)

safe haven (a haven is, by definition, safe)

reiterate again (reiterate means 'go over again')

adequate enough (if something is adequate, there is enough of it)

free gift (a gift is something given freely)

HIV virus (HIV is the Human Immunodeficiency *Virus*)

other alternative (alternative means 'other choice')

past history (history is always in the past)

close proximity (proximity means 'closeness')

tuna fish (there are no tuna birds!)

One instance in which tautology is acceptable is in placenames that combine foreign words with English ones. The best-known example is probably the La Brea tar pits in California – La Brea simply means 'the tar' in Spanish, so the conventional placename actually means 'the the tar tar pits'! As most English speakers don't know the meaning of the Spanish words, however, this tautology is perfectly permissible.

Confusable words

One of the worst pitfalls for any writer or speaker is *malapropism* – using one word as if it were another, with a similar sound. Named after Mrs Malaprop, a character in Sheridan's play *The Rivals* (1775), malapropism can embarrass your listeners or readers – and cause them to regard you as poorly educated or even stupid. It's thus best avoided!

Unfortunately, the vast size of the English vocabulary means that there are many sets of very similar words with entirely different meanings. The following list provides some assistance in negotiating these pitfalls.

aberrant – abhorrent
Aberrant means 'behaving in an abnormal or untypical way'; *abhorrent* means 'repugnant' or 'loathsome'.
> *the erosion of social conventions is blamed for this increase in aberrant behaviour*
> *violent child abusers are, in the view of most people, peculiarly abhorrent.*

abjure – adjure
Abjure means 'to renounce or retract', or 'to abstain from or reject'; *adjure* means 'to command' or 'to appeal earnestly to'.
> *one of the things I did was to abjure fried food – to the benefit of my palate as well as my health*
> *'Hush', his father would adjure, 'George is going to speak'*

accept – except
Accept means 'to take or receive'; *except* means 'to leave out or omit'.
> *train passengers will have to accept expensive fares as the price of an expanding and reliable railway*
> *this shy, indecisive man had never been on a real trip in his life – if we except his visit to the Shima hot springs*

adduce – deduce
To *adduce* something is to cite it as evidence or proof; to *deduce* something is to conclude it by reasoning or inference.
> *the trial judge refused to allow the defendant to adduce evidence that the co-accused had stabbed him*
> *Bogart, having read through the script, was unable to deduce which character had murdered the chauffeur*

adapt – adopt

To *adapt* something is to modify it for a different purpose; to *adopt* something is to take on or assume it.

> *a donation of £50 will help to adapt a standard PC to suit a child with special needs*

> *twelve EU countries will adopt the euro as their currency on January 1*

advice – advise

Advice is recommendation or counsel; to *advise* is to offer advice to someone.

> *formerly politicians used to have to rely for advice on politically neutral civil servants*

> *she was invited to the House of Commons to advise MPs on changes to the prison system.*

affect – effect

To *affect* something is to influence it; to *effect* something is to bring it about.

> *the new rules affect only offshore funds run by life insurers*

> *if thinking murderous thoughts could by itself effect practical results, we would all be orphans.*

afflict – inflict

Afflict means 'to cause suffering or unhappiness to'; *inflict* means 'to impose something unpleasant on'.

> *this is far from the first savage cattle sickness to afflict Britain*

> *we want to live in a country where it is illegal to inflict pain and suffering on wild animals*

affluent – effluent

Affluent means 'rich'; *effluent* is liquid waste.

> *he did not come from an affluent background*

> *by the middle of the 19th century, the human effluent from 2.5 million people was being dumped into the Thames*

allude – elude

To *allude* to something is to refer to it indirectly; to *elude* something is to escape or avoid it.

> *the shows have sparked public debate by showing scenes that allude to sex*

> *he may have changed his appearance to elude would-be captors*

allusion – illusion
An *allusion* to something is a passing reference to it; an *illusion* is a false appearance or impression.
> *'like a marlin,' said Lynch, thinking that the professor would appreciate his allusion to Hemingway*
> *create the illusion of space in your kitchen by using pull-down shutters to hide clutter*

alternate – alternative
Alternate means 'occurring by turns' – first one and then the other; *alternative* means 'presenting a choice'.
> *this is the latest in a series of complementary student briefings that will appear on alternate weeks*
> *duck is the ideal bird for an alternative Christmas feast*

among – between
Among means 'in the midst of'; *between* means 'at a point intermediate to two other points'.
> *the ruin stands desolate among grassy humps and hollows*
> *female bats gather to form maternity roosts between April and September*

amoral – immoral
Amoral means 'with no moral quality, standards, or principles'; *immoral* means 'transgressing moral rules'.
> *the desert is amoral. It doesn't care: you're as useful dead as you are alive*
> *they argue that all forms of animal use by humans are immoral*

appraise – apprise
To *appraise* something is assess its worth or value; to *apprise* someone is to inform them of something.
> *you need to appraise the situation with care as this area of law can be confusing*
> *they promised to apprise him of any developments in the case*

ascent – assent
an *ascent* is a climb or upward slope; *assent* means agreement.
> *it took a day to make the ascent, after which we camped on the crater rim*
> *they are likely to give their assent to the compromise solution*

assure – ensure
Assure means 'to promise or guarantee'; *ensure* means 'to make certain'.

> *I can emphatically assure you that there is no truth whatsoever to this allegation*
> *after all, what is the Treasury for if not to ensure that public spending is good value?*

aural – oral
Aural relates to hearing; *oral* refers to the mouth or speech.
> *after these aural rigours, the trio soothed the audience's ears with a jolly, major-key piece*
> *when you join the scheme, the dentist grades your oral health, then charges you accordingly*

bad – badly
Bad is an adjective; the adverb is *badly*.
> *it was, he said later, such a bad experience that he quit the film business*
> *the ability to play the guitar badly is, in itself, never cool*

blatant – flagrant
If something is *blatant*, then it is glaringly obvious; if something is *flagrant*, then it is openly outrageous. *Flagrant* thus has a negative denotation that blatant does not possess, although *blatant* sometimes has a negative connotation.
> *cinematic homages rarely get more blatant than the scene in which two would-be killers view Hitchcock's 1951 classic* Strangers on a Train *to learn about the mechanics of motiveless murder*
> *the report says the agreement represents a flagrant breach of the United Nations trade embargo*

breach – breech
A *breach* is a crack or rupture; *breech* means the lower portion of something (hence *breeches*, meaning trousers).
> *waiting list fiddles were a major breach of public trust, the audit office said*
> *a breech birth is where the baby is born feet-first.*

bridal – bridle
Bridal means 'relating to a bride or a wedding'; a *bridle* is headgear for a horse
> *the papers are full of bridal fashion spreads and gossip about impending weddings*
> *a former cowboy has invented a horse bridle without a bit*

capital – capitol

The *capital* of a country is the seat of government; the *capitol* is the building that houses a state legislature in the US.

> *there were fresh outbreaks of violence outside the Tajik capital, Dushanbe, this summer*

> *in Austin, he can saunter across the road from his mansion to his office in the spectacular state capitol*

censor – censure

To *censor* something is to cut or ban all or a part of a publication, film etc; to *censure* someone is to criticize him or her severely.

> *the public, by a substantial majority, does not believe we should censor movies for adults*

> *the assembly has the power to censure, though not unseat, the mayor*

certainty – certitude

Certainty is the condition of being certain; *certitude* is confidence.

> *I can predict my arrival time with certainty almost every day*

> *her certitude infused all the small staff*

childish – childlike

Childish means foolish, petty or puerile; *childlike* means innocent or trustful.

> *it amused me to do it, even though it is childish*

> *today, Klee's work is most popular for its childlike qualities*

cleave – cleave

Cleave is an unusual word in that it can mean both 'to split' or 'to cause to split' and 'to cling or adhere to'.

> *using a heavy knife, cleave each drumstick and thigh in two*

> *people cleave to their core beliefs and anchoring facts*

climactic – climatic

Climactic describes something that is coming to a climax; *climatic* refers to climate.

> *this was the climactic concert after six months of workshops*

> *the Americas have the full gamut of climatic zones, from rainforest heat to Arctic cold*

coarse – course

Coarse means rough or indelicate; *course* means a route or direction.

> *it is a myth that frizzy hair is coarse – often it is fine*

> *Hackney foiled the Vikings by building a dam and changing the course of the River Lea: the invaders got lost when next they came*

common – mutual
Something that is *common* belongs to two or more people; something that is *mutual* is, strictly speaking, something that is felt or held by two parties about each other.
> *politics forces people to work together for a common goal*
> *their mutual antagonism is intense and often intensely personal*

compare to – compare with
If you compare something to another thing, you are highlighting the similarities of the two; if you *compare* one thing *with* another, you are drawing attention to the differences between the two.
> *England do not, sadly, have anybody to compare to Shane Warne*
> *many people are needed to plant a paddy field compared with a wheat field*

compliment – complement
A *compliment* is a remark expressing admiration; a *complement* is something that completes another thing.
> *we British find the act of paying a compliment excruciatingly embarrassing*
> *their MBA provides practical experience to complement their academic learning*

comprise – constitute
To *comprise* is to contain or include; to *constitute* is to make up or compose. Note: *comprise* should never be used with of!
> *when the site is completed, it will comprise at least 5,000 homes*
> *the two volumes of autobiography constitute Osborne's most substantial achievement*

confidant – confident
A *confidant* (or *confidante* if female) is someone in whom you confide; *confident* means having confidence.
> *you set yourself up as a mentor and confidant to these young women*
> *kids are so much more confident, and worldly wise these days*

compound – confound
To *compound* something is to intensify it by an added element; to *confound* is to perplex or bewilder.
> *bureaucratic difficulties here that simply compound the problems*
> *will Henman confound his critics by winning a Grand Slam tournament?*

connote – denote

To *connote* is to imply or suggest something other than the literal meaning; to *denote* is to mean literally.

> *red can connote passion in one direction, and in the other, the infernal*
> *'capacity' is used here to denote the power of an engine*

conscience – conscious

Your *conscience* is your sense of right or wrong; to be conscious is to be alert and awake.

> *he says that he wrestled with his conscience before giving evidence*
> *I am conscious of the possibility that an injustice may have been done*

contemptible – contemptuous

To be *contemptible* is to be deserving of contempt; to be *contemptuous* of something is to show contempt for it.

> *morally, the argument was contemptible*
> *he could be contemptuous of colleagues, whom he thought less intelligent*

continual – continuous

Something that is *continual* either recurs frequently or occurs without interruption; something that is *continuous* occurs without interruption.

> *she grew up with continual and violent bullying*
> *the waterfall thunders down in a continuous explosive roaring force*

credible – creditable

Credible means believable; *creditable* means praiseworthy.

> *the police chief said that the FBI had received 'credible threats' of a strike*
> *the team displayed a creditable commitment to attacking football*

criteria – criterion

Criteria is the plural of *criterion*, which means a standard by which something can be judged.

> *looked at objectively they fulfil all the criteria*
> *my first criterion is the overall impression of colour*

data – datum

Data is the plural of *datum*, which means a piece of information.

> *gloomy eurozone data are likely to cast a pall over the smooth launch of euro notes and coins*
> *it is the vital missing datum, without which the whole subject remains a mystery*

demur – demure

To *demur* is to raise objections or to show reluctance; *demure* means reserved or coy.

> *he raised his eyebrows slightly but didn't demur*

> *she doesn't want to get typecast as a demure corset-wearing Edwardian lady*

dependant – dependent

Your *dependants* are people who depend on you for financial support, etc; to be dependent is to *depend* on someone.

> *all proceeds can be passed on to a spouse or dependant free of tax if the investor dies*

> *the bonus payments are dependent on so-called 'performance standards'*

device – devise

A *device* is a machine or tool; to *devise* something is to contrive it or plan it.

> *he found a police bugging device planted in his camper van.*

> *eventually she decided to devise a system that could be accessed centrally*

disassemble – dissemble

To *disassemble* something is to take it apart; to *dissemble* is to conceal one's real motives or feelings, or to pretend.

> *I can disassemble an AK47 – but put it back together?*

> *fear of anger leads us to lie and dissemble*

discreet – discrete

Discreet means tactful; *discrete* means distinct or separate.

> *as befits an upmarket jeweller, Mr Jarvis is discreet about his own clients' names*

> *herbal medicine does not treat mind and body as discrete entities, but holistically*

disinterested – uninterested

To be *disinterested* is to be free from bias; to be *uninterested* in something is to lack interest in it.

> *Watching the conflict through his camera lens, he tried to remain disinterested*

> *Wendy is not only uninterested in football but also actively dislikes it*

economic – economical

In general, *economic* means related to the economy; *economical* means

cheap or unwasteful.
> *the Treasury is required to issue economic forecasts twice a year*
> *the most economical route is via London*

effeminate – effete
If a man is *effeminate*, he is unmanly or womanly; if something is *effete*, it it weak, ineffectual or worn out.
> *some men think it effeminate to care for their hands*
> *they were no longer great warriors; centuries of the soft life had made them effete*

elicit – illicit
To *elicit* something is to give rise to it or to bring it to light; if something is *illicit*, it is against the law.
> *I have phoned press offices to elicit information on obscure topics*
> *further legislation is proposed to clamp down on the illicit trade in ivory*

emigrate – immigrate
To *emigrate* is to leave one country to settle in another; to *immigrate* is to come to a new country to live.
> *he decided to emigrate to America*
> *his grandfather immigrated from Europe in 1890*

eminent – imminent
An *eminent* person is distinguished; if something is *imminent*, it is about to happen.
> *he is Britain's most eminent thinker and writer about war*
> *his enemies have predicted his imminent demise for more than a decade*

empathy – sympathy
Empathy is is the power of imaginatively entering into another person's feelings; *sympathy* is pity or compassion.
> *I feel that many teachers have little empathy with boys*
> *the farmers won sympathy by portraying themselves as little guys*

enormity – enormousness
An *enormity* is an atrocity or great wickedness; *enormousness* is the condition of being very large.
> *the films served to desensitise you to the enormity of killing another person*
> *what hits you first is the gaping enormousness of the place*

ensure – insure
To *ensure* something is to make it certain; to *insure* something is to guarantee it or protect it.
> *it much more difficult for head teachers to ensure good teaching and high standards*
> *kidnapping is on the increase but you can insure against it*

entomology – etymology
Entomology is the study of insects; *etymology* is the study of the origins and development of words.
> *the parsons who collected and classified beetles laid the basis for the science of entomology*
> *cautious lexicographers describe its etymology as 'unknown'*

epigram – epigraph
An *epigram* is a witty remark; an *epigraph* is a quotation at the beginning of a book or chapter, or an inscription.
> *he is a practised raconteur, a master of the Wildean epigram*
> *Boyd takes as his epigraph and title a sentence of Henry James*

especially – specially
Especially means 'exceptionally' or 'in particular'; *specially* means 'in particular' or 'for a particular purpose'. Thus *especially* is a better word to use if you wish to stress that something is noteworthy; *specially* should be preferred if you wish to emphasise that it was designed for a certain purpose.
> *a very romantic spot, almost unearthly – especially after a snowfall*
> *everything is sourced from specially selected farms*

exalt – exult
To *exalt* something is to raise or praise it; to *exult* is to be joyful, jubilant, or triumphant.
> *we exalt freedom and strangle privacy*
> *Rommel was not one to exult or sneer at a fallen enemy*

expedient – expeditious
If something is *expedient*, then it is appropriate in the circumstances; if something is *expeditious*, then it is done promptly and efficiently.
> *IBM realised it was not be politically expedient to upset the powers-that-be*
> *the impeachment inquiry must be seen as fair, expeditious and well-grounded in the facts*

explicit – implicit

If something is *explicit*, it is clearly expressed or graphically detailed; if something is *implicit*, it is implied or indirectly expressed.

> *we think the airline could be more explicit regarding its use of secondary airports*

> *the headlines about the dawn swoops carried the implicit message that those responsible for his murder would soon be brought to book*

extant – extent

Something which is *extant* is still in existence; the *extent* of something is its scope or area.

> *he had been examining the extant manuscripts for decades before I began work*

> *the full extent of the club's problems is slowly sinking in*

extrapolate – interpolate

To *extrapolate* something is to estimate it or infer it; to *interpolate* something is to insert or introduce it.

> *it is unwise to extrapolate too much from one month's figures*

> *the conflicts between Jesus and the leaders of the nation were probably interpolated into the Gospels by later Christians for polemical purposes*

farther – further

Farther is generally used for literal distances; *further* is regarded as more correct for figurative distances, as when referring to amounts or periods of time.

> *the house was a hundred yards farther on down a side street*

> *online bookings attract a further £10 discount*

faze – phase

To *faze* someone is to disconcert or worry them; a *phase* is a distinct period or stage.

> *the prospect of making history does not faze them*

> *the war in Europe had reached its final phase*

fewer – less

Few, fewer and *fewest* refer to countable objects; *little, less* and *least* refer to uncountable objects.

> *there were fewer people there today than yesterday*

> *we drank less wine than last night*

flammable – inflammable
Flammable and *inflammable* mean exactly the same thing; confusion sometimes arises because *inflammable* looks like it might mean the opposite!
> *the poor were huddled together in highly flammable buildings*
> *graffiti removal involved hazardous, inflammable solvents*

flaunt – flout
To *flaunt* something is to show it off; to *flout* something is to show contempt for it.
> *she does not flaunt her status as a billionaire's daughter*
> *they have massive sanctions to fine us if we flout the spirit or the letter of the law*

flounder – founder
To *flounder* is to struggle, or move with difficulty; to *founder* is to break down or fail.
> *the film features Hugh Grant as a blushing chap floundering in a sea of faux pas*
> *their game plan foundered on an inability to win quick ball*

foreboding – forbidding
If something is *forbidding*, it is hostile or unfriendly; if something is *foreboding*, it is ominous.
> *the film has some haunting visual effects and a foreboding atmosphere*
> *a crowd had gathered outside the forbidding 30ft-high walls of the jail*

good – well
Good is an adjective; the adverb is *well*.
> *it was a good game*
> *she played really well*

gorilla – guerrilla
A *gorilla* is a large anthropoid ape; a *guerrilla* (also spelt *guerilla*) is an irregular fighter.
> *They tracked the reclusive silverback gorilla in its natural habitat*
> *two Britons were kidnapped by Colombian guerrillas while searching for new orchids*

grisly – gristly – grizzled – grizzly
If something is *grisly*, it is horrific or gruesome; if meat is *gristly*, it contains cartilage; if something is *grizzled* or *grizzly*, it is grey or

partly grey.
> *it contains some remarkably grisly images for a prewatershed programme*
> *the beef ragout was gristly and thin*
> *Galwey might be a grizzled veteran, but he has maintained the fitness of a much younger man*
> *he produced a smile from beneath the grizzly grey beard*

hanged – hung
If someone is *hanged*, they are killed by being suspended by the neck; if something is *hung* it is attached to, or suspended from, something else.
> *he became the last man to be publicly hanged in Stirling*
> *they sleep under mosquito nets hung from the rotor blades*

hardy – hearty
Hardy means physically tough or robust; *hearty* means warm, vigorous or healthy.
> *the production is a hearty salute to the hardy Cossack spirit*

heroin – heroine
Heroin is a highly addictive narcotic; a *heroine* is a woman with heroic qualities.
> *her daughter died of a heroin overdose in the summer*
> *Iris Murdoch had been a heroine of hers since* A Severed Head

historic – historical
Historic means famous or significant; *historical* means 'concerned with history'.
> *Afghan leaders signed an historic agreement yesterday*
> *the film eschews historical accuracy for sumptuous spectacle*

hoard – horde
A *hoard* is a cache of coins or treasure; a *horde* is a vast crowd.
> *A treasure hunter has found a hoard of Roman coins*
> *on their left was a great horde of Tartar cavalry*

imply – infer
To *imply* something is to express or suggest it by a hint; to *infer* something is to deduce it or conclude it from the available evidence.
> *the boarded-up council houses imply the menace of junkies*
> *perhaps it is unfair to infer so much from his speech*

incipient – insipid
Incipient means starting to happen or beginning; *insipid* means boring or lacking flavour.
> *he has a ponytail sprouting beneath an incipient bald patch*
> *the bread sauce was insipid glue*

incredible – incredulous
Incredible means unbelievable; *incredulous* means unbelieving.
> *he died in an accident that was an almost incredible combination of coincidences*
> *after the talk, we became aware of incredulous looks from the kids*

indeterminable – indeterminate
Something which is *indeterminable* cannot be ascertained or settled; something which is *indeterminate* is uncertain in extent, amount, or nature.
> *she was a substantial woman of an indeterminable age*
> *the government is considering indeterminate sentences for high-risk prisoners*

indict – indite
To *indict* someone is to charge him or her with a crime; to *indite* something is to write it or dictate it.
> *minutes later, prosecutors announced they will indict him on charges of genocide*
> *this ridiculous letter seems to be indited from no deeper source than some tingling volition of the fingertips*

ingenious – ingenuous
Ingenious means skilful or clever; *ingenuous* means naive or innocent.
> *this is an ingenious little scam popular with criminal gangs*
> *the look, the wardrobe and the carefully ingenuous stage persona are undimmed by age*

insidious – invidious
Insidious means stealthy, cunning, or treacherous; *invidious* means 'arousing resentment or unpopularity'.
> *chlamydia is an insidious bacterial infection that has few symptoms*
> *the controversy places the Church of England in an invidious position*

intense – intensive
Intense means extreme in force, strength, degree, or amount; *intensive*

means involving the maximum use of land, time, or some other resource.
> *the flavour was just too intense, not pleasurable at all*
> *much damage to the countryside caused by intensive farm practices.*

intensely – intently
intensely means 'with great force, strength, degree, or amount'; *intently* means purposefully.
> *the Scottish banking marketplace remains intensely competitive*
> *a group of analysts stare intently as they monitor recent movements*

laudable – laudatory
Laudable means praiseworthy; *laudatory* means 'expressing praise'.
> *the scheme is laudable, deserving of consumers' respect*
> *the film's tone is inevitably nostalgic and laudatory*

lay – lie
Lay is a transitive verb – you lay something down; *lie* is an intransitive verb – you lie down. *Lay*, of course, is also the past tense of *lie*.
> *they added a last-minute stop to lay pink carnations at the memorial*
> *when cows are more comfortable they lie down longer and digest better*

loath – loathe
To be *loath* to do something is to hate to have to do it; to *loathe* something is to hate it.
> *John had a little cash put by, which he was loath to put into a pension scheme*
> *viewers loathe it because it's the antithesis of good TV*

loose – lose
If something is *loose*, it is free or not close-fitting; if you *lose* something, you come to be without it.
> *wear loose clothing for added comfort*
> *we can't afford to lose this money*

luxuriant – luxurious
If something is *luxuriant*, it is abundant or lush; if something is *luxurious*, it is extremely comfortable and expensive.
> *a news report falsely suggested that his luxuriant brown hair was dyed*
> *business travel is not luxurious for the majority of travellers*

media – medium

Media is the plural of *medium*.
> *we moved away from that because it's so well catered for in other media*
> *a new medium of linguistic communication does not arrive very often*

metal – mettle

Metal is a hard, shiny substance; *mettle* is courage, spirit, or character.
> *demand for the metal has recently outstripped supply*
> *he had occasion once again to show his mettle during the terrorist attack*

meter – metre

A *meter* is a measuring device; a *metre* is a unit of length.
> *he told the Gestapo that the gas meter in the basement needed replacing*
> *it was a yellowy brown snake-like creature a metre long*

moral – morale

Morals are principles of behaviour; *morale* is confidence or optimism.
> *how different are the morals of 80 years ago from today's*
> *the society's reputation was battered and morale was low*

morbid – moribund

Morbid means unusually interested in death, or gruesome; *moribund* means near death, or stagnant.
> *they were always asking morbid questions about guns and murder*
> *with* The Simpsons, *Groening brought a moribund genre back to life*

oral – verbal

Oral refers to the mouth or to speech; *verbal* refers to words.
Therefore, use *oral* to distinguish the written from the spoken.
> *students make written and oral presentations about their experience,*
> *we took into account provocation from both sides, both verbal and physical*

ordinance – ordnance

An *ordinance* is a regulation or decree; *ordnance* means artillery or munitions. The maps are *Ordnance Survey* (they were originally for military purposes).
> *the government has issued an ordinance under which drug dealers will be sentenced to death*
> *the harsh winter and unexploded ordnance littering the area add to the dangers*

palate – palette – pallet

The *palate* is the roof of the mouth; a *palette* is used for mixing paint; a *pallet* is a straw mattress or bed.

> *babies with a cleft palate often experience feeding problems early on*
> *she began painting from a muted palette, mixing earthy browns and beiges*
> *the boy scrambled from his pallet and pulled on his boots*

parameter – perimeter

A *parameter* is a variable or factor; a *perimeter* is the boundary around something.

> *his absolute ceiling of £25,000 is a tough parameter with which to work*
> *the taxi drivers would ferry the SAS to and from the perimeter of enemy airfields*

persecute – prosecute

To *persecute* people is to oppress or harass them; to *prosecute* someone is to bring criminal action against them.

> *the Church has come a long way since it persecuted Galileo for his scientific discoveries*
> *state officials hunted for laws to prosecute those responsible, but few seemed to apply*

pore – pour

To *pore* over something is to examine it closely; to *pour* something is to cause it to flow out.

> *boys spend less time studying, while girls pore over their books*
> *pour in the juices from the goose's roasting pan*

practicable – practical

If something is *practicable* it is feasible; if something is *practical*, it is useful.

> *this would have been practicable, but extremely expensive*
> *there are lots of hugely practical wine gadgets that make great gifts*

precede – proceed

If one thing *precedes* another, it goes before it; if one *proceeds*, one advances or carries on.

> *all those beautiful dishes that precede the main course are integral to Italian cuisine*
> *good co-ordination is required to perform this exercise correctly, so proceed slowly*

precedence – precedent

Precedence is that act of going before something, or the order of priority; a *precedent* is an earlier example used to justify a similar, later occurrence.

> *the Prince of Wales insisted that King Kalakaua of Hawaii take precedence over the German crown prince*

> *the White House cited ample precedent for its action*

premier – premiere

A *premier* is a prime minister; a *premiere* is the first public performance of a film, play, etc.

> *Bavaria's silver-haired state premier arrived at a film festival*

> *the film receives its world premiere in London tomorrow*

principal – principle

A *principal* is the head of a school or organization; as an adjective, *principal* means 'first' or 'most important'. A *principle* is a standard or rule of personal conduct; *principle* is not an adjective.

> *she has retired from her official position as principal of St Hugh's College*

> *The Times, recognising that an important principle of press freedom was at stake, appealed*

prophecy – prophesy

A *prophecy* is a divine message or a prediction; to *prophesy* is to foretell future events as if by divine intervention.

> *he is reputed to have had supernatural powers of prophecy and healing*

> *she does not preach or prophesy; she merely watches people behave*

prostate – prostrate

The *prostate* is a gland in male mammals that secretes a liquid constituent of semen; *prostrate* means lying face downwards.

> *an alarming 10% of Britons think that women have a prostate gland*

> *spectators hurled objects on to the pitch as Gronkjaer lay prostrate*

purposefully – purposely

Purposefully means determinedly; *purposely* means 'on purpose'.

> *Atta strode purposefully forward*

> *he then accused them of purposely making mischief*

racial – racialist – racist

Racial means 'relating to race'; *racist* means 'relating to the belief that some races are superior to others'; *racialist* is a less common variant of *racist*.

> there is a shortage of suitable donors from minority racial groups
> he was reported to the Press Council for making racialist observations
> she told an employment tribunal that racist jokes and attitudes were rife

rack – wrack

Rack and *wrack* are two of the most difficult homophones to disentangle, as their multiple meanings often overlap. The essential distinction between them is that *rack* means 'to torture' (from *the rack*, the device on which torture victims were stretched) while *wrack* (which is etymologically linked to *wreck*) means 'to ruin'. Thus it is more correct to talk about something being *nerve-racking* than *nerve-wracking*.

> walking to the station, I rack my brains to think if there might be any other solution
> even on his deathbed, wracked by cancer, he was able to laugh

reign – rein

A *reign* is a period of rule; a *rein* is one of two straps used to control a horse (often used figuratively).

> he endured a torrid start to his reign
> a tight rein has been kept on inflation

reluctant – reticent

Reluctant means unwilling or disinclined; *reticent* means uncommunicative, taciturn, or not saying all that one knows.

> people will visit their doctor but are reluctant to spend at the local chemist
> other clients are reticent about admitting they use her services

respectfully – respectively

Respectfully means 'with respect'; *respectively* means 'in the order given'.

> he asked his captain, respectfully, if he could be excused from the embrace
> their daughters were Fanny and Adelaide Kemble, the best actress and the best opera singer (respectively) of their day

review – revue

A *review* is a critical assessment; a *revue* is a form of light entertainment containing sketches, songs, etc. *Revue* is occasionally spelt *review*, however; the opposite does not apply.

> the chancellor needs to conduct an urgent review
> he wrote and produced the famous nude revue Oh! Calcutta

role – roll

A *role* is a part or character in a film or play; a *roll* is cylindrical bundle, a small loaf of bread, or a deep reverberating sound.

> *get them a roll of Sellotape and a ball of string*
> *the role of Tatiana offers a dramatic challenge*

sensual – sensuous

If something is *sensual*, it relates to the body's senses; if something is *sensuous*, it is aesthetically pleasing.

> *the very fact of being in Africa a very powerful sensual experience*
> *at once stately and sensuous, she was likened to a rose, an orchid, a basket of ripe peaches and an alabaster statue*

simple – simplistic

Simple means uncomplicated; *simplistic* means overly simple or naive.

> *it is crucial that the scheme is simple enough for business to use*
> *this strategy has been derided by some as simplistic*

stationary – stationery

If something is *stationary*, it isn't moving; *stationery* is writing materials such as pens and paper.

> *the train remained stationary for a further 10 minutes*
> *you also have to change all your stationery to show the company name*

that – which

That and *which* can be synonyms, as *which* can be a synonym for *that*. But while *which* can be used in place of *that*, *that* cannot always be used instead of *which*. The main difference between the two is that *that* is used as a relative pronoun only in restrictive clauses, where the *that* clause is a key aspect of the thing to which it refers, while *which* is traditionally used in nonrestrictive clauses, describing an incidental aspect of the thing to which the clause refers.

> *he stopped the first car that had a red roof*
> *he stopped the first car, which was driven by a Frenchman*

tortuous – torturous

Tortuous means twisted or winding; *torturous* means 'extremely painful'.

> *he has a hell of a tortuous way of saying it*
> *his training regimes were simply too torturous*

trooper – trouper

A *trooper* is a soldier; a *trouper* is a member of a performing group, or an experienced or dependable member of any group.

> *he was the first special forces trooper to parachute into the Falklands*
> *being the trouper I am, I believe that the show must go on*

turbid – turgid

If something is *turbid*, it is muddy or opaque; if something is *turgid*, it is swollen, congested, or pompous.

> *it was still a turbid brown colour when it reached the taps in my house*
> *he produced turgid and mind-numbing speeches*

unconscionable – unconscious

Unconscionable means unscrupulous or unprincipled; *unconscious* means insensible or unaware.

> *these are barbaric attacks of unconscionable vigilantism*
> *four or five men had beaten his son unconscious and left him for dead*

unexceptionable – unexceptional

If something is *unexceptionable*, it is beyond criticism or objection; if something is *unexceptional*, it is ordinary.

> *the government's position in many respects was unexceptionable*
> *Monday had been an unexceptional news day*

venal – venial

Venal means easily bribed or corruptible; *venial* means easily excused or forgivable.

> *it is a turbulent, venal place, where corruption is the norm*
> *the exemplary heroine is only flawed (if she is flawed at all) by some venial defect*

various – varying

Various means 'several different' or 'of different kinds'; *varying* means changing.

> *he is thought to have access to a number of passports under various aliases*
> *they offer meals of varying quality, depending on the time of evening*

Internet links

The following web pages contain a wealth of useful information for anyone interested in writing, diction, or language in general.

Using the internet safely

The internet contains an inconceivably large amount of information, much of it free, on a vast range of topics. It does not belong to and is not controlled by any single organization, government, or nation. Although the absence of centralized control is occasionally lamented as anarchic, the lack of a top-down structure provides many benefits.

The internet offers the chance for anyone with a computer and a modem to communicate with and learn from any person, group, or organization similarly equipped. Libraries, museums, art galleries, governments, universities, research institutes, and many other bodies provide open access to their data and links to the online resources of other organizations.

This availability of information and the unparalleled potential for communication and the spread of ideas provides internet users with incalculable benefits, but there are downsides. As the internet is unregulated and decentralized there is no quality-control mechanism; the only barrier preventing someone from setting up a website is technical ability. There is much of little merit on the internet.

More worrying is the potential for criminal misuse. The internet's accessibility and inclusiveness is exploited by those who wish to disseminate hate or obscenity or to take advantage of the vulnerable or gullible. As 70 per cent of UK households with school-age children are online it is important that parents and carers are aware of the potential dangers as well as the benefits.

General online language resources

http://www.collins.co.uk/wordexchange/

http://www.collins.co.uk/word_wizard

http://www.britac.ac.uk/portal/

http://www.ilovelanguages.com
http://babel.uoregon.edu/yamada/guides.html

http://www.languagelearn.co.uk

http://www.languages-on-the-web.com

http://www.arels.org.uk

http://www.iatefl.org/newhome.asp

Creative writing

http://www.ideasfactory.com/writing/index.htm

http://www.bbc.co.uk/writersroom/opportunity/

http://www.bbc.co.uk/scotland/arts/writingscotland/

http://www.arvonfoundation.org

http://www.booktrust.org.uk

http://www.branching-out.net

http://www.nald.org

Denotation and connotation

http://www.aber.ac.uk/media/Documents/S4B/semo6.html

http://www.eng.fju.edu.tw/English_Literature/terms/denotation.htm

http://bcs.bedfordstmartins.com/virtualit/poetry/denotate_def.html

http://teenwriting.about.com/library/glossary/bldef-connotation.htm

http://www.bbc.co.uk/education/asguru/english/05languageframeworks/2
2semantics/semantics_4.shtml

Grammar

http://www.ucl.ac.uk/internet-grammar/home.htm

Writing systems

http://www.omniglot.com/writing/atoz.htm

Lexicography

http://www.ims.uni-stuttgart.de/euralex

http://australex.anu.edu.au/

Linguistics

http://www.britac.ac.uk/portal/

http://linguistlist.org/sp/LangAnalysis.html

http://www-nlp.stanford.edu/links/linguistics.html

http://www.phil.uni-passau.de/linguistik/linguistik_urls

Philology

http://www.britac.ac.uk/portal/

Phonetics

http://www2.arts.gla.ac.uk/IPA/ipa.html

http://faculty.washington.edu/dillon/PhonResources

Rhetoric

http://humanities.byu.edu/rhetoric/silva.htm